CHASE'S
Calendar of Events
2006

McGraw·Hill

New York   Chicago   San Francisco   Lisbon   London   Madrid   Mexico City
Milan   New Delhi   San Juan   Seoul   Singapore   Sydney   Toronto

1 2 3 4 5 6 7 8 9 0   QPD/QPD   0 9 8 7 6 5

ISBN 0-07-146110-8 (set)
ISBN 0-07-146111-6 (book)
ISBN 0-07-146112-4 (CD-ROM)
ISSN 0740-5286

Some interior art courtesy of Dover Publications, Inc.

McGraw-Hill books are available at special quantity discounts to use as premiums and sales promotions, or for use in corporate training programs. For more information, please write to the Director of Special Sales, Professional Publishing, McGraw-Hill, Two Penn Plaza, New York, NY 10121-2298. Or contact your local bookstore.

NOTICE
Events listed herein are not necessarily endorsed by the editors or publisher. Every effort has been made to assure the correctness of all entries, but neither the editors nor the publisher can warrant their accuracy. IT IS IMPERATIVE, IF FINANCIAL PLANS ARE TO BE MADE IN CONNECTION WITH DATES OR EVENTS LISTED HEREIN, THAT PRINCIPALS BE CONSULTED FOR FINAL INFORMATION.

This book is printed on acid-free paper.

TABLE OF CONTENTS

How to Use This Book . . . . Inside Front Cover
Introduction 5
Spotlight on 2006 Anniversaries and Events 9
Chronological Calendar of Events: Jan 1–Dec 31 65
    January 65
    February 111
    March 154
    April 200
    May 251
    June 303
    July 352
    August 402
    September 447
    October 504
    November 558
    December 600
Calendar Information for the Years 2006–2008 638
Perpetual Calendar 641
National Days of the World 645
Selected Special Years: 1972–2006 646
Chinese Calendar 646
Wedding Anniversary Gifts 646
World Map of Time Zones 647
Universal, Standard and Daylight Times 648
Leap Seconds 648
Astronomical Phenomena for the Years 2006–2008 649
The Naming of Hurricanes 650
Some Facts about the Presidents 651
Presidential Proclamations 653
Some Facts about the United States 655
State & Territory Abbreviations: United States 656
State Governors/US Senators/US Supreme Court 657
Some Facts about Canada 658
Province & Territory Abbreviations: Canada 658
Some Facts about Mexico 658
2006 Special Months 659
National Film Registry and National Recording Registry 661
Major Awards Presented in 2004–2005 662
Index 672
Order Form for *Chase's* Additional Copies 751
How to Submit a New Entry 752

Introduction

Welcome to *Chase's Calendar of Events 2006*, the 49th edition of this publication. *Chase's* was founded in the summer of 1957 by brothers William D. and the late Harrison V. Chase. The Chases realized then that there was a need for a single reference source for calendar dates—and for authoritative and current information about the various observances throughout the year. Their first publication (for the year 1958) came out in December 1957, and that initial 32-page, 364-entry book has grown to a reference of 752 pages and more than 12,000 entries. Today, *Chase's Calendar of Events* is the most respected and comprehensive reference available on holidays, events and special days, weeks and months.

What's New in 2006

2006 will see a number of special events and anniversaries. We've picked out a selection to highlight in our Spotlight section, but there are many more in the main calendar portion of the book. 2006 marks several birth anniversaries of import, especially the 300th anniversary of Benjamin Franklin's birth and the 250th anniversary of Wolfgang Amadeus Mozart's birth. Both men will be feted the world over but most particularly in Philadelphia, PA, and Austria, respectively. There are more sobering anniversaries as well: the 100th anniversary of the San Francisco earthquake, the 25th anniversary of when AIDS was first remarked in the US, and the 20th anniversaries of the *Challenger* and Chernobyl disasters.

As we have listed every year, there will be thousands of special events and festivals. Particular to 2006 are the World Cup in Germany, Mozart 2006 and the Winter Olympics in Italy (see "Spotlight on 2006 Events").

Types of Entries in *Chase's Calendar of Events*

Astronomical Phenomena

Information about eclipses, equinoxes and solstices, moon phases and other astronomical phenomena is calculated from data prepared by the US Naval Observatory's Nautical Almanac Office and Her Majesty's Nautical Almanac Office. In *Chase's*, universal time has been converted to eastern time.

Religious Observances

Principal observances of the Christian, Jewish, Muslim and Baha'i faiths are presented with background information from their respective calendars. We include anticipated dates for Muslim holidays. When known, religious events of China, Japan and India are also listed. There is no single Hindu calendar and different sects define the Hindu lunar month differently. There is no single lunar calendar that serves as a model for all Buddhists, either. Therefore, we are not able to provide the dates of many religious holidays for these faiths.

National and International Observances and Civic Holidays

Chase's features independence days, national days and public holidays from around the world. Technically, there are no national holidays in the US: holidays proclaimed by the president only apply to federal employees and to the District of Columbia. State governors proclaim holidays for their states. In practice, federal holidays are usually proclaimed by governors as well. Some governors proclaim commemorative days that are unique to their state.

Special Days, Weeks and Months

Whether it's Black History Month, National Police Week or National Grandparents' Day, the annual calendar has loads of special days, weeks and months—and *Chase's* has the most comprehensive listing of them. Until January 1995, Congress had been active in seeing that special observances were commemorated. Members of the Senate and House could introduce legislation for a special observance to commemorate people, events and other activities they thought worthy of national recognition. Because these bills took up a disproportionate amount of time on the part of congressmen and their staffs, Congress decided to discontinue this process in January 1995 when it reviewed and reformed its rules and practices. Congress does from time to time issue commemorative resolutions, which do not have the force of law. The president of the US has the authority to declare any commemorative event by proclamation, but this is done infrequently. (Some state legislatures and governors proclaim special days, as do mayors of cities.)

So where do all these special days, weeks and months come from? The majority come from national organizations who use their observances for public outreach and to plan specific events. For special months regarding health issues, for example, you can expect to see more information disseminated, special commemorative walks and medical screenings during that month. The *Chase's* editorial staff includes a special day, week or month in the annual reference based on the authority of the organization observing it, how many years it has been observed, the amount of promotion and activities that are a part of it, its uniqueness and a variety of other factors. (This year, we've included a list of 2006 special months in our appendix section.)

Presidential Proclamations

As we noted above, the president has the authority to declare any commemorative event by proclamation. A good number of these will be proclamations for which there has been legislation giving continuing authority for a proclamation to be issued each year. Mother's Day, for example, has been proclaimed since 1914 by public resolution. The White House Clerk's Office initiates the issuing of these proclamations each year, since they are mandated by authorizing legislation. Of course, there will be new ones: Patriot Day (in the wake of the Sept 11, 2001, terrorist attacks) and the 2004 death of former president Ronald Reagan are recent examples. In *Chase's* we list proclamations that have continuing authority and those that have been issued consistently since 1995 in the main calendar of the book. In our text, ★ indicates a presidential proclamation. In our appendix, we also offer a complete list of proclamations issued from Jan 9, 2004 to June 16, 2005. (The most recent proclamations can be found at the Federal Register Online: www.access.gpo.gov.)

Events and Festivals

Chase's includes national and international special events and festivals—defined again by their uniqueness and their finite brief length of time. Sporting events; book, film, food and other festivals; seasonal celebrations; folkloric events (Groundhog Day, for example); music outings and more make up these types of entries. These entries are usually sponsored: they have contact information for the general public and all information in the entry comes from the sponsor (see below on sponsored events).

Anniversaries

Anniversaries include historic (creation of states, battles, inventions, publications of note, popular culture events, etc.) and biographical (birth or death anniversaries of notable personages) milestones.

Birthdays Today

Living celebrities in politics, the arts, sports and popular culture are included in the "Birthdays Today" section following each calendar day. If there is a question about the birth day or year, this is noted.

Spotlight

The tinted pages starting off *Chase's Calendar of Events* form the "Spotlight" section. In a book as comprehensive as *Chase's*, the reader may need a little help picking out significant anniversaries and events for the current year, and Spotlight is the answer to that need. For the Spotlight on the Past section, we cover years of the past in a day-by-day format beginning with a year a quarter century from 2005. Significant anniversaries are thus covered on a 25-year basis. For significant anniversaries 5 or 10 years ago, go to the main calendar.

New Style Versus Old Style Dates

Please note: dates for historic events can be assumed to be Gregorian calendar (New Style) dates unless "(OS)" appears after the date. This annotation means that the date in question is an Old Style or Julian date. Most of America's founders were born before 1752, when Great Britain and its colonies adopted the Gregorian calendar. As an example of this, we list George Washington's birthday as Feb 22, 1732, the Gregorian or New Style date. However, when he was born Great Britain and its colonies began the year on Mar 25, not Jan 1, so his Julian birthdate was Feb 11, 1731.

☆ Chase's 2006 Calendar of Events ☆

About Sponsored Events

Events for which there is individual or organizational sponsorship are listed with the name of the event, inclusive dates of observance, a brief description, estimated attendance figures and the sponsor's name and contact information. We obtain information for these events directly from the sponsors. There is no fee to be listed in *Chase's* and sponsors submit events to be chosen at the discretion of the *Chase's* editors. Neither the editors nor the publisher necessarily endorse these events.

Special Notice

Since *Chase's* is compiled months ahead of the year in question, inevitably event information will change. Sponsors may decide to change their dates, they may move or events beyond their control may even force cancellations. IT IS IMPERATIVE, IF FINANCIAL PLANS ARE TO BE MADE IN CONNECTION WITH DATES OR EVENTS LISTED HEREIN, THAT THE SPONSORS BE CONSULTED FOR FINAL INFORMATION. The sponsors are responsible for their own information.

Omissions and "Tentative" Dates

While we make every effort to be as comprehensive as possible, omissions do occur. Most often, these omissions happen because the information as to exact date was not available by press time and we could not list the event. Many fall sporting championships are regretfully not listed in *Chase's* for this reason.

Some sponsors include "tentative" dates in their listings. In these cases, while the sponsors are sure their event will take place and will be probably occur on that date, they realize that factors make them less than 100% sure. For events with tentative dates, be sure to check with the sponsor for final information.

About the CD-ROM

Enclosed is a CD-ROM of the text. For Windows users, this disk provides a quick way to conduct searches—either of a single topic or in combined areas. Search by state, by attendance, by keyword, by type of event and more. Installation instructions are on the disk.

Acknowledgments

A book the size of *Chase's* comes about through the care and attention of many organizations and people. The editors and publisher would like to thank the event sponsors; CVBs; chambers of commerce; tourism agencies; nonprofit organizations; professional and amateur sporting organizations; publicists; festival organizers; historians; museum directors; national, state and local government officials and many others who help us put together this reference every year. As we check and recheck information, the reference staffs of the Chicago, Evanston and Skokie libraries have always been there when we needed them.

Bill and Helen Chase are a continual inspiration as we prepare each new edition. There is no better champion for the unique American passion and pastime of creating holidays than Bill Chase! He continues to offer editorial advice that is always astute.

Our talented 2006 Spotlight essayists are Lee Sullivan (1906, *The Organization Man*, the San Francisco Earthquake and the *Challenger* disaster), Chris Sewell (AIDS in America, the Chernobyl disaster), Johnny Loftus (1956, 1981, Booker T. Washington and the Tuskegee Institute, Sigmund Freud); Scott Belliveau (Benjamin Franklin), Adrienne van den Beemt (Spotlight on People portraits) and Denise Betts Frank (Spotlight on People portraits).

The CD-ROM was created by the powerhouse team at FMA: Rich Shupe (design), Thomas Yeh (programming) and Jodi Rotondo (project management).

Finally, special thanks to our editorial and production colleagues at McGraw-Hill Trade, a division of The McGraw-Hill Companies: Marisa L'Heureux, Terry Stone, Martha Best, Gigi Grajdura, Vilma Peña, Nicole Chaparro, Jeanette Wojtyla, Charles Pelto, Tony Koumas, Arvydas Valiukenas, Karen Jozefowicz, Jeff Barg, Christopher Brown and Denise Duffy Fieldman.

Holly McGuire, Editor in Chief
Kathy Keil, Associate Editor
July 2005

Spotlight *2006 Anniversaries & Events*

The following section focuses on milestone anniversaries in 2006. In Spotlight on the Past we highlight six different years, from 200 years ago to 25 years ago, and provide an overview of the historical, cultural, scientific, economic and sporting activities that were happening in the year in question. In Spotlight on World Anniversaries and Spotlight on American Anniversaries, we give more detailed information on a selection of landmark anniversaries that are being observed in 2006. If observances are planned, addresses are included for further information. Spotlight on People concentrates on milestone birth or death anniversaries— from notable figures becoming centenarians to those even older (in 25-year increments). Finally, Spotlight on 2006 Events highlights noteworthy celebrations taking place this year.

Spotlight *Contents*

Spotlight on the Past **10**
1806 • 1856 • 1906 • 1931 • 1956 • 1981

Spotlight on World Anniversaries **29**
Wolfgang Amadeus Mozart's Birth Anniversary, 250 years • Sigmund Freud's Birth Anniversary, 150 years • Chernobyl Disaster and Legacy, 20 years

Spotlight on American Anniversaries **31**
Benjamin Franklin's Birth Anniversary, 300 years • Booker T. Washington's Birth Anniversary and the Anniversary of the Tuskegee Institute, 150 and 125 years • San Francisco Earthquake and Fire, 100 years • AIDS in America, 25 years • Space Shuttle Challenger Explodes, 20 years

Spotlight on People **36**
World History • American History • Literature • Children's Literature • Journalism • Education • Art • Architecture • Entertainment • Music • Science and Technology • Commerce • Exploration • Sports • Miscellaneous

Spotlight on 2006 Events **58**
FIFA World Cup • Games of the XX Winter Olympiad • IX Paralympic Games • Mozart 2006 • Lewis and Clark Expedition Bicentennial • Benjamin Franklin Tercentenary

Spotlight on the Past *milestone anniversary years*

1806 *200 years ago*

Landmark World Events

Jan 1 Napoleon abolished the French Revolutionary Calendar that had been used since Oct 24, 1793. Each of the 12 months of the calendar were divided into three *décades* of 10 days.

Jan 23 William Pitt the Younger, British prime minister, died in office. He was succeeded by William Wyndham Grenville.

Jan The United Kingdom established the Cape Colony (later to become South Africa).

Aug 6 Francis II abdicated as Holy Roman Emperor, and the Holy Roman Empire ceased to exist after centuries.

Oct 14 The Napoleonic Wars continued. On this day the French engaged the Prussian-Saxon army on two fronts in the Battle of Jena-Auerstädt. The French were victorious, and Prussia was soon conquered.

Nov 21 Napoleon issued the Berlin Decree calling for a blockade of British ports by the French, their allies and neutral parties. Any ship that had visited a British port was subject to seizure at a French-controlled port. Napoleon hoped to paralyze British commerce, and to a certain extent he did, but the blockade was hard to maintain and politically controversial for Napoleon.

Landmark US Events

Jan 1 The Lewis and Clark Expedition greeted the New Year with "the discharge of a volley of small arms" and later had a dinner of boiled elk and wappetoe (an edible tuberous plant). In the expedition journals, they record, "[we solaced] our thirst with our only beverage *pure water*."

Jan 10 President Thomas Jefferson addressed the chiefs of the Cherokee Nation, urging them to promote among their people a settled agrarian lifestyle instead of a nomadic one. He also emphasized US ownership of land west of the Mississippi. Jefferson concluded: "My children, this is what I wished to say to you: To go on in learning to cultivate the earth and to avoid war."

Jan 17 The first child born at the White House was James Madison Randolph—Thomas Jefferson's grandson.

Mar 23 The Lewis and Clark Expedition left Fort Clatsop and began their journey home.

Mar 29 Congress authorized and President Thomas Jefferson signed legislation for construction of the Great National Pike (or National Road). This road, whose first section was begun in 1811 and finished in 1818, would follow Nemacolin's Path (an old Native American trail) and eventually stretched from Cumberland, MD, to Illinois. This was the first federally funded multistate road, and it facilitated settlement in territories west of the Allegheny Mountains.

Apr 17 In the aftermath of the Barbary Wars, the US Senate ratified the Treaty of Tripoli, which dictated terms of peace and resumption of commercial relations. The treaty also reiterated that religion would never disrupt the new détente between the two nations (US and Tripoli).

July 25 William Clark dubbed a rock formation near what is today Billings, MT, "Pompeys Pillar" after Sacagawea's son, whom Clark had playfully nicknamed Pompey. Clark signed the rock and the signature remains today—the only physical souvenir of the expedition.

July US Army lieutenant Zebulon Montgomery Pike led an expedition into the American Southwest to explore the Arkansas and Red rivers. In November, he sighted the mountain in Colorado that would be named for him.

Sept 23 The Lewis and Clark Expedition returned to St. Louis, MO. Wrote Clark in the Corps journals: "We suffered the party to fire off their pieces as a salute to the town. We were met by all the village and received a hearty welcome from its inhabitants." Lewis and Clark journeyed on to Washington, DC, where they were greeted with great fanfare.

Culture

PUBLICATIONS 📖

Fiction

- *The Wild Irish Girl: A National Tale*, Sydney Owenson, Lady Morgan
- Gothic novels were the rage. *Zofloya*, by Charlotte Dacre, and the six-volume *Vicissitudes Abroad*, by Agnes Maria Bennett, were two popular novels of 1806.

Nonfiction

- *A Compendius Dictionary of The English Language*, published by Noah Webster, was his first dictionary—a precursor to his landmark *American Dictionary of the English Language* published in 1828. For the first time, a dictionary reflected America rather than England. There were 38,000 entries and American spellings were included ("center" as opposed to "centre") rather than English ones. Webster was innovative in including scientific and technical terms. A dedicated scholar, Webster wasn't above a little grandstanding: he claimed to be a better lexicographer than Dr. Samuel Johnson.
- *Chironomia*, by Gilbert Austin, was an influential English text on elocution that focused on body movement and persuasive gesture. It was a popular work in the British Isles and America for performers of all kinds and is still referred to today.

Children's Literature

- *Rhymes for the Nursery*, by sisters Ann and Jane Taylor. One featured rhyme was the now classic "Twinkle, Twinkle, Little Star."

Notes

- Future author Washington Irving was admitted to the bar in New York.
- Future poet and novelist Walter Scott became Principle Clerk in Edinburgh, Scotland's Court of Session.

THEATER

NOV 17 The Sans Pareil Theatre opened at London, England. Later renamed the Adelphi Theatre, it is still in operation today.

MUSIC

MAR 29 A revised version of Beethoven's opera *Fidelio* was held at the opera house in Vienna, Austria. At a second performance in April, a dispute over payment resulted in Beethoven's abrupt cancellation of further performances, and the opera was not staged again until 1814.

ART 🎨

- Napoleon commissioned the Arc de Triomphe in Paris to celebrate his victory at the Battle of Austerlitz. It wasn't finished until 1836.
- *Portrait of Napoleon on the Imperial Throne*, Jean-Auguste-Dominique Ingres
- *The Death of Nelson*, Benjamin West
- *Satan Comes to the Gates of Hell*, William Blake

Science and Technology 🧪

JAN 13 Francis Beaufort, a young British naval commander restlessly waiting to embark from Portsmouth Harbor on the storeship *Woolwich*, laid out in his journal the first version of a wind-force scale that, with some improvements, would later become the Beaufort Scale.

- French scientists Louis-Nicolas Vauquelin and Pierre Jean Robiquet isolated the first amino acid, which they named aspargine—since they were studying asparagus.

Commerce and New Products

- Englishman Ralph Wedgwood patented "carbonated paper," which was a piece of paper soaked in ink and then dried that allowed for copies when a stylus was pressed through an overlying piece of paper.
- America's first union, the cordwainer's union of shoemakers (formed in 1805) disbanded. They had been on strike in Philadelphia, PA, and a judge ordered them arrested for criminal conspiracy.

1806 Deaths

- Benjamin Banneker, "first black man of science," surveyor of Washington, DC
- Rétif de la Bretonne, French author
- Charles Augustin Coulomb, French physicist for whom the

unit of electrical charge, the coulomb, is named
- Jean-Honoré Fragonard, French painter
- Jupiter Hammon, first published African-American poet
- Vincenzo Lunardi, Italian balloonist known as the "dare-devil aeronaut" who made the first hydrogen balloon ascent in England; he was a celebrity in Europe and the United Kingdom.
- Mungo Park, Scottish explorer of Africa
- William Pitt the Younger, British prime minister
- George Stubbs, English painter renowned for horse portraiture
- William V of Orange
- George Wythe, first US law professor, mentor to Thomas Jefferson, signer of the Declaration of Independence

1856 *150 years ago*

Landmark World Events

Mar 30 Russia, France, Great Britain, Sardinia-Piedmont and Turkey signed the Treaty of Paris, which ended the Crimean War and recognized the sovereignty of Turkey. The three-year war had taken more than 250,000 lives.

Apr 11 The Costa Rican army successfully prevented the Nicaraguan forces of American strongman William Walker

WILLIAM WALKER

The 19th century abounded with militaristic adventurers seeking to set up their own fiefdoms and colonies in underdeveloped countries. American William Walker, a native of Tennessee, was one. In the early 1850s, he tried to establish a breakaway "republic" in Baja California and Sonora, Mexico. Failing that, he moved his imperialistic schemes to Nicaragua in 1855, aligning himself with a leftist faction. With financing from some rogue American businessmen, Walker controlled Nicaragua until 1857. When his hold on the country collapsed, he surrendered to the US Navy, but still made two more sallies to Central America. In Honduras in 1860, he was executed.

from invading their country in the Battle of Rivas. Apr 11 is now a national holiday commemorating this victory.

July 12 American adventurer William Walker declared himself president of Nicaragua and eked out a presidency until May 1857.

Oct 8 Chinese officials boarded the ship *Arrow* and imprisoned its crew on suspicion that they were pirates. Since the ship may have been flying a British

flag, the British used this as a pretext to reignite military hostilities. Thus began the Second Opium War between China and Britain—with France joining the British (the first Opium War was 1839–1842). Opium was only part of the story: the real battles were over Western access to lucrative Chinese ports and trading. The Second Opium War lasted until 1860.

Landmark US Events

Jan In Ohio, before her pursuers caught her, escaped slave Margaret Garner killed her daughter so that the child would never see bondage again.

Feb 15 The USS *Supply* left Smyrna, Syria, with 21 camels destined for the American West, where they were to be tried out for use instead of horses.

May 19/20 US Senator Charles Sumner of Massachusetts made his famous "On the Crime Against Kansas" speech on the Senate floor. It was a two-day speech.

May 22 Two days after US Senator Charles Sumner denounced the Kansas-Nebraska Act as a swindle, South Carolina Congressman Preston Brooks entered the Senate and beat Sumner with his walking cane until it broke apart. It took Sumner three years to recuperate from his injuries.

The Ravages of Slavery

Margaret Garner, her husband and four children escaped their bondage in Kentucky by crossing into Ohio. But as pursuing US marshals and their slave owner, Archibald Gaines, caught up with them, Garner killed her daughter with a butcher knife and attempted to kill her other children and herself—to prevent their being returned to slavery. The Fugitive Slave Act of 1850 dictated that slaves remained slaves even when in non-slave states. The Garners were returned to their Kentucky owner, who sold them to a slaveholder in New Orleans, LA. The incident sparked national outrage. (American Nobel Literature Laureate Toni Morrison based her 1987 novel *Beloved* on this case.)

May 21–24 The territory of Kansas was a bloody battleground as proslavery and antislavery forces battled over the future state's status as a slave or free state. On May 21, proslavery forces sacked the town of Lawrence, KS. There was only one death—that of a raider. On May 24, abolitionists led by John Brown made a revenge attack at Pottawatomie Creek. Five proslavery men were hacked to death.

June 2 The Democratic presidential convention opened in Cincinnati, OH. Moderate James Buchanan won the nomination.

June 16 America's only crowned king—James Jesse Strang, crowned king of Mormons in 1850—was wounded by assassins at Beaver Island, MI. He died June 19, at Voree, WI.

June 17 In Philadelphia, PA, the new political party, the Republicans, opened their convention and picked their first-ever presidential candidate, John C.

Frémont. The key issue for the Republicans was the abolition of slavery. William Dayton was picked as the vice presidential candidate, winning over a little-known Illinois politician, Abraham Lincoln. The GOP political slogan was "Free Speech. Free Press. Free Soil. Free Men. Frémont and Victory."

Aug 18 The US Copyright Office added dramatic compositions to works protected under US copyright.

Nov 4 Democrat James Buchanan, a supporter of compromise in the growing slavery debate, was elected president, defeating Republican candidate John C. Frémont. Buchanan received 174 electoral votes to Frémont's 114. This was the first election featuring a Republican presidential candidate.

• America's first kindergarten opened at Watertown, WI.

• Auburn University was founded in Alabama.

Culture

Publications

Fiction
• *Madame Bovary*, Gustave Flaubert
• *Dred*, Harriet Beecher Stowe
• *The Piazza Tales*, Herman Melville
• *Rudin*, Ivan Turgenev

Nonfiction
• *Arctic Explorations: The Second Grinnell Expedition in Search of Sir John Franklin*, by explorer Elisha Kent Kane, described his trek of 1853–1855 in search of survivors of the ill-fated Franklin expedition.

Children's Literature
• *The Last of the Huggermuggers*, Christopher Pearse Cranch

Poetry
• *The Panorama*, John Greenleaf Whittier
• "Brahma" and "Two Rivers," Ralph Waldo Emerson
• Walt Whitman published the second edition of *Leaves of Grass*.

Spotlight on the Past *milestone anniversary years*

THEATER

JAN *The Feast at Solhaug*, Henrik Ibsen. This play was the first commercial success for the young playwright.

APR 28 Eight-year-old Ellen Terry—the future great actress—made her stage debut at London, England's Princess's Theatre playing the part of Mamillius in Shakespeare's *A Winter's Tale*.

MUSIC

- German composer Richard Wagner finished *The Valkyrie* and began work on *Siegfried*.

ART

- *The Source*, Jean-Auguste-Dominique Ingres
- *Woman with a Rake*, Jean-François Millet

Photography

- Nadar (Gaspard-Félix Tournachon), the French novelist and pioneering photographer, took the first pictures from a hot-air balloon

Science and Technology

- Skeletal remains of an ancient Ice Age form of human were first found in a cave of the Neander Valley in Germany. Such humans were later termed Neanderthals.
- Augustinian monk and botanist Gregor Mendel began his first experiments with genetics in his Moravian monastery's garden.

- At the request of a businessman whose beer was often turning sour, Louis Pasteur did some analysis and discovered the role of microorganisms (yeast) in the fermentation process.

Commerce and New Products

- Gail Borden received a patent for condensed milk.
- Elisha Otis installed the first passenger elevator in New York City.
- The printing telegraph ticker was patented.
- Henry Bessamer introduced his process for making less expensive steel.
- The New York and Mississippi Valley Printing Telegraph Company, founded in 1851, merged with other telegraph companies to become Western Union Telegraph Company.
- Theodore Woodruff patented the railroad sleeping car.
- The US claimed the four southern islands of Tuvalo in the Pacific in order to mine guano deposits (a fertilizer) there.
- Thomas Burberry founded the company of the same name in Basingstoke, England.

- The sporting goods company Orvis was established in Vermont.

Sports

ARCHERY

- Archery was fast becoming a serious sport in England. In 1856, Horace Ford, a champion English archer, published *Archery, Its Theory and Practice*.

BASEBALL

- In Chicago, IL, the Union Baseball Club was formed.

GOLF

- France's first golf club, the Pau, was founded.

1856 Deaths

- Adolphe Charles Adams, French composer (*Giselle* and "O Holy Night")
- Amadeo Avogadro, Italian scientist, for whom Avogadro's number is named (the number of molecules in one mole)
- Thomas Doughty, American artist
- Heinrich Heine, German poet and critic
- Robert Schumann, German composer
- James Jesse Strang, King of Mormons

1906 *100 years ago*

Landmark World Events

FEB 15 The Labour Representation Committee in Great Britain took the name Labour Party.

APR 7 The Act of Algeciras affirmed international trade rights in Morocco, ending the First Moroccan Crisis, a tense standoff between France and Germany. Alignments established during the months of negotiations foreshadowed First World War alliances.

APR 23 In Russia, Czar Nicholas II enacted the Fundamental Laws, granting limited civil liberties and effectively establishing a constitutional monarchy. The czar had promised reforms in October 1905 to defuse widespread political unrest.

MAY 19 The Simplon Tunnel opened, joining Brig, Switzerland, and Iselle, Italy, with a 12-mile railway line—one of the world's longest railway tunnels.

JUNE 22 Sweden formally adopted its national flag.

JULY 12 A French appeals court officially exonerated Alfred Dreyfus, Jewish army captain wrongly convicted of treason in 1894. The Dreyfus Affair led to separation of church and state in France and caused lasting political divisions between right and left.

JULY 20 Finland established a unicameral parliament elected by universal suffrage, becoming the first nation in Europe to give women the right to vote.

SEPT 18 A typhoon ravaged Hong Kong, killing 10,000.

NOV 3 In Berlin, the Second International Radio Telegraphic Conference proposed a new wireless distress signal: SOS. After its use during the sinking of the *Titanic* in 1912, SOS became the standard distress signal at sea.

• US President Theodore Roosevelt received the Nobel Peace Prize.

Landmark US Events

MAR 19 The US Supreme Court allowed an appeal for Ed Johnson, a black man convicted for raping a white woman in Chattanooga, TN, but that night, a crowd kidnapped him from the city jail, then tortured and lynched him. This challenge to the Supreme Court resulted in a criminal trial in 1909—the first time the Supreme Court held a criminal trial and the first time officers of the law (a sheriff and two deputies) were held responsible for a lynching.

APR 18 A massive earthquake struck San Francisco just before dawn. Fires burned for three days, destroying almost five square miles of the city center. Some 3,000 died in the earthquake and ensuing fires. More than half of the city was left homeless. (See "Spotlight on American Anniversaries.")

MAY 18 Anarchist Alexander Berkman was released from prison after serving a 14-year sentence for attempting to assassinate steel magnate Henry Frick. Berkman and associate Emma Goldman would emerge as leaders of America's anarchist movement.

MAY 19 The Federated Boys' Clubs was founded, later to become the Boys' and Girls' Clubs of America.

JUNE 25 Playboy Harry Thaw shot celebrated architect Stanford White dead at Madison Square Garden. Thaw's wife, showgirl Evelyn Nesbit, was White's former mistress. Newspapers churned the slaying into a scandal, dubbing it the "trial of the century."

JUNE 30 Congress passed the Pure Food and Drugs Act and the Meat Inspection Act, thanks in part to public outcry generated by Upton Sinclair's activist novel *The Jungle* and Samuel Hopkins Adams's exposé *The Great American Fraud*.

SEPT 24 Devils Tower National Monument in Wyoming became the first US national monument to be declared off-limits to developers by US President Theodore Roosevelt.

SEPT 29 William Howard Taft was named provisional governor of Cuba. US forces occupied Cuba in September, intervening against insurgents who were threatening to topple the republic. The occupation would last until 1909.

Nov 14 Theodore Roosevelt became the first US president to travel abroad in office, arriving in Panama to inspect work on the canal. He later boasted, "I took the Isthmus, started the canal and then left Congress not to debate the canal, but to debate me."

Culture

PUBLICATIONS

Fiction

- *The Man of Property*, by John Galsworthy—first novel in The Forsythe Saga
- *The Jungle*, by Upton Sinclair —exposed abuses in the meat-packing industry
- *The Four Million*, by O. Henry —second collection of short stories
- *White Fang*, by Jack London— classic novel of Alaska

Nonfiction

- *The Writings of Henry David Thoreau*—standard edition of his works
- *The Great American Fraud* by Samuel Hopkins Adams— exposé of patent medicines, helped hasten the passage of the Pure Food and Drugs Act

Journalism

- President Theodore Roosevelt coined the term "muckraker" in a speech.

Comics

- *Little Nemo in Slumberland*, by Winsor McKay

Notes

- Italian poet Giosuè Carducci received the Nobel Prize for Literature.

THEATER (INCLUDING OPERA)

- *The Doctor's Dilemma*, by George Bernard Shaw— comedy satirized medicine
- *I quattro rusteghi*, by Ermanno Wolf-Ferrari—comic opera
- *Forty-five Minutes from Broadway*, by George M. Cohan—hit musical

MUSIC

- *Chamber Symphony in E Major*, by Arnold Schoenberg—featured innovative orchestration
- "Anchors Aweigh," by Alfred Miles and Charles Zimmerman —US Navy anthem

ART

- *Portrait of Gertrude Stein* by Pablo Picasso—presaged his embrace of Cubism
- American art collector Charles Lang Freer presented his Oriental art collection to the US government; basis for the Smithsonian's Freer Gallery which opened in 1923.

Science and Technology

FEB 10 HMS *Dreadnought* was launched, ushering in the era of fast, powerful, modern battleships. The British vessel gave its name to a new class of warships, sparking an international arms race.

MAR 18 Romanian inventor Trajan Vuia flew the first monoplane aircraft, staying aloft for a distance of 40 feet.

MAY 22 Orville and Wilbur Wright patented their "flying machine." After their 1903 flight the brothers spent the next three years in relative secrecy, waiting to obtain a patent. Skeptics worldwide disputed their claim to have flown first.

OCT 23 In France, Albert Santos-Dumont was credited with the first observed powered flight in Europe. He piloted his box-kite aircraft for nearly 200 feet.

NOV 20 Greenleaf W. Pickard made radio practical when he patented the crystal detector. Before vacuum tubes, radios relied on crystals to receive broadcasts.

DEC 24 America's first radio program was broadcast by Reginald A. Fessenden from his experimental station in Brant Rock, MA. Ships' wireless operators heard two musical selections and a poetry reading.

Notes

- Joseph John Thomson received the Nobel Prize for Physics; Henri Moissan received the

Nobel Prize for Chemistry; Camillo Golgi and Santiago Ramón y Cajal received the Nobel Prize for Physiology or Medicine.

Commerce and New Products

Jan 12 The Dow Jones Industrial Average closed above 100 for the first time.

Jan 13 Brush salesman Alfred Carl Fuller started the Capital Brush Company in Hartford, CT. Initially, Fuller manufactured brushes between the furnace and coal bin in his sister's basement.

Feb 19 Will Keith Kellogg and Charles D. Brolin incorporated the Battle Creek Toasted Corn Flake Company in Battle Creek, MI.

Mar Henry Ford ordered 2,000 of Harvey Firestone's innovative pneumatic tires to equip his new Model T. The largest tire order ever placed, it marked the beginning of a long relationship between the two companies.

June 6 Frank Gannett purchased a half-interest in the *Elmira Gazette*, a New York newspaper, beginning his media empire.

Sept 17 Lehman Brothers and Goldman, Sachs underwrote the public offering of Sears, Roebuck & Co., financing the burgeoning retailer's expansion.

Oct 15 Benjamin Altman moved his successful Manhattan department store, B. Altman & Co., uptown to Fifth Avenue and 34th Street. Eventually occupying an entire city block, the building would become a New York landmark.

Nov 20 Rolls-Royce, Ltd. was incorporated in England by Charles Stewart Rolls and Frederick Henry Royce.

Sports

Auto Racing

June 26 The first Grand Prix was held, at Le Mans in France. Driving a 90-hp Renault, Hungarian Ferenc Szisz won the two-day, 12-lap event at an average speed of 62.9 mph. Of 32 starters, only 11 were running at the finish.

Baseball

Aug 9 Jack Taylor of the St. Louis Cardinals set a record for pitching complete games, finishing his 187th in a row. Taylor's streak extended over six seasons and ended with his next start on August 13.

Oct 14 In the first crosstown World Series, the Chicago White Sox beat the rival Cubs, four games to two. The "Hitless Wonders" won decisively, despite hitting just .198 for the series.

Bicycling

July 29 Rene Pottier triumphed in the Tour de France with wins in five stages. He would take his own life before the next year's race.

Football

Mar 31 After a slew of gridiron deaths, the Intercollegiate Athletic Association of the United States was organized to improve safety. The body legalized the forward pass to open up play. In 1910, the IAAUS would become the NCAA.

• Undefeated Princeton was crowned national champion with a record of 9-0-1.

Horse Racing

May 2 Sir Huon, ridden by Roscoe Troxler, won the Kentucky Derby by two lengths, with a time of two minutes and eight-and-four-fifths seconds.

Soccer

Apr 21 Everton FC won its first FA Cup, beating favored Newcastle United 1–0 on a goal by Alex "Sandy" Young with 13 minutes left to play.

Tennis

July 5 Dorothea Douglass won her third Wimbledon singles title (of seven); Hugh "Laurie" Doherty won his fifth-straight title the day before.

Yachting

June 11 The inaugural Transpacific Yacht Race from Los Angeles to Honolulu began. Harry Sinclair's *Lurline* won in 12 days and 10 hours, outrunning two other boats over the 2,225-mile distance.

Spotlight on the Past *milestone anniversary years*

1906 Deaths

- Susan Brownell Anthony, reformer and leading advocate of women's suffrage, who was arrested in 1872 for voting (then a criminal act)
- Alexander Johnston Cassatt, early American railroad executive
- Paul Cézanne, influential Postimpressionist painter of still lifes and landscapes
- Pierre Curie, pioneering radioactivity researcher who with his wife, Marie Curie, won the 1903 Nobel Prize for Physics; he was hit by a wagon in a Paris street.
- William "Buck" Ewing, Baseball Hall of Fame catcher considered one of the 19th century's best; credited with being the first to crouch immediately under the batter
- Marshall Field, department store entrepreneur who said, "Give the lady what she wants!"
- Henrik Ibsen, Norwegian playwright considered the father of modern drama
- Samuel Pierpont Langley, American astronomer, physicist, and aviation pioneer for whom Langley Air Force base in Virginia is named
- Russell Sage, financier and railroad speculator who pioneered puts and calls on Wall Street
- Carl Schurz, American journalist, political reformer and Civil War army officer
- Stanford White, American architect who designed many New York landmarks

1931 *75 years ago*

Landmark World Events

Mar Managua, the capital of Nicaragua, was almost completely destroyed by an earthquake and the resulting fires. Some 2,000 residents died.

Apr 14 King Alfonso XIII abdicated and the Second Spanish Republic was created.

Aug 24 As the world's economic crisis worsened, Ramsay MacDonald, British Labour prime minister, resigned in

FOLLOWING A RABBIT-PROOF FENCE

In Australia, Molly Craig, a 14-year-old Aboriginal child taken from her family to a government training institution, escaped from the facility with two young cousins and led them through the Australian desert on a 1,000-mile journey that took nine weeks. The girls followed a "rabbit-proof fence" to find their way home to Jigalong. From 1905 to 1971, Australia forcibly removed Aboriginal children from their families in an effort to assimilate them into mainstream, Anglicized society.

response to his party's ineffectiveness, but governed in a coalition cabinet until 1935.

Sept 8 Nazi party head Adolf Hitler's half-niece, Geli Raubal, committed suicide in his Munich apartment. They were apparently involved in a romance.

Sept 18 Japan invaded Manchuria and within five months controlled the Chinese province.

- The worst flooding disaster in China occurred when the overflowing Hwang Ho (Yellow River) in China killed four million people. The Hwang Ho, which frequently floods, has been dubbed "China's Sorrow."
- China's Yangtze River also flooded in 1931 with devastating results: 400,000 deaths and 50 million homeless.
- Sir Oswald Mosley formed the fascist New Party in Britain.
- Albert the Great (1207–1280) was canonized a Catholic saint.

Landmark US Events

Mar 3 Herbert Hoover signed into law a bill making "The Star-Spangled Banner" the official US national anthem.

Mar 22 Secretary of Commerce Robert P. Lamont declared that the economy was improving and increased employment was on the horizon.

Apr 6 Nine black youths, ages 12 to 20, went on trial at Scottsboro, AL, accused of raping two white women on a freight

THE GREAT DEPRESSION—1931

- US unemployment reached 15.9 percent (in Chicago, it was 40 percent).
- The US GNP fell 8.5 percent. The GNP had declined a total of 17.9 percent since 1929.
- In the US, 2,294 banks failed. On Dec 11, the Bank of the United States in New York collapsed—it was the largest US bank failure in history.
- 28,285 American businesses went bankrupt.
- "Hoover blankets" were newspapers used as covers for the homeless.
- Europe began to feel the adverse affects of the US's Smoot-Hawley Tariff Act of 1930.
- Germany, the United Kingdom and Japan went off the gold standard.
- The Plains states were hit by a severe drought. This was the beginning of the Dust Bowl years.
- Jane Matilda Bolin became the first black woman to graduate from the Yale School of Law (she later because the first black woman judge in the US).
- Construction workers at the RCA Building put up a little Christmas tree. (In 1933, the first formal tree lighting ceremony took place. Today, it's the big Rockefeller Tree Lighting.)

train. Eight of the accused were sentenced to death; the 12-year-old was spared. Hours before the execution date of July 30, the eight were granted a stay after appeals were made on their behalf. The "Scottsboro Boys" were retried in 1933, but the trials dragged on until 1937. None of them were executed.

MAY 1 The Empire State Building officially opened in midtown Manhattan, New York City. President Herbert Hoover "opened" the world's tallest building by pressing a button from the White House that turned on the Empire State's electric lights.

MAY 1 Reno, NV, enacted a law requiring a six-week residency for a divorce.

JULY 1 Aviator Wiley Post and navigator Harold Gatty finished an around-the-world flight that started June 23—setting a new record.

OCT 18 American inventor Thomas Alva Edison died at his home in Glenmount, NJ. On the evening of his funeral, many corporations dimmed their electric lights in respect.

OCT 25 The George Washington Bridge, linking upper Manhattan to New Jersey over the Hudson River, opened. On this day, more than 55,000 vehicles and one horse crossed. The 4,760-foot-long bridge had a lower level that was not opened to traffic until 1962.

NOV 24 Chicago mobster (although his business card said furniture dealer) Al Capone was sentenced to 11 years in a federal prison after being found guilty in October of tax evasion.

DEC 10 Jane Addams was awarded the Nobel Peace Prize at Oslo, Norway, but on this day was being admitted to a hospital.

Culture

PUBLICATIONS 📖

Fiction

- *The Good Earth*, by Pearl S. Buck was America's #1 bestseller
- *The Waves*, Virginia Woolf
- *The Dream Life of Balso Snell*, Nathanael West
- *Sanctuary*, William Faulkner
- *Grand Hotel*, Vicki Baum
- *The Glass Key*, by Dashiell Hammett

Nonfiction

NOV 30 *The Joy of Cooking* was self-published by Irma

Rombauer. The cookbook—America's favorite all-purpose cookbook—was innovative in having an "action format" (chronologically ordered ingredients followed by numbered instructions) that is now commonplace in cookbooks.

- *Contract Bridge Blue Book*, Ely Culbertson

Children's Literature

- *The Story of Babar*, by Jean de Brunhoff, was published in France. It came out in the US two years later.

Comics

Oct 4 Dick Tracy made his comic strip debut in the *Detroit Daily Mirror* in "Plainclothes Tracy."

Notes

- The Nobel Prize for Literature was awarded posthumously to Swedish poet Erik Axel Karlfeldt, who had died Apr 8, 1931. Karlfeldt had refused the award in 1918.

FILM

- *The Champ*, directed by King Vidor, was Hollywood's classic boxing melodrama. It starred Wallace Beery (who shared the 1932 Academy Award for Best Actor with Fredric March) and Jackie Cooper.
- *Dr. Jekyll and Mr. Hyde* starred Oscar-winning Fredric March.
- *The Sin of Madelon Claudet* starred Oscar-winning Helen Hayes.
- *City Lights*, directed by Charlie Chaplin. Despite the prevailing

---

"GOOD TO THE LAST GASP!"

Thursdays aren't usually premier dates for Hollywood pictures, but in 1931, the scheduled Friday debut for *Dracula* fell on the 13th. Director Tod Browning, confessing to a superstitious nature, asked that the film (advertised as "Good to the Last Gasp!") be moved up a day. Consequently, the horror classic opened on Thursday, Feb 12, at the Roxy Theatre in New York. Its star, Bela Lugosi, was a Hungarian actor who had created the stage role of Dracula. He campaigned vigorously to take on the movie role, and his success meant instant stardom but also the straitjacket of only being offered horror roles in the future. *Dracula* was a financial success, helping the shaky standing of Universal Studios. The film also firmly fixed in the popular mind the image of the Count: the tuxedoed and caped, elegant vampire as seducer of women.

---

switch to sound, this film was silent.

- *M*, directed by Fritz Lang, made Peter Lorre famous as a child killer hunted down by the criminal underground.
- *Frankenstein* starred Boris Karloff.
- *Public Enemy* starred James Cagney and Jean Harlow.

Mar 11 The great German director F.W. Murnau died in an auto accident in Hollywood, CA.

RADIO

May 1 Singer Kate Smith made her radio debut with "When the Moon Comes over the Mountain."

Dec 25 The Metropolitan Opera began broadcasting its Saturday matinee. Texaco sponsored the broadcasts from 1931 to 2004—the longest commercial patronage in broadcast history.

THEATER

- *Of Thee I Sing*, George S. Kaufman with Morrie Ryskind and Ira Gershwin (Pulitzer)
- *Cavalcade*, Noël Coward

ART

- *Red, White, and Blue*, Georgia O'Keeffe
- *The Persistence of Memory*, Salvador Dali
- *Frida and Diego Rivera*, Frida Kahlo
- *The Midnight Ride of Paul Revere*, Grant Wood
- *Hotel Room*, Edward Hopper
- *Woman with Yellow Hair*, Pablo Picasso
- Picasso illustrated a new translation of Ovid's *Metamorphoses* with 30 etchings.

Architecture

- The Home Insurance Building, the world's first skyscraper, was demolished in Chicago, IL. The 10-story building, constructed from 1884 to 1885, had a steel frame which carried all the weight. The walls provided no support but hung like curtains on the frame. This method of construction had revolutionized architecture, allowing for taller and taller buildings.

Music

- *Belshazzar's Feast*, William Walton
- American hepcat Cab Calloway took over as house bandleader at Harlem's Cotton Club.
- English composer Edward Elgar was made a baronet. He also composed *Nursery Suite*.

Science and Technology

May 27 The first flight into the stratosphere: Paul Kipfer and Auguste Piccard launched from Augsburg, Germany, in a balloon with a pressurized cabin. They rose almost 10 miles.

Sept Anne and Charles Lindbergh flew across the North Pacific to China, where they viewed the devastation caused by flooding of the Yangtze.

- American chemist Harold Urey discovered deuterium, or heavy hydrogen.

- Max Knott and Ernst Ruska invented the electron microscope.
- The coaxial cable was patented.

Notes

- Friedrick Bergius and Carl Bosch received the Nobel Prize for Chemistry; Otto Warburg received the Nobel Prize for Physiology or Medicine. No prize was awarded in Physics.

Commerce and New Products

Mar 18 The first electric razor was marketed by Schick, Inc.

Oct Waldo Semon, an employee of B.F. Goodrich, patented bubble gum.

Nov 19 Dr. Earle Haas patented the first modern tampon. He later marketed his products under the name Tampax.

Sports 🏀

Auto Racing

May 30 Louis Schneider won the Indianapolis 500.

Baseball

Oct The St. Louis Cardinals triumphed over the Philadelphia Athletics in four games to three in the World Series.

Football

Mar 31 Legendary Notre Dame football coach Knute Rockne died in a plane crash at Bazaar, KS. He was 43 years old. Eulogizing for a shocked nation,

Will Rogers said, "You died one of our national heroes."

Horse Racing

May Twenty Grand won the Kentucky Derby.

Soccer

Sept 5 22-year-old Scottish goalkeeper John Thomson, playing for Glasgow Celtic, was kneed in the head during an opponent's shot on goal and subsequently died.

Tennis

- S.B. Wood was the male Wimbledon champion, while Cilley Aussem was the women's champion.

1931 Deaths

- George Fisher Baker, American financier
- Bix Beiderbecke, American jazz cornettist
- David Belasco, American theatrical impresario, "The Bishop of Broadway"
- Arnold Bennett, English novelist, playwright and critic
- Lizzie Bliss, cofounder of MOMA
- Charles Comiskey, Baseball Hall of Fame first baseman, manager and executive
- Roger Connor, Baseball Hall of Fame outfielder who hit more home runs (136) than any other 19th-century player
- Melvil Dewey, American librarian and creator of the Dewey decimal book classification system
- Charlie Dryden, sportswriter, of the Washington Senators he

once quipped: "First in war, first in peace and last in the American League"

- Thomas Alva Edison, American inventive genius
- Daniel Chester French, American sculptor who carved the huge statue of Abraham Lincoln for the Lincoln Memorial

- Kahlil Gibran, Lebanese-American poet
- Frank Harris, Irish-American journalist
- Ban Johnson, Baseball Hall of Fame executive who transformed the minor Western League into the major American League in 1901
- Erik Axel Karlfeldt, Swedish poet
- André Michelin, French industrialist
- F.W. Murnau, German film director
- Carl Nielsen, Danish composer
- Anna Pavlova, Russian ballerina
- Knute Rockne, legendary Notre Dame football coach
- Arthur Schnitzler, Austrian playwright, novelist and medical doctor
- Ida B. Wells, civil rights crusader
- Eugène-Auguste Ysaÿe, Belgian violinist

1956 *50 years ago*

Landmark World Events

MAR 2 Morocco proclaimed independence from France. On Apr 7, it was granted independence from its other colonial ruler, Spain.

JULY 25 On its way to New York the Italian luxury liner *Andrea Doria* collided with the smaller Swedish liner *Stockholm*, near Nantucket, MA. The *Andrea Doria* sank 11 hours later; 51 passengers died; 1,634 were rescued.

JULY 26 Egyptian president Gamal Abdel Nasser nationalized the Suez Canal, prompting an attack on Oct 29 from Israel and its allies, Great Britain and France.

OCT Construction of Brazil's new capital, Brasília, began.

NOV 4 Hungary's uprising against Soviet occupation was crushed.

NOV 6 President Eisenhower achieved a cease-fire in the Arab-Israeli hostilities, also known as the Suez War. But the political and physical damage done would lead to the Six Day War in 1967.

DEC 2 Fidel Castro and Che Guevara landed in Cuba to fight the Batista dictatorship.

- The Nobel Peace Prize was not awarded this year.
- *Time* magazine's "Man of the Year" award for 1956 went to the Hungarian Patriot, honoring that country's revolt against the Soviet Union.

Landmark US Events

FEB 22 Organizers of the Montgomery, AL, bus boycott and their supporters were arrested after an ultimatum from white city leaders was issued. The boycott ended Nov 13 with a Supreme Court ruling implementing the integration of Montgomery's bus system.

MAY 21 The US tested the world's first hydrogen bomb on the Bikini Atoll (Namu Islet) in the Pacific Ocean.

JUNE 29 President Eisenhower signed a bill providing $33.5 billion for highway construction, effectively creating the country's interstate highway system.

OCT 31 A US Navy team stood at the South Pole—only the third team to do so (after Amundsen and Scott's expeditions in 1912).

NOV President Eisenhower was re-elected. He took 57 percent of the popular vote to defeat Adlai Stevenson.

- President Eisenhower appointed William Brennan to the US Supreme Court.

THE ORGANIZATION MAN

"I was an organization man myself," William H. Whyte admitted in 1986, thirty years after he wrote his groundbreaking social study, which caused a sensation. *The Organization Man* stayed on bestseller lists for a year, selling two million copies in a dozen languages.

Whyte argued that the growth of corporate culture was suppressing individual initiative and creativity, blunting America's competitive edge. His thesis struck a nerve with white collar workers striving to climb the corporate ladder in postwar America.

Like Sloan Wilson's novel *The Man in the Gray Flannel Suit*, Whyte's title became a catchphrase for anonymous conformity. The book joined a stream of 1950s works that challenged middle-class assumptions, such as David Riesman's *The Lonely Crowd*.

An editor at *Fortune* magazine, Whyte drew many of his conclusions from life in the large housing development at Park Forest, IL. Yet he avoided passing judgment on suburban consumerism, insisting, "There will be no strictures in this book against . . . ranch wagons, or television sets, or gray flannel suits."

Instead, *The Organization Man* encouraged corporations to embrace innovation and risk. "I speak of individualism within organization life," Whyte noted. "The fault is not in organization, in short; it is in our worship of it."

Culture

PUBLICATIONS

Fiction

- *Peyton Place*, by Grace Metalious, was a runaway bestseller about the seamy side of a small New England town.
- *Temple of the Golden Pavilion*, Yukio Mishima
- *Seize the Day*, Saul Bellow
- *The Minority Report*, Philip K. Dick
- *Cairo Trilogy*, Naguib Mahfouz
- *Diamonds Are Forever*, Ian Fleming

Nonfiction

JAN 1 *Profiles in Courage*, by Senator John F. Kennedy of Massachusetts, was published to great praise and sales. It won a Pulitzer Prize in 1957.
- *White Negro: Superficial Reflections on the Hipster*, Norman Mailer

Children's Literature

- *Old Yeller*, Fred Gipson

Poetry

- Beat Poet Allen Ginsburg produced *Howl*.

Notes

- The Nobel Prize for Literature was awarded to Spanish poet Juan Ramón Jimènez, author of *Platero y yo (Platero and I)*.

THEATER

MAY 8 *Look Back in Anger*, by 27-year-old playwright John Osborne, premiered at the Royal Court Theatre in England to many scathing reviews. The play revolutionized theater in Britain by turning away from upper-class drawing room sophistications. Influential critic Kenneth Tynan praised it, saying it depicted "postwar youth as it really is."

JULY 24 Popular comedy duo Dean Martin and Jerry Lewis performed together for the last time at New York's Copacabana Club.

- Eugene O'Neill wrote *Long Day's Journey into Night* in the 1940s, but it wasn't published until 1956 (three years after O'Neill's death).

FILM

- *Guys and Dolls* was the year's top-grossing film.
- *Around the World in 80 Days* won Best Picture.
- Best Actor: Yul Brynner, *The King and I*
- Best Actress: Ingrid Bergman, *Anastasia*
- *High Society* starred Frank Sinatra, Bing Crosby, Grace Kelly, Louis Armstrong.
- *The Man Who Knew Too Much*, directed by Alfred Hitchcock, starred Jimmy Stewart and

Doris Day and featured the song "Que Sera, Sera."

- *Love Me Tender* marked Elvis Presley's first foray into film.
- Two glamorous American film stars tied the knot in 1956: **APR 19** Grace Kelly married Prince Rainier III of Monaco. **JUNE 29** Marilyn Monroe married playwright Arthur Miller.

TELEVISION

APR 2 Soap opera "As the World Turns" premiered on CBS.

JUNE 5 Elvis's gyrating hips horrified a nation of squares watching the "Milton Berle Show." Presley performed "Hound Dog."

NOV 3 CBS's "Ford Star Jubilee" aired the film *The Wizard of Oz*—the first time the classic appeared on television.

NOV 5 Popular African-American pianist and singer Nat King Cole premiered his variety show.

NOV 26 Game show "The Price Is Right" premiered with host Bill Cullen and announcer Don Pardo. It is television's longest-running game show; Bob Barker took over hosting duties in 1972.

- The quiz show scandals had their birth when Professor Charles Van Doren agreed to appear on a rigged "Twenty-One" to beat nerdy champion Herb Stempel.
- Chicago's WMAQ became the first TV station to broadcast all local programming in color.

RADIO

APR 7 "Rock 'n' Roll Dance Party" premiered on CBS radio network. Allen Freed was its host.

APR Bob Hope concluded his weekly NBC radio program.

MUSIC

OCT 29 Soprano Maria Callas made her Metropolitan Opera debut at New York City in *Norma*.

DEC 4 Elvis Presley, Jerry Lee Lewis, Johnny Cash and Carl Perkins—"The Million Dollar Quartet"—performed together at Sun Studios in Memphis, TN.

- In 1956 pop music continued its aggressive shift toward rock 'n' roll sounds. Elvis Presley had four charting #1 singles that year: "Heartbreak Hotel" (May 3); "Don't Be Cruel/Hound Dog" (Sept 15); and "Love Me Tender" twice (Nov 17 and Dec 22).

Popular Songs

- "All the Way," Frank Sinatra
- "Be-Bop-a-Lula," Gene Vincent and His Blue Caps
- "The Great Pretender," The Platters
- "Long Tall Sally," Little Richard
- "I'll Be Home," Pat Boone
- "Roll Over Beethoven," Chuck Berry
- "Memories Are Made of This," Dean Martin
- "Tutti-Frutti," Little Richard
- "Whatever Will Be, Will Be (Que Sera, Sera)," Doris Day
- "Why Do Fools Fall in Love," Frankie Lymon and the Teen-agers

Science and Technology

- Scientist John McCarthy organized "The Dartmouth Summer Research Project on Artificial Intelligence," inadvertently coining an important technological term.
- IBM introduced the first hard disk storage system; it held five megabytes.
- The first transatlantic phone call via submarine cable was made.

Notes

- John Bardeen, Walter Brattain and William Shockley received the Nobel Prize for Physics; Sir Cyril Hinshelwood and Nikolay Semenov received the Nobel Prize for Chemistry; André Cournand, Werner Forssmann and Dickinson Richards received the Nobel Prize for Physiology or Medicine.

Commerce and New Products

SEPT IBM announced the debut of the 305 RAMAC and 650 RAMAC data processing machines, which both used magnetic disk memory, a technology introduced by IBM only a year before. The company also brought out the first electronic typewriter and completed development work on the FORTRAN programming language. (It would debut in 1957.)

- Ampex introduced the VRX-1000 videotape recorder. The three major networks put in orders immediately, and tape-delayed broadcasts soon became the norm.
- Calder Hall opened in England; it was the first nuclear power plant built specifically for consumer power.
- Container-based shipping began with *Ideal X*'s sail from Newark, NJ, to Houston, TX.
- Portable black-and-white televisions were brought to market. (By the end of 1956, more than 70 percent of American families owned a TV set.)

- Southdale, the first enclosed shopping mall, opened in suburban Minneapolis.
- Play-Doh was patented.

Sports

- The 1956 Summer Olympics were held at Melbourne, Australia, under the cloud of hostilities in Egypt and Hungary. The world drama was played out in miniature at the Olympics when the Hungarian water polo team met its Soviet counterpart in a semifinal match. Hungary won 4–0, but a brawl erupted during the match over a foul. At both the summer and winter Olympics, the Soviets outmedaled all opponents for the first time.

BASEBALL

APR 17 With President Eisenhower in attendance, Mickey Mantle of the New York Yankees opened the baseball season by hitting two massive home runs against the Washington Senators at Washington's Griffith Stadium.

OCT 8 New York Yankee Don Larson pitched the only perfect game in World Series history, defeating the Brooklyn Dodgers 2–0. The Yankees won the World Series four games to three.

BOXING

APR 27 Boxer Rocky Marciano retired as the first undefeated heavyweight champion. He finished his career with a record of 49–0, with 43 knockouts and six title defenses. His title was claimed by Floyd Patterson on Nov 30, 1956, when Patterson beat Archie Moore.

FOOTBALL

DEC 30 In the NFL Championship game (pre-Super Bowl and pre-AFL formation), the New York Giants steamrolled the Chicago Bears 47–7.

GOLF

SEPT 17 Ann Gregory became the first black woman golfer to play in a USGA national championship when she participated as a woman's amateur at Meridian Hills Country Club in Indianapolis, IN.

HORSE RACING

- Needles won the Kentucky Derby under jockey David Erb.

TENNIS

- Australia's Lew Hoad was men's singles champion at Wimbledon, defeating Ken Rosewall (also from Australia). Ladies' singles was won by Shirley Fry (USA), who defeated Angela Buxton of Great Britain.

1956 Deaths

- Ginger Beaumont, the first player to bat in a World Series (1903)
- Clarence Birdseye, American inventor of flash-frozen foods
- Bertolt Brecht, German playwright, author of *Mother Courage*
- Ralph DePalma, Italian auto racer, winner of 2,557 out of 2,889 races
- Billy Evans, Baseball Hall of Fame umpire and executive
- John Heydler, baseball executive (president of the National League 1918–1934), cofounder of Hall of Fame and source of the designated hitter rule
- Alfred Kinsey, sex researcher
- Charles MacArthur, American playwright
- Connie Mack, Baseball Hall of Fame manager and executive, born Cornelius Alexander McGillicuddy
- H.L. Mencken, American journalist and critic
- Charles Edward Merrill, founder of Merrill Lynch
- A.A. Milne, English author of *Winnie the Pooh* and *House at Pooh Corner*
- George Sessions Perry, American novelist of *Hold Autumn in Your Hand*
- Jackson Pollack, American painter
- Alex Raymond, comic strip artist and creator of Flash Gordon and Jungle Jim
- Juan T. Trippe, founder of Pan Am
- Thomas J. Watson, founder of IBM
- Buck Weaver, one of eight Chicago White Sox players banned for life for conspiring to fix the 1919 World Series
- Babe Didrickson Zaharias, one of the greatest athletes of all time

1981 *25 years ago*

Landmark World Events

MAR 1 Jailed Irish Republican Army member Bobby Sands began a hunger strike that would last until his death on May 5.

MAR 13 Pope John Paul II was shot by escaped terrorist Mehmet Ali Agca. Shot twice, the pope was pronounced recovered on Aug 14.

APR 15 US launched air strikes on Libya.

JULY 29 Longtime bachelor Charles, Prince of Wales, married Lady Diana Spencer in a wedding ceremony televised around the world.

OCT 6 In Cairo, Egypt, Muslim extremists assassinated Egyptian president Anwar Sadat while he reviewed a military parade commemorating the Yom Kippur War. Sadat had shared a Nobel Peace Prize with Israeli prime minister Menachem Begin in 1978.

- The Nobel Peace Prize was awarded to the Office of the United Nations High Commissioner for Refugees.
- Polish Solidarity leader Lech Walesa was *Time* magazine's "Man of the Year."

Landmark US Events

JAN 20 Ronald Reagan was sworn in as president on the West Front of the Capitol—the first time an inauguration had been held there. In his inaugural address, President Ronald Reagan said, "We are a nation that has a government—not the other way around. And this makes us special among the nations of the Earth. Our Government has no power except that granted it by the people. It is time to check and reverse the growth of government which shows signs of having grown beyond the consent of the governed. . . . [I]t is not my intention to do away with government. It is, rather, to make it work—work with us, not over us; to stand by our side, not ride on our back."

JAN 20 The Iran Hostage Crisis ended with the release of 52 US citizens after 444 days of captivity. The deal was announced minutes after the swearing in of President Ronald Reagan.

MAR 30 President Ronald Reagan was shot in the chest by John W. Hinckley, Jr. On June 21, Hinckley was found not guilty by reason of insanity and remitted to St. Elizabeth's Hospital in Washington, DC.

JUNE 27 Centers for Disease Control and Prevention first used the term acquired immune deficiency syndrome (AIDS) to describe the disease caused by the HIV virus. (The virus itself was not identified until 1983.) (See "Spotlight on American Anniversaries.")

Aug 5 President Reagan fired 11,359 striking air traffic controllers.

Sept 25 Sandra Day O'Connor was sworn in as the first woman associate justice on the US Supreme Court.

Culture

PUBLICATIONS

Fiction

- *Midnight's Children*, Salman Rushdie
- *Rabbit Is Rich*, John Updike
- *True Names*, Vernor Vinge
- *Chaneysville Incident*, David Bradley
- *Housekeeping*, Marilynne Robinson
- *World Without End*, Francine du Plessix Gray
- *Flag for Sunrise*, Robert Stone
- *Red Dragon*, Thomas Harris
- *Tar Baby*, Toni Morrison
- *Rights of Passage*, William Golding
- *July's People*, Nadine Gordimer
- *Hotel New Hampshire*, John Irving
- *The Comfort of Strangers*, Ian McEwan
- *The White Hotel*, D.M. Thomas
- *What We Talk About When We Talk About Love*, Raymond Carver

Nonfiction

- *Prisoner Without a Name, Cell Without a Number*, Jacob Timerman
- *Old Glory*, Jonathan Raban
- *Gate of Heavenly Peace*, Jonathan Spence
- *Bad Blood: The Tuskegee Syphilis Experiment*, James H. Jones

Notes

- Nobel Prize for Literature: Elias Canetti, "For writings marked by a broad outlook, a wealth of ideas and artistic power."

THEATER

- *Nohow On*, Samuel Beckett

FILM

- *Raiders of the Lost Ark* was the year's top-grossing film.
- *Chariots of Fire* won Best Picture.
- Best Actor: Henry Fonda, *On Golden Pond*
- Best Actress: Katharine Hepburn, *On Golden Pond*
- *Absence of Malice*
- *The Howling*
- *American Werewolf in London*
- *Mommie Dearest*
- *Heartland*
- *The French Lieutenant's Woman* starred Meryl Streep and Jeremy Irons.
- *Tess*, directed by Roman Polanski

TELEVISION

Jan 12 The lavish prime-time soap "Dynasty" premiered on ABC with stars John Forsythe and Linda Evans.

Jan 15 Stephen Bochco's "Hill Street Blues" premiered on NBC. The grittily realistic police drama would go on to win numerous Emmys and to run for seven seasons.

Mar 6 Walter Cronkite signed off for the last time from the "CBS Evening News."

Aug 1 Music video channel MTV debuted to the sound of the Buggles' "Video Killed the Radio Star."

Nov On the daytime soap "General Hospital," the fictitious wedding of Luke and Laura was a worldwide television event.

MUSIC

- Christopher Cross made it a sweep at the 1981 Grammys, winning the Best New Artist; Album of the Year for his self-titled effort; and both Song of the Year and Record of the Year honors for the single "Sailing."

Albums

- Grandmaster Flash's *Adventures of Grandmaster Flash on the Wheels of Steel* helped to herald the arrival of hip-hop, including DJ scratching.
- *Controversy*, Prince
- *Tattoo You*, The Rolling Stones
- *Sandinista!* The Clash
- *Double Fantasy*, John Lennon and Yoko Ono

Popular Songs

- "Tide Is High," Blondie
- "Celebration," Kool & the Gang

- "Bette Davis Eyes," Kim Carnes
- "9 to 5," Dolly Parton
- "Jessie's Girl," Rick Springfield
- "Physical," Olivia Newton-John
- "America," Neil Diamond (theme from *Jazz Singer*)
- "At This Moment," Billy Vera & the Beaters

Art

May 6 Maya Ying Lin's design for the Vietnam Veterans Memorial in Washington, DC, was unanimously selected.

Science and Technology

Apr 12 NASA launched the space shuttle *Columbia*.

Notes

- Nicolaas Bloembergen, Arthur Schawlow and Kai Siegbahn received the Nobel Prize for Physics; Kenichi Fukui and Roald Hoffmann received the Nobel Prize for Chemistry; David Hubel, Roger Sperry and Torsten Wiesel received the Nobel Prize for Physiology or Medicine.

Commerce and New Products

Feb 2 General Motors announced a loss of $763 million in 1980—the first time since 1921 that the world's largest corporation hadn't announced a profit.

Apr 1 Jack Welch became CEO of General Electric.

July 16 Datsun announced plans to change its nameplates in the US and Canada to Nissan.

Aug 12 IBM introduced its first personal computer with an operating system designed by Bill Gates of Microsoft.

- James Tobin received the Nobel Prize in Economics.
- *Inc.* Magazine listed TSR Hobbies—makers of the Dungeons & Dragons role-playing game—as one of the hundred fastest-growing private companies in America.
- Sony, Philips and PolyGram agreed on technical standards for recording and playback of compact discs. The technology would be released in 1982.
- Visicorp's Vision software package debuted. It combined a word processor with a spreadsheet and database.
- Apple Computer introduced the revised Apple III (256K RAM; $3,495 price tag).
- The burgeoning home video game industry gained even more steam when Intellivision rolled out a $6 million ad campaign promoting its graphical superiority over chief rival Atari. Intellivision would sell 850,000 game consoles by the end of the year.
- The Pac-Man video game debuted; and the Trivial Pursuit board game was trademark registered.
- The food additive aspartame was introduced.

- Stouffer's "Lean Cuisine" line of healthy personal entrees was introduced.

Sports

Auto Racing

May 24 Bobby Unser finished first in the Indy 500, but he was penalized postrace for passing cars illegally under the yellow caution flag. Mario Andretti was given the victory, only to lose again to Unser four months later when the US Auto Club decided the penalty was too severe.

Baseball

Apr 18 Cincinnati Reds pitcher Tom Seaver struck out his 3,000th batter, St. Louis Cardinal Keith Hernandez.

Apr 29 Phillies pitcher Steve Carlton reached 3,000 by striking out the Expos' Tim Wallach.

- In the World Series, the Los Angeles Dodgers beat the New York Yankees four games to two.

Football

Jan 25 Super Bowl XV was held at the Louisiana Superdome in New Orleans. The Oakland Raiders beat the Philadelphia Eagles 27 to 10 behind the passing performance of game MVP Jim Plunkett (13 for 21 pass completions, 261 yards of offense).

Mar 15 NFL outlawed the use of stickum anywhere on the body, uniform or equipment of a player.

HORSE RACING

APRIL 30 Bill Shoemaker rode John Henry to a nose victory to win the inaugural running of the Arlington Million, the first one million dollar horse race.

- Pleasant Colony won the Kentucky Derby with jockey Jorge Velasquez.

TENNIS

- John McEnroe was men's singles champion at Wimbledon, defeating Bjorn Borg. Ladies' singles was won by Chris Evert-Lloyd, who defeated Hana Mandlikova of Czechoslovakia.

1981 Deaths

- Omar Bradley, the "Soldier's General"
- Hoagie Carmichael, American songwriter ("Stardust")
- Harry Chapin, folk singer and songwriter, killed in a Long Island car accident
- Paul Dee "Daffy" Dean, baseball player, less-famous brother of Dizzy Dean
- Will Durant, American author of history and philosophy
- Terry Fox, inspirational runner, ran the "Marathon of Hope" to raise money for cancer research
- Edith Head, legendary Hollywood costume designer
- William Holden, Oscar-winning actor (*Stalag 17*)
- Irving Jaffee, Olympic gold medal speed skater in 1928 and 1932

- John Kieran, *New York Times* sportswriter, 10-year panelist on "Information Please"
- Lotte Lenya, actress, wife of Kurt Weill
- Joe Louis, the "Brown Bomber," greatest boxer of all time
- Bob Marley, Jamaican musician and reggae innovator
- Jeannette Ridlon Piccard, record holder with her husband for balloon ascent into the stratosphere; first woman to be ordained an Episcopal priest
- Mauri Rose, auto racer, winner of the 1941, 1947 and 1948 Indy 500s
- Anwar Sadat, Egyptian president and Nobel Peace Prize recipient
- Albert Speer, Hitler's architect and armaments minister
- Lowell Thomas, journalist and broadcaster
- DeWitt Wallace, founder of *Reader's Digest*
- Natalie Wood, actress; drowned in mysterious circumstances off the California coast

Wolfgang Amadeus Mozart's Birth Anniversary
Jan 27, 1756 • 250 Years

Born at Salzburg, Austria, Johann Chrysostom Wolfgang Amadeus Mozart was one of the greatest musical geniuses of all time.

A child prodigy who quickly gained proficiency at the harpsichord and violin, he began composing at the age of five. He later concentrated his efforts on the pianoforte and under the direction of his father, Mozart and his sister, Maria Anna, began touring Europe in 1762. Throughout the tours, Mozart continued writing music and in 1775 began service under the Archbishop in Salzburg. While in Salzburg he composed *Idomeneo*, the first of his mature operas.

Mozart settled in Vienna in 1781, risking his existence without official patronage. After years of waiting, he was engaged in the service of the emperor, Joseph II, as a chamber composer but at far less wages than his predecessor. Although he enjoyed artistic and popular success, Mozart's finances were never secure. An ardent Freemason, he borrowed extensively from his Masonic brothers, despite the successes of his operas *The Marriage of Figaro, Don Giovanni, Cosi fan tutti* and *The Magic Flute* and his extensive work for the piano.

Mozart became seriously ill in the fall of 1791, and his rapid decline led to speculation that he had been poisoned, although this later was proved false. Mozart died a pauper at Vienna, Austria, Dec 5, 1791.

(For observances of Mozart's 250th birth anniversary, see "Spotlight on 2006 Events.")

Sigmund Freud's Birth Anniversary
May 6, 1856 • 150 Years

Recognized as the founder of psychoanalysis, Sigmund Freud has had a profound and lasting influence on contemporary humanity and culture. Freud's reach has delved as deep into other disciplines (anthropology, for example) as his methods have into the human psyche. His work was debated, as it still is, in scientific and medical circles and was often rejected as selfish, speculative and flawed. But his central theories about sexuality, repressed emotions, the power of dreams and the frustrating autonomy of the human mind have nevertheless become tenets of the self in modern society.

Born in what is now the Czech Republic, Freud and his family moved to Vienna, Austria, when he was still a small boy. Vienna was a major European urban center and reflective of the many changes society faced in the late 19th century. The city was vibrant, romantic and contentious, full of political intrigue, rife with wildly shifting cultural mores and alive with the furious competition of raw scientific thought. Freud studied medicine at the University of

Vienna in the midst of this climate, and its thoughts and theories helped shape his life's work. A primary influence of Freud's formative years was Charles Darwin's *On the Origin of Species*, first published in 1859, putting forth the theory of evolution, a momentous scientific event of the era.

Freud received his medical degree in 1881, and by 1885 was studying in Paris under neurologist Jean-Martin Charcot. The power of hypnosis was his first fascination, and upon returning to Vienna he collaborated with Dr. Josef Breuer on a paper called *On the Physical Mechanism of Hysterical Phenomena* (1893). In it they asserted the treatment of hysteria by hypnosis, which would help patients discharge unresolved emotional energy. Poorly received by the scientific community, the paper did signal the first stirrings of modern psychoanalysis.

Freud was captivated by the human mind, but he was also restless with his own theories about it. Eventually, he began to study free association, a technique for recognizing unresolved emotional issues in the unconscious. In 1902, Freud became an associate professor at the University of Vienna. He also published some of his most famous work in the early 1900s. *Interpretation of Dreams* presented his views about repressed memories surfacing in the volatile subconscious. *Psychopathology of Everyday Life* introduced the now-famous

concept of a Freudian slip, or the way in which menial events and occurrences can reveal the inner workings of our minds. Later, *Three Essays on the Theory of Sexuality* tied the development of the human sex drive to childhood.

Freud's theories were met with skepticism and even hostility, particularly within the conservative mind-set of the era. But he pressed on and found fellow travelers in psychiatrists Alfred Adler, Carl Jung and Eugen Bleuler. They continued to develop psychoanalytical theory. Despite achieving international recognition for the field, their own disagreement on its direction caused friction—most alienating was Freud's continued emphasis on sexuality and Oedipal impulse as root causes for behavior and mental anxiety. By the early 1920s, he'd also developed cancer and he would die from the disease in 1938, after fleeing Nazi-controlled Austria for London. Still, despite discord and disease, it was in 1923 that Freud published what may be his most important work, *The Ego and the Id*. It established a structural view of a mind in three parts—the Id, Ego and Superego—with unique reactions, responsibilities and emotional controls for each. It integrated and streamlined the varying threads and theories Freud had been developing, rejecting and obsessing about for more than 40 years; it was also met with similar peer criticism and has continued to spark debate in the scientific community. Yet there's no debating the incredible influence of Sigmund Freud's central theories on psychoanalysis, as well as humankind's view of ourselves and our minds in the 21st century and beyond.

Chernobyl Disaster and Legacy

Apr 26, 1986 • 20 Years

The worst nuclear accident in history occurred on this day at the Chernobyl nuclear power plant when a forceful explosion caused large amounts of radiation to escape into the atmosphere. Although a relatively small number of people were killed in the blast, the long-term effects of radiation to humans and the environment will be felt for centuries.

The Chernobyl plant is just outside Pripyat, Ukraine, 10 miles from the Ukraine-Belarus border in the former Soviet Union. Shortly after 1:00 AM, a steam explosion during a routine test in the plant's No. 4 reactor triggered a second explosion and a massive fire. Firefighters, rescue workers and clean-up crews who were first to arrive at the scene were unaware that dangerous radiation levels were present and did not wear protective clothing. As a result, 28 of the 31 reported deaths were from exposure to radiation.

The Soviet government was slow to warn the public about

any hazardous radiation that had been released into the air. It wasn't until 36 hours after the explosion that 45,000 residents (mostly from Pripyat) were evacuated from a 10-km area around the plant. Two days later, a 30-km "exclusion zone" was established and more than 100,000 others were evacuated.

In the years since the disaster, the effects of radiation have been devastating. Many babies born in Belarus have multiple holes in their hearts—a condition known as "Chernobyl heart." The number of thyroid cancer cases in people who were younger than 14 at the time of the disaster is also much higher than average.

In addition, many of the 600,000 "liquidators" who for years helped clean up the plant and its surrounding areas, were exposed to high levels of radiation. Numerous health problems have been reported in these people and their children.

The accident contaminated farmlands and threatened water supplies in much of Belarus, Ukraine and Russia. Animal populations also experienced harmful radiation effects initially, but the absence of human beings in the 30-km exclusion zone allowed these populations to flourish in later years.

Today, reactor No. 4 is encased in concrete. Despite radiation warnings, some residents have returned to their homes in the 30-km zone, but no one is permitted to live in the more strictly enforced 10-km zone.

Benjamin Franklin's Birth Anniversary

Birth • Jan 17, 1706 • 300 Years

Born at Boston, MA, Benjamin Franklin had scant formal schooling before going to work in his father's tallow shop at age ten. In 1718, he was apprenticed to a half-brother who owned a print shop and newspaper. Five years later, tiring of his brother's authority, Franklin left for Philadelphia, where he flourished, becoming a prosperous printer and a prominent civic leader.

Franklin formed the Junto, a debating society, which over time developed into the American Philosophical Academy. He helped establish a circulating library, a fire company and the forerunner of the University of Pennsylvania. By 1750, Franklin had left his printing business to a partner and devoted himself to science (he soon gained an international reputation as a serious scientist), civic affairs and politics. Franklin became a member of the Pennsylvania Assembly in 1751 and the deputy postmaster general of the American colonies in 1753. Concerned with the defense of Pennsylvania's western frontier, he proposed in 1754 a union to defend the American colonies against the French.

Franklin's reputation soon was such that he became the London agent of several American colonies, including Pennsylvania, serving from 1757 to 1762 and from 1765 to 1775. Franklin traveled extensively during these years, meeting many famous scientists and thinkers, and immensely enjoyed his social and political activities in London.

Up to this time Franklin had been an ardent British imperialist, but beginning in 1765, gradually he became more convinced of the need to curtail Britain's authority over the American colonies. As he defended the colonists' rights and interests and became an ever-sharper critic of British policy over the next decade— and especially after he became the agent of the increasingly restive Massachusetts in 1770— Franklin endured increasingly bitter personal attacks. In the spring of 1775, he gave up his efforts to reconcile the colonies with the mother country—and also to persuade his loyalist son, William, to join the patriot cause—and Franklin returned to Pennsylvania.

Soon after he arrived home, Pennsylvania selected him as a delegate to the Second Continental Congress. In the summer of 1776, Franklin was on the committee that drafted the Declaration of Independence and was one of its signers. This work alone probably would have secured Franklin's historical reputation. However, it was as one of three colonial emissaries to France (1776–1785) that he performed perhaps his greatest service to his country. By shrewdly cultivating an image of republican simplicity and exploiting his prewar reputation as a scientist and intellectual, Franklin garnered widespread sympathy for the American cause. He thus was able to obtain money and supplies and, in 1778, negotiate an alliance with France that secured French soldiers and warships to help the colonists win their victory over Great Britain. Franklin also was among the American commissioners who negotiated the 1783 Treaty of Paris that officially ended the Revolutionary War.

Back in Philadelphia, Franklin demonstrated an undiminished taste for politics and civic involvement: he became president of Pennsylvania's supreme executive council (1785–1787) and the head of an antislavery society. As a delegate to the 1787 Constitutional Convention, Franklin lent his enormous prestige to the proceedings and was a leading voice of conciliation and compromise. During the process to ratify the Constitution, Franklin was one of its most forceful advocates. He died in April 1790 at age 84.

Like George Washington, the only other truly national figure of the American Revolution and the early republic, Benjamin Franklin still provides Americans an example of selfless service to country and of the boundless opportunities for success and self-improvement that America affords all of its citizens.

(See "Spotlight on 2006 Events" for the many tercentennial events celebrating Franklin.)

Booker T. Washington's Birth Anniversary and the Anniversary of the Tuskegee Institute

1856 and 1881 • 150 and 125 Years

Booker T. Washington was an influential educator, orator and civil rights crusader in a time of great change for the nation and tremendous hardship for black Americans. Born into a Virginia slave settlement, Washington moved with his family after Emancipation to West Virginia, where they labored in the salt mines. Longing for an education, Washington by age 16 had set out on foot for the Hampton Institute, a school for former slaves located hundreds of miles away in Virginia. Ever resourceful, Washington funded his education with a janitor's wages. After leaving his studies in 1875, Washington briefly worked as a schoolteacher in West Virginia but soon returned to Hampton Institute as a full-fledged faculty member.

In 1881, Hampton founder Samuel Chapman Armstrong asked Washington to head up a newly founded school in

Tuskegee, AL, for the practical training of blacks in trades and professions. At the time the school had no staff, a ramshackle classroom building and just a few thousand dollars in funding. The Tuskegee Institute grew under Washington's guidance as its first teacher and the person responsible for developing the curriculum. The 1896 establishment of an agriculture school headed by George Washington Carver added to its stature. The institute also benefited financially from Washington's skills as a speechmaker and a tireless fund-raiser.

At Tuskegee students were urged to become educators themselves in order to spread knowledge through the ranks of the disenfranchised. Vocational trades and farming were also emphasized, and Washington insisted on physical and moral cleanliness. He believed the promotion and support of job skills and strong character in as many blacks as possible would bring economic and social

progress more rapidly than the push for higher education—a course of action encouraged by some of his critics, most notably black statesman W.E.B. DuBois. "The opportunity to earn a dollar in a factory just now," Washington said in his landmark Atlantic Compromise speech (1895), "is worth infinitely more than the opportunity to spend a dollar in an opera house."

Though his theories and opinions were at times contentious, Washington was a role model to African Americans struggling for a voice and footing amidst the racial antagonism of the era, and he remained a tireless and thoughtful advocate for economic progress and social equality. He was president of Tuskegee Institute from 1881 until his death in 1915, when he was buried on its campus. "He lifted the veil of ignorance from his people," his inscription reads, "and pointed the way to progress through education and industry." Tuskegee began as the greatest challenge of Booker T. Washington's already remarkable life; it became his legacy and an enduring tribute to his vision, persevering spirit and passion for education.

(Throughout 2006, Tuskegee University will be observing its 125th founding anniversary and Washington's 150th birthday. Of special notice should be the Apr 2 Founder's Day Convocation/ Official Celebration of the 125th Anniversary at the University Chapel. See the main calendar for more information or go to www.tuskegee.edu.)

San Francisco Earthquake and Fire
Apr 18, 1906 • 100 Years

Shortly before sunrise on Apr 18, 1906, a massive earthquake jolted San Francisco awake, rocking the city for nearly a minute. The time was 5:12 AM. For stunned San Franciscans, a 72-hour ordeal was just beginning.

As the shaking subsided, broken gas lines fueled 30 fires across the city. Blazes raged out of control for the next three days, leaving 500 city blocks— almost five square miles—in smoldering ruin. The central business district burned to the ground. Buildings were dynamited to provide fire breaks. Troops were called in to help keep order and assist firefighters. Citizens were forced to evacuate at bayonet-point. Looters were shot on sight. It was the biggest natural disaster America had ever seen.

"Not in history has a modern imperial city been so completely destroyed," wrote eyewitness Jack London. "San Francisco is gone. Nothing remains of it but memories and a fringe of dwelling-houses on its outskirts. . . . San Francisco, at the present time, is like the crater of a volcano, around which are camped tens of thousands of refugees."

More than half of San Francisco's 400,000 residents were homeless. About 75,000 abandoned the city altogether; others crowded into parks and military installations, living in tents and temporary huts. For months, soldiers and Red Cross workers distributed food and supplies throughout the city. Remarkably, sanitation enforcement prevented widespread outbreaks of disease.

Altogether, the earthquake and fire destroyed 28,000 buildings, killed 3,000 people and left 250,000 homeless. At the time, property losses were reckoned at $250 million. Outside of San Francisco, communities all along the San Andreas fault suffered damage.

Today, the earthquake's magnitude is estimated at anywhere between 7.7 and 8.3 on the Richter scale. Magnitude aside, the 1906 earthquake is also notable for its unprecedented range. Shaking was felt from southern Oregon all the way south of Los Angeles and as far east as central Nevada. The rupture extended roughly 290 miles; displacements as wide as 20 feet were observed.

The 1906 earthquake marked the beginning of American seismic research and preparedness. A landmark state-sponsored study published in 1908 showed the importance of seismic observation and engineering-construction standards. Military and Red Cross cooperation provided a precedent for future disaster relief efforts.

San Franciscans rushed to put the tragedy behind them. By 1915, when San Francisco hosted the Panama-Pacific International Exhibition, most of the city had been rebuilt.

AIDS in America
1981 • 25 Years

On July 3, 1981, the *New York Times* reported a rare form of skin cancer that had appeared in 41 homosexual men in New York City and San Francisco. Although very little was known about the mysterious disease at the time, the article was one of the first to spotlight the now-global AIDS epidemic.

As more gay men died from the strange cancer, a rare form of pneumonia was seen in others. Each case developed because the victim's immune system was weakened and unable to fight off certain infections. In the fall of 1981, the Centers for Disease Control and Prevention (CDC) declared the unknown disease an epidemic.

In 1982, the CDC linked the disease to blood and gave it the name acquired immune deficiency syndrome (AIDS). Even though the CDC had guessed early on that AIDS was transmitted through sex, there was still no clear answer as to what caused the disease or how it was passed from person to person.

By 1983, intravenous drug users, Haitians, hemophiliacs and women who had sex with AIDS-infected men were all considered high-risk groups. But because gay men were the first to show symptoms of the illness, media reports often referred to AIDS as "gay cancer" or gay-related immunodeficiency disease (GRID). These reports led many to mistakenly think AIDS was a "gay disease," which contributed to a social backlash against homosexuals. Some religious groups believed that homosexuality was a sin and that AIDS was a form of punishment. Others unfairly blamed gay men for spreading the disease to hemophiliacs.

In 1984, Dr. Robert Gallo at the National Cancer Institute and Dr. Luc Montagnier at the Pasteur Institute in Paris announced they had codiscovered the virus that caused AIDS. The following year, the name human immunodeficiency virus (HIV) was agreed on.

From a public awareness perspective, HIV/AIDS hit a turning point in 1985 when actor Rock Hudson died from the disease. Even though cases had been reported all over the world by this time, Hudson's death put a notable face on the growing epidemic. Ryan White, an Indiana teenager who contracted AIDS through a blood transfusion and was barred from attending school, also captured the public's attention when he began speaking out against AIDS discrimination. White died in 1990 at the age of 18.

Despite national media attention, public concern and thousands of deaths around the world, the US government did little to treat HIV/AIDS as a national and global health emergency. The government even took steps to block efforts to educate people about the disease. President Ronald Reagan did not mention AIDS publicly until 1987; and Republican Senator

Jesse Helms of North Carolina cut federal funding for AIDS educational materials that "promote or encourage, directly or indirectly, homosexual activities." The so-called "no promo homo" amendment required materials to remove any mention of anal intercourse, which by that time was known to be a primary way in which HIV/AIDS was transmitted.

In his book, *And the Band Played On: People, Politics, and the AIDS Epidemic*, Randy Shilts described the political infighting that hampered efforts to fight HIV/AIDS during the epidemic's first five years. The book was published in 1987 and made into a movie in 1993. Shilts died from AIDS in 1994.

Today, it's estimated that as many as 950,000 are living with HIV in the United States, but fewer Americans are dying of AIDS thanks to new medications and improved funding for education. In parts of the world, however, the epidemic is quite severe. More than 25 million of the estimated 39.4 million people in the world who have HIV live in sub-Saharan Africa.

Space Shuttle *Challenger* Explodes

Jan 28, 1986 • 20 Years

Space travel seemed routine by 1986. The National Aeronautics and Space Administration (NASA) had flown 24 space shuttle missions since April 1981.

Orbiting the earth was becoming commonplace, even boring.

Americans had little reason to believe that the 25th mission, STS 51-L, would be any different. Launch was originally scheduled for Jan 22, from Pad 39-B at the Kennedy Space Center in Cape Canaveral, FL, but weather and technical glitches delayed departure until Jan 28. Most of the nation wasn't even paying attention at 11:38 AM EST, when *Challenger* exploded 73 seconds after liftoff.

All seven astronauts aboard perished.

Replayed over and over on television, the accident stunned America. Ironically, *Challenger*'s mission was intended to rekindle waning interest in space exploration.

During the 1984 presidential campaign, Ronald Reagan had announced that the nation's first civilian in space would be "one of American's finest—a teacher." On July 19, 1985, from among 11,000 applicants NASA selected New Hampshire high school teacher Christa McAuliffe as the primary candidate for the Teacher in Space Project. McAuliffe planned to teach a lesson from orbit. In her honor, the crew included an apple on the mission's official insignia.

Other *Challenger* crew members included commander Francis Scobee; pilot Michael Smith; mission specialists Ronald McNair, Ellison Onizuka and Judith Resnik; and payload specialist Gregory Jarvis.

Losing one of NASA's four shuttles was inconceivable. The

spacecraft was an icon of Reagan's "morning in America," reaffirming national confidence after the troubled 1970s. Outrage followed grief as America demanded answers.

Former secretary of state William Rodgers headed the inquest, which included NASA's first woman in space, Sally Ride. After a four-month investigation, the commission concluded that the explosion was caused by leaking O-ring seals in the spacecraft's right solid-rocket booster. Unseasonable cold had caused the elastic rings to harden, allowing hot exhaust gases to escape and ignite the sealant material, which triggered the explosion.

The commission criticized NASA's decision to launch under severe weather conditions. Safety concerns did not reach administrators in the days leading up to the launch, or they were ignored. Recommendations included new safety procedures, better internal communication and management accountability.

NASA implemented more than 200 improvements by the time *Discovery* resumed flight in September 1988. Shuttles flew safely for 17 more years until February 2003, when *Columbia* broke apart during reentry, killing all aboard. The accident raised many of the same concerns broached in 1986.

Discovery flew again in 2005, but continuing technical problems have again put the shuttle program in limbo.

Spotlight on People

There are many significant people throughout history for whom we celebrate milestone anniversaries in 2006. Provided here is just a selection of people who altered the world in which they lived who would have been 100 years or older in the year 2006. You will find additional famous birth anniversaries in the main calendar section of the book.

World History

MUMTAZ MAHAL

Death • June 17, 1631 • 375 Years

Related to an empress and the daughter of a high-ranking officer, Arjumand Banu Begum was born in India in April 1593. At age 14 she became the third wife of a prince who later ascended the throne with the title Shah Jahan. Renamed Mumtaz Mahal, she was the shah's favorite wife and bore him 14 children, dying in childbirth on June 17, 1631. Shah Jahan was desolate and went into seclusion for a week, during which time it was said that his hair turned completely white. He ordered a tomb built for her in Agra, and it took more than 20 years to complete. Today it stands as an homage to her beauty and virtue: the Taj Mahal.

STAMFORD RAFFLES

Birth • July 6, 1781 • 225 Years

Sir Stamford Raffles, English colonial official and founder of Singapore, was born at sea, off Jamaica. As a teenager, he became a clerk with the East India Company and rapidly rose through its ranks, serving in a variety of posts in the East Indies. During a voyage to Calcutta, he landed on the shores of an island off Malaya on Jan 29, 1819, and created the port of Singapore. Raffles died near London, England, on July 5, 1826.

BENITO PABLO JUAREZ

Birth • Mar 21, 1806 • 200 Years

Born of indigenous parents in Oaxaca, Mexico, Benito Juarez was to rise to become a four-term president of Mexico, transforming his liberal ideas into a political reality. He also led the country through civil war, foreign occupation and economic transformation. As a young man, Juarez was sympathetic to liberal Federalists like the revolutionaries in America and France, believing that capitalism should replace economic monopolies held by the church and the aristocracy. After being exiled with other Federalists in 1853, Juarez returned to Mexico two years later when the Federalists regained control. As minister of justice, Juarez contributed to the Mexican constitution of 1857 which, in an attempt to separate church and state, began to break up large, landed estates. In 1861, the Federalist government collapsed and, as chief justice of the Mexican supreme court,

Juarez became president. The country was bankrupt and struggling to recover after years of civil war; France saw Mexico's vulnerability and attacked in 1862. While marching from Veracruz to Mexico City, the French were routed at Puebla on May 5, 1862. This brief Mexican victory is celebrated today as Cinco de Mayo. The French forces, however, were able to continue on, occupying Mexico City in 1863. Juarez retreated to the border town then called El Paso del Norte (now renamed Ciudad Juarez) while Napoleon III placed Archduke Ferdinand Maximilian of Hapsburg as the emperor of Mexico. France's attention was then drawn back to Europe to fortify its borders against Germany's Otto von Bismarck, and the Mexicans were able to defeat the remaining French troops. In 1867, Emperor Maximilian was executed and Juarez was voted back into the presidency. He worked during this time to revitalize the mining industry, construct railways and create a national state-run educational system. After suffering a stroke in 1870, he was re-elected for a fourth term to the presidency in 1871. He died of a heart attack on July 18, 1872.

JOHN STUART MILL

Birth • May 20, 1806 • 200 Years

Born at London, England, Mill was to become one of the 19th century's leading man of letters—an influential philosopher, ethicist, political scientist and economist who also promoted Utilitarianism. His famous works include *A System of Logic* (1843), *On Liberty* (1859) and *Utilitarianism* (1863). Mill died at Avignon, France, on May 8, 1873. "The worth of a state, in the long run," he wrote in *On Liberty*, "is the worth of the individuals composing it." In *The Subjection of Women* (1869), he said: "Marriage is the only actual bondage known to our law. There remain no legal slaves, except the mistress of every house."

Sigmund Freud

Birth • May 6, 1856 • 150 Years
See Spotlight on World Anniversaries

Mustafa Ataturk

Birth • Mar 12, 1881 • 125 Years
The founder of modern Turkey was born at Salonika, Greece (then part of the Ottoman Empire). After a distinguished educational and army career, he led the Turkish revolution after World War I and was elected Turkey's first president, serving from 1923 to 1938. Under his leadership, Turkey became a democratic state, complete with reformed political, social, legal and educational systems. Women were given the right to vote, conservative religious brotherhoods were outlawed, the practice of polygamy was abolished and the traditional Arabic script was replaced with the Latin alphabet, which gave the Turkish people greater access to the Western world. His death at Istanbul on Nov 10, 1938, was met with an outpouring of grief. Even today, Ataturk's name and likeness are prominently displayed throughout Turkey.

Pope John XXIII

Birth • Nov 25, 1881 • 125 Years
Angelo Roncalli, 261st pope of the Roman Catholic Church, was born at Sotte il Monte, Italy. He was elected pope on Oct 28, 1958, at 71 years of age and served until his death on June 3, 1963, at Rome. He was an incredibly popular pope known for his openness to change, which was first evidenced by his summoning of a general meeting of church bishops, the first in nearly a century. He felt that the Catholic Church was in need of reinvigoration and reform. He sought to heal Christian and Jewish divisions. He also made the Second Vatican Council of 1962 open to observers from Eastern Orthodox, Anglican and Protestant denominations. Unlike his predecessors, he was a familiar presence around Rome, remaining receptive and unaffected despite his stature. He was a tireless promoter of peace and authored *Pacem in Terris*, the first encyclical addressed to all people. His was the voice of caution to US and Russian leaders during the Cuban missile crisis. He was beatified by Pope John Paul II in 2000.

Adolf Eichmann

Birth • Mar 19, 1906 • 100 Years
Adolf Eichmann was a Nazi war criminal tried and sentenced by Israel for his part in the Holocaust. Born at Solingen, Germany, Eichmann joined the Nazi Party in 1932 and rose through the ranks to become chief of the Jewish Office of the Gestapo during World War II. He organized the identification and transportation of Jews throughout occupied Europe to concentration camps, where an incredible number were exterminated. He was captured by US troops, but managed to escape in 1946. He settled in Buenos Aires, Argentina, where Israeli secret service agents arrested him in 1960. Throughout his trial, Eichmann denied involvement in the actual killing of Jews, maintaining that he was simply following orders, not masterminding them. The trial verdict was death; the only death sentence ever ordered by an Israeli court. Eichmann was hanged on May 31, 1962.

William Joyce

Birth • Apr 24, 1906 • 100 Years
Born at New York, NY, Joyce moved to Ireland with his family when he was only three, where he spent several years before going to England. While in college, he became a fascist, established the National Socialist League in 1937 and relocated to Germany in 1939 to support Hitler during World War II. Joyce was a popular and darkly comic Third Reich broadcaster, known as "Lord Haw-Haw,"

who, under the direction of Josef Goebbels, was enterprising in the use of media for propaganda. Although he had never become a British citizen, he was tried for treason and became the last person to be hanged as a traitor by the British government (Jan 3, 1946, at London, England).

LEONID BREZHNEV

Birth • Dec 19, 1906 • 100 Years
Leonid Brezhnev was born at Kamenskoye, Ukraine, and joined the Communist Party in 1931. He served in various political positions under Stalin and Khrushchev. In 1964, Brezhnev helped lead the overthrow of Khrushchev and, shortly thereafter, became the leader of the Communist Party for about 18 years. He expanded and modernized the Soviet Union's military and nuclear power and initiated the policy of détente (from the French for relaxation of tensions) with the United States, but he neglected other aspects of the Soviet economy, including agriculture, consumer goods and health care. He was generally criticized for the resultant decline in Soviet standards of living. Brezhnev died on Nov 10, 1982, at age 75.

American History

BENJAMIN FRANKLIN

Birth • Jan 17, 1706 • 300 Years
See Spotlight on American Anniversaries

MARTHA WASHINGTON

Birth • June 21, 1731 • 275 Years
Martha Washington née Dandridge was the wife of George Washington, first president of the United States. She was born at New Kent County, VA, and grew up among the affluent Virginian plantation families. At age 18, she married Daniel Parke Custis, a wealthy plantation owner who died in 1757, leaving her with two children. Less than a year later, George Washington began to court her and they were married in 1759. During the Revolutionary War, Martha spent winters with her husband, assisting him as necessary. She became first lady in 1789 and was both celebrated as being a genuine and giving person and chastised for entertaining too lavishly. Martha died of "severe fever" on May 22, 1802, and is buried alongside her husband at Mount Vernon, their home in Virginia.

BENJAMIN BANNEKER

Birth • Nov 9, 1731 • 275 Years
Astronomer, mathematician, clock maker, surveyor and almanac author, called the "first black man of science." Born at Ellicott's Mills, MD, to a father who had been a slave, Banneker was a free black tobacco farmer.

A fascination with watches led to his study and mastery of timepieces and accurate clocks. He didn't study astronomy until he was 58 years old, and with his newly gained knowledge, he published an almanac from 1791 to 1802. He assisted in surveying the boundaries for the District of Columbia in 1791 and was able to reconstruct them from memory when city architect Pierre L'Enfant angrily took the plans with him when he quit his post. Banneker died at Baltimore, MD, Oct 9, 1806.

AARON BURR

Birth • Feb 6, 1756 • 250 Years
Born at Newark, NJ, Burr became the third vice president of the United States (1801–1805) after a successful career in law, serving in the New York state assembly and as attorney general. While vice president, Burr challenged political enemy Alexander Hamilton to a duel and mortally wounded him July 11, 1804, at Weehawken, NJ. Indicted for the challenge and for murder, Burr fled to Philadelphia where he and his friend General James Wilkinson planned to invade Mexico and set up an independent government. In 1807, after Wilkinson leaked news of the plan to President Jefferson, Burr was arrested, tried for treason and acquitted. He then left for Europe and tried to convince Napoleon to conquer Florida. Failing in that quest, he returned to his law practice in New York, where he died at Staten Island on Sept 14, 1836.

STAND WATIE

Birth • Dec 12, 1806 • 200 Years

American Indian leader born at Rome, GA, and died there Sept 9, 1871. Watie, a Cherokee chief, signed the Treaty of New Echota, which surrendered his tribe's land in Georgia and forced their relocation to what is now Oklahoma. Though the three other signers of the treaty were murdered by angry Cherokees, Watie escaped and went on to initiate the first volunteer Cherokee regiment for the Confederates in the Civil War. Promoted to brigadier general in 1864, Stand Watie was one of the last Confederate officers to surrender (June 23, 1865).

JAMES ABRAM GARFIELD

Birth • Nov 19, 1831 • 175 Years

The 20th president of the United States (and the first left-handed one) was born in a log cabin at Orange, OH. A dedicated public servant, Garfield started his career as an educator and was president of Hiram College in Ohio before embracing politics. After serving the Union in the Civil War, Garfield was elected to the US House and then the Senate as a member of the young Republican Party. At a divisive Republican convention in 1880, Garfield was nominated as the presidential candidate on the 36th ballot. He served only from Mar 4 to Sept 19, 1881—the second shortest tenure of a president. While walking into the Washington, DC, railway station on the morning of July 2, 1881, Garfield was shot by disap-pointed office seeker Charles J. Guiteau. He survived, in very weak condition, at Elberon, NJ (where he had been taken for recuperation), until Sept 19, 1881, when he succumbed to blood poisoning. Garfield's lingering death put the government in limbo, since up till then no provisions had been made for such a contingency.

BOOKER TALIAFERRO WASHINGTON

Birth • Apr 5, 1856 • 150 Years

See Spotlight on American Anniversaries

LOUIS BRANDEIS

Birth • Nov 13, 1856 • 150 Years

American jurist and the first Jewish associate justice of the US Supreme Court (1916–1939), Brandeis was born at Louisville, KY. Known as the people's attorney, he defended maximum labor hours and minimum wage statutes, devised a system of affordable life insurance for the working class, opposed monopolies and pioneered the "Brandeis brief," in which expert opinions were used to present the historical and future impact on society of the topic at hand. He retired in 1939 and died at Washington, DC, Oct 5, 1941. In 1948, the newly opened Brandeis University at Waltham, MA, was named after him.

WOODROW WILSON

Birth • Dec 28, 1856 • 150 Years

The 28th president of the United States, best remembered for his idealism in the face of the tragic Great War, was born Thomas Woodrow Wilson at Staunton, VA. He was a teacher and scholar before he was a statesman and is the only president to have earned a Ph.D. Wilson became a popular president at Princeton University (1902–1910) and used the attention from his wide-ranging reforms to vault into the governorship of New Jersey in 1910 as a Democrat. It was in his second term as president that a torn Wilson had to say, "The world must be made safe for democracy," as he asked Congress to declare war on Germany in April 1917. Under his administration, the Federal Trade Commission was created and women gained the right to vote. President Wilson was awarded the Nobel Peace Prize in 1919. During an exhaustive tour encouraging ratification of the Treaty of Versailles and of the formation of the League of Nations, Wilson suffered a paralytic stroke on Sept 16, 1919, never regaining his health. His second wife, Edith Wilson, controlled access to him, and there were many speculations about who was running the government during his disability. His second term of office ended in March 1921, and he died at Washington, DC, Feb 3, 1924.

WILLIAM BRENNAN

Birth • Apr 25, 1906 • 100 Years

US Supreme Court associate justice appointed in 1956 by President Dwight Eisenhower. Brennan's liberal leanings and judicial activism raised the ire of

Spotlight on People

many conservatives, even leading Eisenhower to call Brennan's appointment his "worst mistake." Brennan believed that the courts should go beyond strict constructionism and original intent doctrines in interpreting the law. He was responsible for many landmark decisions, such as the one requiring Little Rock, AR, schools to desegregate that contained the controversial assertion that it is not only the Constitution that is the "supreme law of the land" but also the Supreme Court's interpretation of it as well. His legacy also includes major decisions upholding affirmative action, a losing battle to declare the death penalty unconstitutional, decisions broadening free speech and free press guarantees, expansion of the due process guarantees under the 14th Amendment and protection of flag-burning as a form of expression. Brennan's resignation provided President George Bush with an opportunity to swing the balance of the Supreme Court to a more conservative, constructionist majority for the first time since the days of Franklin D. Roosevelt's presidency. Brennan was born at Newark, NJ; he died at Arlington, VA, July 25, 1997.

ANNE MORROW LINDBERGH

Birth • June 22, 1906 • 100 Years

Known primarily as the wife of aviator Charles Lindbergh, Anne Morrow Lindbergh was herself a pioneer in the field of aviation. The daughter of a US ambassador, Lindbergh was taught to fly by her husband, and she became the first American woman to get a glider pilot's license. She flew frequently with her husband, including a 1931 single-engine flight to Japan and China. In 1934, she became the first woman to win the National Geographic Society's Hubbard Gold Medal for distinction in exploration, research and discovery. Anne Morrow Lindbergh also was named to the National Aviation Hall of Fame in 1979. In one of the most heinous crimes of the 20th century, the Lindberghs' firstborn son, Charles Lindbergh III, was kidnapped and murdered in 1933. Lindbergh is also remembered for her inspirational book, *Gift From the Sea*, a 1955 volume about love, marriage and aging, which was a national bestseller and remains popular today. Lindbergh died in rural Vermont on Feb 7, 2001.

SAMUEL ICHIYE HAYAKAWA

Birth • July 18, 1906 • 100 Years

S.I. Hayakawa was born at Vancouver, BC, and came to the United States in 1927. An academic, he was appointed acting president of San Francisco State College in 1968. During student demonstrations on his first day in office, he climbed atop a sound truck and disconnected the wires, silencing the protestors. His actions gained him enormous approval among conservatives, and his presidency was made permanent by Governor Ronald Reagan. As his popularity grew, Hayakawa switched from the Democratic to the Republican Party and in 1976 was elected to the US Senate. He led the successful California initiative in 1986 to declare English the state's official language. Hayakawa wrote nine textbooks on language and semantics. He died Feb 27, 1992, at Greenbrae, CA.

Literature

JOHN DRYDEN

Birth • Aug 9, 1631 • 375 Years

The great man of letters of the Restoration period was born at Aldwinkle, England, to a prosperous squire's family. As the arts thrived with the restoration of the monarchy (Charles II), so did Dryden's fortunes, and he became a revered dramatist, poet and critic. He is credited with creating the mock-epic form of poetry in his savage satire, "MacFlecknoe" (1682). Dryden served as poet laureate of England (1668–1688) until his political fortunes changed. He died at London, England, on May 1, 1700.

ELIZABETH BARRETT BROWNING

Birth • Mar 6, 1806 • 200 Years

This English poet—wife of poet Robert Browning and subject of the play *The Barretts of Wimpole Street*—was born near Durham, England. She wrote her first poem when she was 12 years old. At 14, she was stricken with a lung ailment and at 15, a spinal cord injury from which she would suffer for the rest of her life. In 1826, Elizabeth Barrett anonymously published her first collection of poems, *An Essay on Mind and Other Poems*. Her next volume, *The Seraphim and Other Poems*, came out in 1838. The tyrannical rule of her father and the drowning of her brother led her to become a recluse, refusing to leave her room for five years. In 1844, she published *Poems*, which attracted the attention of fellow poet Robert Browning who then wrote her a letter. Over the next two years, they exchanged nearly 600 letters. Because her father opposed their romance (he did not want any of his children to marry), they eloped to Florence, Italy, in 1846. Elizabeth's *Sonnets from the Portuguese* (1850), dedicated to her husband and written in secret before her marriage, is generally considered her best work. She died at Florence, June 29, 1861.

H. RIDER HAGGARD

Birth • June 22, 1856 • 150 Years
A writer of classic fantasy and adventure stories, Sir H. Rider Haggard was born in England. At age 19, he moved to southern Africa as secretary to the governor of Natal. He traveled extensively among the Zulu people, visiting chieftains and taking notes. He and his wife lived on an ostrich farm in Transvaal, but when the territory was returned to the Dutch in 1881, Haggard went back to England where he began to write novels about Africa. In 1885, his

most famous story, *King Solomon's Mines*, was published. The novel was an instant success; British readers were drawn into the exotic, little-known setting of Africa and its people by Haggard's fast-paced storytelling and imagination. *She* (1886) was loosely based on legends of isolated African tribes ruled by immortal white queens. In all, Haggard wrote more than 50 novels with heroes, heroines and nonstop action set in numerous exotic places, all of which he insisted on personally exploring. He died in London, May 14, 1925.

GEORGE BERNARD SHAW

Birth • July 26, 1856 • 150 Years
Irish playwright, essayist, critic and socialist known for his energetic and engaging speaking manner and wit, who once said, "A fool's brain digests philosophy into folly, science into superstition, and art into pedantry. Hence University education." Shaw was born at Dublin into an atmosphere of genteel poverty and moved to London in 1876 to pursue a writing career. There Shaw cofounded the Fabian Society (1884), a socialist political organization that would come to be influential in establishing the London School of Economics and the Labour Party, and served as the theater critic of the *Saturday Review* from 1895 to 1898, during which time he began writing plays. His major works include *Arms and the Man, Man and Superman, Major Barbara* and *Pygmalion*, which was adapted into the musical *My Fair Lady*. George Bernard Shaw

was awarded the Nobel Prize for Literature in 1925. He died at Ayot St. Lawrence, England, Nov 2, 1950, from injuries incurred when he fell off a ladder while trimming a tree at age 94.

P.G. WODEHOUSE

Birth • Oct 15, 1881 • 125 Years
Pelham Grenville Wodehouse, known later as "Plum," remains one of the best English humorists of the 20th century, having created a host of beloved characters, but none more beloved than the suave, know-it-all butler, Jeeves, and his befuddled, prone-to-trouble master, Bertie Wooster. The prolific writer, who penned about one novel a year for his entire adult life, gently satirized a rapidly disappearing British gentry whose heyday was the 1920s. Wodehouse, who lived in the United States from 1909 on, becoming a citizen in 1955, described his novels as "musical comedies without music." Wodehouse was also a Broadway lyricist (best known for "Bill" from *Showboat*). He was knighted in 1975. Born at Guildford, Surrey, England, P.G. Wodehouse died at Southampton, Long Island, NY, Feb 14, 1975.

ROBERT E. HOWARD

Birth • Jan 22, 1906 • 100 Years
Howard, born at Peaster, TX, was a troubled, reclusive, but prolific writer for pulp fiction magazines like *Weird Tales* and *Action Stories* that paid a penny a word for stories. He began writing for them in the 1920s and his most famous creation was

Spotlight on People

warrior and adventurer Conan the Barbarian, who appeared in *Weird Tales* in December 1932. Conan was a hit, and Howard created tens of stories from 1932 to 1936. Devastated over the decline of his mother's health, Howard shot himself at Cross Plains, TX, on June 11, 1936. He explained his work: "I have lived in the Southwest all my life, yet most of my dreams are laid in cold, giant lands of icy wastes and gloomy skies, and of wild, wind-swept fens and wilderness over which sweep great sea-winds, and which are inhabited by shock-headed savages with light fierce eyes."

SAMUEL BECKETT

Birth • Apr 13, 1906 • 100 Years
Author, critic and playwright concerned with the nature of being, born at Foxrock, County Dublin, Ireland. Samuel Beckett is best remembered for his plays, including *Endgame, Krapp's Last Tape* and *Happy Days*. Beckett settled at Paris, France, in 1937 and served with an underground resistance group during the early years of World War II. In the years following the war he produced—writing in both French and English—the challenging novels *Molloy, Malone Dies* and *The Unnamable* and two plays, *Eleutheria* and *Waiting for Godot*. In January 1953, *Godot* received an acclaimed production at the Theatre de Babylone in Paris, and with it Beckett achieved worldwide renown. He was awarded the Nobel Prize for Literature in 1969. He died Dec 22, 1989, at Paris, France.

TERENCE HANBURY WHITE

Birth • May 29, 1906 • 100 Years
English author of a quartet of novels called *The Once and Future King*, T.H. White was born in Bombay, India. He had an unhappy childhood and occupied himself with learning archery, painting and studying. When he read the 15th century account of King Arthur, Thomas Malory's *Morte d'Arthur*, he found it to be the most perfect tragedy. In 1939, White wrote the first part of his tetralogy that would retell the tale. *The Sword in the Stone* focused on the young Arthur being trained by Merlin the magician and the animals of the nearby forest. White commented later, "It is more or less a kind of wish-fulfillment of the things I should like to have happened to me when I was a boy." In 1940, he published *The Witch in the Wood* (later renamed *The Queen of Air and Darkness*) which set the stage for the tragedy of Arthur's life, as he is seduced by his own half-sister Morgause. *The Ill-Made Knight* (1941) traces Arthur's search for the Holy Grail and shows the members of the Round Table becoming scattered. Lastly, *The Candle in the Wind* (1958) follows Arthur's defeat as Mordred, his son by Morgause, exposes Lancelot and Guenevere's affair and opposes his father in battle. White's story was adapted in 1960 as the musical *Camelot* and in 1963 as a Walt Disney production titled *The Sword in the Stone*. T.H. White died at sea on Jan 17, 1964.

CLIFFORD ODETS

Birth • July 18, 1906 • 100 Years
Playwright Clifford Odets began his career as a poet before turning to acting in a number of minor roles on stage (1923–1930). In 1931, he helped found the Group Theatre in New York City for which he began to write plays of social protest, including *Waiting for Lefty, Awake and Sing!* and *Golden Boy*. His proletarian views helped make him a popular playwright during the Depression years. Odets went to Hollywood in 1936 and wrote screenplays such as *Sweet Smell of Success* (1961). Clifford Odets was born at Philadelphia, PA, and died at Los Angeles, CA, Aug 15, 1963.

HANNAH ARENDT

Birth • Oct 14, 1906 • 100 Years
Political scientist and philosopher Hannah Arendt was born at Hannover, Germany, to Jewish parents. With the Nazi rise to power in 1933, she fled to Paris where she worked with Jewish refugees and orphans. After sailing to the United States (1940), she became the research director for the Conference of Jewish Relations and wrote her first book, *The Origins of Totalitarianism* (1958). This monumental work analyzes the historical circumstances that led to the development of fascism in Europe, tracing its roots to imperialism and anti-Semitism. In 1958, she also published *The Human Condition*, which examined the personal and social alienation of the times. Having established her reputation with

these books and countless articles, she became the first woman professor at Princeton University in 1959. Her most controversial book, *Eichmann in Jerusalem* (1963), suggested that Jewish complicity eventually enabled the Nazis to proceed with the Holocaust and that the Nazi war criminal Adolf Eichmann was just a bureaucrat who had simply lost the ability to think for himself. This epitomized what Arendt called "the fearsome, word-and-thought-defying banality of evil." Her works generated controversy and debate among both her critics and supporters. Hannah Arendt died of a heart attack in New York City, Dec 4, 1975.

JOHN DICKSON CARR

Birth • Nov 30, 1906 • 100 Years
Prolific "Golden Age" mystery novelist who also wrote under the name Carter Dickson. Carr was one of the great writers of "locked room" mysteries—seemingly inexplicable or supernatural murders eventually revealed to have a devious human cause. His first novel, *It Walks by Night*, was published in 1930. Dr. Gideon Fell and Sir Henry Merrivale were two popular detectives he created for several of his novels. In 1949, Carr was

authorized by the estate of Sherlock Holmes's creator to write the biography of Sir Arthur Conan Doyle. Born in Uniontown, PA, and died at Greenville, SC, in 1972.

RICHARD LLEWELLYN

Birth • Dec 8, 1906 • 100 Years
Llewellyn worked in the film and journalism industries, in addition to writing plays and novels. His best-known work is *How Green Was My Valley*, which was made into a movie starring Walter Pidgeon and Maureen O'Hara. Other novels include *None but the Lonely Heart* and *A Night of Bright Stars*. He was born at St. David's, Pembrokeshire, Wales, and died on Nov 30, 1983, at Dublin, Ireland.

Children's Literature

W.W. DENSLOW

Birth • May 5, 1856 • 150 Years
William Wallace Denslow was born at Philadelphia and studied art at The Cooper Union. He became a popular illustrator, known for his posters and theatrical designs for costumes and scenery. His first collaboration with L. Frank Baum, a collection called *Father Goose, His Book*, was published in 1899. The next year, the team produced a fairy tale called *The Wonderful Wizard of Oz*. This wildly successful book had 24 tipped-in color plates, all done by Denslow, and is considered a masterpiece of illustration. However, he had a falling-out

with Baum over copyright and royalty issues and did not illustrate any of the Oz sequels. Denslow never experienced success in his career again, and he died in poverty at New York City in 1915.

L. FRANK BAUM

Birth • May 15, 1856 • 150 Years
Best known as the author of *The Wonderful Wizard of Oz*, L. Frank Baum's love of fairy tales began at a young age. Sickly as a child, he was a voracious reader and showed his creative talents at a young age. He published his own newspaper at 15 and began acting on stage soon thereafter. Baum married and settled into life as a salesman in Syracuse, NY, but after suffering financial reverses, went west and opened a general store in the Dakota Territory. One business venture after another failed, and he eventually drifted back into journalism. He finally found success when he published his take on the rhymes of Mother Goose, a long-favorite topic. *Father Goose, His Book* was published in 1899 with illustrations by W.W. Denslow. Their next collaboration was one of the most successful books in the history of children's literature: *The Wonderful Wizard of Oz* (1900), which of course was the source for the 1939 film. Baum authored 17 sequels; each met with moderate success but none measured up to the original book's wild popularity. Born at Chittenango, NY, Baum died at Hollywood, CA, on May 5, 1919, after decades of poor health.

Spotlight on People

KATE DOUGLAS WIGGIN

See Education

ELEANOR ESTES

Birth • May 9, 1906 • 100 Years

Beloved children's author born in West Haven, CT, Eleanor Ruth Rosenfeld married Rice Estes in 1932 and worked as a children's librarian at the New York Public Library. She published her first novel for children, *The Moffats*, in 1941, and with this simple tale of a family living through World War I, a successful series was created. Follow-up titles included *The Middle Moffat* (1942) and *Rufus M.* (1943), both of which were named Newbery Honor Books by the American Library Association. She won another Newbery Honor in 1945 for perhaps her best-known title, *The Hundred Dresses,* a sad tale of an immigrant girl teased by her classmates. Estes received the Newbery Medal in 1952 for *Ginger Pye.* All of these books remain in print today, having delighted generations of children. Eleanor Estes died at Hamden, CT, July 15, 1988.

MARGRET REY

Birth • May 16, 1906 • 100 Years

Born Margarete Elisabeth Waldstein in Hamburg, Germany, she and her husband, Hans Augusto Rey, are one of the most famous teams of children's authors ever. Living in Paris in the early days of their marriage and career, they were working to expand a minor character from their book *Raffy and the Nine Monkeys* into another book. Both German Jews, they feared for their safety as Hitler's influence spread, and in 1940, they built two bicycles out of spare parts and fled, taking with them only the clothes on their back, a bit of food and five manuscripts. They made their way to Lisbon, then Brazil and eventually New York, where one of those five manuscripts was published in 1941 as *Curious George.* Margret wrote the original seven adventures of George and his friend, the Man with the Yellow Hat, while H.A. created the illustrations. She went on to produce another 28 Curious George titles and released several other picture books as well. She died in 1996.

CROCKETT JOHNSON

Birth • Oct 20, 1906 • 100 Years

Born David Johnson Leisk at New York City, this writer and artist published his work under a pen name that was part childhood nickname, part "easy to pronounce." In the late 1930s, he worked as a political cartoonist and moved on to comic strips by the early 1940s. His popular "Barnaby" chronicles the adventures of Barnaby Baxter and his Fairy Godfather, Mr. O'Malley. The strip was syndicated nationwide and ran for many years. By the 1950s, Johnson was writing and illustrating books for children. His 20+ titles include *The Carrot Seed* (1945), written by his wife, Ruth Krauss, but he is most remembered for *Harold and the Purple Crayon* (1955). This simple story of a small boy's vivid imagination is still a bestseller today. Johnson died on July 11, 1975, at Norwalk, CT.

STERLING NORTH

Birth • Nov 4, 1906 • 100 Years

The author of many books, including the children's classic *Rascal: A Memoir of a Better Era*, was born on a farm in Edgerton, WI. As a child he had many pets—cats, dogs, a crow, skunks and, of course, a raccoon named Rascal who ate at the table and learned to ride on the handlebars of young North's bike. Many of his books draw on his childhood experience and the relationships between humans and animals. North felt that the stories of his youth, a time before television and comic books, were full of values that the modern world was lacking. He said, "In children we have an innocent audience not yet hardened and brutalized and cynical. They look to us trustingly for information and enchantment. How very few of us are worthy of such trust." *Rascal* sold more than two million copies in 14 countries and was adapted as a film by Walt Disney Studios in 1969. Other books include *So Dear to My Heart* (1948), a story of a boy who raises a prize-winning ram; *Wolfling* (1969), a fictional tale about a pioneer family who adopts a half-wolf; and *Abe Lincoln: Log Cabin to White House* (1956). Sterling North died of a stroke on Dec 22, 1974.

Journalism
LOUELLA PARSONS

Birth • Aug 6, 1881 • 125 Years

A legendary Hollywood gossip columnist, the first of her kind, Parsons was born at Freeport, IL, and landed her first newspaper job as drama editor for the *Dixon Morning Star* while still in high school. She eventually went to California where she became a Hearst newspapers' syndicated columnist (1922–1965). In 1934, she created a successful celebrity radio interview program on which movie stars would appear to plug their films in lieu of payment, again, the first of its kind. At the height of her popularity and influence, her column appeared in more than 400 newspapers and was read by approximately 20 million people. Parsons gloried in her power and occasionally used her column in spite, making her a woman feared by many in Hollywood whose careers depended on their reputations and positive publicity. Her famous rivalry with Hedda Hopper was chronicled in an Emmy-nominated, made-for-TV movie, *Malice in Wonderland* (1985), starring Elizabeth Taylor as Parsons. Parsons retired in 1965 and died Dec 9, 1972, at Santa Monica, CA.

FRANKLIN PIERCE ADAMS

Birth • Nov 15, 1881 • 125 Years

Born in Chicago, this newspaper columnist, poet and radio personality primarily wrote under his initials F.P.A. He is best known for his syndicated column, "The Conning Tower," which ran from 1913 to 1937 and featured such contributors as Dorothy Parker and Ring Lardner. In 1938, he joined the panel of experts on the radio show "Information, Please," a move that further established him as a witty and humorous commentator on contemporary America. The first of his 10 books of light verse was published in 1911. His popularity lasted throughout the 1930s, '40s and '50s. Adams died Mar 23, 1960, at New York City.

JOHN CAMERON SWAYZE

Birth • Apr 4, 1906 • 100 Years

This pioneer in television journalism began hosting in 1949 "Camel News Caravan" for NBC, where he was one of the first reporters to do on-air interviews and report on breaking news stories. His catchphrase was "hopscotching the world for headlines." Beginning in 1956, he became a spokesperson for Timex watches and over a span of 20 years made countless television commercials featuring someone performing a stunt that seemed destined to damage his timepiece. However, Swayze assured the public, the Timex watch would always come through unscathed, because "it takes a licking and keeps on ticking." Born at Wichita, KS, he died at Sarasota, FL, Aug 15, 1995.

Education
GRACE HOADLEY DODGE

Birth • May 21, 1856 • 150 Years

Born in New York City to a wealthy family with a history of philanthropic work and business success, Grace Hoadley Dodge devoted her life to the improvement of women's education and well-being, focusing on the concerns of working women. She began by teaching fundamental aspects of cooking, sewing and health care to women who worked in factories. At the same time, she used what she learned from these women to initiate tenement reform. In 1880, she contributed to the formation of the Kitchen Garden Association which supported domestic training and industrial arts in public schools. This association developed into Teachers College in 1889 and became part of Columbia University in 1892. Dodge earned one of the first two seats given to women on the New York City Board of Education where she advocated manual training and evening classes for working women. She organized the New York Traveler's Aid Society as well as the American Social Hygiene Association. In addition, Dodge mediated the merger of two women's groups into the Women's Christian Association (YWCA) in 1905 and served as president until her death in 1914.

Spotlight on People

KATE DOUGLAS WIGGIN

Birth • Sept 28, 1856 • 150 Years

Kate Wiggin was born Kate Douglas Smith at Philadelphia, PA. She helped organize the first free kindergarten on the West Coast in 1878 at San Francisco, and in 1880, she and her sister established the California Kindergarten Training School. After moving back east she devoted herself to writing. Wiggin produced a number of children's books including *The Birds' Christmas Carol* (1887), her first literary success; *Polly Oliver's Problem*; and the hugely popular *Rebecca of Sunnybrook Farm* (1903). She died at Harrow, England, Aug 24, 1923.

ALLEN WALKER READ

Birth • June 2, 1906 • 100 Years

An etymologist, linguist and lexicographer who spent much of his career researching the origins of the phrase "O.K.," the holy grail of etymology. Born at Winnebago, MN, he spent time at Oxford as a Rhodes scholar and returned to the United States to eventually become professor of English at Columbia University for 30 years. Read compiled several dictionaries and wrote approximately 300 papers. His research into the origin of words led him to determine the history of such familiar names as Dixie, Podunk and the Rocky Mountains. The earliest use of O.K. was in the *Boston Morning Post* in 1839 in an article about bad spelling, which said O.K. stood for the phrase "Oll Korrect." Read died Oct 16, 2002.

Art

REMBRANDT

Birth • July 15, 1606 • 400 Years

Dutch painter and etcher, born at Leiden, Holland, one of the undisputed giants of Western art. Rembrandt's paintings feature vibrant color, rich brushwork and dramatic lighting. His numerous paintings, etchings, drawings and prints include portraits, self-portraits, mythical and Biblical themes, still lifes and landscapes. Some famous works are *The Night Watch*, *Danae* and *Anatomy Lesson of Dr. Nicolaes Tulp*. During his time—especially during the 1630s—he was a fashionable portrait painter, although he later lost prestige and prominent commissions, forcing him to go into bankruptcy in 1656. He died in poverty at Amsterdam, Holland, Oct 4, 1669.

JOHN TRUMBULL

Birth • June 6, 1756 • 250 Years

Born at Lebanon, CT, Trumbull is remembered for his paintings of the American Revolution. After a childhood injury, he lost vision in one eye, but this did not prevent him from serving as an aide to George Washington during the Revolutionary War. He studied painting in London under Benjamin West and, with the encouragement of West and Thomas Jefferson, he began work on his famed historical pieces in 1784. His portraits of notable people of his day include George Washington. In 1817, the US Congress commissioned him to create four large paintings to be installed in the rotunda of the Capitol: *Washington Resigning His Commission, The Surrender of Cornwallis, The Surrender of Burgoyne* and *Declaration of Independence*. He died Nov 10, 1843, at New York City.

JOHN SINGER SARGENT

Birth • Jan 12, 1856 • 150 Years

Born in Florence, Italy, of American parents, Sargent became one of the most famous portrait artists of the late Victorian and Edwardian ages in Britain as well as in the United States. Sargent studied in Paris, but his early paintings were not well received. His portrait of Madame Gautreau, *Madame X* (1884), found to be too avant-garde and erotic, caused a scandal at the Paris Salon. Finding it difficult to break into the French market, Sargent moved to England where his work was also considered too eccentric. In fact, *The Misses Vickers* was voted the worst picture of the year by the *Pall Mall Gazette* in 1856. Eventually, the British warmed to him, as did wealthy Americans, and soon he had more portrait commissions than he could handle. His best-known works include *Carnation, Lily, Lily, Rose* (1886) and British actress Ellen Terry as *Lady Macbeth* (1889). While he owed his fame to his success as a portraitist, Sargent said, "I *hate* to paint portraits! I hope to never paint another portrait in my life!" After 1910, he focused on painting landscapes and murals, such as the one in the upper landing of the Boston Public Library and at the Boston

Museum of Fine Arts. John Singer Sargent died of a heart attack on Apr 15, 1925.

PABLO PICASSO

Birth • Oct 25, 1881 • 125 Years

Painter, sculptor, printmaker and ceramicist. This Spanish expatriot's impressive body of work (more than 20,000 pieces) exemplifies modern art and he's generally recognized as the most influential artist of the 20th century. From an early age, Picasso showed an aptitude for drawing and rejected his formal art school training. His early Blue Period (1901–1904) is characterized by paintings in various shades of blue, reflecting moods of despair and depicting outcasts and the downtrodden. Shortly after moving to Paris in 1904, he entered his Rose Period (1904–1906), which is characterized by more traditional, muted and warmer Spanish colors. *Les Demoiselles d'Avignon* was controversial for the way in which the female subjects were portrayed as prostitutes with masklike faces. From 1909 to 1912, Picasso and painter Georges Braque developed Cubism, an analytical style of painting in which a new reality is constructed viewing fractured objects from multiple angles on a single canvas. In the Synthetic phase of his work (1912–1914), Picasso glued paper and other objects onto his canvases, creating works that were a combination of painting and collage. Picasso's reputation as a sculptor came mostly after his death because he kept the majority of his sculpture in his own collection. Throughout his career, Picasso's art was characterized by daring and innovation, lending him an almost mythic status rarely achieved during an artist's lifetime. He is well known for his charm and womanizing, having once described women as either "goddesses or doormats." Born at Malaga, Spain, he died Apr 8, 1973, at Mougins, France.

Architecture

ROBERT MILLS

Birth • Aug 12, 1781 • 225 Years

Born at Charleston, SC, Mills was one of the first professionally trained American architects. He designed more than 50 structures, notably the Treasury Building (1836–1842), the Patent Office, now part of the Smithsonian Institution (1836–1840) and the Washington Monument (1814), all in our nation's capital. Thomas Jefferson, under whom Mills had studied, described the style of architecture they both practiced as using antique, classical forms that nod to those revered democratic republics after which the United States was modeled. Mills died at Washington, DC, on Mar 3, 1855.

LOUIS SULLIVAN

Birth • Sept 3, 1856 • 150 Years

An American architect responsible for the modern, steel-framed skyscraper, his designs are characterized by rich ornamentation, plain outer surfaces and cubic forms. His famous motto was "form follows function." Sullivan produced more than 100 works with his partner Dankmar Adler (1881–1895), including the Transportation Building at the 1893 World's Columbian Exposition held in Chicago, the Auditorium Building in Chicago, the Wainwright Building in St. Louis and the Prudential Building in New York City. Frank Lloyd Wright apprenticed under him for six years but left on bad terms after a quarrel. After the 1893 economic depression resulted in the breakup of the firm, Sullivan established his own practice, which failed, mainly because of his aggressive personality. By 1920, he was being supported financially by friends. Born at Boston, MA, he died Apr 14, 1924, at Chicago, IL.

PHILIP JOHNSON

Birth • July 8, 1906 • 100 Years

Postmodern architect who promoted International Style (post-World War I modern architecture). He was director of the Department of Architecture of New York's Museum of Modern Art, worked with Mies van der Rohe on the Seagram Building at New York City and designed his own "glass house" at New Canaan, CT. Johnson's AT&T headquarters at New York City is an excellent representation of postmodern architecture with its so-called "Chippendale" top. Born at Cleveland, OH, and died Jan 25, 2005, in his home at New Canaan, CT.

Spotlight on People

Entertainment

ANNA PAVLOVA

Birth • Feb 12, 1881 • 125 Years

Russian ballerina Anna Pavlova, thought by some to have been the greatest dancer of all time, was born at St. Petersburg, Russia. After outstanding success with the Ballet Russe and other companies, she formed her own ballet in 1910 and performed on tour for enthusiastic audiences in nearly every country in the world. Pavlova died at The Hague, Netherlands, Jan 23, 1931.

CECIL B. DeMILLE

Birth • Aug 12, 1881 • 125 Years

Film pioneer, born at Ashfield, MA. Cecil Blount DeMille was a showman extraordinaire known for lavish screen spectacles. His more than 70 major films were noted more for their large scale than for their subtle artistry. In 1913, he produced one of the earliest four-reelers, *The Squaw Man*, which boasted the first use of indoor lighting on an actor and was the first picture to publicize the names of its stars. His other innovations included the sneak preview and the idea of producing different versions of a popular film. His work includes *The Crusades, The Sign of the Cross, King of Kings, Cleopatra, The Plainsman, The Buccaneer, Reap the Wild Wind* and *The Ten Commandments*, made in 1923 and then remade in 1956. DeMille was awarded an Oscar for *The Greatest Show on Earth* in 1953. He died Jan 21, 1959, at Hollywood, CA.

LOU COSTELLO

Birth • Mar 6, 1906 • 100 Years

Partner with Bud Abbott in the legendary comedy duo Abbott and Costello. Born at Paterson, NJ, Costello began his career as a burlesque comic, performing with a variety of partners the popular vaudeville routines of the day, of which there were hundreds. He teamed up with Abbott in 1936, playing the patsy to Abbott's straight man. The duo starred in numerous films, including what is generally regarded as their best, *Abbott and Costello Meet Frankenstein* (1948). For years they performed on stage and television such routines as their famous "Who's on First?" bit. Costello died of a heart attack on Mar 3, 1959, at East Los Angeles, CA.

HENNY YOUNGMAN

Birth • Mar 16, 1906 • 100 Years

Born to Russian-Jewish parents who had immigrated to the United States but were living in England at the time (some sources say in 1902), Youngman was known as the "King of the One-Liners." His signature line "Take my wife—please!" for years never failed to get a laugh. Youngman began his career in entertainment as a violin player on the vaudeville circuit. A club owner, impressed by Youngman's witty banter on stage, hired him to work as a comedian, launching his decades-long career. From his appearances on Kate Smith's radio program in the late 1930s he became nationally known. He performed on variety shows throughout the 1950s and was a frequent guest on *Laugh-In*, a 1960s television show. He died Feb 24, 1998, at New York City.

JOSEPHINE BAKER

Birth • June 3, 1906 • 100 Years

The sensation of 1920s Paris, Baker was born into poverty at St. Louis, MO. At age 16, she began working as a dancer and went to Paris in 1925, where her "danse sauvage," in particular her seminude performance in a G-string and bananas, became a hit. In addition to her exotic dance costumes, Baker was well known for her jazz singing. She gained French citizenship in 1937 and was the first American-born woman to be awarded the Croix de Guerre and the Legion of Honor for her Red Cross work during World War II. She briefly retired in 1956 after adopting 12 babies of various nationalities, whom she referred to as her "rainbow tribe," but was forced to return to work for financial reasons. She performed up until her death on Apr 12, 1975, at Paris, France. Josephine Baker also was active in the 1960s civil rights movement in America.

BILLY WILDER

Birth • June 22, 1906 • 100 Years

One of the greatest directors of Hollywood's Golden Age was

born Samuel Wilder at Sucha Beskidzka in the Austro-Hungarian Empire. After a short career in Berlin, Wilder fled Germany in 1933 and eventually landed in Hollywood where he directed and cowrote some of the greatest films of the 20th century. His classics include the film noir works *Double Indemnity* and *Sunset Boulevard*, the searing dramas *Stalag 17* and *The Lost Weekend* and the comic gem *Some Like It Hot*. He received six Oscars (out of 21 nominations), and Best Film Oscars went to *The Lost Weekend* and *The Apartment*. Wilder died at Los Angeles, CA, on Mar 27, 2002.

GEORGE SANDERS

Birth • July 3, 1906 • 100 Years

Sanders, born at St. Petersburg, Russia, to English parents, made a career in Hollywood of playing cynical, sophisticated cads, most famously as the viperish Addison DeWitt in *All About Eve* (1950), for which he won a Best Supporting Actor Oscar. He also appeared in *Rebecca, Foreign Correspondent, Ivanhoe* and as the Saint and the Falcon in a series of midcentury movies. He committed suicide at Barcelona, Spain, on Apr 25, 1972, leaving behind a note that complained of boredom and memorably calling the world a "sweet cesspool."

JOHN HUSTON

Birth • Aug 5, 1906 • 100 Years

This larger-than-life Hollywood figure, son of actor Walter Huston, spent his whole life before or behind the camera as an actor, screenwriter and director, beginning with his stage debut at age three. Huston lived an adventurous, searching life—including becoming California's Amateur Lightweight Boxing Champion and riding with the Mexican Cavalry— before directing his first film: the 1941 detective-noir masterpiece, *The Maltese Falcon,* that catapulted Humphrey Bogart into dark heroic roles and away from gangster parts. Huston and Bogart collaborated on other great movies: *The Treasure of the Sierra Madre* (for which Huston's father Walter won a Best Supporting Actor Oscar in 1948), *Key Largo, The African Queen* and *Beat the Devil*. During World War II, Huston produced for the army three powerful documentaries about the combat soldier. His acting skills are evidenced by his chilling performance as Noah Cross in *Chinatown* (1974). Born at Nevada, MO, the five-time wed, hard-living Huston died Aug 28, 1987, on location at Middletown, RI, not long after completing his final film, *The Dead*.

JANET GAYNOR

Birth • Oct 6, 1906 • 100 Years

This recipient of the first Academy Award for Best Actress was born Laura Gainor at Philadelphia, PA, and moved with her parents to California where at age 20, she was cast as the leading lady in the film *The Johnstown Flood*. Within a year, she was the most sought-after star as audiences were captivated by her wholesome, dimpled sweetness and diminutive stature. In 1929, she became the first winner of the Academy Award for Best Actress for her cumulative work in two 1927 films, *Sunrise* and *Seventh Heaven*, and for 1928's *Street Angel*. Gaynor continued to be a top draw in the film industry; she and Charles Farrell became known as "America's favorite lovebirds." Before her early retirement, her last two successful films were *A Star Is Born* (1937) and *The Young in Heart* (1938). She married costume designer Gilbert Adrian and lived on a ranch in Brazil until his death, occasionally returning to the United States for film and television roles. Gaynor's final appearances were in a Broadway adaptation of *Harold and Maude* (1980) and in an episode of "The Love Boat" TV series. In 1982, she was in a car accident from which she never fully recovered, and Gaynor died of pneumonia on Sept 14, 1984.

LOUISE BROOKS

Birth • Nov 14, 1906 • 100 Years

Born at Cherryvale, KS, Brooks started her career as a dancer before finding fame as an actress in the silent cinema of the 1920s. She is best known for her performances in two 1929 German films: *Pandora's Box* (as Lulu) and *Diary of a Lost Girl*. Would-be flappers the world over copied her trademark hairstyle: a sleek, helmetlike bob. Brooks wrote a well-received book of reminiscences, *Lulu in Hollywood* (1982), before her death on Aug 8, 1985, at Rochester, NY.

Spotlight on People

Music

GEORG PHILIPP TELEMANN

Birth • Mar 14, 1681 • 325 Years

As a child, this German composer was discouraged from pursuing a career in music and was denied music lessons; but while studying law at Leipzig University, Telemann's energy, diligence and musical talent were recognized and allowed to flourish. He reorganized the student musical society, which began to give public concerts to people who had never before been exposed to the music that was traditionally reserved for the court and aristocracy. Telemann became city musical director of Frankfurt am Main (1712–1721) and Hamburg (1721–1767), where he continued to present public concerts and to publish music. He became famous for his church compositions, be they small cantatas or large-scale works involving soloists, choruses and orchestras. In 1722, he declined an offer to become the musical director at Leipzig University; the post was then offered to J.S. Bach. In his lifetime, Telemann composed thousands of works, including concertos, Passions, oratorios, funeral and wedding services, chamber music, operas and overtures. He died in Hamburg on June 25, 1767.

WOLFGANG AMADEUS MOZART

Birth • Jan 27, 1756 • 250 Years

See Spotlight on World Anniversaries

BÉLA BARTÓK

Birth • Mar 25, 1881 • 125 Years

Influential Hungarian composer and pianist of the 20th century, born at Nagyszentmiklos, Hungary. Bartók collected and wove into his own music the folk traditions of Eastern Europe. In the United States, where he fled as the Nazis came to power, he took an academic position that allowed him to do important work documenting more than 6,000 pieces of folk music. Died at New York, NY, Sept 26, 1945.

DMITRI SHOSTAKOVICH

Birth • Sept 25, 1906 • 100 Years

Russian composer born at St. Petersburg. Shostakovich was drawn to avant-garde influences in his compositions, a creative expression that increasingly drew Soviet condemnation after Stalin came to power in 1922. Shostakovich composed 15 well-regarded symphonies and taught at music conservatories, but he was always regarded with displeasure by government authorities. Stalin's death in 1953 eased the pressures somewhat, and Shostakovich was able to finish out his life as Russia's most acclaimed composer. He died at Moscow, USSR, Aug 9, 1975.

Science and Technology

EDMUND HALLEY

Birth • Nov 8, 1656 • 350 Years

Astronomer and mathematician born at London, England. Halley held the position of Astronomer Royal from 1721 until his death Jan 14, 1742, at Greenwich, England. He observed the great comet of 1682 (now named for him), first conceived its periodicity and wrote in his *Synopsis of Comet Astronomy*: "I may venture to foretell that this Comet will return again in the year 1758." It did, and Edmund Halley's memory is kept alive by the once-every-generation appearance of Halley's comet. There have been 28 recorded appearances since 240 BC. Average time between appearances is 76 years. Halley's comet is next expected to be visible in 2061. Halley was the first to catalog stars of the southern hemisphere, the first to publish a meteorological chart, the first to create magnetic charts (reflecting variations in compass readings) and the first gatherer of mortality data (which led to actuarial tables now commonly used).

HENRY CAVENDISH

Birth • Oct 10, 1731 • 275 years

This English physicist and chemist, born at Nice, France, measured the Earth's mass and density using a method that was to become known as the Cavendish experiment. An eccentric and painfully shy man who had no friends or acquaintances outside of his immediate family, he appeared in public only to attend scientific meetings. He was also a misogynist who ordered his female servants never to appear in his presence. As a scientist, Cavendish is best known for his experiments on gases. He was the first to identify hydrogen, and his experiments on carbon dioxide were instrumental for later discoveries of inert gases. In addition, he conducted many unpublished studies of heat and electricity. He died Feb 24, 1810, at London, England.

JOHN LOUDON MCADAM

Birth • Sept 21, 1756 • 250 Years

Born at Ayrshire, Scotland, McAdam invented the macadam road surface. After being appointed a road trustee and wishing to do something about the deplorable local road conditions, he funded his own research that produced this superior road pavement, which was raised to promote water drainage. The popularity of macadamization (later called Tar-Mac) resulted in widespread use of the technique, facilitating travel and communication in Great Britain and the United States. He died Nov 26, 1836.

RENE THEOPHILE HYACINTHE LAENNEC

Birth • Feb 17, 1781 • 225 Years

Famed French physician, author and inventor of the stethoscope (c. 1819), called "father of chest medicine." He wrote extensively about respiratory and heart ailments. Born at Quimper, France, he died there Aug 13, 1826.

GEORGE STEPHENSON

Birth • June 9, 1781 • 225 Years

English inventor, developer of the first practical steam locomotive, born near Newcastle, England. Stephenson built the first passenger train, the *Active*, that ushered in a new age on Sept 27, 1825, when it carried passengers from Darlington to Stockton, England, at 15 mph. Stephenson was commissioned to survey and construct a railway line from Manchester to Liverpool—the Industrial Revolution now could travel. He died near Chesterfield, England, Aug 12, 1848.

DAVID BREWSTER

Birth • Dec 11, 1781 • 225 Years

Born in an obscure village in Scotland, this knighted physicist invented the kaleidoscope (1816). He also discovered what later became known as Brewster's law of polarization, which deals with light refraction and polarizing angles. The British government began to use Fresnel lenses in lighthouses because of his work. Sir David Brewster died on Feb 10, 1868.

MATTHEW FONTAINE MAURY

Birth • Jan 14, 1806 • 200 Years

Naval officer, born at Fredericksburg, VA. Maury established oceanography as a branch of science. As a superintendent of the Naval Observatory (1842–1861), he revolutionized the recording of oceanographic data. In 1855, he authored the first textbook of modern oceanography. Died at Lexington, VA, Feb 1, 1873.

JOHN AUGUSTUS ROEBLING

Birth • June 12, 1806 • 200 Years

Born in Prussia, Roebling was a US civil engineer who designed and built steel suspension bridges, including ones over Niagara Falls and the Ohio River. His most famous design is the Brooklyn Bridge in New York City. Roebling was injured at the site, developed tetanus and died July 22, 1869, before construction was finished. His son, Washington Augustus, completed the project in 1883.

DAVID EDWARD HUGHES

Birth • May 16, 1831 • 175 Years

Born at London, England, Hughes immigrated to the United States with his family when he was a child. He invented a type-printing telegraph instrument, the Hughes Printer, which was adopted by Western Union Telegraph Company and remained popular until the 1930s. He is best known for his invention of the carbon microphone (1878), the predecessor of those still in use today. Hughes was honored with numerous awards for his work. He died Jan 22, 1900, at London, England.

Cullman County Public Library System
200 Clark Street Northeast
Cullman, Alabama 35055

Spotlight on People

JAMES CLERK MAXWELL

Birth • Nov 13, 1831 • 175 Years

British physicist and university professor noted for his research in the field of electricity and magnetism. Born at Edinburgh, Scotland, he died of cancer Nov 5, 1879, at Cambridge, England.

GRANVILLE T. WOODS

Birth • Apr 23, 1856 • 150 Years

Sometimes called the black Thomas Edison, Granville T. Woods was born at Columbus, OH. In 1887, he invented the Synchronous Multiplex Railway Telegraph which allowed dispatchers to communicate with trains in motion, thus decreasing the number of railway accidents. In addition, Woods originated a number of other products: an automotive air brake, a telephone transmitter, many devices for the telegraph. His 1890 invention of an electronically heated egg incubator allowed growers to hatch 50,000 eggs at a time. Still in use today is his overhead conducting system for electric trolleys and rail cars. By the time of his death on Jan 30, 1910, at New York, NY, he had 50 patents to his name.

NIKOLA TESLA

Birth • July 10, 1856 • 150 Years

The inventor and scientist who perfected the use of alternating-current electricity was born in Smiljan, Croatia. After studying and working in Europe, Tesla sailed to the United States in 1884; his few possessions included four cents, some of his own poetry and calculations for a flying machine. He went to work at Thomas Edison's research laboratory in New York City. Edison was committed to direct-current electricity, while Tesla was interested in developing polyphase motors which were based on alternating current. They were unable to overcome their differences and soon parted ways. As owner of his own company, Tesla invented the first efficient polyphase motor that allowed electrical currents to be transmitted over long distances, whereas Edison's direct-current motor could supply electricity only locally. In 1893, George Westinghouse used Tesla's polyphase alternating current to make the Chicago World's Fair the first in history to use electricity. Two years later, Tesla designed the world's first hydroelectric plant at Niagara Falls, which proved the practical application of his polyphase system. Today, alternating current is the standard method of power transmission worldwide. Tesla was also interested in using radio waves to carry electrical energy without wires. He achieved wireless communication in 1897 and demonstrated his radio-controlled boats to a stunned public at Madison Square Garden. Additionally, Tesla discovered terrestrial stationary waves, and he created artificial lightning. Tesla held more than 100 patents, including one for the Tesla coil which is still in use in radio, television and other electronics. Although a highly esteemed member of the scientific community, Tesla became a recluse in his later years, and his body was discovered in his New York City hotel room by a maid on Jan 8, 1943. After his death, he was praised as a scientific visionary and the United States Supreme Court ruled that Nikola Tesla, not Guglielmo Marconi, had invented the radio.

ALEXANDER FLEMING

Birth • Aug 6, 1881 • 125 Years

Born at Lochfield, Scotland, Fleming was a distinguished student, researcher and instructor at St. Mary's Medical School at London University—a stint interrupted by service in World War I. As a research scientist he focused on immunology and bacteriology. In 1928, he noticed a mold growing in a research culture that repelled and killed bacterial virus. Further experiments proved the powerful antibacterial qualities of the mold, which Fleming called penicillin. After development, it was brought into production in the mid-1940s. Fleming's discovery has revolutionized the treatment of infectious illnesses, such as pneumonia, gangrene, blood poisoning and meningitis—many of which were conquered by antibiotics. He received many recognitions, including election to the Royal Society; and in 1944, he was honored with a knighthood. In Spain, the grateful Bullfighting Association (bullfighters were plagued by gangrenous infections) erected a statue in his honor outside a popular stadium. He died at London, England, on Mar 11, 1955.

CLYDE TOMBAUGH

Birth • Feb 4, 1906 • 100 Years

Tombaugh discovered the planet Pluto in 1930. Throughout his extensive career in astronomy he discovered stars and galaxies and made observations of numerous planetary surfaces. Tombaugh held various academic positions at Arizona State College and New Mexico State University and worked as an astronomer at Lowell Observatory at Flagstaff, AZ, and the White Sands Missile Range. Born at Streator, IL, Tombaugh died Jan 17, 1997, at Las Cruces, NM.

MARIA GOEPPERT MAYER

Birth • June 28, 1906 • 100 Years

German American physicist Maria Goeppert Mayer was born at Kattowitz, Germany. A participant in the Manhattan Project, she worked on the separation of uranium isotopes for the atomic bomb. Mayer became the first American woman to win a Nobel Prize when she shared the 1963 prize for physics with J. Hans Daniel Jensen and Eugene P. Wigner for their explanation of the atomic nucleus, known as the nuclear shell theory. Mayer died Feb 20, 1972, at San Diego, CA.

PHILO FARNSWORTH

Birth • Aug 19, 1906 • 100 Years

Farnsworth, an engineer, was a television pioneer who conceived of the idea of TV broadcasting while still in high school and realized his dream at 21. His research into picture transmission led to the establishment of his own company, Farnsworth Radio and Television Corporation, and to his holding about 165 patents. His first transmitted image was of a dollar sign. In addition to being television's inventor, he may also be its first critic. His son Kent has said, "Throughout my childhood his reaction to television was 'There's nothing on it worthwhile, and we're not going to watch it in this household, and I don't want it in your intellectual diet.'" Farnsworth was born at Beaver, UT, and died on Mar 11, 1971, at Salt Lake City, UT.

ALBERT BRUCE SABIN

Birth • Aug 26, 1906 • 100 Years

American medical researcher Albert Bruce Sabin was born at Bialystok, Poland, and immigrated to the United States in 1921. His oral vaccine for polio (1956) provided lifetime protection against the disease and came to replace Jonas Salk's injected vaccine. In 1957, Sabin's vaccine was adopted by the World Health Organization; and in 1971, he was awarded the US National Medal of Science. Sabin died Mar 3, 1993, at Washington, DC.

GRACE HOPPER

Birth • Dec 9, 1906 • 100 Years

Born at New York, NY, Hopper was a mathematician and career military officer. When Rear Admiral Grace Hopper retired from the US Navy at the age of 79, she was the oldest naval officer ever on active duty. She was also a leader in the computer revolution, having developed the computer language COBOL. Hopper died Jan 1, 1992, at Arlington, WV.

Commerce

JOHN BASKERVILLE

Birth • Jan 28, 1706 • 300 Years

Born at Wolverly, England, Baskerville was a printer and typographer whose own elegantly styled typeface lives on today. Baskerville set up his printing establishment in 1757 and created editions of Milton, Virgil and other classic authors. Cambridge University appointed him their printer soon after. His innovations in printing methods (including the "hot presses" method) helped book publishing proceed at a faster pace. Baskerville died Jan 8, 1775, at Birmingham.

GEORGE PULLMAN

Birth • Mar 3, 1831 • 175 Years

Born at Brocton, NY, George Mortimer Pullman was an inventor and industrialist who became famous for his design and production of the Pullman railroad sleeping car, with a folding upper berth (patented in 1864) and a lower berth accomplished with extensible seat

Spotlight on People

cushions (1865). By 1867, Pullman and his partner organized the Pullman Palace Car Company, which became the world's greatest producers of railroad cars. The company also devised dining cars, chair cars and vestibule cars. In 1881, the town of Pullman, IL, south of Chicago, was built by the company to house its employees. Because rents were not lowered when wages were cut, a violent strike took place in May 1894, eventually forcing Pullman to give up control of all property in the town not directly required for manufacturing. George Pullman died Oct 19, 1897, at Chicago, IL.

FREDERICK WINSLOW TAYLOR
Birth • Mar 20, 1856 • 150 Years

Vilified and praised, Frederick Winslow Taylor, changed the face of business forever as the "father of scientific management." Born at Philadelphia, PA, Taylor started out as an innovative athlete who played sports precisely and absolutely by the rules. He was a top amateur tennis player who invented sturdier nets and a golfer who devised an irrigation method for greens and designed several unique golf clubs. He is best known, however, for his scientific approach to worker production. As a chief engineer at Philadelphia's Midvale Steel Company, he introduced time-and-motion studies in 1881, which helped companies find inefficiencies in worker movement and drive out time wasting on the assembly lines.

Henry Ford, in particular, put Taylor's ideas to work, much to his workers' dismay, who complained that they were not machines who performed robotically. Taylor died at Philadelphia, Mar 21, 1915.

EDWARD D. JONES
Birth • Oct 7, 1856 • 150 Years

Born at Worcester, MA, Edward Davis Jones was a Kiernan News Agency reporter alongside Charles Dow and Charles Bergstresser when the three left to found Dow Jones & Company, in 1882, a new business that prepared and distributed bulletins to Wall Street financial houses. Eventually, the publishing enterprise expanded to include the *Wall Street Journal* (1889) and the creation of the Dow Jones Industrial Average, which calculates the average selling price of a given number of stocks. Today, the Dow Jones average is one of the most frequently used indices for US stocks and bonds. Jones retired from the company in 1899 and died Feb 16, 1920, at New York City.

ETTORE ARCO ISADORO BUGATTI
Birth • Sept 15, 1881 • 125 Years

Born at Milan, Italy, Bugatti was a designer and manufacturer of posh racing cars and luxury automobiles, known for the superiority of their construction and design. He is described as an automotive artist for the beauty of his design work. Bugatti was the first to use the concept of modular engineering in the automotive industry, creating parts

that could be used in different styles of a Bugatti car. He survived his son who was to have carried on the family business, which then closed shortly after Ettore Bugatti's death on Aug 21, 1947, at Paris, France.

ARISTOTLE ONASSIS
Birth • Jan 7, 1906 • 100 Years

Billionaire Greek shipping magnate who married Jacqueline Kennedy in 1968. Born in Smyrna (now Izmir), Turkey, Onassis made his first million dollars in cigarette manufacturing and commodities trading in Argentina by the age of 25. During the Great Depression of 1932, he was able to purchase freighters at a relatively low cost, eventually building up a fleet of ships that was so extensive he was able to lease his tankers to the Allies during World War II. His greatest rival was fellow Greek shipping magnate, Stavros Niarchos; and Onassis's first marriage (in 1946) was to the daughter of yet another competitor, Stavros Livanos, which marriage ended in divorce in 1960. He is known for his longtime love affair with opera diva Maria Callas, which is said to have continued throughout his marriage to Jacqueline Onassis, and his celebrated yacht *Christina*, on which he spent much of his time. He died Mar 15, 1975, near Paris, France.

CHARLES REVSON

Birth • Oct 11, 1906 • 100 Years
Revson was the colorful and hard-driving force behind Revlon cosmetics, a company he created in 1932. Revson, who was born at Boston, MA, recognized the backwardness of the cosmetics industry, which was really single vendors with single products, and knew he could do better. His first product was a new kind of opaque nail polish that came in many shades. Revson was known as a color genius who could distinguish between shades of black. By the time of his death, Aug 24, 1975, Revson had built a cosmetics empire and an estate valued at $100 million. His employees feared him, and he is quoted as saying, "Creative people are like a wet towel. You wring them out and pick up another one."

SOICHIRO HONDA

Birth • Nov 17, 1906 • 100 Years
This talented mechanic and businessman founded the Honda Motor Company in September 1948. Soichiro Honda, born at Hamamatsu, Japan, had been an auto racer before World War II. After that, he took advantage of Japan's postwar industrial malaise to find business opportunities, the first of which was creating fuel-efficient motorcycles from extra military engines attached to bicycles. By the 1960s, Honda was the world's biggest motorcycle producer; and in 1962, the company branched

out into automobiles—with its signature Civic appearing in 1972. Soichiro Honda, who retired from his hugely successful company in 1973, died Aug 5, 1991, at Tokyo.

PETER KARL GOLDMARK

Birth • Dec 2, 1906 • 100 Years
Goldmark, an American engineer, invented the first commercial color television system in 1940 and developed the 33⅓-rpm long-playing record in 1948, which had a tremendous impact on the recording industry and dominated record sales for nearly 30 years. Born at Budapest, Hungary, he came to the United States in 1933 and worked for CBS Laboratories (1936–1972), becoming its vice president in 1950. Goldmark developed the system that allowed space photographs of the moon to be taken and also the electronic videocassette recorder. He died Dec 7, 1977, at Westchester County, NY.

Exploration
ROBERT E. PEARY

Birth • May 6, 1856 • 150 Years
Born at Cresson, PA, Peary served as a cartographic draftsman in the US Coast and Geodetic Survey for two years, then joined the US Navy Corps of Civil Engineers in 1881. As subchief of the Inter-Ocean Canal Survey in Nicaragua, he first explored tropical climates. After reading of the inland ice of Greenland, Peary became attracted to the Arctic. He orga-

nized and led eight Arctic expeditions and is credited with the verification of Greenland's island formation, proving that the polar ice cap extended beyond 82° north latitude, and the discovery of the Melville meteorite on Melville Bay, in addition to his famous discovery of the North Pole, Apr 6, 1909. Peary died Feb 20, 1920, at Washington, DC.

Sports
JOHNNY EVERS

Birth • July 21, 1881 • 125 Years
John Joseph (Johnny) Evers, Baseball Hall of Fame second baseman, born at Troy, NY. Evers was a member of the Tinker-to-Evers-to-Chance double-play combination for the Chicago Cubs that first took the field on Sept 13, 1902. For the next eight years this trio was the soul of the powerhouse Cubs—despite the fact that Evers and Joe Tinker stopped speaking to each other in September 1905 (they continued the feud for 33 years). Evers was an aggressive player who never gave an inch. Inducted into the Hall of Fame

Spotlight on People

(with Tinker and Chance) in 1946. Died at Albany, NY, Mar 28, 1947.

BRANCH RICKEY

Birth • Dec 20, 1881 • 125 Years

Born Wesley Branch Rickey at Stockdale, OH, he had an uninspired career as a professional baseball player. He then worked for the St. Louis Cardinals for 25 years as club president and general manager, during which time he developed the "farm system" (1919), the forerunner of today's minor leagues, which was a revolutionary way of developing young players and preparing them for life in the major leagues. Rickey moved to the Brooklyn Dodgers in 1945 and was soon the co-owner of the team. He was instrumental in the integration of baseball, bringing African-American and Latin American players into the farm system, and in 1947, signing Jackie Robinson as the first African-American player on a major-league team. Rickey worked in baseball throughout his life and was elected to the Baseball Hall of Fame in 1967, two years after his death on Dec 9, 1965.

JAMES BRADDOCK

Birth • June 7, 1906 • 100 Years

James Joseph Braddock, boxer, was born at New York City and died at North Bergen, NJ, Nov 29, 1974. Braddock rose from the ranks of undistinguished fighters to win three key bouts in 1934 and 1935 that propelled him to a match for the world heavyweight title. He upset the defending

champion, Max Baer, on June 13, 1935, but remained inactive for two years and then lost his first title defense to Joe Louis.

EARL BASCOM

Birth • June 19, 1906 • 100 Years

Rodeo showman, inventor and pioneer, as well as cowboy artist, Earl W. Bascom was born at Vernal, UT. During his career he developed the first side-delivery rodeo chute (with his brothers, 1916), the first hornless bronco saddle (1922) and the first one-handed bareback rigging (1924). Bascom produced the first rodeo in Mississippi and also the first rodeo held at night under electric lights (1935). This showman also performed on film with fellow cowboy hero Roy Rogers. Bascom died Aug 28, 1995, at Victorville, CA.

SATCHEL PAIGE

Birth • July 7, 1906 • 100 Years

Born Leroy Robert Paige at Mobile, AL, he was one of 11 children in a poor family. Sent out to work early in life, he got his famous nickname at the age of seven from his ability to lug lots of luggage for a railroad. Known

for his incredible pitching ability, Paige was the greatest attraction in the Negro League (1924–1947), playing perhaps 2,500 games and pitching as many as 50 no-hitters, all before moving to the American League at age 42. The Brooklyn Dodgers had signed Jackie Robinson in 1947, and the Cleveland Indians signed Paige in 1948. His color made his six seasons of travel with the team difficult. Despite his status and popularity, Paige often had to sleep in a different hotel and eat separately from his teammates. Called "the greatest arm in baseball," Paige became the first Negro League player to be inducted into the Baseball Hall of Fame in 1971. He died at Kansas City, MO, on June 8, 1982.

GERTRUDE EDERLE

Birth • Oct 23, 1906 • 100 Years

American swimming champion, born at New York City, Ederle was the first woman to swim the English Channel (from Cape Gris-nez, France, to Dover, England). At age 19, she broke the previous world record by swimming this 35-mile distance in 14 hours, 31 minutes, on Aug 6, 1926. During her career she broke many other records and was a gold medal winner at the 1924 summer Olympic Games. She died at Wyckoff, NJ, Nov 30, 2003.

Miscellaneous

BUGSY SIEGEL

Birth • Feb 28, 1906 • 100 Years

Benjamin "Bugsy" Siegel was born in the Hell's Kitchen section of Brooklyn, NY, to poor, Russian-Jewish immigrant parents. He earned his moniker because of his tendency to "go bugs" in sticky situations. From an early age he showed a penchant for crime, extorting money from local street vendors in exchange for refraining to set fire to their stands. He was a contemporary of and in cahoots with Meyer Lansky and Lucky Luciano, running street craps, robbery and extortion operations. Siegel moved his family to Hollywood in 1937 to lie low after committing an impulsive gangland murder. In an attempt to extend the success he'd had with his petty gambling operations, he constructed a hotel and casino, called The Flamingo, in remote Las Vegas, NV, which opened in 1946. Initially the hotel was a failure until Lansky and Luciano poured more money into the venture and managed to get him more time. Siegel was shot and died at the Hollywood home of his girl-friend, Virginia Hill, on June 20, 1947; no one was ever convicted of the murder.

DALE MESSICK

Birth • Apr 11, 1906 • 100 Years
Messick, born at South Bend, IN, was the creator of the intrepid, glamorous globe-trotting reporter Brenda Starr in the comic strip that debuted in June 1940. Messick had to deal with

discrimination as a woman comic-strip artist and thus changed her name to Dale from her birth name of Dalia. Although "Brenda Starr, Reporter" was innovative in featuring an independent working woman, it didn't depict the reality of journalistic life since Starr—modeled on flame-haired Hollywood actress Rita Hayworth—sashayed her way toward scoops in evening gowns and high heels. There have been two film adaptations of this popular comic strip, which is still in syndication. Messick retired from the strip in the 1980s and died at Sonoma County, CA, on Apr 5, 2005.

Spotlight on 2006 Events

In a book that lists more than 6,000 special events, it is difficult to spotlight any one. Here is a selection that will be of particular interest in 2006.

FIFA World Cup

Germany, June 9–July 9

When the officials blow their whistles to start games on June 9, they will be inaugurating the biggest sporting event in the world: the World Cup. This will be the 18th World Cup (there was a 12-year hiatus caused by World War II), which is sponsored by soccer's governing body, Fédération Internationale de Football Association (FIFA). The first World Cup was held in 1930 in Uruguay, when the home team emerged triumphant. Today the event is played on a larger scale with 32 teams competing (up from 16 teams 30 years ago) for the ultimate sports prize.

The matches are really the culmination of four years of preparation, with FIFA's 204 member associations playing in regional qualifying matches. By 2006, the final 32 national teams will represent all regions of the globe and will be divided into eight groups of four. Teams in these groups battle each other in a round-robin before moving into single-elimination semifinals. The international press has noted that there's always one "Group of Death" ("Grupo de muerte" in the language of FIFA) where all four teams are evenly matched for excellent playing ability.

The initial matches will take place in 12 German cities: Berlin, Cologne, Dortmund, Frankfurt, Gelsenkirchen, Hamburg, Hannover, Kaiserslautern, Leipzig, Munich, Nuremberg and Stuttgart. Berlin will do the honors for the final match in its historic Olympiastadion—site of the 1936 Olympics. For Germany, this is the first major event of any kind after its reunification, so hosting the World Cup has special significance. As with any World Cup, there will also be cultural and performing arts events for the international fans coming to Germany during the month of the Cup.

At the 2002 World Cup held in Japan and Korea Republic, more than 49 billion cumulative viewers (on television and in person) watched the matches. For the final match, in which perennial soccer powerhouse Brazil defeated Germany for a record fifth title, there were more than 52.3 million live viewers.

Tickets for this event will be, of course, in hot demand. Sales will occur in five distinct selling periods (two of which will have occurred already by the time *Chase's* is published). Go to the official FIFA website for more information.

For information:

Fédération Internationale de
    Football Association (FIFA)
FIFA House
Hitziweg 11, PO Box 85
Zurich 8030,
Switzerland
Web: fifaworldcup.yahoo.com
(official World Cup site) or
www.fifa.com

For information on the US national team:

US Soccer Federation
1801 S Prairie Ave
Chicago IL 60616
Phone: (312) 808-1300
Web: www.ussoccer.com

Games of the XX Winter Olympiad

Turin, Italy, Feb 10–26

The Olympic games of ancient times date back to 776 BC. In 1896, the first modern Olympiad was held in its birthplace, Greece, and featured 43 events in nine sports. The games were a tremendous success and have been held in various cities around the world since then. In 1896, only men participated, but by the second Olympiad in Paris (1900), women were included. In 1911, the Olympics were separated into winter and summer sessions. During the 1980s, a decision was made to stagger the Winter and Summer Games so that one competition would take place every two years; the 1994 Winter Games at Lillehammer, Norway, were the first to be played under the new schedule, two years early.

During the Winter Games at Turin, 84 medals will be presented over a period of 17 days. More than 2,500 athletes will participate in events held at eight sites in the Turin area: Bardonecchia, Pinerolo, Pragelato, Cesana-Pariol, Cesana-San Sicario, Sauze d'Oulx, Sestriere, Torino. Athletes will take part in biathlon, bobsled, curling, ice hockey, luge, skeleton, speed skating, figure skating and skiing. Officials from 85 national Olympic committees and 650 judges and referees will participate in the games.

The Torch Relay, the traditional lead-up to the games, began Dec 8, 2005, in Rome and will pass through every region and province in Italy. More than 10,000 torchbearers will participate before the Olympic flame reaches Turin on Feb 10, 2006, for the inauguration of the XX Olympic Winter Games. The Olympic cauldron will then be lighted—not to be extinguished until the conclusion of the games.

IX Paralympic Games

March 10–19

Following the Winter Olympics, the Paralympics will be held in the same venues. Some 600 athletes with disabilities will take part in these games that feature 70 medal events in alpine skiing, cross-country, biathlon, ice sledge hockey and a new sport—wheelchair curling (added in 2006 as a medal event for the first time in Paralympic history).

For information:

International Olympic
   Committee
Corso Novara 96
10152
Turin, Italy
Phone: (39) (011) 11-2006
Fax: (39) (011) 11-2222
Web: www.olympic.org

International Paralympic
   Committee
Via Nizza 262/58
10126
Turin, Italy
Phone: (39) (011) 11-2006
Fax: (39) (011) 11-2222
E-mail: Paralympics@torino
2006.it
Web: www.paralympic.org or
www.paralympicgames.torino
2006.org

United States Olympic
   Committee
One Olympic Plaza
Colorado Springs, CO 80909
Phone: (719) 866-4500
E-mail: media@usoc.org
Web: www.usoc.org or www
.olympic-usa.org

Spotlight on 2006 Events

Mozart 2006

Austria, Jan 27–Dec 5

Austria is celebrating the 250th birth anniversary of its famous son with spectacular cultural events throughout the year—beginning with the composer's birthday on Jan 27 and concluding on Dec 5, the day of his death. Although celebrations commence on Jan 1, the official kickoff by the president of Austria will take place Jan 27. Festivities will center around Salzburg—the city of Mozart's birth and youth—and Vienna—the city of his maturity.

Visitors to Austria will be able to hear all Mozart's operas and music, to see historical and biographical exhibitions at national museums and libraries and to experience life in two famous European cities on a grand scale. Some of the international music stars expected to appear and perform in various concerts and festivals are Riccardo Muti, Plácido Domingo, Nikolaus Harnoncourt, Seiji Ozawa and more. Austria's annual cultural festivals will use Mozart as a theme in 2006. No. 5 Domgasse, the only one of Mozart's various Vienna residences to still stand (now called Mozart-Haus), will reopen on Jan 27 after years of extensive renovation and will offer three days of festivities as well as permanent exhibits.

There are more than 1,000 events happening in Austria during the year, but here are a few highlights:

THE OPENING FESTIVAL

Salzburg, Jan 27–29

Salzburg will kick off the Mozart Year with a festival under the motto "All the City's A Stage." Music, dance and literature events will be presented.

MOZART WEEK

Salzburg, Jan 20–Feb 5

Sponsored by the International Mozarteum Foundation, Mozart Week is actually two full weeks of programs featuring world-famous conductors and orchestras, including the Vienna Philharmonic Orchestra.

> International Mozarteum
> Foundation Ticket Office
> E-mail: tickets@mozarteum.at
> Web: www.mozarteum.at

VIENNA STATE OPERA

All year except for June and July

One of the world's premier opera houses will stage Mozart's greatest operas (including *Cosi fan tutte, The Magic Flute, Don Giovanni* and *The Marriage of Figaro*) all season and will conclude celebrations with a special performance of his *Requiem* on Dec 5—the anniversary of his death.

> Vienna State Opera
> Opernring 2
> A-1010 Vienna
> E-mail: information@
> wiener-staatsoper.at

MOZART AT THE SCHÖNBRUNN PALACE ORANGERY

The Magic Flute and the Art of Marionette Theatre

Vienna, Jan 1–Dec 31

Every evening the Schönbrunn Palace Orchestra performs works by Mozart and Strauss in the Orangery, a baroque building where Mozart once played. In the award-winning Schönbrunn Palace Marionette Theatre, the traditional art of string puppetry is celebrated with an enchanting version of *The Magic Flute*.

> Image Performing Arts
> Promotion GmbH
> Orangerie, Schloss Schönbrunn
> A-1130 Vienna
> E-mail: office@imagevienna
> .com

MOZART IN VIENNA'S FINEST CONCERT HALLS

Vienna, Apr 14–Oct 30

Playing in authentic period costumes, the Vienna Mozart Orchestra will re-create the atmosphere of concerts in Mozart's time in various music venues in the city.

MOZART AND MORE WITH THE VIENNA BOYS' CHOIR AT THE MUSIKVEREIN

Vienna, Fridays, Apr 21–Oct 27

The Wiener Sängerknaben (Vienna Boys' Choir) is one of the oldest boys' choirs in the world with its history dating back 500 years. In 2006, they devote their concerts to Mozart.

    Musikverein
    Karlsplatz 6, 1st district
    Vienna
    E-mail: info@mondial.at
    Web: www.musikverein.at

SALZBURG FESTIVAL

Salzburg, Summer

Mozart's musical theater compositions (including all his operas, song plays and other lyric dramas), comprising 22 works, will be staged for the first time within a period of only six weeks.

    Salzburg Festival
    E-mail: tickets@salzburg
    festival.at
    Web: www.salzburgfestival.at

MUSIC FILM FESTIVAL

Vienna, July 1–Sept 3

Using the illuminated City Hall as a backdrop, Vienna's popular outdoor music film festival will focus on Mozart in 2006, showing operas and concerts from around the world on a giant screen. The festival is free. Also included will be child-friendly shows and documentaries.

For information

    Mozart 2006
    Web: www.mozart2006.net

    Austrian National Tourist
      Office
    Margaretenstrasse 1
    A-1040 Vienna
    Phone: (01) 58-866-0
    Fax: (01) 58-866-20
    E-mail: mozart@austria.info
    Web: austria.info

    Wien-Tourismus (Vienna
      Tourist Board)
    Abteilung Markt-und
    Medienmanagement
    Phone: (43) 1-211-14-0
    Fax: (43) 1-216-84-92
    E-mail: markets.media@
    wien.info
    Web: www.wien.info

    Tourismus Salzburg GmbH
      (Tourism Salzburg)
    Marketingabteilung
    Auerspergstrasse 6
    A-5020 Salzburg
    Phone: (43) 662-889-8970
    Fax: (43) 662-889-8732
    E-mail: tourist@salzburg.info
    Web: www.salzburg.info

Lewis and Clark Expedition Bicentennial

2003–2006

The celebration of the bicentennial of the Corps of Discovery concludes this year with the 200th anniversary of their arrival back in St. Louis, MO.

The expedition—which included about 33 members trained in botany, zoology, other scientific disciplines and outdoor survival skills—prepared in St. Louis and set out on May 14, 1804. They traveled up the Missouri River to what is now North Dakota and Montana, then over the Continental Divide and to the Columbia River. The Columbia took them to the Pacific Ocean by November 1805. They were assisted on their journey by trapper and guide Toussaint Charbonneau and his wife Sacagawea, a member of the Shoshone tribe, who interpreted for the explorers and gave them valuable advice on edible and medicinal wild plants. Sacagawea's infant son, called Pompey by Clark, was also part of the group. Despite the hardships of difficult terrain, hunger and sickness, the expedition returned to St. Louis amid much fanfare on Sept 23, 1806, having lost only one man. On that Sept 23, Clark wrote in the Corps journals: "We suffered the party to fire off their pieces as a salute to the town. We were met by all the village and received a hearty welcome from its inhabitants." Lewis and Clark journeyed on to

Spotlight on 2006 Events

Washington, DC, where they were again greeted with acclaim.

From the valuable geographic information gathered from this mission, the US was set to begin migration westward to the Pacific.

While each of the states and communities touched by the Lewis and Clark Expedition have had celebrations during 2003–2006, some observances are designated National Signature Events. As the Bicentennial comes to an end, there are four Signature Events in 2006:

AMONG THE NIIMIIPUU

Lewistown, ID, June 14–17

The Lewis and Clark Expedition entered the Niimiipuu (The Nez Perce) aboriginal homelands in September of 1805; on their return trip eastward in June 1806, the explorers renewed their relationship with the Niimiipuu. The expedition journals describe the Niimiipuu as friendly, hospitable and gracious hosts, qualities that still describe the Niimiipuu today. On June 14–17, the Niimiipuu will commemorate that relationship by hosting a National Signature Event. The world is invited to experience a unique celebration that reflects the diversity of cultures of people.

For information:

Bill Smith
Among the Niimiipuu
17500 Nez Perce Rd
Lewiston, ID 83501
Phone: (208) 843-2253, ext 3511
Fax: (208) 843-7396
E-mail: bill@nezperce.org
Web: www.nezperce.org or lewisandclark200.org

CLARK ON THE YELLOWSTONE

Billings, MT, July 22–25

The Clark on the Yellowstone Signature Event enables modern-day adventurers to rediscover Captain William Clark's travels along the Yellowstone River and also commemorates the 200th anniversary of Clark inscribing his name on Pompeys Pillar, the only remaining physical evidence of the Lewis and Clark Expedition appearing on the trail. Clark, showing his affection for Sacagawea's young son, whom he called "Pomp," named this sandstone pillar at the river's edge in his honor. A National Day of Honor commemorating this event and also recognizing the historic use of the Pillar by Native Americans is set for July 25. Visitors will be greeted in a new interpretive center at the recently created Pompeys Pillar National Monument, which is administered by the Bureau of Land Management. Canoe landings, trail rides, wildlife displays and exhibits at local museums in nearby Billings, MT, will engage people of all ages.

For information:

Robbie Carpenter or Melody Dobson
Clark on the Yellowstone
Billings Chamber of Commerce
815 S 27th St
Billings, MT 59101
Phone: (406) 245-4111, ext 101
E-mail: clarkevents@billings chamber.com
Web: www.clarkontheyellow stone.org or www.lewisand clark200.org

REUNION AT THE HOME OF SAKAKAWEA

New Town, ND, Aug 17–20

Having spent some months split into two groups, on Aug 12, 1806, Lewis and Clark reunited on the Missouri River near the present-day headquarters of the Mandan, Hidatsa and Arikara Nation. The expedition traveled on to the Knife River Hidatsa and Mandan villages and days later, bid farewell to their interpreters Sakakawea and Toussaint Charbonneau. On Aug 20, 1806, the Expedition left what is now North Dakota. In August 2006, the Mandan, Hidatsa and Arikara Nation of North Dakota will commemorate the return of the Corps of Discovery to their homelands and the reunion of Sakakawea at Awatixa, her Hidatsa home. The major themes of this Signature Event will center on Sakakawea and her life before, during and after the expedition; the Missouri River and its impact on the lives of the Mandan, Hidatsa, Arikara and other tribes that hold this river sacred; tribal leadership and the political, social and ceremonial organization of tribes 200 years ago and today; tribal trade networks and international trade. This four-day event will feature scholarly symposia, reenactments, dramatic presentations, an art exhibition and trade fair, indigenous games, land and water parades, singing and traditional dance competition and a fur trade rendezvous.

For information:

Claryca Mandan
Mandan, Hidatsa, Arikara
  Nation
PO Box 610
New Town, ND 58763
Phone: (701) 627-2870
Fax: (701) 627-2873
Web: www.mhanation.com or
www.lewisandclark200.org

CONFLUENCE WITH DESTINY

St. Louis, MO, Sept 23–24

On Sept 23, 1806, the Lewis and Clark Expedition officially ended when the explorers arrived in St. Louis, MO. In commemoration of the bicentennial of this event, a consortium of Missouri and Illinois states, county and local groups will re-create this return: A flotilla of watercraft will originate at various historic sites on the Missouri and Mississippi rivers and converge on the riverfront. A series of programs and events will explore the multicultural composition of the expedition. Representatives from all of the tribal nations encountered by Lewis and Clark will be invited to participate in this final

National Signature Event of the Lewis and Clark Bicentennial.

For information:

Karen Goering
National Council of the Lewis
  and Clark Bicentennial
PO Box 11940
St. Louis, MO 63112-0040
Phone: (314) 454-3160 or
(888) 999-1803
E-mail: info@lewisandclark
200.org
Web: www.lewisandclark
200.org

The Benjamin Franklin Tercentenary 1706–2006

Having only 365 days to commemorate the life of the amazing Benjamin Franklin seems an impossible task, but many organizations and cities are rising to the occasion with an exciting array of programs, seminars, exhibitions, dramatizations and more.

Franklin, a true Renaissance man, touched the fields of commerce (printing, insurance and more), education, safety, science, literature, politics—besides being a Founding Father of the United States.

While the nation and the whole world will be celebrating Franklin's birthday, most events will be focused in Philadelphia. The centerpiece of all tercentennial observances is a major international traveling exhibition entitled "Benjamin Franklin: In Search of a Better World." This exhibit, put together by many organizations around the world, gathers the definitive collection of Frankliniana: his signed copy of the Treaty of Paris, important correspondence, his walking stick, various of his inventions and copies of his *Poor Richard's Almanack.* There will also be hands-on displays that put visitors into Franklin's 18th-century world. The exhibition runs from Dec 15, 2005, to Apr 30, 2006, at the National Constitution Center in Philadelphia, PA, then tours to St. Louis, Houston, Denver, Atlanta and finally Paris, France, during the rest of 2006 on through 2007.

The official website of the tercentenary offers an extensive listing at www.benfranklin300.com. Here is a selection of Franklin events in 2006:

Spotlight on 2006 Events

BEN FRANKLIN'S 300TH BIRTHDAY BASH

The Franklin Institute Science Museum, Philadelphia, PA, Jan 14

This museum celebrates Franklin's birthday every year on the Saturday closest to Jan 17 (his actual birthday). Events include reenactments of Franklin's experiments, giant birthday card signing and cake eating—with an appearance by Ben himself.

BEN'S ELECTRICAL SPECTACULAR

The Franklin Institute Science Museum, Philadelphia, PA, Jan 17–Dec 31

Experience the amazing power of electricity in this live, interactive, high-voltage show—where Franklin's most dramatic experiments are re-created.

PROJECT SPACE: BRIAN TOLLE

Institute of Contemporary Art, Philadelphia, PA, Jan 17–Apr 2

Artist Tolle has been commissioned to create a site-specific work in honor of the tercentenary.

FRANKLIN'S PRINTING PRESS IN ACTION

Lancaster, PA, Jan 19–Feb 5

Exhibition and demonstration of a reproduction of Franklin's printing press.

PHILOMEL BAROQUE ORCHESTRA: FRANKLIN FESTIVAL

Various cities, PA

Jan 20–22 Franklin's Philadelphia
May 5–7 Franklin's France

Philomel is one of the Northeast's premier original instruments ensemble. For the tercentenary, they will offer nine concerts revolving around Franklin's relationship with three cities: London (took place in 2005), Philadelphia and Paris.

THE FULTON OPERA HOUSE

Lancaster, PA

Feb 1, 2006–July 1, 2007, SPARK! (An "Invention" of Benjamin Franklin)

Apr 27–May 14, Lightning Rod

The Fulton Opera House has commissioned and will perform these two works. *SPARK!* is a world-premier play by Barry Kornhauser taking an unconventional look at Franklin's formative years. *Lightning Rod*, by Tim Slover, examines the tense relationship during the American Revolution between Franklin and his son, William, a British loyalist.

THE MEDICAL WORLD OF BENJAMIN FRANKLIN

College of Physicians, Philadelphia, PA, Apr 7, 2006–June 30, 2007

Exhibition on the little-known contributions Franklin made in the realm of health and medicine. A collaboration between the College of Physicians and the Royal Society of Medicine in London.

AMERICAN MUSICAL SALUTE TO BENJAMIN FRANKLIN

National Constitution Center, Philadelphia, PA, Apr 6

Philadelphia will be host to thousands of America's finest young musicians in a historic all-day concert salute to Franklin. The tribute will feature 30-minute performances by bands, choirs, orchestras and other youth performing groups representing states from across America.

FRANKLIN AND THE BOOK

The Library Company of Philadelphia, May 1–Dec 1

This exhibition will explore Franklin's dual relationship to the book as a printer and as an author.

THE KITE AND THE KEY

The Franklin Institute Science Museum, Philadelphia, June 17

A reenactment of Franklin's most famous experiment—with hands-on presentations, indoor kite flying, thunderstorm shows and more.

For more general information on the tercentenary:

Ben Franklin Tercentenary
135 S 18th St, Ste 702
Philadelphia, PA 19103
Phone: (215) 557-0733
E-mail: postmaster@ben franklin300.org
Web: www.benfranklin300 .com

Januarye.

JANUARY 1 — SUNDAY

Day 1 — 364 Remaining

SUNDAY, JANUARY ONE, 2006. Jan 1. First day of the first month of the Gregorian calendar year, Anno Domini 2006, being the second Common Year after Leap Year, and (until July 4th) 230th year of American independence. 2006 will be year 6719 of the Julian Period, a time frame consisting of 7,983 years that began at noon, universal [Greenwich] time, Jan 1, 4714 BC. Astronomers will note that Julian Day number 2,452,644 begins at noon, universal time (representing the number of days since the beginning of the Julian Period). New Year's Day is a public holiday in the US and in many other countries. Traditionally, it is a time for personal stocktaking, for making resolutions for the coming year and sometimes for recovering from the festivities of New Year's Eve. Financial accounting begins anew for businesses and individuals whose fiscal year is the calendar year. Jan 1 has been observed as the beginning of the year in most English-speaking countries since the British Calendar Act of 1751, prior to which the New Year began Mar 25 (approximating the vernal equinox). Earth begins another orbit of the sun, during which it, and we, will travel some 583,416,000 miles in 365.2422 days. New Year's Day has been called "Everyman's Birthday," and in some countries a year is added to everyone's age Jan 1 rather than on the anniversary of each person's birth.

ACADIA NATIONAL PARK ESTABLISHED: ANNIVERSARY. Jan 1, 1919. Maine's Sieur de Monts National Monument, authorized in 1916, was established as Lafayette National Park in 1919. The name was changed to Acadia National Park by an act of Congress in 1929.

AUSTRALIA: COMMONWEALTH FORMED: ANNIVERSARY. Jan 1, 1901. On this day, the six colonies of Victoria, New South Wales, Queensland, South Australia, Western Australia and Northern Territory were united into one nation. The British Parliament had passed the Commonwealth Constitution Bill in the spring of 1900, and Queen Victoria signed the document Sept 17, 1900.

BONZA BOTTLER DAY™. Jan 1. (also Feb 2, Mar 3, Apr 4, May 5, June 6, July 7, Aug 8, Sept 9, Oct 10, Nov 11 and Dec 12). To celebrate when the number of the day is the same as the number of the month. Bonza Bottler Day™ is an excuse to have a party at least once a month. Created by the late Elaine Fremont and continued by her family, Bonza Bottler Day is now celebrated in many countries. Logo buttons are available for $2 (includes postage and handling). For info: Gail M. Berger, Bonza Bottler Day, 14 Fernwood Dr, Taylors, SC 29687. Phone: (864) 609-9874. E-mail: gberger5@aol.com.

BOOK BLITZ MONTH. Jan 1–31. Focuses attention on improving authors' relationships with the media in order to create a best-selling book. Free book PR evaluation available. Annually, the month of January. For info: Barbara Gaughen, Media 21, 7456 Evergreen Dr, Santa Barbara, CA 93117. Phone: (805) 968-8567. Fax: (805) 968-5747. E-mail: bgaughenmu@aol.com. Web: www.goodmorningworld.org.

BRYCE CANYON NATIONAL PARK ESTABLISHED: ANNIVERSARY. Jan 1, 1928. Utah's Bryce Canyon National Monument, created in 1923, was established as a national park and preserve.

CELEBRATION OF LIFE MONTH. Jan 1–31. The month of January, being the first month of the year, signifies the new year, a new beginning, a new life, a new happiness in many lives each year. Every community has a new hope to begin a new page in their lives. Remember always to value the gift of life for all Americans pursuing life, liberty, happiness and justice for all citizens. For info: Judith Natale, NCFA of America, PO Box 493703, Redding, CA 96049-3703. E-mail: childaware@aol.com.

CELEBRATION OF LIFE WEEK. Jan 1–7. The purpose of this week is to impress upon people all over the world the preciousness of life and the importance of all living things. For complete information and many famous quotations about life, send $5 to cover printing, handling and postage. For info: Dr. Stanley Drake, Pres Emeritus, Intl Society of Friendship & Good Will, 8592 Roswell Rd, Ste 251, Atlanta, GA 30350-1867. Phone: (678) 795-1362. E-mail: sjdrake@bellsouth.net. Web: www.friendshipandgoodwill.org.

CERVICAL CANCER SCREENING MONTH. Jan 1–31. During January, the National Cervical Cancer Public Education campaign gives women and their doctors information about what causes cervical cancer and the best ways to prevent or detect it. Women are encouraged to get screened for cervical cancer and pledge their commitment to preventing the disease by visiting the campaign's website at www.cervicalcancercampaign.org. For info: The Gynecologic Cancer Foundation, 230 W Monroe, Ste 2528, Chicago, IL 60606. Phone: (312) 578-1439. Fax: (312) 578-9769. E-mail: info@thegcf.org. Web: www.thegcf.org.

CIRCUMCISION OF CHRIST. Jan 1. Holy day in many Christian churches. Celebrates Jesus's submission to Jewish law; on the octave day of Christmas. See also: "Solemnity of Mary, Mother of God" (Jan 1) for Roman Catholic observance since 1969 calendar reorganization.

COFFEE GOURMET INTERNATIONAL MONTH. Jan 1–31. From the first scent of its aroma when brewing to the last drop rolling off the palate, the pure joy that gourmet coffee evokes is something to be celebrated. This event is dedicated to introducing coffee lovers everywhere to the pleasures of truly gourmet coffee. For info: DiFrances Company, LLC, 208 E Oak Crest Dr, Ste 200, Wales, WI 53183-9700. Phone: (262) 968-9000. Fax: (262) 968-9854. E-mail: gourmetcoffee@difrancesco.com. Web: www.difrancesco.com.

COPYRIGHT REVISION LAW SIGNED: 30th ANNIVERSARY. Jan 1, 1976. The first major revision since 1909 of laws governing intellectual property in the US was signed by President Ford. It took effect two years later on Jan 1, 1978. The act (Public Law 94–553) contains substantial revisions of the principles governing acquisition and duration of copyright and deals with issues that have been raised in recent years concerning photocopying and the use of copyrighted works by public broadcasting and cable television systems.

CUBA: ANNIVERSARY OF THE REVOLUTION. Jan 1. National holiday celebrating the overthrow of the government of Fulgencio Batista in 1959 by the revolutionary forces of Fidel Castro, which had begun a civil war in 1956.

CUBA: LIBERATION DAY. Jan 1. A national holiday that celebrates the end of Spanish rule in 1899. Cuba, the largest island of the West Indies, was a Spanish possession from its discovery by Columbus (Oct 27, 1492) until 1899. Under US military control 1899–1902 and 1906–09, a republican government took over Jan 28, 1909, and controlled the island until overthrown Jan 1, 1959, by Fidel Castro's revolutionary movement.

CZECH-SLOVAK DIVORCE: ANNIVERSARY. Jan 1, 1993. As Dec 31, 1992, gave way to Jan 1, 1993, the 74-year-old state of Czechoslovakia separated into two nations—the Czech Republic and Slovakia. The Slovaks held a celebration through the night in the streets of Bratislava amid fireworks, bell ringing, singing of the new country's national anthem and the raising of the Slovak flag. In the new Czech Republic no official festivities took place, but later in the day the Czechs celebrated with a solemn oath by their parliament. The nation of Czechoslovakia ended peacefully though polls showed that most Slovaks and Czechs would have preferred that it survive. Before the split Czech Prime Minister Vaclav Klaus and Slovak Prime Minister Vladimir Meciar reached an agreement on dividing everything from army troops and gold reserves to the art on government building walls.

DIET RESOLUTION WEEK. Jan 1–7. This week emphasizes the importance of watching your weight by focusing on the type—not the amount—of food you put on your plate. Resolve to consume minimally processed, less-refined carbohydrate foods. Slim down permanently with whole grains, legumes, fresh fruits and vegetables. Eat more but weigh less for life. Delete meat and other animal foods to make miniscule meals and calorie counting obsolete. Start the year off right by eating light with every bite! For info: Vegetarian Awareness Network, Communications Center, PO Box 321, Knoxville, TN 37901-0321. Phone: (877) VEG-DIET or (800) 280-8343.

ELLIS ISLAND OPENED: ANNIVERSARY. Jan 1, 1892. Ellis Island was opened on New Year's Day in 1892. Over the years more than 20 million individuals were processed through the stations. The island was used as a point of deportation as well: in 1932 alone, 20,000 people were deported from Ellis Island. When the US entered WWII in 1941, Ellis Island became a Coast Guard Station. It closed Nov 12, 1954, and was declared a national park in 1956. After years of disuse it was restored and in 1990 it was reopened as a museum.

EMANCIPATION PROCLAMATION TAKES EFFECT: ANNIVERSARY. Jan 1, 1863. Abraham Lincoln, by executive proclamation of Sept 22, 1862, declared that on this date ". . . all persons held as slaves within any state or designated part of a state, the people whereof shall then be in rebellion against the United States, shall be then, thenceforward, and forever, free. . . ." Slaves in the four slave states that had not seceded from the Union (Delaware, Maryland, Kentucky and Missouri) were not freed until the passage of the 13th Amendment in 1865. See also: "Thirteenth Amendment to the US Constitution Ratified" (Dec 6).

ENGLAND: THE NEW YEAR'S DAY PARADE—LONDON. Jan 1. London. The biggest parade of its kind in the world attracts a million people on the streets of the capital. The route starts at noon in Parliament Square, and goes along Whitehall, around Trafalgar Square and up Piccadilly. Dozens of the world's top marching bands, thousands of cheerleaders and the amazing eight-story-high cartoon character balloons all add to the fun. Est attendance: 1,000,000. For info: Mark Phillips, The New Year's Day Parade—London, Research House, Fraser Road, Greenford, Middlesex, England UB6 7AQ. Phone: (44) (20) 8566 8586. Fax: (44) (20) 8566 8494. E-mail: info@londonparade.co.uk. Web: www.londonparade.co.uk.

EURO INTRODUCED: ANNIVERSARY. Jan 1, 1999. The euro, the common currency of members of the European Union, was introduced for use by financial institutions. The value of the currencies of the 11 nations (Austria, Belgium, Finland, France, Germany, Ireland, Italy, Luxembourg, the Netherlands, Portugal and Spain) was locked in at a permanent conversion rate to the euro. Greece joined the eurozone the following year. On Jan 1, 2002, euro bills and coins began circulating; other currencies were phased out as of Feb 28, 2002.

January **2006**	S	M	T	W	T	F	S
	1	2	3	4	5	6	7
	8	9	10	11	12	13	14
	15	16	17	18	19	20	21
	22	23	24	25	26	27	28
	29	30	31				

FAMILY FIT LIFESTYLE MONTH. Jan 1–31. Healthy living is achievable. Try, for one month, to move your body and reduce the fat, sugar and salt in your diet while balancing your meals with healthy nutrition. Use moderation and portion control, and try to prevent many of the diseases associated with high-fat/high-cholesterol diets. Help your kids learn proper nutrition and a regular exercise routine. The first month of the new year is the perfect time to change your life. For info: Family Fit Lifestyle, Inc, 15202 N 50th Pl, Scottsdale, AZ 85254. Phone: (866) 548-3348. E-mail: Jyl@AmericasHealthiestMom.com. Web: www.Americas HealthiestMom.com.

FINANCIAL WELLNESS MONTH. Jan 1–31. For people to establish financial balance after credit card bills pour in from the holidays. This is a time to set new goals for financial freedom and moderation in spending. See a financial advisor. Create money management goals. Set up a savings plan. Figure out how to pay off old loans. Get out of debt. Spend less money. Give up a little luxury and donate the savings to charity. Buy in bulk, shop at discount stores, wait for sales and bargains. Shop garage sales, flea markets and online auctions. For info: Angela Brown, Words for Wellness, PO Box 49266, Charlotte, NC 28277. Phone: (704) 849-2900. Fax: (704) 845-3060. E-mail: angela@wordsofwellness .com. Web: www.wordsofwellness.com.

FIRST BABY BOOMER BORN: 60th ANNIVERSARY. Jan 1, 1946. Kathleen Casey Wilkens, born at one minute after midnight at Philadelphia, PA, was the first of the almost 78 million Baby Boomers born between 1946 and 1964.

FIRST MONDAY TRADE DAYS. Jan 1. (Also the weekend preceding the first Monday of every month.) Jackson County Courthouse Square, Scottsboro, AL. One of the Deep South's oldest and largest trade days where bartering, haggling and swapping of goods have not passed on with time; blend of antique shows, craft fairs, rummage sales. Believed to have begun in the mid-1850s when Jackson County Circuit Court used to meet on the first Monday of each month, thus attracting tradesmen. Est attendance: 7,500. For info: JP Parsons, Tourism Director, The Greater Jackson County Chamber of Commerce, 407 E Willow St, Scottsboro, AL 35768. Phone: (256) 259-5500 or (800) 259-5508. Fax: (256) 259-4447. Web: www.jacksoncountychamber .com.

FORSTER, E.M.: BIRTH ANNIVERSARY. Jan 1, 1879. Edward Morgan Forster, English author born at London, England, is remembered for his six novels: *Where Angels Fear to Tread* (1905), *The Longest Journey* (1907), *A Room with a View* (1908), *Howard's End* (1910), *A Passage to India* (1924) and the posthumously published *Maurice* (1971). He also achieved eminence for his short stories and essays, and he collaborated on the libretto for an opera, Benjamin Britten's *Billy Budd* (1951). Forster died at Coventry, England, June 7, 1970.

GREENBERG, HANK: BIRTH ANNIVERSARY. Jan 1, 1911. Henry Benjamin (Hank) Greenberg, Baseball Hall of Fame first baseman and outfielder, born at New York, NY. One of the game's most prodigious sluggers, Greenberg hit 331 home runs and drove in 1,276 runs in only nine full seasons. Baseball's first Jewish superstar, Greenberg entered the army after playing just 19 games in 1941 and did not return to the Detroit Tigers until midway through the 1945 season. His grand slam on that season's last day won the pennant for the Tigers and propelled them toward a World Series triumph. Inducted into the Hall of Fame in 1956. Died at Beverly Hills, CA, Sept 4, 1986.

HAITI: INDEPENDENCE DAY: ANNIVERSARY. Jan 1. A national holiday commemorating the proclamation of independence in 1804. Haiti, occupying the western third of the island Hispaniola (second largest of the West Indies), was a Spanish colony from the time of its discovery by Columbus in 1492 until 1697, then a French colony until the proclamation of independence in 1804.

HANGOVER HANDICAP RUN. Jan 1. Veteran's Park, Klamath Falls, OR. Two-mile fun run at 9 AM New Year's Day. The first-place male and female finishers each take home a beer can trophy. Est attendance: 100. For info: Hangover Handicap, 1800 Fairmont, Klamath Falls, OR 97601. Phone: (541) 882-6922. Fax: (541) 883-6481.

HOOVER, J. EDGAR: BIRTH ANNIVERSARY. Jan 1, 1895. John Edgar Hoover, born at Washington, DC. He led the Palmer Raids and was director of the FBI from 1924–72. During his time as director, Hoover practiced modern investigative techniques, improved FBI agent training and increased FBI funding from Congress. He died May 2, 1972, at Washington, DC.

INTERNATIONAL BUSINESS RESOLUTIONS MONTH. Jan 1–31. Set in motion a successful year by focusing on PR and marketing efforts guaranteed to make your cash register ring and your bank statements sing. Resolve to get your business and message in front of your target market. For marketing and PR ideas: Raleigh Pinsky. Phone: (800) 249-7322. E-mail: raleigh@promoteyourself.com. Web: www.promoteyourself.com.

INTERNATIONAL CREATIVITY MONTH. Jan 1–31. A month to remind individuals and organizations around the globe to capitalize on the power of creativity. Unleashing creativity and innovation is vital for personal and business success in this age of accelerating change. The first month of the year provides an opportunity to take a fresh approach to problem solving and renew confidence in our creative capabilities. For info: Randall Munson, Pres, Creatively Speaking, 508 Meadow Run Dr SW, Rochester, MN 55902-2337. Phone: (507) 286-1331. Fax: (507) 286-1331. E-mail: Creativity@CreativelySpeaking.com. Web: www.CreativelySpeaking.com.

INTERNATIONAL LIFE BALANCE MONTH. Jan 1–31. Ever feel like a tumbleweed being blown about with no control because of all the demands put on your time? Overwhelmed by all your choices? Those choices can cause stress and isolation. This month is focused not on New Year's resolutions, but on making better strategic decisions yearlong to get your life in balance. Includes the importance of balancing time for self, family and friends. For info: Sheryl Nicholson, 23 Citrus Dr, Palm Harbor, FL 34684. Phone: (727) 937-3322. Fax: (727) 937-4722. Web: www.sheryl.com.

INTERNATIONAL QUALITY OF LIFE MONTH. Jan 1–31. An international recognition of the importance of the quality of life that encompasses family, community, education, work, finances, health, leisure and spirituality. Recognition and achievement of quality of life is a worldwide issue. For info: H. Stanley Jones, Dir, Quality of Life Institute, 590 Farrington, #210, Kapolei, HI 96707. Phone: (808) 672-0777. Fax: (808) 672-0775. E-mail: PRSpeakers@aol.com.

INTERNATIONAL WEALTH MENTALITY MONTH. Jan 1–31. The start of the new year provides a great opportunity to examine your financial position and, more important, your beliefs and behavior regarding your financial goals. The International Center for Strategic Planning hosts this monthlong effort each year to draw attention to the importance of having a wealth mentality (thoughts that encourage and support wealth building) and getting your personal finances in order. For info: Sherrin Ross Ingram, International Center for Strategic Planning, 104 W Chestnut St, #101, Hinsdale, IL 60521. Phone: (800) 962-4750. Fax: (800) 962-0177. E-mail: info@wealthmentality.com. Web: www.wealthmentality.com.

JAPANESE ERA NEW YEAR. Jan 1–3. Celebration of the beginning of the year Heisei Eighteen, the 18th year of Emperor Akihito's reign.

KLIBAN, B(ERNARD): BIRTH ANNIVERSARY. Jan 1, 1935. Cartoonist B. Kliban was born at Norwalk, CT. He was known for his satirical drawings of cats engaged in human pursuits, which appeared in the books *Cat* (1975), *Never Eat Anything Bigger Than Your Head & Other Drawings* (1976) and *Whack Your Porcupine* (1977) and on T-shirts, greeting cards, calendars, bedsheets and other merchandise, creating a $50 million industry before his death at San Francisco, CA, Aug 12, 1990.

MEXICO: ZAPATISTA REBELLION: ANNIVERSARY. Jan 1, 1994. Declaring war against the government of President Carlos Salinas de Gortari, the Zapatista National Liberation Army seized four towns in the state of Chiapas in southern Mexico in 1994. The rebel group, which took its name from the early 20th-century Mexican revolutionary Emiliano Zapata, issued a declaration stating that they were protesting discrimination against the Indian population of the region and against their severe poverty.

MUMMERS PARADE. Jan 1. Philadelphia, PA. World-famous New Year's Day parade of 20,000 spectacularly costumed Mummers in a colorful parade that goes on all day. This celebration has taken place since the 1700s. Est attendance: 100,000. For info: Mummers Parade, 1100 S 2nd St, Philadelphia, PA 19147. Phone: (215) 636-1666. E-mail: parade@mummers.com. Web: www.mummers.com.

NATIONAL BE ON-PURPOSE MONTH. Jan 1–31. An observance to encourage us to start the new year by putting our good intentions into action, personally and professionally, and to trade confusion for clarity as we integrate our lives with more meaning and purpose. For info: Kevin W. McCarthy, CEO, On-Purpose Partners, PO Box 1568, Winter Park, FL 32790-1568. Phone: (407) 657-6000. Fax: (407) 645-1345. E-mail: info@on-purpose.com.

NATIONAL CLEAN UP YOUR COMPUTER MONTH. Jan 1–31. Dedicated to the education of computer users with simple tips and methods to increase the efficiency of their systems. For info: Denise Hall, 24797 State St, PO Box 658, Elberta, AL 36530. Phone: (251) 986-6650. Fax: (251) 986-6652. E-mail: denise@specterweb.com. Web: specterweb.com.

NATIONAL ENVIRONMENTAL POLICY ACT: ANNIVERSARY. Jan 1, 1970. The National Environmental Policy Act of 1969 established the Council on Environmental Quality and made it federal government policy to protect the environment.

NATIONAL GET ORGANIZED MONTH. Jan 1–31. Is your New Year's resolution to get more organized? This is an opportunity to streamline your life, create more time, lower your stress and increase your profit. For info: National Assn of Professional Organizers, 4700 W Lake Ave, Glenview, IL 60025. Phone: (847) 375-4746. E-mail: info@napo.net. Web: www.napo.net.

NATIONAL GLAUCOMA AWARENESS MONTH. Jan 1–31. More than two million Americans age 40 and older suffer from glaucoma. Nearly half do not know they have the disease—it causes no early symptoms. Prevent Blindness America will provide valuable information about this "sneak thief of sight." Organizations are encouraged to educate the community through screenings, forums and programs. For info: Prevent Blindness America®, 211 W Wacker Dr, Ste 1700, Chicago, IL 60606. Phone: (800) 331-2020. E-mail: info@preventblindness.org. Web: www.preventblindness.org.

NATIONAL HOT TEA MONTH. Jan 1–31. To celebrate one of nature's most popular, soothing and relaxing beverages; the only beverage in America commonly served hot or iced, anytime, anywhere, for any occasion. For info: Joseph P. Simrany, Pres, The Tea Council of the USA, 420 Lexington Ave, Ste 825, New York, NY 10170. Phone: (212) 986-6998. Fax: (212) 697-8658. E-mail: info@teausa.org. Web: www.teausa.org.

NATIONAL LOSE WEIGHT/FEEL GREAT WEEK. Jan 1–6. To inspire individuals to incorporate fitness into their daily routine and make exercise a priority, whether to promote weight loss or maintain overall good health and physical condition. For info: Jana Angelakis, PEX Personalized Exercise, 924 Broadway, 3rd Fl, New York, NY 10010. Phone: (212) 254-1915. Fax: (212) 254-7912. E-mail: angelakisjana@cs.com. Web: www.pexinc.com.

NATIONAL MAILORDER GARDENING MONTH. Jan 1–31. There's no better way to beat the winter blahs than by curling up with a few colorful garden catalogs and spending some time dreaming and scheming about next spring's garden. Many catalogs offer tips and information on how to create a beautiful garden. For a listing of more than 135 garden catalogs and magazines, visit our website. For info: Camille Cimino, Exec Dir, Mailorder Gardening Assn, 5836 Rockburn Woods Way, Elkridge, MD 21075. Phone: (410) 540-9830. Fax: (410) 540-9827. E-mail: info@mailordergardening.com. Web: www.mailordergardening.com.

NATIONAL MENTORING MONTH. Jan 1–31. Goals include raising awareness of mentoring in its various forms; recruiting individuals to mentor, especially in programs that have a waiting list of young people; and promoting the rapid growth of mentoring by recruiting organizations to help find mentors for young people. Each January, this monthlong campaign will provide nationwide publicity and information about mentoring programs in various communities that need volunteers. For info: MENTOR/National Mentoring Partnership, 1600 Duke St, Ste 300, Alexandria, VA 22314. Phone: (703) 224-2200. Web: www.mentoring.org.

NATIONAL PERSONAL SELF-DEFENSE AWARENESS MONTH. Jan 1–31. To educate women and teens about realistic self-defense options that could very well save their lives. Sponsored by the National Self-Defense Institute, Inc, a not-for-profit 501(c)(3) corporation. NSDI/SAFE Program™ seminars and related events nationally emphasize being totally prepared by realizing that awareness + risk reduction = 90 percent of self-defense while the other 10 percent is physical and by waking women up to the fact that the key to their own safety lies in themselves. For info: Natl Self-Defense Inst Inc, PO Box 398355, Miami Beach, FL 33239-8355. Phone: (305) 868-NSDI. Fax: (305) 867-6634. E-mail: nsdi@worldnet.att.net. Web: www.nsdi.org.

NATIONAL POVERTY IN AMERICA AWARENESS MONTH. Jan 1–31. To promote public awareness of the continuing existence of poverty and social injustice in America. Individuals are encouraged to support efforts to eradicate poverty by increasing their understanding of the causes and practical solutions and by active participation and support for antipoverty programs. Sponsored by the Catholic Campaign for Human Development, the largest private funder of self-help programs for the poor and disenfranchised in the US, regardless of religion, race or ethnic origin. For info: Barbara Stephenson, CCHD, US Conference of Catholic Bishops, 3211 Fourth St NE, Washington, DC 20017-1194. Phone: (202) 541-3364. Web: www.povertyusa.org.

NATIONAL RADON ACTION MONTH. Jan 1–31. To increase the public's awareness of the effects of radon. For info: Environmental Protection Agency, 1200 Pennsylvania Ave NW, Washington, DC 20460. Phone: (800) SOS-RADON. Web: www.epa.gov.

NATIONAL RETURNS MONTH. Jan 1–31. December is undeniably the busiest shopping month of the year, which leads to the busiest returns month of the year! Celebrate our collective aggravation at the prospect of long lines, cranky salespeople and lost receipts. This month also gives retailers a chance to recognize this last leg of a purchase as a chance to win or keep a customer for life. For info: Newgistics, 2700 Via Fortuna, Ste 450, Austin, TX 78746. Phone: (512) 225-6040. Fax: (512) 225-6001. Web: www.newgistics.com.

NATIONAL YOURS, MINE AND OURS MONTH. Jan 1–31. Blending families and creating positive steprelationships can be one of the most challenging aspects of a couple's remarriage. Each member of the family is affected in different ways. This observance focuses on what parents and children can expect as a step or blended family and offers tips for a smooth transition and enhanced long-term relationships. Annually, the month of January. For info send SASE to: Dale Eshleman, Episcopal Counseling Center, 1021-A E Robinson St, Orlando, FL 32801. Phone: (800) 544-1817.

NEW YEAR'S DAY. Jan 1. Legal holiday in all states and territories of the US and in most other countries. The world's most widely celebrated holiday.

NEW YEAR'S DISHONOR LIST. Jan 1. Since 1976, America's dishonor list of words banished from the Queen's English. Overworked words and phrases (e.g., *metrosexual, red states/blue states, bling-bling, embedded journalist* and *ripped from the headlines*). Send nominations to following address. For info: Public Relations Office, Lake Superior State University, Sault Ste. Marie, MI 49783. Phone: (906) 635-2315. Fax: (906) 635-2623. Web: www.lssu.edu/banished.

NEW YEAR'S RESOLUTIONS WEEK. Jan 1–7. To show people how, why and what resolutions/goals should be set and the necessary action steps to make this new year the best ever! For info: Gary Ryan Blair, The GoalsGuy, 36181 E Lake Rd, Ste 139, Palm Harbor, FL 34685. Phone: (877) GOALSGUY. Fax: (800) 731-GOAL. E-mail: nyrw@goalsguy.com. Web: www.goalsguy.com.

OATMEAL MONTH. Jan 1–31. Celebrate oatmeal, a low-fat, sodium-free, whole grain that when eaten daily as a part of a diet that's low in saturated fat and cholesterol may help reduce the risk of heart disease. Delicious recipes, helpful hints and tips from Quaker® Oats, The Oat Expert, will make enjoying the heart health benefits oatmeal has to offer easy, convenient and, above all, delicious. For info: The Oat Expert. Phone: (312) 629-1234. E-mail: oatexpert@aol.com.

PENGUIN PLUNGE. Jan 1. Mackerel Cove, Jamestown, RI. Annual plunge into the icy waters of Narragansett Bay to benefit Rhode Island Special Olympics. Annually, Jan 1. Est attendance: 2,000. For info: Special Olympics Rhode Island, 33 College Hill Rd, Bldg 31, Warwick, RI 02886. Phone: (401) 823-7411. Fax: (401) 823-7415.

PHILIPPINES: BLACK NAZARENE FIESTA. Jan 1–9. Manila. This traditional nine-day fiesta honors Quiapo district's patron saint. Cultural events, fireworks and parades culminate in a procession with the life-size statue of the Black Nazarene. Procession begins at the historic Quiapo Church.

POETRY CONTEST. Jan 1–Apr 5. El Paso, TX. 16th annual. Every year the El Paso Public Library sponsors a poetry contest for children in grades 1–12. Entries may be submitted Jan 1–Feb 11. Judging will be held Feb 23–26. Award ceremonies will be held on Mar 29 for grades 1–6, Apr 5 for grades 7–12. There are three awards given for each grade in both English and Spanish. Each child receives a new book of poetry in English or Spanish. For info: Laurel Indalecio, El Paso Public Library, 501 N

January 2006	S	M	T	W	T	F	S
	1	2	3	4	5	6	7
	8	9	10	11	12	13	14
	15	16	17	18	19	20	21
	22	23	24	25	26	27	28
	29	30	31				

Oregon, El Paso, TX 79901. Phone/fax: (915) 543-5470. E-mail: indaleciol@elpasotexas.gov. Web: www.elpasolibrary.org.

POLAR BEAR SWIM. Jan 1. Sheboygan Armory, Sheboygan, WI. Each New Year's Day at 1 PM, more than 450 daring swimmers brave Lake Michigan's ice floes. Most are costumed, all are crazy. Refreshments and free live entertainment from 10 AM–6 PM. Est attendance: 2,000. For info: Larry Pratt, Sheboygan Polar Bear Club. Phone: (920) 467-8436. Also: Sheboygan Conv and Visitors Bureau, 712 Riverfront Dr, Ste 101, Sheboygan, WI 53081. Phone: (920) 457-9491. Web: www.sheboygan.org.

PROFILES IN COURAGE PUBLISHED: 50th ANNIVERSARY. Jan 1, 1956. Senator John F. Kennedy of Massachusetts published his book to great praise and sales. It won a Pulitzer Prize in 1957.

REVERE, PAUL: BIRTH ANNIVERSARY. Jan 1, 1735 (OS). American patriot, silversmith and engraver; maker of false teeth, eyeglasses, picture frames and surgical instruments. Best remembered for his famous ride Apr 18, 1775, celebrated in Longfellow's poem "The Midnight Ride of Paul Revere." Born at Boston, MA, died there May 10, 1818. See also: "Paul Revere's Ride: Anniversary" (Apr 18).

ROSS, BETSY: BIRTH ANNIVERSARY. Jan 1, 1752 (OS). According to legend based largely on her grandson's revelations in 1870, needleworker Betsy Ross created the first stars-and-stripes flag in 1775, under instructions from George Washington. Her sewing and her making of flags were well known, but there is little corroborative evidence of her role in making the first stars-and-stripes. The account is generally accepted, however, in the absence of any documented claims to the contrary. She was born Elizabeth Griscom at Philadelphia, PA, and died there Jan 30, 1836.

RUSSIA: NEW YEAR'S DAY OBSERVANCE. Jan 1–2. National holiday. Modern tradition calls for setting up New Year's trees in homes, halls, clubs, palaces of culture and the hall of the Kremlin Palace. Children's parties with Granddad Frost and his granddaughter, Snow Girl. Games, songs, dancing, special foods, family gatherings and exchange of gifts and New Year's cards.

SAINT BASIL'S DAY. Jan 1. St. Basil's or St. Vasily's feast day observed by Eastern Orthodox churches. Special traditions for the day include serving St. Basil cakes, each of which contains a coin. Feast day observed Jan 14 by those churches using the Julian calendar.

SILENT RECORD WEEK. Jan 1–7. To commemorate the anniversary of the invention of the silent record in 1960, which was played on Detroit jukeboxes. The following year a Silent Record Concert and Recording Session featured emcee Henry Morgan, Soupy Sales and the 120-piece Hush Symphonic Band. [Originated by the late W.T. Rabe of Sault Ste. Marie, MI.]

SLOW COOKING MONTH. Jan 1–31. A month that allows slow-cooking enthusiasts to celebrate this useful cooking method and the appliances that make it happen. For time-crunched home cooks, slow cooking and slow cookers offer convenience, ease of preparation, long-lasting delicious aromas (especially in winter) and great taste. Slow cookers use minimal energy and do not heat up the kitchen. They're the ultimate tool for "fix it and forget it" meals. Slow cooking is hot again—use this month to discover a great method and useful machines. Sponsored by General Mills's Betty Crocker Slow Cooker Helper—recipes and other information available. For info: Betty Crocker Slow Cooker Helper, General Mills, Inc, PO Box 9452, Minneapolis, MN 55440. Web: www.bettycrocker.com/products/prod_slowcooker.aspx.

SOLEMNITY OF MARY, MOTHER OF GOD. Jan 1. Holy Day of Obligation in the Roman Catholic Church since calendar reorganization of 1969, replacing the Feast of the Circumcision, which had been recognized for more than 14 centuries. See also: "Circumcision of Christ" (Jan 1).

SUDAN: INDEPENDENCE DAY. Jan 1. National holiday. Sudan was proclaimed a sovereign independent republic in 1956, ending its status as an Anglo-Egyptian condominium (since 1899).

TAIWAN: FOUNDATION DAYS. Jan 1–2. Public holiday. Commemorates the founding of the Republic of China on Jan 1, 1912.

UNITED KINGDOM: NEW YEAR'S HOLIDAY. Jan 1.

UNITED NATIONS: INTERNATIONAL YEAR OF DESERTS AND DESERTIFICATION. Jan 1–Dec 31. On Dec 23, 2003, the General Assembly declared 2006 as the International Year of Deserts and Desertification (resolution 58/211). It invited all countries to establish national committees or focal points and to celebrate the year by arranging appropriate activities. It called upon all relevant international organizations and member states to support the activities related to desertification, including land degradation, to be organized by affected countries, in particular, African countries and least developed countries. For info: United Nations, Dept of Public Info, New York, NY 10017. Web: www.un.org.

WALKER, DOAK: BIRTH ANNIVERSARY. Jan 1, 1927. Ewell Doak Walker, Jr, Pro Football Hall of Fame and Heisman Trophy running back, born at Dallas, TX. Walker won the Heisman Trophy in 1948, playing for SMU, and went on to an outstanding pro career with the Detroit Lions. He was a handsome, humble player during a time when football players could become national heroes. Inducted into the Hall of Fame in 1986. Died at Steamboat Springs, CO, Sept 27, 1998.

WAYNE, "MAD ANTHONY": BIRTH ANNIVERSARY. Jan 1, 1745 (OS). American Revolutionary War general whose daring, sometimes reckless, conduct earned him the nickname "Mad." His courage and shrewdness as a soldier made him a key figure in capturing Stony Point, NY (1779), preventing Benedict Arnold's "delivery" of West Point to the British and subduing hostile Indians of the Northwest Territory (1794). He was born at Waynesboro, PA, and died at Presque Isle, PA, Dec 15, 1796.

WESTERN PACIFIC HURRICANE SEASON. Jan 1–Dec 31. Most hurricanes occur from June 1 through Oct 1, though the season lasts all year. (Western Pacific: West of International Dateline.) Info from: US Dept of Commerce, Natl Oceanic and Atmospheric Admin, Rockville, MD 20852.

Z DAY. Jan 1. To give recognition on the first day of the year to all persons and places whose names begin with the letter *Z* and who are always listed or thought of last in any alphabetized list. For info: Tom Zager. E-mail: tee_zee@excite.com.

BIRTHDAYS TODAY

Valentina Cortese, 81, actress (*The Barefoot Contessa, Juliet of the Spirits*), born Milan, Italy, Jan 1, 1925.

Jon Corzine, 59, US Senator (D, New Jersey), born Taylorville, IL, Jan 1, 1947.

Ernest F. Hollings, 84, retired US Senator (D, South Carolina), born Charleston, SC, Jan 1, 1922.

Michael Imperioli, 40, actor ("The Sopranos"), born Mount Vernon, NY, Jan 1, 1966.

Helmut Jahn, 66, architect, born Nuremberg, Germany, Jan 1, 1940.

Frank Langella, 66, actor (*The Twelve Chairs, Lolita*), born Bayonne, NJ, Jan 1, 1940.

Don Novello, 63, actor, comedian ("The Smothers Brothers Show," "Saturday Night Live": Father Guido Sarducci), born Ashtabula, OH, Jan 1, 1943.

J.D. Salinger, 87, author (*Catcher in the Rye, Franny & Zooey, Seymour: An Introduction*), born New York, NY, Jan 1, 1919.

JANUARY 2 — MONDAY

Day 2 — 363 Remaining

ASIMOV, ISAAC: BIRTH ANNIVERSARY. Jan 2, 1920. Although Isaac Asimov was one of the world's best-known writers of science fiction, his almost 500 books dealt with subjects as diverse as the Bible, works for preschoolers, college textbooks, mysteries, chemistry, biology, limericks, Shakespeare, Gilbert and Sullivan and modern history. During his prolific career he helped to elevate science fiction from pulp magazines to a more intellectual level. Some of his works include the *Foundation Trilogy, The Robots of Dawn, Robots and Empire, Nemesis, Murder at the A.B.A.* (in which he himself was a character), *The Gods Themselves* and *I, Robot,* in which he posited the famous Three Laws of Robotics. His *The Clock We Live On* is an accessible explanation of the origins of calendars. Asimov was born near Smolensk, Russia, and died at New York, NY, Apr 6, 1992.

CAPITAL ONE BOWL. Jan 2. Florida Citrus Bowl Stadium, Orlando, FL. 60th annual. Postseason college football game matching two teams selected from the Big Ten and Southeastern conferences. Sponsor: Capital One. Est attendance: 70,000. For info: Florida Citrus Sports, One Citrus Bowl Pl, Orlando, FL 32805. Phone: (407) 423-2476. Fax: (407) 425-8451. E-mail: contactfcs@fcsports.com. Web: www.fcsports.com.

55-MPH SPEED LIMIT: ANNIVERSARY. Jan 2, 1974. President Richard Nixon signed a bill requiring states to limit highway speeds to a maximum of 55 mph. This measure was meant to conserve energy during the crisis precipitated by the embargo imposed by the Arab oil-producing countries. A plan, used by some states, limited sale of gasoline on odd-numbered days for cars whose plates ended in odd numbers and even-numbered days for even-numbered plates. Some states limited purchases to $2–$3 per auto and lines as long as six miles resulted in some locations. See also: "Arab Oil Embargo Lifted: Anniversary" (Mar 13).

GEORGIA: RATIFICATION DAY. Jan 2, 1788. By unanimous vote, Georgia became the fourth state to ratify the Constitution.

HAITI: ANCESTORS' DAY. Jan 2. Commemoration of the ancestors. Also known as Hero's Day. Public holiday.

HAPPY MEW YEAR FOR CATS DAY. Jan 2. Felines, ever above mere humans in the great chain of being, have a day unto themselves to celebrate the "mewness" of a new time. Annually, Jan 2. [©2003 by WH.] For info: Thomas & Ruth Roy, Wellcat Holidays, 2418 Long Ln, Lebanon, PA 17046. Phone: (717) 279-0184. E-mail: info@wellcat.com. Web: www.wellcat.com.

JAPAN: KAKIZOME. Jan 2. Traditional Japanese festival gets under way when the first strokes of the year are made on paper with the traditional brushes.

MILLER, ROGER: BIRTH ANNIVERSARY. Jan 2, 1936. Country and western singer, songwriter and musician ("King of the Road"), Roger Miller was born at Ft Worth, TX. Miller won 11 Grammy Awards and a Tony (1986 for the score to the Broadway play *Big River*). He died Oct 25, 1992, at Los Angeles, CA.

NOKIA SUGAR BOWL. Jan 2. Louisiana Superdome, New Orleans, LA. 72nd annual. Part of the Bowl Championship Series (BCS). Game time is 7:30 PM, EST. The Sugar Bowl originated in 1935. Est attendance: 75,000. For info: Nokia Sugar Bowl, Louisiana Superdome, Mezzanine Level, 1500 Sugar Bowl Dr, New Orleans, LA 70112. Phone: (504) 525-8573. Fax: (504) 525-4867. E-mail: jeffh@sugarbowl.gs.net. Web: www.nokiasugarbowl.com.

★ ★ ★

January 2006	S	M	T	W	T	F	S
	1	2	3	4	5	6	7
	8	9	10	11	12	13	14
	15	16	17	18	19	20	21
	22	23	24	25	26	27	28
	29	30	31				

OUTBACK BOWL. Jan 2. Raymond James Stadium, Tampa, FL. The Outback Bowl Game brings together top college football teams from the SEC and the Big Ten. Game time is 11 AM, EST. In addition, the bowl is highlighted by a variety of special events, sports activities and private functions. Est attendance: 65,000. For info: Mike Schulze, Tampa Bay Bowl Assn, 4211 W Boy Scout Blvd, Ste 560, Tampa, FL 33607. Phone: (813) 874-2695. Fax: (813) 873-1959. Web: www.outbackbowl.com.

RUSSIA: PASSPORT PRESENTATION. Jan 2. A ceremony for 16-year-olds, who are recognized as citizens of the country. Always on the first working day of the New Year.

SBC COTTON BOWL CLASSIC. Jan 2. Cotton Bowl Stadium, Dallas, TX. Since 1937. Postseason football game matching the #2 team from the Big 12 with the Southeastern Conference (SEC) division champion, division runner-up or a team with a comparable record. Game time is 10 AM, EST. Est attendance: 70,000. For info: Cotton Bowl Athletic Assn, Box 569420, Dallas, TX 75356-9420. Phone: (214) 634-7525 or (888) 792-BOWL. E-mail: coach@sbccottonbowl.com. Web: www.sbccottonbowl.com.

SCOTLAND: NEW YEAR'S BANK HOLIDAY. Jan 2. Public holiday. The working day after New Year's Day.

"SOMEDAY WE'LL LAUGH ABOUT THIS" WEEK. Jan 2–6. We've all used the expression, "Someday we'll laugh about this!" Why wait? It usually takes less than seven days for people to violate 90 percent of their New Year's resolutions. This week helps us to remember the art of laughing at ourselves. This week tickles the yoke and joke of perfectionism while encouraging people to strive for excellence at the same time. This week is a great way to start the new year—laughing at the humorous human condition. For info on the positive power of humor: Dr. Joel Goodman, The Humor Project, Inc, 480 Broadway, Ste 210-C, Saratoga Springs, NY 12866-2288. Phone: (518) 587-8770. E-mail: chase@HumorProject.com. Web: www.HumorProject.com.

SPACE MILESTONE: *LUNA 1* (USSR). Jan 2, 1959. Launch of robotic moon probe that missed the moon and became the first spacecraft from Earth to orbit the sun.

SPAIN CAPTURES GRANADA: ANNIVERSARY. Jan 2, 1492. Spaniards took the city of Granada from the Moors, ending seven centuries of Muslim rule in Spain.

STOCK EXCHANGE HOLIDAY (NEW YEAR'S DAY). Jan 2 (observed). The holiday schedules for the various exchanges are subject to change if relevant rules, regulations or exchange policies are revised. If you have questions, phone: American Stock Exchange (212) 306-1000, Chicago Board of Trade (312) 435-3500, Chicago Board of Options Exchange (312) 786-5600, NASDAQ Stock Market (646) 441-5200, New York Stock Exchange (212) 656-3000, Pacific Stock Exchange (415) 393-4000, Philadelphia Stock Exchange (215) 496-5000.

SWITZERLAND: BERCHTOLDSTAG. Jan 2. Holiday in many cantons. Commemorates the founding of the city of Bern by Duke Berchtold V in the 12th century. Now mainly a children's holiday.

TAFT, HELEN HERRON: BIRTH ANNIVERSARY. Jan 2, 1861. Wife of William Howard Taft, 27th president of the US, born at Cincinnati, OH. Died at Washington, DC, May 22, 1943.

THOMAS, MARTHA CAREY: BIRTH ANNIVERSARY. Jan 2, 1857. The second president of Bryn Mawr College, Martha Carey Thomas gained a reputation for her insistence that the education of women should be as rigorous as that of men. A zealous suffragist, she served as the first president of the National College Women's Equal Suffrage League. Thomas promoted Bryn Mawr's Summer School for Women in Industry (opened in 1921) to provide a liberal education for working women. Born at Baltimore, MD, she died at Philadelphia, PA, Dec 2, 1935.

TOSTITOS FIESTA BOWL. Jan 2. Sun Devil Stadium, Tempe, AZ. Part of the Bowl Championship Series. Game time is 3 PM, MST. Est attendance: 75,000. For info: Fiesta Bowl, 120 S Ash

Ave, Tempe, AZ 85281. Phone: (480) 350-0900. Web: www.tosti tosfiestabowl.com.

TOURNAMENT OF ROSES PARADE. Jan 2. Pasadena, CA. 117th annual parade. Rose Parade starting at 8:00 AM, PST, includes floats, bands and equestrians. Est attendance: 1,000,000. For info: Pasadena Tournament of Roses Assn, 391 S Orange Grove Blvd, Pasadena, CA 91184. Phone: (626) 449-4100. Fax: (626) 449-9066. E-mail: rosepr@earthlink.net. Web: www.tourn amentofroses.com.

WOLFE, JAMES: BIRTH ANNIVERSARY. Jan 2, 1727. English general who commanded the British army's victory over Montcalm's French forces on the Plains of Abraham at Quebec City in 1759. As a result, France surrendered Canada to England. Wolfe was born at Westerham, Kent, England. He died at the Plains of Abraham of battle wounds, Sept 13, 1759.

WOMEN'S SELF-EMPOWERMENT WEEK. Jan 2–8. Women wear many hats these days, and this week is a time to stop, take stock of your life and recognize all that you have accomplished. It's an occasion to pat yourself on the back and feel good about your role in society and the opportunities that have come your way through hard work and dedication. Let it inspire you to establish new goals and reach for the sky. For info: Robin Gorman Newman, The Love Coach, 44 Somerset Dr N, Great Neck, NY 11020. Phone: (516) 773-0911. E-mail: robin@lovecoach.com. Web: www.ibwc.org.

BIRTHDAYS TODAY

Jim Bakker, 67, former TV evangelist, born James Orsen at Muskegon, MI, Jan 2, 1939.

Kate Bosworth, 23, actress (*Blue Crush, Beyond the Sea*), born Los Angeles, CA, Jan 2, 1983.

Brian Boucher, 29, hockey player, born Woonsocket, RI, Jan 2, 1977.

Tia Carrere, 39, actress (*Wayne's World, True Lies*), born Honolulu, HI, Jan 2, 1967.

David Cone, 43, former baseball player, born Kansas City, MO, Jan 2, 1963.

Taye Diggs, 34, model, actor (*How Stella Got Her Groove Back*), born Rochester, NY, Jan 2, 1972.

Christopher Durang, 57, playwright, actor (*The Secret of My Success, Heaven Help Us*), born Montclair, NJ, Jan 2, 1949.

Cuba Gooding, Jr, 38, actor (*Jerry Maguire, As Good As It Gets*), born the Bronx, NY, Jan 2, 1968.

Dennis Hastert, 64, Speaker of the House, born Aurora, IL, Jan 2, 1942.

Edgar Martinez, 43, former baseball player, born New York, NY, Jan 2, 1963.

Wendy Phillips, 54, actress ("Promised Land," "Homefront"), born Brooklyn, NY, Jan 2, 1952.

Renata Tebaldi, 84, opera singer, born Pesaro, Italy, Jan 2, 1922.

Christy Turlington, 37, model, born Walnut Creek, CA, Jan 2, 1969.

JANUARY 3 — TUESDAY
Day 3 — 362 Remaining

ALASKA: ADMISSION DAY: ANNIVERSARY. Jan 3, 1959. Alaska, which had been purchased from Russia in 1867, became the 49th state. The area of Alaska is nearly one-fifth the size of the rest of the US.

ALL STATES PICNIC (FOR SENIOR CITIZENS). Jan 3. Yuma, AZ. Seniors from all over the US and Canada gather for picnic lunch, entertainment and fun. Sponsor: City of Yuma Parks and Recreation Department. Est attendance: 1,000. For info: Yuma Civic Center, 1440 Desert Hills Dr, Yuma, AZ 85365. Phone: (928) 373-5043. Fax: (928) 344-9121. E-mail: ycc@ci .yuma.az.us.

"THE ARSENIO HALL SHOW" TV PREMIERE: ANNIVERSARY. Jan 3, 1989. Arsenio Hall became the first African-American to host a successful syndicated late-night talk show. The show attracted a younger audience than that of Johnny Carson's "The Tonight Show" and effectively limited the impact of CBS's 1989 late-night entry, "The Pat Sajak Show." Hall was successful in booking soul and rap music acts that had rarely been seen on other shows. His was also the show on which presidential candidate Bill Clinton appeared, playing the saxophone in dark glasses. Hall was named by *TV Guide* (June 1990) as its first "TV Person of the Year."

ATTLEE, CLEMENT RICHARD: BIRTH ANNIVERSARY. Jan 3, 1883. English leader of the Labour Party and prime minister (July 1945–October 1951). Born at London, England; died there Oct 8, 1967.

CONGRESS ASSEMBLES. Jan 3. The Constitution provides that "the Congress shall assemble at least once in every year. . . ." and the 20th Amendment specifies "and such meeting shall begin at noon on the third day of January, unless they shall by law appoint a different day." If Jan 3 happens to fall on a weekend, Congress by resolution will meet on the following Monday or Tuesday.

COOLIDGE, GRACE ANNA GOODHUE: BIRTH ANNIVERSARY. Jan 3, 1879. Wife of Calvin Coolidge, 30th president of the US, born at Burlington, VT. Died at Northampton, MA, July 8, 1957.

DAVIES, MARION: BIRTH ANNIVERSARY. Jan 3, 1897. Born at Brooklyn, NY, Marion Cecilia Douras became Marion Davies and made her first appearance on film in 1917. Her romantic and professional involvement with newspaper magnate William Randolph Hearst ensured the type of publicity that would launch her to stardom. Her films included *When Knighthood Was in Flower*, *The Patsy* and *Show People*. Davies died at Hollywood, Sept 23, 1961.

DRINKING STRAW PATENTED: ANNIVERSARY. Jan 3, 1888. A drinking straw made out of paraffin-covered paper was patented by Marvin Stone of Washington, DC. It replaced natural rye straws.

FEDEX ORANGE BOWL. Jan 3. Dolphins Stadium, Miami, FL. Part of the Bowl Championship Series (BCS). Est attendance: 75,000. For info: Orange Bowl Committee, 703 Waterford Way, Ste 590, Miami, FL 33126. Phone: (305) 341-4700. E-mail: info @orangebowl.org. Web: www.orangebowl.org.

FIRST FEMALE CONGRESSIONAL PAGE: ANNIVERSARY. Jan 3, 1939. Gene Cox, 13, served on the House floor as aide to her father, Representative Eugene Cox (D-GA), on opening day of the 76th Congress. She was paid $4 for three hours of work and there were no objections to her one-day service. More than 30 years later, however, there was much debate when Senator Jacob Javits (R-NY) nominated a female to be a real Senate page.

"LOOK UP AND LIVE" TV PREMIERE: ANNIVERSARY. Jan 3, 1954. CBS broadcast this inspirational show on Sunday mornings for 24 years. The Reverend Lawrence McMasters appeared in the early years and Merv Griffin hosted the show in 1955. Pamela Ilott, executive producer, was also director of religious programming for CBS News.

MEMENTO MORI. Jan 3. *Memento, mori,* Latin for "Remember, you die," is also the title of a novel by Muriel Spark. We suggest posting the words at home and at work, not to be morbid, but to remind us to cherish all that we have today . . . for tomorrow may never arrive. [©2003 by WH.] For info: Thomas and Ruth Roy, Wellcat Holidays, 2418 Long Ln, Lebanon, PA 17046. Phone: (717) 279-0184. E-mail: info@wellcat.com. Web: www.wellcat.com.

MOTT, LUCRETIA (COFFIN): BIRTH ANNIVERSARY. Jan 3, 1793. American teacher, minister, antislavery leader and (with Elizabeth Cady Stanton) one of the founders of the women's rights movement in the US. Born at Nantucket, MA, she died near Philadelphia, PA, Nov 11, 1880.

NATIONAL GEOGRAPHIC BEE 2006, SCHOOL LEVEL. Jan 3–13. (Began Nov 14, 2005. Principals must have registered their schools by Oct 15, 2005.) Nationwide contest involving millions of students at the school level. The Bee is designed to encourage the teaching and study of geography. There are three levels of competition. A student must win a school-level Bee in order to win the right to take a written exam. The written test determines the top 100 students in each state who are eligible to go on to the state level. National Geographic brings each state winner and a teacher from their school to Washington for the national level in May. Alex Trebek moderates the national level. For info: Natl Geographic Bee, Natl Geographic Society, 1145 17th St NW, Washington, DC 20036. Phone: (202) 828-6659. Web: www.nationalgeographic.com/geographicbee.

NATIONAL WRITE TO CONGRESS DAY. Jan 3. On this day when Congress convenes for a new session in Washington, American citizens have a unique opportunity to tell our elected representatives and senators how they can best represent us for the coming year. What issues do we care about? What do we hope they will accomplish in this session? One easy way to identify your members of Congress and contact them is at the free website Congress.org. For info: Lara Wyrsta, Capitol Advantage, 2751 Prosperity Ave, 6th Fl, Fairfax, VA 22031. Phone: (703) 289-4670. Fax: (703) 289-4678. E-mail: camarketing@capitoladvantage.com. Web: www.capitoladvantage.com.

"QUEEN FOR A DAY" TV PREMIERE: 50th ANNIVERSARY. Jan 3, 1956. Game show on which prizes were awarded to the contestant who evoked the most sympathy from the studio audience. The show began some 11 years earlier on the radio with Jack Bailey hosting. Five women were chosen from the audience to appear on stage. Each related her story of misfortune and explained what she needed to remedy the situation and the audience would vote by applause. The lucky winner was then given the royal treatment—crown, scepter and red robe—plus a prize to help with her problem. This soon became the top-rated daytime show. In 1969 the show went into syndication with Dick Curtis as host, but it didn't last long.

RAUH, JOSEPH L., JR: BIRTH ANNIVERSARY. Jan 3, 1911. Political activist Joseph L. Rauh, Jr, was born at Cincinnati, OH. In 1947 he cofounded Americans for Democratic Action (ADA), which supports liberal causes. Rauh helped create the minority civil rights plank at the 1948 Democratic National Convention—a foundation for the federal civil rights legislation in the 1960s. He served on the executive board of the NAACP and was general counsel to the Leadership Conference on Civil Rights. He died Sept 3, 1992, at Washington, DC.

SPACE MILESTONE: *MARS EXPLORATION ROVER SPIRIT* **(US).** Jan 3, 2004. After traveling 302.6 million miles from its June 10, 2003, launch at Cape Canaveral Air Force Station, FL, the *Mars Exploration Rover Spirit* landed at Gusev Crater on Mars. The robotic rover's mission was to examine the soil and environment of the red planet. By Jan 6, *Spirit* had taken the sharpest color photograph of Mars ever achieved. *Spirit's* twin rover, *Opportunity*, landed Jan 24, 2004.

STURGES, JOHN: BIRTH ANNIVERSARY. Jan 3, 1911. Motion picture director John Sturges, born at Oak Park, IL, was known for his action movies. He received an Academy Award nomination in 1955 for *Bad Day at Black Rock*. He also directed *Gunfight at the OK Corral* (1956), *The Magnificent Seven* (1960), *The Great Escape* (1963) and his last film *The Eagle Has Landed* (1977). He died Aug 18, 1992, at San Luis Obispo, CA.

TOLKIEN, J.R.R.: BIRTH ANNIVERSARY. Jan 3, 1892. John Ronald Reuel Tolkien, author of *The Hobbit* (1937) and the trilogy *The Lord of the Rings*. Though best known for his fantasies, Tolkien was also a serious philologist. Born at Bloemfontein, South Africa, he died at Bournemouth, England, Sept 2, 1973.

WIND CAVE NATIONAL PARK ESTABLISHED: ANNIVERSARY. Jan 3, 1903. President Theodore Roosevelt signed a bill on this date establishing South Dakota's Wind Cave a national park and preserve. It was the first national park established for the preservation of a cave.

BIRTHDAYS TODAY

Joan Walsh Anglund, 80, author, illustrator of children's books (*Crocus in the Snow, Bedtime Book*), born Hinsdale, IL, Jan 3, 1926.

Dabney Coleman, 74, actor ("Buffalo Bill," *Nine to Five, Tootsie*), born Austin, TX, Jan 3, 1932.

Mel Gibson, 50, actor (*Braveheart, Lethal Weapon*), director (*The Passion of the Christ*), born Peekskill, NY, Jan 3, 1956.

Robert Marvin (Bobby) Hull, 67, Hall of Fame hockey player, born Point Anne, ON, Canada, Jan 3, 1939.

Robert Loggia, 76, actor (*An Officer and a Gentleman, Scarface*), born Staten Island, NY, Jan 3, 1930.

Danica McKellar, 31, actress ("The Wonder Years," *Sidekicks*), born La Jolla, CA, Jan 3, 1975.

Victoria Principal, 56, actress ("Dallas"), born Fukuoka, Japan, Jan 3, 1950.

Stephen Stills, 61, musician, songwriter, born Dallas, TX, Jan 3, 1945.

JANUARY 4 — WEDNESDAY
Day 4 — 361 Remaining

AMNESTY FOR POLYGAMISTS: ANNIVERSARY. Jan 4, 1893. President Benjamin Harrison issued a proclamation granting full amnesty and pardon to all persons who had since Nov 1, 1890, abstained from unlawful cohabitation of a polygamous marriage. This was intended in the main for a specific group of elderly Mormons who had continued in the practice of contracting serial marriages. Amnesty was based on the condition that those pardoned must obey the law in the future or be "vigorously prosecuted." The practice of polygamy was a factor interfering with attainment of statehood for Utah.

BRAILLE, LOUIS: BIRTH ANNIVERSARY. Jan 4, 1809. The inventor of a widely used touch system of reading and writing for the blind was born at Coupvray, France. Permanently blinded at the age of three by a leatherworking awl in his father's saddlemaking shop, Braille developed a system of writing that used, ironically, an awl-like stylus to punch marks in paper that could be felt and interpreted by the blind. The system was largely ignored until after Braille died in poverty, suffering from tuberculosis, at Paris, Jan 6, 1852.

"THE CATHOLIC HOUR" TV PREMIERE: ANNIVERSARY. Jan 4, 1953. Produced in cooperation with the National Council of Catholic Men, this show ran for 17 years, alternating from week to week with "The Eternal Light" and "Frontiers of Faith."

January 2006

S	M	T	W	T	F	S
1	2	3	4	5	6	7
8	9	10	11	12	13	14
15	16	17	18	19	20	21
22	23	24	25	26	27	28
29	30	31				

DIMPLED CHAD DAY. Jan 4. This is a day to commemorate all the dimpled chads of the world, left over from various and sundry contested elections. Chads, roasted in garlic, make an excellent sprinkle topping for salads. [©2003 by WH.] For info: Thomas & Ruth Roy, Wellcat Holidays, 2418 Long Ln, Lebanon, PA 17046. Phone: (717) 279-0184. E-mail: info@wellcat.com. Web: www.wellcat.com.

EARTH AT PERIHELION. Jan 4. At approximately 10 AM, EST, planet Earth will reach Perihelion, that point in its orbit when it is closest to the sun (about 91,400,000 miles). The Earth's mean distance from the sun (mean radius of its orbit) is reached early in the months of April and October. Note that Earth is closest to the sun during Northern Hemisphere winter. See also: "Earth at Aphelion" (July 3).

GENERAL TOM THUMB: BIRTH ANNIVERSARY. Jan 4, 1838. Charles Sherwood Stratton, perhaps the most famous midget in history, was born at Bridgeport, CT. He eventually reached a height of three feet, four inches and a weight of 70 pounds. Discovered by P.T. Barnum in 1842, Stratton, as "General Tom Thumb," became an internationally known entertainer and performed before Queen Victoria and other heads of state. On Feb 10, 1863, he married another midget, Lavinia Warren. Stratton died at Middleborough, MA, July 15, 1883.

GRIMM, JACOB: BIRTH ANNIVERSARY. Jan 4, 1785. Librarian, mythologist and philologist, born at Hanau, Germany. Best remembered for *Grimm's Fairy Tales* (in collaboration with his brother Wilhelm). Died at Berlin, Germany, Sept 20, 1863.

MYANMAR: INDEPENDENCE DAY. Jan 4. National Day. The British controlled the country from 1826 until 1948 when it was granted independence. The country's name was changed from Burma to the Union of Myanmar in 1989 to reflect that the population is made up not just of the Burmese but of many other ethnic groups as well.

NEWTON, ISAAC: BIRTH ANNIVERSARY. Jan 4, 1643. Sir Isaac Newton was the chief figure of the scientific revolution of the 17th century, a physicist and mathematician who laid the foundations of calculus, studied the mechanics of planetary motion and discovered the law of gravitation. Born at Woolsthorpe, England, he died at London, England, Mar 31, 1727. Newton was born before Great Britain adopted the Gregorian calendar. His Julian (Old Style) birth date is Dec 25, 1642.

"NIGHT COURT" TV PREMIERE: ANNIVERSARY. Jan 4, 1984. NBC sitcom set in an urban courtroom. The cast included Harry Anderson as Judge Harry T. Stone, John Larroquette as prosecutor Dan Fielding, Richard Moll as court officer Bull Shannon and Selma Diamond as court officer Selma Hacker. Markie Post joined the cast in 1985 as PD Christine Sullivan. Mel Tormé made a few appearances as himself, Harry's idol. The last telecast was July 1, 1992.

NIXON'S REJECTION OF SENATE ORDER: ANNIVERSARY. Jan 4, 1974. President Richard Nixon rejected the Senate Watergate Committee's subpoenas seeking White House tapes and documents.

POLISH-AMERICAN IN THE HOUSE: ANNIVERSARY. Jan 4, 1977. Maryland Democrat Barbara Mikulski took her seat in the US House of Representatives, the first Polish-American ever to do so. An able voice for female as well as working-class Baltimore constituents of the 3rd District, Ms Mikulski went on to be elected to the US Senate.

POP MUSIC CHART INTRODUCED: 70th ANNIVERSARY. Jan 4, 1936. *Billboard* magazine published the first list of bestselling pop records, covering the week that ended Dec 30, 1935. On the list were recordings by the Tommy Dorsey and the Ozzie Nelson orchestras.

ROSE BOWL GAME. Jan 4. Pasadena, CA. BCS National Championship game. Football conference champions meet in the 92nd Rose Bowl game at 2 PM, PST. Tournament of Roses has been an annual New Year's event since 1890; Rose Bowl football game since 1902. Michigan defeated Stanford 49–0 in what was the first postseason football game. Called the Rose Bowl since 1923, it is preceded each year by the Tournament of Roses Parade. Est attendance: 100,000. For info: Program Coordinator, Tournament of Roses, 391 South Orange Grove Blvd, Pasadena, CA 91184. Phone: (626) 449-ROSE. Fax: (626) 449-9066. Web: www.tournamentofroses.com.

RUSH, BENJAMIN: BIRTH ANNIVERSARY. Jan 4, 1746. Physician, patriot and humanitarian of the American Revolution, born on a plantation at Byberry, PA. Rush was a signer of the Declaration of Independence, and his writings on mental illness earned him the title "Father of Psychiatry." His tract *Inquiry* attacked the common wisdom of the time that alcohol was a positive good. He was the first American to call alcoholism a chronic disease. Benjamin Rush died at Philadelphia, PA, Apr 19, 1813.

SETON, ELIZABETH ANN BAYLEY: FEAST DAY. Jan 4. First American-born saint (beatified Mar 17, 1963; canonized Sept 14, 1975). Born at New York, NY, Aug 28, 1774, Seton was the founder of the American Sisters of Charity, the first American order of Roman Catholic nuns. She died at Baltimore, MD, Jan 4, 1821.

TRIVIA DAY. Jan 4. In celebration of those who know all sorts of facts and/or have doctorates in uselessology. For info: Robert L. Birch, Puns Corps, 3108 Dashiell Rd, Falls Church, VA 22042. Phone: (703) 533-3668.

UTAH: ADMISSION DAY: ANNIVERSARY. Jan 4. Utah became the 45th state in 1896.

BIRTHDAYS TODAY

Dyan Cannon, 69, actress (Oscar nominations for *Heaven Can Wait, Bob and Carol and Ted and Alice*), born Tacoma, WA, Jan 4, 1937.

Patrick Cassidy, 44, actor ("Bay City Blues," *Longtime Companion*), born Los Angeles, CA, Jan 4, 1962.

Dave Foley, 44, actor ("NewsRadio"), born Toronto, ON, Canada, Jan 4, 1962.

Ann Magnuson, 50, performance artist, actress ("Anything but Love," *Clear and Present Danger*), born Charleston, WV, Jan 4, 1956.

Julia Ormond, 41, actress (*Legends of the Fall, Sabrina*), born Surrey, England, Jan 4, 1965.

Floyd Patterson, 71, former boxer, born Waco, NC, Jan 4, 1935.

Barbara Rush, 79, actress ("Peyton Place," *Magnificent Obsession, Hombre*), born Denver, CO, Jan 4, 1927.

Donald Francis (Don) Shula, 76, Hall of Fame football coach and player, born Painesville, OH, Jan 4, 1930.

Michael Stipe, 46, singer (REM), born Decatur, GA, Jan 4, 1960.

Jane Wyman, 92, actress ("Falcon Crest," *Magnificent Obsession*; Oscar for *Johnny Belinda*), born Sarah Jane Faulks, St. Joseph, MO, Jan 4, 1914.

JANUARY 5 — THURSDAY
Day 5 — 360 Remaining

AILEY, ALVIN: BIRTH ANNIVERSARY. Jan 5, 1931. Born at Rogers, TX, Alvin Ailey began his noted career as a choreographer in the late 1950s after a successful career as a dancer. He founded the Alvin Ailey American Dance Theater, drawing from classical ballet, jazz, Afro-Caribbean and modern dance idioms to create the 79 ballets of the company's repertoire. He and his work played a central part in establishing a role for blacks in the world of modern dance. Ailey died Dec 1, 1989, at New York, NY.

"ALL MY CHILDREN" TV PREMIERE: ANNIVERSARY. Jan 5, 1970. This ABC show became TV's top-rated soap opera by the 1978–79 season and still keeps viewers glued to the screen. "All My Children" was created by Agnes Nixon, who had written for several other shows. Set in a place called Pine Valley, NY, the show originally focused on the Tyler and Martin families. The story includes Erica Kane (played by Susan Lucci), one of daytime TV's most popular characters. Lucci has been nominated 21 times for an Emmy, winning only once, in 1999. Other award-winning or longtime cast members include Ruth Warrick as Phoebe Tyler Wallingford, Julia Barr as Brooke English, Michael E. Knight as Tad "The Cad" Martin, David Canary as twin brothers Adam and Stuart Chandler, and John Callahan and Eva LaRue Callahan as Edmund and Maria Grey. The show has also launched the careers of such stars as Kim Delaney, Sarah Michelle Gellar and Kelly Ripa. The 9,000th episode aired Dec 16, 2004.

AMERICAN HISTORICAL ASSOCIATION: ANNUAL MEETING. Jan 5–8. Philadelphia, PA. Approximately 200 sessions will be held covering a wide range of scholarly, professional and pedagogical topics dealing with all areas of history. Est attendance: 5,200. For info: Sharon K. Tune, Convention Director, American Historical Assn, 400 A St SE, Washington, DC 20003. Phone: (202) 544-2422. Fax: (202) 544-8307. E-mail: aha@historians.org. Web: www.historians.org.

CARVER, GEORGE WASHINGTON: DEATH ANNIVERSARY. Jan 5, 1943. Black American agricultural scientist, author, inventor and teacher. Born into slavery at Diamond Grove, MO, probably in 1864. His research led to the creation of synthetic products made from peanuts, potatoes and wood. Carver died at Tuskegee, AL. His birthplace became a national monument in 1953.

DECATUR, STEPHEN: BIRTH ANNIVERSARY. Jan 5, 1779. American naval officer (whose father and grandfather, both also named Stephen Decatur, were also seafaring men) born at Sinepuxent, MD. In a toast at a dinner in Norfolk in 1815, Decatur spoke his most famous words: "Our country! In her intercourse with foreign nations may she always be in the right; but our country, right or wrong." Mortally wounded in a duel with Commodore James Barron, at Bladensburg, MD, on the morning of Mar 22, 1820, Decatur was carried to his home in Washington where he died a few hours later.

ENGLAND: SCHRODERS LONDON BOAT SHOW. Jan 5–15. ExCeL, London's Docklands, London. 52nd show. The show, held in association with the Daily Telegraph, promises to be a great day out with a host of features and a wide range of exhibitors. Est attendance: 200,000. For info: British Marine Federation/Natl Boat Shows Ltd, Marine House, Thorpe Lea Rd, Egham, Surrey, England TW20 8BF. Phone: (44) (1784) 223-600 or (44) (1784) 473-377. Fax: (44) (1784) 439-678. E-mail: info@britishmarine.co.uk. Web: www.britishmarine.co.uk.

FIVE-DOLLAR-A-DAY MINIMUM WAGE: ANNIVERSARY. Jan 5, 1914. Henry Ford announced that all worthy Ford Motor Company employees would receive a minimum wage of $5 a day. Ford explained the policy as "profit sharing and efficiency engineering." The more cynical attributed it to an attempt to prevent unionization and to obtain a docile workforce that would accept job speedups. To obtain this minimum wage an employee had to be of "good personal habits." Whether an individual fit these criteria was determined by a new office created by Ford Motor Company—the Sociological Department.

INTERNATIONAL CONSUMER ELECTRONICS SHOW. Jan 5–8. Las Vegas, NV. The world's largest annual trade show for consumers and America's largest annual trade show of any kind. Exhibitors are manufacturers, developers and suppliers of consumer technology hardware, content, technology delivery systems and related products and services. Attendees representing more than 115 countries include manufacturers, retailers, content providers and creators, broadband developers, wireless carriers, cable and satellite TV providers, installers, engineers, corporate buyers, government leaders, financial analysts and the media from around the world. Held since 1967. Est attendance: 130,000. For info: Consumer Electronics Association, 2500 Wilson Blvd, Arlington, VA 22201-3834. Phone: (866) 233-7968 or (301) 631-3983 (international). Fax: (703) 907-7601. E-mail: CESinfo@CE.org. Web: www.CE.org or www.cesweb.org.

ITALY: EPIPHANY FAIR. Jan 5. Piazza Navona, Rome, Italy. On the eve of Epiphany a fair of toys, sweets and presents takes place among the beautiful Bernini Fountains.

NATIONAL SECONDHAND WARDROBE DAY. Jan 5. Although a secondhand wardrobe is both economically and ecologically sound, buying and wearing used clothing is generally not viewed in a positive light. The purpose of this day is to encourage thrift store donations and to remove the stigma of previously owned clothing and accessories by providing information about the cost benefits, skills required and pleasures of buying secondhand. For info: Cheryl Gorn, PO Box 1746, Latham, NY 12110. E-mail: secondhandwardrobe@hotmail.com.

PICCARD, JEANNETTE RIDLON: BIRTH ANNIVERSARY. Jan 5, 1895. First American woman to qualify as a free-balloon pilot (1934). One of the first women to be ordained as an Episcopal priest (1976). Pilot for record-setting balloon ascent into the stratosphere (from Dearborn, MI, Oct 23, 1934) (57,579 ft) with her husband, Jean Felix Piccard. Identical twin married to identical twin. See also: "Piccard, Jean Felix: Birth Anniversary" (Jan 28). Born at Chicago, IL. Died at Minneapolis, MN, May 17, 1981.

ROMAN CATHOLIC/EASTERN ORTHODOX MEETING: ANNIVERSARY. Jan 5, 1964. Pope Paul VI and Patriarch Athenagoras of Jerusalem met in the Holy Land for the first meeting in five centuries between a Roman Catholic pontiff and an Eastern Orthodox patriarch.

RUFFIN, EDMUND: BIRTH ANNIVERSARY. Jan 5, 1794. Born at Prince George County, VA, Edmund Ruffin was an American agriculturist whose discoveries about crop rotation and fertilizer were influential in the early agrarian culture of the US. He published the *Farmer's Register* from 1833 to 1842, a journal that promoted scientific agriculture. A noted politician as well as a farmer, he was an early advocate of Southern secession whose views were widely circulated in pamphlets. As a member of the Palmetto Guards of Charleston, he was given the honor of firing the first shot on Fort Sumter Apr 12, 1861. According to legend, after the South's defeat he became despondent and, wrapping himself in the Confederate flag, took his own life on June 18, 1865, at Amelia County, VA.

January *2006*	S	M	T	W	T	F	S
	1	2	3	4	5	6	7
	8	9	10	11	12	13	14
	15	16	17	18	19	20	21
	22	23	24	25	26	27	28
	29	30	31				

SAN DIEGO BOAT SHOW. Jan 5–8. San Diego Convention Center, San Diego, CA. Annual show is largest one-stop nautical sports event on the West Coast and features a wide selection of boats and accessories, plus informative boating and fishing seminars. For info: Natl Marine Mfgrs Assn (NMMA), 200 E Randolph St, Ste 5100, Chicago, IL 60601. Phone: (312) 946-6200. Web: www.boatshows.com or www.sandiegoboatshow.com.

TWELFTH NIGHT. Jan 5. Evening before Epiphany. Twelfth Night marks the end of medieval Christmas festivities and the end of Twelfthtide (the 12-day season after Christmas ending with Epiphany). Also called Twelfth Day Eve.

WYOMING INAUGURATES FIRST WOMAN GOVERNOR IN US: ANNIVERSARY. Jan 5, 1925. Nellie Tayloe (Mrs William B.) Ross became the first woman to serve as governor upon her inauguration in Wyoming. She had previously finished out the term of her husband, who had died in office. In 1974 Ella Grasso of Connecticut became the first woman to be elected governor in her own right.

BIRTHDAYS TODAY

Suzy Amis, 44, actress (*Titanic, Judgment Day*), born Oklahoma City, OK, Jan 5, 1962.

Bradley Cooper, 31, actor ("Alias"), born Philadelphia, PA, Jan 5, 1975.

Mike DeWine, 59, US Senator (R, Ohio), born Springfield, OH, Jan 5, 1947.

Warrick Dunn, 31, football player, born Baton Rouge, LA, Jan 5, 1975.

Robert Duvall, 75, actor (*A Civil Action, The Godfather*), born San Diego, CA, Jan 5, 1931.

Umberto Eco, 74, author (*In the Name of the Rose*), born Alessandria, Italy, Jan 5, 1932.

Diane Keaton, 60, actress (Oscar for *Annie Hall; The First Wives Club, The Other Sister*), born Diane Hall at Los Angeles, CA, Jan 5, 1946.

Pamela Sue Martin, 52, actress (*The Poseidon Adventure*, "The Nancy Drew Mysteries," "Dynasty"), born Westport, CT, Jan 5, 1954.

Walter Frederick (Fritz) Mondale, 78, 42nd vice president of the US, former senator, born Ceylon, MN, Jan 5, 1928.

Ed Rendell, 62, Governor of Pennsylvania (D), born New York, NY, Jan 5, 1944.

Charlie Rose, 64, newscaster, TV host, born Henderson, NC, Jan 5, 1942.

W.D. Snodgrass, 80, poet, born Wilkinsburg, PA, Jan 5, 1926.

JANUARY 6 — FRIDAY

Day 6 — 359 Remaining

ARMENIAN CHRISTMAS. Jan 6. Christmas is observed in the Armenian Church, the oldest Christian national church.

CARNIVAL SEASON. Jan 6–Feb 28. A secular festival preceding Lent. A time of merrymaking and feasting before the austere days of Lenten fasting and penitence (40 weekdays between Ash Wednesday and Easter Sunday). The word *carnival* probably is derived from the Latin *carnem levare*, meaning "to remove meat." Depending on local custom, the carnival season may start any time between Nov 11 and Shrove Tuesday. Conclusion of the season is much less variable, being the close of Shrove Tuesday in most places. Celebrations vary considerably, but the festival often includes many theatrical aspects (masks, costumes and songs) and has given its name (in the US) to traveling amusement shows that may be seen throughout the year. Observed traditionally in Roman Catholic countries from Epiphany through Shrove Tuesday.

ELVIS PRESLEY'S BIRTHDAY CELEBRATION. Jan 6–8. Graceland, Memphis, TN. Special birthday proclamation on Jan 8 as well as other Elvis birthday events at Graceland. For info: Graceland, 3734 Elvis Presley Blvd, Memphis, TN 38116. Phone: (800) 238-2000 or (901) 332-3322. E-mail: glsales@elvis.com. Web: www.elvis.com.

EPIPHANY or TWELFTH DAY. Jan 6. Known also as Old Christmas Day and Twelfthtide. On the twelfth day after Christmas, Christians celebrate the visit of the Magi, the first Gentile recognition of Christ. Epiphany of Our Lord, one of the oldest Christian feasts, is observed in Roman Catholic churches in the US on a Sunday between Jan 2 and 8. Theophany of the Eastern Orthodox Church is observed in churches using the Gregorian calendar (Jan 19 in those churches using the Julian calendar). This feast day celebrates the manifestation of the divinity of Jesus at the time of his baptism in the Jordan River by John the Baptist.

GEORGE H.W. AND BARBARA BUSH WEDDING: ANNIVERSARY. Jan 6, 1945. George Herbert Walker Bush was 20 and Barbara Pierce was 19 when they married. They had four sons and two daughters (one of whom died in childhood). Bush served as the 41st president of the US. Their son George W. Bush became the 43rd president of the US.

GIBRAN, KAHLIL: BIRTH ANNIVERSARY. Jan 6, 1883. Lebanese-American poet (*The Prophet*) and artist. Born at Bsherri, Lebanon, he died Oct 10, 1931, at New York, NY.

GRAND AMERICAN COON HUNT. Jan 6–7. County Fairgrounds, Orangeburg, SC. Coon hunters and sportsmen from all over the US and Canada bring their dogs to compete for Grand American Champion. A United Kennel Club qualifying hunt. Est attendance: 35,000. For info: Orangeburg County Chamber of Commerce, PO Box 328, Orangeburg, SC 29116-0328. Phone: (803) 534-6821 or (800) 545-6153. Fax: (803) 531-9435. Web: www.orangeburgchamber.com.

"HALLMARK HALL OF FAME" TV PREMIERE: ANNIVERSARY. Jan 6, 1952. Carried at different times by ABC, CBS, NBC and PBS, this was a top-quality dramatic anthology series. Originally titled "Hallmark Television Playhouse," the program was sponsored by Hallmark Cards and hosted by Sarah Churchill until 1955. A few of the presentations were *Hamlet*, with Maurice Evans and Ruth Chatterton (Apr 26, 1953); *Moby Dick*, with Victor Jory (May 16, 1954); *Macbeth*, with Maurice Evans, Dame Judith Anderson and House Jameson (Nov 28, 1954); *Alice in Wonderland*, with Eva LeGallienne, Elsa Lanchester and Reginald Gardiner (Oct 23, 1955). The list goes on with splendid performances by many highly acclaimed actors and actresses.

ITALY: LA BEFANA. Jan 6. Epiphany festival in which the "Befana," a kindly witch, bestows gifts on children—toys and candy for those who have been good, but a lump of coal or a pebble for those who have been naughty. The festival begins on the night of Jan 5 with much noise and merrymaking (when the Befana is supposed to come down the chimneys on her broom, leaving gifts in children's stockings) and continues with joyous fairs, parades and other activities throughout Jan 6.

JAMAICA: MAROON FESTIVAL. Jan 6. Commemorates the 18th-century Treaty of Cudjoe. While Jamaica was a Spanish colony, its native inhabitants (Arawaks) were exterminated. The Spanish then imported African slaves to work their plantations. When the Spanish were driven out (1655), the black slaves fled to the mountains. The "Maroons" (fugitive slaves) were permitted to settle in the north of the island in 1738.

JOAN OF ARC: BIRTH ANNIVERSARY. Jan 6, 1412. Born at the village of Domrémy, in the Meuse River valley of France (probably in 1412). Turned over to an ecclesiastical court by the British, she was tried for heresy and burned to death at the stake May 30, 1431, at age 19; in reality, she was executed for the military action she'd taken against the British on behalf of Charles VII of France.

JOHNSON, BAN: BIRTH ANNIVERSARY. Jan 6, 1863. Byron Bancroft (Ban) Johnson, Baseball Hall of Fame executive, born at Cincinnati, OH. Johnson transformed the minor league Western League into the major league American League in 1901. He ruled as president with an iron hand and was eased out of power by the league's owners in 1927. Inducted into the Hall of Fame in 1937. Died at St. Louis, MO, Mar 28, 1931.

MALESKA, EUGENE T.: BIRTH ANNIVERSARY. Jan 6, 1916. *New York Times* crossword puzzle editor, Maleska was born at Jersey City, NJ. He invented new puzzle formats and clue styles for crossword puzzles in 1977 after a career in education. Maleska died Aug 3, 1993, at Daytona Beach, FL.

MIX, TOM: BIRTH ANNIVERSARY. Jan 6, 1880. American motion picture actor, especially remembered for western cowboy films. Born at Driftwood, PA. Died near Florence, AZ, Oct 12, 1940.

MOON PHASE: FIRST QUARTER. Jan 6. Moon enters First Quarter phase at 1:56 PM, EST.

NATIONAL SMITH DAY. Jan 6. The commonest surname in the English-speaking world is Smith. There are an estimated 2,900,000 Smiths in the US. This special day honors the birthday in 1580 of Captain John Smith, the leader of the English colonists who settled at Jamestown, VA, in 1607, thus making him one of the first American Smiths. On this special day, all derivatives, such as Goldsmith, Blacksmith, Printsmith, etc., are invited to participate. To alleviate the escalating costs of Eventological® Literature, a charge of $10 must be assessed for each request. Checks are to be made payable to: Adrienne Sioux Koopersmith, 1437 W Rosemont, #1W, Chicago, IL 60660-1319. E-mail: askoopersmith@hotmail.com.

NC RV AND CAMPING SHOW. Jan 6–8. Special Events Center, Greensboro Coliseum Complex, Greensboro, NC. A display of the latest in recreation vehicles and accessories by various dealers. Est attendance: 11,000. For info: Apple Rock Advertising & Promotion, 1200 Eastchester Dr, High Point, NC 27265. Phone: (336) 881-7109. Fax: (336) 883-7198. E-mail: rvshows@apple rock.com. Web: www.applerock.com.

NEVADAPEX COIN AND STAMP EXPO. Jan 6–8 (also Apr 14–16 and Oct 20–22). River Palms Casino, Laughlin, NV. Est attendance: 5,000. For info: Israel Bick, Exec Dir, Intl Stamp & Coin Collectors Society, PO Box 854, Van Nuys, CA 91408. Phone: (818) 997-6496. Fax: (818) 988-4337. E-mail: iibick@sbc global.net. Web: www.bick.net.

NEW MEXICO: ADMISSION DAY: ANNIVERSARY. Jan 6, 1912. Became 47th state in 1912.

PAN AM CIRCLES EARTH: ANNIVERSARY. Jan 6, 1942. A Pan American Airways plane arrived in New York to complete the first around-the-world trip by a commercial aircraft.

SALOMON, HAYM: DEATH ANNIVERSARY. Jan 6, 1785. American Revolutionary War patriot and financier was born at Lissa, Poland, in 1740 (exact date unknown). Salomon died at Philadelphia, PA.

SANDBURG, CARL: BIRTH ANNIVERSARY. Jan 6, 1878. American poet, biographer of Lincoln, historian and folklorist, born at Galesburg, IL. Died at Flat Rock, NC, July 22, 1967.

SMITH, JEDEDIAH STRONG: BIRTH ANNIVERSARY. Jan 6, 1799. Mountain man, fur trader and one of the first explorers of the American West, Smith helped develop the Oregon Trail. He was the first American to reach California by land and the first to travel by land from San Diego up the West Coast to the Canadian border. Smith was born at Jericho (now Bainbridge), NY, and was killed by Comanche Indians along the Santa Fe Trail in what is now Kansas on May 27, 1831.

★   ★   ★

SPACE MILESTONE: *LUNAR EXPLORER* (US). Jan 6, 1998. NASA headed back to the moon for the first time since the *Apollo 17* flight 25 years before. This unmanned probe searched for evidence of frozen water on the moon and found evidence of ice in late 1998.

THOMAS, DANNY: BIRTH ANNIVERSARY. Jan 6, 1912. Comedian Danny Thomas was born Muzyad Yakhoob, later Amos Jacobs, at Deerfield, MI. Thomas began his entertainment career as a radio actor and nightclub comedian and then went on to movies in the late 1940s and early 1950s. His greatest fame came from his television show "Make Room for Daddy" (1953–64) and later as a television producer. He was also a tireless philanthropist who founded St. Jude's Children's Research Hospital at Memphis, TN. Thomas died Feb 6, 1991, at Los Angeles, CA.

THREE KINGS DAY. Jan 6. Major festival of the Christian Church observed in many parts of the world with gifts, feasting, last lighting of Christmas lights and burning of Christmas greens. Twelfth and last day of the Feast of the Nativity. Commemorates the visit of the Three Wise Men (Kings or Magi) to Bethlehem.

"WHEEL OF FORTUNE" TV PREMIERE: ANNIVERSARY. Jan 6, 1975. This daytime quiz show was originally hosted by Chuck Woolery. In 1981 Pat Sajak became host, assisted by Vanna White. A nighttime version was added in 1983. Not to be confused with the human interest show rewarding people who had done good deeds, hosted by Todd Russell, that premiered in 1952.

YOUNG, LORETTA: BIRTH ANNIVERSARY. Jan 6, 1913. Academy Award–winning actress, born at Salt Lake City, UT. She won an Oscar as Best Actress in 1947 for *The Farmer's Daughter* and several Emmys for her television show, "The Loretta Young Show," which ran from 1953 to 1961. She died Aug 12, 2000, at Los Angeles, CA.

BIRTHDAYS TODAY

Joey Lauren Adams, 35, actress (*Chasing Amy, Big Daddy*), born Little Rock, AR, Jan 6, 1971.

Rowan Atkinson, 51, British actor ("Mr Bean"), born Newcastle-upon-Tyne, England, Jan 6, 1955.

E.L. Doctorow, 75, writer (*Ragtime, Welcome to Hard Times*), born New York, NY, Jan 6, 1931.

Bonnie Franklin, 62, actress ("One Day at a Time," *The Kettles in the Ozarks*), born Santa Monica, CA, Jan 6, 1944.

Lou Harris, 85, public opinion analyst, author, born New Haven, CT, Jan 6, 1921.

Louis Leo (Lou) Holtz, 69, former Notre Dame football coach, born Follansbee, WV, Jan 6, 1937.

Howard M. (Howie) Long, 46, sportscaster, Hall of Fame football player, born Somerville, MA, Jan 6, 1960.

Nancy Lopez, 49, Hall of Fame golfer, born Torrance, CA, Jan 6, 1957.

Anthony Minghella, 52, director, writer (*The English Patient, The Talented Mr Ripley*), born Isle of Wight, England, Jan 6, 1954.

Gabrielle Reece, 36, pro volleyball player, born La Jolla, CA, Jan 6, 1970.

Earl Scruggs, 82, musician, born Flint Hill, NC, Jan 6, 1924.

John Singleton, 38, director, screenwriter (*Boyz N the Hood*), born Los Angeles, CA, Jan 6, 1968.

January 2006

S	M	T	W	T	F	S
1	2	3	4	5	6	7
8	9	10	11	12	13	14
15	16	17	18	19	20	21
22	23	24	25	26	27	28
29	30	31				

JANUARY 7 — SATURDAY

Day 7 — 358 Remaining

ADDAMS, CHARLES: BIRTH ANNIVERSARY. Jan 7, 1912. The prolific cartoonist with a macabre sense of humor was born at Westfield, NJ. He became a full-time staff member of *The New Yorker* in 1935 and stayed there for his entire career, producing some 1,300 cartoons. His most famous creation was the ghoulish "Addams Family," who escaped print into television and film. Author of numerous bestselling cartoon collections and the *Charles Addams Mother Goose* (1967), Addams died Sept 29, 1988, at New York, NY. See also: " 'The Addams Family' TV Premiere: Anniversary" (Sept 18).

ARIZONA ANTIQUE SHOW AND SALE. Jan 7–8. Yuma Civic Center, Yuma, AZ. A fine collection of antiques and collectibles. Sponsor: Jack Black Enterprises. Est attendance: 2,000. For info: Marketing Dept, Yuma Civic Ctr, 1440 Desert Hills Dr, Yuma, AZ 85365. Phone: (928) 373-5040. Fax: (928) 344-9121. E-mail: ycc@ci.yuma.az.us.

FILLMORE, MILLARD: BIRTH ANNIVERSARY. Jan 7, 1800. 13th president of the US (July 10, 1850–Mar 3, 1853). Fillmore succeeded to the presidency upon the death of Zachary Taylor, but he did not get the hoped-for nomination from his party in 1852. He ran for president in 1856 as candidate of the "Know-Nothing Party," whose platform demanded, among other things, that *every* government employee (federal, state and local) should be a native-born citizen. Fillmore was born at Summerhill, NY, and died at Buffalo, NY, Mar 8, 1874. Now his birthday is often used as an occasion for parties for which there is no other reason.

FIRST BALLOON FLIGHT ACROSS ENGLISH CHANNEL: ANNIVERSARY. Jan 7, 1785. Dr. John Jeffries, a Boston physician, and Jean-Pierre François Blanchard, French aeronaut, crossed the English Channel from Dover, England, to Calais, France, landing in a forest after being forced to throw overboard all ballast, equipment and even most of their clothing to avoid a forced landing in the icy waters of the English Channel. Blanchard's trousers are said to have been the last article thrown overboard.

FIRST US COMMERCIAL BANK: ANNIVERSARY. Jan 7, 1782. The first commercial bank in the US, the Bank of North America, was opened at Philadelphia.

GARDENIA, VINCENT: BIRTH ANNIVERSARY. Jan 7, 1922. Stage, screen and television performer Vincent Gardenia was born Vincent Scognamiglio at Naples, Italy. Gardenia once estimated he had played 500 parts in his lifetime. He received two Oscar nominations, one for playing a baseball manager in *Bang the Drum Slowly* and again for the role of patriarch of a goofy Brooklyn family in *Moonstruck.* He won a Tony for his part in *The Prisoner of Second Avenue* and an Emmy for his portrayal in *Age Old Friends.* Vincent Gardenia died Dec 9, 1992, at Philadelphia, PA.

GERMANY: MUNICH FASCHING CARNIVAL. Jan 7–Feb 28. Munich. From Jan 7 through Shrove Tuesday is Munich's famous carnival season. Costume balls are popular throughout carnival. The high points of the festival occur on Fasching Sunday (Feb 26) and Shrove Tuesday (Feb 28), with great carnival revelry outside at the Viktualienmarkt and on Pedestrian Mall.

GREAT FRUITCAKE TOSS. Jan 7. Manitou Springs, CO. What do you do with leftover fruitcake? Toss, hurl, launch competitions. Est attendance: 1,000. For info: Manitou Springs Chamber of Commerce, 354 Manitou Ave, Manitou Springs, CO 80829. Phone: (800) 642-2567. Web: www.manitousprings.org.

HARLEM GLOBETROTTERS PLAY FIRST GAME: ANNIVERSARY. Jan 7, 1927. Basketball promoter Abe Saperstein's "New York Globetrotters" took the floor on this date at Hinckley, IL. Despite the "New York" in their name, the Globetrotters (who included Inman Jackson, Lester Johnson and Walter Wright) hailed from Chicago's South Side. The talented African-American players—unable to play in white professional leagues—barnstormed the nation in serious basketball promotional events. They changed to "Harlem Globetrotters" in the 1930s and added humor to their games in the 1940s.

HURSTON, ZORA NEALE: BIRTH ANNIVERSARY. Jan 7, 1891. One of the most important African-American writers of the 20th century was born at Eatonville, FL, to a preacher and former schoolteacher. Hurston attended Barnard College and then became an integral part of the Harlem Renaissance of the 1920s and 1930s. Hurston published four novels in her lifetime, including the classic *Their Eyes Were Watching God* (1937), as well as important anthropological works, short stories, plays and a moving memoir. She was a trailblazer in collecting regional black folklore. Hurston died at Fort Pierce, FL, on Jan 28, 1960.

I'M NOT GOING TO TAKE IT ANYMORE DAY. Jan 7. A day to fight back and take control of all events that happen in one's life. Stand up for your rights—it's so easy to walk away. For info: Bob O'Brien, Consumer Advocate, 1061 Koelle Blvd, Secaucus, NJ 07094. Phone/fax: (201) 865-4775. E-mail: bobtheebest @yahoo.com. Web: www.wtbq.com.

JAPAN: NANAKUSA. Jan 7. Festival dates back to the 7th century and recalls the seven plants served to the emperor that are believed to have great medicinal value—shepherd's purse, chickweed, parsley, cottonweed, radish, hotoke-no-za and aona.

JAPAN: USOKAE (BULLFINCH EXCHANGE FESTIVAL). Jan 7. Dazaifu, Fukuoka Prefecture. "Good Luck" gilded wood bullfinches, mixed among many plain ones, are sought after by the throngs as priests of the Dazaifu Shrine pass them out in the dim light of a small bonfire.

KANE COUNTY FLEA MARKET. Jan 7–8. (also Feb 4–5, Mar 4–5, Apr 1–2, May 6–7, June 3–4, July 1–2, Aug 5–6, Sept 2–3, Sept 30–Oct 1, Nov 4–5 and Dec 2–3). Kane County Fairgrounds, St. Charles, IL. Saturday noon–4; Sunday 7–4. Free parking. Admission $5, children under 12 free. One of the largest antique and collectible flea markets in the Midwest or anywhere. For more than 30 years it has just kept getting bigger and better. If it was ever made, you will probably be able to find it here! Est attendance: 15,000. For info: St. Charles CVB, 311 N Second St, Ste 100, St. Charles, IL 60174. Phone: (800) 777-4373 or (630) 377-6161. Web: www.visitstcharles.com.

MARIAN ANDERSON PERFORMS WITH THE METROPOLITAN OPERA: ANNIVERSARY. Jan 7, 1930. Contralto Marian Anderson made her debut with New York's Metropolitan Opera in Verdi's *Un ballo in maschera,* becoming the first African American to perform with that organization. She was 57 years old. The audience gave her repeated ovations.

MONTGOLFIER, JACQUES ETIENNE: BIRTH ANNIVERSARY. Jan 7, 1745. Merchant and inventor, born at Vidalon-lez Annonay, Ardèche, France. With his older brother, Joseph Michel, in November 1782, conducted experiments with paper and fabric bags filled with smoke and hot air, which led to the invention of the hot-air balloon and a human's first flight. Died at Serrieres, France, Aug 2, 1799. See also: "First Balloon Flight: Anniversary" (June 5); "Aviation History Month" (Nov 1).

NATIONAL WESTERN STOCK SHOW AND RODEO.
Jan 7–22. Denver, CO. 100th annual. It's a rodeo and more! See horse shows, Colorado's largest trade show, Western art and educational displays and the Super Bowl of livestock shows. Est attendance: 640,000. For info: Natl Western Stock Show and Rodeo, 4655 Humboldt St, Denver, CO 80216. Phone: (303) 297-1166 or (800) 336-6977. Fax: (303) 292-1708. Web: www.national western.com.

ONASSIS, ARISTOTLE: 100th BIRTH ANNIVERSARY. Jan 7, 1906. Larger-than-life billionaire Greek shipping magnate who married Jackie Kennedy in 1968. Born in Smyrna (now Izmir), Turkey, Onassis died Mar 15, 1975, near Paris, France.

PENNSYLVANIA FARM SHOW. Jan 7–14. Harrisburg, PA. The largest indoor agricultural event in America. For info: Pennsylvania Dept of Agriculture, State Farm Products Show Commission, 2300 N Cameron St, Harrisburg, PA 17110. Phone: (717) 787-5373. Web: www.agriculture.state.pa.us.

POL POT OVERTHROWN: ANNIVERSARY. Jan 7, 1979. Pol Pot's Cambodian government fell to combined forces of Cambodian rebels and Vietnamese soldiers.

RUSSIA: CHRISTMAS OBSERVANCE. Jan 7. National holiday.

TRANSATLANTIC PHONING: ANNIVERSARY. Jan 7, 1927. Commercial transatlantic telephone service between New York and London was inaugurated. There were 31 calls made the first day.

BIRTHDAYS TODAY

William Blatty, 78, novelist (*The Exorcist*), screenwriter, born New York, NY, Jan 7, 1928.

Nicolas Cage, 42, actor (*Leaving Las Vegas, Con Air*), born Long Beach, CA, Jan 7, 1964.

David Caruso, 50, actor ("NYPD Blue," "CSI: Miami"), born Forest Hills, NY, Jan 7, 1956.

Katie Couric, 49, cohost ("The Today Show"), born Arlington, VA, Jan 7, 1957.

Dustin Diamond, 29, actor ("Saved by the Bell"), born San Jose, CA, Jan 7, 1977.

Eric Gagne, 30, baseball player, born Montreal, QC, Canada, Jan 7, 1976.

Erin Gray, 56, actress ("Buck Rogers in the 25th Century," "Silver Spoons"), born Honolulu, HI, Jan 7, 1950 (some sources say 1952).

Kenny Loggins, 58, singer (Loggins and Messina, "Your Mama Don't Dance"), songwriter ("What a Fool Believes" with Michael McDonald, won three Grammys), born Everett, WA, Jan 7, 1948.

Terry Moore, 77, actress ("Empire," *Gaslight, Come Back Little Sheba*), born Helen Koford at Los Angeles, CA, Jan 7, 1929.

Paul Revere, 68, singer, pianist (Paul Revere & the Raiders), born Harvard, NE, Jan 7, 1938.

Alfonso Soriano, 28, baseball player, born San Pedro de Macoris, Dominican Republic, Jan 7, 1978.

John R. Thune, 45, US Senator (R, South Dakota), born Pierre, SD, Jan 7, 1961.

Jann Wenner, 59, journalist, publisher, *Rolling Stone* magazine, born New York, NY, Jan 7, 1947.

January 2006	S	M	T	W	T	F	S
	1	2	3	4	5	6	7
	8	9	10	11	12	13	14
	15	16	17	18	19	20	21
	22	23	24	25	26	27	28
	29	30	31				

JANUARY 8 — SUNDAY
Day 8 — 357 Remaining

AT&T DIVESTITURE: ANNIVERSARY. Jan 8, 1982. In the most significant antitrust suit since the breakup of Standard Oil in 1911, American Telephone and Telegraph agreed to give up its 22 local Bell System companies ("Baby Bells"). These companies represented 80 percent of AT&T's assets. This ended the corporation's virtual monopoly on US telephone service.

BATTLE OF NEW ORLEANS: ANNIVERSARY. Jan 8, 1815. British forces suffered crushing losses (more than 2,000 casualties) in an attack on New Orleans, LA. Defending US troops were led by General Andrew Jackson, who became a popular hero as a result of the victory. Neither side knew that the War of 1812 had ended two weeks previously with the signing of the Treaty of Ghent, Dec 24, 1814. Battle of New Orleans Day is observed in Louisiana.

BIDDLE, NICHOLAS: BIRTH ANNIVERSARY. Jan 8, 1786. American lawyer, diplomat, statesman and financier who served as president of the Second Bank of the United States. Born at Philadelphia, PA, he died there Feb 27, 1844.

CHOU EN-LAI: 30th DEATH ANNIVERSARY. Jan 8, 1976. Anniversary of the death of Chou En-Lai, premier of the State Council of the People's Republic of China. He was born in 1898 (exact date unknown).

CHRISTMAS EPIPHANY CELEBRATION. Jan 8. St. John's Lutheran Church, Isanti, MN. Celebrate the holiday season through lessons and carols all done in German. A traditional German Christmas tree graces the historic church on the National Register of Historic Sites. We'll heat up the wood stove, but dress warmly. Annually, the Sunday closest to the Epiphany. For info: Kathy McCully, Dir, Isanti County Historical Society, PO Box 525, Cambridge, MN 55008. Phone: (763) 689-4229. Fax: (763) 552-0740. E-mail: ichs@nsatel.net.

COLLINS, WILLIAM WILKIE: BIRTH ANNIVERSARY. Jan 8, 1824. English novelist, author of *The Moonstone* (one of the first examples of detective fiction), *The Woman in White* and *The Dead Secret*. Born at London, England, he died there Sept 23, 1889.

EARTH'S ROTATION PROVED: ANNIVERSARY. Jan 8, 1851. In his Paris home using a device now known as Foucault's pendulum, physicist Jean Foucault demonstrated that the Earth rotates on its axis.

FERRER, JOSE: BIRTH ANNIVERSARY. Jan 8, 1912. Award-winning actor, producer, writer and director was born at Santurce, Puerto Rico. Nominated three times for an Academy Award, he won Best Actor for his role in *Cyrano de Bergerac*. In addition, Ferrer was awarded Tonys and Critics' Circle prizes during half a century in the entertainment world. He died Jan 26, 1992, at Coral Gables, FL.

FOURTEEN POINTS PROPOSED: ANNIVERSARY. Jan 8, 1918. In a speech before a hastily convened joint session of Congress, President Woodrow Wilson presented Fourteen Points for a just peace. The proposal called for reduction of armaments to the lowest point consistent with domestic safety, "open covenants openly arrived at," self-determination of governments and the creation of a League of Nations to preserve peace. Wilson was unable to obtain Allied agreement to his proposals.

GREECE: MIDWIFE'S DAY or WOMEN'S DAY. Jan 8. Midwife's Day or Women's Day is celebrated Jan 8 each year to honor midwives and all women. "On this day women stop their housework and spend their time in cafés, while the men do all the housework chores and look after the children." In some villages, men caught outside "will be stripped . . . and drenched with cold water."

HOME OFFICE SAFETY AND SECURITY WEEK. Jan 8–14. One week each year dedicated to ensuring that the more than 30 million American home offices are safeguarded and protected against break-ins, theft, workplace injury, computer virus and hacking, natural disaster and any other malady that can impact the at-home worker. For info: Jeff Zbar, PO Box 8263, Coral Springs, FL 33075. Phone: (954) 346-4393. E-mail: jeff@chiefhomeofficer.com. Web: www.chiefhomeofficer.com.

NATIONAL JOYGERM DAY. Jan 8. A delightful way to spend the day rejecting pouting and touting Joygerm Fever: that highly contagious, wonderfully incurable disease with prescibed treatment of large daily doses of kindness and courtesy, silliness and sacredness, merriment and mirth, and happiness and humor. Free Joygerm membership cards available; somewhat disorderly quarterly newsletter available by subscription. Become a Joygerm Junkie and get high on happiness! For info: Joygerm Junkie Joan E. White, Founder, Joygerms Unlimited, PO Box 555, Eastwood Station, Syracuse, NY 13206-0555. Phone: (315) 472-2779.

PRESLEY, ELVIS AARON: BIRTH ANNIVERSARY. Jan 8, 1935. Popular American rock singer, born at Tupelo, MS. Although his middle name was spelled incorrectly as "Aron" on his birth certificate, Elvis had it legally changed to "Aaron," which is how it is spelled on his gravestone. Died at Memphis, TN, Aug 16, 1977.

SAINT GUDULA: FEAST DAY. Jan 8. Virgin, patron saint of the city of Brussels. Died Jan 8, probably in the year 712. Her relics were transferred to the church of St. Michael in Brussels.

SHOW AND TELL DAY AT WORK. Jan 8. Since students have show-and-tell at school, adults should get to do the same. [©2003 by WH.] For info: Thomas & Ruth Roy, Wellcat Holidays, 2418 Long Ln, Lebanon, PA 17046. Phone: (717) 279-0184. E-mail: info@wellcat.com. Web: www.wellcat.com.

SIRANI, ELISABETTA: BIRTH ANNIVERSARY. Jan 8, 1638. Born at Bologna, Italy, Elisabetta Sirani was one of the few women Renaissance artists. Among the 190 pieces done by her during her short life was the 1663 *Virgin and Child*, which was chosen by the US Postal Service as the 1994 traditional holiday stamp. While in her twenties Sarani established a painting school for women. When she died at her native Bologna Aug 28, 1665, the entire city went into mourning for her.

SWITZERLAND: MEITLISUNNTIG. Jan 8. On Meitlisunntig, the second Sunday in January, the girls of Meisterschwanden and Fahrwangen, in the Seetal district of Aargau, Switzerland, stage a procession in historical uniforms and a military parade before a female General Staff. According to tradition, the custom dates from the Villmergen War of 1712, when the women of both communes gave vital help that led to victory. Popular festival follows the procession.

UNIVERSAL LETTER-WRITING WEEK. Jan 8–14. The purpose of this week is for people all over the world to get the new year off to a good start by sending letters and cards to friends and acquaintances not only in their own country but to people throughout the world. For complete information and suggestions about writing good letters, send $5 to cover expense of printing, handling and postage. For info: Dr. Stanley Drake, Pres Emeritus, Intl Society of Friendship & Good Will, 8592 Roswell Rd, Ste 251, Atlanta, GA 30350-1867. Phone: (678) 795-1362. E-mail: sjdrake@bellsouth.net. Web: www.friendshipandgoodwill.org.

WAR ON POVERTY: ANNIVERSARY. Jan 8, 1964. President Lyndon Johnson declared a War on Poverty in his State of the Union address. He stressed improved education as one of the cornerstones of the program. The following Aug 20, he signed a $947.5 million antipoverty bill designed to assist more than 30 million citizens.

BIRTHDAYS TODAY

Shirley Bassey, 69, singer ("Goldfinger"), born Cardiff, Wales, Jan 8, 1937.

David Bowie, 59, musician, actor (*The Labyrinth*), born David Robert Jones at London, England, Jan 8, 1947.

Bob Eubanks, 69, game-show host ("The Newlywed Game"), born Flint, MI, Jan 8, 1937.

Vladimir Feltsman, 54, Russian pianist, born Moscow, USSR, Jan 8, 1952.

Jason Giambi, 35, baseball player, born West Covina, CA, Jan 8, 1971.

Stephen Hawking, 64, British physicist, author (*A Brief History of Time*), born Oxford, England, Jan 8, 1942.

Yvette Mimieux, 64, actress (*The Light in the Piazza*, "The Most Deadly Game"), born Hollywood, CA, Jan 8, 1942 (some sources say 1941).

Kathleen Noone, 60, actress ("Party of Five," "Sunset Beach"), born Hillsdale, NJ, Jan 8, 1946.

Charles Osgood, 73, CBS newsman, born New York, NY, Jan 8, 1933.

Soupy Sales, 80, comedian ("The Soupy Sales Show"), born Morton Supman at Wake Forest, NC, Jan 8, 1926.

Bob Taft, 64, Governor of Ohio (R), born Boston, MA, Jan 8, 1942.

JANUARY 9 — MONDAY
Day 9 — 356 Remaining

AVIATION IN AMERICA: ANNIVERSARY. Jan 9, 1793. A Frenchman, Jean-Pierre François Blanchard, made the first manned free-balloon flight in America's history at Philadelphia, PA. The event was watched by President George Washington and many other high government officials. The hydrogen-filled balloon rose to a height of about 5,800 feet, traveled some 15 miles and landed 46 minutes later in New Jersey. Reportedly Blanchard had one passenger on the flight—a little black dog.

CATT, CARRIE LANE CHAPMAN: BIRTH ANNIVERSARY. Jan 9, 1859. American women's rights leader, founder (in 1919) of National League of Women Voters. Born at Ripon, WI, she died at New Rochelle, NY, Mar 9, 1947.

CONNECTICUT RATIFIES CONSTITUTION: ANNIVERSARY. Jan 9, 1788. By a vote of 128 to 40, Connecticut became the fifth state to ratify the Constitution.

ENGLAND: PLOUGH MONDAY. Jan 9. Always the Monday after Twelfth Day. Work on the farm is resumed after the festivities of the 12 days of Christmas. On the preceding Sunday ploughs may be blessed in churches. Celebrated with dances and plays.

FAKE HOWARD HUGHES BIOGRAPHY: ANNIVERSARY. Jan 9, 1972. Reclusive billionaire Howard Hughes held a telephone news conference to state that the biography about him written by Clifford Irving was a fake.

GRAVES' DISEASE AWARENESS WEEK. Jan 9–13. Graves' disease is an abnormality in the autoimmune system, causing production of antibodies that attach to the thyroid, enlargement of the gland and overproduction of thyroid hormone. Similar antibodies may also cause swelling of the eye muscles and swelling in the skin on the front of the lower leg. Graves' disease occurs in less than ¼ of 1 percent of the general population. Most people with Graves' disease are treated and then managed on hormone replacement. Because some people with Graves' disease are misdiagnosed and because it is an illness that occurs in all age groups, education and support continue to be vital. Annually, the second week in January. For info: Graves' Disease Foundation, PO Box 8387, Fleming Island, FL 32006. Phone: (904) 278-9488. Web: www.ngdf.org.

INTIMATE APPAREL MARKET WEEK. Jan 9–13. (Also Feb 27–Mar 3, May 1–5, July 31–Aug 4 and Oct 30–Nov 3.) Market week dates for the intimate apparel industry. For info: Mary Howell, Dir of Specialty Markets, American Apparel &

Footwear Assn, 1601 N Kent St, Ste 1200, Arlington, VA 22209. Phone: (703) 524-1864. Fax: (703) 522-6741. Web: www.apparel andfootwear.org.

"IT TAKES A THIEF" TV PREMIERE: ANNIVERSARY. Jan 9, 1968. ABC's adventure series starred Robert Wagner as Alexander Mundy, an unlikely thief who agrees to conduct secret government missions instead of serving out his prison term. Malachi Throne costarred as Noah Bain, chief of the SIA and Mundy's employer. Fred Astaire made cameo appearances as Mundy's father.

JAPAN: COMING-OF-AGE DAY. Jan 9. National holiday for youth of the country who have reached adulthood during the preceding year. Annually, the second Monday in January.

KIDFILM® FESTIVAL. Jan 9–22. Dallas, TX. 22nd annual. Oldest and largest-attended international children's film festival in the world. Fifty shorts and features shown with filmmakers in attendance. Each year, a major figure in media (for all ages) is honored. Est attendance: 24,000. For info: USA Film Festival, 6116 N Central Expressway, Ste 105, Dallas, TX 75206. Phone: (214) 821-6300 or (214) 821-FILM. Fax: (214) 821-6364. E-mail: info@usafilmfestival.com. Web: www.usafilmfestival.com.

NATIONAL CLEAN-OFF-YOUR-DESK DAY. Jan 9. To provide one day early each year for every desk worker to see the top of the desk and prepare for the following year's paperwork. Annually, the second Monday in January. For info: A.C. Vierow, Box 71, Clio, MI 48420-0071.

NATIONAL THANK GOD IT'S MONDAY! DAY. Jan 9. Besides holidays, such as President's Day, being celebrated on Mondays, people everywhere start new jobs, have birthdays, celebrate promotions and begin vacations on Mondays. A day in recognition of this first day of the week. For info: Dorothy Zjawin, 61 W Colfax Ave, Roselle Park, NJ 07204. Phone: (908) 241-6241.

NATIONAL THANK-YOUR-CUSTOMERS WEEK. Jan 9–13. Business owners should take some time each year to focus on thanking those who make their business possible. Thanking them each January, aside from what is done throughout the year, will strengthen relationships and lead to increased business. Event on Jan 9 at 10 AM, EST, at the Radisson Hotel, Marlborough, MA, to share ideas and techniques, and to teach business owners how to say thank you to their customers. Annually, the first full week in January. Sponsored by the Thank You Institute. For info: Robert Martel, JMB Marketing, 210 Cloverhill St, Marlborough, MA 01752. Phone: (508) 481-8383. Fax: (508) 481-8381. E-mail: bobmartel@jmbmarketing.com. Web: www.thanksabillion.com.

NIXON, RICHARD MILHOUS: BIRTH ANNIVERSARY. Jan 9, 1913. Richard Nixon served as 36th vice president of the US (under President Dwight D. Eisenhower) Jan 20, 1953, to Jan 20, 1961. He was the 37th president of the US, serving Jan 20, 1969, to Aug 9, 1974, when he resigned the presidency while under the threat of impeachment. First US president to resign that office. He was born at Yorba Linda, CA, and died at New York, NY, Apr 22, 1994.

ORGANIZE YOUR HOME DAY. Jan 9. Organize your life by clearing the clutter at home. Start today by organizing your kitchen, kid's room, closets or family room. Devote an entire day to your New Year's resolution of "getting it together!" OrganizedTimes.com, the sponsor, will offer online chat sessions and giveaways. Annually, the second Monday in January. For info: Debbie Williams, OrganizedTimes.com, PO Box 590860, Houston, TX 77259. Phone: (281) 286-9512. E-mail: debbie@organizedtimes.com. Web: www.organizedtimes.com.

January *2006*	S	M	T	W	T	F	S
	1	2	3	4	5	6	7
	8	9	10	11	12	13	14
	15	16	17	18	19	20	21
	22	23	24	25	26	27	28
	29	30	31				

PANAMA: MARTYRS' DAY. Jan 9. Public holiday.

PHILIPPINES: FEAST OF THE BLACK NAZARENE. Jan 9. Culmination of a nine-day fiesta. Manila's largest procession takes place in the afternoon of Jan 9, in honor of the Black Nazarene, whose shrine is at the Quiapo Church.

"RAWHIDE" TV PREMIERE: ANNIVERSARY. Jan 9, 1959. CBS western that kept them dogies [cattle] rollin' home from northern Texas to Sedalia, KS, for seven years. The series featured Eric Fleming as trail boss Gil Favor; Clint Eastwood as Rowdy Yates, ramrod and trail boss after Fleming's departure from the show; Jim Murdock as Mushy; Paul Brinegar as the cook, Wishbone; Steve Raines as Quince; Rocky Shahan as Joe Scarlet; Sheb Wooley as scout Pete Nolan; Robert Cabal as Hey Soos; John Ireland as Jed Colby; David Watson as Ian Cabot; and Raymond St. Jacques as Simon Blake. Also remembered for its rollicking theme song.

ST. PETERSBURG MASSACRE: ANNIVERSARY. Jan 9, 1905. Guards at St. Petersburg's Winter Palace opened fire on some 150,000 unarmed protesting workers, killing at least 200. This event was the major catalyst for revolution in Russia that year, prompting more strikes and uprisings.

"3rd ROCK FROM THE SUN" TV PREMIERE: 10th ANNIVERSARY. Jan 9, 1996. In this Emmy Award–winning comedy a quartet of space aliens who had taken on human form came to Earth to spy on its natives. They were led by Dick Solomon, played by John Lithgow, who fell in love with earthling Mary Albright, played by Jane Curtin. Other cast members included Kristen Johnston, French Stewart and Joseph Gordon-Levitt. The series ended its run after six seasons.

US LANDING ON LUZON: ANNIVERSARY. Jan 9, 1945. US forces began the final push to retake the Philippines by attacking at the same location where the Japanese had begun their invasion nearly four years earlier. General Douglas MacArthur landed 67,000 troops in the Gulf of Lingayen on the western coast of the big island of Luzon. The Japanese offered little opposition to the landing itself but fought fiercely against Allied advancement, particularly around Clarke Field, the major air base in the islands.

VAN CLEEF, LEE: BIRTH ANNIVERSARY. Jan 9, 1925. Actor Lee Van Cleef was born at Somerville, NJ. He appeared in many westerns and action films including *High Noon* (1952), *The Man Who Shot Liberty Valance* (1962), *The Good, the Bad and the Ugly* (1967) and *Escape from New York* (1981). Van Cleef died on Dec 16, 1989, at Oxnard, CA.

WORD NERD DAY. Jan 9. Celebrates writers, editors and all those who enjoy playing with words. Annually, the second Monday in January. For info: Maria Schneider, Writer's Digest, 4700 E Galbraith Rd, Cincinnati, OH 45236. Phone: (513) 531-2690. E-mail: maria.schneider@fwpubs.com. Web: www.writersdigest .com.

YAWM ARAFAT: THE STANDING AT ARAFAT. Jan 9. Islamic calendar date: Dhu-Hijjah 9, 1426. The day when people on the Hajj (pilgrimage to Mecca) assemble for "the Standing" at the plain of Arafat at Mina, Saudi Arabia, near Mecca. This gathering is a foreshadowing of the Day of Judgment. Different methods for "anticipating" the visibility of the new moon crescent at Mecca are used by different Muslim groups. US date may vary. Began at sunset the preceding day.

YORBA LINDA, CALIFORNIA: NIXON BIRTHDAY HOLIDAY. Jan 9. Yorba Linda, the birthplace in 1913 of former president Richard M. Nixon, became the first community officially to declare his birth anniversary a public holiday. In announcing the declaration Sept 20, 1989, Mayor Henry Wedaa said, "We're not here to judge history—we're here to recognize it." The first observance by Yorba Linda's municipal employees took place in 1990.

YOUNG, MURAT BERNARD "CHIC": BIRTH ANNIVERSARY. Jan 9, 1901. The comic strip "Blondie" was created by Murat Bernard "Chic" Young in 1930. Originally about a jazz-age flapper who marries a playboy from a socially prominent family, "Blondie" soon changed its direction: two children and a dog were added to the cast, Dagwood became a working stiff and the strip focused on middle-class family situations and problems. "Blondie" introduced America to the "dagwood," an enormous sandwich made during Dagwood's late-night forays in the refrigerator. Chic Young was born at Chicago, IL, and died at St. Petersburg, FL, Mar 14, 1973.

BIRTHDAYS TODAY

Joan Baez, 65, folksinger, born Staten Island, NY, Jan 9, 1941.
Tyrone Curtis ("Muggsy") Bogues, 41, former basketball player, born Baltimore, MD, Jan 9, 1965.
Bob Denver, 71, actor ("The Many Loves of Dobie Gillis," "Gilligan's Island"), born New Rochelle, NY, Jan 9, 1935.
Richard Allen (Dick) Enberg, 71, sportscaster, born Mount Clemens, MI, Jan 9, 1935.
Sergio Garcia, 26, golfer, born Borriol, Spain, Jan 9, 1980.
Crystal Gayle, 55, singer ("Don't It Make My Brown Eyes Blue"), born Brenda Gayle Webb at Paintsville, KY, Jan 9, 1951.
Mat Hoffman, 34, BMX bike racer, born Oklahoma City, OK, Jan 9, 1972.
Judith Krantz, 78, author (*Dazzle, Scruples*), born Judith Tarcher at New York, NY, Jan 9, 1928.
Dave Matthews, 39, singer, musician (The Dave Matthews Band), born Johannesburg, South Africa, Jan 9, 1967.
Joely Richardson, 41, actress (*The Patriot,* "Nip/Tuck"), born London, England, Jan 9, 1965.
J.K. Simmons, 51, actor ("Law & Order," *Spiderman*), born Detroit, MI, Jan 9, 1955.
Byron Bartlett (Bart) Starr, 72, Hall of Fame football player and former coach, born Montgomery, AL, Jan 9, 1934.
Imelda Staunton, 50, actress (*Vera Drake*), born London, England, Jan 9, 1956.
Susannah York, 65, actress (*Tom Jones; They Shoot Horses, Don't They?; Superman*), born London, England, Jan 9, 1941.

JANUARY 10 — TUESDAY
Day 10 — 355 Remaining

ASARAH B'TEVET. Jan 10. Hebrew calendar date: Tevet 10, 5766. The Fast of the 10th of Tevet begins at first morning light and commemorates the beginning of the Babylonian siege of Jerusalem in the 6th century BC. Began at sundown on Jan 9.

COMMON SENSE PUBLISHED: ANNIVERSARY. Jan 10, 1776. More than any other publication, *Common Sense* influenced the authors of the Declaration of Independence. Thomas Paine's 50-page pamphlet sold 150,000 copies within a few months of its first printing.

EID-AL-ADHA: FEAST OF THE SACRIFICE. Jan 10. Islamic calendar date: Dhu-Hijjah 10, 1426. Commemorates Abraham's willingness to sacrifice his son Ishmael in obedience to God. It is part of the Hajj (pilgrimage to Mecca). The day begins with the sacrifice of an animal in remembrance of the Angel Gabriel's substitution of a lamb as Abraham's offering. One-third of the meat is given to the poor and the rest is shared with friends and family. Celebrated with gifts and general merrymaking, the festival usually continues for several days. It is celebrated as Tabaski in Benin, Burkina Faso, Guinea, Guinea-Bissau, Ivory Coast, Mali, Niger and Senegal; as Hari Raya Hajj in Southeast Asia and as Kurban Bayram in Turkey and Bosnia. Different methods for "anticipating" the visibility of the moon crescent at Mecca are used by different Muslim groups. US date may vary. Began at sunset the preceding day.

FIRST UNITED NATIONS GENERAL ASSEMBLY: 60th ANNIVERSARY. Jan 10, 1946. On the 26th anniversary of the establishment of the unsuccessful League of Nations, delegates from 51 nations met at London, England, for the first meeting of the UN General Assembly.

HENRIED, PAUL: BIRTH ANNIVERSARY. Jan 10, 1908. Actor Paul Henried once estimated that he had played in or directed more than 300 films. Though a staunch anti-Nazi, his early film parts included a number of German roles, including those in *Goodbye Mr Chips* and *Night Train*. He eventually moved away from the German stereotype in such films as *Of Human Bondage, The Four Horsemen of the Apocalypse* and as Victor Laslo in *Casablanca*. His film career cut short by the anti-Communist blacklist in Hollywood during the 1940s, Henried found a second calling as a director, with more than 80 episodes of TV's "Alfred Hitchcock Presents" to his credit. Born at Trieste, Austria, he died Mar 29, 1992, at Pacific Palisades, CA.

JEFFERS, ROBINSON: BIRTH ANNIVERSARY. Jan 10, 1887. American poet and playwright. Born at Pittsburgh, PA, he died at Carmel, CA, Jan 20, 1962.

LEAGUE OF NATIONS FOUNDING: ANNIVERSARY. Jan 10, 1920. Through the Treaty of Versailles, the League of Nations came into existence. Fifty nations entered into a covenant designed to avoid war. The US never joined the League of Nations, which was dissolved Apr 18, 1946.

"MASTERPIECE THEATRE" TV PREMIERE: 35th ANNIVERSARY. Jan 10, 1971. Television at its best, PBS's long-running anthology series consists of many highly acclaimed original and adapted dramatizations. Many are produced by the BBC. Alistair Cooke and Russell Baker have hosted the program. The first presentation was "The First Churchills." Other notable programs include: "The Six Wives of Henry VIII" and "Elizabeth R" (1972); "Upstairs Downstairs" (1974–77); "I, Claudius" (1978); "The Jewel in the Crown" (1984); "The Buccaneers" (1995); and "White Teeth" (2002).

NATIONAL CUT YOUR ENERGY COSTS DAY. Jan 10. A day to educate people on the ways they can stay warm in the winter and cool in the summer while saving money on their energy bills. By following a few easy steps, homeowners and renters can put a reasonable ceiling on their heating and cooling costs and stay comfortable. For info: Tom Peric, National Cut Your Energy Costs Day, 2040 Fairfax Ave, Cherry Hill, NJ 08003.

Phone: (856) 874-0049. Fax: (856) 874-0052. E-mail: tom@cut
yourenergycosts.com. Web: www.cutyourenergycosts.com.

SPACE MILESTONE: *SOYUZ 17* (USSR): ANNIVER-SARY. Jan 10, 1975. Launched on this date, cosmonauts A. Gubarev and G. Grechko completed a 30-day space flight, landing Feb 9. Cosmonauts spent 28 days aboard *Salyut 4*, orbiting space station. With the exception of *Soyuz 19*, the *Soyuz* craft were now used as ferries to the *Salyut* space stations. More than 20 more flights were made.

SPACE MILESTONE: *SOYUZ 27* (USSR). Jan 10, 1978. Launched on this date, cosmonauts Vladimir Dzhanibekov and Oleg Makarov linked with *Salyut 6* space station, which was already occupied by the crew of *Soyuz 26*. Returned to Earth Jan 16 in *Soyuz 26*.

US AND VATICAN REESTABLISH DIPLOMATIC RELATIONS: ANNIVERSARY. Jan 10, 1984. The US and the Vatican established full diplomatic relations after a break of 117 years.

WOMEN'S SUFFRAGE AMENDMENT INTRODUCED IN CONGRESS: ANNIVERSARY. Jan 10, 1878. Senator A.A. Sargent of California, a close friend of Susan B. Anthony, introduced into the US Senate a women's suffrage amendment known as the Susan B. Anthony Amendment. It wasn't until Aug 26, 1920, 42 years later, that the amendment was signed into law.

BIRTHDAYS TODAY

Pat Benatar, 53, singer, born Patricia Andrejewski at Brooklyn, NY, Jan 10, 1953.
George Edward Foreman, 57, boxer, born Marshall, TX, Jan 10, 1949.
Mark Pryor, 43, US Senator (D, Arkansas), born Fayetteville, AR, Jan 10, 1963.
Glenn Robinson, 33, basketball player, born Gary, IN, Jan 10, 1973.
Rod Stewart, 61, singer, musician ("Maggie May," "Do Ya Think I'm Sexy?"), born London, England, Jan 10, 1945.
William Anthony (Bill) Toomey, 67, Olympic gold medal decathlete, born Philadelphia, PA, Jan 10, 1939.

JANUARY 11 — WEDNESDAY
Day 11 — 354 Remaining

CUCKOO DANCING WEEK. Jan 11–17. To honor the memory of Laurel and Hardy, whose theme, "The Dancing Cuckoos," shall be heard throughout the land as their movies are seen and their antics greeted with laughter by old and new fans of these unique masters of comedy. [Originated by the late William T. Rabe of Sault Ste. Marie, MI.]

"DESIGNATED HITTER" RULE ADOPTED: ANNIVERSARY. Jan 11, 1973. American League adopted the "designated hitter" rule, whereby an additional player is used to bat for the pitcher.

FIRST BLACK SOUTHERN LIEUTENANT GOVERNOR: 20th ANNIVERSARY. Jan 11, 1986. L. Douglas Wilder was sworn in as lieutenant governor of Virginia. He was the first black elected to statewide office in the South since Reconstruction. He later served as governor of Virginia.

January	S	M	T	W	T	F	S
2006	1	2	3	4	5	6	7
	8	9	10	11	12	13	14
	15	16	17	18	19	20	21
	22	23	24	25	26	27	28
	29	30	31				

HAMILTON, ALEXANDER: BIRTH ANNIVERSARY. Jan 11, 1755. American statesman, an author of *The Federalist* papers, first secretary of the treasury, born at British West Indies. Engaged in a duel with Aaron Burr the morning of July 11, 1804, at Weehawken, NJ. Mortally wounded there and died July 12, 1804.

HOSTOS, EUGENIO MARIA: BIRTH ANNIVERSARY. Jan 11, 1839. Puerto Rican patriot, scholar and author of more than 50 books. Born at Rio Canas, Puerto Rico, he died at Santo Domingo, Dominican Republic, Aug 11, 1903.

INTERNATIONAL THANK YOU DAYS. Jan 11–18. An eight-day period in which to thank someone from your past or present who did something nice for you. Visit, write, call, fax or e-mail him or her and say thank you. [©1994] Because of the escalating costs of Eventological® Literature, a charge of $10 must be assessed for each request. Checks are to be made payable to: Adrienne Sioux Koopersmith, 1437 W Rosemont, #1W, Chicago, IL 60660-1319. E-mail: askoopersmith@hotmail.com.

JAMES, WILLIAM: BIRTH ANNIVERSARY. Jan 11, 1842. American psychologist and philosopher of distinguished family that included his brother, novelist Henry James. "There is no worse lie," he wrote in *Varieties of Religious Experience* (1902), "than a truth misunderstood by those who hear it." Born at New York City, he died at Chocorua, NH, Aug 26, 1910.

MacDONALD, JOHN A.: BIRTH ANNIVERSARY. Jan 11, 1815. Canadian statesman, first prime minister of Canada. Born at Glasgow, Scotland, he died June 6, 1891, at Ottawa. His birth anniversary is observed in Canada.

MOROCCO: INDEPENDENCE DAY. Jan 11. National holiday. Commemorates the date in 1944 when the Independence Party submitted a memo to the Allied authorities asking for independence under a constitutional regime. Morocco gained independence from France in 1956.

NATIONAL NO-TILLAGE CONFERENCE. Jan 11–14. St. Louis, MO. Attracts innovative farmers interested in reducing tillage to protect the environment and boost profits. Est attendance: 680. For info: Frank Lessiter, Natl No-Tillage Conference, PO Box 624, Brookfield, WI 53008-0624. Phone: (262) 782-4480. Fax: (262) 782-1252. E-mail: info@lesspub.com. Web: www.no-tillfarmer.com.

NEPAL: NATIONAL UNITY DAY. Jan 11. Celebration paying homage to King Prithvinarayan Shah (1723–75), founder of the present house of rulers of Nepal and creator of the unified Nepal of today.

PAUL, ALICE: BIRTH ANNIVERSARY. Jan 11, 1885. Women's rights leader and founder of the National Woman's Party in 1913, advocate of an equal rights amendment to the US Constitution. Born at Moorestown, NJ, she died there July 10, 1977.

THEODOSIUS I: BIRTH ANNIVERSARY. Jan 11, 347. Roman emperor known as Theodosius the Great was born at Cauca, Gallaecia, in Spain. In 379 Theodosius was summoned by the emperor Gratian to become emperor of the East. On Feb 28, 380, without consulting religious authorities, he issued the edict that made the Nicene Creed (in which God the Father, the Son and the Holy Spirit are all of the same substance) binding on all subjects. Only those who accepted it would be considered Christians; this was the first recorded use of that designation. Theodosius engaged in a continuing struggle with the West for power. He prohibited pagan worship, but the emperors of the West had strong connections with pagan aristocracy. The two sides came to blows in 394. His final victory in September of that year was seen as a divine victory in which the Christian god had triumphed over the Roman gods. Theodosius died in January 395.

US SURGEON GENERAL DECLARES CIGARETTES HAZARDOUS: ANNIVERSARY. Jan 11, 1964. US Surgeon General Luther Terry issued the first government report saying that smoking may be hazardous to one's health.

WARMEST YEAR ON RECORD DECLARED: ANNIVERSARY. Jan 11, 1999. NASA declared 1998 the warmest year on record. Global surface temperatures increased by 0.34 of a degree Fahrenheit. The average temperature of 58.496 degrees Fahrenheit eclipsed the previous record set in 1995. The 1998 warmth was associated partly with a strong El Niño, a periodic warming of the Pacific Ocean.

BIRTHDAYS TODAY

Mary J. Blige, 35, pop singer, born the Bronx, NY, Jan 11, 1971.
Jean Chretien, 72, 20th prime minister of Canada, born Shawinigan, QC, Canada, Jan 11, 1934.
Clarence Clemons, 64, musician, singer, born Norfolk, VA, Jan 11, 1942.
Ben Daniel Crenshaw, 54, golfer, born Austin, TX, Jan 11, 1952.
Jim Hightower, 63, radio host, author (*Hard Tomatoes, Hard Times; Eat Your Heart Out*), born Denison, TX, Jan 11, 1943.
Naomi Judd, 60, country singer ("Have Mercy," "Why Not Me"), born Ashland, KY, Jan 11, 1946.
Christine Kaufmann, 61, actress (*Taras Bulba, Bagdad Cafe*), born Lansdorf Graz, Austria, Jan 11, 1945.
Amanda Peet, 34, actress (*Saving Silverman*, "Jack & Jill"), born New York, NY, Jan 11, 1972.
Rod Taylor, 76, actor (*The Birds*, "Masquerade"), born Sydney, Australia, Jan 11, 1930.
Grant Tinker, 80, TV executive, born Stamford, CT, Jan 11, 1926.
Stanley Tucci, 46, actor (*Big Night*, "Murder One"), born Katonah, NY, Jan 11, 1960.

JANUARY 12 — THURSDAY

Day 12 — 353 Remaining

"ALL IN THE FAMILY" TV PREMIERE: 35th ANNIVERSARY. Jan 12, 1971. Based on the success of the British comedy "Till Death Us Do Part," Norman Lear created CBS's controversial sitcom "All in the Family." The series was the first of its kind to realistically portray the prevailing issues and taboos of its time with a wickedly humorous bent. From bigotry to birth control, few topics were considered too sacred to discuss on air. Ultraconservative Archie Bunker (played by Carroll O'Connor) held court from his recliner, spewing invective at any who disagreed with him. Jean Stapleton portrayed Archie's dutiful wife, Edith. Sally Struthers and Rob Reiner rounded out the cast as Archie's liberal daughter and son-in-law, Gloria and Mike "Meathead" Stivic. All three characters often fell victim to Archie's zinging one-liners and insults. The series had a 12-year run.

"BATMAN" TV PREMIERE: 40th ANNIVERSARY. Jan 12, 1966. ABC's crime-fighting show gained a place in Nielsen's top 10 ratings in its first season. The series was based on the DC Comics characters created by Bob Kane in 1939. Adam West starred as millionaire Bruce Wayne and superhero alter ego, Batman. Burt Ward costarred as Dick Grayson/Robin, the Boy Wonder. An assortment of villains guest-starring each week included: Cesar Romero as the Joker, Eartha Kitt and Julie Newmar as Catwoman, Burgess Meredith as the Penguin and Frank Gorshin as the Riddler. Some other stars making memorable appearances included Liberace, Vincent Price, Milton Berle, Tallulah Bankhead

and Ethel Merman. The series played up its comic-strip roots with innovative and sharply skewed camera angles, bright bold colors and wild graphics. Although the last telecast was Mar 14, 1968, "Batman's" memorable theme song, composed by Neal Hefti, can be heard today with some 120 episodes in syndication.

BURKE, EDMUND: BIRTH ANNIVERSARY. Jan 12, 1729. British orator, politician and philosopher, born at Dublin, Ireland. "Superstition is the religion of feeble minds," he wrote in 1790, but best remembered is "The only thing necessary for the triumph of evil is for good men to do nothing," not found in his writings but almost universally attributed to Burke. Died at Beaconsfield, England, July 9, 1797.

CONGRESS AUTHORIZED USE OF FORCE AGAINST IRAQ: 15th ANNIVERSARY. Jan 12, 1991. The US Congress passed a resolution authorizing the president of the US to use force to expel Iraq from Kuwait. This was the sixth congressional vote in US history declaring war or authorizing force on another nation.

"DYNASTY" TV PREMIERE: 25th ANNIVERSARY. Jan 12, 1981. The popular ABC prime-time serial focused on the high-flying exploits of the Denver-based Carrington family. The series had a weekly wardrobe budget of $10,000 with many elegant costumes designed by Nolan Miller. In addition to the juicy storylines, many tuned in worldwide to view the palatial mansions and lavish sets. John Forsythe played patriarch Blake Carrington with Linda Evans as his wife, Krystle. Joan Collins played Alexis, Blake's scheming ex-wife and arch business rival. Other cast members included Kathleen Beller, Pamela Bellwood, Diahann Carroll, Jack Coleman, John James, Heather Locklear, Pamela Sue Martin, Ted McGinley, Michael Nader, Catherine Oxenberg, Emma Samms and Gordon Thomson. Notable guest stars included William Campbell, James Farentino, George Hamilton, Charlton Heston, Rock Hudson, Billy Dee Williams and many others.

FARMER, JAMES: BIRTH ANNIVERSARY. Jan 12, 1920. Civil rights leader, born at Marshall, TX. Farmer was one of the founders of CORE, the Congress of Racial Equality, a volunteer organization established in 1942 to improve race relations and eliminate discriminatory practices. Farmer led the nonviolent fight to desegregate buses and terminals in 1961, known as the Freedom Rides. He received the Presidential Medal of Freedom in 1998. Died at Fredericksburg, VA, July 9, 1999.

FIRST ELECTED WOMAN SENATOR: ANNIVERSARY. Jan 12, 1932. Hattie W. Caraway, a Democrat from Arkansas, was the first woman elected to the US Senate. Born in 1878, Caraway was appointed to the Senate on Nov 13, 1931, to fill out the term of her husband, Senator Thaddeus Caraway, who had died a few days earlier. On Jan 12, 1932, she won a special election to fill the remaining months of his term. Subsequently elected to two more terms, she served in the Senate until January 1945. She was an adept and tireless legislator (once introducing 43 bills on the same day) who worked for women's rights (once cosponsoring an equal rights amendment) and supported New Deal policies. She died Dec 21, 1950, at Falls Church, VA. The first woman appointed to the Senate was Mrs W.H. Felton who, in 1922, served for two days. The first woman to be elected to the Senate without having been appointed first was Margaret Chase Smith of Maine, who had served first in the House. She was elected to the Senate in 1948.

HAYES, IRA HAMILTON: BIRTH ANNIVERSARY. Jan 12, 1922. Ira Hayes was one of six US Marines who raised the American flag on Iwo Jima's Mount Suribachi, Feb 23, 1945, following a US assault on the Japanese stronghold. The event was immortalized by AP photographer Joe Rosenthal's famous photo and later by a Marine War Memorial monument at Arlington, VA. Hayes was born on a Pima Indian Reservation at Arizona. He returned home after WWII a much celebrated hero but was unable to cope with fame. He was found dead of "exposure to freezing weather and overconsumption of alcohol" on the Sacaton Indian Reservation at Arizona, Jan 24, 1955.

ICEBOX DAYS XXVI. Jan 12–15. International Falls, MN. Smoosh racing, 10k and 5k "Freeze Yer Gizzard Blizzard Run," turkey bowling, ski races, mutt races and beach party. Est attendance: 5,000. For info: Kallie L. Briggs, Chamber of Commerce, 301 2nd Ave, International Falls, MN 56649. Phone: (800) 325-5766 or (218) 283-9400. Fax: (218) 283-3572. E-mail: intl fall@intlfalls.org. Web: www.internationalfallsmn.us.

LONDON, JACK: BIRTH ANNIVERSARY. Jan 12, 1876. American author of more than 50 books: short stories, novels and travel stories of the sea and of the far north, many marked by brutal realism. His most widely known work is *The Call of the Wild*, the great dog story published in 1903. London was born at San Francisco, CA. He died of gastrointestinal uremia on Nov 22, 1916, near Santa Rosa, CA.

MISSION SANTA CLARA DE ASIS: FOUNDING ANNIVERSARY. Jan 12, 1777. California mission built by followers of Father Junipero Serra to educate the Indians. In the 1850s, the mission became Santa Clara University, the oldest university in California. The current building, used by the university as its chapel, is a replica of an older building that was destroyed by fire in 1926.

SARGENT, JOHN SINGER: 150th BIRTH ANNIVERSARY. Jan 12, 1856. Born in Florence, Italy, of American parents, Sargent became one of the most famous portrait artists of the late Victorian and Edwardian ages in Britain and the United States. His best-known paintings include *Madame X* (1884), *Carnation, Lily, Lily, Rose* (1885–86) and *Ellen Terry as Lady Macbeth* (1889). Sargent died Apr 15, 1925, at London, England.

TANZANIA: ZANZIBAR REVOLUTION DAY. Jan 12. National day. Zanzibar became independent in December 1963, under a sultan; the sultan was overthrown on this day in 1964.

ULTIMATE FISHING SHOW—DETROIT. Jan 12–15. Rock Financial Showplace, Novi, MI. This event brings together buyers and sellers of boating, fishing and outdoor sporting products. US and Canadian hunting and fishing trips, as well as other vacation travel destinations, are featured. Est attendance: 35,000. For info: Adam Starr, ShowSpan, Inc, 2121 Celebration Dr NE, Grand Rapids, MI 49525. Phone: (616) 447-2860. Fax: (616) 447-2861. E-mail: events@showspan.com. Web: www.showspan.com.

WINGS OVER WILLCOX/SANDHILL CRANE CELEBRATION. Jan 12–15. Willcox, AZ. Tours to the Willcox Playa and Wetlands to see Sandhill Cranes, Hawk Stalk tours, Plovers, Longspurs and much more. Visit Cochise Lake and see the waders. Workshops on wildlife. Seminars on bird-watching by various experts, a banquet, silent auction and a whole lot more. Est attendance: 1,000. For info: Willcox Chamber of Commerce. Phone: (800) 200-2272 or (520) 384-2272. Web: www.wingsover willcox.com or www.willcoxchamber.com.

WINTHROP, JOHN: BIRTH ANNIVERSARY. Jan 12, 1588 (OS). American colonial governor of Massachusetts Bay Colony, born at Edwardston, England. Governor Winthrop kept a diary of events in the Massachusetts Bay Colony, published nearly two centuries later (in 1825–26), titled *The History of New England from 1630 to 1649*. Died at Boston, MA, Mar 26, 1649 (OS).

WOMEN DENIED VOTE: ANNIVERSARY. Jan 12, 1915. The US House of Representatives rejected a proposal to give women the right to vote. Women gained the right to vote in 1920.

BIRTHDAYS TODAY

Kirstie Alley, 51, actress (Emmy for "Cheers"; *Look Who's Talking*, "Veronica's Closet"), born Wichita, KS, Jan 12, 1955.
Jeff Bezos, 42, founder (Amazon.com), born Albuquerque, NM, Jan 12, 1964.
Joe Frazier, 62, former boxer, born Beaufort, SC, Jan 12, 1944.
HAL, 14, computer in *2001: A Space Odyssey*, by Arthur C. Clarke, "born" Urbana, IL, Jan 12, 1992.
Marian Hossa, 27, hockey player, born Stara Lubovna, Czechoslovakia, Jan 12, 1979.
Rush Limbaugh, 55, talk-show host ("The Rush Limbaugh Show"), born Cape Girardeau, MO, Jan 12, 1951.
Oliver Platt, 46, actor ("Huff," "The West Wing," *Dr. Dolittle*), born Windsor, ON, Canada, Jan 12, 1960.
Ray Price, 80, country singer, born Perryville, TX, Jan 12, 1926.
Luise Rainer, 96, actress (Oscars for *The Great Ziegfeld* and *The Good Earth*), born Vienna, Austria, Jan 12, 1910 (some sources say 1912).
Howard Stern, 52, radio and TV personality ("The Howard Stern Show"), born Queens, NY, Jan 12, 1954.

JANUARY 13 — FRIDAY
Day 13 — 352 Remaining

ALGER, HORATIO, JR: BIRTH ANNIVERSARY. Jan 13, 1834. American clergyman and author of more than 100 popular books for boys (some 20 million copies sold). Honesty, frugality and hard work assured that the heroes of his books would find success, wealth and fame. Born at Revere, MA, he died at Natick, MA, July 18, 1899.

ART DECO WEEKEND. Jan 13–15. Miami Beach, FL. 29th annual. Features parade, jazz entertainment and plenty of food. Includes art deco antiques, vendors and artists, from national and local talent. Est attendance: 325,000. For info: Art Deco Weekend, PO Box 190180, Miami Beach, FL 33119. Phone: (305) 672-2014. Fax: (305) 672-4319. Web: www.mdpl.org.

BLAME SOMEONE ELSE DAY. Jan 13. To share the responsibility and the guilt for the mess we're in. Blame someone else! Annually, the first Friday the 13th of the year. For info: A.C. Vierow, Box 71, Clio, MI 48420-0071.

CHASE, SALMON PORTLAND: BIRTH ANNIVERSARY. Jan 13, 1808. American statesman, born at Cornish, NH. US senator, secretary of the treasury and chief justice of the Supreme Court. Salmon P. Chase spent much of his life fighting slavery (he was popularly known as "attorney general for runaway Negroes"). He was one of the founders of the Republican Party and his hopes for becoming candidate for president of the US in 1856 and 1860 were dashed because his unconcealed antislavery views made him unacceptable. Died at New York, NY, May 7, 1873.

DR. MARTIN LUTHER KING, JR, CELEBRATION. Jan 13–15. Hollywood, FL. Saturday Fun Fest features children's activities, DJ and basketball tournament. VIP evening dinner and a Sunday tribute. Est attendance: 3,000. For info: Cynthia Hancock, City of Hollywood, Department of Parks, Recreation & Cultural Arts, 1940 Harrison St, Ste 101, Hollywood, FL 33020. Phone: (954) 921-3404.

ENGLAND: WEST LONDON ANTIQUES AND FINE ART FAIR. Jan 13–15. Kensington Town Hall, London. 60 stands of authenticated antiques and art, 1600–2000. Established 1979. Est attendance: 4,000. For info: Penman Fairs. Phone:

	S	M	T	W	T	F	S
January 2006		1	2	3	4	5	6	7
	8	9	10	11	12	13	14
	15	16	17	18	19	20	21
	22	23	24	25	26	27	28
	29	30	31				

(44) (870) 350-2442. Fax: (44) (870) 350-2443. E-mail: info@pen man-fairs.co.uk.

FRIDAY THE THIRTEENTH. Jan 13. Variously believed to be a lucky or an unlucky day. Every year has at least one Friday the 13th, but never more than three. Two Fridays fall on the 13th in 2006: in January and October. Fear of the number 13 is known as triskaidekaphobia.

FULLER, ALFRED CARL: BIRTH ANNIVERSARY. Jan 13, 1885. Founder of the Fuller Brush Company, born at Kings County, NS, Canada. In 1906 the young brush salesman went into business on his own, making brushes at a bench between the furnace and the coal bin in his sister's basement. Died at Hartford, CT, Dec 4, 1973.

INTERNATIONAL SKEPTICS' DAYS. Jan 13 (also Oct 13). International celebration of the fine art of skepticism. Today, examine those issues which you are most skeptical about. A day to collectively put these issues under a microscope and cut away those attachments that stand in your way of gaining greater success, freedom and independence. Annually, on Friday the 13th. [©1996.] Because of the escalating costs of Eventological® Literature, a charge of $10 must be assessed for each request. Checks are to be made payable to: Adrienne Sioux Koopersmith, 1437 W Rosemont, #1W, Chicago, IL 60660-1319. E-mail: askoop ersmith@hotmail.com.

JOHNNY CASH AT FOLSOM PRISON: ANNIVERSARY. Jan 13, 1968. In a landmark concert, country music star Johnny Cash performed in front of 2,000 inmates at Folsom Prison at Folsom, CA. Backed by the Tennessee Three and accompanied by June Carter, Carl Perkins and the Statler Brothers, Cash performed in the prison cafeteria. The concert was recorded as a live album and was a worldwide hit. Cash's choice to play for prisoners cemented his reputation as a hero to the downtrodden.

LEE-JACKSON DAY IN VIRGINIA. Jan 13. Annually, the Friday in January that precedes Martin Luther King Day. To commemorate the January birthdays of Robert E. Lee and Thomas Jonathan "Stonewall" Jackson.

NORWAY: TYVENDEDAGEN. Jan 13. "20th Day," the traditional end of the Christmas season. Also commemorated as St. Knut's Day (Tjugondag Knut or "The 20th Day of Knut") in Sweden.

RADIO BROADCASTING: ANNIVERSARY. Jan 13, 1910. Radio pioneer and electron tube inventor Lee De Forest arranged the world's first radio broadcast to the public at New York, NY. He succeeded in broadcasting the voice of Enrico Caruso along with other stars of the Metropolitan Opera to several receiving locations in the city where listeners with earphones marveled at wireless music from the air. Though only a few were equipped to listen, it was the first broadcast to reach the public and the beginning of a new era in which wireless radio communication became almost universal. See also: "First Scheduled Radio Broadcast: Anniv" (Nov 2).

RUSSIA: OLD NEW YEAR'S EVE. Jan 13. Although Jan 1 is the official New Year's Day in Russia, some Russians still celebrate on the old Julian date of Jan 13–14. Also celebrated in Belarus and Ukraine.

SEATTLE BOAT SHOW. Jan 13–22. Seahawks Exhibition Center, Seattle, WA. Huge display of new boats, accessories and services. Est attendance: 70,000. For info: Northwest Marine Trade Assn, 1900 N Northlake Way, #233, Seattle, WA 98103. Phone: (206) 634-0911. Fax: (206) 632-0078. Web: www.seattleboatshow.com.

"THE SOPRANOS" TV PREMIERE: ANNIVERSARY. Jan 13, 1999. The thinking viewer's mob drama, "The Sopranos" features James Gandolfini as Tony Soprano, whose panic attacks drive him to seek out a psychiatrist (Lorraine Bracco). The HBO drama revolves around Tony's home and crime lives. *TV Guide* has named the series one of the greatest TV shows of all time.

SOUTHWESTERN EXPOSITION LIVESTOCK SHOW AND RODEO. Jan 13–Feb 5. Fort Worth, TX. Western-flavored extravaganza. World's first indoor professional rodeo began in 1918 (45 acres under one roof). Ranch Rodeo, prize livestock (more than 22,000 head) displays, horse shows, midway, commercial exhibits and quality family-oriented entertainment. Est attendance: 935,000. For info: W.R. Watt, Jr, PO Box 150, Fort Worth, TX 76101-0150. Phone: (817) 877-2400. Fax: (817) 877-2499. Web: www.fwssr.com.

TOGO: LIBERATION DAY: ANNIVERSARY. Jan 13. National holiday. Commemorates 1967 uprising.

VERDON, GWEN: BIRTH ANNIVERSARY. Jan 13, 1926. One of Broadway's premier female dancers and actresses; many of her most successful roles were choreographed by her husband, Bob Fosse. She won Tony Awards for *Can-Can*, *Damn Yankees*, *New Girl in Town* and *Redhead*. She also acted in movies, including *Cocoon* and the film adaptation of *Damn Yankees*. Born at Los Angeles, CA, she died Oct 18, 2000, at Woodstock, VT.

WINTER FEST—VETERAN'S RALLY. Jan 13–15. New Glarus, WI. Bonfire, evening parade, village poker run, silent auction, dance, Veteran's Banquet and much more. Est attendance: 1,700. For info: New Glarus Chamber of Commerce, PO Box 713, New Glarus, WI 53574-0713. Phone: (608) 527-2095 or (800) 527-6838. E-mail: info@swisstown.com. Web: www.swiss town.com.

YUMA HOME SHOW. Jan 13–15. Yuma Civic Center, Yuma, AZ. Public exhibit—home improvement, construction, renovation, remodeling and decorating. Annually, the second weekend in January. Est attendance: 17,000. For info: Yuma Civic Center, 1440 Desert Hills Dr, Yuma, AZ 85365. Phone: (928) 373-5040. Fax: (928) 344-9121. E-mail: ycc@ci.yuma.az.us.

BIRTHDAYS TODAY

Kevin Anderson, 46, actor (*Hoffa, Rising Sun*), born Gurnee, IL, Jan 13, 1960.

Orlando Bloom, 29, actor (*The Lord of the Rings* trilogy), born Canterbury, Kent, England, Jan 13, 1977.

Keith Coogan, 36, actor (*Adventures in Babysitting, Cousins*), born Palm Springs, CA, Jan 13, 1970.

Patrick Dempsey, 40, actor (*Sweet Home Alabama*), born Lewiston, ME, Jan 13, 1966.

Nicole Eggert, 34, actress ("Baywatch," "Charles in Charge"), born Glendale, CA, Jan 13, 1972.

Frank Gallo, 73, artist, sculptor, born Toledo, OH, Jan 13, 1933.

Julia Louis-Dreyfus, 45, actress ("Seinfeld"), born New York, NY, Jan 13, 1961.

Jay McInerney, 51, writer (*Bright Lights, Big City*), born Hartford, CT, Jan 13, 1955.

Penelope Ann Miller, 42, actress (*Adventures in Babysitting, The Freshman, Carlito's Way*), born Los Angeles, CA, Jan 13, 1964.

Richard Moll, 63, actor ("Night Court," *Wicked Stepmother, The Flintstones*), born Pasadena, CA, Jan 13, 1943.

Charles Nelson Reilly, 75, director, actor ("The Ghost and Mrs Muir," "Match Game PM"), born New York, NY, Jan 13, 1931.

Frances Sternhagen, 76, actress (*The Tiger Makes Out, Misery*; stage: *The Good Doctor*), born Washington, DC, Jan 13, 1930.

JANUARY 14 — SATURDAY
Day 14 — 351 Remaining

AFRMA FANCY RAT AND MOUSE ANNUAL SHOW. Jan 14 (tentative—or Jan 21). Riverside, CA. Annual show where trophies are awarded to the winners. Rats and mice are emerging as ideal pets: they provide all the pleasure and satisfaction of a warm, cuddly, intelligent and friendly pet companion. The American Fancy Rat and Mouse Association (AFRMA) was founded in 1983 to promote the breeding and exhibition of fancy rats and mice, to educate the public on their positive qualities as companion animals and to provide information on their proper care. Est attendance: 100. For info: AFRMA (CAE), PO Box 2589, Winnetka, CA 91396-2589. Phone: (951) 685-2350 or (818) 992-5564 or (760) 519-8287. Fax: (818) 592-6590. E-mail: afrma@afrma.org. Web: www.afrma.org.

AKC/EUKANUBA NATIONAL CHAMPIONSHIP. Jan 14–15. St. Pete Times Forum, St. Petersburg, FL, and the Tampa Convention Center, Tampa Bay, FL. At the AKC/Eukanuba National Championship, the top dogs from around the globe compete for the biggest cash prizes offered in the sport. Intense competition, unique awards for breeders and special events for spectators make this the most exciting event in the dog world. For info: American Kennel Club, 260 Madison Ave, New York, NY 10016. Phone: (212) 696-8200. E-mail: invitational@akc.org. Web: www.akc.org.

ARNOLD, BENEDICT: BIRTH ANNIVERSARY. Jan 14, 1741 (OS). American officer who deserted to the British during the Revolutionary War and whose name has since become synonymous with treachery. Born at Norwich, CT. Died June 14, 1801, at London, England.

EAGLE DAYS. Jan 14–15. Milford Nature Center/Fish Hatchery, Junction City, KS. Learn more about the magnificent bird that is our national emblem. Meet both a live bald eagle and a golden eagle! Guides with spotting scopes and binoculars will be waiting to show you eagles as they roost and soar around Milford Lake. Sponsor: Kansas Wildlife and Parks; US Army Corps of Engineers. Est attendance: 700. For info: Milford Nature Center, 3115 Hatchery Dr, Junction City, KS 66441. Phone: (785) 238-5323. Fax: (785) 238-5775.

FIRST CAESAREAN SECTION: ANNIVERSARY. Jan 14, 1794. Dr. Jesse Bennett, of Edom, VA, performed the first successful Caesarean section. The patient was his wife.

MAURY, MATTHEW FONTAINE: 200th BIRTH ANNIVERSARY. Jan 14, 1806. Naval officer, born at Fredericksburg, VA. Maury established oceanography as a branch of science and revolutionized the recording of oceanographic data as a superintendent of the Naval Observatory. Died at Lexington, VA, Feb 1, 1873.

MODEL RAILROAD SHOW. Jan 14–15. Wilson Lodge, Oglebay, Wheeling, WV. Model train enthusiasts will find nearly 80 exhibitors displaying and selling their wide variety of model trains and accessories. Est attendance: 1,700. For info: Steve Mitch, Train Show Mgr, Oglebay Resort, Rt 88 N, Wheeling, WV 26003. Phone: (304) 243-4034. Fax: (304) 243-4110. E-mail: smitch@oglebay-resort.com. Web: www.oglebay-resort.com/specialevents.

MOON PHASE: FULL MOON. Jan 14. Moon enters Full Moon phase at 4:48 AM, EST.

MUSEUM OF AMERICAN GLASS: MID-WINTER EXHIBIT. Jan 14–Mar 5. Wheaton Village, Millville, NJ. "Curator's Choice" exhibit of fine glass items. Est attendance: 6,000. For info: Wheaton Village, 1501 Glasstown Rd, Millville, NJ 08332-1566. Phone: (856) 825-6800 or (800) 998-4552. Fax: (856) 825-2410. E-mail: mail@wheatonvillage.org. Web: www.wheatonvillage.org.

NATIONAL SKATING WEEK. Jan 14–22. During this week, US Figure Skating member clubs and Basic Skill Programs reach out to new members in their community by offering the fundamentals of ice-skating from professionally trained instructors across the US. In 2005, more than 250 member clubs participated in National Skating Week and more than 260 lessons and clinics were held. For info: US Figure Skating, 20 First St, Colorado Springs, CO 80906. Phone: (719) 635-5200. Fax: (719) 635-9548. Web: www.usfsa.org.

OUTCAULT, RICHARD FELTON: BIRTH ANNIVERSARY. Jan 14, 1863. When Richard Felton Outcault was asked by the *New York World*'s Sunday editor to submit drawings for use with their new color printing process, the "funny papers" were born. Outcault's first color drawing, titled "Origin of a New Species," was published Nov 18, 1894. The first regular colored cartoon, "Hogan's Alley," drawn by Outcault, began appearing with its main character's blustery comments written across his yellow nightshirt—thus making him the "Yellow Kid." The term "yellow journalism" was coined for newspapers featuring the Kid. Outcault's strip "Buster Brown" brought him celebrity and fortune. Outcault was born at Lancaster, OH, and died Sept 25, 1928, at Flushing, NY.

PENGUIN AWARENESS DAY. Jan 14. Jenkinson's Aquarium, Point Pleasant Beach, NJ. Learn all about the African penguin families at Jenkinson's Aquarium and the status of penguins in the wild. Children will enjoy penguin storytelling as well as appearances by our mascot, Perky the Penguin. Penguins are fed at 11 AM and 3:30 PM. Free arts and crafts from 1 PM to 4 PM. Est attendance: 800. For info: Jenkinson's Aquarium, 300 Ocean Ave, Point Pleasant Beach, NJ 08742. Phone: (732) 899-1212. Fax: (732) 899-1717. E-mail: jenkinsonsaquarium@comcast.net. Web: www.jenkinsons.com.

RATIFICATION DAY. Jan 14, 1784. Anniversary of the act that officially ended the American Revolution and established the US as a sovereign power. On Jan 14, 1784, the Continental Congress, meeting at Annapolis, MD, ratified the Treaty of Paris, thus fulfilling the Declaration of Independence of July 4, 1776.

ROACH, HAL: BIRTH ANNIVERSARY. Jan 14, 1892. American film writer, director and producer Harold Eugene (Hal) Roach was born at Elmira, NY. He pioneered film comedy as chief of his own studio for nearly 40 years. During that time he produced, and sometimes directed and wrote, nearly 1,000 movies. Roach is noted for originating the *Our Gang* comedies in 1922 and for introducing Laurel and Hardy to film audiences. He won Academy Awards for the short films *The Music Box* (1931) and *Bored of Education* (1936). Roach produced the film version of Steinbeck's novel *Of Mice and Men* in 1939. In 1984 he won an honorary Academy Award for career achievement. Roach died Nov 2, 1992, at Los Angeles, CA.

"SANFORD AND SON" TV PREMIERE: ANNIVERSARY. Jan 14, 1972. NBC sitcom which gained immediate popularity depicting an African-American father and son engaged in the junkyard business. Norman Lear and Bud Yorkin developed the comedy series based on the British "Steptoe and Son." Comedian Redd Foxx played Fred Sanford. His son, Lamont, was played by Demond Wilson. Others appearing on the show were Whitman Mayo as Grady, Slappy White as Melvin, LaWanda Page as Aunt Esther, Gregory Sierra as Julio, Nathaniel Taylor as Rollo, Raymond Allen as Uncle Woody, Don Bexley as Bubba Bexley, Lynn Hamilton as Donna Harris, Howard Platt and Hal Williams as Hoppy and Smitty, Pat Morita as Ah Chew, Marlene Clark as Janet and Edward Crawford as Roger. The last telecast was Sept 2, 1977.

SCHWEITZER, ALBERT: BIRTH ANNIVERSARY. Jan 14, 1875. Alsatian philosopher, musician, physician and winner of the 1952 Nobel Peace Prize was born at Kayserberg, Upper Alsace, and died at Lambarene, Gabon, Sept 4, 1965.

January **2006**

S	M	T	W	T	F	S
1	2	3	4	5	6	7
8	9	10	11	12	13	14
15	16	17	18	19	20	21
22	23	24	25	26	27	28
29	30	31				

SPACE MILESTONE: *SOYUZ 4* (USSR). Jan 14, 1969. First docking of two manned spacecraft (with *Soyuz 5*) and first interchange of spaceship personnel in orbit by means of space walks.

"TODAY" TV PREMIERE: ANNIVERSARY. Jan 14, 1952. NBC program that started the morning news format we know today. Captained by Dave Garroway, the show was segmented with bits and pieces of news, sports, weather, interviews and other features that were repeated so that viewers did not have to stop their morning routine to watch. The segments were brief and to the point. Sylvester Weaver devised this concept to capitalize on television's unusual qualities. What used to take three hours to broadcast live across the country was done in two with videotape on a delayed basis. The addition of chimpanzee J. Fred Muggs in 1953 helped push ratings up. There have been a number of hosts over the years, from John Chancellor and Hugh Downs to Tom Brokaw, Bryant Gumbel and Matt Lauer. Female hosts (originally called "Today Girls") have included Betsy Palmer, Florence Henderson, Barbara Walters, Jane Pauley and Katie Couric.

UZBEKISTAN: ARMY DAY. Jan 14. National holiday.

WELCOME BACK SNOWBIRDS PANCAKE BREAKFAST. Jan 14. El Centro, CA. Annually, the second Saturday in January. Est attendance: 2,500. For info: El Centro Chamber of Commerce, Box 3006, El Centro, CA 92244. Phone: (760) 352-3681. Fax: (760) 352-3246. E-mail: generalinfo@elcentro chamber.com. Web: www.elcentrochamber.com.

WHIPPLE, WILLIAM: BIRTH ANNIVERSARY. Jan 14, 1730. American patriot and signer of the Declaration of Independence. Born at Kittery, ME, he died at Portsmouth, NH, Nov 10, 1785.

BIRTHDAYS TODAY

Jason Bateman, 37, actor ("Arrested Development"), born Rye, NY, Jan 14, 1969.

Julian Bond, 66, legislator, civil rights leader, born Nashville, TN, Jan 14, 1940.

Faye Dunaway, 65, actress (Oscar for *Network*; *Bonnie and Clyde*, *Chinatown*), born Bascom, FL, Jan 14, 1941.

Marjoe Gortner, 61, ex-evangelist, actor, singer, born Long Beach, CA, Jan 14, 1945.

Lawrence Kasdan, 57, filmmaker (*The Bodyguard, The Big Chill, Mumford*), born Miami Beach, FL, Jan 14, 1949.

Shannon Lucid, 63, astronaut, born Shanghai, China, Jan 14, 1943.

Andy Rooney, 87, writer, columnist ("60 Minutes," *Pieces of My Mind*), born Albany, NY, Jan 14, 1919.

Steven Soderbergh, 43, filmmaker (Best Director Oscar for *Traffic; Ocean's Eleven, Erin Brockovich*), born Atlanta, GA, Jan 14, 1963.

Holland Taylor, 63, actress ("The Practice," *The Truman Show*), born Philadelphia, PA, Jan 14, 1943.

Nina Totenberg, 62, broadcast journalist, correspondent ("Nightline"), born New York, NY, Jan 14, 1944.

Emily Watson, 39, actress (*Angela's Ashes, The Boxer*), born London, England, Jan 14, 1967.

Carl Weathers, 58, actor (*Rocky, Happy Gilmore*), born New Orleans, LA, Jan 14, 1948.

JANUARY 15 — SUNDAY
Day 15 — 350 Remaining

ACE, GOODMAN: BIRTH ANNIVERSARY. Jan 15, 1899. Radio and TV writer, actor, columnist and humorist. With his wife, Jane, created and acted in the popular series of radio programs (1928–45) "Easy Aces." Called "America's greatest wit" by Fred Allen. Born at Kansas City, MO; died at New York, NY, Mar 25, 1982, soon after asking that his tombstone be inscribed "No flowers, please, I'm allergic."

ALPHA KAPPA ALPHA SORORITY FOUNDED: ANNIVERSARY. Jan 15, 1908. Founded at Howard University at Washington, DC, by Ethel Hedgeman Lyle, Alpha Kappa Alpha was the first organization of its type for black women. It was incorporated Jan 29, 1913.

BRITISH MUSEUM: ANNIVERSARY. Jan 15, 1759. On this date, the British Museum opened its doors at Montague House in London. Incorporated by an act of Parliament in 1753, following the death of British medical doctor and naturalist Sir Hans Sloane, who had bequeathed his personal collection of books, manuscripts, coins, medals and antiquities to Britain. As the national museum of the United Kingdom, the British Museum houses many of the world's most prized treasures. The national library moved to separate facilities in 1997.

CARLSBAD MARATHON & HALF MARATHON. Jan 15. Plaza Camino Real, Carlsbad, CA. Race open to runners, walkers, race walkers and disabled. Postrace festival with refreshments, entertainment, massages and more. Est attendance: 12,000. For info: Carlsbad Marathon, In Motion, Inc, 6355 Corte del Abeto, Ste C-103, Carlsbad, CA 92009. Phone: (760) 692-2900. E-mail: info@inmotionevents.com. Web: www.sdmarathon.com.

CHAMPION OF THE MONTH. Jan 15. Recognize individuals who live their lives as champions. Nominate your champion at our website between the 15th and the 15th of each month. Each Champion of the Month will be recognized each month in our newsletter and on our radio show (NBC 1190 AM) in Phoenix. For info: Dan Kuschell, 3370 N Hayden, #123-146, Scottsdale, AZ 85251. Phone: (800) 211-4580. E-mail: dan@achampion vision.com. Web: www.achampionvision.com or www.prosperity basedliving.com.

FIRST SUPER BOWL: ANNIVERSARY. Jan 15, 1967. The Green Bay Packers won the first NFL–AFL World Championship Game, defeating the Kansas City Chiefs, 35–10, at the Los Angeles Memorial Coliseum. Packers quarterback Bart Starr was named the game's Most Valuable Player. Pro football's title game later became known as the Super Bowl and is now played on the last Sunday in January.

"HAPPY DAYS" TV PREMIERE: ANNIVERSARY. Jan 15, 1974. This nostalgic comedy set in Milwaukee in the 1950s starred Ron Howard as teenager Richie Cunningham with Anson Williams and Don Most as his friends "Potsie" Weber and Ralph Malph. Tom Bosley played Richie's parents and his sister, Joanie, was played by Erin Moran. The most memorable character was The Fonz—Arthur "Fonzie" Fonzarelli—played by Henry Winkler. "Happy Days" remained on the air until July 12, 1984. "Laverne and Shirley" was a spin-off.

HEALTHY WEIGHT WEEK. Jan 15–21. 13th annual. People who diet the first week in January and binge the second are ready for better living by the third week: Healthy Weight Week. This is a week to promote healthy lifestyle habits that last a lifetime and prevent weight and eating problems (not cause them, as dieting does); a time to move on to Health at Any Size. News release, 2006 awards and consumer handouts available on website. For info: Francie M. Berg, Healthy Weight Network, 402 S 14th St, Hettinger, ND 58639. E-mail: fmberg@healthyweight.net (please put "Berg-Healthy Weight Week" in subject line). Web: www .healthyweight.net.

"HILL STREET BLUES" TV PREMIERE: 25th ANNIVERSARY. Jan 15, 1981. Immensely popular NBC police series created by Stephen Bochco and Michael Kozoll that focused more on police officers than on crime. The show was very realistic and highly praised by real policemen. It won a slew of Emmys and ran for seven seasons. Cast: Daniel J. Travanti as Captain Frank Furillo, Veronica Hamel as public defender Joyce Davenport, Michael Conrad as Sergeant Phil "Let's be careful out there" Esterhaus, Barbara Bosson as Fay Furillo, and as the wonderfully drawn cops, Bruce Weitz (Mick Belker), Taurean Blacque (Neal Washington), Kiel Martin (Johnny LaRue), Joe Spano (Henry Goldblume), James B. Sikking (Howard Hunter), René Enríquez (Ray Calletano), Michael Warren (Bobby Hill), Betty Thomas (Lucy Bates), Ed Marinaro (Joe Coffey) and Charles Haid (Andy Renko). The last telecast was on May 19, 1987.

HOUSTON MARATHON. Jan 15. Houston, TX. 34th annual citywide race. Also features half marathon and 5k run. Est attendance: 20,000. For info: Houston Marathon, 720 N Post Oak Rd, #100, Houston, TX 77024. Phone: (713) 957-3453. Fax: (713) 957-3406. E-mail: marathon@houstonmarathon.com. Web: www.houstonmarathon.com.

HUNT FOR HAPPINESS WEEK. Jan 15–21. Celebrate the 5th annual Hunt for Happiness Week sponsored by the Secret Society of Happy People. Activities, suggestions and ideas for teachers, youth leaders and parents to encourage kids and teens to discover more happy moments are available on our website. Annually, the third full week in January. For info: Secret Society of Happy People, 1315 Riverchase Dr, #2316, Coppell, TX 75019. Phone: (972) 471-1485. E-mail: pjohnson@sohp.com. Web: www.sohp.com.

INTERNATIONAL PRINTING WEEK. Jan 15–21. To develop public awareness of the printing/graphic arts industry. Annually, the week including Ben Franklin's birthday, Jan 17. For info: Kevin P. Keane, Exec Dir, Intl Assn of Printing House Craftsmen, 7042 Brooklyn Blvd, Minneapolis, MN 55429-1370. Phone: (800) 466-4274. Web: www.iaphc.org.

KING, MARTIN LUTHER, JR: BIRTH ANNIVERSARY. Jan 15, 1929. Black civil rights leader, minister, advocate of nonviolence and recipient of the Nobel Peace Prize (1964). Born at Atlanta, GA, he was assassinated at Memphis, TN, Apr 4, 1968. After his death many states and territories observed his birthday as a holiday. In 1983 the Congress approved HR 3706, "A bill to amend Title 5, United States Code, to make the birthday of Martin Luther King, Jr, a legal public holiday." Signed by the president on Nov 2, 1983, it became Public Law 98–144. The law sets the third Monday in January for observance of King's birthday. First observance was Jan 20, 1986. See also: "King, Martin Luther, Jr: Birthday Observed" (Jan 16).

LIVINGSTON, PHILIP: BIRTH ANNIVERSARY. Jan 15, 1716. Merchant and signer of the Declaration of Independence, born at Albany, NY. Died at York, PA, June 12, 1778.

MOLIÈRE DAY: BAPTISM ANNIVERSARY. Jan 15, 1622. Most celebrated of French authors and dramatists, Jean Baptiste Poquelin, baptized at Paris, France, Jan 15, 1622, took the stage name Molière when he was about 22 years old. While playing in a performance of his last play, *Le Malade Imaginaire* (about a hypochondriac afraid of death), Molière became ill and died within a few hours at Paris, Feb 17, 1673.

NATIONAL FRESH SQUEEZED JUICE WEEK. Jan 15–19. Drinking fresh squeezed juice is a great healthy way of living. For info: Bob O'Brien, Consumer Advocate, 1061 Koelle Blvd, Secaucus, NJ 07094. Phone/fax: (201) 865-4775. E-mail: bobtheebest@yahoo.com. Web: www.wtbq.com.

PENTAGON COMPLETED: ANNIVERSARY. Jan 15, 1943. The world's largest office building with 6.5 million square feet of usable space, the Pentagon is located in Virginia across the Potomac River from Washington, DC, and serves as headquarters for the Department of Defense.

SIEGMEISTER, ELIE: BIRTH ANNIVERSARY. Jan 15, 1909. American composer Elie Siegmeister was born at New York, NY. He composed eight symphonies and eight operas and a number of concertos, chamber pieces and orchestral works using folk, jazz and street songs to create a contemporary American classical music. He died Mar 10, 1991, at Manhasset, NY.

SOCIETY FOR THE PRESERVATION & ENCOURAGEMENT OF BARBER SHOP QUARTET SINGING IN AMERICA (SPEBSQSA) MID-WINTER CONVENTION. Jan 15–22. Jacksonville, FL. Members meet for administrative conferences, shows and contest to select national Seniors Quartet Champion. Est attendance: 1,200. For info: Reed Sampson, PR Dir, SPEBSQSA, Inc, 7930 Sheridan Rd, Kenosha, WI 53143. Phone: (800) 876-SING. E-mail: info@spebsqsa.org. Web: www.spebsqsa.org.

TELLER, EDWARD: BIRTH ANNIVERSARY. Jan 15, 1908. Born at Budapest, Hungary, Edward Teller was a physicist who worked on the Manhattan Project at Los Alamos, NM, in the 1940s. He promoted the first hydrogen fusion bomb, work that was considered secondary to the atomic bomb research taking place at the same time. He was a vocal critic of Robert Oppenheimer, director of the Manhattan Project, and his comments eventually destroyed Oppenheimer's career. Teller's hydrogen bomb research ultimately proved feasible but was never used in wartime. Throughout his life he remained a profound influence on America's defense and energy policies. He died at Stanford, CA, Sept 9, 2003.

WORLD RELIGION DAY. Jan 15. To proclaim the oneness of religion and the belief that world religion will unify the peoples of the earth. Baha'i-sponsored observance established in 1950 by the Baha'is of the US. Annually, the third Sunday in January. For info: Baha'is of the US, Office of Communications, 1233 Central St, Evanston, IL 60201. Phone: (847) 733-3411. Fax: (847) 869-0247. E-mail: ooc@usbnc.org. Web: www.us.bahai.org.

BIRTHDAYS TODAY

Ernest J. Gaines, 73, author (*The Autobiography of Miss Jane Pittman, A Lesson Before Dying*), born at River Lake Plantation, Oscar, LA, Jan 15, 1933.

Chad Lowe, 38, actor ("Now and Again," "Life Goes On," *Nobody's Perfect*), born Dayton, OH, Jan 15, 1968.

Rod MacLeish, 80, broadcast journalist, born Bryn Mawr, PA, Jan 15, 1926.

Andrea Martin, 59, actress (*Wag the Dog, Anastasia*, "SCTV"), born Portland, ME, Jan 15, 1947.

Margaret O'Brien, 69, actress (*Little Women, Meet Me in St. Louis*), born San Diego, CA, Jan 15, 1937.

Mario Van Peebles, 49, actor (*Love Kills, Judgment Day*), born Mexico City, Mexico, Jan 15, 1957.

January 2006	S	M	T	W	T	F	S
	1	2	3	4	5	6	7
	8	9	10	11	12	13	14
	15	16	17	18	19	20	21
	22	23	24	25	26	27	28
	29	30	31				

JANUARY 16 — MONDAY
Day 16 — 349 Remaining

APPRECIATE A DRAGON DAY. Jan 16. In school and public libraries everywhere, children will have the opportunity to choose dragons from popular literature and participate in activities to share their enthusiasm for the dragon of their choice. For info: Donita Tompkins, 5031 Stillwater Dr, Colorado Springs, CO 80918. Phone: (719) 635-3940. E-mail: dtompkins@peoplepc .com. Web: www.dragonspell.us.

BOB HOPE CHRYSLER CLASSIC. Jan 16–22. La Quinta, CA. The nation's largest sports event for charity. It features PGA tour pros, celebrities and amateurs. Est attendance: 110,000. For info: Pat Bennett, PR and Production, Bob Hope Chrysler Classic, 39000 Bob Hope Dr, Rancho Mirage, CA 92270. Phone: (760) 346-8184. Fax: (760) 346-6329. E-mail: email@bhcc.com. Web: www.bhcc.com.

BRITISH AIR RAID ON BERLIN: ANNIVERSARY. Jan 16, 1943. In the first bombing of Germany since the Casablanca Conference, the British Royal Air Force began heavy bombing of Germany by day and night to bring about "the progressive destruction and dislocation of the German military, industrial and economic system, and for the undermining of the morale of the German people." The RAF used their new "target indicator" bombs to mark targets for their bombers.

CIVIL SERVICE CREATED: ANNIVERSARY. Jan 16, 1883. The US Congress passed a bill creating the civil service.

COAL CONSERVATION ORDERED: ANNIVERSARY. Jan 16, 1918. In a precursor of things to come, 75 New York schools closed down for lack of coal on Jan 2, 1918. On Jan 16, by order of US Fuel Administrator Harry A. Garfield, all industry east of the Mississippi not crucial to the war effort was shut down. Factories remained closed for five days. In addition, the following nine Mondays became days of leisure for a large segment of the American workforce as further attempts were made to reserve coal for troop transport, ships and merchant vessels.

DEAN, DIZZY: BIRTH ANNIVERSARY. Jan 16, 1911. Jay Hanna "Dizzy" Dean, major league pitcher (St. Louis Cardinals) and Baseball Hall of Fame member was born at Lucas, AR. Following his baseball career, Dean established himself as a radio and TV sports announcer and commentator, becoming famous for his innovative delivery. "He slud into third," reported Dizzy, who on another occasion explained that "Me and Paul [baseball player brother Paul "Daffy" Dean] . . . didn't get much education." Died at Reno, NV, July 17, 1974.

"DONNY AND MARIE" TV PREMIERE: 30th ANNIVERSARY. Jan 16, 1976. ABC show hosted by brother-and-sister act Donny and Marie Osmond. There were seven other talented siblings in the Osmond family who appeared on the show at times along with regulars Jim Connell and Hank Garcia. The sister-and-brother team could sing, dance and perform on ice skates.

EL SALVADOR: NATIONAL DAY OF PEACE. Jan 16, 1992. A peace treaty was signed in Mexico City ending the 12-year civil war that had claimed 75,000 lives. On Feb 1, a cease-fire went into effect.

FOSSEY, DIAN: BIRTH ANNIVERSARY. Jan 16, 1932. Born at San Francisco, CA, Fossey went to the Virunga Mountains at Rwanda, Africa, to study the endangered mountain gorillas. Her work, conducted in isolation among the primates, was groundbreaking in terms of increasing science's understanding of the gorillas' social world. Fossey was a vigorous crusader against the poachers who decimate the gorilla population, and she was probably murdered by them: her body was discovered on Dec 26, 1985, at Mount Visoke, Rwanda.

JAPAN: HARU-NO-YABUIRI. Jan 16. Employees and servants who have been working over the holidays are given a day off.

KING, MARTIN LUTHER, JR: BIRTHDAY OBSERVED. Jan 16. Public Law 98–144 designates the third Monday in January as an annual legal public holiday observing the birth of Martin Luther King, Jr. First observed in 1986. In New Hampshire, this day is designated Civil Rights Day. See also: "King, Martin Luther, Jr: Birth Anniversary" (Jan 15).

MALAWI: JOHN CHILEMBWE DAY. Jan 16. National holiday. Honors a leader for independence who led an uprising against the British in 1915.

★**MARTIN LUTHER KING, JR, FEDERAL HOLIDAY.** Jan 16. Presidential Proclamation has been issued without request each year for the third Monday in January since 1986.

MARTIN LUTHER KING JR DAY. Jan 16. Ash Lawn-Highland, Charlottesville, VA. Special activities focusing on African-American life at Ash Lawn-Highland, home of President James Monroe. For info: Ash Lawn-Highland, 1000 James Monroe Parkway, Charlottesville, VA 22902. Phone: (434) 293-9539. Fax: (434) 293-8000. E-mail: info@ashlawnhighland.org. Web: www .ashlawnhighland.org.

MERMAN, ETHEL: BIRTH ANNIVERSARY. Jan 16, 1909. Musical comedy star famous for her belting voice and brassy style. Born Ethel Agnes Zimmerman on Jan 16, 1909 (or 1912—the date changed the older she got, but most sources say 1909), at Queens, NY. Died Feb 15, 1984, at New York, NY.

MICHELIN, ANDRE: BIRTH ANNIVERSARY. Jan 16, 1853. French industrialist who, along with his brother Edouard, started the Michelin Tire Company in 1888, manufacturing bicycle tires. They were the first to use demountable pneumatic tires on cars. Born at Paris, France; died there Apr 4, 1931.

NATIONAL NOTHING DAY: ANNIVERSARY. Jan 16. Anniversary of National Nothing Day, an event created by newspaperman Harold Pullman Coffin and first observed in 1973 "to provide Americans with one national day when they can just sit without celebrating, observing or honoring anything." Since 1975, though many other events have been listed on this day, lighthearted traditional observance of Coffin's idea has continued. Coffin, a native of Reno, NV, died at Capitola, CA, Sept 12, 1981, at the age of 76.

PEDDLER'S VILLAGE ANNUAL QUILT COMPETITION AND DISPLAY. Jan 16–Apr 2. Peddler's Village, Lahaska, PA. Handmade quilt entries compete for $1,400 in cash prizes in such categories as traditional, Amish, creative, clothing, children's and amateur. A distinguished panel of judges chooses the winners, and quilts are displayed in the Village Gazebo. Open daily to public. Free admission. Est attendance: 250,000. For info: Peddler's Village, Routes 202 & 263, Lahaska, PA 18931. Phone: (215) 794-4000. Fax: (215) 794-4001. Web: www.peddlersvillage .com.

PERSIAN GULF WAR BEGINS: 15th ANNIVERSARY. Jan 16, 1991. Allied forces launched a major air offensive against Iraq to begin the Gulf War. The strike was designed to destroy Iraqi air defenses, command, control and communication centers. As Desert Shield became Desert Storm, the world was able to see and hear for the first time an initial engagement of war as CNN broadcasters, stationed at Baghdad, covered the attack live.

PROHIBITION (EIGHTEENTH) AMENDMENT: ANNIVERSARY. Jan 16, 1919. Nebraska became the 36th state to ratify the prohibition amendment and the 18th Amendment became part of the US Constitution. One year later, Jan 16, 1920, the 18th Amendment took effect and the sale of alcoholic beverages became illegal in the US with the Volstead Act providing for enforcement. This was the first time that an amendment to the Constitution dealt with a social issue. The 21st Amendment, repealing the 18th, went into effect Dec 6, 1933.

RELIGIOUS FREEDOM DAY. Jan 16, 1786. The legislature of Virginia adopted a religious freedom statute that protected Virginians against any requirement to attend or support any church and against discrimination. This statute, which had been drafted by Thomas Jefferson and introduced by James Madison, later was the model for the First Amendment to the US Constitution.

★**RELIGIOUS FREEDOM DAY.** Jan 16. Commemorates the adoption of a religious freedom statute by the Virginia legislature in 1786.

SERVICE, ROBERT WILLIAM: BIRTH ANNIVERSARY. Jan 16, 1874. Canadian poet, born at Preston, England. Lived in the Canadian northwest for many years and perhaps is best remembered for such ballads as "The Shooting of Dan McGrew" and "The Cremation of Sam McGee" and for such books as *Songs of a Sourdough, Rhymes of a Rolling Stone* and *The Spell of the Yukon*. Died at France, Sept 11, 1958.

STOCK EXCHANGE HOLIDAY (MARTIN LUTHER KING DAY). Jan 16. The holiday schedules for the various exchanges are subject to change if relevant rules, regulations or exchange policies are revised. If you have questions, phone: American Stock Exchange (212) 306-1000, Chicago Board of Options Exchange (312) 786-5600, Chicago Board of Trade (312) 435-3500, NASDAQ Stock Market (646) 441-5200, New York Stock Exchange (212) 656-3000, Pacific Stock Exchange (415) 393-4000, Philadelphia Stock Exchange (215) 496-5000.

BIRTHDAYS TODAY

Debbie Allen, 56, dancer, choreographer, singer, actress ("Fame"), born Houston, TX, Jan 16, 1950.

John Carpenter, 58, movie director (*Halloween, The Thing*), born Carthage, NY, Jan 16, 1948.

David Chokachi, 38, actor ("Baywatch"), born Plymouth, MA, Jan 16, 1968.

Anthony Joseph (A.J.) Foyt, Jr, 71, former auto racer, born Houston, TX, Jan 16, 1935.

Marilyn Horne, 72, opera singer, born Bradford, PA, Jan 16, 1934.

William Kennedy, 78, author (*Ironweed, Roscoe*), born Albany, NY, Jan 16, 1928.

Jack Burns McDowell, 40, former baseball player, born Van Nuys, CA, Jan 16, 1966.

Ronnie Milsap, 62, singer ("[There's] No Gettin' Over Me"), born Robinsville, NC, Jan 16, 1944.

Albert Pujols, 26, baseball player, born Santo Domingo, Dominican Republic, Jan 16, 1980.

JANUARY 17 — TUESDAY

Day 17 — 348 Remaining

BENJAMIN FRANKLIN TERCENTENARY. Jan 17–Dec 31. Centering in Philadelphia, PA, the Tercentenary celebrates the life and contributions of Ben Franklin, born Jan 17, 1706. See "Spotlight on 2006 Events" for a partial listing of the many symposia, exhibitions, demonstrations, cultural events and more taking place in 2006. For info: Benjamin Franklin Tercentenary, 135 S 18th St, Ste 702, Philadelphia, PA 19103. Phone: (215) 557-0733. E-mail: postmaster@benfranklin300.org. Web: www.benfranklin300.com.

THE BUSINESS OF AMERICA QUOTATION: ANNIVERSARY. Jan 17, 1925. President Calvin Coolidge, in a speech to the American Society of Newspaper Editors, described America in a way that was to define the country in the 20th century and beyond—not just for the prosperous 1920s. "The chief business of the American people," he said, "is business."

CABLE CAR PATENT: ANNIVERSARY. Jan 17, 1871. Andrew Hallikie received a patent for a cable car system that began service in San Francisco in 1873.

CAPONE, AL: BIRTH ANNIVERSARY. Jan 17, 1899. Gangster Alphonse ("Scarface") Capone was born this date at Brooklyn, NY, to immigrants from Naples, Italy. Capone dominated organized crime in Chicago throughout Prohibition. Targeted by the "Untouchables" after 1929's St. Valentine's Day Massacre (which he allegedly ordered), Capone was finally imprisoned on tax evasion charges. He died Jan 25, 1947, at Miami, FL, after suffering from syphilis.

COIN FLIP FOR BENJAMIN FRANKLIN'S 300th BIRTHDAY. Jan 17. On this day—Benjamin Franklin's 300th birthday—students around the world are invited to commemorate this milestone event by participating in a common scientific enterprise. Students should flip a coin ten times and then enter their data at The Franklin Institute Online. There, their data will merge with the aggregated results from coin flips in classrooms and homes around the world. In this way, students will see how science is a distributed, shared pursuit of knowledge by curious thinkers, a lesson that honors the legacy of Benjamin Franklin. Students should pick the smallest valued coin of their country's coinage (keeping in mind Franklin's famous adage: "A penny saved is a penny earned"). For info: The Franklin Institute Online, 222 N 20th St, Philadelphia, PA 19103. Phone: (215) 448-1200. Web: sln.fi.edu/flip.

CUSTOMER SERVICE DAY. Jan 17. A day to reflect on the importance of providing good customer service—and to commit to learning new skills that will help you provide it. For info: Karen Leland, 180 Harbor Dr, #208, Sausalito, CA 94965. Phone: (415) 331-5200. Fax: (415) 331-5272. E-mail: kleland@scgtraining.com. Web: www.scgtraining.com.

FIRST NUCLEAR-POWERED SUBMARINE VOYAGE: ANNIVERSARY. Jan 17, 1955. At 11 AM, EST, the commanding officer of the world's first nuclear-powered submarine, the *Nautilus*, ordered all lines cast off and sent the historic message: "Under way on nuclear power." Highlights of the *Nautilus*: keel laid by President Harry S Truman June 14, 1952; christened and launched by Mrs Dwight D. Eisenhower Jan 21, 1954; commissioned to the US Navy Sept 30, 1954. It now forms part of the *Nautilus* Memorial Submarine Force Library and Museum at the Naval Submarine Base New London at Groton, CT.

FRANKLIN, BENJAMIN: 300th BIRTH ANNIVERSARY. Jan 17, 1706. "Elder statesman of the American Revolution," oldest signer of both the Declaration of Independence and the Constitution, scientist, diplomat, author, printer, publisher, philosopher, philanthropist and self-made, self-educated man. Author, printer and publisher of *Poor Richard's Almanack* (1733–58). Born at Boston, MA, Franklin died at Philadelphia, PA, Apr 17, 1790. His birthday is commemorated each year by the Poor Richard Club of Philadelphia with graveside observance. In 1728 Franklin wrote a premature epitaph for himself. It first appeared in print in Ames's 1771 almanac: "The Body of BENJAMIN FRANKLIN/Printer/Like a Covering of an old Book/Its contents torn out/And stript of its Lettering and Gilding,/Lies here, Food for Worms;/But the work shall not be lost,/It will (as he believ'd) appear once more/In a New and more beautiful Edition/Corrected and amended/By the Author."

	S	**M**	**T**	**W**	**T**	**F**	**S**
January	1	2	3	4	5	6	7
2006	8	9	10	11	12	13	14
	15	16	17	18	19	20	21
	22	23	24	25	26	27	28
	29	30	31				

"FRONTLINE" TV PREMIERE: ANNIVERSARY. Jan 17, 1983. PBS hour-long independently produced documentaries initially hosted by Jessica Savitch. Judy Woodruff replaced Savitch, who was killed in an auto accident in the fall of 1983. The programs often create controversy, focusing on a variety of political, military and social issues.

"THE GOLDBERGS" TV PREMIERE: ANNIVERSARY. Jan 17, 1949. Originally broadcast by CBS, this show was one of the earliest TV sitcoms. The show centered around a Jewish mother and her family living in the Bronx and later in the suburbs. Gertrude Berg created the hit radio show before she wrote, produced and starred as Molly Goldberg in the television version. Contributing actors and actresses included Philip Loeb, Arlene McQuade, Tom Taylor, Eli Mintz, Menasha Skulnik and Arnold Stang.

HUTCHINS, ROBERT MAYNARD: BIRTH ANNIVERSARY. Jan 17, 1899. American educator, foundation executive and civil liberties activist, born at Brooklyn, NY. He was president and later chancellor of the University of Chicago, where he introduced many educational concepts, including the Great Books program. Died at Santa Barbara, CA, on May 14, 1977.

IKE'S FAREWELL: 45th ANNIVERSARY. Jan 17, 1961. President Dwight D. Eisenhower, in his farewell address to the nation on national radio and television, spoke the sentences that would be the most quoted and remembered of his presidency. In a direct warning, he said, "In the councils of government, we must guard against the acquisition of unwarranted influence, whether sought or unsought, by the military-industrial complex. The potential for the disastrous rise of misplaced power exists and persists."

JAPAN SUFFERS MAJOR EARTHQUAKE: ANNIVERSARY. Jan 17, 1995. Japan suffered its second most deadly earthquake in the 20th century when a 20-second temblor left 5,500 dead and more than 21,600 people injured. The epicenter was six miles beneath Awaji Island at Osaka Bay. This was just 20 miles west of Kobe, Japan's sixth-largest city and a major port that accounted for 12 percent of the country's exports. Measuring 7.2 on the Richter scale, the quake collapsed or badly damaged more than 30,400 buildings and left 275,000 people homeless.

JUDGMENT DAY. Jan 17. No need to wait 'til it's too late. All you need to do to see how you measure up to the standards of your God is simple: look in the mirror. There's your judgment. [©2003 by WH.] For info: Thomas & Ruth Roy, Wellcat Holidays, 2418 Long Ln, Lebanon, PA 17046. Phone: (717) 279-0184. E-mail: info@wellcat.com. Web: www.wellcat.com.

MEXICO: BLESSING OF THE ANIMALS AT THE CATHEDRAL. Jan 17. Church of San Antonio at Mexico City or Xochimilco provide best sights of chickens, cows and household pets gaily decorated with flowers. (Saint's day for San Antonio Abad, patron saint of domestic animals.)

PALOMARES HYDROGEN BOMB ACCIDENT: 40th ANNIVERSARY. Jan 17, 1966. At 10:16 AM, according to villagers, fire fell from the sky over Palomares, Spain. An American B-52 bomber carrying four hydrogen bombs collided with its refueling plane, spilling the bombs (two of which had "chemical explosions," scattering radioactive plutonium over the area). In a cleanup, American soldiers burned crops, slaughtered animals and removed tons of topsoil (which was sent to South Carolina for burial). More than 19 years later, in November 1985, the Nuclear Energy Board permitted villagers to see their medical reports for the first time.

PGA OF AMERICA FOUNDED: 90th ANNIVERSARY. Jan 17, 1916. Golf great Walter Hagen and some 30 other pro golfers met and formed the Professional Golfers' Association of America and also developed the idea for a national championship. Rodman Wanamaker provided the trophy and the $2,580 purse for the first PGA Championship, which was played Apr 10, 1916, at the Siwanoy course at Bronxville, NY. The winner was British golfer Jim Barnes, who also won the second competition—not

held until 1919 because of World War I. In 1921 Walter Hagen became the first American to win, a feat he accomplished four more times—in 1924, '25, '26 and '27.

POLAND: LIBERATION DAY. Jan 17. Celebration of 1945 liberation from Nazi oppression on this day of the city of Warsaw by Soviet troops. Special ceremonies at the Monument to the Unknown Soldier in Warsaw's Victory Square (which had been called Adolf Hitler Platz during the German occupation).

POPEYE DEBUTS: ANNIVERSARY. Jan 17, 1929. In E.C. Segar's newspaper comic strip "Thimble Theatre," a new character, Popeye, appeared on the scene and was an immediate success. Olive Oyl quickly dumped her beau, Ham Gravy, for the colorful sailor. Popeye's signature line was to be "Tha's all I can stands, 'cause I can't stands no more!"

QUARTERLY ESTIMATED FEDERAL INCOME TAX PAYERS' DUE DATE. Jan 17. For those individuals whose fiscal year is the calendar year and who make quarterly estimated federal income tax payments, today would be one of the due dates (Jan 17, Apr 17, June 15 and Sept 15, 2006).

QUEEN LILIUOKALANI DEPOSED: ANNIVERSARY. Jan 17, 1893. Hawaiian Queen Liliuokalani, the last monarch of Hawaii, lost her throne when the monarchy was abolished by the "Committee of Safety," with the foreknowledge of US minister John L. Stevens, who encouraged the revolutionaries. The Queen's supporters were intimidated by the 300 US Marines sent to protect American lives and property. Judge Sanford B. Dole became president of the republic and later was Hawaii's first governor after the US annexed it by joint resolution of Congress on July 7, 1898. Hawaii held incorporated territory status for 60 years. President Dwight D. Eisenhower signed the proclamation making Hawaii the 50th state on Aug 21, 1959.

RID THE WORLD OF FAD DIETS AND GIMMICKS DAY. Jan 17. The 17th annual Slim Chance Awards for the "worst" weight loss products of the year are announced. Diet quackery defrauds, disables and kills. Listing of 2006 awards, diet quackery information and consumer handouts available on website. For info: Francie M. Berg, Healthy Weight Network, 402 S 14th St, Hettinger, ND 58639. E-mail: fmberg@healthyweight.net (please put "Berg-Healthy Weight Week" in subject line). Web: www.healthyweight.net.

RUSH, WILLIAM: DEATH ANNIVERSARY. Jan 17, 1833. First American-born sculptor. William Rush's work in wood and clay included busts of many notables, American and European alike; carved wooden female figureheads for ships; the masks of Tragedy and Comedy seen at the Actor's House outside Philadelphia, PA; and the *Spirit of Schuylkill* in Fairmount Park in Philadelphia. In 1805 Rush and others founded the Pennsylvania Academy of the Fine Arts. Rush was born at Philadelphia in 1756.

SAINT ANTHONY'S DAY. Jan 17. Feast day honoring Egyptian hermit who became the first Christian monk and who established communities of hermits; patron saint of domestic animals and patriarch of all monks. Lived about AD 251–354.

SOUTHERN CALIFORNIA EARTHQUAKE: ANNIVERSARY. Jan 17, 1994. An earthquake measuring 6.6 on the Richter scale struck the Los Angeles area about 4:20 AM. The epicenter was at Northridge in the San Fernando Valley, about 20 miles northwest of downtown Los Angeles. A death toll of 51 was announced Jan 20. Sixteen of the dead were killed in the collapse of one apartment building. More than 25,000 people were made homeless by the quake and 680,000 lost electric power. Many buildings were destroyed and others made uninhabitable due to structural damage. A section of the Santa Monica Freeway, part of the Simi Valley Freeway and three major overpasses collapsed. Hundreds of aftershocks occurred in the following several weeks. Costs to repair the damages were estimated at 15–30 billion dollars.

SOUTHWEST SENIOR INVITATIONAL GOLF CHAMPIONSHIP. Jan 17–20. Yuma Golf and Country Club, Yuma, AZ. 30th annual. A 36-hole medal play tournament, limited to 120 players 50 and older. For info: Caballeros de Yuma, Inc, Box 5987, Yuma, AZ 85366-5987. Phone: (928) 343-1715. Fax: (928) 783-1609. E-mail: caballeros@beamspeed.net. Web: www.caballeros.org.

BIRTHDAYS TODAY

Muhammad Ali, 64, former heavyweight champion boxer, who changed his name after converting to Islam, born Cassius Marcellus Clay, Jr at Louisville, KY, Jan 17, 1942.

Jim Carrey, 44, actor (*Dumb and Dumber, The Truman Show, Ace Ventura*), comedian ("In Living Color"), born Newmarket, ON, Canada, Jan 17, 1962.

James Earl Jones, 75, actor (*The Great White Hope; Roots: The Next Generations*), born Arktabula, MS, Jan 17, 1931.

Eartha Kitt, 79, singer, actress, born North, SC, Jan 17, 1927.

Ruth Ann Minner, 71, Governor of Delaware (D), born Milford, DE, Jan 17, 1935.

Newton Minow, 80, former head of the Federal Communications Commission (1961–63), called television a "vast wasteland," born Milwaukee, WI, Jan 17, 1926.

Sheree North, 73, actress (*Marilyn; How to Be Very, Very Popular*), born Dawn Bethel at Los Angeles, CA, Jan 17, 1933.

Maury Povich, 67, talk-show host, born Washington, DC, Jan 17, 1939.

Vidal Sassoon, 78, hair stylist, born London, England, Jan 17, 1928.

Dwyane Wade, 24, basketball player, born Chicago, IL, Jan 17, 1982.

Betty White, 82, actress ("Mary Tyler Moore," "The Golden Girls"), animal rights activist, born Oak Park, IL, Jan 17, 1924 (some sources say 1922).

Paul Young, 50, singer ("Every Time You Go Away"), born Luton, England, Jan 17, 1956.

Donald William (Don) Zimmer, 75, baseball manager and former player, born Cincinnati, OH, Jan 17, 1931.

JANUARY 18 — WEDNESDAY

Day 18 — 347 Remaining

FIRST BLACK US CABINET MEMBER: 40th ANNIVERSARY. Jan 18, 1966. Robert Clifton Weaver was sworn in as Secretary of Housing and Urban Development, becoming the first black cabinet member in US history. He was nominated by President Lyndon Johnson. Weaver died at New York, NY, July 17, 1997.

FLOOD, CURT: BIRTH ANNIVERSARY. Jan 18, 1938. Curtis Charles (Curt) Flood, baseball player, born at Houston, TX. Flood was one of baseball's best center fielders in the 1960s, batting .293 over 15 seasons and playing spectacular defense. After the 1969 season, he refused to accept a trade from the St. Louis Cardinals to the Philadelphia Phillies. "I am not a piece of property to be bought and sold irrespective of my wishes," he said in a letter to Commissioner Bowie Kuhn. The resulting lawsuit went to the Supreme Court where Flood lost. But his stand, taken because he did not want to switch teams, paved the way for the end of baseball's reserve clause and the advent of free agency. Died at Los Angeles, CA, Jan 20, 1997.

GRANT, CARY: BIRTH ANNIVERSARY. Jan 18, 1904. Known as a romantic leading actor, Grant was born at Bristol, England. For more than three decades Grant entertained with his wit, charm, sophistication and personality. His films include *Topper, The Awful Truth, Bringing Up Baby* and *Holiday*. Died at Davenport, IA, Nov 29, 1986.

HARDY, OLIVER: BIRTH ANNIVERSARY. Jan 18, 1892. Born at Atlanta, GA, Hardy teamed up with Stan Laurel in 1926 to form the comedy team of Laurel and Hardy. Among their most popular films: *From Soup to Nuts, Babes in Toyland, Swiss Miss*. Hardy died at Hollywood, Aug 7, 1957.

ILLINOIS SNOW SCULPTING COMPETITION. Jan 18–21. Rockford, IL. Teams from around the state create enormous works of frozen art, as they compete to represent Illinois in national snow sculpting competition. In case of inclement weather, event may be postponed. Sponsor: Rockford Park District. Est attendance: 75,000. For info: Patricia Hayes, Rockford Park District, 1401 N Second St, Rockford, IL 61107-3086. Phone: (815) 987-8800. Fax: (815) 987-1631. E-mail: rpdmail@RockfordParkDistrict.org. Web: www.snowsculpting.org.

"THE JEFFERSONS" TV PREMIERE: ANNIVERSARY. Jan 18, 1975. CBS sitcom about an African-American family (formerly neighbors of the Bunkers on "All in the Family") who moved to Manhattan's East Side, thanks to the success of George Jefferson's chain of dry cleaning stores. Having a format similar to "All in the Family," the show featured a black bigot, George Jefferson. Cast included Sherman Hemsley as George Jefferson, Isabel Sanford as Louise Jefferson and Marla Gibbs as maid Florence. The last episode aired July 23, 1985.

KAYE, DANNY: BIRTH ANNIVERSARY. Jan 18, 1913. American entertainer Danny Kaye was born David Daniel Kaminski at Brooklyn, NY. Kaye became a star in films, international stage performances and television. His most notable films are *The Secret Life of Walter Mitty* (1947) and *Hans Christian Andersen* (1952), as well as the classic *White Christmas*. He hosted the television show *The Danny Kaye Show* in the 1960s. In addition, Kaye helped raise millions of dollars for the United Nations International Children's Emergency Fund (UNICEF) and musicians' pension plans. He died Mar 3, 1987, at Los Angeles, CA.

LEWIS AND CLARK EXPEDITION COMMISSIONED: ANNIVERSARY. Jan 18, 1803. Seeking information on what lay west of the young United States, President Thomas Jefferson sent a confidential letter to Congress on Jan 18, 1803, requesting funds for an exploratory expedition to be led by Captain Meriwether Lewis and Lieutenant William Clark. After the Louisiana Purchase was signed on Apr 30, 1803, the expedition's mission changed: it became a survey of new American land. The "Corps of Discovery" set off May 14 from St. Louis and returned with much information about the land, the peoples there and the flora and fauna on Sept 23, 1806. (See also May 14, Sept 23 and Nov 16.)

January	S	M	T	W	T	F	S
2006	1	2	3	4	5	6	7
	8	9	10	11	12	13	14
	15	16	17	18	19	20	21
	22	23	24	25	26	27	28
	29	30	31				

NATIONAL SOCCER COACHES ASSOCIATION OF AMERICA NATIONAL CONVENTION. Jan 18-22. Pennsylvania Convention Center, Philadelphia, PA. The NSCAA is the largest single-sport coaching organization in the US. The NSCAA convention is the largest annual gathering of soccer coaches in the world. The convention features clinics, lectures, exhibits and national awards. Est attendance: 7,500. For info: NSCAA, 6700 Squibb Rd, Ste 215, Mission, KS 66202. Phone: (800) 458-0678 or (913) 362-1747. Fax: (913) 362-3439. E-mail: info@nscaa.com. Web: www.nscaa.com.

POOH DAY: A.A. MILNE: BIRTH ANNIVERSARY. Jan 18, 1882. Anniversary of the birth of A(lan) A(lexander) Milne, English author, especially remembered for his children's stories: *Winnie the Pooh* and *The House at Pooh Corner*. Also the author of *Mr Pim Passes By*, *When We Were Very Young* and *Now We Are Six*. Born at London, England, died at Hartfield, England, Jan 31, 1956.

ROGET, PETER MARK: BIRTH ANNIVERSARY. Jan 18, 1779. English physician, best known as author of Roget's *Thesaurus of English Words and Phrases*, first published in 1852. Roget was also the inventor of the "log-log" slide rule. He was born at London and died at West Malvern, Worcestershire, England, Sept 12, 1869.

RUFFIN, DAVIS ELI (DAVID): BIRTH ANNIVERSARY. Jan 18, 1941. American popular singer David Ruffin was born at Meridian, MS. He was one of the original members of the Motown singing group the Temptations, which began in Detroit in the 1960s. Ruffin left the group in 1968 to pursue a solo career. He and the other original members of the Temptations were inducted into the Rock and Roll Hall of Fame in 1989. Ruffin died June 1, 1991, at Philadelphia, PA.

"TED MACK'S ORIGINAL AMATEUR HOUR" TV PREMIERE: ANNIVERSARY. Jan 18, 1948. This immensely popular show, featuring host Ted Mack, introduced amateurs performing their talents on live television. It debuted as a regularly scheduled broadcast on the Dumont network. The show had been a long-running success on radio as "Major Bowes' Original Amateur Hour" until the death of Edward Bowes. Mack became host of the radio show a year later. While a few episodes were televised in 1947, the show did not air weekly until this date. The program ran until 1970 and also continued on radio until 1952.

VERSAILLES PEACE CONFERENCE: ANNIVERSARY. Jan 18, 1919. French President Raymond Poincare formally opened the (World War I) Peace Conference at Versailles, France. It proceeded under the chairmanship of Georges Clemenceau. In May the conference disposed of Germany's colonies and delivered a treaty to the German delegates on May 7, 1919, fourth anniversary of the sinking of the *Lusitania*. Final treaty-signing ceremonies were completed at the palace at Versailles, June 28, 1919.

WEBSTER, DANIEL: BIRTH ANNIVERSARY. Jan 18, 1782. American statesman and orator who said, on Apr 6, 1830, "The people's government, made for the people, made by the people, and answerable to the people." Born at Salisbury, NH; died at Marshfield, MA, Oct 24, 1852.

WEEK OF CHRISTIAN UNITY. Jan 18-25. From the Conversion of St. Peter (Jan 18) to the Conversion of St. Paul (Jan 25).

BIRTHDAYS TODAY

John Boorman, 73, filmmaker (*Deliverance, Excalibur*), born Shepperton, England, Jan 18, 1933.

Kevin Costner, 51, actor (*Field of Dreams, Dances with Wolves* [Oscar for directing], *Bull Durham*), born Lynwood, CA, Jan 18, 1955.

Ray Dolby, 73, inventor of the Dolby Sound System for sound recording, born Portland, OR, Jan 18, 1933.

Jane Horrocks, 42, actress (*Little Voice*, "Absolutely Fabulous"), born Lancashire, England, Jan 18, 1964.

Evelyn Lear, 75, opera singer, born New York, NY, Jan 18, 1931.

Jesse L. Martin, 37, actor ("Law & Order," "Ally McBeal"), born Rocky Mountain, VA, Jan 18, 1969.

Mark Messier, 45, hockey player, born Edmonton, AB, Canada, Jan 18, 1961.

JANUARY 19 — THURSDAY
Day 19 — 346 Remaining

CÉZANNE, PAUL: BIRTH ANNIVERSARY. Jan 19, 1839. Post-Impressionist painter, born at Aix-en-Provence, France. Still lifes and landscapes were his preferred subjects. Cézanne died Oct 23, 1906, at Aix.

CONFEDERATE HEROES DAY IN TEXAS. Jan 19. Also called Confederate Memorial Day, observed on anniversary of Robert E. Lee's birthday. Official holiday in Texas.

ETHIOPIA: TIMKET. Jan 19. National holiday. Epiphany in the Ethiopian and Coptic churches. Occurs some years on Jan 20. Also a holiday in Eritrea.

"48 HOURS" TV PREMIERE: ANNIVERSARY. Jan 19, 1988. CBS prime-time newsmagazine program airing each week with first Dan Rather as host, then Leslie Stahl. Recently, the focus has been on crime mysteries.

GET TO KNOW YOUR CUSTOMER DAY. Jan 19 (also Apr 20, July 20 and Oct 19). Set aside the third Thursday of each quarter to get to know your customers even better. For example, salespeople might plan to take a customer out to lunch, not to sell, but to learn more about their needs and why they like doing business with them. Executives could get out from behind the desk and go into the field. For info: Shep Hyken, Shepard Presentations, LLC, 711 Old Ballas Rd, Ste 215, St. Louis, MO 63141. Phone: (314) 692-2200. Fax: (314) 692-2222. E-mail: Shep@hyken.com. Web: www.hyken.com.

HELMS, EDGAR J.: BIRTH ANNIVERSARY. Jan 19, 1863. Born near Malone, NY, Reverend Dr. Helms became a minister to a parish of poor immigrants in Boston's South End. In that capacity he developed the philosophy and organization that eventually became Goodwill Industries. Helms died Dec 23, 1942, at Boston.

JOPLIN, JANIS: BIRTH ANNIVERSARY. Jan 19, 1943. Possibly the most highly regarded white female blues singer of all time, Janis Joplin was born at Port Arthur, TX. Joplin's appearance with Big Brother and the Holding Company at the Monterey International Pop Festival in August 1967 launched her to superstar status. Among her recording hits were "Get It While You Can," "Piece of My Heart" and "Ball and Chain." She died of a heroin overdose Oct 4, 1970, at Hollywood, CA, at the age of 27.

LEE, ROBERT E.: BIRTH ANNIVERSARY. Jan 19, 1807. Greatest military leader of the Confederacy, son of Revolutionary War General Henry (Light-Horse Harry) Lee. His surrender Apr 9, 1865, to Union General Ulysses S. Grant brought an end to the Civil War. Born at Westmoreland County, VA, he died at Lexington, VA, Oct 12, 1870. His birthday is observed in Florida, Kentucky, Louisiana, South Carolina and Tennessee. Observed on third Monday in January in Alabama, Arkansas and Mississippi.

"THE MILLIONAIRE" TV PREMIERE: ANNIVERSARY. Jan 19, 1955. The CBS drama that had all of America hoping to find Michael Anthony on their doorstep. Mr John Beresford Tipton was a millionaire who made a hobby of giving away million dollar checks anonymously to unknown people to see how they handled the sudden wealth. Michael Anthony, played by Marvin Miller, was Mr Tipton's personal secretary and the star of "The Millionaire." No one ever saw Mr Tipton but his voice would greet Anthony at the opening of each show and issue instructions for delivery of the next check. Anthony would then find the recipient and give him or her the check, explaining that the recipient had to agree never to divulge the amount or how it was acquired.

POE, EDGAR ALLAN: BIRTH ANNIVERSARY. Jan 19, 1809. American poet and story writer, called "America's most famous man of letters." Born at Boston, MA, he was orphaned in dire poverty in 1811 and was raised by Virginia merchant John Allan. In 1836 he married his 13-year-old cousin, Virginia Clemm. A magazine editor of note, he is best remembered for his poetry (especially "The Raven") and for his tales of suspense. Died at Baltimore, MD, Oct 7, 1849.

SLAMDANCE 2006. Jan 19–27. Park City, Utah. 12th annual. Independent film festival "by filmmakers for filmmakers." Feature-length films and shorts. Numerous awards given. Screenplay competition during the year. For info: Slamdance, 5634 Melrose Ave, Los Angeles, CA 90038. Phone: (323) 466-1786. Fax: (323) 466-1784. E-mail: mail@slamdance.com. Web: www.slamdance.com.

SUNDANCE FILM FESTIVAL. Jan 19–29. Park City, UT. "The premier US festival for independent filmmakers." More than 130 feature-length films and more than 90 short films screened. Est attendance: 35,000. For info: Sundance Institute, PO Box 3630, Salt Lake City, UT 84110. Phone: (801) 328-FILM. E-mail: festivalinfo@sundance.org. Web: www.sundance.org.

TIN CAN PATENT: ANNIVERSARY. Jan 19, 1825. Ezra Daggett and Thomas Kensett obtained a patent for a process for storing food in tin cans.

WAR CRIMES TRIBUNAL APPOINTED (JAPAN): 60th ANNIVERSARY. Jan 19, 1946. An international tribunal for the trial of far eastern war criminals was appointed by General Douglas MacArthur on Jan 19, 1946. The trial began at Tokyo on May 3, 1946, and ended more than two years later when the judgments were read, Nov 4–12, 1948. Of the 28 defendants 25 were brought to trial. Seven were sentenced to death by hanging, 16 were sentenced to life imprisonment and two were given lesser prison terms. See also: "Tojo Hideki: Execution Anniversary" (Dec 23).

WATT, JAMES: BIRTH ANNIVERSARY. Jan 19, 1736 (OS). Scottish engineer and inventor, born at Greenock, Scotland. The modern steam engine grew out of his efficiency-improving inventions. Died at Heathfield, England, Aug 25, 1819.

WOMEN'S HEALTHY WEIGHT DAY. Jan 19. A day to honor American women of all sizes and confirm that beauty, talent and love cannot be weighed. Winners of the Women's Healthy Weight Day awards will be announced—businesses that portray size diversity and reject the national obsession with thinness that is shattering the lives of women, young girls and their families. News releases, 2006 awards and consumer handouts available on website. For info: Francie M. Berg, Healthy Weight Network, 402 S 14th St, Hettinger, ND 58639. E-mail: fmberg@healthy weight.net (please put "Berg-Healthy Weight Week" in subject line). Web: www.healthyweight.net.

BIRTHDAYS TODAY

Desi Arnaz, Jr, 53, singer, actor, born Los Angeles, CA, Jan 19, 1953.

Michael Crawford, 64, actor, singer (*Phantom of the Opera*), born Salisbury, Wiltshire, England, Jan 19, 1942.

Drea de Matteo, 34, actress ("The Sopranos," "Joey"), born Queens, NY, Jan 19, 1972.

Phil Everly, 67, singer, with brother Don (The Everly Brothers), born Chicago, IL, Jan 19, 1939.

Shelley Fabares, 64, actress ("The Donna Reed Show," "Coach," sang "Johnny Angel"), born Santa Monica, CA, Jan 19, 1942 (some sources say 1944).

January *2006*	S	M	T	W	T	F	S
	1	2	3	4	5	6	7
	8	9	10	11	12	13	14
	15	16	17	18	19	20	21
	22	23	24	25	26	27	28
	29	30	31				

Richard Lester, 74, director (*The Four Musketeers, Superman II & III*), born Philadelphia, PA, Jan 19, 1932.

Robert MacNeil, 75, broadcast journalist, born Montreal, QC, Canada, Jan 19, 1931.

Dolly Parton, 60, singer ("Jolene"), actress (*Nine to Five*), born Sevier County, TN, Jan 19, 1946.

William Ragsdale, 45, actor ("Brother's Keeper," "Herman's Head"), born El Dorado, AR, Jan 19, 1961.

Simon Rattle, 51, British orchestra conductor, born Liverpool, England, Jan 19, 1955.

Jean Stapleton, 83, actress (*Klute*; Emmy for "All in the Family"), born Jeanne Murray at New York, NY, Jan 19, 1923.

Jeff Van Gundy, 44, basketball coach, born Inkster, MI, Jan 19, 1962.

Shawn Wayans, 35, actor (*Scary Movie*, "In Living Color"), born New York, NY, Jan 19, 1971.

Fritz Weaver, 80, actor (*Holocaust, Marathon Man*), born Philadelphia, PA, Jan 19, 1926.

JANUARY 20 — FRIDAY
Day 20 — 345 Remaining

AQUARIUS, THE WATER CARRIER. Jan 20–Feb 19. In the astronomical/astrological zodiac, which divides the sun's apparent orbit into 12 segments, the period Jan 20–Feb 19 is identified, traditionally, as the sun-sign of Aquarius, the Water Carrier. The ruling planet is Uranus or Saturn.

ARBOR DAY IN FLORIDA. Jan 20. The third Friday in January is Arbor Day in Florida, a ceremonial day.

AZERBAIJAN: MARTYRS' DAY. Jan 20. National holiday. Commemorates the Azeris killed by Soviet troops, Jan 20, 1990, as they fought for independence.

BRAZIL: NOSSO SENHOR DO BONFIM FESTIVAL. Jan 20–30. Salvador, Bahia. Our Lord of the Happy Ending Festival is one of Salvador's most colorful religious feasts. Climax comes with people carrying water to pour over church stairs and sidewalks to cleanse them of impurities.

BRAZIL: SAN SEBASTIAN'S DAY. Jan 20. Patron saint of Rio de Janeiro.

BURNS, GEORGE: BIRTH ANNIVERSARY. Jan 20, 1896. Comedian George Burns was born at New York City. He began in vaudeville without much success until he teamed up with Gracie Allen, who became his wife. As Burns and Allen, the two had a long career on radio, in film and with their hit TV show, "The George Burns and Gracie Allen Show." Later he played the roles of God and the Devil in the *Oh, God!* movies. He lived to be 100 and died Mar 9, 1996, at Los Angeles, CA.

FELLINI, FEDERICO: BIRTH ANNIVERSARY. Jan 20, 1920. Director and screenwriter Federico Fellini was born at Rimini, Italy. Four of Fellini's movies won Oscars for best foreign-language film: *La Strada* (1956), *The Nights of Cabiria* (1957), *8½* (1963) and *Amarcord* (1974). He received an honorary Oscar in 1993 in recognition of his cinematic accomplishments. Fellini died Oct 31, 1993, at Rome.

GRAY, HAROLD LINCOLN: BIRTH ANNIVERSARY. Jan 20, 1894. The creator of "Little Orphan Annie" was born at Kankakee, IL. The comic strip featuring the 12-year-old Annie, her dog, Sandy, and her mentor and guardian Oliver "Daddy" Warbucks began appearing in the *Chicago Tribune* in 1924. While controversial for its strong conservative views, the strip was highly popular for its stories demonstrating the values of perseverance, independence and courage. Gray created the strip for 44 years until his death May 9, 1968, at La Jolla, CA, at age 74.

GUINEA-BISSAU: NATIONAL HEROES DAY. Jan 20. National holiday.

JOHN MARSHALL APPOINTED CHIEF JUSTICE: ANNIVERSARY. Jan 20, 1801. John Marshall was appointed the fourth chief justice of the US Supreme Court.

LEE, RICHARD HENRY: BIRTH ANNIVERSARY. Jan 20, 1732. Signer of the Declaration of Independence. Born at Westmoreland County, VA, he died June 19, 1794, at his birthplace.

LESOTHO: ARMY DAY. Jan 20. Lesotho.

LONGHORN WORLD CHAMPIONSHIP RODEO. Jan 20–22. Tulsa Convention Center, Tulsa, OK. 16th annual. More than 500 cowboys and cowgirls compete in six professional contests ranging from bronc riding to big, bad BONUS bull riding! Free beginners horsemanship clinic 40 minutes before performances. Qualifying rodeo for Longhorn's Championship Finals Rodeo in Murfreesboro, TN. Featuring colorful opening and pageantry. Season opener for Longhorn rodeos nationally. Est attendance: 16,000. For info: W Bruce Lehrke, Pres, Longhorn World Chmpshp Rodeo Inc, PO Box 70159, Nashville, TN 37207. Phone: (615) 876-1016. Fax: (615) 876-4685. E-mail: info@longhornrodeo.com. Web: www.longhornrodeo.com.

MILWAUKEE BOAT SHOW. Jan 20–29. Wisconsin Expo Center, Milwaukee, WI. This event brings together buyers and sellers of sail- and powerboats, including fishing boats, pontoons and boating accessories, as well as vacation property and travel destinations. Est attendance: 25,000. For info: Adam Starr, Show Span, Inc, 2121 Celebration Dr NE, Grand Rapids, MI 49525. Phone: (616) 447-2860. Fax: (616) 447-2861. E-mail: events@showspan.com. Web: www.showspan.com.

NC RV AND CAMPING SHOW. Jan 20–22. Charlotte Merchandise Mart, Charlotte, NC. A display of the latest in recreation vehicles and accessories by various dealers. Est attendance: 11,000. For info: Apple Rock Advertising & Promotion, 1200 Eastchester Dr, High Point, NC 27265. Phone: (336) 881-7100. Fax: (336) 883-7198. E-mail: rvshows@applerock.com. Web: www.applerock.com.

RV WORKERS AND WORKAMPERS DAY. Jan 20–21 (tentative). Idea exchange in conjunction with the Workamper Job Fair in Quartzsite, AZ. Est attendance: 2,500. For info: Jaimie Hall, 127 Rainbow Dr, #2780, Livingston, TX 77399-1027. Phone: (928) 607-3181. Fax: (561) 892-2837. E-mail: calamity jaimie@escapees.com. Web: www.rvsleuths.com.

US HOSTAGES IN IRAN RELEASED: 25th ANNIVERSARY. Jan 20, 1981. The Iran Hostage Crisis ended with the release of 52 US citizens after 444 days of captivity. The deal was announced minutes after the swearing in of President Ronald Reagan.

US REVOLUTIONARY WAR: CESSATION OF HOSTILITIES: ANNIVERSARY. Jan 20, 1783. The British and US Commissioners signed a preliminary "Cessation of Hostilities," which was ratified by England's King George III Feb 14 and led to the Treaties of Paris and Versailles, Sept 3, 1783, ending the war.

BIRTHDAYS TODAY

Edwin "Buzz" Aldrin, 76, former astronaut, one of first three men on moon, born Montclair, NJ, Jan 20, 1930.

James Denton, 43, actor ("The Pretender," "Desperate Housewives"), born Nashville, TN, Jan 20, 1963.

Arte Johnson, 72, comedian, actor (Emmy for "Rowan & Martin's Laugh-In"), born Benton Harbor, MI, Jan 20, 1934 (some sources say 1929).

Lorenzo Lamas, 48, actor ("Falcon Crest," "Renegade"), born Los Angeles, CA, Jan 20, 1958.

David Lynch, 60, director ("Twin Peaks," *Blue Velvet*), writer, producer, born Missoula, MT, Jan 20, 1946.

Bill Maher, 50, comedian, TV host ("Politically Incorrect with Bill Maher"), born New York, NY, Jan 20, 1956.

Patricia Neal, 80, actress (*Breakfast at Tiffany's, Hud, The Subject Was Roses*), born Packard, KY, Jan 20, 1926.

Natan (Anatoly) Scharansky, 58, expatriate Soviet dissident, born Donetsk, USSR, Jan 20, 1948.

Skeet Ulrich, 36, actor (*Scream*), born New York, NY, Jan 20, 1970 (some sources say 1969).

Otis Dewey "Slim" Whitman, 82, singer (first country performer to play at the London Palladium), born Tampa, FL, Jan 20, 1924.

JANUARY 21 — SATURDAY
Day 21 — 344 Remaining

ALLEN, ETHAN: BIRTH ANNIVERSARY. Jan 21, 1738. Revolutionary War hero and leader of the Vermont "Green Mountain Boys." Born at Litchfield, CT, he died at Burlington, VT, Feb 12, 1789.

BALD EAGLE APPRECIATION DAYS. Jan 21–22. River City Mall, Keokuk, IA. Features trained personnel stationed at observation points for viewing the American bald eagle. Indoor activities include a wood-carver's show and a rock, gem and artifact show. Also featuring live eagle demonstrations. Est attendance: 10,000. For info: Kirk Brandenberger, Dir of Tourism, Keokuk Area Conv and Tourism Bureau, 329 Main St, Keokuk, IA 52632. Phone: (800) 383-1219 or (319) 524-5599. E-mail: keokukia@interl.net. Web: www.keokukiowatourism.org.

BALDWIN, ROGER NASH: BIRTH ANNIVERSARY. Jan 21, 1884. Founder of the American Civil Liberties Union, called the "country's unofficial agitator for, and defender of, its civil liberties." Born at Wellesley, MA, he died Aug 26, 1981, at Ridgewood, NJ.

BRECKINRIDGE, JOHN CABELL: BIRTH ANNIVERSARY. Jan 21, 1821. 14th vice president of the US (1857–61), serving under President James Buchanan. Born at Lexington, KY; died there May 17, 1875.

BROWNING, JOHN MOSES: BIRTH ANNIVERSARY. Jan 21, 1855. World-famous gunmaker and inventor who was taught gunsmithing by his Mormon pioneer father, Jonathan Browning, was born at Ogden, UT. Starting the J.M. & M.S. Browning Arms Company with his brother, he designed guns for Winchester, Remington, Stevens and Colt arms companies, as well as American and European armies. Browning had more gun patents than any other gunsmith in the world. He is best known for inventing the machine gun in 1890 and the automatic pistol in 1896. He died suddenly Nov 26, 1926, at age 71, while at Belgium on business. The company he founded, known now as Browning Arms Company, is located at Morgan, UT.

CHINESE NEW YEAR FESTIVAL. Jan 21–Feb 11. San Francisco, CA. North America's largest Chinese community salutes the Year of the Dog, Lunar Year 4704. Activities include Chinatown Flower Fair (Jan 21–22); Miss Chinatown USA Pageant (Feb 4) with Coronation Ball (Feb 10); Chinese New Year Parade (Feb 11); Chinatown Community Street Fair (Feb 11–12). These events showcase the diversity of Chinese culture from Chinese opera and ballet, traditional dance and ancient dynastic costumes to martial arts. Booths feature cooking demonstrations, calligraphy and arts and crafts. Est attendance: 700,000. For info: Chinese Chamber of Commerce, New Year Festival, 730 Sacramento, San Francisco, CA 94108. Phone: (415) 391-9680. Fax: (415) 982-4720. Web: www.chineseparade.com.

CRAB AND STEAK DINNER. Jan 21. Cornelius, OR. Cornelius volunteer firefighters host this 10th annual event featuring Oregon Dungeness crabs and/or 16-ounce New York–cut steaks, clam chowder soup, salad, dinner roll, Oregon strawberries and other refreshments. Proceeds support volunteer firefighter/EMT training, public education programs (CPR) and purchase of firefighting/medical equipment. Annually, the third Saturday in January. Est attendance: 550. For info: Cornelius Firefighter Assn, 1355 N Barlow St, Cornelius, OR 97113-8912. Phone: (503) 357-3840. E-mail: fire@ci.cornelius.or.us. Web: www.corneliusfire.org.

DIOR, CHRISTIAN: BIRTH ANNIVERSARY. Jan 21, 1905. Influential French fashion designer who was the world's premier style maker after World War II up until the 1950s. He was also one of the first designers to utilize licensing to help create his own brand. Born at Granville, France, Dior died on Oct 24, 1957, at Montecatini, Italy.

EAGLE DAY AT THE LAKE. Jan 21. Wyandotte County Lake Park, Kansas City, KS. The public is invited to the environmental learning center to see a live bald eagle presentation and other wildlife presentations. Eagle viewing over the lake and children's activities will be available all day. For info: Mr & Mrs F.L. Schlagle Library, 4051 West Dr, Wyandotte County Lake Park, Kansas City, KS 66109. Phone: (913) 299-2384. Fax: (913) 299-9967. E-mail: aporter@kckpl.lib.ks.us. Web: www.kckpl.lib.ks.us/schlagle.

EAGLE DAYS IN SPRINGFIELD. Jan 21–22. Springfield Conservation Nature Center, Springfield, MO. Celebrate the return of bald eagles to Springfield through indoor programs with a live eagle and outdoor viewing opportunities. Est attendance: 1,000. For info: Springfield Conservation Nature Center, 4600 S Chrisman Ave, Springfield, MO 65804. Phone: (417) 888-4237. Fax: (417) 888-4241. Web: www.missouriconservation.com.

FARMERS MARKET. Jan 21. El Centro, CA. Come enjoy our fresh, locally grown produce. There will also be plenty of crafters, food and entertainment. Est attendance: 25,000. For info: El Centro Chamber of Commerce, Box 3006, El Centro, CA 92244. Phone: (760) 352-3681. Fax: (760) 352-3246. E-mail: generalinfo@elcentrochamber.com. Web: www.elcentrochamber.com.

FIRST CONCORDE FLIGHT: 30th ANNIVERSARY. Jan 21, 1976. The supersonic Concorde airplane was put into service by Britain and France. The Concorde ended flights on Oct 24, 2003—bringing an end to supersonic air travel.

GASPARILLA EXTRAVAGANZA AND PIRATE FEST. Jan 21. Tampa, FL. As any Tampa resident can attest, "Gasparilla" means boats, pirates, parades, merriment and more. The "Extravaganza" is an alcohol-free family event featuring the Children's Gasparilla Parade and one of the largest fireworks displays in the country. The following Saturday, Jan 28, The Southwest Airlines Gasparilla Pirate Fest features 700 citizens, members of Ye Mystic Krewe, reenacting the 1904 invasion of Tampa by a band of pirates. For info: EventMakers Corp of Tampa, 3701 W Azeele St, Tampa, FL 33609. Phone: (813) 353-8108. E-mail: events@Eventmakers-FL.com. Web: www.gasparillapiratefest.com and www.gasparillaextravaganza.com.

January 2006

S	M	T	W	T	F	S
1	2	3	4	5	6	7
8	9	10	11	12	13	14
15	16	17	18	19	20	21
22	23	24	25	26	27	28
29	30	31				

HULA BOWL. Jan 21. Aloha Stadium, Honolulu, Oahu, HI. 60th annual. College senior all-star football classic. Est attendance: 50,000. For info: Hula Bowl. Web: www.hulabowlmaui.com.

JACKSON, THOMAS JONATHAN "STONEWALL": BIRTH ANNIVERSARY. Jan 21, 1824. Confederate general and one of the most famous soldiers of the American Civil War, best known as "Stonewall" Jackson. Born at Clarksburg, VA (now WV). He died of wounds received in battle near Chancellorsville, VA, May 10, 1863.

KIWANIS INTERNATIONAL: ANNIVERSARY. Jan 21, 1915. First Kiwanis Club chartered at Detroit, MI.

LONGWOOD GARDENS WELCOME SPRING. Jan 21–Apr 4. Kennett Square, PA. Indoor conservatory display features thousands of colorful, fragrant spring bulbs, green lawns, orchids and roses. Est attendance: 90,000. For info: Longwood Gardens, PO Box 501, Kennett Sq, PA 19348-0501. Phone: (610) 377-1000. Web: www.longwoodgardens.org.

MARGARET BRENT DEMANDS A POLITICAL VOICE: ANNIVERSARY. Jan 21, 1648. Margaret Brent made her claim as America's first feminist by demanding a voice and vote for herself in the Maryland colonial assembly. Brent came to America in 1638 and was the first woman to own property in Maryland. At the time of her demands she was serving as secretary to Governor Leonard Calvert. She was ejected from the meetings, but when Calvert died she became his executor and acting governor, presiding over the General Assembly.

NATIONAL HUGGING DAY™. Jan 21. Since hugging is something everyone can do and since it is a healthful form of touching, this day should be spent hugging anyone who will accept a hug, especially family and friends. The most "Huggable People" of the year will be announced. Nominations accepted through Jan 10. For more info, please send SASE to: Kevin C. Zaborney, 2023 Vickory Rd, Caro, MI 48723. Phone: (989) 673-6696. E-mail: revkev@avci.net. Web: www.nationalhuggingday.com.

PHILIPPINES: ATI-ATIHAN FESTIVAL. Jan 21–22. Kalibo, Aklan. One of the most colorful celebrations in the Philippines, the Ati-Atihan Festival commemorates the peace pact between the Ati of Panay (pygmies) and the Malays, who were early migrants in the islands. The townspeople blacken their bodies with soot, don colorful and bizarre costumes and sing and dance in the streets. The festival also celebrates the Feast Day of Santo Niño (the infant Jesus). Annually, the third weekend in January.

SQUIRREL APPRECIATION DAY. Jan 21. A day set aside each year to help the public become more aware of wildlife rehabilitation. For info: Christy Hargrove, 25 Jazaka Ridge Ln, Swannanoa, NC 28778. E-mail: christy@wnc-rehab.org. Web: www.wnc-rehab.org.

STONEWALL JACKSON'S BIRTHDAY CELEBRATION. Jan 21. Stonewall Jackson House, Lexington, VA. Celebrates the birthday of Stonewall Jackson. For info: Stonewall Jackson House, 8 E Washington St, Lexington, VA 24450. Phone: (540) 463-2552. E-mail: sjh1@rockbridge.net. Web: www.stonewalljackson.org.

TIP-UP TOWN USA™. Jan 21–22 (also Jan 28–29). Houghton Lake, MI. 56th annual. Michigan's largest winter family festival featuring ice-fishing contests, softball on the ice, polar bear dip, parade, carnival, vendors, arts and crafts, fireworks, Poker Runs & Scavenger Hunts, Radar Runs and much more. Annually, the 3rd and 4th weekends of January. Est attendance: 35,000. For info: Chamber of Commerce, 1625 W Houghton Lake Dr, Houghton Lake, MI 48629. Phone: (800) 248-5253. E-mail: hlcc@iserv.net. Web: www.houghtonlakechamber.org.

WINTERFEST. Jan 21. Burton, MI. All kinds of cans and brewery memorabilia such as steins, coasters, signs, mirrors, bottles, neon signs, etc. $12 general admission includes display table if desired, available on first-come, first-served basis. Also includes food and beverages and door prize raffle tickets. Kids under eight free. Est attendance: 150. For info: Gene Goulet, Pres, Mid-Michigan Chapter, Brewery Collectibles Club of America, 5306 Lippincott, Burton, MI 48519. Phone: (810) 742-5353. E-mail: dave vanh@aol.com. Web: www.bcca.com.

WISCONSIN DELLS FLAKE OUT FESTIVAL. Jan 21–22. Wisconsin Dells, WI. An exciting winter festival featuring Wisconsin's only state-sanctioned snow sculpting competition. Other activities include ice carving demonstrations, live entertainment, snowman making competition, totally tubular snow slide, turkey bowling, Eskimo Pie eating contest, pony rides, sleigh rides, glowing hot-air balloons, food, music and fireworks. Est attendance: 30,000. For info: Wisconsin Dells Visitors & Convention Bureau, PO Box 390, Wisconsin Dells, WI 53965. Phone: (800) 223-3557. E-mail: info@wisdells.com. Web: www.wisdells.com.

WOLFMAN JACK: BIRTH ANNIVERSARY. Jan 21, 1938. Wolfman Jack was born Robert Smith at Brooklyn, NY. He became famous as a disc jockey for radio stations at Mexico in the 1960s. Wolfman Jack was influential as a border radio voice because the Mexican station broadcast at 250,000 watts, five times the legal limit for American stations at the time, and therefore he was heard over a vast part of the US. During his night shift he played blues, hillbilly and other black and white music that wasn't getting a lot of exposure. He later appeared on American radio, movies and television as an icon of 1960s radio. Wolfman Jack died July 1, 1995, at Belvidere, NC.

BIRTHDAYS TODAY

Robby Benson, 50, actor ("Search for Tomorrow," *Ode to Billie Joe*), born Robin Segal, Dallas, TX, Jan 21, 1956.

Geena Davis, 49, actress (Oscar for *The Accidental Tourist; Thelma and Louise*, "Buffalo Bill"), born Ware, MA, Jan 21, 1957.

Mac Davis, 64, actor, songwriter ("The Mac Davis Show," *North Dallas Forty*), born Lubbock, TX, Jan 21, 1942.

Placido Domingo, 65, opera singer, one of the "Three Tenors," born Madrid, Spain, Jan 21, 1941.

Jill Eikenberry, 59, actress ("LA Law"), born New Haven, CT, Jan 21, 1947.

Jack William Nicklaus, 66, golfer, born Columbus, OH, Jan 21, 1940.

Billy Ocean, 56, musician, songwriter, born Leslie Charles at Trinidad, West Indies, Jan 21, 1950.

Hakeem Abdul Olajuwon, 43, former basketball player, born Lagos, Nigeria, Jan 21, 1963.

Detlef Schrempf, 43, former basketball player, born Leverkusen, West Germany, Jan 21, 1963.

Paul Scofield, 84, actor (*A Man for All Seasons, Quiz Show*; stage: *A Man for All Seasons*), born Hurstpierpoint, England, Jan 21, 1922.

JANUARY 22 — SUNDAY
Day 22 — 343 Remaining

ALLIES TAKE NEW GUINEA: ANNIVERSARY. Jan 22, 1943. In the first land victory over the Japanese in World War II, American and Australian soldiers overcame the last pockets of resistance west and south of Sanananda on New Guinea. Three thousand Allies were killed in the battle. The Japanese lost 7,000. Of the 350 prisoners taken, most were Chinese and Korean laborers attached to the Japanese forces. Almost no Japanese allowed themselves to be taken prisoner, preferring to commit hara-kiri.

AMPÈRE, ANDRE: BIRTH ANNIVERSARY. Jan 22, 1775. Physicist, student of electrical and magnetic phenomena, founder of the science of electrodynamics. Born at Lyons, France, from his early childhood, tragedy and depression pursued him. His father was executed during the French Revolution. Ampère died at Marseilles, France, June 10, 1836. The epitaph he selected for his tombstone was *tandem felix* ("happy at last"). The ampere, a unit of electrical current, is named for him.

ANSWER YOUR CAT'S QUESTION DAY. Jan 22. If you will stop what you are doing and take a look at your cat, you will observe that the cat is looking at you with a serious question. Med-

itate upon it, then answer the question! Annually, Jan 22. [©2003 by WH.] For info: Thomas & Ruth Roy, Wellcat Holidays, 2418 Long Ln, Lebanon, PA 17046. Phone: (717) 279-0184. E-mail: info@wellcat.com. Web: www.wellcat.com.

BACON, FRANCIS: BIRTH ANNIVERSARY. Jan 22, 1561 (OS). Statesman and essayist, born at London, England. One may guess that Bacon was of short stature as he wrote (*Apothegms*), "Wise nature did never put her precious jewels into a garret four stories high: and therefore . . . exceeding tall men had ever very empty heads." Died at London, Apr 9, 1626 (OS).

BALANCHINE, GEORGE: BIRTH ANNIVERSARY. Jan 22, 1904. Born Georgi Militonovitch Balanchivadze at St. Petersburg, Russia, George Balanchine became one of the leading influences in 20th-century ballet. He choreographed more than 200 ballets including *Concerto Barocco, Apollo, Orpheus, Firebird, Swan Lake, Waltz Academy* and *The Nutcracker*. In 1933 he was invited to the US by Boston philanthropist Lincoln Kirstein to establish a school for American dancers. Together they founded the School of American Ballet in 1934 and then formed several ballet companies, including the New York City Ballet, which was led by Balanchine. Died at New York, NY, Apr 30, 1983.

BYRON, GEORGE GORDON: BIRTH ANNIVERSARY. Jan 22, 1788. Romantic poet, born at London, England. Described as "Mad, bad, and dangerous to know" by Lady Caroline Lamb. Byron died of fever at Missolonghi, Greece, Apr 19, 1824, while fighting for Greek independence.

CELEBRATION OF LIFE DAY. Jan 22. A time to honor our children and grandchildren in America. Each child and each life is to be held as a precious gift and should be treated with the highest respect and dignity. For info: Judith Natale, Women of Freedom, USA, PO Box 493703, Redding, CA 96049-3703. E-mail: WomenofFreedom@aol.com.

"EMERGENCY!" TV PREMIERE: ANNIVERSARY. Jan 22, 1972. This NBC program was introduced in midseason up against "All in the Family." It surprised everyone by becoming quite popular. The fast-paced action of the fire department paramedics saving lives by giving victims emergency treatment and then taking them to the hospital demonstrated the steps taken during actual emergency situations. The last episode aired Sept 3, 1977.

GRIFFITH, DAVID (LEWELYN) WARK: BIRTH ANNIVERSARY. Jan 22, 1875. D.W. Griffith, pioneer producer-director in the American motion picture industry, best remembered for his film *Birth of a Nation* (1915). Born at LaGrange, KY. Died at Hollywood, CA, July 23, 1948.

HOWARD, ROBERT E.: 100th BIRTH ANNIVERSARY. Jan 22, 1906. Born at Peaster, TX, Howard was to become one of the great and prolific pulp fiction writers of the 1920s and 1930s. He is most famous for creating Conan the Barbarian. Committed suicide at Cross Plains, TX, Jan 11, 1936.

"LAUGH-IN" TV PREMIERE: ANNIVERSARY. Jan 22, 1968. Actually the name of this NBC comedy was "Rowan and Martin's Laugh-In." Funny men Dan Rowan and Dick Martin hosted the show, but they seemed staid next to the show's other regulars, most of whom were young unknowns, including Dennis Allen, Chelsea Brown, Judy Carne, Ruth Buzzi, Ann Elder, Richard Dawson, Teresa Graves, Arte Johnson, Goldie Hawn, Alan Sues, Jo Anne Worley and Lily Tomlin. The show moved fast from gag to gag with heads popping out of bushes or doors in the big wall. The show brought a new energy to comedy as well as new phrases to our vocabulary ("You bet your sweet bippy," "Sock it to me"). The last telecast was May 14, 1973.

MOON PHASE: LAST QUARTER. Jan 22. Moon enters Last Quarter phase at 10:14 AM, EST.

NATIONAL CREATIVE FRUGALITY WEEK. Jan 22–28. Christmas has come and gone and for many Americans the credit card bills are now rolling in. Give your budget a break by participating in National Creative Frugality Week. Participants are encouraged to have fun as they experiment with frugality and resourcefulness. Whether you're new to frugal living or have been doing it for years, use this holiday to challenge yourself to learn a new skill or try a new money-saving technique. For info: Nancy Twigg, Editor, Counting the Cost Newsletter, 8715 Brucewood Ln, Knoxville, TN 37923. Phone: (865) 531-3947. E-mail: editor @countingthecost.com. Web: www.creativefrugality.com.

NATIONAL HANDWRITING ANALYSIS WEEK. Jan 22–28. To inform the public that handwriting is a form of behavior that can be analyzed for personality traits; that handwriting originates in the brain; that handwriting style, like personality, remains constant over a period of time while reflecting development; that personality traits can be changed by making changes in one's handwriting. Annually, a week in January to include National Handwriting Day (John Hancock's birthday, January 23, 1737 [NS]). Sponsor: American Handwriting Analysis Fdtn (AHAF), PO Box 6201, San Jose, CA 95150. Phone: (800) 826-7774. Web: www.handwritingfoundation.org. Additional contact: American Association of Handwriting Analysts, 820 W Maple St, Hinsdale, IL 60521. Phone: (708) 323-5647.

NATIONAL NURSE ANESTHETISTS WEEK. Jan 22–28. To provide recognition for the nation's more than 30,000 certified registered nurse anesthetists (CRNAs), who have been providing safe anesthesia care for more than 100 years. CRNAs administer more than 65 percent of the anesthesia in the US each year. For info: Amer Assn of Nurse Anesthetists, 222 S Prospect, Park Ridge, IL 60068. Phone: (847) 692-7050. Fax: (847) 692-6968. Web: www.aana.com.

"OZARK JUBILEE" TV PREMIERE: ANNIVERSARY. Jan 22, 1955. ABC country and western music show hosted by Red Foley from Springfield, MO. Brenda "(Open Up Your Heart and) Let the Sunshine In" Lee appeared on the show at age 10 as one of the regulars. Other regulars included Smiley Burnette, Bobby Lord, Wanda Jackson, Suzi Arden and Webb Pierce.

PONSELLE, ROSA: BIRTH ANNIVERSARY. Jan 22, 1897. Formerly Rosa Melba Ponzilla, soprano Ponselle was born at Meriden, CT. Her career changed direction from vaudeville to opera when she was discovered by Enrico Caruso at the age of 21. Ponselle made her operatic debut at the Met in Verdi's *La forza del destino*. Her career spanned 19 seasons at the Met and included performances at London and Florence. Ponselle died May 25, 1981, at Baltimore.

QUEEN VICTORIA: DEATH ANNIVERSARY. Jan 22, 1901. Queen Victoria died at age 82 after a reign of 64 years, the longest in British history. She had ruled over the one-quarter of the world that was the British Empire. Born May 24, 1819, at London, she died at Osborne, England.

January *2006*	S	M	T	W	T	F	S
	1	2	3	4	5	6	7
	8	9	10	11	12	13	14
	15	16	17	18	19	20	21
	22	23	24	25	26	27	28
	29	30	31				

***ROE v WADE* DECISION: ANNIVERSARY.** Jan 22, 1973. In the case of *Roe v Wade*, the US Supreme Court struck down state laws restricting abortions during the first six months of pregnancy. In the following decades debate has continued to rage between those who believe a woman has a right to choose whether to continue a pregnancy and those who believe that aborting such a pregnancy is murder of an unborn child.

SAINT VINCENT: FEAST DAY. Jan 22. Spanish deacon and martyr who died AD 304. Patron saint of wine growers. Old weather lore says if there is sun on this day, good wine crops may be expected in the ensuing season.

SOLO–PRENEURING WEEK. Jan 22–28. Control your own destiny by taking charge of your work and your life. This week is set aside to plan and prepare for the work you were meant to do, and to celebrate those who are following a path of their own choosing. Whether you are an employee, a business owner or just contemplating your place in the workforce, resolve to learn how you can do work that is satisfying and fulfilling, create your own job security, prepare for an uncertain future and have fun doing work you love. Free articles available for publishers and webmasters at IdeaLady.com/content.htm. For info: Cathy Stucker, Special Interests Publishing, 4646 Hwy 6, PMB 123, Sugar Land, TX 77478. Phone: (281) 265-7342. E-mail: cathy@ idealady.com. Web: www.idealady.com.

STRINDBERG, AUGUST: BIRTH ANNIVERSARY. Jan 22, 1849. Swedish novelist and dramatist often called Sweden's greatest playwright. Born at Stockholm and died there of cancer on May 14, 1912, at age 63.

UKRAINE: UKRAINIAN DAY. Jan 22. National holiday. Commemorates the proclamation of the Ukrainian National Republic, Jan 22, 1918. Independence was short-lived, however; by 1921 Ukraine had become part of the Soviet Union. It gained its independence from the Soviet Union in 1991.

UPJOHN, RICHARD: BIRTH ANNIVERSARY. Jan 22, 1802. American architect and founder of the American Institute of Architects in 1857. A Gothic revivalist, he designed many churches. Among his works were Trinity Chapel, New York, NY; Corn Exchange Bank Building, New York, NY; Central Congregational Church, Boston, MA. Born at Shaftesbury, England, he died Aug 17, 1878, at Garrison, NY.

VINSON, FRED M.: BIRTH ANNIVERSARY. Jan 22, 1890. The 13th chief justice of the US, born at Louisa, KY. Served in the House of Representatives, appointed director of war mobilization during WWII and secretary of the treasury under Harry Truman. Nominated by Truman to succeed Harlan F. Stone as chief justice of the US Supreme Court. Died at Washington, DC, Sept 8, 1953.

BIRTHDAYS TODAY

Linda Blair, 47, actress (*The Exorcist, Airport*), born Westport, CT, Jan 22, 1959.

Seymour Cassel, 69, actor (*Faces, Dick Tracy, Honeymoon in Vegas*), born Detroit, MI, Jan 22, 1937.

Olivia D'Abo, 39, actress ("The Wonder Years," "The Single Guy"), born London, England, Jan 22, 1967.

Balthazar Getty, 31, actor (*Lost Highway*), born Los Angeles, CA, Jan 22, 1975.

John Hurt, 66, actor ("And the Band Played On," *The Elephant Man*), born Lincolnshire, England, Jan 22, 1940.

Diane Lane, 41, actress (*Unfaithful, A Walk on the Moon, A Little Romance*), born New York, NY, Jan 22, 1965.

Piper Laurie, 74, actress (*Fighting for My Daughter*, "Twin Peaks"), born Rosetta Jacobs at Detroit, MI, Jan 22, 1932.

Christopher Masterson, 26, actor ("Malcolm in the Middle," *My Best Friend's Wedding*), born Long Island, NY, Jan 22, 1980.

Steve Perry, 57, lead singer (Journey), born Hanford, CA, Jan 22, 1949.

Joseph Wambaugh, 69, ex-police officer, author (*The Blooding, Fugitive Nights*), born East Pittsburgh, PA, Jan 22, 1937.

JANUARY 23 — MONDAY

Day 23 — 342 Remaining

"BARNEY MILLER" TV PREMIERE: ANNIVERSARY. Jan 23, 1975. ABC sitcom about a New York precinct captain starred Hal Linden as Captain Barney Miller. The 12th Precinct gang included Barbara Barrie as Miller's wife, Abe Vigoda as Detective Phil Fish, Max Gail as Sergeant Stan Wojciehowicz, Gregory Sierra as Sergeant Chano Amenguale, Jack Soo as Sergeant Nick Yemana, Ron Glass as Detective Ron Harris and a host of others. The last episode aired in 1982.

BETTER BUSINESS COMMUNICATION DAY. Jan 23. This is a day set aside to encourage all workers to acknowledge the importance of effective communication in the workplace. Tips, workshops and seminars will be offered around this day to equip workers with the tools to demonstrate effective communication. Annually, the fourth Monday in January. For info: Corporate Speech Pathology Network (Corspan). Phone: (608) 663-3719. E-mail: info@corspan.org. Web: www.corspan.org.

BLACKWELL, ELIZABETH, AWARDED MD: ANNIVERSARY. Jan 23, 1849. Dr. Elizabeth Blackwell became the first woman to receive an MD degree. The native of Bristol, England, was awarded her degree by the Medical Institution of Geneva, NY.

BULGARIA: BABIN DEN. Jan 23. Celebrated throughout Bulgaria as Day of the Midwives or Grandmother's Day. Traditional festivities.

HANCOCK, JOHN: BIRTH ANNIVERSARY. Jan 23, 1737. American patriot and statesman, first signer of the Declaration of Independence. Born at Braintree, MA, he died at Quincy, MA, Oct 8, 1793. Because of his conspicuous signature on the Declaration, Hancock's name has become part of the American language, referring to any handwritten signature, as in "Put your John Hancock on that!" (Some sources cite Hancock's Old Style birth date of Jan 12, 1736/7.)

HEWES, JOSEPH: BIRTH ANNIVERSARY. Jan 23, 1730. Signer of the Declaration of Independence. Born at Princeton, NJ, he died Nov 10, 1779, at Philadelphia, PA.

"THE KING FAMILY SHOW" TV PREMIERE: ANNIVERSARY. Jan 23, 1965. ABC musical variety show featuring the singing and playing of the King sisters and other descendents of William King Driggs, who organized the family musical group in the 1930s. Including spouses, children, grandchildren and great-grandchildren, some three dozen members of the King family have appeared on camera at one time.

KOVACS, ERNIE: BIRTH ANNIVERSARY. Jan 23, 1919. Comedian and television pioneer, born at Trenton, NJ. Throughout the '40s and '50s Ernie Kovacs made a name for himself hosting his own shows including "The Ernie Kovacs Show" and "Ernie In Kovacsland" and a variety of quiz shows. He died in an automobile accident at Los Angeles, Jan 13, 1962.

MANET, ÉDOUARD: BIRTH ANNIVERSARY. Jan 23, 1832. Painter, born at Paris, France. Among his best-known paintings are *Olympia* and *Déjeuner sur l'herbe.* Manet died Apr 30, 1883, at Paris.

NATIONAL HANDWRITING DAY. Jan 23. Popularly observed on birthday of John Hancock to encourage more legible handwriting. (Some sources cite Hancock's Old Style birth date of Jan 12, 1736/7.)

NATIONAL MEDICAL GROUP PRACTICE WEEK. Jan 23–27. A week to advance and recognize the awareness and understanding of medical group practices as the superior form of health care delivery. This week also honors those physicians, administrators and staff who dedicate their professional careers to the administration of quality health care. Annually, the fourth week of January. For info: Margie Jepson, Medical Group Management Assn, 104 Inverness Terrace E, Englewood, CO 80112. Phone: (303) 799-1111. Fax: (303) 643-4420. E-mail: mpj@mgma .com. Web: www.medicalgrouppracticeweek.com.

SNOWPLOW MAILBOX HOCKEY DAY. Jan 23. It's wintertime and time for snowplow drivers everywhere to see how many rural mailboxes they can knock over. Twenty extra points for boosting one into the next township! [©2003 by WH.] For info: Thomas & Ruth Roy, Wellcat Holidays, 2418 Long Ln, Lebanon, PA 17046. Phone: (717) 279-0184. E-mail: info@wellcat .com. Web: www.wellcat.com.

STENDHAL: BIRTH ANNIVERSARY. Jan 23, 1783. French author Marie Henri Beyle, whose best-known pseudonym was Stendhal. Best remembered are his novels *The Red and the Black* (1831) and *The Charterhouse of Parma* (1839). Born at Grenoble, France, he died at Paris, Mar 23, 1842.

STEWART, POTTER: BIRTH ANNIVERSARY. Jan 23, 1915. Associate justice of the Supreme Court of the US, nominated by President Eisenhower Jan 17, 1959. (Oath of office, May 15, 1959.) Born at Jackson, MI, he retired in July 1981 and died Dec 7, 1985, at Putney, VT, five days after suffering a stroke. Buried at Arlington National Cemetery.

TWENTIETH AMENDMENT TO US CONSTITUTION RATIFIED: ANNIVERSARY. Jan 23, 1933. The 20th Amendment was ratified, fixing the date of the presidential inauguration at the current Jan 20 instead of the previous Mar 4. It also specified that were the president-elect to die before taking office, the vice president-elect would succeed to the presidency. In addition, it set Jan 3 as the official opening date of Congress each year.

TWENTY-FOURTH AMENDMENT TO US CONSTITUTION RATIFIED: ANNIVERSARY. Jan 23, 1964. Poll taxes and other taxes were eliminated as a prerequisite for voting in all federal elections by the 24th Amendment.

USS *PUEBLO* SEIZED BY NORTH KOREA: ANNIVERSARY. Jan 23, 1968. North Korea seized the USS *Pueblo* in the Sea of Japan, claiming the ship was on a spy mission. The crew was held for 11 months. The vessel was confiscated. Accompanying the crew when they were released—on Dec 22, 1968—was the body of Seaman Duane D. Hodges, the only crewman killed.

BIRTHDAYS TODAY

Richard Dean Anderson, 56, actor ("Stargate SG-1," "MacGyver"), born Minneapolis, MN, Jan 23, 1950.

Princess Caroline, 49, born Monte Carlo, Monaco, Jan 23, 1957.

Tom Carper, 59, US Senator (D, Delaware), born Beckley, WV, Jan 23, 1947.

Gil Gerard, 63, actor ("Buck Rogers," "Sidekicks"), born Little Rock, AR, Jan 23, 1943.

Patrick Capper (Pat) Haden, 53, sportscaster, former football player, born Westbury, NY, Jan 23, 1953.

Mariska Hargitay, 42, actress ("Law & Order: Special Victims Unit"), born Los Angeles, CA, Jan 23, 1964.

Rutger Hauer, 62, actor (*Blade Runner*), born Breukelen, Netherlands, Jan 23, 1944.

Frank Lautenberg, 82, US Senator (D, New Jersey), born Paterson, NJ, Jan 23, 1924.

Jeanne Moreau, 78, actress (*Jules and Jim, Viva Maria*), born Paris, France, Jan 23, 1928.

Gail O'Grady, 43, actress ("NYPD Blue"), born Detroit, MI, Jan 23, 1963.

Chita Rivera, 73, singer, actress (*The Kiss of the Spider Woman*, "The New Dick Van Dyke Show"), born Conchita del Rivero at Washington, DC, Jan 23, 1933.

Tiffani-Amber Thiessen, 32, actress ("Beverly Hills 90210," "Saved by the Bell"), born Long Beach, CA, Jan 23, 1974.

JANUARY 24 — TUESDAY

Day 24 — 341 Remaining

ACHELIS, ELISABETH: BIRTH ANNIVERSARY. Jan 24, 1880. Calendar reform advocate, author of *The World Calendar*, born at Brooklyn, NY. Her proposed calendar made every year the same, with equal quarters, each year beginning on Sunday, Jan 1, and each date falling on the same day of the week every year. Died at New York, NY, Feb 11, 1973.

BELUSHI, JOHN: BIRTH ANNIVERSARY. Jan 24, 1949. Actor, comedian ("Saturday Night Live," *Animal House, The Blues Brothers*), born at Chicago, IL. Died Mar 5, 1982, at Hollywood, CA.

BOLIVIA: ALACITIS FAIR. Jan 24–26. La Paz. Traditional annual celebration by Aymara Indians with prayers and offerings to the god of prosperity.

BRICKHOUSE, JACK: BIRTH ANNIVERSARY. Jan 24, 1916. Born John Beasley Brickhouse at Peoria, IL. A legend in Chicago broadcasting, Brickhouse was the play-by-play voice for the first baseball game televised by WGN, an exhibition game between the Cubs and the White Sox on Apr 16, 1948. He broadcast Cubs games for 40 years, Chicago Bears games for 24 years and some Chicago Bulls and White Sox games. In 1983 he received the Ford C. Frick Award. Died at Chicago, IL, Aug 6, 1998.

CALIFORNIA GOLD DISCOVERY: ANNIVERSARY. Jan 24, 1848. James W. Marshal, an employee of John Sutter, accidentally discovered gold while building a sawmill near Coloma, CA. Efforts to keep the discovery secret failed, and the gold rush of 1849 was under way.

FDR's "UNCONDITIONAL SURRENDER" STATEMENT: ANNIVERSARY. Jan 24, 1943. At the end of the Casablanca Conference, 1943, Franklin D. Roosevelt and Winston Churchill held a press conference. Roosevelt stated, "Peace can come to the world only by the total elimination of German and Japanese war power. That means the unconditional surrender of Germany, Italy and Japan." This position calling for "unconditional surrender" has subsequently been criticized by some as having prolonged the war.

GOODSON, MARK: BIRTH ANNIVERSARY. Jan 24, 1915. Producer and creator of TV game shows, Mark Goodson was born at Sacramento, CA. His career in entertainment began in radio where he created his first game show, "Pop the Question." He later teamed with Bill Todman and that partnership led to "I've Got a Secret," "Password," "The Price Is Right," "What's My Line?"and "Family Feud." He died Dec 18, 1992, at New York, NY.

NATIONAL SPEAK UP AND SUCCEED DAY. Jan 24. Fewer than 3 percent of Americans have no fear of public speaking or have never felt shy. Yet, the top-rated skill for success is effective communication skills. On National Speak Up and Succeed Day, face your fear of public speaking and speak out anyway—speak up at a committee meeting, voice your opinion to a group of colleagues, give the toast at a special event, volunteer to chair a program, join Toastmasters. You have nothing to lose and everything to gain. Annually, the fourth Tuesday in January. For info: Mary-Ellen Drummond, Polished Presentations Intl, PO Box 2104, Rancho Santa Fe, CA 92067. Phone: (858) 756-4248. Fax: (858) 756-9621. E-mail: medrummond@aol.com. Web: www .medrummond.com.

SIOUX EMPIRE FARM SHOW. Jan 24–28. Sioux Falls, SD. Winter farm and livestock show featuring all classes of livestock, commercial exhibits and a horse pull. Est attendance: 30,000. For info: Sioux Empire Farm Show, Sioux Falls Area Chamber of Commerce, 200 N Phillips Ave, #102, Sioux Falls, SD 57104. Phone: (605) 373-2016. Fax: (605) 336-6499. E-mail: cchristen sen@siouxfalls.com.

SONORA SHOWCASE. Jan 24–25. Yuma, AZ. A fiesta to promote the state of Sonora, Mexico, features mariachis, folkloric dancers, food and beverage samples, vacation information and curios. Est attendance: 4,500. For info: Yuma Civic Ctr, 1440 Desert Hills Dr, Yuma, AZ 85365. Phone: (928) 373-5043. Fax: (928) 344-9121. E-mail: ycc@ci.yuma.az.us.

SPACE MILESTONE: *COSMOS 954* (USSR) FALLS. Jan 24, 1978. Nuclear-equipped reconnaissance satellite launched Sept 18, 1977, fell into Earth's atmosphere and burned over northern Canada. Some radioactive debris reached ground on Jan 24, 1978.

SPACE MILESTONE: *DISCOVERY* (US). Jan 24, 1985. Space shuttle *Discovery* launched from and returned to Kennedy Space Center, FL, deploying eavesdropping satellite in secret, all-military mission, Jan 24–27, 1985.

WHARTON, EDITH: BIRTH ANNIVERSARY. Jan 24, 1862. American author (*The Age of Innocence, Ethan Frome*) and Pulitzer Prize winner. Born at New York, NY. Died at Pavillon Colombe, France, Aug 11, 1937, of a stroke.

BIRTHDAYS TODAY

Mischa Barton, 20, actress ("The O.C."), born London, England, Jan 24, 1986.

Ernest Borgnine, 89, actor ("McHale's Navy," *Marty*), born Hamden, CT, Jan 24, 1917.

Neil Diamond, 65, singer, composer ("Cracklin' Rosie," "Song Sung Blue"), born Coney Island, NY, Jan 24, 1941.

Nastassja Kinski, 46, actress (*Tess, The Hotel New Hampshire*), born Berlin, Germany, Jan 24, 1960.

Matthew Lillard, 36, actor (*Scream, Scooby-Doo*), born Lansing, MI, Jan 24, 1970.

Aaron Neville, 65, singer, songwriter, born New Orleans, LA, Jan 24, 1941.

Michael Ontkean, 60, actor ("Twin Peaks," *Slap Shot*), born Vancouver, BC, Canada, Jan 24, 1946.

Mary Lou Retton, 38, Olympic gold medal gymnast, born Fairmont, WV, Jan 24, 1968.

Oral Roberts, 88, evangelist, born Tulsa, OK, Jan 24, 1918.

Yakov Smirnoff, 55, comedian ("What a Country," "Night Court"), born Odessa, USSR, Jan 24, 1951.

Maria Tallchief, 81, former ballet dancer, born Fairfax, OK, Jan 24, 1925.

January *2006*	S	M	T	W	T	F	S
	1	2	3	4	5	6	7
	8	9	10	11	12	13	14
	15	16	17	18	19	20	21
	22	23	24	25	26	27	28
	29	30	31				

JANUARY 25 — WEDNESDAY

Day 25 — 340 Remaining

AROUND THE WORLD IN 72 DAYS: ANNIVERSARY. Jan 25, 1890. Newspaper reporter Nellie Bly (pen name used by Elizabeth Cochrane Seaman) set off from Hoboken, NJ, Nov 14, 1889, to attempt to break Jules Verne's imaginary hero Phileas Fogg's record of voyaging around the world in 80 days. She did beat Fogg's record, taking 72 days, 6 hours, 11 minutes and 14 seconds to make the trip, arriving back in New Jersey on Jan 25, 1890.

BOYLE, ROBERT: BIRTH ANNIVERSARY. Jan 25, 1627 (OS). Irish physicist, chemist and author who formulated Boyle's Law in 1662. Born at Lismore, Ireland, he died at London, England, Dec 30, 1691 (OS).

BURNS, ROBERT: BIRTH ANNIVERSARY. Jan 25, 1759. Beloved Scottish poet ("Oh wad some power the giftie gie us/To see oursels as others see us!"). Born at Ayrshire, Scotland, he died at Dumfries, Scotland, July 21, 1796. His birthday is widely celebrated as Burns' Nights, especially in Scotland, England and Newfoundland.

CURTIS, CHARLES: BIRTH ANNIVERSARY. Jan 25, 1860. The 31st vice president of the US (1929–33). Born at Topeka, KS, he died at Washington, DC, Feb 8, 1936.

FIRST SCHEDULED TRANSCONTINENTAL FLIGHT: ANNIVERSARY. Jan 25, 1959. American Airlines opened the jet age in the US with the first scheduled transcontinental flight on a Boeing 707 nonstop from California to New York.

FIRST TELEVISED PRESIDENTIAL NEWS CONFERENCE: 45th ANNIVERSARY. Jan 25, 1961. Beginning a tradition that survives to this day, John F. Kennedy held the first televised presidential news conference five days after being inaugurated the 35th president.

FIRST WINTER OLYMPICS: ANNIVERSARY. Jan 25, 1924. The first Winter Olympic Games opened at Chamonix, France, with athletes representing 16 nations. The ski jump, previously unknown, thrilled spectators. The Olympics offered a boost to skiing, which would make enormous strides in the next decade.

MACINTOSH DEBUTS: ANNIVERSARY. Jan 25, 1984. Apple's Macintosh computer went on sale this day for $2,495. It wasn't until mid-1985, however, that sales began to take off and this computer began to replace the Apple II model.

MAUGHAM, W. SOMERSET: BIRTH ANNIVERSARY. Jan 25, 1874. English short story writer, novelist and playwright, born at Paris, France. Among his best-remembered books: *Of Human Bondage, Cakes and Ale* and *The Razor's Edge.* Died at Cap Ferrat, France, Dec 16, 1965.

MILLS, FLORENCE: BIRTH ANNIVERSARY. Jan 25, 1896. The leading black American singer and dancer of the Jazz Age and the Harlem Renaissance was born Florence Winfree at Washington, DC. She appeared in Langston Hughes's *Shuffle Along* in 1921 and *Plantation Review* on Broadway in 1922, then at the London Pavilion in *Dover Street to Dixie* in 1923. Offered a spot in the *Ziegfeld Follies,* she turned it down and joined in creating a rival show with an all-black cast. Mills was the first black woman to appear as a headliner at the Palace Theatre. She was so revered for her efforts to create opportunities for black entertainers and to bring the unique culture of blacks to Broadway that more than 150,000 people filled the streets of Harlem to mourn her when she died at New York City, Nov 1, 1927, at age 31.

MONTANA WINTER FAIR. Jan 25–29. Lewistown, MT. Fair featuring farm forums, commercial booths, youth education, open exhibits, dog clinic and trials, fiddlers' contest, art swap and shop, 4-H and FFA livestock exhibits and more. Annually, the last full week of January. Est attendance: 10,000. For info: Montana Winter Fair, PO Box 1098, Lewistown, MT 59457. Phone: (406) 538-8841. Fax: (800) 406-8841.

NATIONAL COMPLIMENT DAY. Jan 25. This day is set aside to compliment at least five people. Not only are compliments appreciated by the receiver, they lift the spirit of the giver. Compliments provide a quick and easy way to connect positively with those you come in contact with. Giving compliments forges bonds, dispels loneliness and just plain feels good. For info: Debby Hoffman, Positive Results Seminars, PO Box 3478, Concord, NH 03302-3478. Phone: (603) 783-4446. E-mail: Debby@Debby-Hoffman.com. Or Kathy Chamberlin, Respectful Communication, 724 Park Ave, Contoocook, NH 03229-3089. Phone: (603) 746-3602. E-mail: KathyChamberlin@aol.com. Web: www.complimentday.com.

"ROBOT" ENTERS WORLD LEXICON: 85th ANNIVERSARY. Jan 25, 1921. On this date, the play *R.U.R.* premiered at the National Theater in Prague, Czechoslovakia. "R.U.R." stood for "Rossum's Universal Robots," and the play concerned artificial human workers who rebel against their human masters. Czech dramatist Karel Capek and his brother, Josef Capek, derived "robot" from the Czech noun *robota,* which means "labor" and "servitude." As the play became a hit worldwide (with an English translation published in 1923), the concept of the robot took hold. Capek's robots were chemically created; today's real and fictional robots are metallic machines.

A ROOM OF ONE'S OWN DAY. Jan 25. For anyone who knows or longs for the sheer bliss and rightness of having a private place, no matter how humble, to call one's own. [©2003 by WH.] For info: Thomas & Ruth Roy, Wellcat Holidays, 2418 Long Ln, Lebanon, PA 17046. Phone: (717) 279-0184. E-mail: info@wellcat.com. Web: www.wellcat.com.

SOUTH FLORIDA SENIOR GAMES. Jan 25–Feb 8. Hollywood, FL. 16th annual. Hollywood observance includes paddleball, bocce, shuffleboard, golf and quilting. For info: Cynthia Hancock, City of Hollywood, Dept of Parks, Recreation & Cultural Arts, 1940 Harrison St, Ste 101, Hollywood, FL 33020. Phone: (954) 921-3404.

WOOLF, VIRGINIA: BIRTH ANNIVERSARY. Jan 25, 1882. English writer, critic and novelist, author of *Jacob's Room* and *To the Lighthouse.* Born at London, England. After completing her last novel, *Between the Acts,* she collapsed under the strain and drowned herself in the River Ouse near Rodmell, England, on Mar 28, 1941.

ZEHNDER'S SNOWFEST (WITH ICE CARVING AND STATE OF MICHIGAN SNOW SCULPTING COMPETITIONS). Jan 25–30. Frankenmuth, MI. Annual festival also includes ice demonstrations, snow exhibitions by international teams from 6–10 countries and many children's activities such as a petting zoo, rides and music. Est attendance: 150,000. For info: Linda Kelly, Zehnder's of Frankenmuth, 730 S Main St, Frankenmuth, MI 48734. Phone: (800) 863-7999. Fax: (517) 652-3544. Web: www.zehnders.com.z

ZORA NEALE HURSTON FESTIVAL OF THE ARTS AND HUMANITIES. Jan 25–29. Eatonville, FL (10 miles east of Orlando). Festival celebrates Hurston, her work, her hometown, Eatonville (popularly known as the oldest incorporated African-American municipality in the country) and the cultural contributions Africa-descended people have made to the US and to world culture, with four days of arts and humanities programming highlighting theater, music, folklore and literature through seminars, symposia, master classes, intellectual conversations/dialogues, art exhibitions, workshops, self-tours, concert fare and performances. Festival attracts both "domestic and international travelers looking for 'the other Florida'—the Africa-descendant cultural matrix." Est attendance: 75,000. For info: Assn to Preserve Eatonville, Inc, 227 E Kennedy Blvd, Eatonville, FL 32751. Phone: (407) 647-3307. Fax: (407) 647-3959. E-mail: zora@cs.ucf.edu or zoramuseum2003@yahoo.com. Web: www.zorafestival.com.

BIRTHDAYS TODAY

Corazon "Cory" Aquino, 73, former president of the Philippines, born Tarlac Province, Philippine Islands, Jan 25, 1933.

Conrad Burns, 71, US Senator (R, Montana), born Gallatin, MO, Jan 25, 1935.

Vince Carter, 29, basketball player, born Daytona Beach, FL, Jan 25, 1977.

Chris Chelios, 44, hockey player, born Chicago, IL, Jan 25, 1962.

Ernie Harwell, 88, sportscaster, born Washington, GA, Jan 25, 1918.

Dean Jones, 75, actor (*Tea and Sympathy, The Love Bug, Beethoven*), born Decatur, AL, Jan 25, 1931 (some sources say 1935).

Alicia Keys, 25, musician, singer (*Songs in A Minor*), born Harlem, NY, Jan 25, 1981.

Dinah Manoff, 48, actress (stage: *I Ought to Be in Pictures* [Tony Award]; "Soap," "Empty Nest"), born New York, NY, Jan 25, 1958.

Edwin Newman, 87, journalist, author ("Comet," *A Civil Tongue*), born New York, NY, Jan 25, 1919.

Leigh Taylor-Young, 61, actress ("Peyton Place," "Dallas," *I Love You, Alice B. Toklas*), born Washington, DC, Jan 25, 1945.

JANUARY 26 — THURSDAY

Day 26 — 339 Remaining

AUGUSTA FUTURITY. Jan 26–Feb 4. Augusta, GA. Brings together the top cutting horses and riders in the world to compete for purse and awards of more than $1,000,000. Sponsors: Wrangler, John Deere, Ariat Boots, *Augusta Chronicle*, E-Z-Go Textron, Gist Silversmiths, COMCAST Cable, Circle R Custom Hat Works, Circle Y of Yoakum, Marsh Co, Horsecity.com, Dodge Trucks, Fort Dodge Animal Health, BellSouth, AMVESCAP, Reveal 4-N-1, Quarter Horse News, K.O. Trading Co, Trojan Manufacturing, HorseTrax and Augusta Metro Convention and Visitors Bureau. Est attendance: 45,000. For info: Noell Inman, Dir of Mktg, Augusta Futurity, PO Box 936, Augusta, GA 30903. Phone: (706) 823-3362 or (706) 823-3417. Web: www.augusta futurity.com.

AUSTRALIA: AUSTRALIA DAY—FIRST BRITISH SETTLEMENT: ANNIVERSARY. Jan 26, 1788. A shipload of convicts arrived briefly at Botany Bay (which proved to be unsuitable) and then at Port Jackson (later the site of the city of Sydney). Establishment of an Australian prison colony was to relieve crowding of British prisons. Australia Day, formerly known as Foundation Day or Anniversary Day, has been observed since about 1817 and has been a public holiday since 1838.

COLEMAN, BESSIE: BIRTH ANNIVERSARY. Jan 26, 1893. Born at Atlanta, TX, Bessie Coleman would not take no for an answer, especially where it concerned her dreams of flying. Because of her race and gender, she was denied admission to aviation school programs in the US. She therefore worked as a manicurist earning her way to Paris. There she received an international pilot's license from the Fédération Aéronautique Internationale in 1921. Upon return, "Queen Bess" took part in numerous acrobatic air exhibitions where her stunt-flying and "figure eights" won her many admirers. She avidly encouraged others to follow in her footsteps. Coleman, however, perished in a plane crash during a practice session, at Jacksonville, FL, Apr 30, 1926.

DENTAL DRILL PATENT: ANNIVERSARY. Jan 26, 1875. George F. Green, of Kalamazoo, MI, patented the electric dental drill.

DOMINICAN REPUBLIC: NATIONAL HOLIDAY. Jan 26. An official public holiday celebrates the birth anniversary of Juan Pablo Duarte, one of the fathers of the republic.

"THE DUKES OF HAZZARD" TV PREMIERE: ANNIVERSARY. Jan 26, 1979. This comedy/action show ran for seven seasons and featured car chases. Brothers Bo Duke (John Schneider) and Luke Duke (Tom Wopat) were the good guys, fighting crooked law enforcement in their rural southern community. Other characters included Daisy Duke (Catherine Bach), Uncle Jesse Duke (Denver Pyle), Sheriff Roscoe P. Coltrane (James Best), Deputy Enos Strate (Sonny Shroyer) and Boss Hogg (Sorrell Booke).

FRANKLIN PREFERS TURKEY: ANNIVERSARY. Jan 26, 1784. In a letter to his daughter, Benjamin Franklin expressed his unhappiness over the choice of the eagle as the symbol of America. He preferred the turkey.

GRANT, JULIA DENT: BIRTH ANNIVERSARY. Jan 26, 1826. Wife of Ulysses Simpson Grant, 18th president of the US. Born at St. Louis, MO, died at Washington, DC, Dec 14, 1902.

HITLER YOUTH DEPLOYED: ANNIVERSARY. Jan 26, 1943. Due to the need for more men at the front, the Nazis began manning anti-aircraft batteries within Germany with members of the Hitler Youth who were aged 15 and up. This was 10 days after the British had begun the heavy bombing of Berlin and other German cities. See also: "British Air Raid on Berlin: Anniversary" (Jan 16).

INDIA: REPUBLIC DAY. Jan 26. National holiday. Anniversary of Proclamation of the Republic, Basant Panchmi. In 1929, Indian National Congress resolved to work for establishment of a sovereign republic, a goal that was realized Jan 26, 1950, when India became a democratic republic and its constitution went into effect.

INDIAN EARTHQUAKE: 5th ANNIVERSARY. Jan 26, 2001. An earthquake that struck the state of Gujarat in India left more than 15,000 dead. The quake was estimated to be 7.7 on the Richter scale. India's largest port at Kandla suffered severe damage.

LOTUS 1-2-3 RELEASED: ANNIVERSARY. Jan 26, 1983. This spreadsheet software drove demand for the IBM PC, just as the introduction of VisiCalc had for the Apple II in 1979.

MacARTHUR, DOUGLAS: BIRTH ANNIVERSARY. Jan 26, 1880. US general and supreme commander of Allied forces in Southwest Pacific during World War II. Born at Little Rock, AR, he served as commander of the Rainbow Division's 84th Infantry Brigade in World War I, leading it in the St. Mihiel, Meuse-Argonne and Sedan offensives. Remembered for his "I shall return" prediction when forced out of the Philippines by the Japanese during WWII, a promise he fulfilled. Relieved of Far Eastern command by President Harry Truman on Apr 11, 1951, during the Korean War. MacArthur died at Washington, DC, Apr 5, 1964.

MICHIGAN: ADMISSION DAY: ANNIVERSARY. Jan 26. Became 26th state in 1837.

	S	M	T	W	T	F	S
January		1	2	3	4	5	6	7
2006	8	9	10	11	12	13	14
	15	16	17	18	19	20	21
	22	23	24	25	26	27	28
	29	30	31				

ROCKY MOUNTAIN NATIONAL PARK ESTABLISHED: ANNIVERSARY. Jan 26, 1915. Under President Woodrow Wilson, the area covering more than 1,000 square miles in Colorado became a national park.

TOAD HOLLOW DAY OF ENCOURAGEMENT. Jan 26. A day to give and receive a word of encouragement. For info: Ralph Morrison, Director, Toad Hollow, PO Box 2132, Garden City, MI 48135. Phone: (800) 574-8623.

VAN HEUSEN, JIMMY: BIRTH ANNIVERSARY. Jan 26, 1913. Jimmy Van Heusen was born Edward Chester Babcock at Syracuse, NY. He was a composer of many popular songs with his lyricist partners Johnny Burke and Sammy Cahn. One of his 76 songs that Frank Sinatra recorded was "My Kind of Town." Van Heusen won four Academy Awards for songs in movies such as *Going My Way* (1944). He was inducted into the Songwriters Hall of Fame when it was founded in 1971. Van Heusen died Feb 7, 1990, at Rancho Mirage, CA.

WASHINGTON'S BIRTHDAY CELEBRATION. Jan 26–Feb 19 (tentative). Laredo, TX. Founded in 1898, the event celebrates the cultures of both the US and Mexico with festivities ranging from the Jalapeño Festival to parades, fireworks and a carnival. The largest celebration of George Washington's birthday in the nation. Est attendance: 500,000. For info: Washington's Birthday Celebration Assn, 1819 E Hillside Rd, Laredo, TX 78041. Phone: (956) 722-0589. Fax: (956) 722-5528. E-mail: wbca@wbcalaredo.org.

BIRTHDAYS TODAY

Anita Baker, 48, singer ("Sweet Love," "Rhythm of Love"), born Toledo, OH, Jan 26, 1958.

Father George Harold Clements, 74, Roman Catholic priest, civil rights leader, born Chicago, IL, Jan 26, 1932.

Angela Davis, 62, political activist, born Birmingham, AL, Jan 26, 1944.

Mark Dayton, 59, US Senator (D, Minnesota), born Minneapolis, MN, Jan 26, 1947.

Ellen DeGeneres, 48, comedienne, actress ("Ellen"), talk-show host ("The Ellen DeGeneres Show"), born New Orleans, LA, Jan 26, 1958.

Philip Jose Farmer, 88, science fiction writer, born Peoria, IL, Jan 26, 1918.

Jules Feiffer, 77, cartoonist, writer, born New York, NY, Jan 26, 1929.

Scott Glenn, 64, actor (*The Right Stuff, Silverado*), born Pittsburgh, PA, Jan 26, 1942.

Wayne Gretzky, 45, Hall of Fame hockey player, born Brantford, ON, Canada, Jan 26, 1961.

Paul Newman, 81, actor (Oscar for *The Color of Money; Cat on a Hot Tin Roof, Butch Cassidy and the Sundance Kid*), director (*Rachel, Rachel; The Glass Menagerie*), born Cleveland, OH, Jan 26, 1925.

Andrew Ridgeley, 43, musician, born Bushey, England, Jan 26, 1963.

David Strathairn, 56, actor (*LA Confidential*), born San Francisco, CA, Jan 26, 1950.

Robert George (Bob) Uecker, 71, sportscaster, former baseball player, actor ("Mr Belvedere"), born Milwaukee, WI, Jan 26, 1935.

Eddie Van Halen, 51, guitarist ("Jump," "Right Now"), born Nijmegen, Netherlands, Jan 26, 1955.

JANUARY 27 — FRIDAY
Day 27 — 338 Remaining

ALL THAT JAZZ WEEKEND. Jan 27–29. Asheville, NC. 14th annual. Delve into a world of music with evening and afternoon concerts in the Grand Ballroom and numerous jazz artists performing in the Great Hall all weekend. For info: The Grove Park Inn Resort & Spa, 290 Macon Ave, Asheville, NC 28804. Phone: (800) 438-5800 or (828) 252-2711. Web: www.groveparkinn.com.

AMERICANA INDIAN AND WESTERN ART SHOW AND SALE. Jan 27–29. Yuma, AZ. Indian and Western paintings, rugs and jewelry. Est attendance: 1,800. For info: Yuma Civic Center, 1440 Desert Hills Dr, Yuma, AZ 85365. Phone: (928) 373-5040. Fax: (928) 344-9121. E-mail: ycc@ci.yuma.az.us.

APOLLO I: SPACECRAFT FIRE: ANNIVERSARY. Jan 27, 1967. Three American astronauts, Virgil I. Grissom, Edward H. White and Roger B. Chaffee, died when fire suddenly broke out at 6:31 PM, EST, in *Apollo I* during a launching simulation test, as it stood on the ground at Cape Kennedy, FL. First launching in the Apollo program had been scheduled for Feb 27, 1967.

AUSCHWITZ LIBERATED: ANNIVERSARY. Jan 27, 1945. The Soviet army liberated about 6,000 prisoners of the Nazi concentration camp Auschwitz. It is estimated that 1.5 million inmates were killed at Auschwitz between 1941 and liberation—95 percent of them were Jewish.

AUSTRIA: MOZART 250. Jan 27–Dec 5. Austria is celebrating the 250th birth anniversary of its famous son with some 1,000 spectacular cultural events all during 2006—beginning with Mozart's birthday on Jan 27 and concluding on his death day on Dec 5. The president of Austria will officially kick the year off on Jan 27. The centers of celebration will be in Salzburg—the city of his birth and youth—and Vienna—the city of his maturity. For info: Mozart 2006. Web: www.mozart2006.net. Or Austrian National Tourist Office. E-mail: mozart@austria.info. Web: www.austria.info.

BADGER STATE WINTER GAMES. Jan 27–29 and Feb 3–5. Wausau, WI, and throughout Wisconsin. 18th annual sports festival for Wisconsin residents of all ages and abilities featuring 11 sports and opening ceremonies. More than 6,000 athletes in cross-country skiing, curling, downhill skiing, figure skating, ice hockey, ski jumping, freestyle snowboarding, speedskating and quadrathon. Major sponsors are American Family Insurance, Wisconsin Milk Marketing Board, Mobil, St. Joseph's Hospital. Est attendance: 10,000. For info: Badger State Games, PO Box 7788, Madison, WI 53707-7788. Phone: (608) 226-4780. Fax: (608) 226-9550. E-mail: info@SportsinWisconsin.com. Web: www.SportsinWisconsin.com.

BLACK HILLS STOCK SHOW AND RODEO. Jan 27–Feb 5. Rapid City, SD. Events include PRCA rodeos, ranch rodeo, timed sheepdog trials, cattle cutting, ranch horse competition, livestock shows and sales, buffalo show and sale, team penning, bucking horse and bull sale, stockman banquet and ball and commercial exhibits. Est attendance: 250,000. For info: Black Hills Stock Show & Rodeo, 800 San Francisco, Rapid City, SD 57701. Phone: (605) 355-3861.

BULLNANZA. Jan 27–28 (tentative). Lazy E Arena, Guthrie, OK. Present and past champions, including the top 50 bull riders in the world, compete for the prestigious BULLNANZA Champion title. Est attendance: 14,000. For info: Lazy E Arena, 9600 Lazy E Dr, Guthrie, OK 73044. Phone: (800) 595-RIDE. Fax: (405) 282-3785. E-mail: arena@lazye.com. Web: www.lazye.com.

CANADA: ONTARIO WINTER CARNIVAL BON SOO. Jan 27–Feb 5. Sault Ste. Marie, ON. One of Canada's largest winter carnivals features more than 125 festive indoor and hearty outdoor events for all ages during an annual 10-day winter extravaganza featuring winter sports, festive dances, entertainment, fireworks and the Fantasy Kingdom winter playground. Est attendance: 100,000. For info: Donna Gregg, Bon Soo Winter Carnival Inc, PO Box 781, Sault Ste. Marie, ON, Canada P6A 5N3. Phone: (705) 759-3000 or toll-free (866) 899-1607. Fax:

(705) 759-6950. E-mail: mrbonsoo@bonsoo.on.ca. Web: www
.bonsoo.on.ca.

DODGSON, CHARLES LUTWIDGE (LEWIS CARROLL): BIRTH ANNIVERSARY. Jan 27, 1832. English mathematician and author, better known by his pseudonym, Lewis Carroll, creator of *Alice's Adventures in Wonderland*, was born at Cheshire, England. *Alice* was written for Alice Liddell, daughter of a friend, and first published in 1886. *Through the Looking-Glass*, a sequel, and *The Hunting of the Snark* followed. Dodgson's books for children proved equally enjoyable to adults, and they overshadowed his serious works on mathematics. Dodgson died at Guildford, Surrey, England, Jan 14, 1898.

EAGLES ET CETERA FESTIVAL. Jan 27–29. Bismarck, AR. See bald eagles in the wild and learn about and observe birds of prey. Est attendance: 300. For info: Park Naturalist, DeGray Lake Resort State Park, 2027 State Park Entrance Rd, Bismarck, AR 71929-8194. Phone: (800) 737-8355. Fax: (501) 865-4436. E-mail: degray@arkansas.com. Web: www.degray.com.

FUN AT WORK DAY. Jan 27. Inject some laughter into your workplace by planning a fun and relaxing activity. Do something to encourage enthusiasm and openness and to help build rapport and release tension. When we enjoy our work, we are more productive and creative. Annually, the last Friday of January. For info: Diane C. Decker. Phone: (847) 394-0994. E-mail: dcdecker @msn.com. Web: www.qualitytransitions.com.

GERMANY: DAY OF REMEMBRANCE FOR VICTIMS OF NAZISM. Jan 27. Since 1996 commemorated on this day, the date in 1945 that Soviet soldiers liberated the Auschwitz concentration camp in Poland.

GOMPERS, SAMUEL: BIRTH ANNIVERSARY. Jan 27, 1850. Labor leader, first president of the American Federation of Labor, born at London, England. Died Dec 13, 1924, at San Antonio, TX.

GUNPOWDER PLOT TRIAL: 400th ANNIVERSARY. Jan 27, 1606. The surviving conspirators in the "Gunpowder Treason," a plot to blow up Parliament and the king of England on Nov 5, 1605, were brought to trial and convicted at London, Jan 27, 1606. Four days later they were executed. An inscription on a contemporary engraving states: "The heads of Percy and Catesby after they were dead, were cut off and set upon the ends of Parliament House. Friday the last of Jan, 1606, were executed in Parliament Yard: T. Winter, Rokenvood, Keys and Guido Fawkes, their quarters were placed over London gates and their heads upon London Bridge." See also: "Guy Fawkes Day" (Nov 5).

KERN, JEROME: BIRTH ANNIVERSARY. Jan 27, 1885. American composer born at New York City; died there Nov 11, 1945. In addition to scores for stage and screen, Kern wrote many memorable songs, including "Ol' Man River," "Smoke Gets in Your Eyes," "I Won't Dance," "The Way You Look Tonight," "All the Things You Are" and "The Last Time I Saw Paris."

"LAVERNE AND SHIRLEY" TV PREMIERE: 30th ANNIVERSARY. Jan 27, 1976. This ABC sitcom was a spin-off of the popular TV show "Happy Days" that was also set during the late '50s in Milwaukee, WI. Penny Marshall (sister of series cocreator, Garry Marshall) starred as Laverne DeFazio with Cindy Williams as Shirley Feeney. The two friends worked at a brewery and shared a basement apartment. Also featured in the cast were: Phil Foster as Laverne's father, Frank DeFazio; David L. Lander as Andrew "Squiggy" Squiggman; Michael McKean as Lenny Kosnowski; Betty Garrett as landlady Edna Babish and Eddie Mekka as Carmine Ragusa, Shirley's sometime boyfriend.

	S	M	T	W	T	F	S
January	1	2	3	4	5	6	7
2006	8	9	10	11	12	13	14
	15	16	17	18	19	20	21
	22	23	24	25	26	27	28
	29	30	31				

LENINGRAD LIBERATED: ANNIVERSARY. Jan 27, 1944. The seige of Leningrad began with German bombing of the city on Sept 4, 1941. The bombing continued for 430 hours. The suffering of the people of Leningrad during the 880-day seige was one of the greatest tragedies of World War II. More than half the population of Russia's second largest city died during the winter of 1942. The seige finally ended on Jan 27, 1944.

LONGHORN WORLD CHAMPIONSHIP RODEO. Jan 27–29. US Bank Arena, Cincinnati, OH. More than 200 cowboys and cowgirls compete in six professional contests ranging from bronc riding to big, bad BONUS bull riding. Free beginners horsemanship clinic 40 minutes before performances. Qualifying rodeo for Longhorn's Championship Finals Rodeo in Murfreesboro, TN. Featuring colorful opening and pageantry. 30th annual. Est attendance: 20,000. For info: W. Bruce Lehrke, Pres, Longhorn World Championship Rodeo, Inc, PO Box 70159, Nashville, TN 37207. Phone: (615) 876-1016. Fax: (615) 876-4685. E-mail: info@longhornrodeo.com. Web: www.longhornrodeo.com.

MOZART, WOLFGANG AMADEUS: 250th BIRTH ANNIVERSARY. Jan 27, 1756. Born at Salzburg, Austria, Johann Chrysostom Wolfgang Amadeus Mozart is regarded as one of the greatest musical geniuses of all time. As he gained proficiency at the harpsichord and the violin, he began composing at the age of five. He later concentrated his efforts on the pianoforte and under the direction of his father, Mozart and his sister, Maria Anna, began touring Europe in 1762. Throughout the tours, Mozart continued composing and in 1775 began service under the Archbishop in Salzburg. While in Salzburg he composed *Idomeneo*, the first of his mature operas. Mozart settled in Vienna in 1781, risking his existence without official patronage. After years of waiting, he was engaged in the service of the emperor, Joseph II, as a chamber composer, but at far less wages than his predecessor. Although he enjoyed artistic and popular success, Mozart's finances were never secure. An ardent Freemason, he borrowed extensively from his Masonic brothers, despite the successes of his operas *The Marriage of Figaro, Don Giovanni, Cosi fan tutti* and *The Magic Flute* and his extensive work for the piano. Mozart became seriously ill in the fall of 1791, and his rapid decline led to speculation that he had been poisoned, although this later was proved false. Mozart died a pauper at Vienna, Austria, Dec 5, 1791.

RICKOVER, HYMAN GEORGE: BIRTH ANNIVERSARY. Jan 27, 1900. American naval officer, known as the "Father of the Nuclear Navy." Admiral Rickover directed development of nuclear reactor–powered submarines, the first of which was the *Nautilus*, launched in 1954. Rickover was noted for his blunt remarks: "To increase the efficiency of the Department of Defense," he said, "you must first abolish it." The four-star admiral retired (unwillingly) at the age of 81, after 63 years in the navy. Born in Russia, Rickover died at Arlington, VA, July 9, 1986, and was buried at Arlington National Cemetery.

SAINT PAUL WINTER CARNIVAL. Jan 27–Feb 5. St. Paul, MN. Minnesota's largest tourist attraction and the nation's oldest and largest winter festival. The 120-year-old Saint Paul Winter Carnival provides 10 fun-filled days with more than 75 indoor and outdoor events celebrating the thrills and chills of wintertime fun. Est attendance: 275,000. For info: Saint Paul Festival and Heritage Foundation, 429 Landmark Ctr, 75 W 5th St, St. Paul, MN 55102. Phone: (651) 223-4700. Fax: (651) 223-4707. Web: www.winter-carnival.com.

SUGARLOAF CRAFTS FESTIVAL. Jan 27–29. Dulles Expo Center, Chantilly, VA. This show, now in its eighth year, features more than 350 nationally recognized craft designers and fine artists displaying and selling their original creations. Includes craft demonstrations, live music, specialty foods, hourly gift certificate drawings and more. Est attendance: 26,000. For info: Sugarloaf Mountain Works, 200 Orchard Ridge Dr, #215, Gaithersburg, MD 20878. Phone: (800) 210-9900. Fax: (301) 253-9620. Web: www.sugarloafcrafts.com.

THOMAS CRAPPER DAY: DEATH ANNIVERSARY.
Jan 27, 1910. Born at Thorne, Yorkshire, England, in 1836 (exact date unknown), Crapper is often described as the prime developer of the flush toilet mechanism as it is known today. The flush toilet had been in use for more than 100 years; Crapper perfected it. Founder, London, 1861, of Thomas Crapper & Co, later patentees and manufacturers of sanitary appliances. Died Jan 27, 1910.

UNITED KINGDOM: HOLOCAUST MEMORIAL DAY.
Jan 27. Commemorates the day in 1945 that Soviet troops liberated the Auschwitz concentration camp. For more info: www.holocaustmemorialday.gov.uk.

VIETNAM PEACE AGREEMENT SIGNED: ANNIVERSARY. Jan 27, 1973. US and North Vietnam, along with South Vietnam and the Viet Cong, signed an "Agreement on ending the war and restoring peace in Vietnam." Signed at Paris, France, to take effect Jan 28 at 8 AM Saigon time, thus ending the US combat role in a war that had involved American personnel stationed in Vietnam since defeated French forces had departed under terms of the Geneva Accords in 1954. This was the longest war in US history with more than one million combat deaths (US: 47,366). However, within weeks of the departure of American troops the war between North and South Vietnam resumed. For the Vietnamese, the war didn't end until Apr 30, 1975, when Saigon fell to Communist forces.

BIRTHDAYS TODAY

Mikhail Baryshnikov, 58, ballet dancer, actor (*White Nights, The Turning Point*), born Riga, Latvia, USSR, Jan 27, 1948.
(Anthony) Cris Collinsworth, 47, sportscaster, former football player, born Dayton, OH, Jan 27, 1959.
Mairead Corrigan, 62, pacifist, Nobel Peace Prize winner, born Belfast, Northern Ireland, Jan 27, 1944.
James Cromwell, 64, actor (*The People vs. Larry Flynt, Babe, LA Confidential*), born Los Angeles, CA, Jan 27, 1942.
Alan Cumming, 41, actor (Tony for *Cabaret*; *Spy Kids, The Anniversary Party, Emma*), director, born Perthshire, Scotland, Jan 27, 1965.
Bridget Fonda, 42, actress (*Single White Female, Lake Placid*), daughter of Peter Fonda, born Los Angeles, CA, Jan 27, 1964.
Julie Foudy, 35, former soccer player, born San Diego, CA, Jan 27, 1971.
Skitch Henderson, 88, bandleader ("The Tonight Show"), born Halstad, MN, Jan 27, 1918.
Mimi Rogers, 50, actress (*The Doors, The Rapture*), born Coral Gables, FL, Jan 27, 1956.

JANUARY 28 — SATURDAY

Day 28 — 337 Remaining

"BARNABY JONES" TV PREMIERE: ANNIVERSARY.
Jan 28, 1973. CBS drama about a mild-mannered, milk-drinking private eye who comes out of retirement following his son's murder. Cast included Buddy Ebsen as Barnaby Jones; Lee Meriwether as Barnaby's widowed daughter-in-law, Betty Jones; John Carter as Lieutenant Biddle; and Mark Shera as Jedediah Jones. The last episode aired in 1980.

BROOKFIELD ICE HARVEST. Jan 28. Brookfield, VT. Demonstrations of ice harvesting using the original equipment near the Brookfield Floating Bridge, one of only two such bridges remaining in the US today. Annually, the last Saturday in January. Est attendance: 1,000. For info: Al Wilder, PO Box 405, Brookfield, VT 05036. Phone: (802) 276-3959. Fax: (802) 276-3023.

CANADAFEST 2006. Jan 28–29. Hollywood, FL. Annual event held on the beach and boardwalk featuring Canadian and American entertainment, arts and crafts, community exhibits and international food. Est attendance: 80,000. For info: Roguey Doyle, City of Hollywood, Dept of Parks, Recreation & Cultural Arts, 1940 Harrison St, Ste 101, Hollywood, FL 33020. Phone: (954) 921-3404.

CHALLENGER SPACE SHUTTLE EXPLOSION: 20th ANNIVERSARY. Jan 28, 1986. At 11:39 AM, EST, the Space Shuttle *Challenger* STS-51L exploded, 74 seconds into its flight and about 10 miles above the earth. Hundreds of millions around the world watched television replays of the horrifying event that killed seven people. The billion-dollar craft was destroyed, all shuttle flights suspended and much of the US manned space flight program temporarily halted. Killed were teacher Christa McAuliffe (who was to have been the first ordinary citizen in space) and six crew members: Francis R. Scobee, Michael J. Smith, Judith A. Resnik, Ellison S. Onizuka, Ronald E. McNair and Gregory B. Jarvis.

"FANTASY ISLAND" TV PREMIERE: ANNIVERSARY.
Jan 28, 1978. Ricardo Montalban starred as the prescient guide, Mr Roarke, with Hervé Villechaize as his faithful assistant, Tattoo. Each week, guest stars played characters anxious to live out their fantasies in camp splendor. The show's run of 130 episodes, ending on Aug 18, 1984, was produced by Aaron Spelling and Leonard Goldberg. Best remembered is Tattoo's opening line each week: "De plane, de plane!"

GREAT SEAL OF THE US: AUTHORIZATION ANNIVERSARY. Jan 28, 1782. Congress resolved that the secretary of the Congress should "keep the public seal, and cause the same to be affixed to every act, ordinance or paper, which Congress shall direct. . . ." Although the Great Seal did not exist yet, the Congress recognized the need for it. See also: "Great Seal of the United States: Anniversary" (July 4 and Sept 16).

GREATER SPRINGFIELD GARAGE SALE. Jan 28–29. Ozark Empire Fairgrounds, Springfield, MO. Indoor garage sale featuring more than 400 booths of treasures for shoppers to seek out. For info: Ozark Empire Fair, 3001 N Grant, Springfield, MO 65803. Phone: (417) 833-2660. Fax: (417) 833-3769. Web: www.ozarkempirefair.com.

GROUNDHOG DAYS. Jan 28–Feb 2. Historic Woodstock Square, Woodstock, IL. Thanks to Bill Murray and the *Groundhog Day* movie, Woodstock celebrates with ice-sculpting demonstrations, walking tour of filming sites, breakfast and Woodstock Willie's prognostication. Est attendance: 500. For info: Woodstock Chamber of Commerce, 136 Cass St, Woodstock, IL 60098. Phone: (815) 338-2436. Fax: (815) 338-2927. E-mail: chamber@woodstockilchamber.com Web: www.woodstockilchamber.com.

HOGGETOWNE MEDIEVAL FAIRE. Jan 28–29 (also Feb 3–5). Alachua County Fairgrounds, Gainesville, FL. 20th annual faire features jousting, birds of prey, medieval arts and crafts, food and continuous entertainment on eight stages. Est attendance: 60,000. For info: Linda Piper, City of Gainesville, Dept of Cultural Affairs, PO Box 490 Sta. 30, Gainesville, FL 32602. Phone: (352) 334-5064. Fax: (352) 334-2249. E-mail: piperLr@cityofgainesville.org. Web: www.gvlculturalaffairs.org.

ICE FEST. Jan 28–29. Ligonier, PA. A weekend of ice-carving demonstrations as blocks of ice are turned into works of art. Est attendance: 5,000. For info: Rachel Roehrig, Ligonier Chamber of Commerce, 120 E Main St, Ligonier, PA 15658. Phone: (724) 238-4200. Fax: (724) 238-4610. E-mail: thechamber@ligonier.com.

ISRAELI SIEGE OF SUEZ CITY ENDS: ANNIVERSARY. Jan 28, 1974. The Israeli army lifted its siege of Suez City, freed encircled Egyptian troops and turned over 300,000 square miles of Egyptian territory to the UN, thereby ending the occupation that started during the October 1973 war.

MacKENZIE, ALEXANDER: BIRTH ANNIVERSARY.
Jan 28, 1822. The man who became the first Liberal prime min-

ister of Canada (1873–78) was born at Logierait, Perth, Scotland. He died at Toronto, Apr 17, 1892.

MARTÍ, JOSÉ JULIAN: BIRTH ANNIVERSARY. Jan 28, 1853. Cuban author and political activist, born at Havana, Cuba, Martí was exiled to Spain, where he studied law before coming to the US in 1890. He was killed in battle at Dos Rios, Cuba, May 19, 1895.

NATIONAL COWBOY POETRY GATHERING. Jan 28–Feb 4. Elko, NV. Soulful poetry and music performed by working cowboys. The event, which includes workshops, jam sessions, Western art and buckaroo trappings exhibits, attracts an international audience. For info: Western Folklife Center, 501 Railroad St, Elko, NV 89801. Phone: (775) 738-7508 or (888) 880-5885 for tickets. Fax: (775) 738-2900. E-mail: info@western folklife.org. Web: www.westernfolklife.org.

ORCHID SHOW. Jan 28–Mar 12. Missouri Botanical Garden, St. Louis, MO. Spectacular display of the Garden's vast orchid collection. For info: Missouri Botanical Garden, 4344 Shaw Blvd, St. Louis, MO 63110. Phone: (314) 577-9400 or (800) 642-8842. Web: www.mobot.org.

PICCARD, AUGUSTE: BIRTH ANNIVERSARY. Jan 28, 1884. Scientist and explorer, born at Basel, Switzerland. Made a record-setting balloon ascent into the stratosphere on May 27, 1931, and also ocean-depth descents and explorations. Twin brother of Jean Felix Piccard. Died at Lausanne, Switzerland, Mar 24, 1962. See also: "Piccard, Jean Felix: Birth Anniversary" (Jan 28).

PICCARD, JEAN FELIX: BIRTH ANNIVERSARY. Jan 28, 1884. Scientist, engineer, explorer, born at Basel, Switzerland. Noted for cosmic-ray research and record-setting balloon ascensions into the stratosphere. Reached 57,579 ft in a sealed gondola piloted by his wife, Jeannette, in 1934. Twin brother of Auguste Piccard. Died at Minneapolis, MN, Jan 28, 1963. See also: "Piccard, Jeannette Ridlon: Birth Anniversary" (Jan 5) and "Piccard, Auguste: Birth Anniversary" (Jan 28).

RAILROAD AND HOBBY SHOW. Jan 28–29. West Springfield, MA. Now expanded to three buildings, nearly 5½ acres with dealers, displays, art, more than 30 operating layouts and railroads including Shortline, Tourist, Class 1 and more. Est attendance: 22,000. For info: Amherst Railway Society, PO Box 718, Warren, MA 01083-0718. Phone: (413) 436-0242. Fax: (413) 436-7013. E-mail: ars@samnet.net.

SENIOR BOWL FOOTBALL GAME. Jan 28. Ladd-Peebles Stadium, Mobile, AL. 57th annual. All-star football game featuring the nation's top collegiate seniors on teams coached by National Football League coaching staffs. Proceeds go to charities. Est attendance: 40,700. For info: Senior Bowl, PO Box 1408, Mobile, AL 36633-1408. Phone: (251) 438-2276. Fax: (251) 432-0409. E-mail: srbowl@seniorbowl.com. Web: www.senior bowl.com.

STANLEY, HENRY MORTON: BIRTH ANNIVERSARY. Jan 28, 1841. Explorer, born at Denbigh, Wales, and leader of the expedition to find the missing missionary-explorer David Livingstone, who had not been heard from for more than two years. Stanley began the search in Africa on Mar 21, 1871, finally finding the explorer at Ujiji, near Lake Tanganyika, on Nov 10, 1871, whereupon he asked the now-famous question: "Dr. Livingstone, I presume?" Stanley died at London, England, May 10, 1904.

TEXAS COLLECTORS' GUN & KNIFE SHOW. Jan 28–29. Multi-Purpose Events Center Exhibit Hall, Wichita Falls, TX. The largest gun, knife and shooting sports show and sale in

	S	M	T	W	T	F	S
January	1	2	3	4	5	6	7
2006	8	9	10	11	12	13	14
	15	16	17	18	19	20	21
	22	23	24	25	26	27	28
	29	30	31				

the area. Buy, sell, swap. Est attendance: 5,000. For info: Wichita Falls CVB, 1000 5th St, Wichita Falls, TX 76301. Phone: (940) 716-5500. Fax: (940) 716-5509. E-mail: MPEC@wf.net. Web: www.wichitafalls.org.

UNIVERSITY KIWANIS PANCAKE FESTIVAL. Jan 28. Multi-Purpose Events Center, J.S. Bridwell Center, Wichita Falls, TX. 49th annual. A day of food and fun, featuring the world's "best pancakes." Est attendance: 8,000. For info: Wichita Falls CVB, 1000 5th St, Wichita Falls, TX 76301. Phone: (940) 716-5500. Fax: (940) 716-5509. E-mail: MPEC@wf.net. Web: www.wichita falls.org.

BIRTHDAYS TODAY

Alan Alda, 70, actor (*Paper Lion, The Four Seasons*, "M*A*S*H"), director, born Alphonso D'Abruzzo at New York, NY, Jan 28, 1936.

John Beck, 63, actor ("Dallas", *Sleeper, The Big Bus*), born Chicago, IL, Jan 28, 1943.

Susan Howard, 63, actress ("Dallas"), born Jeri Lynn Mooney, Marshall, TX, Jan 28, 1943.

Harley Jane Kozak, 49, actress (*When Harry Met Sally . . ., Parenthood*), born Wilkes-Barre, PA, Jan 28, 1957.

Sarah McLachlan, 38, folksinger, born Halifax, NS, Canada, Jan 28, 1968.

Kathryn Morris, 37, actress (*Mindhunters*, "Cold Case"), born Cincinnati, OH, Jan 28, 1969.

Claes Oldenburg, 77, artist, sculptor (*Standing Trowel*), born Stockholm, Sweden, Jan 28, 1929.

Elijah Wood, 25, actor (the *Lord of the Rings* trilogy, *The Ice Storm*), born Cedar Rapids, IA, Jan 28, 1981.

JANUARY 29 — SUNDAY
Day 29 — 336 Remaining

CATHOLIC SCHOOLS WEEK. Jan 29–Feb 4. A national celebration focusing on the uniqueness of Catholic schools. Many schools plan special activities celebrating their Catholic heritage. Jointly sponsored by the National Catholic Educational Association and the US Conference of Catholic Bishops. Annually, beginning on the last Sunday in January. For info: Natl Catholic Educational Assn, 1077 30th St NW, Ste 100, Washington, DC 20007-3852. Phone: (202) 337-6232. Web: www.catholicschools week.org.

CHEKHOV, ANTON PAVLOVICH: BIRTH ANNIVERSARY. Jan 29, 1860. Russian playwright and short story writer, especially remembered for *The Sea Gull, The Three Sisters* and *The Cherry Orchard*. Born at Taganrog, Russia; died July 15, 1904, at the Black Forest spa at Badenweiler, Germany.

CHINESE NEW YEAR. Jan 29. Traditional Chinese lunar year 4704 begins at sunset on the day of the second New Moon following the winter solstice. Outside China, the date of the New Year may differ by a day. The New Year can begin any time from Jan 21 through Feb 21. Begins the Year of the Dog. Generally celebrated until the Lantern Festival 15 days later, but merchants usually reopen their stores and places of business on the fifth day of the first lunar month. This holiday is celebrated as Tet in Vietnam. See also: "China: Lantern Festival" (Feb 12).

FIELDS, W.C.: BIRTH ANNIVERSARY. Jan 29, 1880. Stage and motion picture actor (*My Little Chickadee*), screenwriter and expert juggler. Born Claude William Dukenfield at Philadelphia, PA; died Dec 25, 1946, at Pasadena, CA. He wrote his own epitaph: "On the whole, I'd rather be in Philadelphia."

FREETHINKER'S DAY. Jan 29. Annual celebration of the birth of Thomas Paine. For info: Truth Seeker Co, PO Box 28550, San Diego, CA 92198. Phone: (760) 489-5211 or (800) 551-5328. Fax: (760) 489-5311. E-mail: editor@truthseeker.com. Web: truth seeker.com.

GROUNDHOG RUN. Jan 29. Kansas City, MO. 24th annual. The world's only 10k and 5k underground run takes place at the Hunt Midwest SubTropolis. 3,000 runners from across the country participate in this Grand Prix event to benefit Children's TLC Easter Seals. Est attendance: 3,000. For info: Children's TLC Easter Seals, 3101 Main St, Kansas City, MO 64111-1921. Phone: (816) 756-0780. Fax: (816) 756-1677. E-mail: ccarlton@childrens tlc.org. Web: www.childrenstlc.org.

KANSAS: ADMISSION DAY: ANNIVERSARY. Jan 29. Became the 34th state in 1861.

McKINLEY, WILLIAM: BIRTH ANNIVERSARY. Jan 29, 1843. 25th president of the US (1897–1901), born at Niles, OH. Died in office, at Buffalo, NY, Sept 14, 1901, as the result of a gunshot wound by an anarchist assassin Sept 6, 1901, while he was attending the Pan-American Exposition.

MILITARY BAN ON HOMOSEXUALS EASED: ANNIVERSARY. Jan 29, 1993. An interim policy on ending the ban on homosexuals in the US military was announced by President William Clinton. The policy ended the questioning of military recruits regarding their sexual orientation but allowed removal of openly homosexual members from active service. President Clinton's announced policy of "don't ask, don't tell, don't pursue" was intended to allow homosexuals to serve in the armed forces as long as they were discreet.

MOON PHASE: NEW MOON. Jan 29. Moon enters New Moon phase at 9:15 AM, EST.

MORMON BATTALION ARRIVAL IN CALIFORNIA: ANNIVERSARY. Jan 29, 1847. The 500 men of the US Mormon Battalion, along with 50 women and children, arrived at San Diego, CA, on this date, having marched 2,000 miles—the longest march in modern military history—since leaving Council Bluffs, IA, on July 16, 1846, to fight in the war against Mexico. In the course of their trek they established the first wagon route from Santa Fe to southern California. Their historic arrival is commemorated each year with a military parade in San Diego's Old Town.

PAINE, THOMAS: BIRTH ANNIVERSARY. Jan 29, 1737. American Revolutionary leader, a corset-maker by trade, author of *Common Sense*, *The Age of Reason* and many other influential works, was born at Thetford, England. "These are the times that try men's souls" are the well-known opening words of his inspirational tract *The Crisis*. Paine died at New York, NY, June 8, 1809, but 10 years later his remains were moved to England by William Cobbett for reburial there. Reburial was refused, however, and the location of Paine's bones, said to have been distributed, is unknown.

PERIGEAN SPRING TIDES. Jan 29. Spring tides, the highest possible tides, occur when New Moon or Full Moon takes place within 24 hours of the moment the Moon is nearest Earth (perigee) in its monthly orbit. The word *spring* refers not to the season but comes from the German word *springen*, "to rise up."

"THE RAVEN" PUBLISHED: ANNIVERSARY. Jan 29, 1845. One of the most famous poems in American literature was published on this date in New York's *Evening Mirror* newspaper. The author was anonymous, but the poem was such a sensation (it would be reprinted at least 16 times in various periodicals and books that year) that soon the author was revealed as literary critic and author Edgar Allan Poe. Despite the celebrity status Poe enjoyed as a result of "The Raven," it did not relieve his poverty: Poe received $15 for the poem. The classic lines "Once upon a midnight dreary . . ." and "Quoth the Raven, 'Nevermore'" resound in countless anthologies and dramatic readings as well as in parodies.

SANTA CRUZ BRIDAL EXPO. Jan 29. Cocoanut Grove, Santa Cruz, CA. Features more than 60 booths with every aspect needed for that perfect wedding, reception and honeymoon. Est attendance: 2,000. For info: Kate McGuire, Communications Mgr, Santa Cruz Beach Boardwalk, 400 Beach St, Santa Cruz, CA 95060-5491. Phone: (831) 423-5590. Fax: (831) 460-3336. E-mail: publicity@scseaside.com. Web: www.cocoanutgrovesanta cruz.com.

THE SEEING EYE ESTABLISHED: ANNIVERSARY. Jan 29, 1929. The Seeing Eye, North America's first guide dog school, was incorporated on this date at Nashville, TN. The first class took place in February and included Buddy, the "seeing eye" dog brought from Europe. The Seeing Eye was the first program in the US that enabled people with disabilities to be full participants in society. Its mission is to enhance the independence, self-confidence and dignity of people who are blind through the use of Seeing Eye dogs. Since its founding, The Seeing Eye has matched more than 13,000 specially bred dogs with blind people from the US and Canada. In 1931 the school moved to New Jersey, where it continues to breed, raise and train Seeing Eye dogs and instruct blind and visually impaired people in the use and care of their dogs. For info: Melissa Campbell, Mgr of Public Relations, The Seeing Eye, PO Box 375, Morristown, NJ 07963-0375. Phone: (973) 539-4425. Fax: (973) 539-0922. E-mail: info@seeingeye.org. Web: www.seeingeye.org.

SWEDENBORG, EMANUEL: BIRTH ANNIVERSARY. Jan 29, 1688 (OS). Born at Stockholm, Sweden, Swedenborg is remembered as a scientist, inventor, writer and religious leader. Swedenborg made plans for machine guns, submarines and airplanes and published Sweden's first scientific journal. His study of human anatomy and his search for the soul led him to begin thinking about religion. His writings interpreting the scriptures formed the basis of the Church of the New Jerusalem, which was established by his devotees soon after his death. He died at London, England, Mar 29, 1772.

BIRTHDAYS TODAY

John Forsythe, 88, actor ("Bachelor Father," Charlie's voice on "Charlie's Angels," "Dynasty"), born John Freund at Penn's Grove, NJ, Jan 29, 1918.

Sara Gilbert, 31, actress ("Roseanne"), born Santa Monica, CA, Jan 29, 1975.

Heather Graham, 36, actress (*Lost in Space, Boogie Nights*), born Milwaukee, WI, Jan 29, 1970.

Germaine Greer, 67, author (*Daddy We Hardly Knew You, The Female Eunuch*), born Melbourne, Australia, Jan 29, 1939.

Dominik Hasek, 41, former hockey player, born Pardubice, Czechoslovakia, Jan 29, 1965.

Ann Jillian, 55, actress ("It's a Living," *The Ann Jillian Story*), born Cambridge, MA, Jan 29, 1951.

Andrew Keegan, 27, actor (*Independence Day*), born Los Angeles, CA, Jan 29, 1979.

Gregory Efthimios (Greg) Louganis, 46, actor, Olympic gold medal diver, born San Diego, CA, Jan 29, 1960.

Bobbie Phillips, 38, actress ("Murder One," *Red Shoe Diaries*), born Charleston, SC, Jan 29, 1968 (some sources say 1972).

Katharine Ross, 63, actress (*The Graduate*), born Los Angeles, CA, Jan 29, 1943.

Tom Selleck, 61, actor ("Magnum, PI," *Three Men and a Baby, Mr Baseball*), born Detroit, MI, Jan 29, 1945.

Nick Turturro, 44, actor ("NYPD Blue"), born Queens, NY, Jan 29, 1962.

Oprah Winfrey, 52, TV talk-show host (Emmys for "The Oprah Winfrey Show"), actress (*The Color Purple*), producer (owner of Harpo Studios), born Kosciusko, MS, Jan 29, 1954.

JANUARY 30 — MONDAY
Day 30 — 335 Remaining

BEATLES LAST CONCERT: ANNIVERSARY. Jan 30, 1969. On this day the Beatles performed together in public for the last time. The show took place on the roof of their Apple Studios in London, England, but it was interrupted by police after they received complaints from the neighbors about the noise.

BLOODY SUNDAY: ANNIVERSARY. Jan 30, 1972. In Londonderry, Northern Ireland, 13 Roman Catholics were shot dead by British troops during a banned civil rights march. During 1972, the first year of British direct rule, 467 people were killed in the fighting.

BUBBLE WRAP® APPRECIATION DAY. Jan 30. A day to celebrate the joy that Bubble Wrap® brings to our lives. A day to learn the history and snapping etiquette and to gain a new appreciation of the country's favorite shipping material (invented in 1960). Also, a day to snap and share Bubble Wrap® with coworkers, classmates and loved ones. For info: Sealed Air Corp, 301 Mayhill St, Saddlebrook, NJ 07663. Phone: (201) 712-7000. Fax: (201) 712-7019. Web: www.sealedair.com. Also for info: Wake-up Show WVNI with Todd & Denise, PO Box 1628, Bloomington, IN 47402. Phone: (812) 335-9500. Fax: (812) 335-8880. E-mail: todayschristianmusic@spirit95fm.com. Web: www.SPIRIT 95FM.com.

CHARLES I EXECUTION: ANNIVERSARY. Jan 30, 1649. English king beheaded by order of Parliament under Oliver Cromwell on this date; considered a martyr by some.

CHENEY, RICHARD (DICK): BIRTHDAY. Jan 30, 1941. 46th vice president of the US, born at Lincoln, NE.

CRAFT AND HOBBY ASSOCIATION ANNUAL CONVENTION AND TRADE SHOW. Jan 30–Feb 2 (classes begin Jan 29). Las Vegas, NV. The world's largest trade show for the craft and hobby industry. The CHA show also offers extensive educational programs and workshops. Est attendance: 20,000. For info: Craft and Hobby Association, 319 E 54th St, Elmwood Park, NJ 07407. Phone: (201) 794-1133. Fax: (201) 797-0657. E-mail: info@craftandhobby.org. Web: www.chashow.org.

FIRST BRAWL IN THE US HOUSE OF REPRESENTATIVES: ANNIVERSARY. Jan 30, 1798. The first brawl to break out on the floor of the US House of Representatives occurred at Philadelphia, PA. The fight was precipitated by an argument between Matthew Lyon of Vermont and Roger Griswold of Connecticut. Lyon spat in Griswold's face. Although a resolution to expel Lyon was introduced, the measure failed and Lyon maintained his seat.

GANDHI ASSASSINATED: ANNIVERSARY. Jan 30, 1948. Indian religious and political leader, assassinated at New Delhi, India. The assassin was a Hindu extremist, Ram Naturam. See also: "Gandhi, Mohandas Karamchand (Mahatma): Birth Anniversary" (Oct 2).

INANE ANSWERING MESSAGE DAY. Jan 30. Annually, the day set aside to change, shorten, replace or delete those ridiculous and/or annoying answering machine messages that waste the time of anyone who must listen to them. [©2003 by WH.] For info: Thomas & Ruth Roy, Wellcat Holidays, 2418 Long Ln, Lebanon, PA 17046. Phone: (717) 279-0184. E-mail: info@wellcat.com. Web: www.wellcat.com.

	S	M	T	W	T	F	S
January 2006	1	2	3	4	5	6	7
	8	9	10	11	12	13	14
	15	16	17	18	19	20	21
	22	23	24	25	26	27	28
	29	30	31				

JORDAN: KING'S BIRTHDAY. Jan 30. National holiday. Honors King Abdullah II, son of the late King Hussein, who was born Jan 30, 1962, and assumed the throne June 9, 1999.

MARYLAND ADOPTS ARTICLES OF CONFEDERATION: 225th ANNIVERSARY. Jan 30, 1781. Maryland became the last of the 13 original states to adopt the Articles of Confederation.

OSCEOLA: DEATH ANNIVERSARY. Jan 30, 1838. Osceola was a leader during the Second Seminole War (1835–42). During the first two years of the war, he led the fight against removal of the Florida Seminoles to Indian territory. He was captured under a flag of truce in 1837 and imprisoned at Fort Marion in St. Augustine, FL. He was moved to Fort Moultrie at Charleston Harbor, SC, where he died. He was born near present-day Tuskegee, AL, circa 1804.

RAF BOMBS HITLER CELEBRATION: ANNIVERSARY. Jan 30, 1943. British Royal Air Force Mosquito bombers ran a daylight raid on Berlin timed to coincide with a speech being given by Joseph Goebbels in honor of Hitler's 10th year in power.

ROOSEVELT, FRANKLIN DELANO: BIRTH ANNIVERSARY. Jan 30, 1882. 32nd president of the US (Mar 4, 1933–Apr 12, 1945). The only president to serve more than two terms, FDR was elected four times. He supported the Allies in WWII before the US entered the struggle by supplying them with war materials through the Lend-Lease Act; he became deeply involved in broad decision making after the Japanese attack on Pearl Harbor Dec 7, 1941. Born at Hyde Park, NY, he died a few months into his fourth term at Warm Springs, GA, Apr 12, 1945.

TET OFFENSIVE BEGINS: ANNIVERSARY. Jan 30, 1968. After calling for a cease-fire during the Tet holiday celebrations, North Vietnam and the National Liberation Front launched a major offensive throughout South Vietnam on that holiday. Attacks erupted in 36 of the 44 provincial capitals and five of the six major cities. In addition, the Viet Cong attacked the US embassy in Saigon, Tan Son Nhut Air Base, the presidential palace and South Vietnamese general staff headquarters. Costing as many as 40,000 battlefield deaths, the offensive was a tactical defeat for the Viet Cong and North Vietnam. The South Vietnamese held their ground and the US was able to airlift troops into the critical areas and quickly regain control. However, the offensive is credited as a strategic success in that it continued the demoralization of American public opinion. After Tet, American policy toward Vietnam shifted from winning the war to seeking an honorable way out.

THOMAS, ISAIAH: BIRTH ANNIVERSARY. Jan 30, 1749. American printer, editor, almanac publisher, historian and founder of the American Antiquarian Society. Born at Boston, MA; died Apr 4, 1831, at Worcester, MA.

TUCHMAN, BARBARA W.: BIRTH ANNIVERSARY. Jan 30, 1912. Historian and journalist Barbara Tuchman's most famous works were her Pulitzer Prize–winning books *The Guns of August* (1962) and *Stilwell and the American Experience in China, 1911–45* (1971). Tuchman was known for making history lively. Other well-known books included *The Proud Tower* (1966) and *The First Salute* (1988). Barbara Wertheim Tuchman was born at New York, NY, and died at Greenwich, CT, Feb 6, 1988.

TULSA BOAT, SPORT & TRAVEL SHOW. Jan 30–Feb 5. Expo Square, Tulsa, OK. The Southwest's largest selection of boats, RVs and resort information. An annual show that begins the last Monday of January. Est attendance: 60,000. For info: Randy Chrisman, Tulsa Boat, Sport & Travel Show, PO Box 2992, Tulsa, OK 74401. Phone: (918) 486-3318. Fax: (918) 486-3428. E-mail: tbsts1@mindspring.com. Web: www.tulsaboat show.com.

BIRTHDAYS TODAY

John Baldacci, 51, Governor of Maine (D), born Bangor, ME, Jan 30, 1955.

Christian Bale, 32, actor (*Batman Begins, Little Women, Empire of the Sun*), born Pembrokeshire, West Wales, Jan 30, 1974.

Brett Butler, 48, comedienne, actress ("Grace Under Fire"), born Montgomery, AL, Jan 30, 1958.

Richard (Dick) Cheney, 65, 46th vice president of the US, born Lincoln, NE, Jan 30, 1941.

Phil Collins, 55, musician, singer, songwriter, born Chiswick, England, Jan 30, 1951.

Charles S. Dutton, 55, actor ("Roc," *Mississippi Masala, Menace II Society*), born Baltimore, MD, Jan 30, 1951.

Gene Hackman, 76, actor (*The French Connection, Bonnie and Clyde, Unforgiven*), born San Bernardino, CA, Jan 30, 1930.

Davey Johnson, 63, baseball manager and former player, born Orlando, FL, Jan 30, 1943.

Dorothy Malone, 81, actress ("Peyton Place"; Oscar for *Written on the Wind*), born Chicago, IL, Jan 30, 1925.

Dick Martin, 84, comedian, actor (Emmy for "Rowan & Martin's Laugh-In"), born Detroit, MI, Jan 30, 1922.

Vanessa Redgrave, 69, actress (*Mary, Queen of Scots; Julia*), born London, England, Jan 30, 1937.

Jalen Rose, 33, basketball player, born Detroit, MI, Jan 30, 1973.

Louis Rukeyser, 72, financial commentator, former host ("Wall Street Week"), born New York, NY, Jan 30, 1934.

Boris Spassky, 69, former chess player, journalist, born Leningrad, USSR, Jan 30, 1937.

Curtis Strange, 51, golfer, broadcaster, born Norfolk, VA, Jan 30, 1955.

Jody Watley, 47, singer, born Chicago, IL, Jan 30, 1959.

JANUARY 31 — TUESDAY

Day 31 — 334 Remaining

FIRST SOCIAL SECURITY CHECK ISSUED: ANNIVERSARY. Jan 31, 1940. Ida May Fuller of Ludlow, VT, received the first monthly retirement check in the amount of $22.54. Ms Fuller had worked for three years under the Social Security program (which had been established by legislation in 1935). The accumulated taxes on her salary over those three years were $24.75. She lived to be 100 years old, collecting $22,888 in Social Security benefits. See also: "Social Security Act: Anniv" (Aug 14).

GREY, ZANE: BIRTH ANNIVERSARY. Jan 31, 1872. Zane Grey (original name Pearl Grey), American dentist and prolific author of tales of the Old West, was born at Zanesville, OH. Grey wrote more than 80 books that were translated into many languages and sold more than 10 million copies. The novel *Riders of the Purple Sage* (1912) was the most popular. Grey died Oct 23, 1939, at Altadena, CA.

INSPIRE YOUR HEART WITH THE ARTS DAY. Jan 31. A day to experience art in your life. Food sustains you as a human; art inspires you to be divine. Go to an art museum, browse through an art book at the library, enroll in an art class or commission an artist. Read your favorite poem out loud. Go to a music concert or play. Sign up for dance lessons. Today is a day to inspire your heart with the arts! For info: Rev Jayne Howard-Feldman, Angel Heights, PO Box 95, Upperco, MD 21155. Phone: (410) 833-6912. Fax: (410) 429-5425. E-mail: earthangel 4peace@aol.com. Web: www.earthangel4peace.com.

INTERNATIONAL HOOF-CARE SUMMIT. Jan 31–Feb 3. Cincinnati, OH. This annual meeting attracts highly innovative foot care professionals interested in learning new ways to provide quality hoof care. Est attendance: 800. For info: Frank Lessiter, International Hoof-Care Summit, PO Box 624, Brookfield, WI 53008-0624. Phone: (262) 782-4480. Fax: (262) 782-1252. E-mail: info@lesspub.com. Web: www.americanfarriers .com.

ISLAMIC NEW YEAR. Jan 31. Islamic calendar date: Muharram 1, 1427. The first day of the first month of the Islamic calendar. Different methods for "anticipating" the visibility of the new moon crescent at Mecca are used by different groups. US date may vary. Began at sunset the preceding day.

MOORE, GARRY: BIRTH ANNIVERSARY. Jan 31, 1915. American television host Garry Moore was born Thomas Garrison Morfit at Baltimore, MD. His best-known shows were "I've Got a Secret" (1952–67) and "To Tell the Truth" (1969–76). He gave Carol Burnett her break on TV when he made her a regular on "The Garry Moore Show." He died Nov 28, 1993, at Hilton Head Island, SC.

MORRIS, ROBERT: BIRTH ANNIVERSARY. Jan 31, 1734. Signer of the Declaration of Independence, the Articles of Confederation and the Constitution. He was one of only two men who signed all three documents. He was born at Liverpool, England, and died May 7, 1806, at Philadelphia, PA.

NAURU: NATIONAL HOLIDAY. Jan 31. Republic of Nauru. Commemorates independence in 1968 from a UN trusteeship administered by Australia, New Zealand and the UK.

ROBINSON, JACKIE: BIRTH ANNIVERSARY. Jan 31, 1919. Jack Roosevelt Robinson, athlete and business executive, first black to enter professional major league baseball (Brooklyn Dodgers, 1947–56). Voted National League's Most Valuable Player in 1949 and elected to the Baseball Hall of Fame in 1962. Born at Cairo, GA, Jackson died at Stamford, CT, Oct 24, 1972.

SCHUBERT, FRANZ: BIRTH ANNIVERSARY. Jan 31, 1797. Composer, born at Vienna, Austria, and died there of typhus Nov 19, 1828, at age 31. Buried, at his request, near the grave of Beethoven. Schubert last worked on his "Unfinished Symphony" (No 8) in 1822. On the 100th anniversary of his death in 1928 a $10,000 prize was offered to "finish" the work. The protests were so great that the offer was withdrawn.

SCOTLAND: UP HELLY AA. Jan 31. Lerwick, Shetland Islands. Norse galley burned in impressive ceremony symbolizing sacrifice to the sun. Old Viking custom. A festival marking the end of Yule. Annually, the last Tuesday in January. For info: Tourist Information Centre, Market Cross, Lerwick, Shetland, Scotland ZE1 0LU. Phone: (44) (8701) 999-440. Fax: (44) (1595) 695-807. E-mail: info@visitshetland.com. Web: www.visitshetland.com.

SLOVIK, EDDIE D.: EXECUTION ANNIVERSARY. Jan 31, 1945. Anniversary of execution by firing squad of 24-year-old Private Eddie D. Slovik. Born at Detroit, MI, Feb 18, 1920, Slovik was assigned to Company G, 109th Infantry, 28th Division, US Army. His death sentence, the first for desertion since the Civil War, has been a subject of controversy. First buried in France, Slovik's remains were exhumed in 1987 for reburial beside his wife, Antoinette, who died in 1979, after years of effort to clear Slovik's name and have his body returned to the US.

SPACE MILESTONE: *APOLLO 14* (US): 35th ANNIVERSARY. Jan 31, 1971. Launch date of *Apollo 14*. Five days later on Feb 5 astronauts Alan B. Shepard, Jr, and Edgar D. Mitchell landed on the moon (Lunar Module *Antares*). Command Module *Kitty Hawk* was piloted by Stuart A. Roosa. Pacific splashdown on Feb 9.

SPACE MILESTONE: *EXPLORER 1* (US). Jan 31, 1958. The first successful US satellite. Although launched four months later than the Soviet Union's *Sputnik*, *Explorer* reached a higher altitude and detected a zone of intense radiation inside Earth's magnetic field. This was later named the Van Allen radiation belts. More than 65 subsequent *Explorer* satellites were launched through 1984.

SPACE MILESTONE: *LUNA 9* (USSR): 40th ANNIVERSARY. Jan 31, 1966. Launch of unmanned mission that accomplished the first soft landing on the moon three days later on Feb 3. Relayed TV photos of the lunar surface.

SPACE MILESTONE: PROJECT MERCURY TEST (US): 45th ANNIVERSARY. Jan 31, 1961. A test of Project Mercury spacecraft accomplished the first US recovery of a large animal from space. Ham, the chimpanzee, successfully performed simple tasks in space.

Ernest (Ernie) Banks, 75, Hall of Fame baseball player, born Dallas, TX, Jan 31, 1931.

Queen Beatrix, 68, Queen of the Netherlands, born Sostdijk, Netherlands, Jan 31, 1938.

Carol Channing, 83, actress (stage: *Hello, Dolly!; Thoroughly Modern Millie*), born Seattle, WA, Jan 31, 1923.

Minnie Driver, 35, actress (*Gross Pointe Blank, Good Will Hunting*), born London, England, Jan 31, 1971.

Philip Glass, 69, composer, born Baltimore, MD, Jan 31, 1937.

Johnny (Rotten) Lydon, 50, lead singer (Sex Pistols, 1975–77), born near London, England, Jan 31, 1956.

Kelly Lynch, 47, actress (*Mr Magoo, Drugstore Cowboy*), born Minneapolis, MN, Jan 31, 1959.

Norman Mailer, 83, author (*The Executioner's Song, The Naked and the Dead*), born Long Branch, NJ, Jan 31, 1923.

Stuart Margolin, 66, actor, director, writer ("The Rockford Files" [Emmy Awards, 1979, 1980], *The Big Blue, S.O.B.*), born Davenport, IA, Jan 31, 1940.

Suzanne Pleshette, 69, actress ("The Bob Newhart Show"), born New York, NY, Jan 31, 1937.

(Lynn) Nolan Ryan, 59, Hall of Fame baseball player, born Refugio, TX, Jan 31, 1947.

Jean Simmons, 77, actress (*Black Narcissus, The Robe, Elmer Gantry*), born London, England, Jan 31, 1929.

Jessica Walter, 62, actress ("Amy Prentiss," *Play Misty for Me, The Flamingo Kid*), born Brooklyn, NY, Jan 31, 1944.

Februarie.

FEBRUARY 1 — WEDNESDAY
Day 32 — 333 Remaining

AMD/LOW VISION AWARENESS MONTH. Feb 1–28. Macular degeneration is a leading cause of vision loss. Low vision aids can make the most of remaining vision. Information on eye disease warning signs and on low vision aids will be available. For info: Prevent Blindness America ®, 211 W Wacker Dr, Ste 1700, Chicago, IL 60606. Phone: (800) 331-2020. E-mail: info@preventblindness.org. Web: www.preventblindness.org.

★**AMERICAN HEART MONTH.** Feb 1–28. Presidential Proclamation issued each year for February since 1964. (PL88–254 of Dec 30, 1963.)

AMERICAN HEART MONTH. Feb 1–28. During this month, the American Heart Association will focus on women with "Go Red for Women," an educational movement about women and cardiovascular disease. Each year cardiovascular diseases claim the lives of nearly 500,000 women. For all of the women you know who have been affected by cardiovascular disease, participate in Wear Red Day on Friday, Feb 3. For information on American Heart Month and Go Red for Women: American Heart Association, 7272 Greenville Ave, Dallas, TX 75231. Phone: (888) MY-HEART. Fax: (214) 369-3685. Web: www.americanheart.org.

BAKE FOR FAMILY FUN MONTH. Feb 1–28. The Home Baking Association has designated February as "Bake for Family Fun Month," dedicated to the great taste, good nutrition, economy and family fun of traditional home baking. For info: Charlene Patton, 2931 SW Gainsboro Rd, Topeka, KS 66614. Phone: (785) 478-3283. Fax: (785) 478-3024. Web: www.homebaking.org.

BLACK HISTORY MONTH AT TUSKEGEE UNIVERSITY. Feb 1–28. Tuskegee, AL. Events celebrating Tuskegee's 125th anniversary, the 150th anniversary of Booker T. Washington's birth and other great moments in black history. For full schedule of events, contact: Public and Media Affairs, Tuskegee University, 223 Kresge Center, Tuskegee, AL 36088. Phone: (334) 727-8349. E-mail: media@tuskegee.edu. Web: www.tuskegee.edu.

BLACK MARIA STUDIO: ANNIVERSARY. Feb 1, 1893. The first moving picture studio was built at Thomas Edison's laboratory compound at West Orange, NJ, at a cost of less than $700. The wooden structure of irregular oblong shape was covered with black tar paper. It had a sharply sloping roof hinged at one edge so that half of it could be raised to admit sunlight. Fifty feet in length, it was mounted on a pivot enabling it to be swung around to follow the changing position of the sun. There was a stage draped in black at one end of the room. Though the structure was officially called a Kinetographic Theater, it was nicknamed the "Black Maria" because it resembled an old-fashioned police wagon.

BUBBLE GUM DAY. Feb 1. Imagine being able to chew bubble gum at school, while helping a worthy cause! Today children across the country will be doing just that. Kids who donate 50¢ or more get to chew gum at school. The money collected is donated to a charity chosen by the school. Don't forget to get your principal's permission! For info: Ruth Spiro, PO Box 1023, Deerfield, IL 60015. Web: www.bubblegumday.com.

CAR INSURANCE FIRST ISSUED: ANNIVERSARY. Feb 1, 1898. Travelers Insurance Company issued the first car insurance against accidents with horses.

CARAWAY, HATTIE WYATT: BIRTH ANNIVERSARY. Feb 1, 1878. Born at Bakersville, TN, Hattie Caraway became a US Senator from Arkansas in 1931 when her husband died and she was appointed to fill out his term. The following year, she ran for the seat herself and became the first woman elected to the US Senate. She served 14 years there, becoming an adept and tireless legislator (once introducing 43 bills on the same day) who worked for women's rights (once cosponsoring an equal rights amendment), supported New Deal policies as well as Prohibition and opposed the increasing influence of lobbyists. Caraway died at Falls Church, VA, Dec 21, 1950.

FEBRUARY IS FABULOUS FLORIDA STRAWBERRY MONTH. Feb 1–28. Strawberries in February? You bet your snow boots! Though it's cold and dreary in many parts of the country, February is fabulous in Florida where strawberry growers are harvesting their winter crop and shipping handpicked fruit to key markets. Strawberries dipped in chocolate or champagne are a Valentine's Day delight. Consider using the ripe, luscious berry in a variety of recipes from salads to shortbread. For info: Florida Strawberry Growers Assn, PO Drawer 2550, Plant City, FL 33564. Phone: (813) 752-6822. Web: www.straw-berry.org.

FESTIVAL OF CAMELLIAS. Feb 1–28. Massee Lane Gardens, Fort Valley, GA. Focal event of Camellia Days, which run from January through March each year. Annual celebration of the lovely flower, the camellia. Festival events include garden tours and workshops, plant sale and more. Call for more details and ticket prices. Sponsor: The American Camellia Society. Est attendance: 8,000. For info: Massee Lane Gardens, 100 Massee Ln, Fort Valley, GA 31030. Phone: (478) 967-2722. Fax: (478) 967-2083. E-mail: festival@camellias-acs.org. Web: www.camellias-acs.org.

FESTIVAL OF THE NORTH. Feb 1–28. Ketchikan, AK. A cultural event encompassing an annual Wearable Art Show and performing, visual and literary arts, including a myriad of workshops. Annually, the month of February. Est attendance: 2,000. For info: Ketchikan Area Arts and Humanities Council, 716 Totem Way, Ketchikan, AK 99901. Phone: (907) 225-2211. Fax: (907) 225-4330. E-mail: info@ketchikanarts.org.

FIRST SESSION OF SUPREME COURT: ANNIVERSARY. Feb 1, 1790. The Supreme Court of the United States met for the first time in New York City with Chief Justice John Jay presiding.

FLAGSTAFF WINTERFEST. Feb 1–28. Flagstaff, AZ. This festival, now in its 20th year, celebrates the many facets of a Flagstaff winter. Family fun for everyone: concerts, performances, art shows, snow sports, wacky sports, winter workshops, children's events and much more. The fun will go on with or without snow. Est attendance: 20,000. For info: Sarah Whitney, Winterfest Coordinator, Flagstaff Chamber of Commerce, 101 W Rte 66, Flagstaff, AZ 86001. Phone: (928) 774-4505. Fax: (928) 779-1209. E-mail: swhitney@flagstaffchamber.com. Web: www.flagstaffchamber.com.

FORD, JOHN: BIRTH ANNIVERSARY. Feb 1, 1895. Film director John Ford was born at Cape Elizabeth, ME, as Sean Aloysius O'Feeney; he changed his name after moving to Hollywood. Ford won his first Academy Award in 1935 for *The Informer.* Among his many other films: *Stagecoach, Young Mr Lincoln, The Grapes of Wrath, How Green Was My Valley, Rio Grande, What Price Glory?* and *Mister Roberts.* During World War II he served as chief of the Field Photographic Branch of the OSS. Two documentaries made during the war earned him Academy Awards. He died Aug 31, 1973, at Palm Desert, CA.

FREEDOM DAY: ANNIVERSARY. Feb 1, 1865. Anniversary of President Abraham Lincoln's approval of the 13th Amendment to the US Constitution (abolishing slavery): "1. Neither slavery nor involuntary servitude, except as a punishment for crime whereof the party shall have been duly convicted, shall exist within the United States or any place subject to their jurisdiction. 2. Congress shall have power to enforce this article by appropriate legislation." The amendment had been proposed by Congress Jan 31, 1865; ratification was completed Dec 6, 1865.

GABLE, CLARK: BIRTH ANNIVERSARY. Feb 1, 1901. Actor William Clark Gable's first film was *The Painted Desert* in 1931, when talking films were replacing silent films. He won an Academy Award for his role in the comedy *It Happened One Night,* which established him as a romantic screen idol. Other films included *China Seas, Mutiny on the Bounty, Saratoga, Run Silent Run Deep* and *Gone with the Wind,* for which his casting as Rhett Butler seemed a foregone conclusion due to his popularity as the acknowledged "King of Movies." Gable was born at Cadiz, OH, and died Nov 16, 1960, at Hollywood, CA, shortly after completing his last film, Arthur Miller's *The Misfits,* in which he starred with Marilyn Monroe.

"GENERAL ELECTRIC THEATER" TV PREMIERE: ANNIVERSARY. Feb 1, 1953. CBS's half-hour dramatic anthology series was hosted by Ronald Reagan (in between his movie and political careers). Making their television debuts were Joseph Cotten (1954); Fred MacMurray, James Stewart and Myrna Loy (1955); Bette Davis, Anne Baxter, Tony Curtis and Fred Astaire (1957); Sammy Davis, Jr (1958); and Gene Tierney (1960). Other memorable stars who appeared on the series include: Joan Crawford, Harry Belafonte, Rosalind Russell, Ernie Kovacs, the Marx Brothers and Nancy Davis [Reagan], who starred with husband Ronald Reagan in an episode titled "A Turkey for the President" (1958).

"GOOD TIMES" TV PREMIERE: ANNIVERSARY. Feb 1, 1974. A CBS spin-off of "Maude," which was a spin-off of "All in the Family." "Good Times" featured an African-American family living in the housing projects of Chicago and struggling to improve their lot. The cast featured Esther Rolle and John Amos as Florida and James Evans, Jimmie Walker as son J.J., BernNadette Stanis as daughter Thelma, Ralph Carter as son Michael, Johnny Brown as janitor Mr Bookman, Ja'Net DuBois as neighbor Willona Woods, Janet Jackson as Willona's adopted daughter Penny and Ben Powers as Thelma's husband Keith Anderson.

GREENSBORO SIT-IN: ANNIVERSARY. Feb 1, 1960. Commercial discrimination against blacks and other minorities provoked a nonviolent protest. At Greensboro, NC, four students from the Agricultural and Technical College (Ezell Blair, Jr, Franklin McCain, Joseph McNeill and David Richmond) sat down at a Woolworths store lunch counter and ordered coffee. Refused service, they remained all day. The following days similar sit-ins took place at the Woolworths' lunch counter. Before the week was over they were joined by a few white students. The protest spread rapidly, especially in Southern states. More than 1,600 people were arrested before the year was over for participating in sit-ins. Civil rights for all became a cause for thousands of students and activists. In response, equal accommodation regardless of race became the rule at lunch counters, hotels and business establishments in thousands of places.

HUGHES, LANGSTON: BIRTH ANNIVERSARY. Feb 1, 1902. African-American poet and author, born at Joplin, MO. Among his works are the poetry collection *Montage of a Dream Deferred,* plays, a novel, memoirs and short stories. He wrote, "My soul has grown deep like the rivers," and asked, "What happens to a dream deferred?" Hughes died May 22, 1967, at New York, NY.

HULA IN THE COOLA DAY. Feb 1. A day for those longing to escape the winter doldrums to laugh at the cold with a luau party. Put away your winter coats, get out your shorts and flip-flops, play limbo and say aloha! For info: iParty, 270 Bridge St, Ste 301, Dedham, MA 02026. Phone: (888) 4giggles. E-mail: fun @iparty.com. Web: www.iparty.com.

INTERNATIONAL BOOST SELF-ESTEEM MONTH. Feb 1–28. A month to focus on the importance of nurturing and cultivating self-esteem to beat the winter blahs, to boost morale and to inspire yourself and others to seize new challenges. For info: Valla Dana Fotiades, M.Ed., PO Box 133, Waverly, FL 33877. Phone: (863) 875-0759. E-mail: Valladana@cs.com.

INTERNATIONAL EXPECT SUCCESS MONTH. Feb 1–28. If you want good things to happen to you in the new year, you must "Expect Success . . . then work like there is no other option." For details and information on how to make this your most successful year yet by letting the power of positive expectation work for you, contact iExpect Success. For info: Karla Brandau, iExpect Success, 4985 Chartley Circle, Lilburn, GA 30047. Phone: (770) 923-0883. Fax: (770) 931-2530. E-mail: karla@karla speaks.com. Web: www.karlaspeaks.com.

"LATE NIGHT WITH DAVID LETTERMAN" TV PREMIERE: ANNIVERSARY. Feb 1, 1982. This is when it all began: stupid pet tricks, stupid human tricks and the legendary top ten lists. "Late Night" premiered on NBC as a talk/variety show appearing after "The Tonight Show with Johnny Carson." Host David Letterman was known for his irreverent sense of humor and daffy antics. The offbeat show attained cult status among college crowds and insomniacs, as many tuned in to see a Velcro-suited Letterman throw himself against a wall. The show also featured bandleader-sidekick Paul Shaffer, writer Chris Elliott and Calvert DeForest as geezer Larry "Bud" Melman. In 1993 Letterman made a highly publicized exit from NBC and began hosting "The Late Show" on CBS.

LIBRARY LOVERS' MONTH. Feb 1–28. A monthlong celebration of school, public and private libraries of all types. This is a time for everyone, especially library support groups, to recognize the value of libraries and to work to ensure that the nation's libraries will continue to serve. For info: Stephanie Stokes, Friends and Foundations for California Libraries, 11045 Wrightwood Pl, Studio City, CA 91604-3961. Phone: (818) 980-7476. E-mail: librarylovers@librarysupport.net. Web: www.librarysupport.net /librarylovers/.

MARFAN SYNDROME AWARENESS MONTH. Feb 1–28. Volunteers across the country distribute items with a heart theme and educational information about Marfan syndrome and related connective tissue disorders that can result in life-threatening cardiovascular problems as well as orthopedic and ophthalmologic handicaps; it affects about 200,000 Americans. Annually, the month of February. For info: Cathie Tsuchiya, Natl Marfan Foundation, 22 Manhasset Ave, Port Washington, NY 11050. Phone: (800) 862-7326 or (516) 883-8712. Fax: (516) 883-8040. E-mail: ctsuchiya@marfan.org. Web: www.marfan.org.

★**NATIONAL AFRICAN AMERICAN HISTORY MONTH.** Feb 1–28.

NATIONAL BIRD FEEDING MONTH. Feb 1–28. To spread the word of how difficult it can be for birds to survive in North

	S	M	T	W	T	F	S
February				1	2	3	4
2006	5	6	7	8	9	10	11
	12	13	14	15	16	17	18
	19	20	21	22	23	24	25
	26	27	28				

American winters, in 1993 the National Bird-Feeding Society named February National Bird Feeding Month. The widespread awareness generated by this event has contributed to the safe passage of winter for our feathered friends. Providing wild birds with food, water and shelter supplements their natural diet and helps them survive. For info: National Bird Feeding Month, 7370 MacArthur Blvd, Glen Echo, MD 20812. Web: www.birdfeeding.org.

NATIONAL BLACK HISTORY MONTH. Feb 1–28. Traditionally the month containing Abraham Lincoln's birthday (Feb 12) and Frederick Douglass's presumed birthday (Feb 14). Observance of a special period to recognize achievements and contributions by African Americans dates from February 1926, when it was launched by Dr. Carter G. Woodson. 2006 theme: Celebrating Community: Black Fraternal, Social and Civic Institutions. Variously designated Negro History, Black History, Afro-American History, African-American History, the observance period was initially one week, but since 1976 the entire month of February. For info: Assn for the Study of African American Life and History, Inc, Howard University, C.B. Powell Building, 525 Bryant St, Ste C142, Washington, DC 20059. Phone: (202) 865-0053. Fax: (202) 265-7920. E-mail: info@asalh.net. Web: www.asalh.org.

NATIONAL CHERRY MONTH. Feb 1–28. To publicize the colorful red tart cherry. For info: Cherry Marketing Institute, PO Box 30285, Lansing, MI 48909-7785. Fax: (517) 669-3354. E-mail: jdepriest@usacherries.com. Web: www.usacherries.com.

NATIONAL CHILDREN'S DENTAL HEALTH MONTH. Feb 1–28. To increase dental awareness and stress the importance of regular dental care. For info: American Dental Assn, 211 E Chicago Ave, Chicago, IL 60611. Phone: (312) 440-2500. Web: www.ada.org.

NATIONAL GET TO KNOW AN INDEPENDENT REAL ESTATE BROKER MONTH. Feb 1–28. February has been named "National Get to Know an Independent Real Estate Broker Month" by the National Association of Independent Real Estate Brokers. For info: Gary Conner, NAIREB, 7102 Mardyke Ln, Indianapolis, IN 46226. Phone/fax: (317) 549-1709. E-mail: Director@NationalRealEstateBrokers.org. Web: www.NationalRealEstateBrokers.org.

NATIONAL GIRLS AND WOMEN IN SPORTS DAY. Feb 1. Celebrates and honors all girls and women participating in sports. Recognizes the passage of Title IX in 1972, the law that guarantees gender equity in federally funded school programs, including athletics. Sponsored by the American Association of University Women, Girls Incorporated, the Girl Scouts, the National Association for Girls and Women in Sports, the National Women's Law Center, the Women's Sports Foundation and the YWCA. For info: Women's Sports Foundation, Eisenhower Park, East Meadow, NY 11554. Phone: (516) 542-4700 or (800) 227-3988. Web: www.NGWSDcentral.com.

NATIONAL HOT BREAKFAST MONTH. Feb 1–28. Take time out this month to start your day with a good hot breakfast. Sponsored by Jimmy Dean. For info: Marilyn Kroger, Call Center Mgr, Sara Lee Foods, 10151 Carver Rd, Cincinnati, OH 45242-4719. Phone: (513) 936-2199. Fax: (513) 936-2170. E-mail: marilyn.kroger@saralee.com. Web: www.jimmydean.com.

NATIONAL PARENT LEADERSHIP MONTH. Feb 1–28. In order to recognize, honor and celebrate parents for their vital leadership roles in their homes and communities and in state, national and international arenas, Parents Anonymous® Inc has designated the month of February as National Parent Leadership Month. This annual event will acknowledge the strengths of parents as leaders and generate awareness about the important roles parents can play in shaping the lives of their families and communities. Founded in 1969, Parents Anonymous® Inc is dedicated to strengthening families by preventing child abuse and neglect all around the world. For info: Parents Anonymous® Inc, 675 W Foothill Blvd, Ste 220, Claremont, CA 91711. Phone: (909) 621-6184. E-mail: parentsanonymous@parentsanonymous.org. Web: www.parentsanonymous.org.

NATIONAL PATIENT RECOGNITION WEEK. Feb 1–7. The day when health care providers, professionals and personnel make a special effort to recognize their patients through planned interactions and events. Annually, the first seven days of February. For info: John O'Malley, NPRW, 337 Turnberry Rd, Birmingham, AL 35244. Phone: (205) 995-8495. E-mail: jom@mindspring.com. Web: www.nprw.com.

NATIONAL PET DENTAL HEALTH MONTH. Feb 1–28. A nationwide effort cosponsored by veterinary dental groups and Hill's Pet Nutrition, Inc, to educate consumers on the importance of good dental care for pets. For info: Rebecca Hart, 1015 Atlantic Blvd, #272, Atlantic Beach, FL 32233. Phone: (904) 246-7351. Fax: (904) 242-0752. E-mail: rebecca@hartandpartners.com. Web: www.petdental.com.

NATIONAL SENIOR INDEPENDENCE MONTH. Feb 1–28. A month to increase awareness of and celebrate seniors who choose to age with dignity in their own homes and maintain their independence. Per a National Home Instead Senior Care survey, 83 percent of seniors surveyed are very or somewhat likely to remain at home rather than move to a care facility. For info: Nancy Benhardus, CSA, Home Instead Senior Care, 459 N Gilbert Rd, Ste C-120, Gilbert, AZ 85234. Phone: (602) 292-8112. Fax: (480) 827-1101. E-mail: homeinstead195@aol.com. Web: www.homeinstead.com.

NATIONAL TIME MANAGEMENT MONTH. Feb 1–28. This is the month when those noble plans made in January start to go awry. This event is dedicated to renewing those best-laid plans; breaking open those new calendars that have yet to be opened, and reevaluating and reprioritizing harried, out-of-balance lives—making specific commitments to balance them. For info: Sylvia Henderson, Springboard Training, PO Box 588, Olney, MD 20830-0588. Phone: (301) 260-1538. E-mail: admin@springboardtraining.com. Web: www.springboardtraining.com.

NATIONAL WEDDINGS MONTH. Feb 1–28. As the wedding season gets into high gear, this observance is to call attention to the fact that more than 2.5 million weddings are celebrated in the US each year. For info: Gerard J. Monaghan, Pres, Assn of Bridal Consultants, 56 Danbury Rd, Ste 11, New Milford, CT 06776. Phone: (860) 355-0464. Fax: (860) 354-1404. E-mail: pres@bridalassn.com. Web: www.BridalAssn.com.

NORTH CAROLINA SWEETPOTATO MONTH. Feb 1–28. What's the best way to describe North Carolina Sweet-Potatoes? Extreme! Extreme versatility, extreme nutrition, extreme production, extreme availability. Use this month to discover the nutritional benefits of sweet potatoes: they're fat free, cholesterol free, low in sodium and loaded with beta carotene and vitamins A and C. The North Carolina Stroke Association, American Heart Association and American Cancer Society endorse sweet potatoes as a nutritious food helpful in disease prevention. North Carolina is the nation's largest producer. For info: Sue Johnson-Langdon, North Carolina SweetPotato Commission, 1327 N Brightleaf Blvd, Ste H, Smithfield, NC 27577. Phone: (919) 989-7323. Fax: (919) 989-3015. E-mail: ncsweetsue@aol.com. Web: www.ncsweetpotatoes.com.

PLANT THE SEEDS OF GREATNESS MONTH. Feb 1–28. Think globally—build for the future—Plant the Seeds of Greatness. If you're unhappy with your present situation, discover how you can remove the barriers and make a change in your life for the better. Use this month to put to use your own unique prosperity consciousness and plant the seeds for your new career, life objectives or goals. Make a difference for yourself, your family, your business or your community. Get outside of your comfort zone and take action on your ideas and dreams. Info available for $2. For info: Lorrie Walters Marsiglio, Lorimar Communications, PO Box 284-CC, Wasco, IL 60183-0284. Phone: (630) 584-9368.

PUBLICITY FOR PROFIT WEEK. Feb 1–7. Harness the power of free publicity for yourself, your business or your organization. Spend each day this week getting free publicity by doing one task to promote whatever you deem important. For free and easy-to-follow publicity plans, send e-mail request or send SASE. Free publicity newsletter also available. For info: Tom Peric, Publicity for Profit, 2040 Fairfax Ave, Cherry Hill, NJ 08003. Phone: (856) 874-0049. Fax: (856) 874-0052. E-mail: tom@wackydays.com. Web: www.wackydays.com.

RELATIONSHIP WELLNESS MONTH. Feb 1–28. Recapture the spark and zeal of personal relationships. Rekindle the flame with your partner or spouse. Get close, communicate, laugh, love and live. This is a time of forgiveness, harmony and trust. Set new goals as a couple, and establish relationship priorities. Go out on a date once a week. Be irresistible. Be patient. Seek forgiveness. Avoid nagging and complaining. Give bear hugs and gentle kisses. For info: Angela Brown, Words of Wellness, PO Box 49266, Charlotte, NC 28277. Phone: (704) 849-2900. Fax: (704) 845-3060. E-mail: angela@WordsofWellness.com. Web: www.WordsofWellness.com.

RETURN SHOPPING CARTS TO THE SUPERMARKET MONTH. Feb 1–28. A monthlong opportunity to return stolen shopping carts, milk crates, bread trays and ice cream baskets to supermarkets and to avoid the increased food prices that these thefts cause. Annually, the month of February. Sponsor: Illinois Food Retailers Association. For info: Anthony A. Dinolfo, Grocer-Retired, 163 Fairfield Dr, New Lenox, IL 60451-3523. Phone: (815) 463-9136.

ROBINSON CRUSOE DAY. Feb 1, 1709 (OS). Anniversary of the rescue of Alexander Selkirk, a Scottish sailor who had been put ashore (in September 1704) on the uninhabited island Juan Fernandez, at his own request, after a quarrel with his captain. His adventures formed the basis for Daniel Defoe's book *Robinson Crusoe.* A day to be adventurous and self-reliant.

ST. LAURENT, LOUIS STEPHEN: BIRTH ANNIVERSARY. Feb 1, 1882. Canadian lawyer and prime minister, born at Compton, QC. Died at Quebec City, July 25, 1973.

"THE SECRET STORM" TV PREMIERE: ANNIVERSARY. Feb 1, 1954. "The Secret Storm" lathered up homes for 20 years. The first soap on television, it revolved around the Ames family in fictional Woodbridge and featured a variety of actors and actresses who have moved on to bigger things. Among them are: Bibi Besch, Roy Scheider, Diana Muldaur, Nicolas Coster, Robert Loggia, Laurence Luckinbill, Christina Crawford, Diane Ladd, Troy Donahue and Frances Sternhagen.

SOLO DINERS EAT OUT WEEK. Feb 1–7. Treat yourself to a meal in a restaurant—all by yourself. Settle in at a communal table, nab a stool at a counter or opt for a select table for one. Revel in a meal entirely of hors d'oeuvres or even desserts! It's your choice during this special week. For info: Marya Alexander,

	S	M	T	W	T	F	S
February				1	2	3	4
2006	5	6	7	8	9	10	11
	12	13	14	15	16	17	18
	19	20	21	22	23	24	25
	26	27	28				

PO Box 2664, Carlsbad, CA 92018. Phone: (760) 720-1011. Fax: (760) 720-1049. E-mail: editor@solodining.com. Web: www.solodining.com.

SPACE SHUTTLE *COLUMBIA* DISASTER: ANNIVERSARY. Feb 1, 2003. Minutes before space shuttle *Columbia* was due to land after a successful 16-day scientific mission, it disintegrated 40 miles above the state of Texas, killing its seven-member crew. Commander Rick Husband, pilot William McCool, Michael Anderson, David Brown, Kalpana Chawla (first woman astronaut from India), Laurel Clark and Ilan Ramon (first Israeli astronaut) lost their lives and were mourned worldwide. *Columbia* was the first shuttle to fly in space (1981).

US NATIONAL SNOW SCULPTING COMPETITION. Feb 1–5. Lake Geneva, WI. 11th annual. Snow sculpting competition where each three-person team creates a work of art out of a 7-ft × 9-ft block of snow. Several awards given. For info: Lake Geneva Area Conv & Visitors Bureau, 201 Wrigley Dr, Lake Geneva, WI 53147-2004. Phone: (262) 248-4416. E-mail: lgcc@lakegenevawi.com. Web: www.lakegenevawi.com.

WINTER GAMES OF IDAHO. Feb 1–28. Idaho Falls, Sun Valley, Boise, McCall, Donnelly, Salmon and Kellogg, ID. Idaho's official winter sports competition—four weekends of competition in ice hockey, figure skating, alpine skiing, telemark skiing, snowboarding and cross-country skiing with 3,000 participants. For info: Winter Games of Idaho, PO Box 9046, Boise, ID 83707. Phone: (800) 442-3794. Fax: (208) 343-6725. Web: www.wintergamesofidaho.com.

WISE HEALTH CARE CONSUMER MONTH. Feb 1–28. Teaching consumers to make better health care decisions is a proven way to reduce health care costs. For this reason, companies, hospitals and HMOs are offering medical self-care programs for employees, subscribers and patients. Wise Health Care Consumer Marketing packet available. For info: American Institute for Preventive Medicine, 30445 Northwestern Hwy, Ste 350, Farmington Hills, MI 48334. Phone: (248) 539-1800, ext 247. Fax: (248) 539-1808. E-mail: aipm@healthy.net. Web: www.HealthyLife.com.

WOMEN'S HEART HEALTH DAY. Feb 1. As American Heart Month begins, here is a day to promote awareness that heart disease is the number one killer of American women. For info: Charlotte Libov, Founder, Women's Health Hot Line, 28B Heritage Circle, Southbury, CT 06488. Phone: (203) 264-9704. E-mail: char@libov.com. Web: www.libov.com.

WOMEN'S HEART WEEK. Feb 1–7. Women's Heart Foundation's nationally recognized program to raise awareness about the number one killer of American women: heart disease. The program introduces fun activities to promote healthier living. View the Women's Heart Week video online at www.womensheart.org. The turnkey program is designed for health sites around the country to commemorate using the 7 Focus Days for women's heart wellness and provide early intervention using the Women's Aware Kit. The kit includes a risk assessment tool, symptoms awareness brochure and health tracker card. For info: Women's Heart Foundation, PO Box 7827, West Trenton, NJ 08628. Phone: (609) 771-9600. Fax: (609) 771-3778. E-mail: info@womensheart.org. Web: www.womensheart.org.

"YOU ARE THERE" TV PREMIERE: ANNIVERSARY. Feb 1, 1953. The program began as an inventive radio show in 1947. News correspondents would comb the annals of history and "interview" the movers and shakers of times past. Walter Cronkite hosted the series on CBS for four seasons. The show's concept was revived for a season in 1971 with Cronkite gearing the program toward children.

YOUTH LEADERSHIP MONTH. Feb 1–28. This month is dedicated to celebrating young people who take on leadership roles in their lives. It is also dedicated to encouraging those who have not yet done so to consider doing so because they can. Programs that focus on youth leadership opportunities and effective leadership skill building are appropriate for this month. For info: Sylvia Henderson, Springboard Training, PO Box 588, Olney, MD 20830-0588. Phone: (301) 260-1538. E-mail: admin@spring boardtraining.com. Web: www.springboardtraining.com.

BIRTHDAYS TODAY

Michelle Akers, 40, former soccer player, born Santa Clara, CA, Feb 1, 1966.

Michael B. Enzi, 62, US Senator (R, Wyoming), born Bremerton, WA, Feb 1, 1944.

Don Everly, 69, singer, musician ("Bye Bye Love"), with brother Phil (The Everly Brothers), born Brownie, KY, Feb 1, 1937.

Sherilyn Fenn, 41, actress ("Twin Peaks," *Wild at Heart*), born Detroit, MI, Feb 1, 1965.

Sherman Hemsley, 68, actor ("The Jeffersons," "Amen"), born Philadelphia, PA, Feb 1, 1938.

Bob Jamieson, 63, broadcast journalist, born Streator, IL, Feb 1, 1943.

Terry Jones, 64, actor, director ("Monty Python's Flying Circus"), born Colwyn Bay, Wales, Feb 1, 1942.

Garrett Morris, 69, comedian ("Saturday Night Live"), born New Orleans, LA, Feb 1, 1937.

Bill Mumy, 52, actor (*Palm Springs Weekend, Twilight Zone—The Movie*, "The Rockford Files"), born El Centro, CA, Feb 1, 1954.

Lisa Marie Presley, 38, singer, born Memphis, TN, Feb 1, 1968.

Pauly Shore, 36, actor ("Pauly," *What He's Got*), born Los Angeles, CA, Feb 1, 1970.

Stuart Whitman, 77, actor ("Cimarron Strip," *The Seekers*), born San Francisco, CA, Feb 1, 1929.

FEBRUARY 2 — THURSDAY

Day 33 — 332 Remaining

AFRICAN-AMERICAN COACHES DAY. Feb 2. To provide a day each year to educate the African-American community about the value of working with a personal or business coach and to provide an opportunity for coaches and their clients to acknowledge the results and progress made through the coaching process. Annually, the first Tuesday in February. For info: Monique Belton, Ph.D., 35 Dix Hills Rd, Huntington, NY 11743. Phone: (631) 549-7314.

AUDEN, W.H.: BIRTH ANNIVERSARY. Feb 2, 1907. Pulitzer Prize–winning Anglo-American poet was born Wystan Hugh Auden at York, England. "Some books," he wrote in *The Dyer's Hand* (1962), "are undeservedly forgotten; none are undeservedly remembered." Died at Vienna, Austria, Sept 28, 1973.

BAN ON AFRICAN NATIONAL CONGRESS LIFTED: ANNIVERSARY. Feb 2, 1990. The 30-year ban on the African National Congress was lifted by South African President F.W. de Klerk. De Klerk also vowed to free Nelson Mandela and lift restrictions on 33 other opposition groups.

BASEBALL HALL OF FAME'S CHARTER MEMBERS: 70th ANNIVERSARY. Feb 2, 1936. The five charter members of the brand-new Baseball Hall of Fame at Cooperstown, NY, were announced. Of 226 ballots cast, Ty Cobb was named on 222, Babe Ruth on 215, Honus Wagner on 215, Christy Mathewson on 205 and Walter Johnson on 189. A total of 170 votes were necessary to be elected to the Hall of Fame.

BENET, WILLIAM ROSE: BIRTH ANNIVERSARY. Feb 2, 1886. American poet and critic. Born at Fort Hamilton, NY; died at New York, NY, May 4, 1950.

BONZA BOTTLER DAY™. Feb 2. To celebrate when the number of the day is the same as the number of the month. Bonza Bottler Day™ is an excuse to have a party at least once a month. For further information, see Jan 1. For info: Gail M. Berger, 14 Fernwood Dr, Taylors, SC 29687. Phone: (864) 609-9874. E-mail: gberger5@aol.com.

CANDLEMAS DAY or PRESENTATION OF THE LORD. Feb 2. Observed in the Roman Catholic Church. Commemorates presentation of Jesus in the Temple and the purification of Mary 40 days after his birth. Candles have been blessed since the 11th century. This marks the end of the Christmas liturgical season. Formerly called the Feast of Purification of the Blessed Virgin Mary. Old Scottish couplet proclaims: "If Candlemas is fair and clear/There'll be two winters in the year."

GERMAN SURRENDER AT STALINGRAD: ANNIVERSARY. Feb 2, 1943. Two pockets of starving German soldiers remained in Stalingrad on this date. They had received few supplies since Soviet soldiers had encircled the city the previous November. Friedrich von Paulus, whom Hitler had promoted to field marshal only the day before, was forced to seek surrender terms, thereby becoming the first German marshal to surrender. Hitler was furious with von Paulus, believing he should have preferred suicide to surrender. Approximately 160,000 Germans died in the Stalingrad Battle; 34,000 were evacuated by air. Of the 90,000 captured and sent to Siberia on foot, tens of thousands died on the way. This Allied victory is generally considered the psychological turning point of the war.

GETZ, STAN: BIRTH ANNIVERSARY. Feb 2, 1927. American jazz saxophonist Stan Getz was born at Philadelphia, PA. He introduced the cool-jazz style, which became a major movement in the 1950s, and the bossa nova (new wave) style of the 1960s. Getz received 11 Grammy Awards and was the first jazz musician to win the Grammy Award for Record of the Year (1965) for "The Girl from Ipanema." Died at Malibu, CA, June 6, 1991.

GROUNDHOG DAY. Feb 2. Old belief that if the sun shines on Candlemas Day, or if the groundhog sees his shadow when he emerges on this day, six weeks of winter will ensue.

GROUNDHOG DAY IN PUNXSUTAWNEY, PENNSYLVANIA. Feb 2. Widely observed traditional annual Candlemas Day event at which "Punxsutawney Phil, king of the weather prophets," is the object of a search. Tradition is said to have been established by early German settlers. The official trek (which began in 1887) is followed by a weather prediction for the next six weeks. [Phil made his dramatic film debut with Bill Murray in *Groundhog Day*.]

GROUNDHOG DAY IN SUN PRAIRIE, WISCONSIN. Feb 2. Sun Prairie, WI. To predict the weather for the balance of winter. Prognostication at 7:15 AM, EST, to see if Jimmy the Groundhog has seen his shadow. Persons born on this date are eligible for "official" groundhog birth certificate and/or groundhog club membership (for a small fee). Est attendance: 700. For info: Chamber of Commerce, 109 E Main St, Sun Prairie, WI 53590. Phone: (608) 837-4547. Fax: (608) 837-8765. Web: www.sunprairiechamber.com.

GROUNDHOG JOB SHADOW DAY. Feb 2. Students spend part of the day in the workplace "shadowing" an employee as he or she goes through a normal day on the job. Job Shadow Day demonstrates the connection between academics and careers and introduces students to the requirements of professions and industries. Local contacts can be found on the website. Planning kit available. For info: Groundhog Job Shadow Day. Phone: (800) 373-3174. Web: www.jobshadow.org.

HALAS, GEORGE: BIRTH ANNIVERSARY. Feb 2, 1895. George ("Papa Bear") Halas, Pro Football Hall of Fame coach and owner, born at Chicago, IL. After playing football at the University of Illinois and baseball with the New York Yankees, Halas helped to found the National Football League and the Chicago Bears in 1920. As coach of the Bears for 40 years, he compiled a record of 324 wins, 151 losses and 31 ties. Charter member of the Hall of Fame, 1963. Died at Chicago, IL, Oct 31, 1983.

HEDGEHOG DAY. Feb 2. This ancient Roman tradition was the inspiration for Groundhog Day in the United States. Romans observed whether a hedgehog emerging from hibernation could see its shadow in the moonlight—if it could, then six more weeks of winter were expected. Later observed as a folk holiday in Europe and the British Isles.

IMBOLC. Feb 2. (Also called Imbolg, Candlemas, Lupercalia, Feast of Pan, Feast of Torches, Feast of Waxing Light, Brigit's Day and Oimelc.) One of the "Greater Sabbats" during the Wiccan year, Imbolc marks the recovery of the Goddess (after giving birth to the Sun, or the God, at Yule) and celebrates the anticipation of spring. Annually, Feb 2.

JOYCE, JAMES: BIRTH ANNIVERSARY. Feb 2, 1882. Irish novelist and poet, author of *Dubliners, A Portrait of the Artist as a Young Man, Ulysses* and *Finnegans Wake*, was born at Dublin, Ireland. "A man of genius," he wrote in *Ulysses*, "makes no mistakes. His errors are volitional and are portals of discovery." Of *Finnegans Wake* Joyce is reported to have replied to an academic whose letter had asked for clues to its meaning, "If I can throw any obscurity on the subject, let me know." Joyce died at the age of 58 of peritonitis at Zurich, Switzerland, Jan 13, 1941, and was buried there.

LUXEMBOURG: CANDLEMAS. Feb 2. Traditional observance of Candlemas. At night children sing a customary song wishing health and prosperity to their neighbors and receive sweets in return. They carry special candles called *Lichtebengel* symbolizing the coming of spring.

MEXICO: DIA DE LA CANDELARIA. Feb 2. All Mexico celebrates. Dances, processions, bullfights.

RAND, AYN: BIRTH ANNIVERSARY. Feb 2, 1905. Novelist (*The Fountainhead, Atlas Shrugged*), born Alyssa Rosenbaum at St. Petersburg, Russia. Founded the Objectivism school of philosophy. Died Mar 6, 1982, at New York, NY.

THE RECORD OF A SNEEZE: ANNIVERSARY. Feb 2, 1893. One day after Thomas Edison's "Black Maria" studio was completed at West Orange, NJ, a studio cameraman took the first "close-up" in film history. *The Record of a Sneeze*, starring Edison's assistant Fred P. Ott, was also the first motion picture to receive a copyright (1894). See also: "Black Maria Studio: Anniversary" (Feb 1).

SELF-RENEWAL DAY. Feb 2. Provides the opportunity to rise up from the darkness of daily life to look about ourselves and commit to personal growth. For info: Susan Fridy, 33 Steamboat Wharf, Mystic, CT 06355. Phone: (860) 572-1370. Fax: (860) 572-4858. E-mail: susan.fridy@snet.net.

SLED DOGS SAVE NOME: ANNIVERSARY. Feb 2, 1925. When a diphtheria outbreak was diagnosed in Nome, AK (population 1,500), on Jan 21, the nearest large amount of antitoxin serum was in Anchorage. Bitter winter temperatures made air delivery impossible, so a heroic dog sled relay was set up. 300,000 units of serum were delivered by train to Nenana, AK, and on Jan 27—in temperatures of 40–50 degrees below zero—20 mushers drove scores of dogs on a 674-mile journey to Nome in 127 hours. Togo was the lead dog for the first 350 miles, and Balto was the lead dog on the final 53 miles. The frozen serum arrived at 5:30 AM, and once thawed and administered, there were no more diphtheria deaths. Balto became a national hero, and a statue was erected in his honor in New York City's Central Park.

SMOKY MOUNTAINS STORYTELLING FESTIVAL. Feb 2–4. Pigeon Forge, TN. 15th annual. The region's finest yarn-spinners and folklore specialists. Est attendance: 2,500. For info: Office of Special Events, Pigeon Forge Dept of Tourism, 3107 Parkway, PO Box 1390, Pigeon Forge, TN 37868. Phone: (800) 251-9100 or (865) 429-7350. Fax: (865) 429-7392. E-mail: inquire@cityofpigeonforge.com. Web: www.mypigeonforge.com.

TREATY OF GUADALUPE HIDALGO: ANNIVERSARY. Feb 2, 1848. The war between Mexico and the US formally ended with the signing of the Treaty of Guadalupe Hidalgo, signed in the village for which it was named. The treaty provided for Mexico's cession to the US of the territory that became the states of California, Nevada, Utah, most of Arizona, and parts of New Mexico, Colorado and Wyoming, in exchange for $15 million from the US. In addition, Mexico relinquished all rights to Texas north of the Rio Grande. The Senate ratified the treaty Mar 10, 1848.

WALTON, GEORGE: DEATH ANNIVERSARY. Feb 2, 1804. Signer of the Declaration of Independence. Born at Prince Edward County, VA, 1749 (exact date unknown). Died at Augusta, GA.

"WHAT'S MY LINE?" TV PREMIERE: ANNIVERSARY. Feb 2, 1950. This popular game show premiered on CBS and ran for 17 years in prime time. A panel of four celebrities figured out the professions of the contestants and the identities of the mystery guests by asking yes-or-no questions. The first panel consisted of poet Louis Untermeyer, columnist Dorothy Kilgallen, New Jersey Governor Harold Hoffman and psychiatrist Dr. Richard Hoffman. Yankee Phil Rizzuto was the first mystery guest. John Daly hosted.

BIRTHDAYS TODAY

Christie Brinkley, 53, model, born Monroe, MI, Feb 2, 1953.

John Cornyn, 54, US Senator (R, Texas), born Houston, TX, Feb 2, 1952.

Sean Michael Elliott, 38, former basketball player, born Tucson, AZ, Feb 2, 1968.

Farrah Fawcett, 59, actress, model ("Charlie's Angels," *The Burning Bed*), born Corpus Christi, TX, Feb 2, 1947.

Bo Hopkins, 64, actor ("The Rockford Files," "Dynasty," *American Graffiti*), born Greenwood, SC, Feb 2, 1942.

Robert Mandan, 74, actor ("Soap," "Days of Our Lives"), born Clever, MO, Feb 2, 1932.

Graham Nash, 64, musician, singer, born Blackpool, England, Feb 2, 1942.

Liz Smith, 83, journalist, author, born Fort Worth, TX, Feb 2, 1923.

Tom Smothers, 69, comedian, folksinger (brother of Dick Smothers, "The Smothers Brothers Comedy Hour"), born New York, NY, Feb 2, 1937.

Elaine Stritch, 81, singer, actress (*Company, Elaine Stritch at Liberty*), born Birmingham, MI, Feb 2, 1925.

Michael T. Weiss, 44, actor ("The Pretender"), born Chicago, IL, Feb 2, 1962.

February 2006

S	M	T	W	T	F	S
			1	2	3	4
5	6	7	8	9	10	11
12	13	14	15	16	17	18
19	20	21	22	23	24	25
26	27	28				

FEBRUARY 3 — FRIDAY

Day 34 — 331 Remaining

BLACKWELL, ELIZABETH: BIRTH ANNIVERSARY. Feb 3, 1821. First woman physician. Born near Bristol, England, she and several other members of her family were active abolitionists, women's suffrage advocates and pioneers in women's medicine. Her family moved to New York State in 1832, and she received a medical doctor's degree at Geneva, NY, in 1849. She established a hospital in New York City with an all-woman staff, where she recruited and trained nurses for service in the Civil War. Returning to England in 1869, she continued to teach and practice medicine until her death at Hastings, England, May 31, 1910.

CANADA: WINTERLUDE. Feb 3–19. Ottawa, ON. Annual celebration of Canadian winter and traditions for the whole family. Skating on Rideau Canal, the world's longest skating rink; snow and ice sculptures; world-class figure skating; North America's largest snow playground and exciting Winter Triathlon. Est attendance: 700,000. For info: Natl Capital Commission, 202-40 Elgin St, Ottawa, ON, Canada K1P 1C7. Phone: (613) 239-5000 or (800) 465-1867. Web: www.capcan.ca/winterlude.

CIVIL WAR PEACE TALKS: ANNIVERSARY. Feb 3, 1865. Abraham Lincoln and his secretary of state, William Seward, met to discuss peace with Confederate Vice President Alexander Stephens and others at Hampton Roads, VA. The meeting, which took place on board the ship *River Queen*, lasted four hours and produced no positive results. The Confederates sought an armistice first and discussion of reunion later, while Lincoln was insistent that recognition of Federal authority must be the first step toward peace.

"THE DAY THE MUSIC DIED": ANNIVERSARY. Feb 3, 1959. The anniversary of the death of rock-and-roll legend Charles Hardin "Buddy" Holly. "The Day the Music Died," so-called in singer Don McLean's song "American Pie," is the date on which Holly was killed in a plane crash in a cornfield near Mason City, IA, along with J.P. Richardson (otherwise known as "The Big Bopper") and Richie Valens. Holly was born Sept 7, 1936, at Lubbock, TX.

FIFTEENTH AMENDMENT TO US CONSTITUTION RATIFIED: ANNIVERSARY. Feb 3, 1870. The 15th Amendment granted that the right of citizens to vote shall not be denied on account of race, color or previous condition of servitude.

FOUR CHAPLAINS MEMORIAL DAY. Feb 3, 1943. Commemorates four chaplains (George Fox, Alexander Goode, Clark Poling, John Washington) who sacrificed their life belts and lives when the SS *Dorchester* was torpedoed off Greenland during WWII.

GREELEY, HORACE: BIRTH ANNIVERSARY. Feb 3, 1811. Newspaper editor, born at Amherst, NH. Founder of the *New York Tribune* and one of the organizers of the Republican Party, Greeley was an outspoken opponent of slavery. Best remembered for his saying, "Go West, young man." Died Nov 29, 1872, at New York City.

INCOME TAX BIRTHDAY: SIXTEENTH AMENDMENT TO US CONSTITUTION: RATIFICATION: ANNIVERSARY. Feb 3, 1913. The 16th Amendment was ratified, granting Congress the authority to levy taxes on income. (Church bells did not ring throughout the land and no dancing in the streets was reported.)

JAPAN: BEAN-THROWING FESTIVAL (SETSUBUN). Feb 3. Setsubun marks the last day of winter according to the lunar calendar. Throngs at temple grounds throw beans to drive away imaginary devils.

JOHNSTON, JOSEPH: BIRTH ANNIVERSARY. Feb 3, 1807. Born near Farmville, VA, and died Mar 21, 1891, at Washington, DC. Confederate general in the Civil War whose troops were never directly defeated. Long-standing differences with Jefferson Davis, president of the Confederacy, prevented him, however, from reaching his full potential.

KISSIMMEE SLOUGH SHOOTOUT & RENDEZVOUS. Feb 3–5. Ah-Tah-Thi-Ki Museum, Big Cypress Reservation, FL. Seminole War reenactment. Living history camps, Seminole dancing, Indian arts and crafts, pioneer traders and archery contest. Annually, the first weekend in February. Est attendance: 2,000. For info: Brian Zepeda, Ah-Tah-Thi-Ki Museum, HC-61, Box 21A, Clewiston, FL 33440. Phone: (863) 902-1113. Fax: (863) 902-1117. E-mail: bzepeda@semtribe.com. Web: www.seminoletribe.com/museum.

LONGHORN WORLD CHAMPIONSHIP RODEO. Feb 3–4. State Fair Coliseum, Columbus, OH. 32nd annual. More than 350 cowboys and cowgirls compete in six professional contests ranging from bronc riding to big, bad BONUS bull riding. Free beginners horsemanship clinic 40 minutes before performances. Qualifying rodeo for Longhorn's Championship Finals Rodeo in Murfreesboro, TN. Featuring colorful opening ceremonies. Est attendance: 15,000. For info: W. Bruce Lehrke, Pres, Longhorn World Championship Rodeo, Inc, PO Box 70159, Nashville, TN 37207. Phone: (615) 876-1016. Fax: (615) 876-4685. E-mail: info@longhornrodeo.com. Web: www.longhornrodeo.com.

MICHENER, JAMES: BIRTH ANNIVERSARY. Feb 3, 1907. American author, born at New York, NY. His *Tales of the South Pacific* was the basis for the popular musical *South Pacific*. A prolific author, his works included *Sayonara, Iberia, Hawaii, Centennial, Texas* and many others. Died at Austin, TX, Oct 17, 1997.

MOOSESTOMPERS WEEKEND. Feb 3–5. Houlton, ME. Human curling, human dogsled racing, snow balls, giant sliding hill for children, snowmobiling activities, cross-country skiing, skating, bonfire, snowmobile light parade, MooseStompers ball and much more. For info: Greater Houlton Chamber of Commerce, 109 Main St, Houlton, ME 04730. Phone: (207) 532-4216. E-mail: chamber@greaterhoulton.com. Web: www.greaterhoulton.com/moosestompers.

MOZAMBIQUE: HEROES' DAY. Feb 3. National holiday. Honors all heroic citizens, especially Eduardo Mondlane, leader of the fight for independence, assassinated on Feb 3, 1969.

NAUVOO LEGION CHARTERED: ANNIVERSARY. Feb 3, 1841. Created by Illinois Charter and composed of 5,000 Mormon men under the command of Lieutenant General Joseph Smith, the Nauvoo Legion was considered the "largest trained soldiery in the US" except for the US Army.

NORTH AMERICA'S COLDEST RECORDED TEMPERATURE: ANNIVERSARY. Feb 3, 1947. At Snag, in Canada's Yukon Territory, a temperature of 81 degrees below zero (Fahrenheit) was recorded on this date, a record low for all of North America.

ROCKWELL, NORMAN: BIRTH ANNIVERSARY. Feb 3, 1894. American artist and illustrator especially noted for his realistic and homey magazine cover art for the *Saturday Evening Post*. Born at New York, NY, he died at Stockbridge, MA, Nov 8, 1978.

SARANAC LAKE WINTER CARNIVAL. Feb 3–12. Saranac Lake, NY. Come and join the family fun with fireworks, entertainment and much more. For info: Saranac Lake Winter Carnival, Saranac Lake Chamber of Commerce, 39 Main St, Saranac Lake, NY 12983. Phone: (518) 891-1990 or (800) 347-1992. E-mail: BestTown@saranaclake.com.

SPACE MILESTONE: *CHALLENGER STS-10* (US). Feb 3, 1984. Shuttle *Challenger* launched from Kennedy Space Center, FL, with a crew of five (Vance Brand, Robert Gibson, Ronald McNair, Bruce McCandless and Robert Stewart). On Feb 7 two astronauts became the first to fly freely in space (propelled by their backpack jets), untethered to any craft. Landed at Cape Canaveral, FL, Feb 11.

STEIN, GERTRUDE: BIRTH ANNIVERSARY. Feb 3, 1874. Avant-garde expatriate American writer, perhaps best remembered for her poetic declaration (in 1913): "Rose is a rose is a rose." Born at Allegheny, PA; died at Paris, France, July 27, 1946.

VIETNAM: NATIONAL HOLIDAY. Feb 3. National holiday. Anniversary of the founding of the Vietnamese Communist Party, Feb 3, 1930.

WEAR RED DAY. Feb 3. During American Heart Month in February, the American Heart Association will focus on women with "Go Red for Women," an educational campaign about women and cardiovascular disease. Each year cardiovascular diseases claim the lives of nearly 500,000 women. For all of the women you know who have been affected by cardiovascular disease, participate in Wear Red Day. For info: American Heart Foundation, 7272 Greenville Ave, Dallas, TX 75231. Phone: 888-MY-HEART. Web: www.americanheart.org.

WORLD OF WHEELS. Feb 3–5. Multi-Purpose Events Center Exhibit Hall, Wichita Falls, TX. Features spectacular customized, modified and restored vehicles of all sizes, shapes and colors. Famous television stars, exciting entertainment and fun for all ages. Est attendance: 12,000. For info: Wichita Falls Conv & Visitors Bureau, 1000 5th St, Wichita Falls, TX 76301. Phone: (940) 716-5500 or (940) 855-0499. Fax: (940) 716-5509. E-mail: MPEC @wf.net. Web: www.wichitafalls.org.

BIRTHDAYS TODAY

Shelley Berman, 80, comedian ("Mary Hartman, Mary Hartman"), born Chicago, IL, Feb 3, 1926.

Joey Bishop, 88, actor ("The Joey Bishop Show," "Liar's Club"), born Joseph Abraham Gottlieb at New York, NY, Feb 3, 1918.

Thomas Calabro, 47, actor ("Melrose Place"), born Brooklyn, NY, Feb 3, 1959.

Blythe Danner, 63, actress (*Butterflies Are Free, Brighton Beach Memoirs*), born Philadelphia, PA, Feb 3, 1943.

Vlade Divac, 38, basketball player, born Prijepolje, Yugoslavia, Feb 3, 1968.

Morgan Fairchild, 56, actress ("Dallas," "Falcon Crest," "Flamingo Road"), born Patsy McClenny, Dallas, TX, Feb 3, 1950.

Keith Gordon, 45, actor, director (*All That Jazz, Dressed to Kill, A Midnight Clear*), born New York, NY, Feb 3, 1961.

Robert Allen (Bob) Griese, 61, sportscaster, Hall of Fame football player, born Evansville, IN, Feb 3, 1945.

Nathan Lane, 50, actor (Tonys for *A Funny Thing Happened on the Way to the Forum, The Producers; The Birdcage*), born Jersey City, NJ, Feb 3, 1956.

Paul S. Sarbanes, 73, US Senator (D, Maryland), born Salisbury, MD, Feb 3, 1933.

Francis Asbury (Fran) Tarkenton, 66, Hall of Fame football player, born Richmond, VA, Feb 3, 1940.

Maura Tierney, 41, actress ("NewsRadio," "ER"), born Boston, MA, Feb 3, 1965.

February *2006*	S	M	T	W	T	F	S
				1	2	3	4
	5	6	7	8	9	10	11
	12	13	14	15	16	17	18
	19	20	21	22	23	24	25
	26	27	28				

FEBRUARY 4 — SATURDAY
Day 35 — 330 Remaining

ANGOLA: ARMED STRUGGLE DAY. Feb 4. National holiday. Commemorates the beginning of the struggle for independence from Portugal in 1961.

APACHE WARS BEGAN: ANNIVERSARY. Feb 4, 1861. The period of conflict known as the Apache Wars began at Apache Pass, AZ, when Army Lieutenant George Bascom arrested Apache Chief Cochise for raiding a ranch. Cochise escaped and declared war. The wars lasted 25 years under the leadership of Cochise and, later, Geronimo.

COLONIAL FAIRE AND MUSTER. Feb 4–5. Wormsloe Historic Site, Savannah, GA. Experience Colonial life through participation in military and Indian camps, craft demonstrations, vendors, period music and dance. For info: Wormsloe Historic Site, 7601 Skidaway Rd, Savannah, GA 31406. Phone: (912) 353-3023. E-mail: wormsloe@bellsouth.net. Web: www.wormsloe .org.

COWBOY STATE GAMES SPORTS FESTIVAL. Feb 4–5 (also Feb 11–12, 18–20). Casper, WY. The festival features a variety of sporting events for athletes of all ages. Annually, the first three weekends of February including Presidents' Day. Est attendance: 2,500. For info: Eileen Ford, Cowboy State Games, PO Box 3485, Casper, WY 82602. Phone: (307) 577-1125. Fax: (307) 577-8111. E-mail: csg@trib.com.

DOLL SHOW. Feb 4. Yuma Civic Center, Yuma, AZ. Assorted antique, handmade and collector's item dolls on display and for sale. Also, miniature furniture and doll-making supplies on sale. Sponsor: Yuma Doll Club. Annually, the first Saturday in February. Est attendance: 750. For info: Marketing Dept, Yuma Civic Ctr, 1440 Desert Hills Dr, Yuma, AZ 85365. Phone: (928) 782-5797 or (928) 373-5040. Fax: (928) 344-9121. E-mail: ycc @ci.yuma.az.us.

EINSTEIN ON WINE. Feb 4. Tampa, FL. 11th annual benefit. Taste wines from around the world and samples from local restauranteurs. Bid on Tampa's best during our fun and exciting silent auction. All proceeds benefit the Museum of Science & Industry's K+I+D+S education program. Musical entertainment. Sponsored by BEAM (Be Enthusiastic About MOSI) and ABC Fine Wine & Spirits. For tickets, please call (813) 978-6062. Est attendance: 1,500. For info: Museum of Science & Industry, 4801 E Fowler Ave, Tampa, FL 33617-2017. Phone: (813) 987-6062. Fax: (813) 987-6310. E-mail: rsvp@mosi.org. Web: www.mosi.org.

ELGIN MARKET DAYS. Feb 4. Memorial Park, Elgin, TX. (Also Mar 4, Apr 1, May 6, June 3, July 1, Aug 5, Sept 2, Oct 7 and Nov 4.) First Saturday of every month, February–November. Buy and/or sell antiques, crafts and "junque." Vendors welcome. For info: Sharon McCall, 1462 Old Lytton Springs Rd, Lockhart, TX 78644. Phone: (512) 263-2512. E-mail: smccall632@aol.com.

GOLDEN DRAGON PARADE AND CHINESE NEW YEAR FESTIVAL. Feb 4–5. Chinatown, Los Angeles, CA. 107th annual. This traditional, colorful parade is the most popular event of the Chinese New Year celebration activities. The Chinese New Year Festival features stage entertainment including cultural and contemporary performances, food, vendor booths and children's activities. Est attendance: 80,000. For info: Chinese Chamber of Commerce, 977 N Broadway, G/Fl, Ste E, Los Angeles, CA 90012. Phone: (213) 617-0396. Fax: (213) 617-2128. Web: www.lagoldendragonparade.com.

JAMES DEAN BIRTHDAY CELEBRATION. Feb 4–5. Fairmount, IN. The town where James Dean grew up celebrates his birthday with a movie showing, exhibits, refreshments and more. *Rebel Without a Cause* will be screened and the Fairmount Museum will be open all weekend. For info: Fairmount Historical Museum, Inc, 203 E Washington St, PO Box 92, Fairmount, IN 46928. Phone: (765) 948-4555. Web: www.jamesdeanartifacts .com.

KOSCIUSKO, THADDEUS: BIRTH ANNIVERSARY.
Feb 4, 1746. Polish patriot and American Revolutionary War figure. Born at Lithuania, he died at Solothurn, Switzerland, Oct 15, 1817.

LAURA INGALLS WILDER GINGERBREAD SOCIABLE. Feb 4. Pomona, CA. The 39th annual event commemorates the birthday (Feb 7, 1867) of the renowned author of the Little House books. The library has on permanent display the handwritten manuscript of *Little Town on the Prairie* and other Wilder memorabilia. Entertainment by fiddlers, craft displays, apple cider and gingerbread. Annually, the first Saturday in February. Est attendance: 200. For info: Marguerite F. Raybould, Pomona Public Library, 625 S Garey Ave, Pomona, CA 91766. Phone: (909) 620-2043 ext 2. Fax: (909) 620-3713. E-mail: library @ci.pomona.ca.us.

LINDBERGH, CHARLES AUGUSTUS: BIRTH ANNIVERSARY. Feb 4, 1902. American aviator Charles "Lucky Lindy" Lindbergh was the first to fly solo and nonstop over the Atlantic Ocean, New York to Paris, May 20–21, 1927. Born at Detroit, MI; died at Kipahula, Maui, HI, Aug 27, 1974. See also: "Lindbergh Flight: Anniversary" (May 20).

MAI WAH SOCIETY CHINESE LUNAR NEW YEAR PARADE. Feb 4. Butte, MT. The Mai Wah Society, Inc is sponsoring Butte's annual Chinese Lunar New Year celebrations, with Butte's shortest, coldest and loudest parade. Montana's only authentic parade dragon will lead the celebrants through the streets of Uptown Butte, chasing away evil spirits in its path, to the Mai Wah and Wah Chong Tai building. The Society will then light 10,000 firecrackers. Light refreshments will complete our annual celebration! So clean your house, make amends and don't be late! Bring your friends and neighbors and your favorite dog and join us. Est attendance: 500. For info: Leland Greb, Mai Wah Society, PO Box 404, Butte, MT 59703. Phone: (406) 782-3719. Fax: (406) 782-2207. E-mail: info@maiwah.org. Web: www.mai wah.org.

MID-WINTER ANTIQUES AND COLLECTIBLES SHOW AND SALE. Feb 4–5. Millville, NJ. Snow, rain or shine, the sale will go on. Est attendance: 2,000. For info: Wheaton Village, 1501 Glasstown Rd, Millville, NJ 08332. Phone: (800) 998-4552 or (856) 825-6800. Fax: (856) 825-2410. E-mail: mail@wheatonvillage.org. Web: www.wheatonvillage.org.

NATIONAL CITY CLEVELAND HOME AND GARDEN SHOW. Feb 4–12. I-X Center, Cleveland, OH. The largest show of its kind in the country with more than 35 feature gardens, 900 exhibitors and fully decorated and landscaped walk-through model homes. Est attendance: 300,000. For info: Natl City Home and Garden Show, PO Box 550-Edgewater Branch, Cleveland, OH 44107. Phone: (216) 529-1300. Fax: (216) 529-0311. E-mail: expo inc@expoinc.com. Web: www.expoinc.com.

PERRY'S "BRR" (BIKE RIDE TO RIPPEY). Feb 4. Perry, IA. Winter bike riding. Twenty-two miles of frigid fun. Annually, the first Saturday in February. Est attendance: 2,000. For info: Sara Truesdell, Chamber of Commerce, 1226 Second St, Perry, IA 50220. Phone: (515) 465-4601. Fax: (515) 465-2256. E-mail: perrychmbr@aol.com. Web: www.perryia.org.

ROLEX 24 AT DAYTONA GRAND-AM SERIES RACE. Feb 4–5. Daytona International Speedway, Daytona Beach, FL. 44th annual running of the most prestigious endurance race in North America. For info: Daytona Intl Speedway, PO Box 2801, Daytona Beach, FL 32120-2801. Phone: (800) PIT-SHOP. Fax: (386) 947-6791. Web: www.daytonainternationalspeedway.com.

SRI LANKA: INDEPENDENCE DAY: ANNIVERSARY. Feb 4. Democratic Socialist Republic of Sri Lanka observes National Day. Public holiday. On Feb 4, 1948, Ceylon (as it was then known) obtained independence from Great Britain. The country's name was changed to Sri Lanka in 1972.

USO: 65th BIRTHDAY. Feb 4, 1941. To honor the civilian agency founded in 1941 that provides support worldwide for US service people and their families. The United Service Organizations (USO) centers have served as a home away from home for hundreds of thousands of Americans.

WELLS FARGO BOULDER MOUNTAIN TOUR. Feb 4. Galena Lodge, Sun Valley, ID. A 32k cross-country ski race from Galena Lodge to the Sawtooth National Recreation Area (SNRA) headquarters. Annually, the first Saturday of February. For info: Boulder Mountain Tour, PO Box 173, Sun Valley, ID 83353. Phone: (208) 788-1550. E-mail: info@bouldermountaintour.com. Web: www.bouldermountaintour.com.

BIRTHDAYS TODAY

Gabrielle Anwar, 35, actress (*Scent of a Woman*), born Laleham, England, Feb 4, 1971.
Clint Black, 44, country singer, songwriter, born Katy, LA, Feb 4, 1962.
David Brenner, 61, comedian, born Philadelphia, PA, Feb 4, 1945.
Gary Conway, 70, actor ("Burke's Law," *I Was a Teenage Frankenstein*), born Boston, MA, Feb 4, 1936.
Alice Cooper, 58, singer, songwriter, born Vincent Damon Furnier, Detroit, MI, Feb 4, 1948.
Oscar de la Hoya, 33, boxer, born Los Angeles, CA, Feb 4, 1973.
Lisa Eichhorn, 54, actress (*The Vanishing, King of the Hill*), born Reading, PA, Feb 4, 1952.
Pamela Franklin, 56, actress (*The Prime of Miss Jean Brodie, The Legend of Hell House*), born Tokyo, Japan, Feb 4, 1950.
Betty Friedan, 85, author (*The Feminine Mystique*), founder, the National Organization for Women (NOW), born Peoria, IL, Feb 4, 1921.
Michael Goorjian, 35, actor ("Party of Five"), born San Francisco, CA, Feb 4, 1971.
Rosa Lee Parks, 93, civil rights leader who refused to give up her seat on the bus, born Tuskegee, AL, Feb 4, 1913.
J. Danforth (Dan) Quayle, 59, 44th vice president of US, born Indianapolis, IN, Feb 4, 1947.
John Schuck, 66, actor ("McMillan and Wife," *McCabe and Mrs Miller, Dick Tracy*), born Boston, MA, Feb 4, 1940.
Lawrence Taylor, 47, Hall of Fame football player, born Williamsburg, VA, Feb 4, 1959.

FEBRUARY 5 — SUNDAY
Day 36 — 329 Remaining

CARRADINE, JOHN: 100th BIRTH ANNIVERSARY. Feb 5, 1906. American film actor John Carradine was born Richmond Reed Carradine at Greenwich Village, NY. He appeared in more than 200 films. Frequently observed wandering the streets in a velvet suit and satin cape while reciting Shakespeare, he became known as "the Bard of the Boulevard." Died Nov 27, 1988, at Milan, Italy.

CHILDREN'S AUTHORS & ILLUSTRATORS WEEK. Feb 5–11. To celebrate and recognize authors and illustrators who create books for young people and promote literacy by inspiring enjoyment of quality literature. During this week, members of the Children's Authors Network speak at schools, libraries and children's shelters. Motivate children to read and write: invite authors and illustrators to school and venues near you! Annually, the first full week in February. For info: Children's Authors Network! (CAN!), 23291 Mobile St, West Hills, CA 91307. Phone: (818) 615-0857. Web: www.childrensauthorsnetwork.com.

FAMILY-LEAVE BILL: ANNIVERSARY. Feb 5, 1993. President William Clinton signed legislation requiring companies with 50 or more employees (and all government agencies) to allow employees to take up to 12 weeks unpaid leave in a 12-month period to deal with the birth or adoption of a child or to care for a relative with a serious health problem. The bill became effective Aug 5, 1993.

GET PAID TO SHOP WEEK. Feb 5–11. Love to shop? Got those postholiday, maxed-out credit cards, can't go to the mall blues? Start getting paid to go shopping as a mystery shopper. Businesses use thousands of mystery shoppers to tell them what their customers won't—the truth about service, cleanliness and more. And if you work up an appetite shopping, mystery shoppers also get paid to eat out in restaurants. Annually, the first full week in February. For info: Cathy Stucker, 4646 Hwy 6, PMB #123, Sugar Land, TX 77478. Phone: (281) 265-7342. E-mail: cathy@idealady.com. Web: www.idealady.com/shopping.htm.

INTERNATIONAL COACHING WEEK. Feb 5–11. To provide a week each year to educate the public about the value of working with a personal, business or executive coach and to provide an opportunity for coaches and their clients to acknowledge the results and progress made through the coaching process. Annually, the first full week in February. For info: Jerri N. Udelson, MCC, Entrepreneurial Consulting Services, 59 Chestnut St, South Dartmouth, MA 02748. Phone: (508) 990-1999. E-mail: JerriU@aol.com. Web: www.coachfederation.org or www.coachingweek.com.

LEADERSHIP WEEK INTERNATIONAL. Feb 5–11. As leadership is foundational to all organizations, this week is dedicated to the development of leadership that is both great and morally good. Conference themes will include modeling, instructing and mentoring character traits necessary for effective leaders. For info: DiFrances & Assoc, LLC, 208 E Oak Crest Dr, Ste 200, Wales, WI 53183-9700. Phone: (262) 968-9850. Fax: (262) 968-9854. E-mail: leadership@difrances.com. Web: www.difrances.com/leadershipweek.

LONGEST WAR IN HISTORY ENDS: ANNIVERSARY. Feb 5, 1985. The Third Punic War, between Rome and Carthage, started in the year 149 BC. It culminated in the year 146 BC, when Roman soldiers led by Scipio razed Carthage to the ground. The desolated site was cursed and rebuilding forbidden. On this date, 2,131 years after the war began, Ugo Vetere, mayor of Rome, and Chedli Klibi, mayor of Carthage, met at Tunis to sign a treaty of friendship officially ending the Third Punic War.

MEXICO: CONSTITUTION DAY. Feb 5. National holiday. Present constitution, embracing major social reforms, adopted in 1917.

		S	M	T	W	T	F	S
February					1	2	3	4
2006		5	6	7	8	9	10	11
		12	13	14	15	16	17	18
		19	20	21	22	23	24	25
		26	27	28				

MOON PHASE: FIRST QUARTER. Feb 5. Moon enters First Quarter phase at 1:29 AM, EST.

MOVE HOLLYWOOD & BROADWAY TO LEBANON, PENNSYLVANIA DAY. Feb 5. There's lots of room, friendly folks and Amish farms. Lebanon is a safe haven for residents and tourists to serenely indulge in their world-famous bologna and the Wertz family homemade candies. [©2003 by WH.] For info: Thomas & Ruth Roy, Wellcat Holidays, 2418 Long Ln, Lebanon, PA 17046. Phone: (717) 279-0184. E-mail: info@wellcat.com. Web: www.wellcat.com.

★**NATIONAL CONSUMER PROTECTION WEEK.** Feb 5–11.

OCEAN COUNTY BLUEGRASS FESTIVAL. Feb 5. Waretown, NJ. A family-oriented bluegrass festival where no alcoholic beverages or smoking are allowed. Est attendance: 400. For info: Albert Music Hall, PO Box 657, Waretown, NJ 08758. Phone: (609) 971-1593. Web: www.alberthall.org.

PEEL, ROBERT: BIRTH ANNIVERSARY. Feb 5, 1788. English statesman, established the Irish constabulary (known as the "Peelers"). Later, as England's home secretary, he reorganized the London police, thereafter known as "Bobbies." Born at Lancashire, England, he died July 2, 1850, at London from injuries received in a fall from his horse.

STEVENSON, ADLAI EWING: BIRTH ANNIVERSARY. Feb 5, 1900. American statesman, governor of Illinois, Democratic candidate for president in 1952 and 1956, US representative to the UN, 1961–65. Born at Los Angeles, CA. Died at London, England, July 14, 1965. Not to be confused with his grandfather, Vice President Adlai Ewing Stevenson. See also: "Stevenson, Adlai Ewing: Birth Anniversary" (Oct 23).

SUPER BOWL XL. Feb 5. Ford Field, Detroit, MI. The battle between the NFC and AFC champions. For info: PR Dept, The Natl Football League, 280 Park Ave, New York, NY 10017. Phone: (212) 450-2000. Web: www.nfl.com and www.sbxl.org.

SWITZERLAND: HOMSTROM. Feb 5. Scuol. Burning of straw men on poles as a symbol of winter's imminent departure. Annually, the first Sunday in February.

WEATHERMAN'S [WEATHERPERSON'S] DAY. Feb 5. Commemorates the birth of one of America's first weathermen, John Jeffries, a Boston physician who kept detailed records of weather conditions, 1774–1816. Born at Boston, Feb 5, 1744, and died there Sept 16, 1819. See also: "First Balloon Flight Across English Channel: Anniversary" (Jan 7).

WITHERSPOON, JOHN: BIRTH ANNIVERSARY. Feb 5, 1723. Clergyman, signer of the Declaration of Independence and reputed coiner of the word *Americanism* (in 1781). Born near Edinburgh, Scotland. Died at Princeton, NJ, Nov 15, 1794.

BIRTHDAYS TODAY

Henry Louis (Hank) Aaron, 72, Hall of Fame baseball player, baseball executive, all-time home run leader, born Mobile, AL, Feb 5, 1934.

Roberto Alomar, 38, former baseball player, born Ponce, Puerto Rico, Feb 5, 1968.

Bobby Brown, 37, singer, dancer ("My Prerogative," "Every Little Step"), born Roxbury, MA, Feb 5, 1969.

Red Buttons, 87, actor ("The Red Buttons Show," "The Double Life of Henry Phyfe"), born Aaron Chwatt at the Bronx, NY, Feb 5, 1919.

Sara Evans, 35, country singer, born Bookville, MO, Feb 5, 1971.

Jennifer Granholm, 47, Governor of Michigan (D), born Vancouver, BC, Canada, Feb 5, 1959.

Father Andrew Greeley, 78, Roman Catholic priest and author (*Happy Are the Merciful, An Occasion of Sin*), born Oak Park, IL, Feb 5, 1928.

Christopher Guest, 58, writer, comedian (Emmy for writing *Lily Tomlin*; *Spinal Tap, Best in Show*), born New York, NY, Feb 5, 1948.

Barbara Hershey, 58, actress (*Hannah and Her Sisters*), born Barbara Hertzstein at Los Angeles, CA, Feb 5, 1948.

David Alan Ladd, 59, actor, producer (*A Dog of Flanders, The Day of the Locust*), born Los Angeles, CA, Feb 5, 1947.

Jennifer Jason Leigh, 44, actress (*Miami Blues, Rush, Backdraft*), born Los Angeles, CA, Feb 5, 1962.

Laura Linney, 42, actress (*The Truman Show, You Can Count on Me, Kinsey*), born New York, NY, Feb 5, 1964.

Jane Bryant Quinn, 65, financial writer (*Everyone's Money Book*), born Niagara Falls, NY, Feb 5, 1941.

Charlotte Rampling, 60, actress (*Georgy Girl, Farewell My Lovely*), born Sturmer, England, Feb 5, 1946.

David Selby, 65, actor ("Falcon Crest," *Rich and Famous*), born Morgantown, WV, Feb 5, 1941.

Roger Thomas Staubach, 64, Hall of Fame football player, born Cincinnati, OH, Feb 5, 1942.

Darrell Waltrip, 59, auto racer, born Owensboro, KY, Feb 5, 1947.

FEBRUARY 6 — MONDAY
Day 37 — 328 Remaining

ACCESSION OF QUEEN ELIZABETH II: ANNIVERSARY. Feb 6, 1952. Princess Elizabeth Alexandra Mary succeeded to the British throne (becoming Elizabeth II, Queen of the United Kingdom of Great Britain and Northern Ireland and Head of the Commonwealth) upon the death of her father, King George VI, Feb 6, 1952. Her coronation took place June 2, 1953, at Westminster Abbey at London.

BURR, AARON: 250th BIRTH ANNIVERSARY. Feb 6, 1756. 3rd vice president of the US (Mar 4, 1801–Mar 3, 1805). While vice president, Burr challenged political enemy Alexander Hamilton to a duel and mortally wounded him July 11, 1804, at Weehawken, NJ. Indicted for the challenge and for murder, he returned to Washington to complete his term of office (during which he presided over the impeachment trial of Supreme Court Justice Samuel Chase). In 1807 Burr was arrested, tried for treason (in an alleged scheme to invade Mexico and set up a new nation in the West) and acquitted. Born at Newark, NJ, he died at Staten Island, NY, Sept 14, 1836.

FREELANCE WRITERS APPRECIATION WEEK. Feb 6–10. Freelance writers do more than query editors and write and submit articles and books (nonfiction and fiction). They provide overworked editors with material, as well as inform and entertain readers. Annually, the second week of February. Visit www.profitable-pen.com for ideas and discussions, registration is free! For info: Dorothy Zjawin, Dir, 61 W Colfax Ave, Roselle Park, NJ 07204. Phone: (908) 241-6241.

FUNERAL SERVICE EDUCATION WEEK. Feb 6–12. This weeklong event has two purposes: it will educate and prepare the public for the death of a family member and/or loved one—providing an understanding of how to plan a funeral wisely, economically and emotionally; and it will create an awareness of the funeral profession. Annually, the first full week of February. For info: Mark Krause, Krause Funeral Home, 9000 W Capital Dr, Milwaukee, WI 53222. Phone: (414) 464-4640. Fax: (414) 461-3868. E-mail: mark@krausefuneralhome.com. Web: www.krausefuneralhome.com.

JUST SAY NO TO POWERPOINT® WEEK. Feb 6–10. All across America businesspeople are being asked to make presentations without the use of PowerPoint®. We challenge them to communicate with their audiences rather than merely slideswiping them (reading one boring words-only slide after another after another). For info: Nancy Stern. Phone: (800) 280-2666. Fax: (858) 792-2745. E-mail: nancy@nancystern.com. Web: www.nancystern.com.

LINCOLN, ABRAHAM: OREGON BIRTHDAY OBSERVANCE. Feb 6. Observed annually in Oregon on the first Monday in February. See also: "Lincoln, Abraham: Birth Anniversary" (Feb 12).

LOVE A MENSCH WEEK. Feb 6–12. Mensches are decent, responsible men or women. During this week singles look to meet a mensch as well as take time to appreciate how mensches enhance our lives. For info: Robin Gorman Newman, 44 Somerset Dr N, Great Neck, NY 11020. Phone: (516) 773-0911. E-mail: robin@lovecoach.com. Web: www.lovecoach.com.

MARLEY, BOB: BIRTH ANNIVERSARY. Feb 6, 1945. With his group, The Wailers, Bob Marley was one of the most popular and influential performers of reggae music, an "off-beat-accented Jamaican" music closely associated with the political/religious Rastafarian movement (admirers of the late Ethiopian emperor Haile Selassie, who was formerly called Ras Tafari). Marley was born at Rhoden Hall in northern Jamaica. Died of cancer at Miami, FL, May 11, 1981.

MASSACHUSETTS RATIFIES CONSTITUTION: ANNIVERSARY. Feb 6, 1788. By a vote of 187 to 168, Massachusetts became the sixth state to ratify the Constitution.

MIDWINTER'S DAY CELEBRATION. Feb 6. Ann Arbor, MI. To create euphoria by fiat in celebration that winter is half over. For info: Richard Ankli, The Fifth Wheel Tavern, 639 Fifth St, Ann Arbor, MI 48103.

NATIONAL SCHOOL COUNSELING WEEK. Feb 6–10. Promotes school counseling in the school and community. Annually, first full week of February. For info: American School Counselor Assn, 1101 King St, Ste 625, Alexandria, VA 22314. Phone: (800) 306-4722. Fax: (703) 683-1619. E-mail: asca@schoolcounselor.org. Web: www.schoolcounselor.org.

NEW ZEALAND: WAITANGI DAY. Feb 6. National Day. Commemorates signing of the Treaty of Waitangi in 1840 (at Waitangi, Chatham Islands, New Zealand). The treaty, between the native Maori and the European peoples, provided for development of New Zealand under the British Crown.

PAY-A-COMPLIMENT DAY. Feb 6. Practice this simple act of premeditated kindness and pay a compliment to coworkers, family members or a stranger on the street or in the elevator in your office building. Go ahead, make someone feel special and see the difference a sincere compliment makes! [©1995] To alleviate the escalating costs of Eventological® Literature, a charge of $10 must be assessed for each request. Checks are to be made payable to: Adrienne Sioux Koopersmith, 1437 W Rosemont, #1W, Chicago, IL 60660-1319. E-mail: askoopersmith@hotmail.com.

REAGAN, RONALD WILSON: BIRTH ANNIVERSARY. Feb 6, 1911. 40th president of the US (1981–89). Former sportscaster, motion picture actor, governor of California (1967–74); he was the oldest and the first divorced person to become president. Born at Tampico, IL. Married actress Jane Wyman in 1940 (divorced in 1948); married actress Nancy Davis, Mar 4, 1952. The "Great Communicator" ushered in a decade of conservative policies upon his election in 1980 and was an indefatigable critic of communist states; he famously challenged Soviet president Gorbachev to "tear down this wall!" at the Berlin Wall in 1987. He died at his Los Angeles, CA, home on June 5, 2004.

RUTH, "BABE": BIRTH ANNIVERSARY. Feb 6, 1895. One of baseball's greatest heroes, George Herman "Babe" Ruth was born at Baltimore, MD. The left-handed pitcher—"the Sultan of Swat"—hit 714 home runs in 22 major league seasons of play and played in 10 World Series. Died at New York, NY, Aug 16, 1948.

TRUFFAUT, FRANÇOIS: BIRTH ANNIVERSARY. Feb 6, 1932. Born at Paris, France, Truffaut was the most popular and successful French film director of his time. His films include *The 400 Blows, Jules and Jim, The Last Metro* and *The Story of Adele H.* He died at Paris, Oct 21, 1984.

BIRTHDAYS TODAY

Sarah Brady, 64, handgun control activist, born Alexandria, VA, Feb 6, 1942.

Tom Brokaw, 66, journalist, born Yankton, SD, Feb 6, 1940.

Natalie Cole, 56, singer ("This Will Be," "Unforgettable"), born Los Angeles, CA, Feb 6, 1950.

Fabian, 63, singer, actor, born Fabian Forte at Philadelphia, PA, Feb 6, 1943.

Mike Farrell, 67, actor ("M*A*S*H," "Providence"), born St. Paul, MN, Feb 6, 1939.

Zsa Zsa (Sari) Gabor, 87, actress (*Ninotchka, Special Tonight*), born Budapest, Hungary, Feb 6, 1919.

Gayle Hunnicutt, 63, actress ("Dallas," *The Wild Angels, Marlowe*), born Fort Worth, TX, Feb 6, 1943.

Barry Miller, 48, actor (stage: *Biloxi Blues* [Tony Award]; *Saturday Night Fever, The Last Temptation of Christ*), born Los Angeles, CA, Feb 6, 1958.

Kathy Najimy, 49, actress ("Veronica's Closet," *Sister Act*), born San Diego, CA, Feb 6, 1957.

Jim Nicholson, 68, US Secretary of Veteran's Affairs, born Struble, IA, Feb 26, 1938.

Gigi Perreau, 65, actress (*Bonzo Goes to College, Tammy Tell Me True*), born Los Angeles, CA, Feb 6, 1941.

Rip Torn, 75, actor ("The Larry Sanders Show," *Men in Black*), born Elmore Torn, Jr at Temple, TX, Feb 6, 1931.

Robert Townsend, 49, actor, director (*The Five Heartbeats, The Mighty Quinn*), born Chicago, IL, Feb 6, 1957.

Michael Tucker, 62, actor ("LA Law"), born Baltimore, MD, Feb 6, 1944.

Mamie Van Doren, 73, actress (*High School Confidential, Three Nuts in Search of a Bolt*), born Rowena, SD, Feb 6, 1933.

FEBRUARY 7 — TUESDAY

Day 38 — 327 Remaining

BALLET INTRODUCED TO THE US: ANNIVERSARY. Feb 7, 1827. Renowned French danseuse Mme Francisquy Hutin introduced ballet to the US with a performance of *The Deserter*, staged at the Bowery Theater, New York, NY. A minor scandal erupted when the ladies in the lower boxes left the theater upon viewing the light and scanty attire of Mme Hutin and her troupe.

BLAKE, EUBIE: BIRTH ANNIVERSARY. Feb 7, 1883. James Hubert "Eubie" Blake, American composer and pianist, writer of nearly 1,000 songs (including "I'm Just Wild About Harry" and "Memories of You"). Born at Baltimore, MD. Recipient of the Presidential Medal of Freedom in 1981. Last professional performance was in January 1982. Died at Brooklyn, NY, five days after his 100th birthday, Feb 12, 1983.

CHAPLIN'S "TRAMP" DEBUTS: ANNIVERSARY. Feb 7, 1914. Charlie Chaplin, vaudeville star-turned-comedic actor, debuted a new character in *Kid Auto Races at Venice*, a Keystone Studios short released on this date. The mischievous but innocent "Tramp," sporting a tiny mustache and twirling cane and wearing a little derby, tight-fitting jacket, baggy trousers and floppy shoes, was an immediate success with audiences, and soon mass-produced Tramp dolls were selling all over the US and the world.

CONGENITAL HEART DEFECT AWARENESS WEEK. Feb 7–14. Public relations/media campaign, special events in cities throughout the US. For info: Mona Barmash, Congenital Heart Information Network, 1561 Clark Dr, Yardley, PA 19067. Phone: (215) 493-3068. E-mail: mb@tchin.org. Web: www.tchin.org.

DESERT FOOTHILLS MUSICFEST. Feb 7–Mar 12. Carefree/Cave Creek and North Scottsdale, AZ, in four venues. Arizona's premier winter classical music festival celebrates the music of the masters with 12 events over a five-week period. Twelve concerts featuring the Festival Orchestra and guest artists including the Eroica Trio, Orion Weiss, Peter Appleyard, the Los Angeles Guitar Quartet and the Phoenix Symphony Orchestra conducted by Robert Moody and Michael Christie. Est attendance: 7,000. For info: Desert Hills Musicfest, PO Box 5254, Carefree, AZ 85377. Phone: (480) 488-0806. Fax: (480) 488-1401. E-mail: info@azmusicfest.org. Web: www.azmusicfest.org.

DICKENS, CHARLES: BIRTH ANNIVERSARY. Feb 7, 1812. English social critic and novelist, born at Portsmouth, England. Among his most successful books: *Oliver Twist, The Posthumous Papers of the Pickwick Club, A Tale of Two Cities, David Copperfield* and *A Christmas Carol*. Died at Gad's Hill, England, June 9, 1870, and was buried at Westminster Abbey.

DUMP YOUR "SIGNIFICANT JERK" DAY. Feb 7. It's time to take out the garbage and get rid of that "Jerk" boyfriend or girlfriend. This year will be the 13th annual call to arms. Annually, the Tuesday of the week before Valentine's Day. For info: Marcus P. Meleton, Jr, Sharkbait Press, PO Box 11300, Costa Mesa, CA 92627. Phone: (949) 413-3052. E-mail: mm@sharkbait press.com. Web: www.sharkbaitpress.com.

ELEVENTH AMENDMENT TO US CONSTITUTION (SOVEREIGNTY OF THE STATES): RATIFICATION ANNIVERSARY. Feb 7, 1795. The 11th Amendment to the Constitution was ratified, curbing the powers of the federal judiciary in relation to the states. The amendment reaffirmed the sovereignty of the states by prohibiting suits against them.

GRENADA: INDEPENDENCE DAY. Feb 7. National Day. Commemorates independence from Great Britain in 1974.

LEADERSHIP SUCCESS DAY. Feb 7. Honors the CEOs of companies with sales over $20 million where more than 60 percent of company employees voted in the past year that their CEO did not just pay lip service to the statement that "People are our greatest asset." These CEOs demonstrated through their actions on no less than 10 occasions throughout the year that people are their greatest asset. For info: Denis Orme, Leadership Success Institute, Ste 132, 2a Byron Ave, Takapuna, Auckland 1309, New Zealand. E-mail: principal@leader-success.com. Web: www.leader-success.com.

LEWIS, SINCLAIR: BIRTH ANNIVERSARY. Feb 7, 1885. American novelist and social critic. Recipient of Nobel Prize for Literature (1930). Among his novels: *Main Street, Babbitt* and *It Can't Happen Here*. Born Harry Sinclair Lewis at Sauk Center, MN. Died at Rome, Italy, Jan 10, 1951.

	S	M	T	W	T	F	S
February				1	2	3	4
2006	5	6	7	8	9	10	11
	12	13	14	15	16	17	18
	19	20	21	22	23	24	25
	26	27	28				

MORE, SIR THOMAS: BIRTH ANNIVERSARY. Feb 7, 1478. Anniversary of the birth of the lawyer, scholar, author, Lord Chancellor of England, martyr and saint at London, England. Refusing to recognize Henry VIII's divorce from Queen Catherine, the "Man for All Seasons" was found guilty of treason and imprisoned in the Tower of London, Apr 17, 1534. He was beheaded at Tower Hill on July 6, 1535, and his head displayed from Tower Bridge. Canonized in 1935. Memorial observed on June 22.

REJECTION AWARENESS WEEK. Feb 7–14. An annual event celebrating the risk that leads to love. Syndicated advice columnist Harlan Cohen founded RAW in 2003 to help expose the unspoken truth about dating and relationships—that relationship rejection is an unavoidable, normal and natural part of the search for true love. Celebrate RAW 2006 by taking the risk that leads to love. Annually, the week leading up to Valentine's Day. For info: Harlan Cohen, Help Me, Harlan!, 2506 N Clark St, Ste 223, Chicago, IL 60614. Phone: (212) 455-4180. E-mail: raw@helpmeharlan.com. Web: www.helpmeharlan.com.

SPACE MILESTONE: *STARDUST* (US). Feb 7, 1999. *Stardust* began its three-billion-mile journey to collect comet dust on this date. The unmanned mission met up with *Comet Wild-2* on Jan 2, 2004, and the samples it collected will reach Earth in January 2006. This is the first US mission devoted solely to a comet.

WAVE ALL YOUR FINGERS AT YOUR NEIGHBORS DAY. Feb 7. After all the challenges our neighbors and we have faced, it's time to put it all aside for at least one day. Wave "hello" to everybody and mean it. Annually, Feb 7. [©2003 by WH.] For info: Thomas & Ruth Roy, Wellcat Holidays, 2419 Long Ln, Lebanon, PA 17046. Phone: (717) 279-0184. E-mail: info@wellcat.com. Web: www.wellcat.com.

BIRTHDAYS TODAY

Hector Babenco, 60, director (*Ironweed, Kiss of the Spider Woman*), born Buenos Aires, Argentina, Feb 7, 1946.

Oscar Brand, 86, folksinger, born Winnipeg, MB, Canada, Feb 7, 1920.

Garth Brooks, 44, country singer ("Friends in Low Places"), born Tulsa, OK, Feb 7, 1962.

Miguel Ferrer, 52, actor ("Crossing Jordan," "Twin Peaks" *Robo-Cop*), born Santa Monica, CA, Feb 7, 1954.

Juwan Howard, 33, basketball player, born Chicago, IL, Feb 7, 1973.

Herb Kohl, 71, US Senator (D, Wisconsin), born Milwaukee, WI, Feb 7, 1935.

Ashton Kutcher, 28, actor ("That 70s Show," *Hey Dude, Where's My Car?*), born Cedar Rapids, IA, Feb 7, 1978.

Pete Postlethwaite, 61, actor (*Amistad; The Lost World: Jurassic Park; Brassed Off*), born London, England, Feb 7, 1945.

Chris Rock, 40, actor, comedian ("Saturday Night Live," *Beverly Hills Ninja*), born Brooklyn, NY, Feb 7, 1966.

James Spader, 46, actor (*Secretary; Stargate; sex, lies, and videotape*), born Boston, MA, Feb 7, 1960.

Gay Talese, 74, author (*The Kingdom and the Power, Unto the Sons*), born Ocean City, NJ, Feb 7, 1932.

FEBRUARY 8 — WEDNESDAY
Day 39 — 326 Remaining

BOY SCOUTS OF AMERICA FOUNDED: ANNIVERSARY. Feb 8, 1910. The Boy Scouts of America was founded at Washington, DC, by William Boyce, based on the work of Sir Robert Baden-Powell with the British Boy Scout Association.

CANADA: VANCOUVER INTERNATIONAL BOAT SHOW. Feb 8–12. British Columbia Place Stadium, Vancouver, BC. Sail- and powerboats, sailboards, inflatables, canoes, personal watercraft, marine electronics and accessories, marine services, charters, sailing schools, water skis, sporting goods, travel and resort destinations, fishing equipment and Marine Facts Stage. Est attendance: 38,000. For info: NMMA Canada, 8545 Commerce Court, Burnaby, BC, Canada V5A 4N4. Phone: (604) 678-8820. Web: www.discoverboating.com/vancouver/home.asp.

CARLSON, CHESTER F.: 100th BIRTH ANNIVERSARY. Feb 8, 1906. Born at Seattle, WA, Carlson was the inventor in 1938 of the dry-copy machine—something he developed to make quick copies of drawings and technical specifications at his electronics company. This device was to become the first office copier—first offered by Xerox in the mid-1950s. Carlson died Sept 19, 1968.

DEAN, JAMES: BIRTH ANNIVERSARY. Feb 8, 1931. American stage, film and television actor who achieved immense popularity during a brief career. Born at Fairmont, IN. Best remembered for his role in *Rebel Without a Cause*. Died in an automobile accident near Cholame, CA, Sept 30, 1955, at age 24.

THE GRAMMY AWARDS. Feb 8. Staples Center, Los Angeles, CA. 48th annual. Celebrating the best in recording arts and sciences, the Grammys cover 104 categories—from classical to jazz to pop and rock. Awarded by and to artists and technical professionals. For info: National Academy of Recording Arts & Sciences, 3402 Pico Blvd, Santa Monica, CA 90405. Phone: (310) 392-3777. Fax: (310) 392-2778. Web: www.grammy.com.

JAPAN: HA-RI-KU-YO (NEEDLE MASS). Feb 8. Ha-Ri-Ku-Yo, a Needle Mass, may be observed on either Feb 8 or Dec 8. Girls do no needlework; instead they gather old and broken needles, which they dedicate to the Awashima Shrine at Wakayama. Girls pray to Awashima Myozin (their protecting deity) that their needlework, symbolic of love and marriage, will be good. Participation in the Needle Mass hopefully leads to a happy marriage.

JAPAN: SNOW FESTIVAL. Feb 8–12. Sapporo, Hokkaido. Huge, elaborate snow and ice sculptures are erected on the Odori-Koen Promenade.

LAUGH AND GET RICH DAY. Feb 8. Recognition of laughter's power to add to the bottom line. People are more effective and tend to remember things better, and laughter helps to lower the turnover rate. For info: Rick Segel, 1 Wheatland St, Burlington, MA 01803. Phone: (781) 272-9995. Fax: (781) 272-9996. E-mail: rick@ricksegel.com.

LEMMON, JACK: BIRTH ANNIVERSARY. Feb 8, 1925. Stage, screen and television actor, born John Uhler Lemmon III at Boston, MA. Often paired with actor Walter Matthau, he starred in such films as *The Odd Couple, The Fortune Cookie* and *The Front Page*. He was nominated for seven Academy Awards, winning in 1955 for his supporting role in *Mister Roberts* and in 1974 for his leading role in *Save the Tiger*. Other films included *Some Like It Hot, Days of Wine and Roses* and *Grumpy Old Men*. He also starred in television versions of *Inherit the Wind* and *Twelve Angry Men* and won an Emmy in 2000 for the TV movie *Tuesdays with Morrie*. He died at Los Angeles, CA, June 27, 2001.

LOVE MAY MAKE THE WORLD GO 'ROUND, BUT LAUGHTER KEEPS US FROM GETTING DIZZY WEEK. Feb 8–14. This week is dedicated to Victor Borge's notion that "Laughter is the shortest distance between two people" and Joel Goodman's notion that "Seven days without laughter makes one weak." This is a chance to lighten your relationships and to reinforce the connection between "heart" and "hearty laughter." Annually, the week leading up to and including Valentine's Day. For info on the positive power of humor: The HUMOR Project, Inc, 480 Broadway, Ste 210-C, Saratoga Springs, NY 12866-2288. Phone: (518) 587-8770. E-mail: chase@HumorProject.com. Web: www.HumorProject.com.

MARTHA GRIFFITHS SPEAKS OUT AGAINST SEX DISCRIMINATION: ANNIVERSARY. Feb 8, 1964. During the congressional debate over the 1964 Civil Rights Act, Representative Martha Griffiths delivered a memorable speech advocating the prohibition of discrimination based on sex. Her efforts resulted in adding civil rights protection for women to the 1964 Act. She later successfully led the campaign for the Equal Rights Amendment in the House of Representatives.

MARY, QUEEN OF SCOTS: EXECUTION ANNIVERSARY. Feb 8, 1587. Mary Stuart, the queen regent of Scotland, was beheaded at Fotheringhay, England, after being accused of plotting Queen Elizabeth I's death. Mary, the daughter of James V of Scotland by his second wife, Mary of Guise, was born Dec 7 or 8, 1542, at Linlithgow, Scotland, and became queen a week later upon the death of her father, although she did not begin governing until after her mother's death in 1561. Accused of knowingly marrying the alleged murderer of her second husband, Lord Darnley, she was forced to abdicate in favor of her son (James VI) and fled to England for protection, only to find herself a prisoner for the rest of her life—a victim of Elizabethan political intrigue.

NEW ORLEANS BOAT SHOW. Feb 8–12. Louisiana Superdome, New Orleans, LA. Annual show of boat and marine products, fishing equipment and resort info. Informative boating and fishing seminars. For info: Barbara Sclafani, Natl Marine Manufacturers Assn, 3925 N I-10 Service Rd, Ste 209, Metairie, LA 70002. Phone: (504) 780-1818. Fax: (504) 780-1813. E-mail: bsclafani@nmma.org. Web: www.neworleansboatshow.com.

OPERA DEBUT IN THE COLONIES: ANNIVERSARY. Feb 8, 1735. The first opera produced in the colonies was performed at the Courtroom, at Charleston, SC. The opera was *Flora; or the Hob in the Well*, written by Colley Cibber.

REENACTMENT OF COWTOWN'S LAST OLD WEST GUNFIGHT. Feb 8. White Elephant Saloon, Fort Worth, TX. Annual reenactment of Fort Worth's last Old West gunfight, which took place on Feb 8, 1887, between White Elephant Saloon owner Luke Short and former marshal T.I. "Longhaired Jim" Courtright. Annually, Feb 8. Est attendance: 400. For info: Tim Love, Owner, 108 E Exchange Ave, Fort Worth, TX 76106-8210. Phone: (817) 624-9712. Fax: (817) 625-9663. E-mail: info@whiteelephant saloon.com. Web: www.whiteelephantsaloon.com.

SHERMAN, WILLIAM TECUMSEH: BIRTH ANNIVERSARY. Feb 8, 1820. Born at Lancaster, OH, General Sher-

man is especially remembered for his devastating march through Georgia during the Civil War and his statement "War is hell." Died at New York, NY, Feb 14, 1891.

SLOVENIA: CULTURE DAY. Feb 8. National holiday. Honors France Preseren, Slovenia's national poet, who died Feb 8, 1849.

SPACE MILESTONE: *ARABSAT-1*. Feb 8, 1985. League of Arab States communications satellite launched into geosynchronous orbit from Kourou, French Guiana, by the European Space Agency.

SPACE MILESTONE: *BRASILSAT-1* (BRAZIL). Feb 8, 1985. Brazilian communications satellite launched into geosynchronous orbit from Kourou, French Guiana, by the European Space Agency.

VERNE, JULES: BIRTH ANNIVERSARY. Feb 8, 1828. French writer, sometimes called "the father of science fiction," born at Nantes, France. Author of *Around the World in Eighty Days, Twenty Thousand Leagues Under the Sea* and many other novels. Died at Amiens, France, Mar 24, 1905.

BIRTHDAYS TODAY

Brooke Adams, 57, actress (*Days of Heaven, Gas Food Lodging*), born New York, NY, Feb 8, 1949.

Gary Coleman, 38, actor ("Diff'rent Strokes," *The Kid from Left Field*), born Zion, IL, Feb 8, 1968.

Seth Green, 32, actor ("Family Guy," "Greg the Bunny," *Austin Powers*), born Overbrook Park, PA, Feb 8, 1974.

John Grisham, 51, author (*The Firm, The Client*), born Jonesboro, AR, Feb 8, 1955.

Robert Klein, 64, comedian, actor ("Comedy Tonight," *They're Playing Our Song*), born New York, NY, Feb 8, 1942.

Ted Koppel, 66, journalist (anchor of "Nightline"), born Lancashire, England, Feb 8, 1940.

Alonzo Mourning, 36, basketball player, born Chesapeake, VA, Feb 8, 1970.

Nick Nolte, 65, actor (*Affliction, Prince of Tides*, "Rich Man, Poor Man"), born Omaha, NE, Feb 8, 1941.

Mary Steenburgen, 53, actress (*Melvin and Howard, Parenthood, Back to the Future Part III*), born Newport, AR, Feb 8, 1953.

John Williams, 74, pianist, conductor (formerly with Boston Pops), composer (scores for *Jaws, Star Wars, Jurassic Park, Schindler's List*), born New York, NY, Feb 8, 1932.

FEBRUARY 9 — THURSDAY
Day 40 — 325 Remaining

ALLIES RETAKE GUADALCANAL: ANNIVERSARY. Feb 9, 1943. In a major strategic victory, the American 161st and 132nd Regiments retook Guadalcanal in the Solomon Islands on this date after a six-month-long battle. More than 9,000 Japanese and 2,000 Americans were killed. The fierce resistance by the Japanese was an indication to the Allies of things to come. Guadalcanal put the Allies within striking distance of Rabaul, the major Japanese base in the area.

ASHURA: TENTH DAY. Feb 9. Islamic calendar date: Muharram 10, 1427. For Shia Muslims, commemorates death of Muhammad's grandson at the Battle of Karbala. A time of fasting, reflection and meditation. Jews of Medina fasted on the tenth day in remembrance of their salvation from Pharoah. Different methods for "anticipating" the visibility of the new moon crescent at Mecca are used by different groups. US date may vary. Began at sunset the preceding day.

THE BEATLES APPEAR ON "THE ED SULLIVAN SHOW": ANNIVERSARY. Feb 9, 1964. British pop phenomenons The Beatles began the "British Invasion" of America with their appearance on America's top television variety show. They performed five songs before a screaming studio audience of 728. The estimated viewership for that night's show was 73 million people—making it the most viewed US TV program in history up to that time. See also: "Beatles Take Over Music Charts" (Apr 4).

	S	**M**	**T**	**W**	**T**	**F**	**S**
February				1	2	3	4
2006	5	6	7	8	9	10	11
	12	13	14	15	16	17	18
	19	20	21	22	23	24	25
	26	27	28				

BEHAN, BRENDAN: BIRTH ANNIVERSARY. Feb 9, 1923. Irish playwright and poet, born at Dublin, Ireland. Died there Mar 20, 1964.

CANADA: CALGARY BOAT AND SPORTSMEN'S SHOW. Feb 9–12. Roundup Centre, Stampede Park, Calgary, AB. Sail-, power- and fishing boats; hunting, fishing and camping supplies; resort destinations and outdoor recreation; four-wheel-drive vehicles; family entertainment. Est attendance: 25,000. For info: Canadian Natl Sportsmen's Shows, 340 1032-17th Ave SW, Calgary, AB, Canada T2T 0A5. Phone: (403) 245-9008. Fax: (403) 245-5100. Web: www.sportshows.ca.

FLORIDA STATE FAIR. Feb 9–20. Florida State Fairgrounds, Tampa, FL. 102nd annual. The fair features the best arts, crafts, competitive exhibits, equestrian shows, livestock, entertainment and food found in Florida. Also not to be missed is "Cracker Country," where cultural and architectural history has been preserved. Est attendance: 545,000. For info: Sherry Powell, Mktg & Advertising Mgr, Florida State Fair, PO Box 11766, Tampa, FL 33680. Phone: (813) 621-7821 or (800) 345-FAIR. Web: www .floridastatefair.com.

GERMANY: BERLIN INTERNATIONAL FILM FESTIVAL. Feb 9–19. Potsdamer Platz, Berlin. The 56th festival. One of the premier international film festivals since its inaugural opening in 1951. Includes film competition, Children's Film Festival and other special programs. The awarding of Golden and Silver Bears by the International Jury marks the conclusion of the festival. Est attendance: 390,000. For info: Internationale Filmfestspiele Berlin, Potsdamer Strasse 5, D-10785 Berlin, Germany. Phone: (011) (49) (30) 25920. E-mail: info@berlinale.de. Web: www.berlinale.de.

GYPSY ROSE LEE: BIRTH ANNIVERSARY. Feb 9, 1914. American ecdysiast and author whose real name was Rose Louise Hovick, born at Seattle, WA. Her autobiography, *Gypsy*, was made into a Broadway musical and a motion picture. Died at Los Angeles, CA, Apr 26, 1970.

HARRISON, WILLIAM HENRY: BIRTH ANNIVERSARY. Feb 9, 1773. 9th president of the US (Mar 4–Apr 4, 1841). His term of office was the shortest in our nation's history—32 days. He was the first president to die in office (of pneumonia contracted during inaugural ceremonies). Born at Berkeley, VA, he died at Washington, DC, Apr 4, 1841. His grandson, Benjamin Harrison, was the 23rd president of the US.

LEBANON: ST. MARON'S DAY. Feb 9. Holiday of Lebanon's Maronite Christian community. St. Maron was a Syrian hermit of the 4th–5th centuries.

LOWELL, AMY: BIRTH ANNIVERSARY. Feb 9, 1874. American poet born at Brookline, MA. Died there May 12, 1925.

MAYMONT FLOWER & GARDEN SHOW. Feb 9–12. Greater Richmond Convention Center, Richmond, VA. At the 17th annual Maymont Flower and Garden Show, garden lovers will find breathtaking full-scale landscape exhibits, numerous associated shows and the "Great Garden Marketplace." Expert speakers give advice and provide insight into a variety of garden topics. Please contact us for ticket info and a free brochure. Est attendance: 31,000. For info: Maymont Foundation, 1700 Hampton St, Richmond, VA 23220. Phone: (804) 358-7166. E-mail: flowershow@maymont.org. Web: www.maymont.org.

MILWAUKEE/NARI HOME IMPROVEMENT SHOW. Feb 9–12. Wisconsin State Fair Park, West Allis, WI. Cosponsored by Milwaukee/NARI Home Improvement Council and the *Milwaukee Journal Sentinel*, this show is of particular interest to homeowners planning a remodeling project for their home. More than 300 exhibitors in a no-pressure setting. Educational seminars by home improvement experts, a remodeler's showcase with the latest innovations plus guided tours and colorful garden areas. Annually, the second weekend in February. Est attendance: 30,000. For info: Mary Fox-Hagner, Exec Dir, Milwaukee/NARI Home Improvement Council, 11815 W Dearbourn Ave, PO Box 26788, Wauwatosa, WI 53226. Phone: (414) 771-4071. Fax: (414) 771-4077. E-mail: nari@execpc.com. Web: www.milwaukeenari.com.

NEW MEXICO: EXTRATERRESTRIAL CULTURE DAY. Feb 9. New Mexico. A day "to celebrate and honor all past, present and future extraterrestrial visitors in ways to enhance relationships among all citizens of the cosmos, known and unknown." Passed as a memorial (not law) by the New Mexico state legislature in acknowledgment that ever since the Roswell UFO incident of 1947, New Mexico is recognized worldwide as a nexus of sightings and unexplained mysteries. Annually, the second Thursday of February.

RUSK, (DAVID) DEAN: BIRTH ANNIVERSARY. Feb 9, 1909. US diplomat Dean Rusk was born at Cherokee County, GA. He served as US secretary of state from 1961 to 1969, during which time he supported US involvement in the Vietnam War. He died Dec 20, 1994, at Athens, GA.

TUBB, ERNEST: BIRTH ANNIVERSARY. Feb 9, 1914. Country and western singer, born at Crisp, TX. Ernest Tubb was the sixth member to be elected to the Country Music Hall of Fame and the headliner on the first country music show ever to be presented at Carnegie Hall. His first major hit, "Walking the Floor Over You," gained him his first appearance at the Grand Ole Opry in 1942, and he attained regular membership in 1943. He died Sept 6, 1984, at Nashville, TN.

UNION OFFICERS ESCAPE LIBBY PRISON: ANNIVERSARY. Feb 9, 1864. On this date 109 Union officers escaped from Libby Prison at Richmond, VA, in the largest and most dramatic prisoner of war escape of the Civil War. The Libby Prison was the former Libby and Sons candle factory. Forty-eight of the men were recaptured, two drowned and fifty-nine successfully made it back to Federal lines.

VEECK, BILL: BIRTH ANNIVERSARY. Feb 9, 1914. William Louis (Bill) Veeck, Jr, Baseball Hall of Fame executive born at Chicago, IL. Veeck was baseball's premier promoter and showman as an owner of several teams. He integrated the American League, sent a midget to the plate to start a game and, in general, sought to provide fans with entertainment in addition to baseball. Inducted into the Hall of Fame in 1991. Died at Chicago, IL, Jan 2, 1986.

WAR TIME: ANNIVERSARY. Feb 9, 1942. US clocks were advanced one hour at 2 AM as the nation went on War Time to conserve electricity. President Roosevelt had signed this daylight savings bill on Jan 20.

WASHINGTON HOME & GARDEN SHOW. Feb 9–12. The New Washington Convention Center, Washington, DC. Six acres of everything for the home and garden including full-size blooming gardens created by the area's best landscapers. The show also has demonstrations, lectures and a Spring Marketplace where visitors can purchase anything from orchids to a whole new kitchen. For info: Dee Stafford, Washington Home & Garden Show, 6017 Tower Ct, Alexandria, VA 22304. Phone: (703) 823-7960. E-mail: tjsevents@aol.com.

BIRTHDAYS TODAY

Mia Farrow, 61, actress ("Peyton Place," *Rosemary's Baby, Hannah and Her Sisters*), born Maria de Lourdes Villers at Los Angeles, CA, Feb 9, 1945.

Kathryn Grayson, 83, actress (*Kiss Me Kate, The Kissing Bandit*), born Zelma Hedrick at Winston-Salem, NC, Feb 9, 1923.

Vladimir Guerrero, 30, baseball player, born Nizao Bani, Dominican Republic, Feb 9, 1976.

Carole King, 64, singer, songwriter, born Brooklyn, NY, Feb 9, 1942.

Judith Light, 57, actress ("One Life to Live," "Who's the Boss?"), born Trenton, NJ, Feb 9, 1949.

Roger Mudd, 78, journalist (former anchorman "ABC Evening News"), born Washington, DC, Feb 9, 1928.

Joe Pesci, 63, actor (*Raging Bull, Goodfellas, My Cousin Vinny*), born Newark, NJ, Feb 9, 1943.

Shakira, 29, singer, born Shakira Isabelle Mebarak Ripoll at Barranquilla, Colombia, Feb 9, 1977.

Charles Shaughnessy, 51, actor ("Days of Our Lives," "The Nanny"), born London, England, Feb 9, 1955.

Mena Suvari, 27, actress (*American Beauty, Loser*), born Newport, RI, Feb 9, 1979.

Janet Suzman, 67, actress (*Nicholas and Alexandra, A Dry White Season*), born Johannesburg, South Africa, Feb 9, 1939.

Travis Tritt, 43, country and western singer (*Country Club*), born Marietta, GA, Feb 9, 1963.

Alice Walker, 62, author (*The Color Purple, Possessing the Secret of Joy, Meridian*), born Eatonton, GA, Feb 9, 1944.

Ziyi Zhang, 27, actress (*Crouching Tiger, Hidden Dragon; House of Flying Daggers*), born Beijing, China, Feb 9, 1979.

FEBRUARY 10 — FRIDAY

Day 41 — 324 Remaining

"ALL THE NEWS THAT'S FIT TO PRINT": ANNIVERSARY. Feb 10, 1897. The familiar slogan "All the News That's Fit to Print" has appeared on page one of *The New York Times* since Feb 10, 1897. It had first appeared on the editorial page on Oct 25, 1896. Although in 1896 a $100 prize was offered for a slogan, owner Adolph S. Ochs concluded that his own slogan was best.

ANDERSON, DAME JUDITH: BIRTH ANNIVERSARY. Feb 10, 1898. Film and stage actress Dame Judith Anderson was born Frances Margaret Anderson at Adelaide, Australia. She was nominated for an Academy Award in 1941 for her role in Alfred Hitchcock's film *Rebecca*. In 1960 she was made Dame Commander of the British Empire by Queen Elizabeth II. She died Jan 3, 1992, at Santa Barbara, CA.

BRECHT, BERTOLT: BIRTH ANNIVERSARY. Feb 10, 1898. German playwright born at Augsburg, Germany. His plays, such as *Mother Courage*, reflect his Marxist and antimilitary worldview. Also wrote *The Threepenny Opera* in collaboration with composer Kurt Weill. Died at East Berlin, Aug 14, 1956.

CHANEY, LON, JR: 100th BIRTH ANNIVERSARY. Feb 10, 1906. Prolific horror movie actor, son of the famous Lon Chaney, who is best known for his portrayal of the title role in *The Wolf Man* (1941). He was also acclaimed for his performance of Lennie in *Of Mice and Men* (1939). Born Creighton Chaney at Oklahoma City, OK, he died July 12, 1973, at San Clemente, CA.

CHOCOLATE FESTIVAL. Feb 10–12. Galesburg Antiques Mall, Galesburg, IL. A chocolate lover's dream! Homemade and commercially made chocolates, tortes, cakes, pies and creams—all you can eat for a small admission fee. Annually, the weekend closest to Valentine's Day. Est attendance: 1,500. For info: Galesburg Area CVB, PO Box 60, Galesburg, IL 61402-0060. Phone: (309) 343-2485. Fax: (309) 343-2521. E-mail: visitors@visitgalesburg.com. Web: www.visitgalesburg.com.

DEATH OF A SALESMAN PREMIERE: ANNIVERSARY. Feb 10, 1949. Arthur Miller's postwar dramatic masterpiece opened on Broadway's Morosco theater on this day. Elia Kazan was the director and Lee J. Cobb (Willy Loman), Arthur Kennedy (Biff) and Cameron Mitchell (Happy) starred. The play garnered six Tony Awards and was also awarded the 1949 Pulitzer Prize for Drama.

DURANTE, JIMMY: BIRTH ANNIVERSARY. Feb 10, 1893. "The Schnozz," Jimmy Durante, was born at New York City. His first break into show biz came when he was 17 and got a regular job playing ragtime at a saloon at Coney Island. Later his friend Eddie Cantor urged him to try comedy. Durante developed a unique comedic style as a short-tempered but lovable personage. His shtick included slamming down his hat and flapping his arms. His clothing, enormous nose, craggy face, gravelly singing voice and mispronunciations were all part of the persona. Durante, whose career spanned six decades, appeared on TV, stage and screen. His television sign-off, "Good night, Mrs Calabash, wherever you are!" became a trademark. Jimmy Durante died at Santa Monica, CA, Jan 29, 1980.

ENGLAND: PETERSFIELD ANTIQUES FAIR. Feb 10–12 (also Sept 8–10). Festival Hall, Petersfield, Hampshire. 43 stands of good-quality, but affordable, traditional antiques. Est attendance: 3,000. For info: Penman Fairs. Phone: (44) (870) 350-2442. Fax: (44) (870) 350-2443. E-mail: info@penman-fairs.co.uk.

FIRST ACTOR TO PERFORM IN TWO CITIES ON THE SAME DAY: ANNIVERSARY. Feb 10, 1887. Nathaniel Carr Goodwin performed at an 11:30 AM matinee of *Turned Up* at Boston, MA, then, following the closing curtain, he returned to New York City on the 1 PM train and that evening performed in *The Mascot* at the Bijou Theatre at 8 PM.

FIRST COMPUTER CHESS VICTORY OVER HUMAN: 10th ANNIVERSARY. Feb 10, 1996. IBM's Deep Blue computer defeated world champion Garry Kasparov in 34 moves on this date in Philadelphia, PA—the first such victory by a computer in tournament conditions. Kasparov, however, went on to win the tournament, defeating the computer three times (the other two matches were draws). In May 1997, in a six-game rematch, Deep Blue emerged the overall victor. Deep Blue, an RS/6000 supercomputer, can evaluate 200 million chess positions a second, but is not capable of using artificial intelligence to "learn." Kasparov was reigning World Chess Champion from 1985 to 2000.

FIRST WORLD WAR II MEDAL OF HONOR: ANNIVERSARY. Feb 10, 1942. Second Lieutenant Alexander Ramsey ("Sandy") Nininger, Jr, was posthumously awarded World War II's first Medal of Honor for heroism at the Battle of Bataan. He had graduated from West Point in 1941 and was on his first assignment after being commissioned.

GAMES OF THE XX WINTER OLYMPIAD. Feb 10–26. Turin, Italy. More than 2,500 athletes will participate in the 2006 winter Olympics, held at eight sites in the Turin area. For info: International Olympic Committee. Web: www.olympic.org. Or United States Olympic Committee, One Olympic Plaza, Colorado Springs, CO 80909. Phone: (719) 866-4500. E-mail: media@usoc.org. Web: www.usoc.org or www.olympic-usa.org.

	S	M	T	W	T	F	S
February				1	2	3	4
2006	5	6	7	8	9	10	11
	12	13	14	15	16	17	18
	19	20	21	22	23	24	25
	26	27	28				

GOLD RUSH DAYS. Feb 10–12. Wickenburg, AZ. 58th annual communitywide celebration of the Old West: rodeo, parade, carnival, gold panning. Named one of the top 100 events in North America by the American Bus Association. Annually, the second full weekend in February. Est attendance: 50,000. For info: Chamber of Commerce, 216 N Frontier St, Wickenburg, AZ 85390. Phone: (928) 684-5479 or (928) 684-0977. Fax: (928) 684-5470. E-mail: events@wickenburgchamber.com. Web: www.wickenburg chamber.com.

GREAT NORTHEAST HOME SHOW. Feb 10–12. Pepsi Arena and Empire State Plaza, Albany, NY. The annual kickoff to the home-building/remodeling season. Featuring more than 500 exhibits in two buildings and informative seminars. Annually, the first full weekend in February. Sponsor: The Times Union Newspaper. Est attendance: 30,000. For info: Cate Masterson, Ed Lewi Assoc, 6 Chelsea Pl, Clifton Park, NY 12065. Phone: (518) 383-6183. Fax: (518) 383-6755. Web: www.timesunion.com.

ISLAND FALLS WINTERFEST. Feb 10–12. Island Falls, ME. Home of the Log Drivers Cookout, and featuring the "World's Largest Coffee Pot." Radar races, snowmobiling fun, dances, fireworks and fishing derby. Annually, second weekend in February. Est attendance: 1,500. For info: Northern Katahdin Valley Chamber of Commerce. Phone: (207) 463-2077. E-mail: nkvrcc@all maine.com.

LAMB, CHARLES: BIRTH ANNIVERSARY. Feb 10, 1775. Literary critic, poet and essayist, born at London, England. "The greatest pleasure I know," he wrote in 1834, "is to do a good action by stealth, and to have it found out by accident." Died at Edmonton, England, Dec 27, 1834.

LONGHORN WORLD CHAMPIONSHIP RODEO. Feb 10–12. Hara Arena, Dayton, OH. 2nd annual. More than 200 cowboys and cowgirls compete in six professional contests ranging from bronc riding to big, bad BONUS bull riding! Free beginners horsemanship clinic 40 minutes before performances. Qualifying rodeo for Longhorn's Championship Finals Rodeo in Murfreesboro, TN. Featuring colorful opening and pageantry. Est attendance: 12,000. For info: W. Bruce Lehrke, Longhorn World Championship Rodeo, PO Box 70159, Nashville, TN 37207. Phone: (615) 876-1016. Fax: (615) 879-4685. E-mail: info@long hornrodeo.com. Web: www.longhornrodeo.com.

MALTA: FEAST OF ST. PAUL'S SHIPWRECK. Feb 10. Valletta. Holy day of obligation. Commemorates the shipwreck of St. Paul on the north coast of Malta in AD 60.

MOBIUS ADVERTISING AWARDS. Feb 10. Los Angeles, CA. Selection and recognition of the world's most outstanding television and radio commercials, print advertising and package designs. Founded in 1971. The entry deadline is annually on October 1. Est attendance: 200. For info: Lee W. Gluckman, The Mobius Advertising Awards, 713 S Pacific Coast Hwy, Ste A, Redondo Beach, CA 90277-4233. Phone: (310) 540-0959. Fax: (310) 316-8905. E-mail: mobiusinfo@mobiusawards.com. Web: www.mobiusawards.com.

"MY FRIEND FLICKA" TV PREMIERE: 50th ANNIVERSARY. Feb 10, 1956. CBS series about a boy and his horse based on the children's book by Mary O'Hara. The series was set in the early 1900s on the Goose Bar Ranch in Montana. Johnny Washbrook starred as Ken McLaughlin; Gene Evans as Ken's father, Rob; Anita Louise as Ken's mother, Nell; Frank Ferguson as Gus, the ranch hand; and Wahama, the beautiful Arabian horse, as Flicka.

NC RV AND CAMPING SHOW. Feb 10–12. NC State Fairgrounds, Raleigh, NC. A display of the latest in recreational vehicles and accessories by various dealers. Est attendance: 12,000. For info: Apple Rock Advertising & Promotions, 1200 Eastchester Dr, High Point, NC 27265. Phone: (336) 881-7100. Fax: (336) 883-7198. E-mail: rvshows@applerock.com. Web: www.applerock.com.

PASTERNAK, BORIS LEONIDOVICH: BIRTH ANNIVERSARY. Feb 10, 1890. Russian poet and novelist, born at Moscow, Russia. Best-known work: *Doctor Zhivago.* Died at Moscow, May 30, 1960.

PLIMSOLL DAY. Feb 10, 1824. A day to remember Samuel Plimsoll, "The Sailor's Friend," a coal merchant turned reformer and politician, who was elected to the British Parliament in 1868. He attacked the practice of overloading heavily insured ships, calling them "coffin ships." His persistence brought about amendment of Britain's Merchant Shipping Act. The Plimsoll Line, named for him, is a line on the side of ships marking maximum load allowed by law. Born at Bristol, England, Feb 10, 1824. Died at Folkestone, England, June 3, 1898.

SEMINOLE TRIBE FESTIVAL, POWWOW AND PRCA RODEO. Feb 10–12. Hollywood Reservation, Hollywood, FL. The Seminole Tribe of Florida hosts dancers representative of more than 100 tribes from across North America. Featured events include Seminole art show, all-Indian rodeo and seldom-seen deep-water alligator wrestling. Annually, the second weekend in February. Est attendance: 30,000. For info: Seminole Tribe of Florida, 6300 Stirling Rd, Hollywood, FL 33024. Phone: (800) 683-7800. E-mail: tribune@semtribe.com. Web: www.seminole tribe.com.

STAMP EXPO/USA. Feb 10–12. Radisson Hotel, Anaheim, CA. Annual expo. Est attendance: 5,000. For info: Israel Bick, Exec Dir, Intl Stamp & Coin Collectors Society, PO Box 854, Van Nuys, CA 91408. Phone: (818) 997-6496. Fax: (818) 988-4337. E-mail: iibick@sbcglobal.net. Web: www.bick.net.

TILDEN, BILL: BIRTH ANNIVERSARY. Feb 10, 1893. William Tatem (Bill) Tilden, Jr, tennis player, born at Philadelphia, PA. Generally considered one of the greatest players of all time, Tilden won more tournaments than the record books can count. A nearly flawless player, he was also an egotistical showman on the court with an interest in show business. He turned pro in 1930 and continued to win regularly. Died at Hollywood, CA, June 5, 1953.

TREATY OF PARIS ENDS FRENCH AND INDIAN WAR: ANNIVERSARY. Feb 10, 1763. Known in Europe as the Seven Years' War, this conflict ranged from North America to India, with many European nations involved. In North America French expansion in the Ohio River Valley in the 1750s led to conflict with Great Britain. Some Indians fought alongside the French; a young George Washington fought for the British. As a result of the signing of the Treaty of Paris, France lost all claims to Canada and had to cede Louisiana to Spain. Fifteen years later French bitterness over the loss of its North American colonies to Britain contributed to its supporting the colonists in the American Revolution.

TWENTY-FIFTH AMENDMENT TO US CONSTITUTION RATIFIED (PRESIDENTIAL SUCCESSION, DISABILITY): ANNIVERSARY. Feb 10, 1967. Procedures for presidential succession were further clarified by the 25th Amendment, along with provisions for continuity of power in the event of a disability or illness of the president.

WMAS 94.7 FM VALENTINE'S BALL. Feb 10. Springfield, MA. A formal affair for both couples and singles. An evening of music, dancing and prizes. Est attendance: 1,500. For info: Lucie Grondin, PO Box 9500, Springfield, MA 01102. Phone: (413) 737-1414. Fax: (413) 737-1488.

YUMA SQUARE AND ROUND DANCE FESTIVAL. Feb 10–12. Yuma Civic Center, Yuma, AZ. Square and round dance enthusiasts from Southern California and Arizona participate. Est attendance: 2,000. For info: Marketing Dept, Yuma Civic Center, 1440 Desert Hills Dr, Yuma, AZ 85365. Phone: (928) 373-5040. Fax: (928) 344-9121. E-mail: ycc@ci.yuma.az.us.

BIRTHDAYS TODAY

Laura Dern, 39, actress (*Blue Velvet, Rambling Rose*), born Los Angeles, CA, Feb 10, 1967.

Donovan, 60, singer, songwriter, born Donovan P. Leitch at Glasgow, Scotland, Feb 10, 1946.

Leonard Kyle (Lenny) Dykstra, 43, former baseball player, born Santa Ana, CA, Feb 10, 1963.

Roberta Flack, 67, singer, born Black Mountain, NC, Feb 10, 1939.

Frances Moore Lappe, 62, author (*Diet for a Small Planet, Rediscovering America's Values*), born Pendleton, OR, Feb 10, 1944.

Gregory John (Greg) Norman, 51, golfer, born Melbourne, Australia, Feb 10, 1955.

Leontyne Price, 79, opera singer, born Laurel, MS, Feb 10, 1927.

Mark Andrew Spitz, 56, Olympic gold medal swimmer, born Modesto, CA, Feb 10, 1950.

Robert Wagner, 76, actor ("It Takes a Thief," "Hart to Hart"), born Detroit, MI, Feb 10, 1930.

FEBRUARY 11 — SATURDAY
Day 42 — 323 Remaining

AMERICAN COUNCIL ON EDUCATION ANNUAL MEETING. Feb 11–14. Los Angeles, CA. Est attendance: 1,300. For info: Stephanie Marshall, American Council on Education, One Dupont Circle, Washington, DC 20036. Phone: (202) 939-9410. Fax: (202) 939-9557. E-mail: annualmeeting@ace.nche.edu. Web: www.acenet.edu.

ARIZONA RENAISSANCE FESTIVAL. Feb 11–Apr 2. (Saturdays, Sundays and Presidents' Day [Feb 20] only.) Apache Junction, AZ. Enjoy your best day out in history. Find yourself surrounded by medieval merriment with knights, kings, maidens and minstrels. Stroll through acres of amusements, shoppes and nonstop revelry as you join our village celebration. The official sister event to the Robin Hood Festival in Sherwood Forest, England. Est attendance: 265,000. For info: Arizona Renaissance Festival, 12601 E Highway 60, Apache Junction, AZ 85218. Phone: (520) 463-2600. Web: www.renfestinfo.com.

BE ELECTRIFIC DAY. Feb 11. A day to honor the birth of Thomas Alva Edison and recognize his electrical inventions, including the lightbulb. It is also the day to discover our own "body electricity." For information on lectures, demonstrations and packets of information, contact: Carolyn Finch, Electrific Solutions, 51 Cedar Dr, Danbury, CT 06811. Phone: (800) 864-1022 or (203) 792-4833. Fax: (203) 743-5675. E-mail: electrific@comcast.net. Web: www.electrific.com.

BUDWEISER SHOOTOUT AT DAYTONA NEXTEL CUP SERIES RACE. Feb 11. Daytona International Speedway, Daytona Beach, FL. Dash for the cash featuring NASCAR NEXTEL Cup stars. For info: Daytona International Speedway, PO Box 2801, Daytona Beach, FL 32120-2801. Phone: (800) PIT-SHOP. Web: www.daytonainternationalspeedway.com.

CAMEROON: YOUTH DAY. Feb 11. Public holiday.

CANADA: YUKON QUEST INTERNATIONAL 1,000-MILE SLED DOG RACE. Feb 11–27. Fairbanks, AK, and Whitehorse, YT. The 23rd annual running. Two weeks and 1,000 miles through true northern wilderness in the depths of Arctic winter, from Fairbanks, AK, USA, to Whitehorse, YT, Canada. Top mushers from North America and around the world compete for $125,000 in prize money. Est attendance: 10,000. For info: Yukon Quest International Association (Canada), #2-1109 First Ave, Whitehorse, YT Y1A 5G4, Canada. Phone: (867) 668-4711. Fax: (867) 668-6674. E-mail: yukonquest@polarcom.com. Web: www.yukonquest.com.

CHILD, LYDIA MARIA: BIRTH ANNIVERSARY. Feb 11, 1802. Born at Medford, MA. As a writer her works included *Hobomok*, about early Salem and Plymouth life, and *The Rebels*, which described pre-Revolutionary Boston. In addition, she produced several practical works including *The Frugal Housewife*, which enjoyed 21 editions, and *The Mother's Book*. In 1833 she and her husband, David Lee Child, published the controversial abolitionist document "An Appeal in Favor of That Class of Americans Called Africans," which called for educating the slaves. Their work for abolition continued with the weekly newspaper *The National Anti-Slavery Standard*, which they published at New York City from 1840–44. Lydia died Oct 20, 1880, at Wayland, MA.

CORVETTE AND HIGH PERFORMANCE MEET. Feb 11–12. Puyallup, WA. 900-booth swap meet with new and used car parts and automobilia. Vehicles for sale, Corvette invitational display area. Est attendance: 10,000. For info: Larry Johnson, Show Organizer, PO Box 7753, Olympia, WA 98507. Phone: (360) 786-8844. Fax: (360) 754-1498. Web: www.corvhp.com.

DUNNE, PHILIP: BIRTH ANNIVERSARY. Feb 11, 1908. American screenwriter and director Philip Dunne was born at New York, NY. In 1947 he joined directors John Huston and William Wyler to found the Committee for the First Amendment, which campaigned against the "blacklisting" in Hollywood of anyone suspected of being a communist by the House Un-American Activities Committee. He was also a founder of the Screen Writers Guild. Dunne died June 2, 1992, at Malibu, CA.

EARLY AMERICA HISTORICAL FAIR. Feb 11–12. Northbridge Mall, Albert Lea, MN. Reenactors and craftsmen from seven states dress in full costume and sell their colonial period items. Entertainment, kettle korn, food and drink, workshops and demonstrations. Est attendance: 3,000. For info: Big Island Rendezvous & Festivals Inc, 143 W Clark St, Albert Lea, MN 56007. Phone: (800) 658-2526. Fax: (507) 373-0344. E-mail: bigisland@albertalea.org.

EDISON, THOMAS ALVA: BIRTH ANNIVERSARY. Feb 11, 1847. American inventive genius and holder of more than 1,200 patents (including the incandescent electric lamp, phonograph, electric dynamo and key parts of many now-familiar devices such as the movie camera, telephone transmitter, etc). Edison said, "Genius is 1 percent inspiration and 99 percent perspiration." His birthday is now widely observed as Inventor's Day. Born at Milan, OH, and died at Menlo Park, NJ, Oct 18, 1931.

FARM TOY SHOW AND AUCTION. Feb 11. Sauk Centre, MN. More than 30 vendors display farm toy equipment from 9 AM to 3:30 PM, with a consignment auction starting at 4:30 PM. Est attendance: 800. For info: Sauk Centre Chamber of Commerce, PO Box 222, Sauk Centre, MN 56378. Phone: (320)

	S	M	T	W	T	F	S
February				1	2	3	4
2006	5	6	7	8	9	10	11
	12	13	14	15	16	17	18
	19	20	21	22	23	24	25
	26	27	28				

352-5201. Fax: (320) 352-5202. E-mail: chamber@saukcentre chamber.com. Web: www.saukcentrechamber.com.

FIRST WOMAN EPISCOPAL BISHOP: ANNIVERSARY. Feb 11, 1989. The presiding bishop of the Episcopal Church, Bishop Edmond L. Browning, consecrated the Reverend Barbara Clementine Harris as a bishop of the Episcopal Church.

"THE FRENCH CHEF" TV PREMIERE: ANNIVERSARY. Feb 11, 1963. Beginning on this date, Julia Child demystified French cooking and entertained viewers as "The French Chef" on WGBH-TV, Boston, MA. The show was a great success in syndication on PBS stations, and Child filmed 200 programs—always with her trademark trilling voice and at times slapping around the poultry—signing off with a cheery "Bon appetit!" Child's show, along with her book *Mastering the Art of French Cooking* (1961, authored with Simone Beck and Louisette Bertholle), are credited with awakening Americans to the joy of continental cuisine.

FULLER, MELVILLE WESTON: BIRTH ANNIVERSARY. Feb 11, 1833. 8th chief justice of the US Supreme Court. Born at Augusta, ME, he died at Sorrento, ME, July 4, 1910.

ICE FISHING CONTEST. Feb 11. Fort Peck, MT. Annual contest held on Fort Peck Lake. Entry fee of $50 per hole or three holes for $100. Held annually on the second Saturday in February. For info: Glasgow Area Chamber of Commerce, PO Box 832, Glasgow, MT 59230. Phone: (406) 228-2222. Fax: (406) 228-2244. E-mail: chamber@nemontel.net. Web: www.glasgow mt.net.

IRAN: NATIONAL DAY. Feb 11. National holiday. Commemorates the revolution that overthrew the Shah in 1979.

JAPAN: NATIONAL FOUNDATION DAY: ANNIVERSARY. Feb 11. Marks the founding of the Japanese nation. In 1872 the government officially set Feb 11, 660 BC, as the date of accession to the throne of the Emperor Jimmu (said to be Japan's first emperor) and designated the day a national holiday by the name of Empire Day. The holiday was abolished after WWII, but was revived as National Foundation Day in 1966. Ceremonies are held with Their Imperial Majesties the Emperor and Empress, the Prime Minister and other dignitaries attending. National holiday.

MANDELA, NELSON: PRISON RELEASE ANNIVERSARY. Feb 11, 1990. After serving more than 27½ years of a life sentence (convicted, with eight others, of sabotage and conspiracy to overthrow the government), South Africa's Nelson Mandela, 71 years old, walked away from the Victor Verster prison farm at Paarl, South Africa, a free man. He had survived the governmental system of apartheid. Mandela greeted a cheering throng of well-wishers, along with hundreds of millions of television viewers worldwide, with demands for an intensification of the struggle for equality for blacks, who make up nearly 75 percent of South Africa's population.

MANKIEWICZ, JOSEPH L.: BIRTH ANNIVERSARY. Feb 11, 1909. Oscar-winning American film writer, director and producer was born at Wilkes-Barre, PA. He coined the famous W.C. Fields phrase "my little chickadee" in his screenplay for the 1932 film *If I Had a Million*. In 1935 he turned to producing and subsequently made *The Philadelphia Story* and *Woman of the Year*. He began directing in 1946 and his stature grew with such films as *The Late George Apley, The Ghost and Mrs Muir, A Letter to Three Wives, All About Eve, Guys and Dolls, Cleopatra* and *Sleuth*. Mankiewicz won four Academy Awards for directing and screenwriting. He died Feb 5, 1993, at Mount Kisco, NY.

MARRIAGE OF THE PORT CEREMONY. Feb 11. Bryan, TX. Old Portuguese ceremonial tradition in which a superb hearty red wine is fortified by adding brandy to the barrel. After considerable aging the result is gold medal–winning Papa Paulo Port. The ceremony takes place during each $5 tour of the winery and guests are treated to tastings of port and wedding cake. (From Feb 1–11, there are special tours of the winery and demonstrations of the port-making process.) For info: Messina Hof Wine Cellars, 4545 Old Reliance Rd, Bryan, TX 77808. Phone: (979) 778-9463, ext 34. Fax: (979) 778-1729.

NATIONAL SHUT-IN VISITATION DAY. Feb 11. Visit and entertain shut-ins. For info: Natl Shut-In Visitation Day, 237 Franklin St, Reading, PA 19602. Phone: (610) 373-5579.

OCEAN COUNTY WILDFOWL ART AND DECOY SHOW. Feb 11–12. Toms River, NJ. 140 artists and carvers, decoy-carving competitions, decorative and gunning decoys, junior competition; free seminars on decoy carving, decoy painting and flat art painting; etc. Est attendance: 4,000. For info: Janet Sellitto, Show Coord, Ocean County YMCA, 1088 Whitty Rd, Toms River, NJ 08755. Phone: (732) 341-9622. Fax: (732) 341-1629. E-mail: jsellitto@ocymca.org. Web: www.ocymca.org.

PRO SPORTS WIVES DAY. Feb 11. This national day of observance will give polite recognition to sports wives throughout the country for their public service in the estimated $213 billion professional sports industry. Unknown to the public, pro sports wives are the household managers and silent partners who keep their favorite athletes motivated, focused and determined to win and create the feeling of being a winner within us all. Annually, the second Saturday in February. For info: Gena Pitts, Pro Sports Wives, 3528 Old Milton Pkwy, Alpharetta, GA 30005. Phone: (770) 619-0383. Fax: (770) 619-5777. E-mail: gjpitts@pro sportswives.com. Web: www.prosportswives.com.

SATISFIED STAYING SINGLE DAY. Feb 11. As Valentine's Day approaches, some single folks would like to point out that they're quite content buying candy and flowers for no one but themselves. Live it up. Shadow dance! [©2003 by WH.] For info: Thomas & Ruth Roy, Wellcat Holidays, 2418 Long Ln, Lebanon, PA 17046. Phone: (717) 279-0184. E-mail: info@wellcat.com. Web: www.wellcat.com.

SPACE MILESTONE: *ENDEAVOUR* MAPPING MISSION (US). Feb 11, 2000. This manned flight spent 11 days in space creating a 3-D map of more than 70 percent of the Earth's surface. It will be the most accurate and complete topographic map of Earth ever produced.

SPACE MILESTONE: FIRST SOVIET COMMERCIAL SATELLITE MISSION. Feb 11, 1990. Anatoly Solovyov and Aleksandr Balandin departed the Baikonur launching site on the Soviet Union's first satellite mission designed for profit—by producing industrial crystals in the weightlessness of space. The craft arrived at the *Mir* orbital space station on Feb 13. Launching of the *Soyuz TM-9* capsule was witnessed by four American astronauts and televised live. The mission was hailed as initiating a new level of openness of information about Soviet space projects.

SPACE MILESTONE: *OSUMI* (JAPAN). Feb 11, 1970. First Japanese satellite launched. Japan became the fourth nation to send a satellite into space.

VATICAN CITY: INDEPENDENCE ANNIVERSARY. Feb 11, 1929. The Lateran Treaty, signed by Pietro Cardinal Gasparri and Benito Mussolini, guaranteed the independence of the State of Vatican City and recognized the sovereignty of the Holy See over it. Area is about 109 acres.

WHITE SHIRT DAY: ANNIVERSARY. Feb 11, 1937. Anniversary of UAW-GM agreement following 44-day sit-down strike at General Motors' Flint, MI, factories. Blue-collar workers traditionally wear white shirts to work on this day, symbolic of workingman's dignity won. Has been observed by proclamation at Flint, MI.

YALTA AGREEMENT SIGNED: ANNIVERSARY. Feb 11, 1945. President Franklin D. Roosevelt, British Prime Minister Winston Churchill and Soviet leader Joseph Stalin signed an agreement at Yalta, a Soviet city on the Black Sea in the Crimea. The agreement contained plans for new blows at the heart of Germany and for occupying Germany at the end of the war. It also called for a meeting in San Francisco to draft a charter for the United Nations.

BIRTHDAYS TODAY

Jennifer Aniston, 37, actress ("Friends," *The Good Girl*), born Sherman Oaks, CA, Feb 11, 1969.

Paul Bocuse, 80, chef, born Collonges-au-Mont-d'Or, France, Feb 11, 1926.

Brandy, 27, singer, actress ("Cinderella," "Moesha"), born Brandy Norwood at Macomb, MS, Feb 11, 1979.

Jeb Bush, 53, Governor of Florida (R), born Midland, TX, Feb 11, 1953.

Sheryl Crow, 44, singer, musician, born Kennett, MO, Feb 11, 1962.

Virginia Johnson, 81, psychologist, born Springfield, MO, Feb 11, 1925.

Mike Leavitt, 55, US Secretary of Health and Human Services, former Governor of Utah (R), born Cedar City, UT, Feb 11, 1951.

Tina Louise, 72, actress ("Gilligan's Island," *The Stepford Wives*), born New York, NY, Feb 11, 1934.

Carey Lowell, 45, actress ("Law & Order"), born New York, NY, Feb 11, 1961.

Sergio Mendes, 65, musician, bandleader, born Niteroi, Brazil, Feb 11, 1941.

Leslie Nielsen, 84, actor (*Naked Gun* films, *Airplane!*, "Peyton Place"), born Regina, SK, Canada, Feb 11, 1922.

Burt Reynolds, 70, actor (*Hooper, Deliverance, Cannonball Run*, "Evening Shade"), born Waycross, GA, Feb 11, 1936.

Sidney Sheldon, 89, author (*Bloodline, The Doomsday Conspiracy*), born Chicago, IL, Feb 11, 1917.

FEBRUARY 12 — SUNDAY
Day 43 — 322 Remaining

ADAMS, LOUISA CATHERINE JOHNSON: BIRTH ANNIVERSARY. Feb 12, 1775. Wife of John Quincy Adams, 6th president of the US. Born at London, England. Died at Washington, DC, May 14, 1852.

BUD POLE DAY FOR THE DAYTONA 500. Feb 12. Daytona International Speedway, Daytona Beach, FL. Fastest qualifiers have the front row for the Daytona 500. For info: Daytona International Speedway, PO Box 2801, Daytona Beach, FL 32120-2801. Phone: (800) PIT-SHOP. Web: www.daytonainternationalspeedway.com.

CANADA: BANCROFT FROSTY FROLICS. Feb 12–18. "Old Station" and Legion Hall, Bancroft, ON. Events throughout the week include skating, snowmobiling and various community events. The main attraction is the Bancroft Sled Dog Races, a two-day mid-distance race that brings mushers from all over Ontario and the northeastern US. Sprint races, craft show and horse-drawn sleigh rides also round out the final weekend. For info: Bancroft & District Chamber of Commerce, Box 539, 8 Hastings Heritage Way, Unit #1, Bancroft, ON, K0L 1C0, Canada. Phone: (613) 332-1513. Fax: (613) 332-2119. E-mail: chamber@commerce.bancroft.on.ca. Web: www.BancroftDistrict.com.

CELEBRATION OF LOVE WEEK. Feb 12–18. To stress the importance and value of love in making the world a much better place in which to live. For complete info, send $5 to cover expense of printing, handling and postage. Annually, the second full week of February. For info: Dr. Stanley Drake, Pres Emeritus, Intl Society of Friendship & Good Will, 8592 Roswell Rd, Ste 251, Atlanta, GA 30350-1867. Phone: (678) 795-1362. E-mail: sjdrake@bellsouth.net. Web: www.friendshipandgoodwill.org.

CHINA: LANTERN FESTIVAL. Feb 12. Traditional Chinese festival falls on the 15th day of the first month of the Chinese lunar calendar year. Lantern processions mark the end of the Chinese New Year holiday season. Also celebrated in Taiwan and Korea. Date in other countries will differ from China's by up to one day. See also: "Chinese New Year" (Jan 29).

DARWIN, CHARLES ROBERT: BIRTH ANNIVERSARY. Feb 12, 1809. Author and naturalist, born at Shrewsbury, England. Best remembered for his books *On the Origin of Species by Means of Natural Selection, or the Preservation of Favoured Races in the Struggle for Life* and *The Descent of Man and Selection in Relation to Sex*. Died at Down, Kent, England, Apr 19, 1882.

DARWIN DAY. Feb 12. Darwin Day is an international celebration of science and humanity. Events are coordinated around the world to commemorate the life and work of Charles Darwin and the theory of evolution by natural selection, and to recognize the contributions and achievements of science and reason. On a broad scale, the program is an effort to advance science literacy, champion the efforts to humanize science and celebrate the adventurous spirit. Events are held on the anniversary of Darwin's birth. For info: Darwin Day Program, 512 Boland St, Sparta, GA 31087. Phone: (706) 444-5288. E-mail: info@darwinday.org. Web: www.darwinday.org.

***DRACULA* PREMIERE: 75th ANNIVERSARY.** Feb 12, 1931. The horror film classic starring Bela Lugosi premiered on this day at the Roxy Theatre in New York City. It had been slated to premiere on Friday, Feb 13, but director Tod Browning, confessing to a superstitious nature, asked the opening to be moved up a day. *Dracula* made the Hungarian actor Lugosi a star, but at a price: he was only offered horror film roles the rest of his career.

HARRIS, ROY: BIRTH ANNIVERSARY. Feb 12, 1898. Born at Chandler, OK, Harris was one of the most important composers of this century. He was known for his use of Anglo-American folk tunes. He composed more than 200 works, including 13 symphonies, several ballet scores and much chamber and choral music. His best-known work is his *Third Symphony* (1939). He died at Santa Monica, CA, Oct 1, 1979.

HEART FAILURE AWARENESS WEEK. Feb 12–18. To raise awareness and educate health care providers, patients, family members and individuals at risk about heart failure, one of America's silent epidemics. For information visit the Heart Failure Society of America website at www.abouthf.org. For info: Cheryl Yano, HFSA, Court International, Ste 240 South, 2550 University Ave W, St. Paul, MN 55114. Phone: (651) 642-1633. Fax: (651) 642-1502. E-mail: info@hfsa.org. Web: www.abouthf.org.

JELL-O® WEEK. Feb 12–18. Celebrated annually the second full week in February. The first Jell-O® Week was officially declared by the Utah legislature in 2001. For info: Nora Bertucci, Hunter Public Relations, 41 Madison Ave, 5th Fl, New York, NY 10010. Phone: (212) 679-6600. Web: www.hunterpr.com.

	S	M	T	W	T	F	S
February 2006				1	2	3	4
	5	6	7	8	9	10	11
	12	13	14	15	16	17	18
	19	20	21	22	23	24	25
	26	27	28				

LEWIS, JOHN LLEWELLYN: BIRTH ANNIVERSARY. Feb 12, 1889. American labor leader born near Lucas, IA. His parents came to the US from Welsh mining towns, and Lewis left school in the seventh grade to become a miner himself. Became leader of United Mine Workers of America and champion of all miners' causes. Died at Washington, DC, June 11, 1969.

LINCOLN, ABRAHAM: BIRTH ANNIVERSARY. Feb 12, 1809. 16th president of the US (Mar 4, 1861–Apr 15, 1865) and the first to be assassinated (on Good Friday, Apr 14, 1865, at Ford's Theatre at Washington, DC). His presidency encompassed the tragic Civil War. Especially remembered are his Emancipation Proclamation (Jan 1, 1863), his Gettysburg Address (Nov 19, 1863) and his proclamation establishing the last Thursday of November as Thanksgiving Day. Born at Hardin County, KY, he died at Washington, DC, Apr 15, 1865. Lincoln's birthday is observed as part of Presidents' Day in most states, but is a legal holiday in Illinois and an optional bank holiday in Iowa, Maryland, Michigan, Pennsylvania, Washington and West Virginia. See also: "Presidents' Day" (Feb 20).

LINCOLN'S BIRTHPLACE CABIN WREATH LAYING. Feb 12. Abraham Lincoln's Birthplace National Historic Site, Hodgenville, KY. A wreath is placed at the door of the symbolic "Birthplace Cabin" in commemoration of the birth of Abraham Lincoln. Refreshments are also served to park visitors. Est attendance: 75. For info: Sandy Brue, 2995 Lincoln Farm Rd, Hodgenville, KY 42748. Phone: (502) 358-3137. E-mail: Sandy_Brue @NPS.gov.

LOST PENNY DAY. Feb 12. Today is set aside to put all of those pennies stashed in candy dishes, coffee cans, bowls and jars back into circulation. Take those pennies and give them to a shelter or agency that assists the homeless or your local Humane Society. Annually, on President Abraham Lincoln's birthday, the man depicted on the copper penny. [©1995] To alleviate the escalating costs of Eventological® Literature, a charge of $10 must be assessed to each request. Checks are to be made payable to: Adrienne Sioux Koopersmith, 1437 W Rosemont, #1W, Chicago, IL 60660-1319. E-mail: askoopersmith@hotmail.com.

MAN DAY. Feb 12. A day for celebration by friends, family and associates of the men of the world. Annually, the Sunday before Valentine's Day. [©2002 C. Daniel Rhodes.] For info: C. Daniel Rhodes, 1900 Crossvine Rd, Hoover, AL 35244. Phone: (205) 908-6781. E-mail: rhodan@charter.net.

MOON PHASE: FULL MOON. Feb 12. Moon enters Full Moon phase at 11:44 PM, EST.

MYANMAR: UNION DAY. Feb 12. National holiday. Commemorates the founding of the Union of Burma, Feb 12, 1947. The country changed its name to Union of Myanmar in 1989.

NAACP FOUNDED: ANNIVERSARY. Feb 12, 1909. The National Association for the Advancement of Colored People was founded by W.E.B. Du Bois and Ida Wells-Barnett, among others, to wage a militant campaign against lynching and other forms of racial oppression. Its legal wing brought many lawsuits that successfully challenged segregation in the 1950s and '60s.

NATIONAL FAMILY, CAREER AND COMMUNITY LEADERS OF AMERICA WEEK. Feb 12–18. To call the nation's attention to the activities and goals of the FCCLA and to family and consumer sciences education. Theme: "FCCLA: You Got the Power!" For info: Beth Carpenter, Communications Mgr, Family, Career and Community Leaders of America, 1910 Association Dr, Reston, VA 21091. Phone: (703) 476-4900. Fax: (703) 860-2713. E-mail: bcarpenter@fcclainc.org.

OGLETHORPE DAY. Feb 12. General James Edward Oglethorpe (born at London, England, Dec 22, 1696), with some 100 other Englishmen, landed at what is now Savannah, GA, on Feb 12, 1733. Naming the new colony Georgia for England's King George II, Oglethorpe was organizer and first governor of the colony and founder of the city of Savannah. Oglethorpe Day and Georgia Day observed on this date.

PAVLOVA, ANNA: 125th BIRTH ANNIVERSARY. Feb 12, 1881. Russian ballerina Anna Pavlova, thought by some to have been the greatest dancer of all time, was born at St. Petersburg, Russia. After performing with great success with the Ballet Russe and other companies, she formed her own company in 1910 and performed on tour for enthusiastic audiences in nearly every country in the world. Pavlova died at The Hague, Netherlands, Jan 23, 1931.

SAFETYPUP'S® BIRTHDAY. Feb 12. This year Safetypup®, created by the National Child Safety Council, joyously celebrates his birthday by bringing safety awareness/education messages to children and their parents in a positive, nonthreatening manner. Age-appropriate materials available through local law enforcement departments on topics including bike safety, drug abuse prevention, child abduction prevention, farm safety and more. For info: NCSC, Box 1368, Jackson, MI 49204-1368. Phone: (517) 764-6070. E-mail: tlusby@nfcd.org.

SIMENON, GEORGES: BIRTH ANNIVERSARY. Feb 12, 1903. Simenon was the bestselling author of the 20th century, selling more than 500 million copies of his novels in more than 50 languages. The prodigious Simenon wrote up to six novels per year, specializing in dark, intellectual crime works. He garnered worldwide acclaim for his Inspector Maigret novels. He also gained worldwide notoriety in 1977 when he claimed to have had sexual relations with at least 10,000 women. Simenon, born at Liège, Belgium, died at Lausanne, France, on Sept 4, 1989.

UTAH WOMEN GIVEN THE VOTE: ANNIVERSARY. Feb 12, 1870. The women in the Utah Territory were granted the right to vote in political elections—50 years before the 19th Amendment was ratified.

WORLD MARRIAGE DAY. Feb 12. World Marriage Day honors husband and wife as head of the family, the basic unit of society. It salutes the beauty of their faithfulness, sacrifice and joy in daily married life. Sponsored by WorldWide Marriage Encounter since 1981. Annually, second Sunday in February. For info: WorldWide Marriage Encounter, 2210 E Highland, #106, San Bernardino, CA 92404. Phone: (301) 871-1595. Fax: (909) 863-9986. E-mail: office@wwme.org. Web: www.wmd.wwme.org.

WSBA/WARM 103/OLDIES 96.1 EASTER CRAFT SHOW. Feb 12. York, PA. More than 175 quality craft displays will be presented with everything from country to contemporary dolls, jewelry, pottery and much more. Admission fee. Est attendance: 3,500. For info: Joe Alfano, Asst Promo Dir, PO Box 910, York, PA 17402-0910. Phone: (717) 764-1155. Fax: (717) 252-4708. E-mail: jalfano@radioyork.com. Web: www.warm103.com.

BIRTHDAYS TODAY

Maud Adams, 61, actress (*Killer Force, Octopussy*), born Lulea, Sweden, Feb 12, 1945.

Joe Don Baker, 70, actor (*Charlie Varrick, Cool Hand Luke*), born Groesbeck, TX, Feb 12, 1936.

Ehud Barak, 64, former Israeli prime minister, born Mishmar, Hasharon, Israel, Feb 12, 1942.

Judy Blume, 68, author (*Blubber, Superfudge*), born Elizabeth, NJ, Feb 12, 1938.

Josh Brolin, 38, actor (*The Mod Squad, Best Laid Plans*), born Los Angeles, CA, Feb 12, 1968.

Cliff De Young, 59, actor (*Blue Collar, F/X*), born Inglewood, CA, Feb 12, 1947.

Joseph Henry (Joe) Garagiola, 80, sportscaster, former baseball player, born St. Louis, MO, Feb 12, 1926.

Arsenio Hall, 51, comedian, actor (*Coming to America*), former TV talk-show host, born Cleveland, OH, Feb 12, 1955.

Joanna Kerns, 53, actress ("Growing Pains"), former gymnast, born San Francisco, CA, Feb 12, 1953.

Simon MacCorkindale, 54, actor, producer, screenwriter ("Falcon Crest," *Death on the Nile, Jaws 3-D*), born Isle-of-Ely, England, Feb 12, 1952.

Chynna Phillips, 38, singer (Wilson Phillips), born Los Angeles, CA, Feb 12, 1968.

Christina Ricci, 26, actress (*Sleepy Hollow, Ice Storm*), born Santa Monica, CA, Feb 12, 1980.

William Felton (Bill) Russell, 72, Hall of Fame basketball player and former coach, born Monroe, LA, Feb 12, 1934.

Arlen Specter, 76, US Senator (R, Pennsylvania), born Wichita, KS, Feb 12, 1930.

Franco Zeffirelli, 83, film director (*Otello, Romeo and Juliet*), born Florence, Italy, Feb 12, 1923.

FEBRUARY 13 — MONDAY

Day 44 — 321 Remaining

BLACK LOVE DAY. Feb 13. A national, commemorative holiday of observance, celebration, reconciliation and demonstration of love within and for the black community, conceived by Ayo-Handy Kendi in 1993. On this day blacks should perform five specific acts of love—toward the Creator, toward oneself, within the family, in the community and for the race. Whites are encouraged to demonstrate love through acts of service and self-inventory of their attitudes and behavior toward blacks. Annually, Feb 13. For info: African American Holiday Assn, 1855 3rd St, NW, Washington, DC 20001. Phone: (202) 667-2577. E-mail: aaha@aaha-info.org. Web: aaha-info.org.

CHURCHILL, RANDOLPH HENRY SPENCER: BIRTH ANNIVERSARY. Feb 13, 1849. English politician and the father of Winston Churchill. Born at Blenheim, Woodstock, Oxfordshire, England, he died at London, Jan 24, 1895.

DRESDEN FIREBOMBING: ANNIVERSARY. Feb 13, 1945. Dresden, Germany. Allied firebombing caused a firestorm that destroyed the city and killed 135,000 people.

FIRST MAGAZINE PUBLISHED IN AMERICA: ANNIVERSARY. Feb 13, 1741 (OS). Andrew Bradford published *The American Magazine* just three days ahead of Benjamin Franklin's *General Magazine*.

GET A DIFFERENT NAME DAY. Feb 13. For the pity of the millions of us who hate our birth names. On this day we may change our names to whatever we wish and have the right to expect colleagues, family and friends to so address us. [©2003 by WH.] For info: Thomas & Ruth Roy, Wellcat Holidays, 2418 Long Ln, Lebanon, PA 17046. Phone: (717) 279-0184. E-mail: info@wellcat.com. Web: www.wellcat.com.

INTERNATIONAL FLIRTING WEEK. Feb 13–19. Celebrating the ancient art of flirting and recognizing the role it plays in the lives of singles seeking a mate, couples looking to sustain their love and those simply exchanging a playful glance with a stranger, acquaintance, colleague, etc. For info: Robin Gorman Newman, 44 Somerset Dr, N, Great Neck, NY 11020. Phone: (516) 773-0911. E-mail: robin@lovecoach.com. Web: www.lovecoach.com.

February 2006

S	M	T	W	T	F	S
			1	2	3	4
5	6	7	8	9	10	11
12	13	14	15	16	17	18
19	20	21	22	23	24	25
26	27	28				

IRWIN WINS FIRST MEDAL OF HONOR: ANNIVERSARY. Feb 13, 1861. Colonel Bernard Irwin distinguished himself while leading troops in a battle with Chiricahua Apache Indians at Apache Pass, AZ (at the time part of the territory of New Mexico). For those actions Irwin later became the first person awarded the new US Medal of Honor, although he didn't actually receive it until three years later (Jan 24, 1864).

NATIONAL FIELD TRIAL CHAMPIONSHIP. Feb 13–24. (Monday–Friday only.) Ames Plantation, Grand Junction, TN. To select the national champion all-age bird dog. Est attendance: 4,000. For info: R.J. Carlisle, Secy/Treas, Natl Field Trial Champion Assn, Box 389, Grand Junction, TN 38039. Phone: (901) 878-1067. Fax: (901) 878-1068. E-mail: amesplantation@ames plantation.org. Web: www.amesplantation.org.

PIAZZETTA, GIOVANNI BATTISTA: BIRTH ANNIVERSARY. Feb 13, 1682. Prominent 18th-century Venetian painter. Notable among his works are the *Ecstasy of St. Francis* and *Fortune Teller*. Born at Venice, Italy, and died there Apr 28, 1754.

TRUMAN, BESS (ELIZABETH) VIRGINIA WALLACE: BIRTH ANNIVERSARY. Feb 13, 1885. Wife of Harry S Truman, 33rd president of the US. Born at Independence, MO, and died there Oct 18, 1982.

TU B'SHVAT. Feb 13. Hebrew calendar date: Shebat 15, 5766. The 15th day of the month of Shebat in the Hebrew calendar year is set aside as Hamishah Asar (New Year of the Trees or Jewish Arbor Day), a time to show respect and appreciation for trees and plants. Began at sundown on Feb 12.

WESTMINSTER KENNEL CLUB DOG SHOW. Feb 13–14. Madison Square Garden, New York, NY. 130th annual. For info: Westminster Kennel Club, 149 Madison Ave, Ste 803, New York, NY 10016. Web: westminsterkennelclub.org.

WOOD, GRANT: BIRTH ANNIVERSARY. Feb 13, 1892. American artist, especially noted for his powerful realism and satirical paintings of the American scene, was born near Anamosa, IA. He was a printer, sculptor, woodworker and high school and college teacher. Among his best-remembered works are *American Gothic, Fall Plowing* and *Stone City*. Died at Iowa City, IA, Feb 12, 1942.

BIRTHDAYS TODAY

Stockard Channing, 62, actress (*Six Degrees of Separation, The House of Blue Leaves*, "The West Wing"), born Susan Stockard at New York, NY, Feb 13, 1944.

Peter Gabriel, 56, singer, songwriter, born London, England, Feb 13, 1950.

Kelly Hu, 39, actress ("Martial Law," "Nash Bridges"), born Honolulu, HI, Feb 13, 1967.

Carol Lynley, 64, actress (*Harlow, Bunny Lake Is Missing*), born New York, NY, Feb 13, 1942.

Randy Moss, 29, football player, born Rand, WV, Feb 13, 1977.

David Naughton, 55, singer, actor (*An American Werewolf in London, Overexposed*), born Hartford, CT, Feb 13, 1951.

Kim Novak, 73, actress (*Bell, Book and Candle; Vertigo*), born Marilyn Novak at Chicago, IL, Feb 13, 1933.

Eddie Robinson, 87, former college football coach, born Jackson, LA, Feb 13, 1919.

George Segal, 72, actor (*A Touch of Class*, "Just Shoot Me"), born Great Neck, NY, Feb 13, 1934.

Jerry Springer, 62, TV host ("The Jerry Springer Show"), born London, England, Feb 13, 1944.

Bo Svenson, 65, actor (*North Dallas Forty, Heartbreak Ridge*), born Goteborg, Sweden, Feb 13, 1941.

Peter Tork, 62, actor, singer (The Monkees), born Peter Thorkelson at Washington, DC, Feb 13, 1944 (some sources say 1942).

Chuck Yeager, 83, pilot who broke sound barrier, born Myra, WV, Feb 13, 1923.

FEBRUARY 14 — TUESDAY
Day 45 — 320 Remaining

ARIZONA: ADMISSION DAY. Feb 14. Became 48th state in 1912.

BENNY, JACK: BIRTH ANNIVERSARY. Feb 14, 1894. American comedian. Born Benjamin Kubelsky, Jack Benny entered vaudeville at Waukegan, IL, at age 17, using the violin as a comic stage prop. His radio show first aired in 1932 and continued for 20 years with little change in format. He also had a long-running television show. One of his most well-known comic gimmicks was his purported stinginess. Benny was born at Chicago, IL, and died Dec 26, 1974, at Beverly Hills, CA.

BULGARIA: VITICULTURISTS' DAY (TRIFON ZAREZAN). Feb 14. Celebrated since Thracian times. Festivities are based on cult of Dionysus, god of merriment and wine.

ENIAC COMPUTER INTRODUCED: 60th ANNIVERSARY. Feb 14, 1946. J. Presper Eckert and John W. Mauchly demonstrated the Electronic Numerical Integrator and Computer (ENIAC) for the first time at the University of Pennsylvania. This was the first electronic digital computer. It occupied a room the size of a gymnasium and contained nearly 18,000 vacuum tubes. The army commissioned the computer to speed the calculation of firing tables for artillery. By the time the computer was ready, World War II was over. However, ENIAC prepared the way for future generations of computers.

FERRIS WHEEL DAY. Feb 14, 1859. Anniversary of the birth of George Washington Gale Ferris, American engineer and inventor, at Galesburg, IL. Among his many accomplishments as a civil engineer, Ferris is best remembered as the inventor of the Ferris wheel, which he developed for the World's Columbian Exposition at Chicago, IL, in 1893. Built on the Midway Plaisance, the 250-feet-in-diameter Ferris wheel (with 36 coaches, each capable of carrying 40 passengers), proved one of the greatest attractions of the fair. It was America's answer to the Eiffel Tower of the Paris International Exposition of 1889. Ferris died at Pittsburgh, PA, Nov 22, 1896.

FIRST PRESIDENTIAL PHOTOGRAPH: ANNIVERSARY. Feb 14, 1849. President James Polk became the first US president to be photographed while in office. The photographer was Mathew B. Brady, who would become famous for his photography during the American Civil War.

HANCOCK, WINFIELD SCOTT: BIRTH ANNIVERSARY. Feb 14, 1824. Born at Montgomery, PA, died Feb 9, 1886, at Governor's Island, NY. After serving as Union general in the Civil War, his command of the military division of Texas and Louisiana won him much favor from the Democratic Party because he allowed local civil authorities to retain their power. He pleased the Democrats so well they made him their presidential candidate in 1880. He lost to James A. Garfield by a narrow margin.

HINES, GREGORY: BIRTH ANNIVERSARY. Feb 14, 1946. One of the best tap dancers of his generation, Gregory Hines was born at New York, NY. He was a child star, performing regularly at the Apollo Theater in Harlem, NY, by the age of six. As an adult, he turned to acting, working in film, television and on the Broadway stage. He was nominated for several Tony Awards, winning in 1993 for *Jelly's Last Jam*. His films included *Running Scared* and *The Cotton Club,* and he was nominated for several Emmy Awards for his television dance specials. He died at Los Angeles, CA, Aug 9, 2003.

LEAGUE OF WOMEN VOTERS FORMED: ANNIVERSARY. Feb 14, 1920. While meeting in Chicago to celebrate the imminent ratification of the 19th Amendment to the Constitution, leaders of the National American Woman Suffrage Association (NAWSA) approved the formation of a new organization —the League of Women Voters. With the vote for women just a few months away, the new organization was created to help American women exercise their new political rights and responsibilities. For info: League of Women Voters of Illinois, 332 S Michigan Ave, Ste 1142, Chicago, IL 60604. Phone: (312) 939-5935. Web: www.lwv.org.

***THE MALTESE FALCON:* PUBLICATION ANNIVERSARY.** Feb 14, 1930. Ex-Pinkerton agent turned author Dashiell Hammett's crime novel introducing Sam Spade was published on this day by Alfred A. Knopf in New York, NY. (The novel had been serialized in *Black Mask* magazine in the fall of 1929, but Hammett revised the text.) The novel was a milestone in American literature, offering the model by which all "hard-boiled" crime fiction would follow. And in terse tough guy Sam Spade (who "looked rather pleasantly like a blond satan"), the world found a new pop icon. The notably dark-haired Humphrey Bogart played Spade in the 1941 film version directed by John Huston.

NATIONAL CALL IN SINGLE DAY. Feb 14. Singles across the country are encouraged to set aside time for themselves and their love lives in celebration of National Call In Single Day. Singles are invited to extend their lunch hour or take a personal day to gain self-insight and maximize their chances for love. For info: Yahoo! Personals. Phone: (415) 345-4796. Web: www.personals.yahoo.com.

NATIONAL CONDOM WEEK. Feb 14–21. To educate consumers, patients, students and professionals on the prevention of sexually transmitted diseases, AIDS and teenage pregnancies. For info: Frederick S. Mayer, Pres, Pharmacists Planning Service, Inc, 101 Lucas Valley Rd, #210, San Rafael, CA 94903. Phone: (415) 479-8628. Fax: (415) 479-8608. E-mail: ppsi@aol.com. Web: www.ppsinc.org.

NATIONAL HAVE-A-HEART DAY. Feb 14. The goal of this celebration of life is to create a new consciousness concerning the impact of our food choices on the environment, world hunger, animal welfare and human health—especially heart health. A vegetarian lifestyle increases longevity and helps prevent—and even reverse—heart disease. Vegetarians live about 15 years longer than nonvegetarians and they suffer less than one-tenth the heart disease death rate of nonvegetarians. For info: Vegetarian Awareness Network, Communications Center, PO Box 321, Knoxville, TN 37901-0321. Phone: (800) 280-8343. Fax: (423) 539-1078.

OREGON: ADMISSION DAY: ANNIVERSARY. Feb 14. Became 33rd state in 1859.

PROUT, MARY ANN ("AUNT MARY PROUT"): BIRTH ANNIVERSARY. Feb 14, 1801. It is believed most likely that Mary Prout—social activist, humanitarian, educator—was born free on this date at Baltimore, MD. Prout became a teacher and in 1830 founded a day school. Actively involved in her church, she founded a secret society that became the Independent Order of St. Luke to help with the cost of medical care and burial services for needy blacks, an organization that grew to have 1,500 chapters across the nation by 1900. Prout died at Baltimore in 1884.

RACE RELATIONS DAY. Feb 14. A day designated by some churches to recognize the importance of interracial relations. Formerly was observed on Abraham Lincoln's birthday or on the Sunday preceding it. Since 1970 observance has generally been Feb 14.

SALMAN RUSHDIE'S DEATH SENTENCE: ANNIVERSARY. Feb 14, 1989. Iranian leader Ayatollah Ruholla Khomeini, offended by *The Satanic Verses,* called on Muslims to kill the book's British author, Salman Rushdie. On the following day the Ayatollah offered a $1 million reward for execution of his sentence. Rushdie, fearful for his life, went into hiding. Worldwide protests against the efforts to abridge academic and literary freedoms, countered by protests of Muslim and other religious fundamentalists, stimulated the sales of *The Satanic Verses*, but Rushdie remained virtually a prisoner, unable to resume a public life. In 1998 the Iranian government rescinded the death sentence.

SPACE MILESTONE: *NEAR* ORBITS ASTEROID. Feb 14, 2000. The robot spacecraft *Near Earth Asteroid Rendezvous* (now called *NEAR Shoemaker*) finished circling the asteroid Eros for the first time on this day. Eros is called a near-Earth asteroid because its orbit crosses that of Earth and poses a potential collision danger. *NEAR* continued orbiting the asteroid for a year, moving closer to the surface to make more precise measurements and transmit thousands of pictures. In October 2000 it passed within three miles of Eros. Though it was never designed for landing, on Feb 12, 2001, *NEAR* touched down on Eros, history's first landing of an object on an asteroid. *NEAR* was launched from Cape Canaveral, FL, Feb 17, 1996.

SPACE MILESTONE: 100th SPACEWALK. Feb 14, 2001. Two astronauts from the space shuttle *Atlantis* took the 100th spacewalk; the first had been taken by American Edward White in 1965. On their excursion Thomas Jones and Robert Curbeam, Jr, put the finishing touches on the International Space Station's new science lab *Destiny*. See also: "Space Milestone: *Gemini 4*" (June 3).

SPACE MILESTONE: SMM (US). Feb 14, 1980. Unmanned Delta rocket, a "Solar Maximum Mission Observatory," launched on this date. Intended to study solar flares.

VALENTINE'S DAY. Feb 14. St. Valentine's Day celebrates the feasts of two Christian martyrs of this name. One, a priest and physician, was beaten and beheaded on the Flaminian Way at Rome, Italy, Feb 14, AD 269, during the reign of Emperor Claudius II. Another Valentine, the Bishop of Terni, is said to have been beheaded, also on the Flaminian Way at Rome, Feb 14 (possibly in a later year). Both history and legend are vague and contradictory about details of the Valentines and some say that Feb 14 was selected for the celebration of Christian martyrs as a diversion from the ancient pagan observance of Lupercalia. An old legend has it that birds choose their mates on Valentine's Day. Now it is one of the most widely observed unofficial holidays. It is an occasion for the exchange of gifts (usually books, flowers or sweets) and greeting cards with affectionate or humorous messages. See also: "Lupercalia" (Feb 15).

VALENTINE'S DAY MASSACRE: ANNIVERSARY. Feb 14, 1929. Anniversary of Chicago gangland executions, when gunmen posing as police shot seven members of the George "Bugs" Moran gang.

WALLET, SKEEZIX: "BIRTHDAY." Feb 14. Comic strip character in "Gasoline Alley" by Frank King. First cartoon character to grow and age with the years of publication. Foundling child of Walt and Phyllis Wallet, discovered on doorstep Feb 14, 1921. Skeezix grew through childhood, marriage, military service in WWII, returning home to parenthood and business after the war. Comic strip began in the *Chicago Tribune*, Aug 23, 1919.

WORLD AG EXPO. Feb 14–16. Tulare, CA. The largest farm equipment show in North America. For info: Intl Agri-Center, PO Box 1475, 4450 S Laspina, Tulare, CA 93275. Phone: (800) 999-9186 or (559) 688-1751. Fax: (559) 686-5065. E-mail: info @farmshow.org. Web: www.farmshow.org.

February 2006	S	M	T	W	T	F	S
				1	2	3	4
	5	6	7	8	9	10	11
	12	13	14	15	16	17	18
	19	20	21	22	23	24	25
	26	27	28				

BIRTHDAYS TODAY

Carl Bernstein, 62, journalist, author (investigated Watergate story with Bob Woodward), born Washington, DC, Feb 14, 1944.

Drew Bledsoe, 34, football player, born Ellensburg, WA, Feb 14, 1972.

Michael Bloomberg, 64, mayor of New York City (R), born Brighton, MA, Feb 14, 1942.

Enrico Colantoni, 43, actor ("Just Shoot Me"), born Toronto, ON, Canada, Feb 14, 1963.

Hugh Downs, 85, broadcaster ("Today," "20/20"), born Akron, OH, Feb 14, 1921.

Zach Galligan, 42, actor (*Gremlins, Gremlins II*), born New York, NY, Feb 14, 1964.

Judd Gregg, 59, US Senator (R, New Hampshire), born Nashua, NH, Feb 14, 1947.

Milan Hejduk, 30, hockey player, born Usti-nad-Labem, Czechoslovakia, Feb 14, 1976.

Florence Henderson, 72, singer, actress ("The Brady Bunch"), born Dale, IN, Feb 14, 1934.

Andrew Prine, 70, actor (*The Miracle Worker, Chisum*), born Jennings, FL, Feb 14, 1936.

Teller, 58, magician (Penn and Teller), born Raymond Joseph Teller, name legally changed to Teller, born Philadelphia, PA, Feb 14, 1948.

Meg Tilly, 46, actress (*Agnes of God, Two Jakes*), born Long Beach, CA, Feb 14, 1960.

Jessica Yu, 40, filmmaker (Oscar for *Breathing Lessons: The Life and Work of Mark O'Brien*), born Los Altos Hills, CA, Feb 14, 1966.

FEBRUARY 15 — WEDNESDAY
Day 46 — 319 Remaining

AFGHANISTAN: SOVIET TROOP WITHDRAWAL: ANNIVERSARY. Feb 15, 1989. The USSR's target of withdrawal of all Soviet troops from Afghanistan by this date was essentially met, ending more than nine years of intervention in a civil war.

ARLEN, HAROLD: BIRTH ANNIVERSARY. Feb 15, 1905. American composer and songwriter, born at Buffalo, NY. Arlen wrote many popular songs including "Over the Rainbow" (for which he won the 1939 Oscar for Best Song), "That Old Black Magic," "Blues in the Night" and "Stormy Weather." Died at New York, NY, Apr 23, 1986.

BARRYMORE, JOHN: BIRTH ANNIVERSARY. Feb 15, 1882. American actor of famous acting family, brother of Ethel and Lionel. Born John Blythe at Philadelphia, PA, and died at Los Angeles, CA, May 29, 1942.

BIG TEN WOMEN'S SWIMMING AND DIVING CHAMPIONSHIPS. Feb 15–18. Ohio State University, Columbus, OH. Est attendance: 1,500. For info: Big Ten Conference, 1500 W Higgins Rd, Park Ridge, IL 60068-6300. Phone: (847) 696-1010. Fax: (847) 696-1110. Web: www.bigten.org.

CANADA: MAPLE LEAF FLAG ADOPTED: ANNIVERSARY. Feb 15, 1965. The new Canadian national flag was raised at Ottawa, Canada's capital, on this day. The red-and-white flag with a red maple leaf in the center replaced the Red Ensign flag which had the British Union Jack in the upper left-hand corner.

CERMAK, ANTON J.: ASSASSINATION ANNIVERSARY. Feb 15, 1933. At Bay Front Park, Miami, FL, an assassin aiming at President-elect Franklin D. Roosevelt had his aim deflected by a spectator. Cermak, mayor of Chicago, IL, born May 9, 1873, at Kladno, Bohemia, Czechoslovakia, was struck and killed instead. Giuseppe (Joe) Zangara, the 32-year-old assassin, who had emigrated from Italy in 1923, was electrocuted at the Raiford, FL, state prison Mar 20, 1933.

CLARK, ABRAHAM: BIRTH ANNIVERSARY. Feb 15, 1726. Signer of the Declaration of Independence, farmer and lawyer. Born at Elizabethtown, NJ, and died there Sept 15, 1794.

GALILEI, GALILEO: BIRTH ANNIVERSARY. Feb 15, 1564. Physicist and astronomer who helped overthrow medieval concepts of the world, born at Pisa, Italy. He proved the theory that all bodies, large and small, descend at equal speed and gathered evidence to support Copernicus's theory that the Earth and other planets revolve around the sun. Galileo died at Florence, Italy, Jan 8, 1642.

GRAND RAPIDS BOAT SHOW. Feb 15–19. DeVos Place, Grand Rapids, MI. This event brings together buyers and sellers of power- and sailboats, boating accessories, docks, dockominiums and vacation properties. Est attendance: 32,000. For info: Henri Boucher, ShowSpan, Inc, 2121 Celebration Dr NE, Grand Rapids, MI 49525. Phone: (616) 447-2860. Fax: (616) 447-2861. E-mail: events@showspan.com. Web: www.showspan.com.

LUPERCALIA. Feb 15. Anniversary of ancient Roman fertility festival. Thought by some to have been established by Romulus and Remus who, legend says, were suckled by a she-wolf at Lupercal (a cave in Palestine). Goats and dogs were sacrificed. Lupercalia celebration persisted until the fifth century of the Christian era. Possibly a forerunner of Valentine's Day customs.

McCORMICK, CYRUS H.: BIRTH ANNIVERSARY. Feb 15, 1809. Inventor of the reaper, born at Rockbridge County, VA. It is said that Cyrus McCormick's invention of the reaper rates second only to the railroad in the development of the US. Continuing the dream of his father, McCormick constructed a horse-operated reaper which was demonstrated for the first time in a Virginia wheat field in July 1831. He moved his operation to Chicago, IL, in 1847 in order to be closer to the Midwest's expanding wheat fields. His business prospered despite two decades of constant litigation over patent rights. He died May 13, 1884, at Chicago, IL. In 1902–03, his McCormick Harvesting Machine Company was consolidated with other firms to become the International Harvester Company.

MENENDEZ DE AVILES, PEDRO: BIRTH ANNIVERSARY. Feb 15, 1519. Spanish explorer and naval adventurer. Explored Florida coastal regions for king of Spain and established a fort at St. Augustine in September 1565. Died Sept 17, 1574, at Santander, Spain.

REMEMBER THE *MAINE* DAY: ANNIVERSARY. Feb 15, 1898. American battleship *Maine* was blown up while at anchor in Havana Harbor, at 9:40 PM, on this day in 1898. The ship, under the command of Captain Charles G. Sigsbee, sank quickly, and 260 members of its crew were lost. Inflamed public opinion in the US ignored the lack of evidence to establish responsibility for the explosion. "Remember the *Maine*" became the war cry, and a formal declaration of war against Spain followed on Apr 25, 1898.

SHACKLETON, ERNEST: BIRTH ANNIVERSARY. Feb 15, 1874. The Antarctic explorer was born at Kilkea, Ireland. His fame rests not on reaching the South Pole (he tried three times), but on his leadership and bravery. During the British Imperial Trans-Arctic expedition of 1914, the icy seas crushed their ship, *Endurance*, but Shackleton protected his men and buoyed their morale for the two years they were marooned. In 1916 he led a six-man team in a lifeboat on a 17-day, 600-mile journey (with-

out sleep) in search of help. Upon arrival at South Georgia Island, he rounded up a rescue effort and three months later all his men were rescued without a death. Shackleton died Jan 5, 1922, at Grytviken, South Georgia Island, while beginning a fourth expedition to the South Pole.

SPANISH WAR MEMORIAL DAY AND *MAINE* MEMORIAL DAY. Feb 15. Massachusetts.

SUSAN B. ANTHONY DAY. Feb 15. Honors one of the first women's rights advocates, working especially for the right to vote. Anthony was born on this day in 1820 at Adams, MA. She died Mar 13, 1906, at Rochester, NY.

SUTTER, JOHN AUGUSTUS: BIRTH ANNIVERSARY. Feb 15, 1803. Born at Kandern, Germany, Sutter established the first white settlement on the site of Sacramento, CA, in 1839, and owned a large tract of land there, which he named New Helvetia. The first great gold strike in the US was on his property, at Sutter's Mill, Jan 24, 1848. His land was soon overrun by gold seekers who, he claimed, slaughtered his cattle and stole or destroyed his property. Sutter was bankrupt by 1852. Died at Washington, DC, June 18, 1880.

TEXOMA FARM AND RANCH SHOW. Feb 15–16. Multi-Purpose Events Center Exhibit Hall, Wichita Falls, TX. Farmers and ranchers from North Texas and Oklahoma come to see the latest in equipment. Seminars and information in new farming and ranching techniques. Est attendance: 8,000. For info: Wichita Falls CVB, 1000 5th St, Wichita Falls, TX 76301. Phone: (940) 716-5500. Fax: (940) 716-5509. E-mail: MPEC@wf.net. Web: www.wichitafalls.org.

TIFFANY, CHARLES LEWIS: BIRTH ANNIVERSARY. Feb 15, 1812. American jeweler whose name became synonymous with high standards of quality. Born at Killingly, CT, and died at New York, NY, Feb 18, 1902. Father of artist Louis Comfort Tiffany. See also: "Tiffany, Louis Comfort: Birth Anniversary" (Feb 18).

BIRTHDAYS TODAY

Adolfo, 73, fashion designer, born Adolfo F. Sardina at Havana, Cuba, Feb 15, 1933.

Marisa Berenson, 58, actress (*Cabaret, Barry Lyndon*), model, born New York, NY, Feb 15, 1948.

Claire Bloom, 75, actress (*A Doll's House, The Spy Who Came In from the Cold*), born London, England, Feb 15, 1931.

Susan Brownmiller, 71, author, feminist (*Against Our Will, Femininity*), born Brooklyn, NY, Feb 15, 1935.

Matt Groening, 52, cartoonist ("The Simpsons"), born Portland, OR, Feb 15, 1954.

Jaromir Jagr, 34, hockey player, born Kladno, Czechoslovakia, Feb 15, 1972.

Harvey Korman, 79, actor, comedian (two Emmys for "The Carol Burnett Show"; *High Anxiety*), born Chicago, IL, Feb 15, 1927.

Melissa Manchester, 55, singer ("Don't Cry Out Loud"), born the Bronx, NY, Feb 15, 1951.

Kevin McCarthy, 92, actor (*Invasion of the Body Snatchers, Buffalo Bill and the Indians*), born Seattle, WA, Feb 15, 1914.

William Mark Price, 42, former basketball player, born Bartlesville, OK, Feb 15, 1964.

Jane Seymour, 55, actress (Emmy for "East of Eden"; "Dr. Quinn: Medicine Woman"), born Hillingdon, England, Feb 15, 1951.

FEBRUARY 16 — THURSDAY
Day 47 — 318 Remaining

AMERICAN ASSOCIATION FOR THE ADVANCE-MENT OF SCIENCE ANNUAL MEETING. Feb 16–20. St. Louis, MO. 172nd annual meeting. Est attendance: 9,500. For info: AAAS, 1200 New York Ave NW, Washington, DC 20005. Phone: (202) 326-6450. Fax: (202) 289-4021. Web: www.aaas.org/meetings.

BERGEN, EDGAR: BIRTH ANNIVERSARY. Feb 16, 1903. Actor, radio entertainer and ventriloquist, voice of Charlie McCarthy, Mortimer Snerd and Effie Klinker. Father of Emmy Award–winning actress Candice Bergen. Born at Chicago, IL; died at Las Vegas, NV, Sept 30, 1978.

ENGLAND: CHESTER ANTIQUES AND FINE ART SHOW. Feb 16–19 (also Oct 26–29). Chester Racecourse, Cheshire. 60 stands on three floors where all items have been vetted for authenticity and age. Est attendance: 3,500. For info: Penman Fairs. Phone: (44) (870) 350-2442. Fax: (44) (870) 350-2443. E-mail: info@penman-fairs.co.uk.

FLAHERTY, ROBERT JOSEPH: BIRTH ANNIVER-SARY. Feb 16, 1884. American filmmaker, explorer and author, called "father of the documentary film." Born at Iron Mountain, MI; died at Dunnerston, VT, July 23, 1951. Films included *Nanook of the North, Moana* and *Man of Aran.*

GATORADE DUEL QUALIFYING RACES FOR THE DAYTONA 500. Feb 16. Daytona International Speedway, Daytona Beach, FL. 48th annual running. Drivers battle to set the Daytona 500 field. For info: Daytona Intl Speedway, PO Box 2801, Daytona Beach, FL 32120-2801. Phone: (800) PIT-SHOP. Web: www.daytonainternationalspeedway.com.

KENNAN, GEORGE: BIRTH ANNIVERSARY. Feb 16, 1904. US diplomat who coined the phrase "containment policy," Kennan was born at Milwaukee, WI. He served as a diplomat during WWII and was briefly arrested by the Nazis. After the war, he wrote an article for *Foreign Affairs* magazine that had a great influence on America's Cold War foreign policy. The article, entitled "The Sources of Soviet Conduct" and submitted under the pseudonym "Mr. X," called upon the US and its allies to prevent the territorial spread of communism, either by shows of military force or by economic and technological intervention in at-risk nations. Both the Marshall Plan and the Truman Doctrine were heavily influenced by the ideas expressed in the article. Kennan later had a controversial turn as ambassador to the Soviet Union. He died at Princeton, NJ, at the age of 101, Mar 17, 2005.

KING, WAYNE: BIRTH ANNIVERSARY. Feb 16, 1901. American saxophonist and bandleader, widely known as "the Waltz King," born at Savannah, IL. His own composition, "The Waltz You Save for Me," was his theme song. Died at Paradise Valley, AZ, July 16, 1985.

LITHUANIA: INDEPENDENCE DAY. Feb 16. National Day. The anniversary of Lithuania's declaration of independence in 1918 is observed as the Baltic state's Independence Day. In 1940 Lithuania became a part of the Soviet Union under an agreement between Joseph Stalin and Adolf Hitler. On Mar 11, 1990, Lithuania declared its independence from the Soviet Union, the first of the Soviet republics to do so. After demanding independence, Lithuania set up a border police force and aided young men in efforts to avoid the Soviet military draft, prompting then Soviet leader Mikhail Gorbachev to send tanks into the capital of Vilnius and impose oil and gas embargoes. In the wake of the failed coup attempt in Moscow, Aug 19, 1991, Lithuanian independence finally was recognized.

MIAMI INTERNATIONAL BOAT SHOW AND STRICTLY SAIL®. Feb 16–20. Miami Beach Convention Center, Miami Beach, FL. 65th annual boat show, the biggest in the US and considered the main event for product introductions. With more than 3,000 boats, this show offers an unparalleled opportunity to view the sport's latest products. Est attendance: 175,000. For info: NMMA, 200 E Randolph St, Ste 5100, Chicago, IL 60601. Phone: (312) 946-6200. Fax: (312) 946-0388. Web: www.discoverboating.com.

SIMPLOT GAMES. Feb 16–18. Holt Arena, Idaho State University, Pocatello, ID. One of the nation's largest indoor high school track and field events, featuring 2,000 top high school athletes from the US and Canada. Est attendance: 20,000. For info: Carol Lish, Exec Dir, Simplot Games, PO Box 912, Pocatello, ID 83204. Phone: (800) 635-9444. Fax: (208) 235-5669. E-mail: clish@simplot.com. Web: www.simplotgames.com.

SURRENDER OF FORT DONELSON: ANNIVERSARY. Feb 16, 1862. With Confederate troops evacuating Bowling Green, KY, and other points along the Kentucky line, General Ulysses S. Grant's forces encircled Fort Donelson, KY. After hard fighting on land and on the Cumberland River, Grant requested surrender of Fort Donelson, stating that "No terms except unconditional and immediate surrender can be accepted." This earned him the nickname Unconditional Surrender Grant. Confederate General Simon Buckner surrendered the fort, in essence giving the Union army control of Tennessee and Kentucky and the Tennessee and Cumberland rivers. Disruption ensued and civilians attempted to flee the area occupied by Federal troops.

WILSON, HENRY: BIRTH ANNIVERSARY. Feb 16, 1812. 18th vice president of the US (1873–75). Born at Farmington, NH; died at Washington, DC, Nov 22, 1875.

BIRTHDAYS TODAY

Jerome Bettis, 34, football player, born Detroit, MI, Feb 16, 1972.
LeVar Burton, 49, actor, host ("Roots," "Star Trek: The Next Generation," "Reading Rainbow"), born Landsthul, Germany, Feb 16, 1957.
Richard Ford, 62, author (*Independence Day, The Sportswriter*), born Jackson, MS, Feb 16, 1944.
Ice T, 47, rap singer, born Tracy Morrow at Newark, NJ, Feb 16, 1959.
James Ingram, 50, singer ("Baby, Come to Me" [with Patti Austin]), songwriter, born Akron, OH, Feb 16, 1956.
William Katt, 56, actor ("The Greatest American Hero," *Perry Mason Returns, Carrie*), born Los Angeles, CA, Feb 16, 1950 (some sources say 1955 or 1951).
John Patrick McEnroe, Jr, 47, former tennis player, born Wiesbaden, West Germany, Feb 16, 1959.
Barry Primus, 68, actor ("Cagney and Lacey," *Absence of Malice, Down and Out in Beverly Hills*), born New York, NY, Feb 16, 1938.

	S	**M**	**T**	**W**	**T**	**F**	**S**
February				1	2	3	4
2006	5	6	7	8	9	10	11
	12	13	14	15	16	17	18
	19	20	21	22	23	24	25
	26	27	28				

FEBRUARY 17 — FRIDAY

Day 48 — 317 Remaining

BARBER, WALTER LANIER "RED": BIRTH ANNIVERSARY. Feb 17, 1908. One of the first broadcasters inducted into the Baseball Hall of Fame, "Red" Barber was born at Columbus, MS. Barber's first professional play-by-play experience was announcing the Cincinnati Reds opening day on radio in 1934. That game was also the first major league game he had ever seen. He broadcast baseball's first night game (in Brooklyn) on Aug 26, 1939, the 1947 game in which Jackie Robinson broke the color barrier and Roger Maris's 61st home run in 1961. Red Barber died Oct 22, 1992, at Tallahassee, FL.

CHICAGO FLAG EXHIBIT CONTROVERSY: ANNIVERSARY. Feb 17, 1989. An exhibit at the School of the Art Institute of Chicago, titled *What Is the Proper Way to Display a US Flag?*, consisted of a ledger for viewers to write their impressions but required the viewers to stand on a US flag mounted on the floor to reach the ledger. The exhibit by art student Scott Tyler prompted protests from veterans' groups, a failed lawsuit and an introduction of legislation by Senator Bob Dole to make displaying a US flag on the floor or ground a crime. Although that legislation didn't pass, Congress periodically continues to introduce legislation against flag desecration.

CORELLI, ARCANGELO: BIRTH ANNIVERSARY. Feb 17, 1653. Italian composer and virtuoso violinist, born at Fusignano, Italy. From his home in Rome, Corelli made extensive and popular concert tours throughout much of Europe. Died at Rome, Italy, Jan 8, 1713.

CROWN ROYAL INTERNATIONAL RACE OF CHAMPIONS XXX. Feb 17. Daytona International Speedway, Daytona Beach, FL. Best drivers from top stock and open wheel series. Sponsored by Crown Royal. For info: Daytona Intl Speedway, PO Box 2801, Daytona Beach, FL 32120-2801. Phone: (800) PIT-SHOP. Web: www.daytonainternationalspeedway.com.

FORT SUMTER RETURNED TO UNION CONTROL: ANNIVERSARY. Feb 17, 1865. After a siege that lasted almost a year and a half, Fort Sumter in South Carolina returned to Union hands on this date. The site of the first shots fired in the American Civil War on Apr 12, 1861, the fort had become a symbol for both sides. As Union attempts to retake it by shelling diminished the fort's capacity with large bombardments, Southern forces managed to hold out with few casualties.

FRANCE: NICE CARNIVAL. Feb 17–28. Dates from the 14th century and is celebrated each year during the 12 days ending with Shrove Tuesday. Derived from ancient rites of spring, the carnival offers parades, floats, battles of flowers and confetti, a fireworks display lighting up the entire Baie des Anges. King Carnival is burned on his pyre at the end of the event.

GERONIMO: DEATH ANNIVERSARY. Feb 17, 1909. American Indian of the Chiricahua (Apache) tribe was born about 1829 in Arizona. He was the leader of a small band of warriors whose devastating raids in Arizona, New Mexico and Mexico caused the US Army to send 5,000 men to recapture him after his first escape. He was confined at Fort Sill, OK, where he died Feb 17, 1909, after dictating the story of his life for publication.

GREAT BACKYARD BIRD COUNT. Feb 17–20. Thousands of volunteers nationwide track the number and types of birds that live near their homes. Results help researchers monitor species in trouble. Cosponsored by the National Audubon Society and the Cornell University Lab of Ornithology. For info: National Audubon Society, 700 Broadway, 4th Fl, New York, NY 10003. Phone: (212) 979-3000. Web: www.birdsource.org/gbbc.

LAENNEC, RENE THEOPHILE HYACINTHE: 225th BIRTH ANNIVERSARY. Feb 17, 1781. Famed French physician, author and inventor of the stethoscope, called "father of chest medicine." He wrote extensively about respiratory and heart ailments. Born at Quimper, France, he died there Aug 13, 1826.

LEAGUE OF UNITED LATIN AMERICAN CITIZENS (LULAC) FOUNDED: ANNIVERSARY. Feb 17, 1929. Delegates from the Corpus Christi Order of the Sons of America, Knights of America of San Antonio and the League of Latin America Citizens from the Rio Grande Valley met at Obreros Hall, Corpus Christi, TX, to form LULAC. It is now the oldest and largest Hispanic civic organization.

LONGHORN WORLD CHAMPIONSHIP RODEO. Feb 17–19. The Palace of Auburn Hills, Auburn Hills, MI. 42nd annual. More than 250 cowboys and cowgirls compete in six professional contests ranging from bronc riding to big, bad BONUS bull riding! Free beginners horsemanship clinic 40 minutes before performances. Qualifying rodeo for Longhorn's Championship Finals Rodeo in Murfreesboro, TN. Featuring colorful opening ceremonies. Est attendance: 32,000. For info: W. Bruce Lehrke, Pres, Longhorn World Chmpshp Rodeo, Inc, PO Box 70159, Nashville, TN 37207. Phone: (615) 876-1016. Fax: (615) 876-4685. E-mail: info@longhornrodeo.com. Web: www.longhornrodeo.com.

***MADAMA BUTTERFLY* PREMIERE: ANNIVERSARY.** Feb 17, 1904. Giacomo Puccini's *Madama Butterfly* was performed for the first time in Milan. The sold-out crowd, restive at what they saw as Puccini's lack of originality, gave boos, moos, groans and heckling to the extent that the performers couldn't hear the orchestra. Rosina Storchio, the soprano portraying Madama Butterfly, began crying on stage. Puccini, enraged at the opera's reception (saying the opera was "daisies thrown to swine"), nevertheless revised the work, and it had a successful performance on May 24.

MALTHUS, THOMAS: BIRTH ANNIVERSARY. Feb 17, 1766. English economist, author and demographer, born near Dorking, England. Malthusian population theories (especially that population growth exceeds growth of production) provoked great controversy when published in 1798. Died near Bath, England, Dec 23, 1834.

MY WAY DAY. Feb 17. Hundreds of people have their opinions as to who we are. Today is the day we decide who's right. Today we determine our identities all by ourselves. [©2003 by WH.] For info: Thomas & Ruth Roy, Wellcat Holidays, 2418 Long Ln, Lebanon, PA 17046. Phone: (717) 279-0184. E-mail: info@wellcat.com. Web: www.wellcat.com.

NASCAR CRAFTSMAN TRUCK SERIES 250. Feb 17. Daytona International Speedway, Daytona, FL. NASCAR trucks on the Superspeedway. 7th annual. For info: Daytona International Speedway, PO Box 2801, Daytona Beach, FL 32120-2801. Phone: (800) PIT-SHOP. Web: www.daytonainternationalspeedway.com.

NATIONAL DATE FESTIVAL. Feb 17–26. Indio, CA. America's most exotic county fair features Arabian Nights theme, camel and ostrich races, satellite horse wagering, nightly musical pageant, date exhibits and sampling, thousands of competitive exhibits and carnival. Est attendance: 275,000. For info: Riverside County Fair and National Date Fest, PO Box 1180, Riverside, CA 92502. Phone: (760) 863-8247 or (800) 811-FAIR. Web: www.datefest.org.

NATIONAL PTA FOUNDERS' DAY: ANNIVERSARY.
Feb 17, 1897. Celebrates the PTA's founding by Phoebe Apperson Hearst and Alice McLellan Birney. For info: Natl PTA, 541 N Fairbanks, Ste 1300, Chicago, IL 60611-3396. Phone: (312) 670-6782. Fax: (312) 670-6783. E-mail: info@pta.org. Web: www.pta.org.

NBA ALL-STAR WEEKEND. Feb 17–19. Houston, TX. For info: Brian McIntyre, Sr VP, Basketball Communications, Natl Basketball Assn, Olympic Tower, 645 Fifth Ave, New York, NY 10022. Phone: (212) 407-8000. Web: www.nba.com.

NEWPORT WINTER FESTIVAL. Feb 17–26. Newport, RI. More than 160 individual events from food, music and entertainment to skating, hayrides, snow sculptures, ice carving, scavenger hunt and even winter polo demonstrations—fun for all ages. Est attendance: 25,000. For info: Mktg & Events, Inc, 28 Pelham St, Newport, RI 02840. Phone: (401) 847-7666. Web: www.newportevents.com.

NRA/NWRA RODEO FINALS. Feb 17–19. MetraPark Arena, Billings, MT. Rodeo action at its best—31st annual finals. A fun-filled rodeo weekend in cowboy country! Est attendance: 16,000. For info: Northern Rodeo Assn, PO Box 1122, Billings, MT 59103. Phone: (406) 252-1122. Fax: (406) 252-0300.

"A PRAIRIE HOME COMPANION" PREMIERE: ANNIVERSARY. Feb 17, 1979. This popular live variety show debuted locally on Minnesota Public Radio in 1974 and was first broadcast nationally on Feb 17, 1979, as part of National Public Radio's Folk Festival USA. It became a regular Saturday night program in early 1980. Host Garrison Keillor's monologues about the mythical Lake Wobegon and his humorous ads for local businesses such as Bertha's Kitty Boutique, Powdermilk Biscuits and the Chatterbox Cafe were accompanied by various musical groups. Broadcast from the World Theater in St. Paul, MN, the show went off the air in 1986. A series of programs were done for cable TV, and Keillor continues to write works of fiction (*Lake Wobegon Days*). In 1994, "A Prairie Home Companion" went back on the air on Public Radio International.

SECOND HONEYMOON WEEKEND. Feb 17–19. This weekend is set aside for all couples to spend some quality time together away from the routine of their everyday lives. Take your significant other away and experience fun, joy and closeness together. Annually, the weekend immediately after Valentine's Day. [©1996] To alleviate the escalating costs of Eventological® Literature, a charge of $10 must be assessed for each request. Checks are to be made payable to: Adrienne Sioux Koopersmith, 1437 W Rosemont, #1W, Chicago, IL 60660-1319. E-mail: as koopersmith@hotmail.com.

SOUTH COAST WRITER'S CONFERENCE. Feb 17–18. Event Center on the Beach and Gold Beach High School, Gold Beach, OR. Keynote speaker followed by a series of workshops and roundtable discussions concerning writing techniques, publishing guidelines and editorial commentary. Fireman's Fish Fry will take place on Feb 18. Est attendance: 175. For info: Southwestern Oregon Community College, PO Box 590, Gold Beach, OR 97444. Phone: (541) 247-2741. Fax: (541) 247-6247. E-mail: scwc@socc.edu.

SOUTHEASTERN WILDLIFE EXPOSITION. Feb 17–19. Charleston, SC. Spectacular wildlife and nature art exposition showcasing original paintings, prints, sculpture, photography, carvings, collectibles and crafts. Eleven exhibition sites throughout historic Charleston. Est attendance: 40,000. For info: Southeastern Wildlife Exposition, 211 Meeting St, Charleston, SC 29401. Phone: (843) 723-1748. E-mail: sewe@sewe.com. Web: www.sewe.com.

STAMP EXPO. Feb 17–19 (also Aug 25–27 and Nov 24–26). Pasadena Convention Center, Pasadena, CA. Est attendance: 5,000. For info: Israel Bick, Exec Dir, Intl Stamp & Coin Collectors Society, PO Box 854, Van Nuys, CA 91408. Phone: (818) 997-6496. Fax: (818) 988-4337. E-mail: iibick@sbcglobal.net. Web: www.bick.net.

WHISKEY FLAT DAYS. Feb 17–20. Kernville, CA. Whiskey Flat Days commemorates the old Kernville that was called Whiskey Flat until 1860. We turn back the clock as the parade, stores and residents go back to the 1860s. Frog races, craft booths, rodeo, parade, games for small children, carnival, costume and whiskerino contests, melodrama and much more. Est attendance: 40,000. For info: Kernville Chamber of Commerce, PO Box 397, Kernville, CA 93238. Phone: (760) 376-2629 or (866) KERNVILLE. Fax: (760) 376-4371. E-mail: info@kernvillechamber.org. Web: www.kernvillechamber.org.

WORLD HUMAN SPIRIT DAY. Feb 17. Fort Lauderdale, FL. At 3:00 PM, EST, we will hold two minutes of silent meditation throughout the world and beyond, to focus on the true spirit that flows through everything. Please join us in silence to bring the energy of universal healing and peace into the hearts and minds of all humanity. For info: Michael Levy, Point of Life Foundation, PO Box 7, 3032 E Commercial Blvd, Fort Lauderdale, FL 33308. Phone/fax: (954) 785-8439. E-mail: mikmikl@aol.com. Web: www.pointoflife.com or www.polfoundation.org.

BIRTHDAYS TODAY

Vanessa Atler, 24, former gymnast, born Valencia, CA, Feb 17, 1982.

James Nathaniel (Jim) Brown, 70, Hall of Fame football player, activist, actor, born St. Simons Island, GA, Feb 17, 1936.

Ronald DeVoe, 39, singer (Bell Biv DeVoe), born Boston, MA, Feb 17, 1967.

Michelle Forbes, 39, actress ("Homicide: Life on the Street"), born Austin, TX, Feb 17, 1967.

Brenda Fricker, 61, actress (Oscar for *My Left Foot; The Field*), born Dublin, Ireland, Feb 17, 1945.

Joseph Gordon-Levitt, 25, actor ("3rd Rock from the Sun," *Halloween H20*), born Los Angeles, CA, Feb 17, 1981.

Paris Hilton, 25, socialite, television personality ("The Simple Life"), born New York, NY, Feb 17, 1981.

Lee Hoiby, 80, composer, concert pianist, born Madison, WI, Feb 17, 1926.

Hal Holbrook, 81, actor (*Magnum Force, All the President's Men*), born Harold Rowe, Jr at Cleveland, OH, Feb 17, 1925.

Barry Humphries, 72, actor, comedian, aka Dame Edna Everidge (*Spiceworld*), born Melbourne, Australia, Feb 17, 1934.

Michael Jeffrey Jordan, 43, former basketball player, former minor league baseball player, born Brooklyn, NY, Feb 17, 1963.

Richard Karn, 47, actor ("Home Improvement"), game-show host ("Family Feud"), born Seattle, WA, Feb 17, 1959.

Lou Diamond Phillips, 44, actor (*La Bamba, Stand and Deliver*), born Corpus Christi, TX, Feb 17, 1962.

Denise Richards, 35, actress (*Wild Things, The World Is Not Enough*), born Downers Grove, IL, Feb 17, 1971.

Rene Russo, 52, actress (*Lethal Weapon 3, Ransom*), born Burbank, CA, Feb 17, 1954.

Craig Thomas, 73, US Senator (R, Wyoming), born Cody, WY, Feb 17, 1933.

	S	M	T	W	T	F	S
February				1	2	3	4
	5	6	7	8	9	10	11
2006	12	13	14	15	16	17	18
	19	20	21	22	23	24	25
	26	27	28				

FEBRUARY 18 — SATURDAY
Day 49 — 316 Remaining

ALEICHEM, SHOLEM: BIRTH ANNIVERSARY. Feb 18, 1859 (OS). Pen name of Russian-born author and humorist Solomon Rabinowitz. Affectionately known in the US as the "Jewish Mark Twain." Died at New York, NY, May 13, 1916.

BENSON ANTIQUE TRACTOR PULL & ENGINE SHOW. Feb 18–19. Lions Park, Benson, AZ. Garden tractors and peddle tractors will also show, and there will be craft and food vendors and a beer garden. Presented by The Power From The Past and sponsored by the Benson/SPV Chamber of Commerce and the Benson Merchant's Association. Annually, the third weekend in February. Est attendance: 1,500. For info: Benson Chamber of Commerce, PO Box 2255, Benson, AZ 85602. Phone: (520) 586-2842. Fax: (520) 586-1972. E-mail: info@ben sonchamberaz.com. Web: www.bensonchamberaz.com.

COW MILKED WHILE FLYING IN AN AIRPLANE: ANNIVERSARY. Feb 18, 1930. Elm Farm Ollie became the first cow to fly in an airplane. During the flight, which was attended by reporters, she was milked and the milk was sealed in paper containers and parachuted over St. Louis, MO.

DAVIS, JEFFERSON: INAUGURATION ANNIVERSARY. Feb 18, 1861. In the years before the Civil War, Senator Jefferson Davis was the acknowledged leader of the Southern bloc and a champion of states' rights, but he had little to do with the secessionist movement until after his home state of Mississippi joined the Confederacy Jan 9, 1861. Davis withdrew from the Senate that same day. He was unanimously chosen as president of the Confederacy's provisional government and was inaugurated at Montgomery, AL, Feb 18. Within the next year he was elected to a six-year term by popular vote and inaugurated a second time Feb 22, 1862, at Richmond, VA.

LA FIESTA DE LOS VAQUEROS. Feb 18–26. Tucson, AZ. Tucson celebrates its Old West heritage with a parade, a PRCA rodeo and other related rodeo events, including an Extreme bull-riding event. Est attendance: 55,000. For info: Tucson Rodeo Committee, Inc, PO Box 11006, Tucson, AZ 85734. Phone: (520) 741-2233 or (800) 964-5662. Fax: (520) 741-7273. Web: www.tucsonrodeo.com.

GAMBIA: INDEPENDENCE DAY. Feb 18, 1965. National holiday. Independence from Britain granted. Referendum in April 1970 established Gambia as a republic within the Commonwealth.

HERSHEY'S 300 NASCAR BUSCH SERIES RACE. Feb 18. Daytona International Speedway, Daytona Beach, FL. 48th annual race. Busch Series' richest and most competitive event. For info: Daytona Intl Speedway, PO Box 2801, Daytona Beach, FL 32120-2801. Phone: (800) PIT-SHOP. Web: www.daytonainternationalspeedway.com.

KLONDIKE DAYS. Feb 18–19. Eagle River Derby Track, Eagle River, WI. A re-creation of primitive camps used by early buckskinners, pioneers, trappers and traders. Additional attractions include a two-day horse weight-pull reminiscent of Wisconsin's logging days, a chain saw carving competition, a Native American cultural presentation including a ceremonial dance exhibition, lumberjack competition, craft show, dog weight-pull and much more. Wisconsin's premiere multifaceted winter festival. Est attendance: 12,000. For info: Christine Schilling, Exec Dir, Klondike Days, Inc, PO Box 1166, Eagle River, WI 54521. Phone: (800) 359-6315. Web: www.klondikedays.org.

NEPAL: NATIONAL DEMOCRACY DAY. Feb 18. National holiday. Anniversary of the 1952 Constitution.

NEW ENGLAND MID-WINTER SURFING CHAMPIONSHIP. Feb 18. Narragansett Town Beach, Narragansett, RI. 38th annual. Competition in all age categories and specialty events with prizes and trophies. Est attendance: 125. For info: Peter Panagiotis, ESA Dir, 126 Sayles Ave, Pawtucket, RI 02860. E-mail: bicsurf@hotmail.com.

PEABODY, GEORGE: BIRTH ANNIVERSARY. Feb 18, 1795. American merchant and philanthropist, born at South Danvers, MA. He endowed the Peabody Institute in Baltimore, museums at Harvard and Yale and the George Peabody College for Teachers at Nashville, TN. Died at London, England, Nov 4, 1869.

PLANET PLUTO DISCOVERY: ANNIVERSARY. Feb 18, 1930. Pluto, the ninth planet, was discovered by astronomer Clyde Tombaugh at the Lowell Observatory at Flagstaff, AZ. It was given the name of the Roman god of the underworld. Some astronomers don't accept Pluto as a planet.

SHOW OF WHEELS. Feb 18–19. Lea County Fairgrounds, Lovington, NM. Car show presented by the Lovington Chamber of Commerce. Featuring antiques, classics, street rods, motorcycles and minitrucks. Commercial exhibits and games will be an exciting part of the show. RV parking available. For info: Lovington Chamber of Commerce, 201 S Main St, Lovington, NM 88260. Phone: (505) 396-5311 or (505) 396-3661. Fax: (505) 396-2823. E-mail: lchamber@valornet.com. Web: www.lovington.net.

TIFFANY, LOUIS COMFORT: BIRTH ANNIVERSARY. Feb 18, 1848. American artist, son of famed jeweler Charles L. Tiffany. Best remembered for his remarkable work with decorative iridescent "favrile" glass. Born at New York, NY; died there Jan 17, 1933. See also: "Tiffany, Charles Lewis: Birth Anniversary" (Feb 15).

TWIN CITIES' KREWE OF JANUS MARDI GRAS PARADE. Feb 18. Monroe, LA. The streets of Monroe and West Monroe come alive to celebrate Mardi Gras. Bands, music and elaborate floats light up the twin cities with fun for all. For info: Monroe/West Monroe Convention and Visitors Bureau, 601 Constitution Dr, West Monroe, LA 71292. Phone: (800) 843-1872. Fax: (318) 324-1752. E-mail: mwmcvb@monroe-westmonroe.org. Web: www.monroe-westmonroe.org.

WILLKIE, WENDELL LEWIS: BIRTH ANNIVERSARY. Feb 18, 1892. American lawyer, author, public utility executive and politician, born at Elwood, IN. Presidential nominee of the Republican Party in 1940. Remembered for his book, *One World*, published in 1943. Died at New York, NY, Oct 8, 1944.

WINGS OVER THE PLATTE SPRING MIGRATION FESTIVAL. Feb 18–Apr 16. Grand Island, NE. Celebrate the arrival of the world's largest concentration of sandhill cranes. Each spring up to 500,000 cranes gather along the Platte River during their northward migration. Seminars, tours, nature hikes, films. Est attendance: 100,000. For info: Renee Seifert, Grand Island/Hall County Conv and Visitors Bureau, 2424 S Locust St, Ste C, Grand Island, NE 66801. Phone: (800) 658-3178 or (308) 382-4400. Fax: (308) 382-4908. E-mail: info@visitgrandisland.com. Web: www.visitgrandisland.com.

BIRTHDAYS TODAY

Helen Gurley Brown, 84, author (*Sex and the Single Girl*), publisher (*Cosmopolitan*), born Green Forest, AR, Feb 18, 1922.

Aldo Ceccato, 72, conductor, born Milan, Italy, Feb 18, 1934.

Matt Dillon, 42, actor (*My Bodyguard, Drugstore Cowboy*), born Westchester, NY, Feb 18, 1964.

Milos Forman, 74, film director (Oscars for *Amadeus* and *One Flew Over the Cuckoo's Nest*), born Caslaz, Czechoslovakia, Feb 18, 1932.

John Hughes, 56, producer, director, screenwriter (*Sixteen Candles, Pretty in Pink, Home Alone*), born Lansing, MI, Feb 18, 1950.

George Kennedy, 79, actor (Oscar for *Cool Hand Luke*; "The Blue Knight"), born New York, NY, Feb 18, 1927.

Allan Melvin, 83, actor ("The Brady Bunch," "All in the Family"), born Kansas City, MO, Feb 18, 1923.

Toni Morrison, 75, Nobel Prize–winning novelist (*Beloved, Jazz, Tar Baby, Sula*), born Lorain, OH, Feb 18, 1931.

Juice Newton, 54, singer (*Juice, Quiet Lives*), born Judy Cohen at Virginia Beach, VA, Feb 18, 1952.

Yoko Ono, 73, artist, musician, widow of John Lennon, born Tokyo, Japan, Feb 18, 1933.

Jack Palance, 86, actor (Oscar for *City Slickers; Shane*, "Bronk"), born Lattimer, PA, Feb 18, 1920.

Molly Ringwald, 38, actress (*Sixteen Candles, The Breakfast Club, Pretty in Pink*), born Roseville, CA, Feb 18, 1968.

Greta Scacchi, 46, actress (*White Mischief, Presumed Innocent*), born Milan, Italy, Feb 18, 1960.

Cybill Shepherd, 56, actress (*The Last Picture Show*, "Moonlighting," "Cybill"), born Memphis, TN, Feb 18, 1950.

John Travolta, 51, actor (*Pulp Fiction, Urban Cowboy, Saturday Night Fever*, "Welcome Back Kotter"), born Englewood, NJ, Feb 18, 1955.

John William Warner, 79, US Senator (R, Virginia), born Washington, DC, Feb 18, 1927.

Vanna White, 49, TV personality ("Wheel of Fortune"), born Conway, SC, Feb 18, 1957.

FEBRUARY 19 — SUNDAY

Day 50 — 315 Remaining

BOLLINGEN PRIZE: ANNIVERSARY. Feb 19, 1949. On this date, the first Bollingen Prize for poetry was awarded to Ezra Pound for his collection *The Pisan Cantos*. This first award was steeped in controversy because Pound had been charged with treason after making pro-Fascist broadcasts in Italy during World War II.

COPERNICUS, NICOLAUS: BIRTH ANNIVERSARY. Feb 19, 1473. Polish astronomer and priest who revolutionized scientific thought with what came to be called the Copernican theory that placed the sun instead of the Earth at the center of our planetary system. Born at Torun, Poland, he died at East Prussia, May 24, 1543.

DAYTONA 500 NASCAR NEXTEL CUP SERIES RACE. Feb 19. Daytona International Speedway, Daytona Beach, FL. 48th annual running of the "world's greatest race." For info: Daytona Intl Speedway, PO Box 2801, Daytona Beach, FL 32120-2801. Phone: (800) PIT-SHOP. Web: www.daytonainternationalspeedway.com.

THE FEMININE MYSTIQUE PUBLISHED: ANNIVERSARY. Feb 19, 1963. Betty Friedan published *The Feminine Mystique* this month, a call for women to achieve their full potential. Her book generated enormous response and revitalized the women's movement in the US.

February **2006**	S	M	T	W	T	F	S
				1	2	3	4
	5	6	7	8	9	10	11
	12	13	14	15	16	17	18
	19	20	21	22	23	24	25
	26	27	28				

GARRICK, DAVID: BIRTH ANNIVERSARY. Feb 19, 1717. English actor, theater manager and playwright. Born at Hereford, England; died Jan 20, 1779, at London.

INTERNATIONAL FRIENDSHIP WEEK. Feb 19–25. Promotion of international friendship and the international language Esperanto. For complete information, send $5 to cover expense of printing, handling and postage. Annually, the last full week in February. For info: Dr. Stanley Drake, Pres Emeritus, Intl Society of Friendship & Good Will, 8592 Roswell Rd, Ste 251, Atlanta, GA 30350-1867. Phone: (678) 795-1362. E-mail: sjdrake@bellsouth.net. Web: www.friendshipandgoodwill.org.

JAPANESE INTERNMENT: ANNIVERSARY. Feb 19, 1942. As a result of President Franklin Roosevelt's Executive Order 9066, some 110,000 Japanese Americans living in coastal Pacific areas were placed in concentration camps in remote areas of Arizona, Arkansas, inland California, Colorado, Idaho, Utah and Wyoming. The interned Japanese Americans (two-thirds were US citizens) lost an estimated $400 million in property. They were allowed to return to their homes Jan 2, 1945.

KNIGHTS OF PYTHIAS: FOUNDING ANNIVERSARY. Feb 19, 1864. The social and fraternal order of the Knights of Pythias was founded at Washington, DC.

NATIONAL ENGINEERS WEEK. Feb 19–25. The 55th annual observance, cosponsored by more than 140 national engineering societies, federal agencies and major corporations, will feature classroom programs in elementary and secondary schools throughout the US, hands-on activities in science centers and museums, engineering workplace tours, the Future City Competition (see www.furturecity.org) and the annual "Introduce a Girl to Engineering Day." Chair for 2006 is the Society of Women Engineers. For more info call: Natl Engineers Week Headquarters, 1420 King St, Alexandria, VA 22314. Phone: (703) 684-2852. E-mail: eweek@nspe.org. Web: www.eweek.org.

US LANDING ON IWO JIMA: ANNIVERSARY. Feb 19, 1945. Beginning at dawn, the landing of 30,000 American troops took place on the barren 12-square-mile island of Iwo Jima. Initially there was little resistance, but 21,500 Japanese stood ready underground to fight to the last man to protect massive strategic fortifications linked by tunnels. See also: "Iwo Jima Day: Anniversary" (Feb 23).

BIRTHDAYS TODAY

Prince Andrew, 46, Duke of York, born London, England, Feb 19, 1960.

Justine Bateman, 40, actress ("Family Ties," "Men Behaving Badly"), born Rye, NY, Feb 19, 1966.

Lou Christie, 63, singer ("Lightnin' Strikes Again"), born Glen Willard, PA, Feb 19, 1943.

Jeff Daniels, 51, actor (*The Purple Rose of Cairo, Something Wild, Dumb and Dumber*), born Chelsea, MI, Feb 19, 1955.

Benicio Del Toro, 39, actor (Oscar for *Traffic; 21 Grams, The Usual Suspects*), born Santurce, Puerto Rico, Feb 19, 1967.

Jonathan Lethem, 42, author (*Motherless Brooklyn, Fortress of Solitude*), born Brooklyn, NY, Feb 19, 1964.

Stephen Nichols, 55, actor ("Days of Our Lives," "General Hospital"), born Cincinnati, OH, Feb 19, 1951.

Smokey Robinson, 66, singer, songwriter ("Cruisin'," "Being with You"), born William Robinson, Jr at Detroit, MI, Feb 19, 1940.

Seal, 43, singer-songwriter ("Prayer for the Dying"), born Sealhenry Samuel at London, England, Feb 19, 1963.

Andrew Shue, 39, actor ("Melrose Place"), born South Orange, NJ, Feb 19, 1967.

Amy Tan, 54, author (*The Joy Luck Club*), born Oakland, CA, Feb 19, 1952.

FEBRUARY 20 — MONDAY

Day 51 — 314 Remaining

ADAMS, ANSEL: BIRTH ANNIVERSARY. Feb 20, 1902. American photographer, known for his photographs of Yosemite National Park, born at San Francisco, CA. Adams died at Monterey, CA, Apr 22, 1984.

CANADA: FAMILY DAY IN ALBERTA. Feb 20. Annually, the third Monday in February.

CLOSEST APPROACH OF A COMET TO EARTH: ANNIVERSARY. Feb 20, 1491. An unnamed comet came within 860,000 miles (.0094 AU) of Earth on this date in 1491. By comparison, the closest approach that Halley's Comet made to Earth was on Apr 10, 837 AD, at 3 million miles.

DOUGLASS, FREDERICK: DEATH ANNIVERSARY. Feb 20, 1895. American journalist, orator and antislavery leader. Born at Tuckahoe, MD, probably in February 1817. Died at Anacostia Heights, DC. His original name before his escape from slavery was Frederick Augustus Washington Bailey.

GEORGE WASHINGTON BIRTHDAY CELEBRATION PARADE. Feb 20. Alexandria, VA. Nation's largest parade honoring George Washington, staged by his hometown. Floats, bands, antique cars, equestrian and military units and bagpipers. Route through historic district. Sponsor: George Washington Birthday Celebration Committee. Free admission. Est attendance: 50,000. For info: Alexandria Conv and Visitors Assoc, 421 King St, Ste 300, Alexandria, VA 22314. Phone: (703) 838-5005. Fax: (703) 838-4683. Web: www.FunSideofthePotomac.com.

JEFFERSON, JOSEPH: BIRTH ANNIVERSARY. Feb 20, 1829. Distinguished American actor, born at Philadelphia, PA, in a family of actors. Jefferson made his stage debut at the age of three in Kotzebue's *Pizarro*. After many successes, his search for a character both humorous and pathetic centered on Rip Van Winkle, about whom he wrote a short play. Later revised by Dion Boucicault, the play opened with Jefferson in the leading role at London, England, in 1865 and was an immediate success. Rip Van Winkle became the signature role for which he was known. Jefferson died at Palm Beach, FL, Apr 23, 1905. He is remembered each year in Chicago when the Joseph Jefferson (Jeff) Awards are presented to recognize excellence in theatrical productions.

NORTHERN HEMISPHERE HOODIE-HOO DAY. Feb 20. At high noon (local time) citizens are asked to go outdoors and yell "Hoodie-Hoo" to chase away winter and make ready for spring, one month away. [©2003 by WH.] For info: Thomas & Ruth Roy, Wellcat Holidays, 2418 Long Ln, Lebanon, PA 17046. Phone: (717) 279-0184. E-mail: info@wellcat.com. Web: www.wellcat.com.

PISCES, THE FISH. Feb 20–Mar 20. In the astronomical/astrological zodiac, which divides the sun's apparent orbit into 12 segments, the period Feb 20–Mar 20 is identified, traditionally, as the sun sign of Pisces, the Fish. The ruling planet is Neptune.

PRESCOTT, WILLIAM: BIRTH ANNIVERSARY. Feb 20, 1726. American Revolutionary soldier, born at Groton, MA. Died at Pepperell, MA, Oct 13, 1795. Credited with the order "Don't fire until you see the whites of their eyes," at the Battle of Bunker Hill, June 17, 1775.

PRESIDENTS' DAY. Feb 20. Presidents' Day observes the birthdays of George Washington (Feb 22) and Abraham Lincoln (Feb 12). With the adoption of the Monday Holiday Law (which moved the observance of George Washington's birthday from Feb 22 to the third Monday in February), some of the specific significance of the event was lost and added impetus was given to the popular description of that holiday as Presidents' Day. Present usage often regards Presidents' Day as a day to honor all former presidents of the US, though the federal holiday is still Washington's Birthday. Annually, the third Monday in February. See also "Washington, George: Birthday Observance" below.

PRESIDENTS' DAY AT ASH LAWN-HIGHLAND. Feb 20. Ash Lawn-Highland, Charlottesville, VA. Special events to honor our nation's presidents, at the home of President James Monroe. For info: Ash Lawn-Highland, 1000 James Monroe Pkwy, Charlotteville, VA 22902. Phone: (434) 293-9539. Fax: (434) 293-8000. E-mail: info@ashlawnhighland.org. Web: www.ashlawnhighland.org.

PRESIDENTS' DAY: LIVE FROM DELAWARE STREET. Feb 20. Indianapolis, IN. Visit President Benjamin Harrison Home and listen to the conversations and gossip of the day as you enter each room and speak with family members and household staff, whose roles are re-created by actors. For info: PR Dept, President Benjamin Harrison Home, 1230 N Delaware St, Indianapolis, IN 46202. Phone: (317) 631-1888. Fax: (317) 632-5488. Web: www.pbhh.org.

SPACE MILESTONE: *FRIENDSHIP 7* (US): FIRST AMERICAN TO ORBIT EARTH. Feb 20, 1962. John Herschel Glenn, Jr, became the first American, and the third person, to orbit Earth. Aboard the capsule *Friendship 7*, he made three orbits of Earth. Spacecraft was *Mercury-Atlas 6*. In 1998 the 77-year-old Glenn went into space again on the space shuttle *Discovery* to test the effects of aging.

SPACE MILESTONE: *MIR* SPACE STATION (USSR): 20th ANNIVERSARY. Feb 20, 1986. A "third-generation" orbiting space station, *Mir* (Peace), was launched without crew from the Baikonur space center at Leninsk, Kazakhstan. Believed to be 40 feet long, weigh 47 tons and have six docking ports. Both Russian and American crews have used the station. After many equipment failures and financial problems, the Russians took *Mir* out of service Mar 23, 2001. See also: "Space Milestone: *Mir* Abandoned (USSR)" (Mar 23).

STOCK EXCHANGE HOLIDAY (WASHINGTON'S BIRTHDAY). Feb 20 (observed). The holiday schedules for the various exchanges are subject to change if relevant rules, regulations or exchange policies are revised. If you have questions, phone: American Stock Exchange (212) 306-1000, Chicago Board of Trade (312) 435-3500, Chicago Board of Options Exchange (312) 786-5600, NASDAQ Stock Market (646) 441-5200, New York Stock Exchange (212) 656-3000, Pacific Stock Exchange (415) 393-4000, Philadelphia Stock Exchange (215) 496-5000.

STOTZ, CARL E.: BIRTH ANNIVERSARY. Feb 20, 1920. Carl E. Stotz shaped the summers of millions of kids as the founder of Little League baseball. Born at Williamsport, PA, he organized the first three-team league there in 1939. Died at Williamsport, June 4, 1992.

WASHINGTON, GEORGE: BIRTHDAY OBSERVANCE (LEGAL HOLIDAY). Feb 20. Legal public holiday (Public Law 90–363 sets Washington's birthday observance on the third Monday in February each year—applicable to federal employees and to the District of Columbia). Observed in all states. See also: "Washington, George: Birth Anniversary" (Feb 22).

BIRTHDAYS TODAY

Edward Albert, 55, actor (*Butterflies Are Free, Terminal Entry, Guarding Tess*), born Los Angeles, CA, Feb 20, 1951.

Robert Altman, 81, film director (*M*A*S*H, Nashville*), born Kansas City, MO, Feb 20, 1925.

Charles Barkley, 43, former basketball player, born Leeds, AL, Feb 20, 1963.

Brenda Blethyn, 60, actress (*Secrets and Lies, A River Runs Through It*), born Ramsgate, England, Feb 20, 1946.

Cindy Crawford, 40, model, actress, born DeKalb, IL, Feb 20, 1966.

Sandy Duncan, 60, actress (*Funny Face*, "The Hogan Family," *Peter Pan*), born Henderson, TX, Feb 20, 1946.

Ron Eldard, 43, actor ("Men Behaving Badly," "ER"), born Long Island, NY, Feb 20, 1963.

Philip Anthony (Phil) Esposito, 64, hockey executive, former coach and Hall of Fame hockey player, born Sault Ste. Marie, ON, Canada, Feb 20, 1942.

Stephon Marbury, 29, basketball player, born New York, NY, Feb 20, 1977.

Mitch McConnell, 64, US Senator (R, Kentucky), born Colbert County, AL, Feb 20, 1942.

Jennifer O'Neill, 58, actress (*The Summer of '42*, "Cover-Up"), born Rio de Janeiro, Brazil, Feb 20, 1948.

Sidney Poitier, 79, actor (*In the Heat of the Night*; Oscar for *Lilies of the Field*), born Miami, FL, Feb 20, 1927.

Buffy Sainte-Marie, 65, Native-American folksinger ("Mister Can't You See," "He's an Indian Cowboy in the Rodeo"), born Craven, SK, Canada, Feb 20, 1941.

Patty Hearst Shaw, 52, newspaper heiress who was kidnapped by radical group Symbionese Liberation Army; actress (*Cry-Baby*), born San Francisco, CA, Feb 20, 1954.

French Stewart, 42, actor ("3rd Rock from the Sun"), born Albuquerque, NM, Feb 20, 1964.

Peter Strauss, 59, actor ("Rich Man, Poor Man," *Soldier Blue*), born Croton-on-Hudson, NY, Feb 20, 1947.

Lili Taylor, 39, actress ("Six Feet Under," *I Shot Andy Warhol, Ransom, Mystic Pizza*), born Glencoe, IL, Feb 20, 1967.

Robert William (Bobby) Unser, 72, auto racer, born Albuquerque, NM, Feb 20, 1934.

Gloria Vanderbilt, 82, fashion designer, artist, born New York, NY, Feb 20, 1924.

James Wilby, 48, actor (*DreamChild, Howard's End*), born Rangoon, Burma, Feb 20, 1958.

Nancy Wilson, 69, singer ("Yesterday's Love Songs/Today's Blues"), born Chillicothe, OH, Feb 20, 1937.

February *2006*	S	M	T	W	T	F	S
				1	2	3	4
	5	6	7	8	9	10	11
	12	13	14	15	16	17	18
	19	20	21	22	23	24	25
	26	27	28				

FEBRUARY 21 — TUESDAY
Day 52 — 313 Remaining

BANGLADESH: MARTYRS DAY. Feb 21. National mourning day in memory of martyrs of the Bengali Language Movement in 1952. Mourners gather at the Azimpur graveyard.

BATTLE OF VERDUN: 90th ANNIVERSARY. Feb 21, 1916. The German High Command launched an offensive on the Western Front at Verdun, France, which became WWI's single longest battle. An estimated one million men were killed, decimating both the German and French armies, before the battle ended on Dec 15, 1916.

BOMBECK, ERMA: BIRTH ANNIVERSARY. Feb 21, 1927. Humorist and writer, born at Dayton, OH. Authored many books, including *The Grass Is Always Greener Over the Septic Tank*. Bombeck died at San Francisco, CA, Apr 22, 1996.

CIA AGENT ARRESTED AS SPY: ANNIVERSARY. Feb 21, 1994. Aldrich Hazen Ames and his wife, Maria del Rosario Casas Ames, were arrested on charges they had spied for the Soviet Union beginning in 1985 and had continued to spy for Russia after the Soviet collapse in 1991. Ames had worked as a counterintelligence officer for the CIA at its headquarters at Langley, VA. Prosecutors said that the pair had been paid about $2.5 million for their activities and were probably responsible for the deaths of at least 10 CIA agents whom Ames had identified for the Soviets. The government considered this to be one of the most serious spy cases ever uncovered in the US. On Apr 28 Aldrich Ames was sentenced to life in prison. Rosario Ames was sentenced to a 63-month prison term in return for her husband's promise to cooperate with authorities.

MALCOLM X ASSASSINATED: ANNIVERSARY. Feb 21, 1965. Just as he began a speech to his newly formed Organization of Afro-American Unity, black activist leader Malcolm X was gunned down by several men standing among the 400-plus crowd at the Audubon Ballroom in Harlem, New York City. The assassination occurred barely a week after Malcolm X's Queens home was firebombed. Three men were convicted of the murder in 1966 and sentenced to life in prison. See also: "Malcolm X: Birth Anniversary" (May 19).

MOON PHASE: LAST QUARTER. Feb 21. Moon enters Last Quarter phase at 2:17 AM, EST.

***NEW YORKER* PUBLISHED: ANNIVERSARY.** Feb 21, 1925. First issue of the magazine published on this date.

NIXON'S TRIP TO CHINA: ANNIVERSARY. Feb 21, 1972. Richard Nixon became the first US president to visit any country not diplomatically recognized by the US when he went to the People's Republic of China for meetings with Chairman Mao Tse-Tung and Premier Chou En-lai. Nixon arrived at Peking on this date and departed China on Feb 28. The "Shanghai Communique" was issued Feb 27. See also: "Shanghai Communique Anniversary" (Feb 27).

PALMER, ALICE FREEMAN: BIRTH ANNIVERSARY. Feb 21, 1855. Born at Colesville, NY, Alice Freeman Palmer became president of Wellesley College at the age of 27. Under her leadership the school grew into one of the leading women's colleges. She was also instrumental in bringing the women's school Radcliffe College into its association with Harvard University. One of the organizers of the American Association of University Women, she served as its president for two terms. She was appointed the first dean of women at the University of Chicago when it opened in 1892. Palmer died Dec 6, 1902, at Paris.

SANDINO, CESAR AUGUSTO: ASSASSINATION ANNIVERSARY. Feb 21, 1934. Nicaraguan guerrilla leader after whom the Sandinistas of the present day are named. Sandino, born in 1893 (exact date unknown), was murdered along with his brother and several aides at Managua on Feb 21, 1934. He and his followers had eluded the occupying force of US Marines as well as the Nicaraguan National Guard from 1927 until 1933. Regarded by the US as an outlaw and a bandit, he is revered as a martyred patriot hero by many Nicaraguans. His successful resistance and the resulting widespread anti-US feeling were largely responsible for inauguration of a US counteraction—the "Good Neighbor Policy"—toward Latin American nations during the administration of President Franklin D. Roosevelt.

SIMONE, NINA: BIRTH ANNIVERSARY. Feb 21, 1933. The blues and jazz singer was born Eunice Waymon at Tryon, NC. Initially determined to become a concert pianist, Simone instead found a career as a singer of a wide range of musical genres where she could put her uniquely raw and emotional voice on display. She was an ardent supporter of the 1950s and '60s civil rights movement. She died at Carry-le-Rouet, France, on Apr 21, 2003.

SINGLE-TASKING DAY. Feb 21. Multitasking has proven ineffective. Today, do only one thing at a time without feeling guilty. For info: Thesesa Gabriel, PO Box 338, Columbus, NE 68602. Phone: (402) 564-2593. E-mail: trgabe@megavision.com.

UNITED NATIONS: INTERNATIONAL MOTHER LANGUAGE DAY. Feb 21. To help raise awareness among all peoples of the distinct and enduring value of their languages. Annually, on Feb 21. For info: United Nations, Dept of Public Info, New York, NY 10017. Web: www.un.org.

WASHINGTON MONUMENT DEDICATED: ANNIVERSARY. Feb 21, 1885. Monument to the first president was dedicated at Washington, DC.

BIRTHDAYS TODAY

Christopher Atkins, 45, actor ("Dallas," *The Blue Lagoon*), born Rye, NY, Feb 21, 1961.

William Baldwin, 43, actor (*Born on the Fourth of July, Backdraft*), born Massapequa, NY, Feb 21, 1963.

Mary Chapin Carpenter, 48, singer, musician ("Stones in the Road," "Hometown Girl"), born Princeton, NJ, Feb 21, 1958.

Charlotte Church, 20, singer (*Voice of an Angel*), born Cardiff, Wales, Feb 21, 1986.

Tyne Daly, 59, actress ("Judging Amy," Emmy for "Cagney and Lacey"; *Gypsy*), born Madison, WI, Feb 21, 1947.

Christine Ebersole, 53, actress (*Richie Rich, Amadeus*, "Saturday Night Live"), born Chicago, IL, Feb 21, 1953.

David Geffen, 62, record company executive (Geffen Records), born New York, NY, Feb 21, 1944.

Hubert de Givenchy, 79, fashion designer, born Beauvais, France, Feb 21, 1927.

Kelsey Grammer, 51, actor ("Cheers," "Frasier"), born St. Thomas, US Virgin Islands, Feb 21, 1955.

Jennifer Love Hewitt, 27, actress ("Party of Five," "Time of My Life"), born Waco, TX, Feb 21, 1979.

Gary Lockwood, 69, actor (*Splendor in the Grass; 2001: A Space Odyssey*), born Van Nuys, CA, Feb 21, 1937.

Rue McClanahan, 72, actress ("Maude," "The Golden Girls"), born Healdton, OK, Feb 21, 1934.

William Petersen, 53, actor ("C.S.I.," *Manhunter, To Live and Die in LA*), born Evanston, IL, Feb 21, 1953.

Olympia J. Snowe, 59, US Senator (R, Maine), born Augusta, ME, Feb 21, 1947.

FEBRUARY 22 — WEDNESDAY
Day 53 — 312 Remaining

BADEN-POWELL, ROBERT: BIRTH ANNIVERSARY. Feb 22, 1857. British army officer who founded the Boy Scouts and Girl Guides. Born at London, England, he died at Kenya, Africa, Jan 8, 1941.

BIG 12 MEN'S AND WOMEN'S SWIMMING AND DIVING CHAMPIONSHIPS. Feb 22–25. Mizzou Aquatics Center, Columbia, MO. Est attendance: 3,000. For info: Big 12 Conference, 2201 Stemmons Frwy, 28th Fl, Dallas, TX 75207. Phone: (214) 742-1212. Fax: (214) 753-0145. Web: www.big12 sports.com.

CARNIVAL DE PONCE. Feb 22–28. Ponce, PR. Carnival, artisans, parade with floats and colorfully dressed people with papier-mâché masks (vejigantes). Annually, the week before Ash Wednesday. Est attendance: 100,000. For info: Vangie Rivera, Director, Culture and Tourism Office, Municipality of Ponce, PO Box 331709, Ponce, PR 00733-1709. Phone: (787) 841-8044. Fax: (787) 259-1316. E-mail: turponce@coqui.net. Web: ponce web.org.

FLORIDA ACQUIRED BY US: ANNIVERSARY. Feb 22, 1819. Secretary of State John Quincy Adams signed the Florida Purchase Treaty under which Spain ceded Florida to the US. As payment, the US assumed $5 million of claims by US citizens against Spain. Florida became a state in 1845.

INCONVENIENCE YOURSELF DAY. Feb 22. A day to think about others and look for ways to inconvenience yourself while making the lives of others better/easier. Annually, the fourth Wednesday in February. For info: Julie Thompson, 8255 W Sunrise Blvd, #179, Plantation, FL 33322. Phone: (954) 693-4604. Fax: (954) 370-0083. E-mail: julie@inconvenienceyourself.com. Web: www.inconvenienceyourself.com.

IT HAPPENED ONE NIGHT FILM RELEASE: ANNIVERSARY. Feb 22, 1934. Frank Capra's romantic screwball comedy, starring Claudette Colbert as a spoiled runaway heiress and Clark Gable as a cocky reporter on to a good story, was the first film to sweep all the major-category Academy Awards, winning Best Picture, Best Director, Best Actor, Best Actress and Best Screenplay. (A scene in which Clark Gable leans on a fence munching a carrot inspired the Warner Bros. animation team when they were creating Bugs Bunny.)

LOWELL, JAMES RUSSELL: BIRTH ANNIVERSARY. Feb 22, 1819. American essayist, poet and diplomat. Born at Cambridge, MA, he died there Aug 12, 1891.

MILLAY, EDNA ST. VINCENT: BIRTH ANNIVERSARY. Feb 22, 1892. American poet ("My candle burns at both ends . . ."), born at Rockland, ME. She died Oct 19, 1950, at Austerlitz, NY.

MILLS, JOHN: BIRTH ANNIVERSARY. Feb 22, 1908. Popular actor, born at North Elmham, England, who played stalwart, Everyman heroes. His career ranged from 1932 to 2004, and his memorable films included *In Which We Serve* (1942), *Great Expectations* (1946), *Tunes of Glory* (1960) and *Ryan's Daughter* (1970)—for which he received a Best Supporting Actor Oscar. Mills was knighted in 1976. He died Apr 23, 2005, at Denham, England.

MIRACLE ON ICE: US HOCKEY TEAM DEFEATS USSR: ANNIVERSARY. Feb 22, 1980. The US Olympic hockey team upset the team from the Soviet Union, 4–3, at the Lake Placid Winter Games to earn a victory often called the "Miracle on Ice." Led by coach Herb Brooks, the Americans went on to defeat Finland two days later and win the gold medal.

MONTGOMERY BOYCOTT ARRESTS: 50th ANNIVERSARY. Feb 22, 1956. On Feb 20 white city leaders of Montgomery, AL, issued an ultimatum to black organizers of the three-month-old Montgomery bus boycott. They said if the boycott ended immediately there would be "no retaliation whatsoever." If it did not end, it was made clear they would begin arresting black leaders. Two days later, 80 well-known boycotters, including Rosa Parks, Martin Luther King, Jr and E.D. Nixon marched to the sheriff's office in the county courthouse, where they gave themselves up for arrest. They were booked, fingerprinted and photographed. The next day the story was carried by newspapers all over the world.

SAINT LUCIA: INDEPENDENCE DAY. Feb 22. National holiday. Commemorates independence of the island in the West Indies from Britain in 1979.

SCHOPENHAUER, ARTHUR: BIRTH ANNIVERSARY. Feb 22, 1788. Philosopher and author, born at Danzig, Germany, and died at Frankfurt am Main, Germany, Sept 21, 1860. Generally regarded as a misanthrope, the never-married Schopenhauer wrote in 1819, "To marry is to halve your rights and double your duties."

UI LIONEL HAMPTON JAZZ FESTIVAL. Feb 22–25. University of Idaho, Moscow, ID. Each year, college, high school, junior high school and elementary school vocal and instrumental jazz ensembles come from all over the US to compete in the festival and attend concerts and clinics given by the world's greatest jazz artists. Annually, Wednesday–Saturday the last full week of February. Est attendance: 40,000. For info: Dr. Lynn J. Skinner, Exec Dir, UI Lionel Hampton Jazz Fest, PO Box 444257, Moscow, ID 83844-4257. Phone: (208) 885-6765. Fax: (208) 885-6513. E-mail: jazzinfo@uidaho.edu.

WADLOW, ROBERT PERSHING: BIRTH ANNIVERSARY. Feb 22, 1918. Tallest man in recorded history, born at Alton, IL. Though only 9 lbs at birth, by age 10 Wadlow already stood over 6 feet tall and weighed 210 lbs. When Wadlow died at age 22, he was a remarkable 8 feet 11.1 inches tall, 490 lbs. His gentle, friendly manner in the face of constant public attention earned him the name "Gentle Giant." Wadlow died July 15, 1940, at Manistee, MI, of complications resulting from a foot infection.

WASHINGTON, GEORGE: BIRTH ANNIVERSARY. Feb 22, 1732. First president of the US ("First in war, first in peace and first in the hearts of his countrymen" in the words of Henry "Light-Horse Harry" Lee). Born at Westmoreland County, VA, Feb 22, 1732 (New Style). However, the Julian (Old Style) calendar was still in use in the colonies when he was born and the year began in March, so the date on the calendar when he was born was Feb 11, 1731. He died at Mount Vernon, VA, Dec 14, 1799. See also: "Washington, George: Birthday Observance (Legal Holiday)" (Feb 20).

WASHINGTON BOAT SHOW. Feb 22–26. The New Washington Convention Center, Washington, DC. Biggest indoor boat show in the mid-Atlantic region: 400+ boats—from express cruisers to motor yachts to dinghies. Also hundreds of booths with every possible accessory, from electronics and foul-weather gear to marinas and destinations. For info: Dee Stafford, Washington Boat Show, 6017 Tower Ct, Alexandria, VA 22304. Phone: (703) 823-7960. E-mail: tjsevents@aol.com.

WOOLWORTHS FIRST OPENED: ANNIVERSARY. Feb 22, 1879. First chain store, Woolworths, opened at Utica, NY. In 1997 the closing of the chain was announced.

BIRTHDAYS TODAY

Amy Strum Alcott, 50, golfer, born Kansas City, MO, Feb 22, 1956.

George Lee (Sparky) Anderson, 72, Hall of Fame baseball manager and player, born Bridgewater, SD, Feb 22, 1934.

Drew Barrymore, 31, actress (*Charlie's Angels, E.T. The Extra-Terrestrial*), born Los Angeles, CA, Feb 22, 1975.

February 2006	S	M	T	W	T	F	S
				1	2	3	4
	5	6	7	8	9	10	11
	12	13	14	15	16	17	18
	19	20	21	22	23	24	25
	26	27	28				

Michael Te Pei Chang, 34, former tennis player, born Hoboken, NJ, Feb 22, 1972.

Jonathan Demme, 62, director (*Silence of the Lambs*), born Centre, MD, Feb 22, 1944.

Paul Dooley, 78, actor (*Slap Shot, Breaking Away, The Player*), born Parkersburg, WV, Feb 22, 1928.

Julius Winfield ("Dr. J") Erving, 56, Hall of Fame basketball player, born Roosevelt, NY, Feb 22, 1950.

William Frist, 54, US Senator (R, Tennessee), born Nashville, TN, Feb 22, 1952.

Steve Irwin, 44, naturalist, television personality ("The Crocodile Hunter"), born Victoria, Australia, Feb 22, 1962.

Edward Moore (Ted) Kennedy, 74, US Senator (D, Massachusetts), born Boston, MA, Feb 22, 1932.

Kyle MacLachlan, 47, actor ("Twin Peaks," *Blue Velvet, The Flintstones*), born Yakima, WA, Feb 22, 1959.

Miou-Miou, 56, actress (*Entre Nous, La Lectrice*), born Paris, France, Feb 22, 1950.

Jeri Ryan, 38, actress ("Star Trek: Voyager"), born Munich, Germany, Feb 22, 1968.

Kazuhiro Sasaki, 38, baseball player, born Sendai, Japan, Feb 22, 1968.

Vijay Singh, 43, golfer, born Lautoka, Fiji, Feb 22, 1963.

Julie Walters, 56, actress (*Calendar Girls, Billy Elliot, Educating Rita*), born Birmingham, England, Feb 22, 1950.

Jayson Williams, 38, former basketball player, born Ritter, SC, Feb 22, 1968.

FEBRUARY 23 — THURSDAY
Day 54 — 311 Remaining

AMERICAN BIRKEBEINER RACE. Feb 23–25. Cable to Hayward, WI. The largest and most prestigious cross-country ski marathon in North America attracts more than 5,000 participants for the 51k trek. Starting off with the Birkie, skiers of the 23k Kortelopet finish at Telemark Lodge. A Nordic festival of related ski events and activities begins Feb 23. Est attendance: 18,000. For info: American Birkebeiner Ski Foundation, Inc, Box 911, Hayward, WI 54843. Phone: (715) 634-5025. Fax: (715) 634-5663. E-mail: birkie@birkie.com. Web: www.birkie.com.

BIG TEN MEN'S SWIMMING AND DIVING CHAMPIONSHIPS. Feb 23–25. Indiana University, Bloomington, IN. Est attendance: 2,000. For info: Big Ten Conference, 1500 W Higgins Rd, Park Ridge, IL 60068-6300. Phone: (847) 696-1010. Fax: (847) 696-1110. Web: www.bigten.org.

BRUNEI DARUSSALAM: NATIONAL DAY. Feb 23. National holiday observed in Brunei Darussalam, located on the island of Borneo. Commemorates independence from Britain, Feb 23, 1984.

CANADA: MONTREAL HUNTING, FISHING & CAMPING SHOW. Feb 23–26. Place Bonaventure, Montreal, QC. Manufacturers representatives, distributors and retailers of the outdoors, including camping, fishing, hunting, marine (fishing boats, canoes, kayaks, etc), tourism offices, outfitters (lodges), RVs and entertainment. Est attendance: 37,000. For info: Canadian National Sportsmen's Shows, 30 Village Centre Pl, Mississauga, ON, Canada L4Z 1V9. Phone: (905) 361-2677 or (888) 695-2677. Fax: (905) 361-2678. Web: www.sportshows.ca or www.saloncamping.ca.

CANADA: OTTAWA BOAT, SPORTSMEN'S AND COTTAGE SHOW. Feb 23–26. Civic Centre, Coliseum and Aberdeen Pavilion, Lansdowne Park, Ottawa, ON. Boating, hunting, fishing and archery information. Products displayed: powerboats, runabouts, inflatables, personal watercraft, fishing tackle, travel info, cottage products, canoes, kayaks, camping and family entertainment. Est attendance: 30,000. For info: Canadian Natl Sportsmen's Shows, 703 Evans Ave, Ste 202, Toronto, ON, Canada M9C 5E9. Phone: (416) 695-0311. Fax: (416) 695-0381. Web: www.sportshows.ca.

CANADA: YUKON SOURDOUGH RENDEZVOUS. Feb 23–26. Whitehorse, YT. Mad trapper competitions, flour packing, beard-growing contests, old-time fiddle show, sourdough pancake breakfasts, can-can dancers, talent shows, etc. Also, many family-oriented activities. Visitors welcome to participate. Est attendance: 20,000. For info: Yukon Sourdough Rendezvous, Box 31721, Whitehorse, YT, Canada Y1A 6L3. Phone: (867) 667-2148. Fax: (867) 668-6755. E-mail: ysr@polarcom.com. Web: www.yukonrendezvous.com.

CHARRO DAYS FIESTA. Feb 23–26. Brownsville, TX. Two Nations—Twin Cultures, a true example of international harmony and cooperation between Brownsville, Texas, and Matamoros, Mexico. Starts the last Thursday in February. Colorful celebration of the charro horsemen of Mexico, men of great riding skills. Dances, parades and carnival. Est attendance: 150,000. For info: Charro Days, Inc, PO Box 3247, Brownsville, TX 78523-3247. Phone: (956) 542-4245. Fax: (956) 542-6771. E-mail: info@charrodaysfiesta.com. Web: www.charrodaysfiesta.com.

CURLING IS COOL DAY. Feb 23. Offer up a worldwide embrace for an Olympic sport the entire family can play! If you don't get it, you ain't cool. [©2003 by WH.] For info: Thomas & Ruth Roy, Wellcat Holidays, 2418 Long Lane, Lebanon, PA 17046. Phone: (717) 279-0184. Fax: (240) 332-4886. E-mail: info@wellcat.com. Web: www.wellcat.com.

DIESEL ENGINE PATENTED: ANNIVERSARY. Feb 23, 1893. Rudolf Diesel received a patent in Germany for the engine that bears his name. The diesel engine burns fuel oil rather than gasoline and is used in trucks and heavy industrial machinery.

Du BOIS, W.E.B.: BIRTH ANNIVERSARY. Feb 23, 1868. William Edward Burghardt Du Bois, American educator and leader of the movement for black equality. Born at Great Barrington, MA, he died at Accra, Ghana, Aug 27, 1963. "The cost of liberty," he wrote in 1909, "is less than the price of repression."

FIRST CLONING OF AN ADULT ANIMAL: ANNIVERSARY. Feb 23, 1997. Researchers in Scotland announced the first cloning of an adult animal, a lamb they named Dolly with a genetic makeup identical to that of her mother. This led to worldwide speculation about the possibility of human cloning. On Mar 4, President Clinton imposed a ban on the federal funding of human cloning research.

GROUND WAR AGAINST IRAQ BEGINS: 15th ANNIVERSARY. Feb 23, 1991. After an air campaign lasting slightly more than a month, Allied forces launched the ground offensive against Iraqi forces as part of Desert Storm. The relentless air attacks had devastated troops and targets in both Iraq and Kuwait. A world that had watched and anticipated "the mother of all battles" was surprised at the swiftness and ease with which Allied forces were able to subdue Iraqi forces in 100 hours.

GUYANA: ANNIVERSARY OF REPUBLIC. Feb 23. National holiday. Guyana in South America became a republic within the British Commonwealth, Feb 23, 1970.

HANDEL, GEORGE FREDERICK: BIRTH ANNIVERSARY. Feb 23, 1685 (OS). Born at Halle, Saxony, Germany. Handel and Bach, born the same year, were perhaps the greatest masters of Baroque music. Handel's most frequently performed work is the oratorio *Messiah*, which was first heard in 1742. He died at London, England, Apr 14, 1759. See also: "Premiere of Handel's *Messiah*: Anniversary" (Apr 13).

INTRODUCE A GIRL TO ENGINEERING DAY. Feb 23. 7th annual. During National Engineers Week, the engineering community is asked to mobilize women and men engineers to reach more than one million girls and encourage them to pursue the fields that lead to engineering careers. Website includes links for teachers. For info: Natl Engineers Week Headquarters, 1420 King St, Alexandria, VA 22314. Phone: (703) 684-2852. E-mail: eweek@nspe.org. Web: www.eweek.org/site/News/Eweek/girlsday.shtml.

ITALY: FEAST OF THE INCAPPUCCIATI. Feb 23. Gradoli (near Viterbo). On the Thursday before Ash Wednesday the members of the Confraternity of Purgatory make the rounds of the town dressed in traditional hooded robes, bearing a banner and walking to the beat of a drum. They stop at every house to collect foodstuffs in the name of the souls in purgatory; the food is then served at the banquet on Ash Wednesday.

IWO JIMA DAY: ANNIVERSARY. Feb 23, 1945. Anniversary of the day that the US flag was raised on the Pacific island of Iwo Jima by US Marines. Almost 20,000 American soldiers lost their lives before the island was finally taken from the Japanese on Mar 16, 1945.

JAPANESE ATTACK US MAINLAND: ANNIVERSARY. Feb 23, 1942. In the first attack on the US mainland, a Japanese submarine fired 25 shells at an oil refinery at the edge of Ellwood Oil Field 12 miles west of Santa Barbara, CA. One shell made a direct hit of the rigging, causing minor damage. President Roosevelt was giving a fireside chat at the time of the attack.

NATIONAL CHILI DAY. Feb 23. A day to recognize chili as an American staple and to celebrate our love for a great bowl of red—especially in the cold winter months. Annually, the last Thursday in February. For info: Doug Welsh, Hard Times Café, 9731 Ironmaster Dr, Burke, VA 22015. Phone: (703) 608-7725. Fax: (703) 455-2530. E-mail: dougwelsh@aol.com.

PEPYS, SAMUEL: BIRTH ANNIVERSARY. Feb 23, 1633 (OS). Diarist, born at London, England. Wrote Pepys in his diary (Mar 10, 1666): "The truth is, I do indulge myself a little the more in pleasure, knowing that this is the proper age of my life to do it; and, out of my observation that most men that do thrive in the world do forget to take pleasure during the time that they are getting their estate, but reserve that till they have got one, and then it is too late for them to enjoy it." Died at London, England, May 26, 1703 (OS).

RUSSIA: ARMY AND NAVY DAY. Feb 23. Also known as Defender of the Fatherland Day. Wreaths are laid at the Tomb of the Unknown Soldier. Commemorates a 1918 clash with German troops that went down in history as the birthday of the Red Army.

SHIRER, WILLIAM L.: BIRTH ANNIVERSARY. Feb 23, 1904. American journalist and author William L. Shirer was born at Chicago, IL. As the European correspondent from 1927 to 1934 for the *Chicago Tribune* he became a friend of Mohandas K. Gandhi, the leader of India's independence movement. As a result of this he published *Gandhi: A Memoir* in 1980. His best-known book is *The Rise and Fall of the Third Reich* (1960), in which he used his experiences in Europe with the *New York Herald Tribune*, the Universal News Service and CBS Radio. He died Dec 28, 1993, at Boston, MA.

TAYLOR, GEORGE: 225th DEATH ANNIVERSARY. Feb 23, 1781. Signer of the Declaration of Independence. Born 1716 at British Isles (exact date unknown). Died at Easton, PA.

WILLARD, EMMA HART: BIRTH ANNIVERSARY. Feb 23, 1787. Pioneer in higher education for women, born at Berlin, CT. Intent on improving educational opportunities for women, she sent her *Plan for Improving Female Education* to the governor of New York. In it she described her ideal for a girls' school, including the instruction usually offered the girls of her day (music, drawing, penmanship, dancing), as well as adding religious and moral instruction, natural philosophy and domestic science. The New York legislature granted her a charter for the Waterford Academy for Young Ladies. The school later moved to Troy, NY, where it was first named the Troy Female Seminary and later the Emma Willard School. She assisted in the founding of a teachers' training school for girls at Athens, Greece, in 1832. She began the Willard Association for the Mutual Improvement of Female Teachers in 1837, and she authored several textbooks on geography, history and astronomy. Willard died at Troy, NY, Apr 15, 1870.

BIRTHDAYS TODAY

Roberto Martin Antonio (Bobby) Bonilla, 43, former baseball player, born New York, NY, Feb 23, 1963.
Sylvia Chase, 68, newscaster, born Northfield, MN, Feb 23, 1938.
Peter Fonda, 67, actor (*Easy Rider, Ulee's Gold*), born New York, NY, Feb 23, 1939.
Edward Lee ("Too Tall") Jones, 55, former football player and boxer, born Jackson, TN, Feb 23, 1951.
Howard Jones, 51, singer (*Dream into Action*), born Southampton, England, Feb 23, 1955.
Patricia Richardson, 55, actress ("Double Trouble," "Home Improvement"), born Bethesda, MD, Feb 23, 1951.
Johnny Winter, 62, singer, musician, born John Dawson III at Beaumont, TX, Feb 23, 1944.

FEBRUARY 24 — FRIDAY
Day 55 — 310 Remaining

BIG 12 MEN'S AND WOMEN'S INDOOR TRACK CHAMPIONSHIPS. Feb 24–25. Devaney Sports Center, Lincoln, NE. Est attendance: 3,000. For info: Big 12 Conference, 2201 Stemmons Freeway, 28th Fl, Dallas, TX 75207. Phone: (214) 774-1212. Fax: (214) 753-0145. Web: www.big12sports.com.

ESTONIA: INDEPENDENCE DAY. Feb 24. National holiday. Commemorates declaration of independence from Soviet Union in 1918. Independence was brief, however; Estonia was again under Soviet control until 1991.

GREGORIAN CALENDAR DAY: ANNIVERSARY. Feb 24, 1582. Pope Gregory XIII, enlisting the expertise of distinguished astronomers and mathematicians, issued a bull correcting the Julian calendar that was then 10 days in error. The correction was a minor one, changing the rule about leap years. The new calendar named for him, the Gregorian calendar, became effective Oct 4, 1582, in most Catholic countries, in 1752 in Britain and the American colonies, in 1918 in Russia and in 1923 in Greece. It is the most widely used calendar in the world today. See also: "Calendar Adjustment Day: Anniversary" (Sept 2) and "Gregorian Calendar Adjustment: Anniversary" (Oct 4).

GRIMM, WILHELM CARL: BIRTH ANNIVERSARY. Feb 24, 1786. Mythologist and author, born at Hanau, Germany. Best remembered for *Grimm's Fairy Tales,* in collaboration with his brother, Jacob. Died at Berlin, Germany, Dec 16, 1859. See also: "Grimm, Jacob: Birth Anniversary" (Jan 4).

HADASSAH: ANNIVERSARY. Feb 24, 1912. Twelve members of the Daughters of Zion Study Circle met at New York City under the leadership of Henrietta Szold. A constitution was drafted to expand the study group into a national organization called Hadassah (Hebrew for "myrtle" and the biblical name of Queen Esther) to foster Jewish education in America and to create public health nursing and nurses training in Palestine. Hadassah is now the largest women's volunteer organization in the US with 1,500 chapters rooted in health care delivery, education and vocational training, children's villages and services and land reclamation in Israel.

HOMER, WINSLOW: BIRTH ANNIVERSARY. Feb 24, 1836. American artist, born at Boston, MA. Noted for the realism of his work, from the Civil War reportage to the highly regarded rugged outdoor scenes of hunting and fishing. Died at his home at Prout's Neck, ME, Sept 29, 1910.

JOHNSON IMPEACHMENT PROCEEDINGS: ANNIVERSARY. Feb 24, 1867. In a showdown over reconstruction policy following the Civil War, the House of Representatives voted to impeach President Andrew Johnson. During the two years following the end of the war, the Republican-controlled Congress had sought to severely punish the South. Congress passed the Reconstruction Act that divided the South into five military districts headed by officers who were to take their orders from General Grant, the head of the army, instead of from President Johnson. In addition, Congress passed the Tenure of Office Act, which required Senate approval before Johnson could remove any official whose appointment was originally approved by the Senate. Johnson vetoed this act but the veto was overridden by Congress. To test the constitutionality of the act, Johnson dismissed Secretary of War Edwin Stanton, triggering the impeachment vote. On Mar 5, 1868, the Senate convened as a court to hear the charges against the president. The Senate vote of 35–19 fell one vote short of the two-thirds majority needed for impeachment.

LONGHORN WORLD CHAMPIONSHIP RODEO. Feb 24–26. Lawrence-Joel Veterans Memorial Coliseum, Winston-Salem, NC. 35th annual. More than 200 cowboys and cowgirls compete in six professional contests ranging from bronc riding to big, bad BONUS bull riding! Free beginners horsemanship clinic 40 minutes before performances. Qualifying rodeo for Longhorn's Championship Finals Rodeo in Murfreesboro, TN. Featuring colorful opening and pageantry. Est attendance: 16,000. For info: W. Bruce Lehrke, Pres, Longhorn World Chmpshp Rodeo, Inc, PO Box 70159, Nashville, TN 37207. Phone: (615) 876-1016. Fax: (615) 876-4685. E-mail: info@longhornrodeo.com. Web: www.longhornrodeo.com.

LOST DUTCHMAN DAYS. Feb 24–26. Apache Junction, AZ. Arts and crafts show and sale. Three-day rodeo competiton, dance, carnival, parade, business vendors in celebration of the legend of the Superstition Mountains and the Lost Dutchman Mine. Free musical entertainment. Annually, the last full weekend in February. Est attendance: 30,000. For info: Apache Junction Chamber of Commerce, PO Box 1747, Apache Junction, AZ 85217-1747. Phone: (800) 252-3141. Fax: (480) 982-3234. Web: www.apachejunctioncoc.com.

February 2006	S	M	T	W	T	F	S
				1	2	3	4
	5	6	7	8	9	10	11
	12	13	14	15	16	17	18
	19	20	21	22	23	24	25
	26	27	28				

MARDI GRAS FIESTA TROPICALE. Feb 24–28. Hollywood, FL. A New Orleans-style music and food festival featuring music of New Orleans, a Taste of New Orleans, evening parades with bead throws, Arti Gras for Kids Quarter and a season of Fiesta balls presented by individual Mardi Gras krewes. Est attendance: 32,500. For info: Dave Erickson, Fiesta Tropicale of Hollywood, Inc., PO Box 510, Hollywood, FL 33022-0510. Phone: (954) 926-3377. E-mail: david@mardigrasfiesta.com. Web: www.mardigrasfiesta.com.

MEXICO: FLAG DAY. Feb 24. *El Día de la Bandera.* National holiday honoring the Mexican flag, which was created in 1821 after Mexico achieved independence.

***THE NEW YORK TIMES* TRAVEL SHOW.** Feb 24–26. The Javits Convention Center, New York, NY. 3rd annual. "The Ultimate Travel Destination" features 5,000 travel professionals and 500 exhibitors. For the trade and general public, who will learn about the world of travel opportunities open to them. Includes seminars and family entertainment. Est attendance: 28,000. For info: Betsy Areddy, The New York Times. Phone: (212) 556-7633. E-mail: aredde@nytimes.com. Web: www.nytimes.com/travelshow.

NEWPORT SEAFOOD AND WINE FESTIVAL. Feb 24–26. Newport, OR. Central coastal festival featuring seafood and wines from Oregon, Washington, California and Idaho. Arts and crafts exhibits as well. Est attendance: 15,000. For info: Philip K. Hutchinson, Executive Director, Greater Newport Chamber of Commerce, 555 SW Coast Hwy, Newport, OR 97365. Phone: (541) 265-5883. Fax: (541) 265-5589. Web: www.newportchamber.org/swf.

NIMITZ, CHESTER: BIRTH ANNIVERSARY. Feb 24, 1885. Commander of all Allied naval, land and air forces in the southwest Pacific during a portion of WWII, Admiral Chester William Nimitz was born at Fredericksburg, TX. During the final assault on Japan in April 1945, Nimitz resumed command of the entire naval operation in the Pacific which he had shared with MacArthur for some time. Nimitz was one of the signers of the Japanese document of surrender Sept 2, 1945, aboard the USS *Missouri* in Tokyo Bay. Nimitz died Feb 20, 1966, at Treasure Island, San Francisco Bay, CA. The USS *Nimitz* was named in his honor.

OREGON SHAKESPEARE FESTIVAL. Feb 24–Oct 28. An eight-month season of 11 plays by Shakespeare, classic and contemporary playwrights on three stages: the outdoor Elizabethan Stage, the versatile Angus Bowmer Theatre and the intimate New Theatre. Est attendance: 370,000. For info: Oregon Shakespeare Festival, Box 158, Ashland, OR 97520. Phone: (541) 482-4331. Web: www.osfashland.org.

TEXAS COWBOY POETRY GATHERING. Feb 24–26. Sul Ross State University, Alpine, TX. 20th annual. Cowboys from Texas and neighboring states gather for poetry readings and music. Est attendance: 2,000. For info: Betty Tanksley, Texas Cowboy Poetry Gathering Committee, PO Box 395, Alpine, TX 79831. Phone: (432) 364-2490. E-mail: btanksley@overland.net. Web: www.cowboy-poetry.org.

WAGNER, HONUS: BIRTH ANNIVERSARY. Feb 24, 1874. American baseball great, born John Peter Wagner at Carnegie, PA. Nicknamed the "Flying Dutchman," Wagner was among the first five players elected to the Baseball Hall of Fame in 1936. Died at Carnegie, Dec 6, 1955.

WELLS FARGO BANK CUP. Feb 24–26. Winter Park Resort, Winter Park, CO. Elite disabled skiers compete head to head on a dual giant slalom course in the World Disabled Invitational. Amateur races, silent auction and charity dinners benefit the National Sports Center for the Disabled. Est attendance: 10,000. For info: National Sports Center for the Disabled, 1801 Bryant St, Ste 1500, Denver, CO 80204. Phone: (970) 726-1540. E-mail: info@nscd.org. Web: www.nscd.org.

FEBRUARY 25 — SATURDAY
Day 56 — 309 Remaining

BACKUS, JIM: BIRTH ANNIVERSARY. Feb 25, 1913. Born James Gilmore Backus at Cleveland, OH. An actor whose career encompassed radio, television and film, Jim Backus is most remembered as the voice behind the near-sighted bumbler, Mr Magoo, and for his portrayal of Thurston Howell III on the popular TV show "Gilligan's Island." Backus died July 3, 1989, at Santa Monica, CA.

BASCOM, "TEXAS ROSE": BIRTH ANNIVERSARY. Feb 25, 1922. A Cherokee-Choctaw Indian born at Covington County, MS, Rose Flynt married rodeo cowboy Earl Bascom and learned trick roping, becoming known as the greatest female trick roper in the world. She appeared on stage, in movies and on early TV. She toured with the USO during WWII, performing at every military base and military hospital in the US. After the war she entertained servicemen stationed overseas. In 1981 she was inducted into the National Cowgirl Hall of Fame (located at Hereford, TX). She died Sept 23, 1993, at St. George, UT.

BIG TEN MEN'S INDOOR TRACK AND FIELD CHAMPIONSHIPS. Feb 25–26. University of Iowa, Iowa City, IA. Est attendance: 1,500. For info: Big Ten Conference, 1500 W Higgins Rd, Park Ridge, IL 60068-6300. Phone: (847) 696-1010. Fax: (847) 696-1110. Web: www.bigten.org.

BIG TEN WOMEN'S INDOOR TRACK AND FIELD CHAMPIONSHIPS. Feb 25–26. Site TBA. Est attendance: 1,500. For info: Big Ten Conference, 1500 W Higgins Rd, Park Ridge, IL 60068-6300. Phone: (847) 696-1010. Fax: (847) 696-1110. Web: www.bigten.org.

BRAZIL: CARNIVAL. Feb 25–28. Especially in Rio de Janeiro, this carnival is said to be one of the last great folk festivals and the big annual event in the life of Brazilians. Begins on Saturday night before Ash Wednesday and continues through Shrove Tuesday.

BURGESS, ANTHONY: BIRTH ANNIVERSARY. Feb 25, 1917. Author (*A Clockwork Orange*). Born at Manchester, England. Died Nov 25, 1993, at London.

CARUSO, ENRICO: BIRTH ANNIVERSARY. Feb 25, 1873. Operatic tenor of legendary voice and fame, born at Naples, Italy. Died there Aug 2, 1921.

CLAM CHOWDER COOKOFF. Feb 25. Santa Cruz Beach Boardwalk, Santa Cruz, CA. Who makes the world's greatest clam chowder? Up to 60 teams compete to find out. Prizes for best booth encourage wacky costumes and elaborate props! Separate categories for restaurants, media and individuals, Boston and Manhattan style chowder. Free admission. Est attendance: 15,000. For info: Kate McGuire, Communications Mgr, Santa Cruz Beach Boardwalk, 400 Beach St, Santa Cruz, CA 95060-5491. Phone: (831) 423-5590. Fax: (831) 460-3336. E-mail: publicity@scseaside.com. Web: www.beachboardwalk.com.

CLAY BECOMES HEAVYWEIGHT CHAMP: ANNIVERSARY. Feb 25, 1964. Twenty-two-year-old Cassius Clay (later Muhammad Ali) became world heavyweight boxing champion by defeating Sonny Liston. At the height of his athletic career Ali was well known for both his fighting ability and personal style. His most famous saying was "I am the greatest!" Ali is the only fighter to win the heavyweight fighting title three separate times. He defended that title nine times.

FENWICK, MILLICENT HAMMOND: BIRTH ANNIVERSARY. Feb 25, 1910. Former fashion model, author, member NJ General Assembly and US congresswoman, Millicent Fenwick was born at New York, NY. A champion of liberal causes, Fenwick pointed to her sponsorship of the resolution creating the commission to monitor the 1975 Helsinki accords on human rights as her proudest achievement. She fought for civil rights, peace in Vietnam, aid for the poor, reduction of military programs, gun control and restrictions on capital punishment. Fenwick, the inspiration for Garry Trudeau's "Doonesbury" character Lacey Davenport, died at Bernardsville, NJ, Sept 16, 1992.

FIRST NATIONAL BANK CHARTERED BY CONGRESS: ANNIVERSARY. Feb 25, 1791. The First Bank of the US at Philadelphia, PA, was chartered. Proposed as a national bank by Alexander Hamilton, it lost its charter in 1811. The Second Bank of the US received a charter in 1816 which expired in 1836. Since that time, the US has had no central bank. Central banking functions are carried out by the Federal Reserve System, established in 1913. See also: "Federal Reserve System: Anniversary" (Dec 23).

FREER, CHARLES LANG: 150th BIRTH ANNIVERSARY. Feb 25, 1856. American art collector who built and endowed the Freer Gallery, which was presented to the Smithsonian Institution in 1906. Born at Kingston, NY, he died at New York, NY, Sept 25, 1919.

FRENCH WEST INDIES: CARNIVAL. Feb 25–Mar 1. Martinique. For five days ending on Ash Wednesday, business comes to a halt. Streets spill over with parties and parades. A Carnival Queen is elected. On Dimanche Gras, or Fat Sunday, revelers dressed as red devils parade in the streets. King Carnival is "buried" on Ash Wednesday.

HARRISON, GEORGE: BIRTH ANNIVERSARY. Feb 25, 1945. Musician and singer born Liverpool, England, Harrison was the lead guitarist and co-songwriter for The Beatles, alongside John Lennon, Paul McCartney and Ringo Starr. The band is considered to be the most influential rock-and-roll group of all time. Harrison is credited with introducing Eastern musical styles and instrumentation to Western pop. After the breakup of The Beatles, Harrison embarked on a successful solo career, became an independent film producer (*Time Bandits*) and created one of the first charity rock concerts with his Concert for Bangladesh, which brought relief to flood victims of that country. He died at Los Angeles, CA, on Nov 29, 2001.

HATSUME FAIR. Feb 25–26. Morikami Museum and Japanese Gardens, Delray Beach, FL. Celebrates the coming of spring with demonstrations and performances of Japanese taiko drums, folk dancing, martial arts, plants, orchids and bonsai exhibits. Annually, the last weekend in February. Est attendance: 12,000. For info: Marketing Dept, The Morikami Museum and Japanese Gardens, 4000 Morikami Park Rd, Delray Beach, FL 33446. Phone: (561) 495-0233. Fax: (561) 499-2557. Web: www.morikami.org.

HEBRON MASSACRE: ANNIVERSARY. Feb 25, 1994. An American-born Jewish settler in Hebron, Israel, Baruch Goldstein, opened fire with an assault rifle in a crowded mosque, part of a complex sacred to both Jews and Muslims because it is believed to contain the tomb of Abraham and his wife Sarah. Of the more than 400 Muslims gathered for early morning prayers during the holy month of Ramadan, 29 were killed immediately and 150 were wounded. Others, including Goldstein, were crushed in the panic to flee or during subsequent rioting.

HOME AND GARDEN FESTIVAL. Feb 25–26. Multi-Purpose Events Center, Wichita Falls, TX. More than 100 exhibitors providing seminars and demonstrations, home and garden needs and antiques. Est attendance: 15,000. For info: Wichita Falls CVB, 1000 5th St, Wichita Falls, TX 76301. Phone: (940) 716-5500. Fax: (940) 716-5509. E-mail: MPEC@wf.net. Web: www.wichitafalls.org.

KUWAIT: NATIONAL DAY. Feb 25. National holiday. Commemorates the 1978 accession of King Shaykh Sir 'abdullah Al-Salim al-Sabah.

MALTA: CARNIVAL. Feb 25–28. Valletta. Festival dates from 1535 when Knights of St. John of Jerusalem introduced Carnival at Malta. Dancing (featuring the sword dance, or "Parata," and other national dances), bands, decorated trucks and grotesque masks. Annually, the Saturday through Tuesday before Ash Wednesday.

NEW ENGLAND HOME SHOW. Feb 25–Mar 5. World Trade Center, Boston, MA. 56th annual. The oldest and largest home show of its kind in the region. More than 600 exhibits offer the latest ideas for remodeling and redecorating; the most up-to-date information; and product and creative ideas for both home and garden. Est attendance: 150,000. For info: Laurie Myette, Show Mgr, New England Home Show, 45 Braintree Hill Office Park, Ste 302, Braintree, MA 02184. Phone: (781) 849-0990. Fax: (781) 849-7544. E-mail: lauriemyette@us.dmgworldmedia.com. Web: www.newenglandhomeshows.com.

PAUL BUNYAN SLED DOG RACES, SKIJORING AND MUTT RACES. Feb 25–26. Belt City Fairgrounds, Bemidji, MN. 33rd annual competition. For info: Jane McCollom. Phone: (218) 243-3477. Web: www.paulbunyan.net/sleddograce.

RENOIR, PIERRE AUGUSTE: BIRTH ANNIVERSARY. Feb 25, 1841. Impressionist painter, born at Limoges, France. Renoir's paintings are known for their joy and sensuousness as well as the light techniques he employed in them. In his later years he was crippled by arthritis and would paint with the brush strapped to his hand. He died at Cagnes-sur-Mer, Provence, France, Dec 17, 1919.

February *2006*	S	M	T	W	T	F	S
				1	2	3	4
	5	6	7	8	9	10	11
	12	13	14	15	16	17	18
	19	20	21	22	23	24	25
	26	27	28				

SPACE MILESTONE: *SOYUZ 32* (USSR). Feb 25, 1979. Launched from Baikonur space center in Soviet Central Asia. Cosmonauts Vladimir Lyakhov and Valery Ryumin aboard, docked at *Salyut 6* space station Feb 26. Returned to Earth in *Soyuz 34* after what was then a record 175 days in space Aug 19, 1979.

"YOUR SHOW OF SHOWS" TV PREMIERE: ANNIVERSARY. Feb 25, 1950. Sid Caesar and Imogene Coca starred in the NBC 90-minute variety program along with Carl Reiner and Howard Morris. The show included monologues, improvisations, parodies, pantomimes and sketches of varying length. Some of its writers were Mel Tolkin, Lucille Kallen, Mel Brooks, Larry Gelbart, Neil Simon and Woody Allen.

BIRTHDAYS TODAY

Sean Astin, 35, actor (the *Lord of the Rings* trilogy, *Rudy, Courage Under Fire*), born Santa Monica, CA, Feb 25, 1971.
Diane Baker, 68, actress (*Silence of the Lambs*), born Hollywood, CA, Feb 25, 1938.
Tom Courtenay, 69, actor (*The Dresser, The Loneliness of the Long Distance Runner, Otley*), born Hull, England, Feb 25, 1937.
Larry Gelbart, 78, writer, producer ("M*A*S*H"), born Chicago, IL, Feb 25, 1928.
Karen Grassle, 62, actress ("Little House on the Prairie"), born Berkeley, CA, Feb 25, 1944.
Neil Jordan, 56, director, writer (*The Crying Game, Interview with the Vampire*), born County Sligo, Ireland, Feb 25, 1950.
Tea Leoni, 40, actress (*Jurassic Park III, Deep Impact, Flirting with Disaster*), born New York, NY, Feb 25, 1966.
Sally Jessy Raphael, 63, talk-show host, born Easton, PA, Feb 25, 1943.
Bob Schieffer, 69, TV newscaster, born Austin, TX, Feb 25, 1937.
Josh Wolff, 29, soccer player, born Stone Mountain, GA, Feb 25, 1977.

FEBRUARY 26 — SUNDAY
Day 57 — 308 Remaining

AMERICAN CLUB'S TEDDY BEAR AND DOLL CLASSIC. Feb 26. The American Club, Kohler, WI. The creations of 60 teddy bear artists and doll makers from across the country on display—dolls, bears, accessories, clothes, supplies, gifts and demonstrations. Est attendance: 3,500. For info: The American Club, Highland Dr, Kohler, WI 53044. Phone: (800) 344-2838. Fax: (920) 457-4441. Web: www.destinationkohler.com.

CASH, JOHNNY: BIRTH ANNIVERSARY. Feb 26, 1932. The iconic country music star was born J.R. Cash at Kingsland, AR. His career spanned the 1950s through the year he died, and he recorded more than 1,500 songs, including such hits as "I Walk the Line," "Ring of Fire," "Folsom Prison Blues" and "A Boy Named Sue." He was called the Man in Black because he wore a black long-tailed suit in sympathy for those who suffered. The recipient of numerous awards and honors, Cash died at Nashville, TN, on Sept 12, 2003. Cash and Elvis Presley are the only music stars to be inducted into both the Country Music and Rock and Roll halls of fame.

CODY, WILLIAM FREDERIC "BUFFALO BILL": BIRTH ANNIVERSARY. Feb 26, 1846. American frontiersman born at Scott County, IA, who claimed to have killed more than 4,000 buffaloes. Subject of many heroic Wild West yarns, Cody became successful as a showman, taking his acts across the US and to Europe. Died Jan 10, 1917, at Denver, CO.

COMMUNIST MANIFESTO PUBLISHED: ANNIVERSARY. Feb 26, 1848. Written by Karl Marx and Friedrich Engels on the eve of the revolutions of 1848, the *Manifesto* provided ideas for socialist and communist movements.

DAUMIER, HONORE: BIRTH ANNIVERSARY. Feb 26, 1808. French painter and caricaturist famous for his satirical and comic lithographs. Once spent six months in prison for a caricature of Louis Philippe shown as Gargantua consuming the heavy taxes of the citizens. Born at Marseilles, France, he died Feb 11, 1879, at Volmondois, France.

FASCHING SUNDAY. Feb 26. Germany and Austria. The last Sunday before Lent.

FEDERAL COMMUNICATIONS COMMISSION CREATED: ANNIVERSARY. Feb 26, 1934. President Franklin D. Roosevelt ordered the creation of a Communications Commission, which became the FCC. It was created by Congress June 19, 1934, to oversee communication by radio, wire or cable. TV and satellite communication later became part of its charge.

FOR PETE'S SAKE DAY. Feb 26. A world wonders: after all these years, who is Pete and why do we do or not do things for his sake? [©2003 by WH.] For info: Thomas & Ruth Roy, Wellcat Holidays, 2418 Long Ln, Lebanon, PA 17046. Phone: (717) 279-0184. E-mail: info@wellcat.com. Web: www.wellcat.com.

GLEASON, JACKIE: BIRTH ANNIVERSARY. Feb 26, 1916. American musician, comedian and actor, Herbert John "Jackie" Gleason was born at Brooklyn, NY. Best known for his role as Ralph Kramden in the long-running television series "The Honeymooners." Died at Fort Lauderdale, FL, June 24, 1987.

GRAND CANYON NATIONAL PARK ESTABLISHED: ANNIVERSARY. Feb 26, 1919. By an act of Congress, Grand Canyon National Park was established. An immense gorge cut through the high plateaus of northwest Arizona by the raging Colorado River and covering 1,218,375 acres, Grand Canyon National Park is considered one of the most spectacular natural phenomena in the world.

HUGO, VICTOR: BIRTH ANNIVERSARY. Feb 26, 1802. One of the most popular 19th-century authors, born at Besançon, France. His most well-known work was the novel *Les Misérables* and his most famous character was Quasimodo, the Hunchback of Notre Dame. "An invasion of armies can be resisted," Hugo wrote in 1852, "but not an idea whose time has come." Died at Paris, May 22, 1885, and more than two million people thronged to his state funeral.

ITALY: CARNIVAL WEEK. Feb 26–Mar 4. Milan. Carnival week is held according to local tradition, with shows and festive events for children on Tuesday and Thursday. Parades of floats, figures in the costume of local folk characters Meneghin and Cecca, parties and more traditional events are held on Saturday. Annually, the Sunday–Saturday of Ash Wednesday week.

JOE CAIN PROCESSION. Feb 26. Mobile, AL. 40th year. Led by Slacabamorinico IV for the 21st time, it honors the man who revived the Mardi Gras in Mobile in 1866 following the War Between the States. Annually, the Sunday before Shrove Tuesday. Est attendance: 100,000. For info: The Rev Wayne Dean, Sr, VP, Joe Cain Society, 1064 Palmetto St, Mobile, AL 36604-3041. Phone: (251) 432-3960. E-mail: revchief1@peoplepc.com.

NATIONAL EATING DISORDERS AWARENESS WEEK. Feb 26–Mar 4. NEDAW provides opportunities for eating disorders organizations, mental health professionals, families and concerned individuals around the world to join together to distribute information and plan events relating to eating disorders. For info: National Eating Disorders Association, 603 Stewart St, Ste 803, Seattle, WA 98101. Phone: (206) 382-3587. E-mail: info@NationalEatingDisorders.org. Web: www.NationalEatingDisorders.org.

NATIONAL PANCAKE WEEK. Feb 26–Mar 4. Traditional celebration surrounding Shrove, or Pancake, Tuesday to recognize the history and continuing popularity of pancakes. For info: Lori Jones, Bisquick Baking Mix, General Mills, Inc, #1 General Mills Blvd, Minneapolis, MN 55426. Phone/fax: (763) 293-3962. E-mail: lori.jones@genmills.com.

ORTHODOX MEATFARE SUNDAY. Feb 26. Meatfare Sunday begins Meatfare Week, a time of abstaining from meat in preparation for Lent. Some Orthodox communities call this Butterweek.

RANDALL, TONY: BIRTH ANNIVERSARY. Feb 26, 1920. Born Leonard Rosenberg at Tulsa, OK, actor Tony Randall's career spanned five decades. He was a successful film actor, starring in 1957's *Will Success Spoil Rock Hunter?* and 1959's *Pillow Talk*, and performed extensively on the stage. He launched the National Actors Theatre, a company dedicated to performing classic works of theater. He is perhaps best remembered for his role opposite Jack Klugman in television's "The Odd Couple," playing Felix Unger, the tidy, hypochondriac photographer forced by circumstance to share an apartment with slob sportswriter Oscar Madison. The wildly popular series ran from 1970–75. Randall died at New York, NY, May 17, 2004.

SHROVETIDE. Feb 26–28. The three days before Ash Wednesday: Shrove Sunday, Monday and Tuesday—a time for confession and for festivity before the beginning of Lent.

SPECIAL OLYMPICS MARYLAND WINTER GAMES. Feb 26–28. Wisp Ski Resort, McHenry, MD. More than 200 Special Olympics athletes throughout Maryland compete in alpine, cross-country and modified alpine skiing. The three-day festivities include an elaborate opening and closing ceremony featuring the traditional lighting of the Special Olympics cauldron. The Tubes of Fire Reggae Fest and the Deep Creek Dunk are fund-raising events that kick off all festivities. For info: Betsy Jiron, Special Olympics Maryland, 513 Progress Dr, Ste P, Linthicum, MD 21090. Phone: (800) 541-7544 or (410) 789-6677. Fax: (410) 789-5955. E-mail: somdmail@somd.org. Web: www.somd.org.

STRAUSS, LEVI: BIRTH ANNIVERSARY. Feb 26, 1829. Bavarian immigrant Levi Strauss created the world's first pair of jeans—Levi's 501 jeans—for California's gold miners in 1850. Born at Buttenheim, Bavaria, Germany, he died in 1902 at San Francisco.

TELECOMMUTER APPRECIATION WEEK. Feb 26–Mar 4. Sponsored by the American Telecommuting Association, this week is designed to call attention to the benefits of telecommuting: the individual and family as well as the employer and society benefit in a win-win situation. For info: American Telecommuting Assn, 1220 L St, NW, Ste 100, Washington, DC 20005. Phone: (800) ATA-4-YOU. Fax: (800) 465-8638. E-mail: YourATA@knowledgetree.com.

VERCORS, JEAN: BIRTH ANNIVERSARY. Feb 26, 1902. Jean Vercors was the author of the first clandestine novel published during the Nazi occupation of France. Vercors, whose real name was Jean-Marcel de Bruller, was best known for his novel *Silence of the Sea*, which he published with Pierre de Lescure for their publishing house, Les Editions de Minuit, after the Nazis occupied France in 1941. Vercors was born at Paris, France, and died there June 10, 1991.

WORLD TRADE CENTER BOMBING OF 1993: ANNIVERSARY. Feb 26, 1993. A 1,210-lb bomb packed in a van exploded in the underground parking garage of the World Trade Center in New York City, killing six people and injuring more than 1,000 (mostly from smoke inhalation). The powerful blast left a crater 200 feet wide and several stories deep. The cost for damage to the building and disruption of business for the 350 companies with offices in the Center exceeded more than $591 million. Fifteen people—the fundamentalist Muslim cleric Sheik Omar Abdul Rahman and 14 of his followers—were indicted for the bombing. Rahman was given a life sentence and the others received prison terms of up to 240 years each.

	S	M	T	W	T	F	S
February				1	2	3	4
2006	5	6	7	8	9	10	11
	12	13	14	15	16	17	18
	19	20	21	22	23	24	25
	26	27	28				

Erykah Badu, 34, pop singer, born Dallas, TX, Feb 26, 1972.

Fats Domino, 78, singer, songwriter ("Ain't That a Shame," "I'm in Love Again," "Blueberry Hill"), born Antoine Domino at New Orleans, LA, Feb 26, 1928.

Marshall Faulk, 33, football player, born New Orleans, LA, Feb 26, 1973.

Jennifer Grant, 40, actress (*The Evening Star*), born Burbank, CA, Feb 26, 1966.

Betty Hutton, 85, singer, actress (*Annie Get Your Gun*, "The Betty Hutton Show"), born Elizabeth June Thornberg at Battle Creek, MI, Feb 26, 1921.

FEBRUARY 27 — MONDAY
Day 58 — 307 Remaining

ANDERSON, MARIAN: BIRTH ANNIVERSARY. Feb 27, 1897. Born at Philadelphia (some sources say in 1899 or 1902), Anderson's talent was evident at an early age. Her career stonewalled by the prejudice she encountered in the US, she moved to Europe where the magnificence of her voice and her versatility as a performer began to establish her as one of the world's finest contraltos. Preventing Anderson's performance at Washington's Constitution Hall in 1939 on the basis of her color, the Daughters of the American Revolution secured for her the publicity that would lay the foundation for her success in the States. Her performance was rescheduled, and on Apr 9 (Easter Sunday), 75,000 people showed up to hear her sing from the steps of the Lincoln Memorial. The performance was simultaneously broadcast by radio. In 1955 Anderson became the first African American to perform with the New York Metropolitan Opera. The following year President Eisenhower named her a delegate to the United Nations. She performed at President Kennedy's inauguration and in 1963 received the Presidential Medal of Freedom. Anderson died Apr 8, 1993, at Portland, OR.

BENNETT, JOAN: BIRTH ANNIVERSARY. Feb 27, 1910. American film and television actress was born at Palisades, NJ. Her film career was mostly during the 1930s and 1940s in such films as *Father of the Bride* (1950), after which she became a star of the television cult hit "Dark Shadows" (originally broadcast 1966–71). Died Dec 7, 1990, at Scarsdale, NY.

CARNIVAL. Feb 27–28. Period of festivities, feasts, foolishness and gaiety immediately before Lent begins on Ash Wednesday. Ordinarily Carnival includes only Fasching (the Feast of Fools), being the Monday and Tuesday immediately preceding Ash Wednesday. The period of Carnival may also be extended to include longer periods in some areas.

DOMINICAN REPUBLIC: INDEPENDENCE DAY. Feb 27. National Day. Independence gained in 1844 with the withdrawal of Haitians, who had controlled the area for 22 years.

FARRELL, JAMES THOMAS: BIRTH ANNIVERSARY. Feb 27, 1904. American author, novelist and short story writer, best known for his Studs Lonigan trilogy. Born at Chicago, IL, he died at New York, NY, Aug 22, 1979.

FASCHING. Feb 27–28. In Germany and Austria, Fasching, also called Fasnacht, Fasnet or Feast of Fools, is a Shrovetide festival with processions of masked figures, both beautiful and grotesque. Always the two days (Rose Monday and Shrove Tuesday) between Fasching Sunday and Ash Wednesday.

HAMILTON, ALICE: BIRTH ANNIVERSARY. Feb 27, 1869. American pathologist Alice Hamilton was born at New York, NY. She contributed to the workmen's compensation laws by reporting on the dangers to workers of industrial toxic substances. She taught at Harvard Medical School from 1919 until 1935. Hamilton died Sept 22, 1970, at Hadlyme, CT.

ICELAND: BUN DAY. Feb 27. Children invade homes in the morning with colorful sticks and receive gifts of whipped cream buns (on Shrove Monday).

KUWAIT LIBERATED AND 100-HOUR WAR ENDS: 15th ANNIVERSARY. Feb 27, 1991. Allied troops entered Kuwait City, Kuwait, four days after launching a ground offensive. President George Bush declared Kuwait to be liberated and ceased all offensive military operations in the Gulf War. The end of military operations at midnight EST came 100 hours after the beginning of the land attack. Feb 26 is commemorated as Liberation Day in Kuwait.

LONGFELLOW, HENRY WADSWORTH: BIRTH ANNIVERSARY. Feb 27, 1807. American poet and writer, born at Portland, ME. He is best remembered for his classic narrative poems, such as *The Song of Hiawatha, Paul Revere's Ride* and *The Wreck of the Hesperus*. Died at Cambridge, MA, Mar 24, 1882.

MOON PHASE: NEW MOON. Feb 27. Moon enters New Moon phase at 7:31 PM, EST.

PERIGEAN SPRING TIDES. Feb 27. Spring tides, the highest possible tides, occur when New Moon or Full Moon falls within 24 hours of the moment the moon is nearest Earth (perigee) in its monthly orbit. The word *spring* refers not to the season but comes from the German word, *springen*, "to rise up."

READ ME WEEK. Feb 27–Mar 3. National and local celebrities and other volunteers read in classrooms wearing readable clothing with school-appropriate messages. For info: Book 'Em!, 412 Metroplex Dr, Nashville, TN 37211. Phone/fax: (615) 834-7323.

SARAZEN, GENE: BIRTH ANNIVERSARY. Feb 27, 1902. Gene Sarazen, golfer, born Eugenio Saraceni at Harrison, NY. Sarazen was one of the game's greatest players and in his later years one of its greatest goodwill ambassadors. The inventor of the sand wedge, Sarazen was also the first to win the modern grand slam (the Masters, US Open, British Open and PGA), although not in the same year. During the 1935 Masters, he hit one of golf's most famous shots, a four-wood for a double eagle on the par-5 15th hole of the final round. The shot enabled him to tie Craig Wood for the lead and defeat him in a playoff. Sarazen's last shot was the traditional ceremonial tee shot to open the 1999 Masters. Died at Marco Island, FL, May 13, 1999.

SHANGHAI COMMUNIQUE: ANNIVERSARY. Feb 27, 1972. On this day, President Richard Nixon and Premier Chou En-Lai released a joint communique (the Shanghai Communique) after Nixon's weeklong visit to the People's Republic of China. The two nations agreed to work toward normalizing relations. Stopping short of establishing diplomatic relations, this was the first step in that direction. The two nations entered full diplomatic relations on Jan 1, 1979, during the Carter administration.

SHROVE MONDAY. Feb 27. The Monday before Ash Wednesday. In Germany and Austria, this is called Rose Monday.

TERRY, ELLEN: BIRTH ANNIVERSARY. Feb 27, 1847. Popular English actress (Alice) Ellen Terry was born at Coventry, Warwickshire, Feb 27, 1847. Terry was best known for her portrayal of Shakespeare's heroines, especially Portia, and as theatrical partner of English actor Henry Irving. Together she and Irving dominated both the British and American theater of their day. She died at Small Hythe, Kent, July 21, 1928.

TRINIDAD AND TOBAGO: CARNIVAL. Feb 27–28. Port of Spain. Called by islanders "the mother of all carnivals," a special tradition that brings together people from all over the world in an incredibly colorful setting that includes the world's most celebrated calypsonians, steel band players, costume designers and masqueraders. Annually, the two days before Ash Wednesday. For info: Natl Carnival Commission, Corporate Head Office, Queens Park Savannah, Port of Spain, Trinidad, West Indies. Phone: (868) 627-1350. Fax: (868) 623-1391. E-mail: nccmac@tstt.net.tt or tourism-info@tidco.co.tt. Web: www.ncctt.org or www.visittnt.com.

TWENTY-SECOND AMENDMENT TO US CONSTITUTION (TWO-TERM LIMIT): RATIFICATION ANNIVERSARY. Feb 27, 1950. After the four successive presidential terms of Franklin Roosevelt, the 22nd Amendment limited the tenure of presidential office to two terms.

BIRTHDAYS TODAY

Adam Baldwin, 44, actor (*My Bodyguard, Full Metal Jacket*), born Chicago, IL, Feb 27, 1962.

Michael Bolton, 53, singer ("How Am I Supposed to Live Without You"), born New Haven, CT, Feb 27, 1953.

Alan Guth, 59, physicist, born New Brunswick, NJ, Feb 27, 1947.

Howard Hesseman, 66, actor ("WKRP in Cincinnati," "Head of the Class"), born Salem, OR, Feb 27, 1940.

Charlayne Hunter-Gault, 64, broadcast journalist, born Due West, SC, Feb 27, 1942.

Ralph Nader, 72, consumer advocate, lawyer, former presidential candidate, born Winsted, CT, Feb 27, 1934.

Grant Show, 43, actor ("Melrose Place," "Ryan's Hope"), born Detroit, MI, Feb 27, 1963.

Elizabeth Taylor, 74, actress (Oscar for *Who's Afraid of Virginia Woolf?; National Velvet, Cleopatra, Cat on a Hot Tin Roof*), AIDS activist, born London, England, Feb 27, 1932.

Joanne Woodward, 76, actress (Oscar for *The Three Faces of Eve; Mr and Mrs Bridge*), born Thomasville, GA, Feb 27, 1930.

James Ager Worthy, 45, former basketball player, born Gastonia, NC, Feb 27, 1961.

FEBRUARY 28 — TUESDAY

Day 59 — 306 Remaining

BLONDIN, CHARLES: BIRTH ANNIVERSARY. Feb 28, 1824. Daring French acrobat and aerialist (whose real name was Jean François Gravelet), born at St. Omer, France. Especially remembered for his conquest of Niagara Falls on a tightrope. Died Feb 19, 1897, at London. See also: "Charles Blondin's Conquest of Niagara Falls: Anniversary" (June 30).

CANIFF, MILTON: BIRTH ANNIVERSARY. Feb 28, 1907. Creator of the comic strips "Terry and the Pirates®" and "Steve Canyon," Milton Caniff was born at Hillsboro, OH. His strips were noted for their fine draftsmanship and action/adventure story lines. Caniff died Apr 3, 1988, at New York City.

ENGLAND: SHROVETIDE PANCAKE RACE. Feb 28. Olney, Buckinghamshire. The pancake race at Olney has been run since 1445. Competitors must be women over 16 years of age, wearing traditional housewife's costume, including apron and head covering. With a toss and flip of the pancake on the griddle that each must carry, the women dash from the marketplace to the parish church, where the winner receives a kiss from the ringer of the Pancake Bell. Shriving service follows. Annually, on Shrove Tuesday.

FLORAL DESIGN DAY. Feb 28. A day to commemorate floral designing as an art form. Annually, on Feb 28. For info: Dr. Stephen Rittner, Rittners School of Floral Design, 345 Marlborough St, Boston, MA 02115. Phone: (617) 267-3824. E-mail: stevrt @tiac.net. Web: www.floralschool.com.

HECHT, BEN: BIRTH ANNIVERSARY. Feb 28, 1894. In the course of his career Ben Hecht wrote in many genres. His newspaper column, "1001 Afternoons in Chicago," popularized human interest sketches. His play *The Front Page*, written with Charles MacArthur, was a hit on Broadway (1928) and on film (1931). He was a successful reporter and his first novel, *Eric Dorn*, resulted partly from his time reporting from Berlin after World War I. Hecht wrote or cowrote a number of successful movie scripts, including *Notorious* and *Wuthering Heights*. Born at New York City, he died there Apr 18, 1964.

HOUSTON LIVESTOCK SHOW AND RODEO™. Feb 28–Mar 19. Reliant Park, Houston, TX. Livestock show with more than 32,000 entries. Rodeo action and top-name musical entertainment. Est attendance: 1,700,000. For info: Marketing and Presentation Division, Houston Livestock Show and Rodeo, Box 20070, Houston, TX 77225-0070. Phone: (832) 667-1000. Fax: (832) 667-1134. Web: www.rodeohouston.com.

ICELAND: BURSTING DAY. Feb 28. Feasts with salted mutton and thick pea soup. (Shrove Tuesday.)

INTERNATIONAL PANCAKE DAY. Feb 28. Liberal, KS. The 2006 International Pancake Race will be the 57th annual competition between the women of Liberal, KS, and Olney, Buckinghamshire, England. The women, wearing the traditional dress, apron and scarf, run a 415-yard S-shaped course, carrying a pancake in a skillet. Other events taking place include a breakfast, parade, talent show, eating and flipping contests and the Miss Liberal scholarship pageant. Annually on Shrove Tuesday, the day before Ash Wednesday. Est attendance: 5,000. For info: JoAnn Combs, Exec Secy, PO Box 665, Liberal, KS 67905. Phone: (620) 624-6423. Web: www.pancakeday.com.

LYON, MARY: BIRTH ANNIVERSARY. Feb 28, 1797. Mary Lyon, born near Buckland, MA, became a pioneer in the field of higher education for women. She founded Mount Holyoke Seminary (forerunner of Mount Holyoke College) in South Hadley, MA, in 1837 at a time when American women were educated primarily by ministers in classes held in their homes. Mount Holyoke was one of the first permanent women's colleges. Lyon died Mar 5, 1849, at South Hadley.

MARDI GRAS. Feb 28. Celebrated especially at New Orleans, LA, Mobile, AL, and certain Mississippi and Florida cities. Last feast before Lent. Although Mardi Gras (Fat Tuesday, literally) is properly limited to Shrove Tuesday, it has come to be popularly applied to the preceding two weeks of celebration.

"M*A*S*H": THE FINAL EPISODE: ANNIVERSARY. Feb 28, 1983. Concluding a run of 255 episodes, this 2½-hour finale was the most-watched television show at that time—77 per-

cent of the viewing public was tuned in. The show premiered in 1972. See also: "'M*A*S*H' TV Premiere: Anniversary" (Sept 17).

MONTAIGNE, MICHEL DE: BIRTH ANNIVERSARY. Feb 28, 1533. French essayist and philosopher, born at Perigord, France. "And if you have lived a day," he wrote in Book I of his *Essays*, "you have seen everything. One day is equal to all days. There is no other light, no other night. This sun, this moon, these stars, the way they are arranged, all is the very same your ancestors enjoyed and that will entertain your grandchildren. . . ." Died at Montaigne, France, Sept 13, 1592.

NATIONAL TOOTH FAIRY DAY. Feb 28. Why shouldn't the tooth fairy have her own day? Every kid in the country knows about her and every parent is her assistant. Celebrate the hard work she does on the graveyard shift and brush, floss and read books about the tooth fairy in her honor! For info: Katie Davis, PO Box 551, Bedford Hills, NY 10507. Phone/fax: (914) 244-8777. E-mail: katiedavis@katiedavis.com. Web: www.toothfairy day.com.

NATO PLANES DOWN SERB JETS: ANNIVERSARY. Feb 28, 1994. In the first military action by the North Atlantic Treaty Organization (NATO) in the two-year-old Bosnian civil war and the first combat action by NATO in its 45-year history, UN-designated American fighter planes shot down four of six Bosnian Serb jets operating in a no-fly zone.

PACZKI DAY. Feb 28. Food lovers pick this day to enjoy these round, sugar-coated, fruit-filled Polish pre-Lenten pastries, pronounced "poonch-kee," available in bakeries nationwide. Paczki Day coincides with Shrove Tuesday or Fat Tuesday, the day before Ash Wednesday. For info: National Paczki Hotline. Phone: (800) 884-1500.

PALME, OLOF: ASSASSINATION: 20th ANNIVERSARY. Feb 28, 1986. The popular prime minister of Sweden was shot to death as he left a movie theater in Stockholm with his wife. A courageous and dominant figure in Swedish politics, Palme, an aristocrat turned socialist, had earned international respect. On the day of his death he had signed (with five other world leaders) an appeal to the leaders of the United States and the Soviet Union to forgo nuclear testing until the next summit meeting. Born on Jan 30, 1927, Palme was the third European head of government to be assassinated since the beginning of World War II (the others: Prime Minister Armand Calinescu of Romania in 1939 and Prime Minister Luis Carrero Blanco of Spain in 1973).

SAINT OSWALD OF WORCESTER FEAST DAY. Feb 28. Bishop of Worcester, England, from 961, and Archbishop of York from 972. Oswald died Feb 29, 992, but Feb 28 is generally celebrated as his feast day.

SHROVE TUESDAY. Feb 28. Always the day before Ash Wednesday. Sometimes called Pancake Tuesday. This day is a legal holiday in some counties in Florida.

SIEGEL, BUGSY: 100th BIRTH ANNIVERSARY. Feb 28, 1906. The gangster Benjamin "Bugsy" Siegel was born in the Hell's Kitchen section of Brooklyn, NY. He was a contemporary of and in cahoots with Meyer Lansky and Lucky Luciano. Siegel moved to Hollywood, CA, in 1937 to lay low after committing a murder. Expanding on his petty gambling operations, Siegel began to construct a hotel and casino called The Flamingo in remote Las Vegas, NV. The hotel, opened in 1946, was initially a failure, until Lansky and Luciano poured more money into the venture. Siegel was shot and died at his girlfriend Virginia Hill's Hollywood home on June 20, 1947; no one was ever convicted of the murder.

	S	M	T	W	T	F	S
February				1	2	3	4
2006	5	6	7	8	9	10	11
	12	13	14	15	16	17	18
	19	20	21	22	23	24	25
	26	27	28				

SPAY DAY USA. Feb 28. An annual, nationwide campaign to end the tragedy of pet overpopulation by encouraging every humane American to take responsibility for having at least one cat or dog spayed or neutered, be that pet theirs, a neighbor's or a shelter animal. Veterinary clinics, humane societies/shelters, businesses and individuals are encouraged to participate. For info: Doris Day Animal Foundation, Spay Day USA, 227 Massachusetts Ave NE, Ste 100, Washington, DC 20002. Phone: (202) 546-1761. Fax: (202) 546-2193. E-mail: info@ddaf.org. Web: www.spaydayusa.org.

TENNIEL, JOHN: BIRTH ANNIVERSARY. Feb 28, 1820. Illustrator and cartoonist, born at London, England. Best remembered for his illustrations for Lewis Carroll's *Alice's Adventures in Wonderland*. Died at London, Feb 25, 1914.

USS *PRINCETON* EXPLOSION: ANNIVERSARY. Feb 28, 1844. The newly built "war steamer," USS *Princeton*, cruising on the Potomac River with top government officials as its passengers, fired one of its guns (known, ironically, as the "Peacemaker") to demonstrate the latest in naval armament. The gun exploded, killing Abel P. Upshur, secretary of state; Thomas W. Gilmer, secretary of the navy; David Gardiner, of Gardiners Island, NY; and several others. Many were injured. The president of the US, John Tyler, was on board and narrowly escaped death.

BIRTHDAYS TODAY

Svetlana Allilueva, 80, daughter of Joseph Stalin, author (*The Faraway Music*), born Moscow, USSR, Feb 28, 1926.

Mario Gabrielle Andretti, 66, former auto racer, born Montona, Trieste, Italy, Feb 28, 1940.

Charles Durning, 83, actor (*Dog Day Afternoon*, "Evening Shade"), born Highland Falls, NY, Feb 28, 1923.

Frank Gehry, 77, architect, born Toronto, ON, Canada, Feb 28, 1929.

Robert Sean Leonard, 37, actor (*The Manhattan Project, Dead Poets Society*), born Westwood, NJ, Feb 28, 1969.

Eric Lindros, 33, hockey player, born London, ON, Canada, Feb 28, 1973.

Bernadette Peters, 62, singer, actress (*Dames at Sea, Annie Get Your Gun*), born Queens, NY, Feb 28, 1944.

Charles Aaron ("Bubba") Smith, 61, actor, former football player, born Beaumont, TX, Feb 28, 1945.

Jamaal Tinsley, 28, basketball player, born Brooklyn, NY, Feb 28, 1978.

Tommy Tune, 67, actor, singer, dancer (Tony for *My One and Only*; *Will Rogers Follies*, "Dean Martin Presents . . ."), musical theater director, born Wichita Falls, TX, Feb 28, 1939.

John Turturro, 49, actor (*O Brother, Where Art Thou?; Quiz Show*), born Brooklyn, NY, Feb 28, 1957.

MARCH 1 — WEDNESDAY
Day 60 — 305 Remaining

★**AMERICAN RED CROSS MONTH.** Mar 1–31. Presidential Proclamation for Red Cross Month issued each year for March since 1943. Issued as American Red Cross Month since 1987.

THE ARRIVAL OF MARTIN PINZON: ANNIVERSARY. Mar 1, 1493. Martin Alonzo Pinzon (1440–1493), Spanish shipbuilder and navigator (and co-owner of the *Niña* and the *Pinta*), accompanied Christopher Columbus on his first voyage, as commander of the *Pinta*. Storms separated the ships on their return voyage, and the *Pinta* first touched land at Bayona, Spain, where Pinzon gave Europe its first news of the discovery of the New World (before Columbus's landing at Palos). Pinzon's brother, Vicente Yanez Pinzon, was commander of the third caravel of the expedition, the *Niña*.

ARTICLES OF CONFEDERATION RATIFIED: 225th ANNIVERSARY. Mar 1, 1781. This compact made among the original 13 states had been adopted by Congress Nov 15, 1777, and submitted to the states for ratification Nov 17, 1777. Maryland was the last state to approve, Feb 27, 1781, but Congress named Mar 1, 1781, as the day of formal ratification. The Articles of Confederation remained the supreme law of the nation until Mar 4, 1789, when the US Constitution went into effect.

ASH WEDNESDAY. Mar 1. Marks the beginning of Lent. Forty weekdays and six Sundays (Saturday considered a weekday) remain until Easter Sunday. Named for use of ashes in ceremonial penance.

"BELIEVE IT OR NOT" TV PREMIERE: ANNIVERSARY. Mar 1, 1949. The series was originally a radio show based on Robert L. Ripley's comic strips describing curiosities. Both the radio program and the NBC TV show were hosted by Robert Ripley until his death in 1949. Robert St. John became Ripley's successor. ABC re-created the show in 1982 with Jack Palance as host.

BOSNIA AND HERZEGOVINA: INDEPENDENCE DAY. Mar 1. Commemorates independence in 1992.

CRANE WATCH '06. Mar 1–Apr 15. Kearney, NE. "World's Largest Concentration of Cranes." Each spring some 500,000 sandhill cranes (80 percent of the world's population of this species) gather on the Platte River "staging area" during their northward migration. For info: Kearney Visitors Bureau, PO Box

607, Kearney, NE 68848-0607. Phone: (800) 652-9435. Web: www.kearneycoc.org.

ELLISON, RALPH WALDO: BIRTH ANNIVERSARY. Mar 1, 1914. American writer and educator, born at Oklahoma City, OK. Author of the acclaimed novel *Invisible Man* (1952), the story of a young black man's struggle for his own identity in the face of rejection from both whites and blacks. Quickly recognized as a classic of 20th-century literature, it won the National Book Award in 1953. While only one of his novels was published, Ellison published collections of his essays, reviews and stories in *Shadow and Act* (1964) and *Going to the Territory* (1986). He died Apr 16, 1994, at New York City.

FORD CHAMPIONSHIP AT DORAL. Mar 1–5. Doral Golf Resort and Spa, Miami, FL. A PGA Tour golf tournament with a full week of events, including outdoor concerts, celebrity pro-ams and the four-day tournament, which features 144 of the top golfers in the world. More than $10 million raised to date for various South Florida charities. Est attendance: 200,000. For info: South Florida Golf Foundation, 4400 NW 87 Ave, Lodge 8, Miami, FL 33178. Phone: (305) 477-4653. Fax: (305) 477-4914. E-mail: tneville@southfloridagolf.info.

GAINES, WILLIAM M.: BIRTH ANNIVERSARY. Mar 1, 1922. The magazine *Mad*, especially popular in the 1960s and 1970s, was founded and published by William Gaines. Alfred E. Neuman, the loony, freckle-faced mascot of the publication, became a pop-culture hero. The magazine, known for its parodies of movies, comic strips and celebrities as well as its satire of politics and social mores, greatly influenced dozens of humorists. Gaines was born at the Bronx, NY. He died June 3, 1992, at New York City.

HONOR SOCIETY AWARENESS MONTH. Mar 1–31. Promote the students of honor societies and recognize superior scholarship, promote intelligent learning and living and promote equal opportunities for all people. Support the staff, faculty and advisers of honor societies and professional fraternities through the exchange of meaningful ideas, celebration of diversity, understanding and service. For info: Charlin Jones, 6900 N Loop 1604 West, San Antonio, TX 78249. Phone: (210) 458-4155. E-mail: charlin.jones@utsa.edu.

HUMORISTS ARE ARTISTS MONTH (HAAM). Mar 1–31. To recognize the important contributions made by various types of humorists to the high art of living. For info: Lone Star Publications of Humor, 8452 Fredericksburg Rd, PMB 103, San Antonio, TX 78229. E-mail: lspubs@aol.com. Web: members.aol.com/lspubs/lsindex.html.

ICELAND: BEER DAY. Mar 1. Reykjavik. This event began on Mar 1, 1989, when a 75-year-long prohibition of beer was lifted. Features celebrations in pubs and restaurants all over Reykjavik.

INTERNATIONAL IDEAS MONTH. Mar 1–31. Everybody has ideas! Many people need to be encouraged or motivated or need to build skills in order to communicate and get their ideas out in the open for consideration and/or action. This month is dedicated to all ideas—large, small, great, not-so-great, past, current and ideas yet to come. Without constant new ideas, progress and people stagnate. For info: Sylvia Henderson, Springboard Training, 18005 Lafayette Dr, Ste B, Olney, MD 20832-0588. Phone: (301) 260-1538. E-mail: admin@springboardtraining.com. Web: www.springboardtraining.com.

INTERNATIONAL LISTENING AWARENESS MONTH. Mar 1–31. Dedicated to learning more about the impact that listening has on all human activity. To promote the study, development and teaching of effective listening in all settings. For info: James Pratt, PO Box 744, River Falls, WI 54022. Phone: (800) 452-4505 or (715) 425-3377. Fax: (715) 425-9533. E-mail: ilistening@aol.com. Web: www.listen.org.

INTERNATIONAL MIRTH MONTH. Mar 1–31. The merry month of March is set aside to encourage more mirthful moments. Its focus is to show people how to use humor to deal with not-so-funny stuff. Mirth Month was founded by Allen Klein, profes-

	S	M	T	W	T	F	S
March				1	2	3	4
2006	5	6	7	8	9	10	11
	12	13	14	15	16	17	18
	19	20	21	22	23	24	25
	26	27	28	29	30	31	

sional speaker and president of the Association for Applied and Therapeutic Humor (www.aath.org). Free monthly mirth e-mail memo available; request through e-mail listed. For info: Allen Klein, 1034 Page St, San Francisco, CA 94117. Phone: (415) 431-1913. Fax: (415) 431-8600. E-mail: humor@allenklein.com. Web: www.allenklein.com.

★**IRISH-AMERICAN HERITAGE MONTH.** Mar 1–31. Presidential Proclamation called for by House Joint Resolution 401 (PL 103–379).

ITALY: PURGATORY BANQUET. Mar 1. Gradoli (near Viterbo). On Ash Wednesday, gourmands are on hand for the banquet of penitence for the souls in purgatory, held on the premises of the cooperative winery.

JAPAN: OMIZUTORI (WATER-DRAWING FESTIVAL). Mar 1–14. Todaiji, Nara. At midnight, a solemn rite is performed in the flickering light of pine torches. People rush for sparks from the torches, which are believed to have magic power against evil. Most spectacular on the night of Mar 12. The ceremony of drawing water is observed at 2 AM on Mar 13, to the accompaniment of ancient Japanese music.

KOKOSCHKA, OSKAR: BIRTH ANNIVERSARY. Mar 1, 1886. Born at Pochlarn, Austria. Avant-garde artist, playwright, teacher and humanitarian, his work evoked violent reaction. After viewing a 1911 exhibition of Kokoschka's work, the Archduke Franz Ferdinand is reported to have declared, "This man deserves to have every bone in his body broken." Kokoschka's work was featured in a 1937 Nazi exhibit of "Degenerate Art." Died at Montreux, Switzerland, Feb 22, 1980.

KOREA: SAMILJOL or INDEPENDENCE MOVEMENT DAY. Mar 1. Koreans observe the anniversary of the independence movement against Japanese colonial rule in 1919.

LAND MINE BAN: ANNIVERSARY. Mar 1, 1999. A United Nations treaty banning land mines took effect on this date. More than 130 nations signed the treaty; the US, Russia and China did not.

LEARNING DISABILITIES ASSOCIATION OF AMERICA INTERNATIONAL CONFERENCE. Mar 1–4. Hilton New Orleans Riverside, New Orleans, LA. 43rd annual. Est attendance: 2,500. For info: Learning Disabilities Assn of America, 4156 Library Rd, Pittsburgh, PA 15234. Phone: (412) 341-1515. Fax: (412) 344-0224. E-mail: info@ldaamerica.org. Web: www.lda america.org.

LENT. Mar 1–Apr 15. Most Christian churches observe a period of fasting and penitence (40 weekdays and 6 Sundays—Saturday considered a weekday) beginning on Ash Wednesday and ending on the Saturday before Easter. The word *Lent* comes from "lengthen," referring to the lengthening of the day that occurs in the spring.

LINDBERGH KIDNAPPING: ANNIVERSARY. Mar 1, 1932. Twenty-month-old Charles A. Lindbergh, Jr, the son of Charles A. and Anne Morrow Lindbergh, was kidnapped from their home at Hopewell, NJ. Even though the Lindberghs paid a $50,000 ransom, their child's body was found in a wooded area less than five miles from the family home on May 12. Bruno Richard Hauptmann was charged with the murder and kidnapping. He was executed in the electric chair Apr 3, 1936. As a result of the kidnapping and murder of the Lindbergh baby, the Crime Control Act was passed on May 18, 1934. It authorized the death penalty for kidnappers who take their victims across state lines.

MENTAL RETARDATION AWARENESS MONTH. Mar 1–31. To educate the public about the needs of this nation's more than seven million citizens with mental retardation and about ways to prevent retardation. The Arc is a national organization on mental retardation, formerly the Association for Retarded Citizens. For info: The Arc, 1010 Wayne Ave, Ste 650, Silver Spring, MD 20910. Phone: (301) 565-3842. Fax: (301) 565-3542. Web: www.thearc.org.

MILLER, GLENN: BIRTH ANNIVERSARY. Mar 1, 1904. American bandleader and composer (Alton) Glenn Miller was born at Clarinda, IA. He enjoyed great popularity preceding and during World War II. His hit recordings included "Moonlight Serenade," "String of Pearls," "Jersey Bounce" and "Sleepy Lagoon." Major Miller, leader of the US Army Air Force band, disappeared Dec 15, 1944, over the English Channel, on a flight to Paris where he was scheduled to give a show. There were many explanations of his disappearance, but 41 years later, in December 1985, crew members of an aborted RAF bombing said they believed they had seen Miller's plane go down, the victim of bombs being jettisoned by the RAF over the English Channel.

MUSIC IN OUR SCHOOLS MONTH. Mar 1–31. To increase public awareness of the importance of music education as part of a balanced curriculum. Additional information and awareness items are available. For info: MENC: The Natl Assn for Music Education, 1806 Robert Fulton Dr, Reston, VA 20191. Phone: (800) 336-3768. Web: www.menc.org.

NAIA MEN'S AND WOMEN'S SWIMMING AND DIVING NATIONAL CHAMPIONSHIPS. Mar 1–4. St. Peter's Rec-Plex, St. Peters, MO. Individuals compete for the national championship. 26th annual for women; 50th annual for men. For info: Natl Assn of Intercollegiate Athletics, 23500 W 105th St, PO Box 1325, Olathe, KS 66051-1325. Phone: (913) 791-0044. Fax: (913) 791-9555. E-mail: rwiebe@naia.org. Web: www.naia.org.

NATIONAL ATHLETIC TRAINING MONTH. Mar 1–31. This month Certified Athletic Trainers (ATCs) across the nation will be recognized for their dedication and commitment to providing quality health care for athletes at all levels. ATCs are highly educated and can be found everywhere in sports—from high schools to professional ranks. Annually, the month of March. For info: Ellen Satlof, National Athletic Trainers' Assn, 2952 Stemmons Freeway, Dallas, TX 75247. Phone: (214) 637-6282, ext 159. E-mail: ellen@nata.org. Web: www.nata.org.

NATIONAL CAFFEINE AWARENESS MONTH. Mar 1–31. Reduce dependency on caffeine through education. Seminars and other events focus on coffee alternatives and on the harm caffeine causes. For info: CaffeineAwareness.org, PO Box 144, Brooklyn, NY 11224. Phone: (718) 670-7263. E-mail: info@caffeineaware ness.org. Web: www.caffeineawareness.org.

NATIONAL CHRONIC FATIGUE SYNDROME AWARENESS MONTH. Mar 1–31. To educate patients, their families, the public and the medical profession about the nature and impact of CFS, "the Thief of Vitality," and related disorders, as well as to encourage and provide research funding. Annually, the month of March. For info: Natl Chronic Fatigue Syndrome and Fibromyalgia Assn, PO Box 18426, Kansas City, MO 64133. Phone: (816) 313-2000 (24-hour info line). Fax: (816) 524-6782. E-mail: information@ncfsfa.org.

NATIONAL COLLISION AWARENESS MONTH. Mar 1–31. A month of vehicle safety awareness to promote the use of seatbelts, child safety seats, safe driving in inclement weather, obeying speed limits and other safety tips for drivers. For info: Nathan Hostetler, Accurate Autobody, 5550 S Garnett, Ste A, Tulsa, OK 74146. Phone: (918) 270-0100. Fax: (918) 270-0102. E-mail: nathan@44fixit.com.

NATIONAL COLORECTAL CANCER AWARENESS MONTH. Mar 1–31. To generate widespread awareness about colorectal cancer and to encourage people to learn more about how to prevent the disease through a healthy lifestyle and regular screening. Founding partners include the Cancer Research and Prevention Foundation, the American Society for Gastrointestinal Endoscopy, the National Colorectal Cancer Roundtable and The Foundation for Digestive Health and Nutrition. For info: Cancer Research and Prevention Foundation, 1600 Duke St, Alexandria, VA 22314. Phone: (703) 836-4412. Fax: (703) 836-4413. E-mail: Andrea.Untrojb@preventcancer.org. Web: www .preventcancer.org/colorectal.

★**NATIONAL COLORECTAL CANCER AWARENESS MONTH.** Mar 1–31.

NATIONAL CRAFT MONTH. Mar 1–31. Promoting the fun and creativity of hobbies and crafts. For info: National Craft Month, Craft and Hobby Association, PO Box 348, Elmwood Park, NJ 07407. Phone: (201) 794-1133. Fax: (201) 797-0657. E-mail: info@craftandhobby.org. Web: www.craftandhobby.org or www.craftplace.org.

NATIONAL ETHICS AWARENESS MONTH. Mar 1–31. An annual event during March in which ethics organizations and businesses nationwide promote ethics awareness. Ethics is a set of values that consistently guides our behaviors. Today our personal and professional world grows at a pace more rapid than our ability to cope and process the changes, and so looking at how we make our decisions becomes crucial. For info: Patricia Clason, 2437 N Booth St, Milwaukee, WI 53212. Phone: (414) 374-5433. Fax: (414) 374-3997. E-mail: patricia@lightly.com.

NATIONAL EYE DONOR MONTH. Mar 1–31. For info: Eye Bank Association of America, 1015 18th St NW, Ste 1010, Washington, DC 20036. Phone: (202) 775-4999. Web: www.restoresight.org.

NATIONAL FROZEN FOOD MONTH. Mar 1–31. Promotes national awareness of the convenience, quality and nutritional benefits of frozen foods. Annually, the month of March. For info: Julie Henderson, VP Communications, Natl Frozen & Refrigerated Foods Assn, 4755 Linglestown Rd, Ste 300, Harrisburg, PA 17112. Phone: (717) 657-8601. Fax: (717) 657-9862. E-mail: info@nfraweb.org. Web: www.nfraweb.org.

NATIONAL GHOSTWRITERS WEEK. Mar 1–7. Almost 50 percent of all books are written by ghostwriters. This week honors those people who do the work but don't get the credit. One way to celebrate is to do something nice for someone and don't let them know you did it. For info: Mahesh Grossman, 4398 Nicker Ct, Soquel, CA 95073. Phone: (831) 479-7555. Fax: (831) 576-4449. E-mail: GetPublished@AuthorsTeam.com. Web: www.AuthorsTeam.com.

NATIONAL KIDNEY MONTH. Mar 1–31. Kidney disease may often be silent for many years until it has reached an advanced stage. The National Kidney Foundation urges everyone to get regular checkups that include tests for blood pressure, blood sugar, urine protein and kidney function. For info: Ellie Schlam, National Kidney Foundation, 30 E 33rd St, New York, NY 10016. Phone: (800) 622-9010 or (212) 889-2210. Web: www.kidney.org.

NATIONAL MULTIPLE SCLEROSIS EDUCATION AND AWARENESS MONTH. Mar 1–31. This month focuses on raising awareness of and compassion for those diagnosed with multiple sclerosis. A series of national events takes place and educational materials and publications are circulated upon request from the Multiple Sclerosis Foundation. For info: Toni Somma, MS Foundation, 6350 N Andrews Ave, Fort Lauderdale, FL 33309. Phone: (954) 776-6805. Fax: (954) 938-8708. E-mail: toni@msfocus.org. Web: www.msfocus.org.

NATIONAL NUTRITION MONTH®. Mar 1–31. To educate consumers about the importance of good nutrition by providing the latest practical information on how simple it can be to eat healthfully. For info: American Dietetic Assn, 120 S Riverside Plaza, Ste 2000, Chicago, IL 60606-6995. Phone: (312) 899-0040. Fax: (312) 899-4739. E-mail: nnm@eatright.org. Web: www.eatright.org.

NATIONAL ON-HOLD MONTH. Mar 1–31. A month to recognize everyone who has been placed "on hold" after calling a place of business, and to honor those businesses who make this hold time more enjoyable by supplying informative messages and music for their callers waiting on hold. For info: Audiomax, 470 Sentry Pkwy East, Blue Bell, PA 19422. Phone: (800) 284-4653 or (610) 825-9100. Fax: (610) 825-0703. E-mail: kkesler@audiomax.com. Web: www.audiomax.com.

NATIONAL PIG DAY. Mar 1. To accord to the pig its rightful, though generally unrecognized, place as one of man's most intelligent and useful domesticated animals. Annually, Mar 1. For further information send SASE to: Ellen Stanley, 7006 Miami, Lubbock, TX 79413.

NATIONAL TALK WITH YOUR TEEN ABOUT SEX MONTH. Mar 1–31. The importance of frank talk with teenagers about sex is emphasized. Parents are encouraged to provide their teenage children with current, accurate information and open lines for communication, as well as to support their self-esteem, reduce misinformation and guide teenagers toward making responsible decisions regarding sex. Annually, the month of March. For info send SASE to: Dale Eshleman, Episcopal Counseling Center, 1021-A E Robinson St, Orlando, FL 32801. Phone: (800) 544-1817.

NATIONAL UMBRELLA MONTH. Mar 1–31. In honor of one of the most versatile and underrated inventions of the human race, this month is dedicated to the purchase of, use of and conversation about umbrellas. Annually, the month of March. Media: please call at least 24 hrs in advance for interviews. For info: Thomas Edward Knibb, 1654 Colonial Way, Frederick, MD 21702-3919. Phone: (301) 695-7351. E-mail: tomknibb@juno.com.

NATIONAL WOMEN'S HISTORY MONTH. Mar 1–31. A time for reexamining and celebrating the wide range of women's contributions and achievements that are too often overlooked in the telling of US history. For info: Natl Women's History Project, 3343 Industrial Dr, Ste 4, Santa Rosa, CA 95403. Phone: (707) 636-2888. Fax: (707) 636-2909. E-mail: nwhp@aol.com. Web: www.nwhp.org.

NATIONAL WRITE A LETTER OF APPRECIATION WEEK. Mar 1–7. Send a letter expressing your gratitude to others, acknowledging the goodness that we find all around us. For info: Larry McManus, 1504 N Richmond Rd, McHenry, IL 60050-1410. Phone: (815) 344-4934. Fax: (815) 344-4824. E-mail: faithhealer@ameritech.net. Web: www.appreciationweek.org.

NEBRASKA: ADMISSION DAY: ANNIVERSARY. Mar 1. Became 37th state in 1867.

OHIO: ADMISSION DAY: ANNIVERSARY. Mar 1. Became 17th state in 1803.

OPTIMISM MONTH. Mar 1–31. To encourage people to boost their optimism. Research proves optimists achieve more health, prosperity and happiness than pessimists. Use this monthlong celebration to practice optimism and turn optimism into a delightful, permanent habit. Free tip sheets available. For info: Dr. Michael Mercer & Dr. Maryann Troiani, The Mercer Group, Inc, 25597 Drake Rd, Barrington, IL 60010. Phone: (847) 382-0690. E-mail: drmercer@mercersystems.com. Web: www.DrMercer.com.

ORLANDO FAMILY SPRING BREAK®. Mar 1–Apr 30. Orlando, FL. Each year more than 350,000 families gather to experience the Orlando Family Spring Break®, a celebration of reconnecting as a family. The destination offers more than 95 attractions ranging from the largest and most diverse collection of theme parks in the world to a multitude of smaller attractions sure to appeal to everyone in the family. For info: Orlando/Orange County CVB, 6700 Forum Dr, Ste 100, Orlando, FL 32821. Phone: (407) 363-5800. Web: www.orlandoinfo.com.

March 2006	S	M	T	W	T	F	S
				1	2	3	4
	5	6	7	8	9	10	11
	12	13	14	15	16	17	18
	19	20	21	22	23	24	25
	26	27	28	29	30	31	

PARAGUAY: NATIONAL HEROES' DAY. Mar 1. National holiday. Honors those who have died for the country, especially Mariscal Francisco Solano López, who died Mar 1, 1870.

PEACE CORPS FOUNDED: 45th ANNIVERSARY. Mar 1, 1961. Official establishment of the Peace Corps by President John F. Kennedy's signing of executive order. The Peace Corps has sent more than 170,000 volunteers to 136 countries to help people help themselves. The volunteers assist in projects such as health, education, water sanitation, agriculture, nutrition and forestry. For info: Peace Corps, 1111 20th St NW, Washington, DC 20526. Web: www.peacecorps.gov.

PLAN A SOLO VACATION DAY. Mar 1. Wanderlust stirring? Tired of waiting for friends' timetables to coincide with yours? Unable to agree with your spouse on the perfect vacation? This is the day to follow the lead of 34.8 million US adults who have taken a vacation by themselves in the past three years. Indulge yourself by spending the day checking out your growing opportunities for solo travel, including tours, cruises and travel clubs that either match roommates or charge little or no supplement. For info: Marya Alexander, Solo Travel Portal, PO Box 2664, Carlsbad, CA 92018. Phone: (760) 720-1011. Fax: (760) 720-1049. E-mail: editor@solotravelportal.com. Web: www.solo travelportal.com.

PLAY-THE-RECORDER MONTH. Mar 1-31. American Recorder Society members all over the continent will celebrate the organization's annual Play-the-Recorder Month by performing in public places such as libraries, bookstores, museums and shopping malls. Some will offer workshops on playing the recorder or demonstrations in schools. Founded in 1939, the ARS is the membership organization for all recorder players, including amateurs to leading professionals. Annually, the month of March. For info: American Recorder Soc, 1129 Ruth Dr, St. Louis, MO 63122-1019. Phone: (800) 491-9588 or (314) 966-4082. Fax: (314) 966-4649. Web: www.americanrecorder.org.

POISON PREVENTION AWARENESS MONTH. Mar 1-31. To educate parents, grandparents, schoolchildren and PTAs about accidental poisoning and how to prevent it. PPSI is a nonprofit organization. There is a $15 charge for kit materials. Annually, the month of March. For info: Frederick Mayer, Pres, Pharmacists Planning Service, Inc, 101 Lucas Valley Rd, #210, San Rafael, CA 94903. Phone: (415) 479-8628. Fax: (415) 479-8608. E-mail: ppsi@aol.com. Web: www.ppsinc.org.

RAID ON RICHMOND: ANNIVERSARY. Mar 1, 1864. Believing the Confederate capital of Richmond, VA, to be lightly fortified, President Abraham Lincoln ordered a surprise raid to capture the city and free Union prisoners. Federal troops under General Judson Kilpatrick and Colonel Ulric Dahlgren led the attack on this date, but failed when the plan was discovered by Southern forces. In the wake of their retreat, Dahlgren was killed, and two documents were discovered on his body. The incriminating documents contained plans to burn the city and kill Confederate President Jefferson Davis and his cabinet. Confederate General Robert E. Lee complained to the Union commander, George Meade, but a Federal investigation was inconclusive.

RED CROSS MONTH. Mar 1-31. To make the public aware of American Red Cross service in the community. There are nearly 900 Red Cross offices nationwide; each local office plans its own activities. For info on activities in your area, contact your local Red Cross. For info: American Red Cross Natl HQ, Office of Public Inquiry, 2025 E St NW, Washington, DC 20006. Phone: (202) 303-4498. E-mail: info@usa.redcross.org. Web: www.red cross.org.

REFIRED, NOT RETIRED, DAY. Mar 1. This is a day for retirees (or those soon to be retired) to decide that this is the beginning of "Life, Part II," and to make a commitment to make this an exciting adventure. For info: Phyllis May, Refired, 1800 Altlantic Blvd, Ste A-312, Key West, FL 33040. Phone: (305) 295-7501. Fax: (305) 294-7095. E-mail: pmaykeys@bellsouth.net. Web: www.refired.com.

RETURN THE BORROWED BOOKS WEEK. Mar 1-7. To remind you to make room for those precious old volumes that will be returned to you by cleaning out all that worthless trash that your friends are waiting for. Annually, the first seven days of March. For info: Inter-Global Society for Prevention of Cruelty to Cartoonists, Al Kaelin, Secy, 3119 Chadwick Dr, Los Angeles, CA 90032. Phone: (323) 222-7944.

ROZELLE, PETE: BIRTH ANNIVERSARY. Mar 1, 1926. Alvin Ray ("Pete") Rozelle, commissioner of the National Football League, born at South Gate, CA. Rozelle began his career in the public relations department of the Los Angeles Rams, became general manager and was elected commissioner in 1960. He built the NFL into a sporting power through the use of television. He helped engineer the NFL's merger with the American Football League, created the Super Bowl as America's greatest sports extravaganza, conceived the idea for Monday Night Football and persuaded NFL owners to accept revenue sharing. Died at Rancho Santa Fe, CA, Dec 6, 1996.

SAINT-GAUDENS, AUGUSTUS: BIRTH ANNIVERSARY. Mar 1, 1848. Sculptor, born at Dublin, Ireland. His works include the statue of Lincoln in Lincoln Park, Chicago, and of Admiral Farragut in Madison Square, New York. Saint-Gaudens died at Cornish, NH, Aug 3, 1907.

SALEM WITCH HYSTERIA BEGINS: ANNIVERSARY. Mar 1, 1692. The Massachusetts Bay Colony village of Salem had experienced a strange February in which several teenaged girls exhibited bizarre behavior and attributed their ailments to witches. Three women were then arrested on Feb 29, 1692. One of the accused, Tituba, a West Indian slave, broke down under questioning on Mar 1 and admitted to being a witch. Soon the teenaged girls accused four other residents, and by the end of April, 19 women had been accused of witchcraft and were languishing in jail—including a four-year-old child. Massachusetts governor Sir William Phips, seeking to control the growing terror, ordered trials held. In October, the special court was dissolved after growing protests of the trials' unjust proceedings. By then, 19 people had been hung, 5 had died in jail, 1 had been tortured to death and more than 150 had been imprisoned. Two dogs were also executed. On Jan 14, 1697, Judge Samuel Sewall publicly apologized and a court-ordered day of atonement began. In 1711, all those accused of witchcraft were pardoned by the colony's legislature. See also: "Salem Witch Trials Begin: Anniversary" (June 2).

SAVE YOUR VISION MONTH. Mar 1-31. To remind Americans of the importance of eye health and regular exams. For info: American Optometric Assn, 243 N Lindbergh Blvd, St. Louis, MO 63141. Phone: (314) 991-4100, ext 176. Fax: (314) 991-4101. E-mail: jmmahoney@aoa.org. Web: www.aoa.org.

SHORE, DINAH: BIRTH ANNIVERSARY. Mar 1, 1917. American radio and television personality Dinah Shore was born Frances Rose Shore at Winchester, TN. In addition to recording many hit songs in the 1930s and 1940s, she was one of the first women to be successful as a television host, beginning in the 1950s with the "Dinah Shore Chevy Show." She received 10 Emmys before she died Feb 24, 1994, at Beverly Hills, CA.

SLAYTON, DONALD "DEKE" K.: BIRTH ANNIVERSARY. Mar 1, 1924. Deke Slayton, longtime chief of flight operations at the Johnson Space Center, was born at Sparta, WI. Slayton was a member of Mercury Seven, the original group of young military aviators chosen to inaugurate America's sojourn into space. Unfortunately, a heart problem prevented him from participating in any of the Mercury flights. When in 1971 the heart condition mysteriously went away, Slayton flew on the last Apollo mission. The July 1975 flight, involving a docking with a Soviet *Soyuz* spacecraft, symbolized a momentary thaw in relations between the two nations. During his years as chief of flight operations, Slayton directed astronaut training and selected the crews for nearly all missions. He died June 13, 1993, at League City, TX.

SMALL PRESS MONTH. Mar 1–31. Small Press Month honors the quality of work being produced in independent publishing, a part of the industry that is growing at a tremendous rate. The estimated 70,000 US independent publishers create a million-plus books. These publishers are publishing unknown authors, enhancing the careers of established writers, constantly taking risks, exploring innovative ideas and, through their diverse titles, reaching new audiences. Individual expression is the driving force behind these publishers. Manhattan will feature a Small Press Book Fair during this month, and posters and materials about small presses and the month are available. Sponsored by New York's Small Press Center and California's Independent Book Publishers Association. For info: Small Press Month Coordinator, Independent Book Publishers Assn, 627 Aviation Way, Manhattan Beach, CA 90266. Phone: (212) 764-7021 or (310) 372-2732. E-mail: info@smallpress.org. Web: www.smallpress.org.

SPIRITUAL WELLNESS MONTH. Mar 1–31. As spring approaches, this is a time for a new beginning, a time for spiritual renewal and inner peace. Discover a new you as you focus on telling the truth, being honest in all endeavors. Be true to yourself and build your character. Make a list of the values you cherish and work toward incorporating them in your life. Create a life of order, prayer, fasting, faith, learning and respect. For info: Angela Brown, Words of Wellness, PO Box 49266, Charlotte, NC 28277. Phone: (704) 849-2900. Fax: (704) 845-3060. E-mail: Angela@WordsofWellness.com. Web: www.WordsofWellness.com.

STOP THE BAD SERVICE DAY. Mar 1. Celebrates those companies that give exceptional service. Contest for consumers who submit excellent customer service stories. Details at the website. Annually, the first Wednesday of March. For info: Margo Chevers, PO Box 281, Wales, MA 01081. Phone: (413) 267-4500. Fax: (413) 267-4501. E-mail: margo@MargoChevers.com. Web: www.MargoChevers.com.

SWITZERLAND: CHALANDRA MARZ. Mar 1. Engadine. Springtime traditional event when costumed young people, ringing bells and cracking whips, drive away the demons of winter.

UNIVERSAL HUMAN BEINGS WEEK. Mar 1–7. The purpose of this observance is to inspire men and women to become Universal Human Beings in a world that is rapidly becoming a "global village." Annually, Mar 1–7. For complete info send $5 to cover printing, handling and postage. For info: Dr. Stanley Drake, Pres Emeritus, Intl Society of Friendship & Good Will, 8592 Roswell Rd, Ste 251, Atlanta, GA 30350-1867. Phone: (678) 795-1362. E-mail: sjdrake@bellsouth.net. Web: www.friendshipandgoodwill.org.

VULVAR HEALTH AWARENESS MONTH. Mar 1–31. Annual. Become aware of this often misunderstood area of women's health. Learn about self-examination, disorders and vulvar cancer. For info: VHAM, PO Box 6762, Bloomington, IN 47407. E-mail: vulvarhealth@yahoo.com. Web: www.vulvarhealth.org.

WALES: SAINT DAVID'S DAY. Mar 1. Celebrates patron saint of Wales (Dewi Sant). Welsh tradition calls for the wearing of a leek on this day.

★**WOMEN'S HISTORY MONTH.** Mar 1–31.

WORKPLACE EYE HEALTH AND SAFETY MONTH. Mar 1–31. Can you see the dangers at your workplace? Accidents at work are a major cause of preventable blindness. Find out more about Prevent Blindness America®'s workplace safety program, The Wise Owl Club, and find out how to make your work environment easier on your eyes. For info: Prevent Blindness America®, 211 W Wacker Dr, Ste 1700, Chicago, IL 60606. Phone: (800) 331-2020. E-mail: info@preventblindness.org. Web: www.preventblindness.org.

		S	M	T	W	T	F	S
March					1	2	3	4
2006		5	6	7	8	9	10	11
		12	13	14	15	16	17	18
		19	20	21	22	23	24	25
		26	27	28	29	30	31	

YELLOWSTONE NATIONAL PARK ESTABLISHED: ANNIVERSARY. Mar 1, 1872. The first area in the world to be designated a national park, most of Yellowstone is in Wyoming, with small sections in Montana and Idaho. It was established by an act of Congress.

YOUTH ART MONTH. Mar 1–31. To emphasize the value and importance of participation in art in the development of all children and youth. For info: Council for Art Education, Inc, 1280 Main St, PO Box 479, Hanson, MA 02341. Phone: (781) 293-4100. Fax: (781) 294-0808. Web: acminet.org/youthart month.

BIRTHDAYS TODAY

Catherine Bach, 52, actress ("The Dukes of Hazzard"), born Warren, OH, Mar 1, 1954.

Javier Bardem, 37, actor (*The Sea Inside, The Dancer Upstairs*), born Las Palmas de Gran Canaria, Canary Islands, Spain, Mar 1, 1969.

Harry Belafonte, 79, singer ("Mary's Boy Child," "Island in the Sun," "Banana Boat Song"), born New York, NY, Mar 1, 1927.

Robert Conrad, 71, actor ("The Wild Wild West"), born Chicago, IL, Mar 1, 1935.

Roger Daltrey, 62, lead singer (The Who), born London, England, Mar 1, 1944.

Timothy Daly, 50, actor (*Diner*, "Wings"), born New York, NY, Mar 1, 1956.

George Eads, 39, actor ("CSI"), born Fort Worth, TX, Mar 1, 1967.

Ron Francis, 43, hockey player, born Sault Ste. Marie, ON, Canada, Mar 1, 1963.

Mark-Paul Gosselaar, 32, actor ("NYPD Blue," "Saved by the Bell"), born Panorama City, CA, Mar 1, 1974.

Yolanda Griffith, 36, former basketball player, born Chicago, IL, Mar 1, 1970.

Ron Howard, 52, actor ("The Andy Griffith Show," "Happy Days"), director (*A Beautiful Mind, Apollo 13*), born Duncan, OK, Mar 1, 1954.

Judith Rossner, 71, novelist (*Looking for Mr Goodbar*), born New York, NY, Mar 1, 1935.

Alan Thicke, 59, actor ("Growing Pains"), host ("Thicke of the Night"), born Kirkland Lake, ON, Canada, Mar 1, 1947.

Chris Webber, 33, basketball player, born Detroit, MI, Mar 1, 1973.

Richard (Purdy) Wilbur, 85, former poet laureate of the US, born New York, NY, Mar 1, 1921.

MARCH 2 — THURSDAY
Day 61 — 304 Remaining

ARNAZ, DESI: BIRTH ANNIVERSARY. Mar 2, 1917. Born at Santiago, Cuba, as Desidero Alberto Arnaz y Acha III, to a wealthy family. The 1933 revolution sent them (now impoverished) to Miami, FL, and the young Arnaz sought a music career. Arnaz led his own band and introduced the conga line to America. He had several musical hits including "Babalu." He moved into acting, meeting his future wife, Lucille Ball, at RKO. Ball and Arnaz created one of the great TV comedies, "I Love Lucy" (1951–57), and started the innovative Desilu TV production company. Ball and Arnaz divorced in 1960. Arnaz died on Dec 2, 1986, at Del Mar, CA.

BATTLE OF BISMARCK SEA: ANNIVERSARY. Mar 2–4, 1943. Protected by American and Australian fighters, 137 American Flying Fortress and Liberator bombers attacked a Japanese convoy en route from its base at Rabaul to New Guinea on Mar 2, 1943. In the convoy were eight transports carrying 7,000 reinforcements, which were escorted by eight destroyers. All the transports and four of the destroyers were sunk and 3,500 Japanese troops were drowned. Of the 150 Japanese aircraft involved in the fighting, 102 were shot down. The Battle of Bismarck Sea was a major victory for the Allies, ending any efforts by the Japanese to send reinforcements to New Guinea.

BIG TEN WOMEN'S BASKETBALL TOURNAMENT. Mar 2–5. Conseco Fieldhouse, Indianapolis, IN. Est attendance: 2,500. For info: Big Ten Conference, 1500 W Higgins Rd, Park Ridge, IL 60068-6300. Phone: (847) 696-1010. Fax: (847) 696-1110. Web: www.bigten.org.

BIG TEN WRESTLING CHAMPIONSHIPS. Mar 2–4. Indiana University, Bloomington, IN. Est attendance: 1,000. For info: Big Ten Conference, 1500 W Higgins Rd, Park Ridge, IL 60068-6300. Phone: (847) 696-1010. Fax: (847) 696-1110. Web: www.bigten.org.

CORAY, MELISSA BURTON: BIRTH ANNIVERSARY. Mar 2, 1828. Coray was born at Mersey, ON, Canada. At the age of 18 she accompanied her Mormon Battalion soldier husband, William Coray, on a 2,000-mile military march on foot from Council Bluffs, IA, to San Diego, CA, then 1,500 more miles across the Sierra Nevada Mountains and the Nevada desert to Salt Lake City, UT, the only woman to make the entire trip. On July 30, 1994, a mountain peak near Carson Pass was named for her, the second peak in California to be named for a woman.

ETHIOPIA: ADWA DAY. Mar 2. Ethiopian forces under Menelik II inflicted a crushing defeat on the invading Italians at Adwa in 1896.

FLORIDA STRAWBERRY FESTIVAL. Mar 2–12. Plant City, FL. Celebration of winter strawberry harvest. For info: Patsy Brooks, Gen Mgr, Florida Strawberry Fest, PO Drawer 1869, Plant City, FL 33564-1869. Phone: (813) 752-9194 or (813) 754-1996. Fax: (813) 754-4297. Web: www.flstrawberryfestival.com.

FULTON OYSTERFEST. Mar 2–5. Fulton Navigation Park, Fulton, TX. This salute to the oyster industry features oyster-shucking, decorated oyster, raw oyster-eating contests, more than 100 arts and crafts booths, food and fun, live bands and other entertainment. Annually, the first full weekend in March. Est attendance: 30,000. For info: Fulton Oysterfest, PO Box 393, Fulton, TX 78358. Phone: (361) 463-9955 (9 AM to 5 PM) or (361) 790-8362 (after 5 PM). Fax: (361) 729-3248. Email: bgaris@garisfamily.com.

GEISEL, THEODOR "DR. SEUSS": BIRTH ANNIVERSARY. Mar 2, 1904. Theodor Seuss Geisel, the creator of *The Cat in the Hat* and *How the Grinch Stole Christmas*, was born at Springfield, MA. Known to children and parents as Dr. Seuss, his books have sold more than 200 million copies and have been translated into 20 languages. His career began with *And to Think That I Saw It on Mulberry Street*, which was turned down by 27 publishing houses before being published by Vanguard Press. His books included many messages, from environmental consciousness in *The Lorax* to the dangers of pacifism in *Horton Hatches the Egg* and *Yertle the Turtle*'s thinly veiled references to Hitler as the title character. He was awarded a Pulitzer Prize in 1984 "for his contribution over nearly half a century to the education and enjoyment of America's children and their parents." He died Sept 24, 1991, at La Jolla, CA.

HIGHWAY NUMBERS INTRODUCED: ANNIVERSARY. Mar 2, 1925. A joint board of state and federal highway officials created the first system of interstate highway numbering in the US. Standardized road signs identifying the routes were also introduced. Later the system would be improved with the use of odd and even numbers that distinguish between north-south and east-west routes respectively.

HOUSTON, SAM: BIRTH ANNIVERSARY. Mar 2, 1793. American soldier and politician, born at Rockbridge County, VA, is remembered for his role in Texas history. Houston was a congressman (1823–27) and governor (1827–29) of Tennessee. He resigned his office as governor in 1829 and rejoined the Cherokee Indians (with whom he had lived for several years as a teenage runaway), who accepted him as a member of their tribe. Houston went to Texas in 1832 and became commander of the Texan army in the War for Texan Independence, which was secured when Houston routed the much larger Mexican forces led by Santa Anna, Apr 21, 1836, at the Battle of San Jacinto. After Texas's admission to the Union, Houston served as US senator and later as governor of the state. He was deposed in 1861 when he refused to swear allegiance to the Confederacy. Houston, the only person to have been elected governor of two different states, failed to serve his full term of office in either. The city of Houston, TX, was named for him. He died July 26, 1863, at Huntsville, TX.

KING KONG FILM PREMIERE: ANNIVERSARY. Mar 2, 1933. One of the greatest adventure movies of all time premiered on this date at New York City's Radio City Music Hall and the RKO Roxy. It was to be an immediate hit—the biggest film blockbuster up to that time. Directed by Merion Cooper and Ernest Schoedsack, *King Kong* was a variation of "Beauty and the Beast," with the Beast being the 50-ft ape (actually, an 18-in model) and Beauty portrayed by actress Fay Wray, who became known as the "Queen of Scream" after this film. Kong climbing the newly completed Empire State Building clutching Wray as biplanes attack him is one of the iconic images of cinema. Technician Willis O'Brien used state-of-the-art stop-motion photography for the film's special effects.

MOUNT RAINIER NATIONAL PARK ESTABLISHED: ANNIVERSARY. Mar 2, 1899. Located in the Cascade Mountains of Washington State, this is the fourth oldest national park.

NAIA MEN'S AND WOMEN'S INDOOR TRACK AND FIELD NATIONAL CHAMPIONSHIPS. Mar 2–4. Location TBD. Individuals compete for All-America honors while teams compete for the national championship. 41st annual competition for men; 26th annual for women. Est attendance: 2,500. For info: Natl Assn Intercollegiate Athletics, 23500 W 105th St, PO Box 1325, Olathe, KS 66051-1325. Phone: (913) 791-0044. Fax: (913) 791-9555. E-mail: rfeldblum@naia.org. Web: www.naia.org.

NEA'S READ ACROSS AMERICA DAY. Mar 2. A national reading campaign that advocates that all children read a book on Mar 2. Celebrated on Dr. Seuss's birthday. For info: Natl Education Assn, 1201 16th St NW, Washington, DC 20036. Phone: (202) 833-4000. E-mail: readacross@nea.org. Web: www.nea.org/readacross.

OTT, MELVIN (MEL): BIRTH ANNIVERSARY. Mar 2, 1909. Baseball Hall of Fame outfielder, born at Gretna, LA. Playing for the New York Giants, Ott hit 511 home runs, a National League record until Willie Mays surpassed it in 1966. Inducted into the Hall of Fame in 1951. Died at New Orleans, LA, Nov 21, 1958.

POPE PIUS XII: BIRTH ANNIVERSARY. Mar 2, 1876. Eugenio Maria Giovanni Pacelli, 260th pope of the Roman Catholic Church, born at Rome, Italy. Elected pope Mar 2, 1939. Died at Castel Gandolfo, near Rome, Oct 9, 1958.

QCCA REGIONAL LAWN, GARDEN AND FLOWER SHOW. Mar 2–5. QCCA ExpoCenter, Rock Island, IL. "Symphony in Bloom": An extraordinary array of landscape gardens, vignettes, special events, seminars, hands-on workshops and music. Room and patio settings, floral arrangements, an array of lawn and garden products and home accessories. Children's Activity Garden, speakers, silent auction and much more! For info: Phone: (563) 322-0931. Web: www.qcsymphony.com. For info on the Quad Cities: Quad Cities CVB, 102 S Harrison St, Davenport, IA 52801. Phone: (800) 747-7800. Web: www.visitquadcities.com.

RITT, MARTIN: BIRTH ANNIVERSARY. Mar 2, 1914. American film and television director Martin Ritt was born at New York, NY. His best-known films are *Hud* (1963), *Sounder* (1972) and *Norma Rae* (1979). During the 1950s he was blacklisted by McCarthy's anti-Communist crusade. Died Dec 8, 1990, at Santa Monica, CA.

SCHURZ, CARL: BIRTH ANNIVERSARY. Mar 2, 1829. American journalist, political reformer and army officer in Civil War. Born near Cologne, Germany, he died at New York, NY, May 14, 1906.

***THE SOUND OF MUSIC* FILM PREMIERE: ANNIVERSARY.** Mar 2, 1965. The perennially popular family film musical, starring Julie Andrews as Maria Von Trapp, premiered on this date at New York City. Nominated for ten Academy Awards, the film won five Oscars, including awards for Best Picture and Best Director (Robert Wise).

SPACE MILESTONE: *PIONEER 10* (US). Mar 2, 1972. This unmanned probe began a journey on which it passed and photographed Jupiter and its moons, 620 million miles from Earth, in 1973. It crossed the orbit of Pluto, and then in 1983 become the first known Earth object to leave our solar system. On Sept 22, 1987, *Pioneer 10* reached another space milestone at 4:19 PM, when it reached a distance 50 times farther from the sun than the sun is from Earth.

SPACE MILESTONE: *SOYUZ 28* (USSR). Mar 2, 1978. Cosmonauts Alexi Gubarev and Vladimir Remek linked with *Salyut 6* space station Mar 3, visiting crew of *Soyuz 26*. Returned to Earth Mar 10. Remek, from Czechoslovakia, was the first person in space from a country other than the US or USSR.

TEXAS INDEPENDENCE DAY. Mar 2, 1836. Texas adopted Declaration of Independence from Mexico.

UNITED KINGDOM AND IRELAND: WORLD BOOK DAY. Mar 2. The 9th year of this celebration of reading. Aligned with UNESCO's observance that takes place Apr 23, but happening earlier in the UK and Ireland only. World Book Day 2006 in the UK and Ireland is a partnership of publishers, booksellers and interested parties who work together to promote books and reading for the personal enrichment and enjoyment of all. A main aim of World Book Day is to encourage children to explore the pleasures of books and reading by providing them with the opportunity to have a book of their own. For info: World Book Day. E-mail: wbd@education.co.uk or worldbookday@eircom.net. Web: www.worldbookday.com.

BIRTHDAYS TODAY

Jon Bon Jovi, 44, singer, songwriter, actor, born John Bongiovi at Sayreville, NJ, Mar 2, 1962.

John Cullum, 76, actor (stage: *Shenandoah, On the Twentieth Century*; "Northern Exposure"), born Knoxville, TN, Mar 2, 1930.

Russell D. Feingold, 53, US Senator (D, Wisconsin), born Janesville, WI, Mar 2, 1953.

Mikhail Sergeyvich Gorbachev, 75, former Soviet political leader, born Privolnoye, Stavropol, Russia, Mar 2, 1931.

John Irving, 64, author (*Cider House Rules, The World According to Garp*), born Exeter, NH, Mar 2, 1942.

Jennifer Jones, 87, actress (Oscar for *The Song of Bernadette*), born Phyllis Isley at Tulsa, OK, Mar 2, 1919.

March	S	M	T	W	T	F	S
March				1	2	3	4
2006	5	6	7	8	9	10	11
	12	13	14	15	16	17	18
	19	20	21	22	23	24	25
	26	27	28	29	30	31	

Chris Martin, 29, singer, songwriter (Coldplay), born Exeter, Devon, England, Mar 2, 1977.

Eddie Money, 57, musician, born Brooklyn, NY, Mar 2, 1949.

Laraine Newman, 54, comedienne ("Saturday Night Live"), born Los Angeles, CA, Mar 2, 1952.

Ken Salazar, 51, US Senator (D, Colorado), born San Luis Valley, CO, Mar 2, 1955.

Doc Watson, 83, singer, musician (*Riding the Midnight Train, Then and Now*), born Deep Gap, NC, Mar 2, 1923.

Tom Wolfe, 75, author, journalist (*The Bonfire of the Vanities, The Right Stuff*), born Richmond, VA, Mar 2, 1931.

MARCH 3 — FRIDAY
Day 62 — 303 Remaining

ALDO LEOPOLD WEEKEND. Mar 3–5. Statewide, Wisconsin. Communities across Wisconsin come together to demonstrate their individual and combined commitment to the "Land Ethic" put forth by renowned environmentalist Aldo Leopold in his famous book, *A Sand County Almanac*. He wrote, "That land is a community is the basic concept of ecology, but that land is to be loved and respected is an extension of ethics." Annually, the first weekend in March. For info: Jennifer Kobylecky, The Aldo Leopold Foundation, PO Box 77, Baraboo, WI 53913. Phone: (608) 355-0279. Fax: (608) 356-7309. E-mail: jennifer@aldoleopold.org. Web: www.aldoleopold.org.

ALL-NORTHWEST BARBERSHOP BALLAD CONTEST. Mar 3–4. Pacific University, Forest Grove, OR. Barbershop quartets from throughout the Pacific Northwest compete in an 1890s setting. Est attendance: 3,000. For info: Forest Grove Chamber of Commerce, 2417 Pacific Ave, Forest Grove, OR 97116. Phone: (503) 357-3006 or (503) 292-5673. Fax: (503) 357-2367. E-mail: info@fgchamber.org.

BELL, ALEXANDER GRAHAM: BIRTH ANNIVERSARY. Mar 3, 1847. Inventor of the telephone, born at Edinburgh, Scotland, Bell acquired his interest in the transmission of sound from his father, Melville Bell, a teacher of the deaf. Bell's use of visual devices to teach articulation to the deaf contributed to the theory from which he derived the principle of the vibrating membrane used in the telephone. On Mar 10, 1876, Bell spoke the first electrically transmitted sentence to his assistant in the next room: "Mr Watson, come here, I want you." Bell's other accomplishments include a refinement of Edison's phonograph, the first successful phonograph record and the audiometer, and he continued exploring the nature and causes of deafness. He died near Baddeck, NS, Canada, Aug 2, 1922.

BENJAMIN HARRISON DAY. Mar 3. Indiana State Capitol Building, Indianapolis, IN. Presentation of Harrison Day awards, and a reenactment of a Harrison court case in the Supreme Court. For info: President Benjamin Harrison Home, 1230 N Delaware St, Indianapolis, IN 46202. Phone: (317) 631-1888. Fax: (317) 632-5488. E-mail: harrison@presidentbenjaminharrison.org. Web: www.pbhh.org.

BETHUNE, NORMAN: BIRTH ANNIVERSARY. Mar 3, 1890. Canadian physician who worked in the front lines during World War I, the Spanish Civil War and the Chinese Revolution. Bethune was born at Gravenhurst, ON; he died at age 49 at China while treating a soldier of Mao's Eighth Route Army, Nov 11, 1939. He is said to be the only Western man recognized as a hero of the Chinese Revolution.

BONZA BOTTLER DAY™. Mar 3. To celebrate when the number of the day is the same as the number of the month. Bonza Bottler Day™ is an excuse to have a party at least once a month. For more information, see Jan 1. For info: Gail M. Berger, 14 Fernwood Dr, Taylors, SC 29687. Phone: (864) 609-9874. E-mail: gberger5@aol.com.

BULGARIA: LIBERATION DAY. Mar 3. Grateful tribute to the Russian, Romanian and Finnish soldiers and Bulgarian volunteers who, in the Russo-Turkish War, 1877–78, liberated Bulgaria from five centuries of Ottoman rule.

CAMEX. Mar 3–7. Houston, TX. The only national conference and trade exhibit designed exclusively for collegiate retailers. College store buyers and suppliers gather at CAMEX to preview products to be seen on college campuses in the coming year. Est attendance: 7,000. For info: Laura Nakoneczny, Dir of PR, Natl Assn of College Stores (NACS), 500 E Lorain St, Oberlin, OH 44074. Phone: (440) 775-7777 x 2351 or (800) 622-7498 x 2351. E-mail: lnakoneczny@nacs.org. Web: www.camex.org.

CRAFTSMEN'S CLASSIC ARTS & CRAFTS FESTIVAL. Mar 3–5. South Carolina State Fairgrounds, Columbia, SC. 23rd annual. Features work from more than 300 talented artists and craftspeople. All juried exhibitors' work has been handmade by the exhibitors and must be their own original design and creation. See the creative process in action with several exhibitors demonstrating through the weekend. Something for every style, taste and budget with items from the most contemporary to the most traditional. Est attendance: 20,000. For info: Gilmore Enterprises, 1240 Oakland Ave, Greensboro, NC 27403. Phone: (336) 274-5550. E-mail: gilmoreshows@triad.rr.com. Web: www.CraftShow.com or www.gilmoreshows.com.

FLORIDA: ADMISSION DAY: ANNIVERSARY. Mar 3. Became 27th state in 1845.

GODWIN, WILLIAM: 250th BIRTH ANNIVERSARY. Mar 3, 1756. English man of letters, philosopher, political theorist and dissenter, influential in the late 18th century. Married Mary Wollstonecraft in 1797, who died after complications of birthing daughter Mary Godwin. Born at Wisbech, England, Godwin died Apr 7, 1836, at London.

GREEN COUNTRY RV & BOAT SHOW. Mar 3–5. Expo Square, Tulsa, OK. More than seven acres of RVs, boats and camping equipment. Est attendance: 15,000. For info: Randy Chrisman, Green Country RV & Boat Show, PO Box 2992, Tulsa, OK 74101. Phone: (918) 486-3318. Fax: (918) 486-3428. E-mail: tbsts1@mindspring.com. Web: www.tulsaboatshow.com.

I WANT YOU TO BE HAPPY DAY. Mar 3. A day dedicated to reminding people to be thoughtful of others by showing love and concern, even if things are not going well for them. For info: Harriette W. Grimes, Grandmother, PO Box 545, Winter Garden, FL 34777-0545. Fax: (407) 656-2790. E-mail: LAGRIMES@earthlink.net.

JAPAN: HINAMATSURI (DOLL FESTIVAL). Mar 3. This special festival for girls is observed throughout Japan. Annually, Mar 3.

LONGHORN WORLD CHAMPIONSHIP RODEO. Mar 3–5. Von Braun Civic Center, Huntsville, AL. 27th annual. More than 275 cowboys and cowgirls compete in six professional contests ranging from bronco riding to big, bad BONUS bull riding! Free beginners horsemanship clinic 40 minutes before performances. Qualifying rodeo for Longhorn's Championship Finals Rodeo in Murfreesboro, TN. Est attendance: 15,000. For info: W. Bruce Lehrke, Pres, Longhorn World Chmpshp Rodeo, Inc, PO Box 70159, Nashville, TN 37207. Phone: (615) 876-1016. Fax: (615) 876-4685. E-mail: info@longhornrodeo.com. Web: www.longhornrodeo.com.

MALAWI: MARTYR'S DAY. Mar 3. Public holiday in Malawi.

MARYLAND HOME AND GARDEN SHOW. Mar 3–5 (also Mar 10–12). Timonium Fairgrounds, Baltimore, MD. The largest display of home building, remodeling and home decorating exhibits in the Baltimore area. Includes educational exhibits, crafts, plant marketplace and displays of landscaped gardens and floral arrangements. Est attendance: 72,000. For info: S & L Productions Inc, Crain Overlook, 1916 Crain Hwy, Ste 16, Glen Burnie, MD 21061. Phone: (410) 863-1180. Fax: (410) 863-1187. E-mail: jayp@slprod.com.

MIDNIGHT AT THE OASIS. Mar 3–5. Ray Kroc Complex/Desert Sun Stadium, Yuma, AZ. 14th annual. Stroll down memory lane at an incredible nostalgic festival featuring the cars and music of the '50s and '60s. Limited to 850 '72 and older American cars and trucks and foreign classics. Show & Shine, rock 'n' roll concerts and dances, vendors, activities and entertainment for the whole family. Est attendance: 50,000. For info: Caballeros de Yuma, PO Box 5987, Yuma, AZ 85366. Phone: (928) 343-1715. Fax: (928) 783-1609. E-mail: caballeros@beamspeed.net. Web: www.caballeros.org.

MISSOURI COMPROMISE: ANNIVERSARY. Mar 3, 1820. In February of 1819 a bill was introduced into Congress that would admit Missouri to the Union as a state that prohibited slavery. At the time there were 11 free states and 10 slave states. Southern congressmen feared this would upset the balance of power between North and South. As a compromise, on this date Missouri was admitted as a slave state but slavery was forever prohibited in the northern part of the Louisiana Purchase. In 1854 this act was repealed when Kansas and Nebraska were allowed to decide on slave or free status by popular vote.

"MR WIZARD" TV PREMIERE: 55th ANNIVERSARY. Mar 3, 1951. Don Herbert as Mr Wizard explained the mysteries of science while performing experiments in front of wide-eyed children. The series ran on NBC for 14 continuous years. In 1983 Herbert returned to host "Mr Wizard's World" on Nickelodeon.

"MOONLIGHTING" TV PREMIERE: ANNIVERSARY. Mar 3, 1985. Cybill Shepherd and Bruce Willis starred in this ABC comedy-adventure hour about the Blue Moon Detective Agency owned by former model Maddie Hayes (Shepherd) who is partnered with wisecracking detective David Addison (Willis). The two find themselves in a series of madcap adventures. The show featured narrative innovations: having characters directly address the camera, shooting sequences in black and white or by going completely off-concept (as in an episode based on Shakespeare's *The Taming of the Shrew*). Last telecast on May 14, 1989.

NAIA WRESTLING NATIONAL CHAMPIONSHIPS. Mar 3–4. Sioux City, IA. Individuals compete for All-America honors in 10 weight divisions, while teams compete for the national championship. 49th annual competition. Est attendance: 10,000. For info: Natl Assn of Intercollegiate Athletics, 23500 W 105th St, PO Box 1325, Olathe, KS 66051-1325. E-mail: smcclure@naia.org. Web: www.naia.org.

NATIONAL ANTHEM DAY: 75th ANNIVERSARY. Mar 3, 1931. The bill designating "The Star-Spangled Banner" as our national anthem was adopted by the US Senate and went to President Herbert Hoover for signature. The president signed it the same day.

NATIONAL SALESPERSON'S DAY. Mar 3. Salespeople are essential resources for customers today. The talented salesperson filters the vast amount of information that is available to customers and helps businesspeople make the best purchasing decisions. Salespeople also help consumers make better, quicker decisions with the counsel they offer. With the impact of new technologies, the role of the salesperson continually evolves. Annually, first Friday of March. For info: Maura Schreier-Fleming, Best@Selling, 7028 Judi, Dallas, TX 75252. Phone: (972) 380-0200. Fax: (972) 733-0126. E-mail: Maura@BestAtSelling.com. Web: www.BestAtSelling.com.

PULLMAN, GEORGE: 175th BIRTH ANNIVERSARY. Mar 3, 1831. Born at Brocton, NY, George Mortimer Pullman was an inventor and industrialist who became famous for his design and production of the "Pullman" railroad sleeping car. His first attempt at improving railroad sleeping accommodations began in 1858, while working as a contractor for the Chicago &

Alton Railroad at Chicago, IL. His initial model was not adopted, but in 1863 a new design was enthusiastically received. He secured a patent for the folding upper berth design in 1864 and one for the lower berth design in 1865. By 1867 Pullman and his partner organized the Pullman Palace Car Company, which became the greatest railroad car-building organization in the world. In 1881 the town of Pullman, IL, south of Chicago, was formed by Pullman to house his employees. Because rents were not lowered when wages were cut, a strike was initiated against Pullman's company in May 1894. Pullman was eventually forced to give up control of all property in the town not directly required for manufacturing. Pullman died Oct 19, 1897, at Chicago, IL.

RIDGWAY, MATTHEW BUNKER: BIRTH ANNIVERSARY. Mar 3, 1895. American Army officer Matthew Bunker Ridgway was born at Fort Monroe, VA. As major general commanding the newly formed 82nd Airborne Division, he led it in the invasion of Sicily in July 1943 and the invasion of the Italian mainland in 1944. Ridgway replaced MacArthur as commander of the US Eighth Army in Korea in 1951 and succeeded Eisenhower as Supreme Allied Commander of the North Atlantic Treaty Organization in 1952. He became US Army Chief of Staff in 1953. Ridgway died at Fox Chapel, PA, July 26, 1993.

SHABBAT ACROSS AMERICA. Mar 3. More than 600 participating synagogues (Conservative, Orthodox, Reform and Reconstructionist) encourage Jews to observe the Sabbath on this Friday night. Est attendance: 60,000. For info: Natl Jewish Outreach Program, 989 Sixth Ave, 10th Fl, New York, NY 10018. Phone: (888) SHABBAT or (646) 871-4444. Web: www.njop.org.

SOUTH TEXAS RANCHING HERITAGE FESTIVAL. Mar 3–5. Kingsville, TX. Cowboy storytelling, craftsmen, ranching rodeo, chuckwagon cook-off and camp cooking. Est attendance: 10,000. For info: Kingsville CVB, 1501 N Hwy 77, Kingsville, TX 78363. Phone: (800) 333-5032. Fax: (361) 592-3227. E-mail: visitors@kingsvilletexas.com. Web: www.kingsvilletexas.com.

3-A-DAY WEEK. Mar 3–9. 3-A-Day Week begins on the third day of the third month of the third millennium. It's a call to action for families to start eating 3-A-Day of dairy: three servings of milk, cheese and yogurt is a deliciously easy way to build stronger bones and better bodies. Research shows that most Americans are eating only half the recommended three servings of dairy each day. Eating 3-A-Day of calcium-rich milk, cheese and yogurt is the easiest and most wholesome way for families to meet their calcium needs. Try it every day this week! For info: American Dairy Assn/Natl Dairy Council. Phone: (312) 240-2835. Fax: (312) 240-9382. Email: 3aday@rosedmi.com. Web: www.3aday.org.

***TIME* MAGAZINE FIRST PUBLISHED: ANNIVERSARY.** Mar 3, 1923. The first issue of *Time* bore this date. The magazine was founded by Henry Luce and Briton Hadden.

VICTORIAN SHERLOCK HOLMES WEEKEND. Mar 3–5 (also Nov 3–5). Cape May, NJ. A weekend of mystery and intrigue awaits amateur sleuths when Cape May celebrates the works of Sir Arthur Conan Doyle, creator of Sherlock Holmes. Offered twice annually. Est attendance: 200. For info: Mid-Atlantic Center for the Arts, 1048 Washington St, Cape May, NJ 08204. Phone: (609) 884-5404 or (800) 275-4278. Fax: (609) 884-0574. E-mail: mac4arts@capemaymac.org. Web: www.capemaymac.org.

WHAT IF CATS AND DOGS HAD OPPOSABLE THUMBS DAY. Mar 3. We are grateful today that the infinite wisdom of the universe has not allowed cats and dogs to have thumbs. Imagine the cat, able to operate the can opener! Imag-

★ ★ ★

March *2006*	S	M	T	W	T	F	S
				1	2	3	4
	5	6	7	8	9	10	11
	12	13	14	15	16	17	18
	19	20	21	22	23	24	25
	26	27	28	29	30	31	

ine the dog, able to open the refrigerator door! [©2003 by WH.] For info: Thomas & Ruth Roy, Wellcat Holidays, 2418 Long Ln, Lebanon, PA 17046. Phone: (717) 279-0184. E-mail: info@wellcat.com. Web: www.wellcat.com.

WOMAN SUFFRAGE PARADE ATTACKED: ANNIVERSARY. Mar 3, 1913. A parade held by the National American Woman Suffrage Association at Washington, DC, on the day before Woodrow Wilson's inauguration turned into a near riot when people in the crowd began jeering and shoving the marchers. The 5,000 women and their supporters were spit upon, struck in the face and pelted with burning cigar stubs while police looked on and made no effort to intervene. Secretary of War Henry Stimson was forced to send soldiers from Fort Myer to restore order.

WORLD DAY OF PRAYER. Mar 3. An ecumenical event that reinforces bonds among peoples of the world as they join in a global circle of prayer. Annually, the first Friday in March. 119th annual. Sponsor: International Committee for World Day of Prayer. Church Women United is the National World Day of Prayer Committee for the US. For info: Church Women United, 475 Riverside Dr, Ste 1626, New York, NY 10115. Phone: (212) 870-2347 or (800) 298-5551. Fax: (212) 870-2338. Web: www.churchwomen.org.

BIRTHDAYS TODAY

Jessica Biel, 24, actress ("7th Heaven"), born Ely, MN, Mar 3, 1982.

Julie Bowen, 36, actress (*Joe Somebody*, "Ed"), born Baltimore, MD, Mar 3, 1970.

David Faustino, 32, actor ("Married . . . With Children"), born Los Angeles, CA, Mar 3, 1974.

Ira Glass, 47, radio host ("This American Life"), born Baltimore, MD, Mar 3, 1959.

Jacqueline (Jackie) Joyner-Kersee, 44, Olympic gold medal heptathlete, born East St. Louis, IL, Mar 3, 1962.

Tim Kazurinsky, 56, actor, comedian, writer ("Saturday Night Live"), born Johnstown, PA, Mar 3, 1950.

Brian Leetch, 38, hockey player, born Corpus Christi, TX, Mar 3, 1968.

Lee Radziwill, 73, sister of the late Jackie Kennedy Onassis, born Caroline Lee Bouvier at New York, NY, Mar 3, 1933.

Miranda Richardson, 48, actress (*The Crying Game, Enchanted April*), born Lancashire, England, Mar 3, 1958.

Herschel Walker, 44, former football player, born Wrightsville, GA, Mar 3, 1962.

MARCH 4 — SATURDAY

Day 63 — 302 Remaining

ADAMS, JOHN QUINCY: RETURN TO CONGRESS: ANNIVERSARY. Mar 4, 1830. On this day, John Quincy Adams returned to the House of Representatives to represent the district of Plymouth, MA. He was the first former president to do so and served for eight consecutive terms.

BABYSITTER SAFETY DAY. Mar 4. Darien, CT. Special events to promote babysitter safety will include local police sponsors and fire department participation to educate the community. For info: Suzanne Stillwell, The Sitting Service, 1031 Post Rd, #1, Darien, CT 06820. Phone: (203) 655-9783. E-mail: sitserve@aol.com. Web: www.thesittingservice.com.

BIG 12 WRESTLING CHAMPIONSHIP. Mar 4. Hilton Coliseum, Ames, IA. Est attendance: 6,000. For info: Big 12 Conference, 2201 Stemmons Freeway, 28th Fl, Dallas, TX 75207. Phone: (214) 742-1212. Fax: (214) 753-0145. Web: www.big12sports.com.

CITY OF CHICAGO INCORPORATED: ANNIVERSARY. Mar 4, 1837. The Illinois state legislature enacted into law a city charter for Chicago on this date. William B. Ogden became the first mayor of this city of 4,170 people. Chicago had been incorporated as a town on Aug 12, 1833. The name "Chicago" was formed from a Native American word, but its meaning is disputed. It probably means "strong" or "great."

CONGRESS: ANNIVERSARY OF FIRST MEETING UNDER CONSTITUTION. Mar 4, 1789. The first Congress met at New York, NY. A quorum was obtained in the House Apr 1 and in the Senate Apr 5, and the first Congress was formally organized Apr 6. Electoral votes were counted, and George Washington was declared president (69 votes) and John Adams vice president (34 votes).

COURAGEOUS FOLLOWER DAY. Mar 4. We are a country built on the myth of "rugged individualism," in love with the concept of leadership. But all leaders require followers and, in fact, virtually all of us are followers at some times and leaders at others. This day honors the too-often disparaged role of follower. Its purpose is to dispell the myth that followers are passive and to raise awareness that good followership is energetic and at times courageous. In fact, only through active and courageous followership can leaders be counted on to use their power wisely and well. For info: Ira Chaleff, Exec Coaching & Consulting Assoc. Phone: (301) 933-3752. Web: www.exe-coach.com.

"THE DICK CAVETT SHOW" TV PREMIERE: ANNIVERSARY. Mar 4, 1968. Dick Cavett began his television career on ABC with a daytime talk show that subsequently became a late-night program competing with Johnny Carson. Cavett, with his Yale background, had a reputation as an "intellectual" host and was particularly adept at the one-man interview. He has since appeared on the CBS, PBS and USA networks hosting a variety of shows.

DING LING: 20th DEATH ANNIVERSARY. Mar 4, 1986. Writer and champion of women's rights, born at Hunan Province, China, in 1904. Ding was a prolific author, having written nearly 300 novels as well as plays, short stories and essays. She received the 1951 Stalin Prize for Literature for her novel *The Sun Shines Over the Sanggan River* (1949). She fell from favor in the 1950s, was exiled and in 1970 was imprisoned. After the death of Chairman Mao she was freed and during her last years she enjoyed renewed attention and favor. Died at age 82 at Beijing, China.

FAITH CITY KENNEL CLUB DOG SHOW. Mar 4–5. Multi-Purpose Events Center, Wichita Falls, TX. More than 1,000 dogs in competition in the two-day event. Est attendance: 3,600. For info: Wichita Falls CVB, 1000 5th St, Wichita Falls, TX 76301. Phone: (940) 716-5500. Fax: (940) 716-5509. E-mail: MPEC@wf.net. Web: www.wichitafalls.org.

GREENWOOD, JOAN: BIRTH ANNIVERSARY. Mar 4, 1921. British stage and screen actress Joan Greenwood was born at Chelsea, London. With her husky voice she became best known for playing the roles of coquettes. She died Feb 27, 1987, at London.

GROVER CLEVELAND'S SECOND PRESIDENTIAL INAUGURATION: ANNIVERSARY. Mar 4, 1893. Grover Cleveland was inaugurated for a second but nonconsecutive term as president. In 1885 he had become the 22nd president of the US and in 1893 the 24th. Originally a source of some controversy, the Congressional Directory for some time listed him only as the 22nd president. The Directory now lists him as both the 22nd and 24th presidents though some historians continue to argue that one person cannot be both. Benjamin Harrison served during the intervening term, defeating Cleveland in electoral votes, though not in the popular vote.

HOT SPRINGS NATIONAL PARK ESTABLISHED: 85th ANNIVERSARY. Mar 4, 1921. To protect the hot springs of Arkansas the government set aside Hot Springs Reservation on Apr 20, 1832. In 1921 the area became a national park.

HUG A GI DAY. Mar 4. Today is the only calendrical date which is a military command—March Fourth . . . march forth. Therefore, today we honor all of the gallant men and women who serve in all branches of the military. We acknowledge and salute the sacrifices they make to keep this the land of the free and the home of the brave. [©1996] To alleviate the escalating costs of Eventological® Literature, a charge of $10 must be assessed to each request. Checks are to be made payable to: Adrienne Sioux Koopersmith, 1437 W Rosemont, 1W, Chicago, IL 60660-1319. E-mail: askoopersmith@hotmail.com.

IDITAROD TRAIL SLED DOG RACE. Mar 4–19. 34th running of "The Last Great Race on Earth" (first run on Mar 3, 1973). 1,150 miles through Alaskan wilderness from Anchorage to Nome, AK, along the historic Iditarod Trail. More than 60 16-dog teams competing. Awards ceremony on Sunday, Mar 19. Est attendance: 25,000. For info: Iditarod Trail Committee, PO Box 870800, Wasilla, AK 99687. Phone: (907) 376-5155. Fax: (907) 373-6998. Web: www.iditarod.com.

INTERNATIONAL SCRAPBOOKING INDUSTRY DAY. Mar 4. On this day, we celebrate the growth of the scrapbooking industry and the dedicated entrepreneurs who have worked so hard to make it happen. We seek to increase awareness of the scrapbooking industry and to reflect on the ways we can advance this industry to share the gift of scrapbooking with everyone. For info: Sue DiFranco, Fun Facts Publishing, 15 Vermilyea Ave, #43, New York, NY 10034. Phone: (212) 604-4562. Fax: (646) 349-3375. E-mail: info@funfactspublishing.com. Web: www.funfactspublishing.com.

NATIONAL WEEK OF THE OCEAN FESTIVAL SEASON. Mar 4–June 10. Fort Lauderdale, FL. 27th annual. This multiweek celebration includes school marine fair, marine flea market, waterway cleanup, a regatta, Mother Ocean Day and a Reef Sweep. Est attendance: 50,000. For info: Cynthia Hancock, Pres, Natl Week of the Ocean, Inc, PO Box 179, Ft Lauderdale, FL 33302. Phone: (954) 462-5573. Web: www.national-week-of-the-ocean.org.

NATURAL BRIDGE BATTLE REENACTMENT. Mar 4–5. Tallahassee, FL. Reenactment of the Confederate army's victory at the Natural Bridge site, which kept Tallahassee (the state capital) from falling into Union hands. Annually, the first weekend in March. Est attendance: 2,500. For info: Natural Bridge Battlefield Historic State Park, 7502 Natural Bridge Rd, Tallahassee, FL 32305. Phone: (850) 922-6007. Web: www.floridastateparks.org/naturalbridge.

NENANA TRIPOD RAISING FESTIVAL. Mar 4–5. Nenana, AK. Festival centers around the guessing of the exact time of the ice breakup on the Tanana River. Highlights include the raising of the tripod, Nenana Banana Eating, sled dog races, arm wrestling, turkey shoot, craft bazaar and much more. Est attendance: 2,500. For info: Nenana Ice Classic, Box 272, Nenana, AK 99760. Phone: (907) 832-5446. Fax: (907) 832-5888. E-mail: classic@yukontel.com. Web: www.nenanaakiceclassic.com.

OLD INAUGURATION DAY. Mar 4. Anniversary of the date set for beginning the US presidential term of office, 1789–1933. Although the Continental Congress had set the first Wednesday of March 1789 as the date for the new government to convene, a quorum was not present to count the electoral votes until Apr 6. Though George Washington's term of office began on Mar 4, he did not take the oath of office until Apr 30, 1789. All subsequent presidential terms (except successions following the death of an incumbent), until Franklin D. Roosevelt's second term, began Mar 4. The 20th Amendment (ratified Jan 23, 1933) provided that "the terms of the President and Vice President shall end at noon on the 20th day of January . . . and the terms of their successors shall then begin."

PENNSYLVANIA DEEDED TO WILLIAM PENN: 325th ANNIVERSARY. Mar 4, 1681. To satisfy a debt of £16,000, King Charles II of England granted a royal charter, deed and governorship of Pennsylvania to William Penn.

***PEOPLE* MAGAZINE: ANNIVERSARY.** Mar 4, 1974. The popular magazine highlighting celebrities was officially launched with the Mar 4, 1974, issue featuring a cover photo of Mia Farrow.

PERKINS, FRANCES: CABINET APPOINTMENT ANNIVERSARY. Mar 4, 1933. Frances Perkins became the first woman appointed to the president's cabinet when she was appointed secretary of labor by President Franklin D. Roosevelt.

PULASKI, CASIMIR: BIRTH ANNIVERSARY. Mar 4, 1747. American Revolutionary hero, General Kazimierz (Casimir) Pulaski, born at Winiary, Mazovia, Poland, the son of a count. He was a patriot and military leader in Poland's fight against Russia of 1770–71 and went into exile at the partition of Poland in 1772. He came to America in 1777 to join the Revolution, fighting with General Washington at Brandywine and also serving at Germantown and Valley Forge. He organized the Pulaski Legion to wage guerrilla warfare against the British. Mortally wounded in a heroic charge at the siege of Savannah, GA, he died aboard the warship *Wasp* Oct 11, 1779. Pulaski Day is celebrated on the first Monday of March in Illinois.

ROCKNE, KNUTE: BIRTH ANNIVERSARY. Mar 4, 1888. Legendary Notre Dame football coach, born at Voss, Norway. Known for such sayings as "Win one for the Gipper," he died at Cottonwood Falls, KS, Mar 31, 1931.

RONALD AND NANCY REAGAN: WEDDING ANNIVERSARY. Mar 4, 1952. Little Brown Church in the San Fernando Valley, CA. Ronald Reagan was 41 and Nancy Davis (born Anne Frances Robbins) was 30. They were both actors; William Holden served as best man. This was Reagan's second marriage. His first marriage to actress Jane Wyman in 1940 produced daughter Maureen Elizabeth Reagan in 1941, adopted son Michael Edward Reagan (born 1942) in 1945 and daughter Christina Reagan in 1947, who was born prematurely and died within a few days. Nancy and Ronald had two children: Patricia Ann Reagan (Patti Davis), born in 1952, and Ronald Prescott Reagan, in 1958.

SAINT PIRAN'S DAY CELEBRATION. Mar 4. Location available after Jan 1. Celebration in honor of St. Piran, patron saint of Cornwall and Cornish peoples. Held to help preserve history and culture of the Cornish (Celtic). Annually, the Saturday nearest Mar 5. For info: Donald Whitman, Ed, Greater Kansas City Cornish Society, 24 E 68th St, Kansas City, MO 64113-2414. Phone: (816) 361-1956. E-mail: donwhitman1@aol.com.

SOUTHEAST FLORIDA SCOTTISH FESTIVAL AND GAMES. Mar 4. Sportsplex, Coral Springs, FL. 23rd annual. Est attendance: 8,000. For info: Scottish-American Society of Southeast Florida, PO Box 633, Miami Shores, FL 33153. Phone: (954) 476-5559. Web: www.sassf.org.

SPACE MILESTONE: *OGO 5* (US). Mar 4, 1968. Orbiting Geophysical Observatory (OGO) collected data on the sun's influence on Earth. Launched Mar 4, 1968. Six OGOs were launched in all.

TELEVISION ACADEMY HALL OF FAME: FIRST INDUCTEES ANNOUNCED: ANNIVERSARY. Mar 4, 1984. The Television Academy of Arts and Sciences announced the formation of the Television Academy Hall of Fame at Burbank, CA. The first inductees were Lucille Ball, Milton Berle, Paddy Chayefsky, Norman Lear, Edward R. Murrow, William S. Paley and David Sarnoff.

VERMONT: ADMISSION DAY: ANNIVERSARY. Mar 4. Became 14th state in 1791.

BIRTHDAYS TODAY

Landon Donovan, 24, soccer player, born Redlands, CA, Mar 4, 1982.

Emilio Estefan, 53, percussionist for the Miami Sound Machine ("Anything for You"), born Havana, Cuba, Mar 4, 1953.

Patricia Heaton, 47, actress ("Everybody Loves Raymond"), born Bay Village, OH, Mar 4, 1959.

Kevin Johnson, 40, former basketball player, born Sacramento, CA, Mar 4, 1966.

Patsy Kensit, 38, actress (*The Great Gatsby, Blame It on the Bellboy*), born London, England, Mar 4, 1968.

Kay Lenz, 53, actress (*Rich Man, Poor Man*), born Los Angeles, CA, Mar 4, 1953.

Miriam Makeba, 74, actress, singer, anti-apartheid activist, born Johannesburg, South Africa, Mar 4, 1932.

Barbara McNair, 72, singer, actress ("The Barbara McNair Show"), born Racine, WI, Mar 4, 1934.

Catherine O'Hara, 52, comedienne, writer ("SCTV Network 90"), actress (*Home Alone*), born Toronto, ON, Canada, Mar 4, 1954.

Rick Perry, 56, Governor of Texas (R), born Haskell, TX, Mar 4, 1950.

Paula Prentiss, 67, actress ("He & She," *What's New Pussycat?*), born Paula Ragusa at San Antonio, TX, Mar 4, 1939.

Steven Weber, 45, actor ("Wings"), born Queens, NY, Mar 4, 1961.

Mary Wilson, 62, singer (original member of the Supremes with Diana Ross and Florence Ballard), born Detroit, MI, Mar 4, 1944.

MARCH 5 — SUNDAY
Day 64 — 301 Remaining

ACADEMY AWARDS PRESENTATION. Mar 5. Kodak Theatre, Los Angeles, CA. 78th annual. Honoring film achievements of the previous year. Begins at 5:30 PM, PST. Also televised live by ABC. For info: Academy of Motion Picture Arts and Sciences, 8949 Wilshire Blvd, Beverly Hills, CA 90211-1972. Phone: (310) 247-3000. E-mail: www.oscars.org.

BLACKSTONE, WILLIAM: BIRTH ANNIVERSARY. Mar 5, 1595. William Blackstone, born at Durham County, England, was the first settler in what is now Boston, MA, and also the first in what is now Rhode Island. Blackstone came to New England with the Captain Robert Gorges expedition in 1623. When the expedition failed and most returned to England, he stayed and settled on what later became Beacon Hill. In 1634, he sold most of his Boston property and moved to the shores of the river that now bears his name. He died there at what is now Cumberland, RI, May 26, 1675.

BOSTON MASSACRE: ANNIVERSARY. Mar 5, 1770. A skirmish between British troops and a crowd at Boston, MA, became widely publicized and contributed to the unpopularity of the British regime in America before the American Revolution. Five men were killed and six more were injured by British troops commanded by Captain Thomas Preston.

CELEBRATE YOUR NAME WEEK!. Mar 5–11. Who would you be if you didn't have a name? Your name identifies you to

★ ★ ★

	S	M	T	W	T	F	S
March				1	2	3	4
2006	5	6	7	8	9	10	11
	12	13	14	15	16	17	18
	19	20	21	22	23	24	25
	26	27	28	29	30	31	

the world. Celebrate Your Name Week is about not neglecting your name. It's about making sure your name isn't an ignored part of your personhood. Use this week to become connected to your name! See also related events each day this week. Annually, the first full week in March. For info: Jerry Hill. E-mail: allabout names@safe-mail.net. Web: www.jerryhill.com.

CHANNEL ISLANDS NATIONAL PARK ESTABLISHED: ANNIVERSARY. Mar 5, 1980. California's Channel Islands Monument, authorized in 1938 by President Franklin D. Roosevelt, consisted of the islands of Anacapa and Santa Barbara. In 1980 President Jimmy Carter signed a bill establishing the Channel Islands National Park consisting of the islands Anacapa, San Miguel, Santa Barbara, Santa Cruz and Santa Rosa.

CRISPUS ATTUCKS DAY: DEATH ANNIVERSARY. Mar 5, 1770. Honors Crispus Attucks, possibly a runaway slave, who was the first to die in the Boston Massacre.

CULLIGAN, EMMETT J.: BIRTH ANNIVERSARY. Mar 5, 1893. Emmett J. Culligan, founder of the world's largest water treatment organization, was born at Yankton, SD. Culligan first experimented with a water-softening device in the early 1920s—to soften water used to wash his baby's diapers. In 1936 he launched the company from a Northbrook, IL, blacksmith shop. Recipient of the Horatio Alger Award in 1969, Culligan died at San Bernardino, CA, June 3, 1970.

ENGLAND: LONDON BOOK FAIR. Mar 5–7. ExCel Exhibition Centre, London. One of the world's most important publishing events. Est attendance: 25,000. For info: London Book Fair, Oriel House, 26 The Quadrant, Richmond, Surrey, England TW9 1DL. Phone: (44) (20) 8910-7815. Web: www.lbf-virtual.com.

HARRISON, REX: BIRTH ANNIVERSARY. Mar 5, 1908. Born Reginald Carey at Huyton, England. Rex Harrison's career as an actor encompassed more than 40 films and scores of plays. He won both a Tony and an Oscar for the role of Henry Higgins in *My Fair Lady*, perhaps his most famous role. Among other films, he appeared in *Dr. Dolittle, Cleopatra, Blithe Spirit* and *Major Barbara*. He claimed he would never retire from acting, and he was appearing in a Broadway revival of Somerset Maugham's *The Circle* three weeks before his death June 2, 1990, at his home at New York, NY.

HEALING FROM THE INSIDE OUT. Mar 5. Celebrating the innate potential and power we each have to heal. This is a day to recognize the everyday heroes who courageously face crises of mind, body, heart and soul. Through sharing our stories we help each other transform our lives. Annually, the first Sunday in March. For info: The Healing Bridge Project, 505 Monument Ave, Malvern, PA 19355-2634. Phone: (610) 725-9116. Web: www.thehealingbridge.org.

"IRON CURTAIN" SPEECH: 60th ANNIVERSARY. Mar 5, 1946. Winston Churchill, speaking at Westminster College, Fulton, MO, established the cold war boundary with these words: "From Stettin in the Baltic to Trieste in the Adriatic an iron curtain has descended across the continent." Though Churchill was not the first to use the phrase *iron curtain*, his speech gave it a new currency and its usage persisted.

LUXEMBOURG: BÜRGSONNDEG. Mar 5. Young people build a huge bonfire on a hill to celebrate the victorious sun, marking the end of winter. A tradition dating to pre-Christian times. On the Sunday after Ash Wednesday.

MERCATOR, GERHARDUS: BIRTH ANNIVERSARY. Mar 5, 1512. Cartographer-geographer Mercator was born at Rupelmonde, Belgium. His Mercator projection for maps provided an accurate ratio of latitude to longitude and is still used today. He also introduced the term *atlas* for a collection of maps. He died at Duisberg, Germany, Dec 2, 1594.

NAMESAKE DAY. Mar 5. Today is for more than just pondering the existence of your namesakes (people with the same name as you). Consult a telephone directory and/or go online to find namesakes. Make polite, sincere, gentle contact with any namesake(s) you locate. Annually, the Sunday of Celebrate Your Name Week. For info: Jerry Hill. E-mail: allaboutnames@safe-mail.net. Web: www.jerryhill.com.

ORTHODOX CHEESEFARE SUNDAY. Mar 5. The last day for dairy and fish before Clean Monday, which begins Great Lent in the Eastern Orthodox churches.

PHILADELPHIA FLOWER SHOW. Mar 5–12. PA Convention Center, Philadelphia, PA. The largest flower show in the US. The premier event of its kind in the world. Est attendance: 265,000. For info: Pennsylvania Horticultural Society, 100 N 20th St, 5th Fl, Philadelphia, PA 19103-1495. Phone: (215) 988-8800 or (215) 988-8899. Fax: (215) 988-8810. Web: www.theflowershow.com.

PROFESSIONAL PET SITTERS WEEK. Mar 5–11. A week to show appreciation for the pet sitters who work 365 days a year for customers. Annually, the first full week (Sunday through Saturday) in March. For info: Pet Sitters Intl (PSI), 201 E King St, King, NC 27021. Phone: (336) 983-9222. Fax: (336) 983-5266. E-mail: info@petsit.com. Web: www.petsit.com.

READ AN E-BOOK WEEK. Mar 5–11. A week set aside to learn about and/or read an electronic book (e-book). For info: Rita Toews, 9 Esker Pl, East St Paul, MB, Canada, R2E 0K2. Phone: (204) 661-2734. E-mail: r.toews@shaw.ca. Web: www.domokos.com.

SAINT PIRAN'S DAY. Mar 5. Celebrates the birthday of St. Piran, the patron saint of Cornish tinners. Cornish worldwide celebrate this day.

UNITED STATES BANK HOLIDAY: ANNIVERSARY. Mar 5, 1933. On his first full day in office (Sunday, Mar 5, 1933), President Roosevelt proclaimed a national "Bank Holiday" to help save the nation's faltering banking system. Most banks were able to reopen after the 10-day "holiday" (Mar 4–14), but in the meantime, "scrip" had temporarily replaced money in many American households.

BIRTHDAYS TODAY

Samantha Eggar, 67, actress ("Samantha and the King," *The Collector*), born London, England, Mar 5, 1939.

Penn Jillette, 51, magician, born Greenfield, MA, Mar 5, 1955.

Paul Sand, 62, actor ("St. Elsewhere"; Tony Award for *Story Theatre*), born Paul Sanchez at Los Angeles, CA, Mar 5, 1944.

Dean Stockwell, 70, actor (*The Boy with Green Hair*, "Quantum Leap"), born Los Angeles, CA, Mar 5, 1936.

Laurence Tisch, 83, broadcasting executive, born New York, NY, Mar 5, 1923.

Marsha Warfield, 52, actress ("Night Court," "Empty Nest"), born Chicago, IL, Mar 5, 1954.

Michael Warren, 60, actor ("Paris," "Hill Street Blues"), born South Bend, IN, Mar 5, 1946.

Fred Williamson, 68, actor ("Julia," "Half Nelson"), former professional football player, born Gary, IN, Mar 5, 1938.

MARCH 6 — MONDAY
Day 65 — 300 Remaining

AHRMA VINTAGE MOTORCYCLE RACES. Mar 6–7. Daytona Speedway, Daytona Beach, FL. Vintage and historic motorcycles visit the Superspeedway. For info: Daytona International Speedway, PO Box 2801, Daytona Beach, FL 32120-2801. Phone: (800) PIT-SHOP. Web: www.daytonainternationalspeedway.com.

AUSTRALIA: EIGHT HOUR DAY or LABOR DAY. Mar 6. Western Australia and Tasmania. Parades and celebrations commemorate trade union efforts during the 19th century to limit working hours. Their slogan: "Eight hours labor, eight hours recreation, eight hours rest!" Annually, the first Monday in March.

BROWNING, ELIZABETH BARRETT: 200th BIRTH ANNIVERSARY. Mar 6, 1806. English poet, author of *Sonnets from the Portuguese*, wife of poet Robert Browning and subject of the play *The Barretts of Wimpole Street,* was born near Durham, England. She died at Florence, Italy, June 29, 1861.

CHASE'S DEADLINE APPROACHING. Mar 6. Time to plan ahead. Schedule 2007 celebrations and observances and submit information to *Chase's Calendar of Events 2007* by Apr 15, 2006. Sponsors/information suppliers of events in this book should have received confirmation/revision forms for the 2007 edition by this time. To submit new entries for consideration, use a copy of the form on the last page of this book. Send to: Editor, Chase's Calendar of Events, The McGraw-Hill Companies, Contemporary Books, 130 E Randolph St, Ste 900, Chicago, IL 60601.

COSTELLO, LOU: 100th BIRTH ANNIVERSARY. Mar 6, 1906. Born at Paterson, NJ, partner with Bud Abbott in the legendary comedy duo Abbott and Costello. The team formed in 1936 and were popular on radio, TV and film. Films included *Buck Privates* and *Abbott and Costello Meet Frankenstein*. "Who's On First?" was their legendary comedy routine. Costello died Mar 3, 1959, at East Los Angeles, CA.

DRED SCOTT DECISION: ANNIVERSARY. Mar 6, 1857. This was the most famous US Supreme Court decision during the prewar slavery controversy. Dred Scott, a slave, had successfully petitioned for his freedom based on his previous residence in a free state and territory. On this date, the Supreme Court overturned Missouri's Supreme Court decision and declared the 1820 Missouri Compromise unconstitutional. Chief Justice Roger Taney wrote that slaves were property, not citizens, and that Congress had no power to restrict slavery in the territories.

EISNER, WILL: BIRTH ANNIVERSARY. Mar 6, 1917. One of the greatest comic book/graphic artists, William Erwin Eisner was born today at Brooklyn, NY, to Jewish immigrant parents. In a career spanning eight decades, Eisner created the popular and innovative *Spirit* comic book, started an educational comic book business, taught legions of students graphic narrative techniques and created the first graphic novel, *A Contract with God* (1978). He brought cinematic touches—including German Expressionist style—to comics. The Eisner Awards were created in his honor in 1988 to recognize other bright lights in the field. Eisner died Jan 3, 2005, at Fort Lauderdale, FL.

March 2006	S	M	T	W	T	F	S
				1	2	3	4
	5	6	7	8	9	10	11
	12	13	14	15	16	17	18
	19	20	21	22	23	24	25
	26	27	28	29	30	31	

FALL OF THE ALAMO: ANNIVERSARY. Mar 6, 1836. Anniversary of the fall of the Texan fort, the Alamo. The siege, led by Mexican general Santa Anna, began Feb 23 and reached its climax Mar 6, when the last of the defenders was slain. Texans, under General Sam Houston, rallied with the war cry "Remember the Alamo" and, at the Battle of San Jacinto, Apr 21, defeated and captured Santa Anna, who signed a treaty recognizing Texas's independence.

FUN FACTS ABOUT NAMES DAY. Mar 6. Celebrate names today by finding (at a library or online) fun facts about names. Does the doll we call "Barbie" have a last name? Does the dog game piece from Monopoly have a name? What was the name of the White House before it was renamed the White House? Annually, the Monday of Celebrate Your Name Week. For info: Jerry Hill. E-mail: allaboutnames@safe-mail.net. Web: www.jerryhill.com.

GHANA: INDEPENDENCE DAY. Mar 6. National holiday. Commemorates independence from Great Britain in 1957.

GUAM: DISCOVERY DAY or MAGELLAN DAY. Mar 6. Commemorates discovery of Guam in 1521 by Magellan. Annually, the first Monday in March.

HELP SOMEONE SEE WEEK. Mar 6–10. Rockford, OH. Residents and staff at the Laurels of Shane Hill and Maplewood of Shanes Village help the Rockford Lions Club collect used eyeglasses, frames, lenses and cases to be refurbished and distributed to those in need. Residents learn about the guide dog program and diseases and treatments of the eye. More than 200 pairs of glasses and cases were collected in 2005. For info: Brooke Reyman, Activities Dir, Laurels of Shane Hill Nursing Home, 10731 State Rte 118, Rockford, OH 45882-8947. Phone: (419) 363-2620.

"IN THE HEAT OF THE NIGHT" TV PREMIERE: ANNIVERSARY. Mar 6, 1988. NBC's police drama was based on the 1967 movie with the same name. Carroll O'Connor played Mississippi police chief Bill Gillespie who, along with Howard Rollins as Detective Virgil Tibbs, investigated crimes in the rural South. The cast featured Alan Autry as Sergeant Bubba Skinner; Anne-Marie Johnson as Virgil's wife, Althea; David Hart as Deputy Parker William; Hugh O'Connor as Deputy Lonnie Jamison; Christian LeBlanc as Deputy Junior Abernathy; Geoffrey Thorne as Deputy Sweet and Crystal Fox as dispatcher Luanne Corbin. The last telecast aired July 28, 1994, but the program remains popular in reruns.

LARDNER, RING: BIRTH ANNIVERSARY. Mar 6, 1885. Ringgold Wilmer (Ring) Lardner, sportswriter, born at Niles, MI. Lardner wrote about sports for a variety of newspapers, mostly in Chicago. In both his columns and his short stories, he reproduced ballplayers' vernacular speech patterns with great success, thereby laying the groundwork for generations of baseball fiction to come. Lardner abandoned baseball after the Black Sox scandal was exposed. He wrote songs, plays and magazine articles but never the novel that some of his friends thought he should. Taciturn and solemn with a biting sense of humor, Lardner drank and smoked to excess, even after contracting tuberculosis in 1926. Posthumously given the J.G. Taylor Spink Award in 1963 for his baseball writing. Died at East Hampton, NY, Sept 25, 1933.

MICHELANGELO: BIRTH ANNIVERSARY. Mar 6, 1475. Anniversary of the birth, at Caprese, Italy, of Michelangelo di Lodovico Buonarroti Simoni, a prolific Renaissance painter, sculptor, architect and poet who had a profound impact on Western art. Michelangelo's fresco painting on the ceiling of the Sistine Chapel at the Vatican at Rome, Italy, is often considered the pinnacle of his achievement in painting, as well as the highest achievement of the Renaissance. Also among his works were the sculptures *David* and *The Pieta*. Appointed architect of St. Peter's in 1542, a post he held until his death Feb 18, 1564, at Rome.

MOON PHASE: FIRST QUARTER. Mar 6. Moon enters First Quarter phase at 3:16 PM, EST.

NATIONAL CHEERLEADING WEEK. Mar 6–12. Various cheer activites conducted on a daily basis throughout the week. Annually, the first full week in March. For info: Linda Lundy, 59 County Rd 3474, Cleveland, TX 77327. Phone: (281) 399-8357. Fax: (281) 364-1129. E-mail: linda@unitedcheer.com.

NATIONAL PROCRASTINATION WEEK. Mar 6–12. To promote the benefits of relaxing through putting off until tomorrow everything that needn't be done today. For info: Les Waas, Pres, Procrastinators' Club of America Inc, PO Box 712, Bryn Athyn, PA 19009. Phone: (215) 947-9020. Fax: (215) 947-7210. E-mail: procrastinators_club_of_america@yahoo.com. Web: www.geocities.com/procrastinators_club_of_america.

NATIONAL SCHOOL BREAKFAST WEEK. Mar 6–10. To focus on the importance of a nutritious breakfast served in the schools, giving children a good start to their day. Annually, the first full week in March (weekdays). For info: School Nutrition Association, 700 S Washington St, Ste 300, Alexandria, VA 22314. Phone: (703) 739-3900. Fax: (703) 739-3915. E-mail: servicecenter@schoolnutrition.org. Web: www.schoolnutrition.org.

NEWSPAPER IN EDUCATION WEEK. Mar 6–10. A week-long celebration of using newspapers in the classroom as living textbooks. Annually, the first full week in March (weekdays). For info: Zachary Brousseau, Newspaper Assn of America, 1921 Gallows Rd, Ste 600, Vienna, VA 22182-3900. Phone: (703) 902-1698. E-mail: zachary.brousseau@naa.org. Web: www.naafoundation.org.

ORTHODOX GREEN MONDAY. Mar 6. Green, or Clean, Monday is the first Monday of Lent on the Orthodox Christian calendar. Lunch in the fields, with bread, olives and uncooked vegetables and no meat or dairy products.

ORTHODOX LENT. Mar 6–Apr 15. Great Lent or Easter Lent, observed by Eastern Orthodox churches, lasts until Holy Week begins on Orthodox Palm Sunday (Apr 16). The first day is known as Clean Monday which begins the Great Fast when Orthodox Christians abstain from eating meat, dairy and fish.

PEALE, ANNA CLAYPOOLE: BIRTH ANNIVERSARY. Mar 6, 1791. American painter of miniatures and a member of the famous Peale family of artists. Born at Philadelphia, PA; died Dec 25, 1878.

WILLS, BOB: BIRTH ANNIVERSARY. Mar 6, 1905. The Father of Western Swing was born at Kosse, TX. Originally a performer (fiddler) with the Light Crust Doughboys, Wills later formed the popular Texas Playboys. Bob Wills and the Texas Playboys appeared on film and at the Grand Ole Opry and made western swing popular with such hits as "San Antonio Rose." Wills died May 13, 1975, at Fort Worth, TX.

BIRTHDAYS TODAY

Tom Arnold, 47, actor ("Roseanne," *McHale's Navy, True Lies*), born Ottumwa, IA, Mar 6, 1959.

Christopher Samuel Bond, 67, US Senator (R, Missouri), born St. Louis, MO, Mar 6, 1939.

Sarah Caldwell, 82, conductor, born Maryville, MO, Mar 6, 1924.

L. Gordon Cooper, 79, astronaut, born Shawnee, OK, Mar 6, 1927.

Gabriel Garcia-Marquez, 78, Nobel Prize–winning author (*A Hundred Years of Solitude, Love in the Time of Cholera*), born Aracaracca, Colombia, Mar 6, 1928.

Dave Gilmour, 62, singer, musician (member Pink Floyd, *The Dark Side of the Moon*), born Cambridge, England, Mar 6, 1944.

Alan Greenspan, 80, economist, Chairman of the Federal Reserve Board, born New York, NY, Mar 6, 1926.

D.L. Hughley, 43, comedian, actor ("The Hughleys," *The Original Kings of Comedy*), born Los Angeles, CA, Mar 6, 1963.

Kiri Te Kanawa, 62, opera singer, born Gisborne, New Zealand, Mar 6, 1944.

Ed McMahon, 83, actor, TV host ("The Tonight Show," "Star Search"), born Detroit, MI, Mar 6, 1923.

Ben Murphy, 64, actor ("Alias Smith and Jones," *Yours, Mine and Ours*), born Jonesboro, AR, Mar 6, 1942.

Ryan Nyquist, 27, BMX bike racer, born Los Gatos, CA, Mar 6, 1979.

Shaquille Rashan O'Neal, 34, basketball player, born Newark, NJ, Mar 6, 1972.

Amy Pietz, 37, actress ("Caroline in the City"), born Oakcreek, WI, Mar 6, 1969.

Rob Reiner, 59, actor ("All in the Family"), director (*When Harry Met Sally. . . , This Is Spinal Tap*), born New York, NY, Mar 6, 1947 (some sources say 1945).

Valentina Tereshkova-Nikolaeva, 69, cosmonaut, born Maslennikovo, USSR, Mar 6, 1937.

MARCH 7 — TUESDAY
Day 66 — 299 Remaining

ASSOCIATION OF AMERICAN GEOGRAPHERS ANNUAL MEETING. Mar 7–11. Chicago, IL. 102nd annual national meeting of members with workshops, paper and poster sessions and field trips. Est attendance: 3,000. For info: Assn of American Geographers, 1710 16th St NW, Washington, DC 20009-3198. Phone: (202) 234-1450. E-mail: meeting@aag.org. Web: www.aag.org.

BIG 12 WOMEN'S BASKETBALL TOURNAMENT. Mar 7–9, 11. Reunion Arena, Dallas, TX. Est attendance: 30,000. For info: Big 12 Conference, 2201 Stemmons Freeway, 28th Fl, Dallas, TX 75207. Phone: (214) 742-1212. Fax: (214) 753-0145. Web: www.big12sports.com.

BURBANK, LUTHER: BIRTH ANNIVERSARY. Mar 7, 1849. Anniversary of the birth of American naturalist and author, creator and developer of many new varieties of flowers, fruits, vegetables and trees. Luther Burbank's birthday is observed in California as Bird and Arbor Day. Born at Lancaster, MA, he died at Santa Rosa, CA, Apr 11, 1926.

DISTINGUISHED SERVICE MEDAL: ANNIVERSARY. Mar 7, 1918. With US troops fighting in the trenches in France during the First World War, President Woodrow Wilson authorized the creation of a new bronze, beribboned medal to be given to US Army personnel who performed "exceptionally meritorious service."

HOPKINS, STEPHEN: BIRTH ANNIVERSARY. Mar 7, 1707. Colonial governor (Rhode Island) and signer of the Declaration of Independence. Born at Providence, RI, and died there July 13, 1785.

MONOPOLY INVENTED: ANNIVERSARY. Mar 7, 1933. While unemployed during the Depression, Charles Darrow devised this game and he sold it himself for two years. Monopoly was mass marketed by Parker Brothers beginning in 1935. Darrow died a millionaire in 1967.

NATIONAL BE HEARD DAY. Mar 7. Women currently own approximately 9.1 million small businesses in the US and are starting them at twice the rate of their male counterparts. But often, female business owners are less likely to get the media coverage they deserve. National Be Heard Day celebrates and empowers each female business owner and entrepreneur who can find her voice, tell her story and be heard though publicity efforts. More information and a free Be Heard publicity kit is available at www.beheardsolutions.com. For info: Shannon Cherry, Be Heard Solutions, 184 Lancaster St, Albany, NY 12210. Phone: (518) 248-6592. Fax: (408) 539-0324. E-mail: info@beheardsolutions.com. Web: www.beheardsolutions.com.

NORTH DAKOTA WINTER SHOW. Mar 7–12. Valley City, ND. Six-day agricultural expo featuring world's largest crop show, eight-breed cattle show, culinary arts show and competition, style and needlework show and competition, children's area, three-performance PRCA Rodeos, draft horse pulls, old-time tractor pull (tractors built prior to 1955), 80-vendor farm toy show and single performance headliner country concert. Annually, the first week in March. Est attendance: 72,000. For info: Brad Hertel, Mgr, ND Winter Show, PO Box 846, Valley City, ND 58072. Phone: (701) 845-1401 or (800) 437-0218. Fax: (701) 845-3914. E-mail: ndws@northdakotawintershow.com. Web: www.northdakotawintershow.com.

PEACE CORPS DAY. Mar 7. Commemorates the founding of the Peace Corps on Mar 1, 1961, by President John F. Kennedy. Observed on the first Tuesday in March.

REMAGEN BRIDGE CAPTURE: ANNIVERSARY. Mar 7, 1945. On this date in 1945, a small advance force of the US First Army captured the Ludendorff railway bridge across the Rhine River at Remagen (between Bonn and Coblenz)—the only bridge across the Rhine that had not been blown up by the German defenders—thus acquiring the first bridgehead onto the east bank and the beginning of the Allied advance into Germany, a turning point in World War II.

★**SAVE YOUR VISION WEEK.** Mar 7–13. Presidential Proclamation issued for the first week of March since 1964, except 1971 and 1982 when issued for the second week of March. (PL88–1942, of Dec 30, 1963.)

SUEZ CANAL OPENS: ANNIVERSARY. Mar 7, 1869. This waterway across Egypt connecting the Mediterranean and Red seas was built by the French. In 1956 Egyptian president Nasser nationalized the canal, prompting an invasion by the British, French and Israelis. The Six-Day War in 1967 shut down the canal for eight years.

TASTE OF THE TOWN. Mar 7. Multi-Purpose Events Center Exhibit Hall, Wichita Falls, TX. More than 50 restaurants and vendors gather together to show off the best food in town. Benefits the Wichita County Chapter of the Red Cross. Est attendance: 2,000. For info: Wichita Falls Conv & Visitors Bureau, 1000 Fifth St, Wichita Falls, TX 76301. Phone: (940) 716-5500. Fax: (940) 716-5509. Web: www.wichitafalls.org.

TOWN MEETING DAY. Mar 7. Vermont. The first Tuesday in March is an official state holiday in Vermont. Nearly every town elects officers, approves budget items and deals with a multitude of other items in a daylong public meeting of the voters.

UNIQUE NAMES DAY. Mar 7. This is a day for all people to appreciate friends, acquaintances and loved ones who have unique names. This is an opportunity for those of us who can buy mass-produced name items to celebrate the beauty of unique names. Annually, the Tuesday of Celebrate Your Name Week. For info: Jerry Hill. E-mail: allaboutnames@safe-mail.net. Web: www.jerryhill.com.

BIRTHDAYS TODAY

Anthony Armstrong-Jones (Lord Snowdon), 76, photographer, born London, England, Mar 7, 1930.
Bryan Cranston, 50, actor ("Malcolm in the Middle"), born San Fernando Valley, CA, Mar 7, 1956.
Taylor Dayne, 44, singer ("Love Will Send You Back"), born Long Island, NY, Mar 7, 1962.
Michael Eisner, 64, Disney executive, born Mount Kisco, NY, Mar 7, 1942.

	S	M	T	W	T	F	S
March				1	2	3	4
2006	5	6	7	8	9	10	11
	12	13	14	15	16	17	18
	19	20	21	22	23	24	25
	26	27	28	29	30	31	

Janet Guthrie, 68, former auto racer, born Iowa City, IA, Mar 7, 1938.
Franco Harris, 56, Hall of Fame football player, born Fort Dix, NJ, Mar 7, 1950.
John Heard, 60, actor (*The Milagro Beanfield War, Rambling Rose, The Pelican Brief*), born Washington, DC, Mar 7, 1946.
Jeff Kent, 38, baseball player, born Bellflower, CA, Mar 7, 1968.
Ivan Lendl, 46, former tennis player, born Ostrava, Czechoslovakia, Mar 7, 1960.
Willard Herman Scott, 72, weatherman ("The Today Show"), friend of centenarians, born Alexandria, VA, Mar 7, 1934.
Daniel J. Travanti, 66, actor ("Hill Street Blues"), born Kenosha, WI, Mar 7, 1940.
Rachel Weisz, 35, actress (*The Mummy, The Mummy Returns*), born London, England, Mar 7, 1971.
Peter Wolf, 60, lead singer (J. Geils Band, "Centerfold"), born Boston, MA, Mar 7, 1946.

MARCH 8 — WEDNESDAY
Day 67 — 298 Remaining

AMA NATIONAL HOT SHOE DIRT TRACK RACE. Mar 8. Daytona Beach Municipal Stadium, Daytona Beach, FL. Dirt track series race. For info: Daytona Intl Speedway, Box 2801, Daytona Beach, FL 32120-2801. Phone: (800) PIT-SHOP. Web: www.daytonainternationalspeedway.com.

BEAVERS, LOUISE: BIRTH ANNIVERSARY. Mar 8, 1902. The Hollywood career of Louise Beavers spanned 30 years and more than 125 films. Though she was forced to play stereotypical roles, such as those of maids, her authentic talent was always apparent. Her starring role in the film *Imitation of Life* earned her high praise. Beavers was a member of the Black Filmmakers Hall of Fame. She also played the title role in the TV series "Beulah" (1951–53). Born at Cincinnati, OH; died at Los Angeles, Oct 26, 1962.

CAXTON'S *MIRROR OF THE WORLD* TRANSLATION: 525th ANNIVERSARY. Mar 8, 1481. William Caxton, England's first printer, completed the translation from French into English of *The Mirror of the World*, a popular account of astronomy and other sciences. In print soon afterward, *Mirror of the World* became the first illustrated book printed in England.

DAYTONA 200 BY HONDA QUALIFYING DAY. Mar 8–9. Daytona International Speedway, Daytona Beach, FL. For info: Daytona Intl Speedway, PO Box 2801, Daytona Beach, FL 32120-2801. Phone: (800) PIT-SHOP. Web: www.daytonainternationalspeedway.com.

GRAHAME, KENNETH: BIRTH ANNIVERSARY. Mar 8, 1859. Scottish author, born at Edinburgh. His children's book *The Wind in the Willows* has as its main characters a mole, a rat, a badger and a toad. He died July 6, 1932, at Pangbourne, Berkshire.

INTERNATIONAL (WORKING) WOMEN'S DAY. Mar 8. A day to honor women, especially working women. Said to commemorate an 1857 march and demonstration at New York, NY, by female garment and textile workers. Believed to have been first proclaimed for this date at an international conference of women held at Helsinki, Finland, in 1910, "that henceforth Mar 8 should be declared International Women's Day." The 50th anniversary observance, at Peking, China, in 1960, cited Clara Zetkin (1857–1933) as "initiator of Women's Day on Mar 8." This is perhaps the most widely observed holiday of recent origin and is unusual among holidays originating in the US in having been widely adopted and observed in other nations, including socialist countries. In Russia it is a national holiday, and flowers or gifts are presented to women workers.

LEARN WHAT YOUR NAME MEANS DAY. Mar 8. Celebrate your name today by looking up (online or at a library) its meaning. Annually, the Wednesday of Celebrate Your Name Week. For info: Jerry Hill. E-mail: allaboutnames@safe-mail.net. Web: www.jerryhill.com.

LOUISIANA SPORTSMEN'S SHOW. Mar 8–12. Louisiana Superdome, New Orleans, LA. 27th annual. Louisiana's original sportfishing, hunting and boat show also covering Baton Rouge and the Gulf Coast. Est attendance: 100,000. For info: Bob Del Giorno. Phone: (504) 464-7363. Fax: (504) 835-8692. Web: www.sportsmensshow.com.

NAIA DIVISION II MEN'S BASKETBALL NATIONAL CHAMPIONSHIP. Mar 8–14. Point Lookout, MO. 32-team field competes for the national championship. 15th annual. Est attendance: 30,000. For info: Natl Assn of Intercollegiate Athletics, 23500 W 105th St, PO Box 1325, Olathe, KS 66051-1325. Phone: (913) 791-0044. Fax: (913) 791-9555. E-mail: smcclure@naia.org. Web: www.naia.org.

NAIA DIVISION II WOMEN'S BASKETBALL NATIONAL CHAMPIONSHIP. Mar 8–14. Sioux City, IA. 32-team field competes for the national championship. 15th annual. Est attendance: 12,500. For info: Natl Assn of Intercollegiate Athletics, 23500 W 105th St, PO Box 1325, Olathe, KS 66051-1325. Phone: (913) 791-0044. Fax: (913) 791-9555. E-mail: lthomas@naia.org. Web: www.naia.org.

NCAA MEN'S AND WOMEN'S SKIING CHAMPIONSHIPS. Mar 8–11. Mount Werner and Howelsen Hill, Steamboat Springs, CO. Hosted by the University of Colorado, Boulder. Est attendance: 1,500. For info: Natl Collegiate Athletic Assn, 700 W Washington St, PO Box 6222, Indianapolis, IN 46206-6222. Phone: (317) 917-6222. Fax: (317) 917-6888. Web: www.ncaasports.com.

RUSSIA: INTERNATIONAL WOMEN'S DAY. Mar 8. National holiday.

SYRIAN ARAB REPUBLIC: REVOLUTION DAY: ANNIVERSARY. Mar 8, 1963. Official public holiday commemorating assumption of power by Revolutionary National Council.

UNITED NATIONS: DAY FOR WOMEN'S RIGHTS AND INTERNATIONAL PEACE. Mar 8. An international day observed by the organizations of the United Nations system. In some years, known as International Women's Day. For info: United Nations, Dept of Public Info, New York, NY 10017. Web: www.un.org.

UNITED STATES INCOME TAX: ANNIVERSARY. Mar 8, 1913. The Internal Revenue Service began to levy and collect income taxes. The 16th Amendment to the Constitution, ratified Feb 3, 1913, gave Congress the authority to tax income. The US had also levied an income tax during the Civil War. See also: "Lincoln Signs Income Tax" (July 1).

UNIVERSAL WOMEN'S WEEK. Mar 8–14. To remind ourselves and others of the value of women of all ages and classes and of their rights and dignity, and to honor outstanding women in the fields of government, business, industry, science, health, education, social work and the cultural arts by election to Universal Hall of Fame. Please send $5 to cover expense of printing, handling and postage. Annually, Mar 8–14. For info: Dr. Stanley Drake, Pres Emeritus, Intl Society of Friendship & Good Will, 8592 Roswell Rd, Ste 251, Atlanta, GA 30350-1867. Phone: (678) 795-1362. E-mail: sjdrake@bellsouth.net. Web: www.friendshipandgoodwill.org.

VAN BUREN, HANNAH HOES: BIRTH ANNIVERSARY. Mar 8, 1783. Wife of Martin Van Buren, 8th president of the US. Born at Kinderhook, NY, she died at Albany, NY, Feb 5, 1819.

BIRTHDAYS TODAY

George Allen, 54, US Senator (R, Virginia), born Whittier, CA, Mar 8, 1952.

Cyd Charisse, 83, actress (*Silk Stockings*), dancer (*Grand Hotel, Singin' in the Rain*), born Tula Finklea at Amarillo, TX, Mar 8, 1923.

Susan Clark, 66, actress ("Webster," *Babe*), born Sarnia, ON, Canada, Mar 8, 1940.

Micky Dolenz, 61, singer, actor ("The Monkees"), director, born Los Angeles, CA, Mar 8, 1945.

Kathy Ireland, 43, model, born Santa Barbara, CA, Mar 8, 1963.

Camryn Manheim, 45, actress ("The Practice"), born Caldwell, NJ, Mar 8, 1961.

Marcia Newby, 18, gymnast, born Virginia Beach, VA, Mar 8, 1988.

Freddie Prinze, Jr, 30, actor (*Scooby-Doo, She's All That*), born Albuquerque, NM, Mar 8, 1976.

Aidan Quinn, 47, actor (*Desperately Seeking Susan*; stage: *A Streetcar Named Desire*), born Chicago, IL, Mar 8, 1959.

Lynn Redgrave, 63, actress (*Georgy Girl*, "House Calls"), born London, England, Mar 8, 1943.

James Edward (Jim) Rice, 53, former baseball player, born Anderson, SC, Mar 8, 1953.

Carole Bayer Sager, 59, singer, songwriter ("That's What Friends Are For," with Burt Bacharach), born New York, NY, Mar 8, 1947.

Raynoma Gordy Singleton, 69, cofounder of Motown Records, former wife of Berry Gordy, born Detroit, MI, Mar 8, 1937.

James Van Der Beek, 29, actor ("Dawson's Creek"), born Cheshire, CT, Mar 8, 1977.

MARCH 9 — THURSDAY

Day 68 — 297 Remaining

AMA GRAND NATIONAL KICKOFF. Mar 9. Daytona Beach Municipal Stadium, Daytona Beach, FL. Dirt track series race. For info: Daytona Intl Speedway, PO Box 2801, Daytona Beach, FL 32120-2801. Phone: (800) PIT-SHOP. Web: www.daytonainternationalspeedway.com.

BARBIE DEBUTS: ANNIVERSARY. Mar 9, 1959. The popular girls' doll debuted in stores. More than 800 million dolls have been sold.

BELIZE: BARON BLISS DAY. Mar 9. Official public holiday. Celebrated in honor of Sir Henry Edward Ernest Victor Bliss, a great benefactor of Belize.

BIG TEN MEN'S BASKETBALL TOURNAMENT. Mar 9–12. Conseco Fieldhouse, Indianapolis, IN. For info: Big Ten Conference, 1500 W Higgins Rd, Park Ridge, IL 60068-6300. Phone: (847) 696-1010. Fax: (847) 696-1110. Web: www.bigten.org.

BIG 12 MEN'S BASKETBALL CHAMPIONSHIP. Mar 9–12. American Airlines Center, Dallas, TX. Est attendance: 90,000. For info: Big 12 Conference, 2201 Stemmons Freeway, 28th Fl, Dallas, TX 75207. Phone: (214) 742-1212. Fax: (214) 753-0145. Web: www.big12sports.com.

ENGLAND: CRUFTS DOG SHOW. Mar 9–12. National Exhibition Centre, Birmingham, West Midlands. The World's Greatest Dog Show where more than 21,000 top pedigree dogs compete to achieve the title of "Best in Show," the most prestigious award in the world of dogs. Held since 1891. Est attendance: 120,000. For info: Events Department, The Kennel Club, 1 Clarges St, London, England W1J 8AB. Phone: (44) (870) 606-6750. Fax: (44) (207) 518-1050. Web: www.crufts.org.uk.

"FAMILY" TV PREMIERE: 30th ANNIVERSARY. Mar 9, 1976. ABC drama about the Lawrence family living in Pasadena, CA, who stuck together through trials and triumphs. Cast members included Sada Thompson as Kate Lawrence, James Broderick as her husband Douglas, Elayne Heilveil and Meredith Baxter-Birney as their divorced daughter Nancy Maitland, Gary Frank as their son Willie and Kristy McNichol as youngest daughter Buddy (Letitia). The last episode aired on June 25, 1980.

GAGARIN, YURI ALEXSEYEVICH: BIRTH ANNIVERSARY. Mar 9, 1934. Russian cosmonaut Yuri Gagarin, the first person to travel in space, was born at Gzhatsk, USSR. The 27-year-old Soviet Air Force major made his flight Apr 12, 1961, lasting 108 minutes and orbiting Earth in a rocket-propelled, five-ton space capsule, 187 miles above the Earth's surface. Gagarin was killed in an airplane crash near Moscow, USSR, Mar 27, 1968. After his death the town in which he was born was renamed Gagarin, and the Gagarin Museum was established in the frame house where he spent his childhood.

GRANT COMMISSIONED COMMANDER OF ALL UNION ARMIES: ANNIVERSARY. Mar 9, 1864. At Washington, DC, Ulysses S. Grant accepted his commission as Lieutenant General, becoming the commander of all the Union armies.

JOE FRANKLIN DAY. Mar 9. A day to honor the king of radio, television and entertainment for all his contributions on the anniversary of his birth. Franklin appeared on late-night television in New York from 1950–93 and continues to entertain people today. For info: Bob O'Brien, "The Answer Man," 1061 Koelle Ave, Secaucus, NJ 07094. Phone/fax: (201) 865-4775. E-mail: bob theebest@yahoo.com.

JULIA, RAUL: BIRTH ANNIVERSARY. Mar 9, 1940. Born at San Juan, Puerto Rico, Julia won acclaim and four Tony nominations for roles he played on Broadway ranging from Shakespeare's *Proteus* to *Mack the Knife*. Most widely known of his many film roles are Gomez in *The Addams Family* and Valentín in *Kiss of the Spider Woman*. Julia died Oct 24, 1994, at Manhasset, NY.

NAMETAG DAY. Mar 9. Today's celebration of names stipulates that wherever you are, whatever you're doing, you wear a "Hello, I'm [your name here]" nametag. (Note: this event is not for children.) Annually, the Thursday of Celebrate Your Name Week. For info: Jerry Hill. E-mail: allaboutnames@safe-mail.net. Web: www .jerryhill.com.

PANIC DAY. Mar 9. Run around all day in a panic, telling others you can't handle it anymore. [©2003 by WH.] For info: Thomas & Ruth Roy, Wellcat Holidays, 2418 Long Ln, Lebanon, PA 17046. Phone: (717) 279-0184. E-mail: info@wellcat.com. Web: www.wellcat.com.

SAINT FRANCES OF ROME: FEAST DAY. Mar 9. Patron of motorists and model for housewives and widows (1384–1440). After 40 years of marriage she was widowed in 1436 and later joined the community of Benedictine Oblates. Canonized in 1608.

TOKYO BLANKET BOMBING: ANNIVERSARY. Mar 9, 1945. The Japanese capital of Tokyo was bombed by 343 Super-fortresses carrying all the incendiary bombs they could hold. Within the targeted areas of the city, population densities were four times greater than those of most American cities, and homes were made primarily of wood and paper. Carried by the wind, the fires leveled 16 sq miles. More than a quarter million buildings were destroyed. The death toll was 83,000; 41,000 were injured. For the balance of WWII American strategic bombing followed this pattern.

VESPUCCI, AMERIGO: BIRTH ANNIVERSARY. Mar 9, 1454. Italian navigator, merchant and explorer for whom the Americas were named. Born at Florence, Italy (some sources cite his birth year as 1451). He participated in at least two expeditions between 1499 and 1502 which took him to the coast of South America, where he discovered the Amazon and Plata rivers. Vespucci's expeditions were of great importance because he believed that he had discovered a new continent, not just a new route to the Orient. Neither Vespucci nor his exploits achieved the fame of Columbus, but the New World was to be named for Amerigo Vespucci by an obscure German geographer and mapmaker, Martin Waldseemuller. Ironically, in his work as an outfitter of ships, Vespucci had been personally acquainted with Christopher Columbus. Vespucci died at Seville, Spain, Feb 22, 1512. See also: "Waldseemuller, Martin: Remembrance Day" (Apr 25).

VIRGINIA SPRING SHOW. Mar 9–12. Showplace Exhibition Center, Richmond, VA. 19th annual. Features hundreds of artisans and craftspeople, food shops, spring entertainment. Holiday Cooking Theatre. Est attendance: 25,000. For info: Virginia Show Productions, PO Box 305, Chase City, VA 23924. Phone: (434) 372-3996. Fax: (434) 372-3410. E-mail: vashowsinc@aol.com.

BIRTHDAYS TODAY

Juliette Binoche, 42, actress (*The English Patient, Chocolat*), born Paris, France, Mar 9, 1964.

Linda Fiorentino, 46, actress (*Men in Black*), born Philadelphia, PA, Mar 9, 1960.

Robert James (Bobby) Fischer, 63, World Chess Champion (1972), born Chicago, IL, Mar 9, 1943.

Mickey Gilley, 70, singer, musician ("City Lights," "Stand by Me"), cousin of Jerry Lee Lewis, born Natchez, MS, Mar 9, 1936.

Marty Ingels, 70, actor ("I'm Dickens . . . He's Fenster," *A Guide for the Married Man*), born Brooklyn, NY, Mar 9, 1936.

David Hume Kennerly, 59, photographer, born Rosenburg, OR, Mar 9, 1947.

Emmanuel Lewis, 35, actor ("Webster"), born Brooklyn, NY, Mar 9, 1971.

Terence John (Terry) Mulholland, 43, baseball player, born St. Paul, MN, Mar 9, 1963.

Jeffrey Osborne, 58, musician, songwriter, born Providence, RI, Mar 9, 1948.

Benito Santiago, 41, baseball player, born Ponce, Puerto Rico, Mar 9, 1965.

Mickey Spillane, 88, author (*The Killing Man, Vengeance Is Mine*), born Frank Spillane at Brooklyn, NY, Mar 9, 1918.

Trish Van Devere, 63, actress (*Where's Poppa?, One Is a Lonely Number*), born Tenafly, NJ, Mar 9, 1943.

Joyce Van Patten, 72, actress (*Monkey Shines*, "The Goodbye Guys"), born Queens, NY, Mar 9, 1934.

		S	M	T	W	T	F	S
March					1	2	3	4
2006		5	6	7	8	9	10	11
		12	13	14	15	16	17	18
		19	20	21	22	23	24	25
		26	27	28	29	30	31	

MARCH 10 — FRIDAY

Day 69 — 296 Remaining

"BUFFY THE VAMPIRE SLAYER" TV PREMIERE: ANNIVERSARY. Mar 10, 1997. The popular WB show mixed B-movie horror with teen drama. Buffy Summers, played by Sarah Michelle Gellar, is a chosen slayer of vampires, but she still has to get through high school. The witty series was a spin-off of the 1992 film of the same name. After changing networks, the series ended in May 2003.

CRAFTSMEN'S CLASSIC ARTS & CRAFTS FESTI-VAL. Mar 10–12. Richmond Raceway Complex (formerly Virginia State Fairgrounds), Richmond, VA. 22nd annual. Features work from more than 410 talented artists and craftspeople. All juried exhibitors' work has been handmade by the exhibitors and must be their own original design and creation. See the creative process in action with several exhibitors demonstrating throughout the weekend. Something for every style, taste and budget with items from the most contemporary to the most traditional. Est attendance: 20,000. For info: Gilmore Enterprises, Inc, 1240 Oakland Ave, Greensboro, NC 27403. Phone: (336) 274-5550. E-mail: gilmoreshows@triad.rr.com. Web: www.CraftShow.com or www.gilmoreshows.com.

DAYTONA SUPERCROSS BY HONDA. Mar 10. Daytona International Speedway, Daytona Beach, FL. One of the most famous and toughest supercross races in the world. For info: Daytona Intl Speedway, PO Box 2801, Daytona Beach, FL 32120-2801. Phone: (800) PIT-SHOP. Web: www.daytonainternational speedway.com.

ENGLAND: WORDS BY THE WATER: A CUMBRIAN LITERATURE FESTIVAL. Mar 10–19. Lake District. The Theatre by the Lake at Keswick, sitting on the banks of Derwentwater, is the perfect setting for a lively literature festival. Young people's events during the school day complement a stimulating evening and weekend adult program. Program available January 2006. For info: Ways With Words Literature Festival, Dorridge Farm, Dartington, Totnes, Devon, England TQ9 6JQ. Phone: (44) (180) 386-7373. E-mail: office@wayswithwords.co.uk. Web: www.wayswithwords.co.uk.

FORD FIELD HOME AND GARDEN SHOW. Mar 10–12. Ford Field, Detroit, MI. Products and services for home building/remodeling, home furnishings and interior design, lawn and garden and related areas. On-site constructions, theme gardens, seminars and demonstrations, plus The Standard Flower Show sponsored by The Federated Garden Clubs of Michigan, District 1. Est attendance: 45,000. For info: Mike Wilbraham, ShowSpan, Inc, 2121 Celebration Dr NE, Grand Rapids, MI 49525. Phone: (616) 447-2860. Fax: (616) 447-2861. E-mail: events@showspan.com. Web: www.showspan.com.

"THE INCREDIBLE HULK" TV PREMIERE: ANNIVERSARY. Mar 10, 1978. A wonderfully campy action series based on the popular Marvel comic books as well as a modern-day Jekyll and Hyde story. Bill Bixby played the erudite scientist, Dr. David Banner, who accidentally exposed himself to gamma radiation. When provoked, Banner metamorphosed into the shirt-shredding, body-baring, green-skinned, snarling neanderthal Hulk. The 6'5", 275-lb former Mr Universe, Lou Ferrigno, played the largely nonspeaking part of the Hulk.

JUPITER EFFECT: ANNIVERSARY. Mar 10, 1982. The much-talked-about and sometimes-feared planetary configuration of a semi-alignment of the planets on the same side of the sun occurred on this date without causing any of the disasters or unusual natural phenomena that some had predicted.

LONGHORN WORLD CHAMPIONSHIP RODEO. Mar 10–12. UTC Arena, Chattanooga, TN. 24th annual. More than 250 cowboys and cowgirls compete in six professional contests ranging from bronc riding to big, bad BONUS bull riding! Free beginners horsemanship clinic 40 minutes before performances. Qualifying rodeo for Longhorn's Championship Finals Rodeo. Featuring colorful opening and pageantry. Est attendance: 12,000. For info: W. Bruce Lehrke, Pres, Longhorn World Championship Rodeo, Inc, PO Box 70159, Nashville, TN 37207. Phone: (615) 876-1016. Fax: (615) 876-4685. E-mail: info@longhornrodeo.com. Web: www.longhornrodeo.com.

LUCE, CLARE BOOTHE: BIRTH ANNIVERSARY. Mar 10, 1903. Playwright and politician Clare Boothe Luce was born at New York City. Luce wrote for and edited *Vogue* and *Vanity Fair* as well as writing plays, three of which were later adapted into motion pictures—*The Women* (1936), *Kiss the Boys Goodbye* (1938) and *Margin of Error* (1939). She served in the US House of Representatives (1943–47) and as ambassador to Italy (1953–56)—the first woman appointed ambassador to a major country. Luce died Oct 9, 1987, at Washington, DC.

MARIO DAY. Mar 10. A day for all persons named Mario. Using the abbreviation for the month of March, i.e., MAR, with the day, i.e., 10, you get the name spelled out: MAR10. Annually, Mar 10. For info: Mario Fascitelli, 8800 Natalie NE, Albuquerque, NM 87111. Phone: (505) 293-2634. Fax: (505) 323-6333. E-mail: C21Allied@aol.com.

MIDDLE NAME PRIDE DAY. Mar 10. Today's name celebration requires honesty and boldness. Tell three people who don't already know it what your middle name is (even if it's Egbert). Annually, the Friday of Celebrate Your Name Week. For info: Jerry Hill. E-mail: allaboutnames@safe-mail.net. Web: www.jerryhill.com.

MILWAUKEE JOURNAL SENTINEL SPORTS SHOW. Mar 10–19. Milwaukee, WI. Travel and resort exhibits, hunting, fishing, boating, family travel, outdoor recreation. Largest outdoor show in Wisconsin. Est attendance: 150,000. For info: Great Outdoors, LLC, 113 McHenry Rd, #268, Buffalo Grove, IL 60089. Phone: (847) 540-8000 or (800) 472-2070. Fax: (847) 540-8884. E-mail: go2show@msn.com.

NATCHEZ SPRING PILGRIMAGE. Mar 10–Apr 14. Natchez, MS. 74th annual tour of 28 antebellum mansions—many of them private homes of which some have been in the same family for more than 150 years. The owners will be dressed in period costumes to greet visitors. Evening entertainment includes "Southern Exposure," "Southern Road to Freedom" and the "Historic Natchez Pageant." Carriage and bus sightseeing tours daily. Est attendance: 35,000. For info: Natchez Pilgrimage Tours, PO Box 347, Natchez, MS 39121. Phone: (800) 647-6742 or (601) 446-6631. Fax: (601) 446-8687. E-mail: visit@natchezpilgrimage.com. Web: www.natchezpilgrimage.com.

NCAA DIVISION I MEN'S & WOMEN'S INDOOR TRACK AND FIELD CHAMPIONSHIPS. Mar 10–11. Randal Tyson Indoor Track, University of Arkansas, Fayetteville, AR. Annually, the second weekend in March. Est attendance: 7,000. For info: Natl Collegiate Athletic Assn, 700 W Washington Ave, PO Box 6222, Indianapolis, IN 46206-6222. Phone: (317) 917-6222. Fax: (317) 917-6825. Web: www.ncaasports.com.

NETHERLANDS: THE EUROPEAN FINE ART FAIR. Mar 10–19. MECC, Maastricht. Old Master paintings, antiques, textile arts, modern paintings and sculptures, antiquities, books and prints. Annually, in March. Est attendance: 75,000. For info: The European Fine Art Foundation, Broekwal 64, 5268 HD Helvoirt, The Netherlands. Phone: (31) 411 645090. Fax: (31) 411 645091. E-mail: info@tefaf.com. Web: www.tefaf.com.

PARALYMPIC GAMES. Mar 10–19. Turin, Italy. Some 600 athletes with disabilities and 1000 officials will take part in these games that feature medal events such as alpine skiing, nordic skiing and sled hockey. 2006 features the addition of a new sport—wheelchair curling—which is being featured as a medal event for the first time in Paralympic history. For info: International

Olympic Committee. Web: www.olympic.org. Or International Paralympic Committee. E-mail: Paralympics@torino2006.it. Web: www.paralympic.org or www.paralympicgames.torino2006.org.

SALVATION ARMY IN THE US: ANNIVERSARY. Mar 10, 1880. Commissioner George Scott Railton and seven women officers landed at New York to officially begin the work of the Salvation Army in the US.

SOUTH BY SOUTHWEST (SXSW). Mar 10–19. Austin, TX. Annual, internationally recognized music, new media and film conference. Hundreds of music, film and interactive events and panels. Est attendance: 35,000. For info: SXSW Headquarters, Box 4999, Austin, TX 78765. Phone: (512) 467-7979. Fax: (512) 451-0754. E-mail: sxsw@sxsw.com. Web: www.sxsw.com.

SUGARLOAF CRAFTS FESTIVAL. Mar 10–12. Garden State Exhibit Center, Somerset, NJ. This show, now in its 13th year, features 300 nationally recognized craft designers and fine artists displaying and selling their original creations. Includes craft demonstrations, live music, specialty foods, hourly gift certificate drawings and more! Est attendance: 20,000. For info: Sugarloaf Mountain Works, 200 Orchard Ridge Dr, #215, Gaithersburg, MD 20878. Phone: (800) 210-9900. Fax: (301) 253-9620. Web: www.SugarloafCrafts.com.

TELEPHONE INVENTION: ANNIVERSARY. Mar 10, 1876. Alexander Graham Bell transmitted the first telephone message to his assistant in the next room: "Mr Watson, come here, I want you," at Cambridge, MA. See also: "Bell, Alexander Graham: Birth Anniversary" (Mar 3).

TUBMAN, HARRIET: DEATH ANNIVERSARY. Mar 10, 1913. American abolitionist, Underground Railroad leader, born a slave at Bucktown, Dorchester County, MD, about 1820 or 1821. She escaped from a Maryland plantation in 1849 and later helped more than 300 slaves reach freedom. Died at Auburn, NY.

US PAPER MONEY ISSUED: ANNIVERSARY. Mar 10, 1862. The first paper money was issued in the US on this date. The denominations were $5 (Hamilton), $10 (Lincoln) and $20 (Liberty). They became legal tender by Act of Mar 17, 1862.

WORLD'S LARGEST RATTLESNAKE ROUNDUP. Mar 10–12. Sweetwater, TX. Educational programs about rattlesnakes; flea market; gun, knife and coin show; large cook-off; dances; numerous pounds of live rattlesnakes on display; snake meat available to eat and snake articles for sale. Snake hunts and bus tours available. More than 750 booth spaces are available. Annually, the second weekend in March. Est attendance: 30,000. For info: Sweetwater Chamber of Commerce, PO Box 1148, Sweetwater, TX 79556. Phone: (325) 235-5488 or (800) 658-6757. Fax: (325) 235-1026. E-mail: chamber@sweetwatertexas.org. Web: www.sweetwatertexas.org or www.rattlesnakeroundup.com.

BIRTHDAYS TODAY

Edie Brickell, 40, folksinger (New Bohemians), born Oak Cliff, TX, Mar 10, 1966.

Kim Campbell, 59, first woman prime minister of Canada (for five months in 1993), born Vancouver Island, BC, Canada, Mar 10, 1947.

Prince Edward, 42, son of Queen Elizabeth II, born London, England, Mar 10, 1964.

Bob Greene, 59, journalist, born Columbus, OH, Mar 10, 1947.

Jasmine Guy, 42, singer, actress ("A Different World"), born Boston, MA, Mar 10, 1964.

Shannon Miller, 29, former Olympic gymnast, born Rolla, MO, Mar 10, 1977.

	S	M	T	W	T	F	S
March				1	2	3	4
2006	5	6	7	8	9	10	11
	12	13	14	15	16	17	18
	19	20	21	22	23	24	25
	26	27	28	29	30	31	

Chuck Norris, 66, actor (*Missing in Action*, "Walker, Texas Ranger"), born Ryan, OK, Mar 10, 1940.

David Rabe, 66, playwright, born Dubuque, IA, Mar 10, 1940.

Sharon Stone, 48, actress (*Basic Instinct, The Specialist, Casino*), born Meadville, PA, Mar 10, 1958.

Shannon Tweed, 49, actress ("Pacific Blue," *Detroit Rock City*), born St. John's, NF, Canada, Mar 10, 1957.

MARCH 11 — SATURDAY
Day 70 — 295 Remaining

ARTS AND ANTIQUES AT THE AMERICAN CLUB. Mar 11–12. The American Club's Grand Hall of the Great Lakes, Kohler, WI. Discover a wide variety of antiques, furniture, silver and jewelry from fine antique dealers. Carole Carter's Appraisal Service will appraise one item per paid admission daily. For info: The American Club, Highland Drive, Kohler, WI 53044. Phone: (800) 344-2838. Fax: (920) 457-4441. Web: www.destination kohler.com.

BEACH PARTY. Mar 11. Deadwood, SD. 20th annual. Forget Fort Lauderdale for spring break! Head to the beach at the #10. Sand, hot tub, beach hats, music, limbo and wet T-shirt contests. Est attendance: 400. For info: Old Style Saloon #10, 657 Main St, Deadwood, SD 57732. Phone: (605) 578-3346 or (800) 952-9398. Fax: (605) 578-1944. E-mail: saloon10@deadwood.net. Web: www.saloon10.com.

BUREAU OF INDIAN AFFAIRS ESTABLISHED: ANNIVERSARY. Mar 11, 1824. The US War Department created the Bureau of Indian Affairs.

CAMPBELL, MALCOLM: BIRTH ANNIVERSARY. Mar 11, 1885. Record-making British auto racer, the first man to travel five miles a minute (300 mph) in an automobile. Born at Chislehurst, Kent, England, Mar 11, 1885. Died at his home at Surrey, England, Dec 31, 1948.

DAYTONA 200 BY HONDA CLASSIC. Mar 11. Daytona International Speedway, Daytona Beach, FL. 65th annual. For info: Daytona Intl Speedway, PO Box 2801, Daytona Beach, FL 32120-2801. Phone: (800) PIT-SHOP. Web: www.daytonainter nationalspeedway.com.

DREAM 2006 DAY. Mar 11. To focus attention on the new millennium—so that all humans, nations and institutions devote 2006 to unparalleled dreams for a better world and thinking, action, inspiration, determination and love to solve the remaining problems and to achieve a peaceful, united human family on Earth. As envisioned by Robert Muller, called the Millennium Man. For info: Barbara Gaughen-Muller, Pres, Gaughen Global Public Relations, 7456 Evergreen Dr, Santa Barbara, CA 93117. Phone: (805) 968-8567. Fax: (805) 968-5747. E-mail: robert@robertmuller.org. Web: www.robertmuller.org and www.goodmorningworld.org.

GENEALOGY DAY. Mar 11. Join in on one of the world's fastest growing hobbies and celebrate names at the same time. Get genealogy tips, hints and ideas, then begin the journey to knowing your heritage name by name, one ancestor at a time. Annually, the Saturday of Celebrate Your Name Week. For info: Jerry Hill. E-mail: allaboutnames@safe-mail.net. Web: www.jerryhill.com.

HIGHLAND COUNTY MAPLE FESTIVAL. Mar 11–12 (also Mar 18–19). Highland County, VA. 48th annual. Festival welcomes visitors to view the process of syrup making. Large craft shows. Est attendance: 50,000. For info: Highland County Chamber of Commerce, PO Box 223, Monterey, VA 24465. Phone:

(540) 468-2550. Fax: (540) 468-2551. E-mail: highcc@cfw.com. Web: www.highlandcounty.org.

INDIANA FLOWER AND PATIO SHOW. Mar 11–19. Indiana State Fairgrounds, Indianapolis, IN. The oldest show of its kind in the Midwest, featuring more than 30 landscaped gardens and products and services for home, yard and patio. Est attendance: 106,000. For info: Donell Heberer Walton, Show Mgr, HSI Show Productions, Box 502797, Indianapolis, IN 46250. Phone: (317) 576-9933. Fax: (317) 576-9955. Web: www.hsishows.com.

JOHNNY APPLESEED DAY (JOHN CHAPMAN DEATH ANNIVERSARY). Mar 11, 1845. Anniversary of the death of John Chapman, better known as Johnny Appleseed, believed to have been born at Leominster, MA, Sept 26, 1774. The planter of orchards and friend of wild animals was regarded by the Indians as a great medicine man. He died at Allen County, IN. See also: "Appleseed, Johnny: Birth Anniversary" (Sept 26).

LITHUANIA: RESTITUTION OF INDEPENDENCE DAY. Mar 11. National holiday. Commemorates independence from the Soviet Union in 1990. Lithuania had initially declared its independence in 1918 but lost it to the Soviet Union in 1940.

MADRID TRAIN BOMBINGS: ANNIVERSARY. Mar 11, 2004. Ten terrorist bombs exploded on four commuter trains in Spain's busy capital on this date, killing 191 people and injuring 1,800. It was the worst loss of life by violence in Europe since WWII. Nations around the world expressed their sorrow, and demonstrations against terrorism were held in Brussels, Paris, Helsinki, Geneva, Berlin and Stockholm. Spain observed a three-minute period of silence at noon on Mar 15 in order to remember the wounded and slain. Several European countries arrested suspects in the case, and seven militants considered major suspects blew themselves up at Madrid to avoid capture on Apr 3. The terrorists responsible were believed to be allied with Al Qaeda.

PAINE, ROBERT TREAT: 275th BIRTH ANNIVERSARY. Mar 11, 1731. Jurist and signer of the Declaration of Independence. Born at Boston, MA; died there May 11, 1814.

PANDEMIC OF 1918 HITS US: ANNIVERSARY. Mar 11, 1918. The first cases of the "Spanish" influenza were reported in the US when 107 soldiers became sick at Fort Riley, KS. By the end of 1920 nearly 25 percent of the US population had had it. As many as 500,000 civilians died from the virus, exceeding the number of US troops killed abroad in WWI. Worldwide, more than 1 percent of the global population, or 22 million people, had died by 1920. The origin of the virus was never determined absolutely, though it was probably somewhere in Asia. The name "Spanish" influenza came from the relatively high number of cases in that country early in the epidemic. Due to the panic, cancellation of public events was common and many public service workers wore masks on the job. Emergency tent hospitals were set up in some locations due to overcrowding.

RIO GRANDE VALLEY LIVESTOCK SHOW. Mar 11–19. Mercedes, TX. Rodeo, open cattle show and carnival. For the youth of the four counties in the valley to exhibit their projects. Est attendance: 195,000. For info: Jim Beale, Rio Grande Valley Livestock Show Inc, Box 867, Mercedes, TX 78570. Phone: (956) 565-2456. Fax: (956) 565-3005. E-mail: info@rgvlivestockshow.com. Web: www.rgvlivestockshow.com.

TASSO, TORQUATO: BIRTH ANNIVERSARY. Mar 11, 1544. Poet of the late Renaissance, born at Sorrento, Italy. His violent outbursts and acute sensitivity to criticism led to his imprisonment for seven years, during which the "misunderstood genius" continued his literary creativity. Died at Rome, Italy, Apr 25, 1595.

TURKEY VULTURES RETURN TO THE LIVING SIGN. Mar 11–17. Entire Canisteo Valley, Canisteo, NY. Traditionally turkey vultures return on St. Pat's Day to their roosting sites in and around the world-famous living sign. For info: Bill Berry, 6950 Lain Rd, Hornell, NY 14843-9419. Phone: (607) 324-1086. E-mail: thepaperwolf@infoblvd.net.

WELK, LAWRENCE: BIRTH ANNIVERSARY. Mar 11, 1903. Bandleader Lawrence Welk was born at Strasburg, ND. He learned to play the accordion and at 17 formed his first band. After playing all over the Midwest, he moved to Los Angeles where in 1955 his show began its nationwide television broadcast of "Champagne Music." The longest-running program in TV history, "The Lawrence Welk Show" played each Saturday on ABC from 1955 until 1971 when it was dropped because sponsors thought its audience was too old. Welk kept the show on a network of more than 250 independent stations for 11 more years and it still can be seen in reruns. Welk's entertainment empire included the purchase of royalty rights to songs, including the entire collection of songs by Jerome Kern. Welk died at Santa Monica, CA, May 17, 1992.

WILSON, HAROLD: BIRTH ANNIVERSARY. Mar 11, 1916. British statesman and twice prime minister (1964–70 and 1974–76), leader of the Labour Party. Born at Huddersfield, Yorkshire. He died May 24, 1995, at London.

BIRTHDAYS TODAY

Elton Brand, 27, basketball player, born Peekskill, NY, Mar 11, 1979.

Curtis Brown, Jr, 50, astronaut, born Elizabethtown, NC, Mar 11, 1956.

Sam Donaldson, 72, journalist, born El Paso, TX, Mar 11, 1934.

Alex Kingston, 43, actress ("ER"), born London, England, Mar 11, 1963.

Bobby McFerrin, 56, jazz musician, singer, songwriter, conductor, born New York, NY, Mar 11, 1950.

Rupert Murdoch, 75, newspaper publisher (*New York Post, The Boston Herald*), born Melbourne, Australia, Mar 11, 1931.

Gale Norton, 52, US Secretary of the Interior, born Wichita, KS, Mar 11, 1954.

Dominique Sanda, 55, actress (*The Garden of the Finzi-Continis, 1900*), born Paris, France, Mar 11, 1951 (some sources say 1948).

Antonin Scalia, 70, Associate Justice of the US Supreme Court, born Trenton, NJ, Mar 11, 1936.

Jerry Zucker, 56, writer, (*Naked Gun* movies with brother David), producer (*Airplane!*), born Milwaukee, WI, Mar 11, 1950.

MARCH 12 — SUNDAY

Day 71 — 294 Remaining

ATATÜRK, MUSTAFA KEMAL: 125th BIRTH ANNIVERSARY. Mar 12, 1881. The founder of modern Turkey was born at Salonika, Greece (then part of the Ottoman Empire). After a distinguished army career, he led the Turkish revolution after WWI and was elected Turkey's first president. He died at Istanbul, Nov 10, 1938.

AUSTRIA INVADED BY NAZI GERMANY: ANNIVERSARY. Mar 12, 1938. As a test of its own war readiness and of the response of the other major powers, Germany occupied Austria. A year later Germany invaded Czechoslovakia and, in September 1939, Poland, beginning WWII.

BERMUDA COLONIZED BY ENGLISH: ANNIVERSARY. Mar 12, 1609. The ship of Admiral Sir George Somers, taking settlers to Virginia, was wrecked on the reefs of Bermuda. The islands had been discovered in the early 1500s but were uninhabited until 1609.

BOYCOTT, CHARLES CUNNINGHAM: BIRTH ANNIVERSARY. Mar 12, 1832. Charles Cunningham Boycott, born at Norfolk, England, has been immortalized by having his name become part of the English language. In County Mayo, Ireland, the Tenants' "Land League" in 1880 asked Boycott, an estate agent, to reduce rents (because of poor harvest and dire economic conditions). Boycott responded by serving eviction notices on the tenants, who retaliated by refusing to have any dealings with him. Charles Stewart Parnell, then president of the National Land League and agrarian agitator, retaliated against Boycott by formulating and implementing the method of economic and social ostracism that came to be called a "boycott." Boycott died at Suffolk, England, June 19, 1897.

CHURCH OF ENGLAND ORDAINS WOMEN PRIESTS: ANNIVERSARY. Mar 12, 1994. The Church of England for the first time ordained 32 women at Bristol Cathedral. About 700 male members of the clergy and unknown thousands of members indicated they would leave the Church of England and join the Roman Catholic Church. The Catholic Church responded to the ordination by saying that it "constitutes a profound obstacle to every hope of reunion between the Catholic Church and the Anglican Communion." This day's ordinations were not the first. In early 1994 about 1,380 women priests were ordained in churches of the Anglican Communion outside of Great Britain.

FDR'S FIRST FIRESIDE CHAT: ANNIVERSARY. Mar 12, 1933. President Franklin Delano Roosevelt made the first of his Sunday evening "fireside chats" to the American people. Speaking by radio from the White House, he reported rather informally on the economic problems of the nation and on his actions to deal with them.

GABON: NATIONAL DAY. Mar 12. Observes founding of Gabonese Democratic Party on Mar 12, 1968.

GIRL SCOUT WEEK. Mar 12–18. To observe the anniversary of the founding of the Girl Scouts of the USA, the preeminent organization for girls in the world, which began Mar 12, 1912. For info: Media Services, Girl Scouts of the USA, 420 Fifth Ave, New York, NY 10018. Phone: (212) 852-8581. Fax: (212) 852-6514. E-mail: media@girlscouts.org. Web: www.girlscouts.org.

GIRL SCOUTS OF THE USA FOUNDING: ANNIVERSARY. Mar 12, 1912. Juliette Low founded the Girl Scouts of the USA at Savannah, GA.

GREAT BLIZZARD OF '88: ANNIVERSARY. Mar 12, 1888. One of the most devastating blizzards to hit the northeastern US began in the early hours of Monday, Mar 12, 1888. A snowfall of 40–50 inches, accompanied by gale-force winds, left drifts as high as 30–40 feet. More than 400 persons died in the storm (200 at New York City alone). Some survivors of the storm, "The Blizzard Men of 1888," held annual meetings at New York City as late as 1941 to recount personal recollections of the event.

INTERNATIONAL INTERNET MOMS WEEK. Mar 12–18. A week to celebrate the universal bonding and sharing between moms on the Internet. This week is dedicated to showing appreciation of Internet-savvy moms and to encouraging businesses to recognize the power of mom Internet users and forums. Annually, the third week in March. For info: Barb Webb, MOM(dot) COM, PO Box 203, Sharpsburg, GA 30277. Phone: (770) 251-5479. E-mail: bawebbauthor@charter.net. Web: www.mom dotcom.net.

KEROUAC, JACK: BIRTH ANNIVERSARY. Mar 12, 1922. American poet and novelist Jack (Jean-Louis) Kerouac, leader and spokesman for the Beat movement, was born at Lowell, MA. Kerouac is best known for his novel *On the Road*, published in 1957, which celebrates the Beat ideal of nonconformity. Kerouac published *The Dharma Bums* in 1958, followed by *The Subterraneans* the same year, *Doctor Sax* and its sequel *Maggie Cassidy* in 1959, *Lonesome Traveler* in 1960, *Big Sur* in 1962 and *Desolation Angels* in 1965. Kerouac died at St. Petersburg, FL, at age 47, Oct 21, 1969. A previously unpublished part of *On the Road* called *Visions of Cody* was published posthumously in 1972.

LESOTHO: MOSHOESHOE'S DAY. Mar 12. National holiday. Commemorates the great leader Chief Moshoeshoe I, who unified the Basotho people, beginning in 1820.

MAURITIUS: INDEPENDENCE DAY. Mar 12. National holiday commemorates attainment of independent nationhood (within the British Commonwealth) on Mar 12, 1968.

NEWCOMB, SIMON: BIRTH ANNIVERSARY. Mar 12, 1835. Astronomer, born at Wallace, NS, Canada. Newcomb investigated the orbits of Uranus, Neptune and the inner planets and devised planetary tables that were used universally by observatories. Died at Washington, DC, July 11, 1909.

PIERCE, JANE MEANS APPLETON: 200th BIRTH ANNIVERSARY. Mar 12, 1806. Wife of Franklin Pierce, 14th president of the US. Born at Hampton, NH. Died at Concord, NH, Dec 2, 1863.

SAINT PATRICK'S DAY PARADE & FESTIVAL. Mar 12. Hollywood, FL. Traditional parade with pipes and drums, floats, etc, on downtown streets and festival in the park with entertainment stage, Irish food and wares. Est attendance: 10,000. For info: Roguey Doyle, City of Hollywood Dept of Parks, 1940 Harrison St, Ste 101, Hollywood, FL 33020. Phone: (954) 921-3404.

SAVE YOUR HOME WEEK. Mar 12–18. New York, NY. A gathering of members of the National Foreclosure Prevention Associations of America. For info: Bill Young, 64 Wooley St, Southampton, NY 11968. Phone: (877) 291-3642. E-mail: 877 2913642@ureach.com. Web: www.SaveYourHomeLLC.com.

SPAIN: FIESTA DE LAS FALLAS. Mar 12–19. Valencia. This festival of burning effigies and fireworks has been celebrated for more than 150 years.

SUN YAT-SEN: DEATH ANNIVERSARY. Mar 12, 1925. The heroic leader of China's 1911 revolution is remembered on the anniversary of his death at Peking, China. Observed as Arbor Day in Taiwan.

BIRTHDAYS TODAY

Edward Albee, 78, playwright, born Washington, DC, Mar 12, 1928.

Rob Cohen, 57, producer (*Bird on a Wire*), director (*Dragonheart*), born Cornwall-on-Hudson, NY, Mar 12, 1949.

Kent Conrad, 58, US Senator (D, North Dakota), born Bismarck, ND, Mar 12, 1948.

Barbara Feldon, 65, actress ("Get Smart," *Smile*), born Pittsburgh, PA, Mar 12, 1941.

Marlon Jackson, 49, singer (Jackson 5), born Gary, IN, Mar 12, 1957.

Al (Alwin) Jarreau, 66, singer, songwriter, born Milwaukee, WI, Mar 12, 1940.

	S	M	T	W	T	F	S
March				1	2	3	4
2006	5	6	7	8	9	10	11
	12	13	14	15	16	17	18
	19	20	21	22	23	24	25
	26	27	28	29	30	31	

Liza Minnelli, 60, singer, actress (Oscar for *Cabaret; The Sterile Cuckoo, Arthur*), born Los Angeles, CA, Mar 12, 1946.

Raul Mondesi, 35, baseball player, born San Cristobal, Dominican Republic, Mar 12, 1971.

Dale Bryan Murphy, 50, former baseball player, born Portland, OR, Mar 12, 1956.

Mitt Romney, 59, Governor of Massachusetts (R), born Detroit, MI, Mar 12, 1947.

Wally Schirra, 83, former astronaut, born Hackensack, NJ, Mar 12, 1923.

Darryl Eugene Strawberry, 44, former baseball player, born Los Angeles, CA, Mar 12, 1962.

James Taylor, 58, singer, musician ("You've Got a Friend," "Handy Man"), born Boston, MA, Mar 12, 1948.

Andrew Young, 74, civil rights leader, former mayor of Atlanta, GA, born New Orleans, LA, Mar 12, 1932.

MARCH 13 — MONDAY
Day 72 — 293 Remaining

ANNENBERG, WALTER: BIRTH ANNIVERSARY. Mar 13, 1908. Publisher, philanthropist and ambassador, Walter Annenberg was born at Milwaukee, WI. He inherited *The Philadelphia Inquirer* from his father and built the newspaper into the cornerstone of a publishing empire that included newspapers, magazines and radio and television stations. He founded many enduring publications, including *Seventeen* (1944) and *TV Guide* (1953). He served as US ambassador to the United Kingdom 1969–76. As a philanthropist, Annenberg gave billions to charities. He died at Wynnewood, PA, on Oct 1, 2002.

ARAB OIL EMBARGO LIFTED: ANNIVERSARY. Mar 13, 1974. The oil-producing Arab countries agreed to lift their five-month embargo on petroleum sales to the US. During the embargo prices went up 300 percent and a ban was imposed on Sunday gasoline sales. The embargo was in retaliation for US support of Israel during the October 1973 Middle East War.

CAMP FIRE USA BIRTHDAY WEEK. Mar 13–19. To celebrate the 96th anniversary of Camp Fire USA (founded in 1910 as Camp Fire Girls). For info: Camp Fire USA, 4601 Madison Ave, Kansas City, MO 64112. Phone: (816) 756-1950. Fax: (816) 756-2650. E-mail: info@campfireusa.org. Web: www.campfireusa.org.

CLARENCE DARROW DEATH COMMEMORATION. Mar 13. Jackson Park, Chicago, IL. Annually, on the anniversary of his death, a wreath is tossed from the Jackson Park Clarence Darrow Bridge, named in honor of the famed lawyer and civil libertarian at 10 AM. At 11 AM a discussion follows in the Columbian Room of the Museum of Science and Industry, 57th St and South Lake Shore Drive, Chicago. Est attendance: 100. For info: Herb Kraus, 333 N Michigan, Ste 2032, Chicago, IL 60601. Phone: (312) 578-9114. Fax: (312) 726-9520.

DEAF HISTORY MONTH. Mar 13–Apr 15. Observance of three of the most important anniversaries for deaf Americans: Apr 15, 1817, establishment of the first public school for the deaf in America, later known as The American School for the Deaf; Apr 8, 1864, charter signed by President Lincoln authorizing the Board of Directors of the Columbia Institution (now Gallaudet University) to grant college degrees to deaf students; Mar 13, 1988, the victory of the Deaf President Now movement at Gallaudet. For info: Library for Deaf Action, 2930 Craiglawn Rd, Silver Spring, MD 20904-1816. Phone/fax: (301) 572-5168 (TTY). E-mail: alicehagemeyer@aol.com.

DELMONICO, LORENZO: BIRTH ANNIVERSARY. Mar 13, 1813. Famed restaurateur and gastronomic authority. Born at Marengo, Switzerland. Operated a number of restaurants at New York, NY, where he died, Sept 3, 1881.

EARMUFFS PATENTED: ANNIVERSARY. Mar 13, 1887. Chester Greenwood of Maine received a patent for earmuffs.

FILLMORE, ABIGAIL POWERS: BIRTH ANNIVERSARY. Mar 13, 1798. First wife of Millard Fillmore, 13th president of the US. Born at Stillwater, NY. It is said that the White House was without any books until Abigail Fillmore, formerly a teacher, made a room on the second floor into a library. Within a year, Congress appropriated $250 for the president to spend on books for the White House. Died at Washington, DC, Mar 30, 1853.

GOOD SAMARITAN INVOLVEMENT DAY. Mar 13. A day to emphasize the importance of unselfish aid to those who need it. Recognized on the anniversary of the killing of Catherine (Kitty) Genovese, Mar 13, 1964, in the Kew Gardens community, Queens, NY. Reportedly no fewer than 38 of her neighbors, not wanting "to get involved," witnessed and watched for nearly 30 minutes as the fleeing girl was pursued and repeatedly stabbed by her 29-year-old attacker.

HUBBARD, L. RON: BIRTH ANNIVERSARY. Mar 13, 1911. Lafayette Ronald Hubbard, science fiction writer, recluse and founder of the Church of Scientology, was born at Tilden, NE. His best-known book was *Dianetics: The Modern Science of Mental Health*. Died at San Luis Obispo County, CA, Jan 24, 1986.

INTERNATIONAL BRAIN AWARENESS WEEK. Mar 13–19. Brain Awareness Week is an international effort to advance public awareness about the progress, promise and benefits of brain research. The Dana Alliance is joined in the campaign by partners in the US and around the world, including medical and research organizations; patient advocacy groups; the National Institutes of Health and other government agencies; service groups; hospitals and universities; K–12 schools and professional organizations. For info: Dana Alliance for Brain Initiatives, 745 Fifth Ave, Ste 900, New York, NY 10151. Phone: (212) 401-1680. Fax: (212) 593-7623. E-mail: bawinfo@dana.org. Web: www.dana.org/brainweek.

"THE LARRY KING SHOW" TV PREMIERE: ANNIVERSARY. Mar 13, 1983. Radio talk-show host Larry King brought his topical interview program to syndicated TV in 1983. Using a telephone hookup, viewers called in to speak to particular guests. King has been appearing on CNN since 1985 interviewing a variety of newsmakers and celebrities.

LOWELL, PERCIVAL: BIRTH ANNIVERSARY. Mar 13, 1855. American astronomer, founder of the Lowell Observatory at Flagstaff, AZ. Born at Boston, MA, he died at Flagstaff, Nov 12, 1916. Lowell was initiator of the search that resulted (25 years after the search began and 14 years after his death) in discovery of the planet Pluto. The discovery was announced on Lowell's birthday, Mar 13, 1930, by the Lowell Observatory.

MULTIPLE SCLEROSIS AWARENESS WEEK. Mar 13–17. In honor of the 60th anniversary of the founding of the National MS Society, we proclaim this week to raise awareness about multiple sclerosis and the international MS movement. Annually, the week surrounding Mar 11. For info: Becca Kornfeld, National MS Society, 733 Third Ave, New York, NY 10017. Phone: (212) 476-0484. Fax: (212) 989-7981. E-mail: Becca.Kornfeld@nmms.org. Web: www.nationalmssociety.org.

NATIONAL OPEN AN UMBRELLA INDOORS DAY. Mar 13. The purpose of this day is for people to open umbrellas indoors and note whether they have any bad luck. To arrange for an interview, call 24 hours in advance. Annually, Mar 13. For info: Thomas Edward Knibb, 1654 Colonial Way, Frederick, MD 21702-3919. Phone: (301) 695-7351. E-mail: tomknibb@juno.com.

OPERATION FLASH: ANNIVERSARY. Mar 13, 1943. Disillusioned German officers planned to take the life of Adolf Hitler on this date. Hitler was to stop at Smolensk on his way to his headquarters and an officer who was not involved in the plot had been commissioned to deliver a package to Hitler's plane which he was told contained two bottles of liquor for a friend in Rastenburg. A bomb in the package was timed to go off over Minsk, but it reached Rastenburg without detonating. The package was later recovered and a defective detonator was found. See also: "Gersdorff Hitler Assassination Attempt: Anniversary" (Mar 21).

PASSION WEEK. Mar 13–19. The week beginning on the fifth Sunday in Lent; the week before Holy Week.

PLANET URANUS DISCOVERY: 225th ANNIVERSARY. Mar 13, 1781. German-born English astronomer Sir William Herschel discovered the seventh planet from the sun, Uranus.

PRIESTLY, JOSEPH: BIRTH ANNIVERSARY. Mar 13, 1733 (OS). English clergyman and scientist, discoverer of oxygen, born at Fieldhead, England. He and his family narrowly escaped an angry mob attacking their home because of his religious and political views. They moved to the US in 1794. Died at Northumberland, PA, Feb 6, 1804.

SAINT AUBIN, HELEN "CALLAGHAN" CANDAELE: BIRTH ANNIVERSARY. Mar 13, 1929. Helen Candaele Saint Aubin, known as Helen Callaghan during her baseball days, was born at Vancouver, BC, Canada. Saint Aubin and her sister, Margaret Maxwell, were recruited for the All-American Girls Professional Baseball League, which flourished in the 1940s when many major league players were off fighting WWII. She first played at age 15 for the Minneapolis Millerettes, an expansion team that moved to Indiana and became the Fort Wayne Daisies. For the 1945 season the left-handed outfielder led the league with a .299 average and 24 extra base hits. In 1946 she stole 114 bases in 111 games. Her son Kelly Candaele's documentary on the women's baseball league inspired the film *A League of Their Own*. Saint Aubin, known as the "Ted Williams of women's baseball," died Dec 8, 1992, at Santa Barbara, CA.

TA'ANIT ESTHER (FAST OF ESTHER). Mar 13. Hebrew calendar date Adar 13, 5766. Commemorates Queen Esther's fast, in the 6th century BC, to save the Jews of ancient Persia. Began at sundown Mar 12.

UNITED KINGDOM: COMMONWEALTH DAY. Mar 13. Replaces Empire Day observance recognized until 1958. Observed on second Monday in March. Also observed in the British Virgin Islands, Gibraltar and Newfoundland, Canada.

BIRTHDAYS TODAY

Thomas Andrew (Andy) Bean, 53, golfer, born Lafayette, GA, Mar 13, 1953.

Charo, 55, singer, actress ("Chico and the Man"), born Maria Martinez at Murcia, Spain, Mar 13, 1951.

Adam Clayton, 46, musician (U2), born Dublin, Ireland, Mar 13, 1960.

	S	M	T	W	T	F	S
March				1	2	3	4
2006	5	6	7	8	9	10	11
	12	13	14	15	16	17	18
	19	20	21	22	23	24	25
	26	27	28	29	30	31	

Dana Delany, 50, actress ("China Beach," *Moon Over Parador*), born New York, NY, Mar 13, 1956.

Glenne Headly, 49, actress (*The Purple Rose of Cairo, Dick Tracy, Mortal Thoughts*), born New London, CT, Mar 13, 1957 (some sources say 1955).

John Hoeven, 49, Governor of North Dakota (R), born Bismarck, ND, Mar 13, 1957.

William H. Macy, 56, actor (*Fargo, Boogie Nights*, "ER"), born Miami, FL, Mar 13, 1950.

Deborah Raffin, 53, actress ("Foul Play"), born Los Angeles, CA, Mar 13, 1953.

Neil Sedaka, 67, singer, songwriter ("Breaking Up Is Hard to Do," with Howard Greenfield), born Brooklyn, NY, Mar 13, 1939.

MARCH 14 — TUESDAY
Day 73 — 292 Remaining

CARAY, HARRY: BIRTH ANNIVERSARY. Mar 14, 1914. Born Harry Christopher Carabini at St. Louis, MO (some sources say Mar 1, 1920). Caray began his baseball broadcasting career with the St. Louis Cardinals in 1945. He then was the announcer for the Oakland A's, the Chicago White Sox and finally the Chicago Cubs. He became a legend at Wrigley Field with his seventh-inning stretch "Take Me out to the Ball Game" and his quirky phrase "Holy Cow." Caray was inducted into the Broadcasters Hall of Fame in 1989. Died at Rancho Mirage, CA, Feb 18, 1998.

EINSTEIN, ALBERT: BIRTH ANNIVERSARY. Mar 14, 1879. Theoretical physicist best known for his theory of relativity. Born at Ulm, Germany, he won the Nobel Prize in 1921. Died at Princeton, NJ, Apr 18, 1955.

ENGLAND: CHELTENHAM HUNT FESTIVAL. Mar 14–17. Cheltenham Racecourse, Prestbury, Cheltenham, Gloucestershire. "The Olympics of steeplechasing." Est attendance: 150,000. For info: Cheltenham Racecourse, Prestbury Park, Cheltenham, Gloucestershire, England GL50 4SH. Phone: (44) (1242) 513014 or (44) (1242) 226226. Fax: (44) (1242) 224227. Web: www.cheltenham.co.uk.

INDIA: HOLI. Mar 14. In this spring festival people run through the streets smearing each other with brightly hued powders and colored water. This is observed by Indians without regard to caste. Huge bonfires are built on the eve of Holi. Because there is no one universally accepted Hindu calendar, this holiday may be celebrated on a different date in some parts of India but it always falls in February or March.

JONES, CASEY: BIRTH ANNIVERSARY. Mar 14, 1864. Railroad engineer and hero of ballad, whose real name was John Luther Jones. Born near Cayce, KY, he died in a railroad wreck near Vaughn, MS, Apr 30, 1900.

LUNAR ECLIPSE. Mar 14. Penumbral eclipse of the moon. Moon enters penumbra at approximately 4:21 PM EST, reaches the midpoint at 6:47 PM, and leaves penumbra at 9:13 PM. Visible in North America, Central America, South America, Europe, Africa and Asia.

MARSHALL, THOMAS RILEY: BIRTH ANNIVERSARY. Mar 14, 1854. 28th vice president of the US (1913–21). Born at North Manchester, IN, he died at Washington, DC, June 1, 1925.

MOON PHASE: FULL MOON. Mar 14. Moon enters Full Moon phase at 6:35 PM, EST.

MOTH-ER DAY. Mar 14. A day set aside to honor moth collectors and specialists. Celebrated in museums or libraries with moth collections. For info: Bob Birch, Puns Corps Grand Punscorpion, 3108 Dashiell Rd, Falls Church, VA 22042. Phone: (703) 533-3668.

NATIONAL CHILDREN'S CRAFT DAY. Mar 14. To encourage children's creativity through crafts. Celebrate by painting, sculpting or creating arts and crafts projects. For info: S&S Worldwide Arts & Crafts, 75 Mill St, Colchester, CT 06415. Phone: (800) 243-9232. E-mail: hjs@ssww.com. Web: www.ssww.com.

NATIONAL TOAD HOLLOW WEEK. Mar 14–21. A community outreach program encouraging people to nourish their imagination, pursue their dreams and practice old-fashioned values in their relationships with others. For info: Ralph Morrison, Director, Toad Hollow, PO Box 2132, Garden City, MI 48135. Phone: (800) 574-8623.

ORGANIZE YOUR HOME OFFICE DAY. Mar 14. One day each year for the more than 34 million home office households to find files, purge papers and tackle to-do lists. Annually, the second Tuesday in March. For info: Lisa Kanarek, HomeOfficeLife.com, 660 Preston Forest Ctr, #120, Dallas, TX 75230. Phone: (214) 361-0556. Fax: (214) 987-0730. E-mail: info@home officelife.com. Web: www.homeofficelife.com.

PURIM. Mar 14. Hebrew calendar date: Adar 14, 5766. Feasts, gifts, charity and the reading of the Book of Esther mark this joyous commemoration of Queen Esther's intervention, in the 6th century BC, to save the Jews of ancient Persia. Haman's plot to exterminate the Jews was thwarted, and he was hanged on the very day he had set for execution of the Jews. Began at sundown Mar 13.

SEOUL RECAPTURED BY UN FORCES: 55th ANNIVERSARY. Mar 14, 1951. Seoul, Korea, which had fallen to Chinese forces in January 1951, was retaken by United Nations troops during the Korean War.

TAYLOR, LUCY HOBBS: BIRTH ANNIVERSARY. Mar 14, 1833. Lucy Beaman Hobbs, first woman in America to receive a degree in dentistry (Ohio College of Dental Surgery, 1866) and to be admitted to membership in a state dental association. Born at Franklin County, NY. In 1867 she married James M. Taylor, who also became a dentist (after she instructed him in the essentials). Active women's rights advocate. Died at Lawrence, KS, Oct 3, 1910.

"10 MOST WANTED" LIST DEBUTS: ANNIVERSARY. Mar 14, 1950. The Federal Bureau of Investigation instituted the "10 Most Wanted Fugitives" list in an effort to publicize particularly dangerous criminals who were at large. From 1950 to 1998, 454 fugitives appeared on the list; 130 were captured. Generally, the only way to get off the list is to die or be captured. The FBI cooperates with the producers of TV's "America's Most Wanted" to further publicize these fugitives.

BIRTHDAYS TODAY

Frank Borman, 78, former astronaut, airline executive, born Gary, IN, Mar 14, 1928.
Michael Caine, 73, actor (Best Supporting Actor Oscars for *The Cider House Rules* and *Hannah and Her Sisters*), born Maurice Micklewhite, London, England, Mar 14, 1933.
Tom Coburn, 58, US Senator (R, Oklahoma), born Casper, WY, Mar 14, 1948.
Billy Crystal, 59, actor ("Soap," *When Harry Met Sally . . ., City Slickers*), born Long Beach, NY, Mar 14, 1947.
Rick Dees, 55, disc jockey, comedian, born Jacksonville, FL, Mar 14, 1951.
Quincy Jones, 73, composer, producer ("We Are the World"), born Chicago, IL, Mar 14, 1933.
Kirby Puckett, 45, Hall of Fame baseball player, born Chicago, IL, Mar 14, 1961.
Tamara Tunie, 47, actress ("24," "Law & Order: SVU," "As the World Turns"), born McKeesport, PA, Mar 14, 1959.
Rita Tushingham, 64, actress (*Dr. Zhivago, A Taste of Honey*), born Liverpool, England, Mar 14, 1942.

MARCH 15 — WEDNESDAY
Day 74 — 291 Remaining

BELARUS: CONSTITUTION DAY. Mar 15. National holiday. Commemorates the adoption of the constitution on Mar 15, 1994.

BRUTUS DAY. Mar 15. No matter where you work, you must admit there's as much intrigue, plotting and backstabbing as was found in ancient Rome or is found today inside the Washington Beltway. [©2003 by WH.] For info: Thomas & Ruth Roy, Wellcat Holidays, 2418 Long Ln, Lebanon, PA 17046. Phone: (717) 279-0184. E-mail: info@wellcat.com. Web: www.wellcat.com.

CANADA: TORONTO SPORTSMEN'S SHOW. Mar 15–19. National Trade Center, Exhibition Place, Toronto, ON. Fishing manufacturers and retailers, fishing seminars, travel/vacation exhibits, cottages, camping products, boats and marine accessories, wildlife art, pet products and breeders, conservation and outdoor organizations, sporting goods, retriever trials, arena show and family entertainment. Est attendance: 115,000. For info: Canadian Natl Sportsmen's Shows, 703 Evans Ave, Ste 202, Toronto, ON, Canada M9C 5E9. Phone: (416) 695-0311. Fax: (416) 695-0381. E-mail: info@sportshows.ca. Web: www.sport shows.ca.

C.M. RUSSELL AUCTION OF ORIGINAL WESTERN ART. Mar 15–18. Heritage Inn, Great Falls, MT. Western art event features auctions, free seminars, 102 free display/sale rooms with thousands of original artworks for sale, entertainment, elegant receptions and the best of Montana hospitality. Annually, a Wednesday–Saturday in March. Est attendance: 6,000. For info: Donna Camp, Exec Dir, Great Falls Adv Fed, PO Box 634, Great Falls, MT 59403-0634. Phone: (800) 803-3351 or (406) 761-6453. E-mail: gfaf@gfaf.com.

COMMONWEALTH GAMES. Mar 15–26. Melbourne, Australia. The First British Empire Games were in Canada in 1930. The Commonwealth Games began with the Fifth British Empire Games in Vancouver, Canada in 1954. Held every four years, this will be the 18th Commonwealth Games. The nations and territories of the Commonwealth will compete in 24 different disciplines. For info: The Commonwealth Games Federation, 1-2 John Prince's St, London, England W1M 0DH.

"EIGHT IS ENOUGH" TV PREMIERE: ANNIVERSARY. Mar 15, 1977. This one-hour comedy-drama was set in Sacramento and starred Dick Van Patten as Tom Bradford, a columnist for a local paper and a widower with eight children. Diana Hyland played his wife, Joan; she died from cancer after filming five shows. The children were played by Grant Goodeve, Lani O'Grady, Laurie Walters, Susan Richardson, Dianne Kay, Connie Needham, Willie Aames and Adam Rich. In the fall of 1977 Betty Buckley joined the cast as tutor Abby Abbott, who later married Tom. Most of the cast was reunited for Tom's 50th birthday on "Eight Is Enough: A Family Reunion" shown on Oct 18, 1987.

***THE GODFATHER* FILM PREMIERE: ANNIVERSARY.** Mar 15, 1972. Francis Ford Coppola directed what many consider the greatest American film—perhaps only challenged by the sequel released two years later. Based on the Mario Puzo novel that traced the fortunes of the Corleone crime family, *The God-*

father was nominated for 11 Oscars, picking up three for Best Picture, Best Adapted Screenplay and Best Actor (Marlon Brando in a legendary performance). Costars Al Pacino, James Caan and Robert Duvall were all nominated for Best Supporting Actor. *The Godfather: Part II*, which premiered in New York City on Dec 12, 1974, was also nominated for 11 Oscars and won 6, including Best Picture. A third film was released on Dec 25, 1990.

HUNGARY: ANNIVERSARY OF THE 1848 REVOLUTION. Mar 15. National day. Commemorates when the country briefly attained autonomy from Austria.

IDES OF MARCH. Mar 15. In the Roman calendar the days of the month were not numbered sequentially. Instead, each month had three division days: kalends, nones and ides. Days were numbered from these divisions: e.g., IV Nones or III Ides. The ides occurred on the 15th of the month (or on the 13th in months that had less than 31 days). Julius Caesar was assassinated on this day in 44 BC. This system was used in Europe well into the Renaissance. When Shakespeare wrote "Beware the ides of March" in *Julius Caesar* his audience knew what he meant.

JACKSON, ANDREW: BIRTH ANNIVERSARY. Mar 15, 1767. 7th president of the US (Mar 4, 1829–Mar 3, 1837) was born in a log cabin at Waxhaw, SC. Jackson was the first president since George Washington who had not attended college. He was a military hero in the War of 1812. His presidency reflected his democratic and egalitarian values. Died at Nashville, TN, June 8, 1845. His birthday is observed as a holiday in Tennessee.

LIBERIA: J.J. ROBERTS DAY. Mar 15. National holiday. Commemorates the birth in 1809 of the country's first president.

MAINE: ADMISSION DAY: ANNIVERSARY. Mar 15. Became 23rd state in 1820. Prior to this date, Maine had been part of Massachusetts.

NAIA DIVISION I MEN'S BASKETBALL NATIONAL CHAMPIONSHIP. Mar 15–21. Municipal Auditorium, Kansas City, MO. 69th annual tournament. Est attendance: 45,000. For info: Natl Assn of Intercollegiate Athletics, 23500 W 105th St, PO Box 1325, Olathe, KS 66051-1325. Phone: (913) 791-0044. Fax: (913) 791-9555. E-mail: kdee@naia.org. Web: www.naia.org or www.naiahoopskc.org.

NAIA DIVISION I WOMEN'S BASKETBALL NATIONAL CHAMPIONSHIP. Mar 15–21. Jackson, TN. 32-team field competes for the national championship. 26th annual competition. Est attendance: 38,000. For info: Natl Assn of Intercollegiate Athletics, 23500 W 105th St, PO Box 1325, Olathe, KS 66051-1325. Phone: (913) 791-0044. Fax: (913) 791-9555. E-mail: rwiebe@naia.org. Web: www.naia.org.

"THREE'S COMPANY" TV PREMIERE: ANNIVERSARY. Mar 15, 1977. This half-hour comedy featured two girls and a guy sharing an apartment. In order for the landlord to go along with the living arrangements, Jack Tripper, played by John Ritter, had to pretend he was gay. Cast included Joyce DeWitt, Suzanne Somers, Norman Fell, Audra Findley, Richard Kline, Don Knotts and Priscilla Barnes. The last telecast aired on Sept 18, 1984.

TRUE CONFESSIONS DAY. Mar 15. Confession is good for the soul. Go in to work today and tell all. If you plan to stay home, make an appointment with your mirror. [©2003 by WH.] For info: Thomas & Ruth Roy, Wellcat Holidays, 2418 Long Ln, Lebanon, PA 17046. Phone: (717) 279-0184. E-mail: info@wellcat.com. Web: www.wellcat.com.

VAN BROCKLIN, NORM: BIRTH ANNIVERSARY. Mar 15, 1926. Norman Van Brocklin, Pro Football Hall of Fame quarterback and coach, born at Eagle Butte, SD. Van Brocklin played college football at Oregon and then signed with the Los Angeles Rams. He helped the Rams win their only NFL title in 1951. After finishing his playing career with the Philadelphia Eagles, he coached the Minnesota Vikings and the Atlanta Falcons. Inducted into the Pro Football Hall of Fame in 1979. Died at Social Circle, GA, May 2, 1983.

WASHINGTON'S ADDRESS TO CONTINENTAL ARMY OFFICERS: ANNIVERSARY. Mar 15, 1783. George Washington addressed a meeting at Newburgh, NY, of Continental army officers who were dissatisfied and rebellious for want of back pay, food, clothing and pensions. General Washington called for patience, opening his speech with the words "I have grown gray in your service. . . ." Congress later acted to satisfy most of the demands.

"THE WONDER YEARS" TV PREMIERE: ANNIVERSARY. Mar 15, 1988. A coming-of-age tale set in suburbia in the 1960s and 1970s. This drama/comedy starred Fred Savage as Kevin Arnold; Josh Saviano as his best friend, Paul, and Danica McKellar as girlfriend Winnie. Kevin's dad was played by Dan Lauria, his homemaker mom by Alley Mills, his hippie sister by Olivia d'Abo and his bully brother by Jason Hervey. Narrator Daniel Stern was the voice of the grown-up Kevin. The last episode ran Sept 1, 1993, but it remains popular in syndication.

BIRTHDAYS TODAY

Harold Douglas Baines, 47, former baseball player, born St. Michael's, MD, Mar 15, 1959.

Alan Bean, 74, former astronaut, born Wheeler, TX, Mar 15, 1932.

Robert Terrell (Terry) Cummings, 45, former basketball player, born Chicago, IL, Mar 15, 1961.

Fabio, 45, model, born Fabio Lanzoni at Milan, Italy, Mar 15, 1961.

Ruth Bader Ginsburg, 73, Associate Justice of the US Supreme Court, born Brooklyn, NY, Mar 15, 1933.

Judd Hirsch, 71, actor (Emmy for "Taxi"; *Ordinary People*), born New York, NY, Mar 15, 1935.

Eva Longoria, 31, actress ("Desperate Housewives," "The Young and the Restless"), born Corpus Christi, TX, Mar 15, 1975.

Mike Love, 65, singer, musician (Beach Boys), born Los Angeles, CA, Mar 15, 1941.

Mark McGrath, 38, singer (Sugar Ray), born Newport Beach, CA, Mar 15, 1968.

Park Overall, 49, actress ("Empty Nest," *Mississippi Burning*), born Nashville, TN, Mar 15, 1957.

Kim Raver, 37, actress ("Third Watch," "24"), born New York, NY, Mar 15, 1969.

Dee Snider, 51, singer (Twisted Sister), composer, born Massapequa, NY, Mar 15, 1955.

Sly Stone, 62, singer, musician (Sly & the Family Stone), born Sylvester Stewart at Dallas, TX, Mar 15, 1944.

Craig Wasson, 52, actor ("Phyllis," *Body Double, Malcolm X*), born Ontario, OR, Mar 15, 1954.

	S	M	T	W	T	F	S
March				1	2	3	4
2006	5	6	7	8	9	10	11
	12	13	14	15	16	17	18
	19	20	21	22	23	24	25
	26	27	28	29	30	31	

MARCH 16 — THURSDAY

Day 75 — 290 Remaining

ABSOLUTELY INCREDIBLE KID DAY. Mar 16. Camp Fire USA, one of the nation's oldest and largest youth development organizations, sponsors this day of appreciation for America's youth. Celebrate by writing letters of love and encouragement to the absolutely incredible children in your life. For info: Camp Fire USA, 4601 Madison Ave, Kansas City, MO 64112. Phone: (816) 756-1950. Fax: (816) 756-2650. E-mail: kidday@campfireusa.org. Web: www.campfireusa.org.

BLACK PRESS DAY: ANNIVERSARY OF THE FIRST BLACK NEWSPAPER. Mar 16, 1827. Anniversary of the founding of the first black newspaper in the US, *Freedom's Journal*, on Varick Street at New York, NY.

BONHEUR, ROSA: BIRTH ANNIVERSARY. Mar 16, 1822. French painter and sculptor best known for her paintings of animals, Rosa (Marie-Rosalie) Bonheur was born at Bordeaux. With the income from the sale of her art she purchased the castle of By near Fontainebleau at Melun, France, where she died May 25, 1899. Bonheur's *The Horse Fair*, which she painted in 1853, was purchased by the American millionaire Cornelius Vanderbilt for $53,600, a record price at the time. In 1865 Bonheur was awarded the Grand Cross of the Légion d'Honneur, the first woman so honored. An early Bohemian and feminist, Bonheur defied female convention of the day by dressing in pants and smoking cigarettes.

CANADA: QUEBEC CITY HUNTING, FISHING AND CAMPING SHOW. Mar 16–19. Centre de Foires, Quebec City. Major manufacturers, distributors and retailers of the outdoors, including camping, fishing and hunting, marine (fishing boats, canoes, kayaks and other craft), tourism offices, outfitters (lodges) and entertainment. Est attendance: 27,500. For info: Canadian National Sportsmen's Shows, 30 Village Centre Pl, Mississauga, ON, Canada L4Z 1V9. Phone: (905) 361-2677 or (888) 695-2677. Fax: (905) 361-2678. Web: www.sportsmens shows.com.

CLYMER, GEORGE: BIRTH ANNIVERSARY. Mar 16, 1739. Signer of the Declaration of Independence and of the US Constitution. Born at Philadelphia, PA, and died there Jan 24, 1813.

COMPANIES THAT CARE DAY. Mar 16. An annual event, celebrated by companies that prize employees and are committed to ongoing community service. This day encourages employers to highlight and expand their staff and community initiatives as well as highlight their caring activities. Examples of how companies have celebrated the day can be found at our website. For info: Marci Koblenz, Companies That Care, 500 N Dearborn St, 2nd Fl, Chicago, IL 60610. Phone: (312) 286-1547. Fax: (847) 869-2465. E-mail: info@companies-that-care.org. Web: www.com panies-that-care.org.

CURLEW DAY. Mar 16. Traditional arrival date for the long-billed curlew at the Umatilla (Oregon) National Wildlife Refuge. More than 500 of the long-billed curlews have been reported at this location during their nesting season.

FESTIVAL OF HOUSES AND GARDENS. Mar 16–Apr 15. Charleston, SC. Held annually since 1947. Provides a rare opportunity to explore the private dwellings and gardens of historic Charleston. Est attendance: 14,000. For info: Historic Charleston Fdtn Ticket Office, PO Box 1120, Charleston, SC 29402. Phone: (843) 722-3405. Fax: (843) 577-2067. Web: www.historic charleston.org.

FREEDOM OF INFORMATION DAY. Mar 16. The American Library Association supports free and open access to government information created at taxpayer expense. On or near the birthday of James Madison (Mar 16), ALA urges libraries and librarians to join in celebrating the public's "right to know" by sponsoring activities to educate their communities about the importance of promoting and protecting freedom of information. Sponsored by the Freedom Forum and the American Library Association. For info: American Library Assn Washington Office, 1301 Pennsylvania Ave NW, Ste 403, Washington, DC 20004. Phone: (202) 628-8410. E-mail: alawash@alawash.org. Web: www .ala.org.

GODDARD DAY: 80th ANNIVERSARY. Mar 16, 1926. Commemorates first liquid-fuel-powered rocket flight launched by Robert Hutchings Goddard (1882–1945) at Auburn, MA.

"THE GUMBY SHOW" TV PREMIERE: ANNIVERSARY. Mar 16, 1957. This kids' show was a spin-off from "Howdy Doody," where the character of Gumby was first introduced in 1956. Gumby and his horse, Pokey, were clay figures whose adventures were filmed using the process of "claymation." "The Gumby Show," created by Art Clokey, was first hosted by Bobby Nicholson and later by Pinky Lee. It was syndicated in 1966 and again in 1988.

LIPS APPRECIATION DAY. Mar 16. Where would all those lovely teeth we paid a bundle for be without a lovely frame? Do something nice for your lips today. Buy a lip balm. Better yet, kiss somebody! [©2003 by WH.] For info: Thomas & Ruth Roy, Wellcat Holidays, 2418 Long Ln, Lebanon, PA 17046. Phone: (717) 279-0184. E-mail: info@wellcat.com. Web: www.wellcat.com.

MADISON, JAMES: BIRTH ANNIVERSARY. Mar 16, 1751. 4th president of the US (Mar 4, 1809–Mar 3, 1817), born at Port Conway, VA. He was president when British forces invaded Washington, DC, requiring Madison and other high officials to flee while the British burned the Capitol, the president's residence and most other public buildings (Aug 24–25, 1814). Died at Montpelier, VA, June 28, 1836.

MY LAI MASSACRE: ANNIVERSARY. Mar 16, 1968. Most-publicized atrocity of the Vietnam War. According to findings of US Army's investigating team, approximately 300 noncombatant Vietnamese villagers (at My Lai and Mykhe, near the South China Sea) were killed by infantrymen of the American Division.

NATIONAL FESTIVAL OF THE WEST AND LOG HOME SHOW. Mar 16–19. Phoenix/Scottsdale, AZ. Four days of western lifestyle fun with plenty of shopping, log homes, decorative items, clothing, fine art, furniture and more. Four stages of live music, Western Writers of America, movie stars, chuck wagon cookin' competition, historical reenactments. Fun for the whole family. Est attendance: 70,000. For info: Festival of the West, PO Box 12966, Scottsdale, AZ 85267. Phone: (602) 996-4387. Fax: (602) 867-4887. E-mail: info@festivalofthewest .com. Web: www.festivalofthewest.com.

NCAA DIVISION I WOMEN'S SWIMMING AND DIVING CHAMPIONSHIPS. Mar 16–18. Gabrielsen Natatorium, Athens, GA. Est attendance: 3,000. For info: NCAA, 700 W Washington St, PO Box 6222, Indianapolis, IN 46206-6222. Phone: (317) 917-6222. Fax: (317) 917-6888. Web: www.ncaa.org.

NCAA DIVISION I WRESTLING CHAMPIONSHIPS. Mar 16–18. Downtown Arena, Oklahoma City, OK. For info: NCAA, 700 W Washington St, PO Box 6222, Indianapolis, IN 46206-6222. Phone: (317) 917-6222. Web: www.ncaasports.com.

NIXON, THELMA CATHERINE PATRICIA ("PAT") RYAN: BIRTH ANNIVERSARY. Mar 16, 1912. Wife of Richard Milhous Nixon, 37th president of the US. Born at Ely, NV, she died at Park Ridge, NJ, June 22, 1993.

POPE, JOHN: BIRTH ANNIVERSARY. Mar 16, 1822. Pope, a Union general in the Civil War, was born at Louisville, KY, graduated from West Point in 1842 and fought in the Mexican War. During the Civil War President Lincoln put Pope in charge of the Army of Virginia. He led the Union forces at the second Battle of Bull Run (August 1862) to a disastrous defeat, losing about 15,000 troops. He was immediately relieved of his command and sent to Minnesota to handle rioting Sioux Indians. Pope continued to deal with Indian matters until 1883 and eventually espoused the goal of assimilation into white culture. He died at Ohio, Sept 23, 1892.

SAINT URHO'S DAY. Mar 16. Hood River, OR. Join the parade and party to honor the tongue-in-cheek patron saint (invented in 1956) who drove the grasshoppers out of the vineyards in Finland. Est attendance: 150. For info: Camille Hukari, 3009 Dethman Ridge, Hood River, OR 97031. Phone: (541) 386-5785. Fax: (541) 387-4657.

SPACE MILESTONE: *GEMINI 8* (US): 40th ANNIVERSARY. Mar 16, 1966. Executed (with *Agena*) first docking of orbiting spacecraft. Safe emergency landing after malfunction. Launched Mar 16, 1966.

ULTIMATE SPORT AND RV SHOW—GRAND RAPIDS. Mar 16–19. DeVos Place, Grand Rapids, MI. This event brings together buyers and sellers of fishing boats and equipment, RVs, campers and their accessories, as well as other outdoor sporting goods. US and Canadian hunting and fishing trips and other vacation travel destinations are featured. All aspects of fishing, including tackle boats, seminars, demonstrations and displays are emphasized. Est attendance: 45,000. For info: Adam Starr, ShowSpan, Inc, 2121 Celebration Dr NE, Grand Rapids, MI 49525. Phone: (616) 447-2860. Fax: (616) 447-2861. E-mail: events@showspan.com. Web: www.showspan.com.

US MILITARY ACADEMY FOUNDED: ANNIVERSARY. Mar 16, 1802. President Thomas Jefferson signed legislation establishing the US Military Academy to train officers for the army. The college is located at West Point, NY, on the site of the oldest continuously occupied military post in America. Women were admitted to West Point in 1976. The Academy's motto is "Duty, Honor, Country." For more info: www.usma.edu.

BIRTHDAYS TODAY

Bernardo Bertolucci, 65, filmmaker (Oscar for *The Last Emperor; Last Tango in Paris*), born Parma, Italy, Mar 16, 1941.

Erik Estrada, 57, actor ("CHiPS," *Honey Boy*), born New York, NY, Mar 16, 1949.

Victor Garber, 57, actor (*Godspell*, "Alias"), born London, ON, Canada, Mar 16, 1949.

Lauren Graham, 39, actress (*Sweet November*, "The Gilmore Girls"), born Honolulu, HI, Mar 16, 1967.

Alice Hoffman, 54, writer (*Practical Magic, Aquamarine*), born New York, NY, Mar 16, 1952.

Isabelle Huppert, 51, actress (*Violette, Story of Women*), born Paris, France, Mar 16, 1955.

Jerry Lewis, 81, comedian, actor (*My Friend Irma*), director (*The Bellboy*), born Newark, NJ, Mar 16, 1925.

Kate Nelligan, 55, actress (*Eye of the Needle, Frankie and Johnny, The Prince of Tides*), born London, ON, Canada, Mar 16, 1951.

Chuck Woolery, 64, game-show host ("Love Connection," "Scrabble"), born Ashland, KY, Mar 16, 1942.

	S	M	T	W	T	F	S
March 2006				1	2	3	4
	5	6	7	8	9	10	11
	12	13	14	15	16	17	18
	19	20	21	22	23	24	25
	26	27	28	29	30	31	

MARCH 17 — FRIDAY
Day 76 — 289 Remaining

BRIDGER, JIM: BIRTH ANNIVERSARY. Mar 17, 1804. American fur trader, frontiersman and scout, born at Richmond, VA, and died July 17, 1881, near Kansas City, MO. Believed to be the first white man to visit (in 1824) the Great Salt Lake, he also established Fort Bridger in southwestern Wyoming as a fur-trading post and as a way station for pioneers heading west on the Oregon Trail. Bridger National Forest in western Wyoming is named for him.

CAMP FIRE USA: ANNIVERSARY. Mar 17. To commemorate the anniversary of the founding of Camp Fire USA and the service given to children and youth across the nation. Founded in 1910 as Camp Fire Girls. For info: Camp Fire USA, 4601 Madison Ave, Kansas City, MO 64112. Phone: (816) 756-1950. Fax: (816) 756-2650. E-mail: info@campfireusa.org. Web: www.campfireusa.org.

CHARLESTON INTERNATIONAL ANTIQUES SHOW. Mar 17–19. Historic Charleston Foundation Headquarters, Charleston, SC. A world-class antiques show featuring a roster of more than 30 dealers exhibiting museum-quality objects in every category with a concentration on period furnishings and decorative pieces. Est attendance: 3,000. For info: Leigh Handal, Historic Charleston Foundation, PO Box 1120, Charleston, SC 29402. Phone: (843) 722-3405. Fax: (843) 577-2067. E-mail: lhandal@historiccharleston.org. Web: www.historiccharleston.org.

COLE, NAT "KING" (NATHANIEL ADAMS COLE): BIRTH ANNIVERSARY. Mar 17, 1919. Nat King Cole was born at Montgomery, AL, and began his musical career at an early age, playing the piano at age four. He was the first black entertainer to host a national television show. His many songs included "The Christmas Song," "Nature Boy," "Mona Lisa," "Ramblin' Rose" and "Unforgettable." Although he was dogged by racial discrimination throughout his career, including the cancellation of his television show because opposition from Southern white viewers decreased advertising revenue, Cole was criticized by prominent black newspapers for not joining other black entertainers in the civil rights struggle. Cole contributed more than $50,000 to civil rights organizations in response to the criticism. Nat King Cole died Feb 25, 1965, at Santa Monica, CA.

CORBETT-FITZSIMMONS TITLE FIGHT: ANNIVERSARY. Mar 17, 1897. In one of boxing's greatest fights—and the first heavyweight title fight to be filmed—"Gentleman Jim" Corbett lost the world title to "Ruby Robert" Fitzsimmons at Carson City, NV. Fitzsimmons, seemingly a long shot at 34 years of age, hung on for 13 rounds before landing the "solar plexus punch" that felled Corbett. Western legends in attendance were Bat Masterson (overseeing security) and Wyatt Earp.

DOCTOR-PATIENT TRUST DAY. Mar 17. To rekindle the once-revered sanctity of the doctor-patient relationship. For info: Dr. Frank H. Boehm, Vanderbilt Medical Center, B-1000 Medical Center North, Nashville, TN 37232. Phone: (615) 322-2071. E-mail: frank.boehm@vanderbilt.edu. Web: www.dr-boehm.com.

EVACUATION DAY: ANNIVERSARY. Mar 17, 1776. A public holiday at Boston and Suffolk County, MA, celebrates the anniversary of the evacuation from Boston of British troops.

FEMALE RELIEF SOCIETY OF NAUVOO ORGANIZED: ANNIVERSARY. Mar 17, 1842. Twenty Mormon women formally initiated this organization at Nauvoo, IL, which is now known as the Relief Society and has grown to almost four million members. Information furnished by Church of Jesus Christ of Latter-day Saints, Public Affairs Department.

HOWARD, SHEMP: BIRTH ANNIVERSARY. Mar 17, 1895. A member of the original Three Stooges (with Moe Howard and Larry Fine), Howard was born Samuel Horwitz at Brooklyn, NY. He teamed with brother Moe as comic relief with vaudeville entertainer Ted Healy in the early 1920s. In 1925, Larry Fine joined them to create the Three Stooges. Shemp left the trio in

1932—little brother Curly replaced him—and had roles in many films. Upon Curly's retirement in 1946, Shemp rejoined the Stooges until his death on Nov 23, 1955, at Hollywood, CA.

IRELAND: NATIONAL DAY. Mar 17. St. Patrick's Day is observed in the Republic of Ireland as a legal national holiday.

JONES, BOBBY: BIRTH ANNIVERSARY. Mar 17, 1902. Golfing great Robert Tyre Jones, Jr, first golfer to win the grand slam (the four major British and American tournaments in one year). Born at Atlanta, GA, he died there Dec 18, 1971.

MACON, GEORGIA'S INTERNATIONAL CHERRY BLOSSOM FESTIVAL. Mar 17–26. Macon, GA. 24th annual Cherry Blossom Festival features concerts, exhibits, parades, children's events, hot-air balloons, street party, fireworks, food, fun and family entertainment. 275,000 Yoshino cherry trees. Est attendance: 700,000. For info: Samantha Alagna, Macon Cherry Blossom Fest, 794 Cherry St, Macon, GA 31201. Phone: (478) 751-7429. Fax: (478) 751-7408. Web: www.cherryblossom.com.

NORTHEAST GREAT OUTDOORS SHOW. Mar 17–19. Empire State Plaza, Albany, NY. Featuring fishing, hunting, camping and more. Attractions include informative seminars, fly casting pond, archery tournament, turkey and deer calling contests, deer scoring session, bass and other fishing boats, live predatory animals and much more. Annually, the third full weekend in March. Est attendance: 20,000. For info: Cate Masterson, Show Dir, Ed Lewi Assoc, 6 Chelsea Pl, Clifton Park, NY 12065. Phone: (518) 383-6183. Fax: (518) 383-6755. Web: www.edlewi.com.

NORTHERN IRELAND: SAINT PATRICK'S DAY HOLIDAY. Mar 17. National holiday.

NUREYEV, RUDOLF HAMETOVICH: BIRTH ANNIVERSARY. Mar 17, 1938. Rudolf Nureyev, one of the most charismatic ballet stars of the 20th century, was born on a train in southeastern Siberia. Nureyev's defection from the Soviet Union on June 17, 1961, while on tour with the Kirov Ballet, made headlines worldwide. The dancer was known for his ability to combine passion with a high level of perfectionism. His long partnership with Dame Margot Fonteyn of the Royal Ballet was legendary, and he also performed frequently with the Martha Graham Dance Company. Nureyev also choreographed and restaged many classics and served as the Paris Opera Ballet's artistic director. He died Jan 6, 1993, at Levallois, France, a suburb of Paris.

PARKER, GEORGE: DEATH ANNIVERSARY. Mar 17, 1764. George Parker, the second Earl of Macclesfield, was born in 1697 (exact date unknown). The eminent English astronomer was president of the Royal Society from 1752 until his death. He was one of the principal authors of the Bill for Regulating the Commencement of the Year (British Calendar Act of 1751), which was introduced in Parliament by Lord Chesterfield. That act caused the adoption, in 1752, of the "New Style" Gregorian calendar, which is still in use today. Parker died at Shirburn Castle, England.

RUSTIN, BAYARD: BIRTH ANNIVERSARY. Mar 17, 1910. Black pacifist and civil rights leader, Bayard Rustin was an organizer and participant in many of the great social protest marches—for jobs, freedom and nuclear disarmament. He was arrested and imprisoned more than 20 times for his civil rights and pacifist activities. Born at West Chester, PA, Rustin died at New York, NY, Aug 24, 1987.

SAINT PATRICK'S DAY. Mar 17. Commemorates the patron saint of Ireland, Bishop Patrick (AD 389–461) who, about AD 432, left his home in the Severn Valley, England, and introduced Christianity into Ireland. Feast day in the Roman Catholic Church. A national holiday in Ireland and Northern Ireland.

SAINT PATRICK'S DAY PARADE. Mar 17. Fifth Avenue, New York, NY. Held since 1762, the parade of 200,000 begins the two-mile march at 11:00 AM and lasts about six hours. Starts on 44th St and 5th Ave and ends at 86th St and First Ave. Est attendance: 700,000. For info: NYC & Company, 810 7th Ave, 3rd Fl, New York, NY 10019. Phone: (800) NYC-VISIT or (212) 484-1222.

SAINT PATRICK'S DAY PARADE & CELTIC FESTIVAL. Mar 17–19. Roanoke, VA. Sponsors: The Roanoke Special Events Committee. Est attendance: 20,000. For info: City of Roanoke, 210 Reserve Ave SW, Roanoke, VA 24016. Phone: (540) 342-2640. E-mail: katie@RoanokeSpecialEvents.org. Web: www.RoanokeSpecialEvents.org.

SIEGE OF BRIDGEPORT. Mar 17–19. Bridgeport, AL. 11th annual. The largest reenactment in Alabama. The Siege brings history alive as more than 2,000 reenactors thrill thousands of spectators and history buffs with their authentic reenactment of this fateful battle of the Civil War. Also included are period music, authentic encampment and vendors of historical objects and clothing. Est attendance: 15,000. For info: The Greater Jackson County Chamber of Commerce, 407 E Willow St, Scottsboro, AL 35768. Phone: (256) 259-5500 or (800) 259-5508. Web: www.jacksoncountychamber.com.

SOUTH AFRICAN WHITES VOTE TO END MINORITY RULE: ANNIVERSARY. Mar 17, 1992. A referendum proposing ending white minority rule through negotiations was supported by a whites-only ballot. The vote of 1,924,186 (68.6 percent) whites in support of President F.W. de Klerk's reform policies was greater than expected.

SPACE MILESTONE: *VANGUARD 1* (US). Mar 17, 1958. Established "pear shape" of Earth. At only three pounds it was the first solar-powered satellite.

SUGARLOAF CRAFTS FESTIVAL. Mar 17–19. Fort Washington Expo Center, Fort Washington, PA. Now in its 12th year, this show features 350 nationally recognized craft designers and fine artists displaying and selling their original creations. Includes craft demonstrations, live music, specialty foods, hourly gift certificate drawings and more. Est attendance: 25,000. For info: Sugarloaf Mountain Works, 200 Orchard Ridge Dr, #215, Gaithersburg, MD 20878. Phone: (800) 210-9900. Fax: (301) 253-9620. Web: www.SugarloafCrafts.com.

TANEY, ROGER B.: BIRTH ANNIVERSARY. Mar 17, 1777. Fifth chief justice of the Supreme Court, born at Calvert County, MD. Served as attorney general under President Andrew Jackson. Nominated as secretary of the treasury, he became the first presidential nominee to be rejected by the Senate. His rejection centered on his strong stance against the Bank of the United States as a central bank and his role in urging President Jackson to veto the congressional bill extending its charter. A year later, he was nominated to the Supreme Court as an associate justice by Jackson, but his nomination was stalled until the death of Chief Justice John Marshall July 6, 1835. Taney was nominated to fill Marshall's place on the bench and after much resistance he was sworn in as chief justice in March 1836. His tenure on the Supreme Court is most remembered for the Dred Scott decision. He died at Washington, DC, Oct 12, 1864.

BIRTHDAYS TODAY

Daniel Ray (Danny) Ainge, 47, basketball coach, former basketball and baseball player, born Eugene, OR, Mar 17, 1959.

Susie Allanson, 54, singer ("Baby Don't Keep Me Hangin' On"), born Minneapolis, MN, Mar 17, 1952.

Lesley-Anne Down, 52, actress ("Upstairs, Downstairs," *The Pink Panther Strikes Again*), born London, England, Mar 17, 1954.

Patrick Duffy, 57, actor ("Step by Step," "Dallas"), born Townsend, MT, Mar 17, 1949.

Paul Horn, 76, composer, musician, born New York, NY, Mar 17, 1930.

Vicki Lewis, 46, actress ("NewsRadio," *Godzilla*), born Cincinnati, OH, Mar 17, 1960.

Rob Lowe, 42, actor (*St. Elmo's Fire, About Last Night . . .*, "The West Wing"), born Charlottesville, VA, Mar 17, 1964.
Kurt Russell, 55, actor (*Backdraft, Elvis*), born Springfield, MA, Mar 17, 1951.
Gary Sinise, 51, stage and screen actor (*Forrest Gump, Apollo 13*, "CSI: New York"), born Chicago, IL, Mar 17, 1955.

MARCH 18 — SATURDAY
Day 77 — 288 Remaining

ARUBA: FLAG DAY. Mar 18. Aruba national holiday. Display of flags, national music and folkloric events.

AWKWARD MOMENTS DAY. Mar 18. Celebrate the humor in life's uncomfortable situations. Recognize those moments that make us feel unsure and embarrassed, then harness the power of humor, laughter and fun to cope with them. For info: Wayne & Laura Gignac, 30 Slater Ave, Norwich, CT 06360. Phone: (860) 887-7054. Fax: (860) 892-1951. E-mail: wayne@theshow works.com. Web: www.theshowworks.com.

CALHOUN, JOHN CALDWELL: BIRTH ANNIVER-SARY. Mar 18, 1782. American statesman and first vice president of the US to resign that office (Dec 28, 1832). Born at Abbeville District, SC, died at Washington, DC, Mar 31, 1850.

CANADA: MAPLE FESTIVAL OF NOVA SCOTIA. Mar 18–Apr 8 (Saturdays only). Northern Nova Scotia. Promotion of the maple industry. Pancake suppers with entertainment, industry equipment displays and crafts displays. Est attendance: 5,000. For info: Lorna A. Crowe, RR1, Southampton, Cumberland County, NS, Canada B0M 1W0. Phone: (902) 546-2844. Web: www.novascotiamaplesyrup.com.

CLEVELAND, GROVER: BIRTH ANNIVERSARY. Mar 18, 1837. The 22nd and 24th president of the US was born Stephen Grover Cleveland at Caldwell, NJ. Terms of office as president: Mar 4, 1885–Mar 3, 1889, and Mar 4, 1893–Mar 3, 1897. He ran for president for the intervening term and received a plurality of votes cast but failed to win electoral college victory. Only president to serve two nonconsecutive terms. Also the only president to be married in the White House. He married 21-year-old Frances Folsom, his ward. Their daughter, Esther, was the first child of a president to be born in the White House. Died at Princeton, NJ, June 24, 1908.

FIRST ELECTRIC RAZOR MARKETED: 75th ANNIVERSARY. Mar 18, 1931. The first electric razor was marketed by Schick, Inc.

FORGIVE MOM & DAD DAY. Mar 18. Is there a parent alive who has not made mistakes? It's time to let Mom and Dad down off the wedding cake and into the world of mere humans. Besides, you're an alleged grown-up now, and it's time to stop living your life as a reaction to what used to be. [©2003 by WH.] For info: Thomas & Ruth Roy, Wellcat Holidays, 2418 Long Ln, Lebanon, PA 17046. Phone: (717) 279-0184. E-mail: info@wellcat.com. Web: www.wellcat.com.

GREAT AMERICAN MEATOUT. Mar 18–20. America's foremost celebration of meatless eating asks consumers to "kick the meat habit, at least for the day" at 2,000 events across the country. Forty governors and mayors issue supportive proclamations. For info: Farm Animal Reform Movement, Box 30654, Bethesda, MD 20824. Phone: (301) 530-1737 or (800) MEATOUT. Fax: (301) 530-5747. E-mail: info@meatout.org. Web: www.meatout.org.

	S	M	T	W	T	F	S
March				1	2	3	4
2006	5	6	7	8	9	10	11
	12	13	14	15	16	17	18
	19	20	21	22	23	24	25
	26	27	28	29	30	31	

INTERNATIONAL DAY OF THE SEAL CELEBRATION. Mar 18. Jenkinson's Aquarium, Point Pleasant Beach, NJ. Learn all about seals and help us celebrate our seals' birthdays! Seal stories for children will be presented throughout the day. Seals are fed at 10 AM, 1 PM and 4 PM. Free arts and crafts from 1–4 PM. Est attendance: 600. For info: Jenkinson's Aquarium, 300 Ocean Ave, Point Pleasant Beach, NJ 08742. Phone: (732) 899-1212. Fax: (732) 899-1717. E-mail: jenkinsonsaquarium@comcast.net. Web: www.jenkinsons.com.

JOHNSON, WILLIAM H.: BIRTH ANNIVERSARY. Mar 18, 1901. African-American artist, born at Florence, SC; died Apr 13, 1970, at Islip, NY. Johnson spent many years in Europe painting expressionist works. He was strongly influenced by the vivid styles and brushstrokes of Henry O. Tanner, Vincent van Gogh, Paul Gauguin, Edvard Munch and Otto Dix. He left Europe when Hitler began destroying art that had primitivist or African themes. Back in the US, Johnson developed a new, flatter style and delved into subjects of his own experience as well as historical African-American figures and events. *Going to Church* (1940–41) and *Mom and Dad* (1944) are examples of his later work.

MAPLE SYRUP SATURDAY. Mar 18. Gordon Bubolz Nature Preserve, Appleton, WI. Find out how to make maple syrup. Est attendance: 600. For info: Gordon Bubolz Nature Preserve, 4815 N Lynndale Dr, Appleton, WI 54913. Phone: (920) 731-6041. Fax: (920) 731-9593. E-mail: bubolz@dataex.com.

MICHIGAN'S GRANDPARENTS AND GRANDCHILDREN DAY. Mar 18. During this annual observance grandparents are invited into schools across Michigan to join with the children in special programs and events. For info: Luella Davison, Grandparents Anonymous, 900 N Cass Lake Rd, Apt 121, Waterford, MI 48328. Phone: (800) 4AC-HILD or (248) 682-8384.

MILITARY THROUGH THE AGES. Mar 18–19. Jamestown Settlement, Williamsburg, VA. Reenactment groups depicting soldiers and military encounters throughout history join forces with modern-day veterans and active units to demonstrate camp life, tactics and weaponry. For info: Jamestown-Yorktown Foundation, PO Box 1607, Williamsburg, VA 23187. Phone: (757) 253-4838 or (888) 593-4682. Fax: (757) 253-5299. Web: www.historyisfun.org.

NATIONAL BIODIESEL DAY. Mar 18. Birthday of Rudolph Diesel, who invented the diesel engine and unveiled it at the World Fair in 1900. Diesel originally designed the engine to run on peanut oil and was a big believer in the role vegetable oils could play in fueling America. Biodiesel is a cleaner burning petroleum-free alternative to diesel that can be made from any fat or vegetable oil, such as soybean oil. This day honors the man whose vision comes full circle as biodiesel becomes an increasingly popular fuel. For info: Jenna Higgins, National Biodiesel Board, PO Box 104898, Jefferson City, MO 65110-4898. Phone: (573) 635-3893. Fax: (573) 635-7913. E-mail: jhiggins@biodiesel.org. Web: www.biodiesel.org.

NATIONAL QUILTING DAY. Mar 18. 15th annual celebration. Sponsored by NQA since 1992, this day is a grassroots effort to unite quilters and quilt lovers everywhere, not only in this country, but also around the world. Individuals, groups of quilters, shop owners, publishers and the entire community of quiltmaking are invited to join NQA in recognizing and promoting the tradition of quiltmaking. Annually, the third Saturday in March. For info: The Natl Quilting Assn, Inc, PO Box 12190, Columbus, OH 43212-0190. Phone: (614) 488-8520. E-mail: nqaquilts@sbcglobal.net. Web: www.nqaquilts.org.

PLIMPTON, GEORGE: BIRTH ANNIVERSARY. Mar 18, 1927. Born at New York, NY, writer and editor George Plimpton called himself a "participatory" journalist, going to great lengths to research his narratives. After training with the 1963 Detroit Lions, he wrote *Paper Lion* based on his experiences; the book is widely considered one of the best pieces of sports writing ever published. He also founded *The Paris Review*, a highly regarded literary quarterly that published the first works of such writers as Philip Roth and Jack Kerouac. The American Academy of Arts and Letters called him a "central figure in American letters" when they inducted him in 2002. He died at New York, NY, Sept 25, 2003.

SAINT PATRICK'S DAY PARADE. Mar 18. Downtown Hornell, NY. 19th annual. It's a "come as you are" line of march, open to anyone, with no entry fee, no judges, no prizes. Hornell's parade is designed as purely a fun affair, especially for those people who've always wanted to be in a parade but never had the opportunity. It has gotten larger and longer every year, with more and more "would-be Irish" strolling down Main Street. Annually, the Saturday before Saint Patrick's Day except when Saint Patrick's Day is a Thursday or Friday, then, the following Saturday. Est attendance: 4,000. For info: Wolf Berry, 6950 Lain Rd, Hornell, NY 14843-9419. Phone: (607) 324-1086. Fax: (607) 324-2001. E-mail: thepaperwolf@infoblvd.net. Web: www.wkpq.com.

SAINT PATRICK'S DAY PARADE: "THE WEARIN' OF THE GREEN." Mar 18. Baton Rouge, LA. 20th annual parade includes floats, precision marching bands, bagpipers and more. Largest St. Patrick's Day celebration in the region rolls at 10 AM. Est attendance: 135,000. For info: Parade Group, LLC, 6906 Moniteau Ct, Baton Rouge, LA 70809. Phone/fax: (225) 925-8295. E-mail: mabyn@futurebound.com or irishclub@futurebound.com. Web: www.paradegroup.com.

SAVE THE FLORIDA PANTHER DAY. Mar 18. Florida. A ceremonial holiday on the third Saturday in March.

SONGWRITER'S SHOW. Mar 18. Waretown, NJ. Original music written and performed by musicians. No alcoholic beverages or smoking allowed. Est attendance: 400. For info: Songwriter's Show, Albert Music Hall, PO Box 657, Waretown, NJ 08758. Phone: (609) 971-1593. Web: www.alberthall.org.

SPACE MILESTONE: *VOSKHOD 2* (USSR). Mar 18, 1965. Colonel Leonov stepped out of the capsule for 20 minutes in a special space suit, the first man to leave a spaceship. It was two months prior to the first US space walk. See also: "Space Milestone: *Gemini 4* (US)" (June 3).

TAIWAN: BIRTHDAY OF KUAN YIN, GODDESS OF MERCY. Mar 18. A Buddhist deity, Kuan Yin is also the patron goddess of Taiwan. Nineteenth day of Second Moon of the lunar calendar, celebrated at Taipei's Lungshan (Dragon Mountain) and other temples.

"TALES OF WELLS FARGO" TV PREMIERE: ANNIVERSARY. Mar 18, 1957. This half-hour western starred Dale Robertson as Jim Hardie, agent for the Wells Fargo transport company. In the fall of 1961, the show expanded to an hour. Hardie bought a ranch, and new cast members were added including Jack Ging as Beau McCloud, another agent; Virginia Christine as Ovie, a widow owning a nearby ranch; Lory Patrick and Mary Jane Saunders as Ovie's daughters and William Demarest as Jeb, Hardie's ranch foreman. Jack Nicholson appeared in one of his first major TV roles in the episode "The Washburn Girl."

BIRTHDAYS TODAY

Bonnie Blair, 42, Olympic gold medal speed skater, born Cornwall, NY, Mar 18, 1964.

Irene Cara, 47, singer ("Fame," "The Dream"), actress (*Ain't Misbehavin'*), born the Bronx, NY, Mar 18, 1959.

Frederik Willem de Klerk, 70, former president of South Africa, born Johannesburg, South Africa, Mar 18, 1936.

Kevin Dobson, 62, actor ("Kojak," "Knots Landing"), born New York, NY, Mar 18, 1944.

Brad Dourif, 56, actor (*One Flew Over the Cuckoo's Nest, Blue Velvet, Jungle Fever*), born Huntington, WV, Mar 18, 1950.

Peter Graves, 80, actor ("Mission: Impossible," "The Winds of War"), born Peter Aurness at Minneapolis, MN, Mar 18, 1926.

John Kander, 79, composer (*Cabaret, Chicago*), born Kansas City, MO, Mar 18, 1927.

Shashi Kapoor, 68, actor (*Heat and Dust, Sammy and Rosie Get Laid*), born Calcutta, India, Mar 18, 1938.

Queen Latifah, 36, rap artist, actress (*Bringing Down the House, Chicago*), born Dana Owens at East Orange, NJ, Mar 18, 1970.

Wilson Pickett, 65, singer, songwriter ("The Midnight Hour," "It's Too Late"), born Prattville, AL, Mar 18, 1941.

Charley Pride, 68, singer, former minor league baseball player, born Sledge, MS, Mar 18, 1938.

John Updike, 74, author (*Rabbit Run, The Witches of Eastwick*), born Shillington, PA, Mar 18, 1932.

Vanessa Williams, 43, singer, actress (*Bye, Bye Birdie; Kiss of the Spider Woman*), born New York, NY, Mar 18, 1963.

Alexei Yagudin, 26, figure skater, born Leningrad, Russia, Mar 18, 1980.

MARCH 19 — SUNDAY

Day 78 — 287 Remaining

BRADFORD, WILLIAM: BIRTH ANNIVERSARY. Mar 19, 1589 (OS). Pilgrim father, governor of Plymouth Colony. Born at Yorkshire, England, and baptized Mar 19, 1589. Sailed from Southampton, England, on the *Mayflower* in 1620. Died at Plymouth, MA, May 9, 1657 (OS).

BRYAN, WILLIAM JENNINGS: BIRTH ANNIVERSARY. Mar 19, 1860. American political leader, member of Congress, Democratic presidential nominee (1896), "free silver" advocate, assisted in prosecution at Scopes trial, known as "the Silver-Tongued Orator." Born at Salem, IL, he died at Dayton, TN, July 26, 1925.

EARP, WYATT: BIRTH ANNIVERSARY. Mar 19, 1848. Born at Monmouth, IL, and died Jan 13, 1929, at Los Angeles, CA. A legendary figure of the Old West, Earp worked as a railroad hand, saloon keeper, gambler, lawman, gunslinger, miner and real estate investor at various times. Best known for the gunfight at the OK Corral Oct 26, 1881, at Tombstone, AZ.

IRAN: NATIONAL DAY OF OIL. Mar 19. National holiday. Commemorates the nationalization of Iran's oil fields in 1963.

LIVINGSTONE, DAVID: BIRTH ANNIVERSARY. Mar 19, 1813. Scottish physician, missionary and explorer, born at Blantyre, Scotland. Subject of a famous search by Henry M. Stanley, who found him at Ujiji, near Lake Tanganyika in Africa, on Nov 10, 1871. Dr. Livingstone died at Africa, May 1, 1873. See also: "Stanley, Henry Morton: Birth Anniversary" (Jan 28).

McKEAN, THOMAS: BIRTH ANNIVERSARY. Mar 19, 1734. Signer of the Declaration of Independence and governor of Pennsylvania. Born at Chester County, PA, he died June 24, 1817.

METROPOLITAN OPERA NATIONAL COUNCIL AUDITIONS FINALS. Mar 19-26. Metropolitan Opera House, New York, NY. Since 1954, the Metropolitan Opera has held auditions to recognize talented young singers from around the country. Regional winners compete with guidance from the Met artistic staff at the National Semifinals on Sunday, Mar 19, at the Metropolitan Opera House. Approximately ten finalists will compete at the Grand Finals Concert accompanied by the Metropolitan Orchestra on Sunday, Mar 26. As many as five of these finalists will win awards of $15,000. For info: The Metropolitan Opera National Council Auditions, Lincoln Center, New York, NY 10023. Phone: (212) 870-4515. Fax: (212) 870-7606. E-mail: ncouncil@mail.metopera.org. Web: www.metopera.org.

NATIONAL AGRICULTURE WEEK. Mar 19-25. A Celebration of Agriculture. Annually, the week that includes the first day of spring. For info: Agriculture Council of America, 11020 King St, Ste 205, Overland Park, KS 66210. Phone: (913)

491-1895. Fax: (913) 491-6502. E-mail: info@agday.org. Web: www.agday.org.

NATIONAL ANIMAL POISON PREVENTION WEEK Mar 19–25 In conjunction with National Poison Prevention Week, the ASPCA sponsors this important week to educate Americans about common household products, plants and foods that can be dangerous or even deadly to pets. For info: Media Relations, ASPCA, 110 5th Ave, New York, NY 10011. Phone: (212) 876-7700, ext 4655. Fax: (212) 423-9813. E-mail: press@aspca.org. Web: www.aspca.org.

NATIONAL POISON PREVENTION WEEK. Mar 19–25. To aid in encouraging the American people to learn of the dangers of unintentional poisoning and to take preventive measures against it. Annually, the third full week in March. For info: Kim Dulic, Secy, Poison Prevention Week Council, Box 1543, Washington, DC 20013. E-mail: kdulic@cpsc.gov. Web: www.cpsc.gov or www.poisonprevention.org.

★**NATIONAL POISON PREVENTION WEEK.** Mar 19–25. Presidential Proclamation issued each year for the third week of March since 1962. (PL87–319 of Sept 26, 1961.)

OPERATION IRAQI FREEDOM: ANNIVERSARY. Mar 19, 2003. At 9:30 PM, EST, two hours past a deadline for Iraqi dictator Saddam Hussein to step down from power, US and British forces began air strikes against his regime. A ground campaign (adding Australian forces) followed quickly, and by Apr 9, Baghdad was in allied control and Hussein had disappeared. On May 1, President George W. Bush announced the end of major military operations in Iraq, although a peacekeeping force remains and faces violent and fatal attacks from insurgents. Hussein was captured by US forces on Dec 13, 2003. On June 28, 2004, Iraq regained its sovereignty.

ROGERS, EDITH NOURSE: 125th BIRTH ANNIVERSARY. Mar 19, 1881. Edith Nourse Rogers was a YMCA and Red Cross volunteer in France during WWI. In 1925 she was elected to the US Congress to fill the vacancy left by the death of her husband. An able legislator, she was reelected to the House of Representatives 17 times and became the first woman to have her name attached to major legislation. She was a major force in the legislation creating the Women's Army Auxiliary Corps (May 14, 1942) during WWII. Rogers was born at Saco, ME, and died Sept 10, 1960, at Boston.

RUSSELL, CHARLES M.: BIRTH ANNIVERSARY. Mar 19, 1864. Born at St. Louis, MO, Charles M. Russell moved to Montana at about age 16 and became a cowboy. Considered one of the greatest Western artists, he recorded the life of the cowboy in his artwork. He died Oct 26, 1926, at Great Falls, MT.

RYDER, ALBERT PINKHAM: BIRTH ANNIVERSARY. Mar 19, 1847. Painter Albert Pinkham Ryder was born at New Bedford, MA, where he gained a great love for the sea, the subject of many of his works. Ryder was a misanthrope and recluse. He dedicated himself to his painting, working slowly and piling layer after layer of paint on his canvases until he achieved the look he was after. In his lifetime Ryder created only 150 paintings. Three of his best-known works are *The Race Track*, *Toilers of the Sea* and *Siegfried and the Rhine Maidens*. Ryder died Mar 28, 1917, at Elmhurst, NY. Because of his method of painting, many of his works have deteriorated since their creation.

SIRICA, JOHN JOSEPH: BIRTH ANNIVERSARY. Mar 19, 1904. John Sirica, "the Watergate Judge," was born at Waterbury, CT. During two years of trials and hearings, Sirica relentlessly pushed for the names of those responsible for the June 17, 1972, burglary of the Democratic National Committee head-quarters in Washington's Watergate Complex. His unwavering search for the truth ultimately resulted in the toppling of the Nixon administration. Judge John Sirica died Aug 15, 1992, at Washington, DC.

SWALLOWS RETURN TO SAN JUAN CAPISTRANO. Mar 19. Traditional date (St. Joseph's Day), since 1776, for swallows to return to old mission of San Juan Capistrano, CA. See also: "Saint John of Capistrano: Death Anniversary" (Oct 23).

US STANDARD TIME ACT: ANNIVERSARY. Mar 19, 1918. Anniversary of passage by Congress of the Standard Time Act, which authorized the Interstate Commerce Commission to establish standard time zones for the US. The act also established "daylight saving time," to save fuel and to promote other economies in a country at war. Daylight saving time first went into operation on Easter Sunday, Mar 31, 1918. The Uniform Time Act of 1966, as amended in 1986, by Public Law 99–359, now governs standard time in the US. See also: "Daylight Saving Time Begins" (Apr 2).

WARREN, EARL: BIRTH ANNIVERSARY. Mar 19, 1891. American jurist, 14th chief justice of the US Supreme Court. Born at Los Angeles, CA; died at Washington, DC, July 9, 1974.

BIRTHDAYS TODAY

Ursula Andress, 70, actress (*Dr. No, What's New Pussycat?*), born Bern, Switzerland, Mar 19, 1936.

Michael Bergin, 37, actor ("Baywatch"), born Naugatuck, CT, Mar 19, 1969.

Glenn Close, 59, actress (*The Big Chill, Fatal Attraction*; stage: *Sunset Boulevard*), born Greenwich, CT, Mar 19, 1947.

Ornette Coleman, 76, composer, saxophonist, born Fort Worth, TX, Mar 19, 1930.

Patrick McGoohan, 78, director, actor ("The Prisoner"), born New York, NY, Mar 19, 1928.

Philip Roth, 73, author (*The Great American Novel, Portnoy's Complaint*), born Newark, NJ, Mar 19, 1933.

Brent Scowcroft, 81, business executive, consultant, born Ogden, UT, Mar 19, 1925.

Renee Taylor, 71, actress, writer (Emmy for "Acts of Love and Other Comedies"; "Mary Hartman, Mary Hartman," *The Producers, A New Leaf*), born New York, NY, Mar 19, 1935.

Hedo Turkoglu, 27, basketball player, born Hiyadet Turkoglu at Istanbul, Turkey, Mar 19, 1979.

Bruce Willis, 51, actor ("Moonlighting," *The Sixth Sense, Die Hard*), born Idar-Oberstein, West Germany, Mar 19, 1955.

MARCH 20 — MONDAY
Day 79 — 286 Remaining

ACT HAPPY DAY. Mar 20. Method acting techniques are prescribed by physicians to release chemicals in the body which aid health, wealth and friendship. Annually, the third Monday in March. For info: Dale L. Anderson, MD, 2982 W Owasso Blvd, St Paul, MN 55113. Phone: (651) 484-5162. Fax: (651) 486-8860. E-mail: drdla@acthappy.com. Web: www.acthappy.com.

AUSTRALIA: CANBERRA DAY. Mar 20. Australian Capital Territory. Public holiday the third Monday in March.

IBSEN, HENRIK: BIRTH ANNIVERSARY. Mar 20, 1828. Norwegian playwright born at Skien, Norway. Among his best-remembered plays: *Peer Gynt, The Pillars of Society, The Wild Duck, An Enemy of the People* and *Hedda Gabler*. Died at Oslo, Norway, May 23, 1906.

JAPAN: VERNAL EQUINOX DAY. Mar 20. National holiday in Japan.

NATIONAL AGRICULTURE DAY. Mar 20. A day when producers, agricultural associations, corporations, universities, government agencies and countless others across America gather to recognize and celebrate the abundance provided by agriculture. Annually, the first day of spring. Week of celebration: Mar 19–25. For info: Agriculture Council of America, 11020 King St, Ste 205,

	S	M	T	W	T	F	S
March				1	2	3	4
2006	5	6	7	8	9	10	11
	12	13	14	15	16	17	18
	19	20	21	22	23	24	25
	26	27	28	29	30	31	

Overland Park, KS 66210. Phone: (913) 491-1895. Fax: (913) 491-6502. E-mail: info@agday.org. Web: www.agday.org.

NATIONAL BUBBLE WEEK. Mar 20–27. A chance for Americans of all ages to celebrate the classic play and enhancement of bubbles, a favorite hobby in this country for the past 60 years. At the first sign of spring, children and adults alike have headed outside with bubble solution and wands to create the season's first stream of translucent, glimmering bubbles. National Bubble Week was first observed on Mar 20, 2000. Annually, beginning on the first day of spring. For info: Melissa Fogarty, Litzky Public Relations, 88 Garden St, Hoboken, NJ 07030. Phone: (201) 222-9118. Fax: (201) 222-9418. E-mail: mfogarty@litzkypr.com.

NATIONAL SPRING FEVER WEEK. Mar 20–26. Annually, the week including the first day of spring. Recognizing the special socialization rites single people face during this season of revitalization. For info: Robin Gorman Newman, 44 Somerset Dr N, Great Neck, NY 11020. Phone: (516) 773-0911. E-mail: robin@lovecoach.com. Web: www.lovecoach.com.

NERVE GAS ATTACK ON JAPANESE SUBWAY: ANNIVERSARY. Mar 20, 1995. Twelve people were killed and 5,000 injured in a nerve gas attack on the Tokyo subway system during rush hour. Suspected in the attack was the Japanese religious sect Aum Shinrikyo, founded and led by Shoko Asahara (real name Chizuo Matsumoto). The group, which professes belief in a hybrid of Buddhist-Hindu teachings, predicts an apocalypse. In a raid conducted against the sect's main compound in Kamikuishiki on Mar 25, police seized literature that predicted 90 percent of the people in the world would be killed by poison gas. Also seized were two tons of chemicals for making sarin, the poison used in the Mar 20 attack. This cache was reported to contain enough material to kill five million people. In a second raid, Asahara was arrested.

OSTARA. Mar 20. (Also called Alban Eilir.) One of the "Lesser Sabbats" during the Wiccan year, Ostara is a fire and fertility festival that marks the beginning of spring. Annually, on the spring equinox.

PROPOSAL DAY! ®. Mar 20 (also Sept 23). A holiday for those who seek marriage. Single adults who are ready to marry are encouraged to propose marriage to their true love on the days of the vernal equinox and the autumnal equinox. Thousands of men and women are married today as a result of a marriage proposal made on a "Proposal Day!"®, including the creator of the holiday. For info: John Michael O'Loughlin, 3124 Chisolm Trail, Irving, TX 75062. Phone: (972) 258-4996. E-mail: lldjohn@aol.com.

ROGERS, FRED: BIRTH ANNIVERSARY. Mar 20, 1928. Born Fred McFeely Rogers at LaTrobe, PA, Rogers first began producing television for children in 1953. His first program, "The Children's Hour," was the precursor to "Mister Rogers' Neighborhood," which premiered in Canada in 1966 and the US in 1968. The show ran on public television until Rogers' death, and he became known worldwide for his dedication to the well-being of children and for his demonstrations of the importance of kindness, compassion and learning. He authored a number of books for parents and children, wrote more than 200 songs and won dozens of awards, including Emmys, Peabodys and the Presidential Medal of Freedom. He died Feb 27, 2003, at his home in Pittsburgh, PA.

SKINNER, B.F.: BIRTH ANNIVERSARY. Mar 20, 1904. American psychologist Burrhus Frederic Skinner was born at Susquehanna, PA. He was a pioneer in behaviorism and is best known for developing the "Skinner box" (an enclosed experimental environment). He died Aug 18, 1990, at Cambridge, MA.

SNOWMAN BURNING. Mar 20. Reading of poetry heralding the end of winter and the arrival of spring, followed by sacrifice in effigy, toasts and cheers. Annually, on or near the first day of spring. Est attendance: 300. For info: Public Relations Office, Lake Superior State University, Sault Ste. Marie, MI 49783. Phone: (906) 635-2315. Fax: (906) 635-2623. Web: www.lssu.edu.

SPRING. Mar 20–June 21. In the Northern Hemisphere spring begins today with the vernal equinox, at 1:26 PM, EST. Note that in the Southern Hemisphere today is the beginning of autumn. Sun rises due east and sets due west everywhere on Earth (except near poles) and the daylight length (interval between sunrise and sunset) is virtually the same everywhere today: 12 hours, 8 minutes.

TAYLOR, FREDERICK WINSLOW: 150th BIRTH ANNIVERSARY. Mar 20, 1856. Villified and praised, Frederick Winslow Taylor changed the face of business forever as the "Father of Scientific Management." Born at Philadelphia, PA, Taylor was a chief engineer at Philadelphia's Midvale Steel Company, when he introduced time-and-motion studies in 1881, which helped companies find efficiencies in worker movement and drive out time wasting on the assembly lines. Henry Ford, in particular, put Taylor's theories to work. Taylor died at Philadelphia, Mar 21, 1915.

TUNISIA: INDEPENDENCE DAY. Mar 20. Commemorates treaty in 1956 by which France recognized Tunisian autonomy.

WELLDERLY DAY. Mar 20. Celebration and recognition of senior citizens who never act their age. Annually, the third Monday in March. For info: Dale L. Anderson, MD, 2982 W Owasso Blvd, St. Paul, MN 55113. Phone: (651) 484-5162. Fax: (651) 486-8860. E-mail: drdla@acthappy.com. Web: www.acthappy.com.

BIRTHDAYS TODAY

Holly Hunter, 48, actress (Oscar for *The Piano*; *Broadcast News, The Firm*), born Conyers, GA, Mar 20, 1958.

William Hurt, 56, actor (*The Accidental Tourist, Broadcast News*), born Washington, DC, Mar 20, 1950.

Spike Lee, 49, director, producer, writer, actor (*She's Gotta Have It, Do the Right Thing, Malcolm X*), born Atlanta, GA, Mar 20, 1957.

Hal Linden, 75, actor ("Barney Miller," "Blacke's Magic"), born Harold Lipshitz at the Bronx, NY, Mar 20, 1931.

Marian McPartland, 86, jazz pianist (*After Hours, Personal Choice, In My Life*), born Slough, England, Mar 20, 1920.

Brian Mulroney, 67, Canadian statesman and 18th prime minister of Canada, born Baie Comeau, QC, Canada, Mar 20, 1939.

Robert Gordon (Bobby) Orr, 58, Hall of Fame hockey player, born Parry Sound, ON, Canada, Mar 20, 1948.

Jerry Reed, 69, actor, singer, songwriter ("When You're Hot, You're Hot"), born Jerry Hubbard at Atlanta, GA, Mar 20, 1937.

Carl Reiner, 84, actor ("The Dick Van Dyke Show," "Your Show of Shows"), writer, director, born the Bronx, NY, Mar 20, 1922.

Patrick James (Pat) Riley, 61, basketball coach and former player, born Schenectady, NY, Mar 20, 1945.

Theresa Russell, 49, actress (*Straight Time, Black Widow*), born San Diego, CA, Mar 20, 1957.

David Thewlis, 43, actor ("Dinotopia"), born Blackpool, Lancashire, England, Mar 20, 1963.

Paul Junger Witt, 63, producer (*Three Kings*, "Everything's Relative"), director, born New York, NY, Mar 20, 1943.

MARCH 21 — TUESDAY
Day 80 — 285 Remaining

ANN ARBOR FILM FESTIVAL. Mar 21–26. Ann Arbor, MI. Independent digital, 16mm and 35mm film festival in its 44th year. Genres represented include experimental, animation, documentary, narrative, avant-garde. Entry deadline: Nov 15, 2005. $20,000 awarded in prizes. Est attendance: 8,000. For info: Christina Hamilton, Ann Arbor Film Festival, PO Box 8232, Ann Arbor, MI 48107. Phone: (734) 995-5356. Fax: (734) 995-5396. E-mail: info@aafilmfest.org. Web: aafilmfest.org.

ARIES, THE RAM. Mar 21–Apr 19. In the astronomical/astrological zodiac, which divides the sun's apparent orbit into 12 segments, the period Mar 21–Apr 19 is identified, traditionally, as the sun sign of Aries, the Ram. The ruling planet is Mars.

BACH, JOHANN SEBASTIAN: BIRTH ANNIVERSARY. Mar 21, 1685 (OS). Organist and composer, one of the most influential composers in musical history. Born at Eisenach, Germany; he died at Leipzig, Germany, July 28, 1750.

FIRST ROUND-THE-WORLD BALLOON FLIGHT: ANNIVERSARY. Mar 21, 1999. Swiss psychiatrist Bertrand Piccard and British copilot Brian Jones landed in the Egyptian desert on this date, having flown 29,056 miles nonstop around the world in a hot-air balloon. Leaving from Chateau d'Oex in the Swiss Alps on Mar 1, the trip took 19 days, 21 hours and 55 minutes. Piccard is the grandson of balloonist Auguste Piccard, who was the first to ascend into the stratosphere in a balloon. See also: "First Solo Round-the-World Balloon Flight: Anniversary" (July 2) and "Piccard, Auguste: Birth Anniversary" (Jan 28).

GERSDORFF HITLER ASSASSINATION ATTEMPT: ANNIVERSARY. Mar 21, 1943. In a suicide/assassination attempt planned for this date, Major General Baron von Gersdorff was to carry a bomb in the pocket of his greatcoat to the "Heroes Memorial Day" annual dedication to the dead of the First World War. Hitler was to attend this event to inspect some weaponry taken from captured Russian soldiers. The bomb was to go off within 10 minutes of Hitler's arrival at the event as he was not expected to be there for very long. The conspirators were unable to locate the necessary short time fuse and the attempt had to be called off. This was the second serious plan to assassinate Hitler in 1943.

IRANIAN NEW YEAR: NORUZ. Mar 21. National celebration for all Iranians, this is the traditional Persian New Year. (In Iran spring comes Mar 20 or 21.) It is a celebration of nature's rebirth. Every household spreads a special cover with symbols for the seven good angels on it. These symbols are sprouts, wheat germ, apples, hyacinth, fruit of the jujube, garlic and sumac heralding life, rebirth, health, happiness, prosperity, joy and beauty. A fishbowl is also customary, representing the end of the astrological year and wild rue is burnt to drive away evil and bring about a happy New Year. This pre-Islamic holiday, a legacy of Zoroastrianism, is also celebrated as Navruz, Nau-Roz or Noo Roz in Afghanistan, Albania, Azerbaijan, Kazakhstan, Kyrgyzstan, Tajikistan, Turkmenistan and Uzbekistan. For info: Mahvash Tafreshi, Librarian, Farmingdale Public Library, 116 Merritts Rd, Farmingdale, NY 11735. Phone: (516) 249-9090. Fax: (516) 694-9697 or Yassaman Djalali, Librarian, West Valley Branch Library, 1243 San Tomas Aquino Rd, San Jose, CA 95117. Phone: (408) 244-4766.

	S	M	T	W	T	F	S
March				1	2	3	4
2006	5	6	7	8	9	10	11
	12	13	14	15	16	17	18
	19	20	21	22	23	24	25
	26	27	28	29	30	31	

JUAREZ, BENITO: 200th BIRTH ANNIVERSARY. Mar 21. A full-blooded Zapotec Indian, Benito Pablo Juarez was born at Oaxaca, Mexico, in 1806 and grew up to become the president of Mexico. He learned Spanish at age 12. Juarez became judge of the civil court in Oaxaca in 1842, a member of congress in 1846 and governor in 1847. In 1858, following a rebellion against the constitution, the presidency was passed to Juarez. He died at Mexico City, July 18, 1872. A symbol of liberation and of Mexican resistance to foreign intervention, his birthday is a public holiday in Mexico.

LESOTHO: NATIONAL TREE PLANTING DAY. Mar 21. Lesotho.

LEWIS, FRANCIS: BIRTH ANNIVERSARY. Mar 21, 1713. Signer of the Declaration of Independence, born at Wales. Died Dec 31, 1802, at Long Island, NY.

LUNSFORD, BASCOM LAMAR: BIRTH ANNIVERSARY. Mar 21, 1882. Folk song writer and folklorist who authored the folk song "Mountain Dew," Lunsford started the first folk music festival in 1928 at Asheville, NC. This event, which led to the formation of the National Clogging and Hoedown Council, is held to this day. He was known as the "father of clogging dance" and the "king of folk music." He recorded some 320 folk songs, tunes and stories for the Library of Congress. Born at Mars Hill, NC, Lunsford died Sept 4, 1973, at South Turkey Creek, NC.

MEMORY DAY. Mar 21. To encourage awareness of the traditional memory system using pattern t,d = 1; n = 2; m = 3; r = 4; l = 5; j,ch = 6; k,q,g-hard = 7; f,v = 8; b,p = 9. Study historic examples of the use of the memory system in the writings of Milton, Thomas Gray, Longfellow, Lincoln and others. For info: Robert L. Birch, Coord, Puns Corps, 3108 Dashiell Rd, Falls Church, VA 22042. Phone: (703) 533-3668.

NAMIBIA: INDEPENDENCE DAY. Mar 21. National Day. Commemorates independence from South Africa in 1990.

NATIONAL DANCE DAY. Mar 21. Participants across the country will organize events in every community to celebrate the spirit and diversity of dance of all kinds. For info: Sharon Hoge, 480 Park Ave, New York, NY 10022. Phone: (212) 750-6168. Fax: (212) 750-4979. E-mail: skinghoge@aol.com. Web: www.nationaldanceday.org.

NAW-RUZ. Mar 21. Baha'i New Year's Day. Astronomically fixed to commence the year. One of the nine days of the year when Baha'is suspend work. For info: Baha'is of the US, Office of Communications, 1233 Central St, Evanston, IL 60201. Phone: (847) 733-3411. Fax: (847) 869-0247. E-mail: ooc@usbnc.org. Web: www.us.bahai.org.

POCAHONTAS (REBECCA ROLFE): DEATH ANNIVERSARY. Mar 21, 1617. Pocahontas, daughter of Powhatan, born about 1595, near Jamestown, VA, leader of the Indian union of Algonkin nations, helped to foster goodwill between the colonists of the Jamestown settlement and her people. Pocahontas converted to Christianity, was baptized with the name Rebecca and married John Rolfe Apr 5, 1614. In 1616, she accompanied Rolfe on a trip to his native England, where she was regarded as an overseas "ambassador." Pocahontas's stay in England drew so much attention to the Virginia Company's Jamestown settlement that lotteries were held to help support the colony. Shortly before she was scheduled to return to Jamestown, Pocahontas died at Gravesend, Kent, England, of either smallpox or pneumonia.

SECOND BATTLE OF SOMME: ANNIVERSARY. Mar 21–Apr 4, 1918. General Erich Ludendorff launched the Michael offensive, the biggest German offensive of 1918, on Mar 21 with a five-hour artillery barrage. The Central Powers' objective was to drive a wedge between the British and French forces and drive the British to the sea. Although they did not accomplish this objective, in the south they captured Montdidier and advanced to a depth of 40 miles. They managed to create a bulge in the front south of Somme and end what had effectively been a stalemate.

The Allies lost nearly 230,000 men and the Germans almost as many in the Battle of Somme.

SELMA CIVIL RIGHTS MARCH: ANNIVERSARY. Mar 21, 1965. More than 3,000 civil rights demonstrators led by Dr. Martin Luther King, Jr, began a four-day march from Selma, AL, to Montgomery, AL, to demand federal protection of voting rights. There were violent attempts by local police, using fire hoses and dogs, to suppress the march. A march two weeks before on Mar 7, 1965, was called "Bloody Sunday" because of the use of nightsticks, chains and electric cattle prods against the marchers by the police.

SOUTH AFRICA: HUMAN RIGHTS DAY. Mar 21. National holiday. Commemorates the Mar 21, 1960, massacre at Sharpeville and all those who lost their lives in the struggle for equal rights as citizens of South Africa.

STRANG, JAMES JESSE (KING STRANG): BIRTH ANNIVERSARY. Mar 21, 1813. Perhaps America's only crowned king was born at Scipio, NY, and christened Jesse James Strang (which he later changed to James Jesse Strang). He was crowned king of Mormons at Beaver Island, MI, July 8, 1850, and ruled his kingdom until his death. Elected to the Michigan legislature in 1852 and 1854. Wounded by assassins June 16, 1856, at Beaver Island, he died June 19, 1856, at Voree, WI.

UNITED NATIONS: INTERNATIONAL DAY FOR THE ELIMINATION OF RACIAL DISCRIMINATION. Mar 21. Initiated by the United Nations General Assembly in 1966 to be observed annually Mar 21, the anniversary of the killing of 69 African demonstrators at Sharpeville, South Africa, in 1960, as a day to remember "the victims of Sharpeville and those countless others in different parts of the world who have fallen victim to racial injustice" and to promote efforts to eradicate racial discrimination worldwide. For info: United Nations, Dept of Public Info, New York, NY 10017. Web: www.un.org.

UNITED NATIONS: WEEK OF SOLIDARITY WITH THE PEOPLES STRUGGLING AGAINST RACISM AND RACIAL DISCRIMINATION. Mar 21–27. Annual observance initiated by the United Nations General Assembly as part of its program of the Decade for Action to Combat Racism and Racial Discrimination. For info: United Nations, Dept of Public Info, New York, NY 10017. Web: www.un.org.

BIRTHDAYS TODAY

Matthew Broderick, 44, actor (*Godzilla, Inspector Gadget, Election*; stage: *The Producers*), born New York, NY, Mar 21, 1962.

Peter Brook, 81, theater director, born London, England, Mar 21, 1925.

Timothy Dalton, 60, actor (James Bond movies, *Cleopatra, Centennial*), born Colwyn Bay, Wales, Mar 21, 1946.

Al Freeman, Jr, 72, actor (*A Patch of Blue; Roots: The Next Generations*), born San Antonio, TX, Mar 21, 1934.

Rosie O'Donnell, 44, actress (*A League of Their Own*), host ("The Rosie O'Donnell Show"), born Commack, NY, Mar 21, 1962.

Gary Oldman, 48, actor (*Sid and Nancy, JFK*), born South London, England, Mar 21, 1958.

MARCH 22 — WEDNESDAY
Day 81 — 284 Remaining

AS YOUNG AS YOU FEEL DAY. Mar 22. Now more than ever you are as young as you feel. So stop acting your chronological age and get out there and start feeling peppy! [©2003 by WH.] For info: Thomas & Ruth Roy, Wellcat Holidays, 2418 Long Ln, Lebanon, PA 17046. Phone: (717) 279-0184. E-mail: info@wellcat.com. Web: www.wellcat.com.

EQUAL RIGHTS AMENDMENT SENT TO STATES FOR RATIFICATION: ANNIVERSARY. Mar 22, 1972. The Senate passed the 27th Amendment, prohibiting discrimination on the basis of sex, sending it to the states for ratification. Hawaii led the way as the first state to ratify and by the end of the year 22 states had ratified it. On Oct 6, 1978, the deadline for ratification was extended to June 30, 1982, by Congress. The amendment still lacked three of the required 38 states for ratification. This was the first extension granted since Congress set seven years as the limit for ratification. The amendment failed to achieve ratification as the deadline came and passed and no additional states ratified the measure.

FIRST WOMEN'S COLLEGIATE BASKETBALL GAME: ANNIVERSARY. Mar 22, 1893. The first women's collegiate basketball game was played at Smith College at Northampton, MA. Senda Berenson, then Smith's director of physical education and "mother of women's basketball," supervised the game, in which Smith's sophomore team beat the freshman team 5–4. For info: Dir of Media Relations, Smith College, Office of College Relations, Northampton, MA 01063. Phone: (413) 585-2700. Fax: (413) 585-2174. Web: www.smith.edu.

INDIA: NEW YEAR'S DAY. Mar 22. This is the first day of the New Year on the Saka calendar adopted by India after independence from Great Britain. The Saka calendar is a solar calendar with the same Leap Year schedule as the Gregorian calendar. In Leap Years, the New Year falls on Mar 21.

INTERNATIONAL DAY OF THE SEAL. Mar 22. In 1982 Congress declared an International Day of the Seal to draw attention to the cruelty of seal hunts and the virtual inevitability of these creatures' extinction. Zoos and aquariums around the world observe this day with special programs and activities; contact your local affiliate for a schedule of activities.

INTERNATIONAL GOOF-OFF DAY. Mar 22. A day of relaxation and a time to be oneself; a day for some good-humored fun and some good-natured silliness. Everyone needs one special day each year to goof off.

LASER PATENTED: ANNIVERSARY. Mar 22, 1960. The first patent for a laser (light amplification by stimulated emission of radiation) granted to Arthur Schawlow and Charles Townes.

MOON PHASE: LAST QUARTER. Mar 22. Moon enters Last Quarter phase at 2:10 PM, EST.

NATIONAL COMMON COURTESY DAY. Mar 22. Citizens of our country reflect on what it means to demonstrate common courtesy. We live in a society where it seems that we have forgotten how to display such behaviors in our everyday lives, be it at work, home or simply driving down the highway. On National Common Courtesy Day, stories will be collected from individuals who have demonstrated common courtesy or who have been the recipients of such acts. For info: Lefiest H. Galimore, 3139 Plymouth Rd, Ann Arbor, MI 48105. Phone: (734) 995-6816 or (734) 502-5775. Fax: (734) 995-6861. E-mail: lefiest@aol.com.

NJCAA DIVISION II MEN'S BASKETBALL NATIONAL FINALS. Mar 22–25. Danville, IL. Junior College Division II national men's basketball finals tournament. Est attendance: 8,000. For info: Jeanie Cooke, Exec Dir, Danville Area Conv/Visitors Bureau, PO Box 992, Danville, IL 61834. Phone: (800) 383-4386. E-mail: dacvb@cooketech.net.

PUERTO RICO: EMANCIPATION DAY. Mar 22. Holiday commemorates the end of slavery on Mar 22, 1873.

SPACE MILESTONE: RECORD TIME IN SPACE. Mar 22, 1995. Russian cosmonaut Valery Polyakov returned to Earth after setting a record of 438 days in space aboard *Mir*. Previous records include three Soviet cosmonauts who spent 237 days in space at *Salyut 7* space station in 1984, a Soviet cosmonaut who spent 326 days aboard *Mir* in 1987 and two Soviets who spent 366 days aboard *Mir* in 1988. The US space endurance record was set by Carl Walz and Daniel Bursch, who stayed 196 days in space aboard *Endeavor*, completing their mission on June 19, 2002. US astronaut Shannon Lucid set the record for women in space with her 188-day stay on *Mir* in 1996.

TUSKEGEE AIRMEN ACTIVATED: 65th ANNIVERSARY. Mar 22, 1941. This pioneering and highly decorated WWII African-American aviator unit gained their name during training at the US Army airfield near Tuskegee, AL, and at the Tuskegee Institute. They were activated as the 99th Pursuit Squadron and later formed the 332nd Fighter Group (with the 100th, 301st and 302nd squadrons). 992 black pilots emerged from training to fly P-39, P-40, P-47 and P-51 aircraft in more than 15,000 sorties in North Africa, Sicily and Europe. On escort missions, they were the only unit that never lost a US bomber. They shot down 111 enemy planes and destroyed 273 planes on the ground. Lieutenant Colonel Benjamin O. Davis, Jr—later the US Air Force's first black general—was their commander. When President Harry Truman integrated the US military, the all-black group was deactivated. See also: "Davis, Benjamin O., Jr: Birth Anniversary" (Dec 18).

UNITED NATIONS: WORLD DAY FOR WATER. Mar 22. The General Assembly declared this observance (Res 47/193) to promote public awareness of how water resource development contributes to economic productivity and social well-being. Annually, on Mar 22.

BIRTHDAYS TODAY

George Benson, 63, singer, guitarist ("On Broadway," "Give Me the Night"), born Pittsburgh, PA, Mar 22, 1943.

Robert Quinlan (Bob) Costas, 54, sportscaster, born New York, NY, Mar 22, 1952.

Bruno Ganz, 65, actor (*The American Friend, Wings of Desire*), born Zurich, Switzerland, Mar 22, 1941.

Orrin Grant Hatch, 72, US Senator (R, Utah), born Pittsburgh, PA, Mar 22, 1934.

Andrew Lloyd Webber, 58, composer (*Cats, Phantom of the Opera*), born London, England, Mar 22, 1948.

Karl Malden, 92, actor (*A Streetcar Named Desire*, "The Streets of San Francisco"), born Mladen Sekulovich at Gary, IN, Mar 22, 1914 (some sources say 1912 or 1913).

Marcel Marceau, 83, actor, pantomimist (had the only speaking part in *Silent Movie*), born Strasbourg, France, Mar 22, 1923.

Matthew Modine, 47, actor (*Married to the Mob*, "And the Band Played On"), born Loma Linda, CA, Mar 22, 1959.

Allen Neuharth, 82, founder of *USA Today*, born Eureka, SD, Mar 22, 1924.

James Patterson, 59, author (*Kiss the Girls, Along Came a Spider*), born Newburgh, NY, Mar 22, 1947.

Cristen Powell, 27, race car driver, born Portland, OR, Mar 22, 1979.

Pat Robertson, 76, TV evangelist, born Lexington, VA, Mar 22, 1930.

William Shatner, 75, actor ("Star Trek," "Boston Legal"), author (*Tek* novels), born Montreal, QC, Canada, Mar 22, 1931.

Stephen Sondheim, 76, composer (*A Little Night Music*), born New York, NY, Mar 22, 1930.

	S	M	T	W	T	F	S
March				1	2	3	4
2006	5	6	7	8	9	10	11
	12	13	14	15	16	17	18
	19	20	21	22	23	24	25
	26	27	28	29	30	31	

Elvis Stojko, 34, skater, born Newmarket, ON, Canada, Mar 22, 1972.

M. Emmet Walsh, 71, actor (*Serpico, Blood Simple, Raising Arizona*), born Ogdensburg, NY, Mar 22, 1935.

Reese Witherspoon, 30, actress (*The Importance of Being Earnest, Legally Blonde, Election*), born Nashville, TN, Mar 22, 1976.

MARCH 23 — THURSDAY
Day 82 – 283 Remaining

"BEAT THE CLOCK" TV PREMIERE: ANNIVERSARY. Mar 23, 1950. On this game show from the team of Mark Goodson and Bill Todman, couples performed stunts within a specified time period with the winners being given a chance to try a special stunt. Special stunts were very difficult, and the same one was attempted every week until a couple got it right. In 1952, James Dean got his first TV job testing stunts and warming up the audience. Bud Collyer was the host, assisted by Roxanne (real name Dolores Rosedale). A 1969 syndicated version hosted by Jack Narz and then by Gene Wood had celebrities to help the contestants. A 1979 revival was hosted by Monty Hall.

"BIG BERTHA" PARIS GUN: ANNIVERSARY. Mar 23, 1918. Germany initiated use of a terrifying new weapon—the Paris Gun—so called because it was first used against that city. The great gun, with a 25-foot carriage, was first used in combat when it was fired from a wooded location near Laon on Mar 23, 1918. It took 176 seconds for a shell to reach the city from a distance of 75 miles. On that first day 15 shots killed 16 individuals. Ridiculing the designers and manufacturers of the weapon, Parisians nicknamed it "Big Bertha" after the wife of the head of the munitions corporation. On Good Friday, Mar 29, a shell from the armament struck the church of Saint Gervais, which was crowded with worshipers. The casualty toll was 88 dead and 68 injured.

"THE BOLD AND THE BEAUTIFUL" TV PREMIERE: ANNIVERSARY. Mar 23, 1987. A continuing daytime serial created by William Bell and Lee Phillip Bell to be "young and hip." It is set in the fashion industry of Los Angeles with two central families, the Logans and the Forresters. The cast has included, as the Forresters: John McCook, Susan Flannery, Clayton Norcross, Jeff Trachta, Ronn Moss, Teri Ann Linn, Colleen Dion and as the Logans: Robert Pine, Judith Baldwin, Nancy Burnette, Nancy Sloan, Carrie Mitchum, Ethan Wayne, Brian Patrick Clarke, Katherine Kelly Lang and Lesley Woods.

CLARK, BARNEY: DEATH ANNIVERSARY. Mar 23, 1983. Barney Clark died after living almost 112 days with an artificial heart. The heart, made of polyurethane plastic and aluminum, was implanted in Clark at the University of Utah Medical Center, Salt Lake City, Dec 2, 1982. Clark was the first person ever to receive a permanent artificial heart. Born at Provo, UT, Jan 21, 1921, Clark was 62 when he died.

COLFAX, SCHUYLER: BIRTH ANNIVERSARY. Mar 23, 1823. 17th vice president of the US (1869–73). Born at New York, NY. Died Jan 13, 1885, at Mankato, MN.

CRAWFORD, JOAN: BIRTH ANNIVERSARY. Mar 23, 1904. Actress, born Lucille Fay LeSueur at San Antonio, TX. Crawford became a Hollywood star with her performance in *Our Dancing Daughters*. She won an Oscar in 1945 for her role in *Mildred Pierce*. Events of Crawford's life are chronicled in *Mommie Dearest*. Other films included *The Women, Whatever Happened to Baby Jane?* and *Twelve Miles Out*. She died at New York, NY, May 10, 1977.

DICK CLARK RETIRES FROM "AMERICAN BANDSTAND": ANNIVERSARY. Mar 23, 1989. After 33 years, 59-year-old Dick Clark retired from hosting the television program "American Bandstand."

KUROSAWA, AKIRA: BIRTH ANNIVERSARY. Mar 23, 1910. Acclaimed filmmaker (*Rashomon, The Seven Samurai, Kagemusha, Ran*), born at Tokyo, Japan. The ambassador of Japanese cinema to the West, Kurosawa is considered one of the greatest film directors of all time. Died at Tokyo, Sept 6, 1998.

LIBERTY DAY: ANNIVERSARY. Mar 23, 1775. Anniversary of Patrick Henry's speech for arming the Virginia militia at St. John's Church, Richmond, VA. "I know not what course others may take, but as for me, give me liberty or give me death."

NCAA DIVISION I MEN'S SWIMMING AND DIVING CHAMPIONSHIPS. Mar 23–25. Georgia Tech Aquatic Center, Atlanta, GA. For info: NCAA, 700 W Washington St, PO Box 6222, Indianapolis, IN 46206-6222. Phone: (317) 917-6222. Fax: (317) 917-6888. Web: www.ncaa.org.

NEAR MISS DAY. Mar 23, 1989. A mountain-sized asteroid passed within 500,000 miles of Earth, a very close call according to NASA. Impact would have equaled the strength of 40,000 hydrogen bombs, created a crater the size of the District of Columbia and devastated everything for 100 miles in all directions.

NEW ZEALAND: OTAGO AND SOUTHLAND PROVINCIAL ANNIVERSARY. Mar 23. In addition to the statutory public holidays of New Zealand, there is in each provincial district a holiday for the provincial anniversary. This day is observed in Otago and Southland.

"O.K." FIRST APPEARANCE IN PRINT: ANNIVERSARY. Mar 23, 1839. *The Boston Morning Post* printed the first known "o.k." on this day in 1839. It derived from a jovial misspelling of "all correct"—"oll korrect." Etymologist Allen Read doggedly tracked down the word's origin in the 1960s. "O.K." is now used in most languages.

"ORIGINAL" WESTERN MASSACHUSETTS HOME AND GARDEN SHOW. Mar 23–26. West Springfield, MA. The largest home show in New England with more than 700 booths and a large outside area covering more than six acres of exhibits. Annually, third or fourth week of March. For info: Brad Campbell, Home Builders Assn of Western Massachusetts, 240 Cadwell Dr, Springfield, MA 01104. Phone: (413) 733-3126. Fax: (413) 781-8416. E-mail: bcampbell@hbawm.com. Web: www.hbawm.com.

PAKISTAN: REPUBLIC DAY. Mar 23, 1940. National holiday. In 1940 the All-India-Muslim League adopted a resolution calling for a Muslim homeland. On the same day in 1956 Pakistan declared itself a republic.

THE SAVANNAH TOUR OF HOMES AND GARDENS. Mar 23–26. Savannah, GA. Residents of Savannah open their homes to visitors to view 18th- and 19th-century architecture. The beauty of spring makes this tour of homes and gardens even more breathtaking. Est attendance: 4,000. For info: The Savannah Tour of Homes and Gardens, 18 Abercorn St, Savannah, GA 31401. Phone: (912) 234-8054. Fax: (912) 234-2123. E-mail: tourinfo@savannahtourofhomes.org. Web: www.savannahtourofhomes.org.

SPACE MILESTONE: *MIR* ABANDONED (USSR): 5th ANNIVERSARY. Mar 23, 2001. The 140-ton *Mir* space station, launched in 1986, was brought down into the South Pacific near Fiji, about 1,800 miles east of New Zealand, just before 1 AM, EST. Two-thirds of the station burned up during its controlled descent. *Mir's* core component had been aloft for more than 15 years and orbited Earth 86,330 times. Nearly 100 people, seven of them American, had spent some time on *Mir*. See also: "Space Milestone: *Mir* Space Station (USSR)" (Feb 20).

SUWANNEE SPRING FEST. Mar 23–26. Live Oak, FL. Outstanding festival. Previous artists have included Nitty Gritty Dirt Band, Earl Scruggs, Donna the Buffalo, Peter Rowan and more. Also available are vendors and activities for children. Est attendance: 8,000. For info: Spirit of the Suwannee Music Park, 3076 95th Dr, Live Oak, FL 32060. Phone: (386) 364-1683. Fax: (386) 364-2998. E-mail: spirit@musicliveshere.com. Web: www.musicliveshere.com.

UNITED NATIONS: WORLD METEOROLOGICAL DAY. Mar 23. An international day observed by meteorological services throughout the world and by the organizations of the UN system. Annually, on Mar 23. For info: United Nations, Dept of Public Info, New York, NY 10017. Web: www.un.org.

BIRTHDAYS TODAY

Louie Anderson, 53, comedian, actor ("Life with Louie"), born Minneapolis, MN, Mar 23, 1953.

Dr. Roger Bannister, 77, distance runner, broke the 4-minute-mile record in 1954, born Harrow, Middlesex, England, Mar 23, 1929.

Mike Easley, 56, Governor of North Carolina (D), born Nash County, NC, Mar 23, 1950.

Richard Grieco, 41, actor (*Ultimate Deception, Blackheart*), born Watertown, NY, Mar 23, 1965.

Chaka Khan, 53, singer ("Tell Me Something Good," "You Got the Love"), born Yvette Marie Stevens at Chicago, IL, Mar 23, 1953.

Jason Kidd, 33, basketball player, born San Francisco, CA, Mar 23, 1973.

Moses Eugene Malone, 52, Hall of Fame basketball player, born Petersburg, VA, Mar 23, 1954.

Amanda Plummer, 49, actress (Tony for *Agnes of God; The Fisher King*), born New York, NY, Mar 23, 1957.

Keri Russell, 30, actress ("Felicity"), born Fountain Valley, CA, Mar 23, 1976.

MARCH 24 — FRIDAY
Day 83 — 282 Remaining

AMERICAN CROSSWORD PUZZLE TOURNAMENT AND CONVENTION. Mar 24–26. Stamford Marriott Hotel, Stamford, CT. Five hundred solvers from the US and Canada compete on eight puzzles during this 29th annual event. Points are awarded for accuracy and speed. The final puzzle is played on giant white boards for everyone to watch. Prizes are awarded in 21 skill, age and geographical categories and the grand prize is $4,000. The weekend also includes group word games, guest speakers and appearances by celebrity crossword solvers. Solvers can compete at home for fun, either online or by mail, and receive a ranking in all their solving categories. Est attendance: 600. For info: Will Shortz, Dir, American Crossword Puzzle Tournament, 55 Great Oak Lane, Pleasantville, NY 10570. Phone: (732) 296-0246. Web: www.crosswordtournament.com.

BIG TEN MEN'S GYMNASTICS CHAMPIONSHIPS. Mar 24–25. University of Iowa, Iowa City, IA. For info: Big Ten Conference, 1500 W Higgins Rd, Park Ridge, IL 60068-6300. Phone: (847) 696-1010. Fax: (847) 696-1110. Web: www.bigten.org.

CRAFTSMEN'S CLASSIC ARTS & CRAFTS FESTIVAL. Mar 24–26. Dulles Expo and Convention Center, Chantilly, VA. 10th annual. Features work from more than 375 talented artists and craftspeople. All juried exhibitors' work has been handmade by the exhibitors and must be their own original design and creation. See the creative process in action with several exhibitors demonstrating throughout the weekend. Something for every style, taste and budget with items from the most contemporary to the most traditional. Est attendance: 20,000. For info: Gilmore Enterprises, Inc, 1240 Oakland Ave, Greensboro, NC 27403. Phone: (336) 274-5550. E-mail: gilmoreshows@triad.rr.com. Web: www.CraftShow.com or www.gilmoreshows.com.

***EXXON VALDEZ* OIL SPILL: ANNIVERSARY.** Mar 24, 1989. The tanker *Exxon Valdez* ran aground at Prince William Sound, leaking 11 million gallons of oil into one of nature's richest habitats.

HOUDINI, HARRY: BIRTH ANNIVERSARY. Mar 24, 1874. Magician and escape artist. Born at Budapest, Hungary, died at Detroit, MI, Oct 31, 1926. Lecturer, athlete, author, expert on history of magic, exposer of fraudulent mediums and motion picture actor. Was best known for his ability to escape from locked restraints (handcuffs, straitjackets, coffins, boxes and milk cans). Anniversary of his death (Halloween) has been the occasion for meetings of magicians and attempts at communication by mediums.

"LETTER FROM AMERICA" RADIO PREMIERE: 60th ANNIVERSARY. Mar 24, 1946. Acclaimed news correspondent and broadcaster Alistair Cooke began his weekly observations on American life on this date, with a story about British war brides traveling to America on the *Queen Mary*. Broadcast from Radio 4 and the BBC World Service, "Letter from America" would become the world's longest continuous running radio talk program. Cooke created 2,869 "letters." His last broadcast was Feb 20, 2004, and the BBC announced his retirement on Mar 2, 2004.

MELLON, ANDREW W.: BIRTH ANNIVERSARY. Mar 24, 1855. American financier, industrialist, government official (secretary of the treasury), art and book collector, born at Pittsburgh, PA. Died Aug 26, 1937, at Southhampton, NY.

MORRIS, WILLIAM: BIRTH ANNIVERSARY. Mar 24, 1834. English poet, artist and social reformer. Born at Walthamstow, England; died at Hammersmith, London, Oct 3, 1896.

PALMETTO SPORTSMEN'S CLASSIC. Mar 24–26. South Carolina State Fairgrounds, Columbia, SC. Largest family-oriented wildlife show in the Carolinas with information on natural resources education and conservation, hunting, fishing and outdoor recreation. You will find activities for kids and adults throughout the show. Est attendance: 35,000. For info: Mary Pugh, Palmetto Sportsmen's Classic, PO Box 167, Columbia, SC 29202. Phone: (803) 734-4008. E-mail: pughm@dnr.sc.gov.

PHILIPPINE INDEPENDENCE. Mar 24, 1934. President Franklin Roosevelt signed a bill granting independence to the Philippines. The bill, which took effect July 4, 1946, brought to a close almost half a century of US control of the islands.

PITTSBURGH ARTS & CRAFTS SPRING FEVER FESTIVAL. Mar 24–26. Greensburg, PA. Approximately 200 booths, including pottery, flowers, jewelry, quilts, furniture, tole and decorative painting, leather, toys and much more. Find that perfect gift. Est attendance: 21,000. For info: Debbie & Steve Stoner, Family Festivals Assn, PO Box 166, Irwin, PA 15642. Phone/fax: (724) 863-4577. E-mail: familyfestivals@hotmail.com. Web: www.familyfestivals.com.

POWELL, JOHN WESLEY: BIRTH ANNIVERSARY. Mar 24, 1834. American geologist, explorer, ethnologist. He is best known for his explorations of the Grand Canyon by boat on the Colorado River. Born at Mount Morris, NY, he died at Haven, ME, Sept 23, 1902.

RHODE ISLAND VOTERS REJECT CONSTITUTION: ANNIVERSARY. Mar 24, 1788. In a popular referendum, Rhode Island rejected the new Constitution by a vote of 2,708 to 237. The state later ratified the Constitution (May 29, 1790) and the Bill of Rights (June 7, 1790).

SAINT GABRIEL: FEAST DAY. Mar 24. Saint Gabriel the Archangel, patron saint of postal, telephone and telegraph workers.

★   ★   ★

		S	M	T	W	T	F	S
March					1	2	3	4
2006		5	6	7	8	9	10	11
		12	13	14	15	16	17	18
		19	20	21	22	23	24	25
		26	27	28	29	30	31	

SCHMECKFEST. Mar 24–25 (also Mar 31–Apr 1). Freeman, SD. Sausage and sauerkraut, kuchen and pluma moos. These are just a few of the dishes served at this German "festival of tasting" where visitors can also watch cooking and craft demonstrations and an evening musical. Est attendance: 5,000. For info: DelVonna Wentz, Schmeckfest, PO Box S, Freeman, SD 57029. Phone: (605) 660-8369.

STRATTON, DOROTHY CONSTANCE: BIRTH ANNIVERSARY. Mar 24, 1898. Dorothy Constance Stratton, born at Brookfield, MO, was instrumental during WWII in organizing the SPARS, the women's branch of the US Coast Guard (authorized Nov 23, 1942). Under Lieutenant Commander Stratton's command some 10,000 women were trained for supportive noncombat roles in the Coast Guard. SPARS was dissolved in 1946 after the war had ended. Stratton worked with many women's organizations, including the Girl Scouts as national executive director in the '50s.

UNITED NATIONS: WORLD TUBERCULOSIS DAY. Mar 24. Commemorates the day in 1882 when *tubercle bacillus* was discovered by German scientist Robert Koch.

UNITED STATES NATIONAL SNOWSHOE CHAMPIONSHIPS. Mar 24–26. Bolton Valley Resort, Bolton Valley, VT. 6th annual. Men, women and children compete in snowshoe racing at 5k and 10k lengths and at different ability levels. For info: United States Snowshoe Assn, 678 County Rt 25, Corinth, NY 12822. Phone: (518) 654-7648. Web: www.snowshoeracing.com.

BIRTHDAYS TODAY

Lara Flynn Boyle, 36, actress ("Twin Peaks," "The Practice," *Dead Poets Society*), born Davenport, IA, Mar 24, 1970.

R. Lee Ermey, 62, actor (*Full Metal Jacket, Mississippi Burning*), born Emporia, KS, Mar 24, 1944.

Lawrence Ferlinghetti, 87, "Beat" poet, author (*Coney Island of the Mind*), born Yonkers, NY, Mar 24, 1919.

Christine Gregoire, 59, Governor of Washington (D), born Adrian, MI, Mar 24, 1947.

Byron Janis, 78, pianist, born McKeesport, PA, Mar 24, 1928.

Bob Mackie, 66, costume and fashion designer, born Monterey Park, CA, Mar 24, 1940.

Peyton Manning, 30, football player, born New Orleans, LA, Mar 24, 1976.

Donna Pescow, 52, actress (*Saturday Night Fever*, "Angie"), born Brooklyn, NY, Mar 24, 1954.

Star Jones Reynolds, 44, television personality, journalist ("The View"), born Badin, NC, Mar 24, 1962.

Annabella Sciorra, 42, actress (*The Hand That Rocks the Cradle, Jungle Fever*), born Wethersfield, CT, Mar 24, 1964.

MARCH 25 — SATURDAY
Day 84 — 281 Remaining

BARTOK, BELA: 125th BIRTH ANNIVERSARY. Mar 25, 1881. Hungarian composer, born at Nagyszentmiklos (now in Romania). Died at New York, NY, Sept 26, 1945.

BED-IN FOR PEACE: ANNIVERSARY. Mar 25–31, 1969. After their Mar 20 wedding, John Lennon (of The Beatles) and Yoko Ono celebrated their honeymoon with a "happening": a bed-in for peace at their hotel room. In Room 902 of the Hilton Hotel in Amsterdam, pajama-clad Lennon and Ono received the world's print, radio and TV media while sitting up in bed: singing and talking for seven days encouraging the world to choose peace. The couple held another bed-in May 26–June 2 in Montreal, during which "Give Peace a Chance" was recorded.

BIG TEN WOMEN'S GYMNASTICS CHAMPION-SHIPS. Mar 25. Michigan State University, East Lansing, MI. For info: Big Ten Conference, 1500 W Higgins Rd, Park Ridge, IL 60068-6300. Phone: (847) 696-1010. Fax: (847) 696-1110. Web: www.bigten.org.

BIG 12 WOMEN'S GYMNASTICS CHAMPIONSHIP. Mar 25. Devaney Sports Center, Lincoln, NE. Est attendance: 2,000. For info: Big 12 Conference, 2201 Stemmons Freeway, 28th Fl, Dallas, TX 75207. Phone: (214) 742-1212. Fax: (214) 753-0145. Web: www.big12sports.com.

BORGLUM, GUTZON: BIRTH ANNIVERSARY. Mar 25, 1867. American sculptor who created the huge sculpture of four American presidents (Washington, Jefferson, Lincoln and Theodore Roosevelt) at Mount Rushmore National Memorial in the Black Hills of South Dakota. Born John Gutzon de la Mothe Borglum at Bear Lake, ID, the son of Mormon pioneers, he worked the last 14 years of his life on the Mount Rushmore sculpture. He died at Chicago, IL, Mar 6, 1941.

"CAGNEY & LACEY" TV PREMIERE: ANNIVER-SARY. Mar 25, 1982. "Cagney & Lacey" broke new ground as the first TV crime show in which the central characters were both female. The series was based on a made-for-TV movie that aired Oct 8, 1981, starring Loretta Swit and Tyne Daly. Meg Foster played Swit's character, Chris Cagney, but after one season she was replaced by Sharon Gless. Daly and Gless won six Emmys together for their roles. The last telecast aired on Aug 25, 1988.

CHARLIE PARKER AT THE LA PHILHARMONIC: 60th ANNIVERSARY. Mar 25, 1946. One of the most influential solos of jazz alto saxophonist Charlie ("Bird") Parker's career was his rendition of "Lady Be Good," performed at the Los Angeles Philharmonic Auditorium. Every aspect of the performance became part of the language of modern jazz.

CHERRY BLOSSOM FESTIVAL. Mar 25–Apr 9. Various sites in Washington, DC. 94th annual celebration. See more than 6,000 Japanese cherry trees in blossom. Festivities include daily local and international cultural performances, sporting events, arts & crafts, art exhibits and delectable cuisine. Highlights include the National Cherry Blossom Festival Parade® and the Sakuri Matsuri—Japanese Street Festival. For info: Cherry Blossom Festival, 1250 H St NW, Ste 1000, Washington, DC 20005. Phone: (202) 547-1500 or (202) 661-7584. Web: www.nationalcherry blossomfestival.org.

COSELL, HOWARD: BIRTH ANNIVERSARY. Mar 25, 1918. Howard Cosell, broadcaster, born at New York, NY. After earning a law degree, Cosell began his broadcasting career as the host of "Howard Cosell Speaking of Sports." He achieved national prominence and a great deal of notoriety for his support of Muhammad Ali's stand against the Vietnam War and then as cohost of ABC's "Monday Night Football." Died at New York, Apr 23, 1994.

ENGLAND: HEAD OF THE RIVER RACE. Mar 25. Mortlake to Putney, River Thames, London. At 11:30 AM. Processional race for 420 eight-oared crews, starting at 10-second intervals. Est attendance: 7,000. For info: Mr A. Ruddle, 59 Berkeley Ct, Oaklands Dr, Weybridge, Surrey, UK KT13 9HY. Phone: (44) (1932) 220401.

FEAST OF ANNUNCIATION. Mar 25. Celebrated in the Roman Catholic Church in commemoration of the message of the Angel Gabriel to Mary that she was to be the mother of Christ.

GREECE: INDEPENDENCE DAY. Mar 25. National holiday. Celebrates the beginning of the Greek revolt for independence from the Ottoman Empire, Mar 25, 1821 (OS). Greece attained independence in 1829.

★**GREEK INDEPENDENCE DAY: A NATIONAL DAY OF CELEBRATION OF GREEK AND AMERICAN DEMOCRACY.** Mar 25.

LEAN, SIR DAVID: BIRTH ANNIVERSARY. Mar 25, 1908. British film director Sir David Lean was born at London. He directed 16 films and won two Best Director Academy Awards. His films include *Bridge on the River Kwai* (1957), *Lawrence of Arabia* (1962) and *Dr. Zhivago* (1965). He died Apr 16, 1991, at London.

MARYLAND DAY. Mar 25. Commemorates arrival of Lord Baltimore's first settlers at Maryland in 1634.

NATCHEZ POWWOW. Mar 25–26. Natchez, MS. Native American dancing and crafts. Est attendance: 3,000. For info: Grand Village of the Natchez Indians, 400 Jefferson Davis Blvd, Natchez, MS 39120. Phone: (601) 446-6502. Fax: (601) 446-6503. E-mail: gvni@mdah.state.ms.us.

NATO FORCES ATTACK YUGOSLAVIA: ANNIVER-SARY. Mar 25, 1999. After many weeks of unsuccessful negotiations with Serb leader Slobodan Milosevic over the treatment of ethnic Albanians by Serb forces in the Kosovo Province of Yugoslavia, NATO forces began bombing Serbia and Kosovo. In response, the Serb army forced hundreds of thousands of ethnic Albanians to flee Kosovo for neighboring Albania, Macedonia and Montenegro. On June 10, 1999, NATO and Yugoslav officials signed an agreement providing for withdrawal of Serb troops from Kosovo, the end of Allied air strikes and the return of Kosovo refugees.

OLD NEW YEAR'S DAY. Mar 25. In Great Britain and its North American colonies this was the beginning of the new year up through 1751, when with the adoption of the Gregorian calendar the beginning of the year was changed to Jan 1.

PECAN DAY. Mar 25, 1775. Anniversary of the planting by George Washington of pecan trees (some of which still survive) at Mount Vernon. The trees were a gift to Washington from Thomas Jefferson, who had planted a few pecan trees from the southern US at Monticello, VA. The pecan, native to southern North America, is sometimes called "America's own nut." First cultivated by Native Americans, it has been transplanted to other continents but has failed to achieve wide use or popularity outside the US.

ROME EXECUTIONS: ANNIVERSARY. Mar 25, 1944. Nazis occupying Rome during WWII executed 300 Italian priests, Jews, women and two 14-year-old boys in retaliation for the deaths of 33 German soldiers who had been killed by Italian partisans. Hitler demanded 50 Italian lives for each German life that had been taken, but German officials in Italy lowered the number.

SHEEP TO SHAWL FESTIVAL. Mar 25. Oatland Island Education Center, Savannah, GA. This is a popular annual event held at our Heritage Home site where visitors can observe and participate in the creation of a shawl—from sheep shearing to carding, spinning, dying and weaving the wool. Children's activities and refreshments will be available and the Native Animal Nature Trail will be open. Est attendance: 1,900. For info: Oatland Island Education Ctr, 711 Sandtown Rd, Savannah, GA 31410. Phone: (912) 898-3980. Fax: (912) 898-3983. Web: www.oatlandisland.org.

SLAVE TRADE ABOLISHED BY ENGLAND: ANNIVERSARY. Mar 25, 1807. The English Parliament abolished the slave trade after a long campaign against it.

TOSCANINI, ARTURO: BIRTH ANNIVERSARY. Mar 25, 1867. Italian opera and symphony conductor Arturo Toscanini was born at Parma, Italy. He had an all-encompassing repertoire but was famous primarily for the operas of Verdi and the symphonies of Beethoven. Toscanini died at New York City, Jan 16, 1957.

TRIANGLE SHIRTWAIST FIRE: 95th ANNIVERSARY. Mar 25, 1911. At about 4:30 PM, fire broke out at the Triangle Shirtwaist Company at New York, NY, minutes before the seamstresses were to go home. Some workers were fatally burned while others leaped to their deaths from the windows of the 10-story building. The fire lasted only 18 minutes but left 146 workers dead, most of them young immigrant women. Some of the deaths were a direct result of workers being trapped on the ninth floor by a locked door. Labor law forbade locking factory doors while employees were at work, and owners of the company were indicted on charges of first- and second-degree manslaughter. The tragic fire became a turning point in labor history, bringing about reforms in health and safety laws.

WICHITA WEST SPRING ARTS AND CRAFTS SHOW. Mar 25–26. Wichita Falls, TX. Artists/craftspeople from the area display and sell their quality arts and crafts. Free admission to the public. Est attendance: 3,000. For info: Wichita Falls Conv & Visitors Bureau, 1000 5th St, Wichita Falls, TX 76301. Phone: (940) 716-5500 or (940) 691-2738. Fax: (940) 716-5509. E-mail: MPEC@wf.net. Web: www.wichitafalls.org.

BIRTHDAYS TODAY

Bonnie Bedelia, 60, actress (*My Sweet Charlie, Die Hard, Die Hard 2*), born New York, NY, Mar 25, 1946 (some sources say 1952).

Anita Bryant, 66, singer ("The George Gobel Show"; hit song "Paper Roses"), Miss America ('58), born Barnsdall, OK, Mar 25, 1940.

Marcia Cross, 44, actress ("Melrose Place," "Everwood," "Desperate Housewives"), born Marlborough, MA, Mar 25, 1962.

John Ensign, 48, US Senator (R, Nevada), born Roseville, CA, Mar 25, 1958.

Eileen Ford, 84, model agency executive, born New York, NY, Mar 25, 1922.

Aretha Franklin, 64, singer ("Respect," "Think"), born Memphis, TN, Mar 25, 1942.

Paul Michael Glaser, 63, actor ("Starsky and Hutch"), director (*Butterflies Are Free*), born Cambridge, MA, Mar 25, 1943.

Tom Glavine, 40, baseball player, born Concord, MA, Mar 25, 1966.

Cammi Granato, 35, former hockey player, born Maywood, IL, Mar 25, 1971.

March 2006	S	M	T	W	T	F	S
				1	2	3	4
	5	6	7	8	9	10	11
	12	13	14	15	16	17	18
	19	20	21	22	23	24	25
	26	27	28	29	30	31	

Mary Gross, 53, comedienne, actress ("Saturday Night Live"), born Chicago, IL, Mar 25, 1953.

Elton John, 59, musician, singer, songwriter, born Reginald Kenneth Dwight at Pinner, England, Mar 25, 1947.

James Lovell, 78, astronaut, born Cleveland, OH, Mar 25, 1928.

Sarah Jessica Parker, 41, actress (*LA Story, Honeymoon in Vegas*, "Sex and the City"), born Nelsonville, OH, Mar 25, 1965.

Gloria Steinem, 71, feminist (original publisher of *Ms* magazine), journalist, born Toledo, OH, Mar 25, 1935.

John Stockwell, 45, actor, writer, director (*Top Gun, Under Cover*), born Galveston, TX, Mar 25, 1961.

Sheryl Swoopes, 35, basketball player, US Olympic Basketball Team, born Brownfield, TX, Mar 25, 1971.

MARCH 26 — SUNDAY
Day 85 — 280 Remaining

BANGLADESH: INDEPENDENCE DAY. Mar 26. Commemorates East Pakistan's independence in 1971 as the state of Bangladesh. Celebrated with parades, youth festivals and symposia.

BOWDITCH, NATHANIEL: BIRTH ANNIVERSARY. Mar 26, 1773. American mathematician and astronomer, author of the *New American Practical Navigator*. Born at Salem, MA, he died at Boston, MA, Mar 16, 1838.

CAMP DAVID ACCORD SIGNED: ANNIVERSARY. Mar 26, 1979. Israeli Prime Minister Menachem Begin and Egyptian President Anwar Sadat signed the Camp David peace treaty, ending 30 years of war between their two countries. The agreement was fostered by President Jimmy Carter.

DELANO, JANE: BIRTH ANNIVERSARY. Mar 26, 1858. Jane Arminda Delano, dedicated American nurse and teacher, superintendent of the US Army Nurse Corps, chairman of the American Red Cross Nursing Service and recipient (posthumously) of the Distinguished Service Medal of the US, was born near Townsend, NY. While on an official visit to review Red Cross activities, she died Apr 15, 1919, in an army hospital at Savenay, France. Her last words: "What about my work? I must get back to my work." Originally buried at Loire, France, her remains were reinterred at Arlington National Cemetery in 1920.

ENGLAND: MOTHERING SUNDAY. Mar 26. Fourth Sunday of Lent, formerly occasion for attending services at Mother Church, family gatherings and visits to parents. Now popularly known as Mother's Day and a time for visiting and taking gifts to mothers.

EUROPE: SUMMER DAYLIGHT SAVING TIME. Mar 26–Oct 29. All members of the European Union observe daylight saving (summer) time from the last Sunday in March until the last Sunday in October.

FROST, ROBERT LEE: BIRTH ANNIVERSARY. Mar 26, 1874. American poet who tried his hand at farming, teaching, shoemaking and editing before winning acclaim as a poet. Pulitzer Prize winner. Born at San Francisco, CA, he died at Boston, MA, Jan 29, 1963.

LEGAL ASSISTANTS DAY. Mar 26. A day recognizing the many contributions made to the legal profession by legal assistants. For info: Claudia A. Evart, 30 Park Ave, #2-P, New York, NY 10016. Phone: (212) 779-2227. E-mail: paralegalcaevart@earthlink.net.

LUXEMBOURG: BRETZELSONNDEG. Mar 26. The fourth Sunday in Lent is an occasion for boys to give pretzel-shaped cakes to sweethearts who may respond, on Easter Sunday, with a gift of a decorated egg or sweet.

MAKE UP YOUR OWN HOLIDAY DAY. Mar 26. This day is a day you may name for whatever you wish. Reach for the stars! Make up a holiday! Annually, Mar 26. [©2003 by WH.] For info: Thomas & Ruth Roy, Wellcat Holidays, 2418 Long Ln, Lebanon, PA 17046. Phone: (717) 279-0184. E-mail: info@wellcat.com. Web: www.wellcat.com.

MARYLAND DAY. Mar 26. Historic St. Mary's City, MD. Celebrate Maryland's 372nd birthday with pageantry and ceremonies marking the founding of the state in 1634. Est attendance: 500. For info: Visitors Services, Historic St. Mary's City, PO Box 39, St. Mary's City, MD 20686. Phone: (240) 895-4990 or (800) SMC-1634. Fax: (240) 895-4968. Web: www.stmaryscity.org.

NATIONAL CLEANING WEEK. Mar 26–Apr 1. Established by Monica Nassif, founder and president of The Caldrea Company, the manufacturer of upscale cleaning products and cleaning accessories, National Cleaning Week serves as a reminder to tackle spring cleaning. Each day will be dedicated to a specific chore. Annually, the last week in March. For info: Monica Nassif, The Caldrea Company, 420 N 5th St, Ford Centre, Ste 600, Minneapolis, MN 55401. Phone: (612) 371-0003 or (877) 576-8808. Fax: (612) 371-9995. Web: www.caldrea.com.

PRINCE JONAH KUHIO KALANIANOLE DAY. Mar 26. Hawaii. Commemorates the man who, as Hawaii's delegate to the US Congress, introduced the first bill for statehood in 1919. Not until 1959 did Hawaii become a state.

SOVIET COSMONAUT RETURNS TO NEW COUNTRY: ANNIVERSARY. Mar 26, 1992. After spending 313 days in space in the Soviet *Mir* space station, cosmonaut Serge Krikalev returned to Earth and to what was for him a new country. He left Earth May 18, 1991, a citizen of the Soviet Union, but during his stay aboard the space station, the Soviet Union crumbled and became the Commonwealth of Independent States. Originally scheduled to return in October 1991, Krikalev's return was delayed by five months due to his country's disintegration and the ensuing monetary problems.

¡VIVA EL MARIACHI! FESTIVAL. Mar 26. Fresno Convention Center–Selland Arena. Fresno, CA. 24th annual. The longest-running Mariachi festival in the US. Includes workshops, vendor booths and a concert featuring international, state and local mariachis and danzantes. Est attendance: 8,000. For info: Radio Bilingüe, 5005 E Belmont Ave, Fresno, CA 93727. Phone: (559) 455-5777. Web: www.radiobilingue.org.

WILLIAMS, TENNESSEE: BIRTH ANNIVERSARY. Mar 26, 1911. Tennessee Williams was born at Columbus, MS. He was one of America's most prolific playwrights, producing such works as *The Glass Menagerie; A Streetcar Named Desire*, which won a Pulitzer Prize; *Cat on a Hot Tin Roof*, which won a second Pulitzer; *Night of the Iguana; Summer and Smoke; The Rose Tattoo* and *Sweet Bird of Youth*, among others. Williams died at New York, NY, Feb 25, 1983.

WORLD'S LARGEST EASTER EGG HUNT. Mar 26. Searls Park, Rockford, IL. Sponsored by the Rockford Park District and local volunteers, this annual event features over 290,000 plastic Easter eggs filled with candy and prizes. For info: Paul Gorski, 4583 Scenic Dr, Rockford, IL 61109. Phone: (815) 871-6320. E-mail: paul@paulgorski.com.

"THE YOUNG AND THE RESTLESS" TV PREMIERE: ANNIVERSARY. Mar 26, 1973. This daytime serial is generally thought of as TV's most artistic soap and has won numerous Emmys for outstanding daytime drama series. Its original storylines revolved around the Brooks and Foster families, but by the early '80s most of them were gone and the Abbott and Williams families were highlighted. The serial's very large and changing cast has included now-famous actors David Hasselhoff, Tom Selleck, Wings Hauser, Deidre Hall and Michael Damian. In 1980, "Y&R" expanded from a half-hour to an hour. Its theme music is well known as "Nadia's Theme," as it was played during Nadia Comaneci's routine at the 1976 Olympics.

BIRTHDAYS TODAY

Marcus Allen, 46, former football player, TV commentator, born San Diego, CA, Mar 26, 1960.

Alan Arkin, 72, actor (*Catch-22*), director (*Little Murders*), born New York, NY, Mar 26, 1934.

Pierre Boulez, 81, composer, conductor, born Montbrison, France, Mar 26, 1925.

James Caan, 66, actor (*Thief, The Godfather, Mickey Blue Eyes*), born New York, NY, Mar 26, 1940.

Lincoln Chafee, 53, US Senator (R, Rhode Island), born Warwick, RI, Mar 26, 1953.

Elaine Lan Chao, 53, US Secretary of Labor, born Taipei, Taiwan, Mar 26, 1953.

Leeza Gibbons, 49, TV hostess ("Extra"), born Hartsville, SC, Mar 26, 1957.

Jennifer Grey, 46, actress ("It's Like, You Know. . . ," *Dirty Dancing*), born New York, NY, Mar 26, 1960.

John Huntsman, Jr, 46, Governor of Utah (R), born Palo Alto, CA, Mar 26, 1960.

Erica Jong, 64, author, poet (*Fear of Flying, Becoming Light*), born New York, NY, Mar 26, 1942.

Catherine Keener, 46, actress (*Being John Malkovich*), born Miami, FL, Mar 26, 1960.

Keira Knightley, 21, actress (*Bend It Like Beckham, Pirates of the Caribbean*), born Teddington, Middlesex, England, Mar 26, 1985.

Vicki Lawrence, 57, singer, actress ("The Carol Burnett Show," "Mama's Family"), born Inglewood, CA, Mar 26, 1949.

Josh Lucas, 34, actor (*Sweet Home Alabama, American Psycho*), born in Arkansas, Mar 26, 1972.

Leonard Nimoy, 75, actor ("Star Trek"), director (*Three Men and a Baby*), writer, born Boston, MA, Mar 26, 1931.

Sandra Day O'Connor, 76, Associate Justice of the US Supreme Court, born El Paso, TX, Mar 26, 1930.

Teddy Pendergrass, 56, singer, born Philadelphia, PA, Mar 26, 1950.

Diana Ross, 62, singer ("Keep Me Hangin' On," "Ain't No Mountain High Enough"), actress (*Lady Sings the Blues, The Wiz*), born Detroit, MI, Mar 26, 1944.

Martin Short, 56, actor (*The Three Amigos, Inner Space*), comedian ("SCTV Network 90," "Saturday Night Live"), born Hamilton, ON, Canada, Mar 26, 1950.

John Stockton, 44, former basketball player, born Spokane, WA, Mar 26, 1962.

Bob Woodward, 63, journalist (investigated Watergate with Carl Bernstein), born Geneva, IL, Mar 26, 1943.

MARCH 27 — MONDAY
Day 86 — 279 Remaining

CANARY ISLANDS PLANE DISASTER: ANNIVERSARY. Mar 27, 1977. The worst accident in the history of civil aviation. Two Boeing 747s collided on the ground; 570 people lost their lives—249 on the KLM Airlines plane and 321 on the Pan Am plane.

CELEBRATE EXCHANGE: NATIONAL EXCHANGE CLUB: 95th BIRTHDAY. Mar 27, 1911. Anniversary of the day when the first Exchange Club was founded at Detroit, MI, by Charles A. Berkey. Since 1911, Exchange clubs have been working to improve their communities through service projects, by promoting patriotism and pride of country and through their national project, Child Abuse Prevention. Celebrated annually by nearly 32,000 Exchangites in the US and Puerto Rico. For info: The Natl Exchange Club, 3050 Central Ave, Toledo, OH 43606-1700. Phone: (800) 924-2643. Fax: (419) 535-1989. Web: www.nationalexchangeclub.org.

EARTHQUAKE STRIKES ALASKA: ANNIVERSARY. Mar 27, 1964. The strongest earthquake in North American history (8.4 on the Richter scale) struck Alaska, east of Anchorage; 117 people were killed. This was the world's second worst earthquake of the 20th century in terms of magnitude.

★**EDUCATION AND SHARING DAY.** Mar 27. Proclaimed for the last week in March or the first week in April.

FUNKY WINKERBEAN: ANNIVERSARY. Mar 27, 1972. Anniversary of the nationally syndicated comic strip. For info: Tom Batiuk, Creator, 2750 Substation Rd, Medina, OH 44256. Phone: (330) 722-8755.

HILL, PATTY SMITH: BIRTH ANNIVERSARY. Mar 27, 1868. Patty Smith Hill, schoolteacher, author and education specialist, was born at Anchorage (suburb of Louisville), KY. She was author of the lyrics of the song "Good Morning to All," which later became known as "Happy Birthday to You." Her older sister, Mildred J. Hill, composed the melody for the song which was first published in 1893 as a classroom greeting in the book *Song Stories for the Sunday School*. A stanza beginning "Happy Birthday to You" was added in 1924, and the song became arguably the most frequently sung song in the world. Hill died at New York, NY, May 25, 1946. See also: "Happy Birthday to 'Happy Birthday to You' " (June 27).

KITE FLYING DAY. Mar 27. One of the favorite rites of spring is flying kites in the March winds. It has provided fun for families for years. For info: Lindsay Benson, 13116 Frog Hollow Ct, Oak Hill, VA 20171. Phone: (703) 471-5784. E-mail: winniontoe@aol.com.

KRAFT NABISCO CHAMPIONSHIP. Mar 27–Apr 2. Mission Hills Country Club, Rancho Mirage, CA. The first major of the year on the LPGA tour. Held since 1972, this tournament is often called the Master's of women's professional golf. For info: Kraft Nabisco Championship. Phone: (760) 324-4546. Web: www.kraftnabiscochampionship.com.

LUXEMBOURG: OSWEILER. Mar 27. Blessing of horses, tractors and cars.

MYANMAR: RESISTANCE DAY. Mar 27. National holiday. Commemorates the day in 1945 when Burma officially joined the Allies in World War II. Also called Armed Forces Day.

NATIONAL SLEEP AWARENESS WEEK. Mar 27–Apr 2. All Americans are urged to recognize the importance of proper sleep to their health, safety and productivity and the dangers of untreated sleep disorders. For info: Marcia Stein, Natl Sleep Foundation, 1522 K St NW, Ste 500, Washington, DC 20005. Phone: (202) 347-3471, ext 214. Web: www.sleepfoundation.org.

NORTH SEA OIL RIG DISASTER: ANNIVERSARY. Mar 27, 1980. The Alexander L. Keilland Oil Rig capsized during a heavy storm in the Norwegian sector of the North Sea. The pentagon-type, French-built oil rig had about 200 persons aboard, and 123 lives were lost.

QUIRKY COUNTRY MUSIC SONG TITLES DAY. Mar 27. We love those old country music quirky song titles, and it's time to create some new ones. How about "Put me out at the curb darlin', 'cause the recycling truck's a-comin', and you done throwed me out," for starters? [©2003 by WH.] For info: Thomas & Ruth Roy, Wellcat Holidays, 2418 Long Lane, Lebanon, PA 17046. Phone: (717) 279-0184. E-mail: info@wellcat.com. Web: www.wellcat.com.

ROENTGEN, WILHELM KONRAD: BIRTH ANNIVERSARY. Mar 27, 1845. German scientist who discovered X-rays (1895) and won a Nobel Prize in 1901. Born at Lennep, Prussia, he died at Munich, Germany, Feb 10, 1923.

SEWARD'S DAY: ANNIVERSARY OF THE ACQUISITION OF ALASKA. Mar 27. Observed in Alaska near the anniversary of its acquisition from Russia in 1867. The treaty of purchase was signed between the Russians and the Americans Mar 30, 1867, and ratified by the Senate May 28, 1867. The territory was formally transferred Oct 18, 1867. Annually, the last Monday in March.

***SINGIN' IN THE RAIN* FILM PREMIERE: ANNIVERSARY.** Mar 27, 1952. MGM's joyous, comic film musical premiered on this date at New York, NY. Starring Gene Kelly, Debbie Reynolds and Donald O'Connor and featuring the songs "Singin' in the Rain," "Good Morning" and "Make 'Em Laugh," *Singin' in the Rain* depicted a Hollywood romance at the time the talkies arrived. Directed by Kelly and Stanley Donen, and written by Betty Comden and Adolph Green, the film was only nominated for two Oscars, yet is now regarded as one of the greatest movie musicals.

SMITH, THORNE: BIRTH ANNIVERSARY. Mar 27, 1892. Perhaps the most critically neglected popular author of the 20th century, he was born James Thorne Smith, Jr, at Annapolis, MD, educated at Dartmouth, and died at Sarasota, Florida, June 20, 1934. Author of numerous humorous supernatural fantasy novels, including *Rain in the Doorway*, *The Stray Lamb* and *Topper*, he was the master of the pointless conversation. The "Thorne Smith" touch has inspired several motion pictures and television series, including "Bewitched." For info: George H. Scheetz, Executive Secretary, The Thorne Smith Society, 406 Wolcott Lane, Batavia, IL 60510.

SPACE MILESTONE: *VENERA 8* (USSR). Mar 27, 1972. Launched on this date, this unmanned probe made a soft landing on Venus July 22 and sent back radio transmissions of surface data.

STEICHEN, EDWARD: BIRTH ANNIVERSARY. Mar 27, 1879. Celebrated American photographer. Born at Luxembourg, Germany, and died Mar 25, 1973, at West Redding, CT.

SWANSON, GLORIA: BIRTH ANNIVERSARY. Mar 27, 1899. American film actress (*Sunset Boulevard*) and businesswoman. Born Gloria May Josephine Svensson at Chicago, IL. Author of an autobiography, *Swanson on Swanson*, published in 1980. Died at New York, NY, Apr 4, 1983.

UNITED KINGDOM: SUMMER TIME. Mar 27–Oct 29. "Summer Time" (one hour in advance of Standard Time), similar to daylight saving time, is observed from the last Monday in March until the last Sunday in October.

VAUGHAN, SARAH: BIRTH ANNIVERSARY. Mar 27, 1924. Legendary jazz singer, born at Newark, NJ, renowned for her melodic improvising, wide vocal range and extraordinary technique. She began her career by winning an amateur contest at New York's Apollo Theater in 1943. She was hired by Earl Hines to accompany his band as his relief pianist as well as singer. She was given the nickname "The Divine One" by Chicago disc jockey Dave Garroway, a moniker that would remain with her the rest of her life. Died at Los Angeles, CA, Apr 3, 1990.

BIRTHDAYS TODAY

Mariah Carey, 36, singer ("Vision of Love," "I'll Be There"), born Long Island, NY, Mar 27, 1970.

Randall Cunningham, 43, former football player, born Santa Barbara, CA, Mar 27, 1963.

Anthony Lewis, 79, journalist, author (*Gideon's Trumpet; Make No Law: The Sullivan Case and the First Amendment*), born New York, NY, Mar 27, 1927.

Austin Pendleton, 66, actor (*Mr and Mrs Bridge, Guarding Tess*), born Warren, OH, Mar 27, 1940.

Mstislav Leopoldovich Rostropovich, 79, musician, born Baku, USSR, Mar 27, 1927.

	S	M	T	W	T	F	S
March 2006				1	2	3	4
	5	6	7	8	9	10	11
	12	13	14	15	16	17	18
	19	20	21	22	23	24	25
	26	27	28	29	30	31	

Maria Schneider, 54, actress (*Last Tango in Paris*), born Paris, France, Mar 27, 1952.

Quentin Tarantino, 43, actor, director (*Pulp Fiction, Jackie Brown*), born Knoxville, TN, Mar 27, 1963.

William Caleb (Cale) Yarborough, 66, former auto racer, born Timmonsville, SC, Mar 27, 1940.

Michael York, 64, actor (*Cabaret, The Three Musketeers*), born Fulmer, England, Mar 27, 1942.

MARCH 28 — TUESDAY
Day 87 — 278 Remaining

AMERICAN DIABETES ASSOCIATION ALERT DAY. Mar 28. A one-day "wake-up call" to raise awareness about the seriousness of diabetes and its risk factors. The centerpiece of the alert is the diabetes risk test, which is distributed and promoted through national and local media. Annually, the fourth Tuesday in March. For info: 800-DIABETES (342-2383) or www.diabetes.org/alert.

BARTHOLOMEW, FREDDIE: BIRTH ANNIVERSARY. Mar 28, 1924. Child star of the 1930s, Freddie Bartholomew was born Frederick Llewellyn at Great Britain. He appeared in 24 films and became the second-highest paid child star after Shirley Temple. He died Jan 23, 1992, at Sarasota, FL.

BATTLE OF LA GLORIETTA PASS: ANNIVERSARY. Mar 28, 1862. At Pigeon's Ranch, a stagecoach stop on the Santa Fe Trail (about 19 miles southeast of Santa Fe, NM), Confederate forces briefly prevailed over Union troops in what some have called the most important battle of the Civil War in the Southwest. It was feared that if Union troops failed to hold here, the Confederate forces would proceed to Fort Union and on to control the rich gold fields of Colorado and California.

CZECH REPUBLIC: TEACHERS' DAY. Mar 28. Celebrates birth on this day of Jan Amos Komensky (Comenius), Moravian educational reformer (1592–1671).

"GREATEST SHOW ON EARTH" FORMED: 125th ANNIVERSARY. Mar 28, 1881. P.T. Barnum and James A. Bailey merged their circuses to form the "Greatest Show on Earth."

HAIR BROADWAY OPENING: ANNIVERSARY. Mar 28, 1968. The controversial rock musical *Hair*, produced by Michael Butler, opened at the Biltmore Theatre at New York City, after playing off-Broadway. For those who opposed the Vietnam War and the "Establishment," this was a defining piece of work—as evidenced by some of its songs, such as "Aquarius," "Hair" and "Let the Sunshine In."

LAZAR, IRVING ("SWIFTY"): BIRTH ANNIVERSARY. Mar 28, 1907. Hollywood talent agent whose clients included Ernest Hemingway, Lillian Hellman, Cole Porter, Richard Nixon and Humphrey Bogart (who nicknamed him "Swifty" after Lazar met Bogart's challenge to make him five film deals in one day in 1955). He died Dec 30, 1993, at Beverly Hills, CA.

LIBYA: BRITISH BASES EVACUATION DAY. Mar 28. National holiday. Commemorates the closing of British bases on this day in 1970.

SAINT JOHN NEPOMUCENE NEUMANN: BIRTH ANNIVERSARY. Mar 28, 1811. First male saint of the US. Born at Prachatice, Bohemia, came to the US in 1836. As bishop of Philadelphia, he was affectionately known as the "Little Bishop." Died at Philadelphia, PA, Jan 5, 1860. Beatified Oct 13, 1963. Canonized June 19, 1977.

SPACE MILESTONE: NOAA 8 (US): ANNIVERSARY. Mar 28, 1983. Search and Rescue Satellite (SARSAT) launched from Vandenburg Air Force Base, CA, to aid in locating ships and aircraft in distress. *Kosmos 1383*, launched July 1, 1982, by the USSR, in a cooperative rescue effort, is credited with saving more than 20 lives.

THREE MILE ISLAND NUCLEAR POWER PLANT ACCIDENT: ANNIVERSARY. Mar 28, 1979. A series of accidents beginning at 4 AM, EST, at Three Mile Island on the Susquehanna River about 10 miles southeast of Harrisburg, PA, was responsible for extensive reevaluation of the safety of existing nuclear power generating operations. Equipment and other failures reportedly brought Three Mile Island close to a meltdown of the uranium core, threatening extensive radiation contamination.

VIETNAM MORATORIUM CONCERT: ANNIVERSARY. Mar 28, 1970. A seven-hour concert at Madison Square Garden at New York City featured many stars who donated their services for the antiwar cause. Among them were Jimi Hendrix; Dave Brubeck; Harry Belafonte; Peter, Paul and Mary; Judy Collins; the Rascals; Blood, Sweat and Tears and the Broadway cast of *Hair*.

BIRTHDAYS TODAY

Conchata Ferrell, 63, actress ("LA Law," "Hearts Afire," *Edward Scissorhands*), born Charleston, WV, Mar 28, 1943.

Ken Howard, 62, actor ("Crossing Jordan," "The White Shadow"), born El Centro, CA, Mar 28, 1944.

Reba McEntire, 52, singer, actress ("Reba"), born Chockie, OK, Mar 28, 1954.

Frank Hughes Murkowski, 73, Governor of Alaska (R), former US Senator (R, Alaska), born Seattle, WA, Mar 28, 1933.

Earnie Stewart, 37, soccer player, born Veghal, Holland, Mar 28, 1969.

Julia Stiles, 25, actress (*Save the Last Dance, O, 10 Things I Hate About You*), born New York, NY, Mar 28, 1981.

Keith Tkachuk, 34, hockey player, born Melrose, MA, Mar 28, 1972.

Vince Vaughn, 36, actor (*Dodgeball, Old School*), born Minneapolis, MN, Mar 28, 1970.

Dianne Wiest, 58, actress (Oscars for *Hannah and Her Sisters* and *Bullets Over Broadway*; "Law & Order"), born Kansas City, MO, Mar 28, 1948.

MARCH 29 — WEDNESDAY
Day 88 — 277 Remaining

BAILEY, PEARL MAE: BIRTH ANNIVERSARY. Mar 29, 1918. American singer and Broadway musical star Pearl Bailey was born at Newport News, VA. She began her career in vaudeville and won a special Tony Award in 1968 and the Presidential Medal of Freedom in 1988. Bailey died Aug 17, 1990, at Philadelphia, PA.

BIGGS, E. POWER: 100th BIRTH ANNIVERSARY. Mar 29, 1906. Baroque organist who helped establish the organ as a concert instrument. Biggs refused to perform on electronic organs, but sought out and recorded on organs surviving from the era of Johann Sebastian Bach and George Frederick Handel. After arthritis forced him to retire, he published early organ music. Biggs was born at Westcliff-on-Sea, Essex, England, and came to the US in 1930 at the age of 24. He died Mar 10, 1977, at Boston.

CANADA: BRITISH NORTH AMERICA ACT: ANNIVERSARY. Mar 29, 1867. This act of the British Parliament established the Dominion of Canada, uniting Ontario, Quebec, Nova Scotia and New Brunswick. The remaining colonies in Canada were still ruled directly by Great Britain until Manitoba joined the Dominion in 1870, British Columbia in 1871, Prince

Edward Island in 1873, Alberta and Saskatchewan in 1905 and Newfoundland in 1949. Union was proclaimed July 1, 1867. See also: "Canada: Canada Day" (July 1).

CENTRAL AFRICAN REPUBLIC: BOGANDA DAY. Mar 29. National holiday. Commemorates the death of Barthelemy Boganda, the first president, in 1959.

COMMITTEE ON ASSASSINATIONS REPORT: ANNI-VERSARY. Mar 29, 1979. The House Select Committee on Assassinations released on this day the final report on its investigation into the assassinations of President John F. Kennedy, Martin Luther King, Jr, and Robert Kennedy. Based on available evidence, the committee concluded that President Kennedy was assassinated as a result of a conspiracy, although no trail of a conspiracy could be established. They also concluded that on the basis of scientific acoustical evidence two gunmen fired at the President, although no second gunman could be identified. [Note: In December 1980, the FBI released a report discounting the two-gunmen theory, stating that the distinguishable sounds of two separate guns were not proven scientifically.] In addition the committee concluded that the possibility of conspiracy did exist in the cases of Dr. King and Robert Kennedy, although no specific individuals or organizations could be pinpointed as being involved. See also: "Warren Commission Report: Anniversary" (Sept 27).

DOW-JONES TOPS 10,000: ANNIVERSARY. Mar 29, 1999. The Dow-Jones Index of 30 major industrial stocks topped the 10,000 mark for the first time.

HOOVER, LOU HENRY: BIRTH ANNIVERSARY. Mar 29, 1875. Wife of Herbert Clark Hoover, 31st president of the US. Born at Waterloo, IA, she died at Palo Alto, CA, Jan 7, 1944.

KNIGHTS OF COLUMBUS FOUNDER'S DAY. Mar 29. The first Knights of Columbus charter was granted in 1882 by the state of Connecticut. This Catholic, family, fraternal service organization has grown into a volunteer force of Knights and family members totaling nearly six million who annually donate tens of millions of dollars and volunteer hours to countless charitable projects. For info: Robert A. Goossens, Director, Fraternal Services, Knights of Columbus, 1 Columbus Plaza, New Haven, CT 06514.

MADAGASCAR: COMMEMORATION DAY. Mar 29. Memorial Day for the victims of the rebellion in 1947 against French colonization.

MOON PHASE: NEW MOON. Mar 29. Moon enters New Moon phase at 5:15 AM, EST.

NATIONAL MOM AND POP BUSINESS OWNERS DAY. Mar 29. A day recognizing those very special husband-and-wife business owner teams that work and commune together. Take this day to strike a balance between business and love. For info: Rick/Margie Segel, 1 Wheatland St, Burlington, MA 01803. Phone: (781) 272-9995. Fax: (781) 272-9996. E-mail: rick@rick segel.com.

NIAGARA FALLS RUNS DRY: ANNIVERSARY. Mar 29, 1848. A massive assemblage of ice blocks formed upstream of Niagara Falls late on Mar 29, 1848, and by midnight had stopped water flow over the Falls (which are actually three falls: the American, the Horseshoe [or Canadian] and the Bridal Veil). The ice jam held until Apr 1, when the waters of Lake Erie punched through and things got back to normal. Until that happened, hundreds of the curious swarmed into the now-waterless gorge to hunt for geological souvenirs while thousands of spectators

★ ★ ★

March 2006	**S**	**M**	**T**	**W**	**T**	**F**	**S**
				1	2	3	4
	5	6	7	8	9	10	11
	12	13	14	15	16	17	18
	19	20	21	22	23	24	25
	26	27	28	29	30	31	

watched from above. Although the American Falls has stopped flowing before, this 1848 stoppage was the first and only time the entire falls was affected.

QUINLAN, KAREN ANN: BIRTH ANNIVERSARY. Mar 29, 1954. Born at Scranton, PA, Karen Ann Quinlan became the center of a legal, medical and ethical controversy over the right to die. She became irreversibly comatose on Apr 14, 1975. A petition filed by her adoptive parents in New Jersey's Superior Court, Sept 12, 1975, sought permission to discontinue use of a respirator, allowing her to die "with grace and dignity." In 1976 the petition was upheld by New Jersey's Supreme Court. Quinlan lived nearly a decade without the respirator, until June 11, 1985. Her plight brought into focus the ethical dilemmas of advancing medical technology—the need for a new understanding of life and death; the right to die; the role of judges, doctors and hospital committees in deciding when not to prolong life.

SOLAR ECLIPSE. Mar 29. Total eclipse of the sun. Visible as total eclipse in central Africa, Turkey and Russia. Partial phases visible in Europe, Africa and west Africa. Some of eclipse visible from Brazil to Mongolia.

TAIWAN: YOUTH DAY. Mar 29.

TWENTY-THIRD AMENDMENT TO US CONSTITU-TION RATIFIED: 45th ANNIVERSARY. Mar 29, 1961. District of Columbia residents were given the right to vote in presidential elections under the 23rd Amendment.

TYLER, JOHN: BIRTH ANNIVERSARY. Mar 29, 1790. Tenth president of the US (Apr 6, 1841–Mar 3, 1845). Born at Charles City County, VA, Tyler succeeded to the presidency upon the death of William Henry Harrison. Tyler's first wife died while he was president, and he remarried before the end of his term in office, becoming the first president to marry while in office. Fifteen children were born of the two marriages. In 1861 he was elected to the Congress of the Confederate States but died at Richmond, VA, Jan 18, 1862, before being seated. His death received no official tribute from the US government.

WALTON, SAM: BIRTH ANNIVERSARY. Mar 29, 1918. Founder of Wal-Mart discount stores, born at Kingfisher, OK. One of the wealthiest men in America, he died at Little Rock, AR, Apr 5, 1992.

YOUNG, DENTON TRUE (CY): BIRTH ANNIVER-SARY. Mar 29, 1867. Baseball Hall of Fame pitcher, born at Gilmore, OH. Young is baseball's all-time winningest pitcher, having accumulated 511 victories in his 22-year career. The Cy Young Award is given each year in his honor to Major League Baseball's best pitcher. Inducted into the Hall of Fame in 1937. Died at Peoli, OH, Nov 4, 1955.

BIRTHDAYS TODAY

Earl Christian Campbell, 51, Hall of Fame football player, born Tyler, TX, Mar 29, 1955.

Jennifer Capriati, 30, tennis player, born New York, NY, Mar 29, 1976.

Bud Cort, 56, actor (*Harold and Maude, Brewster McCloud*), born New Rochelle, NY, Mar 29, 1950 (some sources say 1948).

Eric Idle, 63, actor ("Monty Python's Flying Circus," "Suddenly Susan"), author, born Durham, England, Mar 29, 1943.

Christopher Lambert, 49, actor (*Greystoke: The Legend of Tarzan, Lord of the Apes; To Kill a Priest*), born New York, NY, Mar 29, 1957.

Lucy Lawless, 38, actress ("Xena"), born Mount Albert, Auckland, New Zealand, Mar 29, 1968.

Elle Macpherson, 42, model, actress (*Sirens*), born Sydney, Australia, Mar 29, 1964.

John Major, 63, former British prime minister, born Brixton, England, Mar 29, 1943.

Eugene McCarthy, 90, former US Senator (anti–Vietnam War presidential candidate in 1968), born Watkins, MN, Mar 29, 1916.

John Joseph McLaughlin, 79, editor, columnist, TV host, born Providence, RI, Mar 29, 1927.

Kurt Thomas, 50, former gymnast, born Miami, FL, Mar 29, 1956.

MARCH 30 — THURSDAY

Day 89 — 276 Remaining

ANESTHETIC FIRST USED IN SURGERY: ANNIVERSARY. Mar 30, 1842. Dr. Crawford W. Long, having seen the use of nitrous oxide and sulfuric ether at "laughing gas" parties, observed that individuals under their influence felt no pain. On this date, he removed a tumor from the neck of a man who was under the influence of ether.

DOCTORS' DAY. Mar 30. Traditional annual observance since 1933 to honor America's physicians on the anniversary of the occasion when Dr. Crawford W. Long became the first acclaimed physician to use ether as an anesthetic agent in a surgical technique, Mar 30, 1842. The red carnation has been designated the official flower of Doctors' Day.

GOYA, FRANCISCO JOSE de: BIRTH ANNIVERSARY. Mar 30, 1746. Spanish painter and etcher. It is estimated that he executed more than 1,800 paintings, drawings and lithographs during his lifetime. Born at Aragon, Spain; died at Bordeaux, France, Apr 16, 1828.

GRASS IS ALWAYS BROWNER ON THE OTHER SIDE OF THE FENCE DAY. Mar 30. A day to honor all of those who did not jump ship, did not quit the same old job, did not leave the same old relationship because things appeared to look better somewhere else. (© 2005 by WH.) For info: Thomas & Ruth Roy, Wellcat Holidays, 2418 Long Ln, Lebanon, PA 17046. Phone: (717) 279-0184. E-mail: wellcat@comcast.net. Web: www.wellcat.com.

"JEOPARDY" TV PREMIERE: ANNIVERSARY. Mar 30, 1964. The "thinking person's" game show, "Jeopardy" has a reputation as an intelligent and classy program. Art Fleming was the original host of the show, in which three contestants won cash by attempting to give the correct question to an answer in six different categories. Contestants go through two rounds and "final jeopardy," where they can wager up to all their earnings on one question. The series returned in 1984 with Alex Trebek as the popular host.

MIAEYC EARLY CHILDHOOD CONFERENCE. Mar 30–Apr 1. Amway Grand Plaza Hotel and DeVos Place, Grand Rapids, MI. This three-day conference sponsored by the Michigan Association for the Education of the Young Child (MiAEYC) focuses on issues affecting children from birth to age eight. Invited are educators, students, advocates and parents; participants can attend one, two or all three days. Each day includes a keynote address, two full-day focus sessions and 75+ workshops. For info: Laurie Nickson, MiAEYC, Beacon Pl, 4572 S Hagadorn Rd, Ste 1-D, East Lansing, MI 48823. Phone: (800) 336-6424. Fax: (517) 336-9790. E-mail: MiAEYC@MiAEYC.org. Web: www.MiAEYC .org.

MULE DAY. Mar 30–Apr 2. Columbia, TN. Started in 1934 as Breeders Day when mules were brought into town to be sold and traded. Today this homecoming is celebrated with arts and crafts, a flea market, a knife show and a huge parade. Est attendance: 150,000. For info: Mule Day, PO Box 66, Columbia, TN 38402. Phone: (931) 381-9557. E-mail: muleday@bellsouth.net.

NICKERSON, CAMILLE ("THE LOUISIANA LADY"): BIRTH ANNIVERSARY. Mar 30, 1888. Camille Nickerson, music arranger, composer, musician and educator, is remembered for her musical talent and her work as a music collector who gathered and transcribed Creole music. Born at the French Quarter, New Orleans. Of Creole extraction herself, Nickerson performed for a time in the US and Europe using the stage name "The Louisiana Lady." She died at Washington, DC, at age 94.

O'CASEY, SEAN: BIRTH ANNIVERSARY. Mar 30, 1880. Irish playwright (*Juno and the Paycock*). Born at Dublin, Ireland, he died at Torquay, England, Sept 18, 1964.

PEDIATRIC NURSE PRACTITIONER WEEK. Mar 30–Apr 2. The National Association of Pediatric Nurse Practitioners, an association of more than 7,000 pediatric nurse practitioners and specialty nurses in advanced practice providing primary health care to infants, children, adolescents and young adults, proclaims this week in honor of nearly 11,000 practitioners dedicated to improving children's health. For info: NAPNAP, 20 Brace Rd, Ste 200, Cherry Hill, NJ 08034. Phone: (856) 857-9700. Fax: (856) 857-1600. E-mail: info@napnap.org. Web: www.napnap.org.

PENCIL PATENTED: ANNIVERSARY. Mar 30, 1858. First pencil with the eraser top was patented by Hyman Lipman.

REAGAN, RONALD: ASSASSINATION ATTEMPT: 25th ANNIVERSARY. Mar 30, 1981. President Ronald Reagan was shot in the chest by a 25-year-old gunman at Washington, DC. Three other persons were wounded. John W. Hinckley, Jr, the accused attacker, was arrested at the scene. On June 21, 1982, a federal jury in the District of Columbia found Hinckley not guilty by reason of insanity and he was committed to St. Elizabeth's Hospital at Washington, DC, for an indefinite time.

TRINIDAD AND TOBAGO: SPIRITUAL BAPTIST LIBERATION SHOUTER DAY. Mar 30. Public holiday. For info: Information Dept, Tourism Div, Tourism and Industrial Development Co, 10-14 Phillips St, Port of Spain, Trinidad, West Indies.

VAN GOGH, VINCENT: BIRTH ANNIVERSARY. Mar 30, 1853. Dutch post-Impressionist painter, especially known for his bold and powerful use of color. Born at Groot Zundert, Holland, he died at Auvers-sur-Oise, France, July 29, 1890.

BIRTHDAYS TODAY

John Astin, 76, actor ("The Addams Family"; stage: *The Three Penny Opera*), director, born Baltimore, MD, Mar 30, 1930.

Brooke Astor, 104, philanthropist, author, 1996 Medal of Freedom recipient, born New York, NY, Mar 30, 1902.

Warren Beatty, 68, actor (*Bonnie and Clyde*), director (*Reds, Dick Tracy*), producer, born Richmond, VA, Mar 30, 1938.

Tracy Chapman, 42, singer ("Fast Car"), born Cleveland, OH, Mar 30, 1964.

Eric Clapton, 61, singer (with Yardbirds, Cream), songwriter ("Layla," with Jim Gordon), born Ripley, England, Mar 30, 1945.

Robbie Coltrane, 56, actor (*GoldenEye*, the Harry Potter films), born Rutherglen, Scotland, Mar 30, 1950 (some sources say Mar 31).

Celine Dion, 38, pop singer, Grammy winner, born Charlemagne, QC, Canada, Mar 30, 1968.

Richard Dysart, 77, actor ("LA Law"), born Augusta, ME, Mar 30, 1929.

M.C. Hammer, 43, rapper, born Stanley Kirk Burrell at Oakland, CA, Mar 30, 1963.

Norah Jones, 27, singer, born New York, NY, Mar 30, 1979.

Frankie Laine, 93, actor, singer ("Frankie Laine Time," *Viva Las Vegas*), born Chicago, IL, Mar 30, 1913.

Peter Marshall, 79, TV host, actor, born Huntington, WV, Mar 30, 1927.

Paul Reiser, 49, actor (*Diner*, "Mad About You"), born New York, NY, Mar 30, 1957.

MARCH 31 — FRIDAY

Day 90 — 275 Remaining

BUNSEN BURNER DAY. Mar 31. A day to honor the inventor of the Bunsen burner, Robert Wilhelm Eberhard von Bunsen, who provided chemists and chemistry students with one of their most indispensable instruments. The Bunsen burner allows the user to regulate the proportions of flammable gas and air to create the most efficient flame. Bunsen was born at Gottingen, Germany, Mar 31, 1811, and was a professor of chemistry at the universities at Kassel, Marburg, Breslau and Heidelberg. He died at Heidelberg, Germany, Aug 16, 1899.

CHAVEZ, CESAR ESTRADA: BIRTH ANNIVERSARY. Mar 31, 1927. Labor leader who organized migrant farm workers in support of better working conditions. Chavez initiated the National Farm Workers Association in 1962, attracting attention to the migrant farm workers' plight by organizing boycotts of products including grapes and lettuce. He was born at Yuma, AZ, and died Apr 23, 1993, at San Luis, AZ. His birthday is a holiday in California.

CHESNUT, MARY BOYKIN MILLER: BIRTH ANNIVERSARY. Mar 31, 1823. Born at Pleasant Hill, SC, and died Nov 22, 1886, at Camden, SC. During the Civil War Chesnut accompanied her husband, a Confederate staff officer, on military missions. She kept a journal of her experiences and observations, which was published posthumously as *A Diary from Dixie*, a perceptive portrait of Confederate military and political leaders and an insightful view of Southern life during the Civil War.

CRAFTSMEN'S CLASSIC ARTS & CRAFTS FESTIVAL. Mar 31–Apr 2. Greensboro Coliseum Complex Special Events Center, Greensboro, NC. 24th annual. Features work from more than 300 talented artists and craftspeople. All juried exhibitors' work has been handmade by the exhibitors and must be their own original design and creation. See the creative process in action with several exhibitors demonstrating throughout the weekend. Something for every style, taste and budget with items from the most contemporary to the most traditional. Est attendance: 20,000. For info: Gilmore Enterprises, Inc, 1240 Oakland Ave, Greensboro, NC 27403. Phone: (336) 274-5550. E-mail: gilmoreshows@triad.rr.com. Web: www.CraftShow.com or www.gilmoreshows.com.

DALAI LAMA FLEES TIBET: ANNIVERSARY. Mar 31, 1959. The Dalai Lama fled Chinese suppression and was granted political asylum in India. In 1950 Tibet had been invaded by China and in 1951 an agreement was signed under which Tibet became a "national autonomous region" of China. Tibetans suffered under China's persecution of Buddhism, and after years of scattered protest a full-scale revolt broke out in 1959. The Dalai Lama fled and with the beginning of the Chinese Cultural Revolution the Chinese took brutal repressive measures against the Tibetans, with the practice of religion banned and thousands of monasteries destroyed. The ban was lifted in 1976 with the end of the Cultural Revolution. The Dalai Lama received the Nobel Peace Prize in 1989 for his commitment to the nonviolent liberation of his country.

DESCARTES, RENE: BIRTH ANNIVERSARY. Mar 31, 1596. French philosopher and mathematician, known as the "father of modern philosophy," born at La Haye, Touraine, France. Cartesian philosophical precepts are often remembered because of his famous proposition "I think, therefore I am" (*Cogito ergo sum* . . .). Died of pneumonia at Stockholm, Sweden, Feb 11, 1650.

EIFFEL TOWER: ANNIVERSARY. Mar 31, 1889. Built for the Paris Exhibition of 1889, the tower was named for its architect, Alexandre Gustave Eiffel, and is one of the world's best-known landmarks.

FITZGERALD, EDWARD: BIRTH ANNIVERSARY. Mar 31, 1809. English author, born at Bredfield, England, perhaps best known for his translation of Omar Khayyam's *Rubaiyat*. Died at Merton, Norfolk, June 14, 1883.

GOGOL, NIKOLAI VASILEVICH: BIRTH ANNIVERSARY. Mar 31, 1809. Russian author of plays, novels and short stories. Born at Sorochinsk, Russia, he died at Moscow, Russia, Mar 4, 1852. Gogol's most famous work was the novel *Dead Souls*.

HAYDN, FRANZ JOSEPH: BIRTH ANNIVERSARY. Mar 31, 1732. "Father of the symphony," born at Rohrau, Austria-Hungary. Composed about 120 symphonies, more than a hundred works for chamber groups, a dozen operas and hundreds of other musical works. Died at Vienna, Austria, May 31, 1809.

JOHNSON, JOHN (JACK) ARTHUR: BIRTH ANNIVERSARY. Mar 31, 1878. In 1908 Jack Johnson became the first black to win the heavyweight boxing championship when he defeated Tommy Burns at Sydney, Australia. Unable to accept a black man's triumph, the boxing world tried to find a white challenger. Jim Jeffries, former heavyweight title holder, was badgered out of retirement. On July 4, 1919, at Reno, NV, the "battle of the century" proved to be a farce when Johnson handily defeated Jeffries. Race riots swept the US, and plans to exhibit the film of the fight were canceled. Johnson was born at Galveston, TX, and died in an automobile accident June 10, 1946, at Raleigh, NC. He was inducted into the Boxing Hall of Fame in 1990. The film *The Great White Hope* is based on his life.

MARVELL, ANDREW: BIRTH ANNIVERSARY. Mar 31, 1621. English poet. Born at Winestead, Yorkshire, England. From his poem "To His Coy Mistress": "Had we but world enough and time/this coyness, lady, were no crime. . . . But at my back I always hear/time's winged chariot drawing near. . . ." Died at London, England, Aug 18, 1678.

MEDIEVAL FAIR. Mar 31–Apr 2. Reaves Park, Norman, OK. Arts and crafts and living history fair. The Middle Ages come alive with dancers, music, theater, jousting, knights in combat and a human chess match. Feasts and follies include games and food "fit for a king." Meet such characters as King Arthur, Sir Lancelot and Merlin. Admission is free. Est attendance: 200,000. For info: Linda Linn, 1700 Asp, Norman, OK 73072. Phone: (405) 288-2536. Fax: (405) 325-7698. E-mail: llinn@ou.edu. Web: www.medievalfair.org.

NATIONAL GEOGRAPHIC BEE, STATE LEVEL. Mar 31. Site is different in each state—many are in the state capital. Winners of school-level competitions who scored in the top 100 in their state on a written test compete in the State Geographic Bees. The winner of each state bee will go to Washington, DC, for the national level in May. Est attendance: 400. For info: Natl

	S	M	T	W	T	F	S
March				1	2	3	4
	5	6	7	8	9	10	11
2006	12	13	14	15	16	17	18
	19	20	21	22	23	24	25
	26	27	28	29	30	31	

Geographic Bee, Natl Geographic Society, 1145 17th St NW, Washington, DC 20036. Phone: (202) 828-6659. Web: www.nationalgeographic.com/geographicbee.

NATIONAL "SHE'S FUNNY THAT WAY" DAY. Mar 31. On this day, individuals will pay tribute to the humorous nature of women, by listing the top five ways in which women in our lives make us laugh. For info: Brenda Meridith, Dahomey Publishing Company, 50 Hall Rd, Winchendon, MA 01475. Phone: (978) 297-1820. Fax: (978) 297-2519. E-mail: BMeridith@aol.com. Web: www.DahomeyPublishing.com.

***OKLAHOMA!* BROADWAY PREMIERE: ANNIVERSARY.** Mar 31, 1943. Rodgers & Hammerstein's landmark musical (their first collaboration) opened at the St. James Theatre on this date in 1943. (It had its world premiere under the title *Away We Go* at the Shubert Theatre in New Haven, CT, on Mar 11, 1943.) *Oklahoma!* is considered significant because it was the first musical in which songs, music, characterization and story are integrated into an emotional whole. It changed musicals forever. It was also the first musical to run more than 2,000 performances and to have a cast album recorded. Agnes de Mille was the choreographer. It received a special Pulitzer Prize for drama on May 2, 1944. In May 1953, "Oklahoma!" became that state's official song.

PEARSE, RICHARD: ANNIVERSARY OF MONOPLANE FLIGHT. Mar 31, 1903. Richard Pearse, a farmer and inventor, flew a monoplane of his own design several hundred yards along a road near Temuka, New Zealand, and then landed it on top of a 12-foot-high hedge. Pearse had built the craft, which consisted of a steerable tricycle undercarriage and an internal combustion engine. A Pearse commemorative medal was issued on Sept 19, 1971, by the Museum of Transport and Technology, Auckland, New Zealand.

RABI' I: THE MONTH OF THE MIGRATION. Mar 31. Begins on Islamic calendar date Rabi' I 1, 1427. The third month of the Islamic calendar, the month of the migration of the Prophet Muhammad from Mecca to Medina in AD 622, the event that was used as the starting year of the Islamic lunar calendar. Different methods for "anticipating" the visibility of the new moon crescent at Mecca are used by different Muslim groups. US date may vary. Began at sunset the preceding day.

ROCKNE, KNUTE: 75th DEATH ANNIVERSARY. Mar 31, 1931. Legendary Notre Dame football coach Knute Rockne died this day in a plane crash at Bazaar, KS. He was 43 years old. Eulogizing for a shocked nation, Will Rogers said, "You died one of our national heroes."

SAINT PETERSBURG FESTIVAL OF STATES. Mar 31–Apr 9. St. Petersburg, FL. To salute civic endeavors. Band shows, art show, parades, open car show, blues festival, kids festival plus concert entertainment, 5k run, fireworks and teen area. Est attendance: 250,000. For info: St. Petersburg Festival of States, 663 6th Ave S, St. Petersburg, FL 33701. Phone: (727) 898-3654. E-mail: festivalofstates@ij.net. Web: festivalofstates.com.

SOVIET GEORGIA VOTES FOR INDEPENDENCE: 15th ANNIVERSARY. Mar 31, 1991. On this date the Soviet Republic of Georgia voted to declare its independence from the Soviet Union. Georgia followed the Baltic states of Lithuania, Estonia and Latvia by becoming the fourth republic to reject Mikhail Gorbachev's new vision of the Soviet Union as espoused in a new Union Treaty. Totals revealed that 98.9 percent of those voting favored independence from Moscow. Hours after the election, troops were dispatched from Moscow to Georgia under a state of emergency.

STAMP EXPO. Mar 31[-]Apr 2. Wilshire Ebell Convention Complex, Los Angeles, CA. Est attendance: 4,000. For info: Israel Bick, Exec Dir, Intl Stamp & Coin Collectors Society, PO Box 854, Van Nuys, CA 91408. Phone: (818) 997-6496. Fax: (818) 988-4337. E-mail: iibick@sbcglobal.net. Web: www.bick.net.

TEMPE SPRING FESTIVAL OF THE ARTS. Mar 31–Apr 2. Downtown Tempe, AZ. Features 500 artists and craftspeople, continuous entertainment and children's activity area. Est attendance: 240,000. For info: Emily Bradley, Festival and Event Mgr, Downtown Tempe Community, PO Box 3084, Tempe, AZ 85280. Phone: (480) 921-2300. Fax: (480) 968-7882. Web: www.tempefestivalofthearts.com.

US VIRGIN ISLANDS: TRANSFER DAY. Mar 31. Commemorates transfer resulting from purchase of the Virgin Islands by the US from Denmark, Mar 31, 1917, for $25 million.

BIRTHDAYS TODAY

Herb Alpert, 71, musician (Tijuana Brass), born Los Angeles, CA, Mar 31, 1935.

Pavel Bure, 35, hockey player, born Moscow, USSR, Mar 31, 1971.

Richard Chamberlain, 71, actor ("Dr. Kildare," *Shogun*), born Los Angeles, CA, Mar 31, 1935.

Liz Claiborne, 77, fashion designer, born Brussels, Belgium, Mar 31, 1929.

William Daniels, 79, actor (Emmy for "St. Elsewhere"; "Boy Meets World"), born Brooklyn, NY, Mar 31, 1927.

Al Gore, 58, 45th vice president of the US, born Albert Gore, Jr, at Washington, DC, Mar 31, 1948.

Gordon (Gordie) Howe, 78, Hall of Fame hockey player, born Floral, SK, Canada, Mar 31, 1928.

John Jakes, 74, author (*North and South*, the Kent Family Chronicles), born Chicago, IL, Mar 31, 1932.

James Earl (Jimmy) Johnson, 68, Hall of Fame football player, born Dallas, TX, Mar 31, 1938.

Shirley Jones, 72, singer, actress ("The Partridge Family," *Elmer Gantry, Oklahoma!*), born Smithton, PA, Mar 31, 1934.

Gabe Kaplan, 60, actor ("Welcome Back Kotter"), born Brooklyn, NY, Mar 31, 1946.

Patrick J. Leahy, 66, US Senator (D, Vermont), born Montpelier, VT, Mar 31, 1940.

Edward Francis (Ed) Marinaro, 56, actor ("Hill Street Blues," "Sisters"), former football player, born New York, NY, Mar 31, 1950.

Marc McClure, 49, actor (*Freaky Friday, Back to the Future*), born San Mateo, CA, Mar 31, 1957.

Ewan McGregor, 35, actor (*Trainspotting, Emma*, Episodes One, Two and Three of the *Star Wars* films), born Crieff, Scotland, Mar 31, 1971.

Rhea Perlman, 58, actress ("Cheers" [three Emmy Awards]; *Carpool*), born Brooklyn, NY, Mar 31, 1948.

Steve Smith, 37, basketball player, born Highland Park, MI, Mar 31, 1969.

Christopher Walken, 63, actor (*The Deer Hunter, Batman Returns*), born Queens, NY, Mar 31, 1943.

Aprill.

APRIL 1 — SATURDAY
Day 91 — 274 Remaining

ALCOHOL AWARENESS MONTH. Apr 1–30. To help raise awareness among community prevention leaders and citizens about the problem of underage drinking. Concentrates on community grassroots activities. For info: Public Info Dept, Natl Council on Alcoholism and Drug Dependence, Inc, 22 Cortlandt St, 8th Fl, New York, NY 10007. Phone: (212) 269-7797. Fax: (212) 269-7510. E-mail: national@ncadd.org. Web: www.ncadd.org.

APPRECIATE DIVERSITY MONTH. Apr 1–30. A new national observance that celebrates all diversity that exists within our workplaces, schools and communitites. For info: ProGroup, One Main St SE, Ste 200, Minneapolis, MN 55414. Phone: (800) 651-4093. Fax: (612) 379-7048. Web: www.appreciatediversity month.org.

APRIL FOOLS' or ALL FOOLS' DAY. Apr 1. April Fools' Day seems to have begun in France in 1564. Apr 1 used to be New Year's Day but the New Year was changed to Jan 1 that year. People who insisted on celebrating the "old" New Year became known as April fools and it became common to play jokes and tricks on them. The general concept of a feast of fools is, however, an ancient one. The Romans had such a day and medieval monasteries also had days when the abbot or bishop was replaced for a day by a common monk, who would order his superiors to do the most menial or ridiculous tasks. "The joke of the day is to deceive persons by sending them upon frivolous and nonsensical errands; to pretend they are wanted when they are not, or, in fact, any way to betray them into some supposed ludicrous situation, so as to enable you to call them 'An April Fool.'"—Brady's *Clavis Calendaria*, 1812.

BATTLE OF OKINAWA BEGINS: ANNIVERSARY. Apr 1, 1945. On Easter Sunday, the US 10th Army began operation *Iceberg*, the invasion of the Ryukyu Islands of Okinawa. Ground troops numbering 180,000 plus 368,000 men in support services made a total of 548,000 troops involved—the biggest amphibious operation of the Pacific war.

BOOMER BONUS DAY. Apr 1. Aging Baby Boomers do not look forward to birthdays. This is a nonthreatening (no extra years added) day to celebrate for the over-50 crowd only! On Apr 1 because the whole thing gets to be a joke—the body goes . . . but the mind still thinks it's 21! For info: Gaye Andersen, Davenport University, 8200 Georgia St, Merrillville, IN 46410. Phone: (219) 650-5218. Fax: (219) 756-8911. E-mail: gaye.andersen@daven port.edu.

		S	M	T	W	T	F	S
April								1
2006		2	3	4	5	6	7	8
		9	10	11	12	13	14	15
		16	17	18	19	20	21	22
		23	24	25	26	27	28	29
		30						

BRIDGE OVER THE NEPONSET: ANNIVERSARY. Apr 1, 1634. The first bridge built in the US spanned the Neponset River between Milton and Dorchester, MA. The authority to build the bridge and an adjoining mill was issued to Israel Stoughton on this date by the Massachusetts General Court.

BULGARIA: SAINT LASARUS'S DAY. Apr 1. Ancient Slavic holiday of young girls, in honor of the goddess of spring and love.

CANADA: ELMIRA MAPLE SYRUP FESTIVAL. Apr 1. Elmira, ON. Tours of maple bush by hay wagon, sugaring-off shanty in operation, Pennsylvania Dutch cuisine, handcrafted goods, arts and crafts and antiques. Est attendance: 60,000. For info: Woolwich Visitor Services, 5 First St E, Elmira, ON, Canada N3B 2E3. Phone: (519) 669-2605. Fax: (519) 669-0503. Web: www.elmiramaplesyrup.com.

CANADA: NUNAVUT INDEPENDENCE: ANNIVERSARY. Apr 1, 1999. Nunavut became Canada's third independent territory. This self-governing territory with an Inuit majority was created from the eastern half of the Northwest Territories.

★**CANCER CONTROL MONTH.** Apr 1–30.

CHANEY, LON: BIRTH ANNIVERSARY. Apr 1, 1883. The "Man of a Thousand Faces" was born Leonidas Chaney at Colorado Springs, CO. One of the biggest box office stars of the silent era, Chaney was a master of disguise and makeup (he kept his transformation tools and methods a closely guarded secret) who specialized in playing tortured, tragic and often menacing characters. He is best known for his gripping portrayals of Quasimodo in *The Hunchback of Notre Dame* (1923) and of the Phantom in *The Phantom of the Opera* (1925). He died of cancer on Aug 26, 1930, at Hollywood, CA—only one month after his first sound film was released. His impact on films was such that all Hollywood studios observed a moment of silence in his honor to commemorate his death.

CHILD ABUSE PREVENTION MONTH. Apr 1–30. In 1979 The National Exchange Club adopted the prevention of child abuse as its national project and established The National Exchange Club Foundation. The Foundation is a chartered nonprofit corporation in Ohio. The Foundation has established nearly 100 Exchange Club Child Abuse Prevention Centers throughout the US. More than 140,000 families and 190,000 children have received services from the Exchange Club Child Abuse Prevention network. "Celebrating 25 years of child abuse prevention." For info: The Natl Exchange Club Foundation, 3050 Central Ave, Toledo, OH 43606-1700. Phone: (419) 535-3232 or (800) 760-3413. Fax: (419) 535-1989. E-mail: info@preventchildabuse.com. Web: www.preventchildabuse.com.

CIGARETTE ADVERTISING BANNED: ANNIVERSARY. Apr 1, 1970. Radio and television ads for cigarettes were banned by legislation signed by President Richard Nixon on this date. The ban went into effect Jan 1, 1971.

CLEAR LAKE CRAWFISH FESTIVAL. Apr 1. Landolt Pavilion, Clear Lake Park, Seabrook, TX. 11th annual. The festival will have crawfish-eating contests, gumbo cook-off, food, games, silent auction and live music. Sponsored by the Clear Lake Area Chamber of Commerce. Proceeds fund the annual July 4th fireworks on Clear Lake. Est attendance: 3,000. For info: Shari Sweeney, Clear Lake Area Chamber of Commerce, 1201 Nasa Rd One, Houston, TX 77058. Phone: (281) 488-7676. Fax: (281) 488-8981. Web: www.clearlakearea.com.

COMMUNITY SPIRIT DAYS. Apr 1–30. During the 30 days of April each community collects items at a central point for distribution to local charities, conducts special projects to help the local populace, congregates the town's nonprofit groups and businesses, thanks all participants and presents the community's Spirit of America Foundation Awards for outstanding volunteerism. For info: Robert Tweedie, Spirit of America Foundation, PO Box 5637, Augusta, ME 04332.

COUPLE APPRECIATION MONTH. Apr 1–30. To show thanks for each other's love and emotional support. Do something special to reinforce and celebrate your relationship. Annually, the month of April. For info: Donald Etkes, PhD, 11693 San Vicente Blvd, #491, Los Angeles, CA 90049. Phone: (310) 281-0123.

DEFEAT AT FIVE FORKS: ANNIVERSARY. Apr 1, 1865. After withdrawing to Five Forks, VA, Confederate troops under George Pickett were defeated and cut off by Union troops. This defeat, according to many military historians, sealed the immediate fate of Robert E. Lee's armies at Petersburg and Richmond. On Apr 2, Lee informed Confederate President Jefferson Davis that he would have to evacuate Richmond. Davis and his cabinet fled by train to Danville, VA.

DESOTO CAVERNS PARK SPRING NATIVE AMERICAN DANCE AND CRAFTS FESTIVAL. Apr 1–2. De-Soto Caverns Park, Childersburg, AL. 31st annual festival. Artists and craftspeople from across the US. Native American dancing includes hoop, traditional, fine, fancy and many more. Est attendance: 10,000. For info: DeSoto Caverns Park, 5181 DeSoto Caverns Pkwy, Childersburg, AL 35044. Phone: (800) 933-2283. E-mail: awm3@desotocavernspark.com. Web: www.desotocaverns park.com.

"THE DOCTORS" TV PREMIERE: ANNIVERSARY. Apr 1, 1963. "The Doctors" premiered on NBC on the same day as ABC's long-running soap "General Hospital," providing viewers with a double dose of medical drama. The show was set at Hope Memorial Hospital and began as an anthology series that was subsequently transformed into a serial in 1964. "The Doctors" ran for 19 years. Ellen Burstyn, Anna Stuart, Nancy Pinkerton, Jonathan Hogan, Julia Duffy and Alec Baldwin are some of its famous alums.

★DONATE LIFE MONTH. Apr 1–30.

EGGSSIBIT. Apr 1–2. Firth Youth Center, Phillipsburg, NJ. 36th annual show to encourage the art of decorating eggshells. Annually, the weekend prior to Palm Sunday. Est attendance: 2,000. For info: Dawn Slifer, Firth Youth Center, 108 Anderson St, Phillipsburg, NJ 08865. Phone: (908) 454-7281.

FRESH FLORIDA TOMATO MONTH. Apr 1–30. To publicize the Florida tomato as a versatile, nutritious, flavorful food. For info: Anita Fial, Lewis & Neale, Inc, 35 E 21st St, 10th Fl, New York, NY 10010. Phone: (212) 420-8808. Fax: (212) 254-2452. E-mail: info@lewis-neale.com.

"GENERAL HOSPITAL" TV PREMIERE: ANNIVERSARY. Apr 1, 1963. "General Hospital," ABC's longest-running soap, revolves around the denizens of fictional Port Charles, NY. "GH" was created by Doris and Frank Hursley. John Beradino, who was with the show from the beginning until his death in May 1996, played the role of Dr. Steve Hardy, upstanding director of medicine and pillar of the community. In the '80s, story lines became unusual with plots involving international espionage, mob activity and aliens. The wedding of supercouple Luke and Laura (Anthony Geary and Genie Francis) was a ratings topper. By the '90s, stories moved away from high-powered action to more conventional romance. Many actors received their big break on the show, including Demi Moore, Janine Turner, Jack Wagner, Richard Dean Anderson, Rick Springfield, John Stamos, Emma Samms, Mark Hamill, Finola Hughes, Ricky Martin and Tia Carrere.

GOLDEN RULE WEEK. Apr 1–7. The purpose of this week is to remind everyone of the importance of the Golden Rule in making this a better world in which we all may live. For a copy of the Golden Rule of 10 religions, send $5 to cover printing and postage. For info: Dr. Stanley Drake, Pres Emeritus, Intl Society of Friendship & Good Will, 8592 Roswell Rd, Ste 251, Atlanta, GA 30350-1867. Phone: (678) 795-1362. E-mail: sjdrake@bell south.net. Web: www.friendshipandgoodwill.org.

GRANGE MONTH. Apr 1–30. State and local recognition for Grange's contribution to rural/urban America. Celebrated at National Headquarters at Washington, DC, and in all states with local, county and state Granges. Begun in 1867, the National Grange is the oldest US rural community service, family-oriented organization with a special interest in agriculture. Annually, the month of April. Est attendance: 3,000. For info: Clyde Berry, The Natl Grange, 1616 H St NW, Washington, DC 20006. Phone: (202) 628-3507 or (888) 4-GRANGE. Fax: (202) 347-1091. E-mail: program_resource@nationalgrange.org. Web: www.nation algrange.org.

HARVEY, WILLIAM: BIRTH ANNIVERSARY. Apr 1, 1578 (OS). Physician, born at Folkestone, England. The first to discover the mechanics of the circulation of the blood. Died at Roehampton, England, June 3, 1657 (OS).

HISTORIC PENDLETON SPRING JUBILEE. Apr 1–2. Pendleton, SC. 29th annual. Come and join the fun in historic Pendleton with arts and crafts displays, food booths, entertainment and much more. Annually, the first full weekend in April. Est attendance: 30,000. For info: Historic Pendleton Spring Jubilee, PO Box 565, Pendleton, SC 29670. Phone: (864) 646-3782 or (800) 862-1795. Fax: (864) 646-2506. E-mail: jomc @bellsouth.net. Web: www.pendleton-district.org.

HOLY HUMOR MONTH. Apr 1–30. To recognize the healing power of Christian joy, humor and celebration; to be "Fools for Christ" on April Fools' Day (Apr 1); to celebrate "Holy Humor Sunday," the Sunday after Easter (Apr 23). Churches and prayer groups nationwide participate. For info: Rev. C. Alan Harvey, The Fellowship of Merry Christians, PO Box 895, Portage, MI 49081-0895. Phone: (863) 294-3121. Fax: (269) 324-3984. E-mail: joyfulnz@aol.com. Web: www.joyfulnoiseletter.com.

HOME IMPROVEMENT TIME. Apr 1–Sept 30. To explain the investment advantages of spending disposable income for home improvement to create better family living and improved community environment. Editorial package includes approximately 100 camera-ready stories and photos free to editors. Also available on disk and website. (May is a promotion focal point.) For info: James A. Stewart, Jr, Home Improvement Time, PO Box 247, Oakdale, PA 15071-0247. Phone: (412) 787-2881. Fax: (412) 787-3233. E-mail: hitdirect@aol.com. Web: homeimprovement time.com.

INFORMED WOMAN MONTH. Apr 1–30. You owe it to yourself to feel happy and fulfilled. To have confidence that you're in charge of your life and you're guiding it in the right direction. You can have whatever you want, but you need to determine what you need to know, where to go and whom to contact. Discover how to enjoy better living today and learn how to become a more informed and aware individual for the future. Ideas and tips for the month available for $2.50. For info: Lorrie Marsiglio, PO Box 284-CC, Wasco, IL 60183-0284. Phone: (630) 584-9368.

INJURY PREVENTION MONTH. Apr 1–30. Move Better, Play Better, Live Better. Learn about preventing orthopaedic injuries and conditions. Throughout the month, orthopaedic surgeons will provide injury prevention information on topics such as preventing playground and sports injuries, osteoporosis, workplace injuries, low back pain and proper shoewear tips. For info: American Academy of Orthopaedic Surgeons, 6300 N River Rd, Rosemont, IL 60018. Phone: (847) 823-7186. Fax: (847) 823-7268. Web: www.aaos.org.

INTERNATIONAL CUSTOMER LOYALTY MONTH. Apr 1–30. We highlight this month to honor and generate customer loyalty! Even though building customer loyalty should be a year-round thing, not just a month, take this month to strategize on how you can improve on relationships with your customers through better service, higher quality, etc. For info: Shep Hyken, Shepard Presentations, LLC, 711 Old Ballas Rd, #215, St. Louis, MO 63141. Phone: (314) 696-2200. E-mail: Shep@hyken.com. Web: www.hyken.com.

INTERNATIONAL DAFFYNITIONS MONTH. Apr 1–30. A celebration of creativity, International Daffynitions Month kicks off each year on April Fool's Day with the Daffynitions Parade. The month features seminars, games and contests designed to encourage creativity and put a smile on the face of the world. Annually, the month of April. For info: Joe Heuer, 2435 Greenwood Dr, Glendale, WI 53209. Phone: (414) 247-0936. E-mail: joe@daffynitions.com. Web: www.daffynitions.com.

INTERNATIONAL TWIT AWARD MONTH. Apr 1–30. Any famous name (celebrity with the worst sense of humor) is eligible for most Tiresome Wit (TWIT) of 2006. For info: Lauren Barnett, Lone Star Publications of Humor, 8452 Fredericksburg Rd, #103, San Antonio, TX 78229. E-mail: lspubs@aol.com. Web: members.aol.com/lspubs/lsindex.html.

IRAN: ISLAMIC REPUBLIC DAY. Apr 1. National holiday. Commemorates the approval of the new constitution of the Islamic Republic of Iran in 1979.

JAZZ APPRECIATION MONTH. Apr 1–30. Every April, Jazz Appreciation Month (JAM) highlights the glories of jazz as both a historical and a living treasure. Here is one special month to draw greater public attention to the extraordinary heritage and history of jazz and its importance to American culture. Musicians, concert halls, schools, colleges, museums, libraries and public broadcasters are encouraged to offer special programs during this month. The Smithsonian Institution's National Museum of American History (which operates the world's most comprehensive set of jazz programs) leads this initiative in concert with a distinguished roster of federal agencies, nongovernmental organizations and broadcasting networks. For info: Timothy Burnside, The Smithsonian Institution, National Museum of American History, PO Box 37012, Washington, DC 20013. Phone: (202) 633-3607. E-mail: burnside@si.edu. Web: www.si.edu.

LAUGH AT WORK WEEK. Apr 1–7. Laughter and humor are an important part of the workplace. Benefits of laughing at work include improved productivity, teamwork, communication, stress relief, job satisfaction and employee retention. This week, which begins on April Fools' Day, focuses on the very serious business of humor. For info: Randall Munson, Creatively Speaking®, 508 Meadow Run Dr SW, Rochester, MN 55902-2337. Phone/fax: (507) 286-1331. E-mail: humor@CreativelySpeaking.com. Web: www.CreativelySpeaking.com.

LUPUS ALERT DAY. Apr 1. Don't be fooled by lupus! To call attention to the confusing characteristics of this potentially fatal autoimmune disease that mimics other, less serious illnesses. For info: Duane Peters, VP of Communications and Advocacy, Lupus Foundation of America, 2000 L St NW, Ste 710, Washington, DC 20036. Phone: (202) 349-1145. Fax: (202) 349-1156. E-mail: peters@lupus.org. Web: www.lupus.org.

MEDICATION SAFETY WEEK. Apr 1–7. Seven focus days to raise awareness about medication safety and offer strategies to reduce risk, including the Cards4Life health care management tool, free on our website. Apr 1 is the day to brown-bag your medicine bottles and herbals that you are taking to your pharmacist to answer any questions or concerns. A Medication Safety PowerPoint program is available on our website for health professionals, pharmacists and nurses to perform outreach in their local communities. For info: Women's Heart Foundation, PO Box 7827, West Trenton, NJ 08628. Phone: (609) 771-9600. Fax: (609) 771-3778. E-mail: info@womensheart.org. Web: www.womensheart.org.

MONTH OF THE YOUNG CHILD®. Apr 1–30. Michigan. To promote awareness of the importance of young children and their specific needs in today's society. Many communities celebrate with special events for children and families. For info: Michigan Assn for Education of Young Children, Beacon Pl, Ste 1-D, 4572 S Hagadorn Rd, East Lansing, MI 48823-5385. Phone: (800) 336-6424 or (517) 336-9700. Fax: (517) 336-9790. E-mail: moyc@miaeyc.org. Web: www.miaeyc.org.

MOUNT HOOD RAILHOOD: A SEASON OF FUN. Apr 1–Dec 31. Hood River, OR. 98-year-old historic railroad offers 44-mile round-trip excursions through the natural beauty of the northwest Columbia River Gorge and foothills of Mount Hood, Oregon's highest peak. Special holiday events, murder mystery, dinner trains and harrowing train robberies throughout the season. For info: Mt Hood Railroad, 110 Railroad Ave, Hood River, OR 97031. Phone: (800) TRAIN-61 or (541) 386-3556. Fax: (541) 386-2140. Web: www.mthoodrr.com.

MS WALK. April 1–2 (tentative). San Jose and Monterey, CA. Looking for a fun family activity? Join the Silicon Valley chapter of the National Multiple Sclerosis Society for the annual MS Walk. Enjoy a delicious breakfast, make new friends and help end the devastating effects of multiple sclerosis. For info: Natl MS Society, 2589 Scott Blvd, Santa Clara, CA 95050. Phone: (408) 988-7557 or (800) FIG-HTMS. Fax: (408) 988-1816. E-mail: cau@nmss.org. Web: www.nationalmssociety.org/cau.

NATCHITOCHES JAZZ FESTIVAL. Apr 1. Natchitoches, LA. The event features numerous bands, continuous music from 11 AM to 9 PM. Annually, the first weekend of April. Est attendance: 25,000. For info: Calendar of Events, Natchitoches Parish Tourism Commission, 781 Front St, Natchitoches, LA 71457. Phone: (318) 352-8072 or (800) 259-1714. Fax: (318) 352-2415. Web: www.natchitoches.net or www.natchjazzfest.com.

NATIONAL AUTISM AWARENESS MONTH. Apr 1–30. A month filled with autism awareness events such as conferences, presentations, displays and media attention. Contact the NJ Center for Outreach & Services for the Autism Community for information on how you can become an "Autism Awareness Ambassador." For info: Julie Abrahamsen, COSAC, 1450 Parkside Ave, Ste 22, Ewing, NJ 08638. Phone: (609) 863-8100. Fax: (609) 883-5509. E-mail: information@njcosac.org. Web: www.njcosac.org.

NATIONAL CAR CARE MONTH. Apr 1–30. A nationwide effort to focus motorists' attention on the importance of vehicle maintenance and care. Annually, the month of April. For info: Car Care Council, 4600 East-West Hwy, Ste 300, Bethesda, MD 20814. Phone: (240) 333-1088. Fax: (301) 654-3299. E-mail: info@carcare.org. Web: www.carcare.org.

★**NATIONAL CHILD ABUSE PREVENTION MONTH.** Apr 1–30.

NATIONAL CHILD ABUSE PREVENTION MONTH. Apr 1–30. For info: Prevent Child Abuse America, 200 S Michigan Ave, 17th Fl, Chicago, IL 60604. Phone: (312) 663-3520. Web: www.preventchildabuse.org.

NATIONAL DECORATING MONTH. Apr 1–30. This month is dedicated to learning more about the many aspects of home decor while promoting the fun and creativity of DIY decorating. For info: Donna Babylon, PO Box 1603, Westminster, MD 21158. Phone: (410) 876-3121. Fax: (410) 848-3293. E-mail: donna@NationalDecoratingMonth.com. Web: www.NationalDecoratingMonth.com.

		S	M	T	W	T	F	S
April								1
2006		2	3	4	5	6	7	8
		9	10	11	12	13	14	15
		16	17	18	19	20	21	22
		23	24	25	26	27	28	29
		30						

NATIONAL DONATE LIFE MONTH. Apr 1–30. Formerly known as National Organ and Tissue Donor Awareness Week, this observance expanded to a full month in 2003. The purpose is to encourage Americans to consider organ and tissue donation and to sign donor cards when getting a driver's license. For info: US Dept of Health and Human Services, 200 Independence Ave SW, Washington, DC 20201. Phone: (877) 696-6775 or (202) 619-0257. Web: www.organdonor.gov.

NATIONAL FUN DAY. Apr 1. A day to laugh and reminisce about the good old days when April 1 meant an exploding pen, a hand buzzer, a nice stick of pepper gum or maybe some fake doggie poo. Play a prank on a friend, family member or coworker to keep the spirit of April Fools' alive. For info: iParty, 270 Bridge St, Ste 301, Dedham, MA 02026. Phone: (888) 4-GIGGLES. E-mail: fun@iparty.com. Web: www.iparty.com.

NATIONAL HUMOR MONTH. Apr 1–30. 30th anniversary. Special events in Canada and the US will focus on the joy and therapeutic value of laughter and how it can reduce stress, improve job performance and enrich the quality of life. For info send 68-cent SASE to: Larry Wilde, Dir, The Carmel Institute of Humor, 25470 Canada Dr, Carmel, CA 93923-8926. Web: www.larrywilde.com.

NATIONAL KITE MONTH. Apr 1–30. Celebrates kiting with more than 600 events throughout the country, including kite festivals, kitemaking classes for kids and adults, kitemaking classes in schools, kite displays in museums and public libraries and "fun flys" at local parks and beaches. For info: Mel Hickman, American Kitefliers Assn, PO Box 1614, Walla Walla, WA 99362. Phone/fax: (800) 252-2550. E-mail: Admin@NationalKiteMonth.org. Web: www.NationalKiteMonth.org.

NATIONAL KNUCKLES DOWN MONTH. Apr 1–30. To recognize and revive the American tradition of playing and collecting marbles and keep it rolling along. Please send SASE with inquiries. For info: Cathy C. Runyan-Svacina, The Marble Lady, 7812 NW Hampton Rd, Kansas City, MO 64152. Phone: (816) 587-8687. Web: www.themarblelady.com.

NATIONAL LANDSCAPE ARCHITECTURE MONTH. April 1–30. Investigate what landscapers do to beautify our grounds—both personal and public. Many architects will have site tours, exhibits, school visits and community projects this week. Annually, during April, as Apr 26 is the birth anniversary of Frederick Law Olmsted. Olmsted is widely regarded as the founder of the profession of landscape architecture in North America. For info: Jeffrey Lofton, APR, ASLA, 636 Eye Street NW, Washington, DC 20001. Phone: (202) 898-2444. Fax: (202) 898-1185. E-mail: jlofton@asla.org. Web: www.asla.org/lamonth/index.html.

NATIONAL LOVE OUR CHILDREN DAY. Apr 1. National Love Our Children Day is like Mother's and Father's Day for children and will be celebrated annually across the US to honor children and strengthen families and raise awareness for efforts to protect children. For info: Ross Ellis, Love Our Children USA, 220 East 57th St, New York, NY, 10022. Phone: (888) 347-KIDS. E-mail: info@loveourchildrenusa.org. Web: www.loveourchildrenusa.org.

NATIONAL OCCUPATIONAL THERAPY MONTH. Apr 1–30. To recognize the services and accomplishments of occupational therapy practitioners and promote awareness of the benefits of occupational therapy. For info: The American Occupational Therapy Assn, Inc, 4720 Montgomery Lane, PO Box 31220, Bethesda, MD 20824-1220. Phone: (301) 652-2682. TDD (800) 377-8555. Fax: (301) 652-7711. E-mail: praota@aota.org. Web: www.aota.org.

NATIONAL PARKINSON'S AWARENESS MONTH. Apr 1–30. To help enhance the public education and awareness about Parkinson's disease by providing information on treatment, medication, support and research, as well as providing these resources to patients with the disease and their caregivers, helping to improve the quality of life for both. For info: Karen Hamilton, Manager of Special Events, Natl Parkinson Foundation, 1501 NW 9th Ave, Miami, FL 33136. Phone: (305) 243-8145 or (800) 327-4545. Fax: (305) 243-1069. Web: www.parkinson.org.

NATIONAL PECAN MONTH. Apr 1–30. A celebration of the great taste, health benefits and versatility of pecans. This delicious tree nut native to North America adds unmistakable flavor, crunch and texture to just about any meal or snack. Pecans have proven cholesterol-lowering properties and contain more than 19 important vitamins and minerals. Almost 90 percent of the fats in pecans are of the heart-healthy, unsaturated variety. For info: Natl Pecan Shellers Assn, 5775 Peachtree-Dunwoody Rd, Ste 500, Bldg G, Atlanta, GA 30342. Phone: (404) 252-3663. Fax: (404) 252-0774. E-mail: info@ilovepecans.org. Web: www.ilovepecans.org.

NATIONAL PET FIRST AID AWARENESS MONTH. Apr 1–30. Sponsored by Pet Tech, Inc, the first national training center for pet first aid and care. To help pet owners everywhere in understanding the importance of knowing the skills and techniques of pet first aid, CPR and care for their pet. For info: Pet Tech, Inc, PO Box 2285, Carlsbad, CA 92018. Phone: (760) 930-0309. E-mail: info@pettech.net. Web: www.pettech.net.

NATIONAL POETRY MONTH. Apr 1–30. Annual observance to pay tribute to the great legacy and ongoing achievement of American poets and the vital place of poetry in American culture. In a proclamation issued in honor of the first observance, President Bill Clinton called it "a welcome opportunity to celebrate not only the unsurpassed body of literature produced by our poets in the past, but also the vitality and diversity of voices reflected in the works of today's American poets. . . . Their creativity and wealth of language enrich our culture and inspire a new generation of Americans to learn the power of reading and writing at its best." Spearheaded by the Academy of American Poets, this is the largest and most extensive celebration of poetry in American history. For info: The Academy of American Poets, 584 Broadway, Ste 604, New York, NY 10012-5243. Phone: (212) 274-0343. Fax: (212) 274-9427. Web: www.poets.org.

NATIONAL PREPARE YOUR HOME TO BE SOLD MONTH. Apr 1–30. April has been declared to be "National Prepare Your Home To Be Sold Month" by the National Association of Independent Real Estate Brokers. For info: Gary Conner, NAIREB, 7102 Mardyke Ln, Indianapolis, IN 46226. Phone: (317) 549-1709. E-mail: info@NationalRealEstateBrokers.org. Web: www.NationalRealEstateBrokers.org.

NATIONAL SEXUAL ASSAULT AWARENESS AND PREVENTION MONTH. Apr 1–30. Every two and a half minutes, somewhere in America, another person is sexually assaulted. During this month, efforts are focused on raising awareness of sexual assault, promoting legislative efforts to address sexual violence, lauding efforts of more than 10,000 volunteers across the US who assist in crisis services and related areas, promoting resources for victims such as the National Sexual Assault Hotline (800-656-HOPE) and, above all, demonstrating solidarity with victims of sexual assault. Celebrated nationally by RAINN, state sexual assault coalitions, local rape crisis centers and other similar organizations. Passed by House/Senate; signed by president. For info: Rape, Abuse & Incest National Network (RAINN), 635-B Pennsylvania Ave SE, Washington, DC 20003. Phone: (202) 544-1034 or (800) 656-HOPE (hotline). Fax: (202) 544-3556. E-mail: info@rainn.org. Web: www.rainn.org.

NATIONAL SEXUALLY TRANSMITTED DISEASES (STDs) EDUCATION AND AWARENESS MONTH. Apr 1–30. To educate consumers, patients, students and professionals about the prevention of sexually transmitted diseases. Kit of materials available for $15. For info: Frederick Mayer, Pharmacists Planning Service, Inc, 101 Lucas Valley Rd, #210, San Rafael, CA 94903. E-mail: ppsi@aol.com. Web: www.ppsinc.org.

NATIONAL YOUTH SPORTS SAFETY MONTH. Apr 1–30. Bringing public attention to the prevalent problem of injuries in youth sports. This event promotes safety in sports activities and is supported by more than 60 national sports and medical organizations. Resource material available on website. For info: Exec Dir, Natl Youth Sports Safety Fdtn, One Beacon St, Ste 3333, Boston, MA 02108. Phone: (617) 367-6677. Fax: (617) 722-9999. E-mail: NYSSF@aol.com. Web: www.nyssf.org.

NCAA DIVISION I MEN'S BASKETBALL CHAMPIONSHIP (FINAL FOUR). Apr 1 & 3. RCA Dome, Indianapolis, IN. For info: Natl Collegiate Athletic Assn, 700 W Washington Ave, PO Box 6222, Indianapolis, IN 46206-6222. Phone: (317) 917-6222. Fax: (317) 917-6827. Web: www.ncaasports.com.

PHARMACISTS' WAR ON DIABETES. Apr 1–30. Educate consumers, patients and health care professionals about prevention of diabetes, especially focusing on "Know Your Numbers for Diabetes" and screening along with awareness and interest in the diabetes epidemic. Kits available for $15. For info: Fred Mayer, Pharmacists Planning Service, Inc (PPSI), c/o the Pharmacy Council on Diabetes Education (PCDE), 101 Lucas Valley Rd, Ste 210, San Rafael, CA 94903. E-mail: ppsi@aol.com. Web: www.ppsinc.org.

PHYSICAL WELLNESS MONTH. Apr 1–30. Time to get in shape for summer! Shed those winter clothes and extra pounds, and rejuvenate your body with healthy eating, restful sleep, vigorous exercise and a new look. Jog, swim, bike, roller-skate, play tennis, go hiking or backpacking. Spend time daily outdoors breathing in fresh air, and take time to relax. Retire to bed early for restful sleep and wake up early feeling refreshed and energized. For info: Angela Brown, Words of Wellness, PO Box 49266, Charlotte, NC 28277. Phone: (704) 849-2900. Fax: (704) 845-3060. E-mail: Angela@WordsofWellness.com. Web: www.WordsofWellness.com.

PREVENTION OF ANIMAL CRUELTY MONTH. Apr 1–30. Sponsored by the ASPCA, this crucial month is designed to educate Americans about animal cruelty and to urge them to report any instances of violence toward animals. For info: ASPCA Media Relations Dept, 110 5th Ave, 2nd Fl, New York, NY 10011. Phone: (212) 876-7700. Fax: (212) 423-9813. E-mail: press@aspca.org. Web: www.aspca.org.

PRO-AM SNIPE EXCURSION AND HUNT. Apr 1. Moultrie, GA. Celebrating the time-honored custom of snipe hunting. The denim snipe has come back from the brink of extinction and will be honored at the 2006 event which will include a Snipe Parade, a Snipe Ball and festivities at the Denim Wing of the Snipe Museum at New Elm, GA. New Snipe-O-Rama racing oval open! Annually, Apr 1. For info: Beth Gay, PO Box 2828, Moultrie, GA 31776. Phone: (229) 985-6540.

RAM, JAGJIVAN: BIRTH ANNIVERSARY. Apr 1, 1908. Indian political leader and coworker with Mohandas K. Gandhi and Jawaharlal Nehru in the fight for Indian independence. Born into a family of "untouchables" at the village of Chandwa, Bihar, India, Ram was one of the first of that class to attend school and university. Known as the champion and spokesman for India's 100 million untouchables, he overcame most of the handicaps of caste. He served in a number of ministerial cabinet posts and twice was a candidate for prime minister. Ram died at New Delhi, India, July 6, 1986.

April 2006	S	M	T	W	T	F	S
							1
	2	3	4	5	6	7	8
	9	10	11	12	13	14	15
	16	17	18	19	20	21	22
	23	24	25	26	27	28	29
	30						

ROBERT THE HERMIT: DEATH ANNIVERSARY. Apr 1, 1832. One of the most famous hermits in American history died in his hermitage at Seekonk, MA. Robert was a bonded slave, the son of an African mother and probably an Anglo-Saxon father. After obtaining his freedom, he was swindled out of it and shipped to a foreign slave market, then later escaped to America. He was separated from his first wife by force and rejected by his second wife after a long sea voyage, before withdrawing from society.

ROSACEA AWARENESS MONTH. Apr 1–31. Rosacea Awareness Month has been designated by the National Rosacea Society to raise awareness and understanding of this increasingly common disease. Rosacea is a facial skin condition that can cause permanent physical and psychological damage if it is not diagnosed and treated. For info: Natl Rosacea Society, 800 S Northwest Hwy, Ste 200, Barrington, IL 60010. Phone: (847) 382-8971 or (888) NO-BLUSH. Fax: (847) 382-5567. E-mail: rosaceas@aol.com. Web: www.rosacea.org.

SCHOOL LIBRARY MEDIA MONTH. Apr 1–30. Celebrates the work of school library media specialists in our nation's elementary and secondary schools. For info: American Assn of School Librarians, American Library Assn, 50 E Huron St, Chicago, IL 60611. Phone: (800) 545-2433. E-mail: AASL@ala.org. Web: www.ala.org/aasl.

SCOTLAND: PITLOCHRY FESTIVAL THEATRE SEASON. Apr 1–Oct 31 (tentative). Pitlochry Festival Theatre, Pitlochry, Perthshire. Year-round venue featuring drama, music, literature and the arts, with plays performed in repertory, plus concerts, exhibitions and fringe events. For info: Pitlochry Festival Theatre, Pitlochry, Perthshire, Scotland PH16 5DR. Phone: (44) (179) 648-4626. Fax: (44) (179) 648-4616. E-mail: boxoffice@pitlochry.org.uk. Web: www.pitlochry.org.uk.

SFCC SPRING ARTS FESTIVAL. Apr 1–2. Gainesville, FL. Artists and craftspeople from all areas of the US display their work. Also, Kids Art Jungle—a complete art fest for kids. Est attendance: 129,000. For info: Santa Fe Community College, Spring Arts Fest, 3000 NW 83rd St, Gainesville, FL 32606. Phone: (352) 395-5355. Fax: (352) 336-2715. E-mail: kathryn.lehman@sfcc.edu.

SKAGIT VALLEY TULIP FESTIVAL. Apr 1–30. Skagit County, La Conner, Mount Vernon, Burlington, WA. To celebrate and share the spectacular beauty of more than 1,000 acres of blooming daffodils and tulips that herald the arrival of spring in the Skagit Valley of Washington state. Est attendance: 350,000. For info: Cindy Verge, SVTF Exec Dir, PO Box 1784, Mount Vernon, WA 98273. Phone: (360) 428-5959. Fax: (360) 428-6753. E-mail: info@tulipfestival.org. Web: www.tulipfestival.org.

SORRY CHARLIE DAY. Apr 1. To honor Charlie the Tuna, who has been rejected for 44 years and still keeps his spunk. A day to recognize anyone who has been rejected and lived through it. Join the "Sorry Charlie, No-Fan-Club-for-You Club" by sending in your best rejection story. Please send SASE with inquiries. For info: Cathy Runyan-Svacina, 7812 NW Hampton Rd, Kansas City, MO 64152. Phone/fax: (816) 587-8687. Web: www.themarblelady.com.

SOUTHERN BELLES MONTH. Apr 1–30. Honoring all Southern Belles, whether born or reborn to the title. For info: Susan Reno-Gilliland, A Southern Belle's Life, 19 Lowry Way, Studio A, Euharlee, GA 30145. Phone: (770) 386-7023. E-mail: southernbelle@susanrenogilliland.com. Web: www.susanrenogilliland.com.

SPRING SWING CITY ELECTRA-QUANAH-WIDE GARAGE SALE. Apr 1. Electra, TX. Sales throughout the

Electra area. 50 miles of garage sales. Chamber of commerce will provide free coffee and maps at 7 AM; sales start at 8 AM. The chamber of commerce office will close at 8 AM so that we too may enjoy all of the bargains. Est attendance: 500. For info: Sherry Strange, Electra Chamber of Commerce, 112 W Cleveland, Electra, TX 76360. Phone: (940) 495-3577. E-mail: electra coc@electratel.net. Web: www.electratexas.org.

STRAW HAT MONTH. Apr 1–30. A month of celebration during which the felt hat is put aside in favor of the straw or fabric hat by both men and women. Local businesses and the media are encouraged to plan hat-related activities. The Headwear Information Bureau hosts events at several venues throughout the month. For info: Casey Bush, Exec Dir, Headwear Info Bureau, 302 W 12 St,, New York, NY 10014. Phone: (212) 627-8333. Web: www.hatsworldwide.com.

STRESS AWARENESS MONTH. Apr 1–30. To promote public awareness of what stress is, what causes it to occur and what can be done about it. A monthlong focus on the dangers of stress, successful coping strategies and the myths about stress that are prevalent in our society. For info: Morton C. Orman, MD, Dir, The Health Resource Network, 908 Cold Bottom Rd, Sparks, MD 21152. Web: www.stresscure.com.

SWITZERLAND: LUCERNE FESTIVAL, OSTERN (EASTER). Apr 1–9. Lucerne. Sacred and concert music at truly unique sites: in the beautiful churches and at the concert hall of the KKL Lucerne. For the period of this festival, the Symphonieorchester des Bayerischen Rundfunks conducted by Mariss Jansons is orchestra-in-residence. For info: Lucerne Festival, PO Box CH-6002, Lucerne, Switzerland. Phone: (41) 226-44-00. Fax: (41) 226-44-60. E-mail: info@lucernefestival.ch. Web: www.lucernefestival.ch.

TESTICULAR CANCER AWARENESS WEEK. Apr 1–7. This public awareness and education program was conceived in 1997 to create a better public understanding of the dangers of undetected testicular cancer in young men ages 15–34. The campaign is designed to promote the importance of early detection, which saves hundreds of young men's lives each year. A free self-exam reminder is available at menstuff-testicular-exam-subscribe @topica.com, so that a monthly self-exam becomes a habit for health. Information is made available to high school and college health centers to ensure correct diagnosis. For info: National Men's Resource Center, PO Box 1080-CH, Brookings, OR 97415-0024. E-mail: tcaw@tcaw.org. Web: www.tcaw.org.

TOUR de CURE. Apr 1–June 30. Thousands of cyclists participate in the American Diabetes Association's annual cycling event to raise money to help find a cure for diabetes and to provide information and resources to improve the lives of all people affected by diabetes. Tours are held in more than 90 communities across America and participants are asked to raise a minimum of $75 in pledges. Contact your local affiliate for the date in your area. For info: (888) 342-2383 or www.diabetes.org.

US AIR FORCE ACADEMY ESTABLISHED: ANNIVERSARY. Apr 1, 1954. President Dwight Eisenhower signed the bill this day that created the US Air Force Academy to train officers for the Air Force. Construction on the Colorado Springs, CO, academy began July 11, 1955, and ended in 1958. The academy was accredited in 1959. Women were admitted in 1976. For more info: www.usafa.edu.

US HOUSE OF REPRESENTATIVES ACHIEVES A QUORUM: ANNIVERSARY. Apr 1, 1789. First session of Congress was held Mar 4, 1789, but not enough representatives arrived to achieve a quorum until Apr 1.

WOMEN'S EYE HEALTH AND SAFETY MONTH. Apr 1–30. Women often manage family health concerns. Do you know how to protect your sight? Hormonal changes, age and even the sun can endanger sight. Information on women's and family eye-health issues will be provided. For info: Prevent Blindness America®, 211 W. Wacker Dr, Ste 1700, Chicago, IL 60606. Phone: (800) 331-2020. E-mail: info@preventblindness.org. Web: www.preventblindness.org.

WORKPLACE CONFLICT AWARENESS MONTH. Apr 1–30. At today's harried pace, workplace conflict is increasing. Many of us try to avoid this conflict, but instead we take it home with us. This month, we try to make people aware that trying to avoid conflict is futile; we must learn to deal with it and manage it. For info: Richard Brenner, 10 Emerson Place, Ste 16A, Boston, MA 02114. Phone: (617) 263-1112. Fax: (617) 263-1113. E-mail: rbrenner@ChacoCanyon.com. Web: www.ChacoCanyon.com.

WORLD HABITAT AWARENESS MONTH. Apr 1–30. A worldwide observance for the need to protect the habitat of all Earth's creatures, to make a conscious effort to preserve nature's ecosystems. Annually, the entire month of April. For info: PALS Foundation, PO Box 1271, San Luis Obispo, CA 93406. Phone: (805) 544-0984. Fax: (805) 544-2027. Web: www.PALS.R8.org.

BIRTHDAYS TODAY

David Eisenhower, 59, author (*Eisenhower at War*), lawyer, grandson of former president Dwight Eisenhower, born West Point, NY, Apr 1, 1947.

Ali MacGraw, 67, actress (*Goodbye, Columbus; Love Story*), born Pound Ridge, NY, Apr 1, 1939.

Annette O'Toole, 53, actress (*Smile, 48Hrs*), born Houston, TX, Apr 1, 1953.

Jane Powell, 77, actress (*Seven Brides for Seven Brothers*), born Suzanne Burce at Portland, OR, Apr 1, 1929.

Debbie Reynolds, 74, actress (*Singin' in the Rain, Mother*), born El Paso, TX, Apr 1, 1932.

Libby Riddles, 50, first woman to win the 1,135-mile Iditarod Alaskan dogsled race, born Madison, WI, Apr 1, 1956.

Glenn Edward ("Bo") Schembechler, Jr, 77, former baseball executive and football coach, born Barberton, OH, Apr 1, 1929.

Daniel Joseph ("Rusty") Staub, 62, former baseball player, born New Orleans, LA, Apr 1, 1944.

APRIL 2 — SUNDAY
Day 92 — 273 Remaining

ANDERSEN, HANS CHRISTIAN: BIRTH ANNIVERSARY. Apr 2, 1805. Author chiefly remembered for his more than 150 fairy tales, many of which are regarded as classics of children's literature. Andersen was born at Odense, Denmark, and died at Copenhagen, Denmark, Aug 4, 1875.

"AS THE WORLD TURNS" TV PREMIERE: 50th ANNIVERSARY. Apr 2, 1956. One of the longest-running soaps currently on the air, "ATWT" premiered on CBS. The series is set in midwestern Oakdale and revolves around the Hughes family and their neighbors. Irma Phillips was the show's creator and head writer. Some of its cast members who made it big are: Meg Ryan, Julianne Moore, Michael Nader, Steven Weber and Swoosie Kurtz.

BARTHOLDI, FREDERIC AUGUSTE: BIRTH ANNIVERSARY. Apr 2, 1834. French sculptor who created *Liberty Enlightening the World* (better known as the Statue of Liberty), which stands at New York Harbor. Also remembered for the *Lion of Belfort* at Belfort, France. Born at Colman, at Alsace, France. Died at Paris, France, Oct 4, 1904.

BREAD RIOT AT RICHMOND: ANNIVERSARY. Apr 2, 1863. Indicative of conditions in the Confederate capital of Richmond, VA, an angry mob's demands for bread from a bakery wagon escalated into the destruction of nearby shops. Confederate president Jefferson Davis, in a bold move, stepped into the angry crowd and stated, "We do not desire to injure anyone, but this lawlessness must stop. I will give you five minutes to disperse, otherwise you will be fired upon." The mob dispersed without bloodshed.

CASANOVA, GIOVANNI GIACOMO GIROLAMO: BIRTH ANNIVERSARY. Apr 2, 1725. Celebrated Italian writer-librarian and, by his own account, philanderer, adventurer, rogue, seminarian, soldier and spy, was born at Venice, Italy. As the Chevalier de Seingalt, he died at Dux, Bohemia, June 4, 1798, while serving as librarian and working on his lively and frank *History of My Life*, a brilliant picture of 18th-century life.

CHECK YOUR BATTERIES DAY. Apr 2. A day set aside for checking the batteries in your smoke detector, carbon monoxide detector, HVAC thermostat, audio/visual remote controls and other electronic devices. This could save your life! Annually, the first Sunday in April.

CONSIDER CHRISTIANITY WEEK. Apr 2–8. A week to encourage Christians to examine the evidence and reasons for their faith and for non-Christians to take another look at the faith that has played such an important role in shaping the history and culture in which we live. Annually, beginning two Sundays before Easter. For info: Hanna Hushbeck, PR, Aletheia, 936 N Lincoln St, Redlands, CA 92374. Phone/fax: (909) 794-8941. E-mail: elgin @consider.org. Web: www.consider.org.

"DALLAS" TV PREMIERE: ANNIVERSARY. Apr 2, 1978. Oil tycoons battled for money, power and prestige in this prime-time CBS drama that ran for nearly 13 years. The Ewings and Barneses were Texas's modern-day Hatfields and McCoys. Larry Hagman starred as the devious, scheming womanizer J.R. Ewing. When J.R. was shot in the 1980 season-ending cliffhanger, the revelation of the mystery shooter was the single-most watched episode of its time (it was Kristin, J.R.'s sister-in-law, played by Mary Crosby). Cast members included Jim Davis, Barbara Bel Geddes, Donna Reed, Ted Shackelford, Joan Van Ark (who, along with Shackelford, starred in the spin-off "Knots Landing"), Patrick Duffy, Linda Gray, Charlene Tilton, David Wayne, Keenan Wynn, Ken Kercheval, Victoria Principal and Steve Kanaly.

DAYLIGHT SAVING TIME BEGINS. Apr 2–Oct 29. Daylight Saving Time begins at 2 AM in the US and Canada. The Uniform Time Act of 1966 (as amended in 1986 by Public Law 99–359), administered by the US Dept of Transportation, provides that Standard Time in each zone be advanced one hour from 2 AM on the first Sunday in April until 2 AM on the last Sunday in October (except where state legislatures provide exemption, as in Hawaii and parts of Arizona and Indiana). Prior to 1986, Daylight Saving Time began on the last Sunday in April. Many use the popular rule "spring forward, fall back" to remember which way to turn their clocks. See also: "Daylight Saving Time Ends; Standard Time Resumes" (Oct 29).

EBSEN, BUDDY: BIRTH ANNIVERSARY. Apr 2, 1908. Born Christian Rudolph Ebsen, Jr, at Belleville, IL. Buddy Ebsen started his career as a vaudeville "song-and-dance" man, then was popular throughout the 1930s on film as well. He almost played the Tin Man in *The Wizard of Oz* (1939), but had a serious allergic reaction to the makeup and was forced to stop filming. In the 1950s, he played Davy Crockett's sidekick on television and film. He played Jed Clampett in "The Beverly Hillbillies" (1962–71), and starred as "Barnaby Jones" (1973–80). He died at Torrance, CA, July 6, 2003.

"THE EDGE OF NIGHT" TV PREMIERE: 50th ANNIVERSARY. Apr 2, 1956. "The Edge of Night" premiered on CBS along with "As The World Turns." Though the plots initially revolved around crime and courtroom drama, the serial's format soon developed along more conventional soap story lines of romance. The soap shifted to ABC in 1975 but was cancelled in 1984. Larry Hagman, Dixie Carter, Lori Loughlin, Willie Aames

and Amanda Blake were some of the show's most prominent players.

ENGLAND: CARE SUNDAY. Apr 2. The fifth Sunday of Lent, also known as Carling Sunday and Passion Sunday. First day of Passiontide, remembering the sorrow and passion of Christ.

FALKLAND ISLANDS WAR: ANNIVERSARY. Apr 2–June 15, 1982. Argentina, claiming sovereignty over the nearby Falkland Islands (called by them the Malvinas), invaded and occupied the British Crown Colony on Apr 2, 1982. British forces defeated the Argentinians on June 15, 1982. About 250 British and 600 Argentine lives were lost in the conflict. In 1986, three military officers, including General Leopoldo Galtieri (who was president of Argentina at the time of the invasion), were convicted and sentenced for the military crime of negligence. Commemorative ceremonies are observed as Malvinas Day on June 13 in Argentina.

FIRST WHITE HOUSE EASTER EGG ROLL: ANNIVERSARY. Apr 2, 1877. The first White House Easter Egg Roll took place during the administration of Rutherford B. Hayes. The traditional event was discontinued by President Franklin D. Roosevelt in 1942 and reinstated Apr 6, 1953, by President Dwight D. Eisenhower.

GUINNESS, SIR ALEC: BIRTH ANNIVERSARY. Apr 2, 1914. Academy Award–winning actor (for *The Bridge on the River Kwai*) born at London, England. An active performer on both stage and screen, his film roles included *Star Wars, A Passage to India* and *Kind Hearts and Coronets*. He died at West Sussex, England, Aug 5, 2000.

INTERNATIONAL CHILDREN'S BOOK DAY. Apr 2. Observes Hans Christian Andersen's birthday and commemorates the international aspects of children's literature. Sponsor: International Board on Books for Young People, Nonnenweg 12, Postfach, CH-4003 Basel, Switzerland. For info: USBBY Secretariat, PO Box 8139, Newark, DE 19714-8139. Phone: (302) 731-1600. E-mail: usbby@reading.org.

NATIONAL BLUE RIBBON WEEK. Apr 2–8. National Blue Ribbon Week encourages all National Exchange Club members to wear and distribute Blue Ribbon pins or cutouts in a national effort to raise awareness and funds for child abuse prevention. The Blue Ribbon symbolizes more than 3.2 million abused children reported each year to Child Protective Services. For info: The Natl Exchange Club Foundation for the Prevention of Child Abuse, 3050 Central Ave, Toledo, OH 43606-1700. Phone: (800) 924-2643. Web: www.preventchildabuse.com.

NATIONAL LIBRARY WEEK. Apr 2–8. A nationwide observance sponsored by the American Library Association. Celebrates libraries and librarians, the pleasures and importance of reading and invites library use and support. For info: American Library Assn, Public Info Office, 50 E Huron St, Chicago, IL 60611. Phone: (312) 280-5044. Fax: (312) 944-8520. E-mail: pio@ala .org. Web: www.ala.org.

NATIONAL MEDICAL PATIENT ADVOCACY WEEK. Apr 2–8. As the medical community continues to grow and get more complex, this one week is intended to create awareness about patient responsibility. The medical consumer should educate him- or herself regarding the physical, emotional, legal and financial concerns encountered before, during and after medical treatment. Patients no longer need to be passive bystanders in dealing with their health care issues, but can be active participants—defining how they receive treatment. Annually, the first full week in April, Sunday through Saturday. For info: Mark S. Vass, 617 N Keller Smithfield Rd, Keller, TX 76248-4229. Phone: (817) 379-5372. E-mail: l.ladybugs@verizon.net.

April 2006	S	M	T	W	T	F	S
							1
	2	3	4	5	6	7	8
	9	10	11	12	13	14	15
	16	17	18	19	20	21	22
	23	24	25	26	27	28	29
	30						

NATIONAL PUBLIC HEALTH WEEK. Apr 2–8. Annually, the first full week in April. For info: American Public Health Assn, 800 I Street NW, Washington, DC 20001-3710. Phone: (202) 777-APHA. E-mail: comments@apha.org. Web: www.apha.org.

NATIONAL WEEK OF THE OCEAN. Apr 2–8. A week focusing on humanity's interdependence with the ocean, asking each of us to appreciate, protect and use the ocean wisely. 23rd annual. For info: Pres/Co-Founder, Cynthia Hancock, Natl Week of the Ocean, Inc, PO Box 179, Ft Lauderdale, FL 33302. Phone: (954) 462-5573. Web: www.national-week-of-the-ocean.org.

NEWSPAPER ASSOCIATION OF AMERICA ANNUAL CONVENTION. Apr 2–5. The Fairmont Chicago, Chicago, IL. For info: Newspaper Association of America, 1921 Gallows Rd, Ste 600, Vienna, VA 22182. Phone: (703) 902-1600. Web: www.naa.org.

NICKELODEON PREMIERE: ANNIVERSARY. Apr 2, 1979. Nickelodeon, the cable TV channel for kids owned by MTV Networks, debuted on this date.

PASCUA FLORIDA DAY. Apr 2. A legal holiday in Florida, designated as State Day. When it falls on a Saturday or Sunday, the governor may declare either the preceding Friday or the following Monday as State Day. Florida also observes Pascua Florida Week from Mar 27–Apr 2. Commemorates the sighting of Florida by Ponce de Leon in 1513. He named the land Pascua Florida because of its discovery at Easter, the "Feast of the Flowers."

PASSIONTIDE. Apr 2–15. The last two weeks of Lent (Passion Week and Holy Week), beginning with the fifth Sunday of Lent (Passion Sunday) and continuing through the day before Easter (Holy Saturday or Easter Even).

PONCE DE LEON DISCOVERS FLORIDA: ANNIVERSARY. Apr 2, 1513. Juan Ponce de Leon discovered Florida, landing at the site that became the city of St. Augustine. He claimed the land for the King of Spain.

POPE JOHN PAUL II: DEATH ANNIVERSARY. Apr 2, 2005. Karol Wojtyla, 264th pope of the Roman Catholic Church, elected Oct 16, 1978, died at The Vatican on Apr 2, 2005.

RECONCILIATION DAY. Apr 2. Columnist Ann Landers wrote, "Since 1989, I have suggested that April 2 be set aside to write that letter or make that phone call and mend a broken relationship. Life is too short to hold grudges. To forgive can be enormously life-enhancing. . . ."

TUSKEGEE UNIVERSITY 125TH ANNIVERSARY CELEBRATION/FOUNDER'S DAY CONVOCATION. Apr 2. Tuskegee University, Tuskegee, AL. Official celebration of Tuskegee University's founding in 1881 and the 150th anniversary of Booker T. Washington's birth. For info: Public and Media Affairs, Tuskegee University, 223 Kresge Center, Tuskegee, AL 36088. Phone: (334) 727-8349. E-mail: media@tuskegee.edu. Web: www.tuskegee.edu.

US MINT: ANNIVERSARY. Apr 2, 1792. The first US Mint was established at Philadelphia, PA, as authorized by an act of Congress.

WEEK OF THE YOUNG CHILD. Apr 2–8. To focus on the importance of quality early childhood education. For info: Natl Assn for the Educ of Young Children, 1509 16th St NW, Washington, DC 20036. Phone: (800) 424-2460. Fax: (202) 328-1846. E-mail: naeyc@naeyc.org. Web: www.naeyc.org.

WHITE, CHARLES: BIRTH ANNIVERSARY. Apr 2, 1918. Renowned African-American artist, born at Chicago, IL; died Oct 3, 1979. Charles White began his professional career by painting murals for the WPA during the Depression. He was influenced by Mexican muralists Diego Rivera and David Alfaro Siqueiros. Among his most notable creations are: *J'Accuse* (1966), a series of charcoal drawings depicting a variety of African Americans from all ages and walks of life; the *Wanted* posters (c. 1969), a series of paintings based on old runaway slave posters; and *Homage to Langston Hughes* (1971).

ZOLA, ÉMILE: BIRTH ANNIVERSARY. Apr 2, 1840. Prolific French novelist of the naturalist school, remembered especially for his role in the Dreyfus case (resulting in retrial and vindication of Alfred Dreyfus). Émile Edouard Charles Antoine Zola was born at Paris, France. Defective venting of a stove flue in his bedroom (which some believed to be the work of political enemies) resulted in his death from carbon monoxide poisoning at Paris, Sept 28, 1902.

BIRTHDAYS TODAY

Emmylou Harris, 59, singer ("Amarillo," "Till I Gain Control Again"), born Birmingham, AL, Apr 2, 1947.
Linda Hunt, 61, actress ("The Practice"; Oscar for *The Year of Living Dangerously*), born Morristown, NJ, Apr 2, 1945.
Christopher Meloni, 45, actor (*Runaway Bride*, "Law & Order: SVU"), born Washington, DC, Apr 2, 1961.
Camille Paglia, 59, literature professor and literary and cultural critic, born Endicott, NY, Apr 2, 1947.
Pamela Reed, 53, actress (*The Right Stuff, Bob Roberts*; stage: *Getting Out* [Drama Desk Award]), born Tacoma, WA, Apr 2, 1953 (some sources say 1949).
Leon Russell, 65, musician, born Lawton, OK, Apr 2, 1941.

APRIL 3 — MONDAY
Day 93 — 272 Remaining

AZALEA FESTIVAL. Apr 3–30. Muskogee, OK. One of the oldest and most celebrated public parks in the southwest: 122 acres, 40 acres of manicured gardens with 30,000 azaleas of 625 varieties. Ranked in the top 100 events by the National Bus Association. Annually in April since 1967. Many related events take place during the month, including a parade and a chili cookoff. Contact Muskogee Convention and Tourism for specific dates and events. Est attendance: 300,000. For info: Ervalene Jenkins, Muskogee Convention and Tourism, PO Box 2361, Muskogee, OK 74402. Phone: (888) 687-6137. Fax: (918) 684-6364. E-mail: tourism@muskogeeonline.org. Web: www.cityofmuskogee.com.

BIRMINGHAM RESISTANCE: ANNIVERSARY. Apr 3, 1962. In retaliation against a black boycott of downtown stores, the Birmingham, AL, city commission voted not to pay the city's $45,000 share of a $100,000 county program which supplied surplus food to the needy. More than 90 percent of the recipients of aid were black. When the NAACP protested the commission's decision, Birmingham Mayor Arthur J. Hanes dismissed their complaint as a "typical reaction from New York Socialist radicals."

BLACKS RULED ELIGIBLE TO VOTE: ANNIVERSARY. Apr 3, 1944. The US Supreme Court, in an 8–1 ruling, declared that blacks could not be barred from voting in the Texas Democratic primaries. The high court repudiated the contention that political parties are private associations and held that discrimination against blacks violated the 15th Amendment.

BOSTON PUBLIC LIBRARY: ANNIVERSARY. Apr 3, 1848. The Massachusetts legislature passed legislation enabling Boston to levy a tax for a public library. This created the funding model for all public libraries in the US. The Boston Public Library opened its doors in 1854.

BRANDO, MARLON: BIRTH ANNIVERSARY. Apr 3, 1924. Born at Omaha, NE, Marlon Brando was perhaps the most influential film actor of his generation. Using the "Method" style of acting as taught by Stella Adler, his powerful performances in *A Streetcar Named Desire* (1951) and *Viva Zapata!* (1952) established his presence as a star, and *On the Waterfront* (1953) earned him an Academy Award. Later films included *Last Tango in Paris* (1972) and *Apocalypse Now* (1979), but he is perhaps best-remembered for his role as Vito Corleone from *The Godfather* (1972), for which he won his second Oscar. Somewhat of a recluse later in his life, he died July 1, 2004, at Los Angeles, CA.

BURROUGHS, JOHN: BIRTH ANNIVERSARY. Apr 3, 1837. American naturalist and author, born at Roxbury, NY. "Time does not become sacred to us until we have lived it," he wrote in 1877. Died en route from California to New York, Mar 29, 1921.

FALL OF RICHMOND: ANNIVERSARY. Apr 3, 1865. After the withdrawal of Robert E. Lee's troops, the Confederate capital of Richmond and nearby Petersburg surrendered to Union forces on this day. Richmond had survived four years of continuous threats from the North. On Apr 4, the city was toured by President Abraham Lincoln.

GRAHAM, CALVIN "BABY VET": BIRTH ANNIVERSARY. Apr 3, 1930. The man who became known as WWII's "baby vet," Calvin Graham was born at Canton, TX, and enlisted in the navy at the age of 12. As a gunner on the USS *South Dakota*, he was struck by shrapnel during the battle of Guadalcanal in 1942 but still helped pull fellow crew members to safety. The navy gave Graham a dishonorable discharge, revoked his disability benefits and stripped him of his decorations, including a Purple Heart and Bronze Star, after discovering his age. Eventually, through congressional efforts, he was granted an honorable discharge and won back all but the Purple Heart. His benefits were restored in 1988. Graham died Nov 6, 1992, at Fort Worth, TX.

GUINEA: ANNIVERSARY OF THE SECOND REPUBLIC. Apr 3. National holiday. Commemorates the establishment of the Second Republic in 1984.

HAUPTMANN EXECUTION: 70th ANNIVERSARY. Apr 3, 1936. Bruno Richard Hauptmann, found guilty of the kidnapping and murder of Charles A. Lindbergh, Jr, was executed on this date in the electric chair. The kidnapping and trial gripped the nation, who mourned the death of aviation heroes Charles and Anne Lindbergh's baby. See also: "Lindbergh Kidnapping: Anniversary" (Mar 1).

HOWARD, LESLIE: BIRTH ANNIVERSARY. Apr 3, 1893. During the return trip from a British government-sponsored tour of Spain, a plane transporting 50-year-old actor Leslie Howard was shot down by German raiders. Rumors that he was serving on a spy mission for his government circulated at the time. In her biography about her father (*A Quite Remarkable Father*) his daughter expressed doubt that her father was the sort to get involved in espionage. Howard's most-remembered film role is that of Ashley Wilkes in *Gone with the Wind*. Born at London, England; died at sea June 1, 1943.

INAUGURATION OF PONY EXPRESS: ANNIVERSARY. Apr 3, 1860. The Pony Express began when the first rider left St. Joseph, MO. The following day another rider headed east from Sacramento, CA. For $5 an ounce letters were delivered within 10 days. There were 190 way stations between 10 and 15 miles apart, and each rider had a "run" of between 75 and 100 miles. The Pony Express lasted less than two years, ceasing operation in October 1861, when the overland telegraph was completed.

IRVING, WASHINGTON: BIRTH ANNIVERSARY. Apr 3, 1783. American author, attorney and one-time US minister to Spain, Irving was born at New York, NY. Creator of *Rip Van Winkle* and *The Legend of Sleepy Hollow*, he was also the author of many historical and biographical works, including *A History of the Life and Voyages of Christopher Columbus* and the *Life of Washington*. Died at Tarrytown, NY, Nov 28, 1859.

ISLE ROYALE NATIONAL PARK ESTABLISHED: ANNIVERSARY. Apr 3, 1940. Isle Royale is the largest of a group of more than 200 islands that make up this national park preserve. To preserve upper Michigan's flora and fauna, Congress authorized a national park in 1931 and it was established in 1940.

LUCE, HENRY: BIRTH ANNIVERSARY. Apr 3, 1898. American editor and publisher, born to missionary parents at Penglai, China. He built his publishing empire with *Time, Fortune, Life* and *Sports Illustrated*. Luce also was involved in broadcasting. Died at Phoenix, AZ, Feb 28, 1967.

MARSHALL PLAN: ANNIVERSARY. Apr 3, 1948. Suggested by Secretary of State George C. Marshall in a speech at Harvard, June 5, 1947, the legislation for the European Recovery Program, popularly known as the Marshall Plan, was signed by President Truman on Apr 3, 1948. After distributing more than $12 billion, the program ended in 1952.

NATIONAL WORKPLACE NAPPING DAY. Apr 3. This is a day for employees to "lie down and be counted" in support of napping at the workplace. This day occurs on the Monday following the advent of daylight saving time. For info: The Napping Co. Inc, 26 Orchard Park Dr, Reading, MA 01867. Phone: (781) 944-3506. E-mail: wanthony@bu.edu. Web: www.napping.com.

RAINEY, MA (GERTRUDE BRIDGET): BIRTH ANNIVERSARY. Apr 3, 1888. Known as the "Mother of the Blues," Gertrude "Ma" Rainey was born at Columbus, GA. She made her stage debut at the Columbus Opera House in 1900 in a talent show called "The Bunch of Blackberries." After touring together as "Rainey and Rainey, the Assassinators of the Blues," she and her husband eventually separated and she toured on her own. She made her first recording in 1923 and her last on Dec 28, 1928, after being told that the rural southern blues she sang had gone out of style. She died Dec 22, 1939, at Columbus, GA.

RAND, SALLY: BIRTH ANNIVERSARY. Apr 3, 1904. American actress, ecdysiast and inventor of the fan dance, which gained fame at the 1933 Chicago World's Fair. Born Helen Gould Beck at Hickory County, MO. Died at Glendora, CA, Aug 31, 1979.

TWEED DAY: ANNIVERSARY. Apr 3, 1823. Day to consider the cost of political corruption. Birthday of William March Tweed, New York City political boss, whose "Tweed Ring" is said to have stolen $30 million to $200 million from the city. Born at New York, NY, Apr 3, 1823, he died in his cell at New York's Ludlow Street Jail, Apr 12, 1878. Cartoonist Thomas Nast deserves much credit for Tweed's arrests and convictions.

***2001: A SPACE ODYSSEY* PREMIERE: ANNIVERSARY.** Apr 3, 1968. Directed by Stanley Kubrick, this influential film has elicited many different interpretations. Sci-fi novelist Arthur C. Clarke based the screenplay on his 1966 book which was prescient in several ways. Written before men had landed on the moon, Clarke describes an expedition launched to Jupiter to track a mysterious signal emanating from the moon. Clarke gave the world's population as six billion (achieved in 1999) and described a space station. During flight, a character reads the news on his electronic newspad. The film starred Keir Dullea, William Sylvester, Gary Lockwood, Daniel Richter and HAL 9000, the creepy computer that had human emotions. The theme music was Richard Strauss's *Also Sprach Zarathrustra*.

April 2006	S	M	T	W	T	F	S
							1
	2	3	4	5	6	7	8
	9	10	11	12	13	14	15
	16	17	18	19	20	21	22
	23	24	25	26	27	28	29
	30						

WOMAN PRESIDES OVER US SUPREME COURT: ANNIVERSARY.
Apr 3, 1995. Supreme Court Justice Sandra Day O'Connor became the first woman to preside over the US high court when she sat in for Chief Justice William H. Rehnquist and second in seniority Justice John Paul Stevens when both were out of town.

BIRTHDAYS TODAY

Alec Baldwin, 48, actor (*The Cooler, The Hunt for Red October*), born Massapequa, NY, Apr 3, 1958.

Amanda Bynes, 20, actress (*Big Fat Liar*, "What I Like About You"), born Thousand Oaks, CA, Apr 3, 1986.

Doris Day, 82, actress, singer ("Young at Heart," *The Man Who Knew Too Much, Pillow Talk*, "The Doris Day Show"), born Doris Von Kappelhoff at Cincinnati, OH, Apr 3, 1924.

Max Frankel, 76, journalist, born Gera, Germany, Apr 3, 1930.

Jennie Garth, 34, actress ("Beverly Hills 90210"), born Champaign, IL, Apr 3, 1972.

Jane Goodall (Baroness Van Lawick-Goodall), 72, anthropologist known for study of chimpanzees, born London, England, Apr 3, 1934.

Jonathan Lynn, 63, writer, actor, director (*Into the Night, Nuns on the Run, My Cousin Vinny*), born Bath, England, Apr 3, 1943.

Marsha Mason, 64, actress (*The Goodbye Girl, Cinderella Liberty*), born St. Louis, MO, Apr 3, 1942.

Eddie Murphy, 45, comedian ("Saturday Night Live"), actor (*Dr. Dolittle, Trading Places, Beverly Hills Cop*), born Brooklyn, NY, Apr 3, 1961.

Wayne Newton, 64, singer ("Danke Schoen," "Daddy Don't You Walk So Fast"), born Norfolk, VA, Apr 3, 1942.

Michael Olowokandi, 31, basketball player, born Lagos, Nigeria, Apr 3, 1975.

Tony Orlando, 62, singer (Tony Orlando and Dawn, "Tie a Yellow Ribbon Round the Old Oak Tree"), born Michael Orlando Cassivitis at New York, NY, Apr 3, 1944.

Bernie Parent, 61, Hall of Fame hockey player, born Montreal, QC, Canada, Apr 3, 1945.

David Hyde Pierce, 47, actor ("Frasier"), born Albany, NY, Apr 3, 1959.

Picabo Street, 35, Olympic skier, born Triumph, ID, Apr 3, 1971.

APRIL 4 — TUESDAY
Day 94 — 271 Remaining

BEATLES TAKE OVER MUSIC CHARTS: ANNIVERSARY.
Apr 4, 1964. On this date The Beatles held the top five positions of the Billboard Hot 100 chart: "Can't Buy Me Love" was number one, followed by (in order) "Twist and Shout," "She Loves You," "I Want To Hold Your Hand" and "Please, Please Me." The Beatles had made their first US appearance barely two months before. In the same week they held the top six places on the Australian music chart.

BONZA BOTTLER DAY™.
Apr 4. To celebrate when the number of the day is the same as the number of the month. Bonza Bottler Day™ is an excuse to have a party at least once a month. For more information, see Jan 1. For info: Gail M. Berger, 14 Fernwood Dr, Taylors, SC 29687. Phone: (864) 609-9874. E-mail: gberger5@aol.com.

BRANSON FEST.
Apr 4–8. Branson, MO. The Branson area's kickoff to a new season of great entertainment! The celebration of Ozarks entertainment, food, arts and culture features some of Branson's best-known performers and a taste of all the Branson area has to offer. For info: Branson/Lakes Area Chamber of Commerce and CVB, PO Box 1897, Branson, MO 65615. Phone: (800) 951-1441. Fax: (417) 334-4139. E-mail: info@bransoncvb.com. Web: www.explorebranson.com.

DIX, DOROTHEA LYNDE: BIRTH ANNIVERSARY.
Apr 4, 1802. American social reformer and author, born at Hampden, ME. Left home at age 10, was teaching at age 14 and founded a home for girls at Boston while still in her teens. In spite of frail health, she was a vigorous crusader for humane conditions in insane asylums, jails and almshouses and for the establishment of state-supported institutions to serve those needs. Named superintendent of women nurses during the Civil War. Died at Trenton, NJ, July 17, 1887.

FLAG ACT OF 1818: ANNIVERSARY.
Apr 4, 1818. Congress approved the first flag of the US.

GIAMATTI, ANGELO BARTLETT: BIRTH ANNIVERSARY.
Apr 4, 1938. Baseball commissioner and former president of Yale University. Born at Boston, MA, Giamatti was the youngest person to be named president of Yale, at the age of 39, in 1978. He became the president of Major League Baseball's National League in 1986 and served in that capacity until he was appointed Commissioner of Baseball Apr 1, 1989. An accomplished author, he moved freely between the worlds of literature and baseball, often linking the two in the many articles he wrote. One week prior to his death, he suspended Pete Rose for life for betting on baseball games. Giamatti died at Martha's Vineyard, MA, Sept 1, 1989.

HATE WEEK.
Apr 4–10. Recognizes the day on which the fictional character Winston Smith started his secret diary and wrote the words "DOWN WITH BIG BROTHER," Wednesday, Apr 4, 1984. From George Orwell's dystopian novel, *1984*, portraying the end of human privacy and the destruction of the individual in a totalitarian state (first published in 1949). "Hates" varied from the daily two-minute concentrated hate to the grand culmination observed during Hate Week.

KING, MARTIN LUTHER, JR: ASSASSINATION: ANNIVERSARY.
Apr 4, 1968. The Reverend Dr. Martin Luther King, Jr, was shot at Memphis, TN. James Earl Ray was serving a 99-year sentence for the crime at the time of his death in 1998. See also: "King, Martin Luther, Jr: Birth Anniversary" (Jan 15).

KING OPPOSES VIETNAM WAR: ANNIVERSARY.
Apr 4, 1967. Speaking before the Overseas Press Club at New York City, Reverend Dr. Martin Luther King, Jr, announced his opposition to the Vietnam War. That same day, at the Riverside Church at Harlem, King suggested that those who saw the war as dishonorable and unjust should avoid military service. He proposed that the US take new initiatives to conclude the war.

LADY BE GOOD LOST: ANNIVERSARY.
Apr 4, 1943. The nine-man crew of the WWII American Liberator bomber *Lady Be Good* bailed out 200 miles off course over the Sahara Desert and disappeared. They were returning to their base in Libya after a raid over southern Italy. On Nov 9, 1958, 15 years after the plane went down and more than 13 years after the war had ended, a pilot flying across the Sahara south of Tobruck sighted wreckage of an aircraft in the sand. Eight skeletons and a diary describing the final days of the crew were recovered near the wreckage. The radio, guns and ammunition in the plane were in working order.

NORTH ATLANTIC TREATY RATIFIED: ANNIVERSARY.
Apr 4, 1949. The North Atlantic Treaty Organization was created by this treaty, which was signed by 12 nations, including the US. (Other countries joined later.) The NATO member nations are united for common defense. The treaty went into effect Apr 24, 1949, and the first session of the North Atlantic Council was held Sept 17, 1949.

PERKINS, ANTHONY: BIRTH ANNIVERSARY. Apr 4, 1932. American actor Anthony Perkins was born at New York, NY. Best known for his movie role as homicidal innkeeper Norman Bates in the film *Psycho* (1960), Perkins appeared in many Broadway plays in addition to his numerous film roles. He received an Oscar nomination for his supporting role in *Friendly Persuasion* (1956). Perkins died Sept 12, 1992, at Hollywood, CA.

SALTER ELECTED FIRST WOMAN MAYOR IN US: ANNIVERSARY. Apr 4, 1887. The first woman elected mayor in the US was Susanna Medora Salter, who was elected mayor of Argonia, KS. Her name had been submitted for election without her knowledge by the Women's Christian Temperance Union, and she did not know she was a candidate until she went to the polls to vote. She received a two-thirds majority vote and served one year for the salary of $1.

SENEGAL: INDEPENDENCE DAY. Apr 4. National holiday. Commemorates independence from France in 1960.

SMOTHERS BROTHERS FIRED: ANNIVERSARY. Apr 4, 1969. CBS canceled the brothers' popular comedy series on this date. The hour-long show strongly influenced television humor during the two years it aired. Tom and Dick, however, frequently found themselves at odds with the censors over material that would be considered tame today. Guests and cast members frequently knocked the Vietnam War and the Nixon Administration. Acts featuring antiwar protestors such as Harry Belafonte were often cut.

SPACE MILESTONE: *CHALLENGER STS-6* (US). Apr 4, 1983. Shuttle *Challenger* launched from Kennedy Space Center, FL, with four astronauts (Paul Weitz, Karol Bobko, Storey Musgrave and Donald Peterson). Four-hour space walk by Musgrave and Peterson. Landed at Edwards Air Force Base, CA, Apr 9.

SWAYZE, JOHN CAMERON: 100th BIRTH ANNIVERSARY. Apr 4, 1906. Pioneering television journalist whose catchphrase was "hopscotching the world for news." Swayze was one of the first reporters to do on-air interviews and report on breaking news stories. Born at Wichita, KS, he died at Sarasota, FL, Aug 15, 1995.

VITAMIN C ISOLATED: ANNIVERSARY. Apr 4, 1932. Vitamin C was first isolated by C.C. King at the University of Pittsburgh.

WATERS, MUDDY: BIRTH ANNIVERSARY. Apr 4, 1915. Born McKinley Morganfield at Rolling Fork, MS, American blues guitarist and singer Muddy Waters played a significant part in developing modern rhythm and blues that came to be known as Chicago or urban blues. It was predominantly from this music that later forms such as rock and roll and soul sprang. Muddy Waters died at Westmont, IL, Apr 30, 1983.

YALE, LINUS: BIRTH ANNIVERSARY. Apr 4, 1821. American portrait painter and inventor of the lock that is named for him was born at Salisbury, NY. He was creator of the Yale Infallible Bank Lock and developer of the cylinder lock. Yale died at New York, NY, Dec 25, 1868.

YAMAMOTO, ISOROKU: BIRTH ANNIVERSARY. Apr 4, 1884. Considered Japan's greatest naval strategist, Admiral Isoroku Yamamoto, who planned the attack on Pearl Harbor, was born at Nagaoka, Honshu. Yamamoto also devised the complex attack on Midway Island which ended in defeat for the Japanese because the Allies had the key to the Imperial fleet code and were prepared for the June 4, 1942, attack. The US intercepted reports of Yamamoto's proposed 1943 tour of the Western Solomons and shot down his plane Apr 18, while he was touring Japanese installations in the area.

BIRTHDAYS TODAY

Maya Angelou, 78, poet, author (*I Know Why the Caged Bird Sings*), born St. Louis, MO, Apr 4, 1928.
David Blaine, 33, magician, born Brooklyn, NY, Apr 4, 1973.
Robert Downey, Jr, 41, actor (*Chaplin, Short Cuts, Natural Born Killers*), born New York, NY, Apr 4, 1965.
Kitty Kelley, 64, author (*Jackie Oh!, Nancy Reagan*), born Hartford, CT, Apr 4, 1942.
Christine Lahti, 56, actress (Emmys for "Chicago Hope"; *Swing Shift*), director (Oscar for "Lieberman in Love"), born Birmingham, MI, Apr 4, 1950.
Heath Ledger, 27, actor (*The Four Feathers, A Knight's Tale, The Patriot*), born Perth, Australia, Apr 4, 1979.
Richard G. Lugar, 74, US Senator (R, Indiana), born Indianapolis, IN, Apr 4, 1932.
Nancy McKeon, 40, actress ("The Facts of Life," "The Division"), born Westbury, NY, Apr 4, 1966.
Dave Mirra, 34, BMX bike racer, born Syracuse, NY, Apr 4, 1972.
Craig T. Nelson, 60, actor ("Coach," *Private Benjamin, Poltergeist, The Killing Fields*), born Spokane, WA, Apr 4, 1946.
Michael Parks, 68, actor ("Then Came Bronson," "Twin Peaks," *The Happening*), born Corona, CA, Apr 4, 1938.
Barry Pepper, 36, actor (*Saving Private Ryan, Enemy of the State*), born Campbell River, BC, Canada, Apr 4, 1970.
Scott Rolen, 31, baseball player, born Evansville, IN, Apr 4, 1975.
Elizabeth Wilson, 81, actress (*The Prisoner of Second Avenue, The Addams Family*; stage: *Taken in Marriage*), born Grand Rapids, MI, Apr 4, 1925.

APRIL 5 — WEDNESDAY
Day 95 — 270 Remaining

ACCELERATE ACL AWARENESS AMONG YOUNG WOMEN DAY. Apr 5. This national AAAYW day will launch an annual campaign targeting parents, young athletes, coaches and all educators with national workshops to educate young women on how to prevent and treat ACL injuries with proper sports training and conditioning programs. Recent studies indicate that the risk of female ACL injuries is five to six times greater than it is for males, and can begin as early as puberty for those who participate in noncontact sports such as soccer, basketball and volleyball. Annually, the first Wednesday in April. For info: Diana Aceti, PO Box 1919, Bridgehampton, NY 11932. Phone/fax: (631) 613-6057. E-mail: dmaceti@aol.com. Web: www.kneehippain.com.

CHINA: QING MING FESTIVAL OR TOMB SWEEPING DAY. Apr 5. This Confucian festival was traditionally celebrated on the fourth or fifth day of the third month but is now on fixed dates (Apr 3, 4 or 5) in China. It is observed by the maintenance of ancestral graves, the presentation of food, wine and flowers as offerings and the burning of paper money at gravesides to help ancestors in the afterworld. People also picnic and gather for family meals. Also observed in Taiwan.

DAVIS, BETTE: BIRTH ANNIVERSARY. Apr 5, 1908. American actress Bette Davis was born Ruth Elizabeth Davis at Lowell, MA. In addition to acting in more than 80 films, earning 10 Academy Award nominations and winning the best actress Academy Award twice, for *Dangerous* (1935) and *Jezebel* (1938), Davis also claimed to have nicknamed the Academy Award "Oscar" after her first husband, Harmon Oscar Nelson, Jr. She died Oct 6, 1989, at Neuilly-sur-Seine, France.

	S	M	T	W	T	F	S
April							1
2006	2	3	4	5	6	7	8
	9	10	11	12	13	14	15
	16	17	18	19	20	21	22
	23	24	25	26	27	28	29
	30						

DISCOTHEQUE BOMBING: 20th ANNIVERSARY. Apr 5, 1986. A bomb exploded at a popular discotheque in West Berlin, Germany, killing two American soldiers and a Turkish woman. Although three groups claimed responsibility for the bombing, American intelligence organizations attributed it to orders from Libyan head-of-state Muammar el-Qaddafi, and President Reagan ordered a retaliatory air strike on Libya. On Apr 14, 1986 (Apr 15, Libyan time), American forces launched a bombing attack on the cities of Tripoli and Benghazi, reportedly killing 37 (including a daughter of Qaddafi). Nearly two years later, on Jan 11, 1988, West German authorities arrested 27-year-old Christine Gabriele Endrigkeit, charging her with the bombing, citing "clues" that it might have been ordered by Syrian agents.

DOGWOOD ARTS FESTIVAL. Apr 5–23. Knoxville, TN. The South's premier celebration with more than 60 miles of dogwood trails and more than 100 events featuring arts, crafts, parades, musical performances and much more. Est attendance: 250,000. For info: Dogwood Arts Festival, 601 W Summit Hill Dr, Knoxville, TN 37902. Phone: (865) 637-4561. Web: www.dogwoodarts.com.

"FIRESIDE THEATRE" TV PREMIERE: ANNIVERSARY. Apr 5, 1949. Gene Raymond and later Jane Wyman hosted this NBC anthology program consisting of 15- and 30-minute dramas. One of its most acclaimed presentations was "The Reign of Amelika Jo" on Oct 12, 1954. It was set in the South Pacific during WW II and had a mostly black and Asian cast.

FIRST US CHAMBER OF COMMERCE FOUNDED: ANNIVERSARY. Apr 5, 1768. The first chamber of commerce in the US was founded at New York City.

HELEN KELLER'S MIRACLE: ANNIVERSARY. Apr 5, 1887. Anne Sullivan went to Tuscumbia, AL, in March 1887 to teach the "unteachable" deaf and blind Helen Keller. Although Keller was resistant, Sullivan was determined, and after only one month she succeeded in reaching her: she placed Keller's hand under a gushing water pump and used sign language to spell "w-a-t-e-r" into her palm. Helen grasped the meaning—spelling the word back into Sullivan's palm—and excitedly learned 30 more words that day. Keller's life changed at that breakthrough moment, as she recalled later: "As the cool stream gushed over one hand . . . I felt a misty consciousness as of something forgotten, a thrill of returning thought, and somehow the mystery of language was revealed to me." Keller would go on to become the first deaf and blind person to graduate from college, write books and crusade for the disabled. See also: "Keller, Helen: Birth Anniversary" (June 27).

LISTER, JOSEPH: BIRTH ANNIVERSARY. Apr 5, 1827. English physician who was the founder of aseptic surgery, born at Upton, Essex, England. Died at Walmer, England, Feb 10, 1912.

"MARRIED . . . WITH CHILDREN" TV PREMIERE: ANNIVERSARY. Apr 5, 1987. This raunchy Fox TV show premiered as the antidote to Cosby-style family shows. Ed O'Neill starred as boorish, luckless shoe salesman Al Bundy, Katey Sagal portrayed Al's big-haired, spandex-clad, sex-starved wife Peggy, Christina Applegate played airheaded bombshell daughter Kelly and David Faustino played hormone-driven son Bud. The last episode aired Apr 20, 1997.

MOON PHASE: FIRST QUARTER. Apr 5. Moon enters First Quarter phase at 8:01 AM, EDT.

NURSING CONFERENCE ON PEDIATRIC PRIMARY CARE. Apr 5–8. Washington, DC. Offers continuing education on clinical practice, professional development and legislative issues relevant to the nursing profession. Est attendance: 1,200. For info: Natl Assn of Pediatric Nurse Practitioners, 20 Brace Rd, Ste 200, Cherry Hill, NJ 08034-2633. Phone: (856) 857-9700. Fax: (856) 857-1600. E-mail: info@napnap.org. Web: www.napnap.org.

PARAPROFESSIONAL APPRECIATION DAY. Apr 5. Originally established several years ago by the governor of Missouri, this holiday honors the contributions of paraprofessionals, especially in education. Annually, the first Wednesday in April. For info: Valerie Pennington, McQuerry Elementary School, 607 S Third St, Odessa, MO 64076. Phone: (816) 633-5334. E-mail: vpenning@odessa.k12.mo.us.

PECK, GREGORY: BIRTH ANNIVERSARY. Apr 5, 1916. Born Eldred Gregory Peck at La Jolla, CA, Gregory Peck was one of Hollywood's most popular and likeable leading men. Nominated five times for best actor, he finally won the Oscar for his role as Atticus Finch in 1962's *To Kill a Mockingbird*. Other popular films included *Roman Holiday, Gentleman's Agreement* and Alfred Hitchcock's *Spellbound*. He also founded the La Jolla Playhouse with Dorothy McGuire and Mel Ferrer in 1947, and appeared there throughout his career. He died at his home in La Jolla on June 11, 2003.

RESNIK, JUDITH A.: BIRTH ANNIVERSARY. Apr 5, 1949. Dr. Judith A. Resnik, the second American woman in space (1984), was born at Akron, OH. The 36-year-old electrical engineer was mission specialist on space shuttle *Challenger*. She perished with all others aboard when *Challenger* exploded Jan 28, 1986. See also: "*Challenger* Space Shuttle Explosion: Anniversary" (Jan 28).

"SECRET AGENT" TV PREMIERE: 45th ANNIVERSARY. Apr 5, 1961. Before Patrick McGoohan became "The Prisoner," he played the role of intelligence agent John Drake on this CBS adventure series. Produced in England by ATV, it also aired there as "Danger Man."

STORIES DAY. Apr 5. A day to share stories with young children and to celebrate the benefits storytelling and reading provide for children and families. The Child Care Coalition of Lake County, IL, and local libraries, child care centers and other organizations declare this day for promoting activities that lead to children's literacy. Events will be held at libraries, child care centers, preschools, schools and many people's homes. Groups and people everywhere are encouraged to share stories with children. Annually, the Wednesday of the Week of the Young Child. For info: The Child Care Coalition of Lake County, 655 Rockland Rd, #4, Lake Bluff, IL 60044. E-mail: info@childcarecoalition.org. Web: www.childcarecoalition.org.

TAIWAN: NATIONAL TOMB-SWEEPING DAY. Apr 5. National holiday since 1972. According to Chinese custom, the tombs of ancestors are swept "clear and bright" and rites honoring ancestors are held. Tomb-Sweeping Day is observed Apr 5, which is also the anniversary of the death of Chiang Kai-Shek.

THANK YOU, SCHOOL LIBRARIAN DAY. Apr 5. Recognizes the unique contribution made by school librarians who are resource people extraordinaire, supporting the myriad educational needs of faculty, staff, students and parents *all year long*! Three cheers to all the public, private and parochial school infomaniacs whose true love of reading and lifelong learning make them great role models for kids of all ages. To help celebrate, take your school librarian to lunch, donate a book in his/her honor to the library, tell your librarian what a difference he/she has made in your life. Sponsor: "Carpe Libris" (Seize the Book), a loosely knit group of underappreciated librarians. For info: Judyth Lessee, Organizer, Carpe Libris, 3645 E Pima St, Tucson, AZ 85716. Phone: (520) 232-8424. E-mail: judyth.lessee@tusd.k12.az.us.

"THE TRACEY ULLMAN SHOW" TV PREMIERE: ANNIVERSARY. Apr 5, 1987. This Emmy award–winning comedy-variety show was one of the Fox network's early critical hits. Tracey Ullman starred with Julie Kavner, Dan Castellaneta, Joe Malone and Sam McMurray. The show, produced by James L. Brooks, contained sketches, songs and satire. Animated snippets in between segments introduced us to the Simpsons, executed by Matt Groening, creator of the "Life in Hell" comic strip. "The Simpsons" spun off from the show in 1990.

TRACY, SPENCER: BIRTH ANNIVERSARY. Apr 5, 1900. Born at Milwaukee, WI, Spencer Tracy was one of the most respected actors in film history. He won Academy Awards for best actor for 1937's *Captains Courageous* and 1938's *Boys Town*, and was nominated seven other times. In 1942, he met actress Katharine Hepburn, and they shared a relationship that lasted until his death, although they never married. Together, they starred in nine films, including *Adam's Rib* in 1949 and *Guess Who's Coming to Dinner* in 1967. Tracy died June 10, 1967, at Hollywood Hills, CA.

WASHINGTON, BOOKER TALIAFERRO: 150th BIRTH ANNIVERSARY. Apr 5, 1856. Black educator and leader born at Franklin County, VA. "No race can prosper," he wrote in *Up from Slavery*, "till it learns that there is as much dignity in tilling a field as in writing a poem." Died at Tuskegee, AL, Nov 14, 1915.

WAYNE STATE UNIVERSITY: FUNERAL FOR OL' MAN WINTER. Apr 5. Detroit, MI. Events include a New Orleans–style procession with band playing Dixieland music. "Miss Spring" and a local TV personality conduct an irreverent burial ceremony. Est attendance: 100. For info: Wayne State University, Detroit, MI 48202. Phone: (313) 577-2424. Web: www.map.wayne.edu/ffomw.html.

BIRTHDAYS TODAY

Jane Asher, 60, actress (*DreamChild, Brideshead Revisited*), born London, England, Apr 5, 1946.

Eric Burdon, 65, singer (*Eric Burdon Declares War, Black Man's Burdon*), songwriter, born Walker-on-Tyne, England, Apr 5, 1941.

Roger Corman, 80, filmmaker (king of B horror movies), born Detroit, MI, Apr 5, 1926.

Max Gail, 63, actor ("Barney Miller," *Pearl*), born Grosse Point, MI, Apr 5, 1943.

Michael Moriarty, 64, actor (*The Last Detail, Bang the Drum Slowly*, "Law & Order"), born Detroit, MI, Apr 5, 1942.

Mitch Pileggi, 54, actor ("The X-Files"), born Portland, OR, Apr 5, 1952.

Colin Luther Powell, 69, former US Secretary of State, general, former Chairman US Joint Chiefs of Staff, born New York, NY, Apr 5, 1937.

Gale Storm, 84, actress ("My Little Margie," "NBC Comedy Hour," "The Gale Storm Show"), born Bloomington, TX, Apr 5, 1922.

		S	M	T	W	T	F	S
April								1
2006		2	3	4	5	6	7	8
		9	10	11	12	13	14	15
		16	17	18	19	20	21	22
		23	24	25	26	27	28	29
		30						

APRIL 6 — THURSDAY

Day 96 — 269 Remaining

"BARNEY & FRIENDS" TV PREMIERE: ANNIVERSARY. Apr 6, 1992. Although most adults find it hopelessly saccharine, this PBS program is hugely popular with preschoolers. Purple dinosaur Barney, his pals, dinosaurs Baby Bop and B.J., and a multi-ethnic group of children sing, play games and learn simple lessons about getting along with one another.

BATTLE OF SHILOH: ANNIVERSARY. Apr 6, 1862. General Ulysess S. Grant's Union forces at Shiloh, or Pittsburgh Landing, TN, were attacked by a large force under General Albert Sidney Johnston on this date. After heavy fighting, the first day of the battle ended without a conclusive victory for either side. Grant was reinforced before the Confederates on the second day and Confederate General Beauregard, in command after Johnston's death the previous day, ordered a retreat back to Corinth, MS, leaving the Federal troops in a stronger position in Tennessee than before the battle. Losses on both sides totaled more than 23,000.

BRIGHAM YOUNG'S LAST MARRIAGE: ANNIVERSARY. Apr 6, 1868. Brigham Young, Mormon Church leader, married his 27th, and last, wife on this day.

CHURCH OF JESUS CHRIST OF LATTER-DAY SAINTS: ANNIVERSARY. Apr 6, 1830. Under the leadership of Joseph Smith, Jr, The Church of Jesus Christ of Latter-day Saints was founded with six members in a log cabin at Fayette, NY. For info: Church of Jesus Christ of Latter-day Saints, Public Affairs Dept, 15 E South Temple St, Salt Lake City, UT 84150. Phone: (801) 240-4395. Fax: (801) 240-1167.

FIRST MODERN OLYMPICS: ANNIVERSARY. Apr 6, 1896. The first modern Olympics formally opened at Athens, Greece, after a 1,500-year hiatus. Thirteen nations participated, represented by 235 male athletes.

FIRST TONY AWARDS PRESENTED: ANNIVERSARY. Apr 6, 1947. The American Theatre Wing bestowed the first annual Tony awards for distinguished service to the theater.

FIRST US CREDIT UNION LAW: ANNIVERSARY. Apr 6, 1909. The St. Canadian credit union of Manchester, NH, was chartered with the help of Alphonse Desjardins, Canadian credit union pioneer.

GANDHI MAKES SALT: ANNIVERSARY. Apr 6, 1930. Mohandas Gandhi, frustrated by British indifference to Indian civil rights demands, planned a symbolic, peaceful protest by conducting a 241-mile march from Sabarmati Ashram to the coast at Dandi. Leaving on Mar 12, Gandhi and his followers arrived at Dandi on Apr 5, and on Apr 6, he made salt by boiling sea water—a violation of the salt law, which granted royal monopoly in its manufacture and levied heavy taxes on its purchasers. His peaceful act and the two-mile-long procession that accompanied it gained worldwide headlines. Besides Gandhi, thousands of Indians were arrested as they, too, made salt in protest.

KINGSVILLE INTERNATIONAL YOUNG PERFORMERS' COMPETITIONS. Apr 6–8. Texas A&M University–Kingsville, TX. 25th annual international music competition for performers of classical music. Prodigies and aspiring concert artists under age 26 compete in separate contests for bowed orchestral instruments. Cash prizes total about $25,000. Performance awards with orchestra. All contest events are free and open to the public. Contestant's entry fee $50; deadline Jan 18, 2006. Sponsor: Music Club of Kingsville, Inc (affiliate of National Federation and Texas Federation of Music Clubs). Est attendance: 1,500. For info: Mary or James Tryer, 1222 W Lee, Kingsville, TX 78363. Phone: (361) 592-2374. E-mail: youngperf@hotmail.com. Web: www.kingsvillemusic.com.

LONESOME RIVER BAND MUSIC FEST. Apr 6–8. Live Oak, FL. Three days of extraordinary music. Previous artists have included The Marksmen, Nothin' Fancy, White Sands, Gary Waldrep Band, Smokey Green and more. Est attendance: 7,000. For info: Spirit of the Suwannee Music Park, 3076 95th Dr, Live Oak, FL 32060. Phone: (386) 364-1683. Fax: (386) 364-2998. E-mail: spirit@musicliveshere.com. Web: www.musicliveshere.com.

MULLIGAN, GERRY: BIRTH ANNIVERSARY. Apr 6, 1927. American jazz saxophonist Gerry Mulligan was born at New York, NY. He performed with many great jazz musicians including Miles Davis, Dave Brubeck, Chet Baker and Duke Ellington, and is credited with helping create the cool-jazz movement with Miles Davis. Mulligan died Jan 20, 1996, at Darien, CT.

NATIONAL ALCOHOL SCREENING DAY. Apr 6. To increase awareness of alcohol's effect on health and connect people with alcohol problems to treatment. Free, anonymous, nationwide. Annually, the Thursday of the first full week in April. For info: Screening for Mental Health, One Washington St, Ste 304, Wellesley Hills, MA 02481-1706. Phone: (781) 239-0071. Fax: (781) 431-7447. Web: www.mentalhealthscreening.org.

NATIONAL FUN AT WORK DAY. Apr 6. Today and every day the workplace should be spiced with fun, laughter and a playful attitude. Morale will increase, productivity will soar and the bottom line will improve. Annually, Apr 1 (or the following Thursday, if April 1 falls on a weekend). For info: Matt Weinstein, Playfair, 2207 Oregon St, Berkeley, CA 94705. Phone: (510) 540-8768. Fax: (510) 540-7638. E-mail: playfair1@aol.com. Web: www.playfair.com.

NCAA DIVISION I MEN'S ICE HOCKEY CHAMPIONSHIP. Apr 6 & 8. Bradley Center, Milwaukee, WI. For info: NCAA, PO Box 6222, Indianapolis, IN 46206-6222. Web: www.ncaasports.com.

NEW YORK STATE MISSING PERSONS DAY. Apr 6. New York State Missing Persons Memorial, Albany, NY. A new memorial will be dedicated on this day. The Center for HOPE sponsors this event for family members and friends of adults and children who have gone missing. Family members participate in a ceremony to remember their missing loved ones; listen to words of hope, comfort and support from other survivors; and share their stories with each other. For info: Doug & Mary Lyall, The Center for HOPE, 20 Prospect St, Ste 103, Chocolate Factory, Ballston Spa, NY 12020. Phone: (518) 884-8761. Web: www.hope4themissing.org.

NORTH POLE DISCOVERED: ANNIVERSARY. Apr 6, 1909. Robert E. Peary reached the North Pole after several failed attempts. The team consisted of Peary, leader of the expedition; Matthew A. Henson, a black man who had served with Peary since 1886 as ship's cook, carpenter and blacksmith, and then as Peary's co-explorer and valuable assistant; and four Eskimo guides—Coquesh, Ootah, Eginwah and Seegloo. They sailed July 17, 1908, on the ship *Roosevelt*, wintering on Ellesmere Island. After a grueling trek with dwindling food supplies, Henson and two of the Eskimos were first to reach the Pole. An exhausted Peary arrived 45 minutes later and confirmed their location. Dr. Frederick A. Cook, surgeon on an earlier expedition with Peary, claimed to have reached the Pole first, but that could not be substantiated and the National Geographic Society credited the Peary expedition.

PORTLAND, OREGON: BIRTHDAY. Apr 6, 1851. "The City of Roses" adds a year today.

RAPHAEL: BIRTH ANNIVERSARY. Apr 6, 1483. Raffaello Santi (Sanzio), Italian painter and architect. Probably born Apr 6, 1483, at Urbino, Italy. Died on his birthday, at Rome, Italy, Apr 6, 1520.

SAVEUR TEXAS HILL COUNTRY WINE & FOOD FESTIVAL. Apr 6–9. Austin, TX. 21st annual. Come on down to Austin and join world-renowned superstar chefs and sommeliers for four days of Texas-flavored events dedicated to the wine and food that have inspired us for more than two decades. Festivities include cooking classes, tastings, kitchen presentations and lots more. For info: Pam Blanton, Blanton Public Relations, 502 Oakland Ave, Ste C, Austin, TX 78703. Phone: (512) 469-0702. Fax:

(512) 469-0706. E-mail: info@texaswineandfood.org. Web: www.texaswineandfood.org.

SCHNEIDERMAN, ROSE: BIRTH ANNIVERSARY. Apr 6, 1882. A pioneer in the battle to increase wages and improve working conditions for women, Rose Schneiderman was born at Saven, Poland, and her family immigrated to the US six years later. At age 16 she began factory work in New York City's garment district and quickly became a union organizer. Opposed to the open-shop policy, which permitted nonunion members to work in a unionized shop, Schneiderman organized a 1913 strike of 25,000 women shirtwaist makers. She worked as an organizer for the International Ladies Garment Workers Union (ILGWU) and for the Women's Trade Union League (WTUL), serving as president for more than 20 years. During the Great Depression President Roosevelt appointed her to his Labor Advisory Board—the only woman member. Died Aug 11, 1972, at New York, NY.

SCOTTSBORO TRIAL: 75th ANNIVERSARY. Apr 6, 1931. In what became a *cause célèbre*, nine black youths went on trial at Scottsboro, AL, accused of raping two white women on a freight train. All were convicted in a hasty trial, but by 1950 were free by parole, appeal or escape.

SWITZERLAND: NAFELS PILGRIMAGE. Apr 6. Canton Glarus. Commemoration of the Battle of Nafels, fought on Apr 9, 1388. Observed annually on first Thursday in April, with processions, prayers, sermon and a reading out of the names of those killed in the battle.

TARTAN DAY. Apr 6. Groups and societies throughout North America take the anniversary of the Declaration of Arbroath (1320) as the day to celebrate their Scottish roots. For more info: www.tartanday.com.

TEFLON INVENTED: ANNIVERSARY. Apr 6, 1938. Polytetraflouroethylene resin was invented by Roy J. Plunkett while he was employed by E.I. Du Pont de Nemours & Co. Commonly known as Teflon, it revolutionized the cookware industry. This substance or something similar coated three-quarters of the pots and pans in America at the time of Plunkett's death in 1994.

THAILAND: CHAKRI DAY. Apr 6. Commemorates the foundation of the present dynasty by King Rama I (1782–1809), who also established Bangkok as the country's capital.

THOMAS, LOWELL: BIRTH ANNIVERSARY. Apr 6, 1892. World traveler, reporter, editor and radio newscaster, whose broadcasts spanned more than half a century, 1925–76. His radio sign-off, "So long until tomorrow," was known to millions of listeners and he is said to have been the first to broadcast from a ship, an airplane, a submarine and a coal mine. Born at Woodington, OH, he died at Pawling, NY, Aug 29, 1981.

TRAGEDY IN RWANDA: ANNIVERSARY. Apr 6, 1994. A plane carrying the presidents of Rwanda and Burundi was shot down near Kigali, the Rwandan capital, exacerbating a brutal ethnic war that led to the massacre of hundreds of thousands. Presidents Juvenal Habyarimana of Rwanda and Cyprien Ntaryamira of Burundi were returning from a summit in Tanzania where they discussed ways of ending the killing in their countries sparked by ethnic rivalries between the Hutu and Tutsi tribes. Following the attack on the two leaders, Rwanda descended into chaos as the two tribes began killing each other in a genocidal battle for power, leading to a mass exodus of civilians caught in the maelstrom.

US ENTERS WORLD WAR I: ANNIVERSARY. Apr 6, 1917. Congress approved a declaration of war against Germany and the US entered WWI, which had begun in 1914. The first US "doughboys" landed in France June 27, 1917.

US SENATE ACHIEVES A QUORUM: ANNIVERSARY. Apr 6, 1789. The US Senate was formally organized after achieving a quorum.

BIRTHDAYS TODAY

Bret Boone, 37, baseball player, born El Cajon, CA, Apr 6, 1969.

Zach Braff, 31, actor ("Scrubs," *Garden State*), born South Orange, NJ, Apr 6, 1975.

Candace Cameron Bure, 30, actress ("Full House"), born Canoga Park, CA, Apr 6, 1976.

Merle Haggard, 69, singer, songwriter ("Okie from Muskogee"), born Bakersfield, CA, Apr 6, 1937.

Marilu Henner, 54, actress ("Taxi," "Evening Shade"), born Chicago, IL, Apr 6, 1952.

Olaf Kolzig, 36, former hockey player, born Johannesburg, South Africa, Apr 6, 1970.

Barry Levinson, 64, director, producer, writer, actor ("The Carol Burnett Show" [writer; Emmy Awards 1974, 1975], *Rain Man, Avalon, Bugsy*), born Baltimore, MD, Apr 6, 1942.

Andre Previn, 77, composer, conductor, born Berlin, Germany, Apr 6, 1929.

John Ratzenberger, 59, actor ("Cheers"), born Bridgeport, CT, Apr 6, 1947.

Paul Rudd, 37, actor (*The Object of My Affection, Clueless*), born Passaic, NJ, Apr 6, 1969.

Roy Thinnes, 68, actor ("The Invaders," "The Outer Limits"), born Chicago, IL, Apr 6, 1938.

James Watson, 78, discoverer (with Francis Crick) of the structure of DNA, born Chicago, IL, Apr 6, 1928.

Billy Dee Williams, 69, actor (*Brian's Song, Lady Sings the Blues, Return of the Jedi*), born New York, NY, Apr 6, 1937.

APRIL 7 — FRIDAY
Day 97 — 268 Remaining

ALCOHOL-FREE WEEKEND. Apr 7–9. Observance to increase public awareness of the problems associated with drinking alcoholic beverages by asking Americans to refrain from drinking them for this weekend. For info: Public Info Office, Natl Council on Alcoholism and Drug Dependence, Inc, 22 Cortlandt St, Ste 801, New York, NY 10007-3128. Phone: (212) 269-7797. Fax: (212) 269-7510. E-mail: national@ncadd.org. Web: www.ncadd.org.

BATTLE OF LYS RIVER: ANNIVERSARY. Apr 7, 1918. Having failed to break through Allied lines at Somme in March, General Erich Ludendorff made another attempt by attacking Flanders along the Lys River. On the hot, misty, sticky mornings of Apr 7 and 8, 1918, the Germans released mustard gas. On Apr 9 the Central Powers began a high explosive bombardment along the 12-mile front from LaBasse to Armentieres. The British managed to avoid a break in their line, and finally Ferdinand Foch sent nine French divisions to take over a portion of it. On Apr 30, realizing that "further attacks promised no success," Ludendorff ended the offensive. As a result of this battle the British were unable to initiate an offensive for three months. The Allies suffered 240,000 casualties while the German losses exceeded 348,000.

BIG MUDDY FOLK MUSIC FESTIVAL. Apr 7–8. Thespian Hall, Boonville, MO. Performing folk festival with instructional workshop by artists appearing. Est attendance: 3,000. For info: Maryellen McVicker, Friends of Historic Boonville, PO Box 1776, Boonville, MO 65233. Phone: (660) 882-7977 or toll-free (888) 588-1477. Fax: (660) 882-9194. E-mail: friends@undata.com.

CAMP, WALTER: BIRTH ANNIVERSARY. Apr 7, 1859. Walter Chauncey Camp, college athlete, coach and administrator, was born at New Britain, CT. Camp played football and several other sports at Yale, but he gained prominence for helping to reshape the rules of rugby football into American football. Among his innovations were reducing the number of players on a side from 15 to 11, introducing the scrimmage, giving one team definite possession of the ball and proposing the downs system. He served as a volunteer coach at Yale and became a national figure as a promoter of football. He selected an All-American team from 1889 until his death. Died at New York, NY, Mar 14, 1925.

CHANNING, WILLIAM ELLERY: BIRTH ANNIVERSARY. Apr 7, 1780. Well-known abolitionist and leader of the Unitarian movement in the US, born at Newport, RI. He stood for religious liberalism and influenced such people as Longfellow, Bryant, Emerson, Lowell and Holmes. Died at Bennington, VT, Oct 2, 1842.

FAIRCHILD, DAVID GRANDISON: BIRTH ANNIVERSARY. Apr 7, 1869. American botanist, government official and explorer, born at East Lansing, MI. Noted for scientific studies on importation of tropical plant species such as avocados and mangoes. Died at Miami, FL, Aug 6, 1954.

HOLIDAY, BILLIE: BIRTH ANNIVERSARY. Apr 7, 1915. Billie Holiday (born Eleanora Fagan, nicknamed "Lady Day") is considered by many jazz critics to have been the greatest jazz singer ever recorded. In her 26-year career, despite having received no formal training, she demonstrated a unique style with sophisticated and dramatic phrasing. Among her best-known songs are "Lover Man," "God Bless the Child," "Don't Explain" and "Strange Fruit." Holiday was born at Philadelphia, PA. She died at New York, NY, July 17, 1959.

HOSPITAL ADMITTING CLERKS DAY. Apr 7. A day set aside to recognize the worthwhile contribution made by admitting clerks in hospitals across the US and Canada. Annually, first Friday in April. For info: Shannon Ouwendyk, 705-6 Ave SE, High River, AB, T1V 1K7 Canada. Phone: (403) 652-4892. E-mail: solo99@shaw.ca.

KING, WILLIAM RUFUS DEVANE: BIRTH ANNIVERSARY. Apr 7, 1786. 13th vice president of the US died on Apr 18, 1853, the 46th day after taking the Oath of Office, of tuberculosis, at Cahaba, AL. The Oath of Office had been administered to King at Havana, Cuba, as authorized by a special act of Congress (the only presidential or vice presidential oath to be administered outside the US). Born on this day at Sampson County, NY, King was the only vice president who had served in both the House of Representatives and the Senate. King's term as vice president was Mar 4–Apr 18, 1853.

McGRAW, JOHN: BIRTH ANNIVERSARY. Apr 7, 1873. John Joseph McGraw, Baseball Hall of Fame third baseman and manager, born at Truxton, NY. Generally regarded as the best manager ever or close to it, McGraw ran the New York Giants with an iron hand from 1902 to 1932. A scrappy ballplayer with the Baltimore Orioles in the 1890s, McGraw demanded and got total effort from his players. Inducted into the Hall of Fame in 1937. Died at New Rochelle, NY, Feb 25, 1934.

MENNONITE RELIEF SALE. Apr 7–8. Kansas State Fair Grounds, Hutchinson, KS. More than 70 Mennonite, Brethren in Christ and Amish congregations in Kansas sponsor this annual festival and benefit auction for the worldwide hunger relief and community aid programs of the Mennonite Central Committee. Auctions of quilts, grandfather clocks, furniture, tools and crafts. Great food and lots more. No vendors. Est attendance: 24,000. For info: Rod Chrystie, 6113 S Broadacres Rd, Hutchinson, KS 67501. Phone: (620) 665-7406. Web: www.kansas.mccsale.org.

	S	**M**	**T**	**W**	**T**	**F**	**S**
April							1
2006	2	3	4	5	6	7	8
	9	10	11	12	13	14	15
	16	17	18	19	20	21	22
	23	24	25	26	27	28	29
	30						

METRIC SYSTEM: ANNIVERSARY. Apr 7, 1795. The metric system was adopted in France, where it had been developed.

NEW YORK SLAVE REVOLT: ANNIVERSARY. Apr 7, 1712. Nine whites were killed in a slave revolt in New York City. Planned by 27 slaves, the rebellion was begun by setting fire to an outhouse; as whites came to put the fire out, they were shot. The state militia was called out to capture the rebels and the city of New York responded to the event by strengthening its slave codes. Twenty-one blacks were executed as participants, and six alleged participants committed suicide. New York outlawed slavery in 1799, though the last slaves were not freed until 1827.

NO HOUSEWORK DAY. Apr 7. No trash. No dishes. No making of beds or washing of laundry. And no guilt. Give it a rest. [©2003 by WH.] For info: Thomas & Ruth Roy, Wellcat Holidays, 2418 Long Ln, Lebanon, PA 17046. Phone: (717) 279-0184. E-mail: info@wellcat.com. Web: www.wellcat.com.

POTEET STRAWBERRY FESTIVAL. Apr 7–9. Poteet, TX. One of the oldest and largest festivals in Texas established to promote Poteet's crop—strawberries. Great food and family entertainment. Est attendance: 100,000. For info: Nita Harvey, Festival Coord, Poteet Strawberry Festival Assn, PO Box 227, Poteet, TX 78065. Phone: (830) 742-8144. Fax: (830) 742-3608. E-mail: nharvey@texas.net. Web: www.strawberryfestival.com.

RWANDA: GENOCIDE REMEMBRANCE DAY. Apr 7. National holiday. Commemorates massacres of 1994.

SCOTLAND: EDINBURGH INTERNATIONAL SCIENCE FESTIVAL. Apr 7–16. Edinburgh. A massive public celebration of science and technology, with more than 150 events at 25 venues. Includes workshops, talks, tours and exhibitions. Est attendance: 120,000. For info: Media Officer, Edinburgh Intl Science Festival, 4 Gayfield Place Ln, Edinburgh, Scotland EH1 3NZ. Phone: (44) 131-558-7666. Fax: (44) 131-557-9177. E-mail: esf@scifest.demon.co.uk. Web: www.sciencefestival.co.uk.

SPACE MILESTONE: *MARS ODYSSEY* (US): 5th ANNIVERSARY. Apr 7, 2001. *Odyssey* was launched on this day and successfully entered Mars's orbit on Oct 23, 2001. The one-way trip is 286 million miles. The two-and-one-half-year mission will monitor space radiation, seek out underground water and identify minerals on the Red Planet.

STUDENT GOVERNMENT DAY IN MASSACHUSETTS. Apr 7. Annually, the first Friday of April.

SUGARLOAF CRAFTS FESTIVAL. Apr 7–9. Montgomery County Fairgrounds, Gaithersburg, MD. This show, now in its 31st year, features more than 450 nationally recognized craft designers and fine artists displaying and selling their original creations. Craft demonstrations, live music, hourly gift certificate drawings, specialty foods and more! Est attendance: 25,000. For info: Sugarloaf Mountain Works, Inc, 200 Orchard Ridge Dr, #215, Gaithersburg, MD 20878. Phone: (800) 210-9900. Fax: (310) 253-9620. Web: www.sugarloafcrafts.com.

UNITED NATIONS: WORLD HEALTH DAY. Apr 7. A UN observance commemorating the establishment of the World Health Organization in 1948. For info: United Nations, Dept of Public Info, New York, NY 10017. Web: www.un.org.

WINCHELL, WALTER: BIRTH ANNIVERSARY. Apr 7, 1897. Journalist, broadcaster, reporter and gossip columnist Walter Winchell was born at New York, NY, and died at Los Angeles, CA, Feb 20, 1972. He was admired for his way with turning a phrase. His show business columns were voraciously read by millions of Americans between 1924 abd 1963.

WORDSWORTH, WILLIAM: BIRTH ANNIVERSARY. Apr 7, 1770. English Lake Poet and philosopher, born at Cumberland, England. "Poetry," he said, "is the spontaneous overflow of powerful feelings: it takes its origin from emotion recollected in tranquility." Wordsworth died Apr 23, 1850, at Rydal Mount, Westmorland.

WORLD HEALTH ORGANIZATION: ANNIVERSARY. Apr 7, 1948. This agency of the UN was founded to coordinate international health systems. It is headquartered at Geneva. Among its achievements is the elimination of smallpox.

WORLD'S LARGEST TRIVIA CONTEST. Apr 7–9. Stevens Point, WI. More than 12,000 players, including more than 500 teams, compete to answer eight questions every hour for 54 hours straight. Prize: Oscar-like trophy. Est attendance: 12,000. For info: Jim Oliva, University of Wisconsin, Rm 101 CAC, WWSP-Radio (89.9 FM), Stevens Point, WI 54481. Phone: (715) 346-3755. E-mail: theoz@dwave.net. Web: www.momsfamilies.com/trivia.

BIRTHDAYS TODAY

(William) Hodding Carter III, 71, television and newspaper journalist, born New Orleans, LA, Apr 7, 1935.

Jackie Chan, 52, martial artist, actor (*Rush Hour, Shanghai Noon, Project A*), born Hong Kong, Apr 7, 1954.

Francis Ford Coppola, 67, filmmaker (*Godfather* movies, *Apocalypse Now*), born Detroit, MI, Apr 7, 1939.

Russell Crowe, 42, actor (*LA Confidential, Gladiator* [Oscar for Best Actor], *A Beautiful Mind*), born Auckland, New Zealand, Apr 7, 1964.

Mitchell Daniels, 57, Governor of Indiana (R), born Monogahela, PA, Apr 7, 1949.

Anthony Drew (Tony) Dorsett, 52, Hall of Fame football player, born Rochester, PA, Apr 7, 1954.

Daniel Ellsberg, 75, author (released the "Pentagon Papers" to *The New York Times*), born Chicago, IL, Apr 7, 1931.

David Frost, 67, entertainer ("That Was the Week That Was"), interviewer, born Tenterden, England, Apr 7, 1939.

James Garner, 78, actor (*Space Cowboys*, "Maverick," "The Rockford Files"), born James Baumgardner at Norman, OK, Apr 7, 1928.

John Oates, 58, singer ("Maneater" with Daryl Hall), songwriter, born New York, NY, Apr 7, 1948.

Wayne Rogers, 73, actor ("M*A*S*H," "House Calls"), born Birmingham, AL, Apr 7, 1933.

Gerhard Schroeder, 62, chancellor of Germany, born Mossenberg, Germany, Apr 7, 1944.

APRIL 8 — SATURDAY
Day 98 — 267 Remaining

BIRTHDAY OF THE BUDDHA: BIRTH ANNIVERSARY. Apr 8. Among Buddhist holidays, this day is the most important as it commemorates the birthday of the Buddha. It is also known as the Day of Vesak. The founder of Buddhism had the given name Siddhartha, the family name Gautama and the clan name Shaka. He is commonly called the Buddha, meaning in Sanskrit "the enlightened one." He is thought to have lived in India from c. 563 BC to 483 BC. Some countries celebrate this holiday on the lunar calendar, so the date changes from year to year but it always occurs in either April or May. This day is a holiday in Indonesia, Korea, Singapore and Thailand.

BLACK SENATE PAGE APPOINTED: ANNIVERSARY. Apr 8, 1965. Sixteen-year-old Lawrence Bradford of New York City was the first black page appointed to the US Senate.

FEDERAL GOVERNMENT SEIZURE OF STEEL MILLS: ANNIVERSARY. Apr 8, 1952. On this date President Harry S. Truman seized control of the nation's steel mills by presidential order in an attempt to prevent a shutdown by strikers. On Apr 29, a US District Court declared the seizure unconstitutional and workers immediately walked out. Production dropped from 300,000 tons a day to less than 20,000. After 53 days the strike ended July 24, with steelworkers receiving a 16¢ hourly wage raise plus a 5.4¢ hourly increase in fringe benefits.

HENIE, SONJA: BIRTH ANNIVERSARY. Apr 8, 1912. Sonja Henie, Olympic gold medal figure skater, born at Oslo, Norway. Henie competed in the 1924 Winter Olympics when she was just 11, but finished last in ladies' singles. She won gold medals at the Winter Games of 1928, 1932 and 1936. She became a professional skater and an actress (*Sun Valley Serenade*). Died Oct 13, 1969.

HOME RUN RECORD SET BY HANK AARON: ANNIVERSARY. Apr 8, 1974. Henry ("Hammerin' Hank") Aaron hit the 715th home run of his career, breaking the record set by Babe Ruth in 1935. Playing for the Atlanta Braves, Aaron broke the record at Atlanta in a game against the Los Angeles Dodgers. He finished his career in 1976 with a total of 755 home runs. This record remains unbroken. At the time of his retirement, Aaron also held records for first in RBIs, second in at-bats and runs scored and third in base hits.

HUNTER, "CATFISH": BIRTH ANNIVERSARY. Apr 8, 1946. James Augustus ("Catfish") Hunter, Baseball Hall of Fame pitcher, born at Hertford, NC. Died Sept 9, 1999, at Hertford.

JAPAN: FLOWER FESTIVAL (HANA MATSURI). Apr 8. Commemorates Buddha's birthday. Ceremonies in all temples.

KNIGHT, O. RAYMOND: BIRTH ANNIVERSARY. Apr 8, 1872. The "Father of Canadian Rodeo," O. Raymond Knight was born at Payson, UT. His father, the Utah mining magnate Jesse Knight, founded the town of Raymond, AB, in 1901. In 1902 Raymond produced Canada's first rodeo, "Raymond Stampede." He also built rodeo's first grandstand and first chute in 1903. O. Raymond Knight died Feb 7, 1947.

LONGWOOD GARDENS EASTER DISPLAY. Apr 8–21. Kennett Square, PA. Fragrant Easter lilies trumpet the season, while brilliant tulips, daffodils, freesias and other colorful plants fill acres of indoor gardens. Est attendance: 40,000. For info: Longwood Gardens, PO Box 501, Kennett Square, PA 19348-0501. Phone: (610) 388-1000. Web: www.longwoodgardens.org.

McRAE, CARMEN: BIRTH ANNIVERSARY. Apr 8, 1920. After winning an amateur contest at Harlem's legendary Apollo Theatre in her hometown New York City, McRae went on to become a noted jazz singer, singing with the Earl Hines, Mercer Ellington and Benny Carter bands among others and recording more than 20 albums. She died Nov 10, 1994, at Beverly Hills, CA.

MORRIS, LEWIS: BIRTH ANNIVERSARY. Apr 8, 1726. Signer of the Declaration of Independence, born at Westchester County, NY. Died Jan 22, 1798, at Morrisania Manor at NY.

POLL TAX OUTLAWED: 40th ANNIVERSARY. Apr 8, 1966. In the last of a series of moves to abolish poll taxes, a three-judge federal court at Jackson, MS, outlawed Mississippi's $2 poll tax as a voting requirement for state and local elections.

April 2006	S	M	T	W	T	F	S
							1
	2	3	4	5	6	7	8
	9	10	11	12	13	14	15
	16	17	18	19	20	21	22
	23	24	25	26	27	28	29
	30						

PRAIRIE DOG CHILI COOKOFF AND WORLD CHAMPIONSHIP OF PICKLED QUAIL-EGG EATING. Apr 8. Traders Village, Grand Prairie, TX. Tongue-in-cheek salute to the official state dish of Texas, chili con carne, or "Texas Red." World championship of pickled quail-egg eating featuring contestants devouring as many of these gourmet delights as possible in the 60-second time limit. Est attendance: 85,000. For info: Allan Hughes, Traders Village, 2602 Mayfield Rd, Grand Prairie, TX 75052-7246. Phone: (972) 647-2331. E-mail: dfwinfo @tradersvillage.com. Web: www.tradersvillage.com.

SEVENTEENTH AMENDMENT TO US CONSTITUTION RATIFIED: ANNIVERSARY. Apr 8, 1913. Prior to the 17th Amendment, members of the Senate were elected by each state's respective legislature. The advent and popularity of primary elections during the last decade of the 19th century and the early 20th century and a string of senatorial scandals, most notably a scandal involving William Lorimer, an Illinois political boss in 1909, forced the Senate to end its resistance to a constitutional amendment requiring direct popular election of senators.

TARPON SPRINGS FINE ARTS FESTIVAL. Apr 8–9. Tarpon Springs, FL. Est attendance: 30,000. For info: Tarpon Springs Chamber of Commerce, 11 E Orange St, Tarpon Springs, FL 34689. Phone: (727) 937-6109. Fax: (727) 937-2879. E-mail: chamber@tarponsprings.com. Web: www.TarponSprings.com.

TUTOR APPRECIATION DAY. Apr 8. A day to express appreciation for the volunteer and paid tutors who help us all be better students and wiser people. Annually, the first Saturday in April, with the exception of Apr 1. For info: Sharon Huntington, 2124 S Highland Dr, Salt Lake City, UT 84121. Phone: (801) 250-6574. E-mail: SHuntington@helpuwrite.com. Web: www.helpuwrite.com.

VOYAGEURS NATIONAL PARK ESTABLISHED: ANNIVERSARY. Apr 8, 1975. Minnesota's Voyageurs land was preserved by Congress on Jan 8, 1971. Four years later, it became the 36th US national park.

WILLIAMS, WILLIAM: 275th BIRTH ANNIVERSARY. Apr 8, 1731. Signer of the Declaration of Independence, born at Lebanon, CT. Died there Aug 2, 1811.

WISCONSIN SPRING GARDEN MARKET. Apr 8–9. The American Club, Kohler, WI. Spring plants, garden ornaments, herbs and unusual varieties of annuals and perennials fill the Grand Hall of the Great Lakes. Lending counsel and a helping hand with seminars, demonstrations and an array of products are more than 70 plant and gardening specialists, landscape designers and artists. Est attendance: 4,000. For info: The American Club, Highland Dr, Kohler, WI 53044. Phone: (800) 344-2838. Web: www.destinationkohler.com.

BIRTHDAYS TODAY

Kofi Annan, 68, UN Secretary General, born Kumasi, Ghana, Apr 8, 1938.

Patricia Arquette, 38, actress ("Medium," *Lost Highway, Flirting with Disaster*), born Chicago, IL, Apr 8, 1968.

Gary Edmund Carter, 52, sportscaster, Hall of Fame baseball player, born Culver City, CA, Apr 8, 1954.

William D. Chase, 84, librarian and chronicler of contemporary civilization as cofounder and coeditor of *Chase's Annual Events*, born Lakeview, MI, Apr 8, 1922.

Elizabeth (Betty) Ford, 88, former First Lady, wife of Gerald Ford, 38th president of the US, born Chicago, IL, Apr 8, 1918.

Shecky Greene, 81, comedian, actor, born Chicago, IL, Apr 8, 1925.

John J. Havlicek, 66, Hall of Fame basketball player, born Lansing, OH, Apr 8, 1940.

Seymour Hersh, 69, journalist, born Chicago, IL, Apr 8, 1937.

Julian Lennon, 43, musician, singer, son of John Lennon, born Liverpool, England, Apr 8, 1963.

Stuart Pankin, 60, actor ("Not Necessarily the News," *Irreconcilable Differences, Arachnophobia*), born Philadelphia, PA, Apr 8, 1946.

Terry Porter, 43, former basketball player, born Milwaukee, WI, Apr 8, 1963.

John Schneider, 52, actor ("Dukes of Hazzard," *Smokey and the Bandit*), born Mount Kisco, NY, Apr 8, 1954 (some sources say 1960).

Robin Wright, 40, actress (*Message in a Bottle, Forrest Gump*), born Dallas, TX, Apr 8, 1966.

APRIL 9 — SUNDAY
Day 99 — 266 Remaining

AFRICAN METHODIST EPISCOPAL CHURCH ORGANIZED: ANNIVERSARY. Apr 9, 1816. The first all-black US religious denomination, the AME church was organized at Philadelphia with Richard Allen, a former slave who had bought his freedom, as the first bishop.

BLACK PAGE APPOINTED TO US HOUSE OF REPRESENTATIVES: ANNIVERSARY. Apr 9, 1965. Fifteen-year-old Frank Mitchell of Springfield, IL, was the first black page appointed to the US House of Representatives.

CIVIL RIGHTS BILL OF 1866: ANNIVERSARY. Apr 9, 1866. The Civil Rights Bill of 1866, passed by Congress over the veto of President Andrew Johnson, granted blacks the rights and privileges of American citizenship and formed the basis for the 14th Amendment to the US Constitution.

CIVIL WAR ENDING: ANNIVERSARY. Apr 9, 1865. At 1:30 PM General Robert E. Lee, commander of the Army of Northern Virginia, surrendered to General Ulysses S. Grant, commander-in-chief of the Union Army, ending four years of civil war. The meeting took place in the house of Wilmer McLean at the village of Appomattox Court House, VA. Confederate soldiers were permitted to keep their horses and go free to their homes, while Confederate officers were allowed to retain their swords and sidearms as well. Grant wrote the terms of surrender. Formal surrender took place at the courthouse on Apr 12. Death toll for the Civil War is estimated at 500,000 men.

DALLAS CUP. Apr 9–16. FC Dallas Stadium Soccer Complex, Frisco, TX. 27th annual. International invitation-only boys' (under 12 to under 19) soccer competition, sanctioned by the USSF and FIFA. In past years, more than 98 countries and all 6 continents have been represented. Many of the world's premier teams participate. Manchester United and Real Madrid will compete in the Super Group. Annually, from Palm Sunday to Easter Sunday. Est attendance: 120,000. For info: Dallas Cup, 12700 Park Central Dr, Ste 507, Dallas, TX 75251-1500. Phone: (214) 221-3636. Fax: (214) 221-4636. E-mail: randy@dallascup.com. Web: www.dallas cup.com.

ECKERT, J(OHN) PRESPER, JR: BIRTH ANNIVERSARY. Apr 9, 1919. Coinventor with John W. Mauchly of ENIAC (Electronic Numerical Integrator and Computer), which was first demonstrated at the Moore School of Electrical Engineering at the University of Pennsylvania at Philadelphia Feb 14, 1946. This is generally considered the birth of the computer age. Originally designed to process artillery calculations for the army, ENIAC was also used in the Manhattan Project. Eckert and Mauchly formed Electronic Control Company, which later became Unisys Corporation. Eckert was born at Philadelphia and died at Bryn Mawr, PA, June 3, 1995.

GREECE: DUMB WEEK. Apr 9–15. The week preceding Holy Week on the Orthodox calendar is known as Dumb Week, as no services are held in churches throughout this period except on Friday, eve of the Saturday of Lazarus.

HOLY WEEK. Apr 9–15. Christian observance dating from the fourth century, known also as Great Week. The seven days beginning on the sixth and final Sunday in Lent (Palm Sunday), consisting of: Palm Sunday, Monday of Holy Week, Tuesday of Holy Week, Spy Wednesday (or Wednesday of Holy Week), Maundy Thursday, Good Friday and Holy Saturday (or Great Sabbath or Easter Even). A time of solemn devotion to and memorializing of the suffering (passion), death and burial of Christ. Formerly a time of strict fasting.

IRAQ: NATIONAL DAY. Apr 9. National holiday commemorating anniversary of dictator Saddam Hussein's fall from power in 2003.

JENKINS'S EAR DAY: 275th ANNIVERSARY. Apr 9, 1731. Spanish *guardacosta* boarded and plundered the British ship *Rebecca* off Jamaica, and, among other outrages, cut off the ear of English master mariner Robert Jenkins. Little notice was taken until seven years later, when Jenkins exhibited the detached ear and described the atrocity to a committee of the House of Commons. In consequence, Britain declared war on Spain in October 1739, a war that lasted until 1743 and is still known as the "War of Jenkins's Ear." Nothing else is known of him.

JUMBO THE ELEPHANT ARRIVES IN AMERICA: ANNIVERSARY. Apr 9, 1882. The most famous elephant in history was captured as a calf near Lake Chad, Africa, in 1861. He was a tremendously popular part of the London Zoo from 1865 to 1882. At London, he gained the name Jumbo (from a West African word for elephant). In 1882, American circus impresario P.T. Barnum bought the 11½-foot tall and seven-ton animal for $10,000. Jumbo arrived at Manhattan, NY, on Easter Sunday. In an amazing spectacle, Jumbo paraded up Broadway in a crate pulled by 16 horses. Jumbo was just as popular in the US as he was in Britain, and his name entered the English language to describe anything oversized.

KING, FRANK: BIRTH ANNIVERSARY. Apr 9, 1883. Created by Frank King in 1919 as a comic strip about men's interest in autos, *Gasoline Alley* had a tremendous jump in popularity in 1921 when its main character Walt adopted a foundling called Skeezix. Devoid of melodrama, this strip sympathetically described the day-to-day lives of Walt, Skeezix and their friends and family, and it was the first American cartoon in which the characters actually aged. Frank King was born at Cashton, WI, and died at Winter Park, FL, June 24, 1969.

LUDENDORFF, ERICH: BIRTH ANNIVERSARY. Apr 9, 1865. German general who, during the last years of WWI, was chiefly responsible for military policy and strategy. Born near Pozen, Prussia, and died at Tutzing, Dec 20, 1937.

MARIAN ANDERSON EASTER CONCERT: ANNIVERSARY. Apr 9, 1939. On this Easter Sunday, black American contralto Marian Anderson sang an open-air concert from the steps of the Lincoln Memorial at Washington, DC, to an audience of 75,000, after having been denied use of the Daughters of the American Revolution (DAR) Constitution Hall. The event became an American antidiscrimination *cause célèbre* and led First Lady Eleanor Roosevelt to resign from the DAR.

MUYBRIDGE, EADWEARD: BIRTH ANNIVERSARY. Apr 9, 1830. English photographer famed for his studies of animals in motion. Born Edward James Muggeridge, at Kingston-on-Thames, England. Died there May 8, 1904.

★**NATIONAL FORMER PRISONER OF WAR RECOGNITION DAY.** Apr 9.

NATIONAL GARDEN WEEK. Apr 9–15. To recognize and honor the 78 million Americans who eagerly garden each year. These American gardeners enhance and improve the environment with their efforts. Annually, the second full week of April. For info: Natl Garden Bureau, 1311 Butterfield Rd, Ste 310, Downers Grove, IL 60515.

NATIONAL WOMEN'S NUTRITION WEEK. Apr 9–15. To recognize the importance and value of health in all phases of a woman's life. A woman's biochemistry needs nutritional support when on the pill, during pregnancy, during lactation, when she is under stress and going through menopause. This week is designed to educate women about the importance of nutrition for their ongoing health and well-being. For info: Dr. Lois M Vanderhoof, Applied Nutrition Concepts, 2828 W Parker Rd, #A205, Plano, TX 75075. Phone: (972) 612-5505. E-mail: drlois@applied nutritionconcepts.com. Web: www.appliednutritionconcepts.com.

PALM SUNDAY. Apr 9. Commemorates Christ's last entry into Jerusalem, when His way was covered with palms by the multitudes. Beginning of Holy (or Great) Week in Western Christian churches.

★**PAN AMERICAN WEEK.** Apr 9–15. Presidential Proclamation customarily issued as "Pan American Day and Pan American Week." Always issued for the week including Apr 14, except in 1965, from 1946 through 1948, 1955 through 1977, and 1979.

PHILIPPINES: ARAW NG KAGITINGAN. Apr 9, 1942. Day of Valor. National observance to commemorate the fall of Bataan. The infamous "Death March" is reenacted at the Mount Samat Shrine, the Dambana ng Kagitingan.

PHILIPPINES: HOLY WEEK. Apr 9–15. National observance. Flagellants in the streets, *cenaculos* (passion plays) and other colorful and solemn rituals mark the country's observance of Holy Week.

PYRAMID FESTIVALS. Apr 9–15 (also June 18–24). This time will be dedicated to all those who were involved in planning, preparation and actual building of the pyramids all over the world. More information and a newsletter are available. For info: Rev Margaret Allbritten, Light Paths, 302 Lincoln St, #21, Roseville, CA 95678. Phone: (916) 446-4961. E-mail: goldenfire@mail.com.

ROBESON, PAUL BUSTILL: BIRTH ANNIVERSARY. Apr 9, 1898. Paul Robeson, born at Princeton, NJ, was an All-American football player at Rutgers University and received his law degree from Columbia University in 1923. After being seen by Eugene O'Neill in an amateur stage production, he was offered a part in O'Neill's play *The Emperor Jones*. His performance in that play with the Provincetown Players established him as an actor. Without ever having taken a voice lesson, he also became a popular singer. His stage credits include *Show Boat, Porgy and Bess, The Hairy Ape* and *Othello*, which enjoyed the longest Broadway run of a Shakespeare play. In 1950 he was denied a passport by the US for refusing to sign an affidavit stating whether he was or ever had been a member of the Communist Party. The action was overturned by the Supreme Court in 1958. His film credits include *Emperor Jones, Show Boat, King Solomon's Mines* and *Song of Freedom*, among others. Robeson died at Philadelphia, PA, Jan 23, 1976.

SPACE MILESTONE: *SOYUZ 35* (USSR). Apr 9, 1980. Two cosmonauts (Valery Ryumin and Leonid Popov) were launched from Baikonur space center at Kazakhstan, USSR. Docked at *Salyut 6* Apr 10. Ryumin and Popov returned to Earth Oct 11, 1980, after setting a new space endurance record of 185 days.

TEXAS PANHANDLE TORNADO: ANNIVERSARY. Apr 9, 1947. A monster tornado clearing a 1.5-mile-long path struck through at least 12 towns in Texas, Oklahoma and Kansas, killing 169 people and causing more than $15 million in damage. The tornado traveled 221 miles across the three states.

TUNISIA: MARTYRS' DAY. Apr 9.

	S	M	T	W	T	F	S
April							1
2006	2	3	4	5	6	7	8
	9	10	11	12	13	14	15
	16	17	18	19	20	21	22
	23	24	25	26	27	28	29
	30						

WINSTON CHURCHILL DAY. Apr 9. Anniversary of enactment of legislation in 1963 that made the late British statesman an honorary citizen of the US.

WSBA/WARM 103/OLDIES 96.1 SPRING CRAFT SHOW. Apr 9. York Fairgrounds, York, PA. More than 160 craft displays, from country to contemporary, Victorian and southwestern, handcrafted furniture, wood carvings, dolls, jewelry, pottery, collectibles, quilts, baskets, garden needs and much more. Admission fee. Est attendance: 3,500. For info: Joe Alfano, Asst Promo Dir, PO Box 910, York, PA 17402-0910. Phone: (717) 764-1155. Fax: (717) 252-4708. E-mail: jalfano@radioyork.com. Web: www.warm103.com.

BIRTHDAYS TODAY

Severiano (Seve) Ballesteros, 49, golfer, born Pedrena, Spain, Apr 9, 1957.

Jean-Paul Belmondo, 73, actor (*Breathless, The Man from Rio, Is Paris Burning?*), born Neuilly-sur-Seine, France, Apr 9, 1933.

Hugh Hefner, 80, founder of *Playboy*, born Chicago, IL, Apr 9, 1926.

Paul Krassner, 74, editor, journalist, born Brooklyn, NY, Apr 9, 1932.

Michael Learned, 67, actress (*The Waltons, Nurses*; stage: *The Sisters Rosenzweig*), born Washington, DC, Apr 9, 1939.

Tom Lehrer, 78, songwriter ("Vatican Rag," "New Math"), pianist, mathematician, born New York, NY, Apr 9, 1928.

Cynthia Nixon, 40, actress ("Sex and the City," *Amadeus*), born New York, NY, Apr 9, 1966.

Keshia Knight Pulliam, 27, actress ("The Cosby Show"), born Newark, NJ, Apr 9, 1979.

Dennis Quaid, 52, actor (*The Rookie, Everybody's All-American*), born Houston, TX, Apr 9, 1954.

Jacques Villeneueve, 35, race car driver, winner of 1995 Indianapolis 500, born St. Jean d'Iberville, QC, Canada, Apr 9, 1971.

APRIL 10 — MONDAY
Day 100 — 265 Remaining

BATAAN DEATH MARCH: ANNIVERSARY. Apr 10, 1942. On this morning American and Filipino prisoners were herded together by Japanese soldiers on Mariveles Airfield on Bataan (in the Philippine islands) and began the Death March to Camp O'Donnell, near Cabanatuan. During the six-day march they were given only one bowl of rice. More than 5,200 Americans and many more Filipinos lost their lives in the course of the march.

THE BEATLES BREAK UP: ANNIVERSARY. Apr 10, 1970. In a press release accompanying promotional copies of his new solo album, Paul McCartney announced that he had no plans for working with the Beatles because of "personal differences, business differences, musical differences." He stated that he didn't know if the break was temporary or permanent, but the years-long tension in the group coupled with their work on solo projects brought about the end of the band that year. McCartney sued to dissolve the Beatles on Dec 31, 1970, and the group was formally dissolved four years later.

BOOTH, WILLIAM: BIRTH ANNIVERSARY. Apr 10, 1829. General William Booth, founder of the movement that became known, in 1878, as the Salvation Army, was born at Nottingham, England. Apprenticed to a pawnbroker at the age of 13, Booth experienced firsthand the misery of poverty. He broke with conventional church religion and established a quasi-military religious organization with military uniforms and ranks. Recruiting from the poor, from converted criminals and from many other social outcasts, his organization grew rapidly and its influence spread from England to the US and to other countries. At revivals in slum areas the itinerant evangelist offered help for the poor, homes for the homeless, sobriety for alcoholics, rescue homes for women and girls, training centers and legal aid. Booth died at London, England, Aug 20, 1912. See also: "Salvation Army Founder's Day" (Apr 10).

BRAHMS "REQUIEM" PREMIERE: ANNIVERSARY. Apr 10, 1868. Composer Johannes Brahms fortified his reputation as one of the leading figures in 19th-century German Romantic music with the success of his *Requiem*, which premiered at Bremen Cathedral on this date. The choral piece, at turns both melancholy and exuberant, is one of the more recognized and often-sung funerary works in the musical canon.

COMMODORE PERRY DAY. Apr 10, 1794. Birth anniversary of Matthew Calbraith Perry, commodore in the US Navy, negotiator of first treaty between US and Japan (Mar 31, 1854). Born at South Kingston, RI. Died Mar 4, 1858, at New York, NY.

CONNORS, CHUCK (KEVIN JOSEPH): BIRTH ANNIVERSARY. Apr 10, 1921. "The Rifleman" of television fame, Chuck Connors played that role from 1958 to 1963. His portrayal of a slave owner in the miniseries *Roots* won him an Emmy nomination. Connors acted in more than 45 films and appeared on many TV series and specials. He played professional basketball and baseball before becoming an actor. Born at Brooklyn, NY; died Nov 10, 1992, at Los Angeles, CA.

EXPLORE YOUR CAREER OPTIONS WEEK. Apr 10–14. Maybe you're aspiring to a new career or merely interested in more opportunities in your present career. Get a fresh start by taking stock of all available options. For info: Dorothy Zjawin, Dir, 61 W Colfax Ave, Roselle Park, NJ 07204. Phone: (908) 241-6241.

FIRST PGA CHAMPIONSHIP: 90th ANNIVERSARY. Apr 10, 1916. The then-recently formed Professional Golfer's Association of America held its first championship at Siwanoy golf course at Bronxville, NY. The trophy and the lion's share of the $2,580 purse were won by British golfer Jim Barnes.

GOOD FRIDAY PEACE AGREEMENT IN NORTHERN IRELAND: ANNIVERSARY. Apr 10, 1998. Protestant and Catholic factions agreed to a power-sharing agreement on Good Friday, 1998. It was endorsed by referenda in Northern Ireland and the Republic of Ireland on May 22, 1998. As a result, a provincial government was established in Northern Ireland to replace direct rule by Britain. The Northern Ireland Assembly met for the first time June 5, 2000. However, the peace remains strained and paramilitaries have yet to be disarmed. The 30-year-old conflict in Northern Ireland has taken more than 3,200 lives.

GROTIUS, HUGO: BIRTH ANNIVERSARY. Apr 10, 1583 (OS). Anniversary of the birth of Hugo Grotius, the Dutch theologian, attorney, scholar and statesman whose beliefs profoundly influenced American thinking, especially with regard to the conscience of humanity. Born at Delft, Holland, he died at Rostock, Germany, Aug 28, 1645 (OS).

NATIONAL NETWORKING WEEK. Apr 10–16. Whether the goal is to grow a business or enrich your personal life, networking is invaluable. One can never meet enough new people, exchange business cards and share one's goals and desires with others who may offer leads. Cameraderie is another benefit that can result from successfully connecting with others through a concerted, consistent effort. For info: Robin Gorman Newman, Independent Business Women's Circle, 44 Somerset Dr N, Great Neck, NY 10020. Phone: (516) 773-0911. E-mail: robin@love coach.com. Web: www.ibwc.org.

NATIONAL SIBLINGS DAY. Apr 10. A commemorative day to honor all brothers and sisters who are here or in the hereafter. Recognizing the bond between brothers and sisters for the special gift it is. A day to hug, honor and enjoy your sibling. Founded by Claudia A. Evart of New York City through her nonprofit charity, Siblings Day Foundation, to honor the memory of her sister Lisette and brother Alan; they both died from accidents early in their lives. Annually, Apr 10. For info: Claudia A. Evart, Siblings Day Foundation, 30 Park Ave, Ste 2-P, New York, NY 10016-3833. Phone: (212) 779-2227. E-mail: siblingsday@earthlink.net. Web: www.siblingsday.org.

ODESSA RETAKEN: ANNIVERSARY. Apr 10, 1944. The Red Army retook the Ukrainian city of Odessa, the port on the northwest coast of the Black Sea that had been in the hands of the Nazis since October 1941.

PERKINS, FRANCES: BIRTH ANNIVERSARY. Apr 10, 1880. First woman member of a US presidential cabinet. Born at Boston, MA, she was married in 1915 to Paul Caldwell Wilson, but used her maiden name in public life. She was appointed secretary of labor by President Franklin D. Roosevelt in 1933, a post in which she served until 1945. Died at New York, NY, May 14, 1965.

PULITZER, JOSEPH: BIRTH ANNIVERSARY. Apr 10, 1847. American journalist and newspaper publisher, founder of the Pulitzer Prizes, born at Budapest, Hungary. Died at Charleston, SC, Oct 29, 1911. Pulitzer Prizes awarded annually since 1917. Write for entry and deadline info. (Please specify Book, Journalism, Drama or Music Competition.) For info: Pulitzer Prize Bd, 709 Journalism, Columbia Univ, New York, NY 10027. Phone: (212) 854-3841. Web: www.pulitzer.org.

ROBERT GRAY BECOMES FIRST AMERICAN TO CIRCUMNAVIGATE THE EARTH: ANNIVERSARY. Apr 10, 1790. When Robert Gray docked the *Columbia* at Boston Harbor, he became the first American to circumnavigate the earth. He sailed from Boston, MA, in September 1787, to trade with Indians of the Pacific Northwest. From there he sailed to China and then continued around the world. His 42,000-mile journey opened trade between New England and the Pacific Northwest and helped the US establish claims to the Oregon Territory.

SAFETY PIN PATENTED: ANNIVERSARY. Apr 10, 1849. Walter Hunt of New York patented the first safety pin.

SALVATION ARMY FOUNDER'S DAY. Apr 10, 1829. Birth anniversary of William Booth, a Methodist minister who began an evangelical ministry in the East End of London in 1865 and established mission stations to feed and house the poor. In 1878 he changed the name of the organization to the Salvation Army. Booth was born at Nottingham, England; he died at London, Aug 20, 1912. See also: "Booth, William: Birth Anniversary" (Apr 10).

SPALDING UNIVERSITY RUNNING OF THE RODENTS. Apr 10–14. Louisville, KY. To celebrate the pre-final exams "Rat Race" that occurs each year, to develop community spirit and to unofficially kick off the Kentucky Derby festivities. Est attendance: 300. For info: Student Life Office, Spalding University, 851 S Fourth St, Louisville, KY 40203. Phone: (502) 585-9911. Web: www.spalding.edu.

WOODWARD, ROBERT BURNS: BIRTH ANNIVERSARY. Apr 10, 1917. Nobel Prize–winning (1965) Harvard University science professor whose special field of study was molecular structure of complex organic compounds. Called "one of the most outstanding scientific minds of the century." Born at Boston, MA, he died at Cambridge, MA, July 8, 1979.

YOUNG PEOPLE'S POETRY WEEK. Apr 10–16. An annual event, sponsored by The Children's Book Council, that highlights poetry for children and young adults and encourages everyone to celebrate poetry—read it, enjoy it, write it—in their homes, child-care centers, classrooms, libraries and bookstores. The CBC is coordinating its promotional efforts with the Academy of American Poets, the sponsor of National Poetry Month in April, and The Center for the Book in the Library of Congress. For info: The Children's Book Council, 12 W 37th St, 2nd Fl, New York, NY 10018-7480. Phone: (800) 999-2160. Fax: (888) 807-9355. E-mail: info@cbcbooks.org. Web: www.cbcbooks.org.

BIRTHDAYS TODAY

Kenneth (Babyface) Edmonds, 49, pop performer and songwriter, born Indianapolis, IN, Apr 10, 1957.

David Halberstam, 72, author (*The Best and the Brightest, The Summer of Forty-Nine*), born New York, NY, Apr 10, 1934.

Dolores Huerta, 76, cofounder, with Cesar Chavez, of the United Farm Workers Union, born Dawson, NM, Apr 10, 1930.

Peter MacNicol, 52, actor ("Ally McBeal," *Ghostbusters II*), born Dallas, TX, Apr 10, 1954.

John Earl Madden, 70, sportscaster, former football coach, born Austin, MN, Apr 10, 1936.

Joe Don Meredith, 68, former sportscaster, actor and football player, born Mount Vernon, TX, Apr 10, 1938.

Harry Morgan, 91, actor (Emmy for "M*A*S*H"; "Dragnet"), born Harry Bratsburg at Detroit, MI, Apr 10, 1915.

Haley Joel Osment, 18, actor (*The Sixth Sense, Bogus*), born Los Angeles, CA, Apr 10, 1988.

Steven Seagal, 55, actor, producer (*Hard to Kill, On Deadly Ground*), born Lansing, MI, Apr 10, 1951.

Omar Sharif, 74, actor (*Lawrence of Arabia, Dr. Zhivago*), born Michael Shalhoub at Alexandria, Egypt, Apr 10, 1932.

Paul Edward Theroux, 65, author (*The Mosquito Coast, Millroy the Magician*), born Medford, MS, Apr 10, 1941.

Max Von Sydow, 77, actor (*The Seventh Seal, The Emigrants*), born Lund, Sweden, Apr 10, 1929.

APRIL 11 — TUESDAY

Day 101 — 264 Remaining

BARBERSHOP QUARTET DAY. Apr 11. Commemorates the gathering of some 26 persons at Tulsa, OK, Apr 11, 1938, and the founding there of the Society for the Preservation and Encouragement of Barbershop Quartet Singing in America.

BLISS, LIZZIE "LILLIE": BIRTH ANNIVERSARY. Apr 11, 1864. Lizzie "Lillie" Bliss was born at Boston, MA. She was one of the three founders (all women) of the Museum of Modern Art at New York City in 1929. She died Mar 12, 1931, at New York City.

BOLIN, JANE MATILDA: BIRTHDAY. Apr 11, 1908. Jane Matilda Bolin, born at Poughkeepsie, NY, was the first black woman to graduate from the Yale School of Law (1931) and went on to become the first black woman judge in the US. She served as assistant corporation counsel for the city of New York before being appointed to the city's Domestic Relations Court and the Family Court of the State of New York.

CHILDREN'S DAY IN FLORIDA. Apr 11. A legal holiday in Florida commemorated on the second Tuesday in April.

CIVIL RIGHTS ACT OF 1968: ANNIVERSARY. Apr 11, 1968. Exactly one week after the assassination of Martin Luther King, Jr, the Civil Rights Act of 1968 (protecting civil rights workers, expanding the rights of Native Americans and providing antidiscrimination measures in housing) was signed into law by President Lyndon B. Johnson, who said: "[T]he proudest moments of my presidency have been times such as this when I have signed into law the promises of a century."

COSTA RICA: JUAN SANTAMARÍA DAY. Apr 11. National holiday. Commemorates the 1856 Battle of Rivas.

CRAFT BREWERS CONFERENCE & BREWEXPO AMERICA®. Apr 11–14. Seattle, WA. This conference (sponsored by the Association of Brewers) is the number-one environment in North America for professional brewers, brewery owners and brewery marketing directors for concentrated, affordable brewing education and idea sharing to improve brewery quality and performance. This is the only industry event that serves both brewpubs and breweries. BrewExpo America allows exhibitors and buyers to develop profitable business relationships and helps them encounter the latest and the best that industry vendors have to offer. Est attendance: 1,200. For info: Brewers Association, 736 Pearl St, Boulder, CO 80302. Phone: (303) 447-0816. Fax: (303) 447-2825. E-mail: cindy@brewersassocia tion.org. Web: www.beertown.org/events/index.html.

HAROLD WASHINGTON ELECTED FIRST BLACK MAYOR OF CHICAGO: ANNIVERSARY. Apr 11, 1983. Harold Washington defeated Bernard Epton and became the first black mayor of Chicago. Of the city's 1.6 million voters a record 82 percent voted. Washington won 51 percent of the votes, which split along racial lines. He was reelected in April 1987, but died suddenly seven months later at his office, Nov 25, 1987.

HUGHES, CHARLES EVANS: BIRTH ANNIVERSARY. Apr 11, 1862. 11th chief justice of the US Supreme Court. Born at Glens Falls, NY. Died at Osterville, MA, Aug 27, 1948.

JULIAN, PERCY: BIRTH ANNIVERSARY. Apr 11, 1899. Percy Julian, producer of a synthetic progesterone using soybeans, was born at Montgomery, AL. He also developed a cheaper method of producing cortisone, a drug to treat glaucoma and a chemical foam to fight petroleum fires. Julian died Apr 19, 1975, at Waukegan, IL.

LIBERATION OF BUCHENWALD CONCENTRATION CAMP: ANNIVERSARY. Apr 11, 1945. Buchenwald, north of Weimar, Germany, was entered by Allied troops. It was the first of the Nazi concentration camps to be liberated. It had been established in 1937, and about 56,000 people died there.

MAWLID AL NABI: THE BIRTHDAY OF THE PROPHET MUHAMMAD. Apr 11. Mawlid al Nabi (Birth of the Prophet Muhammad) is observed on Muslim calendar date Rabi al-Awal 12, 1427. Different methods for calculating the visibility of the new moon crescent at Mecca are used by different Muslim groups. US date may vary. Began at sunset the preceding day.

MESSICK, DALE: 100th BIRTH ANNIVERSARY. Apr 4, 1906. Dalia (Dale) Messick, born at South Bend, IN, was the creator of the intrepid, glamorous globe-trotting reporter Brenda Starr in the comic strip of the same name that debuted in June 1940. It is still syndicated today. Messick, one of the first women to break into comics, retired from the strip in the 1980s and died at Sonoma County, CA, on Apr 5, 2005.

SPACE MILESTONE: *APOLLO 13* (US). Apr 11, 1970. Astronauts Lovell, Haise and Swigert endangered when oxygen tank ruptured. Planned moon landing canceled. Details of accident made public and world shared concern for crew who splashed down successfully in the Pacific Apr 17.

SPELMAN COLLEGE ESTABLISHED: 125th ANNIVERSARY. Apr 11, 1881. Spelman College, with funding from the Rockefeller family, opened its doors for the first time with the purpose of educating young African-American women. The institution, located at Atlanta, GA, was dubbed "the Radcliffe for Negro women."

UGANDA: LIBERATION DAY. Apr 11. Republic of Uganda celebrates anniversary of overthrow of Idi Amin's dictatorship in 1979.

	S	M	T	W	T	F	S
April 2006							1
	2	3	4	5	6	7	8
	9	10	11	12	13	14	15
	16	17	18	19	20	21	22
	23	24	25	26	27	28	29
	30						

BIRTHDAYS TODAY

Tony Brown, 73, journalist, host of "Tony Brown," born Charleston, WV, Apr 11, 1933.

Oleg Cassini, 93, fashion designer, born Paris, France, Apr 11, 1913.

Ellen Goodman, 58, Pulitzer Prize–winning columnist, born Newton, MA, Apr 11, 1948.

Joel Grey, 74, actor (Oscar for *Cabaret; The Seven Per Cent Solution*), born Joe Katz at Cleveland, OH, Apr 11, 1932.

Bill Irwin, 56, actor, choreographer (*The Regard of Flight*), born Santa Monica, CA, Apr 11, 1950.

Ethel Kennedy, 78, widow of Robert Kennedy, born Greenwich, CT, Apr 11, 1928.

Louise Lasser, 67, actress ("Mary Hartman, Mary Hartman"), born New York, NY, Apr 11, 1939.

Peter Riegert, 59, actor (*Local Hero, Crossing Delancey*), born New York, NY, Apr 11, 1947.

Bret William Saberhagen, 42, former baseball player, born Chicago Heights, IL, Apr 11, 1964.

Jean-Claude Servan-Schreiber, 88, journalist, author (*The Chosen and the Choice*), born Paris, France, Apr 11, 1918.

Meshach Taylor, 59, actor ("Dave's World," "Designing Women"), born Boston, MA, Apr 11, 1947.

APRIL 12 — WEDNESDAY

Day 102 — 263 Remaining

ATTACK ON FORT SUMTER: ANNIVERSARY. Apr 12, 1861. After months of escalating tension, Major Robert Anderson refused to evacuate Fort Sumter at Charleston, SC. Confederate troops under the command of General P.T. Beauregard opened fire on the harbor fort at 4:30 AM and continued until Major Anderson surrendered on Apr 13. No lives were lost despite the firing of some 40,000 shells in the first major engagement of the American Civil War.

THE BIG WIND: ANNIVERSARY. Apr 12, 1934. The highest-velocity natural wind ever recorded occurred in the morning at the Mount Washington, NH, Observatory. Three weather observers, Wendell Stephenson, Alexander McKenzie and Salvatore Pagliuca, observed and recorded the phenomenon in which gusts reached 231 miles per hour—"the strongest natural wind ever recorded on the earth's surface." The 50th anniversary was observed at the site in 1984, with the three original observers participating in the ceremony.

CLAY, HENRY: BIRTH ANNIVERSARY. Apr 12, 1777. Statesman, born at Hanover County, VA. Served as the Speaker of the House of Representatives and later became the leader of the new Whig party. He was defeated for the presidency three times. Clay died at Washington, DC, June 29, 1852.

FDR COMMEMORATIVE CEREMONY. Apr 12. Little White House, Warm Springs, GA. Annual ceremony honoring Franklin Delano Roosevelt on the anniversary of his death in Warm Springs. Keynote speaker and Marine color guard highlight this impressive ceremony. Est attendance: 1,000. For info: Mgr, Little White House, 401 Little White House Rd, Warm Springs, GA 31830. Phone: (706) 655-5870.

HALIFAX INDEPENDENCE DAY: ANNIVERSARY. Apr 12, 1776. North Carolina. Anniversary of the resolution adopted by the Provincial Congress of North Carolina at Halifax, NC, authorizing the delegates from North Carolina to the Continental Congress to vote for a Declaration of Independence.

HALL, LYMAN: BIRTH ANNIVERSARY. Apr 12, 1724. Signer of the Declaration of Independence. Born at Wallingford, CT, he died at Burke County, GA, Oct 19, 1790.

MASSACRE AT FORT PILLOW: ANNIVERSARY. Apr 12, 1864. After surrounding Fort Pillow, TN, Confederate General Nathan Bedford Forrest attacked the stronghold on this date. The ensuing Confederate victory led to many casualties, many of them black Union soldiers. Although Forrest claimed that the large amount of casualties was a result of the fort's refusal to surrender, most believe that Forrest's men massacred the defenseless troops after the fort was surrendered. The action inflamed Northern sentiments and is considered one of the most controversial events of the Civil War.

NATIONAL LICORICE DAY. Apr 12. Celebrating black licorice, its history, health benefits and world reknown as a delightful confection. Throughout the entire month of April, Licorice International will present seminars and other special events to educate and entertain the public. For info: Elizabeth Erlandson, Licorice Intl, 803 Q St, Lincoln, NE 68508. Phone: (402) 488-1230. E-mail: elizabeth@licoriceinternational.com. Web: www.licoriceinternational.com.

PASSOVER BEGINS AT SUNDOWN. Apr 12. See "Pesach" (Apr 13).

POLIO VACCINE: ANNIVERSARY. Apr 12, 1955. Anniversary of announcement that the polio vaccine developed by American physician Dr. Jonas E. Salk was "safe, potent and effective." Incidence of the dreaded infantile paralysis, or poliomyelitis, declined by 95 percent following introduction of preventive vaccines. The first mass innoculations of children with the Salk vaccine had begun in Pittsburgh, Feb 23, 1954.

ROOSEVELT, FRANKLIN DELANO: DEATH ANNIVERSARY. Apr 12, 1945. With the end of WWII only months away, the nation and the world were stunned by the sudden death of the president shortly into his fourth term of office. Roosevelt, 32nd president of the US (Mar 4, 1933–Apr 12, 1945), was the only president to serve more than two terms—he was elected to four consecutive terms. He died at Warm Springs, GA.

SPACE MILESTONE: *COLUMBIA STS-1* (US) FIRST SHUTTLE FLIGHT: 25th ANNIVERSARY. Apr 12, 1981. First flight of shuttle *Columbia*. Two astronauts (John Young and Robert Crippen), on first manned US space mission since *Apollo-Soyuz* in July 1976, spent 54 hours in space (36 orbits of Earth) before landing at Edwards Air Force Base, CA, Apr 14.

SPACE MILESTONE: *DISCOVERY* (US). Apr 12, 1985. On its 16th mission (from Kennedy Space Center, FL) shuttle *Discovery* was launched carrying US Senator Jake Garn as a member of its crew of seven.

SPACE MILESTONE: *VOSTOK I*, FIRST MAN IN SPACE: 45th ANNIVERSARY. Apr 12, 1961. Yuri Gagarin became the first man in space when he made a 108-minute voyage, orbiting Earth in a 10,395-lb vehicle, *Vostok I*, launched by the USSR.

TRUANCY LAW: ANNIVERSARY. Apr 12, 1853. The first truancy law was enacted at New York. A $50 fine was charged against parents whose children between the ages of 5 and 15 were absent from school.

WALK ON YOUR WILD SIDE DAY. Apr 12. Time's wasting, friends. It's high time you went out and did some things no one expects you to do. Be unpredictable for once. Go to work dressed like a gorilla, get a master's degree—do something "they" said you'd never ever do. [©2003 by WH.] For info: Thomas & Ruth Roy, Wellcat Holidays, 2418 Long Lane, Lebanon, PA 17046. Phone: (717) 279-0184. E-mail: info@wellcat.com. Web: www.wellcat.com.

"YOUR HIT PARADE" RADIO PREMIERE: ANNIVERSARY. Apr 12, 1935. This program debuted on radio in 1935 with its countdown of the week's top songs. In 1950 it became a TV program. See also: "Your Hit Parade TV Premiere: Anniversary" (Oct 7).

BIRTHDAYS TODAY

David Cassidy, 56, singer ("Cherish"), actor ("The Partridge Family"), born New York, NY, Apr 12, 1950.

Tom Clancy, 59, author (*The Hunt for Red October, Red Storm Rising*), born Baltimore, MD, Apr 12, 1947.

Beverly Cleary, 90, author (*Ramona* series for children; winner of the Newbery Medal for *Dear Mr Henshaw*), born McMinnville, OR, Apr 12, 1916.

Claire Danes, 27, actress (*The Hours, Romeo + Juliet*), born New York, NY, Apr 12, 1979.

Shannen Doherty, 35, actress ("Beverly Hills 90210," *Night Shift, Heathers*), born Memphis, TN, Apr 12, 1971.

Andy Garcia, 50, actor (*The Untouchables; The Godfather, Part III*), born Havana, Cuba, Apr 12, 1956.

Herbie Hancock, 66, musician, born Chicago, IL, Apr 12, 1940.

Dan Lauria, 59, actor ("The Wonder Years," *Stakeout*), born Brooklyn, NY, Apr 12, 1947.

David Letterman, 59, comedian, TV talk-show host ("Late Show with David Letterman"), born Indianapolis, IN, Apr 12, 1947.

Ed O'Neill, 60, actor ("Married . . . With Children," *Deliverance, Wayne's World*), born Youngstown, OH, Apr 12, 1946.

APRIL 13 — THURSDAY

Day 103 — 262 Remaining

BECKETT, SAMUEL: 100th BIRTH ANNIVERSARY. Apr 13, 1906. Author, critic and playwright, born at Foxrock, County Dublin, Ireland. Beckett is best remembered for his plays, including *Waiting for Godot, Endgame, Krapp's Last Tape* and *Happy Days*. Beckett settled at Paris, France, in 1937 and served with an underground resistance group during the early years of WWII. In the years following the war he wrote the challenging novels *Molloy, Malone Dies* and *The Unnamable* and two plays, *Eleutheria* and *Waiting for Godot. Waiting for Godot* received an acclaimed production at Paris in January 1953, and with it Beckett achieved worldwide renown. Awarded the Nobel Prize for Literature in 1969, he died Dec 22, 1989, at Paris, France.

BUTTS, ALFRED M.: BIRTH ANNIVERSARY. Apr 13, 1899. Alfred Butts was a jobless architect in the Depression when he invented the board game Scrabble. The game was just a fad for Butts's friends until a Macy's executive saw the game being played at a resort in 1952, and the world's largest store began carrying it. Manufacturing of the game was turned over to Selchow & Righter when 35 workers were producing 6,000 sets a week. Butts received three cents per set for years. He said, "One-third went to taxes. I gave one-third away, and the other third enabled me to have an enjoyable life." Butts was born at Poughkeepsie, NY. He died Apr 4, 1993, at Rhinebeck, NY.

CASSIDY, BUTCH: BIRTH ANNIVERSARY. Apr 13, 1866. Born Robert Leroy Parker at Beaver, UT, son of Mormon pioneer Maximillian Parker, he became a notorious outlaw of the Old West and leader of The Wild Bunch gang. Some believed he died in a gun battle at Bolivia in 1909, while others are certain he returned and died in the USA.

FIRST BASEBALL STRIKE ENDS: ANNIVERSARY. Apr 13, 1972. Major league baseball players and owners agreed on a settlement in which owners added an additional $500,000 to the players' pension fund. This ended the first baseball strike, which had begun Apr 5 when the season opener was canceled.

GREAT CHICAGO FLOOD: ANNIVERSARY. Apr 13, 1992. On this morning Chicagoans awoke to one of the most unusual disasters of modern times: the Chicago River broke through a rupture in an old underground freight tunnel wall, sending millions of gallons of water flooding into the tunnel system beneath the downtown business district. The water poured into basements of buildings that previously had been connected to the tunnel system. The greater Loop area had to be evacuated as electricity was cut off ahead of the rising water. A hectic effort mounted to plug the leak in the river eventually succeeded. Once the flow of water had stopped, the city began the slow and expensive process of draining the water.

INTERNATIONAL PLANT APPRECIATION DAY. Apr 13. Imagine a world without plants. No coffee, no cereal. No roses, no trees. No cotton t-shirts, no toilet paper. No kidding! People and plants are entwined by threads that are woven tightly into the fabric of life. Celebrate your neighbors, the plants, by giving a houseplant to a friend, kissing a tree, growing tomatoes or wearing cotton. Annually, Apr 13. For info: Marion Owen, PO Box 1694, Kodiak, AK 99615. Phone: (907) 486-5079. E-mail: marion@ptialaska.net. Web: www.upbeetcommunications.com.

ITALY: PROCESSION OF THE ADDOLORATA AND PROCESSION OF THE MYSTERIES. Apr 13-14. Taranto. Procession of the Addolorata is held on Holy Thursday, while the Procession of the Mysteries takes place on Good Friday. Both processions have in common the very slow pace of the participants and their unusual costumes.

JEFFERSON, THOMAS: BIRTH ANNIVERSARY. Apr 13, 1743. 3rd president of the US (Mar 4, 1801–Mar 3, 1809), 2nd vice president (1797–1801), born at Albermarle County, VA. Jefferson, who died at Charlottesville, VA, July 4, 1826, wrote his own epitaph: "Here was buried Thomas Jefferson, author of the Declaration of American Independence, of the statute of Virginia for religious freedom, and father of the University of Virginia." A holiday in Alabama and Oklahoma. See also: "Adams, John, and Jefferson, Thomas: Death Anniversary" (July 4).

★**JEFFERSON, THOMAS: BIRTH ANNIVERSARY.** Apr 13. Presidential Proclamation 2276, of Mar 21, 1938, covers all succeeding years. (Pub Res No. 60 of Aug 16, 1937.)

MAUNDY THURSDAY or HOLY THURSDAY. Apr 13. The Thursday before Easter, originally "dies mandate," celebrates Christ's injunction to love one another, "Mandatus novum do vobis. . . ." ("A new commandment I give to you. . . .")

MOON PHASE: FULL MOON. Apr 13. Moon enters Full Moon phase at 12:40 PM, EDT.

★**NATIONAL D.A.R.E. DAY.** Apr 13. The Drug Abuse Resistance Education (D.A.R.E.) Program, founded in 1983 by the Los Angeles Police Department and the Los Angeles Unified School District, helps give children in grades K–12 the skills they need to avoid involvement in drugs, gangs and violence. Nearly 75 percent of American school districts offer D.A.R.E. training.

PESACH or PASSOVER. Apr 13-20. Hebrew calendar dates: Nisan 15–22, 5766. The first day of Passover begins an eight-day celebration of the delivery of the Jews from slavery in Egypt. Unleavened bread (matzoh) is eaten at this time. Began at sundown Apr 12.

PHILIPPINES: MORIONE'S FESTIVAL. Apr 13-16. Marinduque Island. Provincewide masquerade, Lenten plays and celebrations. Annually, Holy Thursday through Easter Sunday.

★ ★ ★

	S	M	T	W	T	F	S
April							1
2006	2	3	4	5	6	7	8
	9	10	11	12	13	14	15
	16	17	18	19	20	21	22
	23	24	25	26	27	28	29
	30						

PREMIERE OF HANDEL'S *MESSIAH*: ANNIVER-SARY. Apr 13, 1742. In a charity performance at Dublin, Ireland's New Musick Hall on Fishamble Street, George Frederick Handel sat at the harpsichord and conducted the first concert of his masterpiece, *Messiah*. This sacred oratorio became Handel's most popular work and has been performed every year since 1742. Newspapers of the day anticipated the popularity of the first performance and asked ladies not to wear hoops under their skirts and gentlemen not to wear swords so that 700 people could fit into a hall designed for 600. Some years later, King George II stood up in admiration of the Hallelujah Chorus, starting a tradition still followed by audiences to this day.

SILENT SPRING PUBLICATION: ANNIVERSARY. Apr 13, 1962. Rachel Carson's *Silent Spring* warned humankind that for the first time in history every person is subjected to contact with dangerous chemicals from conception until death. Carson painted a vivid picture of how chemicals—used in many ways but particularly in pesticides—have upset the balance of nature, undermining the survival of countless species. This enormously popular and influential book was a soft-spoken battle cry to protect our natural surroundings. Its publication signaled the beginning of the environmental movement.

SRI LANKA: SINHALA AND TAMIL NEW YEAR. Apr 13–14. This New Year festival includes traditional games, the wearing of new clothes in auspicious colors and special foods. Public holiday.

THAILAND: SONGKRAN FESTIVAL. Apr 13–15. Public holiday. Thai New Year Festival (also known as the "Water Festival"). To welcome the new year the image of Buddha is bathed with holy or fragrant water and lustral water is sprinkled on celebrants. Joyous event, especially observed at Buddhist temples.

BIRTHDAYS TODAY

Peabo Bryson, 55, singer ("Just Another Day," "I Can Make It Better"), born Greenville, SC, Apr 13, 1951.

Jack Casady, 62, musician, born Washington, DC, Apr 13, 1944.

Bill Conti, 64, composer (Oscar for *The Right Stuff*; "Falcon Crest," "Inside Edition"), born Providence, RI, Apr 13, 1942.

Tony Dow, 61, actor ("Leave It to Beaver"), born Hollywood, CA, Apr 13, 1945.

Edward Fox, 69, actor (*The Day of the Jackal, Gandhi, The Dresser*), born London, England, Apr 13, 1937.

Al Green, 60, singer ("Let's Stay Together," "You Ought to Be with Me"), born Forrest City, AR, Apr 13, 1946.

Garry Kasparov, 43, International Grandmaster chess player, born Baku, Azerbaijan, Apr 13, 1963.

Davis Love, III, 42, golfer, born Charlotte, NC, Apr 13, 1964.

Ron Perlman, 56, actor (*Hellboy*, "Beauty and the Beast"), born New York, NY, Apr 13, 1950.

Saundra Santiago, 49, actress ("Miami Vice"), born the Bronx, NY, Apr 13, 1957.

Rick Schroder, 36, actor ("Silver Spoons," "NYPD Blue," *The Champ*), born Staten Island, NY, Apr 13, 1970.

Paul Sorvino, 67, actor ("Law & Order"), born Brooklyn, NY, Apr 13, 1939.

Lyle Waggoner, 71, actor ("The Carol Burnett Show," "Wonder Woman"), born Kansas City, KS, Apr 13, 1935.

Max M. Weinberg, 55, musician, bandleader ("Late Night with Conan O'Brien"), born South Orange, NJ, Apr 13, 1951.

APRIL 14 — FRIDAY
Day 104 — 261 Remaining

AFRMA DISPLAY AT AMERICA'S FAMILY PET EXPO. Apr 14–16 (tentative). Costa Mesa, CA. Rats and mice are emerging as ideal pets: they provide all the pleasure and satisfaction of a warm, cuddly, intelligent and friendly pet companion. The American Fancy Rat and Mouse Association (AFRMA) was founded in 1983 to promote the breeding and exhibition of fancy rats and mice, to educate the public on their positive qualities as companion animals and to provide information on their proper care. For info: AFRMA (CAE), PO Box 2589, Winnetka, CA 91396-2589. Phone: (909) 685-2350 or (818) 992-5564 or (626) 966-0350. Fax: (818) 592-6590. E-mail: afrma@afrma.org. Web: www.afrma.org.

CAMPBELL BECOMES FIRST AMERICAN AIR ACE: ANNIVERSARY. Apr 14, 1918. Lieutenant Douglas Campbell became the first American pilot to achieve the designation of ACE when he shot down his fifth German aircraft.

CHILDREN WITH ALOPECIA DAY. Apr 14. If you are a child (or have a child) who is losing hair because of the disease Alopeica Areata, today is your day to stand up and be proud of not having hair. For info: Jeffery Woytovich, The Children's Alopecia Project, PO Box 6036, Wyomissing, PA 19610. Phone: (610) 375-3453. E-mail: jefferywoytovich@yahoo.com. Web: www.childrensalopeciaproject.org.

CHINCOTEAGUE ISLAND EASTER DECOY SHOW. Apr 14–15. Chincoteague Island, VA. Wildfowl carving and wildlife art exhibits. Annually, Easter weekend. Est attendance: 2,000. For info: Chincoteague Chamber of Commerce, 6733 Maddux Blvd, Chincoteague Island, VA 23336. Phone: (757) 336-6161. Fax: (757) 336-1242. E-mail: chincochamber@verizon.net. Web: www.chincoteaguechamber.com.

ENGLAND: BRITISH AND WORLD MARBLES CHAMPIONSHIP. Apr 14. Greyhound Public House, Tinsley Green, West Sussex. Since 1932, more than 100 competitors have vied for team and individual titles in the marbles tournament. Annually, on Good Friday. For info: British Marbles Board of Control. Phone: (44) (1403) 730-602. Fax (44) (1403) 733-877. E-mail: marblesam@hotmail.com. Or Bognor Regis Visitor's Centre, Belmont St, Bognor Regis, West Sussex, England PO21 1BJ. Phone: (44) (1243) 823-140.

ENGLAND: DEVIZES TO WESTMINSTER INTERNATIONAL CANOE RACE. Apr 14–17. 58th year. Starts from Wharf Car Park, Wharf St, Devizes, Wiltshire. Canoes race along 125 miles of the Kennet and Avon canals and the River Thames, ending at County Hall Steps, Westminster Bridge Rd, London. Annually, Good Friday to Easter Monday. Est attendance: 6,000. For info: Competition Secretary, Boscombe Forge, Church Road, Bookham, Surrey, England KT23 3JG. Phone: (44) (020) 7620-0298. Web: www.dwrace.org.uk.

FIRST AMERICAN ABOLITION SOCIETY FOUNDED: ANNIVERSARY. Apr 14, 1775. The first abolition organization formed in the US was The Society for the Relief of Free Negroes Unlawfully Held in Bondage, founded at Philadelphia, PA.

FIRST DICTIONARY OF AMERICAN ENGLISH PUBLISHED: ANNIVERSARY. Apr 14, 1828. Noah Webster published his *American Dictionary of the English Language*.

GIELGUD, SIR JOHN: BIRTH ANNIVERSARY. Apr 14, 1904. Director and actor, born at London, England. A legend of the stage, he played the role of Hamlet more than 500 times. He made his professional film debut in 1924 in *Who Is the Man?*. Other film credits include *Arthur, Murder on the Orient Express* and *Plenty*. He won the Tony Award for best director in 1961 for *Big Fish Little Fish*. He died at Buckinghamshire, England, May 21, 2000.

GOOD FRIDAY. Apr 14. Observed in commemoration of the crucifixion. Oldest Christian celebration. Possible corruption of

"God's Friday." Observed in some manner by most Christian sects and as a public holiday or part holiday in Canada and in Delaware, Florida, Hawaii, Illinois, Indiana, New Jersey, North Carolina, Pennsylvania and Tennessee.

GRAPES OF WRATH PUBLISHED: ANNIVERSARY. Apr 14, 1939. John Steinbeck's novel of the Great Depression, *Grapes of Wrath*, won the 1940 Pulitzer Prize. It chronicled the mass migration to California of dispossessed farmers from the Dust Bowl region of the Great Plains.

HONDURAS: DIA DE LAS AMERICAS. Apr 14. Honduras. Pan-American Day, a national holiday.

HUYGENS, CHRISTIAAN: BIRTH ANNIVERSARY. Apr 14, 1629. Scientist, born at The Hague, Netherlands. He discovered the rings of Saturn and the wave or pulse theory of light. In 1656 he invented the pendulum clock. He died at The Hague, June 8, 1695.

INDIA: VAISAKHI. Apr 14. Sikh holiday that commemorates the founding of the brotherhood of the Khalsa in 1699. A large fair is held at the Golden Temple at Amritsar, the central shrine of Sikhism. While the date may vary in different parts of India, this holiday always falls in April or May.

INTERNATIONAL MOMENT OF LAUGHTER DAY. Apr 14. Laughter is a potent and powerful way to deal with the difficulties of modern living. Since the physical, emotional and spiritual benefits of laughter are widely accepted, this day is set aside for everyone to take the necessary time to experience the power of laughter. For info: Izzy Gesell, Head Honcho of Wide Angle Humor, PO Box 962, Northampton, MA 01061. Phone: (413) 586-2634. Fax: (413) 585-0407. E-mail: izzy@izzyg.com. Web: www.izzyg.com.

LINCOLN, ABRAHAM: ASSASSINATION ANNIVERSARY. Apr 14, 1865. President Abraham Lincoln was shot while watching a performance of *Our American Cousin* at Ford's Theatre, Washington, DC. He died the following day. The assassin was John Wilkes Booth, a young actor.

OZARK UFO CONFERENCE. Apr 14–16. Inn of the Ozarks Conference Center, Eureka Springs, AR. 18th annual meeting of researchers from various states and foreign countries to inform the public of the latest news concerning UFOs. Speakers include authors of books on the subject and people who have investigated UFO cases; program includes audiovisual presentations of UFO evidence. Est attendance: 400. For info: Lucius Farish, Ozark UFO Conference, #2 Caney Valley Dr, Plumerville, AR 72127-8725. Phone: (501) 354-2558. E-mail: ozarkufo@webtv.net. Web: www.ozarkufo.com.

★**PAN-AMERICAN DAY.** Apr 14. Presidential Proclamation 1912, of May 28, 1930, covers every Apr 14 (required by Governing Board of Pan-American Union). Proclamation issued each year since 1948. Commemorates the first International Conference of American States in 1890.

PAN-AMERICAN DAY IN FLORIDA. Apr 14. A ceremonial day in Florida which is observed in the public schools as a day honoring the republics of Latin America. When Apr 14 does not fall on a school day, the governor may designate the preceding Friday or the following Monday as Pan-American Day.

PRESIDENT TAFT OPENS BASEBALL SEASON: ANNIVERSARY. Apr 14, 1910. President William Howard Taft began a sports tradition by throwing out the first baseball of the season at an American League game between Washington and Philadelphia. Washington won 3–0.

STOCK EXCHANGE HOLIDAY (GOOD FRIDAY). Apr 14. The holiday schedules for the various exchanges are subject to change if relevant rules, regulations or exchange policies are revised. If you have questions, phone: American Stock Exchange (212) 306-1000, Chicago Board of Trade (312) 435-3500, Chicago Board of Options Exchange (312) 786-5600, NASDAQ Stock Market (646) 441-5200, New York Stock Exchange (212) 656-3000, Pacific Stock Exchange (415) 393-4000, Philadelphia Stock Exchange (215) 496-5000.

SULLIVAN, ANNE: BIRTH ANNIVERSARY. Apr 14, 1866. Anne Sullivan, born at Feeding Hills, MA, became well known for "working miracles" with Helen Keller, who was blind and deaf. Nearly blind herself, Sullivan used a manual alphabet communicated by the sense of touch to teach Keller to read, write and speak and then to help her go on to higher education. Anne Sullivan died Oct 20, 1936, at Forest Hills, NY.

TOYNBEE, ARNOLD JOSEPH: BIRTH ANNIVERSARY. Apr 14, 1889. English historian, author of monumental *Study of History*. Born at London, England; died at York, England, Oct 22, 1975.

UNITED KINGDOM: GOOD FRIDAY BANK HOLIDAY. Apr 14. Bank and public holiday in England, Wales, Scotland and Northern Ireland.

BIRTHDAYS TODAY

Adrien Brody, 33, actor (Oscar for *The Pianist*), born New York, NY, Apr 14, 1973.

Robert Carlyle, 45, actor (*Angela's Ashes, The Full Monty*), born Glasgow, Scotland, Apr 14, 1961.

Julie Christie, 66, actress (*Dr. Zhivago, Petulia, Shampoo*), born Chukua, India, Apr 14, 1940.

Cynthia Cooper, 43, basketball player, born Chicago, IL, Apr 14, 1963.

Bradford Dillman, 76, actor (*Compulsion*, "Falcon Crest"), born San Francisco, CA, Apr 14, 1930.

Brad Garrett, 46, comedian, actor ("Everybody Loves Raymond"), born Woodland Hills, CA, Apr 14, 1960.

Sarah Michelle Gellar, 29, actress (*Scooby-Doo*, "Buffy the Vampire Slayer"), born New York, NY, Apr 14, 1977.

Anthony Michael Hall, 38, actor, comedian ("Saturday Night Live," *Sixteen Candles, The Breakfast Club*), born Boston, MA, Apr 14, 1968.

David Christopher Justice, 40, baseball player, born Cincinnati, OH, Apr 14, 1966.

Loretta Lynn, 71, singer/songwriter ("Coal Miner's Daughter," "The Pill"), born Butcher's Hollow, KY, Apr 14, 1935.

Gregory Alan (Greg) Maddux, 40, baseball player, born San Angelo, TX, Apr 14, 1966.

Peter Edward (Pete) Rose, 65, former baseball manager and player, born Cincinnati, OH, Apr 14, 1941.

Emma Thompson, 47, actress (Oscar for *Howard's End; Wit, Sense and Sensibility*), screenwriter (Oscar for *Sense and Sensibility*), born London, England, Apr 14, 1959.

	S	M	T	W	T	F	S
April							1
2006	2	3	4	5	6	7	8
	9	10	11	12	13	14	15
	16	17	18	19	20	21	22
	23	24	25	26	27	28	29
	30						

APRIL 15 — SATURDAY
Day 105 — 260 Remaining

ASTRONOMERS FIND NEW SOLAR SYSTEM: ANNIVERSARY. Apr 15, 1999. Astronomers from San Francisco State University working at an observatory in Arizona announced the discovery of the first multiplanet system ever found orbiting around a star other than our own. Three planets orbit the star Upsilon Andromedae, which can be seen with the naked eye. This suggests that the Milky Way probably teems with similar planetary systems.

BENTON, THOMAS HART: BIRTH ANNIVERSARY. Apr 15, 1889. Thomas Hart Benton was an artist whose work was indicative of the American style of painting known as Regionalism. His works of life in the Midwest and South were not always flattering to their subjects, but his style became known as a truly American style of painting. He was born at Neosho, MO, and died at Kansas City, MO, Jan 19, 1975.

"BUCK ROGERS" TV PREMIERE: ANNIVERSARY. Apr 15, 1950. At first a radio show, "Buck Rogers" premiered on ABC with Kem Dibbs. Buck was an average American who woke up from a cave behind Niagara Falls to find himself in the year 2430. The show featured Lou Prentis as Lieutenant Wilma Deering; Harry Sothern as Dr. Huer and Harry Kingston as Black Barney Wade. Buck was later played by Robert Pastene.

BUNNY BOP AND HOP. Apr 15. Aiken, SC. The Bunny Bop and Hop is a children's Easter event with an egg hunt, carnival rides and games at Virginia Acres Soccer Field. Annually, the Saturday before Easter. Est attendance: 400. For info: Bunny Bop and Hop, City of Aiken Parks and Recreation, Odell Weeks Center, PO Box 1177, Aiken, SC 29802. Phone: (803) 642-7631. Fax: (803) 642-7639. E-mail: howeeks@aiken.net.

CHINA: CANTON SPRING TRADE FAIR. Apr 15–May 15. The Guangzhou (Canton) Spring Trade Fair is held on the same dates each year.

CYPRUS: THE PROCESSION OF ICON OF SAINT LAZARUS. Apr 15. Larnaca, Cyprus. The tomb of Lazarus (the man raised from the dead by Christ) resides in the Ayios Lazaros Church—built by Emperor Leo VI in the ninth century. Eight days before the Orthodox Easter Sunday, his icon is taken through the streets of Lanarca.

EASTER BEACH RUN. Apr 15. Daytona Beach, FL. The 39th annual beach run on "the world's most famous beach" includes a four-mile run for 28 age divisions, a two-mile run for youth 11 years old and younger, a two-mile fun run/walk, kids runs for ages 9 and under and a road race division for individuals who are physically challenged. Est attendance: 1,200. For info: Easter Beach Run, Daytona Beach Leisure Services Dept, PO Box 2451, Daytona Beach, FL 32115-2451. Phone: (386) 671-3420 or (386) 322-0835 (Daytona Track Club). Fax: (386) 671-3410. Web: www.easterbeachrun.org.

EASTER EGG HUNT. Apr 15. The Laurels of Shane Hill Nursing Home and Maplewood of Shanes Village Assisted Living Center, Rockford, OH. Residents color Easter eggs to hide for the Egg Hunt held the Saturday before Easter for children and grandchildren of residents, staff and the surrounding community. Pictures with the Easter Bunny are offered for participants. Est attendance: 100. For info: Brooke Reyman, Activities Dir, The Laurels of Shane Hill Nursing Home, 10731 State Rte 118, Rockford, OH 45882-0159. Phone: (419) 363-2620.

EASTER EVEN. Apr 15. The Saturday before Easter. Last day of Holy Week and of Lent.

FIRST MCDONALD'S OPENS: ANNIVERSARY. Apr 15, 1955. The first franchised McDonald's was opened at Des Plaines, IL, by Ray Kroc, who had gotten the idea from a hamburger joint at San Bernardino, CA, run by the McDonald brothers. On opening day a hamburger was 15 cents. The Big Mac was introduced in 1968 for 49 cents and the Quarter Pounder in 1971 for 53 cents. By the late 1990s, there were more than 25,000 McDonald's in 115 countries.

FIRST SCHOOL FOR DEAF FOUNDED: ANNIVERSARY. Apr 15, 1817. Thomas Hopkins Gallaudet and Laurent Clerc founded the first US public school for the deaf, Connecticut Asylum for the Education and Instruction of Deaf and Dumb Persons (now the American School for the Deaf), at Hartford, CT.

GEORGIA RENAISSANCE SPRING FESTIVAL. Apr 15–June 4. Atlanta, GA. A rollicking rendition of a 16th-century English faire. Jousting knights, jugglers, Shakespearean parodies and more than 100 shows daily. Feast like a king and shop like royalty. Saturdays, Sundays and Memorial Day. Est attendance: 200,000. For info: Sarah Petermann, Georgia Renaissance Festival, PO Box 986, Fairburn, GA 30213. Phone: (770) 964-8575. Fax: (770) 964-1477.

HUSBAND APPRECIATION DAY. Apr 15. Wives, show your husbands how much you love and appreciate them. Communicate the difference your husband makes in your life. Annually, the third Saturday in April. For info: Brooke Espinoza. E-mail: kept bythepowerofgod@yahoo.com.

"IN LIVING COLOR" TV PREMIERE: ANNIVERSARY. Apr 15, 1990. Fox's sketch comedy series, created by Keenen Ivory Wayans, was modeled after "Saturday Night Live." Between skits, the Fly Girls would entertain the studio audience with hip-hop dance (choreographed by soon-to-be film actress Rosie Perez). The show featured Wayans, his brothers Damon, Marlon and Shawn, his sister Kim, Tommy Davidson, David Alan Grier, T'Keyah "Crystal" Keymáh, Kelly Coffield, Kim Coles and Jim Carrey before he was Ace Ventura. Some of the most popular recurring characters were Homey, the embittered clown, the flammable Fire Marshall Bill and the effeminate movie critics of "Men on Film."

INCOME TAX PAY DAY—BUT NOT THIS YEAR. Apr 15. A day all Americans need to know—the day by which taxpayers are supposed to make their accounting of the previous year and pay their share of the cost of government. The US Internal Revenue Service provides free forms. But since Apr 15 is a Saturday in 2006, the deadline is extended to Apr 17.

JAMES, HENRY: BIRTH ANNIVERSARY. Apr 15, 1843. Novelist and critic, born at New York, NY. Among his best-known works are *The Portrait of a Lady, Washington Square* and *The Ambassadors.* James died Feb 28, 1916, at London, England.

JOHN WILKES BOOTH ESCAPE ROUTE TOUR. Apr 15 and 29. (Also Sept 9 and 23.) Clinton, MD. A 12-hour bus tour over the route used by Lincoln's assassin. For info: Surratt House Museum, Box 427, Clinton, MD 20735. Phone: (301) 868-1121. Fax: (301) 868-8177. Web: www.surratt.org.

KUUMBA ON THE BEACH. Apr 15. Hollywood, FL. A cultural event celebrating diversity and creativity. Features storytelling, dance and drumming, live music, arts and crafts, car show and motorcycle show. Est attendance: 5,000. For info: Cynthia Hancock, City of Hollywood, 1940 E Harrison St, Ste 101, Hollywood, FL 33020. Phone: (954) 921-3404. Fax: (954) 921-3572. E-mail: chancock@hollywoodfl.org. Web: www.hollywoodfl.org.

LAZARUS SATURDAY. Apr 15. Orthodox celebration of Christ raising Lazarus from the dead. Only time the resurrection liturgy is used on a day other than Sunday.

LONGYEAR, JOHN MUNROE: BIRTH ANNIVERSARY. Apr 15, 1850. American capitalist, landowner, philanthropist, one-time mayor of Marquette, MI. Disapproving of a railway route through Marquette, he caused his home, a stone castle-like showplace, to be torn down in 1903 and moved, stone by stone and stick by stick, in more than 190 freight cars and re-erected at Brookline, MA. Born at Lansing, MI, he died May 28, 1922.

MEGGA HUNT. Apr 15. Lively Park, Springfield, OR. Hunt for 25,000 eggs, play carnival games, enjoy onstage entertainment and ride the Willamalane Train. The valley's biggest egg hunt! Est attendance: 3,500. For info: Willamalane Park and Recreation District, 200 South Mill St, Springfield, OR 97477. Phone: (541) 736-4544. Web: www.willamalane.org.

NATIONAL AUCTIONEERS DAY. Apr 15. Recognizes the auction profession and its contribution to American commerce. Annually, the third Saturday in April. For info: National Auctioneers Association, 8880 Ballentine, Overland Park, KS 66214. Phone: (913) 541-8084. Fax: (913) 894-5281. E-mail: publicrelations@auctioneers.org. Web: www.auctioneers.org.

NATIONAL TAKE A WILD GUESS DAY. Apr 15. The day honoring guesses, hunches, inspirations, speculations and other forms of "intuitive intelligence." For info: Jim Barber, 1101 Marcano Blvd, Fort Lauderdale, FL 33322. Phone: (954) 476-9252. Fax: (954) 424-0309. E-mail: jim@thebarbershop.com. Web: www.thebarbershop.com.

PEALE, CHARLES WILLSON: BIRTH ANNIVERSARY. Apr 15, 1741 (OS). American portrait painter (best known for his many portraits of colonial and American Revolutionary War figures) was born at Queen Anne County, MD. His children Raphaelle, Rembrandt, Titian, Rubens and his niece Sarah were also artists. Died at Philadelphia, PA, Feb 22, 1827.

ROBINSON BREAKS BASEBALL COLOR LINE: ANNIVERSARY. Apr 15, 1947. Jackie Robinson became the first African American to play in the major leagues in the 20th century when he made his debut for the Brooklyn Dodgers against the Boston Braves. Robinson went 0-for-3 but scored the deciding run as the Dodgers prevailed, 5–3. He was later voted 1947's Rookie of the Year.

SIMMS, HILDA: BIRTH ANNIVERSARY. Apr 15, 1920. American stage and film actress, born Hilda Moses at Minneapolis, MN. She joined the American Negro Theater at Harlem, NY, in 1943 and was given the title role in *Anna Lucasta*. When the production moved to Broadway in 1944, it became the first all-black production to be performed on Broadway without a racial theme. Simms was the creative arts director of New York State's human rights division, through which she was instrumental in bringing discrimination against black actors to public attention during the 1960s. She died at Buffalo, NY, Feb 6, 1994.

SINKING OF THE *TITANIC*: ANNIVERSARY. Apr 15, 1912. The "unsinkable" luxury liner *Titanic* on its maiden voyage from Southampton, England, to New York, NY, struck an iceberg just before midnight Apr 14, and sank at 2:27 AM, Apr 15. The *Titanic* had 2,224 persons aboard. Of these, more than 1,500 were lost. About 700 people were rescued from the icy waters off Newfoundland by the liner *Carpathia*, which reached the scene about two hours after the *Titanic* went down. See also: "*Titanic* Discovered: Anniversary" (Sept 1).

SMITH, BESSIE: BIRTH ANNIVERSARY. Apr 15, 1894. The "Empress of the Blues," Bessie Smith, was born at Chattanooga, TN (year varies as late as 1900). She was assisted in her efforts to break into show business by Ma Rainey, the first great blues singer. Her first recording was made in February 1923. Smith died of injuries she sustained in an automobile accident at Clarksdale, MS, Sept 26, 1937.

★ ★ ★

	S	M	T	W	T	F	S
April							1
2006	2	3	4	5	6	7	8
	9	10	11	12	13	14	15
	16	17	18	19	20	21	22
	23	24	25	26	27	28	29
	30						

STRAWBERRY HILL RACES. Apr 15. Colonial Downs, New Kent, VA. Annual steeplechase horse race featuring a week of festivities leading up to the event. Elegant, yet fun, pre-race entertainment and tailgate competition on race day. $68,000 in purses. Sponsored by The State Fair of Virginia. Est attendance: 20,000. For info: Sue Mullins, Race Dir, Strawberry Hill Races, PO Box 26805, Richmond, VA 23261. Phone: (804) 569-3238. Fax: (804) 569-3252. E-mail: smullins@statefair.com.

THAT SUCKS DAY. Apr 15. Today is income tax pay day, quarterly estimated federal income tax payers' due date and the anniversary of the sinking of the *Titanic*. These events and more support a designation for a national THAT SUCKS Day. Visit our website's message boards to commiserate with others. Annually, Apr 15. For info: Bruce Novotny, 5826 Park Circle, Shawnee, KS 66216. Phone: (913) 962-2677. Fax: (913) 962-6926. E-mail: novovet@kcnet.com. Web: www.thatsucks.net.

WASHINGTON, HAROLD: BIRTH ANNIVERSARY. Apr 15, 1922. Illinois legislator and mayor of Chicago (1983–87). Born at Chicago, IL, and died there Nov 25, 1987. Harold Washington was one of the first African Americans to head a major US city. He was instrumental in tearing down Chicago's famed Democratic machine, a holdover from the many decades of domination by the Richard J. Daley administration.

WORLD COW CHIP–THROWING CHAMPIONSHIP® CONTEST. Apr 15. Beaver, OK. 37th annual. A highly specialized international organic sporting event which draws dung flingers from around the world. Also featuring a craft fair, carnival, food vendors and a parade. Est attendance: 2,000. For info: Beaver County Chamber of Commerce, PO Box 878, Beaver, OK 73932-0878. Phone: (580) 625-4726. Web: www.BeaverCountyChamberofCommerce.com.

BIRTHDAYS TODAY

Evelyn Ashford, 49, Olympic gold medal track athlete, born Shreveport, LA, Apr 15, 1957.

Linda Bloodworth-Thomason, 59, producer, writer ("Designing Women," "Evening Shade"), born Poplar Bluff, MO, Apr 15, 1947.

Claudia Cardinale, 68, actress (*The Pink Panther, Once Upon a Time in the West*), born Tunis, Tunisia, Apr 15, 1938.

Roy Clark, 73, singer and guitarist ("Yesterday, When I Was Young," regular on "Hee Haw"), born Meherrin, VA, Apr 15, 1933.

Heloise Cruse Evans, 55, newspaper columnist ("Hints from Heloise"), born Waco, TX, Apr 15, 1951.

Jason Sehorn, 35, football player, born Mt Shasta, CA, Apr 15, 1971.

Emma Watson, 16, actress (the Harry Potter films), born Oxford, England, Apr 15, 1990.

Amy Wright, 56, actress (*Breaking Away, Wise Blood, The Accidental Tourist*), born Chicago, IL, Apr 15, 1950.

APRIL 16 — SUNDAY

Day 106 — 259 Remaining

AMIS, KINGSLEY: BIRTH ANNIVERSARY. Apr 16, 1922. Author (*The Old Devils, Lucky Jim*), born at London, England, and died there Oct 22, 1995.

ANIMAL CRUELTY/HUMAN VIOLENCE AWARENESS WEEK. Apr 16–22. This campaign began in 2000 with the goal to bring more attention to the connection between animal cruelty and interpersonal violence. Each year, The Humane Society of the United States (HSUS) chooses a theme for the week and provides information and suggested ideas for professionals and the general public to get involved. For info: Humane Society of the US, 2100 L St NW, Washington, DC 20037. Phone: (202) 452-1100. E-mail: firststrike@hsus.org. Web: www.hsus.org/firststrike.

CHAPLIN, CHARLES SPENCER: BIRTH ANNIVERSARY. Apr 16, 1889. Celebrated film comedian who portrayed "The Little Tramp" was born at London, England. Film debut in

1914. Knighted in 1975. Died at Vevey, Switzerland, Dec 25, 1977. In his autobiography Chaplin wrote: "There are more valid facts and details in works of art than there are in history books." See also: "Chaplin's 'Tramp' Debuts: Anniversary" (Feb 7).

COCA–COLA SPRING SPLASH. Apr 16. Winter Park Resort, Winter Park, CO. One of Winter Park's most anticipated events, the wet and wild Spring Splash celebrates the joy of spring skiing. Spectators cheer as skiers and snowboarders struggle through a hilarious and challenging obstacle course that includes skimming across a pond of icy water to cross the finish line. Est attendance: 2,000. For info: Winter Park Resort, PO Box 36, Winter Park, CO 80482. Phone: (970) 726-1564. Fax: (970) 726-1572. E-mail: wpinfo@mail.skiwinterpark.com. Web: winter parkresort.com.

CONSUMER AWARENESS WEEK. Apr 16–20. Consumer advocate Bob O'Brien kicks off a weeklong event aimed at advising and helping consumers with their rights. For info: Bob O'Brien, Consumer Advocate, 1061 Koelle Blvd, Secaucus, NJ 07094. Phone/fax: (201) 865-4775. E-mail: bobtheebest@yahoo.com. Web: www.wtbq.com.

DENMARK: QUEEN MARGRETHE II'S BIRTHDAY. Apr 16. Thousands of children gather to cheer the queen (born 1940) at Amalienborg Palace and the Royal Guard wears scarlet gala uniforms.

DIEGO, JOSE de: BIRTH ANNIVERSARY. Apr 16, 1866. Puerto Rican patriot and political leader Jose de Diego was born at Aguadilla, PR. His birthday is a holiday in Puerto Rico. He died July 16, 1918, at New York, NY.

EASTER SUNDAY. Apr 16. Commemorates the Resurrection of Christ. Most joyous festival of the Christian year. The date of Easter, a movable feast, is derived from the lunar calendar: the first Sunday following the first ecclesiastical full moon on or after Mar 21—always between Mar 22 and Apr 25. The Council of Nicaea (AD 325) prescribed that Easter be celebrated on the Sunday after Passover, as that feast's date had been established in Jesus's time. After 1582, when Pope Gregory XIII introduced the Gregorian calendar, Orthodox Christians continued to use the Julian calendar, so Easter can sometimes be as much as five weeks apart in the Western and Eastern churches. Easter in 2007 will be Apr 8; in 2008 it will be Mar 23; in 2009 it will be Apr 12. Many other dates in the Christian year are derived from the date of Easter. See also: "Orthodox Easter Sunday or Pascha." (Apr 23).

EASTER SUNRISE SERVICE. Apr 16. Chimney Rock Park, Chimney Rock, NC. Celebrate the glory of Easter at this 51st annual nondenominational community worship service overlooking beautiful Lake Lure. Gates open at 5:00 AM and close at 6:00 AM for the 6:30 AM service. No admission charge. Est attendance: 1,000. For info: Chimney Rock Park, PO Box 39, Chimney Rock, NC 28720. Phone: (800) 277-9611 or (828) 625-9611. Fax: (828) 625-9610. E-mail: visit@chimneyrockpark.com. Web: www.chimneyrockpark.com.

HAUTE DOG CHARITY EASTER PARADE. Apr 16. Belmont Shore, Long Beach, CA. Just about every breed from bulldog to poodle will take over Belmont Shore for this annual parade. The event has raised thousands of dollars for animal shelters and rescue organizations. About 400 pooches—some colorfully costumed in Easter attire—are expected to pack Livingston Park for a Yappy Hour before beginning their parade down Second Street. Prizes awarded for best outfits and canine bonnets. Annually,

Easter Sunday. Est attendance: 3,000. For info: Justin Rudd. Phone: (562) 439-3316. E-mail: justinrudd@aol.com. Web: www.hautedogs.org.

ITALY: EXPLOSION OF THE CART. Apr 16. Florence. At noon on Easter Sunday in Piazza del Duomo a cart full of fireworks is exploded, perpetuating a ceremony of ancient origin and recalling the fire that used to be kindled during the *Gloria* at Easter mass and was then distributed to all of Florence's households. The tradition is held to date back to the time of the First Crusade, when the valorous Pazzino dei Pazzi was awarded some pieces of flint from the Holy Sepulcher. After his return to Florence the holy fire was kindled with these flints, now preserved in the church of Santi Apostoli.

MANCINI, HENRY: BIRTH ANNIVERSARY. Apr 16, 1924. Born at Cleveland, OH, Mancini made his mark in Hollywood composing film scores and songs. He won 20 Grammy Awards and four Oscars (song "Moon River" and score for *Breakfast at Tiffany's*; song "Days of Wine and Roses" for the film; score for *Victor/Victoria*). He also composed *The Pink Panther*, "Peter Gunn" and "Mr Lucky" themes. Died June 14, 1994, at Beverly Hills, CA.

MARKSVILLE EASTER EGG KNOCKING CONTEST. Apr 16. Marksville, LA. Competition among owners of chicken and guinea eggs which have been boiled and dyed. Annually, on Easter Sunday 9 AM–noon. Est attendance: 500. For info: Chamber of Commerce, Box 767, Marksville, LA 71351. Phone: (318) 253-9222 or (318) 253-0284.

MAROONE HISPANICFEST. Apr 16. Hollywood, FL. Latin festival featuring both folkloric music and dance as well as popular headliners, traditional foods and crafts, community exhibits and children's activities. Est attendance: 25,000. For info: Margaret Delmont-Sanchez, Hispanic Unity of Florida, Inc. Phone: (954) 964-8884. Web: www.hispanicfest.org.

MERRIE MONARCH FESTIVAL (WITH WORLD'S LARGEST HULA COMPETITION). Apr 16–22. Hilo, HI. Cultural event honoring King David Kalakaua. Festival culminates with the world's largest hula competition. Hawaii's finest hula schools compete in ancient and modern divisions. Annually, beginning on Easter Sunday. Est attendance: 6,000. For info: Dorothy Thompson, Hawaii Naniloa Hotel, Merrie Monarch Office, 93 Banyan Dr, Hilo, HI 96720. Phone: (808) 935-9168.

MORAVIAN EASTER RESURRECTION SERVICE. Apr 16. Winston-Salem, NC. Outdoor religious service featuring Moravian brass bands playing in streets to awaken sleepers. Service begins in Salem Square, and concludes in God's Acre, the Moravian Graveyard, at daybreak. Est attendance: 8,000. For info: Salem Congregation, 501 S Main St, Winston-Salem, NC 27101-5314. Phone: (336) 722-6504. Fax: (336) 725-2514. E-mail: facilitiesmgr@mcsp.org.

NATIONAL COIN WEEK. Apr 16–22. 84th annual. Discover the world of money and the hobby of coin collecting. Annually, the third full week of April, Sunday through Saturday. For info: Gail Baker, Dir of Educ, American Numismatic Assn, 818 N Cascade Ave, Colorado Springs, CO 80903. Phone: (719) 632-2646 or (800) 367-9723. Fax: (719) 634-4085. E-mail: Education@money.org. Web: www.money.org.

★**NATIONAL CRIME VICTIMS' RIGHTS WEEK.** Apr 16–22 (tentative). Date varies—a week in April.

★**NATIONAL PARK WEEK.** Apr 16–22.

NATIONAL PERSONAL TRAINING WEEK. Apr 16–23. Personal trainers help build bodies and minds by guiding people through safe strength-building workouts while offering encouragement along the way. Consider personal trainers as guides to better health. Seek out their expertise to get moving and grow stronger and thus enjoy a healthier, more confident life. Annually, the third week in April. For info: Gail Sideman, 8832 N Port Washington Rd, Milwaukee, WI 53217. Phone: (414) 228-0877. E-mail: gsideman@personaltrainingweek.com. Web: www.personaltrainingweek.com.

★**NATIONAL VOLUNTEER WEEK.** Apr 16–22.

NATURAL BRIDGES NATIONAL MONUMENT: ANNIVERSARY. Apr 16, 1908. Utah. Natural Bridges National Monument was established on this date.

ORTHODOX PALM SUNDAY. Apr 16. Celebration of Christ's entry into Jerusalem, when His way was covered with palms by the multitudes. Beginning of Holy Week in the Orthodox Church.

SELENA: BIRTH ANNIVERSARY. Apr 16, 1971. Tejana singer, born Selena Quintanilla at Lake Jackson, TX. Died Mar 31, 1995, at Corpus Christi, TX, murdered by the president of her fan club.

SLAVERY ABOLISHED IN DISTRICT OF COLUMBIA: ANNIVERSARY. Apr 16, 1862. Congress abolished slavery in the District of Columbia. One million dollars was appropriated to compensate owners of freed slaves, and $100,000 was set aside to pay district slaves who wished to emigrate to Haiti, Liberia or any other country outside the US.

SLOANE, HANS: BIRTH ANNIVERSARY. Apr 16, 1660. British medical doctor and naturalist whose personal collection became the nucleus of the British Museum, born at County Down, Ireland. Upon his death at Chelsea, England, Jan 11, 1753, his collections of books, manuscripts, medals and antiquities were bequeathed to Britain and accepted by an act of Parliament that incorporated the British Museum. It was opened to the public at London, England, Jan 15, 1759. It is the national museum of the United Kingdom.

SPACE MILESTONE: *APOLLO 16* (US). Apr 16, 1972. Astronauts John W. Young, Charles M. Duke, Jr and Thomas K. Mattingly II (command module pilot) began an 11-day mission that included 71-hour exploration of moon (Apr 20–23). Landing module named *Orion*. Splashdown in Pacific Ocean within a mile of target, Apr 27.

SYNGE, JOHN MILLINGTON: BIRTH ANNIVERSARY. Apr 16, 1871. Irish dramatist and poet, most of whose plays were written in the brief span of six years before his death at age 37 of lymphatic sarcoma. His best-known work was *The Playboy of the Western World* (1907), which caused protests and rioting at early performances. Synge (pronounced "Sing") was born near Dublin, Ireland, and died there Mar 24, 1909.

TEXAS CITY DISASTER: ANNIVERSARY. Apr 16–17, 1947. The worst industrial disaster in US history. The French-owned *Grandcamp*, docked at the oil and port town of Texas City, TX, and carrying a load of ammonium nitrate, was discovered to have a smoldering fire in her hold. At 9:12 AM, as onlookers gathered and a small firefighting team attempted to extinguish the blaze, the ship exploded with tremendous force, immediately killing everyone at the dock area. The resulting fires destroyed the nearby Monsanto Chemical Company and spread through oil pipelines into the city. At 1:00 AM, another ship, the *High Flyer* exploded. The city was left defenseless due to the deaths of almost the entire fire department. There were 576 known casualties, but most estimate that at least 100 more died in the conflagrations. Thousands were injured. The fires burned for a week. The disaster prompted new regulations on handling chemicals. With thousands of lawsuits, the US Congress passed a special act to settle claims in 1956.

		S	M	T	W	T	F	S
April								1
2006		2	3	4	5	6	7	8
		9	10	11	12	13	14	15
		16	17	18	19	20	21	22
		23	24	25	26	27	28	29
		30						

USTINOV, PETER: BIRTH ANNIVERSARY. Apr 16, 1921. British actor and playwright born at London, Peter Ustinov wrote his first play at age 19. He performed on stage, television and the screen, winning two Oscars (for 1961's *Spartacus* and 1965's *Topkapi*) and several Emmys. He wrote dozens of plays, screenplays and novels, and also directed several films, including the highly regarded 1962 version of *Billy Budd*. He played Agatha Christie's detective Hercule Poirot in several screen adaptations. He was knighted by Queen Elizabeth II and dedicated many years to fund-raising for the United Nation's Children's Fund (UNICEF). He died at Geneva, Switzerland, Mar 28, 2004.

WRIGHT, WILBUR: BIRTH ANNIVERSARY. Apr 16, 1867. Aviation pioneer, born at Millville, IN. Died at Dayton, OH, May 30, 1912. See also: "Wright Brothers First Powered Flight" (Dec 17).

BIRTHDAYS TODAY

Kareem Abdul-Jabbar, 59, Hall of Fame basketball player, born Lewis Ferdinand Alcindor, Jr at New York, NY, Apr 16, 1947.

Edie Adams, 75, singer, actress, born Elizabeth Edith Enke at Kingston, PA, Apr 16, 1931.

Ellen Barkin, 51, actress (*Tender Mercies, Diner*), born New York, NY, Apr 16, 1955.

Jon Cryer, 41, actor ("Partners," *Pretty in Pink, Hot Shots!*), born New York, NY, Apr 16, 1965.

Merce Cunningham, 87, dancer, choreographer, born Centralia, WA, Apr 16, 1919.

Luol Deng, 21, basketball player, born Wow, the Sudan, Apr 16, 1985.

Lukas Haas, 30, actor (*Witness, Rambling Rose*), born West Hollywood, CA, Apr 16, 1976.

Martin Lawrence, 41, comedian, actor (*Bad Boys, Big Momma's House*), born Frankfurt-am-Main, Germany, Apr 16, 1965.

Barry Nelson, 86, actor (*Pete 'n Tillie, The Shining*), born San Francisco, CA, Apr 16, 1920.

Pope Benedict XVI, 79, leader of the Roman Catholic Church, born Joseph Ratzinger at Marktl Am Inn, Germany, Apr 16, 1927.

Jay O. Sanders, 53, actor ("Crime Story," *Tucker: The Man and His Dream*), born Austin, TX, Apr 16, 1953.

Bobby Vinton, 71, singer ("Mr Lonely," "Roses Are Red [My Love]"), born Canonsburg, PA, Apr 16, 1935.

APRIL 17 — MONDAY

Day 107 — 258 Remaining

AMERICAN SAMOA: FLAG DAY: ANNIVERSARY. Apr 17. National holiday commemorating first raising of American flag in what was formerly Eastern Samoa in 1900. Public holiday with singing, dancing, costumes and parades.

ANSON, CAP: BIRTH ANNIVERSARY. Apr 17, 1852. Adrian Constantine ("Cap") Anson, Baseball Hall of Fame player and manager, born at Marshalltown, IA. Anson played professional baseball from 1871 through 1897 and is considered one of the game's greatest first basemen. As a manager, he piloted the Chicago White Stockings (today's Cubs) to five National League pennants and a .575 winning percentage. Inducted into the Hall of Fame in 1939. Died at Chicago, IL, Apr 18, 1922.

BAY OF PIGS INVASION LAUNCHED: 45th ANNIVERSARY. Apr 17, 1961. More than 1,500 Cuban exiles invaded Cuba in an ill-fated attempt to overthrow Fidel Castro.

BIG 12 WOMEN'S GOLF CHAMPIONSHIP. Apr 17–19. Country Club of Lincoln, Lincoln, NE. Est attendance: 1,000. For info: Big 12 Conference, 2201 Stemmons Freeway, 28th Fl, Dallas, TX 75207. Phone: (214) 742-1212. Fax: (214) 742-2046. Web: www.big12sports.com.

BLAH BLAH BLAH DAY. Apr 17. Today's the day to do any of the following, or whatever. Stop smoking, take out the trash, empty the cat litter, lose weight, pick up your clothes, put dirty dishes in the sink, get a job or quit your job. Annually, Apr 17. [©2003 by WH.] For info: Thomas & Ruth Roy, Wellcat Holidays,

2418 Long Ln, Lebanon, PA 17046. Phone: (717) 279-0184. E-mail: info@wellcat.com. Web: www.wellcat.com.

BOSTON MARATHON—110th RUNNING. Apr 17. Boston, MA. The marathon begins in the rural New England town of Hopkinton, winds through eight cities and towns and finishes near downtown Boston. Always the third Monday in April. 20,000 participants. Athletes qualify by meeting time standards which correspond to age. Est attendance: 500,000. For info: Boston Athletic Assn, Boston Marathon, 40 Trinity Place, 4th Fl, Boston, MA 02116. Phone: (617) 236-1652. E-mail: mile27@baa.org. Web: www.baa.org.

CAMBODIA FALLS TO THE KHMER ROUGE: ANNIVERSARY. Apr 17, 1975. Cambodia fell when its capital, Phnom Penh, was captured by the Khmer Rouge. The Pol Pot regime inaugurated "Year One," and the wholesale slaughter of intellectuals, political enemies and peasants began. As many as two million Cambodians perished. See also: "Pol Pot Overthrown: Anniversary" (Jan 7).

CHASE, SAMUEL: BIRTH ANNIVERSARY. Apr 17, 1741. Signer of the Declaration of Independence. Born at Somerset County, MD, he died June 19, 1811.

DOW-JONES TOPS 3,000: 15th ANNIVERSARY. Apr 17, 1991. The Dow-Jones Index of 30 major industrial stocks topped the 3,000 mark for the first time.

EASTER MONDAY. Apr 17. Holiday or bank holiday in many places, including England, Northern Ireland, Wales, Canada and North Carolina in the US.

EGG SALAD WEEK. Apt 17–23. Dedicated to the many delicious uses for all of the Easter eggs that have been cooked, colored, hidden and found. Annually, the full week after Easter. For info: Linda Braun, Consumer Serv Dir, American Egg Bd, 1460 Renaissance Dr, Park Ridge, IL 60068. Web: www.aeb.org.

ELLIS ISLAND FAMILY HISTORY DAY. Apr 17. By official proclamation of our nation's governors, Apr 17 has been designated as "Ellis Island Family History Day." Sponsored by The Statue of Liberty–Ellis Island Foundation, Inc, this annual day recognizes the achievements and contributions made to America by Ellis Island immigrants and their descendants. Historically, Apr 17 marks the day in 1907 when more immigrants were processed through the island than on any other day in its colorful history: 11,747 people. In addition, the Foundation has established the "Ellis Island Family Heritage Awards," which are given annually to a select number of Ellis Island immigrants or their descendants who have made a significant contribution to the American experience. For info: Elizabeth Oravetz, Statue of Liberty–Ellis Island Foundation, Inc, 292 Madison Ave, 14th Fl, New York, NY 10017. Phone: (212) 561-4500. Fax: (212) 779-1990. E-mail: eoravetz@ellisisland.org. Web: www.ellisisland.org.

ENGLAND: HALLATON BOTTLE KICKING. Apr 17. Hallaton, Leicestershire. Ancient custom dating back at least 600 years. Annually, Easter Monday.

FORDYCE ON THE COTTON BELT FESTIVAL. Apr 17–22. Fordyce, AR. 25th annual railroad event includes arts and crafts, quilt show and sale, train rides, musical entertainment, rodeo, parade, railroad displays, beauty pageants, gospel singing and more. Est attendance: 10,000. For info: Chamber of Commerce, PO Box 588, Fordyce, AR 71742. Phone: (870) 352-5125 or (870) 352-3520. Fax: (870) 352-8090. E-mail: fordyce@ipa.net.

"THE FRED WARING SHOW" TV PREMIERE: ANNIVERSARY. Apr 17, 1949. Fred Waring was leader of the big band called the Pennsylvanians, which featured about 65 musicians and singers. The show aired on Sunday nights until 1954.

HERITAGE WEEK. Apr 17–22. New Harmony, IN. Head to this historic village and watch crafters create 19th-century-style candles, baskets and pottery. Annually, Monday through Saturday of the third week in April. Est attendance: 5,000. For info: Education Coordinator, Historic New Harmony, PO Box 579, New Harmony, IN 47631. Phone: (812) 682-4488. Fax: (812) 682-4313. E-mail: jkahle@usi.edu.

HOLDEN, WILLIAM: BIRTH ANNIVERSARY. Apr 17, 1918. William Holden's first starring role was in *Golden Boy*. The actor, born at O'Fallon, IL, won an Oscar for his role in *Stalag 17* in 1953. He was found dead at Los Angeles, CA, Nov 16, 1981.

INCOME TAX PAY DAY: THIS IS REALLY IT. Apr 17. Taxpayers get a temporary reprieve this year. Since Apr 15 fell on a Saturday, we all have had two extra days to procrastinate. But now it's time to face the music and pay the piper—get those returns in the mail by midnight!

INTERNATIONAL FORD MUSTANG DAY. Apr 17. Ford Mustang enthusiasts are encouraged to have car shows, cruises, parties and other events to celebrate the birthday of the Mustang automobile. For info: Mustang Club of America, 4051 Barrancas Ave, PMB 102, Pensacola, FL 32507. Phone: (850) 438-0626. Web: www.mustang.org.

LUXEMBOURG: EMAISHEN. Apr 17. Luxembourg (city). Popular traditional market and festival at the "Marche-aux-Poissons." Young lovers present each other with earthenware articles, sold only on this day. Annually, Easter Monday.

MORGAN, JOHN PIERPONT: BIRTH ANNIVERSARY. Apr 17, 1837. American financier and corporation director, born at Hartford, CT. Morgan died Mar 31, 1913, at Rome, Italy, leaving an estate valued at more than $70 million.

NETHERLANDS AND SCILLY ISLES PEACE: 20th ANNIVERSARY. Apr 17, 1986. The 335-year "state of war" that had existed between the Netherlands and the Scilly Isles came to an end on this date when Dutch ambassador Jonkheer Huydecoper flew to the Scilly Isles to deliver a proclamation terminating the war that had started in 1651. Though hostilities had ceased three centuries earlier, a standing joke in the islands was that no one had bothered to declare an end to the war.

PATRIOT'S DAY IN MASSACHUSETTS AND MAINE. Apr 17. Commemorates Battles of Lexington and Concord, 1775. Annually, the third Monday in April.

QUARTERLY ESTIMATED FEDERAL INCOME TAX PAYERS' DUE DATE. Apr 17. For those individuals whose fiscal year is the calendar year and who make quarterly estimated federal income tax payments, today is one of the due dates (Jan 17, Apr 17, June 15 and Sept 15, 2006).

REASONER, HARRY: BIRTH ANNIVERSARY. Apr 17, 1923. American television journalist Harry Reasoner was born at Dakota City, IA. In 1956 Reasoner joined CBS News, where he anchored the "CBS Sunday News" (1963–70) and was one of the two original anchors, along with Mike Wallace, of the news magazine show "60 Minutes." He was coanchor of the "ABC Evening News" from 1970 until 1978, when he returned to CBS and "60 Minutes." He died Aug 6, 1991, at Norwalk, CT.

SOLIDARITY GRANTED LEGAL STATUS: ANNIVERSARY. Apr 17, 1989. After nearly a decade of struggle and suppression the Polish labor union Solidarity was granted legal status, clearing the way for the downfall of the Polish Communist Party. Solidarity and the Polish people surprised the government by winning 99 of the 100 parliamentary seats in the election. General Wojciech Jaruzelski was elected president on July 19 and nominated Czelaw Kiszczak prime minister, enraging the Lech Walesa–led Solidarity. On Aug 7 Walesa swayed the traditional allies of the Communist Party—the United Peasant and Democratic Parties—to switch sides. Kiszczak resigned as prime minister a week later after failing to form a government, forcing Jaruzelski to accept the principle of a government led by Solidarity.

SOUTH AFRICA: FAMILY DAY. Apr 17. National holiday. Annually, Easter Monday.

STEIGER, ROD: BIRTH ANNIVERSARY. Apr 17, 1925. The magnetic character actor was born at Westhampton, NY. In a 50-year career, Steiger played a wide range of roles for some of the best directors of the day. He won a Best Actor Oscar for *In the Heat of the Night*, and was also nominated for *On the Waterfront* and *The Pawnbroker*. He died at Los Angeles, CA, July 9, 2002.

SWITZERLAND: EGG RACES. Apr 17. Rural northwest Swiss Easter Monday custom. Race among competitors carrying large numbers of eggs while running to neighboring villages.

SYRIAN ARAB REPUBLIC: INDEPENDENCE DAY. Apr 17. Official holiday. Proclaimed independence from League of Nations mandate under French administration in 1946.

UNITED KINGDOM: EASTER MONDAY BANK HOLIDAY. Apr 17. Bank and public holiday in England, Wales and Northern Ireland. (Scotland not included.)

VERRAZANO DAY: ANNIVERSARY. Apr 17, 1524. Celebrates discovery of New York harbor by Giovanni Verrazano, Florentine navigator, 1485–1527.

WHITE HOUSE EASTER EGG ROLL. Apr 17. Traditionally held at executive mansion's south lawn on Easter Monday. Custom said to have started at Capitol grounds about 1810. Transferred to White House lawn in 1870s.

WILDER, THORNTON: BIRTH ANNIVERSARY. Apr 17, 1897. Pulitzer Prize–winning American playwright (*Our Town*) and novelist, born at Madison, WI. Died at Hamden, CT, Dec 7, 1975.

WOC NURSE WEEK. Apr 17. A national observance to honor wound ostomy and continence nurses. Annually, the third week in April. For info: Marilyn Rutkowski, Wound Ostomy and Continence Nurse Society, 4700 W Lake Ave, Glenview, IL 60025. Phone: (847) 375-4830. E-mail: mrutkowski@amctec.com. Web: www.wocn.org.

BIRTHDAYS TODAY

Sean Bean, 48, actor (*Lord of the Rings: Fellowship of the Ring; Stormy Monday, Patriot Games*), born Sheffield, Yorkshire, England, Apr 17, 1958.

Victoria Adams Beckham, 31, actress, singer (Posh Spice of Spice Girls), born Hertfordshire, England, Apr 17, 1975.

Norman Julius ("Boomer") Esiason, 45, broadcaster and former football player, born West Islip, NY, Apr 17, 1961.

Jennifer Garner, 34, actress ("Alias," "Felicity"), born Houston, TX, Apr 17, 1972.

Olivia Hussey, 55, actress (*Romeo and Juliet*), born Buenos Aires, Argentina, Apr 17, 1951.

Don Kirshner, 72, music publisher, promoter, born the Bronx, NY, Apr 17, 1934.

Cynthia Ozick, 78, feminist, writer, born New York, NY, Apr 17, 1928.

Liz Phair, 39, rock singer/songwriter, born New Haven, CT, Apr 17, 1967.

Lela Rochon, 40, actress (*Waiting to Exhale, Boomerang*), born Los Angeles, CA, Apr 17, 1966.

	S	M	T	W	T	F	S
April							1
2006	2	3	4	5	6	7	8
	9	10	11	12	13	14	15
	16	17	18	19	20	21	22
	23	24	25	26	27	28	29
	30						

APRIL 18 — TUESDAY
Day 108 — 257 Remaining

CANADA: CONSTITUTION ACT OF 1982: ANNIVERSARY. Apr 18, 1982. Replacing the British North America Act of 1867, the Canadian Constitution Act of 1982 provided Canada with a new set of fundamental laws and civil rights. Signed by Queen Elizabeth II, at Parliament Hill, Ottawa, Canada, it went into effect at 12:01 AM, Sunday, Apr 19, 1982.

CRAWFORD, SAMUEL EARL "WAHOO SAM": BIRTH ANNIVERSARY. Apr 18, 1880. Major league baseball player with the Detroit Tigers, born at Wahoo, NE. Wahoo Sam played pro ball for 20 years, racking up a career batting average of .309. His record of 312 career triples still stands. He was inducted into the Baseball Hall of Fame in 1957. Crawford died June 15, 1968, at Hollywood, CA.

DARROW, CLARENCE SEWARD: BIRTH ANNIVERSARY. Apr 18, 1857. American attorney often associated with unpopular causes, from the Pullman strike in 1894 to the Scottsboro case in 1932, born at Kinsman, OH. At the Scopes trial, July 13, 1925, Darrow said: "I do not consider it an insult, but rather a compliment, to be called an agnostic. I do not pretend to know where many ignorant men are sure—that is all that agnosticism means." Darrow died at Chicago, IL, Mar 13, 1938.

EIGHTY-NINER CELEBRATION. Apr 18–22. Guthrie, OK. In celebration of its heritage, this historically restored town features Old West gunfights, chuckwagon feed, professional rodeo and Oklahoma's largest parade of bands, floats and roundup clubs from across the state. Est attendance: 30,000. For info: American Legion, Post 58, 123 N 21st St, Guthrie, OK 73044. Phone: (405) 282-2589. E-mail: 89erOK@aol.com. Web: www.guthrieok.com.

FREDERICKSBURG DAY. Apr 18. Fredericksburg, VA. Spring tour of historic homes and gardens. To fund one historic garden restoration in Virginia per year. Est attendance: 2,000. For info: Visitor Center, 706 Caroline St, Fredericksburg, VA 22401. Phone: (800) 678-4748. Fax: (540) 372-6587. E-mail: gboswell@fredericksburgva.gov.

THE HOUSE THAT RUTH BUILT: ANNIVERSARY. Apr 18, 1923. More than 74,000 fans attended Opening Day festivities as the New York Yankees inaugurated their new stadium. Babe Ruth christened it with a game-winning three-run homer into the right-field bleachers. In his coverage of the game for the *New York Evening Telegram* sportswriter Fred Lieb described Yankee Stadium as "The House That Ruth Built," and the name stuck.

JAPAN BOMBED: ANNIVERSARY. Apr 18, 1942. For the first time during WWII, the mainland of Japan was bombed. Brigade General James Doolittle led a squadron of B-25s from the US carrier *Hornet*. Cities bombed included Tokyo, Yokohama, Kobe and Nagoya. Doolittle said they flew so low that "one of our party observed a ball game in progress." Although the bombers did little damage, the psychological victory was enormous.

MARTHA GRAHAM'S FIRST SOLO: 80th ANNIVERSARY. Apr 18, 1926. Martha Graham, dancer and choreographer, performed her first solo, "The Idiom," in New York City. This date is now considered to be the founding date for the Martha Graham Company.

NATIONAL CATHOLIC EDUCATIONAL ASSOCIATION CONVENTION AND EXPOSITION. Apr 18–21. New Orleans, LA. Annual meeting for NCEA members and anyone working in, or interested in, the welfare of Catholic education. For info: Sue Arvo, Conv Dir, Natl Catholic Educational Assn, 1077 30th St NW, Ste 100, Washington, DC 20007. Phone: (202) 337-6232. Fax: (202) 333-6706.

NATIONAL STRESS AWARENESS DAY. Apr 18. To focus public awareness on one of the leading health problems in the world today. Health-related organizations throughout the country are encouraged to sponsor stress education programs and events. Annually, the first day after income taxes due. For info: Morton C. Orman, MD, Dir, The Health Resource Network, 908 Cold Bottom Rd, Sparks, MD 21152. Web: www.stresscure.com.

NATIONAL WEAR YOUR PAJAMAS TO WORK DAY. Apr 18. Relieve that stress and relax after staying up late working on your taxes! Bring the comforts of home to the office for at least one day. Annually, following the day income taxes are due. Sponsored by The PajamaGram Company. For info: The Pajama Gram Company, 6655 Shelburne Rd, Shelburne, VT 05482. Phone: (800) GIVE-PJS. Fax: (802) 985-1382. Web: www.Pajama Gram.com.

PAUL REVERE'S RIDE: ANNIVERSARY. Apr 18, 1775. The "Midnight Ride" of Paul Revere and William Dawes started at about 10 PM to warn American patriots between Boston, MA, and Concord, MA, of the approaching British.

PET OWNERS INDEPENDENCE DAY. Apr 18. Dog and cat owners take the day off from work and the pets go to work in their place, since most pets are jobless, sleep all day and do not even take out the trash. [©2003 by WH.] For info: Thomas & Ruth Roy, Wellcat Holidays, 2418 Long Ln, Lebanon, PA 17046. Phone: (717) 279-0184. E-mail: info@wellcat.com. Web: www.well cat.com.

"REAL PEOPLE" TV PREMIERE: ANNIVERSARY. Apr 18, 1979. Real people do the darnedest things—from making paintings out of lint to making houses out of aluminum cans. NBC developed the program to spotlight the achievements, funny inventions and extraordinary stunts of ordinary Americans. Hosts of the show included Fred Willard, Sarah Purcell, John Barbour, Skip Stephenson, Byron Allen and Peter Billingsley.

SAN FRANCISCO 1906 EARTHQUAKE: 100th ANNIVERSARY. Apr 18, 1906. Business section of San Francisco, some 10,000 acres, destroyed by earthquake. First quake at 5:13 AM, followed by fire. Nearly 4,000 lives lost.

SCOTTSDALE CULINARY FESTIVAL™. Apr 18–23. Scottsdale, AZ. Ten spectacular culinary events including Le Tour Culinaire, a progressive black-tie dinner; Best of the Fest featuring 10 of the valley's best chefs; Great Arizona Picnic featuring 50 of the valley's best restaurants; and more. Proceeds benefit arts education programs for youth in the community. Est attendance: 60,000. For info: Scottsdale Culinary Festival, 15550 N 84th St, #105, Scottsdale, AZ 85260. Phone: (480) 945-7193. Fax: (480) 945-6967. E-mail: karolyn@scottsdaleculinaryfestival .org. Web: www.scottsdaleculinaryfestival.org.

SURRENDER AT DURHAM STATION: ANNIVERSARY. Apr 18, 1865. Union General William Tecumseh Sherman and Confederate General Joseph Johnston signed a broad political peace agreement at Durham Station, NC. The agreement promised a general amnesty for all Southerners and pledged federal recognition of all Southern state governments after their officials took an oath of allegiance to the US. Sherman was roundly criticized for his role in drawing up the agreement, although he based it on an earlier conversation with Lincoln and Grant. The agreement was rejected by President Andrew Johnson, and Sherman and Johnston were forced to reach a new agreement with terms virtually the same as those given Robert E. Lee.

TAX FREEDOM DAY. Apr 18. According to the Tax Freedom Foundation, the average American has to work until today in 2006 to pay federal, state and local taxes. Because state and local taxes vary, this date can vary by almost a whole month depending on the state you live in. Updated information (or information about your state) can be found at www.taxfoundation.org.

"THIRD WORLD" DAY: ANNIVERSARY. Apr 18, 1955. Anniversary of the first use of the phrase "third world," which was by Indonesia's President Sukarno in his opening speech at the Bandung Conference. Representatives of nearly 30 African and Asian countries (2,000 attendees) heard Sukarno praise the American war of independence, "the first successful anticolonial war in history." More than half the world's population, he said, was represented at this "first intercontinental conference of the so-called colored peoples, in the history of mankind." The phrase and the idea of a "third world" rapidly gained currency, generally signifying the aggregate of nonaligned peoples and nations—the nonwhite and underdeveloped portion of the world.

TITAN 34-D ROCKET FAILURE: 20th ANNIVERSARY. Apr 18, 1986. Launched from Vandenburg Air Force Base, CA, the $65 million *Titan* exploded when it was only a few hundred feet into flight, destroying the $500 million KH-11 reconnaissance satellite payload. Poisonous fumes were released by the explosion, causing concern for the safety of people in nearby communities.

ZIMBABWE: INDEPENDENCE DAY. Apr 18. National holiday commemorates the recognition by Great Britain of Zimbabwean independence on this day in 1980. Prior to this, the country had been the British colony of Southern Rhodesia.

BIRTHDAYS TODAY

Barbara Hale, 85, actress ("Perry Mason"), born DeKalb, IL, Apr 18, 1921.

Melissa Joan Hart, 30, actress ("Sabrina the Teenage Witch"), born Long Island, NY, Apr 18, 1976.

Cheryl Ann Haworth, 23, weight lifter, born Savannah, GA, Apr 18, 1983.

Robert Hooks, 69, actor, director, producer (*Star Trek III: The Search for Spock*; stage: *Day of Absence, Where's Daddy?* [Theatre World Awards for both]), born Washington, DC, Apr 18, 1937.

John James, 50, actor ("Search for Tomorrow," "Dynasty"), born Minneapolis, MN, Apr 18, 1956.

Jane Leeves, 45, actress ("Murphy Brown," "Frasier"), born East Grinstead, England, Apr 18, 1961.

Dorothy Lyman, 59, actress ("All My Children," "Mama's Family"), director, born Minneapolis, MN, Apr 18, 1947.

Eric McCormack, 43, actor ("Lonesome Dove," "Will & Grace"), born Toronto, ON, Canada, Apr 18, 1963.

Hayley Mills, 60, actress (*Pollyana, The Parent Trap, The Moon Spinners*), born London, England, Apr 18, 1946.

Rick Moranis, 52, actor, writer (*Ghostbusters, Honey I Shrunk the Kids*), born Toronto, ON, Canada, Apr 18, 1954.

Conan O'Brien, 43, host ("Late Night with Conan O'Brien"), born Brookline, MA, Apr 18, 1963.

John Pankow, 52, actor ("Mad About You"), born St. Louis, MO, Apr 18, 1954.

Eric Roberts, 50, actor (*Runaway Train, Star 80*), born Biloxi, MS, Apr 18, 1956.

James Woods, 59, actor (*Holocaust, The Onion Field*), born Vernal, UT, Apr 18, 1947.

APRIL 19 — WEDNESDAY
Day 109 — 256 Remaining

BATTLE OF LEXINGTON AND CONCORD: ANNIVERSARY. Apr 19, 1775. Massachusetts. Start of the American Revolution as the British fired the "shot heard 'round the world."

BRANCH DAVIDIAN FIRE AT WACO: ANNIVERSARY. Apr 19, 1993. After a 51-day standoff between the Branch Davidians and law-enforcement groups, the compound of the religious cult burned to the ground with 86 of its members inside, near Waco, TX, after federal agents began battering the compound with armored vehicles. Nine people escaped, but the 86 who perished included 17 children and the cult's leader, David Koresh.

EXPLOSION ON THE USS *IOWA*: ANNIVERSARY. Apr 19, 1989. In one of the worst naval disasters since the war in Vietnam, a freak explosion rocked the battleship USS *Iowa*, killing 47 sailors. The explosion occurred in the No. 2 gun turret as the *Iowa* was participating in gunnery exercises about 300 miles northeast of Puerto Rico.

GARFIELD, LUCRETIA RUDOLPH: BIRTH ANNIVERSARY. Apr 19, 1832. Wife of James Abram Garfield, 20th president of the US, born at Hiram, OH. Died at Pasadena, CA, Mar 14, 1918.

INTERNATIONAL WHISTLERS CONVENTION. Apr 19–23. Louisburg, NC. Music festival. Assemblage and contest of professional and amateur whistlers and whistle collectors. Contests for children, teens and adults. Est attendance: 2,500. For info: Allen de Hart, Dir, Franklin County Arts Council, Inc, PO Box 758, Louisburg, NC 27549. Phone: (919) 496-4771. Fax: (919) 496-1191.

JOHN PARKER DAY. Apr 19. Remembering John Parker's order, at Lexington Green, Apr 19, 1775: "Stand your ground. Don't fire unless fired upon; but if they mean to have a war, let it begin here." Parker, revolutionary soldier, captain of minutemen, born at Lexington, MA, July 13, 1729. Died Sept 17, 1775.

MOORE, DUDLEY: BIRTH ANNIVERSARY. April 19, 1935. British comedian, actor and classically trained pianist born at Dagenham, near London. Initially pursuing a career as a concert and jazz pianist, Moore was invited by Peter Cook to join the comedy revue *Beyond the Fringe*. Moore was best known for his movies *10* and *Arthur*, for which he was nominated for an Oscar. Moore died at New Jersey on Mar 27, 2002.

NESS, ELIOT: BIRTH ANNIVERSARY. Apr 19, 1903. The legendary Prohibition Era lawman was born at Chicago, IL. He gained lasting fame as the leader of the "Untouchables": young, dedicated federal agents handpicked by Ness who could not be bribed by the mobsters they were targeting. Ness especially went after Chicago gangster Al Capone's bootlegging business, which was finally brought down in 1931. After stints in other federal and municipal agencies, Ness died May 7, 1957, at Coudersport, PA—just before publication of his memoirs, *The Untouchables*, which went on to inspire a TV series and later a film.

NETHERLANDS–US DIPLOMATIC RELATIONS: ANNIVERSARY. Apr 19, 1782. Anniversary of establishment of America's oldest continuously peaceful diplomatic relations. On this date, the States General of the Netherlands United Provinces admitted John Adams (later to become second president of the US) as minister plenipotentiary of the young American republic. This was the second diplomatic recognition of the US as an independent nation. Within six months Adams had succeeded in bringing about the signing of the first Treaty of Amity and Commerce between the two countries (Oct 8, 1782).

NICARAGUA: CIVIL WAR TRUCE: ANNIVERSARY. Apr 19, 1990. The Contra guerrillas, the leftist Sandinistas and the incoming Chamorro government agreed to a truce, ending a nine-year civil war.

OKLAHOMA CITY BOMBING: ANNIVERSARY. Apr 19, 1995. A car bomb exploded outside the Alfred P. Murrah Federal Building at Oklahoma City, OK, at 9:02 AM, killing 168 people, 19 of them children at a day-care center; a nurse died of head injuries sustained while helping in rescue efforts. The bomb, estimated to have weighed 5,000 pounds, had been placed in a rented truck. The blast ripped off the north face of the nine-story building, leaving a 20-foot-wide crater and debris two stories high. Structurally unsound and increasingly dangerous, the bombed building was razed May 23. Timothy J. McVeigh, a decorated Gulf War army vet who is alleged to have been angered by the Bureau of Alcohol, Tobacco and Firearms (ATF) attack on the Branch Davidian compound at Waco, TX, exactly two years before, was convicted of the bombing and was executed June 11, 2001. The ATF had offices in the OK federal building. Terry L. Nichols, an army buddy of McVeigh, was convicted of murder and conspiracy charges and was sentenced to life in prison.

PATRIOT'S DAY IN FLORIDA. Apr 19. A ceremonial day to commemorate the first blood shed in the American Revolution at Lexington and Concord in 1775.

POPE BENEDICT XVI: ELECTION ANNIVERSARY. Apr 19, 2005. German cardinal Joseph Ratzinger was elected 265th pope of the Roman Catholic Church by a papal conclave of 115 cardinals after the death of Pope John Paul II.

RICARDO, DAVID: BIRTH ANNIVERSARY. Apr 19, 1772. Economist David Ricardo, whose writings greatly influenced later economic theory, was born at London, England. He is recognized as the man who first systematized economics. In his best-known work, *Principles of Political Economy and Taxation* (1817), he discussed wages and rent and the economic relationships among landlords, workers and owners of capital. In 1819 Ricardo purchased his own seat in the House of Commons and became a member of Parliament. He died Sept 11, 1823, at Gatcombe Park, Gloucestershire.

SHERMAN, ROGER: BIRTH ANNIVERSARY. Apr 19, 1721 (OS). American statesman, member of the Continental Congress (1774–81 and 1783–84), signer of the Declaration of Independence and of the Constitution, was born at Newton, MA. He also calculated astronomical and calendar information for an almanac. Sherman died at New Haven, CT, July 23, 1793.

SIERRA LEONE: NATIONAL HOLIDAY. Apr 19. Sierra Leone became a republic in 1971.

SPACE MILESTONE: *SALYUT* (USSR): 35th ANNIVERSARY. Apr 19, 1971. The Soviet Union launched *Salyut*, the first manned orbiting space laboratory. It was replaced in 1986 by *Mir*, a manned space station and laboratory.

SWAZILAND: KING'S BIRTHDAY. Apr 19. National holiday. Commemorates the birth of King Mswati III, born Apr 19, 1968.

URUGUAY: LANDING OF THE 33 PATRIOTS DAY. Apr 19. National holiday. Commemorates the arrival in 1825 of exiles that resulted in independence from Brazil in 1828.

April 2006	S	M	T	W	T	F	S
							1
	2	3	4	5	6	7	8
	9	10	11	12	13	14	15
	16	17	18	19	20	21	22
	23	24	25	26	27	28	29
	30						

WARSAW GHETTO REVOLT: ANNIVERSARY. Apr 19, 1943. A prolonged revolt began at Warsaw, Poland, when German troops tried to resume deportation of Jewish residents of the Warsaw Ghetto to the Treblinka concentration camp. With only 17 rifles and handmade grenades, for almost a month 1,200 Jewish fighters resisted 2,100 German troops who were armed with machine guns. When the uprising ended on May 16, 300 Germans and 7,000 Jews had died and the Warsaw Ghetto lay in ruins.

BIRTHDAYS TODAY

Don Adams, 79, actor (Emmy for "Get Smart"), born New York, NY, Apr 19, 1927 (some sources say Apr 13).

Hayden Christensen, 25, actor (*The Virgin Suicides; Star Wars: Episode II — Attack of the Clones*), born Vancouver, BC, Canada, Apr 19, 1981.

Tim Curry, 60, actor (*The Rocky Horror Picture Show*; stage: *Hair, Amadeus, My Favorite Year*), born Cheshire, England, Apr 19, 1946.

Elinor Donahue, 69, actress ("Father Knows Best," "The Andy Griffith Show"), born Tacoma, WA, Apr 19, 1937.

James Franco, 28, actor (*James Dean, City by the Sea*), born Palo Alto, CA, Apr 19, 1978.

Kate Hudson, 27, actress (*How to Lose a Guy in 10 Days, Almost Famous*), born Los Angeles, CA, Apr 19, 1979.

Ashley Judd, 38, actress (*Double Jeopardy, Kiss the Girls*), born Los Angeles, CA, Apr 19, 1968.

Hugh O'Brian, 76, actor ("The Life and Legend of Wyatt Earp," *Broken Lance, Ten Little Indians*), born Rochester, NY, Apr 19, 1930.

Alan Price, 64, singer, songwriter, born Fairfield, England, Apr 19, 1942.

Maria Sharapova, 19, tennis player, born Nyagan, Russia, Apr 19, 1987.

Al Unser, Jr, 44, auto racer, Indy Car national champion, born Albuquerque, NM, Apr 19, 1962.

APRIL 20 — THURSDAY

Day 110 — 255 Remaining

COLUMBINE HIGH SCHOOL KILLINGS: ANNIVERSARY. Apr 20, 1999. At this high school at Littleton, CO, students Eric Harris and Dylan Klebold killed 12 other students, a teacher and then themselves.

DOGWOOD FESTIVAL. Apr 20–23. Camdenton, MO. This annual rite of spring features music, carnival, food, parade, arts and crafts, art exhibitions and more. For info: Bruce Mitchell, Exec Dir, Camdenton Area Chamber of Commerce, PO Box 1375, Camdenton, MO 65020. Phone: (573) 346-2227 or (800) 769-1004. Fax: (573) 346-3496. E-mail: cchamber@thelake.net.

ENGLAND: CHELSEA ART FAIR. Apr 20–23. London. 45 leading galleries offer contemporary and 20th-century paintings, prints, sculpture and ceramics. Est attendance: 4,000. For info: Caroline Penman. Phone: (44) 1825 744-074. Fax: (44) 1825 744-012. E-mail: info@penman-fairs.co.uk. Web: www.penman-fairs.co.uk.

FRENCH, DANIEL CHESTER: BIRTH ANNIVERSARY. Apr 20, 1850. American sculptor, born at Exeter, NH. One of the most important artists of the 19th and early 20th centuries as a sculptor of public monuments, French is best known for his 1875 "Minute Man" statue at Concord, MA, and his 1922 statue of the seated Abraham Lincoln in the Lincoln Memorial at Washington, DC. French died at Stockbridge, MA, Oct 7, 1931. His home and studio at Stockbridge, MA, were donated to the National Trust for Historic Preservation and are open to the public. For info: Chesterwood, PO Box 827, Stockbridge, MA 01262-0827.

FRENCH QUARTER FESTIVAL. Apr 20–23. New Orleans, LA. 23rd annual. This festival focuses on all that makes the Quarter special—art, antiques, food, music, shopping, lifestyles and the people. Free concerts on 15 stages, historic patio tours, parade, children's activities, fireworks, 5k race and other family activities. Est attendance: 450,000. For info: French Quarter Festivals, Inc, 400 N Peters St, #205, New Orleans, LA 70130. Phone: (504) 522-5730 or (800) 673-5725. Fax: (504) 522-5711. E-mail: feedback@fqfi.org. Web: www.fqfi.org.

HAMPTON, LIONEL: BIRTH ANNIVERSARY. Apr 20, 1908. The jazz great was born at Louisville, KY. Hampton started out on piano and drums, but Louis Armstrong urged him to take up the vibraphone in 1930. Hampton went on to make that his signature instrument. He recorded and played with Armstrong, Benny Goodman, Dizzy Gillespie, Benny Carter and other legends before becoming a bandleader himself. He played almost up until his death on Aug 31, 2002, at New York, NY.

HITLER, ADOLF: BIRTH ANNIVERSARY. Apr 20, 1889. German dictator, obsessed with superiority of the "Aryan race." Hitler was born at Braunau am Inn, Austria. He rose in politics (despite a brief time in prison during which he wrote *Mein Kampf*) quickly as leader of the Nazis, feeding on German anger over the economy and WWI defeat. He also fanned violent anti-Semitism, which later resulted in millions of Jewish deaths in concentration camps. A German plebiscite vested sole executive power in Führer Adolf Hitler Aug 19, 1934. In seeking to increase German power, he started WWII in 1939. Facing certain defeat by the Allied Forces, he shot himself Apr 30, 1945, in a Berlin bunker where he had been hiding for more than three months.

ICELAND: "FIRST DAY OF SUMMER." Apr 20. A national public holiday, *Sumardagurinn fyrsti*, with general festivities, processions and much street dancing, especially at Reykjavik, greets the coming of summer. Flags are flown. Annually, the Thursday between Apr 19 and 25.

LLOYD, HAROLD: BIRTH ANNIVERSARY. Apr 20, 1893. A comic genius of early American film, Harold Lloyd began acting at 20 years of age, and his career took off when he teamed with producer Hal Roach in the comic "Lonesome Luke" shorts (1916–17). Lloyd then created the "glasses" character: the boy-next-door whose distinguishing feature was his round horn spectacles. This character thrilled audiences in "daredevil" comedy featuring dangerous stunts (Lloyd never used a double). Lloyd's hits included *Safety Last* (1923), where he dangled from a building's clock face, *The Freshman* (1925) and *Speedy* (1928). The biggest box-office star of the 1920s, Lloyd survived with lesser success in the talkie 1930s. He was given an honorary Oscar in 1953 for being a "master comedian and good citizen." Born at Burchard, NE, Lloyd died on Mar 8, 1971, at Hollywood, CA.

LUDLOW MINE INCIDENT: ANNIVERSARY. Apr 20, 1914. Miners struggling for recognition of their United Mine Workers Union were attacked at Ludlow, CO, by National Guard troops. The Guardsmen were paid by the mining company. A tent colony was destroyed, five men and one boy were killed by machine-gun fire and eleven children and two women were burned to death.

MOON PHASE: LAST QUARTER. Apr 20. Moon enters Last Quarter phase at 11:28 PM, EDT.

NATIONAL COLLEGIATE WOMEN'S GYMNASTICS. Apr 20–22. Oregon State University, Corvallis, OR. For info: NCAA, PO Box 6222, Indianapolis, IN 46206-6222. Phone: (317) 917-6222. Fax: (317) 917-6826. Web: www.ncaasports.com.

PUENTE, TITO: BIRTH ANNIVERSARY. Apr 20, 1923. The King of the Mambo—or "El Rey"—was born Ernesto Antonio Puente, Jr, at Spanish Harlem, New York City, to Puerto Rican parents. The legendary Puente had a career that spanned more than six decades, starting in 1937. He popularized the timbale, but played many percussion instruments and was also a composer, arranger and bandleader. His album *Dance Mania* (1958) was an international bestseller, and he released more than 100 albums. His song "Oye Como Va" was covered by Carlos Santana and has become a classic. Puente won five Grammys, was inducted into the Jazz and Hispanic halls of fame and received a Smithsonian Lifetime Achievement Award. President Jimmy Carter pronounced him "The Goodwill Ambassador of Latin American Music." Puente died on May 31, 2000, at New York, NY.

PUYALLUP SPRING FAIR. Apr 20–23. Puyallup Fairgrounds, Puyallup, WA. 18th annual. Fair to celebrate spring, including exhibits, animals, flowers, rides, demonstrations, gardening, Kid Zone, recycling, lots of entertainment, food and much more. Est attendance: 100,000. For info: Puyallup Spring Fair, 110 9th Ave SW, Puyallup, WA 98371. Phone: (253) 841-5045. Fax: (253) 841-5390. E-mail: info@thefair.com. Web: www.thefair.com.

SMITH, HOLLAND: BIRTH ANNIVERSARY. Apr 20, 1882. Considered the father of amphibious warfare, Holland "Howling Mad" Smith was born at Hatchechubie, AL. Smith developed techniques for amphibious assaults that involved coordination of land, sea and air forces. During WWII he led troops in assaults in the Marshall and Mariana Islands and also directed forces at Guam, Iwo Jima and Okinawa. Smith died Jan 12, 1967, at San Diego, CA.

TAURUS, THE BULL. Apr 20–May 20. In the astronomical/astrological zodiac that divides the sun's apparent orbit into 12 segments, the period Apr 20–May 20 is identified, traditionally, as the sun sign of Taurus, the Bull. The ruling planet is Venus.

USA FILM FESTIVAL. Apr 20–27. Dallas, TX. 36th annual. Major showcase of new studio and independent films (features and shorts), filmmaker discussions with audience, Master Screen Artist, Great Director and other tributes and retrospectives. Festival is noncompetitive except for Annual National Short Film and Video Competition with cash awards in multiple categories. Est attendance: 15,000. For info: USA Film Festival, 6116 N Central Expressway, Ste 105, Dallas, TX 75206. Phone: (214) 821-6300 or (214) 821-FILM (for 24-hour updates of film programming). Fax: (214) 821-6364. E-mail: usafilmfestival@aol.com. Web: www.usafilmfestival.com.

BIRTHDAYS TODAY

Carmen Electra, 33, actress ("Baywatch," "Singled Out"), born Cincinnati, OH, Apr 20, 1973.

Nina Foch, 82, actress (*Scaramouche*), born Leyden, Holland, Apr 20, 1924.

Crispin Glover, 42, actor (*Back to the Future, The People vs. Larry Flynt*), born New York, NY, Apr 20, 1964.

Jessica Lange, 57, actress (Oscars for *Tootsie* and *Blue Skies*; *Frances, Sweet Dreams*), born Cloquet, MN, Apr 20, 1949.

Joey Lawrence, 30, actor ("Blossom," "Brotherly Love"), born Strawbridge, PA, Apr 20, 1976.

David Leland, 59, actor (*Time Bandits*), writer, director (*Mona Lisa, Wish You Were Here*), born Cambridge, England, Apr 20, 1947.

Donald Arthur (Don) Mattingly, 45, former baseball player, born Evansville, IN, Apr 20, 1961.

Shemar Moore, 36, actor ("The Young and the Restless"), host ("Soul Train"), born Oakland, CA, Apr 20, 1970.

		S	M	T	W	T	F	S
April								1
2006		2	3	4	5	6	7	8
		9	10	11	12	13	14	15
		16	17	18	19	20	21	22
		23	24	25	26	27	28	29
		30						

Ryan O'Neal, 65, actor ("Peyton Place," *Love Story, Paper Moon*), born Los Angeles, CA, Apr 20, 1941.

Pat Roberts, 70, US Senator (R, Kansas), born Topeka, KS, Apr 20, 1936.

Steve Spurrier, 61, football player and Heisman Trophy quarterback, born Miami Beach, FL, Apr 20, 1945.

John Paul Stevens, 86, Associate Justice of the US Supreme Court, born Chicago, IL, Apr 20, 1920.

APRIL 21 — FRIDAY
Day 111 — 254 Remaining

AGGIE MUSTER. Apr 21. Texas A&M University, College Station, TX, and around the world. A ceremony where current and former students (Aggies) of Texas A&M University gather together to recall their days at the university and to honor fellow Aggies who have died in the past year. During the ceremony, a Roll Call for the Absent is read and a comrade answers "here" for the deceased. The school's most sacred and time-honored tradition. First held in 1883, but in 1903 the Muster date was moved to Apr 21—San Jacinto Day. Celebrated on the school campus and at more than 400 locations around the world. Annually, Apr 21. Est attendance: 100,000. For info: The Association of Former Students, 505 George Bush Dr, College Station, TX 77840-2918. Phone: (979) 845-7514. Fax: (979) 845-9263. E-mail: afs@aggienetwork.com. Web: www.aggienetwork.com.

BRASÍLIA INAUGURATED: ANNIVERSARY. Apr 21, 1960. At 9:30 AM, Brazil's new federal capital, Brasília, was inaugurated. The futuristic-looking city, located on the country's central plain and featuring the bold architecture of Oscar Niemeyer and others, was built in four years under the master plan of Lúcio Costa, who won a national contest to create a plan. The former capital was Rio de Janeiro.

BRAZIL: TIRADENTES DAY. Apr 21. National holiday commemorating execution of national hero, dentist Jose da Silva Xavier, nicknamed Tiradentes (tooth-puller), a conspirator in revolt against the Portuguese in 1789.

BRONTË, CHARLOTTE: BIRTH ANNIVERSARY. Apr 21, 1816. English novelist, born at Hartshead, Yorkshire, England. "Conventionality," she wrote in the preface to *Jane Eyre*, "is not morality. Self-righteousness is not religion. To attack the first is not to assail the last." She died Mar 31, 1855, at Haworth, Yorkshire, England.

CIVIL WAR REENACTMENT. Apr 21–23. Rand Park, Keokuk, IA. Battle reenactment, military ball, historic encampment, ladies' tea and style show and Civil War memorial service. Est attendance: 15,000. For info: Kirk Brandenberger, Keokuk Area Conv and Tourism Bureau, 329 Main, Keokuk, IA 52632. Phone: (800) 383-1219 or (319) 524-5599. E-mail: keokukia@interl.net. Web: www.keokukiowatourism.org.

DOROTHY PORTER WESLEY LECTURE. April 21. Moorland-Spingarn Research Center, Howard University, Washington, DC. Annual lecture series in honor of Dorothy Porter Wesley, curator emerita, librarian, bibliophile and historian. Annually, the Friday of Library Week (the third Friday of April). For info: Coni Porter Uzelac, 2400 E Las Olas Blvd, Suite 123, Fort Lauderdale, FL 33301. Phone: (954) 463-7880. Fax: (954) 463-7881. E-mail: coni@dpw-archives.org. Web: www.dpw-archives.org.

FESTIVAL OF RIDVAN. Apr 21–May 2. Annual Baha'i festival commemorating the 12 days (Apr 21–May 2, 1863) when Baha'u'llah, the prophet-founder of the Baha'i faith, resided in a garden called Ridvan (Paradise) in Baghdad, at which time He publicly proclaimed His mission as God's messenger for this age. The first, ninth (Apr 29) and twelfth days are celebrated as holy days and are three of the nine days of the year when Baha'is suspend work. For info: Baha'is of the US, Office of Communications, 1233 Central St, Evanston, IL 60201. Phone: (847) 733-3411. Fax: (847) 869-0247. E-mail: ooc@usbnc.org. Web: www.us.bahai.org.

FIESTA SAN ANTONIO. Apr 21–30. San Antonio, TX. Ten days of culture, heritage, beauty and remembrance. Parades, carnivals, sports, fireworks, music, ethnic feasts, art exhibits, dances—more than 100 events. This colorful fiesta originated in 1891 with the Battle of Flowers parade honoring the memory of Texas heroes who fought against General Santa Anna for Texan independence at the Alamo and San Jacinto. Est attendance: 3,500,000. For info: Fiesta San Antonio Commission, Inc, 2611 Broadway, San Antonio, TX 78215-1022. Phone: (210) 227-5191 or (877) 723-4378. Fax: (210) 227-1139. Web: www.fiesta-sa.org.

FROEBEL, FRIEDRICH: BIRTH ANNIVERSARY. Apr 21, 1782. German educator and author Friedrich Froebel, who believed that play is an important part of a child's education, was born at Oberwiessbach, Thuringia. Froebel invented the kindergarten, founding the first one at Blankenburg, Germany, in 1837. Froebel also invented a series of toys which he intended to stimulate learning. (The American architect Frank Lloyd Wright as a child received these toys [maplewood blocks] from his mother and spoke throughout his life of their value.) Froebel's ideas about the role of directed play, toys and music in children's education had a profound influence in England and the US, where the nursery school became a further extension of his ideas. Froebel died at Marienthal, Germany, June 21, 1852.

HISTORY MEETS THE ARTS. Apr 21–23. Gettysburg, PA. More than 75 historical artists, authors and artisans with original artwork, special tours, historical films, book and print signings. Annually in April. Est attendance: 25,000. For info: Gettysburg CVB, PO Box 4117, Gettysburg, PA 17325. Phone: (717) 334-6274. Fax: (717) 334-1166. E-mail: gettysburgcvb@dejazzd.com. Web: www.gettysburgcvb.com.

HOLIDAY IN DIXIE. Apr 21–30. Shreveport and Bossier City, LA. Ten days in April celebrating the beginning of spring with more than 50 events including carnival, tournaments, a treasure hunt, parades; also Barksdale AFB Open House. Takes place throughout both cities. Est attendance: 200,000. For info: Jeff Ramsey, Executive Director, Holiday in Dixie, 220 Carroll St, Ste C-2, Shreveport, LA 71105. Phone: (318) 865-5555. Fax: (318) 868-9577. E-mail: jeffathid@aol.com. Web: www.holidayindixie.com.

INDONESIA: KARTINI DAY. Apr 21. Republic of Indonesia. Honors the birth in 1879 of Raden Adjeng Kartini, pioneer in the emancipation of the women of Indonesia.

ITALY: BIRTHDAY OF ROME. Apr 21. Celebration of the founding of Rome, traditionally thought to be in 753 BC.

KINDERGARTEN DAY. Apr 21. A day to recognize the importance of play, games and "creative self-activity" in children's education and to note the history of the kindergarten. Observed on the anniversary of the birth of Friedrich Froebel, in 1782, who established the first kindergarten in 1837. German immigrants brought Froebel's ideas to the US in the 1840s. The first kindergarten in a public school in the US was started in 1873, at St. Louis, MO.

MANGANO, SILVANA: BIRTH ANNIVERSARY. Apr 21, 1930. Italian actress Silvana Mangano was born at Rome, Italy. She is best known for her role in the film *Bitter Rice* (1948). Mangano died Dec 16, 1989, at Madrid, Spain.

MUIR, JOHN: BIRTH ANNIVERSARY. Apr 21, 1838. American naturalist, explorer, conservationist and author for whom the 550-acre Muir Woods National Monument (near San Francisco, CA) is named. Muir, born at Dunbar, Scotland, emigrated to the US in 1849, where he urged establishment of national parks and profoundly influenced US forest conservation. Died at Los Angeles, CA, Dec 24, 1914.

NATIONAL YOUTH SERVICE DAYS. Apr 21–23. This 18th annual observance offers thousands of volunteer opportunities in all 50 states for young people, kindergarten and up. More than three million young Americans will serve in 3,000 communities. This is the world's largest volunteer event. More than 55 national organizations serve as partners for this event, which runs in conjunction with Global Youth Service Day. For info: Youth Service America, 1101 15th St NW, Ste 200, Washington, DC 20005-5002. Phone: (202) 296-2992. Web: www.ysa.org/nysd/.

QUINN, ANTHONY: BIRTH ANNIVERSARY. Apr 21, 1915. Actor, sculptor and painter, Anthony Rudolf Oaxaca Quinn was born at Chihuahua, Mexico, and moved to the US as a child. He became a US citizen in 1947. He won Academy Awards for Best Supporting Actor in 1952 for *Viva Zapata!* and in 1956 for *Lust for Life*. His best-remembered role was that of *Zorba the Greek*, for which he was nominated for Best Actor in 1964. He died at Boston, MA, on June 3, 2001.

RED BARON SHOT DOWN: ANNIVERSARY. Apr 21, 1918. German flying ace Baron Manfred von Richthofen was shot down and killed during the Battle of the Somme. The "Red Baron," so named for the color of his Fokker triplane, was credited with 80 kills in less than two years. Royal Flying Corps pilots recovered his body and the Allies buried him with full military honors. Asked about his fighting philosophy he was quoted as saying, "I am a hunter. My brother Lothar is a butcher. When I have shot down an Englishman, my hunting passion is satisfied for a quarter of an hour."

SAN JACINTO DAY. Apr 21. Texas. Commemorates Battle of San Jacinto in 1836, in which Texas won independence from Mexico. A 570-foot monument, dedicated on the 101st anniversary of the battle, marks the site on the banks of the San Jacinto River, about 20 miles from present-day Houston, TX, where General Sam Houston's Texans decisively defeated the Mexican forces led by Santa Anna in the final battle between Texas and Mexico.

SOUTH CAROLINA FESTIVAL OF ROSES. Apr 21–23. Edisto Memorial Gardens, Orangeburg, SC. To celebrate the beauty of the roses and the gardens. Est attendance: 35,000. For info: Orangeburg County Chamber of Commerce, PO Box 328, Orangeburg, SC 29116-0328. Phone: (803) 534-6821 or (800) 545-6153. Fax: (803) 531-9435. E-mail: chamber@orangeburgsc.net. Web: www.festivalofroses.com.

SPACE MILESTONE: *COPERNICUS, OAO 4* (US). Apr 21, 1972. Launch of Orbiting Astronomical Observer, named in honor of the Polish astronomer.

SPRING FESTIVAL. Apr 21–30. Cape May, NJ. Experience and appreciate the Victorian lifestyle with 10 days of spring activities at America's first seashore resort. Special events include a Vintage Dance Weekend, Victorian Murder Mystery Dinners, outdoor crafts, antiques and collectibles shows, free glassblowing demonstrations on the lawn of Cape May's only Victorian House Museum, the 1879 Emlen Physick Estate and much more. Est attendance: 15,000. For info: Mid-Atlantic Center for the Arts, 1048 Washington St, PO Box 340, Cape May, NJ 08204. Phone: (609) 884-5404 or (800) 275-4278. Fax: (609) 884-0574. E-mail: mac4arts@capemaymac.org. Web: www.capemaymac.org.

STAMP & COIN EXPO. Apr 21–23 (also Oct 27–29). Hotel Pennsylvania, New York, NY. Annual expo. Est attendance: 10,000. For info: Israel Bick, Exec Dir, Intl Stamp & Coin Collectors Society, PO Box 854, Van Nuys, CA 91408. Phone: (818) 997-6496. Fax: (818) 988-4337. E-mail: iibick@sbcglobal.net. Web: www.bick.net.

SUGARLOAF ART FAIR. Apr 21–23. New Expo Center, Novi, MI. This show, now in its 12th year, features more than 300 nationally recognized craft designers and fine artists displaying and selling their original creations. Includes craft demonstrations, live music, specialty foods, hourly gift certificate drawings and more. Est attendance: 25,000. For info: Sugarloaf Mountain Works, 200 Orchard Ridge Dr, #215, Gaithersburg, MD 20878. Phone: (800) 210-9900. Fax: (310) 253-9620. Web: www.sugarloafcrafts.com.

BIRTHDAYS TODAY

Ed Belfour, 41, hockey player, born Carman, MB, Canada, Apr 21, 1965.

Tony Danza, 55, actor ("Taxi," "Who's the Boss?"), born Brooklyn, NY, Apr 21, 1951.

Queen Elizabeth II, 80, Queen of the United Kingdom, born London, England, Apr 21, 1926.

Charles Grodin, 71, actor (*Midnight Run, Beethoven*), director, host ("The Charles Grodin Show"), born Pittsburgh, PA, Apr 21, 1935.

Patti LuPone, 57, singer, stage and screen actress (Tony for *Evita; Sunset Boulevard*), born Northport, NY, Apr 21, 1949.

Andie MacDowell, 48, actress (*sex, lies, and videotape; Groundhog Day*), born Gaffney, SC, Apr 21, 1958.

Elaine May, 74, actress, writer (comedy with Mike Nichols), director (*A New Leaf*), born Philadelphia, PA, Apr 21, 1932.

Iggy Pop, 59, singer, born Ann Arbor, MI, Apr 21, 1947.

APRIL 22 — SATURDAY
Day 112 — 253 Remaining

BABE RUTH'S PITCHING DEBUT: ANNIVERSARY. Apr 22, 1914. Babe Ruth made his professional pitching debut, playing for the Baltimore Orioles in his own hometown. Allowing just six hits and contributing two singles himself, Ruth shut out the Buffalo Bisons, 6–0.

BRAZIL: DISCOVERY OF BRAZIL DAY: ANNIVERSARY. Apr 22. Commemorates discovery by Pedro Alvarez Cabral in 1500.

CALIFORNIA POPPY FESTIVAL. Apr 22–23. Lancaster, CA. Celebrating the golden poppy as the state flower of California, the California Poppy Festival features unique homemade crafts, a variety of musical entertainers, delicious food booths and a flower and garden market. Visitors can stop by the Wildflower Information Center to get maps of the best poppy fields. Both kids and adults will enjoy the carnival, games and rides. Est attendance: 55,000. For info: Anne Aldrich, Public Information Officer, City of Lancaster, 44933 Fern Ave, Lancaster, CA 93534. Phone: (661) 723-6053. Fax: (661) 723-6141. Web: cityoflancasterca.org.

CELEBRATE EARTH DAY. Apr 22. Jenkinson's Aquarium, Point Pleasant Beach, NJ. Celebrate Earth Day in a positive way—learn what you can do to help the environment. Free arts and crafts, face painting and storytelling from 1–4 PM. Stories, demonstrations and more throughout the day. Est attendance: 1,200. For info: Jenkinson's Aquarium, 300 Ocean Ave, Point Pleasant Beach, NJ 08742. Phone: (732) 899-1212. Fax: (732) 899-1717. E-mail: jenkinsonsaquarium@comcast.net. Web: www.jenkinsons.com.

COINS STAMPED "IN GOD WE TRUST": ANNIVERSARY. Apr 22, 1864. By Act of Congress, the phrase "In God We Trust" began to be stamped on all US coins.

April *2006*	S	M	T	W	T	F	S
							1
	2	3	4	5	6	7	8
	9	10	11	12	13	14	15
	16	17	18	19	20	21	22
	23	24	25	26	27	28	29
	30						

EARTH DAY. Apr 22. Earth Day, first observed Apr 22, 1970, with message "New Energy for a New Era" and attention to accelerating the transition to renewable energy worldwide. Note: Earth Day activities are held by many groups on various dates, often on the weekends before and after Apr 22. Search for events online. For info: Earth Day Network, 1616 P St NW, Ste 200, Washington, DC 20036. Phone: (202) 518-0044. Fax: (202) 518-8794. Web: www.earthday.net.

FEAST OF THE RAMSON. Apr 22 (tentative). Richwood, WV. A dinner dedicated to the ramp, a wild leek that grows in the mountains. Arts and crafts; mountain song and dance. Est attendance: 2,000. For info: Richwood Area Chamber of Commerce, PO Box 267, Richwood, WV 26261. Phone: (304) 846-6790. E-mail: rwdchamber@richwoodwv.com. Web: www.richwoodwv.com.

FIRST SOLO TRIP TO NORTH POLE: ANNIVERSARY. Apr 22, 1994. Norwegian explorer Borge Ousland became the first person to make the trip to the North Pole alone. The trip took 52 days, during which he pulled a 265-pound sled. Departing from Cape Atkticheskiy at Siberia Mar 2, he averaged about 18½ miles per day over the 630-mile journey. Ousland had traveled to the Pole on skis with Erling Kagge in 1990.

HISTORIC GARDEN WEEK IN VIRGINIA. Apr 22–30. This annual statewide event, celebrating its 73rd anniversary, is billed as "America's Largest Open House." Showcases more than 250 of Virginia's finest homes, gardens, plantations and landmark properties on more than 30 separate tours on different days of the week. A 225-page guidebook will be available in February 2006. Please mail a contribution of $5 to cover postage and handling. Est attendance: 40,000. For info: Historic Garden Week, Garden Club of Virginia, 12 E Franklin St, Richmond, VA 23219. Phone: (804) 644-7776. Fax: (804) 644-7778. E-mail: gdnweek@verizon.net. Web: www.VAGardenweek.org.

KENTUCKY DERBY FESTIVAL. Apr 22–May 6. Louisville, KY. Civic celebration as Louisville warms up for the Kentucky Derby. About 70 events, two-thirds of which are free to the public. Est attendance: 1,500,000. For info: Kentucky Derby Festival, Inc, 1001 S Third St, Louisville, KY 40203. Phone: (502) 584-6383. Fax: (502) 589-4674. E-mail: info@kdf.org. Web: www.kdf.org.

LENIN, NIKOLAI: BIRTH ANNIVERSARY. Apr 22, 1870. Russian socialist and revolutionary leader (real name: Vladimir Ilyich Ulyanov), ideological follower of Karl Marx, born at Simbirst, on the Volga, Russia. Leader of the Great October Socialist Revolution of 1917. Died at Gorky, near Moscow, Jan 21, 1924. His embalmed body, in a glass coffin at the Lenin Mausoleum, has been viewed by millions of visitors to Moscow's Red Square.

LONGWOOD GARDENS ACRES OF SPRING. Apr 22–May 26. Kennett Square, PA. Thousands of spring bulbs, flowering shrubs and trees bloom throughout 1,050 acres of formal gardens, woodlands and meadows. Est attendance: 150,000. For info: Longwood Gardens, PO Box 501, Kennett Square, PA 19348-0501. Phone: (610) 388-1000. Web: www.longwoodgardens.org.

MISSISSIPPI RIVER VALLEY SCENIC DRIVE. Apr 22–23. Mississippi River valley of southeast Missouri. Homemade goodies, quilt shows, history and tours, entertainment, demonstrations; several small towns participate. Annually, the fourth weekend in April. For info: Frank Nickell, One University Plaza, Southeast Missouri State University, Cape Girardeau, MO 63701. Phone: (573) 651-2555. Fax: (573) 651-5114. E-mail: fnickell@semo.edu.

MOSSY CREEK BARNYARD FESTIVAL. Apr 22–23 (also Oct 21–22). Warner Robins, GA. Arts and crafts chosen from best in the nation; heritage crafts, country and folk music and folk tales in relaxed atmosphere. Semiannually, the third weekend of April (usually) and of October. Est attendance: 25,000. For info: Carolyn Chester, Mossy Creek Barnyard Festival, Inc, 106 Anne Dr, Warner Robins, GA 31093. Phone: (478) 922-8265. E-mail: echester@bellsouth.net. Web: www.mossycreekfestival.com.

NAB 2006/NATIONAL BROADCASTERS CONVENTION. Apr 22–27. Las Vegas Convention Center, Las Vegas, NV. World's largest convention of radio, television and other types of multimedia. The awards for the National Broadcasting Hall of Fame are also awarded at the convention. For info: Natl Assn of Broadcasters, 1771 N St NW, Washington, DC 20036-2891. Phone: (202) 429-5300. Fax: (202) 429-4199. E-mail: nab@nab.org. Web: www.nab.org/conventions.

OKLAHOMA DAY. Apr 22. Oklahoma.

OKLAHOMA LAND RUSH: ANNIVERSARY. Apr 22, 1889. At noon a gunshot signaled the start of the Oklahoma land rush as thousands of settlers rushed into the territory to claim land. Under pressure from cattlemen, the federal government opened 1,900,000 acres of central Oklahoma that had been bought from the Creek and Seminole tribes.

POLK COUNTY RAMP TRAMP FESTIVAL. Apr 22. Polk County 4-H Camp, Camp McCroy, near Benton, TN. A tribute to the ramp, a wild leek that grows only in the Appalachian Mountains. Bluegrass music and feast of the ramps. Est attendance: 2,500. For info: Polk Co Ramp Festival, Box 189, Benton, TN 37307. Phone: (423) 338-4503. Web: www.polkagextension.com/ramppage.html.

ROMANCE READER'S LUNCHEON. Apr 22. Portland, OR. A fund-raiser for Oregon Literacy. Come meet your favorite romance authors or hobnob with other readers. Get cool free stuff (lots of books!) at the giveaways and raffles, and have a delicious lunch, all in the name of literacy. $30 to attend, and the book signing is free and open to anyone. Est attendance: 150. For info: Susan Lute, 35725 SE Surface Rd, Estacada, OR 97023. Phone: (503) 630-3473. E-mail: su@susanlute.com. Web: www.rosecityromancewriters.com.

BIRTHDAYS TODAY

Byron Allen, 45, comedian, TV host ("Byron Allen Show," "Real People"), actor (*Case Closed*), born Detroit, MI, Apr 22, 1961.

Glen Campbell, 71, singer ("Gentle on My Mind," "By the Time I Get to Phoenix"), born Billstown, AR, Apr 22, 1935.

Peter Frampton, 56, singer ("Show Me the Way," "Do You Feel Like We Do"), born Beckenham, England, Apr 22, 1950.

Chris Makepeace, 42, actor (*My Bodyguard*), born Montreal, QC, Canada, Apr 22, 1964.

Jack Nicholson, 70, actor (Oscars for *One Flew Over the Cuckoo's Nest, Terms of Endearment* and *As Good As It Gets*), born Neptune, NJ, Apr 22, 1936.

Charlotte Rae, 80, actress ("Diff'rent Strokes," "Facts of Life"), born Milwaukee, WI, Apr 22, 1926.

Aaron Spelling, 78, writer, producer ("Fantasy Island," "Melrose Place"), born Dallas, TX, Apr 22, 1928.

Ryan Stiles, 47, actor ("The Drew Carey Show," "Whose Line Is It Anyway?"), born Seattle, WA, Apr 22, 1959.

John Waters, 60, filmmaker (*Pink Flamingoes*), born Baltimore, MD, Apr 22, 1946.

APRIL 23 — SUNDAY
Day 113 — 252 Remaining

ADMINISTRATIVE PROFESSIONALS WEEK. Apr 23–29. Acknowledgment of the contributions of all administrative professionals and their vital roles in business, industry, education and government. Annually, the last full week (from Sunday–Saturday) in April. Administrative Professionals Day is observed on Wednesday of this week (Apr 26 in 2006). For info: Rick Stroud, Communications Dir, Intl Assn of Administrative Professionals, 10502 NW Ambassador Dr, PO Box 20404, Kansas City, MO 64195-0404. Phone: (816) 891-6600 x 2239. Fax: (816) 891-9118. E-mail: rstroud@iaap-hq.org. Web: www.iaap-hq.org.

"BAYWATCH" TV PREMIERE: ANNIVERSARY. Apr 23, 1989. Set on a California beach, this program starred David Hasselhoff and a changing cast of nubile young men and women as lifeguards. Later the program was moved to Hawaii; the last episode was made in 2001. The most widely viewed TV series in the world, the program aired in 142 countries with an estimated weekly audience of 1.1 billion.

BERMUDA: PEPPERCORN CEREMONY: ANNIVERSARY. Apr 23. St. George. Commemorates the payment of one peppercorn in 1816 to the governor of Bermuda for rental of Old State House by the Masonic Lodge.

BUCHANAN, JAMES: BIRTH ANNIVERSARY. Apr 23, 1791. 15th president of the US, born at Cove Gap, PA, was the only president who never married. He served one term in office, Mar 4, 1857–Mar 3, 1861, and died at Lancaster, PA, June 1, 1868.

CERVANTES SAAVEDRA, MIGUEL DE: DEATH ANNIVERSARY. Apr 23, 1616. Spanish poet, playwright and novelist, died at Madrid, Spain. The exact date of his birth at Alcala de Henares is unknown, but he was baptized Oct 9, 1547. As soldier and tax collector, Cervantes traveled widely. He spent more than five years in prisons in Spain, Italy and North Africa. His greatest creation was Don Quixote, the immortal Knight of La Mancha whose profession was chivalry. Riding his nag, Rozinante, and accompanied by Squire Sancho Panza, Don Quixote tilts at windmills of the mind in the world's best-known novel. Nearly a thousand editions of *Don Quixote* (a bestseller since its first appearance in 1605) have been published, and it has been translated into more languages than any other book except the Bible.

EARTH DAY COMMUNITY FESTIVAL. Apr 23. St. Louis, MO. An educational event with hundreds of exhibitors related to environmental issues and their solutions. Est attendance: 5,000. For info: St. Louis Earth Day, PO Box 19863, St Louis, MO 63144. Phone: (314) 962-5838. E-mail: info@stlouisearthday.org. Web: www.stlouisearthday.org.

FIRST MOVIE THEATER OPENS: ANNIVERSARY. Apr 23, 1896. The first movie was shown at Koster and Bials Music Hall at New York City. Up until this time, people saw films individually by looking into a Kinetoscope, a boxlike "peep show." This was the first time in the US that an audience sat in a theater and watched a movie together.

FIRST PUBLIC SCHOOL IN AMERICA: ANNIVERSARY. Apr 23, 1635 (NS). The Boston Latin School opened—America's oldest public school.

INNOVATION WEEK INTERNATIONAL. Apr 23–29. Innovation raises the standard in every area of human endeavor, whether in products, services or personal performance. Conference themes will focus on how to encourage and nurture innovation at each level of the organization in order to consistently achieve breakthrough results. For info: DiFrances & Assoc., LLC, 208 E Oak Crest Dr, Ste 200, Wales, WI 53187-9700. Phone: (262) 968-9850. Fax: (262) 968-9854. E-mail: innovation@difrances.com. Web: www.difrances.com/innovationweek.

JUST PRAY NO: WORLDWIDE WEEKEND PRAYER. Apr 23–24. 16th annual. Churches throughout the world. Concerts of prayer, fasting, street rallies and marches to gain media attention. Bible studies and sermons concerning alcoholism and drug abuse and revival meetings aimed at those bound by addiction. For info: Just Pray No, Ltd, 1875 Sunset Point Rd, #704, Clearwater, FL 33765. Web: www.justprayno.org.

NATIONAL KARAOKE WEEK. Apr 23–29. Karaoke has grown by leaps and bounds in the US. Once thought to be a fad, more and more people are recognizing the benefits of karaoke—increased self-esteem, confidence and stress release. Annually, the fourth week in April. For info: Visual Perspectives, 1083 W 124th Dr, Westminster, CO 80234-1757. Phone: (303) 452-5140. E-mail: shirai2@comcast.net.

NATIONAL VOLUNTEER WEEK. Apr 23–29. National Volunteer Week has become the official time to recognize and celebrate the efforts of volunteers at the local, state and national levels. It began in 1974 when President Richard Nixon signed an executive order establishing the week as an annual celebration of volunteering. Every president since has signed a proclamation promoting National Volunteer Week, as have governors, mayors and other elected officials. For info: Points of Light Foundation, 1400 I St NW, Ste 800, Washington, DC 20005. E-mail: volunteerweek@pointsoflight.org. Web: www.pointsoflight.org.

NATIONAL WILDLIFE WEEK. Apr 23–29. In 1938 the National Wildlife Federation created National Wildlife Week, a celebration to alert the public to the needs of wildlife and NWF's efforts to preserve wildlife and their habitats. NWF educates students, families and adults about wildlife conservation issues and encourages them to become environmental stewards. For info: National Wildlife Federation, 11100 Wildlife Ctr Dr, Reston, VA 20190. Phone: (703) 438-6000. E-mail: wildlife@nwf.org. Web: www.nwf.org.

NATIONAL WINDOW SAFETY WEEK. April 23–29. Designed to inform parents and caregivers about the critical role played by windows in the safety plans of their homes. Also, to address issues of children falling out windows and using windows as emergency escapes. For info: Jeffrey Lowinski, Window & Door Manufacturers Assn, 1400 E Touhy Ave, Ste 470, Des Plaines, IL 60018. Phone: (847) 299-5200. Fax: (847) 299-1286. E-mail: jlowinski@wdma.com. Web: www.wdma.com.

ORTHODOX EASTER SUNDAY OR PASCHA. Apr 23. Observed by Eastern Orthodox churches on this date. Normally Easter falls on different Sundays in the Eastern and Western churches. See also: "Easter Sunday" (Apr 16).

PEARSON, LESTER B.: BIRTH ANNIVERSARY. Apr 23, 1897. 14th prime minister of Canada, born at Toronto, Canada. He was Canada's chief delegate at the San Francisco conference where the UN charter was drawn up and later served as president of the General Assembly. He wrote the proposal that resulted in the formation of the North Atlantic Treaty Organization (NATO). He was awarded the Nobel Peace Prize. Died at Rockcliffe, Canada, Dec 27, 1972.

PHYSICISTS DISCOVER TOP QUARK: ANNIVERSARY. Apr 23, 1994. Physicists at the Department of Energy's Fermi National Accelerator Laboratory found evidence for the existence of the subatomic particle called the top quark, the last undiscovered quark of the six predicted to exist by current scientific theory. The discovery provides strong support for the quark theory of the structure of matter. Quarks are subatomic particles that make up protons and neutrons found in the nuclei of atoms. The five other quark types that had already been proven to exist are the up quark, down quark, strange quark, charm quark and bottom quark. Further experimentation over many months confirmed the discovery and it was publicly announced Mar 2, 1995.

PLANCK, MAX: BIRTH ANNIVERSARY. Apr 23, 1858. Formulator of the quantum theory which revolutionized physics, born at Kiel, Germany. Einstein's application of quantum theory to light led to the theories of relativity. Planck died at Gottingen, Germany, Oct 3, 1947.

RV LIFESTYLE WEEK. Apr 23–28. Celebrate and raise awareness about the RV lifestyle. Celebrations are planned in Chico, CA, and other locations. For info: Jaimie Hall, RV Hometown, 127 Rainbow Dr, #2780, Livingston, TX 77399. Phone: (928) 607-3181. Fax: (561) 892-2837. E-mail: calamityjaimie@escapees.com. Web: www.rvsleuths.com.

SAINT GEORGE: FEAST DAY. Apr 23. Martyr and patron saint of England, who died Apr 23, AD 303. Hero of the St. George and the dragon legend. The story says that his faith helped him slay a vicious dragon that demanded daily sacrifice after the king's daughter became the intended victim.

SHAKESPEARE, WILLIAM: BIRTH AND DEATH ANNIVERSARY. Apr 23. England's most famous and most revered poet and playwright. He was born at Stratford-on-Avon, England, Apr 23, 1564 (OS), baptized there three days later and died there on his birthday, Apr 23, 1616 (OS). Author of at least 36 plays and 154 sonnets, Shakespeare created the most influential and lasting body of work in the English language, an extraordinary exploration of human nature. His epitaph: "Good frend for Jesus sake forbeare, To digg the dust enclosed heare. Blese be ye man that spares thes stones, And curst be he that moves my bones."

SKY AWARENESS WEEK. Apr 23–29. A celebration of the sky and an opportunity to appreciate its natural beauty, to understand sky and weather processes and to work together to protect the sky as a natural resource (it's the only one we have). Events are held at schools, nature centers, etc, all across the US. For info: Barbara G. Levine & H. Michael Mogil, How The Weatherworks, 301 Creek Valley Ln, Rockville, MD 20850. Phone: (240) 426-2900. Fax: (301) 990-9324. E-mail: skyweek@weatherworks.com. Web: www.weatherworks.com.

SPACE MILESTONE: *SOYUZ 10* **(USSR): 35th ANNIVERSARY.** Apr 23, 1971. Launch date of Soviet mission in which cosmonauts V.A. Shatalov, A.S. Yeliseyev and N.N. Rukavishnikov docked Apr 24 with *Salyut 1* orbital space station. The crew did not enter the space station. Return Earth landing at Kazakhstan, USSR, Apr 24.

SPAIN: BOOK DAY AND LOVER'S DAY. Apr 23. Barcelona. Saint George's Day and the anniversary of the death of Spanish writer Miguel de Cervantes have been observed with special ceremonies in the Palacio de la Disputacion and throughout the city since 1714. Book stands are set up in the plazas and on street corners. This is Spain's equivalent of Valentine's Day. Women give books to men; men give roses to women.

TURKEY: NATIONAL SOVEREIGNTY AND CHILDREN'S DAY: ANNIVERSARY. Apr 23, 1923. Commemorates Grand National Assembly's inauguration.

UNITED NATIONS: WORLD BOOK AND COPYRIGHT DAY. Apr 23. By celebrating this day throughout the world, UNESCO seeks to promote reading, publishing and the protection of intellectual property through copyright. It was a natural choice for UNESCO's General Conference to pay a worldwide tribute to books and authors on Apr 23, because on this date and in the same year of 1616, Cervantes, Shakespeare and Inca Garcilaso de la Vega all died. It is also the date of birth or death of other prominent authors such as Maurice Druon, Halldor Lax-

		S	M	T	W	T	F	S
April								1
2006		2	3	4	5	6	7	8
		9	10	11	12	13	14	15
		16	17	18	19	20	21	22
		23	24	25	26	27	28	29
		30						

ness, Vladimir Nabokov, Josep Pla and Manuel Mejía Vallejo. Observed throughout the United Nations system. For info: United Nations, Dept of Public Info, New York, NY 10017. Web: www .un.org.

WOODS, GRANVILLE T.: 150th BIRTH ANNIVERSARY. Apr 23, 1856. Granville T. Woods was born at Columbus, OH. He invented the Synchronous Multiplex Railway Telegraph which allowed communication between dispatchers and trains while the trains were in motion, which decreased the number of train accidents. In addition, Woods is credited with a number of other electrical inventions. Died Jan 30, 1910, at New York, NY.

BIRTHDAYS TODAY

Valerie Bertinelli, 46, actress ("One Day at a Time," *Silent Witness*), born Wilmington, DE, Apr 23, 1960.

David Birney, 66, actor ("Love Is a Many Splendored Thing," "Bridget Loves Bernie"), born Washington, DC, Apr 23, 1940.

Shirley Temple Black, 78, former ambassador to Ghana, child actress (*Heidi, Curly Top, Little Miss Marker*), TV hostess ("Shirley Temple's Storybook" and "Shirley Temple Theatre"), born Santa Monica, CA, Apr 23, 1928.

Judy Davis, 51, actress (*A Passage to India, Deconstructing Harry*), born Perth, Australia, Apr 23, 1955.

Joyce Dewitt, 57, actress ("Three's Company"), born Wheeling, WV, Apr 23, 1949.

Jan Hooks, 49, actress ("Saturday Night Live," "Designing Women"), born Atlanta, GA, Apr 23, 1957.

Andruw Jones, 29, baseball player, born Wellemstad, Curacao, Netherlands Antilles, Apr 23, 1977.

Melina Kanakaredes, 39, actress ("Providence," "Guiding Light"), born Akron, OH, Apr 23, 1967.

Lee Majors, 66, actor ("The Six Million Dollar Man," "The Fall Guy"), born Wyandotte, MI, Apr 23, 1940.

Bernadette Devlin McAliskey, 59, political activist, born Cookstown, Northern Ireland, Apr 23, 1947.

Michael Moore, 52, author (*Stupid White Men; Dude, Where's My Country?*), filmmaker (*Bowling for Columbine, Fahrenheit 9/11*), born Flint, MI, Apr 23, 1954.

Warren Edward Spahn, 85, Hall of Fame baseball player, born Buffalo, NY, Apr 23, 1921.

Narada Michael Walden, 54, drummer (Mahavishnu Orchestra), singer, songwriter, born Kalamazoo, MI, Apr 23, 1952.

APRIL 24 — MONDAY

Day 114 — 251 Remaining

ARMENIA: ARMENIAN MARTYRS DAY. Apr 24. Commemorates the massacre of Armenians under the Ottoman Turks in 1915. Deportations from Turkey began. Also called Armenian Genocide Memorial Day. Adolf Hitler, in a speech at Obersalzberg, Aug 22, 1939, is reported to have said, "Who today remembers the Armenian extermination?" in an apparent justification of the Nazis' use of genocide.

BASCOM, GEORGE N.: BIRTH ANNIVERSARY. Apr 24, 1836. West Point Graduate Lieutenant George N. Bascom was assigned to search out Apache chief Cochise, believed to be responsible for an 1861 raid on an Arizona ranch. He arrested Cochise at Apache Pass, but the chief escaped and declared war, launching a reign of terror known as the Apache Wars. Bascom was born at Owingsville, KY, and died the year following his Apache adventure when he became a casualty of the Civil War battle at Fort Craig, Valverde, NM, Feb 21, 1862.

BIG 12 MEN'S GOLF CHAMPIONSHIP. Apr 24–25. Southern Hills Country Club, Tulsa, OK. Est attendance: 1,000. For info: Big 12 Conference, 2201 Stemmons Freeway, 28th Fl, Dallas, TX 75207. Phone: (214) 742-1212. Fax: (214) 753-0145. Web: www.big12sports.com.

CANADA: NEWFOUNDLAND: SAINT GEORGE'S DAY. Apr 24. Holiday observed at Newfoundland on Monday nearest Feast Day (Apr 23) of Saint George.

CARTWRIGHT, EDMUND: BIRTH ANNIVERSARY. Apr 24, 1743. English cleric and inventor (developed the power loom and other weaving machines) was born at Nottinghamshire, England. He died at Hastings, Sussex, England, Oct 30, 1823.

CONFEDERATE MEMORIAL DAY IN ALABAMA. Apr 24. On the fourth Monday in April. Other Southern states observe Confederate Memorial Day on different dates.

CONFEDERATE MEMORIAL DAY IN MISSISSIPPI. Apr 24. Annually, on the last Monday in April. Observed on other dates in some states.

ELECTRONIC COMMUNICATIONS WEEK. Apr 24–28. A week dedicated to more effective use of electronic communications devices, with a special focus on etiquette for e-mail, voice-mail and cell phone use. Annually, the fourth week of April, Monday through Friday. For info: Karen Leland, 180 Harbor Dr, #208, Sausalito, CA 94965. Phone: (415) 331-5200. Fax: (415) 331-5272. E-mail: kleland@scgtraining.com. Web: www.scgtraining.com.

FORT MOORE ESTABLISHED: ANNIVERSARY. Apr 24, 1847. At the conclusion of the Mexican War, the Mormon Battalion of the Army of the West established Fort Moore overseeing the pueblo of Los Angeles. The fort was named in honor of their captain who had perished in the Battle of San Pascual.

IRELAND: EASTER RISING: 90th ANNIVERSARY. Apr 24, 1916. Irish nationalists seized key buildings in Dublin and proclaimed an Irish republic. The rebellion collapsed, however, and it wasn't until 1922 that the Irish Free State, the predecessor of the Republic of Ireland, was established.

LIBRARY OF CONGRESS: ANNIVERSARY. Apr 24, 1800. Congress approved an act providing "for the purchase of such books as may be necessary for the use of Congress . . . and for fitting up a suitable apartment for containing them." Thus began one of the world's greatest libraries.

NATIONAL PLAYGROUND SAFETY WEEK. Apr 24–28. An opportunity for families, community parks, schools and child-care facilities to focus on preventing public playground–related injuries. Sponsored by the National Program for Playground Safety (NPPS), this event helps educate the public about the more than 200,000 children (that's one child every 2½ minutes) that require emergency room treatment for playground-related injuries each year. For info: Natl Program for Playground Safety, WRC 205, University of Northern Iowa, Cedar Falls, IA 50614-0618. Phone: (800) 554-PLAY. Fax: (319) 273-7308. Web: www.playgroundsafety.org.

NATIONAL SCOOP THE POOP WEEK. Apr 24–30. Between the snowy storms of winter and the backyard barbecues of summer, now is the perfect time for dog owners to catch up on all those "canine calling cards" that have accumulated during the cold months. Besides creating a nasty mess in your yard, it's a health hazard, it pollutes the groundwater and it annoys the neighbors. It doesn't go away by itself, so get it cleaned up this week. And remind your dog-owning friends! Your family, neighbors and dog will love you for it. Annually, last week of April. For info: Matthew Osborn, PO Box 28412, Columbus, OH 43228. E-mail: scoopweek@pooper-scooper.com. Web: www.pooper-scooper.com.

NATIONAL TV TURNOFF WEEK. Apr 24–30. 12th annual. Encourages Americans to voluntarily turn off their TVs for seven days in order to promote richer, healthier and more connected lives, families and communities. Organizer's kit available. For info: TV-Turnoff Network, 1200 29th St NW, Lower Level #1, Washington, DC 20007. Phone: (202) 333-9220. Fax: (202) 333-9221. E-mail: email@tvturnoff.org. Web: www.tvturnoff.org.

SPACE MILESTONE: *CHINA 1* (PEOPLE'S REPUBLIC OF CHINA). Apr 24, 1970. China became the fifth nation to orbit a satellite with the launch of its own rocket. The satellite broadcast the Chinese song "Tang Fang Hung" ("The East Is Red") and telemetric signals.

THOMAS, ROBERT BAILEY: BIRTH ANNIVERSARY. Apr 24, 1766. Founder and editor of *The Farmer's Almanac* (first issue for 1793) was born at Grafton, MA. Thomas died May 19, 1846, while working on the 1847 edition.

TROLLOPE, ANTHONY: BIRTH ANNIVERSARY. Apr 24, 1815. English novelist (*Barchester Towers*), born at London, England, and died there Dec 6, 1882. "Of the needs a book has," he wrote in his autobiography, "the chief need is that it be readable."

TUCSON INTERNATIONAL MARIACHI CONFERENCE. Apr 24–29. Tucson Convention Center, Tucson, AZ. An exciting festival that showcases the best in baile folklórico and mariachi. There are four events open to the public: the Participant Showcase, the Espectacular Concert, the Mariachi Mass and the Fiesta de Garibaldi. Contact us for the dates, times and locations of these events. The conference also includes workshops giving students of all ages the opportunity to study the music and dance of Mexico and learn from the masters. Est attendance: 50,000. For info: Lolie Gomez, Tucson Intl Mariachi Conference, 502 W 29th St, PO Box 3035, Tucson, AZ 85702. Phone: (520) 838-3908. Fax: (520) 792-9854. E-mail: lgomez@lafrontera.org. Web: www.tucsonmariachi.org.

US ATTEMPT TO FREE IRAN HOSTAGES: ANNIVERSARY. Apr 24, 1980. US Marines attempted to stage a surprise raid to free citizens held at the US embassy in Tehran, Iran, but their helicopters collided at the desert staging area. Eight were killed and five were wounded. No further military rescues were attempted, and the hostages were later released in January 1981 after 444 days of captivity.

WARREN, ROBERT PENN: BIRTH ANNIVERSARY. Apr 24, 1905. American poet, novelist, essayist and critic. America's first official poet laureate, 1986–88, Robert Penn Warren was born at Guthrie, KY. Warren was awarded the Pulitzer Prize for his novel *All the King's Men*, as well as for his poetry in 1958 and 1979. He died of cancer Sept 15, 1989, at Stratton, VT.

WORLD'S BIGGEST FISH FRY. Apr 24–29. Henry County Fairgrounds, Paris, TN. Since 1953. More than 10,000 pounds of catfish will be served. Includes parades, arts and crafts show, auto shows and more. All-you-can-eat dinners are served at the fairgrounds. For info: Paris Chamber of Commerce, 2508 E Wood Rd, PO Box 8, Paris, TN 38242. Phone: (731) 642-3431. E-mail: pariscoc@charterbn.com. Web: paris.tn.org.

BIRTHDAYS TODAY

Eric Balfour, 29, actor (*Rescue Me, No One Would Tell*), musician, born Los Angeles, CA, Apr 24, 1977.

Eric Bogosian, 53, actor (*Under Siege 2*), playwright, performance artist, born Boston, MA, Apr 24, 1953.

Cedric the Entertainer, 42, comedian, actor (*Barbershop, Be Cool*), born Cedric Kyles at Jefferson City, MO, Apr 24, 1964.

A. Paul Cellucci, 58, US ambassador to Canada, former Governor of Massachusetts (R), born Hudson, MA, Apr 24, 1948.

Richard M. Daley, 64, Mayor of Chicago, born Chicago, IL, Apr 24, 1942.

April 2006	S	M	T	W	T	F	S
							1
	2	3	4	5	6	7	8
	9	10	11	12	13	14	15
	16	17	18	19	20	21	22
	23	24	25	26	27	28	29
	30						

Sue Grafton, 66, author (*L Is for Lawless, M Is for Malice*), born Louisville, KY, Apr 24, 1940.

Chipper Jones, 34, baseball player, born DeLand, FL, Apr 24, 1972.

Stanley J. Kauffmann, 90, critic, born New York, NY, Apr 24, 1916.

Shirley MacLaine, 72, author, actress (Oscar for *Terms of Endearment; The Turning Point, Being There*), born Richmond, VA, Apr 24, 1934.

Michael O'Keefe, 51, actor (*The Great Santini, Caddyshack*; stage: *Mass Appeal*), born Larchmont, NY, Apr 24, 1955.

Barbra Streisand, 64, singer, actress (Oscar for *Funny Girl; The Way We Were, Yentl*), director (*Prince of Tides*), born Brooklyn, NY, Apr 24, 1942.

APRIL 25 — TUESDAY
Day 115 — 250 Remaining

ABORTION FIRST LEGALIZED: ANNIVERSARY. Apr 25, 1967. The first law legalizing abortion in the US was signed by Colorado Governor John Arthur Love. The law allowed therapeutic abortions in cases in which a three-doctor panel unanimously agreed.

ANZAC DAY. Apr 25. Australia, New Zealand and Samoa. Memorial day and veterans' observance, especially to mark WWI Anzac landing at Gallipoli, Turkey, in 1915 (ANZAC: Australia and New Zealand Army Corps).

BATTLE OF GALLIPOLI: ANNIVERSARY. Apr 25, 1915–Jan 1916. During WWI the Gallipoli Expedition, or the Dardanelles Campaign, combined Allied naval and military forces tried to capture the Gallipoli peninsula in Turkey in order to effect an open route to Russia via the Black Sea. One French and four British divisions were forced back by a strong Turkish-German defense after almost nine months of fighting. The Australian–New Zealand Army Corps (ANZACS) took much of the brunt of the battle.

BRENNAN, WILLIAM: 100th BIRTH ANNIVERSARY. Apr 25, 1906. US Supreme Court Associate Justice William J. Brennan was appointed to the Supreme Court in 1956 by President Dwight Eisenhower. His liberal leanings and judicial activism raised the ire of many conservatives, even leading Eisenhower to call his appointment his "worst mistake." Brennan believed that the courts should go beyond strict constructionism and original intent doctrines in interpreting the law. He was responsible for many landmark decisions, including the decision requiring the Little Rock, AR, schools to desegregate that included the controversial assertion that it is not only the Constitution that is the "supreme law of the land," but the Supreme Court's interpretation of it as well. His legacy also includes major decisions upholding affirmative action, a losing battle to declare the death penalty unconstitutional, decisions broadening free speech and free press guarantees, expansion of the due process guarantees under the 14th Amendment, and protection of flag burning as a form of expression. Brennan's resignation provided President George Bush with an opportunity to swing the balance of the Supreme Court to a more conservative, constructionist majority for the first time since the days of Franklin D. Roosevelt's presidency. Brennan was born at Newark, NJ; he died at Arlington, VA, July 25, 1997.

EGYPT: SINAI DAY. Apr 25. National holiday celebrating the return of Sinai to Egypt in 1982 after the peace treaty between Egypt and Israel.

FARRAGUT CAPTURES NEW ORLEANS: ANNIVERSARY. Apr 25, 1862. Union forces under the command of Flag Officer David Farragut seized the city of New Orleans, LA, resulting in the surrender of several Confederate forts along the Mississippi in subsequent days. This action removed any Confederate resistance to Northern action on the Mississippi River as far north as New Orleans. General Benjamin Butler arrived on Apr 27 and took command of the management of the captured city.

FIRST LICENSE PLATES: ANNIVERSARY. Apr 25, 1901. New York began requiring license plates on automobiles, the first state to do so.

FITZGERALD, ELLA: BIRTH ANNIVERSARY. Apr 25, 1917. "First Lady of Song," born at Newport News, VA. Jazz singer known for her treatments of Rogers and Hart, Gershwin, Irving Berlin, Cole Porter and Duke Ellington. Fitzgerald died at Beverly Hills, CA, June 15, 1996.

ISRAEL: HOLOCAUST DAY (YOM HASHOAH). Apr 25. Hebrew calendar date: Nisan 27, 5766. A day established by Israel's Knesset as a memorial to the Jewish dead of WWII. Anniversary in Jewish calendar of Nisan 27, 5705 (corresponding to Apr 10, 1945, in the Gregorian calendar), the day on which Allied troops liberated the first Nazi concentration camp, Buchenwald, north of Weimar, Germany, where about 56,000 prisoners, many of them Jewish, perished. Began at sundown Apr 24.

ITALY: LIBERATION DAY. Apr 25. National holiday. Commemorates the liberation of Italy from German troops in 1945.

MARCONI, GUGLIELMO: BIRTH ANNIVERSARY. Apr 25, 1874. Inventor of wireless telegraphy (1895), born at Bologna, Italy. Died at Rome, Italy, July 20, 1937.

NATIONAL TEACH CHILDREN TO SAVE DAY. Apr 25. Thousands of bankers visit classrooms across America to teach children of all ages the importance of saving and making fiscal fitness a lifetime habit. For info: American Bankers Association, 1120 Connecticut Ave NW, Washington, DC 20036. Phone: (202) 663-5473. Fax: (202) 663-5464. E-mail: jhall@aba.com. Web: www.aba.com.

PORTUGAL: LIBERTY DAY. Apr 25. Portugal. Public holiday. Anniversary of the 1974 revolution.

SPACE MILESTONE: HUBBLE SPACE TELESCOPE DEPLOYED (US). Apr 25, 1990. Deployed by *Discovery*, the telescope is the largest on-orbit observatory to date and is capable of imaging objects up to 14 billion light-years away. The resolution of images was expected to be seven to ten times greater than images from Earth-based telescopes, since the Hubble Space Telescope is not hampered by Earth's atmospheric distortion. Launched Apr 12, 1990, from Kennedy Space Center, FL. Unfortunately, the telescope's lenses were defective, so the anticipated high quality of imaging was not possible. In 1993, however, the world watched as a shuttle crew successfully retrieved the Hubble from orbit, executed the needed repair and replacement work and released it into orbit once more. In December 1999 the space shuttle *Discovery* was launched to do extensive repairs on the telescope.

SWAZILAND: NATIONAL FLAG DAY. Apr 25. National holiday.

THEODORE ROOSEVELT NATIONAL PARK ESTABLISHED: ANNIVERSARY. Apr 25, 1947. Located in North Dakota, the Theodore Roosevelt National Park includes two sections of the Badlands on the Missouri River as well as Theodore Roosevelt's Elkhorn Ranch.

TRIBECA FILM FESTIVAL. Apr 25–May 7. New York, NY. 5th annual. For info: Tribeca Film Festival. Phone: (866) 941-FEST. Web: www.tribecafilmfestival.org.

WALDSEEMULLER, MARTIN: REMEMBRANCE DAY. Apr 25, 1507. Little is known about the obscure scholar now called the "godfather of America," the German geographer and mapmaker Martin Waldseemuller, who gave America its name. In a book titled *Cosmographiae Introductio*, published Apr 25, 1507, Waldseemuller wrote: "Inasmuch as both Europe and Asia received their names from women, I see no reason why any one should justly object to calling this part Amerige, i.e., the land of Amerigo, or America, after Amerigo, its discoverer, a man of great ability." Believing it was the Italian navigator and merchant Amerigo Vespucci who had discovered the new continent, Waldseemuller sought to honor Vespucci by placing his name on his map of the world, published in 1507. First applied only to the South American continent, it soon was used for both the American continents. Waldseemuller did not learn about the voyage of Christopher Columbus until several years later. Of the thousand copies of his map that were printed, only one is known to have survived. Waldseemuller probably was born at Radolfzell, Germany, about 1470. He died at St. Die, France, about 1517–20. See also: "Vespucci, Amerigo: Birth Anniversary" (Mar 9).

WWII: EAST MEETS WEST: ANNIVERSARY. Apr 25, 1945. US Army Lieutenant Albert Kotzebue encountered a single Soviet soldier near the German village of Lechwitz, 75 miles south of Berlin. Patrols of General Leonard Gerow's V Corps saluted the advance guard of Marshall Ivan Konev's Soviet 58th Guards Division. Soldiers of both nations embraced and exchanged toasts. The Allied armies of East and West had finally met.

BIRTHDAYS TODAY

Hank Azaria, 42, actor (*The Birdcage*, many voices on "The Simpsons"), born Forest Hills, NY, Apr 25, 1964.

Jeffrey DeMunn, 59, actor (*Ragtime, Frances*), born Buffalo, NY, Apr 25, 1947.

Tim Duncan, 30, basketball player, born St. Croix, Virgin Islands, Apr 25, 1976.

Jon Kyl, 64, US Senator (R, Arizona), born Oakland, NE, Apr 25, 1942.

Meadow George ("Meadowlark") Lemon III, 74, Hall of Fame basketball player, born Lexington, SC, Apr 25, 1932.

Paul Mazursky, 76, director (*Harry and Tonto, An Unmarried Woman, Scenes from a Mall*), born Brooklyn, NY, Apr 25, 1930.

Al Pacino, 66, actor (Oscar for *Scent of a Woman; Dog Day Afternoon, Godfather* movies), born New York, NY, Apr 25, 1940.

Talia Shire, 60, actress (the *Godfather* movies, the *Rocky* movies), born Jamaica, NY, Apr 25, 1946.

Renee Zellweger, 37, actress (Oscar for *Cold Mountain; Chicago, Bridget Jones's Diary*), born Katy, TX, Apr 25, 1969.

APRIL 26 — WEDNESDAY
Day 116 — 249 Remaining

ADMINISTRATIVE PROFESSIONALS DAY. Apr 26. Annually, the Wednesday of Administrative Professionals Week. For info: Rick Stroud, Communications Dir, Intl Assn of Administrative Professionals, 10502 NW Ambassador Dr, PO Box 20404, Kansas City, MO 64195-0404. Phone: (816) 891-6600 x 2239. E-mail: rstroud@iaap-hq.org. Web: www.iaap-hq.org.

AMERICAN QUILTER'S SOCIETY QUILT SHOW. Apr 26–29. Paducah, KY. 22nd annual. More than 400 quilts are exhibited with $100,000 awarded in prizes. Lectures, workshops. Est attendance: 35,000. For info: American Quilter's Society, PO Box 3290, Paducah, KY 42002. Phone: (270) 898-7903. Fax: (270) 898-1173. Web: www.americanquilter.com.

★   ★   ★

AUDUBON, JOHN JAMES: BIRTH ANNIVERSARY.
Apr 26, 1785. American artist and naturalist, best known for his *Birds of America*, born at Haiti. Died Jan 27, 1851, at New York, NY.

CHERNOBYL NUCLEAR REACTOR DISASTER: 20th ANNIVERSARY. Apr 26, 1986. At 1:23 AM, local time, an explosion occurred at the Chernobyl atomic power station at Pripyat in the Ukraine. The resulting fire burned for days, sending radioactive material into the atmosphere. More than 100,000 persons were evacuated from a 300-square-mile area around the plant. Three months later 31 people were reported to have died and thousands exposed to dangerous levels of radiation. Estimates projected an additional 1,000 cancer cases in nations downwind of the radioactive discharge. The plant was encased in a concrete tomb in an effort to prevent the still-hot reactor from overheating again and to minimize further release of radiation.

"CHINA BEACH" TV PREMIERE: ANNIVERSARY. Apr 26, 1988. The stories of "China Beach" revolved around the lives of the women serving at a Da Nang armed forces hospital during the Vietnam War. The theme and background music of the series evoked plenty of nostalgia from the turbulent era. The ABC drama was created by William Boyles, Jr, and John Sacret Young. The cast featured Dana Delany, Michael Boatman, Nancy Giles, Jeff Kober, Robert Picardo, Concetta Tomei, Brian Wimmer, Marg Helgenberger, Chloe Webb, Nan Woods, Megan Gallagher, Ned Vaughn and Ricki Lake.

CONFEDERATE MEMORIAL DAY IN FLORIDA AND GEORGIA. Apr 26. Observed on the anniversary of Confederate General Joseph E. Johnston's surrender to General William T. Sherman in Durham, NC, in 1865. Other Southern states observe this day on different dates.

ETHNIC AWARENESS PROGRAM. Apr 26–29. Macon, GA. To unite, educate and draw this diverse country together and to help its citizens understand one another's cultures, respect one another's differences and share one another's likenesses. Program will include informative films, racial discussions, skits, talent showcases, social events and the 8th annual Ethnic Awards Gala & Film Exposure Feast. For info: Betty Jean Slater, Willis-Slater Productions, 2806 Kent, Macon, GA 31206. Phone: (478) 788-5419.

FAUSET, JESSIE REDMON: BIRTH ANNIVERSARY.
Apr 26, 1882. African-American poet, editor and novelist, born at Fredericksville, NJ, and died in 1961. Fauset, as literary editor of *Crisis* (a publication of the NAACP), was a patron to so many writers of the Harlem Renaissance that her efforts prompted Langston Hughes to dub her the "midwife of the so-called New Negro Literature." Along with W.E.B. Du Bois, Fauset also published and edited the children's magazine *The Brownie Book*. Her novels about the African-American middle-class experience dealt with issues of identity, autonomy and struggles for fulfillment. Her most recognized works include *The Chinaberry Tree* (1931) and *Comedy, American Style* (1933).

	S	M	T	W	T	F	S
April							1
2006	2	3	4	5	6	7	8
	9	10	11	12	13	14	15
	16	17	18	19	20	21	22
	23	24	25	26	27	28	29
	30						

GUERNICA MASSACRE: ANNIVERSARY. Apr 26, 1937. Late in the afternoon, the ancient Basque town of Guernica, in northern Spain, was attacked without warning by German-made airplanes. Three hours of intensive bombing left the town in flames, and citizens who fled to the fields and ditches around Guernica were machine-gunned from the air. This atrocity inspired Pablo Picasso's mural *Guernica*. Responsibility for the bombing was never officially established, but the suffering and anger of the victims and their survivors are still evident at anniversary demonstrations. Intervention by Nazi Germany in the Spanish Civil War has been described as practice for WWII.

HESS, RUDOLF: BIRTH ANNIVERSARY. Apr 26, 1894. One of the most bizarre figures of WWII Germany, Walter Richard Rudolf Hess was born at Alexandria, Egypt. He was a close friend, confidant and personal secretary to Adolf Hitler who had dictated much of *Mein Kampf* to Hess while both were prisoners at Landsberg Prison. Third in command in Nazi Germany, Hess surprised the world on May 10, 1941, by flying alone to Scotland and parachuting from his plane on what he called a "mission of humanity": offering peace to Britain if she would join Germany in attacking the Soviet Union. He was immediately taken prisoner of war. At the Nuremberg Trials (1946), after questions about his sanity, he was convicted and sentenced to life imprisonment at Spandau Allied War Crimes Prison at Berlin, Germany. Outliving all other prisoners there, he was the only inmate from 1955 until he succeeded (in his fourth attempt) in committing suicide. He died at West Berlin, Germany, Aug 17, 1987.

HUG AN AUSTRALIAN DAY. Apr 26. To show our great appreciation for all the love and support the Aussies have given us over the years. [©2003 by WH.] For info: Thomas & Ruth Roy, Wellcat Holidays, 2418 Long Ln, Lebanon, PA 17046. Phone: (717) 279-0184. E-mail: info@wellcat.com. Web: www.wellcat.com.

LOOS, ANITA: BIRTH ANNIVERSARY. Apr 26, 1893. American author and playwright, born at Sisson, CA. She is best remembered for her book *Gentlemen Prefer Blondes*, published in 1925. Loos, a brunette, died at New York, NY, Aug 18, 1981.

MONTGOMERY WARD SEIZED: ANNIVERSARY. Apr 26, 1944. Montgomery Ward Chairman Sewell Avery was physically removed from his office when federal troops seized Ward's Chicago offices after the company refused to obey President Franklin D. Roosevelt's order to recognize a CIO union. Government control ended May 9, shortly before the National Labor Relations Board announced the United Mail Order Warehouse and Retail Employees Union had won an election to represent the company's workers.

OLMSTED, FREDERICK LAW: BIRTH ANNIVERSARY. Apr 26, 1822. Known as the "father of landscape architecture in America," Olmsted participated in the designing of Yosemite National Park, New York City's Central Park and parks for Boston, Hartford and Louisville. Born at Hartford, CT, died at Waverly, MA, Aug 28, 1903. Olmsted's home and studio, Fairsted Estate outside of Boston, is now preserved as a National Historic Site and is open to the public: 99 Warren St, Brookline, MA 02146.

RICHTER SCALE DAY. Apr 26. A day to recognize the importance of Charles Francis Richter's research and his work in development of the earthquake magnitude scale that is known as the Richter scale. Richter, an American author, physicist and seismologist, was born Apr 26, 1900, near Hamilton, OH. An Earthquake Awareness Week was observed in recognition of his work. Richter died at Pasadena, CA, Sept 30, 1985.

ROGER EBERT'S OVERLOOKED FILM FESTIVAL. Apr 26–30. Virginia Theatre, Champaign, IL. Spring film festival hosted by Roger Ebert, University of Illinois journalism graduate and Pulitzer Prize–winning film critic. Ebert selects 12 films representing a cross section of important cinematic works that have been "overlooked" by audiences, critics and distributors. He introduces each film and leads a discussion on stage afterward for general audiences, distributors and international critics. Often in attendance are the films' producers, writers, actors or directors. Festival includes academic panel discussions. Sponsored by the College of Communications, University of Illinois. For info: Mary Susan Britt, University of Illinois, College of Communications, 119 Gregory Hall, MC-462, 810 S Wright St, Urbana, IL 61801. Phone: (217) 244-0552. Fax: (217) 333-9882. E-mail: mar sue@uiuc.edu. Web: www.ebertfest.com.

SIRK, DOUGLAS: BIRTH ANNIVERSARY. Apr 26, 1900. Film director Douglas Sirk was born Detlef Sierck at Hamburg, Germany. His films include *Magnificent Obsession* (1954), *Written on the Wind* (1956) and *Imitation of Life* (1959). He died Jan 14, 1987, at Lugano, Switzerland.

SOUTH AFRICAN MULTIRACIAL ELECTIONS: ANNIVERSARY. Apr 26–29, 1994. For the first time in the history of South Africa, the nation's approximately 18 million blacks voted in multiparty elections. This event marked the definitive end of apartheid, the system of racial separation that had kept blacks and other minorities out of the political process. The election resulted in Nelson Mandela of the African National Congress being elected president and F.W. de Klerk (incumbent president) of the National Party vice president.

TANZANIA: UNION DAY. Apr 26. Celebrates union between mainland Tanzania (formerly Tanganyika) and the islands of Zanzibar and Pemba, in 1964.

US HOLOCAUST MUSEUM OPENS: ANNIVERSARY. Apr 26, 1993. Washington, DC. After the museum opened to the public on this day, more than two million visitors toured the permanent exhibition during its first year of operation.

BIRTHDAYS TODAY

Carol Burnett, 70, actress ("Garry Moore Show," "Carol Burnett Show," *The Four Seasons*), born San Antonio, TX, Apr 26, 1936.
Joan Chen, 45, actress ("Twin Peaks," "Golden Gate"), born Shanghai, China, Apr 26, 1961.
Michael Damian, 44, actor ("Young and the Restless"; stage: *Joseph and the Amazing Technicolor Dreamcoat*), born San Diego, CA, Apr 26, 1962.
Duane Eddy, 68, musician, born Corning, NY, Apr 26, 1938.
Giancarlo Esposito, 48, actor (*Do the Right Thing, Twilight*), born Copenhagen, Denmark, Apr 26, 1958.
Kevin James, 41, actor ("The King of Queens"), born Stony Brook, NY, Apr 26, 1965.
Jet Li, 43, actor (*Romeo Must Die, Once Upon a Time in China*), former martial arts champion, born Li Lian Jie at Beijing, China, Apr 26, 1963.
Boyd Matson, 59, TV journalist (host of "National Geographic Explorer"), born Oklahoma City, OK, Apr 26, 1947.
Bobby Rydell, 64, singer ("Wild One," "Volare"), born Philadelphia, PA, Apr 26, 1942.
Tom Welling, 29, actor ("Smallville"), born New York, NY, Apr 26, 1977.
Gary Wright, 63, musician, born Englewood, NJ, Apr 26, 1943.

APRIL 27 — THURSDAY

Day 117 — 248 Remaining

BABE RUTH DAY: ANNIVERSARY. Apr 27, 1947. Babe Ruth Day was celebrated in every ballpark in organized baseball in the US as well as Japan. Mortally ill with throat cancer, Ruth appeared at Yankee Stadium to thank his former club for the honor.

BIG TEN MEN'S TENNIS CHAMPIONSHIP. Apr 27–30. University of Illinois, Urbana, IL. For info: Big Ten Conference, 1500 W Higgins Rd, Park Ridge, IL 60068-6300. Phone: (847) 696-1010. Fax: (847) 696-1110. Web: www.bigten.org.

BIG TEN WOMEN'S TENNIS CHAMPIONSHIP. Apr 27–30. University of Iowa, Iowa City, IA. For info: Big Ten Conference, 1500 W Higgins Rd, Park Ridge, IL 60068-6300. Phone: (847) 696-1010. Fax: (847) 696-1150. Web: www.bigten.org.

BIG 12 MEN'S AND WOMEN'S TENNIS CHAMPIONSHIPS. Apr 27–30. Baylor Tennis Center, Waco, TX. Est attendance: 3,000. For info: Big 12 Conference, 2201 Stemmons Freeway, 28th Fl, Dallas, TX 75207. Phone: (214) 742-1212. Fax: (214) 753-0145. Web: www.big12sports.com.

DENNIS, SANDY: BIRTH ANNIVERSARY. Apr 27, 1937. American actress Sandy Dennis was born Sandra Dale Dennis at Hastings, NE. In addition to two Tony Awards, she won an Academy Award for her supporting role in *Who's Afraid of Virginia Woolf* (1966). She died Mar 2, 1992, at Westport, CT.

DINING OUT FOR LIFE ATLANTA. Apr 27. Atlanta, GA. Dining Out for Life is an annual fund-raising event involving corporate sponsors and more than 200 Atlanta-area restaurants. An estimated 20 percent of all sales will be donated to Project Open Hand/Atlanta. Project Open Hand cooks, packages and delivers two nutritious meals each day to more than 2,000 Atlantans living with symptomatic HIV/AIDS or other critical illnesses as well as homebound seniors. Annually, the last Thursday of April. Est attendance: 45,000. For info: Michelle Duncan, Project Open Hand, 176 Ottley Dr NE, Atlanta, GA 30324. Phone: (404) 419-3333. Fax: (404) 872-9301. E-mail: mduncan@projectopen hand.org. Web: www.projectopenhand.org.

ENGLAND: HARROGATE SPRING FLOWER SHOW. Apr 27–30. Great Yorkshire Showground, Harrogate, North Yorkshire. Spectacular exhibits and displays at Britain's premier spring show. Est attendance: 60,000. For info: Roger Brownbridge, Show Dir, North of England Horticultural Society, 4A South Park Rd, Harrogate, North Yorkshire, England HG1 5QU. Phone: (44) (1423) 561049. Fax: (44) (1423) 536880. E-mail: info@flower show.org.uk. Web: www.flowershow.org.uk.

FIDDLER'S FROLICS. Apr 27–30. Knights of Columbus Hall, Hallettsville, TX. Competition to determine the Texas state champion fiddler and inductees to the Texas Fiddlers Hall of Fame. Est attendance: 15,000. For info: Kenneth Henneke, Co-chair, PO Box 46, Hallettsville, TX 77964. Phone: (361) 798-5934 or (361) 798-2311. Fax: (361) 798-4365. Web: www.kchall.com.

GIBBON, EDWARD: BIRTH ANNIVERSARY. Apr 27, 1737 (OS). English historian and author. His *History of the Decline and Fall of the Roman Empire* remains a model of historical writing. From his description of the Roman emperor Gordianus II: "Twenty-two acknowledged concubines, and a library of sixty-two thousand volumes, attested the variety of his inclinations; and from the productions which he left behind him, it appears that the former as well as the latter were designed for use rather than for ostentation." Born at Putney, Surrey, England, Gibbon died at London, Jan 6, 1794.

GRANT, ULYSSES SIMPSON: BIRTH ANNIVERSARY. Apr 27, 1822. 18th president of the US (Mar 4, 1869–Mar 3, 1877), born Hiram Ulysses Grant at Point Pleasant, OH. He graduated from the US Military Academy in 1843. President Lincoln promoted Grant to lieutenant general in command of all the Union armies Mar 9, 1864. On Apr 9, 1865, Grant received General Robert E. Lee's surrender, at Appomattox Court House, VA, which he announced to the Secretary of War as follows: "General Lee surrendered the Army of Northern Virginia this afternoon on terms proposed by myself. The accompanying additional correspondence will show the conditions fully." Nicknamed "Unconditional Surrender Grant," he died at Mount McGregor, NY, July 23, 1885, just four days after completing his memoirs. He was buried at Riverside Park, New York, NY, where Grant's Tomb was dedicated in 1897.

INTERNATIONAL HOME FURNISHINGS MARKET. Apr 27–May 3 (also Oct 19–26). High Point and Thomasville, NC. The largest wholesale home furnishings market in the world. (Not open to the general public.) Est attendance: 82,000. For info: Intl Home Furnishings Market Authority, 101 S Main St, High Point, NC 27260. Phone: (336) 869-1000. Fax: (336) 869-6999. Web: www.highpointmarket.org.

LANTZ, WALTER: BIRTH ANNIVERSARY. Apr 27, 1900. Originator of Universal Studios' animated opening sequence for their first major musical film, *The King of Jazz*. Walter Lantz is best remembered as the creator of Woody Woodpecker, the bird with the wacky laugh and the taunting ways. Lantz received a lifetime achievement Academy Award for his animation in 1979. He was born at New Rochelle, NY, and died Mar 22, 1994, at Burbank, CA.

MAGELLAN, FERDINAND: DEATH ANNIVERSARY. Apr 27, 1521. Portuguese explorer Ferdinand Magellan was probably born near Oporto, Portugal, about 1480, but neither the place nor the date is certain. Usually thought of as the first man to circumnavigate the Earth, he died before completing the voyage; thus his coleader, Basque navigator Juan Sebastian de Elcano, became the world's circumnavigator. The westward, 'round-the-world expedition began Sept 20, 1519, with five ships and about 250 men. Magellan was killed by natives of the Philippine island of Mactan.

MATANZAS MULE DAY. Apr 27, 1898. In one of the first naval actions of the Spanish-American War, US naval forces bombarded the Cuban village of Matanzas. It was widely reported that the only casualty of the bombardment was one mule. "The Matanzas Mule" became instantly famous and remains a footnote in the history of the Spanish-American War.

MOON PHASE: NEW MOON. Apr 27. Moon enters New Moon phase at 3:44 PM, EDT.

MORSE, SAMUEL FINLEY BREESE: BIRTH ANNIVERSARY. Apr 27, 1791. American artist and inventor, after whom the Morse code is named, was born at Charlestown, MA, and died at New York, NY, Apr 2, 1872. Graduating from Yale University in 1810, he went to the Royal Academy of London to study painting. After returning to America he achieved success as a portraitist. Morse conceived the idea of an electromagnetic telegraph while on shipboard, returning from art instruction in Europe in 1832, and he proceeded to develop his idea. With financial assistance approved by Congress, the first telegraph line in the US was constructed, between Washington, DC, and Baltimore, MD. The first message tapped out by Morse from the Supreme Court Chamber at the US Capitol building on May 24, 1844, was: "What hath God wrought?"

SERBIA AND MONTENEGRO: NATIONAL DAY. Apr 27. Commemorates the formation of the Yugoslav Federation (consisting of Serbia and Montenegro) by the adoption of a constitution in 1992.

SIERRA LEONE: INDEPENDENCE DAY. Apr 27. National Day. Commemorates independence from Britain in 1961.

		S	M	T	W	T	F	S
April								1
		2	3	4	5	6	7	8
2006		9	10	11	12	13	14	15
		16	17	18	19	20	21	22
		23	24	25	26	27	28	29
		30						

SLOVENIA: INSURRECTION DAY. Apr 27. National holiday. Commemorates the founding of the Liberation Front in 1941 to resist Slovenia's occupation by the Axis powers.

SOUTH AFRICA: FREEDOM DAY. Apr 27. National holiday. Commemorates the day in 1994 when, for the first time, all South Africans had the opportunity to vote.

SULTANA STEAMSHIP EXPLOSION: ANNIVERSARY. Apr 27, 1865. Early in the morning on this day, America's worst steamship disaster occurred. The *Sultana*, heavily overloaded with an estimated 2,300 passengers, exploded in the Mississippi River, just north of Memphis, en route to Cairo, IL. Most of the passengers were Union soldiers who had been prisoners of war and were eagerly returning to their homes. Although there was never an accurate accounting of the dead, estimates range from 1,450 to nearly 2,000. Cause of the explosion was not determined, but the little-known event is unparalleled in US history.

TAKE OUR DAUGHTERS AND SONS TO WORK® DAY. Apr 27. A national public education campaign sponsored by the Ms. Foundation for Women in which children aged 8–12 go to work with adult hosts—parents, grandparents, cousins, aunts, uncles, friends. Nearly 14,000,000 employed Americans participated in 2004 by bringing a boy or girl to work. Annually, the fourth Thursday in April. For info: Take Our Daughters and Sons To Work® Day, Ms. Foundation for Women, 120 Wall St, 33rd Fl, New York, NY 10005. Phone: (800) 676-7780. Fax: (212) 742-1531. E-mail: tods@ms.foundation.org. Web: www.DaughtersandSonstoWork.org.

TOGO: INDEPENDENCE DAY. Apr 27. National holiday. In 1960 Togo gained its independence from French administration under a UN trusteeship.

WASHINGTON STATE APPLE BLOSSOM FESTIVAL. Apr 27–May 7. Wenatchee, WA. To showcase the greater Wenatchee Valley, its people and heritage by producing an ongoing community celebration. Parades, arts and crafts, gem and mineral show, theatrical productions, Youth Day and carnival. More than 40 events. Annually, the last weekend in April through the first weekend in May. Est attendance: 100,000. For info: Washington State Apple Blossom Festival, Box 2836, Wenatchee, WA 98807. Phone: (509) 662-3616. Fax: (509) 665-0347. E-mail: festival@appleblossom.org. Web: www.appleblossom.org.

WOLLSTONECRAFT, MARY: BIRTH ANNIVERSARY. Apr 27, 1759. Writer and advocate of equality for women, Mary Wollstonecraft was born at London, England. Rebelling against her father, she left home at age 18 and served as a lady's companion, opened a school and worked as a governess. Beginning with *Thoughts on the Education of Daughters* in 1787, Wollstonecraft attracted notice as a writer in favor of women's rights. Her *A Vindication of the Rights of Woman* (1792) argued that women should be given an education that would allow them to gain economic independence. She died at London on Sept 10, 1797, eleven days after giving birth to her second daughter (Mary Wollstonecraft Shelley, the author of *Frankenstein*).

BIRTHDAYS TODAY

Anouk Aimee, 72, actress (*A Man and a Woman, The Golden Salamander*), born Paris, France, Apr 27, 1934.

Sheena Easton, 47, singer ("Morning Train"), born Sheena Shirley Orr at Bellshill, Scotland, Apr 27, 1959.

Casey Kasem, 74, radio, TV host ("America's Top 40"), born Detroit, MI, Apr 27, 1932.

Coretta Scott King, 79, lecturer, writer, widow of Martin Luther King, Jr, born Marion, AL, Apr 27, 1927.

Jack Klugman, 84, actor ("The Odd Couple," "Quincy, ME"), born Philadelphia, PA, Apr 27, 1922.

August Wilson, 61, playwright (*Fences, Joe Turner's Come and Gone*), born Pittsburgh, PA, Apr 27, 1945.

APRIL 28 — FRIDAY

Day 118 — 247 Remaining

ARBOR DAY FESTIVAL. Apr 28–30. Nebraska City, NE. To celebrate Arbor Day, the tree planters' holiday, in the hometown of J. Sterling Morton, the founder of Arbor Day. Citywide events include more than 50 artists' and craftsmen's booths, children's environmental festival, parade; tree seedling giveaway, musicians and tree-planting demonstrations. Est attendance: 20,000. For info: Tourism and Events, 806 1st Ave, Nebraska City, NE 68410. Phone: (800) 514-9113. Fax: (402) 873-6701. E-mail: tourism@ nebraskacity.com. Web: www.nebraskacity.com.

ARBOR DAY IN ARIZONA. Apr 28. The last Friday in April is proclaimed as Arbor Day in Arizona. It is not a legal holiday.

BARRYMORE, LIONEL: BIRTH ANNIVERSARY. Apr 28, 1878. Famed American actor of celebrated acting family, Lionel Barrymore was born Lionel Blythe, at Philadelphia, PA. Brother of Ethel and John Barrymore. He died at Van Nuys, CA, Nov 15, 1954.

BIG TEN WOMEN'S GOLF CHAMPIONSHIPS. Apr 28–30. Indiana University, Bloomington, IN. For info: Big Ten Conference, 1500 W Higgins Rd, Park Ridge, IL 60068-6300. Phone: (847) 696-1010. Fax: (847) 696-1110. Web: www.bigten .org.

BIOLOGICAL CLOCK GENE DISCOVERED: ANNIVERSARY. Apr 28, 1994. Northwestern University announced that the so-called biological clock, that gene governing the daily cycle of waking and sleeping called the circadian rhythm, had been found in mice. Never before pinpointed in a mammal, the biological clock gene was found on mouse chromosome #5.

BLUEBERRY HILL OPEN DART TOURNAMENT. Apr 28–30. St. Louis, MO. America's oldest (34th annual) pub dart tournament open to everyone. Est attendance: 200. For info: Joe Edwards, Blueberry Hill, 6504 Delmar, St. Louis, MO 63130. Phone: (314) 727-4444. Web: www.blueberryhill.com.

CANADA: GUELPH SPRING FESTIVAL. Apr 28–May 14. Guelph, ON. Classical and contemporary music featuring outstanding musicians from across Canada and around the world. Est attendance: 5,000. For info: Guelph Spring Festival, 100 Crimea St, Unit B2, Guelph, ON, Canada N1H 2Y6. Phone: (519) 821-3210. Fax: (519) 821-5271. E-mail: info@guelphspringfesti val.org. Web: www.guelphspringfestival.org.

CANADA: NATIONAL DAY OF MOURNING. Apr 28. A national day of mourning for workers killed or injured on the job in Canada. The Canadian Labour Congress first officially recognized the day in 1986. Pointing to the nearly one million workplace injuries each year in Canada, the CLC has called for stricter health and safety regulations and for annual recognition of this day throughout Canada. Federal legislation (Bill D–223) first recognized this day in 1991.

CONNECTICUT STORYTELLING FESTIVAL. Apr 28–30. Connecticut College, New London, CT. 25th annual festival features performances for families and adults, plus workshops and story-sharing by Connecticut and nationally renowned storytellers. Annually, in April. Est attendance: 800. For info: Ann Shapiro, Adm, Connecticut Storytelling Center, Connecticut College Box 5295, 270 Mohegan Ave, New London, CT 06320. Phone: (860) 439-2764. Fax: (860) 439-2895. E-mail: csc@conncoll.edu. Web: www.connstorycenter.org.

DAFFODIL FESTIVAL WEEKEND. Apr 28–30. Nantucket Island, MA. Nantucket's traditional welcome to spring, when more than three million daffodils bloom and turn the countryside into a vivid, yellow tapestry. Events include the annual antique car parade, flower show, tailgate picnic and activities such as hiking, fishing, bird-watching and seal cruises. Est attendance: 1,000. For info: Nantucket Island Chamber of Commerce, 48 Main St, Nantucket, MA 02554-3595. Phone: (508) 228-1700. Web: www.nan tucketchamber.org.

GIBBS, MIFFLIN WISTER: BIRTH ANNIVERSARY. Apr 28, 1828. Mifflin Wister Gibbs was born at Philadelphia, PA. In 1873 he became the first black man to be elected a judge in the US, winning an election for city judge at Little Rock, AR.

HAIRSTYLIST APPRECIATION DAY. Apr 28. The personalized service of hairstylists makes customers look great and feel great about themselves. Hairstyling is the art of creating a self-image to help boost self-esteem while lending an ear to customers' problems, thereby lessening their stress. For info: Anne Camilleri, 1220 Arroyo St, San Carlos, CA 94070. Phone: (650) 593-3733 or (650) 568-0565.

HOMER, LOUISE DILWORTH: BIRTH ANNIVERSARY. Apr 28, 1871. The mesmerizing Louise Dilworth Homer was one of the most formidable contraltos of her time. Her plum roles in *Aïda, Tristan und Isolde, Hänsel und Gretel* and *Samson et Dalilah* (with the legendary Caruso) brought her tremendous acclaim. She was born at Sewickley, PA, and died at Winter Park, FL, May 6, 1947.

JAMES MONROE BIRTHDAY CELEBRATION. Apr 28. Ash Lawn-Highland, home of President James Monroe, Charlottesville, VA. Free admission for local residents. For info: Ash Lawn-Highland, 1000 James Monroe Pkwy, Charlottesville, VA 22902. Phone: (434) 293-9539. Fax: (434) 293-8000. E-mail: info@ashlawnhighland.org. Web: www.ashlawnhighland.org.

MARYLAND CONSTITUTION RATIFICATION: ANNIVERSARY. Apr 28, 1788. Maryland became the seventh state to ratify the Constitution, by a vote of 63 to 11.

MONROE, JAMES: BIRTH ANNIVERSARY. Apr 28, 1758. 5th president of the US was born at Westmoreland County, VA, and served two terms in that office (Mar 4, 1817–Mar 3, 1825). Monrovia, the capital city of Liberia, is named after him, as is the Monroe Doctrine, which he enunciated at Washington, DC, Dec 2, 1823. Last of three presidents to die on US Independence Day, Monroe died at New York, NY, July 4, 1831.

MUSSOLINI EXECUTED: ANNIVERSARY. Apr 28, 1945. Italian partisans shot Benito Mussolini near the lakeside village of Dongo. Leaders of the Fascist Party, several of his friends and his mistress Clara Petacci also were executed. The 23-year-long Fascist rule of Italy was ended.

MUTINY ON THE *BOUNTY*: ANNIVERSARY. Apr 28, 1789. The most famous of all naval mutinies occurred on board HMS *Bounty*. Captain of the *Bounty* was Lieutenant William Bligh, an able seaman and a mean-tempered disciplinarian. The ship, with a load of breadfruit tree plants from Tahiti, was bound for Jamaica. Fletcher Christian, leader of the mutiny, put Bligh and 18 of his loyal followers adrift in a 23-foot open boat. Miraculously Bligh and all of his supporters survived a 47-day voyage of more than 3,600 miles, before landing on the island of Timor, June 14, 1789. In the meantime, Christian had put all of the remaining crew (excepting 8 men and himself) ashore at Tahiti where he picked up 18 Tahitians (6 men and 12 women) and set sail again. Landing at Pitcairn Island in 1790 (probably uninhabited at the time), they burned the *Bounty* and remained undiscovered for 18 years, when an American whaler, the *Topaz*, called at the island (1808) and found only one member of the mutinous crew surviving. However, the little colony had thrived and, when counted by the British in 1856, numbered 194 persons.

NATIONAL ARBOR DAY. Apr 28. Since 1872, a day to honor and plant trees. Observed the last Friday in April (although some states have different dates), which is generally a good planting date throughout the country. First observance of Arbor Day was in Nebraska, Apr 10, 1872, where it is still a state holiday. For info: Natl Arbor Day Foundation, 100 Arbor Ave, Nebraska City, NE 68410. Web: www.arborday.org.

NATIONAL DREAM HOTLINE®. Apr 28–30. Now in its 18th year, the National Dream Hotline® is sponsored by the School of Metaphysics as an educational service to people throughout the world. Faculty and staff of the College and Schools of Metaphysics throughout the Midwest will offer the benefits of more than 30 years of research into the significance and meaning of dreams by manning the hotline phones from 6 PM EDT, Friday until midnight Sunday. Annually, the last weekend in April. For info: Christine Madar, School of Metaphysics, World Headquarters, 163 Moon Valley Rd, Windyville, MO 65783. Phone: (417) 345-8411. Fax: (417) 345-6668. E-mail: som@som.org. Web: www.som.org or www.dreamschool.org.

NATIONAL HAIRBALL AWARENESS DAY. Apr 28. A day to recognize and take steps to eliminate hairballs in cats. Hairballs are more than an inconvenience for cat owners and more than a strain of regurgitated fur—they cause great discomfort and irritation in our cat companions. This pain is easily preventable. Annually, the last Friday in April. For info: Dr. Blake Hawley, 15 Brookhollow Ave, Baalkham Hills BC, NSW 2153, Australia. E-mail: Blake_Hawley@HillsPet.com. Web: www.ScienceDiet.com.

NEW BEGINNING FESTIVAL. Apr 28–29. Coffeyville, KS. A multistate arts and crafts festival, cheese festival, carnival, entertainment, 5k run, car show. Est attendance: 7,000. For info: Chamber of Commerce, Box 457, Coffeyville, KS 67337. Phone: (620) 251-2550. Fax: (620) 251-5448. E-mail: chamber@coffeyville.com.

NEW ORLEANS JAZZ & HERITAGE FESTIVAL. Apr 28–May 7. New Orleans, LA. A two-weekend festival with hundreds of musicians playing. Evening concerts, outdoor daytime activities, Louisiana specialty foods and handmade crafts. Est attendance: 500,000. For info: New Orleans Jazz & Heritage Festival, 1205 N Rampart St, New Orleans, LA 70116. Phone: (504) 522-4786. Web: www.nojazzfest.com.

PANOPLY® 2006. Apr 28–30. Big Spring International Park, Huntsville, AL. Comprehensive arts festival celebrating its 25th year. Showcases the performing arts through a variety of music, theatre and dance. The festival includes five performance stages, family hands-on activities, juried art show and choreography competition. Est attendance: 70,000. For info: The Arts Council, 700 Monroe St, Ste 2, Huntsville, AL 35801. Phone: (256) 519-ARTS. Fax: (256) 533-3811. Web: www.panoply.org.

RATTLESNAKE DERBY. Apr 28–30. Mangum, OK. Hunters stalk these wily reptiles and attempt to bring in the most snakes and the longest snake. Snakeskins and meat will be sold, and entertainment will include live music, a carnival and flea market. Annually, the last full weekend in April. Est attendance: 40,000. For info: Shortgrass Rattlesnake Assn. Phone: (580) 782-2434.

RIVERFEST WEEKEND. Apr 28–30. Columbus, GA. Features fine arts and crafts, children's interactive area, olympigs, hot-air balloons, Native American skills demonstrators, carnival, cornbread cook-off, Riverfest 10k, 5k and 1 Mile Fun Run and a fine arts and folk art show and sale. Also features the Folklife Village with demonstrations by blacksmiths, quilters, basket weavers and potters and the South's most famous barbecue cook-off, the Greater Columbus Pig Jig, an MIM-sanctioned event. Live entertainment on three stages. Annually, the last full weekend in April at the Historic South Commons along the Columbus Riverwalk. Est attendance: 100,000. For info: Riverfest, PO Box 5128, Columbus, GA 31906. Phone: (706) 324-7417. Fax: (706) 323-7979. Web: www.columbusriverfest.com.

SPACE MILESTONE: FIRST TOURIST IN SPACE: 5th ANNIVERSARY. Apr 28, 2001. Millionaire US businessman Dennis Tito reportedly paid the Russian space agency $20 million to accompany *Soyuz TM* to the International Space Station. The rocket with Tito and two Russian cosmonauts was launched this day from the Baikonur launch site in Kazakhstan and arrived at the ISS on Apr 30, 2001. The crew returned to Earth in a week. NASA initially objected to the inclusion of the 60-year-old tycoon on the mission but dropped its opposition.

SPRING FEST. Apr 28–29. Rebel State Park Outdoor Amphitheater, Marthaville, LA. Includes entertainment, food, craft vendors. Admission fee. Est attendance: 2,500. For info: Natchitoches Parish Tourist Commission. Phone: (888) 677-3600 or (800) 259-1714. Web: www.natchitoches.net.

STAMP EXPO: SOUTH. Apr 28–30. Radisson Hotel, Anaheim, CA. Est attendance: 4,000. For info: Israel Bick, Exec Dir, Intl Stamp & Coin Collectors Society, PO Box 854, Van Nuys, CA 91408. Phone: (818) 997-6496. Fax: (818) 988-4337. E-mail: iibick@sbcglobal.net. Web: www.bick.net.

SUGARLOAF CRAFTS FESTIVAL. Apr 28–30. Maryland State Fairgrounds, Timonium, MD. This show, now in its 28th year, features more than 350 nationally recognized craft designers and fine artists displaying and selling their original creations. Includes craft demonstrations, live music, specialty food, hourly gift certificate drawings and more. Est attendance: 21,000. For info: Sugarloaf Mountain Works, Inc, 200 Orchard Ridge Dr, #215, Gaithersburg, MD 20878. Phone: (800) 210-9900. Fax: (310) 253-9620. Web: www.sugarloafcrafts.com.

VERMONT MAPLE FESTIVAL. Apr 28–30. St. Albans, VT. The 40th annual festival includes carnival, talent show, entertainment, arts & crafts, antiques, maple exhibits and demonstrations, sugar house tours and sap run. For info: Vermont Maple Festival, PO Box 255, St. Albans, VT 05478. Phone: (802) 524-5800. Web: www.vtmaplefestival.org.

WARD WORLD CHAMPIONSHIP WILDFOWL CARVING COMPETITION. Apr 28–30. Roland E. Powell Convention Center, Ocean City, MD. 36th annual. Judging of contemporary decoys and wildlife sculpture, fish carvings and paintings. Est attendance: 10,000. For info: Keith Eagle, Special Events Coord, Ward Museum of Waterfowl Art, 909 S Schumaker Dr, Salisbury, MD 21804. Phone: (410) 742-4988. Fax: (410) 742-3107. E-mail: ward@wardmuseum.org. Web: www.wardmuseum.org.

WORKERS MEMORIAL DAY. Apr 28. First proclaimed in 1989 to commemorate the founding of the Occupational Safety and Health Administration on Apr 28, 1970 (signed into law in 1971). In some places this holiday is observed on the fourth Friday of April.

April *2006*	S	M	T	W	T	F	S
							1
	2	3	4	5	6	7	8
	9	10	11	12	13	14	15
	16	17	18	19	20	21	22
	23	24	25	26	27	28	29
	30						

BIRTHDAYS TODAY

Jessica Alba, 25, actress ("Dark Angel," *Sin City*), born Pomona, CA, Apr 28, 1981.

Ann-Margret, 65, actress (*Carnal Knowledge, Tommy*), born Ann-Margret Olsson at Stockholm, Sweden, Apr 28, 1941.

Penelope Cruz, 32, actress (*Vanilla Sky, Captain Corelli's Mandolin, All the Pretty Horses*), born Madrid, Spain, Apr 28, 1974.

John Daly, 40, golfer, born Carmichael, CA, Apr 28, 1966.

Saddam Hussein, 69, former Iraqi dictator, born Tikrit, Iraq, Apr 28, 1937.

Bruno Kirby, 57, actor (*When Harry Met Sally . . ., City Slickers*), born New York, NY, Apr 28, 1949.

Barry Louis Larkin, 42, baseball player, born Cincinnati, OH, Apr 28, 1964.

Harper Lee, 80, author (*To Kill a Mockingbird*), born Nelle Harper at Monroeville, AL, Apr 28, 1926.

Jay Leno, 56, TV talk-show host ("The Tonight Show"), comedian, born New Rochelle, NY, Apr 28, 1950.

Marcia Strassman, 58, actress ("Welcome Back Kotter," *Honey, I Shrunk the Kids*), born New York, NY, Apr 28, 1948.

Chris Young, 35, actor ("Falcon Crest," *The Great Outdoors*), born Chambersburg, PA, Apr 28, 1971.

APRIL 29 — SATURDAY

Day 119 — 246 Remaining

BIG TEN WOMEN'S ROWING CHAMPIONSHIPS. Apr 29. University of Minnesota, Minneapolis, MN. For info: Big Ten Conference, 1500 W Higgins Rd, Park Ridge, IL 60068-6300. Phone: (847) 696-1010. Fax: (847) 696-1150. Web: www.bigten .org.

BOB WILLS DAY. Apr 29. Turkey, TX. Celebration of the creator of western swing, with music, fiddlers contest, parade and barbeque lunch. Appearances by his former band, the Texas Playboys. Annually, the last Saturday in April. Est attendance: 10,000. For info: Bob Wills Foundation, PO Box 306, Turkey, TX 79261. Phone: (806) 423-1253. E-mail: turkey@caprock-spur.com. Web: www.turkeytexas.com.

EARNHARDT, DALE: BIRTH ANNIVERSARY. Apr 29, 1952. Stock car racer, born Kannapolis, NC. He was one of NASCAR's most popular personalities, winning the Winston Cup seven times. He was killed while driving in the Daytona 500 at Daytona Beach, FL, Feb 18, 2001.

ELLINGTON, "DUKE" (EDWARD KENNEDY): BIRTH ANNIVERSARY. Apr 29, 1899. "Duke" Ellington, one of the most influential individuals in jazz history, was born at Washington, DC. Ellington's professional career began when he was 17, and by 1923 he was leading a small group of musicians at the Kentucky Club at New York City who became the core of his big band. Ellington is credited with being one of the founders of big band jazz. He used his band as an instrument for composition and orchestration to create big band pieces, film scores, operas, ballets, Broadway shows and religious music. Ellington was responsible for more than 1,000 musical pieces. He drew together instruments from different sections of the orchestra to develop unique and haunting sounds such as that of his famous "Mood Indigo." Duke Ellington died May 24, 1974, at New York City.

ELLSWORTH, OLIVER: BIRTH ANNIVERSARY. Apr 29, 1745 (OS). Third chief justice of the US Supreme Court, born at Windsor, CT. Died there, Nov 26, 1807.

EWELL, TOM: BIRTH ANNIVERSARY. Apr 29, 1909. Born Samuel Yewell Tompkins at Owensboro, KY, Ewell acted in many films and TV series. He won a Tony Award for his Broadway role as the husband in *The Seven Year Itch*, a role he reprised in the film version costarring Marilyn Monroe. In the '60s he starred in his own TV show, "The Tom Ewell Show." He died Sept 12, 1994, at Woodland Hills, CA.

★ ★ ★

FOXFIELD RACES. Apr 29 (also Sept 24). Charlottesville, VA. Steeplechase horse racing. Est attendance: 20,000. For info: W. Patrick Butterfield, Racing Mgr, Foxfield Racing Assn, PO Box 5187, Charlottesville, VA 22905. Phone: (804) 293-9501. Fax: (804) 293-8169.

HEARST, WILLIAM RANDOLPH: BIRTH ANNIVERSARY. Apr 29, 1863. American newspaper editor and publisher, born at San Francisco, CA. Died at Beverly Hills, CA, Aug 14, 1951.

HERB FESTIVAL. Apr 29. Mattoon, IL. Fresh herbs, everlasting plants, scented geraniums and lots of perennials. Annually, the last Saturday in April. Est attendance: 7,000. For info: The Picket Fence, 901 Broadway, Mattoon, IL 61938. Phone: (217) 258-6364.

HIROHITO MICHI-NO-MIYA, EMPEROR: BIRTH ANNIVERSARY. Apr 29, 1901. Former Emperor of Japan, born at Tokyo. Hirohito's death, Jan 7, 1989, ended the reign of the world's longest-ruling monarch. He became the 124th in a line of monarchs when he ascended to the Chrysanthemum Throne in 1926. Hirohito presided over perhaps the most eventful years in the 2,500 years of recorded Japanese history, including the attempted military conquest of Asia; the attack on the US that brought that country into WWII, leading to Japan's ultimate defeat after the US dropped atomic bombs on Hiroshima and Nagasaki; and the amazing economic restoration following the war that led Japan to a preeminent position of economic strength.

INTERNATIONAL WILDLIFE FILM FESTIVAL. Apr 29–May 6. Missoula, MT. 29th annual juried international wildlife film festival. This eight-day gathering will involve the world's top wildlife filmmakers and producers sharing their ideas, techniques and products to interested members of the public and filmmaking profession. The festival provides films for viewing by people of all ages with special sections for children. Community celebrations such as a wildlife parade, workshops and panel discussions are also part of this annual festival. Festival venues are located at various sites in downtown Missoula. Est attendance: 12,000. For info: Exec Dir, Intl Wildlife Film Festival, 718 S Higgins, Missoula, MT 59801. Phone: (406) 728-9380. Fax: (406) 728-2881. E-mail: iwff@wildlifefilms.org. Web: www.wildlifefilms .org.

JAPAN: GOLDEN WEEK HOLIDAYS. Apr 29–May 5. National holidays. This period includes Greenery Day (Apr 29), Constitution Memorial Day (May 3) and Children's Day (May 5). When a day is between two holidays, like May 4, it becomes a holiday, too.

JAPAN: GREENERY DAY. Apr 29. National holiday. To commemorate the birth of Emperor Hirohito in 1901.

LIBERATION OF DACHAU: ANNIVERSARY. Apr 29, 1945. The Charlie Battery of the 522nd Field Artillery Battalion liberated the concentration camp at Dachau, Germany. The 522nd, part of the legendary 442nd (Go for Broke) regimental combat team, was made up of Nisei—second-generation Japanese Americans.

LOS ANGELES RIOTS: ANNIVERSARY. Apr 29, 1992. A jury in Simi Valley, CA, failed to convict four Los Angeles police officers accused in the videotaped beating of Rodney King, providing the spark that set off rioting, looting and burning at South Central Los Angeles, CA, and other areas across the country. The anger unleashed during and after the violence was attributed to widespread racism, lack of job opportunities and the resulting hopelessness of inner-city poverty.

MAIN STREET FESTIVAL. Apr 29–30. Downtown Franklin, TN. 23rd annual festival features more than 250 of the South's leading craftspersons. Food, entertainment (blues, pop, country, classical and rock), children's area and carnival. Showcases historical downtown. Est attendance: 155,000. For info: Shelly Robertson, Main Street Festival, PO Box 807, Franklin, TN 37065. Phone: (615) 595-1239. Fax: (615) 591-8502. E-mail: srobertson@historicfranklin.com. Web: www.historicfranklin.com.

NATIONAL REBUILDING DAY. Apr 29. 263,500 volunteers come together to rehabilitate the homes of low-income, elderly or disabled people and nonprofit facilities. For info: Rebuilding Together, 1536 16th St NW, Washington, DC 20036-1402. Phone: (202) 483-9083 or (800) 4-REHAB-9. Fax: (202) 483-9081. Web: www.rebuildingtogether.org.

'PEACE' ROSE INTRODUCED TO WORLD: ANNIVERSARY. Apr 29, 1945. The 20th century's most popular rose was publicly released by the Pacific Rose Society at Pasadena, CA, just as Berlin was falling to the Allies. The history of 'Peace' is interwoven with events of WWII, and for many the Hybrid Tea rose has symbolized the hope that grew out of terrible conflict. French rose grower Frances Meilland bred the cream and pink rose (then called 'Mme A. Meilland') in the late 1930s and knew he had something extraordinary. A seedling was smuggled out of France in an American diplomatic pouch on one of the last planes to leave that country before Nazi occupation. American rose company Conrad-Pyle carefully cultivated it. To note Germany's surrender, 'Peace' blooms were presented to all delegates during the first United Nations Conference that May of 1945.

POLICE OFFICERS WHO GAVE THEIR LIVES IN THE LINE OF DUTY WEEK. Apr 29–May 5. A week of events remembering all police officers nationwide who gave their lives to protect others. In addition, lectures on how famous crimes were solved. For info: Bob O'Brien, Consumer Advocate, 1061 Koelle Blvd, Secaucus, NJ 07094. Phone: (201) 865-4775. E-mail: bobtheebest@yahoo.com. Web: www.wtbq.com.

REDBUD TRAIL RENDEZVOUS. Apr 29–30. Rochester, IN. Reenactment of a pre-1840 gathering to trade furs on the Tippecanoe River, featuring tepee and wigwam villages, traditional music and crafts, pioneer and Indian dances, foods cooked over wood fires. Museum, round barn and Living History Village at north end of grounds. For frontier fun, follow the redbuds blooming along the Tippecanoe River. Est attendance: 2,000. For info: Fulton County Historical Society, 37 E 375 N, Rochester, IN 46975. Phone: (574) 223-4436. E-mail: fchs@rtcol.com. Web: www.icss.net/~fchs.

SAINT CATHERINE OF SIENA: FEAST DAY. Apr 29, 1347. St. Catherine of Siena was born at Tuscany, Italy. Patron saint of Italy. She died Apr 29, 1380, at Rome, Italy.

SOUTHERN MARYLAND CELTIC FESTIVAL. Apr 29. Jefferson Patterson Park, St. Leonard, MD. Scottish fiddling championship, bagpipe competition, Scottish heptathlon, Highland dancing competition, Celtic marketplace and crafts, parade of clans and nations, Celtic harp competition, Celtic folk music, demonstrations and Celtic foods. Annually, the last Saturday in April. Est attendance: 15,000. For info: Celtic Society of Southern Maryland, PO Box 209, Prince Frederick, MD 20678. Phone: (443) 404-7319. Web: www.cssm.org.

SPACE MILESTONE: *CHALLENGER STS-51B (US).* Apr 29, 1985. *Challenger* launched from Kennedy Space Center, FL, with a crew of seven and animal menagerie including monkeys and rats. Landed after 111 orbits of Earth on May 6, 1985, at Edwards Air Force Base, CA.

TAIWAN: CHENG CHENG KUNG LANDING DAY. Apr 29. Commemorates landing in Taiwan in 1661 of Ming Dynasty loyalist Cheng Cheng Kung (Koxinga), who ousted Dutch colonists who had occupied Taiwan for 37 years. Main ceremonies held at Tainan, in south Taiwan, where the Dutch had their headquarters and where Cheng is buried.

ZIPPER PATENTED: ANNIVERSARY. Apr 29, 1913. Gideon Sundbach of Hoboken, NJ, received a patent for the zipper.

BIRTHDAYS TODAY

Andre Kirk Agassi, 36, tennis player, born Las Vegas, NV, Apr 29, 1970.

Daniel Day-Lewis, 49, actor (Oscar for *My Left Foot; Gangs of New York, The Unbearable Lightness of Being*), born London, England, Apr 29, 1957.

Nora Dunn, 54, actress (*Passion Fish*, "Saturday Night Live"), born Chicago, IL, Apr 29, 1952.

Robert Gottlieb, 75, editor, born New York, NY, Apr 29, 1931.

Celeste Holm, 87, actress (*All About Eve*; Oscar for *Gentleman's Agreement*), born New York, NY, Apr 29, 1919.

Rod McKuen, 73, poet, singer, born San Francisco, CA, Apr 29, 1933.

Zubin Mehta, 70, conductor, born Bombay, India, Apr 29, 1936.

Kate Mulgrew, 51, actress ("Star Trek: Voyager," "Ryan's Hope"), born Dubuque, IA, Apr 29, 1955.

Michelle Pfeiffer, 48, actress (*What Lies Beneath, Batman Returns, Dangerous Liaisons*), born Santa Ana, CA, Apr 29, 1958.

Eve Plumb, 48, actress ("The Brady Bunch," "Fudge"), born Burbank, CA, Apr 29, 1958.

Jerry Seinfeld, 52, comedian, actor ("Seinfeld"), born Brooklyn, NY, Apr 29, 1954.

Debbie Stabenow, 56, US Senator (D, Michigan), born Clare, MI, Apr 29, 1950.

Uma Thurman, 36, actress (*Henry and June, Pulp Fiction*), born Boston, MA, Apr 29, 1970.

Carnie Wilson, 38, singer, born Bel Air, CA, Apr 29, 1968.

	S	M	T	W	T	F	S
April							1
	2	3	4	5	6	7	8
2006	9	10	11	12	13	14	15
	16	17	18	19	20	21	22
	23	24	25	26	27	28	29
	30						

APRIL 30 — SUNDAY
Day 120 — 245 Remaining

ANNE HUTCHINSON MEMORIAL DAY. Apr 30. Anne Hutchinson Memorial, Founders' Brook Park, Portsmouth, RI. An annual gathering to honor Anne Marbury Hutchinson (1591–1643) cofounder of Pocasset (Portsmouth), RI, in 1638. Wife, mother of 16, midwife, religious leader, she was a caretaker of and spiritual leader to women in Puritan Boston. Anne Hutchinson helped shape the tradition of free speech and religious tolerance that has become so important to modern Americans. Annually, on the Sunday closest to Apr 27, weather permitting. For info: Valerie Debrule, Friends of Anne Hutchinson, 11 Cherry Creek Rd, Newport, RI 02840. Phone: (401) 846-8439. Fax: (401) 848-0373. E-mail: cherrycreek@efortress.com. Or Barbara Finelli. Phone: (401) 846-6101.

BELTANE. Apr 30. (Also called Bealtaine, May Eve, Walpurgis Night, Cyntefyn, Roodmass and Cethsamhain.) One of the "Greater Sabbats" during the Wiccan year, it celebrates the union or marriage of the Goddess and God. In Scotland Beltane was one of the quarter days or terms when rents were due and debts settled. On the eve of Beltane, two fires were built close together and cattle driven between them to ward off disease prior to putting them out to pasture for the new season. Annually, on Apr 30.

BIRD RECORDED: 65th ANNIVERSARY. Apr 30, 1941. The first commercially recorded work of Charlie (Bird) Parker, alto saxophonist and originator of the bebop style of modern jazz, was cut this date at Decca Records. During the recording session, picking up from the last two bars of "Swingmatism," Parker took off into a flowing improvisation that included "Hootie Blues," an example of a Parker blues chorus complete with a characteristic riff figure.

BUGS BUNNY'S DEBUT: ANNIVERSARY. Apr 30, 1938. Warner Bros.' "wascally wabbit" first appeared on screen in the theatrical short "Porky's Hare Hunt," directed by Ben "Bugs" Hardaway and released on this date. Chuck Jones and Tex Avery further developed him into the character we know now—in such cartoons as "A Wild Hare" (1940), in which Bugs asks "What's up, Doc?" for the first time and first kisses perennial foe Elmer Fudd. The rabbit's noisy carrot munching was based on Clark Gable's carrot chewing in the film *It Happened One Night* (1934).

CAMBODIA INVADED BY US: ANNIVERSARY. Apr 30, 1970. President Richard Nixon announced the US was sending troops into Cambodia in an attempt to destroy the "sanctuaries" from which men and materiel were infiltrated into South Vietnam. This sparked widespread protests on the homefront, including a march on Washington and the closure of many American colleges and universities. See also: "Kent State Students' Memorial Day: Anniversay" (May 4).

FIRST PRESIDENTIAL TELECAST: ANNIVERSARY. Apr 30, 1939. Franklin D. Roosevelt became the first president to appear on television when he was televised at the New York World's Fair. However, the appearance was only beamed to 200 TV sets in a 40-mile radius. See also: "First Scheduled Television Broadcast: Anniversary" (July 1).

HARRISON, MARY SCOTT LORD DIMMICK: BIRTH ANNIVERSARY. Apr 30, 1858. Second wife of Benjamin Harrison, 23rd president of the US, born at Honesdale, PA. Died at New York, NY, Jan 5, 1948.

HELENA RAILROAD FAIR. Apr 30. Civic Center, Helena, MT. 26th annual. Largest railroad hobby event in Montana features a mix of scale and tin-plate trains; railroad memorabilia and collectibles; real-life train watching at the MRL Helena depot. Annually, the last Sunday in April. Est attendance: 2,500. For info: Helena Railroad Fair, PO Box 4914, Helena, MT 59604-4914. Phone: (406) 442-2364 or (406) 443-1578. E-mail: rrfair@mt.net.

INTERNATIONAL SCHOOL SPIRIT SEASON. Apr 30–Sept 30. To recognize everyone who has helped to make school spirit better and to provide time to plan improved spirit ideas for the coming school year. For info: Jim Hawkins, Chairman, Pepsters, Committee for More School Spirit, PO Box 122652, San Diego, CA 92112. Phone: (619) 280-0999.

INTERNATIONAL WALK DAYS. Apr 30 (also Dec 26). Today is the day to get primal, leave the magic carpet at home and whenever possible walk to your destination. Touted as the best exercise, walking is an undertaking that is not only aerobically correct, vital for workouts and a great method to pass the time, but it enables a person to get out and enjoy the weather and surroundings. [©1994] To alleviate the escalating costs of Eventological® Literature, a charge of $10 must be assessed to each request. Checks are to be made payable to: Adrienne Sioux Koopersmith, 1437 W Rosemont, #1W, Chicago, IL 60660-1319. E-mail: askoopersmith@hotmail.com.

★**JEWISH HERITAGE WEEK.** Apr 30–May 6. Annually, the week that includes Israeli Independence Day (May 3 in 2006).

LILLY, WILLIAM: BIRTH ANNIVERSARY. Apr 30, 1602 (OS). English astrologer, author and almanac compiler, born at Diseworth, Leicestershire. His almanacs were among the most popular in Britain from 1644 until his death, June 9, 1681 (OS), at Hersham, Surrey, England.

LOUISIANA: ADMISSION DAY: ANNIVERSARY. Apr 30. Became 18th state in 1812.

LOUISIANA PURCHASE DAY: ANNIVERSARY. Apr 30, 1803. One of the greatest real estate deals in history was completed in 1803, when more than 820,000 square miles of the Louisiana Territory were turned over to the US by France, for $15 million. This almost doubled the size of the US, extending its western border to the Rocky Mountains.

MOTHER, FATHER DEAF DAY. Apr 30. A day to honor deaf parents and recognize the gifts of culture and language they give to their hearing children. Annually, the last Sunday of April. Sponsored by Children of Deaf Adults International Inc (CODA). For info: T. Teske, Deaf Awareness Events. E-mail: tteske2724@aol.com.

MUHAMMAD ALI STRIPPED OF TITLE: ANNIVERSARY. Apr 30, 1967. Muhammad Ali was stripped of his world heavyweight boxing championship when he refused to be inducted into military service. Said Ali, "I have searched my conscience, and I find I cannot be true to my belief in my religion by accepting such a call." He had claimed exemption as a minister of the Black Muslim religion. He was convicted of violating the Selective Service Act but the Supreme Court reversed this decision in 1971.

NATIONAL HONESTY DAY (WITH HONEST ABE AWARDS). Apr 30. To celebrate honesty and those who are honest and honorable in their dealings with others. Nominations accepted for most honest people and companies. Winners to be awarded "Honest Abe" awards and given "Abies" on National Honesty Day. Also presented are dishonorable mentions for notables who have been less than honest. Schools and religious organizations are encouraged to make honesty a subject of discussion on or near this day. Annually, Apr 30. For info: M. Hirsh Goldberg, Founder, 3103 Szold Dr, Baltimore, MD 21208. Phone: (410) 486-4150.

NETHERLANDS: QUEEN'S BIRTHDAY. Apr 30. A public holiday in celebration of the birthday of former Queen Juliana and the Dutch National Day. The whole country parties as young and old participate in festivities such as markets, theater, music and games. The current monarch is Queen Beatrix.

ORGANIZATION OF AMERICAN STATES FOUNDED: ANNIVERSARY. Apr 30, 1948. This regional alliance was founded by 21 nations of the Americas at Bogota, Colombia. Its purpose is to further economic development and integration among nations of the Western hemisphere, to promote representative democracy and to help overcome poverty. The Pan-American Union, with offices at Washington, DC, serves as the General Secretariat for the OAS.

SMITH, MICHAEL J.: BIRTH ANNIVERSARY. Apr 30, 1945. Michael J. Smith, 40-year-old pilot of the space shuttle *Challenger* on Jan 28, 1986. It was to have been Commander Smith's first space flight. Born at Beaufort, NC, Smith perished with all others on board when *Challenger* exploded on Jan 28, 1986. See also: "*Challenger* Space Shuttle Explosion Anniversary" (Jan 28).

SOUTH VIETNAM FALLS TO VIETCONG: ANNIVERSARY. Apr 30, 1975. The president of South Vietnam announced the country's unconditional surrender to the Vietcong. Communist troops moved into Saigon and 1,000 Americans in the city were hastily evacuated. Thousands of South Vietnamese also tried to flee. The surrender announcement came 21 years after the 1954 Geneva agreements divided Vietnam into North and South. The last American troops had left South Vietnam in March 1973.

SPANK OUT DAY USA. Apr 30. A day on which all caretakers of children—parents, teachers and day-care workers—are asked not to use corporal punishment as discipline and to become acquainted with positive, effective disciplinary alternatives. For info: Nadine Block, EPOCH-USA, 155 W Main St, Ste 1603, Columbus, OH 43215. Phone: (614) 221-8829. E-mail: nblock@ infinet.com. Web: www.stophitting.org.

SWEDEN: FEAST OF VALBORG. Apr 30. An evening celebration in which Sweden "sings in the spring" by listening to traditional hymns to the spring, often around community bonfires. Also known as Walpurgis Night, the Feast of Valborg occurs annually Apr 30.

SWITZERLAND: LANDSGEMEINDE. Apr 30. In one of the last examples of direct democracy, the citizens of Switzerland's smallest canton, Appenzell Inner Rhoden, gather annually on the last Sunday of April to vote. Uniquely, they don't cast secret ballots but raise their arms in full view of their neighbors. About 2,000 to 3,000 voters of 18 years and older come to the square of the canton capital, Appenzell, after attending a morning church service. Once affairs of the canton are voted on, festivities begin. As part of the tradition, which dates back to the 14th century, men wear swords.

THEATER IN NORTH AMERICA FIRST PERFORMANCE: ANNIVERSARY. Apr 30, 1598. On the banks of the Rio Grande, near present-day El Paso, TX, the first North American theatrical performance was acted. The play was a Spanish commedia featuring an expedition of soldiers. On July 10 of the same year, the same group produced *Moros y Los Cristianos* (*Moors and Christians*), an anonymous play.

VIETNAM: LIBERATION DAY: ANNIVERSARY. Apr 30. National holiday. Commemorates the fall of Saigon to the Communists in 1975, ending the Vietnam War.

WALPURGIS NIGHT. Apr 30. The eve of May Day, which is the feast day of St. Walpurgis, the protectress against the magic arts. According to German legend, witches gather this night and celebrate their sabbath on the highest peak in the Harz Mountains. Celebrated particularly by university students in northern Europe.

WASHINGTON, GEORGE: PRESIDENTIAL INAUGURATION ANNIVERSARY. Apr 30, 1789. George Washington was inaugurated as the first president of the US under the new Constitution at New York, NY. Robert R. Livingston administered the oath of office to Washington on the balcony of Federal Hall, at the corner of Wall and Broad streets.

WILSON, ELLIS: BIRTH ANNIVERSARY. Apr 30, 1899. African-American artist born at Mayfield, KY, and died at New York, NY, Jan 1, 1977. Wilson painted realistic portrayals of African Americans at work and at play. In 1944 he was awarded a Guggenheim fellowship. He visited South Carolina, painting city scenes and fishing towns. In the 1950s, Wilson took a revelatory trip to Haiti which changed the way he painted. Unable to note any facial features on the Haitians he painted from a distance, Wilson began painting flat, stylized silhouettes. *Haitian Funeral Procession* remains Wilson's most popular and accessible painting.

BIRTHDAYS TODAY

Jane Campion, 52, film director (*The Piano*), born Wellington, New Zealand, Apr 30, 1954.

Jill Clayburgh, 62, actress (*Fools Rush In, Luna*), born New York, NY, Apr 30, 1944.

Gary Collins, 68, actor, talk-show host, born Boston, MA, Apr 30, 1938.

Kirsten Dunst, 24, actress (*Spider-Man, Little Women, Interview with the Vampire*), born Point Pleasant, NJ, Apr 30, 1982.

Johnny Galecki, 31, actor ("Roseanne," *Suicide Kings*), born Bree, Belgium, Apr 30, 1975.

Perry King, 58, actor (*Slaughterhouse Five, The Lords of Flatbush, Switch*), born Alliance, OH, Apr 30, 1948.

Cloris Leachman, 76, actress (Oscar for *The Last Picture Show*; "Phyllis"), born Des Moines, IA, Apr 30, 1930.

Willie Nelson, 73, singer ("Always on My Mind," "On the Road Again"), actor (*Honeysuckle Rose*), born Abbott, TX, Apr 30, 1933.

Isiah Thomas, 45, Hall of Fame basketball player, basketball coach, born Chicago, IL, Apr 30, 1961.

Burt Young, 66, writer, actor (*Chinatown, Rocky, Once Upon a Time in America*), born New York, NY, Apr 30, 1940.

Maye.

MAY 1 — MONDAY
Day 121 — 244 Remaining

ADDISON, JOSEPH: BIRTH ANNIVERSARY. May 1, 1672 (OS). English essayist born at Milston, Wiltshire, England. Died at London, June 17, 1719 (OS). "We are," he wrote in *The Spectator*, "always doing something for Posterity, but I would fain see Posterity do something for us."

AMTRAK: 35th ANNIVERSARY. May 1, 1971. Amtrak, the national rail service which combined the operations of 18 passenger railroads, went into service.

★**ASIAN PACIFIC AMERICAN HERITAGE MONTH.** May 1–31. Presidential Proclamation issued honoring Asian Pacific Americans each year since 1979. Public Law 102-450 of Oct 28, 1992, designated the observance for the month of May each year.

ASTRONOMY WEEK. May 1–7. To take astronomy to the people. Astronomy Week is observed during the calendar week in which Astronomy Day falls. See also: "Astronomy Day" (May 6).

AWARENESS OF MEDICAL ORPHANS MONTH. May 1–31. A month dedicated to the awareness of medical orphans—rare disorders/diseases. Includes "Adopt a Medical Orphan" in AmericaCares AmericaCan Project; "Unsolved Cases" spotlighting real stories; publishing of "Hope and Healing" from submissions sent in by the public; and encourages and sponsors internship/study/volunteer programs for credit or noncredit. For info: The ForGoodnessSake! Center, 427 E 7th St, Michigan City, IN 46360. E-mail: ForGood@adsnet.com.

BATMAN DEBUTS: ANNIVERSARY. May 1, 1939. In the May issues of *Detective Comics #27* that appeared on newsstands on this day, a new crime fighter, "The Batman," debuted, created by Bob Kane (collaborating with Bill Finger). The caped hero was an immediate success. See also: "Superman Debuts: Anniversary" (June 1).

BE KIND TO ANIMALS WEEK®. May 1–7. To promote kindness and humane care toward animals. Annually, the first full week of May. Features "Be Kind to Animals Kid Contest" with grand prize. For info: American Humane, 63 Inverness Dr E, Englewood, CO 80112. Phone: (303) 792-9900. Fax: (303) 792-5333. E-mail: info@americanhumane.org. Web: www.americanhumane.org.

BELGIUM: PLAY OF SAINT EVERMAAR. May 1. Annual performance (for more than 1,000 years) of a mystery play, in its original form, by the village inhabitants.

BETTER HEARING AND SPEECH MONTH. May 1–31. A nationwide public information campaign held each May to inform the 41 million Americans with hearing and speech problems that help is available. Annually, the month of May. For info: American Speech-Language-Hearing Assn, 10801 Rockville Pike, Rockville, MD 20852-3279. Phone: (800) 638-8255. Web: www.asha.org.

BREAD PUDDING RECIPE EXCHANGE. May 1–7. A week dedicated to the exchange of creative bread pudding recipes. For sample recipes send SASE. For info: Bread Pudding Update, PO Box 416, Denver, CO 80201. Phone: (303) 575-5676. E-mail: mail@breadpudding.net. Web: www.breadpudding.net.

CANADA: NATIONAL ORGANIZING WEEK. May 1–6. Weeklong celebration designed to educate the public about the importance of getting organized and how professional organizers can assist them in this process. Annually, the first full week in May. For info: Jane Veldhoven, Professional Organizers in Canada, PO Box 82032, 255 Dundas St W, Waterdown, ON, Canada L0R 2M0. Phone: (902) 229-5263. E-mail: pr@organizersincanada.com. Web: www.organizersincanada.com.

CITIZEN KANE PREMIERE: 65th ANNIVERSARY. May 1, 1941. Orson Welles's directorial masterpiece premiered at New York City's RKO Palace. The premiere had been delayed almost three months due to studio jitters about what media magnate William Randolph Hearst's reaction would be—since the film was a thinly disguised version of his life. The film's multiple points of view, deep focus photography and witty script made it a favorite with critics at the time: John O'Hara in *Newsweek* said, "[Y]our faithful bystander reports that he has just seen a picture which he thinks must be the best picture he ever saw. . . ." Nominated for nine Academy Awards, *Citizen Kane* won for best original screenplay by Herman J. Mankiewicz and Welles. The film did not perform well commercially (due in part to Hearst's influence), but is now regarded as the greatest American film.

CLARK, MARK: BIRTH ANNIVERSARY. May 1, 1896. US general who served in both World Wars, Mark Clark was born at Madison Barracks, NY. In November 1942, he commanded the US forces taking part in the invasion of North Africa, and in January 1943, he became commander of the US Fifth Army, which invaded Italy in September 1943, taking Rome in June of 1944. After the Germans capitulated in Italy, Clark was appointed commander of US occupation forces in Austria. He died at Charleston, SC, Apr 17, 1984.

CLEAN AIR MONTH. May 1–31. The American Lung Association releases its annual air quality report, "State of the Air," on May 1. And during this month, local Lung Associations focus on other clean air issues, programs and events. For info: American Lung Assn, 61 Broadway, 6th Fl, New York, NY 10006. Phone: (800) LUNG-USA. E-mail: info@lungusa.org. Web: www.lungusa.org.

COLUMBIAN EXPOSITION OPENING: ANNIVERSARY. May 1, 1893. At 12:08 PM President Grover Cleveland, in the presence of nearly a quarter of a million people, placed his finger on a golden key opening the Columbian Exposition at Chicago, IL. Amid the unfurling of thousands of flags, sounding of trumpets and booming of cannons, the key activated an electromagnetic valve, steam rushed into great cylinders and the immense pump began its enormous burden of pumping 15,000,000 gallons of water a day to supply the 685-acre fair and its visitors with an ample water supply.

CREATIVE BEGINNINGS MONTH. May 1–31. How are you creative? Have you tapped into your full potential? Enjoy the budding month of May while discovering something new about yourself. Enroll in a course, write a poem, plant a garden, coordinate a social event. While developing your gifts, encourage others to also cultivate their own creative beginnings. For info: Christina Bergenholtz, PO Box 301, Grafton, MA 01519. Phone: (508) 839-5139. Fax: (508) 887-9556. E-mail: chrismhb@aol.com.

DENMARK: TIVOLI GARDENS SEASON. May 1–Sept 17. Copenhagen. World famous for its variety of entertainment, symphony concerts, pantomime and ballet. Beautiful flower arrangements and excellent restaurants. Traditional season: May 1 until the third Sunday in September.

EAT DESSERT FIRST WEEK. May 1–7. Forget what your mother told you about eating your dinner before you eat dessert. In May each year, Rowena's, Inc, of Norfolk, VA, encourages you to eat dessert first and enjoy life to its fullest. Life is meant to be lived with gusto. Enjoy! For info: Cameron Foster, Rowena's, Inc, 758 W 22nd St, Norfolk, VA 23517. Phone: (757) 627-8699. Fax: (757) 627-1505. E-mail: cameron@rowenas.com. Web: www.rowenas.com.

EXECUTIVE COACHING DAY. May 1. Workers deserve the best leaders they can get! Our sports stars have skill and strength coaches, our great actors have speech and movement coaches, our politicians have media coaches. Why don't more of our corporate and union executives who are responsible for effectively leading thousands of employees and members utilize the power of coaching? This is a day to applaud all organizational leaders who take their profession seriously enough to improve their skills through coaching. A day to raise the awareness of those who do not utilize coaching as to its power to improve their capacity to effectively lead their organizations. For info: Ira Chaleff, Pres, Exec Coaching & Consulting Assoc. Phone: (301) 933-3752. Web: www.exe-coach.com.

FAMILY WELLNESS MONTH. May 1–31. Spend more time with family and appreciate those closest to you. Hold a family meeting and resolve differences and disputes. Set family goals and share dreams. Call up estranged family and reunite. Remember that your family members are just human, not superhuman, and tell your family members that you love them. For info: Angela Brown, Words of Wellness, PO Box 49266, Charlotte, NC 28277. Phone: (704) 289-2900. Fax: (704) 845-3060. E-mail: Angela@WordsofWellness.com. Web: www.WordsofWellness.com.

FIBROMYALGIA EDUCATION AND AWARENESS MONTH. May 1–31. To promote education and awareness of the dangers of fibromyalgia which is also known as the fibromyalgia syndrome (FSM), fibrositis or chronic muscle pain syndrome. Fibromyalgia affects more than 10 million American women. Kit of materials available for $15. For info: PPSI, c/o Fibromyalgia Council of America, 101 Lucas Valley Rd, San Rafael, CA 94903. Phone: (415) 479-8628. Fax: (415) 479-8608. E-mail: ppsi@aol.com. Web: www.ppsinc.org.

FIRST SKYSCRAPER: ANNIVERSARY. May 1, 1884. Construction was begun on the Home Insurance Company building on this date in Chicago. The 10-story building was completed in 1885. Designed by William Le Baron Jenney, it had a steel frame which carried the weight of the building. The walls provided no support but hung like curtains on the metal frame. This method of construction revolutionized American architecture and allowed architects to build taller and taller buildings. The Home Insurance Building was demolished in 1931.

FREEDOM SHRINE MONTH. May 1–31. The Freedom Shrine is an exclusive program of the National Exchange Club, est 1911. It is a collection of 30 original historic documents photographically reproduced and attractively displayed in thousands of locations across the nation. The purpose of the Freedom Shrine is to remind all Americans that the freedoms, which they enjoy today, are gifts from the past—forged from idealism, determination and the sacrifice of the many courageous men and women who preceded us. It also serves to remind us that so precious a gift as freedom must be continually guarded and protected. For info: The Natl Exchange Club, 3050 Central Ave, Toledo, OH 43606-1700. Phone: (800) 924-2643. Web: www.nationalexchangeclub.org.

FREQUENT FLYER PROGRAM DEBUTS: 25th ANNIVERSARY. May 1, 1981. American Airlines began the first frequent flyer program on this date. Now most airlines offer a frequent flyer program but American is still the industry leader with 45 million members. Today 40 percent of all miles are earned on the ground with affiliated businesses that pay the airlines for the miles, such as hotels, car rental companies, credit card companies, phone companies and retailers.

GET CAUGHT READING MONTH. May 1–31. Celebrities appear in ads appealing to people of all ages to remind them of the joys of reading. Events will be held throughout the country to celebrate reading. For info: Assn of American Publishers, 71 Fifth Ave, New York, NY 10003. Phone: (212) 255-0200. Web: www.publishers.org or www.getcaughtreading.org.

GO FETCH! NATIONAL FOOD DRIVE FOR HOMELESS ANIMALS. May 1–31. An annual, monthlong national food drive to raise awareness about starving and malnourished stray animals. These animals may live on the streets, be abused or neglected, be feral, or be homeless pets living with their homeless families in shelters. For info: Go Fetch!, PALS Foundation, PO Box 1271, San Luis Obispo, CA 93406. Phone: (805) 544-0984. Web: www.SaveAnAnimal.R8.org.

GREAT BRITAIN FORMED: ANNIVERSARY. May 1, 1707 (OS). A union between England and Scotland resulted in the formation of Great Britain. (Wales had been part of England since the 1500s.) Today's United Kingdom consists of Great Britain and Northern Ireland.

HAITIAN HERITAGE MONTH. May 1–31. Boston, MA. A series of events are organized throughout the month of May in the Boston Haitian American community featuring exhibits, flag raisings, concerts, games, parades and presentations. The events are organized to honor Haitian General Toussaint Louverture, to remember the consensus reached by black and mulatto officers to fight for Haitian independence in 1803 and to celebrate the Haitian flag created that same year. The flag-raising ceremony will take place on May 18 and the Haitian-American Unity Day Parade will take place on May 21. For info: Haitian-Americans United, Inc, 10 Fairway St, PO Box 260440, Mattapan, MA 02126. Phone: (617) 298-2976. E-mail: unity@hauinc.org. Web: www.hauinc.org.

HEAL THE CHILDREN MONTH. May 1–31. To encourage survivors of childhood abuse and neglect to speak out. By revealing their painful experiences, they can inspire others to prevent children from suffering the same ordeals. Annually, the month of May. For info: Donald Etkes, PhD, 11693 San Vicente Blvd, #491, Los Angeles, CA 90049. Phone: (310) 281-0123. Web: www.AbuseHealing.com.

HEALTHY VISION MONTH. May 1–31. Although it is believed that half of all blindness can be prevented, the number of people in the US who suffer from vision loss continues to increase. Healthy Vision Month informs the public that preventive eye care is important because eye conditions, diseases and injuries that can rob a person's vision can strike at any time in life, from newborn to old age. For info: American Academy of Ophthalmology, PO Box 7424, San Francisco, CA 94120-7424. Phone: (415) 447-0258. Fax: (415) 561-8533. E-mail: eyemd@aao.org. Web: www.aao.org/eyemd.

HUNTINGTON'S DISEASE AWARENESS MONTH. May 1–31. For info: Huntington's Disease Society of America, 505 Eighth Ave, Ste 902, New York, NY 10018. Phone: (212) 242-1958 or (800) 345-4372. Fax: (212) 239-3430. Web: www.hdsa.org.

INTERNATIONAL BUSINESS IMAGE IMPROVEMENT MONTH. May 1–31. The image of your business sets the tone

May 2006	S	M	T	W	T	F	S
		1	2	3	4	5	6
	7	8	9	10	11	12	13
	14	15	16	17	18	19	20
	21	22	23	24	25	26	27
	28	29	30	31			

for how successful your company will be. Just as we judge others within the first few seconds of meeting, we do the same for a business. Receive more information on how to improve your business image and take the free online business card quiz. For info: Debbie Allen, Pres, Allen & Associates Consulting, Inc, PO Box 27946, Scottsdale, AZ 85255-0149. Phone: (800) 359-4544. Web: www.debbieallen.com.

INTERNATIONAL VICTORIOUS WOMAN MONTH. May 1–31. Victory is foundational to the health, happiness and well-being of a woman. The month of May celebrates the woman who has shaped life's challenges into distinct victories. Acknowledging the victorious woman encourages others to strive toward overcoming difficulties and influences them to achieve their own personal victories. For info: Annmarie Kelly, SkillBuilder Systems. Phone: (610) 738-8225. E-mail: annmarie@victoriouswoman.com. Web: www.victoriouswoman.com.

ITALY: FESTIVAL OF SAINT EFISIO. May 1–4. Cagliari. Said to be one of the biggest and most colorful processions in the world. Several thousand pilgrims on foot, in carts and on horseback wearing costumes dating from the 17th century accompany the statue of the saint through the streets.

JONES, MARY HARRIS (MOTHER JONES): BIRTH ANNIVERSARY. May 1, 1830. Irish-born American labor leader. After the death of her husband and four children (during the Memphis yellow fever epidemic of 1867) and loss of her belongings in the Chicago Fire in 1871, Jones devoted her energies and her life to organizing and advancing the cause of labor. It seemed she was present wherever there were labor troubles. She gave her last speech on her 100th birthday. Born at Cork, Ireland, she died Nov 30, 1930, at Silver Spring, MD.

LABOR DAY. May 1. In 140 countries, May 1 is observed as a workers' holiday. When it falls on a Saturday or Sunday, the following Monday is observed as a holiday. Bermuda, Canada and the US are the only countries that observe Labor Day in September.

★**LAW DAY, USA.** May 1. Presidential Proclamation issued each year for May 1 since 1958 at request. (PL87–20 of Apr 7, 1961.)

LAW ENFORCEMENT APPRECIATION MONTH IN FLORIDA. May 1–31. Law Enforcement Appreciation Day is May 15 in Florida, a ceremonial day.

LEI DAY. May 1. Hawaii. On this special day—the Hawaiian version of May Day—leis are made, worn, given, displayed and entered in lei-making contests. One of the most popular Lei Day celebrations takes place at Honolulu at Kapiolani Park at Waikiki. Includes the state's largest lei contest, the crowning of the Lei Day Queen, Hawaiian music, hula and flowers galore.

LIBRARY LEGISLATIVE DAY. May 1–2. Librarians go to Washington and to their state capitals to talk to legislators about important library issues. For info: Public Information Office, American Library Assn, 1301 Pennsylvania Ave NW, Ste 403, Washington, DC 20004. Phone: (202) 628-8410. E-mail: alawash@alawash.org. Web: ww.ala.org.

LIGHT THE NIGHT FOR SIGHT™. May 1–July 31. Celebrate sight and safety with this national walkathon organized to raise awareness of consumer fireworks dangers and to celebrate the gift of sight. Safe celebrations will be promoted. For info: Prevent Blindness America®, 211 W Wacker Dr, Ste 1700, Chicago, IL 60606. Phone: (800) 331-2020. E-mail: info@preventblindness.org. Web: www.preventblindness.org.

★**LOYALTY DAY.** May 1. Presidential Proclamation issued annually for May 1 since 1959 at request. (PL85–529 of July 18, 1958.) Note that an earlier proclamation was issued in 1955.

MARSHALL ISLANDS, REPUBLIC OF THE: CONSTITUTION DAY. May 1. National holiday.

MAY DAY. May 1. The first day of May has been observed as a holiday since ancient times. Spring festivals, maypoles and maying are still common, but the political importance of May Day

has grown since the 1880s, when it became a workers' day in the US. Now widely observed in countries as a workers' holiday or as Labor Day. (Bermuda, Canada and the US observe Labor Day in September.) In most European countries, when May Day falls on Saturday or Sunday, the Monday following is observed as a holiday, with bank and store closings, parades and other festivities.

MAY IN MONTCLAIR. May 1–31. Montclair Township, NJ. 28th annual monthlong festival celebrating the wealth of cultural, artistic, historic and recreational opportunities in Montclair for residents, merchants and visitors. Est attendance: 4,000. For info: Mary Tetzloff, Chair, May in Montclair, 249 Midland Ave, Montclair, NJ 07042. Phone: (973) 783-5115.

MELANOMA MONDAY. May 1. Also known as National Skin Self-Examination Day. People are encouraged to examine their skin for skin cancer. Annually, the first Monday in May. For info: American Academy of Dermatology, PO Box 4014, Schaumburg, IL 60168-4014. Phone: (847) 330-0230. Fax: (847) 330-0050. Web: www.aad.org.

MELANOMA/SKIN CANCER DETECTION AND PREVENTION MONTH. May 1–31. For info: American Academy of Dermatology, PO Box 4014, Schaumburg, IL 60168-4014. Phone: (847) 330-0230. Web: www.aad.org.

MORE THAN JUST A PRETTY FACE MONTH. May 1–31. Great skin ranges from the scalp down to the soles of the feet. May is a perfect time to begin to prepare skin for the summer. A sun protection cream with an SPF of 15 or higher is to be applied all over the skin daily. Did you know that on average we receive approximately 24 hours a week of accidental sun? This is gathered via windshields, office windows, walking to and from the office or store. Annually, the month of May. For info: Susie Galvez, Faceworks Day Spa, 8502 Patterson Ave, Richmond, VA 23229. Phone: (804) 740-5665. Fax: (804) 741-7203. Web: www.susiegalvez.com.

MOTHER GOOSE DAY. May 1. To re-appreciate the old nursery rhymes. Motto: "Either alone or in sharing, read childhood nursery favorites and feel the warmth of Mother Goose's embrace." Website has ideas for celebrating, including recipes. Annually, May 1. For info: Gloria T. Delamar, Founder, Mother Goose Society. E-mail: mother.goose.society@juno.com. Web: www.delamar.org/mothergoosesociety.htm.

MOTORCYCLE SAFETY MONTH. May 1–31. This month is dedicated to encouraging safe motorcycle riding practices. Learn safe riding practices through state and local motorcycle safety courses and continue improving skills through advanced riding courses. Set a safe environment this month to prepare for a safe riding season. For info: Sylvia Henderson, Springboard Training, PO Box 588, Olney, MD 20830-0588. Phone: (301) 260-1538. E-mail: admin@v-twinvalues.com. Web: www.v-twinvalues.com.

NATIONAL ALLERGY/ASTHMA AWARENESS MONTH. May 1–31. Kit of materials available for $15 from this nonprofit organization. For info: Frederick S. Mayer, Pres, Pharmacist Planning Services, Inc, c/o Allergy Council of America (ACA), 101 Lucas Valley Rd, #210, San Rafael, CA 94903. Phone: (415) 479-8628. Fax: (415) 479-8608. E-mail: ppsi@aol.com. Web: www.ppsinc.org.

NATIONAL ARTHRITIS MONTH. May 1–31. Increases awareness of the more than 100 forms of arthritis and related diseases and increases support for the 66 million Americans with arthritis. During the month, various communities will sponsor Arthritis Walks™ to raise money for education and research. Participants may choose 5k or 1-mile courses, and men, women and children with arthritis will wear special blue "hero" caps to show that they are taking control of their disease. To join an Arthritis Walk in your area, call (877) 232-2898. For info: Arthritis Foundation, 1330 W Peachtree St NW, Ste 100, Atlanta, GA 30309. Phone: (800) 568-4045. Fax: (404) 872-8694. Web: www.arthritis.org.

NATIONAL BARBECUE MONTH. May 1–31. To encourage people to start enjoying barbecuing early in the season when Daylight Saving Time lengthens the day. Annually, the month of May. Sponsor: Hearth, Patio & Barbecue Association. For info: NBM, DHM Group, Inc, 9 Professional Circle, Ste 101, Colts Neck, NJ 07722. Fax: (732) 866-4466. E-mail: hpba@dhmg.com.

NATIONAL BIKE MONTH. May 1–31. 50th annual celebration of bicycling for fun, fitness and transportation. Local activities sponsored by bicycling organizations, environmental groups, PTAs, police departments, health organizations and civic groups. About five million participants nationwide. Annually, the month of May. For info: League of American Bicyclists, 1612 K St, Ste 800, Washington, DC 20006. Phone: (202) 822-1333. Fax: (202) 822-1334. E-mail: bikeleague@bikeleague.org. Web: www.bikemonth.com.

NATIONAL CORRECT POSTURE MONTH. May 1–31. For info: American Chiropractic Assn, 1701 Clarendon Blvd, Arlington, VA 22209. Phone: (800) 986-4636. E-mail: memberinfo@amerchiro.org. Web: www.acatoday.com.

NATIONAL EGG MONTH. May 1–31. Dedicated to the versatility, convenience, economy and good nutrition of "the incredible edible egg™." Annually, the month of May. For info: Linda Braun, American Egg Board, 1460 Renaissance Dr, Park Ridge, IL 60068. Web: www.aeb.org.

NATIONAL FREQUENT FLYER DAY. May 1. May 1, 1981, marks the birthday of today's popular frequent flyer programs, which count millions of members. Frequent flyer miles are often called the second currency for the US for their number (trillions each year) and their popularity. For info: Randy Petersen, 1930 Frequent Flyer Point, Colorado Springs, CO 80915. Phone: (719) 597-8889. Fax: (719) 597-6855. E-mail: randy@insideflyer.com. Web: www.webflyer.com.

NATIONAL GOOD CAR-KEEPING MONTH. May 1–31. To promote increased safety and value through good car maintenance. For info: Sander Allen, Good Car-Keeping Institute, 990 N Lake Shore Dr, Ste 11-A, Chicago, IL 60611.

NATIONAL HAMBURGER MONTH. May 1–31. Sponsored by White Castle, the original fast-food hamburger chain (founded in 1921), to pay tribute to one of America's favorite foods. With or without condiments, on or off a bun or bread, hamburgers have grown in popularity since the early 1920s and are now an American meal mainstay. For info: White Castle Management Co, Marketing Dept, 555 W Goodale St, Columbus, OH 43215-1158. Phone: (614) 228-5781. Fax: (614) 228-8841. Web: www.whitecastle.com.

NATIONAL HEPATITIS AWARENESS MONTH. May 1–31. A month to raise awareness of and increase research for viral hepatitis, while also promoting prevention through schools, health departments, churches, community organizations and other groups. For info: Hepatitis Foundation Intl, 504 Blick Dr, Silver Spring, MD 20904. Phone: (800) 891-0707. E-mail: HFI@comcast.net. Web: www.HepatitisFoundation.org.

NATIONAL MENTAL HEALTH MONTH. May 1–31. For info: Natl Mental Health Assn, 2001 Beauregard St, 12th Floor, Alexandria, VA 22311. Phone: (800) 969-NMHA or (703) 684-7722. E-mail: infoctr@nmha.org. Web: www.nmha.org.

NATIONAL MOVING MONTH. May 1–31. Recognizing America's mobile roots and kicking off the busiest moving season of the year. Each year more than 40 million Americans pack up their belongings and relocate to new homes and communities. More than half these moves take place between May and September. During National Moving Month, moving experts will be educating Americans on how to plan a successful move, to pack efficiently and handle the uncertainties and questions that moving children may have. For info: Allied Van Lines. Web: www.allied.com.

NATIONAL NEUROFIBROMATOSIS AWARENESS MONTH. May 1–31. For info: The Children's Tumor Foundation, 95 Pine St, 16th Fl, New York, NY 10005. Phone: (800) 323-7938 or (212) 344-6633. Fax: (212) 747-0004. E-mail: info@ctf.org. Web: www.ctf.org.

★**NATIONAL OLDER AMERICANS MONTH.** May 1–31. Presidential Proclamation; from 1963 through 1973 this was called "Senior Citizens Month." In May 1974 it became Older Americans Month. In 1980 the title included Senior Citizens Day, which was observed May 8, 1980. Issued annually since 1963.

NATIONAL OSTEOPOROSIS AWARENESS AND PREVENTION MONTH. May 1–31. Osteoporosis is not a natural part of aging. Find out what you can do to prevent and treat it by joining the NOF family. For info: Natl Osteoporosis Foundation, 1232 22nd St NW, Washington, DC 20037. Phone: (202) 223-2226. Fax: (202) 223-2237. E-mail: communications@nof.org. Web: www.nof.org.

NATIONAL PHYSICAL FITNESS AND SPORTS MONTH. May 1–31. Encourages individuals and organizations to promote fitness activities and programs. Popularly known as "May Month," it was established by the President's Council on Physical Fitness and Sports in 1983. For info: President's Council on Physical Fitness and Sports, HHH Building, 200 Independence Ave SW, Room 738H, Washington, DC 20201-0004. Phone: (202) 690-9000. Fax: (202) 690-5211. Web: www.fitness.gov or www.presidentschallenge.org.

NATIONAL PREPARE TO BUY A HOME MONTH. May 1–31. The National Association of Independent Real Estate Brokers would like to encourage prospective home buyers to consult with an independent real estate broker for information about the best ways to buy your new home. For info: Gary Conner, NAIREB, 7102 Mardyke Ln, Indianapolis, IN 46226. Phone/fax: (317) 549-1709. E-mail: info@NationalRealEstateBrokers.org. Web: www.NationalRealEstateBrokers.org.

NATIONAL PRESERVATION MONTH. May 1–31. To draw public attention to historic preservation including neighborhoods, districts, landmark buildings, open space and maritime heritage. For info: Natl Trust for Historic Preservation, 1785 Massachusetts Ave NW, Washington, DC 20036. Phone: (202) 588-6000. Fax: (202) 588-6038. Web: www.nationaltrust.org.

NATIONAL SALSA MONTH. May 1–31. Recognizing salsa as America's favorite way to add flavor to all kinds of food, such as

May 2006	S	M	T	W	T	F	S
		1	2	3	4	5	6
	7	8	9	10	11	12	13
	14	15	16	17	18	19	20
	21	22	23	24	25	26	27
	28	29	30	31			

eggs, burgers, chicken, tacos, chips, potatoes, rice and much more. Celebrates more than 60 years of picante sauce, a salsa created in 1947, and celebrates Cinco de Mayo, a major Mexican holiday now recognized across North America. For info: Pace Foods, c/o Dublin & Associates, 1017 N Main, Ste 201, San Antonio, TX 78212. Phone: (210) 227-0221. Web: www.pacefoods.com.

NATIONAL SCHOLARSHIP MONTH. May 1–31. To recognize organizations, businesses, individuals and communities that have helped and continue to help students with scholarships; to increase awareness of the need for more private sector aid for students; and to focus attention on the impact made by scholarships on students seeking postsecondary educational opportunities. The month kicks off with an annual luncheon at the National Press Club in Washington, DC. An initiative of Scholarship America (formerly Citizens' Scholarship Foundation of America). For info: Office of Public Affairs & Communications, Scholarship America, 7703 Normandale Rd, Ste 110, Minneapolis, MN 55435-5314. Phone: (800) 642-7207. Fax: (952) 830-1929. E-mail: nsm@scholarshipamerica.org. Web: www.nationalscholarshipmonth.org.

NATIONAL SIGHT-SAVING/ULTRAVIOLET AWARENESS MONTH. May 1–31. While the damage ultraviolet (UV) causes to skin is obvious, the damage it can do to eyes may not be. Not enough attention is paid to the damage UV can do to the eyes. Exposure to UV can burn delicate eye tissue and raise the risk of developing cataracts and cancers of the eye. For info: Prevent Blindness America®, 211 W Wacker Dr, Ste 1700, Chicago, IL 60606. Phone: (800) 331-2020. E-mail: info@preventblindness.org. Web: www.preventblindness.org.

NATIONAL SMILE MONTH. May 1–31. Smiling can change your life, which is why the American Academy of Cosmetic Dentistry® (AACD) reminds you to smile all throughout this month. Virtually all Americans say an attractive smile is an important social asset. It has the power to give you more confidence in your job, in your personal relationships and in virtually everything you do. Annually, every May. For info: American Academy of Cosmetic Dentistry, 5401 World Dairy Drive, Madison, WI 53718. Phone: (608) 222-8583 or (800) 543-9220. Fax: (608) 222-9540. E-mail: pr@aacd.com. Web: www.aacd.com.

NATIONAL STROKE AWARENESS MONTH. May 1–31. For info: Natl Stroke Assn, 9707 E Easter Ln, Englewood, CO 80112. Phone: (800) STROKES. Web: www.stroke.org.

NATIONAL WILDFLOWER WEEK. May 1–6. A week "to encourage the observation, cultivation and study of native wildflowers as a means of deepening humankind's relationship, responsibility and commitment to protect and care for the ecological integrity of Mother Earth." Cosponsors: National Council of Women, Environmental Alliance for Senior Involvement, The Groundwater Foundation, Center for Plant Conservation, Franciscans International/North America, North American Coalition on Religion and Ecology, Religious Campaign for Forest Conservation, Penn State University Urban Extension, Eastern Native Tree Society and Tree of Peace Society. Annually, the first full week in May. For info: Damon Waitt, PhD, Lady Bird Johnson Wildflower Center, 4801 La Crosse Ave, Austin, TX 78739-1702. Phone: (512) 292-4200. E-mail: wildflower@wildflower.org. Web: www.wildflower.org.

NEW HOMEOWNER'S DAY. May 1. You have faced all the challenges—now take the time as a new homeowner to stand back and reflect on your new home and savor the feeling. For info: Dorothy Zjawin, Dir, 61 W Colfax Ave, Roselle Park, NJ 07204. Phone: (908) 241-6241.

PAAR, JACK: BIRTH ANNIVERSARY. May 1, 1918. Radio personality, actor and humorist Jack Paar began hosting the "Tonight Show" on NBC in 1957. With his catchphrase, "I kid you not," he revolutionized late-night television, changing the format of traditional late shows from variety hours to talk shows and charming his audience and celebrity guests with a witty interviewing style. Paar introduced dozens of new stars to the American public, including Bill Cosby, Woody Allen, Carol Burnett and the Smothers Brothers. He left the show in 1962, handing it over to Johnny Carson, and retired from show business a few years later. Born at Canton, OH, he died at Greenwich, CT, Jan 27, 2004.

PEN-FRIENDS WEEK INTERNATIONAL. May 1–7. To encourage everyone to have one or more pen-friends not only in their own country but in other countries. For complete information on how to become a good pen-friend and information about how to write good letters, send $5 to cover expense of printing, handling and postage. Annually, May 1–7. For info: Dr. Stanley J. Drake, Pres Emeritus, Intl Soc of Friendship & Good Will, 8592 Roswell Rd, Ste 251, Atlanta, GA 30350-1867. Phone: (678) 795-1362. E-mail: sjdrake@bellsouth.net. Web: www.friendshipandgoodwill.org.

PERSONAL HISTORY MONTH. May 1–31. Members of the Association of Personal Historians donate their services to a variety of community organizations across the US, Canada and beyond, to raise awareness and appreciation for preserving life stories. For info: Sarah White, Marketing Chair, APH, 50 S Fair Oaks Ave, Madison, WI 53714. Phone: (608) 347-7329. Web: www.personalhistorians.org.

PHILIPPINES: FEAST OF OUR LADY OF PEACE AND GOOD VOYAGE. May 1–31. Pilgrimage to the shrine of Nuestra Sra de la Paz y Buen Viaje at Antipolo, Rizal.

PHILIPPINES: SANTACRUZAN. May 1–31. Maytime pageant-procession that recalls the quest of Queen Helena and Prince Constantine for the Holy Cross.

REVISE YOUR WORK SCHEDULE MONTH. May 1–31. To increase awareness, exploration and implementation of nontraditional work schedules such as flextime, telecommuting, job sharing and compressed work weeks. Annually, the month of May. For info: Center for WorkTime Options, 1286 University Ave, #192, San Diego, CA 92103-3312. Phone: (619) 232-0404. E-mail: info@worktimeoptions.com.

RUSSIA: INTERNATIONAL LABOR DAY. May 1–2. Public holiday in Russian Federation. "Official May Day demonstrations of working people."

SAVE THE RHINO DAY. May 1. A new century. An old problem. Rhinos still in danger! Help save the world's remaining rhinos on the verge of extinction! Get involved with local, national and international conservation efforts to stop the senseless slaughter of these gentle pachyderms. Call your local zoo or write Really, Rhinos! For info: Judyth Lessee, Founder, Really, Rhinos!, PO Box 40503, Tucson, AZ 85717-0503. Phone: (520) 327-9048. E-mail: rinophyl@dakotacom.net.

SCHOOL PRINCIPALS' DAY. May 1. A day of recognition for all elementary, middle and high school principals for their leadership and dedication to providing the best education possible for their students. Annually, May 1. For info: Janet M. Dellaria, PO Box 39, Trout Creek, MI 49967. Phone: (906) 852-3539.

SMITH, KATE: BIRTH ANNIVERSARY. May 1, 1909. One of America's most popular singers. Kate Smith, who never took a formal music lesson, recorded more songs than any other performer (more than 3,000), made more than 15,000 radio broadcasts and received more than 25 million fan letters. On Nov 11, 1938, she introduced a new song during her regular radio broadcast, written especially for her by Irving Berlin: "God Bless America." It soon became the unofficial national anthem. Born Kathryn Elizabeth Smith at Greenville, VA, she began her radio career May 1, 1931, with "When the Moon Comes Over the Mountain," a song identified with her throughout her career. She died at Raleigh, NC, June 17, 1986.

SOWERBY, LEO: BIRTH ANNIVERSARY. May 1, 1895. Pulitzer Prize–winning composer of more than 550 compositions, born at Grand Rapids, MI, and died July 7, 1968, at Port Clinton, OH.

STEPMOTHERS DAY. May 1. A day to honor stepmothers who care! Annually, May 1. For info: Susan Wilkins-Hubley, 4 Westwood Blvd Unit 14, Ste 113, Upper Tantallon, NS, B3Z 1H3, Canada. E-mail: secondwivesclub.com@gmail.com. Web: www .secondwivesclub.com.

STRIKE OUT STROKES MONTH. May 1–31. Dedicated to the prevention of strokes. Factors resulting from heredity or natural processes can't be changed but with proper medical treatment and healthful lifestyle adjustments, some risk factors can be eliminated. Kit materials available for $15. For info: Pharmacy Council on Stroke Prevention, c/o PPSI, 101 Lucas Valley Rd, #210, San Rafael, CA 94903. Phone: (415) 479-8628. Fax: (415) 479-8608. E-mail: ppsi@aol.com. Web: www.ppsinc.org.

TEILHARD DE CHARDIN, PIERRE: 125th BIRTH ANNIVERSARY. May 1, 1881. French Jesuit author, paleontologist and philosopher, born at Sarcenat, France. He died at New York, NY, Apr 10, 1955.

TIM & TOM GULLIKSON FOUNDATION WEEK. May 1–8. The Tim & Tom Gullikson Foundation was founded in 1995 by twins Tim and Tom who grew up in Wisconsin and made names for themselves worldwide as tennis players and coaches. Tim Gullikson, then coach to Grand Slam champion Pete Sampras, was diagnosed with brain tumors in 1995 and succumbed to the disease in 1996. The foundation assists brain tumor patients and their families in managing the physical, emotional and social challenges presented by the illness. It also supports and builds programs that visualize success, to make today and tomorrow better for those who face the illness. For info: Tim & Tom Gullikson Foundation, 8000 Sears Tower, Chicago, IL 60606. Phone: (888) GULLIKSON. Fax: (312) 876-7934. Web: www.gulliksonfoundation.org.

UNITED KINGDOM: MAY DAY BANK HOLIDAY. May 1. Bank and public holiday in England, Wales, Scotland and Northern Ireland. Annually, the first Monday in May.

UPDATE YOUR REFERENCES WEEK. May 1–5. A reminder to all career professionals to update their references annually, because people are always moving or changing jobs. Additionally, it reminds former supervisors, etc, of who you are. Keeping an updated list of references means job seekers can be ready when the opportunity presents itself. For info: Laura DeCarlo, Professional Resume Writing & Research Assoc, 1665 Clover Circle, Melbourne, FL 32935. Phone: (800) 715-3442. Fax: (321) 752-7513. E-mail: info@prwra.com. Web: www.prwra .com.

U-2 INCIDENT: ANNIVERSARY. May 1, 1960. On the eve of a summit meeting between US President Dwight D. Eisenhower and Soviet Premier Nikita Khrushchev, a U-2 espionage plane flying at about 60,000 feet was shot down over Sverdlovsk, in central USSR. The pilot, CIA agent Francis Gary Powers, survived the crash, as did large parts of the aircraft, a suicide kit and sophisticated surveillance equipment. The sensational event, which US officials described as a weather reconnaissance flight gone astray, resulted in cancellation of the summit meeting. Pow-

ers was tried, convicted and sentenced to 10 years in prison by a Moscow court. In 1962 he was returned to the US in exchange for an imprisoned Soviet spy. He died in a helicopter crash in 1977. See also: "Powers, Francis Gary: Birth Anniversary" (Aug 17).

VEGETARIAN RESOURCE GROUP'S ESSAY CONTEST FOR KIDS. May 1. Children ages 18 and under are encouraged to submit a two–three-page essay on topics related to vegetarianism. Essays accepted up to May 1. Winners announced Sept 15 and will receive a $50 savings bond. For info: The Vegetarian Resource Group, PO Box 1463, Baltimore, MD 21203. Phone: (410) 366-8343. E-mail: vrg@vrg.org. Web: www .vrg.org.

WILLIAMS, ARCHIE: BIRTH ANNIVERSARY. May 1, 1915. Archie Williams, along with Jesse Owens and others, debunked Hitler's theory of the superiority of Aryan athletes at the 1936 Berlin Olympics. As a black member of the US team Williams won a gold medal by running the 400-meter in 46.5 seconds (.4 second slower than his own record of earlier that year). Williams, who was born at Oakland, CA, earned a degree in mechanical engineering from the University of California–Berkeley in 1939 but had to dig ditches for a time because they weren't hiring black engineers. He became an airplane pilot and for 22 years trained Tuskegee Institute pilots, including the black air corps of WWII. When asked during a 1981 interview about his treatment by the Nazis during the 1936 Olympics, he replied, "Well, over there at least we didn't have to ride in the back of the bus." Archie Williams died June 24, 1993, at Fairfax, CA.

WOMEN'S HEALTH CARE MONTH. May 1–31. To initiate a public education campaign devoted to increasing awareness of the many health concerns unique to women. Focus will be on the prevention of the major causes of death and poor health among women—heart disease, cancer, arthritis, osteoporosis and bone fractures—as well as on depression and alcoholism in women. There is a $15 charge for kit materials. Annually, the month of May. For info: Pharmacists Planning Service, Inc, c/o Pharmacists Council for Women's Health, 101 Lucas Valley Rd, #210, San Rafael, CA 94903. Phone: (415) 479-8628. Fax: (415) 479-8608. E-mail: ppsi@aol.com. Web: www.ppsinc.org.

YOUNG ACHIEVERS MONTH. May 1–31. International Leadership Network's Young Achievers Program recognizes and encourages positive achievement, behavior, leadership and service. Community and national recognition events honor student leaders in grades 5–11. Annually, the month of May. For info: Jim Eichhorst, 1750 S Brentwood Blvd, Ste 502, St Louis, MO 63144. Phone: (314) 961-5978. Fax: (314) 961-8716. E-mail: inleadnet@aol.com. Web: www.YoungAchievers.us.

BIRTHDAYS TODAY

Wes Anderson, 37, film director/screenwriter (*The Royal Tenenbaums, Rushmore, Bottle Rocket*), born Houston, TX, May 1, 1969.

Charles (Chuck) Bednarik, 81, Hall of Fame football player, born Bethlehem, PA, May 1, 1925.

Steve Cauthen, 46, former jockey, born Walton, KY, May 1, 1960.

Judy Collins, 67, singer ("Both Sides Now," "Send In the Clowns"), born Seattle, WA, May 1, 1939.

Rita Coolidge, 61, singer ("[Your Love Has Lifted Me] Higher and Higher," "We're All Alone"), born Nashville, TN, May 1, 1945.

Glenn Ford, 90, actor (*The Blackboard Jungle, The Fastest Gun Alive,* "The Family Holvak"), born Sainte-Christine, QC, Canada, May 1, 1916.

Sonny James, 77, singer ("Young Love"), born Jimmy Loden at Hackleburg, AL, May 1, 1929.

Curtis Martin, 33, football player, born Pittsburgh, PA, May 1, 1973.

Bobbie Ann Mason, 66, writer (*In Country, Spence and Lila*), born Mayfield, KY, May 1, 1940.

Tim McGraw, 39, country singer, born Delhi, LA, May 1, 1967.

Charlie Schlatter, 40, actor ("Diagnosis Murder"), born Englewood, NJ, May 1, 1966.

May **2006**	S	M	T	W	T	F	S
		1	2	3	4	5	6
	7	8	9	10	11	12	13
	14	15	16	17	18	19	20
	21	22	23	24	25	26	27
	28	29	30	31			

MAY 2 — TUESDAY
Day 122 — 243 Remaining

BERLIN SURRENDERS: ANNIVERSARY. May 2, 1945. At 6:45 AM, Soviet Marshall Georgi Zhukov accepted the surrender of Berlin, the German capital. The victory came at a terrible cost for the Red Army, with 304,887 men killed, wounded or missing—10 percent of its soldiers. About 125,000 Berliners died in the siege, many by suicide.

CONTRABAND DAYS (PIRATE FESTIVAL). May 2–14. Lake Charles, LA. A major 13-day festival celebrating the contraband treasures pirates are supposed to have hidden along the shores of Lake Charles. Events include a mock invasion by pirates, a boat parade, concerts, fireworks, water events, children's area. Est attendance: 150,000. For info: Marlene C. Hobbs, Exec Dir, Contraband Days, Inc, PO Box 679, Lake Charles, LA 70602. Phone: (337) 436-5508. Fax: (337) 436-1126. E-mail: contraband@cox-internet.com. Web: www.contrabanddays.com.

ISRAEL: REMEMBRANCE DAY (YOM HA'ZIKKARON). May 2. Hebrew calendar date: Iyar 4, 5766. Honors the more than 20,000 soldiers killed in battle since the start of the nation's war for independence in 1947. Began at sundown May 1.

KING JAMES BIBLE PUBLISHED: ANNIVERSARY. May 2, 1611. King James I had appointed a committee of learned men to produce a new translation of the Bible in English. This version, popularly called the King James Version, is known in England as the Authorized Version.

LEE, PINKY (PINCUS LEFF): BIRTH ANNIVERSARY. May 2, 1907. Born at St. Paul, MN. When young, Leff had dreams of becoming an attorney, but abandoned the idea when classmates laughed at his lisp. His show business debut was in burlesque in the 1930s. He is best remembered for "The Pinky Lee Show," which telecast from Los Angeles in the early 1950s. Pinky Lee died Apr 3, 1993, at Mission Viejo, CA.

LEONARDO DA VINCI: DEATH ANNIVERSARY. May 2, 1519. Italian artist, scientist and inventor. Painter of the famed *Last Supper*, perhaps the first painting of the High Renaissance, and of the *Mona Lisa*. Inventor of the first parachute. Born at Vinci, Italy, in 1452 (exact date unknown), he died at Amboise, France.

PRIMARY DAY: LIVE FROM DELAWARE STREET. May 2. Indianapolis, IN. Visit President Benjamin Harrison Home and listen to the conversations and gossip of the day as you enter each room and meet and speak with all the family members and household staff, whose roles are re-created by exceptional actors. Est attendance: 500. For info: PR Dept, President Benjamin Harrison Home, 1230 N Delaware St, Indianapolis, IN 46202. Phone: (317) 631-1888. Fax: (317) 632-5488. Web: www.pbhh.org.

RAY, SATYAJIT: BIRTH ANNIVERSARY. May 2, 1921. Film director Satyajit Ray was born at Calcutta, India. Possibly India's best known film director, he made more than 30 films and won numerous international awards, including an Academy Award for lifetime achievement. His films include the trilogy *Pather Panchali* (1956), *Aparajito* (1956) and *The World of Apu* (1959). Ray died Apr 23, 1992, at Calcutta.

ROBERT'S RULES DAY. May 2, 1837. Anniversary of the birth of Henry M. Robert (General, US Army), author of *Robert's Rules of Order*, a standard parliamentary guide. Born at Robertville, SC. Died at Hornell, NY, May 11, 1923.

SPOCK, BENJAMIN: BIRTH ANNIVERSARY. May 2, 1903. Pediatrician and author, born at New Haven, CT. His book on childrearing, *Common Sense Book of Baby and Child Care* (later called *Baby and Child Care*), has sold more than 30 million copies. In 1955 he became professor of child development at Western Reserve University at Cleveland, OH. He resigned from this position in 1967 to devote his time to the pacifist movement. Spock died at San Diego, CA, Mar 15, 1998.

Christine Baranski, 54, actress ("Cybill"), born Buffalo, NY, May 2, 1952.

David Beckham, 31, soccer player, born Leytonstone, London, England, May 2, 1975.

Elizabeth Berridge, 44, actress ("The John Larroquette Show"), born Westchester, NY, May 2, 1962.

Theodore Bikel, 82, singer, actor (*Man on the Run, My Fair Lady*), born Vienna, Austria, May 2, 1924.

Larry Gatlin, 57, singer, songwriter ("Broken Lady," "All the Gold in California"), born Odessa, TX, May 2, 1949.

Lesley Gore, 60, singer ("I'll Cry if I Want To"), born Tenafly, NJ, May 2, 1946.

Sarah Hughes, 21, Olympic figure skater, born Manhasset, NY, May 2, 1985.

Bianca Jagger, 61, actress, political activist, ex-wife of Mick Jagger, born Managua, Nicaragua, May 2, 1945.

David Suchet, 60, actor ("The Way We Live Now," "Hercule Poirot Mysteries"), born London, England, May 2, 1946.

Jenna Von Oy, 29, actress ("Blossom"), born Newtown, CT, May 2, 1977.

MAY 3 — WEDNESDAY
Day 123 — 242 Remaining

"CBS EVENING NEWS" TV PREMIERE: ANNIVERSARY. May 3, 1948. The news program began as a 15-minute telecast with Douglas Edwards as anchor. Walter Cronkite succeeded him in 1962 and expanded the show to 30 minutes; Eric Sevareid served as commentator. Dan Rather anchored the newscasts upon Cronkite's retirement in 1981. Rather retired in March 2005.

CROSBY, HARRY LILLIS "BING": BIRTH ANNIVERSARY. May 3, 1903. American singer, composer and actor (*White Christmas, High Society*, various *Road* movies, Oscar for *Going My Way*), born at Tacoma, WA. Died while playing golf near Madrid, Spain, Oct 14, 1977.

DOW-JONES TOPS 11,000: ANNIVERSARY. May 3, 1999. The Dow-Jones Index of 30 major industrial stocks topped the 11,000 mark for the first time.

ISRAEL: INDEPENDENCE DAY (YOM HA'ATZMA'UT): ANNIVERSARY. May 3. Hebrew calendar date: Iyar 5, 5766. Celebrates proclamation of independence from British mandatory rule by Palestinian Jews and establishment of the state of Israel and the provisional government May 14, 1948 (Hebrew calendar date: Iyar 5, 5708). Dates in the Hebrew calendar vary from their Gregorian equivalents from year to year. Began at sundown May 2.

JAPAN: CONSTITUTION MEMORIAL DAY. May 3. National holiday commemorating adoption of constitution in 1947.

LUMPY RUG DAY. May 3. To encourage the custom of teasing bigots and trigots for shoving unwelcome facts under the rug. When many cans of worms have been shoved under the rug, the defenders of the status quo obtain a new rug high enough to cover the unwanted facts. For info: Robert L. Birch, Puns Corps, 3108 Dashiell Rd, Falls Church, VA 22042. Phone: (703) 533-3668.

MACHIAVELLI, NICCOLO: BIRTH ANNIVERSARY. May 3, 1469. Italian writer and statesman, born at Florence, Italy. Author of *The Prince*, a book of advice for a ruler that prescribes strong, absolute government. Died at Florence, June 22, 1527.

MEIR, GOLDA: BIRTH ANNIVERSARY. May 3, 1898. Born at Kiev, Russia, Meir was prime minister of Israel from 1969 to 1974. She died at Jerusalem, Dec 8, 1978.

MEXICO: DAY OF THE HOLY CROSS. May 3. Celebrated especially by construction workers and miners, a festive day during which anyone who is building must give a party for the workers. A flower-decorated cross is placed on every piece of new construction in the country.

NATIONAL ANXIETY DISORDERS SCREENING DAY. May 3. Screenings for anxiety and depressive disorders. For info: NADSD, 308 Seaview Ave, Staten Island, NY 10305. Phone: (718) 351-1717 or (888) 442-2022 for screening locations. Fax: (718) 980-5022. E-mail: fffnadsd@aol.com. Web: freedomfrom fear.org.

NATIONAL MEETING PLANNERS APPRECIATION DAY. May 3. To recognize the important role that meeting and convention planners play in promoting tourism in local communities. For info: Beth Williams, Classic Basket, PO Box 36305, Birmingham, AL 35236. Phone: (205) 424-2275. Fax: (205) 428-3469. E-mail: beth@classicbasket.com. Web: www.classic basket.com.

NATIONAL PUBLIC RADIO FIRST BROADCAST: 35th ANNIVERSARY. May 3, 1971. National noncommercial radio network, financed by Corporation for Public Broadcasting, began programming.

PARANORMAL DAY. May 3. A day for all paranormal enthusiasts to get together and share their unique experiences with each other. Seminars, radio broadcasts and readings will take place worldwide. For info: Bob O'Brien, Consumer Advocate, 1061 Koelle Blvd, Seacaucus, NJ 07094. Phone/fax: (201) 865-4775. E-mail: bobtheebest@yahoo.com. Web: www.wtbq.com.

POLAND: CONSTITUTION DAY (SWIETO TRZE-CIEGO MAJA). May 3. National Day. Celebrates ratification of Poland's first constitution, 1791.

ROBINSON, SUGAR RAY: BIRTH ANNIVERSARY. May 3, 1921. Ray ("Sugar Ray") Robinson, boxer, born Walker Smith, Jr, at Detroit, MI. Generally considered "pound for pound the greatest boxer of all time," Robinson was a welterweight and middleweight champion who won 175 professional fights and lost only 19. A smooth and precise boxer, he fought until he was 45, dabbled in show business and established the Sugar Ray Robinson Youth Foundation to counter juvenile delinquency. To this day, his name connotes class, style and dignity. Died at Los Angeles, CA, Apr 12, 1989.

SUNFEST. May 3–7. West Palm Beach, FL. Florida's largest music, art and waterfront festival features some of the best acts in jazz, rock, blues and more. Family-oriented event includes a juried art show, fireworks, water and youth park activities and fabulous foods. Annually, the first weekend in May. Est attendance: 300,000. For info: SunFest of Palm Beach County, Inc, 525 Clematis St, West Palm Beach, FL 33401. Phone: (561) 659-5980 or (800) SUN-FEST. Fax: (561) 659-3567. E-mail: sunfest@sun-fest.com. Web: www.sunfest.com.

UNITED NATIONS: WORLD PRESS FREEDOM DAY. May 3. A day to recognize that a free, pluralistic and independent press is an essential component of any democratic society and to promote press freedom in the world. For info: United Nations, Dept of Public Info, New York, NY 10017. Web: www.un .org.

★ ★ ★

May	S	M	T	W	T	F	S
2006		1	2	3	4	5	6
	7	8	9	10	11	12	13
	14	15	16	17	18	19	20
	21	22	23	24	25	26	27
	28	29	30	31			

WORDSMITH DAY. May 3. A day dedicated to those who write the promotional prose that markets our goods and services, from copywriters to marketing writers to all-around wordsmiths. For info: Mambo Productions, 14212 164th Ave SE, Ste 303, Renton, WA 98059. Phone: (425) 204-9800. Web: www.wordsmith day.com.

BIRTHDAYS TODAY

James Brown, 73, singer, songwriter ("Papa's Got a Brand New Bag"), born Augusta, GA, May 3, 1933.

Greg Gumbel, 60, TV personality, sportscaster, born New Orleans, LA, May 3, 1946.

Dulé Hill, 32, actor ("The West Wing"), born Orange, NJ, May 3, 1974.

Jeffrey John Hornacek, 43, former basketball player, born Elmhurst, IL, May 3, 1963.

Engelbert Humperdinck, 70, singer ("Release Me," "After the Lovin' "), born Gerry Dorsey at Madras, India, May 3, 1936.

Pete Seeger, 87, folksinger, songwriter ("Where Have All the Flowers Gone?"), born New York, NY, May 3, 1919.

Frankie Valli, 69, singer ("Can't Take My Eyes Off You," "Grease"), born Newark, NJ, May 3, 1937.

David Vitter, 45, US Senator (R, Louisiana), born New Orleans, LA, May 3, 1961.

Ron Wyden, 57, US Senator (D, Oregon), born Wichita, KS, May 3, 1949.

MAY 4 — THURSDAY
Day 124 — 241 Remaining

"ANOTHER WORLD" TV PREMIERE: ANNIVERSARY. May 4, 1964. Created by Irna Phillips and sponsored by P&G, this soap was set in fictional Bay City. It was the first soap to air for a full hour and the first to beget two spin-offs ("Somerset" and "Texas"). Charles Durning, Ted Shackelford, Eric Roberts, Ray Liotta, Kyra Sedgwick, Faith Ford, Morgan Freeman, Jackée Harry, Victoria Wyndham and Valarie Pettiford are some of its well-known alums. The show was cancelled in 1999 and the last episode aired June 25, 1999.

CANADA: CANADIAN TULIP FESTIVAL. May 4–22. Ottawa, ON. The world's largest tulip festival with more than three million tulips in bloom. See a parade of decorated boats, floral displays, nonstop entertainment and fireworks. This event grew out of a thank-you gift of bulbs for providing refuge to the Dutch royal family. Est attendance: 1,000,000. For info: Canadian Tulip Festival, 112 Nelson St, Ste 106, Ottawa, ON, Canada K1N 7R5. Phone: (613) 567-5757. Fax: (613) 567-6216. E-mail: info@tulipfestival.ca. Web: www.tulipfestival.ca.

CANADA: THUNDER BAY CHAMBER OF COMMERCE TRADE SHOW. May 4–6. Thunder Bay, ON. For info: Thunder Bay Chamber of Commerce, 200 Syndicate Ave S, Ste 102, Thunder Bay, ON, Canada P7E 1C9. Phone: (807) 624-2621. Fax: (807) 622-7752. E-mail: nancy@tb-chamber.on.ca. Web: tb-chamber.on.ca.

CHINA: YOUTH DAY. May 4. Annual public holiday "recalls the demonstration on May 4, 1919, by thousands of patriotic students in Beijing's Tiananmen Square to protest imperialist aggression in China."

CINCO DE MAYO FIESTA. May 4–7. Tom McCall Waterfront Park. Portland, OR. A multicultural celebration with ethnic foods, continuous entertainment, dancing, arts and crafts booths. Part of Portland's Sister City program with Guadalajara, Mexico. Est attendance: 300,000. For info: Portland-Guadalajara Sister City Assn. Phone: (503) 232-7550. Web: www.cincodemayo.org.

CURAÇAO: MEMORIAL DAY. May 4. Victims of WWII are honored on this day. Military ceremonies at the War Monument. Not an official public holiday.

DISCOVERY OF JAMAICA BY CHRISTOPHER COLUMBUS: ANNIVERSARY. May 4, 1494. Christopher Columbus discovered Jamaica. The Arawak Indians were its first inhabitants.

ENGLAND: MITSUBISHI MOTORS BADMINTON HORSE TRIALS. May 4–7. Badminton, Gloucestershire. Famous international horse trials consisting of show jumping, cross country and dressage. Est attendance: 200,000. For info: Box Office, Badminton Horse Trials, Badminton, Glos, England GL9 1DF. Phone: (44) (1454) 21-8272. Fax: (44) (1454) 21-8596. E-mail: info@badminton-horse.co.uk. Web: www.badminton-horse.co.uk.

FESTIVAL OF NATIONS. May 4–7. River Centre, St. Paul, MN. Celebration by 90 ethnic groups, each presenting cultural exhibits, food specialties, folk dances and folk arts to the public. Est attendance: 85,000. For info: Intl Institute of Minnesota, 1694 Como Ave, St. Paul, MN 55108. Phone: (651) 647-0191. Fax: (651) 647-9268. Web: www.festivalofnations.com.

FIRST WOMAN BRITISH PRIME MINISTER: ANNIVERSARY. May 4, 1979. With the Conservative Party victory in the British election of May 3, 1979, Margaret Thatcher accepted Queen Elizabeth's appointment as prime minister on May 4. She thus became the first woman prime minister in 700 years of English parliamentary history. Thatcher, dubbed by her party the "Iron Maiden" for her toughness, held the office until forced to resign on Nov 22, 1990.

FREEDOM RIDERS: 45th ANNIVERSARY. May 4, 1961. Militant students joined James Farmer of the Congress of Racial Equality (CORE) to conduct "freedom rides" on public transportation from Washington, DC, across the deep South to New Orleans. The trips were intended to test Supreme Court decisions and Interstate Commerce Commission regulations prohibiting discrimination in interstate travel. In several places riders were brutally beaten by local people and policemen. On May 14, members of the Ku Klux Klan attacked the Freedom Riders in Birmingham, AL, while local police watched. In Mississippi, Freedom Riders were jailed. They never made it to New Orleans. The rides were patterned after a similar challenge to segregation, the 1947 Journey of Reconciliation, which tested the US Supreme Court's June 3, 1946, ban against segregation in interstate bus travel.

HAYMARKET SQUARE RIOT: ANNIVERSARY. May 4, 1886. Labor union unrest at Chicago led to violence when a crowd of unemployed men tried to enter the McCormick Reaper Works, where a strike was under way. Although no one was killed, anarchist groups called a mass meeting in Haymarket Square to avenge the "massacre." When the police advanced on the demonstrators, a bomb was thrown and several policemen were killed. Four leaders of the demonstration were hanged and another committed suicide in jail. Three others were given jail terms. The case aroused considerable controversy around the world. See also: "Haymarket Pardon: Anniversary" (June 26).

HEPBURN, AUDREY: BIRTH ANNIVERSARY. May 4, 1929. Audrey Hepburn, whose first major movie role in *Roman Holiday* (1953) won her an Academy Award as best actress, was born Edda Van Heemstra Hepburn-Rusten near Brussels, Belgium. She made 26 movies during her career and received four additional Oscar nominations. During the latter years of her life Hepburn served as spokesperson for the United Nations Children's Fund, traveling worldwide raising money for the organization. Audrey Hepburn died Jan 20, 1993, at Tolochenaz, Switzerland.

INTERNATIONAL RESPECT FOR CHICKENS DAY. May 4. Launched in 2005, International Respect for Chickens Day is a project of United Poultry Concerns, a nonprofit organization that promotes the compassionate and respectful treatment of domestic fowl. IRCD is a day to celebrate chickens throughout the world by encouraging people to do an ACTION for chickens on May 4, showing the world that chickens matter, too. Ideas include arranging a library display/video presentation, a Respect for Chickens Day school celebration, letters to the editor, radio talk-show participation, showing the movie *Chicken Run*, local mall exhibit, etc. UPC supplies posters, brochures, videos and event ideas. For info: United Poultry Concerns, PO Box 150, Machipongo, VA 23405. Phone: (757) 678-7875. Fax: (757) 678-5070. E-mail: karen@upc-online.org. Web: www.upc-online.org.

KENT STATE STUDENTS' MEMORIAL DAY: ANNIVERSARY. May 4, 1970. Four students (Allison Krause, 19; Sandra Lee Scheuer, 20; Jeffrey Glenn Miller, 20 and William K. Schroeder, 19) were killed by the National Guard during demonstrations against the Vietnam War at Kent (Ohio) State University.

LOYALTY DAYS AND SEAFAIR FESTIVAL. May 4–7. Newport, OR. Celebration of loyalty to America. Parade, queen and court, Navy ships in port and other activities. Est attendance: 3,000. For info: Chamber of Commerce, 555 SW Coast Hwy, Newport, OR 97365. Phone: (541) 265-8801 or (800) 262-7844. Fax: (541) 265-5589. E-mail: chamber@newport.com.

MANN, HORACE: BIRTH ANNIVERSARY. May 4, 1796. American educator, author, public servant, known as the "father of public education in the US," was born at Franklin, MA. Founder of Westfield (MA) State College, president of Antioch College and editor of the influential *Common School Journal*. Mann died at Yellow Springs, OH, Aug 2, 1859.

MARTIN Z. MOLLUSK DAY. May 4. Moorlyn Terrace Beach, Ocean City, NJ. If Martin Z. Mollusk, a hermit crab, sees his shadow at 11 AM, EST, summer comes a week early in Ocean City—if he doesn't, summer begins on time. For info: Mark Soifer, City Hall, 9th St and Asbury Ave, Ocean City, NJ 08226. Phone: (609) 525-9300 or (609) 399-0272. Fax: (609) 399-0374. E-mail: mtsoifer@aol.com.

★ **NATIONAL DAY OF PRAYER.** May 4. Presidential Proclamation always issued for the first Thursday in May since 1981. (PL100–307 of May 5, 1988.) Beginning in 1957, a day in October was designated, except in 1972 and 1975 through 1977.

NATIONAL DAY OF REASON. May 4. The event is used to promote reason and critical thought. Participants across the world are encouraged to celebrate the life of the thoughtful mind and inject rational thought into their actions and behaviors. Annually, the first Thursday in May. For info: American Humanist Assn, 1777 T St NW, Washington, DC 20009-7125. Phone: (202) 238-9088. Fax: (202) 238-9003. E-mail: aha@americanhumanist.org. Web: www.nationaldayofreason.org.

PELLA TULIP TIME FESTIVAL. May 4–6. Pella, IA. To pay homage to the founders of this predominately Dutch community. Activities include coronation of queen, parades, flowers, Dutch singing and dancing. Est attendance: 100,000. For info: Pella Historical Society, 507 Franklin, Pella, IA 50219. Phone: (641) 628-4311. E-mail: info@pellatuliptime.com. Web: www.pellatuliptime.com.

RHODE ISLAND: INDEPENDENCE DAY. May 4. Rhode Island abandoned allegiance to Great Britain in 1776.

SPACE MILESTONE: *ATLANTIS* (US). May 4, 1989. First American planetary expedition in 11 years. Space shuttle *Atlantis* was launched, its major objective to deploy the *Magellan* spacecraft on its way to Venus to map the planet's surface. The shuttle was on its 65th orbit when it landed May 8, mission accomplished.

TYLER, JULIA GARDINER: BIRTH ANNIVERSARY. May 4, 1820. Second wife of John Tyler, tenth president of the US, born at Gardiners Island, NY. Died at Richmond, VA, July 10, 1889.

WADE-DAVIS RECONSTRUCTION BILL PASSES THE HOUSE: ANNIVERSARY. May 4, 1864. Over the objections of President Lincoln, the House of Representatives on this date passed the Wade-Davis Reconstruction bill, containing stiff punitive measures against the South that if put into law would have destroyed Lincoln's more moderate reconstruction aims. The bill was also adamantly opposed by Radical Republicans, led by Thaddeus Stevens for whom it was insufficiently severe in its treatment of the Southern rebels. Lincoln eventually killed the bill by using the pocket veto.

BIRTHDAYS TODAY

Nickolas Ashford, 64, singer, songwriter ("Ain't No Mountain High Enough"), born Fairfield, SC, May 4, 1942.
Maynard Ferguson, 78, bandleader, born Verdun, QC, Canada, May 4, 1928.
Ben Grieve, 30, baseball player, born Arlington, TX, May 4, 1976.
David Guterson, 50, author (*Snow Falling on Cedars*), born Seattle, WA, May 4, 1956.
Jackie Jackson, 55, singer (Jackson 5), born Sigmund Esco Jackson at Gary, IN, May 4, 1951.
Roberta Peters, 76, opera singer (retired), born the Bronx, NY, May 4, 1930.
Dawn Staley, 36, basketball player, born Philadelphia, PA, May 4, 1970.
Randy Travis, 47, country and western musician ("Forever and Ever, Amen"), born Marshville, NC, May 4, 1959.
George F. Will, 65, editor, columnist, baseball executive, born Champaign, IL, May 4, 1941.
Pia Zadora, 50, actress, singer, dancer, born Hoboken, NJ, May 4, 1956.

MAY 5 — FRIDAY
Day 125 — 240 Remaining

AMERICAN MEDICAL ASSOCIATION FOUNDED: ANNIVERSARY. May 5, 1847. The American Medical Association was organized at a meeting at Philadelphia attended by 250 delegates. This was the first national medical convention in the US.

BATTLE OF THE WILDERNESS: ANNIVERSARY. May 5, 1864. The Battle of the Wilderness was the first major encounter between opposing troops under Robert E. Lee and Ulysses S. Grant. So named for the area of dense forest and underbrush of northern Virginia where the battle occurred, the fighting was especially fierce with opposing armies often fighting at point-blank range as the battle lines became obscured in the smoke-filled forest. Both sides suffered heavy casualties totaling more than 28,000, and after the fighting had ceased on the second day, more than 200 wounded Federal troops were trapped and killed by the flames of fires started by the battle.

May 2006	S	M	T	W	T	F	S
		1	2	3	4	5	6
	7	8	9	10	11	12	13
	14	15	16	17	18	19	20
	21	22	23	24	25	26	27
	28	29	30	31			

BEARD, JAMES: BIRTH ANNIVERSARY. May 5, 1903. The Father of American Cooking was born at Portland, OR. In a long and busy culinary career, he penned more than 20 classic cookbooks, appeared on television's first cooking show in 1946 and was an enthusiastic ambassador for the American style of cooking. He died Jan 21, 1985. His Greenwich Village brownstone is America's only culinary historic landmark and serves as the headquarters of the James Beard Foundation.

BIG TEN MEN'S GOLF CHAMPIONSHIPS. May 5–7. Northwestern University, Evanston, IL. For info: Big Ten Conference, 1500 W Higgins Rd, Park Ridge, IL 60068-6300. Phone: (847) 696-1010. Fax: (847) 696-1110. Web: www.bigten.org.

BLY, NELLIE: BIRTH ANNIVERSARY. May 5, 1867. Born at Cochran's Mills, PA. Nellie Bly was the pseudonym used by pioneering American journalist Elizabeth Cochrane Seaman. Like her namesake in a Stephen Foster song, Nellie Bly was a social reformer and human rights advocate. As a journalist, she is best known for her exposé of conditions in what were then known as "insane asylums," where she posed as an "inmate." As an adventurer, she is best known for her 1889–90 around-the-world tour in 72 days, in which she bettered the time of Jules Verne's fictional character Phileas Fogg by eight days. She died at New York, NY, Jan 27, 1922.

BONZA BOTTLER DAY™. May 5. To celebrate when the number of the day is the same as the number of the month. Bonza Bottler Day™ is an excuse to have a party at least once a month. For more information, see Jan 1. For info: Gail M. Berger, 14 Fernwood Dr, Taylors, SC 29687. Phone: (864) 609-9874. E-mail: gberger5@aol.com.

CARTOONISTS DAY. May 5. To honor all cartoonists in the industry: animation, magazines, comic strips, etc. For info: Ken Alvine, Creative Comic Syndicate, 1608 S Dakota Ave, Sioux Falls, SD 57105. Phone: (605) 336-9434. Fax: (605) 338-3501. E-mail: kenalvine@aol.com.

CHINA: BIRTHDAY OF LORD BUDDHA. May 5. Religious observances are held in Buddhist temples and Buddha's statue is bathed. Annually, the eighth day of fourth lunar month. Date in other countries will differ from China's.

DANDELION MAY FEST. May 5–6. Der Marktplatz, Dover, OH. Old-fashioned festival includes finals in a nationwide dandelion recipe contest, live entertainment, slides and presentations about dandelions and food booths featuring dishes made from dandelions, including dandelion coffee ice cream, dandelion pizza, dandelion bread and dandelion omelettes. Also, dandelion wine and jelly tasting, family entertainment and 5k fun run. Festival includes 13th National Dandelion Cook-Off; for entry forms for cook-off call: (800) 843-9463. Est attendance: 15,000. For info: Anita Davis, Coord, Der Marktplatz-Breitenbach Wine Cellars, 5934 Old Route 39 NW, Dover, OH 44622. Phone: (330) 343-3603. Fax: (330) 343-8290. E-mail: amishwine@tusco.net. Web: www.breitenbachwine.com.

EMMETT KELLY CLOWN FESTIVAL. May 5–6. Downtown Houston, MO. Houston was the home of Emmett Kelly, and this festival in his honor features a carnival, clown school, parade on Saturday, arts & crafts, Big Top performances, souvenir sales, clown competition. Appearance by the daughter of Emmett Kelly, Sr, Stasia Kelly, and his grandson, Joey Kelly. Est attendance: 5,000. For info: Houston Area Chamber of Commerce, PO Box 374, Houston, MO 65483. Phone: (417) 967-2220. Fax: (417) 967-2178. E-mail: chamber@train.missouri.org.

ETHIOPIA: PATRIOTS VICTORY DAY. May 5. National holiday. Commemorates the 1941 liberation of Addis Ababa by British and Ethiopian forces.

FASHION SHOW. May 5. Mount Mary College, Milwaukee, WI. Student designer fashion show. Est attendance: 1,200. For info: Mary Cain, Mount Mary College, 2900 N Menomonee River Pkwy, Milwaukee, WI 53222-4597. Phone: (414) 256-1210. Fax: (414) 256-1239. E-mail: mktg@mtmary.edu. Web: www.mtmary.edu.

ISLE OF EIGHT FLAGS SHRIMP FESTIVAL. May 5–7. Fernandina Beach, FL, on beautiful Amelia Island. Florida commemorates Fernandina's role as the birthplace of the modern shrimping industry. Multi-event festival includes juried fine arts and crafts show, entertainment, antiques, pirates, children's fun zone and food. Est attendance: 150,000. For info: Isle of Eight Flags Shrimp Festival, PO Box 6146, Fernandina Beach, FL 32035. Phone: (904) 261-3248 or toll-free (866) 4-AMELIA. E-mail: 4info@shrimpfestival.com. Web: www.shrimpfestival.com.

JAPAN: CHILDREN'S DAY. May 5. National holiday. Observed on the fifth day of the fifth month each year.

JOHNSON, AMY: FLIGHT ANNIVERSARY. May 5, 1930. Yorkshire-born Amy Johnson began the first successful solo flight by a woman from England to Australia. Leaving Croydon Airport in a de Havilland Tiger Moth named *Jason*, she flew 9,960 miles to Port Darwin, Australia, arriving May 28. The song "Amy, Wonderful Amy" celebrated the fame of this "wonder girl of the air," who became a legend in her own lifetime. Serving as an air ferry pilot during WWII, she was lost over the Thames Estuary in 1941.

JOSEY'S WORLD CHAMPION JUNIOR BARREL RACE. May 5–7. Josey's Ranch, Marshall, TX. Youth barrel-racing competition. Annually, the first weekend in May. Est attendance: 4,000. For info: Patsy Dreesen, Dir of Conv and Visitor Development, Marshall Chamber of Commerce, PO Box 520, Marshall, TX 75671. Phone: (903) 935-7868. Fax: (903) 935-9982. E-mail: marshallcvd@hotmail.com. Web: www.marshalltxchamber.com.

KANSAS BARBED WIRE SWAP/SELL. May 5–6. LaCrosse, KS. Barbed Wire Collectors Association show and meeting. Est attendance: 200. For info: Kansas Barbed Wire Collectors Assn, PO Box 578, LaCrosse, KS 67548. Phone: (785) 222-9900.

LANDON AZALEA GARDEN FESTIVAL AND ANTIQUE SHOW. May 5–7. Bethesda, MD. Garden stroll amid 15,000 blooming azaleas. Plant sale, flower show, historic farmhouse tour, lunch, musical entertainment and tons of unique boutique shops and gift vendors. Est attendance: 30,000. For info: Landon School, 6101 Wilson Ln, Bethesda, MD 20817. Phone: (301) 320-1006. Fax: (301) 320-1399. E-mail: claudine_gnall@landon.net. Web: www.landon.net.

LUCKY MAY SHOW AND SALE. May 5–7 (also May 12–14; 19–21; 26–29). Chapel Hill, NC. Each Friday, Saturday and Sunday in May, plus Memorial Day. Unique architectural antiques, featuring an extensive collection of period wrought iron artifacts (especially iron gates, garden art and home embellishments). For info: Gaines Steer, The Last Unicorn, 536 Edwards Ridge Road, Chapel Hill, NC 27517. Phone: (919) 968-8440. E-mail: info@thelastunicorn.com. Web: www.thelastunicorn.com.

MAGIC DRAGON STREET MEET NATIONALS AND EXTREME CAR SHOWS. May 5–7. Lake Ozark, MO. 18th annual meet features more than 700 street rods, customs, trucks, street machines and motorcycles from throughout the US. Always the first weekend in May. Est attendance: 7,000. For info: Lake Area Chamber of Commerce, PO Box 1570, Lake Ozark, MO 65049. Phone: (800) 451-4117 or (573) 964-1008. Fax: (573) 964-1010. E-mail: Candyw@lakeareachamber.com.

MARX, KARL: BIRTH ANNIVERSARY. May 5, 1818. German socialist, founder and father of modern communism, author of *Das Kapital* and (with Friedrich Engels) the *Communist Manifesto*. Born at Treves, Germany, he died at London, England, Mar 14, 1883, at age 64.

MAY DAY. May 5. Lumpkin, GA. Celebration of the planting season with traditional May Day activities and the Maypole Dance. Est attendance: 800. For info: Patty Cannington, PR Dir, Westville Village, PO Box 1850, Lumpkin, GA 31815. Phone: (229) 838-6310 or (888) 733-1850. Web: www.westville.org.

MEXICO: BATTLE OF PUEBLA: ANNIVERSARY. May 5, 1862. The Mexican Army defeated French troops at the city of Puebla. This day is commemorated as a national holiday in Mexico.

MEXICO: CINCO DE MAYO: ANNIVERSARY. May 5. Mexican national holiday recognizing the anniversary of the Battle of Puebla in 1862, in which Mexican troops under General Ignacio Zaragoza, outnumbered three to one, defeated invading French forces of Napoleon III. Anniversary is observed by Mexicans everywhere with parades, festivals, dances and speeches.

MOON PHASE: FIRST QUARTER. May 5. Moon enters First Quarter phase at 1:13 AM, EDT.

NETHERLANDS: LIBERATION DAY. May 5. Marks liberation of the Netherlands from Nazi Germany in 1945.

POWER, TYRONE: BIRTH ANNIVERSARY. May 5, 1913. American actor, best known for his motion picture action-adventure roles, Tyrone Power was born at Cincinnati, OH. He died Nov 15, 1958, at Madrid, Spain.

RICHMOND'S MUSHROOM FESTIVAL. May 5–6. Richmond, MO. Parade, arts and crafts, carnival, bands and stage shows. Est attendance: 5,000. For info: Exec Dir, Chamber of Commerce, 107 N Thornton, Richmond, MO 64085. Phone: (816) 776-6916. Fax: (816) 776-6917. E-mail: cofcommerce@mchsi.com. Web: www.richmondchamber.org.

SOUTH KOREA: CHILDREN'S DAY. May 5. A time for families to take their children on excursions. Parks and children's centers throughout the country are packed with excited and colorfully dressed children. A national holiday since 1975.

SPACE MILESTONE: *FREEDOM 7* (US): 45th ANNIVERSARY. May 5, 1961. First US astronaut in space, second man in space, Alan Shepard, Jr, projected 115 miles into space in suborbital flight reaching a speed of more than 5,000 miles per hour. This was the first piloted Mercury mission.

STAMP EXPO. May 5–7. Radisson Hotel, Anaheim, CA. Est attendance: 4,000. For info: Israel Bick, Exec Dir, Intl Stamp & Coin Collectors Society, PO Box 854, Van Nuys, CA 91408. Phone: (818) 997-6496. Fax: (818) 988-4337. E-mail: iibick@sbcglobal.net. Web: www.bick.net.

STOCK MARKET CRASH OF 1893: ANNIVERSARY. May 5, 1893. Wall Street stock prices took a sudden drop. By the end of the year 600 banks had closed. The Philadelphia and Reading, the Erie, the Northern Pacific, the Union Pacific and the Atchison, Topeka and Santa Fe railroads had gone into receivership; 15,000 other businesses went into bankruptcy. Other than the Great Depression of the 1930s, this was the worst economic crisis in US history; 15–20 percent of the workforce was unemployed.

SUGARLOAF CRAFTS FESTIVAL. May 5–7. Dulles Expo Center, Chantilly, VA. This show, now in its 6th year, features more than 300 nationally recognized craft designers and fine artists displaying and selling their original creations. Includes craft demonstrations, live music, specialty food, hourly gift certificate drawings and more. Est attendance: 15,000. For info: Sugarloaf Mountain Works, 200 Orchard Ridge Dr, #215, Gaithersburg, MD 20878. Phone: (800) 210-9900. Fax: (301) 253-9620. Web: www.sugarloafcrafts.com.

THAILAND: CORONATION DAY. May 5. National holiday. Commemorates the crowning of the current king in 1946.

TOAD SUCK DAZE. May 5–7. Downtown, Conway, AR. 25th annual event features toad jumping contests, concerts, parade, street dancing, carnival, softball tournament, 5k and 10k runs, arts and crafts and more. Annually, the first weekend in May. Est attendance: 160,000. For info: Conway Chamber of Commerce, 900 Oak St, Conway, AR 72032. Phone: (501) 327-7788. Fax: (501) 327-7790. Web: www.toadsuck.org.

TOTALLY CHIPOTLE DAY. May 5. To help trumpet what is proving to be one of the most popular "new" flavors in the US. Totally Chipotle Day helps familiarize the uninitiated with the delectable chipotle—a smoked jalapeño pepper—and its somewhat difficult pronunciation. Celebrated alongside Cinco de Mayo to honor its exclusively Mexican-Indian heritage. For info: M. Larkin. E-mail: info@TotallyChipotle.com. Web: www.TotallyChipotle.com.

BIRTHDAYS TODAY

Pat Carroll, 79, actress (Emmy for "Caesar's Hour"; "The Ted Knight Show"), born Shreveport, LA, May 5, 1927.

Richard E. Grant, 49, actor (*Henry and June, LA Story, The Age of Innocence*), born Mbabane, Swaziland, May 5, 1957.

Lance Henriksen, 63, actor (*Dog Day Afternoon, The Terminator, Near Dark*), born New York, NY, May 5, 1943 (some sources say 1940).

Jean-Pierre Leaud, 62, actor (Truffaut's *The 400 Blows, Love at 20, Stolen Kisses, Bed and Board*), born Paris, France, May 5, 1944.

Michael Murphy, 68, actor (*Nashville, Manhattan, Salvador*), born Los Angeles, CA, May 5, 1938.

Ziggy Palffy, 34, hockey player, born Skalica, Czechoslovakia, May 5, 1972.

Michael Palin, 63, actor, comedian ("Monty Python's Flying Circus," *Life of Brian*), born Sheffield, Yorkshire, England, May 5, 1943.

Tina Yothers, 33, singer, actress ("Family Ties"), born Whittier, CA, May 5, 1973.

MAY 6 — SATURDAY
Day 126 — 239 Remaining

APPLE BLOSSOM FESTIVAL. May 6–7. Gettysburg, PA. An annual event held the first weekend in May at the South Mountain Fairgrounds. Est attendance: 20,000. For info: Gettysburg CVB, PO Box 4117, Gettysburg, PA 17325. Phone: (717) 334-6274. Fax: (717) 334-1166. E-mail: gettysburgcvb@dejazzd.com. Web: www.gettysburgcvb.org.

ASTRONOMY DAY. May 6. To take astronomy to the people. International Astronomy Day is observed on a Saturday near the first quarter moon between mid-April and mid-May. Cosponsored by 13 astronomical organizations. See also: "Astronomy Week" (May 1–7). For info: Gary E. Tomlinson, Coord, Astronomy Day Headquarters, 30 Star Gazer Ln, Comstock Park, MI 49321.

May 2006	S	M	T	W	T	F	S
		1	2	3	4	5	6
	7	8	9	10	11	12	13
	14	15	16	17	18	19	20
	21	22	23	24	25	26	27
	28	29	30	31			

Phone: (616) 784-9518. E-mail: gtomlins@sbcglobal.net. Web: www.astroleague.org.

BABE RUTH'S FIRST MAJOR LEAGUE HOME RUN: ANNIVERSARY. May 6, 1915. George Herman "Babe" Ruth of the Boston Red Sox hit his first major league home run in a game against the New York Yankees in New York.

BANNISTER BREAKS FOUR-MINUTE MILE: ANNIVERSARY. May 6, 1954. Running for the British Amateur Athletic Association in a meet at Oxford University, Roger Bannister broke the four-minute barrier with a time of 3:59.4. Four minutes for a mile at the time was considered not only a physical barrier but also a psychological one.

BARK IN THE PARK. May 6. Lincoln Park, Chicago, IL. In recognition of Be Kind to Animals Week, thousands of paws and feet will hit the ground walking for this 5k event. Entrance fee. Est attendance: 3,500. For info: The Anti-Cruelty Society, 157 W Grand Ave, Chicago, IL 60610. Phone: (312) 329-8726. E-mail: info@anticruelty.org. Web: www.barkinthepark.org.

COMMUNITYWIDE GARAGE SALE. May 6. Elgin, TX. Bargains abound in Elgin. More than 100 garage sales held on the same day. Downtown businesses have sidewalk sales. Visitors and locals can seek out treasures in a historic setting. Annually, the first Saturday in May. Est attendance: 3,000. For info: Sharon McCall, 1462 Old Lytton Springs Rd, Lockhart, TX 78644. Phone: (512) 263-2512. E-mail: smccall632@aol.com.

COTTON PICKIN' FAIR. May 6–7 (also Oct 7–8). Gay, GA. Skilled artisans feature art, antiques and crafts in a 1910-era venue. The Peach Packing Shed, Cotton Gin and Warehouse, 1891 Farmhouse and a number of smaller buildings create a unique backdrop for a great day of family fun in the country. Includes a wonderful variety of great food plus live entertainment on six stages. Biannually: the first weekends of May and October. Est attendance: 35,000. For info: Cotton Pickin' Fair. Phone: (706) 538-6814. E-mail: info@cpfair.com. Web: www.cpfair.com.

DO DAH DAY. May 6. Birmingham, AL. Free music, arts and crafts festival and more to raise funds for the local animal shelters in Birmingham. A mile-long parade kicks off the event. Annually, the first Saturday in May. Est attendance: 50,000. For info: Do Dah Day Committee, PO Box 55951, Birmingham, AL 35255. Phone: (205) 595-3771. Web: www.dodahday.org.

ENGLAND: HELSTON FURRY DANCE. May 6. The world-famous Helston Furry Dance is held each year on May 8 (except when the 8th is a Sunday or Monday, in which case it is held on the preceding Saturday). Dancing around the streets of Helston, Cornwall, begins early in the morning and continues throughout the day. The "Furry" dance leaves Guildhall at the stroke of noon and winds its way in and out of many of the larger buildings.

FISHING CONTEST. May 6. Lake Shenandoah County Park, Lakewood, NJ. Catch the longest fish of a specific species. Novice or expert. Prizes awarded. Bait and Tackle Shop on premises. Picnic area. Rain or shine. Children $1, adults $3. Est attendance: 500. For info: Mickey Coen, Coord, Wells Mills County Park, 905 Wells Mills Rd, Waretown, NJ 08758. Phone: (609) 971-3085. Fax: (609) 971-9540. Web: www.co.ocean.nj.us/parks/default.htm.

4-WHEEL DRIVE JAMBOREE. May 6–7. Ozark Empire Fairgrounds, Springfield, MO. 4-wheel drive truck show, monster trucks, thunder drags, mud races and more. For info: Ozark Empire Fair, 3001 N Grant, Springfield, MO 65803. Phone: (417) 833-2660. Fax: (417) 833-3769. Web: www.ozarkempirefair.com.

FREUD, SIGMUND: 150th BIRTH ANNIVERSARY. May 6, 1856. Austrian physician, born at Freiberg, Moravia. Founder of psychoanalysis. Freud died at London, England, Sept 23, 1939.

GALVESTON HISTORIC HOMES TOUR. May 6–7 (also May 13–14). Galveston Island, TX. Discover Galveston Island's great treasures of Victorian and post-Victorian architecture as privately owned homes are open to the public for tours. Annually, the first two full weekends in May. For info: Galveston Historical Foundation, 502 20th St, Galveston, TX 77550. Phone: (409) 765-7834. Fax: (409) 765-7851. E-mail: foundation@galvestonhistory.org. Web: www.galvestonhistory.org.

HINDENBURG DISASTER: ANNIVERSARY. May 6, 1937. At 7:20 PM, the dirigible *Hindenburg* exploded as it approached the mooring mast at Lakehurst, NJ, after a transatlantic voyage. Of its 97 passengers and crew, 36 died in the accident, which ended the dream of mass transportation via dirigible.

HOLLAND TULIP TIME FESTIVAL. May 6–13. Holland, MI. A celebration of Dutch culture and heritage as well as the queen of the festival, the tulip. Est attendance: 500,000. For info: Holland Tulip Time Festival, Inc, 171 Lincoln Ave, Holland, MI 49423. Phone: (616) 396-4221 or (800) 822-2770. Fax: (616) 396-4545. E-mail: tulip@tuliptime.org. Web: www.tuliptime.org.

INTERNATIONAL PILATES DAY. May 6. An international celebration of the work of Joseph and Clara Pilates and a day to unite the worldwide Pilates community. Annually, the first Saturday of May. For info: The Pilates Method Alliance—Pilates Day, PO Box 370906, Miami, FL 33137-0906. Phone: (866) 573-4945. Fax: (305) 573-4461. E-mail: info@PilatesDay.com. Web: www.PilatesDay.com or www.pilatesmethodalliance.org.

IRELAND: MAY DAY BANK HOLIDAY. May 6. Bank holiday in the Republic of Ireland.

JOIN HANDS DAY. May 6. To bring youth and adults together to improve their own communities. Sponsored by America's Fraternal Benefit Societies and the Points of Light Foundation and the Volunteer Center National Network. Annually, the first Saturday in May. For info: Join Hands Day, 1315 W 22nd St, Ste 400, Oak Brook, IL 60523. Phone: (877) OUR-1DAY. Fax: (630) 522-6327. Web: www.joinhandsday.org.

JOSEPH BRACKETT DAY. May 6. Day honoring the Shaker religious leader, born May 6, 1797, in Cumberland, ME. In 1848 he composed the popular Shaker song "Simple Gifts" (also known as "Tis the Gift To Be Simple") while at the Shaker Community in Alfred, ME. This Shaker dance song became known worldwide after Aaron Copland used it in his score for the ballet "Appalachian Spring" in 1944. Elder Joseph Brackett died at New Gloucester, ME, July 4, 1882. For info: PineTree Productions, 235 Prospect St, Stoughton, MA 02072. E-mail: tunes1342@aol.com. Web: hometown.aol.com/tunes1342/tunelov.htm.

KENTUCKY DERBY. May 6. Churchill Downs, Louisville, KY. The running of America's premier thoroughbred horse race, inaugurated in 1875. First jewel in the "Triple Crown," traditionally followed by the Preakness (second Saturday after the Derby) and the Belmont Stakes (fifth Saturday after the Derby). Annually, the first Saturday in May. Est attendance: 140,000. For info: Churchill Downs, 700 Central Ave, Louisville, KY 40208. Phone: (502) 636-4400. Web: kentuckyderby.com.

LOW COUNTRY SHRIMP FESTIVAL. May 6. McClellanville, SC. Seafood, arts, crafts, civic display, entertainment and Blessing of the Fleet. Annually, the first Saturday in May. Est attendance: 8,000. For info: The Archibald Rutledge Academy, 1011 Old Cemetery Rd, McClellanville, SC 29458. Phone: (843) 887-3323. Web: www.lowcountryshrimpfestival.com.

NATIONAL HEADACHE FOUNDATION FUND-RAISER. May 6. New York, NY. Annual black tie silent auction and dinner serves as the major fund-raiser for the National Headache Foundation. Proceeds from the evening are used for research, education and service. Est attendance: 250. For info: Suzanne E. Simons, Exec Dir, Natl Headache Foundation, 820 N Orleans, Ste 217, Chicago, IL 60610-3132. Phone: (312) 274-2650. Fax: (312) 640-9049.

NATIONAL NURSES DAY AND WEEK. May 6–12. A week to honor the outstanding efforts of nurses everywhere to strengthen the health of the nation. Annually, beginning May 6, National Nurses Day, and ending May 12, Florence Nightingale's birthday. Call or write for a free catalog. For info: American Nurses Assn, 8515 Georgia Ave, Ste 400, Silver Spring, MD 20910. Phone: (301) 628-5000. Fax: (301) 628-5001. Web: www.nursingworld.org.

NATIONAL SCRAPBOOK DAY. May 6. This is a day designated for people in several countries around the world to gather together and create scrapbook photo albums that preserve precious memories. National Scrapbook Day began in 1995 to encourage the value of making and completing photo albums. Annually, the first Saturday in May. For info: Pam Maurus, PR Manager, Creative Memories, 2815 Clearwater Rd, PO Box 1839, St. Cloud, MN 56302. Phone: (320) 529-5493. Fax: (320) 529-5504. E-mail: pmaurus@antioch.com. Web: www.creativememories.com.

NO DIET DAY. May 6. A day to stop dieting, stop hazardous weight-loss attempts. International No Diet Day celebrates a paradigm shift to the nondiet Health at Any Size approach to health and well-being, to acceptance and respect for oneself and others. Discover the Top 10 Reasons Not to Diet and the Risks of Weight Loss on website. For info: Francie M. Berg, Healthy Weight Network, 402 S 14th St, Hettinger, ND 58639. E-mail: fmberg@healthyweight.net (please put "Berg—No Diet Day" in subject line). Web: www.healthyweight.net.

NO HOMEWORK DAY. May 6. Millions of kids, all of them overloaded with homework, get a much-needed night off tonight. Give 'em a break, teachers! These young folks are working harder than Mom 'n' Dad. [©2003 by WH.] For info: Thomas & Ruth Roy, Wellcat Holidays, 2418 Long Ln, Lebanon, PA 17046. Phone: (717) 279-0184. Fax: (240) 332-4886. E-mail: info@wellcat.com. Web: www.wellcat.com.

O. HENRY MUSEUM PUN-OFF (WORLD CHAMPIONSHIP). May 6 (tentative). The O. Henry Museum, Austin, TX. Pundits and punographers match wits for a wordy cause in two separate pun-filled competitions (Punniest of Show and High Lies & Low Puns). Sponsors: The City of Austin Parks and Recreation Dept, Friends of the O. Henry Museum and Punsters United Nearly Yearly (PUNY). Est attendance: 2,000. For info: Valerie Bennett, Curator, O. Henry Museum, 409 E Fifth St, Austin, TX 78701. Phone: (512) 472-1903. Fax: (512) 472-7102. Web: www.ci.austin.tx.us/parks/ohenry.htm or www.ohenryfriends.org.

PEARY, ROBERT E.: 150th BIRTH ANNIVERSARY.
May 6, 1856. Born at Cresson, PA. Peary served as a cartographic draftsman in the US Coast and Geodetic Survey for two years, then joined the US Navy's Corps of Civil Engineers in 1881. He first worked as an explorer in tropical climates as he served as subchief of the Inter-Ocean Canal Survey in Nicaragua. After reading of the inland ice of Greenland, Peary became attracted to the Arctic. He organized and led eight Arctic expeditions and is credited with the verification of Greenland's island formation, proving that the polar ice cap extended beyond 82° north latitude, and the discovery of the Melville meteorite on Melville Bay, in addition to his famous discovery of the North Pole, Apr 6, 1909. Peary died Feb 20, 1920, at Washington, DC.

PENN, JOHN: BIRTH ANNIVERSARY. May 6, 1740. Signer of the Declaration of Independence, born at Caroline County, VA. Died Sept 14, 1788.

SACK OF ROME: ANNIVERSARY. May 6, 1527. The Renaissance ended with the Sack of Rome, which began on this date. As part of a series of wars between the Hapsburg Empire and the French monarchy, German troops killed some 4,000 inhabitants of Rome and looted works of art and libraries. Pope Clement VII, who supported the French, was imprisoned at the Castel St. Angelo. Nearly a year passed before order could be restored in the city.

SEND A KID TO KAMP RADIOTHON. May 6. Paul Laurence Dunbar High School, Lexington, KY. Annually, the first Saturday in May. Est attendance: 5,000. For info: Dennis Smith, 770 AM, WCGW, 3270 Blazer Parkway, Ste 101, Lexington, KY 40509-1847. Phone: (606) 264-9700. Fax: (606) 264-9705. E-mail: dsmith@mortensonradio.com. Web: www.kidtokamp.com.

SEQUIM IRRIGATION FESTIVAL. May 6–13. Sequim, WA. 111th annual. Come and join the fun at this unique festival. Includes amusement rides, a parade, arts and crafts displays, entertainment, food booths and much more. Est attendance: 20,000. For info: Sequim Chamber of Commerce, Sequim Irrigation Festival, PO Box 2073, Sequim, WA 98382. Phone: (360) 683-6197. Fax: (360) 683-6349. Web: www.irrigationfestival.com.

SOUTHERN APPALACHIAN DULCIMER FESTIVAL.
May 6. Tannehill Historical State Park, McCalla, AL. Festival highlighting old-time dulcimer music. Est attendance: 1,500. For info: Tannehill Historical State Park, 12632 Confederate Pkwy, McCalla, AL 35111. Phone: (205) 477-5711. Fax: (205) 477-9400.

SPRING GALA. May 6–7. Lovington, NM. Arts and crafts show at the Lea County Fairgrounds. For info: Libbie Plant, Lea County 4-H, 100 N Main St, Ste 10-C, Lovington, NM 88260. Phone: (505) 396-2819. Fax: (505) 396-2971. E-mail: lplant@nmsu.edu.

STRAWBERRY FESTIVAL. May 6–7. Lahaska, PA. Strawberries served up in various forms—dipped in chocolate, in assorted pastries and shortcake, in jams, in fritters, and fresh and unadorned. Craftspeople gather to show their wares and demonstrate their skills. Live entertainment and pie-eating contests add to the festivities of this traditional spring celebration. Free admission. Est attendance: 18,000. For info: Peddler's Village, Routes 202 & 263, Lahaska, PA 18931. Phone: (215) 794-4000. Fax: (215) 794-4001. Web: www.peddlersvillage.com.

		S	M	T	W	T	F	S
May			1	2	3	4	5	6
2006		7	8	9	10	11	12	13
		14	15	16	17	18	19	20
		21	22	23	24	25	26	27
		28	29	30	31			

TAGORE, RABINDRANATH: BIRTH ANNIVERSARY.
May 6, 1861. Hindu poet, mystic and musical composer was born at Calcutta, India. Received Nobel Prize (literature) in 1913. Died at Calcutta, Aug 7, 1941. His birthday is observed in Bangladesh on the 25th day of the Bengali month of Baishakha (second week of May), when the poet laureate is honored with songs, dances and discussions of his works.

TOWSONTOWN SPRING FESTIVAL. May 6–7. Towson, MD. Five stages with continuous entertainment. 400 food, craft and display vendors on the street. Art and photography exhibit and antique auto display. Annually, the first Saturday and Sunday in May. Est attendance: 250,000. For info: Towsontown Spring Fest, 23 W Chesapeake Ave, Towson, MD 21204. Phone: (410) 825-1144. Fax: (410) 832-5863. Web: www.towsontown springfestival.com.

TYBEE 500. May 6–8. Hollywood, FL. A 540-mile endurance race for catamarans. Hollywood is the official start of the race, which ends at Tybee Island, GA. The public is invited to a meet and greet reception. For info: Cynthia Hancock, City of Hollywood, 1940 E Harrison St, Ste 101, Hollywood, FL 33020. Phone: (954) 921-3404. Fax: (954) 921-3572. E-mail: chancock @hollywoodfl.org. Web: www.hollywoodfl.org.

VALENTINO, RUDOLPH: BIRTH ANNIVERSARY. May 6, 1895. Rodolpho Alfonzo Raffaello Pietro Filiberto Guglielmi Di Valentina D'Antonguolla, whose professional name was Rudolph Valentino, was born at Castellaneta, Italy. Popular cinema actor. For years press reports claimed that "at least one weeping veiled woman in black brought flowers to his tomb" (at Hollywood Memorial Park) every year on the anniversary of his death at New York, NY, Aug 23, 1926.

VIRGINIA GOLD CUP. May 6. Great Meadow, The Plains, VA. Steeplechasing began in Ireland in 1762 when two horsemen held a cross-country match race to a faraway church steeple. Great Meadow is the largest steeplechase course in the country with a spectacular hillside amphitheater. The $50,000 Virginia Gold Cup race is run over a challenging 4-mile post and rail course of 23 fences. Advance tickets only. Annually, the first Saturday in May. Est attendance: 45,000. For info: Virginia Gold Cup Assn, PO Box 840, Warrenton, VA 20188. Phone: (540) 347-2612. Fax: (540) 349-1829. Web: www.vagoldcup.com.

VIRGINIA STATE CHAMPIONSHIP CHILI COOK-OFF. May 6. Historic Market area, Roanoke, VA. Live entertainment, pepper-eating contest, children's festival area, costume contest and the best chili samples from across the US and the Commonwealth of Virginia. All compete for the state title. Est attendance: 40,000. For info: Kathleen Jackson, Greenvale School, 627 Westwood Blvd, Roanoke, VA 24017. Phone: (540) 342-4716. Fax: (540) 344-0876. E-mail: kjackson@greenvale-school.org.

WELLES, ORSON: BIRTH ANNIVERSARY. May 6, 1915. Actor and director born at Kenosha, WI. *Citizen Kane*, which he directed and in which he played the title role, is one of the most influential films ever made. Other films in which he had a role include *The Third Man* and *The Magnificent Ambersons*. Welles died at Los Angeles, CA, Oct 10, 1985.

BIRTHDAYS TODAY

Tom Bergeron, 51, host ("Hollywood Squares"), born Haverhill, MA, May 6, 1955.

Tony Blair, 53, British prime minister, born Edinburgh, Scotland, May 6, 1953.

Martin Brodeur, 34, hockey player, born Montreal, QC, Canada, May 6, 1972.

George Clooney, 45, actor ("ER," *Ocean's Eleven, Three Kings, Batman and Robin*), born Lexington, KY, May 6, 1961.

Roma Downey, 42, actress ("Touched by an Angel"), born Derry, Northern Ireland, May 6, 1964.

Leslie Hope, 41, actress ("24," *Talk Radio*), born Halifax, NS, Canada, May 6, 1965.

Ben Masters, 59, actor (*All That Jazz, Making Mr Right*), born Corvallis, OR, May 6, 1947.

Willie Mays, 75, Hall of Fame baseball player, born Westfield, AL, May 6, 1931.

Bob Seger, 61, musician, singer ("Night Moves," "Travelin' Man"), born Ann Arbor, MI, May 6, 1945.

Richard C. Shelby, 72, US Senator (R, Alabama), born Birmingham, AL, May 6, 1934.

Lynn Whitfield, 53, actress (*Stepmom, Eve's Bayou*), born Baton Rouge, LA, May 6, 1953.

MAY 7 — SUNDAY
Day 127 — 238 Remaining

BEAUFORT SCALE DAY (FRANCIS BEAUFORT BIRTH ANNIVERSARY). May 7, 1774. A day to honor the British naval officer, Sir Francis Beaufort, who devised in 1806 a scale of wind force from 0 (calm) to 12 (hurricane) that was based on observation, not requiring any special instruments. The scale was adopted for international use in 1874 and has since been enlarged and refined. Beaufort was born at Flower Hill, Meath, Ireland, and died at Brighton, England, Dec 17, 1857.

BEETHOVEN'S NINTH SYMPHONY PREMIERE: ANNIVERSARY. May 7, 1824. Beethoven's Ninth Symphony in D Minor was performed for the first time at Vienna, Austria. Known as the *Choral* because of his use of voices in symphonic form for the first time, the Ninth was his musical interpretation of Schiller's *Ode to Joy*. Beethoven was completely deaf when he composed it, and it was said a soloist had to tug on his sleeve when the performance was over to get him to turn around and see the enthusiastic response he could not hear.

BROWNING, ROBERT: BIRTH ANNIVERSARY. May 7, 1812. English poet and husband of poet Elizabeth Barrett Browning, born at Camberwell, near London. Known for his dramatic monologues. Died at Venice, Italy, Dec 12, 1889.

COOPER, GARY: BIRTH ANNIVERSARY. May 7, 1901. Frank James Cooper was born at Helena, MT. He changed his name to Gary at the start of his movie career. He is best known by baseball fans for his portrayal of Lou Gehrig in *The Pride of the Yankees*. Other films included *Wings, The Virginian, The Plainsman, Beau Geste, Sergeant York* (for which he won his first Academy Award), *High Noon* (winning his second Oscar for best actor), *The Court Martial of Billy Mitchell* and *Friendly Persuasion*. He died May 13, 1961, at Hollywood, CA.

DIEN BIEN PHU FALLS: ANNIVERSARY. May 7, 1954. Vietnam's victory over France at Dien Bien Phu ended the Indochina War.

EL SALVADOR: DAY OF THE SOLDIER. May 7. National holiday. Anniversary of the founding of the country's armed forces in 1824.

FIRST PRESIDENTIAL INAUGURAL BALL: ANNIVERSARY. May 7, 1789. Celebrating the inauguration of George Washington, the first Presidential Inaugural Ball was held at New York, NY.

FLEXIBLE WORK ARRANGEMENTS WEEK. May 7–13. To promote experimentation with alternate work schedules and working at home. Annually, the week beginning with the first Sunday in May. For info: Center for WorkTime Options, 1286 University Ave, #192, San Diego, CA 92103-3312. Phone: (619) 232-0404. E-mail: info@worktimeoptions.com.

FRANKENMUTH SKYFEST. May 7. Frankenmuth, MI. 25th annual. To encourage family participation in a healthy outdoor sport that adapts to all age groups. Annually, the first Sunday in May. Est attendance: 4,500. For info: Judy Bergelin, Kite Kraft, 618 S Main St, Frankenmuth, MI 48734. Phone: (989) 652-2961.

GARDEN FESTIVAL. May 7. Chestnut Hill, PA. Lively street festival in charming urban village. Garden-related merchandise and handcrafts, live entertainment, food court and children's activities. Annually, the first Sunday in May. Est attendance: 40,000. For info: Chestnut Hill Business Assn, 8426 Germantown Ave, Philadelphia, PA 19118. Phone: (215) 247-6696. E-mail: info@chestnuthillpa.com. Web: www.chestnuthillpa.com.

GERMANY: HAMBURG HARBOR BIRTHDAY. May 7, 1189. "Hafengeburtstag" celebrates establishment of Hamburg as a free city.

GERMANY'S FIRST SURRENDER: ANNIVERSARY. May 7, 1945. Russian, American, British and French ranking officers crowded into a second-floor recreation room of a small red-brick schoolhouse (which served as Eisenhower's headquarters) at Reims, Germany. Representing Germany, Field Marshall Alfred Jodl signed an unconditional surrender of all German fighting forces. After a signing that took almost 40 minutes, Jodl was ushered into Eisenhower's presence. The American general asked the German if he fully understood what he had signed and informed Jodl that he would be held personally responsible for any deviation from the terms of the surrender, including the requirement that German commanders sign a formal surrender to the USSR at a time and place determined by that government.

GOODWILL INDUSTRIES WEEK. May 7–13. To call international attention to Goodwill Industries as a leader in job training and employment services for people with disabilities and other barriers to employment. Annually, the first full week in May. For info: Goodwill Industries Intl, Communications Dept, 15810 Indianola Dr, Rockville, MD 20855. Phone: (301) 530-6500. Fax: (301) 530-1516. E-mail: contactus@goodwill.org. Web: www.goodwill.org.

"KRAFT TELEVISION THEATRE" TV PREMIERE: ANNIVERSARY. May 7, 1947. Live theatrical programs appearing on both the NBC and ABC networks. The show was a gold mine for discovering new talent. Among the playwrights getting their big breaks were: Rod Serling, Paddy Chayefsky and Tad Mosel. Some of the show's most notable plays included: "The Easy Mark" (1951) with Jack Lemmon, "Double in Ivory" (1953) with Lee Remick, "To Live in Peace" (1953) with Anne Bancroft, "The Missing Years" (1954) with Anthony Perkins and Mary Astor and "A Profile in Courage" (1956) with James Whitmore. The last play was based on a book by Senator John F. Kennedy who appeared on the program to introduce the drama.

LUSITANIA SINKING: ANNIVERSARY. May 7, 1915. British passenger liner *Lusitania*, on its return trip from New York to Liverpool, carrying nearly 2,000 passengers, was torpedoed by a German submarine off the coast of Ireland, sinking within minutes; 1,198 lives were lost. US President Wilson sent note of protest to Berlin on May 13, but Germany, which had issued warning in advance, pointed to *Lusitania*'s cargo of ammunition for Britain. The US maintained neutrality, for the time being.

MacLEISH, ARCHIBALD: BIRTH ANNIVERSARY. May 7, 1892. American poet and Librarian of Congress (1939–44), born at Glencoe, IL. MacLeish, who was also a playwright, Pulitzer Prize winner, editor, lawyer, professor and farmer, died at Boston, MA, Apr 20, 1982.

NATIONAL ALCOHOL AND OTHER DRUG-RELATED BIRTH DEFECTS WEEK. May 7–13. For info: National Council on Alcoholism and Drug Dependence, 20 Exchange Place, Ste 2902, New York, NY 10005. Phone: (212) 269-7797. E-mail: national@ncadd.org. Web: www.ncadd.org.

NATIONAL FAMILY WEEK. May 7–13. Traditionally the first Sunday and the first full week in May are observed as National Family Week in many Christian churches.

NATIONAL HUG HOLIDAY WEEK. May 7–13. Huggers of all ages are invited to make a difference one hug at a time! The Hugs 4 Health movement needs your help to increase hugs, friendship and volunteer support for the elderly living in senior care and residential communities. Send $10 for a "Hugger's Package" that includes an "Official Hugger" button, a Daily Hug Prescription with Proper Hug Etiquette, Hug Tally Sheet, Hugger's Contest registration and more information about this movement. (Include your name, complete address and e-mail to the following address.) For info: Hugs 4 Health—NHHW2006, PO Box 896, Seal Beach, CA 90740-0896. Web: www.hugs4health.org.

NATIONAL INFERTILITY SURVIVAL DAY. May 7. Beat the Mother's Day blues the week *before* Mother's Day. Infertility survivors are encouraged to reach out to those struggling to find resolution to their challenges, through friendship, fund-raising and other supportive and creative endeavors. Infertility Survival Day is for those who want to use their experiences to attain positive outcomes for themselves and others. Annually, the first Sunday in May. For info: Beverly Barna, 10337 Emerald Woods Ave, Orlando, FL 32836. Phone: (407) 248-0452. E-mail: infertility sucks@aol.com. Web: www.infertilitysucks-thebook.com.

NATIONAL PET WEEK. May 7–13. To promote responsible pet ownership and public awareness of veterinary medical service for animal health and care. Annually, the first full week in May. For info: The American Veterinary Medical Assn, 1931 N Meacham Rd, Schaumburg, IL 60173. Phone: (800) 248-2862. Web: www.petweek.org.

NATIONAL POSTCARD WEEK. May 7–13. To advertise use of picture postcards for correspondence and collecting. Annually, the first full week of May since 1984. For info: Jim Ward, Publisher, Journal of the Postcard History Society, 1795 Kleinfeltersville Rd, Stevens, PA 17578-9669. E-mail: midcreek@ptd.net.

NATIONAL PTA TEACHER APPRECIATION WEEK. May 7–13. PTAs across the country conduct activities to strengthen respect and support for teachers and the teaching profession. Founded in 1984. Annually, the first full week of May. For info: Natl PTA, 330 N Wabash Ave, Ste 2100, Chicago, IL 60611. Phone: (312) 670-6782. Fax: (312) 670-6783. E-mail: info @pta.org. Web: www.pta.org.

NATIONAL SPORTING GOODS ASSOCIATION MANAGEMENT CONFERENCE. May 7–10. Hilton Head Marriott Beach & Golf Resort, Hilton Head Island, SC. 42nd annual management conference and 8th annual Team Dealer Summit. The premier educational and networking event for the sporting goods industry. Attracts leading retailers, dealers, manufacturers, agents, media and industry organizations. Est attendance: 400. For info: Larry Weindruch, Dir of Communications, Natl Sporting Goods Assn, 1601 Feehanville Dr, Ste 300, Mt Prospect, IL 60056-6035. Phone: (847) 296-6742. Fax: (847) 391-9827. E-mail: info@nsga.org. Web: www.nsga.org.

"STRIKE IT RICH" TV PREMIERE: 55th ANNIVERSARY. May 7, 1951. The downtrodden and the poverty-stricken showed up on this game show to tell their sob stories. Whoever received the most votes from the studio audience was declared the winner. The losers were able to receive help from sympathetic viewers through a telephone "heart line." The show got in trouble with the New York City Welfare Department in 1954 when 55 of the show's hopeful contestants remained in New York and went on welfare.

TCHAIKOVSKY, PETER ILICH: BIRTH ANNIVERSARY. May 7, 1840. Ranked among the outstanding composers of all time, Peter Ilich Tchaikovsky was born at Vatkinsk, Russia. His musical talent was not encouraged and he embarked upon a career in jurisprudence, not studying music seriously until 1861. Among his famous works are the three-act ballet *Sleeping Beauty*, two-act ballet *The Nutcracker* and the symphony *Pathetique*. Mystery surrounds Tchaikovsky's death. It was believed he had caught cholera from contaminated water, but 20th-century scholars believe he probably committed suicide to avoid his homosexuality being revealed. He died at St. Petersburg, Nov 6, 1893.

TEACHER APPRECIATION WEEK. May 7–13. A day for elementary through high school students to show appreciation to their teachers. Students are urged to thank their teachers for their care and concerned effort, to be extra cooperative with them. For info: Natl Education Assn, 1201 16th St NW, Washington, DC 20036. Phone: (202) 833-4000. Fax: (202) 822-7292. Web: www.nea.org.

TRADITIONAL PLOWING MATCH. May 7. Woodstock, VT. This annual event features a horse- and oxen-drawn plowing competition as well as demonstrations of different plowing techniques. Est attendance: 1,050. For info: Billings Farm and Museum, Rt 12 N and River Rd, Woodstock, VT 05091. Phone: (802) 457-2355. Fax: (802) 457-4663. E-mail: billings.farm@valley.net. Web: www.billingsfarm.org.

TWENTY-SEVENTH AMENDMENT RATIFIED: ANNIVERSARY. May 7, 1992. The 27th amendment to the Constitution was ratified, prohibiting Congress from giving itself midterm pay raises.

UNITAS, JOHNNY: BIRTH ANNIVERSARY. May 7, 1933. Born at Pittsburgh, PA, Johnny Unitas played football for the University of Louisville. After college, he went to work as a construction worker but continued to play football (for $6 per game) for the Bloomfield Rams, a semipro team that played on dirt, not grass. Based on a fan's letter, the Baltimore Colts gave him a conditional contract and soon he was a star. He played 17 seasons for the Colts, was the MVP three times, went to 10 Pro Bowls, and led his team to three NFL championships. He was inducted into the Pro Football Hall of Fame in 1979 and has often been called the greatest quarterback ever to play the game. He died at Baltimore, MD, Sept 11, 2002.

WINTERTHUR POINT-TO-POINT. May 7. Winterthur Museum, Garden and Library, Wilmington, DE. Steeplechase races, antique carriage parade, canine agility competition, kids' activities, tailgating plus much more! Call for pricing. Rain or shine event. Est attendance: 26,000. For info: Greater Wilmington CVB, 100 W 10th St, Ste 20, Wilmington, DE 19801-1661. Phone: (302) 652-4088. E-mail: info@wilmcvb.org. Web: www.visitwilmingtonde.com.

BIRTHDAYS TODAY

Theresa Brewer, 75, singer ("[Open Up Your Heart and] Let the Sun Shine In"), born Toledo, OH, May 7, 1931.
Pete V. Domenici, 74, US Senator (R, New Mexico), born Albuquerque, NM, May 7, 1932.
Amy Heckerling, 52, filmmaker (*Fast Times at Ridgemont High, Look Who's Talking*), born New York, NY, May 7, 1954.
Darren McGavin, 84, actor (*A Christmas Story, The Man with the Golden Arm*), born Spokane, WA, May 7, 1922.
Peter Reckell, 51, actor ("Days of Our Lives"), born Elkhart, IN, May 7, 1955.
Tim Russert, 56, TV news talk-show moderator ("Meet the Press"), born Buffalo, NY, May 7, 1950.

May *2006*	S	M	T	W	T	F	S
		1	2	3	4	5	6
	7	8	9	10	11	12	13
	14	15	16	17	18	19	20
	21	22	23	24	25	26	27
	28	29	30	31			

MAY 8 — MONDAY
Day 128 — 237 Remaining

BATTLE OF THE CORAL SEA: ANNIVERSARY. May 8, 1942. Beginning on this date, the Battle of the Coral Sea impeded Japanese expansion and introduced a new form of naval warfare. None of the surface vessels exchanged fire—the entire battle was waged by aircraft. The US lost a carrier, destroyer and tanker. The Japanese lost seven warships, including a carrier.

CZECH REPUBLIC: LIBERATION DAY. May 8. Commemorates the liberation of Czechoslovakia from the Germans in 1945.

DUNANT, JEAN HENRI: BIRTH ANNIVERSARY. May 8, 1828. Author and philanthropist, founder of the Red Cross Society, was born at Geneva, Switzerland. Nobel Prize winner in 1901. Died at Heiden, Switzerland, Oct 30, 1910.

FRANCE: VICTORY DAY. May 8. Commemorates the surrender of Germany to Allied forces and the cessation of hostilities in 1945.

GERMANY'S SECOND SURRENDER: ANNIVERSARY. May 8, 1945. Stalin refused to recognize the document of unconditional surrender signed at Reims the previous day, so a second signing was held at Berlin. The event was turned into an elaborate formal ceremony by the Soviets who had lost some 20 million lives during the war. As in the Reims document, the end of hostilities was set for 12:01 AM local time on May 9.

GOTTSCHALK, LOUIS MOREAU: BIRTH ANNIVERSARY. May 8, 1829. American pianist of international fame who toured the US during the Civil War. Gottschalk composed for the piano combining American and Creole folk themes and rhythms in his work. Born at New Orleans, LA, he died Dec 18, 1869, at Rio de Janeiro, Brazil.

JOHNSON, ROBERT: BIRTH ANNIVERSARY. May 8, 1911. Born at Hazelhurst, MS, and murdered at age 27, Aug 16, 1938, at Greenwood, MS (poisoned by a jealous husband), in his short life Johnson was a master blues guitarist, a singer and songwriter of great influence. He developed a unique guitar style of such skill that it was said he acquired his ability by selling his soul to the Devil—the film *Crossroads* is based very loosely on this myth. Johnson's only two recording sessions captured the classics "Sweet Home Chicago," "Cross Road Blues," "Me and the Devil Blues" and others. Johnson was inducted posthumously into the Blues Hall of Fame in 1980 and the Rock & Roll Hall of Fame in 1986.

LAVOISIER, ANTOINE LAURENT: EXECUTION ANNIVERSARY. May 8, 1794. French chemist and the "father of modern chemistry." Especially noted for having first explained the real nature of combustion and for showing that matter is not destroyed in chemical reactions. Born at Paris, France, Aug 26, 1743, Lavoisier was guillotined at the Place de la Revolution for his former position as a tax collector. The Revolutionary Tribunal is reported to have responded to a plea to spare his life with the statement: "We need no more scientists in France."

LIFE COACH RECOGNITION WEEK. May 8–14. Coaches love to help people lead joyful, purposeful, successful lives. Whether the goals are to find love, pursue passions, embrace challenges, cultivate a career or achieve personal gratification, a coach's job is to empower, guide and inform. This week is a time to recognize the contributions life coaches make to the well-being of society. For info: Robin Gorman Newman, 44 Somerset Dr N, Great Neck, NY 10020. Phone: (516) 773-0911. E-mail: robin@lovecoach.com. Web: www.lovecoach.com.

LISTON, SONNY: BIRTH ANNIVERSARY. May 8, 1932. Charles ("Sonny") Liston, boxer born at St. Francis County, AR. Liston rose above a record of criminal activity to defeat Floyd Patterson for the heavyweight title on Sept 25, 1962. He defeated Patterson in a rematch but then lost the title to Cassius Clay, who later changed his name to Muhammad Ali. In a rematch Ali knocked out Liston with a punch few observers saw. Died at Las Vegas, NV, Dec 30, 1970.

MOUNT PELÉE ERUPTION: ANNIVERSARY. May 8, 1902. In the worst volcanic disaster of the 20th century, Mount Pelée erupted on the tiny French Caribbean island of Martinique. In minutes, a cloud of ashes, gases and rocks destroyed the thriving port city of Saint-Pierre, killing all but one of its 30,000 inhabitants.

NATIONAL STUTTERING AWARENESS WEEK. May 8–14. Annually, the second full week of May. For info: Stuttering Foundation of America, 3100 Walnut Grove Rd, Ste 603, Memphis, TN 38111-0749. Phone: (800) 992-9392 or (901)452-7343. E-mail: info@stutteringhelp.org. Web: www.stutteringhelp.org or www.tartamudez.org in Spanish.

NO SOCKS DAY. May 8. If we give up wearing socks for one day, it will mean a little less laundry, thereby contributing to the betterment of the environment. Besides, we will all feel a bit freer, at least for one day. Annually, May 8. [©2003 by WH.] For info: Thomas & Ruth Roy, Wellcat Holidays, 2418 Long Ln, Lebanon, PA 17046. Phone: (717) 279-0184. E-mail: info@wellcat.com. Web: www.wellcat.com.

OUIMET, FRANCIS DESALES: BIRTH ANNIVERSARY. May 8, 1893. American amateur golfer who is credited with establishing the popularity of golf in the US. Born at Brookline, MA, his golfing career began as a caddy. In 1913, at age 20, he generated national enthusiasm for the game when he became the first American and first amateur to win the US Open Golf Championship. He won the US Amateur Championship in 1914 and 1931, and was a member of the US Walker Cup team from its first tournament in 1922 until 1949, serving as its nonplaying captain for six of those years. In 1951 he became the first American to be elected Captain of the Royal and Ancient Golf Club of St. Andrews, Scotland. Ouimet died at Newton, MA, Sept 2, 1967.

SLOVAKIA: LIBERATION DAY. May 8. Commemorates the liberation of Czechoslovakia from the Germans in 1945.

TRUMAN, HARRY S: BIRTH ANNIVERSARY. May 8, 1884. The 33rd president of the US, succeeded to that office upon the death of Franklin D. Roosevelt, Apr 12, 1945, and served until Jan 20, 1953. Born at Lamar, MO, Truman was the last of the nine US presidents who did not attend college. Affectionately nicknamed "Give 'em Hell Harry" by admirers. Truman died at Kansas City, MO, Dec 26, 1972. His birthday is a holiday in Missouri.

V-E DAY: ANNIVERSARY. May 8, 1945. Victory in Europe Day commemorates unconditional surrender of Germany to Allied forces. The surrender document was signed by German representatives at General Dwight D. Eisenhower's headquarters at Reims to become effective, and hostilities to end, at one minute past midnight May 9, 1945, which was 9:01 PM EDT on May 8 in the US. President Harry S Truman on May 8 declared May 9, 1945, to be "V-E Day," but it later came to be observed on May 8. A separate German surrender to the USSR was signed at Karlshorst, near Berlin, May 8. See also: "Russia: Victory Day" (May 9).

WORLD RED CROSS DAY. May 8. A day for commemorating the birth of Jean Henry Dunant, the Swiss founder of the International Red Cross Movement in 1863, and for recognizing the humanitarian work of the Red Cross around the world. For info on activities in your area, contact your local Red Cross chapter. For info: American Red Cross Natl Headquarters, 2025 E St NW, Washington, DC 20006. Web: www.redcross.org.

BIRTHDAYS TODAY

David Attenborough, 80, author, naturalist (*Life on Earth, Trials of Life*), born London, England, May 8, 1926.
Peter Benchley, 66, author, journalist (*Rummies, Jaws*), born New York, NY, May 8, 1940.
Bill Cowher, 49, football coach and former player, born Pittsburgh, PA, May 8, 1957.
Melissa Gilbert, 42, actress ("Little House on the Prairie," *The Miracle Worker*), born Los Angeles, CA, May 8, 1964.
Enrique Iglesias, 31, singer, born Madrid, Spain, May 8, 1975.
David Keith, 52, actor (*The Great Santini, An Officer and a Gentleman*), director, born Knoxville, TN, May 8, 1954.
Bobby Labonte, 42, race car driver, born Corpus Christi, TX, May 8, 1964.
Ronald Mandel (Ronnie) Lott, 47, Hall of Fame football player, born Albuquerque, NM, May 8, 1959.
Janet McTeer, 45, actress (*Tumbleweeds*), born Newcastle, England, May 8, 1961.
Thomas Pynchon, 69, writer (*V, Gravity's Rainbow*), born Glen Cove, NY, May 8, 1937.
Don Rickles, 80, comedian, actor (*Blazing Saddles*, "The Dean Martin Show"), born New York, NY, May 8, 1926.
Toni Tennille, 63, singer (with husband Daryl Dragon made up Captain and Tennille), born Montgomery, AL, May 8, 1943.

MAY 9 — TUESDAY
Day 129 — 236 Remaining

BOYD, BELLE: BIRTH ANNIVERSARY. May 9, 1843. Notorious Confederate spy who later became an actress and lecturer was born at Martinsburg, VA. Author of the book *Belle Boyd in Camp and Prison*, she died June 11, 1900, at Kilbourne, WI.

BRITISH CAPTURE ENIGMA MACHINE: 65th ANNIVERSARY. May 9, 1941. During WWII, when a German U-110 submarine attacked a British convoy, two British vessels, the *Bulldog* and *Aubretia*, were able to retaliate so quickly with depth charges that the submarine was disabled and unable to dive. With the submarine captured, British sailors investigated the radio room and discovered the typewriter-like Enigma, a ciphering machine that enabled safe German communication, and documents of tables that helped explain how it worked. The U-110's capture was kept secret, and British cryptographers used this break to begin unraveling German code during the war.

BROWN, JOHN: BIRTH ANNIVERSARY. May 9, 1800. Abolitionist leader born at Torrington, CT, and hanged Dec 2, 1859, at Charles Town, WV. Leader of attack on Harpers Ferry, Oct 16, 1859, which was intended to give impetus to movement for escape and freedom for slaves. His aim was frustrated and in fact resulted in increased polarization and sectional animosity. Legendary martyr of the abolitionist movement.

CHILDHOOD DEPRESSION AWARENESS DAY. May 9. Also known as Green Ribbon Day. Annually, the Tuesday of the first full week in May. For info: Natl Mental Heath Assn, 2001 Beauregard St, 12th Floor, Alexandria, VA 22311. Phone: (800) 969-6642 or (703) 684-7722. Web: www.nmha.org.

May *2006*	S	M	T	W	T	F	S
		1	2	3	4	5	6
	7	8	9	10	11	12	13
	14	15	16	17	18	19	20
	21	22	23	24	25	26	27
	28	29	30	31			

EUROPEAN UNION: ANNIVERSARY OBSERVANCE. May 9, 1950. Member countries of the European Union commemorate the announcement by French statesman Robert Schuman of the "Schuman Plan" for establishing a single authority for production of coal, iron and steel in France and Germany. The European Coal and Steel Community was founded in 1952. This organization was a forerunner of the European Economic Community, founded in 1958, which later became the European Union. At the European Summit at Milan in 1985, this day was proclaimed the Day of Europe.

GONZALES, PANCHO: BIRTH ANNIVERSARY. May 9, 1928. Richard Alonzo ("Pancho") Gonzales, tennis player born at Los Angeles, CA. A self-taught player, Gonzales won the 1948 US National Singles Championship and repeated in 1949. He turned pro and won the world's championship from 1954 through 1962. Gonzales was an aggressive, temperamental player who rarely trained. Died at Las Vegas, NV, July 3, 1995.

HUNTER FREES THE SLAVES: ANNIVERSARY. May 9, 1862. At Hilton Head, SC, General David Hunter, commander of the Department of the South, issued orders freeing slaves in South Carolina, Florida and Georgia. Not having congressional or presidential approval, the orders were countermanded by President Lincoln on May 19.

NATIONAL TEACHER DAY. May 9. To pay tribute to American educators, sponsored by the National Education Association, Teacher Day falls during the National PTA's Teacher Appreciation Week. Local communities and organizations are encouraged to use this opportunity to honor those who influence and inspire the next generation through their work. Annually, the Tuesday of the first full week in May. For info: Natl Education Assn, 1201 16th St NW, #710, Washington, DC 20036. Phone: (202) 833-4000. Web: www.nea.org.

PENINSULA CAMPAIGN INTENSIFIED: ANNIVERSARY. May 9, 1862. Confederate forces at Norfolk, VA, evacuated the city in a costly move, leaving valuable materiel for the Union army. Norfolk and Portsmouth were occupied on May 10 and the naval yard at Gosport, VA, was burned. President Abraham Lincoln was personally involved in this action, supervising the Federal expeditionary force.

RENO, NEVADA: BIRTHDAY. May 9, 1868. First known as Fullers Crossing, then Lakes Crossing, on this date it officially became Reno, known today as "The Biggest Little City in the World." Its six-week residency requirement for divorce became law on May 1, 1931.

RUSSIA: VICTORY DAY. May 9. National holiday observed annually to commemorate the 1945 Allied forces' defeat of Nazi Germany in WWII and to honor the 20 million Soviet people who died in that war. Hostilities ceased and the German surrender became effective at one minute after midnight on May 9, 1945. See also: "V-E Day: Anniversary" (May 8).

UZBEKISTAN: DAY OF MEMORY AND HONOR. May 9. Honors Uzbek citizens killed in WWII. Formerly Victory Day when Uzbekistan was part of the Soviet Union.

"VAST WASTELAND" SPEECH: 45th ANNIVERSARY. May 9, 1961. Speaking before the bigwigs of network TV at the annual convention of the National Association of Broadcasters, Newton Minow, the new chairman of the Federal Communications Commission, exhorted those executives to sit through an entire day of their own programming. He suggested that they "will observe a vast wasteland." Further, he urged them to try for "imagination in programming, not sterility; creativity, not imitation; experimentation, not conformity; excellence, not mediocrity."

BIRTHDAYS TODAY

Candice Bergen, 60, actress (*Starting Over, The Group,* "Murphy Brown"), daughter of ventriloquist Edgar Bergen, born Beverly Hills, CA, May 9, 1946.

James L. Brooks, 66, screenwriter, producer ("Taxi," "The Mary Tyler Moore Show"), born Brooklyn, NY, May 9, 1940.

Rosario Dawson, 27, actress (*He Got Game, Sin City*), born New York, NY, May 9, 1979.

Albert Finney, 70, actor (*Tom Jones, Shoot the Moon, Annie, The Dresser*), born Salford, England, May 9, 1936.

Anthony Keith (Tony) Gwynn, 46, former baseball player, born Los Angeles, CA, May 9, 1960.

Glenda Jackson, 69, actress (Oscars for *Women in Love* and *Touch of Class*), born Cheshire, England, May 9, 1937.

Billy Joel, 57, singer, composer ("It's Still Rock and Roll to Me," "Just the Way You Are"), born Hicksville, NY, May 9, 1949.

Mike Wallace, 88, TV journalist ("60 Minutes"), born Brookline, MA, May 9, 1918.

Steve Yzerman, 41, hockey player, born Cranbrook, BC, Canada, May 9, 1965.

MAY 10 — WEDNESDAY

Day 130 — 235 Remaining

ASTAIRE, FRED: BIRTH ANNIVERSARY. May 10, 1899. Actor, dancer and choreographer, born at Omaha, NE. Astaire began dancing with his sister Adele and in the mid-1930s began dancing with Ginger Rogers. After Astaire's first Hollywood screen test, a producer noted of him: "Can't act. Slightly bald. Can dance a little." Despite this, Astaire starred in more than 40 films including *Holiday Inn, The Gay Divorcee, Silk Stockings* and *Easter Parade*. Died at Los Angeles, CA, June 22, 1987.

ASTOR PLACE RIOT: ANNIVERSARY. May 10, 1849. A riot erupted outside the Astor Place Opera House at New York, NY, where the British actor William Charles Macready was performing. Led by the American actor Edwin Forrest, angry crowds revolted against dress requirements for admission and against Macready's public statements on the vulgarity of American life. On May 8, Macready's performance of *Macbeth* was stopped by Forrest's followers. Two days later, a mob led by Ned Buntline shattered the windows of the theater during a performance. Troops were summoned and they were ordered to fire, killing 22 and wounding 26.

BIG 12 WOMEN'S SOFTBALL CHAMPIONSHIPS. May 10–13. ASA Hall of Fame Stadium, Oklahoma City, OK. Est attendance: 15,000. For info: Big 12 Conference, 2201 Stemmons Frwy, 28th Fl, Dallas, TX 75207. Phone: (214) 742-1212. Fax: (214) 753-0145. Web: www.big12sports.com.

BONNIE BLUE NATIONAL HORSE SHOW. May 10–13. Virginia Horse Center, Lexington, VA. Major all-breed event, "A"-rated show of the American Horse Show Association. For info: Lexington Visitors Bureau, 106 E Washington St, Lexington, VA 24450. Phone: (540) 463-3777. Fax: (540) 463-1105. E-mail: lexington@rockbridge.net. Web: www.horsecenter.org.

CONFEDERATE MEMORIAL DAY IN NORTH AND SOUTH CAROLINA. May 10. Observed on the anniversary of the capture of Jefferson Davis by Union troops in 1865. Other southern states observe Confederate Memorial Day on different dates.

DONATE A DAY'S WAGES TO CHARITY DAY. May 10. All working people are asked to donate the money they make on May 10, 2006, to charity. If unable to afford the donation, they are then asked to take the day off of work and donate their time to charity. Third annual event. For info: E-mail: donatetocharity@yahoo.com.

GOLDEN SPIKE DRIVING: ANNIVERSARY. May 10, 1869. Anniversary of the meeting of Union Pacific and Central Pacific railways at Promontory Point, UT. On that day a golden spike was driven by Leland Stanford, president of the Central Pacific, to celebrate the linkage. The golden spike was promptly removed for preservation. Long called the final link in the ocean-to-ocean railroad, this event cannot be accurately described as completing the transcontinental railroad, but it did complete continuous rail tracks between Omaha and Sacramento. See also: "Transcontinental US Railway Completion: Anniversary" (Aug 15).

MANDELA INAUGURATION: ANNIVERSARY. May 10, 1994. In a dramatic and historic exchange of power, former political prisoner Nelson Mandela was inaugurated as President of South Africa. Long the focal point of apartheid foes' attempts to end the enforced policy of discrimination in South Africa, Mandela handily won the first free election in South Africa despite many attempts by various political factions to either stop the electoral process or alter the outcome.

MICRONESIA, FEDERATED STATES OF: CONSTITUTION DAY. May 10. Proclamation of the Federated States of Micronesia in 1979. National holiday.

NATIONAL NIGHTSHIFT WORKERS DAY. May 10. To honor those workers who reverse their natural circadian rhythm to keep business running 24 hours a day. Annually, the second Wednesday of May. For info: Velcea Kae, 3 Chester Rd, Springfield, VT 05156.

NATIONAL SCHOOL NURSE DAY. May 10. Established to foster a better understanding of the role of school nurses in the educational setting. Annually, the Wednesday of National Nurse Week (May 6–12). For info: NASN, 1416 Park St, Ste A, Castle Rock, CO 80109. Phone: (303) 663-2329. Fax: (303) 663-0403. E-mail: nasn@nasn.org. Web: www.nasn.org.

NATIONAL THIRD SHIFT WORKERS DAY. May 10. To show appreciation for and to honor those often-forgotten workers who toil through the night to keep countless companies and businesses running smoothly. Annually, the second Wednesday in May. For info: Jeff Corbett, PO Box 2, Statesville, NC 28687.

"THE REST OF THE STORY" RADIO PREMIERE: 30th ANNIVERSARY. May 10, 1976. Radio legend Paul Harvey, whose "News and Comment" radio program had been on the air since 1951, spun off a popular segment into its own show on this date. "The Rest of the Story" looks at the story behind the story of famous people and events.

ROOT CANAL APPRECIATION DAY. May 10. A special day whose goal is to reverse common negative misconceptions of a routine dental procedure. The root canal, which has evolved into a simple, painless procedure, should be held in high esteem for the millions of teeth it saves—42 million American teeth this year alone. This day will provide dentists around the country with an opportunity to plan concurrent public educational events. Ceremonies can include performing a root canal filling at various locations around the country. Madison, WI, will serve as the national headquarters for Root Canal Appreciation Day. Annually, the second Wednesday in May. For info: Chris Kammer, DDS, 2275 Deming Way, Middleton, WI 53562. Phone: (608) 827-7650. Fax: (608) 824-9927. E-mail: DrChris@TheSmileExperts.com. Web: www.TheSmileExperts.com.

ROSS, GEORGE: BIRTH ANNIVERSARY. May 10, 1730. Signer of the Declaration of Independence. Born at New Castle, DE, he died July 14, 1779, at Philadelphia.

SINGAPORE: VESAK DAY. May 10. Public holiday. Monks commemorate their Lord Buddha's entry into Nirvana by chanting holy sutras and freeing captive birds.

TRUST YOUR INTUITION DAY. May 10. Today is the day we pay homage to the wonderful gift of sixth sense, "gut" feelings or that still small voice that is sometimes the only clue we have to go on in this ever-changing world. [©1994] Because of the escalating costs of Eventological® Literature, a charge of $10 must be assessed for each request. Checks are to be made payable to: Adrienne Sioux Koopersmith, 1437 W Rosemont, #1W, Chicago, IL 60660-1319. E-mail: askoopersmith@hotmail.com.

BIRTHDAYS TODAY

Bono, 46, singer (U2), humanitarian activist, born Paul Hewson at Dublin, Ireland, May 10, 1960.

Barbara Taylor Bradford, 73, author (*A Woman of Substance, Hold the Dream*), born Upper Armley, Leeds, Yorkshire, England, May 10, 1933.

T. Berry Brazleton, 88, pediatrician, author, born Waco, TX, May 10, 1918.

Jason Brooks, 40, actor ("Days of Our Lives"), born Colorado Springs, CO, May 10, 1966.

Judith Jamison, 62, dancer and choreographer, born Philadelphia, PA, May 10, 1944.

Dave Mason, 60, singer, musician, songwriter ("We Just Disagree," "So High"), born Worcester, England, May 10, 1946.

Gary Owens, 70, actor ("Rowan & Martin's Laugh-In," "The Gong Show"), born Mitchell, SD, May 10, 1936.

Ara Raoul Parseghian, 83, former football coach and sportscaster, born Akron, OH, May 10, 1923.

Marie-France Pisier, 62, actress (*Cousin Cousine, French Postcards*), born Dalat, Vietnam, May 10, 1944.

Rick Santorum, 48, US Senator (R, Pennsylvania), born Winchester, VA, May 10, 1958.

Ronald F. (Rony) Seikaly, 41, former basketball player, born Beirut, Lebanon, May 10, 1965.

MAY 11 — THURSDAY

Day 131 — 234 Remaining

BATTLE OF HAMBURGER HILL: ANNIVERSARY. May 11, 1969. Beginning of one of the most infamous battles that signified the growing frustration with America's involvement in the Vietnam War. Attempting to seize Dong Ap Bia mountain, American troops repeatedly scaled the hill over a 10-day period, often engaging in bloody hand-to-hand combat with the North Vietnamese. After finally securing the objective, American military decision makers chose to abandon it and the North Vietnamese retook it shortly thereafter. The heavy casualties in the struggle to take the hill inspired the name "Hamburger Hill."

BERLIN, IRVING: BIRTH ANNIVERSARY. May 11, 1888. Songwriter born Israel Isidore Baline at Tyumen, Russia. Irving Berlin moved to New York, NY, with his family when he was four years old. After the death of his father, he began singing in saloons and on street corners in order to help his family and worked as a singing waiter as a teenager. Berlin became one of America's most prolific songwriters, authoring such songs as "Alexander's Ragtime Band," "White Christmas," "God Bless America," "There's No Business Like Show Business," "Doin' What Comes Naturally," "Puttin' On the Ritz," "Blue Skies" and "Oh! How I

May 2006	S	M	T	W	T	F	S
		1	2	3	4	5	6
	7	8	9	10	11	12	13
	14	15	16	17	18	19	20
	21	22	23	24	25	26	27
	28	29	30	31			

Hate to Get Up in the Morning" among others. He could neither read nor write musical notation. Berlin died Sept 22, 1989, at New York, NY.

BIG TEN SOFTBALL TOURNAMENT. May 11–13. Site of conference champion. Est attendance: 1,500. For info: Big Ten Conference, 1500 W Higgins Rd, Park Ridge, IL 60068-6300. Phone: (847) 696-1010. Fax: (847) 696-1110. Web: www.bigten.org.

BIRDS & BLOSSOMS SPRING NATURE FESTIVAL. May 11–14. Norfolk Botanical Garden, Norfolk, VA. For beginning to experienced birders and naturalists of all ages. Special guests and keynote speakers, waterfowl boat tours, sunrise birding walks, bird clinics, lectures, butterfly tours and nature walks. For info: Norfolk Botanical Garden, 6700 Azalea Garden Rd, Norfolk, VA 23518-5337. Phone: (757) 441-5838. Fax: (757) 853-8294. Web: www.norfolkbotanicalgarden.org.

DALI, SALVADOR: BIRTH ANNIVERSARY. May 11, 1904. A leading painter in the Surrealist movement, Salvador Dali was equally well known for his baffling antics and attempts to shock his audiences. The largest collection of his works resides in the Salvador Dali Museum at St. Petersburg, FL. Born at Figueras, Spain, Dali died there Jan 23, 1989.

EAT WHAT YOU WANT DAY. May 11. Here's a day you may actually enjoy yourself. Ignore all those on-again/off-again warnings. [©2003 by WH.] For info: Thomas & Ruth Roy, Wellcat Holidays, 2418 Long Ln, Lebanon, PA 17046. Phone: (717) 279-0184. E-mail: info@wellcat.com. Web: www.wellcat.com.

ELKIN, STANLEY: BIRTH ANNIVERSARY. May 11, 1930. Born at Brooklyn, NY, Stanley Elkin became a professor at Washington University at St. Louis, MO, where he lectured on fiction writing for more than 30 years. In addition to his teaching, Elkin was a novelist of particular acclaim. Author of 17 books, he was awarded the National Book Critics Circle Award in 1983 for his novel *George Mills*. Elkin died at St. Louis, MO, May 31, 1995.

ENGLAND: ROYAL WINDSOR HORSE SHOW. May 11–14. Home Park, Windsor, Berkshire. Major annual show jumping event with royal pageantry and color. Est attendance: 60,000. For info: Penelope Henderson, Sec'y, Royal Windsor Horse Show, The Royal Mews, Windsor Castle, Windsor, Berkshire, England SL4 1NG. Phone: (44) (175) 386-0633. Fax: (44) (178) 075-2982. Web: www.rwhs.co.uk.

FAIRBANKS, CHARLES WARREN: BIRTH ANNIVERSARY. May 11, 1852. 26th vice president of the US (1905–09) born at Unionville Center, OH. Died at Indianapolis, IN, June 4, 1918.

GLACIER NATIONAL PARK ESTABLISHED: ANNIVERSARY. May 11, 1910. Located in northwest Montana on the Canadian border. In 1932 Glacier and Waterton Lakes National Park in Alberta were joined together by the governments of the US and Canada as Waterton-Glacier International Peace Park.

GRAHAM, MARTHA: BIRTH ANNIVERSARY. May 11, 1894. Martha Graham was born at Allegheny, PA, and became one of the giants of the modern dance movement in the US. She began her dance career at the comparatively late age of 22 and joined the Greenwich Village Follies in 1923. Her new ideas began to surface in the late '20s and '30s, and by the mid-1930s she was incorporating the rituals of the southwestern American Indians in her work. She is credited with bringing a new psychological depth to modern dance by exploring primal emotions and ancient rituals in her work. She performed until the age of 75 and premiered in her 180th ballet, *The Maple Leaf Rag*, in the fall of 1990. Died Apr 1, 1991, at New York, NY.

HART, JOHN: DEATH ANNIVERSARY. May 11, 1779. Signer of the Declaration of Independence, farmer and legislator, born about 1711 (exact date unknown), at Stonington, CT, died at Hopewell, NJ.

HOMEFEST. May 11–13. Bald Knob, AR. School reunions, homecomings, sports events, antique autos, crafts, parade, beauty pageant and more. Est attendance: 3,000. For info: Bald Knob Area Chamber of Commerce, PO Box 338, Bald Knob, AR 72010. Phone: (501) 724-3140. Fax: (501) 724-8100. E-mail: baldknob chamber@centurytel.net. Web: www.baldknobchamber.com.

JAPAN: CORMORANT FISHING FESTIVAL. May 11–Oct 15. Cormorant fishing on the Nagara River, Gifu. "This ancient method of catching Ayu, a troutlike fish, with trained cormorants, takes place nightly under the light of blazing torches."

MERRIMAC DESTROYED: ANNIVERSARY. May 11, 1862. After a standoff with the Union ironclad *Monitor* on Mar 9, the Confederate ironclad *Merrimac* was destroyed by the Confederate navy on May 11. In the wake of advancing Union troops in the Peninsular Campaign, the South was forced to destroy the valuable vessel to prevent its capture by Union forces. See also: "Battle of Hampton Roads: Anniversary" (Mar 9).

MINNESOTA: ADMISSION DAY: ANNIVERSARY. May 11. Became 32nd state in 1858.

SUTTON HOO SHIP BURIAL DISCOVERED: ANNIVERSARY. May 11, 1939. On this date, in a large mound in rural Suffolk, England, archaeologist Basil Brown discovered an undisturbed royal Anglo-Saxon ship burial. The ship—the largest ever found—was 90 feet long and 14 feet wide (the wood had rotted away, leaving only an outline and rivets). Also discovered were gold, bronze, silver and gemmed artifacts and weapons. The ship burial is believed to be that of King Raedwald of East Anglia, who ruled in the early 600s AD.

BIRTHDAYS TODAY

Louis Farrakhan, 73, Nation of Islam leader, born New York, NY, May 11, 1933.

Bernard Fox, 79, actor ("Bewitched," *Titanic*), born Portalbot, South Wales, May 11, 1927.

Jonathan Jackson, 24, actor (*The Deep End of the Ocean*, "General Hospital"), born Orlando, FL, May 11, 1982.

Robert Jarvik, 60, physician, inventor of artificial heart that went into Barney Clark, born Midland, MI, May 11, 1946.

James M. Jeffords, 72, US Senator (I, Vermont), born Rutland, VT, May 11, 1934.

Natasha Richardson, 43, actress (*The Handmaid's Tale, Nell*), born London, England, May 11, 1963.

Mort Sahl, 79, comic actor (*Don't Make Waves, Doctor You've Got to Be Kidding*), born Montreal, QC, Canada, May 11, 1927.

MAY 12 — FRIDAY
Day 132 — 233 Remaining

ALBANY TULIP FESTIVAL. May 12–14. Washington Park, Albany, NY. A celebration of spring, the Tulip Festival features thousands of tulips abloom throughout the city and honors Albany's Dutch heritage. Events include crowning of a Tulip Queen, arts and crafts vendors, food vendors, entertainment on three stages, children's activities and Dutch dancers in costume. Est attendance: 100,000. For info: Susan T. Cleary, City of Albany Office of Special Events, City Hall, Room 402, Eagle Street, Albany, NY 12207. Phone: (518) 434-2032. Fax: (518) 426-0759. E-mail: info@albanyevents.org. Web: www.albanyevents.org.

BATTLE OF SPOTSYLVANIA: ANNIVERSARY. May 12, 1864. After the Battle of the Wilderness, Grant and Lee next engaged at the Battle of Spotsylvania (VA). Lee had positioned his troops in breastworks along a horseshoe formation utilizing the natural features of the landscape. During Grant's attack on this strong defensive position, both sides suffered losses of more than 12,000 in what became known as "The Bloody Angle." Lee was forced to use every available man in order to protect the position and so ordered his troops to pull back during the night.

BIG TEN MEN'S/WOMEN'S OUTDOOR TRACK AND FIELD CHAMPIONSHIPS. May 12–14. Site TBD. Est attendance: 1,500. For info: Big Ten Conference, 1500 W Higgins Rd, Park Ridge, IL 60068-6300. Phone: (847) 696-1010. Fax: (847) 696-1110. Web: www.bigten.org.

BIG 12 MEN'S AND WOMEN'S OUTDOOR TRACK AND FIELD CHAMPIONSHIPS. May 12–14. Hart-Patterson Track and Field Complex, Waco, TX. For info: Big 12 Conference, 2201 Stemmons Frwy, 28th FL, Dallas, TX 75207. Phone: (214) 742-1212. Fax: (214) 753-0145. Web: www.big12 sports.com.

BLUEGRASS FESTIVAL. May 12–13. Hope, AR. The 10th annual Hope/Hempstead County Chamber of Commerce Free Bluegrass Festival is the only free bluegrass festival in the state of Arkansas. Features local, regional and nationally known bluegrass acts. Est attendance: 3,000. For info: Hope/Hempstead Chamber of Commerce, PO Box 250, Hope, AR 71802. Phone: (870) 777-3640. Fax: (870) 722-6154. E-mail: hopeark@arkansas .net. Web: www.hopemelonfest.com.

DENMARK: COMMON PRAYER DAY. May 12. Public holiday. The fourth Friday after Easter, known as "Store Bededag," is a day for prayer and festivity.

ELECTRA GOAT BBQ COOK-OFF & ARTS AND CRAFTS SHOW. May 12–13. Electra Goat Grounds, Electra, TX. Goat brisket, pork ribs, chicken cook-off, Cow Patty Drop, live band, Jackpot Steak & Beans Competition, tug-of-war, eating contest, children's games and crafts. Little Mr and Miss Goat Competition, Friday night dance and salsa contest. Est attendance: 2,000. For info: Sherry Strange, Electra Chamber of Commerce, 112 W Cleveland, Electra, TX 76360. Phone: (940) 495-3577. E-mail: electracoc@electratel.net. Web: www.electra texas.org.

GEORGE VI'S CORONATION: ANNIVERSARY. May 12, 1937. George VI was crowned at Westminster Abbey at London, following the abdication of his brother, Edward VIII. Born Dec 14, 1895, King George died Feb 6, 1952. He was succeeded by his daughter Elizabeth, the current reigning monarch.

HEPBURN, KATHARINE: BIRTH ANNIVERSARY. May 12, 1907. American actress Katharine Houghton Hepburn was born at Hartford, CT. Nominated for 12 Oscars over the course of her career, she won four times: for 1933's *Morning Glory*, 1967's *Guess Who's Coming to Dinner*, 1968's *The Lion in Winter* and 1981's *On Golden Pond*. She is best remembered for her on- and offscreen pairing with Spencer Tracy. Together, they made 9 films, including *Adam's Rib* and *Woman of the Year*, and enjoyed a 27-year personal relationship. There is often confusion regarding her date of birth: in her 1991 autobiography *Me: Stories of My Life*, she confirmed the May date and admitted often giving out a late brother's birth date as her own. She died at Old Saybrook, CT, June 29, 2003.

LEAR, EDWARD: BIRTH ANNIVERSARY. May 12, 1812. English artist and author, best remembered for his light verse and limericks. Lear was born at Highgate, England, and died at San Remo, Italy, Jan 29, 1888. See also: "Limerick Day" (May 12).

LILAC FESTIVAL. May 12–21. Highland Park, Rochester, NY. Developed by renowned park designer Frederick Law Olmsted, Highland Park is the site of the Lilac Festival, the largest celebration of its kind in North America. In addition to the spectacle of more than 500 varieties of lilacs in bloom, the festival provides free admission, free entertainment, free children's activities and entertainment, a parade, a 10k race, two juried art shows, a senior citizens' day and music festivals. Est attendance: 400,000. For info: Susan LeBeau, Lilac Festival, 171 Reservoir Ave, Rochester, NY 14620. Phone: (585) 256-4960. Fax: (585) 256-4968. E-mail: info@lilacfestival.com. Web: www.lilacfestival.com.

LIMERICK DAY. May 12. Observed on the birthday of one of its champions, Edward Lear. The limerick, which dates from the early 18th century, has been described as the "only fixed verse form indigenous to the English language." It gained its greatest popularity following the publication of Edward Lear's *Book of Nonsense* (and its sequels). Write a limerick today! Example: There was a young poet named Lear/Who said, it is just as I fear/Five lines are enough/For this kind of stuff/Make a limerick each day of the year. See also: "Lear, Edward: Birth Anniversary" (May 12).

NATIONAL RECEPTIONISTS DAY. May 12. Day of recognition for our nation's frontline personnel in business, because you only get one chance to make a good first impression. Receptionists may go by other names such as host/hostess, maitre d', front desk clerk, operator, customer service representative, information desk personnel or anyone responsible for creating or maintaining a favorable image for the company by greeting clients and guests. There are some 892,000 receptionists in the US. Annually, May 12 or the next business day if the 12th falls on a Saturday or Sunday (previously observed on May 14). For info: Jennifer Alexander, Natl Receptionists Association, 22 Lewis St, Milford, CT 06460. Phone: (203) 273-1179. Fax: (203) 283-1888. E-mail: jennifer@nationalreceptionists.com. Web: www.national-receptionists.com.

NATIVE AMERICAN RIGHTS RECOGNIZED: ANNIVERSARY. May 12, 1879. When the US tried to forcibly remove the Poncas from their homeland in Nebraska to an Oklahoma reservation, their chief, Standing Bear, brought suit to prevent it. The US claimed that Standing Bear could not bring suit because as a Native American he had no legal standing in US law. In *Standing Bear v George Crook* at US District Court, Judge J. Dundy ruled on this day that "an Indian is a PERSON within the meaning of the laws of the United States." This landmark decision was appealed by the US to the Supreme Court, who dismissed it. Standing Bear was not forced to move his tribe, but other Native Americans were unable to use the decision to their advantage in other disputes with the US.

May 2006	S	M	T	W	T	F	S
		1	2	3	4	5	6
	7	8	9	10	11	12	13
	14	15	16	17	18	19	20
	21	22	23	24	25	26	27
	28	29	30	31			

NIGHTINGALE, FLORENCE: BIRTH ANNIVERSARY. May 12, 1820. English nurse and public health activist who, through her unselfish devotion to nursing, contributed perhaps more than any other single person to the development of modern nursing procedures and dignity of nursing as a profession. Founder of the Nightingale training school for nurses. Author of *Notes on Nursing*. Born at Florence, Italy. Died at London, England, Aug 13, 1910.

ODOMETER INVENTED: ANNIVERSARY. May 12, 1847. Anniversary of the invention of the first odometer, invented by Mormon pioneer William Clayton while crossing the plains in a covered wagon. Previous to this, mileage was calculated by counting the revolutions of a rag tied to a spoke of a wagon wheel. For info: Museum of Church History and Art, 45 North West Temple, Salt Lake City, UT 84150. Phone: (801) 240-4604.

PENNSYLVANIA ARTS & CRAFTS MOTHER'S DAY FESTIVAL. May 12–14. ExPo Mart, Monroeville, PA. More than 170 exhibits of handcrafted furniture, gift items, children's toys, dolls, dried floral arrangements, clothing, jewelry and much more. Food and entertainment. Est attendance: 15,000. For info: Debbie or Dave Stoner, Family Festivals Assn, Inc, PO Box 166, Irwin, PA 15642. Phone/fax: (724) 863-4577. E-mail: familyfestivals@hotmail.com. Web: www.familyfestivals.com.

PORTUGAL: PILGRIMAGE TO FATIMA: ANNIVERSARY. May 12–13. Commemorates first appearance of the Virgin of the Rosary to little shepherd children May 13, 1917. Pilgrims come to Cova da Iria, religious center, candlelit procession, mass of the sick, for annual observance.

RED, WHITE & BLUEGRASS. May 12–14. Hollywood, FL. Traditional and contemporary bluegrass on three stages. Also features barbeque, contests and arts and crafts vendors. Est attendance: 15,000. For info: Cynthia Hancock, City of Hollywood, 1940 Harrison St, Ste 101, Hollywood, FL 33020. Phone: (954) 921-3404. Fax: (954) 921-3572. E-mail: chancock@hollywoodfl.org. Web: www.hollywoodfl.org.

RHODODENDRON FESTIVAL. May 12–14 (also May 19–21). Georgia Mountain Fairgrounds, Hiawassee, GA. Arts & crafts. Concerts. Est attendance: 15,000. For info: Rhododendron Festival, PO Box 444, Hiawassee, GA 30546. Phone: (706) 896-4191.

SPRING GARDENER'S MARKET AND PLANT SALE. May 12–14. Norfolk Botanical Garden, Norfolk, VA. Gardening enthusiasts can shop from more than 30 specialty growers, plant societies and wholesalers for the best selection of plants. Annually, Mother's Day weekend. Est attendance: 4,000. For info: Norfolk Botanical Garden, 6700 Azalea Garden Rd, Norfolk, VA 23518. Phone: (757) 441-5830. Fax: (757) 853-8294. Web: www.norfolkbotanicalgarden.org.

BIRTHDAYS TODAY

MacKenzie Astin, 33, actor (*The Last Days of Disco*), born Los Angeles, CA, May 12, 1973.

Burt Bacharach, 77, composer ("Walk On By," "Close to You," "Raindrops Keep Fallin' on My Head," many film scores), born Kansas City, MO, May 12, 1929.

Stephen Baldwin, 40, actor (*The Usual Suspects*), born Massapequa, NY, May 12, 1966.

Lawrence Peter (Yogi) Berra, 81, Hall of Fame baseball player, former baseball coach and manager, born St. Louis, MO, May 12, 1925.

Jason Biggs, 28, actor (*American Pie, Loser*), born Pompton Plains, NJ, May 12, 1978.

Bruce Boxleitner, 55, actor (*How the West Was Won*, "Scarecrow and Mrs King"), born Elgin, IL, May 12, 1951.

Gabriel Byrne, 56, actor (*The Usual Suspects*), born Dublin, Ireland, May 12, 1950.

Christian Campbell, 34, actor ("Malibu Shores," *Cold Hearts*), born Toronto, ON, Canada, May 12, 1972.

George Carlin, 69, comedian ("That Girl," "The George Carlin Show"), born New York, NY, May 12, 1937.

Lindsay Crouse, 58, actress (*Slap Shot, The Verdict, Places in the Heart*), born New York, NY, May 12, 1948.

Emilio Estevez, 44, actor (*Breakfast Club, Repo Man*), born New York, NY, May 12, 1962.

Kim Fields, 37, actress ("The Facts of Life," "Living Single"), born Los Angeles, CA, May 12, 1969.

Kim Greist, 48, actress (*Brazil, Throw Momma from the Train*), born Stamford, CT, May 12, 1958.

Tony Hawk, 37, skateboarder, born Carlsbad, CA, May 12, 1969.

Dave Heineman, 58, Governor of Nebraska (R), born Falls City, NE, May 12, 1948.

Jamie Luner, 35, actress ("Melrose Place," "Profiler"), born Los Angeles, CA, May 12, 1971.

Millie Perkins, 68, actress ("Knots Landing," *The Diary of Anne Frank, Wall Street*), born Passaic, NJ, May 12, 1938.

Ving Rhames, 45, actor ("Kojak," *Pulp Fiction*), born New York, NY, May 12, 1961.

Tom Snyder, 70, broadcast journalist, TV personality, born Milwaukee, WI, May 12, 1936.

Frank Stella, 70, artist (*Empress of India*), born Malden, MA, May 12, 1936.

Steve Winwood, 58, musician, singer, born Birmingham, England, May 12, 1948.

MAY 13 — SATURDAY
Day 133 — 232 Remaining

ATTEMPTED ASSASSINATION OF POPE JOHN PAUL II: 25th ANNIVERSARY. May 13, 1981. Pope John Paul II was shot twice at close range while riding in an open automobile at St. Peter's Square at Rome, Italy. Two other persons also were wounded. An escaped terrorist, Mehmet Ali Agca (already under sentence of death for the murder of a Turkish journalist), was arrested immediately and was convicted July 22, 1981, of attempted murder of the pope. After convalescence Pope John Paul II was pronounced recovered by his doctors Aug 14, 1981. In 2000 Agca was released from prison and extradited to Turkey.

CELLULAR SOUTH GUM TREE FESTIVAL. May 13–14. Tupelo, MS. A juried art show with arts, crafts and live entertainment. 10k run. Annually, Mother's Day weekend. Est attendance: 25,000. For info: Tupelo Conv and Visitors Bureau, PO Drawer 47, Tupelo, MS 38802. Phone: (800) 533-0611 or (662) 844-2787. Fax: (662) 844-9751. Web: www.gumtreemuseum.com.

DOUGLAS, VIRGINIA O'HANLON: 35th DEATH ANNIVERSARY. May 13, 1971. Virginia O'Hanlon Douglas lived a long and productive life as an educator and a loving mother. However, to the reading public she is reintroduced year after year at Christmastime as the disheartened eight-year-old who asked the staff of *The New York Sun* whether Santa Claus exists. In a famous 1897 editorial Francis P. Church answered her question and reassured Virginia that yes, indeed "there is a Santa Claus." Douglas died at Valatie, NY, at the age of 81.

INTERNATIONAL MIGRATORY BIRD CELEBRATION. May 13–14. Chincoteague, VA. Three days of walks, talks, workshops, boat tours, children's activities and an art celebration all conducted outdoors with the birds. Annually, Mother's Day weekend. Est attendance: 10,000. For info: Chincoteague Chamber of Commerce, 6733 Maddox Blvd, Chincoteague, VA 23336. Phone: (757) 336-6161. Fax: (757) 336-1242. E-mail: chinco chamber@verizon.net. Web: www.chincoteaguechamber.com.

INTERNATIONAL MIGRATORY BIRD DAY. May 13. To educate the public about migratory birds and the preservation of their habitats in the US and Central America. Annually, the second Saturday in May.

JAMESTOWN LANDING DAY. May 13. Jamestown Settlement, Williamsburg, VA. Maritime demonstrations and interpretative activities exploring contact between European and Virginia Indian cultures mark the 399th anniversary of the founding of America's first permanent English colony. Special programs and events also are held at Historic Jamestown, administered by the Colonial National Historical Park and the Association for the Preservation of Virginia Antiquities. For info: Jamestown-Yorktown Foundation, PO Box 1607, Williamsburg, VA 23187. Phone: (757) 253-4838 or toll-free (888) 593-4682. Fax: (757) 253-5299. Web: www.historyisfun.org.

LIBERACE BIRTHDAY CELEBRATION AND LIBERACE PLAY-A-LIKE COMPETITION. May 13. The Liberace Museum, Las Vegas, NV. To celebrate Liberace's birthday, the museum will host the annual Liberace "Play-a-Like" Competition. Judges pianists on keyboard technique, costume and presentation in two divisions: professional and nonprofessional. Winners receive commemorative awards. Annually, the Saturday before May 16 (Liberace's birthday). Est attendance: 1,000. For info: Liberace Museum, 1775 E Tropicana Ave, Las Vegas, NV, 89119-6529. Phone: (702) 798-5595. Web: www.liberace.org.

LOUIS, JOE: BIRTH ANNIVERSARY. May 13, 1914. World heavyweight boxing champion, 1937–49, nicknamed the "Brown Bomber," Joseph Louis Barrow was born near Lafayette, AL. He died Apr 12, 1981, at Las Vegas, NV. Buried at Arlington National Cemetery. (Louis's burial there, by presidential waiver, was the 39th exception ever to the eligibility rules for burial in Arlington National Cemetery.)

MEET THE ARTISTS AND ARTISANS SHOW. May 13–14. Milford Green, CT. 44th annual. More than 200 juried, award-winning artists and crafters from throughout the nation. For info: Meet the Artists & Artisans Show. Phone: (203) 874-5672. Email: ctlimner@snet.net. Web: www.meettheartists andartisans.com or www.ctlimner.com. For additional info: Greater New Haven Conv & Visitors Bureau, 59 Elm St, New Haven, CT 06510. Phone: (203) 777-8550 or (800) 332-STAY.

MEXICAN WAR DECLARED: ANNIVERSARY. May 13, 1846. Although fighting had begun days earlier, Congress officially declared war on Mexico on this date. The struggle cost the lives of 11,300 American soldiers and resulted in the annexation by the US of land that became parts of Oklahoma, New Mexico, Arizona, Nevada, California, Utah and Colorado. The war ended in 1848. See also: "Treaty of Guadalupe Hidalgo" (Feb 2).

MOON PHASE: FULL MOON. May 13. Moon enters Full Moon phase at 2:51 AM, EDT.

MOTHER OCEAN DAY. May 13. To celebrate the wonder, vastness and beauty of the ocean. Casting of roses into the sea from the beach and from the water. Annually, on the day before Mother's Day. For info: Cynthia Hancock, Pres, Natl Week of the Ocean, Inc, PO Box 179, Ft Lauderdale, FL 33302. Phone: (954) 462-5573. Web: www.national-week-of-the-ocean.org.

MOTHER'S DAY ANNUAL RHODODENDRON SHOW. May 13–14. Crystal Springs Rhododendron Gardens, Portland, OR. Spectacular display of rhododendron and azalea blooms and plant sale. Est attendance: 6,000. For info: Kathy Van Veen, American Rhododendron Society, Portland Chapter, PO Box 86424, Portland, OR 97286. Phone: (503) 777-1734. Fax: (503) 777-2048.

NATIONAL BABYSITTERS DAY. May 13. To give babysitters across the nation appreciation and special recognition for their quality child care. Annually, the Saturday before Mother's Day. For info: Barbara Baldwin RN, Safety Whys, PO Box 1177, Helotes, TX 78023-1177. Phone: (210) 695-9838. Fax: (210) 695-5673. E-mail: bbaldwin@satx.rr.com. Web: www.safetywhys .com.

NATIONAL TOURISM WEEK. May 13–21. 23rd annual week promoting and enhancing awareness of travel and tourism's importance to the economic, social and cultural well-being of the US. For info: Travel Industry Assn of America, 1100 New York Ave NW, Ste 450, Washington, DC 20005-3934. Phone: (202) 408-2182. E-mail: lhorsley@tia.org. Web: www.tia.org.

NETHERLANDS: NATIONAL WINDMILL DAY. May 13. About 950 windmills still survive, and some 300 still are used occasionally and have been designated national monuments by the government. As many windmills as possible are in operation on National Windmill Day for the benefit of tourists. Annually, the second Saturday in May.

OCCONEECHEE STATE PARK NATIVE AMERICAN FESTIVAL AND POW WOW. May 13. Clarksville, VA. Gates open at 10 AM, Grand Entry at 12 PM and continues until 8 PM. Native American artists and crafters show and sell their wares. Dancers, singers and drummers perform intertribal songs and dances. Annually, the second Saturday in May. Est attendance: 3,000. For info: Occoneechee State Park, 1192 Occoneechee Park Rd, Clarksville, VA 23927. Phone: (434) 374-2210. E-mail: occoneechee@dcr.virginia.gov. Web: www.dcr.state.va.us/parks/occoneec.htm.

PHILADELPHIA POLICE BOMBING: ANNIVERSARY. May 13, 1985. During the siege of the radical group MOVE at Philadelphia, PA, police in a helicopter reportedly dropped a bomb containing the powerful military plastic explosive C-4 on the building in which the group was housed. The bomb and the resulting fire left 11 persons dead (including four children) and destroyed 61 homes.

ROAD CHURCH MISSIONARY FAIR. May 13. Road Congregational Church, Pequot Trail, Stonington, CT. Bake sale, crafts, white elephants and more. Homemade luncheon available at noon. 10 AM–2 PM. For info: Libby Kennedy, 21 Roosevelt Ave, Mystic, CT 06355. Phone: (860) 536-1514. E-mail: roadchurch@juno.com. Web: www.roadchurch.org.

SAINT LAWRENCE SEAWAY ACT: ANNIVERSARY. May 13, 1954. President Dwight D. Eisenhower signed legislation authorizing US–Canadian construction of a waterway that would make it possible for oceangoing ships to reach the Great Lakes.

SPACE MILESTONE: *ENDEAVOUR* (US). May 13, 1992. Three astronauts from the shuttle *Endeavour* simultaneously walked in space for the first time.

STAMP OUT HUNGER—NALC NATIONAL FOOD DRIVE. May 13. 14th annual. Every year since 1993, on the second Saturday in May, letter carriers in more than 10,000 cities and towns across the 50 states, the District of Columbia, Puerto Rico, Guam and the Virgin Islands collect nonperishable food items left by mailboxes and in post offices from their postal customers. The National Association of Letter Carriers National Food Drive is the largest one-day food drive in the nation. The US Postal Service, Campbell Soup Company and America's Second Harvest are major sponsors among many others. For info: Drew Von Bergen, Natl Association of Letter Carriers, 100 Indiana Ave NW, Washington, DC 20001-2144. Phone: (202) 662-2489. E-mail: vonbergen@nalc.org. Web: www.nalc.org.

SULLIVAN, ARTHUR: BIRTH ANNIVERSARY. May 13, 1842. English composer best known for light operas (with Sir William Gilbert), born at London, England. Died there Nov 22, 1900.

★   ★   ★

		S	M	T	W	T	F	S
May			1	2	3	4	5	6
2006		7	8	9	10	11	12	13
		14	15	16	17	18	19	20
		21	22	23	24	25	26	27
		28	29	30	31			

SUPER SCOUT SATURDAY. May 13 (tentative). Springfield, MO. Scouts earn nature-oriented badges by visiting programs and stations designed exclusively for scout groups. For info: Linda Chorice, Springfield Conservation Nature Center, 4600 S Chrisman Ave, Springfield, MO 65804. Phone: (417) 888-4237. Fax: (417) 888-4241. Web: www.missouriconservation.com.

TUNIS CAMPAIGN VICTORY: ANNIVERSARY. May 13, 1943. General Sir Harold Alexander telegraphed Winston Churchill, who was in Washington attending a conference, "It is my duty to report that the Tunis campaign is over. All enemy resistance has ceased. We are masters of the North African shores." About 250,000 Germans and Italians surrendered in the last few days of the campaign. This Allied victory in North Africa helped open Mediterranean shipping lanes.

WELLS, MARY: BIRTH ANNIVERSARY. May 13, 1943. Motown's first big star, Mary Wells was born at Detroit, MI. She was known for such hits as "You Beat Me to the Punch," "Two Lovers" and her signature song, "My Guy." She was one of a group of black artists of the '60s who helped end musical segregation by being played on white radio stations. Mary Wells died July 26, 1992, at Los Angeles, CA.

WORLD FAIR TRADE DAY. May 13. A day to promote fair trade as an alternative economic model. "Fair trade" means that trading partnerships are based on reciprocal benefits and mutual respect; that prices paid to producers reflect the work they do; that workers have the right to organize; that national health, safety and wage laws are enforced and that products are environmentally sustainable and conserve natural resources. Celebrated worldwide in 50 countries with a variety of events from live music to symposia. Annually, the second Saturday in May. For info: International Fair Trade Association, Prijssestraat 24, 4101 CR Culemborg, The Netherlands. Phone: (31) (345) 53-59-14. Fax: (31) (847) 47-44-01. E-mail: info@ifat.org. Web: www.ifat.org or www.wftday.org.

YOU GOTTA HAVE PARK. May 13–14. Prospect Park, Brooklyn, NY. This annual weekend-long celebration of Brooklyn's Prospect Park is dedicated to cleaning, greening and bringing the park's neighbors and volunteers together. Annually, the second weekend in May. Est attendance: 20,000. For info: Prospect Park Alliance, Litchfield Villa, 95 Prospect Park W, Brooklyn, NY 11215. Phone: (718) 965-8999. Fax: (718) 965-8926. E-mail: jadelman@prospectpark.org. Web: www.prospectpark.org.

BIRTHDAYS TODAY

Franklyn Ajaye, 57, actor ("Keep on Truckin'," *Car Wash*), born Brooklyn, NY, May 13, 1949.

Beatrice Arthur, 80, actress (*Mame*, "Maude," "Golden Girls"), born Bernice Frankel at New York, NY, May 13, 1926.

Frances Barber, 49, actress (*Sammy and Rosie Get Laid, We Think the World of You*), born Wolverhampton, England, May 13, 1957.

Clive Barnes, 79, critic, born London, England, May 13, 1927.

Mike Bibby, 28, basketball player, born Cherry Hill, NJ, May 13, 1978.

Harvey Keitel, 67, actor (*Mean Streets, Blue Collar, Bugsy, The Piano*), born Brooklyn, NY, May 13, 1939.

Julianne Phillips, 44, actress (*Allie & Me*, "Sisters"), born Lake Oswego, OR, May 13, 1962.

Tim Pigott-Smith, 60, actor ("The Jewel in the Crown," *Remains of the Day*), born Rugby, England, May 13, 1946.

Dennis ("Worm") Rodman, 45, former basketball player, born Trenton, NJ, May 13, 1961.

Darius Rucker, 38, lead singer (Hootie and the Blowfish), born Charleston, SC, May 13, 1968.

Bobby Valentine, 56, former baseball player and manager, broadcaster, born Stamford, CT, May 13, 1950.

Stevie Wonder, 56, singer, musician (19 Grammy Awards; "I Just Called to Say I Love You"), born Steveland Morris Hardaway at Saginaw, MI, May 13, 1950.

MAY 14 — SUNDAY
Day 134 — 231 Remaining

BORNEO RHINO CHALLENGE. May 14–28 (subject to change). Borneo, Malaysia. Fund-raising event to protect the Sumatran rhino. Biathlon consisting of a mountain trek and biking in Borneo. For info: Maggie Heydt, SOS Rhino, 680 N Lake Shore Dr, Ste 807, Chicago, IL 60611. Phone: (312) 222-0440. E-mail: maggie@sosrhino.org. Web: www.sosrhino.org.

CARLSBAD CAVERNS NATIONAL PARK ESTABLISHED: ANNIVERSARY. May 14, 1930. Located in southwestern New Mexico, Carlsbad Caverns was proclaimed a national monument, Oct 25, 1923, and was later established as a national park and preserve.

"ERNIE KOVACS" TV PREMIERE: 55th ANNIVERSARY. May 14, 1951. Comedian Ernie Kovacs first hosted "It's Time for Ernie," a 15-minute afternoon program on NBC in May of 1951 before replacing the "Kukla, Fran and Ollie Show" with "Ernie in Kovacsland." "The Ernie Kovacs Show" debuted on Dec 30, 1952. Kovacs also appeared on a variety of daytime and prime-time series and was a fill-in for Steve Allen on the "Tonight!" show. His early shows featured his wife, Edie Adams.

FAHRENHEIT, GABRIEL DANIEL: BIRTH ANNIVERSARY. May 14, 1686. German physicist whose name is attached to one of the major temperature measurement scales. He introduced the use of mercury in thermometers and greatly improved their accuracy. Born at Danzig, Germany, he died at Amsterdam, Holland, Sept 16, 1736.

FIRST FORMAL FEMALE HOUSE PAGE APPOINTMENT: ANNIVERSARY. May 14, 1973. The House of Representatives received formal approval of the appointment of female pages in 1972. On May 14, 1973, in the 93rd Congress, Felda Looper was appointed as the successor to Gene Cox who, for three hours, had served as the first female page 34 years earlier.

GAINSBOROUGH, THOMAS: BIRTH ANNIVERSARY. May 14, 1727 (OS). English landscape and portrait painter. Among his most remembered works: *The Blue Boy*, *The Watering Place* and *The Market Cart*. Born at Sudbury, Suffolk, England, he was baptized on May 14, 1727 (OS), and he died at London, Aug 2, 1788.

JAMESTOWN, VIRGINIA: FOUNDING ANNIVERSARY. May 14, 1607 (OS). The first permanent English settlement in what is now the US took place at Jamestown, VA (named for England's King James I), on this date. Captains John Smith and Christopher Newport were among the leaders of the group of royally chartered Virginia Company settlers who had traveled from Plymouth, England, in three small ships: *Susan Constant*, *Godspeed* and *Discovery*.

KIWANIS PRAYER WEEK. May 14–20. Encourages Kiwanis Clubs to promote religious activities throughout their communities and to recognize individuals for their contributions to spiritual welfare. Annually, the second full week in May. For info: Kiwanis Intl, Member Services, 3636 Woodview Trace, Indianapolis, IN 46268. E-mail: kiwanismail@kiwanis.org. Web: www.kiwanis.org.

LEWIS AND CLARK EXPEDITION SETS OUT: ANNIVERSARY. May 14, 1804. Charged by President Thomas Jefferson with finding a route to the Pacific, Captain Meriwether Lewis and Lieutenant William Clark left St. Louis with a 33-member group skilled in botany, zoology, outdoor survival and other scientific skills. They arrived at the Pacific coast of Oregon in November 1805 and returned to St. Louis, Sept 23, 1806. (See also Jan 18 and Sept 23.)

MILLION MOM MARCH: ANNIVERSARY. May 14, 2000. Women rallied in Washington, DC, and 60 other US cities to urge Congress to "get serious about commonsense gun legislation." For info: Million Mom March, 1225 Eye St NW, Ste 1100, Washington, DC 20005. Phone: (202) 898-0792. Web: www.millionmommarch.com.

MOTHER'S DAY. May 14. Observed first in 1907 at the request of Anna Jarvis of Philadelphia, PA, who asked her church to hold a service in memory of all mothers on the anniversary of her mother's death. In 1909, two years after her mother's death, Jarvis and friends began a letter-writing campaign to create a Mother's Day observance. Congress passed legislation in 1914 designating the second Sunday in May as Mother's Day. Some say the predecessor of Mother's Day was the ancient spring festival dedicated to mother goddesses: Rhea (Greek) and Cybele (Roman).

★**MOTHER'S DAY.** May 14. Presidential Proclamation always issued for the second Sunday in May. (Pub Res No. 2 of May 8, 1914.)

MOTHERS DAY AT THE WALL. May 14. Washington, DC. Annual observance at the Vietnam Veterans Memorial since 2000 honoring the mothers of those who died in combat. Area schoolchildren offer cards.

MOTHER'S DAY CELEBRATION. May 14. Jenkinson's Aquarium, Point Pleasant Beach, NJ. Calling all kids! Bring your mom for a special day to learn about the roles of mothers in the marine environment. One mother admitted free with each paid child's admission. Est attendance: 800. For info: Jenkinson's Aquarium, 300 Ocean Ave, Point Pleasant Beach, NJ 08742. Phone: (732) 899-1212. Fax: (732) 899-1717. E-mail: jenkinsonsaquarium@comcast.net. Web: www.jenkinsons.com.

MOTHER'S DAY HOUSEWALK. May 14. Evanston, IL. 31st annual tour of historic homes as a fund-raiser for the Evanston Historical Society. Annually, on Mother's Day. Est attendance: 2,000. For info: Evanston Historical Society, 225 Greenwood St, Evanston, IL 60201. Phone: (847) 475-3410. E-mail: evanstonhs@northwestern.edu.

NATIONAL FAMILY MONTH®. May 14–June 18. A month-long national observance to celebrate and promote strong, supportive families. Sponsored by KidsPeace®, a private children's charity that helps kids overcome crisis. Annually, Mother's Day through Father's Day. For info: Kids Peace, 5300 KidsPeace Dr, Orefield, PA 18069. Phone: (800) 25-PEACE. E-mail: jvallone@kidspeace.org. Web: www.familymonth.net.

NATIONAL NURSING HOME WEEK. May 14–20. A community outreach program designed to familiarize the public with long-term care facilities and the services they provide. Activities are conducted locally by individual long-term care facilities. Annually, Mother's Day through the following Saturday. For info: American Health Care Assn, Natl Nursing Home Week, 1201 L St NW, Washington, DC 20005. Phone: (202) 842-4444. Fax: (202) 842-3860. Web: www.ahca.org.

NATIONAL POLICE WEEK. May 14–20. See also: "Peace Officer Memorial Day" (May 15). For info: American Police Hall of Fame and Museum, 6350 Horizon Dr, Titusville, FL 32780. Phone: (321) 264-0911. E-mail: policeinfo@aphf.org. Web: www.aphf.org.

★**NATIONAL TRANSPORTATION WEEK.** May 14–20. Presidential Proclamation issued for week including third Friday in May since 1960. (PL86–475 of May 20, 1960, first requested; PL87–449 of May 14, 1962, requested an annual proclamation.)

NORWAY: MIDNIGHT SUN AT NORTH CAPE. May 14–July 30. North Cape. First day of the season with around-the-clock sunshine. At North Cape, the sun never dips below the horizon from May 14 to July 30, but the night is bright long before and after these dates.

OWEN, ROBERT: BIRTH ANNIVERSARY. May 14, 1771. English progressive owner of spinning works, philanthropist, Utopian socialist, founder of New Harmony, IN, born at Newtown, Wales. Died there Nov 17, 1858.

PHILIPPINES: CARABAO FESTIVAL. May 14–15. Pulilan, Bulacan; Nueva Ecija; Angono, Rizal. Parade of farmers to honor their patron saint, San Isidro, with hundreds of "dressed up" carabaos participating.

★**POLICE WEEK.** May 14–20. Presidential Proclamation 3537 of May 4, 1963, covers all succeeding years. (PL87–726 of Oct 1, 1962.) Always the week including May 15 since 1962.

PREPARE TOMORROW'S PARENTS MONTH. May 14–June 18. To celebrate mothers and fathers, do at least one activity between Mother's Day and Father's Day to help prepare a child or teen to become a better parent in the future. To get ideas for parenting preparation activities for this month and year-round, visit www.preparetomorrowsparents.org which posts easy, fun steps to take at home as well as classroom-ready learning experiences for teachers, parents and youth organization leaders. For info: Prepare Tomorrow's Parents, 454 NE 3rd St, Boca Raton, FL 33432. Phone: (888) PARENTS. E-mail: info@prepare tomorrowsparents.org. Web: www.preparetomorrowsparents.org.

RACE FOR THE CURE®. May 14. Pittsburgh, PA. 5k walk/run and one-mile fun walk to raise awareness of breast cancer and help fund research for a cure. One of 116 races around the country founded by the Susan G. Komen Breast Cancer Foundation. Annually, on Mother's Day. Est attendance: 36,000. For info: Race for the Cure®, 1620 Murray Ave, Pittsburgh, PA 15217. Phone: (412) 521-2873. E-mail: info@pittsburghraceforthecure .org. Web: www.pittsburghraceforthecure.org.

READING IS FUN WEEK. May 14–20. To highlight the importance and fun of reading. For info: Reading Is Fundamental, Inc, 1825 Connecticut Ave NW, Ste 400, Washington, DC 20009. Phone: (202) 673-1526 or (877) RIF-READ. Fax: (202) 673-1635. Web: www.rif.org.

SMALLPOX VACCINE DISCOVERED: ANNIVERSARY. May 14, 1796. In the 18th century, smallpox was a widespread and often fatal disease. Edward Jenner, a physician in rural England, heard reports of dairy farmers who apparently became immune to smallpox as a result of exposure to cowpox, a related but milder disease. After two decades of studying the phenomenon, Jenner injected cowpox into a healthy eight-year-old boy, who subsequently developed cowpox. Six weeks later, Jenner inoculated the boy with smallpox. He remained healthy. Jenner called this new procedure *vaccination*, from *vaccinia*, another term for cowpox. Within 18 months, 12,000 people in England had been vaccinated and the number of smallpox deaths dropped by two-thirds.

SPACE MILESTONE: *SKYLAB* (US). May 14, 1973. The US launched *Skylab*, its first manned orbiting laboratory.

"THE STARS AND STRIPES FOREVER" DAY: ANNIVERSARY. May 14, 1897. Anniversary of the first public performance of John Philip Sousa's march "The Stars and Stripes Forever," at Philadelphia, PA. The occasion was the unveiling of a statue of George Washington, and President William McKinley was present.

UNDERGROUND AMERICA DAY. May 14. Underground America Day is one man's (Malcolm Wells) attempt to get others to think of designing and building structures underground. Mr Wells publishes illustrations and humorous suggestions for celebrating Underground America Day. 32nd anniversary. Annually, May 14. For info: Malcolm Wells, 673 Satucket Rd, Brewster, MA 02631. Phone: (508) 896-6850. Fax: (508) 896-5116. Web: www .malcolmwells.com.

UNIVERSAL FAMILY WEEK. May 14–20. To stress the importance of the fundamental role of good families in strengthening humankind. For complete info, send $5 to cover expense of printing, handling and postage. For info: Dr. Stanley Drake, Pres Emeritus, Intl Soc of Friendship & Good Will, 8592 Roswell Rd, Ste 251, Atlanta, GA 30350-1867. Phone: (678) 795-1362. E-mail: sjdrake@bellsouth.net. Web: www.friendshipandgoodwill.org.

WAAC: ANNIVERSARY. May 14, 1942. During WWII women became eligible to enlist for noncombat duties in the Women's Auxiliary Army Corps (WAAC) by an act of Congress. Women also served as Women Appointed for Voluntary Emergency Service (WAVES), Women's Auxiliary Ferrying Squadron (WAFS) and Coast Guard or Semper Paratus Always Ready Service (SPARS), the Women's Reserve of the Marine Corp.

WORK AT HOME MOMS WEEK. May 14–20. The challenge of motherhood and working at home can be a balancing act. To all women who do it every day, you are applauded this week and always. For info: Robin Gorman Newman, 44 Somerset Dr N, Great Neck, NY 11020. Phone: (516) 773-0911. E-mail: robin@ lovecoach.com. Web: www.menschbaby.com.

BIRTHDAYS TODAY

Cate Blanchett, 37, actress (*Elizabeth, Lord of the Rings*), born Melbourne, Australia, May 14, 1969.

David Byrne, 54, singer (Talking Heads), composer (songs, film scores), born Dumbarton, Scotland, May 14, 1952.

Byron L. Dorgan, 64, US Senator (D, North Dakota), born Dickinson, ND, May 14, 1942.

Meg Foster, 58, actress ("Cagney & Lacey," *The Emerald Forest, They Live*), born Reading, PA, May 14, 1948.

George Lucas, 62, filmmaker (*Star Wars* films), born Modesto, CA, May 14, 1944.

	S	**M**	**T**	**W**	**T**	**F**	**S**
May			1	2	3	4	5	6
2006	7	8	9	10	11	12	13
	14	15	16	17	18	19	20
	21	22	23	24	25	26	27
	28	29	30	31			

Jose Dennis Martinez, 51, former baseball player, born Granada, Nicaragua, May 14, 1955.

Patrice Munsel, 81, opera singer, born Spokane, WA, May 14, 1925.

Ralph Neas, 60, president, People for the American Way, born Brookline, MA, May 14, 1946.

Atanasio (Tony) Perez, 64, Hall of Fame baseball player, born Camaguey, Cuba, May 14, 1942.

Tim Roth, 45, actor (*Pulp Fiction*), born London, England, May 14, 1961.

Valerie Still, 45, basketball player, born Lexington, KY, May 14, 1961.

Amber Tamblyn, 23, actress (*The Ring*, "Joan of Arcadia," "General Hospital"), born Santa Monica, CA, May 14, 1983.

Ronan Tynan, 46, opera singer (The Irish Tenors), born Dublin, Ireland, May 14, 1960.

Robert Zemeckis, 54, director (*Forrest Gump, Back to the Future*), born Chicago, IL, May 14, 1952.

MAY 15 — MONDAY
Day 135 — 230 Remaining

AVEDON, RICHARD: BIRTH ANNIVERSARY. May 15, 1923. Influential photographer born at New York, NY. Avedon began his career with the Merchant Marines, taking personnel identification photos and images of shipwrecks. Later, he worked for *Harper's Bazaar* and *Vogue*, where his artistic style of shooting fashion models against famous backgrounds revolutionized that industry's approach to fashion layouts. He was known for taking memorable, while not necessarily flattering, portraits, and was honored with retrospectives and exhibits at any number of museums. He received the National Medal for the Arts in 2003, and died at New York, NY, Oct 1, 2004.

BAUM, LYMAN FRANK: 150th BIRTH ANNIVERSARY. May 15, 1856. American newspaperman who wrote the Wizard of Oz stories was born at Chittenango, NY. Although *The Wonderful Wizard of Oz* is the most famous, Baum also wrote many other books for children, including more than a dozen about Oz. He died at Hollywood, CA, May 6, 1919.

COTTEN, JOSEPH: BIRTH ANNIVERSARY. May 15, 1905. Stage and screen star Joseph Cotten was born at Petersburg, VA. Among Cotten's movie credits were *Citizen Kane, The Magnificent Ambersons* and *The Third Man*. Among his most noted performances on Broadway were *The Philadelphia Story* and *Once More With Feeling*. Joseph Cotten died Feb 6, 1994, at Los Angeles.

EASTERN PACIFIC HURRICANE SEASON. May 15–Nov 30. Eastern Pacific defined as: Coast to 140 degrees west longitude. Info from: US Dept of Commerce, Natl Oceanic and Atmospheric Admin, Rockville, MD 20852.

FIRST FLIGHT ATTENDANT: ANNIVERSARY. May 15, 1930. Ellen Church became the first airline stewardess (today's flight attendant), flying on a United Airlines flight from San Francisco to Cheyenne, WY.

FRISCH, MAX: BIRTH ANNIVERSARY. May 15, 1911. Max Frisch was one of Europe's leading post–WWII literary figures. His work includes the novels *Homo Faber, I'm Not Stiller, Juerg Reinhardt* and the plays *The Firebugs, Andorra*. In addition to his writing, he was a controversial critic of his native Switzerland. Born at Zurich, he died there Apr 4, 1991.

GEORGE WALLACE SHOT: ANNIVERSARY. May 15, 1972. George Wallace, a former governor of Alabama and a symbol of segregation, was shot by Arthur Bremer while Wallace was at Laurel, MD, campaigning for the US presidency. For the remainder of his life (until he died in 1998), Wallace was paralyzed from the waist down. On Aug 4, 1972, Bremer was sentenced to 67 years in prison for the shooting.

JAPAN: AOI MATSURI (HOLLYHOCK FESTIVAL). May 15. Kyoto. The festival features a pageant reproducing imperial processions of ancient times that paid homage to the shrine of Shimogamo and Kamigamo.

MEXICO: SAN ISIDRO DAY. May 15. Day of San Isidro Labrador celebrated widely in farming regions to honor St. Isidore, the Plowman. Livestock gaily decorated with flowers. Celebrations usually begin about May 13 and continue for about a week.

NAIA MEN'S & WOMEN'S TENNIS NATIONAL CHAMPIONSHIPS. May 15–19. Mobile, AL. 55th annual for men, 25th annual for women. Est attendance: 500. For info: Natl Assn of Intercollegiate Athletics, 23500 W 105th St, PO Box 1325, Olathe, KS 66051-1325. Phone: (913) 791-0044. Fax: (913) 791-9555. E-mail: lthomas@naia.org. Web: www.naia.org.

NATIONAL EFFECTIVENESS WEEK. May 15–19. Neatness and tidiness do not make you effective. On the other hand, messiness does not make you ineffective. What matters is that you get the important things done with a minimum of stress. This week, promote tolerance of different styles of getting things done. Annually, the third full week in May. For info: Jan Jasper. Phone: (212) 465-7472. E-mail: jasper@janjasper.com. Web: www.jan jasper.com.

NYLON STOCKINGS: ANNIVERSARY. May 15, 1940. Nylon hose went on sale at stores throughout the country. Competing producers bought their nylon yarn from E.J. du Pont de Nemours. W.H. Carothers of Du Pont developed nylon, called "Polymer 66," in 1935. It was the first totally man-made fiber and over time was substituted for other materials and came to have widespread application.

OCONALUFTEE INDIAN VILLAGE. May 15–Oct 25. Cherokee Indian Reservation, Cherokee, NC. To portray the Cherokee lifestyle of the 1750 period. Also featuring *Unto These Hills* (mid-June–late-August), a drama portraying history of eastern band of Cherokees. Est attendance: 100,000. For info: Margie Douthit, PR, Cherokee Historical Assn, PO Box 398, Cherokee, NC 28719. Phone: (828) 497-2111. Fax: (828) 497-6987. Web: www.ocona lufteevillage.com.

PARAGUAY: INDEPENDENCE DAY. May 15. Commemorates independence from Spain, attained 1811.

★**PEACE OFFICER MEMORIAL DAY.** May 15. Presidential Proclamation 3537, of May 4, 1963, covers all succeeding years. (PL87-726 of Oct 1, 1962.) Always May 15 of each year since 1963; however, first issued in 1962 for May 14.

PEACE OFFICER MEMORIAL DAY. May 15. An event honored by some 21,000 police departments nationwide. Memorial ceremonies at 10 AM in American Police Hall of Fame and Museum, Titusville, FL. See also: "National Police Week" (May 14–20). Sponsor: National Association of Chiefs of Police. Est attendance: 200. For info: American Police Hall of Fame and Museum, 6350 Horizon Dr, Titusville, FL 32780. Phone: (321) 264-0911. E-mail: policeinfo@aphf.org. Web: www.aphf.org.

PORTER, KATHERINE ANNE: BIRTH ANNIVERSARY. May 15, 1890. American prose writer Katherine Anne Porter was born at Indian Creek, TX. Her one long novel, *Ship of Fools* (1962), is considered by some to be one of the greatest allegorical works in English. She won the Pulitzer Prize and the National Book Award in 1965 for *Collected Short Stories*. Died Sept 18, 1980, at Silver Spring, MD.

SCHNITZLER, ARTHUR: BIRTH ANNIVERSARY. May 15, 1862. Austrian playwright, novelist and medical doctor, Arthur Schnitzler was born at Vienna. Noted for his psychoanalytical examination of Viennese society. Died at Vienna, Oct 21, 1931.

SPACE MILESTONE: *FAITH 7* (US). May 15, 1963. Launched with Major Gordon Leroy Cooper and orbited Earth 22 times.

UNITED NATIONS: INTERNATIONAL DAY OF FAMILIES. May 15. The general assembly (res 47/237) Sept 20, 1993, voted this as an annual observance beginning in 1994. For info: United Nations, Dept of Public Info, New York, NY 10017. Web: www.un.org.

WILSON, ELLEN LOUISE AXSON: BIRTH ANNIVERSARY. May 15, 1860. First wife of Woodrow Wilson, 28th president of the US, born at Savannah, GA. Died at Washington, DC, Aug 6, 1914.

BIRTHDAYS TODAY

Anna Maria Alberghetti, 70, singer, actress (*Cinderfella, Carnival*), born Pesaro, Italy, May 15, 1936.

Madeleine Albright, 69, former US Secretary of State (Clinton administration), born Prague, Czechoslovakia, May 15, 1937.

Eddy Arnold, 88, country singer ("Make the World Go Away"), born Henderson, TN, May 15, 1918.

George Howard Brett, 53, Hall of Fame baseball player, executive, born Glen Dale, WV, May 15, 1953.

David Charvet, 34, actor ("Melrose Place," "Baywatch"), born Lyon, France, May 15, 1972.

David Cronenberg, 63, filmmaker (*The Fly, Naked Lunch*), born Toronto, ON, Canada, May 15, 1943.

Brian Eno, 58, avant-garde musician, born Woodbridge, England, May 15, 1948.

Giselle Fernandez, 45, TV host, actress, born Mexico City, Mexico, May 15, 1961.

Lee Horsley, 51, actor ("Nero Wolfe," "Matt Houston"), born Muleshoe, TN, May 15, 1955.

Jasper Johns, 76, artist (Neo-Dada encaustic and collage composition *Flag*), born Augusta, GA, May 15, 1930.

Lainie Kazan, 64, singer, actress (*My Favorite Year, Beaches*), born New York, NY, May 15, 1942.

Trini Lopez, 69, actor, singer (*Marriage on the Rocks, The Dirty Dozen*), born Dallas, TX, May 15, 1937.

Chazz Palminteri, 55, actor (*Bullets Over Broadway*), playwright, screenwriter (*A Bronx Tale*), born the Bronx, NY, May 15, 1951.

Dan Patrick, 50, sportscaster (ESPN's "SportsCenter"), radio personality, born Zanesville, OH, May 15, 1956.

Kathleen Sibelius, 58, Governor of Kansas (D), born Cincinnati, OH, May 15, 1948.

Emmitt Smith, 37, football player, born Pensacola, FL, May 15, 1969.

John Smoltz, 39, baseball player, born Warren, MI, May 15, 1967.

May 2006	S	M	T	W	T	F	S
		1	2	3	4	5	6
	7	8	9	10	11	12	13
	14	15	16	17	18	19	20
	21	22	23	24	25	26	27
	28	29	30	31			

MAY 16 — TUESDAY
Day 136 — 229 Remaining

BIOGRAPHERS DAY. May 16. Anniversary of the meeting, at London, England, May 16, 1763, of James Boswell and Samuel Johnson, beginning history's most famous biographer-biographee relationship. Boswell's *Journal of a Tour to the Hebrides* (1785) and his *Life of Samuel Johnson* (1791) are regarded as models of biographical writing. Thus, this day is recommended as one on which to start reading or writing a biography.

COMMEMORATION OF THE 1997 PRESIDENTIAL APOLOGY FOR THE UNITED STATES PUBLIC HEALTH SERVICE SYPHILIS STUDY IN TUSKEGEE. May 16–17. Tuskegee University, Tuskegee, AL. All descendants of the study's "survivors" and professionals and leaders in bioethics and health care are invited to attend. Sponsored by the Tuskegee University National Center for Bioethics in Research and Health Care. For info: Public and Media Affairs, Tuskegee University, 223 Kresge Center, Tuskegee, AL 36088. Phone: (334) 724-4612. E-mail: media@tuskegee.edu. Web: www.tuskegee.edu/bioethics.

FIRST ACADEMY AWARDS: ANNIVERSARY. May 16, 1929. About 270 people attended a dinner at the Hollywood Roosevelt Hotel at which the first Academy Awards were given in 12 categories. The silent film *Wings* won Best Picture. A committee of only 20 members selected the winners that year. By the third year, the entire membership of the Academy voted. The Academy Awards were first televised in 1953.

FIRST WOMAN TO CLIMB MOUNT EVEREST: ANNIVERSARY. May 16, 1975. Japanese climber Junko Tabei, leading an all-woman expedition to Mount Everest, became the first woman to reach the summit on this date in 1975. Taking the South-East Ridge route, Tabei was delayed by an avalanche before her last leg up the mountain. "Even after reaching the peak," she later recalled, "instead of shouting with excitement I was simply happy that I didn't have to go any higher!"

FONDA, HENRY: BIRTH ANNIVERSARY. May 16, 1905. American stage, TV and screen actor (*The Grapes of Wrath, Mister Roberts*), Academy Award winner, born Henry Jaynes Fonda at Grand Island, NE. Began his acting career at the Omaha (NE) Playhouse. Fonda died at Los Angeles, CA, Aug 12, 1982.

GWINNETT, BUTTON: DEATH ANNIVERSARY. May 16, 1777. Signer of the Declaration of Independence, born at Down Hatherley, Gloucestershire, England, about 1735 (exact date unknown). Died following a duel at St. Catherine's Island, off of Savannah, GA.

INTERNATIONAL SEA MONKEY DAY. May 16. A day on which we remember our briny friends, the sea monkeys. Annually, May 16 (formerly Feb 15). For info: Susan Barclay, 7520 Queen St, Chilliwack, BC, Canada V2R 1B7. Phone/fax: (604) 824-0678. E-mail: drseamonkey@telus.net. Web: www.seamonkeyworship.com.

LAG B'OMER. May 16. Hebrew calendar date: Iyar 18, 5766. Literally, the 33rd day of the omer (harvest time), the 33rd day after the beginning of Passover. Traditionally a joyous day for weddings, picnics and outdoor activities. Began at sundown May 15.

LIBERACE: BIRTH ANNIVERSARY. May 16, 1919. Wladziu Valentino Liberace, concert pianist who began with a piano, a candelabra, a brother named George and a huge engaging smile, threw in extravagant clothes and jewels and became a Las Vegas headliner and the winner of two Emmy Awards, six gold albums and two stars on the Hollywood Walk of Fame. Liberace was born at West Allis, WI; he died Feb 4, 1987, at Palm Springs, CA.

MARTIN, BILLY: BIRTH ANNIVERSARY. May 16, 1928. Baseball player and manager born at Berkeley, CA. Billy Martin's baseball career included managerial stints with five major league teams: the New York Yankees, Minnesota Twins, Detroit Tigers, Texas Rangers and Oakland Athletics. After a successful playing career, he compiled a record of 1,258 victories to 1,018 losses in his 16 seasons as a manager. His combative style both on and off the field kept him in the headlines, and he will long be remembered for his on-again, off-again relationship with Yankees owner George Steinbrenner, for whom he managed the Yankees five different times. Martin died in an auto accident near Fenton, NY, Dec 25, 1989.

MORTON, LEVI PARSONS: BIRTH ANNIVERSARY. May 16, 1824. 22nd vice president of the US (1889–93) born at Shoreham, VT. Died at Rhinebeck, NY, May 16, 1920.

NAIA MEN'S GOLF NATIONAL CHAMPIONSHIPS. May 16–19. Site TBD. 55th annual. Est attendance: 500. For info: Natl Assn of Intercollegiate Athletics, 23500 W 105th St, PO Box 1325, Olathe, KS 66051-1325. Phone: (913) 791-0044. Fax: (913) 791-9555. E-mail: jrodwell@naia.org. Web: www.naia.org.

PEABODY, ELIZABETH PALMER: BIRTH ANNIVERSARY. May 16, 1804. Born at Billerica, MA, Peabody was an innovative educator, author and publisher. She opened her first school at Lancaster, MA, when only 16. In 1839 Peabody opened a bookstore that quickly became the intellectuals' hangout. With her own printing press Peabody became the first woman publisher of Boston and possibly the US. She published three of her brother-in-law Nathaniel Hawthorne's books. For two years she published and wrote for *The Dial*, the literary magazine and voice of the Transcendental movement. Peabody's enduring accomplishment was the establishment of the first kindergarten in the US, in 1860 at Boston. She created a magazine, *Kindergarten Messenger*, in 1873. Died Jan 3, 1894, at Jamaica Plain, MA.

RAF BOMBS RUHR DAMS: ANNIVERSARY. May 16–17, 1943. Over these two days, Royal Air Force Lancasters attacked three dams in the German Ruhr Valley. They dropped 4.5-ton bombs designed specifically for this mission. The Mohne and the Eder (the largest dam in Europe at the time) were both damaged. These two dams provided drinking water for four million people and supplied 75 percent of the electrical power for industry. Widespread flooding and many deaths resulted.

REY, MARGARET: 100th BIRTH ANNIVERSARY. May 16, 1906. Children's author, born at Hamburg, Germany. Together with her illustrator husband, H.A. Rey, she produced the Curious George series. Rey died at Cambridge, MA, Dec 21, 1996.

BIRTHDAYS TODAY

David Boreanaz, 35, actor ("Angel," "Buffy the Vampire Slayer"), born Philadelphia, PA, May 16, 1971.
Pierce Brosnan, 53, actor ("Remington Steele," James Bond films), born County Meath, Ireland, May 16, 1953.
Jean-Sebastien Giguere, 29, hockey player, born Montreal, QC, Canada, May 16, 1977.
Tracey Gold, 37, actress ("Shirley," "Goodnight Beantown," "Growing Pains"), born New York, NY, May 16, 1969.
Janet Jackson, 40, singer ("What Have You Done for Me Lately"), born Gary, IN, May 16, 1966.
Olga Korbut, 51, Olympic gold medal gymnast, born Grodno, USSR, May 16, 1955.
John Scott (Jack) Morris, 51, former baseball player, born St. Paul, MN, May 16, 1955.
Gabriela Sabatini, 36, former tennis player, born Buenos Aires, Argentina, May 16, 1970.
Joan (Benoit) Samuelson, 49, Olympic gold medal runner, born Cape Elizabeth, ME, May 16, 1957.
Bill Smitrovich, 59, actor ("Crime Story," *Splash, Manhunter*), born Bridgeport, CT, May 16, 1947.
Tori Spelling, 33, actress ("Beverly Hills 90210"), born Beverly Hills, CA, May 16, 1973.
Studs Terkel, 94, author, journalist (*Hard Times, Working*), born Louis Terkel, New York, NY, May 16, 1912.
Mare Winningham, 47, actress (*The Thornbirds, St. Elmo's Fire*), born Phoenix, AZ, May 16, 1959.

MAY 17 — WEDNESDAY
Day 137 — 228 Remaining

BELL, JAMES (COOL PAPA): BIRTH ANNIVERSARY. May 17, 1903. Negro League baseball player James "Cool Papa" Bell was born at Starkville, MS. He played 25 seasons from 1922 to 1946 (one year before Jackie Robinson broke the "color barrier" in major league baseball) with a career average of .338. Regarded as the fastest man ever to play the game—he could round the bases in 13 seconds—he was inducted into the Baseball Hall of Fame in 1974. Bell died Mar 7, 1991, at St. Louis, MO.

***BROWN v BOARD OF EDUCATION* DECISION: ANNIVERSARY.** May 17, 1954. The US Supreme Court ruled unanimously that segregation of public schools "solely on the basis of race" denied black children "equal educational opportunity" even though "physical facilities and other 'tangible' factors may have been equal. Separate educational facilities are inherently unequal." The case was argued before the Court by Thurgood Marshall, who would go on to become the first black appointed to the Supreme Court.

CANNES FILM FESTIVAL. May 17–28. Cannes, France. 59th annual. Premier international film festival, with hundreds of screenings (in competition and out), critical panels, director spotlights, Cannes Market for film distribution and numerous other cultural and artistic activities. Palme d'Or, Caméra d'Or, Grand Prix and other awards presented on the last day of the festival. The festival was first held in September 1946, and there have been only three cancellations since then, in 1948, 1950 and 1968. For info: Assoc Française du Festival Intl du Film, 3, rue Amelie, F-75007 Paris, France. Phone: (33) 0-53-59-61-00. E-mail: festival@festival-cannes.fr. Web: www.festival-cannes.org.

FIRST KENTUCKY DERBY: ANNIVERSARY. May 17, 1875. The first running of the Kentucky Derby took place at Churchill Downs, Louisville, KY. Jockey Oliver Lewis rode the horse Aristides to a winning time of 2:37.25.

FIRST US SAME-SEX MARRIAGES: ANNIVERSARY. May 17, 2004. Massachusetts became the first US state to sanction gay marriage on this date. Hundreds of gay and lesbian couples received licenses and were married.

JENNER, EDWARD: BIRTH ANNIVERSARY. May 17, 1749. English physician, born at Berkeley, England. He was the first to establish a scientific basis for vaccination with his work on smallpox. Jenner died at Berkeley, England, Jan 26, 1823.

NEW YORK STOCK EXCHANGE ESTABLISHED: ANNIVERSARY. May 17, 1792. Some two dozen merchants and brokers agreed to establish what is now known as the New York Stock Exchange. In fair weather they operated under a buttonwood tree on Wall Street, at New York, NY. In bad weather they moved to the shelter of a coffeehouse to conduct their business.

NORWAY: CONSTITUTION DAY OR INDEPENDENCE DAY. May 17. National holiday. Constitution signed and Norway separated from Denmark in 1814. Parades and children's festivities.

TURN BEAUTY INSIDE OUT DAY. May 17. Is beauty only skin-deep? Not if you turn it inside out. This day serves as a reminder that inner beauty is more important than outer beauty. On this day, people challenge the usual definition of beauty as portrayed in popular media and advertising by recognizing the wonderful actions and attitudes of people who are beautiful on the inside. Annually, the third Wednesday in May. For info: Mind on the Media, 710 St Olaf Ave, Ste 200, Northfield, MN 55057. Phone: (952) 210-1625. Web: www.tbio.org.

UNITED NATIONS: WORLD TELECOMMUNICATION DAY. May 17. A day to draw attention to the necessity and importance of further development of telecommunications in the global community. For info: United Nations, Dept of Public Info, New York, NY 10017. Web: www.un.org.

USS *STARK* ATTACKED: ANNIVERSARY. May 17, 1987. The US Navy's guided missile frigate *Stark*, sailing off the Iranian coast in the Persian Gulf, was struck and set afire by two Exocet sea-skimming missiles fired from an Iraqi warplane at 2:10 PM, EDT. Also struck was a Cypriot flag tanker. At least 28 American naval personnel were killed. Only hours earlier a Soviet oil tanker in the Gulf had struck a mine.

BIRTHDAYS TODAY

Mia Hamm, 34, former soccer player, born Selma, AL, May 17, 1972.

Dennis Hopper, 70, actor (*Easy Rider, Giant, Rebel Without a Cause*), born Dodge City, KS, May 17, 1936.

Christian Lacroix, 56, French couturier, born Arles, France, May 17, 1950.

Ray Charles (Sugar Ray) Leonard, 50, former boxer, born Washington, DC, May 17, 1956.

Daniel Ricardo (Danny) Manning, 40, former basketball player, born Hattiesburg, MS, May 17, 1966.

Ben Nelson, 65, US Senator (D, Nebraska), born McCook, NE, May 17, 1941.

Tony Parker, 24, basketball player, born Bruges, Belgium, May 17, 1982.

Bill Paxton, 51, actor (*Aliens, One False Move, Twister*), born Fort Worth, TX, May 17, 1955.

Trent Reznor, 41, singer (Nine Inch Nails), born Mercer, PA, May 17, 1965.

Bob Saget, 50, actor ("Full House"), host ("America's Funniest Home Videos"), born Philadelphia, PA, May 17, 1956.

Debra Winger, 51, actress (*Terms of Endearment, Shadowlands*), born Columbus, OH, May 17, 1955.

MAY 18 — THURSDAY

Day 138 — 227 Remaining

ALLIES CAPTURE MONTE CASSINO: ANNIVERSARY. May 18, 1944. Between Oct 12, 1943, and Jan 17, 1944, there were five Allied attempts to take the German position at the Benedictine abbey at Monte Cassino. Although the abbey had been reduced to rubble, it served as a bunker for the Germans. In the spring of 1944 Marshal Alphonse Pierre Juin devised an operation that crossed the mountainous regions behind the fortresslike structure, using Moroccan troops of the French Expeditionary Force. Specially trained for mountain operations, they climbed 4,850 feet to locate a pass. On May 15, 1944, they attacked the Germans from behind. On May 18, Polish troops attached to this force took Monte Cassino.

ASPENCASH MOTORCYCLE RALLY. May 18–21. Ruidoso, NM. $10,000 cash poker run, trade show, poker run pin. Est attendance: 12,000. For info: Golden Aspen Rally Assn, PO Box 1467, Ruidoso, NM 88355. Phone: (800) 452-8045. E-mail: motorcyclerally@zianet.com. Web: www.motorcyclerally.com.

May *2006*	S	M	T	W	T	F	S
		1	2	3	4	5	6
	7	8	9	10	11	12	13
	14	15	16	17	18	19	20
	21	22	23	24	25	26	27
	28	29	30	31			

BIRTHDAY OF MOTHER'S WHISTLER. May 18. Birthday of the world's most melodious human whistler, who not only duplicates the songs of rare, exotic and extinct birds, but in many cases, does so better than the birds themselves. For info: Mother's Whistler, Warfield and Twin Silo Lanes, Huntingdon Valley, PA 19006. Phone: (215) 947-0500. Fax: (215) 947-7210. E-mail: motherswhistler1@yahoo.com.

CALAVERAS COUNTY FAIR AND JUMPING FROG JUBILEE. May 18–22. Calaveras Fairgrounds, Angels Camp, CA. County fair and reenactment of Mark Twain's "Celebrated Jumping Frog of Calaveras County." This "Superbowl" of the sport of frog jumping attracts more than 2,000 frogs annually from around the country. Est attendance: 45,000. For info: 39th District Agricultural Assn, 101 Frogtown Rd, PO Box 489, Angels Camp, CA 95222. Phone: (209) 736-2561. Fax: (209) 736-2476. E-mail: info@frogtown.org. Web: www.frogtown.org.

CAPRA, FRANK: BIRTH ANNIVERSARY. May 18, 1897. The Academy Award–winning director whose movies were suffused with affectionate portrayals of the common man and the strengths and foibles of American democracy. Capra was born at Palermo, Sicily. He bluffed his way into silent movies in 1922 and, despite total ignorance of moviemaking, directed and produced a profitable one-reeler. He was the first to win three directorial Oscars—for *It Happened One Night* (1934), *Mr Deeds Goes to Town* (1936) and *You Can't Take It with You* (1938). The motion picture academy voted the first and third of these as best picture. Capra said his favorite of the films he made was *It's a Wonderful Life* (1946). He died at La Quinta, CA, Sept 3, 1991.

FONTEYN, MARGOT: BIRTH ANNIVERSARY. May 18, 1919. Born Margaret Hookman at Reigate, Surrey, England, Dame Margot Fonteyn thrilled ballet audiences for 45 years. She emerged from the Sadler's Wells company during the 1930s and 1940s as a solo artist and followed those successes by partnering with Soviet exile Rudolph Nureyev in the 1960s. She died Feb 21, 1991, at Panama City, Panama.

GETTYSBURG BLUEGRASS FESTIVAL. May 18–21. Gettysburg, PA. Granite Hill Campground on Rt 116. Est attendance: 5,000. For info: Gettysburg CVB, PO Box 4117, Gettysburg, PA 17325. Phone: (717) 334-6274. Fax: (717) 334-1166. E-mail: gettysburgcvb@dejazzd.com. Web: www.gettysburgcvb.org.

HAITI: FLAG AND UNIVERSITY DAY. May 18. Public holiday.

INTERNATIONAL MUSEUM DAY. May 18. To pay tribute to museums of the world. "Museums are an important means of cultural exchange, enrichment of cultures and development of mutual understanding, cooperation and peace among people." Annually, May 18. Sponsor: International Council of Museums, Paris, France. For info: AAM/ICOM, 1575 Eye St NW, Ste 400, Washington, DC 20005. Phone: (202) 289-9115. Fax: (202) 289-6578. E-mail: aam-icom@aam-us.org.

MOUNT SAINT HELENS ERUPTION: ANNIVERSARY. May 18, 1980. A major eruption of Mount Saint Helens volcano, in southwestern Washington, blew steam and ash more than 11 miles into the sky. First major eruption of Mount Saint Helens since 1857, though on Mar 26, 1980, there had been a warning eruption of smaller magnitude.

NCAA DIVISION I WOMEN'S TENNIS CHAMPIONSHIPS. May 18–28. Taube Tennis Center, Stanford University, Stanford, CA. For info: Natl Collegiate Athletic Assn, PO Box 6222, Indianapolis, IN 46206-6222. Web: www.NCAAsports.com.

POPE JOHN PAUL II: BIRTH ANNIVERSARY. May 18, 1920. Karol Wojtyla, 264th pope of the Roman Catholic Church, born at Wadowice, Poland. Elected pope Oct 16, 1978, he was the first non-Italian to be elected pope in 456 years and the first Polish pope. His theology was conservative and traditional, and he was known for his worldwide travels to bring the message of the Catholic Church to people around the world. He survived an assassination attempt in 1981, and died at Vatican City on Apr 2, 2005.

SPACE MILESTONE: *APOLLO 10* (US). May 18, 1969. Launched with astronauts Colonel Thomas Stafford and Commander Eugene Cernan, who brought lunar module (LM) "Snoopy" within nine miles of the moon's surface on May 22. *Apollo 10* circled the moon 31 times and returned to Earth May 26.

TURKMENISTAN: REVIVAL AND UNITY DAY. May 18. National holiday. Commemorates the 1992 adoption of the constitution.

URUGUAY: BATTLE OF LAS PIEDRAS DAY. May 18. National holiday. Commemorates battle fought for independence from Spain in 1811.

VISIT YOUR RELATIVES DAY. May 18. A day to renew family ties and joys by visiting often-thought-of-seldom-seen relatives. Annually, May 18. For info: A.C. Vierow, Box 71, Clio, MI 48420-0071.

WILLSON, MEREDITH: BIRTH ANNIVERSARY. May 18, 1902. American musician, playwright and composer best known for *The Music Man*. Born at Mason City, IA, Willson received Oscar nominations for *The Little Foxes* and *The Great Dictator*. Many of his songs, including "It's Beginning to Look a Lot Like Christmas," "Seventy-six Trombones" and "Till There Was You" have become standards. Willson died at Santa Monica, CA, June 15, 1984.

WOMAN INDUCTED INTO NATIONAL INVENTORS HALL OF FAME: 15th ANNIVERSARY. May 18, 1991. Gertrude Belle Elion, corecipient of the 1988 Nobel Prize in Medicine, became the first woman inducted as a member of the National Inventors Hall of Fame. Elion's research led to the development of leukemia-fighting drugs and immunosuppressant Imuran, which is used in kidney transplants.

BIRTHDAYS TODAY

Chow Yun-Fat, 51, actor (*Crouching Tiger, Hidden Dragon; Anna and the King; Bulletproof Monk*), born Lamma Island, Hong Kong, May 18, 1955.

Tina Fey, 36, writer, comedienne ("Saturday Night Live," *Mean Girls*), born Upper Darby, PA, May 18, 1970.

Brad Friedel, 35, soccer player, born Lakewood, OH, May 18, 1971.

Dwayne Hickman, 72, actor ("The Many Loves of Dobie Gillis"), born Los Angeles, CA, May 18, 1934.

Reginald Martinez (Reggie) Jackson, 60, Hall of Fame baseball player, born Wyncote, PA, May 18, 1946.

Jari Kurri, 46, Hall of Fame hockey player, born Helsinki, Finland, May 18, 1960.

Robert Morse, 75, actor (*The Loved One, A Guide for the Married Man*; stage: *How to Succeed in Business Without Really Trying* [Tony Award]), born Newton, MA, May 18, 1931.

Yannick Noah, 46, former tennis player, born Sedan, France, May 18, 1960.

Pernell Roberts, 78, actor (*Ride Lonesome*, "Bonanza," "Trapper John, MD"), born Waycross, GA, May 18, 1928.

Brooks Robinson, 69, Hall of Fame baseball player, born Little Rock, AR, May 18, 1937.

James Stephens, 55, actor ("The Paper Chase"), born Mount Kisco, NY, May 18, 1951.

George Strait, 54, country singer, musician, born Poteet, TX, May 18, 1952.

MAY 19 — FRIDAY

Day 139 — 226 Remaining

ART FAIR AND WINEFEST. May 19–21. Washington, MO. The largest Missouri wine tasting of state wines as well as a juried art show featuring 60 midwestern artists. Art fair is free. Admission to the wine pavilion includes a commemorative wineglass. For info: Downtown Washington Inc, PO Box 144, Washington, MO 63090. Phone: (636) 239-1743. Fax: (636) 239-4832. E-mail: events@downtownwashmo.org. Web: www.downtownwashmo.org.

BARABOO CIRCUS HERITAGE. May 19–21 (tentative). Sauk County Fairgrounds, Baraboo, WI. A weekend of circus fun for Boy Scouts, Girl Scouts, 4-H, church youth groups and other organized youth groups. Hiking, camping, team skills competition, Pinewood Derby race and the Circus World Museum. Est attendance: 2,000. For info: Baraboo Circus Heritage, Boy Scouts of America, Four Lakes Council, 34 Schroeder Ct, Madison, WI 53711-6222. Phone: (608) 273-1005.

BAY TO BREAKERS RACE. May 19–21. San Francisco, CA. Largest footrace in the world attracts 70,000 runners each year, from world-class athletes to fun runners; postrace festival, live concert, food and beverages. Est attendance: 150,000. For info: Bay to Breakers, 1213 Evans Ave, San Francisco, CA 94124. Phone: (415) 359-2800. E-mail: info@baytobreakers.com. Web: www.baytobreakers.com.

BOLEYN, ANNE: EXECUTION ANNIVERSARY. May 19, 1536. Born around 1507, Anne Boleyn captured the eye of England's King Henry VIII in 1527. Her demand that he make her a wife, not a mistress, caused the married Henry's break with the Catholic Church (which wouldn't allow a divorce), which in turn led to decades of religious turmoil in England. Henry had his marriage to Catherine of Aragon annulled and wed Boleyn in 1533. Boleyn's inability to bear a male heir (although her daughter with Henry was to be Queen Elizabeth I) and court intrigue caused her arrest on charges of adultery. She was executed by sword at the Tower of London. The morning of her execution she said, "I heard say the executioner was very good, and I have a little neck."

BOOKEXPO AMERICA TRADE EXHIBIT. May 19–21. The Washington Convention Center, Washington, DC. Publishers display fall titles for booksellers and all interested in reaching the retail bookseller. Book-related items also on display. For info: BookExpo America, 383 Main Ave, Norwalk, CT 06851-1543. Phone: (800) 840-5614. Web: bookexpo.reedexpo.com.

BOYS' CLUBS FOUNDED: 100th ANNIVERSARY. May 19, 1906. The Federated Boys' Clubs, which later became the Boys' and Girls' Clubs of America, was founded.

CELEBRATE YOUR ELECTED OFFICIALS DAY. May 19. We have designated this day to remind Americans that our elected officials are public servants and deserve our thanks for all they do. One easy way to identify and send thanks to your own local, state and national officials is at the free website Congress.org. Annually, the third Friday in May. For info: Lara Wyrsta, Capitol Advantage, 2751 Prosperity Ave, 6th Fl, Fairfax, VA 22031. Phone: (703) 289-4670. Fax: (703) 289-4678. E-mail: royelen@capitoladvantage.com. Web: www.capitoladvantage.com.

COSAC ANNUAL CONFERENCE: ISSUES IN AUTISM 2006. May 19–20. The NJ Center for Outreach & Services for the Autism Community (COSAC) holds its annual autism conference—one of the largest in the nation—featuring educational workshops, exhibitions and an awards reception. Est attendance: 1,300. For info: Madelyn Schiering, Conf Dir, COSAC, 1450 Parkside Ave, Ste 22, Ewing, NJ 08638. Phone: (609) 883-8100. Fax: (609) 883-5509. E-mail: information@njcosac.org. Web: www.njcosac.org.

DARK DAY IN NEW ENGLAND: ANNIVERSARY. May 19, 1780. At midday near-total darkness unaccountably descended on much of New England. Candles were lit, fowls went to roost and many fearful persons believed that doomsday had arrived.

At New Haven, CT, Colonel Abraham Davenport opposed adjournment of the town council in these words: "I am against adjournment. The day of judgment is either approaching or it is not. If it is not, there is no cause for an adjournment. If it is, I choose to be found doing my duty. I wish therefore that candles may be brought." No scientifically verifiable cause for this widespread phenomenon was ever discovered.

DERMOTT'S ANNUAL CRAWFISH FESTIVAL. May 19–20. Dermott, AR. 22nd annual. To publicize and popularize crawfish as a delicacy, to promote the area and to raise funds for industrial expansion. Family fun, arts, crafts, exotic foods, carnival, live music and street dances. Annually, the third weekend in May. Est attendance: 20,000. For info: Dermott Area Chamber of Commerce, Box 147, Dermott, AR 71638. Phone: (870) 538-5656.

DULCIMER DAYS. May 19–21. Coshocton, OH. Dulcimer competition, workshops, exhibits, open stage, jam sessions, Saturday evening concert and more. Annually, the third weekend of May. Est attendance: 1,400. For info: Roscoe Village, 381 Hill St, Coshocton, OH 43812. Phone: (800) 877-1830 or (740) 622-9310. Fax: (740) 623-6555. E-mail: rvmarketing@roscoevillage.com. Web: www.roscoevillage.com.

FISHING HAS NO BOUNDARIES—HAYWARD EVENT. May 19–21. Lake Chippewa Campgrounds, Hayward, WI. A three-day fishing experience for disabled persons. Any disability, age, sex, race, etc, eligible. Fishing with experienced guides on one of the best fishing waters in Wisconsin, attended by 150 participants and 350 volunteers. Advance registration by Apr 28. Est attendance: 2,000. For info: Fishing Has No Boundaries, PO Box 375, Hayward, WI 54843. Phone: (715) 634-3185. Fax: (715) 634-1305. E-mail: hayfhnb@cheqnet.net.

***GONE WITH THE WIND* PUBLISHED: 70th ANNIVERSARY.** May 19, 1936. Margaret Mitchell's epic novel of the Civil War South was published on this date in 1936. It would be awarded the Pulitzer Prize and National Book Award as best novel of 1936. It has been a bestseller since publication, and 40 countries have published translations. See also: "*Gone with the Wind* Film Premiere: Anniversary" (Dec 15).

HANSBERRY, LORRAINE: BIRTH ANNIVERSARY. May 19, 1930. American playwright Lorraine Hansberry was born at Chicago, IL. For her now classic play *A Raisin in the Sun*, she became the youngest American and first black to win the Best Play Award from the New York Critics' Circle. The play, titled after the Langston Hughes poem, deals with issues such as racism, cultural pride and self-respect and was the first stage production written by a black woman to appear on Broadway (1959). *To Be Young, Gifted, and Black*, a book of excerpts from her journals, letters, speeches and plays, was published posthumously in 1969. Lorraine Hansberry died of cancer Jan 12, 1965, at New York, NY.

HO CHI MINH: BIRTH ANNIVERSARY. May 19, 1890. Vietnamese leader and first president of the Democratic Republic of Vietnam, born at Kim Lien, a central Vietnamese village (Nghe An Province), probably May 19, 1890. His original name was Nguyen That Thanh. Died at Hanoi, Vietnam, Sept 3, 1969. The anniversary of his birth is a national holiday in Vietnam as is the anniversary of his death.

HUG YOUR CAT DAY. May 19. Cats act like they don't want or need attention—but they do. Apricat, the pampered star of her own book series, has created a special day for humans to hug their cats without fear of scratches or hisses. For info: Marisa D'Vari, 25 Columbus Circle, Apt ST-55E, New York, NY 10019. E-mail: mdvari@deg.com. Web: www.apricat.com.

May 2006	S	M	T	W	T	F	S
		1	2	3	4	5	6
	7	8	9	10	11	12	13
	14	15	16	17	18	19	20
	21	22	23	24	25	26	27
	28	29	30	31			

LOST IN THE '50s. May 19–21. Sandpoint, ID. Dance and show with '50s & '60s stars, vintage car parade, car show, car rally and 5k run. Est attendance: 10,000. For info: Lost in the '50s, Carolyn Gleason, Chair, 215 S 2nd Ave, Sandpoint, ID 83864. Phone: (208) 263-9321 or (208) 265-LOST. E-mail: lost50s@sandpoint.net.

MAGNOLIA BLOSSOM FESTIVAL. May 19–20. Magnolia, AR. 18th annual. Events include old-fashioned chicken supper, arts and crafts, entertainment and activities for all. World Championship Steak Cook-off (May 20) served under fragrant magnolia trees. Est attendance: 20,000. For info: Magnolia-Columbia County Chamber of Commerce, 202 N Pine, PO Box 866, Magnolia, AR 71754-0866. Phone: (800) 482-3330. E-mail: magcoc@arkansas.net. Web: www. blossomfestival.org.

MAIFEST. May 19–21. MainStrasse Village, Covington, KY. MainStrasse celebrates the German tradition of welcoming the first spring wines and the beginning of the festival season. Artist and craftspeople exhibits, food and drink, live music and entertainment. Est attendance: 175,000. For info: Donna Kremer, Administrative Coord, MainStrasse Village, 406 W 6th St, Ste 201, Covington, KY 41011. Phone: (859) 491-0458. Fax: (859) 655-7932. Web: www.mainstrasse.org.

MALCOLM X: BIRTH ANNIVERSARY. May 19, 1925. Black nationalist and civil rights activist Malcolm X was born Malcolm Little at Omaha, NE. While serving a prison term he resolved to transform his life. On his release in 1952 he changed his name to Malcolm X and worked for the Nation of Islam until he was suspended by Black Muslim leader Elijah Muhammed Dec 4, 1963. Malcolm X later made the pilgrimage to Mecca and became an orthodox Muslim. He was assassinated as he spoke to a meeting at the Audubon Ballroom at New York, NY, Feb 21, 1965.

MAY RAY DAY. May 19. To celebrate the beginning of the warm outside days the sun gives us. Also, a day for people named Ray. Annually, May 19. For info: Richard Ankli, The Fifth Wheel Tavern, 639 Fifth St, Ann Arbor, MI 48103.

MILES CITY BUCKING HORSE SALE. May 19–21. Miles City, MT. Miles City is real "Lonesome Dove" country and its annual bucking horse sale is where rodeo stock operators from around the nation and Canada come to purchase their bucking horses for the coming rodeo season. A festive event, the sale not only involves cowboys trying to ride some of the wildest horses in the country, but Western artists displaying and creating works in a weekend art show, a Western trade show featuring practical and gift items, a Saturday morning parade and Miles City's Western attractions like the Range Riders Museum. (Miles City is the community featured in the novel and two television miniseries about "Lonesome Dove.") Est attendance: 10,000. For info: Miles City Chamber of Commerce, 511 Pleasant, Miles City, MT 59301. Phone: (406) 234-2890.

MINT JULEP SCALE MEET. May 19–21. Rough River Dam State Resort Park, Falls of Rough, KY. A weekend for radio-controlled airplane enthusiasts. Est attendance: 450. For info: Shawn Pickens, Recreation Supervisor, Rough River Dam State Resort Park, 450 Lodge Rd, Falls of Rough, KY 40119. Phone: (270) 257-2311.

MOREL MUSHROOM FESTIVAL. May 19–21. Muscoda, Wisconsin's "Morel Mushroom Capital," celebrates the end of the morel mushroom's two-week peak season. The 24th annual celebration includes the buying and selling of morels, food vendors, Little League baseball tournament, arts & crafts, custom car show, antique tractor pull, flea market, helicopter rides and many fun activities for the whole family. Saturday evening is the annual Fireman's steak feed followed by music and fireworks; Sunday brings a huge parade. Annually, the weekend after Mother's Day. Est attendance: 2,000. For info: Village of Muscoda, Morel Mushroom Fest, PO Box 206, Muscoda, WI 53573-0206. Phone: (608) 739-3182. Fax: (608) 739-3183. E-mail: cljohnson@wppisys.org. Web: www.muscoda.com.

NAIA SOFTBALL NATIONAL CHAMPIONSHIP. May 19–24. Decatur, AL. 26th annual competition. Est attendance: 2,000. For info: Natl Assn of Intercollegiate Athletics, 23500 W 105th St, PO Box 1325, Olathe, KS 66051-1325. Phone: (918) 494-8828. Fax: (918) 494-8841. E-mail: rwiebe@naia.org. Web: www.naia.org.

NATIONAL BIKE TO WORK DAY. May 19. At the state or local level, Bike to Work events are conducted by small and large businesses, city governments, bicycle clubs and environmental groups. About two million participants nationwide. Annually, the third Friday in May. Est attendance: 2,000,000. For info: Patrick McCormick, Communications Dir, League of American Bicyclists, 1612 K St NW, Ste 800, Washington, DC 20006. Phone: (202) 822-1333. Fax: (202) 822-1334. E-mail: bikeleague@bikeleague .org. Web: www.bikeleague.org.

NATIONAL CHILDREN AND POLICE DAY. May 19. A day set aside for the interaction of the local police with schoolchildren so as to build relationships that will increase children's appreciation for the police and other authority figures. Also a day for schoolchildren throughout the US to say "thank you" to the police for all the services rendered throughout the year. Annually, the Friday of National Police Week. For info: BJ Woods, 5126 La Vista Court, Granbury, TX 76049. Phone: (817) 910-2307. Fax: (817) 326-5927. E-mail: bjwoods@granbury.com.

★**NATIONAL DEFENSE TRANSPORTATION DAY.** May 19. Presidential Proclamation customarily issued as "National Defense Transportation Day and National Transportation Week." Issued each year for the third Friday in May since 1957. (PL85–32 of May 16, 1957.)

RHODODENDRON FESTIVAL. May 19–21. Florence, OR. Abundance of springtime rhododendron blooms celebrated with a Grand Floral Parade, arts and crafts show, dance, show & shine, car cruise and carnival. Held annually since 1908. Est attendance: 35,000. For info: Florence Chamber of Commerce, 290 Hwy 101, Florence, OR 97439. Phone: (541) 997-3128 or (800) 524-4864. E-mail: florence@oregonfast.net. Web: www.florencechamber .com.

RHUBARB FESTIVAL. May 19–20. Intercourse, PA. A lighthearted celebration honoring rhubarb, which grows abundantly in the Pennsylvania Dutch country. Food, games and contests all featuring rhubarb—pie baking contest, rhubarb derby, rhubarb pick-up sticks and more—plus entertainment. Annually, the third Friday and Saturday in May. Est attendance: 20,000. For info: Lisa Horn, Kitchen Kettle Village, Box 380, Intercourse, PA 17534. Phone: (800) 732-3538 or (717) 768-8261. Web: www .kitchenkettle.com.

SCOBEE, FRANCIS R.: BIRTH ANNIVERSARY. May 19, 1939. Commander of the ill-fated space shuttle *Challenger*, 46-year-old pilot Francis R. Scobee had been in the astronaut program since 1978 and had been pilot of the *Challenger* in 1984. Born at Cle Elum, WA, Scobee perished with all others on board when the *Challenger* exploded on Jan 28, 1986. See also: "*Challenger* Space Shuttle Explosion Anniversary" (Jan 28).

SIMPLON TUNNEL OPENING: 100th ANNIVERSARY. May 19, 1906. Tunnel from Brig, Switzerland, to Iselle, Italy, officially opened on this day. Construction started in 1898.

SPACE MILESTONE: *MARS 2* AND *MARS 3* (USSR): 35th ANNIVERSARY. May 19 and 28, 1971. Entered Martian orbits on Nov 27 and Dec 2, respectively. *Mars 3* sent down a TV-equipped capsule that soft-landed and transmitted pictures for 20 seconds.

STAMP EXPO. May 19–21. Pasadena Convention Center, Pasadena, CA. Annual expo. Est attendance: 5,000. For info: Israel Bick, Exec Dir, Intl Stamp & Coin Collectors Society, Box 854, Van Nuys, CA 91408. Phone: (818) 997-6496. Fax: (818) 988-4337. E-mail: iibick@sbcglobal.net. Web: www.bick.net.

SWITZERLAND: WORLD OF COFFEE/WORLD BARISTA CHAMPIONSHIP. May 19–21. Berne Exhibition Centre, Berne. Conference, exhibition, championships, educational workshops and more—all on coffee. More than 175 vendors will be exhibiting while the world's top coffee specialists impart their knowledge. Barista certification training available. Among the championships is the World Barista Championship, where nearly 40 competitors from around the world compete for the title of best barista. For info: Specialty Coffee Association of Europe, St. Lawrence, Kingsway, Hullbridge, Hockley, Essex, United Kingdom SS5 6DR. Phone: (44) 1702-232-373. E-mail: secretary@scae.com. Web: www.scae.com or www.worldbarista championship.com. Or Specialty Coffee Association of America. Phone: (562) 624-4100. E-mail: coffee@scaa.org. Web: www.scaa .org.

TEACHER'S DAY IN FLORIDA. May 19. A ceremonial day on the third Friday in May.

TURKEY: YOUTH AND SPORTS DAY. May 19. Public holiday commemorating the beginning of a national movement for independence in 1919, led by Mustafa Kemal Ataturk.

BIRTHDAYS TODAY

Nora Ephron, 65, writer, screenwriter, director (*You've Got Mail, Sleepless in Seattle*), born New York, NY, May 19, 1941.

James Fox, 67, actor (*A Passage to India, The Russia House, Patriot Games*), born London, England, May 19, 1939.

Kevin Garnett, 30, basketball player, born Mauldin, SC, May 19, 1976.

David Hartman, 69, actor, broadcaster (Emmy for "Good Morning America"; *Hello Dolly*), born Pawtucket, RI, May 19, 1937.

Grace Jones, 54, model, singer, actress (*A View to a Kill*), born Spanishtown, Jamaica, May 19, 1952.

William (Bill) Laimbeer, Jr, 49, WNBA coach, former basketball player, born Boston, MA, May 19, 1957.

James Lehrer, 72, journalist, anchor ("The Newshour with Jim Lehrer"), born Wichita, KS, May 19, 1934.

Eric Lloyd, 20, actor ("Jesse," *Dunston Checks In*), born Glendale, CA, May 19, 1986.

Pete Townshend, 61, musician (The Who), born London, England, May 19, 1945.

MAY 20 — SATURDAY
Day 140 — 225 Remaining

AMELIA EARHART ATLANTIC CROSSING: ANNIVERSARY. May 20, 1932. Leaving Harbor Grace, Newfoundland, Canada at 7 PM, Amelia Earhart landed near Londonderry, Ireland. The 2,026-mile flight took 13 hours and 30 minutes. She was the first woman to fly solo across the Atlantic.

★ **ARMED FORCES DAY.** May 20. Presidential Proclamation 5983, of May 17, 1989, covers the third Saturday in May in all succeeding years. Originally proclaimed as "Army Day" for Apr 6, beginning in 1936 (S.Con.Res. 30 of Apr 2, 1936). S.Con.Res. 5 of Mar 16, 1937, requested annual Apr 6 issuance, which was done through 1949. Always the third Saturday in May since 1950. Traditionally issued once by each Administration.

BALZAC, HONORE DE: BIRTH ANNIVERSARY. May 20, 1799. French author of a huge cycle of stories and novels known as *The Human Comedy*, born at Tours, France. "It is easier," Balzac wrote in 1829, "to be a lover than a husband for the simple reason that it is more difficult to be witty every day than to say pretty things from time to time." Died at Paris, Aug 18, 1850.

BEVERLY HILLS: AFFAIRE IN THE GARDENS. May 20–21 (also Oct 21–22). Beverly Gardens Park at Rodeo Drive, Beverly Hills, CA. To foster an appreciation of arts in the community. Juried show; only fine arts and crafts considered. Garden setting. Semiannually, the third weekends in May and October. Est attendance: 40,000. For info: Karen Fitch McLean, Art Show Coordinator, City of Beverly Hills, 501 Doheny Rd, Beverly Hills, CA 90210. Phone: (310) 550-4796. Fax: (310) 858-9238. E-mail: kmclean@beverlyhills.org. Web: www.beverlyhills.org.

CALIFORNIA ARTICHOKE FESTIVAL. May 20–21. Castroville, CA. Annually, in the Artichoke Capital of the World. Events include wine tasting, agro-art contest, vintage car show, 10k run and a recipe contest. Est attendance: 15,000. For info: Castroville Chamber of Commerce, PO Box 744, Castroville, CA 95012. Phone: (831) 633-2465. Fax: (831) 633-0485. Web: www.artichoke-festival.org.

CAMEROON: NATIONAL HOLIDAY. May 20. Republic of Cameroon. Commemorates adoption of constitution in 1972.

CANADA: UPPER CANADA VILLAGE. May 20–Oct 8. Morrisburg, ON (9:30–5 daily). One of Canada's premier attractions. Visitors enter the world of the 1860s. Costumed interpreters bring history to life in this fully operational rural community as they perform period activities as townsfolk or as tradespeople who apply their skills in restored buildings ranging from homes to trade shops. Many special events and programs offered throughout the season. Est attendance: 150,000. For info: Upper Canada Village, Parks of the St. Lawrence, RR 1, Morrisburg, ON, Canada K0C 1X0. Phone: (800) 437-2233 or (613) 543-4328. Web: www.uppercanadavillage.com.

CHEROKEE ROSE FESTIVAL. May 20. Gilmer, TX. Car show, turtle race, children's games, ice cream crank-off, carnival rides and much more. For info: Gilmer Area Chamber of Commerce, PO Box 854, Gilmer, TX 75644. Phone: (903) 843-2413 or (903) 843-3981. Fax: (903) 843-3759. E-mail: upchamber@aol.com. Web: www.gilmerareachamber.com.

COUNCIL OF NICAEA I: ANNIVERSARY. May 20–Aug 25, 325. First ecumenical council of Christian Church, called by Constantine I, first Christian emperor of Roman Empire. Nearly 300 bishops are said to have attended this first of 21 ecumenical councils (latest, Vatican II, began Sept 11, 1962), which was held at Nicaea, in Asia Minor (today's Turkey). The council condemned Arianism (which denied the divinity of Christ), formulated the Nicene Creed and fixed the day of Easter—always on a Sunday.

EAST TIMOR: INDEPENDENCE: ANNIVERSARY. May 20, 2002. East Timor became fully independent from Indonesia on this day. Indonesia had controlled the tiny nation since 1975. It had previously been a colony of Portugal for 450 years.

EIGHTEENTH-CENTURY SPRING MARKET FAIR. May 20–21. McLean, VA. Learn 18th-century crafts, music and games. Period wares, food and drink for sale. Est attendance: 4,000. For info: Claude Moore Colonial Farm at Turkey Run, 6310 Georgetown Pike, McLean, VA 22101. Phone: (703) 442-7557. Fax: (703) 442-0714. Web: www.1771.org.

ELIZA DOOLITTLE DAY. May 20. To honor Miss Doolittle (heroine of George Bernard Shaw's *Pygmalion*) for demonstrating the importance and the advantage of speaking one's native language properly. For info: H.M. Chase, Doolittle Day Committee, 2460 Devonshire Rd, Ann Arbor, MI 48104-2706.

FAIRE ON THE SQUARE ART & CRAFT FAIR. May 20 (also Oct 14). Downtown Baraboo, WI. Biannual outdoor event. Features all handmade work of 150 artists and crafters, local cuisine food stands, farmers' market, live entertainment, community court, carnival and kids' activities. Visit local orchards and browse the unique specialty shops in historic downtown Baraboo. The October Fair is held during the peak fall color time. Est attendance: 10,000. For info: Cindy Doescher, Fan Faire Promotions, LLC, 1801 Jefferson St, Baraboo, WI 53913. Phone: (608) 356-7995. E-mail: fanfaire@chorus.net. Web: www.faireonthesquare.com.

FISHING HAS NO BOUNDARIES. May 20–21. Freeman Lake, Monticello, IN. A two-day event for disabled persons to experience fishing on the lake. Any disability, sex, age, race, etc, are eligible. For info: FHNB, PO Box 325, Battle Ground, IN 47920. Phone: (765) 567-2567. E-mail: smlinder2000@yahoo.com.

GETTYSBURG OUTDOOR ANTIQUE SHOW. May 20. Gettysburg, PA. Features 150 dealers in antiques with exhibits and displays. Annually, a Saturday in May. Est attendance: 25,000. For info: Gettysburg CVB, PO Box 4117, Gettysburg, PA 17325. Phone: (717) 334-6274. Fax: (717) 334-1166. E-mail: gettysburgcvb@dejazzd.com. Web: www.gettysburgcvb.org.

HERZL, THEODOR: BIRTH ANNIVERSARY. May 20, 1860. Founder of the modern Zionist movement, born at Budapest, Hungary. Herzl died at Edlach, Austria, July 3, 1904.

HOMESTEAD ACT: ANNIVERSARY. May 20, 1862. President Lincoln signed the Homestead Act opening millions of acres of government-owned land in the West to settlers or "homesteaders," who had to reside on the land and cultivate it for five years.

LEWIS AND CLARK HERITAGE DAYS. May 20–21. St. Charles, MO. Authentic reenactment of Lewis and Clark's 1804 encampment prior to embarking on the exploration of the Louisiana Purchase. Activities include a parade with fife and drum corps, church service, 19th-century crafts, music, food and demonstrations. Est attendance: 25,000. For info: St. Charles Conv and Visitors Bureau, 230 S Main, St. Charles, MO 63301. Phone: (800) 366-2427 or (636) 946-7776. Web: www.lewisandclarkstcharles.com.

May 2006	S	M	T	W	T	F	S
		1	2	3	4	5	6
	7	8	9	10	11	12	13
	14	15	16	17	18	19	20
	21	22	23	24	25	26	27
	28	29	30	31			

LIBERTY SPRING ON THE SQUARE FESTIVAL. May 20. Historic Downtown Square, Liberty, MO. Handmade crafts, antiques, art and food booths. Annually, the third Saturday in May. Est attendance: 10,000. For info: Bruce Hickam, 1600 S Withers Rd, Liberty, MO 64068. Phone: (816) 792-6009, ext 3316. Fax: (816) 792-6148. E-mail: bhickam@ci.liberty.mo.us. Web: ci.liberty.mo.us.

LINDBERGH FLIGHT: ANNIVERSARY. May 20–21, 1927. Anniversary of the first solo trans-Atlantic flight. Captain Charles Augustus Lindbergh, 25-year-old aviator, departed from rainy, muddy Roosevelt Field, Long Island, NY, alone at 7:52 AM, May 20, 1927, in a Ryan monoplane named *Spirit of St. Louis*. He landed at Le Bourget airfield, Paris, at 10:24 PM Paris time (5:24 PM, NY time), May 21, winning a $25,000 prize offered by Raymond Orteig for the first nonstop flight between New York City and Paris, France (3,600 miles). The "flying fool" as he had been dubbed by some doubters became "Lucky Lindy," an instant world hero. See also: "Lindbergh, Charles Augustus: Birth Anniversary" (Feb 4).

MADISON, DOLLY (DOROTHEA) DANDRIDGE PAYNE TODD: BIRTH ANNIVERSARY. May 20, 1768. Wife of James Madison, 4th president of the US, born at Guilford County, NC. Died at Washington, DC, July 12, 1849.

MAIFEST. May 20–21. Hermann, MO. A German celebration of spring. Winery tours and wine tasting, volksplatz (craft area), parade, museum tours, children's activities, great German food, beer and wine gardens and German bands and dancing. Annually, the third full weekend of May. For info: Hermann Welcome Center, Market St, Hermann, MO 65041. Phone: (800) 932-8687. Fax: (573) 486-8995. Web: www.hermannmo.com.

MECKLENBURG DAY. May 20. North Carolina. Commemorates claimed signing of a declaration of independence from England by citizens of Mecklenburg County on this day, 1775.

MEMORY DAYS. May 20–28. Grayson, KY. Parade, art show and horse show. Est attendance: 10,000. For info: Robert L. Caummisar, Chamber of Commerce, 301 W Main St, Grayson, KY 41143. Phone: (606) 474-9522. Fax: (606) 474-4422.

MOON PHASE: LAST QUARTER. May 20. Moon enters Last Quarter phase at 5:20 AM, EDT.

MOTOR VOTER BILL SIGNED: ANNIVERSARY. May 20, 1993. The latest effort to remove barriers to voter registration resulted in the passage of the Motor Voter Bill, which was signed into law by President William Clinton. This bill requires the states to allow voter registration by mail or when a citizen applies for or renews a driver's license.

NATIONAL SAFE BOATING WEEK. May 20–26. Brings boating safety to the public's attention, decreases the number of boating fatalities and makes the waterways safer for all boaters. Sponsors: National Safe Boating Council and US Coast Guard. For info: Natl Safe Boating Council. E-mail: nsbcdirect@safeboatingcouncil.org. Web: www.safeboatingcouncil.org.

★**NATIONAL SAFE BOATING WEEK.** May 20–26. Presidential Proclamation during May since 1995. From 1958 through 1977, issued for a week including July 4 (PL85–445 of June 4, 1958). From 1981 through 1994, issued for the first week in June (PL96–376 of Oct 3, 1980). From 1995, issued for a seven-day period ending on the Friday before Memorial Day. Not issued from 1978 through 1980.

NORMAN ROCKWELL'S FIRST *SATURDAY EVENING POST* COVER: 90th ANNIVERSARY. May 20, 1916. Norman Rockwell's first cover for the *Post*, depicting a boy having to care for his infant sibling—pushing the baby carriage while his buddies set off to play ball—appeared on the May 20 edition. His last *Post* cover appeared in 1963.

PEC THING. May 20–21 (also Sept 16–17). Pecatonica, IL. Semiannual antique show with more than 400 exhibitors. Est attendance: 20,000. For info: Lisa Rosenkrans, Winnebago Country Fair Assn, PO Box 810, Pecatonica, IL 61063-0670. Phone: (815) 239-1641 or (800) 238-3587. Fax: (815) 239-1653. E-mail: pecthing@winnebagocountyfair.com.

PENNSYLVANIA AVENUE CLOSED: ANNIVERSARY. May 20, 1995. Barricades were erected to close off a two-block stretch of Pennsylvania Avenue, a six-lane street with a sidewalk that passes within 150 feet of the north face of the White House. A review of security procedures had been initiated after an attempt by an unemployed truck driver to land a small airplane on the South Lawn in September of 1994, but the closing of Pennsylvania Avenue was a direct response to the bombing of the Alfred P. Murrah Federal Building at Oklahoma City, OK, Apr 19, 1995.

PREAKNESS STAKES. May 20. Pimlico Race Course, Baltimore, MD. Preakness Stakes, the middle jewel in thoroughbred racing's Triple Crown, was inaugurated in 1873. Annually, the third Saturday in May—two Saturdays after the Kentucky Derby—and followed, three Saturdays later, by the Belmont Stakes. Est attendance: 100,000. For info: Maryland Jockey Club, Pimlico Race Course, Baltimore, MD 21215. Phone: (410) 542-9400. Web: www.preakness.com.

ROUSSEAU, HENRI JULIEN FELIX: BIRTH ANNIVERSARY. May 20, 1844. Henri Rousseau, nicknamed Le Douanier because of his one-time post as customs toll-keeper, was a celebrated French painter born at Laval, Mayenne, France. Painted deceptively "primitive" pictures of exotic foliage, flowers and fruit of the jungle, with stilted human and animal figures. Died at Hospital Necker, Paris, Sept 4, 1910.

SPACE MILESTONE: *PIONEER VENUS I* (US): ANNIVERSARY. May 20, 1978. Launched this date, became first Venus orbiter the following Dec 4.

SPRING CRAFT CELEBRATION. May 20–21. Tyler State Park, Richboro, PA. High-quality juried craft show featuring the work of 175 members of the Pennsylvania Guild of Craftsmen. Demonstrations, seminars, Crafts and Antiques Road Show, festival food, children's activites, musical entertainment. Est attendance: 15,000. For information about tickets, or how to become a member of the PA Guild, contact: Pennsylvania Guild of Craftsmen, 10 Stable Mill Trail, Richboro, PA 18954-1702. Phone: (215) 579-5997. E-mail: pacraft@comcat.com. Web: www.pacrafts.com.

STAGECOACH DAYS. May 20. Marshall, TX. Festival dedicated to transportation during the stagecoach era. Parade, arts and crafts booths and other entertainment. Annually, the third weekend in May. Est attendance: 15,000. For info: Patsy Dreesen, Dir, Convention & Visitor Development, PO Box 520, Marshall, TX 75670. Phone: (903) 935-7868 or (800) 953-7868. Fax: (903) 935-9982. E-mail: chambermfi@hotmail.com. Web: www.marshalltxchamber.com.

STEWART, JIMMY: BIRTH ANNIVERSARY. May 20, 1908. Film actor born James Stewart at Indiana, PA. Best known for his roles in *Mr Smith Goes to Washington* and the Christmas classic *It's a Wonderful Life*, he won an Oscar for *The Philadelphia Story*. Died July 2, 1997, at Beverly Hills, CA.

STORYTELLING HISTORICAL WALK AROUND WASHINGTON. May 20–21. Washington, PA. Sponsored by Washington County Historical Society. Free admission. Est attendance: 180. For info: Washington County Historical Society, 49 E Maiden St, Washington County, PA 15301. Phone: (724) 225-6740. Fax: (724) 225-8495. E-mail: info@wchspa.org. Web: www.wchspa.org.

VIRGINIA WINE FESTIVAL. May 20–21. Ash Lawn-Highland, Home of President James Monroe, Charlottesville, VA. Wineries offering tastings and sales. Commemorative wineglasses as gifts, crafts for sale, food and picnicking, live entertainment and tours of Monroe house and grounds. 12th annual. Est attendance: 1,500. For info: Ash Lawn-Highland, 1000 James Monroe Pkwy, Charlottesville, VA 22902. Phone: (434) 293-9539. Fax: (434) 293-8000. E-mail: info@ashlawnhighland.org. Web: www.ashlawnhighland.org.

WEIGHTS AND MEASURES DAY: ANNIVERSARY. May 20. Anniversary of international treaty, signed May 20, 1875, providing for the establishment of an International Bureau of Weights and Measures. The bureau was founded on international territory at Sèvres, France.

WILDFLOWER FESTIVAL OF THE ARTS. May 20–21. Historic Square, Dahlonega, GA. Springtime in the North Georgia Mountains in a historic 1800s mining town. Visual and performing artists, programs and exhibits on wildflowers of the area, children's art area where children can create their own art. Annually, the third weekend in May. Est attendance: 25,000. For info: Wildflower Festival of the Arts, PO Box 1106, Dahlonega, GA 30533. Phone: (706) 867-6829. Web: www.dahlonega.org/wildflower.

WISCONSIN DELLS AUTOMOTION. May 20–21. Noah's Ark Waterpark, Wisconsin Dells, WI. A showcase of more than 700 cars, including street machines, classics and antiques. Show features swap meet, live entertainment, car cruise, car corral, eight getaway packages valued at approximately $500 each and a car-themed movie at Big Sky Drive-In Theatre on Saturday night. Clowns, mini-tractor pull and model car contests for the kids. For auto buffs and visitors alike. Est attendance: 45,000. For info: Wisconsin Dells Visitor & Convention Bureau, Box 390, Wisconsin Dells, WI 53965. Phone: (800) 223-3557. E-mail: info@wisdells.com. Web: www.wisdells.com.

WORLD CHAMPIONSHIP STEAK COOK-OFF. May 20. Magnolia, AR. Held on the last day of the Magnolia Blossom Festival (May 19–20). Teams prepare and grill more than 2,500 rib-eye steaks to win $2,000 first place and Governor's Silver Cup. Cash prizes for best pit, parade and showmanship. Steak dinners sold to public. Annually, the third Saturday of May. Est attendance: 20,000. For info: Magnolia-Columbia County Chamber of Commerce, 202 N Pine, PO Box 866, Magnolia, AR 71754-0866. Phone: (800) 482-3330. Fax: (870) 234-7937. E-mail: magcoc@arkansas.net. www.blossomfestival.org.

WRIGHT PLUS. May 20. Oak Park, IL. The Frank Lloyd Wright Preservation Trust's annual housewalk features exclusive interior tours of privately owned homes designed by Frank Lloyd Wright and his contemporaries in the historic community of Oak Park, IL. Tickets are limited; they are available beginning Mar 1. Est attendance: 2,500. For info: Wright Plus, Frank Lloyd Wright Preservation Trust, 951 Chicago Ave, Oak Park, IL 60302. Phone: (708) 848-1976 or (708) 848-9518. Fax: (708) 848-1248. E-mail: info@wrightplus.org. Web: www.wrightplus.org.

BIRTHDAYS TODAY

Cher, 60, singer ("Believe"), actress (*Moonstruck*), born Cherilyn Sarkisian at El Centro, CA, May 20, 1946.
Joe Cocker, 62, singer ("You Are So Beautiful"), born Sheffield, England, May 20, 1944.
Michael Crapo, 55, US Senator (R, Idaho), born Idaho Falls, ID, May 20, 1951.

		S	M	T	W	T	F	S
May			1	2	3	4	5	6
2006		7	8	9	10	11	12	13
		14	15	16	17	18	19	20
		21	22	23	24	25	26	27
		28	29	30	31			

Tony Goldwyn, 46, actor (*Ghost, Kiss the Girls*), born Los Angeles, CA, May 20, 1960.
Stan Mikita, 66, Hall of Fame hockey player, born Sokolce, Czechoslovakia, May 20, 1940.
Bronson Pinchot, 47, actor ("Perfect Strangers," "Step by Step"), born New York, NY, May 20, 1959.
Ronald Prescott Reagan, 48, TV host, commentator, son of former President Ronald Reagan, born Los Angeles, CA, May 20, 1958.
Anthony Zerbe, 70, actor ("Harry-O," *Cool Hand Luke, Papillon*), born Long Beach, CA, May 20, 1936.

MAY 21 — SUNDAY
Day 141 — 224 Remaining

AMERICAN RED CROSS: 125th FOUNDING ANNIVERSARY. May 21, 1881. Commemorates the founding of the American Red Cross by Clara Barton, its first president. The Red Cross had been founded in Switzerland in 1864 by representatives from 16 European nations. The organization is a voluntary, not-for-profit organization governed and directed by volunteers and provides disaster relief at home and abroad. 1.1 million volunteers are involved in community services such as collecting and distributing donated blood and blood products, teaching health and safety classes and acting as a medium for emergency communication between Americans and their armed forces.

BURR, RAYMOND WILLIAM STACY: BIRTH ANNIVERSARY. May 21, 1917. Stage, film and TV actor best known for the role of Perry Mason in the long-running series of the same name. His films include *Rear Window* and *Godzilla*, and he was also the star of TV's "Ironside." Born at New Westminster, BC, Canada, Burr died near Healdsburg, CA, Sept 12, 1993.

CAPE MAY MUSIC FESTIVAL. May 21–June 18. Cape May, NJ. 17th annual. Enjoy world-class orchestral and chamber music performances along with internationally acclaimed guest artists. Also features world traditions music: Latin jazz, zydeco, klezmer and more. Est attendance: 10,000. For info: Mid-Atlantic Center for the Arts, 1048 Washington St, Cape May, NJ 08204. Phone: (800) 275-4278 or (609) 884-5404. Fax: (609) 884-0574. E-mail: mac4arts@capemaymac.org. Web: www.capemaymac.org.

CHILE: BATTLE OF IQUIQUE DAY. May 21. Commemorates a naval battle in 1879, part of the War of the Pacific with Peru and Bolivia.

CONCERTS BY THE SPRINGS. May 21 (also June 25, July 30 and Aug 27). Sandy Springs Historic Site, Atlanta, GA. Celebrating its 10th anniversary, this free outdoor concert series features a diversity of music showcasing local entertainers. Coolers and blankets are welcome; concessions are sold. The Williams-Payne House Museum will be open from 5:00 until 6:30 for tours. The concerts begin at 6:30. Est attendance: 4,000. For info: Megan Webb, Heritage Sandy Springs, 135 Hilderbrand Dr, Atlanta, GA 30328. Phone: (404) 851-1328. Fax: (404) 851-9807. E-mail: events@heritagesandysprings.org. Web: www.heritagesandysprings.org.

CURTISS, GLENN HAMMOND: BIRTH ANNIVERSARY. May 21, 1878. American inventor and aviator, born at Hammondsport, NY. The aviation pioneer died at Buffalo, NY, July 23, 1930.

DÜRER, ALBRECHT: BIRTH ANNIVERSARY. May 21, 1471. German painter and engraver, one of the greatest artists of the Renaissance, was born at Nuremberg, Germany, and died there Apr 6, 1528.

FRY, ELIZABETH GURNEY: BIRTH ANNIVERSARY. May 21, 1780. English reformer who dedicated her life to improving the condition of the poor and especially of women in prison, born at Earlham, Norfolk, England. Died at Ramsgate, Oct 12, 1845.

GEMINI, THE TWINS. May 21–June 20. In the astronomical/astrological zodiac, which divides the sun's apparent orbit into 12 segments, the period May 21–June 20 is traditionally identified as the sun sign period of Gemini, the Twins. The ruling planet is Mercury.

HAMMER, ARMAND: BIRTH ANNIVERSARY. May 21, 1898. American industrialist Armand Hammer was born at New York, NY. He built the Occidental Petroleum Company into a $20 billion conglomerate after he invested $100,000 in it in 1956 and it was awarded two oil concessions in Libya. He was a trained physician who was sympathetic to the Soviet people and gave away millions of dollars through philanthropy to cancer research. Hammer died Dec 10, 1990, at Los Angeles, CA.

HUMMEL, SISTER MARIA INNOCENTIA: BIRTH ANNIVERSARY. May 21, 1909. Born at Massing, Bavaria, Sister Maria Innocentia Hummel attended Munich's Academy of Fine Arts. She entered Siessen Convent run by the Sisters of the Third Order of St. Francis and began teaching art to kindergarten children. In 1934 Franz Goebel obtained an exclusive license to translate her drawings into three-dimensional figurines. The first M.I. Hummel figurines were displayed at the Leipzig Trade Fair in 1935; they made their first appearance in the American market in May 1935. She died Nov 6, 1946, at Siessen, Germany. Many M.I. Hummel Clubs across the country commemorate her birth date with special events and fund-raisers for local charities.

"I NEED A PATCH FOR THAT" DAY. May 21. They have patches for nicotine and they have patches for heart patients. How about a patch for runny noses or bad hair? [©2003 by WH.] For info: Thomas & Ruth Roy, Wellcat Holidays, 2418 Long Ln, Lebanon, PA 17046. Phone: (717) 279-0184. E-mail: info@wellcat.com. Web: www.wellcat.com.

NATIONAL DOG BITE PREVENTION WEEK. May 21–27. To promote safety with dogs—especially among children, who are the #1 victims of dog bites. National Association for Humane and Environmental Education (NAHEE), youth education division of The Humane Society of the United States, has developed a dog bite prevention program for kids. Annually, third full week in May. For info: Heidi O'Brien, NAHEE, 67 Norwich Essex Turnpike, East Haddam, CT 06423. Phone: (860) 434-8666, ext 17. Fax: (860) 434-9579. E-mail: obrien@nahee.org. Web: www.nahee.org or www.nodogbites.org.

NATIONAL ETIQUETTE WEEK. May 21–27. A national recognition of proper etiquette in all areas of American life (business, social, dining, international, wedding, computer, etc.). A self-assessment on the current status of civility in the US. Annually, the third week in May starting on Sunday. For info: Sandra Morisset, Protocol Training Services, PO Box 4981, New York, NY 10185. Phone: (212) 802-9098. Web: www.zyworld.com/etiquette.

NATIONAL NEW FRIENDS, OLD FRIENDS WEEK. May 21–27. A week to celebrate and make time for old friends and new friends and remember how vital friends are for our emotional and physical health and well-being and even professional or career success. Friendshifts® is the word coined by author and sociologist Jan Yager to denote the way our ideas about friendships as well as who our friends are may change as we go through different stages of life. But at every stage, friendship is crucial, for children, for teenagers, for young adults, singles, couples, new mothers, the middle-aged and especially for those who are older, retired or widowed. For info: Jan Yager, PhD, PO Box 8038, Stamford, CT 06905-8038. Fax: (203) 968-0193. E-mail: jyager@aol.com. Web: www.JanYager.com/friendship.

NATIONAL STATIONERY SHOW. May 21–24. Javits Center, New York, NY. For info: George Little Management, 10 Bank St, White Plains, NY 10606. Phone: (914) 421-3200. Fax: (914) 948-6088. Web: www.glmshows.com or www.nationalstationeryshow.com.

NATIONAL WAITSTAFF DAY. May 21. A day for restaurant managers and patrons to recognize and to express their appreciation for the many fine and dedicated waitresses and waiters. For info: Gaylord F. Ward, Promotion Dir, 1505 E Bristol Rd, Burton, MI 48529-2214.

NEIGHBOR DAY. May 21. A "Day of Special Observance" in Rhode Island, declared by the General Assembly. Annually, the Sunday prior to Memorial Day weekend. For info: Mary Jane DiMaio, Westerly Town Councilor, 101 Shore Rd, Westerly, RI 02891. E-mail: mjdimaio1@cox.net. Web: townofwesterly.com.

POPE, ALEXANDER: BIRTH ANNIVERSARY. May 21, 1688 (OS). English poet born at London, England. "A man," Pope wrote in 1727, "should never be ashamed to own he has been in the wrong, which is but saying, in other words, that he is wiser today than he was yesterday." Died at Twickenham, May 30, 1744 (OS).

RAJIV GANDHI ASSASSINATED: 15th ANNIVERSARY. May 21, 1991. Former Indian Prime Minister Rajiv Gandhi was assassinated in the midst of a reelection campaign. He was killed when a bomb, hidden in a bouquet of flowers given by admirers, exploded as he approached a dais to begin a campaign rally. He had served as prime minister between 1984 and 1989 after succeeding his mother, Indira Gandhi, who was assassinated in 1984.

ROGATION SUNDAY. May 21. The fifth Sunday after Easter is the beginning of Rogationtide (Rogation Sunday and the following three days before Ascension Day). Rogation Day rituals date from the 5th century.

RURAL LIFE SUNDAY OR SOIL STEWARDSHIP SUNDAY. May 21. With an increase in ecological and environmental concerns, Rural Life Sunday emphasizes the concept that Earth belongs to God, who has granted humanity the use of it, along with the responsibility of caring for it wisely. At the suggestion of the International Association of Agricultural Missions, Rural Life Sunday was first observed in 1929. The day is observed annually by churches of many Christian denominations and includes pulpit exchanges by rural and urban pastors. Under the auspices of the National Association of Soil and Water Conservation Districts, the week beginning with Rural Life Sunday is now widely observed as Soil Stewardship Week, with the Sunday itself alternatively termed Soil Stewardship Sunday. Traditionally, Rural Life Sunday is Rogation Sunday, the Sunday preceding Ascension Day.

SAKHAROV, ANDREI DMITRIYEVICH: BIRTH ANNIVERSARY. May 21, 1921. Soviet physicist, human rights activist and environmentalist Andrei Sakharov was born at Moscow, Russia. A collaborator in producing the first Soviet atomic bomb, and later the hydrogen bomb, Sakharov denounced shortcomings of his country's government and was exiled to Gorky, Russia, 1980–86. He was a formulator of the reform and restructuring concept known as *perestroika* and of *glasnost* (freedom). He was named to the Soviet Congress of Peoples Deputies eight months before his death at Moscow on Dec 14, 1989. As a physicist, he was the developer of destructive weapons; as a humanitarian, he was courageous as a dissident from militarism and an advocate of human rights.

UNITED NATIONS: WORLD DAY FOR CULTURAL DIVERSITY FOR DIALOGUE AND DEVELOPMENT. May 21. Recognizing the need to enhance the potential of culture as a means of achieving prosperity, sustainable development and global peaceful coexistence, the General Assembly, on December 20, 2002, proclaimed May 21 to serve as this day. The Assembly acknowledged the close link between protecting cultural diversity and the larger framework of the dialogue among civilizations. For info: United Nations, Dept of Public Info, New York, NY 10017. Web: www.un.org.

★**WORLD TRADE WEEK.** May 21–27. Presidential Proclamation has been issued each year since 1948 for the third week of May with three exceptions: 1949, 1955 and 1966.

BIRTHDAYS TODAY

Bobby Cox, 65, baseball manager, former executive and player, born Tulsa, OK, May 21, 1941.

Robert Creeley, 80, author, poet (*Have a Heart, Windows*), born Arlington, MA, May 21, 1926.

Janet Dailey, 62, romance novelist (*Tangled Vines*), born Storm Lake, IA, May 21, 1944.

Al Franken, 55, comedian, writer (*Rush Limbaugh Is a Big Fat Idiot and Other Observations*), actor ("Saturday Night Live"), born New York, NY, May 21, 1951.

Heinz Holliger, 67, oboist, composer, conductor, born Langenthal, Switzerland, May 21, 1939.

Ian McEwan, 58, author (*Atonement, Amsterdam*), born Aldershot, Hampstead, England, May 21, 1948.

William "Spike" O'Dell, 53, Chicago radio personality, born Moline, IL, May 21, 1953.

Judge Reinhold, 49, actor (*Beverly Hills Cop*), born Wilmington, DE, May 21, 1957.

Leo Sayer, 58, singer ("You Make Me Feel Like Dancing"), songwriter, born Shoreham, England, May 21, 1948.

Mr T, 54, actor (*Rocky III*, "The A-Team"), born Lawrence Tero or Tureaud at Chicago, IL, May 21, 1952.

MAY 22 — MONDAY

Day 142 — 223 Remaining

CANADA: IMMIGRANTS' DAY. May 22. A day to celebrate and recognize the contributions made by immigrants to Canada and to discuss the Canadian immigration policy and experience. For info: Sergio R. Karas, BA, LLB, Barrister and Solicitor, Karas & Assoc, 65 Queen St W, Ste 1505, Toronto, ON, Canada M5H 2M5. Phone: (416) 506-1800. Fax: (416) 506-1305. E-mail: karas@karas.ca. Web: www.karas.ca.

CANADA: VICTORIA DAY. May 22. Commemorates the birth of Queen Victoria May 24, 1819. Observed annually on the first Monday preceding May 25.

CASSATT, MARY: BIRTH ANNIVERSARY. May 22, 1844. Leading American artist of the Impressionist school, Mary Cassatt was born May 22, 1844 (some sources give 1845), at Allegheny City, PA (now part of Pittsburgh). She settled in Paris in 1874 where she was influenced by Degas and the Impressionists. She was later instrumental in their works becoming well known in the US. The majority of her paintings and pastels were based on the theme of mother and child. After 1900 her eyesight began to fail, and by 1914 she was no longer able to paint. Cassatt died at Chateau de Beaufresne near Paris, France, June 14, 1926.

		S	M	T	W	T	F	S
May			1	2	3	4	5	6
2006		7	8	9	10	11	12	13
		14	15	16	17	18	19	20
		21	22	23	24	25	26	27
		28	29	30	31			

CRATER LAKE NATIONAL PARK ESTABLISHED: ANNIVERSARY. May 22, 1902. One of the world's deepest lakes, Crater Lake was first discovered in 1853. In 1885 William Gladstone Steele saw the Oregon lake and made it his personal goal to establish the lake and surrounding areas as a national park. His goal was attained 17 years later.

DOYLE, SIR ARTHUR CONAN: BIRTH ANNIVERSARY. May 22, 1859. British physician Sir Arthur Conan Doyle is best remembered as a detective story writer, especially for the creation of Sherlock Holmes and Dr. Watson. Doyle was born at Edinburgh, Scotland. He was deeply interested in and lectured on the subject of spiritualism. Died at Crowborough, Sussex, England, July 7, 1930.

JOHNNY CARSON'S FINAL SHOW: ANNIVERSARY. May 22, 1992. After almost 30 years as host of the "Tonight" show, Johnny Carson hosted his last show. Carson became host of the late-night talk show, which began as a local New York program hosted by Steve Allen, Oct 1, 1962. Over the years Carson occasionally made headlines with such extravaganzas as the marriage of Tiny Tim and Miss Vicki. Johnny received Emmys for his work four years in a row, 1976–79. Ed McMahon, his sidekick of 30 years, and Doc Severinsen, longtime bandleader, left the show with Carson. Jay Leno, the show's exclusive guest host, became the new regular host.

"MISTER ROGERS' NEIGHBORHOOD" TV PREMIERE: ANNIVERSARY. May 22, 1967. Presbyterian minister Fred Rogers hosted this long-running PBS children's program. Puppets and human characters interacted in the neighborhood of make-believe. Rogers played the voices of many of the puppets and educated young viewers on a variety of important subjects. The last episodes of the program were made in 2001. Almost 1,000 episodes were produced over the show's history.

NATIONAL BACKYARD GAMES WEEK. May 22–29. Observance to celebrate the unofficial start of summer by fostering social interaction and family togetherness through backyard games. Get outside and be both physically and mentally stimulated, playing classic games of the past while discovering and creating new ways to be active and interact with friends and neighbors. For info: Frank Beres, Patch Products, PO Box 268, Beloit, WI 53511. Phone: (608) 362-6896. Fax: (608) 362-8178. E-mail: patch@patchproducts.com. Web: www.patchproducts.com.

★**NATIONAL MARITIME DAY.** May 22. Presidential Proclamation always issued for May 22 since 1933. (Pub Res No. 7 of May 20, 1933.)

NATIONAL MARITIME DAY. May 22. Anniversary of departure for first steamship crossing of Atlantic from Savannah, GA, to Liverpool, England, by steamship *Savannah* in 1819.

NIXON FIRST AMERICAN PRESIDENT TO VISIT MOSCOW: ANNIVERSARY. May 22, 1972. President Richard Nixon became the first American president to visit Moscow. Four days later on May 26, Nixon and Soviet leader Leonid Brezhnev signed a treaty on antiballistic missile systems and an interim agreement on limitation of strategic missiles.

OLIVIER, LAURENCE: BIRTH ANNIVERSARY. May 22, 1907. Actor, director and theater manager, born at Dorking, England. Thought by many to be the most influential actor of the 20th century, Olivier's theatrical and film career shaped the art forms in which he participated. Honored with nine Academy

Award nominations, three Oscars and five Emmy awards, his repertoire included most of the prime Shakespearean roles and roles in such films as *Rebecca, Pride and Prejudice, Marathon Man* and *Wuthering Heights*. Olivier was an innovative theater manager with London's Old Vic company and the National Theatre of Great Britain. The National Theatre's largest auditorium and Britain's equivalent of Broadway's Tony awards carry his name. He was knighted in 1947 and made a peer of the throne in 1970. Olivier died at Ashurst, England, July 11, 1989.

PGA SENIORS' CHAMPIONSHIP. May 22–28. Oak Tree Golf Club, Edmond, OK. 67th competition for the oldest major championship in senior golf. Conducted by the Professional Golfers' Association of America. For info: Julius Mason, Dir of PR and Media Relations, PGA of America, 100 Avenue of the Champions, Palm Beach Gardens, FL 33418. Phone: (561) 624-8400. Fax: (561) 624-8448. Web: www.pga.com.

RA, SUN: BIRTH ANNIVERSARY. May 22, 1914. Born Herman (Sonny) Blount, Sun Ra was a pioneering and innovative jazz musician whose avant-garde performances mixed elements of theater with his surreal composition and performance style. Ra was born at Birmingham, AL, and died there May 30, 1993.

SRI LANKA: NATIONAL HEROES DAY. May 22. Commemorates the struggle of the leaders of the National Independence Movement to liberate the country from colonial rule in 1971. Public holiday.

STRONGEST EARTHQUAKE OF THE 20th CENTURY: ANNIVERSARY. May 22, 1960. An earthquake of a magnitude 9.5 struck southern Chile, killing 2,000 people and leaving 2,000,000 homeless. The earthquake also caused damage in Hawaii, Japan and the Philippines. While 20th-century earthquakes in Mexico City, Japan and Turkey resulted in far more deaths, this earthquake in Chile was of the highest magnitude.

SUMNER ATTACKED IN THE SENATE: 150th ANNIVERSARY. May 22, 1856. Two days after he decried the "Crime Against Kansas," US Senator Charles Sumner of Massachusetts was attacked with a walking cane by South Carolina Congressman Preston Brooks in the Senate Chamber (the Senate was not in session). Abolitionist Sumner needed three years to recuperate.

SWITZERLAND: PACING THE BOUNDS. May 22. Liestal. Citizens set off at 8 AM and march along boundaries to the beating of drums and firing of pistols and muskets. Occasion for fetes. Annually, the Monday before Ascension Day.

TRUMAN DOCTRINE: ANNIVERSARY. May 22, 1947. Congress approved the Truman Doctrine on this day. In order to contain Communism after WWII, it provided for US aid to Greece and Turkey. A corollary of this doctrine was the Marshall Plan, which began sending aid to war-torn European countries in 1948.

UNITED NATIONS: INTERNATIONAL DAY FOR BIOLOGICAL DIVERSITY. May 22. On Dec 19, 1994, the General Assembly proclaimed this observance for Dec 29, the date of entry into force of the Convention on Biological Diversity (Res 49/119). In 2000 the date was changed to May 22. This day is an opportunity to strengthen people's commitment and actions for the conservation of the world's biological diversity. For info: United Nations, Dept of Public Info, New York, NY 10017. Web: www.un.org.

WAGNER, RICHARD: BIRTH ANNIVERSARY. May 22, 1813. German composer born at Leipzig who made revolutionary changes in the structure of opera. Best known for his Ring Cycle (*Der Ring des Nibelungen*). Died at Italy, Feb 13, 1883.

YEMEN: NATIONAL DAY. May 22. Public holiday. Commemorates the reunification of Yemen in 1990.

BIRTHDAYS TODAY

Charles Aznavour, 82, singer, songwriter, actor (*Shoot the Piano Player, Candy, The Tin Drum*), born Paris, France, May 22, 1924.

Richard Benjamin, 68, actor (*Goodbye Columbus, Diary of a Mad Housewife*, "He & She"), born New York, NY, May 22, 1938.
Naomi Campbell, 36, model, born London, England, May 22, 1970.
Frank Converse, 68, actor ("Movin' On," *Hurry Sundown*), born St. Louis, MO, May 22, 1938.
Judith Crist, 84, critic, born New York, NY, May 22, 1922.
Thomas Edward (Tommy) John, 63, former baseball player, born Terre Haute, IN, May 22, 1943.
A.J. Langer, 32, actress ("My So-Called Life," "Brooklyn South"), born Columbus, OH, May 22, 1974.
Lisa Murkowski, 49, US Senator (R, Alaska), born Ketchikan, AK, May 22, 1957.
Barbara Parkins, 63, actress ("Peyton Place," *Valley of the Dolls*), born Vancouver, BC, Canada, May 22, 1943.
Michael Sarrazin, 66, actor (*The Flim Flam Man, The Reincarnation of Peter Proud*), born Quebec City, QC, Canada, May 22, 1940.
Garry Wills, 72, author (*John Wayne's America, Lincoln at Gettysburg*), born Atlanta, GA, May 22, 1934.

MAY 23 — TUESDAY
Day 143 — 222 Remaining

BONNIE AND CLYDE: DEATH ANNIVERSARY. May 23, 1934. The two-year crime spree of Bonnie Parker and Clyde Barrow, bank robbers accused of at least 12 murders, came to an end when a law enforcement posse led by Texas Ranger Frank Hamer opened fire on the couple in an ambush at Gibsland, LA. The couple had operated in Texas, Oklahoma, Missouri, Louisiana and other states, and had sent ballads to local newspapers chronicling their exploits, making them two of the most notorious—and romanticized—of many Depression-era gangsters. Some 20,000 people lined up to see the body of Clyde Barrow put on display in a mortuary in downtown Dallas, TX.

CLOONEY, ROSEMARY: BIRTH ANNIVERSARY. May 23, 1928. The beloved pop and jazz singer was born at Maysville, KY. She became popular in the 1950s for singing the novelty song "Come-on-a-My House" and pop standards. She also starred in the holiday film *White Christmas* (1954). She died June 29, 2002, at Beverly Hills, CA.

DECLARATION OF THE BAB. May 23. Baha'i commemoration of May 23, 1844, when the Bab, the prophet-herald of the Baha'i Faith, announced in Shiraz, Persia, that he was the herald of a new messenger of God. One of the nine days of the year when Baha'is suspend work. For info: Baha'is of the US, Office of Communications, 1233 Central St, Evanston, IL 60201. Phone: (847) 733-3411. Fax: (847) 869-0247. E-mail: ooc@usbnc.org. Web: www.us.bahai.org.

ENGLAND: CHELSEA FLOWER SHOW. May 23–27. Royal Hospital, Chelsea, London. The world's best flower show with specially designed gardens and spectacular floral displays. Est attendance: 157,000. For info: Shows Marketing Dept, Royal Horticultural Society, 80 Vincent Sq, London, England SW1P 2PE. Phone: (44) (20) 78-43332. E-mail: info@rhs.org.uk. Web: www.rhs.org.uk/chelsea.

FAIRBANKS, DOUGLAS ELTON: BIRTH ANNIVERSARY. May 23, 1883. Douglas Fairbanks was born at Denver, CO. He made his professional debut as an actor at Richmond, VA, Sept 10, 1900, in *The Duke's Jester*. His theatrical career turned to Hollywood, and he became a movie idol appearing in such films as *The Mark of Zorro, The Three Musketeers, Robin Hood, The Thief of Bagdad, The Black Pirate* and *The Gaucho*. He married "America's Sweetheart," Mary Pickford, in 1918, and in 1919 they joined with D.W. Griffith and Charlie Chaplin to form the production company United Artists. He died at Santa Monica, CA, Dec 12, 1939.

FIRST BLACK RECEIVES CONGRESSIONAL MEDAL OF HONOR: ANNIVERSARY. May 23, 1900. Sergeant William H. Carney, of the 54th Massachusetts Colored Infantry, was the first black to win the Congressional Medal of Honor. He was cited for his efforts, although wounded twice, during the Battle of Fort Wagner, SC, June 18, 1863.

FULLER, MARGARET: BIRTH ANNIVERSARY. May 23, 1810. Journalist and author Sarah Margaret Fuller, born at Cambridgeport, MA, began reading Virgil at age six. Her conversational powers won her the admiration of students at Harvard University, and she was befriended by Ralph Waldo Emerson. She shared editorial duties with Emerson on the Transcendentalist quarterly *The Dial* and was hired by Horace Greeley as literary critic for the *New York Tribune*. Her book *Women in the Nineteenth Century*, the first feminist statement by an American writer, brought her international acclaim. In 1846, as a foreign correspondent for the *Tribune*, she became caught up in the Italian revolutionary movement and secretly married a young Roman nobleman, the Marquis Giovanni Angelo Ossoli. En route to the US, Fuller and her husband and child died July 19, 1850, when their ship was wrecked off Fire Island near New York, NY.

MANSFIELD, ARABELLA: BIRTH ANNIVERSARY. May 23, 1846. Arabella Mansfield, born Belle Aurelia Babb near Burlington, IA, was the first woman admitted to the legal profession in the US. In 1869 while teaching at Iowa Wesleyan College, Mansfield was certified as an attorney and admitted to the Iowa bar. According to the examiners, "she gave the very best rebuke possible to the imputation that ladies cannot qualify for the practice of law." Mansfield never did practice law, however, continuing her career as an educator. She joined the faculty of DePauw University, at Greencastle, IN, where she became dean of the schools of art and music. One of the first woman college professors and administrators in the US, Mansfield was also instrumental in the founding of the Iowa Woman Suffrage Society in 1870. She died Aug 2, 1911, at Aurora, IL.

MESMER, FRIEDRICH ANTON: BIRTH ANNIVERSARY. May 23, 1734. German physician after whom Mesmerism was named. Magnetism and hypnotism were used by him in treating disease. Born at Iznang, Swabia, Germany. Died Mar 5, 1815, at Meersburg, Swabia, Germany.

MOROCCO: NATIONAL DAY. May 23. National holiday. Commemorates referendum on the majority of the king in 1980.

NAIA WOMEN'S GOLF NATIONAL CHAMPIONSHIPS. May 23–26. Blackthorn Golf Club, South Bend, IN. 12th annual. Est attendance: 400. For info: Natl Assn of Intercollegiate Athletics, 23500 W 105th St, PO Box 1325, Olathe, KS 66051-1325. Phone: (913) 791-0044. Fax: (913) 791-9555. E-mail: jleavens@naia.org. Web: www.naia.org.

NATIONAL GEOGRAPHIC BEE: NATIONAL FINALS. May 23–24. National Geographic Society Headquarters, Washington, DC. The first-place winner from each state-level competition (that took place on Mar 31) advances to the national level. Alex Trebek of "Jeopardy!" fame moderates the finals, which are televised on the National Geographic Channel and public television stations. They compete for scholarships and prizes totaling more than $50,000. Est attendance: 400. For info: Natl Geographic Bee, Natl Geographic Society, 1145 17th St NW, Washington, DC 20036. Phone: (202) 828-6659. Web: www.nationalgeographic.com/geographicbee.

NCAA DIVISION I WOMEN'S GOLF CHAMPIONSHIPS. May 23–26. Ohio State University, Columbus, OH. For info: NCAA, 700 W Washington Ave, PO Box 6222, Indianapolis, IN 46206-6222. Phone: (317) 917-6222. Fax: (317) 917-6825. Web: www.ncaasports.com.

NEW YORK PUBLIC LIBRARY: ANNIVERSARY. May 23, 1895. New York's then-governor Samuel J. Tilden was the driving force that resulted in the combining of the private Astor and Lenox libraries with a $2 million endowment and 15,000 volumes from the Tilden Trust to become the New York Public Library. The main branch of the library opened to the public on this day in 1911.

SLOVO, JOE: BIRTH ANNIVERSARY. May 23, 1926. South African Communist Party leader Joe Slovo was a longtime friend and ally of Nelson Mandela. The first white to become a member of the African National Congress Executive Committee, he lived in exile from 1963 to 1990, serving as head of the military arm of the ANC during that period. Born at Obelai, Lithuania, he died Jan 6, 1995, at Johannesburg.

SOUTH CAROLINA CONSTITUTION RATIFICATION: ANNIVERSARY. May 23, 1788. By a vote of 149 to 73, South Carolina became the eighth state to ratify the Constitution.

SUPREME COURT UPHOLDS BAN ON ABORTION COUNSELING: 15th ANNIVERSARY. May 23, 1991. In the case *Rust v Sullivan*, the Supreme Court, in a 5–4 ruling, upheld federal regulations that barred federally funded family planning clinics from providing any information about abortion.

SWEDEN: LINNAEUS DAY. May 23. Stenbrohult. Commemorates birth of Carolus Linnaeus (Carl von Linne), Swedish naturalist, born May 23, 1707 (OS) and who died at Uppsala, Sweden, Jan 10, 1778.

WORLD TURTLE DAY. May 23. An observance sponsored by American Tortoise Rescue to help people celebrate and protect turtles and tortoises, as well as their habitat around the world. For info: Susan Tellem, American Tortoise Rescue, 23852 Pacific Coast Highway, Malibu, CA 90265. Phone: (800) 938-3553. E-mail: info@tortoise.com. Web: www.tortoise.com.

BIRTHDAYS TODAY

Mitch Albom, 48, journalist, author (*Tuesdays with Morrie, The Five People You Meet in Heaven*), born Passaic, NJ, May 23, 1958.

Barbara Barrie, 75, actress ("Suddenly Susan," *One Potato, Two Potato; Breaking Away*), born Chicago, IL, May 23, 1931.

Drew Carey, 45, actor ("The Drew Carey Show"), born Cleveland, OH, May 23, 1961 (some sources say 1958).

Joan Collins, 73, actress ("Dynasty"), born London, England, May 23, 1933.

Marvelous Marvin Hagler, 52, former boxer, born Newark, NJ, May 23, 1954.

Jewel, 32, singer, born Jewel Kilcher at Payson, UT, May 23, 1974.

Charles Kimbrough, 70, actor ("Murphy Brown"), born St. Paul, MN, May 23, 1936.

Robert Moog, 72, inventor of first commercially viable keyboard synthesizer, born Flushing, NY, May 23, 1934.

Artie Shaw, 96, musician, bandleader, born New York, NY, May 23, 1910.

May 2006	S	M	T	W	T	F	S
		1	2	3	4	5	6
	7	8	9	10	11	12	13
	14	15	16	17	18	19	20
	21	22	23	24	25	26	27
	28	29	30	31			

MAY 24 — WEDNESDAY
Day 144 — 221 Remaining

ANTI-SALOON LEAGUE FOUNDED: ANNIVERSARY.
May 24, 1893. The Anti-Saloon League was founded by Howard H. Russell at Oberlin, OH. Efforts in that state were so successful that the Anti-Saloon League of America was organized in 1895. The League's permanent home became Otterbein College at Westerville, OH, in 1909.

BASEBALL FIRST PLAYED UNDER LIGHTS: ANNIVERSARY. May 24, 1935. The Cincinnati Reds defeated the Philadelphia Phillies by a score of 2–1, as more than 20,000 fans enjoyed the first night baseball game in the major leagues. The game was played at Crosley Field, Cincinnati, OH.

BELIZE: COMMONWEALTH DAY. May 24. Public holiday.

BIG TEN BASEBALL TOURNAMENT. May 24–27. Site of conference champion. Est attendance: 1,500. For info: Big Ten Conference, 1500 W Higgins Rd, Park Ridge, IL 60068-6300. Phone: (847) 696-1010. Fax: (847) 696-1110. Web: www.bigten .org.

BROOKLYN BRIDGE OPENED: ANNIVERSARY. May 24, 1883. Nearly 14 years in construction, the $16 million Brooklyn Bridge over the East River opened. Designed by John A. Roebling, the steel suspension bridge has a span of 1,595 feet.

BROTHER'S DAY. May 24. Celebration of brotherhood for biological brothers, fraternity brothers, brothers bonded by union affiliation or lifetime experiences. Annually, May 24. [©2001 C. Daniel Rhodes.] For info: C. Daniel Rhodes, 1900 Crossvine Rd, Hoover, AL 35244. Phone: (205) 908-6781. E-mail: rhodan@ charter.net.

BULGARIA: CULTURE DAY. May 24. National holiday festively celebrated by schoolchildren, students, people of science and art.

ECUADOR: BATTLE OF PICHINCHA. May 24. National holiday. Commemorates battle in 1822 that marked the final defeat of Spain in Ecuador.

ERITREA: INDEPENDENCE DAY: ANNIVERSARY. May 24. National Day. Gained independence from Ethiopia in 1993 after 30-year civil war.

INTERNATIONAL TIARA DAY. May 24. A day when all women embrace and celebrate their powers of leadership in their own lives. Real or virtual tiara-wearing is optional. For info: Barbara Bellissimo, PO Box 1303, West Tisbury, MA 02575. Phone: (508) 696-4647. Fax: (508) 696-9648. E-mail: barbara@seasons ofsuccess.com. Web: www.seasonsofsuccess.com.

LEUTZE, EMANUEL: BIRTH ANNIVERSARY. May 24, 1816. Obscure itinerant painter, born at Württemberg, Germany, came to the US when he was nine years old, began painting by age 15. Painted some of the most famous of American scenes, such as *Washington Crossing the Delaware, Washington Rallying the Troops at Monmouth* and *Columbus Before the Queen.* Died July 18, 1868, at Washington, DC.

MORSE OPENS FIRST US TELEGRAPH LINE: ANNIVERSARY. May 24, 1844. The first US telegraph line was formally opened between Baltimore, MD, and Washington, DC. Samuel F.B. Morse sent the first officially telegraphed words "What hath God wrought?" from the Capitol building to Baltimore. Earlier messages had been sent along the historic line during testing, and one, sent May 1 from a meeting in Baltimore, contained the news that Henry Clay had been nominated as president by the Whig party. This message reached Washington one hour prior to a train carrying the same news.

NEWHOUSE, SAMUEL I.: BIRTH ANNIVERSARY. May 24, 1895. Multimillionaire businessman who built family publishing and communications empire. Born to immigrant parents in a New York City tenement, Newhouse became "America's most profitable publisher." He accumulated 31 newspapers, seven magazines, six television stations, five radio stations and 20 cable television systems. He died at New York, NY, Aug 29, 1979.

PALMER, LILLI: BIRTH ANNIVERSARY. May 24, 1914. Stage, screen and television actress Lilli Palmer was born Lillie Marie Peiser, at Poznan, Poland. She also painted and was the author of several novels and an autobiography titled *Change Lobsters—And Dance.* She died at Los Angeles, CA, Jan 27, 1986.

PEALE, JAMES: 175th DEATH ANNIVERSARY. May 24, 1831. American portrait and miniature painter (painted portraits of George and Martha Washington and General Sir Thomas Shirley) was born at Chestertown, MD, in 1749 (exact date unknown). Died at Philadelphia, PA.

SPACE MILESTONE: *AURORA 7* MERCURY SPACE CAPSULE (US). May 24, 1962. With this launch Scott Carpenter became the second American to orbit Earth, circling it three times.

BIRTHDAYS TODAY

DaMarcus Beasley, 24, soccer player, born Fort Wayne, IN, May 24, 1982.

Jim Broadbent, 57, actor (*Moulin Rouge, Topsy-Turvy,* Oscar for *Iris*), born Lincoln, Lincolnshire, England, May 24, 1949.

Gary Burghoff, 63, actor (Emmy for "M*A*S*H"), born Bristol, CT, May 24, 1943.

Tommy Chong, 68, actor (*Up in Smoke, The Corsican Brothers* [also wrote screenplay and directed]), born Edmonton, AB, Canada, May 24, 1938.

Joe Dumars III, 43, former basketball player, born Shreveport, LA, May 24, 1963.

Bob Dylan, 65, composer, singer, born Robert Zimmerman at Duluth, MN, May 24, 1941.

Patti LaBelle, 62, singer ("Since I Don't Have You"), born Patricia Louise Holte at Philadelphia, PA, May 24, 1944.

Tracy McGrady, 27, basketball player, born Bartow, FL, May 24, 1979.

Alfred Molina, 53, actor (*Frida, Chocolat, Letter to Brezhnev*), born London, England, May 24, 1953.

Frank Oz, 62, director, puppeteer, born Hereford, England, May 24, 1944.

Priscilla Beaulieu Presley, 61, actress ("Dallas," *Naked Gun* movies), ex-wife of Elvis, born Brooklyn, NY, May 24, 1945.

Kristin Scott Thomas, 46, actress (*The English Patient, The Horse Whisperer*), born Cornwall, England, May 24, 1960.

MAY 25 — THURSDAY
Day 145 — 220 Remaining

AFRICAN FREEDOM DAY: ANNIVERSARY. May 25. Public holiday in Chad, Zambia and some other African states. Members of the Organization for African Unity (formed May 25, 1963) commemorate their independence from colonial rule. Sports contests, political rallies and tribal dances.

AMERICAN FLIGHT CRASHES AT O'HARE: ANNIVERSARY. May 25, 1979. An American Airlines DC-10 lost an engine upon takeoff and crashed seconds later, killing all 272 aboard and three people on the ground. This is the worst US air disaster in history.

ARGENTINA: REVOLUTION DAY. May 25. National holiday. Commemoration of revolt against Spanish rule in 1810.

ASCENSION DAY. May 25. Commemorates Christ's ascension into heaven. Observed since AD 68. Ascension Day is the 40th day after the Resurrection, counting Easter as the first day.

BELGIUM: PROCESSION OF THE HOLY BLOOD. May 25. Religious historical procession. Recalls adventurous crusaders, including Count Thierry of Alsace, who carried back relics of the Holy Blood. Always on Ascension Day.

CARVER, RAYMOND: BIRTH ANNIVERSARY. May 25, 1938. American poet and short story writer who chronicled the lives of America's working poor. Born at Clatskanie, OR, he died Aug 2, 1988, at his home at Port Angeles, WA, soon after finishing a book of poetry titled *A New Path to the Waterfall.*

CONSTITUTIONAL CONVENTION: ANNIVERSARY. May 25, 1787. At Philadelphia, PA, delegates from seven states, forming a quorum, opened the Constitutional Convention, which had been proposed by the Annapolis Convention Sept 11–14, 1786. Among those who were in attendance: George Washington, Benjamin Franklin, James Madison, Alexander Hamilton and Elbridge Gerry. See also: "1786 Annapolis Convention: Anniversary" (Sept 11).

DAVIS, MILES: BIRTH ANNIVERSARY. May 25, 1926. Jazz trumpeter Miles Davis was born at Alton, IL. He was influenced by the bebop music style of Charlie Parker and Dizzy Gillespie and ended up leaving the Juilliard School of Music to join Parker's quintet in 1945. He experimented with different styles throughout his career, exploring new voicings in jazz with arranger Gil Evans and musicians John Coltrane and Red Garland, delving into "modal" music with Tony Williams and Wayne Shorter and moving into a fusion sound in the '60s. His career was beset with bouts of drug addiction, but in the 1970s his return to the music scene found him creating a sound that melded his bebop origins, modal chord progressions and driving rock rhythms. He died Sept 28, 1991, at Santa Monica, CA.

DOWIE, JOHN ALEXANDER: BIRTH ANNIVERSARY. May 25, 1847. Evangelist and claimant of the title "Elijah the Restorer" was born at Edinburgh, Scotland. He established the Christian Catholic Church at Zion, IL, where some 5,000 followers created a unique community without pharmacies, physicians, theaters or dance halls and where smoking, drinking and the eating of pork were prohibited. Dowie's ostentatiously expensive personal lifestyle and his unsuccessful attempt to convert New York City were partially responsible for the falling away of his followers. He was expelled from the church in 1906 and died at Chicago, IL, Mar 9, 1907.

EMERSON, RALPH WALDO: BIRTH ANNIVERSARY. May 25, 1803. American author and philosopher born at Boston, MA, and died there Apr 27, 1882. It was Emerson who wrote (in his essay "Self-Reliance," 1841), "A foolish consistency is the hobgoblin of little minds, adored by little statesmen and philosophers and divines. With consistency a great soul has simply nothing to do."

GREATEST DAY IN TRACK AND FIELD: JESSE OWENS'S REMARKABLE RECORDS: ANNIVERSARY. May 25, 1935. During the Big Ten Championships at the University of Michigan at Ann Arbor, MI, Jesse Owens, representing Ohio State University, broke three world records and tied a fourth in the space of 45 minutes—from 3:15 PM to 4:00 PM. The "Buckeye Bullet" (who was suffering from an injured back) set records in the running broad jump, the 220-yard dash, the 220-yard hurdles; and tied the record for the 100-yard dash. See also: "Owens, Jesse: Birth Anniversary" (Sept 12).

★ ★ ★

	S	**M**	**T**	**W**	**T**	**F**	**S**
May		1	2	3	4	5	6
2006	7	8	9	10	11	12	13
	14	15	16	17	18	19	20
	21	22	23	24	25	26	27
	28	29	30	31			

GRUBSTAKE DAYS. May 25–29. Yucca Valley, CA. Includes parade, PRCA rodeo, demolition derby, gold panning demonstration, carnival, dances, food and community booths, arts and crafts booths and breakfasts offered by local service organizations. Est attendance: 20,000. For info: Yucca Valley Chamber of Commerce, 56711 29 Palms Hwy, Yucca Valley, CA 92284. Phone: (760) 365-6323. Fax: (760) 365-0763. E-mail: chamber@yuccavalley.org. Web: www.yuccavalley.org.

HERRINFESTA ITALIANA. May 25–29. Herrin Civic Center, Herrin, IL. Authentic Italian food, name Italian and American entertainers, bocce tournament, Midwest Pasta Sauce Contest, road races, grape stomp and more. Est attendance: 55,000. For info: Herrinfesta Italiana, PO Box 2005, Herrin, IL 62948. Phone: (800) ITF-ESTA. Web: www.herrinfesta.com.

IRIS FESTIVAL. May 25–28. Swan Lake, Sumter, SC. In the largest Japanese iris gardens in the world. South Carolina's oldest continuously running festival. Annually, the weekend before Memorial Day beginning on Thursday evening. For info: Sumter Tourism, 32 E Calhoun St, Sumter, SC 29150. Phone: (800) 688-4748. Web: www.sumter-sc-tourism.com.

JORDAN: INDEPENDENCE DAY. May 25. National holiday. Commemorates treaty in 1946, proclaiming independence from Britain and establishing monarchy.

KODIAK CRAB FESTIVAL. May 25–29. Kodiak, AK. A celebration of spring on the Emerald Isle. Delectable food, exciting midway rides and carnival booths and entertaining events such as parades, running and bicycle races, survival suit race, bed races, a blessing of the fleet ceremony and memorial services. Annually, Memorial Day weekend. Est attendance: 15,000. For info: Kodiak Crab Festival, 100 E Marine Way, Ste 300, Kodiak, AK 99615. Phone: (907) 486-5557. Fax: (907) 486-7605. Web: www.kodiak.org/crabfest.html.

MUDBUG MADNESS. May 25–28. Riverfront, Shreveport, LA. The state's delectable crustacean, the crawfish, and Cajun heritage are celebrated during this four-day festival. Est attendance: 150,000. For info: DSU, PO Box 235, Shreveport, LA 71162. Phone: (318) 222-7403. E-mail: mbacon@downtownshreveport.com. Web: www.mudbugmadness.com.

MURRAY, PHILIP: BIRTH ANNIVERSARY. May 25, 1886. American labor leader and founder of the Congress of Industrial Organizations, also active in and a leader of the United Mine Workers, was born near Blantyre, Scotland. Murray died at San Francisco, CA, Nov 9, 1952.

NAIA MEN'S AND WOMEN'S OUTDOOR TRACK AND FIELD NATIONAL CHAMPIONSHIPS. May 25–27. Site TBD. 55th annual men's and 26th annual women's competition. Est attendance: 2,500. For info: Natl Assn of Intercollegiate Athletics, 23500 W 105th St, PO Box 1325, Olathe, KS 66051-1325. Phone: (913) 791-0044. Fax: (913) 791-9555. E-mail: rfeldblum@naia.org. Web: www.naia.org.

NATIONAL MISSING CHILDREN'S DAY. May 25. To promote awareness of the problem of missing children, to offer a forum for change and to offer safety information for children in school and community. Annually, May 25. For info: Child Find of America, Inc, PO Box 277, New Paltz, NY 12561-0277. Phone: (845) 691-4666 or (800) I-AM-LOST. E-mail: information@childfindofamerica.org. Web: www.childfindofamerica.org.

NATIONAL TAP DANCE DAY. May 25. To celebrate this unique American art form that represents a fusion of African and European cultures and to transmit tap to succeeding generations through documentation and archival and performance support. Held on the anniversary of the birth of Bill "Bojangles" Robinson to honor his outstanding contribution to the art of tap dancing on stage and in films through the unification of diverse stylistic and racial elements.

POETRY DAY IN FLORIDA. May 25. In 1947 the legislature decreed this day to be "Poetry Day in all of the public schools of Florida."

ROBINSON, BILL "BOJANGLES": BIRTH ANNIVERSARY. May 25, 1878. Born at Richmond, VA, the grandson of a slave, Robinson is considered one of the greatest tap dancers. He is best known for a routine in which he tap-danced up and down a staircase. He appeared in several films with Shirley Temple and starred in *Stormy Weather*. Died at New York City, Nov 25, 1949.

SIKORSKY, IGOR: BIRTH ANNIVERSARY. May 25, 1889. Aeronautical engineer best remembered for his development of the first successful helicopter in 1939. Also pioneered in multiengine airplanes and large flying boats that made transoceanic air transportation possible. Born at Kiev, Russia, he died Oct 26, 1972, at Easton, CT.

SPACE MILESTONE: *SKYLAB 2* (US). May 25, 1973. Joseph P. Kerwin, Paul J. Weitz and Charles (Pete) Conrad, Jr, spent 28 days in experimentation on this space station, which had been launched May 14. Pacific splashdown occurred June 22.

***STAR WARS* RELEASED: ANNIVERSARY.** May 25, 1977. "May the Force be with you" entered the modern lexicon as a new kind of science fiction film opened at 32 theaters. George Lucas's space epic, starring Mark Hamill as Luke Skywalker, Harrison Ford as Han Solo and Carrie Fisher as Princess Leia, featured stunning special effects and was a smash hit worldwide. It went on to win six Academy Awards out of ten nominations—plus an additional special Academy Award for sound effects. The film was part of a larger saga, and in later years was retitled *Star Wars—Episode IV: A New Hope* as prequels were released.

TITO (JOSIP BROZ): BIRTH ANNIVERSARY. May 25, 1892. Josip Broz, Yugoslavian soldier and political leader, born near Zagreb, Yugoslavia. Died May 4, 1980, at Ljubljana, Yugoslavia (now Slovenia), and was interred in the garden of his home at Belgrade. Tito, a Croat, had managed to keep the many nationalities and religions that made up Yugoslavia in one state, but in the early 1990s the nation broke up as Croats, Serbs and others went to war against each other.

TUNNEY, JAMES JOSEPH (GENE): BIRTH ANNIVERSARY. May 25, 1898. Heavyweight boxing champion, business executive. The famous "long count" occurred in the seventh round of the Jack Dempsey–Gene Tunney world championship fight, Sept 22, 1927, at Soldier Field, Chicago, IL. Tunney was born at New York, NY, and died at Greenwich, CT, Nov 7, 1978.

UNITED NATIONS: WEEK OF SOLIDARITY WITH THE PEOPLE OF NON-SELF-GOVERNING TERRITORIES. May 25–31. On Dec 6, 1999 (Res 54/91) the General Assembly requested the Special Committee on Decolonization to observe this week beginning on May 25, Africa Liberation Day. For info: United Nations, Dept of Public Info, New York, NY 10017. Web: www.un.org.

BIRTHDAYS TODAY

Dixie Carter, 67, actress ("Designing Women," "Family Law"), born McLemoresville, TN, May 25, 1939.

Jessi Colter, 59, singer, songwriter, born Miriam Johnson at Phoenix, AZ, May 25, 1947.

Tom T. Hall, 70, singer ("P.S. I Love You"), songwriter ("Harper Valley PTA"), born Olive Hill, KY, May 25, 1936.

Anne Heche, 37, actress (*Volcano; Six Days, Seven Nights*), born Aurora, OH, May 25, 1969.

Justin Henry, 35, actor (*Kramer v Kramer, Sixteen Candles*), born Rye, NY, May 25, 1971.

Lauryn Hill, 31, singer, actress (*Sister Act 2*), born South Orange, NJ, May 25, 1975.

K.C. Jones, 74, Hall of Fame basketball player, former coach, born Tyler, TX, May 25, 1932.

Jamie Kennedy, 36, actor ("JKX: The Jamie Kennedy Experiment," *Malibu's Most Wanted*), born Upper Darby, PA, May 25, 1970.

Sir Ian McKellen, 67, actor (stage: *Amadeus* [Tony Award]; *Lord of the Rings* trilogy, *Gods and Monsters*), born Burnley, England, May 25, 1939.

Mike Myers, 43, comedian, actor ("Saturday Night Live," *Wayne's World, Austin Powers: International Man of Mystery*), born Scarsborough, ON, Canada, May 25, 1963.

Connie Sellecca, 51, actress ("Hotel," *While My Pretty One Sleeps*), born the Bronx, NY, May 25, 1955.

Beverly Sills, 77, opera singer (retired), born Brooklyn, NY, May 25, 1929.

Gordon Smith, 54, US Senator (R, Oregon), born Pendleton, OR, May 25, 1952.

Leslie Uggams, 63, singer ("Sing Along with Mitch"), actress, born New York, NY, May 25, 1943.

Brian Urlacher, 28, football player, born Lovington, NM, May 25, 1978.

Karen Valentine, 59, actress ("Room 222"), born Sebastopol, CA, May 25, 1947.

MAY 26 — FRIDAY
Day 146 — 219 Remaining

AUSTRALIA: SORRY DAY. May 26. A day to express sorrow for the forced removal of Aboriginal children from their families.

BROOKINGS-HARBOR AZALEA FESTIVAL. May 26–29. Brookings, OR. 67th festival. Parade, street fair, art shows, seafood, 10k run, Bonsai exhibit, regional quilt show, crafts fair, Coast Guard demonstration, live music. Annually, Memorial Day weekend. Est attendance: 12,000. For info: Brookings-Harbor Chamber of Commerce, PO Box 940, Brookings, OR 97415. Phone: (800) 535-9469. Fax: (541) 469-4094. E-mail: chamber@brookingsor.com.

DOWN EAST SPRING BIRDING FESTIVAL. May 26–29. Cobscook Bay area (Eastport, Whiting, Lubec), ME. See more than half Maine's bird species during spring migration and the breeding season—including Atlantic Puffins up close and (almost) touchable! Annually, the Friday through Monday of Memorial Day weekend. For info, write to: Down East Birding Fest, PO Box 42, Whiting, ME 04691. Phone: (207) 733-2201. E-mail: info@cobscookbay.com. Web: www.downeastbirdfest.org.

DUNKIRK EVACUATED: ANNIVERSARY. May 26, 1940. The British Expeditionary Force had become trapped by advancing German armies near this port on the northern coast of France. On this date, the evacuation of 200,000 British and 140,000 French and Belgian soldiers began. Sailing on every kind of transport available, including fishing boats and recreational craft, these men were safely across the English Channel by June 2.

FEAST OF SAINT AUGUSTINE OF CANTERBURY. May 26. Pope Gregory sent Augustine to convert the pagan English. Augustine became the first archbishop of Canterbury. He died May 26, 604 AD.

FLORIDA FOLK FESTIVAL. May 26–28. Stephen Foster Folk Culture Center State Park, White Springs, FL. To celebrate Florida's folk heritage with music, song, dance and stories. Est attendance: 30,000. For info: Stephen Foster Folk Culture Center State Park, Post Office Drawer G, White Springs, FL 32096. Phone: (386) 397-2733 or (877) 6FL-FOLK.

GEORGIA: INDEPENDENCE DAY. May 26. National Day. Commemorates declaration of independence from Russia in 1918. Was absorbed by the Soviet Union in 1922.

GUTHRIE JAZZ BANJO FESTIVAL. May 26–28. Downtown Guthrie, OK. Jazz banjo bands and soloists from all over the US perform music from the gay '90s, as well as the roaring '20s and contemporary selections at various venues around historic Guthrie. Also antique autos on parade. Est attendance: 10,000. For info: National Four String Banjo Museum, 116 E Oklahoma, Guthrie, OK 73044. Phone: (405) 282-1948 or (800) 299-1889 or (800) OK-BANJO.

ISRAEL: JERUSALEM DAY (YOM YERUSHALAYIM). May 26. Hebrew calendar date: Iyar 28, 5766. Commemorates the liberation of the old city, June 7, 1967. Began at sundown May 25.

JOLSON, AL: BIRTH ANNIVERSARY. May 26, 1886. Actor (*The Jazz Singer*) and singer, born Asa Yoelson at St. Petersburg, Russia. Died at San Francisco, CA, Oct 23, 1950.

LEE, PEGGY: BIRTH ANNIVERSARY. May 26, 1920. Singer, songwriter and actress Peggy Lee was born Norma Deloris Egstrom at Jamestown, ND. She got her start singing on a Fargo, ND, radio station and was soon hired by Benny Goodman to sing with his band. Known for her simple, jazzy style as well as her sex appeal, her biggest hits were 1958's "Fever" and 1969's "Is That All There Is?" She is perhaps best remembered for the songs that she cowrote and performed in Disney's *Lady and the Tramp*. She continued to perform until the 1990s, when poor health forced her to retire. She died Jan 21, 2002, at Los Angeles, CA.

MEMORIAL DAY GETAWAY. May 26–29. Live Oak, FL. Fun for the whole family with a variety of entertainment. For info: Spirit of the Suwannee Music Park, 3076 95th Dr, Live Oak, FL 32060. Phone: (386) 364-1683. Fax: (386) 364-2998. E-mail: spirit@musicliveshere.com. Web: www.musicliveshere.com.

MID-AMERICA NATIONAL STREET ROD ASSOCIATION CAR SHOW. May 26–28. Ozark Empire Fairgrounds, Springfield, MO. More than 2,000 pre-1949 street rods on display. More than 80 commercial vendors for shopping. For info: Ozark Empire Fair, 3001 N Grant, Springfield, MO 65803. Phone: (417) 833-2660. Fax: (417) 833-3769. Web: www.ozarkempirefair.com.

MORLEY, ROBERT: BIRTH ANNIVERSARY. May 26, 1908. British actor Robert Morley was born at Semley, England. Among his best known film credits are *Major Barbara* (1939) and *The African Queen* (1951). He died June 3, 1992, at Reading, England.

NAIA BASEBALL WORLD SERIES. May 26–June 2. Lewiston, ID. 50th annual competition. Est attendance: 35,000. For info: Natl Assn of Intercollegiate Athletics, 23500 W 105th St, PO Box 1325, Olathe, KS 66051-1325. Phone: (913) 791-0044. Fax: (913) 791-9555. E-mail: smcclure@naia.org. Web: www.naia.org.

NCAA DIVISION I WOMEN'S LACROSSE CHAMPIONSHIP. May 26 & 28. Nickerson Field, Boston, MA. Hosted by Boston University. Est attendance: 8,000. For info: NCAA, 700 W Washington St, Indianapolis, IN 46206-6222. Phone: (317) 917-6222. Fax: (317) 917-6888. Web: www.ncaasports.com.

NORTHWEST FOLKLIFE FESTIVAL. May 26–29. Seattle Center, Seattle, WA. Ethnic and traditional arts event celebrating world cultures in the Northwest region. Includes music, dance, food, crafts, visual arts exhibits, children's programs, demonstrations, films and more. More than 6,000 performers. Annually, Friday–Monday of Memorial Day weekend. Est attendance: 250,000. For info: Northwest Folklife, 305 Harrison St, Seattle, WA 98109-4623. Phone: (206) 684-7300. Fax: (206) 684-7190. E-mail: folklife@nwfolklife.org. Web: www.nwfolklife.org.

May	S	M	T	W	T	F	S
2006		1	2	3	4	5	6
	7	8	9	10	11	12	13
	14	15	16	17	18	19	20
	21	22	23	24	25	26	27
	28	29	30	31			

RIDE, SALLY KRISTEN: BIRTHDAY. May 26, 1951. Dr. Sally Ride, one of the first women in the US astronaut corps and the first American woman in space, was born at Encino, CA. Her flight aboard the space shuttle *Challenger* was launched from Cape Canaveral, FL, June 18 and landed at Edwards Air Force Base, CA, June 24, 1983. The six-day flight was termed "nearly a perfect mission."

RIVERFEST. May 26–28. Riverfront Park, Little Rock, and North Shore Riverwalk, North Little Rock, AR. 29th annual outdoor festival of the visual and performing arts with 100 acts on five stages, food vendors, visual artists, kid stuff. Est attendance: 225,000. For info: Riverfest, 500 President Clinton Ave, Ste 217, Little Rock, AR 72201. Phone: (501) 255-FEST. Fax: (501) 255-3379. E-mail: director@riverfestarkansas.com. Web: www.riverfestarkansas.com.

SACRAMENTO JAZZ JUBILEE. May 26–29. Sacramento, CA. More than 100 bands from the US, Canada and foreign countries perform American traditional jazz music in approximately 40 venues around Sacramento at the world's largest traditional jazz festival. Est attendance: 100,000. For info: Roger Krum, Exec Dir, Sacramento Traditional Jazz Society, 2787 Del Monte Blvd, Sacramento, CA 95691. Phone: (916) 372-5277. Fax: (916) 372-3429. E-mail: stjs@earthlink.net. Web: www.sacjazz.com.

SHAKER MUSEUM OPENING DAY. May 26. Sabbathday Lake Shaker Village, New Gloucester, ME. The 76th season of the Shaker Museum opens with tours, exhibits and special events. Open through Columbus Day (closed on Sundays). For info: Leonard Brooks, Sabbathday Lake Shaker Village, Route 26, New Gloucester, ME 04260. Phone: (207) 926-4597. E-mail: usshakers@aol.com. Web: www.shaker.lib.me.us.

SPOLETO FESTIVAL USA. May 26–June 11. Charleston, SC. Comprehensive arts festival with a mix of more than 130 performances of opera, dance, theater, chamber and symphonic music, jazz and visual arts set in one of America's most beautiful and historic cities. For info: Spoleto Festival USA, PO Box 157, Charleston, SC 29402. Phone: (843) 579-3100. Web: www.spoletousa.org.

VEGASPEX. May 26–28 (also Dec 8–10). Las Vegas, NV. Coin, stamp, antique watch, jewelry and collectibles expo. Est attendance: 10,000. For info: Israel Bick, Exec Dir, Intl Coin & Stamp Collectors Society, PO Box 854, Van Nuys, CA 91408. Phone: (818) 997-6496. Fax: (818) 988-4337. E-mail: iibick@sbcglobal.net. Web: www.bick.net.

VIETNAM AND US RESUME RELATIONS: ANNIVERSARY. May 26, 1994. Nearly 20 years after the end of the Vietnam War, the US and Vietnam agreed to resume diplomatic relations. In the early 1990s Vietnam had become one of the fastest growing economies in Asia after giving up Communist controls and allowing economic reform. Earlier in 1994 President Bill Clinton had lifted the American embargo that hindered Americans from doing business in Vietnam.

WALES: HAY-ON-WYE FESTIVAL OF LITERATURE. May 26–June 4. Hay-on-Wye, Powys. Largest annual festival of literature takes place in the beautiful market town of Hay-on-Wye in the Black Mountains of the Welsh Marches. Est attendance: 80,000. For info: The Hay Festival, Hay-on-Wye, Wales, UK HR3 5AD. Phone: (44) (870) 990-1299. Fax: (44) (149) 782-1066. E-mail: admin@hayfestival.com. Web: www.hayfestival.com.

WAYNE, JOHN: BIRTH ANNIVERSARY. May 26, 1907. American motion picture actor, born Marion Michael Morrison, at Winterset, IA. The quintessential western actor for five decades. Among his films were *Stagecoach* (1939), *Red River* (1948), *The Searchers* (1956) and *True Grit* (1969), for which he won a Best Actor Oscar. He died at Los Angeles, CA, June 11, 1979. "Talk low, talk slow and don't say too much" was his advice on acting.

WORLD CHAMPIONSHIP OLD-TIME PIANO PLAYING CONTEST. May 26–28. Hotel Père Marquette, Peoria, IL. Competition and festival of ragtime, honky-tonk and old-time music. Includes Old-time Orchestry and dealers rooms. Annually, Memorial Day weekend. Sponsor: Old-Time Music Preservation Association (OMPA) Inc. Est attendance: 1,000. For info: Judy Leschewski, PO Box 4714, Decatur, IL 62525. Phone: (217) 428-2403. Web: oldtimepiano.com.

BIRTHDAYS TODAY

James Arness, 83, actor ("Gunsmoke," "How the West Was Won"), born James Aurness at Minneapolis, MN, May 26, 1923.

Helena Bonham Carter, 40, actress (*A Room with a View, Howard's End*), born London, England, May 26, 1966.

Genie Francis, 44, actress ("General Hospital"), born Englewood, NJ, May 26, 1962.

Pam Grier, 57, actress (*Jackie Brown, Mars Attacks, Something Wicked This Way Comes*), born Winston-Salem, NC, May 26, 1949.

Lenny Kravitz, 42, singer ("Circus"), musician, songwriter ("Justify My Love"), born New York, NY, May 26, 1964.

Brent Musburger, 67, sportscaster, born Portland, OR, May 26, 1939.

Stevie Nicks, 58, singer (with Fleetwood Mac, "Don't Stop"), songwriter ("Edge of Seventeen"), born Phoenix, AZ, May 26, 1948.

Sally K. Ride, 55, astronaut, first American woman in space, born Los Angeles, CA, May 26, 1951.

Philip Michael Thomas, 57, actor ("Miami Vice," *Hair*), born Los Angeles, CA, May 26, 1949.

Hank Williams, Jr, 57, singer ("All for the Love of Sunshine," "I Fought the Law"), born Shreveport, LA, May 26, 1949.

MAY 27 — SATURDAY

Day 147 — 218 Remaining

ALMA HIGHLAND FESTIVAL AND GAMES. May 27–28. Alma College, Alma, MI. 39th annual festival. Old-world pageantry honoring Scottish traditions—Highland dancing, piping, drumming, athletic competitions, clan tents and grand parade. Annually, Memorial Day weekend. Est attendance: 25,000. For info: Alma Highland Festival, 110 W Superior St, PO Box 516, Alma, MI 48801. Phone: (989) 463-8979. Fax: (989) 463-6588. E-mail: highland@almahighlandfestival.com. Web: www.almahighlandfestival.com.

BENNETT, ARNOLD: BIRTH ANNIVERSARY. May 27, 1867. English novelist, playwright and critic (Enoch) Arnold Bennett was born at Hanley, in the pottery-manufacturing district of North Staffordshire, England. Best known of his novels is *The Old Wives' Tale* (1908). His *Journals* from 1896 until near the time of his death in 1931 provide insight into Bennett's thought. "The price of justice," Arnold wrote, "is eternal publicity." He contracted typhoid fever in France and died at London, May 27, 1931.

BLOOMER, AMELIA JENKS: BIRTH ANNIVERSARY. May 27, 1818. American social reformer and women's rights advocate, born at Homer, NY. Her name is remembered especially because of her work for more sensible dress for women and her recommendation of a costume that had been introduced about 1849 by Elizabeth Smith Miller but came to be known as the "Bloomer Costume" or "Bloomers." Amelia Bloomer died at Council Bluffs, IA, Dec 30, 1894.

CARSON, RACHEL (LOUISE): BIRTH ANNIVERSARY. May 27, 1907. American scientist and author, born at Springdale, PA. Author of *Silent Spring* (1962), a book that provoked widespread controversy over the use of pesticides. Died Apr 14, 1964, at Silver Spring, MD.

CELLOPHANE TAPE PATENTED: ANNIVERSARY. May 27, 1930. Richard Gurley Drew received a patent for his adhesive tape, later manufactured by 3M as Scotch tape.

CHESTERTOWN TEA PARTY FESTIVAL. May 27–28. Chestertown, MD. Reenactment of 1774 tea dumping, crafts, music, food and games, 10-mile and 5k runs. Est attendance: 15,000. For info: Chestertown Tea Party Festival, Inc, Box 526, Chestertown, MD 21620. Phone: (410) 778-0416. Web: www.kentcounty.com.

DUNCAN, ISADORA: BIRTH ANNIVERSARY. May 27, 1878. American-born interpretive dancer who revolutionized the entire concept of dance. Barefooted, freedom-loving, liberated woman and rebel against tradition, she experienced worldwide professional success and profound personal tragedy (her two children drowned, her marriage failed and she met a bizarre death when the long scarf she was wearing caught in a wheel of the open car in which she was riding, strangling her). Born at San Francisco, CA; died at Nice, France, Sept 14, 1927.

1836 ENCAMPMENT. May 27–28. Westville-Lumpkin, GA. Reenactment of an encampment of soldiers who had been dispatched to protect local citizens against Indian attacks. An Indian camp will also be demonstrated. Est attendance: 1,500. For info: Patty Cannington, Westville, PO Box 1850, Lumpkin, GA 31815. Phone: (229) 838-6310 or (888) 733-1850. E-mail: director@westville.org. Web: www.westville.org.

FAIRMOUNT ACADEMY 1800s FESTIVAL. May 27. Fairmount, MD. Rain date the following Saturday. Restored school, spelling bees, square dancing, quilt show, folk arts and crafts, music and plenty of good food. Annually, the last Saturday in May. Est attendance: 2,500. For info: Nevette Muir, Fairmount Academy Historical Assn, PO Box 134, Upper Fairmount, MD 21867. Phone: (410) 651-0351 or (410) 651-3945.

FARMINGTON INVITATIONAL BALLOON FESTIVAL. May 27–28. Farmington, NM. Hot-air balloons launch off the banks of Farmington Lake. Famous Splash and Dash and Hare and Hound races included in the two-day event. Est attendance: 2,000. For info: Farmington Conv and Visitors Bureau, 3041 E Main St, Farmington, NM 87402. Phone: (800) 448-1240 or (505) 326-7602. Fax: (505) 327-0577. E-mail: fmncvb@earthlink.net. Web: www.farmingtonnm.org.

FIRST FLIGHT INTO THE STRATOSPHERE: 75th ANNIVERSARY. May 27, 1931. In a balloon launched from Augsburg, Germany, Paul Kipfer and Auguste Piccard became the first to reach the stratosphere. In a pressurized cabin they rose almost 10 miles during their flight.

FIRST RUNNING OF PREAKNESS: ANNIVERSARY. May 27, 1873. The first running of the Preakness Stakes at Pimlico, MD, was won by Survivor with a time of 2:43. The winning jockey was G. Barbee.

GERMANY: BACH FESTIVAL. May 27–June 5. Leipzig. Since 1904, the Festival has been held in Leipzig, where Johann Sebastian Bach lived in his later years and composed some of his best-known works. For info: Bach-Archiv Leipzig, Thomaskirchof 15-16, D-04109 Leipzig, Germany. E-mail: bachfest@bach-leipzig.de. Web: www.bach-leipzig.de.

GOLDEN GATE BRIDGE OPENED: ANNIVERSARY. May 27, 1937. 200,000 people crossed San Francisco's Golden Gate Bridge on its opening day.

GREAT FLOOD OF 1889 COMMEMORATION. May 27–31 (tentative). Johnstown Flood Museum, Johnstown, PA. The Johnstown Flood Museum recreates the May 31, 1889, catastrophe in which 2,209 people died, tens of thousands were left homeless and a prospering city was left a wasteland. "The Johnstown Flood," a 1989 Academy Award–winning documentary, is shown hourly. For info: Johnstown Flood Museum, PO Box 1889, Johnstown, PA 15907-1889. Phone: (814) 539-1889 or (888) 222-1889. Fax: (814) 535-1931. Web: www.jaha.org.

GREAT MISSISSIPPI RIVER ARTS AND CRAFTS FESTIVAL. May 27–28. Mark Twain Historic District, Hannibal, MO. 19th annual art fair featuring 90 exhibitors in the areas of fine art, fine crafts and traditional arts. Concession stands with fried catfish, BBQ pork-chop sandwiches and lemonade, a variety of entertainment groups and creative learning fun in the children's area. Est attendance: 15,000. For info: Hannibal Arts Council, PO Box 1202, Hannibal, MO 63401. Phone: (573) 221-6545. E-mail: arts@nemonet.com. Web: www.hannibalarts.com.

HAMMETT, (SAMUEL) DASHIELL: BIRTH ANNIVERSARY. May 27, 1894. The man who brought realism to the genre of mystery writing, Dashiell Hammett was born at St. Mary's County, MD. His first two novels, *Red Harvest* (1929) and *The Dain Curse* (1929), were based on his eight years spent as a Pinkerton detective. Hammett is recognized as the founder of the "hard-boiled" school of detective fiction. Three of his novels have been made into films: *The Maltese Falcon* (1930), considered by many to be his finest work; *The Thin Man* (1932), which provided the basis for a series of five movies starring William Powell and Myrna Loy; and *The Glass Key* (1931). Hammett was called to testify but refused to name members of an alleged subversive organization during House Un-American Activities Committee hearings. He died Jan 10, 1961, at New York City.

HEAD-OF-THE-MON-RIVER HORSESHOE TOURNAMENT. May 27–29. Fairmont, WV. Open to horseshoe pitchers with a current State/National Horseshoe Pitchers Association membership card. Est attendance: 300. For info: Tri-County Horseshoe Club Dir, Beverly Tiano, 1133 Sunset Dr, Fairmont, WV 26554. Phone: (304) 366-3819. E-mail: btiano1133@aol.com.

HICKOK, WILD BILL: BIRTH ANNIVERSARY. May 27, 1837. Born at Troy Grove, IL, and died Aug 2, 1876, at Deadwood, SD. American frontiersman, legendary marksman, lawman, army scout and gambler. Hickok's end came when he was shot dead at a poker table by a drunk in the Number Ten saloon.

HUMPHREY, HUBERT HORATIO: BIRTH ANNIVERSARY. May 27, 1911. Born at Wallace, SD. The 38th vice president of the US (1965–69). Democratic candidate for president in 1968 who lost to Richard Nixon. Died at Waverly, MN, Jan 13, 1978.

INTERNATIONAL JAZZ DAY. May 27. Jazz lovers worldwide attend local festivals (or can start their own) to celebrate jazz on the Saturday of the Memorial Day weekend. Originated by the New Jersey Jazz Society and sanctioned by the American Federation of Jazz Societies, the United Nations Jazz Society and the Sacramento Traditional Jazz Society. For info: Web: www.geocities.com/BourbonStreet/4270.

IROQUOIS ARTS SHOWCASE. May 27–28 (also Sept 2–4). Iroquois Indian Museum, Howes Cave, NY. Demonstrations of Iroquois arts and crafts including beadwork, cornhusk dolls, pottery and more. Many items for sale by the artists. Children's activities. Iroquois social dancing and nature walks. Annually, Memorial Day weekend and Labor Day weekend. Est attendance: 3,500. For info: Iroquois Indian Museum, PO Box 7, Caverns Rd, Howes Cave, NY 12092. Phone: (518) 296-8949. Fax: (518) 296-8955. E-mail: info@IroquoisMuseum.org.

LOBSTERFEST. May 27–29. Mystic Seaport, Mystic, CT. A New England lobster bake on the banks of the Mystic River over the Memorial Day weekend, put on by the Rotary Club of Mystic. Est attendance: 10,000. For info: Mystic Seaport, 75 Greenmanville Ave, PO Box 6000, Mystic, CT 06355-0990. Phone: (860) 572-5315 or (888) 973-2767. Web: www.mysticseaport.org.

LONGWOOD GARDENS FESTIVAL OF FOUNTAINS. May 27–Sept 2. Kennett Square, PA. A magical mixture of rainbow-hued fountains, alfresco concerts, fireworks and leisurely evenings in the Conservatory. Est attendance: 275,000. For info: Longwood Gardens, PO Box 501, Kennett Square, PA 19348-0501. Phone: (610) 388-1000. Web: www.longwoodgardens.org.

MOON PHASE: NEW MOON. May 27. Moon enters New Moon phase at 1:26 AM, EDT.

PRICE, VINCENT: BIRTH ANNIVERSARY. May 27, 1911. Actor, best known for his portrayal of sinister villains in horror films and as host for the TV series "Mystery!" Born at St. Louis, MO, and died at Los Angeles, CA, Oct 25, 1993.

RMS *QUEEN MARY*: MAIDEN VOYAGE: 70th ANNIVERSARY. May 27, 1936. Anniversary of the maiden voyage from Southampton, England, to New York Harbor. In 1967 the ship sailed to Long Beach, California, where it is permanently berthed and used as a hotel.

ST. PETERSBURG FOUNDED: ANNIVERSARY. May 27, 1703. Czar Peter the Great founded the city of St. Petersburg on the banks of the Neva River by laying the first stone of the Peter and Paul Fortress. It became the capital of Russia in 1712. See also: "St. Petersburg Name Restored: Anniversary" (Sept 6).

SNEAD, SAM: BIRTH ANNIVERSARY. May 27, 1912. The winningest US Tour golfer of the 20th century was born at Hot Springs, VA. He turned pro in 1934 and went on to become the only golfer to win tournaments in six different decades. He won 84 US Tour events and 182 tournaments in total. Snead always wore a snappy straw hat and was a favorite on the Tour. He was one of the founders of the US Senior Tour. Snead died at Hot Springs on May 23, 2002.

TASTE OF CINCINNATI. May 27–29. Cincinnati, OH. Cincinnati is famous for its fine food, from elegant five-star dining to five-way chili. This popular eating extravaganza presents a taste of the most delicious culinary delights available. Annually, Memorial Day weekend. Est attendance: 500,000. For info: Raymond Buse, Cincinnati USA Regional Chamber, 441 Vine St, Ste 300, Cincinnati, OH 45202. Phone: (513) 579-3100. Fax: (513) 579-3101. E-mail: chooven@gccc.com. Web: www.tasteofcincinnati.com.

TIVOLI FEST. May 27–28. Elk Horn, IA. Annual Danish celebration with parade, Danish folk dancers, Danish foods, unique gift shops, historical tours and much more. Annually, Memorial Day weekend. Sponsor: Better Elk Horn Club. Est attendance: 5,000. For info: Lisa Riggs, Danish Windmill, PO Box 245, Elk Horn, IA 51531. Phone: (712) 764-7472 or (800) 451-7960. Fax: (712) 764-7475. E-mail: info@danishwindmill.com. Web: www.danishwindmill.com.

UTICA OLD-FASHIONED ICE CREAM FESTIVAL. May 27–29. Utica, OH. Saluting "America's favorite dessert," ice cream, with a weekend of fun and entertainment: parade, queen contest, arts and crafts, antique gas engines, sheepherding with border collies and plenty of delicious ice cream. Est attendance: 30,000. For info: Utica Ice Cream Festival, St Rt 13, Utica, OH 43080. Phone: (740) 892-3921. Web: www.velveticecream.com.

WAR OF JENKIN'S EAR: LIVING HISTORY. May 27. Wormsloe Historic Site, Savannah, GA. A colonial living history

		S	M	T	W	T	F	S
May			1	2	3	4	5	6
2006		7	8	9	10	11	12	13
		14	15	16	17	18	19	20
		21	22	23	24	25	26	27
		28	29	30	31			

event focusing on the conflict between England and Spain. Features musket demonstrations, military drill, tomahawk throwing and more. Annually, the Saturday of Memorial Day weekend. Est attendance: 500. For info: Wormsloe State Historic Site, 7601 Skidaway Rd, Savannah, GA 31406. Phone: (912) 353-3023. E-mail: wormsloe@bellsouth.net.

WASHINGTON 2006/WORLD PHILATELIC EXHIBITION. May 27–June 3. The Washington Convention Center, Washington, DC. "Stamps—And So Much More." Organized by Washington Philatelic Exhibition, Inc., under the auspices of the American Philatelic Society, and supported by the American Stamp Dealers Association, the Fédération Internationale de Philatélie and the United States Postal Service. Eight days of philatelic adventuring: 3,800 frames of competitive exhibits by collectors from around the world, 500-frame "Court of Honor," including the world's rarest philatelic items, literature competition and special events for children. For info: Washington 2006, PO Box 2006, Ashburn, VA 20146-2006. E-mail: info@washington-2006.org. Web: www.washington-2006.org.

WHIPPOORWILL MORGAN HORSE OPEN BARN. May 27–29. Old Lyme, CT. Visitors can pet newborn foals and watch stallions and mares perform. There will also be an informative and informal introduction to the Morgan Horse. Fall open barn will be Oct 7–9. Est attendance: 900. For info: McCulloch Farm, Whippoorwill Morgan, 100 Whippoorwill Rd, Old Lyme, CT 06371. Phone: (860) 434-7355.

BIRTHDAYS TODAY

Jeff Bagwell, 38, baseball player, born Boston, MA, May 27, 1968.
John Barth, 76, author (*Last Voyage of Somebody the Sailor, Letters*), born Cambridge, MD, May 27, 1930.
Todd Bridges, 41, actor ("Diff'rent Strokes"), born San Francisco, CA, May 27, 1965.
Pat Cash, 41, former tennis player, born Melbourne, Australia, May 27, 1965.
Christopher J. Dodd, 62, US Senator (D, Connecticut), born Willimantic, CT, May 27, 1944.
Joseph Fiennes, 36, actor (*Shakespeare in Love*), born Salisbury, England, May 27, 1970.
Peri Gilpin, 45, actress ("Frasier"), born Waco, TX, May 27, 1961.
Louis Gossett, Jr, 70, actor (Emmy for "Roots"; Oscar for *An Officer and a Gentleman*), born Brooklyn, NY, May 27, 1936.
Henry Kissinger, 83, former secretary of state, author, born Fuerth, Germany, May 27, 1923.
Christopher Lee, 84, actor (*Dracula, The Mummy*), born London, England, May 27, 1922.
Ramsey Lewis, 71, jazz musician, winner of three Grammy awards, born Chicago, IL, May 27, 1935.
Lee Meriwether, 71, actress ("Barnaby Jones," "Batman"), former Miss America ('55), born Los Angeles, CA, May 27, 1935.
Jamie Oliver, 31, chef, television personality ("The Naked Chef"), born Clavering, Essex, England, May 27, 1975.
Richard Schiff, 51, actor ("The West Wing"), born Bethesda, MD, May 27, 1955.
Frank Thomas, 38, baseball player, born Columbus, GA, May 27, 1968.
Bruce Weitz, 63, actor ("Hill Street Blues"), born Norwalk, CT, May 27, 1943.
Herman Wouk, 91, writer (*Marjorie Morningstar, The Winds of War*), born New York, NY, May 27, 1915.

MAY 28 — SUNDAY
Day 148 — 217 Remaining

AGASSIZ, LOUIS: BIRTH ANNIVERSARY. May 28, 1807. Professor of zoology and geology at Harvard, born at Motier, Switzerland. He was a major influence in spawning American interest in natural history and helped to establish the Harvard Museum of Comparative Zoology. "The eye of the trilobite," Agassiz wrote in 1870, "tells us that the sun shone on the old beach where he lived; for there is nothing in nature without a purpose, and when so complicated an organ was made to receive the light, there must have been light to enter it." Died at Cambridge, MA, Dec 14, 1873.

ANTIQUES AT MEMORIAL DAY. May 28. Cape May Convention Hall, Cape May, NJ. Antiques and collectibles dealers from the mid-Atlantic region with a large and varied selection of fine furniture, silver, porcelain, crystal and glass accessories, estate and antique jewelry and vintage clothing. Est attendance: 1,000. For info: Mid-Atlantic Center for the Arts, 1048 Washington St, Cape May, NJ 08204. Phone: (800) 275-4278. Fax: (609) 884-0574. E-mail: mac4arts@capemaymac.org. Web: www.capemaymac.org.

AZERBAIJAN: DAY OF THE REPUBLIC. May 28. Public holiday. Commemorates the declaration of the Azerbaijan Democratic Republic in 1918.

COAL MINER DAYS. May 28–29. Downtown and fairgrounds, Novinger, MO. Turn-of-the-century coal mining boomtown celebrates its heritage with old-time contests, music, dancing and displays. Est attendance: 3,000. For info: Glenna Daniels, Novinger Renewal Inc, 15892 State Hwy 6, Novinger, MO 63559. Phone: (660) 488-5280. E-mail: ddaniels@nemr.net.

DIONNE QUINTUPLETS: BIRTHDAY. May 28, 1934. Five daughters (Marie, Cecile, Yvonne, Emilie and Annette) were born to Oliva and Elzire Dionne, near Callander, ON, Canada. They were the first quints known to have lived for more than a few hours after birth. Emilie died in 1954, Marie in 1970, Yvonne in 2001. The other two sisters are still living.

ETHIOPIA: NATIONAL DAY. May 28. National holiday. Commemorates the downfall of the Dergue, the military government that ruled Ethiopia from 1974 to 1991.

FLEMING, IAN: BIRTH ANNIVERSARY. May 28, 1908. English novelist, creator of the James Bond series. Born at London, died Aug 12, 1964, at Sandwich, England.

GUILLOTIN, JOSEPH IGNACE: BIRTH ANNIVERSARY. May 28, 1738. French physician and member of the Constituent Assembly who urged the use of a machine that was sometimes called the "Maiden" for the execution of death sentences—a less painful, more certain way of dispatching those sentenced to death. The guillotine was first used on Apr 25, 1792, for the execution of a highwayman, Nicolas Jacques Pelletier. Other machines for decapitation had been in use in other countries since the Middle Ages. Guillotin was born at Saintes, France, and died at Paris, Mar 26, 1814.

INDIANAPOLIS 500-MILE RACE. May 28. Indianapolis, IN. Recognized as the world's largest single-day sporting event. First race was in 1911. Annually, the Sunday of Memorial Day weekend. For info: Indianapolis Motor Speedway Corp, 4790 W 16th St, Indianapolis, IN 46222. Phone: (317) 481-8500. Web: www.indy500.com.

ITALY: PALIO DEI BALESTRIERI. May 28. Gubbio. The last Sunday in May is set aside for a medieval crossbow contest between Gubbio and Sansepolcro; medieval costumes, arms.

ITALY: WEDDING OF THE SEA. May 28. Venice. The feast of the Ascension is the occasion of the ceremony recalling the "Wedding of the Sea" performed by Venice's Doge, who cast his ring into the sea from the ceremonial ship known as the *Bucintoro* to symbolize eternal dominion. Annually, on the Sunday following Ascension.

MAD CITY MARATHON. May 28. Madison, WI. Running events include marathon, relays, half-marathon, 10k and 5k run/walks and a kid's race. Health & Fitness Fair on May 27. Annually, on Memorial Day weekend. For info: Keith Peterson, Race Director, Madison Festivals Inc, c/o ASG, 3000 Cahill Main, Ste 216, Madison, WI 53711. Phone: (608) 276-9797, ext 10. Fax: (608) 276-9780. E-mail: events@vymac.com. Web: www.madison festivals.com.

MEMORIAL DAY CEREMONIES. May 28. Andersonville, GA. Ceremonies pay tribute to our country's men and women who paid for our freedom with their lives. Annually, the Sunday before Memorial Day. Est attendance: 500. For info: Lindsey Phillips, Park Ranger, Andersonville National Historic Site, 496 Cemetery Rd, Andersonville, GA 31711. Phone: (229) 924-0343.

PITT, WILLIAM: BIRTH ANNIVERSARY. May 28, 1759. British prime minister from 1783 to 1801 and from 1804 to 1806, Pitt was influenced by Adam Smith's economic theories and reduced England's large national debt caused by the American Revolution. Born at Hayes, Kent, England, he died Jan 23, 1806, at Putney. He was the son of William Pitt, first earl of Chatham, for whom the city of Pittsburgh was named.

SAINT BERNARD OF MONTJOUX: FEAST DAY. May 28. Patron saint of mountain climbers, founder of Alpine hospices of the Great and Little St. Bernard, died at age 85, probably on May 28, 1081.

SIERRA CLUB FOUNDED: ANNIVERSARY. May 28, 1892. Founded by famed naturalist John Muir, the Sierra Club promotes conservation of the natural environment by influencing public policy. It has been especially important in the founding and protection of our national parks. For info: Sierra Club, 85 Second St, 2nd Fl, San Francisco, CA 94105-3441. Phone: (415) 977-5500. Fax: (415) 977-5799. E-mail: information@sierra club.org. Web: www.sierraclub.org.

SLUGS RETURN FROM CAPISTRANO DAY. May 28. It's a little known secret that slimy slugs spend their winters in lovely Capistrano and return to our patios and gardens on this date. Bare feet not a good idea now through first frost. [©2003 by WH.] For info: Thomas & Ruth Roy, Wellcat Holidays, 2418 Long Ln, Lebanon, PA 17046. Phone: (717) 279-0184. E-mail: info@ wellcat.com. Web: www.wellcat.com.

THORPE, JAMES FRANCIS (JIM): BIRTH ANNIVERSARY. May 28, 1888. Jim Thorpe, Pro Football Hall of Famer, distinguished Native American athlete, winner of pentathlon and decathlon events at the 1912 Olympic Games, professional baseball and football player. Born near Prague, OK, and died at Lomita, CA, Mar 28, 1953.

"ZOO PARADE" TV PREMIERE: ANNIVERSARY. May 28, 1950. NBC's half-hour program on animals and animal behavior was hosted by Marlin Perkins and Jim Hurlbut. Initially, it was broadcast from Lincoln Park Zoo in Chicago, but after 1955, the show was broadcast from other locales throughout the country. A successor program, "Mutual of Omaha's Wild Kingdom," was shot almost entirely in the wild and ran into the 1980s.

May 2006	S	M	T	W	T	F	S
		1	2	3	4	5	6
	7	8	9	10	11	12	13
	14	15	16	17	18	19	20
	21	22	23	24	25	26	27
	28	29	30	31			

MAY 29 — MONDAY
Day 149 — 216 Remaining

AMNESTY ISSUED FOR SOUTHERN REBELS: ANNIVERSARY. May 29, 1865. President Andrew Johnson issued a proclamation giving a general amnesty to all who participated in the rebellion against the US. High-ranking members of the Confederate government and military and those who owned more than $20,000 worth of property were excepted and had to apply individually to the President for a pardon. Once an oath of allegiance was taken, all former property rights, except those in slaves, were returned to the former owners.

ASCENSION OF BAHA'U'LLAH: ANNIVERSARY. May 29. Baha'i observance of the anniversary of the death in exile of Baha'u'llah (the prophet-founder of the Baha'i Faith), May 29, 1892. One of the nine days of the year when Baha'is suspend work. For info: Baha'is of the US, Office of Communications, 1233 Central St, Evanston, IL 60201. Phone: (847) 733-3411. Fax: (847) 869-0247. E-mail: ooc@usbnc.org. Web: www.us.bahai .org.

BOLDER BOULDER 10K. May 29. Boulder, CO. A 10k race of walkers, joggers and world-class runners through the streets of Boulder. Annually, on Memorial Day. Est attendance: 50,000. For info: Bolder Boulder, 4571 N Broadway, Boulder, CO 80304. Phone: (303) 444-7223. Fax: (303) 444-6411. E-mail: race@ bolderboulder.com. Web: www.bolderboulder.com.

CHARLES II: RESTORATION ANNIVERSARY. May 29, 1660. Restoration of Charles II to English throne. Also his birthday (May 29, 1630). English monarchy restored after Commonwealth period under Oliver Cromwell.

CHESTERTON, GILBERT KEITH: BIRTH ANNIVERSARY. May 29, 1874. English author and critic born at London, England. Died June 14, 1936, at Beaconsfield, Buckinghamshire, England.

CONSTANTINOPLE FALLS TO THE TURKS: ANNIVERSARY. May 29, 1453. The city of Constantinople was captured by the Turks, who later renamed it Istanbul. This conquest marked the end of the Byzantine Empire; the city became the capital of the Ottoman Empire.

HENRY, PATRICK: BIRTH ANNIVERSARY. May 29, 1736. American Revolutionary leader and orator, born at Studley, VA, and died near Brookneal, VA, June 6, 1799. Especially remembered for his speech (Mar 23, 1775) for arming the Virginia militia, at St. Johns Church, Richmond, VA, when he declared: "I know not what course others may take, but as for me, give me liberty or give me death."

HOPE, BOB: BIRTH ANNIVERSARY. May 29, 1903. The comedic actor was born Leslie Townes Hope at Eltham, England.

Hope had a long career in vaudeville, stage, radio, film and TV. His first film appearance was in *The Big Broadcast of 1938* (in which he sang his signature song, "Thanks for the Memory"). Hope went on to appear in more than 75 films—most memorably with crooner Bing Crosby in their series of *Road* movies. He received five honorary Oscars (among them the Jean Hersholt Humanitarian Award) and numerous other honors. Hope tirelessly entertained US troops during every war from WWII to the Gulf War. President Johnson presented him with the Medal of Freedom and he was knighted in 1998. Hope died July 27, 2003, at Toluca Lake, CA.

KENNEDY, JOHN FITZGERALD: BIRTH ANNIVERSARY. May 29, 1917. 35th president of the US (1961–63), born at Brookline, MA. Assassinated while riding in an open automobile at Dallas, TX, Nov 22, 1963. (Accused assassin Lee Harvey Oswald was killed at the Dallas police station by a gunman, Jack Ruby, two days later.) Kennedy was the youngest man ever elected to the presidency, the first Roman Catholic and the first president to have served in the US Navy. He was the fourth US president to be killed by an assassin, and the second to be buried at Arlington National Cemetery (first was William Howard Taft).

MEMORIAL DAY. May 29. Legal public holiday. (PL90–363 sets Memorial Day on last Monday in May. Applicable to federal employees and District of Columbia.) Also known as Decoration Day because of the tradition of decorating the graves of servicepeople. An occasion for honoring those who have died in battle. (Observance dates from Civil War years in US: first documented observance at Waterloo, NY, May 5, 1866.) See also: "Confederate Memorial Day" (Apr 24, Apr 26, May 10 and June 3).

MEMORIAL DAY PARADE. May 29. Aurora, IL. Annual parade featuring veterans groups, scouts, bands, floats and more. The parade begins at 12:00 PM. Est attendance: 15,000. For info: City of Aurora, Mayor's Office of Special Events, 43 E Downer Place, Aurora, IL 60507. Phone: (630) 844-3640. Fax: (630) 906-7068.

MEMORIAL DAY PARADE AND CEREMONIES. May 29. Gettysburg National Cemetery, Gettysburg, PA. 2,000 schoolchildren scatter flowers over the unknown graves. Memorial services follow parade. For info: Gettysburg CVB, PO Box 4117, Gettysburg, PA 17325. Phone: (717) 334-6274. Fax: (717) 334-1166. E-mail: gettysburgcvb@dejazzd.com. Web: www.gettysburgcvb.org.

MOSCOW COMMUNIQUE: ANNIVERSARY. May 29, 1972. President Richard Nixon and Soviet Party leader Leonid Brezhnev released a joint communique after Nixon's weeklong visit to Moscow. During the visit the two men acknowledged their major differences on the Vietnam War, signed a treaty on antiballistic missile systems as well as an interim agreement on limitation of strategic missiles and an agreement for a joint space flight in 1975. This was the first visit ever to Moscow by a US president (May 22–30, 1972).

MOUNT EVEREST SUMMIT REACHED: ANNIVERSARY. May 29, 1953. New Zealand explorer Sir Edmund Hillary and Tensing Norgay, a Sherpa guide, became the first team to reach the summit of Mount Everest, the world's highest mountain.

★**PRAYER FOR PEACE, MEMORIAL DAY.** May 29. Presidential Proclamation issued each year since 1948. PL81–512 of May 11, 1950, asks President to proclaim annually this day as a day of prayer for permanent peace. PL90–363 of June 28, 1968, requires that beginning in 1971 it will be observed the last Monday in May. Often titled "Prayer for Peace Memorial Day," and traditionally requests the flying of the flag at half-staff "for the customary forenoon period."

RHODE ISLAND: RATIFICATION DAY. May 29. The last of the 13 original states to ratify the Constitution in 1790.

***THE RITE OF SPRING* PREMIERE AND RIOT: ANNIVERSARY.** May 29, 1913. In the most notorious world premiere in any of the arts, Igor Stravinsky's *The Rite of Spring* received a rough reception at the Théatre des Champs-Elysées at Paris, France, on this date. Performed by Serge Diaghilev's Ballets Russes and choreographed by the legendary Vaslav Nijinsky, the ballet and music presented scenes from pagan Russia. The audience began to boo at Stravinsky's challenging and dissonant music, and before long fistfights between different camps of music lovers broke out. The police were called to restore order. Despite its inauspicious beginning, *The Rite of Spring* is now regarded as a masterpiece.

SOCCER TRAGEDY: ANNIVERSARY. May 29, 1985. A riot at Heysel stadium at Brussels, Belgium, killed 39 people. Fans attending the European Cup Final, between Liverpool and Juventus of Turin, clashed before the match started. Some 400 people were injured in the riot. The incident was televised and viewed by millions throughout Europe. More than two years later, Sept 2, 1987, the British government announced that 26 British soccer fans (identified from television tapes) would be extradited to Belgium for trial. Hooliganism at soccer matches became the target of increased security measures for England's professional teams following the 1985 tragedy.

SPENGLER, OSWALD: BIRTH ANNIVERSARY. May 29, 1880. German historian, author of *The Decline of the West*, born at Blankenburg-am-Harz, Germany. Died at Munich, Germany, May 8, 1936.

STOCK EXCHANGE HOLIDAY (MEMORIAL DAY). May 29. The holiday schedules for the various exchanges are subject to change if relevant rules, regulations or exchange policies are revised. If you have questions, phone: American Stock Exchange (212) 306-1000, Chicago Board of Trade (312) 435-3500, Chicago Board of Options Exchange (312) 786-5600, NASDAQ Stock Market (646) 441-5200, New York Stock Exchange (215) 656-3000, Pacific Stock Exchange (415) 393-4000, Philadelphia Stock Exchange (215) 496-5000.

TOUR OF SOMERVILLE. May 29. Somerville, NJ. 61st running. The oldest continuously run major bicycle race in America. Attracts more than 500 top amateur cyclists for four events. Annually, on Memorial Day. Est attendance: 40,000. For info: Dan Puntillo, Middle Earth, PO Box 8045, Bridgewater, NJ 08807. Phone: (908) 725-7223. Fax: (908) 722-5411. Web: www.tourofsomerville.org.

UNITED KINGDOM: SPRING BANK HOLIDAY. May 29. Bank and public holiday in England, Wales, Scotland and Northern Ireland. Annually, the last Monday in May.

UNITED NATIONS: INTERNATIONAL DAY OF UNITED NATIONS PEACEKEEPERS. May 29. The Assembly has designated May 29 of each year as a day to pay tribute to all the men and women who have served in United Nations peacekeeping operations for their high level of professionalism, dedication and courage, and to honor the memory of those who have lost their lives in the cause of peace (Res 57/129, Dec 11, 2002). The Assembly invited all Member States, organizations of the United Nations system, nongovernmental organizations and individuals to observe the day in an appropriate manner. For info: United Nations, Dept of Public Info, New York, NY 10017. Web: www.un.org.

VIRGINIA PLAN PROPOSED: ANNIVERSARY. May 29, 1787. Just five days after the Constitutional Convention met at Philadelphia, PA, the "Virginia Plan" was proposed. It called for establishment of a new governmental organization consisting of a legislature with two houses, an executive (chosen by the legislature) and a judicial branch.

WISCONSIN: ADMISSION DAY: ANNIVERSARY. May 29. Became 30th state in 1848.

BIRTHDAYS TODAY

Carmelo Anthony, 22, basketball player, born New York, NY, May 29, 1984.

Annette Bening, 48, actress (*The American President, Bugsy, The Grifters*), born Topeka, KS, May 29, 1958.

Kevin Conway, 64, actor (*When You Comin' Back, Red Ryder?; Of Mice and Men, Other People's Money*), born New York, NY, May 29, 1942.

Eric Davis, 44, former baseball player, born Los Angeles, CA, May 29, 1962.

Paul Ehrlich, 74, population biologist, born Philadelphia, PA, May 29, 1932.

Melissa Etheridge, 45, singer, guitarist, born Leavenworth, KS, May 29, 1961.

Rupert Everett, 47, actor (*An Ideal Husband, My Best Friend's Wedding*), born Norfolk, England, May 29, 1959.

Anthony Geary, 58, actor ("General Hospital"), born Coalville, UT, May 29, 1948.

Adrian Paul, 47, actor ("Highlander" series), born London, England, May 29, 1959.

Alfred (Al) Unser, Sr, 67, former auto racer, born Albuquerque, NM, May 29, 1939.

Francis Thomas (Fay) Vincent, Jr, 68, former commissioner of baseball, born Waterbury, CT, May 29, 1938.

Lisa Whelchel, 43, actress ("Facts of Life"), born Fort Worth, TX, May 29, 1963.

MAY 30 — TUESDAY

Day 150 — 215 Remaining

BATTLE OF THE ALEUTIAN ISLANDS: ANNIVERSARY. May 30, 1943. The islands of Kiska and Attu in the Aleutian Islands off the coast of Alaska were retaken by the US 7th Infantry Division. The battle (Operation Landgrab) began when an American force of 11,000 landed on Attu May 12. In three weeks of fighting US casualties numbered 552 killed and 1,140 wounded. Only 28 wounded Japanese were taken prisoner. Their dead amounted to 2,352, of whom 500 committed suicide.

BEEF EMPIRE DAYS. May 30–June 11. Finney County Fairgrounds, Garden City, KS. 38th annual celebration of the beef industry. Live and carcass show; PRCA rodeo (three nights); parade; beef tasting for the public; feedlot roping and riding; walk/run; golf, softball and tennis tournaments; children's events. Est attendance: 50,000. For info: Beef Empire Days, PO Box 1197, Garden City, KS 67846-1197. Phone: (620) 275-6807. E-mail: beefempiredays@gcnet.com. Web: www.beefempiredays.com.

CULLEN, COUNTEE: BIRTH ANNIVERSARY. May 30, 1903. One of the leading poets of the Harlem Renaissance (*Color*, 1925). He died at New York City, Jan 9, 1946.

ENGLAND: ROYAL BATH AND WEST SHOW. May 30–June 3. Royal Bath and West Showground, Shepton Mallet, Somerset. One of the largest agricultural shows for the whole family in the country. 229th year. Est attendance: 165,000. For info: Royal Bath and West Society, The Showground, Shepton Mallet, Somerset, England BA4 6QN. Phone: (44) (174) 982-2200. Fax: (44) (174) 982-3169. E-mail: info@bathandwest.co.uk. Web: www.bathandwest.co.uk.

FABERGÉ, CARL: BIRTH ANNIVERSARY. May 30, 1846. The goldsmith, designer and jeweler Peter Carl Fabergé was born on this date at St. Petersburg, Russia. He made the House of Fabergé an internationally known name with fantastical bejeweled decorative objects. His workshop began creating the famous imperial Easter eggs for czars Alexander III and Nicholas II in 1885. After the Russian Revolution, the Bolsheviks shut down the House of Fabergé and the family fled the country. Carl Fabergé died at Lausanne, France, on Sept 24, 1920. (His birth date was May 18 on the Old Style [Julian] calendar.)

FIRST AMERICAN DAILY NEWSPAPER PUBLISHED: ANNIVERSARY. May 30, 1783. *The Pennsylvania Evening Post* became the first daily newspaper published in the US. The paper was published at Philadelphia, PA, by Benjamin Towne.

GOODMAN, BENNY: BIRTH ANNIVERSARY. May 30, 1909. Jazz clarinetist and bandleader, born Benjamin David Goodman at Chicago, IL. The "King of Swing" reigned in popularity especially in the 1930s and 1940s. His band was the first to play jazz at New York's Carnegie Hall. He died June 13, 1986, at New York, NY.

INDIANAPOLIS 500: 95th ANNIVERSARY. May 30, 1911. Ray Harroun won the first Indy 500, averaging 74.6 MPH. The race was created by Carl Fisher, who in 1909 replaced the stone surface of his 2.5-mile racetrack with a brick one—hence the nickname "The Brickyard."

LINCOLN MEMORIAL DEDICATION: ANNIVERSARY. May 30, 1922. The memorial is made of marble from Colorado and Tennessee and limestone from Indiana. It stands in West Potomac Park at Washington, DC. The Memorial was designed by architect Henry Bacon and its cornerstone was laid in 1915. A skylight lets light into the interiors where the compelling statue "Seated Lincoln," by sculptor Daniel Chester French, is situated.

LOOMIS DAY. May 30. To honor Mahlon Loomis, a Washington, DC, dentist who received a US patent on wireless telegraphy in 1872 (before Marconi was born). Titled "An Improvement in Telegraphing," the patent described how to do without wires; this patent was backed up by experiment on the Massanutten Mountains of Virginia. For info: Robert L. Birch, Puns Corps, 3108 Dashiell Rd, Falls Church, VA 22042. Phone: (703) 533-3668.

MEMORIAL DAY (TRADITIONAL). May 30. This day honors the tradition of making memorial tributes to the dead, especially remembering those who have died in battle. Observed as a legal public holiday on the last Monday in May.

PETER I: BIRTH ANNIVERSARY. May 30, 1672. Peter I (Peter the Great), Czar and Emperor of all the Russias. His primary aim was to make Russia a major power equal to its size and potential, and the way he saw to do this was through education and technology. He established printing presses and published translations of foreign books, particularly scientific and technical material. The Russian alphabet was simplified, and Arabic numerals were introduced. Peter encouraged trade with foreign countries, mercantilism within Russia and the entrepreneurial skills of

		S	M	T	W	T	F	S
May			1	2	3	4	5	6
2006		7	8	9	10	11	12	13
		14	15	16	17	18	19	20
		21	22	23	24	25	26	27
		28	29	30	31			

resident foreigners; he allowed industrialists to own serfs, a right previously limited to landholders. He completely overhauled the government, the Russian Orthodox Church, the military system and the structure of taxes, ultimately increasing the power of the monarchy at the expense of the nobility and the national church. Upon his death, Jan 28, 1725, he was succeeded by his wife Catherine.

SAINT JOAN OF ARC: FEAST DAY. May 30. French heroine and martyr, known as the Maid of Orleans, led the French against the English invading army. Captured, found guilty of heresy and burned at the stake in 1431 (at age 19). Innocence declared in 1456. Canonized in 1920.

SPACE MILESTONE: *MARINER 9* (US): 35th ANNIVERSARY. May 30, 1971. Unmanned spacecraft was launched, entering Martian orbit the following Nov 13. The craft relayed temperature and gravitational field information and sent back spectacular photographs of both the surface of Mars and of its two moons. First spacecraft to orbit another planet.

TRINIDAD: INDIAN ARRIVAL DAY. May 30. Port of Spain, West Indies. Public holiday. For info: Info Dept, Tourism Div, Tourism and Industrial Development Co, Trinidad and Tobago Ltd, 10–14 Phillips St, West Indies. Phone: (800) 595-1868.

WORLD TRADE CENTER RECOVERY AND CLEANUP ENDS: ANNIVERSARY. May 30, 2002. New York, NY. A solemn and mostly silent ceremony marked the symbolic end of recovery operations at Ground Zero, the former site of the World Trade Center, after the Sept 11, 2001, terrorist attacks. The last standing steel girder was cut down on May 28. An honor guard carried an empty stretcher draped with an American flag to represent those victims who were not recovered from the ruins. Members of the NYFD, NYPD and city, state and federal workers, as well as family members and Ground Zero recovery teams, participated in the ceremony.

BIRTHDAYS TODAY

Blake Bashoff, 25, actor (*Bushwhacked, Big Bully*), born Philadelphia, PA, May 30, 1981.

Keir Dullea, 70, actor (*David and Lisa, 2001: A Space Odyssey*), born Cleveland, OH, May 30, 1936.

Bob Evans, 88, restaurant executive, born Sugar Ridge, OH, May 30, 1918.

Wynonna Judd, 42, singer (*Wynonna*, "Tell Me Why"), winner of six Grammy awards, born Ashland, KY, May 30, 1964.

Ted McGinley, 48, actor ("Married . . . With Children," *Revenge of the Nerds*), born Newport Beach, CA, May 30, 1958.

Colm Meaney, 53, actor ("Star Trek: The Next Generation," *Last of the Mohicans*), born Dublin, Ireland, May 30, 1953.

Trey Parker, 34, director, creator ("South Park"), born Auburn, AL, May 30, 1972.

Michael J. Pollard, 67, actor (*Bonnie and Clyde*, "Leo & Liz in Beverly Hills"), born Passaic, NJ, May 30, 1939.

Manny Ramirez, 34, baseball player, born Santo Domingo, Dominican Republic, May 30, 1972.

Gale Eugene Sayers, 63, Hall of Fame football player, born Wichita, KS, May 30, 1943.

Stephen Tobolowsky, 55, actor (*The Grifters, Groundhog Day*), born Dallas, TX, May 30, 1951.

Clint Walker, 79, actor (*The Dirty Dozen*, "Cheyenne"), born Hartford, IL, May 30, 1927.

MAY 31 — WEDNESDAY

Day 151 — 214 Remaining

AMECHE, DON: BIRTH ANNIVERSARY. May 31, 1908. Film, stage, radio and TV actor. Born Dominic Felix Amici at Kenosha, WI, and died Dec 6, 1993, at Scottsdale, AZ.

CANADA: ANNAPOLIS VALLEY APPLE BLOSSOM FESTIVAL. May 31–June 5. Windsor to Digby, NS. Annual festival with barbecues, sports events, art show, Princess Tea, coronation ceremonies, dances, concerts, fireworks, craft fair, children's parade, Grand Street Parade and "Sunday in the Park" (family entertainment). Annually, since 1933. Est attendance: 125,000. For info: Mrs Frances Anderson, Annapolis Valley Apple Blossom Fest, 217 Belcher St, Kentville, NS, Canada B4N 1E2. Phone: (902) 678-8322. Fax: (902) 678-3710. E-mail: apple blossom@ns.sympatico.ca. Web: www.appleblossom.com.

CHINA: DRAGON BOAT FESTIVAL. May 31. An important Chinese observance, the Dragon Boat Festival commemorates a hero of ancient China, poet Qu Yuan, who drowned himself in protest against injustice and corruption. It is said that rice dumplings were cast into the water to lure fish away from the body of the martyr, and this is remembered by the eating of zhong zi, glutinous rice dumplings filled with meat and wrapped in bamboo leaves. Dragon boat races are held on rivers. The Dragon Boat Festival is observed in many countries by their Chinese populations (date will differ from China's). Also called Fifth Month Festival or Summer Festival. Annually, the fifth day of the fifth lunar month.

COPYRIGHT LAW PASSED: ANNIVERSARY. May 31, 1790. President George Washington signed the first US copyright law. It gave protection for 14 years to books written by US citizens. In 1891 the law was extended to cover books by foreign authors as well.

GREAT AMERICAN GRUMP OUT. May 31. We are asking America to go 24 hours without being grumpy or crabby. Can YOU meet the challenge? Schoolchildren, parents, businesses and the community will be involved in promoting peace, harmony and lighthearted humor on this day. For info: Janice Hathy, Smile Mania, 1300 N River Rd, S-24, Venice, FL 34293. E-mail: grump out@smilemania.com. Web: www.smilemania.com.

HARRIS, PATRICIA ROBERTS: BIRTH ANNIVERSARY. May 31, 1924. Born at Matoon, IL. The first African-American woman to serve in an ambassadorial post, the first African American to hold a cabinet position (Secretary of Housing and Urban Development) and the first woman to serve as dean of a law school. Died Mar 23, 1985.

JOHNSTOWN FLOOD: ANNIVERSARY. May 31, 1889. Heavy rains caused the Connemaugh River Dam to burst. At nearby Johnstown, PA, the resulting flood killed more than 2,300 people and destroyed the homes of thousands more. Nearly 800 unidentified drowning victims were buried in a common grave at Johnstown's Grandview Cemetery. So devastating was the flood and so widespread the sorrow for its victims that "Johnstown Flood" entered the language as a phrase to describe a disastrous event. The valley city of Johnstown, in the Allegheny Mountains, has been damaged repeatedly by floods. Floods in 1936 (25 deaths) and 1977 (85 deaths) were the next most destructive.

KOREA: TANO DAY. May 31. Fifth day of fifth lunar month. Summer food offered at the household shrine of the ancestors. Also known as Swing Day, since girls, dressed in their prettiest clothes, often compete in swinging matches. The Tano Festival usually lasts from the third through eighth day of the fifth lunar month.

NATIONAL SENIOR HEALTH AND FITNESS DAY. May 31. 1,500 local events held on the same day in all 50 states. 13th annual event to promote the value of fitness and exercise for older adults. During this day—as part of Older Americans Month activities—seniors across the country are involved in locally organized health promotion activities. Call the toll-free number for further info and a list of local sites. Annually, the last Wednesday in May. In 2005 more than 120,000 older adults participated in fitness activities at more than 1,000 events nationwide. Est attendance: 150,000. For info: Tina Godin, Program Mgr, Mature Market Resource Center, 1850 W Winchester Rd, Ste 213, Libertyville, IL 60048. Phone: (800) 828-8225. Fax: (847) 816-8662. E-mail: info@fitnessday.com. Web: www.fitnessday.com.

NATIONAL SPELLING BEE FINALS. May 31–June 1. Washington, DC. Newspapers and other sponsors across the country send 240–250 youngsters to the finals at Washington, DC. Annually, Wednesday and Thursday of Memorial Day week. Est attendance: 1,000. For info: Scripps Natl Spelling Bee, 312 Walnut St, 28th Fl, Cincinnati, OH 45202. Phone: (513) 977-3040. Fax: (513) 977-3800. E-mail: bee@scripps.com. Web: www.spellingbee.com.

NCAA DIVISION I MEN'S GOLF CHAMPIONSHIPS. May 31–June 3. Crosswater Club at Sunriver Resort, Sunriver, OR. For info: NCAA, 700 W Washington Ave, PO Box 6222, Indianapolis, IN 46206-6222. Phone: (317) 917-6222. Fax: (317) 917-6888. Web: www.ncaasports.com.

PEALE, NORMAN VINCENT: BIRTH ANNIVERSARY. May 31, 1898. American religious leader Norman Vincent Peale was born at Bowersville, OH. He is best known for his book *The Power of Positive Thinking* (1952), which combines religion and psychiatry. He was a minister at the Marble Collegiate Church at New York, NY. He died Dec 24, 1993, at Pawling, NY.

POPE PIUS XI: BIRTH ANNIVERSARY. May 31, 1857. Ambrogio Damiano Achille Ratti, 259th pope of the Roman Catholic Church, born at Desio, Italy. Elected pope Feb 6, 1922. Died Feb 10, 1939, at Rome, Italy.

PRINCE RAINIER OF MONACO: BIRTH ANNIVERSARY. May 31, 1923. Born Prince Rainier Louis Henri Maxence Bertrand in the small principality of Monaco, he ascended the throne in 1949. In 1956, he married Hollywood actress Grace Kelly and Monaco soon became the glamour destination for the rich and famous. By changing tax shelter laws and encouraging the casino industry, Rainier changed the destiny of his country, bringing it back from the brink of bankruptcy to become one of the wealthiest nations in Europe. He was Europe's longest-reigning monarch when he died at Monaco on Apr 6, 2005.

"SEINFELD" TV PREMIERE: ANNIVERSARY. May 31, 1990. "Seinfeld"—the show about nothing—premiered on NBC to wide acclaim. The show revolved around the lives and exploits of its four main leads whose story lines were intertwined for some surprising plot twists. Comedian Jerry Seinfeld used his stand-up routines as an introduction to the show; some of the programs concerned relationships, valet parking, annoying dogs and waiting for Chinese food. The cast featured Seinfeld as himself; Julia Louis-Dreyfus as his ex-girlfriend, Elaine Benes; Jason Alexander as his best friend, George Costanza; Wayne Knight as Newman and Michael Richards as his neighbor, Cosmo Kramer. The series ended with the May 14, 1998, episode.

"SURVIVOR" TV PREMIERE: ANNIVERSARY. May 31, 2000. On this immensely popular "reality TV" show, 16 people were sequestered on a deserted island in Malaysia for 39 days. They competed for the right to remain on the island, with the final survivor winning $1,000,000. Hosted by Jeff Probst, the show drew a total audience of 51 million people. On Jan 28, 2001, another group of "Survivor" contestants began their stay in the Australian outback; later that year another group went to Africa.

UNITED NATIONS: WORLD NO-TOBACCO DAY. May 31.

WHAT YOU THINK UPON GROWS DAY. May 31. A day to remind people of the power of positive thinking. For info: Stephanie West Allen, PO Box 9311, Denver, CO 80209. Phone: (303) 742-4790. E-mail: stephanie@allen-nichols.com. Web: www.allen-nichols.com.

WHITMAN, WALT: BIRTH ANNIVERSARY. May 31, 1819. Poet and journalist, born at West Hills, Long Island, NY. Whitman's best known work, *Leaves of Grass* (1855), is a classic of American poetry. His poems celebrated all of modern life, including subjects that were considered taboo at the time. Died Mar 26, 1892, at Camden, NJ.

BIRTHDAYS TODAY

Tom Berenger, 56, actor (*Born on the Fourth of July, Major League, Gettysburg*), born Chicago, IL, May 31, 1950.

Clint Eastwood, 76, actor, director (Oscars for *Unforgiven* and *Million Dollar Baby*), former mayor of Carmel, CA, born San Francisco, CA, May 31, 1930.

Chris Elliott, 46, writer ("Late Night with David Letterman"), actor ("Get a Life"), born New York, NY, May 31, 1960.

Colin Farrell, 30, actor (*Minority Report, The Recruit*), born Castleknock, Dublin, Ireland, May 31, 1976.

Sharon Gless, 63, actress (Emmy for "Cagney & Lacey"), born Los Angeles, CA, May 31, 1943.

Gregory Harrison, 56, actor ("Logan's Run," "Trapper John, MD"), born Avalon, Catalina Island, CA, May 31, 1950.

Kenny Lofton, 39, baseball player, born East Chicago, IN, May 31, 1967.

Roma Maffia, 48, actress ("Chicago Hope," "Nip/Tuck"), born New York, NY, May 31, 1958.

Joseph William (Joe) Namath, 63, Hall of Fame football player, former sportscaster, actor, born Beaver Falls, PA, May 31, 1943.

Kyle Secor, 48, actor ("Homicide: Life on the Streets"), born Tacoma, WA, May 31, 1958.

Brooke Shields, 41, actress (*Pretty Baby, The Blue Lagoon*, "Suddenly Susan"), born New York, NY, May 31, 1965.

Lea Thompson, 45, actress ("Caroline in the City," *Back to the Future, Howard the Duck*), born Rochester, MN, May 31, 1961.

Terry Waite, 67, Church of England special envoy, former hostage in Lebanon (1987–91), born Bollington, Cheshire, England, May 31, 1939.

Peter Yarrow, 68, composer, singer (Peter, Paul and Mary), born New York, NY, May 31, 1938.

Iune.

JUNE 1 — THURSDAY
Day 152 — 213 Remaining

ADOPT-A-SHELTER-CAT MONTH. June 1–30. To promote the adoption of cats from local shelters, the ASPCA sponsors this important observance. "Make Pet Adoption Your First Option®" is a message the organization promotes throughout the year in an effort to end the euthanasia of all adoptable animals. For info: ASPCA Media Relations Dept, 424 E 92nd St, New York, NY 10128. Phone: (212) 876-7700 x 4655. E-mail: press@aspca.org. Web: www.aspca.org.

ALBANY ALIVE AT FIVE. June 1 (also June 8, 15, 22, 29; July 13, 20, 27; Aug 3 and 10). Albany Riverfront Park, Albany, NY. A free summer concert series on Thursday evenings from 5–8 PM. A different theme of music each week, food and refreshment vendors. Est attendance: 80,000. For info: Susan T. Cleary, City of Albany Office of Special Events, Eagle Street, City Hall, 4th Fl, Albany, NY 12207. Phone: (518) 434-2032. Fax: (518) 426-0759. E-mail: info@albanyevents.org. Web: www.albany events.org.

ARTISTS OF AMERICA DAY. June 1. A day to honor all the artists in America—visual, performing or literary—who create the works that make our lives better. Being an artist is hard work and takes great courage. Today we recognize and thank the artists—be they professional, student, hobbyist, children or anyone who uses their creative spirit to express what they want to say to the world. Annually, June 1. For info: Diedre Burke, Artists of America, 741 W 24th St, Ste 33, San Pedro, CA 90731. Phone: (310) 809-5277. Fax: (310) 547-9249. E-mail: dbrke@aol.com. Web: www.artists-of-america.com.

ATLANTIC, CARIBBEAN AND GULF HURRICANE SEASON. June 1–Nov 30. For info: US Dept of Commerce, Natl Oceanic and Atmospheric Admin, Rockville, MD 20852.

BLACK HILLS PASSION PLAY—SOUTH DAKOTA. June 1–Aug 31. Passion Play Amphitheater, Spearfish, SD. Spectacular outdoor drama on a huge stage depicts the last seven days in the life of Christ. It features a professionally led cast of more than 200 and live animals. Annually, Sunday, Tuesday and Thursday evenings. Est attendance: 50,000. For info: Black Hills Passion Play—South Dakota, PO Box 489, Spearfish, SD 57783. Phone: (605) 642-2646 or (800) 457-0160. Fax: (605) 642-7993. E-mail: bhpp@blackhills.com. Web: www.blackhills.com/bhpp.

CANADA: SHELBURNE COUNTY LOBSTER FESTIVAL. June 1–4. Shelburne County, NS. Four days of activities in celebration of the lobster-fishing industry. Local community groups and businesses throughout the county host lobster suppers, sporting events, craft shows, yacht, boat and dorey races and much more. "Shelburne County—The Lobster Capital of Canada." Annually, the first full weekend in June. Est attendance: 5,000. For info: Marilyn Johnston, Lobster Fest Secy, PO Box 280, Shelburne, NS, Canada B0T 1W0. Phone: (902) 875-3544. Fax: (902) 875-1278. E-mail: shelburnemunrec@canada.com.

CANCER FROM THE SUN MONTH. June 1–30. To promote education and awareness of the dangers of skin cancer from too much exposure to the sun. Kit of materials available for $15 from this nonprofit organization. For info: Frederick Mayer, Pres, Pharmacy Council on Dermatology (PCD), 101 Lucas Valley Rd, #210, San Rafael, CA 94903. Phone: (415) 479-8628. Fax: (415) 479-8608. E-mail: ppsi@aol.com. Web: www.ppsinc.org.

CANOE, CAPSTAN & CARGO. June 1–30. Jamestown Settlement, Williamsburg, VA, and Yorktown Victory Center, Yorktown, VA. In the 17th and 18th centuries, Virginians relied on waterways for transportation, food supply and commerce. At Jamestown Settlement, visitors can lend a hand with boatbuilding as well as sail and cargo handling, and learn about the production of lumber for export. Programs at the Yorktown Victory Center will highlight the importance of ships during the American Revolution and in exporting tobacco, Virginia's important cash crop. For info: Jamestown-Yorktown Foundation, PO Box 1607, Williamsburg, VA 23187. Phone: (757) 253-4838. Fax: (757) 253-5299. Web: www.historyisfun.org.

CELIBACY AWARENESS MONTH. June 1–30. A celebration of the "Celibate in the City" club's desire to encourage and reaffirm the Christian commitment to remain celibate until marriage. For info: Audrey Miller, Celibate in the City, 165-08 Liberty Ave, Ste 127, Jamaica, NY 11433. Phone: (877) 422-2782. Fax: (718) 849-4696. E-mail: info@celibateinthecity.com. Web: www.celibateinthecity.com.

CENTRAL PACIFIC HURRICANE SEASON. June 1–Oct 31. Central Pacific is defined as 140° west longitude to the International Date Line (180° west longitude). For info: Natl Dept of Commerce, Natl Oceanic and Atmospheric Admin, Rockville, MD 20852.

CHICAGO BLUES FESTIVAL. June 1–4. Grant Park, Chicago, IL. 23rd annual. Largest free blues festival in the world. Est attendance: 650,000. For info: Mayor's Office of Special Events, City Hall, 121 N LaSalle St, #703, Chicago, IL 60602. Phone: (312) 744-3370. Fax: (312) 744-8523. E-mail: SpecialEvents@city ofchicago.org. Web: www.cityofchicago.org/specialevents.

CHILD VISION AWARENESS MONTH. June 1–30. To better educate and counsel the public on children's vision problems and detection of eye diseases in infants and children, to increase the number of school-aged children who have an eye exam by an eye doctor and to increase the number of children with learning disabilities having a developmental vision exam to rule out vision problems. There is a $15 charge for kit materials. For info: PPSI, c/o Pharmacy Council on Vision Care, 101 Lucas Valley Rd., Ste 210, San Rafael, CA 94903. Phone: (415) 479-8628. Fax: (415) 479-8608. E-mail: ppsi@aol.com. Web: www.ppsinc.org.

CHILDREN'S AWARENESS MONTH. June 1–30. A month-long celebration of America's children in our everyday lives and communities that lovingly remembers all of America's children that we have lost through violence. These could have been our children or grandchildren. We choose to remember the living during the month of June by celebrating the gift of children. For info: Judith Natale, CEO & Founder, NCAC America-USA, PO Box 493703, Redding, CA 96049-3703. E-mail: childaware@aol.com.

CHINA: INTERNATIONAL CHILDREN'S DAY. June 1. Shanghai.

CNN DEBUTED: ANNIVERSARY. June 1, 1980. The Cable News Network, TV's first all-news service, went on the air.

CURWOOD FESTIVAL. June 1–4. Owosso, MI. Homecoming celebration commemorating James Oliver Curwood, Owosso-born author and conservationist (June 12, 1878–Aug 13, 1927). The Curwood castle was built for a studio. Open to the public. 40 events including parades, races and music. Annually, the first full weekend in June. Est attendance: 75,000. For info: Owosso Curwood Festival, Box 461, Owosso, MI 48867. Phone: (989) 723-2161. Fax: (989) 729-6098. E-mail: curwood.festivalinc@verizon.net. Web: www.curwoodfestival.com.

DAIRY ALTERNATIVES MONTH. June 1–30. This event encourages consumers to eliminate dairy products from their diet and explore alternatives made from soybeans, nuts or grains. For info: VEGANET, Natl Headquarters, PO Box 3545, Washington, DC 20027-0045. Phone: (800) 280-8343.

DAYLILY EXTRAVAGANZA. June 1–30. Massee Lane Gardens, Fort Valley, GA. Annual celebration of the flamboyant daylily. Festival events include garden tours and workshops, plant sale and more. Sponsored by the American Camellia Society annually during the month of June. Est attendance: 5,000. For info: Massee Lane Gardens, 100 Massee Ln, Fort Valley, GA 31030. Phone: (478) 967-2722. Fax: (478) 967-2083. Web: www.camellias-acs.org.

EFFECTIVE COMMUNICATIONS MONTH. June 1–30. The most important cog in the wheel of interpersonal relationships is communication. Active listening, verbal language, paralanguage, body language and written communication skills are the essence of how humans relate to each other personally and professionally. This month is dedicated to learning how to, improving upon, and committing to communicating more effectively in our lives. For info: Sylvia Henderson, Springboard Training, PO Box 588, Olney, MD 20830-0588. Phone: (301) 260-1538. E-mail: admin@springboardtraining.com. Web: www.springboardtraining.com.

ENTREPRENEURS "DO IT YOURSELF" MARKETING MONTH. June 1–30. Stand out from your competition and get media attention and more clients, while achieving your goals. Are you looking for better results from your marketing efforts? Would you like to become a new resource the media calls? Remember, your success is a matter of choice, not chance. Discover and apply creative and effective problem-solving marketing ideas that will help you gain the competitive edge. Act now and remove the barriers that are stopping you from achieving your goals. Pamphlet available for $5. For info: Lorrie Walters Marsiglio, Lorimar Communications, PO Box 284-CC, Wasco, IL 60183-0284. Phone: (630) 584-9368.

FIREWORKS SAFETY MONTHS. June 1–July 31. Activities during these months are designed to warn and educate parents and children about the dangers of playing with fireworks. Prevent Blindness America will offer suggestions for safer ways to celebrate the Fourth of July. For info: Prevent Blindness America®, 211 W Wacker Dr, Ste 1700, Chicago, IL 60606. Phone: (800) 331-2020. E-mail: info@preventblindness.org. Web: www.preventblindness.org.

GAY AND LESBIAN PRIDE MONTH. June 1–30. Observed this month because on June 28, 1969, the clientele of a gay bar at New York City rioted after the club was raided by the police. President Clinton issued presidential proclamations for this month, but President Bush has not declared it during his administration to date. See also: "Stonewall Riot: Anniversary" (June 28).

HEIMLICH MANEUVER INTRODUCED: ANNIVERSARY. June 1, 1974. The June issue of the journal *Emergency Medicine* published an article by Dr. Henry Heimlich outlining a better method for aiding choking victims. Instead of the prevailing method of backslaps (which merely pushed foreign objects farther into the airways), Dr. Heimlich advocated "subdiaphragmatic pressure" to force objects out. Three months later, the method was dubbed "the Heimlich Maneuver" by the *Journal of the American Medical Association*.

INTERNATIONAL ACCORDION AWARENESS MONTH. June 1–30. To increase public awareness of this multicultural instrument and its influence and popularity in today's music. For info: Tom Torriglia, All Things Accordion, PO Box 475136, San Francisco, CA 94147-5136. Phone: (415) 440-0800. E-mail: tom@ladyofspain.com. Web: www.ladyofspain.com.

INTERNATIONAL MEN'S MONTH. June 1–30. This program was initiated in 1996 to increase media and local community awareness of the many unique issues that impact men's lives and that are of concern to the people who love them. In an effort to promote positive changes in male roles and relationships, a different issue is addressed each day of the month during June and information and resources on that issue are provided on the website. This free information can be received automatically by signing up at menstuff-subscribe@topica.com. For info: Gordon Clay, Exec Dir, Natl Men's Resource Center, PO Box 1080, Brookings, OR 97415-0024. E-mail: menstuff@menstuff.org. Web: www.menstuff.org.

INTERNATIONAL VOLUNTEERS WEEK. June 1–7. To honor men and women throughout the world who serve as volunteers, rendering valuable service without compensation to the communities in which they live and to honor nonprofit organizations dedicated to making the world a better place in which to live. For complete info, send $5 to cover expense of printing, handling and postage. Annually, the first seven days of June. For info: Dr. Stanley Drake, Pres Emeritus, Intl Soc of Friendship & Good Will, 8592 Roswell Rd, Ste 251, Atlanta, GA 30350-1867. Phone: (678) 795-1362. E-mail: sjdrake@bellsouth.net. Web: www.friendshipandgoodwill.org.

JUNE DAIRY MONTH. June 1–30. Since 1937 the dairy industry has set aside June as a time to pay tribute to the vital role milk and dairy products play in the American diet and the outstanding contribution of America's dairy farmers. For info: Julie Henderson, Natl Frozen & Refrigerated Foods Assn, 4755 Linglestown Rd, Ste 300, Harrisburg, PA 17112. Phone: (717) 657-8601. Fax: (717) 657-9862. E-mail: info@nfraweb.org. Web: www.nfraweb.org.

JUNE IS PERENNIAL GARDENING MONTH. June 1–30. June is the perfect month to celebrate the versatility and beauty of perennial garden plants. We'll offer some good gardening tips on how to keep your perennial garden beautiful all season long and highlight many individual perennials that bloom for the month of June. For info: Steven Still, 3383 Schrirtzinger Rd, Hilliard, OH 43026. Phone: (614) 771-8431. E-mail: ppa@perennialplant.org. Web: www.perennialplant.org.

JUNE IS TURKEY LOVERS' MONTH. June 1–30. Month-long campaign to promote awareness and increase turkey consumption at a nonholiday time. Annually, the month of June. For info: Natl Turkey Federation, 1225 New York Ave NW, Ste 400, Washington, DC 20005. Phone: (202) 898-0100. Fax: (202) 898-0203. E-mail: info@turkeyfed.org. Web: www.eatturkey.com.

KENTUCKY: ADMISSION DAY: ANNIVERSARY. June 1. Became 15th state in 1792.

KENYA: MADARAKA DAY: ANNIVERSARY. June 1. Madaraka Day (Self-Rule Day) is observed as a national public holiday. Commemorates attainment of self-government in 1963.

LITTLE, CLEAVON: BIRTH ANNIVERSARY. June 1, 1939. Best known for his role as the black sheriff who cleaned

		S	M	T	W	T	F	S
June							1	2	3
2006		4	5	6	7	8	9	10
		11	12	13	14	15	16	17
		18	19	20	21	22	23	24
		25	26	27	28	29	30	

up a town of bumbling redneck toughs in the movie *Blazing Saddles*, Cleavon Little was born at Chickasha, OK. Little was the winner of a Tony award for the 1970 musical *Purlie* and an Emmy in 1989 for a guest appearance on the television series "Dear John." Died Oct 22, 1992, near Sherman Oaks, CA.

MAINLY MOZART FESTIVAL: THE 250TH ANNIVERSARY CELEBRATION OF MOZART'S BIRTHDAY. June 1–26. San Diego County and Baja California, Mexico. David Atherton conducts the festival's all-star orchestra and leading soloists and ensembles in a celebration of Mozart's 250th birthday and also the music of his contemporaries in San Diego, La Jolla and Escondito, CA, and Tijuana, Mexico. Chamber orchestra, chamber ensembles and recitals are featured. Est attendance: 50,000. For info: Public Relations, Mainly Mozart, 2802 Juan St, San Diego, CA 92110. Phone: (619) 239-0100. Fax: (619) 233-4292. E-mail: admin@mainlymozart.org. Web: www.mainlymozart.org.

MARQUETTE, JACQUES: BIRTH ANNIVERSARY. June 1, 1637. Father Jacques Marquette (Père Marquette), Jesuit missionary-explorer of the Great Lakes region. Born at Laon, France. Died at Ludington, MI, May 18, 1675.

MONROE, MARILYN: BIRTH ANNIVERSARY. June 1, 1926. American actress and sex symbol of the '50s, born at Los Angeles as Norma Jean Mortensen or Baker. She had an unstable childhood in a series of orphanages and foster homes. Her film career came to epitomize Hollywood glamour. In 1954 she wed Yankee legend "Jolting Joe" DiMaggio, but the marriage didn't last. Monroe remained fragile and insecure, tormented by the pressures of Hollywood life. Her death from an overdose Aug 5, 1962, at Los Angeles shocked the world. Among her films: *The Seven Year Itch, Bus Stop, Some Like It Hot, Gentlemen Prefer Blondes* and *The Misfits*.

NATIONAL APHASIA AWARENESS MONTH. June 1–30. More than one million Americans have acquired aphasia. Aphasia is a language-processing disorder that impairs a person's ability to speak or understand speech. The mission of the National Aphasia Association (NAA) is to reduce the social and emotional consequences of aphasia by raising awareness of and giving a voice to people who cannot use their own. Annually, the month of June. For info: Penny Montgomery-West, Response Center Dir, Natl Aphasia Assn, 7 Dey St, Ste 600, New York, NY 10007. Phone: (800) 922-4622. E-mail: naa@aphasia.org. Web: www.aphasia.org.

NATIONAL CANDY MONTH. June 1–30. Celebrated throughout the confectionary industry. Retailers will host special events in stores, and there will be special promotions and merchandising contests. Get the facts on these fun products: candy is good food and can definitely be enjoyed as a part of a balanced diet. A great month to host a special candy event. Logo available for use. For info: Lisbeth Echeandia, American Consulting Corporation, PO Box 388, Savoy, TX 75479. Phone: (903) 965-9300. Fax: (903) 965-9144. E-mail: lisbeth@texoma.net.

NATIONAL GLBT BOOK MONTH. June 1–30. Created to increase the recognition of gay, lesbian, bisexual and transgender writing. Begun in 1992 by the Publishing Triangle, June was selected in honor of the anniversary of the 1969 Stonewall Riot in New York City. It was this brave resistance to police harassment that kickstarted the gay pride movement in the US. Libraries, bookstores, publishers and bibliophiles everywhere are invited to form a chorus line and celebrate with the community. Annually, the month of June. For info: GLBT Services Committee, Tucson-Pima Public Library, 101 N Stone Ave, Tucson, AZ 85701. Phone: (520) 791-4393. Fax: (520) 791-2672. E-mail: glbt@tucsonaz.gov. Web: www.lib.ci.tucson.az.us/glbt/bookmonth.

NATIONAL ICED TEA MONTH. June 1–30. To celebrate one of the most widely consumed beverages in the world and one of nature's most perfect beverages, and to encourage Americans to refresh themselves with this all-natural, low-calorie, refreshing thirst-quencher. For info: Joseph P. Simrany, Pres, The Tea Council of the USA, 420 Lexington Ave, Ste 825, New York, NY 10170.

Phone: (212) 986-6998. Fax: (212) 697-8658. E-mail: info@teausa.org. Web: www.teausa.org.

NATIONAL RIVERS MONTH. June 1–30. Commemorated by local groups in many states.

NATIONAL ROSE MONTH. June 1–30. To recognize American-grown roses, our national floral emblem. America's favorite flower is grown in all 50 states and more than 1.2 billion fresh-cut roses are sold at retail each year. For info: International Cut Flower Growers. Web: www.rosesinc.org.

NATIONAL SAFETY MONTH. June 1–30. For info: Natl Safety Council, 1121 Spring Lake Dr, Itasca, IL 60143-3201. Phone: (800) 621-7615. Web: www.nsc.org.

NATIONAL SOUL FOOD MONTH. June 1–30. A month to recognize, educate and celebrate the heritage and history of the foods and foodways of African Americans and peoples from the African diaspora. The culinary contributions of this group have had an indelible impact on the menu of the American table and on mainstream American life and culture. For info: Culinary Historians of Chicago, PO Box 805987, Chicago, IL 60680. E-mail: saridgeway0622@yahoo.com. Web: www.culinaryhistorians.org.

NATIONAL STEAKHOUSE MONTH. June 1–30. To celebrate the steakhouse, that uniquely American restaurant, and to recognize and promote the art of expert grilling. Sponsored by Morton's, The Steakhouse, the world's leading fine-dining restaurant brand. For info: Patty Pleuss, VP, Sales & Mktg, Morton's, The Restaurant, 350 W Hubbard St, Chicago IL 60610. Phone: (312) 755-4202. Email: ppleuss@mortons.com. Web: www.mortons.com.

NCAA DIVISION I SOFTBALL CHAMPIONSHIP. June 1–7. University of Oklahoma, Oklahoma City, OK. For info: NCAA, PO Box 6222, Indianapolis, IN 46206-6222. Phone: (317) 917-6222. Fax: (317) 917-6826. Web: www.ncaasports.com.

ORTHODOX ASCENSION DAY. June 1. Observed by Eastern Orthodox Churches.

PHARMACISTS DECLARE WAR ON ALCOHOLISM. June 1–30. To encourage pharmacists, health care professionals and consumers to better educate and counsel the public on alcoholism and other substance abuse illnesses. By promoting alcohol abuse awareness and education to health care professionals and the general public, PCAA strives to break the stereotype surrounding alcoholism that keeps millions of Americans from receiving proper treatment. There is a $15 charge for kit materials. For info: Pharmacists Planning Service, Inc, Pharmacy Council on Alcohol Abuse, 101 Lucas Valley Rd, #210, San Rafael, CA 94903. Phone: (415) 479-8628. Fax: (415) 479-8608. E-mail: ppsi@aol.com. Web: www.ppsinc.org.

PLYMOUTH PLANTATION EARTHQUAKE: ANNIVERSARY. June 1, 1638. The first earthquake in the US to have been recorded and described in writing occurred at Plymouth, MA, at 2 PM. Governor William Bradford described the event in his *History*: ". . . it was very terrible for ye time; and as ye men were set talking in ye house, some women and others were without ye doors, and ye earth shooke with ye violence as they could not stand without catching hold of ye posts . . . but ye violence lasted not long. And about halfe an hower, or less, came an other noyse & shaking, but neither so loud nor strong as ye former, but quickly passed over, and so it ceased."

PORTLAND ROSE FESTIVAL. June 1–30. Portland, OR. 99th annual celebration includes more than 50 events featuring three parades, the Portland Arts Festival, dragon boat races, a waterfront village with amusement rides and Navy fleet visits. Est attendance: 2,000,000. For info: Portland Rose Festival Assn, 5603 SW Hood Ave, Portland, OR 97239. Phone: (503) 227-2681. Fax: (503) 227-6603. E-mail: info@rosefestival.org. Web: www.rosefestival.org.

POTTY TRAINING AWARENESS MONTH. June 1–30. Potty training can be an exciting yet frustrating time for parents. That's why Pull-Ups® Training Pants sponsors this month devoted to educating parents about the potty training process and helping make this milestone in a child's life easier. Toll-free "Potty Training Totline": (877) 4BIG-KID. Annually, the month of June. For info: Anne Marie Bonness, Edelman Public Relations, 200 E Randolph St, 63rd Fl, Chicago, IL 60601. Phone: (312) 616-1601. Fax: (312) 240-1501. E-mail: anne.bonness@edelman.com. Web: www.pull-ups.com.

"THE PRISONER" TV PREMIERE: ANNIVERSARY. June 1, 1968. "The Prisoner" was one of the most imaginative shows on TV, regarded by some as the finest dramatic series in TV history. Patrick McGoohan, who produced and starred in the series, also wrote and directed some episodes. In the series, McGoohan found himself in a self-contained community known as "the village" where he was referred to, not by name, but as Number 6. Number 6 realized he was a prisoner and spent most of the series trying to escape or to learn the identity of the leader, Number 1.

PROFESSIONAL WELLNESS MONTH. June 1–30. Increase your worth in the marketplace. Add value to your company and your customers. Be accessible, reliable and fair. Update your resume, increase your skills and learn your business completely. Become a source of reference: be visible, attend meetings and company or community socials. For info: Angela Brown, Words of Wellness, PO Box 49266, Charlotte, NC 28277. Phone: (704) 849-2900. Fax: (704) 845-3060. E-mail: Angela@WordsofWellness.com. Web: www.WordsofWellness.com.

REBUILD YOUR LIFE MONTH. June 1–30. This is an opportunity for adults neglected and/or abused as children to celebrate their self-worth and discover inner power. They can learn to heal their lives and emotional pain by helping others. For info send SASE: Donald Etkes, PhD, 11693 San Vicente Blvd, #491, Los Angeles, CA 90049. Phone: (310) 281-0123.

SAMOA: INDEPENDENCE DAY. June 1. National holiday. Commemorates independence from New Zealand in 1962. The former Western Samoa changed its name in 1997.

***SGT PEPPER'S LONELY HEARTS CLUB BAND* RELEASED: ANNIVERSARY.** June 1, 1967. After 700 hours of studio work, The Beatles released what many consider one of the greatest rock albums of the 20th century. No singles were released, but the album included such popular tracks as "Lucy in the Sky with Diamonds," "With a Little Help from My Friends," "When I'm Sixty-Four" and "Day in the Life."

SHAVUOT BEGINS AT SUNDOWN. June 1. Jewish Pentecost. See also: "Shavuot" (June 2).

SPORTS AMERICA KIDS MONTH. June 1–30. To encourage the health and well-being of all America's children. Physical fitness and healthy thinking, through the efforts of teamwork with individual self-esteem, can help America's children to appreciate the gift of life and the value of respecting the lives of others. A time for adults and kids to embrace the wonderful outdoors and the benefits of healthy living with physical fitness. For info: Judith Natale, NCAC America-USA, PO Box 493703, Redding, CA 96049-3703. E-mail: childaware@aol.com.

June 2006	S	M	T	W	T	F	S
					1	2	3
	4	5	6	7	8	9	10
	11	12	13	14	15	16	17
	18	19	20	21	22	23	24
	25	26	27	28	29	30	

STEPPARENTS' WEEK. June 1–7. The statistics on family life in the '90s are: 50 percent of all marriages end in divorce and 67 percent of all second marriages end in divorce. This week is in recognition of those courageous souls who flaunt convention and plow forward despite the odds. Annually, the first week in June. [©1996] To alleviate the escalating costs of Eventological® Literature a charge of $10 must be assessed for each request. Checks are to be made payable to: Adrienne Sioux Koopersmith, 1437 W Rosemont, #1W, Chicago, IL 60660-1319. E-mail: askoopersmith@hotmail.com.

STUDENT SAFETY MONTH. June 1–30. Heightening the awareness of safety and making sound decisions following graduations, parties, senior proms and other special events. Encourages young people everywhere not to drink and drive and to use good judgment while celebrating throughout the month. For info: Carole Copeland Thomas, 400 W Cummings Pk, Ste 1725-154, Woburn, MA 01801. Phone: (508) 947-5755 or (800) 801-6599. Fax: (508) 947-3903. E-mail: carole@TellCarole.com. Web: www.TellCarole.com.

SUPERMAN DEBUTS: ANNIVERSARY. June 1, 1938. Ohio teenagers Joe Shuster and Jerry Siegel wowed the comic book world with a new kind of pulp hero: Superman. Superman, a refugee from the planet Krypton with super powers, appeared in the June issue of *Action Comics* #1 (issues probably hit the newsstands in late May of 1938). Now a pop culture icon, Superman was then a smash hit who ushered in many more fantastical superheroes. See also: "Batman Debuts: Anniversary" (May 1).

TENNESSEE: ADMISSION DAY: ANNIVERSARY. June 1. Became 16th state in 1796. Observed as a holiday in Tennessee.

VISION RESEARCH MONTH. June 1–30. While millions of Americans benefit from vision research, many eye diseases have no effective treatments or cures. An overview of vision research successes and the urgent need for future studies will be offered. For info: Prevent Blindness America®, 211 W Wacker Dr, Ste 1700, Chicago, IL 60606. Phone: (800) 331-2020. E-mail: info@preventblindness.org. Web: www.preventblindness.org.

YOUNG, BRIGHAM: BIRTH ANNIVERSARY. June 1, 1801. Mormon church leader born at Whittingham, VT. Known as "the American Moses," having led thousands of religious followers across 1,000 miles of wilderness to settle more than 300 towns in the West. He died at Salt Lake City, UT, Aug 29, 1877, and was survived by 17 wives and 47 children. Utah observes, as a state holiday, the anniversary of his entrance into the Salt Lake Valley, July 24, 1847.

BIRTHDAYS TODAY

Rene Auberjonois, 66, actor (*M*A*S*H*, "Benson"; stage: *Coco* [Tony Award]), born New York, NY, June 1, 1940.

James Hadley Billington, 77, Librarian of Congress, born Bryn Mawr, PA, June 1, 1929.

Lisa Hartman Black, 50, actress ("Tabitha," "Knots Landing"), born Houston, TX, June 1, 1956.

Pat Boone, 72, singer, actor (*State Fair*), author, born Jacksonville, FL, June 1, 1934.

Pat Corley, 76, actor ("Bay City Blues," "Murphy Brown"), born Dallas, TX, June 1, 1930.

Mark Curry, 42, comedian, actor ("Hangin' with Mr Cooper"), born Oakland, CA, June 1, 1964.

Morgan Freeman, 69, stage and film actor (Oscar for *Million Dollar Baby, Driving Miss Daisy*), born Memphis, TN, June 1, 1937.

Andy Griffith, 80, actor ("Matlock," "The Andy Griffith Show"), born Mount Airy, NC, June 1, 1926.

Justine Henin-Hardenne, 24, tennis player, born Liege, Belgium, June 1, 1982.

Alexi Lalas, 36, soccer player, born Detroit, MI, June 1, 1970.

Alanis Morissette, 32, singer, born Ottawa, ON, Canada, June 1, 1974.

Jonathan Pryce, 59, actor (*The Age of Innocence, Glengarry Glen Ross*; stage: *Miss Saigon*; Tony Awards for *Comedians* and *Hamlet*), born Holywell, North Wales, June 1, 1947.

Frederica von Stade, 61, opera mezzo-soprano, born Somerville, NJ, June 1, 1945.

Ron Wood, 59, musician (guitarist with the Rolling Stones), born London, England, June 1, 1947.

Edward Woodward, 76, actor, singer ("The Equalizer," *Wicker Man, Breaker Morant*), born Croydon, England, June 1, 1930.

JUNE 2 — FRIDAY

Day 153 — 212 Remaining

BAHAMAS: LABOR DAY. June 2. Public holiday. First Friday in June celebrated with parades, displays and picnics.

BELGIUM: PROCESSION OF THE GOLDEN CHARIOT. June 2. Mons. Horse-drawn coach carrying a reliquary of St. Waudru circles the town of Mons. Procession commemorates delivery of Mons from the plague in 1349. In the town square, in the afternoon, St. George fights the dragon.

BHUTAN: CORONATION DAY. June 2. National holiday. Commemorates the crowning of the fourth king in 1974.

BUFFALO DAYS CELEBRATION (WITH BUFFALO CHIP THROWING). June 2–4. Luverne, MN. Parade, Arts in the Park, auto shows, free barbecued buffalo burgers (while they last) and unique buffalo chip throwing contest. Annually, the first weekend in June. Est attendance: 12,000. For info: Dave Smith, Exec Dir, Luverne Area Chamber of Commerce, 211 E Main, Luverne, MN 56156. Phone/fax: (507) 283-4061. E-mail: luvernechamber@iw.net. Web: www.luvernemn.com.

BULGARIA: HRISTO BOTEV DAY. June 2. Poet and national hero Hristo Botev fell fighting Turks, 1876.

CHICKEN AND EGG FESTIVAL. June 2–3. Prescott, AR. Two days of athletic events, shows and entertainment for the entire family. Come and watch our famous Cackling and Crowing contest in southwest Arkansas's friendliest city. Other activities include: 5k run and walk, tennis tournament, softball, weight lifting, antique car show, Little Miss Hen and Little Mr Rooster Beauty Pageants and much more. Est attendance: 2,000. For info: Mary Godwin, PO Box 307, Prescott, AR 71857. Phone: (870) 887-2101. Fax: (870) 887-5317. E-mail: mgodwin@iocc.com. Web: partnership.pcfa.org/.

ENGLAND: ENGLISH RIVIERA DANCE FESTIVAL. June 2–10. Torquay, Devon. Demonstrations by world champions and participatory events including Modern, Ballroom, Disco and Latin American dance styles. Est attendance: 2,000. For info: Philip Wylie, 73 Hoylake Crescent, Ickenham, Middlesex, England UB10 8JQ. Phone: (44) (1895) 632-143. Fax: (44) (1895) 635-684. E-mail: holidayanddance@hotmail.com. Web: www.dancesport.co.uk/wylie.

FARMINGTON COUNTRY DAYS. June 2–4. Farmington, MO. Three-day event featuring amusement rides, a free "oldies" concert and a Nashville country star concert, craft show and lots more fun for the whole family. Est attendance: 30,000. For info: Farmington Chamber of Commerce, PO Box 191, Farmington, MO 63640. Phone: (573) 756-3615. Fax: (573) 756-1003. E-mail: ursulak@farmingtonmo.org.

GREAT WISCONSIN CHEESE FESTIVAL. June 2–4. Little Chute, WI. Festival features cheese breakfast, parade, cheese tasting, cheese-carving demo and cheesecake contest. Est attendance: 10,000. For info: Great Wisconsin Cheese Festival, 1940 Buchanan St, Little Chute, WI 54140-1414. Phone: (920) 788-7390. Fax: (920) 788-7820.

HARVARD MILK DAYS™ FESTIVAL. June 2–4. Harvard, IL. This salute to the dairy farmer includes a parade, evening entertainment, arts and crafts fair, Market Place, milk-drinking contest, farm tours, antique farm tractor display, carnival, fireworks, prince and princess contest, 2-mile milk run, 2-mile milk walk, 10k milk run, cattle show, talent show, hot-air balloon launch, helicopter rides and wee farm. Est attendance: 125,000. For info: Harvard Milk Days, Inc, 201 W Front St, PO Box 325, Harvard, IL 60033. Phone: (815) 943-4614. Fax: (815) 943-7404. E-mail: info@milkdays.com. Web: www.milkdays.com.

I LOVE MY DENTIST DAY. June 2. Celebrating going to the dentist to get and keep a happy, healthy smile. Annually, the first Friday in June. For info: Nick Nichols, 6130 W Flamingo Rd, Ste 117, Las Vegas, NV 89103. Phone: (702) 227-5877. Fax: (775) 307-3948. E-mail: info@ilovemydentist.com. Web: www.ilovemydentist.com.

IDAHO SHAKESPEARE FESTIVAL. June 2–Sept 30. Boise, ID. Idaho's renowned professional repertory theater presents a full summer season of The Bard, plus other classical and contemporary playwrights, in its outdoor amphitheater along the Boise River. Join us for our 30th anniversary season. Est attendance: 54,000. For info: Idaho Shakespeare Festival, PO Box 9365, Boise, ID 83707. Phone: (208) 429-9908. Box Office: (208) 336-9221. Fax: (208) 429-8798. E-mail: info@idahoshakespeare.org. Web: www.idahoshakespeare.org.

ITALY: REPUBLIC DAY. June 2. National holiday. Commemorates 1946 referendum in which republic status was selected instead of return to monarchy.

MAINE LAW: ANNIVERSARY. June 2, 1851. America's first statewide statute prohibiting the sale of alcoholic beverages was enacted in the state of Maine. The following Independence Day the mayor of Bangor showed his support of the new law by smashing 10 kegs of confiscated booze.

MARQUIS DE SADE: BIRTH ANNIVERSARY. June 2, 1740. Donatien-Alphonse-François, Comte de Sade, was born at Paris, France. French military man, governor-general and author, who spent much of his life in prison because of his acts of cruelty and violence, outrageous behavior and debauchery. The word *sadism* was created from his name to describe gratification in inflicting pain. He died near Paris, at the Charenton lunatic asylum, Dec 2, 1814.

MUSIC IN THE PARK. June 2–Aug 30. Anchorage, AK. An outdoor summer concert series, free to the public. Every Wednesday and Friday from noon to 1 PM. Live, cross-generational bands perform. This is a fun-for-all event, with a tremendous following! For info: Anchorage Downtown Partnership, Ltd, 245 W 5th St, Anchorage, AK 99501. Phone: (907) 279-5650. Fax: (907) 279-5651. Web: www.anchoragedowntown.org.

NATIONAL BUBBA DAY. June 2. Comedian T. Bubba Bechtol has created a holiday for Bubbas everywhere. Annually, June 2. For info: T. Bubba Bechtol, 339 Panferio Dr, Pensacola Beach, FL 32561. Phone: (850) 932-3162. E-mail: tbubba@tbubba.com. Web: www.tbubba.com.

NATIONAL LEAVE THE OFFICE EARLIER DAY. June 2. Employees commit to working productively all day, so they can get their work done, leave the office earlier and get home to their families. Annually, June 2. For info: John Stack, The Productivity Pro, 9948 S Cottoncreek Dr, Highlands Ranch, CO 80130. Phone: (303) 471-7401. Fax: (303) 471-4702. E-mail: Laura@The ProductivityPro.com. Web: www.TheProductivityPro.com.

SAINT PIUS X: BIRTH ANNIVERSARY. June 2, 1835. Giuseppe Melchiorre Sarto, 257th pope of the Roman Catholic Church, born at Riese, Italy. Elected pope Aug 4, 1903. Died Aug 20, 1914, at Rome. Canonized May 29, 1954.

SALEM WITCH TRIALS BEGIN: ANNIVERSARY. June 2, 1692. As the village of Salem was gripped by terror of witches, Massachusetts Bay Colony governor Sir William Phips ordered a special court created on May 27, 1692, to expedite judgment of the more than 150 people accused of witchcraft. Unpopular resident Bridget Bishop, first accused in April, was the first of the jailed brought to trial on June 2. At her April examination her accusers—teenaged girls—had collapsed in fits as she appeared, but Bishop adamantly denied the charges: "I am no witch—I know not what a witch is." She was convicted June 2 and hung June 10. See also: "Salem Witch Hysteria Begins: Anniversary" (Mar 1).

SHAVUOT or FEAST OF WEEKS. June 2–3. Jewish Pentecost holy days. Hebrew dates, Sivan 6–7, 5766. Celebrates giving of Torah (the Law) to Moses on Mount Sinai. Began at sundown June 1.

SITKA SUMMER MUSIC FESTIVAL. June 2–23. (Tuesdays, Fridays and Saturdays) Sitka, AK. Sitka hosts a highly acclaimed chamber music festival that attracts performers and spectators from around the world. Est attendance: 5,000. For info: Sitka Summer Music Festival, PO Box 201988, Anchorage, AK 99520-1988. Phone: (907) 277-4852. Fax: (907) 277-4842. E-mail: director@sitkamusicfestival.org. Web: www.sitkamusicfestival.org.

SUMMER FARM TOY SHOW. June 2–4. Beckman HS and National Farm Toy Museum, Dyersville, IA. Features tractor parade, tractor pull, citywide garage sales, antique tractors and farm machinery and indoor/outdoor farm toy show. Annually, the first full weekend in June. Est attendance: 5,000. For info: National Farm Toy Museum, 1100 16th Ave Ct SE, Dyersville, IA 52040. Phone: (563) 875-2727. Fax: (563) 875-8391. E-mail: farmtoys@dyersville.com. Web: www.nationalfarmtoymuseum.com.

TELLURIDE BALLOON FESTIVAL. June 2–4. Town Park, Telluride, CO. 23rd annual. A small balloon event with free rides for volunteers; Main Street GLO on Saturday evening. Annually, the first full weekend in June. Est attendance: 2,000. For info: Marilyn Branch, PO Box 1295, Telluride, CO 81435. Phone: (970) 708-2202. Fax: (970) 728-4769. E-mail: balloons@telluridecolorado.net.

UNITED KINGDOM: CORONATION DAY: ANNIVERSARY. June 2. Commemorates the crowning of Queen Elizabeth II in 1953.

US INTERNATIONAL FILM AND VIDEO FESTIVAL AWARDS PRESENTATIONS AND SCREENINGS. June 2. Los Angeles, CA. World's largest awards competition honoring business, television, documentary, informational and industrial productions. Entry deadline is Mar 1. Founded in 1968. Est attendance: 200. For info: Lee W. Gluckman, Jr, Chairman, US Intl Film and Video Festival Awards, 713 S Pacific Coast Hwy, Ste A, Redondo Beach, CA 90277-4233. Phone: (310) 540-0959. Fax: (310) 316-8905. E-mail: filmfestinfo@filmfestawards.com. Web: www.filmfestawards.com.

★ ★ ★

	S	M	T	W	T	F	S
June					1	2	3
2006	4	5	6	7	8	9	10
	11	12	13	14	15	16	17
	18	19	20	21	22	23	24
	25	26	27	28	29	30	

WEISSMULLER, JOHNNY: BIRTH ANNIVERSARY. June 2, 1904. Peter John (Johnny) Weissmuller, actor and Olympic gold medal swimmer, born at Windber, PA. Weissmuller won three gold medals at the 1924 Olympics and two more at the 1928 games. He set 24 world records and in 1950 was voted the best swimmer of the first half of the 20th century. After retiring from amateur competition, he appeared as Tarzan in a dozen movies and as "Jungle Jim" in the movies and on television. Died at Acapulco, Mexico, Jan 20, 1984.

YELL "FUDGE" AT THE COBRAS IN NORTH AMERICA DAY. June 2. Anywhere north of the Panama Canal. In order to keep poisonous cobra snakes out of North America, all citizens are asked to go outdoors at noon, local time, and yell "Fudge." Fudge makes cobras gag and the mere mention of it makes them skedaddle. Annually, June 2. [©2003 by WH.] For info: Thomas & Ruth Roy, Wellcat Holidays, 2418 Long Ln, Lebanon, PA 17046. Phone: (717) 279-0184. E-mail: info@wellcat.com. Web: www.wellcat.com.

BIRTHDAYS TODAY

Diana Canova, 53, actress ("Soap," "I'm a Big Girl Now"), born West Palm Beach, FL, June 2, 1953.

Dana Carvey, 51, comedian, actor (*Wayne's World*, "Saturday Night Live"), born Missoula, MT, June 2, 1955.

Gary Grimes, 51, actor (*Summer of '42, Class of '44*), born San Francisco, CA, June 2, 1955.

Charles Haid, 63, actor ("Hill Street Blues," "Delvecchio"), producer, born San Francisco, CA, June 2, 1943.

Marvin Hamlisch, 62, composer (Oscars for *The Sting, The Way We Were*; Tony for *A Chorus Line*), born New York, NY, June 2, 1944.

Dennis Haysbert, 52, actor ("24," *Waiting to Exhale, Major League*), born San Mateo, CA, June 2, 1954.

Stacy Keach, Jr, 65, actor (*Conduct Unbecoming*, "Mickey Spillane's Mike Hammer"), born Savannah, GA, June 2, 1941.

Sally Kellerman, 70, actress (*M*A*S*H, Back to School*), born Long Beach, CA, June 2, 1936.

Jerry Mathers, 58, actor ("Leave It to Beaver"), born Sioux City, IA, June 2, 1948.

Milo O'Shea, 80, actor (*The Purple Rose of Cairo*), born Dublin, Ireland, June 2, 1926.

Charlie Watts, 65, musician (drummer with the Rolling Stones), born Islington, England, June 2, 1941.

JUNE 3 — SATURDAY
Day 154 — 211 Remaining

BAKER, JOSEPHINE: 100th BIRTH ANNIVERSARY. June 3, 1906. The sensation of 1920s Paris, Baker was born into poverty at St. Louis, MO. She began working as a dancer at age 16 and went to Paris in 1925, where her semi-nude "danse sauvage," became a hit. She was the first American-born woman to be awarded the Croix de Guerre and the Legion of Honor for her Red Cross work during WWII. Baker performed up until her death on Apr 12, 1975, at Paris, France.

BATTLE OF COLD HARBOR: ANNIVERSARY. June 3, 1864. Although Confederate Gen Robert E. Lee had placed his troops behind considerable breastworks, Union Gen Ulysses S. Grant launched an all-out attack on the Southern army in Virginia. More than 7,000 Federal troops were killed within one-half hour of battle on the first attack. After a second unsuccessful attack, Grant's orders for a third assault were all but ignored. Battlefield tradition held that the first commander who sought a truce in order to tend to the wounded was the loser. Grant refused to admit defeat by seeking such a truce and the wounded were left on the ground for three days following the battle. As a consequence, all but two of the thousands of wounded men died either from their wounds, hunger, thirst or exposure.

CAPITOL HILL PEOPLE'S FAIR. June 3–4. Civic Center Park, Denver, CO. More than 500 arts and crafts and other exhibit booths; live entertainment featuring local talent on five stages. Est attendance: 300,000. For info: Capitol Hill United Neighborhoods, 1490 Lafayette, #104, Denver, CO 80218. Phone: (303) 830-1651. Fax: (303) 830-1782. E-mail: info@peoplesfair.com. Web: www.peoplesfair.com.

CHEER COACH DAY. June 3. Show appreciation for the hard work and dedication of those who coach our cheerleaders. Annually, the first Saturday in June. For info: Lindy Lundy, 59 County Rd 3474, Cleveland, TX 77327. Phone: (281) 399-8357. Fax: (281) 364-1129. E-mail: linda@unitedcheer.com.

CHIMBORAZO DAY. June 3. To bring the shape of the Earth into focus by publicizing the fact that Mount Chimborazo, Ecuador, near the equator, pokes farther out into space than any other mountain on earth, including Mount Everest. (The distance from sea level at the equator to the center of the Earth is 13 miles greater than the radius from sea level at the North Pole. This means that New Orleans is about six miles farther from the center of the Earth than is Lake Itasca at the headwaters of the Mississippi, so the Mississippi flows uphill.) For info: Robert L. Birch, Puns Corps, 3108 Dashiell Rd, Falls Church, VA 22042. Phone: (703) 533-3668.

CONFEDERATE MEMORIAL DAY IN KENTUCKY, LOUISIANA AND TENNESSEE. June 3. Ceremonial holiday on the birthday of Jefferson Davis. Also observed as Jefferson Davis Day in Kentucky and Confederate Decoration Day in Tennessee.

DAVIS, JEFFERSON: BIRTH ANNIVERSARY. June 3, 1808. American statesman, US senator, only president of the Confederate States of America. Imprisoned May 10, 1865–May 13, 1867, but never brought to trial, deprived of rights of citizenship after the Civil War. Davis was born at Todd County, KY, and died at New Orleans, LA, Dec 6, 1889. His citizenship was restored, posthumously, Oct 17, 1978, when President Carter signed an Amnesty Bill. This bill, he said, "officially completes the long process of reconciliation that has reunited our people following the tragic conflict between the states." Davis's birth anniversary is observed in Florida, Kentucky and South Carolina on this day, in Alabama on the first Monday in June and in Mississippi on the last Monday in May. Davis's birth anniversary is observed as Confederate Memorial Day in Tennessee.

DEWHURST, COLLEEN: BIRTH ANNIVERSARY. June 3, 1924. Colleen Dewhurst was born at Quebec, Canada. Her 40-year career as an actress spanned stage, screen and television. After making her Broadway debut in Eugene O'Neill's *Desire Under the Elms* in 1952, she became the actress most associated with O'Neill's works in the later part of the 20th century, also performing in *Long Day's Journey into Night; Mourning Becomes Electra; Ah, Wilderness!* and *A Moon for the Misbegotten,* for which she won her second Tony award. At the time of her death, she was president of Actor's Equity Association, the union for professional actors. She won three Emmy awards. She died Aug 22, 1991, at South Salem, NY.

DO-DAH PARADE. June 3. Kalamazoo, MI. "Salute to Silliness." Since 1981 offbeat entries have included a precision grill team (complete with spatulas) and a herbie curbie brigade. Annually, the first Saturday in June. Sponsored by WKMI/WKFR Radio, www.wkfr.com, and Downtown Kalamazoo, Inc. Est attendance: 40,000. For info: Downtown Kalamazoo Inc, 157 S Kalamazoo Mall, Kalamazoo, MI 49007. Phone: (269) 344-0795. Fax: (269) 344-0898. Web: www.central-city.net.

DREW, CHARLES RICHARD: BIRTH ANNIVERSARY. June 3, 1904. African-American physician who discovered how to store blood plasma and who organized the blood bank system in the US and UK during WWII. Born at Washington, DC, he was killed in an automobile accident near Burlington, NC, Apr 1, 1950.

DUKE OF WINDSOR MARRIAGE: ANNIVERSARY. June 3, 1937. The Duke of Windsor who, as King Edward VIII, had abdicated the British throne on Dec 11, 1936, was married to Mrs Wallis Warfield Simpson of Baltimore, MD, at Monts, France. The couple made their home in France after their marriage and had little contact with the royal family. The Duke died at Paris on May 28, 1972, and was buried near Windsor Castle in England. The Duchess died Apr 24, 1986.

FIRST WOMAN RABBI IN US: ANNIVERSARY. June 3, 1972. Sally Jan Priesand was ordained the first woman rabbi in the US. She became assistant rabbi at the Stephen Wise Free Synagogue, New York City, Aug 1, 1972.

FORT SISSETON HISTORICAL FESTIVAL. June 3–4. Fort Sisseton State Park, Lake City, SD. Fort Sisseton comes alive the first weekend in June every year. See life as it was in 1864 when the fort was established. Cavalry drills, military costume ball, Indian dancing, Dakota Dan's medicine show, wagon train, muzzle-loader shoot, rendezvous, draft-horse pulls, fiddlers, square dancing, melodramas and arts and crafts are popular features of the festival. Est attendance: 35,000. For info: Dave Daberkow, Fort Sisseton State Park, Dept of Game, Fish and Parks, 11545 Northside Dr, Lake City, SD 57247-6142. Phone: (605) 448-5701. Fax: (605) 448-5572. Web: www.state.sd.us/gfp/.

GHOST TOURS. June 3–Nov 25. New Hope, PA. (Saturdays, June–November; Fridays in October, plus Halloween.) Tours meet at 8 PM sharp at Main and Ferry streets. No reservations required. Rain or shine. $9 per person. No tours July 4th weekend or Labor Day weekend. For info: Ghost Tours, PO Box 3354, Warminster, PA 18974. Phone: (215) 343-5564. E-mail: ghstofpa@aol.com.

GINSBERG, ALLEN: BIRTH ANNIVERSARY. June 3, 1926. Poet of the Beat Generation ("Howl"), born Newark, NJ. Died Apr 5, 1997, at New York, NY.

HOBART, GARRET AUGUSTUS: BIRTH ANNIVERSARY. June 3, 1844. 24th vice president of the US (1897–99), born at Long Branch, NJ. Died at Paterson, NJ, Nov 21, 1899.

HOT TIMES DOWNTOWN WILBER CAR AND TRUCK SHOW. June 3. Wilber, NE. Car and truck show, live music, door prizes and cash prizes, evening street dance and more. Shop downtown businesses for "Hot Times" sale prices! For info: Joe Carlson, 224 W 4th, PO Box 707, Wilber, NE 68465. Phone: (402) 821-2021. Fax: (402) 821-3144. E-mail: wilberjoechevy@yahoo.com.

INTERNATIONAL CLOTHESLINE WEEK. June 3–10. The public is encouraged to save energy by hanging clothes to dry instead of using their electric dryer. Annually, the first week in June, Saturday to Saturday. For info: Gary Drisdelle, 153 Glenforest Dr, Thornhill, ON, Canada L4J 8K4. Phone: (416) 805-5580. E-mail: gdrisdelle@rogers.com.

IRELAND: BANK HOLIDAY. June 3. National holiday in the Republic of Ireland.

JACK JOUETT'S RIDE: 225th ANNIVERSARY. June 3, 1781. Jack Jouett made a heroic 45-mile ride on horseback during the night of June 3–4, 1781, to warn Virginia Governor Thomas Jefferson and the legislature that the British were coming. Jouett rode from a tavern in Louisa County to Charlottesville,

VA, in about 6½ hours, arriving at Jefferson's home at dawn on June 4. Lieutenant Colonel Tarleton's British forces raided Charlottesville, but Jouett's warning gave the Americans time to escape. Jouett was born at Albemarle County, VA, Dec 7, 1754, and died at Bath, KY, in 1822 (exact date unknown).

KHOMEINI, AYATOLLAH RUHOLLA: DEATH ANNIVERSARY. June 3, 1989. The Ayatollah Ruholla Khomeini, leader of the Islamic Revolution, lifelong foe of the Shah of Iran, was arrested in 1963 after giving a speech accusing the Shah of seeking to destroy Islam. He was exiled to Turkey in 1964, following which he spent 13 years in Iraq and Paris, where he gained exposure to the world press for his cause. On Jan 16, 1979, the Shah of Iran left the country for a supposed vacation, setting the stage for Khomeini's triumphant return on Jan 31. The monarchy fell on Feb 11, 1979. Khomeini proceeded to reorganize the government based on Islamic principles. On Nov 11, 1979, a group of students loyal to Khomeini occupied the American Embassy in Teheran after the Shah was given admittance to the US for medical treatment, placing the Ayatollah at the center of a diplomatic crisis that consumed the presidency of Jimmy Carter. Khomeini focused attention on the US as the "Great Satan" and blamed many of his country's problems on imperialistic intervention. The anniversary of his death is a national holiday in Iran.

LOVELADIES FAIR. June 3–4 (tentative). Loveladies, NJ. 16th annual profusion of Island and mainland merchants and craftspeople. Sponsored by Long Beach Island Foundation of Arts & Sciences. Est attendance: 1,500. For info: Long Beach Island Foundation of Arts & Sciences, 120 Long Beach Blvd, Loveladies, NJ 08008. Phone: (609) 494-1241. Fax: (609) 494-0662.

MALAYSIA: HEAD OF STATE'S OFFICIAL BIRTHDAY. June 3. National holiday. The first Saturday in June.

MARITIME GIG FESTIVAL. June 3. Gig Harbor, WA. This annual family event begins with the parade route that follows the edge of the beautiful harbor with the marina and view of majestic Mount Rainier. The event is jam-packed with family entertainment, a 5-mile run, crafts and games for children, foods of every description, open markets, live music, arts and fine crafts. Est attendance: 40,000. For info: Mary Graves, Event Coordinator, Maritime Gig Festival, PO Box 2424, Poulsbo, WA 98370. Phone: (360) 779-8018. Fax: (360) 779-8019. E-mail: mmgraves 98370@yahoo.com. Web: www.maritimegig.org.

MIGHTY CASEY HAS STRUCK OUT: ANNIVERSARY. June 3, 1888. The famous comic baseball ballad "Casey at the Bat" was printed in the Sunday *San Francisco Examiner*. Appearing anonymously, it was written by Ernest L. Thayer. Recitation of "Casey at the Bat" became part of the repertoire of actor William DeWolf Hopper. The recitation took 5 minutes and 40 seconds. Hopper claimed to have recited it more than 10,000 times, the first being at Wallack's Theater at New York, NY, in 1888. See also: "Thayer, Ernest Lawrence: Birth Anniversary" (Aug 14).

MISSION SAN CARLOS BORROMEO DE CARMELO: FOUNDING ANNIVERSARY. June 3, 1770. California mission to the Indians founded on this date.

MISSOURI STATE CHAMPIONSHIP RACKING HORSE SHOW. June 3. Stoddard County Fairgrounds, Dexter, MO. At this 29th annual event elegant showmanship by both horse and rider provides an afternoon and evening of spectator pleasure. Annually, the first Saturday in June. Est attendance: 500. For info: Missouri State Championship Racking Horse Show, PO Box 21, Dexter, MO 63841. Phone: (573) 624-7458 or (800) 332-8857. Fax: (573) 624-7459.

		S	**M**	**T**	**W**	**T**	**F**	**S**
June							1	2	3
2006		4	5	6	7	8	9	10
		11	12	13	14	15	16	17
		18	19	20	21	22	23	24
		25	26	27	28	29	30	

MOON PHASE: FIRST QUARTER. June 3. Moon enters First Quarter phase at 7:06 PM, EDT.

NATIONAL TRAILS DAY. June 3. National Trails Day celebrates trails and the volunteers who maintain them. The first Saturday of every June more than 3,000 trail organizations, agencies and businesses across the country host a variety of events including new trail dedications, workshops, educational exhibits, equestrian and mountain bike rides, boat paddling, in-line skating, trail maintenance projects and, as always, hikes on backcountry trails in America's wildlands. For info: American Hiking Society, 1422 Fenwick Ln, Silver Spring, MD 20910. Phone: (301) 565-6704, ext 208. E-mail: ntd@americanhiking.org. Web: www.american hiking.org.

OLD TIME SCHOOL. June 3–July 3. West Riverside Historic Site, Cambridge, MN. Children attend school in a one-room schoolhouse from 1898. They dress in the style of Laura Ingalls Wilder, carry their lunch in a pail, play games and learn lessons from the year 1900, do art projects, give a program for parents and actually have homework. There are five one-week sessions beginning in mid-June. Students in grades 1–8 may apply. $40 fee. Est attendance: 300. For info: Kathy McCully, Dir, Isanti County Historical Society, PO Box 525, Cambridge, MN 55008. Phone: (763) 689-4229. Fax: (763) 552-0740. E-mail: ichs@nsa tel.net.

PEDDLER'S VILLAGE FINE ART & CONTEMPORARY CRAFTS SHOW. June 3–4. Juried competition of paintings, prints, photography and more created by fine artists, plus contemporary crafts. Hands-on art activities for children. Shops offer various in-store exhibits and art-related events. Live music, face painting and balloons. Free admission. Est attendance: 12,000. For info: Peddler's Village, Routes 202 & 263, Lahaska, PA 18931. Phone: (215) 794-4000. Fax: (215) 794-4001. Web: www.peddlersvillage.com.

SMALL CRAFT WEEKEND. June 3–4. Mystic Seaport, Mystic, CT. Small craft enthusiasts gather at the museum with their boats. Traditional small boats of every type sail from docks of Mystic Seaport on the Mystic River. Annually, first weekend in June. Est attendance: 4,000. For info: Mystic Seaport, 75 Greenmanville Ave, Box 6000, Mystic, CT 06355. Phone: (860) 572-5315 or (888) 973-2767. Web: www.mysticseaport.org.

SOUTH JERSEY CANOE AND KAYAK CLASSIC. June 3. Ocean County Park, Rt 88, Lakewood, NJ. Canoe and kayak vendors from around the country set up on the beach to show the public the thrill of water sports. You may test paddle the boats of your choice, talk with company reps and attend a clinic or demo. Manufacturers, clubs, paddling accessories and more. Concessions. Free admission ($5 to test paddle). Rain or shine. Annually, the first Saturday in June. Est attendance: 1,200. For info: Michelle Urban, Coord, Wells Mills County Park, 905 Wells Mills Rd, Waretown, NJ 08758. Phone: (609) 971-3085. Fax: (609) 971-9540. Web: www.co.ocean.nj.us/parks/default.htm.

SPACE MILESTONE: *GEMINI 4* (US). June 3, 1965. James McDivitt and Edward White made 66 orbits of Earth. White took the first space walk by an American and maneuvered 20 minutes outside the capsule.

STRAWBERRY FESTIVAL. June 3. Vaile Mansion, Independence, MO. Outdoor Victorian-type festival featuring strawberry treats, crafts, antiques, children's activities, carriage rides, flea market and entertainment. Annually, first Saturday in June. Est attendance: 900. For info: Stephanie Roush, Tourism Dir, 111 E Maple, Independence, MO 64050. Phone: (816) 325-7111. Fax: (816) 325-7932. Web: www.visitindependence.com.

SUMMER READING CLUB. June 3–July 22. El Paso, TX. Every summer the El Paso Public Library has a summer reading club program. The program is open to all children from birth through eighth grade. Children are required to read/have been read to eight books or eight hours during the program to receive a certificate. The 13 libraries plus Bookmobile feature weekly special programs in the libraries for the children. For info: Laurel Indalecio, El Paso Public Library, 501 N Oregon, El Paso, TX 79901. Phone: (915) 543-5470. Fax: (915) 543-5410. E-mail: indaleciol@elpasotexas.gov. Web: www.elpasolibrary.org.

SWAP MEET AND TRACTOR SHOW. June 3–4. Washington, KS. The celebration includes swap meet, flea market, antique tractor and parts auction, antique tractor show, vehicle parade, car races, entertainment, children's games, historic demonstrators, crafts, etc. Est attendance: 5,000. For info: Washington County Travel and Tourism, Courthouse, 214 C St, Washington, KS 66968. Phone: (785) 325-2116. Fax: (785) 325-2830. E-mail: washcott@washingtonks.net.

TOPPENISH MURAL SOCIETY'S "MURAL-IN-A-DAY." June 3. Toppenish, WA. 12 professional artists paint a complete, historically authentic mural in eight hours. Starting at 9 AM they work until finished, usually until 4 PM. Accompanied by an arts and crafts show and a food fair. Annually, the first Saturday in June. Est attendance: 1,200. For info: Toppenish Mural Society, PO Box 1172, Toppenish, WA 98948. Phone: (509) 865-6516. E-mail: chamber@toppenish.net. Web: www.toppenish.net.

ZOOT SUIT RIOTS: ANNIVERSARY. June 3–8, 1943. In Los Angeles, CA, simmering racial unease exploded as 200 white sailors stormed into East LA and began beating Hispanics in response to an earlier altercation between a few sailors and some street kids. The sailors targeted Zoot Suiters—youths outfitted in the defiant, exaggerated suit of their community (long jackets, wide trousers and ankle-length watch chains). The rioting grew as police either stood by or arrested the victims. The media, antagonistic to the Hispanic community, spurred on the violence with sensational headlines. Finally, military brass declared Los Angeles off-limits to its personnel and the LA City Council banned zoot suits. There were no deaths, but the injuries and mayhem were such that a special state committee was convened and First Lady Eleanor Roosevelt fretted in her newspaper column that the riots were symptomatic of a problem with deep roots.

BIRTHDAYS TODAY

Chuck Barris, 77, TV producer ("Dating Game," "Newlywed Game," "Gong Show"), born Philadelphia, PA, June 3, 1929.

Tony Curtis, 81, actor (*Some Like It Hot, The Boston Strangler, The Defiant Ones*), born Bernard Schwartz at New York, NY, June 3, 1925.

Jan-Michael Gambill, 29, tennis player, born Spokane, WA, June 3, 1977.

Charles Hart, 45, lyricist, composer, born London, England, June 3, 1961.

Hale S. Irwin, 61, golfer, born Joplin, MO, June 3, 1945.

Larry McMurtry, 70, author (*Terms of Endearment, Lonesome Dove, The Last Picture Show*), born Wichita Falls, TX, June 3, 1936.

Scott Valentine, 48, actor ("Family Ties"), born Saratoga Springs, NY, June 3, 1958.

Deniece Williams, 55, singer ("Free," "It's Gonna Take a Miracle"), born Gary, IN, June 3, 1951.

JUNE 4 — SUNDAY
Day 155 — 210 Remaining

BATTLE OF MIDWAY: ANNIVERSARY. June 4–6, 1942. A Japanese task force attempted to capture Midway Island in the Central Pacific. American bombers from Midway and from two nearby aircraft carriers sent the Japanese into retreat, having lost four carriers, two large cruisers and three destroyers. Midway was one of the most decisive naval battles of WWII. Japan never regained its margin in carrier strength and the Central Pacific was made safe for American troops.

BLACK SINGLE PARENTS' WEEK. June 4–10. This week is to honor all the black single parents who have successfully raised their sons and daughters despite poor schools, crime and drug-infested neighborhoods to be responsible, self-sufficient (and sometimes famous) citizens. For info: Will Barnes, Exec Dir, The Black Single Parents' Network, 7732 S Cottage Grove, #431, Chicago, IL 60619. Phone: (773) 933-1061. Fax: (773) 933-1059. E-mail: willbar@netzero.net.

"CAVALCADE OF STARS" TV PREMIERE: ANNIVERSARY. June 4, 1949. Although the Dumont network was not very successful, it was around long enough to launch this popular show. The one-hour variety show was hosted by Jack Carter (1949–50), Jackie Gleason (1950–52) and Larry Storch (in the summer of 1952). It also served as a showcase for the soon-to-be immortal "The Honeymooners" with Gleason and Pert Kelton starring as the Kramdens.

CHILDREN'S AWARENESS MEMORIAL DAY. June 4. A day set aside each year to remember all of America's children who have died from violence. A day to bring flowers to the gravesite, have memorial services, spend time with or write a letter to a grieving parent or grandparent. A day to mourn and reach out with healing hands of love to those in need of support. Annually, the first Sunday in June. For info: Judith Natale, NCAC America-USA, PO Box 493703, Redding, CA 96049-3703. E-mail: childaware@aol.com.

CHINA: TIANANMEN SQUARE MASSACRE: ANNIVERSARY. June 4, 1989. After almost a month and a half of student demonstrations for democracy, the Chinese government ordered its troops to open fire on the unarmed protestors at Tiananmen Square at Beijing. The demonstrations began Apr 18 as several thousand students marched to mourn the death of Hu Yaobang, a proreform leader within the Chinese government. A ban was imposed on such demonstrations; Apr 22, 100,000 gathered in Tiananmen Square in defiance of the ban. On May 13, 2,000 of the students began a hunger strike, and on May 20 the government imposed martial law and began to bring in troops. On June 2 the demonstrators turned back an advance of unarmed troops in the first clash with the People's Army. Under the cover of darkness, early June 4, troops opened fire on the assembled crowds and armored personnel carriers rolled into the square crushing many of the students as they lay sleeping in their tents. Although the government claimed that few died in the attack, estimates range from several hundred to several thousand casualties. In the following months thousands of demonstrators were rounded up and jailed.

FINLAND: FLAG DAY. June 4. Finland's armed forces honor the June 4, 1867, birth anniversary of Carl Gustaf Mannerheim.

FIRST FREE FLIGHT BY A WOMAN: ANNIVERSARY. June 4, 1784. Marie Thible, of Lyons, France, accompanied by a pilot (Monsieur Fleurant), became the first woman in history to fly in a free balloon. She drifted across Lyons in a balloon named *Le Gustave* (for King Gustav III of Sweden, who was watching the ascent). The balloon reached a height of 8,500 feet in a flight that lasted about 45 minutes. The event occurred one day short of a year after the first flight in history by a man. See also: "First Balloon Flight: Anniversary" (June 5).

GEORGE III: BIRTH ANNIVERSARY. June 4, 1738. The English king against whom the American Revolution was directed.

Born at London, England, died Jan 29, 1820, at Windsor Castle, near London.

GERMANFEST. June 4–11. Fort Wayne, IN. A celebration of German heritage with folk music, folk dancing, beer tents, German food, beer and wine tastings, Männerchor (men's choir) singing, Gottesdienste (masses), classical organ music, Family Fest, German films, lectures and demonstrations. Est attendance: 80,000. For info: Germanfest Committee, PO Box 10971, Fort Wayne, IN 46855. Phone: (800) 767-7752. Web: www.germanfest.org.

GHANA: REVOLUTION DAY. June 4. National holiday.

INTERNATIONAL CARILLON FESTIVAL. June 4–11. Springfield, IL. A week of recitals by the world's best carillonneurs on Washington Park's carillon of 67 bronze bells. Since it began in 1961, this has become the world's best-known carillon festival. Annually, the first Sunday through the second Sunday in June. Est attendance: 25,000. For info: Karl Keldermans, Springfield Park District, 2500 S 11th St, Springfield, IL 62703. Phone: (217) 753-6219. E-mail: KKRees@Carillon-Rees.org.

ITALY: GIOCO DEL PONTE. June 4. Pisa. The first Sunday in June is set aside for the Battle of the Bridge, a medieval parade and a contest for possession of the bridge.

JAPAN: DAY OF THE RICE GOD. June 4. Chiyoda. Annual rice-transplanting festival observed on first Sunday in June. Centuries-old rural folk ritual revived in 1930s and celebrated with colorful costumes, parades, music, dancing and prayers to the Shinto rice god Wbai-sama.

NATIONAL CANCER SURVIVORS DAY. June 4. More than 700 communities nationwide honor survivors who are living with and beyond cancer. The 19th annual celebration of life. Annually, the first Sunday in June. For info: Natl Cancer Survivors Day Foundation, PO Box 682285, Franklin, TN 37068-2285. Phone: (615) 794-3006. Fax: (615) 794-0179. E-mail: info@ncsdf.org. Web: www.ncsdf.org.

NATIONAL HEADACHE AWARENESS WEEK. June 4–10. Educating the public about the reality and severity of headache pain as a legitimate neuro-biologic disease. Encouraging sufferers to consult with a health care provider for proper diagnosis and treatment, and to let sufferers know that there are new treatments available. For info: Suzanne E Simons, Exec Dir, National Headache Foundation, 820 N Orleans, Ste 217, Chicago, IL 60610-3132. Phone: (312) 274-2651. Fax: (312) 640-9049.

PENTECOST. June 4. The Christian feast of Pentecost commemorates the descent of the Holy Spirit unto the Apostles, 50 days after Easter. Observed on the seventh Sunday after Easter. Recognized since the third century. See also: "Whitsunday" (below).

PULITZER PRIZES FIRST AWARDED: ANNIVERSARY. June 4, 1917. The first Pulitzer Prizes were awarded on this date: for biography, *Julia Ward Howe* by Laura E. Richards and Maude H. Elliott assisted by Florence H. Hall; for history, *With Americans of Past and Present Days* by Jean Jules Jusserand, the French ambassador to the US. Prizes were also awarded for journalistic achievement.

RED CLOUD INDIAN ART SHOW. June 4–Aug 13. Pine Ridge, SD. Encourages Native American artists and gives their artwork exposure to the general public. Juried art show with cash awards. Est attendance: 12,500. For info: Brother C.M. Simon, Red Cloud Indian School, 100 Mission Dr, Pine Ridge, SD 57770. Phone: (605) 867-5491. Fax: (605) 867-1291. E-mail: csimon@redcloudschool.org. Web: www.redcloudschool.org.

	S	M	T	W	T	F	S
June					1	2	3
2006	4	5	6	7	8	9	10
	11	12	13	14	15	16	17
	18	19	20	21	22	23	24
	25	26	27	28	29	30	

ROME LIBERATED: ANNIVERSARY. June 4, 1944. The US 9th Army, commanded by General Mark Clark, entered the southern suburbs of Rome as the last of the German rear guard retreated from Mussolini's former capital. Fearful of a last-ditch effort by the Germans to hold the city, the populace remained behind closed doors as Clark's forces entered the Eternal City.

TONGA: EMANCIPATION DAY. June 4. National holiday. Commemorates independence from Britain in 1970.

UNITED NATIONS: INTERNATIONAL DAY OF INNOCENT CHILDREN VICTIMS OF AGGRESSION. June 4. On Aug 19, 1982, the General Assembly decided to commemorate June 4 of each year as a day to call attention to the urgent need to protect the rights of chidren. It reminds people that throughout the world there are many children suffering from different forms of abuse. For info: United Nations, Dept of Public Info, New York, NY 10017. Web: www.un.org.

WHITSUNDAY. June 4. Whitsunday, the seventh Sunday after Easter, is a popular time for baptism. "White Sunday" is named for the white garments formerly worn by the candidates for baptism and occurs at the Christian feast of Pentecost. See also: "Pentecost" (above).

BIRTHDAYS TODAY

Cecilia Bartoli, 40, opera singer (mezzo-soprano), born Rome, Italy, June 4, 1966.

Keith David, 52, actor (*Platoon, Bird*), born New York, NY, June 4, 1954.

Eldra DeBarge, 45, singer, musician, lead singer (DeBarge), born Grand Rapids, MI, June 4, 1961.

Bruce Dern, 70, actor (*Coming Home, The Burbs*), born Chicago, IL, June 4, 1936.

Freddy Fender, 69, singer/songwriter ("Before the Next Teardrop Falls," "Wasted Days and Wasted Nights"), born Baldemar Huerta at San Benito, TX, June 4, 1937.

Bettina Gregory, 60, journalist, born New York, NY, June 4, 1946.

Andrea Jaeger, 41, former tennis player, born Chicago, IL, June 4, 1965.

Angelina Jolie, 31, actress (Oscar for *Girl, Interrupted*; *Gia*; *Lara Croft: Tomb Raider*), born Los Angeles, CA, June 4, 1975.

Linda Lingle, 53, Governor of Hawaii (R), born St. Louis, MO, June 4, 1953.

Michelle Phillips, 61, singer (with The Mamas and the Papas), actress ("Knots Landing"), born Long Beach, CA, June 4, 1945.

Parker Stevenson, 53, actor ("Falcon Crest," "Baywatch," *Lifeguard*), born Philadelphia, PA, June 4, 1953.

Dennis Weaver, 82, actor ("Gunsmoke," "McCloud"), born Joplin, MO, June 4, 1924.

Dr. Ruth Westheimer, 77, TV, radio host for shows on sexual relationships, born Frankfurt, Germany, June 4, 1929.

Scott Wolf, 38, actor ("Party of Five," *The Evening Star*), born Boston, MA, June 4, 1968.

Noah Wyle, 35, actor (*A Few Good Men*, "ER"), born Hollywood, CA, June 4, 1971.

JUNE 5 — MONDAY
Day 156 — 209 Remaining

AIDS FIRST NOTED: 25th ANNIVERSARY. June 5, 1981. The Centers for Disease Control first described a new illness striking gay men in a newsletter on June 5, 1981. On July 27, 1982, Acquired Immune Deficiency Syndrome was adopted as the official name for the new disease by the CDC. The virus that causes AIDS was identified in 1983 and in May 1985 was named Human Immunodeficiency Virus (HIV) by the International Committee on the Taxonomy of Viruses. The first person killed by this disease in the developed world died in 1959. More than 524,000 Americans have died of AIDS. Worldwide, more than 22 million people have died of AIDS. About 40 million people worldwide are living with HIV/AIDS.

AMERICAN BAHA'I COMMUNITY: ANNIVERSARY. June 5, 1894. The first formal classes on the Baha'i were held at Chicago, IL.

APPLE II COMPUTER RELEASED: ANNIVERSARY. June 5, 1977. The Apple II computer, with 4K of memory, went on sale for $1,298. Its predecessor, the Apple I, was sold largely to electronic hobbyists the previous year. Apple released the Macintosh computer Jan 24, 1984.

BOYD, WILLIAM: BIRTH ANNIVERSARY. June 5, 1895. Born at Hendrysburg, OH, Boyd went to Hollywood in 1919 and got a job as a film extra. In 1935 he got the role of Hopalong Cassidy in a series of popular westerns. He made 66 of these films between 1935 and 1948. Some of them were edited and shown on television; Boyd then made some episodes especially for TV. Died at Hollywood, CA, Sept 12, 1972. See also: "Hopalong Cassidy TV Premiere" (June 24).

DENMARK: CONSTITUTION DAY. June 5. National holiday. Commemorates Denmark's becoming a constitutional monarchy in 1849 and the new constitution adopted in 1953.

ENGLAND: DICING FOR BIBLES. June 5. An old Whitmonday ceremony at All Saints Church, St. Ives, Huntingdonshire. A bequest (in 1675) with the intent of providing Bibles for poor children of the parish required winning them at a dice game played in the church. In recent years the dicing has been moved from the altar to a "more suitable" place. Six Bibles are given on Whitmonday each year.

FIRST BALLOON FLIGHT: ANNIVERSARY. June 5, 1783. The first public demonstration of a hot-air balloon flight took place at Annonay, France, where brothers Joseph and Jacques Montgolfier succeeded in launching the 33-foot-diameter *globe aerostatique* that they had invented. The unmanned balloon rose an estimated 1,500 feet and traveled, wind-borne, about 7,500 feet before landing after a 10-minute flight—the first sustained flight of any object achieved by man.

IRAN: FIFTEENTH OF KHORDAD. June 5. National holiday. Commemorates the deaths of Islamic clerics in a clash with the shah's forces in 1963.

KENNEDY, ROBERT F.: ASSASSINATION ANNIVERSARY. June 5, 1968. Senator Kennedy was shot while campaigning for the Democratic presidential nomination at Los Angeles, CA; he died the following day. Sirhan Sirhan was convicted of his murder.

KEYNES, JOHN MAYNARD: BIRTH ANNIVERSARY. June 5, 1883. British economist born at Cambridge, England. Author of *Treatise on Money* and *The General Theory of Employment, Interest and Money* that focused on "expansionist" economic policy. Died at Firle, England, Apr 21, 1946.

SCARRY, RICHARD McCLURE: BIRTH ANNIVERSARY. June 5, 1919. Author and illustrator of children's books was born at Boston, MA. Two widely known books of the more than 250 Scarry authored are *Richard Scarry's Best Word Book Ever* (1965) and *Richard Scarry's Please & Thank You* (1973). The pages are crowded with small animal characters who live like humans. More than 100 million copies of his books have sold worldwide. Died Apr 30, 1994, at Gstaad, Switzerland.

SHUTTLE CAMP®. June 5–Aug 4. New Mexico Museum of Space History, Alamogordo, NM. Annual series of weeklong residential and day space science camps. Rocket-building classes, field trips and astronomy classes. Est attendance: 750. For info: Shuttle Camp ®, New Mexico Museum of Space History, PO Box 5430, Alamogordo, NM 88311-0533. Phone: (877) 333-6589. Fax: (505) 437-7722. E-mail: LTookey@dca.state.nm.us. Web: www.spacefame.org/camp.html.

SMITH, ADAM: BIRTH ANNIVERSARY. June 5, 1723 (OS). Scottish economist and philosopher, author of *An Enquiry into the Nature and Causes of the Wealth of Nations* (published in 1776), born at Kirkaldy, Fifeshire, Scotland. Died at Edinburgh, Scotland, July 17, 1790. "Consumption," he wrote, "is the sole end and purpose of production; and the interest of the producer ought to be attended to only so far as it may be necessary for promoting that of the consumer."

SPACE MILESTONE: *SOYUZ T-2* (USSR). June 5, 1980. Launched on this date, cosmonauts Yuri Malyshev and Vladimir Aksenov docked at *Salyut 6* on June 6 and returned to Earth June 9. First piloted flight of new T (Transport) spacecraft.

UNITED NATIONS: WORLD ENVIRONMENT DAY. June 5. Observed annually June 5, the anniversary of the opening of the UN Conference on the Human Environment held in Stockholm in 1972, which led to establishment of UN Environment Programme, based in Nairobi. The General Assembly has urged marking the day with activities reaffirming concern for the preservation and enhancement of the environment. For info: United Nations, Dept of Public Info, New York, NY 10017. Web: www.un.org.

UPPERVILLE COLT AND HORSE SHOW. June 5–11. A weeklong "AA-rated" horse show involving hundreds of horse and rider combinations from 8- to 10-year-old children in the pony divisions to leading Olympic and World Cup riders and horses in the Hunter, Jumper and Grand Prix divisions. Sunday's highlight is the prestigious $100,000 Budweiser/Upperville Jumper Classic sponsored by Budweiser. Est attendance: 10,000. For info: Tommy L. Jones, Upperville Colt and Horse Show, PO Box 317, The Plains, VA 20198. Phone: (540) 253-5760. Fax: (540) 253-5761. E-mail: uchs@crosslink.net. Web: www.upperville.com.

WHITMONDAY. June 5. The day after Whitsunday is observed as a public holiday in some countries.

BIRTHDAYS TODAY

Chad Allen, 32, actor ("Dr. Quinn, Medicine Woman"), cartoon voice (Charlie Brown), born Cerritos, CA, June 5, 1974.
Margaret Drabble, 67, British novelist (*The Gates of Ivory*), born Sheffield, Yorkshire, England, June 5, 1939.
Ken Follett, 57, British novelist (*The Eye of the Needle*), born Wales, UK, June 5, 1949.
Brian McKnight, 37, singer, born Buffalo, NY, June 5, 1969.
Bill Moyers, 72, journalist ("Bill Moyers' Journal"), born Hugo, OK, June 5, 1934.
Mark Wahlberg, 35, actor (*Boogie Nights*), also known as rapper Marky Mark (Marky Mark and the Funky Bunch, "Good Vibrations"), born Dorchester, MA, June 5, 1971.

JUNE 6 — TUESDAY
Day 157 — 208 Remaining

BONZA BOTTLER DAY™. June 6. To celebrate when the number of the day is the same as the number of the month. Bonza Bottler Day™ is an excuse to have a party at least once a month. For more information, see Jan 1. For info: Gail M. Berger, 14 Fernwood Dr, Taylors, SC 29687. Phone: (864) 609-9874. E-mail: gberger5@aol.com.

D-DAY: ANNIVERSARY. June 6, 1944. In the early-morning hours Allied forces landed in Normandy on the north coast of France. In an operation that took months of planning, a fleet of 2,727 ships of every description converged from British ports from Wales to the North Sea. Operation *Overlord* involved 2,000,000 tons of war materials, including more than 50,000 tanks, armored cars, jeeps, trucks and half-tracks. The US alone sent 1,700,000 fighting men. The Germans believed the invasion would not take place under the adverse weather conditions of this early June day. But as the sun came up the village of Saint Mère Eglise was liberated by American parachutists, and by nightfall the landing of 155,000 Allies attested to the success of D-Day. The long-awaited second front had at last materialized.

FIRST DRIVE-IN MOVIE OPENS: ANNIVERSARY. June 6, 1933. Richard M. Hollingshead, Jr, opened America's first drive-in movie theater in Camden, NJ, on this date. At the height of their popularity in 1958, there were more than 4,000 drive-ins across America. Today there are fewer than 600 open.

GERMANY: WALDCHESTAG. June 6. Frankfurt. Since the 19th century Frankfurters have spent the Tuesday after Whitsunday in their forest. See also: "Whitsunday" (June 4).

HALE, NATHAN: BIRTH ANNIVERSARY. June 6, 1755. American patriot Nathan Hale was born at Coventry, CT. During the battles for New York in the American Revolution, he volunteered to seek military intelligence behind enemy lines and was captured on the night of Sept 21, 1776. In an audience before General William Howe, Hale admitted he was an American officer and was ordered hanged the following morning. Although some question them, his dying words, "I only regret that I have but one life to lose for my country," have become a symbol of American patriotism. He was hanged Sept 22, 1776, at Manhattan, NY.

KHACHATURIAN, ARAM (ILICH): BIRTH ANNIVERSARY. June 6, 1903. Armenian musician and composer, noted for compositions based on folk music and legend, born at Tbilisi, Georgia, USSR. Died at Moscow, May 1, 1978.

KOREA: MEMORIAL DAY. June 6. Nation pays tribute to the war dead and memorial services are held at the National Cemetery in Seoul. Legally recognized Korean holiday.

NATIONAL HUNGER AWARENESS DAY. June 6. This day was created to increase awareness of the serious problem of hunger in the US. One in five children in this country lives in poverty and is at risk for hunger. One in ten households isn't sure where the next meal is coming from. We hope to enlist your support. For info: America's Second Harvest, 35 E Wacker Dr, #2000, Chicago, IL 60601. Phone: (312) 263-2303. Web: www.secondharvest.org.

PROPOSITION 13: ANNIVERSARY. June 6, 1978. California voters (65 percent of them) supported a primary election ballot initiative to cut property taxes 57 percent. Regarded as a possible omen of things to come across the country—a taxpayer's revolt against high taxes and government spending.

PUSHKIN, ALEXANDER: BIRTH ANNIVERSARY. June 6, 1799. Russian poet (*Eugene Onegin*, a novel in verse), born at Moscow. Died Feb 10, 1837 at St. Petersburg as the result of a duel.

SCOTT, ROBERT FALCON: BIRTH ANNIVERSARY. June 6, 1868. British naval officer and polar explorer, born at Devonport, England. Led the ill-starred expedition to the South Pole that arrived on Jan 18, 1912—one month after Norwegian Roald Amundsen's team became the first humans to set foot on the South Pole. Scott and four team members died on the return journey and their bodies were found November 1912. Scott's diary, with a final entry of Mar 29, 1912, had a message to the public: "Had we lived, I should have had a tale to tell of the hardihood, endurance, and courage of my companions which would have stirred the heart of every Englishman. These rough notes and our dead bodies must tell the tale. . . ."

SECURITIES AND EXCHANGE COMMISSION CREATED: ANNIVERSARY. June 6, 1934. President Franklin D. Roosevelt signed the Securities Exchange Act that established the SEC. Wall Street had operated almost unfettered since the end of the 18th century. However, the stock market crash of 1929 necessitated regulation of the exchanges. The Securities and Exchange Commission is composed of five members appointed by the president of the US.

"SEX AND THE CITY" TV PREMIERE: ANNIVERSARY. June 6, 1998. HBO's modern comedy of manners focused on four fashionable women navigating the perilous waters of New York City's dating scene. Starred Sarah Jessica Parker (Carrie Bradshaw), Kristin Davis (Charlotte York), Kim Cattrall (Samantha Jones) and Cynthia Nixon (Miranda Hobbes). More than 10 million viewers tuned in to watch the 94th and final episode air on Feb 22, 2004.

SPACE MILESTONE: *SOYUZ 11* **(USSR): 35th ANNIVERSARY.** June 6, 1971. Launched with cosmonauts G.T. Dobrovolsky, V.N. Volkov and V.I. Patsayev, who died during the return landing June 30, 1971, after a 24-day space flight. *Soyuz 11* had docked at *Salyut* orbital space station June 7–29; the cosmonauts entered the space station for the first time and conducted scientific experiments. First humans to die in space.

SUSAN B. ANTHONY FINED FOR VOTING: ANNIVERSARY. June 6, 1872. Seeking to test for women the citizenship and voting rights extended to black males under the 14th and 15th Amendments, Susan B. Anthony led a group of women who registered and voted at a Rochester, NY, election. She was arrested, tried and sentenced to pay a fine. She refused to do so and was allowed to go free by a judge who feared she would appeal to a higher court.

SWEDEN: FLAG DAY. June 6. Commemorates the day upon which Gustavus I (Gustavus Vasa) ascended the throne of Sweden in 1523.

"20/20" TV PREMIERE: ANNIVERSARY. June 6, 1978. An hourly newsmagazine developed by ABC to compete with CBS's "60 Minutes." Its original hosts, Harold Hayes and Robert Hughes, were cut after the first show and replaced by Hugh Downs. Barbara Walters became coanchor in 1984. The show consisted of investigative and background reports. Contributors to the show have included Tom Jarriel, Sylvia Chase, Geraldo Rivera, Thomas Hoving, John Stossel, Lynn Sherr and Stone Phillips.

BIRTHDAYS TODAY

Sandra Bernhard, 51, comedienne, actress ("Roseanne"), born Flint, MI, June 6, 1955.

Gary U.S. Bonds, 67, singer ("Quarter to Three"), songwriter, born Gary Anderson at Jacksonville, FL, June 6, 1939.

		S	M	T	W	T	F	S
June						1	2	3
		4	5	6	7	8	9	10
2006		11	12	13	14	15	16	17
		18	19	20	21	22	23	24
		25	26	27	28	29	30	

Bjorn Rune Borg, 50, former tennis player, born Sodertalje, Sweden, June 6, 1956.

Marian Wright Edelman, 67, president of Children's Defense Fund, civil rights activist, born Bennettsville, SC, June 6, 1939.

Harvey Fierstein, 52, playwright, performer (Tony Awards for *Hairspray, Torch Song Trilogy, Tidy Endings*), born Brooklyn, NY, June 6, 1954.

Paul Giamatti, 39, actor (*American Splendor, Sideways*), born New York, NY, June 6, 1967.

Kenny G, 50, sax player, born Kenny Gorelick at Seattle, WA, June 6, 1956.

Amanda Pays, 47, actress ("Max Headroom," *Exposure*), born Berkshire, England, June 6, 1959.

Billie Whitelaw, 74, actress (*The Dressmaker*, "Masterpiece Theater"), born Coventry, England, June 6, 1932.

JUNE 7 — WEDNESDAY
Day 158 — 207 Remaining

APGAR, VIRGINIA: BIRTH ANNIVERSARY. June 7, 1909. Dr. Apgar developed the simple assessment method that permits doctors and nurses to evaluate newborns while they are still in the delivery room to identify those in need of immediate medical care. The Apgar score was first published in 1953, and the Perinatal Section of the American Academy of Pediatrics is named for Dr. Apgar. Born at Westfield, NJ, Apgar died Aug 7, 1974, at New York, NY.

BOONE DAY. June 7. Each year on June 7, the Kentucky Historical Society celebrates the anniversary of the day in 1767 when Daniel Boone, America's most famous frontiersman, reportedly first sighted the land that would become Kentucky. The June 7 date is taken from the book *The Discovery, Settlement and Present State of Kentucky*, by John Filson, published in 1784, with an appendix titled "The Adventures of Colonel Daniel Boone." The information in the appendix supposedly originated with Boone, although Filson is the actual author. The work is not considered completely reliable by historians.

BRADDOCK, JAMES: 100th BIRTH ANNIVERSARY. June 7, 1906. James Walter Braddock, boxer, born at New York, NY. Braddock rose from the ranks of undistinguished fighters to win three key bouts in 1934 and 1935 that propelled him to a match for the heavyweight title. He upset the defending champion, Max Baer, on June 13, 1935, remained inactive for two years and then lost his first title defense to Joe Louis. Died at North Bergen, NJ, Nov 29, 1974.

BRUMMELL, GEORGE BRYAN "BEAU": BIRTH ANNIVERSARY. June 7, 1778. Born at London, England, Beau Brummell was, early in his life, a popular English men's fashion leader, the "arbiter elegantarium" of taste in dress. His extravagance and lack of tact (it was he who reportedly said—indicating the Prince of Wales, later George IV—"Who's your fat friend?") led him from wealth and popularity to poverty and disrepute. Once imprisoned for debt, he became careless of dress and personal appearance. He died in a charitable asylum at Caen, France, Mar 30, 1840.

CANADA: THE NATIONAL TOURNAMENT. June 7–11. Spruce Meadows, Calgary, AB. The National Tournament features the Spruce Meadows Show Jumping Championship, including the Direct Energy Grand Prix Cup and the Shell Cup. Enjoy country atmosphere in the Agrium Country Fair on the Spruce Meadows Plaza. Live entertainment and activities daily. First week of June, Wednesday through Sunday. Est attendance: 85,750. For info: Spruce Meadows, RR 9, Calgary, AB, Canada T2J 5G5. Phone: (403) 974-4200. Fax: (403) 974-4270. E-mail: information@sprucemeadows.com. Web: www.sprucemeadows.com.

GAUGUIN, (EUGENE HENRI) PAUL: BIRTH ANNIVERSARY. June 7, 1848. French painter born at Paris, France. Formerly a stockbroker, he became a painter in his middle age and three years later renounced his life at Paris to move to Tahiti. He is remembered best for his broad, flat tones and bold colors.

Gauguin died May 8, 1903, at Atoana on the island of Hiva Oa in the Marquesas.

INPEX®—AMERICA'S LARGEST INVENTION TRADE SHOW. June 7–10. Greater Pittsburgh ExpoMart, Pittsburgh, PA. INPEX is The Invention/New Product Exposition. Features inventions, new products and innovations. For info: Nicole Hait, INPEX, 217 Ninth St, Pittsburgh, PA 15222. Phone: (412) 288-2136. Fax: (412) 288-2513. E-mail: nhait@inventhelp.com. Web: www.inventionshow.com.

MALTA: NATIONAL DAY. June 7. National day or (in Maltese) Sette Giugno.

MARTIN, DEAN: BIRTH ANNIVERSARY. June 7, 1917. Actor/singer Dean Martin was born Dino Paul Crocetti, at Steubenville, OH. Martin's career was barely moving in 1946, when he met Jerry Lewis. Together they formed an unforgettable comedy act that carried them to dizzying heights of success. When the team broke up, Martin found continued success as a singer as well as a Hollywood film star. He died Dec 25, 1995, at Beverly Hills, CA.

NATIONAL TAILORS DAY. June 7. To honor tailors across the US. Annually, the first Wednesday in June. For info: Doug Foley, Tom James Clothiers, 501 Congressional Blvd, Ste 150, Carmel, IN 46032. Phone: (317) 571-9191. Web: www.tomjamesco.com.

NCAA DIVISION I MEN'S & WOMEN'S OUTDOOR TRACK & FIELD CHAMPIONSHIPS. June 7–10. Alex G. Spanos Sports Complex, Sacramento, CA. Est attendance: 20,000. For info: NCAA, 700 W Washington Ave, PO Box 6222, Indianapolis, IN 46206-6222. Phone: (317) 917-6222. Fax: (317) 917-6825. Web: www.ncaasports.com.

PARTY IN THE PLAZA. June 7–Aug 16 (Wednesdays). Millennium Plaza, Aurora, IL. Weekly music series held every Wednesday from 12:00 PM to 1:30 PM. For info: Lisa Garcia, City of Aurora, Mayor's Office of Special Events, 43 E Downer Place, Aurora, IL 60507. Phone: (630) 844-3640. Fax: (630) 906-7068. E-mail: specialevents@aurora-il.org.

RED RIVER RODEO. June 7–10. Wichita Falls, TX. Professional circuit rodeo held at the Wichita County Mounted Patrol Arena, this event features all of the traditional rodeo attractions as well as a dance. Est attendance: 10,000. For info: Wichita Falls Conv & Visitors Bureau, 1000 5th St, Wichita Falls, TX 76301. Phone: (940) 716-5500. Fax: (940) 716-5509. Web: www.wichitafalls.org.

"THE $64,000 QUESTION" TV PREMIERE: ANNIVERSARY. June 7, 1955. This game show was a big hit, and the first of prime time's big money shows. Contestants, each an expert in one area, answered questions; each time a question was answered correctly, contestants doubled their money and the questions became harder. Players, if successful, could come back the following week. For the $64,000 question, a player could bring along an expert, but if neither got the correct answer, the player left with $4,000. The host was Hal March, assisted by Lynn Dollar and later Pat Donovan, and questions were compiled by Dr. Bergen Evans. Some famous contestants were Dr. Joyce Brothers, Barbara Feldon and Jack Benny (as a joke). The show was dropped in 1958 amid the game show scandals.

SUPREME COURT STRIKES DOWN CONNECTICUT LAW BANNING CONTRACEPTION: ANNIVERSARY. June 7, 1965. In *Griswold v Connecticut*, the Supreme Court guaranteed the right to privacy, including the freedom from government intrusion into matters of birth control.

TRIAL TECHNOLOGY DAY. June 7 (tentative). A day to mark the emerging technologies used for trials. For info: Joyce Mullen, DOAR, 170 Earle Ave, Lynbrook, NY 11563. Phone: (516) 823-3954. Fax: (516) 823-4400. E-mail: joyce@doar.com. Web: www.doar.com.

VCR INTRODUCED: ANNIVERSARY. June 7, 1975. The Sony Corporation released its videocassette recorder, the Betamax, which sold for $995. Eventually, another VCR format, VHS, proved more successful and Sony stopped making the Betamax.

BIRTHDAYS TODAY

Louise Erdrich, 52, author (*Love Medicine, The Beet Queen*), born Little Falls, MN, June 7, 1954.

Allen Iverson, 31, basketball player, born Hampton, VA, June 7, 1975.

Jenny Jones, 60, talk-show host, born London, ON, Canada, June 7, 1946.

Tom Jones, 66, singer ("It's Not Unusual"), born Thomas Woodward at Pontypridd, Wales, UK, June 7, 1940.

Anna Kournikova, 25, tennis player, born Moscow, Russia, June 7, 1981.

Bill Kreutzmann, Jr, 60, drummer, singer, cofounder of The Grateful Dead, born Palo Alto, CA, June 7, 1946.

Mike Modano, 36, hockey player, born Livonia, MI, June 7, 1970.

Liam Neeson, 54, actor (*Excalibur, Ethan Frome, Schindler's List*), born Ballymena, Northern Ireland, June 7, 1952.

Prince, 48, musician, singer, born Prince Rogers Nelson at Minneapolis, MN, June 7, 1958.

John Napier Turner, 77, Canada's 17th prime minister (served June 30, 1984–Sept 17, 1984), born Richmond, Surrey, England, June 7, 1929.

JUNE 8 — THURSDAY

Day 159 — 206 Remaining

AMERICAN HEROINE REWARDED: ANNIVERSARY. June 8, 1697. On Mar 16, 1697, in an attack on Haverhill, MA, Indians captured Hannah Duston and killed her baby, killing or capturing 39 others in addition. After being taken to an Indian camp, she escaped on Apr 29 after killing 10 Indians with a tomahawk and scalping them as proof of her deed. On June 8 her husband was awarded, on her behalf, the sum of 25 pounds for her heroic efforts, the first public award to a woman in America.

ATTACK ON THE USS *LIBERTY*: ANNIVERSARY. June 8, 1967. At 2 PM local time, the unescorted US intelligence ship USS *Liberty*, sailing in international waters off the Egyptian coast, was attacked without warning by Israeli jet planes and three Israeli torpedo boats. It was strafed and hit repeatedly by rockets, cannon, napalm and finally a torpedo. Casualties: out of a crew of 294 Americans, there were 34 dead and 171 wounded. Israel apologized, claiming mistaken identity, but surviving crew members charged deliberate attack by Israel and cover-up by US authorities.

S	**M**	**T**	**W**	**T**	**F**	**S**
				1	2	3
4	5	6	7	8	9	10
11	12	13	14	15	16	17
18	19	20	21	22	23	24
25	26	27	28	29	30	

June 2006

BILL OF RIGHTS PROPOSAL: ANNIVERSARY. June 8, 1789. The Bill of Rights, which led to the first 10 amendments to the US Constitution, was first proposed by James Madison.

CANADA: WINNIPEG INTERNATIONAL CHILDREN'S FESTIVAL. June 8–11. The Forks, Winnipeg, MB. Festival features song, dance, theater, mime, puppetry and music by local, national and international artists. Est attendance: 20,000. For info: Box Office, Winnipeg Intl Children's Fest, 201 Forks Market Rd, Winnipeg, MB, Canada R3C 4L9. Phone: (204) 958-4733 or (800) 527-1515. Fax: (204) 231-7915. Web: www.kidsfest.ca.

COCHISE: DEATH ANNIVERSARY. June 8, 1874. Born around 1810 in the Chiricahua Mountains of Arizona, Cochise became a fierce and courageous leader of the Apache. After his arrest in 1861, he escaped and launched the Apache Wars, which lasted for 25 years. He died 13 years later near his stronghold in southeastern Arizona.

CRICK, FRANCIS: BIRTH ANNIVERSARY. June 8, 1916. Discoverer with James Watson of the structure of DNA in 1953. Born at Northampton, England, Crick died at San Diego, CA, July 28, 2004.

FESTIVAL OF THE BLUEGRASS. June 8–11. Lexington, KY. Bluegrass music in an outdoor setting. Previous artists have included Valerie Smith and Liberty Pike, Honi Deaton and Dream, Dry Branch Fire Squad, Mountain Heart, Seldom Scene and others. Est attendance: 20,000. For info: Spirit of the Suwannee Music Park, 3076 95th Dr, Live Oak, FL 32060. Phone: (904) 364-1683. Fax: (904) 364-2998. Web: www.festivalofthebluegrass.com.

GLENN MILLER BIRTHPLACE SOCIETY FESTIVAL. June 8–11. Clarinda, IA. To commemorate Glenn Miller's contribution to big band music through exhibits, concerts, films, performances by winners of Glenn Miller scholarships and a big band dance. Annually, the second full weekend in June. Est attendance: 5,500. For info: Glenn Miller Birthplace Society, PO Box 61, Clarinda, IA 51632. Phone/fax: (712) 542-2461. E-mail: gmbs@heartland.net. Web: www.glennmiller.org.

ICELAND: LAKI VOLCANO ERUPTION: ANNIVERSARY. June 8, 1783. One of the most violent and important volcanic eruptions of recorded history began on this date. Laki, or Skafta, volcano in southern Iceland continued erupting for eight months, expelling an estimated 4½ cubic miles of lava, ultimately causing a famine and the deaths of nearly 10,000 persons. Acid rain reached western Europe, and other climatic and atmospheric changes were worldwide. English naturalist Gilbert White described some of the "horrible phenomena" of the summer of 1783, including the "peculiar haze, or smokey fog . . . unlike anything known within the memory of man." The effects of this volcanic eruption and its possible long-term consequences are still being studied by scientists. See also: "White, Gilbert: Birth Anniversary" (July 18).

INTERNATIONAL OLD-TIME FIDDLERS' CONTEST. June 8–10. International Peace Garden, Dunseith, ND. The International Old-Time Fiddlers' Contest draws young and old fiddlers alike from both Canada and the US. Contestants compete for two days performing a required list of fiddle music in pursuit of cash prizes and trophies. Est attendance: 1,500. For info: Joseph T. Alme, 1930 23rd Ave SE, Minot, ND 58701-6081. Phone/fax: (701) 838-8472. E-mail: info@internationalmusiccamp.com.

MARDI GRAS IN BRANSON!!! June 8–10. Branson, MO. An authentic Cajun/Zydeco Festival with a Mardi Gras twist. Music, food, arts & crafts from Louisiana. Est attendance: 10,000. For info: Cedric Benoit, Mardi Gras in Branson, 406 Sherry Ln, Branson, MO 65616. Phone: (417) 335-8842. Fax: (417) 336-2502. E-mail: cedric@cedricbenoit.com. Web: www.mardigrasinbranson.com.

MARGARETTA DAYS. June 8–11. Machias, ME. Celebrating the Battle of the Margaretta, the first naval engagement of the American Revolution. Encampment, foot parade, period dress and crafts. Annually, the weekend closest to June 12. Est attendance: 4,000. For info: Louise West, Machias Bay Area Chamber of Commerce, PO Box 606, Machias, ME 04654. Phone: (207) 255-4402. Fax: (207) 255-4128. E-mail: info@machias chamber.org. Web: www.machiaschamber.org.

McKINLEY, IDA SAXTON: BIRTH ANNIVERSARY. June 8, 1847. Wife of William McKinley, 25th president of the US, born at Canton, OH. Died at Canton, OH, May 26, 1907.

MINNESOTA INVENTORS CONGRESS. June 8–11. Redwood Falls, MN. 49th Congress. To promote creativity and development of ideas into marketable products, to educate inventors and to bring the inventor to experts in the appropriate field. Highlights include more than 50–80 inventions from around the world on display, 50 student inventors, the Minnesota Inventors Hall of Fame and the Marketplace with inventions for sale. Also features a Successful Invention Development Workshop on the Thursday preceding the three-day Congress. Est attendance: 5,000. For info: Minnesota Inventors Congress, PO Box 71, Redwood Falls, MN 56283-0071. Phone: (507) 637-2344 or (800) INVENT-1. Fax: (507) 637-4082. E-mail: mic@inventhelper.org. Web: www .inventhelper.org.

MISS IOWA SCHOLARSHIP PAGEANT. June 8–10. North Scott High School Auditorium, Eldridge, IA. Part of the Miss America Organization. For info: Miss Iowa Scholarship Program, PO Box 25, Davenport, IA 52722. Web: www.missiowa .com.

SEA MUSIC FESTIVAL. June 8–11. Mystic, CT. World-famous musicians perform aboard Mystic Seaport's tall ships or in concert. Est attendance: 6,000. For info: Mystic Seaport, 75 Greenmanville Ave, Box 6000, Mystic, CT 06355. Phone: (860) 572-5315 or (888) 973-2767. Web: www.mysticseaport.com.

SPACE MILESTONE: *VENERA 9* AND *10* (USSR). June 8 and 14, 1975. Launched on these dates, unmanned exploration vehicles landed on Venus Oct 22 and 25, respectively. Sent first pictures ever transmitted from Venus, atmospheric analysis and other data.

SUPERMAN CELEBRATION. June 8–11. Metropolis, IL. Weekend full of Super activities. See 15-ft Superman Statue, live entertainment, super museum, road race, carnival, tennis tourney, Supertrek bicycle ride, super car show, washer pitch tournament, weight lifting, arm wrestling, children's games and food fair. Est attendance: 30,000. For info: Metropolis Area Chamber of Commerce, Tourism & Economic Development, PO Box 188, Metropolis, IL 62960. Phone: (618) 524-2714 or (800) 949-5740. Fax: (618) 524-4780. E-mail: metrochamber@hcis.net. Web: www .metropolischamber.com.

TAIWAN: BIRTHDAY OF CHENG HUANG. June 8. Thirteenth day of fifth moon. Celebrated with a procession of actors on stilts doing dragon and lion dances.

TEXAS FOLKLIFE FESTIVAL. June 8–11. San Antonio, TX. Provides an entertaining and historic understanding of the crafts, art, food, music, history and heritage of the more than 40 different cultures and ethnic groups that settled and developed the state of Texas. Est attendance: 70,000. For info: Texas Folklife Festival, Institute of Texan Cultures, 801 S Bowie St, San Antonio, TX 78205-3296. Phone: (210) 458-2390. Fax: (210) 458-2218. Web: www.texasfolklifefestival.org.

UPSY DAISY DAY. June 8. A day to remind people to get up gloriously, gratefully, and gleefully each morning. For info: Stephanie West Allen, PO Box 9311, Denver, CO 80209. Phone: (303) 742-4790. E-mail: stephanie@allen-nichols.com. Web: www .allen-nichols.com.

WHITE, BYRON RAYMOND: BIRTH ANNIVERSARY. June 8, 1917. One of the longest serving justices of the Supreme Court of the US, Byron White was born June 8, 1917, at Fort Collins, CO. He was a football star in college (College Football Hall of Fame) and in the National Football League, as well as an academic standout: he was a Rhodes Scholar among other honors. A graduate of Yale Law School, White was a successful lawyer and director of the Justice Department before being nominated

by President Kennedy for the highest court on Apr 3, 1962. White took the oath of office Apr 16, 1962, and served 31 years before retiring in 1993. He died on April 15, 2002, at Denver, CO.

WRIGHT, FRANK LLOYD: BIRTH ANNIVERSARY. June 8, 1867. American architect born at Richland Center, WI. In his autobiography Wright wrote: "No house should ever be *on* any hill or on anything. It should be *of* the hill, belonging to it, so hill and house could live together each the happier for the other." Wright died at Phoenix, AZ, Apr 9, 1959.

WYTHE, GEORGE: 200th DEATH ANNIVERSARY. June 8, 1806. Signer of the Declaration of Independence. Born at Elizabeth County, VA, about 1726 (exact date unknown). Died at Richmond, VA.

YOUTH COWBOY POETRY GATHERING. June 8–11. Boys Ranch, TX. Youngsters from around the country gather for this educational event featuring such well-known poets and musicians as Don Edwards, Waddie Mitchell, R.W. Hampton, The Gillette Brothers and Wylie & The Wild West. Open to youths of all ages interested in learning western heritage, cowboy values, creative writing and songwriting. Featured guests and other experienced professionals will mentor the young people during open poetry and music sessions and a variety of seminars. Participation is free for all youths. There is a nominal fee for headliner concerts for attending adults and non-participating youth. For info: Cal Farley's Boys Ranch, Attn: Darci Johnson, PO Box 1890, Amarillo, TX 79174. Phone: (806) 322-2635. Fax: (806) 372-6638. E-mail: darcijohnson@calfarley.org. Web: www.cal farley.org.

BIRTHDAYS TODAY

Scott Adams, 49, cartoonist ("Dilbert"), born Windham, NY, June 8, 1957.

Kathy Baker, 56, actress ("Picket Fences," *The Right Stuff*), born Midland, TX, June 8, 1950.

Tim Berners-Lee, 51, inventor of the World Wide Web, born London, England, June 8, 1955.

Barbara Pierce Bush, 81, former First Lady, wife of George H.W. Bush, 41st president of the US, born Rye, NY, June 8, 1925.

Bernie Casey, 67, former football player, actor (*I'm Gonna Git You Sucka, Bill & Ted's Excellent Adventure, Roots: The Next Generations*), born Wyco, WV, June 8, 1939.

Kim Clijsters, 23, tennis player, born Bilzen, Belgium, June 8, 1983.

James Darren, 70, singer ("Goodbye Cruel World"), actor (*Gidget*), born Philadelphia, PA, June 8, 1936.

Lindsay Davenport, 30, tennis player, born Palos Verdes, CA, June 8, 1976.

Griffin Dunne, 51, actor (*Straight Talk*), producer, born New York, NY, June 8, 1955.

Don Grady, 62, actor ("My Three Sons," "Mickey Mouse Club"), born San Diego, CA, June 8, 1944.

Julianna Margulies, 40, actress ("ER"), born Spring Valley, NY, June 8, 1966.

Sara Paretsky, 59, writer (*Killing Orders, Burn Marks*), born Ames, IA, June 8, 1947.

Joan Rivers, 69, comedienne, talk-show host, born New York, NY, June 8, 1937.

Boz Scaggs, 62, singer, musician, songwriter (*Silk Degress, Middle Man*), born Dallas, TX, June 8, 1944.

Nancy Sinatra, 66, singer ("These Boots Are Made for Walkin'," "Something Stupid"), born Jersey City, NJ, June 8, 1940.

Jerry Stiller, 77, comedian, actor (*Hairspray*, "Seinfeld," "The King of Queens"), born Brooklyn, NY, June 8, 1929.

Keenen Ivory Wayans, 48, actor ("In Living Color"), born New York, NY, June 8, 1958.

Andrew Weil, MD, 64, physician and writer on natural healing, born Philadelphia, PA, June 8, 1942.

JUNE 9 — FRIDAY

Day 160 — 205 Remaining

BANANA SPLIT FESTIVAL. June 9–10. JW Denver Williams Memorial Park, Wilmington, OH. 12th annual. A festival celebrating Wilmington as the birthplace of the banana split. Enjoy live concerts, crafters, vendors, great food, games and kids activities and a make-your-own banana split booth. Est attendance: 18,000. For info: Rhonda Henson, Clinton County CVB, 13 N South St, Wilmington, OH 45177. Phone: (877) 428-4748. Fax: (937) 382-1738. E-mail: rhenson@clintoncountyohio.com. Web: www.clintoncountyohio.com.

CARSON CITY RENDEZVOUS. June 9–11. Mills Park, Carson City, NV. A living history event with something for every member of the family. Mountain Men encampment demonstrates black powder shooting and tomahawk and knife throwing. Nevada, Utah and Oregon Civil War volunteers have their own encampments on the Rendezvous grounds. Other features include Pony Express, authentic Indian and Hispanic arts and crafts and dance exhibits, live music and food. Annually, the second full weekend in June. Est attendance: 2,500. For info: Carson City Convention & Visitor's Bureau, 1900 S Carson St, Ste 100, Carson City, NV 89701. Phone: (775) 687-7410 or 800-NEVADA-1. Fax: (775) 687-7416. Web: www.visitcarsoncity.com.

CHICAGO GOSPEL MUSIC FESTIVAL. June 9–11 (tentative). Millenium Park, Chicago, IL. 22nd annual. Largest free outdoor gospel music festival in the world. Features local, national and international performers. Est attendance: 150,000. For info: Mayor's Office of Special Events, City Hall, 121 N LaSalle St, #703, Chicago, IL 60602. Phone: (312) 744-3370. Fax: (312) 744-8523. E-mail: moseinquiry@cityofchicago.org. Web: www.cityofchicago.org/specialevents.

CONNECTICUT EARLY MUSIC FESTIVAL. June 9–25. New London, CT, and nearby towns. Concert series of pre-19th century music performed on period instruments in historically informed styles. Annually, three weekends in June. Est attendance: 1,200. For info: Connecticut Early Music Festival, PO Box 329, New London, CT 06320. Phone: (860) 444-2419. Web: www.ctearlymusic.org.

CRAWFORDSVILLE STRAWBERRY FESTIVAL. June 9–11. Crawfordsville, IN. Festival at historic Lane Place includes three days of arts and crafts, food, music and children's activities. Great music, classic car show (Sunday), softball and tennis tournaments, bike tour, antique tractor exhibits and 4-mile run. All city museums open. Est attendance: 20,000. For info: Montgomery County Visitors & Conv Bureau, Inc, 218 E Pike St, Crawfordsville, IN 47933. Phone: (800) 866-3973. Fax: (317) 362-5215. E-mail: request@crawfordsville.org. Web: www.thestrawberryfestival.com.

CUMMINGS, ROBERT: BIRTH ANNIVERSARY. June 9, 1908. American actor Robert Cummings was born Charles Clarence Robert Orville Cummings at Joplin, MO. His best-known role was in the film *Dial M for Murder* (1954). He won an Emmy for his role in the television version of *Twelve Angry Men* (1954) and starred in the popular comedy "The Bob Cummings Show" (1955–59). He died Dec 2, 1990, at Woodland Hills, CA.

DONALD DUCK: BIRTHDAY. June 9, 1934. Donald Duck was "born."

DOWNTOWN ALIVE! June 9. (also June 16 & 23, July 7, 14 & 21, Aug 4, 11 & 18) Downer Place, Aurora, IL. A summer concert series of events on Friday nights. Local as well as national acts. Family Fun Zone with children's entertainment, classic cars, specialty food and beverages. For info: Gina Moga, Events Coord,

	S	M	T	W	T	F	S
June					1	2	3
	4	5	6	7	8	9	10
2006	11	12	13	14	15	16	17
	18	19	20	21	22	23	24
	25	26	27	28	29	30	

City of Aurora, 43 E Downer Pl, Aurora, IL 60507. Phone: (630) 844-3640. Hotline: (630) 844-4FUN. Fax: (630) 906-7068. E-mail: gmoga@aurora-il.org.

HONG KONG: LEASE SIGNING ANNIVERSARY. June 9, 1898. Hong Kong, consisting of about 400 square miles (islands and mainland) with more than five million persons, was administered as a British Crown Colony after a 99-year lease was signed on June 9, 1898. In 1997 Hong Kong's sovereignty reverted to the People's Republic of China.

JORDAN: ACCESSION DAY. June 9. National holiday. Commemorates the accession to the throne of King Abdullah II in 1999, following the death of his father, King Hussein.

KUSTOM KEMPS OF AMERICA CAR SHOW. June 9–11. Oakside Community Park, Biglerville, PA. Est attendance: 3,500. For info: Gettysburg CVB, PO Box 4117, Gettysburg, PA 17325. Phone: (717) 637-5229. Fax: (717) 334-1166. E-mail: gettysburgcvb@dejazzd.com. Web: www.gettysburgcvb.org.

KUTNER, LUIS: BIRTH ANNIVERSARY. June 9, 1908. Human rights attorney Luis Kutner was born at Chicago, IL. Responsible for the release of many unjustly confined prisoners, he came to be known as "The Springman." He helped free Hungarian Cardinal Josef Mindszenty, poet Ezra Pound and former Congo President Moise Tshombe. He was the author of the living will and founded the World Habeas Corpus. Kutner was nominated nine times for the Nobel Peace Prize. He died Mar 1, 1993, at Chicago, IL.

LILAC FESTIVAL. June 9–18. Mackinac Island, MI. This summer festival provides an excellent chance to see the various lilacs on Mackinac Island. Includes a parade and entertainment. Est attendance: 30,000. For info: Mackinac Island Tourism Bureau, PO Box 451, Mackinac Island, MI 49757. Phone: (906) 847-6418 or (800) 4-LILACS. Fax: (906) 847-3571. Web: www.mackinacisland.org.

LOLOMA, CHARLES: BIRTH ANNIVERSARY. June 9, 1921. Charles Loloma was a major influence on modern Native American art and was famous for changing the look of American Indian jewelry. A painter, sculptor and potter, he was best known for his jewelry, which broke tradition with previous Indian styles using materials such as coral, fossilized ivory, pearls and diamonds. Loloma was born at Hotevilla on the Hopi Indian Reservation and died June 9, 1991, at Scottsdale, AZ.

MISS DELAWARE PAGEANT. June 9–10. Rehoboth Beach Convention Center, Rehoboth Beach, DE. Providing scholarship opportunities for Delaware's young women since 1933. Part of the Miss America Organization. For info: Miss Delaware Scholarship Organization. E-mail: info@missdelaware.org. Web: www.missdelaware.org.

MISS NEW MEXICO SCHOLARSHIP PAGEANT. June 9–10 (tentative). Flickinger Theatre, Alamogordo, NM. Part of the Miss America Organization. Contestants are judged on interviews, lifestyle and fitness, artistic expression, presence and poise. For info: Carol Henry, Executive Director, Miss New Mexico Scholarship Pageant, PO Box 552, Cloudcroft, NM 88317. Phone: (505) 687-2070 or (505) 430-5523. E-mail: carolh@pvtnetworks.net. Web: www.missnewmexico.org.

OK MOZART INTERNATIONAL FESTIVAL. June 9–17. Bartlesville, OK. Festival features world-class artists performing with Solisti New York Orchestra, Ransom Wilson conducting. Est attendance: 15,000. For info: Jacqueline Davis, Public Relations

Director, OK Mozart Intl Festival, Box 2344, Bartlesville, OK 74005. Phone: (918) 336-9900. Fax: (918) 336-9525. Web: www.okmozart.com.

ORPHAN TRAIN HERITAGE SOCIETY OF AMERICA: ANNUAL REUNION. June 9–10. Concordia, KS. Between 1854 and 1929, more than 150,000 homeless children and poor families were transported out of New York City, Boston and Chicago aboard trains accompanied by "agents" for the New York Children's Aid Society who arranged for midwestern families to take the children under a contract agreement. Infants placed by the New York Foundling Hospital were indentured. Annual reunion, plus regional reunions in Oklahoma, Missouri, Kansas, Texas, Iowa, Illinois, Indiana, California, Louisiana, Nebraska and Minnesota bring together survivors of the Orphan Trains era, their descendants and interested persons. All gatherings are open to the public, with a small registration fee charged at each. Books containing stories of the Orphan Train Riders are available at each reunion. Est attendance: 250. For info: OTHSA, PO Box 322, Concordia, KS 66901. E-mail: othsa@msn.com. Web: www .orphantrainriders.com.

PAYNE, JOHN HOWARD: BIRTH ANNIVERSARY. June 9, 1791. American author, actor, diplomat, born at New York, NY. Died at Tunis, Apr 9, 1852. Author of opera libretto (*Clari, or The Maid of Milan*), that contained the song "Home, Sweet Home."

PORTER, COLE: BIRTH ANNIVERSARY. June 9, 1891. Cole Porter published his first song, "The Bobolink Waltz," at the age of 10. His career as a composer and lyricist for Broadway was launched in 1928 when five of his songs were used in the musical play *Let's Do It*. His prolific contributions to the Broadway stage include *Fifty Million Frenchmen, Wake Up and Dream, The Gay Divorcée, Anything Goes, Leave It to Me, Du Barry Was a Lady, Something for the Boys, Kiss Me Kate, Can Can* and *Silk Stockings*. Porter was born at Peru, IN, and died at Santa Monica, CA, Oct 15, 1964.

RIVERBEND FESTIVAL. June 9–17. Chattanooga, TN. Nineday festival on the banks of the Tennessee River includes world-class entertainment, sporting events and an evening finale on the final night featuring musically synchronized fireworks. More than 100 artists perform a variety of musical styles before a diverse audience. Est attendance: 650,000. For info: Friends of the Festival, Inc, 180 Hamm Rd, Chattanooga, TN 37405. Phone: (423) 756-2212. Fax: (423) 756-2719. E-mail: information@riverbend festival.com. Web: www.riverbendfestival.com.

STEPHENSON, GEORGE: 225th BIRTH ANNIVERSARY. June 9, 1781. English inventor, developer of the steam locomotive, born near Newcastle, England. Died near Chesterfield, England, Aug 12, 1848.

TAKE A KID FISHING WEEKEND. June 9–11. St. Paul, MN. Resident adults may fish without a license on these days when fishing with a child under age 16. For info: Ron Payer, Fisheries Management Chief, DNR, Box 20, 500 Lafayette Rd, St. Paul, MN 55155-4020. Web: www.dnr.state.mn.us/.

***TECUMSEH!*: THE EPIC OUTDOOR DRAMA.** June 9–Sept 2 (Mondays through Saturdays). Chillicothe, OH. Witness the spectacular reenactment of the life and death of the great Shawnee leader Tecumseh. Held in the large, tiered amphitheater nestled in the hardwood forest of Sugarloaf Mountain. Take a backstage tour, visit the Prehistoric Museum, dine in the open-air Tecumseh Restaurant Terrace. Est attendance: 60,000. For info: Tecumseh!, PO Box 73, Chillicothe, OH 45601-0073. Phone toll-free Mar 1–Sept 2: (866) 775-0700. Fax: (740) 775-4349. E-mail: tecumseh@bright.net. Web: www.tecumsehdrama.com.

THAYER, SYLVANUS: BIRTH ANNIVERSARY. June 9, 1785. A military engineer and educator, born at Braintree, MA. He was appointed superintendent of West Point at 32 and became known as the "Father of the Military Academy." Thayer died at Braintree, MA, Sept 7, 1872.

WINDSURFING REGATTA/UNVARNISHED MUSIC FESTIVAL. June 9–11. Worthington, MN. Windsurfing on Lake Okabena. Regatta, surfing instruction, swap meet. Traditional music. At sunset, "unvarnished and unamplified" music on the beach. Beach barbecue, food vendors. Est attendance: 8,000. For info: Worthington Conv & Visitors Bureau, 1121 Third Ave, Worthington, MN 56187. Phone: (800) 279-2919 or (507) 372-2919. Fax: (507) 372-2827. E-mail: wcofc@frontiernet.net.

WORLD CUP. June 9–July 9. Germany. The 18th FIFA World Cup, the world's largest sporting event, will be played in 12 cities in Germany: Berlin, Cologne, Dortmund, Frankfurt, Gelsenkirchen, Hanover, Hamburg, Kaiserslautern, Leipzig, Munich, Nuremburg and Stuttgart. Thirty-two national soccer teams representing all regions of the world will compete in eight groups of four. The final match will be in Berlin's Olympiastadion. For info: FIFA, PO Box 85, Zurich 8030, Switzerland. Web: www.fifaworld cup.yahoo.com.

BIRTHDAYS TODAY

Patricia Cornwell, 50, mystery writer (*All That Remains, Postmortem*), born Miami, FL, June 9, 1956.

Johnny Depp, 43, actor (*Pirates of the Caribbean, Chocolat, Ed Wood*), born Owensboro, KY, June 9, 1963.

Michael J. Fox, 45, actor ("Family Ties," "Spin City," *Back to the Future* films), born Edmonton, AB, Canada, June 9, 1961.

Marvin Kalb, 76, educator, journalist, born New York, NY, June 9, 1930.

Jackie Mason, 72, comedian ("Chicken Soup," *The World According to Me*), born Yacov Moshe Maza at Sheboygan, WI, June 9, 1934.

Robert S. McNamara, 90, banker, former cabinet member, born San Francisco, CA, June 9, 1916.

David Gene (Dave) Parker, 55, former baseball player, born Calhoun, MS, June 9, 1951.

Les Paul, 91, musician, singer (with the late Mary Ford; "Hummingbird"), born Waukesha, WI, June 9, 1915.

Natalie Portman, 25, actress (Star Wars saga, Episodes 1–3, *Anywhere But Here, Closer*), born Jerusalem, June 9, 1981.

Ashley Postell, 20, gymnast, born Cheverly, MD, June 9, 1986.

Gloria Reuben, 42, actress ("ER"), born Toronto, ON, Canada, June 9, 1964.

Peja Stojakovic, 29, basketball player, born Predrag Stojakovic at Belgrade, Yugoslavia, June 9, 1977.

Dick Vitale, 67, sportscaster, ESPN and ABC analyst, born East Rutherford, NJ, June 9, 1939.

JUNE 10 — SATURDAY
Day 161 — 204 Remaining

ALCOHOLICS ANONYMOUS: FOUNDING ANNIVERSARY. June 10, 1935. On this day at Akron, OH, Dr. Robert Smith completed his first day of permanent sobriety. "Doctor Bob" and William G. Wilson are considered to have founded Alcoholics Anonymous on that day.

ANTIQUES ON THE DIAMOND. June 10 (also Aug 26). Ligonier, PA. 70 quality antique dealers from six states set up their products along the Diamond. Est attendance: 10,000. For info: Ligonier Chamber of Commerce, 120 E Main St, Ligonier, PA 15658. Phone: (724) 238-4200. Fax: (724) 238-4610. E-mail: thechamber@ligonier.com. Web: www.ligonier.com.

ART FAIR ON THE COURTHOUSE LAWN. June 10. Rhinelander, WI. Original artwork and crafts, food, music and refreshments on the Oneida County Courthouse lawn. Annually, the second Saturday in June. Est attendance: 5,000. For info: Rhinelander Area Chamber of Commerce, PO Box 795, Rhinelander, WI 54501. Phone: (800) 236-4386. Fax: (715) 365-7467. E-mail: info@rhinelanderchamber.com. Web: www.rhinelander chamber.com.

BALLPOINT PEN PATENTED: ANNIVERSARY. June 10, 1943. Hungarian Laszlo Biro patented the ballpoint pen, which he had been developing since the 1930s. He was living at Argentina, where he had gone to escape the Nazis. In many languages, the word for ballpoint pen is *biro*.

BATTLE CREEK CEREAL FESTIVAL (WITH WORLD'S LARGEST BREAKFAST TABLE). June 10. Battle Creek, MI. Featuring a festival parade, arts and crafts, 5k and 10k races, family fun walk, food bank fund-raiser, vendor booths and children's games. The World's Largest Breakfast Table will be from 8 AM–noon, featuring 600 volunteers serving free breakfasts to more than 60,000 people. Est attendance: 60,000. For info: Battle Creek Cereal Festival, Battle Creek CVB, 77 E Michigan Ave, Ste 100, Battle Creek, MI 49017. Phone: (269) 962-2240 or (800) 397-2240. Web: www.battlecreekvisitors.org.

BELLOW, SAUL: BIRTH ANNIVERSARY. June 10, 1915. Born at Lachine, Canada, Bellow would become one of America's great postwar authors, examining the urban anti-heroes at war with the society they live in. His novels included *The Adventures of Augie Marsh* (1953), *Herzog* (1964) and *Mr Sammler's Planet* (1970). Garnered numerous National Book Awards as well as a Pulitzer. Winner of the Nobel Prize for Literature in 1976. Died at Brookline, MA, Apr 5, 2005.

BELMONT STAKES. June 10. Belmont Park, NY. 138th annual. Final race of the "Triple Crown" was inaugurated in 1867. Traditionally run on the fifth Saturday after Kentucky Derby (third Saturday after Preakness). Est attendance: 60,000. For info: Press Office, New York Racing Assn, PO Box 90, Jamaica, NY 11417. Phone: (718) 641-4700. Web: www.nyra.com.

BUZZARD DAY FESTIVAL. June 10. Makoshika State Park, Glendive, MT. Just as the swallows return to Capistrano each year, so do the turkey vultures come back to Makoshika. Festival activities include an 8k run, pancake breakfast, kids fun fest, nature walks, FOLF (frisbee golf) tournament and lots more. Est attendance: 600. For info: Makoshika State Park, Box 1242, Glendive, MT 59330. Phone: (406) 377-6256. Fax: (406) 377-8043. E-mail: makoshika@mt.gov. Web: www.be-quik.com/~makoshika.

CAMBRIDGE POTTERY FESTIVAL AND US POTTERY GAMES. June 10–11. Cambridge, WI. An all-clay event. A nationally recognized art fair featuring potters from all over the US. Professional potters compete in timed events in the US Pottery Games and auction off pottery for charity. The hands-on learning center lets you try your hand at wheel-throwing. Lots of food, fun and Raku firing by the local Clay Guild. Est attendance: 5,000. For info: Cambridge Pottery Festival and US Pottery Games, PO Box 393, Cambridge, WI 53523. Phone: (608) 423-1772. Web: www.cambridgepotteryfestival.org.

CENTER OF THE NATION ALL-CAR RALLY. June 10–11. Belle Fourche, SD. This two-day event includes Saturday's big "Show 'n Shine," held all day in Hermann Park, plus food booths, vendors, live '50s and '60s music. Sunday's events include the State International Chili Society Cook-off. Est attendance: 5,000. For info: Belle Fourche Chamber of Commerce, 415 5th Ave, Belle Fourche, SD 57717. Phone: (605) 892-2676. Fax: (605) 892-4633. E-mail: chamber@bellefourche.org.

	S	M	T	W	T	F	S
					1	2	3
June	4	5	6	7	8	9	10
2006	11	12	13	14	15	16	17
	18	19	20	21	22	23	24
	25	26	27	28	29	30	

CONGO (BRAZZAVILLE): DAY OF NATIONAL RECONCILIATION. June 10. National holiday. Commemorates official conference in 1991.

CZECHOSLOVAKIA: RAPE OF LIDICE: ANNIVERSARY. June 10, 1942. Nazi German troops executed, by shooting, all male inhabitants of the Czechoslovakian village of Lidice (total population about 500 persons), burned every house and deported the women and children to Germany for "re-education." One of the most-remembered atrocities of WWII. June 10, Lidice Memorial Day, is observed in New Jersey.

ENGLAND: THE DERBY. June 10. Epsom Downs. Horse races. Annually, the Saturday after the first Wednesday in June.

ENGLAND: TROOPING THE COLOUR—THE QUEEN'S OFFICIAL BIRTHDAY PARADE. June 10 (tentative). Horse Guards Parade, Whitehall, London. Colorful ceremony with music and pageantry during which Her Majesty The Queen takes the salute from her Household Division. Observance dates from 1805 in the reign of King George III. Starts at 11 AM. When requesting info, send SASE. Trooping the Colour is always the second or third Saturday in June; The Queen's real birthday is Apr 21. Est attendance: 6,500. For info: The Ticket Office, HQ Household Division, Horse Guards, Whitehall, London, England SW1A 2AX. Phone: (44) (020) 7414-2479. Web: www.army.mod.uk/ceremonialandheritage/household.

FIRST MINT IN AMERICA: ANNIVERSARY. June 10, 1652. In defiance of English colonial law, John Hull, a silversmith, established the first mint in America. The first coin issued was the Pine Tree Shilling, designed by Hull.

FOUNDERS' DAY STREET FAIR—THE GOOD LIFE. June 10 (rain date June 11). Toms River, NJ. Street fair for Dover Township nonprofit organizations with a parade, vendor booths, entertainment, prizes, food, literature and games. Crafters welcome. Est attendance: 30,000. For info: Toms River–Ocean County Chamber of Commerce, 1200 Hooper Ave, Toms River, NJ 08753. Phone: (732) 349-0220. Fax: (732) 349-1252. Web: www.oc-chamber.com.

GARLAND, JUDY: BIRTH ANNIVERSARY. June 10, 1922. American actress and singer born Frances Gumm at Grand Rapids, MN. While Garland played in many films and toured widely as a singer, she is probably most remembered for her portrayal of Dorothy Gale in the now-classic *The Wizard of Oz*. Died June 22, 1969, at London, England.

GREAT AMERICAN BRASS BAND FESTIVAL. June 10–11. Centre College Campus, Danville, KY. Brass bands and ensembles from throughout the country in concert Saturday and Sunday. Free to the public. Est attendance: 55,000. For info: Great American Brass Band Festival, PO Box 429, Danville, KY 40422. Phone: (800) 755-0076. Fax: (859) 236-3197. Web: www.danvillekentucky.com.

HERITAGE DAYS FESTIVAL. June 10–11. Cumberland, MD. 38th annual. Held in historic downtown Cumberland, the festival showcases more than 200 arts and crafts booths. Also, music, entertainment, children's activities, carnivals, tours of historic homes and buildings as well as historic reenactments. Annually, the second weekend in June. Est attendance: 25,000. For info: Heritage Days Festival, PO Box 6349, Cumberland, MD 21501. Phone: (301) 722-0037. E-mail: bkcenter@pennswoods.net. Web: www.heritagedaysfestival.com.

HORSERADISH FESTIVAL. June 10–11. Collinsville, IL. Join in the fun at the horseradish capital of the world. "Root Derby" (build a race car out of a horseradish root and win prizes), races, food, great bands and more. For info: Collinsville Chamber of Commerce, 221 W Main St, Collinsville, IL 62234. Phone: (618) 344-2884. E-mail: dcordle@ci.collinsville.il.us.

JORDAN: GREAT ARAB REVOLT AND ARMY DAY. June 10. Commemorates the beginning of the Great Arab Revolt in 1916. National holiday.

McDANIEL, HATTIE: BIRTH ANNIVERSARY. June 10, 1889. Hattie McDaniel was the first African American to win an Academy Award. She won it in 1940 for her role in the 1939 film *Gone with the Wind*. Her career spanned radio and vaudeville in addition to her screen roles in *Judge Priest*, *The Little Colonel*, *Showboat* and *Saratoga*, among others. She was born at Wichita, KS, and died Oct 26, 1952, at Los Angeles, CA.

MELROSE PLANTATION ARTS AND CRAFTS FESTIVAL. June 10–11. Melrose, LA. Held on the grounds of Historic Melrose Plantation, this event features quality handcrafted items from more than 150 juried exhibitors. Food, including famous meat pies and soft drinks will be available. Annually, the second full weekend in June. Est attendance: 20,000. For info: Calendar of Events, Natchitoches Parish Tourist Commission, 781 Front St, Natchitoches, LA 71457. Phone: (318) 379-0055 or (800) 259-1714. Fax: (318) 352-2415. Web: www.natchitoches.net.

ORIGINAL RAGGEDY ANN & ANDY FESTIVAL. June 10–11. Arcola, IL. 17th annual. The whole town celebrates Raggedy Ann & Andy with a parade, arts and crafts, collectibles, food court and entertainment. Est attendance: 10,000. For info: Arcola Chamber of Commerce, PO Box 274, Arcola, IL 61910. Phone: (800) 336-5456. Web: www.arcola-il.org.

PORTUGAL: DAY OF PORTUGAL. June 10. National holiday. Anniversary of the death in 1580 of Portugal's national poet, Luis Vas de Camoes (Camoens), born in 1524 (exact date unknown) at either Lisbon or Coimbra. Died at Lisbon, Portugal.

POTOMAC CELTIC FESTIVAL. June 10–11. Morven Park Equestrian Center, Leesburg, VA. The festival celebrates all Celtic nations: Scotland, Wales, Cornwall, the Isle of Man, Ireland, Brittany (France), Galicia & Asturias (Spain) and North America. Nine stages of live music, dance stage, storytelling, drama, poetry, children's entertainment, workshops, crafts, sports and food. Est attendance: 24,000. For info: Barnaby Council for Celtic Studies, 525-K E Market St, #295, Leesburg, VA 20176. Phone: (703) 938-9779. E-mail: information@pcfest.org. Web: www.PCFest.org.

TURTLE RACES. June 10. Knights of Columbus, Danville, IL. More than 100 turtles compete in 42nd annual races throughout the day. Concessions available. Food and fun. Proceeds go to help people in the area with disabilities. Annually, the second Saturday in June. Est attendance: 3,000. For info: Michael Puhr, President, Turtle Club, 512 W Woodlawn, Danville, IL 61832. Phone: (217) 443-6034 or (217) 260-1983. E-mail: michaelpuhr @sbcglobal.net.

THE WICKET WORLD OF CROQUET®. June 10. President Benjamin Harrison Home, Indianapolis, IN. 24 teams play wearing white in competitive Victorian croquet. Est attendance: 150. For info: President Benjamin Harrison Home, 1230 N Delaware St, Indianapolis, IN 46202. Phone: (317) 631-1888. Fax: (317) 632-5488. E-mail: harrison@presidentbenjaminharrison .org. Web: www.pbhh.org.

BIRTHDAYS TODAY

F. Lee Bailey, 73, lawyer, born Waltham, MA, June 10, 1933.

John Edwards, 53, former vice-presidential candidate, former US Senator (D, North Carolina), born Seneca, SC, June 10, 1953.

Linda Evangelista, 41, model, born St. Catharines, ON, Canada, June 10, 1965.

Jeff Greenfield, 63, author, journalist, born New York, NY, June 10, 1943.

Nat Hentoff, 81, music critic, journalist, born Boston, MA, June 10, 1925.

Elizabeth Hurley, 41, model, actress (*Austin Powers: International Man of Mystery*), born Basingstoke, England, June 10, 1965.

Tara Lipinski, 24, figure skater, born Philadelphia, PA, June 10, 1982.

Doug McKeon, 40, actor (*On Golden Pond*), born Pomptain Plains, NJ, June 10, 1966.

Prince Philip, 85, Duke of Edinburgh, husband of Queen Elizabeth II, born Corfu, Greece, June 10, 1921.

Maurice Sendak, 78, author, illustrator (*Chicken Soup with Rice, Where the Wild Things Are*), born Brooklyn, NY, June 10, 1928.

Leelee Sobieski, 24, actress (*A Soldier's Daughter Never Cries*), born New York, NY, June 10, 1982.

Jeanne Tripplehorn, 43, actress (*The Firm, Waterworld, Mickey Blue Eyes*), born Tulsa, OK, June 10, 1963.

JUNE 11 — SUNDAY

Day 162 — 203 Remaining

ABUSED WOMEN AND CHILDREN'S AWARENESS DAY. June 11. A day to reflect on how we can help stop the violence in America that is destroying the lives and well-being of women and children. A day to prayerfully put an end to violent behavior in American homes, schools, workplaces and communities. Annually, the second Sunday in June. For info: Judith Natale, CEO & Founder, NCAC America-USA, PO Box 493703, Redding, CA 96049-3703. E-mail: childaware@aol.com.

"AMERICAN IDOL" TV PREMIERE: ANNIVERSARY. June 11, 2002. FOX's phenomenally successful talent show was based on a British program. Talented singers compete for a major label record deal while being judged by a panel of (at times) highly critical music experts. The audience participates by phoning in votes for favorites.

BELGIUM: MILITARY MUSIC FESTIVAL. June 11. Tournai. Traditional cultural observance. Annually, the second Sunday in June.

CHILDREN'S DAY IN MASSACHUSETTS. June 11. Annually, the second Sunday in June. The governor proclaims this day each year.

CHILDREN'S SUNDAY. June 11. Traditionally the second Sunday in June is observed as Children's Sunday in many Christian churches.

CONSTABLE, JOHN: BIRTH ANNIVERSARY. June 11, 1776. English landscape painter. Born at East Bergholt, Suffolk, England, he died at London, Mar 31, 1837.

COUSTEAU, JACQUES: BIRTH ANNIVERSARY. June 11, 1910. French undersea explorer, writer and filmmaker born at St. Andre-de-Cubzac, France. He invented the Aqualung, which allowed him and his colleagues to produce more than 80 documentary films about undersea life, two of which won Oscars. This scientist and explorer was awarded the French Legion of Honor for his work in the Resistance in WWII. He died June 25, 1997, at Paris.

GRANT WOOD ART FESTIVAL. June 11. Stone City–Anamosa, IA. Juried art exhibits, demonstrations, stage entertainment, tours of historic Stone City and more. Annually, the second Sunday in June. Est attendance: 8,000. For info: Grant Wood Art Festival, Inc, 124 E Main St, Anamosa, IA 52205. Phone: (319) 462-4267. E-mail: staff@grantwoodartfestival.org. Web: www.grantwoodartfestival.org.

INTERNATIONAL MUSIC CAMP. June 11–Aug 1. International Peace Garden, Dunseith, ND. More than 3,000 students from dozens of countries enjoy the many different programs of IMC. Music camps include concert band, jazz, choir, vocal jazz, orchestra, piano, guitar, marimba and total percussion. Also visual arts, dance, drama and creative-writing sessions. Est attendance: 3,000. For info: Joseph T. Alme, Dir, Intl Music Camp, 1930 23rd Ave SE, Minot, ND 58701-6081. Phone/fax: (701) 838-8472. E-mail: info@internationalmusiccamp.com. Web: www.internationalmusiccamp.com.

JONSON, BEN: BIRTH ANNIVERSARY. June 11, 1572 (OS). English playwright and poet. "Talking and eloquence," he wrote, "are not the same: to speak and to speak well, are two things." Born at London, England, he died there Aug 6, 1637 (OS). The epitaph written on his tombstone in Westminster Abbey: "O rare Ben Jonson."

KING KAMEHAMEHA I DAY. June 11. Designated state holiday in Hawaii honors memory of Hawaiian monarch (1737–1819). Governor appoints state commission to plan annual celebration.

LIBYA: EVACUATION DAY. June 11. National day. Commemorates the closing of US base in 1970.

LOMBARDI, VINCE: BIRTH ANNIVERSARY. June 11, 1913. Vincent Thomas (Vince) Lombardi, Pro Football Hall of Fame coach, born at New York, NY. Lombardi played football for Fordham's famed "Seven Blocks of Granite" line in the mid-1930s, became a teacher and began to coach high school football. He became offensive line coach at West Point in 1949 and moved to the New York Giants in 1954. Five years later, he was named head coach of the Green Bay Packers. His Packers won five NFL titles and two Super Bowls in nine years, and Lombardi was generally regarded as the greatest coach and the finest motivator in pro football history. He retired in 1968, but was lured back to coach the Washington Redskins a year later. Inducted into the Pro Football Hall of Fame in 1971. Died at Washington, DC, Sept 3, 1970.

MOON PHASE: FULL MOON. June 11. Moon enters Full Moon phase at 2:03 PM, EDT.

MOUNT PINATUBO ERUPTS IN PHILIPPINES: 15th ANNIVERSARY. June 11, 1991. Long-dormant volcano Mount Pinatubo erupted with a violent explosion, spewing ash and gases that could be seen for more than 60 miles. The surrounding areas were covered with ash and mud created by rainstorms. US military bases Clark and Subic Bay were also damaged. On July 6, 1992, Ellsworth Dutton of the National Oceanic and Atmospheric Administration's Climate Monitoring and Diagnostics Laboratory announced that a layer of sulfuric acid droplets released into the Earth's atmosphere by the eruption had cooled the planet's average temperature by about 1 degree Fahrenheit. The greatest difference was noted in the Northern Hemisphere with a drop of 1.5 degrees. Although the temperature drop was temporary, the climate trend made determining the effect of greenhouse warming on the Earth more difficult.

MULTICULTURAL AMERICAN CHILD AWARENESS DAY. June 11. Celebrated every second Sunday in June. All children of every culture have been gifted with many talents and uniqueness. As Americans we can all benefit from the sharing of our individual cultural contributions that bring real character and greatness to a nation where all children are precious and deserve our praise. A time to share our many individual talents and treasures. For info: Judith Natale, NCAC America-USA, PO Box 493703, Redding, CA 96049-3703. E-mail: childaware@aol.com.

NATIONAL AUTOMOTIVE SERVICE PROFESSIONALS WEEK. June 11–17. Sponsored by the National Institute for Automotive Service Excellence (ASE), which was incorporated on June 12, 1972. ASE was founded to improve the quality of automotive service through voluntary testing and certification of service professionals. The goal of this week is to recognize mechanics nationwide for their contribution to keeping America's cars and trucks running. The nonprofit organization also serves as an information source for professionals and consumers about automotive repair and related topics. For info: Trish Serratore, 101 Blue Seal Dr, Leesburg, VA 20175. Phone: (703) 669-6600. Fax: (703) 669-6127. E-mail: tserratore@asecert.org. Web: www.ase.com.

★**NATIONAL FLAG WEEK.** June 11–17. Presidential Proclamation issued each year since 1966 for the week including June 14. (PL89–443 of June 9, 1966.) In addition, the president often calls upon the American people to participate in public ceremonies in which the Pledge of Allegiance is recited.

ORTHODOX PENTECOST. June 11. Observed by Eastern Orthodox churches.

RACE UNITY DAY. June 11. Baha'i-sponsored observance promoting racial harmony and understanding and the essential unity of humanity. Annually, the second Sunday in June. Established in 1957 by the Baha'is of the US. For info: Baha'is of the US, Office of Communications, 1233 Central St, Evanston, IL 60201. Phone: (847) 733-3411. Fax: (847) 869-0247. E-mail: ooc@usbnc.org. Web: www.us.bahai.org.

RANKIN, JEANNETTE: BIRTH ANNIVERSARY. June 11, 1880. First woman elected to the US Congress, a reformer, feminist and pacifist, was born at Missoula, MT. She was the only member of Congress to vote against a declaration of war against Japan in December 1941. Died May 18, 1973, at Carmel, CA.

RED ARMY DEPARTS BERLIN: ANNIVERSARY. June 11, 1994. After 49 years, the Russian military occupation of the region once called East Germany ended. At one time there had been 337,800 Soviet troops stationed in Germany. The departure was celebrated with a parade in Wupnsdorf south of Berlin, which was the Soviet Union's military headquarters in the former German Democratic Republic.

STRAUSS, RICHARD GEORG: BIRTH ANNIVERSARY. June 11, 1864. German composer, musician and conductor whose best-remembered works are *Till Eulenspiegel* (1895), *Also Sprach Zarathrustra* (1896) and *Don Quixote* (1898). Born at Munich, he died at Garmisch-Partenkirchen, Germany, after a heart attack Sept 8, 1949, at age 85.

TRINITY SUNDAY. June 11. Christian Holy Day on the Sunday after Pentecost commemorates the Holy Trinity, the three divine persons—Father, Son and Holy Spirit—in one God. See also: "Pentecost" (June 4).

WRITE TO YOUR FATHER DAY. June 11. This is a challenge to all citizens to write a letter to their fathers. Ask, "What do you do (or have you done) that is most exciting to you, most scary, most enjoyable and/or most satisfying?" Don't expect a response, but ask anyway. Annually, the Sunday before Father's Day. For info: Evelyn Cole, 1748 Deer Canyon Rd, Arroyo Grande, CA 93420. Phone: (805) 473-0230. Fax: (805) 481-2688. E-mail: evycole@coles-poetic-license.com. Web: www.coles-poetic-license.com.

June *2006*	S	M	T	W	T	F	S
					1	2	3
	4	5	6	7	8	9	10
	11	12	13	14	15	16	17
	18	19	20	21	22	23	24
	25	26	27	28	29	30	

BIRTHDAYS TODAY

Adrienne Barbeau, 61, actress ("Maude"), born Sacramento, CA, June 11, 1945.

Peter Bergman, 53, actor ("All My Children," "The Young & the Restless"), born Guantanamo Bay, Cuba, June 11, 1953.

Chad Everett, 70, actor ("The Dakotas," "Medical Center"), born Raymond Cramton at South Bend, IN, June 11, 1936.

Joshua Jackson, 28, actor ("Dawson's Creek," *Scream 2*), born Vancouver, BC, Canada, June 11, 1978.

Joseph C. (Joe) Montana, Jr, 50, former sportscaster and Hall of Fame football player, born New Eagle, PA, June 11, 1956.

Jackie Stewart, 67, former auto racer, born Dunbartonshire, Scotland, June 11, 1939.

William Styron, 81, author (*The Confessions of Nat Turner, Sophie's Choice*), born Newport News, VA, June 11, 1925.

Gene Wilder, 67, actor (*The Producers, Willy Wonka & the Chocolate Factory, Blazing Saddles, Young Frankenstein*), director, born Milwaukee, WI, June 11, 1939 (some sources say 1935 or 1933).

JUNE 12 — MONDAY

Day 163 — 202 Remaining

BASEBALL'S FIRST PERFECT GAME: ANNIVERSARY. June 12, 1880. Lee Richmond of the Worcester Ruby Legs (National League) pitched baseball's first perfect game (not allowing a single opposing player to reach first base), 1–0, against the Cleveland Indians.

BIG BEND NATIONAL PARK ESTABLISHED: ANNIVERSARY. June 12, 1944. Area on the "big bend" of the Rio Grande River in western Texas along the Mexican border, authorized June 20, 1935, was established as a national park. For further park info: Big Bend Natl Park, Big Bend Natl Park, TX 79834.

BUSH, GEORGE HERBERT WALKER: BIRTHDAY. June 12, 1924. 41st president of US (1989–93), 43rd vice president of US (1981–89), born at Milton, MA.

CROWDED NEST AWARENESS DAY. June 12. More adult children are coming home due to financial and emotional reasons than ever before. Postparenting survival and support is the key for CNS sufferers. For info: Kathleen Shaputis, PO Box 11056, Olympia, WA 98508. Phone: (360) 791-2041. E-mail: info@crowdednestsyndrome.com. Web: www.crowdednest syndrome.com.

FAMILIES IN BUSINESS WEEK. June 12–16. A variety of activities planned to acknowledge and honor families in business. Annually, the week preceding Father's Day. For info: Chris Bennett, 121 N Mead, Ste 109, Witchita, KS 67202. Phone: (316) 681-0444. Fax: (316) 681-0589. E-mail: cbennett@LegasusGroup .com. Web: www.LegasusGroup.com.

FIRST MAN-POWERED FLIGHT ACROSS ENGLISH CHANNEL: ANNIVERSARY. June 12, 1979. Bryan Allen, 26-year-old Californian, pedaled the 70-lb *Gossamer Albatross* 22 miles across the English Channel, from Folkestone, England, to Cape Gris-Nez, France, in 2 hrs, 49 mins, winning (with the craft's designer, Paul MacCready of Pasadena, CA) the £100,000 prize offered by British industrialist Henry Kremer for the first man-powered flight across the English Channel.

FRANK, ANNE: BIRTH ANNIVERSARY. June 12, 1929. Born at Frankfurt, Germany. Anne Frank's family moved to Amsterdam to escape the Nazis, but after Holland was invaded by Germany, they had to go into hiding. In 1942 Anne began to keep a diary. She died at Bergen-Belsen concentration camp in 1945. After the war, her father published her diary, on which a stage play and movie were later based. See also: "Diary of Anne Frank: The Last Entry: Anniversary" (Aug 1).

LOVING v VIRGINIA: ANNIVERSARY. June 12, 1967. The US Supreme Court decision in *Loving v Virginia* swept away all 16 remaining state laws prohibiting interracial marriages.

MEET A MATE WEEK. June 12–18. To inspire singles seeking a mate to take advantage of summer by pursuing warm-weather meeting opportunities. Options include singles travel, sports activities, New Blood parties and volunteer work. For info: Robin Gorman Newman, 44 Somerset Dr N, Great Neck, NY 11020. Phone: (516) 773-0911. E-mail: robin@lovecoach.com. Web: www.love coach.com.

NATIONAL BASEBALL HALL OF FAME DEDICATED: ANNIVERSARY. June 12, 1939. The National Baseball Hall of Fame and Museum, Inc, was dedicated at Cooperstown, NY. More than 200 individuals have been honored for their contributions to the game of baseball by induction into the Baseball Hall of Fame. The first players chosen for membership (1936) were Ty Cobb, Honus Wagner, Babe Ruth, Christy Mathewson and Walter Johnson. Relics and memorabilia from the history of baseball are housed at this shrine of America's national sport.

★**NATIONAL LITTLE LEAGUE BASEBALL WEEK.** June 12–18. Presidential Proclamation 3296, of June 4, 1959, covers all succeeding years. Always the week beginning with the second Monday in June. (H.Con.Res. 17 of June 1, 1959.)

PARAGUAY: PEACE WITH BOLIVIA DAY. June 12. Commemorates the end of the Chaco War in 1935.

PHILIPPINES: INDEPENDENCE DAY. June 12. National holiday. Declared independence from Spain in 1898.

QUEEN'S OFFICIAL BIRTHDAY. June 12. A holiday in Australia (except for Western Australia), Belize, Cayman Islands, Fiji and Papua New Guinea on the second Monday in June. In New Zealand and Tuvalu it is commemorated on the first Monday in June. Celebrating Queen Elizabeth II's "official" birthday, not the day she was actually born (which is Apr 21).

RUSSIA: INDEPENDENCE DAY. June 12. National holiday. Commemorates the election in 1991 of the first popularly elected leader (Yeltsin) in the 1,000-year history of the Russian state.

SPACE MILESTONE: VENERA 4 (USSR). June 12, 1967. Launched on this date, this instrumental capsule landed on Venus by parachute on Oct 18 and reported a temperature of 536°F.

"TEAR DOWN THIS WALL" SPEECH: ANNIVERSARY. June 12, 1987. US President Ronald Reagan, standing at the Brandenburg Gate and the Berlin Wall, gave one of the most powerful speeches of his career when he challenged Soviet President Mikhail Gorbachev to give liberalization in the Eastern Bloc more than lip service: "General Secretary Gorbachev, if you seek peace, if you seek prosperity for the Soviet Union and Eastern Europe, if you seek liberalization: Come here to this gate! Mr Gorbachev, open this gate! Mr Gorbachev, tear down this wall!" The speech was audible to East Berliners, but East German police made a gathering crowd at the Wall disperse. The State Department had sought to make the speech more conciliatory, but Reagan and his speechwriter, Peter Robinson, refused. The wall was finally opened in 1989. See also: "Berlin Wall Opened: Anniversary" (Nov 9).

BIRTHDAYS TODAY

Marv Albert, 63, sportscaster, born Marvin Philip Aufrichtig at New York, NY, June 12, 1943.

Timothy Busfield, 49, actor ("thirtysomething," *Field of Dreams*), born Lansing, MI, June 12, 1957.

George Herbert Walker Bush, 82, 41st president of the US, born Milton, MA, June 12, 1924.

Chick Corea, 65, musician, born Chelsea, MA, June 12, 1941.

Vic Damone, 78, singer ("On the Street Where You Live"), born Vito Farinola at New York, NY, June 12, 1928.

Hideki Matsui, 32, baseball player, born Ishikawa, Japan, June 12, 1974.

Jim Nabors, 74, actor ("The Andy Griffith Show," "Gomer Pyle, U.S.M.C."), born Sylacauga, AL, June 12, 1932.

Frances O'Connor, 37, actress (*The Importance of Being Earnest, Mansfield Park*), born Oxford, England, June 12, 1969.

David Rockefeller, 91, banker, born New York, NY, June 12, 1915.

JUNE 13 — TUESDAY
Day 164 — 201 Remaining

BOLLES, DON: 30th DEATH ANNIVERSARY. June 13, 1976. Don Bolles, investigative reporter for *The Arizona Republic*, died as a result of injuries received when a bomb exploded in his automobile, June 2, 1976, while he was engaged in journalistic investigation of an alleged Mafia story. Bolles was awarded, posthumously, the University of Arizona's John Peter Zenger Award, Dec 9, 1976.

BURLINGTON STEAMBOAT DAYS/AMERICAN MUSIC FESTIVAL. June 13–18. Mississippi Riverfront at Port of Burlington, IA. 44th annual. Weeklong event offers community and visitors a chance to enjoy top-name entertainment and a carnival setting. Est attendance: 100,000. For info: Steamboat Days, PO Box 271, Burlington, IA 52601. Phone: (319) 754-4334. Fax: (319) 752-1299. Web: www.steamboatdays.com.

EVERS, MEDGAR ASSASSINATED: ANNIVERSARY. June 13, 1963. Civil rights leader Medgar Wiley Evers was active in seeking integration of schools and voter registration. He was assassinated by Byron de la Beckwith. The public outrage following his death was one of the factors that led President John F. Kennedy to propose a comprehensive civil rights law.

FIRST ROLLER COASTER OPENS: ANNIVERSARY. June 13, 1884. The world's first roller coaster opened today in 1884 at Coney Island, Brooklyn, NY. Built and later patented by LaMarcus Thompson, the "Gravity Pleasure Switchback Railway" boasted two parallel 600-foot tracks that descended from 50 feet.

June 2006	S	M	T	W	T	F	S
					1	2	3
	4	5	6	7	8	9	10
	11	12	13	14	15	16	17
	18	19	20	21	22	23	24
	25	26	27	28	29	30	

The cars traveled at six miles per hour. Riders paid five cents for their ride. The roller coaster was a sensation and soon amusement parks all over the US and the world featured them.

GRANGE, RED: BIRTH ANNIVERSARY. June 13, 1903. Harold Edward ("Red") Grange, Pro Football Hall of Fame halfback and broadcaster, born at Forksville, PA. Perhaps the most famous football player of all time, Grange had a spectacular college career at the University of Illinois, being named an All-American in 1923, 1924 and 1925. When Illinois dedicated its Memorial Stadium on Oct 18, 1924, Grange scored four touchdowns against Michigan in the game's first 12 minutes. Known as the "Galloping Ghost," Grange joined the Chicago Bears in 1925 for what amounted to a barnstorming tour, the start of a professional career dictated by Grange and his manager, Charles C. ("Cash and Carry") Pyle. He retired in 1934 following a knee injury, having put pro football on the sports map. Grange entered business and did announcing work on radio and television. In retirement, he lived quietly and humbly. Inducted into the Hall of Fame as a charter member in 1963. Died at Lake Wales, FL, Jan 28, 1991.

HOME OWNERS LOAN ACT: ANNIVERSARY. June 13, 1933. The Federal Savings and Loan Association was authorized with the passage of the Home Owners Loan Act. The purpose of the legislation was to provide a convenient place for investment and to lend money on first mortgages. The first association was the First Federal Savings and Loan Association of Miami, FL, which was chartered on Aug 8, 1933.

MIRANDA DECISION: 40th ANNIVERSARY. June 13, 1966. The US Supreme Court rendered a 5–4 decision in the case of *Miranda v Arizona*, holding that the Fifth Amendment of the Constitution "required warnings before valid statements could be taken by police." The decision has been described as "providing basic legal protections to persons who might otherwise not be aware of their rights." Ernesto Miranda, the 23-year-old whose name became nationally known, was retried after the *Miranda* decision, convicted and sent back to prison. Miranda was stabbed to death in a card game dispute at Phoenix, AZ, in 1976. A suspect in the killing was released by police after he had been read his "Miranda rights." Police procedures now routinely require the reading of a prisoner's constitutional ("Miranda") rights before questioning.

MISSION SAN LUIS REY DE FRANCIA: FOUNDING ANNIVERSARY. June 13, 1798. California mission to the Indians founded on this date. Abandoned by 1846; restoration begun in 1892.

PETIT JEAN ANTIQUE AUTO SHOW AND SWAP MEET. June 13–17. Petit Jean Mountain, Morrilton, AR. 48th annual show and meet with more than 125 antique and classic cars competing for awards, from turn-of-the-century to 1980 models. More than 1,500 vendor spaces filled with antique cars, parts and related items. Also, arts and crafts. Est attendance: 85,000. For info: Buddy Hoelzeman, Museum of Automobiles, 8 Jones Lane, Morrilton, AR 72110. Phone: (501) 727-5427. Fax: (501) 727-6482. E-mail: motaa@ipa.net. Web: www.motaa.com.

SAINT ANTHONY OF PADUA: FEAST DAY: DEATH ANNIVERSARY. June 13. Born at Lisbon, Portugal, Aug 15, 1195, St. Anthony is patron of the illiterate and the poor. Died at Padua, June 13, 1231. Public holiday, Lisbon.

SCOTT, WINFIELD: BIRTH ANNIVERSARY. June 13, 1786. American army general, negotiator of peace treaties with Indians and twice nominated for president (1848 and 1852). Leader of brilliant military campaign in Mexico in 1847. Scott was born at Petersburg, VA, and died at West Point, NY, May 29, 1866.

YEATS, WILLIAM BUTLER: BIRTH ANNIVERSARY. June 13, 1865. Nobel Prize–winning Irish poet and dramatist, born at Dublin, Ireland. He once wrote: "If a poet interprets a poem of his own he limits its suggestibility." Yeats died at France, Jan 28, 1939. After WWII his body was returned, as he had wished, for reburial in a churchyard at Drumcliff, Ireland.

BIRTHDAYS TODAY

Tim Allen, 53, comedian, actor ("Home Improvement," *Galaxy Quest*), born Denver, CO, June 13, 1953.

Christo, 71, conceptual artist (*Running Fence, Valley Curtain*), born Christo Javacheff at Babrovo, Bulgaria, June 13, 1935.

Malcolm McDowell, 63, actor (*A Clockwork Orange, O Lucky Man*), born Leeds, England, June 13, 1943.

Ashley Olsen, 20, actress ("Full House," "Two of a Kind"), born Los Angeles, CA, June 13, 1986.

Mary-Kate Olsen, 20, actress ("Full House," "Two of a Kind"), born Los Angeles, CA, June 13, 1986.

Ally Sheedy, 44, actress (*St. Elmo's Fire, The Breakfast Club*), born New York, NY, June 13, 1962.

Richard Thomas, 55, actor ("The Waltons," *Roots: The Next Generations*), born New York, NY, June 13, 1951.

JUNE 14 — WEDNESDAY

Day 165 — 200 Remaining

ALZHEIMER, ALOIS: BIRTH ANNIVERSARY. June 14, 1864. The German psychiatrist and pathologist Alois Alzheimer was born at Markbreit am Mainz, Germany. In 1907 an article by Alzheimer appeared in *Allgemeine Zeitschrift für Psychiatrie*, first describing the disease that was named for him. It was thought of as a kind of presenile dementia, usually beginning at age 40–60. Alzheimer died Dec 19, 1915, at Breslau, Germany.

BARTLETT, JOHN: BIRTH ANNIVERSARY. June 14, 1820. American editor and compiler (Bartlett's *Familiar Quotations* [1855]) was born at Plymouth, MA. Though he had little formal education, he created one of the most-used reference works of the English language. No quotation of his own is among the more than 22,000 listed today, but in the preface to the first edition he wrote that the object of this work "originally made without any view of publication" was to show "the obligation our language owes to various authors for numerous phrases and familiar quotations which have become 'household words.'" Bartlett died at Cambridge, MA, Dec 3, 1905.

BOURKE-WHITE, MARGARET: BIRTH ANNIVERSARY. June 14, 1904. Margaret Bourke was born at New York City. One of the original photojournalists, she developed her personal style while photographing the Krupp Iron Works in Germany and the Soviet Union during the first Five-Year Plan. Bourke-White was one of the four original staff photographers for *Life* magazine in 1936. The first woman attached to the US armed forces during WWII, she covered the Italian campaign, the siege of Moscow and American soldiers' crossing of the Rhine into Germany, and she shocked the world with her photographs of the concentration camps. Bourke-White photographed Mahatma Gandhi and covered the migration of millions of people after the Indian subcontinent was divided into Hindu India and Muslim Pakistan. She served as a war correspondent during the Korean War. Among her several books, the most famous was her collaboration with her second husband, novelist Erskine Caldwell, a study of rural poverty in the American South called *You Have Seen Their Faces*. She died Aug 27, 1971, at Stamford, CT.

CHICAGO BULLS WIN THIRD STRAIGHT TITLE FOR THE SECOND TIME: ANNIVERSARY. June 14, 1998. The Chicago Bulls defeated the Utah Jazz to win their third consecutive NBA championship. This was their second "three-peat." They had accomplished this feat the first time with wins in 1991, 1992 and 1993.

CRUISIN' DOWNTOWN 2006. June 14 (also July 12, Aug 9 and Sept 13). Toms River, NJ. Enjoy classic automobiles and motorcycles along Washington St. Live entertainment, crafters and food. Est attendance: 2,500. For info: Downtown Toms River, 218 Main St, Toms River, NJ 08753. Phone: (732) 341-8738. Fax: (732) 341-8748. E-mail: trbidstaff@verizon.net. Web: www.downtowntomsriver.com.

FAMILY HISTORY DAY. June 14. Every summer family reunions are so busy with games and activities that most of us forget the true purpose: to share the folklore, legends and myths that bind us together. Each participant should share at least one good recollection (fact or fiction). Don't forget the hot dogs and lemonade. [©2003 by WH.] For info: Thomas & Ruth Roy, Wellcat Holidays, 2418 Long Ln, Lebanon, PA 17046. Phone: (717) 279-0184. E-mail: info@wellcat.com. Web: www.wellcat.com.

FIRST NONSTOP TRANSATLANTIC FLIGHT: ANNIVERSARY. June 14–15, 1919. Captain John Alcock and Lieutenant Arthur W. Brown flew a Vickers Vimy bomber 1,900 miles nonstop from St. Johns, Newfoundland, to Clifden, County Galway, Ireland. In spite of their crash landing in an Irish peat bog, their flight inspired public interest in aviation. See also: "Lindbergh Flight: Anniversary" (May 20).

FIRST US BREACH OF PROMISE SUIT: ANNIVERSARY. June 14, 1623. The first breach of promise suit in the US was filed in the Virginia Council of State, at Charles City, VA. Reverend Greville Pooley brought suit against Cicely Jordan, who had jilted him in favor of another man. (Jordan won the suit.)

★FLAG DAY. June 14. Presidential Proclamation issued each year for June 14. Proclamation 1335, of May 30, 1916, covers all succeeding years. Has been issued annually since 1941. (PL81–203 of Aug 3, 1949.) Customarily issued as "Flag Day and National Flag Week," as in 1986; the president usually mentions "a time to honor America," Flag Day to Independence Day (89 Stat. 211). See also: "National Flag Day USA: Pause for the Pledge" (below).

FLAG DAY: ANNIVERSARY OF THE STARS AND STRIPES. June 14, 1777. John Adams introduced the following resolution before the Continental Congress, meeting at Philadelphia, PA: "Resolved, That the flag of the thirteen United States shall be thirteen stripes, alternate red and white; that the union be thirteen stars, white on a blue field, representing a new constellation." Legal holiday in Pennsylvania.

"THE GONG SHOW" TV PREMIERE: 30th ANNIVERSARY. June 14, 1976. This popular show featured a panel of three celebrities judging amateur and professional acts, from the ordinary to the unusual. At any time, a judge could bang a gong to end the act; this was often done with gusto. Completed acts were then rated and the winner received a cash prize. Chuck Barris created (along with Chris Bearde) and hosted the show for all seasons and in syndication with the exception of one syndicated season hosted by Gary Owens. Celebrities who frequently appeared were Jaye P. Morgan, Rex Reed, Arte Johnson, Phyllis Diller and Jamie Farr.

HOMESTEAD DAYS. June 14–18. Beatrice, NE. This community-wide celebration recognizes the importance of the Homestead Act of 1862 to the settlement of Nebraska. Entertainment, parades and special museum exhibits. Est attendance: 30,000. For info: Homestead Days, Beatrice Chamber of Commerce, 226 S 6th St, Beatrice, NE 68310. Phone: (402) 223-2338 or (800) 755-7745. E-mail: info@beatricechamber.com. Web: www.beatrice chamber.com.

IVES, BURL: BIRTH ANNIVERSARY. June 14, 1909. American singer and actor Burl Icle Ivanhoe Ives was born at Hunt, IL. He helped to reintroduce Anglo-American folk music in the '40s and '50s. Ives won an Academy Award for his supporting role in *The Big Country* (1958), and he is well known for his role as Big Daddy in both the film and Broadway productions of *Cat On a Hot Tin Roof*. He died Apr 14, 1995, at Anacortes, WA.

JAPAN: RICE PLANTING FESTIVAL. June 14. Osaka. Ceremonial transplanting of rice seedlings in paddy field at Sumiyashi Shrine, Osaka.

LEWIS AND CLARK BICENTENNIAL NATIONAL SIGNATURE EVENT: AMONG THE NIIMIIPUU. June 14–17. Lewiston, ID. The Lewis & Clark Expedition entered the Niimiipuu (The Nez Perce) aboriginal homelands in September of 1805. On their return trip eastward, the Lewis & Clark Expedition renewed their relationship with the Niimiipuu in June of 1806. The expedition journals describe the Niimiipuu as friendly, hospitable, and gracious hosts toward the expedition, and it still reflects the Niimiipuu today. On June 14–17, 2006, the Niimiipuu will commemorate that relationship by hosting a National Signature Event. The world is invited to experience a unique commemoration of events that reflect the diversity of cultures of people for those who attend. For info: Bill Smith, 17500 Nez Perce Rd, Lewiston, ID 83501. Phone: (208) 843-2253, ext 3511. Fax: (208) 843-7396. E-mail: bill@nezperce.org. Web: www.nezperce.org or lewisandclark200.org.

MALAWI: FREEDOM DAY. June 14. National holiday. Commemorates free elections in 1994.

MISS OHIO PAGEANT. June 14–17. Renaissance Theatre, Mansfield, OH. Part of the Miss America Organization. For info: Miss Ohio Scholarship Program, PO Box 1818, Mansfield, OH 44901. Phone: (419) 522-6677. Fax: (419) 522-0054. E-mail: info@missohio.org. Web: www.missohio.org.

NATIONAL FLAG DAY USA: PAUSE FOR THE PLEDGE. June 14. Held simultaneously across the country at 7 PM, EDT. PL 99–54 recognizes the Pause for the Pledge as part of National Flag Day ceremonies. The concept of the Pause for the Pledge of Allegiance was conceived as a way for all citizens to share a patriotic moment. National ceremony at Fort McHenry National Monument and Historic Shrine.

OUTDOOR SUMMER THEATER. June 14–Aug 5. Farmington, NM. Performances are held in a natural sandstone amphitheater at the Lion's Wilderness park, with an optional southwest-style dinner served prior to each performance at 6:30 PM. Performances Wednesday through Saturday at 8 PM. Est attendance: 4,000. For info: Farmington Conv and Visitors Bureau, 3041 E Main St, Farmington, NM 87402. Phone: (800) 448-1240 or (505) 326-7602. Fax: (505) 327-0577. E-mail: fmncvb@earthlink.net. Web: www.farmingtonnm.org.

SPACE MILESTONE: *MARINER 5* (US). June 14, 1967. Launched on this date, interplanetary probe established that 72.5–87.5 percent of Venus's atmosphere is carbon dioxide on Oct 18 flyby of the planet.

SPRING SUWANNEE RIVER GOSPEL JUBILEE. June 14–17. Live Oak, FL. Past artists featured have included Dixie Echoes, Florida Boys, Dixie Melody Boys, Perry Sisters and more. Est attendance: 10,000. For info: Spirit of the Suwannee Music Park, 3076 95th Dr, Live Oak, FL 32060. Phone: (386) 364-1683. Fax: (386) 364-2998. E-mail: spirit@musicliveshere.com. Web: www.musicliveshere.com.

STOWE, HARRIET BEECHER: BIRTH ANNIVERSARY. June 14, 1811. American writer Harriet Beecher Stowe, daughter of the Reverend Lyman Beecher and sister of Henry Ward Beecher. Author of *Uncle Tom's Cabin*, an antislavery novel that provoked a storm of protest and resulted in fame for its author. Two characters in the novel attained such importance that their names became part of the English language—the Negro slave, Uncle Tom, and the villainous slaveowner, Simon Legree. The reaction to *Uncle Tom's Cabin* and its profound political impact are without parallel in American literature. It is said that during the Civil War, when Harriet Beecher Stowe was introduced to President Abraham Lincoln, his words to her were, "So you're the little woman who wrote the book that made this great war." Stowe was born at Litchfield, CT, and died at Hartford, CT, July 1, 1896.

UNIVAC COMPUTER: 55th ANNIVERSARY. June 14, 1951. Univac 1, the world's first commercial computer, designed for the US Bureau of the Census, was unveiled, demonstrated and dedicated at Philadelphia, PA. Though this milestone of the computer age was the first commercial electronic computer, it had been preceded by ENIAC (Electronic Numeric Integrator and Computer). It was completed under the supervision of J. Presper Eckert, Jr, and John W. Mauchly at the University of Pennsylvania in 1946.

US ARMY ESTABLISHED BY CONGRESS: ANNIVERSARY. June 14, 1775. Anniversary of Resolution of the Continental Congress establishing the army as the first US military service.

WARREN G. HARDING BECOMES FIRST PRESIDENT TO BROADCAST ON RADIO: ANNIVERSARY. June 14, 1922. Warren G. Harding became the first president to broadcast a message over the radio. The event was the dedication of the Francis Scott Key Memorial at Baltimore, MD. The first official government message was broadcast Dec 6, 1923.

BIRTHDAYS TODAY

Gene Barry, 85, actor (*War of the Worlds*, "Bat Masterson"), born Eugene Klass at New York, NY, June 14, 1921.

Yasmine Bleeth, 38, actress ("Baywatch," "Nash Bridges"), born New York, NY, June 14, 1968.

Boy George, 45, lead singer (Culture Club), born George Alan O'Dowd at London, England, June 14, 1961.

Marla Gibbs, 60, actress ("227," "The Jeffersons"), born Chicago, IL, June 14, 1946 (some sources say 1931 or 1941).

Stephanie Maria (Steffi) Graf, 37, former tennis player, born Bruhl, West Germany, June 14, 1969.

Eric Arthur Heiden, 48, Olympic gold medal speed skater, born Madison, WI, June 14, 1958.

Traylor Howard, 40, actress ("Two Guys and a Girl"), born Orlando, FL, June 14, 1966.

Eddie Mekka, 54, actor ("Laverne and Shirley"), born Worcester, MA, June 14, 1952.

Will Patton, 52, actor (*Silkwood, Desperately Seeking Susan*; stage: *Tourists and Refugees #2* [Obie Award]), born Charleston, SC, June 14, 1954.

Samuel Bruce (Sam) Perkins, 45, former basketball player, born New York, NY, June 14, 1961.

Patricia (Pat) Summitt, 54, college basketball coach and former player, born Clarksville, TN, June 14, 1952.

Donald Trump, 60, real estate mogul, born New York, NY, June 14, 1946.

	S	M	T	W	T	F	S
June					1	2	3
2006	4	5	6	7	8	9	10
	11	12	13	14	15	16	17
	18	19	20	21	22	23	24
	25	26	27	28	29	30	

JUNE 15 — THURSDAY

Day 166 — 199 Remaining

ARKANSAS: ADMISSION DAY: ANNIVERSARY. June 15. Became 25th state in 1836.

BOARDWALK ART SHOW & FESTIVAL. June 15–18. Virginia Beach, VA. 51st annual. The works of approximately 300 artists are displayed along the boardwalk in this nationally ranked fine art show and sale. High-quality evening performances. Annually, on Father's Day weekend. Est attendance: 250,000. For info: Contemporary Art Center of Virginia, 2200 Parks Ave, Virginia Beach, VA 23451. Phone: (757) 425-0000, ext 20. Fax: (757) 425-8186. Web: www.cacv.org.

BROOKFIELD SUMMER FUN DAYS. June 15–18. Brookfield, MO. Celebration of summer with sidewalk sales, craft booths, concession stands, parade, games, carnival, free karaoke, fishing contest, queen contest and baby show. Est attendance: 7,500. For info: Brookfield Chamber of Commerce, 300 N Main, Brookfield, MO 64628. Phone/fax: (660) 258-7255. E-mail: chamber@shighway.com. Web: www.brookfieldmochamber.com.

CANADA: SAM STEELE DAYS. June 15–18. Cranbrook, BC. Parade, Sweetheart Pageant, banquet and ball, railway museum tours, bocce tournament, wild west show, black powder shoot, ball tournament, loggers sports, soccer tournament, live entertainment, climbing wall and children's festival. Est attendance: 19,000. For info: Sam Steele Society, PO Box 115, Cranbrook, BC, Canada V1C 4H6. Phone: (250) 426-4161. Fax: (250) 426-3873. E-mail: cbkchamber@cyberlink.bc.ca.

CORPUS CHRISTI. June 15. Roman Catholic festival celebrated in honor of the Eucharist. A solemnity observed on the Thursday following Trinity Sunday since 1246. In the US Corpus Christi is celebrated on the Sunday following Trinity Sunday. See also: "Corpus Christi (US Observance)" (June 18).

FINLAND: KUOPIO DANCE FESTIVAL. June 15–21. Kuopio, Finland. Some 70 events centering on classical ballet, contemporary dance, folklore plus types depending on the theme for the festival. World-renowned dance and music companies; seminars, lectures, exhibits and films; selection of dance courses with internationally known dance teachers. Est attendance: 45,000. For info: Finnish Tourist Board, 655 Third Ave, New York, NY 10017. Phone: (212) 885-9700. Fax: (358) (17) 368-6220. E-mail: kuopio.dance.festival@travel.fi. Web: www.kuopiodancefestival.fi.

FIRST FATAL AVIATION ACCIDENT: ANNIVERSARY. June 15, 1785. Two French aeronauts, Jean François Pilatre de Rozier and P.A. de Romain, attempting to cross the English Channel from France to England in a balloon, were killed when their balloon caught fire and crashed to the ground—the first fatal accident in aviation history. Pilatre de Rozier was the first man to fly.

FORT UNION TRADING POST RENDEZVOUS. June 15–18. 25 miles SW of Williston, ND. Re-creation of the fur trade era. Fur trade fair, music, blacksmith and craft demonstrations plus Trader's Row. Sponsor: National Park Service, Fort Union Trading Post National Historic Site. Est attendance: 5,000. For info: Fort Union Trading Post NHS, 15550 Hwy 1804, Williston, ND 58801. Phone: (701) 572-9083. Fax: (701) 572-7321. Web: www.nps.gov/fous.

GETTYSBURG BRASS BAND FESTIVAL. June 15–18. Gettysburg, PA. Brass bands, ensembles, drum and bugle corps converge on Gettysburg for many musical events along Gettysburg's "Historical Pathways." Workshops, concerts and performances culminate in one grand finale at the Gettysburg College Stadium on Saturday evening. Est attendance: 8,000. For info: Gettysburg CVB, PO Box 4117, Gettysburg, PA 17325. Phone: (717) 334-6274. Fax: (717) 334-1166. E-mail: gettysburgcvb@dejazzd.com. Web: www.gettysburgcvb.org.

GREAT OBITUARY WRITERS' INTERNATIONAL CONFERENCE. June 15–17 (tentative). Las Vegas, NM. Eighth annual. Members of the International Association of Obituarists gather for their annual meeting. For info: Carolyn Gilbert, International Association of Obituarists, 8409 Pickwick Ln, #312, Dallas, TX 75225. Phone: (972) 980-2868. Fax: (972) 661-5825. E-mail: obituarist@sbcglobal.net. Web: www.ObitPage.com.

GREAT SMOKY MOUNTAINS NATIONAL PARK ESTABLISHED: ANNIVERSARY. June 15, 1934. Area along southern section of Tennessee–North Carolina boundary was authorized May 22, 1926, established for administration and protection only Feb 6, 1930, and finally established for full development as a national park in 1934. For further park info: Great Smoky Mountains Natl Park, Gatlinburg, TN 37738.

GRIEG, EDVARD: BIRTH ANNIVERSARY. June 15, 1843. Pianist, composer, conductor and teacher, the first Scandinavian to compose nationalistic music. Born at Bergen, Norway, and died there Sept 4, 1907.

"HEE HAW" TV PREMIERE: ANNIVERSARY. June 15, 1969. "Hee Haw" has been described as a country-western version of "Laugh-In," composed of fast-paced sketches, silly jokes and songs. Though critics didn't like it, it had popular appeal and did well as a syndicated show. It was cohosted by Buck Owens and Roy Clark, alternating with guest hosts. Regular performers included Louis M. "Grandpa" Jones, Junior Samples, Jeannine Riley, Lulu Roman, David "Stringbean" Akeman, Sheb Wooley, Marianne Gordon, Minnie Pearl and Gordie Tapp.

ICE CREAM DAYS. June 15–18. Le Mars, IA. Art in the park, parade, children's activities and food from the "Ice Cream Capital of the World," home of Wells's Blue Bunny. Est attendance: 10,000. For info: Sue Butcher, Operations Mgr, Le Mars Area Chamber of Commerce, 50 Central Ave SE, Le Mars, IA 51031. Phone: (712) 546-8821. Fax: (712) 546-7218. E-mail: lmchmbr@lemarscomm.net. Web: www.lemarsiowa.com.

JACKSON, RACHEL DONELSON ROBARDS: BIRTH ANNIVERSARY. June 15, 1767. Wife of Andrew Jackson, 7th president of the US, born at Halifax County, NC. Died at Nashville, TN, Dec 22, 1828.

LUDINGTON CAR FERRY FESTIVAL. June 15–18. Ludington, MI. Nautical festival celebrating proud past and prosperous future of Ludington's Harbor. Featuring kids activities, arts & crafts show, tall ship, Coast Guard open house, old-time baseball, entertainment. Est attendance: 30,000. For info: Ludington Area Chamber of Commerce, 5300 W US 10, Ludington, MI 49431. Phone: (800) 542-4600. Fax: (231) 845-6857. E-mail: visitludington@ludington.org. Web: www.ludingtoncvb.com.

MAGNA CARTA DAY: ANNIVERSARY. June 15. Anniversary of King John's sealing, in 1215, of the Magna Carta "in the meadow called Ronimed between Windsor and Staines on the fifteenth day of June in the seventeenth year of our reign." This document is regarded as the first charter of English liberties and one of the most important documents in the history of political and human freedom. Four original copies of the 1215 charter survive.

MISS LOUISIANA PAGEANT. June 15–17. Monroe Civic Center, Monroe, LA. Preliminaries followed by the main event of crowning the new Miss Louisiana. Always culminates on the third Saturday in June. Est attendance: 5,500. For info: Miss Louisiana Organization, PO Box 6003, Monroe, LA 71211. Phone: (318) 387-1658. Fax: (318) 387-6171. E-mail: LKing@jam.rr.com. Web: www.misslouisiana.com.

"MY LITTLE MARGIE" TV PREMIERE: ANNIVERSARY. June 15, 1952. "My Little Margie" was a half-hour sitcom about a "womanizing widower and his meddlesome daughter." Margie was played by Gale Storm and Charles Farrell played her father, Vern Albright.

NATIONAL NURSING ASSISTANTS DAY AND WEEK. June 15–22. 29th annual. Recognizes those nursing assistants who provide care to all ill, elderly and long-term residents in nursing homes and other long-term nursing care centers. Begins on Career Nurse Assistants' Day, June 15, 2006. For info: Natl Network of Career Nursing Assistants, 3577 Easton Rd, Norton, OH

44203. Phone: (330) 825-9342. Fax: (330) 825-9378. E-mail: cnajeni@aol.com. Web: www.cna-network.org.

NATIVE AMERICAN CITIZENSHIP DAY. June 15. Commemorates the day in 1924 when the US Congress passed legislation recognizing the citizenship of Native Americans.

NATURE PHOTOGRAPHY DAY. June 15. A day to promote the art and science of nature photography as a medium of communication, inspiration, nature appreciation and environmental protection. Annually, June 15. For info: North American Nature Photography Association, 10200 W 44th St, Ste 304, Wheat Ridge, CO 80033. Phone: (303) 422-8527. Fax: (303) 422-8894. E-mail: info@nanpa.org. Web: www.nanpa.org.

NORWAY: CELEBRATION OF EDVARD GRIEG'S BIRTH ANNIVERSARY. June 15. Special celebrations at Lofthus on the Hardanger fjord where Grieg's cabin still stands.

PRAIRIE VILLA RENDEZVOUS. June 15–18. Prairie du Chien, WI. Rendezvous with history and learn about life during the fur trading days and experience the fur trader lifestyle firsthand. Many participants come from around the country to display furs, others demonstrate the cumbersome process of loading a rifle with gunpowder and some prepare Indian fry bread and buffalo burgers. Workshops offer information on a variety of subjects including plants and medicines, basket weaving and beadworking. With more than 600 lodges and teepees, this is one of the largest Midwest trading rendezvous. Est attendance: 25,000. For info: Prairie du Chien Area Chamber of Commerce, PO Box 326, Prairie du Chien, WI 53821. Phone: (800) 732-1673. Web: www.prairieduchien.org.

QUARTERLY ESTIMATED FEDERAL INCOME TAX PAYERS' DUE DATE. June 15. For those individuals whose fiscal year is the calendar year and who make quarterly estimated federal income tax payments, today is one of the due dates (Jan 17, Apr 17, June 15 and Sept 15, 2006).

RECESS AT WORK DAY. June 15. The board of directors has declared that all employees should spend some time playing today. That means everyone—even the boss! Call it team building, call it employee morale, call it professional development—just make sure you call it fun. It's time for recess! Annually, the third Thursday in June. For info: Rich DiGirolamo, PO Box 584, Marion, CT 06444. Phone: (203) 879-5970. E-mail: rich@donewhining.com. Web: www.RecessAtWorkDay.com.

TWELFTH AMENDMENT TO US CONSTITUTION RATIFIED: ANNIVERSARY. June 15, 1804. The 12th Amendment to the Constitution was ratified. It changed the method of electing the president and vice president after a tie in the electoral college during the election of 1800. Rather than each elector voting for two candidates with the candidate receiving the most votes elected president and the second-place candidate elected vice president, each elector was now required to designate his choice for president and vice president, respectively.

US LANDING ON SAIPAN: ANNIVERSARY. June 15, 1944. In a continued effort to penetrate the Japanese inner defenses, US amphibious forces invaded the Mariana Islands. A huge fleet of 800 ships from Guadalcanal and Hawaii carried the 2nd and 4th Marine Divisions, consisting of 162,000 men. By the end of the day 20,000 of these men had established a 5½-mile-long beachhead on the island of Saipan. Though the American forces suffered heavy losses during an overnight counterattack, on the morning of June 16 the Marines still held the area they had taken the day before.

June *2006*	S	M	T	W	T	F	S
					1	2	3
	4	5	6	7	8	9	10
	11	12	13	14	15	16	17
	18	19	20	21	22	23	24
	25	26	27	28	29	30	

US OPEN (GOLF) CHAMPIONSHIP. June 15–18. Winged Foot Golf Club, Mamaroneck, NY. For info: US Golf Assn, Golf House, PO Box 708, Championship Dept, Far Hills, NJ 07931. Phone: (908) 234-2300. Fax: (908) 234-9687. E-mail: usga@usga.org. Web: www.usga.org.

WEST ALLIS WESTERN DAYS FAMILY JAMBOREE. June 15–18. West Allis, WI. 42nd annual celebration. This four-day, fun-filled festival kicks off at 7:00 PM on June 15 with one of the largest nonmotorized parades in the world. Live music every day, rodeo, midway, carnival, treats and eats. Est attendance: 75,000. For info: WAWD, c/o West Allis Charities, Inc, PO Box 14544, West Allis, WI 53214. Web: www.westerndays.com.

BIRTHDAYS TODAY

Courteney Cox Arquette, 42, actress ("Friends," *Scream*), born Birmingham, AL, June 15, 1964.

Jim Belushi, 52, actor ("Saturday Night Live," "According to Jim"), born Chicago, IL, June 15, 1954.

Wade Anthony Boggs, 48, former baseball player, born Omaha, NE, June 15, 1958.

Simon Callow, 57, actor (*A Room with a View, Mr and Mrs Bridge, Howards End*); author (*Orson Welles*), born London, England, June 15, 1949.

Julie Hagerty, 51, actress (*Airplane!, Lost in America, Reversal of Fortune*); stage: *The House of Blue Leaves* [Theatre World Award]), born Cincinnati, OH, June 15, 1955.

Neil Patrick Harris, 33, actor ("Doogie Howser, MD," "Stark Raving Mad," *Clara's Heart*), born Albuquerque, NM, June 15, 1973.

Mike Holmgren, 58, football coach, born San Francisco, CA, June 15, 1948.

Helen Hunt, 43, actress ("Mad About You," *Twister*, Oscar for *As Good as It Gets*), born Los Angeles, CA, June 15, 1963.

Justin Leonard, 34, golfer, born Dallas, TX, June 15, 1972.

Nicola Pagett, 61, actress ("Upstairs Downstairs," *There's a Girl in My Soup*), born Cairo, Egypt, June 15, 1945.

Leah Remini, 36, actress ("The King of Queens," "Saved by the Bell"), born Brooklyn, NY, June 15, 1970.

JUNE 16 — FRIDAY
Day 167 — 198 Remaining

ANTIQUES BY THE BAY. June 16–17. St. Ignace, MI. 10th annual show for antique and classic original vehicles 25 years or older. Special tours and awards plus auto world celebrities. For info: Nostalgia Productions, Inc, 268 Hillcrest Blvd, St. Ignace, MI 49781. Phone: (906) 643-8087. Fax: (906) 643-9784. E-mail: ereavie@nostalgia-prod.com. Web: www.nostalgia-prod.com or www.auto-shows.com.

BADGER STATE SUMMER GAMES. June 16–18 and 23–25. Madison, WI. 21st annual sports festival for Wisconsin residents of all ages and abilities, featuring 28 sports and opening ceremonies. Major sponsors: American Family Insurance, Wisconsin Milk Marketing Board, Mobil and St. Joseph's Hospital. Est attendance: 20,000. For info: Badger State Games, PO Box 7788, Madison, WI 53707-7788. Phone: (608) 226-4780. Fax: (608) 226-9550. E-mail: info@SportsinWisconsin.com. Web: www.SportsinWisconsin.com.

BLOOMSDAY: ANNIVERSARY. June 16, 1904. Anniversary of events in Dublin recorded in James Joyce's *Ulysses*, whose central character is Leopold Bloom.

CANADA: NOVA SCOTIA MULTICULTURAL FESTIVAL. June 16–18 (tentative). Dartmouth, NS. 22nd annual. Cultural events include five tents housing exhibits, food booths, children's tent, performances and beer tent with live bands. Est attendance: 47,000. For info: Barbara Campbell, Exec Dir, Multicultural Assn of Nova Scotia, 1113 Marginal Rd, Halifax, NS, Canada B3H 4P7. Phone: (902) 423-6534. Fax: (902) 422-0881. E-mail: info@multifest.ca. Web: www.multifest.ca.

CZECH DAYS. June 16–17. Tabor, SD. 58th annual. Czechs dressed in their festive costumes gather with people from all parts of the world in this gala celebration. Fine Czech foods, dancing, music and entertainment. Est attendance: 15,000. For info: Tabor Area Chamber of Commerce, Inc, PO Box 21, Tabor, SD 57063. Phone: (605) 463-2476. E-mail: czechdays@yahoo.com. Web: www.byelectric.com/~tabor.

DOLLARS AGAINST DIABETES (DAD'S) DAY. June 16–18. DAD's Day is a national fund-raising event conducted in more than 300 cities to help the Diabetes Research Institute find a permanent cure for the disease. Annually, on Father's Day weekend. Sponsor: Building and Construction Trades Dept of the AFL-CIO. Participation 30,000. For info: Dollars Against Diabetes, Building and Construction Trades Dept, 815 16th St NW, Ste 600, Washington, DC 20006. Phone: (888) 883-DADS. E-mail: dadbctd@aol.com. Web: www.dadsday.org.

ENGLAND: EXETER FESTIVAL. June 16–July 2 (tentative). Various venues, Exeter, Devon. A broad ranging eclectic program of classical and contemporary performance in a variety of city venues, featuring the best of British arts and culture. Est attendance: 32,000. For info: David Whitelock, Exeter City Council, Paris Street, Exeter, England EX1 1JJ. Phone: (44) (139) 226-5200. Fax: (44) (139) 226-5366. E-mail: festival@exeter.gov.uk. Web: exeter.gov.uk/festival.

FULTON COUNTY HISTORICAL POWER SHOW. June 16–18. Rochester, IN. Power show will include antique tractors, hit 'n' miss engines, equipment and antique trucks. Also: vendors of swap parts, crafts, food and more. Contests held for exhibitors. Admission fee. Annually, third weekend in June. Est attendance: 3,000. For info: Fulton County Historical Power Assn, c/o Fulton County Historical Society, 37 E 375 N, Rochester, IN 46975. Phone: (574) 223-4436. E-mail: melinda@rtcol.com. Web: icss.net/~fchs.

GRIFFIN, JOHN HOWARD: BIRTH ANNIVERSARY. June 16, 1920. American author and photographer deeply concerned about racial problems in US. To better understand blacks in the American South, Griffin blackened his skin by the use of chemicals and ultraviolet light, keeping a journal as he traveled through the South, resulting in his best-known book, *Black Like Me*. Born at Dallas, TX. Died at Fort Worth, TX, Sept 9, 1980.

HARBORFEST. June 16–18. Riverfront Park, South Haven, MI. Celebrate the harbor with music, arts & crafts, dragon boat races and more. For info: South Haven Chamber of Commerce, 606 Phillips St, South Haven, MI 49090. Phone: (269) 637-5171. Fax: (269) 637-1570. E-mail: cofc@southhavenmi.com. Web: www.shharborfest.com.

HUCK FINN'S JUBILEE. June 16–18. Mojave Narrows Regional Park, Victorville, CA. A Huck Finn celebration with river raft building, country and bluegrass music, hayrides, old-time tent circus, crafts and food, plus Route 66 car show and the California State Arm Wrestling Championships. Annually, on Father's Day weekend. Est attendance: 16,000. For info: Don or Barbara Tucker, PO Box 56419, Riverside, CA 92517. Phone: (951) 780-8810. E-mail: huckfinn@huckfinn.com. Web: www.huckfinn.com.

KIAMICHI OWA-CHITO FESTIVAL OF THE FOREST. June 16–17. Beavers Bend State Park, Broken Bow, OK. A celebration of American Indian culture and of the forest industry. Compete in ax throwing, cross-buck sawing, pole filling and logging to become the "Bull of the Woods." Also kids' games, food booths, Miss Owa-Chito contest, photography contest, golf tour-

nament, canoe races, archery contest, turkey-calling contest, 5k road race, talent contest and more. Annually, the weekend of the third Friday in June. Est attendance: 30,000. For info: Chamber of Commerce, 113 W Martin Luther King, Broken Bow, OK 74728. Phone: (580) 584-3393. Fax: (580) 584-7698. E-mail: bchamber@pine-net.com. Web: www.brokenbowchamber.com.

LADIES' DAY INITIATED IN BASEBALL: ANNIVERSARY. June 16, 1883. The New York Giants hosted the first Ladies' Day baseball game. Both escorted and unescorted ladies were admitted to the game free.

LAUREL, STAN: BIRTH ANNIVERSARY. June 16, 1890. Worked with Oliver Hardy as the comedy team of Laurel & Hardy for more than 30 years. Born at Ulverston, England, Laurel died Feb 23, 1965, at Santa Monica, CA.

LEWIS AND CLARK DAYS. June 16–18. Washburn, ND. Rediscover the land that Lewis and Clark called home in 1804–05. Fur traders of the 1800s hold a rendezvous at Fort Mandan, while downtown Washburn celebrates with a parade, carnival, street dance, family fishing derby, plus many more fun activities. Est attendance: 4,500. For info: (701) 462-8535 or North Dakota Tourism, Century Center, 1600 E Century Ave, Ste 2, Bismarck, ND 58503. Phone: (701) 328-2525 or (800) 435-5663. Web: www.fortmandan.com.

LOCKPORT OLD CANAL DAYS. June 16–18. Lockport, IL. Festival in historic canal community. Crafts, parade, entertainment, food, carnival, contests, beer garden and more. Annually, the third weekend in June. Est attendance: 20,000. For info: Lockport Old Canal Days, PO Box 31, Lockport, IL 60441. Phone: (815) 838-4744.

MEDFORD CRUISE. June 16–18. Medford, OR. Fun Run and Grudge Races on Friday, Show 'n Shine and Cruise on Saturday, pancake breakfast and Show 'n Shine on Sunday. 600 classic pre-1972 cars. Come join the food and fun! Kids activities provided. For info: Medford Cruise, PO Box 629, Medford, OR 97501. Phone: (541) 608-8527. E-mail: vcb@medfordchamber.com.

MISS ALASKA SCHOLARSHIP PAGEANT. June 16–17. Wendy Williamson Auditorium, University of Alaska, Anchorage, AK. Held since 1958. Part of the Miss America Organization. For info: Miss Alaska Scholarship Pageant, Inc, 16823 Schroeder Dr, Eagle River, AK 99577. E-mail: info@missalaskapageant.com. Web: www.missalaskapageant.com.

NCAA DIVISION I MEN'S COLLEGE WORLD SERIES. June 16–26. Rosenblatt Stadium, Omaha, NE. For info: Natl Collegiate Athletic Assn, 700 W Washington Ave, PO Box 6222, Indianapolis, IN 46206-6222. Phone: (317) 917-6222. Web: www.ncaasports.com.

***PSYCHO* FILM PREMIERE: ANNIVERSARY.** June 16, 1960. Millions of filmgoers (and star Janet Leigh) avoided the shower after this thriller's debut in 1960. Alfred Hitchcock's shocker, punctuated by shrieking violins and sudden knife attacks, juxtaposed the old-timey horror of the dark gothic mansion with a new locus of fear: the isolated postwar roadside motel. *Psycho* led the way to the "slasher" films of the 1970s and later. Anthony Perkins starred as motel proprietor and bird lover Norman Bates.

RED RIVER VALLEY FAIR. June 16–25. Fargo, ND. One of the largest fairs in the state with 4-H and commercial exhibits, horse shows, car shows, large carnival midway, free entertainment. Big-name country western and rock entertainers perform every day. Est attendance: 150,000. For info: (701) 282-2200 or North Dakota Tourism, Century Center, 1600 E Century Ave, Ste 2, Bismarck, ND 58503. Phone: (701) 328-2525 or (800) 435-5663. Web: www.redrivervalleyfair.com.

SECRET CITY FESTIVAL. June 16–17. Oak Ridge, TN. A unique event highlighting the genesis of Oak Ridge, TN, as a major site of the Manhattan Project. Oak Ridge was created in 1942 in an almost unknown area in the hills of East Tennessee, specifically for government research. It has grown to be one of this nation's most important technology sites and is a mecca for scientific and technological innovations. Music, arts, WWII reenactments, film festival and more. Est attendance: 12,000. For info: Secret City Festival, PO Box 1, 1403 Oak Ridge Turnpike, Oak Ridge, TN 37830. Phone: (865) 425-3610. Web: www.secretcityfestival.com.

SOUTH AFRICA: YOUTH DAY. June 16. National holiday. Commemorates a student uprising in Soweto against "Bantu Education" and the enforced teaching of Afrikaans in 1976.

SOUTH CAROLINA FESTIVAL OF FLOWERS. June 16–18. Greenwood, SC. Come and see the beautiful flowers of South Carolina. Includes arts and crafts displays, entertainment, sports events and more. Est attendance: 25,000. For info: Greenwood Chamber of Commerce, SC Festival of Flowers, PO Box 980, Greenwood, SC 29648. Phone: (864) 223-8411. Fax: (864) 229-9785. E-mail: frank@greenwoodscchamber.org. Web: www.scfestivalofflowers.org.

SPACE MILESTONE: *VOSTOK 6* **(USSR): FIRST WOMAN IN SPACE.** June 16, 1963. Valentina Tereshkova, 26, former cotton-mill worker, born on collective farm near Yaroslavl, USSR, became the first woman in space when her spacecraft, *Vostok 6*, took off from the Tyuratam launch site. She manually controlled *Vostok 6* during the 70.8-hour flight through 48 orbits of Earth and landed by parachute (separate from her cabin) June 19, 1963. In November 1963 she married cosmonaut Andrian Nikolayev, who had piloted *Vostok 3* through 64 Earth orbits, Aug 11–15, 1962. Their child Yelena (1964) was the first born to space-traveler parents.

STAMP EXPO. June 16–18. Radisson Hotel, Sherman Oaks, CA. Est attendance: 5,000. For info: Israel Bick, Exec Dir, Intl Stamp & Coin Collectors Society, PO Box 854, Van Nuys, CA 91408. Phone: (818) 997-6496. Fax: (818) 988-4337. E-mail: iibick@sbcglobal.net. Web: www.bick.net.

WORK@HOME FATHER'S DAY. June 16. One day each year to honor and celebrate those fathers who have elected to work from home—either as home-based entrepreneurs or teleworkers—as a means to improve family interaction and professional satisfaction. Annually, the Friday before Father's Day. For info: Jeff Zbar, PO Box 8263, Coral Springs, FL 33075. Phone: (954) 346-4393. E-mail: jeff@chiefhomeofficer.com. Web: www.chiefhomeofficer.com.

BIRTHDAYS TODAY

Sonia Braga, 56, actress ("American Family," *Kiss of the Spider Woman*), born Maringá, Paraná, Brazil, June 16, 1950.

Billy "Crash" Craddock, 67, singer ("Don't Destroy Me," "Ruby, Baby"), born Greensboro, NC, June 16, 1939.

Roberto Duran, 55, boxer, born Chorillo, Panama, June 16, 1951.

Cobi Jones, 36, soccer player, played in 1994, 1998 and 2002 World Cups, born Westlake Village, CA, June 16, 1970.

Laurie Metcalf, 51, actress (Emmy for "Roseanne"; "The Norm Show"), born Edwardsville, IL, June 16, 1955.

Phil Mickelson, 36, golfer, born San Diego, CA, June 16, 1970.

Joyce Carol Oates, 68, writer (*Triumph of the Spider Monkey, The Time Traveler*), born Lockport, NY, June 16, 1938.

Irving Penn, 89, photographer, born Plainfield, PA, June 16, 1917.

M. Jodi Rell, 60, Governor of Connecticut (R), born Norfolk, VA, June 16, 1946.

Erich Segal, 69, author (*Acts of Faith, Love Story*), born Brooklyn, NY, June 16, 1937.

Joan Van Ark, 63, actress ("Knots Landing"), born New York, NY, June 16, 1943.

Kerry Wood, 29, baseball player, born Irving, TX, June 16, 1977.

★　★　★

June *2006*	S	M	T	W	T	F	S
					1	2	3
	4	5	6	7	8	9	10
	11	12	13	14	15	16	17
	18	19	20	21	22	23	24
	25	26	27	28	29	30	

JUNE 17 — SATURDAY
Day 168 — 197 Remaining

BELLAMY, RALPH: BIRTH ANNIVERSARY. June 17, 1904. American actor Ralph Rexford Bellamy was born at Chicago, IL. He appeared in more than 100 films and was best known for his stage and film portrayals of President Franklin D. Roosevelt. He was a founder of the Screen Actors' Guild and president of Actors' Equity. Bellamy was awarded an honorary Academy Award in 1987. He died Nov 29, 1991, at Los Angeles, CA.

BUNKER HILL DAY. June 17. Suffolk County, MA. Legal holiday in the county in commemoration of the Battle of Bunker Hill that took place in 1775.

EISENHOWER FIFTIES WEEKEND. June 17–18. Eisenhower National Historic Site, Gettysburg, PA. Revisit the popular culture of the 1950s. See Detroit's finest 1950s cars. Remember rock 'n' roll, the Hula Hoop and more. Ranger programs on the issues of the day. Est attendance: 1,000. For info: Gettysburg CVB, PO Box 4117, Gettysburg, PA 17325. Phone: (717) 334-6274. Fax: (717) 334-1166. E-mail: gettysburgcvb@dejazzd.com. Web: www.gettysburgcvb.org.

FAIN, SAMMY: BIRTH ANNIVERSARY. June 17, 1902. American composer Sammy Fain was born Samuel Feinberg at New York, NY. He won an Academy Award for his song "Secret Love" from *Calamity Jane* (1953) and for "Love Is a Many-Splendored Thing" from the film of the same name (1955). He died Dec 6, 1989, at Los Angeles, CA.

HERITAGE CRAFT AND OLDE-TIME MUSIC FESTIVAL. June 17–18. Coshocton, OH. Old-time musical entertainment; guitar, fiddle, dulcimer and banjo workshops; games and flat-pick guitar contest. Annually, third weekend in June. Est attendance: 5,000. For info: Roscoe Village Fdtn, 381 Hill St, Coshocton, OH 43812. Phone: (800) 877-1830 or (740) 622-9310. Fax: (740) 623-6555. E-mail: rvmarketing@roscoevillage.com. Web: www.roscoevillage.com.

HERSEY, JOHN: BIRTH ANNIVERSARY. June 17, 1914. American novelist, born at Tientsin, China, who wrote *A Bell for Adano*, which won the Pulitzer Prize in 1945. *The Wall* and *Hiroshima* are both based on fact and set in Poland and Japan respectively in WWII. Died at Key West, FL, Mar 24, 1993.

HOOPER, WILLIAM: BIRTH ANNIVERSARY. June 17, 1742. Signer of the Declaration of Independence, born at Boston, MA. Died Oct 14, 1790, at Hillsboro, NC.

ICELAND: INDEPENDENCE DAY. June 17. National holiday. Anniversary of founding of republic and independence from Denmark in 1944 is major festival, especially in Reykjavik. Parades, competitions, street dancing.

KCQ COUNTRY MUSIC FEST. June 17. Saginaw, MI. Country music's hottest artists perform on stage on Ojibway Island. Also featuring a classic car show, art fair and great food, this is mid-Michigan's hottest summer attraction. Free admission. Est attendance: 70,000. For info: WKCQ, PO Box 1776, Saginaw, MI 48605. Phone: (989) 752-8161. Fax: (989) 752-8102. Web: www.98FMKCQ.com.

LAKESTRIDE HALF-MARATHON. June 17. Ludington, MI. Half-marathon race that begins at Lakeshore Drive and Tinkham (by the beach) takes runners along a scenic course through the wooded trails and sand dunes of Lake Michigan at Ludington State Park. Annually, the Saturday of Father's Day weekend. Est attendance: 10,000. For info: Ludington Area CVB, 5300 W US 10, Ludington, MI 49431. Phone: (800) 542-4600. Fax: (231) 845-6857. Web: www.ludington.org.

LONGEST DAM RUN. June 17. Fort Peck, MT. This is a sanctioned 5k and 10k run. There are also 5k walks and a 1-mile run/walk. The run crosses 1.8 miles of Fort Peck Dam. At two miles into the 10k race, the course rises in elevation some 350 feet over a distance of approximately two miles. The 5k is flat. Both distances finish running downhill grade from the top of the dam. Included in the events is a 22-mile bike ride and a 10-mile novice bike ride. Annually, the third weekend in June. Est attendance: 550. For info: Glasgow Chamber of Commerce and Agriculture, Box 832, Glasgow, MT 59230. Phone: (406) 228-2222. Fax: (406) 228-2244. E-mail: chamber@nemontel.net. Web: www .glasgowmt.net.

MARITIME HERITAGE FESTIVAL. June 17. Historic St. Mary's City, St. Mary's City, MD. Big boats, little boats, knots and sea shanties—a celebration of all things maritime. Est attendance: 1,000. For info: Susan Wilkinson, HSMC, Box 39, St. Mary's City, MD 20686. Phone: (240) 895-4967. Fax: (240) 895-4968. Web: www.stmaryscity.org.

MIDNIGHT SUN FESTIVAL. June 17–18. Nome, AK. A celebration of the summer solstice, which is when Nome experiences the midnight sun with more than 22 hours of direct sunlight. The festival usually includes a parade, raft race, folk fest and barbecue. Annually, on the Saturday and Sunday closest to the summer solstice. Est attendance: 500. For info: Nome Conv & Visitors Bureau, PO Box 240, Nome, AK 99762. Phone: (907) 443-6624. Fax: (907) 443-5832. Web: www.nomealaska.org.

NEW OXFORD OUTDOOR ANTIQUE SHOW. June 17. New Oxford, PA. Arts, crafts, antiques and flea market. Annually, the third Saturday in June. Est attendance: 30,000. For info: Gettysburg CVB, PO Box 4117, Gettysburg, PA 17325. Phone: (717) 334-6274. Fax: (717) 334-1166. E-mail: gettysburgcvb@dejazzd .com. Web: www.gettysburgcvb.org.

OIL BOWL FOOTBALL CLASSIC. June 17. Memorial Stadium, Wichita Falls, TX. 67th annual. For more than 60 years, high school all-stars from Texas and Oklahoma tangle in Memorial Stadium, to benefit disadvantaged children. Est attendance: 14,000. For info: Wichita Falls CVB, 1000 5th St, Wichita Falls, TX 76301. Phone: (940) 716-5500. Fax: (940) 716-5509. E-mail: mpec@wf.net. Web: www.wichitafalls.org.

POLAR BEAR SWIM. June 17. Nome, AK. 2 PM on the red sand beaches. More than 100 intrepid swimmers have plunged into the frigid Bering Sea on this day since 1975. The swim may be rescheduled if the ocean ice hasn't sufficiently broken up. For info: Leo B. Rasmussen, Nome Rotary Club, PO Box 275, Nome, AK 99762. Phone: (907) 443-2798 or (907) 443-6022. E-mail: leaknome@alaska.com.

RIVER RAID RENAISSANCE FESTIVAL AND GOETTAFEST. June 17–18. MainStrasse Village, Covington, KY. Step back in time to the Renaissance era with food, art/crafts, demonstrations, costumed villagers, activities and entertainment. Then step out of time and return to present day fun at the MainStrasse Village "Original" Goettafest along the Sixth Street Promenade. Goettafest is a celebration of goetta, a favorite regional food. Est attendance: 25,000. For info: Donna Kremer, MainStrasse Village, 406 West 6th St, Ste 201, Covington, KY 41011. Phone: (859) 491-0458. Fax: (859) 655-7932. E-mail: dkremer@ mainstrasse.org. Web: www.mainstrasse.org.

ROCHESTERFEST. June 17–25. Rochester, MN. This community festival includes Midwestern lumberjack championships, cultural diversity, children's and senior events, gigantic street parade, street vendors with exotic foods, country night, rock and roll night, street dance and breakfast on the farm. Est attendance: 150,000. For info: Carole Brown, Exec Dir, Box 007, Rochester, MN 55903. Phone: (507) 285-8769. Fax: (507) 285-8718. Web: www.rochesterfest.com.

SANDPOINT SADDLE CLUB HORSE SHOW. June 17–18. Sandpoint, ID. English, Western, Parade, Spanish Fiesta classes. Annually, the third weekend in June. For info: Denise Mills, PO Box 243, Sandpoint, ID 83864. Phone: (208) 263-4091. E-mail: deniselm@netw.com. Web: www.sandpointsaddleclub.org.

SOUTH AFRICA REPEALS LAST APARTHEID LAW: 15th ANNIVERSARY. June 17, 1991. The Parliament of South Africa repealed the Population Registration Act, removing the law that was the foundation of apartheid. The law, first enacted in 1950, required the classification by race of all South Africans at birth. It established four compulsory racial categories: white, mixed race, Asian and black. Although this marked the removal of the last of the apartheid laws, blacks in South Africa still could not vote.

STONE MOUNTAIN VILLAGE ARTS AND CRAFTS FESTIVAL. June 17–18. Stone Mountain Village, GA. 34th annual juried arts and crafts show featuring more than 100 of the southeast's finest artists and crafters. The festival will be held in the streets throughout the city. With extraordinary entertainment and the best country cooking around. Est attendance: 3,000. For info: Dir, Village Festivals, PO Box 667, Stone Mountain Village, GA 30086. Phone: (770) 498-2097. Web: www.stone mountainvillage.com.

STRAVINSKY, IGOR FYODOROVICH: BIRTH ANNIVERSARY. June 17, 1882. Russian composer and author, born at Oranienbaum (near Leningrad). Among his best-known music: the ballets *The Firebird, Petrushka* and *The Rite of Spring*; the choral work *Symphony of Psalms*; and *Abraham and Isaac, A Sacred Ballet.* Died at New York, NY, Apr 6, 1971.

UNITED NATIONS: WORLD DAY TO COMBAT DESERTIFICATION AND DROUGHT. June 17. Proclaimed by the General Assembly Dec 19, 1994 (Res 49/115). States were invited to promote public awareness of the need for international cooperation to combat desertification and the effects of drought and the implementation of the UN Convention to Combat Desertification. For info: United Nations, Dept of Public Info, New York, NY 10017. Web: www.un.org.

VINEGAR DAY. June 17. A day set aside to celebrate the virtues of vinegar. All over the world people will conduct vinegar tasting contests and host events connected with vinegar. There will be an International Vinegar Festival in Roslyn, SD, to commemorate. Annually, the third Saturday in June. For info: Lawrence Diggs, Vinegar Connoisseurs Intl, PO Box 41, Roslyn, SD 57261. Phone: (605) 486-4536. E-mail: vinegarday@vinegarman.com. Web: www.vinegarman.com.

WATERGATE DAY: ANNIVERSARY. June 17, 1972. Anniversary of arrests at Democratic Party Headquarters (in Watergate complex, Washington, DC) that led to revelations of political espionage, threats of imminent impeachment of the president and, on Aug 9, 1974, the resignation of President Richard M. Nixon.

WESLEY, JOHN: BIRTH ANNIVERSARY. June 17, 1703. Born at Epworth, England. Wesley, along with his younger brother Charles, was the founder of Methodism. John Wesley died Mar 2, 1791.

WEST QUODDY HEAD LIGHT KEEPERS ASSOCIATION ANNIVERSARY CELEBRATION. June 17. Quoddy Head State Park, Lubec, ME. Anniversary celebration with live entertainment, local food vendors, raffle, museum, art gallery and special lighthouse tower climbing (supervised by the

US Coast Guard). Annually, the third Saturday in June. Est attendance: 750. For info: Judith Ashley, West Quoddy Head Light Keepers Association & Visitor Center, PO Box 378, Lubec, ME 04652. Phone: (207) 733-2180. E-mail: info@westquoddy.com. Web: www.westquoddy.com.

WORLD JUGGLING DAY. June 17. Juggling clubs all over the world hold local festivals to demonstrate, teach and celebrate their art. Annually, the Saturday on or closest to June 17. For info: Intl Jugglers' Assn, PO Box 112550, Carrollton, TX 75011-2550. Web: www.juggle.org.

BIRTHDAYS TODAY

Thomas Haden Church, 45, actor (*Sideways*, "Wings," "Ned & Stacey"), born El Paso, TX, June 17, 1961 (some sources say Mar 31, 1960).

Dermontti Dawson, 41, former football player, born Lexington, KY, June 17, 1965.

Tommy R. Franks, 61, general, US Army, commander-in-chief of US forces during Operation Enduring Freedom in Iraq, born Wynnewood, OK, June 17, 1945.

Elroy Leon ("Crazylegs") Hirsch, 83, Hall of Fame football player, born Wausau, WI, June 17, 1923.

Dan Jansen, 41, former speed skater, sportscaster, born West Allis, WI, June 17, 1965.

Greg Kinnear, 43, actor (*Sabrina, As Good As It Gets*), born Logansport, IN, June 17, 1963.

Mark Linn-Baker, 53, actor ("Perfect Strangers," *My Favorite Year*), born St. Louis, MO, June 17, 1953.

Barry Manilow, 60, singer ("Mandy," "I Write the Songs"), songwriter, born Brooklyn, NY, June 17, 1946.

Joe Piscopo, 55, comedian (former "Saturday Night Live" regular), born Passaic, NJ, June 17, 1951.

Venus Williams, 26, tennis player, born Lynwood, CA, June 17, 1980.

JUNE 18 — SUNDAY

Day 169 — 196 Remaining

APPRECIATE YOUR PLUMBING, HEATING AND COOLING PROFESSIONALS WEEK. June 18–24. Members of the Plumbing-Heating-Cooling Contractors—National Association (PHCC) exhibit professionalism, excellent customer service and high ethical standards as they build, repair and renovate plumbing and HVACR systems for the nation's homes and businesses. Appreciation observances will occur throughout this week to recognize the hard work and dedication of these professionals. PHCC, founded June 20, 1863, is dedicated to the promotion, advancement, education and training of the industry for the protection of our environment and the health, safety and comfort of society. There are 4,000 contractor PHCC members representing more than 79,500 technicians. Annually, the week that includes the June 20 founding anniversary date. For info: Charlotte Perham, PHCC, 180 S Washington St, Falls Church, VA 22046. Phone: (800) 533-7694. Fax: (703) 237-7442. E-mail: perham@naphcc.org. Web: www.phccweb.org.

		S	M	T	W	T	F	S
June						1	2	3
2006		4	5	6	7	8	9	10
		11	12	13	14	15	16	17
		18	19	20	21	22	23	24
		25	26	27	28	29	30	

BATTLE OF WATERLOO: ANNIVERSARY. June 18, 1815. Date of the decisive defeat of Napoleon by British generals Wellington and Blucher, near Waterloo in central Belgium.

CAHN, SAMMY: BIRTH ANNIVERSARY. June 18, 1913. Tin Pan Alley legend Sammy Cahn was born Samuel Cohen at New York City. He was nominated for 26 Academy Awards and won four times for "Three Coins in the Fountain" (1954), "All the Way" (1957), "High Hopes" (1959) and "Call Me Irresponsible" (1963). In the late 1940s he began working with composer Jimmy Van Heusen, and the two in essence were the personal songwriting team for Frank Sinatra. Cahn wrote the greatest number of Sinatra hits, including "Love and Marriage," "The Second Time Around" and "The Tender Trap." Sammy Cahn died Jan 15, 1993, at Los Angeles, CA.

CARPENTER ANT AWARENESS WEEK. June 18–24. Wood-destroying organisms cause Americans to spend $3.5 billion annually. This week will focus attention on the identification, biology and habits of carpenter ants and provide consumers with information on the elimination of these costly pests. Annually, the last full week of June. For info: Jerry Batzner, Pres, Batzner Pest Management, Inc, 16948 W Victor Rd, New Berlin, WI 53151. Phone: (262) 797-4160. Fax: (262) 797-4166. E-mail: JerryB@batzner.com.

CHILTON COUNTY PEACH FESTIVAL. June 18–24. Downtown Clanton, AL. 59th annual. This peach-oriented event features Miss Peach pageants including Little Miss, Young Miss, Junior Miss and Miss Peach; parades, cooking contests, antique car show, motorcycle show, 5k Peach Fun run, American Legion BBQ, a peach auction and much more. Annually, the last full week in June. Est attendance: 10,000. For info: Pennie Broussard, Chilton County Chamber of Commerce, 500 5th Ave N, PO Box 66, Clanton, AL 35045. Phone: (205) 755-2400. Fax: (205) 755-8444. Web: www.chiltoncountychamber.com.

CORPUS CHRISTI (US OBSERVANCE). June 18. A movable Roman Catholic celebration commemorating the institution of the Holy Eucharist. The solemnity has been observed on the Thursday following Trinity Sunday since 1246, except in the US, where it is observed on the Sunday following Trinity Sunday.

EGYPT: EVACUATION DAY. June 18. Public holiday celebrating the anniversary of the withdrawal of the British Army from the Suez Canal area of Egypt in 1954.

FAMILY AWARENESS DAY. June 18. A day to reflect on the important role of fathers in the American family. "Remembering always that every kid needs a Dad." A day and time to reestablish and reaffirm every man's place in our culture. Annually, third Sunday in June. For info: Judith Natale, CEO & Founder, NCAC America-USA, PO Box 493703, Redding, CA 96049-3703. E-mail: childaware@aol.com.

FATHER'S DAY. June 18. Recognition of the third Sunday in June as Father's Day occurred first at the request of Mrs John B. Dodd of Spokane, WA, on June 19, 1910. It was proclaimed for that date by the mayor of Spokane and recognized by the governor of Washington. The idea was publicly supported by President Calvin Coolidge in 1924, but not presidentially proclaimed until 1966. It was assured of annual recognition by PL 92–278 of April 1972. Also celebrated on this day in Britain.

★**FATHER'S DAY.** June 18. Presidential Proclamation issued for third Sunday in June in 1966 and annually since 1971. (PL 92–278 of Apr 24, 1972.)

FATHER'S DAY CELEBRATION. June 18. Jenkinson's Aquarium, Point Pleasant Beach, NJ. Calling all kids! Bring your dad for a special day together to learn about the roles of fathers in the marine environment. One father admitted free with each paid child's admission. Est attendance: 800. For info: Jenkinson's Aquarium, 300 Ocean Ave, Point Pleasant Beach, NJ 08742. Phone: (732) 899-1212. Fax: (732) 899-1717. E-mail: jenkinsons aquarium@comcast.net. Web: www.jenkinsons.com.

FIRST AMERICAN WOMAN IN SPACE: ANNIVERSARY. June 18, 1983. Dr. Sally Ride, 32-year-old physicist and pilot, functioned as a "mission specialist" and became the first American woman in space when she began a six-day mission aboard the space shuttle *Challenger*. The "near-perfect" mission was launched from Cape Canaveral, FL, and landed June 24, 1983, at Edwards Air Force Base, CA. See also: "Ride, Sally Kristen: Birthday" (May 26) and "Space Milestone: *Vostok 6* (USSR): First Woman in Space" (June 16).

FOLGER, HENRY CLAY, JR: BIRTH ANNIVERSARY. June 18, 1857. American businessman and industrialist who developed one of the finest collections of Shakespeareana in the world and bequeathed it (The Folger Shakespeare Library, Washington, DC) to the American people. Born at New York, NY. Died June 11, 1930, at Brooklyn, NY.

HUSBAND CAREGIVER DAY. June 18. Coinciding with Father's Day, today we will honor husbands who give health care to their wives or children. For info: Richard Boyd, MD, 1111 W Spruce St, #30, Yakima, WA 98902. Phone: (509) 575-1922. Fax: (509) 248-2501. E-mail: rboyd@cwmed.com. Web: www.richard boydmd.com.

KYSER, KAY: 100th BIRTH ANNIVERSARY. June 18, 1906. American bandleader whose band, "Kay Kyser's Kollege of Musical Knowledge," enjoyed immense popularity in the swing era. He was born James King Kern Kyser at Rocky Mount, NC. A shrewd showman and performer, he said he never learned to read music or play an instrument. Among his hit recordings were "Three Little Fishes" and "Praise the Lord and Pass the Ammunition," a WWII favorite. Kyser retired from show business in 1951 and died at Chapel Hill, NC, July 23, 1985.

MALLORY, GEORGE LEIGH: BIRTH ANNIVERSARY. June 18, 1886. English explorer and mountain climber born at Mobberley, Cheshire, England. Last seen climbing through the mists toward the summit of the highest mountain in the world, Mount Everest, on the morning of June 8, 1924. Best remembered for his answer when asked why he wanted to climb Mount Everest: "Because it is there." In 1999 Mallory's body was found by an expedition to Mount Everest, 75 years after his death at age 37.

MOON PHASE: LAST QUARTER. June 18. Moon enters Last Quarter phase at 10:08 AM, EDT.

NATIONAL SPLURGE DAY. June 18. Today is the day to go out and do something extraordinarily indulgent. Motto: Have fun! [©1994.] Because of the escalating costs of Eventological® Literature, a charge of $10 must be assessed for each request. Checks are to be made payable to: Adrienne Sioux Koopersmith, 1437 W Rosemont, #1W, Chicago, IL 60660-1319. E-mail: askoopersmith@hotmail.com.

ORTHODOX FESTIVAL OF ALL SAINTS. June 18. Observed by Eastern Orthodox churches on the Sunday following Orthodox Pentecost (June 11 in 2006). Marks the end of the 18-week Triodion cycle.

PORTER, SYLVIA: BIRTH ANNIVERSARY. June 18, 1913. American financial journalist Sylvia Feldman Porter was born at Patchogue, NY. Her column was syndicated by the *Los Angeles Times*, reaching 450 newspapers worldwide. She also wrote more than 20 books and was noted for her ability to turn complex economic language into readable prose. Porter died June 5, 1991, at Pound Ridge, NY.

SEYCHELLES: CONSTITUTION DAY. June 18. National holiday commemorating adoption of constitution in 1993.

SPACE MILESTONE: *CHALLENGER STS-7* (US). June 18, 1983. Shuttle *Challenger* launched from Kennedy Space Center, FL, with crew of five, including Sally K. Ride (first American woman in space), Robert Crippen, Norman Thagard, John Fabian and Frederick Houck. Landed at Edwards Air Force Base, CA, on June 24 after near-perfect six-day mission.

UNIVERSAL FATHER'S WEEK. June 18–24. The purpose of this week, which is celebrated throughout the world the third full week in June, is to stress the importance of fatherhood in family life. For complete info and quotations about the importance

of the father, send $5 to cover expense of printing, handling and postage. For info: Dr Stanley Drake, Pres Emeritus, Intl Soc of Friendship & Good Will, 8592 Roswell Rd, Ste 251, Atlanta, GA 30350-1867. Phone: (678) 795-1362. E-mail: sjdrake@bellsouth .net. Web: www.friendshipandgoodwill.org.

WAR OF 1812: DECLARATION ANNIVERSARY. June 18, 1812. After much debate in Congress between "hawks" such as Henry Clay and John Calhoun and "doves" such as John Randolph, Congress issued a declaration of war on Great Britain. The action was prompted primarily by Britain's violation of America's rights on the high seas and British incitement of Indian warfare on the frontier. War was seen by some as a way to acquire Florida and Canada. The hostilities ended with the signing of the Treaty of Ghent on Dec 24, 1814, at Ghent, Belgium.

BIRTHDAYS TODAY

Lou Brock, 67, Hall of Fame baseball player, born El Dorado, AR, June 18, 1939.

Eddie Cibrian, 33, actor ("Third Watch"), born Burbank, CA, June 18, 1973.

Roger Ebert, 64, Pulitzer Prize–winning film critic, born Urbana, IL, June 18, 1942.

Carol Kane, 54, actress (*Hester Street, The Princess Bride*, "Taxi"), born Cleveland, OH, June 18, 1952.

Donald Keene, 84, literary critic, translator, educator, born New York, NY, June 18, 1922.

Paul McCartney, 64, singer, songwriter (The Beatles, Wings), born Liverpool, England, June 18, 1942.

John D. Rockefeller IV, 69, US Senator (D, West Virginia), born New York, NY, June 18, 1937.

Isabella Rossellini, 54, model, actress (*Blue Velvet, Cousins*), born Rome, Italy, June 18, 1952.

Tom Wicker, 80, journalist, author (*One of Us: Richard Nixon & the American Dream*), born Hamlet, NC, June 18, 1926.

JUNE 19 — MONDAY

Day 170 — 195 Remaining

ASPEN MUSIC FESTIVAL. June 19–Aug 20. Aspen, CO. Nine weeks of concerts performed by highly acclaimed artists. Est attendance: 100,000. For info: Aspen Music Festival, 2 Music School Rd, Aspen, CO 81611. Phone: (970) 925-3254. Fax: (970) 925-3802. E-mail: festival@aspenmusic.org. Web: www.aspen musicfestival.com.

ASSOCIATION WEEK IN CHICAGOLAND. June 19–23. Chicago, IL. The professionals who work for more than 2,000 Chicago-based associations will celebrate their community, learn from each other and recognize excellence. Annually, the third week in June. Est attendance: 2,000. For info: Gary LaBranche, Association Forum of Chicagoland, 20 N Wacker Dr, Ste 3000, Chicago, IL 60606. Phone: (312) 236-2288. E-mail: labranche@ associationforum.org. Web: www.associationforum.org.

BASCOM, EARL W.: 100th BIRTH ANNIVERSARY. June 19, 1906. Rodeo showman and pioneer, Earl W. Bascom was born at Vernal, UT. During his career he developed the first side-delivery rodeo chute (1916), the first hornless bronc saddle (1922) and the first one-handed bareback rigging (1924). He produced the first rodeo in Mississippi and also produced the first rodeo performed at night under electric lights (1935). Bascom died Aug 28, 1995, at Victorville, CA.

BATTLE OF PHILIPPINE SEA: ANNIVERSARY. June 19–20, 1944. Determined to prevent any further advancement by the Allies in Japan's area of inner defense, Vice-Admiral Jisaburo Ozawa ordered the Imperial fleet to the Mariana Islands. Admiral Raymond Spruance, possibly the US's greatest and most successful naval commander, ordered a strike force against the Japanese fleet in the Philippine Sea. A furious battle developed in the skies between US carrier-borne aircraft and Japanese aircraft from their carriers and land bases on the Marianas. The Japanese lost three aircraft carriers (*Shokaku, Taiho* and *Hiyo*), two destroyers and one tanker. Three carriers, one battleship, three cruisers, one destroyer and three tankers were seriously damaged. The Japanese lost at least 400 aircraft, the Americans 130.

DONNA REED PERFORMING ARTS FESTIVAL. June 19–24. Denison, IA. Performing arts festival in Donna Reed's hometown. Focus of the festival is educational workshops in various areas of the performing arts taught by Hollywood and New York professionals. Also included are celebrity golf tournament, auction, beach party, parade, lunch with the stars, 10k run and theatrical performances for the general public. Annually, the third full week in June. Est attendance: 10,000. For info: Gwen Ecklund, Exec Dir, Donna Reed Foundation for the Performing Arts, 1305 Broadway, Denison, IA 51442. Phone: (712) 263-3334. Fax: (712) 263-8026. E-mail: info@donnareed.org. Web: www.donnareed.org.

EMANCIPATION DAY IN TEXAS. June 19, 1865. In honor of the emancipation of the slaves in Texas. See also: "Juneteenth" (June 19).

FIRST RUNNING OF THE BELMONT STAKES: ANNIVERSARY. June 19, 1867. The first running of the Belmont Stakes took place at Jerome Park, NY. The team of jockey J. Gilpatrick and his horse Ruthless finished in a time of 3:05. The Belmont Stakes continued at Jerome Park until 1889, then moved to Morris Park, NY, between 1890–1905, and in 1906 settled at Belmont Park, NY, where it has continued to the present day. The Belmont Stakes is the oldest event of horse racing's Triple Crown.

FORTAS, ABE: BIRTH ANNIVERSARY. June 19, 1910. Abe Fortas was born at Memphis, TN. He was appointed to the Supreme Court by President Lyndon Johnson in 1965. Prior to his appointment he was known as a civil libertarian, having argued cases for government employees and other individuals accused by Senator Joe McCarthy of having communist affiliations. He argued the 1963 landmark Supreme Court case of *Gideon v Wainwright*, which established the right of indigent defendants to free legal aid in criminal prosecutions. In 1968 he was nominated by Johnson to succeed Chief Justice Earl Warren, but his nomination was withdrawn after much conservative opposition in the Senate. In 1969 Fortas became the first Supreme Court Justice to be forced to resign after revelations about questionable financial dealings were made public. He died Apr 5, 1982, at Washington, DC.

GARFIELD: BIRTHDAY. June 19, 1978. America's favorite lasagna-loving cat celebrates his birthday. "Garfield," a modern classic comic strip created by Jim Davis, first appeared in 1978 and has brought laughter to millions. For info: Kim Campbell, Paws, Inc, 5440 E Co Rd 450 N, Albany, IN 47320. Web: www.garfield.com.

GEHRIG, LOU: BIRTH ANNIVERSARY. June 19, 1903. Baseball great Henry Louis Gehrig (lifetime batting average of .341), who played in seven World Series, was born at New York, NY, and died there June 2, 1941, from the degenerative muscle disease amyotropic lateral sclerosis, which has become known as Lou Gehrig's disease.

HOWARD, MOE: BIRTH ANNIVERSARY. June 19, 1897. The head stooge in the Three Stooges, Moe Howard was born Moses Horwitz at Bensonhurst, NY. He died May 4, 1975, at Hollywood, CA. Howard began his show business career at age 12 by running errands at Vitagraph studios. He worked with Ted Healy in various comedy and singing acts, and together they teamed with Shemp Howard and Larry Fine in the mid-1920s for an early Stooges act. In 1930 the Stooges made their film debut in *Soup to Nuts*. Although the members of the Three Stooges changed over the years, Moe Howard was one of the constants. Howard appeared in four feature films without the other Stooges, including *Doctor Death, Seeker of Souls*.

HUBBARD, ELBERT: 150th BIRTH ANNIVERSARY. June 19, 1856. Born at Bloomington, IL, Elbert Green Hubbard, American author and craftsman, founded the Roycroft Press at East Aurora, NY. Best known for his writings were *A Message to Garcia* and a series of essays titled *Little Journeys*. He also became famous for his furniture designs. Hubbard lost his life with the sinking of the *Lusitania*, May 7, 1915.

"I'VE GOT A SECRET" TV PREMIERE: ANNIVERSARY. June 19, 1952. Celebrity panelists tried to guess the guests' secrets on this popular game show; celebrity guests also came on to baffle the panel. Guests whispered their secret to the host and the audience saw it on the screen. Garry Moore hosted the show, followed by Steve Allen and Bill Cullen. Allen Sherman ("My Son the Folk Singer") created the show and most of the celebrity "secrets." Celebrity panelists included Bill Cullen, Betsy Palmer, Henry Morgan, Bess Myerson, Steve Allen and Jayne Meadows.

JUNETEENTH. June 19. Celebrated in Texas to commemorate the day in 1865 when Union General Granger proclaimed the slaves of Texas free. Also proclaimed as Emancipation Day by the Florida legislature. Juneteenth has become an occasion for commemoration by African Americans in many parts of the US.

MARCHAND, NANCY: BIRTH ANNIVERSARY. June 19, 1928. Actress ("Lou Grant," "The Sopranos") born at Buffalo, NY. Died June 18, 2000, at Stratford, CT.

NATIONAL OLD-TIME FIDDLERS' CONTEST AND FESTIVAL. June 19–24. Weiser, ID. 54th anniversary. Largest fiddling event in the world to help perpetuate the old-time fiddling of pioneer America. Annually, the third full week in June. Est attendance: 15,000. For info: National Old-Time Fiddlers' Contest, 115 West Idaho, Weiser, ID 83672. Phone: (800) 437-1280. E-mail: director@fiddlecontest.com. Web: www.fiddlecontest.com.

PASCAL, BLAISE: BIRTH ANNIVERSARY. June 19, 1623. French philosopher, physicist and mathematician born at Clermont-Ferrand and died at Paris, Aug 19, 1662. It was Pascal who said, "Had Cleopatra's nose been shorter, the whole history of the world would have been different." And, in his *Provincial Letters*, he wrote, "I have made this letter longer than usual because I lack the time to make it short."

ROSENBERG EXECUTION: ANNIVERSARY. June 19, 1953. Anniversary of the electrocution of the only married couple ever executed together in the US. Julius (35) and Ethel (37) Rosenberg were executed for espionage at Sing Sing Prison, Ossining, NY. Time for the execution was advanced several hours to avoid conflict with the Jewish Sabbath. Their conviction has been a subject of controversy over the years.

SPACE MILESTONE: *ARIANE* (ESA): 25th ANNIVERSARY. June 19, 1981. Launched from Kourou, French Guiana by the European Space Administration, *Ariane* carried two satellites into orbit: *Meteostat 2*, an ESA weather satellite, and *Apple*, a geostationary communications satellite for India, to be stationed over Sumatra.

June *2006*	S	M	T	W	T	F	S
					1	2	3
	4	5	6	7	8	9	10
	11	12	13	14	15	16	17
	18	19	20	21	22	23	24
	25	26	27	28	29	30	

URUGUAY: ARTIGAS DAY. June 19. National holiday. Commemorates the birth in 1764 of General José Gervasio Artigas, the father of Uruguayan independence.

US VIRGIN ISLANDS: ORGANIC ACT DAY. June 19. Commemorates the enactment by the US Congress, July 22, 1954, of the Revised Organic Act, under which the government of the Virgin Islands is organized. Observed annually on the third Monday in June.

"WAR IS HELL": ANNIVERSARY. June 19, 1879. Addressing the graduating class at Michigan Military Academy, General William Tecumseh Sherman uttered his famous words on war—more than a decade after the Civil War had ended. He said, "War is at best barbarism. . . . Its glory is all moonshine. It is only those who have neither fired a shot nor heard the shrieks and groans of the wounded who cry aloud for blood, more vengeance, more desolation. War is hell."

WORLD SAUNTERING DAY. June 19. A day to revive the lost art of Victorian sauntering and to discourage jogging, lollygagging, sashaying, fast walking and trotting. (Originated by the late W.T. Rabe of Saulte Ste. Marie, MI.)

BIRTHDAYS TODAY

Paula Abdul, 44, singer ("Forever Your Girl"), dancer, choreographer, born Los Angeles, CA, June 19, 1962.

Aung San Suu Kyi, 61, Nobel Peace Prize winner, born Rangoon, Burma, June 19, 1945.

Charles Gwathmey, 68, architect, born Charlotte, NC, June 19, 1938.

Andy Lauer, 41, actor ("Caroline in the City," *I'll Be Home for Christmas*), born Santa Monica, CA, June 19, 1965.

Brian McBride, 34, soccer player, born Arlington Heights, IL, June 19, 1972.

Poppy Montgomery, 34, actress ("Without a Trace"), born Sydney, New South Wales, Australia, June 19, 1972.

Dirk Nowitzki, 28, basketball player, born Wurzburg, West Germany, June 19, 1978.

Marisa Pavan, 74, actress (*The Diary of Anne Frank*), born Cagliari, Sardinia, June 19, 1932.

Phylicia Rashad, 58, actress ("The Cosby Show"), born Houston, TX, June 19, 1948.

Gena Rowlands, 70, actress ("Peyton Place," *A Woman Under the Influence*), born Cambria, WI, June 19, 1936 (some sources say 1943 or 1930).

Salman Rushdie, 59, author (*The Jaguar Smile, Satanic Verses, Midnight's Children*), born Bombay, India, June 19, 1947.

Kathleen Turner, 52, actress (*Body Heat, Peggy Sue Got Married, Romancing the Stone*), born Springfield, MO, June 19, 1954.

Ann Wilson, 55, musician, lead singer (Heart), born San Diego, CA, June 19, 1951.

JUNE 20 — TUESDAY
Day 171 — 194 Remaining

ARGENTINA: FLAG DAY. June 20. National holiday. Commemorates the death in 1820 of Manuel Belgrano, the designer of the Argentine flag.

CHESNUTT, CHARLES W.: BIRTH ANNIVERSARY. June 20, 1858. Born at Cleveland, OH, Chesnutt was considered by many as the first important black novelist. His collections of short stories included *The Conjure Woman* (1899) and *The Wife of His Youth and Other Stories of the Color Line* (1899). *The Colonel's Dream* (1905) dealt with the struggles of the freed slave. His work has been compared to later writers such as William Faulkner, Richard Wright and James Baldwin. He died Nov 15, 1932, at Cleveland.

"THE ED SULLIVAN SHOW" ("TOAST OF THE TOWN") TV PREMIERE: ANNIVERSARY. June 20, 1948. "The Ed Sullivan Show" was officially titled "Toast of the Town" until 1955. It was the longest-running variety show (through 1971) and the most popular for decades. Ed Sullivan, the host, signed all types of acts, both well-known and new, trying to have something to please everyone. Thousands of performers appeared, many making their television debut, such as Irving Berlin, Victor Borge, Hedy Lamarr, Walt Disney, Fred Astaire and Jane Powell. Two acts attracted the largest audience of the time: Elvis Presley and the Beatles.

ENGLAND: ROYAL ASCOT. June 20–23. Ascot, Berkshire. Horse races. Annually, the third Tuesday to Friday in June.

FIRST BALLOON HONEYMOON: ANNIVERSARY. June 20, 1909. Roger Burnham and Eleanor Waring took the first balloon honeymoon, ascending at 12:40 PM in the balloon *Pittsfield*. They began their trip at Woods Hole, Cape Cod, MA, and landed at 4:30 PM in an orchard at Holbrook, MA.

FIRST DOCTOR OF SCIENCE DEGREE EARNED BY A WOMAN: ANNIVERSARY. June 20, 1895. Caroline Willard Baldwin became the first woman to earn a doctor of science degree at Cornell University, Ithaca, NY.

HELLMAN, LILLIAN: BIRTH ANNIVERSARY. June 20, 1905. One of the 20th century's great playwrights, author of such works as *The Children's Hour*, *The Little Foxes* (1939) and *Toys in the Attic* (1960). One of many artists blacklisted by Hollywood in the 1950s. Was the companion for 30 years of novelist Dashiell Hammett. Born at New Orleans, LA, Hellman died June 30, 1984, at Martha's Vineyard, MA.

JAWS FILM RELEASE: ANNIVERSARY. June 20, 1975. With its tagline "Don't go in the water" and its ominous cello music, the Steven Spielberg–directed thriller shocked audiences on this date. Adapted from a Peter Benchley bestseller, *Jaws* showed a great white shark preying on the beachgoers of a New England town. It won three Oscars—best editing, best sound and best original score (by John Williams)—and was a blockbuster success.

LIZZIE BORDEN VERDICT: ANNIVERSARY. June 20, 1893. Spectators at her trial cheered when the "not guilty" verdict was read by the jury foreman in the murder trial of Lizzy Borden on this date. Elizabeth Borden had been accused of and tried for the hacking deaths of her father and stepmother in their Fall River, MA, home, Aug 4, 1892.

MURPHY, AUDIE: BIRTH ANNIVERSARY. June 20, 1924. Born at Kingston, TX, Murphy was the most decorated soldier in WWII and later became an actor in western and war movies. He died May 28, 1971, in a plane crash near Roanoke, VA.

SPANISH-AMERICAN WAR SURRENDER OF GUAM TO US: ANNIVERSARY. June 20, 1898. Not knowing that a war was in progress and having no ammunition on the island, the Spanish commander of Guam surrendered to Captain Glass of the USS *Charleston*.

SWEDISH DAYS—A MIDSOMMAR FESTIVAL. June 20–25. Geneva, IL. Celebrating its 57th anniversary, this grandaddy of all Illinois festivals commemorates Swedish heritage. Six days of entertainment, music competitions, arts, crafts, rosemaling displays, carnival, Kid's Day activities and a parade provide unlimited fun. Food stands throughout the downtown area tempt visitors with Swedish and American menus. Begins annually on the Tuesday after Father's Day. Est attendance: 250,000. For info: Geneva Chamber of Commerce, PO Box 481, 8 S Third St, Geneva, IL 60134. Phone: (630) 232-6060. Fax: (630) 232-6083. E-mail: chamberinfo@genevachamber.com. Web: www.genevachamber.com.

TOAD HOLLOW DAY OF THANK YOU. June 20. A day to say or write a thank-you to the people who have helped us along the way. For info: Ralph Morrison, Director, Toad Hollow, PO Box 2132, Garden City, MI 48135. Phone: (800) 574-8623.

UNITED NATIONS: WORLD REFUGEE DAY. June 20. A day to bring attention to the situation of refugees—their rights, as well as their suffering. First observed on June 20, 2001, the 50th anniversary of the 1951 Convention on the Status of Refugees. Date chosen to coincide with Africa Refugee Day. For info: United Nations, Dept of Public Info, New York, NY 10017. Web: www.un.org.

US WOMEN'S AMATEUR PUBLIC LINKS (GOLF) CHAMPIONSHIP. June 20–26. Walking Stick Golf Course, Pueblo, CO. For info: US Golf Assn, Golf House, PO Box 708, Championship Dept, Far Hills, NJ 07931. Phone: (908) 234-2300. Fax: (908) 234-9687. E-mail: usga@usga.org. Web: www.usga.org or www.uswapl.org.

WEST VIRGINIA: ADMISSION DAY: ANNIVERSARY. June 20, 1863. Became 35th state in 1863. Observed as a holiday in West Virginia. The state of West Virginia is a product of the Civil War. Originally part of Virginia, West Virginia became a separate state when Virginia seceded from the Union.

WESTERN DAYS. June 20–24. Elgin, TX. Events include a parade, horseshoe contest, volleyball tournament, Miss Western Days contest, live music, arts and crafts, rodeo, carnival and cooking, sewing and quilting contests. Est attendance: 20,000. For info: Gena Carter, Elgin Chamber of Commerce, PO Box 408, Elgin, TX 78621. Phone: (512) 285-4515. Web: www.elgintx.com.

WOMAN RUNS THE HOUSE: 85th ANNIVERSARY. June 20, 1921. Alice Robertson of Oklahoma became the first woman to preside in the US House of Representatives. Robertson presided for half an hour.

BIRTHDAYS TODAY

Danny Aiello, Jr, 73, actor ("Lady Blue," *Do the Right Thing*), born New York, NY, June 20, 1933.
LaVar Arrington, 28, football player, born Pittsburgh, PA, June 20, 1978.
Olympia Dukakis, 75, actress, theatrical director (Oscar for *Moonstruck; Steel Magnolias*), born Lowell, MA, June 20, 1931.
John Goodman, 54, actor ("Roseanne," *The Flintstones*), born Afton, MO, June 20, 1952.
Nicole Kidman, 39, actress (Oscar for *The Hours; The Others, Moulin Rouge*), born Honolulu, HI, June 20, 1967.
Martin Landau, 75, actor (*Tucker: The Man and His Dream; Crimes and Misdemeanors;* Oscar for *Ed Wood*), born Brooklyn, NY, June 20, 1931.
Michael Landon, Jr, 42, actor ("Bonanza: The Return," "Bonanza: The Ghosts"), born Encino, CA, June 20, 1964.

June *2006*	S	M	T	W	T	F	S
					1	2	3
	4	5	6	7	8	9	10
	11	12	13	14	15	16	17
	18	19	20	21	22	23	24
	25	26	27	28	29	30	

Cyndi Lauper, 53, singer ("Girls Just Want to Have Fun"), born Brooklyn, NY, June 20, 1953.
John Mahoney, 66, actor ("Frasier"), born Manchester, England, June 20, 1940.
Anne Murray, 61, singer (*Country*, "Snowbird," "Could I Have This Dance"), born Springhill, NS, Canada, June 20, 1945.
Lionel Richie, 57, singer ("Truly"), songwriter, born Tuskegee, AL, June 20, 1949.
Robert Rodriguez, 38, director/screenwriter (*Spy Kids, Desperado*), born San Antonio, TX, June 20, 1968.
James Tolkan, 75, actor (*Serpico, Back to the Future, Dick Tracy*), born Calumet, MI, June 20, 1931.
Bob Vila, 60, handyman, TV show host, born Miami, FL, June 20, 1946.
Andre Watts, 60, pianist, born Nuremburg, Germany, June 20, 1946.
Brian Wilson, 64, singer (The Beach Boys), songwriter, born Hawthorne, CA, June 20, 1942.

JUNE 21 — WEDNESDAY
Day 172 — 193 Remaining

BABY BOOMERS RECOGNITION DAY. June 21. As baby boomers, we'll never forget the Beatles, Vietnam War and other sixties events. However, many of us accomplished a great deal, becoming successful in business, education, medicine and other fields. This special day commemorates our contributions. Annually, June 21. For info: Dorothy Zjawin, 61 W Colfax Ave, Roselle Park, NJ 07204. Phone: (908) 241-6241. Web: www.coolboomers.com (live in December 2005).

BATTLE OF OKINAWA ENDS: ANNIVERSARY. June 21, 1945. With American grenades exploding in the background, inside the Japanese command cave at Mabuni the battle for Okinawa was ended when Major General Isamu Cho and Lieutenant General Mitsuru Ushijima killed themselves in the ceremonial rite of hara-kiri. In the long battle that had begun Apr 1, the American death toll reached enormous proportions by Pacific battle standards—7,613 died on land and 4,907 in the air or from kamikaze attacks. A total of 36 US warships were sunk. More than 70,000 Japanese and 80,000 civilian Okinawans died in the course of the battle.

CANCER, THE CRAB. June 21–July 22. In the astronomical/astrological zodiac, which divides the sun's apparent orbit into 12 segments, the period June 21–July 22 is identified, traditionally, as the sun sign of Cancer, the Crab. The ruling planet is the moon.

GREENLAND: NATIONAL DAY. June 21. National holiday.

HIRSCHFELD, AL: BIRTH ANNIVERSARY. June 21, 1903. Caricature artist known for his inimitable sketches of Broadway and Hollywood stars, Al Hirschfeld was born at St. Louis, MO. His first cartoon appeared in 1926 in the now-defunct *New York Herald Tribune*. Later moving to *The New York Times,* his drawings appeared on the drama page for seven decades. He was known for hiding "Nina" (his daughter's name) somewhere in every caricature that he created after 1945. His art is found in many museums, including the Metropolitan Museum of Art in New York City. He died Jan 20, 2003, at New York, NY.

HURRICANE AGNES: ANNIVERSARY. June 21–26, 1972. Hurricane Agnes hit the eastern seaboard wreaking havoc across seven Atlantic Coast states. Casualties included 118 lives and 116,000 homes, leaving more than 200,000 homeless after Agnes dumped 28.1 trillion gallons of water over 5,000 square miles.

LITTLE BIGHORN DAYS. June 21–25. Hardin, MT. To celebrate the history of the Old West. This annual celebration commemorates the anniversary of Custer's Last Stand (June 25). Activities include carnival, Custer's Last Stand reenactment, trial of George Custer, parade, rodeo, shows, Military Ball and dances. Est attendance: 11,000. For info: Promotions, Hardin Area Chamber of Commerce, 10 E Railway St, Hardin, MT 59034. Phone: (406) 665-1672 or (888) 450-3577. E-mail: hardinchamber@cotcomsol.com. Web: www.custerslaststand.org.

MIDNIGHT SUN BASEBALL GAME. June 21. Fairbanks, AK. To celebrate the summer solstice. Game is played without artificial lights at 10:35 PM. Est attendance: 4,000. For info: Alaska Goldpanners, Box 71154, Fairbanks, AK 99707. Phone: (907) 451-0095. Web: www.goldpanners.com.

MIDSUMMER. June 21. One of the "Lesser Sabbats" during the Wiccan year, celebrating the peak of the Sun God in his annual cycle. Annually, on the summer solstice.

MISS MISSISSIPPI PAGEANT. June 21–24. Vicksburg Convention Center, Vicksburg, MS. Part of the Miss America Organization. For info: The Miss Mississippi Pageant, PO Box 742, Vicksburg, MS 39181. Phone: (601) 638-6746. Fax: (601) 638-8020. E-mail: missmiss@canufly.net. Web: www.missmississippipageant.org.

MISS TENNESSEE PAGEANT. June 21–24. Carl Perkins Civic Center, Jackson, TN. Part of the Miss America Organization. For info: Miss Tennessee Pageant, PO Box 938, Jackson, TN 38302. Phone: (731) 425-8590. Fax: (731) 425-8596. E-mail: MissTnEd@aol.com. Web: www.misstennessee.org.

NEW HAMPSHIRE RATIFIES CONSTITUTION: ANNIVERSARY. June 21, 1788. By a vote of 57 to 47, New Hampshire became the ninth state to ratify the Constitution. With this ratification, the Constitution became effective for all ratifying states, as the approval of nine states was required for the Constitution to go into effect.

PEE ON EARTH DAY. June 21. To reduce toilet-flushing water and divert nitrogen from the waste stream, Pee on Earth Day calls on the world to take their urine outside to apply to healthy aerated soil (such as lawns and forest) or composters. It carries on the tradition of "Pee Outside Day" in Stigomta, Sweden, which saves thousands of gallons of toilet-flushing water and helps return pathogen-free nitrogen (via urine) to the nutrient cycle. Annually, on the summer solstice. For info: Carol Steinfeld, Pee on Earth Day, Ecowaters, PO Box 1330, Concord, MA 01742. Phone: (978) 318-7033. E-mail: info@liquidgoldbook.com.

SARTRE, JEAN-PAUL: BIRTH ANNIVERSARY. June 21, 1905. French philosopher, "father of existentialism," born at Paris, France. In 1964 Sartre rejected the Nobel Prize for Literature when it was awarded to him. He died at Paris, Apr 15, 1980. In *Being and Nothingness*, he wrote: "Man can will nothing unless he has first understood that he must count on no one but himself; that he is alone, abandoned on earth in the midst of his infinite responsibilities, without help, with no other aim than the one he sets for himself, with no other destiny than the one he forges for himself on this earth."

SONOMA-MARIN FAIR. June 21–25. Petaluma Fairgrounds, Petaluma, CA. 67th annual country fair with livestock exhibitions, flowers, ugly dog contest, carnival and entertainment. Est attendance: 67,000. For info: Sonoma-Marin Fair, 175 Fairgrounds Dr, Petaluma, CA 94952. Phone: (707) 283-FAIR. Fax: (707) 283-3250. E-mail: info@sonoma-marinfair.org. Web: www.sonoma-marinfair.org.

SPACE MILESTONE: FIRST MANNED PRIVATE SPACEFLIGHT: ANNIVERSARY. June 21, 2004. Michael Melvill, flying the privately financed SpaceShipOne, flew 62 miles in altitude on this date, leaving the Earth's atmosphere. The spacecraft was designed by Burt Rutan and was financed by Paul Allen, philanthropist and Microsoft cofounder. SpaceShipOne made the flight from Mojave Airport at Mojave, CA.

SUMMER. June 21–Sept 23. In the Northern Hemisphere summer begins today with the summer solstice, at 8:26 AM EDT. Note that in the Southern Hemisphere today is the beginning of winter. Anywhere between the Equator and the Arctic Circle, the sun rises and sets farthest north on the horizon for the year and length of daylight is maximum (12 hours, 8 minutes at equator, increasing to 24 hours at the Arctic Circle).

TANNER, HENRY OSSAWA: BIRTH ANNIVERSARY. June 21, 1859. Henry Ossawa Tanner was one of the first black artists to be exhibited in galleries in the US. He was born at Pittsburgh, PA. He died May 25, 1937, at Paris.

TOMPKINS, DANIEL D.: BIRTH ANNIVERSARY. June 21, 1774. 6th vice president of the US (1817–25), born at Fox Meadows, NY. Died at Staten Island, NY, June 11, 1825.

VEGAN WORLD DAY. June 21. Vegan World Day, celebrated annually on the first day of summer—the day of most light and most hope—is designed to recognize the benefits of the vegan (completely vegetarian) lifestyle and its positive impact on human and environmental health, world hunger and animal suffering. People are asked to go vegan on this day and not consume or wear any animal products and avoid entertainment based on animal exploitation. It is a day to celebrate life! For info: Bob Linden, Go Vegan Radio, PO Box 40246, San Diego, CA 92164. Phone: (818) 623-6477. E-mail: Bob@GoVeganRadio.com. Web: www.GoVeganRadio.com.

WASHINGTON, MARTHA DANDRIDGE CUSTIS: 275th BIRTH ANNIVERSARY. June 21, 1731. Wife of George Washington, first president of the US, born at New Kent County, VA. Died at Mount Vernon, VA, May 22, 1802.

WHITEWATER WEDNESDAY. June 21. Kernville, CA. One-hour and two-hour raft trips on the "Wild and Scenic" Kern River. BBQ lunch included. Fill out reservation form at www.kernvillechamber.org. Est attendance: 1,000. For info: Kernville Chamber of Commerce, PO Box 397, Kernville, CA 93238. Phone: (760) 376-2629 or (866) KERNVILLE. Fax: (760) 376-4371. E-mail: info@kernvillechamber.org.

BIRTHDAYS TODAY

Meredith Baxter, 59, actress ("Bridget Loves Bernie," "Family," "Family Ties"), born Los Angeles, CA, June 21, 1947.

Benazir Bhutto, 53, Pakistani political leader, born Karachi, Pakistan, June 21, 1953.

Berke Breathed, 49, cartoonist ("Bloom County"), born Croatia, June 21, 1957.

Thomas Doane (Tom) Chambers, 47, former basketball player, born Ogden, UT, June 21, 1959.

Derrick D. Coleman, 39, basketball player, born Mobile, AL, June 21, 1967.

Sammi Davis-Voss, 42, actress ("Homefront," *Hope and Glory*), born Kidderminster, Worcestershire, England, June 21, 1964.

Jim Douglas, 55, Governor of Vermont (R), born Springfield, MA, June 21, 1951.

Joe Flaherty, 66, writer, actor ("Second City TV," "SCTV Network 90"), born Pittsburgh, PA, June 21, 1940.

Michael Gross, 59, actor ("Family Ties"), born Chicago, IL, June 21, 1947.

Mariette Hartley, 65, actress ("Peyton Place"), born New York, NY, June 21, 1941.

Richard Jefferson, 26, basketball player, born Los Angeles, CA, June 21, 1980.

Bernie Kopell, 73, actor ("Get Smart," "The Love Boat," "When Things Were Rotten"), born New York, NY, June 21, 1933.

Juliette Lewis, 33, actress (*The Other Sister*, *The Evening Star*), born Los Angeles, CA, June 21, 1973.

Nils Lofgren, 55, musician, singer, songwriter, born Chicago, IL, June 21, 1951.

Monte Markham, 68, actor ("Mr Deeds Goes to Town," "Dallas"), born Manatee, FL, June 21, 1938.

Jane Russell, 85, actress (*The Outlaw, Gentlemen Prefer Blondes*), born Bemidji, MN, June 21, 1921.

Doug Savant, 42, actor ("Melrose Place," "Desperate Housewives"), born Burbank, CA, June 21, 1964.

Maureen Stapleton, 81, actress (Oscar for *Reds*; stage: *The Little Foxes*), born Troy, NY, June 21, 1925.

Rick Sutcliffe, 50, former baseball player, born Independence, MO, June 21, 1956.

Larry Wachowski, 41, filmmaker with brother Andy Wachowski (*The Matrix*), born Chicago, IL, June 21, 1965.

Prince William (William Arthur Philip Louis), 24, son of Prince Charles and Princess Diana, born London, England, June 21, 1982.

JUNE 22 — THURSDAY
Day 173 — 192 Remaining

AMERICAN LIBRARY ASSOCIATION ANNUAL CONFERENCE. June 22–28. New Orleans, LA. The American Library Association (ALA), the oldest and largest library association in the world, holds its annual conference each June. Its attendees include librarians, educators, writers, publishers, friends of libraries, trustees and special guests. More than 2,000 meetings, discussion groups, tours, special events and awards ceremonies (including the presentation of the Newbery and Caldecott medals) are spread throughout the weeklong conference. Est attendance: 25,000. For info: Public Information Office, American Library Assn, 50 E Huron St, Chicago, IL 60611. Phone: (312) 280-5044 or (800) 545-2433. Fax: (312) 944-8520. E-mail: pio@ala.org. Web: www.ala.org.

BLASS, BILL: BIRTH ANNIVERSARY. June 22, 1922. Born at Fort Wayne, IN, William Ralph Blass moved to New York at 17 to study fashion design. After service in WWII, he returned to New York and went to work for Anne Klein. By 1970 he had his own company and put American fashion on the map—favoring a sporty yet classy silhouette. His client list soon included Jacqueline Kennedy, Barbra Streisand and Gloria Vanderbilt, and he became one of the most successful fashion designers in history. He was known as a philanthropist in his later years and died soon after retirement at New Preston, CT, June 12, 2002.

CHESAPEAKE-LEOPARD AFFAIR: ANNIVERSARY. June 22, 1807. One of the events leading to the War of 1812 occurred about 40 miles east of Chesapeake Bay. The US frigate *Chesapeake* was fired upon and boarded by the crew of the British man-of-war *Leopard*. The *Chesapeake*'s commander, James Barron, was court-martialed and convicted of not being prepared for action. Later Barron killed one of the judges (Stephen Decatur) in a duel fought at Bladensburg, MD, Mar 22, 1820.

CIRCUS TRAIN WRECK: ANNIVERSARY. June 22, 1918. A Michigan Central Railroad troop train, after several days shuttling soldiers to New York from Chicago, was deadheading back to the Midwest when it struck the rear of the Hagenbeck–Wallace Circus train. The circus train had stopped to have its brake box overhauled at Ivanhoe, IN. Fifty-three circus performers were killed. Of the circus animals not killed outright, many that were crippled and maimed had to be destroyed by police officers. The performers, of whom only three could be identified, were buried in a mass grave. The engineer, A.K. Sargent, who was accused of falling asleep at the throttle, was tried and acquitted.

★　★　★

	S	M	T	W	T	F	S
June					1	2	3
2006	4	5	6	7	8	9	10
	11	12	13	14	15	16	17
	18	19	20	21	22	23	24
	25	26	27	28	29	30	

CROATIA: ANTIFASCIST STRUGGLE DAY. June 22. National holiday. Commemorates uprising against fascist invaders in 1941.

HELEN KELLER FESTIVAL. June 22–25. Tuscumbia, AL. Commemorates the remarkable life of Helen Keller with stage shows for all ages, arts and crafts fair, free musical entertainment, races, historic tours of Helen Keller's birthplace and other beautiful homes and much more. *The Miracle Worker* play performed evenings during festival and for five weekends following. Annually, the last weekend in June. Est attendance: 105,000. For info: Debbie Wilson, Dir, Florence/Lauderdale Tourism, One Hightower Pl, Florence, AL 35630. Phone: (256) 740-4141 or (888) FLO-TOUR. Fax: (256) 740-4142. E-mail: dwilson@flo-tour.org. Web: www.flo-tour.org.

JOE LOUIS v BRADDOCK/SCHMELING FIGHT ANNIVERSARIES. June 22, 1937/1938. At Chicago's Comiskey Park Joe Louis won the World Heavyweight Championship title by knocking out James J. Braddock (eighth round). Louis retained the title until his retirement in 1949. Exactly one year after the Braddock fight, on June 22, 1938, Louis met Germany's Max Schmeling, at New York City's Yankee Stadium. Louis knocked out Schmeling in the first round.

LINDBERGH, ANNE MORROW: 100th BIRTH ANNIVERSARY. June 22, 1906. American author and aviator, born at Englewood, NJ. Wife of aviator Charles A. Lindbergh, she served as his copilot and navigator when he broke the transatlantic speed record in 1930. A prolific author and poet, in *Gift from the Sea* she wrote: "By and large, mothers and housewives are the only workers who do not have regular time off. They are the great vacationless class." She died Feb 7, 2001, at Passumpsic, VT.

LOUISIANA PEACH FESTIVAL. June 22–25. Ruston, LA. The 56th annual Louisiana Peach Festival will feature rodeo, parade, concerts, cooking contests, sporting events, arts & crafts and more. Est attendance: 30,000. For info: Nancy Bergeron, Ruston/Lincoln Convention & Visitors Bureau, 104 E Mississippi Ave, Ruston, LA 71270. Phone: (800) 392-9032. E-mail: info@rustonlincoln.com. Web: www.rustonlincoln.com.

MALTA: MNARJA. June 22–23. Buskett Gardens. A folk-cum-harvest festival. An all-night traditional Maltese "festa" with folk music, dancing and impromptu Maltese folk singing (ghana). This festival originated in the Middle Ages, and the word *Mnarja* is derived from *luminarja* because the countryside and the bastions around Mdina, Malta's ancient capital, used to be illuminated by "Fjakkoli" (torches made of sand mixed with oil and animal fat) on the eve of and on the feast day itself.

MERAMEC COMMUNITY FAIR. June 22–24. Fairgrounds, Sullivan, MO. 20th annual. Ticket price includes big-name entertainment, huge carnival, truck and tractor pulls, arts and crafts, trick motorcycles, kids games, FFA-4H displays, pageants, Bull Bash and commercial booths. Est attendance: 30,000. For info: Sullivan Chamber of Commerce, PO Box 536, Sullivan, MO 63080. Phone: (573) 468-3314 or (573) 860-2861. E-mail: chamber@sullivanmo.com. Web: www.sullivanmo.com.

MISS ARIZONA PAGEANT. June 22–24. Gilbert, AZ. Part of the Miss America Organization. For info: Miss Arizona Scholarship Foundation, 2800 14th Ave, Douglas, AZ 85607-

2627. Phone: (520) 364-5308. Fax: (520) 364-1137. Web: www
.miss-arizona.org.

MISS VIRGINIA PAGEANT. June 22–24. Roanoke Civic Center Auditorium, Roanoke, VA. Scholarship pageant held since 1953. Miss Virginia then appears in the Miss America pageant. Est attendance: 4,000. For info: The Miss Virginia Pageant, 102 N Mitchell Rd, Vinton, VA 24179. Phone: (540) 989-4531. E-mail: missvirginia@charter.net. Web: www.missva.com.

MISS WISCONSIN PAGEANT. June 22–24. A. Kimball Auditorium, Oshkosh, WI. Part of the Miss America Organization. For info: Miss Wisconsin Organization, 2634 Shorewood Dr, Oshkosh, WI 54901-1625. Phone: (920) 233-1380. E-mail: lcaptain@north net.net. Web: www.misswisconsin.com.

PAPP, JOSEPH: BIRTH ANNIVERSARY. June 22, 1921. Born Yosl Papirofsky at Brooklyn, NY, Joe Papp became one of the leading figures in American theater. At the helm of the New York Public Theatre, Papp produced a wide range of work from the classical to that of the newest American dramatists, including *Hair, Two Gentlemen of Verona, The Pirates of Penzance, The Mystery of Edwin Drood, That Championship Season* and *A Chorus Line.* He began in 1954 with the Shakespeare Theatre Workshop, taking touring productions around the city on a flatbed truck. When the truck broke down in Central Park, Papp turned his touring company into Shakespeare-in-the-Park. Producing and directing more than 400 productions, Papp garnered three Pulitzer Prizes, six New York Critics Circle Awards and 28 Tonys. He died Oct 31, 1991, at New York, NY.

SAINT IGNACE AUTO SHOW. June 22–24. St. Ignace, MI. 31st anniversary. Parade, cruise night and swap meet. Entries from 25 states and Canada. Est attendance: 100,000. For info: Edward K. Reavie, 268 Hillcrest Blvd, St. Ignace, MI 49781. Phone: (906) 643-8087 or (906) 643-1USA. Fax: (906) 643-9784. E-mail: ereavie@nostalgia-prod.com. Web: www.nostalgia-prod .com or www.auto-shows.com.

SHAKESPEARE ON THE GREEN. June 22–25 (also June 29–July 2 and July 5–9). (all dates tentative). Elmwood Park, Univ of Nebraska, Omaha, NE. Nonprofit professional presentations of the works of William Shakespeare in a beautiful outdoor setting for the families of the Great Plains region. One of the largest donation-driven festivals across the country. Includes preshow seminars and workshops. Picnic area and concessions, Elizabethan entertainment featuring music, dancing, singing, juggling and acrobatics. Est attendance: 35,000. For info: Michael Markey, Managing Dir, Nebraska Shakespeare Festival, Dept of Fine Arts, Creighton Univ, Omaha, NE 68178. Phone: (402) 280-2391. E-mail: neshakes@creighton.edu.

SOVIET UNION INVADED: 65th ANNIVERSARY. June 22, 1941. German troops invaded the Soviet Union, beginning a conflict that left 27 million Soviet citizens dead. Ceremonies are held this day in Russia, Belarus and Ukraine, the areas of the former Soviet Union which bore the brunt of the initial invasion.

STUPID GUY THING DAY. June 22. Women are always talking about it, so here's the day to commemorate it! Women everywhere are to make a list of "stupid guy things" and pass it on! [©2004 by WH.] For info: Thomas & Ruth Roy, Wellcat Holidays, 2418 Long Ln, Lebanon, PA 17046. Phone: (717) 279-0184. E-mail: info@wellcat.com. Web: www.wellcat.com.

SWITZERLAND: MORAT BATTLE ANNIVERSARY. June 22, 1476. The little, walled town of Morat played a decisive part in Swiss history. There, the Confederates were victorious over Charles the Bold of Burgundy, laying the basis for French-speaking areas to become Swiss. Now an annual children's festival.

TELLURIDE WINE FESTIVAL. June 22–25. Telluride, CO. This annual festival offers food and wine enthusiasts an unforgettable four-day event with a rare opportunity to meet winemakers, celebrity chefs, experts and authors. It's an unparalleled educational and epicurean experience. Single event tickets and four-day-weekend packages are available. Annually, the last week-

end in June. Est attendance: 4,000. For info: Erin Hass, Telluride Wine Festival, PO Box 1677, Telluride, CO 81435. Phone: (970) 728-3178. Fax: (970) 728-3498. E-mail: info@telluridewinefestival .com. Web: www.telluridewinefestival.com.

US DEPARTMENT OF JUSTICE: ANNIVERSARY. June 22, 1870. Established by an act of Congress, the Department of Justice is headed by the attorney general. Prior to 1870, the attorney general (whose office had been created Sept 24, 1789) had been a member of the president's cabinet but had not been the head of a department.

VANCOUVER, GEORGE: BIRTH ANNIVERSARY. June 22, 1757. English navigator, explorer and author for whom Vancouver Island and the cities of Vancouver (British Columbia and Washington) are named was born at Norfolk, England, and joined the navy at the age of 13. He surveyed the coasts of Australia, New Zealand and western North America and sailed with Captain James Cook to the Arctic in 1780. Vancouver died at Petersham, Surrey, England, May 10, 1798, just as he was correcting the final pages of his *Journal,* which was published at London later that year.

V-MAIL DELIVERY: ANNIVERSARY. June 22, 1942. The first V-Mail (V for victory) was dispatched from New York on this date. The system was devised during WWII to conserve cargo space for war materials and supplies. Special paper was used for writing the letters. At post offices, the letters were opened, censored and photographed in reduced proportions. The film was then transported overseas. A complete roll of film contained 1,600 letters.

WATERMELON THUMP (WITH WORLD CHAMPION SEED-SPITTING CONTEST). June 22–25. Luling, TX. Features World Champion Seed-Spitting Contest, street dance and concert each night, giant parade on Saturday, free live entertainment in the Beer Garden, champion melon auction, arts and crafts exhibit and sales, food, games, fun run and rides. Annually, the last weekend in June (Thursday–Sunday). Est attendance: 45,000. For info: Susan H. Ward, Sec, Luling Watermelon Thump Assn, Box 710, Luling, TX 78648. Phone: (830) 875-3214, ext 2. Fax: (830) 875-2082. E-mail: susan@watermelonthump.com. Web: www.watermelonthump.com.

WILDER, BILLY: 100th BIRTH ANNIVERSARY. June 22, 1906. One of the greatest directors of Hollywood's Golden Age was born Samuel Wilder at Sucha Beskidzka in the Austro-Hungarian Empire. After a short career in Berlin, Wilder fled Germany in 1933 and eventually landed in Hollywood, where he directed and cowrote some of the 20th century's greatest films. His classics include the film noir works *Double Indemnity* and *Sunset Boulevard,* the searing dramas *Stalag 17* and *The Lost Weekend* and the comic gem *Some Like It Hot.* He received six Oscars (out of 21 nominations), and Best Film Oscars went to *The Lost Weekend* and *The Apartment.* Wilder died at Los Angeles, CA, on Mar 27, 2002.

BIRTHDAYS TODAY

Darrell Armstrong, 38, basketball player, born Gastonia, NC, June 22, 1968.

Ed Bradley, 65, broadcast journalist ("60 Minutes"), born Philadelphia, PA, June 22, 1941.

Klaus Maria Brandauer, 62, actor (*Out of Africa, White Fang*), born Altausse, Austria, June 22, 1944.

Amy Brenneman, 42, actress ("Judging Amy"), born Glastonbury, CT, June 22, 1964.

Carson Daly, 33, host ("MTV Live," "Last Call with Carson Daly"), born Santa Monica, CA, June 22, 1973.

Clyde Austin Drexler, 44, basketball coach and former player, born Houston, TX, June 22, 1962.

Dianne Feinstein, 73, US Senator (D, California), born San Francisco, CA, June 22, 1933.

Kris Kristofferson, 70, singer, actor (*Alice Doesn't Live Here Anymore, A Star Is Born*), born Brownsville, TX, June 22, 1936.

Michael Lerner, 65, actor (*The Candidate, Eight Men Out, Barton Fink*), born Brooklyn, NY, June 22, 1941.

Tracy Pollan, 46, actress ("Family Ties," *Bright Lights, Big City*), born New York, NY, June 22, 1960.

Todd Rundgren, 58, singer (*Something/Anything*), producer, born Upper Darby, PA, June 22, 1948.

Meryl Streep, 57, actress (Oscars for *Kramer vs Kramer* and *Sophie's Choice*), born Summit, NJ, June 22, 1949.

Kurt Wagner, 35, football player, born Burlington, IA, June 22, 1971.

Lindsay Wagner, 57, actress ("The Bionic Woman," *The Paper Chase*), born Los Angeles, CA, June 22, 1949.

JUNE 23 — FRIDAY
Day 174 — 191 Remaining

"THE BREAKFAST CLUB" RADIO PREMIERE: ANNIVERSARY. June 23, 1933. "The Breakfast Club with Don McNeil," which hit radio airwaves on this date, had a 35-year run. It was carried by 400 affiliates and tickets became as sought-after as those for a taping of "The Tonight Show" are today. The hour-long show included celebrities such as Fran Allison of "Kukla, Fran and Ollie" fame. Its popularity, however, stemmed mainly from regular features such as "Memory Time," when McNeil read poems and letters from listeners. During WWII "Prayer Time" was started. McNeil's "Call to Breakfast," which was announced every 15 minutes, invited listeners to get up and march around the breakfast table. McNeil died in 1996.

CASH, JUNE CARTER: BIRTH ANNIVERSARY. June 23, 1929. Grammy-winning country-western star born Valerie June Carter at Maces Springs, VA. As a member of the Carter Family, a group that included her mother, sisters and various cousins, she toured as a performer from childhood. She met Johnny Cash on the road in 1961. She cowrote his hit song "Ring of Fire," and they began recording together. They married in 1968, and won two Grammys for their duets. She died May 15, 2004, at Nashville, TN.

CLARKSON CZECH FESTIVAL. June 23–25. Main St, Clarkson, NE. Czech food, entertainment, music, polkas, cooking, demonstrations, carnival, rodeo, arts and crafts. Annually, the fourth full weekend in June. Sponsor: Clarkson Commercial Club. Est attendance: 10,000. For info: Robert Brabec, 515 Elm St, Clarkson, NE 68629. Phone: (402) 892-3331 or (402) 892-3561. Fax: (402) 892-3318.

CLEARWATER CHAMBER OF COMMERCE RODEO. June 23–25. Clearwater, NE. 7:30 PM each day. Annually, the last full weekend of June. Est attendance: 6,000. For info: Clearwater Chamber of Commerce, Box 201, Clearwater, NE 68726.

DALESBURG MIDSUMMER FESTIVAL. June 23. Dalesburg Lutheran Church, rural Vermillion, SD. Celebration of Scandinavian and rural heritage. Programs, dances to raise the Midsummer Pole, a smorgasbord, arts and crafts area, band concert and more. Est attendance: 800. For info: Ronald Johnson, Midsummer Committee, Dalesburg Midsummer Festival, 30595 University Rd, Vermillion, SD 57069-6507. Phone: (605) 253-2575. Web: www.angelfire.com/sd/dalesburg99/.

	S	M	T	W	T	F	S
June					1	2	3
2006	4	5	6	7	8	9	10
	11	12	13	14	15	16	17
	18	19	20	21	22	23	24
	25	26	27	28	29	30	

DELMARVA CHICKEN FESTIVAL. June 23–24. Snow Hill, MD. 58th annual. A family event focusing on chicken, the leading agricultural enterprise on the Delmarva Peninsula. Food, entertainment and consumer information are featured. Est attendance: 25,000. For info: Connie Parvis, Delmarva Poultry Industry, Inc, 16686 County Seat Hwy, Georgetown, DE 19947-4881. Phone: (302) 856-9037. E-mail: dpi@dpichicken.com.

DENMARK: MIDSUMMER EVE. June 23. Celebrated all over the country with bonfires and merrymaking.

DENMARK: VIKING FESTIVAL. June 23–July 2. Frederiksund (about 25 miles northwest of Copenhagen). Famous outdoor plays based on Danish legends. Annually, the next-to-last Friday in June through the first Sunday in July.

ESTONIA: VICTORY DAY. June 23. National holiday. Commemorates victory against Germany in 1919.

FIRST TYPEWRITER: ANNIVERSARY. June 23, 1868. First US typewriter was patented by Luther Sholes.

FOSSE, ROBERT LOUIS (BOB): BIRTH ANNIVERSARY. June 23, 1927. Bob Fosse was born at Chicago, IL. The son of a vaudeville singer, he began his show business career at the age of 13. He was the only director in history to win an Oscar, an Emmy and a Tony for his work. As a choreographer he was known for his unique dance style that focused on explosive angularity of the human body in its movement. His body of work included the plays *Pippin, Sweet Charity, Pajama Game, Chicago* and *Damn Yankees.* His films included *Cabaret, Lenny* and the autobiographical *All That Jazz.* Fosse died Sept 23, 1987, at Washington, DC.

GETTYSBURG CIVIL WAR RELIC AND COLLECTORS SHOW. June 23–25. Gettysburg, PA. Accoutrements, weapons, uniforms and personal effects from American military history, 1865 and earlier. Leading collectors and dealers of Civil War material. Est attendance: 2,000. For info: GBPA, PO Box 4087, Gettysburg, PA 17325. Phone: (717) 334-2350. Fax: (717) 334-3578. E-mail: info@unionddb.com. Web: www.gettysburgcvb.org.

GRANTSVILLE DAYS. June 23–25. Grantsville Park, Grantsville, MD. Three-day annual homecoming weekend. Free entertainment Friday 6:45 PM–Sunday 7 PM. Lion's chicken BBQ, local noncommercial food booths, children's games, horse- and tractor-pulling contests, gospel music, fireworks Friday and Saturday nights. Annually, the last weekend in June. Est attendance: 20,000. For info: Gerry Beachy, PO Box 189, 149 Main St, Grantsville, MD 21536. Fax: (301) 895-3623. E-mail: gbeachy@verizon.net. Web: www.grantsvilledays.com.

KINSEY, ALFRED: BIRTH ANNIVERSARY. June 23, 1894. Born at Hoboken, NJ, Kinsey was a professor of zoology who moved into the study of human sexual behavior in the 1940s at Indiana University's Institute for Sex Research (later renamed after him). Kinsey published two controversial books based on his research: *Sexual Behavior in the Human Male* (1948) and *Sexual Behavior in the Human Female* (1953). Kinsey died Aug 25, 1956, at Bloomington, IN.

LAST FORMAL SURRENDER OF CONFEDERATE TROOPS: ANNIVERSARY. June 23, 1865. The last formal surrender of Confederate troops took place in the Oklahoma Territory. Cherokee leader and Confederate Brigadier General Waite surrendered his command of a battalion formed by Indians.

LET IT GO DAY. June 23. Whatever it is that's bugging you, drop it! It's only eating away at you and providing nothing positive. [©2003 by WH.] For info: Thomas & Ruth Roy, Wellcat Holidays, 2418 Long Ln, Lebanon, PA 17046-1708. Phone: (717) 279-0184. E-mail: info@wellcat.com. Web: www.wellcat.com.

LONG BEACH BAYOU FESTIVAL. June 23–25. Queen Mary Events Park, Long Beach, CA. Celebrate Cajun/Creole cultures with food, live nonstop Cajun, Zydeco and blues music, arts & crafts, activities and a Mardi Gras Parade. Est attendance: 10,000. For info: Phone: (562) 427-3713. Web: www.LongBeach Festival.com.

LUXEMBOURG: NATIONAL HOLIDAY. June 23. Official birthday of His Royal Highness Grand Duke Jean in 1921. Also, Luxembourg's independence is celebrated June 23.

MIDSUMMER DAY/EVE CELEBRATIONS. June 23. Celebrates the beginning of summer with maypoles, music, dancing and bonfires. Observed mainly in northern Europe, including Finland, Latvia and Sweden. Day of observance is sometimes St. John's Day (June 24), with celebration on St. John's Eve (June 23) as well, or June 19. Time approximates the summer solstice. See also: "Summer" (June 21).

NEWPORT FLOWER SHOW. June 23–29. Rosecliff, Newport, RI. New England's premier summertime flower and horticulture show includes judged flower arrangements, a horticultural tent brimming with plants and flowers, demonstrations, lectures and a spectacular garden marketplace in the elegant reception rooms and on the expansive oceanfront lawn of Rosecliff, a Gilded Age mansion. For info: Preservation Society of Newport, 424 Bellevue Ave, Newport, RI 02840. Phone: (401) 847-1000. Web: www.newportmansions.org.

RUDOLPH, WILMA: BIRTH ANNIVERSARY. June 23, 1940. Olympic gold medal sprinter, born at Bethlehem, TN. She won the 100 meters, the 200 meters and the 400-meter relay at the 1960 Rome games, thus becoming the first woman to win three gold medals at the same Olympics. She overcame polio as a child and went on to Tennessee State University to become an athlete. Rudolph won the Sullivan Award in 1961. Died at Brentwood, TN, Nov 12, 1994.

SCANDINAVIAN HJEMKOMST FESTIVAL. June 23–25. Moorhead, MN. 29th annual. Named as "One of North America's Top 100 Events" of 2002 by the American Bus Association. Featuring activities for all ages, including authentic ethnic entertainment, music and folk dancing, a marketplace, foods, exhibitions and demonstrations of arts, fine crafts and ethnic traditions from Denmark, Finland, Iceland, Norway, Sweden and Scandinavian America. Est attendance: 10,000. For info: Festival Director, Scandinavian Hjemkomst Festival, PO Box 926, Fargo, ND 58107. Phone: (218) 299-5452. E-mail: fmshf@ci.moorhead.mn.us. Web: www.scandinavianhjemkomstfestival.org.

SOUTH ST. PAUL KAPOSIA DAYS. June 23–25. South St. Paul, MN. Family-oriented city festival including parades, pageant, children's activities, athletic competitions, craft & flea markets, musical entertainment and fireworks. Annually, the last full weekend in June. For info: South St. Paul Kaposia Days, PO Box 144, South St. Paul, MN 55075. Phone: (651) 451-2266. Fax: (651) 451-0846. E-mail: carol@riverheights.com. Web: www.kaposiadays.com.

STERNWHEELER DAYS. June 23–25. Port Marina Park, Cascade Locks, OR. Home of the sternwheeler *Columbia Gorge*. Salmon Bake, Mountain Men Encampment, bingo, parade, food, arts and crafts, live music. Annually, the last weekend in June. Est attendance: 6,000. For info: Columbia Gorge Lions, PO Box 522, Cascade Locks, OR 97014. Phone: (541) 374-8619. Web: www.cascadelocks.net.

SWEDEN: MIDSUMMER. June 23–24. Celebrated throughout Sweden. Maypole dancing, games and folk music.

TAKE YOUR DOG TO WORK DAY. June 23. A day to celebrate the great companions dogs make and to encourage adoptions from animal shelters. Annually, the first Friday after Father's Day. For info: Pet Sitters Intl, 201 E King St, King, NC 27021. Phone: (336) 983-9222. Fax: (336) 983-5266. E-mail: tydtwd@petsit.com. Web: www.petsit.com.

UNITED NATIONS: PUBLIC SERVICE DAY. June 23. The Assembly designated June 23 of each year as United Nations Public Service Day (resolution 57/277). It encouraged member states to organize special events on that day to highlight the contribution of public service in the development process. For info: United Nations, Dept of Public Info, New York, NY 10017. Web: www.un.org.

WATER SKI DAYS. June 23–25. Lake City, MN. Grand day parade, arts and crafts fair, Venetian boat parade, food, beer tent, live entertainment, carnival and games. Fun for the whole family. Annually, the last full weekend in June. Est attendance: 25,000. For info: Lake City Area Chamber of Commerce, 212 S Washington St, Lake City, MN 55041. Phone: (800) 369-4123. E-mail: lcchamber@earthlink.net.

WORLD CHAMPIONSHIP ROTARY TILLER RACE AND PURPLEHULL PEA FESTIVAL. June 23–24. Emerson, AR. 17th annual festival. World Cup purplehull pea–shelling competition, rotary tiller race, domino tournaments, concessions, arts, crafts, entertainment, children's games, the Great Purplehull Peas and Cornbread Cook-off, Queen's pageant (various ages), 3-on-3 basketball. Est attendance: 10,000. For info: Publicity, Purplehull Pea Fest, PO Box 1, Emerson, AR 71740. Phone: (501) 315-7373. E-mail: purplehull@juno.com. Web: www.purplehull.com.

BIRTHDAYS TODAY

Bryan Brown, 59, actor (*A Town Like Alice, Breaker Morant, F/X*), born Sydney, Australia, June 23, 1947.

James Levine, 63, American conductor and pianist, Metropolitan Opera of New York City, born Cincinnati, OH, June 23, 1943.

Frances McDormand, 49, actress (*Fargo, Mississippi Burning, Almost Famous*), born Chicago, IL, June 23, 1957.

Ted Shackelford, 60, actor ("Knots Landing," "Dallas"), born Oklahoma City, OK, June 23, 1946.

Clarence Thomas, 58, Supreme Court Associate Justice, born Pinpoint, GA, June 23, 1948.

LaDanian Tomlinson, 27, football player, born Waco, TX, June 23, 1979.

JUNE 24 — SATURDAY
Day 175 — 190 Remaining

BAYMEN'S SEAFOOD AND MUSIC FESTIVAL. June 24. Tuckerton Seaport, Tuckerton, NJ. Stroll the Tuckerton Seaport and sample delicious Jersey fresh clams, crabs and shrimp from the finest seafood purveyors. After you satisfy your appetite, move your feet to the beat of live, toe-tapping entertainment. Bring the family and your beach chairs and plan to spend the whole day. Annually, the fourth Saturday in June. Est attendance: 1,600. For info: Karen DeRosa, Tuckerton Seaport, 120 W Main St, PO Box 52, Tuckerton, NJ 08087. Phone: (609) 296-8868. Fax: (609) 296-5810. E-mail: info@tuckertonseaport.org. Web: www.tuckertonseaport.org.

BEARTOOTH RUN. June 24. Red Lodge, MT. 8.2-mile or 4.4-mile footrace up scenic Beartooth Pass. Race will start at 7,000 feet and finish at 9,000 feet. Annually, the last Saturday in June. Est attendance: 350. For info: Denise Parsons, Beartooth Run, Box 988, Red Lodge, MT 59068. Phone: (406) 446-1718. E-mail: information@redlodge.com. Web: www.redlodge.com.

BEECHER, HENRY WARD: BIRTH ANNIVERSARY. June 24, 1813. Famous American clergyman and orator was born at Litchfield, CT. Died Mar 8, 1887, at Brooklyn, NY. His dying words were "Now comes the mystery."

BERLIN AIRLIFT: ANNIVERSARY. June 24, 1948. In the early days of the Cold War the Soviet Union challenged the West's right of access to Berlin. The Soviets created a blockade, and an airlift to supply some 2,250,000 people resulted. The airlift lasted a total of 321 days and brought into Berlin 1,592,787 tons of supplies. Joseph Stalin finally backed down and the blockade ended May 12, 1949.

CANADA: ST. JEAN-BAPTISTE DAY. June 24. Public holiday in Quebec.

CELEBRATION OF THE SENSES. June 24. Treat yourself to a stimulation of the five senses—taste, touch, scent, sight and sound—and you may experience the elevation known to many mystics as the elusive sixth sense. [©2003 by WH.] For info: Thomas & Ruth Roy, Wellcat Holidays, 2418 Long Ln, Lebanon, PA 17046. Phone: (717) 279-0184. E-mail: info@wellcat.com. Web: www.wellcat.com.

CELTIC FLING. June 24–25. Mount Hope Estate & Winery, Manheim, PA. 'Tis but a wee journey to the Scottish Highlands or the Emerald Isle when you dance a jig through the gates of the Pennsylvania Renaissance Faire's annual "Celtic Fling." It's an official Highland Dance competition, Highland Games, 35 acres of authentic Celtic arts and crafts, music and dance, concerts by nationally acclaimed Celtic recording artists and, of course, beer and bagpipes. For info: Thomas Roy, PRF, PO Box 685, Cornwall, PA 17016. Phone: (717) 665-7021. Fax: (717) 664-3466. E-mail: tom@parenfaire.com. Web: www.parenfaire.com.

CHINA: MACAU DAY. June 24. Celebrates defeat of the Dutch invasion forces of 1622 and pays homage to patron saint of Macau, Saint John the Baptist. Macau is a former Portuguese colony that is now part of China.

CIARDI, JOHN: BIRTH ANNIVERSARY. June 24, 1916. American poet, critic, translator, teacher, etymologist and author of children's books, born at Boston, MA. John Anthony Ciardi's criticism and other writings were often described as honest and sometimes as harsh. Died at Edison, NJ, Mar 30, 1986.

COLORADO BREWERS' FESTIVAL. June 24–25. Fort Collins, CO. The kegs will be tapped once again for the annual festival in Old Town Square, Fort Collins, Colorado. Every year more than 40 Colorado breweries, including local favorites Odell's

and New Belgium, come celebrate Colorado's rich brewing history and feature their best native beers. Annually, the last full weekend of June. Est attendance: 30,000. For info: Downtown Fort Collins, 19 Old Town Square, #230, Fort Collins, CO 80524. Phone: (970) 484-6500. E-mail: info@downtownfortcollins.com. Web: www.downtownfortcollins.com.

DEMPSEY, JACK: BIRTH ANNIVERSARY. June 24, 1895. William Harrison Dempsey, known as "The Manassa Mauler," was world heavyweight boxing champion from 1919 to 1926. Following his boxing career Dempsey became a successful New York restaurant operator. Born at Manassa, CO, Dempsey died May 31, 1983, at New York, NY.

DESCENDANTS DAY. June 24–25. The day in each year when all the world's citizens take an accounting of their activities during the preceding year that will impact our descendants and our neighbors across time. Annually, the last weekend in June. For info: Charles A. Howell, Trust for the Future, 2704 12th Ave S, Nashville, TN 37204. Phone: (615) 297-7206. Fax: (615) 269-6268. E-mail: cahowell@edge.net.

EASTERN MUSIC FESTIVAL. June 24–July 29 (tentative). Guilford College, Greensboro, NC. 45th annual summer festival of classical concerts and recitals performed by resident professionals and a corps of talented young students from the US and abroad. Est attendance: 63,000. For info: Eastern Music Festival, PO Box 22026, Greensboro, NC 27420. Phone: (336) 333-7450. Fax: (336) 333-7454. E-mail: info@easternmusicfestival.org. Web: www.easternmusicfestival.org.

GALESBURG RAILROAD DAYS. June 24–25. Galesburg, IL. 29th annual festival celebrating the city's railroad heritage that dates back to 1854. Carnival, street fair, railroad exhibits and displays, 5k run and concerts. Hobby train show with over 200 exhibitions and tables. Includes more than 40 events. Est attendance: 15,000. For info: Galesburg Area CVB, PO Box 60, Galesburg, IL 61402-0060. Phone: (309) 343-2485. Fax: (309) 343-2521. E-mail: visitors@visitgalesburg.com. Web: www.visit galesburg.com.

GETTYSBURG CIVIL WAR HERITAGE DAYS. June 24–July 4. Gettysburg, PA. Commemorates the Battle of Gettysburg. Living history encampment with both Union and Confederate army campsites, concerts, Civil War lecture series, a battle of Gettysburg reenactment, firefighter's festival, encampment church service and Civil War book fair. Est attendance: 350,000. For info: Gettysburg CVB, PO Box 4117, Gettysburg, PA 17325. Phone: (717) 334-6274. Fax: (717) 334-1166. E-mail: gettysburg cvb@dejazzd.com. Web: www.gettysburgcvb.org.

"HOPALONG CASSIDY" TV PREMIERE: ANNIVERSARY. June 24, 1949. A western series starring William Boyd in the title role as a hero who wore black and rode a white horse. The original episodes were segments edited from 66 movie features of Hopalong Cassidy and his sidekick, Red Connors (Edgar Buchanan). The films were so popular that Boyd produced episodes especially for TV.

ITALY: CALCIO FIORENTINO. June 24–28. Florence. Revival of a 16th-century football match in medieval costumes. Fireworks also June 24.

LADIES OF COUNTRY MUSIC SHOW. June 24. Waretown, NJ. Featuring Albert Music Hall's ladies of country and bluegrass. No alcoholic beverages or smoking allowed. For info: Albert Music Hall, PO Box 657, Waretown, NJ 08758. Phone: (609) 971-1593. Web:www.alberthall.org.

LATVIA: JOHN'S DAY (MIDSUMMER NIGHT DAY). June 24. The festival of Jani, which commemorates the summer solstice and the name day of (Janis) John, is one of Latvia's most ancient as well as joyous rituals. This festival is traditionally celebrated in the countryside, as it emphasizes fertility and the beginning of summer. Festivities begin June 23.

MARBLE WEEKEND. June 24–25. Millville, NJ. Marble artists and collectors conference. Rain or shine, the sale will go on. Est attendance: 1,500. For info: Wheaton Village, 1501 Glasstown

	S	M	T	W	T	F	S
June						1	2	3
2006	4	5	6	7	8	9	10
	11	12	13	14	15	16	17
	18	19	20	21	22	23	24
	25	26	27	28	29	30	

Rd, Millville, NJ 08332. Phone: (800) 998-4552 or (856) 825-6800. Fax: (856) 825-2410. E-mail: mail@wheatonvillage.org. Web: www.wheatonvillage.org.

NORSKEDALEN'S MIDSUMMER FEST. June 24–25. Norskedalen Nature and Heritage Center, Coon Valley, WI. Celebrate the summer solstice and Sankt Hans Dag (Saint John's Day) in Scandinavian style. Pioneer crafts and demonstrations; children's activities, entertainment, food and raffle; nature hikes, animal presentations and horse-drawn wagon rides. Woodcarving show and competition, open air museum; artisans demonstrating and selling their works. Est attendance: 1,500. For info: Norskedalen Nature and Heritage Center, Inc, PO Box 235, Coon Valley, WI 54623. Phone: (608) 452-3424. Fax: (608) 452-3157. E-mail: info@norskedalen.org. Web: www.norskedalen.org.

ONIZUKA, ELLISON S.: BIRTH ANNIVERSARY. June 24, 1946. Lieutenant Colonel Ellison S. Onizuka, 39-year-old aerospace engineer, was mission specialist aboard the space shuttle *Challenger* when it exploded Jan 28, 1986 (killing all aboard). Onizuka was born at Kealakekua, Kona, HI. See also: "*Challenger* Space Shuttle Explosion Anniversary" (Jan 28).

PERU: COUNTRYMAN'S DAY. June 24. Half-day public holiday.

PSFCA EAST WEST ALL-STAR GAME. June 24. Mansion Park, Altoona, PA. All-star football game featuring the finest college-bound athletes in Pennsylvania. Come see the "Beasts of the East" take on the "Best of the West" in a must-see, action-packed game. Annually, the last Saturday in June. Est attendance: 7,500. For info: Krista Myers, Allegheny Mountains CVB, One Convention Center Dr, Altoona, PA 16602. Phone: (814) 943-4183. Fax: (814) 943-8094. E-mail: info@amcvb.com. Web: www.east westgame.com.

QUAD CITY AIR SHOW. June 24–25 (tentative). Davenport Municipal Airport, Davenport, IA. 20th annual. Largest family aviation fun-filled weekend in the area featuring the very best of civilian and military aviation. Sat and Sun: gates open at 8 AM, and flying starts at 9 AM with the WWII Dawn Patrol. Action continues nonstop both in the sky and on the ground. For info: Phone: (563) 285-7469. Web: www.quadcityairshow.com. For info on the Quad Cities: Quad Cities CVB. Phone: (800) 747-7800. Web: www.visitquadcities.com.

SAINT JOHN THE BAPTIST DAY. June 24. Celebrates the birth of the saint.

SCOTLAND: BANNOCKBURN DAY. June 24, 1314. Anniversary of the Battle of Bannockburn when Robert the Bruce won independence for Scotland.

SEASPACE. June 24–25. Reliant Arena, Astrodome, Houston, TX. Scuba diving convention featuring seminars, photo and video courses, workshops, photo contest and exhibit, film festivals, halls of exhibits, special kids talk, environmental awareness area, free intro to scuba and snorkeling and receptions. Sponsor: Houston Underwater Club. For more info send SASE. Est attendance: 10,000. For info: Seaspace, PO Box 3753, Houston, TX 77253-3753. Phone: (713) 467-6675. Web: www.seaspace.org.

SNAKE HUNT. June 24–25. Cross Fork, PA. To raise funds for the fire company. Est attendance: 5,000. For info: Barry Gipe, Chmn, Kettle Creek Hose Co #1, 2605 Steward Hill Rd, Cross Fork, PA 17729. Phone: (570) 923-0848.

THORNTON, MATTHEW: DEATH ANNIVERSARY. June 24, 1803. Signer of the Declaration of Independence. Born at Ireland about 1714, he died at Newburyport, MA.

VENEZUELA: BATTLE OF CARABOBO DAY. June 24. National holiday. Commemorates a victory in 1821 that assured Venezuelan independence from Spain.

Nancy Allen, 56, actress (*Carrie, Blow Out, Robocop*), born New York, NY, June 24, 1950.

Claude Chabrol, 76, filmmaker (*La Femme Infidèle, The Cousins*), born Sardent, France, June 24, 1930.

Mick Fleetwood, 64, musician (drummer with Fleetwood Mac, "Dreams," "Don't Stop"), born Cornwall, England, June 24, 1942.

Phyllis George, 57, former sportscaster, former Miss America, born Denton, TX, June 24, 1949.

Juli Inkster, 46, golfer, born Santa Cruz, CA, June 24, 1960.

Michele Lee, 64, actress ("Knots Landing"), born Los Angeles, CA, June 24, 1942.

George Pataki, 61, Governor of New York (R), born Peekskill, NY, June 24, 1945.

Predrag (Preki) Radosavljevic, 43, soccer player, born Belgrade, Yugoslavia, June 24, 1963.

Sherry Stringfield, 39, actress ("NYPD Blue," "ER"), born Colorado Springs, CO, June 24, 1967.

Peter Weller, 59, actor (*Robocop, Naked Lunch*), born Stevens Point, WI, June 24, 1947.

JUNE 25 — SUNDAY

Day 176 — 189 Remaining

AMERICAN NURSES ASSOCIATION CONVENTION. June 25–30. Minneapolis, MN. Informative and useable educational sessions, nurses from around the country and the world, the industry's leading suppliers and employers. The ANA convention occurs every two years and rotates around the country. For info: American Nurses Association, 8515 Georgia Ave, Ste 400, Silver Spring, MD 20910. Phone: (800) 274-4ANA. Web: www.nursingworld.org.

AMERICA'S KIDS DAY. June 25. A day set aside to reach out and teach our children in America the value of life, liberty and the pursuit of happiness. A time to help our kids to learn about the great nation that they live in and to help by demonstrating what it means to be an American. A time to teach them the historical value of their heritage as America's kids. Annually, the fourth Sunday in June. For info: Judith Natale, NCAC America-USA, PO Box 493703, Redding, CA 96049-3703. E-mail: child aware@aol.com.

ARNOLD, HENRY H. "HAP": BIRTH ANNIVERSARY. June 25, 1886. US general and commander of the Army Air Force in all theaters throughout WWII, Arnold was born at Gladwyne, PA. Although no funds were made available, as early as 1938 Arnold was persuading the US aviation industry to step up manufacturing of airplanes. Production grew from 6,000 to 262,000 per year from 1940–44. He supervised pilot training and by 1944 Air Force personnel strength had grown to two million from a prewar high of 21,000. Made a full general in 1944, he became the US Air Force's first five-star general when the Air Force was made a separate military branch equal to the Army and Navy. Arnold died Jan 15, 1950, at Sonoma, CA.

BATTLE OF LITTLE BIGHORN: ANNIVERSARY. June 25, 1876. Lieutenant Colonel George Armstrong Custer, leading military forces of more than 200 men, attacked an encampment of Sioux Indians led by Chiefs Sitting Bull and Crazy Horse near

Little Bighorn River, MT. Custer and all men in his immediate command were killed in the brief battle (about two hours) of Little Bighorn. One horse, named Comanche, is said to have been the only survivor among Custer's forces.

BHUTAN: NATIONAL DAY. June 25. National holiday observed.

CANADA'S FIRST WOMAN PRIME MINISTER: ANNIVERSARY. June 25, 1993. After winning the June 13 election to the leadership of the ruling Progressive-Conservative Party, Kim Campbell became Canada's 19th prime minister and its first woman prime minister. However, in the general election held Oct 25, 1993, the Liberal Party routed the Progressive-Conservatives in the worst defeat for a governing political party in Canada's 126-year history, reducing the former government's seats in the House of Commons from 154 to 2. Campbell was among those who lost their seats.

CBS SENDS FIRST COLOR TV BROADCAST OVER THE AIR: 55th ANNIVERSARY. June 25, 1951. Columbia Broadcast System broadcast the first color television program. The four-hour program was carried by stations at New York City, Baltimore, Philadelphia, Boston and Washington, DC, although no color sets were owned by the public. At the time CBS, itself, owned fewer than 40 color receivers.

CENTRAL CHINA FLOOD: 15th ANNIVERSARY. June 25, 1991. The Huai River flooded its banks and ravaged major portions of the central Chinese province of Anhui. The poor agricultural region was devastated and approximately 3,000 people were killed. The Anhui region sustained enormous damages when the government ordered dikes broken and sluice gates opened in the rural area to prevent flooding of economically important rivers farther downstream.

CIVIL WAR IN YUGOSLAVIA: 15th ANNIVERSARY. June 25, 1991. In an Eastern Europe freed from the iron rule of communism and the USSR, separatist and nationalist tensions suppressed for decades rose to a violent boiling point. The republics of Croatia and Slovenia declared their independence, sparking a fractious and bitter war that spread throughout what was formerly Yugoslavia. Ethnic rivalries between Serbians and Croatians began the military conflicts that spread to Slovenia, and in 1992 fighting began in Bosnia-Herzegovina between Serbians and ethnic Muslims. Although the new republics were recognized by the UN and sanctions passed to stop the fighting, it raged on through 1995 despite the efforts of UN peacekeeping forces.

CONVERGENCE 2006. June 25–July 1. De Vos Place Convention Center, Grand Rapids, MI. Biennial international fiber conference sponsored by Handweavers Guild of America, Inc, offering lectures, seminars, workshops, studio classes, art exhibits and a vendors' hall. For info: Handweavers Guild of America, 1255 Buford Hwy, Ste 211, Suwanee, GA 30024. Phone: (678) 730-0010. Fax: (678) 730-0836. E-mail: hga@weavespindye.org. Web: www.weavespindye.org.

CROATIA: STATEHOOD DAY. June 25. Croatia's national day. Public holiday.

EIGHTEENTH-CENTURY WHEAT HARVEST. June 25. The Claude Moore Colonial Farm at Turkey Run, McLean, VA. Help the colonial farm family cut and bind wheat, the farmer's second most important cash crop. Light refreshments and 18th-century games. Est attendance: 500. For info: The Claude Moore Colonial Farm, Turkey Run, 6310 Georgetown Pike, McLean, VA 22101. Phone: (703) 442-7557. Fax: (703) 442-0714. Web: www.1771.org.

		S	M	T	W	T	F	S
June						1	2	3
2006		4	5	6	7	8	9	10
		11	12	13	14	15	16	17
		18	19	20	21	22	23	24
		25	26	27	28	29	30	

GAY AND LESBIAN PRIDE PARADE. June 25. Chicago, IL. Chicago's 37th annual parade begins at 12 PM. Est attendance: 400,000. For info: Gay and Lesbian Pride Parade, 3712 N Broadway, PMB #544, Chicago, IL 60613. Phone: (773) 348-8243. E-mail: pridechgo@aol.com. Web: www.chicagopride calendar.org.

GILLARS, MILDRED "AXIS SALLY" E.: DEATH ANNIVERSARY. June 25, 1988. Mildred E. Gillars received the nickname "Axis Sally" during WWII, when she broadcast Nazi propaganda to US troops in Europe. An American citizen, born about 1900 at Portland, ME, she was arrested after the war, tried and convicted of treason. She was sentenced to 10 to 30 years in prison and fined $10,000. She was released after 12 years and later taught music in a convent school at Columbus, OH. She died June 25, 1988, at Columbus, OH.

HARRY THAW SHOOTS STANFORD WHITE: 100th ANNIVERSARY. June 25, 1906. Playboy Harry Thaw shot celebrated architect Stanford White dead at Madison Square Garden. Thaw's wife, showgirl Evelyn Nesbit, was White's former mistress. Newspapers churned the slaying into a scandal, dubbing it the "Trial of the Century."

KOREAN WAR BEGAN: ANNIVERSARY. June 25, 1950. Forces from northern Korea invaded southern Korea, beginning a civil war. US ground forces entered the conflict June 30. An armistice was signed at Panmunjom July 27, 1953, formally dividing the country into two—North Korea and South Korea.

LEVITT PAVILION PERFORMING ARTS/MUSIC FESTIVAL. June 25–Aug 27. Levitt Pavilion, Westport, CT. 33rd annual. Performing Arts/Music Festival conducts more than 50 nights of high-quality entertainment offered free to the general public. In addition, a few concerts are presented with a nominal admission charged to raise money to underwrite the free nights of the festival. Est attendance: 60,000. For info: Freda Welsh, Exec Dir, Levitt Pavilion, 260 S Compo Rd, Westport, CT 06880. Phone: (203) 226-7600. Fax: (203) 226-2330. E-mail: levitt@ci.westport.ct.us. Web: www.levittpavilion.com.

LOG CABIN DAY. June 25. Commemorates log cabins with tours, open houses and special festivities throughout the state of Michigan. Est attendance: 4,000. For info: Virginia Handy, Sec/Treas, Log Cabin Society of Michigan, 3503 Rock Edwards Dr, Sodus, MI 49126. Phone: (269) 925-3836. E-mail: logcabincrafts@qtm.net. Web: www.qtm.net/logcabincrafts.

MISS OREGON SCHOLARSHIP PAGEANT. June 25–July 2. Seaside Civic and Convention Center, Seaside, OR. Part of the Miss America Organization. The Miss Oregon Scholarship Program is a not-for-profit corporation established solely to provide contestants with the opportunity to enhance their professional and educational goals and to achieve those pursuits with the assistance of monetary grants and awards. For info: Miss Oregon Scholarship Pageant, 217 Broadway, Seaside, OR 97138. E-mail: miss-or@seasurf.net. Web: www.missoregon.org.

MONTSERRAT: VOLCANO ERUPTS: ANNIVERSARY. June 25, 1997. After lying dormant for 400 years, the Soufriere Hills volcano began to come to life in July 1995. It finally erupted, wiping out the capital city of Plymouth and two-thirds of the rest of this lush Carribean island on June 25, 1997. Two-thirds of the population relocated to other islands or to Great Britain.

MOON PHASE: NEW MOON. June 25. Moon enters New Moon phase at 12:05 PM, EDT.

MOZAMBIQUE: INDEPENDENCE DAY. June 25. National holiday. Commemorates independence from Portugal in 1975.

O'NEILL, ROSE CECIL: BIRTH ANNIVERSARY. June 25, 1874. Rose O'Neill was born at Wilkes-Barre, PA. Her career included work as an illustrator, author and doll designer, the latter gaining her commercial success with the Kewpie Doll. In 1910 *The Ladies Home Journal* devoted a full page to her Kewpie Doll designs, which were a marketing phenomenon for three decades. Died at Springfield, MO, Apr 6, 1944.

ORWELL, GEORGE: BIRTH ANNIVERSARY. June 25, 1903. English satirist, author of *Animal Farm, 1984* and other works, was born at Motihari, Bengal. George Orwell was the pseudonym of Eric Arthur Blair. Died at London, England, Jan 21, 1950.

REVERE, ANNE: BIRTH ANNIVERSARY. June 25, 1903. American actress Anne Revere was born at New York, NY. She won an Academy Award for her supporting role in *National Velvet* (1944) but was barred from films for 20 years after she refused to testify before the House Committee on Un-American Activities in the 1950s. In 1960 she won a Tony Award for her role in *Toys in the Attic*. Revere died Dec 18, 1990, at Locust Valley, NY.

SEVEN DAYS CAMPAIGN: ANNIVERSARY. June 25–July 1, 1862. In an effort to prevent an attack on Richmond, VA, Confederate General Robert E. Lee launched a series of engagements that became known as the Seven Days Campaign. Battles at Oak Grove, Gaine's Mills, Garnett's Farm, Golding's Farm, Savage's Station, White Oak Swamp and finally Malvern Hill left more than 35,000 casualties on both sides. Despite losing the final assault at Malvern Hill, the Confederates succeeded in preventing the Union army from taking Richmond.

SINGING ON THE MOUNTAIN. June 25. Grandfather Mountain, Linville, NC. 82nd annual sing. Modern and traditional gospel music featuring top groups and nationally known speakers. Annually, the fourth Sunday in June. Free admission. Est attendance: 7,000. For info: Grandfather Mountain, US Highway 221 N, PO Box 129, Linville, NC 28646. Phone: (800) 468-7325. Web: www.grandfather.com.

SLOVENIA: NATIONAL DAY. June 25. Public holiday. Commemorates independence from the former Yugoslavia in 1991.

SUPREME COURT ABORTION NOTIFICATION RULING: ANNIVERSARY. June 25, 1990. The Supreme Court ruled, in a 5–4 decision, that it was unconstitutional for a state to require, without providing other options, that a minor notify both her parents before obtaining an abortion.

SUPREME COURT BANS SCHOOL PRAYER: ANNIVERSARY. June 25, 1962. The US Supreme Court ruled that a prayer read aloud in public schools violated the 1st Amendment's separation of church and state. The court again struck down a law pertaining to the 1st Amendment when it disallowed an Alabama law that permitted a daily one-minute period of silent meditation or prayer in public schools June 1, 1985. (Vote 6–3.)

SUPREME COURT UPHOLDS RIGHT TO DIE: ANNIVERSARY. June 25, 1990. In the case *Cruzan v Missouri*, the Supreme Court, in a 5–4 ruling, upheld the constitutional right of a person whose wishes are clearly known to refuse life-sustaining medical treatment.

TWO YUGOSLAV REPUBLICS DECLARE INDEPENDENCE: 15th ANNIVERSARY. June 25, 1991. The republics of Slovenia and Croatia formally declared independence from Yugoslavia. The two northwestern republics did not, however, secede outright.

VIRGINIA: RATIFICATION DAY. June 25. 10th state to ratify the Constitution in 1788.

Linda Cardellini, 31, actress (*Scooby-Doo, Legally Blonde*), born Redmond City, CA, June 25, 1975.

Carlos Delgado, 34, baseball player, born Mayaguez, Puerto Rico, June 25, 1972.

June Lockhart, 81, actress (mom in second "Lassie" series, "Lost in Space"), born New York, NY, June 25, 1925.

Sidney Lumet, 82, director (*12 Angry Men, Serpico, Dog Day Afternoon, Network*), born Philadelphia, PA, June 25, 1924.

George Michael, 43, singer (Wham!, "Wake Me Up Before You Go-Go," "Faith"), born Radlett, England, June 25, 1963.

Dikembe Mutombo, 40, basketball player, born Kinshasa, Zaire, June 25, 1966.

Willis Reed, Jr, 64, Hall of Fame basketball player, basketball executive and former coach, born Hico, LA, June 25, 1942.

Carly Simon, 61, singer ("You're So Vain," "Nobody Does It Better"), songwriter, born New York, NY, June 25, 1945.

Billy Wagner, 35, baseball player, born Tannersville, VA, June 25, 1971.

Jimmie Walker, 58, actor, comedian ("Good Times," "B.A.D. Cats"), born New York, NY, June 25, 1948.

JUNE 26 — MONDAY
Day 177 — 188 Remaining

BAR CODE INTRODUCED: ANNIVERSARY. June 26, 1974. A committee formed in 1970 by US grocers and food manufacturers recommended in 1973 a Universal Product Code (i.e., a bar code) for supermarket items that would allow electronic scanning of prices. On this day in 1974 a pack of Wrigley's gum was swiped across the first checkout scanner at a supermarket in Troy, OH. Today bar codes are used to keep track of everything from freight cars to cattle.

BORDEN, SIR ROBERT LAIRD: BIRTH ANNIVERSARY. June 26, 1854. Canadian statesman and prime minister, born at Grand Pre, Nova Scotia. Died at Ottawa, June 10, 1937.

BUCK, PEARL SYDENSTRICKER: BIRTH ANNIVERSARY. June 26, 1892. American author (*The Good Earth*), noted authority on China and humanitarian. Nobel Prize winner. Born at Hillsboro, WV. Died Mar 6, 1973, at Danby, VT.

CANADA: NEWFOUNDLAND DISCOVERY DAY. June 26. Commemorates the discovery of Newfoundland by John Cabot, June 24, 1497. Commemorated on the Monday nearest June 24.

CN TOWER OPENED: 30th ANNIVERSARY. June 26, 1976. Birthday of the world's tallest building and freestanding structure, the CN Tower, 1,815 feet, 5 inches high, at Toronto, Ontario, Canada. For info: CN Tower, 301 Front St W, Toronto, ON, Canada M5V 2T6. Phone: (416) 360-8500. Fax: (416) 601-4713.

DOUBLEDAY, ABNER: BIRTH ANNIVERSARY. June 26, 1819. Abner Doubleday served in the US Army during the Mexican War and the Seminole War in Florida prior to his service in the American Civil War. His service found him at the battles of Second Bull Run, Antietam, Fredericksburg and as a major general commanding a division at Gettysburg. A commission set up to investigate the origins of baseball by sporting goods manufacturer Albert Spalding credited Doubleday with inventing the game in the year 1839. Subsequent research has debunked the commission's finding. Abner Doubleday was born at Ballston Spa, NY, and died at Mendham, NJ, Jan 26, 1893.

ENGLAND: CITY OF LONDON FESTIVAL. June 26–July 13. London. Annual multi-arts festival held in some of the city's most historically interesting buildings, including St. Paul's Cathedral and the Tower of London. Est attendance: 130,000. For info: City of London Festival, Bishopsgate Hall, 230 Bishopsgate, London, England EC2M 4HW. Phone: (44) (020) 7377-0540. Fax: (44) (020) 7377-1972. Web: www.colf.org.

ENGLAND: LAWN TENNIS CHAMPIONSHIPS AT WIMBLEDON. June 26–July 9. Wimbledon, London. World famous men's and women's singles and doubles championships for the most coveted titles in tennis. Tickets are allocated via public ballot. Send SASE for details between August and December 2005. For info: All England Lawn Tennis and Croquet Club, PO Box 98, Wimbledon, London, England SW19 5AE. Phone: (44) (20) 8944-1066. Fax: (44) (20) 8947-8752. Web: www.wimbledon.org.

FEDERAL CREDIT UNION ACT: ANNIVERSARY. June 26, 1934. Commemorates signing by President Franklin Delano Roosevelt of the Federal Credit Union Act, thus enabling the formation of credit unions anywhere in the US.

"GUIDING LIGHT" TV PREMIERE: ANNIVERSARY. June 26, 1952. "Guiding Light," previously on radio, holds the title of longest-lasting daytime show and longest-lasting series. Set in the fictional midwestern town of Springfield, this soap is still on the air.

HAYMARKET PARDON: ANNIVERSARY. June 26, 1893. Illinois Governor John Peter Altgeld pardoned Samuel Fielden, Michael Schwab and Oscar Neebe, three of the anarchists who had been convicted in the violence connected with the Haymarket Riot on May 4, 1886. At a protest meeting at Haymarket Square an unknown individual threw a bomb which caused the death of several policemen. Eight anarchists were tried and convicted of the bombing. Of those, one committed suicide the day before he was to be hanged; three were hanged; and Fielden, Schwab and Neebe were imprisoned. In 1893 the newly elected Altgeld, at the urging of Clarence Darrow, reviewed the transcripts of the trial of these men and concluded that they had been railroaded. The pardon was widely criticized. It was an act of political suicide for Altgeld.

HUMAN GENOME MAPPED: ANNIVERSARY. June 26, 2000. Biologists J. Craig Venter and Francis S. Collins announced that their research groups had mapped the human genome, a strand of DNA with three billion parts that spells out our genetic code.

MADAGASCAR: INDEPENDENCE DAY. June 26. National holiday. Commemorates independence from France in 1960.

MIDDLETON, ARTHUR: BIRTH ANNIVERSARY. June 26, 1742. American Revolutionary leader and signer of the Declaration of Independence, born near Charleston, SC. Died at Goose Creek, SC, Jan 1, 1787.

		S	M	T	W	T	F	S
June						1	2	3
		4	5	6	7	8	9	10
2006		11	12	13	14	15	16	17
		18	19	20	21	22	23	24
		25	26	27	28	29	30	

MISS SOUTH CAROLINA TEEN COMPETITION. June 26–30. Spartanburg Memorial Auditorium, Spartanburg, SC. For info: Miss South Carolina Organization, 124 W Main St, Liberty, SC 29657. Phone: (864) 843-9090. E-mail: socarpagt@aol.com. Web: www.misssouthcarolina.com.

PIZARRO, FRANCESCO: DEATH ANNIVERSARY. June 26, 1541. Spanish conqueror of Peru, born at Extremadura, Spain, ca 1471. Pizarro died at Lima, Peru.

PLEASE TAKE MY CHILDREN TO WORK DAY. June 26. To recognize and celebrate the tough job that stay-at-home mothers do every day. *Please* Take My Children to Work Day lets stay-at-home moms laugh at themselves while getting a much needed pat on the back. Sponsored by www.MommaSaid.net, the stay-at-home mom's coffee break™. Annually, the last Monday in June. For info: Jen Singer, PO Box 117, Butler, NJ 07405. Phone: (973) 492-8780. E-mail: jensinger@MommaSaid.net. Web: www.MommaSaid.net.

SAINT LAWRENCE SEAWAY DEDICATION: ANNIVERSARY. June 26, 1959. President Dwight D. Eisenhower and Queen Elizabeth II jointly dedicated the St. Lawrence Seaway in formal ceremonies held at St. Lambert, QC, Canada. A project undertaken jointly by Canada and the US, the waterway (which provides access between the Atlantic Ocean and the Great Lakes) had been opened to traffic Apr 25, 1959.

TEXAS-OKLAHOMA JUNIOR GOLF TOURNAMENT. June 26–30. Wichita Falls, TX. More than 1,000 golfers 18 years old and under from 33 states and several foreign countries participate each year. Est attendance: 1,600. For info: Wichita Falls Conv & Visitors Bureau, 1000 5th St, Wichita Falls, TX 76301. Phone: (940) 716-5500. Fax: (940) 716-5509. Web: www.wichitafalls.org.

UNITED NATIONS CHARTER SIGNED: ANNIVERSARY. June 26, 1945. The UN Charter was signed at San Francisco by representatives of 50 nations.

UNITED NATIONS: INTERNATIONAL DAY AGAINST DRUG ABUSE AND ILLICIT TRAFFICKING. June 26. Following a recommendation of the 1987 International Conference on Drug Abuse and Illicit Trafficking, the United Nations General Assembly (Res 42/112) expressed its determination to strengthen action and cooperation for an international society free of drug abuse and proclaimed June 26 as an annual observance to raise public awareness. For info: UN, Dept of Public Info, Public Inquiries Unit, RM GA-57, New York, NY 10017. Phone: (212) 963-4475. E-mail: inquiries@un.org.

UNITED NATIONS: INTERNATIONAL DAY IN SUPPORT OF VICTIMS OF TORTURE. June 26. For info: United Nations, Dept of Public Info, New York, NY 10017. Web: www.un.org.

ZAHARIAS, MILDRED "BABE" DIDRIKSON: BIRTH ANNIVERSARY. June 26, 1914. Born Mildred Ella Didrikson at Port Arthur, TX, the great athlete was nicknamed "Babe" after legendary baseball player Babe Ruth. She was named to the women's All-America basketball team when she was 16. At the 1932 Olympic Games, she won two gold medals and also set world records in the javelin throw and the 80-meter high hurdles; only a technicality prevented her from obtaining the gold in the high jump. Didrikson married professional wrestler George Zaharias in 1938, six years after she began playing golf casually.

In 1946 Babe won the US Women's Amateur tournament, and in 1947 she won 17 straight golf championships and became the first American winner of the British Ladies' Amateur tournament. Turning professional in 1948, she won the US Women's Open in 1950 and 1954, the same year she won the All-American Open. Babe also excelled in softball, baseball, swimming, figure skating, billiards—even football. In a 1950 Associated Press poll she was named the woman athlete of the first half of the 20th century. She died of cancer, Sept 27, 1956, at Galveston, TX.

BIRTHDAYS TODAY

Claudio Abbado, 73, conductor, born Milan, Italy, June 26, 1933.
Paul Thomas Anderson, 36, director/screenwriter (*Punch-Drunk Love, Magnolia, Boogie Nights*), born Studio City, CA, June 26, 1970.
Sean P. Hayes, 36, actor ("Will & Grace"), born Glen Ellyn, IL, June 26, 1970.
Chris Isaak, 50, singer, musician, actor ("The Chris Isaak Show"), born Stockton, CA, June 26, 1956.
Derek Jeter, 32, baseball player, born Pequannock, NJ, June 26, 1974.
Greg LeMond, 45, former cyclist, born Lakewood, CA, June 26, 1961.
Chris O'Donnell, 36, actor (*Scent of a Woman*), born Winnetka, IL, June 26, 1970.
Eleanor Parker, 84, actress (*The Sound of Music*), born Cedarsville, OH, June 26, 1922.
Jason Schwartzman, 26, actor (*Rushmore*), born Los Angeles, CA, June 26, 1980.
Charlotte Zolotow, 91, author (*The Moon Was the Best, Peter and the Pigeons*), born Norfolk, VA, June 26, 1915.

JUNE 27 — TUESDAY
Day 178 — 187 Remaining

BOCA GRANDE TARPON TOURNAMENT ("WORLD'S RICHEST"). June 27–29 (tentative). Boca Grande Pass, Boca Grande, FL. Tarpon fishing; field limited to 60 boats. Est attendance: 1,000. For info: Boca Grande Chamber of Commerce, PO Box 704, Boca Grande, FL 33921. Phone: (941) 964-0568. Fax: (941) 964-0620. E-mail: info@bocagrandechamber.com. Web: www.worldsrichesttarpon.com.

"CAPTAIN VIDEO AND HIS VIDEO RANGERS" TV PREMIERE: ANNIVERSARY. June 27, 1949. "Captain Video" was the first of several TV space shows. The show was set in the 22nd century and starred Richard Coogan as Captain Video, a human who led a squad of agents (the Video Rangers) fighting villains from their own and other worlds. Al Hodge later replaced Coogan. Also featured were Ernest Borgnine, Jack Klugman and Tony Randall as guest villains.

"DARK SHADOWS" TV PREMIERE: 40th ANNIVERSARY. June 27, 1966. This soap opera was completely different from all others because it featured vampires as main characters and had a dark, Gothic feel to it. The show focused on the Collins family living at Collinsport, ME, mainly Barnabas Collins (Jonathan Frid), a 200-year-old vampire. Other cast mem-bers included David Selby, Kate Jackson, Lara Parker and Jerry Lacy. Action shifted between the 1800s and the 1960s. This show was very popular with teenagers and was remade as a short-lived series in 1991.

DECIDE TO BE MARRIED DAY. June 27. To focus attention on the joy of deciding to get married. Based on the poem *Decide to Be Married*: "It's in the deciding to be united in love, to express your joyful oneness to every person you meet, and in every action you take and together a perfect marriage you'll make." For info: Barbara Gaughen-Muller, Pres, Gaughen Global Public Relations, 7456 Evergreen Dr, Santa Barbara, CA 93117. Phone: (805) 968-8567. Fax: (805) 968-5747. E-mail: Barbara@rain.org. Web: www.paradiseearth.us.

DJIBOUTI: INDEPENDENCE DAY. June 27. National day. Commemorates independence from France in 1977.

FINLAND: SATA-HAME ACCORDION FESTIVAL. June 27–July 2. Ikaalinen. Est attendance: 40,000. For info: Finnish Tourist Board, 655 Third Ave, New York, NY 10017. Phone: (212) 885-9700 or (358) (3) 440-0224. E-mail: juhlat@satahamesoi.fi. Web: www.satahamesoi.fi.

HAPPY BIRTHDAY TO "HAPPY BIRTHDAY TO YOU." June 27, 1859. The melody of probably the most often sung song in the world, "Happy Birthday to You," was composed by Mildred J. Hill, a schoolteacher born at Louisville, KY, on this date. Her younger sister, Patty Smith Hill, was the author of the lyrics which were first published in 1893 as "Good Morning to All," a classroom greeting published in the book *Song Stories for the Sunday School*. The lyrics were amended in 1924 to include a stanza beginning "Happy Birthday to You." Now it is sung somewhere in the world every minute of the day. Although the authors are believed to have earned very little from the song, reportedly it later generated about $1 million a year for its copyright owner. The song is expected to enter public domain upon expiration of copyright in 2010. Mildred Hill died at Chicago, IL, June 5, 1916, without knowing that her melody would become the world's most popular song. See also: "Hill, Patty Smith: Birth Anniversary" (Mar 27).

HEARN, LAFCADIO: BIRTH ANNIVERSARY. June 27, 1850. Author, born on the Greek island of Santa Maura. Hearn, who had been a newspaper reporter at Cincinnati, OH, and at New Orleans, LA, went to Japan in 1890 as a magazine writer. Deeply attracted to the country and to the Japanese people, he stayed there as a writer and teacher until his death at Okubo, Japan, Sept 26, 1904. Though his writings are little remembered in America, he remains a popular figure in Japan, where his books are still used, especially in language classes. His home at Matsue is a tourist shrine.

INTERNATIONAL WORKERS OF THE WORLD FOUNDED: ANNIVERSARY. June 27, 1905. With the slogan "One Big Union for All" 43 labor groups merged together to found the IWW at Chicago, IL. Eventually known as the Wobblies, the IWW had a tremendous impact on US labor history.

KEESHAN, BOB: BIRTH ANNIVERSARY. June 27, 1927. Beloved to generations of American children as Captain Kangaroo, Robert J. Keeshan was born at Lynbrook, NJ. He made his acting debut at age 21 as the original Clarabell, the ever-silent clown, sidekick to Buffalo Bob Smith on "The Howdy Doody Show." He was eventually fired from the show but his future as a children's entertainer was secure; on Oct 3, 1955, "Captain Kangaroo" premiered on CBS and it remained on the air for 38 years. Captain Kangaroo was joined by characters Mr Green Jeans, Grandfather Clock, Bunny Rabbit and Mr Moose. His gentle, patient wisdom entertained and educated millions of children over the years. Keeshan died in Vermont on Jan 23, 2004.

KELLER, HELEN: BIRTH ANNIVERSARY. June 27, 1880. Born at Tuscumbia, AL, Helen Keller was left deaf and blind by a disease she contracted at 18 months of age. With the help of her teacher, Anne Sullivan, she graduated from college and had a career as an author and lecturer. She died June 1, 1968, at Westport, CT.

NATIONAL COLUMNIST'S DAY. June 27. Newspaper columnists, who bring you joy all year long, deserve to be celebrated by their readers at least once a year. Now you can send your favorite columnists, local or nationally syndicated, your own wishes for a Happy Columnist's Day and make him or her feel wonderful. Annually, the fourth Tuesday in June. For info: Jim Six, Columnist, *The Gloucester County Times*, 309 S Broad St, Woodbury, NJ 08096. Phone: (856) 845-3300. Fax: (856) 845-5480. E-mail: jimsix@sjnewsco.com.

NATIONAL HIV TESTING DAY. June 27. A nationwide campaign encouraging education, voluntary HIV testing and counseling to people at risk for HIV. For info: Natl Assn of People with AIDS, 8401 Colesville Rd, Ste 750, Silver Spring, MD 20910. Phone: (240) 247-0880. Fax: (240) 247-0574. E-mail: info@napwa .org. Web: www.napwa.org/hivtestinfo/.

NATIONAL PREVENTION OF EYE INJURIES AWARENESS WEEK. June 27–July 5. Information on fireworks safey is available at www.asotonline.org/downloads.html. For info: US Eye Injury Registry, 1201 11th Ave S, Ste 300, Birmingham, AL 35205. Phone: (205) 933-0064. Web: www.useironline.org.

NED KELLY'S LAST STAND: ANNIVERSARY. June 27–29, 1880. Australian folk hero and outlaw Ned Kelly, escaping with his gang from pursuing law officers, made a last stand at Glenrowan—rounding up the townspeople and holing up in a hotel. There he and his mates constructed 90-pound iron body armor. The armor hampered more than it helped, and Kelly's gang—including his brother Dan—were all killed. Kelly was captured and hung on Nov 11, 1880, at Melbourne. The Kelly Gang in their grim armor offered an antihero image that Australians have embraced in film and art.

PARNELL, CHARLES STEWART: BIRTH ANNIVERSARY. June 27, 1846. Irish nationalist leader and home-rule advocate born at Avondale, County Wicklow, Ireland. Politically ruined as a result of an affair with Katherine O'Shea, the estranged wife of a member of Parliament. O'Shea was divorced by her husband (who named Parnell corespondent), and on June 25, 1891, she married Parnell. Less than a month later Parnell was defeated in a by-election. He made his last public speech Sept 27, 1891, and died in the arms of his wife, at Brighton, Oct 6, 1891. Reportedly he was given "a magnificent funeral" by the city of Dublin, where he was buried. The anniversary of Parnell's death is observed by some as Ivy Day when a sprig of ivy is worn on the lapel to remember him. See also: "Ireland: Ivy Day" (Oct 6).

SMITH, JOSEPH, JR, AND HYRUM: DEATH ANNIVERSARY. June 27, 1844. The founding prophet of The Church of Jesus Christ of Latter-day Saints and his brother Hyrum were shot to death by an armed mob in Carthage, IL. At the time, Joseph Smith was the presidential candidate of the National Reform Party, the first US presidential candidate to be assassinated. Joseph Smith was born at Sharon, VT, Dec 23, 1805; Hyrum Smith was born at Tunbridge, VT, Feb 9, 1800.

SMITHSON, JAMES: DEATH ANNIVERSARY. June 27, 1829. Scientist and founder of the Smithsonian Institution, James Smithson was born at Paris, France, in 1765 (exact date unknown). His will, dated Oct 23, 1826, bequeathed his great wealth to a nation he had never visited, to found "at Washington under the name of the Smithsonian Institution, establishment for the increase and diffusion of knowledge among men." In spite of opposition, the Congress approved, on Aug 10, 1846, an act to establish the Smithsonian Institution. Most of Smithson's personal documents, books and collections were destroyed by fire in 1865. Smithson died at Genoa, Italy. His remains were removed from there to Washington, DC, in 1904.

THURGOOD MARSHALL RESIGNS FROM SUPREME COURT: 15th ANNIVERSARY. June 27, 1991. Signaling an end to the era of a liberal Supreme Court, Associate Justice Thurgood Marshall announced his resignation from the US Supreme Court, effective once his successor was confirmed by the US Senate. Marshall was a pioneering civil rights lawyer who helped lead the fight to end racial segregation and served as US Solicitor General prior to his appointment to the high court by President Lyndon Johnson in 1967 as the first black ever to sit on the Supreme Court. As an attorney for the NAACP, he successfully argued the case of *Brown v Board of Education* before the Supreme Court, ending the doctrine of "separate but equal." Marshall's 24-year tenure on the bench was marked by his strong liberal voice championing the rights of criminal defendants and defending abortion rights, his opposition to the death penalty and his commitment to civil rights. On July 1, 1991, President George Bush selected Clarence Thomas, a conservative black jurist, to succeed Marshall. See also: "Marshall, Thurgood: Birth Anniversary" (July 2).

WINDJAMMER DAYS. June 27–28. Boothbay Harbor, ME. The premier maritime event along the coast of Maine. Parades, concerts, waterfront food, interactive children's activities, live music, fireworks, visiting military vessels, windjammers sailing into harbor under full sail and much more. Fun for the whole family. Est attendance: 20,000. For info: Boothbay Harbor Region Chamber of Commerce, PO Box 356, Boothbay Harbor, ME 04538. Phone: (207) 633-2353. Fax: (207) 633-7448. E-mail: sea maine@boothbayharbor.com. Web: www.boothbayharbor.com.

BIRTHDAYS TODAY

Isabelle Adjani, 51, actress (*The Story of Adele H., Camille Claudel*), born Paris, France, June 27, 1955.

Julia Duffy, 55, actress ("Newhart," "Designing Women"), born St. Paul, MN, June 27, 1951.

Shirley-Anne Field, 68, actress (*Alfie, My Beautiful Laundrette, Getting It Right*), born London, England, June 27, 1938.

Norma Kamali, 61, fashion designer, born New York, NY, June 27, 1945.

Tobey Maguire, 31, actor (*Spider-Man, Pleasantville, The Cider House Rules*), born Santa Monica, CA, June 27, 1975.

Anna Moffo, 72, opera singer, born Wayne, PA, June 27, 1934.

Jason Patric, 40, actor (*Speed 2, Sleepers*), born Queens, NY, June 27, 1966.

H. Ross Perot, 76, philanthropist, businessman, 1992 and 1996 presidential candidate, born Texarkana, TX, June 27, 1930.

Chuck Connors Person, 42, former basketball player, born Brantley, AL, June 27, 1964.

	S	M	T	W	T	F	S
June					1	2	3
2006	4	5	6	7	8	9	10
	11	12	13	14	15	16	17
	18	19	20	21	22	23	24
	25	26	27	28	29	30	

JUNE 28 — WEDNESDAY

Day 179 — 186 Remaining

"AMOS 'N' ANDY" TV PREMIERE: 55th ANNIVERSARY. June 28, 1951. This show was based on the popular radio show about black characters played by white dialecticians Freeman Gosden and Charles Correll. In fact, it was the first dramatic series with an all-black cast. The cast included Tim Moore, Spencer Williams, Alvin Childress, Ernestine Wade, Amanda Randolph, Johnny Lee, Nick O'Demus and Jester Hairston. The series was widely syndicated until pressure from civil rights groups, who claimed the show was stereotypical and prejudicial, caused CBS to withdraw it from syndication.

BISCAYNE NATIONAL PARK ESTABLISHED: ANNIVERSARY. June 28, 1980. Including the coral reefs and waters of Biscayne Bay and the area of the Atlantic Ocean that surrounds the northernmost Florida Keys, Biscayne National Monument was authorized Oct 18, 1968. It became a national park in 1980.

BOSTON HARBORFEST. June 28–July 4. Boston, MA. Patriotic festival with reenactments, concerts, chowder competition, Children's Day and much more. Est attendance: 2,500,000. For info: Boston Harborfest, 45 School St, Boston, MA 02108. Phone: (617) 227-1528. Fax: (617) 227-1886. E-mail: festival@boston harborfest.com. Web: www.bostonharborfest.com.

COMECON AND WARSAW PACT DISBAND: 15th ANNIVERSARY. June 28, 1991. The last vestiges of the Cold War–era Soviet bloc, the Council for Mutual Economic Assistance (COMECON) and the Warsaw Pact, formally disbanded on June 28 and July 1, 1991, respectively.

CYPRUS: SAINT PAUL'S FEAST. June 28–29. Kato Paphos, Cyprus. Religious festivities at Kato Paphos at which the archbishop officiates. Procession of the icon of Saint Paul through the streets.

ENGLAND: HENLEY ROYAL REGATTA. June 28–July 2. Henley-on-Thames, Oxfordshire. International rowing event that is one of the big social events of the year. Est attendance: 245,000. For info: The Secretary, Henley Royal Regatta, Regatta Headquarters, Henley-on-Thames, Oxfordshire, England RG9 2LY. Phone: (44) (149) 157-2153. Fax: (44) (149) 157-5509. Web: www.hrr.co.uk.

MAASS, CLARA: BIRTH ANNIVERSARY. June 28, 1876. Commemorates the birth in 1876 of Clara Louise Maass, the heroic nurse who gave her life in the yellow fever experiments of 1901. Maass died at Havana, Cuba, Aug 24, 1901.

MAYER, MARIA GOEPPERT: 100th BIRTH ANNIVERSARY. June 28, 1906. German-American physicist Maria Goeppert Mayer was born at Kattowitz, Germany. A participant in the Manhattan Project, she worked on the separation of uranium isotopes for the atomic bomb. Mayer became the first American woman to win the Nobel Prize when she shared the 1963 prize for physics with J. Hans Daniel Jensen and Eugene P. Wigner for their explanation of the atomic nucleus, known as the nuclear shell theory. Mayer died Feb 20, 1972, at San Diego, CA.

MONDAY HOLIDAY LAW: ANNIVERSARY. June 28, 1968. President Lyndon B. Johnson approved PL 90–363, which amended section 6103(a) of title 5, United States Code, establishing Monday observance of Washington's Birthday, Memorial Day, Labor Day, Columbus Day and Veterans Day. The new holiday law took effect Jan 1, 1971. Veterans Day observance subsequently reverted to its former observance date, Nov 11. See individual holidays for further details.

NATIONAL HANDSHAKE DAY. June 28. Get a grip on a professional handshake today! The handshake is an important part of corporate America, and can make or break a business deal, interview or other encounter. Take this day to perfect your own handshake and put it into practice! For info: Miryam S. Roddy, Brody Communications, 815 Greenwood Ave, Ste 8, Jenkintown, PA 19046. Phone: (800) 726-7936. Fax: (215) 886-1699. E-mail: mroddy@BrodyCommunications.com. Web: www.BrodyCommunications.com.

RADNER, GILDA: BIRTH ANNIVERSARY. June 28, 1946. Actress, comedienne ("Saturday Night Live," *Hanky Panky*), born at Detroit, MI. Died May 20, 1989, at Los Angeles, CA.

ROUSSEAU, JEAN-JACQUES: BIRTH ANNIVERSARY. June 28, 1712. Philosopher, born at Geneva, Switzerland. Died July 2, 1778, at Ermenonville, France. "Man is born free," he wrote in *The Social Contract*, "and everywhere he is in chains."

RUBENS, PETER PAUL: BIRTH ANNIVERSARY. June 28, 1577. Flemish painter and diplomat born at Siegen, Westphalia. Died of gout at Antwerp, Belgium, May 30, 1640.

STONEWALL RIOT: ANNIVERSARY. June 28, 1969. Early in the morning of June 28, 1969, the clientele of a gay bar, the Stonewall Inn at New York City, rioted after the club was raided by police. The riot was followed by several days of demonstrations. Stonewall is now recognized as the start of the gay liberation movement.

TREATY OF VERSAILLES: ANNIVERSARY. June 28, 1919. The signing of the Treaty of Versailles at Versailles, France, formally ended WWI.

BIRTHDAYS TODAY

Kathy Bates, 58, actress (Oscar for *Misery; Fried Green Tomatoes*), born Memphis, TN, June 28, 1948.

Donald Edward (Don) Baylor, 57, baseball manager, former player, born Austin, TX, June 28, 1949.

Danielle Brisebois, 37, actress ("All in the Family," "Knots Landing"), born Brooklyn, NY, June 28, 1969.

Mel Brooks, 78, actor, director (*The Producers, Blazing Saddles*), born Melvyn Kaminsky at New York, NY, June 28, 1928.

John Cusack, 40, actor (*Say Anything, The Grifters, Bullets Over Broadway*), born Chicago, IL, June 28, 1966.

Bruce Davison, 60, actor (*Ulzana's Raid, Longtime Companion, Six Degrees of Separation*), born Philadelphia, PA, June 28, 1946.

John Albert Elway, 46, former football player, born Port Angeles, WA, June 28, 1960.

Mark Grace, 42, former baseball player, born Winston-Salem, NC, June 28, 1964.

Alice Krige, 52, actress (*Chariots of Fire, Barfly*), born Upington, South Africa, June 28, 1954.

Carl Levin, 72, US Senator (D, Michigan), born Detroit, MI, June 28, 1934.

Mary Stuart Masterson, 40, actress (*Fried Green Tomatoes, Benny & Joon*), born New York, NY, June 28, 1966.

JUNE 29 — THURSDAY

Day 180 — 185 Remaining

CANADA: GREAT RENDEZVOUS. June 29–July 3. Fort William Historical Park, Thunder Bay, ON. Join hundreds of reenactors as they celebrate the arrival of the partners, clerks and voyageurs to the inland headquarters of the North West Company. Take part in Rendezvous games and activities with colorful fur trade characters! Est attendance: 4,000. For info: Marty Mascarin, Communications Officer, Vickers Heights Post Office, Thunder Bay, ON, Canada P0T 2Z0. Phone: (807) 473-2326 or (807) 577-8461. Fax: (807) 473-2327. E-mail: info@fwhp.ca. Web: www.fwhp.ca.

DEATH PENALTY BANNED: ANNIVERSARY. June 29, 1972. In a decision that spared the lives of 600 individuals then sitting on death row, the US Supreme Court, in a 5–4 vote, found capital punishment a violation of the Eighth Amendment, which prohibits "cruel and unusual punishment." Later overruling themselves, the court determined on July 2, 1976, that the death penalty was not cruel and unusual punishment and on Oct 4, 1976, lifted the ban on the death penalty in murder cases. On Jan 15, 1977, Gary Gilmore became the first individual executed in the US in more than 10 years.

ELVIS PRESLEY BOULEVARD NAMED: 35th ANNIVERSARY. June 29, 1971. The City of Memphis, TN, voted to name a road in honor of Elvis—a 12-mile portion of the highway that passes Graceland.

GOETHALS, GEORGE WASHINGTON: BIRTH ANNIVERSARY. June 29, 1858. American engineer and army officer, chief engineer of the Panama Canal and first civil governor of the Canal Zone, born at Brooklyn, NY. Died at New York, NY, Jan 21, 1928.

ILLINOIS SHAKESPEARE FESTIVAL. June 29–Aug 12. Ewing Manor, Bloomington, IL. Productions of three Shakespeare plays presented under the stars on alternating nights. Est attendance: 15,000. For info: Illinois Shakespeare Festival, Campus Box 5700, Normal, IL 61790-5700. Phone: (309) 438-8110. Web: www.thefestival.org.

INTERSTATE HIGHWAY SYSTEM BORN: 50th ANNIVERSARY. June 29, 1956. President Dwight Eisenhower signed a bill providing $33.5 billion for highway construction. It was the biggest public works program in history.

LATHROP, JULIA C.: BIRTH ANNIVERSARY. June 29, 1858. A pioneer in the battle to establish child-labor laws, Julia C. Lathrop was the first woman member of the Illinois State Board of Charities and in 1900 was instrumental in establishing the first juvenile court in the US. In 1912 President Taft named Lathrop chief of the newly created Children's Bureau, then part of the US Dept of Commerce and Labor. In 1925 she became a member of the Child Welfare Committee of the League of Nations. Born at Rockford, IL, she died there Apr 15, 1932.

MANISTEE NATIONAL FOREST FESTIVAL. June 29–July 4. Manistee, MI. Grand Parade, a Venetian boat parade, fireworks over Lake Michigan and children's parade. Tours of historic buildings, the Big Manistee River by canoe, North Country Trail and other local attractions. Juried arts and crafts show, entertainment, flea market, races, Twiggy the Water-Skiing Squirrel, high-action bikes, Aquapalooza and a hand wood-carver. Annually, on a weekend near the Fourth of July. Est attendance: 40,000. For info: Manistee Area Chamber of Commerce, 50 Filer St, Ste 224, Manistee, MI 49660. Phone: (231) 723-2575 or (800) 288-2286. E-mail: chamber@manistee.com. Web: www.manistee county.com.

MAYO, WILLIAM JAMES: BIRTH ANNIVERSARY. June 29, 1861. American surgeon, one of the Mayo brothers, establishers of the Mayo Foundation, born at LeSueur, MN. Died July 28, 1939, at Rochester, MN.

June *2006*	S	M	T	W	T	F	S
					1	2	3
	4	5	6	7	8	9	10
	11	12	13	14	15	16	17
	18	19	20	21	22	23	24
	25	26	27	28	29	30	

MESA VERDE NATIONAL PARK ESTABLISHED: 100th ANNIVERSARY. June 29, 1906. Area of southwest Colorado established as a national park. For further park info: Mesa Verde Natl Park, Mesa Verde Natl Park, CO 81330.

OLYMPIC NATIONAL PARK ESTABLISHED: ANNIVERSARY. June 29, 1938. Washington's Mount Olympus National Monument, proclaimed Mar 2, 1909, was transferred from the US Dept of Agriculture's Forest Service to the National Park Service Aug 10, 1933, then established as Olympic National Park five years later. For further park info: Olympic Natl Park, 600 E Park Ave, Port Angeles, WA 98362.

PETER AND PAUL DAY. June 29. Feast day for Saint Peter and Saint Paul. Commemorates dual martyrdom of Christian apostles Peter (by crucifixion) and Paul (by beheading) during persecution by Roman Emperor Nero. Observed since third century.

SAINT PETER'S DAY. June 29. Antakya, Turkey. Peter first preached Christianity at this place. Ceremonies at Saint Peter's Grotto, early Christian cave near Antakya.

SEYCHELLES: INDEPENDENCE DAY. June 29. National holiday. Gained independence from Great Britain in 1976.

SPACE MILESTONE: *ATLANTIS* (US) AND *MIR* (USSR) DOCK. June 29, 1995. An American space shuttle docked with a Russian space station for the first time, resulting in the biggest craft ever assembled in space. The cooperation involved in this linkup was to serve as a steppingstone to building the International Space Station.

SUMMERFEST. June 29–July 9. Milwaukee, WI. Music festival. Est attendance: 1,000,000. For info: Summerfest, 200 N Harbor Dr, Milwaukee, WI 53202. Phone: (800) 273-3378 or (414) 273-2680. Web: www.summerfest.com.

US WOMEN'S OPEN CHAMPIONSHIP. June 29–July 2. Newport Country Club, Newport, RI. For info: USGA, PO Box 708, Far Hills, NJ 07931-0708. Phone: (908) 234-2300. Fax: (908) 234-9687. E-mail: usga@usga.org. Web: www.usga.org.

BIRTHDAYS TODAY

Gary Busey, 62, musician, actor ("The Texas Wheelers," *The Buddy Holly Story*), born Goose Creek, TX, June 29, 1944.

Theo Fleury, 38, hockey player, born Oxbow, SK, Canada, June 29, 1968.

Fred Grandy, 58, former congressman (R, Iowa), former actor ("Love Boat"), born Sioux City, IA, June 29, 1948.

Harmon Clayton Killebrew, 70, Hall of Fame baseball player, born Payette, ID, June 29, 1936.

Sharon Lawrence, 44, actress ("Fired Up," "NYPD Blue"), born Charlotte, NC, June 29, 1962.

JUNE 30 — FRIDAY

Day 181 — 184 Remaining

CHARLES BLONDIN'S CONQUEST OF NIAGARA FALLS: ANNIVERSARY. June 30, 1859. Charles Blondin, a French acrobat and aerialist (whose real name was Jean François Gravelet), in view of a crowd estimated at more than 25,000 persons, walked across Niagara Falls on a tightrope. The walk required only about five minutes. On separate occasions he crossed blindfolded, pushing a wheelbarrow, carrying a man on his back and even on stilts. Blondin was born Feb 28, 1824, at St. Omer, France, and died at London, England, Feb 19, 1897.

COLORADO SHAKESPEARE FESTIVAL. June 30–Aug 12. Boulder, CO. One of the top Shakespeare festivals in the country. Est attendance: 40,000. For info: Richard Devin, Producing Artistic Dir, Colorado Shakespeare Festival Admin Office, University of Colorado, 277 UCB, Boulder, CO 80309-0277. Phone: (303) 492-1527 or box office at (303) 492-0554. Fax: (303) 735-5140. E-mail: shakes@colorado.edu. Web: www.colora doshakes.org.

CONGO (DEMOCRATIC REPUBLIC OF THE): INDEPENDENCE DAY. June 30. National holiday. The Democratic

Republic of Congo was previously known as Zaire. Commemorates independence from Belgium in 1960.

ENGLAND: SHREWSBURY INTERNATIONAL MUSIC FESTIVAL. June 30–July 7. Shrewsbury, Shropshire. 28th annual. Noncompetitive festival that brings together music and dance groups from all over the world. Est attendance: 2,700. For info: Shrewsbury Intl Music Festival, 8 Beach Rd, Hartford, Cheshire, CW8 4BA, England. Email: shrewsbury-fest@iftm.co.uk. For additional info: Professor E. Jon de Revere, Artistic Dir, World Stage Concerts & Tours, 264 Woodbridge Ave, Woodbridge, NJ 07095. Phone: (732) 634-3811. E-mail: shrewsburyfest@aol.com. Web: www.worldstageconcerts.com.

GETTYSBURG CIVIL WAR BOOK FAIR. June 30–July 2. Gettysburg, PA. More than 40 major Civil War book dealers selling new, used, out-of-print and rare books, documents, prints and photographs. Est attendance: 1,000. For info: GBPA, PO Box 4087, Gettysburg, PA 17325.

GUATEMALA: ARMED FORCES DAY. June 30. Public holiday.

LAST HURRAH FOR BRITISH HONG KONG: ANNIVERSARY. June 30, 1997. The crested flag of the British Crown Colony was officially lowered at midnight and replaced by a new flag (marked by the bauhinia flower) representing China's sovereignty and the official transfer of power. Though Britain owned Hong Kong in perpetuity, the land areas surrounding the city were leased from China and the lease expired July 1, 1997. Rather than renegotiate a new lease, Britain ceded its claim to Hong Kong.

LEAP SECOND ADJUSTMENT TIME. June 30. June 30 is one of the times that has been favored for the addition or subtraction of a second from our clock time (to coordinate atomic and astronomical time). The determination to adjust is made by the International Earth Rotation Service of the International Bureau of Weights and Measures, at Paris, France. See also: "Note about Leap Seconds" in appendices.

MONROE, ELIZABETH KORTRIGHT: BIRTH ANNIVERSARY. June 30, 1768. Wife of James Monroe, fifth president of the US, born at New York, NY. Died at their Oak Hill estate at Loudoun County, VA, Sept 23, 1830.

NATIONAL EDUCATION ASSOCIATION MEETING. June 30–July 5. Orlando, FL. Representative Assembly. For info: Natl Education Assn, 1201 16th St NW, Washington, DC 20036-3290. Phone: (202) 833-4000. Web: www.nea.org.

NOW FOUNDED: 40th ANNIVERSARY. June 30, 1966. The National Organization for Women was founded at Washington, DC, by people attending the Third National Conference on the Commission on the Status of Women. NOW's purpose is to take action to bring women into full partnership in the mainstream of American society, exercising all privileges and responsibilities in equal partnership with men. For info: Natl Organization for Women, 1100 H St NW, 3rd Fl, Washington, DC 20005. Phone: (202) 628-8NOW. Fax: (202) 785-8576. E-mail: now@now.org. Web: www.now.org.

OLD-TIME FIDDLERS' JAMBOREE AND CRAFTS FESTIVAL. June 30–July 1. Smithville, TN. Thirty-one categories of old-time bluegrass including clogging, buck dancing, old-time fiddle band, five-string banjo, dulcimer, dobro, flat-top guitar and fiddle-off to decide the Grand Champion Fiddler. Annually, the weekend nearest July 4. Est attendance: 135,000. For info: Smithville Fiddlers' Jamboree, PO Box 83, Smithville, TN 37166.

Phone: (615) 597-8500. Dekalb Chamber of Commerce, phone: (615) 597-4163. Web: www.dekalbtn.com or www.dekalbtn.com/jamboree.

OREGON BACH FESTIVAL. June 30–July 16. Hult Center for the Performing Arts and the University of Oregon, Eugene, OR. Artistic director and conductor Helmuth Rilling leads an international gathering of musicians in choral-orchestral masterworks, intimate concerts and chamber music, informal free concerts and family events, adult education programs and master classes for conductors and composers. Emphasis is on J.S. Bach and his influence on succeeding generations of composers. Est attendance: 30,000. For info: George Evano, Oregon Bach Festival, 1257 University of Oregon, Eugene, OR 97403. Phone: (800) 457-1486 or (541) 346-5666. Fax: (541) 346-5669. Web: www.oregonbachfestival.com.

RIVERFEST. June 30–July 4. Riverside Park, LaCrosse, WI. 24th annual Riverfest—the city's premier summer event! River activities, five stages to provide continuous entertainment, a children's area with games, face painting, etc. Also provided: a food pavilion featuring 16 different vendors, beverage tent, and an arts and crafts area. July 4th features a fireworks display. Est attendance: 40,000. For info: Riverfest, Inc, PO Box 1745, LaCrosse, WI 54602. Phone: (608) 782-6000. Fax: (608) 784-1580. E-mail: riverfest@centurytel.net. Web: www.riverfestlacrosse.com.

SIBERIAN EXPLOSION: ANNIVERSARY. June 30, 1908. Early in the morning, a spectacular explosion occurred over central Siberia. The seismic shock, firestorm, ensuing "black rain" and the illumination that was reportedly visible for hundreds of miles led to speculation that a meteorite was the cause. Said to have been the most powerful explosion in history.

STAMP EXPO. June 30–July 2. Elks Lodge, Pasadena, CA. Est attendance: 4,000. For info: Israel Bick, Exec Dir, Intl Stamp & Coin Collectors Society, Box 854, Van Nuys, CA 91408. Phone: (818) 997-6496. Fax: (818) 988-4337. E-mail: iibick@sbcglobal.net. Web: www.bick.net.

SUDAN: REVOLUTION DAY. June 30. National holiday. Commemorates a bloodless coup in 1989.

WHEELER, WILLIAM ALMON: BIRTH ANNIVERSARY. June 30, 1819. 19th vice president of the US (1877–81), born at Malone, NY. Died there June 4, 1887.

BIRTHDAYS TODAY

Vincent D'Onofrio, 47, actor ("Law & Order: Criminal Intent," *Men in Black*), born Brooklyn, NY, June 30, 1959.

Nancy Dussault, 70, actress ("Too Close for Comfort," "The Ted Knight Show"), born Pensacola, FL, June 30, 1936.

Rupert Graves, 43, actor (*A Room with a View, Maurice*), born Weston-Super-Mare, England, June 30, 1963.

David Alan Grier, 51, actor (*A Soldier's Story, I'm Gonna Git You Sucka*), born Detroit, MI, June 30, 1955.

Lena Horne, 89, singer, actress (*Stormy Weather, Jamaica, Death of a Gunfighter, The Wiz*), born Brooklyn, NY, June 30, 1917.

Mitchell James (Mitch) Richmond, 41, former basketball player, born Ft Lauderdale, FL, June 30, 1965.

Patricia Schroeder, 66, president, Association of American Publishers; former congresswoman, born Portland, OR, June 30, 1940.

Michael Gerard (Mike) Tyson, 40, former heavyweight champion boxer, born New York, NY, June 30, 1966.

Iulye.

JULY 1 — SATURDAY
Day 182 — 183 Remaining

ARAFAT RETURNS TO PALESTINE: ANNIVERSARY.
July 1, 1994. Yasser Arafat, head of the Palestine Liberation Organization (PLO), returned to Palestine for the first time in 33 years. Israel's control of Palestine had prevented his visiting the region because he was a sworn enemy of the State of Israel and was regarded by Israelis as a terrorist. The agreement between Israel and the PLO, signed in September 1993, made possible Arafat's return. He went first to Gaza City in the Gaza Strip, where he was welcomed by a crowd estimated at 200,000. Three days later he flew by helicopter to the city of Jericho. Both areas were granted Palestinian rule by the treaty.

ARTOWN. July 1–31. Reno, NV. More than 200 arts-related events including dance, plays, concerts, fine arts exhibits and demonstrations, hands-on programs for children and film. For info: Artown, 165 W Liberty St, Ste 110, Reno, NV 89501. Phone: (775) 322-1538. Fax: (775) 322-8777. Web: www.renoisartown.com.

BATTLE OF GETTYSBURG: ANNIVERSARY. July 1, 1863. After the Southern success at Chancellorsville, VA, Confederate General Robert E. Lee led his forces on an invasion of the North, initially targeting Harrisburg, PA. As Union forces moved to counter the invasion, the battle lines were eventually formed at Gettysburg, PA, in one of the Civil War's most crucial battles. On the climactic third day of the battle (July 3), Lee ordered an attack on the center of the Union line, later to be known as Pickett's Charge. The 15,000 rebels were repulsed, ending the Battle of Gettysburg. After the defeat, Lee's forces retreated back to Virginia, listing more than one-third of the troops as casualties in the failed invasion. Union General George Meade initially failed to pursue the retreating rebels, allowing Lee's army to escape across the rain-swollen Potomac River. With more than 50,000 casualties, this was the worst battle of the Civil War.

"BIG TOP" TV PREMIERE: ANNIVERSARY. July 1, 1950. Charles Vanda produced this CBS kiddie circus program that broadcast weekly for seven years from Camden, NJ. Jack Sterling played ringmaster. The show also featured Dan Lurie and Ed McMahon (as a clown, in his first TV appearance).

BIOTERRORISM/DISASTER EDUCATION AND AWARENESS MONTH. July 1–31. To educate consumers, health care professionals, nonprofit organizations and health care facilities about being prepared for natural disasters, emergency care, bioterrorism and acts of God. For info: Fred Mayer, PPSI, 101 Lucas Valley Rd, Ste 210, San Rafael, CA 94903. Phone: (415) 479-8628. Fax: (415) 479-8608. E-mail: ppsi@aol.com. Web: www.ppsinc.org.

BLERIOT, LOUIS: BIRTH ANNIVERSARY. July 1, 1872. Louis Bleriot, aviation pioneer and first man to fly an airplane across the English Channel (July 25, 1909), was born at Cambrai, France. He died at Paris, Aug 2, 1936.

BOTSWANA: SIR SERETSE KHAMA DAY. July 1. National holiday. Commemorates the birth in 1921 of the first president of Botswana.

BUREAU OF INTERNAL REVENUE ESTABLISHED: ANNIVERSARY. July 1, 1862. The Bureau of Internal Revenue was established by an act of Congress.

BURUNDI: INDEPENDENCE DAY. July 1. National holiday. Anniversary of establishment of independence from Belgian administration in 1962. Had been part of Ruanda-Urundi.

CANADA: CANADA DAY. July 1. Canada's national day, formerly known as Dominion Day. Observed on following day when July 1 is a Sunday. Commemorates the confederation of Upper and Lower Canada and some of the Maritime Provinces into the Dominion of Canada in 1867.

CANADA: CANADA DAY CELEBRATION. July 1. Ottawa, ON. Annual event celebrating Canada's anniversary. The heart of the capital comes alive at four main sites with shows, street performers, concerts, games and activities for the whole family. In the evening a spectacular show featuring top Canadian performers is staged on Parliament Hill and culminates with a fireworks display. Est attendance: 350,000. For info: Natl Capital Commission, 40 Elgin St, Ste 202, Ottawa, ON, Canada K1P 1C7. Phone: (800) 465-1867 or (613) 239-5000.

CANADA: CANADA DAY CELEBRATIONS. July 1. Squamish, BC. Celebrate Canada's birthday with cake, games and entertainment. For info: Squamish Chamber of Commerce, PO Box 1009, Squamish, BC, Canada V0N 3G0. Phone: (604) 892-9244 or (866) 333-2010. Fax: (604) 892-2034. E-mail: information@squamishchamber.com. Web: www.squamishchamber.com.

CANADA: CANADA DAY PARTY IN THE PARK. July 1. Bancroft, ON. Canada Day fireworks. Craft show, kids' games and local musicians. Est attendance: 5,000. For info: Bancroft and Dist Chmbr of Commerce, PO Box 539, Bancroft, ON, Canada K0L 1C0. Phone: (613) 332-1513. Fax: (613) 332-2119. E-mail: chamber@commerce.bancroft.on.ca. Web: www.BancroftDistrict.com.

CANADA: NOVA SCOTIA INTERNATIONAL TATTOO. July 1–9. Halifax, NS. The Tattoo combines more than 2,000 international military and civilian performers in bands, singing, dancing, marching, gymnastics and comedy. Est attendance: 60,000. For info: The Nova Scotia Intl Tattoo, 1586 Queen St, Halifax, NS, Canada B3J 2J1. Phone: (902) 420-1114 or (800) 563-1114. Fax: (902) 423-6629. E-mail: info@nstattoo.ca. Web: www.nstattoo.ca.

CANADA: YUKON GOLD PANNING CHAMPIONSHIPS. July 1. Dawson City, YT. Yukon residents compete for the honor of Territorial Champion Gold Panner. Dawson visitors can join in and compete for the Cheechako Award. Annually, July 1, Canada Day. Est attendance: 200. For info: Klondike Visitors Assn, PO Box 389, Dawson City, YT, Canada Y0B 1G0. Phone: (867) 993-5575. Fax: (867) 993-6415. E-mail: kva@dawson.net. Web: www.dawsoncity.ca.

CELL PHONE COURTESY MONTH. July 1–31. There are more than 180 million cell phone users in the US. This month is dedicated to encouraging the increasingly unmindful corps of cell phone users to be more respectful of their surroundings and those around them. Annually, the month of July. For info: Jacqueline Whitmore, Etiquette Expert, PO Box 3073, Palm Beach, FL 33480. Phone: (561) 586-9026. Fax: (561) 586-6689. E-mail: info@etiquetteexpert.com. Web: www.etiquetteexpert.com.

July 2006	S	M	T	W	T	F	S
							1
	2	3	4	5	6	7	8
	9	10	11	12	13	14	15
	16	17	18	19	20	21	22
	23	24	25	26	27	28	29
	30	31					

CHINA: HALF-YEAR DAY. July 1. National holiday in China. Midyear Day in Thailand.

CLEMSON, THOMAS GREEN: BIRTH ANNIVERSARY. July 1, 1807. The man for whom Clemson University was named was born at Philadelphia, PA. The mining engineer and agriculturist married John C. Calhoun's daughter, Anna. Clemson bequeathed the old Calhoun plantation to South Carolina, and Clemson Agricultural College (now Clemson University) was founded there in 1889. Clemson died at Clemson, SC, Apr 6, 1888.

CLEVELAND'S SECRET SURGERY: ANNIVERSARY. July 1, 1893. President Grover Cleveland boarded the yacht *Oneida* for surgery to be performed in secret on a cancerous growth in his mouth. As this was during the 1893 depression, secrecy was thought desirable to avoid further panic by the public. The whole left side of Cleveland's jaw was removed as well as a small portion of his soft palate. A second, less extensive operation was performed July 17. He was later fitted with a prosthesis of vulcanized rubber that he wore until his death June 24, 1908. A single leak of the secret was plugged by Cleveland's Secretary of War, Daniel Lamont, the only member of the administration to know about the surgery. The illness did not become public knowledge until an article appeared Sept 22, 1917, in the *Saturday Evening Post*, written by William W. Keen, who assisted in the surgery.

COURT TV DEBUT: 15th ANNIVERSARY. July 1, 1991. The continuing evolution of entertainment brought on by the advent of cable television added another twist on July 1, 1991, with the debut of Court TV. Trials are broadcast in their entirety, with occasional commentary from the channel's anchor desk and switching between several trials in progress. Trials with immense popular interest, such as the Jeffrey Dahmer and O.J. Simpson trials, are broadcast along with more low-profile cases.

CRAFT DAY BY THE BAY. July 1. Harvey Cedars, NJ. More than 100 crafters and artists displaying and selling their hand-crafted goods. Est attendance: 2,000. For info: Harvey Cedars Activity Committee, PO Box 3185, Harvey Cedars, NJ 08008. Phone: (609) 361-7990. Fax: (609) 494-8343. Web: www.harveycedars.org.

THE DAM EXPERIENCE. July 1 (tentative, rain date July 2). Truman Dam, Warsaw, MO. Gigantic fireworks display viewed from land and boat. Est attendance: 15,000. For info: Warsaw Area Chamber of Commerce, PO Box 264, Warsaw, MO 65355. Phone: (800) WARSAW-4. E-mail: warsawcc@iland.net. Web: www.warsawmo.org.

DIANA, PRINCESS OF WALES: BIRTH ANNIVERSARY. July 1, 1961. Former wife of Charles, Prince of Wales, and mother of Prince William and Prince Harry. Born Lady Diana Spencer at Sandringham, England, she died in an automobile accident at Paris, France, Aug 31, 1997.

DIXON, WILLIE: BIRTH ANNIVERSARY. July 1, 1915. Blues legend Willie Dixon was born at Vicksburg, MI. He moved to Chicago in 1936 and began his career as a musician with the Big Three Trio. With the advent of instrument amplification Dixon migrated away from his acoustic upright bass into producing and songwriting with Chess Studios, where he became one of the primary architects of the classic Chicago sound in the 1950s. His songs were performed by Elvis Presley, the Everly Brothers, the Rolling Stones, Led Zeppelin, the Doors, Cream, the Yardbirds, Aerosmith, Jimi Hendrix and the Allman Brothers, among others. Dixon died Jan 29, 1992, at Burbank, CA.

DORSEY, THOMAS A.: BIRTH ANNIVERSARY. July 1, 1899. Thomas A. Dorsey, the father of gospel music, was born at Villa Rica, GA. Originally a blues composer, Dorsey eventually combined blues and sacred music to develop gospel music. It was Dorsey's composition "Take My Hand, Precious Lord" that Reverend Dr. Martin Luther King, Jr, had asked to have performed just moments before his assassination. Dorsey, who composed more than 1,000 gospel songs and hundreds of blues songs in his lifetime, died Jan 23, 1993, at Chicago, IL.

EASTPORT FOURTH OF JULY AND "OLD HOME WEEK CELEBRATION." July 1–5. Eastport, ME. Event features a flea market, craft fair, theater, music, dance, demonstrations and exhibits, fireworks display, public entertainment July 3–4, US naval ship in port and a variety of contests. Eastport, the easternmost city in the US, is bounded by the Atlantic Ocean on the Bay of Fundy and surrounded by Canadian Islands. Canada Day, July 1, is celebrated every year. Est attendance: 10,000. For info: Eastport 4th of July Committee Inc, PO Box 187, Eastport, ME 04631. Phone: (207) 853-6076. E-mail: info@eastport4th.com. Web: www.eastport4th.com.

FAMILY REUNION MONTH. July 1–31. July is the most popular month of the year for families to meet and celebrate the unique history of their family. Trips back to family homesteads, tales of generations gone by and celebrations of generations yet to come are featured again and again as families meet around the country and around the globe. For info: Dina C. Carson, PO Box 999, Niwot, CO 80544. E-mail: info@reunionsolutions.com. Web: www.reunionsolutions.com.

FIRST PHOTOGRAPHS USED IN A NEWSPAPER REPORT: ANNIVERSARY. July 1, 1848. The first instance of photojournalism occurred during the Paris Riots of 1848, when an enterprising French photographer known only as Thibault scrambled to a rooftop to chronicle the events. Taken on June 25 and 26, the two resulting daguerreotypes show first a deserted street, the rue St. Maur, with barricades, then show the same street with insurgents and the military in combat. Wood engravings were made of the daguerreotypes, and on July 1, 1848, the images appeared in the weekly newspaper *L'Illustration Journal Universel*. More than 3,000 Parisians lost their lives during the June revolt.

FIRST SCHEDULED TELEVISION BROADCAST: 65th ANNIVERSARY. July 1, 1941. The National Broadcasting Company (NBC) began broadcasting from the Empire State Building on this day. The Federal Communications Commission had granted the first commercial TV licenses to ten stations on May 2, 1941.

FIRST US POSTAGE STAMPS ISSUED: ANNIVERSARY. July 1, 1847. The first US postage stamps were issued by the US Postal Service, a 5¢ stamp picturing Benjamin Franklin and a 10¢ stamp honoring George Washington. Stamps had been issued by private postal services in the US prior to this date.

FIRST US ZOO: ANNIVERSARY. July 1, 1874. The Philadelphia Zoological Society, the first US zoo, opened. Three thousand visitors traveled by foot, horse and carriage and steamboat to visit the exhibits. Price of admission was 25¢ for adults and 10¢ for children. There were 1,000 animals in the zoo on opening day.

FOURTH OF JULY CELEBRATION. July 1–4. Live Oak, FL. Rock-n-Blues BBQ and kids activities. For info: Spirit of the Suwanee Music Park, 3076 95th Dr, Live Oak, FL 32060. Phone: (386) 364-1683. Fax: (386) 364-2998. E-mail: spirit@musicliveshere.com. Web: www.musicliveshere.com.

FOURTH OF JULY CELEBRATION. July 1–4. Hettinger, ND. Parade, free noon meal, events happening all week long and dances, food, booths and the largest fireworks display in SW North Dakota. Est attendance: 4,000. For info: Community Promotions Office, Box 1031, Hettinger, ND 58639. Phone: (701) 567-2531. Fax: (701) 567-2690. E-mail: adamschmbr@ndsupernet.com. Web: hettingernd.com.

FREEDOM DAYS. July 1–4. Farmington, NM. Celebration with a variety of special events, including spectacular fireworks, food fair, auction, gem and mineral show, parade, triathlon. Est attendance: 70,000. For info: Farmington Conv and Visitors Bureau, 3041 E Main St, Farmington, NM 87402. Phone: (800) 448-1240 or (505) 326-7602. Fax: (505) 327-0577. E-mail: fmncvb@earth link.net. Web: www.farmingtonnm.org.

GHANA: REPUBLIC DAY. July 1. National holiday. Commemorates the inauguration of the Republic in 1960.

THE GREAT INTERNATIONAL CHICKEN WING SOCIETY COOK-OFF. July 1–4. Reno, NV. Festival where bars and restaurants compete to make the best chicken wings. Annually, July 4 weekend. Est attendance: 40,000. For info: Willie Davison, Great Intl Chicken Wing Society, PO Box 190, Sparks, NV 89431. Phone: (775) 358-8376. E-mail: mrdavison@aol.com.

HERBAL/PRESCRIPTION INTERACTION AWARENESS MONTH. July 1–31. To educate health professionals and consumers on dietary supplements, herbs and nutritionals along with mixing those products with prescription drugs. There is a $15 charge for kit materials. For info: PPSI, c/o Pharmacy Council on Dietary Supplements, 101 Lucas Valley Rd, Ste 210, San Rafael, CA 94903. Phone: (415) 479-8628. Fax: (415) 479-8608. E-mail: ppsi@aol.com. Web: www.ppsinc.org.

INTERNATIONAL BLONDIE AND DEBORAH HARRY MONTH. July 1–31. Each July, this special month celebrates the band Blondie and its lead singer, Deborah Harry—and their contributions to popular music. For info: Allan Metz, 333 E Libby Dr, Springfield, MO 65803. Phone: (417) 873-7483. Fax: (417) 873-7432. E-mail: ametz@drury.edu. Web: www.blondiebook .com.

INTERNATIONAL CHERRY PIT SPITTING CHAMPIONSHIP. July 1. Tree-Mendus Fruit Farm, Eau Claire, MI. A nutritious sport—is there a better way to dispose of the pits once you have eaten the cherry? Entrants eat a cherry and then spit the pit as far as possible on a blacktop surface. The entrant who spits the pit the farthest including the roll is the champ. Annually, the first Saturday in July. Est attendance: 1,000. For info: Herb Teichman, Adv and Promo Mgr, Tree-Mendus Fruit Farm, 9351 E Eureka Rd, Eau Claire, MI 49111. Phone: (269) 782-7101. Fax: (269) 461-4187. E-mail: mendus@qtm.net. Web: www.tree mendus-fruit.com.

LAUDER, ESTÉE: BIRTH ANNIVERSARY. July 1, 1908 (some sources say 1906). The cosmetics magnate was born Josephine Esther Mentzer at Corona, Queens, NY. In high school, she took an interest in the work of her uncle, John Schotz, a Hungarian-born chemist who made beauty products for women. She began a business at her kitchen table in 1946 that has gone on to become one of the world's largest, most successful cosmetics companies. The introduction of her breakthrough formula for the bath oil "Youth-Dew" in the 1950s led the way to a company currently worth more than $10 billion. At the time of her death on Apr 24, 2004, at New York, NY, Lauder was among the 500 richest women in the world.

July *2006*	S	M	T	W	T	F	S
							1
	2	3	4	5	6	7	8
	9	10	11	12	13	14	15
	16	17	18	19	20	21	22
	23	24	25	26	27	28	29
	30	31					

"THE LIBERACE SHOW" TV PREMIERE: ANNIVERSARY. July 1, 1952. A pianist known for his outrageous style and a candelabra on his piano, Liberace hosted popular shows in the '50s and '60s. The first premiered on KLAC-TV in Los Angeles and went national in 1953. That did so well that he began a half-hour syndicated series which featured his brother George as violinist and orchestra leader. After a brief leave, he returned to TV in 1958 with a half-hour show. Liberace also hosted a British series and a summer series produced in London.

LINCOLN SIGNS INCOME TAX: ANNIVERSARY. July 1, 1862. President Abraham Lincoln signed into law a bill levying a 3 percent income tax on annual incomes of $600–$10,000 and 5 percent on incomes of more than $10,000. The revenues were to help pay for the Civil War. This tax law actually went into effect, unlike an earlier law passed Aug 5, 1861, making it the first income tax levied by the US. It was rescinded in 1872.

"MAMA" TV PREMIERE: ANNIVERSARY. July 1, 1949. One of TV's first popular sitcoms, "Mama" told the story of a Norwegian family living in San Francisco in 1917. The show aired live through 1956; after it was cancelled, a second, filmed version lasted only 13 weeks. Cast members included Peggy Wood, Judson Laire, Rosemary Rice, Dick Van Patten, Iris Mann, Robin Morgan, Ruth Gates, Malcolm Keen, Carl Frank, Alice Frost, Patty McCormack and Kevin Coughlin. Toni Campbell replaced Robin Morgan in the revival.

MAMMOTH CAVE NATIONAL PARK ESTABLISHED: 65th ANNIVERSARY. July 1, 1941. Area of central Kentucky, originally authorized May 25, 1926, was established as a national park. For more info: Mammoth Cave Natl Park, Mammoth Cave, KY 42259.

MEDICARE: ANNIVERSARY. July 1, 1968. Medicare, the US health insurance program for senior citizens, went into effect. The legislation authorizing the program had been signed by President Lyndon Johnson July 30, 1965. Former President Harry Truman received the first Medicare card.

MESCALERO APACHE MAIDEN'S PUBERTY RITES. July 1–4. Mescalero, NM. Mescalero's longest ceremony is four days long and culminates on the Fourth of July in the dramatic, pre-dawn Maiden's Puberty Rite each year. Visitors are welcome to come and share in this cultural tradition of the Mescalero Apache rite of passage experience, which includes clowns and Crown Dancers. This event is open to the public, but all non-Mescalero Apaches must vacate the reservation ceremony by late evening. For info: Mescalero Apache Tribe Resort Information. Phone: (800) 545-9011. Web: www.innofthemountaingods.com.

MORRILL LAND GRANT ACT PASSED: ANNIVERSARY. July 1, 1862. This federal legislation led to the creation of the Land Grant universities and Agricultural Experiment Stations in each state.

NATIONAL BAKED BEAN MONTH. July 1–31. To pay tribute to one of America's favorite and most healthful and nutritious foods, baked beans, made with dry or canned beans. For info: Chandra Lim, Bean Education & Awareness Network, 35 W Wacker Dr, Chicago, IL 60601. Phone: (312) 861-5200. Fax: (312) 861-5252. E-mail: media@americanbean.org. Web: www.ameri canbean.org.

NATIONAL BLUEBERRIES MONTH. July 1–31. To make the public aware that this is the peak month for fresh blueberries. For info: North American Blueberry Council, 2390 E Bidwell St, Ste 300, Folsom, CA 95630-3873. E-mail: info@blueberry .org. Web: www.blueberry.org.

NATIONAL "DOGHOUSE REPAIRS" MONTH. July 1–31. Celebrate "Doghouse Repairs" Month by staying out of trouble with those you love and care about by doing something extra special. For info: Heidi Richards, Eden Florist and Gift Baskets, 7100 Pembroke Blvd, Miramar, FL 33023. Phone: (954) 981-5515. E-mail: flowers@edenflorist.com. Web: www.edenflorist .com.

NATIONAL GRILLING MONTH. July 1–31. The sizzle, the smoke, and the mouth-watering aromas that come from a grill can be yours if you take the time out this month and enjoy the fun and ease of cooking on a grill—indoor or out! For info: Viking Culinary Arts Center/Viking Home Chef. Web: www.viking culinary.com.

NATIONAL HOME INSPECTOR APPRECIATION MONTH. July 1–31. A month to acknowledge and promote the efforts and contributions of professional home inspectors nationwide. These unique individuals are trusted to evaluate a family's most important investment—their future home. Inspectors indirectly protect their clients from unsafe home conditions. A thorough home inspection is an indispensable component of a well-planned purchase. The month of July is the middle of a busy (and hot!) season for home inspectors—so it's a perfect time to honor their dedication and hard work. For info: Rod Figueroa, Association of New Construction Home Inspectors, PO Box 820846, North Richland Hills, TX 76182. Phone: (817) 590-2630. E-mail: rfig@aol.com.

NATIONAL HORSERADISH MONTH. July 1. What 3,000-year-old plant has been used as an aphrodisiac, a treatment for rheumatism, a bitter herb for Passover Seders and a flavorful accompaniment for beef, chicken and seafood? If you guessed horseradish, you're right. This month, celebrate the healthful and hot horseradish, which has been prized for its medicinal and gastronomic qualities for centuries. For info: National Horseradish Information Council, 5775 Peachtree-Dunwoody Rd, Bldg G, Ste 500, Atlanta, GA 30342. Phone: (404) 252-3663. Fax: (404) 252-0774. Web: www.horseradish.org.

NATIONAL HOT DOG MONTH. July 1–31. Celebrates one of America's favorite hand-held foods with fun facts and new topping ideas. More than 16 billion hot dogs per year are sold in the US. Sponsor: National Hot Dog and Sausage Council. For info: Natl Hot Dog & Sausage Council, 1700 N Moore St, Ste 1600, Arlington, VA 22209. Phone: (703) 841-2400. Web: www.hot-dog .org.

NATIONAL PURPOSEFUL PARENTING MONTH. July 1–31. Encourages parents to incorporate "purpose" in their parenting. Designed to elevate the level of parental effectiveness by building awareness and providing interested participants with tips for positive, conscientious parenting. For info send SASE to: Dale Eshleman, Episcopal Counseling Center, 1021-A E Robinson St, Orlando, FL 32801. Phone: (800) 544-1817.

NATIONAL RECREATION AND PARKS MONTH. July 1–31. To showcase and invite participation in healthy lifestyles for livable communities. For info: Natl Recreation and Park Assn, 22377 Belmont Ridge Rd, Ashburn, VA 20148. Phone: (703) 858-0784. Fax: (703) 858-0794. Web: www.nrpa.org.

NATIONAL TOM SAWYER DAYS (WITH FENCE PAINTING CONTEST). July 1–4. Hannibal, MO. Frog jumping, mud volleyball, Tom and Becky Contest, parade, Tomboy Sawyer Contest, 10k run, arts & crafts show and fireworks launched from the banks of the Mississippi River. Highlight is the National Fence Painting Contest. Sponsor: Hannibal Jaycees. Est attendance: 100,000. For info: Hannibal Visitors Bureau, 505 N 3rd St, Hannibal, MO 63401. Phone: (573) 221-2477. Web: www.hannibaljaycees.org.

NATIONAL UNASSISTED HOMEBIRTH WEEK. July 1–7. Conferences and activities to create awareness and encouragement for couples who intentionally seek to give birth without a midwife or doctor. For info: Lynn M. Griesemer, 4103 Plaza Ln, Fairfax, VA 22033. Phone: (703) 263-2468. E-mail: greeze@ juno.com. Web: www.unassistedhomebirth.com.

NATIONAL WHEELCHAIR BEAUTIFICATION MONTH. July 1–31. Health care centers, hospitals and others participate in this project by using the power of a single flower to brighten the image of an ordinary wheelchair and spread smiles everywhere. Participants attach a florist's water tube with sticky-back Velcro near the top of the chair. These tubes are perfect for living or artificial flowers, and are available at florists for pennies.

For info: Horace Knowles, Founder, National Wheelchair Beautification Project, 1480 Creekside Dr, Apt A206, Walnut Creek, CA 94596. Phone: (925) 287-0256 or (925) 708-5955. E-mail: horaceak@pacbell.net.

NICK AT NITE PREMIERE: ANNIVERSARY. July 1, 1985. The first broadcast of Nick at Nite, the creation of the kids' network Nickelodeon, occurred. Owned and operated by MTV Networks, Nick at Nite presents many of the old classic television series.

OLD RED COURTHOUSE DEDICATION AND OPENING OF OLD RED MUSEUM OF DALLAS COUNTY HISTORY & CULTURE. July 1–7. Old Red Courthouse, Dallas, TX. Rededication of the historic Old Red Courthouse (construction began in 1890) after an extensive restoration. The restored building will house the Old Red Museum of Dallas County History & Culture. For info: David Schulz, Old Red Courthouse, 100 S Houston St, Dallas, TX 75201. Phone: (214) 745-1100. E-mail: david@oldred.org. Web: www.oldred.org.

PEPSI 400 NASCAR NEXTEL CUP SERIES RACE. July 1. Daytona International Speedway, Daytona Beach, FL. 48th running. Drivers battle for Independence Day glory under the lights. For info: Daytona Intl Speedway, PO Box 28014, Daytona Beach, FL 32120-2801. Phone: (800) PIT-SHOP. Web: www.daytonainternationalspeedway.com.

ROCKPORT ART FESTIVAL. July 1–2. Rockport Festival Grounds, Rockport, TX. The work of top artists from across the US lines the waterfront for two days. Music and plenty of good food. Est attendance: 15,000. For info: Rockport Center for the Arts, 902 Navigation Circle, Rockport, TX 78382. Phone: (361) 729-5519. Fax: (361) 729-3551. E-mail: rockart@sbcglobal.net. Web: www.rockportartcenter.org.

ROOTS AND BRANCHES MONTH. July 1–31. Created to inspire others to nurture their roots. An annual observance sponsored by Milford-Haven Enterprises, who believe in the synchronistic links between ourselves and everyone we're intended to meet. For info: Mara Purl, Milford-Haven Enterprises, 4411 Cahuenga Blvd, Ste 8, North Hollywood, CA 91602. Phone: (818) 762-2945. Fax: (818) 508-0299. E-mail: milfordhaven@aol.com. Web: www.milfordhaven.com.

RUSSIAN RUBLE BECOMES CONVERTIBLE: ANNIVERSARY. July 1, 1992. The Russian ruble became convertible with other currencies worldwide. Convertibility had long been held to be an important first move toward bringing the Russian economy into the mainstream of the world's economy. The official rate on July 1 was approximately 125 rubles to the dollar, and authorities hoped that it would eventually stabilize at approximately 80 rubles to the dollar. Previously it was illegal to convert rubles, although they traded briskly on the black market.

RWANDA: INDEPENDENCE DAY. July 1. National holiday. Commemorates independence from Belgium in 1962.

SAND, GEORGE: BIRTH ANNIVERSARY. July 1, 1804. French novelist, author of more than 100 volumes, whose real name was Amandine Aurore Lucile (Dupin) Dudevant, was born at Paris, France. Died at Nohant, France, June 8, 1876. She is better remembered for having been a liberated woman during a romantic epoch than for her literary works.

SEAFAIR. July 1–Aug 6. Seattle, WA. The northwest's largest summer festival. More than 35 events in all highlighted by the Milk Carton Derby, Triathalon Torchlight Run and Torchlight Parade, Unlimited Hydroplane Race and Air Show. Also dozens of community parades and events. Est attendance: 1,000,000. For info: Seafair, 2200 6th Ave, Ste 400, Seattle, WA 98121. Phone: (206) 728-0123. Fax: (206) 728-9506. Web: www.seafair.com.

SECOND HALF OF THE NEW YEAR DAY. July 1. Today is a checkpoint for those who made New Year's resolutions. Celebrate your accomplishments, look at what you did not accomplish and why or set new resolutions. Stay on track to have a healthier, happier and more successful life. Annually, July 1. For info: Cindy Kubica, 414 Parish Pl, Franklin, TN 37067. Phone: (615) 771-3800. E-mail: cindy@cindykubica.com.

SMART IRRIGATION MONTH. July 1–31. Most homeowners over-irrigate their lawns by 30 percent—not only wasting water but washing nutrients into rivers and streams and away from the root zone where the plants can use them. Evaluate your irrigation system this month. For smart irrigation, consider adding a "smart" controller (one that uses weather, plant and soil data to determine when to water) or a rain sensor shut-off device. To find out where your system might be wasting water, seek an irrigation system audit by a qualified irrigation auditor. For info: The Irrigation Association, 6540 Arlington Blvd, Falls Church, VA 22042. Phone: (703) 536-7080. Fax: (703) 536-7019. E-mail: news@irrigation.org. Web: www.irrigation.org.

SOCIAL WELLNESS MONTH. July 1–31. Improve your social and communication skills and learn to act appropriately in prominent situations. Create a positive and lasting first impression. Be distinguished, earn respect, and appear confident under public pressure. For info: Angela Brown, Words of Wellness, PO Box 49266, Charlotte, NC 28277. Phone: (704) 849-2900. Fax: (704) 845-3060. E-mail: Angela@WordsofWellness.com. Web: www.WordsofWellness.com.

SOMALIA DEMOCRATIC REPUBLIC: NATIONAL DAY. July 1. Anniversary of the merger of newly independent British Somaliland and Italian Somaliland on July 1, 1960.

SPACE MILESTONE: *KOSMOS 1383* (USSR). July 1, 1982. First search and rescue satellite—equipped to hear distress calls from aircraft and ships—launched in cooperative project with the US and France.

SPACE MILESTONE: *CASSINI-HUYGENS* REACHES SATURN. July 1, 2004. Launched on Oct 15, 1997, the *Cassini-Huygens* spacecraft, a joint venture of NASA, the European Space Agency (ESA) and the Italian Space Agency, reached Saturn on this date and maneuvered into orbit. The ESA's *Huygens* probe touched down on Saturn's moon Titan on Jan 14, 2005. The purpose of the multibillion-dollar NASA/ESA/ISA mission is to explore the Saturnian system.

SPAMTOWN USA FREEDOM FEST. July 1–4. Austin, MN. 21st annual. Celebrating Austin's sesquicentennial year. Independence Day Parade, salute to veterans, stage entertainment, sports events, fishing contest, classic car cruise, concerts, games, mini-golf, foods galore, two evenings of fireworks and more. Est attendance: 20,000. For info: Cynthia Samuel, Executive Director, Austin's Festival Office, 329 N Main St, Ste 102, Austin, MN 55912. Phone: (507) 437-3448. E-mail: execdir@austincoc.com.

STERLING RENAISSANCE FESTIVAL. July 1–Aug 13 (Saturdays and Sundays only). Sterling, NY. 30th annual re-creation of an English village set in the time period of Queen Elizabeth I. The festival features authentic jousting, more than 80 stage and street performances, music and dance of the period, beautiful arts and handcrafts, unique and delicious foods and drink and much more. Est attendance: 100,000. For info: Festival Office, Sterling Renaissance Festival, 15385 Farden Rd, Sterling, NY 13156. Phone: (800) 879-4446. Web: sterlingfestival.com.

SURINAME: LIBERATION DAY. July 1. National holiday. Commemorates the 1863 abolition of slavery in Dutch territory.

		S	M	T	W	T	F	S
July								1
2006		2	3	4	5	6	7	8
		9	10	11	12	13	14	15
		16	17	18	19	20	21	22
		23	24	25	26	27	28	29
		30	31					

TEN THOUSAND CRESTONIANS. July 1–4. Downtown and McKinley Park, Creston, IA. Parade, fireworks, flea market, talent show, historical village, carnival and food. All to celebrate US founding. Est attendance: 10,000. For info: Creston Chamber of Commerce, PO Box 471, Creston, IA 50801. Phone: (641) 782-7021. E-mail: chamber@crestoniowachamber.com. Web: www.crestoniowachamber.com.

TOUR DE FRANCE. July 1–23. One of the great sporting events in the world. Cycling's best compete for more than 3,427 kilometers in 20 stages in the country of France. Ten stages are flat terrain races, seven are mountain races and three are time-trials (individual and team). For info: Amaury Sport Organisation, 2 rue Rouget de Isle, 92 130 Issy-les-Moulineaux, France. Web: www.letour.fr.

TWENTY-SIXTH AMENDMENT RATIFIED: 35th ANNIVERSARY. July 1, 1971. The 26th Amendment to the Constitution granted the right to vote in all federal, state and local elections to all persons 18 years or older. On the date of ratification the US gained an additional 11 million voters. Up until this time, the minimum voting age was set by the states; in most states it was 21.

UNITED NATIONS: INTERNATIONAL DAY OF COOPERATIVES. July 1. On Dec 16, 1992, the General Assembly proclaimed this observance for the first Saturday of July 1995 (Res 47/60). On Dec 23, 1994, recognizing that cooperatives were becoming an indispensable factor of economic and social development, the Assembly invited governments, international organizations, specialized agencies and national and international cooperative organizations to observe this day annually (Res 49/155). For info: United Nations, Dept of Public Info, New York, NY 10017. Web: www.un.org.

WESTMORELAND ARTS & HERITAGE FESTIVAL. July 1–4. Twin Lakes Park, Greensburg, PA. Celebrating 32 years of arts and humanities. Multicultural celebration including food booths, children's area, crafts, fine art exhibition, continuous entertainment on five stages. Est attendance: 130,000. For info: WAHF, 252 Twin Lakes Rd, Latrobe, PA 15650. Phone: (724) 834-7474. E-mail: info@artsandheritage.com. Web: www.artsandheritage.com.

WOMEN'S MOTORCYCLE MONTH. July 1–31. This month is dedicated to honoring women who ride, co-ride, or wish they could ride motorcycles or their derivatives (sidecar rigs, trikes, etc). For info: Sylvia Henderson, Springboard Training, PO Box 588, Olney, MD 20830-0588. Phone: (301) 260-1538. E-mail: admin@v-twinvalues.com. Web: www.v-twinvalues.com.

ZIP CODES INAUGURATED: ANNIVERSARY. July 1, 1963. The US Postal Service introduced the five-digit zip code on this day.

BIRTHDAYS TODAY

Pamela Anderson, 39, model, actress ("V.I.P.," "Baywatch"), born Ladysmith, BC, Canada, July 1, 1967.

Dan Aykroyd, 54, actor (*Trading Spaces, The Blues Brothers*, "Saturday Night Live"), born Ottawa, ON, Canada, July 1, 1952.

Karen Black, 64, actress (*Five Easy Pieces, Nashville*), born Park Ridge, IL, July 1, 1942.

Andre Braugher, 44, actor ("Homicide," *City of Angels*), born Chicago, IL, July 1, 1962.

Genevieve Bujold, 64, actress (*Choose Me, Trouble in Mind, Dead Ringers*), born Montreal, QC, Canada, July 1, 1942.

Leslie Caron, 75, actress (*Gigi, An American in Paris*), dancer, born Paris, France, July 1, 1931.

Olivia de Havilland, 90, actress (Oscars for *To Each His Own, The Heiress*; *Gone with the Wind*), born Tokyo, Japan, July 1, 1916.

Missy Elliott, 35, singer, born Portsmouth, VA, July 1, 1971.

Jamie Farr, 72, actor ("M*A*S*H," *The Blackboard Jungle*), born Jameel Farah at Toledo, OH, July 1, 1934.

Debbie Harry, 61, lead singer (Blondie, "The Tide Is High"), born Miami, FL, July 1, 1945.

Frederick Carlton (Carl) Lewis, 45, Olympic gold medal track athlete, born Birmingham, AL, July 1, 1961.

Jean Marsh, 72, writer, actress (*Upstairs, Downstairs*), born Stoke Newington, England, July 1, 1934.

Sydney Pollack, 72, filmmaker (*Tootsie, The Way We Were, The Fabulous Baker Boys*), born Lafayette, IN, July 1, 1934.

Alan Ruck, 50, actor ("Spin City," *Ferris Bueller's Day Off*), born Cleveland, OH, July 1, 1956.

Twyla Tharp, 65, dancer, choreographer, born Portland, IN, July 1, 1941.

Liv Tyler, 29, actress (*Lord of the Rings* trilogy, *Armageddon*), born Portland, ME, July 1, 1977.

JULY 2 — SUNDAY
Day 183 — 182 Remaining

AMELIA EARHART DISAPPEARS: ANNIVERSARY. July 2, 1937. In 1937, aviatrix Amelia Earhart planned an around-the-world trip via the equatorial route that would be the longest ever made. Having completed 22,000 miles of her journey, Earhart, accompanied by navigator Fred Noonan, took off on this date from Lae, New Guinea, for the final 7,000 miles over the Pacific. About 800 miles into their flight to tiny Howland Island, radio contact was lost with her craft. Despite a massive search by the US Navy and US Coast Guard, Earhart, Noonan and their plane were never found.

"THE ANDY WILLIAMS SHOW" TV PREMIERE: ANNIVERSARY. July 2, 1957. Singer Andy Williams hosted many variety shows, including "The Andy Williams–June Valli Show," "The Chevy Showroom" and "The Andy Williams Show." His shows featured Dick Van Dyke and the Bob Hamilton Trio, the New Christy Minstrels, the Osmond Brothers, Charlie Callas, Irwin Corey and Janos Prohaska. In 1976 Williams hosted "Andy," a syndicated show.

BE NICE TO NEW JERSEY WEEK. July 2–8. A time to recognize the assets of the state most maligned by American comedians. Annually, the first full week of July. For info: Lauren Barnett, Lone Star Publications of Humor, 8452 Fredericksburg Rd, PMB 103, San Antonio, TX 78229. E-mail: lspubs@aol.com. Web: members.aol.com/lspubs/lsindex.html.

BLACK HILLS ROUNDUP. July 2–4. Roundup Grounds, Belle Fourche, SD. This 87th annual Independence Day celebration includes an exciting PRCA rodeo each day, the Miss Rodeo South Dakota pageant, a big Fourth of July parade downtown at 10 AM and a thrilling carnival and midway. Est attendance: 10,000. For info: Belle Fourche Chamber of Commerce, 415 Fifth Ave, Belle Fourche, SD 57717. Phone: (605) 892-2676. Fax: (605) 892-4633. E-mail: chamber@bellefourche.org. Web: www.bellefourche.org.

CIVIL RIGHTS ACT OF 1964: ANNIVERSARY. July 2, 1964. President Lyndon Johnson signed the Voting Rights Act of 1964 into law, prohibiting discrimination on the basis of race in public accommodations, in publicly owned or operated facilities, in employment and union membership and in the registration of voters. The bill included Title VI, which allowed for the cutoff of federal funding in areas where discrimination persisted.

CONSTITUTION OF THE US TAKES EFFECT: ANNIVERSARY. July 2, 1788. Cyrus Griffin of Virginia, the president of the Congress, announced that the Constitution had been ratified by the required nine states (the ninth being New Hampshire June 21, 1788), and a committee was appointed to make preparations for the change of government.

CRANMER, THOMAS: BIRTH ANNIVERSARY. July 2, 1489. English clergyman, reformer and martyr, born at Aslacton, Nottinghamshire, England. One of the principal authors of *The English Book of Common Prayer*. Archbishop of Canterbury. Tried for treason and burned at the stake at Oxford, England, Mar 21, 1556.

DECLARATION OF INDEPENDENCE RESOLUTION: ANNIVERSARY. July 2, 1776. Anniversary of adoption by the Continental Congress, Philadelphia, PA, of a resolution introduced June 7, 1776, by Richard Henry Lee of Virginia: "Resolved, That these United Colonies are, and of right ought to be, free and independent States, that they are absolved from all allegiance to the British Crown, and that all political connection between them and the State of Great Britain is, and ought to be, totally dissolved. That it is expedient forthwith to take the most effectual measures for forming foreign Alliances. That a plan of confederation be prepared and transmitted to the respective Colonies for their consideration and approbation." This resolution prepared the way for adoption, July 4, 1776, of the Declaration of Independence. See also: "Declaration of Independence Approval and Signing: Anniversary" (July 4).

DENMARK: AALBORG AND REBILD FESTIVAL (AMERICAN INDEPENDENCE DAY CELEBRATION). July 2–4. Aalborg. This celebration of the American Independence Day, at the Rebild National Park, south of Aalborg, Denmark, is described as "the largest single gathering for this occasion in the world." Guest speakers and Danish and American entertainment. Est attendance: 10,000. For info: 4 July Committee, Aalborg Tourist and Convention Bureau, Oesteragade 8, DK-9100 Aalborg, Denmark. Phone: (45) (99) 30-6090. Fax: (45) (98) 16-6922. E-mail: info@visitaalborg.com. Web: www.visitaalborg.com.

DUCKTONA 500. July 2. Riverview Park, Sheboygan Falls, WI. Plastic duck race in the park lagoon, dunk tank, antique car show, craft show, games for children, pancake breakfast, burgers, brats, beverages. Annually, the first Sunday in July. Est attendance: 5,000. For info: Lynn Buehler, Program Director, Sheboygan Falls Chamber Main St Office, 504 Broadway, Sheboygan Falls, WI 53085. Phone: (920) 467-6206. Fax: (920) 467-9571.

FIRST SOLO ROUND-THE-WORLD BALLOON FLIGHT: ANNIVERSARY. July 2, 2002. In his sixth attempt, Steve Fossett became the first person to circumnavigate the world nonstop and in a nonmotorized craft. In his "Spirit of Freedom" balloon, Fossett traveled 19,400 miles. He began his odyssey on June 18, 2002, from Northam, Australia, and arrived at his starting longitude (117° east) on July 2, 2002. (The first balloon flight around the world was accomplished by a two-man team in 1999. See also: "First Round-the-World Balloon Flight: Anniversary" [Mar 21].)

FOURTH OF JULY CELEBRATION. July 2. Eastside Park, Trenton, MO. This event has fun, food, entertainment and fireworks. Each year, something new. Est attendance: 500. For info: Trenton Area Chamber of Commerce, PO Box 84, Trenton, MO 64683. Phone: (660) 359-4324. E-mail: trentonchamber@grundyec.net.

FREEDOM FROM FEAR OF SPEAKING WEEK. July 2–8. This week is dedicated to stamping out the fear monster of public speaking. Priscilla Richardson, President of WriteSpeakforSuccess, has had to tame her own fear monster of public speaking to get her own speaking freedom. For info: Priscilla Richardson, Pres, WriteSpeakforSuccess, PO Box 275, Cloverdale, VA 24077-0275. Phone: (540) 992-1279. E-mail: guru@WriteSpeakforSuccess.com. Web: www.WriteSpeakforSuccess.com.

GARFIELD, JAMES ABRAM: 125th ASSASSINATION ANNIVERSARY. July 2, 1881. President James A. Garfield was shot as he entered the railway station at Washington, DC. He died Sept 19, 1881, never having recovered from the wound. The assassin, Charles J. Guiteau, was hanged June 30, 1882.

HALFWAY POINT OF 2006. July 2. At noon, July 2, 2006, 182 ½ days of the year will have elapsed and 182 ½ will remain before Jan 1, 2007.

I FORGOT DAY. July 2. A day to make up for all the birthdays, anniversaries, new births, graduations, etc, that you forgot to acknowledge with a greeting or gift. Annually, the 182 ½ day of the year—exact center (except for Leap Year). For info: Gaye Andersen, Davenport University, 8200 Georgia St, Merrillville, IN 46410. Phone: (219) 650-5218. Fax: (219) 756-8911. E-mail: gaye .andersen@davenport.edu.

INDEPENDENCE SUNDAY IN IOWA. July 2. Sunday preceding July 4, by proclamation of the governor.

ITALY: PALIO. July 2 (also Aug 16). Siena. Colorful medieval horse race, competing for the banner (Palio).

LACOSTE, RENE: BIRTH ANNIVERSARY. July 2, 1904. Jean Rene Lacoste, tennis player and clothier born at Paris, France. Lacoste, known as the Crocodile, was one-quarter of the great French tennis players in the 1920s known as the Four Musketeers. He won Wimbledon and the US championship twice each, the French Open three times and was ranked No. 1 in the world in 1926–27. He designed the first shirt specifically for tennis, a loose-fitting cotton polo shirt that soon became the standard. He adorned the Lacoste shirt with a small crocodile, the first apparel logo. Died at St. Jean-de-Luz, France, Oct 12, 1996.

LAVALLETTE INDEPENDENCE EXTRAVAGANZA. July 2. Lavallette, NJ. 45-piece orchestra plays patriotic music during an outstanding fireworks display on the bay. Very suitable for boaters to watch from the water. Annually, the first Sunday in July. (Rain date: following Sunday.) Est attendance: 30,000. For info: Lavallette Heritage Committee, Inc, Ocean County Public Affairs, PO Box 2191, Toms River, NJ 08754. Phone: (732) 793-3652. Fax: (732) 854-9038. E-mail: tpgrosko00@aol.com.

"THE LAWRENCE WELK SHOW" TV PREMIERE: ANNIVERSARY. July 2, 1955. This musical series, hosted by accordionist and bandleader Lawrence Welk, lasted for almost three decades. In its early years it was known as "The Dodge Dancing Party." Regulars included the Lennon Sisters, Alice Lon, Norma Zimmer, Tanya Falan, Arthur Duncan, Joe Feeney, Guy Hovis, Jim Roberts, Ralna English, Larry Hooper, Jerry Burke and Bobby Burgess. From 1956–59, this show was on concurrently with either "Lawrence Welk's Top Tunes and New Talent" or "The Plymouth Show Starring Lawrence Welk (Lawrence Welk's Little Band)."

LIVINGSTON ROUNDUP & PRCA RODEO. July 2–4. Park County Fairgrounds, Livingston, MT. Livingston is the trout capital of the world and the Gateway to Yellowstone National Park. Parade on July 2 at 3 PM. Rodeo held nightly. Performances begin at 8 PM each evening. Est attendance: 10,500. For info: Bruce Becker, Pres of Livingston Roundup, PO Box 800, Livingston, MT 59047. Phone: (406) 222-2905. Fax: (406) 222-7725. For tickets: Stacy Sunvison. Phone: (406) 222-6787 or (406) 222-3199.

MARSHALL, THURGOOD: BIRTH ANNIVERSARY. July 2, 1908. Thurgood Marshall, the first African American on the US Supreme Court, was born at Baltimore, MD. For more than 20 years, he served as director-counsel of the NAACP Legal Defense and Educational Fund. He experienced his greatest legal victory May 17, 1954, when the Supreme Court decision on *Brown v Board of Education* declared an end to the "separate but equal" system of racial segregation in public schools in 21 states. Marshall argued 32 cases before the Supreme Court, winning 29 of them, before becoming a member of the high court himself. Nominated by President Lyndon Johnson, he began his 24-year career on the high court Oct 2, 1967, becoming a voice of dissent in an increasingly conservative court. Marshall announced his retirement June 27, 1991, and he died Jan 24, 1993, at Washington, DC.

PUNXSUTAWNEY GROUNDHOG FESTIVAL. July 2–8. Punxsutawney, PA. Provides residents and visitors a festive week of free entertainment. Music, crafts, food, entertainers, contests, live theater. Est attendance: 16,000. For info: c/o Roger Steele, Groundhog Festival Committee, PO Box 1001, Punxsutawney, PA 15767-2017. Web: www.punxsutawneyphil.com/festival.

ROAD TO INDEPENDENCE. July 2–4. Yorktown Victory Center, Yorktown, VA. Salute America during the Fourth of July holiday. This year the annual event will explore America's momentous 1781 Revolutionary War victory at Yorktown 225 years ago. Visitors can observe tactical and artillery exercises, take part in military drills and learn about the sacrifices of our nation's founders, including those who signed the Declaration of Independence. For info: Jamestown-Yorktown Foundation, PO Box 1607, Williamsburg, VA 23187. Phone: (757) 253-4838 or (888) 593-4682. Fax: (757) 253-5299. Web: www.historyisfun .org.

SAINT LOUIS RACE RIOTS: ANNIVERSARY. July 2, 1917. Between 20 and 75 blacks were killed in a race riot in St. Louis, MO; hundreds more were injured. To protest this violence against blacks, W.E.B. DuBois and James Weldon Johnson of the NAACP led a silent march down Fifth Avenue at New York City.

SPECIAL RECREATION FOR DISABLED DAY. July 2. To focus attention on the recreation abilities, aspirations, needs and rights of people with disabilities. See "Special Recreation Week" (July 2–8). For info: John A. Nesbitt, EdD, Pres/CEO, SRDI—Special Recreation for disABLED Intl, 701 Oaknoll Drive, Iowa City, IA 52246. Phone: (319) 466-3192. E-mail: john-nesbitt @uiowa.edu. Also for info: Global Vision for disABLED, web: www.jccniowa.org/~recdsabl or Prevention of Fireworks Disabilities/Deaths, web: www.bailiwick.lib.uiowa.edu/fireworks/.

SPECIAL RECREATION WEEK. July 2–8. To focus attention on the recreation rights, needs, aspirations and abilities of people with disabilities—infants, children, youth, young adults, adults and seniors; living in the community, in residential services and in institutions; in 40 types of play, recreation and leisure pursuits. See "Special Recreation for Disabled Day" (July 2). For info: John A. Nesbitt, Pres/CEO, SRDI—Special Recreation for disABLED Intl, 701 Oaknoll Dr, Iowa City, IA 52246. Phone: (319) 466-3192. E-mail: john-nesbitt@uiowa.edu.

VESEY, DENMARK: DEATH ANNIVERSARY. July 2, 1822. Planner of what would have been the biggest slave revolt in US history, Denmark Vesey was executed at Charleston, SC. He was born around 1767, probably in the West Indies, where he was sold at around age 14 to Joseph Vesey, captain of a slave ship. He purchased his freedom in 1800. In 1818 Vesey and others began to plot an uprising; he held secret meetings, collected

	S	M	T	W	T	F	S
July							1
2006	2	3	4	5	6	7	8
	9	10	11	12	13	14	15
	16	17	18	19	20	21	22
	23	24	25	26	27	28	29
	30	31					

disguises and firearms and chose a date in June 1822. But authorities were warned, and police and the military were out in full force. Over the next two months 130 blacks were taken into custody; 35, including Vesey, were hanged and 31 were exiled. As a result of the plot Southern legislatures passed more rigorous slave codes.

BIRTHDAYS TODAY

José Canseco, Jr, 42, former baseball player, born Havana, Cuba, July 2, 1964.

Sean Casey, 32, baseball player, born Willingsboro, NJ, July 2, 1974.

Vicente Fox Quesada, 64, president of Mexico, born Mexico City, July 2, 1942.

Polly Holliday, 69, actress ("Alice," "Home Improvement"), born Jasper, AL, July 2, 1937.

Lindsay Lohan, 20, actress (*Freaky Friday, Mean Girls*), born New York, NY, July 2, 1986.

Jimmy McNichol, 45, actor ("The Fitzpatricks," "California Fever"), born Los Angeles, CA, July 2, 1961.

Richard Petty, 69, race car driver, born Level Cross, NC, July 2, 1937.

Ron Silver, 60, actor, director (*Silkwood, Enemies: A Love Story*; stage: *Speed-the-Plow*), born New York, NY, July 2, 1946.

JULY 3 — MONDAY

Day 184 — 181 Remaining

AIR CONDITIONING APPRECIATION DAYS. July 3–Aug 15. Northern Hemisphere. During Dog Days, the hottest time of the year in the Northern Hemisphere, to acknowledge the contribution of air conditioning to a better way of life. Annually, July 3–Aug 15. For info: Air-Conditioning and Refrig Institute, 4100 N Fairfax Dr, Ste 200, Arlington, VA 22203. Phone: (703) 524-8800. Fax: (703) 528-3816. E-mail: ari@ari.org. Web: www.ari.org.

ANDREWS 4TH OF JULY FESTIVITIES. July 3–4. Lakeside Park, Andrews, TX. Monday evening features a fireworks display at the Andrews County Rodeo Arena. Tuesday features fun-filled family activities including the egg toss, sack races, and the famous turtle races. Vendors, food, fireworks and live musical entertainment, and also a picnic BBQ catered by the Andrews Mesquite Burners. Est attendance: 1,000. For info: Andrews Chamber of Commerce, 700 W Broadway, Andrews, TX 79714. Phone: (432) 523-2695. Fax: (432) 523-2375. E-mail: achamber @andrewstx.com. Web: www.andrewstx.com.

BELARUS: INDEPENDENCE DAY. July 3. National holiday. Commemorates liberation of Minsk in 1944.

BENNETT, RICHARD BEDFORD: BIRTH ANNIVERSARY. July 3, 1870. Former Canadian prime minister, born at Hopewell Hill, NB. Died at Mickelham, England, June 26, 1947.

CANADA: KIMBERLEY INTERNATIONAL OLD-TIME ACCORDION CHAMPIONSHIPS. July 3–8. Kimberley, BC. World's old-time accordion competitions. Jam session, accordion and dance workshops, family dances, top-notch evening entertainment, pancake breakfasts, BBQ. Est attendance: 15,000. For info: Jean Irvin, PO Box 473, Kimberley, BC, Canada V1A 3B9. Phone: (888) 4-KIOTAC. E-mail: info@kiotac.ca. Web: www.kiotac.ca.

CAPE MAY KIDS PLAYHOUSE. July 3–Aug 17. Cape May Convention Hall, Cape May, NJ. Welcoming kids and their families as jugglers, magicians, puppeteers, clowns and many others perform throughout the summer. At 10 AM and 7 PM on Mondays and Thursdays. Est attendance: 3,000. For info: Mid-Atlantic Center for the Arts, 1048 Washington St, Cape May, NJ 08204. Phone: (800) 275-4278. Fax: (609) 884-0574. E-mail: mac4arts@ capemaymac.org. Web: www.capemaymac.org.

CARIBBEAN OR CARICOM DAY. July 3. The anniversary of the treaty establishing the Caribbean Community (also called the Treaty of Chaguaramas), signed by the prime ministers of Barbados, Guyana, Jamaica and Trinidad and Tobago July 4, 1973. Observed as a public holiday in Guyana and St. Vincent. Annually, the first Monday in July.

COMPLIMENT-YOUR-MIRROR DAY. July 3. Participation consists of complimenting your mirror on having such a wonderful owner and keeping track of whether other mirrors you meet during the day smile at you. For info: Bob Birch, Grand Punscorpion, Puns Corps, 3108 Dashiell Rd, Falls Church, VA 22042. Phone: (703) 533-3668.

DOG DAYS. July 3–Aug 11. Hottest days of the year in Northern Hemisphere. Usually about 40 days, but variously reckoned at 30–54 days. Popularly believed to be an evil time "when the sea boiled, wine turned sour, dogs grew mad, and all creatures became languid, causing to man burning fevers, hysterics and phrensies" (from Brady's *Clavis Calendarium*, 1813). Originally the days when Sirius, the Dog Star, rose just before or at about the same time as sunrise (no longer true owing to precession of the equinoxes). Ancients sacrificed a brown dog at the beginning of Dog Days to appease the rage of Sirius, believing that star was the cause of the hot, sultry weather.

EARTH AT APHELION. July 3. At approximately 7 PM, EDT, planet Earth will reach aphelion, that point in its orbit when it is farthest from the sun (about 94,510,000 miles). The Earth's mean distance from the sun (mean radius of its orbit) is reached early in the months of April and October. Note that Earth is farthest from the sun during Northern Hemisphere summer. See also: "Earth at Perihelion" (Jan 4).

ENGLAND: HAMPTON COURT PALACE FLOWER SHOW CHARITY GALA PREVIEW. July 3. Hampton Court Palace, East Molesey, Surrey. A charity event that launches the world's largest flower show. For info: Royal Horticultural Society, 80 Vincent Square, London SW1P 2PE, England. Phone: (44) (207) 6305-999. Fax: (44) (207) 6308-178. E-mail: galatickets @rhs.org.uk. Web: www.rhs.org.uk/hamptoncourt/2006/gala.

ENNIS RODEO AND PARADE. July 3–4. Ennis, MT. Billed as the fastest two-day rodeo in Montana, this is a nonstop rodeo of excitement. Parade with clowns, bucking broncos and everything imaginable. Annually, July 3–4. Est attendance: 4,000. For info: Pat Hamilton, PR, Ennis Rodeo Club, PO Box 236, Ennis, MT 59729. Phone: (406) 682-4700.

FIREWORKS ON THE FJORD. July 3. Waterfront, Poulsbo, WA. Family event featuring displays, food booths, entertainment and a giant fireworks display on picturesque Liberty Bay. Voted "Best in the West Sound (Puget)"; only fireworks display on July 3 in the Puget Sound area, it's a great way to celebrate Independence Day early! Est attendance: 25,000. For info: Fireworks on the Fjord, Community Events Productions, PO Box 1976, Poulsbo, WA 98370. Phone: (360) 779-8018.

GEORGE WASHINGTON TAKES COMMAND OF THE CONTINENTAL ARMY: ANNIVERSARY. July 3, 1775. George Washington took command of the Continental Army at Cambridge, MA.

HUNTINGTON, SAMUEL: 275th BIRTH ANNIVERSARY. July 3, 1731. President of the Continental Congress, Governor of Connecticut, signer of the Declaration of Independence, born at Windham, CT, died at Norwich, CT, Jan 5, 1796.

IDAHO: ADMISSION DAY: ANNIVERSARY. July 3. Became 43rd state in 1890.

IRAN AIR FLIGHT 655 DISASTER: ANNIVERSARY.
July 3, 1988. At 10:54 AM in the Persian Gulf, the US Navy warship *Vincennes* fired two surface-to-air missiles at Iran Air Flight 655 which destroyed the airbus, killing all 290 passengers aboard. The *Vincennes*, boasting the world's most sophisticated radar detection equipment, reportedly misread radio signals of the airbus, mistaking it for a hostile F-14 fighter plane. A self-conducted military inquiry blamed human failure—stress on the tense crew rather than equipment malfunction—for the disaster. In the summer of 1992 the public learned that the ship had been in Iranian waters at the time in the course of an operation aimed at preventing Iranian boats from laying mines.

KILLDEER MOUNTAIN ROUNDUP RODEO DAYS. July 3–4 (tentative). Killdeer, ND. More than a rodeo, the Western celebration features many events, including parades, contests, dances, musical entertainment, Western art show, animal shows, historical reenactments of the Old West, cultural foods, Native American demonstrations, fireworks and two performances of great rodeo action. Est attendance: 6,000. For info: (701) 573-5254, (701) 764-5641 or North Dakota Tourism, Century Center, 1600 E Century Ave, Ste 2, Bismarck, ND 58503. Phone: (701) 328-2525 or (800) 435-5663.

"MR PEEPERS" TV PREMIERE: ANNIVERSARY. July 3, 1952. This sitcom was broadcast live and focused on mild-mannered junior high school science teacher, Robinson J. Peepers (Wally Cox). The cast also included Tony Randall, Georgann Johnson, Marion Lorne, Reta Shaw, Jack Warden and Ernest Truex. This half-hour series was a summer replacement, but it earned such positive reviews that it was brought back as a regular series. In 1954 *TV Guide* wrote that "'Mr Peepers' . . . comes close to being the perfect TV show."

MOON PHASE: FIRST QUARTER. July 3. Moon enters First Quarter phase at 12:37 PM, EDT.

MORRISON, JIM: 35th DEATH ANNIVERSARY. July 3, 1971. Jim Morrison, charismatic lead singer for the rock group The Doors, was found dead in his bathtub on this date at Paris, France. The probable cause of death was heart failure. Morrison was buried at Paris's famous Cimetière du Père-Lachaise, and his grave quickly became a shrine. See also: "Morrison, Jim: Birth Anniversary" (Dec 8).

MOUNT RUSHMORE FOURTH OF JULY CELEBRATION. July 3–4. Mount Rushmore National Memorial, SD. Fireworks July 3 and musical performances both days. Est attendance: 10,000. For info: Mt Rushmore Natl Memorial, 13000 Highway 244, Bldg 31, Ste 1, Keystone, SD 57751. Phone: (605) 574-2523. Fax: (605) 574-2307. Web: www.nps.gov/moru.

RAID ON ENTEBBE: 30th ANNIVERSARY. July 3, 1976. An Israeli commando unit staged a raid on Entebbe airport in Uganda and rescued 103 hostages on a hijacked Air France airliner. Three of the hostages, seven hijackers and 20 Ugandan soldiers were killed in the raid. The plane had been en route from Tel Aviv to Paris when taken over by the pro-Palestinian guerrillas.

RED, WHITE & BOOM. July 3. Columbus, OH. Central Ohio's Independence Day celebration features one of the largest fireworks displays in the Midwest. Est attendance: 500,000. For info: Michael L. Collins, Exec Dir, Red, White & Boom, Inc, 929 Harrison Ave, Ste 202, Columbus, OH 43215. Phone: (614) 421-BOOM. Fax: (614) 291-9211. Web: www.redwhiteandboom.org.

STAY OUT OF THE SUN DAY. July 3. For health's sake, give your skin a break today. [©2003 by WH.] For info: Thomas & Ruth Roy, Wellcat Holidays, 2418 Long Ln, Lebanon, PA 17046.

July 2006	S	M	T	W	T	F	S
							1
	2	3	4	5	6	7	8
	9	10	11	12	13	14	15
	16	17	18	19	20	21	22
	23	24	25	26	27	28	29
	30	31					

Phone: (717) 279-0184. E-mail: info@wellcat.com. Web: www.wellcat.com.

US VIRGIN ISLANDS: DANISH WEST INDIES EMANCIPATION DAY: ANNIVERSARY. July 3, 1848. Commemorates freeing of slaves in the Danish West Indies. Ceremony at Frederiksted, St. Croix, where actual proclamation was first read by Governor-General Peter Von Scholten.

VICKSBURG SURRENDERS: ANNIVERSARY. July 3, 1863. After weeks of immediate siege at the end of a year-long campaign, Vicksburg, MS, surrendered to General Ulysses S. Grant. Formal surrender was consummated on July 4, and on July 8 the besieged city of Port Hudson also surrendered, giving the Union complete control of the Mississippi River. This cut off the western Confederacy from the rest of the South.

ZAMBIA: HEROES DAY. July 3. First Monday in July is a Zambian national holiday—a memorial day for Zambians who died in the struggle for independence. Political rallies stress solidarity. See also "Zambia: Unity Day" (July 4).

BIRTHDAYS TODAY

Moises Alou, 40, baseball player, born Atlanta, GA, July 3, 1966.

Dave Barry, 59, humorist, author, born Brooklyn, NY, July 3, 1947.

Betty Buckley, 59, actress (*Cats, Sunset Boulevard*, "Eight Is Enough"), born Fort Worth, TX, July 3, 1947.

Tom Cruise, 44, actor (*Eyes Wide Shut, The Color of Money, Born on the Fourth of July*), born Syracuse, NY, July 3, 1962.

Pete Fountain, 76, jazz musician, born New Orleans, LA, July 3, 1930.

Thomas Gibson, 44, actor ("Dharma & Greg"), born Charleston, SC, July 3, 1962.

Teemu Selanne, 36, hockey player, born Helsinki, Finland, July 3, 1970.

Kurtwood Smith, 64, actor ("That '70s Show," *Robocop*), born New Lisbon, WI, July 3, 1942.

Tom Stoppard, 69, playwright (*Travesties, On the Razzle, The Real Thing, Arcadia*), born Zlin, Czechoslovakia, July 3, 1937.

Montel Williams, 50, talk-show host ("The Montel Williams Show"), born Baltimore, MD, July 3, 1956.

JULY 4 — TUESDAY
Day 185 — 180 Remaining

ADAMS, JOHN, AND JEFFERSON, THOMAS: DEATH ANNIVERSARY. July 4, 1826. Former US presidents John Adams and Thomas Jefferson died on the same day, July 4, 1826, the 50th anniversary of adoption of the Declaration of Independence. Adams had once written to Jefferson (1813): "You and I ought not to die before we have explained ourselves to each other." They thus began a spirited correspondence until their deaths. Adams's last words: "Thomas Jefferson still survives." Jefferson's last words: "This is the Fourth?"

"AMERICA THE BEAUTIFUL" PUBLISHED: ANNIVERSARY. July 4, 1895. The poem "America the Beautiful" by Katherine Lee Bates, a Wellesley College professor, was first published in the *Congregationalist*, a church publication.

360

"AMERICAN TOP 40" RADIO PROGRAM: ANNIVERSARY. July 4, 1970. Casey Kasem's hit parade music countdown radio program, "American Top 40," was first broadcast on seven AM stations in the US on July 4, 1970. It is now heard in hundreds of markets around the world. For info: Pete Battistini, 6576 Lake Forest Dr, Avon, IN 46123. Phone: (317) 839-1421. E-mail: at40@aol.com. Web: www.AT4T.com.

ANVIL MOUNTAIN RUN. July 4. Nome, AK. 28th annual running. At 8 AM the 17k run up 1,134-ft Anvil Mountain and return to the City of Nome starts the day's activities. Record time: 1 hr, 11 min, 23 sec. Annually, July 4. Est attendance: 1,500. For info: Rasmussen's Music Mart, PO Box 2, Nome, AK 99762-0002. Phone: (907) 443-2798 or (907) 443-6022. Fax: (907) 443-5777.

ART ARMADA. July 4. Rotary Riverview Park, Sheboygan, WI. The most spectacular and hilarious races of somewhat seaworthy craft ever launched in Wisconsin. Person-powered one-of-a-kind boats compete in various classes for prizes. Awards for the most spirited team, the most beautiful boats, boats following a theme and the most spectacular sinking. Prizes for top finishers. Est attendance: 16,000. For info: John Michael Kohler Arts Center, 608 New York Ave, PO Box 489, Sheboygan, WI 53082-0489. Phone: (920) 458-6144. Fax: (920) 458-4473. Web: www.jmkac.org.

BOOM BOX PARADE. July 4. Main St, Willimantic, CT. Connecticut's unique people's parade. Anyone can march, enter a float or watch; only requirement—bring a radio. No "real" bands allowed. (Marching music broadcast on WILI-AM Radio and played by "boom boxes" along the parade route.) 11 AM. Est attendance: 10,000. For info: Wayne Norman, Prog Dir, WILI-AM, 720 Main St, Willimantic, CT 06226. Phone: (860) 456-1111. Fax: (860) 456-9501. E-mail: wayne@wili.com. Web: www.wili.com/am.

BRISTOL CIVIC, MILITARY AND FIREMEN'S PARADE. July 4. Bristol, RI. The nation's oldest 4th of July parade. Features floats, bands, veteran and patriotic organizations and military units. Patriotic exercises, a tradition dating to 1785, are held prior to the parade. Annually, July 4 except when July 4 is a Sunday, then the parade is held Monday, July 5. Est attendance: 175,000. For info: East Bay Chamber of Commerce, PO Box 588, Warren, RI 02885. Phone: (401) 245-0750. Fax: (401) 245-0110. Web: www.eastbayritourism.com.

CALITHUMPIAN PARADE. July 4. Biwabik, MN. Funny parade, clowns and bands; Biwabik's population of 1,000 jumps to more than 15,000 for a day. Annually, on the Fourth of July. Est attendance: 15,000. For info: 4th of July, Biwabik Area Civic Assn, Box 449, Biwabik, MN 55708. Phone: (218) 865-4183.

CANADA: MINERAL COLLECTING FIELD TRIPS. July 4–Aug 31. Bancroft, ON. Geologist-led mineral collecting field trips visit nearby rock dumps, abandoned mines and collecting sites. Participants are educated about mineral identification, collecting techniques and earth sciences. Annually, every Tuesday, Thursday and Saturday in July and August. Est attendance: 2,500. For info: Bancroft and Dist Chamber of Commerce, PO Box 539, Bancroft, ON, Canada K0L 1C0. Phone: (613) 332-1513. Fax: (613) 332-2119. E-mail: chamber@commerce.bancroft.on.ca. Web: www.bancroftdistrict.com.

CATONSVILLE INDEPENDENCE DAY CELEBRATION. July 4. Catonsville, MD. 60th annual. Children's games and races, concerts, parade and fireworks display. One of the largest parades and fireworks in Maryland. Est attendance: 60,000. For info: Catonsville Celebrations Committee, PO Box 21074, Catonsville, MD 21228.

CELEBRATION ON THE CANE: AN OLD-FASHIONED FOURTH OF JULY. July 4. Natchitoches, LA. Featuring hot dogs, apple pie, lemonade and a variety of traditional Fourth of July fare. Musical entertainment and fireworks over the scenic Cane River Lake. Est attendance: 10,000. For info: Calendar of Events, Natchitoches Parish Tourist Commission, 781 Front St, Natchitoches, LA 71457. Phone: (318) 352-8072 or (800) 259-1714. Fax: (318) 352-2415. Web: www.natchitoches.net.

COOLIDGE, CALVIN: BIRTH ANNIVERSARY. July 4, 1872. The 30th President of the US was born John Calvin Coolidge at Plymouth, VT. He succeeded to the presidency Aug 3, 1923, following the death of Warren G. Harding. Coolidge was elected president once, in 1924, but did "not choose to run for president in 1928." Nicknamed Silent Cal, he is reported to have said, "If you don't say anything, you won't be called on to repeat it." Coolidge died at Northampton, MA, Jan 5, 1933.

DECLARATION OF INDEPENDENCE APPROVAL AND SIGNING: ANNIVERSARY. July 4, 1776. The Declaration of Independence was approved by the Continental Congress: "Signed by Order and in Behalf of the Congress, John Hancock, President, Attest, Charles Thomson, Secretary." The official signing occurred Aug 2, 1776. The manuscript journals of the Congress for that date state: "The declaration of independence being engrossed and compared at the table was signed by the members."

FARM SANCTUARY'S ANNUAL PIGNIC. July 4. Farm Sanctuary, Watkins Glen, NY. Celebrate July 4th by sampling free vegetarian hot dogs and giving a pig a belly rub at the country's premier farm animal shelter. Meet other rescued farm animals, including cows, goats, sheep, turkeys and more. Free farm tours from 11 AM to 3 PM. Est attendance: 200. For info: Education Coord, Farm Sanctuary, PO Box 150, Watkins Glen, NY 14891. Phone: (607) 583-2225. Fax: (607) 583-2041. Web: www.farmsanctuary.org.

FINLAND: TIME OF MUSIC. July 4–9. Viitasaari. Festival in a town of 300 lakes focuses on contemporary music with top international and Finnish artists performing more than 100 works from some of the most interesting composers of our time, many being performed for the first time ever. Est attendance: 8,000. For info: Finnish Tourist Board, 655 Third Ave, New York, NY 10017. Phone: (212) 885-9700, or Time of Music, Kestitie 10, Finland 44500 Viitasaari. Phone: (358) (14) 573195. E-mail: info@timeofmusic.org. Web: www.timeofmusic.org.

FIRESTORM 2006. July 4. Lakemont Park, Altoona, PA. The region's largest Fourth of July celebration with live entertainment on stage all day and a spectacular fireworks show. Free soda! Est attendance: 20,000. For info: Lakemont Park, I-99 Frankstown Rd Exit, Altoona, PA 16602. Phone: (814) 949-7275 or (800) 434-8006. Fax: (814) 949-9207. E-mail: lakemont99@aol.com. Web: www.lakemontparkfun.com.

FIREWORKS CELEBRATION. July 4. Demopolis, AL. Each year the Demopolis Area Chamber of Commerce presents a spectacular array of fireworks in celebration of Independence Day. The fireworks celebration is held at the Demopolis City Landing and begins at 9 PM. Event also includes Best Burger on the River competition, duck race and children's day at Bluff Hall. Est attendance: 15,000. For info: Kelley Smith, Events & Tourism, Demopolis Area Chamber of Commerce, Box 667, Demopolis, AL 36732. Phone: (334) 289-0270. Fax: (334) 289-1382. E-mail: dacc@demopoliscatv.com. Web: www.demopolischamber.com.

FOSTER, STEPHEN: BIRTH ANNIVERSARY. July 4, 1826. Stephen Collins Foster, one of America's most famous and best-loved songwriters, was born at Lawrenceville, PA. Among his nearly 200 songs: "Oh! Susanna," "Camptown Races," "Old Folks at Home" ("Swanee River"), "Jeanie with the Light Brown Hair," "Old Black Joe" and "Beautiful Dreamer." Foster died in poverty at Bellevue Hospital at New York, NY, Jan 13, 1864.

FOURTH OF JULY CELEBRATION. July 4. Aurora Municipal Center, Aurora, CO. In addition to having the largest fireworks display in the metro area, Aurora's Fourth of July Celebration includes performances by the Aurora symphony, other live, interactive entertainment, food and festivities. Annually, the Fourth of July. Est attendance: 3,000. For info: Marie Addleman, City of Aurora, 1298 Peoria St, Aurora, CO 80011. Phone: (303) 326-8615. Fax: (303) 361-2954. E-mail: maddlema @auroragov.org. Web: www.auroragov.org/events.

FOURTH OF JULY PATRIOTIC CONCERT AND FIRE-WORKS. July 4. Aurora, IL. Annual patriotic concert and fireworks display. Concert begins at 8 PM and fireworks display begins at dusk. For info: Lisa Garcia, City of Aurora, Mayor's Office of Special Events, 43 E Downer Pl, Aurora, IL 60507. Phone: (630) 844-3640. Fax: (630) 906-7068. E-mail: lgarcia@aurora-il.org.

FREDERICKSBURG HERITAGE FESTIVAL. July 4. Fredericksburg, VA. To create an awareness of Fredericksburg's historic heritage. Parade, raft race, street festival, country music, jazz, rock and roll and fireworks. Est attendance: 15,000. For info: Visitor Center, 706 Caroline St, Fredericksburg, VA 22401. Phone: (800) 678-4748. Fax: (540) 372-6587. E-mail: gboswell@ fburg.city.state.va.us.

FREEDOM FEST. July 4 (rain date July 5). Lake of the Woods, Mahomet, IL. Annual celebration of patriotism. Family activities capped off by a spectacular fireworks display. Admission charged. Est attendance: 5,000. For info: Andee Chestnut, PR Director, Champaign Co Forest Preserve District, PO Box 1040, Mahomet, IL 61853. Phone: (217) 586-3360. Fax: (217) 586-5724. E-mail: hq@ccfpd.org. Web: www.ccfpd.org.

FREEDOM WEEK. July 4–10. To disseminate throughout the world information about freedom and liberty. For complete info and many famous quotations about freedom and liberty, send $5 to cover expense of printing, handling and postage. Annually, July 4–10. For info: Dr. Stanley Drake, Pres Emeritus, Intl Soc of Friendship & Good Will, 8592 Roswell Rd, Ste 251, Atlanta, GA 30350-1867. Phone: (678) 795-1362. E-mail: sjdrake@bell south.net. Web: www.friendshipandgoodwill.org.

GOLDBERG, RUBE: BIRTH ANNIVERSARY. July 4, 1883. The cartoonist with an engineering degree who put his education to work inventing elaborate machines with involved steps to accomplish ludicrously simple tasks. He is best remembered for the creative inventions of his cartoon character Lucifer Gorgonzola Butts. Born at San Francisco, Goldberg died Dec 7, 1970, at New York City.

GRAND TETON MUSIC FESTIVAL. July 4–Aug 26. Walk Festival Hall, Teton Village, WY. An eight-week summer celebration of classical music in the spectacular setting of Jackson Hole, WY. The festival features the world's finest artists in orchestral and chamber music concerts. Est attendance: 25,000. For info: Grand Teton Music Festival, 4015 W Lake Creek Dr, #1, Wilson, WY 83014. Phone: (307) 733-1128. Fax: (307) 739-9043. E-mail: gtmf@gtmf.org. Web: www.gtmf.org.

GREAT SEAL OF THE US PROPOSED: ANNIVERSARY. July 4, 1776. The Continental Congress, meeting at Philadelphia, PA, after voting to adopt the Declaration of Inde-

pendence, went on to approve the following: "Resolved, that Dr. Franklin, Mr J. Adams and Mr Jefferson, be a committee, to bring in a device for a seal for the United States of America," thus beginning the history of the Great Seal of the US on the first day of independence. The seal wasn't designed and used until 1782.

HAWTHORNE, NATHANIEL: BIRTH ANNIVERSARY. July 4, 1804. Novelist and short-story writer, born at Salem, MA. Works included *The Scarlet Letter, The House of the Seven Gables* and *The Blithedale Romance.* Hawthorne died at Plymouth, NH, May 19, 1864.

HOMETOWN FAMILY FOURTH. July 4. Hollywood, FL. Family event featuring evening popular music at the Hollywood Beach Theater and a spectacular fireworks display offshore Hollywood Beach. Est attendance: 100,000. For info: Roguey Doyle, City of Hollywood, Dept of Parks, Recreation & Cultural Arts, 1940 Harrison St, Ste 101, Hollywood, FL 33020. Phone: (954) 921-3404.

HOOD RIVER OLD-FASHIONED FOURTH OF JULY. July 4. Hood River, OR. Parade, barbecue, fun run, entertainment and fireworks over the Columbia River. Est attendance: 2,000. For info: Hood River County Chamber of Commerce, 405 Portway Ave, Hood River, OR 97031. Phone: (800) 366-3530. Fax: (541) 386-2057. E-mail: hrccc@hoodriver.org. Web: www .hoodriver.org.

ICE CREAM SOCIAL. July 4. Indianapolis, IN. Independence Day celebration. Music, lawn games and living history. Est attendance: 1,000. For info: President Benjamin Harrison Home, PR Dept, 1230 N Delaware St, Indianapolis, IN 46202. Phone: (317) 631-1888. Fax: (317) 632-5488.

INDEPENDENCE DAY (FOURTH OF JULY). July 4, 1776. The US commemorates adoption of the Declaration of Independence by the Continental Congress. The nation's birthday. Legal holiday in all states and territories.

INDEPENDENCE DAY SYMPHONY CONCERT AND FIREWORKS. July 4. Wheeling, WV. Independence Day celebration on the Wheeling waterfront. Est attendance: 30,000. For info: Wheeling Conv and Visitors Bureau, 1401 Main, Wheeling, WV 26003. Phone: (800) 828-3097 or (304) 233-7709. Web: www.wheelingcvb.com/calendar.

INDEPENDENCE-FROM-MEAT DAY. July 4. Don't be a slave to tradition. Declare your freedom from flesh foods. Your fiery Fourth will be fantastic with a good-for-you vegetarian barbecue. Why not fix a freedom feast featuring veggie burgers and veggie dogs for your family and friends? It will be fun for you and your animal friends too! For info: Vegetarian Awareness Network, Communications Center, PO Box 321, Knoxville, TN 37901-0321. Phone: (800) USA-VEGE or (800) 280-8343.

JULY 4th FAMILY CELEBRATION. July 4. Fort Lauderdale, FL. Featuring live music, fireworks and food. Annually, July 4. For info: City of Fort Lauderdale. Phone: (954) 828-5363. Web: www.sunny.org.

KOKO THE GORILLA: 35th BIRTHDAY. July 4, 1971. Koko, a lowland gorilla (full name: Hanabi-Ko, or "Fireworks Child" in Japanese), was born this day at the San Francisco Zoo.

	S	M	T	W	T	F	S
July							1
	2	3	4	5	6	7	8
2006	9	10	11	12	13	14	15
	16	17	18	19	20	21	22
	23	24	25	26	27	28	29
	30	31					

She is probably the most famous gorilla in the world due to her participation in the longest continuous experiment to teach language to animals. She was taught sign language beginning when she was about a year old, and she currently has a vocabulary of 1,000 signs.

LANDERS, ANN: BIRTH ANNIVERSARY. July 4, 1918. Born at Sioux City, IA, the advice columnist Esther Pauline Friedman was beloved worldwide. In 1955 she won a contest to be the new "Ann Landers" columnist for *The Chicago Sun-Times.* For 47 years, with spunky yet compassionate replies that were a refreshing change from prior columnists' styles, she helped everyday people overcome their problems. A trademark admonishment was "40 lashes with a wet noodle." (Her twin sister, Pauline Friedman, followed in her footsteps with a "Dear Abby" column.) By 2002 her column was carried in more than 1,200 newspapers worldwide and had a readership of 30 million. She died June 22, 2002, at Chicago, IL.

MACKINAW CITY'S FOURTH OF JULY FIREWORKS. July 4. State Dock on South Huron Ave, Mackinaw City, MI. Starting at 1:30 PM on the marina lawn, there will be fun and games for all ages. One of the largest fireworks displays in the north will be shot off over the harbor at dusk. For info: Mackinaw City Chamber of Commerce, PO Box 856, Mackinaw City, MI 49701. Phone: (231) 436-5574 or (888) 455-8100. Web: www.mackinaw chamber.com.

MISS SOUTH CAROLINA PAGEANT. July 4–8. Spartanburg Memorial Auditorium, Spartanburg, SC. Part of the Miss America Organization. Televised competition. For info: Miss South Carolina Organization, 124 W Main St, Liberty, SC 29657. Phone: (864) 843-9090. E-mail: socarpagt@aol.com. Web: www .misssouthcarolina.com.

MONETT FOURTH OF JULY CELEBRATION. July 4. Monett South Park, Monett, MO. All-afternoon and evening event includes Li'l Miss & Li'l Mister Liberty Contest; kiddie rides, children's games and contests; gospel, country and other types of music on three stages; patriotic address; food and a fireworks display with a dance following. Annually, the Fourth of July. Est attendance: 5,000. For info: Deborah Schoen, 1304 Hemingway Dr, Monett, MO 65708. Phone: (417) 235-7967. E-mail: dschoen @mo-net.com.

MYSTIC SEAPORT INDEPENDENCE DAY CELEBRATION. July 4. Mystic Seaport, Mystic, CT. Visitors can participate in a re-creation of an 1870s Fourth of July with costumed staff. There are patriotic ceremonies and a parade of the "Antiques and Horribles." Kids' old-fashioned spelling bee. Est attendance: 3,500. For info: Mystic Seaport, 75 Greenmanville Ave, Box 6000, Mystic, CT 06355. Phone: (860) 572-5315 or (888) 973-2767. Web: www.mysticseaport.org.

OLD GLORY JUBILEE. July 4. Elsberry, MO. Old-time picnic, fireworks, parade, entertainment, games, crafts and lots of food. Est attendance: 1,500. For info: Elsberry City Hall, 201 Broadway, Elsberry, MO 63343. Phone: (573) 898-5588. Fax: (573) 898-2249.

OLD VERMONT FOURTH. July 4. Woodstock, VT. A traditional Fourth of July with patriotic speeches and debates, making "1890" flags, a spelling bee for adults, ice cream making, sack race and more. Est attendance: 750. For info: Billings Farm and Museum, Rte 12 North, Woodstock, VT 05091. Phone: (802) 457-2355. Fax: (802) 457-4663. E-mail: billings.farm@valley.net. Web: www.billingsfarm.org.

PEACHTREE ROAD RACE. July 4. Atlanta, GA. 10k run. 55,000-runner limit; advance registration only. Send SASE by Mar 1, 2006. 45,000 entrants on first-come basis and 10,000 selected by lottery from other entries postmarked in March 2006. Est attendance: 55,000. For info: Atlanta Track Club, 3097 E Shadowlawn Ave, Atlanta, GA 30305. Phone: (404) 231-9064. E-mail: atc@atlantatrackclub.org. Web: www.atlantatrackclub.org.

PHILIPPINES: FIL-AMERICAN FRIENDSHIP DAY. July 4. Formerly National Independence Day, when the Philippines were a colony of the US, now celebrated as Fil-American Friendship Day.

PRAIRIE PIONEER DAYS. July 4. Arapahoe, NE. Parade, games for kids, food booths, free swimming, watermelon bust, quilt show, baseball games, fireworks and more. For info: Tammie Middagh, Secy, Arapahoe Chamber of Commerce, PO Box 624, Arapahoe, NE 68922.

"THE SOUPY SALES SHOW" TV PREMIERE: ANNIVERSARY. July 4, 1955. Soupy Sales hosted a number of national and local children's shows from 1955 to 1979. All of his programs included some of these features: jokes, puns, songs, sketches, puppets, silent films and pies in the face. Sales's humor occasionally went over the edge and got him in trouble; for example, in 1965 his show was suspended for a week because he asked his viewers to send him the green paper in their parents' wallets!

SPACE MILESTONE: *DEEP IMPACT* **SMASHES INTO TEMPEL 1 (US).** July 4, 2005. After a six-month journey and 83 million miles, the *Deep Impact* spacecraft smashed—as planned—into the comet Tempel 1. The 820-pound, barrel-shaped craft's purpose is to give scientists more information about comets.

SPACE MILESTONE: *MARS PATHFINDER* **(US).** July 4, 1997. Unmanned spacecraft landed on Mars after a seven-month flight. Carried *Sojourner,* a roving robotic explorer that sent back photographs of the landscape. One of its missions was to find if life ever existed on Mars. See also: "Space Milestone: *Mars Global Surveyor*" (Sept 11).

SPIRIT OF FREEDOM CELEBRATION. July 4. Florence, AL. Celebrate America's birthday on the banks of the beautiful Tennessee River at McFarland Park. Enjoy sunning, swimming, bicycling, golf and entertainment. Playground, picnic tables and campground available. Annually, on July 4. Est attendance: 60,000. For info: Florence/Lauderdale Tourism, One Hightower Place, Florence, AL 35630. Phone: (256) 740-4141 or (888) FLO-TOUR. Fax: (256) 740-4142. E-mail: dwilson@flo-tour.org. Web: www.flo-tour.org.

STAR SPANGLED SPARKS. July 4. Sparks, NV. The biggest firework display in the region. Come to Victorian Square early and get the best viewing spot. Kids area, food, entertainment and crafts start at 3 PM and continue until the fireworks show, which begins around 9:40 PM (weather permitting). For info: John Ascuaga's Nugget, 1100 Nugget Ave, Sparks, NV 89431. Phone: (800) 648-1177. Web: www.janugget.com.

STOCK EXCHANGE HOLIDAY (INDEPENDENCE DAY). July 4. The holiday schedules for the various exchanges are subject to change if relevant rules, regulations or exchange policies are revised. If you have questions, contact: American Stock Exchange (212) 306-1000, Chicago Board of Trade (312) 435-3500, Chicago Board of Options Exchange (312) 786-5600, NASDAQ Stock Market (646) 441-5200, New York Stock Exchange (212) 656-3000, Pacific Stock Exchange (415) 393-4000, Philadelphia Stock Exchange (215) 496-5000.

TRADITIONAL SOUSA CONCERT. July 4. The American Club, Kohler, WI. Celebrate Independence Day on a Great American note with a rousing Sousa Concert performed by the award-winning Kiel Municipal Band. This old-fashioned open-air social recalls the 1919 and 1925 Sousa Concerts in Kohler's Ravine Park. Est attendance: 1,000. For info: The American Club, Highland Dr, Kohler, WI 53044. Phone: (800) 344-2838. Fax: (920) 457-6372. Web: www.destinationkohler.com.

TUSKEGEE INSTITUTE OPENING: 125th ANNIVERSARY. July 4, 1881. Booker T. Washington's famed agricultural-industrial institution was built from the ground up by dedicated students seeking academic and vocational training. The institute started in a shanty before Washington purchased an abandoned plantation at Tuskegee, AL. The students built the dormitories, classrooms and chapel from bricks out of their own kiln.

WALES: LLANGOLLEN INTERNATIONAL MUSICAL EISTEDDFOD. July 4–9. Eisteddfod Field, Llangollen, Denbighshire, North Wales. 60th annual. Thousands of singers and folk dancers from more than 50 countries take part in this annual international music festival. Friendly rivalry among amateur groups performing amid the Welsh rivers and mountains. Est attendance: 80,000. For info: Janet Major, Mktg Dir, Llangollen Intl Musical Eisteddfod, Llangollen, North Wales, UK LL20 8SW. Phone: (44) (1978) 862000. Fax: (44) (1978) 862002. E-mail: info@international-eisteddfod.co.uk. Web: www.international-eisteddfod.co.uk.

WORLD'S GREATEST LIZARD RACE. July 4. Chaparral Park, Lovington, NM. Participants and observers cheer as their lizards and iguanas race down a 16-ft ramp; winners are awarded trophies. Many other lizard events will be held throughout the day. Entertainment and other games are also featured. For info: Lovington Chamber of Commerce, 201 S Main St, Lovington, NM 88260. Phone: (505) 396-5311. Fax: (505) 396-2823. E-mail: lchamber@valornet.com. Web: www.lovington.net.

WSB-TV SALUTE 2 AMERICA PARADE. July 4. Atlanta, GA. One of the largest 4th of July parades in the US. 46th annual parade steps off at 1 PM. Est attendance: 250,000. For info: WSB-TV Salute 2 America Parade, 1601 W Peachtree St NE, Atlanta, GA 30309. Phone: (404) 897-7385. Fax: (404) 897-6236. E-mail: salute2america@wsbtv.com. Web: www.wsbtv.com.

ZAMBIA: UNITY DAY. July 4. Memorial day for Zambians who died in the struggle for independence. Political rallies stressing solidarity throughout country. Annually, the first Tuesday in July.

BIRTHDAYS TODAY

Signy Coleman, 46, actress ("The Young and the Restless"), born Bolinas, CA, July 4, 1960.

Allen (Al) Davis, 77, Hall of Fame football player, executive, born Brockton, MA, July 4, 1929.

Harvey Grant, 41, former basketball player, born Augusta, GA, July 4, 1965.

Horace Grant, 41, former basketball player, born Augusta, GA, July 4, 1965.

Leona Helmsley, 86, former hotel executive, born Brooklyn, NY, July 4, 1920.

Gina Lollobrigida, 78, actress (*Belles de Nuit; Bread, Love and Dreams*), born Auviaco, Italy, July 4, 1928.

Geraldo Rivera, 63, journalist, talk-show host ("Geraldo," *Exposing Myself*), born New York, NY, July 4, 1943.

Eva Marie Saint, 82, actress (Oscar for *On the Waterfront; North by Northwest, Exodus*), born Newark, NJ, July 4, 1924.

Pamela Howard (Pam) Shriver, 44, broadcaster and former tennis player, born Baltimore, MD, July 4, 1962.

Neil Simon, 79, playwright (*The Odd Couple, Barefoot in the Park*), born New York, NY, July 4, 1927.

George Michael Steinbrenner III, 76, baseball executive, born Rocky River, OH, July 4, 1930.

Abigail Van Buren, 88, advice columnist, born Pauline Esther Friedman at Sioux City, IA, July 4, 1918.

★　★　★

July *2006*	S	M	T	W	T	F	S
							1
	2	3	4	5	6	7	8
	9	10	11	12	13	14	15
	16	17	18	19	20	21	22
	23	24	25	26	27	28	29
	30	31					

JULY 5 — WEDNESDAY
Day 186 — 179 Remaining

ALGERIA: INDEPENDENCE DAY. July 5. National holiday. Commemorates the day in 1962 when Algeria gained independence from France.

BARNUM, PHINEAS TAYLOR: BIRTH ANNIVERSARY. July 5, 1810. Promoter of the bizarre and unusual. Barnum's American Museum opened in 1842, promoting unusual acts including the Feejee Mermaid, Chang and Eng (the original Siamese twins) and General Tom Thumb. In 1850 he began his promotion of Jenny Lind, "The Swedish Nightingale," and parlayed her singing talents into a major financial success. Barnum also cultivated a keen interest in politics. A founder of the newspaper *Herald of Freedom*, he wrote outspoken editorials that resulted not only in lawsuits but also in at least one jail sentence. In 1852 he declined the Democratic nomination for governor of Connecticut but did serve two terms in the Connecticut legislature beginning in 1865. He was defeated in a bid for US Congress in 1866 but served as mayor of Bridgeport, CT, from 1875 to 1876. In 1871 "The Greatest Show on Earth" opened at Brooklyn, NY; Barnum merged with his rival J.A. Bailey in 1881 to form the Barnum and Bailey Circus. P.T. Barnum was born at Bethel, CT, and died at Bridgeport, CT, Apr 7, 1891.

BIKINI DEBUTED: 60th ANNIVERSARY. July 5, 1946. The skimpy two-piece bathing suit created by Louis Reard debuted at a fashion show in Paris. It was named after an atoll in the Pacific where the hydrogen bomb was first tested.

CALLAS'S LAST PERFORMANCE: ANNIVERSARY. July 5, 1965. Opera's preeminent soprano, Maria Callas, appeared on the operatic stage for the last time as Tosca at the Royal Opera House at Covent Garden, London. Months of health problems had forced Callas to cancel all but one scheduled performance in London—which was a charity gala with the royal family in attendance—and it turned out to be her last. Marshalling her strength, Callas delivered a performance that thrilled the audience, who asked for close to fifteen curtain calls at the opera's conclusion.

CANADA: THE NORTH AMERICAN TOURNAMENT. July 5–9. Spruce Meadows, Calgary, AB. Show jumping tournament featuring the Spruce Meadows North American Championships. Sun Life Days at Fort Meadows will offer a great variety of entertainment and food kiosks for your enjoyment. Est attendance: 98,000. For info: Spruce Meadows, RR 9, Calgary, AB, Canada T2J 5G5. Phone: (403) 974-4200. Fax: (403) 974-4270. E-mail: information@sprucemeadows.com. Web: www.sprucemeadows.com.

CAPE VERDE: NATIONAL DAY. July 5. Public holiday. Commemorates independence from Portugal in 1975.

FARRAGUT, DAVID: BIRTH ANNIVERSARY. July 5, 1801. Born near Knoxville, TN, and died Aug 14, 1870, at

Portsmouth, NH. Admiral in the American Civil War who was famous for his naval victories. At Mobile Bay, AL, in a disastrous attack on his entire fleet by the Confederates' Fort Morgan, Farragut proclaimed the famous cry, "Damn the torpedoes, full speed ahead!" They escaped the attack and Mobile Bay surrendered.

ISLE OF MAN: TYNWALD DAY. July 5. For more than 1,000 years, the people of the Isle of Man have gathered at Tynwald Hill at St. John's to hear new laws read out, to present petitions and to swear in the island's four coroners. Tynwald (a word of Norse extraction) is the name of the Manx parliament, which is the world's oldest continually held parliament. Held annually on July 5, unless that date falls on a weekend, in which case the event occurs on the following Monday.

NATIONAL LABOR RELATIONS ACT (THE WAGNER ACT): ANNIVERSARY. July 5, 1935. This bill guaranteed workers the right to organize and bargain collectively with their employers. It also prohibited the formation of company unions. An enforcement agency, the National Labor Relations Board, was created by the Act.

RAFFLES, STAMFORD: 225th BIRTH ANNIVERSARY. July 5, 1781. Sir Stamford Raffles, English colonial official, founder of Singapore, where he is supposed to have landed Jan 29, 1819, was born at sea, off Jamaica. He discovered with Joseph Arnold an East Indian fungus that is named after them, *Rafflesia Arnoldi*. Raffles died near London, England, on his birthday, July 5, 1826.

RHODES, CECIL JOHN: BIRTH ANNIVERSARY. July 5, 1853. English-born, South African millionaire politician. Said to have controlled at one time 90 percent of the world's diamond production. His will founded the Rhodes Scholarships at Oxford University for superior scholastic achievers. Rhodesia (now Zimbabwe) was named for him. Born at Bishop's Stortford, Hertfordshire, Rhodes died Mar 26, 1902, at Cape Town, South Africa.

SLOVAKIA: SAINT CYRIL AND METHODIUS DAY. July 5. This day is dedicated to the Greek priests and scholars from Thessalonniki, who were invited by Prince Rastislav of Great Moravia to introduce Christianity and the first Slavic alphabet to the pagan people of the kingdom in AD 863.

VENEZUELA: INDEPENDENCE DAY. July 5. National holiday. Commemorates Proclamation of Independence from Spain in 1811. Independence was not achieved until 1821.

ZETKIN, CLARA: BIRTH ANNIVERSARY. July 5, 1857. Women's rights advocate, born at Wiederau, Germany. Zetkin has been credited with being the initiator of International Women's Day, which has been observed on Mar 8 at least since 1910. She died at Arkhangelskoe, Russia, June 20, 1933. See also: "International (Working) Women's Day" (Mar 8).

BIRTHDAYS TODAY

Edie Falco, 43, actress ("The Sopranos"), born Brooklyn, NY, July 5, 1963.

Eliot Feld, 64, dancer, born Brooklyn, NY, July 5, 1942.

Richard Michael ("Goose") Gossage, 55, former baseball player, born Colorado Springs, CO, July 5, 1951.

Chris Gratton, 31, hockey player, born Brantford, ON, Canada, July 5, 1975.

Katherine Helmond, 72, actress (stage: *The House of Blue Leaves*; "Soap," "Who's the Boss?"), born Galveston, TX, July 5, 1934.

Shirley Knight, 70, actress (stage: *Kennedy's Children* [Tony Award, 1976]; *The Dark at the Top of the Stairs, Sweet Bird of Youth, Petulia*), born Goessel, KS, July 5, 1936.

Huey Lewis, 56, singer (Huey Lewis and the News), born Hugh Anthony Cregg III at New York, NY, July 5, 1950.

James David Lofton, 50, former football player, born Fort Ord, CA, July 5, 1956.

Robbie Robertson, 62, musician (guitarist with The Band), born Toronto, ON, Canada, July 5, 1944.

Janos Starker, 82, musician, born Budapest, Hungary, July 5, 1924.

JULY 6 — THURSDAY
Day 187 — 178 Remaining

BELGIUM: OMMEGANG PAGEANT. July 6. Splendid historic festival of medieval pageantry at the illuminated Grand-Palace in Brussels. The annual event (first Thursday in July) re-creates an entertainment given in honor of Charles V and his court.

BUSH, GEORGE W.: 60th BIRTHDAY. July 6, 1946. 43rd president of the US (2001–). Born at New Haven, CT.

COMOROS: INDEPENDENCE DAY. July 6. Federal and Islamic Republic of Comoros commemorates declaration of independence from France in 1975.

CZECH REPUBLIC: COMMEMORATION DAY OF BURNING OF JOHN HUS. July 6. National holiday. In honor of Bohemian religious reformer John Hus, who was condemned as a heretic and burned at the stake July 6, 1415.

FIRST AIRSHIP CROSSING OF ATLANTIC: ANNIVERSARY. July 6, 1919. The first airship crossing of the Atlantic was completed as a British dirigible landed at New York's Roosevelt Field.

FIRST BLACK US STATE'S ATTORNEY: 45th ANNIVERSARY. July 6, 1961. Cecil Francis Poole became the first black US state's attorney when he was sworn in as US attorney for the Northern District of California. He served until his retirement on Feb 3, 1970.

FIRST SUCCESSFUL ANTIRABIES INOCULATION: ANNIVERSARY. July 6, 1885. Louis Pasteur gave the first successful antirabies inoculation to a boy who had been bitten by an infected dog.

JONES, JOHN PAUL: BIRTH ANNIVERSARY. July 6, 1747 (OS). American naval officer born at Kirkbean, Scotland. Remembered for his victory in the battle of his ship, the *Bonhomme Richard*, with the British frigate *Serapis*, Sept 23, 1779. When Jones was queried: "Do you ask for quarter?" he made his famous reply: "I have not yet begun to fight!" Jones was victorious, but the *Bonhomme Richard*, badly damaged, sank two days later. Jones died at Paris, France, July 18, 1792.

KAHLO, FRIDA: BIRTH ANNIVERSARY. July 6, 1907. The great surrealist painter was born Magdalena Carmen Frida Kahlo Calderón at Coyoacán, Mexico. In 1925 she endured severe injuries in a bus accident that would plague her for the rest of her life (and become artistic subject matter). She turned to art at about this time, encouraged by the great muralist Diego Rivera, whom she married in 1929 (and 1941). She is known almost as much for her tumultuous life (she had an affair with Soviet exile Leon Trotsky and was active in leftist politics) as for her vibrant art works filled with symbols and the flora and fauna of her beloved Mexico. She was one of the first women painters to sell a work to the Louvre. She died at her Casa Azul family home in Coyoacán on July 13, 1954.

LEIGH, JANET: BIRTH ANNIVERSARY. July 6, 1927. Born Jeanette Helen Morrison at Merced, CA, Leigh was signed to a contract by MGM while still a teenager. She starred in *Touch of Evil* with Orson Wells (1958), *The Manchurian Candidate* with Frank Sinatra (1962) and *Bye Bye Birdie* (1963) with Dick Van Dyke. She is best remembered for the scene where she was attacked in the shower by Norman Bates, in Alfred Hitchcock's 1960 classic *Psycho*. She died Oct 3, 2004, at Los Angeles, CA.

LITHUANIA: DAY OF STATEHOOD. July 6. National holiday. Commemorates the 1252 crowning of Mindaugas, who united Lithuania.

LUXEMBOURG: ETTELBRUCK REMEMBRANCE DAY. July 6. In honor of US General George Patton, Jr, liberator of the Grand-Duchy of Luxembourg in 1945, who is buried at the American Military Cemetery at Hamm, Germany, among 5,100 soldiers of his famous Third Army.

MAJOR LEAGUE BASEBALL HOLDS FIRST ALL-STAR GAME: ANNIVERSARY. July 6, 1933. The first midsummer All-Star Game was held at Comiskey Park, Chicago, IL. Babe Ruth led the American League with a home run, as they defeated the National League 4–2. Prior to the summer of 1933, All-Star contests consisted of pre- and postseason exhibitions that often found teams made up of a few stars playing beside journeymen and even minor leaguers.

MALAWI: REPUBLIC DAY. July 6. National holiday. Commemorates attainment of independence from Britain in 1964. Malawi was formerly known as Nyasaland.

MARION COUNTY FAIR. July 6–9. State Fairgrounds, Salem, OR. Exceptional food and entertainment, carnival, talent show, flea market, commercial exhibits, 4-H/FFA exhibits, open class exhibits, Longhorns, horse and llama shows and livestock. Est attendance: 28,000. For info: Marion County Fair, PO Box 7166, Salem, OR 97303. Phone: (503) 585-9998. Fax: (503) 588-1659. E-mail: fair@co.marion.or.us.

MONTANA GOVERNOR'S CUP WALLEYE TOURNAMENT. July 6–8. Fort Peck, MT. Two-person team event, limited to 200 teams. First place award of $15,000 and $20,000 awarded in day money (based on a full field). There is an 80 percent payback of $500 entry fee. Kids' fishing event also. Annually, the second weekend in July. Est attendance: 2,000. For info: Glasgow Area Chamber of Commerce & Agriculture, Box 832, Glasgow, MT 59230. Phone: (406) 228-2222. Fax: (406) 228-2244. E-mail: chamber@nemontel.net. Web: www.mtgovcup.com.

"NAME THAT TUNE" TV PREMIERE: ANNIVERSARY. July 6, 1953. "Name That Tune" was a musical identification show that appeared in different formats in the '50s and the '70s. Red Benson was the host of the NBC series and Bill Cullen (and later George DeWitt) was the CBS host. Two contestants listened while an orchestra played a musical selection, and the first contestant who could identify it raced across the stage to ring a bell. The winner of the round then tried to identify a number of tunes within a specific time period. After 11 years, the show was brought back with Richard Hayes as host. In 1974 new network and syndicated versions appeared.

OPERATION OVERCAST: ANNIVERSARY. July 6, 1945. As the end of the war approached, the US Army had begun to move German scientists and scientific equipment from the German territory designated for Russian occupation. On this date, the American Joint Chiefs of Staff authorized Operation Overcast, under which 350 German and Austrian scientists were transported to the US in a matter of months.

"THE QUIZ KIDS" TV PREMIERE: ANNIVERSARY. July 6, 1949. This show began on radio and continued on TV with the original host, Joe Kelly, and later with Clifton Fadiman. The format was a panel of five child prodigies who answered questions sent in by viewers. Four were regulars, staying for weeks or months, while the fifth was a "guest child." The ages of the panelists varied from 6 to 16.

		S	M	T	W	T	F	S
July								1
2006		2	3	4	5	6	7	8
		9	10	11	12	13	14	15
		16	17	18	19	20	21	22
		23	24	25	26	27	28	29
		30	31					

REPUBLICAN PARTY FORMED: ANNIVERSARY. July 6, 1854. The Republican Party originated at a convention at Ripon, WI, on Feb 28, 1854. A state convention meeting in Michigan formally adopted the name Republican on July 6.

SPACE MILESTONE: *SOYUZ 21* (USSR): 30th ANNIVERSARY. July 6, 1976. Launched this date. Two cosmonauts, Colonel B. Volynov and Lieutenant Colonel V. Zholobov, traveled to *Salyut 5* space station (launched June 22, 1976) to study Earth's surface and conduct zoological-botanical experiments. Forty-eightday stay on space station. Return landing on Aug 24.

TAKE YOUR WEBMASTER TO LUNCH DAY. July 6. Keep the person running your website happy by making sure they're well fed. It makes them feel loved and gives them the energy to fix all the typos that you have on your site. [©2003 by WH.] For info: Thomas & Ruth Roy, Wellcat Holidays, 2418 Long Ln, Lebanon, PA 17046. Phone: (717) 279-0184. E-mail: info@wellcat.com. Web: www.wellcat.com.

US SENIOR OPEN (GOLF) CHAMPIONSHIP. July 6–9. Prairie Dunes Country Club, Hutchinson, KS. For info: US Golf Assn, Golf House, PO Box 708, Championship Dept, Far Hills, NJ 07931. Phone: (908) 234-2300. Fax: (908) 234-9687. E-mail: usga@usga.org. Web: www.usga.org.

WHITE CLOUD DAYS. July 6–10 (tentative). National Buffalo Museum, Jamestown, ND. Annual celebration of the birth of the true albino buffalo, White Cloud, born in Michigan, ND, in July 1996. Included in the celebration are children's activities, a parade, cultural presentations, a street fair and a birthday cake. Est attendance: 1,000. For info: Felicia Sargeant, National Buffalo Museum, PO Box 1712, Jamestown, ND 58402. Phone: (701) 252-8648. Fax: (701) 253-5803. E-mail: director@buffalomuseum.com. Web: www.nationalbuffalomuseum.com.

WILD HORSE STAMPEDE. July 6–8. Wolf Point, MT. The "Granddaddy" of all Montana rodeos features a wild-horse race, three rodeos, two parades and Native American culture. This is the oldest PRCA rodeo in Montana. Est attendance: 12,000. For info: Chairman, Wolf Point Chamber of Commerce, 218 3rd Ave S, Ste B, Wolf Point, MT 59201. Phone: (406) 653-2012. E-mail: wpchmber@nemontel.net.

BIRTHDAYS TODAY

Allyce Beasley, 52, actress ("Moonlighting"), born Brooklyn, NY, July 6, 1954.

Ned Beatty, 69, actor ("Homicide," *Hear My Song, Deliverance*), born Louisville, KY, July 6, 1937.

George W. Bush, 60, 43rd president of the US, former governor of Texas (R), born New Haven, CT, July 6, 1946.

Dalai Lama, 71, Tibet's spiritual leader and Nobel Peace Prize winner, born Taktser, China, July 6, 1935.

Donal Donnelly, 75, actor (*The Knack, The Dead, The Godfather Part III*), born Bradford, England, July 6, 1931.

Pau Gasol, 26, basketball player, born Barcelona, Spain, July 6, 1980.

Grant Goodeve, 54, actor ("Eight Is Enough," "Dynasty"), born New Haven, CT, July 6, 1952.

Merv Griffin, 81, TV host, business executive, born San Mateo, CA, July 6, 1925.

Nancy Davis Reagan, 85, former First Lady, wife of Ronald Reagan, 40th president of the US, born New York, NY, July 6, 1921.

Della Reese, 74, singer ("Don't You Know," "And That Reminds Me"), actress ("Touched by an Angel"), born Deloreese Patricia Early at Detroit, MI, July 6, 1932.

Geoffrey Rush, 55, actor (*Quills, Shakespeare in Love*, Oscar for *Shine*), born Toowoomba, Queensland, Australia, July 6, 1951.

Sylvester Stallone, 60, actor (*Rocky* and *Rambo* films), director, born New York, NY, July 6, 1946.

Burt Ward, 61, actor ("Batman"), born Los Angeles, CA, July 6, 1945.

JULY 7 — FRIDAY
Day 188 — 177 Remaining

AFRMA FANCY RAT & MOUSE DISPLAY AND SHOW. July 7–30. Costa Mesa, CA. American Fancy Rat and Mouse Association exhibits rats and mice of "fancy" species that make good pets. For info: AFRMA, PO Box 2589, Winnetka, CA 91396-2589. Phone: (818) 992-5564 or (951) 685-2350. Fax: (818) 592-6590. E-mail: afrma@afrma.org. Web: www.afrma.org.

BONZA BOTTLER DAY™. July 7. To celebrate when the number of the day is the same as the number of the month. Bonza Bottler Day™ is an excuse to have a party at least once a month. For more information, see Jan 1. For info: Gail M. Berger, 14 Fernwood Dr, Taylors, SC 29687. Phone: (864) 609-9874. E-mail: gberger5@aol.com.

CANADA: ABBOTSFORD BERRY FESTIVAL. July 7–8. Abbotsford, BC. July heralds the height of the Raspberry Capital of Canada's berry season. Sample delicious local strawberry, raspberry and blueberry products. Linger to cheer the top musicians, magicians and clowns; play bingo or mini-golf; thrill to carnival rides and browse through local craft and market-style food stands. Est attendance: 40,000. For info: Abbotsford Downtown Business Assn, 33728 Essendene Ave, Abbotsford, BC, Canada V2S 2G9. Phone: (604) 850-6547. Fax: (604) 859-6507. E-mail: info@abbotsforddowntownbia.bc.ca. Web: www.abbotsforddowntownbia.bc.ca.

CANADA: CALGARY STAMPEDE. July 7–16. Calgary, AB. One of the world's largest rodeos, plus an agricultural fair, entertainment, parade and carnival. Est attendance: 1,218,000. For info: Calgary Exhibition and Stampede, 1410 Olympic Way SE, Calgary, AB, Canada T2P 2K8. Phone: (403) 261-0101. Web: www.calgarystampede.com.

CANADA: CISCO SYSTEMS OTTAWA BLUESFEST. July 7–16. Festival Plaza, Ottawa City Hall, Ottawa, ON. 13th annual. Enjoy a spectacular explosion of blues, gospel, roots, world and popular music in the heart of Canada's national capital. The ten-day festival on multiple stages will offer more than 175 performances. Est attendance: 225,000. For info: Andre Sauve, Cisco Systems Ottawa Bluesfest, 1810 St. Laurent Blvd, Ottawa, ON, Canada K1G 1A2. Phone: (613) 247-1188. Fax: (613) 247-2220. E-mail: ajsauve@ottawa-bluesfest.ca. Web: www.ottawa-bluesfest.ca.

ENGLAND: WAYS WITH WORDS LITERATURE FESTIVAL. July 7–17. Dartington Hall, Dartington, Devon. Some 200 writers give lectures, seminars, interviews, discussions and readings. Book stalls, workshops and plays are also included. Est attendance: 12,000. For info: Steven Bristow, Dir, Ways With Words Literature Festival, Droridge Farm, Dartington, Totnes, Devon, England TQ9 6JQ. Phone: (44) (180) 386-7373. E-mail: admin@wayswithwords.co.uk.

FATHER-DAUGHTER TAKE A WALK TOGETHER DAY. July 7. A special time in the summer for fathers and daughters of all ages to spend time together in the beautiful weather. Annually, July 7. For info: Janet Dellaria, PO Box 39, Trout Creek, MI 49967. Phone: (906) 852-3539.

HAWAII ANNEXED BY US: ANNIVERSARY. July 7, 1898. President William McKinley signed a resolution annexing Hawaii. No change in government took place until 1900, when Congress passed an act making Hawaii an "incorporated" territory of the US. This act remained in effect until Hawaii became a state in 1959.

JAPAN: TANABATA (STAR FESTIVAL). July 7. As an offering to the stars, children set up bamboo branches to which colorful strips of paper bearing poems are tied.

JIMMY AND ROSALYNN CARTER WEDDING: 60th ANNIVERSARY. July 7, 1946. Plains Methodist Church, Plains, GA. James Earl Carter, Jr, was 21 and Eleanor Rosalynn Smith was 18. They have four children: John William "Jack" Carter was born in 1947, James Carl "Chip" Carter, 1950, Donnell Jeffrey Carter, 1952, and Amy Lynn Carter, 1968.

LAURA INGALLS WILDER PAGEANT. July 7–9 (also July 14–16 and 21–23). De Smet, SD. An outdoor pageant on the natural prairie stage depicting scenes historically based on Laura Ingalls Wilder's life and books. Est attendance: 10,000. For info: The Laura Ingalls Wilder Pageant, PO Box 154, De Smet, SD 57231. Phone: (800) 880-3383. Web: www.desmetpageant.org.

LINCOLN ASSASSINATION CONSPIRATORS HANGING: ANNIVERSARY. July 7, 1865. Four persons convicted of complicity with John Wilkes Booth in the assassination of President Abraham Lincoln on Apr 14, 1865, were hanged at Washington, DC. The four: Mary E. Surratt, Lewis Payne, David E. Harold and George A. Atzerodt. Mary Surratt became the first woman executed for a crime in the US. Her conviction was and is a subject of controversy, as the only crime she appeared to have committed was to own the boarding house where John Wilkes Booth planned the assassination.

LITCHFIELD OPEN HOUSE TOUR. July 7–8. Litchfield, CT. Preview tour and cocktail reception on Friday. Open house tour features an assortment of homes as well as additional attractions of historical and architectural significance. Annually, the second weekend in July. Est attendance: 1,500. For info: Connecticut Junior Republic, PO Box 161, Goshen Road, Litchfield, CT 06759. Phone: (860) 567-9423. Fax: (860) 567-8127. E-mail: info@ctjuniorrepublic.org. Web: www.ctjuniorrepublic.org and www.litchfieldct.com/cjr/tour.html.

LONDON TERRORIST BOMBINGS: ANNIVERSARY. July 7, 2005. In the most violent attack on London since WWII, terrorists exploded four bombs in quick succession on three subway cars and one bus, killing more than 50 people and injuring 700. A splinter group of Al Qaeda claimed responsibility.

MAINE POTATO BLOSSOM FESTIVAL. July 7–16. Fort Fairfield, ME. 59th annual. Promotes agricultural history and community activity. Fun for the whole family. Parade, music and much more. Est attendance: 35,000. For info: Fort Fairfield Chamber of Commerce, 232 Main St, Ste 4, Fort Fairfield, ME 04742. Phone: (207) 472-3802. Fax: (207) 472-3886. E-mail: ffcc@mfx.net. Web: www.potatoblossom.org.

MICHIGAN STORYTELLERS FESTIVAL. July 7–8. Flint, MI. Storytelling performances, workshops and swaps come together for family fun and professional support at this 25th annual event. Est attendance: 2,000. For info: Flint Public Library, 1026 E Kearsley, Flint, MI 48502. Phone: (810) 232-7111. Fax: (810) 249-2635. E-mail: drubey@flint.lib.mi.us.

MOTHER FRANCES XAVIER CABRINI CANONIZED: 60th ANNIVERSARY. July 7, 1946. Pope Pius XII presided over the canonization ceremonies for Mother Frances Xavier Cabrini, as she became the first American to be canonized. She was the founder of the Missionary Sisters of the Sacred Heart of Jesus, and her principal shrine is at Mother Cabrini High School, New York, NY. Cabrini was born at Lombardy, Italy, July 15, 1850 and died at Chicago, IL, Dec 22, 1917. Her feast day is celebrated on Dec 22.

NEPAL: BIRTHDAY OF HIS MAJESTY THE KING. July 7. National holiday of Nepal commemorating the birth of King Gyanendra in 1946.

NEWPORT MUSIC FESTIVAL. July 7–23. Newport, RI. Three, four and even five concerts held daily in Newport's fabled mansions featuring unique chamber music programs, American debuts, world-class artists and special events. Est attendance: 27,000. For info: Dr. Mark P. Malkovich III, Gen Dir, The Newport Music Festival, PO Box 3300, Newport, RI 02840-0992. Phone: (401) 846-1133. Box Office Phone: (401) 849-0700. Fax: (401) 849-1857. E-mail: staff@newportmusic.org. Web: www.newportmusic.org.

PAIGE, LEROY ROBERT (SATCHEL): 100th BIRTH ANNIVERSARY. July 7, 1906. Baseball Hall of Fame pitcher born at Mobile, AL. Paige was the greatest attraction in the Negro Leagues and was also, at age 42, the first black pitcher in the American League. Inducted into the Hall of Fame in 1971. Died at Kansas City, MO, June 8, 1982.

PORTLAND HISTORIC RACES. July 7–9. Portland International Raceway, Portland, OR. Featuring racing by some of the most celebrated vintage cars in history. Nearly 250 prestigious cars are divided into groups according to their age and horsepower to compete on the raceway's 1.95-mile track. Annually, the second weekend in July. Est attendance: 10,000. For info: Chris Crabb, Crabbsoup Public Relations, 4906 NE Siskiyou St, Portland, OR 97213. Phone: (503) 314-7583. E-mail: media@portlandhistorics.com. Web: www.portlandhistorics.com.

RIVERWALK FESTIVAL. July 7–8. Riverwalk Plaza, Lowell, MI. A fun-filled family festival featuring the Brian Mead Memorial Cruise-in, a pet parade, pontoon rides, arts & crafts, children's area, historic walking tours and river tour, kayak race and other kayak fun, food booths, live entertainment, a health and fitness fair, parade, $1,500 Duck Race, Riverwalk concert, fireworks and more. Est attendance: 8,000. For info: Lowell Area Chamber of Commerce, PO Box 224, Lowell, MI 49331. Phone: (616) 897-9161. Fax: (616) 897-9101. E-mail: info@lowellchamber.org. Web: www.lowellchamber.org.

"RYAN'S HOPE" TV PREMIERE: ANNIVERSARY. July 7, 1975. This ABC soap ran until 1989 and was set mostly at the fictional Ryan's Tavern or Riverside Hospital at New York City. The show depicted the lives of the ardently Irish Ryan family. The original cast included Faith Catlin, Justin Deas, Bernard Barrow, Helen Gallagher, Michael Hawkins, Ilene Kristen, Malcom Groome and Kate Mulgrew. Marg Helgenberger, Nell Carter, Yasmine Bleeth, Gloria DeHaven, Corbin Bernsen and Grant Show were among the show's other regulars.

SLOW PITCH SOFTBALL TOURNAMENT. July 7–9. Elm Park, Williamsport, PA. 33rd annual charitable tournament with 40 teams. Sponsor: Yuengling Mid-State Beverage Co. Est attendance: 8,500. For info: Don Phillips, 532 Sylvan Dr, South Williamsport, PA 17702. Phone: (570) 322-3331 or (570) 777-0165. E-mail: Phillips828@aol.com.

July *2006*	S	M	T	W	T	F	S
							1
	2	3	4	5	6	7	8
	9	10	11	12	13	14	15
	16	17	18	19	20	21	22
	23	24	25	26	27	28	29
	30	31					

SOLOMON ISLANDS: INDEPENDENCE DAY: ANNIVERSARY. July 7. National holiday. Commemorates independence from Britain in 1978.

SPAIN: RUNNING OF THE BULLS. July 7–14. Pamplona, Spain. Event made famous by Hemingway in his novel *The Sun Also Rises*, in which young men run through the streets of Pamplona chased by bulls from the bull ring. Part of the festival of San Fermin.

STATE GAMES OF OREGON. July 7–9. Portland, OR. Oregon's Olympic-style amateur sports festival. Normally, the first weekend after July 4. Est attendance: 17,500. For info: Dan Duffy, Exec Dir, State Games of Oregon, 4840 SW Western Ave, Ste 900, Beaverton, OR 97005. Phone: (503) 520-1319. Fax: (503) 520-9747. E-mail: info@stategamesoforegon.org. Web: www.stategamesoforegon.org.

TANZANIA: SABA SABA DAY. July 7. Tanzania's mainland ruling party, TANU, was formed on this day in 1954. Saba Saba means "Seven-Seven."

WAYNE CHICKEN DAYS. July 7–8. Wayne, NE. To allow humankind to pay tribute to chickenkind (without laying the proverbial egg). Parade, National Cluck-Off, Hard-Boiled Egg Eating Contest, craft vendors and musical entertainment. Est attendance: 10,000. For info: Wayne Area Chamber of Commerce, 108 W 3rd St, Wayne, NE 68787. Phone: (402) 375-2240. E-mail: waynechamber@hotmail.com. Web: www.chickenshow.com.

BIRTHDAYS TODAY

Billy Campbell, 47, actor ("Once and Again"), born Charlottesville, VA, July 7, 1959.

Pierre Cardin, 84, fashion designer, born Venice, Italy, July 7, 1922.

Shelley Duvall, 57, actress (*Popeye, Nashville, Roxanne*), born Houston, TX, July 7, 1949.

Jorja Fox, 38, actress ("CSI," "ER"), born New York, NY, July 7, 1968.

Michelle Kwan, 26, figure skater, born Torrance, CA, July 7, 1980.

Lisa Leslie, 34, WNBA player, born Inglewood, CA, July 7, 1972.

Gian Carlo Menotti, 95, composer, born Cadigliano, Italy, July 7, 1911.

Joe Sakic, 37, hockey player, born Burnaby, BC, Canada, July 7, 1969.

Ralph Lee Sampson, 46, former basketball player, born Harrisonburg, VA, July 7, 1960.

Doc Severinsen, 79, composer, conductor, musician (former bandleader on "The Tonight Show"), born Arlington, OR, July 7, 1927.

Ringo Starr, 66, singer, musician (The Beatles), born Richard Starkey at Liverpool, England, July 7, 1940.

JULY 8 — SATURDAY
Day 189 — 176 Remaining

ART FAIR ON THE SQUARE. July 8–9. Madison, WI. This is one of the largest and most popular juried art fairs in the Midwest, with nearly 500 artists from around the country selling their works. The fair occupies eight blocks around Madison's state capitol building and attracts large crowds. There's also entertainment and lots of food. For info: Madison Museum of Contemporary Art, 222 W Washington Ave, Ste 350, Madison, WI 53703. Phone: (608) 257-0158. E-mail: artfair@mmoca.org. Web: www.mmoca.org.

ASPINWALL CROSSES US ON HORSEBACK: 95th ANNIVERSARY. July 8, 1911. Nan Jane Aspinwall rode into New York City carrying a letter to Mayor William Jay Gaynor from San Francisco Mayor Patrick Henry McCarthy, becoming the first woman to cross the US on horseback. She began her trip in San Francisco on Sept 1, 1910, and covered 4,500 miles in 301 days.

BON ODORI "FESTIVAL OF THE LANTERNS." July 8. Midwest Buddhist Temple, Chicago, IL. One hundred performers, most clad in colorful kimonos, dance in celebration to music of different prefectures of Japan. The beat of the huge *taiko* (drum) helps keep tempo. Dances are performed outdoors, and public participation is encouraged. 8 PM. Est attendance: 750. For info: Office Secy, Midwest Buddhist Temple, 435 W Menomonee St, Chicago, IL 60614. Phone: (312) 943-7801. Fax: (312) 943-8069.

CANADA: HARRISON FESTIVAL OF THE ARTS. July 8–16. Harrison Hot Springs, BC. A celebration of world music, dance, theater and visual art including a large outdoor art market. Various venues throughout the village. Variety of activities for the entire family. Est attendance: 12,000. For info: Ed Stenson, Gen Mgr, Harrison Fest, Box 399, Harrison Hot Springs, BC, Canada V0M 1K0. Phone: (604) 796-3664. Fax: (604) 796-3694. E-mail: info@harrisonfestival.com. Web: www.harrison festival.com.

CHILDREN'S CELEBRATION. July 8. Island Park, Springfield, OR. Bring your family for a fun-filled day of activity and excitement. Island Park will be transformed into a child's world of life-size characters, creative craft booths, magnificent music, on-stage entertainment and demonstrations and fantastic foods. The dozens of booths and activities range from a petting zoo to exploring the universe. Annually, the second Saturday in July. Est attendance: 6,500. For info: Willamalane Park and Recreation District, 200 South Mill St, Springfield, OR 97477. Phone: (541) 736-4544. Web: www.willamalane.org.

CORN HILL ARTS FESTIVAL. July 8–9. Corn Hill neighborhood, Rochester, NY. Fine arts and crafts show organized by neighborhood residents for more than 37 years. Food and music from around the world, live entertainment, activities for children. All proceeds are reinvested in neighborhood projects. Annually, the first weekend following the 4th of July. Est attendance: 250,000. For info: Corn Hill Arts Festival, 133 S Fitzhugh St, Rochester, NY 14608. Phone: (585) 262-3142. Fax: (585) 546-4788. E-mail: chna@cornhill.org. Web: www.cornhill.org.

DECLARATION OF INDEPENDENCE FIRST PUBLIC READING: ANNIVERSARY. July 8, 1776. Colonel John Nixon read the Declaration of Independence to the assembled residents at Philadelphia's Independence Square.

ECKSTINE, BILLY: BIRTH ANNIVERSARY. July 8, 1914. Bandleader and bass-baritone singer Billy Eckstine was born William Clarence Eckstein at Pittsburgh, PA. After performing with the Earl Hines band for almost 20 years, Eckstine formed his own band in 1944. At one time or another the band's ranks included Charlie Parker, Dizzy Gillespie, Miles Davis, Fats Navarro, Dexter Gordon, Gene Ammons, Art Blakey and vocalist Sarah Vaughan—some of the greatest bebop musicians of all time. Among Eckstine's hits were "Fools Rush In," "Everything I Have Is Yours," "My Foolish Heart," "Blue Moon" and "Body and Soul." Billy Eckstine died Mar 8, 1993, at Pittsburgh, PA.

JOHNSON, PHILLIP: 100th BIRTH ANNIVERSARY. July 8, 1906. Postmodern architect who promoted the International Style. He was director of the Department of Architecture of New York's Museum of Modern Art, worked with Mies van der Rohe on the Seagram Building at New York City and designed his own "Glass House" at New Canaan, CT. Born at Cleveland, OH, and died Jan 25, 2005, in his home at New Canaan, CT.

KIM IL SUNG: DEATH ANNIVERSARY. July 8, 1994. President Kim Il Sung, the only leader in the history of North Korea, died just a few weeks before an historic summit with the president of South Korea was to take place, at Pyongyang, North Korea. A Stalinist-styled dictator, born at Man'gyandae, Korea, Apr 15, 1912, Kim had created a godlike personality cult surrounding himself and his son and presumed heir apparent Kim Jong Il. His death came at a crucial time in world politics. North Korea and the US had recently cooled rhetoric regarding North Korea's nuclear program and had begun further talks just hours prior to the announcement of Kim's death. The North-South Summit and the US–North Korean talks were postponed.

MOULIN, JEAN: DEATH ANNIVERSARY. July 8, 1943. Jean Moulin, a Free French representative, born at Beziers, France, June 20, 1899, was parachuted into occupied France on Jan 1, 1942, with the task of uniting the underground resistance. Moulin had with him (in the false bottom of a matchbox) a personal message of admiration for the resistance from General Charles DeGaulle. On May 27, 1943, the underground agreed to the creation of a National Resistance Council with Moulin as president. A month later he was arrested at Lyon by the Gestapo. He was tortured for 11 days but betrayed no one. Moulin died on a train while being transferred by the Nazis to a concentration camp.

OLIVE BRANCH PETITION: ANNIVERSARY. July 8, 1775. Representatives of New Hampshire, Massachusetts Bay, Rhode Island, Providence, Connecticut, New York, New Jersey, Pennsylvania, Delaware, Maryland, Virginia, North Carolina and South Carolina signed a petition from the Congress to King George III, a final attempt by moderates in the Second Continental Congress to avoid a complete break with England.

ROCKEFELLER, NELSON ALDRICH: BIRTH ANNIVERSARY. July 8, 1908. Born at Bar Harbor, ME. Governor of New York state (1958–73). Nominated as vice president by President Ford, Aug 20, 1974, under provisions of the 25th Amendment. Sworn in Dec 19, 1974, after confirmation by the Senate and served until Jan 20, 1977. Died at New York, NY, Jan 26, 1979. Rockefeller was the second person to become vice president without having been elected (Gerald R. Ford was the first).

SCUD DAY (SAVOR THE COMIC, UNPLUG THE DRAMA). July 8. A day to remind people of the benefits of spending more time in the Comic Zone and less in the Drama Zone. For info: Stephanie West Allen, PO Box 9311, Denver, CO 80209. Phone: (303) 742-4790. E-mail: stephanie@allen-nichols.com. Web: www.allen-nichols.com.

SODBUSTER DAYS. July 8–9. Fort Ransom State Park, Fort Ransom, ND. Remember the way things were done in rural North Dakota during the early 1920s with shelling corn by hand, rope weaving, horse-drawn plowing and haying. Ladies' demonstrations, kids games, live music. Located along the Sheyenne River Valley National Scenic Byway. Est attendance: 3,000. For info: Fort Ransom State Park, 5981 Walt Hjelle Parkway, Ft Ransom, ND 58033-9712. Phone: (701) 973-4331. Fax: (701) 973-4151.

STONE HOUSE DAY. July 8. Hurley, NY. Tour six to nine privately owned, 250-plus-year-old stone houses, six within a 150-yard radius. Annually, the second Saturday in July. Est attendance: 1,000. For info: Stone House Day, Hurley Reformed Church, PO Box 328, Hurley, NY 12443. Phone: (845) 331-4121. E-mail: hrchurch@ulster.net.

THREE RIVERS FESTIVAL. July 8–16. Fort Wayne, IN. A citywide extravaganza of more than 200 events including a parade, food, juried art show, concerts, children's events and fireworks. Est attendance: 500,000. For info: Three Rivers Festival, 102 Three Rivers North, Fort Wayne, IN 46802. Phone: (260) 426-5556. Fax: (260) 420-8611. Web: www.threeriversfestival.org.

TIVOLI-VIKING DAYS AT THE NORDIC HERITAGE MUSEUM. July 8–9. Nordic Heritage Museum, Seattle, WA. A two-day outdoor Scandinavian festival featuring crafts, foods, entertainment and children's activities. Swedish pancake breakfast Saturday and Sunday mornings, salmon dinner Saturday afternoon and food booths throughout both days. Viking crafts and demonstrations. Est attendance: 3,500. For info: Marianne Forssblad, Dir, Nordic Heritage Museum, 3014 NW 67th St, Seattle, WA 98117. Phone: (206) 789-5707. Fax: (206) 789-3271.

TOMS RIVER SEAPORT SOCIETY WOODEN BOAT FESTIVAL. July 8–9. Toms River, NJ. 28th annual. The Wooden Boat Festival is a family event designed to celebrate the glory and history of wooden boats. For info: Toms River Seaport Society & Maritime Museum, PO Box 1111, Toms River, NJ 08754-1111. Phone: (732) 349-9209.

TUPPER LAKE WOODSMEN'S DAYS (WITH CHAINSAW SCULPTURING CONTEST). July 8–9. Tupper Lake, NY. Competitions for woodsmen and lumberjacks—including horse pulls. Includes the annual Northeast Regional Chainsaw Sculpturing Contest. Annually, the second weekend in July. Est attendance: 10,000. For info: Tupper Lake Woodsmen's Assn, PO Box 759, Tupper Lake, NY 12986. Phone: (518) 359-9444. Fax: (518) 359-8244. Web: www.woodsmendays.com.

WORLD FOLKFEST. July 8–15. Springville, UT. 21st annual. Large international folk dance event. Est attendance: 20,000. For info: Springville World Folkfest, PO Box 306, 50 S Main, Springville, UT 84663. Phone: (801) 489-2726. Fax: (801) 489-4811. E-mail: folkfest@springville.org. Web: www.springville.org.

BIRTHDAYS TODAY

Kevin Bacon, 48, actor (*A Few Good Men, Apollo 13*), born Philadelphia, PA, July 8, 1958.

Raffi Cavoukian, 58, children's singer and songwriter, born Cairo, Egypt, July 8, 1948.

Billy Crudup, 38, actor (*Sleepers, Almost Famous*), born Manhasset, NY, July 8, 1968.

Kim Darby, 58, actress ("Rich Man, Poor Man," *True Grit*), born Los Angeles, CA, July 8, 1948.

Cynthia Gregory, 60, ballerina, born Los Angeles, CA, July 8, 1946.

Beck Hansen, 36, rock singer/songwriter, born Beck David Campbell at Los Angeles, CA, July 8, 1970.

Anjelica Huston, 55, actress (Oscar for *Prizzi's Honor; The Addams Family*), born Los Angeles, CA, July 8, 1951.

Steve Lawrence, 71, singer ("Party Doll," "Go Away Little Girl"), born Sidney Liebowitz at New York, NY, July 8, 1935.

Jeffrey Tambor, 62, actor ("Hill Street Blues," "The Larry Sanders Show," *City Slickers*), born San Francisco, CA, July 8, 1944.

Alyce Faye Wattleton, 63, former executive director of Planned Parenthood Federation, born St. Louis, MO, July 8, 1943.

	S	M	T	W	T	F	S
							1
July	2	3	4	5	6	7	8
2006	9	10	11	12	13	14	15
	16	17	18	19	20	21	22
	23	24	25	26	27	28	29
	30	31					

JULY 9 — SUNDAY
Day 190 — 175 Remaining

ALASKA FLAG DAY CELEBRATION. July 9, 1927. This day celebrates the first time Alaska's flag was unfurled over the Jesse Lee Home at Seward, AK. In 1927 Territorial Governor George Parks announced a contest in which children all over Alaska in grades 7–12 were encouraged to design Alaska's flag. The winning flag was designed by John Ben (Benny) Benson, a resident of the Jesse Lee Home, an orphanage. He was the only child in US history to design a state flag. Each year this day is celebrated at Alaska Children's Services (formerly the Jesse Lee Home). Est attendance: 2,000. For info: Alaska Children's Services, 4600 Abbott Rd, Anchorage, AK 99507. Phone: (907) 346-2101. E-mail: akchild@ak.net. Web: www.acs.ak.org.

ARGENTINA: INDEPENDENCE DAY. July 9. Anniversary of establishment of independent republic, with the declaration of independence from Spain in 1816.

EDWARDS, VINCE: BIRTH ANNIVERSARY. July 9, 1928. As Dr. Ben Casey on the 1961 television show "Ben Casey," Edwards's muscular, brooding charm made him an overnight sex symbol. Medical school enrollment increased while he was on the air. After conquering a gambling addiction, he became a real-life hero. Born at Brooklyn, NY, he died at Los Angeles, CA, Mar 11, 1996.

FAMILY, CAREER AND COMMUNITY LEADERS OF AMERICA NATIONAL LEADERSHIP MEETING. July 9–13. Nashville, TN. This meeting is a unique opportunity to gain a national perspective on FCCLA activities and issues, elect officers, receive specialized leadership training and enhance chapter activities. Est attendance: 5,800. For info: Beth Carpenter, Family, Career and Community Leaders of America, Inc, 1910 Association Dr, Reston, VA 20191. Phone: (703) 476-4900. Fax: (703) 860-2713. E-mail: natlhdqtrs@fcclainc.org. Web: www.fcclainc.org.

FIRST OPEN-HEART SURGERY: ANNIVERSARY. July 9, 1893. In Provident Hospital on Chicago's south side, black surgeon Dr. Daniel Hale Williams performed the first successful open-heart surgery.

FOURTEENTH AMENDMENT TO US CONSTITUTION RATIFIED: ANNIVERSARY. July 9, 1868. The 14th Amendment defined US citizenship and provided that no state shall have the right to abridge the rights of any citizen without due process and equal protection under the law. Coming three years after the Civil War, the 14th Amendment also included provisions for barring individuals who assisted in any rebellion or insurrection against the US from holding public office, and releasing federal and state governments from any financial liability incurred in the assistance of rebellion or insurrection against the US.

HIGHEST TSUNAMI IN RECORDED HISTORY: ANNIVERSARY. July 9, 1958. An earthquake registering at 8.3 on the Richter Scale caused a massive landslide at the head of Lituya Bay, AK, which in turn created a tsunami 1,700 feet—higher than the Sears Tower in Chicago (which is 1,450 feet). A 300-foot wave immediately followed, scouring bare about four to five square miles of land on both sides of the bay. Of three boats anchored at this remote spot, one was sunk with the loss of two lives; miraculously, the other two boats with their passengers survived the powerful waves.

HOWE, ELIAS: BIRTH ANNIVERSARY. July 9, 1819. American inventor of the sewing machine. Born at Spencer, MA, he died Oct 3, 1867, at Brooklyn, NY.

MARTYRDOM OF THE BAB. July 9. Baha'i observance of the anniversary of the execution by a firing squad, July 9, 1850, at Tabriz, Persia, of the 30-year-old Siyyid Ali Muhammed, the Bab (prophet-herald of the Baha'i Faith). One of the nine days of the year when Baha'is suspend work. For info: Baha'is of the US, Office of Communications, 1233 Central St, Evanston, IL 60201. Phone: (847) 733-3411. Fax: (847) 869-0247. E-mail: ooc@usbnc.org. Web: www.us.bahai.org.

MOROCCO: YOUTH DAY. July 9. National holiday. On the birthday in 1929 of King Hassan II.

NATIONAL FARRIER'S WEEK. July 9–15. A salute from horse owners to the men and women who keep their horses shod and equine feet and legs in top-notch condition. Annually, the second or third week in July. For info: Frank Lessiter, American Farriers Journal, PO Box 624, Brookfield, WI 53008-0624. Phone: (262) 782-4480. Fax: (262) 782-1252. E-mail: lesspub@aol.com.

NATIONAL THERAPEUTIC RECREATION WEEK. July 9–15. To increase awareness of therapeutic recreation programs and services, and to expand leisure opportunities for individuals with disabilities in their local communities. Annually, the second full week in July. For info: Natl Therapeutic Recreation Society, Ahren's NRPA Institute, 22377 Belmont Ridge Rd, Ashburn, VA 20148. Phone: (703) 858-2153. Web: www.nrpa.org.

OLD MISSION HISTORIC SKILLS FAIR. July 9. Old Mission State Park, Cataldo, ID. An event featuring old-fashioned skills such as spinning, quilting and black powder cannon demonstrations. Annually, the second Sunday of July. Est attendance: 2,000. For info: Bill Scudder, Park Mgr, Old Mission State Park, PO Box 30, Cataldo, ID 83810-0030. Phone: (208) 682-3814. Fax: (208) 682-4032. E-mail: old@idpr.state.id.us.

RADCLIFFE, ANN WARD: BIRTH ANNIVERSARY. July 9, 1764. English novelist famous for her gothic novels (fiction works especially popular in the late 18th and early 19th centuries). Among her works are *The Romance of the Forest, The Mysteries of Udolpho* and *The Italian*. She was born at London, England, and died there Feb 7, 1823.

RESPIGHI, OTTORINO: BIRTH ANNIVERSARY. July 9, 1879. Italian composer (*The Fountains of Rome*) born at Bologna, Italy. He died at Rome, Apr 18, 1936.

RUSSELL-EINSTEIN MANIFESTO: ANNIVERSARY. July 9, 1955. Philosopher Bertrand Russell released this plea, signed by 11 prominent scientists, three months after Albert Einstein's death. Einstein had agreed to put his name to it in his final days. The manifesto urged nations to find peaceful ways to settle differences and to renounce the use of nuclear weapons, which only promised "universal death."

SINCLAIR LEWIS DAYS. July 9–16. Sauk Centre, MN. Parade, kids activities, dance, fireworks, Miss Sauk Centre pageant, flea market, craft sale and Heart of Lakes Bike Tour in Sinclair Lewis's hometown. Est attendance: 10,000. For info: Sauk Centre Chamber of Commerce, PO Box 222, Sauk Centre, MN 56378. Phone: (320) 352-5201. Fax: (320) 352-5202. E-mail: chamber@saukcentrechamber.com. Web: www.saukcentrechamber.com.

SPORTS CLICHÉ WEEK. July 9–15. This week honors the use of sports clichés by fans, athletes, sports announcers and sports writers. Annually, the second week of July. For info: Don Powell, PhD, 30445 Northwestern Hwy, Ste 350, Farmington Hills, MI 48334. Phone: (248) 539-1800. Fax: (248) 539-1808. E-mail: info@bestsportscliches.com. Web: www.bestsportscliches.com.

TAKE CHARGE OF CHANGE WEEK. July 9–15. To increase awareness of the individual's power to control his own destiny, ChangeWorks will sponsor a series of events demonstrating the principles of taking charge of the changes that affect each of us. You can reduce stress and improve the quality of your life when you put yourself in the driver's seat. Learn how to accept the change you cannot control, manage the change you can and make change a positive force in your life. Free articles for publishers and webmasters at IdeaLady.com/content.htm. For info: Cathy Stucker, Special Interests Publishing, 4646 Hwy 6, PMB 123, Sugar Land, TX 77478. Phone: (281) 265-7342. E-mail: cathy@idealady.com. Web: www.idealady.com.

BIRTHDAYS TODAY

Brian Dennehy, 68, actor (Tony for *Long Day's Journey into Night*), born Bridgeport, CT, July 9, 1938.

Margaret Gillis, 53, dancer, choreographer, born Montreal, QC, Canada, July 9, 1953.

Lindsey Graham, 51, US Senator (R, South Carolina), born Pickens County, SC, July 9, 1955.

James Hampton, 70, actor ("F Troop," "Love, American Style"), born Oklahoma City, OK, July 9, 1936.

Tom Hanks, 50, actor (*Saving Private Ryan, Cast Away*; Oscars for *Philadelphia, Forrest Gump*), born Concord, CA, July 9, 1956.

David Hockney, 69, artist, born Bradford, England, July 9, 1937.

Mathilde Krim, 80, geneticist, philanthropist, born Como, Italy, July 9, 1926.

Courtney Love, 41, singer ("Live Through This"), actress (*The People vs. Larry Flynt*), born San Francisco, CA, July 9, 1965.

Kelly McGillis, 49, actress (*Witness, Top Gun, The Accused*), born Newport Beach, CA, July 9, 1957.

Donald Rumsfeld, 74, US Secretary of Defense (Ford and George W. Bush administrations), born Evanston, IL, July 9, 1932.

Fred Savage, 30, actor ("The Wonder Years," "Working," *The Princess Bride*), born Highland Park, IL, July 9, 1976.

Orenthal James (O.J.) Simpson, 59, former sportscaster and actor, Hall of Fame football player, born San Francisco, CA, July 9, 1947.

Jimmy Smits, 51, actor (*Glitz*, "LA Law," "NYPD Blue"), born New York, NY, July 9, 1955.

John Tesh, 54, TV host ("Entertainment Tonight"), composer, born Garden City, NY, July 9, 1952.

JULY 10 — MONDAY

Day 191 — 174 Remaining

ALLIED INVASION OF SICILY: ANNIVERSARY. July 10, 1943. Operation Husky, the Allied infantry attack on Italy, began on the island of Sicily. The British entry into Syracuse was the first Allied success in Europe. General Dwight D. Eisenhower, the Allied Commander-in-Chief, described the invasion as "the first page in the liberation of the European Continent."

ASH LAWN OPERA FESTIVAL. July 10–Aug 15 (tentative). Ash Lawn–Highland, Charlottesville, VA. Established in 1978, Ash Lawn Opera Festival presents opera in English, musical theatre, and concerts at the beautiful Boxwood Gardens of Ash Lawn–Highland, home of President James Monroe. Est attendance: 12,000. For info: Ash Lawn Opera Festival, 2000 Holiday Dr, Ste 100, Charlottesville, VA 22901. Phone: (434) 293-4500. Fax: (434) 293-0736. E-mail: info@ashlawnopera.org. Web: www.ashlawnopera.org.

ASHE, ARTHUR: BIRTH ANNIVERSARY. July 10, 1943. Born at Richmond, VA, Arthur Ashe became a legend for his list of firsts as a black tennis player. Ashe was chosen for the US Davis Cup team in 1963 and became captain in 1980. He won the US men's singles championship and US Open in 1968 and in 1975 the men's singles at Wimbledon. Ashe won a total of 33 career titles. In 1985 he was inducted into the International Tennis Hall of Fame. He helped create inner-city tennis programs for youth and wrote the three-volume *A Hard Road to Glory: A History of the African-American Athlete*. Ashe announced Apr 8, 1992, that he probably contracted HIV through a transfusion during bypass surgery in 1983. In September 1992 he began a $5 million fund-raising effort on behalf of the Arthur Ashe Foundation for the Defeat of AIDS and campaigned for public awareness regarding the AIDS epidemic. He died at New York, NY, Feb 6, 1993, from pneumonia.

BAHAMAS: INDEPENDENCE DAY: ANNIVERSARY.
July 10. Public holiday. At 12:01 AM in 1973 the Bahamas gained their independence after 250 years as a British Crown Colony.

"BASEBALL'S SAD LEXICON" PUBLISHED: ANNIVERSARY. July 10, 1910. Journalist Franklin P. Adams created the second best-known baseball poem (after "Casey at Bat") for the *New York Evening Mail*. Adams extolled the double-play trio of Chicago Cubs Joe Tinker (shortstop), Johnny Evers (second base) and Frank Chance (first base): "These are the saddest of possible words/'Tinker to Evers to Chance.'/Trio of bear cubs, and fleeter than birds,/Tinker and Evers and Chance./Ruthlessly pricking our gonfalon bubble,/Making a Giant hit into a double—/Words that are heavy with nothing but trouble:/'Tinker to Evers to Chance.'" See also: "Mighty Casey Has Struck Out: Anniversary" (June 3) and "Tinker To Evers To Chance: First Double Play Anniversary" (Sept 15).

BETHUNE, MARY McLEOD: BIRTH ANNIVERSARY.
July 10, 1875. Mary Jane McLeod Bethune was born at Mayesville, SC, the first in her family to be born free. Bethune became a teacher and in 1904 founded her own school in Florida, the Daytona Normal and Industrial School for Negro Girls. In 1931 the school merged with a local men's college, Cookman Institute, and was renamed Bethune-Cookman College. An adviser on minority affairs under President Franklin D. Roosevelt, she directed the Division of Negro Affairs of the National Youth Administration. She died May 18, 1955, at Daytona Beach, FL.

BORIS YELTSIN INAUGURATED AS RUSSIAN PRESIDENT: 15th ANNIVERSARY. July 10, 1991. Boris Yeltsin took the oath of office as the first popularly elected president in Russia's 1,000-year history. He defeated the Communist Party candidate resoundingly, establishing himself as a powerful political counterpoint to Mikhail Gorbachev, the president of the Soviet Union, of which Russia was the largest republic. Yeltsin had been dismissed from the Politburo in 1987 and resigned from the Communist Party in 1989. His popularity forced Gorbachev to make concessions to the republics in the new union treaty forming the Confederation of Independent States. Suffering from poor health, Yeltsin resigned as president at the end of 1999.

BRINKLEY, DAVID: BIRTH ANNIVERSARY. July 10, 1920. Born at Wilmington, NC, David Brinkley was one of the most recognizable faces in American broadcast journalism for more than 50 years. He got his start as NBC's first White House correspondent, and his outstanding coverage of the 1956 Democratic and Republican national conventions landed him the anchor job of NBC's nightly TV newscast, paired with Chet Huntley until 1970. In 1981 Brinkley moved to ABC, creating a Sunday morning interview show called "This Week with David Brinkley." His 1995 memoir was titled *David Brinkley: 11 Presidents, 4 Wars, 22 Political Conventions, 1 Moon Landing, 3 Assassinations, 2000 Weeks of News and Other Stuff on Television, and 18 Years of Growing Up in North Carolina*. He died on June 12, 2003, at Houston, TX.

CALVIN, JOHN: BIRTH ANNIVERSARY. July 10, 1509. Theologian, born at Noyon, France. Reformer and founder of Presbyterianism. Calvin died at Geneva, Switzerland, May 27, 1564.

CLERIHEW DAY. July 10. A day recognized in remembrance of Edmund Clerihew Bentley, journalist and author of the celebrated detective thriller *Trent's Last Case* (1912), but perhaps best known for his invention of a popular humorous verse form, the clerihew,

★ ★ ★

	S	M	T	W	T	F	S
July							1
2006	2	3	4	5	6	7	8
	9	10	11	12	13	14	15
	16	17	18	19	20	21	22
	23	24	25	26	27	28	29
	30	31					

consisting of two rhymed couplets of unequal length: Edmund's middle name was Clerihew/A name possessed by very few,/But verses by Mr Bentley/Succeeded eminently. Bentley was born at London, July 10, 1875, and died there, Mar 30, 1956.

DALLAS, GEORGE MIFFLIN: BIRTH ANNIVERSARY.
July 10, 1792. 11th vice president of the US (1845–49), born at Philadelphia, PA. Died there, Dec 31, 1864.

DON'T STEP ON A BEE DAY. July 10. Wellcat Holidays reminds kids and grown-ups that now is the time of year when going barefoot can mean getting stung by a bee. If you get stung tell Mom. [©2003 by WH.] For info: Michael Roy, Wellcat Holidays, 2418 Long Ln, Lebanon, PA 17046. Phone: (717) 279-0184. E-mail: info@wellcat.com. Web: www.wellcat.com.

GILBERT, JOHN: BIRTH ANNIVERSARY. July 10, 1897. Silent film star John Gilbert was born John Pringle at Logan, UT. In 1916 he had his billed screen debut in *Bullets and Brown Eyes*. In the early 1920s Gilbert had leading roles in several films, such as *The Merry Widow* and *The Big Parade*. Although he was a popular leading man, he was unable to succeed when sound came to movies and MGM released him from his contract in 1934. He died Jan 9, 1936, at Los Angeles, CA.

GWYNNE, FREDERICK HUBBARD: BIRTH ANNIVERSARY. July 10, 1926. Stage, screen and TV actor, best known for the TV roles Herman Munster in "The Munsters" and Officer Muldoon in "Car 54, Where Are You?" Gwynne was born at New York, NY, and died at Taneytown, MD, July 2, 1993.

INTERNATIONAL TOWN CRIERS DAY. July 10. A day recognizing the ancient and honorable art and tradition of town crying and the significant contribution town criers make to promoting their respective towns and cities. Annually, the second Monday in July. For info: David Phillips, Official Town Crier, Box 58, Dutton, ON, Canada N0L 1J0. Phone: (519) 762-2862. E-mail: tcrier@hotmail.com.

MOON PHASE: FULL MOON. July 10. Moon enters Full Moon phase at 11:02 PM, EDT.

NUDE RECREATION WEEK. July 10–16. Looking for a way to relax this summer? Why not go barefoot all over? Give nude recreation a try this week by attending special events at a clothing-optional beach, campground or resort near you. For info: The Naturist Society, Box 132, Oshkosh, WI 54903. Phone: (920) 426-5009. Fax: (920) 426-5184. E-mail: naturist@naturistsociety.com. Web: www.naturistsociety.com.

PROUST, MARCEL: BIRTH ANNIVERSARY. July 10, 1871. Famed French author, born at Auteuil, France. He gained an international reputation for his 13-volume masterpiece, *A la Recherche du Temps Perdu* (*Remembrance of Things Past*). "Happiness," he wrote in *The Past Recaptured*, "is beneficial for the body but it is grief that develops the powers of the mind." Proust died Nov 19, 1922, at Paris, France.

RAINBOW WARRIOR SINKING: ANNIVERSARY. July 10, 1985. The 160-ft ship, the *Rainbow Warrior*, operated by Greenpeace, an environmental organization, was sunk and a photographer aboard was killed while the ship was at Auckland, New Zealand. Reportedly a bomb was attached to the underside of the ship by saboteurs. The ship had been scheduled for use in a protest against nuclear tests in the South Pacific Ocean by the French government.

SPACE MILESTONE: *TELSTAR* (US). July 10, 1962. First privately owned satellite (American Telephone and Telegraph Company) and first satellite to relay live TV pictures across the Atlantic was launched.

SWITZERLAND: SEMPACH BATTLE COMMEMORATION. July 10. On the morning of the first Monday after July 4, the Lucerne government, military and student delegations and historical groups make their way in solemn procession to the battlefield of 1386. Commemorative address, battle report and solemn service in the chapel. Also an evening procession.

US AMATEUR PUBLIC LINKS (GOLF) CHAMPIONSHIP. July 10–15. Gold Mountain Golf Course, Bremerton, WA. For info: US Golf Assn, Golf House, PO Box 708, Championship Dept, Far Hills, NJ 07931. Phone: (908) 234-2300. Fax: (908) 234-9687. E-mail: usga@usga.org. Web: www.usga.org.

US LIFTS SANCTIONS AGAINST SOUTH AFRICA: 15th ANNIVERSARY. July 10, 1991. President George H.W. Bush lifted US trade and investment sanctions against South Africa. The sanctions had been imposed through the Comprehensive Anti-Apartheid Act of 1986, which Congress had passed to punish South Africa for policies of racial separation.

WHISTLER, JAMES ABBOTT McNEILL: BIRTH ANNIVERSARY. July 10, 1834. American painter (especially known for painting of his mother) born at Lowell, MA. Died at London, England, July 17, 1903. When a woman declared that a landscape reminded her of Whistler's paintings, he reportedly said, "Yes, madam, Nature is creeping up."

WYOMING: ADMISSION DAY: ANNIVERSARY. July 10. Became 44th state in 1890.

BIRTHDAYS TODAY

Andre Nolan Dawson, 52, former baseball player, born Miami, FL, July 10, 1954.

David Norman Dinkins, 79, former and first black mayor of New York City (D), born Trenton, NJ, July 10, 1927.

Ron Glass, 61, actor ("Barney Miller," voice on "Rugrats"), born Evansville, IN, July 10, 1945.

Arlo Guthrie, 59, singer ("The City of New Orleans," "Alice's Restaurant"), son of Woody Guthrie, born Brooklyn, NY, July 10, 1947.

Brad Henry, 43, Governor of Oklahoma (D), born Shawnee, OK, July 10, 1963.

Jerry Herman, 73, composer, lyricist, born New York, NY, July 10, 1933.

Sue Lyon, 60, actress (*Lolita, The Flim Flam Man*), born Davenport, IA, July 10, 1946.

Lawrence Pressman, 67, actor ("Doogie Howser MD," *The Hanoi Hilton*), born Cynthiana, KY, July 10, 1939.

Eunice Mary Kennedy Shriver, 85, founder of the Special Olympics, born Brookline, MA, July 10, 1921.

Jessica Simpson, 26, singer, television personality ("Newlyweds: Nick & Jessica"), born Abilene, TX, July 10, 1980.

Virginia Wade, 61, former tennis player, born Bournemouth, England, July 10, 1945.

JULY 11 — TUESDAY
Day 192 — 173 Remaining

ADAMS, JOHN QUINCY: BIRTH ANNIVERSARY. July 11, 1767. Sixth president of the US and the son of the second president, John Quincy Adams was born at Braintree, MA. After his single term as president, he served 17 years as a member of Congress from Plymouth, MA. He died Feb 23, 1848, at the House of Representatives (in the same room in which he had taken the presidential Oath of Office Mar 4, 1825). John Quincy Adams was the only president whose father had also been president of the US until George W. Bush became president in January 2001.

ALPENFEST. July 11–15. Gaylord, MI. Swiss-inspired festival that has something for the whole family. Annual traditions include "The World's Largest Coffee Break," Lampion Parade, Burning of the Boogg and a Grand Parade. Free food and entertainment daily, 100 arts & crafts booths, free kids' games, contests and a carnival. Est attendance: 50,000. For info: Kelly Combs, Alpenfest, PO Box 513, Gaylord, MI 49734. Phone: (800) 345-8621. Fax: (989) 732-7990. E-mail: events@gaylordmichigan.net. Web: www.gaylordchamber.com.

BABE RUTH'S DEBUT IN THE MAJORS: ANNIVERSARY. July 11, 1914. Babe Ruth made his debut in major league baseball when he took the mound in Fenway Park for the Boston Red Sox against the Cleveland Indians. Ruth was relieved for the last two innings but was the winning pitcher in a 4–3 game.

BOWDLER'S DAY. July 11. A day to remember the prudish medical doctor, Thomas Bowdler, born near Bath, England, on July 11, 1754. He gave up the practice of medicine and undertook the cleansing of the works of Shakespeare by removing all the words and expressions he considered to be indecent or impious. His *Family Shakespeare*, in 10 volumes, omitted all those words "which cannot with propriety be read aloud in a family." He also "purified" Edward Gibbon's *History of the Decline and Fall of the Roman Empire* and selections from the Old Testament. His name became synonymous with self-righteous expurgation, and the word *bowdlerize* has become part of the English language. Bowdler died at Rhyddings, in South Wales, Feb 24, 1825.

BURR-HAMILTON DUEL: ANNIVERSARY. July 11, 1804. US Vice President Aaron Burr shot and mortally wounded former Secretary of the Treasury (and primary author of *The Federalist Papers*) Alexander Hamilton in a duel at Weehawken, NJ, on this date. Hamilton had insulted Burr and refused to make a public apology. Hamilton died the next day. Although Burr returned to Washington to execute his duties as vice president, the duel ended his political career.

DAY OF THE FIVE BILLION: ANNIVERSARY. July 11, 1987. An eight-pound baby boy, Matej Gaspar, born at 1:35 AM, EST, at Zagreb, Yugoslavia, was proclaimed the five billionth inhabitant of Earth. The United Nations Fund for Population Activities, hoping to draw attention to population growth, proclaimed July 11 as "Day of the Five Billion," noting that 150 babies are born each minute. See also: "Day of the Six Billion: Anniversary" (Oct 12).

FINLAND: JYVASKYLA ARTS FESTIVAL. July 11–16. Jyvaskyla. Annual festival begun in 1955 for the purpose of stimulating discussion of contemporary philosophical and social concerns and building a bridge between different national and ethnic traditions. About 50 events including seminars, music, visual arts and film. Est attendance: 10,000. For info: Finnish Tourist Board, 655 Third Ave, New York, NY 10017. Phone: (212) 885-9700 or (358) (14) 624378. Fax: (358) (14) 214808. E-mail: kesa@jkl.fi. Web: www.jyvaskyla.fi/kesa.

MAJOR LEAGUE BASEBALL ALL-STAR GAME. July 11. PNC Park, Pittsburgh, PA. For info: Major League Baseball. E-mail: fanfeedback@website.mlb.com or tickets@website.mlb.com. Web: www.mlb.com.

MONGOLIA: NAADAM NATIONAL HOLIDAY. July 11. Public holiday. Commemorates overthrow of the feudal monarch in 1921.

NAPALM USED: ANNIVERSARY. July 11, 1945. The US dropped several thousand pounds of the recently developed weapon napalm on Japanese forces still holed up on Luzon in the Philippines. Napalm, which was later used heavily as a defoliant in Vietnam, was a thickener consisting of a mixture of aluminum soaps used to jell gasoline.

NATIONAL ASSOCIATION OF THE DEAF CONFERENCE. July 11–15. New Orleans Marriott, New Orleans, LA. Held biennially. 48th conference. For info: Natl Assn of the Deaf, 814 Thayer Ave, Silver Spring, MD 20910-4500. TTY: (301) 587-1789. Phone: (301) 587-1788. Fax: (301) 587-1791. E-mail: NAD info@nad.org. Web: www.nad.org.

"THE NEWLYWED GAME" TV PREMIERE: 40th ANNIVERSARY. July 11, 1966. Four newly married couples competed for prizes on this game show created by the inimitable Chuck Barris (mastermind of "The Gong Show"). The winners were determined by the couple that could best predict the responses of their respective spouses. Barris, Bob Eubanks and Paul Rodriguez have served as hosts.

NIAGARA MOVEMENT FOUNDED: ANNIVERSARY. July 11, 1905. Led by W.E.B. DuBois, 29 black intellectuals and activists founded the Niagara Movement at Niagara Falls, ON, Canada. The name of their movement alluded both to the location of their founding and to the "mighty current" of protest they hoped to undam. The movement disbanded in 1910, and the NAACP took over its goals.

SMITH, JAMES: 200th DEATH ANNIVERSARY. July 11, 1806. Signer of the Declaration of Independence, born at Ireland about 1719 (exact date unknown). Died at York, PA.

SPACE MILESTONE: *SKYLAB* (US): FALLS TO EARTH. July 11, 1979. The 82-ton spacecraft launched May 14, 1973, re-entered Earth's atmosphere. Expectation was that 20–25 tons probably would survive to hit Earth, including one piece of about 5,000 pounds. This generated intense international public interest in where it would fall. The chance that some person would be hit by a piece of *Skylab* was calculated at one in 152. Targets were drawn and *Skylab* parties were held but *Skylab* broke up and fell to Earth in a shower of pieces over the Indian Ocean and Australia, with no known casualties.

UNITED NATIONS: WORLD POPULATION DAY. July 11. In June 1989 the Governing Council of the United Nations Development Programme recommended that July 11 be observed by the international community as World Population Day. An outgrowth of the Day of the Five Billion (July 11, 1987), the Day seeks to focus public attention on the urgency and importance of population issues, particularly in the context of overall development plans and programs and the need to create solutions to these problems. For info: United Nations, Dept of Public Info, Public Inquiries Unit, RM GA-57, New York, NY 10017. Phone: (212) 963-4475. E-mail: inquiries@un.org.

WHITE, E.B.: BIRTH ANNIVERSARY. July 11, 1899. Versatile author of books for adults and children (*Charlotte's Web*) and *New Yorker* editor. Born at Mount Vernon, NY, White died at North Brooklyn, ME, Oct 1, 1985.

	S	**M**	**T**	**W**	**T**	**F**	**S**
July							1
2006	2	3	4	5	6	7	8
	9	10	11	12	13	14	15
	16	17	18	19	20	21	22
	23	24	25	26	27	28	29
	30	31					

Giorgio Armani, 70, fashion designer, born Romagna, Italy, July 11, 1936.

Harold Bloom, 76, literary critic, born New York, NY, July 11, 1930.

John Henson, 39, TV talk-show host ("Talk Soup"), born Stamford, CT, July 11, 1967.

Tab Hunter, 75, actor (*Damn Yankees*, "The Tab Hunter Show"), born Arthur Gelien at New York, NY, July 11, 1931.

Stephen Lang, 54, actor (*Last Exit to Brooklyn, Tombstone*), born Queens, NY, July 11, 1952.

Mark Lester, 48, actor (*Fahrenheit 451, Oliver*), born Oxford, England, July 11, 1958.

Al MacInnis, 43, hockey player, born Inverness, NS, Canada, July 11, 1963.

Theodore Maiman, 79, physicist, developed first working laser, born Los Angeles, CA, July 11, 1927.

Bonnie Pointer, 55, singer (Pointer Sisters, "Steam Heat"), born East Oakland, CA, July 11, 1951.

Michael Rosenbaum, 34, actor ("Smallville," *Sweet November*), born Oceanside, NJ, July 11, 1972.

Richie Sambora, 46, musician (Bon Jovi), born Amboy, NJ, July 11, 1960.

Leon Spinks, 53, former boxer, born St. Louis, MO, July 11, 1953.

Rod Strickland, 40, basketball player, born the Bronx, NY, July 11, 1966.

Beverly Todd, 60, actress, director, producer (*Baby Boom, Clara's Heart*), born Chicago, IL, July 11, 1946.

Suzanne Vega, 47, singer ("Luka"), born Santa Monica, CA, July 11, 1959.

Sela Ward, 50, actress ("Sisters," "Once and Again"), born Meridian, MS, July 11, 1956.

JULY 12 — WEDNESDAY

Day 193 — 172 Remaining

BATTLE OF KURSK: ANNIVERSARY. July 12, 1943. The largest tank battle in history took place outside the small village of Prohorovka, Russia. Nine hundred Russian tanks attacked an equal number of German Panther and Porsche tanks. Though the German equipment was larger, that advantage was lost in a close-range battle where they lacked maneuverability. When Hitler ordered a cease-fire, 300 German tanks remained strewn over the field.

BERLE, MILTON: BIRTH ANNIVERSARY. July 12, 1908. His nickname was "Mr Television," but Milton Berle had a long career as a vaudeville, film, radio and theater comedian as well. He was born Mendel Berlinger at Harlem, NY. He was popular before becoming the host of NBC's "Texaco Star Theater" in 1948, but that variety show made him a huge national star. Dressing in drag, rattling off corny jokes and drawing the day's biggest stars, "Uncle Miltie" made the show a television event until its end in 1953. He was one of the first seven inductees into the Academy of Television Arts and Sciences' TV Hall of Fame. Berle died Mar 27, 2002, at Los Angeles, CA.

De RITA, JOE: BIRTH ANNIVERSARY. July 12, 1909. American comedian Curly Joe De Rita was the last surviving member of the Three Stooges comedy team. He joined the team in 1959 after Joe Besser left. He appeared in *Have Rocket, Will Travel* (1959), *Snow White and the Three Stooges* (1961) and *The Outlaw Is Coming* (1965). Born at Philadelphia, PA, De Rita died July 3, 1993, at Los Angeles, CA.

DINOSAUR ROUNDUP RODEO. July 12–15. Vernal, UT. 56th annual presentation of one of the top PRCA rodeos, fun for the entire family. Est attendance: 10,000. For info: Vernal Chamber of Commerce, 134 W Main St, Vernal, UT 84078. Phone: (800) 421-9635 or (435) 789-1352.

"EVENING AT POPS" TV PREMIERE: ANNIVERSARY. July 12, 1970. PBS's popular concert series premiered with conductor Arthur Fiedler heading the Boston Pops Orchestra. Conductor/composer John Williams took over the post upon Fiedler's death in 1979; Keith Lockhart is the current conductor.

"FAMILY FEUD" TV PREMIERE: 30th ANNIVERSARY. July 12, 1976. From the production team of Mark Goodson and Bill Todman, this game show sets two families against each other to raise the greater number of points. The contestants have to predict the most common answers to a given survey question. Richard Dawson (TV's famous kissing host), the late Ray Combs, Louie Anderson and Richard Karn have been hosts.

FULLER, BUCKMINSTER: BIRTH ANNIVERSARY. July 12, 1895. Architect, inventor, engineer and philosopher, born Richard Buckminster Fuller at Milton, MA. His geodesic dome is one of the most important structural innovations of the 20th century. He died July 1, 1983, at Los Angeles, CA.

JONES WINS FIRST GRAND SLAM OF GOLF: ANNIVERSARY. July 12, 1930. Bobby Jones won the US Open Championship by two strokes over Macdonald Smith at the Interlachen Country Club at Hopkins, MN. Having already won the British Open, the British Amateur and the US Amateur, Jones became the only golfer to win the Grand Slam (the four major tournaments in one calendar year)—a term that had to be invented by sportswriters since no one had achieved that feat before.

KIRIBATI: INDEPENDENCE DAY. July 12. Republic of Kiribati attained independence from Britain in 1979. Formerly known as the Gilbert Islands.

"NORTHERN EXPOSURE" TV PREMIERE: ANNIVERSARY. July 12, 1990. CBS's comedy-drama was essentially a fish-out-of-water (or rather a New Yorker out of Manhattan) series. Dr. Joel Fleischman (Rob Morrow) was forced to practice medicine in remote Cicely, Alaska, to pay off his student loans. He gradually accepted his lot with the help of the town's quirky citizens who needed him because he was the only doctor in town. The show's cast featured Barry Corbin as Maurice Minnefield, a former NASA astronaut and Cicely's most prominent businessman, Janine Turner as bush pilot Maggie O'Connell, Elaine Miles as Joel's assistant Marilyn, Darren E. Burrows as Ed Chigliak, a half-Indian aspiring filmmaker, John Cullum as tavern owner Holling Vincoeur, Cynthia Geary as Holling's girlfriend and waitress Shelley Tambo, Peg Phillips as store proprietor Ruth-Anne and John Corbett as deejay Chris Stevens. The last episode aired in 1995.

NORTHERN IRELAND: ORANGEMEN'S DAY. July 12. National holiday commemorates Battle of Boyne, July 1 (OS), 1690, in which the forces of King William III of England, Prince of Orange, defeated those of James II, at Boyne River in Ireland. Ordinarily observed July 12. If July 12 is a Saturday or a Sunday the holiday observance is on the following Monday.

SAO TOME AND PRINCIPE: INDEPENDENCE DAY. July 12. National holiday observed. Gained independence from Portugal in 1975.

SPACE MILESTONE: *PHOBOS 2* (USSR). July 12, 1988. Sent back the first close-up photos of Phobos, one of two small moons of Mars. Launched from Soviet space probe in central Asia on July 12, 1988.

THOREAU, HENRY DAVID: BIRTH ANNIVERSARY. July 12, 1817. American author and philosopher, born at Concord, MA. Died there May 6, 1862. In *Walden* he wrote, "I frequently tramped eight or ten miles through the deepest snow to keep an appointment with a beechtree, or a yellow birch, or an old acquaintance among the pines."

TURNER'S FRONTIER ADDRESS: ANNIVERSARY. July 12, 1893. Historian Frederick Jackson Turner delivered his paper, "The Significance of the Frontier in American History," at a meeting of the American Historical Association at Chicago during the Columbian Exposition. Stating that the frontier was a spawning ground for many of the social and intellectual traits that made Americans different from Europeans, Turner saw the end of the frontier as a major break in the psychology of the nation. Turner's formalization of this idea came in part from his reading the *Extra Census Bulletin No. 2: Distribution of Population*

According to Density: 1890, which said that, "Up to and including 1890 the country had a frontier of settlement, but at present the unsettled area has been so broken into by isolated bodies of settlement that there can hardly be said to be a frontier line."

WEDGWOOD, JOSIAH: BIRTH ANNIVERSARY. July 12, 1730. Famed English pottery designer and manufacturer, born at Burslem, Staffordshire, England. Died at Etruria, Staffordshire, England, Jan 3, 1795.

WYANDOTTE STREET ART FAIR. July 12–15. Downtown Wyandotte, MI. More than 350 artists and craftspeople display and sell their wares. Also, music, street entertainers, Children's Emporium and sidewalk sales. Sponsored by Anheuser Busch. Est attendance: 250,000. For info: Leslie Lupo, Dir, 3131 Biddle Ave, Wyandotte, MI 48192. Phone: (734) 324-4506. Fax: (734) 324-4552.

BIRTHDAYS TODAY

Lisa Nicole Carson, 37, actress ("ER," "Ally McBeal"), born Brooklyn, NY, July 12, 1969.

Van Cliburn, 72, pianist, born Harvey Lavan Cliburn, Jr, at Shreveport, LA, July 12, 1934.

Bill Cosby, 68, comedian, actor (Emmys for "I Spy," "The Cosby Show"), born Philadelphia, PA, July 12, 1938.

Paul Guilfoyle, 51, actor ("CSI"), born Boston, MA, July 12, 1955.

Mel Harris, 49, actress ("Something So Right," "thirtysomething"), born Bethlehem, PA, July 12, 1957.

Cheryl Ladd, 54, actress ("Charlie's Angels," "Grace Kelly"), born Huron, SD, July 12, 1952.

Christine McVie, 63, singer, musician (Fleetwood Mac), born Birmingham, England, July 12, 1943.

Denise Nicholas, 61, actress ("Room 222," "In the Heat of the Night," *Let's Do It Again*), born Detroit, MI, July 12, 1945.

Jamey Sheridan, 55, actor ("Law & Order: Criminal Intent," *The House on Carroll Street*), born Pasadena, CA, July 12, 1951.

Richard Simmons, 58, TV personality, weight loss guru, author, born New Orleans, LA, July 12, 1948.

Erik Per Sullivan, 15, actor ("Malcolm in the Middle," *The Cider House Rules*), born Worcester, MA, July 12, 1991.

Rolonda Watts, 47, talk-show host ("Rolonda"), born Winston-Salem, NC, July 12, 1959.

Kristi Tsuya Yamaguchi, 35, Olympic gold medal figure skater, born Hayward, CA, July 12, 1971.

JULY 13 — THURSDAY

Day 194 — 171 Remaining

CANADA: JUST FOR LAUGHS: THE MONTREAL INTERNATIONAL COMEDY FESTIVAL. July 13–23. Montreal, QC. Make the trip to the worldwide capital of comedy! More than 1,000 artists from 19 countries play more than 2,000 shows and performances at indoor and outdoor venues that blanket the entire city. In the past, the Just for Laughs bilingual comedy marathon has featured some of the world's most impressive talent including Tim Allen, Jerry Seinfeld, Drew Carey, Kelsey Grammer, Rowan "Mr Bean" Atkinson, Jim Carrey and David Hyde Pierce, to name but a few. Est attendance: 1,700,000. For info: Just for Laughs Festival, 2101 St-Laurent Blvd, Montreal, QC, Canada H2X 2T5. Phone: (514) 845-3155 or (888) 244-3155. Fax: (514) 845-4140. E-mail: info@hahaha.com. Web: www.hahaha.com.

EMBRACE YOUR GEEKNESS DAY. July 13. Into dungeon games, comic books and doing vampire dress-up? Spend endless hours going strange places on the Internet? You're a geek, and this is the day to roar! [©2003 by WH.] For info: Thomas & Ruth Roy, Wellcat Holidays, 2418 Long Ln, Lebanon, PA 17046. Phone: (717) 279-0184. E-mail: info@wellcat.com. Web: www.wellcat.com.

FAST OF TAMMUZ. July 13. Jewish holiday. Hebrew calendar date: Tammuz 17, 5766. Shiva Asar B'Tammuz begins at first light of day and commemorates the first-century Roman siege that breached the walls of Jerusalem. Begins a three-week time of mourning.

FORREST, NATHAN BEDFORD: BIRTH ANNIVERSARY. July 13, 1821. Confederate cavalry commander whose birthday is observed in schools in Tennessee, Forrest was also one of the founders of the short-lived original Ku Klux Klan. Forrest was born at Bedford County, TN, and died Oct 29, 1877, at Memphis, TN.

FRANCE: NIGHT WATCH or LA RETRAITE AUX FLAMBEAUX. July 13. France. Celebrates eve of the Bastille's fall. On the eve of Bastille Day, there are parades and fireworks.

GRUNTLED WORKERS DAY. July 13. There's so much news about disgruntled workers that today's the day for Gruntled Workers to Unite! Drive to a fast-food restaurant and say, "Thanks, your service is fast, have a nice day." [©2003 by WH.] For info: Thomas & Ruth Roy, Wellcat Holidays, 2418 Long Ln, Lebanon, PA 17046. Phone: (717) 279-0184. E-mail: info@wellcat.com. Web: www.wellcat.com.

HODAG COUNTRY FESTIVAL. July 13–16. Hodag "50" Track, Rhinelander, WI. 29th anniversary country music festival, one of the oldest open-air festivals in the Midwest. Annually, the second full weekend in July. Est attendance: 70,000. For info: Diane Eckert, Hodag Country Fest, PO Box 1184, Rhinelander, WI 54501-1184. Phone: (715) 369-1300. Fax: (715) 362-3919. E-mail: hcf@hodag.com. Web: www.hodag.com.

HOT DOG NIGHT. July 13. Luverne, MN. More than 12,000 hot dogs are served free of charge, and free drink is also provided. Various demonstrations. Est attendance: 5,000. For info: Dave Smith, Exec Dir, Luverne Area Chamber of Commerce, 211 E Main, Luverne, MN 56156. Phone: (507) 283-4061. Fax: (507) 283-4061. E-mail: luvernechamber@iw.net. Web: www.luvernemn.com.

JAPAN: BON FESTIVAL (FEAST OF LANTERNS). July 13–15. Religious rites throughout Japan in memory of the dead, who, according to Buddhist belief, revisit Earth during this period. Lanterns are lighted for the souls. Spectacular bonfires in the shape of the character *dai* are burned on hillsides on the last day of the Bon or O-Bon Festival, bidding farewell to the spirits of the dead.

"LIVE AID" CONCERTS: ANNIVERSARY. July 13, 1985. Concerts at Philadelphia, PA, and London, England (Kennedy and Wembley stadiums) were seen by 162,000 attendees and an estimated 1.5 billion television viewers. Organized to raise funds for African famine relief; the musicians performed without a fee, and nearly $100 million was pledged toward aid to the hungry.

NORTHWEST ORDINANCE: ANNIVERSARY. July 13, 1787. The Northwest Ordinance, providing for government of the territory north of the Ohio River, became law. The ordinance guaranteed freedom of worship and the right to trial by jury, and it prohibited slavery.

OREGON TRAIL DAYS. July 13–16. Gering, NE. Oldest continuing celebration in state of Nebraska commemorating Oregon Trail. Parades, barbecues, street dances, International Food Fair, concert, Nebraska State CASI Chili Cookoff, musical plays and a Western art show highlight the annual celebration. Annually, the second full weekend in July. Est attendance: 30,000. For info: Event Coord, PO Box 222, Gering, NE 69341. Phone: (308) 436-4457. E-mail: info@oregontraildays.com. Web: www.oregontraildays.com.

TURKEY RAMA. July 13–15. McMinnville, OR. This annual event at McMinnville, once known as the Turkey Capital of the world, continues to include Famous Turkey BBQ, Biggest Turkey contest, vendor street sales, 8k fun run, carnival, entertainment. Est attendance: 25,000. For info: McMinnville Area Chamber of Commerce, 417 NW Adams, McMinnville, OR 97128. Phone: (503) 472-6196. Fax: (503) 472-6198. E-mail: chamberinfo@mcminnville.org. Web: www.mcminnville.org.

VIRGINIA LAKE FESTIVAL. July 13–15. Clarksville, VA. Fun-filled weekend with Pig Pickin, opening ceremonies on Friday; arts and crafts show, hot-air balloons, live entertainment for children and adults and fireworks on Saturday. Annually, the third weekend in July. Est attendance: 50,000. For info: Clarksville Lake Country Chamber of Commerce, 105 2nd St, Box 1017, Clarksville, VA 23927. Phone: (434) 374-2436 or (800) 557-5582. E-mail: clarksville@kerrlake.com. Web: www.clarksvilleva.org.

WORLD CUP INAUGURATED: ANNIVERSARY. July 13, 1930. The first World Cup soccer competition was held at Montevideo, Uruguay, with 14 countries participating. On July 30, Uruguay defeated Argentina by a score of 4–2 to take the Cup.

BIRTHDAYS TODAY

Cameron Crowe, 49, director, screenwriter (*Fast Times at Ridgemont High, Jerry Maguire,* Oscar for *Almost Famous*), born Palm Springs, CA, July 13, 1957.

Harrison Ford, 64, actor (*Witness, The Fugitive,* the first Star Wars trilogy, the Indiana Jones films), born Chicago, IL, July 13, 1942.

Robert Forster, 65, actor ("Banyon," *Diamond Men, Jackie Brown*), born Rochester, NY, July 13, 1941.

Jane Hamilton, 49, author (*A Map of the World, The Book of Ruth*), born Oak Park, IL, July 13, 1957.

John French (Jack) Kemp, 71, former US Secretary of Housing and Urban Development, former football player, born Los Angeles, CA, July 13, 1935.

Louise Mandrell, 52, country western singer, born Corpus Christi, TX, July 13, 1954.

Cheech Marin, 60, writer, actor (Cheech and Chong films, "Nash Bridges"), born Los Angeles, CA, July 13, 1946.

Roger McGuinn, 64, musician (The Byrds), born James Joseph McGuinn at Chicago, IL, July 13, 1942.

Erno Rubik, 62, inventor of the Rubik's Cube, born in a hospital air raid shelter, Budapest, Hungary, July 13, 1944.

Wole Soyinka, 72, Nobel Prize–winning author (*The Lion and the Jewel, The Strong Breed*), born Abeokuta, Nigeria, July 13, 1934.

Michael Spinks, 50, former boxer, born St. Louis, MO, July 13, 1956.

Patrick Stewart, 66, actor ("Star Trek: The Next Generation," *Excalibur, LA Story*), born Mirfield, England, July 13, 1940.

David Storey, 73, author, playwright (*The Performance of Small Firms*), born Wakefield, England, July 13, 1933.

Anthony Jerome ("Spud") Webb, 43, former basketball player, born Dallas, TX, July 13, 1963.

	S	M	T	W	T	F	S
July							1
	2	3	4	5	6	7	8
2006	9	10	11	12	13	14	15
	16	17	18	19	20	21	22
	23	24	25	26	27	28	29
	30	31					

JULY 14 — FRIDAY

Day 195 — 170 Remaining

BASCOM, FLORENCE: BIRTH ANNIVERSARY. July 14, 1862. After receiving her third bachelor's degree from the University of Wisconsin in 1884 and a master's degree in 1887, Florence Bascom entered Johns Hopkins University and received a doctorate in 1893. She taught at Ohio State and became a professor at Bryn Mawr. She also was the first woman appointed a geologist with the US Geological Survey, was associate editor of *American Geologist* (1890–1905) and became the first woman elected a Fellow of the Geological Society of America. Born at Williamstown, MA; died at Northampton, MA, June 18, 1945.

BASTILLE DAY CELEBRATION. July 14. Boston, MA. A street celebration with typical Parisian joie de vivre; dining and dancing under the stars. Est attendance: 3,000. For info: The French Library and Cultural Center/Alliance Française, 53 Marlborough St, Boston, MA 02116-2099. Phone: (617) 912-0400. Fax: (617) 912-0450. E-mail: info@frenchlib.org. Web: www.french lib.org.

BEREA CRAFT FESTIVAL. July 14–16. Berea, KY. Craftspeople from 20 states gather to exhibit, demonstrate and sell their work. Est attendance: 10,000. For info: Sandy Chowning, Berea Craft Enterprises, Box 128, Berea, KY 40403. Phone: (859) 986-2818.

BIG SKY STATE GAMES. July 14–16. Billings, MT. An Olympic-styled festival for Montana citizens. This statewide multisport program is designed to inspire people of all ages and skill levels to develop their physical and competitive abilities to the height of their potential through participation in fitness activities. There are 12,000 participants. Est attendance: 30,000. For info: Big Sky State Games, Box 7136, Billings, MT 59103-7136. Phone: (406) 254-7426. Fax: (406) 254-7439. E-mail: info@bigskygames .org. Web: www.bigskygames.org.

CANADA: COUNTRY GOOD TIMES. July 14–16. Wilberforce, ON. Family fun celebrating music and local musicians featuring amateur contest, flea market, carnival midway, vendors and bingo. Annually, the third weekend in July. Est attendance: 5,000. For info: Bancroft and Dist Chamber of Commerce, PO Box 539, Bancroft, ON, Canada K0L 1C0. Phone: (613) 332-1513. Fax: (613) 332-2119. E-mail: chamber@commerce.bancroft.on.ca. Web: www.bancroftdistrict.com.

CANADA: VANCOUVER FOLK MUSIC FESTIVAL. July 14–16. Jericho Beach Park, Vancouver, BC. Come and join in the musical festival which also features food booths, entertainment and much more. Est attendance: 30,000. For info: Vancouver Folk Music Festival, 207 W Hastings St, Ste 1114, Vancouver, BC, Canada V6B 1H7. Phone: (604) 681-5411. Fax: (604) 687-7167. E-mail: info@thefestival.bc.ca. Web: www.thefestival.bc .ca.

CARVEL, TOM: 100th BIRTH ANNIVERSARY. July 14, 1906. American inventor and businessman Tom Carvel was born Thomas Andreas Carvelas at Athens, Greece. He invented the machine that makes soft-serve ice cream (or frozen custard). His chain of ice cream stores began with a $15 loan and grew into the third-largest ice cream chain in America. He died Oct 21, 1990, at Pine Plains, NY.

CELEBRATION OF THE HORSE. July 14–16. Houston, TX. In honor of the human/equine bond and how horses affect people on an individual basis. Annually, the third weekend in July. For info: Tim Raisbeck, Charlotte's Saddlery, 11623A Katy Freeway, Houston, TX 77079. Phone: (281) 596-8225. Fax: (281) 596-8258. E-mail: csadd@charlottes-saddlery.com. Web: www .charlottes-saddlery.com.

CHAMBERSFEST. July 14–30. Chambersburg, PA. Annual Civil War festival including the Ray Depuy Gala Opening, Celebrate the Arts at Old Market Day, Civil War Seminar, Pet Parade and Almost Anything Goes Games. Est attendance: 10,000. For info: Melissa Knepper, Dir of Programs and Events, Greater Chambersburg Chamber of Commerce, 100 Lincoln Way East, Ste A, Chambersburg, PA 17201. Phone: (717) 264-7101. Fax: (717) 267-0399. E-mail: mknepper@chambersburg.org.

CHANCELLOR, JOHN: BIRTH ANNIVERSARY. July 14, 1927. Television broadcast journalist John Chancellor was born at Chicago, IL. He rose through the ranks at the *Chicago Sun-Times*, from copyboy to feature writer. Chancellor spent more than four decades with the NBC network, beginning in 1950. During that time, he took a two-year respite from journalism to serve President Lyndon Johnson as director of the Voice of America. Chancellor retired in 1993, but his distinctive, familiar voice was still heard, for example, when he narrated a PBS documentary in 1996. He died July 12, 1996, at Princeton, NJ.

CHILDREN'S PARTY AT GREEN ANIMALS. July 14. Green Animals Topiary Garden, Portsmouth, RI. Annual party for children and adults at Green Animals, a delightful topiary garden and children's toy museum. Party includes pony rides, games, clowns, refreshments, hot dogs, hamburgers and more. Annually, July 14. Est attendance: 1,500. For info: The Preservation Society of Newport County, 424 Bellevue Ave, Newport, RI 02840. Phone: (401) 847-1000. Web: www.NewportMansions.org.

DECOY AND WILDLIFE ART SHOW. July 14–16. Clayton Recreation Park Arena, Clayton, NY. 38th annual juried show. World championship wildlife carvers, artists, taxidermists, collectors and dealers. Events include hunting decoy contest, gunning rig contest, contemporary painting contest and silent auction. Displays of handcrafted wildlife from wood, silver, gold and pewter. Annually, the third weekend in July. Est attendance: 5,000. For info: Thousand Islands Museum, PO Box 27, Clayton, NY 13624. Phone: (315) 686-5794. Fax: (315) 686-4867. E-mail: info@timuseum.org. Web: www.timuseum.org.

EDWARDS, DOUGLAS: BIRTH ANNIVERSARY. July 14, 1917. American television journalist Douglas Edwards was born at Ada, OK. He began his career in radio, but in 1947 he became the first major announcer to move to television. He was anchor for CBS's first nightly news program, "Douglas Edwards with the News" (1948–62), where he gave memorable on-scene coverage of such events as the sinking of the *Andrea Doria* in 1956. Edwards worked for CBS until his retirement, two years before he died on Oct 13, 1990, at Sarasota, FL.

ENGLAND: BIRMINGHAM RIOT: ANNIVERSARY. July 14, 1791. Following a dinner celebrating the second anniversary of the fall of the Bastille, an angry mob rioted at Birmingham, England. The main target of their wrath was the home of scientist (discoverer of oxygen) Joseph Priestley, who was unpopular because of his religious views and his approval of the American and French revolutionary causes. The mob ruled Birmingham for three days, burning Priestley's home and laboratory as well as the homes of his friends. Priestley, in disguise, and his family narrowly escaped with their lives. They lived for a time at London before moving in 1794 to America. See also: "Priestley, Joseph: Birth Anniversary" (Mar 13).

FORD, GERALD RUDOLPH: BIRTHDAY. July 14, 1913. 38th president of the US (1974–77). Born Leslie King at Omaha, NE, Ford became 41st vice president of the US on Dec 6, 1973, by appointment, following the resignation of Spiro T. Agnew from that office on Oct 10, 1973. Ford became president on Aug 9, 1974, following the resignation from that office on that day of Richard M. Nixon. He was the first nonelected vice president and president of the US.

FRANCE: BASTILLE DAY OR FETE NATIONAL. July 14. Public holiday commemorating the fall of the Bastille at the beginning of the French Revolution, July 14, 1789. Also celebrated or observed in many other countries.

GUTHRIE, WOODROW WILSON "WOODY": BIRTH ANNIVERSARY. July 14, 1912. American folksinger, songwriter ("This Land Is Your Land," "Union Maid," "Hard Traveling"), born at Okemah, OK. Traveled the country by freight train, singing and listening. Died Oct 3, 1967, at New York, NY. Father of Arlo Guthrie.

HANNA, WILLIAM: BIRTH ANNIVERSARY. July 14, 1910. Born at Melrose, NM, William Hanna was the cocreator of such popular characters as Tom and Jerry, Yogi Bear, Snagglepuss and Magilla Gorilla. With partner Joe Barbera, he won seven Academy Awards for his Tom and Jerry cartoon shorts, and another eight works were nominated. The Hanna-Barbera team created the first animated TV sitcom for adults, *The Flintstones* (1960), and such favorites as *The Jetsons* and *Scooby-Doo, Where Are You?* Hanna died at Los Angeles, CA, on Mar 22, 2001.

HERITAGEFEST. July 14–16 (also July 21–23). New Ulm, MN. This unique celebration features European music, family fun, New Ulm's own Concord Singers, five stages, air-conditioned Fest Halle, ethnic food and beverages. Est attendance: 25,000. For info: Heritagefest, Inc, PO Box 461, New Ulm, MN 56073-0461. Phone: (507) 354-8850. E-mail: hfest@newulmtel.net. Web: www.heritagefest.org.

MIDSUMMER NIGHTS' FAIR. July 14–15 (tentative). Lions Park, Norman, OK. 28th annual. Juried and invited artists display their work for show and sale in booths under the stars. Festival foods, free entertainment and free art activities for the whole family, 6:00 PM–11:00 PM. Est attendance: 8,000. For info: Firehouse Art Center, 444 S Flood, Norman, OK 73069. Phone: (405) 329-4523. E-mail: lana@normanfirehouse.com. Web: www.normanfirehouse.com.

MISSION SAN ANTONIO DE PADUA: FOUNDING ANNIVERSARY. July 14. California. Mission to the Indians founded July 14, 1771.

MOZART FESTIVAL. July 14–23. San Luis Obispo County, CA. Variety of music in unique venues celebrating the spirit of Wolfgang Amadeus Mozart. Est attendance: 15,000. For info: Mozart Festival, PO Box 311, San Luis Obispo, CA 93406. Phone: (805) 781-3008. Fax: (805) 781-3011. E-mail: info@mozartfestival.com. Web: www.mozartfestival.com.

MURRAY, KEN: BIRTH ANNIVERSARY. July 14, 1903. American comedian Ken Murray was born at New York, NY. He began in vaudeville, then moved to films and television. He died Oct 12, 1988, at Beverly Hills, CA.

NETHERLANDS: NORTH SEA JAZZ FESTIVAL. July 14–16. Nederlands Congresgebouw (Netherlands Congress Centre), The Hague. Live jazz festival with top-name entertainment. Annually, the second full weekend in July. Est attendance: 13,000. For info: North Sea Jazz Fest, PO Box 3325, 2601 DH Delft, Netherlands. Phone: (31) (15) 215-7756 or fax: (31) (15) 214-8393. For tickets, phone: (31) (10) 591-9000 or fax: (31) (10) 592-6130. E-mail: info@northseajazz.nl. Web: www.northseajazz.nl.

	S	M	T	W	T	F	S
July 2006							1
	2	3	4	5	6	7	8
	9	10	11	12	13	14	15
	16	17	18	19	20	21	22
	23	24	25	26	27	28	29
	30	31					

SAN FRANCISCO SILENT FILM FESTIVAL. July 14–16. San Francisco, CA. 11th annual. A film festival devoted to the unique art form of the silent film. Est attendance: 7,500. For info: San Francisco Silent Film Festival, 833 Market St, Ste 812, San Francisco, CA 94103-1828. Phone: (415) 777-4908. Fax: (415) 777-4904. Web: www.silentfilm.org.

SARTO, ANDREA DEL: BIRTH ANNIVERSARY. July 14, 1486. Celebrated Italian painter was born near Florence, Italy. "Sarto," a nickname referring to his father's trade as a tailor, was the name he chose during his lifetime, though the real surname was probably either Vanucchi or di Francesco. One of the most renowned artists of his time, his paintings hang in the great galleries of the world. He died at Florence, Jan 22, 1531.

THE SCOPES TRIAL. July 14–16. Dayton Courthouse, Dayton, TN. Five performances of an original drama written from the actual transcript of the Scopes trial—"the world's most famous court trial." Also, an arts and crafts fair, an antique car show and much more. Est attendance: 1,500. For info: Cynthia Rodriguez, Dayton Chamber of Commerce, Scopes Festival, 107 Main St, Dayton, TN 37321. Phone: (423) 775-0361. E-mail: chamber@volstate.net. Web: www.bryan.edu.

BIRTHDAYS TODAY

Polly Bergen, 76, actress ("To Tell the Truth," *The Winds of War*), singer, born Knoxville, TN, July 14, 1930.
Ingmar Bergman, 88, filmmaker (*The Seventh Seal, Wild Strawberries, Cries and Whispers*), born Uppsala, Sweden, July 14, 1918.
Gerald Rudolph Ford, 93, 38th president of the US, born Leslie King at Omaha, NE, July 14, 1913.
Matthew Fox, 40, actor ("Lost," "Party of Five"), born Crowheart, WY, July 14, 1966.
Missy Gold, 36, actress ("Benson"), born Great Falls, MT, July 14, 1970.
Roosevelt (Rosey) Grier, 74, actor, former football player, born Cuthbert, GA, July 14, 1932.
Joel Silver, 54, producer (*Lethal Weapon, Die Hard*), born South Orange, NJ, July 14, 1952.
Harry Dean Stanton, 80, actor (*Repo Man; Paris, Texas; Wild at Heart*), born West Irvine, KY, July 14, 1926.
Steven Michael (Steve) Stone, 59, sportscaster, former baseball player, born Euclid, OH, July 14, 1947.
Robin Ventura, 39, baseball player, born Santa Maria, CA, July 14, 1967.

JULY 15 — SATURDAY
Day 196 — 169 Remaining

BANNACK DAYS. July 15–16. Bannack, MT. Montana's first territorial capital, now a living ghost town, comes to life with a celebration of Montana's mining and pioneer history. Wagon rides, main street gunfights, old-time dancing, lots of music and fun are provided during this two-day celebration along Grasshopper Creek each year. Bannack State Park allows visitors to explore the old town and imagine what life was like in the mid-1800s. It is open year-round to the public. Admission fee. Est attendance: 4,000. For info: Dale Carlson, Park Manager, Montana Fish, Wildlife and Parks, 4200 Bannack Rd, Dillon, MT 59725. Phone: (406) 834-3413.

BATTLE OF THE MARNE: ANNIVERSARY. July 15, 1918. General Erich Ludendorff launched Germany's fifth, and last, offensive to break through the Chateau-Thierry salient. This all-out effort involved three armies branching out from Rheims to cross the Marne River. The Germans were successful in crossing the Marne near Chateau-Thierry before American, British and Italian divisions stopped their progress. On July 18 General Foch, Commander-in-Chief of the Allied troops, launched a massive counteroffensive that resulted in a German retreat that continued for four months until they sued for peace in November.

CANADA: SAINT SWITHUN'S SOCIETY ANNUAL CELEBRATION. July 15. Toronto, ON. Goals include the promotion of feelings of goodwill, the encouragement of the celebration of St. Swithun's Day and the patterning of members' lives after the example of our patron. Affiliated with the Friends of Winchester Cathedral. Publishes "The Water Spout" newsletter, free upon request. Annually, July 15. Est attendance: 100. For info: Norman A. McMullen, Pres, St. Swithun's Society, 427 Lynett Crescent, Richmond Hill, ON, Canada L4C 2V6. Phone: (905) 883-0984. E-mail: nmcmullen@rogers.com.

CIRCUS CITY FESTIVAL. July 15–22. Peru, IN. Youth amateur circus performed by children 7 to 21 years of age helping to preserve the circus heritage of Miami County, IN. Circus parade, July 22, 10 AM. Annually, beginning the Saturday before and ending the Saturday after the third Wednesday of July. Est attendance: 75,000. For info: Circus City Festival Inc, 154 N Broadway, Peru, IN 46970. Phone: (765) 472-3918. Fax: (765) 472-2826. Web: www.perucircus.com.

CIVIL WAR REENACTMENT. July 15–16. Coshocton, OH. Features battles, living history scenarios, Civil War artifacts exhibit, style show and outdoor church service. Annually, the third weekend in July. Est attendance: 5,000. For info: Roscoe Village Fdtn, 381 Hill St, Coshocton, OH 43812. Phone: (800) 877-1830 or (740) 622-9310. Fax: (740) 623-6555. E-mail: rvmarketing@roscoevillage.com. Web: www.roscoevillage.com.

COLLECTABLES/ANTIQUES/CRAFT/FLEA MARKET SALE. July 15. Sinclair Lewis City Park, Sauk Centre, MN. 35th year for this sale, sponsored by St. Michael's Auxiliary in conjunction with Sinclair Lewis Days. Sale features 75 exhibitors. The Auxiliary offers lunches at their food stand for a fee, also bake sale and raffle. Annually, the third Saturday in July. Est attendance: 1,500. For info: Joyce C. Lyng, St. Michael's Auxiliary, 750 Railroad Ave, Unit 123, Sauk Centre, MN 56378. Phone: (320) 352-2624. E-mail: gramlyng@hotmail.com.

COLTON COUNTRY DAY. July 15. Colton, NY. Annual flea market, live entertainment, museum exhibits. Special programs to be announced. Annually, the third weekend in July. Sponsor: Colton Historical Society. Est attendance: 1,500. For info: Dennis Eickhoff, Town Historian, 4846-1 State Hwy 56, Colton, NY 13625. Phone: (315) 262-2800. Fax: (315) 386-1013. E-mail: eickhoff@northnet.org.

COW APPRECIATION DAY. July 15. Woodstock, VT. A "cowledge bowl" competition, dairy education programs, butter and ice cream making and more. Est attendance: 300. For info: Billings Farm & Museum, Rte 12 North, Woodstock, VT 05091. Phone: (802) 457-2355. Fax: (802) 457-4663. E-mail: billings.farm@valley.net. Web: www.billingsfarm.org.

DERRIDA, JACQUES: BIRTH ANNIVERSARY. July 15, 1930. Influential French philosopher; proponent of deconstruction. Born at El Biar, Algeria, Derrida died Oct 8, 2004, at Paris, France.

EIGHTEENTH-CENTURY SUMMER MARKET FAIR. July 15–16. McLean, VA. Featuring eighteenth-century games, music, crafts, period food and drink, puppet show and militia drill. Est attendance: 5,000. For info: Claude Moore Colonial Farm at Turkey Run, 6310 Georgetown Pike, McLean, VA 22101. Phone: (703) 442-7557. Fax: (703) 442-0714. Web: www.1771.org.

FINLAND: PORI JAZZ FESTIVAL. July 15–23. Pori. 41st international festival presenting the jazz music of today with top-name performances. Thirteen different venues; some go on all night. Est attendance: 150,000. For info: Finnish Tourist Board, 655 Third Ave, New York, NY 10017. Phone: (212) 885-9700 or (358) (2) 626-2200. Fax: (358) (2) 626-2225. E-mail: festival@porijazz.fi. Web: www.porijazz.fi.

GAY GAMES VII. July 15–22. Chicago, IL. An eight-day sports and cultural festival. Includes 30 sporting competitions, band and choral programs and an arts festival. On July 15, the International Rainbow Memorial Run is the first event of the Gay Games and concludes at Soldier Field to kick off the opening ceremonies. For info: Federation of Gay Games, 584 Castro St, Ste 343, San Francisco, CA 94114. Phone: (415) 695-0222. Fax: (800) 887-1373. Web: www.chicago2006.org or www.gaygames.com.

HIGHLIGHTS® FOUNDATION WRITER'S WORKSHOP. July 15–22. Chautauqua, NY. This workshop is designed to help authors interested in writing for children. Writer workshops offered at beginner, intermediate and advanced levels. Classes offered include Children's Poetry, Book Promotion, Autobiographical Writing, and more. Workshop is held annually. Scholarships are available for first-time attendees. Request application by end of 2005. For info: Highlights Foundation, 814 Court St, Honesdale, PA 18431. Phone: (570) 253-1192. Fax: (570) 253-0179. E-mail: contact@highlightsfoundation.org. Web: www.highlightsfoundation.org.

JOHN MICHAEL KOHLER ARTS CENTER'S OUTDOOR ARTS FESTIVAL. July 15–16. Sheboygan, WI. 36th annual festival. A multiarts extravaganza featuring the works of 145 artists, demonstrations, live entertainment, children's workshops and exhibition tours. Est attendance: 20,000. For info: John Michael Kohler Arts Center, 608 New York Ave, PO Box 489, Sheboygan, WI 53082-0489. Phone: (920) 458-6144. Fax: (920) 458-4473. Web: www.jmkac.org.

KIDSPREE. July 15–16. Bicentennial Park, Aurora, CO. The Denver metro area's only free outdoor festival for kids, featuring more than 50 hands-on activities ranging from educational and recreational to the arts, including local and national children's entertainment. Annually, the third weekend in July. Est attendance: 40,000. For info: Special Events Coordinator, City of Aurora, 1298 Peoria St, Aurora, CO 80011. Phone: (303) 326-8615. E-mail: maddlema@auroragov.org. Web: www.auroraevents.org/kidspree.

MOORE, CLEMENT CLARKE: BIRTH ANNIVERSARY. July 15, 1779. American author and teacher, best remembered for his popular verse "A Visit from Saint Nicholas" (" 'Twas the Night Before Christmas"), which was first published anonymously and without Moore's knowledge in a newspaper, Dec 23, 1823. Moore was born at New York, NY, and died at Newport, RI, July 10, 1863. (In recent years, Moore's authorship of the poem has been challenged, with Henry Livingston, Jr, offered as the creator.)

NATIONAL PERSONAL CHEF DAY. July 15. A national day for clients to honor the hardworking, creative personal chefs who provide them with delicious, affordable, custom-designed meals from fresh ingredients on a regular basis that may be enjoyed in the comfort of the client's own home. Our clients don't have to be celebrities to eat like celebrities! For info: Candy Wallace, 4572 Delaware St, San Diego, CA 92116. Phone: (800) 644-8389. Fax: (619) 294-2823. E-mail: chefcandy@personalchef.com. Web: www.personalchef.com.

NATIONAL RABBIT WEEK. July 15–21. To pay tribute to the rabbit for being a great companion to humans as a house pet. Recognition should also be given to any rabbit that has done something special to help mankind (e.g., saved someone's life, visited patients at a hospital, etc). The public should be informed during this week on the proper care of rabbits and the problems with buying an "Easter" rabbit. For info: Melvin Rabbit, CP 157, Place du Parc, Montreal, QC, Canada H2X 4A4. Phone: (514) 849-0888. E-mail: magician@total.net.

NATIONAL WOODIE WAGON DAY. July 15. The "woodie wagon," made famous in the 1940s and '50s, romanticized the American outing. From Route 66 to the surfer lifestyle, the woodie wagon was there. This national day will be celebrated in individual cities and towns across the US and will pay homage to this great American symbol of freedom and the casual lifestyle. Annually, the third Saturday in July. For info: Historic Preservations, Inc, PO Box 49241, Denver, CO 80249. Phone: (303) 642-1510. Fax: (303) 642-3087. E-mail: gregoryaraymer@yahoo.com.

"ONE LIFE TO LIVE" TV PREMIERE: ANNIVERSARY. July 15, 1968. Set in a fictional Pennsylvania town, the show was created by Agnes Nixon to depict the class and ethnic struggles of the town's denizens. The initial cast featured many Jewish, Polish and African-American characters. The show departed from interethnic storytelling in the 1980s for more fantastic adventures set in locales such as heaven, the old West and a futuristic mountain silo called Eternia. Since then, the show has returned to its strengths of traditional storytelling by featuring Latino and African-American actors as integral characters. Award-winning actress Erika Slezak heads the cast as the venerable Viki Lord Riley Buchanan Carpenter, the town's matron with five alternate personalities. Among those who have appeared on "OLTL" are Tom Berenger, Judith Light, Robert Desiderio, Tommy Lee Jones, Laurence Fishburne, Jameson Parker, Phylicia Rashad, Christine Ebersole, Richard Grieco, Blair Underwood, Joe Lando, Audrey Landers, Christian Slater and Yasmine Bleeth.

RED WINE AND BLUES FESTIVAL. July 15. Tuckerton, NJ. Team up with the Tuckerton Seaport for a perfect afternoon of wine tasting from New Jersey's finest wineries plus live blues entertainment, food, crafts and more. Annually, the third Saturday of July. For info: Karen DeRosa, Tuckerton Seaport, 120 W Main St, PO Box 52, Tuckerton, NJ 08087. Phone: (609) 296-8868. Fax: (609) 296-5810. E-mail: info@tuckertonseaport.org. Web: www.tuckertonseaport.org.

REMBRANDT: 400th BIRTH ANNIVERSARY. July 15, 1606. Dutch painter and etcher, born at Leiden, Holland. One of the undisputed giants of Western art. Known for *The Night Watch* and many portraits and self-portraits, died at Amsterdam, Holland, Oct 4, 1669.

RIVER CITY RUMBLE BOAT RACES. July 15–16. Demopolis City Landing, Demopolis, AL. More than 100 boats from across the Southeast are expected to turn out for these races sponsored by the Outboard Drag Boat Association. Held annually on the third weekend in July, the event also features food vendors and children's activities. Est attendance: 5,000. For info: Kelley Smith, Events & Tourism, Demopolis Area Chamber of Commerce, PO Box 667, Demopolis, AL 36732. Phone: (334) 289-0270. Fax: (334) 289-1382. E-mail: dacc@westal.net. Web: www.demopolischamber.com.

SAINT FRANCES XAVIER CABRINI: BIRTH ANNIVERSARY. July 15, 1850. First American saint, founder of schools, orphanages, convents and hospitals, born at Lombardy, Italy. Died of malaria at Chicago, IL, Dec 22, 1917. Canonized July 7, 1946.

	S	M	T	W	T	F	S
July							1
2006	2	3	4	5	6	7	8
	9	10	11	12	13	14	15
	16	17	18	19	20	21	22
	23	24	25	26	27	28	29
	30	31					

SAINT SWITHIN'S DAY. July 15. Swithun (Swithin), Bishop of Winchester (AD 852–862), died July 2, 862. Little is known of his life, but his relics were transferred into Winchester Cathedral July 15, 971, a day on which there was a heavy rainfall. According to old English belief, it will rain for 40 days thereafter when it rains on this day. "St. Swithin's Day, if thou dost rain, for 40 days it will remain; St. Swithin's Day, if thou be fair, for 40 days, will rain nea mair."

SHARK AWARENESS DAY. July 15. Jenkinson's Aquarium, Point Pleasant Beach, NJ. 10 AM–10 PM. Are sharks dangerous? Learn all about sharks and what you can do to protect them. Free arts & crafts from 1–4 PM. Shark stories for children will be presented throughout the day. You can even touch a live shark in our touch tank. Sharks are fed at 9 PM. Est attendance: 1,200. For info: Jenkinson's Aquarium, 300 Ocean Ave, Point Pleasant Beach, NJ 08742. Phone: (732) 899-1212. Fax: (732) 899-1717. E-mail: jenkinsonsaquarium@comcast.net. Web: www.jenkinsons.com.

SUMMERSWAP. July 15. Heritage Park, Frankenmuth, MI. A beer can collectors and breweriana trade show. Breweriana is the collection of brewery memorabilia, including steins, cans, bottles, signs, coasters, mirrors, neon signs, etc. The show is attended by collectors from a 10–12-state area and Canada. Annually, the third Saturday in July. Est attendance: 350. For info: Dave Van Hine, Show Chairman, Brewery Collectibles Club of America, Mid-Michigan Chapter, 357 N Harvest Lane, Frankenmuth, MI 48734. Phone: (989) 652-9818. E-mail: davevanh@aol.com.

TOSS AWAY THE "COULD HAVES" AND "SHOULD HAVES" DAY. July 15. On this day, everyone will write down their "could haves" and "should haves" on a piece of paper, then throw that list in the trash. Then they will make this resolution: "From this day forward, I choose not to live in the past—the past is history that I can't change. I can do something about the present—I choose to live in the present." Annually, the third Saturday in July. For info: Martha Ross-Rodgers, 2442 Annie Circle, Chesapeake, VA 23323. Phone: (757) 558-4964. Fax: (757) 558-4965. E-mail: MRossrodge@aol.com. Web: www.jireh publishers.com.

BIRTHDAYS TODAY

Willie Aames, 46, actor ("Eight Is Enough," "Charles in Charge"), born Newport Beach, CA, July 15, 1960.

Kim Alexis, 46, model, born Lockport, NY, July 15, 1960.

Julian Bream, 73, musician (classical guitar, lute), born London, England, July 15, 1933.

Lolita Davidovich, 45, actress (*Indictment, Cobb*), born London, ON, Canada, July 15, 1961.

Brian Austin Green, 33, actor ("Beverly Hills 90210"), singer, born Van Nuys, CA, July 15, 1973.

Irene Jacob, 40, actress (*Red, Othello*), born Paris, France, July 15, 1966.

Alex George Karras, 71, former football player, actor ("Webster," *Babe, Victor/Victoria*), born Gary, IN, July 15, 1935.

Ken Kercheval, 71, actor ("Dallas," "Search for Tomorrow"), born Wolcottville, IN, July 15, 1935.

Linda Ronstadt, 60, singer, songwriter, born Tucson, AZ, July 15, 1946.

Richard Russo, 57, author (*Empire Falls, Straight Man, Nobody's Fool*), born Johnstown, NY, July 15, 1949.

Jesse Ventura, 55, former professional wrestler, former Governor of Minnesota (I), born Minneapolis, MN, July 15, 1951.

Jan-Michael Vincent, 62, actor ("The Winds of War," "Airwolf"), born Denver, CO, July 15, 1944.

George V. Voinovich, 70, US Senator (R, Ohio), born Cleveland, OH, July 15, 1936.

Forest Whitaker, 45, actor (*Platoon, Bird, The Crying Game*), director (*Waiting to Exhale*), born Longview, TX, July 15, 1961.

JULY 16 — SUNDAY

Day 197 — 168 Remaining

AMUNDSEN, ROALD: BIRTH ANNIVERSARY. July 16, 1872. Norwegian explorer born near Oslo, Roald Amundsen was the first man to sail from the Atlantic to the Pacific Ocean via the Northwest Passage (1903–05). He discovered the South Pole (Dec 14, 1911) and flew over the North Pole in a dirigible in 1926. He flew, with five companions, from Norway, June 18, 1928, in a daring effort to rescue survivors of an Italian Arctic expedition. No trace of the rescue party or the airplane was ever located. See also: "South Pole: Discovery Anniversary" (Dec 14).

ART FESTIVAL. July 16. Harvey Cedars, NJ. More than 75 artists participate in this festival. Est attendance: 1,500. For info: Harvey Cedars Activity Committee, PO Box 3185, Harvey Cedars, NJ 08008. Phone: (609) 361-7990. Web: www.harvey cedars.org.

ATOMIC BOMB TESTED: ANNIVERSARY. July 16, 1945. In the New Mexican desert at Alamogordo Air Base, 125 miles southeast of Albuquerque, the experimental atomic bomb was set off at 5:30 AM. Dubbed "Fat Boy" by its creator, the plutonium bomb vaporized the steel scaffolding holding it as the immense fireball rose 8,000 ft in a fraction of a second—ultimately creating a mushroom cloud to a height of 41,000 ft. At ground zero the bomb emitted heat three times the temperature of the interior of the sun. All plant and animal life for a mile around ceased to exist. When informed by President Truman at Potsdam of the successful experiment, Winston Churchill responded, "It's the Second Coming in wrath!"

BARN DAY. July 16. Two miles south of Filley, NE. Threshing demonstration, antique farm equipment, entertainment. The barn is on the National Register of Historic Sites and is the largest limestone barn in Nebraska. Est attendance: 300. For info: Lesa Arterburn, Dir, Gage County Historical Society, PO Box 793, Beatrice, NE 68310. Phone: (402) 228-1679. E-mail: gagecounty museum@beatricene.com. Web: www.beatricene.com/gage countymuseum.

BOLIVIA: LA PAZ DAY. July 16, 1548. Founding of city, now capital of Bolivia, on this day, 1548.

★**CAPTIVE NATIONS WEEK.** July 16–22. Presidential proclamation issued each year since 1959 for the third week of July. (PL86–90 of July 17, 1959.)

COMET CRASHES INTO JUPITER: ANNIVERSARY. July 16, 1994. The first fragment of the comet Shoemaker-Levy crashed into the planet Jupiter, beginning a series of spectacular collisions, each unleashing more energy than the combined effect of an explosion of all our world's nuclear arsenal. Video imagery from earthbound telescopes as well as the Hubble telescope provided vivid records of the explosions and their aftereffects. In 1993 the comet had shattered into a series of about a dozen large chunks that resembled "pearls on a string" after its orbit brought it within the gravitational effects of our solar system's largest planet.

CONCOURS d'ELEGANCE. July 16. Forest Grove, OR. Set among the beauty of the Pacific University Campus, this is one of the premier car shows on the West Coast with 300+ beautifully restored vintage autos. A great family event. Annually, the third Sunday in July. Est attendance: 10,000. For info: Forest Grove Rotary Club, PO Box 387, Forest Grove, OR 97116. Phone: (503) 357-2300. Web: www.forestgroveconcours.org.

DIETARY MANAGERS ASSOCIATION ANNUAL MEETING AND EXPO. July 16–20. Milwaukee, WI. 46th annual meeting. Est attendance: 700. For info: Dennis Leopold, VP, Dietary Mgrs Assn, 406 Surrey Woods Dr, St. Charles, IL 60174-2386. Phone: (630) 587-6336. Fax: (630) 587-6308.

DISTRICT OF COLUMBIA ESTABLISHING LEGISLATION: ANNIVERSARY. July 16, 1790. George Washington signed legislation that selected the District of Columbia as the permanent capital of the US. Boundaries of the district were established in 1792. Plans called for the government to remain housed at Philadelphia, PA, until 1800, when the new national capital would be ready for occupancy.

EARTHQUAKE JOLTS PHILIPPINES: ANNIVERSARY. July 16, 1990. An earthquake measuring 7.7 on the Richter scale struck the Philippines, killing an estimated 1,621 persons and leaving approximately 1,000 missing. The quake struck in an area north of Manila, and heavy damage was reported at Cabanatuan, Baguio and on Luzon island. The quake was the worst in the Philippines in 14 years.

EDDY, MARY BAKER: BIRTH ANNIVERSARY. July 16, 1821. Founder of Christian Science; born near Concord, NH, she died at Chestnut Hill, MA, Dec 3, 1910.

FAIRBANKS SUMMER ARTS FESTIVAL. July 16–30. University of Alaska, Fairbanks, AK. A unique study-performance festival involving workshops and master classes in visual and performing arts with more than 80 prestigious guest artists. Performance opportunities in orchestra, jazz band, jazz, choral groups, dance, opera theater, creative writing, healing arts and ice skating. Est attendance: 12,500. For info: Jo Ryman Scott, Fairbanks Summer Arts Festival, Box 80845, Fairbanks, AK 99708. Phone: (907) 474-8869. Fax: (907) 479-4329. E-mail: festival@alaska.net. Web: www.fsaf.org.

ITALY: FEAST OF THE REDEEMER. July 16. Venice. Procession of gondolas and other craft commemorating the end of the epidemic of 1575. Annually, the third Sunday in July.

LUXEMBOURG: BEER FESTIVAL. July 16. At Diekirch an annual beer festival is held on the third Sunday in July.

MISSION SAN DIEGO DE ALCALA: FOUNDING ANNIVERSARY. July 16, 1769. First of 21 California missions to the Indians.

NATIONAL ICE CREAM DAY. July 16. To promote America's favorite dessert, ice cream, on "Sundae Sunday." Annually, the third Sunday in July.

NATIONAL INDEPENDENT RETAILERS WEEK. July 16–22. The week to celebrate and promote those who own and manage the thousands of independent retail businesses around the world. For info: Tom Shay, Profits Plus Seminars, PO Box 1577, St. Petersburg, FL 33731. Phone: (727) 464-2182. Fax: (727) 898-3179. E-mail: TomShay@profitsplus.org. Web: www.profitsplus.org.

REYNOLDS, JOSHUA: BIRTH ANNIVERSARY. July 16, 1723 (OS). English portrait painter whose paintings of 18th-century English notables are among the best of their time. Born at Plympton, Devon, England, Sir Joshua died at London, Feb 23, 1792, at age 68. "He who resolves never to ransack any mind but his own," Reynolds told students of the Royal Academy in 1774, "will be soon reduced, from mere barrenness, to the poorest of all imitations; he will be obliged to imitate himself, and to repeat what he has before often repeated."

ROGERS, GINGER: BIRTH ANNIVERSARY. July 16, 1911. Ginger Rogers is best remembered as Fred Astaire's dance partner in a series of romantic musicals. She appeared in 70 films during her six-decade career, winning an Oscar for her leading role in the 1940 film *Kitty Foyle*. Rogers was born at Independence, MO, and died Apr 25, 1995, at Rancho Mirage, CA.

SAINT CYRIL'S PARISH FESTIVAL. July 16. Kiwanis Park, Sheboygan, WI. Slovenian foods, music, games, raffle 10:30 AM–7 PM. Polka Mass at 10:30 AM, $3,000 bingo at 1 PM under the Big Top tent. Est attendance: 5,000. For info: St. Cyril & Methodius Parish, 822 New Jersey Ave, Sheboygan, WI 53081. Phone: (414) 457-7110.

SANTA FE CHAMBER MUSIC FESTIVAL. July 16–Aug 21 (tentative). St. Francis Auditorium, Museum of Fine Arts and the Lensic Performing Arts Center, Santa Fe, NM. Highly acclaimed chamber music festival celebrates its 34th season. Draws on international talent, featuring works from the baroque, romantic and classical periods, as well as contemporary works, including world premiere performances. Est attendance: 15,000. For info: Santa Fe Chamber Music Festival, PO Box 2227, Santa Fe, NM 87504. Phone: (505) 983-2075. Fax: (505) 986-0251. E-mail: info@sfcmf.org. Web: www.sfcmf.org.

SPACE MILESTONE: *APOLLO 11* (US): MAN SENT TO THE MOON: ANNIVERSARY. July 16, 1969. This launch resulted in man's first moon landing, the first landing on any extraterrestrial body. See also: "Space Milestone: Moon Day" (July 20).

STANWYCK, BARBARA: BIRTH ANNIVERSARY. July 16, 1907. Actress Barbara Stanwyck was born Ruby Stevens at the Flatbush section of Brooklyn, NY. At the age of 18 she won a leading role in the Broadway melodrama *Noose*, appearing for the first time as Barbara Stanwyck. She appeared in 82 films including *Stella Dallas; Double Indemnity; Sorry, Wrong Number; The Lady Eve* and the television series "The Big Valley." In 1944 the government listed her as the nation's highest paid woman, earning $400,000 per year. Stanwyck died at Santa Monica, CA, Jan 21, 1990.

WELLS, IDA B.: BIRTH ANNIVERSARY. July 16, 1862. African American journalist and antilynching crusader Ida B. Wells was born the daughter of slaves at Holly Springs, MS, and grew up as Jim Crow and lynching were becoming prevalent. Wells argued that lynchings occurred not to defend white women but because of whites' fear of economic competition from blacks. She traveled extensively, founding antilynching societies and black women's clubs. Wells's *Red Record* (1895) was one of the first accounts of lynchings in the South. She died Mar 25, 1931, at Chicago, IL.

WSBA/WARM 103/OLDIES 96.1 SUMMER CRAFT SHOW. July 16. York Fairgrounds, York, PA. More than 125 crafts, from country to contemporary, Victorian and southwestern, handcrafted furniture, wood carvings, dolls, jewelry, pottery, collectibles, quilts, baskets and much more. Admission fee. Est attendance: 3,500. For info: Joe Alfano, Asst Promo Dir, PO Box 910, York, PA 17402-0910. Phone: (717) 764-1155. Fax: (717) 252-4708. E-mail: jalfano@radioyork.com. Web: www.warm103.com.

	S	M	T	W	T	F	S
July							1
2006	2	3	4	5	6	7	8
	9	10	11	12	13	14	15
	16	17	18	19	20	21	22
	23	24	25	26	27	28	29
	30	31					

BIRTHDAYS TODAY

Ruben Blades, 58, singer (two Grammy Awards), actor (*Crossover Dreams, The Milagro Beanfield War*), born Panama City, Panama, July 16, 1948.

Phoebe Cates, 43, actress (*Fast Times at Ridgemont High, Gremlins*), born New York, NY, July 16, 1963.

Will Farrell, 39, comedian, actor ("Saturday Night Live," *Elf, Anchorman: The Legend of Ron Burgundy*), born Irvine, CA, July 16, 1967.

Corey Feldman, 35, actor (*Stand by Me, The Lost Boys*), born Reseda, CA, July 16, 1971.

Michael Flatley, 48, dancer (*Lord of the Dance, Feet of Flames*), born Chicago, IL, July 16, 1958.

Alexis Herman, 59, former Secretary of Labor (Clinton administration), born Mobile, AL, July 16, 1947.

Barnard Hughes, 91, actor (*Sisters*, "Doc"), born Bedford Hills, NY, July 16, 1915.

Bess Myerson, 82, former Miss America ('45), former government official, born New York, NY, July 16, 1924.

Barry Sanders, 38, former football player, born Wichita, KS, July 16, 1968.

Pinchas Zukerman, 58, violinist, born Tel Aviv, Israel, July 16, 1948.

JULY 17 — MONDAY
Day 198 — 167 Remaining

ABBOTT, BERENICE: BIRTH ANNIVERSARY. July 17, 1898. Berenice Abbott was born at Springfield, OH, and went on to become a pioneer of American photography. She is best remembered for her black and white photographs of New York City in the 1930s, many of which appeared in the book *Changing New York*. After publishing this collection she began photographing scientific experiments that illustrated the laws and processes of physics. She died at Monson, ME, Dec 11, 1991.

CZAR NICHOLAS II AND FAMILY EXECUTED: ANNIVERSARY. July 17, 1918. Russian Czar Nicholas II; his wife Alexandra; son and heir Alexis; and daughters Anastasia, Tatiana, Olga and Marie were executed by firing squad on this date. The murder of the last of the 300-year-old Romanov dynasty occurred at Yekaterinburg, in the Ural mountains of Siberia where Nicholas had been imprisoned since his abdication in 1917. Local Soviet officials, concerned about advancing promonarchist forces, executed the royal family rather than have them serve as a rallying point for the White Russians. In 1992 two of nine skeletons dug up the previous summer from a pit at Yekaterinburg were identified as the remains of the czar and czarina.

DISNEYLAND OPENED: ANNIVERSARY. July 17, 1955. Disneyland, America's first theme park, opened at Anaheim, CA.

FOLKMOOT USA: THE NORTH CAROLINA INTERNATIONAL FOLK FESTIVAL. July 17–30. Waynesville, NC. A festival of international folk dance featuring groups from 10 countries. Est attendance: 75,000. For info: Folkmoot USA, PO Box 658, Waynesville, NC 28786. Phone: (828) 452-2997 or (877) FOLK-USA. Fax: (828) 452-5762. E-mail: info@folkmoot .com. Web: www.folkmoot.com.

GARDNER, ERLE STANLEY: BIRTH ANNIVERSARY. July 17, 1889. American author of detective fiction, born at Malden, MA. Best remembered for his series about lawyer-detective Perry Mason, Gardner also wrote novels under the pen name A.A. Fair. Gardner died at Temecula, CA, Mar 11, 1970.

GERRY, ELBRIDGE: BIRTH ANNIVERSARY. July 17, 1744. Fifth vice president of the US (1813–14), born at Marblehead, MA. Died at Washington, DC, Nov 23, 1814. His name became part of the language (gerrymander) after he signed a redistricting bill favoring his party while governor of Massachusetts in 1812.

KANSAS CITY HOTEL DISASTER: 25th ANNIVERSARY. July 17, 1981. Anniversary of the collapse of aerial walkways at the Hyatt Regency Hotel at Kansas City, MO. About 1,500 people were attending the popular weekly tea dance when, at about 7 PM, two concrete and steel skywalks that were suspended from the ceiling of the hotel's atrium broke loose and fell on guests in the crowded lobby, killing 114 people. In 1986 a state board revoked the licenses of two engineers convicted of gross negligence for their part in designing the hotel.

KOREA: CONSTITUTION DAY. July 17, 1948. Legal national holiday. Commemorates the proclamation of the constitution of the Republic of Korea in 1948. Ceremonies at Seoul's capitol plaza and all major cities.

MINIMUM LEGAL DRINKING AGE AT 21: ANNIVERSARY. July 17, 1984. Mothers Against Drunk Driving (MADD) helped pass the 21 Minimum Legal Drinking Age (MLDA) law because it makes sense and saves lives. President Ronald Reagan signed MLDA federal legislation making it illegal for anyone under 21 to purchase or publicly possess alcohol. An estimated 1,000 lives are saved each year as a result. For info: MADD. Phone: 800 GET-MADD. Web: www.madd.org.

MOON PHASE: LAST QUARTER. July 17. Moon enters Last Quarter phase at 3:12 PM, EDT.

NATIONAL GET OUT OF THE DOGHOUSE DAY. July 17. In trouble with someone you know and care about? This is the day when anyone can "Get out of the doghouse!" Annually, the third Monday in July. For info: Heidi Richards, Eden Florists and Gift Baskets, 7100 Pembroke Rd, Miramar, FL 33023. Phone: (954) 981-5515. E-mail: flowers@edenflorist.com. Web: www.edenflorist.com.

PUERTO RICO: MUÑOZ-RIVERA DAY. July 17. Public holiday on the anniversary of the birth of Luis Muñoz-Rivera. The Puerto Rican patriot, poet and journalist was born at Barranquitas, Puerto Rico, in 1859. He died at Santurce, a suburb of San Juan, Puerto Rico, Nov 15, 1916.

SPACE MILESTONE: *APOLLO-SOYUZ* TEST PROJECT (US, USSR). July 17, 1975. After three years of planning, negotiation and preparation, the first US–USSR joint space project reached fruition with the linkup in space of *Apollo 18* (crew: T. Stafford, V. Brand, D. Slayton; landed in Pacific Ocean July 24, during 136th orbit) and *Soyuz 19* (crew: A.A. Leonov, V.N. Kubasov; landed July 21, after 96 orbits). *Apollo 18* and *Soyuz 19* were linked for 47 hours (July 17–19) while joint experiments and transfer of personnel and materials back and forth between craft took place. Launch date was July 15, 1975.

SPACE MILESTONE: *SOYUZ T-12* (USSR). July 17, 1984. Cosmonaut Svetlana Savitskaya became the first woman to walk in space (July 25) and the first woman to make more than one space voyage. Docked at *Salyut 7* July 18 and returned to Earth July 29.

STEALTH BOMBER FLIGHT: ANNIVERSARY. July 17, 1989. The B-2 Stealth bomber airplane was flown successfully over the desert near Palmdale, CA, for almost two hours. A decade of work and $22 billion reportedly were spent on the project prior to the first flight. Designed to penetrate Soviet radar, the B-2 Stealth bomber was said to be capable of delivering up to 25 tons of nuclear or other bombs. Average cost of each of the 132 bombers requested by the Air Force was estimated to be $530 million. On this first test flight the plane flew at speeds of up to 180 knots (200 mph) and was put through several types of turns. Higher speeds and retraction of the landing gear were left for subsequent test flights.

"WRONG WAY" CORRIGAN DAY: ANNIVERSARY. July 17, 1938. Douglas Groce Corrigan, an unemployed airplane mechanic, left Brooklyn, NY's Floyd Bennett Field, ostensibly headed for Los Angeles, CA, in a 1929 Curtiss Robin monoplane. He landed 28 hours, 13 minutes later at Dublin, Ireland's Baldonnell Airport after a 3,150-mile nonstop flight without radio or special navigation equipment and in violation of American and Irish flight regulations. Born at Galveston, TX, Jan 22, 1907, Corrigan received a hero's welcome home; he was nicknamed "Wrong

Way" Corrigan because he claimed he accidentally followed the wrong end of his compass needle. Died at New York, NY, Dec 9, 1995.

BIRTHDAYS TODAY

Lucie Arnaz, 55, actress ("Here's Lucy," "The Lucie Arnaz Show," *Lost in Yonkers*), born Los Angeles, CA, July 17, 1951.

Diahann Carroll, 71, singer, actress ("Julia," "Dynasty"), born Carol Diahann Johnson at New York, NY, July 17, 1935.

Phyllis Diller, 89, actress ("The Beautiful Phyllis Diller Show," *Boy, Did I Get a Wrong Number!*), born Phyllis Driver at Lima, OH, July 17, 1917.

David Hasselhoff, 54, actor ("Knight Rider," "Baywatch"), born Baltimore, MD, July 17, 1952.

Jason Jennings, 28, baseball player, born Dallas, TX, July 17, 1978.

Aaron Lansky, 51, founder of National Yiddish Book Center, born New Bedford, MA, July 17, 1955.

Pat McCormick, 72, writer ("The Jack Paar Show," "The Tonight Show"), actor (*Buffalo Bill and the Indians*), born Rocky River, OH, July 17, 1934.

Phoebe Snow, 54, singer ("Poetry Man"), born New York, NY, July 17, 1952.

Donald Sutherland, 71, actor (*M*A*S*H, Klute, Backdraft*), born St. John, NB, Canada, July 17, 1935.

Dawn Upshaw, 46, opera singer, born Nashville, TN, July 17, 1960.

Alex Winter, 41, actor (*Bill & Ted's Excellent Adventure*), born London, England, July 17, 1965.

JULY 18 — TUESDAY
Day 199 — 166 Remaining

CHICAGO GOLF CLUB: ANNIVERSARY. July 18, 1893. The first 18-hole golf course in America, laid out by Charles Blair MacDonald, was incorporated at Wheaton, IL. MacDonald was the architect of many of the early US courses, which he attempted to model on the best in Scotland and England. It was his belief that at each tee a golfer should face a hazard at the average distance of his shot.

EVANS, CHICK: BIRTH ANNIVERSARY. July 18, 1890. Charles (Chick) Evans, Jr, golfer born at Indianapolis, IN. Evans competed as an amateur against the best professionals in the early 20th century, winning the US Open in 1916. In the 1920s he established the Chick Evans Caddie Foundation, later called the Evans Scholarship Fund, which has helped send more than 4,000 people to college. Died at Chicago, IL, Nov 6, 1979.

FIRST PERFECT SCORE IN OLYMPIC HISTORY: 30th ANNIVERSARY. July 18, 1976. At the Montreal Olympics, Romanian gymnast Nadia Comaneci scored the first "10" in Olympic history with her flawless performance of the compulsory exercise on the uneven bars. The scoreboard displayed a "1.00" because it couldn't go up to "10." Comaneci had seven total perfect scores and won five medals, including the gold for all-around performance. Four months previous to the Olympics, Comaneci had scored the first perfect score in international gymnastic competition history.

FULLER, BOBBY: 40th DEATH ANNIVERSARY. July 18, 1966. Bobby Fuller, leader of the rock group Bobby Fuller Four, was found dead in his car at Los Angeles, CA. No definite cause of death was ever proven. The Bobby Fuller Four is best remembered for their 1966 hit song "I Fought the Law," which was written by Sonny Curtis, a member of Buddy Holly's Crickets. Fuller was born Oct 22, 1942, at Baytown, TX.

HAYAKAWA, SAMUEL ICHIYE: 100th BIRTH ANNIVERSARY. July 18, 1906. S.I. Hayakawa was born at Vancouver, BC, and came to the US in 1927. An academic, in 1968 he was appointed acting president of San Francisco State College. During student demonstrations on his first day in office he climbed atop a sound truck and disconnected the wires, silencing the demonstrators. His actions gained him enormous popularity among conservatives and he was promoted to permanent president by Governor Ronald Reagan. As his popularity grew he switched from the Democratic to the Republican party and in 1976 was elected to the US Senate. He led the successful California initiative to declare English the state's official language in 1986. Hayakawa wrote nine textbooks on language and semantics. He died Feb 27, 1992, at Greenbrae, CA.

MANDELA, NELSON: BIRTHDAY. July 18, 1918. Former South African President Nelson Rolihlahla Mandela was born the son of a Tembu tribal chieftain at Qunu, near Umtata, in the Transkei territory of South Africa. Giving up his hereditary rights, Mandela chose to become a lawyer and earned his degree at the University of South Africa. He joined the African National Congress (ANC) in 1944, eventually becoming deputy national president in 1952. His activities in the struggle against apartheid resulted in his conviction for sabotage in 1964. During his 28 years in jail, Mandela remained a symbol of hope to South Africa's nonwhite majority, the demand for his release a rallying cry for civil rights activists. That release finally came Feb 11, 1990, as millions watched via satellite television. In 1994 Mandela was elected President of South Africa in the first all-race election there. See also: "Mandela, Nelson: Prison Release Anniversary" (Feb 11).

NATIONAL BABY FOOD FESTIVAL. July 18–22. Fremont, MI. 16th annual. Baby yourself at this festival in the hometown of Gerber Products. Adults face off in the baby-food-eating contest and tots crawl in races. Top entertainers, two parades, arts and crafts and car shows round out the fun. Est attendance: 125,000. For info: Natl Baby Food Festival, 7 E Main St, Fremont, MI 49412. Phone: (800) 592-BABY. E-mail: nbff@fremontcommerce.com. Web: www.fremontcommerce.com.

ODETS, CLIFFORD: 100th BIRTH ANNIVERSARY. July 18, 1906. Clifford Odets began his writing career as a poet before turning to acting. He helped found the Group Theatre in 1931. In 1935 he returned to writing with works for the Group Theatre such as *Waiting for Lefty, Awake and Sing!* and *Golden Boy*. His proletarian views helped make him a popular playwright during the Depression years. Odets was born at Philadelphia, PA, and died at Los Angeles, CA, Aug 15, 1963.

PRESIDENTIAL SUCCESSION ACT: ANNIVERSARY. July 18, 1947. President Harry S Truman signed an Executive Order determining the line of succession should the president be temporarily incapacitated or die in office. The speaker of the house and president pro tem of the senate are next in succession after the vice president. This line of succession became the 25th Amendment to the Constitution, which was ratified Feb 10, 1967.

PROSPECT PARK FISHING CONTEST. July 18–19. Prospect Park, Brooklyn, NY. A contest for young anglers, 15 and under, sponsored by R.H. Macy's. Prizes awarded daily for the largest or most fish. At the Rustic Shelter Lakeside near the Kate Wollman Rink parking lot. Come learn about fishing and aquatic ecology. Est attendance: 3,000. For info: Jesse Adelman, Public

Info Office, 95 Prospect Park W, Prospect Park, Brooklyn, NY 11215. Phone: (718) 965-8943. E-mail: jadelman@prospectpark .org. Web: www.prospectpark.org.

RESTLESS LEG SYNDROME (RLS) EDUCATION AND AWARENESS WEEK. July 18–25. Over 12 million Americans have severe leg pains called Restless Leg Syndrome (RLS), and this education and awareness week, sponsored by the Pharmacy Council on Women's Health, is a means to educate and to call attention to various treatments and diagnosis to assist patients with this problem. There is a $15 charge for kit materials. For more information, please contact: PPSI, 101 Lucas Valley Rd, Ste 210, San Rafael, CA 94903. Phone: (415) 479-8628. Fax: (415) 479-8608. E-mail: ppsi@aol.com. Web: www.ppsinc .org.

ROCKBRIDGE REGIONAL FAIR. July 18–22. Lexington, VA. Held at the Virginia Horse Center. 4-H Show, rodeo, carnival, exhibits (commercial and crafts), activities of all kinds. For info: Lexington Visitors Bureau, 106 E Washington St, Lexington, VA 24450. Phone: (540) 463-3777. Fax: (540) 463-1105. E-mail: lexington@rockbridge.net.

RUTLEDGE, JOHN: DEATH ANNIVERSARY. July 18, 1800. American statesman, associate justice on the Supreme Court, born at Charleston, SC, in September 1739. Nominated second Chief Justice of the Supreme Court to succeed John Jay and served as Acting Chief Justice until his confirmation was denied because of his opposition to the Jay Treaty. He died at Charleston, SC.

SNAKE RIVER STAMPEDE. July 18–22. Nampa, ID. In its 91st year this is one of the top 15 professional rodeo events in the nation featuring the world's top cowboys and cowgirls in action. Events include bareback bronc riding, saddle bronc riding, bull riding, calf roping, team roping, steer wrestling and barrel racing. Est attendance: 40,000. For info: Jimmie Hurley, Snake River Stampede, PO Box 231, Nampa, ID 83653. Phone: (208) 466-8497. Fax: (208) 465-4438. E-mail: sstampede@earthlink.net.

SPACE MILESTONE: *ROHINI 1* (INDIA). July 18, 1980. First successful launch from India, orbited 77-lb satellite.

SPAIN: CIVIL WAR BEGINS: 70th ANNIVERSARY. July 18, 1936. General Francisco Franco led an uprising of army troops based in North Africa against the elected government of the Spanish Republic. Spain was quickly divided into a Nationalist and a Republican zone. Franco's Nationalists drew support from Fascist Italy and Nazi Germany. On Apr 1, 1939, the Nationalists won a complete victory when they entered Madrid. Franco ruled as dictator in Spain until his death in 1975.

THACKERAY, WILLIAM MAKEPEACE: BIRTH ANNIVERSARY. July 18, 1811. English author, best remembered for his novels *Pendennis* and *Vanity Fair*, was born at Calcutta, India, and died at London, England, Dec 23, 1863.

THOMPSON, HUNTER S.: BIRTH ANNIVERSARY. July 18, 1939. Journalist and author born Louisville, KY, Thompson was one of the first practitioners of "New," or "Gonzo," journalism, a style that featured first-person accounts and scathing criticism of contemporary American society. His most famous work, "Fear and Loathing in Las Vegas," published in *Rolling Stone* magazine in 1972, featured an alter ego character in search of the American Dream via use of hallucinogenic drugs. Other works included *Hell's Angels, The Great Shark Hunt* and *The Proud Highway*. Long hailed as a hero of counterculture, Thompson committed suicide at his home in Woody Creek, CO, Feb 21, 2005.

July 2006	S	M	T	W	T	F	S
							1
	2	3	4	5	6	7	8
	9	10	11	12	13	14	15
	16	17	18	19	20	21	22
	23	24	25	26	27	28	29
	30	31					

URUGUAY: CONSTITUTION DAY. July 18. National holiday. Commemorates the country's first constitution in 1830.

WHITE, GILBERT: BIRTH ANNIVERSARY. July 18, 1720. Born at Selborne, Hampshire, England, Gilbert White has been called the "father of British naturalists." His book *The Natural History of Selborne*, published in 1788, enjoyed immediate success and is said never to have been out of print. White died near his birthplace, June 26, 1793. His home survives as a museum.

BIRTHDAYS TODAY

James Brolin, 65, actor (Emmy for "Marcus Welby, MD"; "Hotel"), born Los Angeles, CA, July 18, 1941.

Richard Totten (Dick) Button, 77, sportscaster, Olympic gold medal figure skater, born Englewood, NJ, July 18, 1929.

Vin Diesel, 39, actor (*XXX, The Fast and the Furious, Pitch Black*), born Mark Vincent at New York, NY, July 18, 1967.

Dion DiMucci, 67, singer (Dion and the Belmonts), born the Bronx, NY, July 18, 1939.

Nick Faldo, 49, golfer, born Welwyn Garden City, England, July 18, 1957.

Steve Forbes, 59, publisher, chairman, Forbes Newspapers, born Morristown, NJ, July 18, 1947.

John Glenn, 85, astronaut, first American to orbit Earth, former US senator (D, Ohio), born Cambridge, OH, July 18, 1921.

Anfernee ("Penny") Hardaway, 34, basketball player, born Memphis, TN, July 18, 1972.

Elizabeth McGovern, 45, actress (*Ordinary People, Racing with the Moon*), born Evanston, IL, July 18, 1961.

Calvin Peete, 63, golfer, born Detroit, MI, July 18, 1943.

Martha Reeves, 65, lead singer (Martha & the Vandellas, "Power of Love"), born Detroit, MI, July 18, 1941.

Ricky Skaggs, 52, musician (bluegrass guitar), singer ("I Don't Care"), born Cordell, KY, July 18, 1954.

Joe Torre, 66, baseball manager and former player, born New York, NY, July 18, 1940.

Yevgeny Yevtushenko, 73, poet, born Zima, USSR, July 18, 1933.

JULY 19 — WEDNESDAY

Day 200 — 165 Remaining

ANN ARBOR SUMMER ART FAIR®. July 19–22. Ann Arbor, MI. Juried art fair with more than 450 of the nation's finest artists and contemporary craftspeople. Free family art activity area, performance areas, artist showcase tent and print tent. Est attendance: 500,000. For info: Debra "Max" Clayton, Exec Dir, Michigan Guild of Artists and Artisans, 118 N Fourth Ave, Ann Arbor, MI 48104-1402. Phone: (734) 662-3382. E-mail: guild@michiganguild.org. Web: www.michiganguild.org.

ATTACK ON FORT WAGNER: ANNIVERSARY. July 19, 1863. In a second attempt to capture Fort Wagner, outside Charleston, SC, Federal troops were repulsed after losing 1,515 men as opposed to Southern losses of only 174. The attack was led by the 54th Massachusetts Colored Infantry, commanded by Colonel Robert Gould Shaw, who was killed in the action. This was the first use of black troops in the war. The film *Glory* was based on the Massachusetts 54th, and this was the attack featured in the film. Fort Wagner was never taken by the Union.

CANADA: WINNIPEG FRINGE THEATRE FESTIVAL. July 19–30. Winnipeg, MB. A 12-day, noon-to-midnight, nonstop theatrical smorgasbord with more than 130 theatre companies from around the world. The Winnipeg Fringe Festival: Pushing the envelope in theatrical entertainment since 1988. Est attendance: 140,000. For info: The Winnipeg Fringe Festival, 174 Market Ave, Winnipeg, MB, Canada R3B 0P8. Fax: (204) 947-3741. E-mail: fringe@mtc.mb.ca. Web: www.winnipegfringe.com.

DEGAS, EDGAR: BIRTH ANNIVERSARY. July 19, 1834. French Impressionist painter, especially noted for his paintings of dancers in motion, was born at Paris, France, and died there Sept 26, 1917.

ELVIS PRESLEY'S FIRST SINGLE RELEASED: ANNIVERSARY. July 19, 1954. "That's All Right (Mama)" backed by "Blue Moon of Kentucky" was released on this date by Sun Records of Memphis, TN. It was 19-year-old Elvis Presley's first professional record. Presley recorded it with guitarist Scotty Moore and bassist Bill Black. Memphis DJ Dewey Phillips previewed the single on July 7—literally two days after it was recorded—on his radio show and his listeners went crazy, demanding that Phillips play it again and again. See also "Elvis Presley's First Concert Appearance: Anniversary" (July 30).

FIRST WOMAN VICE-PRESIDENTIAL CANDIDATE: ANNIVERSARY. July 19, 1984. Congresswoman Geraldine Ferraro was nominated to run with presidential candidate Walter Mondale on the Democratic ticket. They were defeated by the Republican ticket headed by Ronald Reagan.

GEORGIA MOUNTAIN FAIR. July 19–30. Georgia Mountain Fairgrounds, Hiawassee, GA. Authentic mountain demonstrations including corn millin', board splittin', soap and hominy makin' and others. Pioneer village with re-created one-room school, log cabin, barn and corncrib. Nashville talent, clogging, midway, arts and crafts and much more. Est attendance: 130,000. For info: Georgia Mountain Fair, PO Box 444, Hiawassee, GA 30546. Phone: (706) 896-4191.

THE LORD OF THE RINGS: FIRST PART PUBLISHED: ANNIVERSARY. July 19, 1954. *The Fellowship of the Ring*, the first part of J.R.R. Tolkien's epic *The Lord of the Rings* was published on this date in London, England, by George Allen and Unwin. The publishers chose to publish the book in three parts because it was so long. *The Two Towers* was published on Nov 11, 1954, and *The Return of the King* was published on Oct 20, 1955.

MARILYN MONROE'S FIRST SCREEN TEST: 60th ANNIVERSARY. July 19, 1946. Marilyn Monroe was given her first screen test at Twentieth Century-Fox Studios. Even with no sound, this test was all they needed to sign her first contract. Beginning with *Scudda-Hoo! Scudda-Hay!* in 1948 and ending with *The Misfits* in 1961, Monroe made a total of 29 films during her short career.

MAYO, CHARLES HORACE: BIRTH ANNIVERSARY. July 19, 1865. American surgeon, one of the Mayo brothers, founders of the Mayo Clinic and Mayo Foundation, born at Rochester, MN. Died at Chicago, IL, May 26, 1939.

MERRIAM, EVE: BIRTH ANNIVERSARY. July 19, 1916. A poet, playwright and author of more than 50 books for both adults and children. Merriam's works, which often focused on feminism, include *It Doesn't Always Have to Rhyme; After Nora Slammed the Door: The Women's Unfinished Revolution; Mommies at Work* and a book of poems attacked by authorities as glamorizing crime, *The Urban Mother Goose*. Her play *Out of Our Father's House*, portraying the lives of American women, was presented on public television's "Great Performances" series. She also wrote the first documentary on women's rights for network TV, *We the Women*. Born at Philadelphia, PA, she died at New York, NY, Apr 11, 1992.

NICARAGUA: NATIONAL LIBERATION DAY. July 19. Following the National Day of Joy (July 17—anniversary of date in 1979 when dictator Anastasio Somoza Debayle fled Nicaragua) is annual July 19 observance of National Liberation Day, anniversary of day the National Liberation Army claimed victory over the Somoza dictatorship.

SAINT VINCENT DE PAUL: OLD FEAST DAY. July 19. A day remembering the founder of the Vincentian Congregation and the Sisters of Charity, born at Pouy, France, Apr 24, 1581. He died Sept 27, 1660, at Paris, France. His Feast Day was formerly observed on July 19 but is now observed on the anniversary of his death, Sept 27.

WOMEN'S RIGHTS CONVENTION AT SENECA FALLS: ANNIVERSARY. July 19, 1848. A convention concerning the rights of women, called by Lucretia Mott and Elizabeth Cady Stanton, was held at Seneca Falls, NY, July 19–20, 1848. The issues discussed included voting, property rights and divorce. The convention drafted a "Declaration of Sentiments" that paraphrased the Declaration of Independence, addressing man instead of King George, and called for women's "immediate admission to all the rights and privileges which belong to them as citizens of the United States." This convention was the beginning of an organized women's rights movement in the US. The most controversial issue was Stanton's demand for women's right to vote.

YALOW, ROSALYN: BIRTHDAY. July 19, 1921. Medical physicist Rosalyn Yalow was born at New York City. Along with Andrew V. Schally and Roger Guillemin, in 1977 Yalow was awarded the Nobel Prize for Physiology or Medicine. Through her research on medical applications of radioactive isotopes, Yalow developed RIA, a sensitive and simple technique used to measure minute concentrations of hormones and other substances in blood or other body fluids. First applied to the study of insulin concentration in the blood of diabetics, RIA was soon used in hundreds of other applications.

BIRTHDAYS TODAY

Vikki Carr, 65, singer ("It Must Be Him," "With Pen in Hand"), born Florencia Bisenta de Casilla at El Paso, TX, July 19, 1941.

Anthony Edwards, 44, actor ("ER," *Fast Times at Ridgemont High, Top Gun*), born Santa Barbara, CA, July 19, 1962.

Topher Grace, 28, actor ("That 70s Show," *Traffic*), born New York, NY, July 19, 1978.

Clea Lewis, 41, actress ("Ellen," *The Rich Man's Wife*), born Cleveland Heights, OH, July 19, 1965.

George Stanley McGovern, 84, former US senator and '72 Democratic presidential nominee, born Avon, SD, July 19, 1922.

Ilie Nastase, 60, former tennis player, born Bucharest, Romania, July 19, 1946.

Campbell Scott, 44, actor (*Roger Dodger, Singles*), born Westchester County, NY, July 19, 1962.

July *2006*	S	M	T	W	T	F	S
							1
	2	3	4	5	6	7	8
	9	10	11	12	13	14	15
	16	17	18	19	20	21	22
	23	24	25	26	27	28	29
	30	31					

JULY 20 — THURSDAY
Day 201 — 164 Remaining

"ARTHUR MURRAY PARTY" TV PREMIERE: ANNIVERSARY. July 20, 1950. This ballroom dancing show appeared on all four networks (ABC, Dumont, CBS and NBC) and was hosted by Kathryn Murray, wife of famed dance school founder Arthur Murray.

ATTEMPT ON HITLER'S LIFE: ANNIVERSARY. July 20, 1944. During the daily staff meeting at German Headquarters at Rastenburg, an attempt was made to assassinate Adolf Hitler. Count Claus Schenk von Stauffenberg, chosen from a group of German military and civil servants involved in the plot, left a briefcase containing a bomb only six feet from Hitler under the staff table in the briefing room. Four people were killed in the blast, but Hitler's life was saved probably because Colonel Heinz Brandt (who was among those killed) found the briefcase in his way and moved it farther from the German dictator.

BASEBALL DECLARED NONESSENTIAL OCCUPATION: ANNIVERSARY. July 20, 1918. Secretary of War Newton D. Baker ruled that baseball was a nonessential occupation. He stated that all players of draft age should seek "employment to aid successful prosecution of the war or shoulder guns and fight." On July 26, Baker allowed baseball to continue until Sept 1. Nearly 250 ballplayers entered the armed services.

COLOMBIA: INDEPENDENCE DAY. July 20. National holiday. Commemorates the beginning of the independence movement with an uprising against Spanish officials in 1810 at Bogota. Colombia gained independence from Spain in 1819 when Simon Bolivar decisively defeated the Spanish.

CRAFT FAIR OF THE SOUTHERN HIGHLANDS. July 20–23 (also Oct 19–22). Asheville Civic Center, Asheville, NC. In 1948 this fair started the crafts revival so evident today. More than a craft fair, this event includes demonstrations and traditional mountain music—all in addition to the 180 craftspeople representing the finest crafts in a nine-state mountain region. Est attendance: 11,000. For info: Southern Highland Craft Guild, PO Box 9545, Asheville, NC 28815. Phone: (828) 298-7928. Fax: (828) 298-7962. E-mail: info@craftguild.org. Web: www.craftguild.org.

DELAWARE STATE FAIR. July 20–29. Harrington, DE. 87th annual fair will feature major concert and motor events, acres of carnival rides, livestock shows, petting zoos, commercial and competitive events, exotic food and free attractions throughout the grounds. Est attendance: 321,000. For info: Delaware State Fair, PO Box 28, Harrington, DE 19952. Phone: (302) 398-3269. Fax: (302) 398-5030. E-mail: info@delawarestatefair.com. Web: www.delawarestatefair.com.

ENGLAND: THE OPEN CHAMPIONSHIP. July 20–23. The Royal Liverpool Golf Club, Hoylake, Merseyside. Est attendance: 180,000. For info: Ticket Office, The R&A, St. Andrews, Fife, Scotland KY16 9JD, United Kingdom. Phone: (44) (1334) 460-000. Fax: (44) (1334) 460-002. E-mail: tickets@randa.org.

FALCON RIDGE FOLK FESTIVAL. July 20–23. Hillsdale, NY. A four-day community of folk music and dance at the foot of the Berkshires. Mainstage concerts, all-day and into the night dancing, camping, crafts and workshops. Plenty of activities for everyone in the family to enjoy at Long Hill Farm. For info: Falcon Ridge Folk Festival, 74 Modley Rd, Sharon, CT 06069. Phone: (860) 364-0366. Web: www.falconridgefolk.com.

FARGO'S DOWNTOWN STREET FAIR. July 20–22. Fargo, ND. Whether your interest is in baskets, pottery, jewelry, paintings, photography or sculpture, you'll find something at this fair with more than 300 exhibiting artists. Three days of unique arts and crafts, incredible food and free entertainment. Est attendance: 200,000. For info: North Dakota Tourism, Century Center, 1600 E Century Ave, Ste 2, Bismarck, ND 58503. Phone: (701) 241-1570 or (800) 435-5663. Web: www.fmdowntown.com.

GENEVA ACCORDS: ANNIVERSARY. July 20, 1954. An agreement covering cessation of hostilities in Vietnam, signed at Geneva, Switzerland, on behalf of the commanders-in-chief of French forces at Vietnam and the People's Army of Vietnam. A further declaration of the Geneva Conference was released July 21, 1954. Partition, foreign troop withdrawal and elections for a unified government within two years were among provisions.

HILLARY, SIR EDMUND PERCIVAL: BIRTHDAY. July 20, 1919. Explorer, mountaineer born at Auckland, New Zealand. With Tenzing Norgay, a Sherpa guide, became first to ascend summit of highest mountain in the world, Mt Everest (29,028 ft), at 11:30 AM, May 29, 1953. "We climbed because nobody climbed it before," he said.

JAPAN: MARINE DAY. July 20. National holiday.

LOCUST PLAGUE OF 1874: ANNIVERSARY. July 20–30, 1874. The Rocky Mountain locust, long a pest in the American Midwest, became an even bigger threat in the summer of 1874. Beginning in late July, the largest recorded swarm of this insect descended on the Great Plains. It is estimated that 124 billion insects formed a swarm 1,800 miles long and 110 miles wide that ranged from Canada and the Dakotas down to Texas. Contemporary accounts said that the locusts blocked out the sun and devastated farms in mere minutes. The swarms continued in smaller size for the next several years and caused an estimated $200 million in crop destruction.

"POORMAN'S PARADISE" GOLD PANNER CONTEST. July 20. Nome, AK. 106th anniversary. Open to all ages. Contestants pan a coffee can of beach material to free three small gold nuggets. All contestants are timed to determine the fastest gold panner. Trophies for 1st, 2nd and 3rd place overall; 1st, 2nd and 3rd place 12 years and younger; 1st woman. Held on the Red Sand Beaches of the Bering Sea. Est attendance: 500. For info: Rasmussen's Music Mart, PO Box 2, Nome, AK 99762. Phone: (907) 443-2798 or (907) 443-2919. Or, Gold Prospector's Assn of America, 43445 Business Park Dr, Ste 113, Temecula, CA 92590. Phone: (800) 551-9707.

RIOT ACT: ANNIVERSARY. July 20, 1715. To "read the riot act" now usually means telling children to be quiet or less boisterous, but in 18th-century England reading the riot act was a more serious matter. On July 20, 1715, the Riot Act took effect. By law in England, if 12 or more persons were unlawfully assembled to the disturbance of the public peace an authority was required "with a loud voice" to command silence and read the riot act proclamation: "Our sovereign lord the king chargeth and commandeth all persons, being assembled, immediately to disperse themselves, and peaceably to depart to their habitations, or to their lawful business, upon the pains contained in the act made in the first year of King George, for preventing tumults and riotous assemblies. God save the king." Any persons who failed to obey within one hour were to be seized, apprehended and carried before a justice of the peace.

SPACE MILESTONE: MOON DAY. July 20, 1969. Anniversary of man's first landing on the moon. Two US astronauts (Neil Alden Armstrong and Edwin Eugene Aldrin, Jr) landed lunar module *Eagle* at 4:17 PM, EDT and remained on the lunar surface 21 hours, 36 minutes and 16 seconds. The landing was made from the *Apollo XI*'s orbiting command and service module, code named *Columbia*, whose pilot, Michael Collins, remained aboard.

Armstrong was first to set foot on the moon. Armstrong and Aldrin were outside the spacecraft, walking on the moon's surface, approximately 2¼ hours. The astronauts returned to Earth July 24, bringing photographs and rock samples.

SPECIAL OLYMPICS DAY. July 20. Official anniversary of the first ever International Special Olympics Competition, held in 1968 at Soldier Field, Chicago, IL. Special Olympics is an international year-round program of sports training and competition for individuals with mental retardation. More than one million athletes in over 150 countries train and compete in 26 Olympic-style summer and winter sports. Founded in 1968 by Eunice Kennedy Shriver, Special Olympics provides people with mental retardation continuing opportunities to develop fitness, demonstrate courage and experience joy as they participate in the sharing of gifts and friendship with other athletes, their families and the community. For info: Media Relations Mgr, Special Olympics, Inc, 1133 19th St NW, Washington, DC 20036. Phone: (202) 628-3630. Fax: (202) 824-0200. Web: www.specialolympics.org.

BIRTHDAYS TODAY

Ray Allen, 31, basketball player, born Merced, CA, July 20, 1975.

Kim Carnes, 60, singer ("Bette Davis Eyes"), songwriter (cowrote score for *Flashdance*), born Hollywood, CA, July 20, 1946.

Judy Chicago, 67, artist, feminist, born Judy Cohen at Chicago, IL, July 20, 1939.

Larry E. Craig, 61, US Senator (R, Idaho), born Council, ID, July 20, 1945.

John Daley, 21, actor ("Freaks and Geeks"), born New York, NY, July 20, 1985.

Charles Joseph (Chuck) Daly, 76, Hall of Fame basketball coach, sportscaster, born St. Mary's, PA, July 20, 1930.

Donna Dixon, 49, actress ("Bosom Buddies," *Dr. Detroit*), born Alexandria, VA, July 20, 1957.

Peter Forsberg, 33, hockey player, born Ornskoldvik, Sweden, July 20, 1973.

Sir Edmund Hillary, 87, explorer (first to climb Mount Everest), born Auckland, New Zealand, July 20, 1919.

Sally Ann Howes, 76, actress (*Dead of Night, The History of Mr Polly*), singer, born London, England, July 20, 1930.

Michael Ilitch, 77, sports executive, former minor league baseball player, born Detroit, MI, July 20, 1929.

Cormac McCarthy, 73, author (*All the Pretty Horses, The Crossing*), born Providence, RI, July 20, 1933.

Barbara Ann Mikulski, 70, US Senator (D, Maryland), born Baltimore, MD, July 20, 1936.

Claudio Reyna, 33, soccer player, born Livingston, NJ, July 20, 1973.

Diana Rigg, 68, actress (Tony for *Medea; King Lear, Witness for the Prosecution*, "The Avengers"), hostess ("Mystery!"), born Doncaster, Yorkshire, England, July 20, 1938.

Carlos Santana, 59, musician, born Autlan, Mexico, July 20, 1947.

JULY 21 — FRIDAY
Day 202 — 163 Remaining

AEBLESKIVER DAYS. July 21–23. Tyler, MN. A celebration of the city's Danish heritage with Danish food, crafts and folk dancing. Est attendance: 3,000. For info: Tyler Area Community Club, Box Q, Tyler, MN 56178. Phone: (507) 247-3905. Fax: (507) 247-5502. E-mail: tribute@tylertribune.com. Web: www.aebleskiverdays.com.

ARCADIA DAZE. July 21–23. Arcadia, MI. The scenic village of Arcadia is the setting for this midsummer event. Activities include a parade on Sunday at 1:30 PM on Lake Street. An art fair, steak fry, fishing contest, games for the children, pancake breakfast, 5k running race on Saturday and a street dance on Friday and Saturday. Car Show on Saturday. An old-fashioned good time for the whole family. Sponsor: Arcadia Lion's Club. Est attendance: 2,500. For info: Wesley Hull, Arcadia Daze, 3269 Lake St, Arcadia, MI 49613. Phone: (231) 889-5555.

ARTS IN THE PARK. July 21–23. Kalispell, MT. Annual juried arts and crafts show and fair, food and entertainment. Est attendance: 12,000. For info: AIP Coordinator, Hockaday Museum of Art, 302 Second Ave E, Kalispell, MT 59901. Phone: (406) 755-5268. Fax: (406) 755-2023. E-mail: information@hockaday museum.org. Web: www.hockadaymuseum.org.

BATTLE OF BULL RUN: ANNIVERSARY. July 21, 1861. Union Gen Irvin McDowell was defeated by Confederate troops led by Gen Joseph E. Johnston at the first Battle of Bull Run at Manassas, VA. It was the first major engagement of the war. It was during this battle that Confederate Gen T.J. Jackson won the nickname "Stonewall." In the Second Battle of Bull Run, Aug 29–30, 1862, Union Gen John Pope was badly defeated by Gen Robert E. Lee.

BELGIUM: NATIONAL HOLIDAY. July 21. Marks accession of first Belgian king, Leopold I in 1831, after independence from Netherlands.

CHEYENNE FRONTIER DAYS. July 21–30. Frontier Park, Cheyenne, WY. Held annually since 1897, the world's largest outdoor rodeo is the "Daddy of 'em All" with nine rodeos, nine night shows, three free pancake breakfasts, four parades, chuckwagon racing, carnival midway and exhibitors. Annually, the last full week in July. Est attendance: 210,000. For info: Cheyenne Frontier Days, PO Box 2477, Cheyenne, WY 82003. Phone: (800) 227-6336 or (307) 778-7200. Web: www.cfdrodeo.com.

CLEVELAND, FRANCES FOLSOM: BIRTH ANNIVERSARY. July 21, 1864. Wife of Grover Cleveland, 22nd and 24th president of the US, born at Buffalo, NY. She was the youngest First Lady at age 22, and the first to marry a president in the White House. Died at Princeton, NJ, Oct 29, 1947.

EVERS, JOHNNY: 125th BIRTH ANNIVERSARY. July 21, 1881. John Joseph (Johnny) Evers, Baseball Hall of Fame second baseman, born at Troy, NY. Evers was a member of the Tinker–to–Evers–to–Chance double play combination for the Chicago Cubs that first took the field on Sept 13, 1902. Inducted into the Hall of Fame (with Tinker and Chance) in 1946, Evers died at Albany, NY, Mar 28, 1947.

FIRST ROBOT HOMICIDE: ANNIVERSARY. July 21, 1984. The first reported killing of a human by a robot occurred at Jackson, MI. A robot turned and caught a 34-year-old worker between it and a safety bar, crushing him. He died of the injuries July 26, 1984. According to the National Institute for Occupational Safety and Health, it was "the first documented case of a robot-related fatality in the US."

GOLD DISCOVERY DAYS. July 21–23. Custer, SD. Parade, pancake breakfast, bed races, children's fair, fun run, volksmarch and hot-air balloon rally. Est attendance: 6,000. For info: Custer Chamber of Commerce, 615 Washington St, Custer, SD 57730. Phone: (605) 673-2244 or (800) 992-9818. E-mail: info@custersd .com. Web: www.custersd.com.

THE GREAT WELLSVILLE BALLOON RALLY. July 21–23. Island Park, Wellsville, NY. 31st annual. The Great Wellsville Balloon Rally is a great community and western New York state event that boasts four free mass hot-air balloon launches. More than 40 hot-air balloons launch, weather permitting, at 6 PM Friday and Saturday and 6 AM Saturday and Sunday. The weekend's festivities include a huge Wellsville Main Street Merchant Sidewalk Sale, free music, great food, fireworks and afterglow. Est attendance: 50,000. For info: H.M. Bateman, Great Wellsville Balloon Rally, 2584 Trapping Brook Rd, Wellsville, NY 14895. Phone: (585) 593-2426. Web: www.wellsvilleballoonrally .com.

	S	M	T	W	T	F	S
July							1
2006	2	3	4	5	6	7	8
	9	10	11	12	13	14	15
	16	17	18	19	20	21	22
	23	24	25	26	27	28	29
	30	31					

GUAM: LIBERATION DAY. July 21. National holiday. Commemorates US forces' return to Guam in 1944, freeing the island from the Japanese.

HEMINGWAY BIRTHDAY COLLOQUIUM. July 21. Hemingway Museum, Oak Park, IL. Annual celebration of Ernest Hemingway's birth. Includes a lecture and reception. For info: The Ernest Hemingway Foundation of Oak Park, PO Box 2222, Oak Park, IL 60303-2222. Phone: (708) 848-2222. Fax: (708) 386-2952. E-mail: ehfop@sbcglobal.net. Web: www.ehfop.org.

HEMINGWAY, ERNEST: BIRTH ANNIVERSARY. July 21, 1899. American short story writer and novelist born at Oak Park, IL. Made his name with such works as *The Sun Also Rises* (1926), *A Farewell to Arms* (1929), *For Whom the Bell Tolls* (1940) and *The Old Man and the Sea* (1952). He was awarded the Nobel Prize in 1954 and wrote little thereafter; he shot himself July 2, 1961, at Ketchum, ID, having been seriously ill for some time.

IOWA STORYTELLING FESTIVAL. July 21–22 (tentative). City Park, Clear Lake, IA. This 18th annual storytelling event is held in a scenic lakeside setting. Friday evening "Stories After Dark." Two performances Saturday plus story exchange for novice tellers. Est attendance: 800. For info: Jean Casey, Dir, Clear Lake Public Library, 200 N 4th St, Clear Lake, IA 50428. Phone: (641) 357-6133. Fax: (641) 357-4645. E-mail: clplib@netins.net.

KENTUCKY STATE CHAMPIONSHIP OLD-TIME FIDDLER'S CONTEST. July 21–22. Rough River Dam State Resort Park, Falls of Rough, KY. Old-time and bluegrass music competition; Governor's cup trophy is awarded to the champion fiddler. More than $5,000 in prize money. Annually, the third Friday and Saturday in July. Est attendance: 4,000. For info: Brent L. Miller, PO Box 4042, Leitchfield, KY 42755. Phone: (270) 259-3578. Fax: (270) 259-5221. Web: www.kyfiddler.com.

McLUHAN, MARSHALL: BIRTH ANNIVERSARY. July 21, 1911. (Herbert) Marshall McLuhan, university professor and author, called "the Canadian sage of the electronic age," was born at Edmonton, AB, Canada. *Understanding Media* and *The Medium Is the Massage* (not to be confused with his widely quoted aphorism: "The medium is the message"), among other books, were widely acclaimed for their fresh view of communication. McLuhan is reported to have said: "Most people are alive in an earlier time, but you must be alive in our own time." He died at Toronto, ON, Dec 31, 1980.

NATCHITOCHES/NORTHWESTERN STATE UNIVERSITY FOLK FESTIVAL AND THE LOUISIANA STATE FIDDLE CHAMPIONSHIP. July 21–22. Prather Coliseum, Northwestern State University, Natchitoches, LA. The festival is a "purist" folk festival in that folk artists who are reviving a traditional Louisiana folk art or still working a Louisiana tradition are invited. Music, food, crafts and narrative sessions. A four-time winner of the Top Twenty Events in the Southeast, as determined by the Southeast Tourism Society. Est attendance: 5,000. For info: Dr. Lisa Abney, Louisiana Folklife Center, Natchitoches/NSU Folk Fest, NSU PO Box 3663, Natchitoches, LA 71497. Phone: (318) 357-4332 or (800) 259-1714. Fax: (318) 357-4331. E-mail: folklife@nsula.edu. Web: www.nsula.edu/folklife.

NATIONAL WOMEN'S HALL OF FAME: ANNIVERSARY. July 21, 1979. Seneca Falls, NY. Founded to honor American women whose contributions "have been of the greatest value in the development of their country" and located in the community known as the "birthplace of women's rights," where the first Women's Suffrage Movement convention was held in 1848, the Hall of Fame was dedicated with 23 inductees. Earlier National Women's Hall of Fame, honoring "Twenty Outstanding Women of the Twentieth Century," was dedicated at New York World's Fair, on May 27, 1965.

NESHOBA COUNTY FAIR. July 21–28. Philadelphia, MS. Billed as "Mississippi's Giant Houseparty," this is one of the nation's last Campground Fairs. At this 116th annual fair, harness racing, state and national political speaking, crafts, music and amusement are the order each day. Est attendance: 85,000. For info: Neshoba County Fair Assoc, 16800 Hwy 21 South, Philadelphia, MS 39350. Phone: (601) 656-8480. Fax: (601) 656-8461. Web: www.neshobacountyfair.org.

NORTH DAKOTA STATE FAIR. July 21–29. Minot, ND. For nine days the State Fair features the best in big-name entertainment, farm and home exhibits, displays, the Midway and rodeo. Est attendance: 250,000. For info: North Dakota State Fair, Box 1796, Minot, ND 58702. Phone: (701) 857-7620. Fax: (701) 857-7622. E-mail: ndsf@minot.com. Web: www.ndstatefair.com.

SAINT ANN'S ITALIAN STREET FESTIVAL. July 21–25. Hoboken, NJ. 95th annual festival features live entertainment nightly with top stars. Also, rides, games of chance, international foods, crafts and much more. Est attendance: 150,000. For info: Church of St. Ann, 704 Jefferson St, Hoboken, NJ 07030-2010. Phone: (201) 659-1114. Fax: (201) 659-1416. E-mail: churchan@bellatlantic.net. Web: www.st-annchurch.com.

SHERWOOD ROBIN HOOD FESTIVAL. July 21–22. Sherwood, OR. Renaissance group, knighting ceremony, kids and family area, parade, world's only archery contest between Sherwood and Nottingham, England, flower & castle contest, teen dance, music, food and crafts vendors and much more! Annually, the third weekend in July. Est attendance: 18,000. For info: Robin Hood Festival Assn, PO Box 496, Sherwood, OR 97140. Phone: (503) 625-4233.

SONG OF HIAWATHA PAGEANT. July 21–23 (also July 28–30 and Aug 4–6). Pipestone, MN. 58th annual presentation of pageant based on Longfellow's poem, held in a natural outdoor amphitheater. Elaborate lighting, lovely costumes and cast of 200 help make an unforgettable event. Annually, last two weekends in July and first weekend in August. Sponsor: The Hiawatha Club. Est attendance: 9,600. For info: Mick Myers, Exec Dir, Pipestone Chamber of Commerce, PO Box 8 CAE, Pipestone, MN 56164. Phone: (800) 430-4126. Fax: (507) 825-3317. E-mail: hiawathaclub@iw.net. Web: www.songofhiawathapageant.com.

THOUSAND ISLANDS QUILT SHOW. July 21–22. K of C Hall, Clayton, NY. New and old quilts on display in this 12th annual show, "Quilting in the Islands." For info: 1000 Islands Museum, 312 James St, Clayton, NY 13624. Phone: (315) 686-5794. Fax: (315) 686-4867. E-mail: info@timuseum.org. Web: www.timuseum.org.

YARMOUTH CLAM FESTIVAL. July 21–23. Yarmouth, ME. 41st annual. Family-oriented festival featuring clams and more. Annually, starts the third Friday in July. Est attendance: 150,000. For info: Yarmouth Chamber of Commerce, 162 Main St, Yarmouth, ME 04096. Phone: (207) 846-3984. Fax: (207) 846-5419. E-mail: info@clamfestival.com. Web: www.clamfestival.com.

ZIPPO/CASE INTERNATIONAL SWAP MEET. July 21–22. Zippo/Case Visitors Center, Bradford, PA. Annual gathering of fans and collectors of Zippo windproof lighters and Case knives. Hosted by Zippo Manufacturing Company and its subsidiary W.R. Case & Sons Cutlery. Est attendance: 10,000. For info: Communications Coordinator, Zippo Manufacturing Co, 33 Barbour St, Bradford, PA 16701. Phone: (814) 368-2700. Fax: (814) 368-2874. Web: zippo.com or wrcase.com.

BIRTHDAYS TODAY

Brandi Chastain, 38, soccer player, born San Jose, CA, July 21, 1968.

Lance Guest, 46, actor ("Lou Grant," *The Last Starfighter*), born Saratoga, CA, July 21, 1960.

Josh Hartnett, 28, actor (*Pearl Harbor, Halloween H2O*), born San Francisco, CA, July 21, 1978.

Edward Herrmann, 63, actor (*The Paper Chase, Eleanor and Franklin*), born Washington, DC, July 21, 1943.

Norman Jewison, 80, producer, director (*Moonstruck, Fiddler on the Roof*), born Toronto, ON, Canada, July 21, 1926.

Don Knotts, 82, actor, comedian ("The Andy Griffith Show," *The Ghost and Mr Chicken*), born Morgantown, WV, July 21, 1924.

Jon Lovitz, 49, actor (*A League of Their Own*, "NewsRadio"), born Tarzana, CA, July 21, 1957.

Matt Mulhern, 46, actor ("Major Dad," *Biloxi Blues*), born Philadelphia, PA, July 21, 1960.

Janet Reno, 68, former US Attorney General (Clinton administration), born Miami, FL, July 21, 1938.

C.C. Sabathia, 26, baseball player, born Vallejo, CA, July 21, 1980.

Cat Stevens, 58, singer, songwriter, chosen Muslim name is Yusuf Islam, born Stephen Demetri Georgiou at London, England, July 21, 1948.

Garry Trudeau, 57, political cartoonist ("Doonesbury"), born New York, NY, July 21, 1949.

Robin Williams, 54, actor ("Mork and Mindy," *Mrs Doubtfire, Dead Poets Society, Good Will Hunting*), born Chicago, IL, July 21, 1952.

JULY 22 — SATURDAY
Day 203 — 162 Remaining

ALLIES TAKE PALERMO: ANNIVERSARY. July 22, 1943. Two weeks after the July 10 Allied invasion of Sicily, the principal northern town of Palermo was captured. Americans had cut off 50,000 Italian troops in the west, but Germans were escaping to the northeastern corner of the island. After 39 days, on Aug 17, 1943, the entire island of Sicily was under the control of Allied forces. The official total of Germans and Italians captured was put at 130,000. The Germans, however, managed to transfer 60,000 of their 90,000 men back to the Italian mainland.

ANTIQUE AND CLASSIC BOAT RENDEZVOUS. July 22–23. Mystic Seaport, Mystic, CT. Pre-1952 power and sailing yachts on view for Mystic Seaport visitors. Mystic River parade on Sunday. Est attendance: 4,000. For info: Mystic Seaport, 75 Greenmanville Ave, Box 6000, Mystic, CT 06355. Phone: (860) 527-5315 or (888) 973-2767. Web: www.mysticseaport.org.

CALDER, ALEXANDER: BIRTH ANNIVERSARY. July 22, 1898. Internationally acclaimed American abstract artist who invented the mobile. Born at Lawnton, PA, Calder took a degree in mechanical engineering, but was drawn into art in the 1920s. By the 1930s, he was the most famous American artist in the world. Calder created the mobile, a delicate hanging kinetic sculpture whose form changed continuously due to air currents or motors. His stationary abstract sculptures were termed "stabiles," and they influenced many generations of artists to turn to industrial materials and monumental scope for expression as he had (with works like *Flamingo* [1974]). Calder died Nov 11, 1976, at New York, NY.

CANADA: MINERAL CAPITAL ROCK SHOW. July 22. Bancroft, ON. Mineral specimens from central Ontario and Quebec dealers, mineral exhibits, lapidary demonstrations, silent auctions and grand live auction. Est attendance: 1,500. For info: Bancroft and District Chamber of Commerce, PO Box 539, Bancroft, ON, Canada K0L 1C0. Phone: (613) 758-1083. E-mail: chamber@commerce.bancroft.on.ca. Web: www.bancroftdistrict.com.

CANADA: NATIONAL DROWNING PREVENTION DAY. July 22. Drowning is the third leading cause of unintentional death for Canadians under the age of 60—and the majority of these deaths are preventable. The Lifesaving Society urges everyone to please remember the following precautions while out enjoying water activities this summer: always wear a lifejacket while in or near water, take a boating lesson, learn how to swim, keep a close eye on children near or in water, do not consume alcohol while boating and learn rescue skills. For info: Rick Haga, The Lifesaving Society, 287 McArthur Ave, Ottawa, ON, Canada K1L 6P3. Phone: (613) 746-5694. E-mail: experts@lifesaving.ca. Web: www.lifesaving.ca.

DILLINGER, JOHN: DEATH ANNIVERSARY. July 22, 1934. Bank robber, murderer, prison escapee and the first person to receive the FBI's appellation "Public Enemy No. 1" (July 1934). After nine years in prison (1924–33), Dillinger traveled through the Midwest, leaving a path of violent crimes. Reportedly betrayed by the "Lady in Red," he was killed by FBI agents as he left Chicago's Biograph movie theater (where he had watched *Manhattan Melodrama*, starring Clark Gable and Myrna Loy), July 22, 1934. He was born at Indianapolis, IN, June 28, 1902.

GENEVA ARTS FAIR. July 22–23. Geneva, IL. Over 100 artist booths welcome visitors to an open-air Fine Art Show held amid shady trees surrounding the historic Kane County Courthouse. Annually, the fourth Saturday and Sunday in July. Est attendance: 22,000. For info: Geneva Chamber of Commerce, PO Box 481, 8 S Third St, Geneva, IL 60134. Phone: (630) 232-6060. Fax: (630) 232-6083. E-mail: chamberinfo@genevachamber.com. Web: www.genevachamber.com.

HARVEST WEEKENDS. July 22–23. (Also July 29–30, Aug 5–6, 12–13 and 19–20.) Bryan, TX. Step into the romance of winemaking by joining the Harvest Pickers Club and participate in hand-harvesting. A typical harvest weekend begins with a walk through the vines followed by the leisurely hand-harvesting of grapes. Afterward, you're invited to attend a classic European-style harvest luncheon that is followed by a wine and food pairing seminar. Annually, last two weekends of July and first three weekends of August to coincide with the grape harvest. For info: Messina Hof Wine Cellars, 4545 Old Reliance Rd, Bryan, TX 77808. Phone: (979) 778-9463, ext 34. Fax: (979) 778-1729. Web: www.messinahof.com.

LEWIS AND CLARK BICENTENNIAL NATIONAL SIGNATURE EVENT: CLARK ON THE YELLOWSTONE. July 22–25. Billings, MT. The Clark on the Yellowstone Signature Event enables modern day explorers to rediscover Captain William Clark's travels along the Yellowstone River. This event commemorates the 200th anniversary of Clark inscribing his name on Pompeys Pillar, the only remaining physical evidence of the Lewis & Clark Expedition appearing on the trail as it did 200 years ago. Clark, showing his affection for Sacagawea's young son, whom he called "Pomp," named this sandstone pillar at the river's edge in his honor. A National Day of Honor commemorating this event, and recognizing the historic use of the Pillar by Native Americans is set for July 25, 2006. A new interpretive center will greet visitors at the recently created Pompeys Pillar National Monument, administered by the Bureau of Land Management. Canoe landings, trail rides, wildlife displays and exhibits at local museums in nearby Billings, MT, will engage people of all ages. For info: Robbie Carpenter or Melody Dobson, Clark on the Yellowstone, Billings Chamber of Commerce, 815 S 27th St, Billings, MT 59101. Phone: (406) 245-4111, ext 101. E-mail: clarkevents@billingschamber.com. Web: www.clarkonthe yellowstone.org or www.lewisandclark200.org.

MENDEL, GREGOR JOHANN: BIRTH ANNIVERSARY. July 22, 1822. Botanist Gregor Mendel was born of peasant parents at Heinzendorf, Austria. His pioneering work in genetics became the basis for the modern science of genetics and heredity. Around 1856 Mendel began experiments in his small monastery garden, crossing different varieties of the garden pea. The import of Mendel's work was not seen until many years after his death, Jan 6, 1884, at Brünn. In 1900 other European botanists discovered his papers and confirmed and extended his theories, which formed the basis of the study of heredity and genetics.

NATHAN HALE ANCIENT FIFES AND DRUMS COLONIAL ENCAMPMENT AND MUSTER. July 22–23 (tentative). Nathan Hale Homestead, Coventry, CT. Colonial battle reenactments, camp-life demonstrations, colonial fashion show, open-hearth cooking and colonial crafts are highlights on Saturday. On Sunday, in addition to the above there is also a battle of colonial bands when fife and drum corps amass for a muster. Annually, the fourth Saturday and Sunday in July. For info: The Nathan Hale Homestead, 2299 South St, Coventry, CT 06238. Phone: (860) 742-6917.

PIED PIPER OF HAMELIN: ANNIVERSARY—MAYBE. July 22, 1376. According to legend, the German town of Hamelin, plagued with rats, bargained with a piper who promised to, and did, pipe the rats out of town and into the Weser River. Refused payment for his work, the piper then piped the children out of town and into a hole in a hill, never to be seen again. More recent historians suggest that the event occurred in 1284 when young men of Hamelin left the city on colonizing adventures.

RAT-CATCHERS DAY. July 22. A day to recognize the rat-catchers who labor to exterminate members of the genus *Rattus*, disease-carrying rodents that infest most of the "civilized" world. Observed on the anniversary of the legendary feat of the Pied Piper of Hamelin on July 22, 1376 (according to 16th-century chronicler Richard Rowland Verstegen).

RILEY, JAMES WHITCOMB: DEATH ANNIVERSARY. July 22, 1916. American "Hoosier" poet, born at Greenfield, IN, Oct 7, probably in 1853, but possibly several years earlier. Riley died at Indianapolis, IN.

SPACE MILESTONE: *SOYUZ TM-3* **(USSR).** July 22, 1987. Two Soviet cosmonauts, Aleksandr Viktorenko and Aleksandr Aleksandrov, along with the first Syrian space traveler, Mohammed Faris, were launched on a projected 10-day mission. Launched from the Baikonur base in Central Asia, the spacecraft orbited Earth for two days before linking with Soviet space station *Mir*. The *Soyuz TM-3* spacecraft was used as a shuttle to *Mir* into the 1990s.

SPAIN: SAN SEBASTIAN JAZZ FESTIVAL. July 22–27. San Sebastian. This 41st annual festival is the oldest surviving

	S	M	T	W	T	F	S
July							1
	2	3	4	5	6	7	8
2006	9	10	11	12	13	14	15
	16	17	18	19	20	21	22
	23	24	25	26	27	28	29
	30	31					

jazz festival in Europe. Est attendance: 60,000. For info: Festival de Jazz San Sebastian, 2 Calle Camino, 20004 Donostia-San Sebastian, Spain. Phone: (34) (943) 440-034. Fax: (34) (943) 421-117. E-mail: jazzaldia@donostia.org. Web: www.jazzaldia.com.

SPOONER'S DAY (WILLIAM SPOONER BIRTH ANNIVERSARY). July 22. A day named for the Reverend William Archibald Spooner (born at London, England, July 22, 1844, warden of New College, Oxford, 1903–24, died at Oxford, England, Aug 29, 1930), whose frequent slips of the tongue led to coinage of the term *spoonerism* to describe them. A day to remember the scholarly man whose accidental transpositions gave us blushing crow (for crushing blow), tons of soil (for sons of toil), queer old dean (for dear old queen), swell foop (for fell swoop) and half-warmed fish (for half-formed wish).

TAYLOR HORSEFEST. July 22. Taylor, ND. This annual celebration is highlighted by a parade of horses and horse-drawn equipment, ethnic food fest, craft vendors, exhibits, demonstrations, music and cowboy poetry. Horse-drawn taxis provide transportation throughout the town during the day. Est attendance: 3,500. For info: Taylor Horsefest, PO Box 7, Taylor, ND 58656. Phone: (701) 974-4210 or (877) 757-7545. Web: www.taylorhorse fest.com.

BIRTHDAYS TODAY

Orson Bean, 78, actor ("To Tell the Truth," "Mary Hartman, Mary Hartman"), born Dallas Frederick Burroughs at Burlington, VT, July 22, 1928.

Irene Bedard, 39, actress ("Grand Avenue," "Crazy Horse," *Squanto: A Warrior's Tale*; voice of Pocahontas in the Disney film), born Anchorage, AK, July 22, 1967.

Albert Brooks, 59, comedian, director, actor (*Finding Nemo, Broadcast News, Mother*), born Albert Lawrence Einstein at Los Angeles, CA, July 22, 1947.

Willem Dafoe, 51, actor (*Platoon, Mississippi Burning*), born Appleton, WI, July 22, 1955.

Oscar De La Renta, 74, fashion designer, born Santo Domingo, Dominican Republic, July 22, 1932.

Robert J. Dole, 83, former US senator (R, Kansas), born Russell, KS, July 22, 1923.

Rob Estes, 43, actor ("Melrose Place," "Silk Stalkings"), born Norfolk, VA, July 22, 1963.

Danny Glover, 59, actor ("Chiefs," *Lethal Weapon, The Color Purple*), born San Francisco, CA, July 22, 1947.

Don Henley, 59, musician (The Eagles), songwriter (cowrote "The Boys of Summer"), born Linden, TX, July 22, 1947.

Kay Bailey Hutchison, 63, US Senator (R, Texas), born Galveston, TX, July 22, 1943.

Rhys Ifans, 39, actor (*Notting Hill, Dancing at Lughnasa*), born Ruthin, Wales, July 22, 1967.

Keyshawn Johnson, 34, football player, born Los Angeles, CA, July 22, 1972.

John Leguizamo, 41, actor (*Carlito's Way*; stage: *Mambo Mouth* [also writer; Obie Award], *Spic-O-Rama* [also writer; Theatre World Award]), born Bogotá, Colombia, July 22, 1965.

Alan Menken, 57, film score composer (*Pocahontas, Aladdin*), born New Rochelle, NY, July 22, 1949.

Bobby Sherman, 61, singer, actor, born Santa Monica, CA, July 22, 1945.

David Spade, 41, actor ("Saturday Night Live," "Just Shoot Me," *Black Sheep*), born Birmingham, MI, July 22, 1965.

Terence Stamp, 67, actor (*The Limey, Alien Nation, The Collector*), born London, England, July 22, 1939.

Keith Sweat, 45, R&B singer, born New York, NY, July 22, 1961.

Alex Trebek, 66, game-show host ("Concentration," "Jeopardy"), born Sudbury, ON, Canada, July 22, 1940.

Margaret Whiting, 82, singer ("The Money Tree," "The Wheel of Hurt"), born Detroit, MI, July 22, 1924.

JULY 23 — SUNDAY
Day 204 — 161 Remaining

ADMINISTRATIVE PROFESSIONALS INTERNATIONAL ANNUAL CONVENTION AND EDUCATION FORUM. July 23–26. New Orleans, LA. Est attendance: 2,000. For info: Intl Assn for Administrative Professionals, 10502 NW Ambassador Dr, PO Box 20404, Kansas City, MO 64195-0404. Phone: (816) 891-6600, ext 2223. Fax: (816) 891-9118. E-mail: meetings@iaap-hq.org. Web: www.iaap-hq.org.

CHANDLER, RAYMOND: BIRTH ANNIVERSARY. July 23, 1888. The American master of postwar hard-boiled crime fiction didn't begin writing until he lost his management job at an oil company in 1933. After publishing short stories in *Black Mask* and other crime magazines, Chandler published his first novel, *The Big Sleep*, in 1939 to popular and critical acclaim. This and subsequent novels featured Philip Marlowe, a Los Angeles private eye who liked "liquor and women and chess and a few other things." Chandler was known for spare prose that featured gripping similes: "The wet air was as cold as the ashes of love" or "She had eyes like strange sins." Chandler also authored or coauthored three Hollywood screenplays, including the searing *Double Indemnity*. Born at Chicago, IL, Chandler died at La Jolla, CA, on Mar 26, 1959.

DRYSDALE, DON: BIRTH ANNIVERSARY. July 23, 1936. Elected to the Baseball Hall of Fame in 1984, Don Drysdale was a pitcher for the Brooklyn and Los Angeles Dodgers from 1956 to 1969, compiling a won-lost record of 209–166 with a career ERA of 2.95. Following his playing career he became a successful and popular broadcast announcer for the Chicago White Sox and then for the Los Angeles Dodgers. He was born at Van Nuys, CA, and died at Montreal, QC, Canada, July 3, 1993.

EGYPT: REVOLUTION DAY. July 23, 1952. National holiday. Anniversary of the Revolution in 1952, which was launched by army officers and changed Egypt from a monarchy to a republic led by Nasser.

FIRST US SWIMMING SCHOOL OPENED: ANNIVERSARY. July 23, 1827. The first swimming school in the US opened at Boston, MA. Its pupils included John Quincy Adams and James Audubon.

"THE GENE AUTRY SHOW" TV PREMIERE: ANNIVERSARY. July 23, 1950. Popular CBS Western ran for six years starring movie actor Gene Autry. Along with sidekick Pat Buttram, Autry helped bring criminals to justice.

GORGEOUS GRANDMA DAY. July 23. Even though television and the press glamorize youth and make us older folk often feel undervalued, the "senior citizen" label can no longer describe a feeble, antiquated person who is treasured only as a volunteer or a babysitter. Indeed, the majority of us are far from powerless, sickly, frail, helpless and impotent. Today, we empower women to age with style. For info: Alice Solomon, 7385 Cortes Lake Dr, Delray Beach, FL 33446. Phone: (561) 498-3543. Fax: (561) 499-4890. E-mail: GGalice@gorgeousgrandma.com. Web: www .gorgeousgrandma.com.

HOT ENOUGH FOR YA DAY. July 23. We are permitted today to utter the words that suffice when nothing of intelligence comes to mind. "Is it hot enough for ya?" Annually, July 23. [©2003 by WH.] For info: Thomas & Ruth Roy, Wellcat Holidays, 2418 Long Ln, Lebanon, PA 17046-1708. Phone: (717) 279-0184. E-mail: info@wellcat.com. Web: www.wellcat.com.

JAPAN: SOMA NO UMAOI (WILD HORSE CHASING). July 23–25. Hibarigahara, Haramachi, Fukushima Prefecture, Japan. 1,000 horsemen clad in ancient armor compete for possession of three shrine flags shot aloft on Hibarigahara Plain, and men in white costumes attempt to catch wild horses corralled by the horsemen.

LEO, THE LION. July 23–Aug 22. In the astronomical/astrological zodiac, which divides the sun's apparent orbit into 12 segments, the period July 23–Aug 22 is identified, traditionally, as the sun sign of Leo, the Lion. The ruling celestial body is the sun.

★**PARENTS' DAY.** July 23. To pay tribute to the men and women across our country whose devotion as parents strengthens our society and forms the foundation for a bright future for America. Public Law 103-362. Annually, the fourth Sunday in July.

REESE, HAROLD HENRY ("PEE WEE"): BIRTH ANNIVERSARY. July 23, 1918. Hall of Fame shortstop, born at Ekron, KY. Died Aug 14, 1999, at Louisville, KY.

RAGBRAI®—THE *REGISTER'S* ANNUAL GREAT BICYCLE RIDE ACROSS IOWA™. July 23–29. A seven-day, leisurely tour from the western border of Iowa to the Mississippi River enjoying wonderful Iowa scenery and hospitality. RAGBRAI® is the oldest, largest and longest multiday bicycle ride in the United States. The *Des Moines Register* has coordinated this ride that attracts 10,000 riders from across the country (and around the world). Annually, the last full week of July. Est attendance: 10,000. For info: RAGBRAI, PO Box 622, Des Moines, IA 50303-0622. Phone: (800) 474-3342. E-mail: info@ragbrai.org. Web: www.ragbrai.org.

SAINT APOLLINARIS: FEAST DAY. July 23. First bishop of Ravenna, and a martyr, of unknown date. Observed July 23.

SPACE MILESTONE: FIRST FEMALE COMMANDER: *COLUMBIA* (US). July 23, 1999. Colonel Eileen Collins led a shuttle mission to deploy a $1.5 billion x-ray telescope, the Chandra observatory, into space. It is a sister satellite to the Hubble Space Telescope. The observatory is named after Nobel Prize winner Subrahamyar Chandrasekhar.

SPACE MILESTONE: *SOYUZ 37* (USSR). July 23, 1980. Cosmonauts Viktor Gorbatko and, the first non-Caucasian in space, Lieutenant Colonel Pham Tuan (Vietnam), docked at *Salyut 6* July 24. Returned to Earth July 31.

SWITZERLAND: DORNACH BATTLE COMMEMORATION. July 23. The victory at Dornach in 1499 is remembered on the battlefield and in the city of Solothurn on the Sunday nearest to July 22.

July *2006*	S	M	T	W	T	F	S
							1
	2	3	4	5	6	7	8
	9	10	11	12	13	14	15
	16	17	18	19	20	21	22
	23	24	25	26	27	28	29
	30	31					

W.C. HANDY MUSIC FESTIVAL. July 23–29. Florence, AL. A weeklong street-strutting, toe-tapping and hand-clapping celebration of the musical heritage of Florence native W.C. Handy— "the father of the blues"—culminating in a spectacular Saturday evening concert. Also includes athletic events. Est attendance: 150,000. For info: Nancy Gonce, Exec Dir, Music Preservation Society, PO Box 1827, Florence, AL 35631. Phone: (256) 766-7642. Fax: (256) 766-7549. Web: www.wchandymusicfestival.org.

BIRTHDAYS TODAY

Ronny Cox, 68, actor (*Deliverance, Bound for Glory, Total Recall*), born Cloudcroft, NM, July 23, 1938.

Gloria DeHaven, 81, actress (*Two Girls and a Sailor*, "Nakia"), born Los Angeles, CA, July 23, 1925.

Omar Epps, 33, actor (*Love & Basketball*), born Brooklyn, NY, July 23, 1973.

Nicholas Gage, 67, journalist, film producer, writer (*Eleni*), born Lia, Greece, July 23, 1939.

Nomar Garciaparra, 33, baseball player, born Whittier, CA, July 23, 1973.

Woody Harrelson, 45, actor (Emmy for "Cheers"; *White Men Can't Jump, Natural Born Killers*), born Midland, TX, July 23, 1961.

Don Imus, 66, radio talk-show host, media icon and author, born Riverside, CA, July 23, 1940.

Arata Isozaki, 75, architect, born Oita, Japan, July 23, 1931.

Anthony M. Kennedy, 70, Supreme Court Associate Justice, born Sacramento, CA, July 23, 1936.

Eriq La Salle, 44, actor ("ER," *Coming to America*), born Hartford, CT, July 23, 1962.

Edie McClurg, 55, actress ("WKRP in Cincinnati," *Eating Raoul, A River Runs Through It*), born Kansas City, MO, July 23, 1951.

Belinda Montgomery, 56, actress ("The Man from Atlantis," "Doogie Howser, MD"), born Winnipeg, MB, Canada, July 23, 1950.

Gary Dwayne Payton, 38, basketball player, born Oakland, CA, July 23, 1968.

Daniel Radcliffe, 17, actor (the Harry Potter films), born London, England, July 23, 1989 (some sources say July 31).

Marlon Wayans, 34, actor ("In Living Color," *Scary Movie*), born New York, NY, July 23, 1972.

JULY 24 — MONDAY
Day 205 — 160 Remaining

BOLÍVAR, SIMON: BIRTH ANNIVERSARY. July 24, 1783. "The Liberator," born at Caracas, Venezuela. Commemorated in Venezuela and other Latin American countries. Died Dec 17, 1830, at Santa Marta, Colombia. Bolivia is named after him.

COUSINS DAY. July 24. A day to celebrate, honor and appreciate our cousins. For info: Claudia A. Evart, 30 Park Ave, #2P, New York, NY 10016-3833. Phone: (212) 779-2227. E-mail: cevart1@earthlink.net.

DETROIT: ANNIVERSARY. July 24, 1701. Anniversary of the landing at the site of Detroit by Antoine de la Mothe Cadillac in the service of Louis XIV of France. Fort Pontchartrain du Detroit was first settlement on site.

DUMAS, ALEXANDRE: BIRTH ANNIVERSARY. July 24, 1802. French playwright and novelist, born at Villers-Cotterets, France. He is said to have written more than 300 volumes, including *The Count of Monte Cristo* and *The Three Musketeers*. Father of Alexandre Dumas (Dumas fils), also a novelist and playwright (1824–95). Dumas died near Dieppe, France, Dec 5, 1870.

EAA AIRVENTURE OSHKOSH. July 24–30. Wittman Regional Airport, Oshkosh, WI. World's largest sport aviation event. More than 10,000 airplanes annually fly in for this Experimental Aircraft Association event. Daily air shows, special programs, more than 500 forums, workshops and seminars. Est attendance: 750,000. For info: Dick Knapinski, Corporate Communications, Experimental Aircraft Assn, PO Box 3086, Oshkosh, WI 54903-3086. Phone: (920) 426-4800. E-mail: communications @eaa.org. Web: www.eaa.org.

EARHART, AMELIA: BIRTH ANNIVERSARY. July 24, 1897. American aviatrix lost on flight from New Guinea to Howland Island, in the Pacific Ocean, July 2, 1937. First woman to cross the Atlantic solo, second person to cross the Atlantic solo and first person to fly solo across the Pacific from Hawaii to California. Born at Atchison, KS.

JOHNSON COUNTY 4H AND FFA FAIR. July 24–27. Johnson County Fairgrounds, Iowa City, IA. For info: Gene Mohling, Secy, 4265 Oak Crest Hill Rd SE, 4H Fairgrounds, Iowa City, IA 52246. Phone: (319) 337-6592 or (319) 337-5865. E-mail: plichte@iastate.edu.

NATIONAL DRIVE-THRU DAY. July 24. After WW II, California sunshine and a love affair with automobiles spurred the growth of roadside businesses in the Golden State catering specifically to motorists. As America's first major drive-thru hamburger chain, Jack in the Box® restaurants (founded in 1951) helped pave the way for a delicious new dining experience. Annually, on July 24. For info: Brian Luscomb, Jack in the Box, 9330 Balboa Ave, San Diego, CA 92123. Phone: (858) 571-2121. Web: www .jackinthebox.com.

PIONEER DAY: ANNIVERSARY. July 24, 1847. Utah. State holiday. Commemorates the day when Brigham Young and his followers entered the Salt Lake Valley.

RAF JAMS NAZI RADAR IN OPERATION GOMORRAH: ANNIVERSARY. July 24, 1943. On the first of the Royal Air Force Operation Gomorrah raids on Hamburg, Germany, "windows" (bales of 10 ½" strips of aluminum foil) were pushed out of the bombers causing the German radar screens to display a snowstorm of false echo "aircraft" on their screens. As a result only 12 of the 791 bombers sent on the mission were shot down.

VIRGIN ISLANDS: HURRICANE SUPPLICATION DAY. July 24. Legal holiday. Population attends churches to pray for protection from hurricanes. Annually, the fourth Monday in July.

WORLD FOOTBAG CHAMPIONSHIPS. July 24–30. Frankfurt, Germany. 27th annual. Six-day sports event spotlights competition of footskills—the Super Bowl of footbag (also known as Hacky Sack®)! It attracts the world's top footbag competitors from the US and nine other countries. Prize money exceeds $10,000. Sponsors: Sipa Sipa Footbags and The World Footbag Association. Est attendance: 5,000. For info: Bruce Guettich, Dir, World Footbag Assn, PO Box 775208, Steamboat Springs, CO 80477. Phone: (800) 878-8797. Fax: (970) 870-2846. E-mail: wfa @worldfootbag.com. Web: www.worldfootbag.com.

BIRTHDAYS TODAY

Barry Bonds, 42, baseball player, born Riverside, CA, July 24, 1964.

Ruth Buzzi, 70, comedienne, actress ("Rowan & Martin's Laugh-In," "Sesame Street"), born Westerly, RI, July 24, 1936.

Lynda Carter, 55, actress ("Wonder Woman," "Partners in Crime"), former Miss World–USA, singer, born Phoenix, AZ, July 24, 1951.

Kristin Chenoweth, 38, singer, actress (Tony for *You're a Good Man, Charlie Brown*; "Kristin"), born Tulsa, OK, July 24, 1968.

Kadeem Hardison, 41, actor ("A Different World," "The Sixth Man"), born New York, NY, July 24, 1965.

Robert Hays, 59, actor (*Airplane!*, "Starman"), born Bethesda, MD, July 24, 1947.

Julie A. Krone, 43, former jockey, first woman in National Racing Hall of Fame, born Benton Harbor, MI, July 24, 1963.

Jennifer Lopez, 36, singer, actress (*Selena, Blood and Wine*), born the Bronx, NY, July 24, 1970.

Karl Malone, 43, basketball player, born Summerfield, LA, July 24, 1963.

Pat Oliphant, 71, cartoonist, born Adelaide, Australia, July 24, 1935.

Anna Paquin, 24, actress (*The Piano, Fly Away Home*), born Winnipeg, MB, Canada, July 24, 1982.

Chris Sarandon, 64, actor (*Dog Day Afternoon, The Princess Bride*), born Beckley, WV, July 24, 1942.

Peter Serkin, 59, musician, born New York, NY, July 24, 1947.

Billy Taylor, 85, jazz musician, born Greenville, NC, July 24, 1921.

JULY 25 — TUESDAY
Day 206 — 159 Remaining

ANDREA DORIA SINKS: 50th ANNIVERSARY. July 25, 1956. The Italian luxury liner collided with the *Stockholm*, a Swedish liner, on its way to New York. Other ships in the area came to the rescue of the *Andrea Doria*. Some 1,634 people were rescued during the ordeal, including the captain and the crew.

BROOME COUNTY FAIR. July 25–30. Whitney Point, NY. County agricultural fair. Est attendance: 39,000. For info: Rita Smith, Broome County Fair, PO Box 747, Whitney Point, NY 13862. Phone: (607) 692-4149.

COSTA RICA: GUANACASTE DAY. July 25. National holiday. Commemorates the 1814 transfer of the region of Guanacaste from Nicaragua to Costa Rica by Spain.

FIRST AIRPLANE CROSSING OF ENGLISH CHANNEL: ANNIVERSARY. July 25, 1909. Louis Bleriot, after asking from the cockpit, "Where is England?" took off from Les Baraques (near Calais), France, and landed on English soil at Northfall Meadow, near Dover, where he was greeted first by English police and customs officers. This, the world's first international overseas airplane flight, was accomplished in a 28-hp monoplane with a wingspan of 23 ft. See also: "Bleriot, Louis: Birth Anniversary" (July 1).

GERMANY: WAGNER FESTSPIELE. July 25–Aug 28. Bayreuth. The works of Richard Wagner are performed daily at the Festival Theatre, which Wagner had built in 1872–76. For info: Bayreuther Festspiele, Pressebüro, Postfach 100262, Bayreuth, Germany D-95402.

GILFORD, JACK: BIRTH ANNIVERSARY. July 25, 1907. American actor Jack Gilford was born Jacob Gellman at New York, NY. Though he was blacklisted for 10 years following refusal to answer questions before the House Un-American Activities Committee in the 1950s, he appeared in many films, stage productions and television programs including an Academy Award–nominated role opposite Jack Lemmon in *Save the Tiger* (1973) and his best-known role as Hysterium in the stage and film versions of *A Funny Thing Happened on the Way to the Forum*. He died June 4, 1990, at New York, NY.

HARRISON, ANNA SYMMES: BIRTH ANNIVERSARY. July 25, 1775. Wife of William Henry Harrison, ninth president of the US, born at Morristown, NJ. Died at North Bend, IN, Feb 25, 1864.

HEALTH AND HAPPINESS WITH HYPNOSIS DAY. July 25. Participating members of the International Registry of Professional Hypnotherapists offer free seminars, free introductory hypnotherapy sessions, media appearances to publicize how hypnosis can help people be healthier and happier. Annually, the fourth Tuesday in July. For info: Dr. Bryan Knight, Intl Registry of Professional Hypnotherapists, 7306 Sherbrooke St West, Montreal, QC, Canada H4B 1R7. Phone: (514) 332-7902. E-mail: drknight@hypnosis.org. Web: www.hypnosis.org.

MOON PHASE: NEW MOON. July 25. Moon enters New Moon phase at 12:31 AM, EDT.

MUSSOLINI OUSTED: ANNIVERSARY. July 25, 1943. Two weeks after the Allied attack on Sicily began, the Fascist Grand Council met for the first time since December of 1939 and took a confidence vote resulting in Mussolini's being removed from office and placed under arrest. Italy's King Victor Emmanuel ordered Marshal Pietro Badoglio to form a new government.

PUERTO RICO: CONSTITUTION DAY. July 25. Also called Commonwealth Day or Occupation Day. Commemorates proclamation of constitution in 1952.

PUERTO RICO: LOIZA ALDEA FIESTA. July 25–28. Best known of Puerto Rico's patron saint festivities. Villagers of Loiza Aldea, 20 miles east of San Juan, don devil masks and colorful costumes for a variety of traditional activities.

SPAIN: SAINT JAMES DAY. July 25. Holy day of the patron saint of Spain. When this day falls on a Sunday it is a holy year and pilgrims make the pilgrimage to Santiago de Compostela, the site of the saint's tomb. 2010 is the next holy year.

TEST-TUBE BABY: BIRTHDAY. July 25, 1978. Anniversary of the birth of Louise Brown at Oldham, England. First documented birth of a baby conceived outside the body of a woman. Parents: Gilbert John and Lesley Brown, of Bristol, England. Physicians: Patrick Christopher Steptoe and Robert Geoffrey Edwards.

TUNISIA: REPUBLIC DAY. July 25. National holiday. Commemorates the proclamation of the republic in 1957.

BIRTHDAYS TODAY

Midge Decter, 79, journalist, born St. Paul, MN, July 25, 1927.

Illeana Douglas, 41, actress (*Message in a Bottle, Grace of My Heart*), born Boston, MA, July 25, 1965.

Estelle Getty, 82, actress ("Golden Girls"), born New York, NY, July 25, 1924.

Iman, 51, model, actress (*Star Trek VI*), born Iman Mohamed Abdulmajid at Mogadishu, Somalia, July 25, 1955.

Matt LeBlanc, 39, actor ("Friends"), born Newton, MA, July 25, 1967.

Evgeni Nabokov, 31, hockey player, born Kamenogorsk, the former USSR, July 25, 1975.

Brad Renfro, 24, actor (*Telling Lies in America, Tom and Huck*), born Knoxville, TN, July 25, 1982.

Nathaniel (Nate) Thurmond, 65, Hall of Fame basketball player, born Akron, OH, July 25, 1941.

July	S	M	T	W	T	F	S
2006							1
	2	3	4	5	6	7	8
	9	10	11	12	13	14	15
	16	17	18	19	20	21	22
	23	24	25	26	27	28	29
	30	31					

JULY 26 — WEDNESDAY
Day 207 — 158 Remaining

AMERICANS WITH DISABILITIES ACT SIGNED: ANNIVERSARY. July 26, 1990. President George Bush signed the Americans with Disabilities Act, which went into effect two years later. It required that public facilities be made accessible to the disabled.

ARMED FORCES UNIFIED: ANNIVERSARY. July 26, 1947. President Truman signed legislation unifying the two branches of the armed forces into the Department of Defense. The branches merged were the War Department (Army) and the Navy. The Air Force was separated from the Army at the same time and made an independent force. Truman nominated James Forrestal to be the first Secretary of Defense. The legislation also provided for the National Security Council, the Central Intelligence Agency and the Joint Chiefs of Staff.

CATLIN, GEORGE: BIRTH ANNIVERSARY. July 26, 1796. American artist famous for his paintings of Native American life, born at Wilkes-Barre, PA. In 1832 he toured North and South American tribes, recording their lives in his work. He died Dec 23, 1872, at Jersey City, NJ.

CENTRAL MONTANA FAIR. July 26–30. Lewistown, MT. Draft and open-to-all-class horse show, two sessions of rodeo, carnival, 4-H and open exhibits, night shows and AMX & Demolition Derby. Est attendance: 20,000. For info: Central Montana Fair, PO Box 1098, Lewistown, MT 59457. Phone: (406) 538-8841 or (800) 406-8841. Fax: (406) 538-4060. E-mail: cmtfair@tein.net. Web: centralmontanafair.com.

CHINCOTEAGUE PONY PENNING. July 26–27. Chincoteague Island, VA. To round up the 150 wild ponies living on Assateague Island and swim them across the inlet to Chincoteague, where about 80–90 of them are sold. Annually, the last Wednesday and Thursday of July. Est attendance: 50,000. For info: Chincoteague Chamber of Commerce, Box 258, Chincoteague, VA 23336. Phone: (757) 336-6161. Fax: (757) 336-1242. E-mail: chincochamber@verizon.net. Web: www.chincoteaguechamber.com.

CLINTON, GEORGE: BIRTH ANNIVERSARY. July 26, 1739 (OS). Fourth vice president of the US (1805–12), born at Little Britain, NY. Died at Washington, DC, Apr 20, 1812.

CUBA: NATIONAL DAY: ANNIVERSARY OF REVOLUTION. July 26. Anniversary of the 1953 beginning of Fidel Castro's revolutionary "26th of July Movement." He launched a failed attack on the Moncada army barracks, and most involved were killed or captured. He was captured and given a trial, during which he made his famous speech, "History Will Absolve Me." Sentenced to 15 years, he was pardoned after just two.

CURAÇAO: CURAÇAO DAY. July 26. Traditional holiday commemorating Columbus companion Alonso de Ojeda's discovery of the Island of Curaçao in 1499, when he sailed into Santa Ana Bay, the entrance of the harbor of Willemstad. Festivities on this day.

FAIRFEST. July 26–30. Adams County Fairgrounds, Hastings, NE. Annual county fair featuring midway; open-class competitions in culinary arts, needlework, floral culture, woodworking and the visual arts; Adams County 4-H competition, livestock show; strolling acts and live entertainment in the Grand Stand. Est attendance: 82,000. For info: Sandy Himmelberg, Genl Mgr, 947 S Baltimore, Hastings, NE 68901. Phone: (402) 462-3247. Fax: (402) 462-4731. Web: www.adamscountyfairgrounds.com.

GARFIELD COUNTY FAIR. July 26–30. Burwell, NE. County fair, rodeo and commercial and craft concessions. Est attendance: 12,000. For info: Garfield County Frontier Fair Assn, Box 711, Burwell, NE 68823. Phone: (308) 346-5210. Web: www.Burwell Nebr.com.

HOOD RIVER COUNTY FAIR. July 26–29. Hood River, OR. From 4-H activities to the excitement of the carnival, this annual old-fashioned country fair is bustling with things to do! 9 AM to

11:30 PM, Wed and Thurs; 9 AM to 12:30 AM, Fri and Sat EST. Est attendance: 23,000. For info: Hood River County Fair, Box 385, Odell, OR 97044. Phone: (541) 354-2865. Fax: (541) 354-2875.

HUXLEY, ALDOUS: BIRTH ANNIVERSARY. July 26, 1894. English author, satirist, mystic and philosopher, Aldous Leonard Huxley was born at Godalming, Surrey, England. Best known of his works are *Brave New World* and *Point Counter Point.* Huxley died at Los Angeles, CA, Nov 22, 1963.

ITALY: STRESA MUSIC WEEKS. July 26–Aug 6 (also Aug 18–Sept 9) (all dates tentative). Stresa. 46th annual festival. International festival includes concerts by symphonic orchestras, chamber music, recitals and a series by young winners of international musical contests. For info: Settimane Musicali di Stresa del Lago Maggiore, Via Carducci, 38, 28838 Stresa (VB), Italy. Phone: (39) (0323) 31095. Fax: (39) (0323) 33006. E-mail: info@settimane musicali.net. Web: www.settimanemusicali.net.

KUBRICK, STANLEY: BIRTH ANNIVERSARY. July 26, 1928. American film maker, born at the Bronx, NY. Kubrick started out in photography at the age of 16 with *Look* magazine. His first film, *Day of the Fight*, produced in 1950, was a documentary of his photo series about fighter Walter Cartier. His film credits include *Dr. Strangelove, Full Metal Jacket* and *2001: A Space Odyssey. Eyes Wide Shut,* Kubrick's final film, was released posthumously in the summer of 1999. He died at London, England, Mar 7, 1999.

LIBERIA: INDEPENDENCE DAY. July 26. National holiday. Became republic in 1847, under aegis of the US societies for repatriating former slaves in Africa.

MALDIVES: INDEPENDENCE DAY. July 26. National holiday. Commemorates independence from Britain in 1965.

NEW YORK RATIFICATION DAY. July 26, 1788. 11th state to ratify Constitution in 1788.

POTSDAM DECLARATION: ANNIVERSARY. July 26, 1945. As the Potsdam Conference came to a close in Germany, Churchill, Truman and China's representatives fashioned a communique to Japan offering it an opportunity to end the war. It demanded that Japan completely disarm, allowed them sovereignty to the four main islands and to minor islands to be determined by the Allies, and insisted that all Japanese citizens be given immediate and complete freedom of speech, religion and thought. The Japanese would be allowed to continue enough industry to maintain their economy. The communique concluded with a demand for unconditional surrender. Unaware these demands were backed up by an atomic bomb, on July 28 Japanese Prime Minister Admiral Kantaro Suzuki rejected the Potsdam Declaration.

ROBARDS, JASON: BIRTH ANNIVERSARY. July 26, 1922. A staple on the American stage and screen for six decades, Robards was born at Chicago, IL, and was a decorated World War II veteran. He won the Oscar for Best Supporting Actor two years in a row, for 1976's *All the President's Men* and 1977's *Julia.* His most famous stage roles were in the plays of Eugene O'Neill, including *The Iceman Cometh* and *Long Day's Journey into Night.* He won the Tony Award in 1959 for his portrayal of a fictionalized F. Scott Fitzgerald in *The Disenchanted.* He died in Bridgeport, CT, Dec 26, 2000.

SHAW, GEORGE BERNARD: 150th BIRTH ANNIVERSARY. July 26, 1856. Irish playwright, essayist, vegetarian, socialist, antivivisectionist and, he said, ". . . one of the hundred best playwrights in the world." His major works include *Arms and the Man, Man and Superman, Major Barbara* and *Pygmalion.* Born at Dublin, Ireland. Died at Ayot St. Lawrence, England, Nov 2, 1950.

SPACE MILESTONE: *APOLLO 15* **(US): 35th ANNIVERSARY.** July 26, 1971. Launched this date. Astronauts David R. Scott and James B. Irwin landed on moon (lunar module *Falcon*) while Alfred M. Worden piloted command module *Endeavor. Rover 1*, a four-wheel vehicle, was used for further exploration. Departed moon Aug 2, after nearly three days. Pacific landing Aug 7.

US ARMY FIRST DESEGREGATION: ANNIVERSARY. July 26, 1944. During WWII the US Army ordered desegregation of its training camp facilities. Later the same year black platoons were assigned to white companies in a tentative step toward integration of the battlefield. However, it was not until after the War—July 26, 1948—that President Harry Truman signed an order officially integrating the armed forces.

BIRTHDAYS TODAY

Kate Beckinsale, 33, actress (*Pearl Harbor, Van Helsing*), born London, England, July 26, 1973.

Sandra Bullock, 42, actress (*Speed, While You Were Sleeping*), born Arlington, VA, July 26, 1964.

Blake Edwards, 84, producer, writer, director (*Victor/Victoria, The Pink Panther*), born Tulsa, OK, July 26, 1922.

Susan George, 56, actress (*Straw Dogs*), born London, England, July 26, 1950.

Mick Jagger, 63, musician, lead singer (Rolling Stones), born Michael Philip Jagger at Dartford, England, July 26, 1943.

Helen Mirren, 60, actress ("Prime Suspect"; *The Cook, The Thief, His Wife and Her Lover*), born London, England, July 26, 1946.

Jeremy Piven, 42, actor ("Ellen," *Grosse Pointe Blank*), born New York, NY, July 26, 1964.

Kevin Spacey, 47, actor (Oscar for *American Beauty; The Usual Suspects, Working Girl*; stage: *Lost in Yonkers*), born South Orange, NJ, July 26, 1959.

JULY 27 — THURSDAY
Day 208 — 157 Remaining

ATLANTIC TELEGRAPH CABLE LAID: ANNIVERSARY. July 27, 1866. Cable laying successfully completed.

BARBOSA, JOSÉ CELSO: BIRTH ANNIVERSARY. July 27, 1857. Puerto Rican physician and patriot, born at Bayamon, Puerto Rico. His birthday is a holiday in Puerto Rico. He died at San Juan, Puerto Rico, Sept 21, 1921.

BERNE SWISS DAYS. July 27–29. Berne, IN. Discover Switzerland in Indiana with Swiss food, dancing, yodeling and a parade. See quilt show, art show, "stein-toss" contest, polka bands, old-fashioned horse pull, musical, factory tours and more. Est attendance: 75,000. For info: Berne Chamber of Commerce, PO Box 85, Berne, IN 46711. Phone: (260) 589-8080. Web: www.berne swissdays.com.

BIX BEIDERBECKE MEMORIAL JAZZ FESTIVAL. July 27–30. Davenport, IA. 35th annual. Four-day jazz festival honoring the memory of and perpetuating the music of world-renowned cornetist, pianist and composer Bix Beiderbecke. Includes concerts in four venues, food, etc. Est attendance: 12,000. For info: Bix Beiderbecke Memorial Society, PO Box 3688, Davenport, IA 52808. Phone: (563) 324-7170. Fax: (563) 326-1732. E-mail: info@bixsociety.org. Web: www.bixsociety.org or www.visitquadcities.com.

CANADA: CALGARY FOLK MUSIC FESTIVAL. July 27–30. Calgary, AB. Celebration of local, national and international folk music. Est attendance: 45,000. For info: Kerry Clarke, Assoc Producer, Folk Festival Society of Calgary, PO Box 2897 Station M, Calgary, AB, Canada T2P 3C3. Phone: (403) 233-0904. E-mail: info@calgaryfolkfest.com. Web: www.calgary folkfest.com.

CANADA: ROCKHOUND GEMBOREE. July 27–30. Bancroft, ON. Daily expeditions to prime mineral locations; dealers, demonstrations and displays, swapping. Est attendance: 16,000. For info: Bancroft and District Chamber of Commerce, PO Box 539, Bancroft, ON, Canada K0L 1C0. Phone: (613) 332-1513. Fax: (613) 332-2119. E-mail: chamber@commerce.bancroft.on.ca. Web: www.bancroftdistrict.com.

DUMAS, ALEXANDRE (DUMAS FILS): BIRTH ANNIVERSARY. July 27, 1824. French novelist and playwright, as was his father. Author of *La Dame aux Camélias.* Dumas fils was born at Paris and died at Marly-le-Roi, France, Nov 27, 1895.

DUROCHER, LEO: BIRTH ANNIVERSARY. July 27, 1905. Leo Durocher was born at West Springfield, MA. He began his major league baseball career with the New York Yankees in 1925. He also played for the St. Louis Cardinals' "Gashouse Gang" and the Brooklyn Dodgers, where he first served as player-manager in 1939. On July 6, 1946, he used the phrase "Nice guys finish last," which would become his trademark. As a manager, he guided the New York Giants into two World Series. Following a five-year period away from baseball, he resurfaced as a coach with the Los Angeles Dodgers in 1961. In 1966 he signed with the Chicago Cubs as manager. After leaving the Cubs, he spent one season with the Houston Astros, then retired from baseball in 1973. He died Oct 7, 1991, at Palm Springs, CA.

GREAT TEXAS MOSQUITO FESTIVAL. July 27–29. Clute, TX. More than 100 booth spaces: arts and crafts, food, entertainment, novelty games and carnival. Meet "Willie Man Chew," a 26-ft inflatable mosquito dressed in cowboy boots and hat. Annually, the last weekend in July. Est attendance: 17,000. For info: The Great Texas Mosquito Festival, City of Clute Pks and Rec Dept, PO Box 997, Clute, TX 77531. Phone: (979) 265-8392 or (800) 371-2971. Fax: (979) 265-8767. E-mail: buzz@mosquitofestival.com. Web: www.mosquitofestival.com.

INSULIN FIRST ISOLATED: 85th ANNIVERSARY. July 27, 1921. Dr. Frederick Banting and his assistant at the University of Toronto Medical School, Charles Best, gave insulin to a dog whose pancreas had been removed. In 1922 insulin was first administered to a diabetic 14-year-old boy.

KOREAN WAR ARMISTICE: ANNIVERSARY. July 27, 1953. Armistice agreement ending war that had lasted three years and 32 days was signed at Panmunjom, Korea (July 26, US time) by US and North Korean delegates. Both sides claimed victory at conclusion of two years, 17 days of truce negotiations.

★**NATIONAL KOREAN WAR VETERANS ARMISTICE DAY.** July 27.

NEBRASKA'S BIG RODEO. July 27–29. Fairgrounds, Burwell, NE. Professional rodeo. Contestants compete in four exciting performances in historic, outdoor rodeo arena. Added thrills: chuckwagon races, wild horse races, Dinnerbell Derby, bull fighting Burwell-style. Also, quilt and art shows, parade, flea market, beef and longhorn cattle show, country and western music and dancing. Est attendance: 12,000. For info: Garfield County Frontier Fair Assn, Box 711, Burwell, NE 68823. Phone: (308) 346-5210. Web: www.BurwellNebr.com.

OREGON BREWERS FESTIVAL. July 27–30. Tom McCall Waterfront Park, Portland, OR. 72 microbreweries from across the country showcase their handcrafted brews to beer lovers. Annually, the last full weekend in July. Est attendance: 50,000. For info: Chris Crabb, Crabbsoup Public Relations, 4906 NE Siskiyou St, Portland, OR 97213. Phone: (503) 778-5917. Fax: (503) 274-1907. E-mail: chrisc@oregonbrewfest.com. Web: www.oregonbrewfest.com.

QUILT ODYSSEY 2006. July 27–30. Hershey, PA. Judged quilt competition; antique and special quilt exhibits. Large merchants' mall. Classes and lectures by nationally known professional quilters. Est attendance: 7,000. For info: Quilt Odyssey, 15004 Burnt Mill Rd, Shippensburg, PA 17257. Phone: (717) 423-5148. E-mail: quiltodyssey@supernet.com.

TAKE YOUR HOUSEPLANTS FOR A WALK DAY. July 27. Walking your plants around the neighborhood enables them to know their environment, thereby providing them with a sense of knowing, bringing on wellness. [©2003 by WH.] For info: Thomas & Ruth Roy, Wellcat Holidays, 2418 Long Ln, Lebanon, PA 17046. Phone: (717) 279-0184. E-mail: info@wellcat.com. Web: www.wellcat.com.

TINKER, JOE: BIRTH ANNIVERSARY. July 27, 1880. Born at Muscotah, KS, shortstop Joseph Bert Tinker was part of the Chicago Cubs' famous Tinker-to-Evers-to-Chance double play combination that first took the field on Sept 13, 1902. For the next eight years this trio was the soul of the powerhouse Cubs—despite the fact that Tinker and Johnny Evers stopped speaking to each other in September 1905 (they continued the feud for 33 years). Tinker played with the Cincinnati Reds after the Cubs, played and managed in the Federal League and then managed the Cubs. Inducted into the Hall of Fame (with Evers and Chance) in 1946. Died at Orlando, FL, July 27, 1948. See also: "Tinker to Evers to Chance: First Double Play Anniversary" (Sept 15).

US DEPARTMENT OF STATE FOUNDED: ANNIVERSARY. July 27, 1789. The first presidential cabinet department, called the Department of Foreign Affairs, was established by the Congress. Later the name was changed to Department of State.

WALK ON STILTS DAY. July 27. A day to walk on stilts, providing a chance to develop self-confidence through mastery of balance and coordination. A chance to enjoy the challenge of childhood no matter your age. A celebration of daring accomplishments at homes, circuses and theme parks everywhere. For info: Bill "Stretch" Coleman, Stiltwalker.com, 930 S Decatur St, Denver, CO 80219. Phone: (303) 922-4655. E-mail: stretch@stiltwalker.com. Web: www.stiltwalker.com.

BIRTHDAYS TODAY

Peggy Gale Fleming, 58, Olympic gold medal figure skater, sportscaster, born San Jose, CA, July 27, 1948.

Bobbie Gentry, 64, singer, songwriter ("Ode to Billie Joe"), born Roberta Streeter at Chicasaw County, MS, July 27, 1942.

Courtney Kupets, 20, gymnast, born Bedford, TX, July 27, 1986.

Norman Lear, 84, TV scriptwriter, producer ("All in the Family," "Maude"), born New Haven, CT, July 27, 1922.

Maureen McGovern, 57, singer ("The Morning After"), actress, born Youngstown, OH, July 27, 1949.

Julian McMahon, 38, actor ("Charmed," "Nip/Tuck"), born Sydney, New South Wales, Australia, July 27, 1968.

Alex Rodriguez, 31, baseball player, born New York, NY, July 27, 1975.

Maya Rudolph, 34, actress, comedienne ("Saturday Night Live"), born Gainesville, FL, July 27, 1972.

Betty Thomas, 58, director, actress ("Hill Street Blues"), born St. Louis, MO, July 27, 1948.

Jerry Van Dyke, 75, actor ("Coach," "Teen Angel"), born Danville, IL, July 27, 1931.

James Victor, 67, actor (*Fuzz, Stand and Deliver*), born Santiago, Dominican Republic, July 27, 1939.

July 2006	S	M	T	W	T	F	S
							1
	2	3	4	5	6	7	8
	9	10	11	12	13	14	15
	16	17	18	19	20	21	22
	23	24	25	26	27	28	29
	30	31					

JULY 28 — FRIDAY
Day 209 — 156 Remaining

AMERICAN LEGACY. July 28–30 (tentative). Fort Abraham Lincoln State Park, Mandan, ND. Frontier Army reenactments of military life. Activities and demonstrations, as well as the Mandan Indian Nu-eta Corn Festival. Events will include noted speakers and authors presenting frontier military and Native American topics. Est attendance: 5,000. For info: Jeff Hoffer, Park Historian, Fort Abraham Lincoln State Park, 4480 Fort Lincoln Rd, Mandan, ND 58554. Phone: (701) 667-6350. Fax: (701) 667-6349.

ANNIE OAKLEY DAYS. July 28–30. Greenville, OH. To keep alive the memory of Annie Oakley. Large antique and collectibles market. Annually, the last full weekend in July. Est attendance: 60,000. For info: Annie Oakley Days Committee, Inc, PO Box 129, Greenville, OH 45331. Phone: (937) 548-1582. Web: www .AnnieOakleyFestival.org.

ANTIQUE POWER EXHIBITION. July 28–30. Burton, OH. More than 100 old-time engines toot whistles and puff smoke as they demonstrate yesterday's feats such as wood sawing and grain threshing. Daily parades, slow races, tractor pulls. Est attendance: 2,600. For info: Century Village Museum, PO Box 153, Burton, OH 44021. Phone: (440) 834-1492. Fax: (440) 834-4012.

BANGOR STATE FAIR. July 28–Aug 6. Bass Park Complex, Bangor, ME. For info: Bangor State Fair, 100 Dutton St, Bangor, ME 04401. Phone: (207) 947-5555. Fax: (207) 947-5105. E-mail: info@bangorstatefair.com. Web: www.bangorstatefair.com.

BELE CHERE. July 28–30 (tentative). Asheville, NC. A community celebration featuring three food courts, eight music stages, regional and national artists, children's area and events. The largest free outdoor street festival in the Southeast. Est attendance: 350,000. For info: Paul Clarke, Festival Coord, Asheville Parks & Rec/Festival Division, PO Box 7148, Asheville, NC 28802. Phone: (828) 259-5800. Web: www.belechere.com.

CANADA: ANNUAL NOVA SCOTIA BLUEGRASS AND OLDTIME MUSIC FESTIVAL. July 28–30. Stewiacke, NS. 35th annual family event featuring acoustic music by groups from the US and Canada's Atlantic area. Annually, the last full weekend in July. Est attendance: 3,000. For info: Nova Scotia Bluegrass Oldtime Music Festival, 48 Boxwood Crescent, Lower Sackville, NS, Canada B4C 3Z0. E-mail: wgraves@acncanada.net.

CENTRAL NEBRASKA ETHNIC FESTIVAL. July 28–30. Downtown Grand Island, NE. The streets come alive with color, music and foods from all ethnic cultures in the Central Nebraska area. Singing, dancing, eating, laughter and enjoyment for the whole family. Annually, the fourth weekend in July. Est attendance: 40,000. For info: Central Nebraska Ethnic Fest, PO Box 1306, Grand Island, NE 68802. Phone: (308) 385-5444. Fax: (308) 385-5423. Web: www.grand-island.com/ethnic.

DODGE CITY DAYS. July 28–Aug 6. Dodge City, KS. Western heritage celebration with concerts, arts and crafts, parades, PRCA rodeo, street dances, cookouts, art show, classic car show. Est attendance: 90,000. For info: Dodge City Conv & Visitors Bureau, Third & W Wyatt Earp, PO Box 1474, Dodge City, KS 67801. Phone: (800) OLD-WEST. Fax: (620) 225-8268. E-mail: cvb@ dodgecity.org. Web: www.visitdodgecity.org.

FOX, TERRY: BIRTH ANNIVERSARY. July 28, 1958. With cancer requiring amputation of his right leg at age 18, Fox was determined to devote his life to a fight against the disease. His "Marathon of Hope," a planned 5,200-mile run westward across Canada, started Apr 12, 1980, at St. John's, NF, and continued 3,328 miles to Thunder Bay, ON, Sept 1, 1980, when he was forced to stop by spread of the disease. During the run (on an artificial leg) he raised $24 million for cancer research and inspired millions with his courage. Terry Fox was born at Winnipeg, MB, and died at New Westminster (near Vancouver), BC, Canada, June 28, 1981.

GILROY GARLIC FESTIVAL. July 28–30. Gilroy, CA. Midsummer harvest celebration in the "Garlic Capital of the World." Great garlic recipe contest/cook-off. Ethnic foods, continuous entertainment on three stages, arts, crafts and children's area. Annually, the last full weekend of July, Friday through Sunday. Est attendance: 130,000. For info: Gilroy Garlic Festival Assn, PO Box 2311, Gilroy, CA 95021. Phone: (408) 842-1625. Web: www.gilroygarlicfestival.com.

HAMBURG FIRESTORM: ANNIVERSARY. July 28, 1943. More than 42,000 civilians were killed when 2,326 tons of bombs, predominantly incendiaries, were dropped on Hamburg, Germany, by the Allies on this date. At the center of the firestorm the winds uprooted trees, and flames burned eight square miles in the eight hours the fire lasted. A firestorm occurs when the fires in a given area become so intense they devour all the oxygen nearby and suck more into themselves creating hurricane-force winds which feed the fires and move them at great speeds.

HANOVER DUTCH FESTIVAL. July 28–29. Hanover, PA. Handmade crafts, ethnic foods, music, entertainment, children's carnival, antique car show. Demonstrations Friday evening. Annually, the last Friday and Saturday in July. Est attendance: 10,000. For info: Hanover Area Chamber of Commerce, 146 Carlisle St, Hanover, PA 17331. Phone: (717) 637-6130. Web: www.hanover chamber.com.

HEYWARD, THOMAS: BIRTH ANNIVERSARY. July 28, 1746. American Revolutionary soldier, signer of the Declaration of Independence. Died Mar 6, 1809.

LOGGING MUSEUM FESTIVAL DAYS. July 28–29. Rangeley, ME. Bean-hole beans, Logger's Hall of Fame, Miss Woodchip Contest, parade, logging competition. Sponsor: Logging Museum. Est attendance: 1,500. For info: Rangeley Logging Museum, Box 154, Rangeley, ME 04970. Phone: (207) 864-5595.

LUMBERJACK WORLD CHAMPIONSHIPS 2006. July 28–30. Hayward, WI. The "Olympics of the Forest" welcomes the world's best lumberjacks competing in a variety of competitions, including log rolling, tree climbing, cutting with saws and chainsaws and axe chopping. Annually, the last weekend in July. For info: Lumberjack World Championships, PO Box 666, Hayward, WI 54843. Phone: (715) 634-2484. E-mail: info@lumberjack worldchampionships.com. Web: www.lumberjackworldchampion ships.com.

MONTANA STATE FAIR. July 28–Aug 5. Great Falls, MT. Mighty Thomas Carnival, night shows, PRCA rodeo, Xtreme Bullriding, demolition derby, free acts, food fair, 4-H, exhibits and much more. Est attendance: 150,000. For info: Montana State Fair, Box 1888, Great Falls, MT 59403. Phone: (406) 727-8900. Fax: (406) 452-8955. E-mail: info@goexpopark.com.

NEWBERRY LIBRARY'S ANNUAL BOOK FAIR. July 28–30. Chicago, IL. 22nd annual. More than 100,000 books have been sorted into 50 categories for your browsing convenience. With many books priced at a dollar, it's easy to restock your library with titles ranging from classics to pulp fiction. Est attendance: 7,000. For info: The Newberry Library, 60 W Walton St, Chicago, IL 60610. Phone: (312) 255-3510. Web: www.newberry.org.

ONASSIS, JACQUELINE LEE BOUVIER KENNEDY: BIRTH ANNIVERSARY. July 28, 1929. Editor, widow of John Fitzgerald Kennedy (35th president of the US), born at Southampton, NY. Later married (Oct 20, 1968) Greek shipping magnate Aristotle Socrates Onassis, who died Mar 15, 1975. The widely admired and respected former First Lady died May 19, 1994, at New York City.

OZARK EMPIRE FAIR. July 28–Aug 6. Springfield, MO. Regional fair with carnival, exhibits, livestock and entertainment. Est attendance: 215,000. For info: Ozark Empire Fair, 3001 N Grant, Springfield, MO 65803. Phone: (417) 833-2660. Fax: (417) 833-3769. Web: www.ozarkempirefair.com.

PERU: INDEPENDENCE DAY. July 28. San Martin declared independence from Spain on this day in 1821. After the final defeat of Spanish troops by Simon Bolivar in 1824, Spanish rule ended.

POTTER, (HELEN) BEATRIX: BIRTH ANNIVERSARY. July 28, 1866. Author and illustrator of the Peter Rabbit stories for children, born at London, England. Died at Sawrey, Lancashire, Dec 22, 1943.

"THE SAMMY KAYE SHOW" TV PREMIERE: 55th ANNIVERSARY. July 28, 1951. CBS's musical program hosted by bandleader Sammy Kaye swayed audiences to swinging tunes on Saturday nights.

SINGING TELEGRAM: ANNIVERSARY. July 28, 1933. Anniversary of the first singing telegram, said to have been delivered to singer Rudy Vallee on his 32nd birthday. Early singing telegrams often were delivered in person by uniformed messengers on bicycle. Later they were usually sung over the telephone.

SNOWBIRD, UTAH JAZZ & BLUES FESTIVAL. July 28–29. Snowbird, UT. Come and join the fun with plenty of jazz and blues music. Festival also includes food booths and much more. Annually, the last weekend in July. Est attendance: 4,000. For info: Snowbird & Ski Summer Resort, PO Box 92900, Snowbird, UT 84092-9000. Phone: (801) 742-2222. Fax: (801) 933-2298. E-mail: info@snowbird.com. Web: www.snowbird.com.

SPACE MILESTONE: *SKYLAB 3* (US). July 28, 1973. Alan L. Bean, Owen K. Garriott and Jack R. Lousma started 59-day mission in the space station to test man's space flight endurance. Pacific splashdown Sept 25.

STATE CRAFT FAIR. July 28–30. Franklin & Marshall College, Lancaster, PA. 60th annual fair. High-quality juried craft show featuring the work of more than 250 members of the Pennsylvania Guild of Craftsmen. Demonstrations, seminars, Crafts and Antiques Road Show, food available. Indoors and air conditioned! For information about tickets, or how to become a member, contact the PA Guild. Est attendance: 18,000. Pennsylvania Guild of Craftsmen, 10 Stable Mill Trail, Richboro, PA 18954. Phone: (215) 579-5997. E-mail: pacraft@comcat.com. Web: www.pacrafts.com.

THAT FAMOUS PRESTON NIGHT RODEO. July 28–30. Preston, ID. The second under-the-lights rodeo in America, this PRCA-approved rodeo has top national cowboys. Est attendance: 20,000. For info: Preston Chamber of Commerce, 49 N State, Ste A, Preston, ID 83263. Phone: (208) 852-2703. Fax: (208) 852-1475. E-mail: pacc@dcdi.net. Web: www.prestonidaho.org.

July 2006	S	M	T	W	T	F	S
							1
	2	3	4	5	6	7	8
	9	10	11	12	13	14	15
	16	17	18	19	20	21	22
	23	24	25	26	27	28	29
	30	31					

VALLEE, RUDY: BIRTH ANNIVERSARY. July 28, 1901. American singer, saxophone player and radio idol of millions during the 1930s. Born Hubert Prior Vallee, at Island Pond, VT, the crooner used a megaphone to amplify his voice and introduced his performances with the salutation, "Heigh-ho-everybody!" Vallee appeared in a number of movies, including *How to Succeed in Business Without Really Trying*. Among his best-remembered songs are "I'm Just a Vagabond Lover," "Say It Isn't So" and his signature song, "My Time Is Your Time." Vallee died at age 84 at North Hollywood, CA, July 3, 1986.

VETERANS BONUS ARMY EVICTION: ANNIVERSARY. July 28, 1932. Some 15,000 unemployed veterans of WWI marched on Washington, DC, in the summer of 1932, demanding payment of a war bonus. After two months' encampment in Washington's Anacostia Flats, eviction of the bonus marchers by the US Army was ordered by President Herbert Hoover. Under the leadership of General Douglas MacArthur, Major Dwight D. Eisenhower and Major George S. Patton, Jr (among others), cavalry, tanks and infantry attacked. Fixed bayonets, tear gas and the burning of the veterans' tents hastened the end of the confrontation. One death was reported.

WORLD FUTURE SOCIETY ANNUAL CONFERENCE. July 28–30. Toronto, ON, Canada. For info: World Future Society, 7910 Woodmont Ave, Ste 450, Bethesda, MD 20814. Phone: (800) 989-8274 or (301) 656-8274. Fax: (301) 951-0394. E-mail: sechard@wfs.org. Web: www.wfs.org.

WORLD WAR I BEGINS: ANNIVERSARY. July 28, 1914. Archduke Francis Ferdinand of Austria-Hungary and his wife were assassinated at Sarajevo, Bosnia, by a Serbian nationalist June 28, 1914, touching off the conflict that became WWI. Austria-Hungary declared war on Serbia July 28, the formal beginning of the war. Within weeks, Germany entered the war on the side of Austria-Hungary and Russia, France and Great Britain on the side of Serbia.

BIRTHDAYS TODAY

William Warren (Bill) Bradley, 63, former US senator, Hall of Fame basketball player, born Crystal City, MO, July 28, 1943.

Jim Davis, 61, cartoonist ("Garfield"), born Marion, IN, July 28, 1945.

Darryl Hickman, 75, actor ("The Americans," *The Tingler*), born Los Angeles, CA, July 28, 1931.

Linda Kelsey, 60, actress ("Lou Grant"), born Minneapolis, MN, July 28, 1946.

Lori Loughlin, 42, actress ("Full House," *Back to the Beach*), born Long Island, NY, July 28, 1964.

Jacques Piccard, 84, inventor, explorer, born Brussels, Belgium, July 28, 1922.

Sally Struthers, 58, actress ("All in the Family"), born Portland, OR, July 28, 1948.

Rick Wright, 61, singer, musician (keyboard player with Pink Floyd), born London, England, July 28, 1945.

JULY 29 — SATURDAY

Day 210 — 155 Remaining

ALL-AMERICAN SOAP BOX DERBY. July 29. Derby Downs, Akron, OH. A weeklong festival culminating in world championship race by regional champs from US, New Zealand, Germany, Japan and the Philippines. 69th annual derby. Est attendance: 20,000. For info: Jeff Iula, General Manager, Intl Soap Box Derby, Inc, PO Box 7225, Derby Downs, Akron, OH 44306. Phone: (330) 733-8723. Fax: (330) 733-1370. E-mail: soapbox@aasbd.org. Web: www.aasbd.com.

ARTS AND CRAFTS FESTIVAL. July 29–30. Loveladies, NJ. 12th annual. Featuring juried arts and crafts displays, entertainment, food and more. For info: Long Beach Island Foundation of the Arts and Sciences, 120 Long Beach Blvd, Loveladies, NJ 08008. Phone: (609) 494-1241. Fax: (609) 494-0662.

CURTIS CUP. July 29–30. Bandon Dunes Golf Resort, Bandon, OR. Biennial competition (officially named "The Women's International Cup") between teams of women amateur golfers from the US and the UK. Named after British golfing sisters Harriot and Margaret Curtis. Contested in even-numbered years since 1932 (except during WWII). Sponsored by the USGA and Ladies Golf Union. For info: US Golf Assn, Golf House, Far Hills, NJ 07931. Phone: (908) 234-2300. Fax: (908) 234-9687. E-mail: usga@usga.org. Web: www.usga.org.

ENGLAND: SKANDIA COWES WEEK. July 29–Aug 5. Cowes, Isle of Wight. Yachting festival for 35 classes of yacht racing. Est attendance: 14,000. For info: Cowes Combined Clubs Ltd, 18 Bath Rd, Cowes, Isle of Wight, England PO31 7QN. Phone: (44) (198) 329-5744. Fax: (44) (198) 329-5329. E-mail: ccc@cowesweek.co.uk. Web: www.cowesweek.co.uk.

HOT AUGUST NIGHTS. July 29–Aug 6. Reno and Sparks, NV. Celebration of the music and cars of the '50s and '60s features show and shine, parade, cruises, proms and concerts by the entertainers of the era. For info: Hot August Nights, 1425 E Greg St, Sparks, NV 89431. Phone: (775) 356-1956. Web: www.hotaugustnights.net.

***INDIANAPOLIS* SUNK: ANNIVERSARY.** July 29, 1945. After delivering the atomic bomb to Tinian Island, the American cruiser *Indianapolis* was headed for Okinawa to train for the invasion of Japan when it was torpedoed by a Japanese submarine. Of 1,196 crew members, more than 350 were immediately killed in the explosion or went down with the ship. There were no rescue ships nearby, and those fortunate enough to survive endured the next 84 hours in ocean waters. By the time they were spotted by air on Aug 2, only 318 sailors remained alive, the others either having drowned or been eaten by sharks. This is the US Navy's worst loss at sea.

ISLAND FALLS SUMMERFEST. July 29–Aug 6. Island Falls, ME. Cookout, craft and trade fair, pageants, tournaments and a parade. For info: Northern Katahdin Valley Chamber of Commerce, PO Box 374, Island Falls, ME 04747-0374. Phone: (207) 463-2077. E-mail: nkvrcc@allmaine.com. Or MaineLee Promotions. Phone: (207) 463-2498.

MID-SUMMER ANTIQUES AND COLLECTIBLES SHOW AND SALE. July 29–30. Millville, NJ. Rain or shine. Est attendance: 2,000. For info: Wheaton Village, 1501 Glasstown Rd, Millville, NJ 08332. Phone: (856) 825-6800 or (800) 998-4552. Fax: (856) 825-2410. E-mail: mail@wheatonvillage.org. Web: www.wheatonvillage.org.

MUSSOLINI, BENITO: BIRTH ANNIVERSARY. July 29, 1883. Italian Fascist leader, born at Dovia, Italy. Self-styled "Il Duce" (the leader), Mussolini governed Italy, first as prime minister and later as absolute dictator, 1922–43. It was Mussolini who said: "War alone . . . puts the stamp of nobility upon the peoples who have the courage to face it." But military defeat of Italy in World War II was Mussolini's downfall. Repudiated and arrested by the Italian government, he was temporarily rescued by German paratroops in 1943. Later, as they attempted to flee in disguise to Switzerland, he and his mistress, Clara Petacci, were killed by Italian partisans near Lake Como, Italy, Apr 28, 1945.

NASA ESTABLISHED: ANNIVERSARY. July 29, 1958. President Eisenhower signed a bill creating the National Aeronautics and Space Administration to direct US space policy.

NORFOLK PUBLIC LIBRARY LITERATURE FESTIVAL. July 29. Lifelong Learning Center, Norfolk, NE. Presentations by award-winning, nationally known authors, book reviews, book displays and sales and autograph sessions. Est attendance: 300. For info: Karen Drevo, Youth Services Librarian, Norfolk Public Library, 308 Prospect Ave, Norfolk, NE 68701. Phone: (402) 844-2100. Fax: (402) 844-2102. E-mail: kdrevo@ci.norfolk.ne.us.

NORWAY: OLSOK EVE. July 29. Commemorates Norway's Viking king St. Olav, who fell in battle at Stiklestad near Trondheim, Norway, July 29, 1030. Bonfires, historical pageants.

QUILT SHOW. July 29–Sept 10. Woodstock, VT. A juried showing of quilts made by Windsor County quilters, displayed with selected 19th-century Vermont quilts. Daily quilting demonstrations and activities. Est attendance: 9,700. For info: Billings Farm and Museum, Rte 12 North, Woodstock, VT 05091. Phone: (802) 457-2355. Fax: (802) 457-4663. E-mail: billings.farm@valley.net. Web: www.billingsfarm.org.

RAIN DAY AT WAYNESBURG, PENNSYLVANIA. July 29. Legend has it that rain will fall at Waynesburg, PA, on July 29 as it has most years for the last century, according to local records in this community, which was laid out in 1796 and incorporated in 1816.

ROOSEVELT, ALICE HATHAWAY LEE: BIRTH ANNIVERSARY. July 29, 1861. First wife of Theodore Roosevelt, 26th president of the US, whom she married in 1880. Born at Chestnut Hill, MA, she died at New York, NY, Feb 14, 1884.

TARKINGTON, BOOTH: BIRTH ANNIVERSARY. July 29, 1869. American novelist (*The Magnificent Ambersons*), born at Indianapolis, IN. Died there May 19, 1946.

TIDEWATER ARCHAEOLOGY DIG. July 29–30. St. Mary's City, MD. Hands-on opportunity to dig at an archaeology site at Maryland's first capital. Special behind-the-scenes tours. Annually, usually the last weekend in July. Est attendance: 500. For info: Visitors Services, Historic St. Mary's City, PO Box 39, St. Mary's City, MD 20686. Phone: (240) 895-4990 or (800) SMC-1634. Fax: (240) 895-4968. Web: www.stmaryscity.org.

TOCQUEVILLE, ALEXIS DE: BIRTH ANNIVERSARY. July 29, 1805. French politician and author whose 1831 trip to the United States inspired *Democracy in America*, one of the most insightful books written on the US. "America is a land of wonders," he wrote, "in which everything is in constant motion and every change seems an improvement." Born at Verneuil, France, Tocqueville died at Cannes on Apr 16, 1859.

WHITE RIVER WATER CARNIVAL. July 29–Aug 5. Batesville, AR. Public receptions, Miss White River pageant, bass classic tournament, four-mile run, four-ball golf tournament, arts, crafts, parade, children's activities, entertainment in the park, ski show, car and bike show. Est attendance: 9,000. For info: Batesville Area Chamber of Commerce, 409 Vine, Batesville, AR 72501. Phone: (870) 793-2378. Fax: (870) 793-3061. E-mail: batesvillechamber@cox-internet.com. Web: watercarnival.com.

BIRTHDAYS TODAY

Debbie Black, 40, basketball player, born Philadelphia, PA, July 29, 1966.

Ken Burns, 53, documentary filmmaker ("Civil War" series), born New York, NY, July 29, 1953.

Elizabeth Hanford Dole, 70, US Senator (R, North Carolina), former president, American Red Cross, former secretary of transportation and secretary of labor, born Salisbury, NC, July 29, 1936.

Martina McBride, 40, country singer, born Sharon, KS, July 29, 1966.

Alexandra Paul, 43, actress ("Baywatch," *Dragnet*), born New York, NY, July 29, 1963.

Patty Scialfa, 50, singer, born Deal, NJ, July 29, 1956.

Paul Taylor, 76, dancer, choreographer, born Allegheny, NY, July 29, 1930.

David Warner, 65, actor ("Holocaust," *Tron*), born Manchester, England, July 29, 1941.

Wil Wheaton, 34, actor ("Star Trek: The Next Generation," *Stand by Me*), born Burbank, CA, July 29, 1972.

JULY 30 — SUNDAY
Day 211 — 154 Remaining

BRONTË, EMILY: BIRTH ANNIVERSARY. July 30, 1818. English novelist, one of the Brontë sisters, best known for *Wuthering Heights*. Born at Thornton, Yorkshire, England. Died Dec 19, 1848, at Haworth, Yorkshire, England.

CHURCH AND SYNAGOGUE LIBRARY ASSOCIATION CONFERENCE. July 30–Aug 1. Greensboro, NC. Est attendance: 200. For info: Judith Janzen, Administrator, Church and Synagogue Library Assn, Box 19357, Portland, OR 97280-0357. Phone: (503) 244-6919 or (800) LIB-CSLA. Fax: (503) 977-3734. E-mail: csla@worldaccessnet.com. Web: www.worldaccessnet.com/~csla.

ELVIS PRESLEY'S FIRST CONCERT APPEARANCE: ANNIVERSARY. July 30, 1954. Elvis Presley appeared in concert for the first time at Overton Park Orchestra Shell in Memphis, TN. He was billed third and country crooner Slim Whitman was the headliner. Presley, only 19 years old, nervously began gyrating his leg and a legend was born. See also: "Elvis Presley's First Single Released: Anniversary" (July 19).

FORD, HENRY: BIRTH ANNIVERSARY. July 30, 1863. Industrialist Henry Ford, whose assembly-line method of automobile production revolutionized the industry, was born at Wayne County, MI, on the family farm. His Model T made up half of the world's output of cars during its years of production. Ford built racing cars until in 1903 he and his partners formed the Ford Motor Company. In 1908 the company presented the Model T, which was produced until 1927, and in 1913 Ford introduced the assembly line and mass production. This innovation reduced the time it took to build each car from 12½ hours to only 1½. This enabled Ford to sell cars for $500, making automobile ownership a possibility for an unprecedented percentage of the population. He is also remembered for introducing a $5-a-day wage for automotive workers and for his statement: "History is bunk." Died Apr 7, 1947, at age 83 at Dearborn, MI, where his manufacturing complex was located.

HOFFA, JAMES: DISAPPEARANCE: ANNIVERSARY. July 30, 1975. Former Teamsters Union leader, 62-year-old James Riddle Hoffa was last seen on this date outside a restaurant in Bloomfield Township, near Detroit, MI. His 13-year federal prison sentence had been commuted by former President Richard M. Nixon in 1971. On Dec 8, 1982, seven years and 131 days after his disappearance, an Oakland County judge declared Hoffa officially dead as of July 30, 1982.

LAVALLETTE HERITAGE ARTS AND CRAFTS SHOW. July 30 (rain date Aug 6). Lavallette, NJ. Juried arts, crafts and antiques show. Only the best of the best welcome to exhibit. One of the best shows on the eastern seaboard. 10 AM to dusk. Ribbon and cash awards given in both categories. Annually, the last Sunday in July. Est attendance: 20,000. For info: Joy Grosko, Heritage Committee of Lavallette, 13 Camden Ave, Lavallette, NJ 08735. Phone: (732) 793-3652. Fax: (732) 854-9038. E-mail: tpgrosko00@aol.com.

MOORE, HENRY: BIRTH ANNIVERSARY. July 30, 1898. English sculptor born at Castleford, Yorkshire. Died at Hertfordshire, Aug 31, 1986.

PAPERBACK BOOKS INTRODUCED: ANNIVERSARY. July 30, 1935. Although books bound in soft covers were first introduced in 1841 at Leipzig, Germany, by Christian Bernhard Tauchnitz, the modern paperback revolution dates to the publication of the first Penguin paperback by Sir Allen Lane at London in 1935. Penguin Number 1 was *Ariel*, a life of Shelley by Andre Maurois.

STENGEL, CHARLES DILLON (CASEY): BIRTH ANNIVERSARY. July 30, 1890. Baseball Hall of Fame outfielder and manager born at Kansas City, MO. His success as manager of the New York Yankees (10 pennants and 7 World Series titles in 12 years) made him one of the game's enduring stars. Inducted into the Hall of Fame in 1966. Died at Glendale, CA, Sept 29, 1975.

VANUATU: INDEPENDENCE DAY. July 30. Vanuatu became an independent republic in 1980 (from France and the UK) and observes its national holiday.

VEBLEN, THORSTEIN: BIRTH ANNIVERSARY. July 30, 1857. American economist, born at Valders, WI, and died at Menlo Park, CA, Aug 3, 1929. "Conspicuous consumption," he wrote in *The Theory of the Leisure Class*, "of valuable goods is a means of reputability to the gentleman of leisure."

BIRTHDAYS TODAY

Lamar Alexander, 66, US Senator (R, Tennessee), born Maryville, TN, July 30, 1940.

Paul Anka, 65, singer, songwriter ("Diana," "My Way" for Frank Sinatra), born Ottawa, ON, Canada, July 30, 1941.

William Atherton, 59, actor (*The Day of the Locust, Ghostbusters, Die Hard, Die Hard 2*), born New Haven, CT, July 30, 1947.

Peter Bogdanovich, 67, producer, director (*The Last Picture Show, Paper Moon*), born Kingston, NY, July 30, 1939.

Delta Burke, 50, actress ("Designing Women"), former Miss Florida, born Orlando, FL, July 30, 1956.

Kate Bush, 48, singer ("The Man with the Child in His Eyes"), songwriter, born Lewisham, England, July 30, 1958.

Edd Byrnes, 73, actor ("77 Sunset Strip," *Darby's Rangers*), born New York, NY, July 30, 1933.

Laurence Fishburne, 45, actor (*Boyz N the Hood, What's Love Got to Do with It, Higher Learning*; stage: *Two Trains Running* [Tony Award]), born Augusta, GA, July 30, 1961.

Anita Faye Hill, 50, law professor, born on an Oklahoma farm, July 30, 1956.

Lisa Kudrow, 43, actress ("Friends," *Romy and Michele's High School Reunion*), born Encino, CA, July 30, 1963.

Christopher Paul (Chris) Mullin, 43, former basketball player, born New York, NY, July 30, 1963.

July *2006*	S	M	T	W	T	F	S
							1
	2	3	4	5	6	7	8
	9	10	11	12	13	14	15
	16	17	18	19	20	21	22
	23	24	25	26	27	28	29
	30	31					

Ken Olin, 52, actor ("LA Doctors," "thirtysomething"), born Chicago, IL, July 30, 1954.

David Sanborn, 61, saxophonist, composer, born Tampa, FL, July 30, 1945.

Arnold Schwarzenegger, 59, Governor of California (R), bodybuilder, actor (*The Terminator, Twins, True Lies*), born Graz, Austria, July 30, 1947.

Allan Huber ("Bud") Selig, 72, Commissioner of Baseball, born Milwaukee, WI, July 30, 1934.

Hilary Swank, 32, actress (Oscar for *Boys Don't Cry*), born Lincoln, NE, July 30, 1974.

JULY 31 — MONDAY
Day 212 — 153 Remaining

CHINA: DOUBLE SEVEN FESTIVAL. July 31. Also called Chinese Valentine's Day. Observed on seventh day of seventh lunar month. From a folktale in which two lovers (a cowherd and a weaver) are separated by the Milky Way. They are able to meet once a year when all the world's magpies form a bridge for the lovers.

FEAST OF SAINT IGNATIUS OF LOYOLA. July 31. 1491–1556. Founder of the Society of Jesus (Jesuits). Canonized in 1622.

FIRST INDIAN SAINT: ANNIVERSARY. July 31, 2002. In Mexico City, Mexico, Pope John Paul II canonized the Roman Catholic Church's first Indian saint, Juan Diego. In 1531 Diego claimed to have seen the Virgin of Guadalupe, whose rose-framed image later appeared on his cloak. See also: "Day of Our Lady of Guadalupe" (Dec 12).

FIRST US GOVERNMENT BUILDING: ANNIVERSARY. July 31, 1792. The cornerstone of the Philadelphia Mint, the first US government building, was laid on this day.

KENNEDY INTERNATIONAL AIRPORT DEDICATION: ANNIVERSARY. July 31, 1948. New York's International Airport at Idlewild Field was dedicated by President Harry S Truman. It was later renamed John F. Kennedy International Airport.

MELVILLE MARATHON. July 31–Aug 1. Mystic Seaport, Mystic, CT. Marathon reading of the classic *Moby-Dick* in celebration of Herman Melville's birthday. Reading takes place on deck and in fo'c'sle of the last wooden whaler, *Charles W. Morgan*. Annually, 24-hour reading from noon July 31 to noon Aug 1. Est attendance: 6,000. For info: Mystic Seaport, 75 Greenmanville Ave, PO Box 6000, Mystic, CT 06355-0990. Phone: (860) 572-5315 or (888) 973-2767. Web: www.mysticseaport.org.

PRESIDENT'S ENVIRONMENTAL YOUTH AWARD NATIONAL COMPETITION DEADLINE. July 31. Young people in all 50 states are invited to participate in the President's Environmental Youth Awards program, which offers them, individually and collectively, an opportunity to be recognized for environmental efforts in their community. The program encourages individuals, school classes, schools, summer camps and youth organizations to promote local environmental awareness and positive community involvement. The annual deadline is always July 31, and applications should be returned to EPA regional offices. Regional contacts can be found at www.epa.gov/enviroed. For additional info: Office of Environmental Education, US Environmental Protection Agency, 1200 Pennsylvania Ave NW (MC 1704A), Washington, DC 20460. Phone: (202) 564-0443. Fax: (202) 564-2754. Web: www.epa.gov/enviroed.

SALVADOR, FRANCIS: DEATH ANNIVERSARY. July 31, 1776. The first Jew to die in the American Revolution, Salvador was also the first Jew elected to office in Colonial America. He was voted a member of the South Carolina Provincial Congress in January 1775.

"THE SHADOW" RADIO PREMIERE: ANNIVERSARY. July 31, 1930. "Who knows what evil lurks in the hearts of men? The Shadow knows!" This popular crime and suspense program premiered on CBS radio. Originally, the Shadow was just the narrator of the changing stories, but later he became a character with his own adventures—with the alter ego of Lamont Cranston. Orson Welles was the first Shadow.

US PATENT OFFICE OPENS: ANNIVERSARY. July 31, 1790. The first US Patent Office opened its doors and the first US patent was issued to Samuel Hopkins of Vermont for a new method of making pearlash and potash. The patent was signed by George Washington and Thomas Jefferson.

BIRTHDAYS TODAY

Dean Cain, 40, actor ("Lois & Clark: The New Adventures of Superman"), born Mount Clemens, MI, July 31, 1966.

Geraldine Chaplin, 62, actress (*Nashville, Roseland, Chaplin*), born Santa Monica, CA, July 31, 1944.

Susan Flannery, 63, actress ("The Bold & the Beautiful," "Dallas"), born Jersey City, NJ, July 31, 1943.

Milton Friedman, 94, economist, journalist, born Brooklyn, NY, July 31, 1912.

Evonne Goolagong, 55, former tennis player, born Griffith, Australia, July 31, 1951.

Sherry Lansing, 62, producer (*Fatal Attraction, The Accused*), born Chicago, IL, July 31, 1944.

Gary Lewis, 60, singer ("This Diamond Ring"), born New York, NY, July 31, 1946.

Don Murray, 77, actor (*Bus Stop*, "Knots Landing"), born Hollywood, CA, July 31, 1929.

France Nuyen, 67, actress ("St. Elsewhere"), born Marseilles, France, July 31, 1939.

Jonathan Ogden, 32, football player, born Washington, DC, July 31, 1974.

J.K. Rowling, 41, author (the Harry Potter series), born Joanne Rowling at Bristol, England, July 31, 1965.

Wesley Snipes, 44, actor (*Blade, US Marshals, Jungle Fever, White Men Can't Jump*), born Orlando, FL, July 31, 1962.

August.

AUGUST 1 — TUESDAY
Day 213 — 152 Remaining

AMERICAN HISTORY ESSAY CONTEST. Aug 1–Dec 15. American History Committee activities are promoted throughout the year with the essay contest conducted in grades 5–8 beginning in August. Essays are submitted for judging by Dec 15, with the winners announced in April at the Daughters of the American Revolution Continental Congress. Events vary, but include programs, displays, spot announcements and recognition of essay writers. Essay topic can be obtained from DAR Headquarters. For info: Natl Society of Daughters of the American Revolution, Office of the Historian-General, Admin Bldg, 1776 D St NW, Washington, DC 20006-5392. Phone: (202) 628-1776. Web: www .dar.org.

BENIN: INDEPENDENCE DAY. Aug 1. Public holiday. Commemorates independence from France in 1960. Benin at that time was known as Dahomey.

BLACK BUSINESS MONTH. Aug 1–31. Six months after Black History Month, the focus on and awareness of black-owned and operated enterprises needs a boost. This month is dedicated to starting, maintaining, growing, buying from and committing to black-owned businesses and entrepreneurs. For info: Sylvia Henderson, Springboard Training, PO Box 588, Olney, MD 20830-0588. Phone: (301) 260-1538. E-mail: admin@spring boardtraining.com. Web: www.springboardtraining.com.

BURK, MARTHA (CALAMITY JANE): DEATH ANNIVERSARY. Aug 1, 1903. Known as a frontierswoman and companion to Wild Bill Hickok, Calamity Jane Burk was born Martha Jane Cannary at Princeton, MO, in May 1852. As a young girl living in Montana, she became an excellent markswoman. She went to the Black Hills of South Dakota as a scout for a geological expedition in 1875. Several opposing traditions account for her nickname, one springing from her kindness to the less fortunate, while another attributes it to the harsh warnings she would give men who offended her. She died at Terry, SD, and was buried at Deadwood, SD, next to Wild Bill Hickok.

CATARACT AWARENESS MONTH. Aug 1–31. Cataract is the leading cause of blindness in the world. There are close to 20.5 million Americans age 40 and older with cataracts. More than half of all Americans will have cataracts by age 80. For info: Prevent Blindness America®, 211 W Wacker Dr, Ste 1700, Chicago, IL 60606. Phone: (800) 331-2020. E-mail: info@prevent blindness.org. Web: www.preventblindness.org.

	S	M	T	W	T	F	S
August			1	2	3	4	5
2006	6	7	8	9	10	11	12
	13	14	15	16	17	18	19
	20	21	22	23	24	25	26
	27	28	29	30	31		

CHILDREN'S EYE HEALTH AND SAFETY MONTH. Aug 1–31. Information will be available about amblyopia, a condition that can affect 2 to 3 percent of children and cause permanent vision loss. Also, get tips about preventing eye injuries in children, signs of possible eye problems and general eye health. For info: Prevent Blindness America, 211 W Wacker Dr, Ste 1700, Chicago, IL 60606. Phone: (800) 331-2020. E-mail: info@prevent blindness.org. Web: www.preventblindness.org.

CHILDREN'S VISION AND LEARNING MONTH. Aug 1–31. Researchers estimate that 1 out of 4 children have an undiagnosed vision problem that is interfering with their ability to read and learn. Since 80% of learning is dependent upon vision, it is vital that parents and educators ensure they understand the signs of vision problems. With children getting ready to go back to school, August is the perfect month for education. For info: College of Optometrists in Vision Development, 243 N Lindbergh Blvd, Ste 310, St. Louis, MO 63141. Phone: (314) 991-4007. E-mail: covded@sbcglobal.net. Web: www.covd.org.

CLARK, WILLIAM: BIRTH ANNIVERSARY. Aug 1, 1770. The soldier, explorer and public servant was born at Caroline County, VA. He served seven years in the US Army and then gained his lasting fame when Meriwether Lewis asked him to join an expedition exploring the Louisiana Territory (1803–06). Clark was an able leader, and contributed detailed maps and animal illustrations on the journey. A grateful President Thomas Jefferson made Clark brigadier general of militia for the Louisiana Territory (1807–13) and superintendent of Indian Affairs (1807–38). Clark was also governor of the Missouri Territory (1813–20) and surveyor general for Illinois, Missouri and Arkansas (1824–25). Clark foresaw the tension between US interests and the native peoples of the western US, and he urged that the US treat western tribes with respect. Clark died at St. Louis, MO, on Sept 1, 1838.

COLORADO: ADMISSION DAY: ANNIVERSARY. Aug 1, 1876. Colorado admitted to the Union as the 38th state. The first Monday in August is celebrated as Colorado Day.

DIARY OF ANNE FRANK: THE LAST ENTRY: ANNIVERSARY. Aug 1, 1944. To escape deportation to concentration camps, the Jewish family of Otto Frank hid for two years in the warehouse of his food products business at Amsterdam. Gentile friends smuggled in food and other supplies during their confinement. Thirteen-year-old Anne Frank, who kept a journal during the time of their hiding, penned her last entry in the diary Aug 1, 1944: "[I] keep on trying to find a way of becoming what I would like to be, and what I could be, if . . . there weren't any other people living in the world." Three days later (Aug 4, 1944) Grüne Polizei raided the "Secret Annex" where the Frank family was hidden. Anne and her sister were sent to Bergen-Belsen concentration camp where Anne died at age 15, two months before the liberation of Holland. Young Anne's diary, later found in the family's hiding place, has been translated into 30 languages and has become a symbol of the indomitable strength of the human spirit. See also: "Frank, Anne: Birth Anniversary" (June 12).

EMANCIPATION OF 500: ANNIVERSARY. Aug 1, 1791. Virginia planter Robert Carter III confounded his family and friends by filing a deed of emancipation for his 500 slaves. One of the wealthiest men in the state, Carter owned 60,000 acres over 18 plantations. The deed included the following words: "I have for some time past been convinced that to retain them in Slavery is contrary to the true principles of Religion and Justice and therefore it is my duty to manumit them." The document established a schedule by which 15 slaves would be freed each Jan 1, over a 21-year period, plus slave children would be freed at age 18 for females and 21 for males. It is believed this was the largest act of emancipation in US history and predated the Emancipation Proclamation by 70 years.

FAMILY MEAL MONTH. Aug 1–31. Dedicated to bringing dinner back to the table. During the month, families are encouraged to eat dinner together. Several studies have shown family dinners have a positive impact on children in such areas as nutrition, communication and school performance. Family Meal Month focuses on families sharing and enjoying a home-cooked meal and meaningful conversation together. For info: Keri Willenborg, 2356 South 156th Circle, Omaha, NE 68130. Phone: (402) 933-4521. Fax: (402) 614-5900. E-mail: keri.willenborg@supper thymeusa.com. Web: www.supperthymeusa.com.

FIRST US CENSUS: ANNIVERSARY. Aug 1, 1790. The first census revealed that there were 3,939,326 citizens in the 16 states and the Ohio Territory. The US has taken a census every 10 years since 1790. The next one will be in 2010.

GARCIA, JERRY: BIRTH ANNIVERSARY. Aug 1, 1942. Jerome John Garcia was born at San Francisco, CA. Country, bluegrass and folk musician, a guitar player of remarkable ability, Garcia was the leading force behind the legendary Grateful Dead, the band that sustained a veritable industry for its legion of followers. He died Aug 9, 1995, at Forest Knolls, CA, ending a musical career that spanned more than three decades.

GET READY FOR KINDERGARTEN MONTH. Aug 1–31. This is a celebration to support a happy entry into kindergarten for the almost 2 million children in the US. Going to kindergarten is a life-changing event not only for the child, but also for parents, siblings, and educators. Tips are provided to help smooth the way for an easy transition. For info: Katie Davis, PO Box 551, Bedford Hills, NY 10507. Phone: (914) 244-8777. E-mail: katie davis@katiedavis.com. Web: www.kindergartenrocks.net.

GIRLFRIEND'S DAY. Aug 1. Celebrate this special day by taking your girlfriend(s) shopping, to a play, to the movies, out to eat, to the spa and/or to the park. A fun slumber party is also recommended. Annually, Aug 1. For info: Thema Martin. Phone: (404) 849-1249. E-mail: thema_martin@hotmail.com. Web: www .cosmocompany.com.

HAPPINESS HAPPENS MONTH. Aug 1–31. This 7th annual month, sponsored by the Secret Society of Happy People, encourages people to express happiness and discourages parade-raining. Visit our website to find out about activities. For info: Secret Society of Happy People, 1315 Riverchase Dr #2316, Coppell, TX 75019. Phone: (972) 471-1485. E-mail: pjohnson@sohp.com. Web: www.sohp.com.

HAWAII VOLCANOES NATIONAL PARK ESTABLISHED: 90th ANNIVERSARY. Aug 1, 1916. Area of Hawaii's Hawaii Island, including active volcanoes Kilauea and Mauna Loa, was established as Hawaii National Park in 1916 but its name was changed to Hawaii Volcanoes National Park in 1961. For further park info: Hawaii Volcanoes Natl Park, Hawaii Natl Park, HI 96718.

JAMAICA: ABOLITION OF SLAVERY. Aug 1, 1838. National day. Spanish settlers introduced the slave trade into Jamaica in 1509 and sugar cane in 1640. Slavery continued until Aug 1, 1838, when it was abolished by the British.

KEY, FRANCIS SCOTT: BIRTH ANNIVERSARY. Aug 1, 1779. American attorney, social worker, poet and author of the US national anthem. While on a legal mission, Key was detained on shipboard off Baltimore, during the British bombardment of Fort McHenry on the night of Sept 13–14, 1814. Thrilled to see the American flag still flying over the fort at daybreak, Key wrote the poem "The Star Spangled Banner." Printed in the *Baltimore American* Sept 21, 1814, it was soon popularly sung to the music of an old English tune, "Anacreon in Heaven." It did not become the official US national anthem until 117 years later when, on Mar 3, 1931, President Herbert Hoover signed into law an act for that purpose. Key was born at Frederick County, MD, and died at Baltimore, MD, Jan 11, 1843.

LUGHNASADH. Aug 1. (Also called August Eve, Lammas Eve, Lady Day Eve and Feast of Bread.) One of the "Greater Sabbats" during the Wiccan year, Lughnasadh marks the first harvest. Annually, Aug 1.

MELVILLE, HERMAN: BIRTH ANNIVERSARY. Aug 1, 1819. American author, best known for his novel *Moby-Dick*, born at New York, NY, and died there Sept 28, 1891.

MITCHELL, MARIA: BIRTH ANNIVERSARY. Aug 1, 1818. An interest in her father's hobby and an ability for mathematics resulted in Maria Mitchell's becoming the first female professional astronomer. In 1847, while assisting her father in a survey of the sky for the US Coast Guard, Mitchell discovered a new comet and determined its orbit. She received many honors because of this, including being elected to the American Academy of Arts and Sciences—its first woman. Mitchell joined the staff at Vassar Female College in 1865—the first US female professor of astronomy—and in 1873 was a cofounder of the Association for the Advancement of Women. Born at Nantucket, MA, Mitchell died June 28, 1889, at Lynn, MA.

MTV PREMIERE: 25th ANNIVERSARY. Aug 1, 1981. The all-music-video channel debuted on this date. VH1, another music channel owned by MTV Networks that is aimed at older pop music fans, premiered in 1985.

NATIONAL IMMUNIZATION AWARENESS MONTH. Aug 1–31. Immunization is critical to maintaining health and preventing life-threatening diseases among people of all ages and cultures throughout the US. Each year in the US, tens of thousands of people die because of vaccine-preventable diseases or their complications, and even more experience pain, suffering and disability. This month calls attention to the importance of infant, child, adolescent and adult immunization, and seeks to reduce disparities in vaccine use while maintaining public trust in their value and safety. National Immunization Awareness Month promotional materials are available. For info: National Partnership for Immunization, 121 N Washington St, Ste 300, Alexandria, VA 22314. Phone: (703) 836-6110. Fax: (703) 836-3470. E-mail: npi@hmhb.org. Web: www.partnersforimmunization.org.

NATIONAL INVENTORS' MONTH®. Aug 1–31. To educate the American public about the value of creativity and inventiveness and the importance of inventions and inventors to the quality of our lives. This will be accomplished by specially designed displays for libraries, an interactive website and through the placement of media stories about living inventors in most of the top national, local and trade publications. Sponsored by the United Inventors Association of the USA (UIA-USA), the Academy of Applied Science and *Inventors' Digest.* For info: Joanne Hayes-Rines, Inventors' Digest. Phone: (617) 367-4540. Fax: (617) 723-6988. E-mail: joanne@inventorsdigest.com. Web: www .inventorsdigest.com.

NATIONAL NIGHT OUT. Aug 1. Designed to heighten crime prevention awareness and to promote police-community partnerships. Annually, the first Tuesday in August. For info: Matt A. Peskin, Dir, Natl Assn of Town Watch, PO Box 303, Wynnewood, PA 19096. Phone: (610) 649-7055 or (800) 648-3688. Fax: (610) 649-5456. E-mail: info@natw.org. Web: www.nationalnightout .org.

NATIONAL WIN WITH CIVILITY MONTH. Aug 1–31. When we are civil to each other we confirm our worth and acknowledge the worth of others. We can move in and out of all levels of society confident that we are always doing the "right thing." We gain recognition for civility and we secure the respect of our fellow human beings. For info: Thomas Danaher, PO Box 85193, Las Vegas, NV 89185. Phone: (702) 384-7376. E-mail: thomasdanaher@yahoo.com.

NORTH CENTRAL MISSOURI FAIR. Aug 1–6. North Central Missouri Fairgrounds, Trenton, MO. Carnival rides, professional vendors, parade, livestock, dairy demo. Art exhibits. Nightly events, such as Demolition Derby, bull riding, Mud Run and other entertainment. Est attendance: 2,500. For info: North Central Missouri Fair, PO Box 245, Trenton, MO 64683.

OAK RIDGE ATOMIC PLANT BEGUN: ANNIVERSARY. Aug 1, 1943. Ground was broken at Oak Ridge, TN, for the first plant built to manufacture the uranium 235 needed to build an atomic bomb. The plant was largely completed by July of 1944 at a final cost of $280 million. By August 1945 the total cost for development of the A-bomb ran to $1 billion.

RESPECT FOR PARENTS DAY. Aug 1. A day set aside to think of positive things parents contribute to society. Annually, Aug 1. For info: Marilyn Dalrymple, PO Box 1563, Lancaster, CA 93539. Phone: (661) 945-2360. Web: members.tripod.com/MarilynDalrymple/index-4.html.

ROUNDS RESOUNDING DAY. Aug 1. To sing rounds, catches and canons in folk contrapuntal tradition. Motto: "As rounds re-sound and resound, all the world's joined in a circle of harmony." Annually, Aug 1. For info: Gloria T. Delamar, Founder, Rounds Resounding Society. E-mail: Rounds.Resounding.Society@juno.com. Web: www.delamar.org/roundsresounding.htm.

"THE RUSH LIMBAUGH SHOW" NATIONAL RADIO PREMIERE: ANNIVERSARY. Aug 1, 1988. Conservative political commentator and radio personality Rush Limbaugh began his nationally syndicated show on this date with 56 stations. It quickly became the nation's top-rated show and rejuvenated the radio talk format. Today, more than 645 stations carry the program to an estimated 20 million listeners.

SEED TO STALK. August 1–31. Jamestown Settlement, Williamsburg, VA, and Yorktown Victory Center, Yorktown, VA. Explore American agriculture of the 17th and 18th centuries. Compare Powhatan and European planting and cultivation methods and learn which crops were grown for sustenance and which were for profit. Throughout the month, visitors can try their hand at tending and watering gardens, and learn about the many practical uses of herbs and plants. For info: Jamestown-Yorktown Foundation, PO Box 1607, Williamsburg, VA 23187. Phone: (757) 253-4838 or toll-free (888) 593-4682. Fax: (757) 253-5299. Web: www.historyisfun.org.

SIMPLIFY YOUR LIFE WEEK. Aug 1–7. A week to encourage people to simplify their lives and reduce clutter, thereby reducing stress and acquiring a happier and more peaceful lifestyle. For information about this worldwide organization and 100 ways to simplify one's life, send $5 to cover expenses of printing, handling and postage. For info: Dr. Stanley Drake, Pres Emeritus, Intl Soc of Friendship & Good Will, 8592 Roswell Rd, Ste 251, Atlanta, GA 30350-1867. Phone: (678) 795-1362. E-mail: sjdrake@bellsouth.net. Web: www.friendshipandgoodwill.org.

SPINAL MUSCULAR ATROPHY AWARENESS MONTH. Aug 1–31. To promote awareness of this congenital disease. For info: Families of Spinal Muscular Atrophy, PO Box 196, Libertyville, IL 60048. Phone: (800) 886-1762. E-mail: info@fsma.org. Web: www.curesma.com or www.fsma.org.

SWITZERLAND: CONFEDERATION DAY. Aug 1. National holiday. Anniversary of the founding of the Swiss Confederation. Commemorates a pact made in 1291. Parades, patriotic gatherings, bonfires and fireworks. Young citizens' coming-of-age ceremonies. Observed since 600th anniversary of Swiss Confederation was celebrated in 1891.

August 2006	S	M	T	W	T	F	S
			1	2	3	4	5
	6	7	8	9	10	11	12
	13	14	15	16	17	18	19
	20	21	22	23	24	25	26
	27	28	29	30	31		

TEXAS COUNTY FAIR/OLD SETTLERS REUNION. Aug 1–5. Fair Grounds, Houston, MO. A fun festival with family night, cowboy night and health fair night. Featuring arts and crafts, carnival midway, music concerts, bluegrass and country bands, demolition derby, bull ride, livestock exhibit and sale. Est attendance: 8,000. For info: Texas County Fair/Old Settlers Reunion, PO Box 374, Houston, MO 65483. Phone: (417) 967-2220. Fax: (417) 967-2178. E-mail: chamber@train.missouri.org.

TRINIDAD AND TOBAGO: EMANCIPATION DAY. Aug 1. Public holiday. Slavery was abolished in all British colonies on this day in 1834. Also called Discovery Day.

US CUSTOMS: ANNIVERSARY. Aug 1, 1789. "The first US customs officers began to collect the revenue and enforce the Tariff Act of July 4, 1789, on this date. Since then, the customhouse and the customs officer have stood as symbols of national pride and sovereignty at ports of entry along the land and sea borders of our country." (From Presidential Proclamation 4306.)

WARSAW UPRISING: ANNIVERSARY. Aug 1, 1944. Having received radio reports from Moscow promising aid from the Red Army, the Polish Home Army rose up against the Nazi oppressors. At 5 PM thousands of windows were thrown open and Polish patriots, 40,000 strong, began shooting at German soldiers in the streets. The Germans responded by throwing eight divisions into the battle. Despite appeals from the London-based Polish government-in-exile, no assistance was forthcoming from the Allies, and after two months of horrific fighting the rebellion was quashed.

WORLD BREASTFEEDING WEEK. Aug 1–7. Commemoration of signing of Innocenti Declaration. Includes a World Walk for Breastfeeding. Breastfeeding advocates, health care professionals and social service agencies focus attention on the importance and benefits of breastfeeding. Fairs, picnics, fund-raising and government proclamations highlight the week. Annually, the first seven days of August. For info: La Leche League Intl, 1400 N Meacham, Schaumburg, IL 60168-4079. Phone: (847) 519-7730. Fax: (847) 519-0035. E-mail: PRManager@llli.org or PRAssociate@llli.org. Web: www.lalecheleague.org.

WORLD WIDE WEB: ANNIVERSARY. Aug 1, 1990. The creation of what would become the World Wide Web was suggested this month in 1990 by Tim Berners-Lee and Robert Cailliau at CERN, the European Laboratory for Particle Physics at Switzerland. By October they had designed a prototype Web browser. They also introduced HTML (Hypertext Markup Language) and the URL (Universal Resource Locator). Mosaic, the first graphical Web browser, was designed by Marc Andreessen and released in 1993. By early 1993 there were 50 Web servers worldwide.

BIRTHDAYS TODAY

Tempestt Bledsoe, 33, talk-show host, actress ("Tempestt," "The Cosby Show"), born Chicago, IL, Aug 1, 1973.

Robert Cray, 53, singer, guitarist, songwriter, born Columbus, GA, Aug 1, 1953.

Dom DeLuise, 73, comedian, actor (*Cannonball Run*), born Brooklyn, NY, Aug 1, 1933.

Giancarlo Giannini, 64, actor (*Swept Away . . . , Seven Beauties*), born La Spezia, Italy, Aug 1, 1942.

Arthur Hill, 84, actor (*Harper, The Andromeda Strain*, "Owen Marshall"), born Melfort, SK, Canada, Aug 1, 1922.

Yves Saint Laurent, 70, fashion designer, born Oran, Algeria, Aug 1, 1936.

Tom Wilson, 75, cartoonist ("Ziggy"), born Grant Town, WV, Aug 1, 1931.

AUGUST 2 — WEDNESDAY
Day 214 — 151 Remaining

BALDWIN, JAMES: BIRTH ANNIVERSARY. Aug 2, 1924. Black American author noted for descriptions of black life in the US. Born at New York, NY. His best-known work, *Go Tell It on the Mountain*, was published in 1953. Died at Saint Paul-de-Vence, France, Nov 30, 1987.

COSTA RICA: FEAST OF OUR LADY OF ANGELS. Aug 2. National holiday.

DECLARATION OF INDEPENDENCE: OFFICIAL SIGNING: ANNIVERSARY. Aug 2, 1776. Contrary to widespread misconceptions, the 56 signers did not sign as a group and did not do so July 4, 1776. John Hancock and Charles Thomson signed only draft copies that day, the official day the Declaration was adopted by Congress. The signing of the official declaration occurred Aug 2, 1776, when 50 men probably took part. Later that year, five more apparently signed separately and one added his name in a subsequent year. (From "Signers of the Declaration . . ." US Dept of the Interior, 1975.) See also: "Declaration of Independence Approval and Signing: Anniversary" (July 4).

IRAQ INVADES KUWAIT: ANNIVERSARY. Aug 2, 1990. On orders of President Saddam Hussein, the Iraqi army invaded Kuwait. Hussein claimed that Kuwait presented a serious threat to Iraq's economic existence by overproducing oil and driving prices down on the world market. After conquering the capital, Kuwait City, Hussein installed a military government in Kuwait, prior to annexing it to Iraq on the claim that Kuwait was historically part of Iraq. This led to the 100-hour war against Iraq, Operation Desert Storm.

L'ENFANT, PIERRE CHARLES: BIRTH ANNIVERSARY. Aug 2, 1754. The architect, engineer and Revolutionary War officer who designed the plan for the city of Washington, DC, L'Enfant was born at Paris, France. He died at Prince Georges County, MD, June 14, 1825.

LOY, MYRNA: BIRTH ANNIVERSARY. Aug 2, 1905. America's favorite leading lady of the 1930s, Loy was born Myrna Adele Williams near Helena, MT. She soared to fame as the madcap New York sophisticate Nora Charles in the "Thin Man" movies with William Powell (Nick Charles). She also starred in the critically acclaimed *The Best Years of Our Lives* (1946). After a career spanning seven decades, she was awarded an honorary Oscar in 1991, and died at New York, NY, Dec 14, 1993.

MACEDONIA: NATIONAL DAY: ANNIVERSARY. Aug 2. Commemorates the nationalist uprising against the Ottoman Empire in 1903. Called Prophet Elias Day or Illinden. (See also "Saint Elias Day (Illinden): Macedonian Uprising: Anniversary" below.)

MAINE LOBSTER FESTIVAL. Aug 2–6. Rockland, ME. Annual celebration and promotion of the lobster industry featuring lobster dinners, arts, crafts, exhibits, live entertainment, parade, contests and a road race. Est attendance: 100,000. For info: Maine Lobster Festival, PO Box 552, Rockland, ME 04841. Phone: (207) 596-0376 or (800) LOB-CLAW. Fax: (207) 596-6549. E-mail: info@mainelobsterfestival.com. Web: www.mainelobsterfestival.com.

McHENRY COUNTY FAIR. Aug 2–6 (tentative). Woodstock, IL. Rides, food, entertainment, animal and antique competitions, talent and queen contests, demolition derby, exhibits, livestock judging and more. Est attendance: 125,000. For info: McHenry County Fairgrounds, PO Box 375, Woodstock, IL 60098. Phone: (815) 338-5315. Fax: (815) 338-5310. Web: www.mchenrycounty fair.com.

MISS CRUSTACEAN USA BEAUTY PAGEANT AND OCEAN CITY CREEP. Aug 2. 6th Street Beach, Ocean City, NJ. Participants are hermit tree crabs. To determine the most beautiful and fastest tree crab on Earth. Begins at 1 PM, EST. Est attendance: 500. For info: Mark Soifer, PR Dir, City of Ocean City, City Hall, Ocean City, NJ 08226. Phone: (609) 525-9300. Fax: (609) 399-0374. E-mail: MTSoifer@aol.com.

MOON PHASE: FIRST QUARTER. Aug 2. Moon enters First Quarter phase at 4:46 AM, EDT.

O'CONNOR, CARROLL: BIRTH ANNIVERSARY. Aug 2, 1924. Television, stage and screen actor born in New York, NY. He was best known for his portrayal of the bigoted, blue-collar Archie Bunker on "All in the Family." He played the role of Bunker from 1971 to 1979, and was nominated for eight Emmy Awards, winning four. He won a fifth Emmy in 1989 for "In the Heat of the Night." He was also inducted into the Television Hall of Fame in 1989. He died at Culver City, CA, on June 21, 2001.

OHIO STATE FAIR. Aug 2–13. Columbus, OH. Family fun, amusement rides, games, food booths, parades, entertainment, agriculture exhibits and educational displays. Est attendance: 850,000. For info: Ohio State Fair, 717 E 17th Ave, Columbus, OH 43211. Phone: (614) 644-4000. Fax: (614) 644-4031. Web: www.ohiostatefair.com.

SAINT ELIAS DAY (ILLINDEN): MACEDONIAN UPRISING: ANNIVERSARY. Aug 2, 1903. Most sacred, honored and celebrated day of the Macedonian people. Anniversary of the uprising of Macedonians against the Ottoman Empire. Turkish reprisals against the insurgents were ruthless, including the destruction of 105 villages and the execution of more than 1,700 noncombatants.

SCOTLAND: ABERDEEN INTERNATIONAL YOUTH FESTIVAL. Aug 2–12. Aberdeen. Talented young people from all areas of the performing arts come from around the world to participate in this festival. Est attendance: 30,000. For info: Stephen Stenning, Linksfield Community Centre, 520 King St, Aberdeen, Scotland AB24 5SS. Phone: (44) (1224) 494400. Fax: (44) (1224) 494114. E-mail: info@aiyf.org. Web: www.aiyf.org.

SEASHORE OPEN HOUSE TOUR. Aug 2. Loveladies, NJ. 40th annual. Come and enjoy the fabulous shoreline houses. For info: Long Beach Island Foundation of the Arts and Sciences, 120 Long Beach Blvd, Loveladies, NJ 08008. Phone: (609) 494-1241. Fax: (609) 494-0662.

US VIRGIN ISLANDS NATIONAL PARK ESTABLISHED: 50th ANNIVERSARY. Aug 2, 1956. The US Virgin Islands, including areas on St. John and St. Thomas, were established as a national park and preserve. On Oct 5, 1962, the Virgin Islands National Park was enlarged to include offshore areas, including coral reefs, shorelines and sea grass beds.

BIRTHDAYS TODAY

Joanna Cassidy, 62, actress ("Buffalo Bill," *Under Fire*), born Camden, NJ, Aug 2, 1944.

Wes Craven, 67, writer, director (*The Nightmare on Elm Street, Scream*), born Cleveland, OH, Aug 2, 1939.

James Fallows, 57, journalist, former editor (*US News & World Report*), born Philadelphia, PA, Aug 2, 1949.

Edward Furlong, 29, actor (*Before and After, Terminator 2*), born Glendale, CA, Aug 2, 1977.

Kathryn Harrold, 56, actress ("I'll Fly Away," "The Larry Sanders Show," *Modern Romance*), born Tazewell, VA, Aug 2, 1950.

Lamar Hunt, 74, Hall of Fame football executive, Hall of Fame soccer executive, born El Dorado, AR, Aug 2, 1932.

Victoria Jackson, 47, actress ("Saturday Night Live," *I Love You to Death*), born Miami, FL, Aug 2, 1959.

Peter O'Toole, 73, actor (*Lawrence of Arabia, Becket*), born Connemara, Ireland, Aug 2, 1933.

Mary-Louise Parker, 42, actress (Tony Award for *Proof*; "The West Wing," *Fried Green Tomatoes*), born Fort Jackson, SC, Aug 2, 1964.

John Snow, 67, US Secretary of the Treasury, born Toledo, OH, Aug 2, 1939.

Michael Weiss, 30, figure skater, born Washington, DC, Aug 2, 1976.

AUGUST 3 — THURSDAY

Day 215 — 150 Remaining

ADAMS COUNTY FAIR/RODEO. Aug 3–6. Hettinger, ND. 7th annual fair with booths, exhibits and special events. Est attendance: 2,500. For info: Community Promotions Office, PO Box 1031, Hettinger, ND 58639. Phone: (701) 567-2531. E-mail: adamschmbr@ndsupernet.com. Web: hettingernd.com.

CANADA: AGRIFAIR. Aug 3–7. Abbotsford, BC. Fun for everyone with attractions like draft horses, dairy, beef and poultry; hands-on milking display; motor sports; my marketplace trade show; antique farm display bursting with antique toys; midway; plus everything from national and international stage entertainment to a pro rodeo and fireworks. Est attendance: 57,000. For info: Harvey Carroll, Abbotsford Agrifair, PO Box 2334, Abbotsford, BC, Canada V2T 4X2. Phone: (604) 852-6674. Fax: (604) 852-6631. E-mail: agrifair@telus.net.

COLUMBUS SAILS FOR THE NEW WORLD: ANNIVERSARY. Aug 3, 1492. Christopher Columbus, "Admiral of the Ocean Sea," set sail half an hour before sunrise from Palos, Spain, Aug 3, 1492. With three ships, *Niña*, *Pinta* and *Santa Maria*, and a crew of 90, he sailed "for Cathay" but found instead a New World of the Americas, first landing at Guanahani (San Salvador Island in the Bahamas) Oct 12. See also: "Columbus Day" (Oct 12).

EQUATORIAL GUINEA: ARMED FORCES DAY. Aug 3. National holiday.

FESTIVAL AT SANDPOINT. Aug 3–6 (also Aug 10–13). Sandpoint, ID. Summer music concert series featuring classical, country, jazz, pop, world, blues and folk. Est attendance: 20,000. For info: Dyno Wahl, Exec Dir, Festival at Sandpoint, PO Box 695, Sandpoint, ID 83864. Phone: (888) 265-4554. Fax: (208) 263-6858. E-mail: festival@sandpoint.net. Web: www.festivalatsandpoint.com.

GUINEA-BISSAU: COLONIZATION MARTYR'S DAY. Aug 3. National holiday. Also called Pidjiguiti Martyrs' Day.

August 2006	S	M	T	W	T	F	S
			1	2	3	4	5
	6	7	8	9	10	11	12
	13	14	15	16	17	18	19
	20	21	22	23	24	25	26
	27	28	29	30	31		

KUHN, MARGARET (MAGGIE): BIRTH ANNIVERSARY. Aug 3, 1905. When she was forced into retirement because she'd reached the age of 65, Maggie Kuhn founded the Gray Panthers organization to fight age discrimination. Subsequently she waged a battle that resulted in mandatory retirement being banned. Born at Buffalo, NY, Kuhn died Apr 22, 1995, at Philadelphia, PA.

MOUNTAIN DANCE AND FOLK FESTIVAL. Aug 3–5. Asheville, NC. 79th annual festival. More than 400 performers in this three-day fest, which celebrates the cultural heritage of the Southern Appalachian Mountains. Includes dance teams, mountain fiddlers, banjo pickers, old-time string bands, storytellers, bluegrass bands and dulcimer sweepers. Oldest of its kind, founded in 1928 by Bascom Lamar Lunsford. Est attendance: 1,500. For info: Asheville Area Chamber of Commerce, Folk Heritage, PO Box 1010, Asheville, NC 28802. Phone: (828) 258-6101. Web: www.folkheritage.org.

NIGER: INDEPENDENCE DAY. Aug 3. Niger gained its independence from France on this day in 1960.

"PRIMETIME LIVE" TV PREMIERE: ANNIVERSARY. Aug 3, 1989. Sam Donaldson and Diane Sawyer were the first hosts of this magazine show that features investigative and consumer reports as well as human interest stories.

PYLE, ERNEST TAYLOR: BIRTH ANNIVERSARY. Aug 3, 1900. Ernie Pyle was born at Dana, IN, and began his career in journalism in 1923. After serving as managing editor of the Washington *Daily News*, he returned to his first journalistic love of working as a roving reporter in 1935. His column was syndicated by nearly 200 newspapers and often focused on figures behind the news. His reports of the bombing of London in 1940 and subsequent reports from Africa, Sicily, Italy and France earned him a Pulitzer Prize in 1944. He was killed by machine-gun fire at the Pacific island of Ie Shima, Apr 18, 1945.

RIBFEST. Aug 3–5. Kalamazoo, MI. Features the smell of sizzling ribs as rib-burners from throughout the US tantalize the taste buds of West Michigan. Festival will feature live entertainment, family-oriented events, food booths and the "Sponsors Choice Award" for best ribs. Annually, the first full weekend in Aug (including Thursday). Est attendance: 30,000. For info: Deborah Droppers, Community Advocates for Persons with Developmental Disabilities, 814 S Westnedge St, Kalamazoo, MI 49008-1162. Phone: (269) 388-2830. E-mail: eventkzoo@chartermi.net. Web: www.eventkalamazoo.com.

SANTA CRUZ BEACH BOARDWALK LOOFF CAROUSEL: 95th ANNIVERSARY. Aug 3, 1911. Danish woodcarver Charles I.D. Looff delivered the classic carousel on Aug 3, 1911. A furniture-maker by trade, Looff began carving carousel animals as a hobby after immigrating to America. His first carousel was installed at Coney Island in New York in 1875. The Boardwalk carousel features jeweled horses and a 342-pipe Ruth band organ built in 1894. The carousel and the park's Giant Dipper roller-coaster were designated National Historic Landmarks by the US National Park Service in June 1987.

SATCHMO SUMMERFEST. Aug 3–6. New Orleans, LA. The spirit of "Satchmo" lives with this annual birthday celebration of Louis "Satchmo" Armstrong's music, legacy and cultural contributions. The free event, centered around the Louisiana State Museum's Old US Mint (400 Esplanade Ave) will include a jazz-filled music festival, children's activities, seminars and panels, photo exhibits and cultural displays, a jazz mass and Satchmo-inspired New Orleans cuisine served up in "Red Bean Alley." It's all part of New Orleans' ongoing tribute to the "International Ambassador of Jazz" in the birthplace of jazz. Est attendance: 45,000. For info: French Quarter Festivals, Inc, 400 N Peters St, #205, New Orleans, LA 70130. Phone: (800) 673-5725 or (504) 522-5730. E-mail: feedback@fqfi.org. Web: www.fqfi.org.

SCOPES, JOHN T.: BIRTH ANNIVERSARY. Aug 3, 1900. Central figure in a cause célèbre (the "Scopes Trial" or the "Monkey Trial"), John Thomas Scopes was born at Paducah, KY. An obscure 24-year-old schoolteacher at the Dayton, TN, high school in 1925, he became the focus of world attention. Scopes never uttered a word at his trial, which was a contest between two of America's best-known lawyers, William Jennings Bryan and Clarence Darrow. The trial, July 10–21, 1925, resulted in Scopes's conviction. He was fined $100 "for teaching evolution" in Tennessee. The verdict was upset on a technicality and the statute he was accused of breaching was repealed in 1967. Scopes died at Shreveport, LA, Oct 21, 1970.

TISHA B'AV OR FAST OF AB. Aug 3. Hebrew calendar date: Ab 9, 5766. Commemorates and mourns the destruction of the first and second Temples in Jerusalem (586 BC and AD 70). Began at sundown Aug 2.

URIS, LEON: BIRTH ANNIVERSARY. Aug 3, 1924. American novelist born to a family of Russian Jews at Baltimore, MD. His most successful novels were those that chronicled the Holocaust (1960's *Mila 18*) and the founding of Israel (1958's *Exodus*). His novels sold millions and were made into several feature films. Later titles included *QB VII*, a fictionalized account of his own trial for libel, and *Trinity*, which followed the life of three generations of an Irish family. Uris died June 21, 2003, at Shelter Island, NY.

WISCONSIN STATE FAIR. Aug 3–13. State Fair Park, Milwaukee, WI. Wisconsin celebrates its rural heritage at the state's most popular and most historic annual event. Features numerous midway rides, 28 free stages of entertainment, hundreds of animals, wide variety of food and beverages and top-name entertainment. (Call 24-hour recorded information line at 1-800-884-FAIR for up-to-date information.) Est attendance: 910,000. For info: PR Dept, Wisconsin State Fair Park, PO Box 14990, West Allis, WI 53214-0990. Phone: (414) 266-7000. Fax: (414) 266-7007. E-mail: wsfp@sfp.state.wi.us. Web: www.wistatefair .com.

BIRTHDAYS TODAY

Tony Bennett, 80, singer ("I Left My Heart in San Francisco"), born Anthony Dominick Benedetto at New York, NY, Aug 3, 1926.

Steven Berkoff, 69, actor, director, writer (*A Clockwork Orange, Beverly Hills Cop*), born London, England, Aug 3, 1937.

Tom Brady, 29, football player, born San Mateo, CA, Aug 3, 1977.

P.D. James, 86, mystery novelist (*Devices and Desires, Innocent Blood*), born Phyllis Dorothy James at Oxford, England, Aug 3, 1920.

Evangeline Lilly, 27, actress ("Lost"), born Fort Saskatchewan, AB, Canada, Aug 3, 1979.

John McGinley, 47, actor (*Platoon, Born on the Fourth of July,* "Scrubs"), born New York, NY, Aug 3, 1959.

Martin Sheen, 66, actor (*Apocalypse Now*, "The West Wing"), born Ramon Estevez at Dayton, OH, Aug 3, 1940.

Martha Stewart, 65, lifestyle consultant, TV personality, writer, born Nutley, NJ, Aug 3, 1941.

Blaine Wilson, 32, gymnast, born Columbus, OH, Aug 3, 1974.

AUGUST 4 — FRIDAY
Day 216 — 149 Remaining

ARMSTRONG, LOUIS: BIRTH ANNIVERSARY. Aug 4, 1900 (or 1901). Jazz musician extraordinaire born at New Orleans, LA. Died at New York, NY, July 6, 1971. Armstrong often said he was born on the 4th of July, but documents in the Louis Armstrong Archives of Queens College, Flushing, NY, indicate that he was actually born Aug 4, 1900 or 1901. Asked to define jazz, Armstrong reportedly replied, "Man, if you gotta ask, you'll never know." The trumpet player was also known as Satchmo. He appeared in many films. Popular singles included "What a Wonderful World" and "Hello, Dolly" (with Barbra Streisand).

BLUEBERRY FESTIVAL. Aug 4–5. Library Lawn and Village Green, Montrose, PA. 27th annual fund-raiser for the Susquehanna County Library and Historical Society. Two days filled with food, fun and festivity. Raffles, book sale, children's games, silent auction, hand-stitched quilts, commemorative items and more. Annually, the first Friday and Saturday in August. Est attendance: 5,000. For info: Hilary Caws-Elwitt, Susquehanna County Library, 2 Monument Sq, Montrose, PA 18801. Phone: (570) 278-1881. Fax: (570) 278-9336. E-mail: sctylibrary@stny.rr.com. Web: www .susqcolibrary.org/bf.htm.

BOOM DAYS. Aug 4–6. Leadville, CO. The city's oldest annual celebration features a large parade, street races, mining events, pack burro race and arts and crafts. Fun for the whole family. Est attendance: 35,000. For info: Chamber of Commerce, PO Box 861, Leadville, CO 80461. Phone: (719) 486-3900 or (800) 933-3901. Fax: (719) 486-8478. E-mail: leadville@leadvilleusa.com. Web: www.leadvilleusa.com.

BRAHAM PIE DAY. Aug 4. Freedom Park, Braham, MN. Celebrate Braham's status as "Homemade Pie Capital of Minnesota" during this one-day festival. Visitors will find homemade pies, craft displays, pie-eating contests, a pie auction, a pie race and performing artists in Braham's main street park. Activities also include an exotic pie-eating contest, a pi R squared contest, a pie art show and the "Pie-alluia" chorus. Est attendance: 5,000. For info: Andrea Downing, Braham City Hall, 2nd St SW, PO Box 383, Braham, MN 55006. Phone: (320) 396-4956. E-mail: dandrea@ecenet.com. Web: www.braham.com.

BURKINA FASO: REVOLUTION DAY: ANNIVERSARY. Aug 4. National holiday. Commemorates 1983 coup.

CANADA: BIG VALLEY JAMBOREE. Aug 4–7. Camrose, AB. Canada's premier country music festival, featuring top-name entertainers and more than 25 acts. Beer gardens, trade shows, unserviced camping and parking. Est attendance: 70,000. For info: Glen Vinet, 4238-37 St, Camrose, AB, Canada T4V 4L6. Phone: (780) 672-0224 or (888) 404-1234. Fax: (780) 672-9530. E-mail: bvj@bigvalleyjamboree.com. Web: www.bigvalleyjamboree .com.

CANADA: CANADA'S NATIONAL UKRAINIAN FESTIVAL. Aug 4–6. Dauphin, MB. Experience the richness and flavors of Ukrainian culture. From the colorful, energized dancers to the powerful folk songs of Ukraine, there is something for everyone to enjoy. Est attendance: 7,000. For info: Canada's National Ukrainian Festival, Box 368, Dauphin, MB, Canada R7N 2V2. Phone: (204) 622-4600. Fax: (204) 622-4606. E-mail: cnuf @mts.net. Web: www.cnuf.ca.

CANADA: PIONEER DAYS. Aug 4–7. Mennonite Heritage Village, Steinbach, MB. Pioneer demonstrations and related activities in a heritage village setting. Est attendance: 14,500. For info: Jim Penner, Exec Dir, 231 PTH 12N, Steinbach, MB, Canada R5G 1T8. Phone: (204) 326-9661 or toll-free (866) 280-8741. Fax: (204) 326-5046. E-mail: info@mennoniteheritagevillage.com. Web: www.mennoniteheritagevillage.com.

CIVIL RIGHTS WORKERS FOUND SLAIN: ANNIVERSARY. Aug 4, 1964. After disappearing on June 21, three civil rights workers were found murdered and buried in an earthen dam outside Philadelphia, MS. The three young men were workers on the Mississippi Summer Project organized by the Student Nonviolent Coordinating Committee (SNCC) to increase black voter registration. Prior to their disappearance, James Chaney, Andrew Goodman and Michael Schwerner were detained by Neshoba County police on charges of speeding. When their car was found, burned, on June 23, President Johnson ordered an FBI search for the men.

COAST GUARD DAY. Aug 4. Celebrates anniversary of founding of the Revenue Cutter Service in 1790, which merged with the Life Saving Service in 1915 to become the US Coast Guard.

CRAFTSMEN'S CLASSIC ARTS & CRAFTS FESTIVAL. Aug 4–6. Myrtle Beach Convention Center, Myrtle Beach, SC. 24th annual. Features work from more than 260 talented artists and craftspeople. All juried exhibitors' work has been handmade by the exhibitors and must be their own original design and creation. See the creative process in action with several exhibitors demonstrating throughout the weekend. Something for every style, taste, and budget with items from the most contemporary to the most traditional. Est attendance: 15,000. For info: Gilmore Enterprises, Inc, 1240 Oakland Ave, Greensboro, NC 27403. Phone: (336) 274-5550. E-mail: gilmoreshows@triad.rr.com. Web: www.CraftShow.com or www.gilmoreshows.com.

CUNNINGHAM, GLENN: BIRTH ANNIVERSARY. Aug 4, 1909. Glenn Clarence Cunningham, the "Kansas Ironman," American track athlete and 1934–37 world-record holder for the mile, member of the US Olympic teams in 1932 and 1936, was born at Atlanta, KS. On June 16, 1934, at Princeton, NJ, Cunningham set a world record for the mile (4:06.7 min). Cunningham died at Menifee, AR, Mar 10, 1988.

DECATUR CELEBRATION. Aug 4–6. Decatur, IL. The largest free family street festival in Illinois, within 22 city blocks of fun there are 13 entertainment stages, 110 arts and crafts vendors, 46 commercial vendors, and 69 one-of-a-kind food vendors. Annually, the first weekend in August. Est attendance: 300,000. For info: Decatur Celebration, 227 S Main St, Decatur, IL 62523. Phone: (217) 423-4222. Fax: (217) 423-4271. Web: decaturcelebration.com.

GIFT OF THE WATERS PAGEANT & ART FESTIVAL IN THE PARK. Aug 4–6. Hot Springs State Park, Thermopolis, WY. Indian dance demonstrations and pageant, powwow, parade, arts & crafts festival, craft demonstrations. Est attendance: 3,000. For info: Toddi Darlington, Thermopolis Chamber of Commerce, 119 South 6th St, Thermopolis, WY 82443. Phone: (307) 864-3192. E-mail: thercc@rtconnect.net. Web: www.thermopolis.com.

GIGGLEFEET DANCE FESTIVAL. Aug 4 & 6. Ketchikan, AK. Two evening performances celebrating dance in the community, including jazz, tap, ballet, modern, hip-hop, Native Alaskan, breakdance and more. Annually, the first Friday and Sunday in August, part of the Blueberry Arts Festival. Est attendance: 1,000. For info: Ketchikan Area Arts & Humanities Council, 716 Totem Way, Ketchikan, AK 99901. Phone: (907) 225-2211. Fax: (907) 225-4330. E-mail: info@ketchikanarts.org.

GREAT ARKANSAS PIG-OUT. Aug 4–5. Morrilton, AR. 18th annual pig-out. Focus is on food of all kinds: barbecue, chicken-on-a-stick, funnel cakes, hamburgers. Activities include pig chase, hog calling, children's pig-tail, arts, crafts, games, entertainment, Tour de Oink, 5k fun run. Est attendance: 25,000. For info: Great Arkansas Pig-Out Committee, PO Box 101, Morrilton, AR 72110. Phone: (501) 354-5400. Web: www.pigout.org.

INDIAN ARTIFACT SHOW. Aug 4–6. Owensboro, KY. To promote the art and culture of prehistoric Indians and to display outstanding collections of relics; buying, selling and trading. Est attendance: 3,000. For info: Kathy Pohl Finley, Box 93, Cannelton, IN 47520-0093. Phone: (812) 547-3255. Fax: (812) 547-2525. E-mail: kpohl@psci.net.

INTERNATIONAL HYPNOSIS FEDERATION CONFERENCE. Aug 4–6. Los Angeles, CA. "It's All About You" Conference for mind, body and spirit. Includes world class speakers, fun, friends—and you. Everyone is welcome. Continuing education for helpers, parents, counselors, hypnotists, acupuncturists, RN's, teachers and healers. Annually, the first weekend in August. Est attendance: 2,000. For info: Shelley Stockwell, PhD, Intl Hypnosis Federation, 30819 Casilina Dr, Rancho Palos Verdes, CA 90275. Phone: (310) 541-4844. E-mail: ihf@cox.net. Web: www.hypnosisfederation.com.

MANDELA, NELSON: ARREST ANNIVERSARY. Aug 4, 1962. Nelson Rolihlahla Mandela, charismatic black South African leader, was born in 1918, the son of the Tembu tribal chief, at Umtata, Transkei territory of South Africa. A lawyer and political activist, Mandela, who in 1952 established the first black law partnership in South Africa, had been in conflict with the white government there much of his life. Acquitted of a treason charge after a trial that lasted from 1956 to 1961, he was apprehended again by security police Aug 4, 1962. The subsequent trial, widely viewed as an indictment of white domination, resulted in Mandela's being sentenced to five years in prison. In 1963 he was taken from the Pretoria prison to face a new trial—for sabotage, high treason and conspiracy to overthrow the government—and in June 1964 he was sentenced to life in prison. See also: "Mandela, Nelson: Prison Release Anniversary" (Feb 11).

MUSIKFEST. Aug 4–13. Bethlehem, PA. Entertainment, ethnic foods and music—more than 300 performers on 13 indoor and outdoor stages. Est attendance: 1,000,000. For info: ArtsQuest, 25 W Third St, Bethlehem, PA 18015-1238. Phone: (610) 861-0678. Fax: (610) 861-2644. E-mail: info@fest.org. Web: www.musikfest.org.

NATIONAL CZECHOSLOVAKIAN FESTIVAL. Aug 4–6. Wilber, NE. Festival to promote preservation of Czech culture, foods, traditions—accordion, polka and Czech band music, three parades, national queen contest, museum, art show, Czech dinners, programs, contests, fellowship, reunions. Annually, the first weekend in August. Sponsored by Nebraska Czechs of Wilber. Est attendance: 50,000. For info: Wilber Chamber of Commerce, PO Box 1164, Wilber, NE 68465. Phone: (888) 4-WILBER.

NEW JERSEY STATE FAIR/SUSSEX COUNTY FARM AND HORSE SHOW. Aug 4–13. Sussex County Fairgrounds, Augusta, NJ. The state's largest livestock and horse show also includes educational exhibits, amusements, commercial exhibits and entertainment. Located off Rt 206 Plains Rd. Gate opens 10 AM Friday and closes 5 PM Sunday. Est attendance: 200,000. For info: New Jersey State Fair, PO Box 2456, Branchville, NJ 07826. Phone: (973) 948-5500. Fax: (973) 948-0147. E-mail: thefair@njstatefair.com. Web: www.njstatefair.com.

QUEEN ELIZABETH THE QUEEN MOTHER: BIRTH ANNIVERSARY. Aug 4, 1900. One of the most beloved members of the English royal family, the Queen "Mum" saw England through some of its most trying times in the 20th century. She was born Elizabeth Angela Marguerite Bowes-Lyon at London, England, and married the then Duke of York in 1923. When her husband was unexpectedly crowned King George IV in 1936 (after

	S	**M**	**T**	**W**	**T**	**F**	**S**
August			1	2	3	4	5
2006	6	7	8	9	10	11	12
	13	14	15	16	17	18	19
	20	21	22	23	24	25	26
	27	28	29	30	31		

the abdication of Edward VIII), she became his strong and guiding support. She won the undying gratitude of her subjects, moreover, when she refused to remove the royal family to the safety of the countryside during the German bombing of London in World War II. After the King's death in 1952, she took on a different role, that of the Queen Mother, but kept up a busy schedule of public duties almost until her death. She died Mar 30, 2002.

RICHARD, MAURICE ("ROCKET"): BIRTH ANNIVERSARY. Aug 4, 1921. Hockey Hall of Fame right wing, born at Montreal, QC, Canada. Died May 27, 2000, at Montreal.

SCALIGER, JOSEPH JUSTUS: BIRTH ANNIVERSARY. Aug 4, 1540 (OS). French scholar who has been called the founder of scientific chronology. Born at Agen, France, the son of classical scholar Julius Caesar Scaliger. In 1582 he suggested a new system for measuring time and numbering years. His "Julian Period" (named for his father), which consisted of 7,980 consecutive years (beginning Jan 1, 4713 BC), is still in use by astronomers. He died at Leiden, Netherlands, Jan 21, 1609 (OS).

SCHUMAN, WILLIAM HOWARD: BIRTH ANNIVERSARY. Aug 4, 1910. American composer who won the first Pulitzer Prize for composition and founded the Juilliard School of Music, born at New York. His compositions include *American Festival Overture, New England Triptych,* the baseball opera *The Mighty Casey* and *On Freedom's Ground,* written for the centennial of the Statue of Liberty in 1986. He was instrumental in the conception of the Lincoln Center for the Performing Arts and served as its first president. In 1985 he was awarded a special Pulitzer Prize for his contributions. He also received a National Medal of Arts in 1985 and a Kennedy Center Honor in 1989. Schuman died at New York City, Feb 15, 1992.

SCOTLAND: EDINBURGH MILITARY TATTOO: THE MAIN EVENT. Aug 4–26. Edinburgh Castle, Edinburgh, Lothian. Display of military color and pageantry held at night on the flood-lit esplanade of Edinburgh Castle. A unique blend of music, ceremony, entertainment and theater. Est attendance: 217,000. For info: The Edinburgh Military Tattoo, The Tattoo Office, 32 Market St, Edinburgh, Scotland EH1 1QB. Phone: (44) (131) 225-1188. Fax: (44) (131) 225-8627. E-mail: edintattoo@edintattoo.co.uk. Web: www.edintattoo.co.uk.

SHELLEY, PERCY BYSSHE: BIRTH ANNIVERSARY. Aug 4, 1792. Poet Percy Bysshe Shelley, one of the leading English Romantic poets and embodiment of a free spirit, was born at Warnham, Sussex. He lived abroad in Italy until his death at sea off the coast of Viareggio, just a month before his 30th birthday, July 8, 1822. Shelley's important works include "Ozymandias," published in 1818; "Ode to the West Wind," "The Cloud," "To a Skylark" and *Prometheus Unbound* in 1819; and *Adonais* (an elegy for John Keats) in 1821.

TELLURIDE JAZZ CELEBRATION. Aug 4–6. Telluride, CO. 30th anniversary celebration. Some of jazz's hottest rising stars and most accomplished musicians team up in the town park by day and in intimate nightclubs at night. Annually, the first weekend in August. Est attendance: 9,000. For info: Telluride Mountain Village CVB, PO Box 1009, Telluride, CO 81435. Phone: (88) TELLURIDE. Fax: (970) 728-6475. E-mail: info@visittelluride.com. Web: www.visittelluride.com.

TWINS DAY FESTIVAL. Aug 4–6. Twinsburg, OH. 31st festival. According to *Guinness Book of World Records,* this is the world's largest gathering of twins. Annually, the first full weekend in August. For info: Twins Day Festival Committee, PO Box 29, Twinsburg, OH 44087. Phone: (330) 425-3652. E-mail: info@twinsdays.org. Web: www.twinsdays.org.

WHITE OAK RENDEZVOUS. Aug 4–6. Deer River, MN. 100 tipis and white canvas lodges placed around a North West Company Fur Post from 1798. Blacksmith shop, clerk's quarters and store, birchbark canoe–building shed, Ojibwe village. Live music, dance, storytelling and nature trail with plants labeled to explain their use in 1798 for medicine, shelter or food. 18th-century craft demonstrations and sales. Also, specialty foods from the fur trade

period. RV and tent campground available. Est attendance: 3,000. For info: White Oak Society, 33155 State Highway 6, Deer River, MN 56636. Phone: (218) 246-9393. Fax: (218) 246-9393. E-mail: whiteoak@paulbunyan.net. Web: www.whiteoak.org.

WORK LIKE A DOG DAY. Aug 4. A celebration (during the Dog Days of summer) of the professional and personal satisfaction experienced by entrepreneurs and small businesses that work like a dog to be successful. Take this day to lap up and celebrate the rewards of your success. Stop by a spa: just because you work like a dog, it doesn't mean you have to look like one. Annually, the first Friday of August. For info: Aida Rodriguez, Evil Twin Productions, 5201 Fulton Ave, Los Angeles, CA 91401. Phone: (818) 986-8551. E-mail: Aida@eviltwinproductions.com. Web: www.eviltwinproductions.com.

WORLD FREEFALL CONVENTION. Aug 4–13. Rantoul, IL. More than 5,400 skydivers converge in Rantoul and fill the skies with their brilliant-colored parachutes. Spectators can enjoy the sights and take part in helicopter rides and hot-air balloon rides. Those wishing to skydive may purchase a tandem skydive or take lessons and skydive on their own. Est attendance: 100,000. For info: World Freefall Convention, 1659 Hwy 104, Quincy, IL 62305. Phone: (217) 222-5867. Fax: (217) 885-3141. E-mail: wffc@freefall.com. Web: www.freefall.com.

BIRTHDAYS TODAY

Richard Belzer, 62, comedian, actor ("Law & Order: SVU," "Homicide: Life on the Street"), born Bridgeport, CT, Aug 4, 1944.

(William) Roger Clemens, 44, baseball player, born Dayton, OH, Aug 4, 1962.

Alberto Gonzales, 51, US Attorney General, born San Antonio, TX, Aug 4, 1955.

Jeff Gordon, 35, race car driver, born Pittsboro, IN, Aug 4, 1971.

Barack Obama, 45, US Senator (D, Illinois), born Honolulu, HI, Aug 4, 1961.

Kristoffer Tabori, 54, actor ("Seventh Avenue," "Chicago Story"), born Los Angeles, CA, Aug 4, 1952.

Helen Thomas, 86, journalist (longtime White House correspondent), born Winchester, KY, Aug 4, 1920.

Billy Bob Thornton, 51, actor (*The Man Who Wasn't There, A Simple Plan*), director, screenwriter (Oscar for *Sling Blade*), born Hot Springs, AR, Aug 4, 1955.

AUGUST 5 — SATURDAY

Day 217 — 148 Remaining

AIKEN, CONRAD: BIRTH ANNIVERSARY. Aug 5, 1899. American poet, short-story writer, critic and Pulitzer Prize winner (poetry, 1930). He was born at Savannah, GA, and died there Aug 17, 1973.

"AMERICAN BANDSTAND" TV PREMIERE: ANNIVERSARY. Aug 5, 1957. "American Bandstand" and Dick Clark are synonymous; he hosted the show for more than 30 years. "AB" started out as a local show at Philadelphia, PA, in 1952. Clark, then a disk jockey, took over as host at the age of 26. The format was simple: teens dancing, performers doing their latest hits, Clark introducing songs and listing the top 10 songs each week. This hour-long show was not only TV's longest-running musical series, but also the first one devoted exclusively to rock and roll. The show was cancelled six months after Clark turned over the hosting duties to David Hirsch in 1989.

BATTLE OF BUSHY RUN REENACTMENT. Aug 5–6. Harrison City, PA. This reenactment commemorates the decisive battle of Pontiac's War on Aug 5 and 6, 1763. Event includes a guided tour through the battle's historic camps and demonstrations of military crafts. Est attendance: 2,000. For info: David Miller, Bushy Run Battlefield, PO Box 468, Harrison City, PA 15636-0468. Phone: (724) 527-5584. E-mail: davmiller@state.pa.us.

BATTLE OF MOBILE BAY: ANNIVERSARY. Aug 5, 1864. A Union fleet under Admiral David Farragut attempted to run past three Confederate forts into Mobile Bay, AL. After coming under fire, the Union fleet headed into a maze of underwater mines, known at that time as torpedos. The ironclad *Tecumseh* was sunk by a torpedo, after which Farragut is said to have exclaimed, "Damn the torpedos, full steam ahead." The Union fleet was successful and Mobile Bay was secured.

BAY HARBOR SUMMER ART FAIR. Aug 5–6. Village of Bay Harbor, MI. 7th annual fine art and fine craft show, located in the Marina District, near Charlevoix and Petoskey. Est attendance: 10,000. For info: Audree Levy, 1809 Morning Glory, Carrollton, TX 75007. E-mail: audree@levyartfairs.com. Web: www.levyartfairs.com.

BLUEBERRY ARTS FESTIVAL. Aug 5. State Office Building, Methodist Church and Mainstay Gallery, Ketchikan, AK. A street fair featuring arts and crafts, food, games and contests for all ages, performing arts events and poetry and prose reading. Annually, the first Saturday in August. Est attendance: 7,000. For info: Ketchikan Area Arts and Humanities Council, 716 Totem Way, Ketchikan, AK 99901. Phone: (907) 225-2211. Fax: (907) 225-4330. E-mail: info@ketchikanarts.org.

BURKINA FASO: REPUBLIC DAY. Aug 5. Burkina Faso (formerly Upper Volta) gained autonomy from France in 1960.

CANADA: CANMORE FOLK MUSIC FESTIVAL. Aug 5–7. Centennial Park, Canmore, AB. 29th annual. Alberta's longest-running folk festival. Featuring food and craft booths, entertainment, workshops and free pancake breakfast on Monday. Est attendance: 13,000. For info: Canmore Folk Music Festival, PO Box 8098, Canmore, AB, Canada T1W 2T8. Phone: (403) 678-2524. Fax: (403) 678-2524. E-mail: info@canmorefolkfestival.com. Web: www.canmorefolkfestival.com.

CROATIA: HOMELAND THANKSGIVING DAY. Aug 5. National holiday.

ELIOT, JOHN: BIRTH ANNIVERSARY. Aug 5, 1604 (OS). American "Apostle to the Indians," translator of the Bible into an Indian tongue (the first Bible to be printed in America), was born at Hertfordshire, England. He died at Roxbury, MA, May 21, 1690 (OS).

E.P. "TOM" SAWYER STATE PARK/LOUISVILLE LANDSHARKS TRIATHLON XXV. Aug 5. Tom Sawyer State Park, Louisville, KY. Participants swim ½ mile, bicycle 14 miles and run 5k. Est attendance: 500. For info: Gary M. Parsons, Recreation Supervisor, E.P. "Tom" Sawyer State Park, 3000 Freys Hill Rd, Louisville, KY 40241-2172. Phone: (502) 429-7270.

FANCY FARM PICNIC. Aug 5. Downtown Fancy Farm, KY. Southern hospitality at its best. The small community volunteers its time to entertain with games, prizes and great fun. Raffle for a brand new car. Bingo with wonderful prizes. Down home country dinners including the famous Fancy Farm Picnic Barbeque. Annually, the first Saturday in August. Est attendance: 20,000. For info: Sharon Hayden, c/o Fancy Farm Picnic, 2759 Carrico Rd, Fancy Farm, KY 42039. Phone: (270) 623-6129. E-mail: todd hayden@wk.net.

	S	M	T	W	T	F	S
August			1	2	3	4	5
2006	6	7	8	9	10	11	12
	13	14	15	16	17	18	19
	20	21	22	23	24	25	26
	27	28	29	30	31		

FARM SANCTUARY HOEDOWN. Aug 5–6. Farm Sanctuary, Watkins Glen, NY. America's premier shelter for farm animals hosts a fun and educational weekend of farm tours, hayrides, lectures, exhibits, music, food and more, all located on a beautiful 175-acre animal shelter with hundreds of cows, pigs, turkeys and other animals. Est attendance: 200. For info: Education Coord, Farm Sanctuary, PO Box 150, Watkins Glen, NY 14891. Phone: (607) 583-2225. Fax: (607) 583-2041.

FIRST ENGLISH COLONY IN NORTH AMERICA: ANNIVERSARY. Aug 5, 1583. Sir Humphrey Gilbert, English navigator and explorer, aboard his sailing ship, the *Squirrel*, sighted the Newfoundland coast and took possession of the area around St. John's harbor in the name of the Queen, thus establishing the first English colony in North America. Gilbert was lost at sea, in a storm off the Azores, on his return trip to England.

HUSTON, JOHN: 100th BIRTH ANNIVERSARY. Aug 5, 1906. This larger-than-life Hollywood figure, son of the actor Walter Huston, spent his whole life before or behind the camera as an actor, writer and director. His first film, 1941's masterpiece of detective-noir, *The Maltese Falcon*, catapulted Humphrey Bogart away from gangster roles into dark heroic roles. Huston and Bogart collaborated on other great films: *The Treasure of the Sierra Madre* (which featured Huston's father in a Best Supporting Actor role), *Key Largo*, *The African Queen* and *Beat the Devil*. Born at Nevada, MO, Huston died Aug 28, 1987, at Middletown, RI, not long after completing his final film, *The Dead* (1987).

IRELAND: BANK HOLIDAY. Aug 5. Bank holiday in the Republic of Ireland.

KRXL CAR CRUISE. Aug 5. Kirksville, MO. Motorcycles, cars, antiques, hot rods, classics, originals and street rods. Est attendance: 1,000. For info: Steve Lloyd, General Mgr, KRXL, PO Box 130, Kirksville, MO 63501. Phone: (660) 665-9841.

LEAGUE OF NEW HAMPSHIRE CRAFTSMEN ANNUAL CRAFTSMEN'S FAIR. Aug 5–13. Mount Sunapee Resort, Newbury, NH. "America's oldest crafts fair"— 73rd annual fair. More than 200 crafts booths, Living with Crafts exhibit, CraftWear exhibit, New Hampshire Art Association exhibit, daily performing arts, children's activities and more. Est attendance: 40,000. For info: League of NH Craftsmen, 205 N Main St, Concord, NH 03301. Phone: (603) 224-3375. Fax: (603) 225-8452. Web: www.nhcrafts.org.

LYNCH, THOMAS: BIRTH ANNIVERSARY. Aug 5, 1749. Signer, Declaration of Independence, born Prince George's Parish, SC. Died 1779 (lost at sea, exact date of death unknown).

NATIONAL MUSTARD DAY. Aug 5. Mustard lovers across the nation pay tribute to the king of condiments by slathering their favorite mustard on hot dogs, pretzels, circus peanuts and all things edible. The Mount Horeb Mustard Museum holds the world's largest collection of prepared mustards and mustard memorabilia. Activities include the mustard games, street music, and lots of great food (with mustard, of course!). Join in the mustard college fight song with the "POUPON U" marching band. Annually, the first Saturday in August. Est attendance: 4,000. For info:

Barry M. Levenson, Curator, The Mount Horeb Mustard Museum, 100 W Main St, Mount Horeb, WI 53572. Phone: (608) 437-3986. Fax: (608) 437-4018. E-mail: curator@mustardmuseum.com. Web: www.mustardmuseum.com.

OMARR, SIDNEY: BIRTH ANNIVERSARY. Aug 5, 1926. Born Sidney Kimmelman at Philadelphia, PA, this world-famous astrologer became fascinated by numerology and astrology, and changed his name to "Sydney Omarr" at the age of 15. He began contributing to astrology magazines, and eventually became well known in Hollywood. He wrote dozens of books, an average of thirteen per year, that sold more than 50 million copies. His newspaper astrology column was syndicated in more than 200 newspapers. He died Jan 16, 2003, at Santa Monica, CA.

SHARON ON THE GREEN ARTS AND CRAFTS FAIR. Aug 5. Sharon, CT. A high-quality, juried art show with 100 regional artists and crafters offering a broad range of unique handmade items of glass, ceramics, pewter, jewelry, quilts, woodcrafts, photos, paintings, art-to-wear and gourmet items. 10:00 AM to 5:00 PM. Est attendance: 1,500. For info: Sharon Rec/Youth, PO Box 385, Sharon, CT 06069. Phone: (860) 364-1400. E-mail: sharon.rec.ctr@snet.net.

SIDEWALK ART FESTIVAL. Aug 5. Bangor, ME. Sponsored by WLBZ-2, this 17th annual festival is one of Maine's largest urban art festivals, featuring more than 100 artists with work for sale. From Broad St to Merchant's Plaza, streets are closed to vehicular traffic. Annually, the first Saturday in August. Est attendance: 25,000. For info: Charlene Belanger, WLBZ-2, 329 Mt Hope Ave, Bangor, ME 04401. Phone: (207) 828-6666. Fax: (207) 828-6620. E-mail: charlene.belanger@wcsh6.com. Web: www.wlbz2.com.

SIZZLIN' SUMMER GARAGE SALE. Aug 5. Spirit of the Suwannee Music Park, Live Oak, FL. Gigantic garage sale held throughout the park, with fun for all ages. With vendors and live music. For info: Spirit of the Suwannee Music Park, 3076 95th Dr, Live Oak, FL 32060. Phone: (386) 364-1683. Fax: (386) 364-2998. E-mail: spirit@musicliveshere.com. Web: www.musicliveshere.com.

TALL TIMBER DAYS FESTIVAL. Aug 5–6. Grand Rapids, MN. Festival features the Sheer Brothers Lumberjack Show, chainsaw carvers, arts and crafts, Applecords Quartet, competitions, YMCA run and bed racing. Families welcome. Annually, the first full weekend in August. Est attendance: 30,000. For info: Tall Timber Days, PO Box 134, Grand Rapids, MN 55744. Phone: (218) 326-5618. E-mail: talltimberdays@hotmail.com.

WALES: NATIONAL EISTEDDFOD OF WALES. Aug 5–12. Swansea. In 1880 the National Eisteddfod association was formed and charged with the responsibility of staging an annual festival to be held in North and South Wales alternately, and with the exception of 1914 and 1940, this target has been successfully achieved. The National Eisteddfod of Wales is a cultural event with competitive festivals of music, drama, literature, art and crafts. All events conducted in Welsh with simultaneous translation into English available. Est attendance: 160,000. For info: Natl Eisteddfod of Wales, 40 Parc Ty Glas, Llanishen, Cardiff, Wales, UK CF14 5WU. Phone: (44) (2920) 763777. Fax: (44) (2920) 763737. Web: www.eisteddfod.org.uk.

WALLENBERG, RAOUL: BIRTH ANNIVERSARY. Aug 5, 1912. Swedish architect Raoul Gustaf Wallenberg was born at Stockholm, Sweden. He was the second person in history (Winston Churchill was the first) to be granted honorary American citizenship (US House of Representatives voted 396–2, Sept 22, 1981). He is credited with saving 100,000 Jews from almost certain death at the hands of the Nazis during WWII. Wallenberg was arrested by Soviet troops at Budapest, Hungary, Jan 17, 1945, and, according to the official Soviet press agency Tass, died in prison at Moscow, July 17, 1947.

WOMEN'S PRO FOOTBALL DAY. Aug 5. A day to honor all the women who've played American full-contact football from the 1920s to today. Annually, the first Saturday in August. For info: Jody Taylor, Media Relations, Women's Professional Football League, 232 Belmont St, Hurst, TX 76053. Phone: (866) WPFL-NOW. E-mail: info@womensprofootball.com. Web: www.womensprofootball.com.

AUGUST 6 — SUNDAY
Day 218 — 147 Remaining

AMERICAN FAMILY DAY IN ARIZONA. Aug 6. Observed in Arizona on the first Sunday in August. The observance date is designated by statute.

ATOMIC BOMB DROPPED ON HIROSHIMA: ANNIVERSARY. Aug 6, 1945. At 8:15 AM, local time, an American B-29 bomber, the *Enola Gay*, dropped an atomic bomb named "Little Boy" over the center of the city of Hiroshima, Japan. The bomb exploded about 1,800 ft above the ground, killing more than 105,000 civilians and destroying the city. It is estimated that another 100,000 persons were injured and died subsequently as a direct result of the bomb and the radiation it produced. This was the first time in history that such a devastating weapon had been used by any nation.

BALL, LUCILLE: BIRTH ANNIVERSARY. Aug 6, 1911. Film and television pioneer and comedienne born at Jamestown, NY. In addition to her many film and television credits, Lucille Ball always will be remembered for her role in the 1950's CBS sitcom "I Love Lucy." As Lucy Ricardo, the wife of bandleader Ricky Ricardo (her real-life husband Desi Arnaz), she exhibited a comedic style that became a trademark of early television comedy. She died Apr 26, 1989, at Los Angeles, CA.

BOLIVIA: INDEPENDENCE DAY. Aug 6. National holiday. Gained freedom from Spain in 1825. Named after Simon Bolivar.

BURRO RACE. Aug 6. Leadville, CO. International Pack Burro Race leaves from Main Street up Mosquito Pass and back. Est attendance: 3,500. For info: Chamber of Commerce, Box 861, Leadville, CO 80461. Phone: (719) 486-3900 or (800) 933-3901. Fax: (719) 486-8478. E-mail: leadville@leadvilleusa.com. Web: www.leadvilleusa.com.

CANADA: FOLKLORAMA—CANADA'S CULTURAL CELEBRATION. Aug 6–19. Winnipeg, MB. 37th festival. More than 40 pavilions representing various cultures offer traditionally prepared cuisine, exhilarating entertainment and captivating cultural displays for 14 prairie summer nights. Folklorama is the largest multicultural celebration of its kind in the world and has been named the Internationally Known Super Event by the American Bus Association. Est attendance: 450,000. For info: David Sherman, Exec Dir, Folklorama, 183 Kennedy St, 2nd Fl, Winnipeg, MB, Canada R3C 1S6. Phone: (204) 982-6210 or (800) 665-0234. Fax: (204) 943-1956. E-mail: folkarts@folklorama.ca. Web: www.folklorama.ca.

ELECTROCUTION FIRST USED TO CARRY OUT DEATH PENALTY: ANNIVERSARY. Aug 6, 1890. At Auburn Prison, Auburn, NY, William Kemmler of Buffalo, NY, became the first man to be executed by electrocution. He had been convicted of the hatchet murder of his common-law wife, Matilde Ziegler, on Mar 28, 1889. This first attempt at using electrocution to carry out the death penalty was a botched affair. As reported by George Westinghouse, Jr, "It has been a brutal affair. They could have done better with an axe."

FINLAND: LAHTI ORGAN FESTIVAL. Aug 6–11. Lahti. Annual festival emphasizing organ music. Also, choirs, orchestras, instrumental groups and solo artists. Plus master classes, seminars and panel discussions. Est attendance: 6,000. For info: Finnish Tourist Board, 655 Third Ave, New York, NY 10017. Phone: (212) 885-9700 or (358) (3) 782-3184. Or Lahti Organ Festival, Kirkkokatu 5, 15110 Lahti, Finland. Fax: (358) (3) 783-2190. E-mail: office@lahtiorgan.fi. Web: www.lahtiorgan.fi.

FIRST WOMAN SWIMS THE ENGLISH CHANNEL: 80th ANNIVERSARY. Aug 6, 1926. The first woman to swim the English Channel was 19-year-old Gertrude Ederle of New York, NY. Her swim was completed in 14 hours and 31 minutes.

FLEMING, ALEXANDER: 125th BIRTH ANNIVERSARY. Aug 6, 1881. Sir Alexander Fleming, Scottish bacteriologist, discoverer of penicillin and 1945 Nobel Prize recipient, was born at Lochfield, Scotland. He died at London, England, Mar 11, 1955.

HIROSHIMA DAY: ANNIVERSARY. Aug 6. Memorial observances in many places for victims of the first atomic bombing of a populated place, which occurred at Hiroshima, Japan, in 1945, when an American B-29 bomber dropped an atomic bomb over the center of the city. More than 205,000 civilians died either immediately in the explosion or subsequently of radiation.

ITALY: JOUST OF THE QUINTANA. Aug 6. Ascoli/Piceno. The first Sunday in August is set aside for the Torneo della Quintana, an historical pageant with 15th-century costumes.

	S	M	T	W	T	F	S
August			1	2	3	4	5
2006	6	7	8	9	10	11	12
	13	14	15	16	17	18	19
	20	21	22	23	24	25	26
	27	28	29	30	31		

JAPAN: PEACE FESTIVAL. Aug 6. Hiroshima. The festival held annually at Peace Memorial Park is observed in memory of the victims of the Aug 6, 1945, atomic bomb explosion there.

JUDGE CRATER DISAPPEARANCE: ANNIVERSARY. Aug 6, 1930. Anniversary of mysterious disappearance at age 41, on Aug 6, 1930, of Joseph Force Crater, justice of the New York State Supreme Court. Never seen or heard from after disappearance on this date. Declared legally dead in 1939.

MITCHUM, ROBERT: BIRTH ANNIVERSARY. Aug 6, 1917. Film actor (*The Night of the Hunter, The Story of GI Joe*), born at Bridgeport, CT. Died July 1, 1997, at Santa Barbara County, CA.

NATIONAL FRESH BREATH DAY. Aug 6. Offensive breath wafts across all boundaries of age, income and intelligence. It manifests itself at the worst possible times: breaking business deals, stopping love in its tracks and just ruining otherwise fine relationships. National Fresh Breath Day is an educational awareness day designed to bring attention to the importance of fresh breath as an integral part of your overall health and wellness, as well as the impact it has on your personal and professional image. For info: Carol Meyer, Personal Breath Consultants, PO Box 65, Westhampton Beach, NY 11978-0065. Phone: (631) 288-7285. E-mail: Breathlady@hotmail.com.

NATIONAL KIDSDAY. Aug 6. A day to celebrate and honor children by spending meaningful time with them. Sponsored by KidsPeace® and the Boys and Girls Clubs of America. Annually, the first Sunday in August. For info: National Kidsday Mgmt, c/o Boys & Girls Clubs of America, 1230 W Peachtree St, Atlanta, GA 30309. Phone: (404) 487-5700. Fax: (404) 487-5787. E-mail: kidsday@bgca.org. Web: www.kidsday.net.

O'CONNELL, DANIEL: BIRTH ANNIVERSARY. Aug 6, 1775. Irish Catholic political leader Daniel O'Connell, known as "the Liberator" for his role in achieving the right of Catholics to sit in Parliament, was born near Cahirciveen, County Kerry. He died at age 81, May 15, 1847, at Genoa, Italy.

PARSONS, LOUELLA: 125th BIRTH ANNIVERSARY. Aug 6, 1881. A legendary Hollywood gossip columnist, the first of her kind, Parsons was born at Freeport, IL. At the height of her popularity and power—from the 1930s to the 1950s, her column appeared in more than 400 newspapers and was read by approximately 20 million people. She gloried in her power and occasionally used her column in spite, making her a woman feared by many in Hollywood whose careers depended on their reputations and positive publicity. Parsons retired in 1965 and died Dec 9, 1972, at Santa Monica, CA.

PSYCHIC SUNDAY. Aug 6. A day to develop your intuition and put the natural back into supernatural. Annually, the first Sunday in August. For info: International Hypnosis Federation, 30819 Casilina Dr, Rancho Palos Verdes, CA 90275. Phone: (310) 541-4844. E-mail: ihf@cox.net. Web: www.hypnosisfederation.com.

ROOSEVELT, EDITH KERMIT CAROW: BIRTH ANNIVERSARY. Aug 6, 1861. Second wife of Theodore Roosevelt, 26th president of the US, whom she married in 1886. Born at Norwich, CT, she died at Long Island, NY, Sept 30, 1948.

SISTERS' DAY®. Aug 6. Celebrating the spirit of sisterhood—sisters nationwide show appreciation and give recognition to one another for the special relationship they share. Send a card, make a phone call, share memories, photos, flowers, candy, etc. Sisters may include biological sisters, sorority sisters, sisterly friends, etc. Annually, the first Sunday in August. Please call for a press kit. For info: Tricia Eleogram, 5112 Normandy Ave, Memphis, TN 38117. Phone: (901) 681-2145 or (901) 755-0751. Fax: (901) 754-9923. E-mail: MySistersDay@aol.com.

SPACE MILESTONE: *VOSTOK 2* (USSR): 45th ANNIVERSARY. Aug 6, 1961. Launched on Aug 6, 1961, Gherman Titov orbited Earth 17 times over a period of 25 hours, 18 minutes. Titov broadcast messages in passage over countries, controlled spaceship manually for two hours.

TENNYSON, ALFRED, LORD: BIRTH ANNIVERSARY. Aug 6, 1808. English poet born at Somersby, Lincolnshire, England. His most celebrated works include the poems "The Lady of Shalott" and "The Lotos-Eaters" and the verse novelettes *Maud, Enoch Arden, In Memoriam, Locksley Hall Sixty Years After* and *The Idylls of the King.* Appointed English poet laureate in 1850 in succession to William Wordsworth and made a peer in 1884. Died at Aldworth, England, Oct 6, 1892.

VOLKSFEST. Aug 6. New Glarus, WI. Celebration of Swiss Independence Day. Annually, the first Sunday in August. Est attendance: 2,000. For info: Volksfest, Box 713, New Glarus, WI 53574. Phone: (608) 527-2095 or (800) 527-6838. E-mail: info@swisstown.com. Web: www.swisstown.com.

VOTING RIGHTS ACT OF 1965 SIGNED: ANNIVERSARY. Aug 6, 1965. Signed into law by President Lyndon Johnson, the Voting Rights Act of 1965 was designed to thwart attempts to discriminate against minorities at the polls. The act suspended literacy and other disqualifying tests, authorized appointment of federal voting examiners and provided for judicial relief on the federal level to bar discriminatory poll taxes. Congress voted to extend the Act in 1975, 1984 and 1991.

WARHOL, ANDY: BIRTH ANNIVERSARY. Aug 6, 1928. The artist, filmmaker and provocateur was born Andrew Warhola to Czech immigrant parents at Forest City, PA. (Some sources cite his birth year as 1927.) A leader of the Pop art movement, Warhol challenged the definitions of art. After a stint as a commercial artist, Warhol gained attention in 1962 with paintings of ordinary commercial products—most famously, Campbell's Soup cans—and pop culture figures. He moved on to silk-screen portraits (of subjects like Marilyn Monroe, Elvis Presley and Mao Tse-Tung) and experimental film projects (*Empire* [1964] was a static depiction of the Empire State Building that ran more than eight hours). Warhol was the center of New York's celebrity scene, and in 1968 it was he who claimed, "In the future everyone will be world-famous for fifteen minutes." Warhol died Feb 22, 1987, at New York, NY.

BIRTHDAYS TODAY

Peter Bonerz, 68, actor ("The Bob Newhart Show," "9 to 5"), director, born Portsmouth, NH, Aug 6, 1938.

Soleil Moon Frye, 30, actress ("Punky Brewster"), born Glendora, CA, Aug 6, 1976.

Melissa George, 30, actress ("Alias"), born Perth, Western Australia, Australia, Aug 6, 1976.

Dorian Harewood, 56, actor (*The Falcon and the Snowman, Full Metal Jacket*), born Dayton, OH, Aug 6, 1950.

Catherine Hicks, 55, actress (*Marilyn, Peggy Sue Got Married*), born Scottsdale, AZ, Aug 6, 1951.

Shirley Ann Jackson, 60, first woman to chair US Nuclear Regulatory Commission, born Washington, DC, Aug 6, 1946.

Freddie Laker, 84, former airline executive, born Kent, England, Aug 6, 1922.

David Maurice Robinson, 41, basketball player, born Key West, FL, Aug 6, 1965.

Michelle Yeoh, 44, actress (*Crouching Tiger, Hidden Dragon; Tomorrow Never Dies*), born Yang Zi Chong at Ipoh, Perak, Malaysia, Aug 6, 1962.

AUGUST 7 — MONDAY

Day 219 — 146 Remaining

ANTIGUA AND BARBUDA: AUGUST MONDAY. Aug 7–8. The first Monday in August and the day following form the August Monday Public Holiday.

AUSTRALIA: PICNIC DAY. Aug 7. The first Monday in August is a bank holiday in New South Wales and Picnic Day in Northern Territory, Australia.

BAHAMAS: EMANCIPATION DAY. Aug 7. Public holiday in Bahamas. Annually, the first Monday in August. Commemorates the emancipation of slaves by the British in 1834.

BUNCHE, RALPH JOHNSON: BIRTH ANNIVERSARY. Aug 7, 1904. American statesman, UN official, Nobel Peace Prize recipient (the first black to win the award), born at Detroit, MI. Died Dec 9, 1971, at New York, NY. See also: "Ralph Bunche Awarded Nobel Peace Prize: Anniversary" (Dec 10).

CANADA: CIVIC HOLIDAY. Aug 7. The first Monday in August is observed as a holiday in seven of Canada's 10 provinces. Civic holiday in Manitoba, New Brunswick, Northwest Territories, Ontario and Saskatchewan, British Columbia Day in British Columbia and Heritage Day in Alberta.

COLOMBIA: BATTLE OF BOYACÁ DAY. Aug 7. National holiday. Commemorates victory over Spanish forces in 1819.

COLORADO DAY. Aug 7. Colorado. Annually, the first Monday in August. Commemorates Admission Day, Aug 1, 1876, when Colorado became the 38th state.

CÔTE D'IVOIRE: NATIONAL DAY. Aug 7. Commemorates the independence of the Ivory Coast from France in 1960.

DESERT SHIELD: ANNIVERSARY. Aug 7, 1990. Five days after the Iraqi invasion of Kuwait, US President George H.W. Bush ordered the military buildup that would become known as Desert Shield to prevent further Iraqi advances.

DON'T WAIT—CELEBRATE! WEEK. Aug 7–13. A week dedicated to spontaneous and frequent celebrations of non-milestone events. Celebration is good for you, your health and your relationships. For info: Patty Sachs, 2300 Twelve Oaks Dr, #K-13, Orange Park, FL 32065. Phone: (904) 272-0959. Fax: (801) 217-1573. E-mail: pattysachs@prodigy.net.

EXHIBITOR APPRECIATION WEEK. Aug 7–11. An opportunity for trade/consumer show organizers to recognize and appreciate the thousands of exhibitors who make their events possible. For info: Susan Friedmann, CSP, The Tradeshow Coach, 2301 Saranac Ave, Lake Placid, NY 12946. Phone: (518) 523-1320. E-mail: susan@thetradeshowcoach.com. Web: www.thetradeshowcoach.com.

GREENE, NATHANIEL: BIRTH ANNIVERSARY. Aug 7, 1742 (OS). Born at Patowomut, RI, American Revolutionary War General Nathaniel Greene was described as the "ablest military officer of the Revolution under Washington." Greene died at Savannah, GA, June 19, 1786.

GRENADA: EMANCIPATION DAY. Aug 7. Grenada observes a public holiday annually on the first Monday in August. Commemorates the emancipation of slaves by the British in 1834.

GULF OF TONKIN RESOLUTION: ANNIVERSARY. Aug 7, 1964. Congress approved the "Gulf of Tonkin Resolution," pertaining to the war in Vietnam, which gave President Lyndon Johnson authority "to take all necessary measures to repel any armed attack against the forces of the United States and to prevent further aggression."

HATFIELD-McCOY FEUD ERUPTS: ANNIVERSARY. Aug 7–9, 1882. The long-simmering tension between two Appalachian families who lived by Tug Fork on the Kentucky–West Virginia border erupted into full-scale violence on Election Day 1882. Brothers Tolbert, Pharmer and Randolph McCoy knifed and shot Ellison Hatfield. The Hatfield family captured the three McCoys. When Ellison Hatfield died on Aug 9, the Hatfields executed the brothers. The feud continued with much loss of life. In 1888, when Kentucky authorities sought to detain feud murder suspects and West Virginia authorities complained, the dispute went all the way to the US Supreme Court, who decided in Kentucky's favor. The feud sputtered out by the end of the century.

ICELAND: AUGUST HOLIDAY. Aug 7. National holiday. The first Monday in August. Commemorates Iceland's constitution of 1874.

ISING, RUDOLF C.: BIRTH ANNIVERSARY. Aug 7, 1903. Rudolf C. Ising, cocreator with Hugh Harmon of "Looney Tunes" and "Merrie Melodies," was born at Kansas City, MO. Ising and Harmon's initial production, "Bosko the Talk-Ink Kid" (1929), was the first talkie cartoon synchronizing dialogue on the soundtrack with the action on screen. Ising received an Academy Award in 1940 for *Milky Way*, a cartoon about three kittens. During WWII he headed the animation division for the Army Air Corps movie unit developing training films. Rudolf Ising died July 18, 1992, at Newport Beach, CA.

JAMAICA: INDEPENDENCE DAY. Aug 7. National holiday observing achievement of Jamaican independence from Britain Aug 6, 1962. Annually, the first Monday in August.

MATA HARI: BIRTH ANNIVERSARY. Aug 7, 1876. Mata Hari (child of the dawn) was born Margaret Gertrude Zelle at Leewarden, Netherlands. Her spectacular career as a dancer, courtesan and spy made her known around the world. Probably an ineffective double agent, she nevertheless fascinated royalty and high officials of several countries. Arrested as a German spy (Agent H-21) in a Paris hotel, Feb 13, 1917, she was tried, convicted and sentenced to death. The greatest of her many roles was the final one—when she refused a blindfold and threw a kiss to the firing squad at Vincennes, France, Oct 15, 1917.

OLD FIDDLERS' CONVENTION. Aug 7–12. Galax, VA. 71st annual event features dance, folk songs and old-time and bluegrass music competition. Est attendance: 25,000. For info: Thomas L Jones Jr, Box 655, Galax, VA 24333. Phone: (276) 236-8541.

PARTICULARLY PREPOSTEROUS PACKAGING DAY. Aug 7. Buy anything lately? Did you succeed in getting the durn thing open? What do older people do when even mainstream society can't open a simple bottle of aspirin, let alone a milk carton? Annually, Aug 7. [©2003 by WH.] For info: Thomas & Ruth Roy, Wellcat Holidays, 2418 Long Ln, Lebanon, PA 17046. Phone: (717) 279-0184. E-mail: info@wellcat.com. Web: www.wellcat.com.

PROFESSIONAL SPEAKERS DAY. Aug 7. A day celebrating the consummate professionals who help people through their oratorical skills. For info: Jim Barber, 1101 Marcano Blvd, Plantation, FL 33322. Phone: (954) 476-9252. Fax: (954) 424-0309. E-mail: jim.barber@thebarbershop.com. Web: www.professionalspeakersday.com.

PSYCHIC WEEK. Aug 7–11. To utilize the power of the psyche to bring peace, find lost individuals and concentrate "psychic power" on beneficial causes. Annually, the first week in August (Monday–Friday). [Created by the late Richard R. Falk.]

PURPLE HEART: ANNIVERSARY. Aug 7, 1782. At Newburgh, NY, General George Washington ordered the creation of a Badge of Military Merit. The badge consisted of a purple cloth heart with silver braided edge. Only three are known to have been awarded during the Revolutionary War. The award was reinstituted on the bicentennial of Washington's birth, Feb 22, 1932, and recognizes those wounded in action.

SCOTLAND: SUMMER BANK HOLIDAY. Aug 7. Bank and public holiday in Scotland. The first Monday in August.

	S	M	T	W	T	F	S
August			1	2	3	4	5
2006	6	7	8	9	10	11	12
	13	14	15	16	17	18	19
	20	21	22	23	24	25	26
	27	28	29	30	31		

SPACE MILESTONE: FIRST PICTURE OF EARTH FROM SPACE. Aug 7, 1959. US satellite *Explorer VI* transmitted the first picture of Earth from space. For the first time we had a likeness of our planet based on more than projections and conjectures.

STURGIS RALLY. Aug 7–13. Sturgis, SD. The granddaddy of all motorcycle rallies and races. For 65 years the small community of Sturgis has welcomed motorcycle enthusiasts from around the world to a week of varied cycle racing, tours of the beautiful Black Hills, trade shows and thousands of bikes on display. Annually, beginning the Monday after the first full weekend in August. Est attendance: 350,000. For info: Sturgis Bike Week Productions, PO Box 999, Sturgis, SD 57785. Phone: (605) 347-0200. Fax: (605) 347-8888. E-mail: jr@sbwproductions.com. Web: www.sturgisrallynews.com.

US WAR DEPARTMENT ESTABLISHED: ANNIVERSARY. Aug 7, 1789. The second presidential cabinet department, the War Department, was established by Congress.

US WOMEN'S AMATEUR (GOLF) CHAMPIONSHIP. Aug 7–13. Pumpkin Ridge Golf Club, North Plains, OR. For info: US Golf Assn, Golf House, PO Box 708, Championship Dept, Far Hills, NJ 07931. Phone: (908) 234-2300. Fax: (908) 234-9687. E-mail: usga@usga.org. Web: www.usga.org.

ZAMBIA: YOUTH DAY. Aug 7. National holiday. Youth activities are order of the day. Focal point is Lusaka's Independence Stadium. Annually, the first Monday in August.

BIRTHDAYS TODAY

Lana Cantrell, 63, singer, actress, born Sydney, Australia, Aug 7, 1943.

David Duchovny, 46, actor ("The X-Files"), born New York, NY, Aug 7, 1960.

Stan Freberg, 80, satirist, born Pasadena, CA, Aug 7, 1926.

John Glover, 62, actor (stage: *Great God Brown; Julia, Melvin and Howard*), born Salisbury, MD, Aug 7, 1944.

Garrison Keillor, 64, humorist, producer (host "The Prairie Home Companion"), writer (*Lake Wobegon Days*), born Anoka, MN, Aug 7, 1942.

DeLane Matthews, 45, actress ("Dave's World"), born Rockledge, FL, Aug 7, 1961.

Alberto Salazar, 49, marathon runner, born Havana, Cuba, Aug 7, 1957.

Charlize Theron, 31, actress (*Monster, The Cider House Rules*), born Benoni, South Africa, Aug 7, 1975.

Billy Joe (B.J.) Thomas, 64, singer ("Raindrops Keep Falling on My Head"), born Houston, TX, Aug 7, 1942.

AUGUST 8 — TUESDAY

Day 220 — 145 Remaining

BAHAMAS: FOX HILL DAY. Aug 8. Nassau. Annually, the second Tuesday in August.

BONZA BOTTLER DAY™. Aug 8. To celebrate when the number of the day is the same as the number of the month. Bonza Bottler Day™ is an excuse to have a party at least once a month. For more information, see Jan 1. For info: Gail M. Berger, 14 Fernwood Dr, Taylors, SC 29687. Phone: (864) 609-9874. E-mail: gberger5@aol.com.

CHINA: FESTIVAL OF HUNGRY GHOSTS. Aug 8. Important Chinese festival, also known as the Chung Yuan Festival. According to Chinese legend, during the seventh lunar month the souls of the dead are released from purgatory to roam the Earth. Joss sticks are burned in homes; prayers, food and "ghost money" are offered to appease the ghosts. Market stallholders combine to hold celebrations to ensure that their businesses will prosper in the coming year. Wayang (Chinese street opera) and puppet shows are performed, and fruit and Chinese delicacies are offered to the spirits of the dead. Chung Yuan is observed on the 15th day of the 7th lunar month. Date in other countries will differ from China's.

THE DATE TO CREATE. Aug 8. A day to increase awareness of individual and organizational potential to solve problems and make things happen. All of us have this potential but may not realize it. Learn your innovative capacity and plan activities that increase it. Rediscover your creative spark. Annually, Aug 8. For info: Diane Decker. Phone: (847) 394-0994. E-mail: dcdecker@ msn.com. Web: www.qualitytransitions.com.

ELVIS WEEK. Aug 8–16. Memphis, TN. Each year Elvis fans from around the world visit Memphis as Aug 16 marks the anniversary of Elvis Presley's death (Aug 16, 1977) at his beloved home, Graceland Mansion. Events occur throughout the city with special events sponsored by Graceland. A commemoration of the music, magic and memories associated with the legacy of Elvis Presley. Est attendance: 75,000. For info: Graceland, 3734 Elvis Presley Blvd, Memphis, TN 38116. Phone: (800) 238-2000 or (901) 332-3322. Web: www.elvis.com.

HAPPINESS HAPPENS DAY. Aug 8. This day celebrates the 8th birthday of the Secret Society of Happy People by encouraging the expression of happiness and discouraging parade-raining. Suggested celebration activities are available on our website. For info: Secret Society of Happy People, 1315 Riverchase Dr, #2316, Coppell, TX 75019. Phone: (972) 471-1485. E-mail: pjohnson@sohp.com. Web: www.sohp.com.

HENSON, MATTHEW A.: BIRTH ANNIVERSARY. Aug 8, 1866. African-American explorer, born at Charles County, MD. He met Robert E. Peary while working in a Washington, DC, store in 1888 and was hired to be Peary's valet. He accompanied Peary on his seven subsequent Arctic expeditions. During the successful 1908–09 expedition to the North Pole, Henson and two of the four Eskimo guides reached their destination Apr 6, 1909. Peary arrived minutes later and verified the location. Henson's account of the expedition, *A Negro Explorer at the North Pole*, was published in 1912. In addition to the Congressional medal awarded all members of the North Pole expedition, Henson received the Gold Medal of the Geographical Society of Chicago and, at 81, was made an honorary member of the Explorers Club at New York, NY. Died Mar 9, 1955, at New York, NY.

MARCH, FREDRIC: BIRTH ANNIVERSARY. Aug 8, 1897. Award–winning actor Fredric March was born Frederick McIntyre Bickel at Racine, WI. Over the course of his long and distinguished career, March performed on both the stage and screen. He made more than 65 movies and was nominated for five Academy Awards, winning in 1932 for his role in *Dr. Jekyll and Mr Hyde* and in 1947 for *The Best Years of Our Lives*. In 1956 he appeared on stage in the world premiere of Eugene O'Neill's *Long Day's Journey into Night*. He received the Tony Award for that performance. He died Apr 14, 1975, at Los Angeles, CA.

MARKERT, RUSSELL: BIRTH ANNIVERSARY. Aug 8, 1899. American choreographer Russell Markert was born at Jersey City, NJ. He founded and directed the Radio City Music Hall Rockettes from 1932 to 1971. He died Dec 1, 1990, at Waterbury, CT.

MORRIS, ESTHER HOBART McQUIGG: BIRTH ANNIVERSARY. Aug 8, 1814. Esther Hobart McQuigg Morris was born at Tioga County, NY, but eventually moved to the Wyoming Territory, where she worked in the women's rights movement and had a key role in getting a women's suffrage bill passed. Morris became justice of the peace of South Pass City, WY, in 1870, one of the first times a woman held public office in the US. She represented Wyoming at the national suffrage convention in 1895. She died Apr 2, 1902, at Cheyenne, WY.

ODIE: BIRTHDAY. Aug 8, 1978. Commemorates the birthday of Odie, Garfield's sidekick, who first appeared in the Garfield comic strip Aug 8, 1978. For info: Kim Campbell, Paws, Inc, 5440 E Co Rd, 450 N, Albany, IN 47320. Web: www.garfield.com.

RAWLINGS, MARJORIE KINNAN: BIRTH ANNIVERSARY. Aug 8, 1896. American short-story writer and novelist (*The Yearling*), born at Washington, DC. Rawlings died at St. Augustine, FL, Dec 14, 1953.

SECOND BATTLE OF AMIENS: ANNIVERSARY. Aug 8, 1918. Two days after the Battle of Marne ended, the British Fourth Army mounted an offensive at Amiens with the objective of freeing the Amiens-Paris railway from bombardment by the German Second and Eighteenth Armies. More than 16,000 German prisoners were taken in two hours of fighting the first day. The German forces were forced back to the Hindenburg line by Sept 3. This battle is considered a turning point by many historians because of its impact on the psyche of Germany. Aug 8 was described by General Erich Ludendorff as a "Black Day" for Germany.

SHILTS, RANDY: BIRTH ANNIVERSARY. Aug 8, 1951. Journalist known for his reporting on the AIDS epidemic. One of the first openly homosexual journalists to work for a mainstream newspaper and the author of *And the Band Played On: Politics, People and the AIDS Epidemic*. Born at Davenport, IA, and died at Guerneville, CA, Feb 17, 1994.

SIOUX EMPIRE FAIR. Aug 8–13. W.H. Lyon Fairgrounds, Sioux Falls, SD. Grandstand concerts, free entertainment, livestock exhibits, 4-H activities, flower and vegetable displays and craft exhibits. Camping available, with full hook-ups. Est attendance: 261,000. For info: Sioux Empire Fair, W.H. Lyon Fairgrounds, 4000 W 12th St, Sioux Falls, SD 57107. Phone: (605) 367-7178. Fax: (605) 367-7886. E-mail: info@siouxempirefair .com. Web: www.siouxempirefair.com.

SNEAK SOME ZUCCHINI ONTO YOUR NEIGHBORS' PORCH NIGHT. Aug 8. Due to overzealous planting of zucchini, citizens are asked to drop off baskets of the squash on neighbors' doorsteps. Annually, Aug 8. [©2003 by WH.] For info: Thomas & Ruth Roy, Wellcat Holidays, 2418 Long Ln, Lebanon, PA 17046. Phone: (717) 279-0184. E-mail: info@wellcat.com. Web: www.wellcat.com.

SPACE MILESTONE: *GENESIS* (US): 5th ANNIVERSARY. Aug 8, 2001. The robotic explorer *Genesis* was launched on a mission to gather tiny particles of the sun. Its three-year, 20-million-mile round-trip mission was to shed light on the origin of the solar system. It traveled to a spot where the gravitational pulls of the sun and the Earth are equal and gathered atoms from the solar wind hurtling by. But on Sept 8, 2004, the *Genesis* return capsule crashed in a western US desert and most of its solar samples were destroyed.

SPACE MILESTONE: *PIONEER VENUS* MULTIPROBE (US). Aug 8, 1978. Second craft in *Pioneer Venus* program. Split into five and probed Venus atmosphere Dec 9. Launched on Aug 8, 1978.

TANZANIA: FARMERS' DAY. Aug 8. National holiday. Also called "Nane Nane" (8–8).

BIRTHDAYS TODAY

Keith Carradine, 56, actor (*Nashville, Will Rogers Follies*), singer, born San Mateo, CA, Aug 8, 1950.

Dino De Laurentiis, 87, producer, born Torre Annunziata, Italy, Aug 8, 1919.

The Edge, 45, musician (U2), born David Evans at East London, England, Aug 8, 1961.

Dustin Hoffman, 69, actor (Oscars for *Rain Man* and *Kramer vs. Kramer; The Graduate, Midnight Cowboy, Outbreak*), born Los Angeles, CA, Aug 8, 1937.

Deborah Norville, 48, TV host ("Inside Edition"), born Dalton, GA, Aug 8, 1958.

Roberta Cooper Ramo, 64, first woman president of the American Bar Association, born Denver, CO, Aug 8, 1942.

Connie Stevens, 68, actress ("Hawaiian Eye"), born Brooklyn, NY, Aug 8, 1938.

Mel Tillis, 74, singer, songwriter, born Pahokee, FL, Aug 8, 1932.

Esther Williams, 83, swimmer, actress (*Take Me Out to the Ball Game, Dangerous When Wet*), born Los Angeles, CA, Aug 8, 1923.

AUGUST 9 — WEDNESDAY
Day 221 — 144 Remaining

ATOMIC BOMB DROPPED ON NAGASAKI: ANNIVERSARY. Aug 9, 1945. Three days after the atomic bombing of Hiroshima, an American B-29 bomber named *Bock's Car* left its base on Tinian Island carrying a plutonium bomb nicknamed "Fat Man." Its target was the Japanese city of Kokura, but because of clouds and poor visibility the bomber headed for a secondary target, Nagasaki, where at 11:02 AM, local time, it dropped the bomb, killing an estimated 70,000 persons and destroying about half the city. Memorial services are held annually at Nagasaki and also at Kokura, where those who were spared because of the bad weather also grieve for those at Nagasaki who suffered in their stead.

CANADA: CANADIAN OPEN FIDDLE CHAMPIONSHIP. Aug 9–13. Shelburne, ON. 56th annual competition. Est attendance: 10,000. For info: Shelburne Rotary Club, PO Box 27, Shelburne, ON, Canada L0N 1S0. Phone: (519) 925-2600, ext 252. Fax: (519) 925-1105. E-mail: cindy.sabo@sympatico.ca. Web: www.shelburnefiddlecontest.on.ca.

COCHRAN, JACQUELINE: DEATH ANNIVERSARY. Aug 9, 1980. American pilot Jacqueline Cochran was born at Pensacola, FL, about 1910. She began flying in 1932 and by the time of her death she had set more distance, speed and altitude records than any other pilot, male or female. She was founder

and head of the WASPs (Women's Air Force Service Pilots) during WWII; she won the Distinguished Service Medal in 1945 and the US Air Force Distinguished Flying Cross in 1969. She died at Indio, CA.

FILIPINA-AMERICAN RECOGNITION DAY. Aug 9. Honoring the contributions and accomplishments of American women of Filipino heritage. Annually, the second Wednesday in August. For info: Cantara Christopher, 204 E 11th St, #171, New York, NY 10003. Phone: (917) 674-7560. E-mail: filipina@anamerican romantic.com. Web: www.anamericanromantic.com.

INDIANA STATE FAIR. Aug 9–20. Indiana State Fairgrounds, Indianapolis, IN. Top-rated livestock exhibition, world-class harness racing, top music and entertainment, giant midway and Pioneer Village. Est attendance: 900,000. For info: Andy Klotz, Public Relations Dir, Indiana State Fair, 1202 E 38th St, Indianapolis, IN 46205-2869. Phone: (317) 927-7524. Fax: (317) 927-7578. Web: www.indianastatefair.com.

JAPAN: MOMENT OF SILENCE. Aug 9. Nagasaki. Memorial observance held at Peace Memorial Park for victims of second atomic bomb, which was dropped on Nagasaki by an American bomber Aug 9, 1945.

LASSEN VOLCANIC NATIONAL PARK ESTABLISHED: 90th ANNIVERSARY. Aug 9, 1916. California's Lassen Peak and Cinder Cone National Monument, proclaimed May 6, 1907, and other wilderness land were combined and established as a national park. For further park info: Lassen Volcanic Natl Park, Mineral, CA 96063.

MICHIGAN STATE FAIR. Aug 9–20 (tentative). State Fairgrounds, Detroit, MI. Est attendance: 450,000. For info: State Fairgrounds, Eight Mile Road and Woodward Ave, Detroit, MI 48203. Phone: (313) 369-8250. Fax: (313) 369-8410. Web: www.michiganstatefair.com.

MOON PHASE: FULL MOON. Aug 9. Moon enters Full Moon phase at 6:54 AM, EDT.

NATIONAL UNDERWEAR DAY. Aug 9. Each August, underwear ambassadors storm the streets of New York City, modeling some of today's hottest brands and conducting surveys on undergarment choices. Enthusiastic New Yorkers caught in the grip of underwear frenzy join in—men drop their pants and women flash their bras in support, while passersby are asked to sign a petition for official recognition of National Underwear Day. Visit Freshpair.com to electronically sign the petition yourself! For info: PR Dept, Freshpair, LLC, 611 Broadway, Ste 605, New York, NY 10012. Phone: (212) 505-6900 or (866) FRESH-PAIR. Fax: (212) 202-4754. E-mail: press@freshpair.com. Web: www.nationalunderwearday.com or www.freshpair.com.

NIXON RESIGNS: ANNIVERSARY. Aug 9, 1974. The resignation from the presidency of the US by Richard Milhous Nixon, which had been announced in a speech to the American people the night before, became effective at noon. Nixon, under threat of impeachment as a result of the Watergate scandal, became the first US president to resign.

PERSEID METEOR SHOWERS. Aug 9–13. Among the best-known and most spectacular meteor showers are the Perseids, peaking about Aug 10–12. As many as 50–100 may be seen in a single night. Wish upon a "falling star"!

August *2006*	S	M	T	W	T	F	S
			1	2	3	4	5
	6	7	8	9	10	11	12
	13	14	15	16	17	18	19
	20	21	22	23	24	25	26
	27	28	29	30	31		

SINGAPORE: NATIONAL DAY. Aug 9, 1965. Most festivals in Singapore are Chinese, Indian or Malay, but celebration of national day is shared by all to commemorate the withdrawal of Singapore from Malaysia and its becoming an independent state in 1965. Music, parades, dancing.

SOUTH AFRICA: NATIONAL WOMEN'S DAY. Aug 9. National holiday. Commemorates the march of women in Pretoria to protest the pass laws in 1956.

SWEDEN: CRAYFISH PREMIERE. Aug 9. Crayfish may be sold and served in restaurants the following day after the season opens. Annually, the second Wednesday in August.

UNITED NATIONS: INTERNATIONAL DAY OF THE WORLD'S INDIGENOUS PEOPLE. Aug 9. On Dec 23, 1994, the General Assembly decided that the International Day of the World's Indigenous People shall be observed Aug 9 every year during the International Decade of the World's Indigenous People (1994–2004) (Res 49/214). The date marks the anniversary of the first day of the meeting in 1992 of the Working Group on Indigenous Populations of the Subcommission on Prevention of Discrimination and Protection of Minorities. For info: United Nations, Dept of Public Info, Public Inquiries Unit, RM GA-57, New York, NY 10017. Phone: (212) 963-4475. E-mail: inquiries @un.org.

VEEP DAY. Aug 9. Commemorates the day in 1974 when Richard Nixon's resignation let Gerald Ford succeed to the presidency of the US. This was the first time the new Constitutional provisions for presidential succession took effect. For info: Bob Birch, The Puns Corps, 3108 Dashiell Rd, Falls Church, VA 22042. Phone: (703) 533-3668.

WALTON, IZAAK: BIRTH ANNIVERSARY. Aug 9, 1593 (OS). English author of classic treatise on fishing, *The Compleat Angler,* published in 1653, was born at Stafford, England. Died at Winchester, England, Dec 15, 1683 (OS). "Angling," Walton wrote, "may be said to be so like the mathematics, that it can never be fully learnt."

WEBSTER-ASHBURTON TREATY SIGNED: ANNIVERSARY. Aug 9, 1842. The treaty delimiting the eastern section of the Canadian-American border was negotiated by the US Secretary of State, Daniel Webster, and Alexander Baring, president of the British Board of Trade. The treaty established the boundaries between the St. Croix and Connecticut rivers, between Lake Superior and the Lake of the Woods and between Lakes Huron and Superior. The treaty was signed at Washington, DC.

BIRTHDAYS TODAY

Gillian Anderson, 38, actress ("The X-Files," *The House of Mirth*), born Chicago, IL, Aug 9, 1968.

Amanda Bearse, 48, actress ("Married . . . With Children"), born Winter Park, FL, Aug 9, 1958.

Robert Joseph (Bob) Cousy, 78, Hall of Fame basketball player, former coach, born New York, NY, Aug 9, 1928.

Sam Elliott, 62, actor ("Mission Impossible," *Gettysburg*), born Sacramento, CA, Aug 9, 1944.

Melanie Griffith, 49, actress (*Working Girl, Something Wild, Milk Money*), born New York, NY, Aug 9, 1957.

Chamique Holdsclaw, 29, former basketball player, born Astoria, NY, Aug 9, 1977.

Whitney Houston, 43, singer ("And I Will Always Love You"), actress (*Waiting to Exhale*), born Newark, NJ, Aug 9, 1963.

Brett Hull, 42, hockey player, born Belleville, ON, Canada, Aug 9, 1964.

Rodney George (Rod) Laver, 68, former tennis player, born Rockhampton, Australia, Aug 9, 1938.

Kenneth Howard (Ken) Norton, Sr, 61, former boxer, born Jacksonville, IL, Aug 9, 1945.

Deion Sanders, 39, former football player, former baseball player, born Fort Myers, FL, Aug 9, 1967.

David Steinberg, 64, comedian ("The David Steinberg Show"), born Winnipeg, MB, Canada, Aug 9, 1942.

AUGUST 10 — THURSDAY

Day 222 — 143 Remaining

AMERICAN PSYCHOLOGICAL ASSOCIATION ANNUAL MEETING. Aug 10–13. New Orleans, LA. For info: Convention Office, American Psychological Assn, 750 First St NE, Washington, DC 20002-4242. Phone: (202) 336-6020. E-mail: convention.office@apa.org. Web: www.apa.org.

AMISH ACRES ARTS & CRAFTS FESTIVAL. Aug 10–13. Nappanee, IN. Displays of traditional arts and crafts including furniture and other objects. Also features a variety of entertainment. Est attendance: 70,000. For info: Amish Acres Arts & Crafts Festival, 1600 W Market St, Nappanee, IN 46550. Phone: (574) 773-4188 x 215. Fax: (574) 773-4180. E-mail: JenniWysong@ AmishAcres.com. Web: www.amishacres.com.

CANADA: EDMONTON FOLK MUSIC FESTIVAL. Aug 10–13. Gallagher Park, Edmonton, AB. Folk music and fun for the entire family highlighting blues, country, Celtic, traditional folk and bluegrass music, arts and crafts displays and a food fair. Est attendance: 85,000. For info: Edmonton Folk Music Festival Society, PO Box 4130, Edmonton, AB, Canada T6E 4T2. Phone: (780) 429-1899. E-mail: fadmin@efmf.ab.ca. Web: www.edmontonfolkfest.org.

CANADA: HALIFAX INTERNATIONAL BUSKER FESTIVAL. Aug 10–20 (tentative). Halifax, NS. Street performers and artists from around the world, vaudeville nights and entertainment tent. Annually, the first Thursday after Natal Day (first Monday in August). Est attendance: 500,000. For info: Halifax Intl Busker Fest, c/o Pickford & Black, 1869 Upper Water St, 5th Fl, Halifax, NS, Canada B3J 1S9. Phone: (902) 429-3910. Fax: (902) 429-7554. E-mail: debbie@espproductions.ca.

"CANDID CAMERA" TV PREMIERE: ANNIVERSARY. Aug 10, 1948. This show—which appeared at various times on the big three networks and in syndication—was created and hosted by Allen Funt. The show was initially an Armed Forces Radio program based on Funt's success in recording and broadcasting soldiers' gripes. The show's modus operandi was to catch people unawares on camera—either as part of a practical joke or just being themselves. It spawned numerous imitators.

ECUADOR: INDEPENDENCE DAY. Aug 10. National holiday. Celebrates declaration of independence in 1809. Freedom from Spain was attained May 24, 1822.

ENGLAND: JERSEY BATTLE OF FLOWERS. Aug 10–11. St. Helier, Jersey Channel Islands. Colorful parade of floats decorated with hundreds of flowers. First held in 1902 to mark the coronation of Edward VII and Queen Alexandra. Annually, the second Thursday in August. Est attendance: 27,500. For info: The Jersey Battle of Flowers Assn, Meadow Bank, St. Lawrence, Jersey, Channel Islands, England JE3 1EE. Phone: (44) (153) 463-9000. E-mail: battle@battleofflowers.com. Web: www.battleofflowers.com.

HOOVER, HERBERT CLARK: BIRTH ANNIVERSARY. Aug 10, 1874. The 31st president of the US (1929–33) was born at West Branch, IA. Hoover was the first president born west of the Mississippi River and the first to have a telephone on his desk (installed Mar 27, 1929). "Older men declare war. But it is youth that must fight and die," he said at Chicago, IL, at the Republican National Convention, June 27, 1944. Hoover died at New York, NY, Oct 20, 1964. The Sunday nearest Aug 10th is observed in Iowa as Herbert Hoover Day.

HOPE WATERMELON FESTIVAL. Aug 10–13. Hope, AR. An event in which the entire family can participate while promoting the city of Hope and having fun. Hope is the birthplace of the 42nd president of the US, Bill Clinton. Annually, in August. Est attendance: 40,000. For info: Mktg Dept, Hope–Hempstead County Chamber of Commerce, PO Box 250, Hope, AR 71802-0250. Phone: (870) 777-3640. Fax: (870) 722-6154. E-mail: hopeark@arkansas.net. Web: www.hopemelonfest.com.

IOWA STATE FAIR. Aug 10–20. Iowa State Fairgrounds, Des Moines, IA. One of America's oldest and largest state fairs. A grand showcase of Iowa agriculture, talent and tradition. The Fair boasts one of the world's largest livestock shows, ten-acre carnival, superstar grandstand stage shows, track events, spectacular free entertainment. 160-acre campgrounds. Est attendance: 1,054,000. For info: Lori Chappell, Mktg Dir, Iowa State Fair, PO Box 57130, Des Moines, IA 50317-0003. Phone: (515) 262-3111. Fax: (515) 262-6906. E-mail: info@iowastatefair.org. Web: www.iowastatefair.org.

JAPAN'S UNCONDITIONAL SURRENDER: ANNIVERSARY. Aug 10, 1945. A gathering to discuss surrender terms took place in Emperor Hirohito's bomb shelter; the participants were stalemated. Hirohito settled the question, believing continuation of the war would only result in further loss of Japanese lives. A message was transmitted to Japanese ambassadors in Switzerland and Sweden to accept the terms issued at Potsdam July 26, 1945, except that the Japanese emperor's sovereignty must be maintained. The Allies devised a plan under which the emperor and the Japanese government would administer under the rule of the Supreme Commander of the Allied Powers and the Japanese surrendered.

"LIL" MARGARET'S BLUEGRASS AND OLD-TIME MUSIC FESTIVAL. Aug 10–12. Leonardtown, MD. Bluegrass music, crafts, old-time cars and tractors, plenty of home-cooked meals and lots of fun. Annually, the second weekend in August. Est attendance: 1,000. For info: Joseph H. Goddard, Lil Margaret's Bluegrass, 20529 White Point Rd, Leonardtown, MD 20650. Phone: (301) 475-8191. Web: www.gotech.com.

MISSOURI: ADMISSION DAY: ANNIVERSARY. Aug 10. Became 24th state in 1821.

MISSOURI STATE FAIR. Aug 10–20. Sedalia, MO. Livestock shows, commercial and competitive exhibits, horse show, car races, tractor pulls, carnival and headline musical entertainment. Economical family entertainment. Est attendance: 375,000. For info: Kimberly Allen, PR Dir, Missouri State Fair, 2503 W 16th, Sedalia, MO 65301. Phone: (660) 827-8150 or (800) 422-FAIR. Fax: (660) 827-8160. Web: www.mostatefair.com.

NATIONAL BLUEBERRY FESTIVAL. Aug 10–13. South Haven, MI. At the World's Highbush Blueberry Capital, enjoy events such as concerts, a parade, pie-eating contests, craft fair, children's fun and much more on the shores of Lake Michigan. Est attendance: 50,000. For info: South Haven Chamber of Commerce, 606 Philips, South Haven, MI 49090. Phone: (269) 637-5171 or (269) 637-5252. Web: www.blueberryfestival.com.

NATIONAL DURAN DURAN APPRECIATION DAY. Aug 10. This is a day for everyone to enjoy the underrated beauty of '80s rock icons, Duran Duran. For info: Matt Kennedy. E-mail: xprufrock@yahoo.com.

		S	M	T	W	T	F	S
August				1	2	3	4	5
2006		6	7	8	9	10	11	12
		13	14	15	16	17	18	19
		20	21	22	23	24	25	26
		27	28	29	30	31		

NATIONAL HOBO CONVENTION. Aug 10–13. Britt, IA. Held since 1900, the National Hobo Convention celebrates current and retired hoboes and the independent lifestyle they lead. Events include the crowning of the Hobo King and Queen, storytelling, flea market, carnival, parade, live entertainment, antique and classic car show, and consumption of the traditional mulligan stew. For info: Britt Chamber of Commerce, PO Box 63, Britt, IA 50423. Phone: (641) 843-3867. E-mail: brittcoc@ncn.net.

SKOWHEGAN STATE FAIR. Aug 10–19. Fairgrounds, Skowhegan, ME. 188th annual. Huge fair with horse pulling, tractor pulls, harness racing, carnival midway, exhibits, flower show, grandstand shows, coliseum events, truck pulls, demolition derby and much more. Annually, beginning three weeks before Labor Day. Est attendance: 100,000. For info: Skowhegan State Fair Assn, PO Box 39, Skowhegan, ME 04976. Phone: (207) 474-2947.

SMITHSONIAN INSTITUTION FOUNDED: ANNIVERSARY. Aug 10, 1846. Founding of the Smithsonian Institution at Washington, DC. For info: Smithsonian Institution, 900 Jefferson Dr SW, Washington, DC 20560. Phone: (202) 357-2700.

BIRTHDAYS TODAY

Ian Anderson, 59, musician, lead singer (Jethro Tull), born Blackpool, England, Aug 10, 1947.
Rosanna Arquette, 47, actress (*Desperately Seeking Susan, New York Stories*), born New York, NY, Aug 10, 1959.
Antonio Banderas, 46, actor (*Spy Kids, The Mask of Zorro, Desperado*), born Malaga, Spain, Aug 10, 1960.
Riddick Bowe, 39, boxer, born Brooklyn, NY, Aug 10, 1967.
Jimmy Dean, 78, singer ("Big Bad John," "P.T. 109"), born Seth Ward at Plainview, TX, Aug 10, 1928.
Eddie Fisher, 78, singer ("Heart," "Cindy, Oh Cindy"), born Philadelphia, PA, Aug 10, 1928.
Rhonda Fleming, 83, actress ("Stage Door," *The Best of Broadway*), born Marilyn Lewis at Los Angeles, CA, Aug 10, 1923.
Angie Harmon, 34, actress ("Law & Order," "Baywatch Nights"), born Dallas, TX, Aug 10, 1972.
Betsy Johnson, 64, fashion designer, born Wethersfield, CT, Aug 10, 1942.

AUGUST 11 — FRIDAY
Day 223 — 142 Remaining

ATCHISON, DAVID R.: BIRTH ANNIVERSARY. Aug 11, 1807. Missouri legislator who was president of the US for one day. Born at Frogtown, KY, Atchison's strong pro-slavery opinions made his name prominent in legislative debates. He served as president pro tempore of the Senate a number of times, and he became president of the US for one day—Sunday, Mar 4, 1849—pending the swearing in of President-elect Zachary Taylor on Monday, Mar 5, 1849. The city of Atchison, KS, and the county of Atchison, MO, are named for him. He died at Gower, MO, Jan 26, 1886.

BLUEGRASS FESTIVAL. Aug 11–13. Grand Targhee Ski and Summer Resort, Alta, WY. 19th annual. Set in a beautiful outdoor venue on a pristine mountainside on the gorgeous western slopes of the Grand Teton Mountains, this festival is three days of incredible bluegrass music featuring national, regional and local talent such as Alison Krauss, Del McCoury Band, Peter Rown and David Grisman. Also, arts and crafts, food and beverages. Est attendance: 7,000. For info: Grand Targhee Resort, PO Box SKI, Alta, WY 83414. Phone: (800) TAR-GHEE. Fax: (307) 353-8148. E-mail: info@grandtarghee.com. Web: www.grandtarghee.com.

BOND, CARRIE JACOBS: BIRTH ANNIVERSARY. Aug 11, 1862. American composer of well-known songs, including "I Love You Truly" and "A Perfect Day," and of scores for motion pictures, Carrie Jacobs Bond was born at Janesville, WI. She died at Hollywood, CA, at age 84, Dec 28, 1946.

CALIFORNIA STATE FAIR. Aug 11–Sept 4. Sacramento, CA. Top-name entertainment, fireworks, California counties exhibits, livestock nursery, culinary delights, carnival rides and award-winning wines and microbrews. For info: California State Fair, PO Box 15649, Sacramento, CA 95852. Phone: (916) 263-FAIR. Web: www.bigfun.org.

CANADA: ABBOTSFORD INTERNATIONAL AIRSHOW. Aug 11–13 (tentative). Abbotsford Airport, Abbotsford, BC. "Canada's National Airshow," 44th annual. Leading air show in North America attracts the world's top aeronautical performers. Thrill to the grace of the Canadian Snowbirds, the raw power of the international air demonstration squadrons, dramatic teams of daring performers and soloists. Static displays and food booths. Open daily 8–6; aerial show 10–5. Airshow camping facilities. Est attendance: 160,000. For info: Abbotsford Intl Airshow, 1276 Tower St, Unit #4, Abbotsford, BC, Canada V2T 6H5. E-mail: info@abbotsfordairshow.com. Web: www.abbotsfordairshow.com.

CHAD: INDEPENDENCE DAY. Aug 11. National holiday. Commemorates independence from France in 1960.

FINLAND: TURKU MUSIC FESTIVAL. Aug 11–20. Turku. One of Finland's oldest music festivals in its oldest city. Music ranges from the medieval era to present day, performed by world-famous artists and groups in halls with fine acoustics, churches and even museums. Est attendance: 17,000. For info: Finnish Tourist Board, 655 Third Ave, New York, NY 10017. Phone: (212) 885-9700. Or Turku Music Festival, Uudenmaankatu 1, 20500 Turku, Finland. Phone: (358) (2) 251-1162. Fax: (358) (2) 231-3316. E-mail: info@turkumusicfestival.fi. Web: www.turkumusicfestival.fi.

FREDERICK DOUGLASS SPEAKS: ANNIVERSARY. Aug 11, 1841. Having escaped from slavery only three years earlier, Frederick Douglass was legally a fugitive when he first spoke before an audience. At an antislavery convention on Nantucket Island, Douglass spoke simply but eloquently about his life as a slave. His words were so moving that he was asked to become a full-time lecturer for the Massachusetts Anti-Slavery Society. Douglass became a brilliant orator, writer and abolitionist who championed the rights of blacks as well as the rights of all humankind.

GINZA HOLIDAY: JAPANESE CULTURAL FESTIVAL. Aug 11–13. Midwest Buddhist Temple, Chicago, IL. Experience the Waza (National Treasures tradition) by viewing 300 years of Edo craft tradition and seeing it come alive as master craftspeople from Tokyo demonstrate their arts. Japanese folk and classical dancing, martial arts, taiko (drums), flower arrangements and cultural displays. Chicken teriyaki, sushi, udon, shaved ice, corn on the cob and refreshments. Annually, the second weekend in August. Est attendance: 15,000. For info: Office Secretary, Midwest Buddhist Temple, 435 W Menomonee St, Chicago, IL 60614. Phone: (312) 943-7801. Fax: (312) 943-8069.

GREAT RIVER TUG FEST. Aug 11–13. Port Byron, IL, and LeClaire, IA. 20th annual. The Tug is the only tug-of-war across the mighty Mississippi River or any other moving body of water in the world. For two hours barge traffic, pleasure boats, gambling and paddle boats yield the right of way to a 400-ft, 680-lb rope that stretches between Illinois and Iowa. At 1 PM Saturday, the first team of 20 tuggers grip the rope, the crowd counts down and dirt starts flying! Festivals on both sides of the river Friday and Saturday. Fireworks Friday evening. Annually, the second weekend in August. For info: Phone: (563) 289-3946 or (309) 523-3734. Web: www.tugfest.org or www.qconline.com/tugfest. For info on the Quad Cities: Quad Cities CVB. Phone: (800) 747-7800. Web: www.visitquadcities.com.

HALEY, ALEX PALMER: BIRTH ANNIVERSARY. Aug 11, 1921. Born at Ithaca, NY, Alex Palmer Haley was raised by his grandmother at Henning, TN. In 1939 he entered the US Coast Guard and served as a cook, but eventually he became a writer and college professor. His interview with Malcolm X for *Playboy* led to his first book, *The Autobiography of Malcolm X*, which sold six million copies and was translated into eight languages. *Roots*, his Pulitzer Prize–winning novel published in 1976, sold millions, was translated into 37 languages and was made into an eight-part TV miniseries in 1977. The story generated an enormous interest in family ancestry. Haley died at Seattle, WA, Feb 13, 1992.

ILLINOIS STATE FAIR. Aug 11–20. Springfield, IL. Amusement rides, food booths, parade, various types of entertainment, and tractor pulls. Est attendance: 700,000. For info: Illinois State Fair, PO Box 19427, Springfield, IL 62794. Phone: (217) 782-6661. Fax: (217) 782-9115. Web: www.illinoisstatefair.info.

KOOL-AID DAYS. Aug 11–13. Hastings, NE. Family festival in the town where Kool-Aid was invented. Large inflatable games, live entertainment, festival foods, commemoratives, games for kids. Purchase a mug and receive free Kool-Aid all day from the world's largest Kool-Aid stand where we pour more than a gallon a minute of 22 flavors. Annually, the second weekend in August. Est attendance: 8,000. For info: Kool-Aid Days, PO Box 541, Hastings, NE 68902-0541. E-mail: info@kool-aiddays.com. Web: www.kool-aiddays.com.

MONTGOMERY COUNTY AGRICULTURAL FAIR. Aug 11–19. Gaithersburg, MD. 58th annual. Maryland's largest county fair, family-oriented entertainment, farm animals, arts and crafts exhibits of all types, many contests, carnival rides, grandstand entertainment to include demolition derby, horse events and musical performances. Est attendance: 250,000. For info: Montgomery County Agricultural Fair, 16 Chestnut St, Gaithersburg, MD 20877. Phone: (301) 926-3100. Fax: (301) 926-1532. Web: www.mcagfair.com.

SAINT CLARE OF ASSISI: FEAST DAY. Aug 11, 1253. Chiara Favorone di Offreduccio, a religious leader inspired by St. Francis of Assisi, was the first woman to write her own religious order rule. Born at Assisi, Italy, July 16, 1194, she died there Aug 11, 1253. A "Privilege of Poverty" freed her order from any constraint to accept material security, making the "Poor Clares" totally dependent on God.

SAINT JOHNS MINT FESTIVAL. Aug 11–13. St. Johns, MI. Arts & crafts, flea market, collectibles, sports events, parade, mint tours and two evening concerts. Annually, the second weekend in August. Est attendance: 75,000. For info: St. Johns Area Chamber of Commerce, Box 61, St. Johns, MI 48879. Phone: (989) 224-7248. Fax: (989) 224-7667. E-mail: stjohnschamber@power-net.net. Web: www.stjohnschamber.org.

SHANTY DAYS: CELEBRATION OF THE LAKE. Aug 11–13. Legion Park, Algoma, WI. Three-day festival to celebrate lakeshore heritage. Entertainment, ethnic food, arts and crafts, street fair, 5k walk/run, fishing contest, kids' area, book sale, community parade, photo contest and fireworks finale. Est attendance: 23,000. For info: Pam Ritchie, Algoma Area Chamber of Commerce, 1226 Lake St, Algoma, WI 54201. Phone: (920) 487-2041 or (800) 498-4888. Fax: (920) 487-5519. E-mail: chamber@itol.com. Web: www.algoma.org.

SPACE MILESTONE: *VOSTOK 3* (USSR). Aug 11, 1962. Launched on this date, Andrian Nikolayev orbited Earth 64 times over a period of 94 hours, 25 minutes, covering a distance of 1,242,500 miles. Achieved radio communication with *Vostok 4* and telecast from spacecraft.

SWITZERLAND: LUCERNE FESTIVAL, SOMMER. Aug 11–Sept 17. Lucerne. Featuring 100 events and directed by Michael Haefliger since 1999, the summer festival has been restructured and now intensively focuses on specific festival topics. Important artistic accents are set by each year's "artistes étoile," composers-in-residence and orchestras-in-residence as well as the concert cycles "Moderne," "Debut" and "Children's Corner." For info: Lucerne Festival, PO Box CH-6002, Lucerne, Switzerland. Phone: (41) 226-4400. Fax: (41) 226-4460. E-mail: info@lucernefestival.ch. Web: www.lucernefestival.ch.

TETONKAHA RENDEZVOUS. Aug 11–13. Hole in the Mountain County Park, Lake Benton, MN. Presents the fur-trading atmosphere of the 1840s. Muzzle-loader contest, tomahawk and knife throw, log sawing, canoe races, kids' games. Est attendance: 300. For info: Dave Huebner, Brookings Renegade Muzzle Loaders, 47826 Main St, Bushnell, SD 57276. Phone: (605) 693-4589.

WATTS RIOT: ANNIVERSARY. Aug 11, 1965. A minor clash between the California Highway Patrol and two young blacks set off six days of riots in the Watts area of Los Angeles. Thirty-four deaths were reported and more than 3,000 people were arrested. Damage to property was listed at $40 million. The less-immediate cause of the disturbance and the others that followed was racial tension between whites and blacks in American society.

WEST VIRGINIA STATE FAIR. Aug 11–20. Lewisburg, WV. For info: The State Fair of West Virginia, PO Drawer 986, Lewisburg, WV 24901. Phone: (304) 645-1090. E-mail: publicrelations@statefairofwv.com. Web: www.statefairofwv.com.

ZIMBABWE: HEROES' DAY. Aug 11. National holiday. Followed by Defense Forces Day on August 12.

BIRTHDAYS TODAY

Joanna Coles, 62, children's author, born Newark, NJ, Aug 11, 1944.

Arlene Dahl, 78, actress ("One Life to Live," "Fantasy Island"), born Minneapolis, MN, Aug 11, 1928.

Mike Douglas, 81, TV host, singer, born Michael Delaney Dowd, Jr, at Chicago, IL, Aug 11, 1925.

Jerry Falwell, 73, clergyman (head of Moral Majority PAC), born Lynchburg, VA, Aug 11, 1933.

Will Friedle, 30, actor ("Boy Meets World"), born Hartford, CT, Aug 11, 1976.

Hulk Hogan, 53, wrestler, actor, born Terry Gene Bollea at Augusta, GA, Aug 11, 1953.

Joe Jackson, 51, musician, songwriter, born Burton-on-Trent, England, Aug 11, 1955.

Anna Massey, 69, actress (*Bunny Lake Is Missing, A Doll's House*), born Thankeham, England, Aug 11, 1937.

Marilyn vos Savant, 60, columnist ("Ask Marilyn"), claims world's highest IQ, born St. Louis, MO, Aug 11, 1946.

Stephen Wozniak, 56, Apple computer cofounder, born Sunnyvale, CA, Aug 11, 1950.

	S	M	T	W	T	F	S
August			1	2	3	4	5
2006	6	7	8	9	10	11	12
	13	14	15	16	17	18	19
	20	21	22	23	24	25	26
	27	28	29	30	31		

AUGUST 12 — SATURDAY
Day 224 — 141 Remaining

ANTIQUE SHOW. Aug 12. Somerset, PA. 36th annual. More than 100 vendors dealing in quality antiques and collectibles. Est attendance: 5,000. For info: Sandy Berkebile, Somerset County Chamber of Commerce, 601 N Center Ave, Somerset, PA 15501. Phone: (814) 445-6431. E-mail: info@somersetcountychamber.com.

BEWICK, THOMAS: BIRTH ANNIVERSARY. Aug 12, 1753. English artist, wood engraver and author, remembered especially for his book illustrations in *General History of Quadrupeds*, *A History of British Birds* and *Aesop's Fables*. Born at Cherryburn, Northumberland, and died at Gateshead, Durham, England, Nov 8, 1828.

BON FESTIVAL. Aug 12. Morikami Museum, Delray Beach, FL. Traditional Japanese summer festival welcomes the ancestral spirits back to Earth with folk dancing, music, games and amusements, culminating with the floating of paper lanterns on Morikami pond at dusk and a fireworks display. Est attendance: 7,000. For info: The Morikami Museum, 4000 Morikami Park Rd, Delray Beach, FL 33446. Phone: (561) 495-0233. Fax: (561) 499-2557. Web: www.morikami.org.

CANADA: SIEGE AT KANATA. Aug 12–13. Kanata Iroquoian Village, Brantford, ON, Canada. Civil War battle re-enactment of the Iroquois Confederate Nations against the British. Event includes storytelling, aboriginal dancing, traditional fare and more. For info: Jean Hawke, 440 Mohawk St, Brantford, ON, Canada N3T 5L9. Phone: (519) 751-9900. Fax: (519) 751-2617. E-mail: kanata@kanatavillage.net. Web: www.kanatavillage.net.

CANTINFLAS: BIRTH ANNIVERSARY. Aug 12, 1911. Mexico's most famous comic actor, Cantinflas, was born at Mexico City as Mario Moreno Reyes. Particularly popular with the poor of Mexico because he most often portrayed the underdog, Cantinflas got his start in Mexico City *carpas*, the equivalent of vaudeville. He became internationally known for his role in *Around the World in 80 Days*. The name Cantinflas was invented by the comic to prevent his parents from learning he was in show business, which they considered a shameful endeavor. Died Apr 20, 1993, at Mexico City.

CRATER LAKE RIM RUNS AND MARATHON. Aug 12. Crater Lake National Park, OR. 31st annual. One of the toughest and most spectacular races you'll ever run! Race routes are around Crater Lake, the deepest lake in the US. Included are a 6.7-mile walk and 6.7-mile run, a 13-mile and a full marathon. The field is limited to 500 competitors. For info: Crater Lake Rim Runs, 5830 Mack Ave, Klamath Falls, OR 97603. Phone: (541) 884-6939. E-mail: rimruns@aol.com or info@craterlakerimruns.com.

De MILLE, CECIL B.: 125th BIRTH ANNIVERSARY. Aug 12, 1881. Film pioneer, born at Ashfield, MA. Cecil Blount De Mille was a film showman extraordinaire known for lavish screen spectacles. He produced more than 70 major films which were noted more for their large scale than for their subtle artistry. He produced one of the earliest four-reel films, *The Squaw Man*, in 1913, which boasted the first use of indoor lighting on an actor and was the first film to publicize the names of its stars. His other innovations included the sneak preview and the idea of producing different versions of a popular film. His films include *The Crusades, The Sign of the Cross, King of Kings, Cleopatra, The Plainsman, The Buccaneer, Reap the Wild Wind* and *The Ten Commandments*, which was made in 1923 and then in a new version in 1956. De Mille was awarded an Oscar for *The Greatest Show on Earth* in 1953. He died Jan 21, 1959, at Hollywood, CA.

ELEANOR ROOSEVELT DAY. Aug 12–14. Menlo, WA. Celebration of this great lady's life. Sponsored by Willapa DAWN (Domestic Abuse Women's Net). Annually, the long weekend culminating in the second Monday in August. Established in 1995 by the National Grange. For info: Anne Louise Grimm, 434

6th St, #206, Raymond, WA 98577-1804. Phone: (360) 942-4596. E-mail: anne@willapabay.org. Web: www.willapadawn .org/eleanor.htm.

ELVIS PRESLEY REMEMBERED. Aug 12. St. Louis, MO. Singer Elvis Presley, his entire family and Colonel Tom Parker are impersonated in a live display titled "From Tupelo to Graceland" to mark the anniversary week of his death. Later a two-hour live music show featuring Steve Davis and the TCB Band will be held in the Duck Room at Blueberry Hill. Est attendance: 400. For info: Blueberry Hill, 6504 Delmar, St. Louis, MO 63130. Phone: (314) 727-4444. Web: www.blueberryhill.com.

FLOOD VICTIMS RECEIVE $6.2 BILLION: ANNIVERSARY. Aug 12, 1993. President Bill Clinton signed a bill Aug 12, 1993, providing $6.2 billion in federal relief to victims of floods in July and August for nine states from North Dakota to Missouri. Due to the record rains in the spring of up to 200 percent above average, the Midwest suffered 50 deaths, 70,000 left homeless and an estimated $12 billion in damage as of Aug 9, 1993.

GREATER PITTSBURGH RENAISSANCE FESTIVAL. Aug 12–13. (also Aug 19–20, 26–27, Sept 2–4, 9–10, 16–17 and 23–24.) West Newton, PA. A re-creation of a 16th-century marketplace where the king and queen come on holiday. Featured are more than 100 craft shops, six themed stages, games, food and armoured contact jousting. Est attendance: 60,000. For info: Lori Hughes, Greater Pittsburgh Renaissance Festival, 112 Renaissance Ln, West Newton, PA 15089.

HOME SEWING MACHINE PATENTED: ANNIVERSARY. Aug 12, 1851. Isaac Singer developed the sewing machine for use in homes.

IBM PERSONAL COMPUTER INTRODUCED: 25th ANNIVERSARY. Aug 12, 1981. IBM's first personal computer was released. The computer cost the equivalent of $3,000 in today's currency. Although IBM was one of the pioneers in making mainframe and other large computers, this was the company's first foray into the desktop computer market. Eventually, more IBM-compatible computers were manufactured by IBM's competitors than by IBM itself.

INTER-STATE FAIR AND RODEO. Aug 12–20. Coffeyville, KS. "Largest outdoor fair and rodeo event in southeast Kansas and northeast Oklahoma." Includes truck & tractor pull, concerts, demo derby, four nights of PRCA rodeo and livestock shows. Est attendance: 75,000. For info: Montgomery County Fair Assn, Box 457, Coffeyville, KS 67337. Phone: (620) 251-2550. Fax: (620) 251-5448. E-mail: fairandrodeo@coffeyville.com. Web: www .coffeyville.com.

JOURS DE FÊTE (DAYS OF CELEBRATION). Aug 12–13. Ste. Genevieve, MO. Celebration of town's French heritage. Tours of historic homes dating to the 1700s that exemplify some of the finest French Creole architecture. Also more than 600 arts and crafts booths and colonial crafts demonstrations by authentically costumed crafters. Annually, the second weekend of August. Est attendance: 40,000. For info: Ste. Genevieve Tourist Info Center, 66 S Main, Ste. Genevieve, MO 63670. Phone: (573) 883-7097 or (800) 373-7007. E-mail: sgtourism@ brick.net.

KING PHILIP ASSASSINATION: ANNIVERSARY. Aug 12, 1676. Native American, Philip, son of Massasoit, chief of the Wampanog tribe, was killed near Mt Hope, RI, by a renegade Indian of his own tribe, bringing to an end the first and bloodiest war between American Indians and white settlers of New England, a war that had raged for nearly two years and was known as King Philip's War.

KNIGHTS OF COLUMBUS FAMILY WEEK. Aug 12–19. Held annually in August as a celebration of the importance of the family. Local councils throughout the countries in which the K of C is present hold family-oriented activities throughout this observance. The birth (Aug 12) and death (Aug 14) anniversaries of Father Michael J. McGivney, founder of the Knights of Colum-

bus, fall during this event. For info: Robert A. Goossens, Director, Fraternal Services, Knights of Columbus, 1 Columbus Plaza, New Haven, CT 06510-3326.

KUNTA KINTE HERITAGE FESTIVAL. Aug 12–13. Anne Arundle Fair Grounds, Crownsville, MD. A two-day celebration featuring an arts and crafts village, children's village, an education village, two stages of entertainment, workshops, health screenings, public service and corporate displays and a pictorial history of Alex Haley's country of Gambia. Annually, the second weekend in August. Est attendance: 10,000. For info: David Arthur, Kunta Kinte Heritage Festival, 1517 Ritchie Hwy, Ste L-5, Arnold, MD 21012. Phone: (410) 349-0338. Fax: (410) 349-0069. E-mail: kuntakinte@prodigy.net. Web: www.kuntekinte .org.

LEADVILLE TRAIL 100 BIKE RACE. Aug 12. Leadville, CO. Some 600 cyclists compete in this 100-mile off-road bike race over Colorado's high peaks—out 50 miles to a peak above Twin Lakes and back to Leadville. Sponsor: Leadville Trail 100, Inc. Est attendance: 5,000. For info: Leadville Chamber of Commerce, PO Box 861, Leadville, CO 80461. Phone: (719) 486-3900 or (800) 933-3901. Fax: (719) 486-8478. E-mail: leadville@lead villeusa.com. Web: www.leadvilleusa.com.

LEITERSBURG PEACH FESTIVAL. Aug 12–13. Leitersburg Ruritan Community Park, Leitersburg, MD. This peach-oriented event features crafts, pony rides, petting zoo, antique tractor display, a barrel cart train, Civil war re-enactors, a variety of food stands, oldies and country music and a quilt raffle. Annually, the second weekend in August. Est attendance: 10,000. For info: Ray Johns, 19211 Woodhaven Dr, Hagerstown, MD 21742. Phone: (301) 797-4419.

MATHEWSON, CHRISTY: BIRTH ANNIVERSARY. Aug 12, 1880. Famed American baseball player Christopher (Christy) Mathewson, one of the first players named to Baseball's Hall of Fame, was born at Factoryville, PA. Died at Saranac Lake, NY, Oct 7, 1925. He pitched three complete games during the 1905 World Series without allowing opponents to score a run. In 17 years he won 372 games while losing 188 and striking out 2,499 players.

MINNESOTA RENAISSANCE FESTIVAL. Aug 12–Sept 24 (weekends, Labor Day and Friday, Sept 22). Shakopee, MN. A celebration of 16th-century Renaissance Europe with entertainment on 12 lively stages, food, arts and crafts, games and live jousting. Est attendance: 300,000. For info: Minnesota Renaissance Festival, 1244 S Canterbury Rd, Ste 306, Shakopee, MN 55379. Phone: (800) 966-8215 or (952) 445-7361. Fax: (952) 445-7380. Web: www.renaissancefest.com.

MOUNT OGURA PLANE CRASH: ANNIVERSARY. Aug 12, 1985. A Japan Airlines plane crashed into the side of Mount Ogura, Japan, claiming 520 lives. The worst air disaster involving a single plane. See also: "Canary Islands Plane Disaster: Anniversary" (Mar 27).

NATIONAL GARAGE SALE DAY. Aug 12. A day to turn the nation into a giant shopping mall! Annually, the second Saturday in August. For info: C. Daniel Rhodes, 1900 Crossvine Rd, Hoover, AL 35244. Phone: (205) 908-6781. E-mail: rhodan@charter.net.

PENNSYLVANIA RENAISSANCE FAIRE. Aug 12–Oct 29 (Saturdays, Sundays, Labor Day). Manheim, PA. Re-creation of 16th-century Elizabethan village. Lords and ladies, mongers, merchants, jousting, human chess match, medieval foods and crafts. Est attendance: 200,000. For info: Thomas Roy, Mount Hope Estate and Winery, PO Box 685, Cornwall, PA 17016. Phone: (717) 665-7021. Fax: (717) 664-3466. E-mail: Tom@parenfaire.com. Web: www.parenfaire.com.

RIVER REGALIA. Aug 12. Hot Springs State Park, Thermopolis, WY. River-floating parade starting at the Wedding of the Waters at 11 AM for floaters and 1PM for racers. Decorate any legal flotation device, including inner tube, raft and canoe, and join the floating fun traveling approximately 8 miles to the Hot Springs State Park. Prizes will be awarded in several class divisions. Est attendance: 800. For info: Toddi Darlington, Thermopolis Chamber of Commerce, 119 South 6th St, Thermopolis, WY 82443. Phone: (307) 864-3192. E-mail: thercc@rtconnect.net. Web: www.thermopolis.com.

SPACE MILESTONE: *ECHO I* (US). Aug 12, 1960. First successful communications satellite in Earth's orbit to relay voice and TV signals from one ground station to another was launched.

SPACE MILESTONE: *ENTERPRISE* (US). Aug 12, 1977. Reusable orbiting vehicle (space shuttle) makes first successful flight on its own within Earth's atmosphere. Launched from Boeing 747 on Aug 12, 1977.

STREETSCENE. Aug 12. Covington, VA. Car Show, open to all types of vehicles! 10–4. Entertainment throughout the day. Annually, the second Saturday in August. Est attendance: 8,000. For info: Kars Unlimited, Inc, PO Box 851, Covington, VA 24426. Phone: (540) 962-3642.

THAILAND: BIRTHDAY OF THE QUEEN. Aug 12. The entire kingdom of Thailand celebrates the birthday of Queen Sirikit.

UNITED NATIONS: INTERNATIONAL YOUTH DAY. Aug 12. Day to increase public awareness of the World Programme of Action for Youth to the Year 2000 and Beyond, which calls for action in 10 priority areas: education, employment, hunger and poverty, health, environment, drug abuse, juvenile delinquency, leisure-time activities, girls and young women, and full and effective participation of youth (15 to 24 years old) in the life of society and in decision making. For info: United Nations, Dept of Public Info, New York, NY 10017. Web: www.un.org.

VINYL RECORD DAY. Aug 12. We all need a reminder sometimes that life is good, regardless of national news and daily challenges. Favorite songs can bring back fond memories, and Vinyl Record Day encourages celebrating these music memories with family and friends. The day also seeks to recognize the tremendous cultural influence that vinyl records and album covers have had for more than 60 years. Annually, on Aug 12—the day Thomas Edison invented the phonograph in 1877. For info: Gary Freiberg, 1107 11th St, Los Osos, CA 93402. Phone: (888) 644-4567. Fax: (805) 528-1365. E-mail: gary@VinylRecordDay.org. Web: www.VinylRecordDay.org.

WATERMELON FESTIVAL. Aug 12. Rush Springs, OK. Beginning with watermelon judging and ending with the crowning of the festival queen, the highlight of the celebration is the serving of 50,000 pounds of free watermelon at Jeff Davis Park. Annually, the second Saturday in August. Est attendance: 20,000. For info: Rush Springs Lions Club, Box 298, Rush Springs, OK 73082. Phone: (580) 476-3277 or (580) 476-3255.

WYOMING STATE FAIR AND RODEO. Aug 12–19. Douglas, WY. Recognizing the products, achievements and cultural heritage of the people of Wyoming. Bringing together rural and urban citizens for an inexpensive, entertaining and educational experience. Features Livestock Shows for beef, goats, swine, sheep and horses; Junior Livestock Shows for beef, swine, sheep, horses, goats, dogs, poultry and rabbits; competitions and displays for culinary arts, needlework, visual arts, and floriculture; 4-H and FFA County/Chapters State qualification competitions; Demo Derby, live entertainment, carnival, PRCA Rodeo, Ranch Rodeo and an All Women Rodeo (rough stock). Est attendance: 47,000. For info: Wyoming State Fair, PO Drawer 10, Douglas, WY 82633. Phone: (307) 358-2398. Fax: (307) 358-6030. E-mail: wsf@netcommander.com. Web: www.wystatefair.com.

BIRTHDAYS TODAY

William Goldman, 75, writer (*The Princess Bride, Marathon Man*), born Chicago, IL, Aug 12, 1931.

George Hamilton, 67, actor (*Love at First Bite, Act One*, "The Survivors"), born Memphis, TN, Aug 12, 1939.

Sam J. Jones, 52, actor (*Flash Gordon, 10*), born Chicago, IL, Aug 12, 1954.

Michael Kidd, 87, choreographer, born Milton Greenwald at Brooklyn, NY, Aug 12, 1919.

Peter Krause, 41, actor ("Six Feet Under," "Sports Night"), born Minneapolis, MN, Aug 12, 1965.

Ann Martin, 51, author (The Baby-Sitter's Club series), born Princeton, NJ, Aug 12, 1955.

Pat Metheny, 52, jazz guitarist ("Song X," "Letter from Home"), born Lee's Summit, MO, Aug 12, 1954.

Alvis Edgar ("Buck") Owens, 77, singer ("Hee Haw," "Act Naturally"), songwriter, born Sherman, TX, Aug 12, 1929.

Pete Sampras, 35, tennis player, born Washington, DC, Aug 12, 1971.

George Soros, 76, billionaire, financier, philanthropist in Eastern Europe and the US, born Budapest, Hungary, Aug 12, 1930.

Porter Wagoner, 76, singer ("The Carroll County Accident"), born West Plains, MO, Aug 12, 1930.

Antoine Walker, 30, basketball player, born Chicago, IL, Aug 12, 1976.

Jane Wyatt, 93, actress (Emmy Awards for "Father Knows Best"; *Lost Horizon*), born New York, NY, Aug 12, 1913.

AUGUST 13 — SUNDAY
Day 225 — 140 Remaining

BERLIN WALL ERECTED: 45th ANNIVERSARY. Aug 13, 1961. Early in the morning, the East German government closed the border between east and west sectors of Berlin with barbed wire fence to discourage further population movement to the west. Telephone and postal services were interrupted, and, later in the week, a concrete wall was built to strengthen the barrier between official crossing points. The dismantling of the wall began Nov 9, 1989. See also: "Berlin Wall Opened: Anniversary" (Nov 9).

August 2006	S	M	T	W	T	F	S
			1	2	3	4	5
	6	7	8	9	10	11	12
	13	14	15	16	17	18	19
	20	21	22	23	24	25	26
	27	28	29	30	31		

CAXTON, WILLIAM: BIRTH ANNIVERSARY. Aug 13, 1422. First English printer, born at Kent, England. Died at London, England, 1491. Caxton produced his first book printed in English (while he was still at Bruges), the *Recuyell of the Histories of Troy*, in 1476, and in the autumn of 1476 set up a print shop at Westminster, becoming the first printer in England.

CENTRAL AFRICAN REPUBLIC: INDEPENDENCE DAY. Aug 13. Commemorates Proclamation of Independence from France in 1960.

HERBERT HOOVER DAY. Aug 13. Iowa. Annually, the Sunday nearest Aug 10th, the birthday of Herbert Hoover.

HITCHCOCK, ALFRED (JOSEPH): BIRTH ANNIVERSARY. Aug 13, 1899. English film director and master of suspense born at London. Hitchcock's career as a filmmaker dates back to the silent film era when he made *The Lodger* in 1926, based on the tale of Jack the Ripper. American audiences were introduced to the Hitchcock style in 1935 with *The Thirty-Nine Steps* and *The Lady Vanishes* in 1938, after which he went to Hollywood. There he produced a string of classics including *Rebecca, Suspicion, Notorious, Rear Window, To Catch a Thief, The Birds, Psycho* and *Frenzy*, in addition to his TV series "Alfred Hitchcock Presents." He died Apr 29, 1980, at Beverly Hills, CA.

HOGAN, BEN: BIRTH ANNIVERSARY. Aug 13, 1912. Golfer born at Dublin, TX. Hogan was one of only four players to win all four major professional championships, and his 63 career victories rank him third after Sam Snead and Jack Nicklaus. Died at Ft Worth, TX, July 25, 1997.

HOLLYWOOD BEACH LATIN FESTIVAL. Aug 13. Hollywood, FL. 13th annual. Festival features Latin entertainment, arts and crafts, food and health court. Est attendance: 35,000. For info: Roguey Doyle, City of Hollywood, Dept of Parks, Recreation & Cultural Arts, 1940 Harrison St, Ste 101, Hollywood, FL 33020. Phone: (954) 921-3404.

ITALY: PALIO DEL GOLFO. Aug 13. La Spezia. A rowing contest over a 2,000-meter course is held on the second Sunday in August.

KRUPP, ALFRIED von BOHLEN und HALBACH: BIRTH ANNIVERSARY. Aug 13, 1907. As sole owner of the massive Krupp industries, Alfried Krupp took over the factories of German-occupied countries and used them for the Nazi war machine. Sometimes he had complete facilities dismantled and reassembled inside Germany. He used prisoners of war, civilians from occupied countries and inmates of concentration camps as forced labor in his factories. Found guilty as a war criminal by the Military Court at Nuremberg in 1948, he regained his property after serving three years of a twelve-year sentence. He was named Alfried von Bohlen und Halbach at birth, but the family was authorized by Emperor Wilhelm II to add the mother's maiden name of Krupp to their own. Born at Essen, Germany, he died there July 30, 1967.

NATIONAL RESURRECT ROMANCE WEEK. Aug 13–19. Event focuses on celebrating creative romance. Encourages men and women to find ways to be romantic every day this week by using their hearts. For info: Michael Webb, Romance Expert and Author, PO Box 1567, Cary, NC 27512. Phone: (919) 462-0900. E-mail: chase@theromantic.com. Web: www.TheRomantic.com.

OAKLEY, ANNIE: BIRTH ANNIVERSARY. Aug 13, 1860. Annie Oakley was born at Darke County, OH. She developed an eye as a markswoman early as a child, becoming so proficient that she was able to pay off the mortgage on her family farm by selling the game she killed. A few years after defeating vaudeville marksman Frank Butler in a shooting match, she married him and they toured as a team until joining Buffalo Bill's Wild West Show in 1885. She was one of the star attractions for 17 years. She died Nov 3, 1926, at Greenville, OH.

SCOTLAND: EDINBURGH INTERNATIONAL FESTIVAL. Aug 13–Sept 3. Edinburgh, Lothian. Now in its 60th year, this is one of the world's largest arts festivals, attracting many international stars. The festival includes symphonic music, opera, theater and dance. Est attendance: 420,000. For info: Edinburgh Intl Festival, The Hub, Castlehill, The Royal Mile, Edinburgh, Scotland EH1 2NE. Phone: (44) (131) 473 2000. Fax: (44) (131) 473 2002. E-mail: eif@eif.co.uk. Web: www.eif.co.uk.

SPACE MILESTONE: *HELIOS* SOLAR WING: 5th ANNIVERSARY. Aug 13, 2001. The solar-powered plane *Helios* broke the altitude records for propeller-driven aircraft and non-rocket planes on this date, soaring higher than 96,500 feet. The plane has a wingspan longer than a Boeing 747 and uses solar-powered motors to power 14 propellers, flying at speeds as high as 170 MPH. NASA plans to develop similar craft for unmanned flights on Mars.

STONE, LUCY: BIRTH ANNIVERSARY. Aug 13, 1818. American women's rights pioneer, born near West Brookfield, MA, Lucy Stone dedicated her life to the abolition of slavery and the emancipation of women. Although she graduated from Oberlin College, she had to finance her education by teaching for nine years because her father did not favor college education for women. An eloquent speaker for her causes, she headed the list of 89 men and women who signed the call to the first national Woman's Rights Convention, held at Worcester, MA, October 1850. On May 1, 1855, she married Henry Blackwell. She and her husband aided in the founding of the American Suffrage Association, taking part in numerous referendum campaigns to win suffrage amendments to state constitutions. She died Oct 18, 1893, at Dorchester, MA.

THANKS FOR ALL THE GIFTS WEEK. Aug 13–19. Designed for procrastinators, this is a time to catch up on all the thank-you notes and cards for birthdays, graduations, weddings, etc, that you forgot to send. Annually, the third week in August. For info: Eva Rosenberg, Giftech Corp, 2961 Industrial Rd, Ste 731, Las Vegas, NV 89109. Phone: (800) 594-9829. Web: www.giftsurf.com.

TUNISIA: WOMEN'S DAY. Aug 13. General holiday. Celebration of independence of women.

BIRTHDAYS TODAY

Kathleen Battle, 58, opera soprano, born Portsmouth, OH, Aug 13, 1948.

Danny Bonaduce, 47, radio personality, actor ("The Partridge Family"), born Broomall, PA, Aug 13, 1959.

Fidel Castro, 79, President of Cuba, former amateur baseball player, born Mayari, Oriente Province, Cuba, Aug 13, 1927.

Quinn Cummings, 39, actress (*The Goodbye Girl*, "Family"), born Los Angeles, CA, Aug 13, 1967.

Dan Fogelberg, 55, composer, singer ("Same Old Lang Syne," "Leader of the Band"), born Peoria, IL, Aug 13, 1951.

Pat Harrington, Jr, 77, actor, comedian ("The Jack Paar Show," "One Day at a Time"), born New York, NY, Aug 13, 1929.

Don Ho, 76, singer ("Tiny Bubbles"), born Oahu, HI, Aug 13, 1930.

Kevin Tighe, 62, actor ("Emergency," *The Graduate, What's Eating Gilbert Grape?*), born Los Angeles, CA, Aug 13, 1944.

AUGUST 14 — MONDAY

Day 226 — 139 Remaining

ATLANTIC CHARTER SIGNING: 65th ANNIVERSARY. Aug 14, 1941. The eight-point agreement was signed by US President Franklin D. Roosevelt and British Prime Minister Winston S. Churchill. The charter grew out of a three-day conference aboard ship in the Atlantic Ocean, off the Newfoundland coast, and stated policies and hopes for the future agreed to by the two nations.

CANADA: YUKON DISCOVERY DAY. Aug 14. In the Klondike region of the Yukon, at Bonanza Creek (formerly known as Rabbit Creek), George Washington Carmack discovered gold Aug 16 or 17, 1896. During the following year more than 30,000 people joined the gold rush to the area. Anniversary is celebrated as a holiday (Discovery Day) in the Yukon, on nearest Monday.

CHENEY, LYNNE: BIRTHDAY. Aug 14, 1941. Wife of Vice President Richard (Dick) Cheney, born at Casper, WY. Former chairman of the National Endowment for the Humanities (1986–93).

COLOGNE CATHEDRAL COMPLETION: ANNIVERSARY. Aug 14, 1880. The largest Gothic church in northern Europe, the Cologne Cathedral at Cologne, Germany, was completed Aug 14, 1880, just 632 years after rebuilding began on Aug 14, 1248. In fact, there had been a church on its site since 873, but a fire in 1248 made rebuilding necessary. The cathedral was again damaged, by bombing, during World War II.

JUST, ERNEST E.: BIRTH ANNIVERSARY. Aug 14, 1883. American marine biologist Ernest E. Just was born at Charleston, SC. He was the first recipient of the NAACP's Spingarn Medal and was a professor at Howard University from 1907 to 1941, where he was head of physiology at the medical school (1912–20) and head of zoology (1912–41). He died Oct 27, 1941, at Washington, DC.

NATIONAL AVIATION WEEK. Aug 14–20. A celebration of flight designed to increase public awareness, knowledge and appreciation of aviation. Annually, the week of Orville Wright's birthday, Aug 19. For info: Lafayette Natural History Museum and Planetarium, 433 Jefferson St, Lafayette, LA 70501. Phone: (337) 291-5547. Fax: (337) 291-5464.

PAKISTAN: INDEPENDENCE DAY. Aug 14, 1947. Gained independence from Britain in 1947.

PGA CHAMPIONSHIP. Aug 14–20. Medinah, IL. The 88th championship conducted by the Professional Golfers' Association of America. Est attendance: 150,000. For info: PGA of America, 100 Avenue of the Champions, Palm Beach Gardens, FL 33418. Phone: (561) 624-8495. Fax: (561) 624-8429. Web: www.pga.com.

SCOTTS BLUFF COUNTY FAIR. Aug 14–20. County Fairgrounds, Mitchell, NE. County fair including stock displays and shows, special events such as large-name country and western concert, largest amateur rodeo in Nebraska, tractor pull, free stage acts, grounds act, rubber-check races, demolition derby. Est attendance: 47,000. For info: Diane Wurdeman, Manager, Scotts Bluff County Fair, Box 157, Mitchell, NE 69357. Phone: (308) 623-1828. Fax: (308) 623-1328. E-mail: sbcofair@nebmail.com. Web: www.scbcountyfair.com.

SOCIAL SECURITY ACT: ANNIVERSARY. Aug 14, 1935. President Franklin D. Roosevelt signed the Social Security Act, which contained provisions for the establishment of a Social Security Board to administer federal old-age and survivors' insurance in the US. By signing the bill into law, Roosevelt was fulfilling a 1932 campaign promise.

THAYER, ERNEST LAWRENCE: BIRTH ANNIVERSARY. Aug 14, 1863. The man who wrote the famous comic baseball ballad "Casey at the Bat" was born at Lawrence, MA. He wrote a series of comic poems for the *San Francisco Examiner*, of which "Casey at the Bat" was the last. It was published Sunday, June 3, 1888, and Thayer received $5 in payment for it. Thayer, who regarded the poem's fame as a nuisance and whose other writings are largely forgotten, died at Santa Barbara, CA, Aug 21, 1940.

365-INNING SOFTBALL GAME: 30th ANNIVERSARY. Aug 14–15, 1976. The Gager's Diner softball team played the Bend'n Elbow Tavern in a 365-inning softball game. Starting at 10 AM Aug 14, the game was called because of rain and fog at 4 PM, Aug 15. The 70 players, including 20 women, raised $4,000 for construction of a new softball field and for the Monticello, NY, Community General Hospital. The Gagers beat the Elbows 491–467. To date, this remains the longest softball game on record.

VICTORY DAY. Aug 14. Rhode Island. State holiday commemorating President Truman's announcement of the surrender of the Japanese to the Allies on Aug 14, 1945. Annually, the second Monday in August.

V-J DAY: ANNIVERSARY. Aug 14, 1945. Anniversary of President Truman's announcement that Japan had surrendered to the Allies, setting off celebrations across the nation. Official ratification of surrender occurred aboard the USS *Missouri* at Tokyo Bay, Sept 2 (Far Eastern time).

WEIRD CONTEST WEEK. Aug 14–18. Music Pier, Ocean City, NJ. One contest daily. Contests include artistic pie eating (chewing something meaningful out of a TastyKake Pie), saltwater taffy sculpting, french fry sculpting, wet T-shirt throwing, Little Miss and Little Mister Chaos and Miss Miscellaneous Contest. 11 AM. Annually, the third week in August. Sponsors: The City of Ocean City, TastyKake Baking Company, Shriver's Saltwater Taffy, The Promenade. Est attendance: 4,500. For info: Mark Soifer, PR Dir, City of Ocean City, City Hall, 9th Asbury Ave, Ocean City, NJ 08226. Phone: (609) 525-9300. Fax: (609) 399-0374. E-mail: MTSoifer@aol.com.

BIRTHDAYS TODAY

Russell Baker, 81, journalist, author, TV host ("Masterpiece Theatre"), born Loudoun County, VA, Aug 14, 1925.

Catherine Bell, 38, actress ("JAG"), born London, England, Aug 14, 1968.

Halle Berry, 38, actress (*Die Another Day, X-Men*, Oscar for *Monster's Ball*), born Cleveland, OH, Aug 14, 1968.

Lynne Cheney, 65, wife of Dick Cheney, 46th vice president of the US, born Casper, WY, Aug 14, 1941.

David Crosby, 65, singer (Crosby, Stills & Nash), songwriter, born Los Angeles, CA, Aug 14, 1941.

Antonio Fargas, 60, actor (*Shaft, I'm Gonna Git You Sucka!, Car Wash*), born the Bronx, NY, Aug 14, 1946.

Alice Ghostley, 80, actress ("Designing Women," "Bewitched"), born Eve, MO, Aug 14, 1926.

Buddy Greco, 80, singer ("Mr Lonely"), composer, musician, born Philadelphia, PA, Aug 14, 1926.

Marcia Gay Harden, 47, actress (Oscar for *Pollock; Space Cowboys*), born La Jolla, CA, Aug 14, 1959.

Terin Humphrey, 20, gymnast, born St. Louis, MO, Aug 14, 1986.

Earvin ("Magic") Johnson, Jr, 47, former basketball player, born Lansing, MI, Aug 14, 1959.

Mila Kunis, 23, actress ("That 70s Show," "Family Guy"), born Kiev, Ukraine, Aug 14, 1983.

Arthur Betz Laffer, 66, economist (The Laffer Curve), born Youngstown, OH, Aug 14, 1940.

Gary Larson, 56, cartoonist ("The Far Side"), born Tacoma, WA, Aug 14, 1950.

August 2006

S	M	T	W	T	F	S
		1	2	3	4	5
6	7	8	9	10	11	12
13	14	15	16	17	18	19
20	21	22	23	24	25	26
27	28	29	30	31		

Steve Martin, 61, comedian, actor ("Saturday Night Live," *LA Story, Roxanne, Parenthood*), born Waco, TX, Aug 14, 1945.

Susan Saint James, 60, actress ("MacMillan and Wife," "Kate and Allie"), born Long Beach, CA, Aug 14, 1946.

Danielle Steel, 59, author (*Vanished, Wanderlust*), born New York, NY, Aug 14, 1947.

Rusty Wallace, 50, auto racer, born St. Louis, MO, Aug 14, 1956.

AUGUST 15 — TUESDAY
Day 227 — 138 Remaining

ALLIED LANDINGS IN SOUTH OF FRANCE: ANNIVERSARY. Aug 15, 1944. After several postponements, Allied forces began Operation Dragoon, the landing on the south coast of France. More than 2,000 transports and landing craft transported 94,000 men to an area between Toulon and Cannes, with only 183 Allied losses. They encountered minimal opposition, and by the end of August the French coast from the mouth of the Rhone to Nice was in Allied hands.

ASSUMPTION OF THE VIRGIN MARY. Aug 15. Greek and Roman Catholic churches celebrate Mary's ascent to Heaven. In Orthodox Churches called the Dormition of the Theotokos and commemorated on Aug 15 or 28. A holiday in many Christian countries.

BARRYMORE, ETHEL: BIRTH ANNIVERSARY. Aug 15, 1879. Celebrated award-winning actress of stage, screen and television, born Ethel Blythe at Philadelphia, PA. Sister of John and Lionel Barrymore. Died at Beverly Hills, CA, June 18, 1959.

BEST FRIEND'S DAY. Aug 15. Celebrate this special day by doing something fun with your best friend. Go shopping, go to the movies, go to a park or restaurant, play a game or just hang out and be together. For info: Thema Martin. Phone: (404) 849-1249. E-mail: thema_martin@hotmail.com. Web: www.cosmocompany.com.

BONAPARTE, NAPOLEON: BIRTH ANNIVERSARY. Aug 15, 1769. Anniversary of birth of French emperor Napoleon Bonaparte on the island of Corsica. He died in exile at 5:49 PM, May 5, 1821, on the island of St. Helena. Public holiday at Corsica, France.

CHAUVIN DAY. Aug 15. A day named for Nicholas Chauvin, French soldier from Rochefort, France, who idolized Napoleon and who eventually became a subject of ridicule because of his blind loyalty and dedication to anything French. Originally referring to bellicose patriotism, chauvinism has come to mean blind or absurdly intense attachment to any cause. Observed on Napoleon's birth anniversary because Chauvin's birth date is unknown.

CHILD, JULIA: BIRTH ANNIVERSARY. Aug 15, 1912. America's beloved food authority, who didn't take a cooking lesson until she was in her thirties, was born at Pasadena, CA. Child's cookbooks and television shows (most famously, "The French Chef") encouraged Americans to cook and eat well and to be skeptical of food fads and diet strictures. "Cooking is not a chore, it is a joy," Child believed. She died at Santa Barbara, CA, Aug 12, 2004.

COEUR D'ALENE TRIBAL PILGRIMAGE. Aug 15. Old Mission State Park, Cataldo, ID. The annual Feast of the Assumption pilgrimage by the Coeur d'Alene Indians. Annually, Aug 15. Est attendance: 1,800. For info: Bill Scudder, Park Mgr, Old Mission State Park, PO Box 30, Cataldo, ID 83810-0030. Phone: (208) 682-3814. Fax: (208) 682-4032. E-mail: old@idpr.state.id.us.

CONGO (BRAZZAVILLE): NATIONAL DAY. Aug 15. National day of the People's Republic of the Congo. Commemorates independence from France in 1960.

DORMITION OF THEOTOKOS. Aug 15. Orthodox observance. According to New Calendar (Gregorian), the Dormition Fast is observed Aug 1–14, followed by Dormition of Theotokos Aug 15.

EQUATORIAL GUINEA: CONSTITUTION DAY. Aug 15. National holiday. Commemorates the 1982 revision of the original constitution of 1968.

FERBER, EDNA: BIRTH ANNIVERSARY. Aug 15, 1887. Edna Ferber was born at Kalamazoo, MI. She wrote her first novel, *Dawn O'Hara*, in 1911 and became a prolific writer, producing many popular magazine stories. Her novel *So Big* brought her commercial success in 1924 as well as a Pulitzer Prize. Her other novels include *Show Boat, Cimarron, Saratoga Trunk, Giant* and *Ice Palace*, all of which were made into successful films. Ferber collaborated with George Kaufman in writing for the stage on *The Royal Family, Dinner at Eight, Stage Door* and *Bravo*. Ferber died at New York, NY, Apr 16, 1968.

HARDING, FLORENCE KLING DeWOLFE: BIRTH ANNIVERSARY. Aug 15, 1860. Wife of Warren Gamaliel Harding, 29th president of the US, born at Marion, OH, Aug 15, 1860. Died at Marion, OH, Nov 21, 1924.

INDIA: INDEPENDENCE DAY. Aug 15. National holiday. Anniversary of Indian independence from Britain in 1947.

KOREA: INDEPENDENCE DAY. Aug 15. National holiday commemorates acceptance by Japan of Allied terms of surrender in 1945, thereby freeing Korea from 36 years of Japanese domination. Also marks formal proclamation of the Republic of Korea in 1948. Military parades and ceremonies throughout country.

LIECHTENSTEIN: NATIONAL DAY. Aug 15. Public holiday on Assumption Day.

MOON PHASE: LAST QUARTER. Aug 15. Moon enters Last Quarter phase at 9:51 PM, EDT.

NATIONAL RELAXATION DAY. Aug 15. Hold the phones, call in sick, or just take a nap. Today is the perfect excuse to reduce stress and improve your lifestyle by relaxing. Spend a few minutes learning or sharing the art of relaxation with family, friends and co-workers. Annually, Aug 15. For info: Sean M. Moeller, PO Box 593, Jenison, MI 49429-0593.

PANAMA CANAL OPENS: ANNIVERSARY. Aug 15, 1914. After ten years of construction and much multination diplomacy, the Panama Canal opened for operation. A self-propelled crane boat made the first passage through the canal, a 50-mile waterway connecting the Atlantic and Pacific oceans, on Jan 7, 1914. The first ocean steamer, the SS *Ancon*, passed through Aug 3, 1914, and the canal officially opened Aug 15, 1914.

PANAMA: PANAMA CITY FOUNDATION DAY. Aug 15. Traditional annual cultural observance recognizes foundation of Panama City.

PENN STATE'S AGRI PROGRESS DAYS. Aug 15–17. The Larson Agricultural Research Center, Rock Springs, PA. To provide the public with the latest information on agricultural industries and developments Penn State has made in the field of agriculture. More than 350 commercial exhibitors. Est attendance: 50,000. For info: Robert Oberheim, Penn State Univ, 420 Agricultural Admin Bldg, University Park, PA 16802. Phone: (814) 865-2081. Fax: (814) 865-1677. Web: apd.cas.psu.edu.

SCOTT, SIR WALTER: BIRTH ANNIVERSARY. Aug 15, 1771. Born at Edinburgh, Scotland. Famed poet and novelist.

"But no one shall find me rowing against the stream," he wrote in the introduction to *The Fortunes of Nigel*; "I care not who knows it—I write for the general amusement." Died at Abbotsford, Scotland, Sept 21, 1832.

TRANSCONTINENTAL US RAILWAY COMPLETION: ANNIVERSARY. Aug 15, 1870. The Golden Spike ceremony at Promontory Point, UT, May 10, 1869, was long regarded as the final link in a transcontinental railroad track reaching from an Atlantic port to a Pacific port. In fact, that link occurred unceremoniously on another date in another state. Diaries of engineers working at the site establish "the completion of a transcontinental track at a point 928 feet east of today's milepost 602, or 3,812 feet east of the present Union Pacific depot building at Strasburg (formerly Comanche)," CO. The final link was made at 2:53 PM, Aug 15, 1870. Annual celebration at Strasburg, CO, on a weekend in August. See also: "Golden Spike Driving: Anniversary" (May 10).

WOODSTOCK: ANNIVERSARY. Aug 15, 1969. The Woodstock Music and Art Fair opened on this day on an alfalfa field on or near Yasgur's Farm at Bethel, NY. The three-day rock concert featured 24 bands and drew a crowd of more than 400,000 people.

WORLD DAY OF REIKI. Aug 15. A day to unite all Reiki practitioners in commemoration of the birthday of Dr. Mikao Usui (Aug 15, 1865) and his legacy of Reiki. For info: Rinda-Mary Payne, RMT, The-Reiki-Works, 30 Gardner Rd #4H, Brookline, MA 02445. Phone: (617) 734-1219. E-mail: TheReikiWorks1@aol.com.

BIRTHDAYS TODAY

Ben Affleck, 34, actor (*Good Will Hunting, Forces of Nature*), born Berkeley, CA, Aug 15, 1972.

Princess Anne, 56, Princess Royal of the UK, horsewoman, born London, England, Aug 15, 1950.

Stephen G. Breyer, 68, US Supreme Court justice, born San Francisco, CA, Aug 15, 1938.

Mike Connors, 81, actor ("Mannix"), born Krekor Ohanian at Fresno, CA, Aug 15, 1925.

Linda Ellerbee, 62, journalist, born Bryan, TX, Aug 15, 1944.

Zeljko Ivanek, 49, actor ("24," *Donnie Brasco*), born Ljubljana, Slovenia, Aug 15, 1957.

Vernon Jordan, Jr, 71, civil rights leader, born Atlanta, GA, Aug 15, 1935.

Debra Messing, 38, actress ("Will & Grace"), born Brooklyn, NY, Aug 15, 1968.

Phyllis Stewart Schlafly, 82, conservative spokeswoman, author, born St. Louis, MO, Aug 15, 1924.

Eugene (Gene) Upshaw, 61, Hall of Fame football player, union executive, born Robstown, TX, Aug 15, 1945.

Kathryn Whitmire, 60, first woman mayor of Houston, Texas, born Houston, TX, Aug 15, 1946.

August 2006	S	M	T	W	T	F	S
			1	2	3	4	5
	6	7	8	9	10	11	12
	13	14	15	16	17	18	19
	20	21	22	23	24	25	26
	27	28	29	30	31		

AUGUST 16 — WEDNESDAY
Day 228 — 137 Remaining

ARTISTS IN THE PARK. Aug 16. Cate Park, Wolfeboro, NH. 27th annual juried exhibit and sale including 41 artists and craftspeople, demonstrations throughout the day and family entertainment. Held rain or shine, 10 AM–4 PM. Sponsors: Governor Wentworth Arts Council. Est attendance: 4,000. For info: Deborah Hopkins, Chair, PO Box 1379, Wolfeboro, NH 03894. Phone: (603) 569-4994.

BATTLE OF CAMDEN: ANNIVERSARY. Aug 16, 1780. Revolutionary War battle fought near Camden, SC. American troops led by General Horatio Gates suffered disastrous losses. Nearly 1,000 Americans killed and another 1,000 captured by the British. British losses about 325. One of America's worst defeats in the war.

BEGIN, MENACHEM: BIRTH ANNIVERSARY. Aug 16, 1913. Born at Brest-Litovsk, Poland. A militant Zionist and anticommunist, he fled to Russia in 1939 ahead of the advancing Nazis; he was soon arrested and sent to Siberia. Freed in 1941, he went to Palestine and became a leader in the Jewish underground, fighting for Israel's independence; by 1943 he headed the national military organization. Elected Prime Minister of Israel in 1977, he signed the historic peace treaty between Israel and Egypt with President Anwar el Sadat of Egypt and US President Jimmy Carter at Camp David in 1979. He died Mar 9, 1992, at Tel Aviv, Israel.

BENNINGTON BATTLE DAY: ANNIVERSARY. Aug 16, 1777. Anniversary of battle is legal holiday in Vermont.

DOMINICAN REPUBLIC: RESTORATION OF THE REPUBLIC. Aug 16. The anniversary of the Restoration of the Republic in 1863 is celebrated as an official public holiday.

HARMONIC CONVERGENCE: ANNIVERSARY. Aug 16, 1987. At about 20 designated "sacred sites" around the world (including Lake Titicaca, Bolivia; Boulder, CO; Niagara Falls and the Grand Canyon in the US) believers gathered to meditate about peace and to ward off any impending doom. The harmonic convergence, projected from ancient Mayan and Aztec calendars to begin on this date, was said to signal the beginning of a period of cleansing that would last until 1992, in preparation for alien intelligence to be confronted in the next century.

JOE MILLER'S JOKE DAY. Aug 16. A day to tell a joke in honor of the English comic actor Joseph (or Josias) Miller, who was born in 1684 (exact date unknown). Miller acted at the Drury Lane Theatre at London and was a popular favorite. He died at London, Aug 16, 1738. A book with which Miller had no direct connection, *Joe Miller's Jests*, was compiled by John Mottley and first published in 1739. It contained 247 jokes. Revised and expanded hundreds of times, it contained more than 1,500 jokes in the ensuing two centuries. From *Joe Miller's Jests*, London, 1739: "A melting Sermon being preached in a country Church, all fell a weeping but one Man, who being asked, why he did not weep with the rest? O! said he. I belong to another Parish."

KLONDIKE GOLD DISCOVERY: ANNIVERSARY. Aug 16, 1896. According to the oral tradition of the Tagish First Nations People, Skookum Jim, Dawson Charlie and George Carmack found gold in Rabbit Creek, a tributary of the Klondike River, lying "thick between the flaky slabs like cheese sandwiches." This event that led to the great Klondike Gold Rush is celebrated in the Yukon each year with a public holiday, Discovery Day, observed on the nearest Monday.

LAWRENCE (OF ARABIA), T.E.: BIRTH ANNIVERSARY. Aug 16, 1888. British soldier, archaeologist and writer, born at Tremadoc, North Wales. During WWI, led the Arab revolt against the Turks and served as a spy for the British. His book, *Seven Pillars of Wisdom*, is a personal account of the Arab revolt. He was killed in a motorcycle accident at Dorset, England, May 19, 1935.

MacFADDEN, BERNARR: BIRTH ANNIVERSARY. Aug 16, 1868. Physical culture enthusiast and publisher, born at Mill Springs, MO. He was publisher of *Physical Culture Magazine, True Story Magazine, True Romances, True Detective Mysteries Magazine* and many others. MacFadden made parachute jumps on his 81st, 83rd and 84th birthdays. He died at Jersey City, NJ, of jaundice, following a three-day fast, Oct 12, 1955.

MEANY, GEORGE: BIRTH ANNIVERSARY. Aug 16, 1894. American labor leader George Meany was born at New York, NY. A plumber by trade, he became president of the AFL (American Federation of Labor) in 1952, and when he merged the AFL with the CIO (Congress of Industrial Organizations) he became the leading labor spokesperson in the US. In 1957 he expelled Jimmy Hoffa's Teamsters Union from the AFL-CIO and lost the United Auto Workers in 1967. His tenure as president lasted until 1979. He died Jan 10, 1980, at Washington, DC.

MICHIGAN FIBER FESTIVAL. Aug 16–20. Allegan County Fairgrounds, Allegan, MI. A unique opportunity to see and learn about natural fibers and the animals and plants that produce them. Includes classes and displays of fiber animals and processes of fiber into garments or décor. Est attendance: 8,000. For info: Michigan Fiber Festival, PO Box 744, Hastings, MI 49058. Phone: (269) 948-2497. E-mail: mff@iserv.net. Web: www.michiganfiberfestival.org.

PRESLEY, ELVIS: DEATH ANNIVERSARY. Aug 16, 1977. One of America's most popular singers, Elvis Presley was pronounced dead at the Memphis Baptist Hospital at 3:30 PM, Aug 16, 1977, at age 42. The anniversary of his death is an occasion for pilgrimages by admirers to Graceland, his home and gravesite at Memphis, TN. See also: "Presley, Elvis: Birth Anniversary" (Jan 8).

RUTH, BABE: DEATH ANNIVERSARY. Aug 16, 1948. Baseball fans of all ages and all walks of life mourned when the great Bambino died of cancer at New York City at the age of 53. Born Feb 6, 1895, at Baltimore, MD, the left-handed pitcher and "Sultan of Swat" hit 714 home runs in 22 major league seasons of play and played in 10 World Series. His body lay in state at the main entrance of Yankee Stadium where people waited in line for hours to march past the coffin. On Aug 19, countless people surrounded St. Patrick's Cathedral for the funeral mass and lined the streets along the route to the cemetery as America bade farewell to one of baseball's greatest legends.

STAGG, AMOS ALONZO: BIRTH ANNIVERSARY. Aug 16, 1862. Amos Alonzo Stagg, football player and coach born at West Orange, NJ. Stagg played baseball and football at Yale and then forsook the ministry for physical education. He built the football program at the University of Chicago as an integral part of William Rainey Harper's plan to build a great university. Over 40 years at Chicago, he became the game's greatest innovator and master strategist. When Chicago de-emphasized football, he moved to the College of the Pacific, finishing his career with a record of 314-181-15. Died at Stockton, CA, Mar 17, 1965.

BIRTHDAYS TODAY

Angela Bassett, 48, actress (*Malcolm X, What's Love Got to Do with It, Waiting to Exhale*), born New York, NY, Aug 16, 1958.

James Cameron, 52, director (Oscar for *Titanic; True Lies*), born Kapuskasing, ON, Canada, Aug 16, 1954.

Robert Culp, 76, actor ("I Spy," *Bob and Carol and Ted and Alice*), born Berkeley, CA, Aug 16, 1930.

Frank Newton Gifford, 76, sportscaster, Hall of Fame football player, born Santa Monica, CA, Aug 16, 1930.

Kathie Lee Gifford, 53, TV personality, singer, born Paris, France, Aug 16, 1953.

Eydie Gorme, 74, singer ("Blame It on the Bossa Nova"), born Edith Gormezano at New York, NY, Aug 16, 1932.

Timothy Hutton, 46, actor (*Sunshine State*, Oscar for *Ordinary People*), born Malibu, CA, Aug 16, 1960.

Laura Innes, 46, actress ("ER," "Wings"), born Pontiac, MI, Aug 16, 1960.

Madonna, 48, singer, actress (*Desperately Seeking Susan, Evita*), born Madonna Louise Veronica Ciccone at Bay City, MI, Aug 16, 1958.

Julie Newmar, 71, actress (Cat Woman on TV's "Batman," *Li'l Abner*), born Hollywood, CA, Aug 16, 1935.

Fess Parker, 79, actor ("Daniel Boone," *Davy Crockett*), born Fort Worth, TX, Aug 16, 1927.

Jeff Perry, 51, actor ("Nash Bridges"), founder of Chicago's Steppenwolf Theater, born Highland Park, IL, Aug 16, 1955.

Seth Peterson, 36, actor ("Providence"), born the Bronx, NY, Aug 16, 1970.

Reginald VelJohnson, 54, actor (*Ghostbusters, Die Hard, Die Hard 2*), born Queens, NY, Aug 16, 1952.

Lesley Ann Warren, 60, actress (*Victor/Victoria, Choose Me*, "Cinderella"), born New York, NY, Aug 16, 1946.

AUGUST 17 — THURSDAY
Day 229 — 136 Remaining

ARGENTINA: DEATH ANNIVERSARY OF SAN MARTÍN. Aug 17. National holiday. Commemorates the death in 1850 of the hero of the struggle for independence.

BALLOON CROSSING OF ATLANTIC OCEAN: ANNIVERSARY. Aug 17, 1978. Three Americans—Maxie Anderson, 44, Ben Abruzzo, 48, and Larry Newman, 31—all of Albuquerque, NM, became first to complete a transatlantic trip in a balloon. Starting from Presque Isle, ME, Aug 11, they traveled some 3,200 miles in 137 hours, 18 minutes, landing at Miserey, France (about 60 miles west of Paris), in their craft, named the *Double Eagle II*.

CANADA: EDMONTON INTERNATIONAL FRINGE THEATRE FESTIVAL. Aug 17–27. Edmonton, AB. A ten-day extravaganza of new plays, old plays, dance, music, mime and street entertainment. More than 1,000 performances of 135 productions in 30 indoor and outdoor theatres. Performers from around the world. Regarded as the largest and most exciting festival of alternative theatre in North America. Est attendance: 500,000. For info: Fringe Theatre Adventures, 10330-84 Ave, Edmonton, AB, Canada T6E 2G9. Phone: (780) 448-9000. Web: www.fringetheatreadventures.ca.

CHASE, HARRISON V.: BIRTH ANNIVERSARY. Aug 17, 1913. Cofounder and coeditor of *Chase's Annual Events*, professor at Florida State University, born at Big Rapids, MI. Died Feb 6, 2000, at Tallahassee, FL.

CLINTON'S "MEANING OF 'IS' IS": ANNIVERSARY. Aug 17, 1998. During grand jury hearings that sought to clarify President Bill Clinton's relationship with Monica Lewinsky, Clinton engaged in some semantic fine-tuning: "It depends on what your meaning of 'is' is. If 'is' means 'is and never has been' that's one thing—if it means 'there is none,' that was a completely true statement." Clinton also parsed the meanings of "alone," "sexual relations" and "sex." His testimony was later televised to the nation on Sept 21.

CROCKETT, DAVID "DAVY": BIRTH ANNIVERSARY. Aug 17, 1786. American frontiersman, adventurer and soldier, born at Hawkins County, TN. Died during final heroic defense of the Alamo, Mar 6, 1836, at San Antonio, TX. In his *Autobiography* (1834), Crockett wrote, "I leave this rule for others when I'm dead, Be always sure you're right—then go ahead."

FORT SUMTER SHELLED BY NORTHERN FORCES: ANNIVERSARY. Aug 17, 1863. In what would become a long siege, Union forces began shelling Fort Sumter at Charleston, SC. The site of the first shots fired during the Civil War on Apr 12, 1861, Sumter endured the siege for a year and a half before being returned to Union hands.

FULTON SAILS STEAMBOAT: ANNIVERSARY. Aug 17, 1807. Robert Fulton began the first American steamboat trip between Albany and New York, NY, on a boat later called the *Clermont*. After years of promoting submarine warfare, Fulton engaged in a partnership with Robert R. Livingston, the US minister to France, allowing Fulton to design and construct a steamboat. His first success came in August 1803 when he launched a steam-powered vessel on the Seine. That same year the US Congress granted Livingston and Fulton exclusive rights to operate steamboats on New York waters during the next 20 years. The first Albany–to–New York trip took 32 hours to travel the 150-mile course. Although his efforts were labeled "Fulton's Folly" by his detractors, his success allowed the partnership to begin commercial service the next year, Sept 4, 1808.

GABON: INDEPENDENCE DAY. Aug 17. National holiday. Commemorates independence from France in 1960.

GOLDWYN, SAMUEL: BIRTH ANNIVERSARY. Aug 17, 1882. Motion picture producer and industry pioneer, born Samuel Goldfish, at Warsaw, Poland. Goldwyn died at Los Angeles, CA, Jan 31, 1974. Attributed to Goldwyn is the observation: "Anybody who goes to see a psychiatrist ought to have his head examined."

INDONESIA: INDEPENDENCE DAY. Aug 17. National holiday. Republic proclaimed in 1945. It was only after several years of fighting, however, that Indonesia was formally granted its independence by the Netherlands, Dec 27, 1949.

KENTUCKY STATE FAIR (WITH WORLD'S CHAMPIONSHIP HORSE SHOW). Aug 17–27. Kentucky Fair and Expo Center, Louisville, KY. Midway, concerts by nationally known artists and the World's Championship Horse Show. Since 1904. Est attendance: 650,000. For info: Media Office, KY Fair and Expo Ctr, Box 37130, Louisville, KY 40233. Phone: (502) 367-5000 or (502) 367-5180. Web: www.kyfairexpo.org or www .kystatefair.org.

LEWIS AND CLARK BICENTENNIAL NATIONAL SIGNATURE EVENT: REUNION AT THE HOME OF SAKAKAWEA. Aug 17–20. New Town, ND. On Aug 12, 1806, Lewis and Clark reunited on the Missouri River near the present-day headquarters of the Mandan, Hidatsa and Arikara Nation. The expedition traveled on to the Knife River Hidatsa and Mandan villages and days later, bid farewell to their interpreters Sakakawea and Toussaint Charbonneau. On Aug 20, 1806, the Expedition left what is now North Dakota. In August 2006, the Mandan, Hidatsa and Arikara Nation of North Dakota will commemorate the return of the Corps of Discovery to their homelands and the reunion of Sakakawea at Awatixa, her Hidatsa home. The major themes of this signature event will center on Sakakawea and her life before, during and after the expedition; the Missouri River and its impact on the lives of the Mandan, Hidatsa, Arikara and other tribes that hold this river sacred; tribal leadership and the political, social, and ceremonial organization of tribes 200 years ago and today; tribal trade networks and international trade. This four-day event will feature scholarly symposia, re-enactments, dramatic presentations, an art exhibition and trade fair, indigenous games, land and water parades, singing and traditional dance competition and a fur trade rendezvous. For info:

Claryca Mandan, Mandan, Hidatsa, Arikara Nation, PO Box 610, New Town, ND 58763. Phone: (701) 627-2870. Fax: (701) 627-2873. Web: www.mhanation.com or www.lewisandclark200.org.

MACHIAS WILD BLUEBERRY FESTIVAL. Aug 17–20. Machias, ME. Harvest festival includes crafts sale, lobster boil, five-mile race, entertainment, children's parade, blueberry foods and a wild blueberry pie-eating contest. Annually, the third weekend in August. Est attendance: 22,000. For info: Machias Wild Blueberry Festival, PO Box 265, Machias, ME 04654. Phone: (207) 255-6665. Web: www.machiasblueberry.com.

MILWAUKEE IRISH FEST. Aug 17–20. Milwaukee, WI. 26th annual. World's largest Irish music and cultural event, with the best of Irish and Irish American music, dance and theater on 15 stages. Activities include a cultural village, sports, contests, parades, displays, food, marketplace and children's activities. Weeklong summer school (open to the public) precedes the festival. Annually, the third weekend in August. Est attendance: 130,000. For info: Milwaukee Irish Fest, 1532 Wauwatosa Ave, Milwaukee, WI 53213. Phone: (414) 476-3378. E-mail: ifest@ execpc.com. Web: www.irishfest.com.

NEVADA STATE FAIR. Aug 17–20 (dates subject to change). Reno Livestock Events Center, Reno, NV. State entertainment and carnival, with creative living, agriculture and commercial exhibits. Est attendance: 60,000. For info: Nevada State Fair, 1350-A N Wells Ave, Reno, NV 89512. Phone: (775) 688-5767. Fax: (775) 688-5763. E-mail: info@nvstatefair.com. Web: www.nv statefair.com.

POWERS, FRANCIS GARY: BIRTH ANNIVERSARY. Aug 17, 1929. One of America's most famous aviators, Francis Gary Powers was born at Jenkins, KY. The CIA agent, pilot of a U-2 overflight across the Soviet Union, was shot down May 1, 1960, near Sverdlovsk, USSR. He was tried, convicted and sentenced to 10 years' imprisonment, at Moscow, USSR, in August 1960. Returned to the US in 1962, in exchange for an imprisoned Soviet spy (Colonel Rudolf Abel), he found an unwelcoming homeland. Powers died in a helicopter crash near Los Angeles, CA, Aug 2, 1977.

SANDCASTLE DAY. Aug 17. Making sandcastles at the beach is a time-honored family tradition. Today is a day to recognize this tradition and celebrate it at beaches everywhere! For info: David Benson, 13116 Frog Hollow Ct, Oak Hill, VA 20171. Phone: (703) 471-5784. E-mail: David.C.Benson@saic.com.

SOLDIERS' REUNION CELEBRATION. Aug 17. Newton, NC. Parade climaxes the 117th annual soldiers' reunion celebration—"oldest patriotic event of its kind in the US, honoring all veterans." Annually, the third Thursday in August. Concerts, arts, crafts, food and games. Est attendance: 31,000. For info: Soldiers' Reunion Committee, Box 267, Newton, NC 28658. Phone: (828) 464-2383.

SUN PRAIRIE'S SWEET CORN FESTIVAL. Aug 17–20. Sun Prairie, WI. Family-oriented fun. Carnival, midget auto races, parade, beer, brats, food, exhibits, entertainment, craft fair and tons of hot, buttered sweet corn. Est attendance: 100,000. For info: Chamber of Commerce, 109 E Main, Sun Prairie, WI 53590. Phone: (608) 837-4547. Fax: (608) 837-8765. E-mail: sprairie@ merr.com. Web: www.sunprairiechamber.com.

SWEDEN: SOUR HERRING PREMIERE. Aug 17. By ordinance, the year's supply of sour herring may begin to be sold on the third Thursday in August.

	S	M	T	W	T	F	S
August			1	2	3	4	5
2006	6	7	8	9	10	11	12
	13	14	15	16	17	18	19
	20	21	22	23	24	25	26
	27	28	29	30	31		

TELLURIDE MUSHROOM FESTIVAL. Aug 17–20. Telluride, CO. To educate people about the types of wild mushrooms—edible, poisonous, psychoactive—and their cultivation. Est attendance: 250. For info: Fungophile, Inc, Box 480503, Denver, CO 80248-0503. Phone: (303) 296-9359. Fax: (303) 296-9359. E-mail: lodomyco@earthlink.net. Web: www.shroom festival.com.

TURKISH EARTHQUAKE: ANNIVERSARY. Aug 17, 1999. A quake with a magnitude of 7.4 struck northwestern Turkey where 45 percent of the population lives. More than 17,000 died and thousands more remained missing. Many of the deaths were due to the shoddy construction of apartment houses. Aftershocks in the region through September 1999 resulted in more deaths. On Nov 12, 1999, a magnitude 7.2 earthquake struck Turkey, killing more than 800 people. Also in 1999 there were earthquakes in Greece (139 dead) and Taiwan (2,200 dead and many missing).

BIRTHDAYS TODAY

Belinda Carlisle, 48, singer (The Go-Go's, "Mad About You"), born Hollywood, CA, Aug 17, 1958.

Norm Coleman, 57, US Senator (R, Minnesota), born Brooklyn, NY, Aug 17, 1949.

Robert De Niro, 63, actor (Oscars for *Raging Bull, The Godfather Part II; Taxi Driver*), born New York, NY, Aug 17, 1943.

W. Mark Felt, 93, former Associate Director of the Federal Bureau of Investigation (Nixon administration), born at Twin Falls, ID, Aug 17, 1913.

Jonathan Franzen, 47, author (*The Corrections*), born Western Springs, IL, Aug 17, 1959.

Robert Joy, 55, actor (*Atlantic City, Desperately Seeking Susan, Longtime Companion*), born Montreal, QC, Canada, Aug 17, 1951.

Christian Laettner, 37, NBA forward, member of the Dream Team in the 1992 Olympics, born Angola, NY, Aug 17, 1969.

Maureen O'Hara, 86, actress (*Miracle on 34th Street, The Hunchback of Notre Dame*), born Dublin, Ireland, Aug 17, 1920.

Sean Penn, 46, actor (Oscar for *Mystic River, Dead Man Walking*), born Santa Monica, CA, Aug 17, 1960.

Nelson Piquet, 54, former auto racer, born Brasilia, Brazil, Aug 17, 1952.

Guillermo Vilas, 54, former tennis player, born Mar del Plata, Argentina, Aug 17, 1952.

Donnie Wahlberg, 37, actor ("Band of Brothers," *Diamond Men*), former singer (New Kids on the Block), born Boston, MA, Aug 17, 1969.

AUGUST 18 — FRIDAY

Day 230 — 135 Remaining

AMERICAN NEUTRALITY APPEAL: ANNIVERSARY. Aug 18, 1914. President Woodrow Wilson followed his Aug 4th Proclamation of Neutrality with an appeal to the American people to remain impartial in thought and deed with respect to the war that was raging in Europe (World War I).

BAD POETRY DAY. Aug 18. After all the "good" poetry you were forced to study in school, here's a chance for a payback. Invite some friends over, compose some really rotten verse and send it to your old high school English teacher. [©2003 by WH.] For info: Thomas & Ruth Roy, Wellcat Holidays, 2418 Long Ln, Lebanon, PA 17046. Phone: (717) 279-0184. E-mail: info@well cat.com. Web: www.wellcat.com.

BIRTH CONTROL PILLS SOLD: ANNIVERSARY. Aug 18, 1960. The first commercially produced oral contraceptives were marketed by the G.D. Searle Company of Illinois. The pill, developed by Gregory Pincus, had been undergoing clinical trials since 1954.

CANADA: COE HILL AGRICULTURAL FAIR. Aug 18–19. Coe Hill, ON. Competitions for best vegetables and animals, along with kids' games, auto thrill show and music. Est attendance: 5,000. For info: Bancroft and District Chamber of Commerce, PO Box 539, Bancroft, ON, Canada K0L 1C0. Phone: (613) 332-1513. Fax: (613) 332-2119. E-mail: chamber@commerce.ban croft.on.ca. Web: www.bancroftdistrict.com.

CANADA: NOVA SCOTIA'S GEM AND MINERAL SHOW. Aug 18–20. Parrsboro, NS. Only gem and mineral show in the Maritime Provinces. US and Canadian dealers bring rocks, minerals, beads, jewelry and jewelry findings as well as other items made from rocks and minerals. Take a geological walk, tour the exhibits, take part in workshops and demonstrations or watch the professionals do their work. Est attendance: 2,000. For info: Carol Corbett, PO Box 640, 162 Two Island Rd, Parrsboro, NS, Canada B0M 1S0. Phone: (866) 856-DINO or (902) 254-3814. Fax: (902) 254-3666. E-mail: corbettc@gov.ns.ca. Web: museum.gov.ns.ca/fgm.

CANADA: YUKON RIVER BATHTUB RACE. Aug 18–20 (tentative). Beginning in Whitehorse, YT. Annual 462-mile bathtub race from Whitehorse to Dawson. Est attendance: 1,500. For info: Yukon Sourdough Rendezvous Society, Box 31721, Whitehorse, YT, Canada Y1A 6L3. Phone: (867) 667-2148. Fax: (867) 668-6755. E-mail: ysr@polarcom.com. Web: www.tubrace.com.

CLEMENTE, ROBERTO: BIRTH ANNIVERSARY. Aug 18, 1934. National League baseball player, born at Carolina, Puerto Rico. Drafted by the Pittsburgh Pirates in 1954, he played his entire major league career with them. Clemente died in a plane crash Dec 31, 1972, while on a mission of mercy to Nicaragua to deliver supplies he had collected for survivors of an earthquake. He was elected to the Baseball Hall of Fame in 1973.

COBBLESTONE FESTIVAL. Aug 18–20. Falls City, NE. Includes games, sporting events, contests, draft horse pull, bull riding, carnival rides, flea market, food concessions, fishing contest, parade, craft demos and more. Est attendance: 5,000. For info: Chamber of Commerce, 1705 Stone St, Falls City, NE 68355. Phone: (402) 245-4228. Fax: (402) 245-4228. E-mail: fcchamber@sentco.net.

DARE, VIRGINIA: BIRTH ANNIVERSARY. Aug 18, 1587 (OS). Virginia Dare, the first child of English parents to be born in the New World, was born to Ellinor and Ananias Dare, at Roanoke Island, NC, Aug 18, 1587. When a ship arrived to replenish their supplies in 1591, the settlers (including Virginia Dare) had vanished, without leaving a trace of the settlement.

ELWOOD GLASS FESTIVAL. Aug 18–20. Elwood, IN. Glass factory tours, parade, craft market, flea market, quilt show, entertainment, carnival, helicopter rides, kids activities and more. Est attendance: 20,000. For info: Chamber of Commerce, 108 S Anderson St, Elwood, IN 46036. Phone: (765) 552-0180. E-mail: elwoodchamber@yahoo.com.

FESTIVAL OF THE LITTLE HILLS. Aug 18–20. Frontier Park and Historic Main, St. Charles, MO. The largest festival of the year. Includes more than 350 craft booths, live music and food and beverage booths. Annually, the third weekend in August. Est attendance: 300,000. For info: St. Charles Conv and Visitors Bureau, 230 S Main, St. Charles, MO 63301. Phone: (800) 366-2427 or (636) 946-7776. Web: www.festivalofthelittlehills.com.

HAWAII ADMISSION DAY HOLIDAY. Aug 18. The third Friday in August is observed as a state holiday each year, recognizing the anniversary of Hawaii's statehood. Hawaii became the 50th state Aug 21, 1959.

LEADVILLE TRAIL 100 ULTRAMARATHON. Aug 18–19. Leadville, CO. One of the toughest 100-mile foot races in the country, the course goes through the Rocky Mountains 50 miles to the ghost town of Winfield and back. Runners begin at 4 AM and must complete the race in 30 hours. All race applications mailed by Jan 2. Sponsor: Leadville Trail 100, Inc. Est attendance: 5,000. For info: Leadville Chamber of Commerce, PO Box 861, Leadville, CO 80461. Phone: (719) 486-3900 or (800) 933-3901. Fax: (719) 486-8478. E-mail: leadville@leadvilleusa.com. Web: www.leadvilleusa.com.

LEWIS, MERIWETHER: BIRTH ANNIVERSARY. Aug 18, 1774. American explorer (of Lewis and Clark expedition), born at Albemarle County, VA. Died Oct 11, 1809, near Nashville, TN.

LITTLE LEAGUE BASEBALL WORLD SERIES. Aug 18–27. Williamsport, PA. Sixteen teams from the US and foreign countries compete for the World Championship. Est attendance: 315,000. For info: Little League International, Box 3485, Williamsport, PA 17701. Phone: (570) 326-1921. Web: www.little league.org.

MAIL-ORDER CATALOG: ANNIVERSARY. Aug 18, 1872. The first mail-order catalog was published by Montgomery Ward. It was only a single sheet of paper. By 1904 the Montgomery Ward catalog weighed four pounds. In 1985 Montgomery Ward closed its catalog operation; in 2000 it announced the closing of its retail stores.

MOUNTAIN MAN RENDEZVOUS. Aug 18–20. Old Mission State Park, Cataldo, ID. 1800s fur trappers and traders, in period clothing. Features a primitive bow shoot. Est attendance: 2,500. For info: Roger Howard, Old Mission State Park, PO Box 30, Cataldo, ID 83810-0030. Phone: (208) 682-3814. Fax: (208) 682-4032. E-mail: old@idpr.state.id.us.

MUDDY FROGWATER COUNTRY CLASSIC FESTIVAL. Aug 18–20. Yantis Park, Milton-Freewater, OR. Arts, crafts, food, karaoke, country music, frog jumping contest, book sale, square dancing, firefighters' water fight, 3-on-3 basketball tournament, corn roast, watermelon feed and softball tournament. Annually, the third weekend in August. Est attendance: 5,000. For info: Milton-Freewater Area Chamber of Commerce, 505 Ward St, Milton-Freewater, OR 97862. Phone: (541) 938-5563. Fax: (541) 938-5564. E-mail: mfmdfrog@oregontrail.net. Web: www.mfchamber.com.

NINETEENTH AMENDMENT TO US CONSTITUTION RATIFIED: ANNIVERSARY. Aug 18, 1920. The 19th Amendment extended the right to vote to women.

NORTHEASTERN WISCONSIN ANTIQUE POWER AND MACHINERY SHOW THRESHEREE. Aug

August 2006	S	M	T	W	T	F	S
			1	2	3	4	5
	6	7	8	9	10	11	12
	13	14	15	16	17	18	19
	20	21	22	23	24	25	26
	27	28	29	30	31		

18–20. Sturgeon Bay, WI. Continuous display of operating antique machinery, antique tractor pull, barefoot horse pull, crafts, games for kids, food and refreshments. Annually, the third weekend in August. Est attendance: 3,000. For info: Bernie Geisel. Phone: (920) 743-4859. Or Josie Bochek. Phone: (920) 743-5251. E-mail: coldcomfortfarms@hotmail.com.

POTATO FEAST DAYS. Aug 18–20. Houlton, ME. Potato Feast supper, Parade of Dolls, potato games for kids, entertainment, townwide sales, fun run, classic car show, arts and crafts fair, potato-barrel rolling contest and much more. For info: Greater Houlton Chamber of Commerce, 109 Main St, Houlton, ME 04730. Phone: (207) 532-4216. E-mail: chamber@greaterhoulton.com. Web: www.greaterhoulton.com.

TEXAS RANCH ROUNDUP. Aug 18–19. MPEC Exhibit Hall & Kay Yeager Coliseum, Wichita Falls, TX. Cowboys from prestigious ranches in Texas compete in the events that make up their daily work. Cattle roping and penning and other rodeo-type events plus ranch cooking contests, ranch talent contests. Est attendance: 18,000. For info: Wichita Falls Conv and Visitors Bureau, 1000 5th St, Wichita Falls, TX 76301. Phone: (800) 799-6732 or (940) 716-5500. Fax: (940) 716-5509. Web: www.wichitafalls.org.

TRAILS WEST!® Aug 18–20. Civic Center Park, St. Joseph, MO. Arts festival celebrating St. Joseph's unique cultural heritage. Fine arts, crafts and folk art, wide variety of taste-tempting food, beer and wine garden, children's activities and four entertainment stages. Est attendance: 80,000. For info: Marketing Manager, Allied Arts Council, 118 S 8th, St. Joseph, MO 64501. Phone: (800) 216-7080 or (816) 233-0231. Fax: (816) 233-6704. E-mail: artstaff@stjoearts.org. Web: www.StJoeArts.org.

WESTERN IDAHO FAIR. Aug 18–27. Boise, ID. 109th annual. Largest fair in the state, including four stages of entertainment on the grounds with local and regional talent, three nights of grandstand concerts, carnival midway and 70 food booths. Est attendance: 254,000. For info: Bob Batista, Mgr, Western Idaho Fair, 5610 Glenwood, Boise, ID 83714. Phone: (208) 287-5650. Fax: (208) 375-9972. Web: www.idahofair.com.

BIRTHDAYS TODAY

Elayne Boosler, 54, comedienne, born Brooklyn, NY, Aug 18, 1952.

Rosalynn (Eleanor) Smith Carter, 79, former First Lady, wife of Jimmy Carter, 38th president of the US, born Plains, GA, Aug 18, 1927.

Bobby Higginson, 36, baseball player, born Philadelphia, PA, Aug 18, 1970.

Mike Johanns, 56, US Secretary of Agriculture, former Governor of Nebraska (R), born Osage, IA, Aug 18, 1950.

Luc Montagnier, 74, virologist, discovered the AIDS virus in 1983, born Chabris, France, Aug 18, 1932.

Martin Mull, 63, actor, comedian ("Sabrina, the Teenage Witch," "Roseanne"), born Chicago, IL, Aug 18, 1943.

Edward Norton, 37, actor (*Primal Fear, American History X*), born Boston, MA, Aug 18, 1969.

Roman Polanski, 73, filmmaker (*Rosemary's Baby, Macbeth, Chinatown*), born Paris, France, Aug 18, 1933.

Robert Redford, 69, actor (*Butch Cassidy and the Sundance Kid, The Sting, The Natural*), director (*A River Runs Through It*, Oscar for *Ordinary People*), born Santa Monica, CA, Aug 18, 1937.

Christian Slater, 37, actor (*Heathers, Broken Arrow, Pump Up the Volume*), born New York, NY, Aug 18, 1969.

Madeleine Stowe, 48, actress (*The Last of the Mohicans, Short Cuts*), born Los Angeles, CA, Aug 18, 1958.

Patrick Swayze, 52, dancer, actor ("North and South," *Dirty Dancing*), born Houston, TX, Aug 18, 1954.

Malcolm-Jamal Warner, 36, actor ("The Cosby Show"), born Jersey City, NJ, Aug 18, 1970.

Shelley Winters, 84, actress (Oscars for *A Patch of Blue, The Diary of Anne Frank*), born Shelly Schrift at St. Louis, MO, Aug 18, 1922.

AUGUST 19 — SATURDAY
Day 231 — 134 Remaining

AFGHANISTAN: INDEPENDENCE DAY. Aug 19. National day. Gained independence from British control, Treaty of Rawalpindi in 1919.

AMERICAN SOCIETY OF ASSOCIATION EXECUTIVES ANNUAL MEETING AND EXPOSITION. Aug 19–22. Boston, MA. Major meeting for ASAE members, nonmembers and suppliers including education sessions, trade show, speakers and networking events. Est attendance: 5,000. For info: American Society of Assn Executives, 1575 I St NW, Washington, DC 20005. Phone: (202) 626-2723. Fax: (202) 371-8825. E-mail: pr@asaenet.org. Web: www.asaenet.org.

ANTIQUE MARINE ENGINE EXPOSITION. Aug 19–20. Mystic Seaport, Mystic, CT. Collectors from across the US and Canada gather for an annual exposition of pre–World War II marine engines and engine models. For info: Mystic Seaport, 75 Greenmanville Ave, PO Box 6000, Mystic, CT 06355-0990. Phone: (860) 572-5315 or (888) 973-2767. Web: www.mystic seaport.org.

BATTLE OF BLUE LICKS CELEBRATION. Aug 19–20. Blue Licks Battlefield State Park, Mount Olivet, KY. Commemorates the anniversary of Revolutionary War Battle of Blue Licks (which involved Daniel Boone). Living-history demonstrations, arts, crafts, games, competitions and battle reenactment. Annually, the third weekend in August. Est attendance: 3,000. For info: Doug Price, Park Mgr, Blue Licks Battlefield State Resort Pk, PO Box 66, Mt Olivet, KY 41064-0066. Phone: (859) 289-5507. Fax: (859) 289-5409. Web: www.state.ky.us/agencies/parks/bluelick .htm.

BIKE VAN BUREN. Aug 19–20. Van Buren County, IA. A laid-back bicycle tour of the villages, landmarks and landscape of this rural Iowa county. The "red carpet of hospitality" is rolled out for the bikers as they pass through. Annually, the third weekend in August. Est attendance: 500. For info: Villages of Van Buren, Inc, PO Box 9, Keosauqua, IA 52565. Phone: (800) 868-7822. Fax: (319) 293-7116. E-mail: info@villagesofvanburen.com. Web: www .villagesofvanburen.com.

"BLACK COW" ROOT BEER FLOAT CREATED: ANNIVERSARY. Aug 19, 1893. Frank J. Wisner, owner of Cripple Creek Brewing, served the first root beer float in Cripple Creek, CO. Inspired by the moon-lit view of snow-capped Cow Mountain, he added a scoop of ice cream to his Myers Avenue Red root beer and began serving it as the "Black Cow Mountain." Kids loved it and shortened the name to "Black Cow." Cripple Creek Brewing still sells beverages based on the original formulas. For info: Michael Lynn, Cripple Creek Brewing, 23244 Rebecca Ct, Naperville, IL 60564. Phone: (630) 904-0022. E-mail: lbartl6415@aol.com. Web: www.cripplecreekbrewing.com.

BLUE CLAW CRAB CRAFT SHOW & CRAB RACE. Aug 19. Harvey Cedars, NJ. Crafters displaying their goods at Sunset Park. Crab race determines fastest crab on Long Beach Island. For info: Harvey Cedars Activity Committee, PO Box 3185, Harvey Cedars, NJ 08008. Phone: (609) 361-7990. Fax: (609) 494-8343. Web: www.harveycedars.org.

CANADA: OJIBWA KEESHIGUN. Aug 19–20. Fort William Historical Park, Thunder Bay, ON. A celebration of native culture. Taste historic foods, enjoy unique demonstrations and join in crafts and games. Experience the atmosphere with traditional singing and dancing. Annually, late August. Est attendance: 3,000. For info: Marty Mascarin, Communications Officer, Vickers Heights PO, Thunder Bay, ON, Canada P0T 2Z0. Phone: (807) 473-2326 or (807) 577-8461. Fax: (807) 473-2327. E-mail: info @fwhp.ca. Web: www.fwhp.ca.

CHANEL, COCO: BIRTH ANNIVERSARY. Aug 19, 1883. The most important fashion designer of the 20th century was born Gabrielle Chanel in rural Saumur, France. After starting out in a millinery shop, she began a fashion revolution when moving on to couture fashion in the late teens: using men's clothing (pants) for women's wear; creating simple, comfortable clothing that was nonetheless elegant; making dramatic use of costume jewelry (especially ropes of pearls) and popularizing the "little black dress" and sportswear. She was the first couturier to put her name on a signature perfume: Chanel No. 5 (created in 1921, it was an immediate sensation and today sells every 30 seconds around the world). After closing her shop with the outbreak of World War II, Chanel reopened it in 1954 and introduced her signature suit of collarless, bias-trimmed jacket with skirt. "Elegance does not consist in putting on a new dress," she once stated. The fashion icon died on Jan 10, 1971, at Paris, France.

CLASSIC BOAT SHOW. Aug 19–20. Tuckerton, NJ. Join the Tuckerton Seaport and the Philadelphia Chapter of the Antique and Classic Boat Society for two splendid days of classic wood and glass boat exhibitors, demonstrations, and entertainment. Watch the parent/child boat building contest or take a cruise up Tuckerton Creek. The Classic Boat Show is fun for the whole family. Annually, the third weekend in August. Est attendance: 2,500. For info: Karen DeRosa, Tuckerton Seaport, 120 W Main St, PO Box 52, Tuckerton, NJ 08087. Phone: (609) 296-8868. Fax: (609) 296-5810. E-mail: info@tuckertonseaport.org. Web: www.tuckertonseaport.org.

CLINTON, WILLIAM JEFFERSON (BILL): 60th BIRTHDAY. Aug 19, 1946. The 42nd US president (1993–2001), born at Hope, AR.

COSHOCTON CANAL FESTIVAL. Aug 19–20. Coshocton, OH. Celebrates the arrival of first canal boat at Port Roscoe. Crafts, demonstrations and live entertainment. Annually, the third weekend in August. Est attendance: 14,000. For info: Roscoe Village Fdtn, 381 Hill St, Coshocton, OH 43812. Phone: (800) 877-1830 or (740) 622-9310. Fax: (740) 623-6555. E-mail: rv marketing@roscoevillage.com. Web: www.roscoevillage.com.

COUP ATTEMPT IN THE SOVIET UNION: 15th ANNIVERSARY. Aug 19, 1991. A Soviet coalition of hard-line communists staged a coup d'état, removing President Mikhail Gorbachev from power. Gorbachev had been on vacation in the Crimea and was due to return to Moscow the next day to sign a treaty that would have taken much of the power away from the central USSR government and given it to the republics signing the treaty. On the third day, Aug 21, in the face of massive public resistance, the conspirators gave up, flew to the Crimea hoping to negotiate with Gorbachev and were taken into custody, but Gorbachev returned to Moscow in an extremely weakened position. The independence of the republics, the dissolution of the Soviet Union and the loss of power by Gorbachev soon followed.

FARNSWORTH, PHILO: 100th BIRTH ANNIVERSARY. Aug 19, 1906. Farnsworth was a television pioneer who conceived of the idea of television broadcasting while still in high school and realized his dream at 21. His first transmitted image was of a dollar sign. Farnsworth was born at Beaver, UT, and died on Mar 11, 1971, at Salt Lake City, UT.

FORBES, MALCOLM: BIRTH ANNIVERSARY. Aug 19, 1919. Publisher, born at New York, NY. Malcolm Forbes was an unabashed proponent of capitalism, and his beliefs led to his colorful and successful climb to the top of the magazine-publishing industry. Known as much for his lavish lifestyle as his publishing acumen, Forbes was also an avid motorcyclist and hot-air balloonist. He died Feb 24, 1990, at Far Hills, NJ.

GERMAN PLEBISCITE: ANNIVERSARY. Aug 19, 1934. In a plebiscite, 89.9 percent of German voters approved giving Chancellor Adolf Hitler the additional office of president, placing the Führer in uncontestable supreme command of that country's destiny.

LARDNER, RING, JR: BIRTH ANNIVERSARY. Aug 19, 1915. Born Chicago, IL, Aug 19, 1915, son of fabled baseball writer and humorist Ring Lardner. Lardner, Jr, was an Academy Award–winning screenwriter (Oscar for *Woman of the Year*; *M*A*S*H*), and he also wrote for television. He was a member of the Hollywood Ten, a group of film industry executives sent to federal prison in 1950 for their refusal to tell the House Un-American Activities Committee if they were members of the Communist Party. He served nine months, and was blacklisted for many years. Died at New York, NY, Oct 31, 2000.

MAINE HIGHLAND GAMES. Aug 19. Thomas Point Beach, Brunswick, ME. 28th annual. Presented by the Saint Andrew's Society of Maine. Bagpipe bands, Highland and Scottish dancing, Scottish arts and crafts fair, folksingers, Scottish fiddling, children's games, adult athletics including tossing of the caber, wheat sheaf toss and putting of the stone, Border collie herding demonstrations, Highland cattle and individual piping contests. American and Scottish foods galore. The only Scottish event of its kind held in Maine! Scots and non-Scots will enjoy the color, pageantry and friendly atmosphere. Est attendance: 8,000. For info: Thomas Point Beach, 29 Meadow Rd, Brunswick, ME 04011. Phone: (207) 725-6009. Web: www.thomaspointbeach.com.

NASH, OGDEN: BIRTH ANNIVERSARY. Aug 19, 1902. American writer, best remembered for his humorous verse. Born at Rye, NY; died May 19, 1971, at Baltimore, MD.

★**NATIONAL AVIATION DAY.** Aug 19. Presidential Proclamation 2343, of July 25, 1939, covers all succeeding years. Always Aug 19 of each year since 1939. Observed annually on anniversary of birth of Orville Wright, who piloted "first self-powered flight in history," Dec 17, 1903. First proclaimed by President Franklin D. Roosevelt.

NATIONAL HOMELESS ANIMALS DAY AND CANDLELIGHT VIGILS. Aug 19. A day to call attention to the fact that millions of healthy dogs and cats are killed each year in the US in animal shelters because of overpopulation—a problem that has a solution: Spay/Neuter! It stops the killing! The vigils memorialize the animals killed in the preceding year and sympathize with the caring shelter personnel who must take the lives of the animals. Vigils will be held throughout the US and beyond. For info: Intl Society for Animal Rights, Inc, Susan Dapsis, Pres, 965 Griffin Pond Rd, Clarks Summit, PA 18411-9214. Phone: (570) 586-2200. Fax: (570) 586-9580. E-mail: contact@ISAR online.org.

NEW WEST FEST. Aug 19–20. Fort Collins, CO. More than 300 artists showcase their creations during this festival, also featuring a carnival, kids activities, food booths, a beer garden, and three stages of local bands, singers, and dancers in "Old Town" Fort Collins. For info: Downtown Fort Collins Business Assoc, 19 Old Town Square, #230, Fort Collins, CO 80524. Phone: (970) 484-6500. E-mail: info@downtownfortcollins.com. Web: www .downtownfortcollins.com.

ROCKBRIDGE COMMUNITY FESTIVAL. Aug 19. Lexington, VA. Fun for all ages—crafts, exhibits, live music, food and games. For info: Lexington Visitors Bureau, 106 E Washington St, Lexington, VA 24450. Phone: (540) 463-3777. Fax: (540) 463-1105. E-mail: lexington@rockbridge.net.

RODDENBERRY, GENE: BIRTH ANNIVERSARY. Aug 19, 1921. The creator of the popular TV series "Star Trek," Gene Roddenberry was born at El Paso, TX. Turning from his first career as an airline pilot to writing, he created one of the most successful TV science fiction series ever. The original series, which ended its run in 1969, lives on in reruns, and led to other popu-

lar spin-off series. Ten films also have been spawned from the original concept. Roddenberry died Oct 24, 1991, at Santa Monica, CA.

SANDCASTLE & SCULPTURE DAY. Aug 19. Jetties Beach, Nantucket, MA. Islanders and visitors create masterpiece sandcastles and sand sculptures on the beach. This 33rd annual contest will last all afternoon and ribbons will be awarded in various categories. For info: Nantucket Chamber of Commerce, 48 Main St, Nantucket, MA 02554. Phone: (508) 228-1700. E-mail: info @nantucketchamber.org. Web: www.nantucketchamber.org.

SPACE MILESTONE: *SOYUZ T-7* (USSR). Aug 19, 1982. Launched from Tyuratam, USSR, with second woman in space (test pilot Svetlana Savitskaya) and two other cosmonauts. Docked at *Salyut 7* and visited the cosmonauts who had been in residence there for the three previous months before returning to Earth on Aug 27 in the *Soyuz T-5* vehicle that had been docked there. The *Soyuz T-7* returned to Earth Dec 10 with the remaining two cosmonauts.

SPACE MILESTONE: *SPUTNIK 5* (USSR). Aug 19, 1960. Space menagerie satellite with dogs Belka and Strelka, mice, rats, houseflies and plants launched. These passengers became first living organisms recovered from orbit when the satellite returned safely to Earth the next day.

WRIGHT, ORVILLE: BIRTH ANNIVERSARY. Aug 19, 1871. Aviation pioneer born at Dayton, OH, and died there Jan 30, 1948. See also: "Wright Brothers First Powered Flight: Anniversary" (Dec 17).

BIRTHDAYS TODAY

Adam Arkin, 50, actor ("Chicago Hope," "Northern Exposure"), born Brooklyn, NY, Aug 19, 1956.

William Jefferson Clinton, 60, 42nd president of the US, born Hope, AK, Aug 19, 1946.

Kevin Dillon, 41, actor (*Platoon, The Doors*), born Mamaroneck, NY, Aug 19, 1965.

Peter Gallagher, 51, actor (*sex, lies and videotape; Short Cuts*, "The O.C."), born New York, NY, Aug 19, 1955.

Tipper Gore, 58, wife of Al Gore, 45th vice president of the US, advocate for the homeless, mental health and children's causes, born Mary Elizabeth Aitcheson at Washington, DC, Aug 19, 1948.

Frank McCourt, 75, author (*Angela's Ashes, 'Tis*), born Brooklyn, NY, Aug 19, 1931.

Gerald McRaney, 58, actor ("Simon & Simon," "Major Dad"), born Collins, MS, Aug 19, 1948.

Diana Muldaur, 68, actress ("Star Trek: The Next Generation," "LA Law," *The Swimmer*), born New York, NY, Aug 19, 1938.

(Franklin) Storey Musgrave, 71, former astronaut, born Boston, MA, Aug 19, 1935.

Cindy Nelson, 51, former alpine skier, born Lutsen, MN, Aug 19, 1955.

Matthew Perry, 37, actor ("Friends," *Fools Rush In*), born Williamstown, MA, Aug 19, 1969.

Jill St. John, 66, actress (*Diamonds Are Forever*), born Jill Oppenheim at Los Angeles, CA, Aug 19, 1940.

Kyra Sedgwick, 41, actress (*Phenomenon, Born on the Fourth of July*), born New York, NY, Aug 19, 1965.

John Stamos, 43, actor ("General Hospital," "Full House"), born Los Angeles, CA, Aug 19, 1963.

Fred Thompson, 64, former US Senator (R, Tennessee), actor ("Law & Order," *In the Line of Fire*), born Sheffield, AL, Aug 19, 1942.

August 2006	S	M	T	W	T	F	S
			1	2	3	4	5
	6	7	8	9	10	11	12
	13	14	15	16	17	18	19
	20	21	22	23	24	25	26
	27	28	29	30	31		

AUGUST 20 — SUNDAY

Day 232 — 133 Remaining

BAMBOO CELEBRATION DAY. Aug 20. Honoring the unique group of garden lovers who are planting bamboo in the United States. Strict government restrictions enacted on Aug 20, 1912 have been loosened, allowing for limited American planting. This is an excellent day for seeking information on bamboo plants and celebrating their beauty and tenacity in gardens and their impressive symbolism in feng shui design. Annually, Aug 20. For info: Carol MacKenzie, 1805 Ironwood Way, Kissimmee, FL 34746. Phone: (407) 414-1605. E-mail: fengshuigardenassociation@msn.com.

DOG DAY ROAD RACE. Aug 20. Harvey Cedars, NJ. 28th annual. More than 800 runners will participate in this five-mile run. Sponsored by the High Point Volunteer Fire Company. For info: Art Ballinger, Dog Day Race, High Point Fire Co, PO Box 3219, Harvey Cedars, NJ 08008. Phone: (609) 361-9364. Web: www.harveycedars.org.

GUEST, EDGAR ALBERT: 125th BIRTH ANNIVERSARY. Aug 20, 1881. Newspaperman and author of folksy, homespun verse that enjoyed great popularity and was syndicated in more than 100 newspapers. Born at Birmingham, England; died at Detroit, MI, Aug 5, 1959. "Eddie Guest Day" usually proclaimed on birth anniversary in Detroit.

HARRISON, BENJAMIN: BIRTH ANNIVERSARY. Aug 20, 1833. The 23rd president of the US, born at North Bend, OH. He was the grandson of William Henry Harrison, 9th president of the US. His term of office, Mar 4, 1889–Mar 3, 1893, was preceded and followed by the presidential terms of Grover Cleveland (who thus became the 22nd and 24th president of the US). Harrison died at Indianapolis, IN, Mar 13, 1901.

HUNGARY: ST. STEPHEN'S DAY. Aug 20. National holiday. Commemorates the canonization of St. Stephen, king and founder of the state, in 1083. Under the Communists, commemorated as Constitution Day.

LOVECRAFT, H.P.: BIRTH ANNIVERSARY. Aug 20, 1890. Howard Phillips Lovecraft, American author of horror tales of the supernatural, a pioneering science fiction writer and a notable epistolarian, was born at Providence, RI, and died there Mar 15, 1937.

LUXEMBOURG: SCHUEBERMESS SHEPHERD'S FAIR. Aug 20–Sept 2. Fair dates from 1340. (Two weeks beginning on the next to last Sunday of August.)

MOROCCO: REVOLUTION OF THE KING AND THE PEOPLE: ANNIVERSARY. Aug 20. National holiday. Commemorates the response of the people to Sultan (later King) Sidi Muhammed being sent into exile in 1953 by the French.

NATIONAL SAVE YOUR SMILE WEEK. Aug 20–26. A week dedicated to the prevention of adult tooth loss. Seeing the mouth as part of the whole body, correct selection of dental professionals and most important reversing gum disease naturally. For info: S. Senzon, RDH, 32 Bridies Path, Southampton, NY 11968. Phone: (516) 287-6671. Fax: (516) 287-9737. E-mail: S.Senzon961@aol.com. Web: www.tooth.qpg.com.

O'HIGGINS, BERNARDO: BIRTH ANNIVERSARY. Aug 20, 1778. First ruler of Chile after its declaration of independence. Called the "Liberator of Chile." Born at Chillan, Chile. Died at Lima, Peru, Oct 24, 1842.

PLUTONIUM FIRST WEIGHED: ANNIVERSARY. Aug 20, 1942. University of Chicago scientist Glen Seaborg and his colleagues first weighed plutonium, the first man-made element.

PRESIDENT BENJAMIN HARRISON'S BIRTHDAY CELEBRATION. Aug 20. Indianapolis, IN, Harrison's hometown. Also free tours of the Victorian mansion. Est attendance: 500. For info: PR Dept, President Benjamin Harrison Home, 1230 N Delaware St, Indianapolis, IN 46202. Phone: (317) 631-1888. Fax: (317) 632-5488. E-mail: harrison@presidentbenjaminharrison.org. Web: www.pbhh.org.

REEVES, JIM: BIRTH ANNIVERSARY. Aug 20, 1924. Country music star Jim Reeves was born at Galloway, Panola County, TX, and died at Nashville, TN, July 31, 1964, when the single-engine plane in which he was traveling crashed in a dense fog. Reeves's biggest hit was "He'll Have to Go" (1959), and he was inducted into the Country Music Hall of Fame in 1967.

SAARINEN, EERO: BIRTH ANNIVERSARY. Aug 20, 1910. Born at Kirkkonummi, Finland, but raised in the United States by his architect father Eliel and sculptor mother, Saarinen was a leading postwar architect and furniture designer whose sculptural designs were in contrast to the reigning International Style. Saarinen died Sept 1, 1961, at Ann Arbor, MI.

SAARINEN, ELIEL: BIRTH ANNIVERSARY. Aug 20, 1873 (OS). Famed architect. Born at Helsinki, Finland. Died at Bloomfield Hills, MI, July 1, 1950.

SOUTH KOREA: INTERNATIONAL FEDERATION OF LIBRARY ASSOCIATIONS ANNUAL CONFERENCE. Aug 20–24. Seoul, South Korea. The theme for the 72nd annual conference is "Libraries: Dynamic Engines for the Knowledge and Information Society." For info: International Federation of Library Assns Conference, WLIC 2006 Seoul, Korean Library Assn, International Affairs, 60-1, Banpo-Dong, Seocho-Gu, Seoul, 137-702, South Korea. Phone: (82) 2-5354868. Fax: (82) 2-5355616. E-mail: wlic@ifla2006seoul.org. Web: www.ifla.org.

SPACE MILESTONE: *VIKING 1* AND *2* (US). Aug 20 and Sept 9, 1975. Sister ships launched toward Mars from Cape Canaveral, FL, on Aug 20 and Sept 9, 1975. *Viking 1*'s lander touched down on Mars July 20, 1976, and *Viking 2*'s lander on Sept 3, 1976. Sent back to Earth high-quality photographs, analysis of atmosphere, weather information and results of sophisticated experiments intended to determine whether life may be present on Mars.

SPACE MILESTONE: *VOYAGER 2* (US). Aug 20, 1977. This unmanned spacecraft journeyed past Jupiter in 1979, Saturn in 1981, Uranus in 1986 and Neptune in 1989, sending photographs and data back to scientists on Earth.

BIRTHDAYS TODAY

Joan Allen, 50, actress (*Searching for Bobby Fischer, Nixon, The Contender*), born Rochelle, IL, Aug 20, 1956.

Andy Benes, 39, former baseball player, born Evansville, IN, Aug 20, 1967.

Connie Chung, 60, journalist, born Constance Yu-Hwa at Washington, DC, Aug 20, 1946.

Tara Dakides, 31, snowboarder, born Mission Viejo, CA, Aug 20, 1975.

Isaac Hayes, 64, musician, singer, songwriter, born Covington, TN, Aug 20, 1942.

Todd Helton, 33, baseball player, born Knoxville, TN, Aug 20, 1973.

Donald (Don) King, 75, boxing promoter, born Cleveland, OH, Aug 20, 1931.

Mark Edward Langston, 46, former baseball player, born San Diego, CA, Aug 20, 1960.

Alfonso Raymond (Al) Lopez, 98, Hall of Fame baseball player and manager, born Tampa, FL, Aug 20, 1908.

Robert Plant, 58, singer, born Bromwich, England, Aug 20, 1948.

Al Roker, 52, meteorologist ("Today Show"), born Brooklyn, NY, Aug 20, 1954.

Theresa Saldana, 51, actress ("The Commish"), born Brooklyn, NY, Aug 20, 1955.

AUGUST 21 — MONDAY

Day 233 — 132 Remaining

AMERICAN BAR ASSOCIATION FOUNDING: ANNIVERSARY. Aug 21, 1878. Organized at Saratoga, NY.

AQUINO, BENIGNO: ASSASSINATION ANNIVERSARY. Aug 21, 1983. Filipino opposition leader Benigno S. Aquino, Jr, was shot and killed at the Manila airport on his return to the Philippines on Aug 21, 1983. The killing precipitated greater anti-Marcos feeling and figured significantly in the Feb 7, 1986, election that brought about the collapse of the government administration of Ferdinand E. Marcos and the inauguration of Corazon C. Aquino, widow of the slain man, as president.

BEARDSLEY, AUBREY VINCENT: BIRTH ANNIVERSARY. Aug 21, 1872. English artist and illustrator born at Brighton. Died at Menton, France, Mar 16, 1898.

CHAMBERLAIN, WILT: BIRTH ANNIVERSARY. Aug 21, 1936. Basketball Hall of Fame center, born at Philadelphia, PA. Died Oct 12, 1999, at Los Angeles, CA.

HAWAII: ADMISSION DAY: ANNIVERSARY. Aug 21, 1959. President Dwight Eisenhower signed a proclamation admitting Hawaii to the Union. The statehood bill had passed the previous March with a stipulation that statehood should be approved by a vote of Hawaiian residents. The referendum passed by a huge margin in June and Eisenhower proclaimed Hawaii the 50th state on Aug 21.

ISRA AL MI'RAJ: ASCENT OF THE PROPHET MUHAMMAD. Aug 21. Islamic calendar date: evening after Rajab 26, 1427. Commemorates the journey of the Prophet Muhammad from Mecca to Jerusalem, his ascension into the Seven Heavens and his return on the same night. Muslims believe that on that night Muhammad prayed together with Abraham, Moses and Jesus in the area of the Al-Aqsa Mosque in Jerusalem. The rock from which he is believed to have ascended to heaven to speak with God is the one inside The Dome of the Rock. Different methods for "anticipating" the visibility of the new moon crescent at Mecca are used by different Muslim groups. US date may vary. Began at sunset the preceding day.

POET'S DAY. Aug 21. A day for all poets to celebrate their special talents and the vision that makes them so wonderful and dear. Poet's Day is a time to share special thoughts about poets and poetry. (©2001 C. Daniel Rhodes) For info: C. Daniel Rhodes or Natalie Danielle Rhodes, 1900 Crossvine Rd, Hoover, AL 35244. Phone: (205) 908-6781. E-mail: rhodan@charter.net.

QUANTRILL'S RAID ON LAWRENCE, KANSAS: ANNIVERSARY. Aug 21, 1863. Confederate raider William Clarke Quantrill launched a predawn terrorist raid on Lawrence, KS, leaving 150 civilians dead and much of the town ruined. Quantrill had been denied a commission in the Southern army for his barbaric approach to war.

SEMINOLE TRIBE OF FLORIDA LEGALLY ESTABLISHED: ANNIVERSARY. Aug 21, 1957. In 1953 Congress adopted a proposal to terminate assistance to non-recognized Indian tribes. Seminole leaders and tribal members began to fight the proposal by drafting a constitution and charter for the Seminole Tribe. These were later approved by the Secretary of the Interior. On this date, a majority of tribal members voted to establish the Seminole Tribe of Florida. Today, 2,200 Seminoles live on five reservations in Florida.

★ ★ ★

	S	M	T	W	T	F	S
August			1	2	3	4	5
2006	6	7	8	9	10	11	12
	13	14	15	16	17	18	19
	20	21	22	23	24	25	26
	27	28	29	30	31		

SPACE MILESTONE: *GEMINI 5* (US). Aug 21, 1965. Launched on this date, this craft carrying astronauts Lieutenant Colonel Cooper and Lieutenant Commander Conrad orbited Earth 128 times for new international record of eight days.

SWEDISH LANGUAGE AND CULTURE DAY CAMP. Aug 21–25. West Riverside Historic Site, Cambridge, MN. Children learn to speak Swedish and understand Swedish culture through songs, games, language classes and craft classes. Families can see what the children have learned through a program at the end of the week. Fee is $50 per student. For info: Kathy McCully, Dir, Isanti County Historical Society, PO Box 525, Cambridge, MN 55008. Phone: (763) 689-4229. Fax: (763) 552-0740. E-mail: ichs@nsatel.net.

US AMATEUR (GOLF) CHAMPIONSHIP. Aug 21–27. Hazeltine National Golf Club, Chaska, MN. For info: US Golf Assn, Golf House, PO Box 708, Championship Dept, Far Hills, NJ 07931. Phone: (908) 234-2300. Fax: (908) 234-9687. E-mail: usga@usga.org. Web: www.usga.org.

BIRTHDAYS TODAY

Steve Case, 48, founder of America Online, born Oahu, HI, Aug 21, 1958.

Kim Cattrall, 50, actress ("Sex and the City," *Mannequin*), born Liverpool, England, Aug 21, 1956.

Jackie DeShannon, 62, singer, songwriter ("Put a Little Love in Your Heart"), born Hazel, KY, Aug 21, 1944.

James Robert (Jim) McMahon, 47, former football player, born Jersey City, NJ, Aug 21, 1959.

Kenny Rogers, 68, singer ("Lucille," "Lady"), born Houston, TX, Aug 21, 1938.

Melvin Van Peebles, 74, playwright (*Ain't Supposed to Die a Natural Death*), born Chicago, IL, Aug 21, 1932.

Peter Weir, 62, director (*Dead Poets Society, Gallipoli, The Truman Show*), born Sydney, Australia, Aug 21, 1944.

Clarence Williams III, 67, actor ("The Mod Squad," *Purple Rain*), born New York, NY, Aug 21, 1939.

Alicia Witt, 31, actress ("Cybill"), born Worcester, MA, Aug 21, 1975.

AUGUST 22 — TUESDAY

Day 234 — 131 Remaining

BATTLE OF STALINGRAD BEGINS: ANNIVERSARY. Aug 22, 1942. Having captured Sevastopol on the Crimea on July 2, after an eight-month seige, the Germans began an offensive to capture Stalingrad. During this five-month-long battle the city of 500,000 people dwindled to a population of 1,515. In the fighting Russia lost 750,000 troops, the Germans 400,000, the Romanians nearly 200,000 and the Italians 130,000—a total of 1,480,000. The last German strongholds at Stalingrad surrendered to the Russian Army on Feb 2, 1943.

BE AN ANGEL DAY. Aug 22. A day to do "one small act of service for someone. Be a blessing in someone's life." Annually, Aug 22. For info: Angel Heights Healing Center, Rev Jayne M. Howard-Feldman, PO Box 95, Upperco, MD 21155. Phone: (410) 833-6912. E-mail: earthangel4peace@aol.com. Web: earthangel4peace.com.

CAMEROON: VOLCANIC ERUPTION: 20th ANNIVERSARY. Aug 22, 1986. Deadly fumes from a presumed volcanic eruption under Lake Nios at Cameroon killed more than 1,500 persons. A similar occurrence two years earlier had killed 37 persons.

CARTIER-BRESSON, HENRI: BIRTH ANNIVERSARY. Aug 22, 1908. Pioneering photojournalist who cofounded the Magnum photo agency. Probably the most respected 20th-century photographer. Famous for looking for "the decisive moment." Born at Chanteloup, France, he died Aug 2, 2004, at I'lle-sur-Sorgue, France.

DEBUSSY, CLAUDE: BIRTH ANNIVERSARY. Aug 22, 1862. (Achille) Claude Debussy, French musician and composer, especially remembered for his impressionistic "tone poems," was born at St. Germain-en-Laye, France. He died at Paris, France, Mar 25, 1918.

HERRIMAN, GEORGE: BIRTH ANNIVERSARY. Aug 22, 1880. In 1910 when George Herriman introduced a cat and mouse as subplot characters to his comic strip "The Dingbat Family," their non-sequitur dialogue gained enough attention to result in a spin-off strip of their own. The superbly drafted "Krazy Kat and Ignatz" had as its central theme unrequited love. Kat loved Ignatz, but the malevolent mouse took every opportunity to throw bricks at the devoted cat. "Krazy Kat" was popular with a mass audience as well as artists and intellectuals, and it remained enormously popular after Herriman's death. Born at New Orleans, LA, he died at Hollywood, CA, Apr 25, 1944.

INTERNATIONAL YACHT RACE: ANNIVERSARY. Aug 22, 1851. A silver trophy (then known as the "Hundred Guinea Cup," and offered by the Royal Yacht Squadron) was won in a race around the Isle of Wight by the US yacht *America*. The trophy, later turned over to the New York Yacht Club, became known as the America's Cup.

KGB FOUNDER STATUE DISMANTLED: 15th ANNIVERSARY. Aug 22, 1991. In the wake of the popular revolt that smashed the right-wing Soviet coup, a crowd of 10,000 Muscovites watched as cranes dismantled a 14-ton statue of Felix Dzerzhinsky, a Polish intellectual tapped by Vladimir Lenin to organize the fledgling Soviet Union's secret police. After trucks had hauled away the massive likeness of Dzerzhinsky, Moscow residents adorned the statue's pedestal and the nearby KGB headquarters with graffiti.

LANGLEY, SAMUEL PIERPONT: BIRTH ANNIVERSARY. Aug 22, 1834. American astronomer, physicist and aviation pioneer for whom Langley Air Force Base, VA, is named. Born at Roxbury, MA, Langley died at Aiken, SC, Feb 27, 1906.

MORMON CHOIR FIRST PERFORMANCE: ANNIVERSARY. Aug 22, 1847. What would later become the world-famous Mormon Tabernacle Choir gave its first public performance at Salt Lake City, UT, for an outdoor meeting of The Church of Jesus Christ of Latter-day Saints. Widely known for its concert tours, recordings and weekly radio and television broadcasts from Temple Square, the choir's radio program "Music and the Spoken Word" is the longest continuously running radio program in network history, dating back to 1929.

RIEFENSTAHL, LENI: BIRTH ANNIVERSARY. Aug 22, 1902. Controversial actress and filmmaker who directed the infamous Nazi propaganda films *Triumph of the Will* (1934) and *Olympia* (1936). Both films are noted for innovative filming techniques. Born at Berlin, Germany, Riefenstahl died at Pöcking, Germany, on September 8, 2003.

SPAIN: INTERNATIONAL CONGRESS OF MATHEMATICIANS: MADRID 2006. Aug 22–30. Palacio Municipal de Congresos, Madrid. A major scientific event bringing together mathematicians from all over the world and demonstrating the vital role that mathematics play in our society. For info: International Congress of Mathematicians, International Math Union, Institute for Advanced Study, Einstein Dr, Prince-ton, NJ 08540. Fax: (609) 683-7605. E-mail: icm2006@uni congress.com. Web: www.icm2006.org or www.mathunion.org.

VIETNAM CONFLICT BEGINS: ANNIVERSARY. Aug 22, 1945. Less than a week after the Japanese surrender ended WWII, a team of Free French parachuted into southern Indochina in response to a successful coup by a Communist guerrilla named Ho Chi Minh in the French colony.

WILLARD, ARCHIBALD M.: BIRTH ANNIVERSARY. Aug 22, 1836. American artist, best known for his painting *The Spirit of '76*, was born at Bedford, OH. Willard died at Cleveland, OH, Oct 11, 1918.

BIRTHDAYS TODAY

Tori Amos, 43, musician, singer, songwriter, born Newton, NC, Aug 22, 1963.
Ray Bradbury, 86, author (*The Toynbee Convector, Fahrenheit 451*), born Waukegan, IL, Aug 22, 1920.
Gerald Paul Carr, 74, former astronaut, born Denver, CO, Aug 22, 1932.
Valerie Harper, 65, actress ("The Mary Tyler Moore Show," "Rhoda"), born Suffern, NY, Aug 22, 1941.
Steve Kroft, 61, coeditor, correspondent ("60 Minutes"), born Kokomo, IN, Aug 22, 1945.
Paul Leo Molitor, 50, former baseball player, born St. Paul, MN, Aug 22, 1956.
Duane Charles (Bill) Parcells, 65, football coach, born Englewood, NJ, Aug 22, 1941.
E. Annie Proulx, 71, author (*The Shipping News, Accordian Crimes*), born Norwich, CT, Aug 22, 1935.
Norman H. Schwarzkopf, 72, retired army general, born Trenton, NJ, Aug 22, 1934.
Cindy Williams, 58, actress (*American Graffiti*, "Laverne & Shirley"), born Van Nuys, CA, Aug 22, 1948.
Carl Michael Yastrzemski, 67, Hall of Fame baseball player, born Southampton, NY, Aug 22, 1939.

AUGUST 23 — WEDNESDAY

Day 235 — 130 Remaining

AMERICAN QUILTER'S SOCIETY QUILT EXPOSITION. Aug 23–26. Gaylord Opryland Resort, Nashville, TN. Contest quilts and special quilt exhibits. Workshops, lectures. Est attendance: 25,000. For info: American Quilter's Society, PO Box 3290, Paducah, KY 42002. Phone: (270) 898-7903. E-mail: shows@AQSquilt.com. Web: www.americanquilter.com.

FIRST MAN-POWERED FLIGHT: ANNIVERSARY. Aug 23, 1977. At Schafter, CA, Bryan Allen pedaled the 70-lb *Gossamer Condor* for a mile at a "minimal altitude of two pylons" in a flight certified by the Royal Aeronautical Society of Britain, winning a £50,000 prize offered by British industrialist Henry Kremer. See also: "First Man-Powered Flight Across English Channel: Anniversary" (June 12).

KELLY, GENE: BIRTH ANNIVERSARY. Aug 23, 1912. Actor, dancer, director, choreographer born at Pittsburgh, PA. His movies included the musicals *Singin' in the Rain* and *An American in Paris*. Kelly died at Beverly Hills, CA, Feb 2, 1996.

MASTERS, EDGAR LEE: BIRTH ANNIVERSARY. Aug 23, 1869. American poet, author of the *Spoon River Anthology*, was born at Garnett, KS. He died at Melrose Park, PA, Mar 5, 1950.

MOON PHASE: NEW MOON. Aug 23. Moon enters New Moon phase at 3:10 PM, EDT.

PERRY, OLIVER HAZARD: BIRTH ANNIVERSARY. Aug 23, 1785. American naval hero, born at South Kingston, RI. Died Aug 23, 1819, at sea. Best remembered is his announcement of victory at the Battle of Lake Erie, Sept 10, 1813: "We have met the enemy, and they are ours."

ROMANIA SURRENDER TO USSR: ANNIVERSARY. Aug 23, 1944. Romanian King Michael I removed pro-German Premier Jon Antonescue from his position, dismissed his entire government and broadcast to the people of Romania that all hostilities had ceased and that he had accepted all peace terms demanded by the Allies. Most important, the Ploesti oil fields would be secured by the Allies.

SACCO-VANZETTI MEMORIAL DAY: ANNIVERSARY. Aug 23, 1927. Nicola Sacco and Bartolomeo Vanzetti were electrocuted at the Charlestown, MA, prison on this date. Convicted of a shoe factory payroll robbery during which a guard had been killed, Sacco and Vanzetti maintained their innocence to the end. Six years of appeals marked this American cause célèbre during which substantial evidence was presented to show that both men were elsewhere at the time of the crime. On the 50th anniversary of their execution, Massachusetts governor Michael S. Dukakis proclaimed Aug 23, 1977, a memorial day, noting that the 1921 trial had been "permeated by prejudice."

SOUTH MOUNTAIN FAIR. Aug 23–27. Gettysburg, PA. Display of agricultural products, arts, crafts and industrial and agricultural exhibits. Est attendance: 12,500. For info: Gettysburg CVB, PO Box 4117, Gettysburg, PA 17325. Phone: (717) 334-6274. Fax: (717) 334-1166. Web: www.gettysburgcvb.org.

SOUTHERN HEMISPHERE HOODIE-HOO DAY. Aug 23. Long awaited by our Southern-half friends, this is the day to go outdoors at high noon and yell "Hoodie-Hoo" to chase winter and make ready for spring, only one month away. [©2003 by WH.] For info: Thomas & Ruth Roy, Wellcat Holidays, 2418 Long Ln, Lebanon, PA 17046. Phone: (717) 279-0184. E-mail: info@wellcat.com. Web: www.wellcat.com.

SPACE MILESTONE: *INTELSAT-4 F-7 (US).* Aug 23, 1973. International Communications Satellite Consortium's *Intelsat* launched Aug 23, 1973, to relay communications from North and South America to Europe and Africa.

"STOCKHOLM SYNDROME" BANK ROBBERY: ANNIVERSARY. Aug 23–28, 1973. In a botched bank robbery at Stockholm, Sweden, Jan Erik Olsson took four hostages and barricaded himself with them and a friend, Clark Olofsson, in the vault. After a six-day siege, the police piped in gas and the hostages were freed. Afterwards, it emerged that the hostages were more afraid of the police than of their captors, and Swedish professor Nils Bejerot coined the term "Stockholm Syndrome" to explain the phenomena of hostages identifying and sympathizing with their captors.

TENNESSEE WALKING HORSE NATIONAL CELEBRATION. Aug 23–Sept 2. Celebration Grounds, Shelbyville, TN. More than 5,000 entries compete for more than $650,000 in prizes and awards—and the World Grand Championship titles. An 11-day festival for the whole family, plus trade show. Est attendance: 250,000. For info: Chip Walters, Dir Public & Media Relations, Tennessee Walking Horse Natl Celebration, Calhoun and Evans, PO Box 1010, Shelbyville, TN 37162. Phone: (931) 684-5915. Fax: (931) 684-5949. E-mail: twhnc@twhnc.com. Web: www.twhnc.com.

August	S	M	T	W	T	F	S
2006			1	2	3	4	5
	6	7	8	9	10	11	12
	13	14	15	16	17	18	19
	20	21	22	23	24	25	26
	27	28	29	30	31		

UNITED NATIONS: INTERNATIONAL DAY FOR THE REMEMBRANCE OF THE SLAVE TRADE AND ITS ABOLITION. Aug 23. For info: United Nations, Dept of Public Info, New York, NY 10017. Web: www.un.org.

VALENTINO MEMORIAL SERVICE. Aug 23. Hollywood Cathedral Mausoleum, Hollywood Forever Cemetery, Los Angeles, CA. Since 1927 annual memorial service celebrating the life of the silent screen's biggest male star, Rudolph Valentino. Held each year on the anniversary of his 1926 death at 12:10 PM—the time he died (in New York City). Attendees include the "Lady in Black." For info: Hollywood Forever Cemetery, 6000 Santa Monica Blvd, Los Angeles, CA, 90038.

VIRGO, THE VIRGIN. Aug 23–Sept 22. In the astronomical/astrological zodiac, which divides the sun's apparent orbit into 12 segments, the period Aug 23–Sept 22 is identified, traditionally, as the sun sign of Virgo, the Virgin. The ruling planet is Mercury.

BIRTHDAYS TODAY

Tony Bill, 66, actor (*You're a Big Boy Now*), director (*My Bodyguard*), born San Diego, CA, Aug 23, 1940.

Kobe Bryant, 28, basketball player, born Philadelphia, PA, Aug 23, 1978.

Barbara Eden, 72, actress ("I Dream of Jeannie," *Harper Valley P.T.A.*), born Barbara Huffman at Tucson, AZ, Aug 23, 1934.

Sonny Jurgensen, 72, Hall of Fame football player, born Wilmington, NC, Aug 23, 1934.

Cortez Kennedy, 38, former football player, born Osceola, AR, Aug 23, 1968.

Shelley Long, 57, actress ("Cheers," *Irreconcilable Differences*), born Fort Wayne, IN, Aug 23, 1949.

Patricia McBride, 64, dancer, born Teaneck, NJ, Aug 23, 1942.

Vera Miles, 76, actress (*The Wrong Man, Psycho*), born Boise City, OK, Aug 23, 1930.

Jay Mohr, 36, actor (*Jerry Maguire, Picture Perfect*, "Action"), comedian, born Verona, NJ, Aug 23, 1970.

Antonia Novello, 62, first woman and first Hispanic US Surgeon General (1990–93), born Fajardo, Puerto Rico, Aug 23, 1944.

Mark Russell, 74, political comedian, born Mark Ruslander at Buffalo, NY, Aug 23, 1932.

Richard Sanders, 66, actor ("WKRP in Cincinnati," "Berrengers"), born Harrisburg, PA, Aug 23, 1940.

Rik Smits, 40, former basketball player, born Eindhoven, Netherlands, Aug 23, 1966.

Rick Springfield, 57, singer, actor, born Sydney, Australia, Aug 23, 1949.

AUGUST 24 — THURSDAY
Day 236 — 129 Remaining

ACTON FAIR. Aug 24–27. Acton, ME. A country fair featuring horse and ox pulls, antique tractor pull, firemen's muster, 4-H projects, flowers, arts and crafts, stage shows and handicraft. Vendors call Douglas Roberts at (207) 324-1250. Est attendance: 15,000. For info: Lista C. Staples, Secy, 178 Nason Rd, Shapleigh, ME 04076. Phone: (207) 636-2026.

ALASKA STATE FAIR. Aug 24–Sept 4. Palmer, AK. Cows and critters, music and dancing, rides, excitement and family fun at the state's largest summer extravaganza. See 100-lb cabbages, native art, more than 500 events including demonstrations, high-caliber entertainment, rodeos, horse shows, crafts and agricultural exhibits. Est attendance: 300,000. For info: Alaska State Fair, Inc, 2075 Glenn Hwy, Palmer, AK 99645. Phone: (907) 745-4827 or (800) 850-FAIR. Fax: (907) 746-2699. Web: www.alaskastatefair.org.

ARAFAT, YASSER: BIRTH ANNIVERSARY. Aug 24, 1929. Controversial Middle Eastern leader who for almost 50 years was the face of the Palestinian cause. Reviled by some as a terrorist (as leader of Al-Fatah and the PLO) and cheered by others as a freedom fighter, Arafat shared the 1994 Nobel Peace

Prize with Shimon Peres and Yitzhak Rabin. Born Muhammad Abdul Raouf Arafat al-Qudwa al-Husseini at Cairo, Egypt (some sources say Jerusalem or Gaza), Arafat died Nov 11, 2004, in a hospital near Paris, France.

BORGES, JORGE LUIS: BIRTH ANNIVERSARY. Aug 24, 1899. Argentinean author, critic and poet who created intellectually fantastical tales (collected in *Ficciones* and *The Aleph and Other Stories*). "There are so many futures," he said, "[all] quite different from each other." Born at Buenos Aires, Borges died June 14, 1986, at Geneva, Switzerland.

BRANTFORD'S ELVIS FESTIVAL. Aug 24–27. Sanderson Centre for the Performing Arts, Brantford, ON, Canada. Grab your hound dog, put on your blue suede shoes, grease back that hair and set your sights on Brantford as the city gets ready to shake, rattle and roll at the 7th annual Brantford tribute to the King! For info: Jean Hawke, 399 Wayne Gretzky Parkway, Brantford, ON, Canada N3R 8B4. Phone: (800) 265-6299. Fax: (519) 751-2617. E-mail: jhawke@brantford.ca. Web: www.memphis motion.com.

CANADA: OTTAWA FOLK FESTIVAL. Aug 24–26. Britannia Park, Ottawa, ON. A four-day celebration of acoustic music on the banks of the Ottawa River, featuring North America's finest folk performers. Est attendance: 23,000. For info: Ottawa Folk Festival, 107A-858 Bank St, Ottawa, ON, Canada K1S 3W3. Phone: (613) 230-8234. E-mail: festival@ottawafolk.org. Web: www.ottawafolk.org.

"THE FACTS OF LIFE" TV PREMIERE: ANNIVERSARY. Aug 24, 1979. This NBC sitcom was spun off from "Dif'rent Strokes" with Drummond family housekeeper Edna Garrett (Charlotte Rae) moving to Peekskill, NY, to take over as housemother at Eastland, a boarding school for girls. During the first season, the cast included John Lawlor as Headmaster Steven Bradley, Jenny O'Hara as Miss Mahoney, Lisa Whelchel as Blair Warner, Mindy Cohn as Natalie Green, Kim Fields as Dorothy "Tootie" Ramsey, Felice Schachter as Nancy Olson, Julie Piekarski as Sue Ann Weaver, Julie Anne Haddock as Cindy Webster and Molly Ringwald as Molly Parker. The last episode aired in 1986.

GETTYSBURG FALL BLUEGRASS FESTIVAL. Aug 24–27. Gettysburg, PA. Granite Hill Campground on Rt 116. Features some of the country's best stars of bluegrass music. Est attendance: 5,000. For info: Gettysburg CVB, PO Box 4117, Gettysburg, PA 17325. Phone: (717) 334-6274. Fax: (717) 332-1166. E-mail: gettysburgcvb@dejazzd.com. Web: www.gettysburgcvb.org.

HOTTER 'N HELL HUNDRED BIKE RACE/FESTIVAL. Aug 24–27. Wichita Falls, TX. Cyclists of all ages participate in the largest sanctioned century ride in the US. Treks of 100, 50 or 25 miles. Est attendance: 10,000. For info: Wichita Falls CVB, 1000 5th St, Wichita Falls, TX 76301. Phone: (940) 716-5500 or (940) 322-3223. Fax: (940) 716-5509. E-mail: hh100@wf.net. Web: www.hh100.org.

JARVIS, GREGORY B.: BIRTH ANNIVERSARY. Aug 24, 1944. Gregory B. Jarvis, a civilian engineer with Hughes Aircraft Co, was born at Detroit, MI. He was the 41-year-old payload specialist who perished with other crew members and Christa McAuliffe in the Space Shuttle *Challenger* explosion on Jan 28, 1986. See also: "*Challenger* Space Shuttle Explosion: Anniversary" (Jan 28).

KAHANAMOKU, DUKE: BIRTH ANNIVERSARY. Aug 24, 1890. Duke Paoa Kahanamoku, Olympic gold medal swimmer and "Father of International Surfing," born at Honolulu, HI. Kahanamoku won gold medals in the 100-meter freestyle at the 1912 Olympics and at the 1920 Olympics. In total, he won five medals in four Olympics. Credited with inventing the flutter kick, he enjoyed a long career, not retiring from competition until age 42. Kahanamoku was also Hawaii's ambassador of surfing, popularizing the sport around the world. In 1917, on a 16-foot, 114-pound board, he rode a wave off Waikiki for 1.75 miles. The "Duke" acted in movies and served as sheriff of Honolulu, running alternately on the Republican and Democratic tickets. Died

at Honolulu, Jan 22, 1968. Hawaii has honored him with a statue on Waikiki Beach, on which fans place leis.

LIBERIA: FLAG DAY. Aug 24. National holiday.

MINNESOTA STATE FAIR. Aug 24–Sept 4. St. Paul, MN. Twelve days of fun ending on Labor Day. Major entertainers, agricultural displays, arts, crafts, food, carnival rides, animal judging and performances. Est attendance: 1,700,000. For info: Minnesota State Fair, 1265 Snelling Ave N, St. Paul, MN 55108-3099. Phone: (651) 288-4400. E-mail: fairinfo@mnstatefair.org. Web: www.mnstatefair.org.

NEW YORK STATE FAIR. Aug 24–Sept 4. Syracuse, NY. Agricultural and livestock competitions, top-name entertainment, the International Horse Show, business and industrial exhibits, the midway and ethnic presentations. Est attendance: 1,000,000. For info: Joseph LaGuardia, Dir of Mktg, NY State Fair, 581 State Fair Blvd, Syracuse, NY 13209. Phone: (315) 487-7711. Fax: (315) 487-9260.

RE/MAX BALLUNAR LIFTOFF FESTIVAL. Aug 24–26. NASA/Johnson Space Center, Clear Lake Area, Houston, TX. Featuring more than 100 hot-air balloons, sky diving competitions, arts and crafts, midway game area, food, music and other entertainment. Sponsored by NASA/Johnson Space Center, Clear Lake Area Chamber of Commerce, ReMax and Space Center Houston. For info: Clear Lake Area Chamber of Commerce, 1201 NASA Rd One, Houston, TX 77058. Phone: (281) 488-7676. Fax: (281) 488-8981.

SAINT BARTHOLOMEW'S DAY MASSACRE: ANNIVERSARY. Aug 24, 1572. Anniversary of the massacre in Paris and throughout France of thousands of Protestant Huguenots. The massacre began when the church bells tolled at dawn on St. Bartholomew's Day, Aug 24, 1572, and continued for several days. Pope Gregory XIII ordered a medal struck to commemorate the event, but Protestant countries abhorred the killings, estimated at 2,000 to 70,000.

SOUTHERN CYCLONE: ANNIVERSARY. Aug 24, 1893. A hurricane hit Savannah, GA, and Charleston, SC, killing between 1,000 and 2,000 people.

SPACE MILESTONE: *VOYAGER 2* (US) REACHES NEPTUNE. Aug 24, 1989. Launched in 1977, *Voyager 2* had its first close encounter with Neptune.

UKRAINE: INDEPENDENCE DAY. Aug 24. National day. Commemorates independence from the former Soviet Union in 1991.

VESUVIUS DAY. Aug 24, AD 79. Anniversary of the eruption of Vesuvius, an active volcano in southern Italy, which destroyed the cities of Pompeii, Stabiae and Herculaneum. Pliny the Younger, who escaped the disaster, wrote of it to the historian Tacitus: "[B]lack and horrible clouds, broken by sinuous shapes of flaming winds, were opening with long tongues of fire . . ."

WARNER WEATHER QUOTATION: ANNIVERSARY. Aug 24, 1897. Charles Dudley Warner, American newspaper editor for the *Hartford Courant*, published this now-famous and oft-quoted sentence, "Everybody talks about the weather, but nobody does anything about it." The quotation is often mistakenly attributed to his friend and colleague Mark Twain. Warner and Twain were part of the most notable American literary circle during the late 19th century. Warner was a journalist, essayist, novelist, biographer and author who collaborated with Mark Twain in writing *The Gilded Age* in 1873.

WASHINGTON, DC: INVASION ANNIVERSARY. Aug 24–25, 1814. British forces briefly invaded and raided Washington, DC, burning the Capitol, the president's house and most other public buildings. President James Madison and other high US government officials fled to safety until British troops (not knowing the strength of their position) departed the city two days later.

BIRTHDAYS TODAY

Gerry Cooney, 50, former boxer, born New York, NY, Aug 24, 1956.

Stephen Fry, 49, actor (*Gosford Park*, *Wilde*, "Jeeves and Wooster"), novelist, born Hampstead, London, England, Aug 24, 1957.

Rafael Furcal, 28, baseball player, born Loma de Cabrera, Dominican Republic, Aug 24, 1978.

Rupert Grint, 18, actor (*Harry Potter and the Sorcerer's Stone*), born Hertfordshire, England, Aug 24, 1988.

Kenny Guinn, 70, Governor of Nevada (R), born Garland, AR, Aug 24, 1936.

Steve Guttenberg, 48, actor ("Billy," *Three Men and a Baby*), born Brooklyn, NY, Aug 24, 1958.

Oscar Hijuelos, 55, author (*Mambo Kings Play Songs of Love*), born New York, NY, Aug 24, 1951.

Mike Huckabee, 51, Governor of Arkansas (R), born Hope, AR, Aug 24, 1955.

Craig Kilborn, 44, TV host ("The Late Late Show"), born Hastings, MN, Aug 24, 1962.

Joe Manchin III, 59, Governor of West Virginia (D), born Farmington, WV, Aug 24, 1947.

Marlee Matlin, 41, actress (Oscar for *Children of a Lesser God*), born Morton Grove, IL, Aug 24, 1965.

Reginald Wayne (Reggie) Miller, 41, basketball player, born Riverside, CA, Aug 24, 1965.

Chad Michael Murray, 25, actor ("One Tree Hill," "Dawson's Creek," *House of Wax*), born Buffalo, NY, Aug 24, 1981.

Michael Richards, 56, actor ("Seinfeld," *Trial and Error*), born Culver City, CA, Aug 24, 1950.

Calvin Edward (Cal) Ripken, Jr, 46, former baseball player, born Havre de Grace, MD, Aug 24, 1960.

Louis Teicher, 82, pianist (Ferrante and Teicher), composer, born Wilkes-Barre, PA, Aug 24, 1924.

Mason Williams, 68, composer, born Abilene, TX, Aug 24, 1938.

AUGUST 25 — FRIDAY
Day 237 — 128 Remaining

BE KIND TO HUMANKIND WEEK. Aug 25–31. 18th annual observance. All of the negative news that you read and hear about in the media is disheartening—but the truth is the positive stories outweigh the negative stories by a long shot! We just don't hear about them as often. Take heart—most people are caring individuals! Show you care by being kind. Daily affirmations: Motorist Consideration Monday. Touch-a-Heart Tuesday. Willing to Lend a Hand Wednesday. Thoughtful Thursday. Forgive Your Foe Friday. Speak Kind Words Saturday. Sacrifice Our Wants for Others' Needs Sunday. For info: Lorraine Jara, PO Box 586, Island Heights, NJ 08732-0586. Phone: (732) 255-0553. E-mail: Lsays BeKind@comcast.net.

BERNSTEIN, LEONARD: BIRTH ANNIVERSARY. Aug 25, 1918. American conductor and composer Leonard Bernstein was born at Lawrence, MA. One of the greatest conductors in American music history, he first conducted the New York Philharmonic Orchestra at age 25 and was its director from 1959 to 1969. His musicals include *West Side Story* and *On the Town*, and his operas and operettas include *Candide*. He died five days after his retirement, Oct 14, 1990, at New York, NY.

CANADA: MORDEN CORN AND APPLE FESTIVAL. Aug 25–27. Morden, MB. It's fun and it's free! Est attendance: 50,000. For info: Morden Chamber of Commerce, 311 N Railway St, Morden, MB, Canada R6M 1S9. Phone: (204) 822-5630. Fax: (204) 822-2041. E-mail: chamber@mordenmb.com.

COLORADO STATE FAIR. Aug 25–Sept 4. State Fairgrounds, Pueblo, CO. Colorado's largest single event. For info: Colorado State Fair. www.coloradostatefair.com.

CORVETTE SHOW. Aug 25–26. State Dock, Mackinaw City, MI. Show and visitor viewing, awards and Boat Cruise on Friday, parade across the Mackinaw Bridge on Saturday at 7 PM. Est attendance: 4,000. For info: Corvette Show, PO Box 856, Mackinaw City, MI 49701. Phone: (231) 436-5574 or (888) 455-8100. Web: www.mackinawchamber.com.

ENGLAND: BEATLES FESTIVAL. Aug 25–30. Liverpool, Merseyside. Music and entertainment connected with Liverpool's own, the Beatles. Est attendance: 300,000. For info: Mr Bill Heckle, Cavern City Tours Ltd, The Cavern Club, 10 Mathew St, Liverpool, Merseyside, England L2 6RE. Phone: (44) (151) 236-9091. Fax: (44) (151) 236-8081.

GIBSON, ALTHEA: BIRTH ANNIVERSARY. Aug 25, 1927. Born at Silver, SC, Althea Gibson learned paddle tennis by chance as a child when her block of West 143rd St in New York was designated as a Police Athletic League play street. She overcame great financial and social adversity, and eventually won ten consecutive national titles in the American Tennis Association, a league for black players. On Aug 28, 1950, she became the first black player to compete in the national tennis championship at Forest Hills, NY. A few years later, she became the first black woman to win the singles championship at Wimbledon. In her prime, she was ranked as high as 7th in the United States, winning titles at the French Open, Wimbledon and US Nationals at Forest Hills. She died at East Orange, NJ, Sept 28, 2003.

HARTE, BRET: BIRTH ANNIVERSARY. Aug 25, 1836. Francis Bret(t) Harte, journalist, poet, printer, teacher and novelist, especially remembered for his early stories of California ("The Luck of Roaring Camp," "The Outcasts of Poker Flat" and "How Santa Claus Came to Simpson's Bar"), was born at Albany, NY. He died at London, England, May 5, 1902.

KELLY, WALT: BIRTH ANNIVERSARY. Aug 25, 1913. American cartoonist and creator of the comic strip "Pogo" was born at Philadelphia, PA. It was Kelly's character Pogo who paraphrased Oliver Hazard Perry to say, "We has met the enemy, and it is us." Kelly died at Hollywood, CA, Oct 18, 1973. See also: "Perry, Oliver Hazard: Birth Anniversary" (Aug 23).

KISS-AND-MAKE-UP-DAY. Aug 25. A day to make amends and for relationships that need mending! For info: Jacqueline V. Milgate, 121 Little Tree Ln, Hilton, NY 14468.

MAKAH DAYS. Aug 25–27. Neah Bay, WA. Makah Day originated Aug 26, 1913, with the presentation of the American Flag to the Makah Tribe. Flag-raising honors were shared by three tribal members whose present-day descendants still carry on this Makah's Day tradition. Makahs proud to be American citizens celebrate with traditional dance and song, canoe races, salmon bake, parade, fireworks, and Sla-Hal, or "Bone Games," an Indian form of gambling. Makah Day has expanded to Makah Days, and the Makah are proud to share their rich heritage with the rest of the world. Annually, on the weekend closest to Aug 26. For info: Leonard A. Denney, Jr, PO Box 115, Neah Bay, WA 98357. Phone: (360) 645-3281. Fax: (360) 645-2033. E-mail: mtcbic@olypen.com. Web: www.makah.com.

MARYLAND STATE FAIR. Aug 25–Sept 4. Timonium, MD. Home arts, agricultural and livestock presentations, midway rides, live entertainment and thoroughbred horse racing. Est attendance: 500,000. For info: Maryland State Fair, Publicity Dept, State Fairgrounds, PO Box 188, Timonium, MD 21094. Phone: (410)

August 2006	S	M	T	W	T	F	S
			1	2	3	4	5
	6	7	8	9	10	11	12
	13	14	15	16	17	18	19
	20	21	22	23	24	25	26
	27	28	29	30	31		

252-0200. E-mail: msfair@msn.com. Web: www.marylandstate fair.com.

MEXICAN FIESTA INTERNACIONAL. Aug 25–27. Milwaukee, WI. Mexican Fiesta brings the sounds and tastes of Mexico to Milwaukee's lakefront. Three days of fun, food, Mariachi and fiesta for everyone. Plus the traditional jalapeño-eating contest, national and international entertainment and the best Mexican cuisine. Est attendance: 70,000. For info: Mexican Fiesta, 1220 W Windlake Ave, Milwaukee, WI 53215. Phone: (414) 383-7066. Fax: (414) 383-6677. E-mail: info@mexicanfiesta.org. Web: www.mexicanfiesta.org.

MISSOURI RIVER FESTIVAL OF THE ARTS. Aug 25–27. Thespian Hall, Boonville, MO. Performing arts festival with major symphony, jazz, children's program, Broadway music, dance and contemporary music. Est attendance: 5,000. For info: Maryellen H. McVicker, Executive Director, Friends of Historic Boonville, PO Box 1776, Boonville, MO 65233. Phone: (660) 882-7977 or toll-free (888) 588-1477. Fax: (660) 882-9194. E-mail: friends@undata.com.

OREGON STATE FAIR. Aug 25–Sept 4. Salem, OR. Exhibits, products and displays illustrate Oregon's role as one of the nation's major agricultural and recreational states. Floral gardens, carnival, entertainment, horse show and food. Est attendance: 400,000. For info: Oregon State Fair, 2330 17th St NE, Salem, OR 97303-3201. Phone: (503) 947-3247. Web: www.oregonstate fair.com.

OZARK ANTIQUE AUTO CLUB SWAP MEET. Aug 25–27. Ozark Empire Fairgrounds, Springfield, MO. Hundreds of booths fill the fairgrounds with antique auto parts to buy, sell and swap. For info: Ozark Empire Fair, 3001 N Grant, Springfield, MO 65803. Phone: (417) 833-2660. Fax: (417) 833-3769. Web: www.ozarkempirefair.com.

PARIS LIBERATED: ANNIVERSARY. Aug 25, 1944. As dawn broke, the men of the 2nd French Armored Division entered Paris, ending the long German occupation of the City of Light. That afternoon General Charles de Gaulle led a parade down the Champs Elysées. Though Hitler had ordered the destruction of Paris, German occupying-officer General Dietrich von Choltitz refused that order and instead surrendered to French Major General Jacques Le Clerc.

PINKERTON, ALLAN: BIRTH ANNIVERSARY. Aug 25, 1819. Scottish-born American detective, founder of detective agency at Chicago, IL, in 1850, first chief of US Army's secret service, remembered now because of his strike-breaking and his lack of sympathy for working people. Pinkerton was born at Glasgow, Scotland, and died at Chicago, IL, July 1, 1884.

PRAIRIE VILLAGE JAMBOREE. Aug 25–27. Prairie Village, Madison, SD. Come and join the fun with 40 restored buildings, parades, tractor pulls, threshing, plowing, wagon trains, flea market, train and carousel rides, entertainment and much more. Est attendance: 15,000. For info: Prairie Village Jamboree, PO Box 256, Madison, SD 57042. Phone: (800) 693-3644. E-mail: prairiev@rapidnet.com. Web: www.prairievillage.org.

ROCKY MOUNTAIN BALLOON FESTIVAL. Aug 25–27. Chatfield State Park, Denver, CO. Hot-air balloon festival and outdoor celebration. Fun family event with dawn balloon ascensions and Saturday sunset "Lites in the Nite" mass balloon illumination. Annually, the weekend before Labor Day weekend. Est attendance: 50,000. For info: Rocky Mountain Balloon Festival. Phone: (303) 697-1039. E-mail: info@rockymountainballoonfestival.com. Web: www.rockymountainballoonfestival.com.

URUGUAY: INDEPENDENCE DAY. Aug 25. National holiday. Declared independence from Brazil in 1825. Independence granted in 1828.

***THE WIZARD OF OZ* RELEASED: ANNIVERSARY.** Aug 25, 1939. This motion-picture classic directed by Victor Fleming was a musical adaptation of the L. Frank Baum children's book with both black-and-white and color sequences. It starred Judy Garland as Dorothy as well as Frank Morgan as the Wizard (and four other characters), Ray Bolger as the Scarecrow, Bert Lahr as the Lion, Jack Haley as the Tin Man and Margaret Hamilton as the Wicked Witch of the West. Nominated for six Academy Awards, it won two for best original music score and best song, "Over the Rainbow" (Harold Arlen music and E.Y. Harburg lyrics).

BIRTHDAYS TODAY

Martin Amis, 57, author (*The Information, London Fields*), critic, born Oxford, England, Aug 25, 1949.

Anne Archer, 59, actress ("Falcon Crest"; stage: *A Couple of White Chicks Sitting Around Talking*), born Los Angeles, CA, Aug 25, 1947.

Albert Belle, 40, former baseball player, born Shreveport, LA, Aug 25, 1966.

Cornelius O'Landa Bennett, 40, former football player, born Birmingham, AL, Aug 25, 1966.

Tim Burton, 48, director (*Edward Scissorhands, The Nightmare Before Christmas*), born Burbank, CA, Aug 25, 1958.

Sean Connery, 76, actor (James Bond movies; *The Man Who Would Be King*), born Edinburgh, Scotland, Aug 25, 1930.

Elvis Costello, 52, singer, songwriter born Declan McManus at Paddington, London, England, Aug 25, 1954.

Billy Ray Cyrus, 45, country singer ("Achy Breaky Heart"), born Flatwoods, KY, Aug 25, 1961.

Mel Ferrer, 89, actor (*Scaramouche, The Sun Also Rises*), born Elberon, NJ, Aug 25, 1917.

Frederick Forsyth, 68, author (*The Day of the Jackal*), born Ashford, Kent, England, Aug 25, 1938.

Monty Hall, 83, former TV host ("Let's Make a Deal"), born Winnipeg, MB, Canada, Aug 25, 1923.

Anthony Heald, 62, actor (*The Silence of the Lambs, Searching for Bobby Fischer*), born New Rochelle, NY, Aug 25, 1944.

Regis Philbin, 73, TV show host ("Live with Regis & Kelly," "Who Wants to Be a Millionaire?"), born New York, NY, Aug 25, 1933.

John Savage, 57, actor (*The Deer Hunter, Hair*), born Long Island, NY, Aug 25, 1949.

Claudia Schiffer, 36, model, born Rheinberg, Germany, Aug 25, 1970.

Wayne Shorter, 73, jazz musician ("High Life"), born Newark, NJ, Aug 25, 1933.

Gene Simmons, 57, cofounder of KISS, actor, born Chaim Witz at Haifa, Israel, Aug 25, 1949.

Tom Skerritt, 73, actor ("Picket Fences," *Steel Magnolias*), born Detroit, MI, Aug 25, 1933.

Blair Underwood, 42, actor ("One Life to Live," "LA Law"), born Tacoma, WA, Aug 25, 1964.

Ally Walker, 45, actress ("The Profiler"), born Tullahoma, TN, Aug 25, 1961.

Joanne Whalley, 42, actress ("The Singing Detective"; stage: *What the Butler Saw*), born Manchester, England, Aug 25, 1964.

AUGUST 26 — SATURDAY
Day 238 — 127 Remaining

CHAMPLAIN VALLEY FAIR. Aug 26–Sept 4. Essex Junction, VT. Vermont's largest fair. Agricultural exhibits and competitions, variety of entertainment, arts and crafts, midway rides, commercial exhibits, great food and much more. Est attendance: 300,000. For info: George Rousseau, Dir of Sales and Mktg, PO Box 209, Essex Junction, VT 05453. Phone: (802) 878-5545. Fax: (802) 879-5404. E-mail: info@cvfair.com. Web: www.cvfair.com.

CHILDREN'S DAY. Aug 26. Woodstock, VT. Traditional farm activities from corn shelling to sawing firewood—19th-century games, traditional spelling bee, ice cream and butter making, wagon rides. For info: Billings Farm Museum, Rte 12 North, Woodstock, VT 05091. Phone: (802) 457-2355. Fax: (802) 457-4663. E-mail: billings.farm@valley.net. Web: www.billingsfarm.org.

COUNTRY FEST AND AUCTION. Aug 26. Garrett County Fairgrounds, Deep Creek Lake, McHenry, MD. Family-oriented activities, demonstrations, crafts, baked goods, horse-and-buggy and pony rides, farm animal petting zoo, gospel music, chicken BBQ and an auction featuring handcrafted wood items, locally made hand-quilted quilts and much more. Event sponsored by the Bittinger Mennonite Church. Annually, the fourth Saturday in August. Est attendance: 2,500. For info: Country Fest & Auction, 1705 Foy Rd, Accident, MD 21520. Phone: (301) 245-4564 or (301) 245-4326. E-mail: countryfest@juno.com. Web: www.countryfest.org.

De FOREST, LEE: BIRTH ANNIVERSARY. Aug 26, 1873. American inventor of the electron tube, radio knife for surgery and the photoelectric cell and a pioneer in the creation of talking pictures and television. Born at Council Bluffs, IA, De Forest was holder of hundreds of patents but perhaps best remembered by the moniker he gave himself in the title of his autobiography, *Father of Radio*, published in 1950. So unbelievable was the idea of wireless radio broadcasting that De Forest was accused of fraud and arrested for selling stock to underwrite the invention that later was to become an essential part of daily life. De Forest died at Hollywood, CA, June 30, 1961.

DENMARK: HO SHEEP MARKET. Aug 26. The village of Ho, near Esbjerg, holds its annual sheep market on the last Saturday in August, when some 50,000 people visit the fair.

FIESTA LA BALLONA. Aug 26–27. Veterans Park, Culver City, CA. A Culver City community celebration since 1951. This 54th Fiesta La Ballona features carnival rides, arts and crafts booths, nonprofit booths, local business booths and more. Culver City is known as the "Heart of Screenland" and is the historical site of the MGM and Hal Roach studios. Annually, the last weekend in August. Est attendance: 12,000. For info: Marty Nicholson, Culver City Parks & Recreation Dept, 4117 Overland Ave, Culver City, CA 90230-3733. Phone: (310) 253-6650. Fax: (310) 253-6666. E-mail: marty.nicholson@culvercity.org. Web: fiestalaballona.org.

FIRST BASEBALL GAMES TELEVISED: ANNIVERSARY. Aug 26, 1939. WXBS television, at New York City, broadcast the first major league baseball games—a doubleheader between the Cincinnati Reds and the Brooklyn Dodgers at Ebbets Field. Announcer Red Barber interviewed Leo Durocher, manager of the Dodgers, and William McKechnie, manager of the Reds, between games.

ISHERWOOD, CHRISTOPHER: BIRTH ANNIVERSARY. Aug 26, 1904. Author of short stories, plays and novels, Christopher William Isherwood was born at High Lane, Cheshire, England. The play and motion picture *I Am a Camera* and the musical *Cabaret* were based on the short story "Sally Bowles" in his collection from the 1930s titled *Goodbye to Berlin*, which contained the line "I am a camera with its shutter open, quite passive, recording, not thinking." Isherwood died at Santa Monica, CA, Jan 4, 1986.

KRAKATOA ERUPTION: ANNIVERSARY. Aug 26, 1883. Anniversary of the biggest explosion in historic times. The eruption of the Indonesian volcanic island Krakatoa (Krakatau) was heard 3,000 miles away, created tidal waves 120 ft high (killing 36,000 persons), hurled five cubic miles of earth fragments into the air (some to a height of 50 miles) and affected the oceans and the atmosphere for years.

MARYLAND RENAISSANCE FESTIVAL. Aug 26–Oct 22 (Saturdays, Sundays and Labor Day). Annapolis, MD. A 16th-century English festival with Henry VIII, sword swallowers, magicians, authentic jousting, juggling, music, theater, games, food and crafts. Est attendance: 298,000. For info: Jules Smith, Maryland Renaissance Festival, PO Box 315, Crownsville, MD 21032. Phone: (410) 266-7304. Fax: (410) 573-1508. E-mail: rennfest@erols.com. Web: www.rennfest.com.

MONTGOLFIER, JOSEPH MICHEL: BIRTH ANNIVERSARY. Aug 26, 1740. French merchant and inventor, born at Vidalonlez-Annonay, France, who, with his brother Jacques Etienne in November 1782, conducted experiments with paper and fabric bags filled with smoke and hot air, which led to invention of the hot-air balloon and man's first flight. Died at Balaruc-les-Bains, France, June 26, 1810. See also: "Montgolfier, Jacques Etienne: Birth Anniversary" (Jan 7), "First Balloon Flight: Anniversary" (June 5) and "Aviation History Month" (Nov 1).

NAMIBIA: HEROES' DAY. Aug 26. National holiday. Commemorates beginning of struggle for independence in 1966.

NATIONAL DOG DAY. Aug 26. More people have dogs for pets than any other animal in the country. Why? Because they are loving and loyal companions. They treat us better than we treat each other. Here is one day to recognize and honor them for their love, loyalty and life saving skills. Annually, Aug 26. For info: National Dog Day Foundation, PO Box 1364, Port Townsend, WA 98368. Phone: (206) 284-2676. E-mail: info@nationaldogday.com. Web: www.nationaldogday.com.

NEBRASKA STATE FAIR. Aug 26–Sept 4. Lincoln, NE. Showcasing Nebraska pride, people and products. Food booths, variety of entertainment, amusement rides, concerts, livestock shows, tractor pulls and monster truck shows. Est attendance: 300,000. For info: Nebraska State Fair, PO Box 81223, Lincoln, NE 68501. Phone: (402) 474-5371. Fax: (402) 473-4114. E-mail: nestatefair@statefair.org. Web: www.statefair.org.

POCONO STATE CRAFT FAIR. Aug 26–27. Sun Mountain Recreation Club, Shawnee-on-the-Delaware, PA. High-quality juried craft show featuring the work of 80 members of the Pennsylvania Guild of Craftsmen. Enjoy a day in this lakeside setting with festival food, craft demonstrations, children's activities, and strolling musical entertainment. Est attendance: 5,000. For information about tickets, or how to become a member of the PA Guild, contact PGC at: PGC, 10 Stable Mill Trail, Richboro, PA 18954. Phone: (215) 579-5997. E-mail: pacraft@comcat.com. Web: www.pacrafts.com.

	S	M	T	W	T	F	S
August			1	2	3	4	5
2006	6	7	8	9	10	11	12
	13	14	15	16	17	18	19
	20	21	22	23	24	25	26
	27	28	29	30	31		

SABIN, ALBERT BRUCE: 100th BIRTH ANNIVERSARY. Aug 26, 1906. American medical researcher Albert Bruce Sabin was born at Bialystok, Poland. He is most noted for his oral vaccine for polio, which replaced Jonas Salk's injected vaccine because Sabin's provided lifetime protection. He was awarded the US National Medal of Science in 1971. Sabin died Mar 3, 1993, at Washington, DC.

SIDEWALK ART FESTIVAL. Aug 26. Portland, ME. Sponsored by WCSH 6, this 41st annual festival is Maine's largest and oldest one-day art show. More than 300 artists from around the Northeast with works for sale. On Congress St, from Park St to Elm St (closed to vehicular traffic). Annually, the fourth Saturday in August. For info: Community Relations, WCSH 6, One Congress Square, Portland, ME 04101. Phone: (207) 828-6666. Fax: (207) 828-6620. E-mail: communityrelations@WCSH6.com. Web: WCSH6.com.

SNOWBIRD OKTOBERFEST. Aug 26–27. (Also Sept 2–4, 9–10, 16–17, 23–24, Sept 30–Oct 1, Oct 7–8). Snowbird, UT. Festival includes traditional European music, shopping, dancing and food. For info: Snowbird & Ski Summer Resort, PO Box 929000, Snowbird, UT 84092-9000. Phone: (801) 742-2222. Fax: (801) 933-2298. E-mail: info@snowbird.com. Web: www .snowbird.com.

SPACE MILESTONE: *SOYUZ 31* (USSR). Aug 26, 1978. Launched on Aug 26, Valery Bykovsky and Sigmund Jaehn docked at *Salyut 6* on Aug 27, stayed for a week, then returned to Earth in *Soyuz 29* vehicle, leaving their *Soyuz 31* docked at space station. Earth landing on Sept 3.

VIVA! CHICAGO LATIN MUSIC FESTIVAL. Aug 26–27 (tentative). Grant Park, Chicago, IL. 18th annual. The spectrum of Latin music: cumbias, tropical, merengue, salsa, norteñas, ranchero and mariachi. Est attendance: 160,000. For info: Mayor's Office of Special Events, City Hall, 121 N LaSalle St, #703, Chicago, IL 60602. Phone: (312) 744-3370 (hotline). Fax: (312) 744-8523. Web: www.cityofchicago.org/specialevents.

★**WOMEN'S EQUALITY DAY.** Aug 26. Presidential Proclamation issued in 1973 and 1974 at request and since 1975 without request.

WOMEN'S EQUALITY DAY. Aug 26. Anniversary of certification as part of US Constitution, in 1920, of the 19th Amendment, prohibiting discrimination on the basis of sex with regard to voting. Congresswoman Bella Abzug's bill to designate Aug 26 of each year as "Women's Equality Day" in August 1974 became Public Law 93-382.

BIRTHDAYS TODAY

Benjamin Crowninshield Bradlee, 85, journalist, editor, born Boston, MA, Aug 26, 1921.
Christopher Burke, 41, actor ("Life Goes On"), born New York, NY, Aug 26, 1965.
Macaulay Culkin, 26, actor (*Home Alone, My Girl*), born New York, NY, Aug 26, 1980.
Geraldine Ferraro, 71, first woman vice-presidential candidate, born Newburgh, NY, Aug 26, 1935.
Irving R. Levine, 84, broadcast journalist, born Pawtucket, RI, Aug 26, 1922.
Branford Marsalis, 46, musician, born Beaux Bridge, LA, Aug 26, 1960.

AUGUST 27 — SUNDAY
Day 239 — 126 Remaining

BARNEGAT BAY CRAB RACE AND FESTIVAL. Aug 27. Seaside Heights, NJ. Crab race, festival and craft fair. Annually, the last Sunday in August. Est attendance: 5,000. For info: Lucy Greene, Pres, Barbara Morgan, Admin Asst, Toms River–Ocean Co Chmbr of Com, 1200 Hooper Ave, Toms River, NJ 08753. Phone: (732) 349-0220. Fax: (732) 349-1252. Web: www .oc-chamber.com.

BELGIUM: WEDDING OF THE GIANTS. Aug 27. Traditional cultural observance. Annually, the fourth Sunday in August.

DAWES, CHARLES GATES: BIRTH ANNIVERSARY. Aug 27, 1865. Thirtieth vice president of the US (1925–1929), born at Marietta, OH. Won the Nobel Peace Prize in 1925 for the Dawes Plan for German reparations. Died at Evanston, IL, Apr 23, 1951.

DREISER, THEODORE: BIRTH ANNIVERSARY. Aug 27, 1871. American novelist Theodore Dreiser was born at Terre Haute, IN. He was an exponent of American naturalism in literature. His first novel, *Sister Carrie* (1900), was suppressed by his publisher on moral grounds. Dreiser's finest achievement is widely considered to be his novel *An American Tragedy* (1925). He died Dec 28, 1945, at Hollywood, CA.

"THE DUCHESS" WHO WASN'T DAY. Aug 27. At least once on Aug 27 repeat the following now-famous quotation from the novel *Molly Bawn*: "Beauty is in the eye of the beholder." Margaret Wolfe Hungerford often wrote under the pseudonym "The Duchess," which was the title of her most popular novel—hence the name of this event. A popular romance novelist with about 40 books published, Hungerford was born at Rosscarbery, County Cork, Ireland, on Aug 27, 1850; she died at Bandon, County Cork, in 1897. For info: Peggy Shirley, 3800 Treyburn Dr, #4402, Williamsburg, VA 23185. Phone: (757) 220-6870.

FAMILY DAY IN TENNESSEE. Aug 27. Observed annually on the last Sunday in August.

FIRST COMMERCIAL OIL WELL: ANNIVERSARY. Aug 27, 1859. W.A. "Uncle Billy" Smith discovered oil in a shaft being sunk by Colonel E.L. Drake at Titusville, in western Pennsylvania. Drilling had reached 69 ft, 6 inches when Smith saw a dark film floating on the water below the derrick floor. Soon 20 barrels of crude were being pumped each day. The first oil was refined to make kerosene for lighting, replacing whale oil. Later it was refined to make gasoline for cars. The first gas station opened in 1907.

FIRST PLAY PRESENTED IN NORTH AMERICAN COLONIES: ANNIVERSARY. Aug 27, 1655. Acomac, VA, was the site of the first play presented in the North American colonies. The play was *Ye Bare and Ye Cubb*, by Phillip Alexander Bruce. Three local residents were arrested and fined for acting in the play. At the time, most colonies had laws prohibiting public performances; Virginia, however, had no such ordinance.

"GOOD SEX! WITH DR. RUTH WESTHEIMER" TV PREMIERE: ANNIVERSARY. Aug 27, 1984. This program premiered on the Lifetime Cable Channel with sex therapist Ruth Westheimer counseling actors appearing as her patients. The show's format later changed to include celebrity and physician interviews and call-ins.

HAMLIN, HANNIBAL: BIRTH ANNIVERSARY. Aug 27, 1809. Fifteenth vice president of the US (1861–65) born at Paris, ME. Died at Bangor, ME, July 4, 1891.

JOHNSON, LYNDON BAINES: BIRTH ANNIVERSARY. Aug 27, 1908. The 36th president of the US succeeded to the presidency following the assassination of John F. Kennedy. Johnson's term of office: Nov 22, 1963–Jan 20, 1969. In 1964, he said: "The challenge of the next half-century is whether we have the wisdom to use [our] wealth to enrich and elevate our national life—and to advance the quality of American civilization."

Johnson was born near Stonewall, TX, and died at San Antonio, TX, Jan 22, 1973. His birthday is observed as a holiday in Texas.

MOLDOVA: INDEPENDENCE DAY. Aug 27. Republic of Moldova. Moldova declared its independence from the Soviet Union in 1991.

MOTHER TERESA: BIRTH ANNIVERSARY. Aug 27, 1910. Albanian Roman Catholic nun born Agnes Gonxha Bojaxhiu at Skopje, Macedonia. She founded the Order of the Missionaries of Charity, which cared for the destitute of Calcutta, India. She won the Nobel Peace Prize in 1979. She died at Calcutta, Sept 5, 1997.

MOUNTBATTEN, LOUIS: ASSASSINATION ANNIVERSARY. Aug 27, 1979. Lord Mountbatten (Louis Francis Albert Victor Nicholas Mountbatten), celebrated British war hero, cousin of Queen Elizabeth II, last viceroy of India, was killed by bomb, along with his 14-year-old grandson and two others, while on his yacht in Donegal Bay off the coast of Ireland, on Aug 27, 1979. Provisional Irish Republican Army claimed responsibility for the explosion and for the killing of 18 British soldiers later the same day, deepening the crisis and conflict between Protestants and Catholics and between England and Ireland. Lord Mountbatten was born at Windsor, England, June 25, 1900.

PHILIPPINES: NATIONAL HEROES' DAY. Aug 27. National holiday. The last Sunday in August. Commemorates the Aug 26, 1896, beginning of the Philippine fight for independence from Spain.

PONY EXPRESS FESTIVAL. Aug 27. Hollenberg Pony Express Station, State Historic Site, Hanover, KS. Reenactment of Pony Express ride with mochila exchange, pioneer living-history demonstrations, 1860s historic dress group, circuit-rider church service and a noon meal on the grounds. Annually, the last Sunday in August. Sponsor: Kansas State Historical Society, Friends of Hollenberg Station. Est attendance: 2,000. For info: Duane Durst, Curator, Hollenberg Pony Express Station, State Historic Site, RR1, 2889 23rd Rd, Hanover, KS 66945. Phone: (785) 337-2635. Fax: (785) 337-2309. E-mail: hollenberg@kshs.org.

RAYE, MARTHA: BIRTH ANNIVERSARY. Aug 27, 1916. Born at Butte, MT, Martha Raye began singing when she was three. Raye performed for American servicemen during three wars and received the Jean Hersholt Humanitarian Award from the Academy of Motion Picture Arts and Sciences (1969) for that service. She appeared in her first film, *Rhythm on the Range*, in 1936. She had several TV shows, including "The Martha Raye Show" (1955–56). In 1993 Raye was awarded the Presidential Medal of Freedom. Martha Raye died Oct 19, 1994, at Los Angeles, CA.

TOBACCO HARVEST. Aug 27. McLean, VA. Help cut and hang tobacco to dry and enjoy 18th-century games. Est attendance: 400. For info: Claude Moore Colonial Farm at Turkey Run, 6310 Georgetown Pike, McLean, VA 22101. Phone: (703) 442-7557. Fax: (703) 442-0714. Web: www.1771.org.

BIRTHDAYS TODAY

Sarah Chalke, 30, actress ("Roseanne," "Scrubs"), born Ottawa, ON, Canada, Aug 27, 1976.

Daryl Dragon, 64, musician (Captain and Tennille), songwriter, born Studio City, CA, Aug 27, 1942.

Carlos Moya, 30, tennis player, born Palma, Majorca, Spain, Aug 27, 1976.

Paul Rubens (Pee-wee Herman), 54, actor, writer ("Pee-wee's Playhouse," *Pee-wee's Big Adventure*), born Peekskill, NY, Aug 27, 1952.

August 2006	S	M	T	W	T	F	S
			1	2	3	4	5
	6	7	8	9	10	11	12
	13	14	15	16	17	18	19
	20	21	22	23	24	25	26
	27	28	29	30	31		

Tommy Sands, 69, singer ("Teen-Age Crush," "Goin' Steady"), born Chicago, IL, Aug 27, 1937.

Jim Thome, 36, baseball player, born Peoria, IL, Aug 27, 1970.

Tuesday Weld, 63, actress ("The Many Loves of Dobie Gillis," *Looking for Mr Goodbar*), born Susan Kerr at New York, NY, Aug 27, 1943.

AUGUST 28 — MONDAY
Day 240 — 125 Remaining

BOYER, CHARLES: BIRTH ANNIVERSARY. Aug 28, 1889. Film star (*Mayerling, Gaslight*), born at Figeac, France. Died at Scottsdale, AZ, Aug 26, 1978.

FEAST OF SAINT AUGUSTINE. Aug 28. Bishop of Hippo, author of *Confessions* and *The City of God*, born Nov 13, 354, at Tagaste, in what is now Algeria. Died Aug 28, 430, at Hippo, also in North Africa.

GOETHE, JOHANN WOLFGANG von: BIRTH ANNIVERSARY. Aug 28, 1749. German author, poet, dramatist and philosopher, born at Frankfurt. Died Mar 22, 1832, at Weimar, Germany. Best known for the novels *The Sorrows of Young Werther* and *Wilheim Meister* and the play *Faust*.

HAYES, LUCY WARE WEBB: 175th BIRTH ANNIVERSARY. Aug 28, 1831. Wife of Rutherford Birchard Hayes, 19th president of the US, born at Chillicothe, OH. Died at Fremont, OH, June 25, 1889. She was nicknamed "Lemonade Lucy" because she and the president, both abstainers, served no alcoholic beverages at White House receptions.

HONG KONG: LIBERATION DAY. Aug 28. Public holiday to celebrate liberation from the Japanese in 1945. Annually, the last Monday in August.

MARCH ON WASHINGTON: ANNIVERSARY. Aug 28, 1963. More than 250,000 people attended this Civil Rights rally at Washington, DC, at which Reverend Dr. Martin Luther King, Jr, made his famous "I have a dream" speech.

NATIONAL OLD-TIME COUNTRY MUSIC CONTEST, FESTIVAL & EXPO. Aug 28–Sept 3. Harrison County Fairgrounds, Missouri Valley, IA. Country music fans come from all around to hear their favorites. Also many arts and crafts displays, other musical entertainment and food booths. Est attendance: 50,000. For info: Natl Old-Time Country Music Contest, Fest & Expo, PO Box 492, Anita, IA 50020. Phone: (712) 762-4363. E-mail: bobeverhart@yahoo.com. Web: www.oldtimemusic.bigstep.com.

O'CONNOR, DONALD: BIRTH ANNIVERSARY. Aug 28, 1925. Singer, dancer and vaudeville performer Donald O'Connor was born into a family of circus performers at Chicago, IL, Aug 28, 1925. He joined the family's vaudeville act at a very young age, and was soon under contract with Universal Studios. He appeared in *Beau Geste*, portraying Gary Cooper's character as a child, and continued to work steadily. He starred opposite Frances the Mule in a string of very successful film comedies throughout the 1950s, but is best remembered for his role opposite Gene Kelly and Debbie Reynolds in 1952's *Singin' in the Rain*. His solo number "Make 'Em Laugh" is considered one of Hollywood's finest moments. O'Connor died Sept 28, 2003, at Woodland Hills, CA.

PETERSON, ROGER TORY: BIRTH ANNIVERSARY. Aug 28, 1908. Naturalist, author of *A Field Guide to Birds*, born at Jamestown, NY. Peterson died at Old Lyme, CT, July 28, 1996.

PORT ROYAL HURRICANE: ANNIVERSARY. Aug 28, 1722. The hapless Jamaican town of Port Royal was devastated twice within a 30-year span by two natural disasters—an earthquake in 1692 and a hurricane in 1722. The hurricane killed 400 townspeople and sunk 26 merchant ships.

RACE YOUR MOUSE AROUND THE ICONS DAY. Aug 28. While you're waiting for any number of endless items to finally come up on your screen, don't just sit there. Race your mouse in and around the icons! You'll feel peppy for doing it. [©2003 by WH.] For info: Thomas & Ruth Roy, Wellcat Holidays, 2418 Long Ln, Lebanon, PA 17046. Phone: (717) 279-0184. E-mail: info@wellcat.com. Web: www.wellcat.com.

RADIO COMMERCIALS: ANNIVERSARY. Aug 28, 1922. Broadcasters realized radio could earn profits from the sale of advertising time. WEAF in New York ran a commercial "spot," which was sponsored by the Queensboro Realty Corporation of Jackson Heights to promote Hawthorne Court, a group of apartment buildings at Queens. The commercial rate was $100 for 10 minutes.

TILL, EMMETT: DEATH ANNIVERSARY. Aug 28, 1955. Emmett Till, a 14-year-old African-American teenager from Chicago visiting relatives in Money, MS, was murdered on this date by a group of white men angry at Till's reported flirtation with a white woman. The Till murder and the acquittal of two of the men involved brought the nation's attention to racial tensions in the South and helped spark civil rights protests later that year—most famously, Rosa Parks's refusal to give up her seat to a white man on a municipal bus in Montgomery, AL, in December of that year.

UNITED KINGDOM: SUMMER BANK HOLIDAY. Aug 28. Bank and public holiday in England, Wales and Northern Ireland. (Scotland not included.) Annually, the last Monday in August.

BIRTHDAYS TODAY

Mamadou Diallo, 35, soccer player, born Dakar, Senegal, Aug 28, 1971.

Ben Gazzara, 76, actor (*Anatomy of a Murder*, "Run for Your Life"), born New York, NY, Aug 28, 1930.

Ronald Ames (Ron) Guidry, 56, former baseball player, born Lafayette, LA, Aug 28, 1950.

Scott Hamilton, 48, Olympic gold medal figure skater, born Toledo, OH, Aug 28, 1958.

Paul Martin, 68, 21st prime minister of Canada, born Windsor, ON, Canada, Aug 28, 1938.

Noriyuki ("Pat") Morita, 74, actor ("Sanford and Son," "Happy Days," *The Karate Kid*), born Isleton, CA, Aug 28, 1932.

Lou Piniella, 63, baseball manager and former player, born Tampa, FL, Aug 28, 1943.

Jason Priestley, 37, actor ("Beverly Hills 90210," *Tombstone*), born Vancouver, BC, Canada, Aug 28, 1969.

LeAnn Rimes, 24, country and western singer, born Jackson, MS, Aug 28, 1982.

Rick Rossovich, 49, actor (*The Terminator, Roxanne*), born Palo Alto, CA, Aug 28, 1957.

Emma Samms, 46, actress ("General Hospital," "Dynasty"), born Emma Samuelson at London, England, Aug 28, 1960.

David Soul, 60, actor ("Starsky and Hutch," *Salem's Lot*), born Chicago, IL, Aug 28, 1946.

Daniel Stern, 49, actor (*City Slickers, Home Alone*), born Bethesda, MD, Aug 28, 1957.

Shania Twain, 41, country singer, born Eileen Twain at Windsor, ON, Canada, Aug 28, 1965.

AUGUST 29 — TUESDAY
Day 241 — 124 Remaining

"ACCORDING TO HOYLE" DAY (EDMOND HOYLE DEATH ANNIVERSARY). Aug 29, 1769. A day to remember Edmond Hoyle and a day for fun and games *according to the rules*. He is believed to have studied law. For many years he lived at London, England, and gave instructions in the playing of games. His "Short Treatise" on the game of whist (published in 1742) became a model guide to the rules of the game. Hoyle's name became synonymous with the idea of correct play according to the rules, and the phrase "according to Hoyle" became a part of the English language. Hoyle was born at London about 1672 and died there.

AMISTAD SEIZED: ANNIVERSARY. Aug 29, 1839. In January 1839, 53 Africans were seized near modern-day Sierra Leone, taken to Cuba and sold as slaves. While being transferred to another part of the island on the ship *Amistad*, led by the African, Cinque, they seized control of the ship, telling the crew to take them back to Africa. However, the crew secretly changed course and the ship landed at Long Island, NY, where it and its "cargo" were seized as salvage. The *Amistad* was towed to New Haven, CT, where the Africans were imprisoned and a lengthy legal battle began to determine if they were property to be returned to Cuba or free men. John Quincy Adams took their case all the way to the Supreme Court, where on Mar 9, 1841, it was determined that they were free and could return to Africa.

BERGMAN, INGRID: BIRTH ANNIVERSARY. Aug 29, 1915. One of cinema's greatest actresses. Bergman was born at Stockholm, Sweden, and died at London, England, on her 67th birthday, Aug 29, 1982. Three-time Academy Award winner for *Gaslight, Anastasia, Murder on the Orient Express*. Controversy over her personal life made her and her films unpopular to American audiences during an interval of several years between periods of awards and adulation.

HOLMES, OLIVER WENDELL: BIRTH ANNIVERSARY. Aug 29, 1809. Physician and author, father of Supreme Court justice Oliver Wendell Holmes, born at Cambridge, MA. Died at Boston, MA, Oct 7, 1894. "A moment's insight," he wrote, "is sometimes worth a life's experience."

LOCKE, JOHN: BIRTH ANNIVERSARY. Aug 29, 1632 (OS). English philosopher, founder of philosophical liberalism, born at Wrington, England. His ideas influenced the American colonists and were enshrined in the Constitution. Locke died at Essex, England, Oct 28, 1704 (OS).

MORE HERBS, LESS SALT DAY. Aug 29. It's healthier, zestier and lustier! [©2003 by WH.] For info: Thomas & Ruth Roy, Wellcat Holidays, 2418 Long Ln, Lebanon, PA 17046. Phone: (717) 279-0184. E-mail: info@wellcat.com. Web: www.wellcat.com.

PARKER, CHARLIE: BIRTH ANNIVERSARY. Aug 29, 1920. Jazz saxophonist Charlie Parker was born at Kansas City, KS. He earned the nickname "Yardbird" (later "Bird") from his habit of sitting in the backyard of speakeasies, fingering his saxophone. His career as a jazz saxophonist took him from jam sessions in Kansas City to New York, where he met Dizzy Gillespie and others who were creating a style of music that would become known as bop or bebop. Although his musical genius was unquestioned, Parker's addiction to heroin haunted his life. He died at Rochester, NY, Mar 12, 1955, at the age of 34.

ROYAL GEORGE SINKS: ANNIVERSARY. Aug 29, 1792. Prized British battleship *Royal George* sank due to fatal human error in one of the worst maritime disasters in history. While the ship was being repaired at Spithead, the port side was tilted too close to the waterline. A gust of wind lowered the ship even further, allowing tons of water to flood into its open gunports. The ship sank within minutes before many of the 1,300 on board realized what was happening and more than 900 people drowned.

SHAYS REBELLION: ANNIVERSARY. Aug 29, 1786. Daniel Shays, veteran of the battles of Lexington, Bunker Hill, Ticonderoga and Saratoga, was one of the leaders of more than 1,000 rebels who sought redress of grievances during the depression days of 1786–87. They prevented general court sessions and on Sept 26 they prevented Supreme Court sessions at Springfield, MA. On Jan 25, 1787, they attacked the federal arsenal at Springfield; Feb 2, Shays's troops were routed and fled. Shays was sentenced to death but pardoned June 13, 1788. Later he received a small pension for services in the American Revolution.

SLOVAKIA: NATIONAL UPRISING DAY. Aug 29. National holiday. Commemorates resistance to Nazi occupation in 1944.

SOVIET COMMUNIST PARTY SUSPENDED: 15th ANNIVERSARY. Aug 29, 1991. The Supreme Soviet, the parliament of the USSR, suspended all activities of the Communist Party, seizing its property and bringing to an end the institution that ruled the Soviet Union for nearly 75 years. The action followed an unsuccessful coup Aug 19–21 that sought to overthrow the government of Soviet President Mikhail Gorbachev but instead prompted a sweeping wave of democratic change. Gorbachev quit as party leader Aug 24.

BIRTHDAYS TODAY

Sir Richard Attenborough, 83, filmmaker (*In Which We Serve, The Great Escape*), born Cambridge, England, Aug 29, 1923.

Rebecca De Mornay, 44, actress (*Risky Business, The Hand That Rocks the Cradle*), born Santa Rosa, CA, Aug 29, 1962.

William Friedkin, 67, filmmaker (Oscar for *The French Connection; The Exorcist*), born Chicago, IL, Aug 29, 1939.

Richard Gere, 57, actor (*An Officer and a Gentleman, Pretty Woman*), born Philadelphia, PA, Aug 29, 1949.

Elliott Gould, 68, actor (*M*A*S*H, The Long Goodbye*), born Elliott Goldstein at Brooklyn, NY, Aug 29, 1938.

Michael Jackson, 48, singer, songwriter, born Gary, IN, Aug 29, 1958.

Robin Leach, 65, TV host ("Lifestyles of the Rich and Famous"), born London, England, Aug 29, 1941.

Pablo Mastrioeni, 30, soccer player, born Mendoza, Argentina, Aug 29, 1976.

John Sidney McCain III, 70, US Senator (R, Arizona), born Panama Canal Zone, Aug 29, 1936.

Mark Morris, 50, choreographer, dancer, born Seattle, WA, Aug 29, 1956.

Roy Oswalt, 29, baseball player, born Kosciusko, MS, Aug 29, 1977.

William Edward (Will) Perdue III, 41, former basketball player, born Melbourne, FL, Aug 29, 1965.

Pierre Turgeon, 37, hockey player, born Rouyn, QC, Canada, Aug 29, 1969.

AUGUST 30 — WEDNESDAY

Day 242 — 123 Remaining

ARTHUR, ELLEN LEWIS HERNDON: BIRTH ANNIVERSARY. Aug 30, 1837. Wife of Chester Alan Arthur, 21st president of the US, born at Fredericksburg, VA. Died at New York, Jan 12, 1880.

BOOTH, SHIRLEY: BIRTH ANNIVERSARY. Aug 30, 1898. American actress Shirley Booth was born Thelma Booth Ford at New York, NY. She won a Tony Award and an Oscar for her roles in the stage (1950) and film (1952) productions of *Come Back, Little Sheba*, but she is best known for her title role in the television program "Hazel" (1961–66). She died at Chatham, MS, Oct 16, 1992.

COLUMBIA COUNTY FAIR. Aug 30–Sept 4. Chatham, NY. Midway and agricultural exhibits for the family to enjoy. For info: Columbia County Tourism Dept, 401 State St, Hudson, NY 12534. Phone: (800) 724-1846. Web: www.columbiacountyny.org or www.columbiafair.com.

CORN PALACE FESTIVAL. Aug 30–Sept 4. Mitchell, SD. Celebration of the harvest and the annual redecoration of the world's only Corn Palace (with ears of corn). Midway and carnival rides, games, specialty vendors, food and top-name entertainment on the stage of the Corn Palace. Est attendance: 40,000. For info: Corn Palace, 612 N Main, Mitchell, SD 57301. Phone: (605) 995-8427. Fax: (605) 995-8443. E-mail: mschilling.cityofmitchell@midconetwork.com. Web: www.cornpalacefestival.com.

FIRST WHITE HOUSE PRESIDENTIAL BABY: BIRTH ANNIVERSARY. Aug 30, 1893. Frances Folsom Cleveland (Mrs Grover Cleveland) was the first presidential wife to have a baby at the White House when she gave birth to a baby girl (Esther). The first child ever born in the White House was a grandson to Thomas Jefferson in 1806.

HUEY P. LONG DAY. Aug 30. A legal holiday in Louisiana.

MacMURRAY, FRED: BIRTH ANNIVERSARY. Aug 30, 1908. Fred MacMurray was born at Kankakee, IL. His film and television career included a wide variety of roles, ranging from comedy (*The Absent-Minded Professor, Son of Flubber, The Shaggy Dog, The Happiest Millionaire*) to serious drama (*The Caine Mutiny, Fair Wind to Java, Double Indemnity*). During 1960–72 he portrayed the father on "My Three Sons," which was second only to "Ozzie and Harriet" as network TV's longest running family sitcom. He died Nov 5, 1991, at Santa Monica, CA.

NATIONAL HOLISTIC PET DAY. Aug 30. A day to celebrate the growing interest in natural/holistic medicine and the animals who are treated holistically. For info: Shawn Messonnier, 2145 W Park, Plano, TX 75075. Phone: (972) 867-8800. Fax: (972) 985-9216. E-mail: shawnvet@sbcglobal.net.

PERU: SAINT ROSE OF LIMA DAY. Aug 30. Saint Rose of Lima was the first saint of the Western Hemisphere. She lived at the time of the colonization by Spain in the 16th century. Patron saint of the Americas and the Philippines. Public holiday in Peru.

RUTHERFORD, ERNEST: BIRTH ANNIVERSARY. Aug 30, 1871. Physicist, born at Nelson, New Zealand. He established the nuclear nature of the atom, the electrical structure of matter and achieved the transmutation of elements, research which later resulted in the atomic bomb. Rutherford died at Cambridge, England, Oct 19, 1937.

SHELLEY, MARY WOLLSTONECRAFT: BIRTH ANNIVERSARY. Aug 30, 1797. English novelist Mary Shelley, daughter of the philosopher William Godwin and the feminist Mary Wollstonecraft and wife of the poet Percy Bysshe Shelley, was born at London and died there Feb 1, 1851. In addition to being the author of the famous novel *Frankenstein*, Shelley is important in literary history for her work in the editing and publishing of her husband's unpublished work after his early death.

SPACE MILESTONE: *CHALLENGER STS-8* (US). Aug 30, 1983. Shuttle *Challenger* with five astronauts (Richard Truly, Daniel Brandenstein, Guion Bluford, Jr, Dale Garner and William Thornton) was launched from Kennedy Space Center, FL, on this date. Return landing six days later on Sept 5 at Edwards Air Force Base, CA.

SPACE MILESTONE: *DISCOVERY* (US). Aug 30, 1984. Space shuttle *Discovery* was launched from Kennedy Space Center, FL, for its maiden flight with six-member crew. During the flight the crew deployed three satellites and used a robot arm before landing at Edwards Air Force Base, CA, Sept 5.

SPAIN: LA TOMATINA. Aug 30. Buñol (near Valencia). The world's biggest food fight takes place today as 35,000 revelers hurl 120 tons of tomatoes at each other (and the town) for two hours. La Tomatina ("Tomato Festival") occurs annually the last Wednesday of August. Festivities kick off with a competition to see who can reach a ham at the top of a greased pole. With the ham secured, the trucks arrive with tomatoes.

STRAITH, CLAIRE, MD: BIRTH ANNIVERSARY. Aug 30, 1891. Innovator in plastic and cosmetic surgery, born at Southfield, MI. After attending an international meeting at Paris, France, at the end of World War I to share information regarding reconstructive surgical techniques used on the battlefield, Straith dedicated his career to the new field of plastic surgery. He developed many of the techniques used in plastic and cosmetic

August 2006	S	M	T	W	T	F	S
			1	2	3	4	5
	6	7	8	9	10	11	12
	13	14	15	16	17	18	19
	20	21	22	23	24	25	26
	27	28	29	30	31		

surgery, designed new surgical instruments and led a campaign that convinced automakers, in 1930, to use safety glass and remove dangerous projections from the interior of cars. Straith died July 13, 1958.

TURKEY: VICTORY DAY. Aug 30. Commemorates victory in War of Independence in 1922. Military parades, performing of the Mehtar band (the world's oldest military band), fireworks.

WILKINS, ROY: BIRTH ANNIVERSARY. Aug 30, 1901. Roy Wilkins, grandson of a Mississippi slave, civil rights leader, active in the National Association for the Advancement of Colored People (NAACP), retired as its executive director in 1977. Born at St. Louis, MO. Died at New York, NY, Sept 8, 1981.

WILLIAMS, TED: BIRTH ANNIVERSARY. Aug 30, 1918. Born Theodore Samuel Williams at San Diego, CA, Ted Williams played his first major league baseball game for the Boston Red Sox on Apr 22, 1939. In the years that followed, he became known as perhaps the best hitter ever to play the game. His career batting average was .344, and his record average of .406 set during the 1941 season stands unsurpassed. He played 19 seasons for the Red Sox, but during the prime of his career, missed three full seasons while serving as a Navy pilot in WWII, and most of two seasons serving as a Marine pilot in the Korean War. He was elected to the Baseball Hall of Fame in 1966. He died July 5, 2002, at Inverness, FL.

BIRTHDAYS TODAY

Elizabeth Ashley, 65, actress (*Agnes of God, Cat on a Hot Tin Roof*, "Evening Shade"), born Elizabeth Ann Cole, Ocala, FL, Aug 30, 1941.

Lewis Black, 58, comedian ("The Daily Show"), born Silver Springs, MD, Aug 30, 1948.

Timothy Bottoms, 55, actor (*The Last Picture Show, The Paper Chase*), born Santa Barbara, CA, Aug 30, 1951.

Michael Chiklis, 43, actor (Emmy and Golden Globe for "The Shield"), born Lowell, MA, Aug 30, 1963.

Cameron Diaz, 34, actress (*My Best Friend's Wedding, There's Something About Mary*), born San Diego, CA, Aug 30, 1972.

Jean-Claude Killy, 63, Olympic gold medal alpine skier, born Saint Cloud, France, Aug 30, 1943.

Peggy Lipton, 59, actress (Golden Globe Award for "The Mod Squad"; "Twin Peaks"), born New York, NY, Aug 30, 1947.

Michael Michele, 40, actress ("Homicide: Life on the Street," "ER"), born Evansville, IN, Aug 30, 1966.

Robert Lee Parish, 53, former basketball player, born Shreveport, LA, Aug 30, 1953.

David Paymer, 52, actor (*City Slickers, Mr Saturday Night*), born Long Island, NY, Aug 30, 1954.

Andy Roddick, 24, tennis player, born Omaha, NE, Aug 30, 1982.

Kitty Wells, 87, singer ("Jealousy"), born Muriel Deason at Nashville, TN, Aug 30, 1919.

AUGUST 31 — THURSDAY

Day 243 — 122 Remaining

"ALICE" TV PREMIERE: 30th ANNIVERSARY. Aug 31, 1976. Linda Lavin played the title role in this CBS comedy that was based on the 1975 film *Alice Doesn't Live Here Anymore*. Alice Hyatt was the new girl in town—a widow raising her son while trying to make ends meet by waitressing at a diner. She had dreams of making it big as a singer. Nine years later, Alice was able to leave her "temp" job for a gig. Lavin's co-stars included Vic Tayback as diner owner Mel Sharples, Philip McKeon as Alice's son Tommy, Beth Howland as waitress Vera Gorman, Polly Holliday as sassy waitress Flo Castleberry. The last telecast aired on July 2, 1985.

BLUE HILL FAIR. Aug 31–Sept 4. Blue Hill, ME. A "down-to-earth" country fair. Annually, Labor Day weekend. Est attendance: 35,000. For info: Blue Hill Fair, PO Box 390, Blue Hill, ME 04614. Phone: (207) 374-3701. Fax: (207) 374-3702. Web: www.bluehillfair.com.

CHARLESTON EARTHQUAKE: ANNIVERSARY. Aug 31, 1886. Charleston, SC. The first major earthquake in the recorded history of the eastern US occurred on this date. It is believed that about 100 persons perished in the quake, centered near Charleston but felt up to 800 miles away. Though a number of smaller eastern US quakes had been described and recorded since 1638, this affected persons living in an area of some 2 million square miles.

CHICAGO JAZZ FESTIVAL. Aug 31–Sept 3 (tentative). Grant Park, Chicago, IL. 28th annual. International line-ups on three stages. Free. Est attendance: 315,000. For info: Mayor's Office of Special Events, City Hall, 121 N LaSalle St, #703, Chicago, IL 60602. Phone: (312) 744-3370. Fax: (312) 744-8523. E-mail: moseinquiry@cityofchicago.org. Web: www.cityofchicago.org/specialevents.

COBURN, JAMES: BIRTH ANNIVERSARY. Aug 31, 1928. Academy Award–winning actor born at Laurel, NE. He rose to fame as the knife thrower in *The Magnificent Seven* and became known for his tough-guy roles in films such as *The Great Escape* and *Our Man Flint*. He received an Oscar for his supporting role in 1999's *Affliction*. He died at Los Angeles, CA, Nov 18, 2002.

"CRANKSHAFT": ANNIVERSARY. Aug 31. Celebrating the anniversary of the nationally syndicated comic strip that premiered Aug 31, 1987. For info: Tom Batiuk, 2750 Substation Rd, Medina, OH 44256. Phone: (330) 722-8755.

KAZAKHSTAN: CONSTITUTION DAY. Aug 31. National holiday. Commemorates the constitution of 1995.

KLONDIKE ELDORADO GOLD DISCOVERY: ANNIVERSARY. Aug 31, 1896. Two weeks after the Rabbit/Bonanza Creek claim was filed, gold was discovered on Eldorado Creek, a tributary of Bonanza. More than $30 million worth of gold (worth some $600–$700 million in today's dollars) was mined from the Eldorado Claim in 1896.

KYRGYZSTAN: INDEPENDENCE DAY. Aug 31. National holiday. Commemorates independence from the former Soviet Union in 1991.

LITTLE BALKANS DAYS. Aug 31–Sept 3. Pittsburg, KS. This event in downtown Pittsburg features approximately 100 craft vendors as well as concessions, tournaments, live entertainment, street dances, quilt show, doll show, baby contest, car show and much more! Annually, Labor Day weekend. Est attendance: 30,000. For info: Pam Henderson, Pittsburg Chamber of Commerce, PO Box 1933, Pittsburg, KS 66762. Phone: (620) 231-1000 or (800) 879-1212. Fax: (620) 231-3178. E-mail: cvb@pittsburgkschamber.com. Web: www.pittsburgkschamber.com.

LOUISIANA SHRIMP AND PETROLEUM FESTIVAL AND FAIR. Aug 31–Sept 4. Morgan City, LA. Free admission to this event that recognizes and celebrates the importance of the shrimp and petroleum industry to the area. Arts, crafts, water and street parades, Cajun culinary classic, music in the park, unique children's village (a magical adventureland), gospel tent, coronation pageant and ball, carnival, blessing of the fleet. Chosen as the American Bus Association's "Festival of the Year" for the past four years. Est attendance: 175,000. For info: Louisiana Shrimp and Petroleum Festival and Fair Assn, Box 103, Morgan City, LA 70381. Phone: (504) 385-0703. Fax: (504) 384-4628. E-mail: info@shrimp-petrofest.org.

LOVE LITIGATING LAWYERS DAY. Aug 31. Lawyer jokes abound, but when push comes to shove, these are the folks who can end up saving the day. [©2003 by WH.] For info: Thomas & Ruth Roy, Wellcat Holidays, 2418 Long Ln, Lebanon, PA 17046. Phone: (717) 279-0184. E-mail: info@wellcat.com. Web: www.wellcat.com.

MALAYSIA: FREEDOM DAY. Aug 31. National holiday. Commemorates independence from Britain in 1957.

MOLDOVA: NATIONAL LANGUAGE DAY. Aug 31. National holiday. Also called Mother Tongue Day. Commemorates the replacement of the Cyrillic alphabet with the Latin alphabet in 1991.

MONTESSORI, MARIA: BIRTH ANNIVERSARY. Aug 31, 1870. Italian physician and educator, born at Chiaraville, Italy. Founder of the Montessori method of teaching children. Montessori died at Noordwijk, Holland, May 6, 1952.

MOON PHASE: FIRST QUARTER. Aug 31. Moon enters First Quarter phase at 6:56 PM, EDT.

NATIONAL SWEETCORN FESTIVAL. Aug 31–Sept 4. McFerron Park, Hoopeston, IL. Annual festival includes 29 tons of free corn on the cob, nationally sanctioned beauty pageant, carnival, flea market, horse show, demolition derby, bands and talent shows. Est attendance: 50,000. For info: Jeanie Cooke, Exec Dir, Danville Area Conv/Visitors Bureau, PO Box 992, Danville, IL 61834. Phone: (217) 442-2096.

NUGGET BEST IN THE WEST RIB COOK-OFF. Aug 31–Sept 4. Victorian Square, Sparks, NV. Rib cookers from across the country compete for the title of Nugget Best in the West Rib Cooker. Competing cookers sell ribs to the crowd over the Labor Day weekend. Free concerts nightly feature groups like BTO, War and Terri Clark. Other music groups presented throughout the day—all free. Hundreds of craft booths and activities for the whole family. Est attendance: 300,000. For info: John Ascuaga's Nugget, 1100 Nugget Ave, Sparks, NV 89431. Phone: (800) 648-1177. Web: www.janugget.com.

OLD THRESHERS REUNION. Aug 31–Sept 4. McMillan Park, Mount Pleasant, IA. The reunion began in 1950. Old Threshers is a celebration of our rich agricultural heritage. Attractions range from displays of steam engines and agricultural exhibits to turn-of-the-century living and antique cars, tractors and gas engines. There are also steam trains, trolleys, crafts, museums, music and camping. Annually, five days ending on Labor Day. Est attendance: 100,000. For info: Midwest Old Threshers, 405 E Threshers Rd, Mt Pleasant, IA 52641. Phone: (319) 385-8937. Fax: (319) 385-0563. Web: www.oldthreshers.org.

ON THE WATERFRONT. Aug 31–Sept 3. Rockford, IL. Illinois's largest music festival. Nine music stages, more than 150 performers, more than 50 specialty foods, and dozens of special events. Est attendance: 350,000. For info: On the Waterfront, Inc, 308 W State St, Ste 115, Rockford, IL 61101. Phone: (815) 964-4388 or (815) 963-4FUN. E-mail: 4fun@onthewaterfront.com. Web: www.onthewaterfront.com.

POLAND: SOLIDARITY FOUNDED: ANNIVERSARY. Aug 31, 1980. The Polish trade union Solidarity was formed at the Baltic Sea port of Gdansk, Poland. Outlawed by the government, many of its leaders were arrested. Led by Lech Walesa, Solidarity persisted in its opposition to the Communist-controlled government, and Aug 19, 1989, Polish president Wojciech Jaruzelski astonished the world by nominating for the post of prime minister Tadeusz Mazowiecki, a deputy in the Polish Assembly, 1961–72, and editor-in-chief of Solidarity's weekly newspaper, bringing to an end 42 years of Communist Party domination.

SAROYAN, WILLIAM: BIRTH ANNIVERSARY. Aug 31, 1908. American writer of Armenian descent, author of *The Human Comedy* and of the Pulitzer Prize–winning play *The Time of Your Life*, was born at Fresno, CA, and died there May 18, 1981. In April 1981 he gave reporters a final statement for publication after his death: "Everybody has got to die, but I have always believed an exception would be made in my case. Now what?"

SHAWN, WILLIAM: BIRTH ANNIVERSARY. Aug 31, 1907. William Shawn, editor of *The New Yorker* for 35 years, was born at Chicago, IL. He was virtual dictator of editorial policy for the magazine, which in turn had an impact on the literary and reportorial styles of writers throughout the country. Nonfiction pieces in *The New Yorker* contributed to public opinion on important issues during Shawn's tenure. Shawn died Dec 8, 1992, at New York, NY.

THOMAS POINT BEACH BLUEGRASS FESTIVAL. Aug 31–Sept 3. Brunswick, ME. 28th annual festival. Featuring world-class bluegrass musicians on the southern coast of Maine. Swimming, playground, picnic area, snack bar, free camping, Sunday morning worship service on the beach. Fun for the whole family! Enjoy an end-of-summer family outing and terrific bluegrass music. Est attendance: 4,000. For tickets and info: Thomas Point Beach, 29 Meadow Rd, Brunswick, ME 04011. Phone: (207) 725-6009 or (877) TPB-4321. E-mail: summer@thomaspointbeach.com. Web: www.thomaspointbeach.com.

TRINIDAD AND TOBAGO: INDEPENDENCE DAY. Aug 31. National holiday. Became an independent nation within the British Commonwealth on this day in 1962. Trinidad became a republic, Sept 24, 1976.

WHITECHAPEL MURDERS BEGIN: ANNIVERSARY. Aug 31, 1888. At 3:40 AM, the body of Mary Ann Nichols was found in the impoverished Whitechapel district of London, England. This was (debatably) the first in a series of brutal murders that autumn that claimed the lives of at least five women, perhaps more, by a serial killer who has come to be known as "Jack the Ripper" because of the mutilations he inflicted on his victims. The ferocity of the Whitechapel killings created an "Autumn of Terror" in which the entire populace of London was terrified and where mobs frequently tried to mete out justice to suspects they picked. Mary Kelly, found Nov 9, is considered the last victim. No suspect was ever tried for the murders. See also: "'Jack the Ripper' Letter: Anniversary" (Sept 27).

BIRTHDAYS TODAY

Jennifer Azzi, 38, basketball player, born Oak Ridge, TN, Aug 31, 1968.

Debbie Gibson, 36, singer ("Only in My Dreams," "Foolish Beat"), born Brooklyn, NY, Aug 31, 1970.

Van Morrison, 61, singer, songwriter ("Brown Eyed Girl," "Domino"), born Belfast, Northern Ireland, Aug 31, 1945.

Edwin Corley Moses, 51, Olympic gold medal track athlete, born Dayton, OH, Aug 31, 1955.

Hideo Nomo, 38, baseball player, born Osaka, Japan, Aug 31, 1968.

Itzhak Perlman, 61, violinist, born Tel Aviv, Israel, Aug 31, 1945.

Frank Robinson, 71, Hall of Fame baseball player, former baseball executive and manager, born Beaumont, TX, Aug 31, 1935.

Daniel Schorr, 90, journalist, born New York, NY, Aug 31, 1916.

G.D. Spradlin, 86, actor (*The Godfather Part II, North Dallas Forty, The War of the Roses*), born Garvin County, OK, Aug 31, 1920.

Jack Thompson, 66, actor (*The Chant of Jimmie Blacksmith, Breaker Morant*), born Sydney, Australia, Aug 31, 1940.

Glenn Tilbrook, 49, singer, musician, born London, England, Aug 31, 1957.

Chris Tucker, 34, actor (*Rush Hour, The Fifth Element*), born Decatur, GA, Aug 31, 1972.

September.

SEPTEMBER 1 — FRIDAY
Day 244 — 121 Remaining

"ART LINKLETTER'S HOUSE PARTY" TV PREMIERE: ANNIVERSARY. Sept 1, 1952. Television's longest-running daytime variety show was hosted by Art Linkletter. This blend of talk and audience participation started on radio. In 1968 the show was renamed "The Linkletter Show" and moved from the afternoon to a morning slot. The series was well known for its daily interview with four schoolchildren.

ATTENTION DEFICIT HYPERACTIVITY DISORDER MONTH. Sept 1–30. To educate healthcare groups, children and family organizations, teachers, parents and others interested in childhood health issues by providing information on effective treatments for ADHD. Some treatments have been scientifically validated, tested and proven to reduce the severity of ADHD symptoms and thereby reduce adverse consequences in the child's current and future life. There is a $15 charge for kit materials. For info: PPSI, c/o Pharmacy Council on Children's Health, 101 Lucas Valley Rd, Ste 210, San Rafael, CA 94903. Phone: (415) 479-8628. Fax: (415) 479-8608. E-mail: ppsi@aol.com. Web: www.ppsinc.org.

BABY SAFETY MONTH. Sept 1–30. The Juvenile Products Manufacturers Association, Inc (JPMA), a national trade organization of juvenile product manufacturers devoted to helping parents keep baby safe, is disseminating information to parents, grandparents and other child caregivers about baby safety. The information from JPMA pertains to safe selection of juvenile products through the Association's Safety Certification Program and tips on correct use of products such as cribs, car seats, infant carriers and decorative accessories. For a free copy of JPMA's brochure "Safe and Sound for Baby," write to the address below and mark ATTN: JPMA Safety Brochure. Enclose a SASE and specify whether you want the brochure in English or Spanish. For info: JPMA, 15000 Commerce Pkwy, Ste C, Mt Laurel, NJ 08054. E-mail: jpma@ahint.com.

BACKPACK SAFETY AMERICA MONTH. Sept 1–30. Thousands of school-age children are straining in pain under backpacks that are too heavy for their growing bodies. This month is set aside to remind students, parents and teachers about the safe and proper ways to choose, pack, lift and carry a backpack. Annually, the month of September. For info: John Carroll, PO Box 2430, Mt Pleasant, SC 29465. Phone: (800) 672-4277. Fax: (843) 881-6746. E-mail: info@backpacksafe.com. Web: www.backpacksafe.com.

BE KIND TO EDITORS AND WRITERS MONTH. Sept 1–30. A time for editors and writers to show uncommon courtesy toward each other. For info: Lauren Barnett, Lone Star Publications of Humor, 8452 Fredericksburg Rd, PMB 103, San Antonio, TX 78229. E-mail: lspubs@aol.com. Web: members.aol.com/lspubs/lsindex.html.

BENTON NEIGHBOR DAY. Sept 1–2. Benton, MO. Large festival that includes exhibits, greased pole climb, amusement park, Little Mr and Miss Contest, Queen Contest, Jr Miss Contest, greased pig chase, live bands, antique car show, horseshoe tournament, sky divers, kid tractor pull, parade and talent show. Antique tractor pull, outdoor games for kids and adults. Annually, the Friday and Saturday before Labor Day. Est attendance: 3,000. For info: Benton Chamber of Commerce, PO Box 477, Benton, MO 63736. Phone: (573) 545-3125.

BRAZIL: INDEPENDENCE WEEK. Sept 1–7. The independence of Brazil from Portugal in 1822 is commemorated with civic and cultural ceremonies promoted by federal, state and municipal authorities. On Sept 7, a grand military parade takes place and the National Defense League organizes the Running Race in Honor of the Symbolic Torch of the Brazilian Nation.

BRITT DRAFT HORSE SHOW. Sept 1–3. Hancock County Fairgrounds, Britt, IA. One of the largest draft horse hitch shows in North America, featuring 18 six-horse hitches from the US and Canada representing the very best of the Belgian, Percheron and Clydesdale performance horses. Annually, Labor Day weekend. Est attendance: 10,000. For info: Randel or Melodie Hiscocks, Britt Draft Horse Assn, PO Box 312, Britt, IA 50423. Phone: (641) 843-4181.

BUMBERSHOOT: THE SEATTLE ARTS FESTIVAL. Sept 1–4. Seattle Center, Seattle, WA. Celebrates the arts in every genre; includes kids' activities. Annually, Labor Day weekend. Est attendance: 250,000. For info: One Reel, PO Box 9750, Seattle, WA 98109. Phone: (206) 281-8111. E-mail: info@onereel.org. Web: www.bumbershoot.org.

BURROUGHS, EDGAR RICE: BIRTH ANNIVERSARY. Sept 1, 1875. US novelist (*Tarzan of the Apes*), born at Chicago, IL. Correspondent for the *Los Angeles Times*, died at Encino, CA, Mar 19, 1950.

CANADA: CLASSIC BOAT FESTIVAL. Sept 1–3. Victoria, BC. Classic sail and power vessels from all over the west coast of the US, Canada and beyond gather in Victoria's Inner Harbour. View these lovingly restored and maintained boats with their polished brass fittings and rich teak and oak decks and hulls. Schooner races, sail-past, steamboat parade. Sponsored by Victoria Real Estate Board and Monday Publications. For info: Classic Boat Festival, 3035 Nanaimo St, Victoria, BC, Canada V8T 4W2. Phone: (604) 385-7766. Fax: (604) 385-8773. E-mail: vreb@vreb.org. Web: www.classicboatfestival.ca.

CANADA: MAYNOOTH MADNESS AND LOGGERS GAMES. Sept 1–2. Maynooth, ON. An exciting, fun-filled weekend for the whole family, with loggers' games and parade, children's activities, petting zoo, pony rides and a craft show featuring original arts and crafts. Est attendance: 7,000. For info: Bancroft and District Chamber of Commerce, PO Box 539, Bancroft, ON, Canada K0L 1C0. Phone: (613) 332-1513. Fax: (613) 332-2119. E-mail: chamber@commerce.bancroft.on.ca. Web: www.bancroftdistrict.com.

CARTIER, JACQUES: DEATH ANNIVERSARY. Sept 1, 1557. French navigator and explorer who sailed from St. Malo, France, Apr 20, 1534, in search of a northwest passage to the Orient. Instead, he discovered the St. Lawrence River, explored Canada's coastal regions and took possession of the country for France. Cartier was born at St. Malo, about 1491 (exact date unknown) and died there.

CHICKEN BOY'S BIRTHDAY. Sept 1. Chicken Boy is a 22-ft statue of a boy with a chicken's head, holding a bucket of chicken. Formerly the mascot for the restaurant for which he is named, he was rescued from destruction when the restaurant went out of business by Future Studio of Los Angeles, a graphic design studio. Chicken Boy has since become a pop culture icon. (Some call him the Statue of Liberty of Los Angeles.) For info: Amy Inouye, Future Studio, PO Box 292000, Los Angeles, CA 90029. Phone: (323) 254-4565. Fax: (323) 254-2010. E-mail: amy@futurestudio.com. Web: www.chickenboy.com.

CHILDREN'S GOOD MANNERS MONTH™. Sept 1–30. Starts the school year with a national program of teachers and parents encouraging good manners in children. The year-long program includes monthly objectives that work in conjunction with a reinforcing home program. For info: "Dr. Manners," Fleming Allaire, PhD, 35 Eastfield St, Manchester, CT 06040. Phone: (860) 643-0051. E-mail: dr.manners@cox.net. Web: www.good mannersclub.com.

CHILE: NATIONAL MONTH. Sept 1–30. A month of special significance in Chile: arrival of spring, a Day of Unity on the first Monday in September, Independence of Chile anniversary (proclaimed Sept 18, 1810) and celebration of the 1980 Constitution and Army Day, Sept 19.

COLLEGE SAVINGS MONTH. Sept 1–30. Encourages families to plan ahead for the cost of college attendance. College savings programs make it easy and affordable for the average family to save and are available in most states. The programs offer affordable, flexible and tax-advantaged savings options that deliver the dream of education to our most precious resources—the children of America. Sponsored by the College Savings Plan Network of the National Association of State Treasurers. For info: College Savings Plan Network, PO Box 11910, Lexington, KY 40578-1910. Phone: (859) 244-8175. Fax: (859) 244-8053. E-mail: cspn@csg.org. Web: www.collegesavings.org.

DANIEL BOONE PIONEER FESTIVAL. Sept 1–3. Winchester, KY. Take yourself back to the days of Daniel Boone and the pioneers. Features street dance, fireworks, 5k run, arts and crafts displays and food booths. Est attendance: 35,000. For info: Daniel Boone Pioneer Festival, 2 S Maple St, Winchester, KY 40391. Phone: (859) 744-0556. Fax: (859) 744-9229. E-mail: info@tourwinchester.com.

EMMA M. NUTT DAY. Sept 1. A day to honor the first woman telephone operator, Emma M. Nutt, who reportedly began her professional career at Boston, MA, Sept 1, 1878, and continued working as a telephone operator for some 33 years.

ENGLAND: BLACKPOOL ILLUMINATIONS. Sept 1–Nov 5. The Promenade, Blackpool, Lancashire. "A five-mile spectacle of lighting." Est attendance: 3,000,000. For info: Blackpool Tourism, 1 Clifton St, Blackpool, Lancashire, England FY1 1LY. Phone: (44) 1253 478203. Fax: (44) 1253 478210. E-mail: tourism@blackpool.gov.uk. Web: www.visitblackpool.com.

EVERLY BROTHERS/CENTRAL CITY ROCK 'N ROLL CRUISE-IN & CONCERT. Sept 1–2. Central City, KY. Cruise the "famous Central City Strip" in your street rod or muscle car. Enjoy the concert on Sept 2. Lots of concessions, booths and fun. Est attendance: 10,000. For info: Central City Music Festival, 208 N First St, Central City, KY 42330. Phone: (270) 754-2360. Fax: (270) 754-2365. Web: www.centralcityky.com or www.centralcitykytourism.

FALL HAT MONTH. Sept 1–30. A month of celebration during which the straw hat is put aside in favor of the felt or fabric hat by both men and women. Local businesses and the media are encouraged to plan hat-related activities. The Headwear Information Bureau hosts events at several venues throughout the month. For info: Casey Bush, Exec Dir, Headwear Info Bureau, 302 W 12th St, New York, NY 10014. Phone: (212) 627-8333. Web: www.hatsworldwide.com.

	S	M	T	W	T	F	S
September						1	2
2006	3	4	5	6	7	8	9
	10	11	12	13	14	15	16
	17	18	19	20	21	22	23
	24	25	26	27	28	29	30

FALL IN LOVE WITH FOND DU LAC! Sept 1–Oct 31. Fond du Lac, WI. Hike, bike or bird-watch in the Horicon National Wildlife Refuge, home to more than 260 species of birds, including the world's largest flock of migrating Canada geese. Horicon Marsh viewing area is located 12 miles south of Fond du Lac on Hwy 49. Also explore colorful Kettle Moraine State Forest. Enjoy orchard hayrides, art galleries, farm markets, ranch tours, country roads co-guided tours and more. Annually, September and October. Est attendance: 4,500. For info: Fond du Lac Area Conv and Visitors Bureau, 171 S Pioneer Rd, Fond du Lac, WI 54935. Phone: (800) 937-9123 x92. Fax: (920) 929-6846. E-mail: market@fdl.com. Web: www.fdl.com.

FESTIVAL OF CHILDREN. Sept 1–30. South Coast Plaza, Costa Mesa, CA. The festival includes more than 65 local charities and Southern California organizations hosting live performances, free workshops, activities and special guest appearances. Est attendance: 2,000,000. For info: Festival of Children, South Coast Plaza, Carousel Court, 3333 Bristol St, Costa Mesa, CA 92626. Phone: (714) 546-0110. Web: www.festivalofchildren.org.

FORT BRIDGER RENDEZVOUS. Sept 1–4. Fort Bridger, WY. Come and join in the family fun with entertainment, food booths, merchandise exhibits and much more. Est attendance: 30,000. For info: Traci Hardy, Fort Bridger Rendezvous Assn, PO Box 9, Woodruff, UT 84086. Phone: (435) 793-4570. E-mail: fbrainc@hotmail.com. Web: www.fortbridgerrendezvous.net.

GERMANY: CAPITAL RETURNS TO BERLIN: ANNIVERSARY. Sept 1, 1999. In July the monthlong process of moving the German government from Bonn to Berlin began, eight years after Parliament had voted to return to its prewar seat. Berlin officially became the capital of Germany on Sept 1, 1999, and Parliament reconvened at the newly restored Reichstag on Sept 7, 1999.

GO WILD DURING CALIFORNIA WILD RICE MONTH. Sept 1–30. To promote greater appreciation and use of cultivated wild rice. California wild rice growers want America to know that wild rice is no longer simply hiding inside a holiday turkey. This versatile grain can add a gourmet touch to meals year-round. Stuff it inside pork chop pockets and chicken breasts or toss it into soups, salads, stir-frys and even pancake and muffin batters. Let your imagination run wild! Annually, the month of September. For info: The Thacker Group, 4550 Post Oak Pl, Ste 307, Houston, TX 77027. Phone: (713) 355-1242. Fax: (713) 355-1952. E-mail: julie@thackergroup.com. Web: www.cawildrice.com.

GREAT AMERICAN LOW-CHOLESTEROL, LOW-FAT PIZZA BAKE. Sept 1–30. Pizza parlors, restaurants and volunteer agencies nationwide create healthy pizza recipes to increase the public's awareness of the benefits of controlling high cholesterol levels through diet. For info: Frederick S. Mayer, Pres, Cholesterol Council of America, c/o PPSI, 101 Lucas Valley Rd, #210, San Rafael, CA 94903. Phone: (415) 479-8628. Fax: (415) 479-8608. E-mail: ppsi@aol.com. Web: www.ppsinc.org.

GYNECOLOGIC CANCER AWARENESS MONTH. Sept 1–30. During September, women are encouraged to learn more about gynecologic cancers—how they can be detected and prevented before they become fatal. For more information, please visit the Gynecologic Cancer Foundation at www.thegcf.org or the Women's Cancer Network at www.wcn.org. For info: Gynecologic Cancer Foundation, 230 W Monroe, Ste 2528, Chicago, IL 60606. Phone: (312) 578-1439. Fax: (312) 578-9769. E-mail: info@thegcf.org. Web: www.thegcf.org.

HOG CAPITAL OF THE WORLD FESTIVAL. Sept 1–4. Kewanee, IL. World's largest pork chop BBQ. Also features professional entertainment, carnival, flea market, Model T races, parade, four-mile run (Hog Stampede) and the Hogatta Regatta. Annually, Labor Day weekend. Est attendance: 60,000. For info: Mark Mikenas, Exec VP, Kewanee Chamber of Commerce, 113 E 2nd St, Kewanee, IL 61443. Phone: (309) 852-2175. Fax: (309) 852-2176. E-mail: chamber@kewanee-il.com. Web: www.kewanee-il.com or www.kewaneehogdays.com.

HOISINGTON CELEBRATION. Sept 1–4. Bicentennial Park, Hoisington, KS. Annual event includes dances, demolition derby, parade, car show, carnival, kiddie events, baby contest, float contest. Annually, Labor Day weekend. Est attendance: 25,000. For info: Hoisington Labor Day Committee, 123 N Main, Hoisington, KS 67544. Phone: (620) 653-4311.

INTERNATIONAL ENTHUSIASM WEEK. Sept 1–7. Display genuine enthusiasm to every person, every project, every possibility that comes your way. It will change your week, your month, your year, your life. For info: Carolyn Stein, 1901 S Oak Haven Circle, Miami, FL 33179. Phone: (305) 931-3237. Fax: (305) 682-1416. E-mail: carolyn@carolynstein.com. Web: www.carolynstein.com.

INTERNATIONAL PEOPLE SKILLS MONTH. Sept 1–30. Get a better job, improve the office atmosphere and increase rapport with your family. How? By refining your people skills and learning how to "de-puzzle" human behavior. More information is available on resolving conflicts, gaining influence and encouraging others. For info: Karla Brandau, Pres, People Skills Intl, 4985 Chartley Circle, Lilburn, GA 30047. Phone: (770) 923-0883. Fax: (770) 931-2530. E-mail: karla@karlaspeaks.com. Web: www.4peopleskills.com.

INTERNATIONAL SELF-AWARENESS MONTH. Sept 1–30. Cathcart Institute Inc of Lake Sherwood, CA, hosts this month each year to draw attention to the value of knowing oneself. Taking Socrates's advice "Know Thyself," this effort is targeted to identify, highlight and explore all the various means and models people use for improved understanding. Jim Cathcart, founder, is one of the premier professional speakers on self-awareness. For info: Jim Cathcart, Cathcart Institute Inc, 2324 Crombie Ct, Lake Sherwood, CA 91361-5322. Phone: (800) 222-4883. Fax: (805) 777-7013. E-mail: info@cathcart.com. Web: www.cathcart.com.

INTERNATIONAL STRATEGIC THINKING MONTH. Sept 1–30. A monthlong effort to bring awareness of the universal need to improve thinking skills. The International Center for Strategic Planning hosts this month each year to draw attention to the value of proactively seeking to expand individual views of the world and to remove thought barriers that prevent professional achievement, personal fulfillment, cultural awareness and tolerance. For info: Sherrin Ross Ingram, Intl Center for Strategic Planning, 104 W Chestnut St, #101, Hinsdale, IL 60521. Phone: (800) 962-4750. Fax: (800) 962-0177. E-mail: info@icfsp.com. Web: www.icfsp.com.

JAPAN: KANTO EARTHQUAKE MEMORIAL DAY: ANNIVERSARY. Sept 1, 1923. A day to remember the 57,000 people who died during Japan's greatest earthquake.

JOHNSON CITY FIELD DAYS. Sept 1–4. Northside Park, Johnson City, NY. Amusement rides, game booths, live entertainment, food concessions, area's largest fireworks display. The annual celebration benefits many nonprofit organizations in Johnson City. Annually, Labor Day weekend. For info: Johnson City Celebration Committee, 243 Main St, Johnson City, NY 13790. Phone: (607) 798-7861. Fax: (607) 798-7865. E-mail: jcmayor@stny.rr.com.

KOREAN AIR LINES FLIGHT 007 DISASTER: ANNIVERSARY. Sept 1, 1983. Korean Air Lines Flight 007, en route from New York, NY, to Seoul, Korea, reportedly strayed more than 100 miles off course, flying over secret Soviet military installations on the Kamchatka Peninsula and Sakhalin Island. Two and one half hours after it was said to have entered Soviet airspace, a Soviet interceptor plane destroyed the Boeing 747 with 269 persons on board which then crashed in the Sea of Japan. There were no survivors. President Reagan, in Proclamation 5093, named Sunday, Sept 11, 1983, as a National Day of Mourning as "homage to the memory of those who died."

LABOR DAY PICNIC. Sept 1–4. Live Oak, FL. Great family weekend for outdoor and kid activities. With live music! For info: Spirit of the Suwannee Music Park, 3076 95th Dr, Live Oak, FL

32060. Phone: (386) 364-1683. Fax: (386) 364-2998. E-mail: spirit@musicliveshere.com. Web: www.musicliveshere.com.

LIBRARY CARD SIGN-UP MONTH. Sept 1–30. This observance was launched in 1987 to meet the challenge of then Secretary of Education William J. Bennett who said, "Let's have a national campaign. . . . every child should obtain a library card—and use it." Since then, thousands of public and school libraries join each fall in a national effort to ensure every child does just that. Annually, the month of September. For info: American Library Assn, Public Information Office, 50 E Huron St, Chicago, IL 60611. Phone: (312) 280-5043 or (312) 280-5042. E-mail: pio@ala.org. Web: www.ala.org.

LIBYA: REVOLUTION DAY. Sept 1. Commemorates the revolution in 1969 when King Idris I was overthrown by Colonel Qaddafi. National holiday.

MARCIANO, ROCKY: BIRTH ANNIVERSARY. Sept 1, 1923. Rocky Marciano, boxer born Rocco Francis Marchegiano at Brockton, MA. Marciano used superb conditioning to fashion an impressive record that propelled him to fight against Jersey Joe Walcott for the heavyweight title on Sept 23, 1952. Marciano knocked Walcott out and in 1956 he retired as the only undefeated heavyweight champion. Died in a plane crash at Newton, IA, Aug 31, 1969. The film *Somebody Up There Likes Me* recounts his life story.

MARSHALL COUNTY BLUEBERRY FESTIVAL. Sept 1–4. Plymouth, IN. More than 600 craft and commercial booths, parade, carnival, fireworks, 15k run, antique car show, horse pull and luscious blueberry treats. Est attendance: 500,000. For info: Marshall County Blueberry Festival, 220 N Center St, PO Box 639, Plymouth, IN 46563-0639. Phone: (574) 936-5020 or (888) 936-5020. Fax: (574) 936-9845. E-mail: blueberrymail@blueberryfestival.org. Web: www.blueberryfestival.org.

MENOPAUSE AWARENESS MONTH. Sept 1–30. More than 1,500 American women reach menopause every day. This is the month to make an appointment with your healthcare provider and take charge of your health during and after menopause. For info: American Menopause Foundation, 350 Fifth Ave, Ste 2822, New York, NY 10118. Phone: (212) 714-2398. E-mail: menopause@earthlink.net. Web: www.americanmenopause.org.

METAPHYSICAL AWARENESS MONTH. Sept 1–30. A time to review our holistic lifestyle and reconnect to the source of all living and nonliving things, which we are and are not aware of, which constantly keeps us healthy and safe. A newsletter is available. For info: Rev Margaret Allbritten, Light Paths, 302 Lincoln St #21, Roseville, CA 95678. Phone: (916) 446-4961. E-mail: goldenfire@mail.com.

MEXICO: PRESIDENT'S STATE OF THE UNION ADDRESS. Sept 1. National holiday.

MILLION MINUTE FAMILY CHALLENGE™. Sept 1–Dec 31. 6th annual. A national effort to bring family, friends and neighbors together through board games. Goal is one million minutes of game playing. Add your minutes to the running total at www.millionminute.com. Special teacher material and media information available, including press kits, interviews, etc. Annually, September through December. For info: Frank Beres, Million Minute Family Challenge, PO Box 268, Beloit, WI 53512-0268. Phone: (800) 524-4263. Fax: (608) 362-8178. E-mail: millionminute@patchproducts.com. Web: www.millionminute.com.

MISSION SAN LUIS OBISPO DE TOLOSA: FOUNDING ANNIVERSARY. Sept 1, 1772. California mission to the Indians.

NATIONAL ALCOHOL AND DRUG ADDICTION RECOVERY MONTH. Sept 1–30. An initiative of the US Department of Health and Human Services and Substance Abuse and Mental Health Services Administration. Celebrated in local communities throughout the nation, this celebration lauds the contributions of drug and alcohol abuse treatment providers and promotes the message that recovery from drug and alcohol use in all its forms is possible. For info: Natl Alcohol and Drug Addiction Recovery Month, 1 Choke Cherry Rd, Room 8-1054, Rockville, MD 20857. Phone: (240) 276-1660. Fax: (240) 276-1670. Web: www.recoverymonth.gov.

NATIONAL BISCUIT MONTH. Sept 1–30. To promote usage of biscuits in restaurants and other food service outlets. Biscuits are a classic American food, good at any time of day—morning, noon or night. They're great alone and make a perfect partner to all sorts of dishes. For info: Tom O'Brien, Bakery Chef, Inc. Phone: (312) 372-6142.

NATIONAL CHAMPIONSHIP CHUCKWAGON RACES. Sept 1–3. Clinton, AR. 21st annual. Five divisions of chuckwagon races, bronc fanning, Snowy River race, live entertainment, trail rides, barn dance, Western show, Western art, saddles, tack-clothing vendors. Annually, Labor Day weekend. Est attendance: 25,000. For info: Dan Eoff, 2848 Shake Rag Rd, Clinton, AR 72031. Phone: (501) 745-8407. Fax: (501) 745-4416. E-mail: chuckwag@artelco.com. Web: www.chuckwagonraces.com.

NATIONAL CHICKEN MONTH. Sept 1–30. Focuses food shoppers' and restaurant customers' attention on chicken as the most healthy, convenient, economical and versatile food available; in short, "America's favorite." For info: Bill Roenigk, Sr VP, Natl Chicken Council, 1015 15th St NW, Ste 930, Washington, DC 20005. Phone: (202) 296-2622. Fax: (202) 293-4005. E-mail: WRoenigk@chickenUSA.org. Web: www.eatchicken.com or www.nationalchickencouncil.com.

NATIONAL CHILDHOOD INJURY PREVENTION WEEK. Sept 1–7. Injuries continue to be the #1 killer of American children. This week promotes prevention and intervention of unintentional injuries to children and emphasizes community involvement. Although money cannot buy social change, no significant change can happen without it. We invite you to join our mission. "Because the worst kind of childhood injury is the one that could have been prevented."® For info on our strategic partnership and sponsorship opportunities to help us mobilize the necessary human and financial resources to accomplish our objectives, contact The As Safe As Possible Campaign, PO Box 715, Richboro, PA 18954. E-mail: nobooboos@AsSafeAsPossible.org. Web: www.AsSafeAsPossible.org.

NATIONAL CIVICS AWARENESS MONTH. Sept 1–30. A national observance month to promote citizen participation in programs, activities and events pertaining to civic awareness and to encourage continued acknowledgment of historical civic events. This focused initiative is to inspire local communities to celebrate established activities during this month such as Library Card Sign Up Month, Patriot Day, National POW/MIA Recognition Day, Constitution Week and Citizenship Day. Also to initiate new civic related activities such as local voters registration drives, selective service drives, school children identification drives and other significant civic activities, events and programs. For info: Tracy Baulding, Natl Civics Awareness Month, PO Box 1775, Pittsburgh, PA 15230. E-mail: tabaulding@yahoo.com.

September 2006

	S	M	T	W	T	F	S
						1	2
	3	4	5	6	7	8	9
	10	11	12	13	14	15	16
	17	18	19	20	21	22	23
	24	25	26	27	28	29	30

NATIONAL COUPON MONTH. Sept 1–30. Sponsored by the Coupon Council of the Promotional Marketing Association and celebrates the nearly four billion dollar savings American consumers receive each year by redeeming coupons for their favorite brands. Contests and fun activities are planned on a national level to raise the awareness of coupons and their redemption value. For info: Sherry Lauderback, Valassis, 19775 Victor Parkway, Livonia, MI 47152. Phone: (734) 591-7374. Fax: (734) 591-4503. E-mail: lauderbacks@valassis.com. Web: www.couponmonth.com.

NATIONAL 5-A-DAY MONTH. Sept 1–30. To encourage all Americans to increase the amount of fruits and vegetables they eat to five to nine servings per day, to better their health and reduce their risk of cancer and other chronic diseases. For info: Produce for Better Health Foundation, 5341 Limestone Rd, Wilmington, DE 19808-1249. Phone: (302) 235-ADAY or (800) 4-CANCER. Web: www.5aday.org.

NATIONAL HARD CRAB DERBY AND FAIR. Sept 1–3. Somers Cover Marina grounds, Crisfield, MD. 58th annual. An annual Labor Day weekend tradition celebrating Chesapeake Bay's favorite crustacean. Features the famous crab races, crab feast, Miss Crustacean beauty contest, fishing contest, crab picking contest, boat parades, great food and lots more. For info: Crisfield Chamber of Commerce, PO Box 292, Crisfield, MD 21817. Phone: (410) 968-2500 or (800) 782-3913. Fax: (410) 968-0524. Web: www.crisfieldchamber.com/crabderby.htm.

NATIONAL HONEY MONTH. Sept 1–30. To honor the US's 211,600 beekeepers and 2.63 million colonies of honeybees, which produce more than 220 million pounds of honey each year. For info: Natl Honey Bd, 390 Lashley St, Longmont, CO 80501-6045. Phone: (303) 776-2337. Web: www.honey.com.

NATIONAL MUSHROOM MONTH. Sept 1–30. To promote the greater appreciation and use of fresh mushrooms. For info: Ruth Lowenberg, Lewis & Neale, Inc, 35 E 21st St, New York, NY 10010. Phone: (212) 420-8808. Fax: (212) 254-2452. E-mail: ruth@lewis-neale.com. Web: www.mushroominfo.com.

NATIONAL ORGANIC HARVEST MONTH. Sept 1–30. National celebration to educate all ages about organic agriculture and products sponsored by Organic Trade Association. Local and regional events organized by retailers, manufacturers, distributors and consumer groups include food fairs, tastings, farm tours, cooking demonstrations and meet-the-farmer days. Annually, the month of September. For info: Holly Givens, Organic Trade Assn, PO Box 547, Greenfield, MA 01302. Phone: (413) 774-7511. Fax: (413) 774-6432. E-mail: info@ota.com. Web: www.theorganicreport.org.

NATIONAL OSTEOPATHIC MEDICINE MONTH. Sept 1–30. Celebrated by the American Osteopathic Association to raise public awareness of osteopathic medicine. Activities may include a health fair, blood drive, public advertising campaigns and more. For info: American Osteopathic Assn, 142 E Ontario St, Chicago, IL 60611. Phone: (312) 202-8045. Fax: (312) 202-8345. Web: www.osteopathic.org.

★**NATIONAL OVARIAN CANCER AWARENESS MONTH.** Sept 1–30.

NATIONAL PEDICULOSIS PREVENTION MONTH. Sept 1–30. To promote awareness of how to prevent pediculosis and protect against unnecessary and potentially harmful pesticide treatments for head lice. For info: Natl Pediculosis Assn, 50 Kearney Rd, Needham, MA 02494. Phone: (781) 449-NITS. Fax: (781) 449-8129. Web: www.headlice.org or www.licemeister.org.

NATIONAL PIANO MONTH. Sept 1–30. Recognizes America's most popular instrument and its more than 20 million players; also encourages piano study by people of all ages. For info: Donald W. Dillon, Exec Dir, Natl Piano Foundation, 13140 Coit Rd, Ste 320, LB 120, Dallas, TX 75240-5737. Phone: (972) 233-9107. Fax: (972) 490-4219. E-mail: don@dondillon.com. Web: www.pianonet.com.

NATIONAL POTATO MONTH. Sept 1–30. To celebrate the taste, variety and nutrition of potatoes. This month is dedicated to the celebration of one of America's most popular foods—the potato. For info: Cape Cod Potato Chips, 100 Breed's Hill Rd, Hyannis, MA 02601. Phone: (508) 775-3358. Web: www.capecodchips.com.

NATIONAL PREPAREDNESS MONTH. Sept 1–30. A nationwide coordinated effort held each September to promote emergency preparedness in the home, workplace, school and community. The US Department of Homeland Security and a wide variety of public and private sector organizations will participate in events and activities to highlight the importance of emergency preparedness. For info: US Department of Homeland Security, Office of Public Affairs, Washington, DC 20528. Phone: (202) 282-8010.

NATIONAL RICE MONTH. Sept 1–30. To focus attention on the importance of rice to the American diet and to salute the US rice industry. For info: Molly Johnson, Mgr Retail Trade Development, USA Rice Federation, 4301 North Fairfax Dr, Arlington, VA 22203. Phone: (703) 236-2300. Web: www.usarice.com or www.nationalricemonth.com.

NATIONAL SCHOOL SUCCESS MONTH. Sept 1–30. Today's young people have many distractions from school and are sometimes overwhelmed when it comes to academics. Parents are often unskilled at effectively redirecting the attention of their children, especially their teenagers. This observance is to recognize parents who want to support and encourage their children to succeed in school and to explore ways to do that. Annually, the month of September. For info send SASE to: Dale Eshleman, Episcopal Counseling Center, 1021-A E Robinson St, Orlando, FL 32801. Phone: (800) 544-1817.

NATIONAL SKIN CARE AWARENESS MONTH. Sept 1–30. This special month focuses on providing education on caring for your skin. Topics include protecting your skin from the dangers of the sun, how diet and lifestyle affect your skin, developing a proper skin care routine and myths and facts about skin care products. All important knowledge for great-looking skin. For info: Renee Rouleau Skin Care, 4025 Preston Rd, Ste 606, Dallas, TX 75093. Phone: (972) 378-6655. Web: www.reneerouleau.com.

NATIONAL VERY IMPORTANT PARENTS (VIP) MONTH™. Sept 1–30. Family Information Services (FIS) is an organization serving professionals who provide information and support about parenting, child guidance, and family relationships in their communities. VIP Month celebrates the crucial role parents play in the growth and development of their children, and focuses on a different important area of parenting each year. Free ready-to-copy master page for promoting VIP Month is available. Annually, in September. For info, send SASE to: Family Information Services, 12565 Jefferson St NE, Ste 102, Minneapolis, MN 55434-2102. Phone: (800) 852-8112 or (763) 755-6233. Fax: (763) 755-7355. E-mail: staff@familyinfoserv.com. Web: www.familyinfoserv.com.

NORTH CAROLINA APPLE FESTIVAL. Sept 1–4. Hendersonville, NC. Festival includes arts and crafts displays, entertainment, food booths, sports events and much more. Est attendance: 200,000. For info: North Carolina Apple Festival, PO Box 886, Hendersonville, NC 28793. Phone: (828) 697-4557.

OATMEAL FESTIVAL. Sept 1–2. Bertram/Oatmeal, TX. Annual festival to honor Oatmeal, the community and the cereal, and to have a weekend of family fun, good food and a whole lot of foolishness. Annually, Friday and Saturday before Labor Day. Est attendance: 7,000. For info: Oatmeal Fest, PO Box 70, Bertram/Oatmeal, TX 78605. Phone: (512) 355-2197. Fax: (512) 355-3182.

ODYSSEY—A GREEK FESTIVAL. Sept 1–4. Orange, CT. An indoor/outdoor festival celebrating Greek culture, featuring authentic Greek cuisine, live music and marketplace. Est attendance: 15,000. For info: St. Barbara Greek Orthodox Church, 480 Racebrook Rd, Orange, CT 06477. Phone: (203) 795-1347. Web: www.saintbarbara.org. Or: Greater New Haven Conv & Visitors Bureau, One Long Wharf Dr, New Haven, CT, 06511. Phone: (203) 777-8550 or (800) 332-STAY. Fax: (203) 782-7755.

OREGON TRAIL RODEO. Sept 1–3. Hastings, NE. PRCA-sponsored rodeo. Annually, Friday–Sunday of Labor Day weekend. Est attendance: 9,000. For info: Sandy Himmelberg, Genl Mgr, Oregon Trail Rodeo, 947 S Baltimore, Hastings, NE 68901. Phone: (402) 462-3247. Fax: (402) 462-4731. Web: www.adamscountyfairgrounds.com.

OVARIAN CANCER AWARENESS MONTH. Sept 1–30. For info: Natl Ovarian Cancer Coalition, 500 NE Spanish River Blvd, Ste 8, Boca Raton, FL 33431. Phone: (888) OVA-RIAN. E-mail: nocc@ovarian.org. Web: www.ovarian.org.

PAYSON GOLDEN ONION DAYS. Sept 1–4. Payson, UT. This unique festival includes amusement rides, fireworks, a parade, arts and crafts displays, entertainment, food booths, a demolition derby and much more. Annually, Labor Day weekend. Est attendance: 13,000. For info: Payson Community Services Dir, 439 W Utah Ave, Payson, UT 84651. Phone: (801) 465-5226. Fax: (801) 465-5208. E-mail: oniondays@payson.org. Web: www.payson.org.

PEDIATRIC CANCER AWARENESS MONTH. Sept 1–30. Bear Necessities Pediatric Cancer Foundation is dedicated to eliminating pediatric cancer and to provide hope and support to those touched by it. Pediatric cancer is the #1 cause of death by disease in children. For info: Bear Necessities Pediatric Cancer Foundation, 23 W Hubbard St, 3rd Fl, Chicago, IL 60610. Phone: (312) 836-BEAR. Fax: (312) 836-1284. Web: www.bearnecessities.org.

PENNSYLVANIA ARTS & CRAFTS COLONIAL FESTIVAL. Sept 1–4. Westmoreland Fairgrounds, Greensburg, PA. Step back to Colonial times with more than 200 exhibits of handcrafted furniture, floral arrangements, ceramics, tole, decorative paintings and wrought iron. Civil War encampment, fife and drum music and food booths. Est attendance: 30,000. For info: Debbie & Dave Stoner, Family Festivals Assn, Inc, PO Box 166, Irwin, PA 15642. Phone: (724) 863-4577. Fax: (724) 863-4577. E-mail: familyfestivals@hotmail.com. Web: www.familyfestivals.com.

PHILLIS WHEATLEY'S POETRY COLLECTION PUBLISHED: ANNIVERSARY. Sept 1, 1773. On this date in 1773, the first book of poetry composed by an African American was published. Phillis Wheatley's *Poems on Various Subjects, Religious and Moral* was published at London, England. This publication came only 12 years after her arrival in America as a child slave from Senegal. In those 12 years, she learned to read and write English and studied literature in English and Latin. Feted in America and England, Wheatley eventually gained her freedom but died in poverty. See also: "Wheatley, Phillis: Death Anniversary" (Dec 5).

PICATINNY PEAK FALL HAWKWATCH. Sept 1–Nov 30. Picatinny Arsenal, Dover, NJ. Fall hawkwatch to count migrating raptors. Between 9,000 and 12,000 raptors per year are counted. Member site of Hawk Migration Association of North America (HMANA). Annually, Sept 1 through Dec 1. For info: John J. Reed, 31 Croft Rd, Lake Hopatcong, NJ 07849-1023. Phone: (201) 724-2703. E-mail: eagle76@verizon.net.

PLEASURE YOUR MATE MONTH. Sept 1–30. To promote love and show appreciation to your mate. Look for new ways to create happiness together. Use this event to establish a lifelong habit of sharing pleasure. Annually, the month of September. For info: Donald Etkes, PhD, 11693 San Vincente Blvd, #491, Los Angeles, CA 90049. Phone: (310) 281-0123.

REUNION PLANNING MONTH. Sept 1–30. September is the month when family, class, military, association and corporate reunion committees meet to start planning their upcoming reunions. This is the month to start locating members of your reunion group, organizing your committee, finding a place to meet and designing a reunion that your members will remember for years to come. For info: Dina Carson, PO Box 999, Niwot, CO 80544. E-mail: info@reunionsolutions.com. Web: www.reunionsolutions.com.

REUTHER, WALTER PHILIP: BIRTH ANNIVERSARY. Sept 1, 1907. American labor leader who began work in a steel factory at age 16 and later became president of the United Automobile Workers (UAW) and the Congress of Industrial Organizations (CIO). Born at Wheeling, WV, Reuther worked for two years in a Russian automobile factory. Often at the center of controversy, he was the target of an assassin in 1948. Reuther and his wife died in an airplane crash May 9, 1970, at Black Lake, MI. The UAW Family Education Center, a project which he had cherished, was later named for Walter and May Reuther.

SANTA-CALI-GON DAYS FESTIVAL. Sept 1–4. Historic Square, Independence, MO. Regional celebration for the three trails—Santa Fe, California, Oregon—which all started in Independence. Huge arts and crafts show, live Nashville performers, large carnival midway and free admission. Largest Labor Day weekend event in Kansas City metropolitan area. Est attendance: 150,000. For info: Santa-Cali-Gon Days, 210 W Truman Rd, Independence, MO 64051. Phone: (816) 252-4745. Web: www.santacaligon.com.

SEA CADET MONTH. Sept 1–30. Nationwide year-round youth program for boys and girls 11–17 teaches leadership and self-discipline with emphasis on nautically oriented training without military obligation. Various events will take place during the month, nationwide. Est attendance: 10,000. For info: US Naval Sea Cadet Corps, 2300 Wilson Blvd, Arlington, VA 22201. Phone: (703) 243-6910. Fax: (703) 243-3985. E-mail: mford@NAVYLEAGUE.org. Web: www.seacadets.org.

SELF-IMPROVEMENT MONTH. Sept 1–30. To disseminate information about the importance of lifelong learning and self-improvement. For complete information and lists of books, materials and cassettes, send $5 to cover expense of printing, handling and postage. Annually, the month of September. For info: Dr. Stanley Drake, Pres Emeritus, Intl Soc of Friendship & Good Will, 8592 Roswell Rd, Ste 251, Atlanta, GA 30350-1867. Phone: (678)

795-1362. E-mail: sjdrake@bellsouth.net. Web: www.friendshipandgoodwill.org.

SELF-UNIVERSITY WEEK. Sept 1–7. Reminds adults (in or out of school) that each of us has a responsibility to help shape the future by pursuing lifelong learning. Committed to self-education as the lifeblood of democracy and the key to living life to its fullest. Dedicated to furthering education not as something you get but as something you take. We assert that America's greatest treasures are found not in our shopping malls but in our libraries. Annually, the first seven days of September. For info: Charles Hayes, Publisher, Autodidactic Press, PO Box 872749, Wasilla, AK 99687. Phone: (907) 376-2932. Fax: (907) 376-2932. E-mail: autpress@alaska.net. Web: www.autodidactic.com.

SEPTEMBER IS HEALTHY AGING® MONTH. Sept 1–30. Annual health observance designed to focus national attention on the positive aspects of growing older. This month is part of the Healthy Aging® Campaign, a national, ongoing health promotion designed to broaden awareness of the positive aspects of aging and to provide inspiration for adults, ages 50+, to improve their physical, mental, social and financial health. The Campaign is developed and produced by Educational Television Network, Inc. (ETNET), a nonprofit corporation based in Pennsylvania. For info: The Healthy Aging® Campaign, PO Box 442, Unionville, PA 19375. Phone: (610) 793-0979. E-mail: info@healthyaging.net. Web: www.healthyaging.net.

SHAMELESS PROMOTION MONTH. Sept 1–30. This is the month for you to go out and promote yourself, your business, your book or your product shamelessly. For outrageous tips, visit our website. For info: Marisa D'Vari, 25 Columbus Circle, Apt ST-55E, New York, NY 10019. E-mail: mdvari@deg.com. Web: www.buildingbuzz.com.

SLOVAKIA: CONSTITUTION DAY. Sept 1. Anniversary of the adoption of the Constitution of the Slovak Republic in 1992.

SONOMA VALLEY HARVEST WINE AUCTION. Sept 1–3. Sonoma Mission Inn & Spa, Sonoma, CA. Winery dinners, a vintner & grower picnic, live and silent auctions and the main event charity auction, which has raised more than $3.6 million during the first 12 years. For info or tickets: Sonoma Valley Vintners & Growers Alliance. Phone: (707) 935-0803. Web: www.sonomavalleywine.com.

SOUTHERN GOSPEL MUSIC MONTH. Sept 1–30. To promote the growth, enjoyment and awareness nationwide of Southern Gospel music, a cherished American art form, by promoting radio airplay, concert attendance and retail awareness. For info: Southern Gospel Music Guild, PO Box 3722, Brentwood, TN 37024-3722. E-mail: info@sgmg.org. Web: www.sgmg.org.

SPORTS AND HOME EYE HEALTH AND SAFETY MONTH. Sept 1–30. There are thousands of eye injuries each year related to common household products and sports. Tips on how to protect yourself and your children from such eye injuries will be discussed. For info: Prevent Blindness America®, 211 W Wacker Dr, Ste 1700, Chicago, IL 60606. Phone: (800) 331-2020. E-mail: info@preventblindness.com. Web: www.preventblindness.org.

September 2006	S	M	T	W	T	F	S
						1	2
	3	4	5	6	7	8	9
	10	11	12	13	14	15	16
	17	18	19	20	21	22	23
	24	25	26	27	28	29	30

SUBLIMINAL COMMUNICATIONS MONTH. Sept 1–30. Not getting the results you want? Make a change for the positive and learn how to maximize your effectiveness. Learn how to put to use your entrepreneurial thinking to achieve your goals and increase your visibility socially or in the corporate world. Recognize and apply prosperity-building opportunities for increasing your networking, marketing and publicity goals through the use of color, scents and language. Finish the last quarter of the year successfully by using the powerful resources you already possess. It's your choice! For tips and suggestions send $2.50 to Lorrie Walters Marsiglio, Lorimar Communications, PO Box 284-CC, Wasco, IL 60183-0284. Phone: (630) 584-9368.

A TASTE OF COLORADO. Sept 1–4. Denver, CO. The Rocky Mountain region's largest free outdoor festival, this four-day food and entertainment extravaganza over Labor Day weekend features 50 Colorado area restaurants. Musical entertainment on six outdoor stages, gourmet cooking demonstrations, 280 arts and crafts vendors and children's music and activities. Friday, Saturday and Sunday 11 AM–10:30 PM. Monday 11 AM–8:30 PM. Est attendance: 500,000. For info: Susan Rogers Kark, Event Mgr, Downtown Denver Partnership, Inc, 511 16th St, Ste 200, Denver, CO 80202. Phone: (303) 534-6161 or (303) 478-7878 (Hotline). Fax: (303) 534-2803. E-mail: susan@downtowndenver.com. Web: www.atasteofcolorado.com.

TELLURIDE FILM FESTIVAL. Sept 1–4. Telluride, CO. 33rd film festival attracts film lovers, artists and scholars from all over the globe. National and international premieres, world archive treasures, filmmaker discussions, innovative or experimental filmmaking and retrospectives. 8 venues. Annually, Labor Day weekend. Est attendance: 5,000. For info: Telluride Film Festival, The Natl Film Preserve, 379 State St, Portsmouth, NH 03801. Phone: (603) 433-9202. Fax: (603) 433-9206. Web: www.telluridefilmfestival.org.

TITANIC DISCOVERED: ANNIVERSARY. Sept 1, 1985. Almost 75 years after the *Titanic* sank in the North Atlantic after striking an iceberg, a joint American-French expedition force led by marine geologist Dr. Robert Ballard located the wreck. The luxury liner was resting on the ocean floor 12,500 feet down—about 350 miles southeast from Newfoundland, Canada. In July 1986 Ballard returned in an expedition aboard the *Atlantis II* to explore the ship with underwater robots. Two memorial bronze plaques were left on the deck. See also: "Sinking of the *Titanic*: Anniversary" (Apr 15).

TOY TIPS EXECUTIVE TOY TEST. Sept 1. New York, NY. Annual event where senior executives of various companies test toys and learn how to use creativity in the workplace. For info: Toy Tips, Inc, 3611 Jerelin Dr, Franklin, WI 53132. Phone: (414) 421-9668. Fax: (414) 421-9778. Web: www.toytips.com.

TWITTY, CONWAY: BIRTH ANNIVERSARY. Sept 1, 1933. Country and western music star who began his career as a rock and roll performer in the style of Elvis Presley, born at Friars Point, MS. Died June 5, 1993, at Springfield, MO.

UNITED PLANET MONTH. Sept 1–30. Sponsored by United Planet, a Boston-based, international nonprofit public charity. A monthlong holiday dedicated to the promotion of cross-cultural understanding, friendship, world unity and peace. During the month of September, United Planet sponsors a diverse and creative range of events and initiatives to celebrate these ideals. Come join the fun in the celebration of a global community beyond borders! Annually, every September. For info: David Santulli, United Planet, 11 Arlington St, Boston, MA 02116. Phone: (617) 267-7763. Fax: (617) 267-7764. E-mail: quest@unitedplanet.org. Web: www.unitedplanet.org.

UPDATE YOUR RESUME MONTH. Sept 1–30. The Professional Resume Writing and Research Association is an international group of resume writing and career coaching professionals who are "Setting the Standard for Resume Excellence" by encouraging the updating and maintenance of resumes for every employed individual. For info: Laura DeCarlo, Professional Resume Writing and Research Assn, 1665 Clover Circle, Melbourne, FL 32935. Phone: (800) 715-3442. Fax: (321) 752-7513. E-mail: info@prwra.com. Web: www.prwra.com.

UZBEKISTAN: INDEPENDENCE DAY. Sept 1. National holiday. Commemorates independence upon the dissolution of the Soviet Union in 1991.

VERMONT STATE FAIR. Sept 1–10. Fairgrounds, Rutland, VT. Est attendance: 100,000. For info: Vermont State Fair, 175 S Main St, Rutland, VT 05701. Phone: (802) 775-5200. E-mail: vtstfair@sover.net. Web: www.vermontstatefair.net.

WEST VIRGINIA ITALIAN HERITAGE FESTIVAL. Sept 1–3. Clarksburg, WV. Includes Pasta Cook-off—participants cook a pasta dish to compete for prizes. Est attendance: 150,000. For info: West Virginia Italian Heritage Festival Office, Box 1632, Clarksburg, WV 26302. Phone: (304) 622-7314. Fax: (304) 622-5727. E-mail: benvenuto79@wvihf.com. Web: www.wvihf.com.

WILHELM TELL FESTIVAL. Sept 1–3. New Glarus, WI. Presentation of Schiller's drama *Wilhelm Tell* in German and English in natural outdoor theater. Alpine festival with Swiss entertainment. Annually, Labor Day weekend. Est attendance: 2,000. For info: New Glarus Chamber, PO Box 713, New Glarus, WI 53574. Phone: (800) 527-6838. E-mail: info@swisstown.com. Web: www.swisstown.com.

WISCONSIN STATE COW-CHIP THROW. Sept 1–2. Prairie du Sac, WI. Cow-Chip Throw, 5k and 10k runs, arts and crafts fair, live music and parade. Annually, the Friday night and Saturday of Labor Day weekend. Est attendance: 50,000. For info: Wisconsin State Cow-Chip Throw, PO Box 3, Prairie du Sac, WI 53578. Phone: (608) 643-4317. Fax: (608) 643-5421. E-mail: marietta@merr.com.

WOODSTOCK FAIR. Sept 1–4. Woodstock, CT. Annually, Labor Day weekend. Est attendance: 250,000. For info: Woodstock Fair, PO Box 1, South Woodstock, CT 06267. Phone: (860) 928-3246.

WORLD WAR II BEGINS: GERMANY INVADES POLAND: ANNIVERSARY. Sept 1, 1939. After securing a nonagression pact with the USSR (which secretly allowed for the partition of Poland by the Soviet Union and Germany) on Aug 23, Germany invaded Poland without a declaration of war at 4:45 AM. Two days later, Britain and France declared war, with Canada, Australia, New Zealand and South Africa soon following with their own declarations. Poland, overwhelmed by German air and land power, was in German and Soviet hands before the month concluded.

BIRTHDAYS TODAY

Yvonne De Carlo, 84, actress ("The Munsters," *Salome*), born Peggy Yvonne Middleton at Vancouver, BC, Canada, Sept 1, 1922.

Alan Dershowitz, 68, attorney, author, born Brooklyn, NY, Sept 1, 1938.

Gloria Estefan, 49, singer (Miami Sound Machine, "Don't Want to Lose You"), born Havana, Cuba, Sept 1, 1957.

Barry Gibb, 60, singer (with the Bee Gees, "Staying Alive"), songwriter, born Manchester, England, Sept 1, 1946.

Timothy Duane (Tim) Hardaway, 40, former basketball player, born Chicago, IL, Sept 1, 1966.

Dr. Phil McGraw, 56, psychologist, author, television personality ("The Oprah Winfrey Show," "Dr. Phil"), born Vinita, OK, Sept 1, 1950.

Seiji Ozawa, 71, conductor, born Hoten, Japan, Sept 1, 1935.

Don Stroud, 69, actor ("Mike Hammer," *The Buddy Holly Story*, *License to Kill*), born Honolulu, HI, Sept 1, 1937.

Lily Tomlin, 67, actress ("Laugh-In," *The Search for Signs of Intelligent Life in the Universe*), comedienne, born Detroit, MI, Sept 1, 1939.

☆ *Chase's 2006 Calendar of Events* ☆

SEPTEMBER 2 — SATURDAY
Day 245 — 120 Remaining

BISON-TEN-YELL DAY. Sept 2. Honoring the "bicentennial" of the birth of Bison-Ten-Yell, imaginary inventor of a set of ten battle yells as signals, based on the traditional memory aid system eventually adopted by football players. For info: Bob Birch, Grand Punscorpion, Puns Corps, 3108 Dashiell Rd, Falls Church, VA 22042. Phone: (703) 533-3668.

CAL FARLEY'S BOYS RANCH RODEO. Sept 2–3. Boys Ranch, TX. For young stick-horse riders to more experienced bareback bronc riders, the two-day event provides recognition and rewards for children living at Cal Farley's Boys Ranch, Girlstown, USA and Family Program. Winners in each event are presented with rodeo belt buckles. Special awards are given to the All-Around Cowboy, the All-Around Cowgirl and the Junior All-Around Cowboy. Annually, Labor Day weekend. Est attendance: 10,000. For info: Cal Farley's Boys Ranch, PO Box 1890, Amarillo, TX 79174. Phone: (806) 372-2341. Fax: (806) 372-6638. Web: www.calfarley.org.

CALENDAR ADJUSTMENT DAY: ANNIVERSARY. Sept 2. Pursuant to the British Calendar Act of 1751, Britain (and the American colonies) made the "Gregorian Correction" in 1752. The Act proclaimed that the day following Wednesday, Sept 2, should become Thursday, Sept 14, 1752. There was rioting in the streets by those who felt cheated and who demanded the 11 days back. The Act also provided that New Year's Day (and the change of year number) should fall Jan 1 (instead of Mar 25) in 1752 and every year thereafter. As a result, 1751 only had 282 days. See also: "Gregorian Calendar Adjustment: Anniversary" (Feb 24, Oct 4).

CLEVELAND NATIONAL AIR SHOW. Sept 2–4. Burke Lakefront Airport, Cleveland, OH. Country's oldest air show, featuring extensive military and foreign aircraft participation. Est attendance: 80,000. For info: Cleveland Natl Air Show, Burke Lakefront Airport, Cleveland, OH 44114. Phone: (216) 781-0747. Fax: (216) 781-7810. E-mail: info@clevelandairshow.com. Web: www.clevelandairshow.com.

CLOTHESLINE FAIR. Sept 2–4. Prairie Grove Battlefield State Park, Prairie Grove, AR. 54th annual fair with more than 200 arts and crafts exhibitors; parade; folk, bluegrass, gospel and country music; square-dancing exhibitions and competitions; living history programs and tours. Annually, Labor Day weekend. Est attendance: 45,000. For info: Rhonda Escobedo, Prairie Grove Battlefield State Park, PO Box 306, Prairie Grove, AR 72753. Phone: (479) 846-2990. Fax: (479) 846-4035.

EASTERN IDAHO STATE FAIR. Sept 2–9. Blackfoot, ID. Family fun, amusement rides, food booths, entertainment, tractor pulls and more. Est attendance: 212,000. For info: Manager, Eastern Idaho State Fair, PO Box 250, Blackfoot, ID 83221. Phone: (208) 785-2480. Fax: (208) 785-2483. E-mail: theFair@idaho-state-fair.com. Web: www.idaho-state-fair.com.

FORTEN, JAMES: BIRTH ANNIVERSARY. Sept 2, 1766. James Forten was born of free black parents at Philadelphia, PA. As a powder boy on an American Revolutionary warship, he escaped being sold as a slave when his ship was captured due to the intervention of the son of the British commander. While in England he became involved with abolitionists. On his return to Philadelphia, he became an apprentice to a sailmaker and eventually purchased the company for which he worked. He was active in the abolition movement, and in 1816 his support was sought by the American Colonization Society for the plan to settle American blacks at Liberia. He rejected their ideas and their plans to make him the ruler of the colony. From the large profits of his successful sailmaking company, he contributed heavily to the abolitionist movement and was a supporter of William Lloyd Garrison's anti-slavery journal, *The Liberator*. Died at Philadelphia, PA, Mar 4, 1842.

FRANKFORT FALL FESTIVAL. Sept 2–4. Frankfort, IL. One of the largest arts and crafts festivals in the Midwest, featuring 300 crafters, carnival, entertainment tent, community parade and civic food booths. Annually, on Labor Day weekend. Est attendance: 200,000. For info: Lynne Doogan, Exec Dir, Frankfort Chamber of Commerce, 123 Kansas St, Frankfort, IL 60423. Phone: (877) 469-3356. Fax: (815) 469-4352. E-mail: Lynne@frankfortchamber.com. Web: www.frankfortchamber.com.

GREAT FIRE OF LONDON: ANNIVERSARY. Sept 2–5, 1666 (OS). The fire generally credited with bringing about our system of fire insurance started Sept 2, 1666 (OS), in the wooden house of a baker named Farryner, at London's Pudding Lane, near the Tower. During the ensuing three days more than 13,000 houses were destroyed, though it is believed that only six lives were lost in the fire.

HISTORIC MARATHON RUNS: ANNIVERSARY. Sept 2–9, 490 BC. Anniversary of the event during the Persian Wars from which the marathon race is derived. Phidippides, "an Athenian by profession and practice a trained runner," according to Herodotus, was dispatched from Marathon to Sparta (26 miles), Sept 2 to seek help in repelling the invading Persian army. Help being unavailable by religious law until after the next full moon, Phidippides ran the 26 miles back to Marathon Sept 4. Without Spartan aid, the Athenians defeated the Persians at the Battle of Marathon Sept 9. According to legend Phidippides carried the news of the battle to Athens and died as he spoke the words, "Rejoice, we are victorious." The marathon race was revived at the 1896 Olympic Games at Athens. Course distance, since 1924, is 26 miles, 385 yards. See also: "Battle of Marathon: Anniversary" (Sept 9).

IROQUOIS INDIAN FESTIVAL. Sept 2–4. Iroquois Indian Museum, Howes Cave, NY. 25th annual celebration of Iroquois arts. Performing artists, craft demonstrations, speakers, storytellers, native foods, children's activities, Nature Park walks and fine-quality Iroquois art market. Est attendance: 2,000. For info: Iroquois Indian Museum, PO Box 7, Howes Cave, NY 12092. Phone: (518) 296-8949. Fax: (518) 296-8955. E-mail: info@iroquoismuseum.org.

JAPANESE FESTIVAL. Sept 2–4. Missouri Botanical Garden, St. Louis, MO. Japanese cultural activities including taiko (drumming), bon odori festival dancing, bonsai demonstrations, martial arts, tea ceremonies, cooking demonstrations, craft demos, ikebana, karaoke, kimono fashion show, Zen lectures and much more. For info: Missouri Botanical Garden, 4344 Shaw Blvd, St. Louis, MO 63110. Phone: (314) 577-9400 or (800) 642-8842. Web: www.mobot.org.

JUBILEE DAYS FESTIVAL. Sept 2–4. Zion, IL. 58th annual communitywide festival featuring arts and crafts, Queen's Pageant, Illinois's largest Labor Day parade and fireworks. Annually, Labor Day weekend. Est attendance: 10,000. For info: Richard Walker, Exec Dir, Jubilee Days Fest, Inc, PO Box 23, Zion, IL 60099. Phone: (847) 746-5500.

KANSAS CITY RENAISSANCE FESTIVAL. Sept 2–Oct 15 (weekends, Labor Day and Columbus Day). Bonner Springs, KS. Re-creation of a 16th-century harvest fair featuring more than 160 artisans selling handcrafted wares and continuous enter-

September 2006	S	M	T	W	T	F	S
						1	2
	3	4	5	6	7	8	9
	10	11	12	13	14	15	16
	17	18	19	20	21	22	23
	24	25	26	27	28	29	30

tainment on 12 stages. Food, special events and the Children's Realm are highlights. Est attendance: 200,000. For info: The Kansas City Renaissance Festival. Phone: (800) 373-0357. E-mail: renfest@kcrenfest.com. Web: www.kcrenfest.com.

MANAHAWKIN GOOD OL' DAYS. Sept 2. Manahawkin Lake Park, Manahawkin, NJ. Craft show, food court, games, pony rides and all-day entertainment. Est attendance: 4,000. For info: Linda Morris, 265 W 9th St, Ship Bottom, NJ 08008. Phone: (609) 494-7211. Fax: (609) 494-5807. E-mail: event@discover southernocean.com.

McAULIFFE, CHRISTA: BIRTH ANNIVERSARY. Sept 2, 1948. Christa McAuliffe, a 37-year-old Concord, NH, high school teacher, was to have been the first "ordinary citizen" in space. Born Sharon Christa Corrigan at Boston, MA, she perished with six crew members in the Space Shuttle *Challenger* explosion Jan 28, 1986. See also: "Challenger Space Shuttle Explosion: Anniversary" (Jan 28).

OLD TIME ANTIQUES & COLLECTIBLES FAIRE. Sept 2. Toms River, NJ. More than 100 vendors of primitive kitchen wares, books, postcards, vintage textiles, jewelry, furniture, collectibles galore, craft demonstrations, appraisals, antique cars and engines, museum displays and refreshments. 25th annual. Est attendance: 5,000. For info: Ocean County Historical Society, 26 Hadley Ave, PO Box 2191, Toms River, NJ 08754-2191. Phone: (732) 341-1880. Web: www.oceancountyhistory.org.

POWERS' CROSSROADS COUNTRY FAIR AND ART FESTIVAL. Sept 2–4. Newnan, GA. 300 top US artists and craftsmen. Old plantation skills revived including gristmill, blacksmithing; entertainment, continuous music and down-home cooking. Est attendance: 45,000. For info: Coweta Festivals, Inc, 4766 W Hwy 34, Newnan, GA 30263. Phone: (770) 253-2011. Fax: (770) 253-8180. E-mail: cowetafestivals@charter.net.

SCOTLAND: BRAEMAR ROYAL HIGHLAND GATHERING. Sept 2. Princess Royal and Duke of Fife Memorial Park, Braemar, Grampian. Kilted clansmen from all over the world gather. Traditional activities including tossing cabers, dancing and playing bagpipes. Est attendance: 18,000. For info: Mr. W.A. Meston, Secretary, Coilacriech, Ballater, Aberdeenshire, Scotland AB35 5UH. Phone/fax: (44) (133) 975-5377. E-mail: info@braemargathering.org.

SHERMAN ENTERS ATLANTA: ANNIVERSARY. Sept 2, 1864. After a four-week siege, Union General William Tecumseh Sherman entered Atlanta, GA. The city had been evacuated on the previous day by Confederate troops under General John B. Hood. Hood had mistakenly assumed Sherman was ending the siege Aug 27, when actually Sherman was beginning the final stages of his attack. Hood then sent troops to attack the Union forces at Jonesboro. Hood's troops were defeated, opening the way for the capture of Atlanta.

SOUTH DAKOTA STATE FAIR. Sept 2–9. Huron, SD. Grandstand entertainment nightly, two free stages with multiple shows daily, hundreds of commercial exhibits and thousands of livestock exhibits. One of the largest agricultural fairs in the US. Est attendance: 110,000. For info: South Dakota State Fair, PO Box 1275, Huron, SD 57350-1275. Phone: (605) 353-7340 or (800) 529-0900. Fax: (605) 353-7348. E-mail: jodi.burma@state.sd.us.

STA-BIL NATIONALS CHAMPIONSHIP LAWN MOWER RACE. Sept 2–3. Mansfield, OH. Five classes of races for winners of regional races held across the US. Mowers will travel at speeds ranging from 10 mph to more than 50 mph. Est attendance: 2,000. For info: US Lawn Mower Racing Assn, 1812 Glenview Rd, Glenview, IL 60025. Phone: (847) 729-7363. E-mail: letsmow@aol.com. Web: www.letsmow.com.

TASTE OF MADISON. Sept 2–3. Capitol Square, Madison, WI. Food and entertainment festival, including booths from more than 80 restaurants, five stages, waiters' race and Kiddie Korner. Est attendance: 175,000. For info: Keith Peterson, Events Manager, Madison Festivals, Inc, c/o ASG, 3000 Cahill Main, Ste 216, Madison, WI 53711. Phone: (608) 276-9797, ext 23. Fax: (608) 276-9780. E-mail: events@vymac.com. Web: www.madison festivals.com.

TOOLS AND SKILLS THAT BUILT THE COLONY. Sept 2. Wormsloe Historic Site, Savannah, GA. Living history demonstrations relating to the tools and skills that were used to build the colony. These will include woodworking, blacksmithing, spinning, candlemaking and more. Museum, film and trails. 11 AM to 4 PM. Annually, the Saturday before Labor Day. Est attendance: 500. For info: Wormsloe State Historic Site, 7601 Skidaway Rd, Savannah, GA 31406. Phone: (912) 353-3023. E-mail: wormsloe @bellsouth.net.

TOTAH FESTIVAL. Sept 2–3. Farmington, NM. Native American arts and crafts show and marketplace—highlighted by an Indian rug auction. Est attendance: 13,000. For info: Farmington Conv and Visitors Bureau, 3041 E Main St, Farmington, NM 87402. Phone: (800) 448-1240 or (505) 326-7602. Fax: (505) 327-0577. E-mail: fmncvb@earthlink.net. Web: farmingtonnm.org.

US TREASURY DEPARTMENT: ANNIVERSARY. Sept 2, 1789. The third presidential cabinet department, the Treasury Department, was established by Congress.

VIETNAM: INDEPENDENCE DAY. Sept 2. Ho Chi Minh formally proclaimed the independence of Vietnam from France and the establishment of the Democratic Republic of Vietnam on this day in 1945. National holiday.

V-J DAY: ANNIVERSARY. Sept 2, 1945. Official ratification of Japanese surrender to the Allies occurred aboard the USS *Missouri* at Tokyo Bay Sept 2 (Far Eastern time) in 1945, thus prompting President Truman's declaration of this day as Victory-over-Japan Day. Japan's initial, informal agreement of surrender was announced by Truman and celebrated in the US Aug 14.

WESTFEST. Sept 2–3. West, TX. West celebrates its Czech heritage with folk dances, Czech pastries, sausage, polka music, arts and crafts, children's area, 5k run, parade. Est attendance: 35,000. For info: Westfest, Box 65, West, TX 76691. Phone: (254) 826-5058. Web: www.westfest.com.

WORLD CHAMPIONSHIP BARBECUE GOAT COOK-OFF AND ARTS AND CRAFTS FAIR. Sept 2. Richards Park, Brady, TX. 33rd annual cook-off to promote Brady/McCulloch County and the sheep and goat industry. Arts and crafts fair featuring local and statewide artists. Annually, the Saturday before Labor Day. Est attendance: 30,000. For info: Brady/McCulloch County Chamber of Commerce, 101 E First St, Brady, TX 76825. Phone: (325) 597-3491. Fax: (325) 792-9181. E-mail: bradychamber@hotmail.com. Web: www.bradytx.com.

BIRTHDAYS TODAY

Nathaniel ("Tiny") Archibald, 58, Hall of Fame basketball player, born New York, NY, Sept 2, 1948.

Terry Paxton Bradshaw, 58, sportscaster, Hall of Fame football player, born Shreveport, LA, Sept 2, 1948.

Marge Champion, 83, dancer, actress ("Marge and Gower Champion Show," *Show Boat*), born Los Angeles, CA, Sept 2, 1923.

Jimmy Connors, 54, former tennis player, born East St. Louis, IL, Sept 2, 1952.

Jim DeMint, 55, US Senator (R, South Carolina), born Greenville, SC, Sept 2, 1951.

Eric Dickerson, 46, Hall of Fame football player, broadcaster, born Sealy, TX, Sept 2, 1960.

Mark Harmon, 55, actor ("St. Elsewhere," "Chicago Hope"), born Burbank, CA, Sept 2, 1951.

Salma Hayek, 40, actress (*Fools Rush In, Frida*), born Veracruz, Mexico, Sept 2, 1966.

Linda Purl, 51, actress ("Happy Days," "Matlock"), born Greenwich, CT, Sept 2, 1955.

Keanu Reeves, 42, actor (*The Matrix, Speed*), born Beirut, Lebanon, Sept 2, 1964.

John Thompson, 65, college basketball coach, former player, born Washington, DC, Sept 2, 1941.

Peter Victor Ueberroth, 69, former commissioner of baseball and Olympic organizer, born Evanston, IL, Sept 2, 1937.

Carlos Valderrama, 45, soccer player, born Santa Marta, Colombia, Sept 2, 1961.

SEPTEMBER 3 — SUNDAY

Day 246 — 119 Remaining

BEGINNING OF THE PENNY PRESS: ANNIVERSARY.
Sept 3, 1833. Benjamin H. Day launched the *New York Sun* on this date, the first truly successful penny newspaper in the US. The *Sun* was sold on sidewalks by newspaper boys. By 1836 the paper was the largest seller in the country with a circulation of 30,000. It was possibly Day's concentration on human interest stories and sensationalism that made his publication a success while efforts at penny papers at Philadelphia and Boston had failed.

BRITAIN DECLARES WAR ON GERMANY: ANNIVERSARY.
Sept 3, 1939. British ultimatum to Germany, demanding halt to invasion of Poland (which had started at dawn on Sept 1), expired at 11 AM, GMT, Sept 3, 1939. At 11:15 AM, in a radio broadcast, Prime Minister Neville Chamberlain announced the declaration of war against Germany. France, Canada, Australia, New Zealand and South Africa quickly issued separate declarations of war. Winston Churchill was named First Lord of the Admiralty. See also: "World War II Begins: Germany Invades Poland" (Sept 1).

CRANDALL, PRUDENCE: BIRTH ANNIVERSARY.
Sept 3, 1803. Born to a Quaker family at Hopkinton, RI, this American schoolteacher sparked controversy in the 1830s with her efforts to educate black girls. When her private academy for girls was boycotted because she admitted a black girl, she started a school for "young ladies and misses of colour." Died Jan 28, 1890, at Elk Falls, KS.

DOUGLASS'S ESCAPE TO FREEDOM: ANNIVERSARY.
Sept 3, 1838. Dressed as a sailor and carrying identification papers borrowed from a retired merchant seaman, Frederick Douglass boarded a train at Baltimore, MD, a slave state, and rode to Wilmington, DE, where he caught a steamboat to the free city of Philadelphia. He then transferred to a train headed for New York City where he entered the protection of the Underground Railway network. Douglass later became a great orator and one of the leaders of the antislavery struggle.

September 2006	S	M	T	W	T	F	S
						1	2
	3	4	5	6	7	8	9
	10	11	12	13	14	15	16
	17	18	19	20	21	22	23
	24	25	26	27	28	29	30

FILENE, EDWARD ALBERT: BIRTH ANNIVERSARY.
Sept 3, 1860. American merchant and philanthropist, born at Salem, MA, who established the US credit union movement in 1921. Died at Paris, France, Sept 26, 1937.

FIRST SECRET SERVICE AGENT TO DIE IN THE LINE OF DUTY: ANNIVERSARY.
Sept 3, 1902. While on duty protecting President Theodore Roosevelt, William Craig was killed when a streetcar collided with the carriage carrying the president (who suffered some cuts). The United States Secret Service was founded in 1865 as a branch of the Treasury Department entrusted with foiling counterfeiting, but was given the additional role of protecting the US president upon the assassination of William McKinley. Craig, born in Glasgow, Scotland, in 1855, was also a bodyguard for Queen Victoria before moving to Chicago. Roosevelt affectionately called Craig his "shadow."

HARVEST WINE CELEBRATION.
Sept 3-4. Livermore, CA. The Harvest Wine Celebration is an open-house event offering the public an opportunity to visit 30 wineries, sample wines, learn more about this historic wine region, enjoy entertainment and shop for arts and crafts. Shuttle bus service is available between the wineries. Annually, Labor Day weekend. Est attendance: 10,000. For info: Livermore Valley Winegrowers Assn, 3585 Greenville Rd, Ste 4, Livermore, CA 94550. Phone: (925) 447-9463. Fax: (925) 447-0433. E-mail: lvwa@livermorewine.com.

ITALY: HISTORICAL REGATTA.
Sept 3. Venice. Traditional competition among two-oar racing gondolas, preceded by a procession of Venetian ceremonial boats of the epoch of the Venetian Republic. Annually, the first Sunday in September.

ITALY: JOUST OF THE SARACEN.
Sept 3. Arezzo. The first Sunday in September is set aside for the Giostra del Saracino, a tilting contest of the 13th century, with knights in armor.

ITALY SURRENDERS: ANNIVERSARY.
Sept 3, 1943. General Giuseppe Castellano signed three copies of the "short armistice," effectively surrendering "unconditionally" for the Italian government. That same day the British Eighth Army, commanded by General Bernard Montgomery, invaded the Italian mainland.

JERRY LEWIS MUSCULAR DYSTROPHY ASSOCIATION TELETHON.
Sept 3-4. The annual Labor Day TV broadcast to raise money for 40 neuromuscular diseases. For info: Muscular Dystrophy Assn, 3300 E Sunrise Dr, Tucson, AZ 85718. Phone: (800) 572-1717. Web: www.mdausa.org.

NATIONAL WAFFLE WEEK.
Sept 3-9. A celebration of the wonderful, crispy breakfast orb and its contributions to American society. Annually, the first week of September. For info: Waffle House, Attention: Pat Warner, PO Box 6450, Norcross, GA 30091. Phone: (770) 729-5842. Fax: (770) 729-5999. Web: www.waffleweek.com.

QATAR: INDEPENDENCE DAY.
Sept 3. National holiday. Commemorates the severing in 1971 of treaty with Britain, which had handled Qatar's foreign relations.

SAN MARINO: NATIONAL DAY.
Sept 3. Public holiday. Honors St. Marinus, the traditional founder of San Marino.

SCANDINAVIAN FEST.
Sept 3. NJ Convention and Exposition Center, Edison, NJ. Celebrate and sample the cultures, traditions and contemporary life of the Nordic countries: Denmark, Estonia, Finland, Iceland, Norway and Sweden through food, entertainment, music, dancing, handicrafts and lectures. Annually, the Sunday before Labor Day. Est attendance: 6,000. For info: Carl Anderson, PO Box 5103, Bethlehem, PA 18015. Phone: (610) 868-7525. E-mail: info@ScanFest.org. Web: www.ScanFest.org.

"SEARCH FOR TOMORROW" TV PREMIERE: 55th ANNIVERSARY.
Sept 3, 1951. This soap lasted for 35 years. It began as a 15-minute program and expanded to 30 minutes in 1968, when performances began to be videotaped instead of airing live. "Search" was set in the town of Henderson, and its central character was Joanne Gardner Barron Tate Vincente

Tourneur (played by Mary Stuart). Other notable cast members have included: Don Knotts, Robert Mandan, Ken Kercheval, Jill Clayburgh, Natalie Schafer, Susan Sarandon, Robert Loggia, Hal Linden, Morgan Fairchild, Joe Morton, Robby Benson, Kevin Kline, Cynthia Gibb and Olympia Dukakis.

SULLIVAN, LOUIS: 150th BIRTH ANNIVERSARY.
Sept 3, 1856. An American architect responsible for the modern, steel-framed skyscrapers, his designs are characterized by rich ornamentation, plain outer surfaces and cubic forms. His famous motto was, "form follows function." Frank Lloyd Wright was a student of Sullivan before the two quarreled. Born at Boston, MA, Sullivan died Apr 14, 1924, at Chicago, IL.

TREATY OF PARIS ENDS AMERICAN REVOLUTION: ANNIVERSARY. Sept 3, 1783. Treaty between Britain and the US, ending the Revolutionary War, signed at Paris, France. American signatories: John Adams, Benjamin Franklin and John Jay.

WAIKIKI ROUGHWATER SWIM. Sept 3 (tentative). Waikiki Beach, Honolulu, HI. The 37th annual swim is 2.4 miles from Sans Souci Beach to Duke Kahanamoku Beach. "The World's Most Prestigious Open Water Swimming Event." Preregistration is required. Est attendance: 1,000. For info: Jim Anderson, One Keahole Place #1607, Honolulu, HI 96825-3414. Phone: (808) 396-8866. Fax: (808) 396-8868. E-mail: waikikijim@aol.com. Web: www.WaikikiRoughwaterSwim.com.

BIRTHDAYS TODAY

Eileen Brennan, 69, actress (*The Last Picture Show, Private Benjamin*), born Los Angeles, CA, Sept 3, 1937.
Kitty Carlisle, 91, actress (*A Night at the Opera*, "To Tell the Truth"), singer, born New Orleans, LA, Sept 3, 1915.
Pauline Collins, 66, actress ("Upstairs, Downstairs"; stage: *Shirley Valentine* [Olivier and Tony awards]), born Exmouth, England, Sept 3, 1940.
Anne Jackson, 80, actress (*Lovers and Other Strangers*), born Allegheny, PA, Sept 3, 1926.
Alison Lurie, 80, author (*Foreign Affairs, The War Between the Tates*), born Chicago, IL, Sept 3, 1926.
Valerie Perrine, 63, actress (*Lenny, W.C. Fields and Me*), born Galveston, TX, Sept 3, 1943.
Charlie Sheen, 41, actor (*Platoon, Hot Shots!*), born Carlos Irwin Estevez at New York, NY, Sept 3, 1965.
Damon Stoudamire, 33, basketball player, born Portland, OR, Sept 3, 1973.
Mort Walker, 83, cartoonist ("Beetle Bailey"), born Mortimer Walker Addison at El Dorado, KS, Sept 3, 1923.

SEPTEMBER 4 — MONDAY
Day 247 — 118 Remaining

BRUCKNER, ANTON: BIRTH ANNIVERSARY. Sept 4, 1824. Austrian composer born at Ansfelden, Austria. Died at Vienna, Austria, Oct 11, 1896.

BUHL DAY. Sept 4. Buhl Farm, Sharon, PA. To honor the laboring man. Observed annually on Labor Day. Est attendance: 25,000. For info: Karen Campman-Emmett, 36 Dogwood Ln, West Middlesex, PA 16159. Phone: (724) 528-1071. E-mail: kpemmett@verizon.net.

BURNHAM, DANIEL: BIRTH ANNIVERSARY. Sept 4, 1846. American architect and city planner born at Henderson, NY. Daniel Hudson Burnham was an advocate of tall, fireproof buildings, probably the first to be called "sky-scrapers." In 1909 he proposed a long-range city plan for Chicago, IL, that was a key factor in the "forever open, clear and free" policy which resulted in Chicago having the most beautiful lakefront of any major city in the US. Died June 1, 1912, at Heidelberg, Germany.

CANADA: LABOR DAY. Sept 4. Annually, the first Monday in September.

"CAPTAIN MIDNIGHT" TV PREMIERE: ANNIVERSARY. Sept 4, 1954. A children's show starring Richard Webb as Captain Midnight, a World War I flying ace who battled crime as part of the Secret Squadron. Webb was joined by Sid Melton as Ichabod (Ikky) Mudd, his assistant, and Olan Soule as Tut, an eccentric scientist. "Captain Midnight" moved to TV from radio, where it was sponsored by Ovaltine. In reruns the name was changed to "Jet Jackson, Flying Commando" because Ovaltine owned the rights to the Captain Midnight name.

CHATEAUBRIAND, FRANCOIS RENE DE: BIRTH ANNIVERSARY. Sept 4, 1768. French poet, novelist, historian, explorer and statesman, witness to the French Revolution. Born at St. Malo, France, he died at Paris, France, July 4, 1848.

COLUMBIA RIVER CROSS CHANNEL SWIM. Sept 4. Hood River, OR. The annual swim across the mighty Columbia River draws 550 contestants each year to swim the approximately one-mile distance for fun. Annually, on Labor Day. Est attendance: 1,000. For info: Columbia River Cross Channel Swim, Hood River County Chamber of Commerce, 405 Portway Ave, Hood River, OR 97031. Phone: (800) 366-3530. E-mail: hrccc@hoodriver.org. Web: www.hoodriver.org.

CURAÇAO: ANIMALS' DAY. Sept 4. In Curaçao the Association for the Protection of Animals organizes an animal show for this day and the best-kept animals are awarded prizes.

FIRST ELECTRIC LIGHTING: ANNIVERSARY. Sept 4, 1882. Four hundred electric lights came on in offices on Spruce, Wall, Nassau and Pearl streets in lower Manhattan as Thomas Edison hooked up light bulbs to an underground cable carrying direct current electrical power. Edison had demonstrated his first incandescent light bulb in 1879. See also: "Incandescent Lamp Demonstrated: Anniversary" (Oct 21).

GREAT BATHTUB RACE. Sept 4. Nome, AK. 29th annual. Bathtubs mounted on wheels are raced down Front Street. Each team has five members, one in the tub, with bubbles apparent in the bath water. Tub must be full of water at beginning and have at least 10 gallons at the finish line. The other four team members must wear large-brim hats and suspenders and carry either a bar of soap, washcloth, towel or bath mat for the entire race. Winning team claims trophy: a statue of Miss Piggy and Kermit taking a bath, which is handed down from year to year. Annually, at noon on Labor Day. Est attendance: 1,500. For info: Rasmussen's Music Mart, PO Box 2, Nome, AK 99762-0002. Phone: (907) 443-2798 or (907) 443-2919. Fax: (907) 443-5777.

LABOR DAY. Sept 4. Legal public holiday. Public Law 90–363 sets Labor Day on the first Monday in September. Observed in all states. First observance believed to have been a parade on Tuesday, Sept 5, 1882, at New York, NY, probably organized by Peter J. McGuire, a Carpenters and Joiners Union secretary. In 1883 a union resolution declared "the first Monday in September of each year a Labor Day." By 1893 more than half of the states were observing Labor Day on one or another day and a bill to establish Labor Day as a federal holiday was introduced in Congress. On June 28, 1894, President Grover Cleveland signed into law an act making the first Monday in September a legal holiday for federal employees and the District of Columbia. Canada also celebrates Labor Day on the first Monday in September. In most other countries, Labor Day is observed May 1.

LITTLE ROCK NINE: ANNIVERSARY. Sept 4, 1957. Governor Oval Faubus called out the Arkansas National Guard to turn away nine black students who had been trying to attend Central High School in Little Rock. President Eisenhower sent in troops to enforce the law allowing the students to integrate the school.

LOS ANGELES, CALIFORNIA, FOUNDED: 225th ANNIVERSARY. Sept 4, 1781. Los Angeles founded by decree and called "El Pueblo de Nuestra Senora La Reina de Los Angeles de Porciuncula." The City of Los Angeles was incorporated on Apr 4, 1850.

MACKINAC BRIDGE WALK. Sept 4. St. Ignace, MI. 49th annual event. This is the only day of the year pedestrians are permitted to walk across the five-mile-long span, one of the world's longest suspension bridges, connecting Michigan's two peninsulas. Walk is from St. Ignace to Mackinaw City. Est attendance: 50,000. For info: Mackinac Bridge Authority, 333 Interstate 75, St. Ignace, MI 49781. Phone: (906) 643-7600. Fax: (906) 643-7668. Web: www.mackinacbridge.org.

NATIONAL PAYROLL WEEK. Sept 4–8. Founded in 1996 by the American Payroll Association to recognize the important partnership of America's workers and the payroll professionals who pay them on time and accurately. Provides an annual opportunity to proudly proclaim "America Works Because We're Working for America!" For info: Mark Coindreau, American Payroll Assn, 660 N Main Ave, Ste 100, San Antonio, TX 78205. Phone: (210) 226-4600. Fax: (210) 224-2028. E-mail: mcoindreau@americanpayroll.org. Web: www.nationalpayrollweek.com.

NATIONAL STEARMAN FLY-IN DAYS. Sept 4–10. Galesburg, IL. The largest gathering of Stearman airplanes—the biplane trainers that gave wings to more military pilots than any other series of aircraft in the world. Est attendance: 7,500. For info: Galesburg Area CVB, PO Box 60, Galesburg, IL 61402-0060. Phone: (309) 343-2485. Fax: (309) 343-2521. E-mail: visitors@visitgalesburg.com. Web: www.visitgalesburg.com.

NEWSPAPER CARRIER DAY. Sept 4. Anniversary of the hiring of the first "newsboy" in the US, 10-year-old Barney Flaherty, who is said to have answered the following classified advertisement, which appeared in *The New York Sun* in 1833: "To the Unemployed—a number of steady men can find employment by vending this paper. A liberal discount is allowed to those who buy to sell again."

POLK, SARAH CHILDRESS: BIRTH ANNIVERSARY. Sept 4, 1803. Wife of James Knox Polk, 11th president of the US. Born at Murfreesboro, TN, and died at Nashville, TN, Aug 14, 1891.

SNAKE RIVER DUCK RACE. Sept 4. Nome, AK. Since 1992 thousands of plastic ducks have negotiated the historic Snake River to Nome's power plant. 2 PM. For info: Leo B. Rasmussen, Nome Rotary Club, PO Box 275, Nome, AK 99762. Phone: (907) 443-2798 or (907) 443-6022. E-mail: leaknome@alaska.com.

STOCK EXCHANGE HOLIDAY (LABOR DAY). Sept 4. The holiday schedules for the various exchanges are subject to change if relevant rules, regulations or exchange policies are revised. If you have questions, phone: American Stock Exchange (212) 306-1000, Chicago Board of Trade (312) 435-3500, Chicago Board of Options Exchange (312) 786-5600, NASDAQ Stock Market (646) 441-5200, New York Stock Exchange (212) 656-3000, Pacific Stock Exchange (415) 393-4000, Philadelphia Stock Exchange (215) 496-5000.

WRIGHT, RICHARD: BIRTH ANNIVERSARY. Sept 4, 1908. Novelist and short story writer whose works included *Native Son, Uncle Tom's Children* and *Black Boy*, born at Natchez, MS. Wright died at Paris, France, Nov 28, 1960.

BIRTHDAYS TODAY

Mitzi Gaynor, 75, singer, dancer, actress (*South Pacific*), born Franchesca Mitzi Marlene de Charney von Gerber at Chicago, IL, Sept 4, 1931.
Paul Harvey, 88, broadcaster, commentator ("The Rest of the Story"), born Tulsa, OK, Sept 4, 1918.
Judith Ivey, 55, actress (*Compromising Positions, Brighton Beach Memoirs*; stage: *Steaming*), born El Paso, TX, Sept 4, 1951.
Beyoncé Knowles, 25, singer, actress (*Austin Powers in Goldmember*), born Houston, TX, Sept 4, 1981.
Michael Joseph (Mike) Piazza, 38, baseball player, born Norristown, PA, Sept 4, 1968.
Jennifer Salt, 62, actress ("Soap"), born Los Angeles, CA, Sept 4, 1944.
Ione Skye, 36, actress (*Say Anything . . .; Gas, Food, Lodging*), born Hertfordshire, England, Sept 4, 1970.
Thomas Sturges (Tom) Watson, 57, golfer, born Kansas City, MO, Sept 4, 1949.
Damon Wayans, 46, actor, comedian ("In Living Color"), born New York, NY, Sept 4, 1960.

SEPTEMBER 5 — TUESDAY
Day 248 — 117 Remaining

ANOTHER LOOK UNLIMITED DAY. Sept 5. Your house, garage, barn, shed, attic or yard. Encourages everyone to look over their possessions and give surplus to charity or reuse in other projects. Lessen the flow to landfills. Annually, the day after Labor Day. For info: ENVIRA MYNYTL, PO Box 220, Holts Summit, MO 65043. E-mail: envira-myntyl@cal-a-co.com.

BABE RUTH'S FIRST PRO HOMER: ANNIVERSARY. Sept 5, 1914. Babe Ruth hit his first home run as a professional while playing for Providence in the International League, a type of minor league affiliate of the Boston Red Sox. He pitched a one-hit shutout against Toronto.

BE LATE FOR SOMETHING DAY. Sept 5. To create a release from the stresses and strains resulting from a consistent need to be on time. For info: Les Waas, Pres, Procrastinators' Club of America, Inc, Box 712, Bryn Athyn, PA 19009. Phone: (215) 947-9020. Fax: (215) 947-7210. E-mail: procrastinators_club_of_america@yahoo.com. Web: www.geocities.com/procrastinators_club_of_america.

CAGE, JOHN: BIRTH ANNIVERSARY. Sept 5, 1912. Avant-garde American composer John Cage was born at Los Angeles, CA. He pioneered the experimental music and performance art schools. He used non-traditional instruments such as flower pots and cowbells in innovative situations, such as performances governed by chance, in which the *I Ching* was consulted to determine the direction of the performance. In 1978 he was elected to the American Academy of Arts and Sciences, and in 1982 was awarded France's highest honor for cultural contributions, *Commandeur de l'Ordre des Arts et des Lettres*. He died Aug 12, 1992, at New York, NY.

CARNOVSKY, MORRIS: BIRTH ANNIVERSARY. Sept 5, 1897. American actor Morris Carnovsky was born at St. Louis, MO. In 1931 with actor Lee Strasberg and others he founded the Group Theater at New York, NY. He was blacklisted in the 1950s by the House Un-American Activities Committee, but was still

September 2006	S	M	T	W	T	F	S
						1	2
	3	4	5	6	7	8	9
	10	11	12	13	14	15	16
	17	18	19	20	21	22	23
	24	25	26	27	28	29	30

asked by John Houseman to perform in the American Shakespeare Festival in 1956 and began a successful Shakespearean career. He was elected to the Theater Hall of Fame in 1979. Carnovsky died Sept 1, 1992, at Easton, CT.

FIRST CONTINENTAL CONGRESS ASSEMBLY: ANNIVERSARY. Sept 5, 1774. The first assembly of this forerunner of the US Congress took place at Philadelphia, PA. Peyton Randolph, delegate from Virginia, was elected president.

GERALD FORD: ASSASSINATION ATTEMPT: ANNIVERSARY. Sept 5, 1975. Lynette A. "Squeaky" Fromme, a follower of convicted murderer Charles Manson, attempted to shoot President Gerald Ford. On Sept 22 of the same year, another attempt on Ford's life occurred when Sara Jane Moore shot at him.

ISRAELI OLYMPIAD MASSACRE: ANNIVERSARY. Sept 5–6, 1972. Eleven members of the Israeli Olympic Team were killed in an attack on the Olympic Village at Munich and attempted kidnapping of team members. Four of seven guerrillas, members of the Black September faction of the Palestinian Liberation Army, were also killed. In retaliation, Israeli jets bombed Palestinian positions at Lebanon and Syria on Sept 8, 1972.

JAMES, JESSE: BIRTH ANNIVERSARY. Sept 5, 1847. Western legend and bandit Jesse Woodson James was born at Centerville (now Kearney), MO. His criminal exploits were glorified and romanticized by writers for Eastern readers looking for stories of Western adventure and heroism. After the Civil War, James and his brother, Frank, formed a group of eight outlaws who robbed banks, stagecoaches and stores. In 1873 the James gang began holding up trains. The original James gang was put out of business Sept 7, 1876, while attempting to rob a bank at Northfield, MN. Every member of the gang except for the James brothers was killed or captured. The brothers formed a new gang and resumed their criminal careers in 1879. Two years later, the governor of Missouri offered a $10,000 reward for their capture, dead or alive. On Apr 3, 1882, at St. Joseph, MO, Robert Ford, a member of the gang, shot 34-year-old Jesse in the back of the head and claimed the reward.

KOESTLER, ARTHUR: BIRTH ANNIVERSARY. Sept 5, 1905. Born at Budapest, Hungary, Koestler is best known for his novel about his disillusionment with Communism, *Darkness at Noon*, and for *The God That Failed*. Died at London, England, Mar 3, 1983.

"THE MacNEIL–LEHRER NEWSHOUR" TV PREMIERE: ANNIVERSARY. Sept 5, 1983. Originally, this PBS news show was called "The MacNeil-Lehrer Report" and was on every weeknight for a half hour starting in 1976. Robert MacNeil and Jim Lehrer were joined by Charlayne Hunter-Gault and Judy Woodruff. In 1983 the show was expanded to an hour and became TV's first regularly scheduled daily hour news show. The show has been praised for its depth and objectivity. In 1995 Robert MacNeil retired and the show was retitled "The Newshour with Jim Lehrer."

MICHIGAN'S GREAT FIRE OF 1881: 125th ANNIVERSARY. Sept 5, 1881. According to Michigan Historical Commission, "Small fires were burning in the forests of the 'Thumb area of Michigan,' tinder-dry after a long, hot summer, when a gale swept in from the southwest on Sept 5, 1881. Fanned into an inferno, the fire raged for three days. A million acres were devastated in Sanilac and Huron counties alone. At least 125 persons died, and thousands more were left destitute. The new American Red Cross won support for its prompt aid to the fire victims. This was the first disaster relief furnished by this great organization."

NIELSEN, ARTHUR CHARLES: BIRTH ANNIVERSARY. Sept 5, 1897. Marketing research engineer, founder of AC Nielsen Company, in 1923, known for radio and TV audience surveys, was born at Chicago, IL, and died there June 1, 1980.

PLAY DAYS. Sept 5–9. In a world filled with downsizing, rightsizing and shaftsizing, we need humor to reaffirm our humanity and sanity. In the week after Labor Day, the HUMOR Project will playfully spread the word on 1,001 ways to add humor to your life and work. Jest for success—humor works—the funny line and bottom line intersect! Annually, the Tuesday through Saturday after Labor Day. For info: The HUMOR Project, 480 Broadway, Ste 210-C, Saratoga Springs, NY 12866-2288. Phone: (518) 587-8770. E-mail: chase@HumorProject.com. Web: www.Humor Project.com.

POTATO BOWL USA. Sept 5–10. Grand Forks, ND. Includes the World's Largest French Fry Feed. For info: Grand Forks Conv and Visitors Bureau, 4251 Gateway Dr, Grand Forks, ND 58203. Phone: (800) 866-4566 or (701) 746-0444. E-mail: info@visit grandforks.com. Web: www.visitgrandforks.com.

SPACE MILESTONE: *VOYAGER 1* (US). Sept 5, 1977. Twin of *Voyager 2*, which was launched Aug 20. On Feb 18, 1998, *Voyager 1* set a new distance record when after more than 20 years in space it reached 6.5 billion miles from Earth.

SWITZERLAND: SAINT GOTTHARD AUTOMOBILE TUNNEL OPENING: ANNIVERSARY. Sept 5, 1980. The longest underground motorway in the world, the St. Gotthard Auto Tunnel in Switzerland, was opened to traffic. More than 10 miles long, requiring $417,000,000 and 10 years for construction, it became the most direct route from Switzerland to the southern regions of the continent. The St. Gotthard Pass, the main passage since the Middle Ages, was closed much of every year by massive snow drifts.

ZANUCK, DARRYL F.: BIRTH ANNIVERSARY. Sept 5, 1902. Born at Wahoo, NE, Darryl F. Zanuck became a celebrated—and controversial—movie producer. He was also a cofounder of Twentieth Century Studios, which later merged with Fox. His film credits include *The Jazz Singer* (the first sound picture), *Forever Amber, The Snake Pit* and *The Grapes of Wrath*. He died Dec 21, 1979, at Palm Springs, CA.

BIRTHDAYS TODAY

Kristian Alfonso, 42, actress ("Days of Our Lives," "Melrose Place"), born Brockton, MA, Sept 5, 1964.

William Devane, 67, actor ("24," "Knots Landing"), born Albany, NY, Sept 5, 1939.

Dennis Dugan, 60, actor, director (*Big Daddy, Problem Child*), born Wheaton, IL, Sept 5, 1946.

Cathy Lee Guisewite, 56, cartoonist ("Cathy"), born Dayton, OH, Sept 5, 1950.

Carol Lawrence, 71, singer, actress (*West Side Story*), born Carol Maria Laraia at Melrose Park, IL, Sept 5, 1935.

Rose McGowan, 33, actress (*Jawbreaker*, "Charmed"), born Florence, Italy, Sept 5, 1973.

Bob Newhart, 77, comedian ("The Bob Newhart Show," "Newhart"), born Chicago, IL, Sept 5, 1929.

Brian Schweitzer, 51, Governor of Montana (D), born Havre, MT, Sept 5, 1955.

Raquel Welch, 64, actress (*The Three Musketeers, Woman of the Year*), model, born Chicago, IL, Sept 5, 1942.

Dweezil Zappa, 37, singer, actor ("Normal Life"), born Hollywood, CA, Sept 5, 1969.

☆ *Chase's 2006 Calendar of Events* ☆

SEPTEMBER 6 — WEDNESDAY

Day 249 — 116 Remaining

ADDAMS, JANE: BIRTH ANNIVERSARY. Sept 6, 1860. American worker for peace, social welfare, rights of women, founder of Hull House (Chicago), cowinner of Nobel Prize, 1931. Born at Cedarville, IL, she died May 21, 1935, at Chicago, IL.

BALTIC STATES' INDEPENDENCE RECOGNIZED: 15th ANNIVERSARY. Sept 6, 1991. The Soviet government recognized the independence of the Baltic states—Latvia, Estonia and Lithuania. The action came 51 years after the Baltic states were annexed by the Soviet Union. All three Baltic states had earlier declared their independence, and many nations had already recognized them diplomatically, including the US, Sept 2, 1991.

BEECHER, CATHARINE ESTHER: BIRTH ANNIVERSARY. Sept 6, 1800. Catharine Esther Beecher was born at East Hampton, NY. In addition to teaching herself mathematics, philosophy and Latin, Beecher had been formally educated in art and music. An early advocate for equal education for women, she founded the Hartford Female Seminary, which was widely recognized for its advanced curriculum. She was also instrumental in the founding of women's colleges in Iowa, Illinois and Wisconsin. Beecher died May 12, 1878, at Elmira, NY.

BULGARIA: UNIFICATION DAY. Sept 6. National holiday. Commemorates the anniversary of the reunification of the southern part of Bulgaria with the rest of the country in 1885.

CANADA: THE MASTERS. Sept 6–10. Spruce Meadows, Calgary, AB. International show jumping competition, along with Equi-Fair, TELUS Battle of the Breeds and the BP Amoco Festival of Nations. Featured events are the EnCana Cup, the ATCO Electric Circuit "Six-Bar," the BMO Financial Group Nations' Cup and the CN International. Est attendance: 175,000. For info: Spruce Meadows, RR 9, Calgary, AB, Canada T2J 5G5. Phone: (403) 974-4200. Fax: (403) 974-4270. E-mail: information@sprucemeadows.com. Web: www.sprucemeadows.com.

DALTON, JOHN: BIRTH ANNIVERSARY. Sept 6, 1766. English chemist, physicist, teacher and developer of atomic theory, was born at Eaglesfield, near Cockermouth, England. Dalton died at Manchester, England, July 27, 1844.

DEFEAT OF JESSE JAMES DAYS. Sept 6–10. Northfield, MN. Bank raid reenactment, 5k and 15k runs, arts, crafts, bike race, parade and professional rodeo. Est attendance: 150,000. For info: Northfield Chamber of Commerce, PO Box 198, Northfield, MN 55057. Phone: (507) 645-5604. Fax: (507) 663-7782. Web: www.defeatofjessejamesdays.org.

DO IT! DAY (aka FIGHT PROCRASTINATION DAY). Sept 6. Feeling overwhelmed? Too many things left undone? Hard to focus? Today is your day to turn your Do Its into Did Its! Annually, the first Wednesday after Labor Day. For info: Productivity Coach Ethel Cook, 4 Hilda Rd, Bedford, MA 01730. Phone: (781) 275-2326. Fax: (781) 275-7136. E-mail: coachethel@ethelcook.com.

FARMERS AND THRESHERMENS JUBILEE. Sept 6–10. New Centerville, PA. Many steam engines, threshing demonstrations using manpower, horses and steam, quilt show, crafts, truck and tractor pulls. Live entertainment, good food. Est attendance: 25,000. For info: Farmers & Threshermens Jubilee, 1428 Casselman Rd, Rockwood, PA 15557. Phone: (814) 926-3142.

★ ★ ★

	S	M	T	W	T	F	S
September						1	2
2006	3	4	5	6	7	8	9
	10	11	12	13	14	15	16
	17	18	19	20	21	22	23
	24	25	26	27	28	29	30

FIRST RADIO BROADCAST OF A PRIZEFIGHT: ANNIVERSARY. Sept 6, 1920. In the first boxing match broadcast on radio, Jack Dempsey knocked out Billy Miske in the third round of a scheduled 10-round fight.

LAFAYETTE, MARQUIS DE: BIRTH ANNIVERSARY. Sept 6, 1757. The French general and aristocrat, whose full name was Marie-Joseph-Paul-Yves-Roch-Gilbert du Motier, came to America to assist in the revolutionary cause. Lafayette, who had convinced Louis XVI to send 6,000 French soldiers to assist the Americans, was given command of an army at Virginia and was instrumental in forcing the surrender of Lord Cornwallis at Yorktown. He was called "The Hero of Two Worlds" and was appointed a brigadier general on his return to France in 1782. He became a leader of the liberal aristocrats during the early days of the French revolution. As the commander of the newly formed national guard of Paris, he rescued Louis XVI and Marie-Antoinette from a crowd that stormed Versailles Oct 6, 1789. His popularity waned after his guards opened fire on angry demonstrators demanding abdication of the king in 1791. He fled to Austria with the overthrow of the monarchy in 1792, returning when Napoleon Bonaparte came to power. Born at Chavaniac, he died at Paris, May 20, 1834.

PAKISTAN: DEFENSE OF PAKISTAN DAY. Sept 6. National holiday. Commemorates the Indo-Pakistan War of 1965.

ROSE, BILLY: BIRTH ANNIVERSARY. Sept 6, 1899. Billy Rose (William S. Rosenberg), American theatrical producer, author, songwriter and husband of Fanny Brice, was born at New York, NY. His songs include: "That Old Gang of Mine," "Me and My Shadow," "Without a Song," "It's Only a Paper Moon" and hundreds of others. Rose died at Montego Bay, Jamaica, Feb 10, 1966.

SAINT PETERSBURG NAME RESTORED: 15th ANNIVERSARY. Sept 6, 1991. Russian legislators voted to restore the name Saint Petersburg to the nation's second largest city. The city had been known as Leningrad for 67 years in honor of the Soviet Union's founder, Vladimir I. Lenin. The city, founded in 1703 by Peter the Great, has had three names in the 20th century with Russian leaders changing its German-sounding name to Petrograd at the beginning of WWI in 1914 and Soviet Communist leaders changing its name to Leningrad in 1924 following their leader's death.

SWAZILAND: INDEPENDENCE DAY: ANNIVERSARY. Sept 6. National holiday. Commemorates attainment of independence from Britain in 1968. Also called Somhlolo Day in honor of the great 19th-century Swazi leader.

UNITED NATIONS: MILLENNIUM SUMMIT: ANNIVERSARY. Sept 6–8, 2000. More than 150 world leaders met at the United Nations in New York City, the largest gathering of such leaders in history. Among the kings, prime ministers, presidents and generals attending were US President Bill Clinton, Fidel Castro and Yasser Arafat. These leaders adopted a declaration which committed them to promote democracy, strengthen respect for human rights, reverse the spread of AIDS, cut poverty, protect the planet and improve the ability of the UN to keep the peace.

"WYATT EARP" TV PREMIERE: ANNIVERSARY. Sept 6, 1955. Officially titled "The Life and Legend of Wyatt Earp," this half-hour series marked the beginning of the trend toward "adult Westerns." It was loosely based on fact, with Hugh O'Brian as Earp, marshall of Dodge City, KS, and later of Tombstone, AZ.

TEA PLANT,   SUGAR CANE,   COFFEE PLANT.

BIRTHDAYS TODAY

Jane Curtin, 59, actress ("Saturday Night Live," "3rd Rock from the Sun"), comedienne, born Cambridge, MA, Sept 6, 1947.

Jeff Foxworthy, 48, comedian (*You Know You're a Redneck*), actor ("The Jeff Foxworthy Show"), author (*No Shirt, No Shoes . . . No Problem*), born Atlanta, GA, Sept 6, 1958.

Tim Henman, 32, tennis player, born Oxford, England, Sept 6, 1974.

Swoosie Kurtz, 62, actress ("Sisters," *The World According to Garp*; Tony for *The House of Blue Leaves*), born Omaha, NE, Sept 6, 1944.

Rosie Perez, 42, actress (*King of the Jungle, White Men Can't Jump*), born Brooklyn, NY, Sept 6, 1964.

Justin Whalin, 32, actor ("Charles in Charge," "Lois & Clark"), born San Francisco, CA, Sept 6, 1974.

Jo Anne Worley, 69, comedienne, actress ("Rowan & Martin's Laugh-In"), born Lowell, IA, Sept 6, 1937.

SEPTEMBER 7 — THURSDAY
Day 250 — 115 Remaining

BRAZIL: INDEPENDENCE DAY. Sept 7. Declared independence from Portugal in 1822. National holiday.

CANADA: TORONTO INTERNATIONAL FILM FESTIVAL. Sept 7–16. Toronto, ON. 31st annual. A 10-day festival of contemporary Canadian and international cinema at various downtown theatres. Call or write for info or to be put on mailing list. Est attendance: 250,000. For info: Toronto Intl Film Festival, 2 Carlton St, Ste 1600, Toronto, ON, Canada M5B 1J3. Phone: (416) 968-FILM. Fax: (416) 967-9477. E-mail: tiffg@torfilmfest.ca. Web: www.bell.ca/filmfest.

CORBETT-SULLIVAN PRIZE FIGHT: ANNIVERSARY. Sept 7, 1892. John L. Sullivan was knocked out by James J. Corbett in the 21st round of a prize fight at New Orleans, LA. It was the first major fight under the Marquess of Queensberry Rules.

THE 59 MINUTE 37 SECOND ANVIL MOUNTAIN CHALLENGE. Sept 7. Nome, AK. 11th annual running event that starts at the base of Anvil Mountain, where runners must run 834 ft up the face of the mountain and return in less than 59 minutes and 37 seconds or be disqualified from the competition. Trophies awarded for first–third finishers, first woman finisher and first finisher 16 years of age and under. Record time is 25 minutes 37 seconds. Est attendance: 1,000. For info: Rasmussen's Music Mart, PO Box 2, Nome, AK 99762-0002. Phone: (907) 443-2798 or (907) 443-2919. Fax: (907) 443-5777.

"THE FLYING NUN" TV PREMIERE: ANNIVERSARY. Sept 7, 1967. This sitcom about a nun at a convent in Puerto Rico who discovers that she can fly starred Sally Field as Elsie Ethrington (Sister Bertrille) and featured Madeleine Sherwood, Marge Redmond, Shelley Morrison, Alejandro Rey and Vito Scotti.

GOOGLE FOUNDED: ANNIVERSARY. Sept 7, 1998. Sergey Brin and Larry Page incorporated the Internet search engine company Google on this date at Menlo Park, CA. Although still in beta, Google.com was receiving 10,000 queries a day at that time. Within a year, the company was doing 3 million searches a day. Before long, Google entered the pop culture zeitgeist by becoming a verb for Internet searching.

GRANDMA MOSES DAY. Sept 7. Anna Mary (Robertson) Moses, modern primitive American painter born at Greenwich, NY, Sept 7, 1860. Started painting at the age of 78. Her 100th birthday was proclaimed Grandma Moses Day in New York state. Died at Hoosick Falls, NY, Dec 13, 1961.

GREAT PEANUT TOUR. Sept 7–10. Skippers, VA. Assorted bicycle rides from 13 to 100 miles. Special peanut tour ride to examine peanuts growing, method of harvesting and a sampling of more than 40 peanut goodies. Unique water stops, nature walks, music, campfires with marshmallow roast. Annually, the weekend following Labor Day. Est attendance: 1,200. For info: Robert C. Wrenn, Emporia Bicycle Club, PO Box 668, Emporia, VA 23847. Phone: (800) 449-2453. Fax: (804) 348-4020. E-mail: rcw@telpage.net. Web: www.greatpeanuttour.com.

HARVEST MOON. Sept 7. So called because the full moon nearest the autumnal equinox extends the hours of light into the evening and helps the harvester with his long day's work. Moon enters Full Moon phase at 2:42 PM, EDT.

HOLLY, BUDDY: BIRTH ANNIVERSARY. Sept 7, 1936. American popular music performer, composer and bandleader. Called one of the most innovative and influential musicians of his time, he was a pioneer of rock 'n' roll. His hits included "That'll Be the Day" and "Peggy Sue." Born Charles Harden Holley, at Lubbock, TX, he died at age 22 in an airplane crash near Mason City, IA, Feb 3, 1959.

KAZAN, ELIA: BIRTH ANNIVERSARY. Sept 7, 1909. Born Elia Kazanjoglou at Constantinople, Turkey, Elia Kazan was one of the most influential directors in history of American stage and film. He directed the Broadway premieres of Arthur Miller's *Death of a Salesman* and Tennessee Williams's *A Streetcar Named Desire* as well as many other Williams plays. He won directing Oscars for the films *On the Waterfront* and *Gentleman's Agreement*. He discovered and promoted actors such as Marlon Brando, Warren Beatty and James Dean, who he directed in *East of Eden*. In 1952 he angered much of Hollywood by testifying before the House Un-American Activities Committee, naming persons he thought to be members of the Communist Party. Kazan died at New York, NY, Sept 7, 2003.

LAWRENCE, JACOB: BIRTH ANNIVERSARY. Sept 7, 1917. African American painter, born at Atlantic City, NJ. Lawrence was best known for his series of historical paintings on John Brown and on the migration of African Americans out of the South. A recipient of the NAACP's Spingarn Medal, he won many other awards during his lifetime. Lawrence died June 9, 2000, at Seattle, WA.

LONGS PEAK SCOTTISH/IRISH HIGHLAND FESTIVAL. Sept 7–10. Estes Park, CO. 30th annual Scottish-Irish celebration festival with pipe bands, Highland and Irish dancing, jousting and gathering of the clans. Featuring professional Scottish and Irish entertainers, "Dogs of the British Isles" dog competition, professional Scottish athletes and vendors with imported and handcrafted merchandise. Annually, the first weekend after Labor Day. Est attendance: 70,000. For info: Longs Peak Scottish/Irish Highland Festival, Inc, Box 1820, Estes Park, CO 80517. Phone: (800) 903-7837. Fax: (970) 586-5328. E-mail: info@scotfest.com. Web: www.scotfest.com.

LUNAR ECLIPSE. Sept 7. Partial of the moon. Moon enters penumbra at 12:42 PM, EDT, reaches middle of eclipse at 2:51 PM and leaves penumbra at 5:00 PM. Visible in Europe, Africa, Asia and Australia.

MARION POPCORN FESTIVAL. Sept 7–9. Marion, OH. Performances by nationally known entertainers every evening; parade, athletic and popcorn cooking competitions, arts and crafts. 11 AM to midnight daily. Est attendance: 350,000. For info: Marion Popcorn Festival, PO Box 1101, Marion, OH 43301-1101. Phone: (740) 387-3378. Web: www.popcornfestival.com.

MOON PHASE: FULL MOON. Sept 7. Moon enters Full Moon phase at 2:42 PM, EDT.

"NEITHER SNOW NOR RAIN" DAY: ANNIVERSARY.
Sept 7, 1914. Anniversary of the opening to the public on Labor Day 1914 of the New York Post Office Building at Eighth Avenue between 31st and 33rd streets. On the front of this building was an inscription supplied by William M. Kendall of the architectural firm that planned the building. The inscription, a free translation from Herodotus, reads: "Neither snow nor rain nor heat nor gloom of night stays these couriers from the swift completion of their appointed rounds." This has long been believed to be the motto of the US Post Office and Postal Service. They have, in fact, no motto . . . but the legend remains. [Info from: New York Post Office, Public Info Office and US Postal Service.]

PERIGEAN SPRING TIDES. Sept 7. Spring tides, the highest possible tides, occur when New Moon or Full Moon falls within 24 hours of the moment the Moon is nearest Earth (perigee) in its monthly orbit at 1 PM, EDT. These tides are not named for the season of spring but for the German *springen*, "to leap up."

QUEEN ELIZABETH I: BIRTH ANNIVERSARY. Sept 7, 1533. Queen of England, daughter of Henry VIII and Anne Boleyn, after whom the Elizabethan era was named, was born at Greenwich Palace. She ascended the throne in 1558 at the age of 25. During her reign, the British defeated the Spanish Armada in July 1588, the Anglican Church was essentially established and England became a world power. She died at Richmond, England, Mar 24, 1603.

"TRUTH OR CONSEQUENCES" TV PREMIERE: ANNIVERSARY. Sept 7, 1950. This game show lasted for many years on both radio and TV. The half-hour show was based on a parlor game: contestants who failed to answer a question before the buzzer (nicknamed Beulah) went off had to perform stunts (i.e., pay the consequences). Ralph Edwards created and hosted the show until 1954, then it became a prime-time show hosted by Jack Bailey. Bob Barker succeeded him in 1966 and hosted it through its syndicated run. In 1977 the show was revived as "The New Truth or Consequences" with Bob Hilton as host.

UNITED TRIBES POWWOW. Sept 7–10. United Tribes Technical College, Bismarck, ND. Enjoy one of the largest international powwows in the nation. This colorful pageant includes Native Americans from across the country singing and dancing in friendly competition. Indian foods, artifacts and jewelry are sold on the premises. Est attendance: 20,000. For info: (701) 255-3285 or North Dakota Tourism, Century Center, 1600 E Century Ave, Ste 2, Bismarck, ND 58503. Phone: (701) 328-2525 or (800) 435-5663. Web: www.unitedtribespowwow.com.

UTAH STATE FAIR. Sept 7–17. Utah State FairPark, Salt Lake City, UT. Exhibits, livestock, family contests, cook-offs, concerts and entertainment. Annually, beginning the first Thursday after Labor Day. Est attendance: 277,000. For info: Utah State Fair-Park, 155 N 1000 W, Salt Lake City, UT 84116. Phone: (801) 538-8400. Fax: (801) 538-8455. E-mail: utstfair@fiber.net.

WILLIAMSBURG OLD-FASHIONED TRADING DAYS.
Sept 7–9. Courthouse Square, Williamsburg, KY. Arts and crafts, bluegrass and gospel singing, antique car show and more. Annually, the first Thursday, Friday and Saturday after Labor Day. Est attendance: 25,000. For info: Joyce Bird, Coordinator, PO Box 2, Williamsburg, KY 40769. Phone: (606) 549-0530. Fax: (606) 539-0095.

YELLOW DAISY FESTIVAL. Sept 7–10. Stone Mountain Park, Stone Mountain, GA. Arts and crafts festival with more than 475 exhibitors. Continuous entertainment and foods. Annually, the weekend after Labor Day. Est attendance: 225,000. For info: Special Events Office, Stone Mountain Park, PO Box 778, Stone Mountain, GA 30086. Phone: (770) 498-5633. Fax: (770) 413-5059. E-mail: cchadwick@stonemountainpark.com. Web: www.stonemountainpark.com.

BIRTHDAYS TODAY

Corbin Bernsen, 52, actor ("LA Law," "Ryan's Hope," *Major League*), born North Hollywood, CA, Sept 7, 1954.
Susan Blakely, 56, actress (*The Way We Were, The Lords of Flatbush, Shampoo*), born Frankfurt, Germany, Sept 7, 1950.
Michael DeBakey, 98, distinguished heart surgeon, born Lake Charles, LA, Sept 7, 1908.
Michael Feinstein, 50, singer, pianist, born Columbus, OH, Sept 7, 1956.
Arthur Ferrante, 85, pianist (Ferrante and Teicher), composer, born New York, NY, Sept 7, 1921.
Chrissie Hynde, 55, lead singer (Pretenders), songwriter, born Akron, OH, Sept 7, 1951.
Daniel Ken Inouye, 82, US Senator (D, Hawaii), born Honolulu, HI, Sept 7, 1924.
Julie Kavner, 55, actress (*Radio Days*, "Rhoda," Marge Simpson's voice on "The Simpsons"), born Los Angeles, CA, Sept 7, 1951.
John Philip Law, 69, actor (*The Russians Are Coming, the Russians Are Coming; Barbarella*), born Hollywood, CA, Sept 7, 1937.
Richard Roundtree, 64, actor (*Shaft, Q, Once upon a Time When We Were Colored*), born New Rochelle, NY, Sept 7, 1942 (some sources say 1939).
Devon Sawa, 28, actor (*Wild America, The Boy's Club*), born Vancouver, BC, Canada, Sept 7, 1978.
Briana Scurry, 35, soccer player, born Minneapolis, MN, Sept 7, 1971.

SEPTEMBER 8 — FRIDAY
Day 251 — 114 Remaining

ANDORRA: NATIONAL HOLIDAY. Sept 8. Honors our Lady of Meritxell.

ARCOLA BROOM CORN FESTIVAL. Sept 8–10. Arcola, IL. The whole town celebrates. Free entertainment, arts and crafts, flea markets, food. Est attendance: 60,000. For info: Arcola Chamber of Commerce, PO Box 274, Arcola, IL 61910. Phone: (800) 336-5456. Web: www.arcola-il.org.

BALD IS BEAUTIFUL CONVENTION. Sept 8–10. Morehead City, NC. To cultivate a sense of pride for all bald-headed men (folks) everywhere and eliminate the vanity associated with the loss of one's hair. As seen on national television; Bald is Beautiful Contests, family events. Annually, the second weekend in September. Est attendance: 250. For info: John T. Capps III, Founder, Bald Headed Men of America, 102 Bald Dr, Morehead City, NC 28557. Phone/fax: (252) 726-1823. E-mail: jcapps4102@aol.com. Web: members.aol.com/BaldUSA.

CLINE, PATSY: BIRTH ANNIVERSARY. Sept 8, 1932. Country and western singer, born Virginia Patterson Hensley at Winchester, VA. Patsy Cline got her big break in 1957 when she won an Arthur Godfrey Talent Scout show, singing "Walking After Midnight." Her career took off and she became a featured singer at the Grand Ole Opry, attaining the rank of top female country singer. She died in a plane crash Mar 5, 1963, at Camden, TN, along with singers Hawkshaw Hawkins and Cowboy Copas.

	S	M	T	W	T	F	S
September 2006						1	2
	3	4	5	6	7	8	9
	10	11	12	13	14	15	16
	17	18	19	20	21	22	23
	24	25	26	27	28	29	30

CLINTON COUNTY CORN FESTIVAL. Sept 8–10. Clinton County Fairgrounds, Wilmington, OH. 29th annual. Help us celebrate our agricultural heritage as we honor one of the area's biggest industries. The festival features antique farm machinery, a parade (Saturday at 10 AM), games, all types of food made from corn, a quilt show, music, antiques, crafts and the Corn Olympics. This is an event not to miss in Clinton County! For info: Rhonda Henson, Clinton County CVB, 13 N South St, Wilmington, OH 45177. Phone: (877) 428-4748. Fax: (937) 382-1738. E-mail: rfhenson@clintoncountyohio.com. Web: www.clintoncountyohio.com.

FESTIVAL OF THE VINE. Sept 8–10. Geneva, IL. Flavors of fall are celebrated with music, wine tasting, antique carriage rides, arts and crafts, entertainment and specialties of Geneva's fine restaurants. Est attendance: 75,000. For info: Geneva Chamber of Commerce, 8 S Third St, PO Box 481, Geneva, IL 60134. Phone: (630) 232-6060. Fax: (630) 232-6083. E-mail: chamber-info@genevachamber.com. Web: www.genevachamber.com.

GALVESTON HURRICANE: ANNIVERSARY. Sept 8, 1900. The worst national disaster in US history in terms of lives lost. More than 6,000 people were killed when a hurricane struck Galveston, TX, with winds of more than 120 mph, followed by a huge tidal wave. More than 2,500 buildings were destroyed.

GOAT DAYS. Sept 8–10. USA Stadium, Millington, TN. Goat contests with large cash prizes and trophies, children's area, camping, fishing, goat races, dancing, music, food, rodeo, crafts, Cabrito Challenge Cook-Off, Dutch-oven cook-offs, ice cream making and National Anvil Shoot. Huge display of antique engines and tractors and national stock dog trials. Est attendance: 20,000. For info: Goat Days Intl, 4880 Navy Rd, Millington, TN 38053. Phone: (901) 872-4559. Fax: (901) 872-7700. E-mail: goatdays@bigriver.net.

KANSAS STATE FAIR. Sept 8–17. Hutchinson, KS. Commercial and competitive exhibits, entertainment, carnival, car racing and other special attractions. Annually, beginning the first Friday after Labor Day. Est attendance: 400,000. For info: Denny Stocklein, Gen Mgr, Kansas State Fair, 2000 N Poplar St, Hutchinson, KS 67502. Phone: (620) 669-3600. E-mail: info@kansasstatefair.com. Web: www.kansasstatefair.com.

KEYSTONE COUNTRY FESTIVAL. Sept 8–10. Blair County Convention Center, Altoona, PA. Arts and crafts vendors display their wares throughout the weekend. Attractions include an ethnic food village, sports café, children's activities and live entertainment. For info: Allegheny Mountains Convention and Visitors Bureau, One Convention Center Dr, Altoona, PA 16602. Phone: (814) 943-4183. Fax: (814) 943-8094. E-mail: info@amcvb.com. Web: www.visitcentralpa.com.

LIGONIER HIGHLAND GAMES. Sept 8–9. Ligonier, PA. Scottish bagpipe bands on parade, Highland dancers and athletes in daylong performances. Clan gatherings, dog show. Offers imported woolens, china, jewelry, records and foods. Mail SASE for schedule of events. Est attendance: 10,000. For info: David L. Peet, Ligonier Highland Games, PO Box 884, Bethel Park, PA 15102-0884. Phone: (412) 851-9900. E-mail: ligdir@icubed.com. Web: www.ligoniergames.org.

MACEDONIA: INDEPENDENCE DAY. Sept 8. National holiday. Commemorates independence from the Yugoslav Union in 1991.

MALTA: SIEGE BROKEN: ANNIVERSARY. Sept 8. "Two Sieges and Regatta Day" festivities now commemorate victory over the Turks, Sept 8, 1565, when the siege that began in May 1565 was broken by the Maltese and the Knights of St. John after a loss of nearly 10,000 lives. Also commemorated is survival of the 1943 siege by the Axis Powers. Parades, fireworks, boat races, etc, especially at the capital, Valleta, and the Grand Harbour.

MARIGOLD FESTIVAL. Sept 8–10. Pekin, IL. Parade, arts, crafts, golf, carnival, Festive Foods and other family-oriented activities. Est attendance: 100,000. For info: Chamber of Commerce, PO Box 636, Pekin, IL 61555-0636. Phone: (309) 346-2106. Fax: (309) 346-2104. E-mail: chamber@pekin.net.

McGWIRE BREAKS HOME RUN RECORD: ANNIVERSARY. Sept 8, 1998. Mark McGwire of the St. Louis Cardinals hit his 62nd home run, breaking Roger Maris's 1961 record for the most home runs in a single season. McGwire hit his homer at Busch Stadium at St. Louis against pitcher Steve Trachsel of the Chicago Cubs as the Cardinals won, 6–3. McGwire finished the season with 70 home runs. On Oct 5, 2001, Barry Bonds hit his 71st home run, breaking McGwire's record. Bonds finished the season with 73 homers.

MISS AMERICA FIRST CROWNED: 85th ANNIVERSARY. Sept 8, 1921. Margaret Gorman of Washington, DC, was crowned the first Miss America at the end of a two-day pageant at Atlantic City, NJ.

MISSION SAN GABRIEL ARCHANGEL: FOUNDING ANNIVERSARY. Sept 8, 1771. California mission to the Indians founded on this date.

NATIONAL CHAMPIONSHIP INDIAN POWWOW. Sept 8–10. Traders Village, Grand Prairie, TX. Hundreds of Indians gather for colorful traditional dance contests, Indian arts and crafts shows and Indian food. Est attendance: 90,000. For info: Dallas–Fort Worth Inter-Tribal Assn, Traders Village, 2602 Mayfield Rd, Grand Prairie, TX 75052-7246. Phone: (972) 647-2331. E-mail: dfwinfo@tradersvillage.com. Web: www.tradersvillage.com.

NIXON PARDONED: ANNIVERSARY. Sept 8, 1974. Anniversary of the "full, free, and absolute pardon unto Richard Nixon, for all offenses against the United States which he, Richard Nixon, has committed or may have committed or taken part in during the period from January 20, 1969, through August 9, 1974." (Presidential Proclamation 4311, Sept 8, 1974, by Gerald R. Ford.)

NORDICFEST. Sept 8–10. Libby, MT. Scandinavian festival with food booths, dinners, cultural exhibits, craft shows, quilt show, art show, folk dance performances, entertainment and the international fjord horse show. Parade showcases a contingent of Norwegian fjord horses plus a variety of floats. Est attendance: 10,000. For info: Libby Nordicfest, Inc, Box 791, Libby, MT 59923. Phone: (800) 785-6541. E-mail: smokesignal@libby.org. Web: www.libbynordicfest.org.

NORTHERN PACIFIC RAILROAD COMPLETED: ANNIVERSARY. Sept 8, 1883. After 19 years of construction, the Northern Pacific Railroad became the second railroad to link the two coasts. The Union Pacific and Central Pacific lines met at Utah in 1869.

NORWALK SEAPORT OYSTER FESTIVAL. Sept 8–10. Norwalk, CT. Huge festival with vintage ships on display, 225 juried crafters, main stage entertainment, oyster shucking and slurping contests and Kids Cove (children's entertainment). Annually, the weekend following Labor Day. Est attendance: 82,000. For info: Norwalk Seaport Assn, 132 Water St, Norwalk, CT 06854. Phone: (203) 838-9444. Fax: (203) 855-1017. E-mail: nseaport@snet.net. Web: www.seaport.org.

OHIO RIVER STERNWHEEL FESTIVAL. Sept 8–10. Ohio River Levee, Marietta, OH. A three-day riverfront extravaganza. More than two dozen sternwheelers line the Ohio River shore in Marietta, OH. Continuous musical entertainment for all ages, food concessions, queen coronation, sternwheel races, fireworks. Annually, the weekend following Labor Day. Est attendance: 85,000. For info: Ohio River Sternwheel Festival Committee, 316 Third St, Marietta, OH 45750. Phone: (740) 373-5178 or (740) 374-4913. Fax: (740) 374-4959. E-mail: info@mariettaohio.org. Web: www.mariettaohio.org.

OKTOBERFEST. Sept 8–10. MainStrasse Village, Covington, KY. Celebration of the German "storybook wedding reception" kicks off with a beer-tapping ceremony. Features include German and American food, live Bavarian music and dancing, arts and crafts, children's rides and much more. Est attendance: 250,000. For info: Donna Kremer, Administrative Coordinator, MainStrasse Village, 406 W 6th St, Ste 201, Covington, KY 41011. Phone: (859) 491-0458. Fax: (859) 655-7932. E-mail: dkremer@main strasse.org. Web: www.mainstrasse.org.

"THE OPRAH WINFREY SHOW" TV PREMIERE: 20th ANNIVERSARY. Sept 8, 1986. This daytime talk show was the top-rated talk show for years and also has the distinction of being the first talk show hosted by a black woman, Oprah Winfrey. Her show is taped in front of a studio audience who are solicited for their questions and feedback. In the mid-1990s, fed up with the plethora of trashy talk shows that had sprung up everywhere, Winfrey decided to upgrade the quality of topics that her show presented. Her book club feature has been a popular element of her show, and chosen books usually become best-sellers.

PEPPER, CLAUDE DENSON: BIRTH ANNIVERSARY. Sept 8, 1900. US Representative and Senator, born near Dudleyville, AL. Pepper's career in politics spanned 53 years and 10 presidents, and he became the champion for America's senior citizens. He was elected to the US Senate in 1936, where he was a principal architect of many of the nation's "safety net" social programs including Social Security, the minimum wage and medical assistance for the elderly and for handicapped children. After a 14-year career in the Senate, he returned to Congress in the House of Representatives where he served 14 terms. He served as chairman of the House Select Committee on Aging, drafted legislation banning forced retirement and fought against cutting Social Security benefits. Pepper died at Washington, DC, May 30, 1989.

PUYALLUP FAIR. Sept 8–24. Puyallup, WA. Entertainment, animals, rides, displays and food. The 106th fair. Est attendance: 1,100,000. For info: Western Washington Fair, 110 Ninth Ave SW, Puyallup, WA 98371. Phone: (253) 841-5045. Fax: (253) 841-5390. E-mail: info@thefair.com. Web: www.thefair.com.

SAILFEST. Sept 8. Pavilion, Island Heights, NJ. A sailboat race and street fair that benefits the Rotary Club of Toms River. Annually, the Saturday after Labor Day. Est attendance: 12,000. For info: Len Adams, PO Box 747, 21 Central Venue, Island Heights, NJ 08732. Phone: (732) 929-0011. Fax: (732) 506-6341. E-mail: cprintr@aol.com.

SELLERS, PETER: BIRTH ANNIVERSARY. Sept 8, 1925. Award-winning British comedian and film star, born Richard Henry Sellers at Southsea, Hampshire, England. Sellers is remembered for his multiple roles in *Dr. Strangelove*, his Oscar-nominated role as Chance the Gardener in *Being There* and for his role as the bumbling Inspector Clouseau in the *Pink Panther* films. Died at London, England, July 24, 1980.

STAMP EXPO. Sept 8–10. Radisson Hotel, Anaheim, CA. Est attendance: 4,000. For info: Israel Bick, Exec Dir, Intl Stamp & Coin Collectors Society, PO Box 854, Van Nuys, CA 91408. Phone: (818) 997-6496. Fax: (818) 988-4337. E-mail: iibick@sbcglobal.net. Web: www.bick.net.

"STAR TREK" TV PREMIERE: 40th ANNIVERSARY. Sept 8, 1966. The first of 79 episodes of the TV series "Star Trek" was aired on the NBC network. Although the science fiction show set in the future only lasted a few seasons, it has remained enormously popular through syndication reruns. It has been given new life through many motion pictures, a cartoon TV series and popular spin-off TV series such as "Star Trek: The Next Generation," "Enterprise" and others. It has consistently ranked among the biggest titles in the motion picture, television, home video and licensing divisions of Paramount Pictures.

SUGARLOAF CRAFTS FESTIVAL. Sept 8–10. Prince William County Fairgrounds, Manassas, VA. This show, now in its 26th year, features 300 nationally recognized craft designers and fine artists displaying and selling their original creations. Craft demonstrations, live music, food, hourly gift certificate drawings and more. Est attendance: 21,000. For info: Sugarloaf Mountain Works, 200 Orchard Ridge Dr, #215, Gaithersburg, MD 20878. Phone: (800) 210-9900. Fax: (301) 253-9620. Web: www.sugarloafcrafts.com.

"TARZAN" TV PREMIERE: 40th ANNIVERSARY. Sept 8, 1966. This hour adventure series was based on Edgar Rice Burroughs's character, who appeared for the first time on TV. Tarzan, an English lord who preferred the jungle, was played by Ron Ely. Manuel Padilla, Jr, was Jai, a jungle orphan, Alan Caillou was Jason Flood, Jai's tutor, and Rockne Tarkington was Rao, a veterinarian. There was no Jane.

TENNESSEE STATE FAIR. Sept 8–17. Nashville, TN. A huge variety of exhibits, carnival midway, animal and variety shows, live stage presentations, livestock, agricultural and craft competitions and food and game booths. Annually, beginning the first Friday after Labor Day. Est attendance: 200,000. For info: Tennessee Fair Office, PO Box 40208, Melrose Station, Nashville, TN 37204. Phone: (615) 862-8980. Fax: (615) 862-8992. E-mail: tsf@nashville.gov. Web: www.tennesseestatefair.org.

"THAT GIRL" TV PREMIERE: 40th ANNIVERSARY. Sept 8, 1966. "That Girl" was a half-hour sitcom starring Marlo Thomas as Ann Marie, an independent aspiring actress in New York City. Ted Bessell also starred as her boyfriend Don Hollinger. They were finally engaged in 1970. Also featured were Lew Parker, Rosemary De Camp and Bonnie Scott. Well-known performers who appeared on the show include Dabney Coleman, George Carlin and Bernie Kopell.

UNITED NATIONS: INTERNATIONAL LITERACY DAY. Sept 8. An international day observed by the organizations of the United Nations system. For info: United Nations, Dept of Public Info, New York, NY 10017. Web: www.un.org.

ZIEGLER KETTLE MORAINE JAZZ FESTIVAL. Sept 8–9. Riverside Park, West Bend, WI. Features nationally recognized jazz musicians and vocalists. Past performers have included Richard Elliott, Chris Botti and Rick Braun. Est attendance: 5,500. For info: Dave Amoroso, Ron Sonntag Public Relations, 9406 N 107th St, Milwaukee, WI 53224. Phone: (877) 271-6903. Fax: (414) 354-5317. E-mail: dave@rspr.com. Web: www.kmjazz.com.

BIRTHDAYS TODAY

David Arquette, 35, actor (*Scream, Muppets from Space*), born Winchester, VA, Sept 8, 1971.

Sid Caesar, 84, comedian, actor ("Your Show of Shows"), born Yonkers, NY, Sept 8, 1922.

Alan Feinstein, 65, actor ("Edge of Night," "Love of Life," "Search for Tomorrow"), born New York, NY, Sept 8, 1941.

Marilyn Mims, 52, opera singer, born Collins, MS, Sept 8, 1954.

Latrell Sprewell, 36, basketball player, born Milwaukee, WI, Sept 8, 1970.

Heather Thomas, 49, actress ("The Fall Guy"), born Greenwich, CT, Sept 8, 1957.

Henry Thomas, 35, actor (*E.T. The Extra-Terrestrial, Legends of the Fall*), born San Antonio, TX, Sept 8, 1971.

Jonathan Taylor Thomas, 25, actor ("Home Improvement"), born Bethlehem, PA, Sept 8, 1981.

Rogatien (Rogie) Vachon, 61, former hockey executive and player, born Palmarolle, QC, Canada, Sept 8, 1945.

★   ★   ★

	S	M	T	W	T	F	S
September						1	2
2006	3	4	5	6	7	8	9
	10	11	12	13	14	15	16
	17	18	19	20	21	22	23
	24	25	26	27	28	29	30

SEPTEMBER 9 — SATURDAY

Day 252 — 113 Remaining

ALBANY RIVERFRONT JAZZ FESTIVAL. Sept 9. Riverfront Amphitheater, Albany, NY. A daylong celebration of traditional and smooth jazz music. Great food and beverages, as well as children's activities, make for a great free festival. Est attendance: 15,000. For info: Albany Special Events, City Hall, 4th Fl, Eagle St, Albany, NY 12207. Phone: (518) 434-2032. Fax: (518) 426-0759. E-mail: info@albanyevents.org. Web: www.albany events.org.

ARTIST RECEPTION & ART IN THE GARDEN. Sept 9–10. Washington, PA. Est attendance: 1,200. For info: Joyce Mullen, Washington County Historical Society, 49 E Maiden St, Washington, PA 15317. Phone: (724) 225-6740. Fax: (724) 225-8495. E-mail: info@wchspa.org. Web: www.wchspa.org.

BATTLE OF MARATHON: ANNIVERSARY. Sept 9. On the day of the ninth month's full moon in the year 490 BC, the numerically superior invading army of Persia was met and defeated on the Plain of Marathon by the Athenian army, led by Miltiades. More than 6,000 men died in the day's battle, which drove the Persians to the sea. The mound of earth covering the dead is still visible at the site. This date is in dispute. See also: "Historic Marathon Runs: Anniversary" (Sept 2) for the legendary running of Phidippides and the origin of the marathon race.

BATTLE OF SALERNO: ANNIVERSARY. Sept 9–16, 1943. US General Mark Clark's Fifth Army made an amphibious assault on Salerno, Italy (Operation Avalanche), at 3:30 AM. The British 1st Airborne Division seized the southern Italian port of Taranto (Operation Slapstick) without opposition. Initial gains along the western coast of Italy were checked by strong German forces by Sept 12. In some places the Allied forces were pushed back to within two miles of the coast. On Sept 15 US 82nd Airborne and British 7th Armoured counter-attacked and on Sept 16 units of the American 5th Army and the British 8th Army joined up near Vallo di Lucania.

BONZA BOTTLER DAY™. Sept 9. To celebrate when the number of the day is the same as the number of the month. Bonza Bottler Day™ is an excuse to have a party at least once a month. For more information, see Jan 1. For info: Gail M. Berger, 14 Fernwood Dr, Taylors, SC 29687. Phone: (864) 609-9874. E-mail: gberger5@aol.com.

BOONESBOROUGH DAYS. Sept 9–10. Shafer Memorial Park, Boonsboro, MD. Crafts, antiques, living history, demonstrations, food. Boonesborough was the original spelling of the town's name. Est attendance: 10,000. For info: Boonsboro Historical Society, PO Box 213, Boonsboro, MD 21713. Phone: (301) 432-5889.

CALIFORNIA: ADMISSION DAY: ANNIVERSARY. Sept 9. Became 31st state in 1850.

CHADDS FORD DAYS. Sept 9–10. Chadds Ford, PA. Open-air colonial fair with 18th-century craft demonstrations, Brandywine Valley art, live old-time music, country rides and games, colonial and contemporary crafts for sale, good food. Est attendance: 8,000. For info: Chadds Ford Historical Society, Box 27, Chadds Ford, PA 19317. Phone: (610) 388-7376. Web: www .chaddsfordhistory.org.

CIVIL WAR DAYS. Sept 9–10. Chesapeake Public Library, Chesapeake, VA. 14th annual living history event. Skirmish both days, encampment drills, demonstrations, speakers, displays, children's activities and much more. Music groups and food vendors on site. Est attendance: 20,000. For info: Rhonda Riddick, Chesapeake Public Library, 298 Cedar Rd, Chesapeake, VA 23322. Phone: (757) 382-6579. Fax: (757) 382-8301. E-mail: rriddick@ chesapeake.lib.va.us. Web: www.chesapeake.lib.va.us.

"FAT ALBERT AND THE COSBY KIDS" TV PREMIERE: ANNIVERSARY. Sept 9, 1972. This cartoon series was hosted by Bill Cosby, with characters based on his childhood friends at Philadelphia. Its central characters—Fat Albert, Weird Harold, Mush Mouth and Donald—were weird-looking but very human. The show sent messages of tolerance and harmony. In 1979 the show was renamed "The New Fat Albert Show."

FLAX SCUTCHING FESTIVAL. Sept 9–10. Stahlstown, PA. Demonstrations of the art of making linen from the flax plant. Second oldest continuous complete flax demonstration festival in the world. Annually, the second full weekend in September. Est attendance: 15,000. For info: Frank Newell, Flax Scutching Festival, 3932 Route 130, Stahlstown, PA 15687. Phone: (724) 593-2119 or (724) 238-9244.

GARDENFEST AT LONGWOOD GARDENS. Sept 9–Oct 3. Kennett Square, PA. Longwood celebrates September beauty and bounty with harvest displays, flower shows, gardening demonstrations, family entertainment, and a miniature garden railway. Est attendance: 50,000. For info: Longwood Gardens, PO Box 501, Kennett Square, PA 19348-0501. Phone: (610) 388-1000. Web: www.longwoodgardens.org.

HANG AROUND VICTOR DAY. Sept 9. Victor, NY. 30th annual festival with artists, craftsmen, antique dealers, civic and social organizations, family entertainment, pet parade and pet contest, cloggers, magicians, clowns and food vendors. Annually, the first Saturday after Labor Day. Est attendance: 25,000. For info: Susan Stehling, Victor Chamber of Commerce, PO Box 86, Victor, NY 14564. Phone: (585) 742-1476. Fax: (585) 924-0523.

HERITAGE DAY FESTIVAL. Sept 9 (rain date Sept 10). Lavallette, NJ. Clowns, antique cars, four live bands, games, food, children's games, train rides and finale with Ocean County String Band performing. 10 AM–dusk. Annually, the first Saturday after Labor Day. Est attendance: 30,000. For info: Joy Grosko, Dir, Heritage Committee Inc, 13 Camden Ave, Lavallette, NJ 08735. Phone: (732) 793-3652 or (908) 793-3652. Fax: (732) 854-9038. E-mail: tpgrosko00@aol.com.

HILLTOP FESTIVAL. Sept 9–10. Huntington Museum of Art, Huntington, WV. Book fair, arts and crafts and demonstrations, children's activities and food booths. HMA is fully accessible. Annually, first weekend after Labor Day. Est attendance: 3,000. For info: Huntington Museum of Art, 2033 McCoy Rd, Huntington, WV 25701. Phone: (304) 529-2701. Fax: (304) 529-7447. Web: www.hmoa.org.

JAPAN: CHRYSANTHEMUM DAY. Sept 9. Traditional chrysanthemum festival.

KOREA, DEMOCRATIC PEOPLE'S REPUBLIC OF: NATIONAL DAY. Sept 9. National holiday in the Democratic People's Republic of [North] Korea.

LITTLE FALLS ARTS AND CRAFTS FAIR. Sept 9–10. Little Falls, MN. 820 artists, craftspeople and hobbyists displaying and selling their items. Est attendance: 100,000. For info: Chamber of Commerce, 200 NW First St, Little Falls, MN 56345. Phone: (320) 632-5155. Fax: (320) 632-2122. E-mail: artsand crafts@littlefallsmnchamber.com. Web: www.littlefallsmnchamber .com.

LOUISIANA FOLKLIFE FESTIVAL. Sept 9–10. Monroe, LA. A festival of Louisiana's culture, heritage and music, featuring five entertainment stages, craft demonstrations and food. For info: Mike Luster. Phone: (318) 324-1665. Web: www.louisianafolklife fest.org.

LUXEMBOURG: LIBERATION CEREMONY: ANNIVERSARY. Sept 9. Petange. Commemoration of liberation of Grand-Duchy by the Allied forces in 1944. Ceremony at monument of the American soldier.

MAO TSE-TUNG: 30th DEATH ANNIVERSARY. Sept 9, 1976. People's Republic of China pays tribute to memory of the Chinese revolutionary leader, who died at Beijing. Memorial Hall, where his flag-draped body lies encased in crystal, was opened at Tiananmen Square at Beijing on the first anniversary of his death. Mao was born Dec 26, 1893, at Hunan Province, China.

MUSHROOM FESTIVAL. Sept 9–10. Downtown Kennett Square, PA. Weekend of fun, food and fungi at the mushroom capital of the world! Help taste and judge the soup cook-off, attend cooking or growing demos. Also mushroom judging, art show, car show, WineFest, Street Festival with entertainment and mushroom farm tours. Est attendance: 80,000. For info: The Mushroom Festival, PO Box 1000, Kennett Square, PA 19348. Phone: (888) 440-9920. E-mail: info@mushroomfestival.org. Web: www.mushroomfestival.org.

NANTICOKE INDIAN POWWOW. Sept 9–10. Millsboro, DE. Annual gathering of Native Americans during which Native American dances, music and storytelling are presented and Native American foods and arts and crafts are sold. 40 different tribes participate. Dance sessions: Saturday, noon–5 PM, Sunday, 2–5 PM. Sunday worship service, 10:30 AM–noon. Annually, the weekend after Labor Day. Est attendance: 40,000. For info: Nanticoke Indian Assn, 27073 John J. William Hwy, Millsboro, DE 19966. Phone: (302) 945-3400. E-mail: nanticok@bellatlantic.net.

PENDLETON ROUND-UP. Sept 9–16. Pendleton, OR. America's classic rodeo. A 95-year-old Western tradition, with participating Indian tribes from the Pacific Northwest. Plus historical Happy Canyon, an outdoor pageant each evening. Kickoff parade and concert plus professional bull riding events early in the week. Est attendance: 48,000. For info: Pendleton Round-Up Assn, Box 609, Pendleton, OR 97801. Phone: (800) 457-6336. Web: www.pendletonroundup.com.

POTATO DAY FESTIVAL. Sept 9. Centennial Village Museum, Greeley, CO. Living history demonstrations, musical entertainment, square dancing, children's activities spread over five-acre site. Free baked potato and trimmings. Ages 12 and over $5. Children free. Est attendance: 2,200. For info: Greeley Museums, 714 8th St, Greeley, CO 80631. Phone: (970) 350-9220. Fax: (970) 350-9700. Web: www.greeleymuseums.com.

PRAIRIE DAY. Sept 9. Diamond, MO. A celebration of life on the Missouri prairie. Prairie walks, wagon rides, basket weaving, candle-making, dutch oven cooking and numerous other activities. For info: George Washington Carver National Monument, 5646 Carver Rd, Diamond, MO 64840. Phone: (417) 325-4151. Fax: (417) 325-4231. E-mail: superintendent@nps.gov. Web: www.nps.gov/gwca.

QUADRANGLE FESTIVAL. Sept 9–10. Downtown Texarkana, TX and AR. 25th annual festival features 5k BiState Race on the Texas-Arkansas state line. Also, three stages of entertainment, more than 150 artists and craftsmen, antique autos, pet shows; country/rock, traditional and contemporary music; street dancing and food vendors. Est attendance: 35,000. For info: Dir of Mktg, Texarkana Museums System, PO Box 2343, Texarkana, TX 75504. Phone: (903) 793-4831. Fax: (903) 793-7108. Web: www.texarkanamuseums.com.

SANDERS, COLONEL HARLAND DAVID: BIRTH ANNIVERSARY. Sept 9, 1890. Founder of Kentucky Fried Chicken, born near Henryville, IN. Died Dec 16, 1980, at Shelbyville, KY.

SCOTT COUNTY COURTFEST. Sept 9. Downtown Courthouse, Scottsburg, IN. 26th annual. A fundraising activity where the biggest men in the area compete for the title and crown of ugliest "woman." Money raised goes to the winner's favorite charity. "Ugly Women" compete in various categories, including costume and stage presence, trivia and fundraising success. Also arts & crafts and a free concert featuring a national entertainer. Always the first weekend after Labor Day. For info: Executive Director, Scott County Visitors Commission, 5809 W Oak Hill Road, Scottsburg, IN 47170. Phone: (812) 752-9211. Fax: (812) 752-0151. E-mail: kstonebob@aol.com. Web: www.greatscottindiana.org.

SODBUSTER DAYS—THE HARVEST. Sept 9–10. Sunne Farm, Fort Ransom State Park, Fort Ransom, ND. Demonstrations of life on a small family farm of the 1920s during the fall harvest. Activities include threshing, fall field work, gathering prairie hay, ladies' demonstrations, kids games, food, music. Most farm machinery is horse drawn. Annually, the weekend after Labor Day. Located along the Sheyenne River Valley National Scenic Byway. Est attendance: 2,000. For info: Fort Ransom State Park, 5981 Walt Hjelle Pkwy, Fort Ransom, ND 58033-9712. Phone: (701) 973-4331. Fax: (701) 973-4151.

SOUTHEAST MISSOURI DISTRICT FAIR. Sept 9–16. Arena Park Fairgrounds, Cape Girardeau, MO. Oldest outdoor fair in the state. Celebrating its 151st year with beauty pageants, livestock exhibition, horse show, entertainment, carnival, food and 4-H and FFA displays. Annually, starts the Saturday after Labor Day and continues to the next Saturday. Est attendance: 100,000. For info: SEMO District Fair Assn, PO Box 234, Cape Girardeau, MO 63702-0234. Phone: (800) 455-FAIR or (573) 334-9250. E-mail: info@semofairs.com. Web: www.semofair.com.

TAJIKISTAN: INDEPENDENCE DAY. Sept 9. National holiday commemorating independence from the Soviet Union in 1991.

TASTE OF THE BLUE RIDGE BLUES & JAZZ FESTIVAL. Sept 9–10. Roanoke, VA. Sponsors: The Roanoke Special Events Committee. Est attendance: 10,000. For info: Taste of the Blue Ridge Blues and Jazz Festival, PO Box 8276, Roanoke, VA 24014. Phone: (540) 342-2640. E-mail: info@roanokefestival.org. Web: www.tobr.org.

TOLSTOY, LEO: BIRTH ANNIVERSARY. Sept 9, 1828. Russian novelist and moral philosopher, born at Tula Province, Russia. Best known for his novels (*War and Peace, Anna Karenina*), Tolstoy also wrote short stories, plays and essays. A member of the nobility, in his moral and religious writings he condemned private property and championed nonviolent protest. Died Nov 20, 1910, at Astapovo, Russia.

US MID-AMATEUR (GOLF) CHAMPIONSHIP. Sept 9–14. Forest Highlands Golf Club, Flagstaff, AZ. For info: US Golf Assn, Golf House, PO Box 708, Championship Dept, Far Hills, NJ 07931. Phone: (908) 234-2300. Fax: (908) 234-9687. Web: www.usga.org.

September *2006*	S	M	T	W	T	F	S
						1	2
	3	4	5	6	7	8	9
	10	11	12	13	14	15	16
	17	18	19	20	21	22	23
	24	25	26	27	28	29	30

VALPARAISO POPCORN FESTIVAL. Sept 9. Valparaiso, IN. Celebration of popcorn with a parade, the Popcorn Panic and Little Kernel Puff running races, arts, crafts, food booths, music and entertainment, kiddie carnival and a hot-air balloon show. Annually, the first Saturday after Labor Day. Est attendance: 65,000. For info: Glennas Kueck, Exec Dir, 162 W Lincolnway, Valparaiso, IN 46383. Phone: (219) 464-8332. Fax: (219) 464-2343. E-mail: popcorn@netnitco.net. Web: www.popcornfest.org.

"WELCOME BACK, KOTTER" TV PREMIERE: ANNIVERSARY. Sept 9, 1975. In this half-hour sitcom, Gabe Kotter (Gabe Kaplan) returned to James Buchanan High School, his alma mater, to teach the "sweathogs," a group of hopeless underachievers. Other cast members included Marcia Strassman, John Travolta, Robert Hegyes, Ron Palillo, Lawrence Hilton-Jacobs and John Sylvester White. The theme song, "Welcome Back," was sung by John Sebastian. The last telecast was Aug 10, 1979.

WHIPPOORWILL MORGAN HORSE VERSATILITY EVENT. Sept 9. Old Lyme, CT. Morgan horses in performance. Carriage, dressage, reining, bareback riders—a day of free fun for the whole family. Est attendance: 700. For info: McCulloch Farm, Whippoorwill Morgan, 100 Whippoorwill Rd, Old Lyme, CT 06371. Phone: (860) 434-7355.

WILLIAM, THE CONQUEROR: DEATH ANNIVERSARY. Sept 9, 1087. William I, The Conqueror, King of England and Duke of Normandy, whose image is portrayed in the Bayeux Tapestry, was born about 1028 at Falaise, Normandy. Victorious over Harold at the Battle of Hastings (the Norman Conquest) in 1066, William was crowned King of England at Westminster Abbey on Christmas Day of that year. Later, while waging war in France, William met his death at Rouen, Sept 9, 1087.

WILLOW TREE FESTIVAL. Sept 9–10. Gordon, NE. This festival is a cornucopia of arts and crafts, three quality performing stages including a children's stage, children's activities, fun and food. Annually, the second weekend in September. Est attendance: 4,600. For info: Willow Tree Festival, PO Box 303, Gordon, NE 69343-0303. Phone: (308) 282-2464. E-mail: barth@gpcom.net.

WONDERFUL WEIRDOS DAY. Sept 9. All of us are blessed with one or two wonderful weirdos in our lives. These are the folks who remind us to think outside the box, to be a little more true to ourselves. Today's the day to thank them. So give them a hug, and say "I love you, you weirdo!" [©2003 by WH.] For info: Thomas & Ruth Roy, Wellcat Holidays, 2418 Long Lane, Lebanon, PA 17046. Phone: (717) 279-0184. E-mail: info@wellcat.com. Web: www.wellcat.com.

WOODLAND INDIAN DISCOVERY DAY. Sept 9. St. Mary's City, MD. Explore the lifeways of the Yaocomaco Indian people at the Woodland Indian Hamlet. Hands-on demonstrations, storytelling and more. Est attendance: 800. For info: Visitors Services, Historic St. Mary's City, PO Box 39, St. Mary's City, MD 20686. Phone: (240) 895-4990 or (800) SMC-1634. Fax: (240) 895-4968. Web: www.stmaryscity.org.

WYANDOTTE HERITAGE DAYS. Sept 9–10. Bishop Park Area, Wyandotte, MI. Outdoor craft show, living history encampments, Teddy Bear picnic, costume show, Historic Home and Church Tours and Colonial dinners. Est attendance: 10,000. For info: Museum Director, 2610 Biddle Ave, Wyandotte, MI 48192. Phone: (734) 324-7297. Fax: (734) 324-7283.

Benjamin Roy (BJ) Armstrong, 39, former basketball player, born Detroit, MI, Sept 9, 1967.
Shane Battier, 28, basketball player, born Birmingham, MI, Sept 9, 1978.
Angela Cartwright, 54, actress ("Lost in Space," *The Sound of Music*), born Cheshire, England, Sept 9, 1952.
Hugh Grant, 46, actor (*Notting Hill, About a Boy, Four Weddings and a Funeral*), born London, England, Sept 9, 1960.
Mike Hampton, 34, baseball player, born Brooksville, FL, Sept 9, 1972.
Rachel Hunter, 37, model, born New Zealand, Sept 9, 1969.
Kazuhiro Ishii, 33, baseball player, born Chiba, Japan, Sept 9, 1973.
Michael Keaton, 55, actor (*Batman, Beetlejuice, My Life*), born Michael Douglas at Pittsburgh, PA, Sept 9, 1951.
Daniel Lewis (Dan) Majerle, 41, basketball player, born Traverse City, MI, Sept 9, 1965.
Sylvia Miles, 72, actress (*Midnight Cowboy; Farewell, My Lovely*), born New York, NY, Sept 9, 1934.
Billy Preston, 60, musician, songwriter, singer ("Nothing from Nothing"), born Houston, TX, Sept 9, 1946.
Cliff Robertson, 81, actor ("Falcon Crest," *Brainstorm, Charly, PT-109*), born La Jolla, CA, Sept 9, 1925.
Adam Sandler, 40, actor, comedian ("Saturday Night Live," *The Wedding Singer*), born Brooklyn, NY, Sept 9, 1966.
Joseph Robert (Joe) Theisman, 57, sportscaster, Hall of Fame football player, born New Brunswick, NJ, Sept 9, 1949.
Goran Visnjic, 34, actor ("ER," *The Deep End*), born Sibenik, Croatia, Sept 9, 1972.
Michelle Williams, 26, actress ("Dawson's Creek," *Dick*), born Kalispell, MT, Sept 9, 1980.
Tom Wopat, 55, actor ("The Dukes of Hazzard," "Cybill," *Annie Get Your Gun*), born Lodi, WI, Sept 9, 1951.

SEPTEMBER 10 — SUNDAY
Day 253 — 112 Remaining

BELGIUM: HISTORICAL PROCESSION. Sept 10. Tournai. Traditional cultural observance. Annually, the Sunday closest to Sept 8.

BELIZE: SAINT GEORGE'S CAYE DAY. Sept 10. Public holiday celebrated in honor of the battle between the European Baymen Settlers and the Spaniards for the territory of Belize.

BRAXTON, CARTER: BIRTH ANNIVERSARY. Sept 10, 1736. American revolutionary statesman and signer of the Declaration of Independence. Born at Newington, VA, he died Oct 10, 1797, at Richmond, VA.

CATONSVILLE ARTS & CRAFTS FESTIVAL. Sept 10. Catonsville, MD. Fall festival featuring handmade items by 200 artisans and crafters in the revitalized village of Catonsville. Continuous music, children's entertainment and local food vendors. Annually, the Sunday after Labor Day. Est attendance: 30,000. For info: Greater Catonsville Chamber of Commerce, PO Box 21100, Catonsville, MD 21228. Phone: (410) 719-9609.

FESTIVAL-IN-THE-PARK. Sept 10 (rain date Sept 24). Memorial Park, Nutley, NJ. 33rd annual festival, a craft and collectibles show to benefit the Nutley Historical Society and the Historic Restoration Trust. Annually, the first Sunday after Labor Day. Est attendance: 16,000. For info: Douglas J. Eisenfelder, Festival-in-the-Park, 51 Enclosure, Nutley, NJ 07110. Phone: (973) 667-3013.

"GENTLE BEN" TV PREMIERE: ANNIVERSARY. Sept 10, 1967. This show was about the adventures of a boy, Mark Wedloe (Clint Howard) and his pet bear, Ben. Also featured were Dennis Weaver as his father Tom, a game warden, Beth Brickell as his mother Ellen, Jack Worley as Tom's friend Spencer and Angelo Rutherford as his friend Willie. It was filmed on location in Florida.

GOULD, STEPHEN JAY: BIRTH ANNIVERSARY. Sept 10, 1941. Evolutionary biologist and influential writer for academic and lay audiences. With colleague Niles Eldredge, he proposed the theory of punctuated equilibrium to explain sudden changes (and lack of) in fossil records. He died in his birthplace city, New York, NY, on May 20, 2002.

"GUNSMOKE" TV PREMIERE: ANNIVERSARY. Sept 10, 1955. "Gunsmoke" was TV's longest-running Western, moving from radio to TV. John Wayne turned down the role of Marshall Matt Dillon but recommended James Arness, who got the role. Other regulars included Amanda Blake as Kitty Russell, saloon-owner; Dennis Weaver as Chester B. Goode, Dillon's deputy; and Milburn Stone as Doc Adams. In 1962 a fifth character was added—the "rugged male." Burt Reynolds played Quint Asper, followed by Roger Ewing as Thad Greenwood, and Buck Taylor as Newly O'Brien. In 1964 Ken Curtis was added as funnyman Festus Haggen, the new deputy. "Gunsmoke" was the number-one rated series for four seasons, and a top ten hit for six seasons. The last telecast was Sept 1, 1975.

HABITAT FOR HUMANITY INTERNATIONAL'S BUILDING ON FAITH WEEK. Sept 10–17. An opportunity to celebrate Habitat for Humanity's partnerships with churches and other faith groups around the world building houses as a global witness to faith in action. Uniting people of diverse faiths in the common cause of eliminating poverty housing and rebuilding communities, Habitat for Humanity affiliates around the country are reaching out to families in need by holding multifaith builds. For info: Habitat for Humanity Intl, 121 Habitat St, Americus, GA 31709-3498. Phone: (800) HAB-ITAT or (229) 924-6935. E-mail: publicinfo@hfhi.org. Web: www.habitat.org.

HOMESTEADER HARVEST FESTIVAL. Sept 10. Beaver Creek Nature Area, Brandon, SD. This is a re-creation of the harvest and celebration that went with it back in the pioneer days. Annually, the Sunday after Labor Day. Est attendance: 1,200. For info: Palisades State Park, 25495 485th Ave, Garretson, SD 57030-6117. Phone: (605) 594-3824.

ITALY: GIOSTRA DELLA QUINTANA. Sept 10. Foligno. A revival of a 17th-century joust of the Quintana, featuring 600 knights in full costume. Annually, the second Sunday in September.

KURALT, CHARLES: BIRTH ANNIVERSARY. Sept 10, 1934. TV journalist ("On the Road with Charles Kuralt") born at Wilmington, NC. Died at New York, NY, July 4, 1997.

LISCO OLD-TIMERS DAY. Sept 10. Lisco, NE. Local talent puts on program and skits about an honored old-timer or couple. Parade, barbecue (free-will offering), horseshoe tournament, antique tractor pull and more. Annually, Sunday after Labor Day. Sponsor: Lisco Old-Timers Day Committee. Est attendance: 2,000. For info: Lisco State Bank, Lisco Old-Timers Day Committee, Lisco, NE 69148.

MARIS, ROGER: BIRTH ANNIVERSARY. Sept 10, 1934. Roger Eugene Maris, baseball player born Roger Eugene Maras at Hibbing, MN. In 1961 Maris surpassed the mark set by Babe Ruth in 1927, hitting 61 home runs, a record which wasn't broken until 1998. He won the American League MVP award in 1960 and 1961 and finished his career with the St. Louis Cardinals. Died at Houston, TX, Dec 14, 1985.

★**MINORITY ENTERPRISE DEVELOPMENT WEEK.** Sept 10–16 (tentative). Presidential Proclamation issued without request since 1983.

NATIONAL ASSISTED LIVING WEEK. Sept 10–16. A weeklong observance designed to raise awareness of the role assisted living plays in serving the nation's elderly. Annually, Grandparents' Day through the following Saturday. For info: Natl Center for Assisted Living, 1201 L St NW, Washington, DC 20005. Phone: (202) 842-4444. Fax: (202) 842-3860.

NATIONAL GRANDPARENTS' DAY. Sept 10. To honor grandparents, to give grandparents an opportunity to show love for their children's children and to help children become aware of the strength, information and guidance older people can offer. Annually, the first Sunday after Labor Day.

NATIONAL SUICIDE PREVENTION WEEK. Sept 10–16. For info: American Assn of Suicidology, 4201 Connecticut Ave NW, Ste 408, Washington, DC 20009. Phone: (202) 237-2280. Web: www.suicidology.org.

NORTHEAST MISSOURI TRIATHLON. Sept 10. Thousand Hills State Park, Kirksville, MO. Swim 3/4 mile, bike 18 miles, run 5 miles. USA Triathlon sanctioned. Qualifier for International Course Nationals. Annually, the Sunday after Labor Day. Est attendance: 350. For info: ATSU-TCC, 210 S Osteopathy, Kirksville, MO 63501. Phone: (660) 626-2213. Fax: (660) 626-2071. E-mail: lcrossgrove@atsu.edu. Web: www.nemotriathlon.org.

OCEAN COUNTY BLUEGRASS FESTIVAL. Sept 10. Waretown, NJ. A family-oriented bluegrass festival where no alcoholic beverages or smoking is allowed. Est attendance: 400. For info: Albert Music Hall, PO Box 657, Waretown, NJ 08758. Phone: (609) 971-1593. Web: www.alberthall.org.

SCHIAPARELLI, ELSA: BIRTH ANNIVERSARY. Sept 10, 1890. Born in Rome, Italy, Elsa Schiaparelli was one of the world's leading fashion designers from the late 1920s through the 1950s. Based in Paris, France, Schiaparelli created striking, often surrealistic designs in collaboration with such artists as Salvador Dali and Jean Cocteau. She introduced the shoulder pad to women's fashion, named "shocking pink" (hot pink) and worked with man-made materials. A white evening dress bedecked with a lobster and a hat that appeared to be a giant shoe were some of her avant-garde looks. "If you define fashion as time moving . . ." she wrote, "then you are not fully alive unless you are moving with it." Schiaparelli died at Paris on Nov 13, 1973.

SEW BE IT! DAY. Sept 10. Celebrating the anniversary of the patent on the sewing machine on Sept 10, 1846. Recognizing that when a hem loosens or a button pops off, Sew Be It! [©1995]. Because of the escalating costs of Eventological® Literature, a charge of $10 must be assessed for each request. Checks are to be made payable to: Adrienne Sioux Koopersmith, 1437 W Rosemont, #1W, Chicago, IL 60660-1319. E-mail: askoopersmith@hotmail.com.

SWAP IDEAS DAY. Sept 10. To encourage people to explore ways in which their ideas can be put to work for the benefit of humanity, and to encourage development of incentives that will encourage use of creative imagination. For info: Robert L. Birch, Puns Corps, 3108 Dashiell Rd, Falls Church, VA 22042. Phone: (703) 533-3668.

UNITED KINGDOM: BATTLE OF BRITAIN WEEK. Sept 10–16. Annually, the week of September containing Battle of Britain Day (Sept 15).

		S	M	T	W	T	F	S
September							1	2
2006		3	4	5	6	7	8	9
		10	11	12	13	14	15	16
		17	18	19	20	21	22	23
		24	25	26	27	28	29	30

WERFEL, FRANZ: BIRTH ANNIVERSARY. Sept 10, 1890. Austrian author (*The Song of Bernadette, The Forty Days of Musa Dagh*), born at Prague, Czechoslovakia. Died at Hollywood, CA, Aug 26, 1945.

"THE X-FILES" TV PREMIERE: ANNIVERSARY. Sept 10, 1993. "The Truth Is Out There" was the mantra of FOX's scary and brainy sci-fi drama. Special FBI agents Fox Mulder (David Duchovny) and Dana Scully (Gillian Anderson) solved the cases too weird for the Bureau and also uncovered a vast conspiracy involving aliens and human-alien hybrids. *TV Guide* named "The X-Files" one of the greatest TV shows of all time. A feature-length film was created as well. The series ended in 2002.

BIRTHDAYS TODAY

José Feliciano, 61, singer, musician ("Light My Fire," "Hi-Heel Sneakers"), born Lares, Puerto Rico, Sept 10, 1945.

Colin Firth, 46, actor (*Shakespeare in Love, Valmont*, "Pride and Prejudice"), born Grayshott, Hampshire, England, Sept 10, 1960.

Judy Geeson, 58, actress (*To Sir with Love, The Eagle Has Landed*), born Arundel, Sussex, England, Sept 10, 1948.

Matt Geiger, 37, former basketball player, born Salem, MA, Sept 10, 1969.

Amy Irving, 53, actress (*Carrie, Crossing Delancey*, "Alias"), born Palo Alto, CA, Sept 10, 1953.

Clark Johnson, 42, actor ("Homicide"), born Philadelphia, PA, Sept 10, 1964.

Randy Johnson, 43, baseball player, born Walnut Creek, CA, Sept 10, 1963.

Karl Lagerfeld, 68, fashion designer, born Hamburg, Germany, Sept 10, 1938.

Joe Nieuwendyk, 40, hockey player, born Oshawa, ON, Canada, Sept 10, 1966.

Arnold Palmer, 77, golfer, born Latrobe, PA, Sept 10, 1929.

Yma Sumac, 78, singer, born Ichocan, Peru, Sept 10, 1928.

John Sununu, 42, US Senator (R, New Hampshire), born Boston, MA, Sept 10, 1964.

Robert Wise, 92, filmmaker (*The Curse of the Cat People, The Sound of Music*), born Winchester, IN, Sept 10, 1914.

SEPTEMBER 11 — MONDAY

Day 254 — 111 Remaining

ATTACK ON AMERICA: 5th ANNIVERSARY. Sept 11, 2001. Terrorists hijacked four planes, piloting two of them into the World Trade Center's twin towers in New York City and one into the Pentagon in Washington, DC. Passengers on the fourth plane appear to have attempted to overcome the hijackers, causing the plane to crash in western Pennsylvania instead of reaching its target in Washington. The twin towers at the WTC collapsed about an hour after being hit. More than 3,000 people died as a result of the attacks. The hijackers were agents of the Al Qaeda terrorist group led by Islamic extremist Osama bin Laden, who was headquartered in Afghanistan. In response, the US began unprecedented internal security measures and launched a war on terrorism with the support of many nations. See also: "The Fall of Kabul: Anniversary" (Nov 13) and "World Trade Center Recovery and Cleanup Ends: Anniversary" (May 30).

BATTLE OF BRANDYWINE: ANNIVERSARY. Sept 11, 1777. The largest engagement of the American Revolution, between the Continental Army led by General George Washington and British troops led by General William Howe. General Howe was marching to take Philadelphia when Washington chose to try and stop the British advance at the Brandywine River near Chadds Ford, PA. The American forces were defeated and the British went on to take Philadelphia Sept 26. They spent the winter in the city while Washington's troops suffered at their encampment at Valley Forge, PA.

"THE CAROL BURNETT SHOW" TV PREMIERE: ANNIVERSARY. Sept 11, 1967. This popular comedy/variety show starred comedienne Carol Burnett, who started the show by taking questions from the audience and ended with an ear

tug. Sketches and spoofs included recurring characters like "The Family" (later to be spun off as "Mama's Family") and "As the Stomach Turns." Regular cast members included Harvey Korman, Lyle Waggoner and Vicki Lawrence. Later, Tim Conway joined the cast. Dick Van Dyke briefly joined after Korman left in 1977.

ETHIOPIA: NEW YEAR'S DAY. Sept 11. In the year 2006, this day will start the year 2000 on the Ethiopian calendar. On the Coptic Orthodox calendar, it begins the year 1723.

FOOD STAMPS AUTHORIZED: ANNIVERSARY. Sept 11, 1959. Congress passed a bill authorizing food stamps for low-income Americans.

LAWRENCE, DAVID HERBERT: BIRTH ANNIVERSARY. Sept 11, 1885. English novelist, author of *Lady Chatterley's Lover*. Born at Eastwood, Nottinghamshire, England, D.H. Lawrence died Mar 2, 1930, at Vence, France.

LIBRARIES REMEMBER. Sept 11. Libraries represent the sum of all human knowledge. They also represent equal access to that knowledge as well as freedom of expression, celebration of diversity, preservation of heritage and commitment to the future. Libraries represent everything that is antithetical to the fanaticism responsible for the terrorist events of Sept 11, 2001. Libraries Remember encourages libraries across the United States to remain open for the entire 24 hours of Sept 11 as remarkable symbols of freedom, tolerance and hope. For info: Bill Erbes, Bensenville Community Public Library, 200 S Church Rd, Bensenville, IL 60106. Phone: (630) 766-4642. Fax: (630) 595-9171. E-mail: billerbes@aol.com. Web: www.bensenville.lib.il.us.

LIND, JENNY: US PREMIERE: ANNIVERSARY. Sept 11, 1850. Jenny Lind, the "Swedish Nightingale," gave her first American performance in the Castle Garden Theatre, New York, NY, on this day.

"LITTLE HOUSE ON THE PRAIRIE" TV PREMIERE: ANNIVERSARY. Sept 11, 1974. This hour-long family drama was based on books by Laura Ingalls Wilder. It focused on the Ingalls family and their neighbors living at Walnut Grove, MN: Michael Landon as Charles (Pa), Karen Grassle as Caroline (Ma), Melissa Sue Anderson as daughter Mary, Melissa Gilbert as daughter Laura, from whose point of view the stories were told, Lindsay and Sidney Greenbush as daughter Carrie and Wendi and Brenda Turnbaugh as daughter Grace. In its last season (1982), the show's name was changed to "Little House: A New Beginning." Landon appeared less often and the show centered around Laura and her husband.

MARCOS, FERDINAND EDRALIN: BIRTH ANNIVERSARY. Sept 11, 1917. Former ruler of the Philippines, born at Sarrat, Philippines. Ferdinand Marcos served as head of state from 1966 until his ouster in 1986. His authoritarian regime was marred by widespread corruption and suppression of democratic processes. After the assassination of Benigno Aquino, Jr, in 1983, anti-government protests increased and Marcos called for an election in 1986, hoping to reassert his mandate. Although he defeated Corazon Aquino in the election, it was widely asserted he did so through massive vote fraud, leading to a decline in support, and Corazon Aquino became the new president of the Philippines. Marcos died in exile Sept 28, 1989, at Honolulu, HI.

NATIONAL BOSS/EMPLOYEE EXCHANGE DAY. Sept 11. To help bosses and employees appreciate each other by sharing each other's point of view for a day. Annually, the first Monday after Labor Day. For info: A.C. Vierow, Box 71, Clio, MI 48420-0071.

NATIONAL INVISIBLE CHRONIC ILLNESS AWARENESS WEEK. Sept 11–17. San Diego, CA. Activities include online events and outreach to communities and churches, encouraging them to participate in calling attention to reaching out to those with chronic illness. For info: Lisa Copen, PO Box 502928, San Diego, CA 92150. Phone: (888) 751-7378. Fax: (800) 933-1078. E-mail: rest@restministries.org. Web: www.invisible illness.com.

NATIONAL NO BULLY WEEK. Sept 11–15. A week in which no one is bullied in school, at work or in society! For info: Andy Tomko, 2142 Englewood SE, Grand Rapids, MI 49506. Phone: (616) 855-2571. E-mail: andy@youbigbully.com. Web: www.youbig bully.com.

O. HENRY (WILLIAM S. PORTER): BIRTH ANNIVERSARY. Sept 11, 1862. William Sydney Porter, American author, who wrote under the pen name O. Henry. Best known for his short stories, including "Gift of the Magi." Born at Greensboro, NC, he died at New York, NY, June 5, 1910.

PAKISTAN: FOUNDER'S DEATH ANNIVERSARY. Sept 11. Pakistan observes the death anniversary in 1948 of Qaid-e-Azam Mohammed Ali Jinnah (founder of Pakistan) as a national holiday. His birth date of Dec 25 is also a national holiday.

PATRIOT DAY. Sept 11. On Dec 18, 2001, a joint resolution of Congress amended Title 36, Chapter 1, Sec. 144 of the US Code to permit the president to declare Sept 11 of each year as Patriot Day, in commemoration of the terrorist attacks on the United States on Sept 11, 2001. The resolution requests that all state and local governments observe this day "with appropriate programs and activities," that the flag be displayed at half-staff from sunrise till sundown, and that a moment of silence be observed in honor of those who lost their lives in the attacks.

PEDDLER'S VILLAGE SCARECROW CONTEST AND OUTDOOR DISPLAY. Sept 11–Oct 29. Peddler's Village, Lahaska, PA. Contestants compete for $5,600 in cash prizes. Categories include: "A Scarecrow Whirligig"—a scarecrow that makes noise and moves with the wind; "An Extraordinary Contemporary Scarecrow"—an imaginative piece created to give a good scare in the garden; "A Traditional Scarecrow"—an outstanding example of the American Scarecrow; and "The Amateur Scarecrow"—for those who haven't won previously. Free admission. Est attendance: 650,000. For info: Peddler's Village, Routes 202 and 263, Lahaska, PA 18931. Phone: (215) 794-4000. Fax: (215) 794-4001. Web: www.peddlersvillage.com.

PENNSYLVANIA RV & CAMPING SHOW. Sept 11–17. Hersheypark® Entertainment Complex, Hershey, PA. 38th annual. America's largest RV show, with more than 1,200 RVs on display. The equivalent of 26 football fields of RVs! Est attendance: 40,000. For info: PRVCA, 4000 Trindle Rd, Camp Hill, PA 17011. Phone: (888) 303-2887. Fax: (717) 303-0297. E-mail: rvcamping@prvca.org. Web: www.LargestRVShow.com.

1786 ANNAPOLIS CONVENTION: ANNIVERSARY. Sept 11–14, 1786. Twelve delegates from New York, New Jersey, Delaware, Pennsylvania and Virginia met at Annapolis, MD, to discuss commercial matters of mutual interest. The delegates voted, on Sept 14, to adopt a resolution prepared by Alexander Hamilton asking all states to send representatives to a convention at Philadelphia, PA, in May 1787 "to render the constitution of the Federal Government adequate to the exigencies of the Union."

SPACE MILESTONE: *MARS GLOBAL SURVEYOR* (US). Sept 11, 1997. Launched Nov 7, 1996, this unmanned vehicle was put into orbit around Mars. It was designed to compile global maps of Mars by taking high-resolution photos. This mission inaugurated a new series of Mars expeditions in which NASA launched pairs of orbiters and landers to Mars. *Mars Global Surveyor* was paired with the lander *Mars Pathfinder*. See also: "Space Milestone: *Mars Pathfinder*" (July 4).

TYLER'S CABINET RESIGNS: ANNIVERSARY. Sept 11, 1841. In protest of President John Tyler's veto of the Banking Bill all of his cabinet except Secretary of State Daniel Webster resigned on this day.

BIRTHDAYS TODAY

Daniel K. Akaka, 82, US Senator (D, Hawaii), born Honolulu, HI, Sept 11, 1924.

Harry Connick, Jr, 39, singer (Grammy for *We Are in Love*), actor (*When Harry Met Sally. . .*), born New Orleans, LA, Sept 11, 1967.

Brian De Palma, 66, filmmaker (*The Untouchables, Bonfire of the Vanities, Carrie*), born Newark, NJ, Sept 11, 1940.

Lola Falana, 63, actress ("The New Bill Cosby Show," "Ben Vereen—Comin' at Ya"), born Camden, NJ, Sept 11, 1943.

Donna Lopiano, 60, women's sports executive and former softball player, born Stamford, CT, Sept 11, 1946.

Amy Madigan, 55, actress (*Places in the Heart, Field of Dreams, Uncle Buck*), born Chicago, IL, Sept 11, 1951.

Virginia Madsen, 43, actress (*Sideways, Dune, The Hot Spot*), born Winnetka, IL, Sept 11, 1963.

Kristy McNichol, 44, actress ("Empty Nest," *Little Darlings, Summer of My German Soldier*, Emmys for "Family"), born Los Angeles, CA, Sept 11, 1962.

Moby, 41, rock singer/songwriter, born Richard Melville Hall at New York, NY, Sept 11, 1965.

SEPTEMBER 12 — TUESDAY
Day 255 — 110 Remaining

BATTLE OF SAINT-MIHIEL: ANNIVERSARY. Sept 12, 1918. Under the command of General John J. Pershing, the 1st US Army attacked the Germans at the Saint-Mihiel salient. This was the first major US offensive of WWI. Sixteen army divisions, coupled with French II Colonial Corps tanks and artillery support, forced back the Germans after 36 hours of heavy fighting and reclaimed 200 square miles of French territory that had been in the hands of the Germans since 1914. The 1st US Army lost about 7,000 soldiers in the Battle of Saint-Mihiel.

CHARLES LEROUX'S LAST JUMP: ANNIVERSARY. Sept 12, 1889. American aeronaut of French extraction, born in New York, NY, about 1857, achieved world fame as a parachutist. After his first public performance (Philadelphia, PA, 1887) he toured European cities, where his parachute jumps attracted wide attention. Credited with 238 successful jumps. On Sept 12, 1889, he jumped from a balloon over Tallinn, Estonia, and perished in the Bay of Reval.

CZECH REPUBLIC: PRAGUE AUTUMN INTERNATIONAL MUSIC FESTIVAL. Sept 12–Oct 1. Symphonic and chamber orchestras, instrumental concerts. For info: Prague Autumn International Music Festival, 130 00 - CZ, Prague 3, Pribenicka 20, Czech Republic. Phone: (42 2) 22 540 484. Fax: (42 2) 22 540 415. E-mail: festival@pragueautumn.cz. Web: pragueautumn.cz.

DEFENDERS DAY. Sept 12. Maryland. Public holiday. Annual reenactment of bombardment of Fort McHenry in 1814 that inspired Francis Scott Key to write the "Star-Spangled Banner."

September 2006

S	M	T	W	T	F	S
					1	2
3	4	5	6	7	8	9
10	11	12	13	14	15	16
17	18	19	20	21	22	23
24	25	26	27	28	29	30

"FRAGGLE ROCK" TV PREMIERE: ANNIVERSARY. Sept 12, 1987. This children's show was a cartoon version of the live Jim Henson puppet production on HBO. It was set in the rock underneath a scientist's house and featured characters such as the Fraggles, the Doozers and the Gorgs.

GUINEA-BISSAU: NATIONAL HOLIDAY. Sept 12. Amilcar Cabral's birthday, Sept 12, is observed as a national holiday.

HUSKER HARVEST DAYS. Sept 12–14. Grand Island, NE. The largest irrigated working agricultural show on a permanent site in the United States. 80 acres of exhibits, 700 acres of field demonstrations and more. Annually, the Tuesday–Thursday of the second full week of September. Est attendance: 50,000. For info: Renee Seifert, Grand Island/Hall County CVB, 2424 S Locust St, Ste C, Grand Island, NE 68801. Phone: (308) 382-4400. Fax: (308) 382-4908. E-mail: info@visitgrandisland .com. Web: www.visitgrandisland.com.

"LASSIE" TV PREMIERE: ANNIVERSARY. Sept 12, 1954. This long-running series was originally about a boy and his courageous and intelligent dog, Lassie (played by more than six different dogs, all male). For the first few seasons, Lassie lived on the Miller farm. The family included Jeff (Tommy Rettig), his widowed mother Ellen (Jan Clayton) and George Cleveland as Gramps. Throughout the years there were many format and cast changes, as Lassie was exchanged from one family to another in order to have a variety of new perils and escapades. Other featured performers included Cloris Leachman, June Lockhart and Larry Wilcox.

"MAUDE" TV PREMIERE: ANNIVERSARY. Sept 12, 1972. Bea Arthur's character, Maude Findlay, was first introduced as Edith Bunker's cousin on "All in the Family." She was a loud, opinionated liberal, living with her fourth husband Walter (Bill Macy). Other characters on the show were her divorced daughter by a previous marriage, Carol Trainer (Adrienne Barbeau), Conrad Bain as Dr. Arthur Harmon, Rue McClanahan as Arthur's wife Vivian, Esther Rolle as Florida Evans, Maude's maid, and John Amos as her husband, Henry. This was one of the first shows to tackle the controversial issue of abortion.

MENCKEN, HENRY LOUIS: BIRTH ANNIVERSARY. Sept 12, 1880. American newspaperman, lexicographer and critic, "the Sage of Baltimore" was born at Baltimore, MD, and died there Jan 29, 1956. "If, after I depart this vale," he wrote in 1921 (Epitaph, *Smart Set*), "you ever remember me and have thought to please my ghost, forgive some sinner and wink your eye at some homely girl."

"THE MONKEES" TV PREMIERE: 40th ANNIVERSARY. Sept 12, 1966. Featuring a rock group that was supposed to be an American version of the Beatles, this half-hour show featured a blend of comedy and music. Four young actors were chosen from more than 400 to play the group members: Micky Dolenz, Davy Jones, Mike Nesmith and Peter Tork. Dolenz and Jones had previous acting experience and Tork and Nesmith had previous musical experience. The music that they performed on the show proved to be immensely popular; at first they sang with a studio band but later insisted on writing and performing their own music. They released several albums and toured several times. In 1986, the Monkees, except for Nesmith, were reunited for a 20th Anniversary tour and the show was broadcast in reruns on MTV. The Monkees sans Nesmith also toured in 1996 for the 30th reunion celebration.

OWENS, JESSE: BIRTH ANNIVERSARY. Sept 12, 1913. James Cleveland (Jesse) Owens, American athlete, winner of four gold medals at the 1936 Olympic Games at Berlin, Germany, was born at Oakville, AL. Owens set 11 world records in track and field. During one track meet, at Ann Arbor, MI, May 23, 1935, Owens, representing Ohio State University, broke three world records and tied a fourth in the space of 45 minutes. Died at Tucson, AZ, Mar 31, 1980.

SPACE MILESTONE: *LUNA 2* (USSR). Sept 12, 1959. First spacecraft to land on moon was launched.

TEXAS-OKLAHOMA FAIR. Sept 12–17. Multi-Purpose Events Center, Wichita Falls, TX. Largest fair in the North Texas area. Exhibits, carnival, food, arts and crafts, animal barn, special entertainment. Est attendance: 80,000. For info: Wichita Falls Conv & Visitors Bureau, 1000 5th St, Wichita Falls, TX 76301. Phone: (940) 716-5500. Fax: (940) 716-5509. Web: www.wichitafalls.org.

VIDEO GAMES DAY. Sept 12. A day for kids who love video games to celebrate the fun they have playing them and to thank their parents for all the cartridges and quarters they have provided to indulge this enthusiasm.

WARNER, CHARLES DUDLEY: BIRTH ANNIVERSARY. Sept 12, 1829. American newspaperman, born at Plainfield, MA, authored many works, but is perhaps best remembered for a single sentence (in an editorial, *Hartford Courant*, Aug 24, 1897): "Everybody talks about the weather, but nobody does anything about it." The quotation is often mistakenly attributed to his friend, Mark Twain. Died at Hartford, CT, Oct 20, 1900.

BIRTHDAYS TODAY

Sam Brownback, 50, US Senator (R, Kansas), born Garnett, KS, Sept 12, 1956.

Irene Dailey, 86, actress ("Another World"), born New York, NY, Sept 12, 1920.

Linda Gray, 65, actress ("Dallas," "Melrose Place"), born Santa Monica, CA, Sept 12, 1941.

Ian Holm, 75, actor (*The Sweet Hereafter*, Academy Award for *Chariots of Fire*), born Goodmayes, England, Sept 12, 1931.

George Jones, 75, singer ("White Lightning," "Race Is On," "He Stopped Loving Her Today"), born Saratoga, TX, Sept 12, 1931.

Benjamin McKenzie, 28, actor ("The O.C."), born Austin, TX, Sept 12, 1978.

Yao Ming, 26, basketball player, born Shanghai, China, Sept 12, 1980.

Maria Muldaur, 63, singer ("Midnight at the Oasis," "I'm a Woman"), born New York, NY, Sept 12, 1943.

Joe Pantoliano, 52, actor (*Risky Business, The Fugitive*; stage: *Orphans*), born Jersey City, NJ, Sept 12, 1954.

Emmy Rossum, 20, actress (*The Day After Tomorrow, The Phantom of the Opera*), born New York, NY, Sept 12, 1986.

Peter Scolari, 52, actor ("Bosom Buddies," "Newhart"), born New Rochelle, NY, Sept 12, 1954.

Rachel Ward, 49, actress ("The Thorn Birds," *Against All Odds*), born London, England, Sept 12, 1957.

Amy Yasbeck, 43, actress (*The Mask*, "Wings"), born Cincinnati, OH, Sept 12, 1963.

SEPTEMBER 13 — WEDNESDAY
Day 256 — 109 Remaining

ANDERSON, SHERWOOD: BIRTH ANNIVERSARY. Sept 13, 1876. American author and newspaper publisher, born at Camden, OH. His best remembered book is *Winesburg, Ohio.* Anderson died at Colon, Panama, Mar 8, 1941.

BARRY, JOHN: DEATH ANNIVERSARY. Sept 13, 1803. Revolutionary War hero John Barry, first American to hold the rank of commodore, died at Philadelphia, PA. He was born at Tacumshane, County Wexford, Ireland, in 1745. He has been called the "Father of the American Navy."

COLBERT, CLAUDETTE: BIRTH ANNIVERSARY. Sept 13, 1903. Actress and comedienne Colbert, born Lily Claudette Chauchoin at Paris, France, was a beloved movie star of the '30s. She was best known for her films *Midnight, Cleopatra* and *It Happened One Night,* for which she won an Oscar in 1934. In addition to more than 60 movies, she appeared in Broadway shows and won a Golden Globe Award for her role in the 1986 miniseries "The Two Mrs Grenvilles." She also received a Life Achievement Award from the Kennedy Center for Performing Arts in 1989. She died July 30, 1996, at Bridgetown, Barbados.

DAHL, ROALD: BIRTH ANNIVERSARY. Sept 13, 1916. Author (*Charlie and the Chocolate Factory, James and the Giant Peach*), born at Llandaff, South Wales, Great Britain. Died Nov 23, 1990, at Oxford, England.

FORTUNE COOKIE DAY. Sept 13. San Francisco, CA. San Francisco—birthplace of the fortune cookie—is the Fortune Cookie Capital of the World. Celebrate good fortune and family fun today! For info: Margaret Speaker Yuan, 17 Mt Darwin Ct, San Rafael, CA 94903. Phone: (415) 492-1074. E-mail: books4women@yahoo.com. Web: www.fortunecookieday.com.

GOLDEN ASPEN MOTORCYCLE RALLY. Sept 13–17. Ruidoso, NM. Trade show, bike shows, riding tours, skill events, parade, awards banquet, stunt shows and thousands in prizes. Est attendance: 35,000. For info: Golden Aspen Rally Assn, PO Box 1467, Ruidoso, NM 88355. Phone: (800) 452-8045. E-mail: motorcyclerally@zianet.com. Web: www.motorcyclerally.com.

KENTUCKY BOURBON FESTIVAL. Sept 13–17. Bardstown, KY. Visit the "Bourbon Capital of the World" and celebrate the history and making of Kentucky's finest product, Kentucky bourbon. Enjoy tours, displays, music, food, competitions and much more. For info: Kentucky Bourbon Festival, One Court Square, Bardstown, KY 40004. Phone: (502) 348-3623. Fax: (502) 349-0804. E-mail: info@kybourbonfestival.com. Web: www.kybourbonfestival.com.

"LAW & ORDER" TV PREMIERE: ANNIVERSARY. Sept 13, 1990. Filmed on location at New York City, "Law & Order" shows the interaction between the police and the district attorney's office in dealing with a crime. Almost the entire cast has changed over the life of this program and has included Michael Moriarty (Assistant District Attorney Benjamin Stone), Sam Waterston (ADA Jack McCoy), Jerry Orbach (Detective Lennie Briscoe), Christopher Noth (Detective Mike Logan), Jesse L. Martin (Detective Edward Green) and many others. "Law & Order" has spun off two other series: "Law & Order: Special Victims Unit" and "Law & Order: Criminal Intent."

MORTON PUMPKIN FESTIVAL. Sept 13–16. Morton, IL. Carnival, parade, entertainment and fantastic food to celebrate the pumpkin in the "Pumpkin Capital of the World." Est attendance: 70,000. For info: Morton Chamber of Commerce, 415 W Jefferson St, Morton, IL 61550. Phone: (888) 765-6588. Fax:

September 2006	S	M	T	W	T	F	S
						1	2
	3	4	5	6	7	8	9
	10	11	12	13	14	15	16
	17	18	19	20	21	22	23
	24	25	26	27	28	29	30

(309) 263-2401. E-mail: chamber@mtco.com. Web: www.pumpkincapital.com.

"THE MUPPET SHOW" TV PREMIERE: 30th ANNIVERSARY. Sept 13, 1976. This comedy-variety show was hosted by Kermit the Frog of "Sesame Street." The new Jim Henson puppet characters included Miss Piggy, Fozzie Bear and The Great Gonzo. Many celebrities appeared as guests on the show, which was broadcast in more than 100 countries. The show ran until 1981. "Muppet Babies" was a Saturday morning cartoon that ran from 1984 until 1992. *The Muppet Movie* (1979) was the first of five films based on "The Muppet Show." In 1996 a new show, "Muppets Tonight!," was created.

NATIONAL CHAMPIONSHIP AIR RACES. Sept 13–17. Reno, NV. Six classes of races—Unlimited, Sport, Jet, Formula One, T-6 and Biplane—compete. The event includes thrilling aerobatics and displays of military, vintage and contemporary aircraft. Est attendance: 223,000. For info: National Championship Air Races, 14501 Mt Anderson St, Reno, NV 89506. Phone: (775) 972-6663. Web: www.airrace.org.

PERSHING, JOHN J.: BIRTH ANNIVERSARY. Sept 13, 1860. US Army general who commanded the American Expeditionary Force (AEF) during World War I, Pershing was born at Laclede, MO. The AEF, as part of the inter-Allied offensive, successfully assaulted the Saint-Mihiel salient in September 1918 and later that month quickly regrouped for the Meuse-Argonne operation that led to the Armistice of Nov 11, 1918. Pershing died July 15, 1948, at Washington, DC.

REED, WALTER: BIRTH ANNIVERSARY. Sept 13, 1851. American army physician (especially known for his Yellow Fever research). Born at Gloucester County, VA, he served as an army surgeon for more than 20 years and as a professor at the Army Medical College. He died at Washington, DC, Nov 22, 1902. The US Army's general hospital at Washington, DC, is named in his honor.

"SCOOBY-DOO, WHERE ARE YOU?" TV PREMIERE: ANNIVERSARY. Sept 13, 1969. A tremendously popular Saturday morning cartoon, Hanna-Barbera's show featured four wacky kids and lovable Great Dane Scooby-Doo solving spooky (and often hilarious) mysteries. Fred, Daphne and Velma usually do the work, while Shaggy (originally voiced by radio personality Casey Kasem) and Scooby-Doo look for something to eat. A live-action feature film was released in 2002 starring Freddie Prinze, Jr, Sarah Michelle Gellar, Matthew Lillard, Linda Cardellini and a digital Scooby.

"SOAP" TV PREMIERE: ANNIVERSARY. Sept 13, 1977. "Soap" was a prime-time comedy that parodied soap operas. It had plots that were funny (e.g., Corinne's baby is possessed by the devil), controversial (e.g., Billy joins a cult) and downright bizarre (e.g., Burt is abducted by aliens). The show focused on two families, the wealthy Tates and the middle-class Campbells. It starred Katherine Helmond, Robert Mandan, Jennifer Salt, Diana Canova, Jimmy Baio, Robert Guillaume, Cathryn Damon, Richard Mulligan, Ted Wass, Billy Crystal, Richard Libertini, Kathryn Reynolds, Robert Urich, Arthur Peterson, Roscoe Lee Browne and Jay Johnson. Rod Roddy was the announcer who recapped what had happened on the previous episode.

"STAR-SPANGLED BANNER" INSPIRED: ANNIVERSARY. Sept 13–14, 1814. On the night of Sept 13, Francis Scott Key was aboard a ship that was delayed in Baltimore harbor by the British attack there on Fort McHenry. Key had no choice but to anxiously watch the battle. That experience and seeing the

American flag still flying over the fort the next morning inspired him to pen the verses that, coupled with the tune of a popular drinking song, became our official national anthem in 1931, 117 years after the words were written.

US CAPITAL ESTABLISHED AT NEW YORK CITY: ANNIVERSARY.
Sept 13, 1788. Congress picked New York, NY, as the location of the new US government in place of Philadelphia, which had served as the capital up until this time. In 1790 the capital moved back to Philadelphia for ten years, before moving permanently to Washington, DC.

BIRTHDAYS TODAY

Fiona Apple, 29, singer, born New York, NY, Sept 13, 1977.

Jacqueline Bisset, 62, actress (*Rich & Famous, The Deep*), born Weybridge, England, Sept 13, 1944.

Peter Cetera, 62, singer (former lead singer of Chicago; solo hit "Glory of Love"), songwriter, born Chicago, IL, Sept 13, 1944.

Robert Indiana, 78, artist (*As I Opened Fire*), born New Castle, IA, Sept 13, 1928.

Michael Johnson, 39, track athlete, born Dallas, TX, Sept 13, 1967.

Richard Kiel, 67, actor (*The Longest Yard, Silver Streak, The Spy Who Loved Me*), born Detroit, MI, Sept 13, 1939.

Judith Martin, 68, author, journalist ("Miss Manners"), born Washington, DC, Sept 13, 1938.

Stella McCartney, 35, fashion designer, born London, England, Sept 13, 1971.

Ben Savage, 26, actor ("Boy Meets World"), born Chicago, IL, Sept 13, 1980.

Fred Silverman, 69, TV producer, born New York, NY, Sept 13, 1937.

Jean Smart, 47, actress ("Designing Women"), born Seattle, WA, Sept 13, 1959.

Bernabe ("Bernie") Williams, 38, baseball player, born San Juan, Puerto Rico, Sept 13, 1968.

SEPTEMBER 14 — THURSDAY
Day 257 — 108 Remaining

ANTIQUE AND CLASSIC CAR SHOW.
Sept 14–16. Bennington, VT. Classic cars, Woodies. A flea market with auto-related parts and memorabilia entices collectors seeking that elusive fender or gas running lamp. A display and demonstration of antique motorcycles, tractor and farm machinery are also featured. Live entertainment. Annually, the second weekend after Labor Day. Est attendance: 10,000. For info: Bennington Area Chamber of Commerce, 100 Veterans Memorial Dr, Bennington, VT 05201. Phone: (802) 447-3311. Fax: (802) 447-1163. E-mail: chamber@bennington.com. Web: www.bennington.com.

DANTE ALIGHIERI: DEATH ANNIVERSARY.
Sept 14, 1321. Italian poet, author of the *Divine Comedy*, died at Ravenna, Italy. He was born in May 1265 (exact date unknown) at Florence, Italy.

"THE GOLDEN GIRLS" TV PREMIERE: ANNIVERSARY.
Sept 14, 1985. This comedy starred Bea Arthur, Betty White, Rue McClanahan and Estelle Getty as four divorced/widowed women sharing a house in Florida during their golden years. The last episode aired Sept 14, 1992, but the show remains popular in syndication.

"HAVE GUN WILL TRAVEL" TV PREMIERE: ANNIVERSARY.
Sept 14, 1957. "Have Gun, Will Travel . . ." So read the business card of Paladin (Richard Boone), a loner whose professional services were available for a price. This half-hour Western also featured Kam Tong as his servant, Hey Boy. The show was extremely popular and ranked in the top five for most of its run.

HUMMER/BIRD CELEBRATION.
Sept 14–17. Rockport and Fulton, TX. To celebrate the spectacular fall migration of the ruby-throated hummingbird and other birds from their summer nesting grounds in the north along the eastern Gulf Coast on the way to their winter grounds in Mexico and Central America, and its 500-mile journey across the Gulf. There are programs, workshops, booths, concessions, bus and boat tours. Est attendance: 10,000. For info: Rockport Fulton Area Chamber of Commerce, Hummer/Bird Celebration, 404 Broadway, Rockport, TX 78382. Phone: (800) 242-0071 or (361) 729-6445. Fax: (361) 729-7681. E-mail: tourism@1rockport.org. Web: www.rockport-fulton.org.

"IRONSIDE" TV PREMIERE: ANNIVERSARY.
Sept 14, 1967. This crime series starred Raymond Burr as Robert T. Ironside, Chief of Detectives for the San Francisco Police Department (he was in a wheelchair, paralyzed from an assassination attempt). Also featured were Don Galloway as his assistant, Detective Sergeant Ed Brown; Barbara Anderson as Officer Eve Whitfield; Don Mitchell as Mark Sanger, Ironside's personal assistant; Gene Lyons as Commissioner Dennis Randall; Elizabeth Baur as Officer Fran Belding and Joan Pringle as Diana, Mark's wife.

McKINLEY, WILLIAM: DEATH ANNIVERSARY.
Sept 14, 1901. President William McKinley was shot at Buffalo, NY, Sept 6, 1901. He died eight days later. Assassin Leon Czolgosz was executed Oct 29, 1901.

MOON PHASE: LAST QUARTER.
Sept 14. Moon enters Last Quarter phase at 7:15 AM, EDT.

MOTLEY, CONSTANCE BAKER: BIRTHDAY.
Sept 14, 1921. New York's first black woman state senator and federal judge, and the first woman elected borough president of Manhattan, Constance Baker Motley became interested in law and civil rights when she was barred from a public beach at age 15. She went on to become one of the top civil rights lawyers of the '50s and '60s. She presented arguments before the US Supreme Court for seven cases and won them all. Motley was born at New Haven, CT.

NATIONAL GUITAR FLAT-PICKING CHAMPIONSHIPS AND WALNUT VALLEY FESTIVAL.
Sept 14–17. Cowley County Fairgrounds, Winfield, KS. The Walnut River is the site of this 35th annual family event featuring four stages with eight contests, at least 14 workshops and many first-class concerts. The Walnut Valley Arts and Crafts Festival features handmade instruments and a large variety of arts and crafts items, both ornamental and functional. All-weather facilities. Est attendance: 45,000. For info: Walnut Valley Assn, Bob Redford, PO Box 245, Winfield, KS 67156. Phone: (620) 221-3250. Fax: (620) 221-3109. E-mail: hq@wvfest.com. Web: www.wvfest.com.

NEWPORT INTERNATIONAL BOAT SHOW.
Sept 14–17. Newport, RI. More than 400 new sail and power boats in the water and displays of accessories, equipment and services. New product information, TrawlerPort program, seminars, etc. Est attendance: 42,000. For info: Newport Exhibition Group, PO Box 360, Newport, RI 02840. Phone: (401) 846-1115. Web: www.newportboatshow.com.

NICARAGUA: BATTLE OF SAN JACINTO DAY.
Sept 14. National holiday. Commemorates the 1856 defeat of US invader William Walker.

OKLAHOMA STATE FAIR.
Sept 14–24. State Fair Park, Oklahoma City, Oklahoma. One of the top state fairs in North America includes six buildings of commercial exhibits, ten barns for livestock and horse competitions, Disney on Ice, PRCA championship rodeo, live entertainment and motor sports events. Est attendance: 900,000. For info: Oklahoma State Fair, PO Box 74943, Oklahoma City, OK 73147. Phone: (405) 948-6700. Fax: (405) 948-6828. E-mail: mail@oklahomastatefair.com. Web: www.oklahomastatefair.com.

SANGER, MARGARET (HIGGINS): BIRTH ANNIVERSARY. Sept 14, 1879. Feminist, nurse and founder of the birth control movement in the US. Born at Corning, NY. (Note: birth year not entirely certain because, apparently, Sanger often used a later date when obliged to divulge her birthday. Best evidence now points to Sept 14, 1879, rather than the frequently used 1883 date.) She died at Tucson, AZ, Sept 6, 1966.

SETON, ELIZABETH ANN: CANONIZATION: ANNIVERSARY. Sept 14, 1975. Elizabeth Ann Seton became the first native-born American to be canonized. She was declared a saint in 1974 by Pope Paul VI.

SOLO TRANSATLANTIC BALLOON CROSSING: ANNIVERSARY. Sept 14–18, 1984. Joe W. Kittinger, 56-year-old balloonist, left Caribou, ME, in a 10-story-tall helium-filled balloon named *Rosie O'Grady's Balloon of Peace* Sept 14, 1984, crossed the Atlantic Ocean and reached the French coast, above the town of Capbreton, in bad weather Sept 17 at 4:29 PM, EDT. He crash-landed amid wind and rain near Savone, Italy, at 8:08 AM, EDT, Sept 18. Kittinger suffered a broken ankle when he was thrown from the balloon's gondola during the landing. His nearly 84-hour flight, covering about 3,535 miles, was the first solo balloon crossing of the Atlantic Ocean and a record distance for a solo balloon flight.

"THE WALTONS" TV PREMIERE: ANNIVERSARY. Sept 14, 1972. This epitome of the family drama spawned nearly a dozen knock-offs during its nine-year run on CBS. The drama was based on creator/writer Earl Hamner Jr's experiences growing up during the Depression in rural Virginia. It began as the TV movie "The Homecoming," which was turned into a weekly series covering the years 1933–43. The cast went through numerous changes through the years; the principals were: Michael Learned as Olivia Walton, mother of the clan; Ralph Waite as John Walton, father; Richard Thomas as John-Boy, eldest son; Jon Walmsley as son Jason; Judy Norton-Taylor as daughter Mary Ellen; Eric Scott as son Ben; Mary Beth McDonough as daughter Erin; David W. Harper as son Jim-Bob and Kami Cotler as daughter Elizabeth. The Walton grandparents were played by Ellen Corby and Will Geer. The last telecast aired Aug 20, 1981.

WILSON, JAMES: BIRTH ANNIVERSARY. Sept 14, 1742. Signer of the Declaration of Independence and one of the first associate justices of the US Supreme Court. Born at Fifeshire, Scotland, he died Aug 21, 1798, at Edenton, NC.

BIRTHDAYS TODAY

Zoe Caldwell, 73, actress (*Medea, The Prime of Miss Jean Brodie*), born Melbourne, Australia, Sept 14, 1933.
Dan Cortese, 39, actor ("Veronica's Closet," *Public Enemies*), born Sewickley, PA, Sept 14, 1967.
Mary Crosby, 47, actress ("Dallas," *Tapeheads*), born Los Angeles, CA, Sept 14, 1959.
Faith Ford, 42, actress ("Murphy Brown"), born Alexandria, LA, Sept 14, 1964.
Joey Heatherton, 62, actress (*Cry Baby, Bluebeard,* "Dean Martin and the Golddiggers"), born Rockville Centre, NY, Sept 14, 1944.
Walter Koenig, 70, actor, writer, director, producer ("Star Trek" and *Star Trek* movies), born Chicago, IL, Sept 14, 1936.
Kate Millett, 72, feminist, writer (*Sexual Politics, Flying*), born St. Paul, MN, Sept 14, 1934.
Sam Neill, 59, actor (*My Brilliant Career, Jurassic Park, The Piano*), born Northern Ireland, Sept 14, 1947.
Nicol Williamson, 68, actor (*Robin and Marian, Excalibur*), born Hamilton, Scotland, Sept 14, 1938.

	S	M	T	W	T	F	S
September						1	2
2006	3	4	5	6	7	8	9
	10	11	12	13	14	15	16
	17	18	19	20	21	22	23
	24	25	26	27	28	29	30

SEPTEMBER 15 — FRIDAY
Day 258 — 107 Remaining

ACUFF, ROY: BIRTH ANNIVERSARY. Sept 15, 1903. Grand Ole Opry "King of Country Music" Roy Acuff was born at Maynardville, TN. Singer and fiddler Acuff (who was cofounder of Acuff-Rose Publishing Company, the leading publisher of country music) was a regular host on weekly Grand Ole Opry broadcasts. He frequently appeared at the Opry with his group, the Smoky Mountain Boys. In December of 1991 Acuff became the first living member elected to the Country Music Hall of Fame. Some of his more famous songs were "The Wabash Cannonball" (his theme song), "Pins and Needles (In My Heart)" and "Night Train to Memphis." Roy Acuff died Nov 23, 1992, at Nashville, TN.

"BACHELOR FATHER" TV PREMIERE: ANNIVERSARY. Sept 15, 1957. John Forsythe (Bentley Gregg) and Noreen Corcoran (Kelly Gregg) starred in this sitcom about a bachelor attorney's life turning upside-down after his orphaned niece moves in with him. The last episode aired Sept 25, 1962. Supporting players included: Sammee Tong as Peter Tong, the butler, and Jimmy Boyd as Kelly's boyfriend, Howard Meechim.

THE BIG E. Sept 15–Oct 1. West Springfield, MA. New England's autumn tradition and one of the nation's largest fairs. Each September, The Big E features all free entertainment including top-name talent, a big-top circus and horse show. Also children's attractions, daily parade with custom-built Mardi Gras floats, historic village, Avenue of States, Better Living Center and much more. Annually, beginning the second Friday after Labor Day. Est attendance: 1,250,000. For info: Eastern States Exposition, 1305 Memorial Ave, West Springfield, MA 01089. Phone: (413) 737-2443. Fax: (413) 787-0127. E-mail: info@thebige.com. Web: www.thebige.com.

"CHiPS" TV PREMIERE: ANNIVERSARY. Sept 15, 1977. A popular action-packed NBC police series depicting cases and chases of the motorcycle-riding California Highway Patrol. The show starred Erik Estrada as Francis "Ponch" Poncherello and Larry Wilcox as Jon Baker, two quick-witted cops. Wilcox left the show, and Estrada's new partner, Bobby "Hot Dog" Nelson, was played by Tom Reilly. The last telecast aired July 17, 1983.

CHRISTIE, AGATHA: BIRTH ANNIVERSARY. Sept 15, 1890. English author of nearly a hundred books (mysteries, drama, poetry and nonfiction), born at Torquay, England. Died at Wallingford, England, Jan 12, 1976. "Every murderer," she wrote, in *The Mysterious Affair at Styles*, "is probably somebody's old friend."

"COLUMBO" TV PREMIERE: 35th ANNIVERSARY. Sept 15, 1971. "Columbo," based on a 1968 made-for-TV movie, entered the lineup of NBC's "Mystery Movie" series on this date. Peter Falk starred as one of TV's great characters, Lieutenant Columbo, the crime-solving policeman dressed in rumpled raincoat and bearing a chewed up cigar. In almost every episode, Columbo latches himself onto the main suspect, usually a polished sophisticate in comparison to Columbo's seeming simpleness, and nags him or her to death with questions and comments such as "But one thing bothers me, sir." The series ended in 1978, but reemerged in the form of periodic movies beginning in 1989.

COOPER, JAMES FENIMORE: BIRTH ANNIVERSARY. Sept 15, 1789. American novelist, historian and social critic, born at Burlington, NJ, James Fenimore Cooper was one of the earliest American writers to develop a native American literary tradition. His most popular works are the five novels comprising *The Leatherstocking Tales,* featuring the exploits of one of the truly unique American fictional characters, Natty Bumppo. These novels, *The Deerslayer, The Last of the Mohicans, The Pathfinder, The Pioneers* and *The Prairie,* chronicle Natty Bumppo's continuing flight away from the rapid settlement of America. Other works, including *The Monikins* and *Satanstoe,* reveal him as an astute critic of American life. He died Sept 14, 1851, at Cooperstown, NY, the town founded by his father.

COSTA RICA: INDEPENDENCE DAY. Sept 15. National holiday. Gained independence from Spain in 1821.

CRESTON/SOUTHWEST IOWA BALLOON DAYS. Sept 15–17. Creston, IA. Hare and hound races held at sunrise and sunset; parade and marching band contest; craft market; food and much more. Annually, the third weekend in September. Est attendance: 9,500. For info: Creston Chamber of Commerce, PO Box 471, Creston, IA 50801. Phone: (641) 782-7021. E-mail: chamber@crestoniowachamber.com. Web: www.crestoniowachamber.com.

EL SALVADOR: INDEPENDENCE DAY. Sept 15. National holiday. Gained independence from Spain in 1821.

ENGLAND: CHELSEA ANTIQUES FAIR. Sept 15–24. Chelsea Old Town Hall, King's Rd, London. Traditional, prestigious event now modernizing its style, but retaining top-quality items. Est attendance: 6,000. For info: Penman Antiques Fair. Phone: (44) (870) 350-2442. Fax: (44) (870) 350-2443. E-mail: info@penman-fairs.co.uk.

ENGLAND: HARROGATE AUTUMN FLOWER SHOW. Sept 15–17. Great Yorkshire Showground, Harrogate, N Yorkshire. See Britain's finest blooms, talk to the experts and witness the giants in the National Onion Championship. Est attendance: 35,000. For info: Roger Brownbridge, North of England Horticultural Society, 4A South Park Rd, Harrogate, North Yorkshire, England HG1 5QU. Phone: (44) (1423) 561049. Fax: (44) (1423) 536880. E-mail: info@flowershow.org.uk. Web: www.flowershow.org.uk.

FIRST NATIONAL CONVENTION FOR BLACKS: ANNIVERSARY. Sept 15, 1830. The first national convention for blacks was held at Bethel Church, Philadelphia, PA. The convention was called to find ways to better the condition of black people and was attended by delegates from seven states. Bishop Richard Allen was elected as the first convention president.

FRIENDS OF LAKE FOREST LIBRARY ANNUAL BOOK SALE. Sept 15–17. Lake Forest, IL. A three-day sale of used books in excellent condition set up in 20 categories. Est attendance: 5,000. For info: Kaye Grabbe, Lake Forest Library, 360 E Deerpath, Lake Forest, IL 60045. Phone: (847) 234-0636. Fax: (847) 234-1453. E-mail: kgrabbe@lfl.alibrary.com. Web: lfkhome.northstarnet.org/FriendsofLFL.html.

GREENPEACE FOUNDED: 35th ANNIVERSARY. Sept 15, 1971. The environmental organization Greenpeace, committed to a green and peaceful world, was founded by 12 members of the Don't Make a Wave committee of Vancouver, BC, Canada, when the boat *Phyllis Cormack* sailed to Amchitka, AK, to protest US nuclear testing. Greenpeace's basic principle is "that determined individuals can alter the actions and purposes of even the overwhelmingly powerful by 'bearing witness'—drawing attention to an environmental abuse through their mere unwavering presence, whatever the risk."

GUATEMALA: INDEPENDENCE DAY. Sept 15. National holiday. Gained independence from Spain in 1821.

HODAG MUSKIE CHALLENGE. Sept 15–17. Rhinelander, WI. Catch and release muskie tournament. Guaranteed $20,000 first-place grand prize based on full capacity of 200 teams. Annually, the third weekend in September. For info: Rhinelander Area Chamber of Commerce, PO Box 795, Rhinelander, WI 54501. Phone: (800) 236-4386. Fax: (715) 365-7467. E-mail: info@rhinelanderchamber.com. Web: www.rhinelanderchamber.com.

HONDURAS: INDEPENDENCE DAY. Sept 15. National holiday. Gained independence from Spain in 1821.

"I SPY" TV PREMIERE: ANNIVERSARY. Sept 15, 1965. Bill Cosby made television history as the first African American actor starring in a major dramatic role in this spy series. Cosby played Alexander "Scotty" Scott, an intellectual spy with a cover as a tennis trainer. Robert Culp played Kelly Robinson, the "tennis pro" and Scotty's partner in espionage. The series was notable for filming worldwide.

INTERNATIONAL SING-OUT DAY™. Sept 15. Break out in song today like they do in the musicals. After all, it is better to break OUT than to break up. Sing out (loud and strong) your words in conversations instead of speaking them. You can even add a few dance steps if you like. To alleviate the escalating costs of Eventological® Literature, a charge of $10 must be assessed for each request. Checks are to be made payable to: Adrienne Sioux Koopersmith, 1437 W Rosemont, #1W, Chicago, IL 60660. E-mail: askoopersmith@hotmail.com.

JAPAN: RESPECT FOR THE AGED DAY. Sept 15. National holiday to honor Japan's senior citizens—especially those who are centenarians.

"THE LONE RANGER" TV PREMIERE: ANNIVERSARY. Sept 15, 1949. This character was created for a radio serial in 1933 by George W. Trendle. The famous masked man was the alter ego of John Reid, a Texas Ranger who was the only survivor of an ambush. He was nursed back to health by his Native American friend, Tonto. Both men traveled around the West on their trusty steeds, Silver and Scout, fighting injustice. Clayton Moore played the Lone Ranger/John Reid and Jay Silverheels costarred as Tonto. The theme music was Rossini's "William Tell Overture." The last episode aired Sept 12, 1957.

MONTEREY JAZZ FESTIVAL. Sept 15–17. Monterey, CA. Celebrating its 49th year, the country's oldest continuous jazz festival features the sounds of some of the world's finest jazz musicians. Est attendance: 40,000. For info: Monterey Jazz Festival, PO Box Jazz, Monterey, CA 93942. Phone: (925) 275-9255 (tickets and info) or (831) 373-3366 (corporate offices). Web: www.montereyjazzfestival.org.

★**NATIONAL HISPANIC HERITAGE MONTH.** Sept 15–Oct 15. Presidential Proclamation. Beginning in 1989, always issued for Sept 15–Oct 15 of each year (PL100–402 of Aug 17, 1988). Previously issued each year for the week including Sept 15 and 16 since 1968 at request (PL90–498 of Sept 17, 1968).

★**NATIONAL POW/MIA RECOGNITION DAY.** Sept 15. Annually, the third Friday of September.

NICARAGUA: INDEPENDENCE DAY. Sept 15. National holiday. Gained independence from Spain in 1821.

ON THE WATERFRONT SWAP MEET AND CAR SHOW. Sept 15–17. Downtown St. Ignace, MI. 16th anniversary. Car show, toy show, truck display and swap meet. Est attendance: 10,000. For info: Ed Reavie, President, Nostalgia Prod, Inc, 268 Hillcrest Blvd, St. Ignace, MI 49781. Phone: (906) 643-8087 or (906) 643-1USA. Fax: (906) 643-9784. E-mail: ereavie@nostalgia-prod.com. Web: www.nostalgia-prod.com or www.auto-shows.com.

OSAGE RIVER MOUNTAIN MAN FESTIVAL AND BLACK POWDER SHOOT. Sept 15–17. Lake Ozark, MO. 19th annual. Mountain men, Indians, musicians, storytellers in authentic attire gather to reenact a pre-1840s wilderness rendezvous. Annually, the third full weekend in September. Est attendance: 6,000. For info: Lake Area Chamber of Commerce, PO Box 1570, Lake Ozark, MO 65049. Phone: (800) 451-4117 or (573) 964-1008. Fax: (573) 964-1010. E-mail: candyw@lakearea chamber.com. Web: lakeareachamber.com.

QUARTERLY ESTIMATED FEDERAL INCOME TAX PAYERS' DUE DATE. Sept 15. For those individuals whose fiscal year is the calendar year and who make quarterly estimated federal income tax payments, today is one of the due dates. (Jan 17, Apr 17, June 15 and Sept 15, 2006.)

RICHARD CRANE MEMORIAL TRUCK SHOW. Sept 15–17. St. Ignace, MI. 11th annual show featuring 18-wheeler competition. $2,000 cash Best of Show. Parade of Lights across the Mackinac Bridge. Est attendance: 10,000. For info: Nostalgia Productions, Inc, 268 Hillcrest Blvd, St. Ignace, MI 49781. Phone: (906) 643-8087 or (906) 643-1USA. Fax: (906) 643-9784. E-mail: ereavie@nostalgia-prod.com. Web: www.nostalgia-prod .com or www.auto-shows.com.

ROCHESTER FAIR. Sept 15–24. Rochester, NH. Agricultural Fair. Est attendance: 150,000. For info: Rochester Fair Assn, 72 Lafayette St, Rochester, NH 03867. Phone: (603) 332-6585. Fax: (603) 332-1896. Web: rochesterfair.com.

SEVEN SWEETS AND SOURS FESTIVAL. Sept 15–16. Intercourse, PA. The biggest time of the year is when we put up our fruits and vegetables for the long winter. The whole village is invaded with wonderful end-of-the-garden creations. Est attendance: 30,000. For info: Lisa Horn, Kitchen Kettle Village, Box 380, Intercourse, PA 17534. Phone: (800) 732-3538 or (717) 768-8261. Web: www.kitchenkettle.com.

16th STREET BAPTIST CHURCH BOMBING: ANNIVERSARY. Sept 15, 1963. In a horrific episode of the civil rights struggle, a bomb blast in the basement of the 16th Street Baptist Church in Birmingham, AL, killed four girls preparing for church: Denise McNair, Carole Robertson, Cynthia Wesley and Addie Mae Collins. Previously, the church had been the center for marches led by Dr. Martin Luther King, Jr. Three suspects were brought to trial in 1977, 2001 and 2002 and found guilty.

SOMEDAY. Sept 15. You know all those things you're going to do "someday"—lose weight, start a business, learn another language, skydive, whatever. Well, someday is here! This is the day to tackle new challenges and experience the joy of accomplishment. Free articles available for publishers and webmasters at IdeaLady.com/content.htm. For info: Cathy Stucker, Special Interests Publishing, 4646 Hwy 6, PMB 123, Sugar Land, TX 77478. Phone: (281) 265-7342. E-mail: cathy@idealady.com. Web: www .idealady.com.

SPACE MILESTONE: *ARIANE-3* (ESA). Sept 15, 1987. European Space Agency rocket carrying two (Australian and European) communications satellites into Earth's orbit marked the re-entry of western nations into commercial space projects. Launched this date from Kourou, French Guiana, with Arianespace, a private company operating the rocket for the 13-nation European Space Agency.

STARMAN FAMILY-CON 2006. Sept 15–17. Hollywood, CA. Ninth biennial international "family reunion" of the people who created/appreciated the TV series "Starman" (and the movie on which it was based). This year we celebrate the 20th anniversary of the TV show's premiere on Sept 19, 1986. Though it lasted only one season, this TV show touched many souls and helped people change their lives in positive ways. See also: "International Starman Month (Oct 1)." For info: Vicki Werkley, 16563 Ellen Springs Dr, Lower Lake, CA 95457-9477. Phone: (707)

September 2006	S	M	T	W	T	F	S
						1	2
	3	4	5	6	7	8	9
	10	11	12	13	14	15	16
	17	18	19	20	21	22	23
	24	25	26	27	28	29	30

995-1228. E-mail: Spotlight_Starman@bigfoot.com (put "SFC2K6" in subject line). Web: www.starmanet.com.

STREET MACHINE FALL NATIONALS. Sept 15–17. Ozark Empire Fairgrounds, Springfield, MO. Car & truck show with Family Fun Zone and Performance Market Place. For info: Ozark Empire Fair, 3001 N Grant, Springfield, MO 65803. Phone: (417) 833-2660. Fax: (417) 833-3769. Web: www.ozarkempirefair.com.

SUMMERSET FESTIVAL. Sept 15–17. Clement Park, Littleton, CO. A family-oriented event, held for the purpose of saying good-bye to summer. There is something for everyone: car show, arts & crafts, business and nonprofit exhibitors, fishing derby, food concessions, kids areas, softball tournament, entertainment and loads of family fun! Est attendance: 50,000. For info: Lora Knowlton, Summerset Festival, PO Box 621788, Littleton, CO 80162-1788. Phone: (303) 973-1209. Fax: (303) 948-5550. E-mail: summersetfest@aol.com. Web: www.summersetfest.com.

TAFT, WILLIAM HOWARD: BIRTH ANNIVERSARY. Sept 15, 1857. The 27th president of the US was born at Cincinnati, OH. His term of office was Mar 4, 1909–Mar 3, 1913. Following his presidency he became a law professor at Yale University until his appointment as Chief Justice of the US Supreme Court in 1921. Died at Washington, DC, Mar 8, 1930, and was buried at Arlington National Cemetery.

TELLURIDE BLUES & BREWS FESTIVAL. Sept 15–17. Telluride, CO. Three-day blues festival with 20 nationally touring bands and 3-hour grand tasting with 50 microbreweries on the Saturday of the festival. Includes Rainbow Kids area, late-night juke joints, four-day blues camp and free acoustic concerts. Est attendance: 8,000. For info: Telluride Blues & Brews Festival, PO Box 2966, Telluride, CO 81435. Phone: (970) 728-8037. Fax: (970) 728-1350. E-mail: info@tellurideblues.com. Web: www .tellurideblues.com.

TINKER TO EVERS TO CHANCE: FIRST DOUBLE PLAY ANNIVERSARY. Sept 15, 1902. Chicago Cubs' shortstop Joe Tinker, second baseman Johnny Evers and first baseman Frank Chance recorded their first double play together on this date. This was two days after they took the field for the first time in this configuration, and the Cubs went on to beat the Cincinnati Reds, 6–3. The threesome were later immortalized in Franklin Adams's poem "Baseball's Sad Lexicon." Tinker, Evers and Chance were inducted together into the Baseball Hall of Fame in 1946. See also: "'Baseball's Sad Lexicon' Published: Anniversary" (July 10).

UNITED KINGDOM: BATTLE OF BRITAIN DAY. Sept 15. Commemorates end of biggest daylight bombing raid of Britain by German Luftwaffe, in 1940. Said to have been the turning point against Hitler's siege of Britain in WWII.

US TROOPS ENTER GERMANY: ANNIVERSARY. Sept 15, 1944. US troops of the VII and V Corps reached the southwestern frontier of Germany. The war had finally moved into the Third Reich's backyard.

USA TODAY FIRST PUBLISHED: ANNIVERSARY. Sept 15, 1982. Media corporation Gannett published a new kind of daily—the "Nation's Newspaper"—that featured general interest articles for a national audience on this date.

WIZARD OF OZ FESTIVAL. Sept 15–17. Chesterton, IN. 25th annual festival. Parade, costumed Oz characters, original Munchkins, arts and crafts, food. Est attendance: 80,000. For info: Lake Shore Festivals & Events, Inc, PO Box 2138, Chesterton, IN 46304. Phone: (219) 983-1691. Web: www.wizardofoz festival.org.

WO-ZHA-WA DAYS FALL FESTIVAL. Sept 15–17. Wisconsin Dells, WI. Celebrates the beginning of the fall season. Arts, crafts, 100-unit parade, Maxwell Street Days, Wo-Zha-Wa Run and antique flea market. Est attendance: 100,000. For info: Wisconsin Dells Visitors Bureau, PO Box 390, Wisconsin Dells, WI 53965. Phone: (800) 223-3557. E-mail: info@wisdells.com. Web: www.wisdells.com.

WRAY, FAY: BIRTH ANNIVERSARY. Sept 15, 1907. Hollywood's "Scream Queen" was born in Alberta, Canada, on this day. The star of numerous silent films (notably Erich von Stroheim's *The Wedding March*), Wray made her mark in 1930s thrillers—and then became a pop culture icon through her role as Ann Darrow, the giant ape's obsession in the 1933 film *King Kong*. Wray died at New York City, Aug 8, 2004. See also: "*King Kong* Film Premiere: Anniversary" (Mar 2).

BIRTHDAYS TODAY

Jackie Cooper, 84, actor (*Our Gang* shorts, "The People's Choice"), producer, born Los Angeles, CA, Sept 15, 1922.

Norm Crosby, 79, comedian, host ("The Comedy Shop"), born Boston, MA, Sept 15, 1927.

Sherman Douglas, 40, former basketball player, born Washington, DC, Sept 15, 1966.

Prince Harry (Henry Charles Albert David), 22, second son of Prince Charles and Princess Diana, born London, England, Sept 15, 1984.

Tommy Lee Jones, 60, actor (Oscar for *The Fugitive*; *Coal Miner's Daughter*), born San Saba, TX, Sept 15, 1946.

Daniel Constantine (Dan) Marino, Jr, 45, former football player, born Pittsburgh, PA, Sept 15, 1961.

Carmen Maura, 61, actress (*Women on the Verge of a Nervous Breakdown*), born Madrid, Spain, Sept 15, 1945.

Jessye Norman, 61, soprano, opera singer, born Augusta, GA, Sept 15, 1945.

Merlin Jay Olsen, 66, Hall of Fame football player, sportscaster, actor ("Little House on the Prairie"), born Logan, UT, Sept 15, 1940.

Gaylord Jackson Perry, 68, Hall of Fame baseball player, born Williamston, NC, Sept 15, 1938.

Oliver Stone, 60, director (*Platoon, JFK, Wall Street*), screenwriter, born New York, NY, Sept 15, 1946.

SEPTEMBER 16 — SATURDAY

Day 259 — 106 Remaining

AEROSPACE WALK OF HONOR. Sept 16. Lancaster, CA. In the tradition of the aerospace industry of the Antelope Valley, the City of Lancaster Aerospace Walk of Honor attracts visitors to Lancaster Boulevard to the unveiling of granite monuments honoring Edwards Air Force Base test pilots whose aviation careers are marked by significant achievements. Honorees such as Neil Armstrong, Chuck Yeager and William "Pete" Knight are selected because they have soared above the rest. Est attendance: 6,500. For info: Anne Aldrich, Public Information Officer, City of Lancaster, 44933 Fern Ave, Lancaster, CA 93534. Phone: (661) 723-6053. Fax: (661) 723-6141. Web: www.cityoflancaster ca.org.

ALABAMA COASTAL CLEANUP. Sept 16. Mobile, Baldwin and Escambia counties, AL. 19th annual. Volunteers convene to "get the trash out of the splash" by cleaning up Alabama's beaches and waterways. This event provides participants with a firsthand experience that improves the ecosystem. Annually, the third Saturday in September. Est attendance: 3,000. For info: Alabama Dept of Conservation & Natural Resources, State Lands Division Coastal Section, Stonebrook Executive Complex, Ste B-1, 23210 Highway 98, Fairhope, AL 36532. Phone: (251) 929-0900. Fax: (251) 990-9293. Web: www.alabamacoastalcleanup.com.

AMERICAN DIETETIC ASSOCIATION FOOD & NUTRITION CONFERENCE & EXPO. Sept 16–19. Honolulu, HI. Est attendance: 10,000. For info: Public Relations, American Dietetic Assn, 120 S Riverside Plaza, Ste 2000, Chicago, IL 60606-6995. Phone: (312) 899-0040. Fax: (312) 899-0008. E-mail: mtgsinfo@eatright.org. Web: www.eatright.org.

ANNE BRADSTREET DAY. Sept 16. An official date proclaimed by the governor of the Commonwealth of Massachusetts to honor Anne Bradstreet, America's first poet, who is also recognized as the first published woman poet in the English language. Anne Bradstreet was born in 1612 in England and came to America in 1630. Unbeknownst to Anne, her brother-in-law took some of her poetry back to England where it was published in 1630 as *The Tenth Muse Lately Sprung Up in America*. Subsequent editions were also published in Boston. She died at Old Andover, MA, Sept 16, 1672. For info: Sue Ellen Holmes, Dir, Stevens Memorial Library, PO Box 8, North Andover, MA 01845. Phone: (978) 688-9505. Fax: (978) 688-9507. E-mail: SHolmes @mailserv.mvlc.lib.ma.us.

APPLEJACK FESTIVAL. Sept 16–17. Nebraska City, NE. To promote local orchards and their abundant apple harvest through craft shows, children's festivals, music, food and fun. Fantastic parade with many marching bands on Saturday. Plenty of good times for the whole family. Est attendance: 40,000. For info: Nebraska City Tourism & Events, 806 First Ave, Nebraska City, NE 68410. Phone: (402) 873-3000 or (800) 514-9113. Fax: (402) 873-6701. E-mail: tourism@nebraskacity.com. Web: www.nebras kacity.com.

BELLE MEADE PLANTATION FALL FEST. Sept 16–17. Belle Meade Plantation, Nashville, TN. Annual fundraiser, crafts, antiques, art, food, market, fine jewelry, garage treasures and children's fest. Annually, the third weekend of September. Est attendance: 10,000. For info: Belle Meade Plantation, 5025 Harding Rd, Nashville, TN 37205. Phone: (615) 356-0501 or (800) 270-3991. Fax: (615) 356-2336. Web: www.bellemeadeplantation.com.

BIG MAC SHORELINE FALL SCENIC BIKE TOUR & RIDE ACROSS THE MACKINAC BRIDGE. Sept 16–17. Mackinaw City Public School, Mackinaw City, MI. A one-of-a-kind bike tour that has become a tradition for many bikers in Michigan and surrounding states. On Saturday, more than 600 participants ride 25-, 50-, 75- or 100-mile bike tours along the shores of Lake Michigan. The routes are clearly marked and a number of rest areas dot the course. SAG Safety Wagons also circle the route to ensure safety for riders. For those who participate on Saturday, there is a beautiful ride across Mackinac Bridge on Sunday at 7 AM. Est attendance: 600. For info: Kelly Vieau, Mackinaw Chamber of Commerce, PO Box 856, Mackinaw City, MI 49701. Phone: (231) 436-5574. Fax: (231) 436-7989. E-mail: info@mackinawchamber.com. Web: www.mackinawchamber.com.

BIG WHOPPER LIAR'S CONTEST. Sept 16. Murphy Auditorium, New Harmony, IN. Thirty "storytellers" compete to see who can tell the BIGGEST whopper. Annually, the third Saturday in September. Est attendance: 425. For info: Jeff Fleming, PO Box 598, Olney, IL 62450. Phone: (618) 395-8491. Fax: (618) 392-3174.

CAPE MAY FOOD & WINE FESTIVAL. Sept 16–20. Cape May, NJ. Come see why *The New York Times* calls Cape May "the restaurant capital of New Jersey." Take classes and seminars taught by Cape May chefs. Attend workshops and tours that invite visitors into the kitchens of Cape May's critically acclaimed restaurants. Enjoy special dinner and lunch meal packages and visit the Gourmet Marketplace, featuring the People's Choice Chowder Contest. For info: Mid-Atlantic Center for the Arts, 1048 Washington St, Cape May, NJ 08204. Phone: (800) 275-4278. Fax: (609) 884-0574. E-mail: mac4arts@capemaymac.org. Web: www.capemaymac.org.

CHAUTAUQUA OF THE ARTS. Sept 16–17. Greensburg, IN. Fine artists and craftsmen gather to demonstrate and sell their works. Annually, the third weekend in Sept. Est attendance: 10,000. For info: Chautauqua of the Arts, 1119 W Main St, Madison, IN 47250-3013. Phone: (812) 265-5080. Fax: (812) 265-5080. E-mail: james@chautauquaofthearts.com. Web: www.chautauquaofthearts.com.

CHEROKEE STRIP CELEBRATION. Sept 16. Perry, OK. To commemorate the opening of the Cherokee Strip to settlement on Sept 16, 1893. Annually, the Saturday or weekend nearest Sept 16. Est attendance: 8,000. For info: Carolyn Briegge, Chamber of Commerce, Box 426, Perry, OK 73077. Phone: (580) 336-4684. Fax: (580) 336-3522. E-mail: information@perrychamber.org.

CHEROKEE STRIP DAY: ANNIVERSARY. Sept 16, 1893. Optional school holiday, Oklahoma. Greatest "run" for Oklahoma land in 1893.

COMMENCEMENT BAY MARITIME FEST. Sept 16–17. Thea's Park, Tacoma, WA. Maritime festival celebrating Tacoma's working waterfront. Tugboat, dragon boat and sailboat races, salmon bakes, juried art shows, beer gardens, food and craft vendors, Port of Tacoma boat tours and Tacoma Rail train rides. Activities for children of all ages. A project of the Youth Marine Foundation. Annually, the third weekend in Sept. Est attendance: 12,000. For info: Julie Coggins, CBMF, 1118 East D St, Tacoma, WA 98421. Phone: (253) 318-2210. Fax: (253) 404-1950. E-mail: maritime_fest@yahoo.com. Web: www.maritimefest.org.

COVERED BRIDGE FESTIVAL. Sept 16–17. Washington and Greene County, PA. Arts and crafts, entertainment and lots of homestyle food at each of eight covered bridges. Annually, the third weekend in September. Est attendance: 110,000. For info: Washington Co Tourism, 273 S Main St, Washington, PA 15301. Phone: (800) 531-4114 or (724) 228-5520. E-mail: info@washpatourism.org. Web: www.washpatourism.org.

EISENHOWER WORLD WAR II WEEKEND. Sept 16–17. Eisenhower National Historic Site, Gettysburg, PA. A living history encampment featuring Allied soldiers, German prisoners of war, tanks and military vehicles of that time. Annually, the third weekend in September. Est attendance: 2,500. For info: Gettysburg CVB, PO Box 4117, Gettysburg, PA 17325. Phone: (717) 334-6274. Fax: (717) 334-1166. E-mail: gettysburgcvb@dejazzd.com. Web: www.gettysburgcvb.org.

September 2006

S	M	T	W	T	F	S
					1	2
3	4	5	6	7	8	9
10	11	12	13	14	15	16
17	18	19	20	21	22	23
24	25	26	27	28	29	30

FALL FEST. Sept 16. Monett, MO. Street festival in historic downtown featuring live entertainment, including line dancing, cloggers, storytelling, and pancake breakfast, pork steak barbecue, car show with antique and classic vehicles from four states, food and craft booths, full carnival, children's rides, carriage rides, ARTExpo display, karaoke, Little Miss & Mr Oktoberfest, best downtown window display contest and more. Annually, on the third Saturday of September. For info: Monett Chamber of Commerce, 705 E Broadway, Monett, MO 65708. Phone: (417) 235-7919 or (417) 235-3349.

FESTIVAL OF ADVENTURES. Sept 16–17. Aitkin, MN. This annual festival celebrates the area's fur-trading history. Rendezvous at the City Park with trappers, traders, ethnic dancers, music and food. Est attendance: 5,000. For info: Aitkin Area Chamber of Commerce, PO Box 127, Aitkin, MN 56431. Phone: (218) 927-2316 or (800) 526-8342. Fax: (218) 927-4494. E-mail: upnorth@aitkin.com. Web: www.aitkin.com.

FESTIVAL OF THE SEA. Sept 16. Point Pleasant Beach, NJ. Come join the fun with arts, crafts, food, games for the kids, pony rides, antiques, nonprofit and commercial exhibits. Free admission. Est attendance: 55,000. For info: Point Pleasant Beach Chamber of Commerce, 517A Arnold Ave, Point Pleasant Beach, NJ 08742. Phone: (732) 899-2424. Fax: (732) 899-0103. E-mail: info@pointpleasantbeachnj.com. Web: www.pointpleasantbeachnj.com.

FESTIVAL 2006: FESTIVAL OF FINE ARTS AND FINE CRAFTS. Sept 16–17. Downtown, Dalton, GA. 43rd annual. Fine arts and fine crafts festival includes outdoor artist booths, food vendors, children's arts festival, entertainment for adults and children, cash awards. Est attendance: 7,000. For info: Creative Arts Guild, Box 1485, Dalton, GA 30722-1485. Phone: (706) 278-0168. Fax: (706) 278-6996. E-mail: cagarts@creativeartsguild.org.

"FRASIER" TV PREMIERE: ANNIVERSARY. Sept 16, 1993. In this acclaimed spin-off of "Cheers," psychiatrist Dr. Frasier Crane (Kelsey Grammer) has moved to Seattle, where he dispenses advice on the radio, produced by Roz Doyle (Peri Gilpin). He lives with his ex-cop father Martin (John Mahoney) and Martin's physical therapist Daphne Moon (Jane Leeves). His brother, Dr. Niles Crane (David Hyde Pierce), frequently asks for Frasier's advice about his love life. The show, which was a five-time Emmy winner for Outstanding Comedy Series (not to mention numerous Emmys for cast and crew), finished its run in 2004.

GENERAL MOTORS: FOUNDING ANNIVERSARY. Sept 16, 1908. The giant automobile manufacturing company was founded by William Crapo "Billy" Durant, a Flint, MI, entrepreneur.

GREAT SEAL OF THE US: FIRST USE ANNIVERSARY. Sept 16, 1782. On this date the Great Seal of the United States was, for the first time, impressed upon an official document. That document authorized George Washington to negotiate a prisoner of war agreement with the British. See also: "Great Seal of the United States: Anniversary" (Jan 28 and July 4).

HANKFEST. Sept 16–17. Chicago, IL. Celebrating the life and music of Hank Williams, Sr. This annual event features live bands and guest musicians, "Ghost Writers in the Sky" original songwriting contest, plus a jambalaya cook-off (in honor of one of Hank's best songs). For info: M. Larkin, Hankfest, 1924 W Montrose, Ste 117, Chicago, IL 60613. E-mail: contact@hankfest.com. Web: www.hankfest.com.

HERITAGE DAY. Sept 16. Houston, MO. Arts and crafts, demonstrations of old-time crafts. Heritage parade and free entertainment, delicious food booths and free music shows. Street dance on Saturday night. For info: Houston Area Chamber of Commerce, PO Box 374, Houston, MO 65483. Phone: (417) 967-2220. Fax: (417) 967-2178. E-mail: chamber@train.missouri.org.

INTERNATIONAL EAT AN APPLE DAY. Sept 16. To promote the beginning of fall with its vivid color and crispness, celebrate by eating an apple, the fruit of the fall season. Annually, the third Saturday in September. For info: Apple Berry Farm Market, 360 LaHave St, Bridgewater, NS, Canada, B4V 2T7. Phone: (902) 543-6622. Fax: (902) 527-1470. Web: www.appleberry.ca.

INTERNATIONAL COASTAL CLEANUP. Sept 16. A million volunteers remove and tabulate 12 million pieces of trash on 21,000 miles of beaches as well as below the water in 100 countries. Annually, the third Saturday in Sept. For info: The Ocean Conservancy, 1725 DeSales St NW, Washington, DC 20036. Phone: (202) 429-5609. Fax: (202) 872-0619. E-mail: cleanup@oceanconservancyva.org. Web: www.oceanconservancy.org.

JOHNNY APPLESEED FESTIVAL. Sept 16–17. Fort Wayne, IN. A return to the pioneer spirit of the early 1800s, at the gravesite of John Chapman, known as "Johnny Appleseed," who planted hundreds of apple orchards along the early Indiana frontier. Crafts, music, food and demonstrators. Annually, the third full weekend in September. Est attendance: 350,000. For info: Johnny Appleseed Festival, Inc, 1502 Harry Baals Dr, Fort Wayne, IN 46805. Phone: (260) 427-6003. Fax: (260) 427-6020. Web: johnnyappleseedfest.com.

KING TURKEY DAYS (WITH TURKEY RACE). Sept 16. Worthington, MN. Community celebration that includes live turkey race between Paycheck, Worthington, MN, and Ruby Begonia, Cuero, TX. Also included are a grand parade, live entertainment, free pancake breakfast and family activities. Est attendance: 15,000. For info: King Turkey Days, Inc, 1121 Third Ave, Worthington, MN 56187. Phone: (800) 279-2919 or (507) 372-2919. Fax: (507) 372-2827. E-mail: wcofc@frontiernet.net.

"MANNIX" TV PREMIERE: ANNIVERSARY. Sept 16, 1967. Mike Connors starred as Joe Mannix, a Los Angeles private investigator working for the computer organization Intertect, in this long-running CBS crime series. Joseph Campanella played his boss, Lou Wickersham, during the first season. The show then changed format with Mannix setting up his own agency. The new cast members were Gail Fisher as Peggy Fair, his secretary, Robert Reed as Lieutenant Adam Tobias and Ward Wood as Lieutenant Art Malcolm.

MAYFLOWER DAY: ANNIVERSARY. Sept 16, 1620. Anniversary of the departure of the *Mayflower* from Plymouth, England, with 102 passengers and a small crew. Vicious storms were encountered en route, which caused serious doubt about the wisdom of continuing, but the ship reached Provincetown, MA, Nov 21, and discharged the Pilgrims at Plymouth, MA, Dec 26, 1620.

MEXICO: INDEPENDENCE DAY. Sept 16. National Day. The official celebration begins at 11 PM, Sept 15 and continues through Sept 16. On the night of the 15th, the president of Mexico steps onto the balcony of the National Palace at Mexico City and voices the same "El Grito" (Cry for Freedom) that Father Hidalgo gave on the night of Sept 15, 1810, that began Mexico's rebellion from Spain.

MUSEUM OF CONTEMPORARY ART STUDIO TOUR. Sept 16–17. Fort Collins, CO., 6th annual. The MOCA Studio

Tour is a public tour of artists' private studios. Each year the Museum of Contemporary Art organizes more than 50 artists in the Fort Collins/Loveland area to participate in the tour. During the tour artists sell artwork and demonstrate their art techniques at their private studios. For info: Jeanne Shoaff, 201 South College Ave, Fort Collins, CO 80524. Phone: (970) 482-2787. E-mail: info@fcmoca.org. Web: www.fcmoca.org.

OLD IRONSIDES SAVED BY POEM: ANNIVERSARY. Sept 16, 1830. Alarmed by a newspaper report that Congress was to have the USS *Constitution* (popularly known as "Old Ironsides") sent to a scrap yard, law student Oliver Wendell Holmes dashed off a poem in protest. The poem began "Ay, tear her tattered ensign down!/Long has it waved on high,/And many an eye has danced to see/That banner in the sky." "Old Ironsides," published anonymously this day in the *Boston Daily Advertisor*, was to stir up national outrage as newspaper after newspaper reprinted it. Congress instead appropriated money for the frigate's reconstruction, and Old Ironsides still floats today. (Some historians think that Holmes never actually saw the ship he saved.) See also: "Old Ironsides Launched: Anniversary" (Oct 21).

"OWEN MARSHALL: COUNSELOR AT LAW" TV PREMIERE: 35th ANNIVERSARY. Sept 16, 1971. "Owen Marshall" was an hour-long ABC drama with Arthur Hill as the title character, a widowed attorney in Santa Barbara. Lee Majors, Reni Santoni and David Soul played his associates. Also featured were Joan Darling as Marshall's secretary and Christine Matchett as his daughter.

PALESTINIAN MASSACRE: ANNIVERSARY. Sept 16, 1982. Christian militiamen (the Phalangists) entered Sabra and Shatila, two Palestinian refugee camps in West Beirut. They began open shooting and by Sept 18 hundreds of Palestinians, including elderly men, women and children, were dead. Phalangists had demanded blood of Palestinians since the assassination of their president, Bashir Gemayel, on Sept 14. Survivors of the massacre said they had not seen Israeli forces inside the camp; however, they claimed Israelis sealed off boundaries to the camps and allowed Christian militiamen to enter.

PANIZZI, ANTHONY: BIRTH ANNIVERSARY. Sept 16, 1797. Sir Anthony Panizzi, the only librarian ever hanged in effigy, was born Antonio Genesio Maria Panizzi at Brescello, Italy. As a young man he joined a forbidden Italian patriotic society that advocated the overthrow of the oppressive Austrians who then controlled most of northern Italy. Tried in absentia by an Austrian court in 1820, he was sentenced to death and all his property was confiscated. He fled to England in 1823, learned the language and by 1831 was employed in the British Museum where, in 1856, he was named principal librarian. Later described as the "prince of librarians," Panizzi died at London, England, Apr 8, 1879.

PAPUA NEW GUINEA: INDEPENDENCE DAY. Sept 16. National holiday. Commemorates independence from Australian administration in 1975.

PARKMAN, FRANCIS: BIRTH ANNIVERSARY. Sept 16, 1823. American historian, author of *The Oregon Trail*, was born at Boston, MA, and died there Nov 8, 1893.

PEDDLER'S VILLAGE SCARECROW FESTIVAL. Sept 16–17. Peddler's Village, Lahaska, PA. Weekend festival includes scarecrow making, pumpkin-painting workshops, musical entertainment and scarecrow competition display. Free admission and free live entertainment, charge for workshops. Est attendance: 16,000. For info: Peddler's Village, Routes 202 & 263, Lahaska, PA 18931. Phone: (215) 794-4000. Fax: (215) 794-4001. Web: www.peddlersvillage.com.

ROAD CHURCH COUNTRY FAIR. Sept 16. Road Congregational Church, Pequot Trail, Stonington, CT. White elephants, bake table, harvest table, crafts and children's midway. Famous Barnes's Chowder Luncheon at noon (served in Civil War kettles). 10 AM–3 PM. Est attendance: 300. For info: Libby Kennedy, 21 Roosevelt Ave, Mystic, CT 06355. Phone: (860) 536-1514. E-mail: roadchurch@juno.com. Web: www.roadchurch.org.

SANDY SPRINGS FESTIVAL. Sept 16–17. Sandy Springs Historic Site, Atlanta, GA. Now in its 21st year, the Sandy Springs Festival has grown from a small, picnic-style gathering to an event drawing more than 20,000. This neighborhood event welcomes new families and friends. Celebrating community and tradition, there is something for everyone. Annually, the third weekend of September. Est attendance: 20,000. For info: Megan Webb, Sandy Springs Festival, 135 Hilderbrand Dr, Atlanta, GA 30328. Phone: (404) 851-1328. Fax: (404) 851-9807. E-mail: info@sandysprings festival.com. Web: www.sandyspringsfestival.com.

"SKY KING" TV PREMIERE: 55th ANNIVERSARY. Sept 16, 1951. This half-hour children's adventure series began on radio in 1947. Kirby Grant starred as Schuyler J. (Sky) King, owner of the Flying Crown Ranch, who used his plane, *The Song-bird*, to help victims and capture criminals. To help him was a cast that included Gloria Winters as his niece, Penny; Ron Hagerthy as his nephew, Clipper; Ewing Mitchell as the sheriff, Mitch; Norman Ollstead as Bob Carey and Gary Hunley as Mickey.

TORQUEMADA, TOMAS DE: DEATH ANNIVERSARY. Sept 16, 1498. One of history's most malevolent persons, feared and hated by millions. As Inquisitor-General of Spain, he ordered burning at the stake for more than 10,000 persons and burning in effigy for another 7,000 (according to 18th-century estimates). Torquemada persuaded Ferdinand and Isabella to rid Spain of the Jews. More than a million families were driven from the country and Spain suffered a commercial decline from which it never recovered. Torquemada was born at Valladolid, Spain, in 1420 (exact date unknown) and died at Avila, Spain.

TRAIL OF COURAGE LIVING-HISTORY FESTIVAL. Sept 16–17. Rochester, IN. Portrayal of life in frontier Indiana when it was Indian territory. Historic skits, two stages with music and dancing, historic encampments for Revolutionary War, French and Indian War, Voyageurs, Western Fur Trade and Plains Indians; re-created 1832 Chippeway Village, also Woodland Indian Village, pioneer foods and crafts, muzzle-loading and tomahawk contests, canoe rides. Museum, round barn and Living History Village on grounds. Special honored Potawatomi family from Indiana's history each year. Est attendance: 18,000. For info: Fulton County Historical Society, 37 E 375N, Rochester, IN 46975. Phone: (574) 223-4436. E-mail: fchs@rtcol.com. Web: www.icss.net/~fchs.

TRAIL OF TEARS COMMEMORATION AND MOTOR-CYCLE RIDE. Sept 16. Waterloo, AL. A day to gather and remember the tragic Trail of Tears when Native Americans were removed from their homes in the 1830s and forced to walk a trail to the West. Arts and crafts, museum exhibits and great entertainment. An organized motorcycle ride begins at Chattanooga the same morning and arrives in Waterloo for afternoon activities. Est attendance: 100,000. For info: Debbie Wilson, Florence/Lauderdale Tourism, One Hightower Place, Florence, AL 35630. Phone: (256) 740-4141 or (888) FLO-TOUR. Fax: (256) 740-4142. E-mail: dwilson@flo-tour.org. Web: www.flo-tour.org.

UNITED NATIONS: INTERNATIONAL DAY FOR THE PRESERVATION OF THE OZONE LAYER. Sept 16. On Dec 19, 1994, the General Assembly proclaimed this day to commemorate the date in 1987 on which Montreal Protocol on Substances that Deplete the Ozone Layer was signed (Res 49/114). States are invited to devote the Day to promote, at the national level, activities in accordance with the objectives of the Protocol. The ozone layer filters sunlight and prevents the adverse effects of ultraviolet radiation from reaching the Earth's surface, thereby preserving life on the planet. For info: United Nations, Dept of Public Info, Public Inquiries Unit, Rm GA-57, New York, NY 10017. Phone: (212) 963-4475. E-mail: inquiries@un.org. Web: www.un.org.

USGA SENIOR AMATEUR (GOLF) CHAMPIONSHIP. Sept 16–21. Victoria National Golf Club, Newburgh, IN. For info: US Golf Assn, Golf House, PO Box 708, Championship Dept, Far Hills, NJ 07931. Phone: (908) 234-2300. Fax: (908) 234-9687. E-mail: usga@usga.org. Web: www.usga.org.

WIFE APPRECIATION DAY. Sept 16. Husbands, show your wives how much you love and appreciate them. Communicate the difference your wife makes in your life. Annually, the third Saturday in September. For info: Brooke Espinoza. E-mail: kept bythepowerofgod@yahoo.com.

WINGS 'N' WATER FESTIVAL. Sept 16–17. Wetlands Institute, Stone Harbor, NJ. Coastal arts celebration of the environment throughout seaside towns of Stone Harbor and Avalon. 24th annual award-winning festival features Wildlife, Duck Stamp, Maritime & Landscape art. Plus bird and fish carvings, decoys, photography, crafts, quilts, music, retriever demos, live animals, boat cruises, kayaking, seafood and more. Est attendance: 5,000. For info: Nancy Morrow, Wetlands Institute, 1075 Stone Harbor Blvd, Stone Harbor, NJ 08247-1424. Phone: (609) 368-1211. Fax: (609) 368-3871. Web: www.wetlandsinstitute.org.

BIRTHDAYS TODAY

Marc Anthony, 37, singer, actor (*Bringing Out the Dead*), born New York, NY, Sept 16, 1969.

Lauren Bacall, 82, actress (*Applause, Woman of the Year, Key Largo*), born Betty Joan Perske at New York, NY, Sept 16, 1924.

Elgin Gay Baylor, 72, Hall of Fame basketball player, former coach, born Washington, DC, Sept 16, 1934.

Ed Begley, Jr, 57, actor ("St. Elsewhere"), born Los Angeles, CA, Sept 16, 1949.

Alexis Bledel, 24, actress ("Gilmore Girls"), born Houston, TX, Sept 16, 1982.

David Copperfield, 50, illusionist, born David Kotkin at Metuchen, NJ, Sept 16, 1956.

Peter Falk, 79, actor (*The Great Race*, "Columbo"), born New York, NY, Sept 16, 1927.

Anne Francis, 74, actress (*Bad Day at Black Rock, Blackboard Jungle, Forbidden Planet*), born Ossining, NY, Sept 16, 1932.

Henry Louis Gates, Jr, 56, professor of African American studies at Harvard, editor of the *Norton Anthology of African American Literature*, born Keyser, WV, Sept 16, 1950.

Orel Leonard Hershiser IV, 48, former baseball player, born Buffalo, NY, Sept 16, 1958.

B.B. King, 81, singer ("Rock Me Baby," "The Thrill Is Gone"), born Itta Bena, MS, Sept 16, 1925.

Richard Marx, 43, singer, born Chicago, IL, Sept 16, 1963.

Mark McEwen, 52, weatherman, music editor, born San Antonio, TX, Sept 16, 1954.

Janis Paige, 83, singer, actress (stage: *The Pajama Game, Silk Stockings*), born Tacoma, WA, Sept 16, 1923.

Amy Poehler, 35, actress, comedienne ("Saturday Night Live," "Upright Citizen's Brigade"), born Burlington, MA, Sept 16, 1971.

Tim Raines, 47, former baseball player, born Sanford, FL, Sept 16, 1959.

Mickey Rourke, 50, actor (*9 ½ Weeks, Bar Fly*), born Schenectady, NY, Sept 16, 1956.

Susan Ruttan, 56, actress ("LA Law"), born Oregon City, OR, Sept 16, 1950.

Molly Shannon, 42, actress ("Saturday Night Live"), born Shaker Heights, OH, Sept 16, 1964.

Jennifer Tilly, 45, actress (*Johnny Be Good, Made in America*), born Los Angeles, CA, Sept 16, 1961.

Robin R. Yount, 51, Hall of Fame baseball player, born Danville, IL, Sept 16, 1955.

September 2006

S	M	T	W	T	F	S
					1	2
3	4	5	6	7	8	9
10	11	12	13	14	15	16
17	18	19	20	21	22	23
24	25	26	27	28	29	30

SEPTEMBER 17 — SUNDAY
Day 260 — 105 Remaining

ANGOLA: DAY OF THE NATIONAL HERO. Sept 17. National holiday.

ARTS/QUINCY RIVERFEST. Sept 17. Quincy, IL. Celebration of the arts and the Mississippi River in the riverfront parks. Fine arts and crafts and a children's area featuring hands-on activities and performances. Annually, the third Sunday in September. Est attendance: 5,000. For info: Quincy Society of Fine Arts, 300 Civic Center Plaza, Ste 244, Quincy, IL 62301-4162. Phone: (217) 222-3432. Fax: (217) 228-2787. E-mail: art@artsqcy.org. Web: www.artsqcy.org.

BATTLE OF ANTIETAM: ANNIVERSARY. Sept 17, 1862. This date has been called America's bloodiest day in recognition of the high casualties suffered in the Civil War battle between General Robert E. Lee's Confederate forces and General George McClellan's Union army. Estimates vary, but more than 25,000 Union and Confederate soldiers were killed or wounded in this battle on the banks of the Potomac River at Maryland.

"BEWITCHED" TV PREMIERE: ANNIVERSARY. Sept 17, 1964. This sitcom centered around blonde-haired witch Samantha Stephens (Elizabeth Montgomery). Although she promises not to use her witchcraft in her daily life, Samantha finds herself twitching her nose in many situations. Her husband, Darrin Stephens, was played by Dick York and Dick Sargent, and her daughter, Tabitha Stephens, was played by Erin and Diane Murphy. The last episode aired July 1, 1972. Other cast members included Agnes Moorehead, David White, Alice Ghostley, Bernard Fox and Paul Lynde.

BOTTLED WATER WEEK. Sept 17–23. An education effort designed to increase awareness and appreciation of the epicurean and cultural qualities that characterize fine bottled waters. Annually, the third week in September. For info: Michael Mascha, FineWaters Media LLC, 6244 Damask Ave, Los Angeles, CA 90056. Phone/fax: (323) 295-5750. E-mail: michael@finewaters.com. Web: www.finewaters.com.

BUILD A BETTER IMAGE WEEK. Sept 17–23. In order to be a success, you need to look like one. This week is set aside for people to evaluate their professional image and take the steps necessary to improve on it. For "10 Steps to a Better Image" tip sheet, send #10 SASE. Annually, the third full week of September. For info: Marlys K. Arnold, ImageSpecialist, PO Box 901808, Kansas City, MO 64190-1808. Phone: (816) 746-7888. E-mail: marnold@imagespecialist.com. Web: www.imagespecialist.com.

BURGER, WARREN E.: BIRTH ANNIVERSARY. Sept 17, 1907. Former Chief Justice of the US Supreme Court, Warren E. Burger was born at St. Paul, MN. A conservative on criminal matters, but a progressive on social issues, he had the longest tenure (1969–86) of any chief justice in the 20th century. Appointed by President Nixon, he voted in the majority on *Roe v Wade* (1973), which upheld a woman's right to an abortion, and on *US v Nixon* (1974), which forced Nixon to surrender audiotapes to the Watergate special prosecutor. He died June 25, 1995, at Washington, DC.

CHRISTIAN LEADERSHIP WEEK INTERNATIONAL. Sept 17–23. Nowhere is exemplary leadership expected more than in Christian organizations, whether the church or parachurch. This event is dedicated to developing Christian leaders in all areas of life and to establishing an example of great and morally good leadership for both secular and faith-based organizations. For info: DiFrances & Assoc, LLC, 208 E Oak Crest Dr, Ste 200, Wales, WI 53183-9700. Phone: (262) 968-9850. Fax: (262) 968-9854. E-mail: christianleadership@difrances.com. Web: www.difrances.com/christianleadershipweek.

★**CITIZENSHIP DAY.** Sept 17. Presidential Proclamation always issued for Sept 17 at request (PL82–261 of Feb 29, 1952). Customarily issued as "Citizenship Day and Constitution Week." Replaces Constitution Day.

CONNOLLY, MAUREEN: BIRTH ANNIVERSARY. Sept 17, 1934. Maureen ("Little Mo") Catherine Connolly Brinker, tennis player born at San Diego, CA. Connolly became the second-youngest woman to win the US National championship at Forest Hills, NY, when she captured that title in 1951. She repeated in 1952 and won Wimbledon as well. In 1953 she became the first woman to win the Grand Slam, taking the US, French, Australian and Wimbledon championships. After winning a second straight French title and a third straight Wimbledon, she suffered a crushed leg in a horseback riding accident and never competed again. Died at Dallas, TX, June 21, 1969.

CONSTITUTION COMMEMORATION DAY IN ARIZONA. Sept 17. Arizona. This state holiday commemorates the signing of the US Constitution on Sept 17, 1787.

CONSTITUTION OF THE US: ANNIVERSARY. Sept 17, 1787. Delegations from 12 states (Rhode Island did not send a delegate) at the Constitutional Convention at Philadelphia, PA, voted unanimously to approve the proposed document. Thirty-nine of the 42 delegates present signed it and the Convention adjourned, after drafting a letter of transmittal to the Congress. The proposed constitution stipulated that it would take effect when ratified by nine states. This day is a legal holiday in Florida.

★**CONSTITUTION WEEK.** Sept 17–23. Presidential Proclamation always issued for the period of Sept 17–23 each year since 1955 (PL84–915 of Aug 2, 1956).

FOSTER, ANDREW (RUBE): BIRTH ANNIVERSARY. Sept 17, 1879. Rube Foster's efforts in baseball earned him the title of "The Father of Negro Baseball." He was a manager and star pitcher, pitching 51 victories in one year. In 1919, he called a meeting of black baseball owners and organized the first black baseball league, the Negro National League. He served as its president until his death in 1930. Foster was born at Calvert, TX, the son of a minister. He died Dec 9, 1930, at Kankakee, IL.

FOUNDER'S DAY CORN ROAST. Sept 17. Pacific University, Forest Grove, OR. 1–5 PM. Mountain men, interactive pioneer displays, native and other entertainment, buffalo burgers, family activities and lots of CORN!!! Est attendance: 2,000. For info: Forest Grove Chamber of Commerce, 2417 Pacific Ave, Forest Grove, OR 97116. Phone: (503) 357-3006. Fax: (503) 357-2367. E-mail: info@fgchamber.org. Web: www.fgchamber.org.

"THE FUGITIVE" TV PREMIERE: ANNIVERSARY. Sept 17, 1963. A nail-biting adventure series on ABC. Dr. Richard Kimble (David Janssen) was wrongly convicted and sentenced to death for his wife's murder, but escaped from his captors in a train wreck. This popular program aired for four years detailing Kimble's search for the one-armed man (Bill Raisch) who had killed his wife, Helen (Diane Brewster). In the meantime Kimble himself was being pursued by Lieutenant Philip Gerard (Barry Morse). The final episode aired Aug 29, 1967, and featured Kimble extracting a confession from the one-armed man as they struggled from the heights of a water tower in a deserted amusement park. That single episode was the highest-rated show ever broadcast until 1976. The TV series generated a hit movie in 1993 with Harrison Ford as Kimble and Oscar-winner Tommy Lee Jones as Gerard.

HENDRICKS, THOMAS ANDREWS: BIRTH ANNIVERSARY. Sept 17, 1819. Twenty-first vice president of the US (1885) born at Muskingum County, OH. Died at Indianapolis, IN, Nov 25, 1885.

HERZOG, CHAIM: BIRTH ANNIVERSARY. Sept 17, 1918. President of Israel, an ex-general and chief delegate to the UN, author, lawyer, born at Belfast, Northern Ireland. He was a British army officer in World War II. Died at Tel Aviv, Israel, Apr 17, 1997.

"HOME IMPROVEMENT" TV PREMIERE: 15th ANNIVERSARY. Sept 17, 1991. This comedy was a TV program about a TV program. Tim Taylor, played by Tim Allen, was host of the popular fix-it show "Tool Time." His wife Jill, played by Patricia Richardson, was a housewife going back to school to get a degree in psychology. The couple's three sons were played by Zachery Ty Bryan, Jonathan Taylor Thomas and Taran Noah Smith. Other cast members included Richard Karn as Tim's TV assistant, and Earl Hindman, Debbe Dunning and Pamela Anderson. The last episode aired May 25, 1999.

INTERNATIONAL DAY OF PRAYER AND ACTION FOR HUMAN HABITAT. Sept 17. This day is set aside to encourage churches to pray for those in need of shelter and guidance in what God would have them do to help eliminate poverty housing. Annually, the third Sunday in September (which is also the end of Building on Faith Week). For info: Habitat for Humanity Intl, 121 Habitat St, Americus, GA 31709-3498. Phone: (800) HAB-ITAT or (229) 924-6935. E-mail: publicinfo@hfhi.org. Web: www.habitat.org.

MacNELLY, JEFF: BIRTH ANNIVERSARY. Sept 17, 1947. Pulitzer prize–winning editorial cartoonist, comic strip cartoonist ("Shoe"), born at New York, NY. Died June 9, 2000, at Baltimore, MD.

"M*A*S*H" TV PREMIERE: ANNIVERSARY. Sept 17, 1972. This popular CBS series was based on the 1970 Robert Altman movie and a book by Richard Hooker. Set during the Korean War, the show aired for 11 years (lasting longer than the war). It followed the lives of doctors and nurses on the war front with both humor and pathos. The cast included: Alan Alda as Captain Benjamin Franklin "Hawkeye" Pierce, Wayne Rogers as Captain John "Trapper John" McIntyre, McLean Stevenson as Lieutenant Colonel Henry Blake, Loretta Swit as Major Margaret "Hot Lips" Houlihan, Larry Linville as Major Frank Burns, Gary Burghoff as Corporal Walter "Radar" O'Reilly, William Christopher as Father Francis Mulcahy, Jamie Farr as Corporal Max Klinger, Harry Morgan as Colonel Sherman Potter and Mike Farrell as Captain B.J. Hunnicut. The show won numerous awards during its run. Its final episode, "Goodbye, Farewell and Amen" was the highest-rated program of all time, topping the "Who Shot J.R.?" revelation on "Dallas." See also: "M*A*S*H: The Final Episode: Anniversary" (Feb 28). The show generated two spin-offs: "Trapper John, MD" and "After M*A*S*H."

"MISSION: IMPOSSIBLE" TV PREMIERE: 40th ANNIVERSARY. Sept 17, 1966. This action-adventure espionage series was produced by Bruce Geller, appearing on CBS for seven years. The premise of the show was simple: each week the IMF (Impossible Missions Force) leader would receive instructions on a super-secret mission to be carried out by the crew. Steven Hill played the first IMF leader, Dan Briggs. He was replaced by Peter Graves, who played Jim Phelps. The crew included: Martin Landau as Rollin Hand, master of disguise; Barbara Bain, real-life wife of Landau, as Cinnamon Carter; Greg Morris as Barney Collier, technical expert; Peter Lupus as Willy Armitage, tough guy; Leonard Nimoy as Hand's replacement,

Paris; Lesley Ann Warren as Dana Lambert; Sam Elliott as Doug; Lynda Day George as Lisa Casey and Barbara Anderson as Mimi Davis. The show was remade for ABC in 1988; it lasted two seasons.

NATIONAL CLEAN HANDS WEEK. Sept 17–23. Established by the Clean Hands Coalition, a unified alliance of public and private partners, working together to create and support coordinated, sustained initiatives to significantly improve health and save lives through clean hands. Activities will be held nationwide to raise awareness about the importance of good hand hygiene. Annually, the third full week in September. For info: E-mail: cleanhandscoalition@wiu.edu. Web: www.cleanhandscoalition.org.

NATIONAL CONSTITUTION CENTER CONSTITUTION WEEK. Sept 17–23. To celebrate and commemorate the signing of the US Constitution Sept 17, 1787. The National Constitution Center sponsors special events and activities. Annually, Sept 17–23. Est attendance: 150,000. For info: Natl Constitution Center, 525 Arch St, Independence Mall, Philadelphia, PA 19106. Phone: (215) 409-6600. Web: www.constitutioncenter.org.

★**NATIONAL FARM AND RANCH SAFETY AND HEALTH WEEK.** Sept 17–23. Presidential Proclamation issued since 1982 for the third week in September. Previously, from 1944, for one of the last two weeks in July.

NATIONAL FARM ANIMALS AWARENESS WEEK. Sept 17–23. Because the world has become more urban and industrialized, millions of people literally have never had any contact with farm animals. What they know about these animals comes from dubious sources: storybooks and advertising campaigns that foster misconceptions about the nature of these animals and how they are raised. The purpose of this week is to dispel many of these inaccuracies, and to help educate the public about what farm animals are really like. The Humane Society of the United States believes that once people understand the complex and sensitive nature of these animals, they will insist that farm animals be treated humanely. They will show compassion for all animals, not just those we keep as companions. Annually, the third full week in September. For info: Miyun Park, The Humane Society of the US, Farm Animal Section, 2100 L St NW, Washington, DC 20037. Phone: (301) 548-7706. E-mail: mpark@hsus.org. Web: www.hsus.org.

NATIONAL FOOTBALL LEAGUE FORMED: ANNIVERSARY. Sept 17, 1920. The National Football League was formed at Canton, OH.

★**NATIONAL HISTORICALLY BLACK COLLEGES AND UNIVERSITIES WEEK.** Sept 17–23 (tentative).

NATIONAL LOVE YOUR FILES WEEK. Sept 17–23. A good filing system can be a powerful asset. Filing gets a bad rap because people do it the hard way. If a filing system is set up correctly, it's easy to maintain and a pleasure to use. Annually, the third full week in September. For info: Jan Jasper. Phone: (212) 465-7472. E-mail: jasper@janjasper.com. Web: www.janjasper.com.

September 2006	S	M	T	W	T	F	S
						1	2
	3	4	5	6	7	8	9
	10	11	12	13	14	15	16
	17	18	19	20	21	22	23
	24	25	26	27	28	29	30

NATIONAL REHABILITATION AWARENESS CELE-BRATION. Sept 17–23. The observance salutes the determination of the more than 50 million Americans with disabilities. It is a time to applaud the efforts of rehab professionals, provide a forum for education and offer an occasion to call upon our citizens to find new ways to fulfill needs that still exist. Annually, the third full week in Sept. For info: Natl Rehabilitation Awareness Foundation, PO Box 71, Scranton, PA 18501. Phone: (570) 341-4637 or (800) 943-6723. Fax: (570) 341-4331. Web: www.nraf-rehabnet.org.

NATIONAL SINGLES WEEK. Sept 17–23. To celebrate single life and to recognize singles and their contributions to society. For info: Rich Gosse, Chairman, American Singles, 205 Mark Twain Ave, San Rafael, CA 94903. Phone: (415) 479-3800. E-mail: rich@richgosse.com.

PROSTATE CANCER AWARENESS WEEK. Sept 17–23. Free or low-cost prostate cancer screenings for all men over the age of 40 and men in high-risk groups such as African American men and Hispanics over age 35. Annually, the third week in September. For info: Prostate Cancer Education Council, 5299 DTC Blvd, Ste 345, Greenwood Village, CO 80111. Phone: (303) 316-4685. Web: www.pcaw.com.

SELFRIDGE, THOMAS E.: DEATH ANNIVERSARY. Sept 17, 1908. Lieutenant Thomas E. Selfridge, 26-year-old passenger in 740-lb biplane piloted by Orville Wright, was killed when, after four minutes in the air, the plane fell from a height of 75 feet. Nearly 2,000 spectators witnessed the crash at Fort Myer, VA. The plane was being tested for possible military use by the Army Signal Corps. Orville Wright was seriously injured in the crash. Selfridge Air Force Base, MI, was named after the young lieutenant, a West Point graduate, who was the first fatality of powered airplane travel.

SHEEP HERDING WITH BORDER COLLIES. Sept 17. Billings Farm and Museum, Woodstock, VT. This daylong event focuses on the many aspects of wool production, including sheep herding, as well as many hands-on activities for all ages to enjoy. These activities include carding wool, drop spindle spinning, weaving, knitting and rug hooking. Border collie demonstrations will show how these natural shepherds efficiently round up sheep, drive them from one area to another and corral them. Est attendance: 1,000. For info: Billings Farm & Museum, Rte 12 North, Woodstock, VT 05091. Phone: (802) 457-2355. Fax: (802) 457-4663. E-mail: billings.farm@valley.net. Web: www.billingsfarm.org.

SPACE MILESTONE: *PEGASUS 1* **(US).** Sept 17, 1978. 23,000-pound research satellite broke up over Africa and fell to Earth. Major pieces are believed to have fallen into Atlantic Ocean off the coast of Angola. The satellite had been orbiting Earth for more than 13 years since being launched Feb 16, 1965.

TOLKIEN WEEK. Sept 17–23. To promote appreciation and enjoyment of the works of J.R.R. Tolkien. Annually, the week that includes Hobbit Day (Sept 22). For info: Amalie Helms, American Tolkien Society, PO Box 7871, Flint, MI 48507-0871. E-mail: americantolkiensociety@yahoo.com.

VFW LADIES AUXILIARY ORGANIZED: ANNIVER-SARY. Sept 17, 1914. This organization is loyal to the issues and actions affecting America's heroes. Its members offer assistance in addition to supporting veterans' issues in Congress. Part of the organization's mission, according to its charter, is "to assist the Posts and members thereof . . . to foster true patriotism; and to preserve and defend the United States from all her enemies, whomsoever." For info: Veterans of Foreign Wars of the US, Women's Auxiliary, 406 W 34th St, Kansas City, MO 64111. Phone: (816) 561-8655. Fax: (816) 931-4753. Web: www.ladiesauxvfw.com.

VON STEUBEN, BARON FRIEDRICH: BIRTH ANNI-VERSARY. Sept 17, 1730. Prussian-born general who volunteered to serve in the American Revolution. He died at Remsen, NY, Nov 28, 1794. Von Steuben Day is commemorated on this day, on the following Saturday or on the 4th Sunday in September.

WILLIAMS, HANK, SR: BIRTH ANNIVERSARY. Sept 17, 1923. Hiram King Williams, country and western singer, born at Georgia, AL. He achieved his first hit with "Lovesick Blues," which brought him a contract with the Grand Ole Opry. His string of hits included "Cold, Cold Heart," "Honky Tonk Blues," "Jambalaya," "Your Cheatin' Heart," "Take These Chains from My Heart" and "I'll Never Get Out of This World Alive," which was released prior to his death Jan 1, 1953, at Oak Hill, VA.

WOMEN'S FRIENDSHIP DAY. Sept 17. Every woman has special friends she can't live without; those women to whom she tells everything, friends who will always listen and who know just what to say. Women's Friendship Day provides the perfect opportunity for women to acknowledge the special women in their lives. Annually, the third Sunday in September. For info: Kappa Delta Sorority, 3205 Players Ln, Memphis, TN 38125. Phone: (901) 748-1897. Fax: (901) 748-0949. E-mail: commspec@kappadelta.org. Web: www.kappadelta.org.

BIRTHDAYS TODAY

Paul Benedict, 68, actor ("The Jeffersons," many stage roles), born Silver City, NM, Sept 17, 1938.

George Blanda, 79, Hall of Fame football player, born Youngwood, PA, Sept 17, 1927.

Mark Brunell, 36, football player, born Los Angeles, CA, Sept 17, 1970.

Kyle Chandler, 41, actor ("Early Edition," "Homefront"), born Buffalo, NY, Sept 17, 1965.

Charles Grassley, 73, US Senator (R, Iowa), born New Hartford, IA, Sept 17, 1933.

Philip D. (Phil) Jackson, 61, basketball coach, former player, born Deer Lodge, MT, Sept 17, 1945.

Dorothy Loudon, 73, actress, singer ("The Garry Moore Show"), born Boston, MA, Sept 17, 1933.

Cassandra Peterson, 55, actress (movie hostess Elvira), born Manhattan, KS, Sept 17, 1951.

Rita Rudner, 50, comedienne, actress (*Peter's Friends*), born Miami, FL, Sept 17, 1956.

David H. Souter, 67, Associate Justice of the US Supreme Court, born Melrose, MA, Sept 17, 1939.

Rasheed Wallace, 32, basketball player, born Philadelphia, PA, Sept 17, 1974.

SEPTEMBER 18 — MONDAY
Day 261 — 104 Remaining

"THE ADDAMS FAMILY" TV PREMIERE: ANNIVER-SARY. Sept 18, 1964. Charles Addams's quirky *New Yorker* cartoon creations were brought to life in this ABC sitcom about a family full of oddballs. John Astin played lawyer Gomez Addams; with Carolyn Jones as his morbid wife Morticia; Ken Weatherwax as son Pugsley; Lisa Loring as daughter Wednesday; Jackie Coogan as Uncle Fester; Ted Cassidy as both Lurch, the butler, and Thing, a disembodied hand; Blossom Rock as Grandmama and Felix Silla as Cousin Itt. The last episode aired Sept 2, 1966. In 1991, *The Addams Family* movie was released, followed by a sequel. Both starred Anjelica Huston as Morticia, Raul Julia as Gomez, Christopher Lloyd as Uncle Fester, Jimmy Workman as Pugsley and Christina Ricci as Wednesday.

BALANCE AWARENESS WEEK. Sept 18–23. To develop public awareness of balance and disorders of balance system (vestibular disorders); to unite professionals, educators, support groups, medical facilities in a week-long effort to focus attention of the public and the media. Annually, the third full week in Sept. For info: Vestibular Disorders Assn, PO Box 13305, Portland, OR 97213. Phone: (800) 837-8428. Fax: (503) 229-8064. E-mail: veda@vestibular.org. Web: www.vestibular.org.

BRAZZI, ROSSANO: BIRTH ANNIVERSARY. Sept 18, 1916. Hollywood actor Rossano Brazzi was born at Bologna, Italy. A leading romantic figure in the 1950s and 1960s, he appeared in more than 200 films (*South Pacific, Summertime*). He died Dec 24, 1994, at Rome, Italy.

CHILE: INDEPENDENCE DAY. Sept 18. National holiday. Declared independence from Spain in 1810. Sept 19 is commemorated as Armed Forces Day in Chile.

COLUMBUS'S LAST VOYAGE TO THE NEW WORLD: ANNIVERSARY. Sept 18, 1502. Columbus landed at Costa Rica on his fourth and last voyage to the New World. He returned to Spain in 1504 and died there in 1506.

DeMILLE, AGNES: BIRTH ANNIVERSARY. Sept 18, 1905. Dancer, choreographer for ballet and Broadway shows such as *Oklahoma*, born at New York, NY. DeMille died at New York, NY, Oct 7, 1993.

DIEFENBAKER, JOHN: BIRTH ANNIVERSARY. Sept 18, 1895. Canadian lawyer, statesman and Conservative prime minister (1957–63). Born at Normandy Township, ON, Canada, he died at Ottawa, ON, Aug 16, 1979. Diefenbaker was a member of the Canadian Parliament from 1940 until his death.

GARBO, GRETA: BIRTH ANNIVERSARY. Sept 18, 1905. International film actress Greta Garbo was born Greta Lovisa Gustafsson at Stockholm, Sweden. A famous recluse, she retired temporarily, then permanently, from films after 19 years and 27 films, which spanned the late silent era and beginning of sound movies. Her on-screen roles were characterized by an image of a seductress involved in tragic love affairs. She died Apr 15, 1990, at New York, NY.

GEIGER, RAY: BIRTH ANNIVERSARY. Sept 18, 1910. Born at Irvington, NJ, Ray Geiger became editor of the *Farmer's Almanac* in 1934, shortly after graduating from Notre Dame. He remained editor until completing the 1994 edition in the fall of 1993 (when his son Peter became editor), the longest running almanac editor in American history. He died Apr 1, 1994, at Auburn, ME. The *Farmer's Almanac* offices are in Lewiston, ME.

"GET SMART" TV PREMIERE: ANNIVERSARY. Sept 18, 1965. A spy-thriller spoof appearing on both NBC (1965–69) and CBS (1969–70). Don Adams starred as bumbling CONTROL Agent 86, Maxwell Smart. His mission was to thwart the evildoings of the KAOS organization. Agent Smart was usually successful with the help of his friends: Barbara Feldon as Agent 99 (whom Smart eventually married), Edward Platt as The Chief, Robert Karvelas as Agent Larrabee, Dick Gautier as Hymie the Robot and David Ketchum as Agent 13.

HULL HOUSE OPENS: ANNIVERSARY. Sept 18, 1889. This settlement house was founded in Chicago by Jane Addams and Ellen Gates Starr. It soon became the heart of one of the country's most influential social reform movements, offering a mix of cultural and education programs to new immigrants. See also: "Addams, Jane: Birth Anniversary" (Sept 6).

IRON HORSE OUTRACED BY HORSE: ANNIVERSARY. Sept 18, 1830. In a widely celebrated race, the first locomotive built in America, the Tom Thumb, lost to a horse. Mechanical difficulties plagued the steam engine over the nine-mile course between Riley's Tavern and Baltimore, MD, and a boiler leak prevented the locomotive from finishing the race. In the early days of trains, engines were nicknamed "Iron Horses."

JOHNSON, SAMUEL: BIRTH ANNIVERSARY. Sept 18, 1709 (OS). English lexicographer and literary lion, creator of the first great dictionary of the English language (1755) and author of poems, novels and essays. Johnson was born at Lichfield, Staffordshire, England, and died at London, England, Dec 13, 1784. Johnson, master of the quip, stated, "Patriotism is the last refuge of a scoundrel."

"LOVE IS A MANY SPLENDORED THING" TV PREMIERE: ANNIVERSARY. Sept 18, 1967. A soap opera created by veteran writer Irna Phillips, airing on CBS for five years. It was based on the 1955 film starring William Holden and Jennifer Jones. Irna Phillips left the show after the network nixed interracial romance in favor of political storylines. David Birney, Bibi Besch and Donna Mills appeared on the show.

LUNCH PROWL WEEK. Sept 18–22. A week dedicated to teaching women how to use their lunch hour to find single men. This event introduces women to a new method of mate-searching that is based on the compatability of a man's profession with hers. Women will learn how to follow simple techniques to maximize their mate-searching efforts. For info: Nancy Fagan, MS. E-mail: AskDrRomance@aol.com. Web: www.ExpertDatingAdvice.com.

***THE NEW YORK TIMES* FIRST PUBLISHED: ANNIVERSARY.** Sept 18, 1851. The *Times* debuted as *The New-York Daily Times*. The name was changed to the current one in 1857.

PCOS AWARENESS DAY. Sept 18. National day of awareness for polycystic ovarian syndrome (PCOS). PCOS is the most common endocrine disorder of women of child-bearing age. Between 5–10% of all women suffer from PCOS, causing weight gain, infertility, acne, hair loss and other health issues. PCOS increases risk of heart disease, diabetes and cancer. Annually, the third Monday in September For info: Julie Callaway. Phone: (801) 231-5024. E-mail: julie@pcoscoach.com. Web: www.pcoscoach.com.

READ, GEORGE: BIRTH ANNIVERSARY. Sept 18, 1733. Lawyer and signer of the Declaration of Independence, born at Cecil County, MD. Died Sept 21, 1798, at New Castle, DE.

"SHIRLEY TEMPLE THEATRE" TV PREMIERE: ANNIVERSARY. Sept 18, 1960. An NBC children's anthology of specials appearing on Sundays, hosted by Shirley Temple. Reruns were broadcast on ABC on the following Mondays. "Beauty and the Beast," "Rumplestiltskin," "Rapunzel," "Mother Goose," "The Land of Oz" and "Babes in Toyland" were among the stories presented.

STORY, JOSEPH: BIRTH ANNIVERSARY. Sept 18, 1779. Associate justice of the US Supreme Court (1811–45) was born at Marblehead, MA. "It is astonishing," he wrote a few months before his death, "how easily men satisfy themselves that the Constitution is exactly what they wish it to be." Story died Sept 10, 1845, at Cambridge, MA, having served 33 years on the Supreme Court bench.

SUBSTITUTE TEACHER APPRECIATION WEEK. Sept 18–22. Although substitute teachers get no sick days or respect, they teach when the regular teacher cannot and continually adjust

September 2006	S	M	T	W	T	F	S
						1	2
	3	4	5	6	7	8	9
	10	11	12	13	14	15	16
	17	18	19	20	21	22	23
	24	25	26	27	28	29	30

to different classroom situations. Annually, the third week of September. For info: Dorothy Zjawin, Dir, 61 W Colfax Ave, Roselle Park, NJ 07204. Phone: (908) 241-6241.

US AIR FORCE ESTABLISHED: ANNIVERSARY. Sept 18, 1947. Although its heritage dates back to 1907 when the Army first established military aviation, the US Air Force became a separate military service on this date. Responsible for providing an Air Force that is capable, in conjunction with the other armed forces, of preserving the peace and security of the US, the department is separately organized under the Secretary of the Air Force and operates under the authority, direction and control of the Secretary of Defense.

US CAPITOL CORNERSTONE LAID: ANNIVERSARY. Sept 18, 1793. President George Washington laid the Capitol cornerstone at Washington, DC, in a Masonic ceremony. That event was the first and last recorded occasion at which the stone with its engraved silver plate was seen. In 1958, during the extension of the east front of the Capitol, an unsuccessful effort was made to find it.

US TAKES OUT ITS FIRST LOAN: ANNIVERSARY. Sept 18, 1789. The first loan taken out by the US was negotiated and secured by Alexander Hamilton on Feb 17, 1790. After beginning negotiations with the Bank of New York and the Bank of North America on Sept 18, 1789, Hamilton obtained the sum of $191,608.81 from the two banks in what became known as the Temporary Loan of 1789. The loan was obtained without authority of law and was used to pay the salaries of the president, senators, representatives and officers of the first Congress. Repayment was completed on June 8, 1790.

"WAGON TRAIN" TV PREMIERE: ANNIVERSARY. Sept 18, 1957. "Wagon Train" was a popular western on NBC and ABC, airing for eight years with its last telecast Sept 5, 1965. Each week travelers on a journey along the wagon trail from Missouri to California encountered new surroundings and interacted with different guest stars. Ward Bond played wagonmaster Major Seth Adams until his death in 1960. He was replaced by John McIntire as Chris Hale. Other regulars were: Robert Horton (scout Flint McCullough), Frank McGrath (cook Charlie Wooster), Terry Wilson (Bill Hawks), Denny (Scott) Miller (scout Duke Shannon), Michael Burns (Barnaby West) and Robert Fuller as scout Cooper.

WHITE WOMAN MADE AMERICAN INDIAN CHIEF: ANNIVERSARY. Sept 18, 1891. Harriet Maxwell Converse was made a chief of the Six Nations Tribe at the Tonawanda Reservation, NY. She was given the name Ga-is-wa-noh, which means "The Watcher." She had been adopted as a member of the Seneca tribe in 1884 in appreciation of her efforts on behalf of the tribe.

BIRTHDAYS TODAY

Lance Armstrong, 35, cyclist, national and world champion, two-time Olympian, seven-time winner of the Tour de France, born Plano, TX, Sept 18, 1971.

Frankie Avalon, 67, singer ("Venus"), actor (teen flicks with Annette Funicello), born Philadelphia, PA, Sept 18, 1939.

Robert F. Bennett, 73, US Senator (R, Utah), born Salt Lake City, UT, Sept 18, 1933.

Robert Blake, 68, actor ("Baretta," *In Cold Blood, Little Rascals*), born Michael Gubitosi at Nutley, NJ, Sept 18, 1938.

Scotty Bowman, 73, Hall of Fame hockey coach, born Montreal, QC, Canada, Sept 18, 1933.

James Gandolfini, 45, actor ("The Sopranos"), born Westwood, NJ, Sept 18, 1961.

Jada Pinkett Smith, 35, actress (*The Nutty Professor, Menace II Society*), born Baltimore, MD, Sept 18, 1971.

Ryne Dee Sandberg, 47, former baseball player, born Spokane, WA, Sept 18, 1959.

Aisha Tyler, 36, television host, actress ("Talk Soup," "24," "CSI"), born San Francisco, CA, Sept 18, 1970.

Jack Warden, 86, actor ("NYPD Blue," "Bad News Bears," "Crazy Like a Fox"), born Newark, NJ, Sept 18, 1920.

SEPTEMBER 19 — TUESDAY
Day 262 — 103 Remaining

BROUGHAM, HENRY PETER: BIRTH ANNIVERSARY. Sept 19, 1778. Scottish jurist and orator born at Edinburgh, Scotland. Died at Cannes, France, May 7, 1868. The Brougham carriage was named after him. "Education," he said, "makes a people easy to lead, but difficult to drive; easy to govern, but impossible to enslave."

CARROLL, CHARLES: BIRTH ANNIVERSARY. Sept 19, 1737 (OS). American Revolutionary leader and signer of the Declaration of Independence, born at Annapolis, MD. The last surviving signer of the Declaration, he died Nov 14, 1832, at Baltimore, MD.

"ER" TV PREMIERE: ANNIVERSARY. Sept 19, 1994. This medical drama takes place in the emergency room of the fictional County General Hospital in Chicago. Doctors and nurses care for life-and-death cases while experiencing their personal traumas as well. Cast has included Anthony Edwards, George Clooney, Sherry Stringfield, Noah Wyle, Laura Innes, Gloria Reuben, Eriq La Salle, Maura Tierney, Goran Visnjic and Alex Kingston. On May 8, 2003, the 200th episode aired.

"FLIPPER" TV PREMIERE: ANNIVERSARY. Sept 19, 1964. An adventure series starring Flipper, the intelligent, communicative and helpful dolphin. The human cast members included Brian Kelly as Chief Ranger Porter Ricks, Luke Halpin as his son Sandy, Tommy Norden as his son Bud and Ulla Strömstedt as biochemist Ulla Norstrand. The last telecast of this series was Sept 1, 1968. The series was briefly re-created under the same title in the '90s.

GOLDING, SIR WILLIAM: BIRTH ANNIVERSARY. Sept 19, 1911. Born at Columb Minor at Cornwall, England, this celebrated author was recognized for his contributions to literature with a Nobel Prize in 1983. His first and most popular novel was *Lord of the Flies*. He died June 19, 1993, near Truro, Cornwall.

"ICEMAN" MUMMY DISCOVERED: 15th ANNIVERSARY. Sept 19, 1991. At 10,531 feet in the Austrian-Italian Alps, two hikers discovered a 5,300-year-old frozen mummy from late Neolithic times. The man carried rough bow and arrows as well as a copper axe, and wore a grass cloak for warmth. His shoes were made from bearskin, deer hide and tree bark. He now rests as a frozen exhibit at the South Tyrol Museum of Archaeology at Bolzano, Italy. The "Iceman" was gently thawed in September 2000 in order for scientists to conduct valuable DNA analysis and determine his last meal.

INTERNATIONAL WOMEN'S ECOMMERCE DAY. Sept 19. This day will celebrate women around the globe and their economic impact and purchasing power. The schedule of events (subject to change) includes encouraging women around the world to make an online purchase today, sending information to the media on all continents, coordinating with more than 160 partnering organizations (made up of 100,000 members) to spread the word and culminating in a World Congress to be held in New York City on Sept 18–21. For info: Heidi Richards, Women's Ecommerce Association, Intl, 7100 Pembroke Rd, Miramar, FL 33023. Phone: (945) 981-5515. E-mail: heidi@wecai.org. Web: www.wecai.org.

JACKSON COUNTY APPLE FESTIVAL. Sept 19–23. Jackson County, OH. Mountains of apples and barrels of cider. Homemade apple butter, apple pies and candy apples. Est attendance: 225,000. For info: Jackson County Apple Festival, Inc, PO Box 8, Jackson, OH 45640-0008. Phone: (740) 286-1339. Web: www.jacksonapplefestival.com.

JAMESTOWN BURNED BY BACON'S REBELLION: ANNIVERSARY. Sept 19, 1676. In the Virginia colony every adult male could vote. When Charles II was restored to the English throne, he sought to exploit the colony to the fullest. Virginia Governor Sir William Berkeley, supporting the king, adopted new laws to facilitate these efforts including measures allowing only property holders to vote, raising taxes and raising the cost of shipping while lowering the price for tobacco. The resulting discontent exploded when the frontier of the colony was attacked by Indians and the governor refused to defend the settlers. Nathaniel Bacon, a colonist on the governor's council, was made leader for the frontier farmers, and his troops successfully defeated the Indians. Denounced by Berkeley as rebels, Bacon and his men occupied Jamestown, forcing the governor to call an election, the first in 15 years. The Berkeley laws were repealed and election and tax reforms were instituted. While Bacon and his troops were gone on a raiding party against the Indians, Berkeley again denounced them. They returned and attacked Berkeley's forces, defeating them and burning Jamestown on Sept 19, 1676. Berkeley fled and Bacon became ruler of Virginia. When he died suddenly a short time later, the rebellion collapsed. Berkeley returned to power and Bacon's followers were hunted down, some executed and their property confiscated. Berkeley was replaced the next year and peace was restored.

LUYTS, JAN: 350th BIRTH ANNIVERSARY. Sept 19, 1655. Dutch scholar, physicist, mathematician and astronomer, Jan Luyts was born at Hoorn in western Netherlands. Little remembered except for his books: *Astronomica Institutio . . .* (1689) and *Introductio ad Geographiam . . .* (1690).

"THE MARY TYLER MOORE SHOW" TV PREMIERE: ANNIVERSARY. Sept 19, 1970. This show—one of the most popular sitcoms of the '70s—combined good writing, an effective supporting cast and contemporary attitudes. The show centered around the two most important places in Mary Richards's (Mary Tyler Moore) life—the WJM-TV newsroom and her apartment at Minneapolis. At home she shared the ups and downs of life with her friend Rhoda Morgenstern (Valerie Harper) and the manager of her apartment building, Phyllis Lindstrom (Cloris Leachman). At work, as the associate producer (later producer) of "The Six O'Clock News," Mary struggled to function in a man's world. Figuring in her professional life were her irascible boss Lou Grant (Ed Asner), levelheaded and softhearted news writer Murray Slaughter (Gavin MacLeod) and narcissistic anchorman Ted Baxter (Ted Knight). In the last of 168 episodes (Mar 19, 1977), the unthinkable happened: everyone in the WJM newsroom except the inept Ted was fired.

MEXICO CITY EARTHQUAKE: ANNIVERSARY. Sept 19–20, 1985. Nearly 10,000 persons perished in the earthquakes (8.1 and 7.5 respectively, on the Richter scale) that devastated Mexico City. Damage to buildings was estimated at more than $1 billion, and 100,000 homes were destroyed or severely damaged.

NETHERLANDS: PRINSJESDAG. Sept 19. Official opening of parliament at The Hague. The queen of the Netherlands, by tradition, rides in a golden coach to the hall of knights for the annual opening of parliament. Annually, on the third Tuesday in September.

September 2006	S	M	T	W	T	F	S
						1	2
	3	4	5	6	7	8	9
	10	11	12	13	14	15	16
	17	18	19	20	21	22	23
	24	25	26	27	28	29	30

POWELL, LEWIS F., JR: BIRTH ANNIVERSARY. Sept 19, 1907. Former associate justice of the Supreme Court of the US, nominated by President Nixon Oct 21, 1971. (Took office Jan 7, 1972.) Justice Powell was born at Suffolk, VA. In 1987, he announced his retirement from the Court. He died Aug 25, 1998, at Richmond, VA.

ROYKO, MIKE: BIRTH ANNIVERSARY. Sept 19, 1932. Syndicated columnist to more than 600 newspapers nationwide, Pulitzer Prize–winner and author (*Boss, Slats Grobnick*). Born at Chicago, IL, he died there, Apr 29, 1997.

SAINT CHRISTOPHER (SAINT KITTS) AND NEVIS: INDEPENDENCE DAY: ANNIVERSARY. Sept 19. National holiday. Commemorates independence from Britain in 1983.

SAINT JANUARIUS (GENNARO): FEAST DAY. Sept 19. Fourth-century bishop of Benevento, martyred near Naples, Italy, whose relics in the Naples Cathedral are particularly famous because on his feast days the blood in a glass vial is said to liquefy in response to prayers of the faithful. In September 1979, the Associated Press reported that some 5,000 persons gathered at the cathedral at dawn, and that "the blood liquefied after 63 minutes of prayers." This phenomenon is said to occur also on the first Saturday in May.

TALK LIKE A PIRATE DAY. Sept 19. A day when people everywhere can swash their buckles and add a touch of larceny to their dialogue by talking like pirates: for example, "Arr, matey, it be a fine day." While it's inherently a guy thing, women have been known to enjoy the day because they have to be addressed as "me beauty." Arr! Annually, Sept 19. For info: John Baur. Phone: (541) 928-3513. Also: Mark Summers. Email: capnslappy@talklikeapirate.com. Web: www.talklikeapirate.com.

TITAN II MISSILE EXPLOSION: ANNIVERSARY. Sept 19, 1980. The third major accident involving America's most powerful single weapon occurred near Damascus, AR. The explosion, at 3 AM, came nearly 11 hours after a fire had started in the missile silo. The multimegaton nuclear warhead (a hydrogen bomb) reportedly was briefly airborne, but came to rest a few hundred feet away. One dead, 21 injured in accident. Previous major Titan Missile accidents: Aug 9, 1965, near Searcy, AR (53 dead); and Aug 24, 1978, near Rock, KS (2 dead, 29 injured).

UNITED NATIONS: OPENING DAY OF GENERAL ASSEMBLY. Sept 19. The 61st session. Annually, the third Tuesday in September. For info: United Nations, Dept of Public Info, New York, NY 10017. Web: www.un.org.

"THE VIRGINIAN" TV PREMIERE: ANNIVERSARY. Sept 19, 1962. TV's first 90-minute Western starred James Drury as the Virginian, a foreman trying to come to terms with the westward expansion of civilization. It was set on the Shiloh Ranch, in Wyoming. Key players included Doug McClure (with Drury, the only cast member to stay for the entire run), Lee J. Cobb, Roberta Shore, Pippa Scott, Gary Clarke, David Hartman and Tim Matheson. In the last season, the title was changed to "The Men from Shiloh," and Stewart Granger and Lee Majors joined the cast.

BIRTHDAYS TODAY

James Anthony (Jim) Abbott, 39, former baseball player, born Flint, MI, Sept 19, 1967.
Jimmy Fallon, 32, comedian, actor ("Saturday Night Live," *Fever Pitch*), born Brooklyn, NY, Sept 19, 1974.
Kevin Hooks, 48, actor, director ("The White Shadow," *Sounder*), born Philadelphia, PA, Sept 19, 1958.

Jeremy Irons, 58, actor (Oscar for *Reversal of Fortune; Lolita, Dead Ringers*), born Cowes, Isle of Wight, England, Sept 19, 1948.

Nick Johnson, 28, baseball player, born Sacramento, CA, Sept 19, 1978.

Joan Lunden, 55, broadcast journalist (former cohost of "Good Morning America"), born Sacramento, CA, Sept 19, 1951.

Randolph Mantooth, 61, actor ("Emergency"), born Sacramento, CA, Sept 19, 1945.

David McCallum, 73, actor ("The Man from U.N.C.L.E.," *The Great Escape*), born Glasgow, Scotland, Sept 19, 1933.

Joe Morgan, 63, broadcaster, Hall of Fame baseball player, born Bonham, TX, Sept 19, 1943.

Twiggy, 57, actress (*The Boy Friend, The Blues Brothers*), model, born Leslie Hornby at London, England, Sept 19, 1949.

Adam West, 78, actor ("Batman," "The Last Precinct"), born Walla Walla, WA, Sept 19, 1928 (some sources say 1929 or 1930).

Paul Williams, 66, singer, composer ("Love Boat" theme song), born Omaha, NE, Sept 19, 1940.

Trisha Yearwood, 42, singer, born Monticello, GA, Sept 19, 1964.

SEPTEMBER 20 — WEDNESDAY
Day 263 — 102 Remaining

BILLIE JEAN KING WINS THE "BATTLE OF THE SEXES": ANNIVERSARY. Sept 20, 1973. Billie Jean King defeated Bobby Riggs in the nationally televised "Battle of the Sexes" tennis match in three straight sets.

BLACK WALNUT FESTIVAL. Sept 20–23. Stockton, MO. 46th annual. Tours of the largest black walnut processing plant in the world. Also included are a parade, craft demonstrations, queen contest, carnival and musical entertainment. Est attendance: 30,000. For info: Stockton Area Chamber of Commerce, PO Box 410, Stockton, MO 65785. Phone: (417) 276-5213. E-mail: scofc@microcore.net. Web: www.stocktonmochamber.com.

"THE COSBY SHOW" TV PREMIERE: ANNIVERSARY. Sept 20, 1984. This Emmy Award–winning comedy set in New York City revolved around the members of the Huxtable family. Father Dr. Heathcliff Huxtable was played by Bill Cosby; his wife Clair, an attorney, was played by Phylicia Rashad. Their four daughters were played by Sabrina Le Beauf (Sondra), Lisa Bonet (Denise), Tempestt Bledsoe (Vanessa) and Keshia Knight Pulliam (Rudy); Malcolm-Jamal Warner played son Theo. By the end of the series in 1992, the two oldest daughters had finished college and were married. "A Different World" was a spin-off set at historically black Hillman College where Denise was a student.

EQUAL RIGHTS PARTY FOUNDING: ANNIVERSARY. Sept 20, 1884. The Equal Rights Party was formed at San Francisco, CA. Its candidate for president, nominated in convention, was Mrs Belva Lockwood. The vice presidential candidate was Marietta Stow.

FINANCIAL PANIC OF 1873: ANNIVERSARY. Sept 20, 1873. For the first time in its history, the New York Stock Exchange was forced to close because of a banking crisis. Although the worst of the panic and crisis was over within a week, the psychological effect on businessmen, investors and the nation at large was more lasting.

"THE LORETTA YOUNG SHOW" TV PREMIERE: ANNIVERSARY. Sept 20, 1953. NBC half-hour dramatic anthology series (initially titled "Letter to Loretta") hosted by and frequently starring Oscar-winning actress Loretta Young. At the beginning of each episode Young would swirl through a door in a spectacular gown. Young garnered two Emmys during the show's eight-year run. In 1972 it was reported that Young had been awarded $559,000 in a suit against NBC for syndicating reruns of the show without her permission. Young did not want them shown because her clothes and hairstyles in the shows were long out of date by the '70s.

MORTON, FERDINAND "JELLY ROLL": BIRTH ANNIVERSARY. Sept 20, 1885. American jazz pianist, composer and orchestra leader, was born at New Orleans, LA (some scholars believe in 1890). Morton, subject of a biography titled *Mr Jelly Roll* by Alan Lomax, died July 10, 1941, at Los Angeles, CA.

NATIONAL RESEARCH COUNCIL: FIRST MEETING: 90th ANNIVERSARY. Sept 20, 1916. Anniversary of first meeting of National Research Council, at New York, NY. Formed at request of President Woodrow Wilson for " . . . encouraging the investigation of natural phenomena . . . ." for American business and national security.

PETIT JEAN FALL ANTIQUE AUTO SWAP MEET. Sept 20–23. Petit Jean Mountain, Morrilton, AR. 9th annual antique auto swap meet, car corral, flea market and arts and crafts. Military vehicle show Friday and Saturday. More than 1,400 vendor spaces. Est attendance: 30,000. For info: Buddy Hoelzeman, Museum of Automobiles, 8 Jones Ln, Morrilton, AR 72110. Phone: (501) 727-5427. Fax: (501) 727-6482. E-mail: moa@ipa.net. Web: museumofautos.com.

"THE PHIL SILVERS SHOW" TV PREMIERE: ANNIVERSARY. Sept 20, 1955. This popular half-hour sitcom starred Phil Silvers as Sergeant Ernie Bilko, a scheming but good-natured con man whose schemes rarely worked out. Guest stars included Fred Gwynne, Margaret Hamilton, Dick Van Dyke and Alan Alda in his first major TV role.

ROCK OF CHICKAMAUGA: ANNIVERSARY. Sept 20, 1863. After disastrous moves by Union General William Starke Rosecrans, Confederate forces appeared to be carrying the day at the Battle of Chickamauga in Tennessee. With Rosecrans in flight to Chattanooga, Union General Henry Thomas and his men maintained their position and repeatedly turned back Southern attacks until they were reinforced. Thomas's actions saved the Union forces from a complete rout and earned him the nickname "Rock of Chickamauga." Rosecrans was relieved of his command.

SINCLAIR, UPTON (BEALL): BIRTH ANNIVERSARY. Sept 20, 1878. American novelist and politician born at Baltimore, MD. He worked for political and social reforms, and his best-known novel, *The Jungle*, prompted one of the nation's first pure food laws. Died at Bound Brook, NJ, Nov 25, 1968.

BIRTHDAYS TODAY

Arnold Jacob ("Red") Auerbach, 89, Hall of Fame basketball coach, born Brooklyn, NY, Sept 20, 1917.

Joyce Brothers, 78, psychologist, author, born New York, NY, Sept 20, 1928.

Donald A. Hall, 78, poet, author (*Lucy's Christmas, Ox Cart Man*), born New Haven, CT, Sept 20, 1928.

Kristen Johnston, 39, actress ("3rd Rock from the Sun"), born Washington, DC, Sept 20, 1967.

Guy Damien LaFleur, 55, Hall of Fame hockey player, born Thurso, QC, Canada, Sept 20, 1951.

Sophia Loren, 72, actress (*Black Orchid, Marriage Italian Style*, "Brief Encounter," Oscar for *Two Women*), born Sofia Scicoloni at Rome, Italy, Sept 20, 1934.

Anne Meara, 77, actress ("Fame"), comedienne (Stiller and Meara), born New York, NY, Sept 20, 1929.

SEPTEMBER 21 — THURSDAY

Day 264 — 101 Remaining

ARMENIA: INDEPENDENCE DAY. Sept 21. Public holiday. Commemorates independence from Soviet Union in 1991.

BARNESVILLE PUMPKIN FESTIVAL. Sept 21–24. Downtown Barnesville, OH. This 43rd annual festival features King Pumpkin contest, Queen Pageant, Giant Pumpkin Parade, classic car show, banjo & fiddle contest and more. Annually, the last full weekend of September. Est attendance: 100,000. For info: Tom Michelli, President, Barnesville Pumpkin Festival, Inc, PO Box 5, Barnesville, OH 43713. Phone: (740) 425-2593. Fax: (740) 425-1755. E-mail: bacc@1st.net.

BELIZE: INDEPENDENCE DAY. Sept 21. National holiday. Commemorates independence of the former British Honduras from Britain in 1981.

HOPKINSON, FRANCIS: BIRTH ANNIVERSARY. Sept 21, 1737. Signer of the Declaration of Independence. Born at Philadelphia, PA, he died there May 9, 1791.

HURRICANE HUGO HITS AMERICAN COAST: ANNIVERSARY. Sept 21, 1989. After ravaging the Virgin Islands, Hurricane Hugo hit the American coast at Charleston, SC. In its wake, Hugo left destruction totaling at least $8 billion.

INTERNATIONAL DAY OF PEACE. Sept 21. Annual worldwide concert and media event to celebrate the wonderful world we live in and to pause, calm down, be nice and plant a seed. Not-for-profit. Annually, Sept 21—on United Nations' International Day of Peace. For info: Paul Sladkus, 126 Fifth Ave, Ste 3D, New York, NY 10011. Phone: (212) 647-1212. Fax: (212) 647-1216. E-mail: goodnews@goodnewsbroadcast.com. Web: www.good newsbroadcast.com.

JONES, CHUCK: BIRTH ANNIVERSARY. Sept 21, 1912. Born at Spokane, WA, Chuck Jones worked as a child extra in Hollywood in the 1920s. After attending art school, he landed a job washing animation cels for famed Disney animator Ub Iwerks. He learned the craft, and by 1962 he headed his own unit at Warner Bros. Animation. He created the characters Road Runner and Wile E. Coyote, Marvin the Martian and Pepe le Pew. He worked on the development of Bugs Bunny, Elmer Fudd, Daffy Duck and Porky Pig, and also produced, directed and wrote the screenplay for the animated 1966 television classic "Dr. Seuss' How the Grinch Stole Christmas." He won several Academy Awards for his work, and his cartoon "What's Opera, Doc?" is in the National Film Registry. He died on Feb 22, 2002, at Corona del Mar, CA.

JOSEPH, CHIEF: DEATH ANNIVERSARY. Sept 21, 1904. Admirable Nez Percé chief, whose Indian name was In-Mut-Too-Yah-Lat-Lat, was born about 1840 at Wallowa Valley, Oregon Territory, and died on the Colville Reservation at Washington. Faced with war or resettlement to a reservation, Chief Joseph led a dramatic attempt to escape to Canada. After three months and more than 1,000 miles, he and his people were surrounded 40 miles from Canada and sent to a reservation at Oklahoma. Though the few survivors were later allowed to relocate to another reservation at Washington, they never regained their ancestral lands.

MALTA: INDEPENDENCE DAY. Sept 21. National Day. Commemorates independence from Britain in 1964.

"MONDAY NIGHT FOOTBALL" TV PREMIERE: ANNIVERSARY. Sept 21, 1970. Following the complete merger of the American Football League and the National Football League, ABC joined CBS and NBC in televising weekly games with the debut of "Monday Night Football." The show began as an experiment but soon became an institution. Announcers Howard Cosell, Keith Jackson and Don Meredith called the first game, a 31–21 victory by the Cleveland Browns over the New York Jets.

"NYPD BLUE" TV PREMIERE: ANNIVERSARY. Sept 21, 1993. This gritty New York City police drama has had a large and changing cast. The central characters were partners Detective Bobby Simone (who later died), played by Jimmy Smits, and Detective Andy Sipowicz, played by Dennis Franz. Other cast members have included Kim Delaney as Detective Diane Russell, James McDaniel as Lieutenant Arthur Fancy, Gordon Clapp as Detective Gregory Medavoy, Rick Schroder as Detective Danny Sorenson, Nicholas Turturro as Detective James Martinez, Mark-Paul Gosselaar as Detective John Clark and Esai Morales as Lieutenant Tony Rodriguez. The series ended in 2005.

"PERRY MASON" TV PREMIERE: ANNIVERSARY. Sept 21, 1957. Raymond Burr will forever be associated with the character of Perry Mason, a criminal lawyer who won the great majority of his cases. Episodes followed a similar format: the action took place in the first half, with the killer's identity unknown, and the courtroom drama took place in the latter half. Mason was particularly adept at eliciting confessions from the guilty parties. Regulars and semi-regulars included Barbara Hale, William Hopper, William Talman and Ray Collins. Following the series' end, with the last telecast on Jan 27, 1974, a number of successful "Perry Mason" TV movies aired and the show remains popular in reruns.

POWERED PARACHUTE FLY-IN. Sept 21–24. Columbus, KS. Largest powered parachute fly-in in the world. More than 320 machines participating. World Record Launch on Saturday morning. Annually, begins the third Thursday in Sept. Est attendance: 8,000. For info: Jean Pritchett, Columbus Chamber of Commerce, 320 E Maple, Columbus, KS 66725. Phone: (620) 429-1492. Fax: (620) 429-1674. E-mail: columbuschamber@ columbus-ks.com. Web: www.columbus-ks.com.

STATE FAIR OF VIRGINIA. Sept 21–Oct 1. Richmond Raceway Complex, Richmond, VA. It's the Big Red Barn, racing pigs, the State Fair Animal Nursery, the famous State Fair Duck Slide and more! Get up close and personal with more than 5,000 farm animals in Virginia's largest outdoor classroom. Enjoy 11 days of rides, thrills and fun for the whole family with blue ribbon competitions, exhibits, midway rides and shows. There's daily entertainment on the MusicFest Stage and in the Classic Amphitheatre. It's a Virginia tradition and the only place to get that delicious State Fair food. Est attendance: 350,000. For info: Mike Fritzsche, Fair Mgr, PO Box 26805, Richmond, VA 23261-6805. Phone: (804) 569-3200. Fax: (804) 569-3252. Web: www.statefair.com.

TAYLOR, MARGARET SMITH: BIRTH ANNIVERSARY. Sept 21, 1788. Wife of Zachary Taylor, 12th president of the US, born at Calvert County, MD. Died Aug 18, 1852.

"THE TEXACO STAR THEATER" TV PREMIERE: ANNIVERSARY. Sept 21, 1948. Also known as "The Milton Berle Show" and sponsored by Texaco until 1953, this popular variety show was a good sign for the fledgling TV industry. Milton Berle became a superstar. The show featured singing and comedy, especially sight gags and outrageous costumes, and guest stars. Changes were made in the fourth season: Berle cut back his appearances, new writers and a new director were added and the format was changed to a show-within-a-show. Ruth Gilbert,

September 2006	S	M	T	W	T	F	S
						1	2
	3	4	5	6	7	8	9
	10	11	12	13	14	15	16
	17	18	19	20	21	22	23
	24	25	26	27	28	29	30

Fred Clark and Arnold Stang were featured, along with the new pitchman, ventriloquist Jimmy Nelson and his dummy Danny O'Day.

UNITED NATIONS: INTERNATIONAL DAY OF PEACE. Sept 21. The General Assembly proclaimed the International Day of Peace in 1981, "devoted to commemorating and strengthening the ideals of peace both within and among all nations and peoples." In 2001, the Assembly decided that, beginning in 2002, the International Day of Peace would be observed on Sept 21 each year (resolution 55/282) as a day of global ceasefire and nonviolence, an invitation to all nations and people to honor a cessation of hostilities throughout the day. For info: United Nations, Dept of Public Info, New York, NY 10017. Web: www .un.org.

WELLS, HERBERT GEORGE: BIRTH ANNIVERSARY. Sept 21, 1866. English novelist and historian, born at Bromley, Kent, England. Among his books: *The Time Machine, The Invisible Man, The War of the Worlds* and *The Outline of History*. H.G. Wells died at London, Aug 13, 1946. "Human history," he wrote, "becomes more and more a race between education and catastrophe."

WORLD BEEF EXPO/HARVEST FAIR. Sept 21–24. Milwaukee, WI. World-class cattle shows and sales representing 14 beef cattle breeds. Trade show featuring agribusinesses catering to the beef industry. Also includes activities for children and adults, such as Taste of Beef, Supreme Champion Drive, microbrewery sampling, scarecrow making and Harvest Fair. Est attendance: 50,000. For info: World Beef Expo, Wisconsin State Fair Park, 640 S 84th St, PO Box 14990, West Allis, WI 53214-0990. Phone: (800) 884-FAIR or (414) 266-7000. Web: www.worldbeefexpo .com.

BIRTHDAYS TODAY

Ethan Coen, 49, writer, producer (*Fargo*), born Minneapolis, MN, Sept 21, 1957.
Leonard Cohen, 72, singer, songwriter, born Montreal, QC, Canada, Sept 21, 1934.
David James Elliott, 46, actor ("JAG"), born Toronto, ON, Canada, Sept 21, 1960.
Cecil Grant Fielder, 43, former baseball player, born Los Angeles, CA, Sept 21, 1963.
Fannie Flagg, 62, actress, writer (*Fried Green Tomatoes*), born Birmingham, AL, Sept 21, 1944.
Henry Gibson, 71, comedian ("Rowan and Martin's Laugh-In"), actor (*Nashville*), born Germantown, PA, Sept 21, 1935.
Artis Gilmore, 57, former basketball player, born Chipley, FL, Sept 21, 1949.
Larry Hagman, 75, actor ("I Dream of Jeannie," "Dallas"), born Fort Worth,TX, Sept 21, 1931.
Faith Hill, 39, country singer, born Jackson, MS, Sept 21, 1967.
Stephen King, 59, author (*Christine, Pet Sematary, The Shining, Misery, The Stand*), born Portland, ME, Sept 21, 1947.
Bill Kurtis, 66, TV journalist ("Investigative Reports"), born Pensacola, FL, Sept 21, 1940.
Ricki Lake, 38, talk-show host, actress (*Hairspray, Serial Mom*), born New York, NY, Sept 21, 1968.
Rob Morrow, 44, actor ("Northern Exposure," *Quiz Show*), born New Rochelle, NY, Sept 21, 1962.

Bill Murray, 56, comedian ("Saturday Night Live"), actor (*Lost in Translation, Groundhog Day, Caddyshack*), born Evanston, IL, Sept 21, 1950.
Nicole Richie, 25, television personality ("The Simple Life"), born Berkeley, CA, Sept 21, 1981.
Nancy Travis, 45, actress ("Almost Perfect," *Married to the Mob, Chaplin*), born New York, NY, Sept 21, 1961.
Luke Wilson, 35, actor (*The Royal Tenenbaums, Legally Blonde*), born Dallas, TX, Sept 21, 1971.

SEPTEMBER 22 — FRIDAY

Day 265 — 100 Remaining

AMERICAN BUSINESS WOMEN'S DAY. Sept 22. A day set forth by Congress on which all Americans can recognize the important contributions more than 57 million American working women have made and are continuing to make to this nation. Annually, Sept 22. For info: Elizabeth Kennedy, American Business Women's Assn, 9100 Ward Pkwy, Kansas City, MO 64114. Phone: (816) 361-6621. Fax: (816) 361-4991. E-mail: abwa@abwa .org. Web: www.abwa.org.

"CHARLIE'S ANGELS" TV PREMIERE: 30th ANNIVERSARY. Sept 22, 1976. This extremely popular show of the '70s featured three attractive women solving crimes. Sabrina Duncan (Kate Jackson), Jill Munroe (Farrah Fawcett-Majors) and Kelly Garrett (Jaclyn Smith) signed on with detective agency Charles Townsend Associates. Their boss was never seen, only heard (the voice of John Forsythe); messages were communicated to the women by his associate John Bosley (David Doyle). During the course of the series, Cheryl Ladd replaced Fawcett, Shelley Hack and Tanya Roberts succeeded Kate Jackson. The show went off the air in 1981 but feature films were made in 2000 and 2003.

COMMON GROUND COUNTRY FAIR. Sept 22–24. MOFGA's Common Ground, Unity, ME. Old-time country fair celebrating rural life with the revival of forgotten skills and demonstrations of technology appropriate for the future. Features Maine-produced food, crafts, entertainment, farming demonstrations and talks, a very special children's area with daily and ongoing participatory activities. Annually, the third weekend after Labor Day. Sponsor: Maine Organic Farmers and Gardeners Assn. Est attendance: 60,000. For info: Barbara Luce, Fair Dir, Common Ground Country Fair, PO Box 170, Unity, ME 04988. Phone: (207) 568-4142. Fax: (207) 568-4141. E-mail: cgcf@mofga .org. Web: www.mofga.org.

DEAR DIARY DAY. Sept 22. Put it on paper. You'll feel better. No need to be a professional writer. [©2003 by WH.] For info: Thomas & Ruth Roy, Wellcat Holidays, 2418 Long Ln, Lebanon, PA 17046. Phone: (717) 279-0184. E-mail: info@wellcat.com. Web: www.wellcat.com.

ELEPHANT APPRECIATION DAY. Sept 22. Celebrate the earth's largest, most interesting and most noble endangered land animal. Free info kit from: Wayne Hepburn, Mission Media, Inc, PO Box 50095, Sarasota, FL 34232. Phone: (941) 355-4552. Fax: (941) 355-6592. Web: www.himandus.net/elephanteria.

EMANCIPATION PROCLAMATION: ANNIVERSARY. Sept 22, 1862. One of the most important presidential proclamations of American history is that of Sept 22, 1862, in which Abraham Lincoln, by executive proclamation, freed the slaves in the rebelling states. "That on . . . [Jan 1, 1863] . . . all persons held as slaves within any state or designated part of a state, the people whereof shall then be in rebellion against the United States, shall be then, thenceforward, and forever, free. . . ." See also: "13th Amendment Anniversary" (Dec 18) for abolition of slavery in all states.

FAIRMOUNT MUSEUM DAYS/REMEMBERING JAMES DEAN FESTIVAL. Sept 22–24. Fairmount, IN. The town where James Dean grew up honors Dean and other celebrated former citizens such as Jim Davis, creator of Garfield, journalist Phil Jones and Robert Sheets, retired director of the National Hurricane Center. The Fairmount Museum boasts "the

Authentic James Dean Exhibit" of memorabilia and personal items of Dean's and it sponsors the festival that also includes a parade, James Dean Look-Alike Contest, custom car show featuring the James Dean Run for pre-1970 autos, Garfield Cat Photo and Art Contest, Garfield Great Run, carnival, booths, live '50s entertainment and more. Annually, the last full weekend in September. Est attendance: 40,000. For info: Fairmount Historical Museum, Inc, 203 E Washington St, PO Box 92, Fairmount, IN 46928. Phone: (765) 948-4555. Web: www.jamesdeanartifacts .com.

FALL FIESTA. Sept 22–24. Andrews Airport Grounds, Andrews, TX. 6th annual event featuring trade show, classic car show, motorcycle display, antique farm equipment and tractor show, airplane display, food concessions, rides and live entertainment. For info: Andrews Chamber of Commerce, 700 W Broadway, Andrews, TX 79714. Phone: (432) 523-2695. E-mail: achamber @andrewstx.com. Web: www.andrewstx.com.

"FAMILY TIES" TV PREMIERE: ANNIVERSARY. Sept 22, 1982. This popular '80s sitcom was set at Columbus, OH, and focused on the Keaton family: Ex-hippies Elyse (Meredith Baxter-Birney), an architect, and Steven (Michael Gross), a station manager of the local public TV station, Alex (Michael J. Fox), their smart, conservative and financially driven son, Mallory (Justine Bateman), their materialistic, ditzy daughter and Jennifer (Tina Yothers), their tomboy youngest daughter. Later in the series Elyse gave birth to Andrew (Brian Bonsall). Marc Price played Irwin "Skippy" Handleman, the nerdy next-door neighbor who adored the Keatons, and Mallory in particular. The last episode aired Sept 17, 1989.

FARADAY, MICHAEL: BIRTH ANNIVERSARY. Sept 22, 1791. English scientist and early experimenter with electricity, born at Newington, Surrey, England. Died at Hampton Court, Aug 25, 1867.

FIRST ALL-WOMAN JURY EMPANELED IN COLONIES: 350th ANNIVERSARY. Sept 22, 1656. The General Provincial Court at Patuxent, MD, empaneled the first all-woman jury in the colonies to hear the case of Judith Catchpole, accused of murdering her child. The defendant claimed she had never even been pregnant, and after all the evidence was heard, the jury acquitted her.

"FRIENDS" TV PREMIERE: ANNIVERSARY. Sept 22, 1994. This hugely popular NBC comedy brought together six single friends and the issues in their personal lives, ranging from their jobs to their romances. The cast was Courteney Cox Arquette, Lisa Kudrow, Jennifer Aniston, Matthew Perry, David Schwimmer and Matt Le Blanc. The show concluded its run in 2004, with a finale in which 51.1 million viewers tuned in, making its finale the fourth most-watched TV program in history.

HOBBIT DAY. Sept 22. To commemorate the birthdays of Frodo and Bilbo Baggins and their creator J.R.R. Tolkien. For info: American Tolkien Society, PO Box 7871, Flint, MI 48507-0871. E-mail: americantolkiensociety@yahoo.com.

HOUSEMAN, JOHN: BIRTH ANNIVERSARY. Sept 22, 1902. American actor and producer John Houseman was born Jacques Haussmann at Bucharest. He is best known for his collaboration with Orson Welles on the 1938 radio production of *War of the Worlds* and for his role as Professor Kingsfield in the film and television version of *The Paper Chase.* He won an Oscar for that film role in 1974 and helped establish the Juilliard drama school and the Acting Company repertory group. He died Oct 30, 1988, at Malibu, CA.

ICE CREAM CONE: ANNIVERSARY. Sept 22, 1903. Italo Marchiony emigrated from Italy in the late 1800s and soon thereafter went into business at New York, NY, with a pushcart dispensing lemon ice. Success soon led to a small fleet of pushcarts, and the inventive Marchiony was inspired to develop a cone, first made of paper, later of pastry, to hold the tasty delicacy. On Sept 22, 1903, his application for a patent for his new mold was filed, and US Patent No 746971 was issued to him Dec 15, 1903.

IRAN-IRAQ WAR: ANNIVERSARY. Sept 22, 1980. Iraq invaded western Iran on this date, starting an eight-year war. This deadly war saw one million casualties, the use of chemical weapons and extensive damage to each nation's economy.

LIBERTY FALL FESTIVAL. Sept 22–23. Liberty, MO. Arts and crafts booth, food booths, children's activities, a carnival, a parade, car show, entertainment provided throughout the two-day festival. Annually, the fourth weekend in September. Est attendance: 30,000. For info: Liberty Area Chamber of Commerce, 9 S Leonard St, Liberty, MO 64068. Phone: (816) 781-5200. Fax: (816) 781-4901. E-mail: info@libertychamber.com. Web: www.lib ertychamber.com.

LONG COUNT DAY: ANNIVERSARY. Sept 22, 1927. Anniversary of world championship boxing match between Jack Dempsey and Gene Tunney, at Soldier Field, Chicago, IL. It was the largest fight purse ($990,446) in the history of boxing to that time. Nearly half the population of the US is believed to have listened to the radio broadcast of this fight. In the seventh round of the 10-round fight, Tunney was knocked down. Following the rules, Referee Dave Barry interrupted the count when Dempsey failed to go to the farthest corner. The count was resumed and Tunney got to his feet at the count of nine. Stopwatch records of those present claimed the total elapsed time from the beginning of the count until Tunney got to his feet at 12–15 seconds. Tunney, awarded seven of the 10 rounds, won the fight and claimed the world championship. Dempsey's appeal was denied and he never fought again. Tunney retired the following year after one more (successful) fight.

MALI: INDEPENDENCE DAY. Sept 22. National holiday commemorating independence from France in 1960. Mali, in West Africa, was known as the French Sudan while a colony.

MARION COUNTY COUNTRY HAM DAYS. Sept 22–24. Lebanon, KY. Country ham breakfast served under a tent in downtown Lebanon. Pokey pig 5k run, PIGasus parade, more than 125 arts and crafts booths and free entertainment. Est attendance: 50,000. For info: Kathy Browning, Lebanon-Marion County Chamber of Commerce, 239 N Spalding Ave, Ste 201, Lebanon, KY 40033. Phone: (270) 692-9594. Fax: (270) 692-2661. E-mail: chamber@hamdays.com. Web: www.hamdays.com.

"MAVERICK" TV PREMIERE: ANNIVERSARY. Sept 22, 1957. This popular Western starred James Garner as Bret Maverick, a clever man who preferred card playing to fighting. A second Maverick was introduced when production was behind schedule—Jack Kelly played his brother Bart. Garner and Kelly played most episodes separately, and when Garner left in 1961, Kelly was in almost all the episodes. Other performers included Roger Moore, Robert Colbert and Diane Brewster. This Western distinguished itself by its light touch and parody of other Westerns.

MID-SOUTH FAIR. Sept 22–Oct 1. Fairgrounds, Memphis, TN. Regional fair featuring concerts, free entertainment, midway, rodeo, livestock, exhibits and special events. Est attendance: 500,000. For info: Misty Craft, Mid-South Fair, 940 Early Maxwell Blvd, Memphis, TN 38104. Phone: (901) 274-8800. Fax: (901) 274-8804. E-mail: mcraft@midsouthfair.com. Web: www.midsouth fair.com.

September *2006*	S	M	T	W	T	F	S
						1	2
	3	4	5	6	7	8	9
	10	11	12	13	14	15	16
	17	18	19	20	21	22	23
	24	25	26	27	28	29	30

MITCHELL PERSIMMON FESTIVAL. Sept 22–30. Main Street, Mitchell, IN. 60th annual. Persimmon pudding and novelty contests, parade, carnival, arts and crafts, fine arts and photography shows, antique autos and machinery, pioneer village candlelight tour, free entertainment nightly. Annually, the last full week in September. Est attendance: 90,000. For info: Greater Mitchell Chamber of Commerce, PO Box 216, Mitchell, IN 47446. Phone: (800) 580-1985. E-mail: mitchell@kiva.net. Web: www.persimmonfestival.org.

MOON PHASE: NEW MOON. Sept 22. Moon enters New Moon phase at 7:45 AM, EDT.

MOUNT PLEASANT GLASS & ETHNIC FESTIVAL. Sept 22–24. Mount Pleasant, PA. Large outdoor street festival featuring glass blowing demos, arts and crafts, two parades, national and regional entertainment and ethnic foods. Free entertainment on three stages, fireworks, a carnival and unique activities. Est attendance: 45,000. For info: Jeff Landy, Mount Pleasant Glass and Ethnic Festival, Municipal Bldg, 1 Etze Ave, Mt Pleasant, PA 15666. Phone: (724) 547-7738. Fax: (724) 547-0115. Web: www.mtpleasantglassandethnicfestival.com.

NEW HAMPSHIRE HIGHLAND GAMES. Sept 22–24. Hopkinton Fair Grounds, Contoocook, NH. From the tossing of the caber to the lilting melodies of the clarsach plus massed pipe bands on parade, there's something for everyone at New Hampshire's Highland Games: a three-day Scottish festival crammed with music, dance, crafts, athletic events, Scottish food and more. For those of Scottish heritage, there's also a chance to look up one's clan connection, as more than 60 Scottish clans and societies have tents with displays. Admission charged. Est attendance: 42,000. For info: New Hampshire Highland Games, PO Box 4197, Concord, NH 03302-4197. Phone: (603) 229-1975. Fax: (603) 223-6678. E-mail: info@nhscot.org. Web: www.nhscot.org.

PLEDGE ACROSS AMERICA. Sept 22. On the Friday of Constitution Week, every school is invited to join a synchronized recitation of the Pledge of Allegiance coast to coast, 8 AM Hawaiian time to 2 PM Eastern time. Supported by the US Department of Education, this event enables our nation's youth to unite for a patriotic observance. The original 1892 National School Celebration, declared by President Benjamin Harrison, was the event for which the Pledge of Allegiance was written. Free resources for schools available from Farmers Insurance and Celebration USA. For info: Paula Burton, President, Celebration USA, 17853 Santiago Blvd, Ste 107, Villa Park, CA 92861. Phone: (714) 283-1892. Web: www.americanpromise.com or www.celebration usa.org.

RELIGIOUS FREEDOM WEEK. Sept 22–Oct 1. This date commemorates the anniversary of the Bill of Rights and the right to believe and practice the religion of one's own choice as laid out in the First Amendment. Annually, the week including the anniversary date, Sept 25. For info: Rev Susan Taylor, Religious Freedom Week Committee, c/o Church of Scientology, 1701 20th St NW, Washington, DC 20009. Phone: (202) 667-6404. Fax: (202) 667-6314. E-mail: suetaylor1@juno.com.

ROSH HASHANAH BEGINS AT SUNDOWN. Sept 22. Jewish New Year. See also: "Rosh Hashanah" (Sept 23).

RYDER CUP MATCHES. Sept 22–24. Kildare Golf and Country Club, Straffan, Ireland. Held every two years, this match pits American golfers against a European team. First held in 1927, this is the 36th match. For info: Professional Golfers' Association of America, 100 Ave of the Champions, Palm Beach Gardens, FL 33418. Phone: (561) 630-1737. Fax: (561) 624-8448. Web: www.pga.com.

SOLAR ECLIPSE. Sept 22. Annular eclipse of the sun. Visible in South America, West Africa and Antarctica.

STANHOPE, PHILIP DORMER: BIRTH ANNIVERSARY. Sept 22, 1694 (OS). Philip Dormer Stanhope, the 4th Earl of Chesterfield, was born at London, England. He was a brilliant politician and orator. On Feb 20, 1751, he brought a bill into the House of Lords that caused the "New Style" Gregorian calendar to replace the "Old Style" Julian calendar in 1752. His influential political career was eclipsed by the fame of the letters he wrote to his son Philip, giving shrewd counsel on manners, morals and the ways of the world. Published less than a year after his own death at London, Mar 24, 1773, the *Letters* became immensely popular, were translated and republished in many editions. The Chesterfield, a kind of sofa, is said to be named for him.

TACA FALL CRAFT FAIR. Sept 22–24. Centennial Park, Nashville, TN. 27th annual fair. Festival of fine crafts featuring 190 selected American craft artists. Annually, the last weekend in September. Est attendance: 40,000. For info: Alice C. Merritt, Exec Dir, Tennessee Assn of Craft Artists, PO Box 120066, Nashville, TN 37212. Phone: (615) 385-1904. Web: www.tennesseecrafts.org.

US POSTMASTER GENERAL ESTABLISHED: ANNIVERSARY. Sept 22, 1789. Congress established office of Postmaster General, following the Departments of State, War and Treasury.

VIRGINIA PEANUT FESTIVAL. Sept 22–23. Emporia, VA. Annual celebration promoting peanuts and harvesting. Features musical concerts, arts and crafts, parade, corporate village, luncheon/fashion show, carnival, car show and fireworks. Sponsored by Emporia-Greensville Chamber of Commerce. Est attendance: 20,000. For info: Virginia Peanut Festival, Attn: Lisa Council, PO Box 956, Emporia, VA 23847. Phone: (434) 634-5405. E-mail: cor@ci.emporia.va.us.

WARRENS CRANBERRY FESTIVAL. Sept 22–24. Warrens, WI. 34th annual. A community celebration of the ruby-red fruit at the "Cranberry Capital of Wisconsin." More than 1,250 vendors in three miles of booths offer arts and crafts, antiques, local produce and cranberries. Events include cranberry marsh tours and contests for "Biggest Berry" and best recipes. Est attendance: 100,000. For info: Warrens Cranberry Festival, Inc, PO Box 146, Warrens, WI 54666. Phone: (608) 378-4200. Fax: (608) 378-4250. E-mail: cranfest@cranfest.com. Web: www.cranfest.com.

BIRTHDAYS TODAY

Scott Baio, 45, actor ("Happy Days," "Diagnosis Murder," "Charles in Charge"), born Brooklyn, NY, Sept 22, 1961.
Shari Belafonte-Harper, 52, model, actress, born New York, NY, Sept 22, 1954.
Debbie Boone, 50, singer ("You Light Up My Life," "Baby, I'm Yours"), born Hackensack, NJ, Sept 22, 1956.
Bonnie Hunt, 42, actress (*Jerry Maguire, Jumanji*), born Chicago, IL, Sept 22, 1964.
Joan Jett, 46, singer ("I Love Rock 'n' Roll," "Crimson and Clover"), musician, born Philadelphia, PA, Sept 22, 1960.
Thomas Charles (Tommy) Lasorda, 79, Hall of Fame baseball manager and former player, born Norristown, PA, Sept 22, 1927.
Paul Le Mat, 61, actor (*American Graffiti, Melvin and Howard, Strange Invaders*), born Rahway, NY, Sept 22, 1945.
Catherine Oxenberg, 45, actress ("Dynasty"), born New York, NY, Sept 22, 1961.
Mike Richter, 40, hockey player, born Philadelphia, PA, Sept 22, 1966.
Ronaldo, 30, Brazilian soccer player, born Ronaldo Luiz Nazario de Lima at Rio de Janeiro, Brazil, Sept 22, 1976.
Arthur O. Sulzberger, 55, publisher (*The New York Times*), born Mount Kisco, NY, Sept 22, 1951.
Junko Tabei, 67, mountaineer (first woman to climb Mount Everest), born Fukushima Prefecture, Japan, Sept 22, 1939.

SEPTEMBER 23 — SATURDAY

Day 266 — 99 Remaining

APPLE SATURDAYS. Sept 23 (also Sept 30 and Oct 7). Sabbathday Lake Shaker Village, New Gloucester, ME. Guided tours of the Shaker orchard exhibit and walks to the Shaker orchard for pick-your-own apples! For info: Leonard Brooks, Sabbathday Lake Shaker Village, 707 Shaker Rd, New Gloucester, ME 04260. Phone: (207) 926-4597. E-mail: usshakers@aol.com. Web: www .shaker.lib.me.us.

AUTUMN. Sept 23–Dec 22. In the Northern Hemisphere, autumn begins today with the autumnal equinox, at 12:03 AM, EDT. Note that in the Southern Hemisphere today is the beginning of spring. Everywhere on Earth (except near the poles) the sun rises due east and sets due west and daylight length is nearly identical—about 12 hours, 8 minutes.

BANNED BOOKS WEEK—CELEBRATING THE FREEDOM TO READ. Sept 23–30. Brings to the attention of the general public the importance of the freedom to read and the harm censorship causes to our society. Sponsors: American Library Association, American Booksellers Association, American Booksellers Association for Free Expression, American Society of Journalists and Authors, Association of American Publishers, National Association of College Stores. For info: Judith F. Krug, American Library Assn, Office for Intellectual Freedom, 50 E Huron St, Chicago, IL 60611. Phone: (312) 280-4220. Fax: (312) 280-4227. E-mail: bbe@ala.org. Web: www.ala.org/bbooks.

BASEBALL'S GREATEST DISPUTE: ANNIVERSARY. Sept 23, 1908. In the decisive game between the Chicago Cubs and the New York Giants, the National League pennant race erupted in controversy during the bottom of the ninth with the score tied 1–1, at the Polo Grounds, New York, NY. New York was at bat with two men on. The batter hit safely to center field, scoring the winning run. Chicago claimed that the runner on first, Fred Merkle, seeing the winning run scored, headed toward the dugout without advancing to second base, thus invalidating the play. The Chicago second baseman, Johnny Evers, attempted to get the ball and tag Merkle out, but was prevented by the fans streaming onto the field. Days later Harry C. Pulliam, head of the National Commission of Organized Baseball, decided to call the game a tie. The teams were forced to play a postseason play-off game, which the Cubs won 4–2. Fans invented the terms "boner" and "bonehead" in reference to the play and it has gone down in baseball history as "Merkle's Boner."

CHARLES, RAY: BIRTH ANNIVERSARY. Sept 23, 1930. Born at Albany, GA, Ray Charles Robinson began losing his sight at age 5. He began formal music training at the St. Augustine School for the Deaf and Blind, and by age 15 was earning a living as a musician. He went on to become one of the most influential performers of all time. As a pianist, singer, songwriter, band leader and producer, he played country, jazz, rock, gospel and standards. His renditions of "Georgia on My Mind," "I Can't Stop Loving You" and "America the Beautiful" are considered true American classics. He died at Beverly Hills, CA, June 10, 2004.

CHECKERS DAY: ANNIVERSARY. Sept 23. Anniversary of the nationally televised "Checkers Speech" by then vice presidential candidate Richard M. Nixon, on Sept 23, 1952. Nixon was found "clean as a hound's tooth" in connection with a private fund for political expenses, and he declared he would never give back the cocker spaniel dog, Checkers, which had been a gift to his daughters. Other dogs prominent in American politics: Abraham Lincoln's dog, Fido; Franklin D. Roosevelt's much-traveled terrier, Fala; Harry S. Truman's dogs, Mike and Feller; Dwight D. Eisenhower's dog, Heidi; Lyndon Johnson's beagles, Him and Her; Ronald Reagan's dogs, Lucky and Rex; and George H.W. Bush's dog, Millie.

DESOTO CAVERNS PARK FALL NATIVE AMERICAN DANCE AND CRAFTS FESTIVAL. Sept 23–24. DeSoto Caverns Park, Childersburg, AL. 31st annual event, featuring Native American dancing, singing and lifeways demonstrations. Arts and crafts and great food. Est attendance: 8,000. For info: DeSoto Caverns Park, 5181 DeSoto Caverns Pkwy, Childersburg, AL 35044. Phone: (205) 378-7252 or (800) 933-2283. E-mail: fun@desotocavernspark.com. Web: www.DeSotoCavernsPark .com.

DYERSVILLE FESTIVAL OF THE ARTS. Sept 23–24. Beckman High School, Dyersville, IA. The "Farm Toy Capital of the World," near the site of the movie *Field of Dreams*. Features the Dyersville Quilt & Craft Show, with hundreds of quilts and hundreds of crafts, all handmade. Entertainment and food. Annually, the last full weekend in September. Est attendance: 3,000. For info: Dyersville Area Chamber of Commerce, 1100 16th Ave Ct SE, Dyersville, IA 52040. Phone: (563) 875-2311 or (866) DYERSVILLE. Fax: (563) 875-8391. E-mail: dyersvillechamber@ dyersville.org. Web: www.dyersville.org.

FALL FESTIVAL OF THE ARTS AND CRAFTS. Sept 23–24. Washington, MO. Juried festival featuring the creative talents of two- and three-dimensional artists and crafters. Free children's area, beer and wine area, specialty foods, music and live entertainment. For info: Downtown Washington, Inc, PO Box 144, Washington, MO 63090. Phone: (636) 239-1743. Fax: (636) 239-4832. E-mail: events@downtownwashmo.org. Web: down townwashmo.org.

FALLASBURG FALL FESTIVAL. Sept 23–24. Fallasburg Park, Lowell, MI. Unique event with 80 artists displaying and selling their work. Historical setting, arts, entertainment, kids activities and food. Annually, the last full weekend in September. For info: Michelle Ellison, Lowell Area Arts Council, 149 S Hudson, Lowell, MI 49331. Phone: (616) 897-8545. Fax: (616) 897-3061. E-mail: info@lowellartscouncil.org.

FIESTA BULLWHACKER/WILD WEST SHOW. Sept 23–24. Mahaffie Stagecoach Stop and Farm, Olathe, KS. A multicultural celebration of Olathe's Santa Fe Trail heritage with 1800s-period demonstrations, Mexican and American music, children's games and stagecoach rides. The Mahaffie Farmstead on the Santa Fe and Oregon Trails served warm meals for travelers as a stagecoach stop from 1863 to 1869. "Bullwhackers" were the men who drove teams of oxen. Est attendance: 6,000. For info: Tim Talbott, Mahaffie Stagecoach Stop, 1100 Kansas City Rd, Olathe, KS 66061. Phone: (913) 971-5111. Web: www .mahaffie.com.

FISH AMNESTY DAY. Sept 23. Give animals a break by not fishing. Fish are intelligent animals who feel pain just like the dogs and cats who share our homes. Annually, the fourth Saturday in September. For info: Karin Robertson, 501 Front St, Norfolk, VA 23510. Phone: (757) 622-7382.

GENEVA AREA GRAPE JAMBOREE. Sept 23–24. Geneva, OH. Grape harvest and products. 43rd annual Jamboree. Annually, the last full weekend in September. Est attendance: 250,000. For info: Geneva Grape Jamboree, Box 92, Geneva, OH 44041. Phone: (440) 466-5262. Web: www.grapejamboree.com.

	S	M	T	W	T	F	S
September						1	2
2006	3	4	5	6	7	8	9
	10	11	12	13	14	15	16
	17	18	19	20	21	22	23
	24	25	26	27	28	29	30

GETTYSBURG OUTDOOR ANTIQUE SHOW. Sept 23. Gettysburg, PA. More than 150 dealers displaying their wares on the sidewalk. Annually, the fourth Saturday in September. Est attendance: 25,000. For info: Gettysburg Conv & Visitors Bureau, PO Box 4117, Gettysburg, PA 17325. Phone: (717) 334-6274. Fax: (717) 334-1166. E-mail: gettysburgcvb@dejazzd.com. Web: www.gettysburgcvb.org.

JAPAN: AUTUMNAL EQUINOX DAY. Sept 23. National holiday in Japan.

"THE JETSONS" TV PREMIERE: ANNIVERSARY. Sept 23, 1962. "Meet George Jetson. His boy Elroy. Daughter Judy. Jane, his wife. . . ." These words introduced us to the Jetsons, a cartoon family living in the twenty-first century, the Flintstones of the Space Age. We followed the exploits of George and his family, as well as his work relationship with his greedy, ruthless boss Cosmo Spacely. Voices were provided by George O'Hanlon as George, Penny Singleton as Jane, Janet Waldo as Judy, Daws Butler as Elroy, Don Messick as Astro, the family dog, and Mel Blanc as Spacely. New episodes were created in 1985 which also introduced a new pet, Orbity.

KIWANIS KIDS' DAY. Sept 23. To honor and assist youth—our greatest resource. Annually, the fourth Saturday in September. For info: Kiwanis Intl, Member Services, 3636 Woodview Trace, Indianapolis, IN 46268. E-mail: kiwanismail@kiwanis.org. Web: www.kiwanis.org.

LAVITSEF. Sept 23–24. Norfolk, NE. Concerts, pet show, quilt show, pancake feed, craft fair, ice cream social, museum events, car show, BBQ, German dinner, kids fun events. Parade at 10 AM on Saturday. Est attendance: 15,000. For info: LaVitsef, Inc, PO Box 1512, Norfolk, NE 68702-1512. Web: www.lavitsef.com.

LEWIS & CLARK EXPEDITION RETURNS: 200th ANNIVERSARY. Sept 23, 1806. After more than two years in the American West, the Corps of Discovery returned to St. Louis amid much fanfare. They had traveled—with the assistance of guides Toussaint Charbonneau and his wife Sacagawea (a member of the Shoshone tribe)—to what is now North Dakota and Montana, over the Continental Divide and to the Columbia River, which took them to the Pacific (Nov 1805). They lost only one man from the 33-member group. Their valuable findings on western tribes, geography, plants and animals dispelled many longstanding myths about the region. (See also Jan 18 and May 14.)

LEWIS AND CLARK BICENTENNIAL NATIONAL SIGNATURE EVENT: CONFLUENCE WITH DESTINY. Sept 23–24. St. Louis, MO. On Sept 23, 1806, the Lewis and Clark Expedition officially ended when the explorers arrived in St. Louis, MO. In commemoration of the bicentennial of this event, a consortium of Missouri and Illinois state, county and local groups will re-create this return: A flotilla of watercraft will originate at various historic sites on the Missouri and Mississippi rivers and converge on the riverfront. A series of programs and events will explore the multicultural composition of the expedition. Representatives from all of the Tribal Nations encountered by Lewis and Clark will be invited to participate in this final national signature event of the Lewis and Clark Bicentennial. For info: Karen Goering, Natl Council of the Lewis and Clark Bicentennial, PO Box 11940, St. Louis, MO 63112-0040. Phone: (314) 454-3160 or (888) 999-1803. E-mail: info@lewisandclark200.org. Web: www.lewisandclark200.org.

LIBRA, THE BALANCE. Sept 23–Oct 22. In the astronomical/astrological zodiac that divides the sun's apparent orbit into 12 segments, the period Sept 23–Oct 22 is identified traditionally as the sun sign of Libra, the Balance. The ruling planet is Venus.

LIPPMANN, WALTER: BIRTH ANNIVERSARY. Sept 23, 1889. American journalist, political philosopher and author. Born at New York, NY, he died there Dec 14, 1974. As a syndicated newspaper columnist he was the foremost and perhaps the most influential commentator in the nation. "Without criticism," he said in an address to the International Press Institute in 1965,

"and reliable and intelligent reporting, the government cannot govern."

MABON. Sept 23. (Also called Alban Elfed.) One of the "Lesser Sabbats" during the Wiccan year, Mabon marks the second harvest as Nature prepares for the coming of winter. Annually, on the autumnal equinox.

McGUFFEY, WILLIAM HOLMES: BIRTH ANNIVERSARY. Sept 23, 1800. American educator and author of the famous *McGuffey Readers*, born at Washington County, PA. Died at Charlottesville, VA, May 4, 1873.

★**NATIONAL HUNTING AND FISHING DAY.** Sept 23. Presidential Proclamation 4682, of Sept 11, 1979, covers all succeeding years. Annually, the fourth Saturday of September.

NORSKEDALEN'S THRESHING BEE. Sept 23. Norskedalen Nature and Heritage Center, Coon Valley, WI. Antique engines and pioneer demonstrations, such as winnowing, threshing, corn shredding, shelling and grinding; cream separating and butter-making; horse-drawn wagon rides, rope braiding, sawmill, quilt show and farm tool displays. Threshers' meal served, reservations required. Est attendance: 500. For info: Norskedalen Nature and Heritage Center, Inc, PO Box 235, Coon Valley, WI 54623. Phone: (608) 452-3424. Fax: (608) 452-3157.

NORTHEAST MONTANA THRESHING BEE AND ANTIQUE SHOW. Sept 23–24. Culbertson, MT. See how grandma and grandpa worked and lived. At the threshing grounds one mile southeast of town. Annually, the fourth full weekend in September. Est attendance: 2,000. For info: Rodney Iverson or David Krogedal, Northeast Montana Threshing Bee/Antique Show, Culbertson, MT 59218. Phone: (406) 787-5265. E-mail: elk1@nemontel.net.

PAULUS, FRIEDRICH: BIRTH ANNIVERSARY. Sept 23, 1890. The German commander of the Sixth Army who led the advance on Stalingrad in 1942, Friedrich von Paulus was born at Breitenau, Germany. Paulus's troops succeeded in taking most of Stalingrad in November 1942, but eventually became trapped within the city they had captured. Paulus surrendered to the Russians Jan 31, 1943, the same day that Hitler promoted him to field marshal. He appeared as a key witness for the Soviet prosecution at the Nuremberg trials. Paulus died Feb 1, 1957, at Dresden, East Germany.

PIDGEON, WALTER: BIRTH ANNIVERSARY. Sept 23, 1897. Actor Walter Pidgeon was born at East St. John, NB, Canada. He died at age 87, Sept 25, 1984, at Santa Monica, CA. He made his film debut in 1925 in *Mannequin*. Among his films are *Saratoga* and *Mrs Miniver*.

PLANET NEPTUNE DISCOVERY: ANNIVERSARY. Sept 23, 1846. Neptune is 2,796,700,000 miles from the sun (about 30 times as far from the sun as Earth). Eighth planet from the sun, Neptune takes 164.8 years to revolve around the sun. Diameter is about 31,000 miles compared to Earth at 7,927 miles. Discovered by German astronomer Johann Galle.

R.E.A.D. IN AMERICA DAY. Sept 23. National Mall, Washington, DC. R.E.A.D. stands for "Reading helps Everyone Accomplish Dreams." An annual event, R.E.A.D. in America Day is sponsored by the CheeREADing program. The day's motto is "anything is possible if you read." It is through the power of reading that goals are set and dreams are realized. It is important we encourage our youth to pick up a book and start reading. The day's purpose is to raise awareness about youth literacy and to encourage the power of daily reading for our youth. The day's activities will include: a rally for reading (with local heroes and celebrities stopping by to read a book and share how reading has changed their lives), local bookstore "Power of One Hour" reading sessions and local school events. Annually, the fourth Saturday in September. For info: Ashley Anderson, CheeREADing, 5230 Norborne Ln, Houston, TX 77069. Phone: (281) 583-8440. E-mail: cheereadingprogram@yahoo.com.

ROSH HASHANAH or JEWISH NEW YEAR. Sept 23–24. Jewish holy day observed on two consecutive days. Hebrew calendar date: Tishri 1–2, 5767. Rosh Hashanah (literally "Head of the Year") is the beginning of ten days of repentance and spiritual renewal. (Began at sundown Sept 22.)

SAUDI ARABIA: KINGDOM UNIFICATION. Sept 23. National holiday. Commemorates unification in 1932.

SHEYENNE VALLEY ARTS & CRAFTS FESTIVAL. Sept 23–24. Fort Ransom, ND. This 39th annual festival is one of the oldest and best in the area. Artists and crafters from several states join local people in offering 200 displays, church bazaar and dinner, turkey barbecue—all in a rustic historic atmosphere. Annually, the last full weekend in September. Sponsor: Sheyenne Valley Arts and Crafts Assn, Inc, a nonprofit organization. Est attendance: 10,000. For info: SVACA, PO Box 21, Fort Ransom, ND 58033. Phone: (701) 973-4461. E-mail: svaca@drtel.net.

TASTE OF MORGAN HILL. Sept 23–24. Downtown Morgan Hill, CA. 17th annual family festival featuring fine arts and quality crafts, entertainment, wine and beer garden, local restaurants and food booths, custom and classic car show, and kids zone. Annually, the last full weekend in Sept. Est attendance: 50,000. For info: Michele Naylor, Morgan Hill Chamber of Commerce, PO Box 786, Morgan Hill, CA 95038. Phone: (408) 779-9444. Fax: (408) 779-5405. E-mail: mhcc@morganhill.org. Web: www .morganhill.org.

WOODHULL, VICTORIA CHAFLIN: BIRTH ANNIVERSARY. Sept 23, 1838. American feminist, reformer and first female candidate for the presidency of the US. Born at Homer, OH, she died at Norton Park, Bremmons, Worcestershire, England, June 10, 1927.

BIRTHDAYS TODAY

Jason Alexander, 47, actor ("Seinfeld," *Pretty Woman; Bye, Bye, Birdy*; stage: *Jerome Robbins' Broadway*), born Newark, NJ, Sept 23, 1959.

Ani DiFranco, 36, folk-punk singer and songwriter, born Buffalo, NY, Sept 23, 1970.

Julio Iglesias, 63, singer ("To All the Girls I've Loved Before" with Willie Nelson), songwriter, born Madrid, Spain, Sept 23, 1943.

Tony Joseph Mandarich, 40, former football player, born Oakville, ON, Canada, Sept 23, 1966.

Larry Hogan Mize, 48, golfer, born Augusta, GA, Sept 23, 1958.

Elizabeth Peña, 45, actress (*Rush Hour, Lone Star, Jacob's Ladder*), born Elizabeth, NJ, Sept 23, 1961.

Paul Petersen, 61, actor ("The Donna Reed Show," *Houseboat*), born Glendale, CA, Sept 23, 1945.

Mary Kay Place, 59, writer, actress ("Mary Hartman, Mary Hartman," *The Big Chill*), born Tulsa, OK, Sept 23, 1947.

Mickey Rooney, 86, actor (*Andy Hardy* movies, *The Black Stallion*), born Joe Yule, Jr, at Brooklyn, NY, Sept 23, 1920.

Bruce Springsteen, 57, singer, songwriter ("Born in the USA"), born Freehold, NJ, Sept 23, 1949.

September **2006**	S	M	T	W	T	F	S
						1	2
	3	4	5	6	7	8	9
	10	11	12	13	14	15	16
	17	18	19	20	21	22	23
	24	25	26	27	28	29	30

SEPTEMBER 24 — SUNDAY
Day 267 — 98 Remaining

ALL ABOUT APPLES. Sept 24. Billings Farm and Museum, Woodstock, VT. Learn more about this most basic American fruit that boasts hundreds of varieties. Activities include cider pressing, making apple butter in the farmhouse kitchen, apples-on-a-string, and wagon rides. For info: Billings Farm and Museum, Rte 12 North, Woodstock, VT 05091. Phone: (802) 457-2355. Fax: (802) 457-4663. E-mail: billings.farm@valley.net. Web: www .billingsfarm.org.

AMERICAN HERITAGE QUILT SHOW. Sept 24–Oct 1. Frontier Culture Museum, Staunton, VA. View the 6th annual show presenting a wide variety of quilting styles and traditions. These works of art demonstrate both hand and machine quilting. Some antique quilts will also be on display. For info: Frontier Culture Museum, 1290 Richmond Rd, PO Box 810, Staunton, VA 24401. Phone: (540) 332-7850. Fax: (540) 332-9989. Web: www .frontier.virginia.gov.

CAMBODIA: CONSTITUTIONAL DECLARATION DAY: ANNIVERSARY. Sept 24. National holiday. Commemorates the new constitution of 1993.

"DANIEL BOONE" TV PREMIERE: ANNIVERSARY. Sept 24, 1964. A successful show based loosely on the life of pioneer Daniel Boone, who helped settle Kentucky in the 1770s. Fess Parker starred as the American hero. Ed Ames played Mingo, Boone's friend, an educated Cherokee and Pat Blair played his wife, Rebecca. Also featured were Albert Salmi, Jimmy Dean, Roosevelt Grier, Darby Hinton, Veronica Cartwright and Dallas McKennon.

DEAF AWARENESS WEEK. Sept 24–30. Nationwide celebration to promote deaf culture, American Sign Language and deaf heritage. Activities might include library displays, interpreted story hours, open houses in residential schools and mainstream programs, exhibit booths in shopping malls with "Five Minute Sign Language Lessons," material distribution. Annually, the last full week of September. For info: Natl Assn of the Deaf, 814 Thayer Ave, Silver Spring, MD 20910-4500. Fax: (301) 587-1791. E-mail: nadinfo@nad.org. Web: www.nad.org.

FANEUIL HALL OPENED TO THE PUBLIC: ANNIVERSARY. Sept 24, 1742. On this date Faneuil Hall at Boston, MA, opened to the public. Designed by painter John Smibiert, it was enlarged in 1805 according to plans by Charles Bulfinch. Today it is on the Freedom Trail, as part of the Boston Historical Park administered by the National Park Service.

FESTIFALL. Sept 24. Friendship Hill National Historic Site, Point Marion, PA. To celebrate the 19th-century arts, crafts and music of the Allegheny Plateau. Historic foods are available for purchase. Annually, the last Sunday in September. Est attendance: 3,000. For info: Friendship Hill Natl Historic Site, 223 New Geneva Rd, Point Marion, PA 15474. Phone: (724) 725-9190. Fax: (724) 725-1999. Web: www.nps.gov/frhi/.

FITZGERALD, F. SCOTT: BIRTH ANNIVERSARY. Sept 24, 1896. American short story writer and novelist; author of *This Side of Paradise, The Great Gatsby* and *Tender Is the Night.* Born Francis Scott Key Fitzgerald, at St. Paul, MN, he died at Hollywood, CA, Dec 21, 1940.

★**GOLD STAR MOTHER'S DAY.** Sept 24. Presidential Proclamation always for last Sunday of each September since 1936. Proclamation 2424 of Sept 14, 1940, covers all succeeding years.

GUINEA-BISSAU: INDEPENDENCE DAY: ANNIVERSARY. Sept 24. National holiday. Commemorates declaration of independence from Portugal in 1973.

HENSON, JIM: BIRTH ANNIVERSARY. Sept 24, 1936. Puppeteer, born at Greenville, MS. Jim Henson created a unique family of puppets known as the Muppets. Kermit the Frog, Big Bird, Rowlf, Bert and Ernie, Gonzo, Animal, Miss Piggy and Oscar the Grouch are a few of the puppets that captured the hearts of children and adults alike in television and film productions including "Sesame Street," "The Jimmy Dean Show," "The Muppet Show," *The Muppet Movie, The Muppets Take Manhattan, The Great Muppet Caper* and *The Dark Crystal.* Henson began his career in 1954 as producer of the TV show "Sam and Friends" at Washington, DC. He introduced the Muppets in 1956. His creativity was rewarded with 18 Emmy Awards, seven Grammy Awards, four Peabody Awards and five ACE Awards from the National Cable Television Association. Henson died unexpectedly May 16, 1990, at New York, NY.

INNERGIZE DAY. Sept 24. A day set aside for anyone who has said "I don't have time to do the personal things I want to do for myself." Today is the day to set time aside for yourself to do anything you want to do. Annually, the day after autumn. For info: Michelle Porchia, Inner Dimensions, 4 Daniels Farm Rd, Ste 137, Trumbull, CT 06611. Phone: (203) 924-1012. Fax: (203) 924-1012. Web: www.michelleporchia.com.

"THE LOVE BOAT" TV PREMIERE: ANNIVERSARY. Sept 24, 1977. This one-hour comedy-drama featured guest stars aboard a cruise ship, the *Pacific Princess.* All stories had to do with finding or losing love. The ship's crew were the only regulars: Gavin MacLeod as Captain Merrill Stubing, Bernie Kopell as Doctor Adam Bricker, Fred Grandy as assistant purser Burl "Gopher" Smith, Ted Lange as bartender Isaac Washington and Lauren Tewes as cruise director Julie McCoy. The series ended with the last telecast on Sept 5, 1986, but special TV movies were broadcast in later years.

"LOVE OF LIFE" TV PREMIERE: 55th ANNIVERSARY. Sept 24, 1951. This serial, which began as a 15-minute show, ran for 28 years. The story lines shifted from a focus on two sisters to a larger number of characters. The diverse cast included such notables as Christopher Reeve, Karen Grassle, Roy Scheider, Dana Delaney, John Aniston, Marsha Mason, Bert Convy, Warren Beatty and Barnard Hughes.

MARSHALL, JOHN: BIRTH ANNIVERSARY. Sept 24, 1755. Fourth Chief Justice of Supreme Court, born at Germantown, VA. Served in House of Representatives and as secretary of state under John Adams. Appointed by President Adams to the position of chief justice in January 1801, he became known as "The Great Chief Justice." Marshall's court was largely responsible for defining the role of the Supreme Court and basic organizing principles of government in the early years after adoption of the Constitution in such cases as *Marbury v Madison, McCulloch v Maryland, Cohens v Virginia* and *Gibbons v Ogden.* He died at Philadelphia, PA, July 6, 1835.

MOZAMBIQUE: ARMED FORCES DAY. Sept 24. National holiday. Commemorates the beginning of the war for independence in 1964.

"THE MUNSTERS" TV PREMIERE: ANNIVERSARY. Sept 24, 1964. "The Munsters" was a half-hour sitcom about an unusual family who thought they were ordinary. Each family member resembled a different type of monster: Herman Munster (Fred Gwynne) was Frankenstein's monster; Lily, his wife (Yvonne DeCarlo), and Grandpa, her father (Al Lewis), were vampires and his son Eddie (Butch Patrick) was a werewolf. Only their niece, Marilyn (Beverly Owen and Pat Priest), looked normal, and they considered her the unattractive family member. Most of the show's laughs came from the family's interactions with outsiders. The last telecast was on Sept 1, 1966.

NATIONAL ADULT IMMUNIZATION AWARENESS WEEK. Sept 24–30. Thousands of deaths occur each year—deaths which could be easily prevented by today's available vaccines. NAIAW emphasizes the importance of appropriately vaccinating adults against measles, mumps, rubella, hepatitis A, hepatitis B, tetanus, diphtheria, influenza, pneumococcal disease and varicella. A campaign kit of materials is available. For info: Natl Coalition for Adult Immunization, 4733 Bethesda Ave, Ste 750, Bethesda, MD 20814-5278. Phone: (301) 656-0003. Fax: (301) 907-0878. E-mail: ncai@nfid.org. Web: www.NFID.org.

NATIONAL CHIMNEY SAFETY WEEK. Sept 24–30. Each year CSIA Certified Chimney Sweeps work to raise awareness of chimney safety. For a list of Certified Chimney Sweeps in your state, call CSIA at (800) 536-0118. Annually, the week prior to National Fire Prevention Week. For info: CSIA, 2155 Commercial Dr, Plainfield, IN 46168. Phone: (317) 837-5362. Fax: (317) 837-5365. E-mail: office@csia.org. Web: www.csia.org.

NATIONAL GOOD NEIGHBOR DAY. Sept 24. To build a nation and world that cares by increasing appreciation and understanding of our fellow man. Start a memorable tradition: plan a family block party with your good neighbors. Annually, the fourth Sunday in September. For info: Natl Good Neighbor Day Fdtn, Box 379, Lakeside, MT 59922. Phone: (406) 844-3000. Web: www.natgoodneighborday.org.

NATIONAL KEEP KIDS CREATIVE WEEK. Sept 24–30. More than ever before, kids today need encouragement to be imaginative. Their busy, task-oriented schedules in home and school give children little room for creative play. Set aside time this week to celebrate the inventive minds of kids. Encourage a child to make up a story, draw, even look for animals in cloud shapes—let their imaginations soar. Annually, the last week in September. For info: Bruce Van Patter, Let's Get Creative! Phone: (570) 524-9770. Web: www.brucevanpatter.com/keepkidscreative .html.

NATIONAL PUNCTUATION DAY. Sept 24. A celebration of the lowly comma, the correctly used quote and other proper uses of periods, semicolons and the ever mysterious ellipsis. For info: Jeff Rubin, Put It in Writing Newsletter Publishers, 1517 Buckeye Court, Pinole, CA 94564. Phone: (510) 724-9507 or toll-free (877) 588-1212. Fax: (510) 741-8698. E-mail: jeff@put-it-in-writing .com. Web: www.put-it-in-writing.com.

RAMADAN: THE ISLAMIC MONTH OF FASTING. Sept 24–Oct 23. Begins on Islamic lunar calendar date Ramadan 1, 1427. Ramadan, the ninth month of the Islamic calendar, is holy because it was during this month that the Holy Qur'an [Koran] was revealed. All adults of sound body and mind fast from dawn (before sunrise) until sunset to achieve spiritual and physical purification and self-discipline, abstaining from food, drink and intimate relations. It is a time for feeling a common bond with the poor and needy, a time of piety and prayer. Different methods for "anticipating" the visibility of the new moon crescent at Mecca are used by different Muslim groups. US date may vary. Began at sunset the preceding day.

SCHWENKFELDER THANKSGIVING. Sept 24. On this day in 1734 members of the Schwenkfelder Society gave thanks for their deliverance from Old World persecution as they prepared to take up new lives in the Pennsylvania-Dutch counties of Pennsylvania. Still celebrated.

"60 MINUTES" TV PREMIERE: ANNIVERSARY. Sept 24, 1968. TV's longest-running prime-time program was originally hosted by Harry Reasoner and Mike Wallace. Dan Rather and Diane Sawyer were also reporters on TV's first newsmagazine. Today the show's correspondents include Ed Bradley, Steve Kroft, Lesley Stahl, Morley Safer, Andy Rooney and Mike Wallace.

SOUTH AFRICA: HERITAGE DAY. Sept 24. A celebration of South African nationhood, commemorating the multicultural heritage of this rainbow nation.

BIRTHDAYS TODAY

Gordon Clapp, 58, actor ("NYPD Blue"), born North Conway, NH, Sept 24, 1948.

Morgan Hamm, 24, gymnast, born Ashland, WI, Sept 24, 1982.

Paul Hamm, 24, gymnast, born Ashland, WI, Sept 24, 1982.

Sheila MacRae, 83, singer, actress, born London, England, Sept 24, 1923.

Jim McKay, 85, sportscaster, born James Kenneth McManus at Philadelphia, PA, Sept 24, 1921.

Rafael Corrales Palmeiro, 42, baseball player, born Havana, Cuba, Sept 24, 1964.

Kevin Sorbo, 48, actor ("Hercules"), born Mound, MN, Sept 24, 1958.

Nia Vardalos, 44, screenwriter, actress (*My Big Fat Greek Wedding*), born Winnipeg, MB, Canada, Sept 24, 1962.

SEPTEMBER 25 — MONDAY
Day 268 — 97 Remaining

"BEAUTY AND THE BEAST" TV PREMIERE: ANNIVERSARY. Sept 25, 1987. This updated version of the fairy tale was a romantic hit and acquired a cult following. It followed the experiences of Catherine Chandler (Linda Hamilton), a Manhattan lawyer who is beaten and abandoned and subsequently found and cared for by Vincent (Ron Perlman), a man-beast living under the city. Other cast members included Roy Dotrice, Jay Acovone, Ren Woods, Cory Danziger and David Greenlee. Hamilton left the series at the beginning of the third season; the series ended shortly thereafter.

FAMILY DAY—A DAY TO EAT DINNER WITH YOUR CHILDREN. Sept 25. A national event meant to remind Americans of the value of parental engagement and to encourage them to make family dinners a regular feature of their lives. Research by the National Center on Addiction and Substance Abuse (CASA) at Columbia University has shown that the more often children eat dinner with their families, the less likely they are to smoke, drink or use illegal drugs. Materials available on how to regularly eat dinner with your children and address tough issues. Annually, the fourth Monday of September. For info: Family Day Coord, CASA, 633 Third Ave, 19th Fl, New York, NY 10017. Phone: (212) 841-5200. Fax: (212) 956-8020. Web: www.casafamilyday.org.

September 2006	S	M	T	W	T	F	S
						1	2
	3	4	5	6	7	8	9
	10	11	12	13	14	15	16
	17	18	19	20	21	22	23
	24	25	26	27	28	29	30

FAST OF GEDALYA. Sept 25. Jewish holiday. Hebrew calendar date: Tishri 3, 5767. Tzom Gedalya begins at first light of day and commemorates the 6th-century BC assassination of Gedalya Ben Achikam. Began at sundown Sept 24.

FAULKNER, WILLIAM CUTHBERT: BIRTH ANNIVERSARY. Sept 25, 1897. American novelist and short story writer William Faulkner (born Falkner) was born at New Albany, MS. A Nobel Prize–winner who changed the style and structure of the American novel, he died at Byhalia, MS, on July 6, 1962. Faulkner's first novel, *Soldiers' Pay*, was published in 1926. His best-known book, *The Sound and the Fury*, appeared in 1929. Shunning literary circles, Faulkner moved to a pre–Civil War house on the outskirts of Oxford, MS, in 1930. From 1930 until the onset of World War II he published an incredible body of work. In June 1962 Faulkner published his last novel, *The Reivers*.

FIRST AMERICAN NEWSPAPER PUBLISHED: ANNIVERSARY. Sept 25, 1690. The first (and only) edition of *Publick Occurrences Both Foreign and Domestick* was published by Benjamin Harris, at the London-Coffee-House, Boston, MA. Authorities considered this first newspaper published in the US offensive and ordered immediate suppression.

FIRST WOMAN SUPREME COURT JUSTICE: 25th ANNIVERSARY. Sept 25, 1981. Sandra Day O'Connor was sworn in as the first woman associate justice on the US Supreme Court on this date. She had been nominated by President Ronald Reagan in July 1981.

GREENWICH MEAN TIME BEGINS: ANNIVERSARY. Sept 25, 1676 (OS). Two very accurate clocks were set in motion at the Royal Observatory at Greenwich, England. Greenwich Mean Time (now known as Universal Time) became the standard for England; in 1884 it became the standard for the world.

MAJOR LEAGUE BASEBALL'S FIRST DOUBLEHEADER: ANNIVERSARY. Sept 25, 1882. The first major league baseball doubleheader was played between the Providence and Worcester teams.

NATIONAL ONE-HIT WONDER DAY. Sept 25. Honors the one-hit wonders of rock'n' roll. Anyone who ever had a hit single deserves eternal remembrance. For info: Steven Rosen, 1944 S Glendon Ave, #105, Los Angeles, CA 90025. Phone: (310) 441-5102. E-mail: srosenone@aol.com.

PACIFIC OCEAN DISCOVERED: ANNIVERSARY. Sept 25, 1513. Vasco Núñez de Balboa, a Spanish conquistador, stood high atop a peak in the Darien, in present-day Panama, becoming the first European to look upon the Pacific Ocean, claiming it as the South Sea in the name of the King of Spain.

PROWSE, JULIET: BIRTH ANNIVERSARY. Sept 25, 1936. Dancer, actress, born Bombay, India. Died Sept 14, 1996.

RAMEAU, JEAN PHILLIPPE: BIRTH ANNIVERSARY. Sept 25, 1683. French composer Jean Phillippe Rameau was baptised at Dijon, France, Sept 25, 1683. Called by some the greatest French composer and musical theorist of the 18th century, Rameau died at Paris, France, Sept 12, 1764.

REEVE, CHRISTOPHER: BIRTH ANNIVERSARY. Sept 25, 1952. Born at New York, NY, this actor was best known for his portrayal of the title character in *Superman* (1978) and three sequels during the 1980s. After being paralyzed in a horseback riding accident, he was confined to a wheelchair and became an activist for spinal-cord research and awareness. He died at Mount Kisco, NY, Oct 10, 2004.

RWANDA: REPUBLIC DAY. Sept 25. National holiday. Marks the 1961 abolition of the monarchy.

SEQUOIA AND KINGS CANYON NATIONAL PARK ESTABLISHED: ANNIVERSARY. Sept 25, 1890. Area in central California established as a national park. For further park info: Sequoia Natl Park, Three Rivers, CA 93271.

SHOSTAKOVICH, DMITRI: 100th BIRTH ANNIVERSARY. Sept 25, 1906. Russian composer born at St. Petersburg, Russia. Died at Moscow, USSR, Aug 9, 1975.

SMITH, WALTER WESLEY "RED": BIRTH ANNIVERSARY. Sept 25, 1905. Pulitzer Prize–winning sports columnist and newspaperman for 54 years, Walter Wesley (Red) Smith was born at Green Bay, WI. Called the "nation's most respected sportswriter," Smith's columns appeared in some 500 newspapers. He died at Stamford, CT, Jan 15, 1982.

UNITED NATIONS: WORLD MARITIME DAY. Sept 25 (day varies by nation, but always last week in Sept). A day to stress the importance of shipping safety and the maritime environment. For info: United Nations, Dept of Public Info, New York, NY 10017. Web: www.un.org.

BIRTHDAYS TODAY

Tate Donovan, 43, actor ("Friends," "Partners"), born New York, NY, Sept 25, 1963.

Michael Douglas, 62, actor ("The Streets of San Francisco," *Fatal Attraction, Basic Instinct*), director, born New York, NY, Sept 25, 1944.

Mark Hamill, 55, actor ("General Hospital," *Star Wars*), born Oakland, CA, Sept 25, 1951.

Heather Locklear, 45, actress ("T.J. Hooker," "Dynasty," "Melrose Place"), born Los Angeles, CA, Sept 25, 1961.

Michael Madsen, 47, actor (*Species, Reservoir Dogs*), born Chicago, IL, Sept 25, 1959.

Scottie Pippen, 41, basketball player, born Hamburg, AR, Sept 25, 1965.

Philip Francis (Phil) Rizzuto, 89, Hall of Fame baseball player, born New York, NY, Sept 25, 1917.

Will Smith, 38, actor (*Independence Day*, "The Fresh Prince of Bel-Air"), singer, born Philadelphia, PA, Sept 25, 1968.

Robert Walden, 63, actor ("Lou Grant," *All the King's Men*), born New York, NY, Sept 25, 1943.

Barbara Walters, 75, journalist, interviewer, TV host ("20/20"), born Boston, MA, Sept 25, 1931.

Catherine Zeta-Jones, 37, actress (*The Mask of Zorro, Chicago*), born Swansea, Glamorgan, Wales, Sept 25, 1969.

SEPTEMBER 26 — TUESDAY
Day 269 — 96 Remaining

APPLESEED, JOHNNY: BIRTH ANNIVERSARY. Sept 26, 1774. John Chapman, better known as Johnny Appleseed, believed to have been born at Leominster, MA. Died at Allen County, IN, Mar 11, 1845. Planter of orchards and friend of wild animals, he was regarded as a great medicine man by the Indians.

BATTLE OF MEUSE–ARGONNE FOREST: ANNIVERSARY. Sept 26, 1918. As part of four major efforts to break the Hindenburg line, a Franco-American offensive began on this date, with the US First Army striking between the Meuse River and the Argonne Forest and the French Fourth Army to their west. After four taxing weeks of attack, the Germans were gradually pushed back. By Oct 31, the Americans had advanced 10 miles, the French had reached the Aisne River 20 miles away and the Argonne Forest was rid of the Central Power forces. This was the final great battle of World War I.

"THE BEVERLY HILLBILLIES" TV PREMIERE: ANNIVERSARY. Sept 26, 1962. This half-hour comedy was one of the most successful "rural" comedies on TV; in addition, according to Nielsen, the eight most-watched half-hour shows are episodes of this series. "The Beverly Hillbillies" was about an Appalachian man, Jed Clampett (Buddy Ebsen), who found oil on his property, so he moved his family to a better life in Beverly Hills, CA. Most of its jokes were based on its fish-out-of-water premise. Also in the cast were Irene Ryan as Granny, Jed's mother-in-law; Donna Douglas as his daughter Elly May; Max Baer, Jr, as his nephew Jethro Bodine; Raymond Bailey as neurotic Milburn Drysdale, Jed's neighbor; Nancy Kulp as Jane Hathaway, Drysdale's secretary; and Harriet MacGibbon as Margaret Drysdale, Milburn's wife.

"THE BRADY BUNCH" TV PREMIERE: ANNIVERSARY. Sept 26, 1969. This popular sitcom starred Robert Reed as widower Mike Brady who has three sons and is married to Carol (played by Florence Henderson), who has three daughters. Housekeeper Alice was played by Ann B. Davis. Sons Greg (Barry Williams), Peter (Christopher Knight) and Bobby (Mike Lookinland) and daughters Marcia (Maureen McCormick), Jan (Eve Plumb) and Cindy (Susan Olsen) experienced the typical crises of youth. The program steered clear of social issues and portrayed childhood as a time of innocence. The last episode was telecast on Aug 30, 1974. The program continues to be popular in reruns, and there were also many spin-offs: a cartoon, a variety series, a sitcom, a short-lived dramatic series and films.

COMAL COUNTY FAIR. Sept 26–Oct 1. Comal County Fairgrounds, New Braunfels, TX. Local and surrounding community festival with exhibits of livestock, arts and crafts, antiques, agricultural products, poultry, handwork, baked goods and horticulture. 113th annual fair. Est attendance: 80,000. For info: Comal County Fair Assn, PO Box 310223, New Braunfels, TX 78131. Phone: (830) 625-1505 or (830) 609-2860. Web: www.comalcountyfair.org.

DONIZETTI'S *LUCIA DI LAMMERMOOR* PREMIERE: ANNIVERSARY. Sept 26, 1835. *Lucia di Lammermoor*, one of opera's greatest tragic love stories, premiered in Naples, Italy. The opera was composed by Gaetano Donizetti with a libretto by Salvatore Cammarano. The plot was based on Sir Walter Scott's *The Bride of Lammermoor* and takes place in 17th-century Scotland. Lucia, thwarted by a blood feud from marrying the man she loves, kills her husband and then herself.

ELIOT, T.S.: BIRTH ANNIVERSARY. Sept 26, 1888. Thomas Stearns Eliot, Nobel Prize winner, poet, playwright and critic, was born at St. Louis, MO. "There never was a time," he believed, "when those that read at all, read so many more books by living authors than books by dead authors; there never was a time so completely parochial, so shut off from the past." Eliot died at London, England, Jan 4, 1965.

FIRST TELEVISED PRESIDENTIAL DEBATE: ANNIVERSARY. Sept 26, 1960. The debate between presidential candidates John F. Kennedy and Richard Nixon was televised from WBBM-TV, a Chicago TV studio. Howard K. Smith was the moderator.

GERSHWIN, GEORGE: BIRTH ANNIVERSARY. Sept 26, 1898. American composer remembered for his many enduring songs and melodies, including: "The Man I Love," "Strike Up the Band," "Funny Face," "I Got Rhythm" and the opera *Porgy and Bess*. Many of his works were in collaboration with his brother, Ira. Born at Brooklyn, NY, he died of a brain tumor at Beverly Hills, CA, July 11, 1937. See also: "Gershwin, Ira: Birth Anniversary" (Dec 6).

"GILLIGAN'S ISLAND" TV PREMIERE: ANNIVERSARY. Sept 26, 1964. Seven people set sail aboard the *Minnow* for a three-hour tour and became stranded on an island. They used the resources on the island for food, shelter and entertainment. The cast included Bob Denver as Gilligan, Alan Hale, Jr, as the Skipper, Jim Backus as Thurston Howell III, Natalie Schafer as Mrs "Lovey" Howell, Russell Johnson as the Professor, Dawn Wells as Mary Ann and Tina Louise as Ginger Grant, the movie star. The last telecast aired on Sept 4, 1967.

"HAWAII FIVE-O" TV PREMIERE: ANNIVERSARY. Sept 26, 1968. "Book 'em, Dano" became a national catchphrase after this CBS crime series began airing. It starred the granite-jawed Jack Lord as Steve McGarrett, leader of a special Hawaiian state police force that only answered to the governor. His officers included Danny "Dano" Williams (James MacArthur), Chin Ho Kelly (Kam Fong), Duke Lukela (Herman Wedemeyer) and others. Filmed on location at Oahu, Hawaii, and featuring a popular theme song by the Ventures, the show was a huge hit until it concluded in 1980. "Hawaii Five-O" did garner criticism for its violence.

POPE PAUL VI: BIRTH ANNIVERSARY. Sept 26, 1897. Giovanni Battista Montini, 262nd pope of the Roman Catholic Church, born at Concesio, Italy. Elected pope June 21, 1963. Died at Castel Gandolfo, near Rome, Italy, Aug 6, 1978.

SHAMU'S BIRTHDAY. Sept 26, 1985. Shamu was born at Sea World at Orlando, FL, and is the first killer whale born in captivity to survive. Shamu is now living at Sea World's Texas park.

BIRTHDAYS TODAY

Lynn Anderson, 59, singer ("Rose Garden"), born Grand Forks, ND, Sept 26, 1947.

Melissa Sue Anderson, 44, actress ("Little House on the Prairie"), born Berkeley, CA, Sept 26, 1962.

Bryan Ferry, 61, lead singer (Roxy Music, "Heart on My Sleeve"), songwriter, born Durham, England, Sept 26, 1945.

Linda Hamilton, 49, actress (*Terminator, Terminator 2*), born Salisbury, MD, Sept 26, 1957.

Mary Beth Hurt, 58, actress (*The World According to Garp, Six Degrees of Separation*), born Marshalltown, IA, Sept 26, 1948.

Olivia Newton-John, 58, singer ("Physical"), actress (*Grease*), born Cambridge, England, Sept 26, 1948.

Jane Smiley, 57, author (*A Thousand Acres, Moo*), born Los Angeles, CA, Sept 26, 1949.

Christine T. Whitman, 60, former administrator of the Environmental Protection Agency, former Governor of New Jersey (R), born New York, NY, Sept 26, 1946.

Serena Williams, 25, tennis player, born Saginaw, MI, Sept 26, 1981.

SEPTEMBER 27 — WEDNESDAY

Day 270 — 95 Remaining

ADAMS, SAMUEL: BIRTH ANNIVERSARY. Sept 27, 1722. Revolutionary leader and Massachusetts state politician Samuel Adams, cousin to President John Adams (1797–1801), was born at Boston. He died there Oct 2, 1803. As a delegate to the First and Second Continental Congresses Adams urged a vigorous stand against England. He signed the Declaration of Independence and the Articles of Confederation and supported the war for independence. Adams served as lieutenant governor of Massachusetts under John Hancock from 1789 to 1793 and then as governor until 1797.

ANCESTOR APPRECIATION DAY. Sept 27. A day to learn about and appreciate one's forebears. For info: AAD Assn, 2460 Devonshire Rd, Ann Arbor, MI 48104-2706.

BATTLE OF CAMBRAI–SAINT QUENTIN: ANNIVERSARY. Sept 27, 1918. British General Sir Douglas Haig moved his armies toward Cambrai and St. Quentin as part of four major efforts to break the Hindenburg line in the German salient that extended from Verdun to the sea. To the south the New Zealand and Canadian divisions smashed through the Hindenburg line on Oct 6. German General Erich Ludendorff resigned Oct 16, and the line was taken between Oct 18 and 20.

CRUIKSHANK, GEORGE: BIRTH ANNIVERSARY. Sept 27, 1792. English illustrator, especially known for caricatures and for illustration of Charles Dickens's books. Born at London, England, and died there Feb 1, 1878.

DAVIDSON FELLOWS AWARD RECEPTION. Sept 27. Library of Congress, Washington, DC. Each year, the Davidson Institute for Talent Development honors our nation's brightest young minds, students under the age of 18, who have completed prodigious works in science, mathematics, technology, music, literature and/or philosophy. These students are recognized as Davidson Fellows Award recipients and receive up to a $50,000 scholarship to attend an accredited institute of learning. The Davidson Institute is a national nonprofit foundation dedicated to supporting America's most intelligent young people. Annually, the last Wednesday in September. For info: Tacie Moessner, Davidson Institute, 9665 Gateway Dr, Ste B, Reno, NV 89521. Phone: (775) 852-3483, ext 423. Fax: (775) 852-2184. E-mail: davidsonfellows@ditd.org. Web: www.davidsonfellows.org.

ETHIOPIA: TRUE CROSS DAY. Sept 27. National holiday. Commemorates the finding of the true cross (*Maskal*). Also a holiday in Eritrea.

"JACK THE RIPPER" LETTER: ANNIVERSARY. Sept 27, 1888. In the midst of the "Autumn of Terror" in which London, England, was convulsed over the crimes of a brutal serial killer, the city's Central News Agency received a letter written in red ink purporting to be written by the killer. He dubbed himself "Jack the Ripper" and threatened more killings. Police at the time and most historians today believe(d) the letter to be a hoax by an irresponsible journalist, but the name took hold in the public imagination and is forever associated with the Whitechapel murders of 1888. See also: "Whitechapel Murders Begin: Anniversary" (Aug 31).

NAST, THOMAS: BIRTH ANNIVERSARY. Sept 27, 1840. American political cartoonist born at Landau, Germany, best known for his cartoons attacking New York's Tweed ring. Died Dec 7, 1902, at Guayaquil, Ecuador.

NATIONAL WOMEN'S HEALTH AND FITNESS DAY. Sept 27. 5th annual event to promote the value of health and fitness for women of all ages. More than 700 local women's health events will be held across the country on the same day. Call the toll-free number for further info and a list of local events. Annually, the last Wednesday in September. Est attendance: 70,000. For info: Tina Godin, Program Mgr, Health Information Resource Center, 1850 W Winchester Rd #213, Libertyville, IL 60048. Phone: (800) 828-8225. Fax: (847) 816-8662. E-mail: info@fitnessday.com. Web: www.fitnessday.com.

SAINT VINCENT DE PAUL: FEAST DAY. Sept 27. French priest, patron of charitable organizations, and cofounder of the Sisters of Charity. Canonized 1737 (lived 1581?–1660).

SEMMES, RAPHAEL: BIRTH ANNIVERSARY. Sept 27, 1809. Born at St. Charles County, MD, and died Aug 30, 1877, at Mobile, AL. Daring Confederate naval officer, best known for his incredible raids on Union merchant ships during the middle two years of the Civil War. As commander of the *Alabama*, he captured, sank or burned 82 Union ships valued at more than $6,000,000.

SPACE MILESTONE: *SOYUZ 12* (USSR): ANNIVERSARY. Sept 27, 1973. Because of the death of the crew of *Soyuz 11* upon reentry, it was decided that cosmonauts must wear pressurized space suits on takeoff and landing. Thus there was no longer room for three cosmonauts on a flight. Two Soviet cosmonauts (V.G. Lazarev and O.G. Makarov) made the two-day flight launched on this date.

September 2006	S	M	T	W	T	F	S
						1	2
	3	4	5	6	7	8	9
	10	11	12	13	14	15	16
	17	18	19	20	21	22	23
	24	25	26	27	28	29	30

"THE TONIGHT SHOW" TV PREMIERE: ANNIVERSARY. Sept 27, 1954. "The Tonight Show" has gone through numerous changes over the years, yet it has remained a top-rated show that set the standards for all variety/talk shows to come. Steve Allen served as host from 1954–57. He introduced the format of the show with an opening monologue, games or segments for the studio audience, and then the interview on a simple desk and couch set. Jack Paar hosted from 1957–62 and Johnny Carson reigned as the king of comedy from 1962–92. Comedian Jay Leno serves as its current host.

WARREN COMMISSION REPORT: ANNIVERSARY. Sept 27, 1964. On this day, the Warren Commission issued a report stating that Lee Harvey Oswald acted alone in the assassination of President John F. Kennedy on Nov 22, 1963. Congress reopened the investigation and in 1979 the House Select Committee on Assassinations issued a report stating a conspiracy was most likely involved. See also: "Committee on Assassinations Report: Anniversary" (Mar 29).

WORLD TOURISM DAY. Sept 27. Observed on the anniversary of the adoption of the World Tourism Organization Statutes in 1970. Annually, Sept 27. For info: World Tourism Organization, Calle Capitan Haya 42, 28020 Madrid, Spain. Phone: (34) 91 5678100. Fax: (34) 91 571373. Web: www.world-tourism.org.

BIRTHDAYS TODAY

Wilford Brimley, 72, actor (*Cocoon*, "Our House"), born Salt Lake City, UT, Sept 27, 1934.
Shaun Cassidy, 47, singer ("Da Doo Ron Ron"), actor ("The Hardy Boys," "General Hospital"), born Los Angeles, CA, Sept 27, 1959.
Claude Jarman, Jr, 72, actor (*The Yearling, Rio Grande*), born Nashville, TN, Sept 27, 1934.
Stephan Jenkins, 41, musician (Third Eye Blind), born Southern CA, Sept 27, 1965.
Steve Kerr, 41, basketball player, born Beirut, Lebanon, Sept 27, 1965.
Jayne Meadows, 82, actress ("I've Got a Secret," "The Steve Allen Show," *Lady in the Lake*), born Chang, China, Sept 27, 1924.
Meat Loaf, 59, singer, musician (*The Rocky Horror Picture Show*), born Marvin Lee Aday at Dallas, TX, Sept 27, 1947.
Arthur Heller Penn, 84, filmmaker (*Bonnie and Clyde, The Miracle Worker*), born Philadephia, PA, Sept 27, 1922.
Michael Jack (Mike) Schmidt, 57, Hall of Fame baseball player, born Dayton, OH, Sept 27, 1949.
Delores Taylor, 67, actress, writer, producer (*Billy Jack, The Trial of Billy Jack*), born Winner, SD, Sept 27, 1939.
Sada Thompson, 77, actress (*Twigs*, "Family"), born Des Moines, IA, Sept 27, 1929.

SEPTEMBER 28 — THURSDAY

Day 271 — 94 Remaining

CABRILLO DAY: ANNIVERSARY OF DISCOVERY OF CALIFORNIA. Sept 28, 1542. California. Commemorates discovery of California by Portuguese navigator Juan Rodríguez Cabrillo, who reached San Diego Bay. Cabrillo died at San Miguel Island, CA, Jan 3, 1543. His birth date is unknown. The Cabrillo National Monument marks his landfall and Cabrillo Day is still observed in California (in some areas on the Saturday nearest Sept 28).

CAPP, AL: BIRTH ANNIVERSARY. Sept 28, 1909. The creator of the fictitious village of Dogpatch, KY, Al Capp was born Alfred Gerald Caplin at New Haven, CT. The comic strip "Li'l Abner" appeared in daily newspapers from 1934 until its final episode was published Nov 13, 1977. Along with the misadventures of Abner Yokum, Capp lampooned famous public figures. The minor American institution of "Sadie Hawkins Day" made its debut in "Li'l Abner." Al Capp died Nov 5, 1979, at Cambridge, MA.

GERALDINE R. DODGE POETRY FESTIVAL. Sept 28–Oct 1. NJ location TBD. Twelfth biennial Geraldine R. Dodge Poetry Festival will include the participation of more than 100 poets and will offer dozens of simultaneous poetry readings and discussions. Est attendance: 15,000. For info: Geraldine R. Dodge Foundation, 163 Madison Ave, PO Box 1239, Morristown, NJ 07962-1239. Phone: (973) 540-8443 x 139. E-mail: festival@grdodge.org. Web: grdodge.org/poetry/.

FIRST NIGHT FOOTBALL GAME: ANNIVERSARY. Sept 28, 1892. The first night football game in America was played between Mansfield State Normal School (now Mansfield University) and Wyoming Seminary.

GREAT AMERICAN BEER FESTIVAL. Sept 28–30. Denver, CO. Annual festival holds the Guinness World Record for most beers tapped in one location with 1,400 beers on tap. More than 320 US breweries will be found on the festival floor. Also featuring live music and Beer Garden and Food Marketplace. In the cooking demonstration area you can learn to cook with beer and pair a beer style with a particular food. Est attendance: 28,000. For info: Cindy Jones, Brewers Association, 736 Pearl St, Boulder, CO 80302. Phone: (303) 447-0816. Fax: (303) 447-2825. E-mail: cindy@brewersassociation.org. Web: www.gabf.org.

"HAZEL" TV PREMIERE: 45th ANNIVERSARY. Sept 28, 1961. "Hazel" was based on a comic strip of the same name about a maid working for the Baxter family who gets into everyone's business. Hazel was played by Shirley Booth, and the Baxters were played by Don DeFore, Whitney Blake and Bobby Buntrock. "Hazel" moved from NBC to CBS after the third season and Hazel switched families from George to younger brother Steve Baxter. These Baxters were played by Ray Fulmer, Lynn Borden and Julia Benjamin. This successful series also featured Mala Powers and Ann Jillian.

MASTROIANNI, MARCELLO: BIRTH ANNIVERSARY. Sept 28, 1924. One of the great international stars of cinema, born at Fontana Liri, Italy. Mastroianni worked with the master directors of the mid-20th century, among them Federico Fellini and Luchino Visconti. Two of his most famous roles were the world-weary journalist of *La Dolce Vita* (1960) and the in-crisis movie director of *8½* (1963)—both films directed by Fellini. He was nominated for Oscars three times and twice won the Best Actor Award at the Cannes Film Festival. Died at Paris, France, Dec 19, 1996.

NATIONAL WOMEN'S LEADERSHIP CONFERENCE. Sept 28–30. Anaheim, CA. Businesswomen gather to learn, network and elect ABWA's national board of directors for the coming year. Seminars, speakers and the announcement of the Top Ten Business Women of ABWA and the American Business Woman of ABWA are featured. Est attendance: 3,000. For info: Mary Solis, American Business Women's Assn, 9100 Ward Parkway, PO Box 8728, Kansas City, MO 64114-0728. Phone: (816) 361-6621. Fax: (816) 361-4991. E-mail: abwa@abwa.org. Web: www.abwa.org.

PRESTON COUNTY BUCKWHEAT FESTIVAL. Sept 28–Oct 1. Kingwood, WV. Celebrating the fall harvest, with coronations, parades, exhibits, arts and crafts, antique cars, livestock, carnival, country music and Buckwheat Cake Dinners. Annually, beginning the last Thursday in September. Est attendance: 100,000. For info: Lucille H. Crogan, Fest Secy, Kingwood Volunteer Fire Dept, PO Box 74, Kingwood, WV 26537. Phone: (304) 329-0021. Fax: (304) 329-0021. Web: www.buckwheatfest.com.

RIVER CITY ROUNDUP. Sept 28–Oct 1. Omaha, NE. Take a moment to reflect on the Midwest's proud past. A celebration of Omaha's agricultural and Western heritage; PRCA rodeo, barbecue contest, trail rides, western/wildlife art show, dances, the world's largest 4-H Livestock Expo and a downtown parade. Est attendance: 300,000. For info: Annie Olson, Event Coordinator,

River City Roundup and Rodeo, 302 S 36th, Ste 800, Omaha, NE 68114. E-mail: olsona@aksarben.org. Web: www.rivercity roundup.org.

SCHMELING, MAX: BIRTH ANNIVERSARY. Sept 28, 1905. First European boxer to hold the world heavyweight boxing title (1930–32). Best known for fighting American great Joe Louis twice: the first time defeating him; the second time losing. The Nazi government tried to use Schmeling—to his dismay—as a propaganda tool to demonstrate the superiority of the Aryan race. Schmeling rejected that role, never joined the Nazi party and was punished by being given dangerous WWII combat duties. Schmeling saved two Jewish boys during the November 1939 Kristallnacht terrors. Schmeling and Louis developed a strong friendship outside the ring and Schmeling paid for Louis's funeral. Born at Klein Luckow, Germany, Schmeling died Feb 2, 2005, at Hollenstedt, Germany.

SULLIVAN, ED: BIRTH ANNIVERSARY. Sept 28, 1901. Known as the "King of TV Variety," born at New York, NY. Sullivan started his media career in 1932 as a sportswriter for the *Daily News* in New York. His popular variety show, "The Ed Sullivan Show" ("Toast of the Town"), ran from 1948 until 1971. It included such sensational acts as Elvis Presley and the Beatles. He died at New York, NY, Oct 13, 1974.

TAIWAN: CONFUCIUS'S BIRTHDAY AND TEACHERS' DAY. Sept 28. National holiday, designated as Teachers' Day. Confucius is the Latinized name of Kung-futzu, born at Shantung province on the 27th day of the tenth moon (lunar calendar) in the 22nd year of Kuke Hsiang of Lu (551 BC). He died at age 72, having spent some 40 years as a teacher. Teachers' Day is observed annually on Sept 28.

WIGGIN, KATE DOUGLAS: 150th BIRTH ANNIVERSARY. Sept 28, 1856. Kate Wiggin was born Kate Douglas Smith at Philadelphia, PA. She helped organize the first free kindergarten on the West Coast in 1878 at San Francisco and in 1880 she and her sister established the California Kindergarten Training School. After moving back east she devoted herself to writing, producing a number of children's books including *The Birds' Christmas Carol, Polly Oliver's Problem* and *Rebecca of Sunnybrook Farm*. She died at Harrow, England, Aug 24, 1923.

WILLARD, FRANCES ELIZABETH CAROLINE: BIRTH ANNIVERSARY. Sept 28, 1839. American educator and reformer, president of the Women's Christian Temperance Union, 1879–98, and women's suffrage leader, born at Churchville, NY. Died at New York, NY, Feb 18, 1898.

BIRTHDAYS TODAY

Brigitte Bardot, 72, actress (*And God Created Woman, Viva Maria*), animal rights activist, born Camille Javal at Paris, France, Sept 28, 1934.

Jerry Clower, 80, comedian ("Nashville on the Road"), born Liberty, MS, Sept 28, 1926.

Hilary Duff, 19, actress (*A Cinderella Story,* "Lizzie McGuire"), born Houston, TX, Sept 28, 1987.

Janeane Garofalo, 42, actress (*Reality Bites, The Truth About Cats and Dogs*), born Newton, NJ, Sept 28, 1964.

Jeffrey Jones, 59, actor (*Beetlejuice, Stay Tuned*), born Buffalo, NY, Sept 28, 1947.

Ben E. King, 68, singer, musician ("There Goes My Baby"), born Henderson, NC, Sept 28, 1938.

Steve M. Largent, 52, Hall of Fame football player, born Tulsa, OK, Sept 28, 1954.

Emeka Okafor, 24, basketball player, born Houston, TX, Sept 28, 1982.

September 2006	S	M	T	W	T	F	S
						1	2
	3	4	5	6	7	8	9
	10	11	12	13	14	15	16
	17	18	19	20	21	22	23
	24	25	26	27	28	29	30

Se Ri Pak, 29, golfer, born Daejeon, South Korea, Sept 28, 1977.

Gwyneth Paltrow, 33, actress (*Emma, Shakespeare in Love*), born Los Angeles, CA, Sept 28, 1973.

Brian Rafalski, 33, hockey player, born Dearborn, MI, Sept 28, 1973.

William Windom, 83, actor ("Murder She Wrote," Emmy for "My World and Welcome to It"), born New York, NY, Sept 28, 1923.

SEPTEMBER 29 — FRIDAY
Day 272 — 93 Remaining

BAYFEST. Sept 29–Oct 1 (tentative). Corpus Christi, TX. Plenty of fun at this waterfront festival. Includes amusement rides, games, arts and crafts displays, various musical entertainment, food booths, merchandise exhibitors and much more. Est attendance: 165,000. For info: Bayfest, PO Box 1858, Corpus Christi, TX 78403. Phone: (361) 887-0868. Fax: (361) 887-9773. E-mail: lidia bayfest@interconnect.net. Web: www.bayfesttexas.com.

CABRILLO FESTIVAL. Sept 29–Oct 1. San Diego, CA. Colorful pageant reenacts the historic landing of explorer Juan Rodríguez Cabrillo, who sailed into San Diego Bay on Sept 28, 1542. Kumeyaay basket-weaving, acorn grinding and flint knapping demonstrations. Knot-tying exhibition. Reenactment of Spanish soldier encampment. Portuguese, Spanish, Native American and Mexican dances and food. Pageant takes place annually on the Sunday on or following Sept 28. Est attendance: 6,000. For info: Cabrillo Natl Monument, 1800 Cabrillo Memorial Dr, San Diego, CA 92106. Phone: (619) 557-5450. Fax: (619) 226-6311. Web: www.nps.gov/cabr.

CELTIC CLASSIC HIGHLAND GAMES & FESTIVAL. Sept 29–Oct 1. Bethlehem, PA. America's largest highland games and festival, celebrating Celtic culture with three free days of Celtic music, Irish dance, world-class highland athletic competitions, Border Collie exhibitions, pipe band and drum major competitions, art and history workshops, foods, crafts, entertainment and much more. For info: Celtic Cultural Alliance, Celtic Classic, 532 Main St, 2nd Fl, Bethlehem, PA 18018. Phone: (610) 868-9599. Fax: (610) 868-9730. E-mail: info@celticculturalalliance.org. Web: www.celticculturalalliance.org.

CRAFTSMEN'S CLASSIC ARTS & CRAFTS FESTIVAL. Sept 29–Oct 1. Roanoke Civic Center, Roanoke, VA. 19th annual. Features work from more than 250 talented artists and craftspeople. All juried exhibitors' work has been handmade by the exhibitors and must be their own original design and creation. See the creative process in action with several exhibitors demonstrating throughout the weekend. Something for every style, taste, and budget with items from the most contemporary to the most traditional. Est attendance: 20,000. For info: Gilmore Enterprises, 1240 Oakland Ave, Greensboro, NC 27403. Phone: (336) 274-5550. E-mail: gilmoreshows@triad.rr.com. Web: www.CraftShow.com or www.gilmoreshows.com.

FABULOUS 1890s WEEKEND. Sept 29–30. Mansfield, PA. Night football in America began in 1892 with a game between Mansfield University and Wyoming Seminary. Annually, Mansfield celebrates a "Fabulous 1890s Weekend" to commemorate the event. Motorless parade, period exhibits, crafts and other events, including the re-creation of the first night football game. Sponsors: Mansfield University of Pennsylvania and Greater Area Mansfield Chamber of Commerce. Est attendance: 10,000. For info: Dennis Miller, Dir PR, Mansfield University, Beecher House,

Mansfield, PA 16933. Phone: (570) 662-4293. Fax: (570) 662-4965. E-mail: dmiller@mansfield.edu. Web: www.mansfield.edu.

FERMI, ENRICO: BIRTH ANNIVERSARY. Sept 29, 1901. Nuclear physicist, born at Rome, Italy. Played a prominent role in the splitting of the atom and the construction of the first American nuclear reactor. Died at Chicago, IL, Nov 28, 1954.

HOWARD, TREVOR: BIRTH ANNIVERSARY. Sept 29, 1916. British actor Trevor Howard was born at Cliftonville, England. He appeared in more than 70 films including *The Third Man* (1950) and *Mutiny on the Bounty* (1962). He died Jan 7, 1988, at Bushey, England.

"MAKE ROOM FOR DADDY" TV PREMIERE: ANNIVERSARY. Sept 29, 1953. Danny Thomas starred as Danny Williams, a nightclub singer and comedian, in this family sitcom. The series was renamed "The Danny Thomas Show" in 1956 after Jean Hagen (who played his wife, Margaret) left the show. Thomas's co-stars were: Sherry Jackson and Penney Parker as Danny's daughter Terry; Rusty Hamer as son Rusty; Amanda Randolph as housekeeper Louise; Horace McMahon as Danny's agent, Phil Arnold; Jesse White as agent Jesse Leeds; Sid Melton as Charlie Halper, owner of the Copa Club; Ben Lessy as Danny's pianist, Ben; Mary Wickes as his publicist, Liz O'Neal; Hans Conried as Uncle Tonoose; Nan Bryant as Danny's mother-in-law and Marjorie Lord as his new wife Kathy. Many cast members returned for the show's sequel, "Make Room for Granddaddy," in 1970.

MICHAELMAS. Sept 29. The feast of St. Michael and All Angels in the Greek and Roman Catholic Churches.

NATIONAL ATTEND YOUR GRANDCHILD'S BIRTH DAY. Sept 29. Bonding with your grandchild should begin at birth. This day is set aside to encourage grandparents to participate in their grandchild's birth as well as his/her life. Annually, on Sept 29. For info: Carolynn Zorn, PO Box 744, Agoura, CA 91376. Phone: (818) 889-8377. E-mail: carolynn@attendingthe birth.com. Web: www.attendingthebirth.com.

NELSON, HORATIO: BIRTH ANNIVERSARY. Sept 29, 1758. English naval hero of the Battle of Trafalgar, born at Burnham Thorpe, Norfolk, England. Died during a battle at sea off Cape Trafalgar, Spain, Oct 21, 1805.

NEPTUNE FESTIVAL BOARDWALK WEEKEND. Sept 29–Oct 1. Virginia Beach, VA. A major mid-Atlantic regional festival. Events include sand sculpture contests, a parade, wine-tasting, sport events and more. Est attendance: 750,000. For info: Neptune Festival Boardwalk Weekend, 265 Kings Grant Rd, #102, Virginia Beach, VA 23452. Phone: (757) 498-0215. Web: www.neptunefestival.com.

NEW YORK FILM FESTIVAL. Sept 29–Oct 15. Lincoln Center, New York City. The 44th annual film festival presented by the Film Society of Lincoln Center. 17-day showcase of the newest and most important films from around the world. All features are US premieres, and more than 20 nations are represented. For info: New York Film Festival, The Film Society of Lincoln Center, 70 Lincoln Center Plaza, New York, NY 10023-6595. E-mail: webmaster@filmlinc.com. Web: www.filmlinc.com.

OHIO SWISS FESTIVAL. Sept 29–30. Sugarcreek, OH. Swiss music, games, costumes, parades. Continuous entertainment and tons of Swiss cheese. Annually, the fourth Friday and Saturday following Labor Day. Est attendance: 50,000. For info: Patricia Kaser, Info Coord, Ohio Swiss Festival, PO Box 158, Sugarcreek, OH 44681. Phone: (330) 852-4113 or (888) 609-7592.

PARAGUAY: BOQUERÓN DAY. Sept 29. National holiday. Commemorates a battle during the 1932 Chaco War.

SCOTLAND YARD FIRST APPEARANCE: ANNIVERSARY. Sept 29, 1829. The first public appearance of Greater London's Metropolitan Police occurred amid jeering and abuse from disapproving political opponents. Public sentiment turned to confidence and respect in the ensuing years. The Metropolitan Police had been established by an act of Parliament in June 1829, at the request of Home Secretary Sir Robert Peel, after whom the London police officers became more affectionately known as "bobbies." Scotland Yard, the site of their first headquarters near Charing Cross, soon became the official name of the force.

SPACE MILESTONE: *DISCOVERY* (US). Sept 29, 1988. Space Shuttle *Discovery*, after numerous reschedulings, launched from Kennedy Space Center, FL, with a five-member crew on board, and landed Oct 3 at Edwards Air Force Base, CA. It marked the first American manned flight since the *Challenger* tragedy in 1986. See also: "*Challenger*, Space Shuttle Explosion: Anniversary" (Jan 28).

SPACE MILESTONE: *SALYUT 6* (USSR). Sept 29, 1977. Soviet space station launched this date. *Salyut* stayed in space for four years, during which 31 spacecraft docked with the space station. Burned up when it reentered Earth's atmosphere after nearly five years on July 29, 1982.

STATE FAIR OF TEXAS. Sept 29–Oct 22. Fair Park, Dallas, TX. Features a Broadway musical, college football games, new car show, concerts, livestock shows and traditional events and entertainment including exhibits, creative arts and parades. Est attendance: 3,000,000. For info: Public Relations, State Fair of Texas, PO Box 150009, Dallas, TX 75315. Phone: (214) 421-8715. Fax: (214) 421-8710. E-mail: pr@bigtex.com. Web: www.bigtex.com.

"THIRTYSOMETHING" TV PREMIERE: ANNIVERSARY. Sept 29, 1987. This ABC drama series about a group of seven baby boomers was created by Ed Zwick and Marshall Herskovitz. It depicted the struggles of the show's characters—such as the death of a parent, illness, singlehood, marriage, divorce, career setbacks and the birth of a child. The cast featured Ken Olin as Michael Steadman; Mel Harris as his wife, Hope; Timothy Busfield as Michael's business partner, Elliot Weston; Patricia Wettig as Elliot's wife, Nancy; Polly Draper as Hope's friend Ellyn Warren; Melanie Mayron as Michael's cousin, Melissa Steadman and Peter Horton as family friend Gary Shepherd. The last telecast was Sept 3, 1991.

VETERANS OF FOREIGN WARS ESTABLISHED: ANNIVERSARY. Sept 29, 1899. This organization is loyal to the issues and actions affecting America's heroes. Its members offer assistance in addition to supporting veterans issues in Congress. Part of the organization's mission, according to its charter, is "to preserve and strengthen comradeship among its members; to foster true patriotism; and to preserve and defend the United States from all her enemies, whomsoever." For info: Veterans of Foreign Wars of the United States, 406 W 34th St, Kansas City, MO 64111. Phone: (816) 756-3390. Fax: (816) 968-1149. Email: info@vfw.org. Web: www.vfw.org.

BIRTHDAYS TODAY

Michelangelo Antonioni, 94, filmmaker (*Blow-Up, Zabriskie Point*), born Ferrara, Italy, Sept 29, 1912.

Anita Ekberg, 75, actress (*La Dolce Vita*), born Malmo, Sweden, Sept 29, 1931.

Bryant Gumbel, 58, TV host ("Today," "The Public Eye," "CBS This Morning"), sportscaster, born New Orleans, LA, Sept 29, 1948.

Hersey R. Hawkins, Jr, 40, former basketball player, born Chicago, IL, Sept 29, 1966.

Patricia Hodge, 60, actress ("Rumpole of the Bailey," *The Elephant Man, Betrayal*), born Cleethorpes, Lincolnshire, England, Sept 29, 1946.

Jerry Lee Lewis, 71, singer, musician ("Whole Lot of Shakin' Goin' On," "Great Balls of Fire"), born Ferriday, LA, Sept 29, 1935.

Emily Lloyd, 36, actress (*Wish You Were Here, In Country, A River Runs Through It*), born North London, England, Sept 29, 1970.

Ian McShane, 64, actor ("Deadwood," *The Last of Sheila*), born Blackburn, England, Sept 29, 1942.

Bill Nelson, 64, US Senator (D, Florida), born Miami, FL, Sept 29, 1942.

John MacBeth Paxson, 46, former basketball player, born Dayton, OH, Sept 29, 1960.

Lech Walesa, 63, Polish labor leader, Solidarity founder, born Popowo, Poland, Sept 29, 1943.

Dave Wilcox, 64, Hall of Fame football player, born Ontario, OR, Sept 29, 1942.

SEPTEMBER 30 — SATURDAY
Day 273 — 92 Remaining

ALBUQUERQUE INTERNATIONAL BALLOON FIESTA. Sept 30–Oct 8. Balloon Fiesta Park, Albuquerque, NM. Held since 1972, the largest hot air balloon gathering in the world features more than 750 hot air and gas balloons, mass ascensions, balloon glows and specially shaped balloons. The ten-day event includes entries from more than 28 countries. Annually, the first through second weekends in October. For info: Albuquerque Intl Balloon Fiesta, Inc, 4401 Alameda NE, Albuquerque, NM 87113. Phone: (505) 821-1000 or (888) 422-7277. Fax: (505) 828-2887. E-mail: balloons@balloonfiesta.com. Web: www.balloonfiesta.com.

BRIGG'S AND AL'S RUN & WALK FOR CHILDREN'S HOSPITAL. Sept 30. Milwaukee, WI. Choose from an 8k run, 5-mile walk or 3-mile walk along the lake and through the streets. Benefit fundraiser for Children's Hospital of Wisconsin. Finish line party on Summerfest grounds with free entertainment and fitness expo. Est attendance: 17,000. For info: Children's Hospital Foundation, PO Box 1997 MS#3050, Milwaukee, WI 53201. Phone: (414) 266-6320. Fax: (414) 266-6139. Web: www.alsmemorialrun.com.

BABE RUTH SETS HOME RUN RECORD: ANNIVERSARY. Sept 30, 1927. George Herman "Babe" Ruth hit his 60th home run of the season off Tom Zachary, of the Washington Senators. Ruth's record for the most homers in a single season stood for 34 years—until Roger Maris hit 61 in 1961. Maris's record was broken in 1998 by Mark McGwire with 62 home runs. Barry Bonds broke McGwire's record on Oct 5, 2001.

BABE RUTH'S LAST GAME AS YANKEE: ANNIVERSARY. Sept 30, 1934. On this date Babe Ruth played his last game for the New York Yankees. Soon after, while watching the fifth game of the World Series (between the St. Louis Cardinals and Detroit Tigers) and angry that he was not to be named Yankees manager, Ruth told Joe Williams, sports editor of the Scripps-Howard newspapers, that after 15 seasons he would no longer be playing for the Yankees.

BOTSWANA: INDEPENDENCE DAY. Sept 30. National holiday. The former Bechuanaland Protectorate (British Colony) became the independent Republic of Botswana in 1966.

BUFFALO ROUNDUP ARTS FESTIVAL. Sept 30–Oct 2. Custer, SD. South Dakota artists and craftsmen display and sell their arts and crafts. Also Western and Native American entertainment, pancake feeds, chili cook-off and much more. 13th annual. Est attendance: 15,000. For info: Craig Pugsley, Visitor Services Coord, Custer State Park, HC 83, Box 70, Custer, SD 57730. Phone: (605) 255-4515. Fax: (605) 255-4460. E-mail: craig.pugsley@state.sd.us. Web: www.custerstatepark.info.

September 2006	S	M	T	W	T	F	S
						1	2
	3	4	5	6	7	8	9
	10	11	12	13	14	15	16
	17	18	19	20	21	22	23
	24	25	26	27	28	29	30

CAPOTE, TRUMAN: BIRTH ANNIVERSARY. Sept 30, 1924. American novelist and literary celebrity, was born Truman Streckfus Persons at New Orleans, LA. He later took the name of his stepfather to become Truman Capote. Among his best-remembered books: *Other Voices, Other Rooms; Breakfast at Tiffany's* and *In Cold Blood.* He was working on a new novel, *Answered Prayers,* at the time of his death at Los Angeles, CA, Aug 25, 1984.

"CHEERS" TV PREMIERE: ANNIVERSARY. Sept 30, 1982. NBC sitcom revolving around the owner, employees and patrons of a Beacon Street bar at Boston. Original cast: Ted Danson as owner Sam Malone, Shelley Long and Rhea Perlman as waitresses Diane Chambers and Carla Tortelli, Nicholas Colasanto as bartender Ernie "Coach" Pantusso, John Ratzenberger as mailman Cliff Clavin and George Wendt as accountant Norm Peterson. Later cast members: Woody Harrelson as bartender Woody Boyd, Kelsey Grammer as Dr. Frasier Crane, Kirstie Alley as Rebecca Howe and Bebe Neuwirth as Dr. Lilith Sternin Crane. The theme song "Where Everybody Knows Your Name," was sung by Gary Portnoy. The last episode aired Aug 19, 1993.

DEAN, JAMES: DEATH ANNIVERSARY. Sept 30, 1955. Rising young film star James Dean died in an auto accident near Cholame, CA, two hours after getting a speeding ticket. He was 24 years old. His final films, *Rebel Without a Cause* and *Giant,* were released posthumously in 1956. See also "Dean, James: Birth Anniversary" (Feb 8).

EVERYBODY'S DAY FESTIVAL. Sept 30. Thomasville, NC. A downtown street festival for "everybody." Crafts, food vendors and live entertainment. Annually, the last Saturday in Sept. Est attendance: 82,000. For info: Thomasville Area Chamber of Commerce, Box 1400, Thomasville, NC 27361. Phone: (336) 475-6134. Fax: (336) 475-4802. E-mail: tvillecoc@northstate.net. Web: www.everybodysday.com.

FAMILY HEALTH AND FITNESS DAY—USA. Sept 30. 10th annual national event promoting family health and fitness. Families across the country will be involved in locally organized health promotion activities at hundreds of locations all on the same day. Always held the last Saturday in September. Est attendance: 25,000. For info: Pat Henze, Program Mgr, Health Info Resource Center, 1850 Winchester Rd, Ste 213, Libertyville, IL 60048. Phone: (800) 828-8225. Fax: (847) 816-8662. E-mail: info @fitnessday.com. Web: www.fitnessday.com.

FEAST OF SAINT JEROME. Sept 30. Patron saint of scholars and librarians.

FIRST ANNUAL FAIR IN AMERICA: ANNIVERSARY. Sept 30, 1641. According to the Laws and Ordinances of New Netherlands (now New York and New Jersey), on Sept 30, 1641, authorities declared that "henceforth there shall be held annually at Fort Amsterdam" a Cattle Fair (Oct 15) and a Hog Fair (Nov 1), and that "whosoever hath any things to sell or buy can regulate himself accordingly."

FIRST CRIMINAL EXECUTION IN AMERICAN COLONIES: ANNIVERSARY. Sept 30, 1630. John Billington, one of the first Pilgrims to land in America, was hanged for murder, becoming the first criminal to be executed in the American colonies.

"THE FLINTSTONES" TV PREMIERE: ANNIVERSARY. Sept 30, 1960. This Hanna Barbera cartoon comedy was set in prehistoric times. Characters included two Stone Age families, Fred and Wilma Flintstone and neighbors Barney and Betty Rubble. In 1994 *The Flintstones* movie was released, starring John Goodman, Rick Moranis and Rosie O'Donnell.

GUADALUPE MOUNTAINS NATIONAL PARK ESTABLISHED: ANNIVERSARY. Sept 30, 1972. Area in western Texas along Texas–New Mexico border, originally authorized Oct 15, 1966, was established as a national park. For further park info: Guadalupe Mountains Natl Park, HC 60, Box 400, Salt Flat, TX 79847-9400.

GUTENBERG BIBLE PUBLISHED: ANNIVERSARY.
Sept 30, 1452. The first section of the Gutenberg Bible, the first book printed from movable type, was published at Mainz, Germany. Johann Gutenberg was the printer. The book was completed by 1456.

HALEAKALA NATIONAL PARK ESTABLISHED: ANNIVERSARY. Sept 30, 1960. Summit of a volcano on Maui in the Hawaiian Islands was authorized as a part of Hawaii National Park on Aug 1, 1916. In 1960 Haleakala was established as a separate national park. The park was expanded in 1969 to include the Kipahulu Valley. For further park info: Haleakala Natl Park, PO Box 369, Makawao, HI 96768.

KWXX HO'OLAULE'A IN DOWNTOWN HILO. Sept 30. Hilo, HI. East Hawaii's largest music block party. This annual free event features three stages with more than 15 of Hawaii's premiere local musicians, playing into the night. Food and craft vendors line the street. Family event, all ages welcome! Est attendance: 15,000. For info: New West Broadcasting Corp, 1145 Kilauea Ave, Hilo, HI 96720. Phone: (808) 935-5461. E-mail: chris@kwxx.com.

LONG BEACH ISLAND CHOWDER COOK-OFF. Sept 30–Oct 1. Bayfront Park, Beach Haven, NJ. Weekend-long festival featuring unlimited tasting of up to 30 different red/white clam chowders prepared by area restaurants. Entertainment; other food/beverages available. Annually, the weekend before Columbus Day weekend. Est attendance: 24,000. For info: Southern Ocean County Chamber of Commerce, 265 W 9th St, Ship Bottom, NJ 08008. Phone: (800) 292-6372 or (609) 494-7211. Fax: (609) 494-5807. E-mail: event@discoversouthernocean.com. Web: www.chowderfest.com.

MEREDITH ENROLLS AT OLE MISS: ANNIVERSARY.
Sept 30, 1962. Rioting broke out when James Meredith became the first black to enroll in the all-white University of Mississippi. President Kennedy sent US troops to the area to force compliance with the law. Three people died in the fighting and 50 were injured. On June 6, 1966, Meredith was shot while participating in a civil rights march at Mississippi. On June 25 Meredith, barely recovered, rejoined the marchers near Jackson, MS.

MOON PHASE: FIRST QUARTER. Sept 30. Moon enters First Quarter phase at 7:04 AM, EDT.

"MURDER, SHE WROTE" TV PREMIERE: ANNIVERSARY. Sept 30, 1984. Angela Lansbury starred as crime novelist Jessica Fletcher from Cabot Cove, Maine, who traveled the country solving murders. This top-rated detective show also featured Tom Bosley as Sheriff Amos Tupper and William Windom as Dr. Seth Hazlett. The program aired for 12 years and is still in syndication.

NATCHEZ FALL PILGRIMAGE. Sept 30–Oct 14. Natchez, MS. Tours of 18 antebellum mansions furnished with fine antiques and surrounded by lovely gardens. Carriage and bus sightseeing tours, evening entertainment. Est attendance: 10,000. For info: Natchez Pilgrimage Tours, PO Box 347, 640 S Canal St, Natchez, MS 39121. Phone: (800) 647-6742 or (601) 446-6631. Fax: (601) 446-8687. E-mail: visit@natchezpilgrimage.com. Web: www.natchezpilgrimage.com.

OCEAN COUNTY DECOY AND GUNNING SHOW. Sept 30–Oct 1 (tentative). Pinelands High and Middle Schools, Tip Seaman County Park and Tuckerton Seaport, Tuckerton, NJ. 24th annual. Gathering to celebrate the local waterfowling heritage. Emphasizes traditional skills such as decoy carving, working decoy rigs, sneakbox building, gunning, retrieving and goose- and duck-calling contests. Wildlife art and crafts, outdoor clothing and gear, hunting and fishing supplies. More than 500 vendors. Free. Rain or shine. Est attendance: 35,000. For info: Wells Mills Co Park. Phone: (609) 971-3085. Web: www.co.ocean.nj.us/parks/default.htm.

OCTOBERFEST. Sept 30. Lawrence University, Appleton, WI. Come enjoy a family event with ethnic foods, arts & crafts, fun and entertainment. Annually, the last Saturday in September. Est attendance: 150,000. For info: Campus Activities, Lawrence University, PO Box 599, Appleton, WI 54912.

PUMPKIN DAY. Sept 30. Woodstock, VT. Learn about the many uses and varieties of pumpkin through activities and programs and take home a miniature pumpkin. Also harvest activities and wagon rides. First day of the annual pumpkin sale! For info: Billings Farm & Museum, Rte 12 North, Woodstock, VT 05091. Phone: (802) 457-2355. Fax: (802) 457-4663. E-mail: billings.farm@valley.net. Web: www.billingsfarm.org.

"THE RED SKELTON SHOW" TV PREMIERE: 55th ANNIVERSARY. Sept 30, 1951. Vaudevillian and radio performer Red Skelton hosted several popular variety shows on NBC and CBS in a career that spanned 20 years. He was a gifted comedian, famous for his loony characters, sight gags, pantomimes and ad-libs. His show was also notable for introducing Johnny Carson and the Rolling Stones to a national audience.

TACA FALL CRAFT FAIR. Sept 30–Oct 1. Coolidge Park, Chattanooga, TN. 11th annual fair. Marketing the creative work of the hand by 100 select American craft artists. Annually, the first weekend in October. Est attendance: 10,000. For info: Alice C. Merritt, Exec Director, Tennessee Assn of Craft Artists, PO Box 120066, Nashville, TN 37212. Phone: (615) 385-1904. Web: www.tennesseecrafts.org.

TOMS RIVER CANOE RACE. Sept 30. Old Toms River Bus Terminal, Toms River, NJ. 8½-mile race, 16 categories, every skill level. Prizes awarded. Pre-registration to enter the contest, or pay a late registraton fee if you register the morning of the race. Or just come and observe! Est attendance: 500. For info: Mickey Coen, Coord, Wells Mills County Park, 905 Wells Mills Rd, Waretown, NJ 08758. Phone: (609) 971-3085. Fax: (609) 971-9540. Web: www.co.ocean.nj.us/parks/default.htm.

TRI-STATE BAND FESTIVAL. Sept 30. Luverne, MN. 56th annual festival with more than 2,500 high school students from Minnesota, South Dakota and Iowa; trophies awarded in four classes. Annually, the last Saturday in September. Est attendance: 10,000. For info: Dave Smith, Exec Dir, Luverne Area Chamber of Commerce, 211 E Main, Luverne, MN 56156. Phone: (507) 283-4061. Fax: (507) 283-4061. E-mail: luvernechamber@iw.net. Web: www.luvernemn.com.

BIRTHDAYS TODAY

Deborah Allen, 53, singer ("Baby I Lied"), songwriter ("Don't Worry 'Bout Me"), born Memphis, TN, Sept 30, 1953.

Crystal Bernard, 42, actress ("Wings"), born Garland, TX, Sept 30, 1964.

Angie Dickinson, 75, actress (Emmy for "Police Woman"; *Dressed to Kill*), born Angeline Brown at Kulm, ND, Sept 30, 1931.

Fran Drescher, 49, actress ("The Nanny," *Jack*), born Flushing, NY, Sept 30, 1957.

Jenna Elfman, 35, actress ("Dharma & Greg," "Townies"), born Los Angeles, CA, Sept 30, 1971.

Martina Hingis, 26, former tennis player, born Kosice, Slovakia, Sept 30, 1980.

Deborah Kerr, 85, actress (*From Here to Eternity, The King and I*), born Helensburgh, Scotland, Sept 30, 1921.

Blanche Lambert Lincoln, 46, US Senator (D, Arkansas), born Helena, MT, Sept 30, 1960.

Johnny Mathis, 71, singer ("It's Not for Me to Say," "Chances Are"), born Gilmer, TX, Sept 30, 1935.

Marilyn McCoo, 63, singer (Fifth Dimension, "Up, Up and Away"), actress, born Jersey City, NJ, Sept 30, 1943.

Dominique Moceanu, 25, gymnast, born Hollywood, CA, Sept 30, 1981.

Eric Stoltz, 45, actor (*Fast Times at Ridgemont High, Pulp Fiction*), born Los Angeles, CA, Sept 30, 1961.

Victoria Tennant, 53, actress ("Winds of War," *All of Me, LA Story*), born London, England, Sept 30, 1953.

Elie Wiesel, 78, author, human rights activist, Nobel Peace Prize recipient, founder of the Elie Wiesel Foundation for Humanity, born Sighet, Romania, Sept 30, 1928.

October.

OCTOBER 1 — SUNDAY
Day 274 — 91 Remaining

ADOPT-A-SHELTER-DOG MONTH. Oct 1–31. To promote the adoption of dogs from local shelters, the ASPCA sponsors this important observance. "Make pet adoption your first option®" is a message the organization promotes throughout the year in an effort to end the euthanasia of all adoptable animals. For info: ASPCA Media Relations Dept, 110 5th Ave, 2nd Fl, New York, NY 10011. Phone: (212) 876-7700 ext 4655. E-mail: press @aspca.org. Web: www.aspca.org.

APPLE FESTIVAL. Oct 1. Old Prairie Town at Ward-Meade Historic Site, Topeka, KS. Celebration of harvest and heritage of Kansas located in 5½-acre historical park. Ethnic foods, live entertainment, special shows, turn-of-the-century town square activities, nearly 100 craft booths. Annually, the first Sunday in October. Est attendance: 10,000. For info: Sara Leeth, Old Prairie Town at Ward-Meade Historic Site, 124 NW Fillmore, Topeka, KS 66606. Phone: (785) 368-3888. Fax: (785) 368-3890.

BABE RUTH CALLS HIS SHOT?: ANNIVERSARY. Oct 1, 1932. In the fifth inning of game three of the World Series, with a count of two balls and two strikes and with hostile Cubs fans shouting epithets at him, Babe Ruth pointed to the center field bleachers in Chicago's Wrigley Field and followed up by hitting a soaring home run high above the very spot to which he had just gestured. With that homer Ruth squashed the Chicago Cubs' hopes of winning the game, and the Yankees went on to sweep the Series with four straight victories. For more than half a century the question has remained: Did Ruth actually call his shot that day? Even eyewitnesses disagree. Joe Williams of *The New York Times* wrote, "In no mistaken motions, the Babe notified the crowd that the nature of his retaliation would be a wallop right out of the confines of the park." But Cubs pitcher Charlie Root said, "Ruth did *not* point at the fence before he swung. If he'd made a gesture like that, I'd have put one in his ear and knocked him on his ass." Ruth's daughter has said that he denied it. But the Babe himself also claimed he had. Fact or folklore? Either way, legend!

	S	M	T	W	T	F	S
October	1	2	3	4	5	6	7
2006	8	9	10	11	12	13	14
	15	16	17	18	19	20	21
	22	23	24	25	26	27	28
	29	30	31				

BILLIARD AWARENESS MONTH. Oct 1–31. Sponsored by the Billiard Congress of America, a national nonprofit organization, Billiard Awareness Month celebrates the historic, recreational and educational aspects of cue sports. Cue sports are recognized as part of amateur and professional competitive sports, but more importantly promote camaraderie among participants of all ages and abilities. Throughout this month, BCA will highlight the skills learned at billiards: hand-eye coordination, physics, sportsmanship, strategy, discipline, concentration and goal-setting. For info: Amy Long, Billiard Congress of America, 4345 Beverly St, Colorado Springs, CO 80918. Phone: (719) 264-8300, ext 104. Fax: (719) 264-0900. E-mail: amy@bca-pool.com. Web: www.bca-pool .com.

BLESSING OF THE FISHING FLEET. Oct 1. Church of Saints Peter and Paul and Fisherman's Wharf, San Francisco, CA. Annually, the first Sunday in October.

BRAZIL: FESTIVAL OF PENHA. Oct 1–31. Rio de Janeiro. Pilgrimages, especially on Saturdays during October, to the Church of Our Lady of Penha, which is built on top of a rock, requiring a climb of 365 steps (representing the days of the year), or ride in car on inclined plane (for children, invalids and aged), for those troubled and sick who seek hope or cure.

BUFFALO WALLOW CHILI COOK-OFF. Oct 1. Custer State Park, Custer, SD. Musical entertainment, art fair and lots of chili cooking and tasting. Est attendance: 4,000. For info: Custer Area Chamber of Commerce, 615 Washington St, Custer, SD 57730. Phone: (800) 992-9818. Fax: (605) 673-3726.

CARTER, JIMMY: BIRTHDAY. Oct 1, 1924. 39th president of US (1977–81), Nobel Peace Prize recipient, born James Earl Carter, Jr, at Plains, GA.

CATTUS ISLAND NATURE FESTIVAL. Oct 1. Cattus Island County Park, Toms River, NJ. 26th annual environmental organizations fair with natural history programs throughout the day. Annually, the first Sunday in October. Est attendance: 1,700. For info: Christopher Claus, Cattus Island Park, 1170 Cattus Island Blvd, Toms River, NJ 08753. Phone: (732) 270-6960. E-mail: cclaus@co.ocean.nj.us.

CD PLAYER DEBUTS: ANNIVERSARY. Oct 1, 1982. The first compact disc player, developed jointly by Sony, Philips and Polygram, went on sale. It cost $625.

CELEBRATE SUN DRIED TOMATOES MONTH. Oct 1–31. Celebrate all that's great about sun dried tomatoes—it's more than taste! Before modern canning methods were available, Italians dried tomatoes on their tile roofs for use in winter when fresh tomatoes were not available. These nutrient-dense tomatoes contain lycopene, a phytochemical and antioxidant that fights free radicals in the body and can help reduce the risk factors for many types of cancer and heart disease. To obtain recipes and health info: Mooney Farms, 1220 Fortress St, Chico, CA 95973. Phone: (530) 899-2661. Fax: (530) 899-7746. E-mail: Mooney Farm@aol.com. Web: www.mooneyfarms.com.

CELIAC DISEASE AWARENESS MONTH. Oct 1–31. For info: Celiac Sprue Assn/USA, PO Box 31700, Omaha, NE 68131-0700. Phone: (402) 643-4101 or (877) CSA-4CSA. Fax: (402) 643-4108. E-mail: celiacs@csaceliacs.org. Web: www.csaceliacs .org.

CHILDREN'S MAGAZINE MONTH. Oct 1–31. Nationwide literacy initiative to raise awareness and create interest in children's magazines. For info: Children's Magazine Month, 66 Witherspoon St, #207, Princeton, NJ 08542. E-mail: info@cmm .magazineliteracy.org. Web: www.childmagmonth.org.

CHINA, PEOPLE'S REPUBLIC OF: NATIONAL DAY. Oct 1. Commemorates the founding of the People's Republic of China in 1949.

CHRISTMAS SEAL CAMPAIGN®. Oct 1–Dec 31. An American tradition dating back to 1907 when the first Christmas Seals® were made available in the US, the annual campaign is a major support of American Lung Association programs dedicated to fighting lung diseases such as asthma, emphysema, tuberculosis and lung cancer, as well as their causes. For info: American Lung Assn, 61 Broadway, 6th Fl, New York, NY 10006. Phone: (800) LUNG-USA. Web: www.lungusa.org.

CHURCH SAFETY AND SECURITY MONTH. Oct 1–31. A yearly reminder to churches that there are easy and inexpensive ways to protect themselves from intruders, accidents, injuries and other tragedies that could impact the church's vitality. Topics addressed include playground safety, transportation safety, fire prevention and protection, food safety in church kitchens, how to deal effectively with crisis situations and general building security. The GuideOne Center for Risk Management will provide churches across the country free tips, materials and resources to help protect faithful congregations. For info: The GuideOne Center for Risk Management, 1111 Ashworth Rd, West Des Moines, IA 50265. Phone: (515) 267-5709. Fax: (515) 267-2250. E-mail: eabbas@guideone.com. Web: www.guideonecenter.com.

CLASS REUNION MONTH. Oct 1–31. Every October, classmates from around the country and the world will gather to reconnect, reminisce and remember those carefree days of youth. For info: Dina C. Carson, PO Box 999, Niwot, CO 80544. E-mail: info@reunionsolutions.com. Web: www.reunionsolutions.com.

COUNTRY INN, BED AND BREAKFAST DAY. Oct 1. In Florida, Pennsylvania, West Virginia and British Columbia, Canada, several country inns and bed & breakfasts will welcome visitors with information, special events, special treats (home-baked goodies) and good fellowship. The weekend will also introduce people to the world of inns and B&Bs. Annually, the first Sunday of October. For info: Tina Czarnota. Phone: (561) 487-6917. E-mail: tczarnot@bellsouth.net. Web: www.tinaczarnota.com.

"CYBERSPACE" COINED: *NEUROMANCER* PUBLICATION ANNIVERSARY. Oct 1, 1984. The groundbreaking science fiction novel *Neuromancer*, by William Gibson, was published on this day and featured a word now commonplace in popular culture: "cyberspace." The novel was a winner of the Hugo, Nebula and Philip K. Dick awards.

CYPRUS: INDEPENDENCE DAY. Oct 1. National holiday. Commemorates independence from Britain in 1960.

DISNEY WORLD OPENED: 35th ANNIVERSARY. Oct 1, 1971. Disney's second theme park opened at Orlando, FL. See also "Disneyland Opened: Anniversary" (July 17).

DIVERSITY AWARENESS MONTH. Oct 1–31. Celebrating, promoting and appreciating the diversity of our society. Also, a month to foster and further our understanding of the inherent value of all races, genders, nationalities, age groups, religions, sexual orientations, classes and physical disabilities. Annually, in October. For info: Carole Copeland Thomas, C. Thomas & Assoc, 400 W Cummings Park, Ste 1725-154, Woburn, MA 01801. Phone: (800) 801-6599 or (508) 947-5755. Fax: (508) 947-3903. E-mail: Carole@TellCarole.com. Web: www.TellCarole.com.

DOMESTIC VIOLENCE AWARENESS MONTH. Oct 1–31. Commemorated since 1987, this month attempts to raise awareness of efforts to end violence against women and their children. The Domestic Violence Awareness Month Project is a collaborative effort of the National Resource Center on Domestic Violence, Family Violence Prevention Fund, National Coalition Against Domestic Violence, National Domestic Violence Hotline and the National Network to End Domestic Violence. For info: NCADV, PO Box 18749, Denver, CO 80218. Phone: (303) 839-1852. Web: www.ncadv.org.

EAT BETTER, EAT TOGETHER MONTH. Oct 1–31. Time to encourage families to eat together. Research indicates that children who eat with their families not only have better nutrition, but they do better in school and have fewer behavior problems. A tool kit has been created to show how family meals can be simple, easy and nutritious. Call for the top ten ways to eat better, eat together. For info: Nutrition Education Network of Washington State, Cooperative Extension, Washington State University,

7612 Pioneer Way E, Puyallup, WA 98317-4989. Phone: (253) 761-2757. Web: nutrition.wsu.edu/ebet/index.html.

EMOTIONAL WELLNESS MONTH. Oct 1–31. Get more out of every day with laughter and enjoyment. This is a time to reduce stress and seek moderation in mood swings. Balance your activities to support your emotional state, and keep your positive attitude in check. Take an anger management course to learn how to control explosive tempers. Seek the help of a therapist. Distance yourself from drama and chaos. Create a humor file with clipped columns and cartoons, and watch comedy on TV and film. Lighten up and learn to laugh at yourself. For info: Angela Brown, Words of Wellness, PO Box 49266, Charlotte, NC 28277. Phone: (704) 849-2900. Fax: (704) 845-3060. E-mail: angela@wordsofwellness.com. Web: www.wordsofwellness.com.

ENERGY MANAGEMENT IS A FAMILY AFFAIR— IMPROVE YOUR HOME. Oct 1–Mar 31, 2007. Replace energy-consuming units with new efficient home conveniences and remodel to prevent heating and cooling loss. Editorial package includes approximately 100 camera-ready stories and photos free to editors. Also available on disk and website. For info: James A. Stewart, Jr, Home Improvement Time Inc, PO Box 247, Oakdale, PA 15071-0247. Phone: (412) 787-2881. Fax: (412) 787-3233. E-mail: hitdirect@aol.com. Web: homeimprovementtime.com.

FALL ON NANTUCKET. Oct 1–Nov 30. Nantucket Island, MA. Includes the Nantucket Arts Festival, Chowder Contest, Cranberry Harvest, Harvest Fair and more. Est attendance: 2,000. For info: Nantucket Island Chamber of Commerce, 48 Main St, Nantucket, MA 02554-3595. Phone: (508) 228-1700. Web: www.nantucketchamber.org.

FIREPUP'S® BIRTHDAY. Oct 1. Firepup spends his time teaching fire and burn prevention and life safety awareness to children and their parents in a fun-filled and non-threatening manner. Materials are available through local fire departments. For info: Natl Fire Safety Council, Inc, PO Box 378, Michigan Center, MI 49254-0378. Phone: (517) 764-2811. E-mail: tlusby@nfcd.org.

FRYEBURG FAIR. Oct 1–8. Rte 5, Fryeburg, ME. Agricultural exposition, draft horse competitions, oxen and horse pulling, midway, country shows each evening, harness racing, Woodsmen's Day (always Monday), tractor pulling, baking contests, Forestry Resource Center, Fireman's Muster, sheepdog trials and juried crafts show. Annually, the week that includes the first Wednesday in October. Est attendance: 350,000. For info: June Hammond, Secy, PO Box 78, Fryeburg, ME 04037. Phone: (207) 935-3268. Fax: (207) 935-3662. E-mail: info@fryeburgfair.com.

GAY AND LESBIAN HISTORY MONTH. Oct 1–31. October was selected to commemorate the first two lesbian and gay marches on Washington in October 1979 and 1987.

GERMAN-AMERICAN HERITAGE MONTH. Oct 1–31. A month celebrating America's German heritage. Numerous historical programs, museum and library exhibits, cultural events, genealogical workshops and more planned. For info: Dr. Don Heinrich Tolzmann, Dir, German-American Studies Program, University of Cincinnati, PO Box 210113, Cincinnati, OH 45221-0113. Phone: (513) 556-1955. Fax: (513) 556-2113. E-mail: don.tolzmann@uc.edu.

GERMANY: ERNTEDANKFEST. Oct 1. A harvest thanksgiving festival, or potato harvest festival, Erntedankfest (or Erntedanktag) is generally observed on the first Sunday in October.

GO HOG WILD—EAT COUNTRY HAM MONTH. Oct 1–31. Suuu-eee! It's not just a word, it's a state of mind. For more than 200 years, Americans have been curing and eating country ham. The custom of curing that began in the state of Virginia during the mid-1700s continues today from Georgia to Missouri and points in between. Discover the difference between "city ham" and "country ham" and get some great recipes to boot during Eat Country Ham Month. For info: Natl Country Ham Assn, PO Box 948, Conover, NC 28613. Phone: (800) 820-4HAM. E-mail: eatham@countryham.org. Web: www.countryham.org.

HALLOWEEN SAFETY MONTH. Oct 1–31. There are steps you can take to make it a safe Halloween for children and teens. Information about the dangers of cosmetic contact lenses will be included, as the use of these lenses increases at this time of the year. For info: Prevent Blindness America®, 211 W Wacker Dr, Ste 1700, Chicago, IL 60606. Phone: (800) 331-2020. E-mail: info@preventblindness.org. Web: www.prevent-blindness.org.

HARRIS, RICHARD: BIRTH ANNIVERSARY. Oct 1, 1930. Born at Limerick, Ireland, Richard Harris became known as a stage actor on the London theater scene in the 1950s. Although his first love was the stage, it was in films that he earned his highest degree of success. He was unforgettable as King Arthur in the film version of *Camelot* (1967) and was twice nominated for best actor Oscars: for 1963's *This Sporting Life* and 1991's *The Field*. He portrayed headmaster Albus Dumbledore in the first two Harry Potter films in 2001 and 2002. He died Oct 25, 2002, at London, England.

HARRISON, CAROLINE LAVINIA SCOTT: BIRTH ANNIVERSARY. Oct 1, 1832. First wife of Benjamin Harrison, twenty-third president of the US, born at Oxford, OH. Died at Washington, DC, Oct 25, 1892. She was the second First Lady to die in the White House.

HEALTH LITERACY MONTH. Oct 1–31. Promoting understandable health information around the world. For info: Health Literacy Consulting, 31 Highland St, Ste 201, Natick, MA 01760. Phone: (508) 653-1199. E-mail: Helen@healthliteracy.org. Web: www.healthliteracymonth.org.

HOROWITZ, VLADIMIR: BIRTH ANNIVERSARY. Oct 1, 1904. Virtuoso pianist, born at Berdichev, Russia. Horowitz was widely hailed as one of the world's greatest pianists, renowned for his masterful technique. His debut was at Kiev in 1920, and at the age of 20 he played a series of 23 recitals at Leningrad, performing a total of more than 200 works with no duplications. He made his US debut in 1928 with the New York Philharmonic. He settled in the US in 1940 and became a citizen in 1944. His career swung full circle Apr 20, 1986, when he performed his first concert in his native Russia after a self-imposed absence of 60 years. He died Nov 5, 1989, at New York, NY.

INTERGENERATION DAY. Oct 1. Connecting generations through communication, celebration and education. Annually, the first Sunday in October, culminating Intergeneration Activities Week. For info: Intergeneration Foundation, 430 N Tejon St, Ste 300, Colorado Springs, CO 80903. Phone: (719) 471-3691. Fax: (719) 471-3696. E-mail: information@intergenerationday.org. Web: www.intergenerationday.org.

INTERNATIONAL STARMAN MONTH. Oct 1–31. Celebrates the TV series "Starman," which first aired in 1986 and inspired many people around the world to change their lives in positive ways. Spotlight Starman International is a group of people who appreciate the quality, consciousness and themes of the show and continue to gather annually to celebrate that spirit while raising funds for environmental, social and/or educational causes. (The organization is open to all without membership dues.) See also "Starman Family-Con 2006 (Sept 15)." For info: Vicki Werkley, Spotlight Starman Intl, 16563 Ellen Springs Dr, Lower Lake, CA 95457-9477. Phone: (707) 995-1228. E-mail: spotlight_starman@bigfoot.com (put "Starman" in subject line). Web: www.starmanet.com.

INTERNATIONAL STRATEGIC PLANNING MONTH. Oct 1–31. The start of the final quarter of the year provides a great opportunity for businesses and individuals to review the results of their efforts to date, make adjustments to meet this year's goals, and begin thinking about next year's goals. Strategic planning is a systematic and continuous process of evaluation, decision, implementation and measuring. For info: Sherrin Ross Ingram, Intl Center for Strategic Planning, 104 W Chestnut St, #101, Hinsdale, IL 60521. Phone: (800) 962-4750. Fax: (800) 962-0177. E-mail: info@icfsp.com. Web: www.icfsp.com.

JAPAN: NEWSPAPER WEEK. Oct 1–7. During this week newspapers make an extensive effort to acquaint the public with their functions and attempt to carry out the role of a newspaper in a free society. Annually, the first week in October.

JOHNNY APPLESEED DAYS. Oct 1–2. Lake City, MN. Apple pie, arts and crafts fair, silent auction, games. Annually, the first full weekend in October. Est attendance: 6,500. For info: Lake City Area Chamber of Commerce, 212 S Washington St, Lake City, MN 55041. Phone: (800) 369-4123. E-mail: lcchambr@earthlink.net.

THE JOY OF SEX: PUBLICATION ANNIVERSARY. Oct 1, 1972. English publisher Mitchell Beazely released Dr. Alex Comfort's landmark book this month in 1972. Published in the midst of the western world's sexual revolution, *The Joy of Sex* was an immediate bestseller and to date has sold almost 10 million copies.

"KUNG FU" TV PREMIERE: ANNIVERSARY. Oct 1, 1972. David Carradine starred in this unusual ABC western as Kwai Chang Caine, a half-Chinese martial arts master drifter who was exiled from China. Appearing in flashback were: Keye Luke as Master Po, Philip Ahn as Master Kan and Radames Pera as the younger Caine. The show ran for three years. "Kung Fu" returned as a 1986 TV movie introducing the late Brandon Lee as Caine's son. A sequel series currently appears in syndication starring a much older Carradine.

LAST WEEK TO REGISTER TO VOTE IN US GENERAL ELECTIONS. Oct 1–7. This is the last week that every state in the nation still allows US citizens to register to vote for the November general elections. After this week, different states' deadlines will pass each day. One easy way to register to vote is at the free website Congress.org, where you can fill out an application, print, sign and mail it to the appropriate address. Annually, the seven days ending the 5th Saturday before the general election (which is the first Tuesday after the first Monday in November). For info: Lara Wyrsta, Capitol Advantage, 2751 Prosperity Ave, 6th Fl, Fairfax, VA 22031. Phone: (703) 289-4670. Fax: (703) 289-4678. E-mail: lamarketing@capitoladvantage.com. Web: www.capitoladvantage.com.

October 2006	S	M	T	W	T	F	S
	1	2	3	4	5	6	7
	8	9	10	11	12	13	14
	15	16	17	18	19	20	21
	22	23	24	25	26	27	28
	29	30	31				

LAWRENCE, JAMES: 225th BIRTH ANNIVERSARY. Oct 1, 1781. Brilliant American naval officer, whose last battle was a defeat, but whose dying words became a most honored naval motto. Lawrence, born at Burlington, NJ, was captain of the *Chesapeake* when she engaged in a naval duel with HMS *Shannon* off Boston, June 1, 1813. The *Chesapeake* was captured and towed to Halifax as a British prize. Lawrence was mortally wounded by a musket ball during the engagement and uttered his famous last words, "Don't give up the ship," as he was being carried off the ship's deck.

LITTLE RED SCHOOL HOUSE ANNUAL ART FAIR. Oct 1. Willow Springs, IL. Over 75 artists participate in the outdoor event with a "Nature in Cook County/Northern Illinois" theme. Est attendance: 5,000. For info: Little Red School House Nature Center, Forest Preserve Dist of Cook County, 9800 Willow Springs Rd, Willow Springs, IL 60480. Phone: (708) 839-6897. Web: www.fpdcc.com.

LONG TERM CARE PLANNING MONTH. Oct 1–31. As lifespans increase and family structures change, this month promotes awareness and discussion of how to meet the challenge of providing compassionate long term care. Raising awareness of the importance of long term care planning in everyone's retirement plan. Annually, the month of October. For info: Marilee Driscoll, Long Term Care Learning Institute, PO Box 956, Plymouth, MA 02362. Phone: (508) 830-9975. Fax: (508) 830-9976. E-mail: mdriscoll@LTCmonth.com. Web: www.LTCmonth.com.

LUPUS AWARENESS CAMPAIGN. Oct 1–Nov 15. To promote public awareness of lupus symptoms to aid in early diagnosis and treatment of this disease. For info: Duane Peters, VP of Communications & Advocacy, Lupus Foundation of America, 2000 L St NW, Ste 710, Washington, DC 20036. Phone: (202) 349-1145. Fax: (202) 349-1156. E-mail: peters@lupus.org. Web: www.lupus.org.

MARIS BREAKS RUTH HOME RUN RECORD: 45th ANNIVERSARY. Oct 1, 1961. Roger Maris of the New York Yankees hit his 61st home run, breaking Babe Ruth's record for the most home runs in a season. Maris hit his homer against pitcher Tracy Stallard of the Boston Red Sox as the Yankees won, 1–0. Controversy over the record arose because the American League had adopted a 162-game schedule in 1961, and Maris played in 161 games. In 1927, when Ruth set his record, the schedule called for 154 games, and Ruth played in 151. On Sept 8, 1998, Mark McGwire of the St. Louis Cardinals hit his 62nd home run, breaking Maris's record. On Oct 5, 2001, Barry Bonds of the San Francisco Giants broke McGwire's record.

MATTHAU, WALTER: BIRTH ANNIVERSARY. Oct 1, 1920. Actor (*The Odd Couple*, *Grumpy Old Men*), born at New York, NY. Died July 1, 2000, at Santa Monica, CA.

MENTAL ILLNESS AWARENESS WEEK. Oct 1–7. To increase public awareness of the causes of, symptoms of and treatments for mental illnesses. Annually, the first full week in October. For info: Div of Public Affairs, American Psychiatric Assn, 1000 Wilson Blvd, Ste 1825, Arlington, VA 22209-3901. Phone: (703) 907-7300. E-mail: apa@psych.org. Web: www.psych.org.

"THE MERV GRIFFIN SHOW" TV PREMIERE: ANNIVERSARY. Oct 1, 1962. Singer and game show king Merv Griffin's first effort as an afternoon talk-show host premiered on NBC but was later dropped for syndication. The afternoon show continued until 1969 when Griffin was tapped to host a late-night program on CBS to compete with "The Tonight Show with Johnny Carson."

MODEL T INTRODUCED: ANNIVERSARY. Oct 1, 1908. Ford introduced the Model T at a price of $850 but by 1924 the basic model sold for as little as $260. Between 1908 and 1927 Ford sold 15,007,033 Model Ts in the US. Although the first Model Ts were not built on an assembly line, the demand for the cars was so high that Ford developed a system where workers remained at their stations and cars came to them. This enabled Ford to turn out a Model T every 10 seconds.

MYSTERY SERIES WEEK. Oct 1–7. A celebration of continuing characters in mystery fiction. Two-thirds of all new mysteries each year feature a series detective. The series tradition has been alive and well for more than 100 years. Series readers today can choose from more than 12,500 adult mysteries featuring more than 2,500 continuing characters from living writers. Mystery Series Week will celebrate fictional cops, private eyes and amateur sleuths from all walks of life—solving crimes from 55 BC to the 22nd century. Annually, the first full week in October. For info: Purple Moon Press, 3319 Greenfield Rd, #317, Dearborn, MI 48120-1212. Phone: (313) 593-1033. Fax: (313) 593-4087. E-mail: info@purplemoonpress.com. Web: www.mysteryseriesweek.com.

NATIONAL ANIMAL SAFETY AND PROTECTION MONTH. Oct 1–31. Observance to promote the appropriate ways to protect and care for domestic and wild animals and help people strengthen skills for staying safe around animals. For info: PALS Foundation, PO Box 1271, San Luis Obispo, CA 93406. Phone: (805) 544-0984. Fax: (805) 544-2027. Web: www.PALS.R8.org.

NATIONAL BOOK MONTH. Oct 1–31. When the world demands more and more of our time, National Book Month invites everyone in America to take time out to treat themselves to a unique pleasure: reading a good book. Readers participate in National Book Month annually through literary events held at schools, bookstores, libraries, community centers and arts organizations. The organization also sponsors the annual National Book Awards. For info: Natl Book Foundation, 95 Madison Ave, Ste 709, New York, NY 10016. Phone: (212) 685-0261. Fax: (212) 235-6570. E-mail: nationalbook@nationalbook.org. Web: www.nationalbook.org.

NATIONAL BREAST CANCER AWARENESS MONTH. Oct 1–31. Entering its second decade of public and professional education and awareness. This month is promoted by 17 major national nonprofit cancer organizations working in partnership to raise awareness of breast cancer and to provide access to screening services. The third Friday in October (Oct 20 in 2006) is National Mammography Day. For info: call the Natl Breast Cancer Awareness Month Program toll-free at (877) 88-NBCAM. Web: www.nbcam.org.

★**NATIONAL BREAST CANCER AWARENESS MONTH.** Oct 1–31.

NATIONAL CARRY A TUNE WEEK. Oct 1–7. This week celebrates favorite tunes from the past by performing them in a concert, at school, at church or at home. The purpose is to remember tunes from America's past and keep them alive. Annually, the week nearest the birthday of William Billings (born Oct 7, 1746), America's first important tune composer ("Chester"). Sponsor: Tune Lovers Society. For info: Pine Tree Productions, 235 Prospect St, Stoughton, MA 02072. Phone: (781) 344-6954. E-mail: tunes1342@aol.com. Web: hometown.aol.com/tunes1342/tunelov3.htm.

NATIONAL CHILI MONTH. Oct 1–31. National observance and celebration of chili, one of the most historical and traditional American dishes. For info: Williams Foods, Inc, 13301 W 99th St, Lenexa, KS 66215. E-mail: 2chilicooks@williamsfoods.com.

NATIONAL COMMUNICATE WITH YOUR KID MONTH. Oct 1–31. The generation gap—parents and teens are often on different wavelengths and complain that they cannot talk to each other. The purpose of this observance is to open the doors to better communication between parents and teens and to build positive teen/parent relationships. Annually, the month of October. For info send SASE to: Dale Eshleman, Episcopal Counseling Center, 1021-A E Robinson St, Orlando, FL 32801. Phone: (800) 544-1817.

NATIONAL CONSTRUCTION TOY MONTH. Oct 1–31. A monthlong celebration of the creativity and educational value children gain from building with construction toys. For info: Knex Industries, Inc, 2990 Bergey Rd, Hatfield, PA 19440. Phone: (215) 997-7722. Fax: (215) 996-4222. E-mail: email@knex.com. Web: www.knexeducation.com.

NATIONAL COOKIE MONTH. Oct 1–31. Remember the aroma and tradition of fresh-baked cookies? Remember how the delicious scent filled the house? Celebrate the All-American favorite treat, the cookie, during National Cookie Month. Make, bake or buy a batch of fresh homemade cookies in any of your favorite flavors this month. Share a little love today—share a fresh-baked cookie! For info: Cookies For You, 117 S Main, Minot, ND 58701. Phone: (701) 839-4975 or (800) 814-5334. Web: www.cookiesforyou.com.

NATIONAL CRIME PREVENTION MONTH. Oct 1–31. During Crime Prevention Month, individuals can commit to working on at least one of three levels—family, neighborhood or community—to drive violence and drugs from our world. It is also a time to honor individuals who have accepted personal responsibility for their neighborhoods and groups who work for the community's common good. Annually, every October. For info: Natl Crime Prevention Council, 1000 Connecticut Ave NW, 13th Fl, Washington, DC 20036. Phone: (202) 466-6272. Fax: (202) 296-1356. Web: www.weprevent.org or www.ncpc.org.

NATIONAL DENTAL HYGIENE MONTH. Oct 1–31. To increase public awareness of the importance of preventive oral health care and the dental hygienist's role as the preventive professional. Annually, during the month of October. For info: Public Relations, American Dental Hygienists' Assn, 444 N Michigan Ave, Ste 3400, Chicago, IL 60611. Phone: (312) 440-8900 or (800) 243-ADHA. Fax: (312) 440-1702. E-mail: media@adha.net. Web: www.adha.org.

NATIONAL DEPRESSION EDUCATION AND AWARENESS MONTH. Oct 1–31. A nonprofit campaign to educate patients, the elderly and professionals about depression disorders. Kit of materials available for $15. Annually, the month of October. For info: PPSI, c/o Pharmacy Council on Depression Education, 101 Lucas Valley Rd, #210, San Rafael, CA 94903. Phone: (415) 479-8628. Fax: (415) 479-8608. E-mail: ppsi@aol.com. Web: www.ppsinc.org.

October 2006	**S**	**M**	**T**	**W**	**T**	**F**	**S**
	1	2	3	4	5	6	7
	8	9	10	11	12	13	14
	15	16	17	18	19	20	21
	22	23	24	25	26	27	28
	29	30	31				

NATIONAL DISABILITY EMPLOYMENT AWARENESS MONTH. Oct 1–31. To foster the full integration of people with disabilities into the workforce. For info: US Dept of Labor, Office of Disability Employment Policy, 200 Constitution Ave NW, Rm S1303, Washington, DC 20210-0002. Phone: (202) 693-7880. Fax: (202) 693-7888. E-mail: infoODEP@dol.gov. Web: www.dol.gov/odep.

★**NATIONAL DISABILITY EMPLOYMENT AWARENESS MONTH.** Oct 1–31. Presidential Proclamation issued for the month of October (PL100–630, Title III, Sec 301a of Nov 7, 1988). Previously issued as "National Employ the Handicapped Week" for a week beginning during the first week in October since 1945.

★**NATIONAL DOMESTIC VIOLENCE AWARENESS MONTH.** Oct 1–31.

NATIONAL DOWN SYNDROME MONTH. Oct 1–31. To promote better understanding of Down Syndrome. For info: Natl Down Syndrome Congress, 1370 Center Dr, Ste 102, Atlanta, GA 30338. Phone: (800) 232-NDSC. E-mail: info@ndsccenter.org. Web: www.ndsccenter.org.

NATIONAL FAMILY SEXUALITY EDUCATION MONTH. Oct 1–31. A national coalition effort to support parents as the first and primary sexuality educators of their children by providing information for parents and young people. For info: Planned Parenthood Federation of America, Education Dept, 434 W 33rd St, New York, NY 10001. Phone: (212) 261-4628. Fax: (212) 247-6269. E-mail: education@ppfa.org. Web: www.plannedparenthood.org.

NATIONAL "GAIN THE INSIDE ADVANTAGE" MONTH. Oct 1–31. Gaining "The Inside Advantage" is how ordinary people accomplish extraordinary things. It refers to taking control of your life from the inside out. It means learning how to live deeply, joyfully and successfully. For info: Cathy W. Lauro. Phone: (800) 215-3644. E-mail: mind@CWLauro.com. Web: www.CWLauro.com.

NATIONAL GO ON A FIELD TRIP MONTH. Oct 1–31. A month to highlight the importance of the field trip as a way to help children learn. Studies show that children learn 40–60 percent more outside the classroom, and the field trip is a great way to teach valuable life skills and career education. For info: Field Trip Factory, 2211 N Elston, Ste 304, Chicago, IL 60614. Phone: (800) 987-6409. Web: www.fieldtripfactory.com.

NATIONAL MEDICAL LIBRARIANS MONTH. Oct 1–31. Recognizes and celebrates the importance and the achievements of health sciences information professionals. Medical librarians offer efficient access to quality print and online medical and health-related information within a wide variety of health-care settings. Librarians representing 23 specialty groups and 14 regional chapters of the Medical Library Association (MLA) sponsor several events and educational opportunities throughout the month of October. For info: Medical Library Assn, 65 E Wacker Place, Ste 1900, Chicago, IL 60601. Phone: (312) 419-9094. Fax: (312) 419-8950. E-mail: info@mlahq.org. Web: www.mlanet.org.

NATIONAL NEWSPAPER WEEK. Oct 1–7. To emphasize the importance of newspapers to the public. Annually, the first full week in October. For info: Newspaper Assn Managers, Inc, 70 Washington St, Salem, MA 01970. Phone: (978) 744-8940. Fax: (978) 744-0333. E-mail: mlp@nenews.org. Web: www.nammanagers.com.

NATIONAL ORTHODONTIC HEALTH MONTH. Oct 1–31. A beautiful, healthy smile is only the most obvious benefit of orthodontic treatment. Orthodontic care plays an important role in dental health, overall physical health and emotional well-being. National Orthodontic Health Month is sponsored by the American Association of Orthodontists (AAO), the oldest and largest dental specialty organization in the world, established in 1900. The AAO supports research and education leading to quality patient care, as well as increased public awareness of the need for and benefits of orthodontic treatment. For info: Pam Paladin,

American Assn of Orthodontists, 401 N Lindbergh Blvd, St. Louis, MO 63141-7816. Phone: (314) 993-1700 or (800) STRAIGHT. E-mail: ppaladin@aaortho.org. Web: www.braces.org.

NATIONAL PAJAMA MONTH. Oct 1–31. October is National Pajama Month—THE month to hold pajama parties with your girlfriends to celebrate friendship. It's a chance to slow down and get comfortable. All pajama parties held this month are in honor of the fight against breast cancer. Sponsored by Tide with a touch of Downy in benefit of the Susan G. Komen Breast Cancer Foundation. Annually, the month of October. For info: Elexis Mariash, Fleishman-Hillard New York. E-mail: mariashe@fleishman.com. Web: www.komen.org.

NATIONAL PHYSICAL THERAPY MONTH. Oct 1–31. To increase awareness of the role of physical therapy in health care, thousands of physical therapists nationwide celebrate by hosting special activities such as fitness clinics, open houses, hotlines, athletic events, health seminars and exhibits. Annually, the month of October. For info: The American Physical Therapy Assn, 1111 N Fairfax St, Alexandria, VA 22314. Phone: (800) 999-2782 or (703) 706-3248. Web: www.apta.org.

NATIONAL POPCORN POPPIN' MONTH. Oct 1–31. To celebrate the wholesome, economical, natural food value of popcorn, America's native snack. For info: The Popcorn Board, 401 N Michigan Ave, Chicago, IL 60611-4267. Phone: (312) 644-6610. Web: www.popcorn.org.

NATIONAL PORK MONTH. Oct 1–31. The National Pork Board, in cooperation with state pork producers associations, celebrates October as National Pork Month. While pork promotions are conducted throughout the year, special emphasis is placed on Pork: The Other White Meat® during October. For info: National Pork Board, PO Box 9114, Des Moines, IA 50306. Phone: (515) 223-2600. Fax: (515) 223-2646. E-mail: porkboard@porkboard.org. Web: www.porkboard.org or www.theotherwhitemeat.com.

NATIONAL READING GROUP MONTH. Oct 1–31. Reading group members celebrate the joy of a book shared and inspire individuals who do not belong to a reading group to join one or start their own. Organizations, bookstores and libraries are encouraged to sponsor reading group events during this month. For info: Martha Burns, 41 Park Ln, Essex Fells, NJ 07021. E-mail: mlbwrite@aol.com. Alternate contact: Alice Dillon. Email: AJDdesign@aol.com.

NATIONAL ROLLER SKATING MONTH. Oct 1–31. A monthlong celebration recognizing the health benefits and recreational enjoyment of this long-loved pastime. Also includes in-line skating and an emphasis on safe skating. For info: Roller Skating Assn, 6905 Corporate Dr, Indianapolis, IN 46278. Phone: (317) 347-2626. Fax: (317) 347-2636. E-mail: rsa@rollerskating.com. Web: www.rollerskating.com.

NATIONAL RSV AWARENESS MONTH. Oct 1–31. Most babies get Respiratory Syncytial Virus (RSV) before they turn two, and it generally has symptoms much like a common cold. However, other children who get RSV, especially those born early or with ongoing lung problems, may develop serious complications associated with it, such as pneumonia or bronchiolitis. Each year, 125,000 babies are hospitalized because of complications with RSV and some of these babies die. There are things we can do to help protect our babies. A free booklet on RSV is available. For info: PreemieCare, c/o MOST (Mothers of Supertwins), PO Box 306, East Islip, NY 11730-0306. Phone: (631) 859-1110. E-mail: info@PreemieCare.org. Web: www.PreemieCare.org.

NATIONAL SARCASTICS AWARENESS MONTH. Oct 1–31. To help people everywhere understand the positive and negative aspects of sarcasm. For info: Dr. Virginia Tooper, Dir of Barbs, Sarcastics Anonymous, 100 Bay Pl, #2112, Oakland, CA 94610. Phone: (510) 891-8479. E-mail: vtooper@ix.netcom.com.

NATIONAL SEAFOOD MONTH. Oct 1–31. To promote the taste, variety and nutrition of fish and shellfish. For info and recipes: Natl Fisheries Institute, 7918 Jones Branch Dr, Ste 700, McLean, VA 22102. Phone: (703) 524-8880. E-mail: gthomas@nfi.org. Web: www.nfi.org.

NATIONAL SPINA BIFIDA AWARENESS MONTH. Oct 1–31. Promoting public awareness of current scientific, medical and educational issues related to spina bifida—the most frequently occuring permanently disabling birth defect. For info: Natl Resource Center, Natl Spina Bifida Assn of America, 4590 McArthur Blvd NW, Ste 250, Washington, DC 20007-4226. Phone: (202) 944-3285 or (800) 621-3141. E-mail: sbaa@sbaa.org. Web: www.sbaa.org.

NATIONAL SPINAL HEALTH MONTH. Oct 1–31. For info: American Chiropractic Assn, 1701 Clarendon Blvd, Arlington, VA 22209. Phone: (800) 986-4636. E-mail: memberinfo@amerchiro.org. Web: www.acatoday.com.

NATIONAL SUDDEN INFANT DEATH SYNDROME AWARENESS MONTH. Oct 1–31. Monthlong focus on sudden infant death syndrome (also called crib death), the nation's major cause of death for infants beyond one month of age. The BACK TO SLEEP CAMPAIGN hopes to increase public awareness and funds available for medical research and family services. For info: First Candle/SIDS Alliance, 1314 Bedford Ave, Ste 210, Baltimore, MD 21208. Phone: (800) 221-7437. Fax: (410) 653-8709. E-mail: info@firstcandle.org. Web: www.firstcandle.org.

NATIONAL TOILET TANK REPAIR MONTH. Oct 1–31. Monthlong observance dedicated to the value and benefits of a properly tuned toilet with special emphasis on do-it-yourself repairs and water conservation. For info: Greg Wisner, Mktg Mgr, Fluidmaster Inc, 30800 Rancho Viejo Rd, San Juan Capistrano, CA 92675. Phone: (949) 728-2000. Fax: (949) 728-2805.

NATIONAL WORK FROM HOME WEEK. Oct 1–7. A week to celebrate the trends, technology and tactics that allow millions of Americans to work from home as entrepreneurs and corporate teleworkers. For info: Jeff Zbar, PO Box 8263, Coral Springs, FL 33075-8263. Phone: (954) 346-4393. E-mail: jeff@chiefhomeofficer.com. Web: www.chiefhomeofficer.com.

NIGERIA: INDEPENDENCE DAY. Oct 1. National holiday. Became independent of Great Britain in 1960 and a republic in 1963.

NUCLEAR MEDICINE WEEK. Oct 1–7. Dedicated to recognizing the professionals devoted to using nuclear medicine as an integral part of patient care. This is the perfect time to promote the value and safety of nuclear medicine to patients, referring physicians and your community. Promotional items will be available through SNM. For info: Society of Nuclear Medicine. Phone: (703) 708-9000. Web: www.snm.org/nmw.

OCTOBER FROZEN & REFRIGERATED FOODS FESTIVAL. Oct 1–31. Promotes a national awareness of the convenience, quality and nutritional benefits of frozen and refrigerated foods. Annually, the month of October. For info: Julie Henderson, VP Communications, Natl Frozen & Refrigerated Foods Assn, 4755 Linglestown Rd, Ste 300, Harrisburg, PA 17112. Phone: (717) 657-8601. Fax: (717) 657-9862. E-mail: info@nfraweb.org. Web: www.nfraweb.org.

ORGANIZE YOUR MEDICAL INFORMATION MONTH. Oct 1–31. This month is dedicated to learning how to acquire, understand, utilize and store pertinent medical information and knowledge enabling each of us to become a more informed and active participant in our own medical care. This organization leads to fewer medical errors, shorter hospital stays, increased positive outcomes, the motivation to seek preventive care and the skills to negotiate the health care system. For info: Lynda Shrager. Phone/fax: (518) 475-1792. E-mail: LShrager@otherwisehealthy.com. Web: www.otherwisehealthy.com.

POLISH AMERICAN HERITAGE MONTH. Oct 1–31. A national celebration of Polish history, culture and pride, in cooperation with the Polish American Congress and Polonia Across America. For info: Michael Blichasz, Chair, Polish American Cultural Center, Natl HQ, 308 Walnut St, Philadelphia, PA 19106. Phone: (215) 922-1700. Fax: (215) 922-1518. E-mail: mail@polish americancenter.org. Web: www.polishamericancenter.org.

POSITIVE ATTITUDE MONTH. Oct 1–31. Sometimes it just comes down to attitude! Zig Ziglar says that attitude, more than aptitude, affects altitude. Keith Harrell says attitude is everything. Atta-tude is a self-reflection of who you think you are. This month is dedicated to establishing, boosting, or forcing ourselves to adopt positive attitudes and discovering and/or creating positive self-images. For info: Sylvia Henderson, Springboard Training, PO Box 588, Olney, MD 20830-0588. Phone: (301) 260-1538. E-mail: admin@springboardtraining.com. Web: www.springboard training.com.

PULASKI DAY PARADE. Oct 1. Philadelphia, PA. Parade honoring the Polish patriot known as the "Father of the American Cavalry." Begins at 20th and Benjamin Franklin Pkwy and ends at 19th and Benjamin Franklin Pkwy. For info: Polish American Congress, Eastern Pennsylvania District, 308 Walnut St, Philadelphia, PA 19106. Phone: (215) 739-3408. Fax: (215) 922-1518. Web: www.polishamericancongress.com.

"REMINGTON STEELE" TV PREMIERE: ANNIVERSARY. Oct 1, 1982. Laura Holt (played by Stephanie Zimbalist, daughter of Efrem Zimbalist, Jr), an imaginative private detective, could not get a case of her own—until she made up a partner, Remington Steele, who was conveniently out of the office when clients came calling. Then she met the suave stranger (Pierce Brosnan) with a foreign accent who called himself Remington Steele. They began a working partnership . . . which ended in marriage. The show aired on NBC, with the last telecast on Mar 9, 1987, and costarred James Read, Janet DeMay and Doris Roberts.

RETT SYNDROME AWARENESS MONTH. Oct 1–31. To promote awareness of this neurological disease. For info: Intl Rett Syndrome Assn, 9121 Piscataway Rd, Clinton, MD 20735. Phone: (301) 856-3334 or (800) 818-RETT. E-mail: irsa@rettsyndrome .org. Web: www.rettsyndrome.org.

RIGHT-BRAINERS RULE MONTH. Oct 1–31. Right-brainers are often ridiculed and reprimanded for their unorthodox and creative ways of doing things. The month of October is a chance to show how the right-brained person can survive and thrive in a very left-brained world. For info: Lee Silber, Creative Lee Speaking, 822 Redondo Ct, San Diego, CA 92109. Phone: (858) 488-4249. E-mail: leesilber@earthlink.net. Web: www.creativelee .com.

SELF-PROMOTION MONTH. Oct 1–31. Learn how to toot your own horn and promote your business to another level of success. Unique marketing strategies with a twist are shared by some of the most successful marketing gurus in the nation. Discover some of these insightful and low cost marketing strategies for yourself! Sign up for Debbie Allen's marketing expertise newsletter free. For info: Debbie Allen, Allen & Assoc Consulting, Inc, PO Box 27946, Scottsdale, AZ 85255-0149. Phone: (800) 359-4544. Web: www.confessionsofshameless.com.

SOUTH KOREA: ARMED FORCES DAY. Oct 1. Marked by many colorful military parades, aerial acrobatics and honor guard ceremonies, held around the reviewing plaza at Yoido, an island in the Han River.

★ ★ ★

October 2006	S	M	T	W	T	F	S
							1
	1	2	3	4	5	6	7
	8	9	10	11	12	13	14
	15	16	17	18	19	20	21
	22	23	24	25	26	27	28
	29	30	31				

SPINACH LOVERS MONTH. Oct 1–31. Spinach has finally become "the darling of vegetables": from its delectable taste to the breaking news on its lutein content for the prevention of macular degeneration. "Spinach—it's not just for breakfast anymore!" For info: Burgundy L. Olivier, "The Spinach Lady," PO Box 61952, Dept C, Lafayette, LA 70596. E-mail: email@ilovespinach .com. Web: www.ilovespinach.com.

SQUIRREL AWARENESS WEEK (SAW). Oct 1–7. Set aside to honor one of our friendliest forms of wildlife, squirrels. "I SAW a squirrel today." Annually, the first Sunday in October through the following Saturday. For info: Gregg Bassett, The Squirrel Lover's Club, 318 W Fremont Ave, Elmhurst, IL 60126. Phone: (630) 833-1117. E-mail: sqrlman@thesquirrelloversclub .com. Web: www.thesquirrelloversclub.com.

STOCKTON, RICHARD: BIRTH ANNIVERSARY. Oct 1, 1730. Lawyer and signer of the Declaration of Independence, born at Princeton, NJ. Died there, Feb 8, 1781.

TALK ABOUT PRESCRIPTIONS MONTH. Oct 1–31. For info: Natl Council on Patient Information and Education, 4915 Saint Elmo Ave, Ste 505, Bethesda, MD 20814-6082. Phone: (301) 656-8565. Fax: (301) 656-4464. E-mail: ncpie@ncpie.info. Web: www.talkaboutrx.org or www.bemedwise.org.

"THIS IS YOUR LIFE" TV PREMIERE: ANNIVERSARY. Oct 1, 1952. Ralph Edwards hosted this program that lured unsuspecting guests on the show and surprised them by detailing their lives and achievements with their family and friends. It began as a radio show in 1948.

"TOM CORBETT, SPACE CADET" TV PREMIERE: ANNIVERSARY. Oct 1, 1950. This space show was set in the 2350s at the Space Academy and starred Frankie Thomas in the title role as an eager cadet. "Tom Corbett" was one of the few shows to be aired on all four major networks, including running on two different networks (NBC and ABC) at the same time.

TUVALU: NATIONAL HOLIDAY: ANNIVERSARY. Oct 1. Gained independence from Britain on this day in 1978.

UNITED NATIONS: INTERNATIONAL DAY OF OLDER PERSONS. Oct 1. Designated by the General Assembly on Dec 14, 1990 (originally "International Day for the Elderly," the name was changed later on Dec 21, 1995). A day to encourage all societies to better integrate aging issues into the larger context of development. States are encouraged to do everything in their power to enable all men and women to age with security and dignity. For info: United Nations, Dept of Public Info, Public Inquiries Unit, Rm GA-57, New York, NY 10017. Phone: (212) 963-4475. E-mail: inquiries@un.org. Web: www.un.org.

UNIVERSAL CHILDREN'S WEEK. Oct 1–7. To disseminate throughout the world info on the needs of children and to distribute copies of the Declaration of the Rights of the Child. For complete info, send $5 to cover expense of printing, handling and postage. Annually, the first seven days of October. For info: Dr. Stanley Drake, Pres Emeritus, Intl Soc of Friendship & Good Will, 8592 Roswell Rd, Ste 251, Atlanta, GA 30350-1867. Phone: (678) 795-1362. E-mail: sjdrake@bellsouth.net. Web: www.friend shipandgoodwill.com.

UNIVERSITY OF CHICAGO FIRST DAY OF CLASSES: ANNIVERSARY. Oct 1, 1892. The University of Chicago opened with an enrollment of 594 and a faculty of 103, including eight former college presidents.

US 2007 FEDERAL FISCAL YEAR BEGINS. Oct 1, 2006–Sept 30, 2007.

VEGETARIAN MONTH. Oct 1–31. This educational event advances awareness of the many surprising ethical, environmental, economic, health, humanitarian and other benefits of the increasingly popular vegetarian lifestyle. (Formerly Vegetarian Awareness Month.) For info: Vegetarian Awareness Network, Communications Center, PO Box 321, Knoxville, TN 37901-0321. Phone: (800) USA-VEGE or (800) 280-8343.

WOMEN'S SMALL BUSINESS MONTH. Oct 1–31. National events celebrate women's small businesses. Seminars, award ceremonies and prize giveaways annually every October. For info: Linda Hollander, 4214 Glencoe Ave, Marina Del Rey, CA 90292. Phone: (310) 337-1430. Fax: (310) 641-5823. E-mail: info@womenssmallbusinessexpo.com. Web: www.womenssmallbusinessexpo.com.

WORKPLACE POLITICS AWARENESS MONTH. Oct 1–31. Workplace politics often seems to be a moral morass and a collosal waste of time. Many of us try to avoid participating, but too often, we seem to be inevitably drawn in. This month, we try to increase awareness that trying to avoid workplace politics is futile—instead we can learn to deal with it. For info: Richard Brenner, 10 Emerson Pl, Ste 16A, Boston, MA 02114. Phone: (617) 263-1112. Fax: (617) 263-1113. E-mail: rbrenner@Chaco Canyon.com. Web: www.ChacoCanyon.com.

WORLD COMMUNION SUNDAY. Oct 1. Communion is celebrated by Christians all over the world. Annually, the first Sunday in October.

WORLD VEGETARIAN DAY. Oct 1. Celebration of vegetarianism's benefits to humans, animals and our planet. In addition to individuals, participants include libraries, schools, colleges, restaurants, food services, health-care centers, health food stores, workplaces and many more. For info: North American Vegetarian Soc, PO Box 72, Dolgeville, NY 13329. Phone: (518) 568-7970. Fax: (518) 568-7979. E-mail: navs@telenet.net. Web: www.navs-online.org.

YOM KIPPUR BEGINS AT SUNDOWN. Oct 1. Jewish Day of Atonement. See "Yom Kippur" (Oct 2).

YOSEMITE NATIONAL PARK ESTABLISHED: ANNIVERSARY. Oct 1, 1890. Yosemite Valley and Mariposa Big Tree Grove, granted to the State of California June 30, 1864, were combined and established as a national park. For further park info: Yosemite Natl Park, PO Box 577, Yosemite Natl Park, CA 95389.

BIRTHDAYS TODAY

Julie Andrews, 71, actress, singer (Emmy for "The Julie Andrews Hour"; Oscar for *Mary Poppins*), born Julia Wells at Walton-on-Thames, England, Oct 1, 1935.

Tom Bosley, 79, actor ("Happy Days," "Father Dowling Mysteries"), born Chicago, IL, Oct 1, 1927.

Rodney Cline (Rod) Carew, 61, Hall of Fame baseball player, born Gatun, Panama Canal Zone, Oct 1, 1945.

Jimmy Carter, 82, 39th president of the US, born James Earl Carter, Jr, at Plains, GA, Oct 1, 1924.

Stephen Collins, 59, actor ("7th Heaven," *All the President's Men*), born Des Moines, IA, Oct 1, 1947.

Mark McGwire, 43, former baseball player, born Pomona, CA, Oct 1, 1963.

Esai Morales, 44, actor ("American Family," "NYPD Blue"), born Brooklyn, NY, Oct 1, 1962.

Philippe Noiret, 76, actor (*The Day of the Jackal, Coup de Torchon, Il Postino*), born Lille, France, Oct 1, 1930.

Tim O'Brien, 60, author (*In the Lake of the Woods, Going After Cacciato*), born Austin, MN, Oct 1, 1946.

Randy Quaid, 56, actor (*The Last Picture Show, Dead Solid Perfect*), born Houston, TX, Oct 1, 1950.

William Hubbs Rehnquist, 82, Chief Justice of the US Supreme Court, born Milwaukee, WI, Oct 1, 1924.

Stella Stevens, 70, actress ("Ben Casey," "Flamingo Road"), born Hot Coffee, MS, Oct 1, 1936.

Grete Waitz, 53, marathoner, born Oslo, Norway, Oct 1, 1953.

OCTOBER 2 — MONDAY
Day 275 — 90 Remaining

"ALFRED HITCHCOCK PRESENTS" TV PREMIERE: ANNIVERSARY. Oct 2, 1955. Alfred Hitchcock was already an acclaimed director when he began hosting this mystery anthology series that aired on CBS and NBC for 10 years. Each episode began with an introduction by Hitchcock, the man with the world's most recognized profile. Hitchcock directed about 22 episodes of the series; Robert Altman also directed. Among the many stars who appeared on the show were: Barbara Bel Geddes, Brian Keith, Gena Rowlands, Dick York, Cloris Leachman, Joanne Woodward, Steve McQueen, Peter Lorre, Dick Van Dyke, Robert Redford and Katherine Ross.

BUFFALO ROUNDUP. Oct 2. Custer, SD. 41st annual. To round up, brand and separate 1,500 buffalo before auction in November. Est attendance: 8,500. For info: Craig Pugsley, Custer State Park, HC 83, Box 70, Custer, SD 57730. Phone: (605) 255-4515. Fax: (605) 255-4460. E-mail: craig.pugsley@state.sd.us. Web: www.custerstatepark.info.

CALIFORNIA RIDESHARE WEEK. Oct 2–6. Reduce pollution and traffic! Form a carpool to take to work, or try public transportation. Annually, the first full business week in October. For info: Donna Blanchard, MTA, One Gateway Pl, Los Angeles, CA 90012. Phone: (213) 922-5614. Fax: (213) 236-5640. E-mail: blanchardd@metro.net. Web: www.metro.net.

★**CHILD HEALTH DAY.** Oct 2. Presidential Proclamation always issued for the first Monday of October. Proclamation has been issued since 1928. In 1959 Congress changed celebration day from May 1 to the present observance (Pub Res No. 46 of May 18, 1928, and PL86–352 of Sept 22, 1959).

FINANCIAL PLANNING WEEK. Oct 2–8. Everyone needs objective advice to make smart financial decisions and when seeking the advice of a financial planner, the planner should be a CFP® professional. Financial Planning Week is designed to help the public discover the value of financial planning and advance the financial planning profession. Many of FPA's 100 chapters hold free events in their communities to promote financial literacy and provide resources for the public. Annually, the first full week of October. For info: Beau Ballinger, The Financial Planning Assn, 4100 E Mississippi Ave, Ste 400, Denver, CO 80246. Phone: (303) 759-4900. Fax: (303) 759-0749. E-mail: beau.ballinger@fpanet.org. Web: www.fpanet.org/public.

GANDHI, MOHANDAS KARAMCHAND (MAHATMA): BIRTH ANNIVERSARY. Oct 2, 1869. Indian political and spiritual leader who achieved world honor and fame for his advocacy of nonviolent resistance as a weapon against tyranny was born at Porbandar, India. He was assassinated in the garden of his home at New Delhi, Jan 30, 1948. On the anniversary of Gandhi's birth (Gandhi Jayanti) thousands gather at the park on the Jumna River at Delhi where Gandhi's body was cremated. Hymns are sung, verses from the Gita, the Koran and the Bible are recited and cotton thread is spun on small spinning wheels (one of Gandhi's favorite activities). Other observances held at his birthplace and throughout India on this public holiday.

"THE GEORGE GOBEL SHOW" TV PREMIERE: ANNIVERSARY. Oct 2, 1954. George Gobel hosted this comedy-variety show for five years on NBC. Chanteuse Peggy King and Jeff Donnell were also on the show, with Eddie Fisher as "permanent guest star." In 1959 Gobel switched networks to CBS and appeared for a year with Joe Flynn, Anita Bryant and Harry von Zell.

GREENE, GRAHAM: BIRTH ANNIVERSARY. Oct 2, 1904. British author Graham Greene was born at Berkhamsted, Hertfordshire, England. He centered his works around characters facing salvation and damnation in a world of chaos, often with complex Catholic settings. His works include *The Power and the Glory* (1940) and *The Third Man* (1950). He died Apr 3, 1991, at Vevey, Switzerland.

GUINEA: INDEPENDENCE DAY: ANNIVERSARY. Oct 2. National Day. Guinea gained independence from France in 1958.

GUNN, MOSES: BIRTH ANNIVERSARY. Oct 2, 1929. The 1981 winner of the NAACP Image Award for his performance as Booker T. Washington in the film *Ragtime* was born at St. Louis, MO. His appearances on stage ranged from the title role in *Othello* to Jean Genet's *The Blacks*. He received an Emmy nomination for his role in *Roots* and was awarded several Obies for off-Broadway performances. On film he appeared in *Shaft* and *The Great White Hope*. He died Dec 17, 1993, at Guilford, CT.

HULL, CORDELL: BIRTH ANNIVERSARY. Oct 2, 1871. American statesman who served in both houses of the Congress and as secretary of state was born at Pickett County, TN. Noted for his contributions to the "Good Neighbor" policies of the US with regard to countries of the Americas and to the establishment of the United Nations. Hull died at Bethesda, MD, July 23, 1955.

INDIA: DASSEHRA (VIJAYA DASAMI). Oct 2. Hindu holiday. Marks the triumph of Lord Rama over the demon king, Ravana, or the victory of good over evil. Effigies of Ravana are burned. Because there is no one universally accepted Hindu calendar, this holiday may be celebrated on a different date in some parts of India but it always occurs in September or October.

"THE JIMMY DURANTE SHOW" TV PREMIERE: ANNIVERSARY. Oct 2, 1954. Affectionately known as "The Schnozz," Durante hosted a Saturday night variety show with his former vaudeville partner, Eddie Jackson. It alternated with "The Donald O'Connor Show" on NBC and aired for two years.

MARSHALL, THURGOOD, SWORN IN TO SUPREME COURT: ANNIVERSARY. Oct 2, 1967. Thurgood Marshall was sworn in as the first black associate justice to the US Supreme Court. On June 27, 1991, he announced his resignation, effective upon the confirmation of his successor. See also: "Marshall, Thurgood: Birth Anniversary" (July 2).

MARX, GROUCHO: BIRTH ANNIVERSARY. Oct 2, 1890. Born Julius Henry Marx at New York, NY. Comedian who along with his brothers constituted the famous Marx Brothers. The Marx Brothers began as a singing group and then acted in such movies as *Duck Soup* and *Animal Crackers*. During the '40s and '50s, Groucho was the host of the television and radio show "You Bet Your Life." Died at Los Angeles, CA, Aug 19, 1977.

McFARLAND, GEORGE (SPANKY): BIRTH ANNIVERSARY. Oct 2, 1928. Chubby child star of the "Our Gang" comedy film shorts. Born at Dallas, TX, and died at Grapevine, TX, June 30, 1993.

	S	M	T	W	T	F	S
October	1	2	3	4	5	6	7
	8	9	10	11	12	13	14
2006	15	16	17	18	19	20	21
	22	23	24	25	26	27	28
	29	30	31				

NATIONAL CUSTODIAL WORKERS DAY. Oct 2. A day to honor all custodial workers—those who clean up after us. For info: Bette Tadajewski, Saint John the Baptist Church, 2425 Frederick, Alpena, MI 49707. Phone: (517) 354-3019.

NO SALT WEEK. Oct 2–9. Give no-salt cooking and food preparation a try! This celebration will help with recipes and combinations. Annually, the first week in October. For ideas send a large self-addressed stamped envelope. For info: Make It Tasty Spice Co, Box 416, Denver, CO 80201. Phone: (303) 575-5676. E-mail: starsuccess@excite.com.

NORTH CASCADES NATIONAL PARK ESTABLISHED: ANNIVERSARY. Oct 2, 1968. Located in Washington state.

NORTHEAST KINGDOM FALL FOLIAGE FESTIVAL. Oct 2–8. Walden, Cabot, Plainfield, Peacham, Barnet, Groton and St. Johnsbury, VT. Seven towns welcome visitors during Vermont's famous fall foliage season. Est attendance: 2,500. For info: Northeast Kingdom Chamber of Commerce, Fall Festival, 51 Depot Square, Ste 3, St. Johnsbury, VT 05819. Phone: (802) 748-3678 or (800) 639-6379. E-mail: nekinfo@nekchamber.com. Web: www.nekchamber.org.

NORWAY: PAGEANTRY IN OSLO. Oct 2. The Storting (Norway's Parliament) convenes on first weekday in October, when it decides date for the ceremonial opening of the Storting—usually the following weekday—and the parliamentary session is then opened by King Harald V in the presence of Corps Diplomatique, preceded and followed by a military procession between the Royal Palace and the Storting.

"PEANUTS" DEBUTS: ANNIVERSARY. Oct 2, 1950. This comic strip by Charles Schulz featured Charlie Brown, Lucy, Linus, Sally, Peppermint Patty and Charlie's dog Snoopy. The last new "Peanuts" strip was published Feb 13, 2000.

PHILEAS FOGG'S WAGER DAY: ANNIVERSARY. Oct 2, 1872. Anniversary, from Jules Verne's *Around the World in Eighty Days*, of the famous wager upon which the book is based: "I will bet twenty thousand pounds against any one who wishes, that I will make the tour of the world in eighty days or less." Then, consulting a pocket almanac, Phileas Fogg said: "As today is Wednesday, the second of October, I shall be due in London, in this very room of the Reform Club, on Saturday, the twenty-first of December, at a quarter before nine PM; or else the twenty thousand pounds . . . will belong to you." See also: "Phileas Fogg Wins a Wager Day" (Dec 21).

REDWOOD NATIONAL PARK ESTABLISHED: ANNIVERSARY. Oct 2, 1968. California's Redwood National Park was established. For further park info: Redwood Natl Park, 1111 Second St, Crescent City, CA 95531.

SPINNING AND WEAVING WEEK. Oct 2–8. To celebrate the timeless craft of weaving and spinning and to honor craftspeople past and present who perpetuate a legacy of fine handmade textiles. Annually, the first full week in October, Monday–Sunday. For info: Handweavers Guild of America, Inc, 1255 Buford Hwy, Ste 211, Suwanee, GA 30024. Phone: (678) 730-0010. E-mail: hga@weavespindye.org. Web: www.weavespindye.org.

STREETER, RUTH CHENEY: BIRTH ANNIVERSARY. Oct 2, 1895. Born at Brookline, MA, Ruth Cheney Streeter was the first director of the US Marine Corps Women's Reserve. She was active in unemployment relief, public health, welfare and old-age assistance in New Jersey during the 1930s. A student of aeronautics, she learned to fly while serving as an adjutant of a flight group in the Civil Air Patrol during the early years of World War II. She died Sept 30, 1990, at Morristown, NJ.

SUPREME COURT 2006–2007 TERM BEGINS. Oct 2. Traditionally, the Supreme Court's annual term begins on the first Monday in October and continues with seven two-week sessions of oral arguments. Between the sessions are six recesses during which the opinions are written by the justices. Ordinarily, all cases are decided by the following June or July.

"THE TWILIGHT ZONE" TV PREMIERE: ANNIVERSARY. Oct 2, 1959. "The Twilight Zone" went on the air with these now-familiar words: "There is a fifth dimension, beyond that which is known to man. It is a dimension as vast as space and as timeless as infinity. It is the middle ground between light and shadow, between science and superstition, and it lies between the pit of man's fear and the summit of his knowledge. This is the dimension of imagination. It is an area which we call The Twilight Zone." The anthology program ran five seasons for 154 installments, with a one-year hiatus between the third and fourth seasons. Created and hosted by Rod Serling, it is now considered to have been one of the best dramas to appear on television. The last episode was telecast on Sept 31, 1965.

UNITED NATIONS: WORLD HABITAT DAY. Oct 2. The United Nations General Assembly, by a resolution of Dec 17, 1985, has designated the first Monday of October each year as World Habitat Day—a day to reflect on the living conditions of human beings and for actions to be taken to address the shortcomings of those conditions. The first observance of this day, Oct 5, 1986, marked the 10th anniversary of the first international conference on the subject. For info: United Nations, Dept of Public Info, Public Inquiries Unit, Rm GA-57, New York, NY 10017. Phone: (212) 963-4475. E-mail: inquiries@un.org. Web: www.un .org.

WORLD FARM ANIMALS DAY. Oct 2. Celebrated on Gandhi's birthday. To expose and memorialize the needless suffering and death of billions of innocent, sentient animals in factories, farms and slaughterhouses. Local actions include memorial services, vigils, street theater, picketing, leafletting and information tables. For info: Farm Animal Reform Movement, Box 30654, Bethesda, MD 20824. Phone: (301) 530-1737. Fax: (301) 530-5747. E-mail: info@wfad.org. Web: www.wfad.org.

YOM KIPPUR or DAY OF ATONEMENT. Oct 2. Holiest Jewish observance. A day for fasting, repentance and seeking forgiveness. Hebrew calendar date: Tishri 10, 5767. Began at sundown on Oct 1.

BIRTHDAYS TODAY

Lorraine Bracco, 51, actress ("The Sopranos," *Goodfellas*), born Brooklyn, NY, Oct 2, 1955.

Clay S. Felker, 78, publisher, born St. Louis, MO, Oct 2, 1928.

Donna Karan, 58, fashion designer, born Forest Hills, NY, Oct 2, 1948.

Don McLean, 61, singer ("Crying"), songwriter ("American Pie," "Vincent"), born New Rochelle, NY, Oct 2, 1945.

Rex Reed, 67, movie critic, born Fort Worth, TX, Oct 2, 1939.

Kelly Ripa, 36, actress ("All My Children"), TV host ("Live with Regis & Kelly"), born Stratford, NJ, Oct 2, 1970.

Sting, 55, musician, lead singer (Police), songwriter ("Every Breath You Take"), actor (*Dune*), born Gordon Sumner at London, England, Oct 2, 1951.

OCTOBER 3 — TUESDAY
Day 276 — 89 Remaining

"THE ANDY GRIFFITH SHOW" TV PREMIERE: ANNIVERSARY. Oct 3, 1960. Marks the airing of the first of 249 episodes. Set in rural Mayberry, NC, the show starred Griffith as Sheriff Andy Taylor, Ron Howard as his son Opie, Frances Bavier as Aunt Bee Taylor and Don Knotts as Deputy Barney Fife. Although the last telecast aired Sept 16, 1968, more than 12,000 members of "The Andy Griffith Show" Rerun Watchers Club and others celebrate this day with festivities every year.

BANCROFT, GEORGE: BIRTH ANNIVERSARY. Oct 3, 1800. American historian, known as "The Father of American History," born at Worcester, MA. Died at Washington, DC, Jan 27, 1891.

"CAPTAIN KANGAROO" TV PREMIERE: ANNIVERSARY. Oct 3, 1955. On the air until 1985, this was the longest-running children's TV show until it was surpassed by "Sesame Street." Starring Bob Keeshan as Captain Kangaroo, it was broadcast on CBS and PBS. Other characters included Mr Green Jeans, Grandfather Clock, Bunny Rabbit, Mr Moose and Dancing Bear. Keeshan was an advocate for excellence in children's programming and even supervised which commercials would appear on the program. In 1997 "The All New Captain Kangaroo" debuted, starring John McDonough.

"THE DICK VAN DYKE SHOW" TV PREMIERE: 45th ANNIVERSARY. Oct 3, 1961. This Carl Reiner–created sitcom wasn't an immediate success but soon became a hit. It starred Dick Van Dyke as Rob Petrie, a TV show writer, and Mary Tyler Moore as his wife Laura, a former dancer. This was one of the first shows revolving around the goings-on at a TV series. Other cast members included: Morey Amsterdam, Rose Marie, Richard Deacon, Carl Reiner, Jerry Paris, Ann Morgan Guilbert and Larry Matthews. The last episode aired Sept 7, 1966, but the show remains popular in reruns.

GERMAN REUNIFICATION: ANNIVERSARY. Oct 3, 1990. After 45 years of division, East and West Germany reunited just four days short of East Germany's 41st founding anniversary (Oct 7, 1949). The new united Germany took the name the Federal Republic of Germany, the formal name of the former West Germany, and adopted the constitution of the former West Germany. Today is a national holiday in Germany, Tag der Deutschen Einheit (Day of German Unity).

GORGAS, WILLIAM CRAWFORD: BIRTH ANNIVERSARY. Oct 3, 1854. Physician and sanitary engineer, born at Toulminville, AL. He eradicated yellow fever from Havana and the Panama Canal, allowing the completion of the canal. Gorgas died at London, England, July 4, 1920.

HERRIOT, JAMES: BIRTH ANNIVERSARY. Oct 3, 1916. Author and veterinarian born James Alfred Wight at Glasgow, Scotland. Under the pen name Herriot he wrote more than 12 books chronicling his life as a veterinarian in northern England. His *All Creatures Great and Small* (1974) was made into a TV series that was an international hit. He was made a member of the Order of the British Empire in 1979. Herriot died Feb 23, 1995, at Yorkshire, England.

HONDURAS: FRANCISCO MORAZÁN HOLIDAY. Oct 3. Public holiday in honor of Francisco Morazán, national hero, who was born in 1799.

KOREA: NATIONAL FOUNDATION DAY. Oct 3. National holiday also called Tangun Day, as it commemorates day when legendary founder of the Korean nation, Tangun, established his kingdom of Chosun in 2333 BC.

KURTZMAN, HARVEY: BIRTH ANNIVERSARY. Oct 3, 1902. Cartoonist and founder of *Mad* magazine, Harvey Kurtzman was born at Brooklyn, NY. At the age of 14 he had his first cartoon published, and he began his career in comic books in 1943. His career led him to EC (Educational Comics), and with the support of William Gaines, he created *Mad* magazine, which first appeared in 1952. He died Feb 21, 1993, at Mount Vernon, NY.

"LA LAW" TV PREMIERE: 20th ANNIVERSARY. Oct 3, 1986. Set in the Los Angeles law firm of McKenzie, Brackman, Chaney and Kuzak, this drama had a large cast. Divorce lawyer Arnie Becker was played by Corbin Bernsen, public defender Victor Sifuentes by Jimmy Smits and managing partner Douglas Brackman by Alan Rachins. Other cast members included Harry Hamlin as Michael Kuzak, Richard Dysart as Leland McKenzie, Susan Dey as Grace Van Owen, Jill Eikenberry as Ann Kelsey, Michael Tucker as Stuart Markowitz and Susan Ruttan as Roxanne Melman. The last telecast was May 19, 1994.

MANSON, PATRICK: BIRTH ANNIVERSARY. Oct 3, 1844. British parasitologist and surgeon sometimes called the "father of tropical medicine." Manson's research into insects as carriers of parasites was instrumental in later understanding of mosquitoes as transmitters of malaria. Born at Aberdeen, Scotland, Manson died Apr 9, 1922, at London, England.

"MICKEY MOUSE CLUB" TV PREMIERE: ANNIVERSARY. Oct 3, 1955. This afternoon show for children was on ABC. Among its young cast members were Mouseketeers Annette Funicello and Shelley Fabares. A later version, "The New Mickey Mouse Club," starred Keri Russell, Christina Aguilera and Britney Spears.

NETHERLANDS: RELIEF OF LEIDEN DAY. Oct 3. Celebration of the liberation of Leiden in 1574.

NOBEL CONFERENCE 42. Oct 3–4. Gustavus Adolphus College, St. Peter, MN. Annual two-day scientific symposium (42nd year), and the first one sanctioned by the Nobel Foundation, Stockholm. Annually, the first Tuesday and Wednesday in October. Est attendance: 6,000. For info: Dean Wahlund, Dir of Special Events, Gustavus Adolphus College, 800 W College Avenue, St. Peter, MN 56082-1498. Phone: (507) 933-7520.

"OUR MISS BROOKS" TV PREMIERE: ANNIVERSARY. Oct 3, 1952. This half-hour sitcom began on the radio, and unlike many radio programs that moved to TV, most of the original radio cast was retained. It was about a favorite high school English teacher named Connie Brooks (played by Eve Arden). Also featured were Gale Gordon, Richard Crenna, Gloria McMillan and Jane Morgan.

"OZZIE AND HARRIET" TV PREMIERE: ANNIVERSARY. Oct 3, 1952. "Ozzie and Harriet" was TV's longest-running sitcom. The successful radio-turned-TV show about the Nelson family starred the real-life Nelsons—Ozzie, his wife Harriet and their sons David and Ricky. Officially titled "The Adventures of Ozzie and Harriet," this show was set in the family's home. The boys were one reason the show was successful, and Ricky used the advantage to become a pop star. David and Rick's real-life wives—June Blair and Kris Nelson—also joined the cast. The show was canceled at the end of the 1965–66 season after 435 episodes, 409 of which were in black and white and 26 in color. The last episode aired Sept 3, 1966.

"THE PAT BOONE SHOW" TV PREMIERE: ANNIVERSARY. Oct 3, 1957. Clean-cut singer Pat Boone hosted three shows between 1957 and 1969. The first was a prime-time variety series with the McGuire Sisters and the Mort Lindsey Orchestra as regulars. The second show featured the Paul Smith Orchestra and was a daytime variety and talk show. "Pat Boone in Hollywood" was the title of the third, a 90-minute talk show.

"QUINCY" TV PREMIERE: 30th ANNIVERSARY. Oct 3, 1976. This medically oriented crime show starred Jack Klugman as Dr. Raymond Quincy, a medical examiner for the L.A.

coroner's office. Quincy's curiosity about his cases led to investigative work that often solved them. Later in the series, the show focused on social issues that were unrelated to forensic medicine. The last telecast aired on Sept 5, 1983.

"THE REAL McCOYS" TV PREMIERE: ANNIVERSARY. Oct 3, 1957. This first successful rural comedy program was one of the most popular, predating similar shows such as "The Beverly Hillbillies" by many seasons. It was set in rural California and featured the McCoys, played by Walter Brennan, Richard Crenna, Kathleen Nolan, Michael Winkelman and Lydia Reed.

ROBINSON NAMED BASEBALL'S FIRST BLACK MAJOR LEAGUE MANAGER: ANNIVERSARY. Oct 3, 1974. The only major league player selected most valuable player in both the American and National Leagues, Frank Robinson was hired by the Cleveland Indians as baseball's first black major league manager. During his playing career Robinson represented the American League in four World Series playing for the Baltimore Orioles, led the Cincinnati Reds to a National League pennant and hit 586 home runs in 21 years of play.

"SCARECROW AND MRS KING" TV PREMIERE: ANNIVERSARY. Oct 3, 1983. A one-hour adventure series starring Bruce Boxleitner as Lee Stetson (code name "Scarecrow"), a government agent working with Mrs Amanda King (Kate Jackson), a housewife-turned-agent. Mr King, played by Sam Melville, appeared once, but he was out of the picture when Mrs King and Scarecrow were married in the final season.

WORLD DAIRY EXPO. Oct 3–7. Madison, WI. World's largest dairy cattle exhibition and trade show features more than 680 commercial exhibitors and 2,000 head of cattle in seven breed shows at the Dane County Expo Center. About 200 animals offered for sale in five cattle breed sales. Educational forum. Open to the public. Est attendance: 70,525. For info: World Dairy Expo, 3310 Latham Dr, Madison, WI 53713. Phone: (608) 224-6455. Fax: (608) 224-0300. E-mail: wde@wdexpo.com. Web: www.world-dairy-expo.com.

BIRTHDAYS TODAY

Jeff Bingaman, 63, US Senator (D, New Mexico), born El Paso, TX, Oct 3, 1943.

Lindsey Buckingham, 59, singer, songwriter (with Fleetwood Mac, "Go Your Own Way"), born Palo Alto, CA, Oct 3, 1947.

Neve Campbell, 33, actress ("Party of Five," *Scream*), born Guelph, ON, Canada, Oct 3, 1973.

Chubby Checker, 65, musician, singer ("The Twist"), born Ernest Evans at Philadelphia, PA, Oct 3, 1941.

Fred Couples, 47, golfer, born Seattle, WA, Oct 3, 1959.

Dennis Lee Eckersley, 52, former baseball player, born Oakland, CA, Oct 3, 1954.

Janel Maloney, 37, actress ("From the Earth to the Moon," "The West Wing"), born Woodland Hills, CA, Oct 3, 1969.

Clive Owen, 42, actor (*Closer, Sin City, King Arthur*), born Keresley, Coventry, Warwickshire, England, Oct 3, 1964.

Madlyn Rhue, 72, actress (*It's a Mad Mad Mad Mad World*, "Executive Suite"), born Washington, DC, Oct 3, 1934.

Bob Riley, 62, Governor of Alabama (R), born Ashland, AL, Oct 3, 1944.

Gwen Stefani, 37, singer (No Doubt), born Anaheim, CA, Oct 3, 1969.

Gore Vidal, 81, author (*Burr, Myra Breckinridge*), born West Point, NY, Oct 3, 1925.

Jack P. Wagner, 47, actor ("Melrose Place," "General Hospital"), born Washington, MO, Oct 3, 1959.

David Mark (Dave) Winfield, 55, Hall of Fame baseball player, born St. Paul, MN, Oct 3, 1951.

	S	M	T	W	T	F	S
October		1	2	3	4	5	6	7
2006	8	9	10	11	12	13	14
	15	16	17	18	19	20	21
	22	23	24	25	26	27	28
	29	30	31				

OCTOBER 4 — WEDNESDAY
Day 277 — 88 Remaining

"THE ALVIN SHOW" TV PREMIERE: 45th ANNIVERSARY. Oct 4, 1961. This prime-time cartoon was based on Ross Bagdasarian's novelty group The Chipmunks, which began as recordings with speeded-up vocals. In the series, the three chipmunks, Alvin, Simon and Theodore, sang and had adventures along with their songwriter-manager David Seville. Bagdasarian supplied the voices. "Alvin" was more successful as a Saturday morning cartoon. It returned in reruns in 1979 and also prompted a sequel, "Alvin and the Chipmunks," in 1983.

BALLOONS AROUND THE WORLD. Oct 4. Balloon twisting and sculpting artists donate an hour or more to a charity of their choice in their community. Annually, the first Wednesday in October. For info: Jeff Brown, 135 W Second St, Juneau, AK 99801. Phone: (907) 586-1670. E-mail: jbrown@alaska.net. Web: www.balloonsaroundtheworld.com.

CORSICA LIBERATED: ANNIVERSARY. Oct 4, 1943. The Island of Corsica became the first French territory in Europe freed from Nazi control when Free French troops entered the city of Bastia, the culmination of a French uprising that had begun on the island on Sept 19.

DICK TRACY DEBUTS: 75th ANNIVERSARY. Oct 4, 1931. Square-jawed detective Dick Tracy made his comic strip debut in the *Detroit Daily Mirror* in "Plainclothes Tracy."

ENGLAND: NOTTINGHAM GOOSE FAIR. Oct 4–7. Forest Recreation Ground, Nottingham. Held annually since 1284 (except during the Great Plague in 1665 and the two World Wars), the fair formerly lasted three weeks and boasted as many as 20,000 geese on display. Now lasting four days, the Nottingham Goose Fair always operates in early October. A traditional fair with modern amusements. For info: Markets Division, Victoria Market Offices, Glasshouse St, Nottingham, England NG1 3LP. Phone: (44) (115) 915-6970 or (44) (115) 915-6973. E-mail: tourist.information@nottinghamcity.gov.uk. Web: www.nottinghamgoosefair.co.uk.

FALL SUWANNEE RIVER GOSPEL JUBILEE. Oct 4–7. Live Oak, FL. Featuring well-known musical groups for a weekend of music in this beautiful park. Previous artists featured include Naomi and the Segos, Bibletones, Jody Brown Indian Family and more. Est attendance: 5,000. For info: Spirit of the Suwannee Music Park, 3076 95th Dr, Live Oak, FL 32060. Phone: (386) 364-1683. E-mail: spirit@musicliveshere.com. Web: www.musicliveshere.com.

GERMANY: FRANKFURT BOOK FAIR. Oct 4–8. Fairgrounds, Frankfurt. World's largest international book fair; also important event for electronic media. Best place for international rights and licenses. Open to trade for three days and to the public for two. Est attendance: 270,000. For info: Frankfurt Book Fair, Reinecksstr. 3, D-60313 Frankfurt am Main, Germany. Phone: (49) 69-2102-0. Fax: (49) 69-2102-227. E-mail: info@book-fair.com. Web: www.book-fair.com.

GREGORIAN CALENDAR ADJUSTMENT: ANNIVERSARY. Oct 4, 1582. Pope Gregory XIII issued a bulletin that decreed that the day following Thursday, Oct 4, 1582, should be Friday, Oct 15, 1582, thus correcting the Julian Calendar, then 10 days out of date relative to the seasons. This reform was effective in most Catholic countries; the Julian Calendar continued in use in Britain and the American colonies until 1752, in Russia until 1918 and in Greece until 1923. See also: "Gregorian Calendar Adjustment: Anniversary" (Feb 24) and "Calendar Adjustment Day: Anniversary" (Sept 2).

HAYES, RUTHERFORD BIRCHARD: BIRTH ANNIVERSARY. Oct 4, 1822. Rutherford Birchard Hayes, 19th president of the US (Mar 4, 1877–Mar 3, 1881), was born at Delaware, OH. In his inaugural address, Hayes said: "He serves his party best who serves the country best." He died at Fremont, OH, Jan 17, 1893.

JOHNSON, ELIZA McCARDLE: BIRTH ANNIVERSARY. Oct 4, 1810. Wife of Andrew Johnson, 17th president of the US, born at Leesburg, TN. Died at Greeneville, TN, Jan 15, 1876.

KEATON, BUSTER: BIRTH ANNIVERSARY. Oct 4, 1895. Born Joseph Francis Keaton at Piqua, KS, Buster Keaton (supposedly nicknamed by Harry Houdini) would become one of America's greatest filmmakers. He became a star on the vaudeville stage by age 6 in a family show with his parents, but moved on to films at age 21, costarring in several comic shorts with Roscoe "Fatty" Arbuckle, then starring, writing, directing and producing his own shorts—which featured improbable stunts and physical gags along with Keaton's deadpan expression. His full-length silent films are regarded as masterpieces of American comedy, especially *Sherlock, Jr* (1924) and the Civil War epic *The General* (1927)—both of which are on the Library of Congress's National Film Registry. Alcoholism and troubled relations with the MGM studio sidelined his career in the 1930s and '40s, but he later began a quieter career writing gags, making comic cameos in such films as *Around the World in Eighty Days*, appearing on TV's "Candid Camera" and even performing as a clown in Paris's Cirque Medrano. Keaton died on Feb 1, 1966, at Los Angeles, CA.

"LEAVE IT TO BEAVER" TV PREMIERE: ANNIVERSARY. Oct 4, 1957. This family sitcom was a stereotypical portrayal of American family life. It focused on Theodore "Beaver" Cleaver (Jerry Mathers) and his family: his patient, understanding and all-knowing father Ward (Hugh Beaumont), impeccably dressed housewife and mother June (Barbara Billingsley) and Wally (Tony Dow), Beaver's good-natured, all-American brother. The "perfectness" of the Cleaver family was balanced by other, less-than-perfect characters played by Ken Osmond, Frank Bank, Richard Deacon, Diane Brewster, Sue Randall, Rusty Stevens and Madge Blake. The last episode aired Sept 12, 1963. "Leave It to Beaver" remained popular in reruns.

LESOTHO: INDEPENDENCE DAY. Oct 4. National holiday. Commemorates independence from Britain in 1966. Formerly Basutoland.

MISSISSIPPI STATE FAIR. Oct 4–15. Jackson, MS. Features nightly professional entertainment, livestock show, midway carnival, domestic art exhibits. Begins on the first Wednesday of October. Est attendance: 620,000. For info: Mississippi Fair Commission, PO Box 892, Jackson, MS 39205. Phone: (601) 961-4000. Fax: (601) 354-6545.

REMINGTON, FREDERIC S.: BIRTH ANNIVERSARY. Oct 4, 1861. Born at Canton, NY. Artist and writer Frederic Remington was devoted to the outdoors of New York's North Country and the rugged characters and landscapes of the Old West. He began as an illustrator for popular magazines and worked to become a fine artist and sculptor, capturing images of Native Americans, Buffalo Soldiers, cowboys, horses and Western adventure. Died Dec 26, 1909, at age 48, at Ridgefield, CT, following an appendectomy. Illustrations, watercolors, oil paintings, sketches, bronzes on display at the Frederic Remington Art Museum. For museum info: Frederic Remington Art Museum, 303 Washington St, Ogdensburg, NY 13669. Phone: (315) 393-2425. E-mail: info@fredericremington.org. Web: www.fredericremington.org.

RUNYAN, DAMON: BIRTH ANNIVERSARY. Oct 4, 1884. American newspaperman and author, born at Manhattan, KS, and died at New York, NY, Dec 10, 1946. The musical *Guys and Dolls* was based on one of his short stories. "Always try to rub up against money," he wrote, "for if you rub up against money long enough, some of it may rub off on you."

SAINT FRANCIS OF ASSISI: FEAST DAY. Oct 4. Giovanni Francesco Bernardone, religious leader, founder of the Friars Minor (Franciscan Order), born at Assisi, Umbria, Italy, in 1181. Died at Porziuncula, Oct 3, 1226.

SPACE MILESTONE: *LUNA 3* (USSR). Oct 4, 1959. First satellite to photograph moon's distant side was launched on this date.

SPACE MILESTONE: *SPUTNIK* (USSR). Oct 4, 1957. Anniversary of launching of first successful man-made earth satellite. *Sputnik I* ("satellite") weighing 184 lbs was fired into orbit from the USSR's Tyuratam launch site. Transmitted radio signal for 21 days, decayed Jan 4, 1958. Beginning of Space Age and man's exploration beyond Earth. This first-in-space triumph by the Soviets resulted in a stepped-up emphasis on the teaching of science in American classrooms.

STRATEMEYER, EDWARD L.: BIRTH ANNIVERSARY. Oct 4, 1862. American author of children's books, Stratemeyer was born at Elizabeth, NJ. He created numerous series of popular children's books including The Bobbsey Twins, The Hardy Boys, Nancy Drew and Tom Swift. He and his Stratemeyer Syndicate, using 60 or more pen names, produced more than 800 books. More than four million copies were in print in 1987. Stratemeyer died at Newark, NJ, May 10, 1930.

TEN-FOUR DAY. Oct 4. The fourth day of the tenth month is a day of recognition for radio operators, whose code words, "Ten-Four," signal an affirmative reply.

UNITED NATIONS: WORLD SPACE WEEK. Oct 4–10. To celebrate the contributions of space science and technology to the betterment of the human condition. The dates recall the launch, on Oct 4, 1957, of the first artificial satellite, *Sputnik*, and the entry into force, on Oct 10, 1967, of the Treaty on Principles Governing the Activities of States in the Exploration and Use of Outer Space. For info: United Nations, Dept of Public Info, New York, NY 10017. Web: www.un.org.

BIRTHDAYS TODAY

Armand Assante, 57, actor (*Belizaire the Cajun, The Mambo Kings, Fatal Instinct*), born New York, NY, Oct 4, 1949.
Jackie Collins, 65, author (*Lucky*), born London, England, Oct 4, 1941.
Rachael Leigh Cook, 27, actress (*She's All That*, "The Baby-Sitter's Club"), born Minneapolis, MN, Oct 4, 1979.
Clifton Davis, 61, singer, actor ("That's My Mama," "Amen"), composer, born Chicago, IL, Oct 4, 1945.
Anita L. DeFrantz, 54, Olympics executive and former rower, born Philadelphia, PA, Oct 4, 1952.
Charles (Chuck) Hagel, 60, US Senator (R, Nebraska), born North Platte, NE, Oct 4, 1946.
Charlton Heston, 84, actor (*The Ten Commandments, Ben-Hur, Planet of the Apes*), born Evanston, IL, Oct 4, 1922.
Tony La Russa, Jr, 62, baseball manager and former player, born Tampa, FL, Oct 4, 1944.
Jan Murray, 89, comedian (emcee of "Dollar a Second," "Treasure Hunt"), born Murry Janofsky at New York, NY, Oct 4, 1917.
Anne Rice, 65, novelist (*Interview with the Vampire*), born New Orleans, LA, Oct 4, 1941.

	S	M	T	W	T	F	S
October		1	2	3	4	5	6	7
2006	8	9	10	11	12	13	14
	15	16	17	18	19	20	21
	22	23	24	25	26	27	28
	29	30	31				

Susan Sarandon, 60, actress (Oscar for *Dead Man Walking; Atlantic City, Thelma and Louise, Lorenzo's Oil*), born Susan Tomaling at New York, NY, Oct 4, 1946.
Alicia Silverstone, 30, actress (*Clueless, Batman & Robin*), born San Francisco, CA, Oct 4, 1976.
Alvin Toffler, 78, author (*Future Shock, Power Shift*), born New York, NY, Oct 4, 1928.
Jimy Williams, 63, baseball manager and former player, born Santa Maria, CA, Oct 4, 1943.

OCTOBER 5 — THURSDAY
Day 278 — 87 Remaining

ARTHUR, CHESTER ALAN: BIRTH ANNIVERSARY. Oct 5, 1829. The 21st president of the US, Chester Alan Arthur, was born at Fairfield, VT, and succeeded to the presidency following the death of James A. Garfield. Term of office: Sept 20, 1881–Mar 3, 1885. Arthur was not successful in obtaining the Republican party's nomination for the following term. He died at New York, NY, Nov 18, 1886.

BONDS BREAKS HOME RUN RECORD: 5th ANNIVERSARY. Oct 5, 2001. Barry Bonds of the San Francisco Giants broke Mark McGwire's 1998 home run record when he hit his 71st homer of the season in a game against the Los Angeles Dodgers at Pacific Bell Park. Later in the game he hit another homer. The Dodgers beat the Giants, 11–10, eliminating them from the playoffs. On Oct 7 Bonds hit one more homer to finish the season with 73. He also broke Babe Ruth's slugging record of .847 with .863.

CHICAGO INTERNATIONAL FILM FESTIVAL. Oct 5–19 (tentative). Chicago, IL. North America's oldest competitive film festival. Some of cinema's greatest filmmakers have been introduced at this festival. Gold and Silver Hugos awarded at its conclusion. For info: Chicago Intl Film Fest, 32 W Randolph St, Ste 600, Chicago, IL 60601. Phone: (312) 683-0121. E-mail: info@chicagofilmfestival.com. Web: www.chicagofilmfestival.com.

CHIEF JOSEPH SURRENDER: ANNIVERSARY. Oct 5, 1877. After a 1,700-mile retreat, Chief Joseph and the Nez Percé Indians surrendered to US Cavalry troops at Bear's Paw near Chinook, MT, Oct 5, 1877. Chief Joseph made his famous speech of surrender, "From where the sun now stands, I will fight no more forever."

CIVIL WAR "SUBMARINE" ATTACK: ANNIVERSARY. Oct 5, 1863. In an attempt to disrupt the Union blockade of Charleston Harbor, the Confederate semi-submersible *David* rammed the federal ironclad *New Ironsides* with a spar torpedo. This was the first successful Southern attack using a submersible craft. Although both sides experimented with submarine warfare during the Civil War, the results were far from encouraging, as the submarines caused more fatalities to their own crews than to the opposing side.

COWBOY HALL OF FAME CEREMONY AND BANQUET. Oct 5. Willcox Community Center, Willcox, AZ. The Cowboy Hall of Fame events lead into the Rex Allen Days celebration. Open house 6 PM, dinner 7 PM. Includes "Cowboy Hall of Fame" induction ceremony, favorite son/daughter award. Sponsored by the Willcox Chamber of Commerce & Agriculture. Est attendance: 340. For info: (520) 384-2272 or (800) 200-2272. Web: www.willcoxchamber.com.

EAST TEXAS POULTRY FESTIVAL. Oct 5–7. Shelby County Courthouse Square, Center, TX. County fair–style festival featuring carnival rides, food booths run by local charities, art and craft exhibits, live entertainment, chicken clucking contest, street dance, 4-H broiler show and auction. Annually, the first Thursday, Friday and Saturday of October. Est attendance: 15,000. For info: Shelby County Chamber of Commerce, 100 Court House Square, Center, TX 75935. Phone: (936) 598-3682. Web: www.shelbycountychamber.com.

EDWARDS, JONATHAN: BIRTH ANNIVERSARY. Oct 5, 1703 (OS). The great theologian and leader of the "Great Awakening," the religious revival in the Colonies, was born at East Windsor, CT. His "Sinners in the Hands of an Angry God" is the most famous sermon in American history. He later became president of Princeton College (then the College of New Jersey). Edwards died at Princeton, NJ, Mar 22, 1758, when he contracted smallpox from an inoculation.

ENRICO FERMI ATOMIC POWER PLANT ACCIDENT: 40th ANNIVERSARY. Oct 5, 1966. A radiation alarm and Class I alert at 3:09 PM, EST, signaled a problem at the Enrico Fermi Atomic Power Plant, Lagoona Beach, near Monroe, MI. The accident was contained, but nearly a decade was required to complete the decommissioning and disassembly of the plant.

FINE, LARRY: BIRTH ANNIVERSARY. Oct 5, 1902. The fuzzy-haired Stooge, many times a victim of the mean-tempered Moe, was born Louis Fienberg at Philadelphia, PA. He started his show business career in vaudeville with a joke-and-violin act (he was a prolific musician). Fine was an orginal member of the Three Stooges, formed in 1925. Fine died Jan 24, 1975, at Woodland Hills, CA.

GODDARD, ROBERT HUTCHINGS: BIRTH ANNIVERSARY. Oct 5, 1882. The "father of the Space Age," born at Worcester, MA. Largely ignored or ridiculed during his lifetime because of his dreams of rocket travel, including travel to other planets. Launched a liquid-fuel-powered rocket Mar 16, 1926, at Auburn, MA. Died Aug 10, 1945, at Baltimore, MD. See also: "Goddard Day" (Mar 16).

HASENFUS, EUGENE, CAPTURED: 20th ANNIVERSARY. Oct 5, 1986. A plane carrying arms for the Nicaraguan rebels (contras) was shot down over Nicaragua on Oct 4. The only survivor was Eugene Hasenfus, ex–US Marine, of Marinette, WI, who parachuted from the doomed plane and was captured by Nicaraguan Sandinistas. The US administration at first denied any link to the mission. Hasenfus was put on trial for violating Nicaraguan security laws. He was convicted and sentenced to 30 years in prison on Nov 15, 1986. On request of President Daniel Ortega, the Nicaraguan National Assembly pardoned Hasenfus on Dec 17, 1986, and he was flown back to the US. This episode commenced the unravelling and exposure of covert operations and possible violations of US law, which led to Congressional "Iran Contra" hearings and investigation by a special prosecutor.

IG® NOBEL PRIZE CEREMONY. Oct 5 (tentative). Sanders Theatre, Harvard University, Cambridge, MA. The "Sixteenth 1st Annual." Honors achievements that make people laugh and then make them think. Prizes awarded by Nobel laureates. Sponsored by the science humor magazine *Annals of Improbable Research*. Annually, first Thursday in October, pending theater availability. For info: Marc Abrahams, Annals of Improbable Research, PO Box 380853, Cambridge, MA 02238. Phone: (617) 491-4437. E-mail: marca@chem2.harvard.edu. Web: www.improbable.com.

INDIANAPOLIS SENIOR EXPO. Oct 5. Indiana State Fairgrounds, Marsh Blue Ribbon Pavilion, Indianapolis, IN. An annual, free event for seniors and their families. There will be dozens of local vendors, an entertainment stage, free antique appraisals, health screenings and much more! Est attendance: 3,000. For info: Kirstin Offenbacher, Indianapolis Senior Expo, 41 E Washington St, Ste 200, Indianapolis, IN 46204. Phone: (317) 472-5230. Fax: (317) 263-5259. E-mail: koffenbacher@ibj .com. Web: www.SeniorExpos.com.

LUMIÈRE, LOUIS: BIRTH ANNIVERSARY. Oct 5, 1864. Born at Besançon, France, Louis Lumière with brother Auguste were film pioneers who created the first movie, "Workers Leaving the Lumière Factory" (1895). He died at Bandol, France, on June 6, 1948.

"MONTY PYTHON'S FLYING CIRCUS" TV PREMIERE: ANNIVERSARY. Oct 5, 1969. This wacky comedy series debuted on BBC-1 in Great Britain and aired until 1974. The cast was made up of Graham Chapman, John Cleese, Eric Idle, Terry Jones, Michael Palin and American Terry Gilliam. John Phillip Sousa's "Liberty Bell March" got the show started, and viewers were treated to surreal animation and such skits as "The Spanish Inquisition" and "The Ministry of Silly Walks." On October 6, 1974, "Monty Python's Flying Circus" began airing in the US. The cast members also made four films together.

NATIONAL DEPRESSION SCREENING DAY. Oct 5. Offers free, anonymous education and screening for depression, bipolar disorder, generalized anxiety disorder and post-traumatic stress disorder. The screenings connect people in need with treatment and provide support and resources for friends and family members. For info: Screening for Mental Health, One Washington St, Ste 304, Wellesley Hills, MA 02481-1706. Phone: (781) 239-0071. Fax: (781) 431-7447. Web: www.mentalhealthscreening .org.

PORTUGAL: REPUBLIC DAY. Oct 5. National holiday. Commemorates establishment of the republic in 1910.

"SCHLITZ PLAYHOUSE OF STARS" TV PREMIERE: 55th ANNIVERSARY. Oct 5, 1951. This half-hour dramatic anthology on CBS gave many actors their first dramatic or TV role, including Amanda Blake (first major TV role), Lee Van Cleef (first major TV role), James Dean (last dramatic TV appearance), Gene Kelly (TV dramatic debut) and Janet Leigh (first dramatic American TV role). For several seasons Irene Dunne was the host; Robert Paige succeeded her.

SOUTH CAROLINA STATE FAIR. Oct 5–15. Columbia, SC. Conklin Shows, rides, musical entertainment, food booths and children's activities. Begins on the first Thursday of October. Est attendance: 576,000. For info: South Carolina State Fair, PO Box 393, Columbia, SC 29202. Phone: (803) 799-3387. Fax: (803) 799-1760. E-mail: geninfo@scstatefair.org.

SPACE MILESTONE: *CHALLENGER STS 41-G*. Oct 5, 1984. Space shuttle *Challenger*'s sixth mission with crew of seven, including two women. Launched from Kennedy Space Center, FL, on this date and landed there on Oct 13, 1984. Kathryn D. Sullivan became the first American woman to walk in space.

STONE, THOMAS: DEATH ANNIVERSARY. Oct 5, 1787. Signer of the Declaration of Independence, born 1743 (exact date unknown) at Charles County, MD. Died at Alexandria, VA.

TECUMSEH: DEATH ANNIVERSARY. Oct 5, 1813. Shawnee Indian chief and orator, born at Old Piqua near Springfield, OH, in March 1768. Tecumseh was one of the greatest of Native American leaders. He came to prominence between the years 1799 and 1804 as a powerful orator, defending his people against whites. He denounced as invalid all treaties by which Indians ceded their lands and condemned the chieftains who had entered into such agreements. With his brother Tenskwatawa, the Prophet, he established a town on the Tippecanoe River near

Lafayette, IN, and then embarked on a mission to organize an Indian confederation to stop white encroachment. Although he advocated peaceful methods and negotiation, he did not rule out war as a last resort as he visited tribes throughout the country. While he was away, William Henry Harrison defeated the Prophet at the Battle of Tippecanoe Nov 7, 1811, and burned the town. Tecumseh organized a large force of Indian warriors and assisted the British in the War of 1812. Tecumseh was defeated and killed at the Battle of the Thames, Oct 5, 1813.

UNITED NATIONS: WORLD TEACHERS' DAY. Oct 5. A day to honor teachers and their contributions to learning. For info: United Nations, Dept of Public Info, New York, NY 10017. Web: www.un.org.

"YOU BET YOUR LIFE" TV PREMIERE: ANNIVER-SARY. Oct 5, 1950. This funny game show began on radio in 1947 and moved to TV with Groucho Marx as host and George Fenneman as announcer and scorekeeper. Players tried to answer questions in the category of their choice, but Groucho's impro-vised interviews stole the show. Many guests appeared, including Phyllis Diller and Candice Bergen, who would later become famous. Players could also win money by uttering the secret word, an everyday word suspended above the stage on a duck that dropped when the word was spoken. This was one of the few shows to be filmed, because the interviews needed to be edited. Two short-lived revivals of the series aired, with Buddy Hackett as host in 1980, and with Bill Cosby in 1992.

"ZANE GREY THEATER" TV PREMIERE: 50th ANNI-VERSARY. Oct 5, 1956. Officially titled "Dick Powell's Zane Grey Theater," this western anthology series was hosted by Pow-ell and featured both stories by Grey and original telecasts. Pow-ell occasionally starred in an episode. Guest stars included Hedy Lamarr (in her only dramatic TV role), Ginger Rogers, Claudette Colbert and Esther Williams.

BIRTHDAYS TODAY

Karen Allen, 55, actress (*The Wanderers, Raiders of the Lost Ark, Starman*), born Carrollton, IL, Oct 5, 1951.

Michael Andretti, 44, race car driver, son of Mario Andretti, born Bethlehem, PA, Oct 5, 1962.

Raymond Lester ("Trace") Armstrong, 41, football player, born Bethesda, MD, Oct 5, 1965.

Josie Bissett, 36, actress ("Melrose Place"), born Seattle, WA, Oct 5, 1970.

Jeff Conaway, 56, actor ("Taxi," *Grease*), born New York, NY, Oct 5, 1950.

Bill Dana, 82, actor, comedian ("The Steve Allen Show," "The Bill Dana Show"), born Quincy, MA, Oct 5, 1924.

Laura Davies, 43, golfer, 1994 LPGA Championship winner, born Coventry, England, Oct 5, 1963.

Bob Geldof, 55, singer (Boomtown Rats), social activist, born Dublin, Ireland, Oct 5, 1951.

Vaclav Havel, 70, dramatist, President of the Czech Republic, born Prague, Czechoslovakia, Oct 5, 1936.

Grant Hill, 34, basketball player, born Dallas, TX, Oct 5, 1972.

Glynis Johns, 83, actress (*Mary Poppins, The Ref, A Little Night Music*), born Pretoria, South Africa, Oct 5, 1923.

Bil Keane, 84, cartoonist ("Family Circus"), born Philadelphia, PA, Oct 5, 1922.

Mario Lemieux, 41, Hall of Fame hockey player, hockey execu-tive, born Montreal, QC, Canada, Oct 5, 1965.

Bernie Mac, 48, actor ("The Bernie Mac Show," *The Original Kings of Comedy*), born Chicago, IL, Oct 5, 1958.

October 2006	S	M	T	W	T	F	S
	1	2	3	4	5	6	7
	8	9	10	11	12	13	14
	15	16	17	18	19	20	21
	22	23	24	25	26	27	28
	29	30	31				

Steve Miller, 63, musician, singer (Steve Miller Band, "The Joker," "Abracadabra"), born Dallas, TX, Oct 5, 1943.

Parminder K. Nagra, 31, actress (*Bend It Like Beckham*, "ER"), born Leicester, Leicestershire, England, Oct 5, 1975.

Patrick Roy, 41, former hockey player, born Quebec City, QC, Canada, Oct 5, 1965.

Kate Winslet, 31, actress (*Titanic*), born Reading, England, Oct 5, 1975.

OCTOBER 6 — FRIDAY
Day 279 — 86 Remaining

ALABAMA NATIONAL FAIR. Oct 6–15. Garrett Coli-seum/Fairgrounds, Montgomery, AL. A midway filled with excit-ing rides and games, arts and crafts, exhibits, livestock shows, racing pigs, a circus, a petting zoo, food and entertainment. Est attendance: 225,000. For info: Russell Melton, Alabama National Fair, PO Box 3304, Montgomery, AL 36109-0304. Phone: (334) 272-6831. Fax: (334) 272-6835. Web: www.alnationalfair.org.

AMERICAN LIBRARY ASSOCIATION FOUNDING: ANNIVERSARY. Oct 6, 1876. Founded at Philadelphia, PA, by 103 librarians attending the Centennial Exposition.

CANADA: OKTOBERFEST. Oct 6–14. Kitchener and Water-loo, ON. "The second largest Oktoberfest in the world." More than 70 events and festhalls, including one of the premier parades in Canada on Canadian Thanksgiving morning. Est attendance: 700,000. For info: Kitchener-Waterloo Oktoberfest Inc, 17 Ben-ton St, Kitchener, ON, Canada N2G 3G9. Phone: (519) 570-4267 or (888) 294-HANS. E-mail: info@oktoberfest.ca. Web: www .oktoberfest.ca.

CHINA: MOON FESTIVAL (OR MID-AUTUMN FESTI-VAL). Oct 6. According to folk legend this day is the birthday of the earth god T'u-ti Kung. The festival indicates the year's hard work in the fields will soon end with the harvest. People express gratitude to heaven as represented by the moon and to earth as symbolized by the earth god for all good things from the pre-ceding year. Special harvest foods are eaten, especially "moon cakes." Observed on the 15th day of the eighth month of the Chi-nese lunar calendar, this festival is called by different names in different places, but is widely recognized throughout the Far East, including Taiwan, Korea, Singapore and Hong Kong. Date here is for China; date in other countries will differ.

COHOCTON FALL FOLIAGE FESTIVAL. Oct 6–8. Cohoc-ton, NY. 39th annual. World-famous tree-sitting contest. Parade, more than 100 food, antiques, arts and crafts booths. Annually, the first weekend in October. Est attendance: 50,000. For info: Tom Cox, PO Box 306, Cohocton, NY 14826. Phone: (585) 384-5287.

COLUMBUS DAY FESTIVAL AND HOT AIR BALLOON REGATTA. Oct 6–8. Downtown square and Industrial Park, Columbus, KS. Hot Air Balloon Regatta starts with Balloon Glow Friday evening; prizes are awarded for both Saturday and Sun-day races. Also, car show, arts and crafts fair, entertainment, chil-dren's festival and more. Est attendance: 15,000. For info: Jean Pritchett, Mgr, Columbus Chamber of Commerce, 320 E Maple, Columbus, KS 66725. Phone: (620) 429-1492. Fax: (620) 429-1674. E-mail: columbuschamber@columbus-ks.com. Web: www.columbus-ks.com/chamber.

COME AND TAKE IT FESTIVAL. Oct 6–8. Gonzales, TX. This celebration commemorating the first shot fired for Texas independence in 1835 is named for the defiant battle cry of the colonists when the Mexican military demanded the return of a cannon. Est attendance: 30,000. For info: Chamber of Commerce, Box 134, Gonzales, TX 78629. Phone: (830) 672-6532. Fax: (830) 672-6533. E-mail: info@gonzalestexas.com. Web: www .gonzalestexas.com.

"CSI: CRIME SCENE INVESTIGATION" TV PREMIERE: ANNIVERARY. Oct 6, 2000. CBS's consistently top-rated mystery drama focuses on the Las Vegas Police forensics team led by preternaturally calm Gil Grissom (William Petersen). "CSI" brings science to the foreground, with close-up looks at technology and lab techniques. The 100th episode aired Nov 18, 2004. The show spawned equally successful spin-offs: "CSI: Miami" and "CSI: New York."

DALTON DEFENDERS DAY. Oct 6–7. Coffeyville, KS. Event to honor citizens killed during Dalton Gang's robbery of two banks on Oct 5, 1892. Est attendance: 5,000. For info: Coffeyville Area Chamber of Commerce, PO Box 457, Coffeyville, KS 67337. Phone: (620) 251-2550 or (800) 626-3357. Fax: (620) 251-5448. E-mail: chamber@coffeyville.com.

EGYPT: ARMED FORCES DAY: ANNIVERSARY. Oct 6. The Egyptian Army celebrates crossing into Sinai in 1973.

EL-SADAT, ANWAR: 25th ASSASSINATION ANNIVERSARY. Oct 6, 1981. Egyptian president and Nobel Peace Prize recipient Anwar el-Sadat was killed by assassins at Cairo while he was reviewing a military parade commemorating the 1973 Egyptian-Israeli War. At least eight other persons were reported killed in the attack on Sadat. Anwar el-Sadat was born Dec 25, 1918, at Mit Abu Al-Kom, a village near the Nile River delta.

GAYNOR, JANET: 100th BIRTH ANNIVERSARY. Oct 6, 1906. Born Laura Gainor at Philadelphia, PA, in 1929, she became the first winner of the Academy Award for Best Actress for her cumulative work in two 1927 films, *Sunrise* and *Seventh Heaven*, and for 1928's *Street Angel*. Gaynor died Sept 14, 1984, at Palm Springs, CA.

GEORGIA NATIONAL FAIR. Oct 6–15. Georgia National Fairgrounds, Perry, GA. Traditional state agricultural fair features thousands of entries in horse, livestock, horticultural, youth, home and fine arts categories. Family entertainment, education and fun. Sponsored by the State of Georgia. Annually, beginning the fifth Friday after Labor Day. Est attendance: 395,000. For info: Michele B. Treptow, Dir of Communcations, Georgia Natl Fair, PO Box 1367, Perry, GA 31069. Phone: (478) 987-3247. Fax: (478) 987-7218. E-mail: mtreptow@gnfa.com. Web: www.georgia nationalfair.com.

HEYERDAHL, THOR: BIRTH ANNIVERSARY. Oct 6, 1914. The anthropologist and explorer was born at Larvik, Norway. Seeking to prove the plausibility of South American peoples having settled Polynesia, he embarked on an epic raft ride with five companions in 1947. The "Kon-Tiki" made the 4,300-mile voyage from Peru to Raroia in 101 days. Heyerdahl's book chronicling the adventure became an international best-seller. He continued his travels (including a solo 1970 trip in a reed boat from North Africa to Barbados) and writing until his death. He died at Italy on Apr 18, 2002.

HISTORY ALIVE! Oct 6–8 (tentative). Norfolk Botanical Garden, Norfolk, VA. Features historical groups from various periods, with reenactors participating in field maneuvers and constructing encampments and featuring display areas with equipment, clothing, food and bedding authentic to the era they represent. Interpreters at each site explain the life and times of the characters, providing an accurate and exciting chronicle of our past. Est attendance: 2,000. For info: Norfolk Botanical Garden, 6700 Azalea Garden Rd, Norfolk, VA 23518. Phone: (757) 441-5838. Fax: (757) 853-8294. Web: www.norfolkbotanical garden.org.

HUNTER'S MOON. Oct 6. The full moon following Harvest Moon. So called because the moon's light in evening extends day's length for hunters. Moon enters Full Moon phase at 11:13 PM, EDT.

IRELAND: IVY DAY. Oct 6. The anniversary of the death of Irish nationalist leader and Home Rule advocate Charles Stewart Parnell is observed, especially in Ireland, as Ivy Day. A sprig of ivy is worn on the lapel to remember Parnell. James Joyce's short story "Ivy Day in the Committee Room," published in the collection titled *Dubliners*, addresses this event. See also: "Parnell, Charles Stewart: Birth Anniversary" (June 27).

JACKIE MAYER REHAB DAY. Oct 6. Sandusky, OH. Known as Sandusky's "favorite daughter," Jacquelyn Jeanne Mayer, Miss America 1963 and stroke survivor since 1970, is honored on Oct 6, the anniversary of the 1997 renaming of Providence Hospital's rehab and nursing facility as the Jackie Mayer Rehab Center. After seven years of self-directed rehab to regain her speech and mobility, Jackie has been a motivational speaker and tireless advocate on behalf of stroke survivors across the US and Canada. For info: Dr. Nancy Linenkugel, OSF, Chatfield College, 20918 State Rte 251, St. Martin, OH 45118-9705. Phone: (513) 875-3344. Fax: (513) 875-3912. Web: www.jackiemayer.com. To contact Ms Mayer, phone (419) 627-5476.

KENTUCKY APPLE FESTIVAL. Oct 6–7. Paintsville, KY. Apple blossom beauty pageants, country music show, arts and crafts, flea market, antique car show, Corvette show, Apple Bowl, Terrapin Trot, amusement rides, food booths, clogging and square dancing. Annually, the first Friday and Saturday in October. Est attendance: 75,000. For info: Kentucky Apple Festival, Inc, Ray Tosti, Chmn, PO Box 1245, Paintsville, KY 41240-5245. Phone: (606) 789-4355 or (800) 542-5790.

KOREA: CHUSOK. Oct 6. Gala celebration by Koreans everywhere. Autumn harvest thanksgiving moon festival. Observed on 15th day of eighth lunar month (eighth full moon of lunar calendar) each year. Koreans pay homage to ancestors and express gratitude to guarding spirits for another year of rich crops. A time to visit tombs, leave food and prepare for the coming winter season. Traditional food is the "moon cake," made on the eve of Chusok, with rice, chestnuts and jujube fruits. Games, dancing and gift exchanges. Observed since Silla Dynasty (beginning of First Millennium).

LEE COUNTY COTTON FESTIVAL AND AGRICULTURAL FAIR. Oct 6–7. Bishopville, SC. Join the festivities with amusement rides, parade, entertainment, sports events, food booths and much more. Annually, the first weekend in October. Est attendance: 20,000. For info: Lee County Chamber of Commerce, Lee County Cotton Festival, PO Box 187, Bishopville, SC 29010. Phone: (803) 484-5145. Fax: (803) 484-4270. E-mail: kingcotton@ftc-i.net. Web: www.ebishopville.com.

LEE NATIONAL DENIM DAY®. Oct 6. Lee Jeans invites companies nationwide to participate by allowing employees to wear denim to work in exchange for a contribution of $5 to the Susan G. Komen Breast Cancer Foundation. Since 1996 this program has raised more than $52 million—and the foundation receives 100 percent of these donations. Sponsored by Lee Jeans. For info: Lee Jeans, One Lee Dr, Merriam, KS 66202. Phone: (800) 521-5533. Fax: (888) 254-4794. E-mail: denimday@vfc.com. Web: www.denimday.com.

LIND, JENNY: BIRTH ANNIVERSARY. Oct 6, 1820. Opera singer known as the "Swedish Nightingale," born at Stockholm, Sweden. She died at Malvern, England, Nov 2, 1887.

LITERALLY, A HAUNTED HOUSE. Oct 6–7 (also Oct 13–14, 20–21, 27–28). New Albany, IN. Friends of Culbertson Mansion fundraiser. Est attendance: 7,500. For info: Culbertson Mansion, 914 E Main, New Albany, IN 47150. Phone: (812) 944-9600. E-mail: culbertson@disknet.com. Web: www.indiana museum.org.

MAKOTI THRESHING BEE SHOW. Oct 6–8. Makoti, ND. To acquire, rebuild and maintain antique farm machinery and motor vehicles. Threshing and other demonstrations. Annually, the first weekend in October. Est attendance: 7,000. For info: Loren Quandt, Makoti Threshers, Inc, PO Box 124, Makoti, ND 58756. Phone: (701) 726-5649.

MOODY, HELEN WILLS: BIRTH ANNIVERSARY. Oct 6, 1905. One of the greatest tennis players of the twentieth century was born at Centreville, CA. Moody, 1921's US national junior champion, had a phenomenal professional career: with a .919 winning average, she won 52 out of 92 tournaments between 1919 and 1938. She won Wimbledon eight out of nine tries, the US Open seven times and the French Open four times. Amazingly, from 1927 to 1932, she did not lose one single set in any singles competition. A 1924 Olympic gold-medal winner for singles and doubles, Moody also became in 1928 the first player to win a Grand Slam. "Little Miss Poker Face" (as she was nicknamed for her no-nonsense style) was inducted into the International Tennis Hall of Fame in 1969. She died Jan 1, 1998, at Carmel, CA.

MOON PHASE: FULL MOON. Oct 6. Moon enters Full Moon phase at 11:13 PM, EDT.

NATIONAL DIVERSITY DAY. Oct 6. A day to celebrate and embrace who we are, despite our differences, no matter what race, religion, gender, sexual orientation, age, nationality or disability. A day to reflect on and learn about different cultures and ideologies. A day to vow acceptance and tolerance. A day to consciously address these areas at educational and religious institutions, as well as in the workplace and at home. Our slogan: "Embrace diversity, embrace our world." Annually, the first Friday in October. For info: Leo Parvis, 991 Carriage Ln, Chaska, MN 55318. Phone: (612) 386-7102. E-mail: drparvis@mn.rr.com. Web: www.nationaldiversityday.com.

★**NATIONAL GERMAN-AMERICAN DAY.** Oct 6. Celebration of German heritage and contributions German Americans have made to the building of the nation. A Presidential Proclamation has been issued each year since 1987. Annually, Oct 6.

NATIONAL GERMAN-AMERICAN DAY. Oct 6. Annual day celebrated since the 19th century that honors the contributions of German immigrants to US culture and history. Celebrated on the day in 1683 when 13 Mennonite families disembarked near Philadelphia, PA, from Krefeld. These families later founded Germantown, PA. The day is celebrated by all those who are culturally German from all parts of Europe. This special day had a boost in popularity when President Ronald Reagan became the first US president to proclaim it in 1987.

NATIONAL STORYTELLING FESTIVAL. Oct 6–8. Jonesborough, TN. Tennessee's oldest town plays host to the most dynamic storytelling event dedicated to the oral tradition. This three-day celebration showcases storytellers, stories and traditions from across America and around the world. Annually, the first full weekend in October. Est attendance: 10,000. For info: International Storytelling Center, 116 W Main, Jonesborough, TN 37659. Phone: (800) 952-8392. Fax: (423) 913-8219. E-mail: info @storytellingcenter.net. Web: www.storytellingcenter.net.

OCEAN COUNTY COLUMBUS DAY PARADE AND ITALIAN FESTIVAL. Oct 6–8. Seaside Heights, NJ. Parade features bands, floats, groups, organizations, antique cars and special performers from Italy. The festival features ethnic and traditional foods, entertainment, exhibits and performances from our special guests. Est attendance: 65,000. For info: Ocean County Columbus Day Parade Committee, PO Box 1492, 500 Christopher Columbus Blvd, Seaside Heights, NJ 08751. Phone: (732) 477-6507. Web: www.ameri-com.com/columbus.

OKTOBERFEST. Oct 6–7 (also Oct 13–14). New Ulm, MN. Celebrating New Ulm's German heritage, with musical entertainment, food, craft shows and dancing. Est attendance: 6,000. For info: New Ulm Chamber of Commerce, Box 384, New Ulm, MN 56073. Phone: (507) 233-4300 or (888) 4NEW-ULM. E-mail: nuchamber@newulmtel.net. Web: www.newulm.com.

OZARK FALL FARMFEST. Oct 6–8. Ozark Empire Fairgrounds, Springfield, MO. The largest agricultural trade show in the Ozarks. Exhibits fill the grounds and all buildings. Free admission and free parking. For info: Ozark Empire Fair, 3001 N Grant, Springfield, MO 65803. Phone: (417) 833-2660. Fax: (417) 833-3769. Web: www.ozarkempirefair.com.

PAUL BUNYAN SHOW. Oct 6–8. Hocking College Campus, Nelsonville, OH. Live demonstrations of forestry equipment, lumberjack contests, professional timber harvester competitions, forest industry trade show, chainsaw sculptors, Robbins Crossing interpretive history program, activities and steam show exhibits. Est attendance: 60,000. For info: Judy Sinnott, Public Info Dir, Hocking College, 3301 Hocking Pkwy, Nelsonville, OH 45764. Phone: (740) 753-3591 x 2102. Fax: (740) 753-9018. E-mail: sinnott_j@hocking.edu.

PERIGEAN SPRING TIDES. Oct 6. Spring tides, the highest possible tides, which occur when New Moon or Full Moon takes place within 24 hours of the moment the Moon is nearest Earth (perigee) in its monthly orbit at 6 PM, EST. These tides are not named for the season of spring but for the German *springen*, "to leap up."

PHYSICIAN ASSISTANTS (PA) WEEK. Oct 6–12. To acknowledge the unique contribution of physician assistants in providing access to medical care on the anniversary of the graduation of the first class of PAs from Duke University. For info: American Academy of Physician Assistants, 950 N Washington St, Alexandria, VA 22314-1534. Phone: (703) 836-2272. Fax: (703) 684-1924. E-mail: aapa@aapa.org. Web: www.aapa.org.

REX ALLEN DAYS. Oct 6–8. Willcox, AZ. Annual celebration honors hometown boy the late Rex Allen, who gained fame as a singer, cowboy movie star and narrator for Walt Disney Productions. Celebration also honors Rex Allen, Jr, famed singer, who appeared on TNN's "Yesteryears" and "Statler Brothers' Show." Activities include golf tournament, parade, country fair, rodeo, General Willcox Turtle Race, arts and crafts, country western concert, carnival, softball tournament, cowboy dances. Est attendance: 20,000. For info: Willcox Chamber of Commerce, 1500 N Circle I Rd, Willcox, AZ 85643. Phone: (520) 384-2272 or (800) 200-2272. Fax: (520) 384-0293. Web: www.rexallendays .com or www.willcoxchamber.com.

October **2006**	S	M	T	W	T	F	S
	1	2	3	4	5	6	7
	8	9	10	11	12	13	14
	15	16	17	18	19	20	21
	22	23	24	25	26	27	28
	29	30	31				

RHINELANDER'S OKTOBERFEST. Oct 6–8. Rhinelander, WI. The entire weekend enjoy German music, dancers and food. Est attendance: 9,000. For info: Rhinelander Area Chamber of Commerce, PO Box 795, Rhinelander, WI 54501. Phone: (800) 236-4386. Fax: (715) 365-7467. Web: www.rhinelanderchamber.com.

ROCKPORT SEAFAIR. Oct 6–8. Ski Basin area, Rockport, TX. Features fresh-from-the-bay seafood, gumbo cook-off, ongoing live musical entertainment, crab races, arts and crafts booths and land parade on Saturday. Annually, Columbus Day weekend. Est attendance: 20,000. For info: Rockport Seafair, 404 Broadway, Rockport, TX 78382. Phone: (800) 242-0071 or (361) 729-6445. E-mail: leadership@1rockport.org. Web: www.rockport-fulton.org.

ROCKTOBER GEODE FEST. Oct 6–8. Keokuk, IA. A celebration of the geode! Fest includes daily contests for prettiest, most unusual and largest geode. Guided hunts, geode cracking and swap area. Annually, first weekend in October. For info: Kirk Brandenberger, Keokuk Area CTB, 329 Main St, Keokuk, IA 52632. Phone: (319) 524-5599. E-mail: keokukia@interl.net. Web: www.keokukiowatourism.org.

ST. CHARLES SCARECROW FESTIVAL. Oct 6–8. St. Charles, IL. More than 100 handcrafted scarecrows invade St. Charles along with live musical entertainment, carnival, children's activities, great food, huge craft show and much more. Est attendance: 100,000. For info: St. Charles CVB, 311 N Second St, Ste 100, St. Charles, IL 60174. Phone: (630) 377-6161 or (800) 777-4373. Fax: (630) 513-0566. Web: www.scarecrowfest.com.

SEIBERT, FLORENCE: BIRTH ANNIVERSARY. Oct 6, 1897. American physician Florence B. Seibert was born at Easton, PA. She developed the test for tuberculosis that was adopted by the US and used worldwide by the World Health Organization. She died Aug 23, 1991, at St. Petersburg, FL.

SPRINGS FOLK FESTIVAL. Oct 6–7. Springs, PA. 49th annual festival during the peak of fall foliage in Amish country. 140 craftsmen, Dutch food and continuous live music. Est attendance: 15,000. For info: Springs Folk Festival, PO Box 293, Springs, PA 15562. Phone: (814) 662-4158. Web: www.springspa.org.

STAMP EXPO. Oct 6–8. Radisson Hotel, Anaheim, CA. Est attendance: 4,000. For info: Israel Bick, Exec Dir, Intl Stamp & Coin Collectors Society, PO Box 854, Van Nuys, CA 91408. Phone: (818) 997-6496. Fax: (818) 988-4337. E-mail: iibick@sbcglobal.net. Web: www.bick.net.

SUGARLOAF CRAFTS FESTIVAL. Oct 6–8. Maryland State Fairgrounds, Timonium, MD. This show, now in its 30th year, features more than 350 nationally recognized fine artists and craft designers displaying and selling their original creations. Includes craft demonstrations, live music, specialty food, hourly gift certificate drawings and more. Est attendance: 26,500. For info: Sugarloaf Mountain Works, 200 Orchard Ridge Dr, #215, Gaithersburg, MD 20878. Phone: (800) 210-9900. Fax: (301) 253-9620. Web: www.sugarloafcrafts.com.

SUKKOT BEGINS AT SUNDOWN. Oct 6. Jewish Feast of Tabernacles. See "Sukkot" (Oct 7).

SWAPPIN' MEETIN'. Oct 6–7. Southeast Community College, Cumberland, KY. A celebration of the rich heritage of the mountain people. Handmade goods such as quilts and woodwork are displayed; demonstrations include lye soap making, sorghum molasses making and folk singing. Est attendance: 10,000. For info: Michael Corriston, Facility Dir, Appalachian Cntr, 700 College Rd, Cumberland, KY 40823. Phone: (606) 589-2145, ext 13137. Fax: (606) 589-3181. E-mail: michael.corriston@kctcs.edu. Web: www.state.ky.us.

TENNESSEE VALLEY OLD TIME FIDDLERS CONVENTION. Oct 6–7. Athens State University, Athens, AL. This convention annually attracts thousands of old time music fans and brings some 200 contestants to the grounds of historic Athens State University. Over $11,000 in cash prizes is awarded and the fiddle champion takes home $1,000 plus a trophy. There is competition in 16 categories at this, the "Granddaddy of Mid-South Fiddlers Conventions." Annually, the first full weekend in October. Est attendance: 20,000. For info: Rick Mould, Athens State University, 300 N Beaty St, Athens, AL 35611. Phone: (256) 233-8215. Fax: (256) 230-2565. E-mail: mouldrl@athens.edu. Web: www.athens.edu.

US OPEN STOCK DOG TRIALS & FARM FESTIVAL. Oct 6–8. Hubert Bailey Farm, Dawsonville, GA. In the foothills of the Appalachian mountains, handlers from across the country will work both sheep and cattle. Also a petting zoo for children. Est attendance: 10,000. For info: Dawson County Chamber of Commerce, PO Box 299, Dawsonville, GA 30534. Phone: (706) 265-6278. Fax: (706) 265-6279. E-mail: info@dawson.org. Web: www.dawson.org.

VICTORIAN WEEK. Oct 6–15. Cape May, NJ. Hailed as "A Top 100 Event in North America," the 34th annual Victorian Week is a 10-day celebration of Cape May's Victorian heritage, with self-guided tours of Victorian homes, antiques and crafts shows, brass band concerts, wine schools, chocolate fantasy events, murder mystery dinners, Victorian fashion shows, workshops, tours and lectures. Annually, 10 days beginning the Friday before Columbus Day. Est attendance: 20,000. For info: Mid-Atlantic Center for the Arts, 1048 Washington St, Cape May, NJ 08204. Phone: (800) 275-4278. Fax: (609) 884-0574. E-mail: mac4arts@capemaymac.org. Web: www.capemaymac.org.

WESTINGHOUSE, GEORGE: BIRTH ANNIVERSARY. Oct 6, 1846. Engineer and inventor of the air brake for trains, born at Central Bridge, NY. He was the first employer to give his employees paid vacations. Westinghouse died at New York, NY, Mar 12, 1914.

WORLD SMILE DAY. Oct 6. A day dedicated to good works and good cheer throughout the world. The official theme for the day is "Do an act of kindness. Help one person smile." The symbol for the day is the world-famous "smiley face" icon, created in 1963 by Harvey Ball of Worcester, MA. This icon is now the international symbol of happiness and goodwill. Annually, the first Friday in October. For info: Charles P. Ball, President, World Smile Corp, 22 Front St, PO Box 171, Worcester, MA 01614. Web: www.worldsmileday.com.

YOM KIPPUR WAR: ANNIVERSARY. Oct 6–25, 1973. A surprise attack by Egypt and Syria pushed Israeli forces several miles behind the 1967 cease-fire lines. Israel was caught off guard, partly because the attack came on the holiest Jewish religious day. After 18 days of fighting, hostilities were halted by the UN Oct 25. Israel partially recovered from the initial setback but failed to regain all the land lost in the fighting.

BIRTHDAYS TODAY

Britt Ekland, 64, actress (*The Night They Raided Minsky's*), born Stockholm, Sweden, Oct 6, 1942.

Rebecca Lobo, 33, basketball player, born Southwick, MA, Oct 6, 1973.

Elisabeth Shue, 43, actress (*Adventures in Babysitting, Leaving Las Vegas*), born Wilmington, DE, Oct 6, 1963.

Fred Travalena, 64, actor ("Keep on Truckin'," "ABC Comedy Hour"), born New York, NY, Oct 6, 1942.

Stephanie Zimbalist, 50, actress ("Remington Steele"), born Encino, CA, Oct 6, 1956.

David Zucker, 59, writer, producer (*Naked Gun* movies, *Airplane!*), born Milwaukee, WI, Oct 6, 1947.

OCTOBER 7 — SATURDAY
Day 280 — 85 Remaining

APPLE BUTTER FESTIVAL. Oct 7–8. Berkeley Springs, WV. Fall festival with spicy apple butter simmering in copper kettles in the town square. A parade, two days of mountain music and old-fashioned contests. Fine crafts, farmer's market, down-home cooking and fall foliage. Annually, Columbus Day weekend. Est attendance: 40,000. For info: Apple Butter Festival, 127 Fairfax St, Berkeley Springs, WV 25411. Phone: (304) 258-3738. Web: www.berkeleysprings.com.

APPLE HARVEST FESTIVAL. Oct 7–8 (also Oct 14–15). South Mountain Fairgrounds, Gettysburg, PA. 42nd annual celebration includes tours of orchards, apple-butter boiling and antique cider press. Est attendance: 100,000. For info: Gettysburg CVB, PO Box 4117, Gettysburg, PA 17325. Phone: (717) 334-6274. Fax: (717) 334-1166. E-mail: gettysburgcvb@dejazzd.com. Web: www.gettysburgcvb.org.

BATTLE OF GERMANTOWN REENACTMENT. Oct 7. Philadelphia, PA. Annual reenactment of the Oct 4, 1777, Battle of Germantown. Featured are more than 400 authentically costumed troops re-creating the original battle at noon and at 3 PM. Shuttles run throughout the day between battle site and six other participating historical sites. Annually, the first Saturday in October. Est attendance: 4,000. For info: Public Relations, Cliveden of the National Trust, 6401 Germantown Ave, Philadelphia, PA 19144. Phone: (215) 848-1777. Fax: (215) 438-2892. Web: www.cliveden.org.

BIG ISLAND RENDEZVOUS AND FESTIVAL. Oct 7–8. Bancroft Bay City Park, Albert Lea, MN. Midwest's largest early American re-enactment with 1,000 costumed participants—including New Ulm Battery Civil War group. With old-time bluegrass and country music, black powder shoot, tipi village, Colonial crafts for sale, workshops, traditional and ethnic foods. Est attendance: 13,000. For info: Big Island Rendezvous and Festival, Inc, 143 W Clark St, Albert Lea, MN 56007-2547. Phone: (800) 658-2526. Fax: (507) 373-0344. E-mail: bigisland@albertlea.org. Web: www.bigislandfestival.org.

BUTTERFIELD OVERLAND STAGE DAYS. Oct 7–8. Benson, AZ. Commemorates when Benson was a stop for the Overland Stage and the Southern Pacific Railroad came through to make Benson a "Hub City" for three major rail lines. Parade, food booths and arts and crafts. Est attendance: 2,000. For info: Benson–San Pedro Valley C of C, PO Box 2255, Benson, AZ 85602. Phone: (520) 586-2842. Fax: (520) 586-1972.

CANADA: HERITAGE DAYS—"THE FAIRE AT THE FORKS." Oct 7–8. Chatham, ON. A family-oriented, historical "faire" and reenactment of the Battle of the Thames where the great native leader Tecumseh was killed during the War of 1812. Est attendance: 10,000. For info: Jim Gilbert, Chair of the Faire, 508 King St W, Chatham, ON, Canada N7M 1G9. Phone: (519) 351-2058. Fax: (519) 351-5059. E-mail: jgilbert@ciaccess.com.

CARSON CITY LIBRARY FOUNDATION OKTOBERFEST. Oct 7. Pony Express Pavillion, Mills Park, Carson City, NV. Live oompah music, polka dancing, beer-grilled sausages, craft faire, book sale and fun for the entire family amidst the colorful autumn season. This annual fundraiser, benefitting the Carson City Library, is held the first Saturday in October. Est attendance: 2,500. For info: Andrea Moore, Carson City Library,

★   ★   ★

October 2006	S	M	T	W	T	F	S
	1	2	3	4	5	6	7
	8	9	10	11	12	13	14
	15	16	17	18	19	20	21
	22	23	24	25	26	27	28
	29	30	31				

900 N Roop St, Carson City, NV 89701. Phone: (775) 887-2244. Fax: (775) 887-2273. E-mail: awmoore@clan.lib.nv.us.

CATS PREMIERES: ANNIVERSARY. Oct 7, 1982. The longest-running production in Broadway history opened this day. *Cats* was based on a book of poetry by T.S. Eliot and had a score by Andrew Lloyd Webber. More than 10 million theatergoers saw the New York City production, which closed Sept 10, 2000, after 7,485 performances. *Cats* was also produced in 30 other countries.

DOW-JONES INDUSTRIAL AVERAGE: ANNIVERSARY. Oct 7, 1896. Dow Jones began reporting an average of the prices of 12 industrial stocks in the *Wall Street Journal* on this day. In the early years these were largely railroad stocks. In 1928 Mr Dow expanded the number of stocks to 30, where it remains today. Today, the large, frequently traded stocks in the DJIA represent about a fifth of the market value of all US stocks.

FALL CITYWIDE GARAGE SALE. Oct 7. Electra, TX. Sales throughout the Electra area. Chamber of Commerce will provide free coffee and maps at 7 AM. The Chamber of Commerce office will close at 8 AM so that they, too, may enjoy all of the bargains. Est attendance: 500. For info: Sherry Strange, Electra Chamber of Commerce, 112 W Cleveland, Electra, TX 76360. Phone: (940) 495-3577. E-mail: electracoc@electratel.net. Web: www.electratexas.org.

FEAST OF THE HUNTERS' MOON. Oct 7–8. Fort Ouiatenon Historic Park, Lafayette, IN. Re-creation of French and Native American life at mid-1700s fur-trading outpost. 8,000 participants. Est attendance: 65,000. For info: Angela Bowen, Tippecanoe County Historical Assn, 909 South St, Lafayette, IN 47901. Phone: (765) 476-8402. Fax: (765) 476-8414. E-mail: feast-info@tcha.mus.in.us. Web: www.tcha.mus.in.us.

FELL'S POINT FUN FESTIVAL. Oct 7–8. Fell's Point National Historic District, Baltimore, MD. 40th annual popular outdoor street festival held in Baltimore's original seaport. 400+ arts and crafts vendors, antique market, carnival rides, Hispanic area, five stages featuring rock and roll, bluegrass, jazz, blues, folk, gospel, dancing, etc, family and children's area, three beer gardens, international bazaar retail area, 40+ food vendors in three food courts and much more. Annually, the first full weekend in October. Sponsor: The Preservation Society. Est attendance: 700,000. For info: Fell's Point Fun Festival, 812 S Ann St, Baltimore, MD 21231. Phone: (410) 675-6756. Fax: (410) 675-6769. Web: www.preservationsociety.com.

FESTIVAL OF FINE CRAFT. Oct 7–8. Millville, NJ. Snow, rain or shine, the show will go on. Est attendance: 10,000. For info: Wheaton Village, 1501 Glasstown Rd, Millville, NJ 08332. Phone: (856) 825-6800, ext 104, or (800) 998-4552, ext 104. Fax: (856) 825-2410. E-mail: mail@wheatonvillage.org. Web: www.wheatonvillage.org.

HARVEST WEEKEND. Oct 7–8. Woodstock, VT. Traditional celebration of the harvest featuring a husking bee and barn dance. Also, farm harvest activities including food preservation, traditional toy making and cider pressing. Est attendance: 1,600. For info: Billings Farm and Museum, Rte 12 North, Woodstock, VT 05091. Phone: (802) 457-2355. Fax: (802) 457-4663. E-mail: billings.farm@valley.net. Web: www.billingsfarm.org.

INTERNATIONAL FRUGAL FUN DAY. Oct 7. A day to celebrate that having fun doesn't have to be costly. Do at least one fun thing for yourself and/or your family that is free of cost or under $5 a person: a concert or play, a hike, a meal out, a picnic, an art gallery or museum tour, a day trip, a boat ride. Annually, the first Saturday in October. For info: Shel Horowitz, 16 Barstow Ln, Hadley, MA 01035. Phone: (413) 586-2388. E-mail: shel@frugalfun.com. Web: www.frugalfun.com/frugalfundayideas.html.

ISSAQUAH SALMON DAYS FESTIVAL. Oct 7–8. Issaquah, WA. To celebrate the return of the spawning salmon to the hatchery. Annually, the first weekend in October. Est attendance: 150,000. For info: Issaquah Salmon Days Festival, 155 NW Gilman Blvd, Issaquah, WA 98027. Phone: (425) 392-0661. Fax: (425) 392-8101. E-mail: info@salmondays.org. Web: www.salmon days.org.

JAY PEAK ANNUAL ARTS AND CRAFTS FAIR. Oct 7–8. Jay Peak Ski Resort, Jay, VT. This annual event features primarily Vermont artists and artisans. The show is juried, providing many crafters the opportunity to display their wares such as jewelry, woodworking, painting, slate, maple syrup and other food products, clothing, quilting, candle making, toys, dolls, pottery, glass, just to name a few. Fall foliage tramway rides, hiking, brunch both Sat & Sun, buffets. Annually, the Saturday and Sunday before Columbus Day. Est attendance: 6,000. For info: Jay Peak Ski Resort, Rte 242, Jay, VT 05859. Phone: (802) 327-2198. Fax: (802) 988-4049. E-mail: bkeet@jaypeakresort.com. Web: www.jaypeakresort.com.

JONES, EDWARD D.: 150th BIRTH ANNIVERSARY. Oct 7, 1856. Born at Worcester, MA, Edward Davis Jones was a Kiernan News Agency reporter alongside Charles Dow and Charles Bergstresser when the three left to form a new company, Dow Jones & Company, in 1897. Their new business prepared and distributed bulletins to Wall Street financial houses. They eventually expanded their publishing enterprise to include the *Wall Street Journal* and the creation of the Dow Jones Industrial Average. Jones retired from the company in 1899 and died Feb 16, 1920, at New York City.

KNOX COUNTY SCENIC DRIVE. Oct 7–8 (also Oct 14–15). Knox County, IL. A self-conducted 100-mile driving tour through rural Spoon River Valley resplendent with fall colors. Different attractions at every stop feature food, crafts, art, antiques, fresh produce, old skills demonstrations, flea markets or games. Est attendance: 75,000. For info: Galesburg Area CVB, PO Box 60, Galesburg, IL 61402-0060. Phone: (309) 343-2485. Fax: (309) 343-2521. E-mail: visitors@visitgalesburg.com. Web: www.visit galesburg.com.

LONG BEACH ISLAND SURF FISHING TOURNAMENT. Oct 7–Nov 19. Long Beach Island, NJ. 52nd annual LBI Surf Fishing Tournament. Thousands of dollars in daily, weekly and grand prizes for bluefish and striped bass. Always starts the Saturday of Columbus Day weekend. For info: Southern Ocean County Chamber of Commerce, 265 W 9th St, Ship Bottom, NJ 08008. Phone: (800) 292-6372. Fax: (609) 494-5807. E-mail: socccmanager@comcast.net. Web: www.LBIFT.com.

LONGWOOD GARDENS AUTUMN'S COLORS. Oct 7–27. Kennett Square, PA. Outdoor display features a harvest rainbow of brilliant foliage on 1,050 acres. Est attendance: 50,000. For info: Longwood Gardens, PO Box 501, Kennett Square, PA 19348-0501. Phone: (610) 388-1000. Web: www.long woodgardens.org.

MORRO BAY HARBOR FESTIVAL. Oct 7–8. Morro Bay, CA. Celebrates a working waterfront at play! Showcases seafood, fishing industry and diversity of marine life and coastal lifestyles. Features California Seafood Faire, wine and premium beer tasting, and a flotilla of family-oriented attractions. Annually, the first full weekend in October. Phone in California: (800) 366-6043. Est attendance: 25,000. For info: Exhibits Coord, Morro Bay Harbor Festival, Inc, PO Box 1869, Morro Bay, CA 93443. Phone:

(805) 772-1155. Fax: (805) 772-2107. E-mail: exhibits@mbharbor fest.com. Web: www.mbhf.com.

NORTHEAST MARBLE MEET. Oct 7–8. Radisson Inn, Marlborough, MA. Auction, exhibits; dealers and collectors buy, sell and trade marbles. Est attendance: 1,000. For info: Bert Cohen, 169 Marlborough St, Boston, MA 02116. Phone: (617) 247-4754. Fax: (617) 266-0895. E-mail: marblebert@aol.com. Web: www.marblebert.com.

OKTOBERFEST. Oct 7–8. St. Charles, MO. A citywide celebration of German heritage. Activities include a parade, German bands, foods, beer gardens, antique car show and children's area and crafts. Annually, the first full weekend in October. Est attendance: 40,000. For info: Convention and Visitors Bureau, 230 S Main St, St. Charles, MO 63301. Phone: (800) 366-2427 or (636) 946-7776. Web: www.historicstcharles.com.

OYSTER FESTIVAL. Oct 7. Chincoteague Island, VA. Oysters fixed every way possible—all you can eat. Annually, Saturday of Columbus Day weekend. Tickets can be obtained in advance by contacting Chincoteague Chamber of Commerce. Est attendance: 2,700. For info: Chincoteague Chamber of Commerce, 6733 Maddox Blvd, Chincoteague Island, VA 23336. Phone: (757) 336-6161. Fax: (757) 336-1242. E-mail: chincochamber@verizon .net. Web: www.chincoteaguechamber.com.

PINE BARRENS JAMBOREE. Oct 7. Wells Mills County Park, Waretown, NJ. Celebrate the culture and natural history of the New Jersey Pinelands. Live folk and country music, crafts, wood carvers, nature walks, canoeing, children's activities, food and more. Includes exhibits featuring traditional industries of the Pinelands. Free rain or shine. Est attendance: 1,500. For info: Amanda Adis, Coordinator, Wells Mills County Park, 905 Wells Mills Rd, Waretown, NJ 08758. Phone: (609) 971-3085. Fax: (609) 971-9540. Web: www.co.ocean.nj.us/Parks.

RODNEY, CAESAR: BIRTH ANNIVERSARY. Oct 7, 1728 (OS). Signer of the Declaration of Independence who cast a tie-breaking vote. Born near Dover, DE, he died June 26, 1784. Rodney is on the Delaware quarter issued by the US Mint in 1999, the first in a series of quarters that will commemorate each of the 50 states.

SEA HARVEST. Oct 7–9. Mystic Seaport, Mystic, CT. Columbus Day weekend. A riverfront festival of New England chowders. Est attendance: 9,000. For info: Mystic Seaport, 75 Greenmanville Ave, PO Box 6000, Mystic, CT 06355-0990. Phone: (860) 572-5315 or (888) 973-2767. Web: www.mysticseaport.org.

SEDONA ARTS FESTIVAL. Oct 7–8. Sedona, AZ. Annual celebration of visual, performing and culinary arts. Creative artisans present a unique collection of fine arts, crafts, foods, music and entertainment, surrounded by the scenic grandeur of towering red rocks. Application deadline: April 15. Admission $7; children 12 and under free with paid adult. Proceeds will benefit the cultural arts of Sedona. Rated best arts festival in Northern Arizona. Est attendance: 6,000. For info: Sedona Arts Festival, PO Box 2729, Sedona, AZ 86339-2729. Phone: (928) 204-9456. Fax: (928) 204-9456.

SPOON RIVER VALLEY SCENIC DRIVE. Oct 7–8 (also Oct 14–15). Fulton County, IL. Fall festival in 15 villages with fall foliage, arts and crafts, antiques and collectibles, demonstrations, exhibits, food and the beauty of the 100-mile-long Spoon River Valley. Performance of *Spoon River Anthology* in Lewistown. Annually, the first two weekends in October. Est attendance: 100,000. For info: Spoon River Valley Scenic Drive, PO Box 525, Canton, IL 61520. Phone: (309) 647-8980. Web: www.spoon riverdrive.org.

SUKKOT, SUCCOTH or FEAST OF TABERNACLES, FIRST DAY. Oct 7. Hebrew calendar date: Tishri 15, 5767, begins nine-day festival in commemoration of Jewish people's 40 years of wandering in the desert and thanksgiving for the fall harvest. This high holiday season closes with Shemini Atzeret (see entry on Oct 14) and Simchat Torah (see entry on Oct 15). Began at sundown Oct 6.

VERMONT APPLE FESTIVAL. Oct 7–8. Riverside Middle School, Springfield, VT. Craft fair, apples, games and other family entertainment. Annually, Columbus Day weekend. Est attendance: 6,000. For info: Springfield Chamber of Commerce, 14 Clinton St, Springfield, VT 05156. Phone: (802) 885-2779. E-mail: spfldcoc@vermontel.com.

WALLACE, HENRY AGARD: BIRTH ANNIVERSARY. Oct 7, 1888. Thirty-third vice president of the US (1941–45) born at Adair County, IA. Died at Danbury, CT, Nov 18, 1965.

WINFIELD ART-IN-THE-PARK FESTIVAL. Oct 7. Scenic Island Park, Winfield, KS. More than 100 artists and craftspersons display and sell their wares. Entertainment; food services available. $2 contribution for those over 12 years of age. Annually, the first Saturday in October. Est attendance: 6,000. For info: Debra Carr, Program Coord, Winfield Arts and Humanities Council, 700 Gary, Stes A & B, Winfield, KS 67156-3731. Phone: (620) 221-2161. Fax: (620) 221-0587. E-mail: wahc@iwinfield.net.

WISE, THOMAS J.: BIRTH ANNIVERSARY. Oct 7, 1859. English bibliophile and literary forger, born at Gravesend, England. One of England's most distinguished bibliographic experts, he was revealed, in 1934, to have forged dozens of "first editions" and "unique" publications over a period of more than 20 years. Many of them had been sold at high prices to collectors and libraries. The forgeries in some cases purported to predate the real first editions. Wise died at Hampstead, England, May 13, 1937.

WOOFSTOCK. Oct 7. Wichita, KS. An annual celebration of peace, love and pets, Woofstock invites canines and their owners to participate in activities catered exclusively for them, including a one-mile mutt strut, two-mile fun run, pet trick and costume contests and much more. Silent auction, more than 60 pet-friendly vendors, demonstrations of dog agility, canine search and rescue, water retrieval and sheep herding. All proceeds benefit the Kansas Humane Society and the 13,500 animals it receives each year. Est attendance: 8,000. For info: Kansas Humane Society, 4218 Southeast Blvd, Wichita, KS 67210. Phone: (316) 524-1590. Fax: (316) 554-0356. Web: www.kshumane.org.

"YOUR HIT PARADE" TV PREMIERE: ANNIVERSARY. Oct 7, 1950. "Your Hit Parade" began as a radio show in 1935. When it finally made it to TV, the format was simple: the show's cast performed the week's top musical hits. To sustain interest, since many of the same songs appeared weekly, eye-catching production sequences were created. "YHP" was the starting point for many famous choreographers and dancers, including Peter Gennaro and Bob Fosse. Regulars included Dorothy Collins, Eileen Wilson, Snooky Lanson and Sue Bennett. The show was overhauled many times and switched networks before leaving the air in 1959. A summer revival in 1974 was short-lived. See also: " 'Your Hit Parade' Radio Premiere: Anniversary" (Apr 12).

October *2006*	S	M	T	W	T	F	S
		1	2	3	4	5	6	7
	8	9	10	11	12	13	14
	15	16	17	18	19	20	21
	22	23	24	25	26	27	28
	29	30	31				

June Allyson, 89, actress (*Little Women, The Shrike*, "The June Allyson Show"), born Ella Geisman at Lucerne, NY, Oct 7, 1917.

Imamu Amiri Baraka, 72, poet, dramatist, born Leroi Jones at Newark, NJ, Oct 7, 1934.

Joy Behar, 63, comedienne, television personality ("The View"), born Brooklyn, NY, Oct 7, 1943.

Toni Braxton, 39, singer, born Severn, MD, Oct 7, 1967.

Charles Dutoit, 70, Swiss conductor, born Lausanne, Switzerland, Oct 7, 1936.

Thomas Keneally, 71, novelist (*Schindler's List*), born New South Wales, Australia, Oct 7, 1935.

Yo-Yo Ma, 51, cellist, born Paris, France, Oct 7, 1955.

Al Martino, 79, actor, singer (*Hello Dolly, Phantom of the Opera*), born Alfred Cini at Philadelphia, PA, Oct 7, 1927.

John Mellencamp, 55, singer (*American Fool, Uh-Huh*), born Seymour, IN, Oct 7, 1951.

Oliver Laurence North, 63, US Marine Corps Lieutenant Colonel (retired), center of Iran-Contra controversy, born San Antonio, TX, Oct 7, 1943.

Vladimir Putin, 54, Russian president, born St. Petersburg, Russia, Oct 7, 1952.

Desmond Tutu, 75, South African archbishop, Nobel Peace Prize winner, born Klerksdorp, South Africa, Oct 7, 1931.

OCTOBER 8 — SUNDAY
Day 281 — 84 Remaining

ALVIN C. YORK DAY. Oct 8, 1918. Sergeant Alvin C. York (while in the Argonne Forest, France, and separated from his patrol) killed 20 enemy soldiers and captured a hill, 132 enemy soldiers and 35 machine guns. He was awarded the US Medal of Honor and French Croix de Guerre. Ironically, York had petitioned for exemption from the draft as a conscientious objector, but was turned down by his local draft board.

BRAZIL: CIRIO DE NAZARE. Oct 8–21. Greatest festival of northern Brazil, the Feast of Cirio starts on second Sunday of October in city of Belem (St. Mary of Bethlehem), capital of the state of Para. Festival lasts two weeks.

BUILD YOUR BUSINESS WITH BUSINESS CARDS WEEK. Oct 8–14. Celebrate the power of the world's most portable, affordable and versatile marketing tool—the business card. An excellent reason to contact previous customers and cultivate new relationships. Event ideas and materials available. Annually, the week beginning with the second Sunday in October. For info: Diana Ratliff. E-mail: diana@businesscarddesign .com. Web: www.businesscardweek.com.

BURGOO FESTIVAL. Oct 8. Downtown, North Utica, IL. Only the "Burgoomeister" knows the secret recipe for this pioneer stew, burgoo, served outdoors at this annual Utica festival. Other events include arts and crafts, antiques, food, and a reenactment of Civil War living conditions by uniformed volunteers. Annually, the Sunday of Columbus Day Weekend. Est attendance: 30,000. For info: Burgoo Chairman, LaSalle Co Historical Museum, PO Box 278, Utica, IL 61373. Phone: (815) 667-4861. Web: www .lasallecountymuseum.org/burgoo.

COSMOPOLITE'S DAY. Oct 8. Celebrate this cosmopolitan day by eating at an upscale restaurant, staying at a luxury hotel or resort, going shopping at a boutique, going for a spa treatment and/or attending a sophisticated cocktail party. Annually, Oct 8. For info: Thema Martin. Phone: (404) 849-1249. E-mail: thema_martin@hotmail.com. Web: www.cosmocompany.com.

EMERGENCY NURSES WEEK. Oct 8–14. Sponsored by the Emergency Nurses Association (ENA) since 1989, this is a week-long celebration recognizing emergency nurses for their dedication, service and commitment to their patients and communities. Special focus is given on Wednesday, which is Emergency Nurses Day (Oct 11), to honor nursing professionals who provide care to those whose lives have been touched by life's tragedies. For info: Emergency Nurses Assoc Headquarters, 915 Lee St, Des Plaines, IL 60016. Phone: (800) 900-9659. E-mail: pr@ena.org. Web: www.ena.org.

★**FIRE PREVENTION WEEK.** Oct 8–14. Presidential Proclamation issued annually for the first or second week in October since 1925. For many years prior to 1925, National Fire Prevention Day was observed in October. Sponsored by the National Fire Protection Association. Annually, the Sunday-through-Saturday period during which the Oct 9 anniversary date falls.

FIRE PREVENTION WEEK. Oct 8–14. To increase awareness of the dangers of fire and to educate the public on how to stay safe from fire. For info: Natl Fire Protection Assn, One Batterymarch Park, Quincy, MA 02169. Phone: (617) 770-3000. E-mail: public_affairs@nfpa.org. Web: www.nfpa.org.

GRANDMOTHER'S DAY IN FLORIDA. Oct 8. A ceremonial day on the second Sunday in October.

GREAT CHICAGO FIRE: ANNIVERSARY. Oct 8, 1871. Great fire of Chicago began, according to legend, when Mrs O'Leary's cow kicked over the lantern in her barn on DeKoven Street. The fire leveled 3 ½ sq miles, destroying 17,450 buildings and leaving 98,500 people homeless and about 250 people dead. Financially, the loss was $200 million. On the same day a fire destroyed the entire town of Peshtigo, WI, killing more than 1,100 people.

HISPANIC HERITAGE FESTIVAL. Oct 8. Dade County, Miami, FL. A series of special, cultural, educational and sporting events to celebrate and enhance Hispanic culture and traditions. Est attendance: 350,000. For info: Eduardo Mendoza, Hispanic Heritage Council, Inc, 5040 NW 7 St, Ste 417, Miami, FL 33126. Phone: (305) 461-1014. Fax: (305) 461-1015. Web: www.hispanicfestival.com.

HOME-BASED BUSINESS WEEK. Oct 8–14. To celebrate, recognize and promote the home-based entrepreneur. Annually, the week including the second Tuesday of October. For info: Beverley Williams, The Home Business Advocate. E-mail: bevspeaks@earthlink.net. Web: www.beverleywilliams.com.

NATIONAL CHESTNUT WEEK. Oct 8–14. A celebration of the chestnut throughout the US. Events to include farm visits, chestnut roasts, grower displays and more. Annually, the second full week of October. For info: Ray Young, PO Box 841, Ridgefield, WA 98642. Phone: (360) 887-3669. E-mail: Ray@ChestnutsOnLine.com. Web: www.wcga.net.

NATIONAL METRIC WEEK. Oct 8–14. To maintain an awareness of the importance of the metric system as the primary system of measurement for the US. Annually, the week of the tenth month containing the tenth day of the month. For info: US Metric Assn, 10245 Andasol Ave, Northridge, CA 91325-1504. Phone: (818) 363-5606. Web: www.metric.org.

★**NATIONAL SCHOOL LUNCH WEEK.** Oct 8–14. Presidential Proclamation issued for the week beginning with the second Sunday in October since 1962 (PL87–780 of Oct 9, 1962). Note: Not issued in 1981.

NORMAN ROCKWELL'S SELF-PORTRAIT: ANNIVERSARY. Oct 8, 1938. For the *Saturday Evening Post* cover for this date Norman Rockwell chose to portray himself in a quandary he frequently had to grapple with—trying to come up with a cover for the *Post* on deadline.

"OZZIE AND HARRIET SHOW" RADIO DEBUT: ANNIVERSARY. Oct 8, 1944. Ozzie and Harriet Nelson made their CBS Radio debut in "The Adventures of Ozzie and Harriet." Although their sons David and Ricky were referred to frequently on air and eventually played by others, it was not until Feb 20, 1949, that David (age 12) and Rick (age 8) first appeared playing themselves on the show. "The Adventures of Ozzie and Harriet" hit television airwaves Oct 3, 1952, on ABC.

PESHTIGO FOREST FIRE: ANNIVERSARY. Oct 8, 1871. One of the most disastrous forest fires in history began at Peshtigo, WI, the same day the Great Chicago Fire began. The Wisconsin fire burned across six counties, killing more than 1,100 people.

RICKENBACKER, EDWARD V.: BIRTH ANNIVERSARY. Oct 8, 1890. American auto racer, war hero and airline executive (Eastern Airlines). Dubbed "America's Ace of Aces" for his victories as a pilot in the 94th Aero Squadron during WWI. Recipient of the Congressional Medal of Honor, the Distinguished Service Medal and the French Croix de Guerre. Born at Columbus, OH, Rickenbacker died July 23, 1973, at Zurich, Switzerland.

SAMOA AND AMERICAN SAMOA: WHITE SUNDAY. Oct 8. The second Sunday in October. For the children of Samoa and American Samoa, this is the biggest day of the year. Traditional roles are reversed, as children lead church services, are served special foods and receive gifts of new church clothes and other special items. All the children dress in white. The following Monday is an official holiday.

SCHUTZ, HEINRICH: BIRTH ANNIVERSARY. Oct 8, 1585. German musician and composer sometimes called the father of German music. Born at Kostritz, Saxony, Schutz died at Dresden, Germany, Nov 6, 1672. His works enjoyed renewed attention on the occasions of the bicentennials (1885) and tricentennials (1985) of two of his most devoted followers: George Frederick Handel and Johann Sebastian Bach.

BIRTHDAYS TODAY

Rona Barrett, 70, gossip columnist, born New York, NY, Oct 8, 1936.

Chevy Chase, 63, comedian, actor ("Saturday Night Live," *Caddyshack*), born Cornelius Crane at New York, NY, Oct 8, 1943.

Clodagh, 69, designer, born Clodagh Aubry at Galway, Ireland, Oct 8, 1937.

Matt Damon, 36, actor (*Good Will Hunting, The Rainmaker*), born Cambridge, MA, Oct 8, 1970.

Bill Elliott, 51, race car driver, born Dawsonville, GA, Oct 8, 1955.

Darrell Hammond, 46, comedian, actor ("Saturday Night Live"), born Melbourne, FL, Oct 8, 1960.

Paul Hogan, 67, actor, writer (*Crocodile Dundee, Crocodile Dundee II*), born Lightning Ridge, Australia, Oct 8, 1939.

Jesse Jackson, 65, clergyman, civil rights leader ("I am somebody," "Keep hope alive"), born Greenville, NC, Oct 8, 1941.

Sarah Purcell, 58, TV personality ("Real People"), born Richmond, IN, Oct 8, 1948.

Faith Ringgold, 76, artist, writer (*Tar Beach, My Dream of Martin Luther King*), born New York, NY, Oct 8, 1930.

Rashaan Salaam, 32, former football player, born San Diego, CA, Oct 8, 1974.

R.L. Stine, 63, author (Goosebumps series), born Columbus, OH, Oct 8, 1943.

Sigourney (Susan) Weaver, 57, actress (*Ghostbusters, Gorillas in the Mist, Alien*), born New York, NY, Oct 8, 1949.

OCTOBER 9 — MONDAY
Day 282 — 83 Remaining

AMERICAN INDIAN HERITAGE DAY (ALABAMA). Oct 9. First declared in 2000, this state holiday will also be observed as Columbus Day in Alabama. Annually, the second Monday in October.

CANADA: THANKSGIVING DAY. Oct 9. Observed on second Monday in October each year.

CHASE'S CALENDAR OF EVENTS 2007 PUBLISHED. Oct 9. The 2007 *Chase's* is now available. Buy a copy on our website at www.chases.com or through your favorite book retailer.

★**COLUMBUS DAY.** Oct 9. Presidential Proclamation always the second Monday in October. Observed on Oct 12 from 1934 to 1970 (Pub Res No 21 of Apr 30, 1934). PL90–363 of June 28, 1968, required that beginning in 1971 it would be observed on the second Monday in October.

COLUMBUS DAY OBSERVANCE. Oct 9. Public Law 90–363 sets observance of Columbus Day on the second Monday in October. Applicable to federal employees and to the District of Columbia, but observed also in most states. Commemorates the landfall of Columbus in the New World, Oct 12, 1492. See also: "Columbus Day (Traditional)" (Oct 12).

DISCOVERERS' DAY IN HAWAII. Oct 9. Honors all discoverers, including Pacific and Polynesian navigators. Second Monday in October.

ICELAND: LEIF ERIKSON DAY. Oct 9. Celebrates discovery of North America in the year 1000 by Norse explorer.

IMPROVE YOUR HOME OFFICE WEEK. Oct 9–13. Spend the week improving the way you work from home—find the best place to work, equip your office with the right technology, make your home office fit your work style. Annually, the second week in October. For info: Lisa Kanarek, HomeOfficeLife.com, 660 Preston Forest Center, #120, Dallas, TX 75230. Phone: (214) 361-0556. E-mail: info@homeofficelife.com. Web: www.home officelife.com.

JAPAN: HEALTH-SPORTS DAY. Oct 9. National holiday to encourage physical activity for building sound body and mind. Created in 1966 to commemorate the day of the opening of the 18th Olympic Games at Tokyo, Oct 10, 1964. Annually, the second Monday in October.

KOREA: ALPHABET DAY (HANGUL). Oct 9. Celebrates anniversary of promulgation of Hangul (24-letter phonetic alphabet) by King Sejong of the Yi Dynasty in 1446.

★**LEIF ERIKSON DAY.** Oct 9. Presidential Proclamation always issued for Oct 9 since 1964 (PL88–566 of Sept 2, 1964) at request.

LEIF ERICSON DAY CELEBRATION. Oct 9. Statue of Thorfin Karlsefne, Philadelphia, PA. Celebration honoring the first European to set foot on the North American continent. Event also seeks to promote knowledge about and a realistic historic image of the Viking people as merchants, navigators, shipbuilders, artists, explorers and warriors. Sponsored by the Leif Ericson Viking Ship, Inc, and the Leif Ericson Society. Annually, Oct 9.

For info: Leif Ericson Viking Ship, Inc, 4919 Township Line Rd, Ste 303, Drexel Hill, PA 19026. Phone: (410) 275-8516. Fax: (410) 275-2633. E-mail: info@vikingship.org. Web: www.viking ship.org.

LENNON, JOHN: BIRTH ANNIVERSARY. Oct 9, 1940. John Winston Lennon, English composer, musician and member of The Beatles, the sensationally popular group of musical performers who captivated audiences first in England and Germany, and later throughout the world. A fervent activist for peace. Born at Liverpool, England, Lennon was murdered at New York City, Dec 8, 1980.

MISSION DELORES FOUNDING: ANNIVERSARY. Oct 9, 1776. The oldest building at San Francisco, CA. Formerly known as Mission San Francisco de Asis, the mission survived the great earthquake and fire of 1906.

NATIONAL KICK-BUTT DAY. Oct 9. On this day we commit to kicking ourselves in the butt to take action on goals we've set and not achieved, actions we've committed to and not taken, promises we've made and not kept, excuses we've created that have us stalled and difficulties we've faced and not overcome. This is the day we get our butts in gear and move forward in our lives. No butts about it! Annually, the second Monday of October. For info: Sylvia Henderson, Springboard Training, PO Box 588, Olney, MD 20830-0588. Phone: (301) 260-1538. E-mail: admin@springboardtraining.com. Web: www.springboardtraining .com.

NATIONAL SCHOOL LUNCH WEEK. Oct 9–13. To celebrate good nutrition and healthy, safe school lunches. Annually, the second full week in October. For info: Service Center, American School Food Service Assn, 700 S Washington St, Ste 300, Alexandria, VA 22314-4287. Phone: (703) 739-3900. Web: www .asfsa.org.

NATIVE AMERICANS' DAY (SOUTH DAKOTA). Oct 9. Observed in the state of South Dakota as a legal holiday, dedicated to the remembrance of the great Native American leaders who contributed so much to the history of South Dakota. Annually, the second Monday in October.

PERU: DAY OF NATIONAL HONOR: ANNIVERSARY. Oct 9. Public holiday. Commemorates nationalization of the oil fields in 1968.

UGANDA: INDEPENDENCE DAY. Oct 9. National holiday commemorating achievement of autonomy from Britain in 1962.

UNITED NATIONS: WORLD POST DAY. Oct 9. An annual special observance of Postal Administrations of the Universal Postal Union (UPU). For info: United Nations, Dept of Public Info, Public Inquiries Unit, Rm GA-57, New York, NY 10017. Phone: (212) 963-4475. E-mail: inquiries@un.org. Web: www.un .org.

VIRGIN ISLANDS–PUERTO RICO FRIENDSHIP DAY. Oct 9. Columbus Day (second Monday in October) also celebrates historical friendship between peoples of Virgin Islands and Puerto Rico.

YORKTOWN VICTORY DAY. Oct 9. Observed as a holiday in Virginia. Annually, the second Monday in October. Commemorates the Revolutionary War battle fought in 1781.

October 2006	S	M	T	W	T	F	S
	1	2	3	4	5	6	7
	8	9	10	11	12	13	14
	15	16	17	18	19	20	21
	22	23	24	25	26	27	28
	29	30	31				

BIRTHDAYS TODAY

Scott Bakula, 52, actor ("Enterprise," "Quantum Leap"), born St. Louis, MO, Oct 9, 1954.

Jackson Browne, 56, singer, songwriter ("Running on Empty," "Lawyers in Love"), born Heidelberg, Germany, Oct 9, 1950.

Zachery Ty Bryan, 25, actor ("Home Improvement"), born Aurora, CO, Oct 9, 1981.

Trent Lott, 65, US Senator (R, Mississippi), born Duck Hill, MS, Oct 9, 1941.

Russell Myers, 68, cartoonist ("Broom Hilda"), born Pittsburg, KS, Oct 9, 1938.

Michael Pare, 47, actor (*Streets of Fire, The Philadelphia Experiment*), born Brooklyn, NY, Oct 9, 1959.

Joseph Anthony (Joe) Pepitone, 66, former baseball player, born New York, NY, Oct 9, 1940.

Tony Shalhoub, 53, actor ("Monk," "Wings," *Big Night*), born Green Bay, WI, Oct 9, 1953.

Donald Sinden, 83, actor (*The Day of the Jackal*), born Plymouth, England, Oct 9, 1923.

Michael (Mike) Singletary, 48, Hall of Fame football player, born Houston, TX, Oct 9, 1958.

Annika Sorenstam, 36, golfer, born Stockholm, Sweden, Oct 9, 1970.

Robert Wuhl, 55, writer, actor (*Bull Durham, Cobb*), born Union, NJ, Oct 9, 1951.

OCTOBER 10 — TUESDAY

Day 283 — 82 Remaining

AGNEW RESIGNATION: ANNIVERSARY. Oct 10, 1973. Spiro Theodore Agnew became the second person to resign the office of vice president of the United States. Agnew entered a plea of no contest to a charge of income tax evasion (on contract kickbacks received while he was governor of Maryland and after he became vice president). He was sentenced to pay a $10,000 fine and serve three years' probation. Agnew was elected vice president twice, serving under President Richard M. Nixon. See also "Agnew, Spiro: Birth Anniversary" (Nov 9).

"THE BOB NEWHART SHOW" TV PREMIERE: ANNIVERSARY. Oct 10, 1962. This half-hour variety series was hosted by Bob Newhart, a successful stand-up comedian famous for his trademark "telephone conversation" monologues. The show was critically acclaimed, winning both an Emmy and a Peabody in its short time on the air. Newhart later starred in situation comedies. In "The Bob Newhart Show," which aired 1972–78, he played a psychologist. See also: "Newhart TV Premiere: Anniversary" (Oct 25).

BONZA BOTTLER DAY™. Oct 10. To celebrate when the number of the day is the same as the number of the month. Bonza Bottler Day™ is an excuse to have a party at least once a month. For more information, see Jan 1. For info: Gail M. Berger, 14 Fernwood Dr, Taylors, SC 29687. Phone: (864) 609-9874. E-mail: gberger5@aol.com.

CUBA: BEGINNING OF INDEPENDENCE WARS DAY. Oct 10. National holiday. Commemorates the beginning of struggle against Spain in 1868.

DOUBLE TENTH DAY: 95th ANNIVERSARY. Oct 10, 1911. Tenth day of 10th month, Double Tenth Day, is observed by many Chinese as the anniversary of the outbreak of the revolution against the imperial Manchu dynasty, Oct 10, 1911. Sun Yat-sen and Huan Hsing were among the revolutionary leaders. This is a holiday in Taiwan.

FIJI: INDEPENDENCE DAY. Oct 10. National holiday. Commemorates independence from Britain in 1970.

HAYES, HELEN: BIRTH ANNIVERSARY. Oct 10, 1900. Actress Helen Hayes, often called the First Lady of the American Theater, was born at Washington, DC. Hayes's greatest stage triumph was her role as the long-lived British monarch Queen Victoria in the play *Victoria Regina*. Her first great success was in *Coquette* (1927). She won an Academy Award for best actress for her first major film role in *The Sin of Madelon Claudet* (1931) and won best supporting actress for her role in *Airport* (1971). Helen Hayes died Mar 17, 1993, at Nyack, NY.

NORSK HOSTFEST. Oct 10–14. State Fairgrounds, Minot, ND. The Northern Plains' biggest ethnic festival draws thousands of people to Minot for Scandinavian and American entertainment, Scandinavian delicacies, arts and crafts exhibits and dignitaries representing Sweden, Norway, Denmark, Iceland and Finland with big-name entertainment nightly. Est attendance: 60,000. For info: (701) 852-2368 or North Dakota Tourism, Century Center, 1600 E Century Ave, Ste 2, Bismarck, ND 58503. Phone: (701) 328-2525 or (800) 435-5663. Web: www.hostfest.com.

OKLAHOMA HISTORICAL DAY. Oct 10. Oklahoma.

PEARL, DANIEL: BIRTH ANNIVERSARY. Oct 10, 1963. Born at Princeton, NJ, Daniel Pearl was a foreign correspondent for the *Wall Street Journal* when he was assassinated by a terrorist group in Pakistan. His body was found in Karachi, Pakistan, where he had been researching terrorist threats against America. British-born Islamic militant Ahmed Omar Sheikh, a leader of the National Movement for the Restoration of Pakistani Sovereignty, was convicted of Pearl's kidnapping and murder. Pearl was 38 at the time he was kidnapped, on Jan 23, 2002.

TAIWAN: DOUBLE TENTH DAY. Oct 10. Commemorates the proclamation of the Chinese Republic in 1911.

TUXEDO CREATED: ANNIVERSARY. Oct 10, 1886. Griswold Lorillard of Tuxedo Park, NY, fashioned the first tuxedo for men by cutting the tails off a tailcoat.

UNITED NATIONS: WORLD MENTAL HEALTH DAY. Oct 10. For info: United Nations, Dept of Public Info, New York, NY 10017. Web: www.un.org.

"UPSTAIRS, DOWNSTAIRS" TV PREMIERE: 35th ANNIVERSARY. Oct 10, 1971. The 52 episodes of this "Masterpiece Theatre" series covered the years 1903 to 1930 in the life of a wealthy London family ("Upstairs") and their many servants ("Downstairs"). Produced by London Weekend Television, cast members included Angela Baddeley, Pauline Collins, Gordon Jackson and Jean Marsh. Won a Golden Globe for Best Drama TV Show in 1975 and an Emmy for Outstanding Limited Series in 1976. The last episode aired May 1, 1977, though the series has been rerun several times on PBS.

US NAVAL ACADEMY FOUNDED: ANNIVERSARY. Oct 10, 1845. A college to train officers for the navy was established at Annapolis, MD. Women were admitted in 1976. The Academy's motto is "Honor, Courage, Commitment." For more info: www.usna.edu.

VERDI, GIUSEPPI: BIRTH ANNIVERSARY. Oct 10, 1813. Italian composer, born at Le Roncole, Italy. His 26 operas include *Rigoletto*, *Il Trovatore*, *La Traviata* and *Aida*, and are among the most popular of all operatic music today. Died at Milan, Italy, Jan 27, 1901.

BIRTHDAYS TODAY

Bob Burnquist, 30, skateboarder, born Rio de Janiero, Brazil, Oct 10, 1976.

Charles Dance, 60, actor (*The Jewel in the Crown, White Mischief*), born Worcestershire, England, Oct 10, 1946.

Dale Earnhardt, Jr, 32, race car driver, born Concord, NC, Oct 10, 1974.

Brett Favre, 37, football player, born Gulfport, MS, Oct 10, 1969.

Jessica Harper, 57, actress (*Stardust Memories, Pennies from Heaven, My Favorite Year*), born Chicago, IL, Oct 10, 1949.

Mario Lopez, 33, actor ("Saved by the Bell," "Pacific Blue"), born San Diego, CA, Oct 10, 1973.

Harold Pinter, 76, director (*Butley*), playwright (*Betrayal, The Birthday Party*), born London, England, Oct 10, 1930.

Chris Pronger, 32, hockey player, born Dryden, ON, Canada, Oct 10, 1974.

Nora Roberts, 56, author (*Birthright, Hidden Riches, Rising Tides*), born Silver Springs, MD, Oct 10, 1950.

David Lee Roth, 51, singer, musician (Van Halen, "Jump," *Eat 'Em and Smile*), born Bloomington, IN, Oct 10, 1955.

Tanya Tucker, 48, singer ("Delta Dawn," "Lizzie and the Rain Man"), born Seminole, TX, Oct 10, 1958.

Ben Vereen, 60, actor, singer, dancer (Tony for *Pippin; Roots, All That Jazz*, "Webster"), born Miami, FL, Oct 10, 1946.

OCTOBER 11 — WEDNESDAY

Day 284 — 81 Remaining

AMERICAN MASSAGE THERAPY ASSOCIATION® NATIONAL CONVENTION. Oct 11–14. Hilton Atlanta, Atlanta, GA. Annual meeting and convention of the American Massage Therapy Association (established 1943), the largest association of professional massage therapists and massage schools, representing more than 52,000 members from throughout the US. Includes continuing education classes, association governance and current massage research. Exhibit area of products and services pertinent to the profession. Est attendance: 800. For info: American Massage Therapy Assn, 500 Davis Center, Ste 900, Evanston, IL 60201-4444. Phone: (847) 864-0123. Fax: (847) 864-1178. E-mail: media@amtamassage.org. Web: www.amtamassage.org.

BILL AND HILLARY CLINTON WEDDING: ANNIVERSARY. Oct 11, 1975. William Jefferson (Blythe) Clinton was 29 and Hillary Rodham was 27 when they wed on this date at Fayetteville, AR. They have one child, Chelsea Victoria Clinton, born in 1980.

BLAKEY, ART: BIRTH ANNIVERSARY. Oct 11, 1919. Born at Pittsburgh, PA, jazz musician Blakey recorded many albums with his group, The Jazz Messengers. Died at New York, NY, Oct 16, 1990.

EMERGENCY NURSES DAY. Oct 11. Sponsored by the Emergency Nurses Association (ENA) since 1989, this day serves to recognize emergency nurses for their dedication, service and commitment to their patients and communities. It honors nursing professionals who provide care to those whose lives have been touched by life's tragedies. For info: Emergency Nurses Assoc Headquarters, 915 Lee St, Des Plaines, IL 60016. Phone: (800) 900-9659. E-mail: pr@ena.org. Web: www.ena.org.

★**GENERAL PULASKI MEMORIAL DAY.** Oct 11. Presidential Proclamation always issued for Oct 11 since 1929. Requested by Congressional Resolution each year from

		S	M	T	W	T	F	S
October		1	2	3	4	5	6	7
2006		8	9	10	11	12	13	14
		15	16	17	18	19	20	21
		22	23	24	25	26	27	28
		29	30	31				

1929–1946. (Since 1947 has been issued by custom.) Note: Proclamation 4869, of Oct 5, 1981, covers all succeeding years.

NATIONAL BRING YOUR TEDDY BEAR TO WORK DAY. Oct 11. A celebration and observation of the help, stress relief and joy that teddy bears bring into the lives of people of all ages and stages! Annually, the second Wednesday in October. For info: Susan E. Schwartz, Teddies Are the Answer, 454 26th Ave, San Mateo, CA 94403. Phone: (650) 349-3184. Fax: (650) 345-4944. E-mail: suwho2@rcn.com.

NATIONAL COMING OUT DAY. Oct 11. A project of the Human Rights Campaign. An international day of visibility for the lesbian, gay, bisexual and transgender community since 1988. Local community groups sponsor activities and events which in the past have included "coming out" dances, rallies and demonstrations, educational films, fairs and workshops, literature drops, fundraisers, and religious blessings of lesbian and gay couples and families. Annually, Oct 11. For info: Natl Coming Out Project, 1640 Rhode Island Ave NW, Washington, DC 20036. Phone: (800) 866-6263. Fax: (202) 347-5323. E-mail: ncop@hrc.org. Web: www.hrc.org.

PATENT ISSUED FOR FIRST ADDING MACHINE: ANNIVERSARY. Oct 11, 1887. A patent was granted to Dorr Eugene Felt for the Comptometer, which was the first adding machine known to be absolutely accurate at all times.

REVSON, CHARLES: 100th BIRTH ANNIVERSARY. Oct 11, 1906. Revson, born at Boston, MA, was the colorful and hard-driving force behind Revlon cosmetics, a company he created in 1932. Revson was fond of saying, "Creative people are like a wet towel. You wring them out and pick up another one." By the time of his death, Aug 24, 1975, Revson had an estate valued at $100 million and a cosmetics empire.

ROBBINS, JEROME: BIRTH ANNIVERSARY. Oct 11, 1918. Choreographer and ballet dancer, born at New York, NY. Robbins choreographed several Broadway musicals including *Fiddler on the Roof, The King and I* and *On the Town*. He died at New York, NY, July 29, 1998.

ROBINSON, ROSCOE, JR: BIRTH ANNIVERSARY. Oct 11, 1928. The first black American to achieve the Army rank of four-star general. Born at St. Louis, MO, and died at Washington, DC, July 22, 1993.

ROOSEVELT, (ANNA) ELEANOR: BIRTH ANNIVERSARY. Oct 11, 1884. Wife of Franklin Delano Roosevelt, 32nd president of the US, was born at New York, NY. She led an active and independent life and was the first wife of a president to give her own news conference in the White House (1933). Widely known throughout the world, she was affectionately called "the first lady of the world." She served as US delegate to the United Nations General Assembly for a number of years before her death at New York, NY, Nov 7, 1962. A prolific writer, she wrote in *This Is My Story*, "No one can make you feel inferior without your consent."

"SATURDAY NIGHT LIVE" TV PREMIERE: ANNIVERSARY. Oct 11, 1975. Through the years this weekly show has been through numerous cast, writing and producing staff changes, but its format has remained the same: skits, commercial parodies and news parodies, with a different guest host and musical guest performing—live. Originally titled "NBC's Saturday Night," its first guest host was comedian George Carlin. Notable cast members have included: Chevy Chase, Dan Aykroyd, John Belushi, Jane Curtin, Garrett Morris, Laraine Newman, Gilda Radner, Bill Murray, Joe Piscopo, Eddie Murphy, Billy Crystal, Martin Short, Christopher Guest, Harry Shearer, Joan Cusack, Robert Downey, Jr, Nora Dunn, Jon Lovitz, Dana Carvey, Phil Hartman, Jan Hooks, Dennis Miller, Chris Farley, Mike Myers, Adam Sandler, Will Ferrell, Molly Shannon and Tina Fey.

SPACE MILESTONE: *DISCOVERY STS-92*: 100th SHUTTLE FLIGHT. Oct 11, 2000. *Discovery* was launched on its 28th flight. This marked the shuttle program's 100th mission. On this flight, *Discovery* headed to the International Space Station, where it docked on Oct 13. On earlier flights, the shuttles *Columbia, Challenger, Endeavour, Atlantis* and *Discovery* had launched the Hubble Space Telescope and Chandra X-Ray Observatory, docked with the *Mir* space station, and supported scientific research. The first shuttle flight took place in 1981. Since the first mission, space shuttles have carried 261 individuals and nearly 3 million pounds of payload, logging an estimated 350 million miles. See: "Space Milestone: Columbia STS-1" (Apr 12).

STONE, HARLAN FISKE: BIRTH ANNIVERSARY. Oct 11, 1872. Former associate justice and later chief justice of the US Supreme Court who wrote more than 600 opinions and dissents for that court, Stone was born at Chesterfield, NH. He served on the Supreme Court from 1925 until his death, at Washington, DC, Apr 22, 1946.

TENNESSEE FALL HOMECOMING. Oct 11–15. Museum of Appalachia, Norris, TN. A celebration of the culture and heritage of Appalachian, pioneer, mountain and rural life. Four stages provide continuous musical performances by more than 260 old-time musicians and legendary greats. Scores of traditional mountain activities such as molasses making, sheep herding, rail splitting, soap making and sawmilling are demonstrated to help preserve the old ways in an interesting and educational manner. For info: John Rice Irwin or Elaine Irwin Meyer, Museum of Appalachia, PO Box 1189, Norris, TN 37828. Phone: (865) 494-0514 or (865) 494-7680. Web: www.museumofappalachia.com.

UNITED NATIONS: INTERNATIONAL DAY FOR NATURAL DISASTER REDUCTION. Oct 11. The General Assembly made this designation for the second Wednesday of October each year as part of its efforts to foster international cooperation in reducing the loss of life, property damage and social and economic disruption caused by natural disasters. For info: United Nations, Dept of Public Info, New York, NY 10017. Web: www.un.org.

VATICAN COUNCIL II: ANNIVERSARY. Oct 11, 1962. The 21st ecumenical council of the Roman Catholic Church was convened by Pope John XXIII. It met in four annual sessions, concluding Dec 8, 1965. It dealt with the renewal of the Church and introduced sweeping changes, such as the use of the vernacular rather than Latin in the Mass.

WEEMS, PARSON (MASON LOCKE): BIRTH ANNIVERSARY. Oct 11, 1759. Mason Locke Weems was born at Anne Arundel County, MD. An Episcopal clergyman and traveling bookseller, Weems is remembered for the fictitious stories he presented as historical fact. Best known of his "fables" is the story describing George Washington cutting down his father's cherry tree with a hatchet. Weems's fictionalized histories, however, delighted many readers who accepted them as true. They became immensely popular and were bestsellers for many years. Weems died May 23, 1825, at Beaufort, SC.

WEST, DOTTIE: BIRTH ANNIVERSARY. Oct 11, 1932. American singer Dottie West was born at McMinnville, TN. In 1964 she won the first Grammy ever by a country vocalist for "Here Comes My Baby." She died Sept 4, 1991, at Nashville, TN.

BIRTHDAYS TODAY

Joan Cusack, 44, actress (*Working Girl, In & Out*), born Evanston, IL, Oct 11, 1962.

Robert Gale, 61, physician, cofounder of the International Bone Marrow Registry, born Brooklyn Heights, NY, Oct 11, 1945.

Daryl Hall, 58, singer, musician (Hall and Oates), born Pottstown, PA, Oct 11, 1948.

Orlando Hernandez, 37, baseball player, known as "El Duque," born Villa Clara, Cuba, Oct 11, 1969.

Ron Leibman, 69, actor (*Norma Rae*; stage: *We Bombed in New Haven, Angels in America* [Tony Award]), born New York, NY, Oct 11, 1937.

Elmore Leonard, 81, writer (*Glitz, Get Shorty*), born New Orleans, LA, Oct 11, 1925.

David Morse, 53, actor ("St. Elsewhere," *The Indian Runner*), born Beverly, MA, Oct 11, 1953.

Patty Murray, 56, US Senator (D, Washington), born Seattle, WA, Oct 11, 1950.

Luke Perry, 40, actor ("Beverly Hills 90210," *Buffy the Vampire Slayer*), born Fredricktown, MO, Oct 11, 1966.

Steve Young, 45, former football player, born Salt Lake City, UT, Oct 11, 1961.

OCTOBER 12 — THURSDAY
Day 285 — 80 Remaining

BAHAMAS: DISCOVERY DAY. Oct 12. Commemorates the landing of Columbus in the Bahamas in 1492.

BALI TERRORIST BOMBING: ANNIVERSARY. Oct 12, 2002. Two bombs detonated in Kuta on the Indonesian island of Bali killed more than 200 people and injured hundreds. The bombs were placed at bars where vacationing tourists were known to gather. Although the terrorist group Al Qaeda claimed responsibility, suspects who later confessed to the crime stated that they were working independently.

BELIZE: COLUMBUS DAY. Oct 12. Public holiday.

"THE BOB HOPE SHOW" TV PREMIERE: ANNIVERSARY. Oct 12, 1953. Premiere funnyman, well-known and loved Bob Hope made monthly appearances on TV in the 1950s. During the first season he hosted "The Colgate Comedy Hour," and during the later seasons his show was seen replacing and then alternating with Milton Berle (and in 1955–56 with Martha Raye and Dinah Shore). Leo Robin and Ralph Rainger wrote Hope's trademark show-closing song, "Thanks for the Memory."

BOER WAR: ANNIVERSARY. Oct 12, 1899. The Boers of the Transvaal and Orange Free State in southern Africa declared war on the British. The Boer states were annexed by Britain in 1900 but guerrilla warfare on the part of the Boers caused the war to drag on. It was finally ended May 31, 1902 by the Treaty of Vereeniging.

"THE BURNS AND ALLEN SHOW" TV PREMIERE: ANNIVERSARY. Oct 12, 1950. The comedic husband and wife duo of George Burns and Gracie Allen starred as themselves in this comedy series in which Burns was the straight man and Allen was known for her ditziness. The show employed the technique of speaking directly to the camera ("breaking the fourth wall"); Burns often commented on the plot, told jokes or tried to make sense of Allen's actions and statements. Also on the show were their real-life son, Ronnie Burns; Bea Benaderet; Hal March; John Brown (until blacklisted by McCarthyites in the "red scare"); Fred Clark; Larry Keating; Bill Goodwin and Harry von Zell. The show was done live for the first two seasons and included vaudeville scenes at the end of each episode.

CANADA: TORONTO SKI, SNOWBOARD AND TRAVEL SHOW. Oct 12–15. Exhibition Place, Toronto, ON. Ski manufacturers (equipment, fashions, accessories), retailers, ski resorts, hotels, travel agencies, tourist bureaus, ski clinics and demonstrations, ski clubs, associations, movies and live entertainment. Catering to all ski disciplines—alpine, cross country and snowboarding. Est attendance: 35,000. For info: Canadian Natl Sportsmen's Shows, 703 Evans Ave, Ste 202, Toronto, ON, Canada M9C 5E9. Phone: (416) 695-0311. Fax: (416) 695-0381. Web: www.torontoskishow.com or www.snowboardshow.ca.

COLUMBUS DAY (TRADITIONAL). Oct 12. Public holiday in most countries in the Americas and in most Spanish-speaking countries. Observed under different names (Dia de la Raza or Day of the Race) and on different dates (most often, as in US, on the second Monday in October). Anniversary of Christopher Columbus's arrival, Oct 12, 1492, after a dangerous voyage across "shoreless Seas," at the Bahamas (probably the island of Guanahani), which he renamed El Salvador and claimed in the name of the Spanish crown. In his *Journal*, he wrote: "As I saw that they (the natives) were friendly to us, and perceived that they could be much more easily converted to our holy faith by gentle means than by force, I presented them with some red caps, and strings of beads to wear upon the neck, and many other trifles of small value, wherewith they were much delighted, and becamed wonderfully attached to us." See also: "Columbus Day Observance" (Oct 9).

DAY OF THE SIX BILLION: ANNIVERSARY. Oct 12, 1999. According to the United Nations, the population of the world reached six billion on this date. More than one-third of the world's people live in China and India. It wasn't until 1804 that the world's population reached one billion; now a billion people are added to the population about every 12 years. See also: "Day of the Five Billion" (July 11).

EQUATORIAL GUINEA: INDEPENDENCE DAY: ANNIVERSARY. Oct 12. National holiday. Gained independence from Spain in 1968.

GORDONE, CHARLES: BIRTH ANNIVERSARY. Oct 12, 1925. First black playwright to win the Pulitzer Prize for drama, for his play *No Place to Be Somebody*. Born at Cleveland, OH. Died Nov 17, 1995, at College Station, TX.

INTERNATIONAL MOMENT OF FRUSTRATION SCREAM DAY. Oct 12. To share any or all of our frustrations, all citizens of the world will go outdoors at twelve hundred hours Greenwich time and scream for 30 seconds. We will all feel better or Earth will go off its orbit. Annually, Oct 12. [©2003 by WH.] For info: Thomas & Ruth Roy, Wellcat Holidays, 2418 Long Ln, Lebanon, PA 17046. Phone: (717) 279-0184. E-mail: info@wellcat.com. Web: www.wellcat.com.

MacDONALD, ANNE THOMPSON: DEATH ANNIVERSARY. Oct 12, 1993. Born in 1896, MacDonald founded a nonprofit organization, Recording for the Blind, that produces audio tapes of books to benefit blind and learning disabled people. MacDonald founded the organization in 1948; its library currently contains more than 80,000 titles. She died at Huntington, NY.

McNAIR, RONALD E.: BIRTH ANNIVERSARY. Oct 12, 1950. Ronald E. McNair, a 35-year-old physicist, was the second black American astronaut in space (February 1984). He was born at Lake City, SC. As mission specialist for the crew, he perished in the space shuttle *Challenger* explosion Jan 28, 1986. See also: "Challenger Space Shuttle Explosion: Anniversary" (Jan 28).

MEXICO: DIA DE LA RAZA. Oct 12. Columbus Day is observed as the "Day of the Race," a fiesta time to commemorate the discovery of America as well as the common interests and cultural heritage of the Spanish and Indian peoples and the Hispanic nations.

"SNEAK PREVIEWS" TV PREMIERE: ANNIVERSARY. Oct 12, 1978. This show with film critics Gene Siskel and Roger Ebert got its start on public television in Chicago in 1975. In 1978 it went national on PBS. In 1981 the program moved to network TV and the name was changed to "At the Movies." After Siskel's death in 1999, a rotating panel of critics joined Ebert and in 2000 journalist Richard Roeper was named the permanent co-host. The title was changed to "Ebert & Roeper and the Movies."

SPAIN: NATIONAL HOLIDAY. Oct 12. Called Hispanity Day or Day of Spanish Consciousness. Honors Christopher Columbus and the Spanish conquerors of Latin America.

TRUMBULL, JONATHAN: BIRTH ANNIVERSARY. Oct 12, 1710. American patriot, counselor and friend of George Washington, governor of Connecticut Colony, born at Lebanon, CT. Died there, Aug 17, 1785.

VAUGHAN WILLIAMS, RALPH: BIRTH ANNIVERSARY. Oct 12, 1872. English composer and conductor Ralph Vaughan Williams was born at Down Ampney, Gloucestershire. He is considered England's first great truly national composer, having rooted "modern" composition techniques in traditional English folk and Tudor music and themes to create a uniquely English style. Among his many works are nine symphonies, church and choral music, film and stage music and several operas. His major compositions include the *Mass in G Minor* and the opera *The Pilgrim's Progress*. He died Aug 26, 1958, at London.

BIRTHDAYS TODAY

Susan Anton, 56, singer ("Killin' Time" with Fred Knoblock), actress (*Goldengirl*), born Yucaipa, CA, Oct 12, 1950.

Carlos Bernard, 44, actor ("24"), born Evanston, IL, Oct 12, 1962.

Kirk Cameron, 36, actor ("Growing Pains," "Kirk"), born Panorama City, CA, Oct 12, 1970.

Chris Chandler, 41, football player, born Everett, WA, Oct 12, 1965.

Dave Freudenthal, 56, Governor of Wyoming (D), born Thermopolis, WY, Oct 12, 1950.

Dick Gregory, 74, comedian, author, activist, born St. Louis, MO, Oct 12, 1932.

	S	M	T	W	T	F	S
October							
	1	2	3	4	5	6	7
	8	9	10	11	12	13	14
2006	15	16	17	18	19	20	21
	22	23	24	25	26	27	28
	29	30	31				

Marion Jones, 31, track runner, born Los Angeles, CA, Oct 12, 1975.

Anthony Christopher (Tony) Kubek, 70, sportscaster, former baseball player, born Milwaukee, WI, Oct 12, 1936.

Jean Nidetch, 83, founder of Weight Watchers, born Brooklyn, NY, Oct 12, 1923.

Luciano Pavarotti, 71, opera singer, one of the "Three Tenors," born Modena, Italy, Oct 12, 1935.

Adam Rich, 38, actor ("Eight Is Enough"), born Brooklyn, NY, Oct 12, 1968.

Chris Wallace, 59, broadcaster ("Dateline"), White House correspondent, born Chicago, IL, Oct 12, 1947.

OCTOBER 13 — FRIDAY
Day 286 — 79 Remaining

ALGONQUIN MILL FALL FESTIVAL. Oct 13–15. Four miles south of Carrollton, OH. Presented by the Carroll County Historical Society. An 1800s pioneer festival featuring steam-powered grist and sawmill in operation. Also featured are antique tools and farm machinery and quilting, spinning and weaving demonstrations. Log buildings include a book store, print shop, souvenir shop and a two-story home. A one-room school and a railroad station are on exhibit. More than 70 quality craftsmen selling their products. Est attendance: 35,000. For info: Jeanie Stevens, 3007 Mayham Rd NE, Carrollton, OH 44615. Phone: (330) 627-2946 or (330) 627-5910. Web: www.carrollcountyohio.com.

AMERICAN ROSE SOCIETY FALL NATIONAL CONVENTION. Oct 13–16. Dallas, TX. Amateur rose growers from all over the US display thousands of their roses in this major competition. Hobbyists from all over the country come together to talk shop, attend seminars and show their roses. Est attendance: 800. For info: American Rose Society, PO Box 30000, Shreveport, LA 71130. Phone: (800) 637-6534. E-mail: ars@ars-hq.org. Web: www.ars.org.

APPLE BUTTER MAKIN' DAYS. Oct 13–15. Mt Vernon, MO. A huge festival highlighting the making of apple butter in large copper kettles on the courthouse lawn. Also, 375 crafters displaying and selling handmade goods, free entertainment all three days, apple pie eating contest, hairy legs contest, log sawing contest, bubble gum blowing contest, nail driving contest, pet parade, terrapin race and fiddlers. Annually, the second full weekend in October. Est attendance: 60,000. For info: Chamber of Commerce, PO Box 373, Mt Vernon, MO 65712. Phone: (417) 466-7654.

ARKANSAS STATE FAIR AND LIVESTOCK SHOW. Oct 13–22. Barton Coliseum and State Fairground, Little Rock, AR. Est attendance: 400,000. For info: Arkansas State Fair, 2600 Howard St, Little Rock, AR 72206. Phone: (501) 372-8341. Fax: (501) 372-4197. Web: www.arkfairgrounds.com.

BROWN, JESSE LEROY: BIRTH ANNIVERSARY. Oct 13, 1926. Jesse Leroy Brown was the first black American naval aviator and also the first black naval officer to lose his life in combat when he was shot down over Korea, Dec 4, 1950. On Mar 18, 1972, USS *Jesse L. Brown* was launched as the first ship to be named in honor of a black naval officer. Brown was born at Hattiesburg, MS.

BRUCE, LENNY: BIRTH ANNIVERSARY. Oct 13, 1925. Born Leonard Alfred Schneider at New York, NY, Lenny Bruce was an innovative, hip and searing stand-up comedian whose material touched on adult themes. His satiric and sometimes shocking routines gained him the wrath of public officials, and he was arrested multiple times on obscenity charges. His trials became celebrated calls to arms to protect first amendment rights. By the time of his death by morphine overdose on Aug 3, 1966, at Hollywood Hills, CA, Bruce was banned in many US cities, Australia and England, and from comedy clubs who feared legal action.

BURUNDI: ASSASSINATION OF THE HERO OF THE NATION DAY. Oct 13. National holiday. Commemorates the assassination of Prince Louis Rwagasore in 1961.

FOOTHILLS ART FESTIVAL. Oct 13–15. Jackson, OH. Visual arts exhibits with more than 600 works by 150 artists from the tri-state area. Also live music and arts activities for the entire family. Est attendance: 4,000. For info: Barbara Summers, Southern Hills Arts Council, PO Box 149, Jackson, OH 45640. Phone/fax: (740) 286-6355. E-mail: shac@zoomnet.net.

FORT LIGONIER DAYS. Oct 13–15. Ligonier, PA. Commemorates the Battle of Ligonier. Reenactments, parade, outdoor entertainment, craft booths and food booths. For info: Rachel Roehrig, Ligonier Chamber of Commerce, 120 E Main St, Ligonier, PA 15658. Phone: (724) 238-4200. Fax: (724) 238-4610. E-mail: thechamber@ligonier.com.

MEDFORD JAZZ JUBILEE. Oct 13–15. Medford, OR. 17 nationally known bands will play in downtown Medford locations. More than 100 performances along with fun, food and music for all ages. Est attendance: 6,000. For info: Medford Jazz Jubilee, PMB 201, 221 N Central, Medford, OR 97501. Phone: (541) 770-6972 or (800) 599-0039. E-mail: info@medfordjazz.org. Web: www.medfordjazz.org.

MISSISSINEWA 1812. Oct 13–15. Marion, IN. Largest War of 1812 living history event in US includes reenactment of battle. Military, trappers, woodland Indians, settlers, food purveyors and musicians, living as they did 190 years ago. Est attendance: 30,000. For info: Mississinewa Battlefield Society, PO Box 1812, Marion, IN 46952. Phone: (800) 822-1812. Fax: (765) 662-1809. E-mail: war1812@aol.com.

MONTAND, YVES: BIRTH ANNIVERSARY. Oct 13, 1921. French actor Yves Montand was born Ivo Livi at Monsummano Alto, Italy. His career was successful in both France and America, including more than 50 films. He died Nov 9, 1991, at Senlis, France.

MOON PHASE: LAST QUARTER. Oct 13. Moon enters Last Quarter phase at 8:25 PM, EDT.

NAVY BIRTHDAY. Oct 13. Since 1972 a Navywide celebration (for members of the active forces and reserves, as well as retirees and dependents) recognizing the authorization of the Continental Navy on this date in 1775. The celebration is meant "to enhance a greater appreciation of [the] Navy heritage and to provide a positive influence toward pride and professionalism in the naval service." See also: "US Navy: Authorization Anniversary." For info: www.history.navy.mil.

NORTH CAROLINA STATE FAIR. Oct 13–22. State Fairgrounds, Raleigh, NC. Agricultural fair with livestock, arts and crafts, home arts, entertainment and carnival. Est attendance: 750,000. For info: Wesley Wyatt, Mgr, North Carolina State Fair, 1025 Blue Ridge Blvd, Raleigh, NC 27607. Phone: (919) 821-7400. Fax: (919) 733-5079. Web: www.ncstatefair.org.

OZ FEST. Oct 13–15. Liberal, KS. A three-day festival that will have you remembering the classic 1939 movie *The Wizard of Oz* (a few of the original cast members attend each year). Royal Procession, look-alike contests, games and dinner with Munchkins, Glinda, Toto, the Wicked Witch, Auntie Em and of course Dorothy. Follow the yellow brick road to Oz Fest! Annually the second weekend in October. Est attendance: 3,000. For info: Sherry Taylor, 567 East Cedar, Liberal, KS 67901. Phone: (620) 624-7624.

Fax: (620) 624-7656. E-mail: schs@swko.net. Web: www.seward countymuseum.com.

PARKE COUNTY COVERED BRIDGE FESTIVAL. Oct 13–22. Rockville, IN. Covered bridge capital of the world, 32 historic covered bridges. Headquarters: Courthouse Lawn, Rockville. Guided bus tours on covered bridge routes. Hundreds of booths of arts, crafts, demonstrations, old-fashioned homemade foods and a farmers' market. Annually, beginning on the second Friday in October. Est attendance: 2,000,000. For info: Covered Bridge Capital, PO Box 165, Rockville, IN 47872-0165. Phone: (765) 569-5226. Fax: (765) 569-3900. E-mail: pci@ticz.com. Web: www .coveredbridges.com.

PITCHER, MOLLY: BIRTH ANNIVERSARY. Oct 13, 1754. "Molly Pitcher," heroine of the American Revolution, was a water carrier at the Battle of Monmouth (Sunday, June 28, 1778), where she distinguished herself by loading and firing a cannon after her husband, William Hays, was wounded. Affectionately known as "Sergeant Molly" after General Washington issued her a warrant as a noncommissioned officer. Her real name was Mary Hays McCauley (née Ludwig). Born near Trenton, NJ, she died at Carlisle, PA, Jan 22, 1832.

SAINT EDWARD, THE CONFESSOR: FEAST DAY. Oct 13. King of England, 1042–66, Edward was the son of King Ethelred the Unready. Born at Islip, England, in 1003, he died Jan 5, 1066, at London, England. On Oct 13, 1163, his remains were transported in a ceremony that was of national interest. Since then Oct 13 has been observed as his principal feast day.

SOUTHERN FESTIVAL OF BOOKS: A CELEBRATION OF THE WRITTEN WORD. Oct 13–15. Cook Convention Center, Memphis, TN. To promote reading, writing, the literary arts and a broader understanding of the language and culture of the South, this annual festival will feature readings, talks and panel discussions by more than 200 authors, exhibit booths of publishing companies and bookstores, autographing sessions, a comprehensive children's program and a Cafe Stage, which is a performance corner for authors, storytellers and musicians. Annually, the second weekend in October. Est attendance: 30,000. For info: Serenity Gerbman, Dir, Southern Festival of Books, Humanities Tennessee, 306 Gay St, Nashville, TN 37201. Phone: (615) 770-0006. Fax: (615) 770-0007. E-mail: serenity@tn-humanities .org. Web: www.humanitiestennessee.org.

SUGARLOAF CRAFTS FESTIVAL. Oct 13–15. Montgomery County Fairgrounds, Gaithersburg, MD. This show, now in its sixth year, features more than 450 nationally recognized craft designers and fine artists displaying and selling their original creations. Includes craft demonstrations, live music, specialty food, hourly gift certificate drawings and more. Est attendance: 25,000. For info: Sugarloaf Mountain Works, 200 Orchard Ridge Dr, #215, Gaithersburg, MD 20878. Phone: (800) 210-9900. Fax: (310) 253-9620. Web: www.sugarloafcrafts.com.

THATCHER, MARGARET HILDA ROBERTS: BIRTHDAY. Oct 13, 1925. First woman prime minister in 700 years of English parliamentary history. Election of May 3, 1979, gave Conservative Party victory, and Thatcher accepted Queen Elizabeth's appointment as prime minister on May 4. She held the office until forced to resign on Nov 22, 1990. She was given a life peerage as Baroness Thatcher of Kesteven, June 5, 1992, a position that entitles her to a seat in the House of Lords, where she remains an active Tory voice. Mrs Thatcher was born at Grantham, Lincolnshire.

★   ★   ★

		S	M	T	W	T	F	S
October			1	2	3	4	5	6	7
2006		8	9	10	11	12	13	14
		15	16	17	18	19	20	21
		22	23	24	25	26	27	28
		29	30	31				

US NAVY: AUTHORIZATION ANNIVERSARY. Oct 13, 1775. Commemorates legislation passed by Second Continental Congress authorizing the acquisition of ships and establishment of a navy.

VIRCHOW, RUDOLF: BIRTH ANNIVERSARY. Oct 13, 1821. German political leader, scientist, teacher and author. Called "the founder of cellular pathology." Born at Schivelbein, Prussia, died at Berlin, Sept 5, 1902.

WHITE HOUSE CORNERSTONE LAID: ANNIVERSARY. Oct 13, 1792. The presidential residence at 1600 Pennsylvania Ave NW, Washington, DC, designed by James Hoban (q.v.), observes its birthday Oct 13. The cornerstone was laid; the first presidential family to occupy it was that of John Adams, in November 1800. With three stories and more than 100 rooms, the White House is the oldest building at Washington. First described as the "presidential palace," it acquired the name "White House" about 10 years after construction was completed. Burned by British troops in 1814, it was reconstructed, refurbished and reoccupied by 1817.

WORLD EGG DAY. Oct 13. Dedicated to the global appeal of the billions of nutritious eggs produced worldwide. Annually, the second Friday of October. For info: Lin Jackowski, State Promotion Coordinator, American Egg Board, 1460 Renaissance Dr, Park Ridge, IL 60068. E-mail: aeb@aeb.org. Web: www.aeb.org.

BIRTHDAYS TODAY

Ashanti, 26, singer, actress (*The Muppets' Wizard of Oz*), born Ashanti Sequoiah Douglas at Long Island, NY, Oct 13, 1980.

Maria Cantwell, 48, US Senator (D, Washington), born Indianapolis, IN, Oct 13, 1958.

Chris Carter, 49, creator of "The X-Files," born Bellflower, CA, Oct 13, 1957.

Melinda Dillon, 67, actress (*Close Encounters of the Third Kind, Absence of Malice, A Christmas Story*), born Hope, AR, Oct 13, 1939.

Sammy Hagar, 57, singer, musician ("Your Love Is Driving Me Crazy"), born Monterrey, CA, Oct 13, 1949.

Nancy Kerrigan, 37, figure skater, born Woburn, MA, Oct 13, 1969.

Jermaine O'Neal, 28, basketball player, born Columbia, SC, Oct 13, 1978.

Marie Osmond, 47, actress, singer ("Donny and Marie"), born Ogden, UT, Oct 13, 1959.

Paul Pierce, 29, basketball player, born Oakland, CA, Oct 13, 1977.

Kelly Preston, 44, actress (*Christine, Twins*), born Honolulu, HI, Oct 13, 1962.

Jerry Lee Rice, 44, football player, born Starkville, MS, Oct 13, 1962.

Glenn Anton ("Doc") Rivers, 45, basketball coach and former player, born Maywood, IL, Oct 13, 1961.

Nipsey Russell, 82, comedian, actor, born Atlanta, GA, Oct 13, 1924.

Paul Simon, 65, singer, songwriter (with Art Garfunkel: "The Sounds of Silence," "Mrs Robinson"; solo album: *Graceland*), born Newark, NJ, Oct 13, 1941.

Margaret Hilda Roberts Thatcher, 81, former Prime Minister of England, born Grantham, England, Oct 13, 1925.

Pamela Tiffin, 64, actress (*Harper*; stage: *Dinner at Eight* [Theatre World Award]), born Oklahoma City, OK, Oct 13, 1942.

OCTOBER 14 — SATURDAY

Day 287 — 78 Remaining

"THE ADVENTURES OF ELLERY QUEEN" TV PREMIERE: ANNIVERSARY. Oct 14, 1950. The first of many series to portray fictional detective Ellery Queen, it began on the Dumont network and later moved to ABC. Queen was played by Richard Hart. In the next four series, he would also be played by Lee Bowman, Hugh Marlowe, George Nadar, Lee Philips, Peter Lawford and Jim Hutton. In each series Queen talked to the home audience at the show's climax to see if they were able to identify the killer. Future series were titled "Ellery Queen" and "The Further Adventures of Ellery Queen." The last telecast aired on Sept 5, 1976.

BE BALD AND BE FREE DAY. Oct 14. For those who are bald and who either do wear or do not wear a wig or toupee, this is the day to go "shiny" and be proud. Annually, Oct 14. [©2003 by WH.] For info: Thomas & Ruth Roy, Wellcat Holidays, 2418 Long Ln, Lebanon, PA 17046. Phone: (717) 279-0184. E-mail: info@wellcat.com. Web: www.wellcat.com.

CATOCTIN COLORFEST ARTS AND CRAFTS SHOW. Oct 14–15. Thurmont, MD. Live music, food, 350 arts and crafts booths featuring artists from Maryland, Virginia, West Virginia and Pennsylvania. Annually, the second weekend in October. Est attendance: 100,000. For info send a SASE to: Catoctin ColorFest, Inc, Box 33, Thurmont, MD 21788. Phone: (301) 271-4432. Web: www.colorfest.org.

COLONIAL DAY. Oct 14. Celebrate the unique traditions of our colonial past with crafts, games and special demonstrations including weaving, basket making, and blacksmithing. Annually, the second Saturday in October. For info: Karen DeRosa, Tuckerton Seaport, 120 W Main St, PO Box 52, Tuckerton, NJ 08087. Phone: (609) 296-8868. Fax: (609) 296-5810. E-mail: info@tuckertonseaport.org. Web: www.tuckertonseaport.org.

DOW-JONES TOPS 6,000: 10th ANNIVERSARY. Oct 14, 1996. The Dow-Jones Index of 30 major industrial stocks topped the 6,000 mark for the first time.

EISENHOWER, DWIGHT DAVID: BIRTH ANNIVERSARY. Oct 14, 1890. The 34th president of the US, Dwight David Eisenhower, was born at Denison, TX. Serving two terms as president, Jan 20, 1953–Jan 20, 1961, Eisenhower was the first president to be baptized after taking office (Sunday, Feb 1, 1953). Nicknamed "Ike," he held the rank of five-star general of the army (resigned in 1952, and restored by act of Congress in 1961). He served as supreme commander of the Allied forces in western Europe during WWII. In his Farewell Address (Jan 17, 1961), speaking about the "conjunction of an immense military establishment and a large arms industry," he warned: "In the councils of government, we must guard against the acquisition of unwarranted influence, whether sought or unsought, by the military-industrial complex. The potential of the disastrous rise of misplaced power exists and will persist." An American hero, Eisenhower died at Washington, DC, Mar 28, 1969.

ELDON TURKEY FESTIVAL. Oct 14. Eldon, MO. A celebration of Miller County's state and national ranking as a top producer of wild and domestic turkeys. Event includes more than 200 crafters and exhibitors, turkey events, food, quilt show and old-time machinery show. Annually, the second Saturday in October. Est attendance: 12,000. For info: Eldon Chamber of Commerce, PO Box 209, Eldon, MO 65026. Phone: (573) 392-3752. Fax: (573) 392-0634. Web: www.eldonchamber.com.

FIREANT FESTIVAL. Oct 14–15. Marshall, TX. Arts and crafts, chili cook-off, Tour de FireAnt bike ride, 5k run, fireant calling contest, fireant roundup, rubber chicken chunking, gurning contest (ugly face), Diaper Derby Contest (crawling), parade, men's crazy leg contest and street dance. Est attendance: 50,000. For info: Marshall Chamber of Commerce, PO Box 520, Marshall, TX 75671. Phone: (903) 935-7868. Fax: (903) 935-9982. E-mail: chambermfi@hotmail.com. Web: www.marshalltxchamber.com.

FODOR, EUGENE: BIRTH ANNIVERSARY. Oct 14, 1905. Travel writer Eugene Fodor was born at Leva, Hungary. His first travel book was published in 1936, after which he published more than 140, bringing to them a human element previously lacking in travel books. He died Feb 18, 1991, at Torrington, CT.

FOREST CRAFT/SCENIC DRIVE FESTIVAL. Oct 14–15. Van Buren County, IA. Scenic landscapes, historic architecture, wood carvers, buckskinners camp, flea market, arts festival, crafts and more. Annually, the second full weekend in October. Est attendance: 18,000. For info: Villages of Van Buren, Inc, PO Box 9, Keosauqua, IA 52565. Phone: (800) 868-7822. Fax: (319) 293-7116. E-mail: info@villagesofvanburen.com. Web: www.villagesofvanburen.com.

GISH, LILLIAN: BIRTH ANNIVERSARY. Oct 14, 1893. American actress Lillian Diana Gish was born at Springfield, OH. Her film and stage career spanned more than 85 years, 100 films, the silent and sound eras of film and numerous stage productions. She was awarded an honorary Oscar in 1970 and made her last film appearance in *The Whales of August* (1987). She died Feb 27, 1993, at New York, NY.

IRONMAN TRIATHLON WORLD CHAMPIONSHIP. Oct 14 (tentative). Kailua-Kona, HI. The world's most famous triathlon: a 2.4-mile swim, 112-mile bike ride and 26.2-mile run that the 2,000 competitors have 17 hours to finish. More than 50 million people worldwide watch the event on TV. Est attendance: 35,000. For info: World Triathlon Corporation/Ironman, 43309 US Hwy 19 N, Tarpon Springs, FL 34689. E-mail: kona@ironmanlive.com. Web: www.ironmanlive.com.

JAPAN: MEGA KENKA MATSURI or ROUGHHOUSE FESTIVAL. Oct 14–15. Himeji. Palanquin bearers jostle one another to demonstrate their skill and balance in handling their burdens.

KING AWARDED NOBEL PEACE PRIZE: ANNIVERSARY. Oct 14, 1964. Martin Luther King, Jr, became the youngest recipient of the Nobel Peace Prize when awarded the honor. Dr. King donated the entire $54,000 prize money to furthering the causes of the civil rights movement.

LAILAT UL QADR: THE NIGHT OF POWER. Oct 14 (also Oct 16, 18, 20 or 22). "The Night of Power" falls on one of the last 10 days of Ramadan on an odd-numbered night (Islamic calendar dates: Ramadan 21, 23, 25, 27 or 29, 1427). It commemorates the night of the first revelation of the Holy Qur'an to Muhammad by the angel Gabriel. The Holy Qur'an states that praying on this night is better than praying 1,000 months. Since it is not known which day it is, Muslims feel it is best to pray on each of the possible nights. Different methods for "anticipating" the visibility of the new moon crescent at Mecca are used by different Muslim sects or groups. US date may vary.

LEE, FRANCIS LIGHTFOOT: BIRTH ANNIVERSARY. Oct 14, 1734. Signer of the Declaration of Independence. Born at Westmoreland County, VA, he died Jan 11, 1797, at Richmond County, VA.

MONSTER MYTHS BY MOONLIGHT. Oct 14. Milford State Park, Milford, KS. Learn the truth about spiders, snakes, bats, vultures, owls and other Halloween "monsters." Meet the real creatures as you walk our nature trail and learn the truth about them from witches, snake charmers and Little Red Riding Hood. Wear costumes. Cookies and cider served by Mother Nature. Sponsored by Friends of Milford Nature Center and State Park. Est attendance: 650. For info: Milford Nature Center, 3115 Hatchery Dr, Junction City, KS 66441. Phone: (785) 238-5323. Fax: (785) 238-5775.

MOUNTAIN GLORY FESTIVAL. Oct 14. Marion, NC. A celebration of mountain heritage in western North Carolina. Arts, crafts, children's area and continuous entertainment. Annually, the second Saturday in October. Est attendance: 20,000. For info: Mountain Glory Festival, PO Drawer 700, Marion, NC 28752. Phone: (828) 652-3551. Fax: (828) 652-1983. E-mail: info@mtngloryfestival.com. Web: www.mtngloryfestival.com.

NATCHITOCHES HISTORIC PILGRIMAGE. Oct 14–15. Natchitoches, LA. Tour of homes in the National Historic Landmark District and plantation homes in Cane River Country. Est attendance: 5,000. For info: Natchitoches Parish Tourist Commission, 781 Front St, Natchitoches, LA 71457. Phone: (318) 352-8072 or 800-259-1714. Fax: (318) 352-2415. Web: www.natchitoches.net.

PENN, WILLIAM: BIRTH ANNIVERSARY. Oct 14, 1644. Founder of Pennsylvania, born at London, England. Penn died July 30, 1718, at Buckinghamshire, England. Presidential Proclamation 5284 of Nov 28, 1984, conferred honorary citizenship of the USA upon William Penn and his second wife, Hannah Callowhill Penn. They were the third and fourth persons to receive honorary US citizenship (following Winston Churchill and Raoul Wallenberg).

PUMPKIN FEST. Oct 14. DeLaney Farm, Aurora, CO. Aurora's award-winning fall festival, featuring the Jack-o-Launch, family entertainment and practically every activity you can think of having to do with pumpkins. Annually, the second Saturday of October. Est attendance: 26,000. For info: Marie Addleman, Pumpkin Fest, 1298 Peoria St, Aurora, CO 80011. Phone: (303) 326-8615. Fax: (303) 361-2954. E-mail: maddlema@auroragov.org. Web: www.auroragov.org/pumpkinfest.

SHEMINI ATZERET. Oct 14. Hebrew calendar date: Tishri 22, 5767. The eighth day of Solemn Assembly, part of the Sukkot Festival (see entry on Oct 7), with memorial services and cycle of Biblical readings in the synagogue. Began at sundown on Oct 13.

SOUND BARRIER BROKEN: ANNIVERSARY. Oct 14, 1947. Flying a Bell X-1 at Muroc Dry Lake Bed, CA, Air Force pilot Chuck Yeager broke the sound barrier, ushering in the era of supersonic flight.

TAMARACK TIME! Oct 14. Bigfork, MT. Old-fashioned village celebration of harvest and autumn. Local chefs prepare their specialties for a taste treat. No vendors. Est attendance: 600. For info: Elna Darrow, Box 400, Bigfork, MT 59911-0400. Phone: (406) 837-4400. E-mail: crossbow@cyberport.net.

	S	M	T	W	T	F	S
October	1	2	3	4	5	6	7
	8	9	10	11	12	13	14
2006	15	16	17	18	19	20	21
	22	23	24	25	26	27	28
	29	30	31				

OCTOBER 15 — SUNDAY
Day 288 — 77 Remaining

ACHIEVE FINANCIAL INDEPENDENCE WEEK. Oct 15–21. A week dedicated to helping people improve their financial position so they can enjoy a better life. Inspired by the proven philosophies and practices of James E. Stowers, self-made billionaire, founder and chairman of the board of American Century Investments, Inc. Includes strategies and concepts for people at every life stage—from children to newlyweds to retirees. Annually, beginning the third Sunday in October. Sponsored by Stowers Innovation, Inc, an education-focused company. For info: Sam Goller, 4500 Main, Kansas City, MO 64111. Phone: (816) 753-7787. E-mail: sam_goller@americancentury.com.

AIDS WALK ATLANTA. Oct 15. Piedmont Park, Atlanta, GA. AIDS Walk Atlanta is a 10-kilometer fundraising walkathon benefiting AID Atlanta and other AIDS service and education providers around metro Atlanta. Annually, the third Sunday in October. Est attendance: 15,000. For info: Claudia Zevallos-Byers, 1438 W Peachtree St, Ste 100, Atlanta, GA 30309. Phone: (404) 876-9255. Fax: (404) 877-9496. E-mail: claudia@aidswalkatlanta.com. Web: www.aidswalkatlanta.com.

ASSOCIATION FOR DRESSINGS & SAUCES ANNUAL MEETING. Oct 15–17. Grove Park Inn, Asheville, NC. For info: Jacque Knight, Assn for Dressings & Sauces, 5775 Peachtree-Dunwoody Rd, Bldg G, Ste 500, Atlanta, GA 30342. Phone: (404) 252-3663. Fax: (404) 252-0774. E-mail: ads@kellencompany.com. Web: www.dressings-sauces.org.

CHINA: CANTON AUTUMN TRADE FAIR. Oct 15–Nov 15. The Guangzhou (Canton) Autumn Trade Fair is held during the same dates each year.

CROW RESERVATION OPENED FOR SETTLEMENT: ANNIVERSARY. Oct 15, 1892. By Presidential Proclamation 1.8 million acres of Crow Indian reservation were opened to settlers. The government had induced the Crow to give up a portion of their land in the mountainous western area in the state of Montana, for which they received 50 cents per acre.

FIRST MANNED FLIGHT: ANNIVERSARY. Oct 15, 1783. Jean Francois Pilatre de Rozier and Francois Laurent, Marquis d'Arlandes became the first people to fly when they ascended in a Montgolfier hot-air balloon at Paris, France, less than three months after the first public balloon flight demonstration (June 5, 1783), and only a year after the first experiments with small paper and fabric balloons by the Montgolfier brothers, Joseph and Jacques, in November 1782. The first manned free flight lasted about 4 minutes and carried the passengers at a height of about 84 feet. On Nov 21, 1783, they soared 3,000 feet over Paris for 25 minutes.

GETTING THE WORLD TO BEAT A PATH TO YOUR DOOR WEEK. Oct 15–21. To focus attention on improving "public relationships" in order to create success for companies, products and individuals. Free self-evaluation available. Annually, the third week in October. For info: Barbara Gaughen, Pres, Gaughen Global Public Relations, 7456 Evergreen Dr, Santa Barbara, CA 93117. Phone: (805) 968-8567. Fax: (805) 968-5747. E-mail: bgaughenmu@aol.com. Web: www.robertmuller.org.

"I LOVE LUCY" TV PREMIERE: 55th ANNIVERSARY. Oct 15, 1951. This enormously popular sitcom, TV's first smash hit, starred the real-life husband and wife team of Cuban actor/bandleader Desi Arnaz and talented redheaded actress/comedienne Lucille Ball. They played Ricky and Lucy Ricardo, a New York bandleader and his aspiring actress/homemaker wife who was always scheming to get on stage. Costarring were William Frawley and Vivian Vance as Fred and Ethel Mertz, the Ricardos' landlords and good friends who participated in the escapades and dealt with the consequences of Lucy's often well-intentioned plans. Famous actors guest-starred on the show, including Harpo Marx, Rock Hudson, William Holden, Hedda Hopper and John Wayne. This was the first sitcom to be filmed live before a studio audience, and it did extremely well in the ratings both the first time around and in reruns. The last telecast ran Sept 24, 1961.

INTERNATIONAL CREDIT UNION WEEK. Oct 15–21. Worldwide observance to recognize the contribution of credit unions to the development and practice of democracy. For info: Public Relations, Credit Union Natl Assn, PO Box 431, Madison, WI 53701-0431. Phone: (608) 231-5794. Fax: (608) 231-4370.

INTERNATIONAL GOLD CUP. Oct 15. Great Meadow, The Plains, VA. A day of steeplechasing in the heart of Virginia's hunt country, to promote steeplechase racing and to encourage open-space land preservation. Gates open at 10 AM. Corporate and private hospitality packages available. Est attendance: 30,000. For info: Virginia Gold Cup Assn, PO Box 840, Warrenton, VA 20188. Phone: (540) 347-2612. Fax: (540) 349-1829. Web: www.vagoldcup.com.

MANN, MARTY: BIRTH ANNIVERSARY. Oct 15, 1904. American social activist and author was born at Chicago, IL. She was founder in 1944 of the National Committee for Education on Alcoholism and author of *A New Primer on Alcoholism*. She died at Bridgeport, CT, July 22, 1980.

★**NATIONAL CHARACTER COUNTS WEEK.** Oct 15–21. One of the greatest building blocks of character is citizen service. The future belongs to those who have the strength of character to live a life of service to others.

NATIONAL FOOD BANK WEEK. Oct 15–21. Educates and recognizes efforts of food banks, their donors and volunteers to alleviate hunger in the US. Observed at local food banks around the country. Annually, the week encompassing World Food Day (Oct 16). For info on activities in your area, go to Second Harvest's website at www.secondharvest.org and do a zipcode search.

★**NATIONAL FOREST PRODUCTS WEEK.** Oct 15–21. Presidential Proclamation always issued for the week beginning with the third Sunday in October since 1960 (PL86–753 of Sept 13, 1960).

NATIONAL GROUCH DAY. Oct 15. Honor a grouch; all grouches deserve a day to be recognized. Annually, Oct 15. For info: Alan R. Miller, Carter Middle School, 300 Upland Dr, Room 207, Clio, MI 48420. Phone: (810) 591-0503.

NATIONAL SCHOOL BUS SAFETY WEEK. Oct 15–21. This week is set aside to focus attention on school bus safety—from the standpoint of the bus drivers, students and the motoring public. The theme for 2006 is "I See The Driver, The Driver Sees Me!" Annually, the third full week of October, starting on Sunday. For info: Natl Assn for Pupil Transportation, 1840 Western Ave, Albany, NY 12203. Phone: (800) 989-6278. E-mail: sbsw@napt.org. Web: www.napt.org.

NIETZSCHE, FRIEDRICH WILHELM: BIRTH ANNIVERSARY. Oct 15, 1844. Influential German philosopher born at Rocken. Especially remembered among his philosophical beliefs are contempt for the weak and expected ultimate triumph of a superman. Nietzsche died at Weimar, Aug 25, 1900, a decade after suffering a mental breakdown.

SIMCHAT TORAH. Oct 15. Hebrew calendar date: Tishri 23, 5767. Rejoicing in the Torah concludes the nine-day Sukkot Festival (see entry on Oct 7). Public reading of the Pentateuch is completed and begun again, symbolizing the need for ever-continuing study. Began at sundown on Oct 14.

SPACE MILESTONE: *CASSINI* (US). Oct 15, 1997. The plutonium-powered spacecraft was launched to arrive at Saturn in July 2004. It arrived on schedule, passing between the rings of the planet on June 30, 2004, and sending back photographs of the moons. It will orbit the planet, continue to take pictures of its 18 known moons and dispatch a probe to Titan, the largest of these moons.

SUNDAY SCHOOL TEACHER APPRECIATION DAY. Oct 15. Established in 1993, this is a day set aside for churches to honor the 15 million men and women who faithfully serve as Sunday School teachers—one of the largest volunteer forces in America. For info: Gospel Light, 1957 Eastman Ave, Ventura, CA 93003. Phone: (800) 354-4224. Fax: (805) 677-6818. E-mail: hillarywiens@regalbooks.com. Web: www.mysundayschoolteacher.com.

TEEN READ WEEK. Oct 15–21. The teen years are a time when many kids reject reading as being just another dreary assignment. The goal of Teen Read Week is to encourage young adults to read for the fun of it. Also to remind parents, teachers, booksellers and others that reading for fun is important for teens as well as young children and to increase awareness of the resources available at libraries. More than 1,400 school and public libraries are registered to participate. For info: Young Adult Library Services Assn, American Library Assn, 50 E Huron St, Chicago, IL 60611. Phone: (800) 545-2433 x 4390. E-mail: yalsa@ala.org. Web: www.ala.org/teenread.

★**WHITE CANE SAFETY DAY.** Oct 15. Presidential Proclamation always issued for Oct 15 since 1964 (PL88–628 of Oct 6, 1964).

WILSON, EDITH BOLLING GALT: BIRTH ANNIVERSARY. Oct 15, 1872. Second wife of Woodrow Wilson, 28th president of the US, born at Wytheville, VA. Died at Washington, DC, Dec 28, 1961.

WISHBONES FOR PETS. Oct 15–Nov 30. This is a voluntary program designed for professional pet sitters to host a pet goods or fund drive in their community around Thanksgiving with all proceeds going to their favorite local pet-related charity. For info: Janet Depathy, Wishbones for Pets, PO Box 777, Plymouth, MA 02362. Phone: (508) 747-4259. E-mail: paws@adelphia.net. Web: www.wishbonesforpets.com.

WODEHOUSE, PELHAM GRENVILLE: 125th BIRTH ANNIVERSARY. Oct 15, 1881. English author, lyricist ("Bill"), humorist, creator of Bertie Wooster and Jeeves. Born at Guildford, Surrey, England, P.G. Wodehouse died at Southampton, Long Island, NY, Feb 14, 1975.

WSBA/WARM 103/OLDIES 96.1 HOLIDAY CRAFT SHOW. Oct 15. York Fairgrounds, York, PA. More than 170 craft displays, from country to contemporary, Victorian and southwestern, handcrafted furniture, wood carvings, dolls, jewelry, pottery, collectibles, quilts, baskets, fine arts and much more. Admission fee. Est attendance: 3,500. For info: Joe Alfano, Asst Promo Dir, PO Box 910, York, PA 17402-0910. Phone: (717) 764-1155. Fax: (717) 252-4807. E-mail: jalfano@radioyork.com. Web: www.warm103.com.

YWCA WEEK WITHOUT VIOLENCE. Oct 15–21. Celebrated the third full week in October, this annual campaign seeks to make people aware of the violence in their communities and suggest alternatives to it. For info: YWCA USA, 1015 18th St NW, Ste 1100, Washington, DC 20036. Phone: (202) 467-0801. Fax: (202) 467-0802. Web: www.ywca.org.

BIRTHDAYS TODAY

Victor Banerjee, 60, actor (*A Passage to India, The Home and the World*), born Calcutta, India, Oct 15, 1946.

Paige Davis, 37, actress, television personality ("Trading Spaces"), born Philadelphia, PA, Oct 15, 1969.

Sarah Ferguson, 47, Duchess of York (former wife of Prince Andrew), born London, England, Oct 15, 1959.

John Kenneth Galbraith, 98, economist, diplomat, author, born Iona Station, ON, Canada, Oct 15, 1908.

Lee Iacocca, 82, former automobile executive (Ford and Chrysler), born Allentown, PA, Oct 15, 1924.

Tito Jackson, 53, singer, musician (Jackson 5), born Toriano Adaryll Jackson at Gary, IN, Oct 15, 1953.

Linda Lavin, 67, actress (Tony for *Broadway Bound*; "Alice"), born Portland, ME, Oct 15, 1939.

Penny Marshall, 64, director (*Big, A League of Their Own*), actress ("Laverne & Shirley"), born New York, NY, Oct 15, 1942.

James Alvin (Jim) Palmer, 61, Hall of Fame baseball player, sportscaster, born New York, NY, Oct 15, 1945.

Arthur Meier Schlesinger, Jr, 89, historian, author, born Columbus, OH, Oct 15, 1917.

	S	M	T	W	T	F	S
October	1	2	3	4	5	6	7
2006	8	9	10	11	12	13	14
	15	16	17	18	19	20	21
	22	23	24	25	26	27	28
	29	30	31				

OCTOBER 16 — MONDAY
Day 289 — 76 Remaining

AMERICAN DENTAL ASSOCIATION ANNUAL SESSION. Oct 16–19. Las Vegas, NV. Est attendance: 31,000. For info: James P. Donovan, American Dental Assn, 211 E Chicago Ave, Ste 200, Chicago, IL 60611. Fax: (312) 440-2707. E-mail: annualsession@ada.org. Web: www.ada.org/goto/session.

AMERICA'S FIRST DEPARTMENT STORE: ANNIVERSARY. Oct 16, 1868. Salt Lake City, UT. America's first department store, "ZCMI" (Zion's Co-Operative Mercantile Institution), is still operating at Salt Lake City. It was founded under the direction of Brigham Young. For info: Museum of Church History and Art, 45 North West Temple, Salt Lake City, UT 84150. Phone: (801) 240-4604.

BEN-GURION, DAVID: BIRTH ANNIVERSARY. Oct 16, 1886. First prime minister of the state of Israel. Born at Plonsk, Poland, died at Tel Aviv, Israel, Dec 1, 1973.

BIRTH CONTROL CLINIC OPENED: 90th ANNIVERSARY. Oct 16, 1916. Margaret Sanger, Fania Mindell and Ethel Burne opened the first birth control clinic in the US at 46 Amboy St, Brooklyn, NY. Sanger believed that the poor should be able to control the size of their families.

CELEBRATE MICRO SMALL & HOME BUSINESS WEEK. Oct 16–22. A week of events, contests and awareness celebrating the growing importance of micro small and home businesses to the national economy and local communities. The week will culminate in The Micro Small & Home Business Expo and Small Biz Games Awards Banquet, October 20–22 in Las Vegas, NV. Co-founded by Michael Brooks, CEO of The Small Biz Games, and Stephanie Chandler, owner of Book Lovers Bookstore in Sacramento, CA. For info: Michael Brooks, 2200 Lonesome Dove, Boise, ID 82642. Phone: (208) 884-5263. E-mail: marketsparkmedia@aol.com. Web: www.smallbizgames.com or www.BusinessInfoGuide.com.

CRIMEAN WAR: ANNIVERSARY. Oct 16, 1853. The Ottoman Empire declared war on Russia on this day to stem Russian expansionist policies in the Empire. Britain, France and parts of Italy allied themselves with the Turks against Russia. A battle in this war was immortalized in Tennyson's poem, "The Charge of the Light Brigade." Health conditions for soldiers were scandalous, leading Florence Nightingale to work in the British hospital at Istanbul. This was the first war to be observed firsthand by newspaper reporters and photographers.

DICTIONARY DAY. Oct 16. The birthday of Noah Webster, American teacher and lexicographer, is occasion to encourage every person to acquire at least one dictionary—and to use it regularly.

DOUGLAS, WILLIAM ORVILLE: BIRTH ANNIVERSARY. Oct 16, 1898. American jurist, world traveler, conservationist, outdoorsman and author. Born at Maine, MN, he served as justice of the US Supreme Court longer than any other (36 years). Died at Washington, DC, Jan 19, 1980.

FREEDOM FROM BULLIES WEEK. Oct 16–22. A time for courage, support, inspiration and peace for people suffering health-endangering bullying and for others who witness the mistreatment. For info: Bullying Institute, PO Box 29915, Bellingham, WA 98228. Phone: (360) 656-6630. E-mail: wbti@bullying institute.org. Web: www.bullybusters.org or www.bullyinginstitute.org.

INFECTION PREVENTION WEEK. Oct 16–22. To promote awareness of prevention and treatment of infection. Annually, the third week in October. For info: Assn for Professionals in Infection Control and Epidemiology, 1275 K St NW, Ste 1000, Washington, DC 20005-4006. Phone: (202) 789-1890. Fax: (202) 789-1899. E-mail: APICinfo@apic.org. Web: www.apic.org.

JAMAICA: NATIONAL HEROES DAY. Oct 16. National holiday established in 1969. Always observed on third Monday of October.

JOHN BROWN'S RAID: ANNIVERSARY. Oct 16, 1859. White abolitionist John Brown, with a band of about 20 men, seized the US Arsenal at Harpers Ferry, WV. Brown was captured and the insurrection put down by Oct 19. Brown was hanged at Charles Town, WV, Dec 2, 1859.

MARIE ANTOINETTE: EXECUTION ANNIVERSARY. Oct 16, 1793. Queen Marie Antoinette, whose extravagance and "let them eat cake" attitude toward the starving French underclass made her a target of the French Revolution, was beheaded on this date.

MILLION MAN MARCH: ANNIVERSARY. Oct 16, 1995. Hundreds of thousands of black men met at Washington, DC, for a "holy day of atonement and reconciliation" organized by Louis Farrakhan, leader of the Nation of Islam. Marchers pledged to take responsibility for themselves, their families and their communities.

NATIONAL BOSS DAY. Oct 16. For all employees to honor their bosses. Annually, the weekday closest to Oct 16. Mrs Patricia Bays Haroski originated this event. For info: Edward A. Haroski, 1315 Forestwood Dr, Lewisville, NC 27023.

NATIONAL BUSINESS WOMEN'S WEEK. Oct 16–20. Celebrates the contributions of working women to American society, the economy and the family. It is commemorated nationwide by special activities. Annually, starting the third Monday in October. For info: Business and Professional Women/USA, 1900 M St NW, #310, Washington, DC 20036. Phone: (202) 293-1100. E-mail: editor@bpwusa.org. Web: www.bpwusa.org.

NATIONAL HEALTH EDUCATION WEEK. Oct 16–20. Annually, the third week in October. For info: Ray Marks, National Center for Health Education, 375 Hudson St, New York, NY 10014. Phone: (212) 463-4053. E-mail: ray@nche.org. Web: www.nche.org.

O'NEILL, EUGENE GLADSTONE: BIRTH ANNIVERSARY. Oct 16, 1888. American playwright (*Long Day's Journey into Night, Ah, Wilderness*), recipient of Pulitzer and Nobel Prize. Born at New York, NY, he died at Boston, MA, Nov 27, 1953.

UNITED NATIONS: WORLD FOOD DAY. Oct 16. Annual observance to heighten public awareness of the world food problem and to strengthen solidarity in the struggle against hunger, malnutrition and poverty. Date of observance is anniversary of founding of Food and Agriculture Organization (FAO), Oct 16, 1945, at Quebec, Canada. For info: United Nations, Dept of Public Info, New York, NY 10017. Web: www.un.org.

VIRGIN ISLANDS: HURRICANE THANKSGIVING DAY. Oct 16. Third Monday of October is a legal holiday celebrating the end of hurricane season.

WAR CRIMINALS (GERMAN) EXECUTION: 60th ANNIVERSARY. Oct 16, 1946. The War Crimes Trials of Berlin and Nuremberg had sentenced 12 of the 22 defendants to death by hanging. They were: Hermann Goering, Joachim von Ribbentrop, Wilhelm Keitel, Ernst Kaltenbrunner, Alfred Rosenberg, Hans Frank, Wilhelm Frick, Julius Streicher, Fritz Sauckel, Alfred Jodl, Martin Bormann and Arthur von Seyss-Inquart. Goering committed suicide a few hours before his scheduled execution, and Martin Bormann had not been found (he was tried in absentia). The remaining 10 were hanged at Nuremberg Prison on this date.

WEBSTER, NOAH: BIRTH ANNIVERSARY. Oct 16, 1758. American teacher and journalist whose name became synonymous with the word "dictionary" after his compilations of the earliest American dictionaries of the English language. Born at West Hartford, CT, he died at New Haven, CT, May 28, 1843.

WILDE, OSCAR: BIRTH ANNIVERSARY. Oct 16, 1854. Irish wit, poet and playwright Oscar (Fingal O'Flahertie Wills) Wilde was born at Dublin, Ireland. At the height of his career he was imprisoned for two years on a morals offense, during which time he wrote "A Ballad of Reading Gaol." Best known of his plays is *The Importance of Being Earnest.* "We are all in the gutter," he wrote in *Lady Windermere's Fan*, "but some of us are looking at the stars." Wilde died at Paris, France, Nov 30, 1900.

WORLD FOOD DAY. Oct 16. To increase awareness, understanding and informed action on hunger. Annually, on the founding date of the UN Food and Agriculture Organization. For info: Patricia Young, US Natl Committee for World Food Day, 2175 K St NW, Washington, DC 20437. Phone: (202) 653-2404. Web: www.worldfooddayusa.org.

WORLD RAINFOREST WEEK. Oct 16–22. Rainforest activists worldwide will sponsor events to increase public awareness of rainforest destruction and motivate people to protect the Earth's rainforests, and support the rights of their inhabitants. The global rate of destruction of rainforests is 2.4 acres per second—equivalent to two US football fields. For info: Grassroots Coord, Rainforest Action Network, 221 Pine St, 5th Fl, San Francisco, CA 94104. Phone: (415) 398-4404. E-mail: grassroots@ran.org. Web: www.ran.org.

YALE UNIVERSITY FOUNDED: ANNIVERSARY. Oct 16, 1701 (OS). The Collegiate School was founded at Branford, CT, by Congregationalists dissatisfied with the growing liberalism at Harvard. In 1716, the school was moved to New Haven, CT, where it became Yale College, named after Elihu Yale, a governor of the East India Company. The first degrees were awarded in 1716. Yale became a university in 1887. Founded as a school for men, Yale began admitting women undergraduates in 1969.

BIRTHDAYS TODAY

Melissa Louise Belote, 50, Olympic gold medal swimmer, born Washington, DC, Oct 16, 1956.

Manute Bol, 44, former basketball player, born Gogrial, Sudan, Oct 16, 1962.

Barry Corbin, 66, actor ("Northern Exposure," *Stir Crazy, Any Which Way You Can*), born Dawson County, TX, Oct 16, 1940.

Juan Gonzalez, 37, baseball player, born Vaga Baja, Puerto Rico, Oct 16, 1969.

Gunter Grass, 79, author (*The Tin Drum, Dog Years*), born Danzig, Germany, Oct 16, 1927.

Paul Kariya, 32, hockey player, born Vancouver, BC, Canada, Oct 16, 1974.

Angela Lansbury, 81, actress ("Murder She Wrote," *National Velvet*; Tony for *Sweeney Todd*), born London, England, Oct 16, 1925.

Kellie Martin, 31, actress ("Life Goes On," "ER"), born Riverside, CA, Oct 16, 1975.

Tim Robbins, 48, actor (*Shawshank Redemption, The Player*), director, born West Covina, CA, Oct 16, 1958.

Suzanne Somers, 60, actress ("Three's Company," "Step by Step," *American Graffiti*), born San Bruno, CA, Oct 16, 1946.

Kordell Stewart, 34, football player, born New Orleans, LA, Oct 16, 1972.

Bob Weir, 59, cofounder (The Grateful Dead), born San Francisco, CA, Oct 16, 1947.

OCTOBER 17 — TUESDAY
Day 290 — 75 Remaining

ARTHUR, JEAN: BIRTH ANNIVERSARY. Oct 17, 1900. American actress Jean Arthur was born Gladys Georgianna Greene at Plattsburg, NY. Her films included *Mr Deeds Goes to Town* (1936), *Mr Smith Goes to Washington* (1939) and *Shane* (1953). She died June 19, 1991, at Carmel, CA.

FOOD AND DRUG INTERACTION EDUCATION AND AWARENESS WEEK. Oct 17–24. This campaign has been designed to help educate health professionals, patients and consumers on the problems of certain foods mixed with prescription drugs, over-the-counter drugs and herbal/alternative medicines. There is a $15 charge for kit materials. For info: PPSI, 101 Lucas Valley Rd, Ste 210, San Rafael, CA 94903. Phone: (415) 479-8628. Fax: (415) 479-8608. E-mail: ppsi@aol.com. Web: www .ppsinc.org.

HAMMON, JUPITER: BIRTH ANNIVERSARY. Oct 17, 1711. America's first published black poet, whose birth anniversary is celebrated annually as Black Poetry Day, was born into slavery, probably at Long Island, NY. He was taught to read, however, and as a trusted servant was allowed to use his master's library. "With the publication on Christmas Day, 1760, of the 88-line broadside poem 'An Evening Thought,' Jupiter Hammon, then 49, became the first black in America to publish poetry." Hammon died around 1806. The exact date and place of his death are unknown.

"THE HOLLYWOOD SQUARES" TV PREMIERE: 40th ANNIVERSARY. Oct 17, 1966. On this game show, nine celebrities sat in a giant grid. Two contestants played tic-tac-toe by determining if an answer given by a celebrity was correct. Peter Marshall hosted the show for many years with panelists Paul Lynde, Rose Marie, Cliff Arquette, Wally Cox, John Davidson and George Gobel among others. John Davidson took over as host in 1986 for a new version of the game show with Joan Rivers and, later, Shadoe Stevens at center square. In 1998 "Hollywood Squares" appeared again with Tom Bergeron as host and Whoopi Goldberg as the center square.

JOHNSON, RICHARD MENTOR: BIRTH ANNIVERSARY. Oct 17, 1780. Ninth vice president of the US (1837–41). Born at Floyd's Station, KY. Died at Frankfort, KY, Nov 19, 1850.

MILLER, ARTHUR: BIRTH ANNIVERSARY. Oct 17, 1915. Born at New York, NY, Miller began writing plays in college and also published several novels and collections of short stories. He won the Pulitzer Prize in 1949 for *Death of a Salesman*, one of the most significant works in American literature. The play won the Tony Award twice: once in 1949, and again in 1999 when it won for best revival. Miller also received a Tony for *The Crucible*, a drama about the Salem witch trials, and a lifetime achievement award in 1999. He was married to actress Marilyn Monroe in the 1950s and wrote the 1963 play *After the Fall* about their relationship. Miller died at Roxbury, CT, Feb 11, 2005.

MULLIGAN DAY. Oct 17. A day for giving yourself or another a second chance; a day for a "do-over." For info: C. Daniel Rhodes, 1900 Crossvine Rd, Hoover, AL 65244. Phone: (205) 908-6781. E-mail: rhodan@charter.net.

POPE JOHN PAUL I: BIRTH ANNIVERSARY. Oct 17, 1912. Albino Luciani, 263rd pope of the Roman Catholic Church. Born at Forno di Canale, Italy, he was elected pope Aug 26, 1978. Died at Rome, 34 days after his election, Sept 28, 1978. Shortest papacy since Pope Leo XI (Apr 1–27, 1605).

October *2006*	S	M	T	W	T	F	S
							1
	1	2	3	4	5	6	7
	8	9	10	11	12	13	14
	15	16	17	18	19	20	21
	22	23	24	25	26	27	28
	29	30	31				

SAN FRANCISCO 1989 EARTHQUAKE: ANNIVERSARY. Oct 17, 1989. The San Francisco Bay area was rocked by an earthquake registering 7.1 on the Richter scale at 5:04 PM, EDT, just as the nation's baseball fans settled in to watch the 1989 World Series. A large audience was tuned in to the pregame coverage when the quake hit and knocked the broadcast off the air. The quake caused damage estimated at $10 billion and killed 67 people, many of whom were caught in the collapse of the double-decked Interstate 80, at Oakland, CA.

UNITED NATIONS: INTERNATIONAL DAY FOR THE ERADICATION OF POVERTY. Oct 17. The General Assembly proclaimed this observance (Res 47/196) to promote public awareness of the need to eradicate poverty and destitution in all countries, particularly the developing nations. For info: United Nations, Dept of Public Info, New York, NY 10017. Web: www.un.org.

BIRTHDAYS TODAY

Ernie Els, 37, golfer, born Johannesburg, South Africa, Oct 17, 1969.

Eminem, 34, musician, rapper (*The Slim Shady LP, The Marshall Mathers LP*), born Marshall Bruce Mathers III at Kansas City, MO, Oct 17, 1972.

Beverly Garland, 80, actress ("My Three Sons," "Scarecrow and Mrs King"), born Santa Cruz, CA, Oct 17, 1926.

Mae Jemison, 50, scientist, astronaut, host ("Susan B. Anthony Slept Here"), born Decatur, AL, Oct 17, 1956.

Margot Kidder, 58, actress (Lois Lane in *Superman* movies), born Yellowknife, NT, Canada, Oct 17, 1948.

Robert Craig ("Evel") Knievel, 68, motorcycle stunt performer, born Butte, MT, Oct 17, 1938.

Norm Macdonald, 43, comedian, actor ("Saturday Night Live," "Norm"), born Quebec City, QC, Canada, Oct 17, 1963.

Michael McKean, 59, actor ("Laverne & Shirley," *This Is Spinal Tap*), born New York, NY, Oct 17, 1947.

Tom Poston, 79, actor ("Grace Under Fire," Emmy for "The Steve Allen Show," *Soldier in the Rain*), born Columbus, OH, Oct 17, 1927.

Richard Roeper, 47, newspaper columnist, film reviewer ("At the Movies" with Roger Ebert), born Chicago, IL, Oct 17, 1959.

George Wendt, 58, actor ("Cheers," "The Naked Truth"), born Chicago, IL, Oct 17, 1948.

OCTOBER 18 — WEDNESDAY
Day 291 — 74 Remaining

ALASKA DAY. Oct 18. Alaska. Anniversary of transfer of Alaska on Oct 18, 1867, from Russia to the US. The transfer became official on Sitka's Castle Hill. This is a holiday in Alaska; when it falls on a weekend it is observed on the following Monday.

ANDREE, SALOMON AUGUSTE: BIRTH ANNIVERSARY. Oct 18, 1854. Swedish explorer and balloonist born at Grenna, Sweden. His North Pole expedition of 1897 attracted world attention but ended tragically. With two companions, Andree left Spitzbergen, July 11, 1897, in a balloon, hoping to place the Swedish flag at the North Pole. The last message from Andree, borne by carrier pigeons, was dated noon, July 13, 1897. The frozen bodies of the explorers were found 33 years later by another polar expedition in the summer of 1930. Diaries, maps and exposed photographic negatives also were found. The photos were developed successfully, providing a pictorial record of the ill-fated expedition.

AZERBAIJAN: INDEPENDENCE DAY. Oct 18. National holiday. Commemorates declaration of independence from the Soviet Union in 1991.

BERGSON, HENRI: BIRTH ANNIVERSARY. Oct 18, 1859. French philosopher, Nobel Prize winner and author of *Creative Evolution*, born at Paris, France. Died there Jan 4, 1941.

BLACK POETRY DAY. Oct 18 (tentative). To recognize the contribution of black poets to American life and culture and to honor Jupiter Hammon, first black in America to publish his own verse. Jupiter Hammon of Huntington, Long Island, NY, was born Oct 17, 1711. The celebration includes a poetry reading by an important black poet. Est attendance: 200. For info: Black Poetry Day Committee, EOP Office, Algonquin Hall, SUNY-Plattsburgh, Plattsburgh, NY 12901-2681. Phone: (518) 564-2263. E-mail: marlene.fields@plattsburgh.edu.

BROOKS, JAMES DAVID: 100th BIRTH ANNIVERSARY. Oct 18, 1906. Born at St. Louis, MO, during the Depression Brooks worked as a muralist in the Federal Art Project of the Works Progress Administration. His best-known work of that period was "Flight," a mural on the rotunda of the Marine Air Terminal at La Guardia National Airport in New York. It was painted over during the 1950s but restored in 1980. Brooks served with the US Army from 1942 to 1945. When he returned to New York, his interest shifted to abstract expressionism. His paintings were exhibited in the historic "Ninth Street Exhibition" as a part of the Museum of Modern Art's exhibits "Twelve Americans" and "New American Painting," among others. He died Mar 8, 1992, at Brookhaven, NY.

CANADA: PERSONS DAY. Oct 18. A day to commemorate the anniversary of the 1929 ruling that declared women to be persons in Canada. Prior to this ruling English common law prevailed ("Women are persons in matters of pains and penalties, but are not persons in matters of rights and privileges"). The celebrated cause, popularly known as the "Persons Case," was brought by five women of Alberta, Canada; leader of the courageous "Famous Five" was Emily Murphy (1868–1933). This ruling by the Judicial Committee of England's Privy Council, Oct 18, 1929, overturned a 1928 decision of the Supreme Court of Canada. Fifty years after the Persons Case decision, in 1979, the Governor General's Awards in Commemoration of the Persons Case were established to recognize deserving persons who have made outstanding contributions to the quality of life of women in Canada.

CANALETTO, GIOVANNI ANTONIO: BIRTH ANNIVERSARY. Oct 18, 1697. Italian painter Giovanni Antonio Canaletto (born Canale), who is best known for his detailed landscapes of Venice and London, was born at Venice and died there at age 70, Apr 20, 1768. He was known for his accurate use of perspective, shadow and light. He went to England in 1746 and expanded his range of subjects to include English landscapes and country homes.

CHINA: BIRTHDAY OF CONFUCIUS. Oct 18. Observed on 27th day of eighth lunar month.

CIRCLEVILLE PUMPKIN SHOW. Oct 18–21. Circleville, OH. More than 100,000 pounds of pumpkins, squash and gourds. Est attendance: 300,000. For info: Hugh Dresbach, Secy, Pumpkin Show Inc, 159 E Franklin St, Circleville, OH 43113. Phone: (740) 474-7000. Fax: (740) 474-6611. Web: www.pumpkinshow.com.

DAY OF NATIONAL CONCERN ABOUT YOUNG PEOPLE AND GUN VIOLENCE. Oct 18. Students across America are asked to voluntarily sign a "Student Pledge Against Gun Violence," a solemn promise never to bring a gun to school, never to use a gun to settle a personal problem or dispute and to discourage their friends from using guns inappropriately. Formerly issued as a presidential proclamation. Since 1996, more than 10 million students have participated. For info: Student Pledge Against Gun Violence, 112 Nevada St, Northfield, MN 55057. Phone: (507) 645-5378. Web: www.pledge.org.

EAST TEXAS YAMBOREE. Oct 18–21. Gilmer, TX. Est attendance: 100,000. For info: Joan Small, Exec Dir, Gilmer Area Chamber of Commerce, Box 854, Gilmer, TX 75644. Phone: (903) 843-2413 or (903) 843-3981. Fax: (903) 843-3759. E-mail: upchamber@aol.com. Web: www.yamboree.com.

EDISON, THOMAS ALVA: 75th DEATH ANNIVERSARY. Oct 18, 1931. Great American inventor Thomas Alva Edison died at his home in Glenmount, NJ. On the evening of his funeral, many corporations dimmed their electric lights in respect.

FIRST NEWSPAPER COMIC STRIP: ANNIVERSARY. Oct 18, 1896. Although cartoons had appeared in newspapers for many years, the comic strip—a narrative told in cartoons over several panels—took its main form with the appearance of "The Yellow Kid Takes a Hand at Golf" in the *New York Journal's* weekly supplement *American Humorist*. The creator was Richard Fenton Outcault. In March 1897 the *Yellow Kid Magazine* gathered the strips and became the first published collection of a comic strip—setting the stage for the first comic books in the late 1920s. See also: "Outcault, Richard Fenton: Birth Anniversary" (Jan 14).

FRENCH POLYNESIA: HAWAIKI NUI VA'A RACE. Oct 18. Spectacular, three-day, open water traditional outrigger canoe race. More than 2,000 racers in more than 100 canoes battle for 78 miles, traveling from Huahine to Raiatea to Tahaa to Bora Bora. *Va'a* is the Tahitian word for canoe. Held since 1992, the race begins the third Wednesday of October every year. For info: Tahiti Tourisme, Immeuble Paofi, Batiment D - Boulevard Pomare, B P 65 Papeete, French Polynesia. Phone: (689) 50-57-00. Fax: (689) 43-66-19. E-mail: tahiti-tourisme@mail.pf or ftvaa@mail.pf. Web: www.hawaikinuivaa.pf.

LIEBLING, A.J.: BIRTH ANNIVERSARY. Oct 18, 1904. American journalist and author who said, "Freedom of the press belongs to those who own one." Abbott Joseph Liebling was born at New York, NY, and died there Dec 28, 1963.

MERCOURI, MELINA: BIRTH ANNIVERSARY. Oct 18, 1922. Greek actress and politician Melina Mercouri was born Maria Amalia Mercouri at Athens, Greece, Oct 18, 1922 or 1925 (both reported). Of her more than 70 films and plays she is most known for her role in *Never on Sunday* (1960). In 1977 she was elected to Greece's parliament and became the first woman in Greece's senior cabinet when appointed by Premier Andreas Papandreou to the position of minister of culture in 1981. She died Mar 6, 1994, at New York, NY.

MISSOURI DAY. Oct 18. Observed by teachers and pupils of schools with appropriate exercises throughout state of Missouri. Annually, the third Wednesday of October.

NATIONAL SUPPORT YOUR LOCAL CHAMBER OF COMMERCE DAY. Oct 18. A day to honor the local chamber of commerce. If your company is a COC member, make a donation, upgrade your membership, recruit a new member or buy a sponsorship of a chamber ad. Join a local chamber if your company is not yet a member. Send flowers or chocolates to your local chamber office. Annually, the third Wednesday in October. For info: Joy McCarthy-Sessing, Warsaw Kosciusko Chamber of Commerce, 313 S Buffalo St, Warsaw, IN 46580. Phone: (800) 776-6311. Fax: (574) 267-7762. E-mail: jmccarthy-sessing@wkchamber.com. Web: www.wkchamber.com.

NORTHERN INTERNATIONAL LIVESTOCK EXPOSITION. Oct 18–21. MetraPark, Billings, MT. PRCA rodeo, trade show exhibits, horse clinics, cattle, sheep, swine and horse sales. Est attendance: 25,000. For info: Joyce Laughery, Genl Mgr, NILE Office, PO Box 1981, Billings, MT 59103. Phone: (406) 256-2495. Fax: (406) 256-2494. E-mail: joyce@thenile.org. Web: www.thenile.org.

"ROSEANNE" TV PREMIERE: ANNIVERSARY. Oct 18, 1988. This comedy showed the blue-collar Conner family trying to make ends meet. Rosanne played wise-cracking Roseanne Conner, John Goodman played her husband Dan and Laurie Metcalf played her sister Jackie. The Conner children were played by Sara Gilbert (Darlene), Alicia Goranson and Sarah Chalke (Becky) and Michael Fishman (D.J.). The last episode aired Nov 14, 1997, but it remains popular in reruns.

SAINT LUKE: FEAST DAY. Oct 18. Patron saint of doctors and artists, himself a physician and painter, authorship of the third Gospel and Acts of the Apostles is attributed to him. Died about AD 68. Legend says that he painted portraits of Mary and Jesus.

SILVERSTEIN, SHEL: BIRTH ANNIVERSARY. Oct 18, 1932. Cartoonist and children's author, best remembered for his poetry that included *A Light in the Attic* and *The Giving Tree*. Silverstein won the Michigan Young Reader's Award for *Where the Sidewalk Ends*. Also a songwriter, he wrote "The Unicorn Song" and "A Boy Named Sue" for Johnny Cash. Born at Chicago, IL, he died at Key West, FL, May 9, 1999.

TRUDEAU, PIERRE ELLIOTT: BIRTH ANNIVERSARY. Oct 18, 1919. Prime Minister of Canada 1968–79, 1980–84. Born at Montreal, QC, Canada on Oct 18, 1919, he died there Sept 28, 2000.

WATER POLLUTION CONTROL ACT: ANNIVERSARY. Oct 18, 1972. Overriding President Nixon's veto, Congress passed a $25 billion Water Pollution Control Act.

WORLD MENOPAUSE DAY. Oct 18. The World Menopause Day challenge calls on every nation to make menopausal health a principal issue in their research and public health agendas in order to help women prevent unpleasant symptoms that can affect productivity and quality of life, as well as reduce rates of osteoporosis, heart disease, colon cancer and other aging- and hormone-related diseases. For info: Intl Menopause Society, PO Box 687, Wray, Lancaster, LA2 8WY United Kingdom. Phone: (44) (1524) 221-190. Web: www.imsociety.org.

BIRTHDAYS TODAY

Chuck Berry, 80, singer, songwriter ("Johnny B. Goode," "Roll Over Beethoven"), musician, born Charles Edward Anderson at St. Louis, MO, Oct 18, 1926.

Peter Boyle, 73, actor (*Medium Cool, The Dream Team*, "Everybody Loves Raymond"), born Philadelphia, PA, Oct 18, 1933.

Pam Dawber, 55, actress ("Mork & Mindy," "My Sister Sam"), born Farmington, MI, Oct 18, 1951.

October 2006

S	M	T	W	T	F	S
1	2	3	4	5	6	7
8	9	10	11	12	13	14
15	16	17	18	19	20	21
22	23	24	25	26	27	28
29	30	31				

Mike Ditka, 67, Hall of Fame football player, former coach, sportscaster, born Carnegie, PA, Oct 18, 1939.

Jesse Helms, 85, retired five-term US Senator (R, North Carolina), born Monroe, NC, Oct 18, 1921.

Wynton Marsalis, 45, jazz musician, born New Orleans, LA, Oct 18, 1961.

Terry McMillan, 55, author (*How Stella Got Her Groove Back, Waiting to Exhale*), born Port Huron, MI, Oct 18, 1951.

Erin Moran, 45, actress ("Happy Days," "Joanie Loves Chachi"), born Burbank, CA, Oct 18, 1961.

Joe Morton, 59, actor (*The Brother from Another Planet, Trouble in Mind, City of Hope*), born New York, NY, Oct 18, 1947.

Martina Navratilova, 50, former tennis player, born Martina Subertova at Prague, Czechoslovakia, Oct 18, 1956.

Ntozake Shange, 58, dramatist, poet, born Paulette L. Williams at Trenton, NJ, Oct 18, 1948.

Vincent Spano, 44, actor (*Baby, It's You; Rumblefish*), born New York, NY, Oct 18, 1962.

Jim Talent, 50, US Senator (R, Missouri), born Des Peres, MO, Oct 18, 1956.

Jean-Claude Van Damme, 46, actor (*Kickboxer*), born Brussels, Belgium, Oct 18, 1960.

Wendy Wasserstein, 56, playwright (*The Heidi Chronicles, The Sisters Rosenzweig*), born Brooklyn, NY, Oct 18, 1950.

OCTOBER 19 — THURSDAY
Day 292 — 73 Remaining

BIKETOBERFEST®. Oct 19–22. Daytona Beach, FL. Bikers return to Daytona Beach for that last chance to ride before winter. Parades, concerts and expos highlight the weekend. Est attendance: 100,000. For info: Daytona Beach Area CVB, 126 E Orange Ave, Daytona Beach, FL 32114. Phone: (866) 296-8970. Fax: (386) 255-5478. E-mail: info@daytonabeach.com. Web: www.biketoberfest.org.

BOO AT THE ZOO. Oct 19–22 (also Oct 26–29). Cleveland Metroparks Zoo, Cleveland, OH. Eight nights of spooky but not too scary Halloween fun at Cleveland Metroparks Zoo. Safe family fun takes place after-hours at the zoo, with seasonal entertainment for all ages to enjoy. Many of your favorite zoo animals will be on exhibit. Est attendance: 40,000. For info: Cleveland Metroparks Zoo, 3900 Wildlife Way, Cleveland, OH 44109. Phone: (216) 661-6500 or TDD (216) 661-1090. Fax: (216) 661-3312. E-mail: zooinfo@clevelandmetroparks.com. Web: clemetzoo.com.

BROWNE, THOMAS: BIRTH ANNIVERSARY. Oct 19, 1605 (OS). Physician, scholar and author, Thomas Browne was born at London, England. At age 55 he wrote: "The long habit of living indisposeth us for dying." His most famous work, *Religio Medici*, was published in 1642. Browne died at Norwich, England, Oct 19, 1682 (OS).

DOW-JONES BIGGEST DROP: ANNIVERSARY. Oct 19, 1987. The Dow-Jones Industrial Average plunged 508 points, or 22.6 percent, after frenzied selling, the largest percentage drop in history.

FALL CYCLE SCENE MOTORCYCLE RACES. Oct 19–22. Daytona International Speedway, Daytona Beach, FL. For info: Daytona International Speedway, PO Box 2801, Daytona Beach, FL 32120-2801. Phone: (800) PIT-SHOP. Web: www.daytonainternationalspeedway.com.

GET SMART ABOUT CREDIT DAY. Oct 19. Thousands of bankers visit high schools across America today to teach youth the importance of establishing and maintaining good credit. Annually, the third Thursday of October. For info: American Bankers Assn, 1120 Connecticut Ave NW, Washington, DC 20036. Phone: (800) BANKERS. E-mail: EduFoun@aba.com. Web: www.aba.com.

INTERNATIONAL CREDIT UNION DAY. Oct 19. A celebration of the credit union movement's significant points in history. On Jan 17, 1927, the Credit Union League of Massachusetts celebrated the first official holiday for credit union members and staff on the birthday of Benjamin Franklin, America's apostle of thrift. In 1948, the 100th anniversary of the credit union movement, Credit Union National Association (CUNA) set aside the third Thursday in October as the day of observance. More than 40,000 credit unions, representing 123 million people in 84 countries, celebrate the credit union difference on this day and during International Credit Union Week (Oct 15–21). For info: Joe Day, CUNA and Affiliates, PO Box 431, Madison, WI 53701. Phone: (608) 231-5794. Fax: (608) 231-4370.

JEFFERSON, MARTHA WAYLES SKELTON: BIRTH ANNIVERSARY. Oct 19, 1748. Wife of Thomas Jefferson, third president of the US. Born at Charles City County, VA, she died at Monticello, VA, Sept 6, 1782.

LUMIÈRE, AUGUSTE: BIRTH ANNIVERSARY. Oct 19, 1862. Born at Besançon, France, Auguste Lumière with brother Louis were film pioneers who created the first movie, "Workers Leaving the Lumière Factory" (1895). He died at Lyon, France, on Apr 10, 1954.

MAGNOLIA FEST. Oct 19–22. Live Oak, FL. Music festival. Previous artists have included Bela Fleck Acoustic Trio, David Grisman Quintet, Peter Rowan, Tony Rice, Vassar Clements, Laura Love Band and many more. Also available are workshops, vendors and activities for children. Est attendance: 8,000. For info: Spirit of the Suwannee Music Park, 3076 95th Dr, Live Oak, FL 32060. Phone: (386) 364-1683. Fax: (386) 364-2998. E-mail: spirit@musicliveshere.com. Web: www.musicliveshere.com.

MISSOURI DAY FESTIVAL. Oct 19–22. North Central Missouri Fairgrounds, Trenton, MO. Annual festival in conjunction with high school marching band competitions. Features a parade, car show, baby show, quilt show, craft booths, flea market, food vendors and entertainment of all kinds. Est attendance: 20,000. For info: Missouri Day Festival, Trenton Chamber of Commerce, PO Box 22, Trenton, MO 64683. Phone: (660) 359-4324. E-mail: trentonchamber@grundyec.net.

PECK, ANNIE S.: BIRTH ANNIVERSARY. Oct 19, 1850. World-renowned mountain climber Annie S. Peck won an international following in 1895 when she climbed the Matterhorn in the Swiss Alps. Peck climbed the Peruvian peak Huascaran (21,812 ft), giving her the record for the highest peak climbed in the Western Hemisphere by an American man or woman, and at age 61 she climbed Mt Coropuna in Peru (21,250 ft) and placed a "Votes for Women" banner at its pinnacle. Annie Peck died July 18, 1935, at New York City.

YORKTOWN DAY: "AMERICA'S REAL INDEPENDENCE DAY." Oct 19. Yorktown, VA. Representatives of the US, France and other nations involved in the American Revolution gather to celebrate the anniversary of the victory (Oct 19, 1781) that assured American independence. Parade and commemorative ceremonies. Annually, Oct 19. Est attendance: 2,000. For info: Public Affairs Officer, Colonial Natl Historical Park, Box 210, Yorktown, VA 23690. Phone: (757) 898-2410. Web: www.nps.gov/colo.

YORKTOWN DAY: 225th ANNIVERSARY. Oct 19, 1781. More than 7,000 English and Hessian troops, led by British General Lord Cornwallis, surrendered to General George Washington at Yorktown, VA, effectively ending the war between Britain and her American colonies. There were no more major battles, but the provisional treaty of peace was not signed until Nov 30, 1782, and the final Treaty of Paris, Sept 3, 1783.

BIRTHDAYS TODAY

Jack Anderson, 84, journalist, columnist, author (*Japan Conspiracy, Stormin' Norman*), born Long Beach, CA, Oct 19, 1922.

Michael Gambon, 66, actor ("The Singing Detective," *The Cook, The Thief, His Wife & Her Lover*), born Dublin, Ireland, Oct 19, 1940.

Evander Holyfield, 44, boxer, born Atlanta, GA, Oct 19, 1962.

Patricia Ireland, 61, feminist, social activist, former president of National Organization for Women, born Oak Park, IL, Oct 19, 1945.

John LeCarré, 75, author (*Tinker, Tailor, Soldier, Spy; Little Drummer Girl*), born David John Moore Cornwell at Poole, Dorset, England, Oct 19, 1931.

John Lithgow, 61, actor (*Don Quixote, Harry & the Hendersons*, "3rd Rock from the Sun"), born Rochester, NY, Oct 19, 1945.

Peter Max, 69, artist, designer, born Berlin, Germany, Oct 19, 1937.

Ty Pennington, 41, carpenter, television personality ("Trading Spaces," "Extreme Makeover: Home Edition"), born Atlanta, GA, Oct 19, 1965.

Simon Ward, 65, actor (*The Three Musketeers, The Four Musketeers*), born London, England, Oct 19, 1941.

OCTOBER 20 — FRIDAY
Day 293 — 72 Remaining

APPLE BUTTER STIRRIN'. Oct 20–22. Coshocton, OH. Kettles of apple butter simmer over open fires; demonstrations, craft show, contests in Roscoe Village, a restored canal town. Also, live musical entertainment. Annually, the third weekend of October. Est attendance: 35,000. For info: Roscoe Village Fdtn, 381 Hill St, Coshocton, OH 43812. Phone: (800) 877-1830 or (740) 622-9310. Fax: (740) 623-6555. E-mail: rvmarketing@roscoevillage.com. Web: www.roscoevillage.com.

BIRTH OF THE BAB: ANNIVERSARY. Oct 20, 1819. Baha'i observance of anniversary of the birth in Shiraz, Persia, of Siyyid Ali Muhammad, who later took the title "the Bab"; the Bab was the prophet-herald of the Baha'i Faith. One of the nine days of the year when Baha'is suspend work. For info: Baha'is of the US, Office of Communications, 1233 Central St, Evanston, IL 60201. Phone: (847) 733-3411. Fax: (847) 869-0247. E-mail: ooc@usbnc.org. Web: www.us.bahai.org.

CRAFTSMEN'S CLASSIC ARTS & CRAFTS FESTIVAL. Oct 20–22. Dulles Expo and Convention Center, Chantilly, VA. 11th annual. Features work from more than 400 talented artists and craftspeople. All juried exhibitors' work has been handmade by the exhibitors and must be their own original design and creation. See the creative process in action with several exhibitors demonstrating throughout the weekend. Something for every style, taste, and budget with items from the most contemporary to the most traditional. Est attendance: 30,000. For info: Gilmore Enterprises, Inc, 1240 Oakland Ave, Greensboro, NC 27403. Phone: (336) 274-5550. E-mail: gilmoreshows@triad.rr.com. Web: www.CraftShow.com or www.gilmoreshows.com.

DEWEY, JOHN: BIRTH ANNIVERSARY. Oct 20, 1859. American psychologist, philosopher and educational reformer born at Burlington, VT. His philosophical views of education have been termed pragmatism, instrumentalism and experimentalism. Died at New York, NY, June 1, 1952.

FALL FESTIVAL OF LEAVES. Oct 20–22. Bainbridge, Ross County, OH. Celebrating the beauty of the season and region. Folk arts, crafts, music, antique car show, log sawing contest, flea markets and parades. To obtain a map of self-guided scenic tours send SASE to sponsor. For info: Fall Festival of Leaves, Box 571, Bainbridge, Ross County, OH 45612. Phone: (740) 634-3173. Web: www.fallfestivalofleaves.com.

FANTASY FEST. Oct 20–29. Key West, FL. Ten-day adult costume festival with street parties, masked balls and nighttime grand parade. Est attendance: 75,000. For info: Fantasy Fest, Linda O'Brien, Box 230, Key West, FL 33041. Phone: (305) 296-1817. Fax: (305) 294-3335. Web: www.fantasyfest.net.

GUATEMALA: REVOLUTION DAY: ANNIVERSARY. Oct 20. Public holiday. Commemorates the overthrow of dictator Jorge Ubico Castañada in 1944.

HOOD RIVER VALLEY HARVEST FEST. Oct 20–22. Hood River, OR. The valley welcomes visitors for three days of continuous entertainment, crafts, fresh locally grown produce and fruits. Est attendance: 30,000. For info: Hood River County Chamber of Commerce, 405 Portway Ave, Hood River, OR 97031. Phone: (800) 366-3530. E-mail: hrccc@hoodriver.org. Web: www.hoodriver.org.

KENYA: KENYATTA DAY. Oct 20. Public holiday.

LUGOSI, BELA: BIRTH ANNIVERSARY. Oct 20, 1882. Born Bela Ferenc Denzso Blasko at Lugos, Hungary. Known best for his role as Count Dracula in *Dracula*. Lugosi died of a heart attack at Los Angeles, CA, Aug 16, 1956.

MacARTHUR RETURNS: US LANDINGS ON LEYTE, PHILIPPINES: ANNIVERSARY. Oct 20, 1944. In mid-September of 1944 American military leaders made the decision to begin the invasion of the Philippines on Leyte, a small island north of the Surigao Strait. With General Douglas MacArthur in overall command, US aircraft dropped hundreds of tons of bombs in the area of Dulag. Four divisions were landed on the east coast, and after a few hours General MacArthur set foot on Philippine soil for the first time since he was ordered to Australia Mar 11, 1942, thus fulfilling his promise, "I shall return."

MANN, JAMES ROBERT: 150th BIRTH ANNIVERSARY. Oct 20, 1856. American lawyer and legislator, born near Bloomington, IL, Republican member of Congress from Illinois from 1896 until his death, Nov 30, 1922, at Washington, DC. Mann was the author and sponsor of the "White Slave Traffic Act," also known as the "Mann Act," passed by Congress on June 25, 1910. The act prohibited, under heavy penalties, the interstate transportation of women for immoral purposes.

MANTLE, MICKEY: BIRTH ANNIVERSARY. Oct 20, 1931. Baseball Hall of Famer, born at Spavinaw, OK. Died Aug 13, 1995, at Dallas, TX.

MISS AMERICAN ROSE DAY. Oct 20. Miss American Rose is a pageant devoted to high achievement and community service for girls and women of all ages. On this day, treat the women in your life like beautiful American roses, and/or perform a community service project. For info: Lynanne White, Miss American Rose Pageants, 19689 7th Av, PMB 323, Poulsbo, WA 98370. E-mail: miss@americanrose.com. Web: www.americanrose.com.

MOSCOW SOCCER TRAGEDY: ANNIVERSARY. Oct 20, 1982. The world's worst soccer disaster occurred at Moscow when 340 sports fans were killed during a game between Soviet and Dutch players. Details of the event, blaming police for the tragedy in which spectators were crushed to death in an open staircase, were not published until nearly seven years later (July 1989) in *Sovietsky Sport*.

NATIONAL MAMMOGRAPHY DAY. Oct 20. On this day, or throughout the month of October, radiologists provide discounted or free screening mammograms. Annually, the third Friday of October. For info: Web: www.nbcam.org.

★   ★   ★

October 2006

S	M	T	W	T	F	S
1	2	3	4	5	6	7
8	9	10	11	12	13	14
15	16	17	18	19	20	21
22	23	24	25	26	27	28
29	30	31				

ORBACH, JERRY: BIRTH ANNIVERSARY. Oct 20, 1935. Actor born at the Bronx, NY, he starred in the original Broadway productions of *The Fantasticks, 42nd Street* and *Chicago*. He won a Best Actor Tony Award for *Promises, Promises* in 1969. Films included *Dirty Dancing* and the voice of Lumiere in Disney's *Beauty and the Beast*. His most popular role was that of wisecracking homicide detective Lennie Briscoe on television's "Law & Order," a role he played from 1998 until his death at New York, NY, on Dec 28, 2004.

PENNSYLVANIA ARTS & CRAFTS CHRISTMAS FESTIVAL. Oct 20–22 (also Oct 28–29). Washington County Fairgrounds, Washington, PA. More than 165 exhibits of handcrafted furniture, gift items, children's toys, dolls, dried floral arrangements and clothing. Holiday food and entertainment. Est attendance: 30,000. For info: Debbie & Dave Stoner, Family Festivals Assn, Inc, PO Box 166, Irwin, PA 15642. Phone: (724) 863-4577. Fax: (724) 863-4577. E-mail: familyfestivals@hotmail.com. Web: www.familyfestivals.com.

SATURDAY NIGHT MASSACRE: ANNIVERSARY. Oct 20, 1973. Anniversary of dramatic turning point in the Watergate affair. On Oct 20, 1973, the White House announced at 8:24 PM, EDT, that President Richard M. Nixon had discharged Archibald Cox (special Watergate prosecutor) and William B. Ruckelshaus (deputy attorney general) and that Attorney General Elliot L. Richardson had resigned. Immediate and widespread demands for impeachment of the president ensued and were not stilled until President Nixon resigned, Aug 9, 1974.

"THE SIX MILLION DOLLAR MAN" TV PREMIERE: ANNIVERSARY. Oct 20, 1973. This action-adventure series based on the novel "Cyborg" was a monthly feature on "The ABC Suspense Movie" before becoming a regular series in 1974. Lee Majors starred as astronaut Steve Austin, who, after an accident, was "rebuilt" with bionic legs, arms and an eye. He worked for the Office of Strategic Information (OSI) carrying out sensitive missions. Also in the cast were Richard Anderson, Alan Oppenheimer and Martin E. Brooks. "The Bionic Woman," starring Lindsay Wagner, was a spin-off from this show, and the two main characters were paired for several made-for-TV sequels.

SUGARLOAF ART FAIR. Oct 20–22. New Expo Center, Novi, MI. This show, now in its 12th year, features more than 300 nationally recognized craft designers and fine artists displaying and selling their original creations. Includes craft demonstrations, live music, specialty foods, hourly gift certificate drawings and more. Est attendance: 25,000. For info: Sugarloaf Mountain Works, 200 Orchard Ridge Dr, #215, Gaithersburg, MD 20878. Phone: (800) 210-9900. Fax: (310) 253-9620. Web: www.sugarloafcrafts.com.

WREN, CHRISTOPHER: BIRTH ANNIVERSARY. Oct 20, 1632 (OS). Sir Christopher Wren, English architect, astronomer and mathematician, was born at East Knoyle, Wiltshire, England. Died Feb 25, 1723 (OS), at London, England. His epitaph, written by his son, is inscribed over the interior of the north door at St. Paul's Cathedral, London: "Si monumentum requiris, circumspice." ("If you would see his monument, look about you.")

BIRTHDAYS TODAY

Art Buchwald, 81, columnist, author (*While Reagan Slept*), born Mount Vernon, NY, Oct 20, 1925.

William Christopher, 74, actor ("M*A*S*H," *With Six You Get Eggroll*), born Evanston, IL, Oct 20, 1932.

Keith Hernandez, 53, former baseball player, born San Francisco, CA, Oct 20, 1953.

Eddie Jones, 35, basketball player, born Pompano Beach, FL, Oct 20, 1971.

Melanie Mayron, 54, actress (Emmy for "thirtysomething"; *Car Wash, My Blue Heaven*), born Philadelphia, PA, Oct 20, 1952.

Viggo Mortensen, 48, actor (*The Lord of the Rings* trilogy), born New York, NY, Oct 20, 1958.

Tom Petty, 53, musician, singer ("Stop Draggin' My Heart Around"), born Gainesville, FL, Oct 20, 1953.

OCTOBER 21 — SATURDAY

Day 294 — 71 Remaining

ADAI CADDO INDIAN NATION POW WOW. Oct 21. Marthaville, LA. Held on the grounds of historic St. Anne Catholic Church. Celebrate the Adai Caddo Indian heritage through music, dance, arts and crafts, and food. Admission. Est attendance: 2,500. For info: Natchitoches Parish Tourist Commission. Phone: (800) 259-1714. Web: www.natchitoches.net.

ALABAMA RENAISSANCE FAIRE. Oct 21–22. Florence, AL. Celebration in grand 16th-century style with music, arts and crafts, costumes, theater and dance. Listen to minstrels, dulcimers and autoharps, watch as knights in shining armor transform Wilson Park into "Fountain-on-the-Green," the scene of a 16th-century faire. Est attendance: 30,000. For info: Debbie Wilson, Dir, Florence/Lauderdale Tourism, One Hightower Pl, Florence, AL 35630. Phone: (256) 740-4141 or (800) 888-FLO-TOUR. Fax: (256) 740-4142. E-mail: dwilson@flo-tour.org. Web: www.flo-tour .org.

AUTUMN HISTORIC FOLKLIFE FESTIVAL. Oct 21–22. Downtown Historic District, Hannibal, MO. The Hannibal Arts Council sponsors its 30th annual festival celebrating heritage and tradition of the 1800s. Artisans demonstrate the folk arts of the mid-1800s, vendors prepare food and drink over wood fires and street performers play traditional tunes. Also living history and children's areas with many activities. Est attendance: 25,000. For info: Hannibal Arts Council, PO Box 1202, Hannibal, MO 63401. Phone: (573) 221-6545. E-mail: arts@nemonet.com. Web: www .hannibalarts.com.

BATTLE OF TRAFALGAR: ANNIVERSARY. Oct 21, 1805. This famous naval action between the British Royal Navy and the combined French and Spanish fleets removed the threat of Napoleon's invasion of England. The British victory, off Trafalgar on the coast of Spain, guaranteed the fame of Viscount Horatio Nelson, who died in the battle.

BRIDGE DAY. Oct 21. New River Gorge Bridge, Fayetteville, WV. 27th annual. World's biggest extreme sports event and West Virginia's largest festival. Up to 500 BASE jumpers leap off North America's longest single span bridge at a height of 876 feet. Annually, the third Saturday in October. Est attendance: 250,000. For info: Fayette County Chamber of Commerce, 310 Oyler Av, Oak Hill, WV 25901. Phone: (800) 927-0263 or (304) 465-5617. Web: www.newrivercvb.com or www.officialbridgeday.com.

CARLETON, WILL: BIRTH ANNIVERSARY. Oct 21, 1845. Anniversary of the birth of poet Will Carleton, observed (by 1919 statute) in Michigan schools, where poems of Carleton must be read on this day. Best known of his poems: "Over the Hill to the Poorhouse." Carleton died in 1912.

COLERIDGE, SAMUEL TAYLOR: BIRTH ANNIVERSARY. Oct 21, 1772. English poet ("The Rime of the Ancient Mariner") and essayist born at Ottery St. Mary, Devonshire, England. Died at Highgate, England, July 25, 1834. In *Table Talk*, he wrote: "I wish our clever young poets would remember my homely definitions of prose and poetry; that is, prose = words in their best order; poetry = the *best* words in the best order."

COUNTRY AFFAIR. Oct 21–22. Ben Franklin School, Menomonee Falls, WI. Community League's 24th annual fair features timeless treasures and today's trends. More than 100 exhibitors; a Country Luncheon of homemade food and desserts; a Quilt Raffle; a "Pastries 'n' More" and silent auction. Admission charged. Est attendance: 5,000. For info: Jeanne Verbsky, Community League, Inc, Publicity—ACA, PO Box 101, Menomonee Falls, WI 53052. Phone: (414) 297-9446.

CRUZ, CELIA: BIRTH ANNIVERSARY. Oct 21, 1924. The Grammy Award–winning singer was dubbed the "Queen of Salsa" by her adoring fans. Born as Celia de la Caridad Cruz Alonso at Havana, Cuba (some sources cite her birth year as 1925 or 1929), Cruz had a career spanning six decades and recorded some 70 albums. Her energetic performances were punctuated by her call of "Azucar!" ("Sugar!") and flamboyant costumes. President Bill Clinton awarded her the National Medal of Arts in 1994. Cruz died at New York, NY, on July 16, 2003.

DEUTSCH COUNTRY DAYS. Oct 21–22. Luxenhaus Farm, Marthasville, MO. 25th annual. An authentic re-creation of early German life in Missouri as 85 costumed artisans present log hewing, kloppolei, bee keeping, broom making, wood turning, quilting and more. Period music, meals, a sorghum press driven by Missouri mules and a steam-powered sawmill add to the festivities. Est attendance: 9,000. For info: Lois Mueller, Deutsch Country Days, Historic Luxenhaus Farm, 18055 State Hwy O, Marthasville, MO 63357. Phone: (636) 433-5669. E-mail: info@ deutschcountrydays.org. Web: www.deutschcountrydays.org.

EIGHTEENTH-CENTURY AUTUMN MARKET FAIR. Oct 21–22. McLean, VA. Crafts, games, music and dancing. Period food and wares. Est attendance: 5,500. For info: Claude Moore Colonial Farm at Turkey Run, 6310 Georgetown Pike, McLean, VA 22101. Phone: (703) 442-7557. Fax: (703) 442-0714. Web: www.1771.org.

FILLMORE, CAROLINE CARMICHAEL McINTOSH: BIRTH ANNIVERSARY. Oct 21, 1813. Second wife of Millard Fillmore, 13th president of the US, born at Morristown, NJ. Died at New York, Aug 11, 1881.

GILLESPIE, JOHN BIRKS "DIZZY": BIRTH ANNIVERSARY. Oct 21, 1917. Dizzy Gillespie, trumpet player, composer, bandleader and one of the founding fathers of modern jazz, was born at Cheraw, SC. In the early 1940s Gillespie and alto saxophonist Charlie (Yardbird) Parker created bebop. In the late '40s he created a second music revolution by incorporating Afro-Cuban music into jazz. In 1953 someone fell on Gillespie's trumpet and bent it. Finding he could hear the sound better, he kept it that way; his puffed cheeks and bent trumpet became his trademarks. He won a Grammy in 1975 for *Oscar Peterson and Dizzy Gillespie* and again in 1991 for *Live at the Royal Festival Hall*. He died Jan 6, 1993, at Englewood, NJ.

GRAND MILITIA MUSTER. Oct 21. St. Mary's City, MD. The largest gathering of 17th-century military reenactment groups in the US. Tacticals, contests of skill and camp life demonstrations. Est attendance: 500. For info: Visitors Services, Historic St. Mary's City, PO Box 39, St. Mary's City, MD 20686. Phone:

(240) 895-4990 or (800) SMC-1634. Fax: (240) 895-4968. Web: www.stmaryscity.org.

HARTVILLE ANNUAL FALL FESTIVAL. Oct 21. Hartville, MO. Annual festival includes local entertainment, parade, games, rides for the kids and craft booths. A day of fun for all—young and old. Est attendance: 2,500. For info: Hartville Area Chamber of Commerce, PO Box 307, Hartville, MO 65667. Phone: (417) 741-7777. Fax: (417) 741-7741.

INCANDESCENT LAMP DEMONSTRATED: ANNIVERSARY. Oct 21, 1879. Thomas A. Edison demonstrated the first incandescent lamp that could be used economically for domestic purposes. This prototype, developed at his Menlo Park, NJ, laboratory, could burn for 13 ½ hours.

INDIA: DIWALI (DEEPAVALI). Oct 21. Diwali, the five-day festival of lights that begins today, is the prettiest of all Indian festivals. It celebrates the return of Lord Rama to Ayodhya after a 14-year exile. Thousands of flickering lights illuminate houses and transform urban landscapes while fireworks add color and noise. The goddess of wealth, Lakshmi, is worshipped in Hindu homes on Diwali. Houses are whitewashed and cleaned and elaborate designs drawn on thresholds with colored powder to welcome the fastidious goddess. Because there is no one universally accepted Hindu calendar, this holiday may be celebrated on a different date in some parts of India but it always falls in the months of October or November.

NOBEL, ALFRED BERNHARD: BIRTH ANNIVERSARY. Oct 21, 1833. Swedish chemist and engineer who invented dynamite was born at Stockholm, Sweden, and died at San Remo, Italy, Dec 10, 1896. His will established the Nobel Prize.

OLD IRONSIDES LAUNCHED: ANNIVERSARY. Oct 21, 1797. The USS *Constitution* was launched and christened by Captain James Sever on this date at Boston, making this frigate the oldest commissioned warship afloat in the world. Congress had commissioned *Constitution* and five other ships in 1794. The *Constitution* earned her nickname and place in America's heart through valiant service in the War of 1812: in a fight with Britain's HMS *Guerriere* on Aug 19, 1812, sailors reported a British shot repelled by the side of the ship and declared that her sides were made of iron. No enemy ever boarded her in her days of active service. She now rests at Boston Harbor. See also: "Old Ironsides Saved by Poem: Anniversary" (Sept 16).

QUINCY PRESERVES FALL ARCHITECTURAL TOUR. Oct 21. Quincy, IL. 10AM–4PM. Tour historic homes decked out in their finest. Homes range in size from Quincy's grandest mansions to quaint cottages. Inside each home, ticket holders are awed by the architectural splendors. Annually, the third Saturday in October. Est attendance: 1,000. For info: Fran Cook, Quincy Preserves, 310 S 16th St, Quincy, IL 62301. Phone: (217) 224-2587.

REPTILE AWARENESS DAY. Oct 21. Jenkinson's Aquarium, Point Pleasant Beach, NJ. Learn how alligators, snakes and turtles are related. Meet our live reptiles up close! Reptile stories for children will be presented thoughout the day. Alligators are fed at 1:30 PM. Free arts and crafts and face painting 1–4 PM. Est attendance: 700. For info: Jenkinson's Aquarium, 300 Ocean Ave, Point Pleasant Beach, NJ 08742. Phone: (732) 899-1212. Fax: (732) 899-1717. E-mail: jenkinsonsaquarium@comcast.net. Web: www.jenkinsons.com.

RICHMOND HIGHLAND GAMES AND CELTIC FESTIVAL. Oct 21–22. Richmond, VA. 12th annual celebration of Scottish and Celtic heritage features "Music. Food. Large Men Throwing Stuff." Athletic competition, two entertainment stages, parade of dogs of the British Empire, fiddle, harp and dance competitions, food, drink and more. Est attendance: 20,000. For info: Richmond Highland Games & Celtic Fest, Richmond Raceway Complex, PO Box 26805, Richmond, VA 23261. Phone: (804) 569-3200. Fax: (804) 569-3252.

ROMP IN THE SWAMP FUN WALK. Oct 21. Gordon Bubolz Nature Preserve, Appleton, WI. Choose to hike ¼-, 1½-, 2½- or 4-mile distances on the Preserve's beautiful trail system. Food and activities at rest stops along the way. Est attendance: 600. For info: Joann Engel, Naturalist, 4815 N Lynndale Dr, Appleton, WI 54913. Phone: (920) 731-6041. Fax: (920) 731-9593. E-mail: bubolz@dataex.com.

SAINT MARY'S COUNTY MD OYSTER FESTIVAL. Oct 21–22. Fairgrounds, Leonardtown, MD. Oysters served every style, national oyster shucking contest and national oyster cook-off. Est attendance: 18,000. For info: David L. Taylor, Admin, Oyster Fest Office, Box 766, California, MD 20619-0766. Phone: (301) 863-5015. Fax: (301) 863-7789. Web: www.usoysterfest .com.

SHAWN, TED: BIRTH ANNIVERSARY. Oct 21, 1891. Named Edwin Myers Shawn at birth, Ted Shawn was born at Kansas City, MO. Partially paralyzed by diphtheria, Shawn was introduced to ballet for therapeutic purposes and became a professional dancer by the age of 21. The Denishawn School of Dancing was established with the help of his wife, Ruth St. Denis, and became the epicenter of much innovation in 20th-century dance and choreography. Among his many achievements is Jacob's Pillow Dance Festival, which he inaugurated and directed for the remainder of his years, and such modern ballets as *Osage-Pawnee*, *Labor Symphony* and *John Brown*. He died Jan 9, 1972.

SOLTI, GEORG: BIRTH ANNIVERSARY. Oct 21, 1912. Conductor born at Budapest, Hungary. Sir Georg conducted orchestras at London (for which he was knighted), Paris and Chicago. He died at Antibes, France, Sept 5, 1997.

SWEETEST DAY. Oct 21. Around 1922, a candy company employee named Herbert Birch Kingston decided that it would be a wonderful thing to distribute candy to the sick, shut-ins, and orphans of Cleveland, OH. Thus, Sweetest Day was born. Do something nice for someone today, something that will make them say, "Oh, that's so sweet!" Annually, the third Saturday in October.

TAIWAN: OVERSEAS CHINESE DAY. Oct 21. Thousands of overseas Chinese come to Taiwan for this and other occasions that make October a particularly memorable month.

VALLE COUNTY FAIR. Oct 21. VC Conference Center, Valle Crucis, NC. An overgrown church bazaar set in the center of one of the most picturesque valleys in the North Carolina mountains. Features include 135 craft booths, mountain music, BBQ, Brunswick Stew, jams & jellies, freshly pressed apple cider and apple butter. Annually, the third Saturday in October. For info: Catherine Morton, Valle County Fair, Holy Cross Episcopal Church, PO Box 543, Valle Crucis, NC 28691. Phone: (828) 733-2013. Fax: (828) 733-2608. E-mail: cmorton@grandfather .com. Web: www.vallecountyfair.org.

October 2006	S	M	T	W	T	F	S
	1	2	3	4	5	6	7
	8	9	10	11	12	13	14
	15	16	17	18	19	20	21
	22	23	24	25	26	27	28
	29	30	31				

VIETNAM WAR PROTESTORS STORM PENTAGON: ANNIVERSARY. Oct 21, 1967. Some 250 protestors were arrested when thousands of the 50,000 participants in a rally against the Vietnam War at Washington, DC, crossed the Potomac River and stormed the Pentagon. No shots were fired, but many demonstrators were struck with nightsticks and rifle butts.

WISCONSIN DELLS AUTUMN HARVEST FEST. Oct 21–22. Wisconsin Dells, WI. Celebration of the autumn harvest season. A variety of events for the entire family including fall color tours, Dells on Tap, craft fair, live entertainment, straw dig, scarecrow stuffing, pumpkin decorating contests, Kid's Kookie Corner, petting zoo, hayrides, pony rides, caricatures, face painting and clowns for the kids. Est attendance: 25,000. For info: Wisconsin Dells Visitor & Convention Bureau, PO Box 390, Wisconsin Dells, WI 53965. Phone: (800) 223-3557. E-mail: info@wisdells.com. Web: www.wisdells.com.

WOOLLY WORM FESTIVAL. Oct 21–22. Banner Elk, NC. Annual woolly worm races, mountain entertainment, crafts and food. Third full weekend in October. Est attendance: 25,000. For info: Chamber of Commerce, PO Box 335, Banner Elk, NC 28604. Phone: (828) 898-5605. Fax: (828) 898-8287. E-mail: chamber@averycounty.com. Web: www.averycounty.com.

BIRTHDAYS TODAY

Sir Malcolm Arnold, 85, composer, born Northampton, England, Oct 21, 1921.
Elvin Bishop, 64, musician, born Glendale, CA, Oct 21, 1942.
Carrie Fisher, 50, actress (*Star Wars, Shampoo*), novelist (*Postcards from the Edge*), born Beverly Hills, CA, Oct 21, 1956.
Frances Fitzgerald, 66, journalist, author (*The Fire in the Lake*), born New York, NY, Oct 21, 1940.
Edward Charles ("Whitey") Ford, 78, Hall of Fame baseball player, born New York, NY, Oct 21, 1928.
Ursula K. LeGuin, 77, author (*The Wind's Twelve Quarters, A Wizard of Earthsea*), born Berkeley, CA, Oct 21, 1929.
Ken Watanabe, 47, actor (*The Last Samurai*), born Kansaku Watanabe at Koide, Niigata, Japan, Oct 21, 1959.

OCTOBER 22 — SUNDAY
Day 295 — 70 Remaining

BEADLE, GEORGE: BIRTH ANNIVERSARY. Oct 22, 1903. Born on a farm near Wahoo, NE, Beadle began his professional career as a professor of genetics at Harvard, eventually becoming president of the University of Chicago. Dr. Beadle won many international prizes, including the Nobel Prize for Medicine in 1958 for his work in genetic research, as well as the National Award of the American Cancer Society in 1959 and the Kimber Genetica Award of the National Academy of Science in 1960. Beadle demonstrated how the genes control the basic chemistry of the living cell. Because of his work, he has been termed "the man who did most to put modern genetics on its chemical basis." Beadle died June 9, 1989, at Pomona, CA.

CAPA, ROBERT: BIRTH ANNIVERSARY. Oct 22, 1913. Born Andrei Friedmann at Budapest, Hungary, Capa was one of the great photojournalists in the 20th century, best known for his gritty, close-up battle photography from the five wars he covered in his brief life—most notably the Spanish Civil War, WWII and the early Vietnam War. His handful of images from the midst of the D-Day invasion are legendary, as is his shot of a Spanish loyalist soldier who has just been killed in 1936. Cofounder of the elite Magnum Photos agency, Capa was killed by a land mine on May 25, 1954, at Thai Binh, Vietnam.

CUBAN MISSILE CRISIS: ANNIVERSARY. Oct 22, 1962. President John F. Kennedy, in a nationwide television address Oct 22, 1962, demanded the removal from Cuba of Soviet missiles, launched equipment and bombers and imposed a naval "quarantine" to prevent further weaponry from reaching Cuba. On Oct 28, the USSR announced it would remove the weapons in question. In return, the US removed missiles from Turkey that were aimed at the USSR.

HOLY SEE: NATIONAL HOLIDAY. Oct 22. The state of Vatican City and the Holy See observe Oct 22 as a national holiday.

HOWARD, CURLY: BIRTH ANNIVERSARY. October 22, 1903. Howard, born Jerome Lester Horwitz at Brooklyn, NY, was the brother of Stooges Moe and Shemp. The two older brothers groomed Curly for a life in show business and he got his big break in 1932 when brother Shemp left the Stooges. Curly took his place, and his manic style of slapstick comedy (with trademark "n'yuk-n'yuks") quickly made him popular. On May 6, 1946, while shooting his 97th Three Stooges film, Howard suffered a stroke and subsequently retired. He died Jan 18, 1952, at San Gabriel, CA.

INTERNATIONAL STUTTERING AWARENESS DAY. Oct 22. For info: National Stuttering Assn, 119 W 40th St, 14th Fl, New York, NY 10018. Phone: (800) 364-1677. Web: www.nsastutter.org or www.stutteringhomepage.com.

KIDS CARE WEEK. Oct 22–28. You're never too young to volunteer! This week is dedicated to recognizing the power of kids to reach out and help others in their local and global community. During the week young people focus their compassion on a specific social issue by participating in a national service project.. For info: Points of Light Foundation, 1400 I St NW, Ste 800, Washington, DC 20005. Phone: (203) 656-8052 or (202) 729-8156. Fax: (202) 729-8100. Web: www.kidscare.org.

THE LASALLE BANK CHICAGO MARATHON. Oct 22. Grant Park, Chicago, IL. The world's fastest 26.2-mile marathon attracts an international field of top athletes. Est attendance: 40,000. For info: The LaSalle Bank Chicago Marathon, PO Box 5709, Chicago, IL 60680-5709. Phone: (312) 904-9800. Fax: (312) 904-9820. Web: www.chicagomarathon.com.

LEARY, TIMOTHY: BIRTH ANNIVERSARY. Oct 22, 1920. Timothy Francis Leary was born at Springfield, MA. Prominent psychologist and professor at Harvard, Leary became an icon of the countercultural movement in the 1960s. He lost his professorship after giving a hallucinogenic drug, psilocybin, to students. Leary was arrested numerous times, and on one occasion, while being held at a California prison, he was forced to submit to a personality test that he had designed himself several years earlier. He continued to advocate the use of LSD in the pursuit of spiritual and political freedom and simply for the fun of it, until his death, of prostate cancer, May 31, 1996, at Beverly Hills, CA.

LISZT, FRANZ: BIRTH ANNIVERSARY. Oct 22, 1811. Hungarian pianist and composer (*Hungarian Rhapsodies*). Born at Raiding, Hungary. Died July 31, 1886, at Bayreuth, Germany.

METROPOLITAN OPERA HOUSE: OPENING ANNIVERSARY. Oct 22, 1883. Grand opening of the original New York Metropolitan Opera House was celebrated with a performance of Gounod's *Faust*.

MOON PHASE: NEW MOON. Oct 22. Moon enters New Moon phase at 1:14 AM, EDT.

MOTHER-IN-LAW DAY. Oct 22. Traditionally, the fourth Sunday in October is occasion to honor mothers-in-law for their contribution to the success of families and for their good humor in enduring bad jokes.

NATIONAL CHEMISTRY WEEK. Oct 22–28. To celebrate the contributions of chemistry to modern life and to help the public understand that chemistry affects every part of our lives. Activities include an array of outreach programs such as open houses, contests, workshops, exhibits and classroom visits. 2006 theme: "It's Your Home: It's All Built on Chemistry." 10 million participants nationwide. For info: Office of Community Activities, American Chemical Society, 1155 16th St NW, Washington, DC 20036. Phone: (800) 227-5558. Fax: (202) 776-8258. E-mail: ncw@acs.org. Web: www.chemistry.org/ncw.

NATIONAL COLOR DAY. Oct 22. Making people aware of how color affects them and how their names are color coded. Fashion show will show how this color philosophy works. Est attendance: 250. For info: D.G. Rolliet, PO Box 21, Crockett, CA 94525. E-mail: dgrolliet@aol.com. Web: www.namecolorology.com.

NATIONAL MASSAGE THERAPY AWARENESS WEEK®. Oct 22–28. Sponsored by the American Massage Therapy Association® (AMTA) to increase public awareness of the value of massage therapy in health and wellness. Results of an annual national survey of consumer usage of and attitudes about massage are released. Special attention is given to research confirming the efficacy of massage for relief of stress. AMTA provides information about how to locate and choose a qualified massage therapist and AMTA chapters emphasize the importance of legislation in states that do not yet regulate the profession. Annually, the last full week of October. For info: American Massage Therapy Assn (AMTA), 500 Davis Center, Ste 900, Evanston, IL 60201. Phone: (847) 864-0123. Fax: (847) 864-1178. E-mail: media@amtamassage.org. Web: www.amtamassage.org.

PASTORAL CARE WEEK. Oct 22–28. Honors clergy of all faiths who provide pastoral care in congregations and in such specialized settings as hospitals, correctional facilities, mental health systems, the military and counseling centers. For info: Pastoral Care Week. Web: www.pastoralcareweek.org.

RANDOLPH, PEYTON: DEATH ANNIVERSARY. Oct 22, 1775. First president of the Continental Congress, died at Philadelphia, PA. Born about 1721 (exact date unknown), at Williamsburg, VA.

SYNERGY WEEK INTERNATIONAL. Oct 22–28. Synergy enables organizations to consistently achieve exponential outcomes through the optimal integration of all of their resources. Conference themes will promote awareness of methods for achieving synergy within organizations. For info: DiFrances & Assoc, LLC, 208 E Oak Crest Dr, Ste 200, Wales, WI 53183-9700. Phone: (262) 968-9850. Fax: (262) 968-9854. E-mail: synergy@difrances.com. Web: www.difrances.com/synergyweek.

WORLD'S END DAY: ANNIVERSARY. Oct 22, 1844. Anniversary of the day set as the one on which the world would end by followers of William Miller, religious leader and creator of a movement known as Millerism. Stories about followers disposing of all earthly possessions and climbing to high places on that date are believed to be apocryphal. (Miller was born at Pittsfield, MA, Feb 15, 1782. Died at Low Hampton, NY, Dec 20, 1849.)

BIRTHDAYS TODAY

Haley Barbour, 59, Governor of Mississippi (R), born Yazoo County, MS, Oct 22, 1947.

Brian Anthony Boitano, 43, Olympic gold medal figure skater, born Mountain View, CA, Oct 22, 1963.

Jan De Bont, 63, director (*Speed, Twister*), born Amsterdam, the Netherlands, Oct 22, 1943.

	S	M	T	W	T	F	S
October		1	2	3	4	5	6	7
2006	8	9	10	11	12	13	14
	15	16	17	18	19	20	21
	22	23	24	25	26	27	28
	29	30	31				

Catherine Deneuve, 63, actress (*Repulsion, Indochine*), born Catherine Dorleac at Paris, France, Oct 22, 1943.

Annette Funicello, 64, singer, actress ("Mickey Mouse Club," Beach Party movies), born Utica, NY, Oct 22, 1942.

Jeff Goldblum, 54, actor (*The Big Chill, The Fly, Jurassic Park*), born Pittsburgh, PA, Oct 22, 1952.

Valeria Golino, 40, actress (*Big Top Pee-wee, Hot Shots!, Hot Shots! Part Deux*), born Naples, Italy, Oct 22, 1966.

Derek Jacobi, 68, actor ("I Claudius," *The Day of the Jackal*), born London, England, Oct 22, 1938.

Christopher Lloyd, 68, actor ("Taxi," *Back to the Future, Who Framed Roger Rabbit?*), born Stamford, CT, Oct 22, 1938.

Bill Owens, 56, Governor of Colorado (R), born Fort Worth, TX, Oct 22, 1950.

Robert Rauschenberg, 81, artist (*Monogram*), born Port Arthur, TX, Oct 22, 1925.

Tony Roberts, 67, actor (*Victor/Victoria, Annie Hall*), born New York, NY, Oct 22, 1939.

Ichiro Suzuki, 33, baseball player, born Kasugai, Japan, Oct 22, 1973.

OCTOBER 23 — MONDAY
Day 296 — 69 Remaining

APPERT, NICOLAS: BIRTH ANNIVERSARY. Oct 23, 1752. Also known as "Canning Day," this is the anniversary of the birth of French chef, chemist, confectioner, inventor and author Nicolas Appert, at Chalons-Sur-Marne. Appert, who also invented the bouillon tablet, is best remembered for devising a system of heating foods and sealing them in airtight containers. Known as the "father of canning," Appert won a prize of 12,000 francs from the French government in 1809, and the title "Benefactor of Humanity" in 1812, for his inventions, which revolutionized our previously seasonal diet. Appert died at Massy, France, June 3, 1841.

BATTLE OF LEYTE GULF: ANNIVERSARY. Oct 23–26, 1944. In response to the Allied invasion of the Philippines at Leyte, the Japanese initiated Sho-Go ("Operation Victory"), an attempt to counter the Allies' next invasion by heavy air attacks. Four carriers were sent south from Japanese waters to lure the US aircraft carriers away from Leyte Gulf. At the same time Japanese naval forces from Singapore were sent to Brunei Bay, split up into two groups and converged on Leyte Gulf from the north and southwest. The group in the north, under Vice Admiral Kurita Takeo, was to enter the Pacific through the San Bernardino Strait between the Philippine islands of Samar and Luzon. On Oct 23 Kurita lost two of his heavy cruisers to US submarine attack, and one of Japan's greatest battleships, the *Musashi*, was sunk in an aerial attack the next day, but Kurita made his way unopposed through the San Bernardino Strait on Oct 25. The southern group commanded by Vice Admiral Nishimura Teiji was detected on its way to the Surigao Strait and was practically annihilated by the US 7th Fleet as it entered the Leyte Gulf on Oct 25. Kurita, as a result, was forced to turn back from his planned rendezvous with Nishimura. Japan's Sho-Go, rather than inflicting damage on the Americans, resulted in serious losses for the Japanese.

BEIRUT TERRORIST ATTACK: ANNIVERSARY. Oct 23, 1983. A suicidal terrorist attack on American forces at Beirut, Lebanon, killed 240 US personnel when a truck loaded with TNT was driven into and exploded at US Headquarters there. A similar attack on French forces killed scores more.

CAMBODIA: PEACE TREATY DAY. Oct 23. National holiday. Commemorates peace treaty of 1991.

CARSON, JOHNNY: BIRTH ANNIVERSARY. Oct 23, 1925. Television talk show host, born in Corning, IA. He worked for various radio and television shows, including "Who Do You Trust?" He first appeared on "The Tonight Show" in 1958, and was named the permanent host in 1962 with the resignation of Jack Paar. He remained on the air for more than 30 years, and along with sidekick Ed McMahon and bandleader Doc Severinsen, basically invented the TV talk show format as we know it today. When he retired from television in 1992, he was regarded as a national institution. Carson died at Los Angeles, CA, Jan 23, 2005.

CELEBRATE JOB LOSS WEEK. Oct 23–27. To inspire and empower you to turn job loss upside down by guiding you with a step-by-step plan to celebrate and move on after getting fired or laid off. Annually, the fourth week in October. For info: Ann T. Ulrich, BOLD! Companies, 5505 W Danube Rd, Minneapolis, MN 55432. Phone: (763) 502-0878. Fax: (763) 502-9290. E-mail: annuinc@aol.com.

EDERLE, GERTRUDE: 100th BIRTH ANNIVERSARY. Oct 23, 1906. American swimming champion, born at New York City, Gertrude Caroline Ederle was the first woman to swim the English Channel (from Cape Gris-nez, France, to Dover, England). At age 19 she broke the previous world record by swimming the 35-mile distance in 14 hours, 31 minutes, on Aug 6, 1926. During her swimming career she broke many other records and was a gold medal winner at the 1924 summer Olympic Games. She died at Wyckoff, NJ, Nov 30, 2003.

GIVE WILDLIFE A BRAKE! WEEK. Oct 23–29. As daylight savings time ends, it's time to Give Wildlife a Brake! At this time of year, many of us are now driving to and from work in near darkness, just as large animals such as deer are entering mating season, and others are active in preparing for the long winter ahead. Scan the road as you drive, watching the edges for wildlife about to cross. Not only will this help you avoid killing harmless wildlife, but it will also make you aware of other hazards such as bicyclists, children at play and slow-moving vehicles. Be alert! For info: Humane Society of the US, 2100 L St NW, Washington, DC 20037. Phone: (202) 452-1100. E-mail: wildlife@hsus.org. Web: www.hsus.org/wildlife.

HUNGARY: ANNIVERSARY OF 1956 REVOLUTION. Oct 23. National holiday. Also called Uprising Day of Remembrance. Commemorates revolt against Soviet domination, which was crushed on Nov 4, 1956.

HUNGARY DECLARES INDEPENDENCE: ANNIVERSARY. Oct 23, 1989. Hungary declared itself an independent republic, 33 years after Russian troops crushed a popular revolt against Soviet rule. The announcement followed a weeklong purge by Parliament of the Stalinist elements from Hungary's 1949 constitution, which defined the country as a socialist people's republic. Acting head of state Matyas Szuros made the declaration in front of tens of thousands of Hungarians at Parliament Square, speaking from the same balcony from which Imre Nagy addressed rebels 33 years earlier. Nagy was hanged for treason after Soviet intervention. Free elections held in March 1990 removed the Communist party to the ranks of the opposition for the first time in four decades.

THE MAGIC OF DIFFERENCES™ WEEK. Oct 23–29. All wars, divorces and child abuse are rooted in feeling threatened by differences. Yet, each individual and each culture or nationality has been created to be different from all others. The Magic of Differences™ Week is devoted to affirming the wondrous discovery and adventure, learning and expansion that are only possible through experiencing the value of our differences. School and church programs, public workshops, premarital seminars and media events will celebrate the power of differences to transform society for the better. For info: Judith Sherven and James Sniechowski, PO Box 975, Windham, NY 12496. Phone: (518) 734-3657. E-mail: shervsniec@aol.com. Web: www.themagicof differences.com.

NATIONAL MOLE DAY. Oct 23. Celebrated on Oct 23 each year from 6:02 AM to 6:02 PM in observance of the "mole." The "mole" is a way of counting the Avogadro number, 6.02×10 to the 23rd power of anything (just like a "dozen" is a way of counting 12 of anything). Mole Day owes its existence to an early 19th-century Italian physics professor named Amedeo Avogadro. He discovered that the number of molecules in a mole is the same for all substances. Because of this, chemists are able to precisely measure quantities of chemicals in the laboratory. Mole Day is celebrated to help all persons, especially chemistry students, become enthused about chemistry, which is the central science. Individual teachers develop their own ways of observing Mole Day. For 2006 the Mole Day theme is "Mole Madness." For info: Tom Tweedle, Executive Director, National Mole Day Foundation, PO Box 602, Millersport, OH 43046. E-mail: mole@avolve.net. Web: moleday.org.

NATIONAL SAVE YOUR BACK WEEK. Oct 23–29. To educate the population on proper back care. For info: Daniel S. Romm, MD, c/o VAMC (117), Rehab Medicine Dept, 400 Veteran's Ave, Biloxi, MS 39531. Phone: (228) 523-4557. Fax: (228) 523-4517. E-mail: Daniel.Romm@med.va.gov.

NEW ZEALAND: LABOR DAY. Oct 23. National holiday on the fourth Monday in October.

SAINT JOHN OF CAPISTRANO: 550th DEATH ANNIVERSARY. Oct 23, 1456. Giovanni da Capistrano, Franciscan lawyer, educator and preacher, was born at Capistrano, Italy, in 1386, and died of plague on Oct 23, 1456. Feast Day is Mar 28.

SCORPIO, THE SCORPION. Oct 23–Nov 22. In the astronomical/astrological zodiac that divides the sun's apparent orbit into 12 segments, the period Oct 23–Nov 22 is identified, traditionally, as the sun sign of Scorpio, the Scorpion. The ruling planet is Pluto or Mars.

STEVENSON, ADLAI EWING: BIRTH ANNIVERSARY. Oct 23, 1835. Twenty-third vice president of the US (1893–97) born at Christian County, KY. Died at Chicago, IL, June 14, 1914. He was grandfather of Adlai E. Stevenson, the Democratic candidate for president in 1952 and 1956. See also: "Stevenson, Adlai Ewing: Birth Anniversary" (Feb 5).

SWALLOWS DEPART FROM SAN JUAN CAPISTRANO. Oct 23. Traditional date for swallows to depart for the winter from old mission of San Juan Capistrano, CA. See also: "Swallows Return to San Juan Capistrano" (Mar 19).

THAILAND: CHULALONGKORN DAY. Oct 23. Annual commemoration of the death of King Chulalongkorn the Great, who died Oct 23, 1910, after a 42-year reign. King Chulalongkorn abolished slavery at Thailand. Special ceremonies with floral tributes and incense at the foot of his equestrian statue in front of Bangkok's National Assembly Hall.

TV TALK-SHOW HOST DAY. Oct 23. To celebrate the many TV talk-show hosts whose personalities and intellects enable them to bring out the best in their guests. For info: Glenn Rothenberger, Blue Collar Show, 541 Clinton St, Ste 2B, Brooklyn, NY 11231. Phone: (718) 802-1689. E-mail: gnlroth@aol.com.

ZAMBIA: INDEPENDENCE DAY. Oct 23. Zambia. National holiday commemorates the independence of what was then Northern Rhodesia from Britain in 1964. Celebrations in all cities, but main parades of military, labor and youth organizations are at capital, Lusaka. The fourth Monday in October.

BIRTHDAYS TODAY

Jim Bunning, 75, US Senator (R, Kentucky), born Southgate, KY, Oct 23, 1931.

Michael Crichton, 64, writer (*Jurassic Park, Rising Sun*), born Chicago, IL, Oct 23, 1942.

Douglas Richard (Doug) Flutie, 44, football player, born Manchester, MD, Oct 23, 1962.

Ang Lee, 52, director (Oscar for *Crouching Tiger, Hidden Dragon; Sense and Sensibility, The Ice Storm*), born Taiwan, Oct 23, 1954.

Melquiades (Mel) R. Martinez, 60, US Senator (R, Florida), former US Secretary of Housing and Urban Development, born Sagua la Grande, Cuba, Oct 23, 1946.

Tiffeny Milbrett, 34, soccer player, born Portland, OR, Oct 23, 1972.

Pelé, 66, former soccer player, born Edson Arantes do Nascimento at Tres Coracoes, Brazil, Oct 23, 1940.

Juan ("Chi-Chi") Rodriguez, 72, golfer, born Rio Piedras, Puerto Rico, Oct 23, 1934.

Michael John (Mike) Tomczak, 44, former football player, born Calumet City, IL, Oct 23, 1962.

Keith Van Horn, 31, basketball player, born Fullerton, CA, Oct 23, 1975.

Alfred Matthew ("Weird Al") Yankovic, 47, singer, satirist, born Lynwood, CA, Oct 23, 1959.

Dwight Yoakam, 50, country singer, actor (*Sling Blade*), born Pikeville, KY, Oct 23, 1956.

OCTOBER 24 — TUESDAY

Day 297 — 68 Remaining

BATTLE OF VITTORIO VENETO: ANNIVERSARY. Oct 24–Nov 3, 1918. Italian forces, commanded by General Armando Diaz, began the last offensive against Austrian troops in upper Italy on this date. The battle began north of the Piave River, and on Oct 30 the Austrian headquarters at Vittorio Veneto was taken. By Nov 1 Austrian troops were breaking up into deserting mobs. A truce was signed at Villa Giusti on Nov 3, which provided for fighting to end the next day. This Allied victory led to the collapse of the Austro-Hungarian Empire.

EID-AL-FITR: CELEBRATING THE FAST. Oct 24. Islamic calendar date: Shawwal 1, 1427. This feast/festival celebrates the completion of the Ramadan fasting and usually lasts for several days. Everyone wears new clothes; children receive gifts from parents and relatives; children are allowed to stay up late and participate in games, folktales, plays, puppet shows, trips to amusement parks. This holiday is known as Seker Bayram in Turkey and Hari Raya Puasa in southeast Asia. Different methods for "anticipating" the visibility of the new moon crescent at Mecca are used by different Muslim groups. US date may vary. Began at sunset the preceding day.

LOCKWOOD, BELVA A. BENNETT: BIRTH ANNIVERSARY. Oct 24, 1830. Belva Lockwood, an educator, lawyer and advocate for women's rights, was born at Royalton, NY. In 1879 she was admitted to practice before the US Supreme Court—the first woman to do so. While practicing law at Washington, DC, she secured equal property rights for women. By adding amendments to statehood bills, Lockwood helped to provide voting rights for women in Oklahoma, New Mexico and Arizona. In 1884 she was the first woman formally nominated for the US presidency. Died May 19, 1917, at Washington, DC.

PRESCRIPTION ERRORS EDUCATION AND AWARENESS WEEK. Oct 24–31. According to a Harvard study, over 107,000 Americans take their prescription medications incorrectly, resulting in hospitalization or death. This week focuses on educating patients and consumers about serious drug interactions, adverse drug events, allergies, and the mixing of prescription drugs with herbals and over-the-counter medications. There is a $15 charge for kit materials. To find out more, please contact: PPSI, 101 Lucas Valley Rd, Ste 210, San Rafael, CA 94903. Phone: (415) 479-8628. Fax: (415) 479-8608. E-mail: ppsi@aol .com. Web: www.ppsinc.org.

SHERMAN, JAMES SCHOOLCRAFT: BIRTH ANNIVERSARY. Oct 24, 1855. Twenty-seventh vice president of the US (1909–12), born at Utica, NY. Died there Oct 30, 1912.

STOCK MARKET PANIC: ANNIVERSARY. Oct 24, 1929. After several weeks of a downward trend in stock prices, investors began panic selling on Black Thursday, Oct 24, 1929. More than 13 million shares were dumped. Desperate attempts to support the market brought a brief rally. See also: "Stock Market Crash: Anniversary" (Oct 29).

★**UNITED NATIONS DAY.** Oct 24. Presidential Proclamation. Always issued for Oct 24 since 1948. (By unanimous request of the UN General Assembly.)

UNITED NATIONS DAY: ANNIVERSARY OF FOUNDING. Oct 24, 1945. Official United Nations holiday commemorates founding of the United Nations and effective date of the United Nations Charter. In 1971 the General Assembly recommended this day be observed as a public holiday by UN Member States (Res 2782/xxvi). For info: United Nations, Dept of Public Info, Public Inquiries Unit, Rm GA-57, New York, NY 10017. Phone: (212) 963-4475. Fax: (212) 963-0071. E-mail: inquiries@ un.org. Web: www.un.org.

UNITED NATIONS: DISARMAMENT WEEK. Oct 24–30. In 1978 the General Assembly called on member states to highlight the danger of the arms race, propagate the need for its cessation and increase public understanding of the urgent task of disarmament. Observed annually, beginning on the anniversary of the founding of the UN. For info: United Nations, Dept of Public Info, New York, NY 10017. Web: www.un.org.

UNITED NATIONS: WORLD DEVELOPMENT INFORMATION DAY. Oct 24. Anniversary of 1970 adoption by United Nations General Assembly of the International Development Strategy for the Second United Nations Development Decade. Object is to "draw the attention of the world public opinion each year to development problems and the necessity of strengthening international cooperation to solve them." For info: United Nations, Dept of Public Info, New York, NY 10017. Web: www.un.org.

October 2006	S	M	T	W	T	F	S
	1	2	3	4	5	6	7
	8	9	10	11	12	13	14
	15	16	17	18	19	20	21
	22	23	24	25	26	27	28
	29	30	31				

BIRTHDAYS TODAY

F. Murray Abraham, 66, actor (Oscar for *Amadeus*), born El Paso, TX, Oct 24, 1940.

Kevin Kline, 59, actor (Oscar for *A Fish Called Wanda; Silverado*), born St. Louis, MO, Oct 24, 1947.

Kweisi Mfume, 58, NAACP president, born Baltimore, MD, Oct 24, 1948.

Monica, 26, singer, born Monica Arnold at Atlanta, GA, Oct 24, 1980.

David Nelson, 70, actor ("The Adventures of Ozzie and Harriet"), born New York, NY, Oct 24, 1936.

Mike Rounds, 52, Governor of South Dakota (R), born Huron, SD, Oct 24, 1954.

Yelberton Abraham (Y.A.) Tittle, Jr, 80, Hall of Fame football player, born Marshall, TX, Oct 24, 1926.

Bill Wyman, 70, musician (Rolling Stones), born William Perks at London, England, Oct 24, 1936.

OCTOBER 25 — WEDNESDAY
Day 298 — 67 Remaining

CARTOONISTS AGAINST CRIME DAY™. Oct 25. A day in honor of all those cartoonists, graphic designers and illustrators who join together to promote the prevention of crime through the art and medium of cartooning. Motto: "Cartoonists Against Crime: We Draw Cartoons—Not Guns!" CAC's slogan is to "Toon Out Crime" by employing comic art as an educational tool for implanting seeds of safety prevention into the minds of viewers/readers. To alleviate the escalating costs of Eventological® Literature, a charge of $10 must be assessed for each request. Checks are to be made payable to: Adrienne Sioux Koopersmith, Cartoonists Against Crime, 1437 W Rosemont, #1W, Chicago, IL 60660-1319. E-mail: askoopersmith@hotmail.com.

CHAUCER, GEOFFREY: DEATH ANNIVERSARY. Oct 25, 1400. English poet and the best-known English writer of the Middle Ages, was born at London, England, probably about 1340. His greatest work, *Canterbury Tales*, consists of some 17,000 poetic lines. Unfinished at his death, it tells the stories of 23 pilgrims. Among his lesser-known prose writings was a treatise on the Astrolabe titled *Brede and Milke for Children* (1387), written for "little Lewis, my son." Chaucer died at London and is buried at Westminster Abbey.

FIRST FEMALE FBI AGENTS: ANNIVERSARY. Oct 25, 1972. The first women to become FBI agents completed training at Quantico, VA. The new agents, Susan Lynn Roley and Joanne E. Pierce, graduated from the 14-week course with a group of 45 men.

GRENADA INVADED BY US: ANNIVERSARY. Oct 25, 1983. Some 2,000 US Marines and Army Rangers invaded the Caribbean island of Grenada, taking control after a political coup the previous week had made the island a "Soviet-Cuban colony," according to President Reagan. Commemorated as Thanksgiving Day in Grenada, a public holiday.

INTERNATIONAL MAGIC WEEK. Oct 25–31. A week to celebrate the world of magic and the magicians who create it. Annually, Oct 25–31—culminating on Oct 31, the anniversary of Harry Houdini's death and Magic Day. For info: Sir Nemo Turner, The Protocol Institute, CP 157, Place du Parc, Montreal, QC, Canada, H2X 4A4. Phone: (514) 849-0888. E-mail: magician@total.net.

KAZAKHSTAN: INDEPENDENCE DAY. Oct 25. National Day. Commemorates independence from the Soviet Union in 1991.

LOUISIANA YAMBILEE. Oct 25–29. Opelousas, LA. Sweet potato, corn, rice and soybean shows, cooked foods contest, yam auction, "yum-yum contest," carnival, grand parade and the crowning of King Will Yam and Queen Marigold and the 2006 Louisiana Yambilee Queen. Est attendance: 50,000. For info: Sheryl Badeaux, Louisiana Yambilee, Inc, 1939 W Landry St, #103, Opelousas, LA 70570-2010. Phone: (800) 210-5298. Fax: (337) 948-4331. E-mail: yambilee1@aol.com.

MACAULAY, THOMAS BABINGTON: BIRTH ANNIVERSARY. Oct 25, 1800. English essayist and historian, born at Rothley Temple, Leicestershire, England. Died at Campden Hill, London, England, Dec 28, 1859. "Nothing," he wrote, "is so useless as a general maxim."

"NEWHART" TV PREMIERE: ANNIVERSARY. Oct 25, 1982. Bob Newhart starred in this sitcom as Dick Loudon, an author of "how-to" books who moved with his wife, Joanna (Mary Frann), to Vermont to take over the Stratford Inn. Regulars included Tom Poston as George Utley, caretaker of the inn; Julia Duffy as Stephanie Vanderkellen, the reluctant maid; Peter Scolari as Michael Harris, producer of Dick's talk show and Stephanie's squeeze; and, as the owners of the Minute Man Café, William Sanderson as Larry and Tony Papenfuss and John Volstad as his silent brothers, both named Darryl. The last telecast was Sept 8, 1990.

PEACE, FRIENDSHIP AND GOOD WILL WEEK. Oct 25–31. To encourage and foster international understanding, good human relations, friendship, good will and peace throughout the world. For complete info, send $5 to cover expense of printing, handling and postage. Annually, the last seven days in October. For info: Dr. Stanley Drake, Pres Emeritus, Intl Soc of Friendship & Good Will, 8592 Roswell Rd, Ste 251, Atlanta, GA 30350-1867. Phone: (678) 795-1362. E-mail: sjdrake@bellsouth.net. Web: www.friendshipandgoodwill.org.

PEARL, MINNIE: BIRTH ANNIVERSARY. Oct 25, 1912. Comedian, Grand Ole Opry star born at Centerville, TN. Pearl died at Nashville, TN, Mar 4, 1996.

PICASSO, PABLO RUIZ: 125th BIRTH ANNIVERSARY. Oct 25, 1881. Called by many the greatest artist of the 20th century, Pablo Picasso excelled as a painter, sculptor and engraver. He is said to have commented once: "I am only a public entertainer who has understood his time." Born at Málaga, Spain, he died Apr 8, 1973, at Mougins, France.

SAINT CRISPIN'S DAY. Oct 25. Martyr in the reign of Diocletian. Saint Crispin's Day is famous as the day in 1415 when King Henry V defeated the superior forces of France at the Battle of Agincourt. A passage in Shakespeare's *Henry V* notes this.

SOUREST DAY. Oct 25. To emphasize the balance of things in nature. A day for sour (Sauer) people. For info: Richard Ankli, The Fifth Wheel Tavern, 639 Fifth St, Ann Arbor, MI 48103.

SOUTHERN CALIFORNIA FIRESTORMS: ANNIVERSARY. Oct 25, 1993. The Southern California fire season began viciously when fires swept from the celebrity-studded beachfront homes of Malibu to the Mexican border. Blown out of the desert by the fierce Santa Anna winds, the fires destroyed suburban enclaves south of L.A. at Laguna Beach and northeast of L.A. at Altadena. As winds died down, firefighters appeared to gain control as the flames reached the Santa Monica Mountains, but the winds roared again, spreading the fire into Malibu—often jumping the Pacific Coast Highway to destroy the beachfront homes of the wealthy celebrities who lived there. Damage from the fires was estimated at more than $1 billion.

TACOMA HOLIDAY FOOD AND GIFT FESTIVAL. Oct 25–29. Tacoma Dome, Tacoma, WA. Gifts, crafts, gourmet foods and more amidst this glittering extravaganza, which transforms the Tacoma Dome into a fairyland of twinkling lights, trees and Christmas cheer. Est attendance: 50,000. For info: Showcase Events, Inc, PO Box 2815, Kirkland, WA 98083. Phone: (425) 889-9494 or (800) 521-7469. Fax: (425) 889-8165. E-mail: tacoma@showcaseevents.org. Web: www.showcaseevents.org.

TAIWAN EXPELLED FROM UN: 35th ANNIVERSARY. Oct 25, 1971. The United Nations General Assembly voted to admit mainland China and expel Taiwan. This was after many years of debate about which government was the "official" government of China. In 1979 the US accorded diplomatic recognition to mainland China.

TAIWAN: RETROCESSION DAY. Oct 25. Commemorates restoration of Taiwan to Chinese rule in 1945, after half a century of Japanese occupation.

BIRTHDAYS TODAY

Anthony Franciosa, 78, actor ("The Name of the Game," "Wheels"), born Anthony Papaleo at New York, NY, Oct 25, 1928.

Brian Kerwin, 57, actor ("Lobo," "The Blue and the Gray"), born Chicago, IL, Oct 25, 1949.

Robert Montgomery (Bobby) Knight, 66, college basketball coach and former player, born Orrville, OH, Oct 25, 1940.

Pedro Martinez, 35, baseball player, born Manoguyabo, Dominican Republic, Oct 25, 1971.

Midori, 35, violinist, born Osaka, Japan, Oct 25, 1971.

Helen Reddy, 64, singer, songwriter ("I Am Woman"), born Melbourne, Australia, Oct 25, 1942.

Marion Ross, 70, actress ("Happy Days," *The Evening Star*), born Albert Lea, MN, Oct 25, 1936.

Anne Tyler, 65, author (*The Accidental Tourist, Breathing Lessons*), born Minneapolis, MN, Oct 25, 1941.

OCTOBER 26 — THURSDAY
Day 299 — 66 Remaining

AUSTRIA: NATIONAL DAY. Oct 26. National holiday. Commemorates the withdrawal of Soviet troops in 1955.

ERIE CANAL: ANNIVERSARY. Oct 26, 1825. The Erie Canal, first US major man-made waterway, was opened, providing a water route from Lake Erie to the Hudson River. Construction started July 4, 1817, and the canal cost $7,602,000. Cannons fired and celebrations were held all along the route for the opening.

FORT LAUDERDALE INTERNATIONAL BOAT SHOW. Oct 26–30. Fort Lauderdale, FL. Everything from small boats to mega-yachts to boating equipment. Visitors attend from all over the world. For info: Greater Ft Lauderdale Conv/Visitors Bureau, 100 E Broward Blvd, Ste 200, Ft Lauderdale, FL 33301. Phone: (954) 765-4466 or (954) 764-7642. Web: www.sunny.org.

GUNFIGHT AT THE OK CORRAL: 125th ANNIVERSARY. Oct 26, 1881. At 2:30 PM, the Earp brothers and gambler/dentist Doc Holliday confronted the Clanton and McLaury brothers at a vacant lot behind the OK Corral in Tombstone, AZ. After 30 seconds of gunfire, three deaths and decades of romanticizing, the incident would become the most notorious of the Old West. Marshal Virgil Earp and Deputy Marshals Wyatt and Morgan Earp attempted to disarm the Clanton faction when gunfire erupted, although some witnesses claimed that the Clantons and McLaurys threw up their hands when ordered to. Billy Clanton and Frank and Thomas McLaury died. Virgil and Morgan Earp were wounded. After a 30-day murder trial, the presiding judge dismissed the charges stating that the Earps and Holliday had acted in self-defense.

HANSOM, JOSEPH: BIRTH ANNIVERSARY. Oct 26, 1803. English architect and inventor Joseph Aloysius Hansom registered his "Patent Safety Cab" in 1834. The two-wheeled, one-horse, enclosed cab, with driver seated above and behind the passengers, quickly became a familiar and favorite vehicle for public transportation. Hansom was born at York, England, and died at London, June 29, 1882.

October 2006	S	M	T	W	T	F	S
	1	2	3	4	5	6	7
	8	9	10	11	12	13	14
	15	16	17	18	19	20	21
	22	23	24	25	26	27	28
	29	30	31				

JACKSON, MAHALIA: BIRTH ANNIVERSARY. Oct 26, 1911. Born at New Orleans, LA, Jackson was the most famous gospel singer of her time. After moving to Chicago in 1928, Jackson sang with the Johnson Gospel Singers. Thomas A. Dorsey, the father of gospel music, was her advisor and accompanist from 1937 to 1946. By the 1950s, Jackson could be heard in concert halls around the world. She sang at the inauguration of President John F. Kennedy and at the 1963 March on Washington rally. Dr. Martin Luther King, Jr, described her voice as "one heard once in a millennium." She died at Chicago, IL, on Jan 27, 1972, and was buried in New Orleans, where her funeral procession was thronged with mourners.

MULE DAY. Oct 26. Anniversary of the first importation of Spanish jacks to the US, a gift from King Charles III of Spain. Mules are said to have been bred first in this country by George Washington from a pair delivered at Boston, Oct 26, 1785.

ROCKEFELLER, ABBY GREENE ALDRICH: BIRTH ANNIVERSARY. Oct 26, 1874. A philanthropist and art patron, Abby Rockefeller was one of the three founders of the New York Museum of Modern Art in 1929. Born at Providence, RI, she died Apr 5, 1948, at New York City.

"ST. ELSEWHERE" TV PREMIERE: ANNIVERSARY. Oct 26, 1982. A popular one-hour medical drama set in St. Eligius Hospital at Boston. Among its large and changing cast were Ed Flanders; William Daniels; Ed Begley, Jr; David Morse; Howie Mandel; Christina Pickles; Denzel Washington; Norman Lloyd; David Birney; G.W. Bailey; Kavi Raz; Stephen Furst; Mark Harmon and Alfre Woodard. The last episode of the series aired on Aug 10, 1988.

SCARLATTI, DOMENICO: BIRTH ANNIVERSARY. Oct 26, 1685. Italian keyboard composer, born at Naples, Italy. Died July 23, 1757, at Madrid, Spain.

SPACE MILESTONE: *SOYUZ 3* (USSR). Oct 26, 1968. After the crash of *Soyuz 1* and the death of its cosmonaut, *Soyuz 3* was launched this date with Colonel Georgi Beregovoy. It orbited Earth 64 times, rendezvousing but not docking with unmanned *Soyuz 2*, which had been launched the day before. Both vehicles returned to Earth under ground control. *Soyuz* means "union."

STATE FAIR OF LOUISIANA. Oct 26–Nov 12. Fairgrounds, Shreveport, LA. Educational, agricultural, commercial exhibits, entertainment. Est attendance: 350,000. For info: Sam Giordano, Pres/Genl Mgr, Louisiana State Fairgrounds, 3701 Hudson St, Shreveport, LA 71109. Phone: (318) 635-1361. Fax: (318) 631-4909.

BIRTHDAYS TODAY

Tom Cavanagh, 38, actor ("Ed"), born Ottawa, ON, Canada, Oct 26, 1968.

Hillary Rodham Clinton, 59, US Senator (D, New York), former First Lady, wife of Bill Clinton, 42nd president of the US, born Park Ridge, IL, Oct 26, 1947.

Sasha Cohen, 22, figure skater, born Westwood, CA, Oct 26, 1984.

Nick Collison, 26, basketball player, born Orange City, IA, Oct 26, 1980.

Pat Conroy, 61, writer (*The Prince of Tides, The Lords of Discipline*), born Atlanta, GA, Oct 26, 1945.

Cary Elwes, 44, actor (*The Princess Bride, Glory, Bram Stoker's Dracula*), born London, England, Oct 26, 1962.

Bob Hoskins, 64, actor (*Mona Lisa, Who Framed Roger Rabbit?*), born Bury St. Edmonds, Suffolk, England, Oct 26, 1942.

Dylan McDermott, 44, actor ("The Practice"), born Waterbury, CT, Oct 26, 1962.

Natalie Merchant, 43, singer, born Jamestown, NY, Oct 26, 1963.

Jeff Probst, 44, TV host ("Survivor," "Rock and Roll Jeopardy"), born Wichita, KS, Oct 26, 1962.

Ivan Reitman, 60, filmmaker (*Ghostbusters* movies), born Komarno, Czechoslovakia, Oct 26, 1946.

Pat Sajak, 60, TV personality ("Wheel of Fortune"), born Chicago, IL, Oct 26, 1946.

Jaclyn Smith, 59, actress ("Charlie's Angels"), former Breck Girl, born Houston, TX, Oct 26, 1947.

OCTOBER 27 — FRIDAY
Day 300 — 65 Remaining

COOK, JAMES: BIRTH ANNIVERSARY. Oct 27, 1728 (OS). English sea captain of the ship *Endeavour* and explorer who brought Australia and New Zealand into the British Empire. Born at Marton-in-Cleveland, Yorkshire, England, he was killed Feb 14, 1779, at the Hawaiian Islands, which he discovered.

CRANKY COWORKERS DAY. Oct 27. Because all of us have bad days (some more than others), here's a day when crankiness at work is actually encouraged. [©2003 by WH.] For info: Thomas & Ruth Roy, Wellcat Holidays, 2418 Long Ln, Lebanon, PA 17046. Phone: (717) 279-0184. E-mail: info@wellcat.com. Web: www.wellcat.com.

EDGAR ALLAN POE EVERMORE. Oct 27–Nov 12. Mount Hope Estate, Manheim, PA. Friday, Saturday and Sunday evenings. Nights of suspense featuring the spine-chilling short stories of Edgar Allan Poe. Professionals from the Pennsylvania Renaissance Faire Actors Conservatory perform, wine served. Est attendance: 10,000. For info: Thomas Roy, Mount Hope Estate and Winery, PO Box 685, Cornwall, PA 17016. Phone: (717) 665-7021. Fax: (717) 664-3466. E-mail: Tom@parenfaire.com. Web: www.parenfaire.com/.

FEDERALIST PAPERS: ANNIVERSARY. Oct 27, 1787. The first of the 85 "Federalist" papers appeared in print in a New York City newspaper, Oct 27, 1787. These essays, written by Alexander Hamilton, James Madison and John Jay, argued in favor of adoption of the new Constitution and the new form of federal government. The last of the essays was completed Apr 4, 1788.

FRANKENSTEIN FRIDAY. Oct 27. This holiday has been designed to honor and celebrate the "mother" and "father" of Frankenstein, Mary Shelley and Boris Karloff. Every year a different venue will be used to celebrate this occasion. In years past it has included a torch lighting ceremony, film festival and awarding of THE FRANKY. A special celebration is planned for 2006 to commemorate the 75th anniversary of the original film. Annually, the last Friday in October. For info: Ron MacCloskey. E-mail: ronmac55@optonline.net.

FRIENDLY FOREST HALLOWEEN HIKE. Oct 27–28. Savannah, GA. A safe, not-so-scary, fun-filled alternative suited for young children. Adults will walk with their children while they trick-or-treat along a short portion of our trail to visit some lovable, huggable critters. Children are encouraged to wear their costumes and comfortable walking shoes. Treat bags will be provided at the admissions counter. Children must be accompanied by an adult. Food concessions and other attractions and activities will be available. There is a fee for this event. Est attendance: 1,200. For info: Oatland Island Education Center. Phone: (912) 898-3980. Web: www.oatlandisland.org.

GHOST TALES OF THE WHITE HOUSE. Oct 27–29. President Benjamin Harrison Home, Indianapolis, IN. Tour the home of the 23rd president and learn about the ghosts of the White House. Est attendance: 600. For info: President Benjamin Harrison Home, 1230 N Delaware St, Indianapolis, IN 46202. Phone:

(317) 631-1888. Fax: (317) 632-5488. E-mail: harrison@president benjaminharrison.org. Web: www.pbhh.org.

GHOSTLY GATHERING. Oct 27–28. Sandy Springs Historic Site, Atlanta, GA. Spooky storytellers, enchanting magicians, and costume contests set the stage for Ghostly Gathering. Young children enjoy the Bubbling Brook and Ghostly Walk, and older children get thrills from the Fortune Teller and spine-chilling Witch. For info: Megan Webb, Heritage Sandy Springs, 135 Hilderbrand Dr, Atlanta, GA 30328. Phone: (404) 851-1328. Fax: (404) 851-9807. E-mail: events@heritagesandysprings.org. Web: www.heritagesandysprings.org.

HUMORESILIENCE: TICKLING STRESS BEFORE IT TICKLES YOU. Oct 27–29. Lake George, NY. This 30th annual workshop, which draws participants from around the world, is designed to help you move from "grim and bear it" to "grin and share it." Led by Margie Ingram and Joel Goodman, this program is fun but not for fun. Attendees laugh while learning practical ideas and skills they can use both personally as well as on the job. For info: The HUMOR Project, Inc, 480 Broadway, Ste 210-C, Saratoga Springs, NY 12866-2288. Phone: (518) 587-8770. E-mail: Chase@HumorProject.com. Web: www.Humor Project.com.

HURRICANE MITCH: ANNIVERSARY. Oct 27, 1998. More than 7,000 people were killed at Honduras by flooding caused by Hurricane Mitch. Thousands more were killed in other Central American countries, especially Nicaragua.

LICHTENSTEIN, ROY: BIRTH ANNIVERSARY. Oct 27, 1923. Pop artist who used comic strips and other elements of pop culture in his paintings. Born at New York City, he died there Sept 29, 1997.

NAVY DAY. Oct 27. Established in 1922 to honor the "past and present services" of the US Navy to the nation. Also honored Theodore Roosevelt, whose birth date is Oct 27 (and who had been assistant secretary of the Navy early in his public career). Not a national holiday, it was last observed in 1949.

NEW YORK CITY SUBWAY: ANNIVERSARY. Oct 27, 1904. Running from City Hall to West 145th Street, the New York City subway began operation. It was privately operated by the Interborough Rapid Transit Company and later became part of the system operated by the New York City Transit Authority.

PAGANINI, NICOLO: BIRTH ANNIVERSARY. Oct 27, 1782. Hailed as the greatest violin virtuoso of all time, Paganini was born at Genoa, Italy. Unusually long arms contributed to his legendary Mephisthelian appearance—and probably to his unique skills as a performer. His immensely popular concerts brought him great wealth, but his compulsive gambling repeatedly humbled the genius. Paganini died at Nice, France, May 27, 1840.

ROOSEVELT, THEODORE: BIRTH ANNIVERSARY. Oct 27, 1858. Twenty-sixth president of the US, succeeded to the presidency on the death of William McKinley. His term of office: Sept 14, 1901–Mar 3, 1909. Roosevelt was the first president to ride in an automobile (1902), to submerge in a submarine (1905) and to fly in an airplane (1910). Although his best-remembered quote was perhaps, "Speak softly and carry a big stick," he also said: "The first requisite of a good citizen in this Republic of ours is that he shall be able and willing to pull his weight." Born at New York, NY, Roosevelt died at Oyster Bay, NY, Jan 6, 1919. His last words: "Put out the light."

SAINT VINCENT AND THE GRENADINES: INDEPENDENCE DAY. Oct 27. National Day commemorating independence from Britain in 1979.

SUGARLOAF CRAFTS FESTIVAL. Oct 27–29. Fort Washington Expo Center, Fort Washington, PA. This show, now in its 12th year, features more than 350 nationally recognized craft designers and fine artists displaying and selling their original creations. Includes craft demonstrations, live music, specialty foods, hourly gift certificate drawings and more. Est attendance: 25,500. For info: Sugarloaf Mountain Works, 200 Orchard Ridge Dr,

#215, Gaithersburg, MD 20878. Phone: (800) 210-9900. Fax: (301) 253-9620. Web: www.sugarloafcrafts.com.

TEXAS BOOK FESTIVAL. Oct 27–29. State Capitol and Capitol Extension, Austin, TX. Eleventh annual fair benefiting the public libraries of Texas. More than 150 authors will give readings, participate in panel discussions and sign books. Outdoor book fair with displays by publishers and booksellers. Free. For info: Texas Book Festival, 610 Brazos St, Ste 200, Austin, TX 78701. Phone: (512) 477-4055. Fax: (512) 322-0722. Web: www.texas bookfestival.org.

THOMAS, DYLAN MARLAIS: BIRTH ANNIVERSARY. Oct 27, 1914. Welsh poet and playwright, born at Swansea, Wales. Died at New York, NY, Nov 9, 1953.

TURKMENISTAN: INDEPENDENCE DAY. Oct 27. National holiday. Commemorates independence from the Soviet Union in 1991.

"WALT DISNEY" TV PREMIERE: ANNIVERSARY. Oct 27, 1954. This highly successful and long-running show appeared on different networks under different names but was essentially the same show. It was the first ABC series to break the Nielsen's Top Twenty and the first prime-time anthology series for kids. "Walt Disney" was originally titled "Disneyland" to promote the park and upcoming Disney releases. When it switched networks, it was called "Walt Disney's Wonderful World of Color" to highlight its being broadcast in color. Presentations included edited versions of previously released Disney films and original productions (including natural history documentaries, behind-the-scenes at Disney shows and dramatic shows, including the popular Davy Crockett segments that were the first TV miniseries). The show went off the air in December 1980 after 25 years, making it the longest-running series in prime-time TV history. In 1997 ABC revived the series as "Wonderful World of Disney."

BIRTHDAYS TODAY

Roberto Benigni, 54, actor, director (Oscar for *Life Is Beautiful*), born Arezzo, Italy, Oct 27, 1952.

John Cleese, 67, actor, writer ("Monty Python's Flying Circus," *A Fish Called Wanda*), born Weston-Super-Mare, England, Oct 27, 1939.

Ruby Dee, 82, actress ("Ossie and Ruby," *Zora Is My Name, Do the Right Thing*), born Cleveland, OH, Oct 27, 1924.

Nanette Fabray, 86, actress (Emmy for "Caesar's Hour"; "One Day at a Time," *Our Gang* comedies), born San Diego, CA, Oct 27, 1920.

Simon LeBon, 48, singer (Duran Duran), born Bushey, England, Oct 27, 1958.

Fran Lebowitz, 56, magazine columnist famous for essays on urban life (*Social Studies*), born Morristown, NJ, Oct 27, 1950.

Marla Maples, 43, model, actress, born Dalton, GA, Oct 27, 1963.

October 2006	S	M	T	W	T	F	S
	1	2	3	4	5	6	7
	8	9	10	11	12	13	14
	15	16	17	18	19	20	21
	22	23	24	25	26	27	28
	29	30	31				

OCTOBER 28 — SATURDAY
Day 301 — 64 Remaining

BLUE RIDGE FOLKLIFE FESTIVAL. Oct 28. Ferrum College/Blue Ridge Institute and Museum, Ferrum, VA. The largest celebration of authentic folkways in Virginia featuring food, crafts, music and exhibits. Annually, the fourth Saturday in October. Est attendance: 20,000. For info: Roddy Moore, BRI Dir, Ferrum College/BRI, PO Box 1000, Rte 40 West, Ferrum, VA 24088. Phone: (540) 365-4416. Fax: (540) 365-4419. E-mail: bri@ferrum.edu. Web: www.blueridgeinstitute.org.

CZECH REPUBLIC: INDEPENDENCE DAY. Oct 28. National Day, anniversary of the bloodless revolution at Prague in 1918 resulting in independence from the Austro-Hungarian Empire, after which the Czechs and Slovaks united to form Czechoslovakia (a union they dissolved without bloodshed in 1993).

DONNER PARTY FAMINE: ANNIVERSARY. Oct 28, 1846–Apr 21, 1847. The pioneering Donner Party, a group of 90 people consisting of immigrants, families and businessmen led by George and Jacob Donner and James F. Reed, headed toward California in 1846 from Springfield, IL, in hopes of beginning a new life. They experienced the normal travails of caravan travel until their trip took several sensational twists. Indian attacks and winter weather, which forced them to interrupt their journey, led to famine and outright cannibalism, which took their toll on members of the party, whose numbers dwindled to 48 by journey's end.

EMMA CRAWFORD FESTIVAL AND MEMORIAL COFFIN RACE. Oct 28. Manitou Springs, CO. Ghost tours, 5k, coffin races and parade. Annually, the Saturday before Halloween. Est attendance: 3,000. For info: Manitou Springs Chamber of Commerce, 354 Manitou, Manitou Springs, CO 80829. Phone: (800) 642-2567. Fax: (719) 685-0355. Web: www.manitou springs.org.

ERASMUS, DESIDERIUS: BIRTH ANNIVERSARY. Oct 28, 1467. Dutch author and scholar Desiderius Erasmus was born at Rotterdam, probably Oct 28, 1467. Best known of his writings is *Encomium Moriae* (*In Praise of Folly*). Erasmus died at Basel, Switzerland, July 12, 1536.

ESCOFFIER, GEORGES AUGUSTE: BIRTH ANNIVERSARY. Oct 28, 1846. Celebrated French chef and author, inventor of the peche Melba (honoring the operatic singer Dame Nellie Melba), Escoffier became known as the "king of chefs and the chef of kings." Born at Villeneuve-Loubet, France. He was awarded the Legion d'Honneur in recognition of his contribution to the international reputation of French cuisine and his service at the Savoy and Carlton hotels at London, England, brought him world fame. He died at Monte Carlo, Monaco, Feb 12, 1935.

FIRST WOMAN US AMBASSADOR APPOINTED: ANNIVERSARY. Oct 28, 1949. Helen Eugenie Moore Anderson became the first woman to hold the post of US ambassador when she was sworn in by President Harry S. Truman on this date. She served as Ambassador to Denmark.

GERMAN REVOLUTION OF 1918: ANNIVERSARY. Oct 28, 1918. On this date in the final days of World War I, crews of six German battleships protested a series of planned cruiser raids. A mutiny broke out in the fleet at Kiel. All but one of the ships remaining in port ran up the red flag of revolution, 600 sailors were arrested and imprisoned on shore. The uprising spread to Hamburg, Bremen and Lubeck. On Nov 9 a general strike at Berlin brought the administration to a halt. The abdication of Kaiser Wilhelm began to be seen as the only way to avoid a full-scale revolution.

GREECE: "OCHI DAY." Oct 28. National holiday commemorating Greek resistance and refusal to open her borders when Mussolini's Italian troops attacked Greece, Oct 28, 1940. *Ochi* means "no." Celebrated with military parades, especially at Athens and Thessaloniki.

HANSON, HOWARD: BIRTH ANNIVERSARY. Oct 28, 1896. Born at Wahoo, NE, Howard Hanson in 1921 became the first American to win the Prix de Rome. In 1924 he became head of the Eastman School of Music at the University of Rochester, NY, where he served for 40 years. Best known for the music he composed, Hanson was awarded the Pulitzer Prize as outstanding contemporary composer in 1944 for his composition *Symphony No. 4*, the George Foster Peabody Award in 1946, the Laurel Leaf of the American Composers Alliance in 1957 and the Huntington Hartford Foundation Award in 1959. He died at Rochester, Feb 26, 1981.

HARVARD UNIVERSITY FOUNDED: ANNIVERSARY. Oct 28, 1636 (OS). Harvard University founded at Cambridge, MA, when the Massachusetts General Court voted to provide £400 for a "schoale or colledge."

HAUNTED SEAPORT. Oct 28. Tuckerton, NJ. Pirates and sea captains long lost at sea wander the boardwalk for a night of screams. Annually, the fourth Saturday in October. For info: Karen DeRosa, Tuckerton Seaport, 120 W Main St, PO Box 52, Tuckerton, NJ 08087. Phone: (609) 296-8868. Fax: (609) 296-5810. E-mail: info@tuckertonseaport.org. Web: www.tuckertonseaport.org.

HOGEYE FESTIVAL. Oct 28. Elgin, TX. Day's events include Road Hog Car Show, pork and bean cook-off, crowning of King Hog or Queen Sowpreme, handmade arts & crafts, kids activities and Elgin's famous hot sausage and live music. Annually, the fourth Saturday in October. Est attendance: 20,000. For info: Hogeye Festival, PO Box 591, Elgin, TX 78621. Phone: (512) 285-5721, ext 17. Fax: (512) 285-5962. E-mail: hogeye@totalaccess.net. Web: www.elgintx.com.

IRELAND: BANK HOLIDAY. Oct 28. Bank holiday in the Republic of Ireland.

"THE JACK BENNY PROGRAM" TV PREMIERE: ANNIVERSARY. Oct 28, 1950. One of radio's favorite comedians, Jack Benny made the transition to favorite TV personality with this situation comedy–variety show in 1950. Regulars included Eddie Anderson, Don Wilson, Dennis Day, Mel Blanc, Mary Livingstone (Benny's real-life wife) and Frank Nelson. Benny also had guest stars, including Ken Murray, Frank Sinatra, Claudette Colbert, Basil Rathbone and TV newcomers Johnny Carson, Marilyn Monroe and Humphrey Bogart. Famous for his cheapness, Benny had a guard for his vaults, which created many laughs.

LONGWOOD GARDENS CHRYSANTHEMUM FESTIVAL. Oct 28–Nov 19. Kennett Square, PA. 17,000 chrysanthemums are featured in indoor displays accompanied by performances and activities throughout this late autumn festival. Est attendance: 50,000. For info: Longwood Gardens, PO Box 501, Kennett Square, PA 19348-0501. Phone: (610) 388-1000. Web: www.longwoodgardens.org.

MAKE A DIFFERENCE DAY. Oct 28. This national day of community service is sponsored by *USA Weekend* Magazine. Volunteer projects are judged by well-known celebrities. Selected projects receive $10,000 charitable awards to further their good work. Key projects are honored in April during National Volunteer Week. More than three million people nationwide participate. For info: Make A Difference Day, *USA Weekend* Magazine, 7950 Jones Branch Dr, McLean, VA 22107. Phone: (800) 416-3824. Web: www.makeadifferenceday.com.

SAINT JUDE'S DAY. Oct 28. St. Jude, the saint of hopeless causes, was martyred along with St. Simon at Persia, and their feast is celebrated jointly. St. Jude was supposedly the brother of Jesus, and, like his brother, a carpenter by trade. He is most popular with those who attempt the impossible and with students, who often ask for his help on exams.

SALK, JONAS: BIRTH ANNIVERSARY. Oct 28, 1914. Dr. Jonas Salk, developer of the Salk polio vaccine, was born at New York, NY. Salk announced his development of a successful vaccine in 1953, the year after a polio epidemic claimed some 3,300 lives in the US. Polio deaths were reduced by 95 percent after the introduction of the vaccine. Salk spent the last 10 years of his life doing AIDS research. He died June 23, 1995, at La Jolla, CA.

SCARED SILLY: HALLOWEEN IN PROSPECT PARK. Oct 28. Prospect Park, Brooklyn, NY. Celebrate Halloween with a haunted walk through the Ravine and a full carnival on the Nethermead. Hear scary stories at Lefferts Historic house—even ride a haunted carousel! Est attendance: 5,000. For info: Marketing Office, Prospect Park Alliance, 95 Prospect Park West, Brooklyn, NY 11215. Phone: (718) 965-8943. E-mail: jadelman@prospectpark.org. Web: www.prospectpark.org.

SEA WITCH HALLOWEEN & FIDDLERS FESTIVAL. Oct 28–30. Rehoboth Beach/Dewey Beach, DE. Fiddler's Festival, costume parade and contest, Sea Witch Hunt, horse show on the beach, best costumed pet contest, spook shows, horse-drawn hayrides and entertainment. Annually, the last full weekend in October. Est attendance: 100,000. For info: Elizabeth Beck, Festival Dir, PO Box 216, Rehoboth Beach, DE 19971. Phone: (800) 441-1329. Fax: (302) 227-8351. E-mail: rehoboth@beach-fun.com. Web: www.beach-fun.com.

SEPARATION OF CHURCH & STATE DAY. Oct 28. Eighth annual recognition of this day, now proclaimed jointly by two separate national groups, American Atheists, Inc, and the Freedom From Religion Foundation. The purpose of the day is to honor James Madison's "Remonstrance Against Taxes for Religious Uses," Thomas Jefferson's "Virginia Statute for Religious Freedom" and the Establishment Clause of the First Amendment of the Constitution of the United States. For info: John Simpson, American Atheist Publications, 1352 Hunter Ave, Columbus, OH 43201-2773. Phone: (614) 299-1036. E-mail: tgp@ams.org.

SORGHUM DAY FESTIVAL. Oct 28. Wewoka, OK. The autumn air fills with the sweet-smelling aroma of sorghum during this old-time festival and fall tradition. Visitors can witness sorghum-making, a quilt show, antique car show and pioneer demonstrations and visit more than 100 craft booths. Annually, the fourth Saturday in October. Est attendance: 40,000. For info: Wewoka Chamber of Commerce, PO Box 719, Wewoka, OK 74884. Phone: (405) 257-5485. Fax: (405) 257-2662. E-mail: wewokachamber@sbcglobal.net.

SPACE MILESTONE: INTERNATIONAL SPACE RESCUE AGREEMENT. Oct 28, 1970. US and USSR officials agreed upon space rescue cooperation.

STATUE OF LIBERTY: DEDICATION ANNIVERSARY. Oct 28, 1886. Frederic Auguste Bartholdi's famous sculpture, the statue of *Liberty Enlightening the World*, on Bedloe's Island in New York Harbor, was dedicated. Ground breaking for the structure was in April 1883. A sonnet by Emma Lazarus, inside the pedestal of the statue, contains the words: "Give me your tired, your poor, your huddled masses yearning to breathe free, the wretched refuse of your teeming shore. Send these, the homeless, tempest-tost to me, I lift my lamp beside the golden door!"

WILSON'S VOLSTEAD PROHIBITION ACT VETO OVERRIDDEN: ANNIVERSARY. Oct 28, 1919. Woodrow Wilson's veto of the Volstead Prohibition Act was overridden by Congress.

WMAS 94.7 FM ANNUAL HALLOWEEN BALL. Oct 28. Springfield, MA. Our annual listener appreciation ball, where listeners come dressed in their wildest and most creative costumes. Lots of prize categories in which people can win trips, VCRs, TVs, jewelry and more. Est attendance: 3,500. For info: Lucie Gronelin, PO Box 9500, Springfield, MA 01102. Phone: (413) 737-1414. Fax: (413) 737-1488.

BIRTHDAYS TODAY

Jane Alexander, 67, actress (*The Great White Hope, Kramer v Kramer*), former chair of the National Endowment for the Arts, born Jane Quigley at Boston, MA, Oct 28, 1939.

Charlie Daniels, 70, musician, singer, songwriter ("Devil Went Down to Georgia"), born Wilmington, NC, Oct 28, 1936.

Jeremy Davies, 37, actor (*Saving Private Ryan*), born Rockford, IA, Oct 28, 1969.

Terrell Davis, 34, football player, born San Diego, CA, Oct 28, 1972.

Dennis Franz, 62, actor ("Hill Street Blues," "NYPD Blue"), born Maywood, IL, Oct 28, 1944.

Bill Gates, 51, computer software executive (Microsoft), born Seattle, WA, Oct 28, 1955.

Jami Gertz, 41, actress ("ER," *Twister*), born Chicago, IL, Oct 28, 1965.

Lauren Holly, 43, actress (*Dumb & Dumber, Sabrina*), born Geneva, NY, Oct 28, 1963.

Telma Hopkins, 58, singer, actress ("Family Matters"), born Louisville, KY, Oct 28, 1948.

William Bruce Jenner, 57, sportscaster, Olympic gold medal decathlete, born Mount Kisco, NY, Oct 28, 1949.

Bowie Kent Kuhn, 80, former commissioner of baseball, born Tacoma Park, MD, Oct 28, 1926.

Annie Potts, 54, actress ("Designing Women," *Ghostbusters, Pretty in Pink*), born Nashville, TN, Oct 28, 1952.

Andy Richter, 40, former cohost ("Late Night with Conan O'Brien"), born Grand Rapids, MI, Oct 28, 1966.

Julia Roberts, 39, actress (Oscar for *Erin Brockovich; My Best Friend's Wedding*), born Smyrna, GA, Oct 28, 1967.

OCTOBER 29 — SUNDAY

Day 302 — 63 Remaining

BIG TEN MEN'S AND WOMEN'S CROSS COUNTRY CHAMPIONSHIPS. Oct 29. Indiana University, Bloomington, IN. For info: Big Ten Conference, 1500 W Higgins Rd, Park Ridge, IL 60068-6300. Phone: (847) 696-1010. Fax: (847) 696-1110. Web: www.bigten.org.

BOSWELL, JAMES: BIRTH ANNIVERSARY. Oct 29, 1740 (OS). Scottish biographer, born at Edinburgh, Scotland. Died at London, England, May 19, 1795. "I think," he wrote in his monumental biography, *Life of Samuel Johnson*, "no innocent species of wit or pleasantry should be suppressed: and that a good pun may be admitted among the smaller excellencies of lively conversation."

DAYLIGHT SAVING TIME ENDS; STANDARD TIME RESUMES. Oct 29–Apr 1, 2007. Standard Time resumes at 2 AM on the last Sunday in October in each time zone, as provided by the Uniform Time Act of 1966 (as amended in 1986 by Public Law 99–359). Many use the popular rule: "spring forward, fall back" to remember which way to turn their clocks. See also: "Daylight Saving Time" (Apr 2).

EMMETT, DANIEL DECATUR: BIRTH ANNIVERSARY. Oct 29, 1815. Creator of words and music for the song "Dixie's Land" ("Dixie"), which became a fighting song for Confederate troops and unofficial anthem of the South. Emmett was born at Mount Vernon, OH, and died there June 28, 1904.

A FAMILY HALLOWEEN. Oct 29. Billings Farm and Museum, Woodstock, VT. Mystery stories, doughnuts on a string, pumpkin carving, costume parades, plus wagon rides. Children in costume

★ ★ ★

	S	M	T	W	T	F	S
October	1	2	3	4	5	6	7
2006	8	9	10	11	12	13	14
	15	16	17	18	19	20	21
	22	23	24	25	26	27	28
	29	30	31				

accompanied by an adult admitted free. For info: Billings Farm and Museum, Rte 12 North, Woodstock, VT 05091. Phone: (802) 457-2355. Fax: (802) 457-4663. E-mail: billings.farm@valley.net. Web: www.billingsfarm.org.

"GIMME A BREAK!" TV PREMIERE: 25th ANNIVERSARY. Oct 29, 1981. Half-hour sitcom starring singer Nell Carter as Nell Harper, housekeeper, surrogate parent and confidante to a gruff cop, Carl Kanisky (Dolph Sweet) and his three daughters: Katie (Kari Michaelsen), Julie (Lauri Hendler) and Samantha (Lara Jill Miller). Also featured were Joey Lawrence and Telma Hopkins. Sweet's death in 1985 was incorporated into the storyline. Other changes included the marriage of Julie, Samantha going off to college and moving the setting to New York. The series ended with the last telecast May 12, 1987.

GOEBBELS, PAUL JOSEF: BIRTH ANNIVERSARY. Oct 29, 1897. German Nazi leader, born at Rheydt, Germany, who became Hitler's minister of propaganda, had earlier been rejected by the military because of a limp caused by infantile paralysis. Killed himself, his wife and children May 1, 1945, in Hitler's bunker in Berlin as Russian forces advanced into the city.

HAUTE DOG CHARITY HOWL'OWEEN PARADE. Oct 29. Belmont Shore, Long Beach, CA. Just about every breed from boxer to poodle—even a potbellied pig—will take over Belmont Shore for the annual Haute Dog Howl'oween Parade. The event has raised thousands of dollars for animal shelters and rescue organizations. About 400 pooches—mostly colorfully costumed for Halloween—are expected to pack Livingston Park for a Yappy Hour before beginning their parade down Second Street. Prizes awarded for the best canine costumes. Annually, the Sunday before Halloween. Est attendance: 3,000. For info: Justin Rudd. Phone: (562) 439-3316. E-mail: justinrudd@aol.com. Web: www.hautedogs.org.

INTERNET CREATED: ANNIVERSARY. Oct 29, 1969. The first connection on what would become the Internet was made on this day when bits of data flowed between computers at UCLA and the Stanford Research Institute. This was the beginning of ARPANET, the precurser to the Internet developed by the Department of Defense. By the end of 1969 four sites were connected: UCLA, the Stanford Research Institute, the University of California at Santa Barbara and the University of Utah. By the next year there were 10 sites and soon there were applications like e-mail and file transfer utilities. The @ symbol was adopted in 1972 and a year later 75 percent of ARPANET traffic was e-mail. ARPANET was decommissioned in 1990 and the National Science Foundation's NSFnet took over the role of backbone of the Internet.

MOON PHASE: FIRST QUARTER. Oct 29. Moon enters First Quarter phase at 4:25 PM, EST.

NISSAN XTERRA WORLD CHAMPIONSHIP. Oct 29. Makena, Maui, HI. Heralded as the hot new king of multisport, the Nissan Xterra World Championship is the culmination of more than 100 events held across the globe. Includes 1.5k roughwater swim, 30k mountain bike race and 11k cross-country run. $130,000 pro purse. CBS one-hour television feature. Est attendance: 8,000. For info: TEAM Unlimited, 500 Ala Moana Blvd, 2-Waterfront Plaza, #302, Honolulu, HI 96813. Phone: (808) 521-4322. Fax: (808) 538-0314. E-mail: info@xterraplanet.com. Web: www.xterraplanet.com.

REFORMATION SUNDAY. Oct 29. Many Protestant churches commemorate Reformation Day (Oct 31—anniversary of the day on which Martin Luther nailed his 95 theses to the door of Wittenberg's Palace church, protesting the sale of papal indulgences, in 1517) on the Sunday preceding Oct 31, each year or on the 31st, if a Sunday.

SPACE MILESTONE: OLDEST MAN IN SPACE: *DISCOVERY* (US). Oct 29, 1998. Former astronaut and senator John Glenn became the oldest man in space when he traveled on the space shuttle *Discovery* at the age of 77. In 1962 on *Friendship 7* Glenn had been the first American to orbit Earth. See "Space Milestone: *Friendship 7*" (Feb 20).

STOCK MARKET CRASH: ANNIVERSARY. Oct 29, 1929. Prices on the New York Stock Exchange plummeted and virtually collapsed four days after President Herbert Hoover had declared "The fundamental business of the country . . . is on a sound and prosperous basis." More than 16 million shares were dumped and billions of dollars were lost. The boom was over and the nation faced nearly a decade of depression. Some analysts had warned that the buying spree, with prices 15 to 150 times above earnings, had to stop at some point. Frightened investors ordered their brokers to sell at whatever price. The resulting Great Depression, which lasted until about 1939, involved North America, Europe and other industrialized countries. In 1932 one out of four US workers was unemployed.

TURKEY: REPUBLIC DAY: ANNIVERSARY. Oct 29. Anniversary of the founding of the republic in 1923.

BIRTHDAYS TODAY

Richard Dreyfuss, 59, actor (*American Graffiti, Jaws*; Oscar for *The Goodbye Girl*), born Brooklyn, NY, Oct 29, 1947.

Joely Fisher, 41, actress ("Ellen"), born Los Angeles, CA, Oct 29, 1965.

Finola Hughes, 46, actress ("Blossom," "Pacific Palisades"), born London, England, Oct 29, 1960.

Kate Jackson, 58, actress ("Charlie's Angels," "Scarecrow and Mrs King"), born Birmingham, AL, Oct 29, 1948.

Randy Jackson, 45, singer (Jackson 5), born Steven Randall Jackson at Gary, IN, Oct 29, 1961.

Dirk Kempthorne, 55, Governor of Idaho (R), born San Diego, CA, Oct 29, 1951.

Melba Moore, 61, singer ("You Stepped into My Life"), actress ("Melba"), born New York, NY, Oct 29, 1945.

Winona Ryder, 35, actress (*Beetlejuice, Edward Scissorhands, Little Women*), born Winona, MN, Oct 29, 1971.

Gabrielle Union, 34, actress (*Bring It On, The Honeymooners*), born Omaha, NE, Oct 29, 1972.

OCTOBER 30 — MONDAY
Day 303 — 62 Remaining

ADAMS, JOHN: BIRTH ANNIVERSARY. Oct 30, 1735. Second president of the US (term of office: Mar 4, 1797–Mar 3, 1801), had been George Washington's vice president, and was the father of John Quincy Adams (sixth president of the US). Born at Braintree, MA, he once wrote in a letter to his wife Abigail: "I must study politics and war that my sons may have liberty to study mathematics and philosophy." Adams and Thomas Jefferson died on the same day, July 4, 1826. Adams died at Quincy, MA. See also: "Adams, John, and Jefferson, Thomas: Death Anniversary" (July 4).

ATLAS, CHARLES: BIRTH ANNIVERSARY. Oct 30, 1893. Charles Atlas (ex-97-lb weakling), whose original name was Angelo Siciliano, was born at Acri, Calabria, Italy. A bodybuilder and physical culturist, he created a popular mail-order body-building course. The legendary sand-kicking episode used later in advertising for his course occurred at Coney Island when a lifeguard kicked sand in Atlas's face and stole his girlfriend. Three generations of comic book fans read his advertisements. He died Dec 24, 1972, at Long Beach, NY.

CHINA: CHUNG YEUNG FESTIVAL (OR DOUBLE NINE FESTIVAL). Oct 30. This festival relates to the old story of the Han Dynasty, when a soothsayer advised a man to take his family to a high place on the ninth day of the ninth moon for 24 hours in order to avoid disaster. The man obeyed and found, on returning home, that all living things had died a sudden death in his absence. Part of the celebration is climbing to high places. Date in other countries will differ from China's.

CLOSING OF COLUMBIAN EXPOSITION: ANNIVERSARY. Oct 30, 1893. After a rousing success, the Columbian Exposition held "American Cities Day" Oct 28, and Chicago Mayor Carter Harrison gave a speech before the visiting mayors. After he arrived home, Harrison's doorbell rang. When the mayor answered the door he was shot by Patrick Eugene Pendergast, who had been disappointed when his request for a position with the city as corporation counsel was turned down. Instead of the elaborate ceremony that had been planned to close the exposition on Oct 30, a single speech was given and the flags lowered to half-mast.

CREATE A GREAT FUNERAL DAY. Oct 30. A day to remind people of all the benefits of creating their own unique funerals or memorial services, regardless of age or state of health. For info: Stephanie West Allen, PO Box 9311, Denver, CO 80209. Phone: (303) 742-4790. Fax: (303) 935-8842. E-mail: stephanie@allen-nichols.com. Web: www.allen-nichols.com.

DEVIL'S NIGHT. Oct 30. Formerly a "Mischief Night" on the evening before Halloween and an occasion for harmless pranks, chiefly observed by children. However, in some areas of the US, the destruction of property and endangering of lives has led to the imposition of dusk-to-dawn curfews during the last two or three days of October. Not to be confused with "Trick or Treat," or "Beggar's Night," usually observed on Halloween. See also: "Hallowe'en" (Oct 31).

HALSEY, WILLIAM "BULL" FREDERICK: BIRTH ANNIVERSARY. Oct 30, 1882. American admiral and fleet commander who played a leading role in the defeat of the Japanese in the Pacific naval battles of WWII, William Halsey was born at Elizabeth, NJ. In April 1942, aircraft carriers under his command ferried Jimmy Doolittle's B-25s to within several hundred miles of Japan's coast. From that location the aircraft were launched from the decks of the carriers for a raid on Tokyo. In October 1942, as commander of all the South Pacific area, Halsey led naval forces in the defeat of Japan at Guadalcanal, and in November 1943, he directed the capture of Bougainville. He supported the landings in the Philippines in June 1944. In the great naval battle of Leyte (Oct 23–25, 1944) he assisted in an overwhelming defeat of the Japanese. On Sept 2, 1945, Japan's final instrument of surrender was signed in Tokyo Bay aboard Halsey's flagship, the USS *Missouri*. Halsey died at Fishers Island, NY, Aug 16, 1959.

HAUNTED REFRIGERATOR NIGHT. Oct 30. Who knows what evil lurks in the refrigerators of men and women. It's time to be afraid, very afraid. Gather friends, open the refrigerator door and venture unto the realm of the lower shelf, rear. That "thing" inside that container is much more horrifying than any haunted hayride. Annually, Oct 30. [©2003 by WH.] For info: Thomas & Ruth Roy, Wellcat Holidays, 2418 Long Ln, Lebanon, PA 17046. Phone: (717) 279-0184. E-mail: info@wellcat.com. Web: www.wellcat.com.

MALLE, LOUIS: BIRTH ANNIVERSARY. Oct 30, 1932. Born at Thumeries, France, film director Louis Malle was known for his experimental approach to filmmaking and his investigation of controversial topics. *Le Souffle Au Coeur* (1971), *Lancombe, Lucien* (1974) and *Pretty Baby* (1978), for instance, dealt with the issues of incest, the collaboration of France with its Nazi occupiers and child prostitution, respectively. Of all his films, Malle wished most to be remembered for *Au Revoir Les Enfants* (1987). Died Nov 23, 1995, at Beverly Hills, CA.

POST, EMILY: BIRTH ANNIVERSARY. Oct 30, 1872. Emily Post was born at Baltimore, MD. Published in 1922, her book *Etiquette: The Blue Book of Social Usage* instantly became the American bible of manners and social behavior and established Post as the household name in matters of etiquette. It was in its 10th edition at the time of her death Sept 25, 1960, at New York, NY. *Etiquette* inspired a great many letters asking Post for advice on manners in specific situations. She used these letters as the basis for her radio show and her syndicated newspaper column, which eventually appeared in more than 200 papers.

POUND, EZRA LOOMIS: BIRTH ANNIVERSARY. Oct 30, 1885. Modernist poet, editor and critic, born at Hailey, ID. His success as a poet began in 1909 with the publication of *Personae*. In 1912 Pound initiated the Imagist movement, edited its first anthology in 1914 and collaborated with James Joyce and T.S. Eliot. He moved to Italy in 1924. As a result of his pro-Fascist radio broadcasts from Italy Pound was indicted for treason July 26, 1943, and arrested near Genoa by the US Army. He was confined to St. Elizabeth's Hospital, Washington, DC, from 1946 to 1958. Considered mentally unable to stand trial, he was never tried for treason. Pound died at Venice, Italy, Nov 1, 1972.

SHERIDAN, RICHARD BRINSLEY: BIRTH ANNIVERSARY. Oct 30, 1751. Dramatist, born at Dublin, Ireland. Died at London, England, July 7, 1816. Sheridan is said to have extended the following invitation to a young lady: "Won't you come into the garden? I would like my roses to see you."

SISLEY, ALFRED: BIRTH ANNIVERSARY. Oct 30, 1839. French impressionist painter, born at Paris, France. One of the most influential artists of his time, he died near Fontainbleau, Jan 29, 1899.

"WAR OF THE WORLDS": BROADCAST ANNIVERSARY. Oct 30, 1938. As part of a series of radio dramas based on famous novels, Orson Welles with the Mercury Players produced H.G. Wells's *War of the Worlds*. Near panic resulted when listeners believed the simulated news bulletins, which described a Martian invasion of New Jersey, to be real.

ZERO-TASKING DAY. Oct 30. Today is the day daylight savings time ends—when we turn our clocks back and "gain" an hour. Instead of filling that extra 60 minutes with more work and stress, use that hour to do nothing but take a breath, relax, re-energize, refresh and de-load (opposite of overload). For info: Nancy Christie, PO Box 4505, Austintown, OH 44515. Phone: (330) 793-3675. Fax: (330) 793-5653. E-mail: nancy@nancychristie.com.

BIRTHDAYS TODAY

Robert A. Caro, 71, author (3-volume biography of Lyndon B. Johnson), born New York, NY, Oct 30, 1935.

Dick Gautier, 69, actor (*Bye Bye Birdie*, "Here We Go Again"), born Los Angeles, CA, Oct 30, 1937.

Harry Hamlin, 55, actor ("LA Law," "Studs Lonigan"), born Pasadena, CA, Oct 30, 1951.

Ed Lauter, 66, actor (*The Longest Yard, Fat Man and Little Boy*), born Long Beach, NY, Oct 30, 1940.

Diego Armando Maradona, 46, former soccer player, born Lanus, Argentina, Oct 30, 1960.

Andrea Mitchell, 60, news correspondent, born New York, NY, Oct 30, 1946.

Kevin Pollak, 48, actor (*A Few Good Men, Grumpy Old Men*), born San Francisco, CA, Oct 30, 1958.

October 2006	S	M	T	W	T	F	S
	1	2	3	4	5	6	7
	8	9	10	11	12	13	14
	15	16	17	18	19	20	21
	22	23	24	25	26	27	28
	29	30	31				

Grace Slick, 67, singer (Jefferson Airplane, "White Rabbit"), born Chicago, IL, Oct 30, 1939.

Charles Martin Smith, 53, actor (*American Graffiti, The Buddy Holly Story, The Untouchables*), director, born Los Angeles, CA, Oct 30, 1953.

Dick Vermeil, 70, football coach, born Calistoga, CA, Oct 30, 1936.

Henry Winkler, 61, actor ("Happy Days"), children's author, born New York, NY, Oct 30, 1945.

OCTOBER 31 — TUESDAY
Day 304 — 61 Remaining

BOOKS FOR TREATS DAY. Oct 31. San Jose, CA. The Books for Treats cause gives gently read children's books at Halloween instead of candy. "Feed kids' minds, not their cavities. Give them brain candy." Supported by the city of San Jose and numerous community institutions. For info: Rebecca Morgan, Books for Treats, 1440 Newport Ave, San Jose, CA 95125. Phone: (408) 998-7977. E-mail: rebecca@rebeccamorgan.com. Web: www.BooksforTreats.org.

CANDY, JOHN: BIRTH ANNIVERSARY. Oct 31, 1950. Comedic actor who got his start in Second City improvisation at Toronto and graduated to film stardom (*Uncle Buck, Home Alone*). Born at Toronto, ON, Canada, and died Mar 4, 1994, while on location for a film at Chupederos, Mexico.

"CAR TALK" NATIONAL RADIO PREMIERE: ANNIVERSARY. Oct 31, 1987. "Car Talk," the irreverent talk show that diagnoses auto ills, premiered nationally on National Public Radio on this date. Hosted by brothers Ray and Tom Magliozzi (also known as "Click and Clack, the Tappet Brothers"), "Car Talk" originally debuted in Boston in 1977. Today, almost 4 million listeners tune in to the Peabody Award–winning show on 550 NPR stations.

CHIANG KAI-SHEK: BIRTH ANNIVERSARY. Oct 31, 1887. Chinese soldier and statesman, born at Chekiang, China. Educated at the Wampoa Military Academy, Chiang led the KMT (nationalist) forces in the struggle against the Communist army led by Mao Tse-Tung and eventually had to flee mainlaind China. He died at Taipei, Taiwan, Apr 5, 1975.

FIRST BLACK PLAYS IN NBA GAME: ANNIVERSARY. Oct 31, 1950. Earl Lloyd became the first black ever to play in an NBA game when he took the floor for the Washington Capitols at Rochester, NY. Lloyd was actually one of three blacks to become an NBA player in the 1950 season, the others being Nat "Sweetwater" Clifton, who was signed by the New York Knicks, and Chuck Cooper, who was drafted by the Boston Celtics (and debuted the night after Lloyd).

HALLOWEEN IN ARAPAHOE. Oct 31. Arapahoe, NE. Merchants and business personnel dress in Halloween costumes, children's parade and prizes. Est attendance: 200. For info: Secretary, Chamber of Commerce, PO Box 624, Arapahoe, NE 68922.

HALLOWE'EN or ALL HALLOW'S EVE. Oct 31. An ancient celebration combining Druid autumn festival and Christian customs. Hallowe'en (All Hallow's Eve) is the beginning of Hallowtide, a season that embraces the Feast of All Saints (Nov 1) and the Feast of All Souls (Nov 2). The observance, dating from the sixth or seventh century, has long been associated with thoughts of the dead, spirits, witches, ghosts and devils. In fact, the ancient Celtic Feast of Samhain, the festival that marked the beginning of winter and of the New Year, was observed Nov 1. See also: "Trick or Treat or Beggar's Night" (Oct 31).

HALLOWEEN PARADE. Oct 31. Toms River, NJ. Reported as the second largest Halloween parade in the nation with 8,000 participants, 118 prizes and 100,000 spectators. Parade covers a one-mile route. Est attendance: 100,000. For info: Carl Weingroff, c/o Toms River Fire Co. 1, PO Box 1035, Toms River, NJ 08754. Phone: (732) 349-0144. Fax: (732) 349-5024. E-mail: trfdno1@aol.com.

HOUDINI, HARRY: 80th DEATH ANNIVERSARY. Oct 31, 1926. Harry Houdini (whose real name was Ehrich Weisz), magician, illusionist and escape artist, died at Grace Hospital, Detroit, MI, of peritonitis following an Oct 19 blow to the abdomen. Houdini's death anniversary, on Halloween, is occasion for meetings of magicians. See also: "Houdini, Harry: Birth Anniversary" (Mar 24).

KEATS, JOHN: BIRTH ANNIVERSARY. Oct 31, 1795. One of England's greatest poets, born at London, England. Keats wrote to Fanny Brawne (in 1820): "If I should die . . . I have left no immortal work behind me—nothing to make my friends proud of my memory—but I have loved the principle of beauty in all things, and if I had had time I would have made myself remembered." Died at the age of 25 at Rome, Italy, Feb 23, 1821.

LANDON, MICHAEL: BIRTH ANNIVERSARY. Oct 31, 1936. American actor, born Eugene Maurice Orowitz, at Forest Hills, NY. He is best known for his roles in the television series "Bonanza" (1959–73), "Little House on the Prairie" (1974–83) and "Highway to Heaven" (1984–89). He died July 1, 1991, at Malibu, CA.

LOW, JULIET GORDON: BIRTH ANNIVERSARY. Oct 31, 1860. Founded Girl Scouts of the USA Mar 12, 1912, at Savannah, GA. Born at Savannah, Low died there Jan 17, 1927.

MAGIC DAY. Oct 31. Traditionally observed on the anniversary of the death of Harry Houdini in 1926.

MOUNT RUSHMORE COMPLETION: 65th ANNIVERSARY. Oct 31, 1941. The Mount Rushmore National Memorial was completed after 14 years of work. First suggested by Jonah Robinson of the South Dakota State Historical Society, the memorial was dedicated in 1925, and work began in 1927. The memorial contains sculptures of the heads of presidents George Washington, Thomas Jefferson, Abraham Lincoln and Theodore Roosevelt. The 60-foot-tall sculptures represent, respectively, the nation's founding, political philosophy, preservation, expansion and conservation.

NATIONAL KNOCK-KNOCK DAY. Oct 31. Celebrated in tandem with Halloween, National Knock-Knock Day answers the age-old question "who's there?" A day for kids of all ages to try out their best knock-knock jokes (i.e., Knock Knock/Who's there?/Weirdo/Weirdo who?/Weirdo you keep all your Halloween candy? I'm starving!). For a list of Halloween Knock-Knock Jokes, contact children's joke book authors Matt Rissinger and Philip Yates. Annually, on October 31. For info: Matt Rissinger/Philip Yates. Phone: (610) 650-9136. E-mail: mrissinger@aol.com or laugharoni@msn.com.

NATIONAL PARK OF AMERICAN SAMOA AUTHORIZED: ANNIVERSARY. Oct 31, 1988. An area of American Samoa was authorized to be developed as a national park. For further park info: Natl Park of American Samoa, c/o Pacific Area Office, PO Box 50165, Honolulu, HI 96850.

★**NATIONAL UNICEF DAY.** Oct 31. Presidential Proclamation 3817, of Oct 27, 1967, covers all succeeding years. Annually, Oct 31.

NEVADA: ADMISSION DAY: ANNIVERSARY. Oct 31, 1864. Became 36th state in 1864. Observed as a holiday in Nevada.

PACA, WILLIAM: BIRTH ANNIVERSARY. Oct 31, 1740. Signer of the Declaration of Independence and governor of Maryland. Born near Abingdon, MD, he died Oct 13, 1799, at Talbot County, MD.

REFORMATION DAY: ANNIVERSARY. Oct 31, 1517. Anniversary on which Martin Luther nailed his 95 theses to the door of Wittenberg's Palace church, denouncing the selling of papal indulgences—the beginning of the Reformation in Germany. Observed by many Protestant churches on Reformation Sunday, on this day if it is a Sunday or on the Sunday before Oct 31.

SAMHAIN. Oct 31. (Also called November Eve, Hallowmas, Hallowe'en, All Hallow's Eve, Feast of Souls, Feast of the Dead, Feast of Apples and Calan Gaeaf.) One of the "Greater Sabbats" during the Wiccan year, Samhain or "Summer's end" marks the death of the Sun-God, who then awaits his rebirth from the Mother Goddess at Yule (Dec 21 in 2006). In the Celtic tradition, the feast of Samhain was also celebrated as New Year's Eve, as their new year began on Nov 1. Annually, Oct 31.

SCARE A FRIEND DAY. Oct 31. Have some innocent fun by scaring friends and family. Watch a horror movie, visit a haunted house attraction, play a harmless prank or do anything that gets the old blood pumping. Have a screaming good time! For info: Christopher Cook, Fearmakers Studios, 387 E Weber Rd, Columbus, OH 43202. Phone: (614) 262-9573. E-mail: ccook@fearmakers.com. Web: www.fearmakers.com.

SLEIDANUS, JOHANNES: 450th DEATH ANNIVERSARY. Oct 31, 1556. German historian, born at Schleiden in 1506. His *Famous Chronicle of Oure Time*, called *Sleidanes Comentaires*, was first translated into English in 1560. The translator spoke thus to the book: "Go forth my painful Boke, Thou art no longer mine. Eche man may on thee loke, The Shame and praise is thine." He died at Strasbourg, Oct 31, 1556.

TAIWAN: CHIANG KAI-SHEK DAY: ANNIVERSARY. Oct 31. National holiday to honor the memory of Generalissimo Chiang Kai-Shek, the first constitutional president of the Republic of China, born Oct 31, 1887.

TRICK OR TREAT or BEGGAR'S NIGHT. Oct 31. A popular custom on Hallowe'en, in which children wearing costumes visit neighbors' homes, calling out "Trick or treat" and "begging" for candies or gifts to place in their beggars' bags. In recent years there has been increased participation by adults, often parading in elaborate or outrageous costumes and also requesting candy.

WATERS, ETHEL: BIRTH ANNIVERSARY. Oct 31, 1896. Married when she was 13, Ethel Waters began her singing career at the urging of friends. At age 17 she was singing at Baltimore, billing herself as Sweet Mama Stringbean. Her career took her to New York, where she divided her work between the stage, nightclubs and films. She made her Broadway debut in 1927 in the revue *Africana*, and her other stage credits included *Blackbirds* and *Thousands Cheer*. Her memorable stage roles in *Cabin in the Sky* and *A Member of the Wedding* (for which she won the Drama Critics' Award) were re-created for film. Born at Chester, PA, she died Sept 9, 1977, at Chatsworth, GA.

BIRTHDAYS TODAY

Michael Collins, 75, former astronaut, born Rome, Italy, Oct 31, 1931.

Deidre Hall, 58, actress ("Our House," "Days of Our Lives"), born Lake Worth, FL, Oct 31, 1948.

Peter Jackson, 45, director (the *Lord of the Rings* trilogy), born Pukerua Bay, North Island, New Zealand, Oct 31, 1961.

Frederick Stanley (Fred) McGriff, 43, baseball player, born Tampa, FL, Oct 31, 1963.

Larry Mullen, 45, musician (drummer with U2; Grammy for *The Joshua Tree*), born Dublin, Ireland, Oct 31, 1961.

Dermot Mulroney, 43, actor (*Young Guns, Longtime Companion*), born Alexandria, VA, Oct 31, 1963.

Jane Pauley, 56, TV personality, born Indianapolis, IN, Oct 31, 1950.

Dan Rather, 75, journalist (former anchor "CBS Evening News"), born Wharton, TX, Oct 31, 1931.

Stephen Rea, 63, actor (*The Crying Game, Michael Collins*), born Belfast, Northern Ireland, Oct 31, 1943.

Ron Rifkin, 67, actor (*L.A. Confidential*, "Alias"), born New York, NY, Oct 31, 1939.

Rob Schneider, 43, actor ("Saturday Night Live," "Men Behaving Badly"), born San Francisco, CA, Oct 31, 1963.

David Ogden Stiers, 64, actor ("M*A*S*H," *North and South*), born Peoria, IL, Oct 31, 1942.

Vanilla Ice, 39, rapper, actor, born Robert Van Winkle at Miami, FL, Oct 31, 1967.

Nouember.

NOVEMBER 1 — WEDNESDAY
Day 305 — 60 Remaining

ALGERIA: REVOLUTION DAY. Nov 1. National holiday. Commemorates beginning of revolt against France in 1954.

ALL HALLOWS or ALL SAINTS' DAY. Nov 1. Roman Catholic Holy Day of Obligation. Commemorates the blessed, especially those who have no special feast days. Observed on Nov 1 since Pope Gregory IV set the date of recognition in 835. All Saints' Day is a legal holiday in Louisiana. Halloween is the evening before All Hallows Day.

AMERICAN DIABETES MONTH. Nov 1–30. American Diabetes Month is designed to communicate the seriousness of diabetes and the importance of proper diabetes control and treatment to those diagnosed with the disease and their families. Throughout the month, the American Diabetes Association holds special events and programs on a variety of topics related to diabetes care and treatment. For info contact: American Diabetes Assn at (800) DIABETES or www.diabetes.org.

ANTIGUA AND BARBUDA: INDEPENDENCE DAY. Nov 1. National holiday. Commemorates independence from Britain in 1981.

AVIATION HISTORY MONTH. Nov 1–30. Anniversary of aeronautical experiments in November 1782 (exact dates unknown) by Joseph Michel Montgolfier and Jacques Etienne Montgolfier, brothers living at Annonay, France. Inspired by Joseph Priestley's book *Experiments Relating to the Different Kinds of Air*, the brothers experimented with filling paper and fabric bags with smoke and hot air, leading to the invention of the hot air balloon, man's first flight and the entire science of aviation and flight.

CAMELLIA SASANQUA DAYS. Nov 1–22 (also Nov 24–30). Massee Lane Gardens, Fort Valley, GA. An annual celebration of the lovely fall-blooming *Camellia sasanqua*. Festival events include garden tours and workshops, plant sale and more. Sponsored by The American Camellia Society. For info: Massee Lane Gardens, 100 Massee Ln, Fort Valley, GA 31030. Phone: (478) 967-2358. Fax: (478) 967-2083. Web: www.camellias-acs.com.

CANADA: BANFF MOUNTAIN BOOK FESTIVAL. Nov 1–3. Banff, AB. An international mountain book competition that features guest speakers, readings, seminars, book signings, book launches and a book fair. Est attendance: 3,000. For info: Banff Mountain Book Festival, The Banff Centre, Box 1020, Banff, AB, Canada T1L 1H5. Phone: (403) 762-6369. Fax: (403) 762-6277.

November 2006	S	M	T	W	T	F	S
				1	2	3	4
	5	6	7	8	9	10	11
	12	13	14	15	16	17	18
	19	20	21	22	23	24	25
	26	27	28	29	30		

E-mail: banffmountainbooks@banffcentre.ca. Web: www.banffmountainfestivals.ca.

CELEBRATE EMPTY NESTER MONTH. Nov 1–30. A time for empty nesters to enjoy the advantages of their new stage in life. Although it can be jarring for parents to watch their children leave the nest, this special month encourages them to reconnect with each other as spouses, discover new hobbies, travel and take time to enjoy their favorite foods. For info: Mary Jo Exley, Padilla Speer Beardsley, 1101 W River Pkwy, Minneapolis, MN 55415. Phone: (612) 455-1776. Fax: (612) 455-1060. E-mail: mexley@psbpr.com.

CRANE, STEPHEN: BIRTH ANNIVERSARY. Nov 1, 1871. American author (*The Red Badge of Courage*), born at Newark, NJ. Died June 5, 1900, at Badenweiler, Germany.

DIABETIC EYE DISEASE MONTH. Nov 1–30. Can people with diabetes prevent the onset of diabetic eye disease? During this observance Prevent Blindness America® tells how early detection and treatment of diabetes can help save sight. For info: Prevent Blindness America®, 211 W Wacker Dr, Ste 1700, Chicago, IL 60606. Phone: (800) 331-2020. E-mail: info@preventblindness.org. Web: www.preventblindness.org.

EPILEPSY AWARENESS MONTH. Nov 1–30. To increase public awareness that despite dramatic gains in treatment, epilepsy is a serious and chronic health condition for which there is no cure. Annually, the month of November. For info: PR Dept, Epilepsy Foundation, 4351 Garden City Dr, Landover, MD 20785. Phone: (800) 332-1000. Web: www.epilepsyfoundation.org.

EUROPEAN UNION ESTABLISHED: ANNIVERSARY. Nov 1, 1993. The Maastricht Treaty went into effect this day, formally establishing the European Union. The treaty was drafted in 1991. By 1993, 12 nations had ratified it. In 1995 three more nations ratified the treaty. The European Union grew out of the European Economic Community (also known as the Common Market), which was established in 1958.

FAMILY STORIES MONTH. Nov 1–30. November starts out with crisper weather and ends with the gathering of family and friends around the table, which makes it the perfect month to start telling and saving family stories. For info: Joanna Campbell Slan, 7 Ailanthus Ct, Chesterfield, MO 63005. Phone: (636) 519-1612. Fax: (636) 519-1583. E-mail: savetales@aol.com. Web: www.scrapbookstorytelling.com.

GUATEMALA: KITE FESTIVAL OF SANTIAGO SACATEPEQUEZ. Nov 1. Long ago, when evil spirits disturbed the good spirits in the local cemetery, a magician told the townspeople a secret way to get rid of the evil spirits—by flying kites (because the evil spirits were frightened by the noise of wind against paper). Since then, the kite festival has been held at the cemetery each year on Nov 1 or Nov 2, and it is said that "to this day no one knows of bad spirits roaming the streets or the cemetery of Santiago Sacatepequez," a village about 20 miles from Guatemala City. Nowadays, the youth of the village work for many weeks to make the elaborate and giant kites to fly on All Saints' Day (Nov 1) or All Souls' Day (Nov 2).

HOCKEY MASK INVENTED: ANNIVERSARY. Nov 1, 1959. Tired of stopping hockey pucks with his face, Montreal Canadiens goalie Jacques Plante, having received another wound, reemerged from the locker room with seven new stitches—and a face mask he had made from fiberglass and resin. Although Cliff Benedict had tried a leather mask back in the '20s, the idea didn't catch on, but after Plante wore his, goalies throughout the NHL began wearing protective plastic face shields.

I AM SO THANKFUL MONTH. Nov 1–30. This month is dedicated to giving thanks and counting your blessings daily. Share with others the things you are thankful for! For info: Nancy J. Lewis, MS, PHR, PO Box 342, Fayetteville, GA 30214. Phone: (404) 559-7614. Fax: (770) 306-8237. E-mail: nancyjlewis@bell south.net. Web: www.nancyjlewis.com.

INTERNATIONAL MICROFINANCE MONTH. Nov 1–30. Microfinance is the practice of extending small loans to people in developing countries to start self-sustaining businesses—helping them escape poverty. This month celebrates the millions of lives that have been transformed through microfinance and the people who support them. For info: Grameen Foundation USA, 1029 Vermont Ave NW, Ste 400, Washington, DC 20005-3517. Phone: (888) 764-3872. E-mail: michelle@tennant.org. Web: www .gfusa.org.

LISBON EARTHQUAKE: ANNIVERSARY. Nov 1, 1755. A powerful earthquake struck Lisbon, Portugal, on this day in 1755. The earthquake probably had a Richter scale magnitude of 9 and caused a large tsunami to sweep over the capital. In the resulting deluge and fires, more than 75 percent of Lisbon was destroyed. Some 90,000 people died in Portugal, and an additional 10,000 people died in other parts of the Mediterranean.

LUNG CANCER AWARENESS MONTH. Nov 1–30. A month created to increase awareness of the need for screening, early detection, more research and compassion for lung cancer survivors. ALCASE is the only organization in the world solely dedicated to helping people at risk for and living with lung cancer. Support and education resources are available free of charge by phone, mail or Internet. For info: The Lung Cancer Alliance, 888 16th St NW, Ste 800, Washington, DC 20006. Phone: (202) 463-2080. E-mail: info@lungcanceralliance.org. Web: www.lung canceralliance.org.

MEDICAL SCHOOL FOR WOMEN OPENED AT BOSTON: ANNIVERSARY. Nov 1, 1848. Founded by Samuel Gregory, a pioneer in medical education for women, the Boston Female Medical School opened as the first medical school exclusively for women. The original enrollment was 12 students. In 1874 the school merged with the Boston University School of Medicine and formed one of the first coed medical schools in the world.

MEXICO: DAY OF THE DEAD. Nov 1–2. Observance begins during last days of October when "dead men's bread" is sold in bakeries—round loaves, decorated with sugar skulls. Departed souls are remembered not with mourning but with a spirit of friendliness and good humor. Cemeteries are visited and graves are decorated.

MISSION SAN JUAN CAPISTRANO: FOUNDING ANNIVERSARY. Nov 1, 1776. California mission founded on this date, collapsed during the 1812 earthquake. The swallows of Capistrano nest in the ruins of the old mission church, departing each year on Oct 23, and returning the following year on or near St. Joseph's Day (Mar 19).

NATIONAL ADOPTION MONTH. Nov 1–30. To commemorate the success of three kinds of adoption—infant, special needs and intercountry—through a variety of special events. For info: Natl Council for Adoption, 225 N Washington St, Alexandria, VA 22314-2561. Phone: (703) 299-6633. Fax: (703) 299-6004. E-mail: ncfa@adoptioncouncil.org. Web: www.adoptioncouncil .org.

★**NATIONAL ADOPTION MONTH.** Nov 1–30.

NATIONAL AIDS AWARENESS MONTH. Nov 1–30. To educate consumers, patients, students and professionals on the prevention of AIDS and sexually transmitted diseases. Kit of materials available for $15. For info: Frederick Mayer, Pres, Pharmacists Planning Service, Inc, 101 Lucas Valley Rd, #210, San Rafael, CA 94903. Phone: (415) 479-8628. Fax: (415) 479-8608. E-mail: ppsi@aol.com. Web: www.ppsinc.org.

NATIONAL ALZHEIMER'S DISEASE MONTH. Nov 1–30. To increase awareness of Alzheimer's disease and what the Alzheimer's Association is doing to advance research and help patients, their families and their caregivers. For info: Alzheimer's Assn, 225 N Michigan, 17th Fl, Chicago, IL 60601. Phone: (312) 335-8700. Fax: (312) 335-1110. E-mail: info@alz.org. Web: www .alz.org.

★**NATIONAL AMERICAN INDIAN HERITAGE MONTH.** Nov 1–30.

NATIONAL ASSOCIATION FOR GIFTED CHILDREN CONVENTION. Nov 1–5. Charlotte Convention Center, Charlotte, NC. Educational sessions for administrators, counselors, coordinators, teachers and parents. Est attendance: 4,000. For info: Natl Assn for Gifted Children, 1707 L St NW, Ste 550, Washington, DC 20036. Phone: (202) 785-4268. Fax: (202) 785-4248. E-mail: nagc@nagc.org. Web: www.nagc.org.

NATIONAL AUTHORS' DAY. Nov 1. This observance was adopted by the General Federation of Women's Clubs in 1929 and in 1949 was given a place on the list of special days, weeks and months prepared by the US Dept of Commerce. The resolution states: "by celebrating an Authors' Day as a nation, we would not only show patriotism, loyalty, and appreciation of the men and women who have made American literature possible, but would also encourage and inspire others to give of themselves in making a better America. . . ." It was also resolved "that we commemorate an Authors' Day to be observed on November First each year."

NATIONAL COPD AWARENESS MONTH. Nov 1–30. Established by EFFORTS (Emphysema Foundation for Our Right to Survive) to raise public awareness about the prevalence of chronic obstructive pulmonary disease and the serious problems associated with the disease. Annually, the month of November. For info: Gary Bain, EFFORTS, Claycomo Plaza, 239 NE US Highway 69, Ste D, Claycomo, MO 64119. Phone: (816) 452-3132. Fax: (816) 413-0176. E-mail: 1efforts@emphysema.net. Web: www.emphysema.net.

NATIONAL FAMILY CAREGIVERS MONTH. Nov 1–30. A nationwide month of recognition for the millions of family caregivers. For info: Suzanne Geffen Mintz, Pres, Natl Family Caregivers Assn, 10400 Connecticut Ave, Ste 500, Kensington, MD 20895-3944. Phone: (800) 896-3650. Fax: (301) 942-2302. E-mail: info@thefamilycaregiver.org. Web: www.thefamilycaregiver .org.

★**NATIONAL FAMILY CAREGIVERS MONTH.** Nov 1–30. To honor family members who care for aging relatives or those with disabilities.

NATIONAL FAMILY LITERACY DAY®. Nov 1. Celebrated all over the country with special activities and events that showcase the importance of family literacy programs. Family literacy programs bring parents and children together in the classroom to learn and support each other in efforts to further their education and improve their life skills. Sponsored by the National Center for Family Literacy and Toyota. Annually, Nov 1. For info: Natl Center for Family Literacy, 325 W Main St, Ste 300, Louisville, KY 40202. Phone: (502) 584-1133 or (877) FAMLIT 1. Fax: (502) 584-0172. E-mail: ncfl@famlit.org. Web: www.famlit.org.

NATIONAL FIG WEEK. Nov 1–7. To celebrate the completion of the California fig harvest and encourage consumers to use California figs as part of their diet for the taste, high fiber and nutritional value. For info: California Fig Advisory Board, 7395 N Palm Bluffs Ave, Ste 106, Fresno, CA 93711. Phone: (800) 588-2344. Fax: (559) 438-5405. E-mail: info@californiafigs.com. Web: www.californiafigs.com.

NATIONAL GEORGIA PECAN MONTH. Nov 1–30. To herald the Georgia pecan harvest and recognize Georgia's status as the nation's top pecan-producing state, providing 50 percent of the nation's supply. For info: Marcia Crowley, Georgia Agricultural Commodity Commission for Pecans (GACCP), Commodities Promotion Div, GA Dept of Agriculture, 328 Agriculture Bldg, Capitol Square, Atlanta, GA 30334. Phone: (404) 656-3678. Fax: (404) 656-9380.

NATIONAL HOSPICE MONTH. Nov 1–30. To promote greater awareness of hospice care and the advantages it offers; to educate physicians and other health care professionals about the concept of hospice; to honor patients and family members, as well as the thousands of dedicated professionals and volunteers who devote their time, love and support to the terminally ill and their families; and to educate public officials to ensure hospice care remains a key component in the health care delivery system. For info: Public Relations, Hospice Assn of America, 228 Seventh St SE, Washington, DC 20003. Phone: (202) 546-4759. Fax: (202) 547-3540. Web: www.nahc.org/.

NATIONAL INSPIRATIONAL ROLE MODELS MONTH. Nov 1–30. To acknowledge the impact contemporary and historic role models have on our lives. Individuals chosen for recognition may include celebrities, historic figures, relatives, friends, colleagues, associates, etc. Celebrate with creative projects and activities featuring historic role models and by spending time with contemporary role models. For info: Darlene House, House of Communications, PO Box 23598, Detroit, MI 48223. Phone: (313) 255-6274. Web: www.houseofcommunications.com.

NATIONAL LIFEWRITING MONTH. Nov 1–30. An opportunity to celebrate ourselves and our families by committing our life stories to writing. Preserving our autobiographies in writing allows us to know ourselves better and to share our stories with future generations. For info: Soleil Lifestory Network, 95 Gould Rd, #33, Lisbon Falls, ME 04252. Phone: (207) 353-5454. E-mail: lifewritingmonth@turningmemories.com.

NATIONAL MARROW AWARENESS MONTH. Nov 1–30. More than 30,000 Americans are diagnosed each year with leukemia or another life-threatening blood disease for which a bone marrow or blood stem cell transplant offers hope for survival. The National Marrow Donor Program maintains a computerized registry of nearly 4,000,000 volunteer donors. For info: Natl Marrow Donor Program, 3001 Broadway St NE, Ste 500, Minneapolis, MN 55413-2197. Phone: (800) MAR-ROW2. Web: www.marrow.org.

NATIONAL POMEGRANATE MONTH. Nov 1–30. Fresh pomegranates are one of the few fruits that are seasonal—and their season coincides with the festive season! Grown in California, pomegranates are only available from October through January. This month, celebrate them in eating, snacking and decorating. For info: Fiona Posell, POM Wonderful, LLC, 11444 W Olympic Blvd, Los Angeles, CA 90064. Phone: (310) 966-5800. E-mail: pr@pomwonderful.com. Web: www.pomwonderful.com.

NATIONAL ROASTING MONTH. Nov 1–30. From roasted leg of lamb to perfectly cooked roast beef, learn this tried-and-true method of cooking in your own oven. For info: Viking Culinary Arts Center/Viking Home Chef. Web: www.vikingculinary.com.

OZARK MOUNTAIN CHRISTMAS/BRANSON AREA FESTIVAL OF LIGHTS. Nov 1–Dec 31. Branson, MO. A tradition for more than 1.4 million visitors, who relish the opportunity to celebrate a traditional Christmas ambiance with a dash of dazzle as only Branson can offer. The area is illuminated in twinkling lights, special holiday events and shows galore. For info: Branson Area CVB, PO Box 1897, Branson, MO 65615. Phone: (888) 886-3637. Fax: (417) 334-4139. E-mail: info@bransoncvb.com. Web: www.explorebranson.com.

PEANUT BUTTER LOVERS' MONTH. Nov 1–30. Celebration of America's favorite food and #1 sandwich. For info: Peanut Advisory Board, 1025 Sugar Pike Way, Canton, GA 30115. Web: www.peanutbutterlovers.com.

PREMATURITY AWARENESS MONTH. Nov 1–30. Sponsored by the March of Dimes to alert Americans to the common, serious and costly problem of premature birth (before 37 weeks). One in eight babies is born prematurely in this country, many without warning and with no known cause. Prematurity is the leading cause of newborn death (before the first month in life) and babies who do survive often face chronic health and developmental disabilities for the rest of their lives. For info: March of Dimes, 1275 Mamaroneck Ave, White Plains, NY 10605. Phone: (914) 997-4533. Fax: (914) 997-4585. Web: www.marchofdimes.com/prematurity.

PRESIDENT OCCUPIES THE WHITE HOUSE: ANNIVERSARY. Nov 1, 1800. Philadelphia had served as the nation's capital from 1790 to 1800. On Nov 1, 1800, President John Adams and his family moved into the newly completed White House, as Washington, DC, became the new capital.

PRIME MERIDIAN SET: ANNIVERSARY. Nov 1, 1884. Delegates from 25 nations met in October at Washington, DC, at the International Meridian Conference to set up time zones for the world. On this day the treaty adopted by the conference took effect, making Greenwich, England, the Prime Meridian (i.e., zero° longitude) and setting the International Date Line at 180° longitude in the Pacific. Every 15° of longitude equals one hour and there are 24 meridians. While some countries do not strictly observe this system (for example, while China stretches over five time zones, it is the same time everywhere in China), it has brought predictability and logic to time throughout the world.

SEABISCUIT DEFEATS WAR ADMIRAL: ANNIVERSARY. Nov 1, 1938. In a special match race at Pimlico, Seabiscuit, ridden by George Wolff, defeated favored War Admiral before a crowd of 40,000. Seabiscuit captured the winner-take-all purse of $15,000.

US VIRGIN ISLANDS: LIBERTY DAY. Nov 1. Officially "D. Hamilton Jackson Memorial Day," commemorating establishment of the first press in the Virgin Islands in 1915.

VEGAN MONTH. Nov 1–30. This outreach event encourages everyone to GO VEGAN! Vegans choose to neither eat nor use any animal products (eg, meat, poultry, seafood, dairy products, eggs, gelatin, leather, fur, etc). A growing number of caring, compassionate people are adopting this conscientious lifestyle. Primarily ethical reasons, but also health and environmental concerns, motivate them to GO VEGAN. For info: VEGANET,

November 2006	S	M	T	W	T	F	S
				1	2	3	4
	5	6	7	8	9	10	11
	12	13	14	15	16	17	18
	19	20	21	22	23	24	25
	26	27	28	29	30		

PO Box 3545, Washington, DC 20027-0045. Phone: (877) GO-VEGAN or (800) 280-8343.

WORLD COMMUNICATION WEEK. Nov 1-7. To stress the importance of communication among the more than six billion human beings in the world who speak more than 3,000 languages and to promote communication by means of the international language, Esperanto. For complete info, send $5 to cover expense of printing, handling and postage. Annually, the first seven days of November. For info: Dr. Stanley Drake, Pres Emeritus, Intl Society of Friendship & Good Will, 8592 Roswell Rd, Ste 251, Atlanta, GA 30350-1867. Phone: (678) 795-1362. E-mail: sjdrake@bellsouth.net. Web: www.friendshipandgoodwill.org.

BIRTHDAYS TODAY

Toni Collette, 34, actress (*The Sixth Sense, About a Boy, Muriel's Wedding*), born Sidney, New South Wales, Australia, Nov 1, 1972.

Larry Claxton Flynt, 64, publisher, born Magoffin County, KY, Nov 1, 1942.

James Jackson Kilpatrick, 86, journalist (conservative side of "60 Minutes" Point-Counterpoint segment), born Oklahoma City, OK, Nov 1, 1920.

Lyle Lovett, 49, country and western singer ("Cowboy Man"), born Klein, TX, Nov 1, 1957.

Jenny McCarthy, 34, model, actress ("Jenny"), born Chicago, IL, Nov 1, 1972.

Betsy Palmer, 80, actress ("I've Got a Secret," "Knots Landing," "Today"), born Patricia Bromek at East Chicago, IN, Nov 1, 1926.

Tim Pawlenty, 46, Governor of Minnesota (R), born St. Paul, MN, Nov 1, 1960.

Gary Jim Player, 71, golfer, born Johannesburg, South Africa, Nov 1, 1935.

Rachel Ticotin, 48, actress (*Total Recall, Natural Born Killers*), born the Bronx, NY, Nov 1, 1958.

Fernando Anguamea Valenzuela, 46, former baseball player, born Navojoa, Sonora, Mexico, Nov 1, 1960.

NOVEMBER 2 — THURSDAY
Day 306 — 59 Remaining

ALL SOULS' DAY. Nov 2. Commemorates the faithful departed. Catholic observance.

BIG TEN WOMEN'S SOCCER TOURNAMENT. Nov 2-5. University of Iowa, Iowa City, IA. Est attendance: 1,000. For info: Big Ten Conference, 1500 W Higgins Rd, Park Ridge, IL 60068-6300. Phone: (847) 696-1010. Fax: (847) 696-1110. Web: www.bigten.org.

BOONE, DANIEL: BIRTH ANNIVERSARY. Nov 2, 1734 (NS). American frontiersman, explorer and militia officer, born at Berks County, near Reading, PA. In February 1778, he was captured at Blue Licks, KY, by Shawnee Indians, under Chief Blackfish, who adopted Boone when he was inducted into the tribe as "Big Turtle." Boone escaped after five months, and in 1781 was captured briefly by the British. He experienced a series of personal and financial disasters during his life, but continued a rugged existence, hunting until his 80s. Boone died at St. Charles County, MO, Sept 26, 1820. The bodies of Daniel Boone and his wife, Rebecca, were moved to Frankfort, KY, in 1845.

FIRST SCHEDULED RADIO BROADCAST: ANNIVERSARY. Nov 2, 1920. Station KDKA at Pittsburgh, PA, broadcast the results of the presidential election. The station got its license to broadcast Nov 7, 1921. By 1922 there were about 400 licensed radio stations in the US.

HARDING, WARREN GAMALIEL: BIRTH ANNIVERSARY. Nov 2, 1865. Twenty-ninth president of the US was born at Corsica, OH. His term of office: Mar 4, 1921–Aug 2, 1923 (died in office). His undistinguished administration was tainted by the Teapot Dome scandal, and his sudden death in San Francisco, CA, while on a western speaking tour prompted many rumors.

LANCASTER, BURT: BIRTH ANNIVERSARY. Nov 2, 1913. Distinguished American actor, born Burton Stephen Lan-

caster, who began his career in show business as a circus acrobat. In a career spanning 45 years, he appeared in nearly 80 films. Some of his more memorable roles are in *From Here to Eternity* (1953), *The Bird Man of Alcatraz* (1962) and *The Leopard* (1963); he received an Academy Award for his performance in the title role of *Elmer Gantry* (1961). Some of his later popular movies include *Atlantic City* (1981), *Local Hero* (1983) and *Field of Dreams* (1989). Born at New York City, he died Oct 20, 1994, at Los Angeles.

NATIONAL MEN MAKE DINNER DAY. Nov 2. One day set aside for "Non-Cooking Men Only" in the kitchen. Give wives a break and let the men whip up some culinary delight with no help from family members. In the true spirit of Men Make Dinner Day, barbecues are not allowed! For info: Sandy Sharkey, 939 BOB-FM Radio, 87 George St, Ottawa, ON, Canada K1N 9H7. Phone: (613) 738-2372. Fax: (613) 739-4040. E-mail: ssharkey@939bobfm.com. Web: www.menmakedinnerday.com.

NATIONAL TRAFFIC DIRECTORS DAY. Nov 2. A day honoring radio and TV traffic departments, who schedule programs and announcements on the nation's broadcast stations. For info: Traffic Directors Guild of America, 26000 Avenida Aeropuerto, #114, San Juan Capistrano, CA 92675. Phone: (949) 429-7063. Fax: (509) 471-5765. E-mail: tdga@earthlink.net. Web: www.tdga.org.

NEW YORK SUBWAY ACCIDENT: ANNIVERSARY. Nov 2, 1918. The Brighton Beach Express, exceeding its speed limit five times over (going 30 mph) while approaching the station near Malbone Street tunnel at Brooklyn, jumped the tracks, killing 97 people and injuring 100. The supervisor-engineer, taking the place of a striking motorman of the Brotherhood of Locomotive Engineers, was tried and acquitted of charges of negligence.

NORTH DAKOTA: ADMISSION DAY: ANNIVERSARY. Nov 2. Became 39th state in 1889.

PLAN YOUR EPITAPH DAY. Nov 2. Dedicated to the proposition that a forgettable gravestone is a fate worse than death, and that everyone can be in the same league with William Shakespeare and W.C. Fields. Annually, coincides with the Day of the Dead. For info: Lance Hardie, Dead or Alive, PO Box 4595, Arcata, CA 95518. Phone: (707) 822-6924. E-mail: sunrise@hardiehouse.org. Web: www.hardiehouse.org/epitaph.

POLK, JAMES KNOX: BIRTH ANNIVERSARY. Nov 2, 1795. The 11th president of the US was born at Mecklenburg County, NC. His term of office: Mar 4, 1845–Mar 3, 1849. A compromise candidate at the 1844 Democratic Party convention, Polk was awarded the nomination on the ninth ballot. He declined to be a candidate for a second term and declared himself to be "exceedingly relieved" at the completion of his presidency. He died shortly thereafter at Nashville, TN, June 15, 1849.

SENECA FALLS CONVENTION SURVIVOR VOTES: ANNIVERSARY. Nov 2, 1920. The only woman who attended the historic Seneca Falls Women's Rights Convention in 1848 who lived long enough to exercise her right to vote under the 19th Amendment, Charlotte Woodward voted at Philadelphia in the general election Nov 2, 1920.

SOUTH DAKOTA: ADMISSION DAY: ANNIVERSARY. Nov 2. Became 40th state in 1889.

SPACE MILESTONE: INTERNATIONAL SPACE STATION INHABITED. Nov 2, 2000. On Oct 31, 2000, a *Soyuz* shuttle left with the first crew to live in the International Space Station, consisting of American commander Bill Shepherd and two Russians cosmonauts. The flight left from the same site in Central Asia where *Sputnik* was launched in 1957, beginning the Space Age. The astronauts stayed on board the International Space Station (ISS) until March 2001, when they were replaced by a crew that arrived on the shuttle *Discovery*. Sixteen nations are participating in the ISS project. The construction of the station will be complete in 2006.

SPRUCE GOOSE FLIGHT: ANNIVERSARY. Nov 2, 1947. The mammoth flying boat *Hercules*, then the world's largest airplane, was designed, built and flown (once) by Howard Hughes. Its first and only flight was about one mile and at an altitude of 70 feet over Long Beach Harbor, CA. The $25 million, 200-ton plywood craft was nicknamed the "Spruce Goose." It is now displayed at the Evergreen Aviation Museum in McMinnville, OR.

VIRGINIA CHRISTMAS SHOW. Nov 2–5. Showplace Exhibition Center and Annex, Richmond, VA. 21st annual show featuring 450 artisans and crafters, Christmas gourmet food shops and Christmas Holiday Theatre, entertainment, legendary "Sgt Santa." Est attendance: 40,000. For info: Virginia Show Productions, PO Box 305, Chase City, VA 23924. Phone: (434) 372-3996. Fax: (434) 372-3410. E-mail: vashowsinc@aol.com.

BIRTHDAYS TODAY

Patrick Buchanan, 68, political commentator, born Washington, DC, Nov 2, 1938.

Shere Hite, 64, author (*The Hite Report, Women and Love*), born St. Joseph, MO, Nov 2, 1942.

k.d. lang, 45, singer, born Kathryn Dawn Lang at Consort, AB, Canada, Nov 2, 1961.

Stefanie Powers, 64, actress ("Hart to Hart"), born Hollywood, CA, Nov 2, 1942.

David Knapp (Dave) Stockton, 65, golfer, born San Bernardino, CA, Nov 2, 1941.

NOVEMBER 3 — FRIDAY
Day 307 — 58 Remaining

AUSTIN, STEPHEN FULLER: BIRTH ANNIVERSARY. Nov 3, 1793. A principal founder of Texas, for whom its capital city was named, Austin was born at Wythe County, VA. He first visited Texas in 1821 and established a settlement there the following year, continuing a colonization project started by his father, Moses Austin. Thrown in prison when he advocated formation of a separate state (Texas still belonged to Mexico), he was freed in 1835, lost a campaign for the presidency (of the Republic of Texas) to Sam Houston (q.v.) in 1836 and died (while serving as Texas secretary of state) at Austin, TX, Dec 27, 1836.

BIG TEN FIELD HOCKEY TOURNAMENT. Nov 3–5. University of Michigan, Ann Arbor, MI. Est attendance: 1,000. For info: Big Ten Conference, 1500 W Higgins Rd, Park Ridge, IL 60068-6300. Phone: (847) 696-1010. Fax: (847) 696-1110. Web: www.bigten.org.

BRONSON, CHARLES: BIRTH ANNIVERSARY. Nov 3, 1921. Movie tough guy Charles Bronson was born Charles Buchinsky at Ehrenfeld, PA. One of 15 children, he was raised in poverty and was working in the coal mines by age 16. He discovered acting after a stint in the army and was soon making low-budget films, usually violent. His best-known films included *The Magnificent Seven* (1960), *The Great Escape* (1963), *Death Wish* (1974) and four *Death Wish* sequels. He died at Los Angeles, CA, Sept 6, 2003.

BRYANT, WILLIAM CULLEN: BIRTH ANNIVERSARY. Nov 3, 1794. American poet (*Thanatopsis*), born at Cummington, MA. Died at New York, NY, June 12, 1878.

CANADA: BANFF MOUNTAIN FILM FESTIVAL. Nov 3–5. Banff, AB. The 31st annual festival brings the best films and videos on mountain subjects to the town of Banff. The weekend's activities, which take place at The Banff Centre, include continuous film screenings, guest speakers, public forums on mountain issues, a climbing wall, adventure fair, trade fair and a mountain art and craft sale. Presented by National Geographic and Dunham Bootmakers. Est attendance: 8,000. For info: Sharlene Mentanko, Marketing Officer, Mountain Film Festival, PO Box 1020, Station 38, Banff, AB, Canada T1L 1H5. Phone: (403) 762-6446. Fax: (403) 762-6277. E-mail: mountainculture@banffcentre.ca. Web: www.banffmountainfestivals.ca.

CANADA: NEW INUIT TERRITORY APPROVED: ANNIVERSARY. Nov 3, 1992. Canada's Inuit people voted to accept a federal land-claim package granting them control over a new territory, Nunavut, to be carved out of the existing Northwest Territories by 1999. The voting on Nov 3–5, 1992, indicated that 69 percent of the 9,648 eligible Inuit voters accepted the settlement. In exchange for the new territory, approximately 135,000 square miles, the Inuits gave up their rights to a territory of 775,000 square miles. See also: "Canada: Nunavut Independence" (Apr 1).

CHRISTMAS MAGIC. Nov 3–5. Multi-Purpose Events Center, Wichita Falls, TX. "A Christmas marketplace," with vendors from Texas and other states. Food, gift items, arts and crafts, entertainment. Est attendance: 10,000. For info: Wichita Falls CVB, 1000 5th St, Wichita Falls, TX 76301. Phone: (940) 716-5500 or (800) 799-6732. Fax: (940) 716-5509. E-mail: MPEC@wf.net. Web: www.wichitafalls.org.

CLICHÉ DAY. Nov 3. Use clichés as much as possible today. Hey, why not? Give it a shot! Win some, lose some. You'll never know 'til you try it. Annually, Nov 3. [©2003 by WH.] For info: Thomas & Ruth Roy, Wellcat Holidays, 2418 Long Ln, Lebanon, PA 17046-1708. Phone: (717) 279-0184. E-mail: info@wellcat.com. Web: www.wellcat.com.

COLORADO COUNTRY CHRISTMAS HOLIDAY GIFT SHOW. Nov 3–5. Denver Merchandise Mart, Denver, CO. More than 400 booths of holiday gifts. Exhibitors from 25 states participate. Event includes local entertainment and free child care by Kindercare. Free parking. Annually, the first weekend in November. Est attendance: 25,000. For info: Susie O'Brien Borer, Showcase Events, PO Box 2815, Kirkland, WA 98083. Phone: (800) 521-7469. Fax: (425) 889-8165. E-mail: denver@showcaseevents.org. Web: www.showcaseevents.org or www.holidaygiftshows.com.

CRAFTSMEN'S CHRISTMAS CLASSIC ARTS & CRAFTS FESTIVAL. Nov 3–5. Richmond Raceway Complex, Richmond, VA. 27th annual. Features work from more than 500 talented artists and craftspeople. All juried exhibitors' work has been handmade by the exhibitors and must be their own original design and creation. See the creative process in action with several exhibitors demonstrating throughout the weekend. Visit Christmas Tree Village to view the uniquely decorated Christmas trees by some of our exhibitors. Something for every style, taste and budget with items from the most contemporary to the most traditional. Est attendance: 35,000. For info: Gilmore Enterprises Inc, 1240 Oakland Ave, Greensboro, NC 27403. Phone: (336) 274-5550. E-mail: gilmoreshows@triad.rr.com. Web: www.CraftShow.com or www.gilmoreshows.com.

"DEWEY DEFEATS TRUMAN" HEADLINE: ANNIVERSARY. Nov 3, 1948. This headline in the *Chicago Tribune* notwithstanding, Harry Truman defeated Republican candidate Thomas E. Dewey for the US presidency.

November 2006	S	M	T	W	T	F	S
				1	2	3	4
	5	6	7	8	9	10	11
	12	13	14	15	16	17	18
	19	20	21	22	23	24	25
	26	27	28	29	30		

DOMINICA: NATIONAL DAY: ANNIVERSARY. Nov 3. National holiday. Commemorates independence from Britain in 1978.

GUMBO FESTIVAL. Nov 3–5 (tentative). Bridge City, LA. To promote Cajun-French culture and provide the opportunity for people from everywhere to enjoy continuous Cajun entertainment on an outdoor stage and cuisine. Gumbo cooking contests and 5k Bridge Run. Est attendance: 150,000. For info: Rev Msgr J. Anthony Luminais, Pastor, Holy Guardian Angels Church, Box 9069, Bridge City, LA 70096. Phone: (504) 436-4712. Fax: (504) 436-4070. E-mail: gumbofestival@aol.com.

HOLIDAY MARKET. Nov 3–5. Greensboro Coliseum Complex Special Events Center, Greensboro, NC. 16th annual commercial holiday gift show. Celebrate the season at Holiday Market, a true feast for all the senses. Of course there is shopping with a capital SHOP! Enjoy the singing of the Victorian-costumed strolling carolers and let the children visit with Santa. You'll come away with ideas, recipes, samples, beauty makeovers and lots of holiday gifts and ideas. Est attendance: 25,000. For info: Gilmore Enterprises, Inc, 1240 Oakland Ave, Greensboro, NC 27403. Phone: (336) 274-5550. E-mail: gilmoreshows@triad.rr.com. Web: www.gilmoreshows.com or www.CraftShow.com.

JAPAN: CULTURE DAY. Nov 3. National holiday.

MICRONESIA, FEDERATED STATES OF: INDEPENDENCE DAY. Nov 3. National holiday commemorating independence from US in 1980.

NAGURSKI, BRONKO: BIRTH ANNIVERSARY. Nov 3, 1908. Bronislau ("Bronko") Nagurski, College Football Hall of Fame and charter member of the Pro Football Hall of Fame. Born at Rainy River, ON, Canada, he played football at the University of Minnesota, earning All-American honors at both tackle and fullback, and for the Chicago Bears. After retiring from football, Nagurski wrestled professionally. He died at International Falls, MN, Jan 7, 1990.

NATIONAL FARM TOY SHOW. Nov 3–5. Beckman HS, National Farm Toy Museum and The Commercial Club Park, Dyersville, IA. This "granddaddy" of farm toy shows features tours of farm toy manufacturers, auction, craft bazaar, pedal pull and more than 400 vendors dealing in farm toys and implements. Annually, the first full weekend in November. Est attendance: 15,000. For info: Dyersville Area Chamber of Commerce, 1100 16th Ave Ct SE, Dyersville, IA 52040. Phone: (563) 875-2311. Fax: (563) 875-8391. E-mail: dyersvillechamber@dyersville.org. Web: www.dyersville.org.

PACIFIC DANCESPORT CHAMPIONSHIPS. Nov 3–5. Los Angeles, CA. Launched in 1990, the Pacific DanceSport Championships, which is a part of the DanceSport Super Bowl Series, captures the best that ballroom has to offer. It is now considered one of the most prestigious and largest ballroom dance events west of the Mississippi. Competitors arrive from around the world to vie for a $100,000 purse. For info: A. Marashi, Pacific DanceSport Championships, 924 Bellevue Way NE, Ste 200, Bellevue, WA 98004. Phone: (425) 688-1010 or (877) 553-5735. Fax: (425) 688-7484. E-mail: info@pacificdancesport.com. Web: www.pacificdancesport.com.

PANAMA: INDEPENDENCE DAY: ANNIVERSARY. Nov 3. Independence Day. Panama declared itself independent of Colombia in 1903.

PUBLIC TELEVISION DEBUTS: ANNIVERSARY. Nov 3, 1969. A string of local educational TV channels united on this day under the Public Broadcasting System banner. Today there are more than 350 PBS stations.

SAMOA: ARBOR DAY. Nov 3. The first Friday in November is observed as Arbor Day in Samoa (formerly Western Samoa).

SANDWICH DAY: BIRTH ANNIVERSARY OF JOHN MONTAGUE. Nov 3, 1718. A day to recognize the inventor of the sandwich, John Montague, Fourth Earl of Sandwich, born at London, England. England's first lord of the admiralty, secretary of state for the northern department, postmaster general and the man after whom Captain Cook named the Sandwich Islands in 1778. A rake and a gambler, he is said to have invented the sandwich as a time-saving nourishment while engaged in a 24-hour-long gambling session in 1762. He died at London, England, Apr 30, 1792.

SOS ADOPTED: 100th ANNIVERSARY. Nov 3, 1906. Today the Second International Radio Telegraphic Conference at Berlin, Germany, proposed a new wireless distress signal: SOS. After its use during the sinking of the *Titanic* in 1912, SOS became the standard distress signal at sea.

SPACE MILESTONE: *SPUTNIK 2* (USSR). Nov 3, 1957. A dog named Laika became the first animal sent into space. Total weight of craft and dog was 1,121 lbs. The satellite was not capable of returning the dog to Earth and she died when her air supply was gone. Nicknamed "Muttnik" by the American press.

SUGARLOAF CRAFTS FESTIVAL. Nov 3–5. Meadowlands Exposition Center, Secaucus, NJ. This new show features more than 300 nationally recognized craft designers and fine artists displaying and selling their original creations. Includes craft demonstrations, live music, specialty foods, hourly gift certificate drawings and more. Est attendance: 20,000. For info: Sugarloaf Mountain Works, 200 Orchard Ridge Dr, #215, Gaithersburg, MD 20878. Phone: (800) 210-9900. Fax: (301) 253-9620. Web: www.sugarloafcrafts.com.

WALSH INVITATIONAL RIFLE TOURNAMENT. Nov 3–5 (also Nov 10–12 and 17–18). Xavier University, Cincinnati, OH. To promote marksmanship and sportsmanship in the competitive spirit of collegiate athletics. International air rifle match open to all competitors. Recognized as "the largest indoor rifle match in the nation." Sponsor: Xavier University Athletic Department. Est attendance: 300. For info: Pete Holterman, Office of Sports Info, Dept of Athletics, Xavier Univ, 3800 Victory Pkwy, Cincinnati, OH 45207-7530. Fax: (513) 745-2825.

WHITE, EDWARD DOUGLASS: BIRTH ANNIVERSARY. Nov 3, 1845. Ninth Chief Justice of the Supreme Court, born at La Fourche Parish, LA. During the Civil War, he served in the Confederate Army after which he returned to New Orleans to practice law. Elected to the US Senate in 1891, he was appointed to the Supreme Court by Grover Cleveland in 1894. He became Chief Justice under President William Taft in 1910 and served until 1921. He died at Washington, DC, May 19, 1921.

BIRTHDAYS TODAY

Adam Ant, 52, singer ("Goody Two Shoes"), born Stewart Goddard at London, England, Nov 3, 1954.

Ken Berry, 73, actor ("F Troop," "Mayberry RFD," "Mama's Family"), singer, dancer, born Moline, IL, Nov 3, 1933.

Kate Capshaw, 53, actress ("Duke of Groove," *How to Make an American Quilt*), born Fort Worth, TX, Nov 3, 1953.

Michael S. Dukakis, 73, former Governor of Massachusetts (D), 1988 presidential candidate, born Brookline, MA, Nov 3, 1933.

Robert William Andrew (Bob) Feller, 88, Hall of Fame baseball player, born Van Meter, IA, Nov 3, 1918.

Kathy Kinney, 52, actress ("The Drew Carey Show"), born Stevens Point, WI, Nov 3, 1954.

Steve Landesberg, 61, actor ("Barney Miller," "Friends and Lovers"), born the Bronx, NY, Nov 3, 1945.

Dolph Lundgren, 47, actor (*A View to a Kill, Rocky IV*), born Stockholm, Sweden, Nov 3, 1959.

Dennis Miller, 53, comedian, actor ("Saturday Night Live," "The Dennis Miller Show"), born Pittsburgh, PA, Nov 3, 1953.

Evgeny Plushenko, 24, figure skater, born Vologograd, Russia, Nov 3, 1982.

Roseanne, 53, comedienne, actress ("Roseanne," *She-Devil*), born Roseanne Barr at Salt Lake City, UT, Nov 3, 1953.

Philip (Phil) Simms, 50, sportscaster, former football player, born Lebanon, KY, Nov 3, 1956.

Monica Vitti, 73, actress (*The Red Desert*), born Monica Luisa Ceciarelli at Rome, Italy, Nov 3, 1933.

NOVEMBER 4 — SATURDAY

Day 308 — 57 Remaining

APPLE FESTIVAL. Nov 4–5. Peddler's Village, Lahaska, PA. Craftspeople gather to show their wares and demonstrate their skills. Enjoy country apple butter, cider, fritters and dumplings. Live entertainment and pie-eating contests add to the festivities of this traditional fall celebration. Free admission. For info: Andrea Wheatley, Peddler's Village, Rtes 202 & 263, PO Box 218, Lahaska, PA 18931. Phone: (215) 794-4000. Fax: (215) 794-4001. E-mail: awheatley@peddlersvillage.com. Web: www.peddlersvillage.com.

BREEDERS' CUP WORLD THOROUGHBRED CHAMPIONSHIPS. Nov 4 (subject to change). Churchill Downs, Louisville, KY. Since 1982, the Breeders' Cup World Thoroughbred Championships has brought together the world's best horses to compete in eight sensational races. The Breeders' Cup culminates the racing season and crowns the fleetest sprinters, the most promising two-year-olds, the best turf horses. The right to be called the best of the best belongs to the winner of the day's final and richest race: the $4 million Breeders' Cup Classic. For info: Breeders' Cup Limited, PO Box 4230, Lexington, KY 40544-4230. Phone: (859) 223-5444. Fax: (859) 223-3945. E-mail: breederscup@breederscup.com. Web: www.breederscup.com.

BUSH, LAURA: 60th BIRTHDAY. Nov 4, 1946. First Lady, wife of President George W. Bush, born Laura Welch at Midland, TX.

CARNEY, ART: BIRTH ANNIVERSARY. Nov 4, 1918. Born at Mount Vernon, NY, this comedian and actor got his start on the vaudeville circuit. He appeared in dozens of Broadway shows and feature films, winning the Oscar for *Harry and Tonto* in 1974, but will always be best remembered for his role of sewer worker Ed Norton on the television classic "The Honeymooners." He played Jackie Gleason's upstairs neighbor on this show for many years, winning six Emmys. He died at Chester, CT, Nov 9, 2003.

DOWNTOWN FESTIVAL AND ART SHOW. Nov 4–5. Downtown Gainesville, FL. 25th annual. 250 fine artists display one-of-a-kind art for purchase. Two full days of live music on three stages, with children's activity area and food vendors. Blues music on Friday night and jazz music on Saturday night. Est attendance: 115,000. For info: Linda Piper, City of Gainesville, Dept of Cultural Affairs, PO Box 490, Gainesville, FL 32602. Phone: (352) 334-5064. Fax: (352) 334-2249. E-mail: piperLr@cityofgainesville.org. Web: www.gvlculturalaffairs.org.

★ ★ ★

	S	M	T	W	T	F	S
November				1	2	3	4
2006	5	6	7	8	9	10	11
	12	13	14	15	16	17	18
	19	20	21	22	23	24	25
	26	27	28	29	30		

FALL COUNTRY JAMBOREE. Nov 4–5. Pioneer Settlement for the Creative Arts, Barberville, FL. A celebration of pioneer life and food. More than 100 demonstrating crafters and tradespeople, three continuous musical stages featuring more than 75 noted artists. Historical displays include Indian and Cracker camps, antique autos, flywheelers and model railroaders. Annually, the first Saturday and Sunday in November. Est attendance: 20,000. For info: Pioneer Settlement for the Creative Arts, PO Box 6, Barberville, FL 32105. Phone: (386) 749-2959. E-mail: pioneersettle@bellsouth.net.

GREAT NY STATE SNOW & TRAVEL EXPO. Nov 4–6. Empire State Plaza, Albany, NY. Top-of-the-line equipment, apparel and destinations for the outdoor winter sports enthusiast. Annually, the first full weekend in November. Sponsor: Alpine Haus. Est attendance: 20,000. For info: Cate Masterson, Ed Lewi Associates, 6 Chelsea Pl, Clifton Park, NY 12065. Phone: (518) 383-6183. Fax: (518) 383-6755. E-mail: cmasterson@edlewi.com. Web: www.edlewi.com.

ITALY: VICTORY DAY. Nov 4. Commemorates the signing of a WWI treaty by Austria in 1918, which resulted in the transfer of Trentino and Trieste from Austria to Italy.

KING TUT TOMB DISCOVERY: ANNIVERSARY. Nov 4, 1922. In 1922, one of the most important archaeological discoveries of modern times occurred at Luxor, Egypt. It was the tomb of Egypt's child-king, Tutankhamen, who became pharaoh at the age of nine and died, probably in the year 1352 BC, when he was 19. Perhaps the only ancient Egyptian royal tomb to have escaped plundering by grave robbers, it was discovered more than 3,000 years after Tutankhamen's death by English archaeologist Howard Carter, leader of an expedition financed by Lord Carnarvon. The priceless relics yielded by King Tut's tomb were placed in Egypt's National Museum at Cairo.

LOVINGTON FALL ARTS AND CRAFTS FESTIVAL. Nov 4–5. Lea County Fairgrounds, Lovington, NM. 29th annual. Displays from more than 100 local and regional crafters. No commercially manufactured items allowed. Annually, the first weekend in November. Est attendance: 10,000. For info: Lovington Chamber of Commerce, 201 S Main St, Lovington, NM 88260. Phone: (505) 396-5311. Fax: (505) 396-2823. E-mail: lchamber@valornet.com. Web: www.lovington.net.

MAPPLETHORPE, ROBERT: BIRTH ANNIVERSARY. Nov 4, 1946. Born at Floral Park, NY, Mapplethorpe was one of photography's most controversial artists, known initially for his photographs of sadomasochistic rituals and later for his still lifes, nudes and portraits. Mapplethorpe died at Boston, Mar 9, 1989. Exhibits of his work sparked controversy in 1989 and 1990, leading to intense political debate about the funding practices of the National Endowment for the Arts when its charter was up for renewal by Congress. An exhibition of his work in Cincinnati led to the arrest of the museum's curator, causing an additional uproar over First Amendment freedoms and obscenity issues.

MISCHIEF NIGHT. Nov 4. Observed in England, Australia and New Zealand. Nov 4, the eve of Guy Fawkes Day, is occasion for bonfires and firecrackers to commemorate failure of the plot to blow up the Houses of Parliament Nov 5, 1605. See also: "England: Guy Fawkes Day" (Nov 5).

NATIONAL CHICKEN LADY DAY. Nov 4. Miami Shores, FL. The Chicken Lady has helped thousands to learn the art of public speaking through her nonprofit organization The Professional Speakers Network, Inc. Each year as a thank-you, people come out and have a celebration to show their appreciation for what she has done to help them. Fifty-three of them, thanks to the Chicken Lady, have published their own books. For info: Dr. Marthenia "Tina" Dupree, The Chicken Lady, PO Box 9906, Fort Lauderdale, FL 33310. Phone: (866) SPEAK-2U or (954) 485-5100. E-mail: chickenlady@prodigy.net. Web: www.thechickenlady.com.

NATIONAL TRAIL RIDE GATHERING. Nov 4–8. Live Oak, FL. Dust off your boots and be prepared for a grand time including daily trail rides, auctions, dances and much more! For info: Spirit of the Suwannee Music Park, 3076 95th Dr, Live Oak, FL 32060. Phone: (386) 364-1683. Fax: (386) 364-2998. E-mail: spirit@musicliveshere.com. Web: www.musicliveshere.com.

PANAMA: FLAG DAY. Nov 4. Public holiday.

ROGERS, WILL: BIRTH ANNIVERSARY. Nov 4, 1879. William Penn Adair Rogers, American writer, actor, humorist and grassroots philosopher, born at Oologah, Indian Territory (now Oklahoma). With aviator Wiley Post, he was killed in an airplane crash near Point Barrow, AK, Aug 15, 1935. "My forefathers," he said, "didn't come over on the *Mayflower*, but they met the boat."

SADIE HAWKINS DAY. Nov 4. Widely observed in US, usually on the first Saturday in November. Tradition established in "Li'l Abner" comic strip in 1930s by cartoonist Al Capp. A popular occasion when women and girls are encouraged to take the initiative in inviting the man or boy of their choice for a date. A similar tradition is associated with Feb 29 in leap years.

SEIZURE OF US EMBASSY IN TEHERAN: ANNIVERSARY. Nov 4, 1979. About 500 Iranians seized the US Embassy in Teheran, taking some 90 hostages, of whom about 60 were Americans. They vowed to hold the hostages until the former Shah, Mohammed Reza Pahlavi (in the US for medical treatments), was returned to Iran for trial. The Shah died July 27, 1980, in an Egyptian military hospital near Cairo. The remaining 52 American hostages were released and left Teheran on Jan 20, 1981, after 444 days of captivity. The release occurred on America's Presidential Inauguration Day, during the hour in which the American presidency was transferred from Jimmy Carter to Ronald Reagan.

STEEPLECHASE AT CALLAWAY GARDENS. Nov 4. Pine Mountain, GA. A six-race steeplechase "meet" where riders match their horses for speed and split-second timing over brush jumps. Box seating and infield tailgating spaces available. Est attendance: 10,000. For info: The Steeplechase at Callaway Gardens, PO Box 2311, Columbus, GA 31902. Phone: (706) 324-6252. Fax: (706) 324-3651. Web: www.steeplechaseatcallaway.org.

SWEDEN: ALL SAINTS' DAY. Nov 4. Honors the memory of deceased friends and relatives. Annually, the Saturday following Oct 30.

UNESCO: 60th ANNIVERSARY. Nov 4, 1946. The United Nations Educational, Scientific and Cultural Organization was formed.

VERBOORT SAUSAGE AND KRAUT DINNER. Nov 4. Visitation Parish, Forest Grove, OR. 72nd annual event features crafts, Bingo, raffles, beer garden, local produce, home-baked goods and, of course, famous Verboort sausage and kraut. Annually, the first Saturday in November. Est attendance: 8,000. For info: Visitation Parish, 4285 NW Visitation Rd, Forest Grove, OR 97116. Phone: (503) 357-6990. Web: www.verboort.org/dinner.

WILL ROGERS DAY. Nov 4. Oklahoma.

BIRTHDAYS TODAY

Laura Bush, 60, First Lady, wife of George W. Bush, 43rd president of the US, born Midland, TX, Nov 4, 1946.

Sean ("Puffy") Combs, 36, rapper known as Puff Daddy, born New York, NY, Nov 4, 1970.

Walter Leland Cronkite, Jr, 90, journalist (former anchor for "CBS Evening News"), born St. Joseph, MO, Nov 4, 1916.

Kathy Griffin, 40, comedienne, actress ("Suddenly Susan"), born Chicago, IL, Nov 4, 1966.

Carlos Gutierrez, 53, US Secretary of Commerce, born Havana, Cuba, Nov 4, 1953.

Ralph Macchio, 44, actor ("Eight Is Enough," *The Karate Kid*), born Huntington, NY, Nov 4, 1962.

Andrea McArdle, 43, singer, actress (Broadway's *Annie*), born Philadelphia, PA, Nov 4, 1963.

Matthew McConaughey, 37, actor (*Dazed and Confused, A Time to Kill*), born Uvalde, TX, Nov 4, 1969.

Orlando Pace, 31, football player, born Sandusky, OH, Nov 4, 1975.

Markie Post, 56, actress ("Night Court," "Hearts Afire"), born Palo Alto, CA, Nov 4, 1950.

Doris Roberts, 76, actress ("Everybody Loves Raymond," "Remington Steele"), born St. Louis, MO, Nov 4, 1930.

Loretta Swit, 69, actress ("M*A*S*H"), born Passaic, NJ, Nov 4, 1937.

NOVEMBER 5 — SUNDAY
Day 309 — 56 Remaining

BRANSON VETERANS HOMECOMING 2006. Nov 5–11. Branson, MO. An areawide celebration honoring America's veterans. Annually, the seven days in November ending with the 11th. Est attendance: 50,000. For info: Bill Groninger, Branson Veterans Task Force, PO Box 128, Branson, MO 65615. Phone: (417) 337-8387. E-mail: bvtf1@sofnet.com. Web: www.bransonveterans.com.

DEAR SANTA LETTER WEEK. Nov 5–9. Consumer advocate Bob O'Brien answers "Dear Santa" letters for the holiday season. For info: Bob O'Brien, Consumer Advocate, 1061 Koelle Blvd, Secaucus, NJ 07094. Phone/fax: (201) 860-4775. E-mail: bobtheebest@yahoo.com. Web: www.wtbq.com.

DEBS, EUGENE VICTOR: BIRTH ANNIVERSARY. Nov 5, 1855. American politician, first president of the American Railway Union, founder of the Social Democratic Party of America and Socialist Party candidate for president of the US in 1904, 1908, 1912 and 1920, sentenced to 10-year prison term in 1918 (for sedition) and pardoned by President Harding in 1921. Debs was born at Terre Haute, IN, and died at Elmhurst, IL, Oct 20, 1926.

DURANT, WILL: BIRTH ANNIVERSARY. Nov 5, 1885. American author and popularizer of history and philosophy. Among his books: *The Story of Philosophy* and *The Story of Civilization* (a 10-volume series of which the last four were coauthored by his wife, Ariel). Born at North Adams, MA, and died Nov 7, 1981, at Los Angeles, CA.

EL SALVADOR: DAY OF THE FIRST SHOUT FOR INDEPENDENCE. Nov 5. National holiday. Commemorates the first Central American battle for independence in 1811.

ENGLAND: GUY FAWKES DAY. Nov 5. United Kingdom. Anniversary of the "Gunpowder Plot." Conspirators planned to blow up the Houses of Parliament and King James I, Nov 5, 1605 (OS). Twenty barrels of gunpowder, which they had secreted in a cellar under Parliament, were discovered on the night of Nov 4, the very eve of the intended explosion, and the conspirators were arrested. They were tried and convicted, and Jan 31, 1606, eight (including Guy Fawkes) were beheaded and their heads displayed on pikes at London Bridge. Though there were at least 11 conspirators, Guy Fawkes is most remembered. In 1606, the Parliament, which was to have been annihilated, enacted a law establishing Nov 5 as a day of public thanksgiving. It is still observed, and on the night of Nov 5, "the whole country lights up with bonfires and celebration." "Guys" are burned in effigy and the old verses repeated: "Remember, remember the fifth of November,/Gunpowder treason and plot;/I see no reason why Gunpowder Treason/Should ever be forgot."

ENGLAND: LONDON TO BRIGHTON VETERAN CAR RUN. Nov 5. London. A 60-mile run for approximately 500 veteran cars, along the A23 road from Hyde Park, London, to Madeira Drive, Brighton. Only cars (three wheels or more) built before Dec 31, 1904, are eligible to participate. Celebrates the November 1896 English law raising the speed limit of "light locomotives" from 4 mph to 14 mph. Annually, the first Sunday in November. For info: Motion Works UK Ltd, 10 High St, Brackley, Northamptonshire, NN13 7DT England. Phone: (44) (1280) 841-062. Fax: (44) (1280) 841-067. E-mail: info@LBVCR.com. Web: www.LBVCR.com.

FIRST SHATTERED BACKBOARD: 60th ANNIVERSARY. Nov 5, 1946. Chuck Connors of the Boston Celtics became the first NBA player to shatter a backboard, doing so during the pregame warm-up in Boston Garden. Connors also played major league baseball with the Brooklyn Dodgers and the Chicago Cubs and gained fame as star of the television series "The Rifleman."

GEORGE W. AND LAURA BUSH WEDDING: ANNIVERSARY. Nov 5, 1977. George W. Bush and Laura Welch were married at Midland, TX. They have twin daughters, Barbara Pierce Bush and Jenna Welch Bush, born in 1981.

INDIA: GURU NANAK'S BIRTH ANNIVERSARY. Nov 5. According to the Hindu solar calendar, this is the birth anniversary of Guru Nanak, the founder of Sikhism.

INTERNATIONAL IRRIGATION SHOW. Nov 5–7. San Antonio, TX. The 27th annual conference and show is the largest collection of irrigation equipment and services under one roof. More than 300 exhibits display irrigation-related products and services for agriculture, golf courses and the landscape. Technical conference looks at emerging irrigation technology, and meetings bring together leaders in the irrigation industry to discuss relevant issues, including the latest, most efficient irrigation technology. Industry tours provide a close-up view of unique irrigation operations in the San Antonio area. Irrigation Association awards are presented at the annual Keynote Breakfast on Nov 7. Irrigation classes and certification exams are offered Nov 3–8. Est attendance: 6,000. For info: The Irrigation Association, 6540 Arlington Blvd, Falls Church, VA 22046. Phone: (703) 536-7080. Fax: (703) 536-7019. E-mail: news@irrigation.org. Web: www.irrigation.org.

LOEWY, RAYMOND: BIRTH ANNIVERSARY. Nov 5, 1893. Raymond Fernand Loewy, the "father of streamlining," an inventor, engineer and industrial designer whose ideas changed the look of 20th-century life, was born at Paris, France. His designs are evident in almost every area of modern life—the US Postal Service logo, the president's airplane, *Air Force One*, in streamlined automobiles, trains, refrigerators and pens. "Between two products equal in price, function and quality," he said, "the better looking will outsell the other." Loewy died at Monte Carlo, July 14, 1986.

MAXWELL, ROBERT: 15th DEATH ANNIVERSARY. Nov 5, 1991. Media mogul Robert Maxwell's mysterious death added more controversy to his already controversial and intriguing larger-than-life story. Born Jan Ludwig Hoch to a poor farm family in the Carpathian mountains of Czechoslovakia, he ended his life a billionaire with a media empire that included TV stations in France, Macmillan Publishing Company in the US, newspapers in Hungary and the former East Germany, MTV Europe, the only official English language newspaper in China and two of the biggest tabloids in the English-speaking world: New York's *Daily News* and London's *Daily Mirror*. He earned his first million publishing scientific books. After a brief career as a member of Parliament, he began his rise as a media baron. Maxwell died after falling overboard from his yacht near the Canary Islands. After his death, his empire was found to be in significant financial disrepair.

McCREA, JOEL: BIRTH ANNIVERSARY. Nov 5, 1905. American actor Joel McCrea was born at South Pasadena, CA. His more than 80 films include *Wells Fargo* (1937), *Union Pacific* (1939), *Sullivan's Travels* (1941) and *Foreign Correspondent* (1940). He died Oct 20, 1990, at Los Angeles, CA.

MOON PHASE: FULL MOON. Nov 5. Moon enters Full Moon phase at 7:58 AM, EST.

"THE NAT KING COLE SHOW" TV PREMIERE: 50th ANNIVERSARY. Nov 5, 1956. Popular African-American pianist and singer Cole hosted his own variety show for NBC. The Nelson Riddle Orchestra and the Randy Van Horne Singers also appeared as regulars on the show. It began as a 15-minute show, which was expanded to half an hour. The show was dropped as a result of lack of sponsorship and because many affiliates declined to carry it.

NATIONAL ANIMAL SHELTER APPRECIATION WEEK. Nov 5–11. This is a week to focus on and recognize the indispensable role that animal shelters play in maintaining the safety and health of a community, for all of its residents. Through celebration and promotion of the week, animal shelters and other humane organizations can educate the public about the important services they provide. It's also a great opportunity for individuals or groups to volunteer their time or resources to help the animal shelter care for the community's homeless and abused animals. For info: Humane Society of the US, 2100 L St NW, Washington, DC 20037. Phone: (202) 452-1100. E-mail: asi@hsus.org. Web: www.hsus.org/shelters.

NEW YORK CITY MARATHON. Nov 5. New York, NY. 37,000 runners from all over the world gather to compete with more than 2.5 million spectators watching from the sidelines. Sponsored by ING. For info: Phone: (212) 423-2249. Web: www.nycmarathon.org.

***NEW YORK WEEKLY JOURNAL* FIRST ISSUE: ANNIVERSARY.** Nov 5, 1733. John Peter Zenger, colonial American printer and journalist, published the first issue of the *New*

November 2006	S	M	T	W	T	F	S
				1	2	3	4
	5	6	7	8	9	10	11
	12	13	14	15	16	17	18
	19	20	21	22	23	24	25
	26	27	28	29	30		

York Weekly Journal newspaper. He was arrested and imprisoned on Nov 17, 1734, for libel. The trial remains an important landmark in the history of the struggle for freedom of the press. See also: "Zenger, John P.: Arrest Anniversary" (Nov 17).

ROGERS, ROY: BIRTH ANNIVERSARY. Nov 5, 1912. Known as the "King of the Cowboys," Rogers was born Leonard Slye at Cincinnati, OH. His many songs included "Don't Fence Me In" and "Happy Trails to You." He made his acting debut in *Under Western Stars* in 1935 and later hosted his own show, "The Roy Rogers Show," in 1951. Rogers died at Apple Valley, CA, July 6, 1998. See also: "The Roy Rogers Show" TV Premiere: Anniversary (Dec 30).

TARBELL, IDA M.: BIRTH ANNIVERSARY. Nov 5, 1857. American writer born at Erie County, PA. She edited the muckraking journal *McClure's Magazine*, which exposed the political and industrial corruption of the day and emphasized the need for reform. Died at Bethel, CT, Jan 6, 1944.

BIRTHDAYS TODAY

Bryan Adams, 47, singer ("Heaven," "Summer of '69"), songwriter ("Everything I Do"), born Vancouver, BC, Canada, Nov 5, 1959.

Arthur (Art) Garfunkel, 65, singer (Simon and Garfunkel), actor (*Carnal Knowledge*), born Forest Hills, NY, Nov 5, 1941.

Ted Kulongoski, 66, Governor of Oregon (D), born in rural Missouri, Nov 5, 1940.

Javy Lopez, 36, baseball player, born Ponce, Puerto Rico, Nov 5, 1970.

Corin Nemec, 35, actor ("Parker Lewis Can't Lose," *Tucker: The Man and His Dream*), born Little Rock, AR, Nov 5, 1971.

Tatum O'Neal, 43, actress (Oscar for *Paper Moon*; *Bad News Bears*), born Los Angeles, CA, Nov 5, 1963.

Sam Shepard, 63, dramatist, actor (*Buried Child, The Right Stuff*), born Samuel Shepard Rogers at Fort Sheridan, IL, Nov 5, 1943.

Elke Sommer, 65, actress (*A Shot in the Dark, The Prize*), born Elke Schletze at Berlin, Germany, Nov 5, 1941.

Jerry Stackhouse, 32, basketball player, born Kinston, NC, Nov 5, 1974.

Ike Turner, 75, singer (Ike and Tina Turner Revue), born Clarksdale, MS, Nov 5, 1931.

Bill Walton, 54, broadcaster, Hall of Fame basketball player, born Mesa, CA, Nov 5, 1952.

Geoffrey Wolff, 69, author (*The Duke of Deception, The Age of Consent*), born Los Angeles, CA, Nov 5, 1937.

NOVEMBER 6 — MONDAY
Day 310 — 55 Remaining

AUSTRALIA: RECREATION DAY. Nov 6. The first Monday in November is observed as Recreation Day at Northern Tasmania, Australia.

"GOOD MORNING AMERICA" TV PREMIERE: ANNIVERSARY. Nov 6, 1975. This ABC morning program, set in a living room, is a mixture of news reports, features and interviews with newsmakers and people of interest. It was the first program to compete with NBC's "Today" show and initially aired as "A.M. America." Hosts have included David Hartman, Nancy Dussault, Sandy Hill, Charles Gibson, Joan Lunden, Lisa McRee, Kevin Newman and Diane Sawyer.

KIDS' GOAL SETTING WEEK. Nov 6–10. Encourages parents, teachers and coaches to foster goal-setting habits in children's lives so that the children can make their dreams come true. For info: Gary Ryan Blair, The GoalsGuy, 36181 E Lake Rd, Ste 139, Palm Harbor, FL 34685. Phone: (877) GOALSGUY. Fax: (800) 731-GOAL. E-mail: info@goalsguy.com. Web: www.goalsguy.com.

"MEET THE PRESS" TV PREMIERE: ANNIVERSARY. Nov 6, 1947. "Meet the Press" holds the distinction of being the oldest program on TV. It originally debuted on radio in 1945. The show has changed its format little since it began: a well-known guest (usually a politician) is questioned on current, relevant issues by a panel of journalists. The moderators throughout the years have included Martha Rountree, Lawrence E. Spivak, Ned Brooks, Bill Monroe, Marvin Kalb, Chris Wallace and Garrick Utley with the current host being Tim Russert.

MOROCCO: ANNIVERSARY OF THE GREEN MARCH. Nov 6. National holiday. Commemorates the march into the Spanish Sahara in 1975 to claim the land for Morocco.

NAISMITH, JAMES: BIRTH ANNIVERSARY. Nov 6, 1861. Inventor of the game of basketball was born at Almonte, ON, Canada. Died at Lawrence, KS, Nov 28, 1939. Inducted into the Basketball Hall of Fame in 1959. Basketball became an Olympic sport in 1936.

PADEREWSKI, IGNACE JAN: BIRTH ANNIVERSARY. Nov 6, 1860. Polish composer, pianist, patriot born at Kurylowka, Podolia, Poland. He died at New York, NY, June 29, 1941. When Poland fell into the hands of the Soviets after WWII, his family decided he would remain buried in Arlington National Cemetery. In May 1963, President John F. Kennedy dedicated a plaque to Paderewski's memory and declared that the pianist would rest in Arlington until Poland was free. Paderewski's remains were returned to his native country on June 29, 1992, the 51st anniversary of his death, after Poland held its first parliamentary election following its independence from the Soviet Union.

"THE PHIL DONAHUE SHOW" TV PREMIERE: ANNIVERSARY. Nov 6, 1967. The forerunner of Oprah, Jerry, Montel, etc, this first talk show with audience participation went on the air on this date at Dayton, OH. The first guest interviewed by host Phil Donahue was atheist Madalyn Murray O'Hair. In 1970 the program went national; it moved to Chicago in 1974 and to New York in 1985. In later years the program was titled "Donahue." After winning 19 Emmy Awards, the show left daytime TV in 1996. Phil Donahue briefly aired a show on the MSNBC cable network, but it was canceled after six months Feb 25, 2003.

SAXOPHONE DAY (ADOLPHE SAX BIRTH ANNIVERSARY). Nov 6. A day to recognize the birth anniversary of Adolphe Sax, Belgian musician and inventor of the saxophone and the saxotromba. Born at Dinant, Belgium, in 1814, Antoine Joseph Sax, later known as Adolphe, was the eldest of 11 children of a musical instrument builder. Sax contributed an entire family of brass wind instruments for band and orchestra use. He was accorded fame and great wealth, but business misfortunes led to bankruptcy. Sax died in poverty at Paris, Feb 7, 1894.

SOUSA, JOHN PHILIP: BIRTH ANNIVERSARY. Nov 6, 1854. American composer and band conductor, remembered for stirring marches such as "The Stars and Stripes Forever," "Semper Fidelis," "El Capitan," born at Washington, DC. Died at Reading, PA, Mar 6, 1932. See also: "The Stars and Stripes Forever Day: Anniversary" (May 14).

SWEDEN: GUSTAVUS ADOLPHUS DAY. Nov 6. Honors Sweden's King and military leader killed in 1632.

UNITED NATIONS: INTERNATIONAL DAY FOR PREVENTING THE EXPLOITATION OF THE ENVIRONMENT IN WAR AND ARMED CONFLICT. Nov 6. A day calling attention to the irreparable damage to ecosystems and natural resources caused by armed conflict. For info: United Nations, Dept of Public Info, New York, NY 10017. Web: www.un.org.

BIRTHDAYS TODAY

Sally Field, 60, actress (Oscars for *Norma Rae, Places in the Heart*; Emmy for *Sybil*), born Pasadena, CA, Nov 6, 1946.

Glenn Frey, 58, musician, songwriter, singer ("The Heat Is On"), born Detroit, MI, Nov 6, 1948.

Nigel Havers, 57, actor (*Chariots of Fire, Empire of the Sun*), born London, England, Nov 6, 1949.

Ethan Hawke, 36, actor (*Training Day, Dead Poets Society*), novelist, born Austin, TX, Nov 6, 1970.

Lance Kerwin, 46, actor ("James at 15," "The Family Holvak"), born Newport Beach, CA, Nov 6, 1960.

Thandie Newton, 34, actress (*Beloved, Mission Impossible II*), born in Zambia, Nov 6, 1972.

Mike Nichols, 75, comedian, actor, theater producer, director, filmmaker (Oscar for *The Graduate; Working Girl*), born Michael Igor Peschkowsky at Berlin, Germany, Nov 6, 1931.

Rebecca Romijn, 34, model, host (MTV's "House of Style"), actress (*X-Men*), born Berkeley, CA, Nov 6, 1972.

Maria Owings Shriver, 51, First Lady of California, broadcast journalist ("Today"), born Chicago, IL, Nov 6, 1955.

NOVEMBER 7 — TUESDAY

Day 311 — 54 Remaining

BANGLADESH: SOLIDARITY DAY. Nov 7. National holiday. Commemorates a coup in 1975.

CAMUS, ALBERT: BIRTH ANNIVERSARY. Nov 7, 1913. French writer and philosopher, winner of the Nobel Prize for Literature in 1957, was born at Mondavi, Algeria. "The struggle to reach the top is itself enough to fulfill the heart of man. One must believe that Sisyphus is happy," he wrote, in *Le Mythe de Sisyphe*. Camus was killed in an automobile accident in France, Jan 4, 1960.

CANADIAN PACIFIC RAILWAY: TRANSCONTINENTAL COMPLETION ANNIVERSARY. Nov 7, 1885. At 9:30 AM the last spike was driven at Craigellachie, British Columbia, completing the Canadian Pacific Railway's 2,980-mile transcontinental railroad track between Montreal, Quebec, in the east and Port Moody, British Columbia, in the west.

CONTINENT-SIZED WINDSTORMS DISCOVERED: 15th ANNIVERSARY. Nov 7, 1991. A satellite that had been launched from the space shuttle *Discovery* on Sept 15, 1991, discovered large windstorms in Earth's upper atmosphere. The satellite's 10 instruments became functional on Nov 7 and detected the continent-sized windstorms, which measured up to 200 MPH velocities in areas that are 600 to 6,000 miles wide in the mesosphere. The largest storm was discovered in the Southern hemisphere and reached from western Australia eastward to points halfway across the Atlantic Ocean.

CURIE, MARIE SKLODOWSKA: BIRTH ANNIVERSARY. Nov 7, 1867. Polish chemist and physicist, born at Warsaw, Poland. In 1903 she was awarded, with her husband, the Nobel Prize for physics for their discovery of the element radium. Died near Sallanches, France, July 4, 1934.

"FACE THE NATION" TV PREMIERE: ANNIVERSARY. Nov 7, 1954. The CBS counterpart to NBC's "Meet the Press," this show employed a similar format: panelists interviewed a well-known guest. In 1983 the panel was changed to include experts in addition to journalists. Though usually produced at Washington, DC, the show occasionally interviewed people elsewhere (such as Khrushchev in Moscow in 1957).

FIRST BLACK GOVERNOR ELECTED: ANNIVERSARY. Nov 7, 1989. L. Douglas Wilder was elected governor of Virginia, becoming the first elected black governor in US history. Wilder had previously served as lieutenant governor of Virginia, becoming the first black elected to statewide office in the South since Reconstruction.

GENERAL ELECTION DAY. Nov 7. Annually, the Tuesday after the first Monday in November. Many state and local government elections are held on this day, as well as presidential and congressional elections in the appropriate years. All US congressional seats and one-third of US senatorial seats are up for election in even-numbered years. Presidential elections are held in even-numbered years that can be divided equally by four. This day is a state holiday in 12 states.

GREAT OCTOBER SOCIALIST REVOLUTION: ANNIVERSARY. Nov 7, 1917. This holiday in the old Soviet Union was observed for two days with parades, military displays and appearances by Soviet leaders. In the mid-1990s, President Yeltsin issued a decree renaming the holiday the "Day of National Reconciliation and Agreement." According to the old Russian calendar, the revolution took place Oct 25, 1917. Soviet calendar reform causes observance to fall Nov 7 (Gregorian). The Bolshevik Revolution began at Petrograd, Russia, on the evening of Nov 6 (Gregorian), 1917. A new government headed by Nikolai Lenin took office the following day under the name Council of People's Commissars. Leon Trotsky was commissar for foreign affairs and Josef Stalin became commissar of national minorities.

JAGGER, DEAN: BIRTH ANNIVERSARY. Nov 7, 1903. American actor Dean Jagger was born at Columbus Grove, OH. Predominantly a character actor, he appeared in more than 120 films, including *Twelve O'Clock High* (1950), for which he won an Oscar for best supporting actor. He died Feb 5, 1991, at Santa Monica, CA.

NIXON'S "LAST" PRESS CONFERENCE: ANNIVERSARY. Nov 7, 1962. Richard M. Nixon, having been narrowly defeated in his bid for the presidency by John F. Kennedy in the 1960 election, returned to politics two years later as a candidate for governor of California in the election of Nov 6, 1962. Defeated again (this time by incumbent governor Edmund G. Brown), Nixon held his "last" press conference with assembled reporters in Los Angeles at mid-morning the next day at which he said: ". . . just think how much you're going to be missing. You won't have Nixon to kick around anymore, because, gentlemen, this is my last press conference."

OLD STOUGHTON MUSICAL SOCIETY: ANNIVERSARY. Nov 7, 1786. Founded at Stoughton, MA, the Stoughton Musical Society is the oldest choral society in the US. Originally consisting of 25 men, it now includes both men and women. The society performed at the Chicago World's Columbian Exposition in 1893.

REPUBLICAN SYMBOL: ANNIVERSARY. Nov 7, 1874. Thomas Nast used an elephant to represent the Republican Party in a satirical cartoon in *Harper's Weekly*. Today the elephant is still a well-recognized symbol for the Republican Party in political cartoons.

	S	M	T	W	T	F	S
November 2006				1	2	3	4
	5	6	7	8	9	10	11
	12	13	14	15	16	17	18
	19	20	21	22	23	24	25
	26	27	28	29	30		

ROOSEVELT ELECTED TO FOURTH TERM: ANNIVERSARY. Nov 7, 1944. Defeating Thomas Dewey, Franklin D. Roosevelt became the first, and only, person elected to four terms as President of the US. Roosevelt was inaugurated the following Jan 20 but died in office Apr 12, 1945, serving only 53 days of the fourth term.

RUSSIA: OCTOBER REVOLUTION. Nov 7. National holiday in Russia and Ukraine. Commemorates the Great Socialist Revolution, which occurred in October 1917 under the Old Style calendar. In 1997, the holiday was renamed the "Day of National Reconciliation and Agreement."

BIRTHDAYS TODAY

Billy Graham, 88, evangelist, born William Franklin Graham at Charlotte, NC, Nov 7, 1918.

Keith Lockhart, 47, Boston Pops conductor, born Poughkeepsie, NY, Nov 7, 1959.

Jeremy London, 34, actor ("I'll Fly Away," "Party of Five"), born San Diego, CA, Nov 7, 1972.

Joni Mitchell, 63, singer, songwriter ("Both Sides Now," "Big Yellow Taxi," "Woodstock"), born Roberta Joan Anderson at McLeod, AB, Canada, Nov 7, 1943.

Barry Newman, 68, actor ("Petrocelli," *Vanishing Point*), born Boston, MA, Nov 7, 1938.

Johnny Rivers, 64, singer ("Poor Side of Town," "Secret Agent Man"), born John Ramistella at New York, NY, Nov 7, 1942.

Joan Sutherland, 80, opera singer, born Sydney, Australia, Nov 7, 1926.

Mary Travers, 69, composer, singer (Peter, Paul and Mary, "Blowin' in the Wind"), born Louisville, KY, Nov 7, 1937.

NOVEMBER 8 — WEDNESDAY

Day 312 — 53 Remaining

ABET AND AID PUNSTERS DAY. Nov 8. Laugh instead of groan at incredibly dreadful puns. All-time greatest triple pun: "Though he's not very humble, there's no police like Holmes," from the register of worst puns of Punsters Unlimited. (Originated by Earl Harris, retired, and the late William Rabe.)

BARNARD, CHRISTIAAN: BIRTH ANNIVERSARY. Nov 8, 1922. Pioneering heart surgeon, born at Beaufort West, South Africa. Dr. Barnard performed the first human heart transplant on Dec 3, 1967, after years of practicing the procedure, mainly on dogs. The patient, Mr. Louis Washkansky, lived for 18 days before dying from an infection. Today, heart transplants are performed regularly and with good success. Barnard died at Paphos, Cyprus, Sept 2, 2001, of heart failure.

CHRISTMAS GIFT AND HOBBY SHOW. Nov 8–12. West Pavilion, Indiana State Fairgrounds, Indianapolis, IN. 57th annual event. Selling show of arts, crafts, collectibles and other gift items. Est attendance: 60,000. For info: Donell Heberer Walton, Executive Dir, HSI Show Productions, Box 502797, Indianapolis, IN 46250. Phone: (317) 576-9933. Fax: (317) 576-9955. Web: www.hsishows.com.

COOK SOMETHING BOLD AND PUNGENT DAY. Nov 8. Especially for those of us who have tightly closed up the house against chill weather for the next six months. Now is the time to create the heavenly, homey odor of pungently bold cooking. Don't forget the sauerkraut and garlic! [©2003 by WH.] For info: Thomas & Ruth Roy, Wellcat Holidays, 2418 Long Ln, Lebanon, PA 17046. Phone: (717) 279-0184. E-mail: info@wellcat.com. Web: www.wellcat.com.

CORTÉS CONQUERS MEXICO: ANNIVERSARY. Nov 8, 1519. After landing on the Yucatán peninsula in April, Spaniard Hernan Cortés and his troops marched into the interior of Mexico to the Aztec capital and took the Aztec emperor Montezuma hostage.

"DAYS OF OUR LIVES" TV PREMIERE: ANNIVERSARY. Nov 8, 1965. This popular daytime serial, like many others, has gone through many changes throughout its run. It expanded from 30 minutes to an hour; it went to number one in the ratings and slipped to nine out of 12 in the 1980s; and it dropped or deemphasized older characters, which angered its audience. The soap is set in Salem and centers around the Horton and Brady families. Notable cast members included Mary Frann, Joan Van Ark, Susan Oliver, Mike Farrell, Kristian Alfonso, Garry Marshall, John Aniston, Josh Taylor, Wayne Northrop, John DeLancie, Andrea Barber, Deidre Hall, Thaao Penghlis, Jason Bernard, Marilyn McCoo, Charles Shaughnessy, Peter Reckell, Francis Reid, Patsy Pease and Genie Francis.

HALLEY, EDMUND: 350th BIRTH ANNIVERSARY. Nov 8, 1656 (OS). Astronomer and mathematician born at London, England. Astronomer Royal, 1721–42. Died at Greenwich, England, Jan 14, 1742 (OS). He observed the great comet of 1682 (now named for him), first conceived its periodicity and wrote in his *Synopsis of Comet Astronomy*: ." . . I may venture to foretell that this Comet will return again in the year 1758." It did, and Edmund Halley's memory is kept alive by the once-every-generation appearance of Halley's Comet. There have been 28 recorded appearances of this comet since 240 BC. Average time between appearances is 76 years. Halley's Comet is next expected to be visible in 2061.

MITCHELL, MARGARET: BIRTH ANNIVERSARY. Nov 8, 1900. American novelist who won a Pulitzer Prize (1937) for her only book, *Gone with the Wind*, a romantic novel about the Civil War and Reconstruction. *Gone with the Wind* sold about 10,000,000 copies and was translated into 30 languages. Born at Atlanta, GA, Mitchell died there after being struck by an automobile Aug 16, 1949.

MONTANA: ADMISSION DAY: ANNIVERSARY. Nov 8. Became 41st state in 1889.

MOUNT HOLYOKE COLLEGE FOUNDED: ANNIVERSARY. Nov 8, 1837. The first college for women in the United States was founded as Mt Holyoke Seminary in 1837 at South Hadley, MA. While many colleges for women became coeducational institutions in the 1970s and 1980s, Mt Holyoke remains a women's college.

NATIONAL PARENTS AS TEACHERS DAY. Nov 8. To pay tribute to the more than 3,000 Parents as Teachers programs located nationwide and around the world. These programs give all parents of very young children support and information on their developing child so all children will learn, grow and develop to realize their full potential. For info: Parents as Teachers National Center, 2228 Ball Dr, St. Louis, MO 63146. Phone: (866) PAT-4YOU. Fax: (314) 432-8963. E-mail: info@ParentsAsTeachers.org. Web: www.ParentsAsTeachers.org.

PURSUIT OF HAPPINESS WEEK. Nov 8–14. The purpose of this week is to remind everyone, as stated in the Declaration of Independence, that all men and women are "endowed by their Creator with certain unalienable rights, that among them are life, liberty and the pursuit of happiness." For complete info and quotations about happiness by famous people, send $5 to cover expense of printing, handling and postage. For info: Dr. Stanley Drake, Pres Emeritus, Intl Society of Friendship & Good Will, 8592 Roswell Rd, Ste 251, Atlanta, GA 30350-1867. Phone: (678)

795-1362. E-mail: sjdrake@bellsouth.net. Web: www.friendship andgoodwill.org.

X-RAY DISCOVERY DAY: ANNIVERSARY. Nov 8, 1895. Physicist Wilhelm Conrad Roentgen (q.v.) discovered X-rays, beginning a new era in physics and medicine. Although X-rays had been observed previously, it was Roentgen, a professor at the University of Wurzburg (Germany), who successfully repeated X-ray experimentation and who is credited with the discovery.

BIRTHDAYS TODAY

Edgardo Alfonzo, 33, baseball player, born St. Teresa, Venezuela, Nov 8, 1973.

Mary Hart, 55, TV host, born Madison, SD, Nov 8, 1951.

June Havoc, 90, actress (*Gentleman's Agreement, Brewster's Millions*), born Vancouver, BC, Canada, Nov 8, 1916.

Christie Hefner, 54, business executive (*Playboy*), daughter of Hugh Hefner, born Chicago, IL, Nov 8, 1952.

Ricki Lee Jones, 52, singer, musician ("Chuck E.'s in Love"), born Chicago, IL, Nov 8, 1954.

Virna Lisi, 69, actress (*How to Murder Your Wife, The Secret of Santa Vittoria*), born Ancona, Italy, Nov 8, 1937.

Patti Page, 79, singer ("The Doggie in the Window," "Allegheny Moon"), born Clara Ann Fowler at Clarence, OK, Nov 8, 1927.

Parker Posey, 38, actress (*Personal Velocity, The House of Yes, Party Girl*), born Baltimore, MD, Nov 8, 1968.

Bonnie Raitt, 57, singer ("Sweet Forgiveness"), actress, daughter of John Raitt, born Los Angeles, CA, Nov 8, 1949.

Tara Reid, 31, actress (*American Pie, Josie & the Pussycats*), born Wyckoff, NJ, Nov 8, 1975.

Morley Safer, 75, journalist ("60 Minutes"), born Toronto, ON, Canada, Nov 8, 1931.

Courtney Thorne-Smith, 39, actress ("Melrose Place," "Ally McBeal"), born San Francisco, CA, Nov 8, 1967.

Alfre Woodard, 53, actress (*Cross Creek, Miss Evers' Boys, How to Make an American Quilt*), born Tulsa, OK, Nov 8, 1953.

NOVEMBER 9 — THURSDAY

Day 313 — 52 Remaining

AGNEW, SPIRO THEODORE: BIRTH ANNIVERSARY. Nov 9, 1918. 39th vice president of the US, born at Baltimore, MD. Twice elected vice president (1968 and 1972), Agnew became the second person to resign that office Oct 10, 1973. Agnew entered a plea of no contest to a charge of income tax evasion (on contract kickbacks received while he was governor of Maryland and after he became vice president). He died Sept 17, 1996, at Berlin, MD. See also: "Vice Presidential Resignation: Anniversary" (Dec 28) and "Calhoun, John Caldwell: Birth Anniversary" (Mar 18).

BANNEKER, BENJAMIN: 275th BIRTH ANNIVERSARY. Nov 9, 1731. American astronomer, mathematician, clockmaker, surveyor and almanac author, called "first black man of science." Took part in original survey of city of Washington. Banneker's *Almanac* was published 1792–97. Born at Elliott's Mills, MD, he died at Baltimore, MD, Oct 9, 1806. A fire that started during his funeral destroyed his home, library, notebooks, almanac calculations, clocks and virtually all belongings and documents related to his life.

BERLIN WALL OPENED: ANNIVERSARY. Nov 9, 1989. After 28 years as a symbol of the Cold War, the Berlin Wall was opened on this evening, and citizens of both sides walked freely through the barrier as others danced atop the structure to celebrate the end of an historic era. Coming amidst the celebration of East Germany's 40-year anniversary, pro-democracy demonstrations led to the resignation of Erich Honecker, East Germany's head of state and party chief. It was Honecker who had supervised the construction of the 27.9-mile wall across the city during the night of Aug 13, 1961, because US President John Kennedy had ordered a troop buildup in response to the blockade of West Berlin by the Soviets.

BIG TEN MEN'S SOCCER CHAMPIONSHIP. Nov 9–12. Michigan State University, East Lansing, MI. For info: Big Ten Conference, 1500 W Higgins Rd, Park Ridge, IL 60068-6300. Phone: (847) 696-1010. Fax: (847) 696-1110. Web: www.bigten.org.

BOSTON FIRE: ANNIVERSARY. Nov 9, 1872. Though Boston had experienced several damaging fires, the worst one started on this Saturday evening in a dry-goods warehouse. Spreading rapidly in windy weather, it devastated several blocks of the business district, destroying nearly 800 buildings. Damage was estimated at more than $75 million. It was said that the fire caused a bright red glare in the sky that could be seen from nearly 100 miles away. The Boston fire came one year, one month and one day after the Great Chicago Fire of Oct 8, 1871.

CAMBODIA: INDEPENDENCE DAY. Nov 9. National Day. Declared independence from France in 1949.

DANDRIDGE, DOROTHY: BIRTH ANNIVERSARY. Nov 9, 1923. Actress and singer Dandridge was a child star, born at Cleveland, OH, who toured with her sisters, Vivian and Etta Jones, as The Dandridge Sisters. They played at the Cotton Club, sharing the stage with artists such as Cab Calloway and W.C. Handy. Dandridge went solo in 1941 to perform in Hollywood movies and on stage with the Desi Arnaz Band. Her big break came with the lead role in Otto Preminger's musical, *Carmen Jones*. Dandridge received an Oscar nomination for her performance. Unfortunately, she could not overcome Hollywood's racism and tendency to typecast and her career foundered. She died at West Hollywood, CA, Sept 8, 1965.

EAST COAST BLACKOUT: ANNIVERSARY. Nov 9, 1965. Massive electric power failure starting in western New York state at 5:16 PM cut electric power to much of northeastern US and Ontario and Quebec in Canada. More than 30 million people in an area of 80,000 square miles were affected. The experience provoked studies of the vulnerability of 20th-century technology.

FULBRIGHT, J. WILLIAM: BIRTH ANNIVERSARY. Nov 9, 1905. US Senator, born at Sumner, MO. He sponsored the legislation that created the Fulbright scholarships for international study for graduate students, faculty and researchers. Died Feb 9, 1995.

INTERNATIONAL GIFT FESTIVAL. Nov 9–11. Fairfield, PA. Traditional handcrafts, home decor, pottery, baskets, textiles, oriental rugs, jewelry and toys from more than 30 countries around the world. Est attendance: 4,500. For info: Gettysburg CVB, PO Box 4117, Gettysburg, PA 17325. Phone: (717) 334-6274. Fax: (717) 334-1166. E-mail: gettysburgcvb@dejazzd.com. Web: www.gettysburgcvb.com.

KRISTALLNACHT (CRYSTAL NIGHT): ANNIVERSARY. Nov 9–10, 1938. During the evening of Nov 9 and into the morning of Nov 10, 1938, mobs in Germany destroyed thousands of shops and homes carrying out a pogrom against Jews. Synagogues were burned down or demolished. There were bonfires in every Jewish neighborhood, fueled by Jewish prayer

	S	**M**	**T**	**W**	**T**	**F**	**S**
November				1	2	3	4
2006	5	6	7	8	9	10	11
	12	13	14	15	16	17	18
	19	20	21	22	23	24	25
	26	27	28	29	30		

books, Torah scrolls and volumes of philosophy, history and poetry. More than 30,000 Jews were arrested and 91 killed. The night got its name from the smashing of glass store windows.

THE LINKS, INC: 60th ANNIVERSARY. Nov 9, 1946. In Philadelphia, PA, Margaret Roselle Hawkins and Sarah Strickland Scott founded a nonpartisan, volunteer organization called The Links, "linking" their friendship and resources in an effort to better the lives of disadvantaged African Americans after WWII. From a first group of nine, The Links grew to an incorporated organization of 8,000 women in 240 local chapters in 40 states plus the District of Columbia and two foreign countries. The Links promotes educational, cultural and community activities through a variety of projects here and in Africa. In May of 1985 The Links became an official Non-Governmental Organization of the UN.

LONGHORN CHAMPIONSHIP FINALS RODEO. Nov 9–11. Murfreesboro, TN. 41st annual. Best 72 of 1,200+ qualifiers compete each performance in six contests for the 2006 Championships. Awards include gold and silver diamond-studded trophy belt buckles and hand-tooled trophy saddles. Large Western Trade Show will include retail vendor booths and Texas-style cowboy meals served off a genuine ranch chuckwagon. Free beginners horsemanship clinic 40 minutes before each performance. Contests include Big, Bad BONUS bull riding! Est attendance: 15,000. For info: W. Bruce Lehrke, Longhorn World Chmpshp Rodeo, Inc, PO Box 70159, Nashville, TN 37207. Phone: (615) 876-1016. Fax: (615) 876-4685. E-mail: info@longhornrodeo.com. Web: www.longhornrodeo.com.

LOVEJOY, ELIJAH P.: BIRTH ANNIVERSARY. Nov 9, 1802. American newspaper publisher and abolitionist born at Albion, ME. Died Nov 7, 1837, at Alton, IL, in a fire started by a mob angry about his antislavery views.

NATIONAL CHILD SAFETY COUNCIL FOUNDED: ANNIVERSARY. Nov 9, 1955. National Child Safety Council (NCSC) at Jackson, MI, is the oldest and largest nonprofit organization in the US dedicated solely to child safety. Distributes comprehensive safety education materials to children and adults through local law enforcement, and the Council's mascot, Safetypup®. For info: NCSC, Box 1368, Jackson, MI 49204-1368. Phone: (517) 764-6070. E-mail: tlusby@nfcd.org.

"OMNIBUS" TV PREMIERE: ANNIVERSARY. Nov 9, 1952. This eclectic series deserved its name, offering a variety of presentations, including dramas, documentaries and musicals for more than 10 years. Alistair Cooke hosted the program, which was the first major TV project to be underwritten by the Ford Foundation. Notable presentations included: James Agee's "Mr Lincoln"; "Die Fledermaus," with Eugene Ormandy conducting the Metropolitan Opera Orchestra; Agnes DeMille's ballet "Three Virgins and the Devil" (presented as "Three Maidens and the Devil"); and documentaries from underwater explorer Jacques Cousteau.

RETURN DAY. Nov 9. Georgetown, DE. The day when officially tabulated election returns are read from the balcony of Georgetown's red brick, Greek Revival courthouse to the throngs of voters assembled below. Always the second day after a general election. An official "half-holiday" in Sussex County. Reportedly Return Day has become so popular "that it is for all intents and purposes a state holiday as well."

SAGAN, CARL: BIRTH ANNIVERSARY. Nov 9, 1934. Astronomer, biologist, author (*Broca's Brain, Cosmos*), born at New York, NY. Died at Seattle, WA, Dec 20, 1996.

VIETNAM VETERANS MEMORIAL STATUE UNVEILING: ANNIVERSARY. Nov 9, 1984. The Vietnam Veterans Memorial was completed by the addition of a statue, "Three Servicemen" (sculpted by Frederick Hart), which was unveiled on this date. The statue faces the black granite wall on which are inscribed the names of more than 58,000 Americans who were killed or missing in action in the Vietnam War.

WHITE, STANFORD: BIRTH ANNIVERSARY. Nov 9, 1853. American architect who designed the old Madison Square Garden, the Washington Square Arch, and the Players, Century and Metropolitan Clubs at New York City. Stanford White was born at New York City and was shot to death on the roof of the Madison Square Garden by Harry Thaw, June 25, 1906.

WILHELM II ABDICATES: ANNIVERSARY. Nov 9, 1918. As WWI was coming to a close and it became clear their cause was lost, a revolt broke out in Germany. The Kaiser was advised by his military staff that the loyalty of the army could not be guaranteed. On Nov 9, 1918, it was announced in Berlin that Kaiser Wilhelm II had abdicated his throne. The former leader then fled to Holland. Philip Scheidemann, a Socialist leader, proclaimed a German Republic and became its first chancellor.

BIRTHDAYS TODAY

Adam Dunn, 27, baseball player, born Houston, TX, Nov 9, 1979.
David Duval, 35, golfer, born Jacksonville, FL, Nov 9, 1971.
Lou Ferrigno, 55, actor (*Pumping Iron*, "The Incredible Hulk"), former bodybuilder, born Brooklyn, NY, Nov 9, 1951.
Robert (Bob) Gibson, 71, Hall of Fame baseball player, born Omaha, NE, Nov 9, 1935.
Nick Lachey, 33, singer (98 Degrees), television personality ("Newlyweds: Nick & Jessica"), born Harlan, KY, Nov 9, 1973.
Thomas Quasthoff, 47, opera singer, born Hanover, Germany, Nov 9, 1959.
Thomas Daniel (Tom) Weiskopf, 64, broadcaster, former golfer, born Massillon, OH, Nov 9, 1942.

NOVEMBER 10 — FRIDAY
Day 314 — 51 Remaining

AREA CODES INTRODUCED: 55th ANNIVERSARY. Nov 10, 1951. The 10-digit North American Numbering Plan, which provides area codes for Canada, the US, and many Caribbean nations, was devised in 1947 by AT&T and Bell Labs. Eighty-four area codes were assigned. However, all long-distance calls at that time were operator-assisted. On this date in 1951, the mayor of Englewood, NJ (area code 201), direct-dialed the mayor of Alameda, CA. By 1960 all telephone customers could dial long-distance calls. Because of the proliferation of faxes, modems and cell phones, the US could run out of area codes as early as 2007. The system is administered by the North American Numbering Plan Administration. For more info: www.nanpa.com.

BADLANDS NATIONAL PARK ESTABLISHED: ANNIVERSARY. Nov 10, 1978. South Dakota's Badlands National Monument, authorized Mar 4, 1929, was established as a national park and preserve.

BURTON, RICHARD: BIRTH ANNIVERSARY. Nov 10, 1925. Welsh-born stage and film actor. Richard Burton was never knighted and never an Oscar winner, but he was generally regarded as one of the great acting talents of his time. Born Richard Jenkins at Pontrhydyfen, South Wales, the son of a coal miner, he later took the name of his guardian, schoolmaster Philip Burton. His films include *Cleopatra, Becket, Who's Afraid of Virginia Woolf?, Anne of the Thousand Days* and *Equus*. An intense and tempestuous personal life and career suggested a self-destructive bent. Burton died at Geneva, Switzerland, Aug 5, 1984.

CHRISTKINDL MARKT. Nov 10–12. Cultural Center for the Arts, Canton, OH. 35th annual. Fine arts and crafts show and sale. Sponsored by the Canton Fine Arts Associates to benefit the

Canton Museum of Art. Est attendance: 6,000. For info: Christkindl Market, 1001 Market Ave N, Canton, OH 44702. Phone: (330) 453-7666. Fax: (330) 453-1034. Web: www.canton art.org.

CRAFTSMEN'S CHRISTMAS CLASSIC ARTS & CRAFTS FESTIVAL. Nov 10–12. South Carolina State Fairgrounds, Columbia, SC. 31st annual. Features work from more than 300 talented artists and craftspeople. All juried exhibitors' work has been handmade by the exhibitors and must be their own original design and creation. See the creative process in action with several exhibitors demonstrating throughout the weekend. Visit Christmas Tree Village to view the uniquely decorated Christmas trees by some of our exhibitors. Something for every style, taste and budget with items from the most contemporary to the most traditional. Est attendance: 35,000. For info: Gilmore Enterprises, Inc, 1240 Oakland Ave, Greensboro, NC 27403. Phone: (336) 274-5550. E-mail: gilmoreshows@triad.rr .com. Web: www.CraftShow.com or www.gilmoreshows.com.

***EDMUND FITZGERALD* MEMORIAL BEACON LIGHTING.** Nov 10. Noon–6 PM, Split Rock Lighthouse, Two Harbors, MN. Includes information on *Edmund Fitzgerald* and other shipwrecks on Lake Superior; beacon lighting at dusk in memory of the 29 men lost on the *Edmund Fitzgerald* on Nov 10, 1975, and of all those who lost their lives in other Great Lakes shipwrecks. Lighthouse open. Est attendance: 1,000. For info: Lee Radzak, 3713 Split Rock Lighthouse Rd, Two Harbors, MN 55616. Phone: (218) 226-6372. E-mail: splitrock@mnhs.org.

***EDMUND FITZGERALD* SINKING: ANNIVERSARY.** Nov 10, 1975. The ore carrier *Edmund Fitzgerald* broke in two during a heavy storm in Lake Superior (near Whitefish Point). There were no survivors of this, the worst Great Lakes ship disaster of the decade, which took the lives of 29 crew members.

FOUR CORNER STATES BLUEGRASS FESTIVAL. Nov 10–12. Wickenburg, AZ. 26th annual old-time fiddle, banjo, mandolin, flat-pick guitar championships. Includes gospel music. Special entertainment by nationally known bands as well as 13 competitive events. Annually, the second weekend in November. Est attendance: 5,000. For info: J Brooks, Exec Dir, Chamber of Commerce, 216 N Frontier Street, Wickenburg, AZ 85390. Phone: (928) 684-5479 or (928) 684-0977. Fax: (928) 684-5470. E-mail: events@wickenburgchamber.com. Web: www.wickenburg chamber.com.

GOLDSMITH, OLIVER: BIRTH ANNIVERSARY. Nov 10, 1728. Irish writer, author of the play *She Stoops to Conquer*. Born at Pallas, County Longford, Ireland, he died Apr 4, 1774, at London. "A book may be amusing with numerous errors," he wrote (Advertisement to *The Vicar of Wakefield*), "or it may be very dull without a single absurdity."

GREAT AMERICAN WARM-UP. Nov 10–12. Just as the weather outside begins to change, this weekend is set aside to clean out those closets and take your warm, wearable coats, jackets, scarves, hats and mittens that you no longer use and donate them to a homeless shelter or agency for distribution. Do it now, before it gets even colder outside. Annually, the second full weekend in November. [© 1995] To alleviate the escalating costs of Eventological® Literature, a charge of $10 must be assessed for each request. Checks are to be made payable to: Adrienne Sioux Koopersmith, 1437 W Rosemont, #1W, Chicago, IL 60660-1319. E-mail: askoopersmith@hotmail.com.

GREATER PITTSBURGH ARTS & CRAFTS HOLIDAY SPECTACULAR. Nov 10–12. Expo Center at Greengate Mall, Greensburg, PA. Approximately 200 booths including pottery,

jewelry, quilts, furniture, tole and decorative painting, leather, toys and much more. Find that perfect gift for the holidays. Est attendance: 30,000. For info: Debbie & Dave Stoner, PO Box 166, Irwin, PA 15642. Phone/fax: (724) 863-4577. E-mail: family festivals@hotmail.com. Web: www.familyfestivals.com.

HOGARTH, WILLIAM: BIRTH ANNIVERSARY. Nov 10, 1697. English painter and engraver, famed for his satiric series of engravings (*A Harlot's Progress, A Rake's Progress, Four Stages of Cruelty*, etc). Born at London, England, he died there, Oct 26, 1764.

KIRTLAND, JARED: BIRTH ANNIVERSARY. Nov 10, 1793. American physician and naturalist, Dr. Jared Potter Kirtland (for whom Kirtland's Warbler is named) was born at Wallingford, CT. The first of the now rare Kirtland's Warblers to be identified and studied was found on his farm near Cleveland, OH, in 1851. Dr. Kirtland died at Rockport, near Cleveland, Dec 10, 1877.

LUTHER, MARTIN: BIRTH ANNIVERSARY. Nov 10, 1483. Augustinian monk who was a founder and leader of the Protestant Reformation was born at Eisleben, Saxony. Luther tacked his 95 Theses "On the Power of Indulgences" on the door of Wittenberg's castle church, on Oct 31, 1517, the eve of All Saints' Day. Luther asserted that the Bible was the sole authority of the church, called for reformation of abuses by the Roman Catholic Church and denied the supremacy of the Pope. Tried for heresy by the Roman Church, threatened with excommunication and finally banned by a papal bull (Jan 2, 1521), he responded by burning the bull. In 1525 he married Katherine von Bora, one of nine nuns who had left the convent due to his teaching. Luther died near his birthplace, at Eisleben, Feb 18, 1546.

MARINE CORPS BIRTHDAY: ANNIVERSARY. Nov 10, 1775. Commemorates the Marine Corps' establishment in 1775. Originally part of the navy, it became a separate unit July 11, 1789.

MICROSOFT RELEASES WINDOWS: ANNIVERSARY. Nov 10, 1983. In 1980 Microsoft signed a contract with IBM to design an operating system, MS-DOS, for a personal computer that IBM was developing. On Nov 10, 1983, Microsoft released Windows, an extension of MS-DOS with a graphical user interface. Windows 3.1 was released Apr 6, 1992.

NATIONAL DONOR SABBATH. Nov 10–12. To increase awareness about the dire need for organs and tissues for transplantation and to dispel fears that religion and tissue and organ donation are incompatible. Annually, the Friday, Saturday and Sunday two weekends before Thanksgiving. For info: Health Resources and Services Admin, US Dept of Health and Human Services. Phone: (301) 443-7577. Web: www.organdonor.gov.

PANAMA: FIRST SHOUT OF INDEPENDENCE. Nov 10. National holiday. Commeorates Panama's first battle for independence from Spain in 1821.

SALT LAKE'S FAMILY CHRISTMAS GIFT SHOW. Nov 10–12. Sandy, UT. A delightful holiday experience. Shoppers will find gifts and decorations from vendors across the nation. A festive shopping atmosphere with music, entertainment, Santa Claus and a Specialty Food area for all to enjoy. Est attendance: 21,000. For info: Showcase Events, Inc, PO Box 2815, Kirkland, WA 98083. Phone: (800) 521-SHOW. E-mail: saltlake@showcase events.org. Web: www.showcaseevents.org.

	S	M	T	W	T	F	S
November				1	2	3	4
2006	5	6	7	8	9	10	11
	12	13	14	15	16	17	18
	19	20	21	22	23	24	25
	26	27	28	29	30		

"SESAME STREET" TV PREMIERE: ANNIVERSARY. Nov 10, 1969. An important, successful long-running children's show, "Sesame Street" educates children while they have fun. It takes place along a city street, featuring a diverse cast of humans and puppets. Through singing, puppetry, film clips and skits, kids are taught letters, numbers, concepts and other lessons. Shows are "sponsored" by letters and numbers. Human cast members have included: Loretta Long, Matt Robinson, Roscoe Orman, Bob McGrath, Linda Bove, Buffy Sainte-Marie, Ruth Buzzi, Will Lee, Northern J. Calloway, Emilio Delgado and Sonia Manzano. Favorite Jim Henson Muppets include Ernie, Bert, Grover, Oscar the Grouch, Kermit the Frog, the Cookie Monster, Big Bird and Mr Snuffleupagus.

STAMP EXPO: AMERICA. Nov 10-12. Radisson Hotel, Anaheim, CA. Est attendance: 4,000. For info: Israel Bick, Exec Dir, Intl Stamp & Coin Collectors Society, PO Box 854, Van Nuys, CA 91408. Phone: (818) 997-6496. Fax: (818) 988-4337. E-mail: iibick@sbcglobal.net. Web: www.bick.net.

STANLEY FINDS LIVINGSTONE: ANNIVERSARY. Nov 10, 1871. Having begun his search the previous March for the then two-years-missing explorer-missionary David Livingstone, explorer Henry M. Stanley found him on this day at Ujiji (Africa) and uttered those now immortal words, "Dr. Livingstone, I presume?"

WATERFOWL FESTIVAL. Nov 10-12. Easton, MD. A family wildlife art adventure, featuring paintings, carvings, sculpture, decoys, photography and crafts in gallery and shop venues throughout town. Lots of food, music and kids activities. Also, retriever, shooting and fly-fishing demonstrations, World Championship Goose and Mason-Dixon Duck Calling contests, Antique Decoy Auction. Annually, the second full weekend in November. Proceeds contributed to wildlife conservation. Est attendance: 18,000. For info: Waterfowl Festival, PO Box 929, Easton, MD 21601. Phone: (410) 822-4567. Fax: (410) 820-9286. E-mail: facts @waterfowlfestival.org. Web: www.waterfowlfestival.org.

WISCONSIN HOLIDAY MARKET. Nov 10-12. The American Club, Kohler, WI. More than 100 artists and craftspeople display their specialties in a glittering holiday market setting. Christmas shoppers can browse for crafts and collectibles to find the perfect holiday gift. Est attendance: 6,000. For info: The American Club, Highland Dr, Kohler, WI 53044. Phone: (800) 344-2838. Fax: (920) 457-4441. E-mail: kay.miller@kohler.com. Web: www.destinationkohler.com.

BIRTHDAYS TODAY

Vanessa Angel, 43, actress (*Spies Like Us, Kingpin*), born London, England, Nov 10, 1963.

Isaac Bruce, 34, football player, born Ft Lauderdale, FL, Nov 10, 1972.

Saxby Chambliss, 63, US Senator (R, Georgia), born Warrenton, NC, Nov 10, 1943.

Roland Emmerich, 51, director, producer (*The Day After Tomorrow, Independence Day*), born Stuttgart, Germany, Nov 10, 1955.

Donna Fargo, 57, singer ("Funny Face"), songwriter, born Yvonne Vaughan at Mount Airy, NC, Nov 10, 1949.

Russell Charles Means, 66, Native American rights activist, born Pine Ridge, SD, Nov 10, 1940.

Brittany Murphy, 29, actress (*Girl, Interrupted; 8 Mile; Sin City*), born Atlanta, GA, Nov 10, 1977.

Mackenzie Phillips, 47, actress ("One Day at a Time," *American Graffiti*), daughter of John Phillips of the Mamas and Papas, born Alexandria, VA, Nov 10, 1959.

Ann Reinking, 57, choreographer (Tony for *Chicago*), director, dancer, actress (*Goodtime Charley*), born Seattle, WA, Nov 10, 1949.

Tim Rice, 62, Tony Award–winning lyricist (*Aida, Evita, Jesus Christ Superstar*), born Amersham, England, Nov 10, 1944.

Roy Scheider, 71, actor (*Jaws, All That Jazz*, "Seaquest DSV"), born Orange, NJ, Nov 10, 1935.

Sinbad, 50, actor (*Unnecessary Roughness*, "A Different World"), born David Adkins at Benton Harbor, MI, Nov 10, 1956.

NOVEMBER 11 — SATURDAY
Day 315 — 50 Remaining

ANGOLA: INDEPENDENCE DAY. Nov 11. National holiday. Angola gained its independence from Portugal in 1975.

ANN ARBOR WINTER ART FAIR. Nov 11-12. Ann Arbor, MI. 32nd annual. Fine art and selected craft show. Some of the best artists and craftspersons in the country. Est attendance: 10,000. For info: Audree Levy, 1809 Morning Glory, Carrollton, TX 75007. Phone: (972) 394-5236. Fax: (972) 394-6236. E-mail: audree@levyartfairs.com. Web: www.levyartfairs.com.

BONZA BOTTLER DAY™. Nov 11. To celebrate when the number of the day is the same as the number of the month. Bonza Bottler Day™ is an excuse to have a party at least once a month. For more information, see Jan 1. For info: Gail M. Berger, 14 Fernwood Dr, Taylors, SC 29687. Phone: (864) 609-9874. E-mail: gberger5@aol.com.

CANADA: REMEMBRANCE DAY. Nov 11. Honors those who died in WWI and WWII. Public holiday.

COLOMBIA: CARTAGENA INDEPENDENCE DAY. Nov 11. National holiday. Commemorates declaration of independence from Spain of the city of Cartagena in 1811.

DEATH/DUTY DAY. Nov 11. Honoring soldiers on both sides who died on Nov 11, 1918, the armistice day that ended the fighting in the First World War of 1914-18. The order was to stop fighting at 11 AM, rather than on receipt of the order. For info: Bob Birch, Punscorpion, The Puns Corps, 3108 Dashiell Rd, Falls Church, VA 22042. Phone: (703) 533-3668.

DOSTOYEVSKY, FYODOR MIKHAILOVICH: BIRTH ANNIVERSARY. Nov 11, 1821. Russian novelist, author of *The Brothers Karamazov, Crime and Punishment* and *The Idiot*, was born at Moscow, and died at St. Petersburg, Feb 9, 1881. A political revolutionary, he was arrested, tried, convicted and sentenced to death, but instead of execution he served a sentence in a Siberian prison and later served in the army there.

ENGLAND: LORD MAYOR'S SHOW. Nov 11. The City of London. Each year a colorful parade steps off at 11 AM from the Guildhall to the Royal Courts of Justice to mark the inauguration of the new Lord Mayor, who pledges allegiance to the Crown. Annually, the second Saturday in November. Est attendance: 500,000. For info: Pageantmaster, The Lord Mayor's Show, The Barge, Hindringham Rd, Great Walsingham, Norfolk, England NR22 6DR. Phone: (44) (1328) 824-420. Fax: (44) (1328) 824-422. E-mail: show@reidandreid.com. Web: www.lordmayorshow .org.

"GOD BLESS AMERICA" FIRST PERFORMED: ANNIVERSARY. Nov 11, 1938. Irving Berlin wrote this song especially for Kate Smith. She first sang it during her regular radio broadcast. It quickly became a great patriotic favorite of the nation and one of Smith's most requested songs.

MALDIVES: REPUBLIC DAY: ANNIVERSARY. Nov 11. National holiday. Commemorates the abolition of the sultanate in 1968.

MARTINMAS. Nov 11. The Feast Day of St. Martin of Tours, who lived about AD 316-397. A bishop, he became one of the most popular saints of the Middle Ages. The period of warm weather often occurring about the time of his feast day is sometimes called St. Martin's Summer (especially in England).

PATTON, GEORGE S., JR: BIRTH ANNIVERSARY. Nov 11, 1885. American military officer, graduate of West Point (1909), George Smith Patton, Jr, was born at San Gabriel, CA. Ambitious and flamboyant, he lived for combat. He served in the punitive expedition into Mexico (1916), in Europe in WWI and in North Africa and Europe in WWII. He received world attention and official censure in 1943 for slapping a hospitalized shell-shocked soldier. While a full general, owing to his critical public statements, he was relieved of his command in 1945. He died at Heidelberg, Germany, Dec 21, 1945, of injuries received in an automobile accident.

POLAND: INDEPENDENCE DAY. Nov 11. Poland regained independence in 1918, after having been partitioned among Austria, Prussia and Russia for more than 120 years.

SPACE MILESTONE: *COLUMBIA STS-5* (US). Nov 11, 1982. Shuttle *Columbia* launched from Kennedy Space Center, FL, with four astronauts: Vance Brand, Robert Overmyer, William Lenoir and Joseph Allen. "First operational mission" delivered two satellites into orbit for commercial customers. *Columbia* landed at Edwards Air Force Base, CA, Nov 16, 1982.

SPACE MILESTONE: *GEMINI 12* (US): 40th ANNIVERSARY. Nov 11, 1966. Last Project Gemini manned Earth orbit launched. Buzz Aldrin spent five hours on a space walk, setting a new record.

SWEDEN: SAINT MARTIN'S DAY. Nov 11. Originally in memory of St. Martin of Tours; also associated with Martin Luther, who is celebrated the day before. Marks the end of the autumn's work and the beginning of winter activities.

SWITZERLAND: MARTINMAS GOOSE (MARTINI-GIANS). Nov 11. Sursee, Canton Lucerne. At 3 PM on Martinmas (the day on which interest is due), the "Gansabhauet" is staged in front of Town Hall. Blindfolded participants try to bring down, with a single sword stroke, a dead goose suspended on a wire.

★**VETERANS DAY.** Nov 11. Presidential Proclamation. Formerly called Armistice Day and proclaimed each year since 1926 for Nov 11. PL 83–380 of June 1, 1954, changed the name to Veterans Day. PL 90–363 of June 28, 1968, required that beginning in 1971 it would be observed the fourth Monday in October. PL 94–97 of Sept 18, 1975, required that effective Jan 1, 1978, the observance would revert to Nov 11.

VETERANS DAY. Nov 11. Veterans Day was observed on Nov 11 from 1919 through 1970. Public Law 90–363, the "Monday Holiday Law," provided that, beginning in 1971, Veterans Day would be observed on "the fourth Monday in October." This movable observance date, which separated Veterans Day from the Nov 11 anniversary of World War I Armistice, proved unpopular. State after state moved its observance back to the traditional Nov 11 date, and finally Public Law 94–97 of Sept 18, 1975, required that, effective Jan 1, 1978, the observance of Veterans Day revert to Nov 11. As Armistice Day this is a holiday in Belgium, France and other European countries. "At the eleventh hour of the eleventh day of the eleventh month" fighting ceased in WWI.

VETERANS DAY CELEBRATION. Nov 11. Mamou, LA. Memorial services, a patriotic parade and speeches. Sponsor: American Legion Post 123. Est attendance: 1,000. For info: Danzel D. Marcantel, Sr, Commander, PO Box 123, Mamou, LA 70554-123. Phone: (337) 468-3153.

VICTOR EMMANUEL III: BIRTH ANNIVERSARY. Nov 11, 1869. Last king of Italy Victor Emmanuel III was born at Naples, Italy, and became king upon the assassination of his father in July 1900. For the first 20 years of his reign, Victor Emmanuel followed Italy's constitutional custom of selecting a prime minister based on the parliamentary majority, but with parliament in disarray after WWI, he named Benito Mussolini to form a cabinet and then failed to prevent Mussolini and the Fascists from seizing power. The king became little more than a figurehead. In 1946 Victor Emmanuel abdicated the throne, and he and the Crown Prince went into exile. He died at Alexandria, Egypt, Dec 28, 1947.

VIETNAM WOMEN'S MEMORIAL DEDICATION: ANNIVERSARY. Nov 11, 1993. In recognition of the 11,500 women who served in the Vietnam war, the bronze sculpture erected at Washington, DC, was dedicated this day.

VOX POPULI DAY. Nov 11. Vox Populi is the Latin term for "People's Voice." Today is the day to make your voice count. Speak up and out for social change on impending cultural issues in international, national, regional and local news via the mediums of print, radio, TV, the Internet and open assemblies. [©1994] To alleviate the escalating costs of Eventological® Literature, a charge of $10 must be assessed for each request. Checks are to be made payable to: Adrienne Sioux Koopersmith, 1437 W Rosemont, #1W, Chicago, IL 60660-1319. E-mail: askoopersmith@hotmail.com.

WASHINGTON: ADMISSION DAY: ANNIVERSARY. Nov 11. Became 42nd state in 1889.

WORLD WAR I ARMISTICE: ANNIVERSARY. Nov 11, 1918. Anniversary of armistice between Allied and Central Powers ending WWI, signed at 5 AM, Nov 11, 1918, in Marshal Foch's railway car in the Forest of Compiegne, France. Hostilities ceased at 11 AM. Recognized in many countries as Armistice Day, Remembrance Day, Veterans Day, Victory Day or World War I Memorial Day. Many places observe silent memorial at the 11th hour of the 11th day of the 11th month each year. See also: "Veterans Day" (Nov 11).

BIRTHDAYS TODAY

Bibi Andersson, 71, actress (*Story of a Woman*), born Birgitta Anderson at Stockholm, Sweden, Nov 11, 1935.

Barbara Boxer, 66, US Senator (D, California), born Brooklyn, NY, Nov 11, 1940.

Leonardo DiCaprio, 32, actor (*Catch Me If You Can, Titanic, The Aviator*), born Hollywood, CA, Nov 11, 1974.

Calista Flockhart, 42, actress ("Ally McBeal"), born Freeport, IL, Nov 11, 1964.

Philip McKeon, 42, actor ("Alice"), born Westbury, NY, Nov 11, 1964.

Demi Moore, 44, actress ("General Hospital," *Ghost, GI Jane*), born Roswell, NM, Nov 11, 1962.

Reynaldo Ordonez, 34, baseball player, born Havana, Cuba, Nov 11, 1972.

Kurt Vonnegut, Jr, 84, novelist (*Slaughterhouse Five, Cat's Cradle*), born Indianapolis, IN, Nov 11, 1922.

Jonathan Winters, 81, comedian, actor ("The Jonathan Winters Show," "Mork & Mindy"), born Dayton, OH, Nov 11, 1925.

Frank Urban ("Fuzzy") Zoeller, 55, golfer, born New Albany, IN, Nov 11, 1951.

NOVEMBER 12 — SUNDAY

Day 316 — 49 Remaining

AMERICAN EDUCATION WEEK. Nov 12–18. Focuses attention on the importance of education and all that it stands for. Annually, the week preceding the week of Thanksgiving. For info: Natl Education Assn (NEA), 1201 16th St NW, Washington, DC 20036. Phone: (202) 833-4000. Web: www.nea.org.

ARCHES NATIONAL PARK ESTABLISHED: 35th ANNIVERSARY. Nov 12, 1971. Area of natural wind-eroded formations in eastern Utah, originally proclaimed a national monument Apr 12, 1929, was established as a national park. For further park info: Arches Natl Park, PO Box 907, Moab, UT 84532.

BIRTH OF BAHA'U'LLAH. Nov 12, 1817. Baha'i observance of anniversary of the birth of Baha'u'llah (born Mirza Husayn Ali)

November *2006*	S	M	T	W	T	F	S
				1	2	3	4
	5	6	7	8	9	10	11
	12	13	14	15	16	17	18
	19	20	21	22	23	24	25
	26	27	28	29	30		

at Nur, Persia. Baha'u'llah was prophet-founder of the Baha'i Faith. One of the nine days of the year when Baha'is suspend work. For info: Baha'is of the US, Office of Communications, 1233 Central St, Evanston, IL 60201. Phone: (847) 733-3411. Fax: (847) 869-0247. E-mail: ooc@usbnc.org. Web: www.us.bahai .org.

BLACKMUN, HARRY A.: BIRTH ANNIVERSARY. Nov 12, 1908. Former associate justice of the Supreme Court of the US, nominated by President Nixon Apr 14, 1970. He retired from the Court Aug 3, 1994. Justice Blackmun was born at Nashville, IL, and died at Arlington, VA, Mar 4, 1999.

ENGLAND: REMEMBRANCE SUNDAY. Nov 12. Cenotaph, Whitehall, London. Wreath-laying ceremony to commemorate the dead of both World Wars by Her Majesty The Queen, members of the Royal Family, government and service organizations. Annually, the Sunday closest to Nov 11. For info: Public Info Office, HQ London District Military, Horse Guards, Whitehall, London, England SW1A 2AX.

KELLY, GRACE PATRICIA: BIRTH ANNIVERSARY. Nov 12, 1929. American award-winning actress (Oscar for *The Country Girl*; *Rear Window*, *To Catch a Thief*) who became Princess Grace of Monaco when she married that country's ruler, Prince Rainier III, in 1956. Born at Philadelphia, PA, she died of injuries sustained in an automobile accident, Sept 14, 1982, at Monte Carlo, Monaco.

MEXICO: POSTMAN'S DAY. Nov 12. Every year on "Día del cartero," Mexicans show their appreciation for their postal carriers by leaving a little something in their mailboxes.

MOON PHASE: LAST QUARTER. Nov 12. Moon enters Last Quarter phase at 12:45 PM, EST.

PERIOPERATIVE (OR) NURSE WEEK. Nov 12–18. To inform health care consumers that the nurse in the operating room cares for patients before, during and after surgery. Annually, the week including Nov 14. For info: PR Mgr, AORN, 2170 S Parker Rd, Ste 300, Denver, CO 80231-5711. Phone: (303) 755-6300. Fax: (303) 338-4838. E-mail: jpaulson@aorn.org. Web: www.aorn.org.

RODIN, AUGUSTE: BIRTH ANNIVERSARY. Nov 12, 1840. French sculptor (*The Kiss, The Thinker*), born at Paris, France. Died Nov 17, 1917, near Paris.

SPACE MILESTONE: *COLUMBIA STS-2* (US): 25th ANNIVERSARY. Nov 12, 1981. Shuttle *Columbia*, launched from Kennedy Space Center, FL, with Joe Engle and Richard Truly on board, became first spacecraft launched from Earth for a second orbiting mission. Landed at Edwards Air Force Base, CA, Nov 14, 1981.

STANTON, ELIZABETH CADY: BIRTH ANNIVERSARY. Nov 12, 1815. American woman suffragist and reformer, Elizabeth Cady Stanton was born at Johnstown, NY. "We hold these truths to be self-evident," she said at the first Women's Rights Convention, in 1848, "that all men and women are created equal." She died at New York, NY, Oct 26, 1902.

SUN YAT-SEN: BIRTH ANNIVERSARY (TRADITIONAL). Nov 12. Although his actual birth date in 1866 is not known, Dr. Sun Yat-Sen's traditional birthday commemoration is held Nov 12. Heroic leader of China's 1911 revolution, he died at Peking, Mar 12, 1925. A holiday in Taiwan. His death

anniversary is also widely observed. See also: "Sun Yat-Sen: Death Anniversary" (Mar 12).

TUNISIA: TREE FESTIVAL. Nov 12. National agricultural festival. Annually, the second Sunday in November.

TYLER, LETITIA CHRISTIAN: BIRTH ANNIVERSARY. Nov 12, 1790. First wife of John Tyler, tenth president of the US, born at New Kent County, VA. Died at Washington, DC, Sept 10, 1842.

BIRTHDAYS TODAY

Nadia Comaneci, 45, Olympic gold medal gymnast, born Onesti, Romania, Nov 12, 1961.
Ernie Fletcher, 54, Governor of Kentucky (R), born Mount Sterling, KY, Nov 12, 1952.
Tonya Harding, 36, figure skater, born Portland, OR, Nov 12, 1970.
Norman Mineta, 75, US Secretary of Transportation, born San Jose, CA, Nov 12, 1931.
Megan Mullally, 48, actress ("Will & Grace," *How to Succeed in Business Without Really Trying*), born Los Angeles, CA, Nov 12, 1958.
Jack Reed, 57, US Senator (D, Rhode Island), born Providence, RI, Nov 12, 1949.
David Schwimmer, 40, actor ("Friends"), born Queens, NY, Nov 12, 1966.
Sammy Sosa, 38, baseball player, born San Pedro de Macoris, Dominican Republic, Nov 12, 1968.
Neil Young, 61, singer (Buffalo Springfield and Crosby, Stills, Nash & Young), songwriter, born Toronto, ON, Canada, Nov 12, 1945.

NOVEMBER 13 — MONDAY
Day 317 — 48 Remaining

BOOTH, EDWIN (THOMAS): BIRTH ANNIVERSARY. Nov 13, 1833. Famed American actor and founder of the Players Club, born near Bel Air, MD. His brother, John Wilkes Booth, assassinated President Lincoln. Died at New York, NY, June 7, 1893.

BRANDEIS, LOUIS DEMBITZ: 150th BIRTH ANNIVERSARY. Nov 13, 1856. American jurist, associate justice of US Supreme Court (1916–39), born at Louisville, KY. Died at Washington, DC, Oct 5, 1941.

CHILDREN'S BOOK WEEK. Nov 13–19. An annual event, sponsored by The Children's Book Council, to encourage the enjoyment of reading for young people. For info: The Children's Book Council, Inc, 12 W 37th St, 2nd Fl, New York, NY 10018. Phone: (800) 999-2160. Fax: (888) 807-9355. E-mail: info@cbc-books.org. Web: www.cbcbooks.org.

FALL OF KABUL: 5th ANNIVERSARY. Nov 13, 2001. Northern Alliance troops opposing the Islamic extremist regime of the Taliban moved into the capital of Afghanistan on this date— the first major victory in the war on terrorism prompted by the Sept 11, 2001, attacks on America. After fleeing Kabul (which they had controlled since 1996), the Taliban regime quickly collapsed. The US had demanded that the Taliban regime give up Al Qaeda terrorists and their leader, Osama bin Laden, or face reprisals. Upon the Taliban's prevarication, the US led a multinational force in support of the Northern Alliance that began with a bombardment and then ground warfare in Afghanistan. The fall of Kabul was the first major step to destroying Al Qaeda's Afghanistan stronghold. See also "Attack on America: Anniversary" (Sept 11).

HOLLAND TUNNEL: ANNIVERSARY. Nov 13, 1927. The Holland Tunnel, running under the Hudson River between New York, NY, and Jersey City, NJ, was opened to traffic. The tunnel was built and operated by the New York–New Jersey Bridge and Tunnel Commission. Comprised of two tubes, each large enough for two lanes of traffic, the Holland was the first underwater tunnel built in the US.

MAXWELL, JAMES CLERK: 275th BIRTH ANNIVERSARY. Nov 13, 1831. British physicist noted for his work in the field of electricity and magnetism. Born at Edinburgh, Scotland, he died of cancer Nov 5, 1879, at Cambridge, England.

THE NATIONAL GINGERBREAD HOUSE COMPETITION. Nov 13. The Grove Park Inn Resort & Spa, Asheville, NC. Hundreds of totally edible and highly decorative entries adorn the resort's grand ballroom as celebrity judges determine the grand prize champion. Est attendance: 500. For info: The Grove Park Inn Resort & Spa, 290 Macon Ave, Asheville, NC 28804. Phone: (800) 438-5800 or (828) 252-2711. Fax: (828) 252-6040. Web: www.groveparkinn.com.

STEVENSON, ROBERT LOUIS: BIRTH ANNIVERSARY. Nov 13, 1850. Scottish author, born at Edinburgh, Scotland, known for his *Child's Garden of Verses* and novels such as *Treasure Island* and *Kidnapped*. Died at Samoa, Dec 3, 1894.

STOKES BECOMES FIRST BLACK MAYOR IN US: ANNIVERSARY. Nov 13, 1967. Carl Burton Stokes became the first black in the US elected mayor when he won the Cleveland, OH, mayoral election Nov 13, 1967. Died Apr 3, 1996.

TRELAWNEY, EDWARD JOHN: BIRTH ANNIVERSARY. Nov 13, 1792. English traveler and author, friend of Shelley and Byron, born at London. He died at Sompting, Sussex, Aug 13, 1881, and was buried at Rome, next to Shelley.

TRIPLE CROWN OF SURFING. Nov 13–Dec 20. Oahu, HI. The 24th annual Triple Crown includes three professional big wave surf meets on Oahu's North Shore that mark the conclusion of the yearlong Association of Surfing Professionals (ASP) world tour. Following the Triple Crown the ASP Men's and Women's Champions are crowned. Est attendance: 20,000. For info: Randy Rarick, 59-063-A Hoalua St, Haleiwa, HI 96712. Phone: (808) 638-7266. Fax: (808) 638-7764. E-mail: surfpro@hawaii.rr.com. Web: www.triplecrownofsurfing.com.

WORLD KINDNESS DAY. Nov 13. The Kindness Movement has gone global! The World Kindness Movement grew out of a series of Kindness Conferences convened by the Japanese Small Kindness Movement in 1996. The Random Acts of Kindness Foundation, USA has been a part of these conferences along with representatives from Japan, Singapore, Australia, Canada, Thailand and England. This day represents the pledge of each of these countries to join together to build a kinder and more compassionate world. For info: Random Acts of Kindness Foundation, 1727 Tremont Pl, Denver, CO 80202. Phone: (800) 660-2811. E-mail: rakinfo@actsofkindness.org. Web: www.actsofkindness.org.

November 2006

S	M	T	W	T	F	S
			1	2	3	4
5	6	7	8	9	10	11
12	13	14	15	16	17	18
19	20	21	22	23	24	25
26	27	28	29	30		

Sheila E. Frazier, 58, actress (*Super Fly, I'm Gonna Git You Sucka*), born the Bronx, NY, Nov 13, 1948.

Whoopi Goldberg, 57, comedienne, actress (Oscar for *Ghost; Sister Act, The Color Purple*), born Caryn Elaine Johnson at New York, NY, Nov 13, 1949.

Jimmy Kimmel, 39, late night talk-show host, comedian ("The Man Show," "Jimmy Kimmel Live"), born Brooklyn, NY, Nov 13, 1967.

Joe Mantegna, 59, actor (stage: Tony for *Glengarry Glen Ross; House of Games, Things Change*), born Chicago, IL, Nov 13, 1947.

Garry Marshall, 72, producer, director (*Beaches, Pretty Woman*), actor ("Murphy Brown"), born New York, NY, Nov 13, 1934.

Chris Noth, 49, actor ("Sex and the City," "Law & Order," *Burnzy's Last Call*), born Madison, WI, Nov 13, 1957.

Tracy Scoggins, 47, actress ("The Colbys," *Some Kind of Hero*), born Galveston, TX, Nov 13, 1959.

Madeline Sherwood, 84, actress ("The Flying Nun"), born Montreal, QC, Canada, Nov 13, 1922.

Vincent Frank (Vinny) Testaverde, 43, football player, born New York, NY, Nov 13, 1963.

Steve Zahn, 38, actor (*National Security, Sahara*), born Marshall, MN, Nov 13, 1968.

NOVEMBER 14 — TUESDAY
Day 318 — 47 Remaining

BROOKS, LOUISE: 100th BIRTH ANNIVERSARY. Nov 14, 1906. Born at Cherryvale, KS, Brooks started out as a dancer before finding fame as an actress in the 1920s silent cinema. She is best known for her performances in two 1929 German films: *Pandora's Box* (as Lulu) and *Diary of a Lost Girl*. Would-be flappers the world over copied her trademark hairstyle: a sleek helmet-like bob. Brooks wrote a well-received book of reminiscences, *Lulu in Hollywood* (1982), before her death on Aug 8, 1985, at Rochester, NY.

COPLAND, AARON: BIRTH ANNIVERSARY. Nov 14, 1900. American composer Aaron Copland was born at Brooklyn, NY. Incorporating American folk music and, later, the 12-tone system, he strove to create an American music style that was both popular and artistic. He composed ballets, film scores and orchestral works including *Fanfare for the Common Man* (1942), *Appalachian Spring* (1944) (for which he won the Pulitzer Prize) and the score for *The Heiress* (1948) (for which he won an Oscar). He died Dec 2, 1990, at North Tarrytown, NY.

DOW-JONES TOPS 1,000: ANNIVERSARY. Nov 14, 1972. The Dow-Jones Index of 30 major industrial stocks topped the 1,000 mark for the first time.

EISENHOWER, MAMIE DOUD: BIRTH ANNIVERSARY. Nov 14, 1896. Wife of Dwight David Eisenhower, 34th president of the US, born at Boone, IA. Died Nov 1, 1979, at Gettysburg, PA.

FULTON, ROBERT: BIRTH ANNIVERSARY. Nov 14, 1765. Inventor of the steamboat, born at Little Britain, PA. Died Feb 24, 1815, at New York, NY.

GUINEA-BISSAU: READJUSTMENT MOVEMENT'S DAY. Nov 14. National holiday.

INDIA: CHILDREN'S DAY. Nov 14. Holiday observed throughout India.

JORDAN: KING HUSSEIN: BIRTH ANNIVERSARY. Nov 14. H.M. King Hussein's birthday is honored each year on the anniversary of his birth in 1935. He died in Jordan Feb 7, 1999.

LOOSEN UP, LIGHTEN UP DAY. Nov 14. A day to remind people of all the benefits of joy and laughter. For info: Stephanie West Allen, PO Box 9311, Denver, CO 80209. Phone: (303) 742-4790. Fax: (303) 935-8842. E-mail: stephanie@allen-nichols.com. Web: www.allen-nichols.com.

MONET, CLAUDE: BIRTH ANNIVERSARY. Nov 14, 1840. French Impressionist painter (*Water Lillies*), born at Paris. Died at Giverny, France, Dec 5, 1926.

"MURPHY BROWN" TV PREMIERE: ANNIVERSARY. Nov 14, 1988. This intelligent, often acerbic sitcom set in Washington, DC, starred Candice Bergen as an egotistical, seasoned journalist working for the fictitious TV news show "FYI." Featured were Grant Shaud, as the show's high-strung producer, Miles Silverberg (later replaced by Lily Tomlin); Faith Ford as the former Miss America-turned-anchor, Corky Sherwood; Joe Regalbuto as neurotic reporter Frank Fontana; Charles Kimbrough as uptight anchorman, Jim Dial; Pat Corley as Phil, owner of the local watering hole and Robert Pastorelli as Eldin Bernecky, perfectionist housepainter and aspiring artist. The show often blurred the line between reality and fiction by dealing with topical issues and including real-life journalists as guest stars playing themselves. The series ended with the May 31, 1998, episode.

NATIONAL AMERICAN TEDDY BEAR DAY. Nov 14. The Vermont Teddy Bear Company® annually celebrates the birth of America's most beloved companion, the teddy bear. The legend goes that President Theodore Roosevelt spared the life of a bear cub while on a big game hunt in Mississippi in 1902. Clifford Berryman, a political cartoonist, recorded the incident. President Theodore Roosevelt was most often depicted alongside a teddy bear and thus America's love affair with the teddy bear began. For info: The Vermont Teddy Bear Company®, 6655 Shelburne Rd, Shelburne, VT 05482. Phone: (800) 829-BEAR. Web: www.VermontTeddyBear.com.

NATIONAL YOUNG READER'S DAY. Nov 14. Pizza Hut and the Center for the Book in the Library of Congress established National Young Reader's Day to remind Americans of the joys and importance of reading for young people. Schools, libraries, families and communities nationwide use this day to celebrate youth reading in a variety of creative and educational ways. Ideas on ways you can celebrate this special day available. For info: Shelley Morehead, The BOOK IT! Program, PO Box 2999, Wichita, KS 67201. Phone: (800) 426-6548. Fax: (316) 685-0977. Web: www.bookitprogram.com.

NEHRU, JAWAHARLAL: BIRTH ANNIVERSARY. Nov 14, 1889. Indian leader and first prime minister after independence. Born at Allahabad, India, he died May 27, 1964, at New Delhi.

SALISBURY, HARRISON: BIRTH ANNIVERSARY. Nov 14, 1908. American journalist Harrison Evans Salisbury was born at Minneapolis, MN. *New York Times* Moscow correspondent from 1949 to 1954. Salisbury won the Pulitzer Prize in 1955 for a series of articles on the Soviet Union. He died July 5, 1993, at Providence, RI.

SPACE MILESTONE: *APOLLO 12* (US). Nov 14, 1969. Launched this date. This was the second manned lunar landing—in Ocean of Storms. First pinpoint landing. Astronauts Conrad, Bean and Gordon visited *Surveyor 3* and took samples. Earth splashdown Nov 24.

STEIG, WILLIAM: BIRTH ANNIVERSARY. Nov 14, 1907. Prolific cartoonist, satirist and illustrator, William Steig was born at Brooklyn, NY. *The New Yorker* published more than 1,600 of his drawings, including 117 covers, and he wrote more than 25 books for children. He won the Caldecott Medal in 1970 for *Sylvester and the Magic Pebble*, and received two Newbery Honors, for *Abel's Island* and *Dr. De Soto*. Other favorites include *The Amazing Bone, Brave Irene, CDB* and *Shrek,* the basis for the 2001 animated film featuring Mike Myers. Steig died at Boston, MA, Oct 3, 2003.

BIRTHDAYS TODAY

Boutros Boutros-Ghali, 84, former Secretary-General of the UN, born Cairo, Egypt, Nov 14, 1922.
Prince Charles, 58, Prince of Wales, heir to the British throne, born London, England, Nov 14, 1948.
Condoleezza Rice, 52, US Secretary of State, former US National Security Adviser, born Birmingham, AL, Nov 14, 1954.
Laura San Giacomo, 44, actress (*sex, lies and videotape*, "Just Shoot Me"), born Hoboken, NJ, Nov 14, 1962.
Curt Schilling, 40, baseball player, born Anchorage, AK, Nov 14, 1966.
Joseph ("Run") Simmons, 42, rapper (*Run D.M.C.*), born Queens, NY, Nov 14, 1964.
Don Stewart, 71, singer, actor ("Guiding Light"), born Staten Island, NY, Nov 14, 1935.
D.B. Sweeney, 45, actor (*Spawn, The Cutting Edge*), born Shoreham, Long Island, NY, Nov 14, 1961.
Yanni, 52, New Age composer, born Yanni Chrysomalis at Kalamata, Greece, Nov 14, 1954.

NOVEMBER 15 — WEDNESDAY
Day 319 — 46 Remaining

AMERICA RECYCLES DAY. Nov 15. To promote recycling and recycled products. More than 40 states will participate. Annually, every Nov 15. For info: Natl Program Mgr, America Recycles Day, 1325 G St NW, Ste 1025, Washington, DC 20005. Phone: (202) 347-0450. Web: www.americarecyclesday.org.

BELGIUM: DYNASTY DAY. Nov 15. National holiday in honor of Belgian monarchy.

BRAZIL: REPUBLIC DAY. Nov 15. Commemorates the Proclamation of the Republic in 1889. Celebrated on the Monday nearest Nov 15.

GATEWAY FARM EXPO. Nov 15–16. Buffalo County Fairgrounds, Kearney, NE. Est attendance: 6,000. For info: Kearney Area Chamber of Commerce, PO Box 607, Kearney, NE 68848. Phone: (877) 720-4885. Web: www.gatewayfarmexpo.org.

GEORGE SPELVIN DAY. Nov 15. Believed to be the anniversary of George Spelvin's theatrical birth—in Charles A. Gardiner's play *Karl the Peddler* on Nov 15, 1886, in a production at New York, NY. The name (or equivalent Georgina, Georgetta, etc) is used in play programs to conceal the fact that an actor is performing in more than one role. The fictitious Spelvin is said to have appeared in more than 10,000 Broadway performances. See also: "England: Walter Plinge Day" (Dec 2) for British equivalent.

GYPSY CONDEMNATION ORDER: ANNIVERSARY. Nov 15, 1943. An order was issued by Heinrich Himmler for nomadic Gypsies and part-Gypsies to be placed in concentration camps. In cases of doubt, it was up to local heads of police to determine who was a Gypsy. Some estimates put the number of Gypsies killed in the Holocaust as high as half a million.

I LOVE TO WRITE DAY. Nov 15. New York City, Los Angeles, Boston, Chicago, Philadelphia and other major cities across the US. I Love To Write Day encourages people of all ages to write something: a poem, a short story, a letter to the editor or to start or finish a novel—the possibilities are endless! Special writing events and activities take place in more than 15,000 schools, libraries, bookstores and community centers all across the US. Annually, Nov 15. For info: John Riddle, 6 Basset Pl, Bear, DE 19701. Phone: (302) 834-3055. E-mail: johnriddle@sprintmail.com. Web: www.ilovetowriteday.org.

JAPAN: SHICHI-GO-SAN. Nov 15. Annual children's festival. The *Shichi-Go-San* (Seven-Five-Three) rite is "the most picturesque event in the autumn season." Parents take their three-year-old children of either sex, five-year-old boys and seven-year-old girls to the parish shrines dressed in their best clothes. There the guardian spirits are thanked for the healthy growth of the children and prayers are offered for their further development.

LEMAY, CURTIS: 100th BIRTH ANNIVERSARY. Nov 15, 1906. Born at Columbus, OH, LeMay was a WWII hero whose bombing strategies for the US helped push the Axis powers toward surrender. He later oversaw the Berlin airlift in 1948 and headed the US Strategic Air Command (1948–57). In 1968, he ran as vice presidential candidate in the American Independent Party headed by George Wallace. LeMay died Oct 1, 1990, at March AFB, CA.

NAIA MEN'S & WOMEN'S SOCCER NATIONAL CHAMPIONSHIPS. Nov 15–21. Daytona Beach, FL (men's); Olathe, KS (women's). 20-team fields compete for national championships. 48th annual for men; 23rd annual for women. For info: Natl Assn of Intercollegiate Athletics, 23500 W 105th St, PO Box 1325, Olathe, KS 66051-1325. Phone: (913) 791-0044. Fax: (913) 791-9555. E-mail: smcclure@naia.org (men's) or rfeldblum @naia.org (women's). Web: www.naia.org.

NATIONAL EDUCATIONAL SUPPORT PROFESSIONALS DAY. Nov 15. A mandate of the delegates to the 1987 National Education Association Representative Assembly called for a special day during American Education Week to honor the contributions of school support employees. Local associations and school districts salute support staff on this 19th annual observance, the Wednesday of American Education Week. For info: Natl Education Assn (NEA), 1201 16th St NW, Washington, DC 20036. Phone: (202) 833-4000. Fax: (202) 822-7974. Web: www.nea.org.

O'KEEFFE, GEORGIA: BIRTH ANNIVERSARY. Nov 15, 1887. Described as one of the greatest American artists of the 20th century, Georgia O'Keeffe was born at Sun Prairie, WI. In 1924, she married the famous photographer Alfred Stieglitz. His more than 500 photographs of her have been called "the greatest love poem in the history of photography." She painted desert landscapes and flower studies. She died at Santa Fe, NM, Mar 6, 1986.

ROMMEL, ERWIN: BIRTH ANNIVERSARY. Nov 15, 1891. Field marshal and commander of the German Afrika Korps in WWII, Erwin Rommel was born at Heidenheim, in Württemberg, Germany. Rommel commanded the Seventh Panzer Division in the Battle of France. Considered an excellent commander, Rommel's early success in Africa made him a legend as the "Desert Fox," but in early 1943 he was outmaneuvered by Field Marshal Bernard Montgomery, and Germany surrendered Tunis in May of that year. Implicated in July 1944 in an attempted assassination of Hitler, he was given the choice of suicide or a trial and chose the former. Rommel died by his own hand at age 52, Oct 14, 1944, near Ulm, Germany.

SPACE MILESTONE: *BURAN* (USSR). Nov 15, 1988. The Soviet Union's first reusable space plane, *Buran*, landed on this date, completing a smooth, unmanned mission at approximately 1:25 AM, EST, after orbiting the Earth twice in 3 hours, 25 minutes. Launched at Baikonur, Soviet central Asia. The importance of this mission was in its computer-controlled liftoff and return.

★ ★ ★

November 2006

	S	M	T	W	T	F	S
				1	2	3	4
	5	6	7	8	9	10	11
	12	13	14	15	16	17	18
	19	20	21	22	23	24	25
	26	27	28	29	30		

Ed Asner, 77, actor ("The Mary Tyler Moore Show," "Lou Grant," *Roots*), born Kansas City, MO, Nov 15, 1929.

Daniel Barenboim, 64, musician, conductor, born Buenos Aires, Argentina, Nov 15, 1942.

Joanna Barnes, 72, actress ("The Trials of O'Brien"), born Boston, MA, Nov 15, 1934.

Petula Clark, 74, singer ("Downtown," "I Know a Place," "This Is My Song"), actress, born Ewell, Surrey, England, Nov 15, 1932.

Beverly D'Angelo, 52, actress (*Hair, Coal Miner's Daughter*), born Columbus, OH, Nov 15, 1954.

Kevin Eubanks, 49, "The Tonight Show" bandleader, born Philadelphia, PA, Nov 15, 1957.

Yaphet Kotto, 69, actor ("Homicide," *Nothing but a Man, Blue Collar, Midnight Run*), born New York, NY, Nov 15, 1937.

Jonny Lee Miller, 34, actor (*Dracula 2000, Behind the Lines, Mansfield Park*), born Kingston, England, Nov 15, 1972.

Bill Richardson, 59, Governor of New Mexico (D), former Secretary of Energy (Clinton Administration), born Pasadena, CA, Nov 15, 1947.

Joseph Wapner, 87, television personality ("People's Court"), retired judge, born Los Angeles, CA, Nov 15, 1919.

Sam Waterston, 66, actor (*The Killing Fields, The Great Gatsby*, "I'll Fly Away," "Law & Order"), born Cambridge, MA, Nov 15, 1940.

NOVEMBER 16 — THURSDAY
Day 320 — 45 Remaining

AMERICAN SPEECH-LANGUAGE-HEARING ASSOCIATION CONVENTION. Nov 16–18. Miami, FL. Scientific sessions held on language, speech disorders, hearing science and hearing disorders and matters of professional interest to speech-language pathologists and audiologists. Est attendance: 15,000. For info: American Speech-Language-Hearing Assn, 10801 Rockville Pike, Rockville, MD 20852-3279. Phone: (301) 897-5700. Web: www.asha.org.

ESTONIA: DAY OF NATIONAL REBIRTH: ANNIVERSARY. Nov 16. National holiday. Commemorates the 1988 Declaration of Sovereignty. Became independent from the Soviet Union in 1991.

GREAT AMERICAN SMOKEOUT. Nov 16. A day observed annually to celebrate smoke-free environments. Annually, the third Thursday in November. For info: American Cancer Society. Phone: (800) ACS-2345. Web: www.cancer.org.

HANDY, WILLIAM CHRISTOPHER: BIRTH ANNIVERSARY. Nov 16, 1873. American composer, bandleader, "Father of the Blues," W.C. Handy was born at Florence, AL. He died at New York, NY, Mar 28, 1958.

LEWIS AND CLARK EXPEDITION REACHES PACIFIC OCEAN: ANNIVERSARY. Nov 16, 1805. Lewis and Clark's Corps of Discovery reached the Pacific Ocean on this date. They had glimpsed it on Nov 7, moving Clark to write in his journal: "Great joy in camp! We are in view of the Ocean, this great Pacific Ocean which we have been so anxious to see. And the roaring or noise of the waves breaking on the rocky shores . . . may be heard distinctly."

MADD'S TIE ONE ON FOR SAFETY HOLIDAY RIBBON CAMPAIGN. Nov 16–Dec 31. TOOFS is a drunk driving awareness campaign created by Mothers Against Drunk Driving that encourages the public to tie a MADD red ribbon to their vehicle as a pledge to drive safe and sober and buckle up seat belts throughout the holidays and year-round. For info: MADD. Phone: (800) GET-MADD. Web: www.madd.org.

MEREDITH, BURGESS: BIRTH ANNIVERSARY. Nov 16, 1907. Actor (*Of Mice and Men, Rocky*) born at Cleveland, OH. Some sources give his year of birth as 1908 or 1909. Died at Malibu, CA, Sept 9, 1997.

★NATIONAL GREAT AMERICAN SMOKEOUT DAY. Nov 16.

OKLAHOMA: ADMISSION DAY: ANNIVERSARY. Nov 16. Became 46th state in 1907.

RIEL, LOUIS: HANGING ANNIVERSARY. Nov 16, 1885. Born at St. Boniface, MB, Canada, Oct 23, 1844, Louis Riel, leader of the Metis (French/Indian mixed ancestry), was elected to Canada's House of Commons in 1873 and 1874, but never seated. Confined to asylums for madness (feigned or falsely charged, some said), Riel became a US citizen in 1883. In 1885 he returned to western Canada to lead the North West Rebellion. Defeated, he surrendered and was tried for treason, convicted and hanged, at Regina, NT, Canada. Seen as a patriot and protector of French culture in Canada, Riel's life and death became a legend and a symbol of the problems between French and English Canadians.

ROMAN CATHOLICS ISSUE NEW CATECHISM: ANNIVERSARY. Nov 16, 1992. For the first time since 1563, the Roman Catholic Church issued a new universal catechism, which addressed modern-day issues.

SAINT EUSTATIUS, WEST INDIES: STATIA AND AMERICA DAY. Nov 16, 1776. St. Eustatius, Leeward Islands. To commemorate the first salute to an American flag by a foreign government, from Fort Oranje in 1776. Festivities include sports events and dancing. During the American Revolution St. Eustatius was an important trading center and a supply base for the colonies.

SPACE MILESTONE: *SKYLAB 4* (US). Nov 16, 1973. 30th manned US space flight launched with three astronauts, G.P. Carr, W.R. Page and E.G. Gibson, who spent 84 days on the space station. Space walks totaled 22 hours. Returned to Earth on Feb 8, 1974.

SPACE MILESTONE: *VENERA 3* (USSR). Nov 16, 1965. Launched this date, this unmanned space probe crashed into Venus, Mar 1, 1966. First man-made object on another planet.

SUGARLOAF CRAFTS FESTIVAL. Nov 16–19. Montgomery County Fairgrounds, Gaithersburg, MD. This show, now in its 31st year, features more than 500 nationally recognized craft designers and fine artists displaying and selling their original creations. Includes craft demonstrations, live music, specialty foods, hourly gift certificate drawings and more. Est attendance: 37,500. For info: Sugarloaf Mountain Works, 200 Orchard Ridge Dr, #215, Gaithersburg, MD 20878. Phone: (800) 210-9900. Fax: (301) 253-9620. Web: www.sugarloafcrafts.com.

UNITED NATIONS: INTERNATIONAL DAY FOR TOLERANCE. Nov 16. On Dec 12, 1996, the General Assembly established the International Day for Tolerance, to commemorate the adoption by UNESCO member states of the Declaration of Principles on Tolerance in 1995. For info: United Nations, Dept of Public Info, New York, NY 10017. Web: www.un.org.

Oksana Baiul, 29, Olympic gold medal figure skater, born Dniepropetrovsk, Ukraine, Nov 16, 1977.
Lisa Bonet, 39, actress ("The Cosby Show," "A Different World," *Angel Heart*), born San Francisco, CA, Nov 16, 1967.
Elizabeth Drew, 71, journalist, born Cincinnati, OH, Nov 16, 1935.
Dwight Eugene Gooden, 42, former baseball player, born Tampa, FL, Nov 16, 1964.
Maggie Gyllenhaal, 29, actress (*Secretary, Donnie Darko*), born New York, NY, Nov 16, 1977.
Marg Helgenberger, 48, actress ("CSI," "China Beach"), born Fremont, NE, Nov 16, 1958.
Diana Krall, 42, jazz singer, born Nanaimo, BC, Canada, Nov 16, 1964.
Martha Plimpton, 36, actress (*The Libertine*), born New York, NY, Nov 16, 1970.

NOVEMBER 17 — FRIDAY
Day 321 — 44 Remaining

COLORADO RIVER CROSSING BALLOON FESTIVAL. Nov 17–19. Cibola High School, Yuma, AZ. 16th annual. 55 balloons. Sunrise balloon liftoffs on Saturday and Sunday at Cibola High School. Sunset balloon glow and fireworks on Saturday evening at Ray Kroc Complex/Desert Sun Stadium. Entertainment, food, vendors. Free admission. Est attendance: 17,000. For info: Caballeros de Yuma, Inc, PO Box 5987, Yuma, AZ 85366. Phone: (928) 343-1715. Fax: (928) 783-1609. E-mail: caballeros@beamspeed.net. Web: www.caballeros.org.

FANTASY OF LIGHT PARADE. Nov 17. Wheeling, WV. Night parade with more than 100 lighted floats and musical units. Est attendance: 80,000. For info: Wheeling Conv and Visitors Bureau, 1401 Main St, Wheeling, WV 26003. Phone: (800) 828-3097 or (304) 233-7709. Fax: (304) 233-1470. Web: www.wheelingcvb.com/calendar.

GRAND ILLUMINATION. Nov 17. Lahaska, PA. Santa switches on the village's outdoor light display on Friday at 6:15 PM to kick off the holiday season. Free cider and toasted marshmallows. Preview of new gift ideas in shops. Free admission. Est attendance: 5,000. For info: Peddler's Village, Rtes 202 & 263, Lahaska, PA 18931. Phone: (215) 794-4000. Fax: (215) 794-4001. Web: www.peddlersvillage.com.

HOLIDAY FOLK FAIR INTERNATIONAL. Nov 17–19. Wisconsin State Fair Park, Milwaukee, WI. International festival featuring costumes, dancing, entertainment, exhibits, workshops, folk wares and cuisine from 65 cultures. Also children's activities. Annually, the weekend before Thanksgiving. Est attendance: 65,000. For info: Holiday Folk Fair International, Intl Institute of Wisconsin, 1110 N Old World Third St, Ste 420, Milwaukee, WI 53203. Phone: (414) 225-6220. Fax: (414) 225-6235. E-mail: folkfair@execpc.com.

HOMEMADE BREAD DAY. Nov 17. A day for the family to remember and enjoy the making, baking and eating of nutritious homemade bread. For info: Homemade Bread Day Committee, PO Box 3, Montague, MI 49437-0003.

HONDA, SOICHIRO: 100th BIRTH ANNIVERSARY. Nov 17, 1906. Born at Hamamatsu, Japan, Honda was the enterprising auto racer turned businessman who founded the Honda Motor Company, a great part of Japan's postwar emergence as an economic power. Honda retired in 1973 and died Aug 5, 1991, at Tokyo.

MÖBIUS, AUGUST: BIRTH ANNIVERSARY. Nov 17, 1790. German astronomer, mathematician, teacher and author, August Ferdinand Möbius was born at Schulpforte, Germany. Möbius was a pioneer in the field of topology, and first described the Möbius net and the Möbius strip. He died at Leipzig, Sept 26, 1868.

MONTGOMERY, BERNARD LAW: BIRTH ANNIVERSARY. Nov 17, 1887. Bernard Law Montgomery, who commanded the British Eighth Army to victory at El Alamein in North Africa in 1943, was born at St. Mark's Vicarage, Kennington Oval, London, England. He also led the Eighth Army in the Sicilian and Italian campaigns and commanded all ground forces in the 1944 Normandy landing. Montgomery died Mar 24, 1976, at Alton, Hampshire, England.

★ **NATIONAL FARM-CITY WEEK.** Nov 17–23. Presidential Proclamation issued for a week in November since 1956, customarily for the week ending with Thanksgiving Day. Requested by congressional resolutions from 1956–58; since 1959 issued annually without request.

NCAA DIVISION III FIELD HOCKEY CHAMPIONSHIP. Nov 17–18. McCooey Memorial Field, Geneva, NY. Hosted by William Smith College. Est attendance: 1,000. For info: Natl Collegiate Athletic Assn, 700 W Washington St, PO Box 6222, Indianapolis, IN 46206-6222. Phone: (317) 917-6222. Fax: (317) 917-6888. Web: www.ncaasports.com.

PEDDLER'S VILLAGE GINGERBREAD HOUSE COMPETITION & DISPLAY. Nov 17–Jan 4, 2007. Lahaska, PA. More than 100 gingerbread house entries from throughout the US compete for more than $3,400 in cash prizes in such categories as: Traditional, Authentic Reproduction of a Significant Building, Amateur, Incredibly Unusual 3-Dimensional and Children's (12 and under; 13–18). The creative masterpieces are displayed throughout the holiday season in the Village Gazebo. Free admission. Est attendance: 850,000. For info: Peddler's Village, Rtes 202 & 263, Lahaska, PA 18931. Phone: (215) 794-4000. Fax: (215) 794-4001. Web: www.peddlersvillage.com.

LA POSADA de KINGSVILLE: A CELEBRATION OF LIGHTS. Nov 17–Dec 16. Kingsville, TX. While a celebration of lights recaptures the joy and spirit of Christmas as businesses and neighborhoods twinkle with lights from the weekend before Thanksgiving, many holiday events with a South Texas flavor are scheduled: special activities for children, nighttime parade with lighted floats and holiday music and much more. Call for dates of specific events. Est attendance: 50,000. For info: Kingsville Conv and Visitors Bureau, 1501 N Hwy 77, Kingsville, TX 78364-1562. Phone: (800) 333-5032. Fax: (361) 592-3227. Web: www.kingsvilletexas.com.

QUEEN ELIZABETH I: ACCESSION ANNIVERSARY. Nov 17, 1558. Anniversary of accession of Elizabeth I to English throne; celebrated as a holiday in England for more than a century after her death in 1603.

SILVER BELLS IN THE CITY. Nov 17. Lansing, MI. Michigan's capital city sparkles with hospitality on the streets of downtown Lansing's business district for this celebration of lights, music and holiday cheer including an electric light parade, lighting of the State of Michigan Holiday Tree and a fireworks display (weather permitting) over the state capitol dome. Annually, the Friday before Thanksgiving. Coordinated by Arts Council of Greater Lansing, Inc. Est attendance: 50,000. For info: Arts Council of Greater Lansing, Inc, Center for the Arts, 425 S Grand Ave, Lansing, MI 48933. Phone: (517) 372-4636, x 6. Fax: (517) 484-2564. Web: www.lansingarts.org.

SOUTH TEXAS WILDLIFE AND BIRDING FESTIVAL. Nov 17–19. Kingsville, TX. Birding and wildlife field trips, speakers, demonstrations and a nature marketplace. Est attendance: 3,000. For info: Kingsville Conv & Visitors Bureau, 1501 N Hwy 77, Kingsville, TX 78363. Phone: (800) 333-5032. Fax: (361) 592-3227. E-mail: visitors@kingsvilletexas.com. Web: www.kingsvilletexas.com.

STAMP EXPO: CALIFORNIA. Nov 17–19. Pasadena Convention Center, Pasadena, CA. Est attendance: 4,000. For info: Israel Bick, Exec Dir, Intl Stamp & Coin Collectors Society, PO Box 854, Van Nuys, CA 91408. Phone: (818) 997-6496. Fax: (818) 988-4337. E-mail: iibick@sbcglobal.net. Web: www.bick.net.

SUEZ CANAL: ANNIVERSARY. Nov 17, 1869. Formal opening of the Suez Canal. It had taken 1.5 million men a decade to dig the 100-mile canal. It shortened the sea route from Europe to India by 6,000 miles. An Anglo-French commission ran the canal until 1956, when Egypt's President Gamal Abdel Nasser seized it.

TELLABRATION! A WEEKEND OF STORYTELLING FOR GROWN-UPS. Nov 17–19. Many sites throughout Connecticut. Simultaneous storytelling concerts for adults. Annually, the weekend before Thanksgiving. Est attendance: 1,000. For info: Ann Shapiro, Adm, Connecticut Storytelling Center, Connecticut College, Box 5295, 270 Mohegan Ave, New London, CT 06320. Phone: (860) 439-2764. Fax: (860) 439-5431. E-mail: csc@conncoll.edu. Web: www.connstorycenter.com.

YORK INTERNATIONAL POSTCARD FAIR. Nov 17–18. York Fairgrounds, York, PA. Est attendance: 1,000. For info: Mary Martin Ltd, 4899 Pulaski Hwy, Rt 40, Perryville, MD 21903. Phone: (410) 642-3581. Fax: (410) 642-2053.

ZENGER, JOHN PETER: ARREST ANNIVERSARY. Nov 17, 1734. Colonial printer and journalist who established the *New York Weekly Journal* (first issue, Nov 5, 1733). Zenger was arrested Nov 17, 1734, for libel against the colonial governor, but continued to edit his newspaper from jail. Trial was held during August 1735. Zenger's acquittal was an important early step toward freedom of the press in America. Zenger was born at Germany in 1697, came to the US in 1710 and died July 28, 1746, at New York, NY.

BIRTHDAYS TODAY

Justin Cooper, 18, actor ("Brother's Keeper," *Liar, Liar*), born Southern California, Nov 17, 1988.

Howard Dean, 58, former Governor of Vermont (D), former Presidential candidate, born East Hampton, NY, Nov 17, 1948.

Danny DeVito, 62, actor ("Taxi," *Twins*), director (*Throw Mama from the Train*), born Neptune, NJ, Nov 17, 1944.

Daisy Fuentes, 40, MTV veejay, host ("America's Funniest Home Videos"), born Havana, Cuba, Nov 17, 1966.

Isaac Hanson, 26, singer (Hanson), born Tulsa, OK, Nov 17, 1980.

Lauren Hutton, 62, model, actress (*American Gigolo*), born Charleston, SC, Nov 17, 1944.

James M. Inhofe, 72, US Senator (R, Oklahoma), born Des Moines, IA, Nov 17, 1934.

Gordon Lightfoot, 68, singer ("Sundown"), songwriter ("Early Morning Rain"), born Orilla, ON, Canada, Nov 17, 1938.

Sophie Marceau, 40, actress (*Braveheart*), born Paris, France, Nov 17, 1966.

Mary Elizabeth Mastrantonio, 48, actress (*The Color of Money, Thieves*), born Oak Park, IL, Nov 17, 1958.

Robert Bruce (Bob) Mathias, 76, former congressman, Olympic gold medal decathlete, born Tulare, CA, Nov 17, 1930.

Lorne Michaels, 62, producer ("Saturday Night Live"), born Toronto, ON, Canada, Nov 17, 1944.

RuPaul, 46, model, actor ("The RuPaul Show"), born RuPaul Andre Charles at San Diego, CA, Nov 17, 1960.

Martin Scorsese, 64, director (*Mean Streets, The Color of Money, Raging Bull, Goodfellas*), born Flushing, NY, Nov 17, 1942.

George Thomas (Tom) Seaver, 62, Hall of Fame baseball player, broadcaster, born Fresno, CA, Nov 17, 1944.

Dylan Walsh, 43, actor ("Nip/Tuck"), born Los Angeles, CA, Nov 17, 1963.

November 2006	S	M	T	W	T	F	S
				1	2	3	4
	5	6	7	8	9	10	11
	12	13	14	15	16	17	18
	19	20	21	22	23	24	25
	26	27	28	29	30		

NOVEMBER 18 — SATURDAY
Day 322 — 43 Remaining

APPALACHIAN POTTERS MARKET. Nov 18. McDowell High School, Marion, NC. One-day display and sale of clay work by 60 potters. Annually, the third Saturday in November. Sponsor: McDowell Arts Council. Est attendance: 1,600. For info: Appalachian Potters Market, c/o MACA, PO Box 1387, Marion, NC 28752. Phone: (828) 652-8610.

CANADA: RALLY OF THE TALL PINES. Nov 18. Bancroft, ON. Combining winter road surfaces with the scenic, winding backroads of the Canadian Shield makes this event of the Canadian Rally Car Race Circuit one of the most popular. For info: Bancroft & District Chamber of Commerce, Box 539, Bancroft, ON, K0L 1C0, Canada. Phone: (613) 332-1513. Fax: (613) 332-2119. E-mail: chamber@commerce.bancroft.on.ca. Web: www.BancroftDistrict.com.

CUSTER STATE PARK BUFFALO AUCTION. Nov 18. Custer, SD. A live sale at 10 AM, MST, of 300–400 surplus buffalo (calves, yearlings, mature cows and two-year-old bulls). Est attendance: 600. For info: Ron Walker, Custer State Park, HC 83, Box 70, Custer, SD 57730. Phone: (605) 255-4515. Fax: (605) 255-4460. E-mail: ron.walker@state.sd.us.

DAGUERRE, LOUIS JACQUES MANDE: BIRTH ANNIVERSARY. Nov 18, 1789. French tax collector, theater scene-painter, physicist and inventor, was born at Cormeilles-en-Parisis, France. He is remembered for his invention of the daguerreotype photographic process—one of the earliest to permit a photographic image to be chemically fixed to provide a permanent picture. The process was presented to the French Academy of Science Jan 7, 1839. Daguerre died near Paris, France, July 10, 1851.

GILBERT, SIR WILLIAM SCHWENCK: BIRTH ANNIVERSARY. Nov 18, 1836. English author of libretto for the famed Gilbert and Sullivan comic operas, born at London, England. Died May 29, 1911, at Harrow Weald, Middlesex, England, as a result of a heart attack experienced while saving a woman from drowning.

GRAY, ASA: BIRTH ANNIVERSARY. Nov 18, 1810. Botanist and natural history professor at Harvard, born at Paris, NY. Gray was known as a pioneer in the field of plant geography and a chief advocate of Darwin. Died at Cambridge, MA, Jan 30, 1888.

HAITI: ARMY DAY: ANNIVERSARY. Nov 18, 1803. Commemorates the Battle of Vertiéres, Nov 18, 1803, in which Haitians defeated the French.

HOLIDAYS IN THE CITY GRAND ILLUMINATION PARADE. Nov 18. Norfolk, VA. A cherished tradition, the buildings of downtown Norfolk and Olde Towne Portsmouth illuminate their profiles to create a picture-postcard skyline. On the first evening of the illumination a downtown lighted street parade kicks off the celebration of the season. All of the floats, bands and entries in this nighttime parade are lighted. Annually, the Saturday before Thanksgiving. Est attendance: 100,000. For info: Parade Mgr, Downtown Norfolk Council, 201 Granby St, Ste 101, Norfolk, VA 23510. Phone: (757) 623-1757. Fax: (757) 623-1756. E-mail: dnc@downtownnorfolk.org. Web: www.downtownnorfolk.org.

HOMEPLACE FESTIVAL. Nov 18. Waretown, NJ. Featuring families playing country, bluegrass and traditional music. No alcoholic beverages or smoking allowed. For info: Albert Music Hall, PO Box 657, Waretown, NJ 08758. Phone: (609) 971-1593. Web: www.alberthall.org.

"HOWARD STERN SHOW" RADIO PREMIERE: ANNIVERSARY. Nov 18, 1985. Radio's pioneering shock jock, Howard Stern, began broadcasting with sidekick Robin Quivers on New York radio station WXRK-FM. With outrageous humor and a gleeful disregard for taste, Stern quickly became popular nationally, but many remain outraged at his show elements. The FCC has frequently fined his broadcasting company. Radio listeners today number around 25 million.

JONESTOWN MASSACRE: ANNIVERSARY. Nov 18, 1978. On this date, Indiana-born, 47-year-old Reverend Jim Jones, leader of the "People's Temple," was reported to have directed the suicides of more than 900 persons at Jonestown, Guyana. US Representative Leo J. Ryan, of California, and four members of his party were killed in ambush at Port Kaituma airstrip on Nov 18, 1978, when they attempted to leave after an investigative visit to the remote jungle location of the religious cult. On the following day, Jones and his mistress killed themselves after watching the administration of Kool-Aid laced with the deadly poison cyanide to members of the cult. At least 912 persons died in the biggest murder-suicide in history.

LATVIA: INDEPENDENCE DAY. Nov 18. National holiday. Commemorates the declaration of an independent Latvia from Germany and Russia in 1918.

LOMBROSO, CESARE: BIRTH ANNIVERSARY. Nov 18, 1836. Italian founder of criminology, born at Verona, Italy. A professor of psychiatry, Lombroso believed that criminality could be identified with certain physical types of people. He died at Turin, Oct 19, 1909.

MARRIED TO A SCORPIO SUPPORT DAY. Nov 18. A worldwide day of remembrance to honor all those married to Scorpios and who suffer greatly. Assert yourself today! Hide their household flowcharts. Annually, Nov 18. [©2003 by WH.] For info: Thomas & Ruth Roy, Wellcat Holidays, 2418 Long Ln, Lebanon, PA 17046. Phone: (717) 279-0184. E-mail: info@wellcat.com. Web: www.wellcat.com.

MERCER, JOHN HERNDON (JOHNNY): BIRTH ANNIVERSARY. Nov 18, 1909. American songwriter, singer, radio performer and actor, born at Savannah, GA. Johnny Mercer wrote lyrics (and often the music) for some of the great American popular music from the 1930s through the 1960s, including "Autumn Leaves," "One for My Baby," "Satin Doll," "On the Achison, Topeka, and the Santa Fe," "You Must Have Been a Beautiful Baby," "Come Rain or Come Shine," "Hooray for Hollywood," "Jeepers Creepers" and countless more. Mercer died June 25, 1976, at Bel Air, CA.

MESSINA HOF'S WINE PREMIERE. Nov 18 (tentative). Bryan, TX. Traditional celebration of the new vintages. Wine aficionados' palates are treated to the premiere of all the new wines, and also the prize-winning wine label from our Texas Artist Competition earlier in the year. There are several wine-related activities like the Winemaker's Blending Lab and wine and food pairing seminars. In the evening a new vintage reception will be followed by an elegant gourmet wine premiere dinner. Est attendance: 2,500. For info: Messina Hof Wine Cellars, 4545 Old Reliance Rd, Bryan, TX 77808. Phone: (979) 778-9463, ext 34. Fax: (979) 778-1729. E-mail: wine@messinahof.com. Web: www.messinahof.com.

MICKEY MOUSE'S BIRTHDAY. Nov 18. The comical activities of squeaky-voiced Mickey Mouse first appeared in 1928, on the screen of the Colony Theatre at New York City. The film, Walt Disney's "Steamboat Willie," was the first animated cartoon talking picture.

NAIA MEN'S AND WOMEN'S CROSS COUNTRY NATIONAL CHAMPIONSHIPS. Nov 18. EP Tom Sawyer

State Park, Louisville, KY. Men compete on an 8k course and women compete on a 5k course with the top 25 individual finishers in each championship receiving All-America honors. 51st men's championship; 27th women's. For info: Natl Assn of Intercollegiate Athletics, 23500 W 105th St, PO Box 1325, Olathe, KS 66051-1325. Phone: (913) 791-0044. Fax: (913) 791-9555. E-mail: rfeldblum@naia.org. Web: www.naia.org.

NATCHITOCHES FESTIVAL OF LIGHTS. Nov 18–Jan 6, 2007. Natchitoches, LA. A fairyland of multicolored lights, created by 170,000 Christmas bulbs strung along city streets and incorporated into 72 unique set pieces along Cane River Lake. Est attendance: 500,000. For info: Natchitoches Parish Tourist Commission, Calendar of Events, 781 Front St, Natchitoches, LA 71457. Phone: (318) 352-8072 or (800) 259-1714. Fax: (318) 352-2415. Web: www.natchitoches.net.

NATIONAL FAMILY VOLUNTEER DAY. Nov 18. To encourage and mobilize families in community-oriented projects. Designed to showcase the benefits of families working together, support organizations and businesses engaging family volunteers and encourage those who haven't yet made the commitment to volunteer with their family to begin doing so. Strategically occurring the Saturday before Thanksgiving Day, National Family Volunteer Day is the perfect way for families and those who work with them to kick off a caring and giving holiday season. For info: Points of Light Foundation, 1400 I St NW, Ste 800, Wahington, DC 20005. Phone: (202) 729-8000. Fax: (202) 729-8100. E-mail: YouthandFamily@PointsofLight.org. Web: www.FamilyCares.org or www.PointsofLight.org.

NORDIC YULEFEST. Nov 18–19. Seattle, WA. A Scandinavian holiday extravaganza with typical Nordic Christmas foods, music and dance. Crafts throughout the museum, kid's room for decoration making, one-of-a-kind gifts. Est attendance: 5,000. For info: Marianne Forssblad, Dir, Nordic Heritage Museum, 3014 NW 67th St, Seattle, WA 98117. Phone: (206) 789-5707. Fax: (206) 789-3271.

OMAN: NATIONAL HOLIDAY. Nov 18. Sultanate of Oman celebrates its national day, the birthday in 1942 of Sultan Qaboos bin Said.

PUSH-BUTTON PHONE DEBUTS: ANNIVERSARY. Nov 18, 1963. Push-button telephones went into service as an alternative to rotary-dial phones. Touch-tone service was available as an option at an extra charge. This option was only available in two Pennsylvania cities.

RANCH HAND BREAKFAST. Nov 18. King Ranch, Kingsville, TX. A breakfast cooked and served outdoors at the world-famous King Ranch. See longhorn cattle and real cowboys on horseback. Annually, the Saturday before Thanksgiving. Est attendance: 7,000. For info: Kingsville Convention & Visitors Bureau, 1501 N Hwy 77, Kingsville, TX 78364-1562. Phone: (800) 333-5032. Fax: (361) 592-3227. E-mail: visitors@kingsvilletexas.com. Web: www.kingsvilletexas.com.

REMEMBRANCE DAY. Nov 18. Gettysburg, PA. An annual event held in conjunction with the Lincoln Observance, with a parade of Civil War troops to the High Water Mark and then to the Albert Woolson Monument for a wreath-laying ceremony. Civil War Ball held in the evening at Eisenhower Inn & Conference Center. Sponsored by the Sons of Union Veterans. Est attendance: 5,000. For info: Gettysburg CVB, PO Box 4117, Gettysburg, PA 17325. Phone: (717) 334-6274. Fax: (717) 334-1166. E-mail: gettysburgcvb@dejazzd.com. Web: www.gettysburgcvb.org.

"SEE IT NOW" TV PREMIERE: 55th ANNIVERSARY. Nov 18, 1951. "See It Now" was a high-quality and significant public affairs show of the 1950s. Known for using its own film footage, unrehearsed interviews and no dubbing, "See It Now" covered many relevant and newsworthy stories of its time, including desegregation, lung cancer and anti-Communist fervor. One of the most notable shows focused on Senator Joseph McCarthy, leading to McCarthy's appearance on the show which damaged his credibility. The show was hosted by Edward R. Murrow, who also produced it jointly with Fred W. Friendly. Its premiere was the first live commercial coast-to-coast broadcast. The show had premiered on radio the year before as "Hear It Now."

SHEPARD, ALAN: BIRTH ANNIVERSARY. Nov 18, 1923. Former astronaut and the first American in space (in 1961), Shepard was born at East Derry, NH. He was one of only 12 Americans who have walked on the moon and was America's only lunar golfer, practicing his drive in space with a six iron. He was awarded the Medal of Honor in 1979. Shepard died near Monterey, CA, July 21, 1998.

SOUTH AFRICA ADOPTS NEW CONSTITUTION: ANNIVERSARY. Nov 18, 1993. After more than 300 years of white majority rule, basic civil rights were finally granted to blacks in South Africa. The constitution providing such rights was approved by representatives of the ruling party, as well as members of 20 other political parties.

THAILAND: ELEPHANT ROUNDUP AT SURIN. Nov 18. Elephant demonstrations in morning, elephant races and tug-of-war between 100 men and one elephant. Observed since 1961 on third Saturday in November. Special trains from Bangkok on previous day.

US UNIFORM TIME ZONE PLAN: ANNIVERSARY. Nov 18, 1883. Charles Ferdinand Dowd, a college professor and one of the early advocates of uniform time, proposed a time zone plan of the US (four zones of 15 degrees), which he and others persuaded the railroads to adopt and place in operation on this date. Because it didn't involve the enactment of any law, some localities didn't change their clocks. A year later an international conference applied the same procedure to create time zones for the entire world. US time zones weren't nationally legalized until 1918, with the passage of the Standard Time Act. See also: "Prime Meridian Set: Anniversary" (Nov 1) and "US Standard Time Act: Anniversary" (Mar 19).

WARM SPRINGS THANKSGIVING. Nov 18. Little White House, Warm Springs, GA. Dr. Tom Wentland portrays Pres Franklin D. Roosevelt in this presentation of what it was like when FDR spent the holiday here. Antique cars, harvest decor. Annually, the Saturday before Thanksgiving. Est attendance: 800. For info: Frankie Mewborn, Mgr, FDR's Little White House, 401 Little White House Rd, Warm Springs, GA 31830. Phone: (706) 655-5870. Fax: (706) 655-5872.

WEBER, CARL MARIA VON: BIRTH ANNIVERSARY. Nov 18, 1786. Composer, founder of the German romantic school, was born at Eutin, Germany. Member of a musical family, he is remembered mainly for his operas, especially the immensely popular *Der Freischutz* (1821). He died at London, England, June 5, 1826, at age 39.

BIRTHDAYS TODAY

Margaret Eleanor Atwood, 67, author (*Cat's Eye, The Handmaid's Tale*), born Ottawa, ON, Canada, Nov 18, 1939.

Dante Bichette, 43, former baseball player, born West Palm Beach, FL, Nov 18, 1963.

	S	M	T	W	T	F	S
November				1	2	3	4
2006	5	6	7	8	9	10	11
	12	13	14	15	16	17	18
	19	20	21	22	23	24	25
	26	27	28	29	30		

Linda Evans, 64, actress ("Dynasty," "Big Valley"), born Hartford, CT, Nov 18, 1942.

Wilma Mankiller, 61, Chief of the Cherokee Nation 1985–95, born Tahlequah, OK, Nov 18, 1945.

Andrea Marcovicci, 58, actress ("Trapper John, MD"), singer, born New York, NY, Nov 18, 1948.

Harold Warren Moon, 50, former football player, born Los Angeles, CA, Nov 18, 1956.

Kevin Nealon, 53, comedic actor ("Champs," "Saturday Night Live"), born St. Louis, MO, Nov 18, 1953.

Jameson Parker, 59, actor ("Simon and Simon," *A Small Circle of Friends*), born Baltimore, MD, Nov 18, 1947.

Elizabeth Perkins, 46, actress (*About Last Night . . ., Big, The Flintstones*), born Queens, NY, Nov 18, 1960.

Katey Sagal, 50, actress ("Married . . . With Children," "8 Simple Rules for Dating My Teenage Daughter"), born Los Angeles, CA, Nov 18, 1956.

Gary Sheffield, 38, baseball player, born Tampa, FL, Nov 18, 1968.

Ted Stevens, 83, US Senator (R, Alaska), born Indianapolis, IN, Nov 18, 1923.

Susan Sullivan, 62, actress ("Falcon Crest," "Dharma & Greg"), born New York, NY, Nov 18, 1944.

Brenda Vaccaro, 67, actress (*Cactus Flower, How Now Dow Jones, The Goodbye People*), born Brooklyn, NY, Nov 18, 1939.

Owen Wilson, 38, actor (*Starsky and Hutch, Behind Enemy Lines, Bottle Rocket*), screenwriter, born Dallas, TX, Nov 18, 1968.

NOVEMBER 19 — SUNDAY
Day 323 — 42 Remaining

BELIZE: GARIFUNA DAY. Nov 19. Public holiday celebrating the first arrival of Black Caribs from St. Vincent and Rotan to southern Belize in 1823.

CAMPANELLA, ROY: BIRTH ANNIVERSARY. Nov 19, 1921. Roy Campanella, one of the first black major leaguers and a star of one of baseball's greatest teams, the Brooklyn Dodgers' "Boys of Summer," was born at Philadelphia, PA. He was named the National League MVP three times in his 10 years of play, in 1951, 1953 and 1955. Campanella had his highest batting average in 1951 (.325), and in 1953 he established three single-season records for a catcher—most putouts (807), most home runs (41) and most runs batted in (142)—as well as having a batting average of .312. His career was cut short on Jan 28, 1958, when an automobile accident left him paralyzed. Campanella gained even more fame after his accident as an inspiration and spokesman for the handicapped. He was named to the Baseball Hall of Fame in 1969. Roy Campanella died June 26, 1993, at Woodland Hills, CA.

CLARK, GEORGE ROGERS: BIRTH ANNIVERSARY. Nov 19, 1752. American soldier and frontiersman, born at Albemarle County, VA. Died at Louisville, KY, Feb 13, 1818.

COLD WAR FORMALLY ENDED: ANNIVERSARY. Nov 19–21, 1990. A summit was held at Paris with the leaders of the Conference on Security and Cooperation in Europe (CSCE). The highlight of the summit was the signing of a treaty to dramatically reduce conventional weapons in Europe, thereby ending the Cold War.

EIGHTEENTH-CENTURY THRESHING DAY. Nov 19. McLean, VA. Help the farm family thresh wheat, make yeast cakes and celebrate the end of the season with light refreshment. Annually, the third Sunday in November. Est attendance: 500. For info: Claude Moore Colonial Farm at Turkey Run, 6310 Georgetown Pike, McLean, VA 22101. Phone: (703) 442-7557. Fax: (703) 442-0714. Web: www.1771.org.

FIRST AUTOMATIC TOLL COLLECTION MACHINE: ANNIVERSARY. Nov 19, 1954. At the Union Toll Plaza on New Jersey's Garden State Parkway motorists dropped 25¢ into a wire mesh hopper and a green light would flash. The first modern toll road was the Pennsylvania Turnpike, which opened in 1940.

FIRST PRESIDENTIAL LIBRARY: ANNIVERSARY. Nov 19, 1939. President Franklin D. Roosevelt laid the cornerstone for his presidential library at Hyde Park, NY. He donated the land, but public donations provided funds for the building, which was dedicated on June 30, 1941.

GARFIELD, JAMES ABRAM: 175th BIRTH ANNIVERSARY. Nov 19, 1831. Twentieth president of the US (and the first left-handed president) was born at Orange, OH. Term of office: Mar 4–Sept 19, 1881. While walking into the Washington, DC, railway station on the morning of July 2, 1881, Garfield was shot by disappointed office seeker Charles J. Guiteau. He survived, in very weak condition, until Sept 19, 1881, when he succumbed to blood poisoning at Elberon, NJ (where he had been taken for recuperation). Guiteau was tried, convicted and hanged at the jail at Washington, June 30, 1882.

GERMANY: VOLKSTRAUERTAG. Nov 19. Memorial Day and national day of mourning in all German states for victims of National Socialism and the dead of both world wars. Observed on the Sunday before Totensonntag. See also: "Germany: Totensonntag" (Nov 26).

GETTYSBURG ADDRESS MEMORIAL CEREMONY. Nov 19. Gettysburg, PA. The 143rd anniversary of Lincoln's Gettysburg Address is celebrated with brief memorial services at the Soldiers' National Monument in Gettysburg National Cemetery. Est attendance: 2,000. For info: Gettysburg CVB, PO Box 4117, Gettysburg, PA 17325. Phone: (717) 334-6274. Fax: (717) 334-1166. E-mail: gettysburgcvb@dejazzd.com. Web: www.gettysburgcvb.org.

"HAVE A BAD DAY" DAY. Nov 19. For those who are filled with revulsion at being told endlessly to "have a nice day," this day is a brief respite. Store and business owners are to ask workers to tell customers to "have a bad day." Annually, Nov 19. [©2003 by WH.] For info: Thomas & Ruth Roy, Wellcat Holidays, 2418 Long Ln, Lebanon, PA 17046. Phone: (717) 279-0184. E-mail: info@wellcat.com. Web: www.wellcat.com.

LINCOLN'S GETTYSBURG ADDRESS: ANNIVERSARY. Nov 19, 1863. In 1863, 17 acres of the battlefield at Gettysburg, PA, were dedicated as a national cemetery. Noted orator Edward Everett spoke for two hours; the address that Lincoln delivered in less than two minutes was later recognized as one of the most eloquent of the English language. Five manuscript copies in Lincoln's hand survive, including the rough draft begun in ink at the executive Mansion at Washington and concluded in pencil at Gettysburg on the morning of the dedication (kept at the Library of Congress).

MONACO: NATIONAL HOLIDAY. Nov 19.

MOTHER GOOSE PARADE. Nov 19. El Cajon, CA. "A celebration of children." Floats depict Mother Goose rhymes and fairy tales and/or annual theme. Bands, equestrians and clowns. Traditionally, the Sunday before Thanksgiving. Est attendance: 250,000. For info: Mother Goose Parade Assn, 480 N Magnolia Ave, Ste 106, El Cajon, CA 92020. Phone: (619) 444-8712. Fax: (619) 444-3971. E-mail: mothergooseparade@sbcglobal.net. Web: www.mothergooseparade.com.

NATIONAL BIBLE WEEK. Nov 19–26. An interfaith campaign to promote reading of the Bible. Free resources available. Governors and mayors across the country proclaim National Bible Week observance to their constituencies. Annually, from the Sunday preceding Thanksgiving to the following Sunday. For info: Tamara Collins, VP for Programs, Natl Bible Assn, 1865 Broadway, New York, NY 10023. Phone: (212) 408-1390. Fax: (212) 408-1448. E-mail: tcollins@nationalbible.org. Web: www.national bible.org.

★**NATIONAL FAMILY WEEK.** Nov 19–25.

NATIONAL GAME & PUZZLE WEEK™. Nov 19–25. 12th annual event to increase appreciation of board games and puzzles while preserving the tradition of investing time with family and friends. Part of The Million Minute Family Challenge™, conducted Sept 1–Dec 31. Special teacher material and media information available, including press kits, interviews, etc. Annually, the Sunday through Saturday of Thanksgiving week. For info: Frank Beres, National Game & Puzzle Week, PO Box 268, Beloit, WI 53512-0268. Phone: (800) 524-4263. Fax: (608) 362-8178. E-mail: patch@patchproducts.com. Web: www.millionminute.com.

PASADENA DOO DAH PARADE. Nov 19. Pasadena, CA. Held in Old Pasadena, this spoof of the more traditional parade is a wacky and humorous celebration that attracts thousands. Includes entries like the precision marching Briefcase Drill Team. Annually, the Sunday before Thanksgiving. For info: Light Bringer Project, 64 N Raymond Ave, Pasadena, CA 91103. Phone: (626) 440-7379. Web: www.pasadenadoodahparade.com.

PELÉ SCORES 1,000th GOAL: ANNIVERSARY. Nov 19, 1969. Playing for the Santos team, legendary Brazilian soccer player Pelé scored his 1,000th goal in competition on a penalty kick against the team Vasco de Gama. Pelé dedicated this emotional and tremendous feat to Brazil's poor children and its elderly and suffering. By the time Pelé retired in 1977, he had scored an astounding 1,281 goals in 1,363 matches—a world record that still stands.

PUERTO RICO: DISCOVERY DAY. Nov 19. Public holiday. Columbus discovered Puerto Rico in 1493 on his second voyage to the New World.

"ROCKY AND HIS FRIENDS" TV PREMIERE: ANNIVERSARY. Nov 19, 1959. This popular cartoon featured the adventures of a talking squirrel, Rocky (Rocket J. Squirrel), and his friend Bullwinkle, a flaky moose. The tongue-in-cheek dialogue contrasted with the simple plots in which Rocky and Bullwinkle tangled with Russian bad guys Boris Badenov and Natasha (who worked for Mr Big). Other popular segments on the show included "Fractured Fairy Tales," "Bullwinkle's Corner" and the adventures of Sherman and Mr Peabody (an intelligent talking dog). In 1961 the show was renamed "The Bullwinkle Show," but the cast of characters remained the same.

SUFFRAGISTS' VOTING ATTEMPT: ANNIVERSARY. Nov 19, 1868. Testing the wording of the 14th Amendment that says "no State shall make or enforce any law which shall abridge the privileges or immunities of citizens of the United States," 172 New Jersey suffragists, including four black women, attempted to vote in the presidential election. Denied, they cast their votes instead into a women's ballot box overseen by 84-year-old Quaker Margaret Pryer.

SUNDAY, BILLY: BIRTH ANNIVERSARY. Nov 19, 1862. Born William Ashley Sunday at Ames, IA, Sunday rose from poverty to become a professional baseball player with the Chicago White Stockings in 1883. He quit baseball in 1891 to devote himself to evangelism after hearing gospel singers at a Chicago mission. Sunday's fiery, athletic sermons—especially against demon rum—made him a star in the early 1900s, and at each revival he attracted around 100,000 listeners. At a typical revival in Detroit, MI, Sunday exhorted, "Help me, Jesus, help me save all in Detroit who are rushing to hell so fast that you can't see them for the dust." Sunday died Nov 6, 1935, at Chicago, IL.

WOMEN'S CHRISTIAN TEMPERANCE UNION ORGANIZED: ANNIVERSARY. Nov 19, 1874. Developed out of the Women's Temperance Crusade of 1873, the Women's Christian Temperance Union was organized at Cleveland, OH. The Crusade had swept through 23 states with women going into saloons to sing hymns, pray and ask saloonkeepers to stop selling liquor. Today the temperance group, headquartered at Evanston, IL, includes more than a million members with chapters in 72 countries and continues to be concerned with educating people on the potential dangers of the use of alcohol, narcotics and tobacco.

ZION NATIONAL PARK ESTABLISHED: ANNIVERSARY. Nov 19, 1919. Utah's Mukuntuweap National Monument, proclaimed July 31, 1909, and later incorporated in Zion National Monument by proclamation Mar 18, 1918, was established as Zion National Park in 1919.

BIRTHDAYS TODAY

Dick Cavett, 70, entertainer ("The Dick Cavett Show"), born Gibbon, NE, Nov 19, 1936.

Eileen Collins, 50, first female space shuttle commander, Lieutenant Colonel USAF, born Elmira, NY, Nov 19, 1956.

Gail Devers, 40, Olympic gold medal sprinter, born Seattle, WA, Nov 19, 1966.

Peter Drucker, 97, management and business theorist, born Vienna, Austria, Nov 19, 1909.

Terry Farrell, 43, actress ("Star Trek: Deep Space Nine," "Becker"), born Cedar Rapids, IA, Nov 19, 1963.

Jodie Foster, 44, actress (Oscars for *The Accused, The Silence of the Lambs; Taxi Driver*), director (*Home for the Holidays*), born Los Angeles, CA, Nov 19, 1962.

Savion Glover, 33, dancer, choreographer (*Bring in 'Da Noise, Bring in 'Da Funk*), born Newark, NJ, Nov 19, 1973.

Thomas R. Harkin, 67, US Senator (D, Iowa), born Cumming, IA, Nov 19, 1939.

Scott Jacoby, 50, actor (*The Little Girl Who Lives Down the Lane, Return to Horror High*), born Chicago, IL, Nov 19, 1956.

Allison Janney, 46, actress (*American Beauty*, "The West Wing"), born Dayton, OH, Nov 19, 1960.

Larry King, 73, talk-show host ("Larry King Live"), born Brooklyn, NY, Nov 19, 1933.

Calvin Klein, 64, fashion designer, born New York, NY, Nov 19, 1942.

Glynnis O'Connor, 51, actress (*Ode to Billy Joe, Johnny Dangerously*), born New York, NY, Nov 19, 1955.

Kathleen Quinlan, 52, actress (*Twilight Zone: The Movie; The Doors*), born Pasadena, CA, Nov 19, 1954.

Ahmad Rashad, 57, sportscaster, former football player, born Bobby Moore at Portland, OR, Nov 19, 1949.

Meg Ryan, 45, actress (*When Harry Met Sally . . ., Sleepless in Seattle*), born Fairfield, CT, Nov 19, 1961.

Kerri Strug, 29, Olympic gymnast, born Tucson, AZ, Nov 19, 1977.

Ted Turner, 68, baseball, basketball and cable TV executive, born Cincinnati, OH, Nov 19, 1938.

Garrick Utley, 67, journalist, born Chicago, IL, Nov 19, 1939.

Jack Welch, 71, ex-chairman of GE, born Peabody, MA, Nov 19, 1935.

November 2006

S	M	T	W	T	F	S
			1	2	3	4
5	6	7	8	9	10	11
12	13	14	15	16	17	18
19	20	21	22	23	24	25
26	27	28	29	30		

NOVEMBER 20 — MONDAY
Day 324 — 41 Remaining

BATTLE OF TARAWA-MAKIN: ANNIVERSARY. Nov 20, 1943. The US began its offensive against Japan in the Central Pacific (Operation Galvanic) by attacking the Gilbert Islands, particularly the islets of Betio and Makin. The Japanese had heavily fortified the Tarawa chain of atolls, especially Tarawa, with pillboxes, blockhouses and ferroconcrete bombproofs. In the eight days it took the 5th Amphibious Corps, 2nd Marine Division and the 27th Infantry Division to take the Tarawa and Makin Islands, 1,000 US soldiers were killed and 2,311 wounded. The Japanese loss was tallied at 4,700 men killed, 17 wounded and captured and 129 Koreans surrendered. The US public, who through censorship previously had been kept in the dark about the human cost of the war, was appalled by casualty figures and photographs from this battle.

BETTER CONVERSATION WEEK. Nov 20–26. This week supports rich, meaningful conversation among family members, gatherings of friends and across generations. Simple, clear guidelines and conversation starters assure that. This holiday week can deepen personal relationships and strengthen family bonds through meaningful talk. Check the website below for articles, book references and other resources for better conversation. For info: Dr. Loren Ekroth. Phone: (702) 214-6782. E-mail: loren@conversation-matters.com. Web: www.conversation-matters.com.

BILL OF RIGHTS: ANNIVERSARY OF FIRST STATE RATIFICATION. Nov 20, 1789. New Jersey became the first state to ratify 10 of the 12 amendments to the US Constitution proposed by Congress Sept 25. These 10 amendments came to be known as the Bill of Rights.

CANADA: CANADIAN WESTERN AGRIBITION. Nov 20–25. Regina, SK. Canada's premier international livestock show and marketplace featuring North America's finest livestock genetics. More than 4,000 cattle, sheep, goats, llamas and horses are on display to the public at this trade show featuring more than 400 exhibitors. Major attractions include indoor pro rodeo, Grain and Forage showcase, Prairie Cuisine, draft horse events, light horse competitions, our award-winning Agri-ed program for youth and the Agribition grandstand, featuring cowboy poetry and musical performers. Est attendance: 140,000. For info: Canadian Western Agribition, Box 3535, Regina, SK, Canada S4P 3J8. Phone: (306) 565-0565. Fax: (306) 757-9963. E-mail: info@agribition.com. Web: www.agribition.com.

CHATTERTON, THOMAS: BIRTH ANNIVERSARY. Nov 20, 1752. English poet Thomas Chatterton was born at Bristol, England, and killed himself at age 17 by taking arsenic at his London garret, Aug 24, 1770. A gifted but lonely child, before he reached his teens Chatterton had created a fantasy poet-priest, Thomas Rowley, who lived in the 16th century. With his own pen, Chatterton created enough verses "by" Rowley to fill more than 600 printed pages. Chatterton's fantasy-forgery poems attracted little attention during his short life, but they were later admired by Wordsworth, Coleridge, Shelley, Keats and Byron. In addition, he became the subject of at least one play, an opera and a novel.

COOKE, ALISTAIR: BIRTH ANNIVERSARY. Nov 20, 1908. Broadcast journalist and author Alfred Alistair Cooke was born at Salford, England. He came to the US in the 1930s and eventually became an American citizen. His program "Letter from America" was broadcast in more than 50 countries by BBC Radio for an astonishing 58 years. He was the chief American correspondent for *The Guardian* for 26 years, and he hosted PBS's "Masterpiece Theatre" for more than 20 years. Highly regarded for his sophisticated grace and style in both writing and broadcasting, he continued to broadcast "Letter from America" until his death at New York, NY, Mar 30, 2004.

GOULD, CHESTER: BIRTH ANNIVERSARY. Nov 20, 1900. In 1931, Chester Gould created comic strip character Dick Tracy, the clean-cut, square-jawed, plainclothed detective who represented the code that "crime doesn't pay." The strip first appeared Oct 4, 1931, in the *Detroit Daily Mirror* and later was syndicated in nearly 1,000 newspapers worldwide. *Dick Tracy* (originally called *Plainclothes Tracy*) featured Tess Trueheart (later Mrs Tracy) and a host of bad guys with ugly names and faces to match their ugly ways—Mole, Pruneface, Flat Top, B-B Eyes, Mumbles and others. Closely following actual police methods of crime prevention, it included a "Crimestopper Notebook" with tips on self-protection. More violent than most comic strips, *Dick Tracy* was a combination of realism and science fiction. Chester Gould was born at Pawnee, OK, and died May 11, 1985, at Woodstock, IL.

HUBBLE, EDWIN POWELL: BIRTH ANNIVERSARY. Nov 20, 1889. American astronomer Edwin Hubble was born at Marshfield, MO. His discovery and development of the concept of an expanding universe has been described as the "most spectacular astronomical discovery" of the 20th century. As a tribute, the Hubble Space Telescope, deployed Apr 25, 1990, from US space shuttle *Discovery*, was named for him. The Hubble Space Telescope, with a 240-centimeter mirror, was to allow astronomers to see farther into space than they had ever seen from telescopes on Earth. Hubble died at San Marino, CA, Sept 28, 1953.

KENNEDY, ROBERT FRANCIS: BIRTH ANNIVERSARY. Nov 20, 1925. US Senator and younger brother of John F. Kennedy (35th president) was born at Brookline, MA. An assassin shot him at Los Angeles, CA, June 5, 1968, while he was campaigning for the presidential nomination. He died the next day. Sirhan Sirhan was convicted of his murder.

LAGERLOF, SELMA: BIRTH ANNIVERSARY. Nov 20, 1858. Swedish author, member of the Swedish Academy and the first woman to receive the Nobel Prize for literature (1909) was born at Sweden's Varmland Province. She died there Mar 16, 1940.

LANDIS, KENESAW MOUNTAIN: BIRTH ANNIVERSARY. Nov 20, 1866. Baseball Hall of Fame executive born at Millville, OH. Landis, a federal judge, was named the first commissioner of baseball in 1920. He ruled with an absolutely firm hand and imposed his view of how baseball should operate upon owners and players alike. Inducted into the Hall of Fame in 1944. Died at Chicago, IL, Nov 25, 1944.

LAURIER, SIR WILFRED: BIRTH ANNIVERSARY. Nov 20, 1841. Canadian statesman (premier, 1896–1911), born at St. Lin, Quebec. Died Feb 17, 1919, at Ottawa, ON.

LIVE: FAMILY CHRISTMAS AT THE BENJAMIN HARRISON HOME. Nov 20. Indianapolis, IN. Guided tour of the 23rd president's home decorated in seasonal Victorian style. For info: PR Dept, President Benjamin Harrison Home, 1230 N Delaware St, Indianapolis, IN 46202-2598. Phone: (317) 631-1888. Fax: (317) 632-5488. E-mail: harrison@presidentbenjaminharrison.org. Web: www.pbhh.org.

MARRIAGE OF ELIZABETH AND PHILIP: ANNIVERSARY. Nov 20, 1947. The Princess Elizabeth Alexandra Mary was wed to Philip Mountbatten on Nov 20, 1947. Elizabeth was the first child of King George VI and Queen Elizabeth. Philip, the former Prince Philip of Greece, had become a British subject nine months earlier and the title Duke of Edinburgh was bestowed on him. The bride later became Elizabeth II, Queen of the United

Kingdom of Great Britain and Northern Ireland and Head of the Commonwealth, upon the death of her father on Feb 6, 1952, her coronation taking place at Westminster Abbey on June 2, 1953.

MEXICO: REVOLUTION DAY. Nov 20. Anniversary of the social revolution launched by Francisco I. Madero in 1910. National holiday.

MOON PHASE: NEW MOON. Nov 20. Moon enters New Moon phase at 5:18 PM, EST.

NAME YOUR PC DAY. Nov 20. Hey, why not? People name their boats! There are a lot more PCs than boats these days. "Binky" is already taken. Annually, Nov 20. [©2003 by WH.] For info: Thomas & Ruth Roy, Wellcat Holidays, 2418 Long Ln, Lebanon, PA 17046. Phone: (717) 279-0184. E-mail: info@wellcat .com. Web: www.wellcat.com.

NUREMBERG WAR CRIMES TRIAL: ANNIVERSARY. Nov 20, 1945. The first session of the German war crimes trials started at Berlin with indictments against 24 former Nazi leaders. Later sessions were held at Nuremberg, starting Nov 20, 1945. One defendant committed suicide during the trial, and another was excused because of his physical and mental condition. The trial lasted more than 10 months, and delivery of the judgment was completed on Oct 1, 1946. Twelve were sentenced to death by hanging, three to life imprisonment, four to lesser prison terms and three were acquitted.

THE SHEIK FILM RELEASE: 85th ANNIVERSARY. Nov 20, 1921. The silent film that catapulted Rudolph Valentino into stardom was given a general release on this date after premieres in New York and Los Angeles. The romantic melodrama, about a prince of the desert's obsession with an Englishwoman, was a hit that actually had women fainting in theaters. The film was scandalously frank for the times about sexual desire. "Sheik" even became slang for a man women couldn't resist. While the film made Valentino a reluctant sex symbol, it also typecast him—to his frustration. A sequel, *The Son of the Sheik*, was released in September 1926 a few weeks after Valentino's sudden death.

TIERNEY, GENE: BIRTH ANNIVERSARY. Nov 20, 1920. Known best for the title role in the film *Laura*, actress Gene Tierney was born at Brooklyn, NY. Her other films include *Heaven Can Wait, A Bell for Adano, Advise and Consent* and her last film, *The Pleasure Seekers*. She died Nov 6, 1991, at Houston, TX.

UNITED NATIONS: AFRICA INDUSTRIALIZATION DAY. Nov 20. The General Assembly proclaimed this day for the purpose of mobilizing the commitment of the international community to the industrialization of the continent (Res 44/237, Dec 22, 1989). For info: United Nations, Dept of Public Info, New York, NY 10017. Web: www.un.org.

UNITED NATIONS: UNIVERSAL CHILDREN'S DAY. Nov 20. Designated by the United Nations General Assembly as Universal Children's Day. First observance was in 1953. A time to honor children with special ceremonies and festivals and to make children's needs known to governments. Observed on different days and in different ways in more than 120 nations. For info: United Nations, Dept of Public Info, New York, NY 10017. Web: www.un.org.

WOLCOTT, OLIVER: BIRTH ANNIVERSARY. Nov 20, 1726. Signer of the Declaration of Independence, governor of Connecticut, born at Windsor, CT. Died Dec 1, 1797, at Litchfield, CT.

BIRTHDAYS TODAY

Joseph (Joe) Robinette Biden, Jr, 64, US Senator (D, Delaware), born Scranton, PA, Nov 20, 1942.

Matt Blunt, 36, Governor of Missouri (R), born Strafford, MO, Nov 20, 1970.

Robert C. Byrd, 89, US Senator (D, West Virginia), born North Wilkesboro, NC, Nov 20, 1917.

Steve Dahl, 52, Chicago radio personality, born La Canada, CA, Nov 20, 1954.

Richard Dawson, 74, actor, TV game-show host ("Hogan's Heroes"; Emmy for "Family Feud"), born Gosport, England, Nov 20, 1932.

Don DeLillo, 70, author (*White Noise, Underworld*), born New York, NY, Nov 20, 1936.

Bo Derek, 50, actress (*10, Bolero, Tarzan, A Change of Seasons*), born Cathleen Collins at Long Beach, CA, Nov 20, 1956.

Nadine Gordimer, 83, writer (*July's People, Lifetimes Under Apartheid*), born Springs, South Africa, Nov 20, 1923.

Veronica Hamel, 63, actress ("Hill Street Blues"), born Philadelphia, PA, Nov 20, 1943.

Ruth Laredo, 69, concert pianist, born Detroit, MI, Nov 20, 1937.

Sabrina Lloyd, 36, actress (*Sliders*), born Mount Dora, FL, Nov 20, 1970.

Richard Masur, 58, actor ("One Day at a Time," *Who'll Stop the Rain, Under Fire, Heartburn*), born New York, NY, Nov 20, 1948.

Ricardo Montalban, 86, actor ("Fantasy Island," *Star Trek II: The Wrath of Khan*), born Mexico City, Mexico, Nov 20, 1920.

Estelle Parsons, 79, actress ("Roseanne," *Bonnie and Clyde, Dick Tracy*; stage: *Next Time I'll Sing to You* [Obie], *In the Summer House* [Obie]), born Marblehead, MA, Nov 20, 1927.

Dick Smothers, 67, comedian, folksinger (with brother Tom, "The Smothers Brothers Comedy Hour"), born New York, NY, Nov 20, 1939.

Ming-Na Wen, 39, actress ("ER," *One Night Stand*), born Macau, China, Nov 20, 1967.

Judy Woodruff, 60, journalist, author, born Tulsa, OK, Nov 20, 1946.

Sean Young, 47, actress (*Blade Runner, No Way Out*), born Louisville, KY, Nov 20, 1959.

NOVEMBER 21 — TUESDAY
Day 325 — 40 Remaining

BARTLETT, JOSIAH: BIRTH ANNIVERSARY. Nov 21, 1729. Signer of the Declaration of Independence. Born at Amesbury, MA, he died at Kingston, NH, May 19, 1795.

BEAUMONT, WILLIAM: BIRTH ANNIVERSARY. Nov 21, 1785. US Army surgeon whose contribution to classic medical literature and world fame resulted from another man's shotgun wound. When Canadian fur trapper Alexis St. Martin received a wound June 6, 1822—a nearly point-blank blast to the abdomen—Dr. Beaumont began observing his stomach and digestive processes through an opening in his abdominal wall. His findings were published in 1833 in *Experiments and Observations on the Gastric Juice and the Physiology of Digestion*. St. Martin returned to Canada in 1834 and resisted Beaumont's efforts to have him return for further study. He outlived his doctor by 20 years and was buried at a depth of eight feet to discourage any attempt at posthumous examination. Beaumont, born at Lebanon, CT, died Apr 25, 1853, at St. Louis, MO.

CARRS/SAFEWAY GREAT ALASKA SHOOTOUT. Nov 21–25. Sullivan Arena, Anchorage, AK. Top NCAA basketball

	S	M	T	W	T	F	S
November 2006				1	2	3	4
	5	6	7	8	9	10	11
	12	13	14	15	16	17	18
	19	20	21	22	23	24	25
	26	27	28	29	30		

action as eight men's and four women's Division I teams from around the country compete. Est attendance: 48,000. For info: Univ of Alaska–Anchorage, Athletic Dept, 3211 Providence Dr, Anchorage, AK 99508. Phone: (907) 786-1250. Fax: (907) 563-4565. E-mail: tim@uaa.alaska.edu. Web: www.goseawolves .com.

CONGRESS FIRST MEETS AT WASHINGTON: ANNIVERSARY. Nov 21, 1800. Congress met at Philadelphia from 1790 to 1800, when the north wing of the new Capitol at Washington, DC, was completed. The House and the Senate had been scheduled to meet in the new building Nov 17, 1800, but a quorum wasn't achieved until Nov 21, 1800.

DOW-JONES TOPS 5,000: ANNIVERSARY. Nov 21, 1995. The Dow-Jones Index of 30 major industrial stocks topped the 5,000 mark for the first time.

ELLA FITZGERALD WINS APOLLO AMATEUR NIGHT: ANNIVERSARY. Nov 21, 1934. A shy, impoverished teenager, dressed in borrowed clothes and men's shoes, stepped on the stage of Harlem, NY's Apollo Theater for Amateur Night on this date. Ella Fitzgerald, in her stage debut, was so nervous that she fumbled her first song, but prompted to restart, she sang "Object of My Affection" and "Judy" to a crowd that exploded with applause. She won the contest. Bandleader Benny Carter, whose orchestra was backing the amateurs that night, helped Fitzgerald make music industry connections, and, in 1935, she began to find success as a singer.

FRENCHMAN ROWS ACROSS PACIFIC: 15th ANNIVERSARY. Nov 21, 1991. Gerard d'Aboville completed a four-month solo journey across the Pacific Ocean on this date. D'Aboville began rowing across the Pacific on July 11 when he left Choshi, Japan. His journey ended at Ilwaco, WA.

GREEN, HETTY: BIRTH ANNIVERSARY. Nov 21, 1835. Henrietta Howland Robinson Green, better known as Hetty Green, reported to have been the richest woman in America, was born at New Bedford, MA. She was an able financier who managed her own wealth, which was estimated to have been in excess of $100 million. Died at New York, NY, July 3, 1916.

NORTH CAROLINA: RATIFICATION DAY. Nov 21. 12th state to ratify Constitution in 1789.

POPE BENEDICT XV: BIRTH ANNIVERSARY. Nov 21, 1854. Giacomo dela Chiesa, 258th pope of the Roman Catholic Church, born at Pegli, Italy, and elected pope Sept 3, 1914. Died at Rome, Italy, Jan 22, 1922.

PUMPKIN PIE DAY. Nov 21. Making pumpkin pies is a family tradition that goes back generations. People associate the sweet smell of pumpkin pie with the late fall. For info: Cindy Benson, 13116 Frog Hollow Ct, Oak Hill, VA 20171. Phone: (703) 471-5784. E-mail: benson1984@aol.com.

PURCELL, HENRY: DEATH ANNIVERSARY. Nov 21, 1695. (OS). English composer of the early Baroque period was born at London circa 1659. Purcell's work includes more than 100 songs, the opera *Dido and Aeneas* and *The Fairy Queen*, incidental music for a version of Shakespeare's *A Midsummer Night's Dream*. Purcell died at London.

SWITZERLAND: LUCERNE FESTIVAL, PIANO. Nov 21–26. Lucerne. This piano festival focusing on keyboards is unique in Europe for the compact range of piano music it offers, ranging from classical to jazz music, performed on modern and historical instruments. Exhibitions, workshops, films and more on the topic of keyboard instruments will additionally expand the range of events. Piano Off-Stage!, a festival of bar-piano music, will take place simultaneously in the beautiful restaurants, hotels and bars of Lucerne. For info: Lucerne Festival, PO Box CH-6002, Lucerne, Switzerland. Phone: (41) 226-44-00. Fax: (41) 226-44-60. E-mail: info@lucernefestival.ch. Web: www.lucerne festival.ch.

UNITED NATIONS: WORLD TELEVISION DAY. Nov 21. On Dec 17, 1996, the General Assembly proclaimed this day as World Television Day, commemorating the date in 1996 on which the first World Television Forum was held at the UN. For info: United Nations, Dept of Public Info, New York, NY 10017. Web: www.un.org.

VOLTAIRE, JEAN FRANÇOIS MARIE: BIRTH ANNIVERSARY. Nov 21, 1694. French author and philosopher to whom is attributed (perhaps erroneously) the statement: "I disapprove of what you say, but I will defend to the death your right to say it." His most famous work is the novel *Candide*. Born at Paris, he died there May 30, 1778.

WORLD HELLO DAY. Nov 21. 34th annual observance. Everyone who participates greets 10 people. People in 180 countries have participated in this annual activity for advancing peace through personal communication. Heads of state of 114 countries have expressed approval of the event. For info: Michael McCormack, The McCormack Brothers, PO Box 15592, Beverly Hills, CA 90209. Web: www.worldhelloday.org.

BIRTHDAYS TODAY

Troy Aikman, 40, former football player, born West Covina, CA, Nov 21, 1966.

Bjork, 41, singer, actress, born Björk Godmundsdóttir at Reykjavik, Iceland, Nov 21, 1965.

Phil Bredesen, 63, Governor of Tennessee (D), born Shortsville, NY, Nov 21, 1943.

Marcy Carsey, 62, television producer, born South Weymouth, MA, Nov 21, 1944.

James (Anderson) DePreist, 70, conductor (Oregon Symphony), born Philadelphia, PA, Nov 21, 1936.

Richard J. Durbin, 62, US Senator (D, Illinois), born East St. Louis, IL, Nov 21, 1944.

George Kenneth (Ken) Griffey, Jr, 37, baseball player, born Donora, PA, Nov 21, 1969.

Goldie Hawn, 61, actress ("Rowan & Martin's Laugh-In," *Private Benjamin*; Oscar for *Cactus Flower*), born Washington, DC, Nov 21, 1945.

Laurence Luckinbill, 72, actor ("The Delphi Bureau," *The Boys in the Band, Star Trek V*), born Fort Smith, AR, Nov 21, 1934.

Lorna Luft, 54, singer, actress, born Los Angeles, CA, Nov 21, 1952.

Juliet Mills, 65, actress ("Nanny and the Professor," "Passions," *So Well Remembered, Carry on Jack*), born London, England, Nov 21, 1941.

Stanley Frank ("Stan the Man") Musial, 86, Hall of Fame baseball player, born Donora, PA, Nov 21, 1920.

Harold Ramis, 62, actor, director, writer, producer (*Ghostbusters, Back to School*), born Chicago, IL, Nov 21, 1944.

Cynthia Rhodes, 50, actress, dancer (*Flashdance, Dirty Dancing*), born Nashville, TN, Nov 21, 1956.

Tasha Schwikert, 22, gymnast, born Las Vegas, NV, Nov 21, 1984.

Nicollette Sheridan, 43, actress ("Desperate Housewives," "Knots Landing"), born Worthing, Sussex, England, Nov 21, 1963.

Marlo Thomas, 68, actress ("That Girl"), author (*Free to Be . . . You and Me*), born Detroit, MI, Nov 21, 1938.

NOVEMBER 22 — WEDNESDAY

Day 326 — 39 Remaining

ADAMS, ABIGAIL SMITH: BIRTH ANNIVERSARY. Nov 22, 1744. Wife of John Adams, second president of the US, and mother of John Quincy Adams, sixth president of the US. An intelligent woman very interested in politics and current affairs, she was a prodigious letter writer and an influence on her husband. Adams argued to her husband that Congress "should remember the ladies" as the new American government took form. Born at Weymouth, MA, Adams died Oct 28, 1818, at Quincy, MA.

BRITTEN, (EDWARD) BENJAMIN: BIRTH ANNIVERSARY. Nov 22, 1913. English composer born at Lowestoft, Suffolk, England. Lord Britten, Baron Britten of Aldeburgh, died at Aldeburgh, Dec 4, 1976.

CARMICHAEL, HOAGIE: BIRTH ANNIVERSARY. Nov 22, 1899. Hoagland Howard Carmichael, attorney who gave up the practice of law to become an actor and songwriter, was born at Bloomington, IN. Among his many popular songs: "Stardust," "Lazybones," "Two Sleepy People" and "Skylark." Carmichael died at Rancho Mirage, CA, Dec 27, 1981.

CHINA CLIPPER: ANNIVERSARY. Nov 22, 1935. A Pan American Martin 130 "flying boat" called the *China Clipper* began regular trans-Pacific mail service on Nov 22, 1935. The plane, powered by four Pratt and Whitney Twin Wasp engines, took off from San Francisco. It reached Manila, Philippines, 59 hours and 48 minutes later. About 20,000 persons watched the historic take-off. Commercial passenger service was established the following year (Oct 21, 1936).

De GAULLE, CHARLES ANDRE MARIE: BIRTH ANNIVERSARY. Nov 22, 1890. President of France from December 1958 until his resignation in April 1969, Charles de Gaulle was born at Lille, France. A military leader, he wrote *The Army of the Future* (1934) in which he predicted just the type of armored warfare that was used against his country by Nazi Germany in WWII. After France's defeat at the hands of the Germans, he declared the existence of "Free France" and made himself head of that organization. When the French Vichy government began to collaborate openly with the Germans, the French citizenry looked to de Gaulle for leadership. His greatest moment of triumph was when he entered liberated Paris on Aug 26, 1944. De Gaulle died at Colombey-les-Deux-Eglises, France, Nov 19, 1970.

ELIOT, GEORGE: BIRTH ANNIVERSARY. Nov 22, 1819. English novelist George Eliot, whose real name was Mary Ann Evans, was born at Chilvers Coton, Warwickshire, England. Her works include *Silas Marner* and *Middlemarch*. She died at Chelsea, Dec 22, 1880.

GARNER, JOHN NANCE: BIRTH ANNIVERSARY. Nov 22, 1868. Thirty-second vice president of US (1933–41) born at Red River County, TX. Died at Uvalde, TX, Nov 7, 1967.

GERMANY: BUSS UND BETTAG. Nov 22. Buss und Bettag (Repentance Day) is observed on the Wednesday before the last Sunday of the church year. A legal public holiday in all German states except Bavaria (where it is observed only in communities with predominantly Protestant populations).

THE HUMANE SOCIETY OF THE UNITED STATES: ANNIVERSARY. Nov 22. In 1954, when The Humane Society of the United States (HSUS) was founded by a handful of dedicated visionaries, the modern concept of "animal welfare" barely existed. A half-century later, The HSUS has become the nation's largest animal protection organization, with a constituency of millions, and a leader in the parallel rise of the modern animal welfare movement. The HSUS mission is to create a humane and sustainable world for all animals, including people, through education, advocacy and the promotion of respect and compassion. For info: Humane Society of the US, 2100 L St NW, Washington, DC 20037. Phone: (202) 452-1100. Web: www.hsus.org.

KENNEDY, JOHN F.: ASSASSINATION ANNIVERSARY. Nov 22, 1963. President John F. Kennedy was slain by a sniper while riding in an open automobile at Dallas, TX. Accused assassin Lee Harvey Oswald was killed by Jack Ruby while in police custody awaiting trial.

LEBANON: INDEPENDENCE DAY: ANNIVERSARY. Nov 22. National Day. Gained independence from France in 1943.

***ON THE ORIGIN OF SPECIES* PUBLISHED: ANNIVERSARY.** Nov 22, 1859. Charles Darwin's monumental work, *On the Origin of Species by Means of Natural Selection, or the Preservation of Favoured Races in the Struggle for Life,* was published on this date by London publisher John Murray. The print run of 1,250 (priced at 15 shillings) sold out the same day. A second print run of 3,000 in December also sold quickly. The book immediately generated a firestorm of public and private discussion. The word "evolution" did not appear until the 1872 (last) edition of *Origin.*

POST, WILEY: BIRTH ANNIVERSARY. Nov 22, 1898. Barnstorming aviator, stunt parachutist and adventurer, Wiley Post was born at Grand Plain, TX. Post, who taught himself to fly, and his plane, the *Winnie Mae,* were the center of world attention in the 1930s. He was coauthor (with his navigator, Harold Gatty) of *Around the World in Eight Days.* In 1935, Post and friend Will Rogers started on a flight to Asia. Their plane crashed near Point Barrow, AK, Aug 15, 1935; both were killed.

SAGITTARIUS, THE ARCHER. Nov 22–Dec 21. In the astronomical/astrological zodiac that divides the sun's apparent orbit into 12 segments, the period Nov 22–Dec 21 is identified, traditionally, as the sun sign of Sagittarius, the Archer. The ruling planet is Jupiter.

SAINT CECILIA: FEAST DAY. Nov 22. Roman virgin, Christian martyr and patron of music and musicians lived during the second or third century. Survived sentence of suffocation by steam, but succumbed to sentence of beheading. Subject of poetry and musical compositions and her feast day is still an occasion for musical events.

WHAT DO YOU LOVE ABOUT AMERICA DAY. Nov 22. One day to talk about what's great about our country and its people. In the midst of cynicism, let's talk to each other about what we love. Annually, the day before Thanksgiving. For info: Chuck Sutherland, 6906 Waggoner Pl, Dallas, TX 75230. Phone: (214) 696-9214. Fax: (214) 722-1266. E-mail: sutherla@swbell.net.

WONDERLAND OF LIGHTS. Nov 22–Dec 31. Marshall, TX. More than 10 million tiny white lights cover the city. Features JC's lighted Christmas parade, candlelight home tours. Outdoor ice-skating on the square and live entertainment on the square Tuesdays, Thursdays, Fridays and Saturdays. First Saturday (Dec 2), Cowboy Christmas Celebration with breakfast, entertainment, stick-horse races, mule rides, carriage rides, bus tours and Santa Claus. Est attendance: 500,000. For info: Patsy Dreesen, Dir of Conv & Visitors Dvmt, Greater Marshall Chamber of Commerce, PO Box 520, Marshall, TX 75671. Phone: (903) 935-7868. Fax: (903) 935-9982. E-mail: chambermfi@hotmail.com. Web: www.marshalltxchamber.com.

November *2006*	S	M	T	W	T	F	S
				1	2	3	4
	5	6	7	8	9	10	11
	12	13	14	15	16	17	18
	19	20	21	22	23	24	25
	26	27	28	29	30		

BIRTHDAYS TODAY

Boris Becker, 39, former tennis player, born Leimen, Germany, Nov 22, 1967.

Guion S. Bluford, Jr, 64, first black astronaut in space, born West Philadelphia, PA, Nov 22, 1942.

Tom Conti, 65, actor (*Reuben, Reuben*), born Paisley, Scotland, Nov 22, 1941.

Jamie Lee Curtis, 48, actress (*True Lies, Halloween, A Fish Called Wanda*), born Los Angeles, CA, Nov 22, 1958.

Harry Edwards, 64, sports sociologist, born St. Louis, MO, Nov 22, 1942.

Allen Garfield, 67, actor (*Bananas, The Conversation, Dick Tracy*), born Newark, NJ, Nov 22, 1939.

Stephen Geoffreys, 47, actor (*Heaven Help Us, 976-EVIL*), born Cincinnati, OH, Nov 22, 1959.

Terry Gilliam, 66, actor, writer ("Monty Python's Flying Circus," *Life of Brian*), director (*Brazil*), born Minneapolis, MN, Nov 22, 1940.

Mariel Hemingway, 45, actress (*Manhattan, Personal Best, Superman IV*), born Ketchum, ID, Nov 22, 1961.

Scarlett Johansson, 22, actress (*Ghost World, Lost in Translation*), born New York, NY, Nov 22, 1984.

Richard Kind, 49, actor ("Spin City," "Mad About You"), born Trenton, NJ, Nov 22, 1957.

Billie Jean King, 63, former tennis player, born Long Beach, CA, Nov 22, 1943.

Robert Vaughn, 74, actor ("The Man From U.N.C.L.E.," *The Magnificent Seven*), born New York, NY, Nov 22, 1932.

NOVEMBER 23 — THURSDAY

Day 327 — 38 Remaining

ASHFORD, EMMETT LITTLETON: BIRTH ANNIVERSARY. Nov 23, 1914. Emmett Littleton Ashford, born at Los Angeles, CA, was the first black to officiate at a major league baseball game. Ashford began his pro career calling games in the minors in 1951 and went to the majors in 1966. He was noted for his flamboyant style when calling strikes and outs as well as for his dapper dress, which included cufflinks with his uniform. He died Mar 1, 1980, at Marina del Rey, CA.

ATLANTA MARATHON AND ATLANTA HALF MARATHON. Nov 23. Atlanta, GA. 26.2-mile and 13.1-mile races (USATF certified). Advance registration only; entry forms available in July; please send SASE. Est attendance: 8,000. For info: Atlanta Track Club, Atlanta Marathon, 3097 E Shadowlawn Ave, Atlanta, GA 30305. Phone: (404) 231-9064, ext 17. Fax: (404) 364-0708. E-mail: atc@atlantatrackclub.org. Web: www.atlanta trackclub.org.

BILLY THE KID: BIRTH ANNIVERSARY. Nov 23, 1859. Legendary outlaw of western US. Probably named Henry McCarty at birth (New York, NY), he was better known as William H. Bonney. Ruthless killer, a failure at everything legal, he escaped from jail at age 21 while under sentence of hanging. Recaptured at Stinking Springs, NM, and returned to jail, he again escaped, only to be shot through the heart by pursuing Lincoln County Sheriff Pat Garrett at Fort Sumner, NM, during the night of July 14, 1881. His last words, answered by two shots, reportedly were "Who is there?"

DAYTONA TURKEY RUN. Nov 23–26. Daytona International Speedway, Daytona Beach, FL. 33rd annual car show of all makes of 1980 and older collector vehicles. Show includes display of classics, street rods, muscle cars, race cars, customs and special trucks on the speedway infield with a large swap meet (4,400 vendors) of auto parts and accessories and car sales corral. Also a craft sale. Annually, Thanksgiving weekend. Est attendance: 150,000. For info: Ron Baynton, Mgr of Show Operations, Daytona Beach Racing and Recreational Facilities District, PO Box 1958, Daytona Beach, FL 32115-1958. Phone: (386) 255-7355. Fax: (386) 255-5755. Web: www.turkeyrun.com.

"DR. WHO" TV PREMIERE: ANNIVERSARY. Nov 23, 1963. First episode of "Dr. Who" premiered on British TV with William Hartnell as the first doctor. Traveling through time and space in the TARDIS (an acronym for Time and Relative Dimensions in Space), the doctor and his companions found themselves in mortal combat with creatures such as the Daleks. The series aired until 1989, with a special film in 1996. "Dr. Who" didn't air in the US until Sept 29, 1975.

FIRST PLAY-BY-PLAY FOOTBALL GAME BROADCAST: ANNIVERSARY. Nov 23, 1919. The first play-by-play football game radio broadcast in the US took place on this day. Texas A&M blanked the University of Texas 7–0.

FOODS & FEASTS OF COLONIAL VIRGINIA. Nov 23–25. Jamestown Settlement, Williamsburg, VA, and Yorktown Victory Center, Yorktown, VA. Explore the 17th- and 18th-century culinary practices of Virginia at this three-day event starting on Thanksgiving Day. At Jamestown Settlement, learn how food was gathered, preserved and prepared on land and at sea by Virginia's English colonists and Powhatan Indians. At Yorktown Victory Center, learn about typical soldiers' fare during the American Revolution and trace the bounty of a 1780s farm from field to kitchen. For info: Jamestown-Yorktown Foundation, PO Box 1607, Williamsburg, VA 23187. Phone: (757) 253-4838 or toll-free (888) 593-4682. Fax: (757) 253-5299. Web: www.historyisfun.org.

GARDEN OF LIGHTS. Nov 23–Jan 1, 2007. Honor Heights Park, Muskogee, OK. Park sparkles and shimmers with more than one million lights. Three graceful doves with 12-ft wingspans; four lighted nature exhibits; lighted waterfall with sound effects is 200 ft long with a family of deer resting nearby. Lights all over! Est attendance: 280,000. For info: Ervalene Jenkins, Muskogee Convention & Tourism, 425 Boston, Muskogee, OK 74402-0797. Phone: (888) 687-6137. Fax: (918) 684-6364. E-mail: tourism@ muskogeeonline.org. Web: www.cityofmuskogee.com.

GARDEN OF LIGHTS. Nov 23–Jan 1, 2007. Norfolk Botanical Garden, Norfolk, VA. This holiday festival includes more than 500,000 twinkling lights along a 2.5-mile route through the Garden. Proceeds to benefit the Norfolk Botanical Garden Society, a nonprofit organization. Est attendance: 100,000. For info: Norfolk Botanical Garden, 6700 Azalea Garden Rd, Norfolk, VA 23518. Phone: (757) 441-5830. Fax: (757) 853-8294. Web: www .norfolkbotanicalgarden.org.

GILBERT ISLANDS TAKEN: ANNIVERSARY. Nov 23, 1943. The US Second Marine Division took control of the Gilbert Islands after fierce fighting on the heavily fortified Tarawa Atoll. In the 76-hour battle the Marines beat back a "death charge" in which the Japanese ran directly at the American guns. American troops sustained 3,500 killed and wounded. The Japanese suffered 5,000 killed and 17 wounded and captured. (The Gilbert Islands are the westernmost of the Polynesians, midway between Australia and Hawaii and today are part of the nation of Kiribati.)

HOLIDAY LIGHTS ON THE LAKE. Nov 23–Jan 7, 2007. Lakemont Park, Altoona, PA. Drive-through displays of more than 51 acres of animated holiday lights, plus a holiday gift shop, food, model train displays and visits from Santa Claus. Est attendance: 75,000. For info: Lakemont Park, 1-99 Frankstown Exit, Altoona, PA 16602. Phone: (814) 949-7275 or (800) 434-8006. Fax: (814) 949-9207. E-mail: lakemontparkfun@hotmail.com. Web: www .lakemontparkfun.com.

JAPAN: LABOR THANKSGIVING DAY. Nov 23. National holiday.

KARLOFF, BORIS: BIRTH ANNIVERSARY. Nov 23, 1887. Born William Henry Pratt at London, England. An actor known for his portrayal of ghoulish figures, his movies included *Frankenstein, The Body Snatcher* and *The Bride of Frankenstein.* Karloff died Feb 2, 1969, at Sussex, England.

***LIFE* MAGAZINE DEBUTS: 70th ANNIVERSARY.** Nov 23, 1936. The illustrated magazine *Life* debuted on this day. The first cover featured a dramatic photograph by Margaret Bourke-White of Fort Peck Dam.

LONGWOOD GARDENS CHRISTMAS DISPLAY. Nov 23–Jan 7, 2007. Kennett Square, PA. Indoor conservatory display of thousands of poinsettias and decorated trees. Outdoors, more than 400,000 lights and holiday fountain displays. Est attendance: 200,000. For info: Longwood Gardens, PO Box 501, Kennett Square, PA 19348-0501. Phone: (610) 388-1000. Web: www .longwoodgardens.org.

MACY'S THANKSGIVING DAY PARADE. Nov 23. New York, NY. 80th annual parade. Starts at 9 AM, EST, in Central Park West. A part of everyone's Thanksgiving, the parade grows bigger and better each year. Featuring floats, giant balloons, marching bands and famous stars, the parade is televised for the whole country. For info: New York Conv/Visitors Bureau, 810 7th Ave, 3rd Fl, New York, NY 10019. Phone: (212) 484-1222. Web: www.nycvisit.com.

MARX, HARPO: BIRTH ANNIVERSARY. Nov 23, 1893. Harpo (Adolph Arthur) Marx was born at New York, NY. He was the second born of the famed Marx brothers who were a popular comedy team of stage, screen and radio for 30 years. The silent brother, Harpo wore a red curly wig and communicated by honking a taxi horn at the most inopportune moments. He was a self-taught and expert player of the harp. Marx died Sept 28, 1964, at Hollywood, CA. Other family members who participated in the comedy team were Groucho (Julius), Chico (Leonard) and, briefly, Zeppo (Herbert) and Gummo (Milton).

OLD TYME FARM DAYS. Nov 23–25. Live Oak, FL. You will experience the past in the present, from cane syrup making and mule-pulled wagon rides to a living old tyme village and an old tyme gospel sing. There will be vendors selling all kinds of old tyme wares. Est attendance: 5,000. For info: Spirit of the Suwannee Music Park, 3076 95th Dr, Live Oak, FL 32060. Phone: (386) 364-1683. Fax: (386) 364-2998. E-mail: spirit@musicliveshere .com. Web: www.musicliveshere.com.

PIERCE, FRANKLIN: BIRTH ANNIVERSARY. Nov 23, 1804. The 14th president of the US was born at Hillsboro, NH. Term of office: Mar 4, 1853–Mar 3, 1857. Not nominated until the 49th ballot at the Democratic party convention in 1852, he was refused his party's nomination in 1856 for a second term. Pierce died at Concord, NH, Oct 8, 1869.

PLAZA LIGHTS. Nov 23–mid-January, 2007. Country Club Plaza, Kansas City, MO. Annual lighting ceremony heralds the beginning of the holiday season. More than 200,000 jewel-colored lights, spanning 80 miles, illuminate the outline of every tower, balcony and courtyard of a 14-square block area. Christmas shopping against a backdrop of the Plaza Lights is a Kansas City tradition that began with a single strand of lights over a store entrance in 1925. Est attendance: 250,000. For info: Highwoods Properties, 310 Ward Pkwy, Kansas City, MO 64112. Phone: (816) 753-0100. Fax: (816) 753-4625. Web: www.countryclubplaza .com.

★ ★ ★

November 2006

S	M	T	W	T	F	S
			1	2	3	4
5	6	7	8	9	10	11
12	13	14	15	16	17	18
19	20	21	22	23	24	25
26	27	28	29	30		

RUTLEDGE, EDWARD: BIRTH ANNIVERSARY. Nov 23, 1749. Signer of the Declaration of Independence, governor of South Carolina, born at Charleston, SC. Died there Jan 23, 1800.

SCOTLAND: SCOTTISH INTERNATIONAL BADMINTON CHAMPIONSHIP. Nov 23–26. Kelvin Hall International Sports Arena, Glasgow. A European Badminton Union Grand Prix Tournament. Est attendance: 7,000. For info: Badminton Scotland, Cockburn Centre, 40 Bogmoor Pl, Glasgow, Scotland G51 4TQ. Phone: (44) (141) 445-1218. Fax: (44) (141) 425-1218. E-mail: enquiries@badmintonscotland.org.uk. Web: www.badmintonscotland.org.uk.

STOCK EXCHANGE HOLIDAY (THANKSGIVING DAY). Nov 23. The holiday schedules for the various exchanges are subject to change if relevant rules, regulations or exchange policies are revised. If you have questions, phone: American Stock Exchange (212) 306-1000, Chicago Board of Trade (312) 435-3500, Chicago Board of Options Exchange (312) 786-5600, NASDAQ Stock Market (646) 441-5200, New York Stock Exchange (212) 656-3000, Pacific Stock Exchange (415) 393-4000, Philadelphia Stock Exchange (215) 496-5000.

★**THANKSGIVING DAY.** Nov 23. Presidential Proclamation. Always issued for the fourth Thursday in November. See also: "First US Holiday by Presidential Proclamation: Anniversary" (Nov 26).

THANKSGIVING DAY. Nov 23. Legal public holiday. (Public Law 90–363 sets Thanksgiving Day on the fourth Thursday in November.) Observed in all states. In most states, the Friday after Thanksgiving is also a holiday; in Nevada it is called Family Day.

TURKEY-FREE THANKSGIVING. Nov 23. This is a time for you to take turkey off your table, forgoing flesh foods "cold turkey" and having a harvest of health. Why not carve a compassionate celebration centerpiece—a tasty mock turkey made from tofu, tempeh or seitan? The turkeys will thank you for having a humane holiday! For info: Vegetarian Awareness Network, Communications Center, PO Box 321, Knoxville, TN 37901-0321. Phone: (800) USA-VEGE or (800) 280-8343.

BIRTHDAYS TODAY

Susan Anspach, 61, actress (*Five Easy Pieces, Play It Again Sam, Montenegro*), born New York, NY, Nov 23, 1945.

Vin Baker, 35, basketball player, born Lake Wales, FL, Nov 23, 1971.

Jerry Bock, 78, composer ("Fiddler on the Roof," "Fiorello"), born New Haven, CT, Nov 23, 1928.

Jim Doyle, 61, Governor of Wisconsin (D), born Madison, WI, Nov 23, 1945.

Steve Harvey, 50, comedian, actor (*The Original Kings of Comedy*, "The Steve Harvey Show"), born Welch, WV, Nov 23, 1956.

Mary L. Landrieu, 51, US Senator (D, Louisiana), born Arlington, VA, Nov 23, 1955.

Krzysztof Penderecki, 73, composer, born Debica, Poland, Nov 23, 1933.

Charles E. Schumer, 56, US Senator (D, New York), born Brooklyn, NY, Nov 23, 1950.

NOVEMBER 24 — FRIDAY

Day 328 — 37 Remaining

BARKLEY, ALBEN WILLIAM: BIRTH ANNIVERSARY.
Nov 24, 1877. Thirty-fifth vice president of the US (1949–53), born at Graves County, KY. Died at Lexington, VA, Apr 30, 1956.

BATTLE OF CHATTANOOGA: ANNIVERSARY. Nov 24, 1863. After reinforcing the besieged Union army at Chattanooga, TN, General Ulysses S. Grant launched the Battle of Chattanooga on this date. Falsely secure in the knowledge that his troops were in an impregnable position on Lookout Mountain, Confederate General Braxton Bragg and his army were overrun by the Union forces, Bragg himself barely escaping capture. The battle is famous for the Union army's spectacular advance up a heavily fortified slope into the teeth of the enemy guns.

BELSNICKEL CRAFT SHOW. Nov 24–25. Boyertown, PA. Sale of juried crafts with folk art emphasis. Annually, the first Friday and Saturday after Thanksgiving. Est attendance: 5,000. For info: Lindsay Dieroff, Collection Dir, Boyertown Area Historical Society, 43 S Chestnut St, Boyertown, PA 19512. Phone: (610) 367-5255. E-mail: boyertownhistory@juno.com or mdmarkley@aol.com.

BLACK FRIDAY. Nov 24. The traditional beginning of the Christmas shopping season on the Friday after Thanksgiving. Called "Black Friday" because traditionally retailers were in the "black" by this day of the year.

BUY NOTHING DAY. Nov 24. A 24-hour moratorium on consumer spending. A celebration of simplicity, about getting our runaway consumer culture back onto a sustainable path. Annually, on the first shopping day after Thanksgiving. For info: The Media Foundation, 1243 W 7th Ave, Vancouver, BC, Canada V6H 1B7. Phone: (800) 663-1243 or (604) 736-9401. Fax: (604) 737-6021. E-mail: bnd@adbusters.org. Web: www.adbusters.org.

CARNEGIE, DALE: BIRTH ANNIVERSARY. Nov 24, 1888. American inspirational lecturer and author, Dale Carnegie was born at Maryville, MO. His best-known book, *How to Win Friends and Influence People*, published in 1936, sold nearly five million copies and was translated into 29 languages. Carnegie died at New York, NY, Nov 1, 1955.

CHRISTMAS AT UNION STATION. Nov 24–Jan 7, 2007. Omaha, NE. Celebration of the Christmas holiday around a giant 50-ft Christmas tree in the splendor of Omaha's historic Union Station. Est attendance: 26,000. For info: Durham Western Heritage Museum, 801 S 10th St, Omaha, NE 68108-3299. Phone: (402) 444-5701. Fax: (402) 444-5397. E-mail: info@dwhm.org. Web: www.dwhm.org.

CHRISTMAS CANDLELIGHT TOUR. Nov 24–25 (also Dec 1–2 and 8–9). My Old Kentucky Home State Park, Bardstown, KY. Christmas in the style and flavor of the 1800s. Annually, the first three weekends after Thanksgiving. Est attendance: 10,000. For info: My Old Kentucky Home State Pk, PO Box 323, Hwy 150, Bardstown, KY 40004. Phone: (800) 323-7803 or (502) 348-3502. Fax: (502) 349-0054. Web: www.kystateparks.com.

CHRISTMAS IN ROSELAND. Nov 24–Dec 30 (closed Dec 25). American Rose Center, Shreveport, LA. A fantasyland featuring millions of twinkling lights, live entertainment, fascinating railroad and model train display and unique gift shop. Est attendance: 25,000. For info: American Rose Center, 8877 Jefferson-Paige Rd, Shreveport, LA 71119. Phone: (318) 938-5402, ext 3011. Fax: (318) 938-5405. E-mail: ars@ars-hq.org. Web: www.ars.org.

CHRISTMAS TRADITIONS. Nov 24–Dec 23. St. Charles, MO. Holiday festivities include caroling, chestnut roasting and authentically costumed Santas from around the world. Enjoy candlelight shopping on Wednesdays and Fridays. "Las Posadas," a traditional reenactment of Mary and Joseph seeking shelter, is Saturday, Dec 2. Annually, after Thanksgiving until Christmas. Est attendance: 50,000. For info: St. Charles CVB, 230 S Main St, St. Charles, MO 63301. Phone: (800) 366-2427. Web: www.stcharleschristmas.com.

CRAFTSMEN'S CHRISTMAS CLASSIC ARTS & CRAFTS FESTIVAL. Nov 24–26. Greensboro Coliseum Complex Special Events Center, Greensboro, NC. 33rd annual. Features work from more than 500 talented artists and craftspeople. All juried exhibitors' work has been handmade by the exhibitors and must be their own original design and creation. See the creative process in action as many exhibitors demonstrate throughout the weekend. Visit Christmas Tree Village to view the uniquely decorated Christmas trees by some of our exhibitors. Something for every style, taste and budget with items from the most contemporary to the most traditional. Est attendance: 35,000. For info: Gilmore Enterprises, 1240 Oakland Ave, Greensboro, NC 27403. Phone: (336) 274-5550. E-mail: gilmoreshows@triad.rr.com. Web: www.CraftShow.com or www.gilmoreshows.com.

CUT YOUR OWN CHRISTMAS TREE. Nov 24–Dec 24. Charlottesville, VA. Est attendance: 100. For info: Ash Lawn–Highland, Home of President James Monroe, 1000 James Monroe Parkway, Charlottesville, VA 22902. Phone: (434) 293-9539. Fax: (434) 293-8000. E-mail: info@ashlawnhighland.org. Web: www.ashlawnhighland.org.

"D.B. COOPER" HIJACKING: 35th ANNIVERSARY. Nov 24–25, 1971. A middle-aged man whose plane ticket was made out to "D.B. Cooper" parachuted from a Northwest Airlines 727 jetliner on Nov 25, 1971, carrying $200,000 which he had collected from the airline as ransom for the plane and passengers as a result of threats made during his Nov 24 flight from Portland, OR, to Seattle, WA. He jumped from the plane over an area of wilderness south of Seattle and was never apprehended. Several thousand dollars of the marked ransom money turned up in February 1980, along the Columbia River, near Vancouver, WA.

DICKENS OF A CHRISTMAS AT MOUNT HOPE MANSION. Nov 24–Dec 23 (Fridays, Saturdays, Sundays). Mount Hope Estate and Winery, Manheim, PA. An open house in colorfully decorated Mount Hope Mansion: wine sampling in the billiards room, actors portraying such Dickens favorites as Tiny Tim, Oliver Twist and Ebenezer Scrooge. Est attendance: 10,000. For info: Thomas Roy, Mgr, Mount Hope Estate and Winery, PO Box 685, Cornwall, PA 17016. Phone: (717) 665-7021, ext 127. Fax: (717) 664-3466. E-mail: tom@parenfaire.com. Web: www.parenfaire.com.

DICKENS VILLAGE FESTIVAL. Nov 24–26 (also Dec 1–2 and Dec 8–9). Garrison, ND. Walk the streets of downtown and eat delicious hot baked potatoes and sausages on a stick, warm up with a cup of English tea, shop the English Market for Victorian treasures and English gifts. In the evening be outside for a parade of lights led by Christmas carolers and then attend the nightly performance of Dickens's *A Christmas Carol*. Est attendance: 4,000. For info: North Dakota Tourism, Century Center, 1600 E Century Ave, Ste 2, Bismarck, ND 58503. Phone: (800) 799-4242 or (800) 435-5663. Web: www.dickensfestival.com.

DUFF, HOWARD: BIRTH ANNIVERSARY. Nov 24, 1913. American actor Howard Duff was born at Bremerton, WA. He played detective Sam Spade on radio in the 1940s and then went on to films and television ("Knots Landing"). He died July 8, 1990, at Santa Barbara, CA.

FAMILY DAY IN NEVADA. Nov 24. Observed annually on the Friday following the fourth Thursday in November.

GETTYSBURG HOLIDAY FESTIVAL. Nov 24–26. (Also Dec 1–3, 8–10, 15–17, 22–24, 29–31.) Gettysburg, PA. Tours of decorated historic homes, live nativity scene, caroling and handbell choirs, Christmas parade, community concerts, holiday dessert tasting, tuba fest, candlelight walking tour and Adams County New Year's Eve Bash with fireworks. Annually, the last weekend in November, weekends in December and New Year's Eve. Est attendance: 10,000. For info: Gettysburg CVB, PO Box 4117, Gettysburg, PA 17325. Phone: (717) 334-6274. Fax: (717) 334-1166. E-mail: gettysburgcvb@dejazzd.com. Web: www.gettysburgcvb.org.

HEARTH AND HOME IN EARLY MARYLAND. Nov 24–25. St. Mary's City, MD. From everyday meals to feasts, join us as we examine the colonial table. Demonstrations of food preservation and hearth cooking. 10 AM–5 PM. Est attendance: 500. For info: Visitors Services, Historic St. Mary's City, PO Box 39, St. Mary's City, MD 20686. Phone: (240) 895-4990 or (800) SMC-1634. Fax: (240) 895-4968. Web: www.stmaryscity.org.

HOLIDAY MAGIC. Nov 24. Galena Blvd in downtown Aurora, IL. Annual celebration as Santa Claus arrives in our Parade of Lights, followed by the annual lighting of the City Christmas tree and fireworks. For info: City of Aurora, Mayor's Office of Special Events, 43 E Downer Pl, Aurora, IL 60507. Phone: (630) 844-3640. Fax: (630) 906-7068.

JOPLIN, SCOTT: BIRTH ANNIVERSARY. Nov 24, 1868. American musician and composer famed for his piano rags, born at Texarkana, TX. Died at New York, NY, Apr 1, 1917.

JULE FEST. Nov 24–26. Elk Horn, IA. Danish Christmas festival. Est attendance: 3,000. For info: Lisa Riggs, Danish Windmill, PO Box 245, Elk Horn, IA 51531. Phone: (712) 764-7472 or (800) 451-7960. Fax: (712) 764-7475. E-mail: info@danishwindmill.com. Web: www.danishwindmill.com.

MANSTEIN, ERICH VON: BIRTH ANNIVERSARY. Nov 24, 1887. Considered by many to be the greatest strategist of WWII, Erich von Manstein was born at Berlin, Germany. His plan for the invasion of France in 1940 was a complete success. He was dismissed by Hitler in March 1944. Manstein died at Irschenhausen, Germany, June 10, 1973.

MAYOR'S CHRISTMAS TREE. Nov 24. Crown Center Square, Kansas City, MO. The lighting of the nation's tallest Christmas tree celebrates Kansas City's 99-year-old tradition of holiday giving. Local celebrities, musical entertainment, costume characters and outdoor ice-skating are all part of the evening's

festivities. The Mayor's Christmas Tree stands 100 ft tall and shines with thousands of white lights and colorful ornaments. Each evening throughout the holiday season, more than 55,000 lights illuminate Crown Center Square, creating a holiday atmosphere beyond compare. Est attendance: 15,000. For info: Crown Center, 2405 Grand Blvd, Ste 200, Kansas City, MO 64108-2519. Phone: (816) 274-8444 or (800) 721-STAY. Fax: (816) 274-4567. Web: www.crowncenter.com.

MYSTIC SEAPORT FIELD DAYS. Nov 24–25. Mystic Seaport, Mystic, CT. Families enjoy special Thanksgiving weekend activities including wagon rides, food, entertainment and outdoor games on the green. Est attendance: 3,000. For info: Mystic Seaport, 75 Greenmanville Ave, PO Box 6000, Mystic, CT 06355-0990. Phone: (860) 572-5315 or (888) 973-2767. Web: www.mysticseaport.org.

NATIONAL FLOSSING DAY. Nov 24. Americans are encouraged to consider the role flossing has played in their lives, and make plans to help spread "Peace of Mouth" in their own lives and the lives of others around them, in ways with and without floss. On this day, our children should also be made aware of the richness and health that flossing can bring to life. For info: National Flossing Council, 533 4th St SE, Washington, DC 20003. Phone: (202) 544-0711. E-mail: nfd@flossing.org. Web: www.flossing.org.

SINKIE DAY. Nov 24. "Sinkies" (people who occasionally dine over the kitchen sink and elsewhere) are encouraged to celebrate this time-honored, casual-yet-tasteful cuisine culture. This is a particularly appropriate day to become acquainted with the sinkie style of dining. Christmas shopping and Thanksgiving leftovers provide the perfect reasons to enjoy a quick meal. Also the day the annual list of "Six Prominent Suspected Closet-Sinkies" is announced. Annually, the day after Thanksgiving. If it has anything to do with having a quick bite, it has everything to do with being a sinkie. For info: Norm Hankoff, Founder, Intl Assn of People Who Dine Over the Kitchen Sink, PO Box 221413, Sacramento, CA 95822. E-mail: normh@sinkie.com. Web: www.sinkie.com.

SPINOZA, BARUCH: BIRTH ANNIVERSARY. Nov 24, 1632 (OS). Dutch philosopher, born at Amsterdam. Died at The Hague, Feb 21, 1677 (OS). "Peace is not an absence of war," wrote Spinoza, in 1670, "it is a virtue, a state of mind, a disposition for benevolence, confidence, justice."

STERNE, LAURENCE: BIRTH ANNIVERSARY. Nov 24, 1713. Novelist, born at Clonmel, Ireland. Died at London, England, Mar 18, 1768. In his dedication to *Tristram Shandy*, Sterne wrote: "I live in a constant endeavour to fence against the infirmities of ill health, and other evils of life, by mirth; being firmly persuaded that every time a man smiles—but much more so, when he laughs, that it adds something to this Fragment of Life."

TAYLOR, ZACHARY: BIRTH ANNIVERSARY. Nov 24, 1784. The soldier who became 12th president of the US was born at Orange County, VA. Term of office: Mar 4, 1849–July 9, 1850. He was nominated at the Whig party convention in 1848, but, the story goes, he did not accept the letter notifying him of his nomination because it had postage due. He cast his first vote in 1846, when he was 62 years old. Becoming ill July 4, 1850, he died at the White House, July 9. His last words: "I am sorry that I am about to leave my friends."

TOULOUSE-LAUTREC, HENRI DE: BIRTH ANNIVERSARY. Nov 24, 1864. French painter and designer of posters. Born at Albi, France, he died Sept 9, 1901, at Bordeaux, France.

US MILITARY LEAVES PHILIPPINES: ANNIVERSARY. Nov 24, 1992. The Philippines became a US colony at the turn of the last century when it was taken over from Spain after the Spanish-American War. Though President Franklin D. Roosevelt signed a bill Mar 24, 1934, granting the Philippines independence to be effective July 4, 1946, before that date Manila and Washington signed a treaty allowing the US to lease military

	S	M	T	W	T	F	S
November				1	2	3	4
2006	5	6	7	8	9	10	11
	12	13	14	15	16	17	18
	19	20	21	22	23	24	25
	26	27	28	29	30		

bases on the island. In 1991 the Philippine Senate voted to reject a renewal of that lease, and Nov 24, 1992, after almost 100 years of military presence on the island, the last contingent of US marines left Subic Base.

VICTORIAN CHRISTMAS CELEBRATION. Nov 24–Dec 30. Gordon-Roberts House, Cumberland, MD. Victorian Christmas tea and candlelight tours with musical entertainment. Various workshops and children's programs. Theme decorating in an 1867 Victorian mansion museum. Est attendance: 1,500. For info: Sharon Nealis, Admin, Gordon-Roberts House, 218 Washington St, Cumberland, MD 21502. Phone: (301) 777-8678. Web: www .historyhouse.allconet.org.

WORLD FAMOUS FISH HOUSE PARADE. Nov 24. Aitkin, MN. 16th annual special parade of uniquely and humorously decorated fish houses used for ice fishing during the winter. Annually, the Friday after Thanksgiving. Est attendance: 6,000. For info: Carroll Kukowski, Exec Dir, Aitkin Area Chamber of Commerce, PO Box 127, Aitkin, MN 56431. Phone: (800) 526-8342. Fax: (218) 927-4494. E-mail: upnorth@aitkin.com. Web: www.aitkin.com.

WORLD'S CHAMPIONSHIP DUCK-CALLING CONTEST AND WINGS OVER THE PRAIRIE FESTIVAL. Nov 24–25. Stuttgart, AR. Annually, Thanksgiving weekend. Duck-calling contests, duck gumbo cook-off, carnival, 10k race, arts and crafts, beauty pageant, concessions, sporting collectibles, Sportsman's Dinner and Dance, commercial exhibitors, fun shoot. Est attendance: 65,000. For info: Stuttgart Chamber of Commerce, 507 S Main, Stuttgart, AR 72160. Phone: (870) 673-1602. Fax: (870) 673-1604. Web: www.stuttgart arkansas.com.

YOU'RE WELCOMEGIVING DAY. Nov 24. The day after Thanksgiving, to create a four-day weekend. For info: Richard Ankli, The Fifth Wheel Tavern, 639 Fifth St, Ann Arbor, MI 48103-4840.

BIRTHDAYS TODAY

William Frank Buckley, Jr, 81, editor (*The National Review*), author (*God and Man at Yale*), born New York, NY, Nov 24, 1925.
Stanley Livingston, 56, actor ("My Three Sons"), born Los Angeles, CA, Nov 24, 1950.
Keith Primeau, 35, hockey player, born Toronto, ON, Canada, Nov 24, 1971.
Oscar Palmer Robertson, 68, Hall of Fame basketball player, born Charlotte, TN, Nov 24, 1938.
Dwight Schultz, 59, actor ("Star Trek: The Next Generation," *Fat Man and Little Boy*), born Baltimore, MD, Nov 24, 1947.
Brad Sherwood, 42, comedian, actor ("Whose Line Is It Anyway?"), born Chicago, IL, Nov 24, 1964.
Rudolph (Rudy) Tomjanovich, 58, basketball coach and former player, born Hamtramck, MI, Nov 24, 1948.

NOVEMBER 25 — SATURDAY
Day 329 — 36 Remaining

ALASCATTALO DAY. Nov 25. Anchorage, AK. To honor humor in general and Alaskan humor in particular. Event is named after "alascattalo," said to be the genetic cross between a moose and a walrus. For info: Steven C. Levi, Parsnackle Press, PO Box 241467, Anchorage, AK 99524. Phone/fax: (907) 337-2021. E-mail: scl@parsnackle.com.

AUTOMOBILE SPEED REDUCTION: ANNIVERSARY. Nov 25, 1973. Anniversary of the presidential order requiring a cutback from the 70 MPH speed limit. The 55 MPH National Maximum Speed Limit (NMSL) was established by Congress in January 1974 (PL 93–643). The National Highway Traffic Administration reported that "analysis of available data shows that the 55 mph NMSL forestalled 48,310 fatalities through 1980. There were also reductions in crash-related injuries and property damage." Motor fuel savings were estimated at 2.4 billion gallons per year. Notwithstanding, in 1987 Congress permitted states to increase speed limits on rural interstate highways to 65 MPH.

BOSNIA AND HERZEGOVINA: NATIONAL DAY. Nov 25. National holiday. Commemorates the declaration of statehood within the federation of Yugoslavia in 1943.

CARNEGIE, ANDREW: BIRTH ANNIVERSARY. Nov 25, 1835. American financier, philanthropist and benefactor of more than 2,500 libraries, was born at Dunfermline, Scotland. Carnegie Hall, Carnegie Foundation and the Carnegie Endowment for International Peace are among his gifts. Carnegie wrote in 1889, "Surplus wealth is a sacred trust which its possessor is bound to administer in his lifetime for the good of the community. . . . The man who dies . . . rich dies disgraced." Carnegie died at his summer estate, Shadowbrook, MA, Aug 11, 1919.

DiMAGGIO, JOSEPH PAUL (JOE): BIRTH ANNIVERSARY. Nov 25, 1914. Baseball Hall of Fame outfielder, born at Martinez, CA. In 1941 he was on "the streak," getting a hit in 56 consecutive games. He was the American League MVP for three years, was the batting champion in 1939 and led the league in RBIs in both 1941 and 1948. DiMaggio was married to actress Marilyn Monroe in 1954, but they later divorced. He died at Harbour Island, FL, Mar 8, 1999.

GERMANY: FRANKFURT CHRISTMAS MARKET. Nov 25–Dec 23. "Weinachtsmarkt auf dem Romerberg," the Christmas market in Frankfurt, is one of Germany's best. Bells are rung simultaneously from nine downtown churches. Glockenspiels are sounded by hand and trumpets blown from the old St. Nicolas Church.

INTERNATIONAL AURA AWARENESS DAY. Nov 25. A day to increase awareness of the human energy body, or aura. Annually, the fourth Saturday in November. For info: Cynthia Larson, PO Box 7393, Berkeley, CA 94707. Phone: (510) 528-2044. E-mail: cynthia@realityshifters.com. Web: realityshift ers.com/pages/auraday.html.

KENNEDY, JOHN F., JR: BIRTH ANNIVERSARY. Nov 25, 1960. Lawyer, editor (*George* magazine), born at Washington, DC. Son of John F. Kennedy (35th president of the US) and Jacqueline Bouvier Kennedy. He died along with his wife, Carolyn, and his sister-in-law, Lauren Bessette, when the plane he was piloting crashed off of Cape Cod, MA, July 16, 1999.

"THE LIGHT OF THE WORLD" CHRISTMAS PAGEANT. Nov 25–26 (also Dec 3). Courthouse square, Minden, NE. 60th annual. Pageant presented on two sides of the courthouse square with around 115 local citizens performing in beautiful costumes. At the climax some 12,000 Christmas lights are turned on around the downtown square. 7 PM; free admission. Annually, the first Saturday after Thanksgiving and the next two Sundays. Est attendance: 1,000. For info: Dena Beck, Mgr, Minden Chamber of Commerce, PO Box 375, Minden, NE 68959. Phone: (308) 832-1811. E-mail: mindenchamber@gtmc.net. Web: www.mindenne.org.

MEXICO: GUADALAJARA INTERNATIONAL BOOK FAIR. Nov 25–Dec 3. Latin America's largest book fair with exhibitors from all over the Spanish-speaking world. Est attendance: 425,000. For info: David Unger, Guadalajara Book Fair–US Office, Div of Hum, NAC 5225, City College, New York, NY 10031. Phone: (212) 650-7925. Fax: (212) 650-7912. E-mail: filny@aol.com.

MIRABEL SISTERS MURDERED: ANNIVERSARY. Nov 25, 1960. On this date Maria, Teresa and Minerva Mirabel, political activists in the Dominican Republic, were assassinated on orders of dictator Rafael Trujillo. The anniversary of their deaths is now observed as International Day for the Elimination of Violence Against Women by the United Nations.

NATION, CARRY AMELIA MOORE: BIRTH ANNIVERSARY. Nov 25, 1846. American temperance leader, famed as hatchet-wielding smasher of saloons, born at Garrard County, KY. Died at Leavenworth, KS, June 9, 1911.

POPE JOHN XXIII: 125th BIRTH ANNIVERSARY. Nov 25, 1881. Angelo Roncalli, 261st pope of the Roman Catholic Church, born at Sotte il Monte, Italy. Elected pope, Oct 28, 1958. Died June 3, 1963, at Rome, Italy.

SAINT CATHERINE'S DAY. Nov 25. Patron saint of maidens, mechanics and philosophers, as well as of all who work with wheels.

SHOPPING REMINDER DAY. Nov 25. One month before Christmas, a reminder to shoppers that after today there are only 28 more shopping days (excluding Christmas Eve) until Christmas.

SURINAME: INDEPENDENCE DAY. Nov 25. Holiday. Gained independence from the Netherlands in 1975.

TERRITORIAL CHRISTMAS CELEBRATION. Nov 25–Dec 30. Guthrie, OK. Take a step back in time and celebrate Christmas in grand Victorian style. Enjoy the Pollard's production of "A Territorial Christmas Carol," the Victorian Walk, Bed & Breakfast Home Tour, Lion's Club Christmas Parade, Christmas light tour on the trolley, street carolers, peanut vendors, Christmas Tree Auction and Reception and Election of the Territorial Governor. Est attendance: 13,000. For info: Guthrie Conv & Visitors Bureau, PO Box 995, Guthrie, OK 73044-0995. Phone: (800) 299-1889 or (405) 282-1947. Fax: (405) 282-0061. E-mail: info@guthrieok.com. Web: www.guthrieok.com.

UNITED NATIONS: INTERNATIONAL DAY FOR THE ELIMINATION OF VIOLENCE AGAINST WOMEN. Nov 25. Observed by the United Nations since 1993 on the anniversary of the 1960 murders of the Mirabal sisters in the Dominican Republic. In 2004, UN Secretary-General Kofi Annan said, "Let us be encouraged that there is a growing understanding of the problem. But let us also pledge to do our utmost to protect women, banish such violence and build a world in which women enjoy their rights and freedoms on an equal basis with men." Annually, Nov 25. For more info: www.un.org.

BIRTHDAYS TODAY

Christina Applegate, 35, actress ("Married . . . With Children," "Jesse"), born Hollywood, CA, Nov 25, 1971.

Cris Carter, 41, former football player, born Troy, OH, Nov 25, 1965.

Bucky Dent, 55, former baseball player and manager, born Russell Earl O'Dey at Savannah, GA, Nov 25, 1951.

Robert Ehrlich, Jr, 49, Governor of Maryland (R), born Baltimore, MD, Nov 25, 1957.

Joe Jackson Gibbs, 66, Hall of Fame football coach, sportscaster, born Mocksville, NC, Nov 25, 1940.

Amy Grant, 46, singer ("Baby, Baby"), born Augusta, GA, Nov 25, 1960.

Jill Hennessy, 37, actress ("Law & Order," "Crossing Jordan"), born Edmonton, AB, Canada, Nov 25, 1969.

Bernie Joseph Kosar, Jr, 43, former football player, born Boardman, OH, Nov 25, 1963.

John Larroquette, 59, actor (Emmy for "Night Court"; "Payne," "The John Larroquette Show"), born New Orleans, LA, Nov 25, 1947.

John Lynch, 54, Governor of New Hampshire (D), born Waltham, MA, Nov 25, 1952.

Lenny Moore, 73, Hall of Fame football player, born Reading, PA, Nov 25, 1933.

Ben Stein, 62, actor, game-show host ("Win Ben Stein's Money"), born Washington, DC, Nov 25, 1944.

NOVEMBER 26 — SUNDAY

Day 330 — 35 Remaining

CASABLANCA PREMIERE: ANNIVERSARY. Nov 26, 1942. Due to the landing of the Allies in North Africa on Nov 8, the premiere and release of the film were moved up from June 1943 to Nov 26, 1942, when it premiered at New York City on Thanksgiving Day. The general nationwide release followed on Jan 23, 1943, during the Roosevelt-Churchill conferences in Casablanca.

CHRISTMAS ON THE RIVER. Nov 26–Dec 2. Demopolis, AL. Fun with arts and crafts, children's parade, Alabama State BBQ Cook-off and a riverboat parade. Annually, the week concluding with the first Saturday of December. Est attendance: 40,000. For info: Kelley Smith, Events & Tourism, Demopolis Area Chamber of Commerce, Box 667, Demopolis, AL 36732. Phone: (334) 289-0270. Fax: (334) 289-1382. E-mail: dacc@demopoliscatv.com. Web: www.demopolischamber.com.

CUSTER BATTLEFIELD BECOMES LITTLE BIGHORN BATTLEFIELD: 15th ANNIVERSARY. Nov 26, 1991. The US Congress approved a bill renaming Custer Battlefield National Monument as Little Bighorn Battlefield National Monument. The bill also authorized the construction of a memorial to the Native Americans who fought and died at the battle known as Custer's Last Stand. Introduced by then Representative Ben Nighthorse Campbell, the only Native American in Congress, the bill was signed into law by President George H.W. Bush.

FIRST US HOLIDAY BY PRESIDENTIAL PROCLAMATION: ANNIVERSARY. Nov 26, 1789. President George Washington proclaimed Nov 26, 1789, to be Thanksgiving Day. Both Houses of Congress, by their joint committee, had requested him to recommend "a day of public thanksgiving and prayer, to be observed by acknowledging with grateful hearts the many and signal favors of Almighty God, especially by affording them an opportunity to peaceably establish a form of government for their safety and happiness." Proclamation issued Oct 3, 1789. Next proclaimed by President Lincoln in 1863 for the last Thursday in November. In 1939 President Roosevelt moved Thanksgiving to the fourth Thursday in November.

GERMANY: TOTENSONNTAG. Nov 26. In Germany, Totensonntag is the Protestant population's day for remembrance of the dead. It is celebrated on the last Sunday of the church year (the Sunday before Advent).

	S	M	T	W	T	F	S
November				1	2	3	4
2006	5	6	7	8	9	10	11
	12	13	14	15	16	17	18
	19	20	21	22	23	24	25
	26	27	28	29	30		

GRIMKE, SARAH MOORE: BIRTH ANNIVERSARY. Nov 26, 1792. American antislavery and women's rights advocate along with her sister Angelina. Born at Charleston, SC, and died Dec 23, 1873, at Hyde Park, MA.

JAPAN AGREES TO END USE OF DRIFT NETS: 15th ANNIVERSARY. Nov 26, 1991. Japan agreed to comply with a 1989 United Nations moratorium on the use of huge fishing nets in the Northern Pacific Ocean. The large nets extend up to 40 miles and have been criticized as "walls of death," causing widespread destruction of marine life, including whales, turtles, birds and many varieties of fish. Japan agreed to end half of its drift-net fishing by the June 30, 1992, deadline, and the remainder by the end of 1992.

JOHN HARVARD DAY: BIRTH ANNIVERSARY. Nov 26, 1607. English clergyman and scholar. Born in England, he died Sept 24, 1638, at the Massachusetts Bay Colony. Harvard bequeathed part of his estate to a local college, which renamed itself Harvard in his honor.

MONGOLIA: REPUBLIC DAY. Nov 26. National holiday. Commemorates the declaration of the republic in 1924.

"THE PRICE IS RIGHT" TV PREMIERE: 50th ANNIVERSARY. Nov 26, 1956. This popular show is also TV's longest-running daily game show, surviving changes in format, networks, time slots and hosts. It began in 1956 with Bill Cullen as host, Don Pardo as announcer; four contestants had to bid on an item and the one who bid closest to the manufacturer's suggested price without going over won the item. In 1972, after a seven-year hiatus, "The Price Is Right" came back in two versions. Bob Barker was the host of the network version, which expanded to an hour and which he hosts to this day. Johnny Olsen was the announcer until his death in 1985; Rod Roddy took his place. Also on the show are attractive women who model the prizes to be won and help set up the price-guessing games. "Price" contestants are drawn from the studio audience.

QUEEN ELIZABETH II AGREES TO PAY TAXES: ANNIVERSARY. Nov 26, 1992. Prime Minister John Major announced that Britain's monarch, Queen Elizabeth, had decided to begin paying taxes on her personal income.

RADIOLOGICAL SOCIETY OF NORTH AMERICA SCIENTIFIC ASSEMBLY AND ANNUAL MEETING. Nov 26–Dec 1. McCormick Place, Chicago, IL. 92nd annual. Est attendance: 61,000. For info: Radiological Society of North America, 820 Jorie Blvd, Oak Brook, IL 60523-2251. Phone: (630) 571-2670. Fax: (630) 571-7837.

SCHULZ, CHARLES: BIRTH ANNIVERSARY. Nov 26, 1922. Cartoonist, born at Minneapolis, MN. Created the "Peanuts" comic strip that debuted on Oct 2, 1950. The strip included Charlie Brown, his sister Sally, his dog Snoopy, friends Linus and Lucy and a variety of other characters. Schulz's last daily strip was published Jan 3, 2000, and his last Sunday strip was published Feb 13, 2000. The strip ran in more than 2,500 newspapers in many different countries. Schulz won the Reuben Award in both 1955 and 1964 and was named International Cartoonist of the Year in 1978. Several TV specials were spin-offs of the strip including "It's the Great Pumpkin Charlie Brown" and "You're a Good Man Charlie Brown." Schulz died at Santa Rosa, CA, Feb 12, 2000. See also "Peanuts Debuts: Anniversary" (Oct 2).

SEVAREID, ERIC: BIRTH ANNIVERSARY. Nov 26, 1912. American journalist Eric (Arnold) Sevareid was born at Velva, ND. He worked for CBS News as a radio reporter during WWII, appeared regularly on "The CBS News with Walter Cronkite" from 1964 to 1977, won the Peabody Award for news interpretations (1950, 1964 and 1967) and earned two Emmys in 1973. He died July 9, 1992, at Washington, DC.

TRAVELERS WITH DISABILITIES AWARENESS WEEK. Nov 26–Dec 3. To promote the economic well-being of Americans with disabilities who travel and to create an environment free of obstacles throughout the tourism and travel industry for Americans with disabilities. Annually, the week following Thanksgiving. For info: Society for Accessible Travel and Hospitality, 347 Fifth Ave, Ste 610, New York, NY 10016. Phone: (212) 447-7284. E-mail: SATHTRAVEL@aol.com. Web: www.sath.org.

TRUTH, SOJOURNER: DEATH ANNIVERSARY. Nov 26, 1883. A former slave who had been sold four different times, Sojourner Truth became an evangelist who argued for abolition and women's rights. After a troubled early life, she began her evangelical career in 1843, traveling through New England until she discovered the utopian colony called the Northampton Association of Education and Industry. It was there she was exposed to, and became an advocate for, the cause of abolition, working with Frederick Douglass, Wendell Phillips, William Lloyd Garrison and others. In 1850 she befriended Lucretia Mott, Elizabeth Cady Stanton and other feminist leaders and actively began supporting calls for women's rights. In 1870 she attempted to petition Congress to create a "Negro State" on public lands in the west. Born at Ulster County, NY, about 1790, with the name Isabella Van Wagener, she died Nov 26, 1883, at Battle Creek, MI.

"TWENTY QUESTIONS" TV PREMIERE: ANNIVERSARY. Nov 26, 1949. This game show was based on the old guessing game. A celebrity panel had to guess the identity of an object (at the start they were told only if it was animal, vegetable or mineral) by asking up to 20 questions. Bill Slater hosted two network versions of the show on NBC and Dumont. Jay Jackson took over when it switched from NBC to ABC. "Twenty Questions" first began on radio. Regular panelists included Fred Van Deventer, Florence Rinard, Herb Polesie and Johnny McPhee.

WALKER, MARY EDWARDS: BIRTH ANNIVERSARY. Nov 26, 1832. American physician and women's rights leader, born at Oswego, NY. First female surgeon in US Army (Civil War). Spent four months in Confederate prison. First and only woman ever to receive Medal of Honor (Nov 11, 1865). Two years before her death, on June 3, 1916, a government review board asked that her award be revoked. She continued to wear it, in spite of official revocation, until her death, Feb 21, 1919, at Oswego. On June 11, 1977, the secretary of the army posthumously restored the Medal of Honor to Dr. Walker.

BIRTHDAYS TODAY

Garcelle Beauvais-Nilon, 40, actress ("NYPD Blue," *Bad Company*), born St. Marc, Haiti, Nov 26, 1966.

Samuel Bodman, 68, US Secretary of Energy, born Chicago, IL, Nov 26, 1938.

Shannon Dunn, 34, Olympic snowboarder, born Arlington Heights, IL, Nov 26, 1972.

Robert Goulet, 73, entertainer, actor (*Camelot, Naked Gun 2½*), born Lawrence, MA, Nov 26, 1933.

Dale Jarrett, 50, race car driver, born Conover, NC, Nov 26, 1956.

Shawn Kemp, 37, basketball player, member of Dream Team II, born Elkhart, IN, Nov 26, 1969.

Richard (Rich) Caruthers Little, 68, impressionist, born Ottawa, ON, Canada, Nov 26, 1938.

Tina Turner, 68, singer (with Ike: "A Fool in Love"; solo: "What's Love Got to Do With It"), born Nutbush, TN, Nov 26, 1938.

NOVEMBER 27 — MONDAY
Day 331 — 34 Remaining

AGEE, JAMES: BIRTH ANNIVERSARY. Nov 27, 1909. Poet, critic, novelist (*A Death in the Family*), social historian (*Let Us Now Praise Famous Men*), scriptwriter, born at Knoxville, TN. Died at New York, NY, May 16, 1955.

BANK BAILOUT BILL: 15th ANNIVERSARY. Nov 27, 1991. Both houses of Congress approved legislation authorizing $70 billion in additional borrowing authority for the Federal Deposit Insurance Corporation (FDIC) because of the record number of savings and loan failures.

BEARD, CHARLES A.: BIRTH ANNIVERSARY. Nov 27, 1874. American historian Charles Austin Beard who wrote many books in collaboration with his wife, Mary R. Beard, was born near Knightstown, IN. He died at New Haven, CT, Sept 1, 1948.

"THE DINAH SHORE SHOW" TV PREMIERE: 55th ANNIVERSARY. Nov 27, 1951. Dinah Shore hosted a successful 15-minute musical show until 1957 and then an hour variety show from 1957 to 1962, one of the few females to have done so. The music show was sponsored by Chevrolet (and was officially known as "The Dinah Shore Chevy Show") and featured a backup group called the Skylarks. Shore also starred in specials and hosted a variety series with a guest host filling in for her every fourth week. She later moved on to hosting a talk show.

DUBCEK, ALEXANDER: BIRTH ANNIVERSARY. Nov 27, 1921. The man who attempted to give his country "socialism with a human face," Alexander Dubcek was born at Uhrocev, a village in western Slovakia. As first secretary of the Czechoslovak Communist Party during the "Prague Spring" of 1968, he moved to achieve the "widest possible democratization" and to loosen the dominant influence of the Soviet Union. As a result, Czechoslovakia was invaded by armed forces of the Warsaw Pact on Aug 21, 1968. Dubcek died Nov 7, 1992, at Prague.

GINGERBREAD ON PARADE. Nov 27–Dec 24. Mormon Trail Center at Historic Winter Quarters Visitors Center, Omaha, NE. View more than 200 gingerbread exhibits of every shape and size delightfully decorated for the holidays. Est attendance: 22,000. For info: Director, Mormon Trail Center, 3215 State St, Omaha, NE 68112. Phone: (402) 453-9372.

HENDRIX, JIMI: BIRTH ANNIVERSARY. Nov 27, 1942. American musician and songwriter Jimi Hendrix was born at Seattle, WA. One of the greatest rock guitarists in history, he revolutionized the guitar sound with heavy use of feedback and incredible fretwork. His success first came in England, then in the US after his appearance at the Monterey Pop Festival (1967). His albums included *Are You Experienced?*, *Electric Ladyland* and *Band of Gypsys*. He died Sept 18, 1970, at London, England.

KEMBLE, FANNY: BIRTH ANNIVERSARY. Nov 27, 1809. Frances Anne Kemble, English actress, born at London, England, and died there Jan 15, 1893.

LEE, BRUCE: BIRTH ANNIVERSARY. Nov 27, 1940. The actor and martial artist was born at San Francisco, CA, but raised in Hong Kong. In 1959, he returned to the US to teach martial arts, opening schools in Seattle, WA, and Oakland, CA. Spotted at a competition by a TV producer, Lee was cast as Kato in TV's *The Green Hornet* in 1966. He moved on to film, where he displayed an intense charisma that would make him a star. Before he could enjoy this new success, Lee died of a cerebral edema on July 20, 1973, at Hong Kong. His films included *Fists of Fury* (1972) and *Enter the Dragon* (1973).

	S	M	T	W	T	F	S
November				1	2	3	4
2006	5	6	7	8	9	10	11
	12	13	14	15	16	17	18
	19	20	21	22	23	24	25
	26	27	28	29	30		

LIVINGSTON, ROBERT R.: BIRTH ANNIVERSARY. Nov 27, 1746 (OS). Member of the Continental Congress, farmer, diplomat and jurist, was born at New York, NY. It was Livingston who administered the oath of office to President George Washington in 1789. He died at Clermont, NY, Feb 26, 1813.

MASTERSON, BAT: BIRTH ANNIVERSARY. Nov 27, 1853. Old American West gambler, saloonkeeper, lawman and newswriter/editor. Born at Henryville, QC, Canada; died Oct 25, 1921, at New York, NY.

SPACE MILESTONE: *SOYUZ T-3* (USSR). Nov 27, 1980. Launched this date with three cosmonauts, O. Makarov, L. Kizim and G. Strekalov, docked at *Salyut 6* space station on Nov 28. Returned to Earth, Dec 10, 1980. This was the first Soviet crew of three since 1971.

SWITZERLAND: ONION MARKET (ZIBELEMARIT). Nov 27. Berne. Best known and most popular of Switzerland's many autumn markets. Great heaps of onions in front of Federal Palace. Fourth Monday in November commemorates granting of market right to people after great fire of Berne in 1405.

WEIZMANN, CHAIM: BIRTH ANNIVERSARY. Nov 27, 1874. Israeli statesman born near Pinsk, Byelorussia. He played an important role in bringing about the British government's Balfour Declaration, calling for the establishment of a national home for Jews at Palestine. He died at Tel Aviv, Israel, Nov 9, 1952.

BIRTHDAYS TODAY

Richard J. Codey, 60, Governor of New Jersey (D), born Orange, NJ, Nov 27, 1946.

Robin Givens, 42, actress ("Head of the Class," *A Rage in Harlem*), born New York, NY, Nov 27, 1964.

Jimmy Rollins, 28, baseball player, born Oakland, CA, Nov 27, 1978.

Gail Henion Sheehy, 69, author, journalist (*The Silent Passage: Menopause; Pathfinders*), born Mamaroneck, NY, Nov 27, 1937.

Fisher Stevens, 43, actor (*The Brother from Another Planet, Bob Roberts*), born Chicago, IL, Nov 27, 1963.

Nick Van Exel, 35, basketball player, born Kenosha, WI, Nov 27, 1971.

Jaleel White, 30, actor ("Family Matters"), born Los Angeles, CA, Nov 27, 1976.

NOVEMBER 28 — TUESDAY
Day 332 — 33 Remaining

ALBANIA: INDEPENDENCE DAY. Nov 28. Commemorates independence from the Ottoman Empire in 1912.

ALSTON, CHARLES H.: BIRTH ANNIVERSARY. Nov 28, 1907. African-American painter and sculptor born at Charlotte, NC, and died at New York, NY, Apr 27, 1977. Throughout his career, Alston experimented with styles ranging from realism to abstraction. His realistic WPA murals at Harlem Hospital depict a narrative in the style of Diego Rivera. The Cubist painting of *The Family* (1955) is an excellent example of Alston's early work, influenced by Italian artist Amedeo Modigliani. *Black Man, Black Woman USA* has a decidedly Egyptian style of portraiture. *Walking* (1958), which depicts a silent crowd, almost prophesied the turmoil and social agitation of the Civil Rights Movement.

BLAKE, WILLIAM: BIRTH ANNIVERSARY. Nov 28, 1757. English poet (*Songs of Innocence*), artist and philosopher, born at London, England. Died there Aug 12, 1827.

BUNYAN, JOHN: BIRTH ANNIVERSARY. Nov 28, 1628 (OS). English cleric and author of *A Pilgrim's Progress*, born at Elstow, Bedfordshire. Died at London, Aug 31, 1688 (OS).

CHAD: REPUBLIC DAY: ANNIVERSARY. Nov 28. National holiday. Commemorates proclamation of the republic in 1958.

LULLY, JEAN BAPTISTE: BIRTH ANNIVERSARY. Nov 28, 1632. Versatile musician and composer, born at Florence, Italy, who chose France for his homeland. Noted for his quick temper, it is said that he struck his own foot with a baton while in a rage. The resulting wound led to blood poisoning, from which he died, at Paris, France, Mar 22, 1687.

MAURITANIA: INDEPENDENCE DAY. Nov 28. National holiday. Attained sovereignty from France in 1960.

MOON PHASE: FIRST QUARTER. Nov 28. Moon enters First Quarter phase at 1:29 AM, EST.

PANAMA: INDEPENDENCE FROM SPAIN. Nov 28. Public holiday. Commemorates the independence of Panama (which at the time was part of Colombia) from Spain in 1821.

ROCKEFELLER CENTER CHRISTMAS TREE: ANNUAL LIGHTING. Nov 28 (tentative). New York, NY. Lighting of the huge Christmas tree in Rockefeller Center signals the opening of the holiday season at New York City. More than 30,000 lights are strung on five miles of electric wire. In 1933 the first formal tree lighting ceremony took place with 700 lights. Date is usually the Tuesday or Wednesday after Thanksgiving.

SPACE MILESTONE: *COLUMBIA STS-9* (US). Nov 28, 1983. Shuttle *Columbia* launched from Kennedy Space Center, FL, with five astronauts (John Young; Brewster Shaw, Jr; Owen Garriot; Robert Parker; Byron Lichtenberg) and German physicist Ulf Merbold. Landed Edwards Air Force Base, CA, on Dec 8.

SPACE MILESTONE: *MARINER 4* (US). Nov 28, 1964. The first successful mission to Mars. Approached within 6,118 miles of Mars on July 14, 1965. Took photographs and instrument readings.

TEHERAN CONFERENCE: ANNIVERSARY. Nov 28–Dec 1, 1943. President Franklin D. Roosevelt, British Prime Minister Winston Churchill and Soviet Premier Joseph Stalin met at Teheran, Iran, to formulate a plan for an Allied assault, a second front, in western Europe. The resulting plan was "Operation Overlord," which commenced with the landing on Normandy's beaches on June 6, 1944 ("D-Day").

BIRTHDAYS TODAY

Michael Chertoff, 53, US Secretary of Homeland Security, born Elizabeth, NJ, Nov 28, 1953.

Berry Gordy, Jr, 77, record and motion picture executive (cofounder of Motown), born Detroit, MI, Nov 28, 1929.

Ed Harris, 56, actor (*The Hours, Pollock, The Right Stuff*), born Englewood, NJ, Nov 28, 1950.

Gary Hart, 68, former senator, former presidential candidate, born Gary Hartpence at Ottawa, KS, Nov 28, 1938.

Hope Lange, 73, actress ("The Ghost and Mrs Muir," *Bus Stop*), born Reading Ridge, CT, Nov 28, 1933.

S. Epatha Merkerson, 54, actress ("Law & Order"), born Detroit, MI, Nov 28, 1952.

Judd Nelson, 47, actor (*The Breakfast Club, St. Elmo's Fire*, "Suddenly Susan"), born Portland, ME, Nov 28, 1959.

Randy Newman, 63, singer, songwriter ("Short People"), composer (film scores *Ragtime, The Natural*), born New Orleans, LA, Nov 28, 1943.

Paul Shaffer, 57, bandleader ("Late Night with David Letterman"), comedian, born Thunder Bay, ON, Canada, Nov 28, 1949.

Jon Stewart, 44, writer, comedian ("The Daily Show"), born Jonathan Stuart Leibowitz at New York, NY, Nov 28, 1962.

Matt Williams, 41, baseball player, born Bishop, CA, Nov 28, 1965.

NOVEMBER 29 — WEDNESDAY
Day 333 — 32 Remaining

ALCOTT, LOUISA MAY: BIRTH ANNIVERSARY. Nov 29, 1832. American author, born at Philadelphia, PA. Died at Boston, MA, Mar 6, 1888. Her most famous novel was *Little Women*, the classic story of Meg, Jo, Beth and Amy.

BERKELEY, BUSBY: BIRTH ANNIVERSARY. Nov 29, 1895. William Berkeley Enos was born at Los Angeles, CA. After serving in WWI as an entertainment officer, he changed his name to Busby Berkeley and began a career as an actor. He turned to directing in 1921, and his lavish Broadway and Hollywood creations include *Forty-Second Street, Gold Diggers of 1933, Footlight Parade, Stage Struck, Babes in Arms, Strike Up the Band, Girl Crazy* and *Take Me Out to the Ball Game*. He retired in 1962 and returned to Broadway in 1970 to supervise a revival of *No, No, Nanette*. He died Mar 14, 1976, at Palm Springs, CA.

CZECHOSLOVAKIA ENDS COMMUNIST RULE: ANNIVERSARY. Nov 29, 1989. Czechoslovakia ended 41 years of one-party communist rule when the Czechoslovak parliament voted unanimously to repeal the constitutional clauses giving the Communist Party a guaranteed leading role in the country and promoting Marxism-Leninism as the state ideology. The vote came at the end of a 12-day revolution sparked by the beating of protestors Nov 17. Although the Communist Party remained in power, the tide of reform led to its ouster by the Civic Forum, headed by playwright Vaclav Havel. The Civic Forum demanded free elections with equal rights for all parties, a mixed economy and support for foreign investment. In the first free elections in Czechoslovakia since WWII, Vaclav Havel was elected president.

ELECTRONIC GREETINGS DAY. Nov 29. Save a letter carrier, save a tree, save a stamp! Today's the day to send your greetings the free, electronic way, via the Internet! (©2003 by WH.) For info: Thomas & Ruth Roy, Wellcat Holidays, 2418 Long Ln, Lebanon, PA 17046. Phone: (717) 279-0184. E-mail: info@well cat.com. Web: www.wellcat.com.

FIRST ARMY-NAVY GAME: ANNIVERSARY. Nov 29, 1890. Army played Navy for the first time in football, and Navy won, 24–0. Red Emrich scored four touchdowns (worth four points each) and kicked two field goals (worth two points each), and Moulton Johnson added the other touchdown to account for all the scoring.

"KUKLA, FRAN AND OLLIE" TV PREMIERE: ANNIVERSARY. Nov 29, 1948. This popular children's show featured puppets created and handled by Burr Tillstrom and was equally popular with adults. Fran Allison was the only human on the show. Tillstrom's lively and eclectic cast of characters, called the "Kuklapolitans," included the bald, high-voiced Kukla, the big-toothed Oliver J. Dragon (Ollie), Fletcher Rabbit, Cecil Bill, Beulah the Witch, Colonel Crackie, Madame Ooglepuss and Dolores Dragon. Most shows were performed without scripts.

LEWIS, C.S. (CLIVE STAPLES): BIRTH ANNIVERSARY. Nov 29, 1898. British scholar, novelist and author (*The Screwtape Letters, Chronicles of Narnia*), born at Belfast, Ireland, died at Oxford, England, Nov 22, 1963.

ROSS, NELLIE TAYLOE: BIRTH ANNIVERSARY. Nov 29, 1876. Nellie Tayloe Ross became the first female governor in the US when she was chosen to serve out the last month and two days of her husband's term as governor of Wyoming after he died in office. She was elected in her own right in the Nov 4, 1924, election but lost the 1927 race. Ross was appointed vice chairman of the Democratic National Committee in 1926 and named director of the US Mint by President Franklin D. Roosevelt in 1933. She served in that capacity for 20 years. Born at St. Joseph, MO, she died Dec 20, 1977, at Washington, DC.

THOMSON, CHARLES: BIRTH ANNIVERSARY. Nov 29, 1729. America's first official record keeper. Chosen secretary of the First Continental Congress Sept 5, 1774, Thomson recorded proceedings for 15 years and delivered his journals together with tens of thousands of records to the federal government in 1789. Born in Ireland, he died Aug 16, 1824. It was Thomson who notified George Washington of his election as president.

UNITED NATIONS: INTERNATIONAL DAY OF SOLIDARITY WITH THE PALESTINIAN PEOPLE. Nov 29. Annual observance proclaimed by UN General Assembly in 1977. At request of the assembly, observance is organized by secretary-general in consultation with Committee on the Exercise of the Inalienable Rights of the Palestinian People. Recommendations include a plan for return of the Palestinians to their homes and the establishment of an "independent Palestinian entity." For info: United Nations, Dept of Public Info, New York, NY 10017. Web: www.un.org.

WAITE, MORRISON R.: BIRTH ANNIVERSARY. Nov 29, 1816. Seventh Chief Justice of the Supreme Court, born at Lyme, CT. Appointed Chief Justice by President Ulysses S. Grant Jan 19, 1874. The Waite Court is remembered for its controversial rulings that did much to rehabilitate the idea of states' rights after the Civil War and early Reconstruction years. Waite died at Washington, DC, Mar 23, 1888.

BIRTHDAYS TODAY

Don Cheadle, 42, actor (*Hotel Rwanda, Ocean's Eleven*), born Kansas City, MO, Nov 29, 1964.
Jacques Rene Chirac, 74, President of France, born Paris, France, Nov 29, 1932.
Joel Coen, 52, producer, screenwriter (*Fargo*), born Minneapolis, MN, Nov 29, 1954.
Kim Delaney, 45, actress ("NYPD Blue"), born Philadelphia, PA, Nov 29, 1961.
Diane Ladd, 74, actress (*Alice Doesn't Live Here Anymore, Ramblin' Rose, The Cemetery Club*), born Rose Diane Ladner at Meridian, MS, Nov 29, 1932.
Madeleine L'Engle, 88, writer (*A Wrinkle in Time, Summer of the Great-Grandmother*), born New York, NY, Nov 29, 1918.
Howie Mandel, 51, comedic actor ("Howie Mandel's Sunny Skies," "Bobby's World"), born Toronto, ON, Canada, Nov 29, 1955.
Chuck Mangione, 66, musician, composer (Grammy for "Bellavia"), born Rochester, NY, Nov 29, 1940.
John Mayall, 73, musician, bandleader (The Bluesbreakers), born Manchester, England, Nov 29, 1933.
Andrew McCarthy, 44, actor (*Pretty in Pink, Weekend at Bernie's*), born Westfield, NJ, Nov 29, 1962.
Cathy Moriarty, 46, actress (*Raging Bull, The Mambo Kings*), born the Bronx, NY, Nov 29, 1960.
Janet Napolitano, 49, Governor of Arizona (D), born Pittsburgh, PA, Nov 29, 1957.
Mariano Rivera, 37, baseball player, born Panama City, Panama, Nov 29, 1969.
Vincent Edward (Vin) Scully, 79, sportscaster, born New York, NY, Nov 29, 1927.
Garry Shandling, 57, comedian ("The Larry Sanders Show"), born Chicago, IL, Nov 29, 1949.

November 2006	S	M	T	W	T	F	S
				1	2	3	4
	5	6	7	8	9	10	11
	12	13	14	15	16	17	18
	19	20	21	22	23	24	25
	26	27	28	29	30		

NOVEMBER 30 — THURSDAY
Day 334 — 31 Remaining

ANDREWS CHAMBER OF COMMERCE HOLLY JOLLY WEEKEND. Nov 30–Dec 3. Andrews, TX. The Holly Jolly Weekend kicks off with the 12th annual Chow-Down at the James Roberts Center. Festivities continue on Friday, Dec 1, with Christmas tree lighting and caroling at Lakeside Park. The 30th annual Christmas Bazaar runs Dec 2–3. For info: Andrews Chamber of Commerce, 700 W Broadway, Andrews, TX 79714. Phone: (432) 523-2695. E-mail: achamber@andrewstx.com. Web: www.andrewstx.com.

ARTICLES OF PEACE BETWEEN GREAT BRITAIN AND THE US: ANNIVERSARY. Nov 30, 1782. These provisional articles of peace, which were to end America's War of Independence, were signed at Paris, France. The refined and definitive treaty of peace between Great Britain and the US was signed at Paris, on Sept 3, 1783. In it "His Britannic Majesty acknowledges the said United States . . . to be free, sovereign and independent states; that he treats them as such; and for himself, his heirs and successors, relinquishes all claims to the government, propriety and territorial rights of the same, and every part thereof. . . ."

BARBADOS: INDEPENDENCE DAY. Nov 30. National holiday. Gained independence from Great Britain in 1966.

CHISHOLM, SHIRLEY: BIRTH ANNIVERSARY. Nov 30, 1924. Born at Brooklyn, NY, Shirley St. Hill Chishom was an educator, author and politician who was the first African-American woman elected to the US House of Representatives. A liberal Democrat, she was known for her strong opinions and outspoken nature as she represented the Bedford-Stuyvesant neighborhood of New York City in Congress from 1974–82. She fought against poverty and discrimination, and ran for the 1972 Democratic nomination for president just to prove that she could. She retired from politics in the 1980s, and died at Ormond Beach, FL, Jan 1, 2005.

CHURCHILL, WINSTON: BIRTH ANNIVERSARY. Nov 30, 1874. Winston Leonard Spencer Churchill, British statesman and the first man to be made an honorary citizen of the US (by an act of Congress, Apr 9, 1963), born at Blenheim Palace, Oxfordshire, England. Died Jan 24, 1965, at London, England. Dedicated to Britain and total victory over Germany, Churchill as minister of defense and prime minister was a strong leader during WWII. A stirring public speaker, Churchill said upon becoming prime minister in 1940, "I have nothing to offer but blood, toil, tears and sweat."

CLEMENS, SAMUEL LANGHORNE (MARK TWAIN): BIRTH ANNIVERSARY. Nov 30, 1835. Celebrated American author, whose books include: *The Adventures of Tom Sawyer*, *The Adventures of Huckleberry Finn* and *The Prince and the Pauper*. Born at Florida, MO, Twain is quoted as saying, "I came in with Halley's Comet in 1835. It is coming again next year, and I expect to go out with it." He did. Twain died at Redding, CT, Apr 21, 1910 (just one day after Halley's Comet perihelion).

COMPUTER SECURITY DAY. Nov 30. The use of computers and the concern for security increases daily. This annual observance reminds people to protect their computers, programs and data at home and at work. More than 1,500 companies participate worldwide. For info: Assn for Computer Security Day, PO Box 39110, Washington, DC 20016. E-mail: computer_security_day@acm.org. Web: www.computersecurityday.com or www.geocities.com/a4csd.

HOFFMAN, ABBOT (ABBIE): BIRTH ANNIVERSARY. Nov 30, 1936. Political activist, born at Worcester, MA, Abbie Hoffman rose to prominence during the 1968 Democratic National Convention at Chicago and at his subsequent trial as a member of the Chicago Seven, a group of radicals accused of conspiring to disrupt the convention. Combining politics and street theater was a Hoffman trait. During the 1967 march on the Pentagon, he sought a permit to allow 1,200 demonstrators to encircle and levitate the military headquarters in an attempt to end the war in Vietnam. He, Jerry Rubin and Paul Krassner conceived the Yippie movement as a youth festival of life to run concurrently with the 1968 convention. Hoffman fled underground in 1974 to avoid trial on cocaine-possession charges and remained a fugitive for nearly seven years. Surrendering to authorities in 1980, he served his sentence in a work-release program. Hoffman died Apr 12, 1989, at New Hope, PA.

THE JOY OF COOKING: 75th PUBLICATION ANNIVERSARY. Nov 30, 1931. America's favorite all-purpose cookbook was self-published on this date by Irma Rombauer (1877–1962). Rombauer was a comforting voice for cooks during the Depression, and the book grew into an institution. The first commercial edition of the book appeared in 1936, and it offered a revolutionary "action format" (chronologically ordered ingredients followed by instructions) now commonplace in cookbooks. The numerous editions overseen by Rombauer and later her daughter and grandson sold more than 14 million copies.

NAIA WOMEN'S NATIONAL VOLLEYBALL CHAMPIONSHIP. Nov 30–Dec 3. Point Loma Nazarene University, San Diego, CA. 20 teams compete in a pool play tournament to determine the national champion. 27th annual championship, cohosted by Point Loma Nazarene University with the San Diego International Sports Council. Est attendance: 3,000. For info: Natl Assn of Intercollegiate Athletics, 23500 W 105th St, PO Box 1325, Olathe, KS 66051-1325. Phone: (913) 791-0044. Fax: (913) 791-9555. E-mail: lthomas@naia.org. Web: www.naia.org.

PHILIPPINES: BONIFACIO DAY. Nov 30. Also known as National Heroes' Day. Commemorates birth of Andres Bonifacio, leader of the 1896 revolt against Spain. Bonifacio was born in 1863.

SAINT ANDREW'S DAY. Nov 30. Feast day of the apostle and martyr, Andrew, who died about AD 60. Patron saint of Scotland.

SAINT OLAF CHRISTMAS FESTIVAL. Nov 30–Dec 3. St. Olaf College, Northfield, MN. Annually since 1912. This celebration of the Christmas season brings together 600 student musicians (a 90-piece symphony orchestra and 500 singers) to perform sacred and folk songs from around the world. Annually, the weekend after Thanksgiving, Thurs–Sun. Est attendance: 12,000. For info: Bob Johnson, St. Olaf College, 1520 St. Olaf Ave, Northfield, MN 55057-1098. Phone: (507) 646-3179. Web: www.stolaf.edu.

SIDNEY, PHILIP: BIRTH ANNIVERSARY. Nov 30, 1554. English poet, statesman and soldier was born at Penshurst, Kent, England. Best known of his poems is *Arcadia* (1580). Mortally wounded as he led an English detachment aiding the Dutch near Zutphen, Sept 22, 1586, Sidney gave his water bottle to another dying soldier with the words "Thy necessity is yet greater than mine." He died at Arnhem, Oct 17, 1586, and all England mourned his death.

STATUE OF RAMSES II UNEARTHED: ANNIVERSARY. Nov 30, 1991. Egyptian construction workers in the ancient provincial town of Akhimim, 300 miles south of Cairo, unearthed a statue of Ramses II. Akhimim was an important provincial district that included the city of Ipu, a mecca for worshippers of the fertility god Min. The statue was uncovered during an excavation to prepare a foundation for a post office. An additional statue was uncovered 33 feet away, but the identity of its subject was unknown.

STAY HOME BECAUSE YOU'RE WELL DAY. Nov 30. So we can call in "well," instead of faking illness, and stay home from work. [©2003 by WH.] For info: Thomas & Ruth Roy, Wellcat Holidays, 2418 Long Ln, Lebanon, PA 17046. Phone: (717) 279-0184. E-mail: info@wellcat.com. Web: www.wellcat.com.

SWIFT, JONATHAN: BIRTH ANNIVERSARY. Nov 30, 1667 (OS). Clergyman and satirist born at Dublin, Ireland. Died there Oct 19, 1745 (OS). Author of *Gulliver's Travels*. "I never saw, heard, nor read," Swift wrote in *Thoughts on Religion*, "that the clergy were beloved in any nation where Christianity was the religion of the country. Nothing can render them popular but some degree of persecution."

BIRTHDAYS TODAY

Richard Burr, 51, US Senator (R, North Carolina), born Charlottesville, VA, Nov 30, 1955.

Dick Clark, 77, longtime host of "American Bandstand," entertainer, producer, born Mount Vernon, NY, Nov 30, 1929.

Joan Ganz Cooney, 77, founder of the Children's Television Workshop and creator of "Sesame Street," born Phoenix, AZ, Nov 30, 1929.

Elisha Cuthbert, 24, actress ("24," "Are You Afraid of the Dark?"), born Calgary, AB, Canada, Nov 30, 1982.

Des'ree, 36, singer (*I Ain't Movin'*), born London, England, Nov 30, 1970.

Robert Guillaume, 79, actor ("Soap," "Benson"), born St. Louis, MO, Nov 30, 1927.

Billy Idol, 51, singer ("Mony Mony," "Eyes Without a Face"), songwriter, born Surrey, England, Nov 30, 1955.

Vincent Edward ("Bo") Jackson, 44, former baseball player, former football player, born Bessemer, AL, Nov 30, 1962.

G. Gordon Liddy, 76, convicted Watergate coconspirator, radio talk-show host, born New York, NY, Nov 30, 1930.

David Mamet, 59, dramatist (*American Buffalo, Oleanna, Things Change*), born Chicago, IL, Nov 30, 1947.

Colin Mochrie, 49, comedian, actor ("Whose Line Is It Anyway?"), born Ayrshire, Scotland, Nov 30, 1957.

Sandra Oh, 36, actress (*Under the Tuscan Sun, Sideways*, "Grey's Anatomy"), born Nepean, ON, Canada, Nov 30, 1970.

Gordon Parks, 94, photographer, author, born Fort Scott, KS, Nov 30, 1912.

Mandy Patinkin, 54, actor (Tony for *Evita; Sunday in the Park with George*, "Chicago Hope"), born Chicago, IL, Nov 30, 1952.

Ivan ("Pudge") Rodriguez, 35, baseball player, born Vega Baja, Puerto Rico, Nov 30, 1971.

Ridley Scott, 69, director (*Alien, Blade Runner, Gladiator*), born Northumberland, England, Nov 30, 1937.

Margaret Spellings, 49, US Secretary of Education, born in Michigan, Nov 30, 1957.

Ben Stiller, 41, actor, director (*Starsky and Hutch, Meet the Parents, Reality Bites*), born New York, NY, Nov 30, 1965.

Noel Paul Stookey, 69, singer, songwriter (Peter, Paul and Mary), born Baltimore, MD, Nov 30, 1937.

Lawrence Summers, 52, president, Harvard University, former US Secretary of the Treasury (Clinton administration), born New Haven, CT, Nov 30, 1954.

Efrem Zimbalist, Jr, 83, actor ("The F.B.I.," *Airport*), born New York, NY, Nov 30, 1923.

December.

DECEMBER 1 — FRIDAY

Day 335 — 30 Remaining

BASKETBALL CREATED: ANNIVERSARY. Dec 1, 1891. James Naismith was a teacher of physical education at the International YMCA Training School at Springfield, MA. To create an indoor sport that could be played during the winter months, he nailed up peach baskets at opposite ends of the gym and gave students soccer balls to toss into them. Thus was born the game of basketball.

BIFOCALS AT THE MONITOR LIBERATION DAY. Dec 1. Our hearts fill with compassion today for coworkers stuck wearing bifocals at the PC. Shed a tear as their heads bob up and down, in and out, trying to read the monitor, trying to decide which set of lenses to use. Annually, Dec 1. [©2003 by WH.] For info: Thomas & Ruth Roy, Wellcat Holidays, 2418 Long Ln, Lebanon, PA 17046. Phone: (717) 279-0184. E-mail: info@wellcat.com. Web: www.wellcat.com.

BINGO'S BIRTHDAY MONTH. Dec 1–31. To celebrate the innovation and manufacture of the game of Bingo in 1929 by Edwin S. Lowe. Bingo has grown into a five-billion-dollar-a-year charitable fund-raiser. For info: Tara Snowden, Pres, Bingo Bugle, Inc, Box 527, Vashon, WA 98070. Phone: (800) 327-6437 or (206) 463-5656. E-mail: tara@bingobugle.com.

CANADA: YUKON ORDER OF PIONEERS: ANNIVERSARY. Dec 1, 1894. The Yukon Order of Pioneers held its founding meeting on this date at Fortymile, Yukon. It began as a vigilante police force to deter claim jumping and later inaugurated Discovery Day (Aug 17), a statutory Yukon holiday commemorating the discovery of gold on Bonanza Creek in 1896.

CHRISTMAS CRAFT SHOW. Dec 1–2. H.O. Weeks Recreation Center, Aiken, SC. 36th annual. This show consists of more than 150 Christmas exhibits and other items from the Southeast's top craftspeople. The displays range from woodwork to fine porcelain sculpture. Est attendance: 7,000. For info: City of Aiken Park & Rec Dept, PO Box 1177, Aiken, SC 29802. Phone: (803) 642-7631. Fax: (803) 642-7639. E-mail: howeeks@aiken.com.

CHRISTMAS FESTIVAL OF LIGHTS. Dec 1–2. Natchitoches, LA. 80th annual. Featuring a parade, fireworks, food, entertainment, a fun run/walk and Christmas lighting. Listed as one of the "Top 100 Events in North America" by the American Bus Association. Est attendance: 150,000. For info: Natchitoches

★   ★   ★

	S	M	T	W	T	F	S
December						1	2
2006	3	4	5	6	7	8	9
	10	11	12	13	14	15	16
	17	18	19	20	21	22	23
	24	25	26	27	28	29	30
	31						

Parish Tourist Commission, 781 Front St, Natchitoches, LA 71457. Phone: (318) 352-8072 or (800) 259-1714. Fax: (318) 352-2415. Web: www.natchitoches.net or www.christmasfestival.com.

CHRISTMAS GREENS SHOW. Dec 1–3. Jackman-Long Building, State Fairgrounds, Salem, OR. Half the building houses decorated trees, large Christmas displays, hundreds of floral arrangements, wreaths and wall hangings. The other half houses 106 handcrafters and their wares, also fresh greens and wreaths. Food available. Proceeds benefit community projects. Annually, the second Friday, Saturday and Sunday after Thanksgiving. Est attendance: 15,000. For info: Linda Nelson, Willamette Christmas Assn, 543 Lakefair Pl, N, Keizer, OR 97303. Phone: (503) 393-4439. For application write to: Willamette Christmas Assn, PO Box 20817, Keizer, OR 97307.

CHRISTMAS NEW ORLEANS STYLE. Dec 1–31. New Orleans, LA. Cathedral Christmas concerts, caroling in Jackson Square, holiday parades with Papa Noel, cooking demonstrations, Celebration in the Oaks, Christmas Day Concert, tours of 19th-century houses in holiday dress, Reveillon dinners and Papa Noel hotel rates. For info: French Quarter Festivals, Inc, 400 N Peters St, #205, New Orleans, LA 70130. Phone: (800) 673-5725 or (504) 522-5730. E-mail: feedback@fqfi.org. Web: www.fqfi.org.

CHRISTMAS STROLL WEEKEND. Dec 1–3. Nantucket Island, MA. Christmas trees, costumed carolers, theatrical performances. Santa arrives via Coast Guard boat and is driven up Main Street in a horse-drawn carriage. Est attendance: 7,000. For info: Nantucket Island Chamber of Commerce, 48 Main St, Nantucket, MA 02554-3595. Phone: (508) 228-1700. Web: www.nantucketchamber.org.

CHRISTMAS WALK AND HOUSE TOUR. Dec 1–2. Geneva, IL. A special holiday tradition emphasizing the warmth and hospitality of our town. Spend the day touring charming homes aglow with holiday decorations. In the evening Santa Lucia, the Swedish symbol of the season, arrives, and Santa Claus opens his house for children's visits. Merchants graciously serve traditional holiday refreshments, including roasted chestnuts, as carolers fill the air with the sounds of the season. Est attendance: 35,000. For info: Geneva Chamber of Commerce, PO Box 481, 8 S Third St, Geneva, IL 60134. Phone: (630) 232-6060. Fax: (630) 232-6083. E-mail: chamberinfo@genevachamber.com. Web: www.genevachamber.com.

CIVIL AIR PATROL FOUNDED: ANNIVERSARY. Dec 1, 1941. The Director of Civilian Defense, former New York Mayor Fiorello H. LaGuardia, signed a formal order creating the Civil Air Patrol, a US Air Force Auxiliary. The CAP has a three-part mission: to provide an aerospace education program, a CAP cadet program and an emergency services program. For info: Civil Air Patrol, 105 S Hansell St, Maxwell AFB, AL 36112-6332. Phone: (205) 953-5463.

COLORECTAL CANCER EDUCATION AND AWARENESS MONTH. Dec 1–31. To educate consumers, patients and professionals regarding the need for early diagnosis and treatment of colorectal cancer. For info: PPSI, c/o Pharmacy Council on Colorectal Cancer Education, 101 Lucas Valley Rd, #210, San Rafael, CA 94903. Phone: (415) 479-8628. Fax: (415) 479-8608. E-mail: ppsi@aol.com. Web: www.ppsinc.org.

COOKIE CUTTER WEEK. Dec 1–7. The international cookie cutter collectors club celebrates a special time of baking cookies and collecting cutters. And what better time than the first week of December—baking season? For info: Paula W. Mullins, 207 Ash, Box 8, Lawrenceburg, KY 40342. Phone: (502) 839-4929.

DAY WITH(OUT) ART. Dec 1. An annual observance about the impact of AIDS on the visual arts. Events to increase public awareness through the visual arts, direct services to artists living with HIV/AIDS. For info: Visual AIDS, 526 W 26th St, #510, New York, NY 10001. Phone: (212) 627-9855. Fax: (212) 627-9815. E-mail: info@visualaids.org. Web: www.visualaids.org.

DICKENS ON THE STRAND. Dec 1–3. Galveston, TX. Victorian Christmas celebration focuses on the 19th-century architecture of Galveston's Strand National Historic Landmark District and ties to Charles Dickens's 19th-century London. Annually, the first weekend in December. Est attendance: 50,000. For info: Galveston Historical Foundation, 502 20th St, Galveston, TX 77550. Phone: (409) 765-7834. Fax: (409) 765-7851. E-mail: foundation@galvestonhistory.org. Web: www.dickensonthestrand .org or www.galvestonhistory.org.

ETHNIC HOLIDAY FESTIVAL. Dec 1. Omaha, NE. Experience cultures from around the world by sampling ethnic holiday foods, viewing traditional crafts and observing ethnic performances. Also, experience entertainment from distant lands, view a display of miniature Christmas trees decorated in the fashion of many nations, and much more. For info: Durham Western Heritage Museum, 801 S 10th St, Omaha, NE 68108-3299. Phone: (402) 444-5701. Fax: (402) 444-5397. E-mail: info@dwhm.org. Web: www.dwhm.org.

FANTASY OF LIGHTS. Dec 7–Jan 1, 2007. Wichita Falls, TX. A spectacular light and toyland display on the Midwestern State University campus. A Wichita Falls Christmas tradition! Est attendance: 250,000. For info: Wichita Falls Conv & Visitors Bureau, 1000 Fifth St, Wichita Falls, TX 76301. Phone: (940) 716-5500. Fax: (940) 716-5509. E-mail: MPEC@wf.net. Web: www.wichita falls.org.

HOLIDAY ALE FESTIVAL. Dec 1–3. Pioneer Courthouse Square, Portland, OR. The only beer festival in the Northwest to be held outdoors in the dark, cold and often wet month of December, the Holiday Ale Festival is truly distinctive. Despite chilly temperatures and often-inclement weather outside, attendees stay warm and dry under a large clear tent that covers the venue while allowing for views of the city lights. Twenty-five potent winter ales are featured at the event. Est attendance: 12,000. For info: Chris Crabb, Crabbsoup Public Relations, 4906 NE Siskiyou St, Portland, OR 97213. Phone: (503) 314-7583. E-mail: crabbsoup@ comcast.net. Web: www.holidayale.com.

ICELAND: UNIVERSITY STUDENTS' CELEBRATION: ANNIVERSARY. Dec 1, 1918. Marks the day in 1918 when Iceland became an independent state from Denmark (but still remained under the king of Denmark).

IDENTITY THEFT PREVENTION AND AWARENESS MONTH. Dec 1–31. A month to increase awareness and prevention of identity theft—especially during the holidays. For info: Johnny May, PO Box 7754, Bloomfield Hills, MI 48302. Phone: (248) 745-0286. E-mail: secres@prodigy.net. Web: www.identity theftinfo.com.

LANTERN LIGHT TOURS. Dec 1–23. Mystic, CT. Step into Christmas past. You may find yourself riding in a horse-drawn omnibus, kicking up your heels with revelers in the tavern or spying on silver-haired St. Nick. Est attendance: 7,000. For info: Mystic Seaport, 75 Greenmanville Ave, Box 6000, Mystic, CT 06355. Phone: (860) 572-5315 or (888) 973-2767. Web: www.mysticsea port.org.

LIGHTS OF BLACKLANDS. Dec 1–31. Various sites around Texas. Lighted parades, holiday concerts, strolling carolers, Santa Claus and free hot chocolate attract folks from all over to visit the eight communities participating in this holiday showcase. The towns of Elgin, Bartlett, Lexington, Thrall, Hutto, Taylor, Granger and Thorndale display lights and banners during the month of December. Est attendance: 5,000. For info: Greater Elgin Chamber of Commerce, PO Box 408, Elgin, TX 78621. Phone: (512) 285-4515. Fax: (512) 281-3393. Web: elgintx.com.

MARTIN, MARY: BIRTH ANNIVERSARY. Dec 1, 1913. American stage star was born Mary Virginia Martin at Weatherford, TX. She is best known for her title role in the Broadway and television productions of *Peter Pan*. She won Tony awards for her starring roles in *South Pacific* and *Peter Pan*. She died Nov 3, 1990, at Rancho Mirage, CA.

MOORE, JULIA A. DAVIS: BIRTH ANNIVERSARY. Dec 1, 1847. Julia Moore, known as the "Sweet Singer of Michigan," was born in a log cabin at Plainfield, MI. A writer of homely verse and ballads, Moore enjoyed remarkable popularity and gave many public readings before realizing that her public appearances were occasions for laughter and ridicule. Her poems were said to be "so bad, her subjects so morbid and her naivete so genuine" that they were actually gems of humorous genius. At her final public appearance she told her audience: "You people paid 50 cents to see a fool, but I got $50 to look at a house full of fools." Moore died June 17, 1920, near Manton, MI.

NATIONAL APLASTIC ANEMIA AWARENESS WEEK. Dec 1–7. Annually, Dec 1–7. For info: Marilyn Baker, Aplastic Anemia & MDS Intl Foundation, Inc, PO Box 613, Annapolis, MD 21404-0613. Phone: (800) 747-2820. E-mail: help@aamds .org. Web: www.aamds.org.

★**NATIONAL DRUNK AND DRUGGED DRIVING PREVENTION MONTH.** Dec 1–31.

NATIONAL SIGN UP FOR SUMMER CAMP MONTH. Dec 1–31. Every year more than ten million children continue a national tradition by attending day or resident camps. Building self-confidence, learning new skills and making memories that last a lifetime are just a few examples of what makes camp special and why camp does children a world of good. To find the right program, parents begin looking at summer camps during this month—and sign their children up while there are still vacancies. For a guide to accredited camps, call (800) 428-CAMPS. For info: Public Relations, American Camping Assn, 5000 State Rd 67N, Martinsville, IN 46151. Phone: (765) 342-8456. E-mail: pr@aca camps.org. Web: www.ACAcamps.org.

NATIONAL STRESS-FREE FAMILY HOLIDAYS MONTH. Dec 1–31. The holidays are so fraught with busy schedules that families often miss out on quality time together because outside demands have left them virtually drained. This observance is a reminder for parents to strive for more stress-free holidays for their families. Annually, the month of December. For info send SASE to: Dale Eshleman, Episcopal Counseling Center, 1021-A E Robinson St, Orlando, FL 32801. Phone: (800) 544-1817.

NATIONAL TIE MONTH. Dec 1–31. Annually in December. 20 percent of all ties sold are bought as Christmas gifts. Celebrate the tie and promote its proper use this month. For info: Sir Nemo Turner, The Protocol Institute, CP 157, Place du Parc, Montreal, QC, H2X 4A4 , Canada. Phone: (514) 849-0888. E-mail: magician @total.net.

NCAA DIVISION I MEN'S SOCCER CHAMPIONSHIP—THE COLLEGE CUP. Dec 1 & 3. Site TBD. For info: Natl Collegiate Athletic Assn, 700 W Washington Ave, PO Box 6222, Indianapolis, IN 46206-6222. Phone: (317) 917-6222. Web: www.ncaasports.com.

NCAA DIVISION I WOMEN'S SOCCER CHAMPIONSHIP—THE COLLEGE CUP. Dec 1 & 3. Site TBD. For info: Natl Collegiate Athletic Assn, 700 W Washington Ave, PO Box 6222, Indianapolis, IN 46206-6222. Phone: (317) 917-6222. Web: www.ncaasports.com.

NORTH STAR CLASSIC. Dec 1–3. Valley City, ND. Three-day livestock show and sale featuring 11 breeds of cattle shows and 5 breed sales, plus shows for swine, a Bull-o-rama and a junior livestock show. Also a commercial exhibit area that features only items and equipment related to livestock production. Est attendance: 15,000. For info: Brad Hertel, Mgr, North Star Classic, PO Box 846, Valley City, ND 58072. Phone: (701) 845-1401 or (800) 437-0218. Fax: (701) 845-3914. E-mail: ndws@northdakota wintershow.com. Web: www.northdakotawintershow.com.

OPERATION SANTA PAWS. Dec 1–22. During the holiday season extra help is needed for abused and abandoned animals in the care of local animal shelters. One local grassroots organization, "Operation Santa Paws," is helping by spearheading a canine/feline toy/treat drive to benefit less fortunate pets this season. Justin Rudd, organizer of this holiday effort, is encouraging animal lovers to purchase a new dog or cat toy, treat or supply that will be delivered in time for Christmas to local shelters and rescue organizations. For info: Justin Rudd. Phone: (562) 439-3316. E-mail: justinrudd@aol.com. Web: www.santapaws .info.

PEGGY V. HELMERICH DISTINGUISHED AUTHOR AWARD PRESENTATION. Dec 1–2. Central Library, Tulsa, OK. The award is given annually by the Tulsa Library Trust to a nationally acclaimed author who has written a distinguished body of work and made a major contribution to the field of literature and letters. The award consists of a $25,000 cash prize and an engraved crystal book. The winning author will be the keynote speaker at this black-tie dinner in his or her honor. Past recipients include Shelby Foote (2003), Joyce Carol Oates (2002) and William Kennedy (2001). Est attendance: 1,000. For info: Larry Bartley, Trust and Development Mgr, Tulsa Public Library, 400 Civic Center, Tulsa, OK 74103. Phone: (918) 596-7985. Fax: (918) 596-7990.

***PLAYBOY* FIRST PUBLISHED: ANNIVERSARY.** Dec 1, 1953. *Playboy* magazine was launched at Chicago by publisher Hugh Hefner.

PORTUGAL: INDEPENDENCE DAY. Dec 1. Public holiday. Became independent of Spain in 1640.

QATAR: ASIAN GAMES—DOHA 2006. Dec 1–15. Doha. The 45 member nations of the Olympic Council of Asia will celebrate the 15th Asian Games. More than 20,000 athletes will participate in 40 sports at 30 sports facilities. For info: Doha Asian Games Organizing Committee (DAGOC), PO Box 32006, Doha, Qatar. Phone: (974) 448-2006. Fax: (974) 447-9761. E-mail: info @dagoc2006.org. Web: www.doha-2006.com/en.

RECIPE GREETINGS FOR THE HOLIDAYS. Dec 1–8. A week in which to send recipes as great greetings. Create your own or send a large SASE for ideas. For info: Recipe Greetings Update, PO Box 416, Denver, CO 80201. Phone: (303) 575-5676. E-mail: mail@contentprovidermedia.com.

ROMANIA: NATIONAL DAY. Dec 1. National holiday. Marks unification of Romania and Transylvania in 1918 and the overthrow of the communist regime in 1989.

ROSA PARKS DAY: ANNIVERSARY OF ARREST. Dec 1, 1955. Anniversary of the arrest of Rosa Parks, at Montgomery, AL, for refusing to give up her seat and move to the back of a municipal bus. Her arrest triggered a yearlong boycott of the city bus system and led to legal actions that ended racial segregation on municipal buses throughout the southern US. The event has been called the birth of the modern civil rights movement. Rosa McCauley Parks was born at Tuskegee, AL, Feb 4, 1913.

	S	M	T	W	T	F	S
December						1	2
	3	4	5	6	7	8	9
2006	10	11	12	13	14	15	16
	17	18	19	20	21	22	23
	24	25	26	27	28	29	30
	31						

SAFE TOYS AND GIFTS MONTH. Dec 1–31. What toys are dangerous to children's eyesight? Tips on how to choose age-appropriate toys will be distributed. For info: Prevent Blindness America®, 211 W Wacker Dr, Ste 1700, Chicago, IL 60606. Phone: (800) 331-2020. E-mail: info@preventblindness.org. Web: www.preventblindness.org.

SPIRITUAL LITERACY MONTH. Dec 1–31. Promoting respect for and among the world's religions by engaging people in exploring the sacred texts of humankind. Discussions are held at libraries, community centers, civic clubs, coffee houses, houses of worship and private homes. Participants are invited to download free booklets containing selections from the text under study and open-ended questions derived from the text to encourage dialogue. Separate leader's guides are also available to assist those facilitating a discussion. Sponsored by the One River Foundation, a not-for-profit educational organization devoted to the study of the world's religions. For info: Rabbi Rami Shapiro, One River Foundation, 2441-Q Old Fort Parkway, Ste 412, Murfreesboro, TN 37128. Phone: (615) 653-5041. E-mail: rabbirami@earth-link.net. Web: www.one-river.org.

SUWANNEE LIGHTS. Dec 1–25. Spirit of the Suwannee Music Park and Campground, Live Oak, FL. Monthlong light display, scenes and animation of the wonder of Christmas. Share your childhood memories with your family. Visit Santa and craft villages. For info: Spirit of the Suwannee Music Park, 3076 95th Dr, Live Oak, FL 32060. Phone: (386) 364-1683. Web: www .musicliveshere.com.

TOLERANCE WEEK. Dec 1–7. The purpose of this week is to promote the importance of tolerance among human beings as a means of reducing bigotry and prejudice toward those of a different religion, race or creed. For a copy of quotations about tolerance by famous people, as well as a frameable copy of the Golden Rule of ten religions, send $5 to cover printing, handling and postage. For info: Dr. Stanley Drake, Pres Emeritus, Intl Soc of Friendship & Good Will, 8592 Roswell Rd, Ste 251, Atlanta, GA 30350-1867. Phone: (678) 795-1362. E-mail: sjdrake@bell south.net. Web: www.friendshipandgoodwill.org.

TWELVE VILLAGES OF CHRISTMAS. Dec 1–23. Each of 12 cities in Washington County, KS, organizes events including special lighting of entire county, craft festivals, drawings, special musical programs, retail open houses. Some towns have a Christmas tree in every yard. Annually, the three weekends before Christmas. Est attendance: 7,000. For info: Washington County Travel and Tourism, Courthouse, 214 C St, Washington, KS 66968. Phone: (785) 325-2116. Fax: (785) 325-2830. E-mail: washcott@washingtonks.net.

UNITED NATIONS: WORLD AIDS DAY. Dec 1. In 1988 the World Health Organization of the UN declared Dec 1 as World AIDS Day, an international day of awareness and education about AIDS. The WHO is the leader in global direction and coordination of AIDS prevention, control, research and education. A program called UN-AIDS was created to bring together the skills and expertise of the World Bank, UNDP, UNESCO, UNICEF, UNFPA and the WHO to strengthen and expand national capacities to respond to the pandemic. For info: United Nations, Dept of Public Info, New York, NY 10017. Web: www.un.org.

UNIVERSAL HUMAN RIGHTS MONTH. Dec 1–31. To disseminate throughout the world information about human rights and distribute copies of the Universal Declaration of Human Rights in English and other languages. Please send $5 to cover expense of printing, handling and postage. Annually, the month of December. For info: Dr. Stanley Drake, Pres Emeritus, Intl Soc of Friendship & Good Will, 8592 Roswell Rd, Ste 251, Atlanta, GA 30350-1867. Phone: (678) 795-1362. E-mail: sjdrake@bell south.net. Web: www.friendshipandgoodwill.org.

VICTORIAN CHRISTMAS HOME TOUR AND MINER'S BALL. Dec 1–2. Leadville, CO. 22nd annual. Highlight of the holiday season—annual showing off of Leadville's historic homes and buildings bedecked in Christmas trimmings. Locals and guests alike dress in period fashions. Activities include the National Mining Hall of Fame brunch. Est attendance: 350. For info: Chamber of Commerce, Box 861, Leadville, CO 80461. Phone: (719) 486-3900 or (800) 933-3901. Fax: (719) 486-8478. E-mail: leadville@leadvilleusa.com. Web: www.leadvilleusa.com.

VICTORIAN SLEIGHBELL PARADE & OLD CHRISTMAS WEEKEND. Dec 1–3. Manistee, MI. Re-creation of Manistee history. No motorized vehicles, no amplification. Horse-drawn entries, walking entries, singers, animals and St. Nick. Parade on Dec 2. Est attendance: 10,000. For info: Manistee Area Chamber of Commerce, 11 Cypress St, Manistee, MI 49660. Phone: (231) 723-2575 or (800) 288-2286. E-mail: chamber@manistee.com. Web: www.manisteecountychamber.com.

WINTERFEST. Dec 1–3. Luverne, MN. Christmas Light Parade, Parade of Homes, craft show, historical tours, dinner theater. For info: Dave Smith, Exec Dir, Luverne Area Chamber of Commerce, 211 E Main, Luverne, MN 56156. Phone/fax: (507) 283-4061. E-mail: luvernechamber@iw.net. Web: www.luvernemn.com.

WOLF POINT'S ANNUAL CHRISTMAS PARADE. Dec 1. Wolf Point, MT. The city comes alive with the Christmas spirit in this magical and enchanting evening, which features a parade in which all the floats are illuminated with lights, Santa is the master of ceremonies and awards for floats are given in three categories. This event will make you remember what Christmas looks like through the eyes of a child. Est attendance: 1,000. For info: Wolf Point Chamber of Commerce, 218 3rd Ave S, Ste B, Wolf Point, MT 59201. Phone: (406) 653-2012. E-mail: wpchmber@nemontel.net.

★**WORLD AIDS DAY.** Dec 1.

BIRTHDAYS TODAY

Woody Allen, 71, filmmaker (Oscar for *Annie Hall; Manhattan, Hannah and Her Sisters*), actor, born Allen Stewart Konigsberg at Brooklyn, NY, Dec 1, 1935.

Carol Alt, 46, model, born New York, NY, Dec 1, 1960.

Nestor Carbonell, 39, actor ("Suddenly Susan"), born New York, NY, Dec 1, 1967.

Bette Midler, 61, singer ("You Are the Wind Beneath My Wings"), actress (*Beaches, For the Boys, Down and Out in Beverly Hills*), born Paterson, NJ, Dec 1, 1945.

Richard Pryor, 66, actor, comedian (*Blue Collar, Stir Crazy*, "The Richard Pryor Show"), born Peoria, IL, Dec 1, 1940.

Lou Rawls, 71, blues singer ("A Natural Man," "You've Made Me So Very Happy"), actor, born Chicago, IL, Dec 1, 1935.

Reggie Sanders, 39, baseball player, born Florence, SC, Dec 1, 1967.

Lee Buck Trevino, 67, golfer, born Dallas, TX, Dec 1, 1939.

Larry Walker, 40, baseball player, born Maple Ridge, BC, Canada, Dec 1, 1966.

Treat Williams, 54, actor (*Hair, Smooth Talk*), born Rowayton, CT, Dec 1, 1952.

DECEMBER 2 — SATURDAY
Day 336 — 29 Remaining

ADELPHIAN CLUB CHRISTMAS BAZAAR. Dec 2. American Legion Building, Kennett, MO. Huge sale of arts and crafts with more than 100 exhibitors, plus a bake sale. Free admission. Annually, the first Saturday in December. For info: Adelphian Civic Club, 301 S Everett, Kennett, MO 63857. Phone: (573) 888-9472.

ARTIFICIAL HEART TRANSPLANT: ANNIVERSARY. Dec 2, 1982. Barney C. Clark, 61, became the first recipient of a permanent artificial heart. The operation was performed at the University of Utah Medical Center at Salt Lake City. Near death at the time of the operation, Clark survived almost 112 days after the implantation. He died Mar 23, 1983.

BROWN, JOHN: EXECUTION ANNIVERSARY. Dec 2, 1859. Abolitionist leader who is remembered for his raid on the US Arsenal at Harper's Ferry was hanged for treason at Charles Town, WV.

CALLAS, MARIA: BIRTH ANNIVERSARY. Dec 2, 1923. American opera singer born at New York, NY. Died at Paris, Sept 16, 1977.

CAMBRIDGE COUNTRY CHRISTMAS. Dec 2–3. Cambridge, WI. The Dickens-inspired festival offers carriage rides, roasted chestnuts, hot apple cider, strolling carolers, live nativity scene and a beautifully decorated village to truly enjoy the season. Est attendance: 3,500. For info: Cambridge Chamber of Commerce, PO Box 572, Cambridge, WI 53523. Phone: (608) 423-3780. Web: www.cambridgewi.com.

CHESTER GREENWOOD DAY PARADE. Dec 2. Farmington, ME. Celebration of Farmington's famous inventor of the earmuff. An earmuff-themed parade with flag raising. Annually, the first Saturday in December. Est attendance: 1,500. For info: Farmington-Wilton Chamber of Commerce, 575 Wilton Rd, Farmington, ME 04938. Phone: (207) 778-4215.

CHIMNEYVILLE CRAFTS FESTIVAL. Dec 2–3. Jackson, MS. The finest crafts for sale by more than 150 craftsmen: wood-carving, blown glass, weaving, leather, baskets, stained glass, pottery. Est attendance: 6,500. For info: Kit Davis Barksdale, Exec Dir, Craftsmen's Guild of Mississippi, Inc, 1150 Lakeland Dr, Jackson, MS 39216. Phone: (601) 981-0019. Fax: (601) 981-0488. E-mail: mscraftsmen@aol.com. Web: www.mscraftsmensguild.org.

CHRISTMAS CANDLELIGHT HOUSE TOURS. Dec 2 (also Dec 9 and 16). Throughout Cape May, NJ. More than 20 bed and breakfast inns, guesthouses, hotels and churches open their festively decorated doors to reveal the charm, holiday cheer and Victorian interiors that make Christmas in Cape May a truly special time. These self-guided tours are from 5:30 to 8:30 PM and cost $22 for adults, $11 for children ages 3-12; advance reservations strongly recommended. 33rd annual. Est attendance: 6,000. For info: Mid-Atlantic Center for the Arts, 1048 Washington St, Cape May, NJ 08204. Phone: (800) 275-4278. Fax: (609) 884-0574. E-mail: mac4arts@capemaymac.org. Web: www.capemaymac.org.

CHRISTMAS CANDLELIGHTINGS. Dec 2 (also Dec 9 and 16). Roscoe Village, Coshocton, OH. Nineteenth-century holiday atmosphere, 51-room country inn, hot mulled cider in village. Candlelighting ceremony on the first three Saturdays in December. Special weekend activities including Christmas carriage rides, strolling carolers, visits with Santa Claus. Annually, the first three Saturdays of December. Est attendance: 6,500. For info: Roscoe Village Foundation, 381 Hill St, Coshocton, OH 43812. Phone: (740) 622-9310 or (800) 877-1830. Fax: (740) 623-6555. E-mail: rvmarketing@roscoevillage.com. Web: www.roscoevillage.com.

CHRISTMAS IN THE VILLAGES. Dec 2–3. Van Buren County, IA. Event features tour of homes, English high tea, cookie walk, Festival of Trees, horse-drawn carriage rides, bake sales, lighting contests and displays, soup suppers and the natural beauty of the season that is found throughout the county. Est attendance: 5,000. For info: Villages of Van Buren, Inc, PO Box 9, Keosauqua, IA 52565. Phone: (800) 868-7822. Fax: (319) 293-7116. E-mail: info@villagesofvanburen.com. Web: www.villagesofvanburen.com.

CHRISTMAS ON THE PRAIRIE. Dec 2–3. Saunders County Museum, Wahoo, NE. Old-fashioned Christmas featuring entertainment by local groups, lots of period costumes, special postal cancellation, children's activities common to the 1800s and demonstrations in the historical village decorated in the 1800s style. Annually, the first weekend of December. Sponsor: Christmas on the Prairie Steering Committee. Est attendance: 3,000. For info: Curator, Saunders County Museum, 240 N Walnut, Wahoo, NE 68066-1858. Phone: (402) 443-3090. Web: www.visitsaunderscounty.org.

COATS AND TOYS FOR KIDS DAY. Dec 2. Charity drive and live television broadcast from seven locations across Maine. More than 12,000 new and gently used children's winter coats and new, unwrapped toys are collected in a giant one-day pep rally. The holiday campaign collects more than 40,000 coats annually. For info: Community Relations, WCSH 6, One Congress Square, Portland, ME 04101. Phone: (207) 828-6666. Fax: (207) 828-6620. E-mail: communityrelations@WCSH6.com. Web: WCSH6.com.

ENGLAND: WALTER PLINGE DAY. Dec 2. A day to recognize Walter Plinge, said to have been a London pub landlord in 1900. His generosity to actors led to the use of his name as an actor in play programs to conceal the fact that an actor was playing more than one role. See also: "George Spelvin Day" (Nov 15) for US equivalent.

ENRON FILES FOR BANKRUPTCY: 5th ANNIVERSARY. Dec 2, 2001. The once high-flying Houston, TX, energy services company filed for bankruptcy on this date. Subsequent investigations revealed questionable accounting practices and unethical dealings, to the extent that "Enron" became the buzzword for corporate malfeasance of the late 1990s and into the 21st century. Many other corporations were found to have questionable financial statements after the Enron scandal (in which thousands of employees lost their jobs and retirement savings), and investor confidence in the US stock market was shaken. Federal Reserve chairman Alan Greenspan, in a July 16, 2002, report to the Senate Banking Committee, indicted such corporate misbehavior: "An infectious greed seemed to grip much of our business community [in the 1990s]."

December 2006	S	M	T	W	T	F	S
						1	2
	3	4	5	6	7	8	9
	10	11	12	13	14	15	16
	17	18	19	20	21	22	23
	24	25	26	27	28	29	30
	31						

FIRST SELF-SUSTAINING NUCLEAR CHAIN REACTION: ANNIVERSARY. Dec 2, 1942. Physicist Enrico Fermi led a team of scientists at the University of Chicago in producing the first controlled, self-sustaining nuclear chain reaction. Their first simple nuclear reactor was built under the stands of the University's football stadium.

HERITAGE CHRISTMAS. Dec 2 (also Dec 9). Old Mill Museum Complex, Lindsborg, KS. A celebration of Christmas past with the music, drama and costumes of a traditional pioneer Christmas on the Kansas prairie. Annually, the first two Saturday evenings in December. Est attendance: 1,200. For info: McPherson County Old Mill Museum, PO Box 94, Lindsborg, KS 67456. Phone: (785) 227-3595. E-mail: info@oldmillmuseum.org. Web: www.oldmillmuseum.com.

HOLIDAY HAPPINESS. Dec 2. Upper Arlington Public Library, Upper Arlington, OH. Holiday crafts, music and activities, including a visit from Santa Claus, for the whole family to enjoy. Annually, the first Saturday of December. For info: Upper Arlington Public Library, 2800 Tremont Rd, Upper Arlington, OH 43221. Phone: (614) 486-9621. Fax: (614) 486-4530. Web: www.ualibrary.org.

HOLLYWOOD BEACH CANDY CANE PARADE. Dec 2. Hollywood, FL. More than 200 floats and marching units line the Hollywood Beach Boardwalk during this popular evening event. Est attendance: 40,000. For info: Roguey Doyle, City of Hollywood, Dept of Parks, Recreation & Cultural Arts, 1940 Harrison St, Ste 101, Hollywood, FL 33020. Phone: (954) 921-3404.

HOMESTEADERS HOLIDAY. Dec 2. Centennial Village Museum, Greeley, CO. Pioneer holiday family festival with candledipping, cowboy Santa, live reindeer, telegrams to North Pole, living history demos, musical entertainment, decorated homes, craft activities and food. Est attendance: 1,200. For info: Greeley Museums, 714 8th St, Greeley, CO 80631. Phone: (970) 350-9220. Fax: (970) 350-9700. Web: www.greeleymuseums.com.

"IMUS IN THE MORNING" RADIO PREMIERE: 35th ANNIVERSARY. Dec 2, 1971. Award-winning radio broadcaster Don Imus signed on to New York City's WNBC on this date. Today, "Imus in the Morning" is heard nationwide via radio and cable TV and focuses on current affairs.

LAOS: NATIONAL DAY. Dec 2. National holiday commemorating declaration of the republic in 1975.

LEMOYNE HOUSE CANDLELIGHT CHRISTMAS TOURS. Dec 2–3 (also Dec 9–10). Washington, PA. Candlelight tours of the beautifully decorated LeMoyne House. Volunteers dressed in period costume guide visitors through this historic home. Est attendance: 500. For info: Joyce Mullen, Washington County Historical Society, 49 E Maiden St, Washington, PA 15317. Phone: (724) 225-6740. Fax: (724) 225-8495. E-mail: info@wchspa.org. Web: www.wchspa.org.

MADRIGAL DINNER AND CONCERT. Dec 2–3. Mount Mary College, Milwaukee, WI. Saturday dinner concert and Sunday dessert concert. Est attendance: 300. For info: Mary Cain, PR Office, Mount Mary College, 2900 N Menomonee River Pkwy, Milwaukee, WI 53222-4597. Phone: (414) 256-1210. Fax: (414) 256-1239. E-mail: mktg@mtmary.edu. Web: www.mtmary.edu.

McCARTHY SILENCED BY SENATE: ANNIVERSARY. Dec 2, 1954. On Feb 9, 1950, Joseph McCarthy, a relatively obscure senator from Wisconsin, announced during a speech in Wheeling, WV, that he had a list of Communists in the State Department. Over the next two years he made increasingly sensational charges and in 1953 McCarthyism reached its height as he held Senate hearings in which he bullied defendants. In 1954 McCarthy's tyranny was exposed in televised hearings during which he took on the Army and on Dec 2, 1954, the Senate voted to censure him. McCarthy died May 2, 1957.

MONROE DOCTRINE: ANNIVERSARY. Dec 2, 1823. President James Monroe, in his annual message to Congress, enunciated the doctrine that bears his name and that was long hailed as a statement of US policy. ". . . In the wars of the European powers in matters relating to themselves we have never taken any part . . . we should consider any attempt on their part to extend their system to any portion of this hemisphere as dangerous to our peace and safety. . . ."

NATIONAL PARKS ESTABLISHED IN ALASKA: ANNIVERSARY. Dec 2, 1980. Eight national parks were established in Alaska on this date. Mount McKinley National Park, which was established Feb 26, 1917, and Denali National Monument, which was proclaimed Dec 1, 1978, were combined as Denali National Park and Preserve. Gates of the Arctic National Monument, proclaimed Dec 1, 1978; Glacier Bay National Monument, proclaimed Feb 25, 1925; and Katmai National Monument, proclaimed Sept 24, 1918, were established as national parks and preserves. Kenai Fjords National Monument, proclaimed Dec 1, 1978, and Kobuk Valley National Monument, proclaimed Dec 1, 1978, were established as national parks. Lake Clark National Monument, proclaimed Dec 1, 1978, and Wrangell–St. Elias National Monument, proclaimed Dec 1, 1978, were established as national parks and preserves. For info: www.nps.gov.

NORSKEDALEN'S OLD-FASHIONED CHRISTMAS. Dec 2–3. Coon Valley, WI. Celebrate an old-fashioned Christmas with decorated pioneer log homes to view, entertainment, a la carte ethnic foods, raffle, horse-drawn wagon/sleigh rides and outdoor activities. Fun for all ages. 10 AM–4 PM. Est attendance: 500. For info: Norskedalen Nature and Heritage Center, Inc, PO Box 235, Coon Valley, WI 54623. Phone: (608) 452-3424. Fax: (608) 452-3157. E-mail: info@norskedalen.org. Web: www.norske dalen.org.

NORWEGIAN CHRISTMAS. Dec 2–3. Brooklyn Park, MN. Old-fashioned farm Christmas with late 19th-century decorations, carolers, making of traditional gifts, lefse and other Norwegian delicacies, a visit by St. Nicholas and sled or hayrides. Est attendance: 1,000. For info: Kay Grotenhuis, Site Mgr, Brooklyn Park Historical Farm, 4345 101st Ave N, Brooklyn Park, MN 55443. Phone: (763) 493-4604 or (763) 493-8333. Web: www.brook lynpark.org/recreation.

PALM HARBOR ART, CRAFT AND MUSIC FESTIVAL. Dec 2–3. Palm Harbor, FL. 32nd annual juried arts and crafts show with some 150 exhibitors from all over the US. Artists' cash awards: $16,000. Annually, the first weekend in December. Est attendance: 30,000. For info: Connie Davis, Exec Dir, Palm Harbor Chamber of Commerce, 1151 Nebraska Ave, Palm Harbor, FL 34683. Phone: (727) 784-4287. Fax: (727) 786-2336. E-mail: phchamber@palmharborcc.org. Web: www.palmharborcc.org.

PARADE OF LIGHTS. Dec 2. Kingsville, TX. Breakfast with Santa kicks off a fun-filled day of holiday activities for children ending with an illuminated nighttime parade for children of all ages in historic downtown Kingsville. Est attendance: 3,000. For info: Kingsville CVB, 1501 N Hwy 77, Kingsville, TX 78363. Phone: (800) 333-5032. Fax: (361) 592-3227. E-mail: visitors@ kingsvilletexas.com. Web: www.kingsvilletexas.com.

SAFETY RAZOR PATENTED: ANNIVERSARY. Dec 2, 1901. American King Camp Gillette designed the first razor with disposable blades. Up until this time, men shaved with a straight-edge razor that they sharpened on a leather strap.

SANTA BY STAGECOACH PARADE. Dec 2. El Centro, CA. Annually, the first Saturday in December. Est attendance: 25,000. For info: El Centro Chamber of Commerce, Box 3006, El Centro, CA 92244. Phone: (760) 352-3681. Fax: (760) 352-3246. Web: www.elcentrochamber.com.

SEURAT, GEORGES PIERRE: BIRTH ANNIVERSARY. Dec 2, 1859. French Neo-Impressionist painter born at Paris, France. Died there Mar 29, 1891. Seurat is known for his style of painting with small spots of color, called pointillism, as in *Sunday Afternoon on the Island of Grand Jatte*.

SHAKER CHRISTMAS FAIR. Dec 2. Sabbathday Lake Shaker Village, New Gloucester, ME. Traditional holiday church fair featuring home-baked foods. Nine rooms of the 1816 Trustee's Office are filled with holiday items for all ages. For info: Leonard Brooks, Sabbathday Lake Shaker Village, 707 Shaker Rd, New Gloucester, ME 04260. Phone: (207) 926-4597. E-mail: usshakers @aol.com. Web: www.shaker.lib.me.us.

SPECIAL EDUCATION DAY. Dec 2. Celebrate the anniversary of the first US special education law—Dec 2, 1975. A time to reflect and move forward. Where were we when President Ford signed the groundbreaking legislation? Where are we now? And where do we need to be tomorrow? A day to visit schools, honor progress and dialogue. For info: Special Education Day. E-mail: info@specialeducationday.com. Web: www.specialeducationday .com.

TAMALE FIESTA. Dec 2. Bucklin Park, El Centro, CA. Tamale contest plus various arts & crafts and entertainment. Annually, the first Saturday in December. Est attendance: 4,000. For info: El Centro Chamber of Commerce, PO Box 3006, El Centro, CA 92244. Phone: (760) 352-3681. Fax: (760) 352-3246. E-mail: generalinfo@elcentrochamber.com. Web: www.elcentrochamber .com.

UNITED ARAB EMIRATES: NATIONAL DAY. Dec 2. Anniversary of the day in 1971 when a federation of seven sheikdoms known as the Trucial States declared independence from the UK and became known as the United Arab Emirates.

UNITED NATIONS: INTERNATIONAL DAY FOR THE ABOLITION OF SLAVERY. Dec 2. Recalls the date of adoption by the General Assembly in 1949 of the Convention for the Suppression of the Traffic in Persons and the Exploitation of Others. For info: United Nations, Dept of Public Info, New York, NY 10017. Web: www.un.org.

BIRTHDAYS TODAY

Wayne Allard, 63, US Senator (R, Colorado), born Fort Collins, CO, Dec 2, 1943.

T. Coraghessan Boyle, 58, author (*Riven Rock, The Tortilla Curtain*), born Peekskill, NY, Dec 2, 1948.

Dan Butler, 52, actor ("Frasier"), born Huntington, IN, Dec 2, 1954.

Dennis Christopher, 51, actor (*Sweet Dreams, Breaking Away*), born Philadelphia, PA, Dec 2, 1955.

Cathy Lee Crosby, 58, actress ("That's Incredible," *Coach*), born Los Angeles, CA, Dec 2, 1948.

Randy Gardner, 48, figure skater, born Marina del Rey, CA, Dec 2, 1958.

Julie Harris, 81, actress ("Knots Landing," *I Am a Camera, The Member of the Wedding*), born Grosse Pointe, MI, Dec 2, 1925.

Lucy Liu, 39, actress ("Ally McBeal," *Charlie's Angels*), born Queens, NY, Dec 2, 1967.

Garry Meier, 57, Chicago radio personality, born Chicago, IL, Dec 2, 1949.

Stone Phillips, 52, anchor ("Dateline," "20/20"), born Texas City, TX, Dec 2, 1954.

Harry Reid, 67, US Senator (D, Nevada), born Searchlight, NV, Dec 2, 1939.

Monica Seles, 33, tennis player, born Novi Sad, Yugoslavia, Dec 2, 1973.

Britney Spears, 25, singer, born Kentwood, LA, Dec 2, 1981.

William Wegman, 63, artist, photographer, born Holyoke, MA, Dec 2, 1943.

DECEMBER 3 — SUNDAY
Day 337 — 28 Remaining

ADORATION PARADE. Dec 3. Branson, MO. The 58th annual Adoration Parade will present a celebration of Christmas—the traditional values of faith, family and friendliness. For info: Branson Area CVB, PO Box 1897, Branson, MO 65615. Phone: (888) 886-3637. Fax: (417) 334-4139. E-mail: info@bransoncvb.com. Web: www.explorebranson.com.

ADVENT, FIRST SUNDAY. Dec 3. Advent includes the four Sundays before Christmas, Dec 3, Dec 10, Dec 17 and Dec 24 in 2006.

BCHS CHRISTMAS OPEN HOUSE AND GINGERBREAD CONTEST. Dec 3. Ainsworth, NE. Displays, gingerbread houses, refreshments, sing-along at 2 PM. Annually, the first Sunday in December. Est attendance: 100. For info: Carol Larson, Brown County Historical Society, HC 65 Box 158, Ainsworth, NE 69210. E-mail: Carolarson10@hotmail.com.

BHOPAL POISON GAS DISASTER: ANNIVERSARY. Dec 3, 1984. At Bhopal, India, a leak of deadly gas (methyl isocyanate) at a Union Carbide Corp plant killed more than 4,000 persons and injured more than 200,000 in the world's worst industrial accident.

CHRISTMAS TO REMEMBER. Dec 3. Laurel, MT. To officially open the Christmas season in Laurel, this daylong celebration includes the arrival of Santa, a community bazaar, children's craft activities, musical entertainment, lighting ceremony, parade of lights and fireworks. Annually, the first Sunday of December. Est attendance: 5,000. For info: Christmas to Remember Committee, Jean Carroll Thompson, PO Box 463, Laurel, MT 59044. Phone: (406) 248-8557.

CLERC-GALLAUDET WEEK. Dec 3–9. Week in which to celebrate the birth anniversaries of Laurent Clerc (Dec 26, 1785) and Thomas Hopkins Gallaudet (Dec 10, 1787). Clerc and Gallaudet pioneered education for the deaf in the US. Library activities will include a lecture on Clerc and Gallaudet and their contemporaries, storytelling for all ages and a display of books, videos, magazines, newspapers and posters. For info: Library for Deaf Action, 2930 Craiglawn Rd, Silver Spring, MD 20904-1816. Phone/fax: (301) 572-5168 (TTY). E-mail: alicehagemeyer@aol.com.

CONRAD, JOSEPH: BIRTH ANNIVERSARY. Dec 3, 1857. English novelist, born Jozef Korzeniowski to Polish parents at Berdichev in the Ukraine. He learned English as a sailor on British ships. Author of *Lord Jim* and *Heart of Darkness*, among others. Died Aug 3, 1924, at Bishopsbourne, Kent, England.

DICKENS' CHRISTMAS EXTRAVAGANZA. Dec 3–5. Cape May, NJ. This three-day celebration features the sights and sounds, tastes and scents of the Dickens era, with lectures, performances, tours and feasts in various locations. For info: Mid-Atlantic Center for the Arts, 1048 Washington St, Cape May, NJ 08204. Phone: (800) 275-4278. Fax: (609) 884-0574. E-mail: mac4arts@capemaymac.org. Web: www.capemaymac.org.

FIRST HEART TRANSPLANT: ANNIVERSARY. Dec 3, 1967. Dr. Christiaan Barnard, a South African surgeon, performed the world's first successful heart transplantation at Cape Town, South Africa. See also: "Barnard, Christiaan Neethling: Birthday" (Nov 8).

ILLINOIS: ADMISSION DAY: ANNIVERSARY. Dec 3. Became 21st state in 1818.

★ ★ ★

	S	M	T	W	T	F	S
December 2006						1	2
	3	4	5	6	7	8	9
	10	11	12	13	14	15	16
	17	18	19	20	21	22	23
	24	25	26	27	28	29	30
	31						

JINGLEBELL JOURNEY. Dec 3. Mount Wolf, PA. Enjoy a special holiday tour of seven creatively decorated homes and a historical landmark. They are all decked out in their holiday finery and say WELCOME to all. Enjoy more holiday atmosphere as the Northeastern Senior Community Center opens its doors and provides visitors with musical entertainment, a seniors art show, handmade crafts, homemade tea breads, cookies and wassail. Proceeds from the tour provide funding to the Senior Center to supply and improve services offered to the area's senior citizens. Annually, the third Sunday before Christmas. For info: Northeastern Senior Community Center, 131 Center St, PO Box 386, Mt Wolf, PA 17347. Phone: (717) 266-1400. E-mail: seniorstars@nassc.org. Web: www.nassc.org.

MONTOYA, CARLOS: BIRTH ANNIVERSARY. Dec 3, 1903. Guitarist and composer renowned for popularizing flamenco guitar music. His solo performances of the Spanish folk form lifted flamenco from its traditional accompaniment role. Montoya never learned to read music and relied on the traditional improvisational nature of flamenco rooted in the Andalusian Gypsy form of music that stressed rhythms and harmonic patterns. He was born at Madrid, Spain, and died Mar 3, 1993, at Wainscott, NY.

NETHERLANDS: MIDWINTER HORN BLOWING. Dec 3–Jan 6, 2007. Twente and several other areas in the Netherlands. Midwinter horn blowing, folklore custom of announcing the birth of Christ, begins with Advent and continues until Epiphany (Jan 6) of the following year.

***A STREETCAR NAMED DESIRE* BROADWAY OPENING: ANNIVERSARY.** Dec 3, 1947. Tennessee Williams's drama opened on Broadway at the Ethel Barrymore Theatre with Jessica Tandy (as Blanche Du Bois) and newcomer Marlon Brando (as Stanley Kowalski). Williams was already a Broadway star with his first play, *Glass Menagerie*, and *Streetcar* was to be equally successful: it ran for two years and won the Pulitzer Prize for Drama. Marlon Brando's performance, using his Method style, was a sensation to audience members and critics. Tandy won the Tony Award for Best Actress in a Play.

STUART, GILBERT CHARLES: BIRTH ANNIVERSARY. Dec 3, 1755. American portrait painter whose most famous painting is that of George Washington. He also painted portraits of Madison, Monroe, Jefferson and other important Americans. Stuart was born near Narragansett, RI, and died July 9, 1828, at Boston, MA.

UNITED NATIONS: INTERNATIONAL DAY OF DISABLED PERSONS. Dec 3. On Oct 14, 1992 (Res 47/3), at the end of the Decade of Disabled Persons, the General Assembly proclaimed Dec 3 to be an annual observance to promote the continuation of integrating the disabled into general society. For info: United Nations, Dept of Public Info, New York, NY 10017. Web: www.un.org.

BIRTHDAYS TODAY

Brian Bonsall, 25, actor ("Family Ties," *Blank Check*), born Torrance, CA, Dec 3, 1981.

Bruno Campos, 32, actor ("Jesse"), born Rio de Janeiro, Brazil, Dec 3, 1974.

Holly Marie Combs, 33, actress ("Picket Fences," "Charmed"), born San Diego, CA, Dec 3, 1973.

Brendan Fraser, 38, actor (*Mummy, The Quiet American*), born Indianapolis, IN, Dec 3, 1968.

Jean Luc Godard, 76, filmmaker (*Breathless, Weekend*), born Paris, France, Dec 3, 1930.

Daryl Hannah, 45, actress (*Splash, Grumpy Old Men*), born Chicago, IL, Dec 3, 1961.

Ferlin Husky, 79, singer ("Gone," "On the Wings of a Dove"), born Flat River, MO, Dec 3, 1927.

Bucky Lasek, 34, skateboarder, born Baltimore, MD, Dec 3, 1972.

Rick Ravon Mears, 55, former auto racer, born Wichita, KS, Dec 3, 1951.

Julianne Moore, 45, actress (*The Hours, Far from Heaven*), born Fort Bragg, Fayetteville, NC, Dec 3, 1961.

Jaye P. Morgan, 74, singer ("That's All I Want from You," "The Longest Walk"), born Mancos, CO, Dec 3, 1932.

Sven Vilhem Nykvist, 84, cinematographer (*The Unbearable Lightness of Being*), born Moheda, Sweden, Dec 3, 1922.

Ozzy Osbourne, 58, singer, songwriter (originally lead singer for Black Sabbath), born Birmingham, England, Dec 3, 1948.

Andy Williams, 76, singer (platinum album *Love Story*, 13 gold albums), born Wall Lake, IA, Dec 3, 1930.

Katarina Witt, 41, Olympic figure skater, born Karl-Marx-Stadt, East Germany, Dec 3, 1965.

DECEMBER 4 — MONDAY

Day 338 — 27 Remaining

BUTLER, SAMUEL: BIRTH ANNIVERSARY. Dec 4, 1835. English author (*Erewhon, The Way of All Flesh*), born at Bingham, Nottinghamshire, England. Died at London, June 18, 1902.

CARLYLE, THOMAS: BIRTH ANNIVERSARY. Dec 4, 1795. Scottish essayist and historian, born at Ecclefechan, Scotland. Died at London, Feb 4, 1881. "A well-written Life is almost as rare as a well-spent one," Carlyle wrote in his *Critical and Miscellaneous Essays*.

CENTRAL AFRICAN REPUBLIC: NATIONAL DAY OBSERVED. Dec 4. Commemorates Proclamation of the Republic Dec 1, 1958. Usually observed on the first Monday in December.

CHASE'S CALENDAR OF EVENTS: BIRTHDAY. Dec 4, 1957. Today in 1957 the first copies of the first edition of *Chase's Calendar of Annual Events* (for the year 1958) were delivered by the printer at Flint, MI. Two thousand copies, consisting of 32 pages and listing 364 events, were printed. Now annual editions are more than 700 pages long and list more than 12,000 events. It has several offspring, including *The Teacher's Calendar*, which debuted in 1999.

ELECTRIC LIGHT PARADE. Dec 4. Downtown Lovington, NM. Christmas shines in Lovington with more than 60 entries including floats, motorhomes, cars and motorcycles decorated with Christmas lights. Annually, early December. Est attendance: 7,000. For info: Lovington Chamber of Commerce, 201 S Main St, Lovington, NM 88260. Phone: (505) 396-5311. E-mail: lchamber@valornet.com. Web: www.lovington.net.

EXTRAORDINARY WORK TEAM RECOGNITION DAY. Dec 4. To recognize business teams that work extraordinarily well together, producing significant results/accomplishments for their company or organization. Team leaders and management "champions" are encouraged to recognize exceptional team performance and submit their stories for a chance to win an extraordinary prize for their team! Annually, on Dec 4. For info: Kristin J. Arnold, Quality Process Consultants, Inc, 11304 Megan Dr, Fairfax, VA 22030. Phone: (703) 278-0892. Fax: (703) 278-0891. E-mail: karnold@qpcteam.com. Web: www.qpcteam.com.

"FALCON CREST" TV PREMIERE: 25th ANNIVERSARY. Dec 4, 1981. This nighttime serial was set in California wine country and originally focused on Angela Channing's determined efforts to gain control of the Falcon Crest vineyard and winery; later in the nine-year run the emphasis turned to crime. Famous actors who were a part of the cast at one time or another include: Jane Wyman, Lorenzo Lamas, Billy R. Moses, Cliff Robertson, Lana Turner, Gina Lollobrigida, Parker Stevenson, Anne Archer, Apollonia, Cesar Romero, Morgan Fairchild, Ken Olin and Mary Ann Mobley. In the season finale, Angela received Falcon Crest and everyone was happy.

LAST AMERICAN HOSTAGE RELEASED IN LEBANON: 15th ANNIVERSARY. Dec 4, 1991. A sad chapter of US history came to a close when Terry Anderson, an Associated Press correspondent, became the final American hostage held in Lebanon to be freed. Anderson had been held since Mar 16, 1985, one of 15 Americans who were held hostage for from two months to as long as six years and eight months. Three of the hostages, William Buckley, Peter Kilburn and Lieutenant Colonel William Higgins, were killed during their captivity. The other hostages, released previously one or two at a time, were Jeremy Levin, Benjamin Weir, the Reverend Lawrence Martin Jenco, David Jacobsen, Thomas Sutherland, Frank Herbert Reed, Joseph Cicippio, Edward Austin Tracy, Alan Steen, Jesse Turner and Robert Polhill.

MISSION SANTA BARBARA: FOUNDING ANNIVERSARY. Dec 4, 1786. Franciscan Mission to the Indians founded at Santa Barbara, CA. Present structure is the fourth to stand on same site. Last one destroyed by 1812 earthquake.

MOON PHASE: FULL MOON. Dec 4. Moon enters Full Moon phase at 7:25 PM, EST.

NATIONAL DICE DAY. Dec 4. A day for everyone to enjoy playing the game of dice. The goal of the game is to get to 10,000 points. Each player rolls 5 dice. If you roll a 5, it counts for 500 points. If you roll a 1, it counts for 100 points. If you roll neither, you lose your turn. If you roll 3-of-a-kind, it will count for the number x 100. If you roll 4-of-a-kind, double the number; 5-of-a-kind, double the number. If you roll a straight 12345 or 23456, you earn 1,500 points. Once someone reaches 10,000 points, they have to make every die count; once they do that everyone else has a chance to beat their score. For info: Julia Chase, 2681 Balmoral Ct, Ann Arbor, MI 48103.

NATIONAL GRANGE FOUNDING: ANNIVERSARY. Dec 4, 1786. The anniversary of the National Grange, the first organized agricultural movement in the US.

RUSSELL, LILLIAN: BIRTH ANNIVERSARY. Dec 4, 1861. American singer and actress who in 1881 gained fame in the comic opera *The Great Mogul*. Born Helen Louise Leonard at Clinton, IA, she died June 6, 1922, at Pittsburgh, PA.

SAINT BARBARA'S DAY. Dec 4. On this day, traditionally the feast day of St. Barbara, a young girl places a twig from a cherry tree in a glass of water. If it blooms by Christmas Eve, she is certain to marry the following year. Because the narratives of her life and martyrdom are legendary, St. Barbara was dropped from the Roman Catholic Calendar of Saints in 1970.

SPACE MILESTONE: INTERNATIONAL SPACE STATION LAUNCH (US): ANNIVERSARY. Dec 4, 1998. The shuttle *Endeavour* took a US component of the space station named *Unity* into orbit 220 miles from Earth where spacewalking astronauts fastened it to a component launched by the Russians Nov 20, 1998. On July 25, 2000, the Russian service module *Zvezda* docked with the station. It will take a total of 45 Russian and US launches over the next five years before the space station is complete. When finished, it will be 356′ across and 290′ long and will support a crew of up to seven. On Oct 31, 2000, NASA launched the first expedition with a three-man crew to stay aloft for four months.

BIRTHDAYS TODAY

Max Baer, Jr, 69, actor ("The Beverly Hillbillies"), producer (*Ode to Billy Joe*), born Oakland, CA, Dec 4, 1937.

Tyra Banks, 33, model, actress ("Soul Train Lady of Soul Awards"), born Los Angeles, CA, Dec 4, 1973.

Jeff Bridges, 57, actor (*The Contender, Starman, The Last Picture Show*), born Los Angeles, CA, Dec 4, 1949.

Helen M. Chase, 82, retired chronicler of contemporary civilization as coeditor of *Chase's Annual Events*, born Whitehall, MI, Dec 4, 1924.

Deanna Durbin, 85, actress (*It Started with Eve, Can't Help Singing*), born Winnipeg, MB, Canada, Dec 4, 1921.

Chris Hillman, 64, musician (the Byrds, the Desert Rose Band), born Los Angeles, CA, Dec 4, 1942.

Stewart Rawlings Mott, 69, philanthropist, born Flint, MI, Dec 4, 1937.

Marisa Tomei, 42, actress (*The Flamingo Kid, My Cousin Vinny*), born Brooklyn, NY, Dec 4, 1964.

Patricia Wettig, 55, actress ("St. Elsewhere," *City Slickers*; Emmys for "thirtysomething"), born Cincinnati, OH, Dec 4, 1951.

Cassandra Wilson, 51, jazz singer, born Jackson, MS, Dec 4, 1955.

December 2006

S	M	T	W	T	F	S
					1	2
3	4	5	6	7	8	9
10	11	12	13	14	15	16
17	18	19	20	21	22	23
24	25	26	27	28	29	30
31						

DECEMBER 5 — TUESDAY
Day 339 — 26 Remaining

"THE ABBOTT AND COSTELLO SHOW" TV PREMIERE: ANNIVERSARY. Dec 5, 1952. Bud Abbott and Lou Costello made 52 half-hour films for television incorporating many of their best burlesque routines. The show ran for two seasons, until 1954. Costello was born at Paterson, NJ, Mar 6, 1906, and died at East Los Angeles, CA, Mar 3, 1959. In 1966 Hanna-Barbera Productions produced an animated cartoon based on the characters of Abbott and Costello. Abbott supplied his own voice while Stan Irwin imitated Costello. Bud Abbott was born at Asbury Park, NJ, Oct 2, 1895, and died at Woodland Hills, CA, Apr 24, 1974.

AFL-CIO FOUNDED: ANNIVERSARY. Dec 5, 1955. The American Federation of Labor and the Congress of Industrial Organizations joined together in 1955, following 20 years of rivalry, to become the nation's leading advocate for trade unions.

AUSTRIA: KRAMPUSLAUF. Dec 5. Salzburg region. On the eve of St. Nicholas's Day, Austrians celebrate the Krampuslauf (Krampus Run). In folklore, the Krampus is a devilish companion of St. Nicholas who punishes bad children just as St. Nicholas rewards good ones. The Krampus, represented by costumed revelers, is usually depicted as a dark, hairy, cloven-hoofed beast with red horns, a leering mouth, chains and a switch. Children are invited to throw snowballs at the Krampus. Also known as Krampus Day.

BATHTUB PARTY DAY. Dec 5. Almost everyone nowadays takes showers, so here's a day to recall some of the warm water luxury of days gone by. Invite a few friends. [©2003 by WH.] For info: Thomas & Ruth Roy, Wellcat Holidays, 2418 Long Ln, Lebanon, PA 17046. Phone: (717) 279-0184. E-mail: info@wellcat.com. Web: www.wellcat.com.

CLUTE'S CHRISTMAS IN THE PARK. Dec 5–8. Clute Municipal Park, Clute, TX. A Christmas event with nightly entertainment, Santa's Land, a beautifully decorated Christmas tree forest and a marshmallow roasting pit. Great family fun for all ages. Food and crafts. Est attendance: 4,500. For info: Clute Parks and Recreation, PO Box 997, Clute, TX 77531. Phone: (800) 371-2971 or (979) 265-8392. Fax: (979) 265-8767.

DISNEY, WALT: BIRTH ANNIVERSARY. Dec 5, 1901. Animator, filmmaker, theme park developer, born at Chicago, IL. Disney died at Los Angeles, CA, Dec 15, 1966.

GRANT'S SPEECH OF APOLOGY: ANNIVERSARY. Dec 5, 1876. President Ulysses S. Grant delivered his speech of apology to Congress claiming mistakes he made while he was president were due to his inexperience. His errors, he said, were "errors of judgment, not intent." While Grant's personal integrity was never formally questioned, he was closely associated with many government scandals, which became public during his presidency. He unwittingly aided Jay Gould in an attempt to corner the gold market during his first term. During the second, the Credit Mobilier affair involving many of the president's friends aired, while significant fraud was discovered in the Treasury Department and Indian Service.

HAITI: DISCOVERY DAY: ANNIVERSARY. Dec 5. Commemorates the discovery of Haiti by Christopher Columbus in 1492. Public holiday.

"IRRATIONAL EXUBERANCE" ENTERS LEXICON: 10th ANNIVERSARY. Dec 5, 1996. In a speech to the Washington, DC–based American Enterprise Institute for Policy Research, Federal Reserve Chairman Alan Greenspan uttered a new catchphrase that the media quickly saw as a warning about the high-flying 1990s stock market. He asked, "How do we know when irrational exuberance has unduly escalated asset values. . . . And how do we factor that assessment into monetary policy?" Those two words, buried in an academic speech, nonetheless sparked panic in markets fearing the Fed would raise interest rates. The Tokyo, Hong Kong, Frankfurt, London and US markets dropped 2–4 percent after his speech. Most economists thought Greenspan was simply suggesting that markets needed to slow down a bit. But "irrational exuberance" lives on as Greenspan's most famous quote.

MONTGOMERY BUS BOYCOTT BEGINS: ANNIVERSARY. Dec 5, 1955. Rosa Parks was arrested at Montgomery, AL, for refusing to give up her seat on a bus to a white man. In support of Parks, and to protest the arrest, the black community of Montgomery organized a boycott of the bus system. The boycott lasted from Dec 5, 1955, to Dec 20, 1956, when a US Supreme Court ruling was implemented at Montgomery, integrating the public transportation system.

NATIONAL COMMUNICATE WITH YOUR BABY DAY. Dec 5. A day that promotes open and ongoing communication between parents and children with a special emphasis on communicating with preverbal babies through sign language. Annually, Dec 5. For info: Diane Ryan, KinderSigns, 8707 Mill Creek Ln, Bayonet Point, FL 34667. E-mail: info@kindersigns.com. Web: www.kindersigns.com.

PICKETT, BILL: BIRTH ANNIVERSARY. Dec 5, 1870. American rodeo cowboy, born at Williamson County, TX; died Apr 21, 1932, at Tulsa, OK. Inventor of bulldogging, the modern rodeo event that involves wrestling a running steer to the ground.

ROSSETTI, CHRISTINA: BIRTH ANNIVERSARY. Dec 5, 1830. Great English poet of beautiful yet melancholy verses who is best known for her lyrical fable "Goblin Market." Born at London, where she died on Dec 29, 1894.

THAILAND: KING'S BIRTHDAY AND NATIONAL DAY. Dec 5. Celebrated throughout the kingdom with colorful pageantry. Stores and houses decorated with spectacular illuminations at night. Public holiday.

THURMOND, STROM: BIRTH ANNIVERSARY. Dec 5, 1902. The longest serving senator in American history, James Strom Thurmond was born at Edgefield, SC. The only senator ever elected by a write-in vote, he joined the US Senate in 1954. He was elected as both a Democrat and a Republican, and is remembered for his record-breaking filibuster protesting pending civil rights legislation. He did not yield the floor for 24 hours, 18 minutes over Aug 28–29, 1957, although the legislation did pass less than 2 hours later. He served in the Senate until Nov 19, 2002, just a few weeks shy of his 100th birthday. He died at Edgefield on June 26, 2003.

TWENTY-FIRST AMENDMENT TO THE US CONSTITUTION RATIFIED: ANNIVERSARY. Dec 5, 1933. Prohibition ended with the repeal of the 18th Amendment, as the 21st Amendment was ratified. Congress proposed repeal of Amendment XVIII (" . . . the manufacture, sale, or transportation of intoxicating liquors, within, the importation thereof into, or the exportation thereof from the United States and all territory subject to the jurisdiction thereof, for beverage purposes is hereby prohibited. . . .") Feb 20, 1933. By Dec 5, 1933, the repeal amendment had been ratified by the required 36 states and went into effect immediately as Amendment XXI to the US Constitution.

UNITED NATIONS: INTERNATIONAL VOLUNTEER DAY FOR ECONOMIC AND SOCIAL DEVELOPMENT. Dec 5. In a resolution of Dec 17, 1985, the United Nations General Assembly recognized the desirability of encouraging the work of all volunteers. It invited governments to observe annually on Dec 5 the "International Volunteer Day for Economic and Social Development, urging them to take measures to heighten awareness of the important contribution of volunteer service." A day commemorating the establishment in December 1970 of the UN Volunteers program and inviting world recognition of volunteerism in the international development movement. For info: United Nations, Dept of Public Info, Public Inquiries Unit, Rm GA-57, New York, NY 10017. Phone: (212) 963-4475. E-mail: inquiries@un.org. Web: www.un.org.

VAN BUREN, MARTIN: BIRTH ANNIVERSARY. Dec 5, 1782. The eighth president of the US (term of office: Mar 4, 1837–Mar 3, 1841) was the first to have been born a citizen of the US. He was a widower for nearly two decades before he entered the White House. His daughter-in-law, Angelica, served as White House hostess during an administration troubled by bank and business failures, depression and unemployment. Van Buren was born at Kinderhook, NY, and died there July 24, 1862.

WHEATLEY, PHILLIS: DEATH ANNIVERSARY. Dec 5, 1784. Born at Senegal, West Africa, about 1753 or 1754, Phillis Wheatley was brought to the US in 1761 and purchased as a slave by a Boston tailor named John Wheatley. She was allotted unusual privileges for a slave, including being allowed to learn to read and write. She wrote her first poetry at age 14, and her first work was published in 1770. Wheatley's fame as a poet spread throughout Europe as well as the US after her *Poems on Various Subjects, Religious and Moral* was published at England in 1773. She was invited to visit George Washington's army headquarters after he read a poem she had written about him in 1776. Phillis Wheatley died at about age 30, at Boston, MA.

BIRTHDAYS TODAY

Morgan Brittany, 56, actress ("Dallas," "Glitter"), born Suzanne Cupito at Hollywood, CA, Dec 5, 1950.

José Carreras, 60, opera singer, one of the "Three Tenors," born Barcelona, Spain, Dec 5, 1946.

Margaret Cho, 38, actress ("All-American Girl"), comedienne, born San Francisco, CA, Dec 5, 1968.

Joan Didion, 72, author, journalist (*After Henry, Run River, The White Album*), born Sacramento, CA, Dec 5, 1934.

Jeroen Krabbe, 62, actor (*A World Apart, King of the Hill, The Fugitive*), born Amsterdam, the Netherlands, Dec 5, 1944.

Little Richard, 71, singer ("Tutti Frutti," "Long Tall Sally"), songwriter, born Richard Penniman at Macon, GA, Dec 5, 1935.

Jim Messina, 59, singer ("Your Mama Don't Dance"), songwriter, born Maywood, CA, Dec 5, 1947.

Chad Mitchell, 70, lead singer (Chad Mitchell trio, "Lizzie Borden"), born Spokane, WA, Dec 5, 1936.

Art Monk, 49, former football player, born White Plains, NY, Dec 5, 1957.

Frankie Muniz, 21, actor ("Malcolm in the Middle," *My Dog Skip*), born Ridgewood, NJ, Dec 5, 1985.

Calvin Trillin, 71, author (*American Stories, Remembering Denny*), born Kansas City, MO, Dec 5, 1935.

DECEMBER 6 — WEDNESDAY
Day 340 — 25 Remaining

ALTAMONT CONCERT: ANNIVERSARY. Dec 6, 1969. A free concert featuring performances by the Rolling Stones; Jefferson Airplane; Santana; Crosby, Stills, Nash and Young and the Flying Burrito Brothers turned into tragedy. The "thank-you" concert for 300,000 fans was marred by overcrowding, drug overdoses and the fatal stabbing of a spectator by a member of the Hell's Angels motorcycle gang, who had been hired as security guards for the event. The concert was held at the Altamont Speedway, Livermore, CA.

ECUADOR: DAY OF QUITO. Dec 6. Commemorates founding of city of Quito by Spaniards in 1534.

EISENSTAEDT, ALFRED: BIRTH ANNIVERSARY. Dec 6, 1898. American photojournalist Alfred Eisenstaedt was born at Dirschau, Prussia. One of the greatest photojournalists in US history, he is best known for his 86 photos that were used on covers of *Life* magazine, including the iconic image of a sailor kissing a nurse in New York's Times Square at the end of WWII. He died Aug 23, 1995, at Martha's Vineyard, MA.

EVERGLADES NATIONAL PARK ESTABLISHED: ANNIVERSARY. Dec 6, 1947. Part of vast marshland area on southern Florida peninsula, originally authorized May 30, 1934, was established as a national park.

FINLAND: INDEPENDENCE DAY. Dec 6. National holiday. Declaration of independence from Russia in 1917.

GERALD FORD SWEARING-IN AS VICE PRESIDENT: ANNIVERSARY. Dec 6, 1973. Gerald Ford was sworn in as vice president under Richard Nixon, following the resignation of Spiro Agnew who pled no contest to a charge of income tax evasion. See also "Agnew, Spiro Theodore: Birth Anniversary" (Nov 9) and "Ford, Gerald Rudolph: Birthday" (July 14).

GERSHWIN, IRA: BIRTH ANNIVERSARY. Dec 6, 1896. Pulitzer Prize–winning American lyricist and author who collaborated with his brother, George, and with many other composers. Among his Broadway successes: *Lady Be Good, Funny Face, Strike Up the Band* and such songs as "The Man I Love," "Someone to Watch Over Me," "I Got Rhythm" and hundreds of others. Born at New York, NY, he died at Beverly Hills, CA, Aug 17, 1983.

HALIFAX, NOVA SCOTIA, DESTROYED: ANNIVERSARY. Dec 6, 1917. More than 1,650 people were killed at Halifax when the Norwegian ship *Imo* plowed into the French munitions ship *Mont Blanc*. *Mont Blanc* was loaded with 4,000 tons of TNT, 2,300 tons of picric acid, 61 tons of other explosives and a deck of highly flammable benzene, which ignited and touched off an explosion. In addition to those killed, 1,028 were injured. A tidal wave caused by the explosion washed much of the city out to sea.

HOLIDAY TOUR OF HOMES. Dec 6 (also Dec 8–9, 13, 15–16). Natchitoches, LA. Come join us for the magic and the beauty of Christmas in historic Natchitoches. Christmas will be brought to life this holiday season during the Christmas by Candlelight tour. Each tour day will have three homes on tour. Come join us for this wonderful experience. Admission. Est attendance: 2,500. For info: Natchitoches Parish Tourist Commission. Phone: (800) 259-1714. Web: www.natchitoches.net.

	S	M	T	W	T	F	S
December						1	2
2006	3	4	5	6	7	8	9
	10	11	12	13	14	15	16
	17	18	19	20	21	22	23
	24	25	26	27	28	29	30
	31						

KILMER, JOYCE (ALFRED): BIRTH ANNIVERSARY. Dec 6, 1886. American poet most famous for his poem "Trees," which was published in 1913, was born at New Brunswick, NJ. Kilmer was killed in action near Ourcy, France, in WWI, July 30, 1918. Camp Kilmer was named for him.

LEVINE, CHARLES A.: 15th DEATH ANNIVERSARY. Dec 6, 1991. Charles A. Levine, whose efforts to beat Charles Lindbergh across the Atlantic by plane were stymied by a lawsuit, nevertheless became the first air passenger to cross the Atlantic Ocean. Levine's 225-horsepower plane, *The Columbia*, was grounded when one of his copilots filed a suit hours after Lindbergh took off from Roosevelt Field. Not to be overshadowed by Lindbergh's success, Levine announced that his flight, leaving June 4, 1927, would fly beyond Paris to Berlin, with himself as a passenger. Piloted by Clarence Chamberlin, the plane exhausted its fuel and landed at Eisleben, Germany, June 6, 100 miles short of his goal. The flight set a new record of 3,911 miles in 43 hours of nonstop flight, besting Lindbergh by approximately 300 miles. Levine was born at North Adams, MA, in 1897, and died at Washington, DC.

MISSOURI EARTHQUAKES: ANNIVERSARY. Dec 6, 1811. New Madrid, MO. Most prolonged series of earthquakes in US history occurred not in California, but in the Midwest. Lasted until Feb 12, 1812. There were few deaths because of the sparse population. These were the most severe earthquakes in the contiguous US; those higher on the Richter scale have all occurred in Alaska.

NATIONAL PAWNBROKERS DAY. Dec 6. Celebrated on St. Nicholas Day, the patron saint of pawnbroking. Designed to acknowledge the valuable lending and retail services the pawnbroker provides his or her clientele. For info: Michael Goldstein, Empire Loan, 1130 Washington St, Boston, MA 02118. Phone: (617) 423-9366.

ROBERT-HOUDIN, JEAN EUGÈNE: ANNIVERSARY. Dec 6, 1805. The founder of modern magic who was the first to use electricity in his illusions. Robert-Houdin also popularized wearing evening attire (instead of wizard's robes) on stage. He inspired scores of younger magicians, including Harry Houdini, whose stage name saluted Robert-Houdin's name. Born at Blois, France, Robert-Houdin died at St. Gervais, France, on June 13, 1871.

SAINT NICHOLAS DAY. Dec 6. One of the most venerated saints of both Eastern and Western Christian churches, of whose life little is known, except that he was Bishop of Myra (in what is today's Turkey) in the fourth century, and that from early times he has been especially noted for his charity. Santa Claus and the presentation of gifts is said to derive from St. Nicholas.

SPAIN: CONSTITUTION DAY. Dec 6. National holiday. Commemorates the voters' approval of a new constitution in 1978.

SPECIAL KIDS DAY. Dec 6. Elmhurst, IL. Established in 1990 to honor children who are developmentally delayed or physically challenged—building on UN resolution #47/3, which also sets aside Dec 3 as a day to promote integrating the disabled into society. This free, community-wide holiday party features food and gifts distributed to all special needs children and their siblings and family photo sessions. Special Kids Day is a not-for-profit corporation. Est attendance: 400. For info: Rich Rosenberg, Special Kids Day, 111 Linden, Elmhurst, IL 60126. Phone: (630) 530-8000. Fax: (630) 530-8800. E-mail: info@specialkidsday.org. Web: www.specialkidsday.org.

"TALENT SCOUTS" TV PREMIERE: ANNIVERSARY. Dec 6, 1948. Officially titled "Arthur Godfrey's Talent Scouts," this TV show was created when host Arthur Godfrey took his radio show to TV in 1948. On this talent show, celebrity guests introduced amateur and young professional acts. It was a weekly show until 1958. For several years beginning in 1960 it was a summer replacement series called "Celebrity Talent Scouts" and "Hollywood Talent Scouts." Hosts included Sam Levenson, Jim Backus, Merv Griffin and Art Linkletter. Pat Boone, Shari Lewis and the McGuire Sisters got their start here.

THIRTEENTH AMENDMENT TO THE US CONSTITUTION RATIFIED: ANNIVERSARY. Dec 6, 1865. The 13th Amendment to the Constitution was ratified, abolishing slavery in the US. "Neither slavery nor involuntary servitude, save as a punishment for crime whereof the party shall have been duly convicted, shall exist within the United States, or any place subject to their jurisdiction." This amendment was proclaimed Dec 18, 1865. The 13th, 14th and 15th amendments are considered the Civil War Amendments. See also: "Emancipation Proclamation: Anniversary" (Jan 1) for Lincoln's proclamation freeing slaves in the rebelling states.

BIRTHDAYS TODAY

Dave Brubeck, 86, jazz musician, born Concord, CA, Dec 6, 1920.
Otto Graham, 85, Hall of Fame football player, former coach, born Waukegan, IL, Dec 6, 1921.
Macy Gray, 37, singer, born Canton, OH, Dec 6, 1969.
Thomas Hulce, 53, actor (*Amadeus, Parenthood*), born Plymouth, MI, Dec 6, 1953.
James Naughton, 61, actor (*The Paper Chase, The Good Mother*; stage: *Long Day's Journey into Night*), born Middletown, CT, Dec 6, 1945.
Janine Turner, 44, actress ("Northern Exposure," *Cliffhanger*), born Lincoln, NE, Dec 6, 1962.
JoBeth Williams, 53, actress (*The Big Chill*, "Payne"), born Houston, TX, Dec 6, 1953.
Steven Wright, 51, comedian, born New York, NY, Dec 6, 1955.

DECEMBER 7 — THURSDAY
Day 341 — 24 Remaining

ARMENIAN EARTHQUAKE OF 1988: ANNIVERSARY. Dec 7, 1988. An earthquake measuring 6.9 on the Richter scale rocked the Soviet province of Armenia killing upward of 60,000 people. Many of the deaths were blamed on poor construction practices as many homes had been made of adobe, mud or stones; had unreinforced masonry or were prefabricated structures made of loosely connected concrete slabs. In the quake's aftermath, Soviet President Mikhail Gorbachev cut short his trip to the US to fly home and head the massive worldwide relief efforts.

BELGIUM: LOVER'S FAIR. Dec 7. Arlon, Belgium. Traditional cultural observance. Annually, the first Thursday in December.

CATHER, WILLA SIBERT: BIRTH ANNIVERSARY. Dec 7, 1873. American author born at Winchester, VA. Died at New York, NY, Apr 24, 1947. Best known for her novels about the development of early 20th-century American life, such as *O Pioneers!* and *My Ántonia*. She won a Pulitzer Prize in 1922 for her book *One of Ours*.

CHAPIN, HARRY: BIRTH ANNIVERSARY. Dec 7, 1942. Folksinger/songwriter Harry Chapin was one of only five songwriters to receive the Special Congressional Gold Medal for his devotion to the issue of hunger throughout the world. Born at New York, NY, he was killed in a car accident July 16, 1981, at Long Island, NY.

CÔTE D'IVOIRE: COMMEMORATION DAY. Dec 7. National holiday. Commemorates the death of the first president, Félix Houphouët-Boigny, in 1993.

DELAWARE RATIFIES CONSTITUTION: ANNIVERSARY. Dec 7, 1787. Delaware became the first state to ratify the proposed Constitution. It did so by unanimous vote.

LIBERACE MUSEUM CHRISTMAS TREE LIGHTING CEREMONY. Dec 7. The Liberace Museum, Las Vegas, NV. Santa wearing Liberace's gold lamé Santa suit will pull the switch to light the tree with music of the season provided by Liberace scholars. Free admission to all who donate a new toy or nonperishable food item, which will be given to the Salvation Army for distribution to the needy. Annually, the first Thursday in December. Est attendance: 1,000. For info: Liberace Museum, 1775 E Tropicana Ave, Las Vegas, NV, 89119-6529. Phone: (702) 798-5595. Web: www.liberace.org.

NATIONAL FIRE SAFETY COUNCIL: FOUNDING ANNIVERSARY. Dec 7, 1979. Founded to promote fire and burn prevention and life safety awareness. Council distributes comprehensive material to children and adults through local fire departments and the Council's mascot, Firepup®. For info: Natl Fire Safety Council Inc, PO Box 378, Michigan Center, MI 49254-0378. Phone: (517) 764-2811. E-mail: tlusby@nfcd.org.

★**NATIONAL PEARL HARBOR REMEMBRANCE DAY.** Dec 7.

PEARL HARBOR DAY: 65th ANNIVERSARY. Dec 7, 1941. At 7:55 AM (local time) Dec 7, 1941, "a date that will live in infamy," nearly 200 Japanese aircraft attacked Pearl Harbor, Hawaii, long considered the US "Gibraltar of the Pacific." The raid, which lasted little more than one hour, left nearly 3,000 dead. Nearly the entire US Pacific Fleet was at anchor there and few ships escaped damage. Several were sunk or disabled, while 200 US aircraft on the ground were destroyed. The attack on Pearl Harbor brought about immediate US entry into WWII, a declaration of war being requested by President Franklin D. Roosevelt and approved by the Congress Dec 8, 1941.

SPACE MILESTONE: *APOLLO 17* (US). Dec 7, 1972. Launched this date with three-man crew—Eugene A. Cernan, Harrison H. Schmidt, Ronald E. Evans—who explored the moon, Dec 11–14. Lunar landing module named *Challenger*. Pacific splashdown, Dec 19. This was the last manned mission to the moon.

SPACE MILESTONE: *GALILEO* (US). Dec 7, 1995. Launched Oct 18, 1989, by the space shuttle *Atlantis*, the spacecraft *Galileo* entered the orbit of Jupiter after a six-year journey. It has been orbiting Jupiter ever since, sending out probes to study three of its moons. Organic compounds, the ingredients of life, were found on them. On May 25, 2001, it passed within 86 miles of Callisto, one of Jupiter's moons.

TUSSAUD, MARIE GROSHOLTZ: BIRTH ANNIVERSARY. Dec 7, 1761. Creator of Madame Tussaud's waxwork museum, born at Strasbourg, France. Some of the wax figures she created are still on view at Madame Tussaud's at London. She died at London, Apr 15, 1850.

UNITED NATIONS: INTERNATIONAL CIVIL AVIATION DAY. Dec 7. On Dec 6, 1996, the General Assembly proclaimed Dec 7 as International Civil Aviation Day. On Dec 7, 1944, the Convention on International Civil Aviation, which established the International Civil Aviation Organization, was signed. For info: United Nations, Dept of Public Info, New York, NY 10017. Web: www.un.org.

BIRTHDAYS TODAY

Johnny Lee Bench, 59, Hall of Fame baseball player, born Oklahoma City, OK, Dec 7, 1947.
Larry Joe Bird, 50, Hall of Fame basketball player, former coach, born West Baden, IN, Dec 7, 1956.
Ellen Burstyn, 74, actress (*Alice Doesn't Live Here Anymore; The Exorcist; Same Time, Next Year*), born Edna Rae Gilhooley at Detroit, MI, Dec 7, 1932.
Thad Cochran, 69, US Senator (R, Mississippi), born Pontotoc, MS, Dec 7, 1937.

Susan M. Collins, 54, US Senator (R, Maine), born Caribou, ME, Dec 7, 1952.

Edd Hall, 48, announcer ("The Tonight Show with Jay Leno"), born Boston, MA, Dec 7, 1958.

C. Thomas Howell, 40, actor ("Two Marriages," *Soul Man, Tank*), born Los Angeles, CA, Dec 7, 1966.

Tino Martinez, 39, baseball player, born Tampa, FL, Dec 7, 1967.

Tom Waits, 57, singer, songwriter ("I Never Talk to Strangers"), actor (*Down by Law, Short Cuts*), born Pomona, CA, Dec 7, 1949.

Eli Wallach, 91, actor (*The Tiger Makes Out*; Emmy for "The Poppy Is Also a Flower"), born New York, NY, Dec 7, 1915.

DECEMBER 8 — FRIDAY
Day 342 — 23 Remaining

AMERICA ENTERS WORLD WAR II: 65th ANNIVERSARY. Dec 8, 1941. One day after the surprise Japanese attack on Pearl Harbor, Congress declared war against Japan and the US entered WWII.

AMERICAN FEDERATION OF LABOR (AFL) FOUNDED: ANNIVERSARY. Dec 8, 1886. Originally founded at Pittsburgh, PA, as the Federation of Organized Trades and Labor Unions of the United States and Canada in 1881, the union was reorganized in 1886 under the name American Federation of Labor (AFL). The AFL was dissolved as a separate entity in 1955 when it merged with the Congress of Industrial Organizations to form the AFL-CIO. See also: "AFL-CIO Founded: Anniversary (Dec 5)."

CHINESE NATIONALISTS MOVE TO FORMOSA: ANNIVERSARY. Dec 8, 1949. The government of Chiang Kai-Shek moved to Formosa (Taiwan) after being driven out of Mainland China by the Communists led by Mao Tse-Tung.

DAVIS, SAMMY, JR: BIRTH ANNIVERSARY. Dec 8, 1925. Born at New York, NY, Sammy Davis, Jr, was the son of vaudevillians and first appeared on the stage at the age of four. He made his first film appearance in *Rufus Jones for President* in 1931. He joined the Will Mastin Trio, a song-and-dance team popular on the night club circuit; as Davis matured, his singing, dancing and impersonations became the center of the act. Davis began performing on his own in the 1950s, headlining club engagements, appearing on television variety shows and making numerous records. His Broadway debut came in 1956 in the hit musical *Mr Wonderful*, and in the late '50s and early '60s he starred in a number of films, including a series with Frank Sinatra and the Rat Pack. Davis died at Los Angeles, CA, May 16, 1990.

DURANT, WILLIAM CRAPO: BIRTH ANNIVERSARY. Dec 8, 1861. "Billy" Durant, a leading producer of carriages at Flint, MI; promoter of the Buick car; cofounder of Chevrolet and founder, in 1908, of General Motors. He lost, regained and again lost control of GM, after which he founded Durant Motors, went bankrupt in the Depression and operated a Flint bowling alley in his last working years. Durant was born at Boston, MA, and died at New York, NY, Mar 18, 1947.

FEAST OF THE IMMACULATE CONCEPTION. Dec 8. Roman Catholic Holy Day of Obligation. A public holiday in Nicaragua.

FIRST STEP TOWARD A NUCLEAR-FREE WORLD: ANNIVERSARY. Dec 8, 1987. The former Soviet Union and the US signed a treaty at Washington eliminating medium-range and shorter-range missiles. This was the first treaty completely doing away with two entire classes of nuclear arms. These missiles, with a range of 500 to 5,500 kilometers, were to be scrapped under strict supervision within three years of the signing.

GUAM: LADY OF CAMARIN DAY. Dec 8. Declared a legal holiday by Guam legislature, Mar 2, 1971.

HOBAN, JAMES: 175th DEATH ANNIVERSARY. Dec 8, 1831. Irish-born architect who designed the US President's Executive Mansion, later known as the White House. He was born at Callan, County Kilkenny, Ireland, in 1762 (exact date unknown) and died at Washington, DC. The cornerstone for the White House, Washington's oldest public building, was laid in 1792.

JOHN LENNON SHOT: ANNIVERSARY. Dec 8, 1980. On this date deranged gunman Mark David Chapman shot and killed rock star John Lennon outside his apartment building as he returned from a recording session. The death of the former Beatle, who was an international peace activist, shocked the world. His widow, Yoko Ono, asked for 10 minutes of silence at 2 PM, EST on the following Sunday, Dec 14, and many US and international radio stations observed it. See also: "Lennon, John: Birth Anniversary" (Oct 9).

MORRISON, JIM: BIRTH ANNIVERSARY. Dec 8, 1943. Songwriter, poet, lead singer of The Doors, Jim Morrison is considered to be one of the fathers of contemporary rock. The bacchic Morrison, known as "The Lizard King," brought avant-garde theatrics to his musical performances and mystical influences to his songs. Born at Melbourne, FL, and died at Paris, France, July 3, 1971.

NAFTA SIGNED: ANNIVERSARY. Dec 8, 1993. President Clinton signed the North American Free Trade Agreement, which cut tariffs and eliminated other trade barriers between the US, Canada and Mexico. The agreement went into effect Jan 1, 1994.

RIVERA, DIEGO: BIRTH ANNIVERSARY. Dec 8, 1886. Mexican painter whose murals became center of political controversy, born at Guanajuato, Mexico. Died in his studio at San Angel, near Mexico City, Nov 25, 1957.

SEGAR, ELZIE CRISLER: BIRTH ANNIVERSARY. Dec 8, 1894. Popeye creator Elzie Crisler Segar was born at Chester, IL. Originally called *Thimble Theater*, the comic strip that came to be known as *Popeye* had the unusual format of a one-act play in cartoon form. Centered on the Oyl family, especially daughter Olive, the strip introduced a new central character in 1929. A one-eyed sailor with bulging muscles, Popeye became the strip's star attraction almost immediately. Popeye made it to the silver screen in animated form and in 1980 became a movie with Robin Williams playing the lead. Segar died Oct 13, 1938, at Santa Monica, CA.

SOVIET UNION DISSOLVED: 15th ANNIVERSARY. Dec 8, 1991. The Union of Soviet Socialist Republics ceased to exist, as the republics of Russia, Byelorussia and Ukraine signed an agreement at Minsk, Byelorussia, creating the Commonwealth of Independent States. The remaining republics, with the exception of Georgia, joined in the new commonwealth as it began the slow and arduous process of removing the yoke of Communism and dealing with strong separatist and nationalistic movements within the various republics.

December 2006	S	M	T	W	T	F	S
						1	2
	3	4	5	6	7	8	9
	10	11	12	13	14	15	16
	17	18	19	20	21	22	23
	24	25	26	27	28	29	30
	31						

SUGARLOAF CRAFTS FESTIVAL. Dec 8–10. Dulles Expo Center, Chantilly, VA. This new show features more than 300 nationally recognized craft designers and fine artists displaying and selling their original creations. Includes craft demonstrations, live music, specialty foods, hourly gift certificate drawings, and more. Est attendance: 15,000. For info: Sugarloaf Mountain Works, 200 Orchard Ridge Dr, #215, Gaithersburg, MD 20878. Phone: (800) 210-9900. Fax: (301) 253-9620. Web: www.sugarloafcrafts.com.

THURBER, JAMES: BIRTH ANNIVERSARY. Dec 8, 1894. James Grover Thurber, American humorist and artist, longtime contributor to the *New Yorker*, born at Columbus, OH. Died at New York, NY, Nov 2, 1961.

UZBEKISTAN: CONSTITUTION DAY. Dec 8. National holiday. Commemorates the constitution of 1991.

WASSAIL CELEBRATION. Dec 8–10. Woodstock, VT. Activities include a horse rider and carriage parade, Santa comes to town, house tours, concert by The Ten Men's Vocal Choir, caroling, burning the yule log on the Village Green and additional events each year. Est attendance: 5,000. For info: Executive Director, Woodstock Area Chamber of Commerce, 18 Central St, PO Box 486, Woodstock, VT 05091. Phone: (802) 457-3555 or (888) 496-6378. E-mail: office@woodstockvt.com. Web: www.woodstockvt.com.

WHITNEY, ELI: BIRTH ANNIVERSARY. Dec 8, 1765. Inventor of the cotton gin, born at Westboro, MA. Died at New Haven, CT, Jan 8, 1825.

BIRTHDAYS TODAY

Gregg Allman, 59, singer ("Ramblin' Man"), actor (*Rush*), born Nashville, TN, Dec 8, 1947.

Kim Basinger, 53, actress (Oscar for *L.A. Confidential*; *Batman, The Natural*), born Athens, GA, Dec 8, 1953.

Gordon Arthur ("Red") Berenson, 65, former hockey player and coach, born Regina, SK, Canada, Dec 8, 1941.

David Carradine, 66, actor (*Boxcar Bertha*, "Kung-Fu" series), born Hollywood, CA, Dec 8, 1940.

Ann Coulter, 45, political commentator, author (*Slander: Liberal Lies About the American Right*), born New Canaan, CT, Dec 8, 1961 (some sources say 1963).

James Galway, 67, flutist, born Belfast, Northern Ireland, Dec 8, 1939.

Jeff George, 39, former football player, born Indianapolis, IN, Dec 8, 1967.

Teri Hatcher, 42, actress ("Desperate Housewives," "Lois & Clark"), born Sunnyvale, CA, Dec 8, 1964.

James MacArthur, 69, actor ("Hawaii Five-O"), born Los Angeles, CA, Dec 8, 1937.

Dominic Monaghan, 30, actor (*The Lord of the Rings* trilogy, "Lost"), born Berlin, Germany, Dec 8, 1976.

Mike Mussina, 38, baseball player, born Williamsport, PA, Dec 8, 1968.

Sinead O'Connor, 40, singer, songwriter, born Dublin, Ireland, Dec 8, 1966.

Maximilian Schell, 76, actor (*Judgment at Nuremberg, The Odessa File*), producer, born Vienna, Austria, Dec 8, 1930.

Mary Woronov, 60, actress (*Rock 'n' Roll High School, Eating Raoul*), born Brooklyn, NY, Dec 8, 1946.

DECEMBER 9 — SATURDAY
Day 343 — 22 Remaining

AMERICA'S FIRST FORMAL CREMATION: ANNIVERSARY. Dec 9, 1792. The first formal cremation of a human body in America took place near Charleston, SC. Henry Laurens, Colonial statesman and signer of the Treaty of Paris ending the Revolutionary War, in his will provided: "I do solemnly enjoin it on my son, as an indispensable duty, that as soon as he conveniently can, after my decease, he cause my body to be wrapped in twelve yards of tow cloth and burned until it be entirely consumed, and then, collecting my bones, deposit them wherever he may think proper." Laurens died Dec 8, 1792, at his plantation, and was cremated there.

BIRDSEYE, CLARENCE: BIRTH ANNIVERSARY. Dec 9, 1886. American industrialist who developed a way of deep-freezing foods. He was marketing frozen fish by 1925 and was one of the founders of General Foods Corporation. Born at Brooklyn, NY, he died at New York City, Oct 7, 1956.

CHRISTMAS CANDLELIGHT TOUR. Dec 9–10. Fredericksburg, VA. To instill the spirit of Christmases past by opening historic homes to the public. Eighteenth-century music, street dancers, carriage rides throughout the tour. Est attendance: 10,000. For info: Visitor Center, 706 Caroline St, Fredericksburg, VA 22401. Phone: (800) 678-4748. Fax: (540) 372-6587. E-mail: gboswell@fredericksburgva.gov.

DICKENS OF A CHRISTMAS. Dec 9–10. Downtown Franklin, TN. 21st annual festival features living characters from *A Christmas Carol* as well as other Victorian characters including Father and Mother Christmas. Street vendors sell roasted chestnuts, plum pudding and hot chocolate. Horse-drawn carriage rides, musical, dramatic performances and town sing. Local artists and crafters create "living windows" by demonstrating their skills in shop windows and on the historic square. Est attendance: 50,000. For info: Shelly Robertson, Heritage Foundation, PO Box 807, Franklin, TN 37065. Phone: (615) 595-1239. Fax: (615) 591-8502. E-mail: srobertson@historicfranklin.com. Web: www.historicfranklin.com.

FOXX, REDD: BIRTH ANNIVERSARY. Dec 9, 1922. Born John Elroy Sanford at St. Louis, MO, Redd Foxx plied his comedic trade on vaudeville stages, in nightclubs, on television, in films and on record albums. His talents reached a national audience with the TV sitcom "Sanford and Son." He died after collapsing during a rehearsal for a new TV sitcom, "The Royal Family," at Los Angeles, CA, Oct 11, 1991.

GENOCIDE CONVENTION: ANNIVERSARY. Dec 9, 1948. The United Nations General Assembly unanimously approved the Convention on Prevention and Punishment of the Crime of Genocide on Dec 9, 1948. It took effect Jan 12, 1951, when ratification by 20 nations had been completed. President Truman sent it to the US Senate for approval on June 16, 1949; it was supported by presidents Kennedy, Johnson, Nixon, Ford, Carter and Reagan. Thirty-seven years after its submission, and after approval by more than 90 nations, the Senate approved it, Feb 19, 1986, by a vote of 83–11.

HARRIS, JOEL CHANDLER: BIRTH ANNIVERSARY. Dec 9, 1848. American author, creator of the "Uncle Remus" stories, born at Eatonton, GA. Died July 3, 1908, at Atlanta, GA.

HOPPER, GRACE: 100th BIRTH ANNIVERSARY. Dec 9, 1906. Born at New York, NY. When she retired from the US Navy at the age of 79, she was the oldest naval officer ever on active duty. She attained the rank of rear admiral and was a leader in the computer revolution, having developed the computer language COBOL. Grace Hopper died Jan 1, 1992, at Arlington, WV.

INTERNATIONAL SHAREWARE DAY. Dec 9. A day to take the time to reward the efforts of thousands of computer programmers who trust that if we try their programs and like them, we will pay for them. Unfortunately, very few payments are received, thus stifling the programmers' efforts. This observance is meant to prompt each of us to inventory our PCs and Macs, see if we are using any shareware and then take the time in the holiday spirit to write payment checks to the authors. Hopefully this will keep shareware coming. Annually, the second Saturday in December. For info: David Lawrence, Online Today, Net Music Countdown, 145 S Glenoaks Blvd, Ste 336, Burbank, CA 91501. Phone: (818) 563-3123. E-mail: david@onlinetonight.net. Web: onlinetonight.net.

KELLY, EMMETT: BIRTH ANNIVERSARY. Dec 9, 1898. American circus clown and entertainer, born at Sedan, KS. Kelly was best known for "Weary Willie," a clown dressed in tattered clothes, with a beard and large nose. Died at Sarasota, FL, Mar 28, 1979.

MILTON, JOHN: BIRTH ANNIVERSARY. Dec 9, 1608. English poet, historian, civil servant and defender of freedom of the press born at Bread Street, Cheapside, London. Considered one of the greatest poets of the English language, second only to William Shakespeare. Author of the great verse epics *Paradise Lost* (1667) and *Paradise Regained* (1671). Died from gout, Nov 8, 1674, at London, England. "No man who knows aught," he wrote, "can be so stupid to deny that all men naturally were born free."

NATIONAL DAY OF THE HORSE. Dec 9. The horse is a living link to the heritage and history of our nation, and represents a common bond among all peoples who led the way in building our country. Today, the horse industry contributes more than $112 billion annually to the American economy. Therefore, the California State Legislature (as well as the US Senate) has declared the second Saturday of December to be the Day of the Horse in honor of these magnificent creatures.

PETRIFIED FOREST NATIONAL PARK ESTABLISHED: ANNIVERSARY. Dec 9, 1962. Arizona's Petrified Forest National Monument, proclaimed Dec 8, 1906, was established as a national park. For further park info: Petrified Forest Natl Park, Petrified Forest Natl Park, AZ 86028.

POLISH CHRISTMAS OPEN HOUSE. Dec 9. Polish American Cultural Center Museum, Philadelphia, PA. Sw. Mikolaj (Polish St. Nicholas) will greet everyone with gifts for the children. Polish Christmas Tree and entertainment. Free admission. For info: Polish American Cultural Center Museum, 308 Walnut St, Philadelphia, PA 19106. Phone: (215) 922-1700. Fax: (215) 922-1518. E-mail: mail@polishamericancenter.org. Web: www.polishamericancenter.org.

SANDYS, EDWIN: BIRTH ANNIVERSARY. Dec 9, 1561. Sir Edwin Sandys, English statesman and one of the founders of the Virginia Colony (treasurer, the Virginia Company, 1619–20), born at Worcestershire, England. Died at Kent, England, in October 1629 (exact date unknown).

TANZANIA: INDEPENDENCE AND REPUBLIC DAY. Dec 9. Tanganyika became independent of Britain in 1961. The republics of Tanganyika and Zanzibar joined to become one state (Apr 27, 1964), renamed (Oct 29, 1964) the United Republic of Tanzania.

December 2006

S	M	T	W	T	F	S
					1	2
3	4	5	6	7	8	9
10	11	12	13	14	15	16
17	18	19	20	21	22	23
24	25	26	27	28	29	30
31						

34th STREET EXPRESS. Dec 9. Chartered Amtrak train leaves from Boston, MA. Christmas shopping special to New York City also takes in the Radio City Christmas Spectacular. Annually, the second Saturday in December. Est attendance: 300. For info: Mystic Valley Railway Society, Inc, PO Box 365486, Hyde Park, MA 02136-0009. Phone: (617) 361-4445. Fax: (617) 361-4445*51 (dial all as one number). Web: www.mysticvalleyrs.org.

VICTORIAN CHRISTMAS TOURS AT FRANK LLOYD WRIGHT HOME. Dec 9 (also Dec 16). Oak Park, IL. A wonderful Christmas tradition, the Frank Lloyd Wright Preservation Trust presents FREE Victorian Christmas tours of Wright's home in Oak Park. These tours feature stories of how the Wright family celebrated the holidays at the turn of the 20th century and are led by Junior Interpreters: specially trained middle and high school students who bring a new perspective to the tour experience. Annually, the second and third Saturdays of Dec. For info: Frank Lloyd Wright Preservation Trust, 931 Chicago Ave, Oak Park, IL 60302. Phone: (708) 848-1976. Web: www.wrightplus.org.

BIRTHDAYS TODAY

Joan Armatrading, 56, singer, songwriter (*Me, Myself, I*), born Saint Kitts, West Indies, Dec 9, 1950.

Reiko Aylesworth, 34, actress ("24," "One Life to Live"), born Chicago, IL, Dec 9, 1972.

Beau Bridges, 65, actor ("James Brady Story," *The Fabulous Baker Boys*), born Los Angeles, CA, Dec 9, 1941.

Richard Marvin (Dick) Butkus, 64, Hall of Fame football player, sportscaster, actor, born Chicago, IL, Dec 9, 1942.

Thomas Daschle, 59, former US Senator (D, South Dakota), born Aberdeen, SD, Dec 9, 1947.

Judi Dench, 72, actress (*Mrs Brown, Iris*; Oscar for *Shakespeare in Love*), born York, England, Dec 9, 1934.

Kirk Douglas, 90, actor (*Champion, Lust for Life*), author, born Issur Danielovitch Demsky at Amsterdam, NY, Dec 9, 1916.

David Anthony Higgins, 45, actor ("Ellen," "Malcolm in the Middle"), born Des Moines, IA, Dec 9, 1961.

Felicity Huffman, 44, actress ("Sports Night," "Desperate Housewives"), born Bedford, NY, Dec 9, 1962.

Thomas O. (Tom) Kite, Jr, 57, golfer, born Austin, TX, Dec 9, 1949.

Joe Lando, 45, actor ("Dr. Quinn, Medicine Woman"), born Chicago, IL, Dec 9, 1961.

John Malkovich, 53, actor (*The Killing Fields, The Sheltering Sky*), filmmaker, born Christopher, IL, Dec 9, 1953.

Dina Merrill, 81, actress (*Desk Set, Operation Petticoat*), born New York, NY, Dec 9, 1925.

Jesse Metcalfe, 28, actor ("Desperate Housewives," "Passions"), born Waterford, CT, Dec 9, 1978.

Michael Nouri, 61, actor ("Search for Tomorrow," *Flashdance*), born Washington, DC, Dec 9, 1945.

Donny Osmond, 49, actor, singer, born Ogden, UT, Dec 9, 1957.

Dick Van Patten, 78, actor ("Eight Is Enough," "Mama"), born Richmond Hill, NY, Dec 9, 1928.

DECEMBER 10 — SUNDAY
Day 344 — 21 Remaining

COLONIAL CHRISTMAS AT WORMSLOE. Dec 10. Wormsloe Historic Site, Savannah, GA. Join us for caroling, burning of the Yule log and other holiday observances of the Colonial Period, including games and refreshments. For info: Wormsloe Historic Site, 7601 Skidaway Rd, Savannah, GA 31406. Phone: (912) 353-3023. E-mail: wormsloe@bellsouth.net. Web: www.wormsloe.org.

DEWEY, MELVIL: BIRTH ANNIVERSARY. Dec 10, 1851. American librarian and inventor of the Dewey decimal book classification system was born at Adams Center, NY. Born Melville Louis Kossuth Dewey, he was an advocate of spelling reform, urged use of the metric system and was interested in many other education reforms. Dewey died at Highlands County, FL, Dec 26, 1931.

DICKINSON, EMILY: BIRTH ANNIVERSARY. Dec 10, 1830. One of America's greatest poets, Emily Dickinson was born at Amherst, MA. She was reclusive, mysterious and frail in health. Seven of her poems were published during her life, but after her death her sister, Lavinia, discovered almost 2,000 more poems written on the backs of envelopes and other scraps of paper locked in her bureau. They were published gradually, over 50 years, beginning in 1890. She died May 15, 1886, at Amherst, MA. The little-known Emily Dickinson who was born, lived and died at Amherst now is recognized as one of the most original poets of the English-speaking world.

EIGHTEENTH-CENTURY CHRISTMAS WASSAIL. Dec 10. McLean, VA. Greet the winter solstice and Christmas season with a toast to the apple trees. Caroling and warm refreshments. Bring pots or other noisemakers to frighten off evil spirits threatening next year's apple crop. Est attendance: 800. For info: Claude Moore Colonial Farm at Turkey Run, 6310 Georgetown Pike, McLean, VA 22101. Phone: (703) 442-7557. Fax: (703) 442-0714. Web: www.1771.org.

FIRST GRAND OLE OPRY BROADCAST: ANNIVERSARY. Dec 10, 1927. Grand Ole Opry made its first radio broadcast from Nashville, TN.

FIRST US HEAVYWEIGHT CHAMP DEFEATED IN ENGLAND: ANNIVERSARY. Dec 10, 1810. Tom Molineaux, the first unofficial heavyweight champion of the US, was a freed slave from Virginia. He was beaten in the 40th round by Tom Cribb, the English champion, in a boxing match at Copthall Common at London.

FIRST US SCIENTIST RECEIVES NOBEL PRIZE: ANNIVERSARY. Dec 10, 1907. University of Chicago professor Albert Michelson, eminent physicist known for his research on the speed of light and optics became the first US scientist to receive the Nobel Prize.

GALLAUDET, THOMAS HOPKINS: BIRTH ANNIVERSARY. Dec 10, 1787. A hearing educator who, with Laurent Clerc, founded the first public school for deaf people, Connecticut Asylum for the Education and Instruction of Deaf and Dumb Persons (now the American School for the Deaf), at Hartford, CT, Apr 15, 1817. Gallaudet was born at Philadelphia, PA, and died Sept 9, 1851, at Hartford, CT.

HISTORICAL SOCIETY'S CHRISTMAS TOUR OF HOMES. Dec 10. Crawfordsville, IN. A walking tour of fine Victorian homes at Crawfordsville. Sponsor: Montgomery County Historical Society. Est attendance: 400. For info: Montgomery County Visitors & Conv Bureau, Inc, 218 E Pike St, Crawfordsville, IN 47933. Phone: (800) 866-3973. Fax: (765) 362-5215. E-mail: mcvcb@tctc.com. Web: www.crawfordsville.org.

HOLIDAY HOUSE TOURS. Dec 10–31. Ash Lawn–Highland, Home of President James Monroe, Charlottesville, VA. House decorated inside and out with fresh greens, fruits and woodland seed pods. 11AM–5PM. Evening candlelight openings. Est attendance: 1,000. For info: Ash Lawn–Highland, 1000 James Monroe Pkwy, Charlottesville, VA 22902. Phone: (434) 293-9539. Fax: (434) 293-8000. E-mail: info@ashlawnhighland.org. Web: www.ashlawnhighland.org.

★**HUMAN RIGHTS DAY.** Dec 10. Presidential Proclamation 2866, of Dec 6, 1949, covers all succeeding years. Customarily issued as "Bill of Rights Day, Human Rights Day and Week."

★**HUMAN RIGHTS WEEK.** Dec 10–16. Presidential Proclamation issued since 1958 for the week of Dec 10–16, except in 1986. See also: "Human Rights Day" (Dec 10) and "Bill of Rights Day" (Dec 15).

LAMOUR, DOROTHY: BIRTH ANNIVERSARY. Dec 10, 1914. Singer, actress (*The Hurricane, Road to Singapore*), born New Orleans, LA. Died Sept 22, 1996, at Los Angeles, CA.

"THE MIGHTY MOUSE PLAYHOUSE" TV PREMIERE: ANNIVERSARY. Dec 10, 1955. An all-time favorite of the Saturday-morning crowd (including adults). CBS had a hit with their pint-sized cartoon character Mighty Mouse, who was a tongue-in-cheek version of Superman. The show had other feature cartoons such as "The Adventures of Gandy Goose."

MISSISSIPPI: ADMISSION DAY: ANNIVERSARY. Dec 10. Became 20th state in 1817.

NATIONAL CHILDREN'S MEMORIAL DAY AND WORLDWIDE CANDLE LIGHTING. Dec 10. A day to remember the more than 79,000 children who die in the US every year. Annually, the second Sunday in December. For info: The Compassionate Friends, PO Box 3696, Oak Brook, IL 60522-3696. Phone: (877) 969-0010. E-mail: nationaloffice@compassionatefriends.org. Web: www.compassionatefriends.org.

NOBEL PRIZE AWARDS CEREMONIES. Dec 10. Oslo, Norway and Stockholm, Sweden. Alfred Nobel, Swedish chemist and inventor of dynamite who died in 1896, provided in his will that income from his $9 million estate should be used for annual prizes—to be awarded to people who are judged to have made the most valuable contributions to the good of humanity. The Nobel Peace Prize is awarded by a committee of the Norwegian parliament and the presentation is made at the Oslo City Hall. Five other prizes, for physics, chemistry, medicine, literature and economics, are presented in a ceremony at Stockholm, Sweden. Both ceremonies traditionally are held on the anniversary of the death of Alfred Nobel. First awarded in 1901, the current value of each prize is about $1,000,000. To date, more than 250 Americans have won Nobel prizes. See also "Nobel, Alfred Bernhard: Birth Anniversary" (Oct 21).

NORTON, MARY: BIRTH ANNIVERSARY. Dec 10, 1903. British author Mary Norton was born at London, England. An author of children's books, she is best known for *Bedknob and Broomstick* (1957). She died Aug 29, 1992, at Hartland, England.

QUINCY PRESERVES CHRISTMAS CANDLELIGHT TOUR. Dec 10. Quincy, IL. Tour historic homes decked out in their Christmas finest. Each year this walking tour features a different neighborhood. Homes range in size from grand mansions to quaint cottages. Annually, the second Sunday in December. Est attendance: 1,000. For info: Fran Cook, Quincy Preserves, 310 S 16th St, Quincy, IL 62301. Phone: (217) 224-2587.

RALPH BUNCHE AWARDED NOBEL PEACE PRIZE: ANNIVERSARY. Dec 10, 1950. Dr. Ralph Johnson Bunche became the first black man awarded the Nobel Peace Prize. Bunche was awarded the prize for his efforts in mediation between Israel and neighboring Arab states in 1949.

RED CLOUD: DEATH ANNIVERSARY. Dec 10, 1909. Sioux Indian chief Red Cloud was born in 1822 (exact date unknown), near North Platte, NE. A courageous leader and defender of Indian rights, Red Cloud was the son of Lone Man and Walks as She Thinks. His unrelenting determination caused US abandonment of the Bozeman trail and of three forts that interfered with Indian hunting grounds. Red Cloud died at Pine Ridge, SD.

SPACE MILESTONE: *SOYUZ 26* (USSR). Dec 10, 1977. Launched this date with cosmonauts Yuri Romanenko and Georgi Grechko who linked it with *Salyut 6* space station on Dec 11, after the unsuccessful attempt by *Soyuz 25* earlier that year. Returned to Earth in *Soyuz 27*, Mar 16, 1978, after record-setting 96 days in space.

TAKE A NEW YEAR'S RESOLUTION TO STOP SMOKING (TANYRSS). Dec 10–Feb 17, 2007. 18th annual. To educate consumers/patients, health care professionals to take a New Year's resolution to stop smoking. Kit materials available for $15. For info: Fred Mayer, RPh, MPH, Pharmacists Planning Service Inc, c/o Pharmacy Council on Tobacco Dependence, 101 Lucas Valley Rd, Ste 210, San Rafael, CA 94903. E-mail: ppsi@aol.com. Web: www.ppsinc.org.

THAILAND: CONSTITUTION DAY. Dec 10. National holiday. Commemorates the constitution of 1932, the nation's first.

TREATY OF PARIS ENDS SPANISH-AMERICAN WAR: ANNIVERSARY. Dec 10, 1898. Following the conclusion of the Spanish-American War in 1898, American and Spanish ambassadors met at Paris, France, to negotiate a treaty. Under the terms of this treaty, Spain granted the US the Philippine Islands and the islands of Guam and Puerto Rico, and agreed to withdraw from Cuba. Senatorial debate over the treaty centered on the US's move toward imperialism by acquiring the Philippines. A vote was taken Feb 6, 1899, and the treaty passed by a one-vote margin. President William McKinley signed the treaty Feb 10, 1899.

UNITED NATIONS: HUMAN RIGHTS DAY. Dec 10. Official United Nations observance day. Date is the anniversary of adoption of the "Universal Declaration of Human Rights" in 1948. The Declaration sets forth basic rights and fundamental freedoms to which all men and women everywhere in the world are entitled. For info: United Nations, Dept of Public Info, New York, NY 10017. E-mail: inquiries@un.org. Web: www.un.org.

WSBA/WARM 103/OLDIES 96.1 CHRISTMAS CRAFT SHOW. Dec 10. York Fairgrounds, York, PA. More than 250 craft displays, from country to contemporary, Victorian and southwestern, handcrafted furniture, wood carvings, dolls, jewelry, pottery, collectibles, quilts, baskets, fine arts and much more. Admission fee. Est attendance: 3,500. For info: Joe Alfano, Asst Promo Dir, PO Box 910, York, PA 17402-0910. Phone: (717) 764-1155. Fax: (717) 252-4807. E-mail: jalfano@radioyork.com. Web: www.warm103.com.

BIRTHDAYS TODAY

Rod Blagojevich, 50, Governor of Illinois (D), born Chicago, IL, Dec 10, 1956.

Kenneth Branagh, 46, actor (*Shackleton*), director (*Hamlet, Henry V*), born Belfast, Northern Ireland, Dec 10, 1960.

Susan Dey, 54, model, actress ("The Partridge Family," "LA Law,"), born Pekin, IL, Dec 10, 1952.

Harold Gould, 83, actor ("Rhoda," "Under One Roof"), born Schenectady, NY, Dec 10, 1923.

Gloria Loring, 60, singer, actress ("Days of Our Lives"), born New York, NY, Dec 10, 1946.

December 2006

S	M	T	W	T	F	S
					1	2
3	4	5	6	7	8	9
10	11	12	13	14	15	16
17	18	19	20	21	22	23
24	25	26	27	28	29	30
31						

DECEMBER 11 — MONDAY
Day 345 — 20 Remaining

BUELL, MARJORIE H.: BIRTH ANNIVERSARY. Dec 11, 1904. Cartoonist, creator of comic strip character Little Lulu, Marjorie Buell was considered a pioneer for creating a female character that outsmarted the neighborhood boys. She was born at Philadelphia, PA, and died May 30, 1993, at Elyria, OH.

BURKINA FASO: NATIONAL DAY. Dec 11. Gained independence within the French community, 1958.

CANNON, ANNIE JUMP: BIRTH ANNIVERSARY. Dec 11, 1863. American astronomer and discoverer of five stars, was born at Dover, DE. Author and winner of the National Academy of Science Draper Medal, she died at Cambridge, MA, Apr 13, 1941.

EDWARD VIII ABDICATION: 70th ANNIVERSARY. Dec 11, 1936. Christened Edward Albert Christian George Andrew Patrick David, King Edward VIII was born at Richmond Park, England, on June 12, 1894, and became Prince of Wales in July 1911. He ascended to the English throne upon the death of his father, George V, on Jan 20, 1936, but coronation never took place. He abdicated on Dec 11, 1936, in order to marry "the woman I love," twice-divorced American Wallis Warfield Simpson. They were married in France, June 3, 1937. Edward was named Duke of Windsor by his brother-successor, George VI. The duke died at Paris, May 28, 1972, but was buried in England, near Windsor Castle.

INDIANA: ADMISSION DAY: ANNIVERSARY. Dec 11. Became 19th state in 1816.

LA GUARDIA, FIORELLO HENRY: BIRTH ANNIVERSARY. Dec 11, 1882. Popularly known as the "Little Flower," Fiorello H. La Guardia was not too busy as mayor of New York City to read the "funnies" to radio listeners during the New York newspaper strike. He said of himself: "When I make a mistake it's a beaut!" La Guardia was born at New York, NY, and died there Sept 20, 1947.

"MAGNUM, PI" TV PREMIERE: ANNIVERSARY. Dec 11, 1980. Premiered on CBS television network, starring Tom Selleck, John Hillerman, Roger E. Mosley and Larry Manetti. Each year on this anniversary, "Magnum" fans turn to the international fan organization "Magnum Memorabilia by David Romas" as the center of observances worldwide. For info: David Romas, Magnum Memorabilia, 438 Leroy St, Ferndale, MI 48220. E-mail: ac2942@wayne.edu.

UNITED NATIONS: INTERNATIONAL MOUNTAIN DAY. Dec 11. With mountains covering one-quarter of the Earth's land surface and home to 12 percent of the world's population, mountain people are affected by conflict out of all proportion to their numbers and the land they occupy. The UN General Assembly declared Dec 11 International Mountain Day as a result of the successful observance of the UN International Year of Mountains in 2002, which increased global awareness of the importance of mountains, stimulated the establishment of national committees in 78 countries and strengthened alliances through promoting the creation of the Mountain Partnership. For info: United Nations, Dept of Public Info, New York, NY 10017. Web: www.un.org or www.mountainpartnership.org.

UNITED NATIONS: UNICEF'S 60th ANNIVERSARY. Dec 11, 1946. Anniversary of the establishment by the United Nations General Assembly of the United Nations International Children's Emergency Fund (UNICEF). For info: United Nations, Dept of Public Info, New York, NY 10017. Web: www.unicef.org.

BIRTHDAYS TODAY

Max Baucus, 65, US Senator (D, Montana), born Helena, MT, Dec 11, 1941.

Jay Bell, 41, baseball player, born Pensacola, FL, Dec 11, 1965.

Mos Def, 33, rapper, actor (*The Italian Job, Something the Lord Made*), born Dante Terrell Smith at Brooklyn, NY, Dec 11, 1973.

Gary Dourdan, 40, actor ("CSI"), born Philadelphia, PA, Dec 11, 1966.

Teri Garr, 57, actress (*Young Frankenstein, Tootsie, The Black Stallion*), born Lakewood, OH, Dec 11, 1949.

David Gates, 66, singer, songwriter, born Tulsa, OK, Dec 11, 1940.

Tom Hayden, 66, journalist, activist, politician, born Royal Oak, MI, Dec 11, 1940.

Jermaine Jackson, 52, singer, musician (Jackson 5), born Gary, IN, Dec 11, 1954.

John F. Kerry, 63, US Senator (D, Massachusetts), born Denver, CO, Dec 11, 1943.

Brenda Lee, 62, singer ("I'm Sorry," "All Alone Am I"), born Brenda Mae Tarpley at Atlanta, GA, Dec 11, 1944.

Donna Mills, 63, actress ("Knots Landing," "Melrose Place"), born Chicago, IL, Dec 11, 1943.

Rita Moreno, 75, singer, actress (Oscar for *West Side Story*; Tony for *The Ritz*), born Hunacao, Puerto Rico, Dec 11, 1931.

Carlo Ponti, 93, producer, born Milan, Italy, Dec 11, 1913.

Susan Seidelman, 54, filmmaker (*Desperately Seeking Susan, Making Mr Right*), born Philadelphia, PA, Dec 11, 1952.

Aleksandr Isayevich Solzhenitsyn, 88, author (*Cancer Ward, One Day in the Life of Ivan Denisovich, The Gulag Archipelago*), born Kislovodsk, USSR, Dec 11, 1918.

Rider Strong, 27, actor ("Boy Meets World"), born San Francisco, CA, Dec 11, 1979.

Ken Wahl, 53, actor ("Wiseguy," *The Wanderers, Fort Apache: The Bronx*), born Chicago, IL, Dec 11, 1953.

Curtis Williams, 44, musician, singer (Penguins, "Earth Angel"), born Buffalo, NY, Dec 11, 1962.

DECEMBER 12 — TUESDAY
Day 346 — 19 Remaining

BONZA BOTTLER DAY™. Dec 12. To celebrate when the number of the day is the same as the number of the month. Bonza Bottler Day™ is an excuse to have a party at least once a month. For more information, see Jan 1. For info: Gail M. Berger, 14 Fernwood Dr, Taylors, SC 29687. Phone: (864) 609-9874. E-mail: gberger5@aol.com.

DAY OF OUR LADY OF GUADALUPE. Dec 12. The legend of Guadalupe tells how in December 1531, an Indian, Juan Diego, saw the Virgin Mother on a hill near Mexico City, who instructed him to go to the bishop and have him build a shrine to her on the site of the vision. After his request was initially rebuffed, the Virgin Mother appeared to Juan Diego three days later. She instructed him to pick roses growing on a stony and barren hillside nearby and take them to the bishop as proof. Although flowers do not normally bloom in December, Juan Diego found the roses and took them to the bishop. As he opened his mantle to drop the roses on the floor, an image of the Virgin Mary appeared among them. The bishop built the sanctuary as instructed. Our Lady of Guadalupe became the patroness of Mexico City and by 1746 was the patron saint of all New Spain and by 1910 of all Latin America.

FIRST BLACK SERVES IN US HOUSE OF REPRESENTATIVES: ANNIVERSARY. Dec 12, 1870. Joseph Hayne Rainey of Georgetown, SC, was sworn in as the first black to serve in the US House of Representatives. Rainey filled the seat of Benjamin Franklin Whittemore, which had been declared vacant by the House. He served until Mar 3, 1879.

FLAUBERT, GUSTAVE: BIRTH ANNIVERSARY. Dec 12, 1821. French author whose works include one of the greatest French novels, *Madame Bovary*, was born at Rouen. Flaubert died at Croisset, France, May 8, 1880.

GARRISON, WILLIAM LLOYD: BIRTH ANNIVERSARY. Dec 12, 1805. American antislavery leader, poet and journalist, was born at Newburyport, MA. Garrison died at New York, NY, May 24, 1879.

GINGERBREAD HOUSE DAY. Dec 12. One of the best activities of the Christmas season is the making of gingerbread houses. It's pure fun for all involved. Spend time with your family and create one today! For info: Allison Benson, 13116 Frog Hollow Ct, Oak Hill, VA 20171. Phone: (703) 471-5784. E-mail: Firebird 121212@aol.com.

JAY, JOHN: BIRTH ANNIVERSARY. Dec 12, 1745 (OS). American statesman, diplomat and first chief justice of the US Supreme Court (1789–95), coauthor (with Alexander Hamilton and James Madison) of the influential *Federalist* papers, was born at New York, NY. Jay died at Bedford, NY, May 17, 1829.

KENYA: JAMHURI DAY: ANNIVERSARY. Dec 12. Jamhuri Day (Independence Day) is Kenya's official National Day, commemorating proclamation of the republic and independence from Britain in 1963.

MEXICO: GUADALUPE DAY. Dec 12. One of Mexico's major celebrations. Honors the "Dark Virgin of Guadalupe," the republic's patron saint. Parties and pilgrimages, with special ceremonies at the Shrine of Our Lady of Guadalupe at Mexico City.

MOON PHASE: LAST QUARTER. Dec 12. Moon enters Last Quarter phase at 9:32 AM, EST.

PENNSYLVANIA RATIFIES CONSTITUTION: ANNIVERSARY. Dec 12, 1787. Pennsylvania became the second state to ratify the US Constitution, by a vote of 46 to 23, in 1787.

POINSETTIA DAY (JOEL ROBERTS POINSETT: DEATH ANNIVERSARY). Dec 12. A day to enjoy poinsettias and to honor Dr. Joel Roberts Poinsett, the American diplomat who introduced the Central American plant which is named for him into the US. Poinsett was born at Charleston, SC, Mar 2, 1799. He also served as a member of Congress and as secretary of war. He died near Statesburg, SC, Dec 12, 1851. The poinsettia has become a favorite Christmas season plant.

PUERTO RICO: LAS MAÑANITAS. Dec 12. Ponce, Puerto Rico. Procession at 5 AM honoring our patron saint, Virgen de la Guadalupe. Mass with music from a mariachi band; free breakfast afterward. Annually, on Dec 12. For info: Vangie Rivera, Director, Culture and Tourism Office, PO Box 331709, Ponce, PR 00733-1709. Phone: (787) 841-8044 or (787) 284-4141. Fax: (787) 259-1316. E-mail: turponce@coqui.net. Web: www.ponce web.org.

RUSSIA: CONSTITUTION DAY: ANNIVERSARY. Dec 12. National holiday commemorating the adoption of a new constitution in 1993.

SINATRA, FRANK: BIRTH ANNIVERSARY. Dec 12, 1915. Born at Hoboken, NJ, Frank Sinatra matured from a teen idol to the premier singer of American popular music. Known as the "Chairman of the Board" to his fans, he made more than 200 albums. His signature songs included "All the Way," "New York, New York" and "My Way." His film career included musicals (*On the Town* and *Pal Joey*) and two gritty films: *From Here to Eternity* (Oscar for Best Supporting Actor) and *The Man with the Golden Arm* (Oscar nomination). Died May 14, 1998, at Los Angeles, CA.

SUPREME COURT RULES FOR BUSH: ANNIVERSARY. Dec 12, 2000. The Supreme Court ruled by a vote of 5 to 4 that there could be no further counting of Florida's disputed presidential votes, ending deliberations over the 2000 presidential election. After five weeks of conflict over this pivotal vote count in Florida, Democratic candidate Al Gore conceded the election to George W. Bush. While Bush won the electoral vote to become the nation's 43rd president, Gore won the popular vote. Bush was only the fourth president in American history to be elected without winning the popular vote.

TURKMENISTAN: NEUTRALITY DAY. Dec 12. National holiday. Commemorates the UN's recognition of Turkmenistan's neutrality in 1995.

WATIE, STAND: 200th BIRTH ANNIVERSARY. Dec 12, 1806. Born at Rome, GA, and died there Sept 9, 1871. Cherokee chief who, by signing the treaty of New Echota, surrendered his people's land in Georgia, forcing relocation to Oklahoma. Though the three other signers were murdered, Watie escaped and went on to initiate the first volunteer Cherokee regiment for the Confederates in the Civil War. Promoted to brigadier general, he was active in destroying the property of other Native Americans who supported the Union.

BIRTHDAYS TODAY

Tracy Ann Austin, 44, former tennis player, born Rolling Hills Estates, CA, Dec 12, 1962.

Bob Barker, 83, TV personality, game-show host (Emmy for "The Price Is Right"), born Darrington, WA, Dec 12, 1923.

Mayim Bialik, 31, actress ("Blossom"), born San Diego, CA, Dec 12, 1975.

Jennifer Connelly, 36, actress (*Hulk,* Oscar for *A Beautiful Mind*), born Catskill Mountains, NY, Dec 12, 1970.

Sheila E, 47, singer, musician ("The Glamorous Life"), born Sheila Escoveda at San Francisco, CA, Dec 12, 1959.

Connie Francis, 68, singer ("Where the Boys Are"), born Constance Franconero at Newark, NJ, Dec 12, 1938.

Edward Irwin Koch, 82, former mayor of New York City, born New York, NY, Dec 12, 1924.

Robert Lindsay, 57, actor (*Me and My Girl* [Olivier, Tony, Theatre World and Drama Desk Awards]), born Derbyshire, England, Dec 12, 1949.

Robert Lee (Bob) Pettit, Jr, 74, Hall of Fame basketball player, born Baton Rouge, LA, Dec 12, 1932.

Cathy Rigby, 54, former Olympic gymnast, born Long Beach, CA, Dec 12, 1952.

Dionne Warwick, 65, singer ("I Say a Little Prayer for You," "This Girl's in Love with You"), born East Orange, NJ, Dec 12, 1941.

Tom Wilkinson, 58, actor (*In the Bedroom, The Full Monty*), born Leeds, West Yorkshire, England, Dec 12, 1948.

December **2006**	S	M	T	W	T	F	S
						1	2
	3	4	5	6	7	8	9
	10	11	12	13	14	15	16
	17	18	19	20	21	22	23
	24	25	26	27	28	29	30
	31						

DECEMBER 13 — WEDNESDAY
Day 347 — 18 Remaining

BROOKS, PHILLIPS: BIRTH ANNIVERSARY. Dec 13, 1835. American clergyman and composer born at Boston, MA. Best remembered for his lyrics for the Christmas carol "O Little Town of Bethlehem." Brooks died at Boston, Jan 23, 1893.

HEINE, HEINRICH: BIRTH ANNIVERSARY. Dec 13, 1797. German poet and critic, born at Dusseldorf. Died at Paris, France, Feb 17, 1856.

LINCOLN, MARY TODD: BIRTH ANNIVERSARY. Dec 13, 1818. Wife of Abraham Lincoln, 16th president of the US, born at Lexington, KY. Died at Springfield, IL, July 16, 1882.

MALTA: REPUBLIC DAY. Dec 13. National holiday. Malta became a republic in 1974.

MOORE, ARCHIE: BIRTH ANNIVERSARY. Dec 13, 1913. Born Archibald Lee Wright at Benoit, MS. One of the most colorful fighters ever, Moore boxed from the mid-1930s to 1963, holding the light-heavyweight title for a record nine years. For much of his career, he fought an average of once a month. Moore let an aura of celebrity surround him: he lied about his age, ate an unusual diet, married five times and spoke out on a variety of political and social issues. Died at San Diego, CA, Dec 9, 1998.

NEW ZEALAND FIRST SIGHTED BY EUROPEANS: ANNIVERSARY. Dec 13, 1642. Captain Abel Tasman of the Dutch East India Company first sighted New Zealand but was kept from landing by Maori warriors. In 1769 Captain James Cook landed and claimed formal possession for Great Britain.

NORTH AND SOUTH KOREA END WAR: 15th ANNIVERSARY. Dec 13, 1991. North and South Korea signed a treaty of reconciliation and nonaggression, formally ending the Korean War—38 years after fighting ceased in 1953. This agreement was not hailed as a peace treaty, and the armistice that was signed July 27, 1953, between the UN and North Korea, was to remain in effect until it could be transformed into a formal peace.

SWEDEN: SANTA LUCIA DAY. Dec 13. Nationwide celebration of festival of light, honoring St. Lucia. Many hotels have their own Lucia, a young girl attired in a long, flowing white gown, who serves guests coffee and lussekatter (saffron buns) in the early morning.

BIRTHDAYS TODAY

Steve Buscemi, 48, actor (*Ghost World, Fargo, Reservoir Dogs*), born Brooklyn, NY, Dec 13, 1958.

John Davidson, 65, singer, actor (*Edward Scissorhands,* "Hollywood Squares"), born Pittsburgh, PA, Dec 13, 1941.

Sergei Fedorov, 37, hockey player, born Pskov, Russia, Dec 13, 1969.

Jamie Foxx, 39, actor (Oscar for *Ray,* "The Jamie Foxx Show"), born Dallas, TX, Dec 13, 1967.

Wendie Malick, 56, actress ("Just Shoot Me"), born Buffalo, NY, Dec 13, 1950.

Ted Nugent, 57, singer ("Cat Scratch Fever"), born Detroit, MI, Dec 13, 1949.

Christopher Plummer, 77, actor (Emmy for "The Moneychangers"; *The Sound of Music, Dolores Claiborne*), born Toronto, ON, Canada, Dec 13, 1929.

Robert Prosky, 76, actor ("Hill Street Blues," "Veronica's Closet"), born Philadelphia, PA, Dec 13, 1930.

Dick Van Dyke, 81, comedian, actor (*Mary Poppins,* "The Dick Van Dyke Show," "Diagnosis Murder"), born West Plains, MO, Dec 13, 1925.

Tom Vilsack, 56, Governor of Iowa (D), born Pittsburgh, PA, Dec 13, 1950.

DECEMBER 14 — THURSDAY

Day 348 — 17 Remaining

ALABAMA: ADMISSION DAY: ANNIVERSARY. Dec 14. Became 22nd state in 1819.

DOOLITTLE, JAMES HAROLD: BIRTH ANNIVERSARY. Dec 14, 1896. American aviator and WWII hero General James Doolittle was born at Alameda, CA. A lieutenant general in the US Army Air Force, he was the first person to fly across North America in less than a day. On Apr 18, 1942, Doolittle led a squadron of 16 B-25 bombers, launched from aircraft carriers, on the first US aerial raid on Japan of WWII. He was awarded the Congressional Medal of Honor for this accomplishment. Doolittle also headed the Eighth Air Force during the Normandy invasion. He died Sept 27, 1993, at Pebble Beach, CA.

NOSTRADAMUS: BIRTH ANNIVERSARY. Dec 14, 1503. French physician, best remembered for his astrological predictions (written in rhymed quatrains), was born Michel de Notredame, at St. Rémy, Provence, France. Many believed that his book of prophecies actually foretold the future. Nostradamus died at Salon, France, July 2, 1566.

REMICK, LEE: BIRTH ANNIVERSARY. Dec 14, 1935. American actress Lee Remick was born at Quincy, MA. Her films include *A Face in the Crowd* (1957), *Anatomy of a Murder* (1959) and *Days of Wine and Roses* (1963). She died July 2, 1991, at Los Angeles, CA.

SMITH, MARGARET CHASE: BIRTH ANNIVERSARY. Dec 14, 1897. American politician Margaret Madeline Chase Smith was born at Skowhegan, ME. As the first woman to be elected to both houses of Congress (1941 to the House and 1949 to the Senate), she was also one of seven Republican senators to issue a "declaration of conscience" to denounce Senator Joseph R. McCarthy's communist witch hunt. She died May 29, 1995, at Skowhegan, ME.

SOUTH POLE DISCOVERY: 95th ANNIVERSARY. Dec 14, 1911. The elusive object of many expeditions dating from the seventh century, the South Pole was located and visited by Roald Amundsen with four companions and 52 sled dogs. All five men and 12 of the dogs returned to base camp safely. Next to visit the South Pole, Jan 17, 1912, was a party of five led by Captain Robert F. Scott, all of whom perished during the return trip. A search party found their frozen bodies 11 months later. See also: "Amundsen, Roald: Birth Anniversary" (July 16).

THOMASVILLE'S VICTORIAN CHRISTMAS. Dec 14–15. Thomasville, GA. Downtown Thomasville relives Christmas past as it celebrates the Victorian era of the late 1800s. Costumed strollers and carolers, horse-drawn carriages, bell-ringers and colorful characters from the past fill the streets of downtown. Victorian-clad merchants welcome shoppers with hot cider and confections and street vendors offer Christmas delicacies. Free—wonderful family event. Est attendance: 30,000. For info: Thomasville Victorian Christmas, Thomasville Main Street, PO Box 1540, Thomasville, GA 31799. Phone: (229) 227-3310. E-mail: mainstrt@rose.net. Web: www.downtownthomasville .com.

BIRTHDAYS TODAY

Craig Biggio, 41, baseball player, born Smithtown, NY, Dec 14, 1965.

Jane Birkin, 60, actress (*Blow-Up, Death on the Nile, Evil Under the Sun*), born London, England, Dec 14, 1946.

Leonardo Boff, 68, Catholic theologian, born Concordia, Brazil, Dec 14, 1938.

William Joseph (Bill) Buckner, 57, former baseball player, born Vallejo, CA, Dec 14, 1949.

Patty Duke, 60, actress (Oscar for *The Miracle Worker*; Emmy for *My Sweet Charlie*), born New York, NY, Dec 14, 1946.

Don Hewitt, 84, TV news producer ("60 Minutes"), born New York, NY, Dec 14, 1922.

Michael Owen, 27, soccer player, born Chester, England, Dec 14, 1979.

Dee Wallace Stone, 58, actress (*10, E.T. The Extra-Terrestrial*), born Kansas City, MO, Dec 14, 1948.

DECEMBER 15 — FRIDAY

Day 349 — 16 Remaining

BATTLE OF SAN PIETRO: ANNIVERSARY. Dec 15, 1943. A German panzer battalion inflicted heavy casualties on American forces trying to take the 700-year-old Italian village of San Pietro, before withdrawing from the town. San Pietro was reduced almost entirely to rubble. The American movie director John Huston, serving as an Army lieutenant, filmed the battle for the military. So graphic was the film that it was described as anti-war by the military brass at the War Department. The film was cut from five to three reels before censors allowed it to be released in 1944. It was later re-edited for the television series "The Big Picture."

BILL OF RIGHTS: ANNIVERSARY. Dec 15, 1791. The first 10 amendments to the US Constitution, known as the Bill of Rights, became effective following ratification by Virginia. The anniversary of ratification and of effect is observed as Bill of Rights Day.

★**BILL OF RIGHTS DAY.** Dec 15. Presidential Proclamation. Has been proclaimed each year since 1962, but was omitted in 1967 and 1968. (Issued in 1941 and 1946 at Congressional request and in 1947 without request.) Since 1968 has been included in Human Rights Day and Week Proclamation.

CAT HERDERS DAY. Dec 15. If you can say that your job—or even your life—is like trying to herd cats, then this day is for you—with our sympathy. (© 2003 by WH.) For info: Thomas & Ruth Roy, Wellcat Holidays, 2418 Long Ln, Lebanon, PA 17046. Phone: (717) 279-0184. E-mail: wellcat@comcast.net. Web: www .wellcat.com.

CURAÇAO: KINGDOM DAY AND ANTILLEAN FLAG DAY. Dec 15. This day commemorates the Charter of Kingdom, signed in 1954 at the Knight's Hall at The Hague, granting the Netherlands Antilles complete autonomy. The Antillean flag was hoisted for the first time on this day in 1959.

"DAVY CROCKETT" TV PREMIERE: ANNIVERSARY. Dec 15, 1954. This show, a series of five segments, can be considered TV's first miniseries. Shown on Walt Disney's "Disneyland" show, it starred Fess Parker as American western hero Davy Crockett and was immensely popular. The show spawned Crockett paraphernalia, including the famous coonskin cap (even after we found out that Crockett never wore a coonskin cap).

EIFFEL, ALEXANDRE GUSTAVE: BIRTH ANNIVERSARY. Dec 15, 1832. Eiffel, the French engineer who designed the 1,000-ft-high, million-dollar, open-lattice wrought-iron Eiffel Tower, and who participated in designing the Statue of Liberty, was born at Dijon, France. The Eiffel Tower, weighing more than 7,000 tons, was built for the Paris International Exposition of 1889. Eiffel died at Paris, France, Dec 23, 1923.

GAL, UZI: BIRTH ANNIVERSARY. Dec 15, 1923. Inventor of the 9-millimeter submachine gun that bears his name, Uziel Gal was born in Germany but spent most of his life in Israel. A mechanical engineer, he fought in the 1948 Arab-Israeli war, to which he brought a homemade submachine gun. He went on to design the Uzi, and by 1956 it was being manufactured by Israeli Military Industries, whose management named it for him against his own wishes. The gun itself revolutionized automatic weaponry, and is currently found in the arsenals of armies, secret-service organizations, bodyguards, etc, worldwide. Gal died at Philadelphia, PA, on Sept 2, 2002.

GONE WITH THE WIND FILM PREMIERE: ANNIVERSARY. Dec 15, 1939. One of the 20th century's biggest film blockbusters premiered on this date in Atlanta, GA. Based on Margaret Mitchell's bestselling and Pulitzer Prize–winning novel of Civil War passions, the film starred Vivian Leigh and Clark Gable and was produced by the dynamic David O. Selznick. It won an unprecedented eight Academy Awards, including best picture. Hattie McDaniel won a best supporting actress Oscar—the first time an African-American actor had won or been nominated. No film would touch its Oscar achievement or monetary grosses for decades. At the chilly Atlanta premiere, more than 300,000 people lined the streets to catch sight of the film's stars arriving at the Loew's Grand Theater. See also "Gone with the Wind Published: Anniversary" (May 19).

HALCYON DAYS. Dec 15-29. Traditionally, the seven days before and the seven days after the winter solstice. To the ancients a time when fabled bird (called the halcyon—pronounced hal-cee-on) calmed the wind and waves—a time of calm and tranquility.

INTERNATIONAL LANGUAGE WEEK. Dec 15-21. To disseminate information about mankind's quest for an international language to solve the communication problem of humans, and to supply information about the international language, Esperanto. Esperanto was created in 1887 by Dr. L.L. Zamenhof as a solution to the world's language problem. For complete info, send $5 to cover expense of printing, handling and postage. Annually, Dec 15-21. For info: Dr. Stanley Drake, Pres Emeritus, Intl Society of Friendship & Good Will, 8592 Roswell Rd, Ste 251, Atlanta, GA 30068. Phone: (678) 795-1362. E-mail: sjdrake@bellsouth.net. Web: www.friendshipandgoodwill.org.

MILITARY DICTATORSHIP ENDED IN CHILE: ANNIVERSARY. Dec 15, 1989. In an election on this date, Patricio Aylwin defeated General Augusto Pinochet's former finance minister, Hernan Buchi, bringing the military dictatorship of Pinochet to an end. Fourteen months previously, Pinochet suffered defeat in a national plebiscite on eight more years of his rule. This defeat prompted democratic elections and crippled the Pinochet regime. Pinochet came to power when the military overthrew a democratically elected government and killed Marxist president Salvador Allende in a 1973 coup. Patricio Aylwin avoided a two-candidate runoff by achieving 55.2 percent of the vote. He was inaugurated on Mar 11, 1990.

PUERTO RICO: NAVIDADES. Dec 15-Jan 6. Traditional Christmas season begins mid-December and ends on Three Kings Day. Elaborate nativity scenes, carolers, special Christmas foods and trees from Canada and US. Gifts on Christmas Day and on Three Kings Day.

SITTING BULL: DEATH ANNIVERSARY. Dec 15, 1890. Famous Sioux Indian leader, medicine man and warrior of the Hunkpapa Teton band. Known also by his native name, Tatanka-yatanka, Sitting Bull was born on the Grand River, SD. He first accompanied his father on the warpath at the age of 14 against the Crow and thereafter rapidly gained influence within his tribe. In 1866 he led a raid on Fort Buford. His steadfast refusal to go to a reservation led General Phillip Sheridan to initiate a campaign against him, which led to the massacre of Lieutenant Colonel George Custer's men at the Little Bighorn, after which Sitting Bull fled to Canada, remaining there until 1881. Although many in his tribe surrendered on their return, Sitting Bull remained hostile until his death in a skirmish with the US soldiers along the Grand River.

SPACE MILESTONE: VEGA 1 (USSR). Dec 15, 1984. Craft launched this date to rendezvous with Halley's Comet in March

1986. *Vega 2*, launched Dec 21, 1984, was part of same mission, which, in cooperation with the US, carried US-built "comet-dust" detection equipment.

UNDERDOG DAY. Dec 15. To salute, before the year's end, all of the underdogs and unsung heroes—the Number Two people who contribute so much to the Number One people we read about. (Sherlock Holmes's Dr. Watson and Robinson Crusoe's Friday are examples.) Observed annually on the third Friday in December since its founding in 1976 by the late Peter Moeller, THE Chief Underdog. For info: A.C. Vierow, Underdogs Intl, Box 71, Clio, MI 48420-0071.

US FORCES LAND IN MINDORO, PHILIPPINES: ANNIVERSARY. Dec 15, 1944. After the usual barrage from naval guns, the US 24th Division landed on Mindoro, the largest of the islands immediately south of Luzon (the most important island of the Philippines). American soldiers easily advanced eight miles inland, took the perimeter of their beachhead and started construction of an airfield. Japanese kamikaze counterattacks, however, sank two motor torpedo boats and damaged the escort carrier *Marcus Island*, two destroyers and a third motor torpedo boat, making Mindoro a more costly conquest than the island of Leyte had been.

BIRTHDAYS TODAY

Kathleen Babineaux Blanco, 64, Governor of Louisiana (D), born Iberia Parish, AL, Dec 15, 1942.
Adam Brody, 27, actor ("The O.C.," *Growing Up Brady*), born San Diego, CA, Dec 15, 1979.
Nicholas (Nick) Buoniconti, 66, former football player, born Springfield, MA, Dec 15, 1940.
Dave Clark, 64, musician (leader of the Dave Clark Five, "I Like It Like That"), born London, England, Dec 15, 1942.
Tim Conway, 73, comedian, actor ("McHale's Navy," "The Carol Burnett Show"), born Willoughby, OH, Dec 15, 1933.
Don Johnson, 57, actor ("Miami Vice," "Nash Bridges"), born Flatt Creek, MO, Dec 15, 1949.
Edna O'Brien, 75, author (*Country Girls Trilogy, Time and Tide*), born Tuamgraney, Ireland, Dec 15, 1931.
Helen Slater, 43, actress (*City Slickers, The Secret of My Success*), born Long Island, NY, Dec 15, 1963.
Alexandra Stevenson, 26, tennis player, born San Diego, CA, Dec 15, 1980.
Garrett Wang, 38, actor ("Star Trek: Voyager"), born Riverside, CA, Dec 15, 1968.
Mark Warner, 52, Governor of Virginia (D), born Indianapolis, IN, Dec 15, 1954.

DECEMBER 16 — SATURDAY
Day 350 — 15 Remaining

AUSTEN, JANE: BIRTH ANNIVERSARY. Dec 16, 1775. English novelist (*Pride and Prejudice, Sense and Sensibility*), born at Steventon, Hampshire, England. Died July 18, 1817, at Winchester, England.

BAHRAIN: INDEPENDENCE DAY. Dec 16. National holiday. Commemorates independence from British protection in 1971.

BANGLADESH: VICTORY DAY. Dec 16. National holiday. Commemorates victory over Pakistan in 1971. The former East Pakistan became Bangladesh.

	S	M	T	W	T	F	S
December 2006						1	2
	3	4	5	6	7	8	9
	10	11	12	13	14	15	16
	17	18	19	20	21	22	23
	24	25	26	27	28	29	30
	31						

BARBIE AND BARNEY BACKLASH DAY. Dec 16. If we have to explain this to you, you don't have kids. It's one day each year when Mom and Dad can tell the kids that Barbie and Barney don't exist. [©2003 by WH.] For info: Thomas & Ruth Roy, Wellcat Holidays, 2418 Long Ln, Lebanon, PA 17046. Phone: (717) 279-0184. E-mail: info@wellcat.com. Web: www.wellcat.com.

BATTLE OF NASHVILLE: ANNIVERSARY. Dec 16, 1864. On the second day of battle at Nashville, Union troops defeated Confederate forces under General John B. Hood, essentially knocking the Confederate Army of Tennessee out of the war.

BATTLE OF THE BULGE: ANNIVERSARY. Dec 16, 1944. A German offensive was launched in the Belgian Ardennes Forest, where Hitler had managed to concentrate 250,000 men. The Nazi commanders, hoping to minimize any aerial counterattack by the Allies, chose a time when foggy, rainy weather prevailed and the initial attack by eight armored divisions along a 75-mile front took the Allies by surprise, the 5th Panzer Army penetrating to within 20 miles of crossings on the Meuse River. US troops were able to hold fast at bottlenecks in the Ardennes, but by the end of December the German push had penetrated 65 miles into the Allied lines (though their line had narrowed from the initial 75 miles to 20 miles). By that time the Allies began to respond and the Germans were stopped by Montgomery on the Meuse and by Patton at Bastogne. The weather then cleared and Allied aircraft began to bomb the German forces and supply lines by Dec 26. The Allies reestablished their original line by Jan 21, 1945.

BEETHOVEN, LUDWIG VAN: BIRTH ANNIVERSARY. Dec 16, 1770. Regarded by many as the greatest orchestral composer of all time, Ludwig van Beethoven was born at Bonn, Germany. Impairment of his hearing began before he was 30, but even total deafness did not halt his composing and conducting. His last appearance on the concert stage was to conduct the premiere of his *Ninth Symphony*, at Vienna, May 7, 1824. He was unable to hear either the orchestra or the applause. Often in love, he never married. Of a stormy temperament, he is said to have died during a violent thunderstorm Mar 26, 1827, at Vienna.

BOSTON TEA PARTY: ANNIVERSARY. Dec 16, 1773. Anniversary of Boston patriots' boarding of British vessel at anchor at Boston Harbor. Contents of nearly 350 chests of tea were dumped into the harbor.

CALABRIA EARTHQUAKE: ANNIVERSARY. Dec 16, 1857. Calabria—an especially quake-prone region near Naples, Italy—experienced a devastating earthquake of great magnitude that left more than 10,000 people dead and entire villages destroyed. Between 1783 (the last big quake) and 1857, about 111,000 people lost their lives in the unstable region.

CHANUKAH. Dec 16–23. Feast of Lights or Feast of Dedication. Festival lasting eight days commemorates victory of Maccabees over Syrians (165 BC) and rededication of Temple of Jerusalem. Begins on Hebrew calendar date Kislev 25, 5767. Began at sundown on Dec 15.

A COLONIAL CHRISTMAS. Dec 16–31. Jamestown Settlement, Williamsburg, VA, and Yorktown Victory Center, Yorktown, VA. Experience 17th- and 18th-century holiday traditions. At Jamestown Settlement, a film and special guided tours compare and contrast English Christmas customs of the period with how the season may have been observed in the difficult early years of the Jamestown colony. At the Yorktown Victory Center, hear accounts of Christmas and winter in military encampments during the American Revolution, and glimpse holiday preparations on a 1780s Virginia farm. For info: Jamestown-Yorktown Foundation, PO Box 1607, Williamsburg, VA 23187. Phone: (757) 253-4838 or toll-free (888) 593-4682. Fax: (757) 253-5299. Web: www.historyisfun.org.

COWARD, NOËL: BIRTH ANNIVERSARY. Dec 16, 1899. English playwright, actor and wit known for his sophisticated comedies *Private Lives* (1930), *Design for Living* (1933), *Blithe Spirit* (1941) and others—many of which were later filmed. He is also known for such songs as "Mad Dogs and Englishmen." He advised actors: "Learn the lines and don't bump into the furniture." Born at Teddington, England, Coward died at St. Mary, Jamaica, on Mar 26, 1973.

"DRAGNET" TV PREMIERE: 55th ANNIVERSARY. Dec 16, 1951. This famous crime show stressed authenticity, and episodes were supposedly based on real cases. It starred Jack Webb as stoic and determined Sergeant Joe Friday, a man whose life was his investigative police work and who was recognized by his recurring line, "Just the facts, ma'am." Friday had many partners: Barton Yarborough played Sergeant Ben Romero for three episodes; for the rest of the season Barney Phillips played Sergeant Ed Jacobs and Ben Alexander played his comedic sidekick, Officer Frank Smith. A new version appeared in 1967 with Webb and his new partner, Officer Bill Gannon (Harry Morgan). "Dragnet" is also known for its theme music and its narrative epilogue describing the fate of the bad guys.

MEAD, MARGARET: BIRTH ANNIVERSARY. Dec 16, 1901. American anthropologist and author, especially known for her studies of peoples of the southwest Pacific area, and for her forthright manner in speaking and writing. Born at Philadelphia, PA, Mead died at New York, NY, Nov 15, 1978.

MEXICO: POSADAS. Dec 16–24. A nine-day annual celebration throughout Mexico. Processions of "pilgrims" knock at doors asking for posada (shelter), commemorating the search by Joseph and Mary for a shelter in which the infant Jesus might be born. Pilgrims are invited inside, and fun and merrymaking ensue with blindfolded guests trying to break a "piñata" (papier-mâché decorated earthenware utensil filled with gifts and goodies) suspended from the ceiling. Once the piñata is broken, the gifts are distributed and celebration continues.

NAIA FOOTBALL NATIONAL CHAMPIONSHIP GAME. Dec 16. Hardin County, TN. 16-team field competes, ending with the final two teams vying for the national championship. 51st annual game. For info: Natl Assn of Intercollegiate Athletics, 23500 W 105th St, PO Box 1325, Olathe, KS 66051-1325. Phone: (913) 791-0044. Fax: (913) 791-9555. E-mail: rwiebe@naia.org. Web: www.naia.org.

NEW WORLD SYMPHONY PREMIERE: ANNIVERSARY. Dec 16, 1893. Anton Dvořák's *New World Symphony* premiered at the newly erected Carnegie Hall with the New York Philharmonic playing. The composer attended and enjoyed enthusiastic applause from the audience. The symphony contains snatches from black spirituals and American folk music. Dvořák, a Bohemian, had been in the US only a year when he composed it as a greeting to his friends in Europe.

"ONE DAY AT A TIME" TV PREMIERE: ANNIVERSARY. Dec 16, 1975. This sitcom about a divorced mother raising two girls in Indianapolis starred Bonnie Franklin as Ann Romano, Mackenzie Phillips and Valerie Bertinelli as daughters Julie and Barbara Cooper. Other regulars included: Pat Harrington, Jr, as tool-belt-wearing maintenance man Dwayne Schneider; Richard Masur as David Kane, Ann's boyfriend; and Nanette Fabray as Ann's mother. All three female leads got married and Ann opened her own ad agency before the series ended in 1984.

PHILIPPINES: PHILIPPINE CHRISTMAS OBSERVANCE. Dec 16–Jan 6. Philippine Islands. Said to be world's longest Christmas celebration.

PHILIPPINES: SIMBANG GABI. Dec 16–25. Nationwide. A nine-day novena of predawn masses, also called "Misa de Gallo." One of the traditional Filipino celebrations of the holiday season.

SANTAYANA, GEORGE: BIRTH ANNIVERSARY. Dec 16, 1863. Philosopher and author born at Madrid, Spain. At the age of nine he emigrated to the US where he attended and later taught at Harvard University. In 1912 he returned to Europe and traveled extensively. It was Santayana who said, "Those who cannot remember the past are condemned to repeat it." He died at Rome, Italy, Sept 26, 1952.

SOUTH AFRICA: RECONCILIATION DAY. Dec 16. National holiday. Celebrates the spirit of reconciliation, national unity and peace among all citizens.

UNITED NATIONS REVOKES RESOLUTION ON ZIONISM: 15th ANNIVERSARY. Dec 16, 1991. The United Nations voted 111 to 25 to revoke Resolution 3379, which equated Zionism with racism. Resolution 3379 was approved Nov 10, 1975, with 72 countries voting in favor, 35 against and 32 abstentions. The largest block of changed votes came from the former Soviet Union and Eastern Europe.

WINTERFEST BOAT PARADE. Dec 16. More than 100 decorated yachts sail up Fort Lauderdale's Intracoastal Waterway starting at Port Everglades. Winterfest Black Tie Ball is Dec 9, Intracoastal Decorating is Dec 13 and Celebrity Reception is Dec 15. Est attendance: 850,000. For info: Winterfest, 512 NE 3rd Ave, Fort Lauderdale, FL 33301. Phone: (954) 767-0686. Fax: (954) 767-0665. E-mail: boats@winterfestparade.com. Web: www.winterfestparade.com.

BIRTHDAYS TODAY

Bruce N. Ames, 78, biochemist, cancer researcher, born New York, NY, Dec 16, 1928.

Steven Bochco, 63, TV writer, producer ("Hill Street Blues," "NYPD Blue"), born New York, NY, Dec 16, 1943.

Benjamin Bratt, 43, actor ("Law & Order"), born San Francisco, CA, Dec 16, 1963.

Donald Carcieri, 64, Governor of Rhode Island (R), born East Greenwich, RI, Dec 16, 1942.

Arthur Charles Clarke, 89, author (*2001: A Space Odyssey, Islands in the Sky*), born Minehead, England, Dec 16, 1917.

Alison La Placa, 47, actress ("The John Laroquette Show"), born Lincolnshire, IL, Dec 16, 1959.

William ("The Refrigerator") Perry, 44, former football player, born Aiken, SC, Dec 16, 1962.

Clifford (Cliff) Ralph Robinson, 40, basketball player, born Buffalo, NY, Dec 16, 1966.

Lesley Stahl, 65, journalist ("60 Minutes," former White House correspondent), born Lynn, MA, Dec 16, 1941.

Jon Tenney, 45, actor ("Brooklyn South"), born Princeton, NJ, Dec 16, 1961.

Liv Johanne Ullmann, 67, actress (*The Immigrants, Scenes from a Marriage*), born Tokyo, Japan, Dec 16, 1939.

	S	M	T	W	T	F	S
December 2006						1	2
	3	4	5	6	7	8	9
	10	11	12	13	14	15	16
	17	18	19	20	21	22	23
	24	25	26	27	28	29	30
	31						

DECEMBER 17 — SUNDAY
Day 351 — 14 Remaining

AZTEC CALENDAR STONE DISCOVERY: ANNIVERSARY. Dec 17, 1790. One of the wonders of the western hemisphere—the Aztec Calendar or Solar Stone—was found beneath the ground by workmen repairing Mexico City's Central Plaza. The centuries-old, intricately carved stone, 11 ft, 8 inches in diameter and weighing nearly 25 tons, proved to be a highly developed calendar monument to the sun. Believed to have been carved in the year 1479, this extraordinary time-counting basalt tablet originally stood in the Great Temple of the Aztecs. Buried along with other Aztec idols, soon after the Spanish conquest in 1521, it remained hidden until 1790. Its 52-year cycle had regulated many Aztec ceremonies, including grisly human sacrifices to save the world from destruction by the gods.

BOLÍVAR, SIMÓN: DEATH ANNIVERSARY. Dec 17, 1830. Commemorated in Venezuela and other Latin American countries. Bolívar, called "The Liberator," was born July 24, 1783, at Caracas, Venezuela, and died Dec 17, 1830, at Santa Marta, Colombia.

CLEAN AIR ACT PASSED BY CONGRESS: ANNIVERSARY. Dec 17, 1967. A sweeping set of laws passed to protect the nation from air pollution. This was the first legislation to place pollution controls on the automobile industry.

COMMUNITY CAROL SING. Dec 17. Mystic, CT. Lift up your voice in song to celebrate the season. Museum admission is free when you bring a canned good to be donated to charity. A brass quartet and the Mystic Seaport carolers lead an afternoon of joyous musical cheer. Est attendance: 1,000. For info: Mystic Seaport, 75 Greenmanville Ave, Box 6000, Mystic, CT 06355. Phone: (860) 572-5315 or (888) 973-2767. Web: www.mysticseaport.org.

FIRST FLIGHT ANNIVERSARY CELEBRATION. Dec 17. Kill Devil Hills, NC. Each year since 1928, on the anniversary of the Wright brothers' first successful heavier-than-air flight at Kitty Hawk, NC, Dec 17, 1903, a celebration has been held at the Wright Brothers National Memorial, with wreaths, flyover and other observances—regardless of weather.

FLOYD, WILLIAM: BIRTH ANNIVERSARY. Dec 17, 1734. Signer of the Declaration of Independence, member of Congress, born at Brookhaven, Long Island. Died at Westernville, NY, Aug 4, 1821.

HENRY, JOSEPH: BIRTH ANNIVERSARY. Dec 17, 1797. Scientist Joseph Henry was born at Albany, NY. One of his great discoveries was the principle of self-induction; the unit used in the measure of electrical inductance was named "the henry" in his honor. In 1831 Henry constructed the first model of an electric telegraph with an audible signal. This formed the basis of nearly all later work on commercial wire telegraphy. In 1832 Henry was named professor of natural philosophy at the College of New Jersey, now Princeton University. Henry was involved in the planning of the Smithsonian Institution and became its first secretary in 1846. President Lincoln named Henry as one of the original 50 scientists to make up the National Academy of Sciences in 1863. He served as that organization's president from 1868 until his death May 13, 1878, at Washington, DC.

KING, W.L. MACKENZIE: BIRTH ANNIVERSARY. Dec 17, 1874. Former Canadian prime minister, born at Berlin, Ontario. Served 21 years, the longest term of any prime minister in the English-speaking world. Died at Kingsmere, July 22, 1950.

LIBBY, WILLARD FRANK: BIRTH ANNIVERSARY. Dec 17, 1908. American educator, chemist, atomic scientist and Nobel Prize winner was born at Grand Valley, CO. He was the inventor of the carbon-14 "atomic clock" method for dating ancient and prehistoric plant and animal remains and minerals. Died at Los Angeles, CA, Sept 8, 1980.

SAMPSON, DEBORAH: BIRTH ANNIVERSARY. Dec 17, 1760. Born at Plympton, MA, Deborah Sampson spent her childhood as an indentured servant. In 1782, wishing to participate in the Revolutionary War, she disguised herself as a man and enlisted in the Continental Army's 4th Massachusetts Regiment under the name Robert Shurtleff. Her identity was unmasked and she was dismissed from the army in 1783. In 1802 Sampson became perhaps the first woman to lecture professionally in the US when she began giving public speeches on her experiences. Deborah Sampson died Apr 29, 1827, at Sharon, MA. Full military pension was provided for her heirs by an act of Congress in 1838.

SATURNALIA. Dec 17–23. Ancient Roman festival honoring Saturnus, the god of agriculture. It was a time of merriment at the end of harvesting and wine-making. Presents were exchanged, sacrifices offered, and masters served their slaves. Approximates the winter solstice. Some say that the date for the observance of the nativity of Jesus was selected by the early Christian church leaders to fall on Dec 25 partly to counteract the popular but disapproved-of pre-Christian Roman festival of Saturnalia.

"THE SIMPSONS" TV PREMIERE: ANNIVERSARY. Dec 17, 1989. TV's hottest animated family, "The Simpsons," premiered as a half-hour weekly sitcom. The originator of Homer, Marge, Bart, Lisa and Maggie is cartoonist Matt Groening. The show's 300th episode, "Barting Over," aired Feb 16, 2003.

WHITTIER, JOHN GREENLEAF: BIRTH ANNIVERSARY. Dec 17, 1807. Poet and abolitionist, born at Haverhill, Essex County, MA. Whittier's books of poetry include *Legends of New England* and *Snowbound*. Died at Hampton Falls, NH, Sept 7, 1892.

★**WRIGHT BROTHERS DAY.** Dec 17. Presidential Proclamation always issued for Dec 17 since 1963 (PL88–209 of Dec 17, 1963). Issued twice earlier at Congressional request in 1959 and 1961.

WRIGHT BROTHERS FIRST POWERED FLIGHT: ANNIVERSARY. Dec 17, 1903. Orville and Wilbur Wright, brothers, bicycle shop operators, inventors and aviation pioneers, after three years of experimentation with kites and gliders, achieved the first documented successful powered and controlled flights of an airplane. The flights, near Kitty Hawk, NC, piloted first by Orville then by Wilbur Wright, were sustained for less than one minute but represented man's first powered airplane flight and the beginning of a new form of transportation. Orville Wright was born at Dayton, OH, Aug 19, 1871, and died there Jan 30, 1948. Wilbur Wright was born at Millville, IN, Apr 16, 1867, and died at Dayton, OH, May 30, 1912.

BIRTHDAYS TODAY

Christopher Cazenove, 61, actor (*Zulu Dawn, Eye of the Needle*), born Winchester, England, Dec 17, 1945.

Bob Guccione, 76, publisher, born Brooklyn, NY, Dec 17, 1930.

Bernard Hill, 62, actor (*Gandhi, Shirley Valentine*), born Manchester, England, Dec 17, 1944.

Ernie Hudson, 61, actor (*Ghostbusters, Ghostbusters II, The Hand That Rocks the Cradle*), born Benton Harbor, MI, Dec 17, 1945.

Eugene Levy, 60, comedian, writer, actor (*American Pie, Best in Show*, "Second City TV"), born Hamilton, ON, Canada, Dec 17, 1946.

Bill Pullman, 52, actor (*Independence Day, While You Were Sleeping*), born Delphi, NY, Dec 17, 1954.

William Safire, 77, author, journalist (*Coming to Terms, Words of Wisdom*), born New York, NY, Dec 17, 1929.

Tommy Steele, 70, actor (*The Happiest Millionaire, Half a Sixpence*), born London, England, Dec 17, 1936.

Sean Patrick Thomas, 36, actor (*Save the Last Dance*, "The District"), born Wilmington, DE, Dec 17, 1970.

DECEMBER 18 — MONDAY
Day 352 — 13 Remaining

BELGIUM: NUTS FAIR. Dec 18. Bastogne. Traditional cultural observance. Annually, the third Monday in December.

BRANDT, WILLY: BIRTH ANNIVERSARY. Dec 18, 1913. Former West German chancellor Willy Brandt was born Herbert Ernst Karl Frahm at Lubeck, Germany. An anti-Nazi exile during WWII, he won the Nobel Peace Prize in 1971 for seeking better East-West relations. He died Oct 8, 1992, at Unkel, Germany.

CAPITOL REEF NATIONAL PARK ESTABLISHED: 35th ANNIVERSARY. Dec 18, 1971. Area of outstanding geological features, colorful canyons, prehistoric Fremont petroglyphs and Mormon historic fruit orchards and buildings in south central Utah, originally proclaimed a national monument Aug 2, 1937, was established as a national park. For further park info: Capitol Reef Natl Park, Box 15, Torrey, UT 84775. E-mail: care-interpretation@nps.gov. Web: www.nps.gov/care.

COBB, TYRUS RAYMOND "TY": BIRTH ANNIVERSARY. Dec 18, 1886. Famed American baseball player born at Narrows, GA. Died at Atlanta, GA, July 17, 1961. Lifetime batting average of .367 compiled over 24 years during which he played in more than 3,000 games. Cobb was among the first five players inducted into the National Baseball Hall of Fame in 1936.

DAVIS, BENJAMIN O., JR: BIRTH ANNIVERSARY. Dec 18, 1912. The WWII hero was born at Washington, DC, to the Army's first black general. Davis had a distinguished career serving the US: he was the first African American to graduate from West Point in the 20th century; he led the first all-black air unit, the 99th Pursuit Squadron (the Tuskegee Airmen), in WWII; he helped plan the integration of the US Air Force in 1948–49 and he was the Air Force's first black general (1954). He died at Washington, DC, on July 4, 2002. See also "Tuskegee Airmen Activated: Anniversary" (Mar 22).

DAVIS, OSSIE: BIRTH ANNIVERSARY. Dec 18, 1917. Born at Cogdell, GA, Davis began his career as an actor with the Rose McClendon Players in Harlem, NY, in the 1940s. He became involved with civil rights, counting among his friends W.E.B. DuBois, Richard Wright and Langston Hughes, and worked to promote African Americans in the entertainment industry throughout his life. Often sharing the stage or screen with wife Ruby Dee, he was featured in dozens of stage productions and feature films. He died at Miami Beach, FL, Feb 4, 2005.

GRIMALDI, JOSEPH: BIRTH ANNIVERSARY. Dec 18, 1778. Known as the "greatest clown in history" and the "king of pantomime," Joseph Grimaldi began his stage career at age two. He was an accomplished singer, dancer and acrobat. Born at London, England, he is best remembered as the original "Joey the Clown" and for the innovative humor he brought to the clown's role in theater. Illness forced his early retirement in 1823, and he died at London, May 31, 1837.

MEXICO: FEAST OF OUR LADY OF SOLITUDE. Dec 18. Oaxaca. Pilgrims venerate the patron of the lonely.

NEW JERSEY RATIFICATION DAY: ANNIVERSARY. Dec 18, 1787. New Jersey became the third state to ratify the Constitution (following Delaware and Pennsylvania). It did so unanimously.

NIGER: REPUBLIC DAY: ANNIVERSARY. Dec 18. National holiday. Gained autonomy within the French community in 1958.

STRADIVARI, ANTONIO: DEATH ANNIVERSARY. Dec 18, 1737. Celebrated Italian violin maker was born probably in the year 1644, and died at Cremona, at about age 93.

"TO TELL THE TRUTH" TV PREMIERE: 50th ANNIVERSARY. Dec 18, 1956. This long-running popular game show was a production of the Mark Goodson-Bill Todman team. A celebrity panel (and the home audience) tried to guess which of three guests claiming to be the same person was telling the truth. Panelists took turns questioning the guests, and, at the conclusion, the identity of the person was revealed. Hosts have included Bud Collyer, Garry Moore, Joe Garagiola, Robin Ward, Gordon Elliott and Alex Trebek. Celebrity panelists included Dick Van Dyke, Tom Poston, Peggy Cass, Kitty Carlisle and Bill Cullen.

UNITED NATIONS: INTERNATIONAL MIGRANTS DAY. Dec 18. Recognizes the contributions that millions of migrant workers make to the global economy and seeks to draw attention to the precarious state of their rights. For info: United Nations, Dept of Public Info, New York, NY 10017. Web: www.un.org.

BIRTHDAYS TODAY

Christina Aguilera, 26, singer, born Staten Island, NY, Dec 18, 1980.

Katie Holmes, 28, actress ("Dawson's Creek"), born Toledo, OH, Dec 18, 1978.

Ray Liotta, 51, actor (*Unforgettable, Goodfellas, Field of Dreams, Something Wild*), born Newark, NJ, Dec 18, 1955.

Leonard Maltin, 56, movie critic, author (*Maltin's Guide*), born New York, NY, Dec 18, 1950.

Charles Oakley, 43, basketball player, born Cleveland, OH, Dec 18, 1963.

Brad Pitt, 42, actor (*Ocean's Eleven, Interview with the Vampire, A River Runs Through It*), born Shawnee, OK, Dec 18, 1964.

Keith Richards, 63, musician, singer (Rolling Stones), born Dartford, England, Dec 18, 1943.

Steven Spielberg, 59, producer, director (*E.T. The Extra-Terrestrial, Indiana Jones* movies, *Close Encounters of the Third Kind, Jurassic Park, The Color Purple*; Oscars for *Schindler's List, Saving Private Ryan*), born Cincinnati, OH, Dec 18, 1947.

December 2006	S	M	T	W	T	F	S
						1	2
	3	4	5	6	7	8	9
	10	11	12	13	14	15	16
	17	18	19	20	21	22	23
	24	25	26	27	28	29	30
	31						

DECEMBER 19 — TUESDAY
Day 353 — 12 Remaining

BREZHNEV, LEONID: 100th BIRTH ANNIVERSARY. Dec 19, 1906. Leader of the Soviet Union after the overthrow of Nikita Khrushchev in 1964 (which he had a part in). He expanded and modernized Soviet military and nuclear power at the cost of the country's economic health. Born at Kamenskoye, Ukraine, Brezhnev died at Moscow, Russia, Nov 10, 1982.

CHRISTMAS GREETINGS FROM SPACE: ANNIVERSARY. Dec 19, 1958. At 3:15 PM, EST, the US Earth satellite *Atlas* transmitted the first radio voice broadcast from space, a 58-word recorded Christmas greeting from President Dwight D. Eisenhower: "to all mankind America's wish for peace on earth and good will toward men everywhere." The satellite had been launched from Cape Canaveral Dec 18.

FISKE, MINNIE MADDERN: BIRTH ANNIVERSARY. Dec 19, 1865. American theater actress with a long, distinguished career. First stage appearance at the age of three as "Little Minnie Maddern." Born at New Orleans, LA, she died Feb 15, 1932, at Hollis, NY.

LIVERMORE, MARY ASHTON: BIRTH ANNIVERSARY. Dec 19, 1821. American reformer and women's suffrage leader, born at Boston, MA. Died May 23, 1905, at Melrose, MA.

PARRY, WILLIAM: BIRTH ANNIVERSARY. Dec 19, 1790. British explorer Sir William Edward Parry was born at Bath, England. Remembered for his Arctic expeditions and for his search for a Northwest Passage, Parry died at Ems, Germany, July 8, 1855.

SPACE MILESTONE: *INTELSAT 4 F-3* (US): 35th ANNIVERSARY. Dec 19, 1971. Communications satellite launched by NASA on contract with COMSAT. Mission involved intercontinental relay phone and TV communications.

SUSSKIND, DAVID: BIRTH ANNIVERSARY. Dec 19, 1920. American television producer David (Howard) Susskind was born at New York, NY. In 1952 he started his own television production company and soon was producing more live programs than the three networks combined. He began to host talk shows in 1958 and was widely respected for focusing on serious matters. He died Feb 22, 1987, at New York, NY.

***TITANIC* RELEASED: ANNIVERSARY.** Dec 19, 1997. The most expensive film made (up to that time) at $200 million was released in theaters on this date. *Titanic*, written and directed by James Cameron, featured the drama of star-crossed lovers (Leonardo DiCaprio and Kate Winslet) paired with the amazing special effects re-creation of the doomed 1912 ocean liner's first and last voyage. The film won 11 Academy Awards, including best picture, which tied it with 1959's *Ben-Hur*. It is widely considered one of the most successful films ever made.

WOODSON, CARTER GODWIN: BIRTH ANNIVERSARY. Dec 19, 1875. Historian who introduced black studies to colleges and universities, born at New Canton, VA. His scholarly works included *The Negro in Our History, The Education of the Negro Prior to 1861*. Known as the father of Black history, he inaugurated Negro History Week. Woodson was working on a six-volume *Encyclopaedia Africana* when he died at Washington, DC, Apr 3, 1950.

BIRTHDAYS TODAY

Jennifer Beals, 43, actress (*Flashdance, The Bride, Into the Soup*), born Chicago, IL, Dec 19, 1963.

Janie Fricke, 54, country singer ("It Ain't Easy"), born Whitney, IN, Dec 19, 1952.

Tom Gugliotta, 37, basketball player, born Huntington Station, NY, Dec 19, 1969.

Jake Gyllenhaal, 26, actor (*Moonlight Mile, October Sky*), born Los Angeles, CA, Dec 19, 1980.

Richard E. Leakey, 62, anthropologist, born Nairobi, Kenya, Dec 19, 1944.

Kevin Edward McHale, 49, Hall of Fame basketball player, born Hibbing, MN, Dec 19, 1957.

Alyssa Milano, 34, actress ("Charmed," "Melrose Place"), born Brooklyn, NY, Dec 19, 1972.

Tim Reid, 62, actor ("Frank's Place," "WKRP in Cincinnati"), born Norfolk, VA, Dec 19, 1944.

Kristy Swanson, 37, actress (*Buffy the Vampire Slayer*), born Mission Viejo, CA, Dec 19, 1969.

Cicely Tyson, 67, actress (Emmy for *The Autobiography of Miss Jane Pittman*; *Sounder*), born New York, NY, Dec 19, 1939.

DECEMBER 20 — WEDNESDAY
Day 354 — 11 Remaining

AMERICAN POET LAUREATE ESTABLISHMENT: ANNIVERSARY. Dec 20, 1985. A bill empowering the Librarian of Congress to name, annually, a poet laureate/consultant in poetry was signed into law by President Ronald Reagan. In return for a stipend as poet laureate and a salary as the consultant in poetry, the person named will present at least one major work of poetry and will appear at selected national ceremonies. The first poet laureate of the US was Robert Penn Warren, appointed to that position by the Librarian of Congress Feb 26, 1986. See also: "Warren, Robert Penn: Birth Anniversary" (Apr 24).

CATHODE-RAY TUBE PATENTED: ANNIVERSARY. Dec 20, 1938. The kinescope, today known as the cathode-ray tube, was patented by Russian immigrant Vladimir Zworykin. It is still used today in computer monitors and television sets.

CLINTON IMPEACHMENT PROCEEDINGS: ANNIVERSARY. Dec 20, 1998. President William Clinton was impeached by a House of Representatives that was divided along party lines. He was convicted of perjury and obstruction of justice stemming from a sexual relationship with a White House intern. He was then tried by the Senate in January 1999. On Feb 12, 1999, the Senate acquitted him on both charges. Clinton was only the second US president to undergo impeachment proceedings. Andrew Johnson was impeached by the House in 1868, but the Senate voted against impeachment and he finished his term of office. See also: "Johnson Impeachment Proceedings" (Feb 24).

"THE DATING GAME" TV PREMIERE: ANNIVERSARY. Dec 20, 1965. Another game show developed by Chuck Barris, it typically featured a "bachelorette" who questioned three men who were hidden from her view and decided, based on their answers, which guy appealed to her the most. The couple was then sent on a date, courtesy of the show. Occasionally, a bachelor would question three women. Jim Lange was the host of the network series and two syndicated ones. Elaine Joyce and Jeff MacGregor hosted one season each on the retitled "The New Dating Game."

FIRESTONE, HARVEY S.: BIRTH ANNIVERSARY. Dec 20, 1868. American industrialist, businessman and founder of the Firestone Tire and Rubber Company, Harvey Samuel Firestone was born at Columbiana County, OH. A close friend of Henry Ford, Thomas Edison and John Burroughs, Firestone died at Miami Beach, FL, Feb 7, 1938.

IT'S A WONDERFUL LIFE FILM PREMIERE: 60th ANNIVERSARY. Dec 20, 1946. America's favorite Christmas drama premiered on this date at New York, NY. Directed by Frank Capra and starring James Stewart (George Bailey), Donna Reed (Mary Bailey), Henry Travers (as Clarence Oddbody, trying to earn his angel wings) and Lionel Barrymore (as villainous Mr Potter), the film was nominated for five Academy Awards.

LANGER, SUSANNE K.: BIRTH ANNIVERSARY. Dec 20, 1895. Susanne Langer, a leading American philosopher, author of *Philosophy in a New Key: A Study in the Symbolism of Reason, Rite, and Art*, was born at New York, NY. Her studies of aesthetics and art exerted a profound influence on thinking in the fields of psychology, philosophy and the social sciences. She died at Old Lyme, CT, July 17, 1985.

MACAU REVERTS TO CHINESE CONTROL: ANNIVERSARY. Dec 20, 1999. Macau, a tiny province on the southeast coast of China, reverted to Chinese rule. It had been a Portuguese colony since 1557.

MENZIES, ROBERT GORDON: BIRTH ANNIVERSARY. Dec 20, 1894. Australian statesman and conservative leader, born at Jeparit, Victoria, Australia, Sir Robert died at Melbourne, Australia, May 14, 1978, at age 83.

MONTGOMERY BUS BOYCOTT ENDS: 50th ANNIVERSARY. Dec 20, 1956. The US Supreme Court ruling of Nov 13, 1956, calling for integration of the Montgomery, AL, public bus system was implemented. Since Dec 5, 1955, the black community of Montgomery had refused to ride on the segregated buses. The boycott was in reaction to the Dec 1, 1955, arrest of Rosa Parks for refusing to relinquish her seat on a Montgomery bus to a white man.

MOON PHASE: NEW MOON. Dec 20. Moon enters New Moon phase at 9:01 AM, EST.

MUDD DAY. Dec 20, 1833. A day to remember Dr. Samuel A. Mudd (born near Bryantown, MD, Dec 20, 1833), sentenced to life imprisonment for giving medical aid to disguised John Wilkes Booth, fleeing assassin of Abraham Lincoln. Imprisoned four years before being pardoned by President Andrew Johnson. Died on Jan 10, 1883.

RICKEY, BRANCH: 125th BIRTH ANNIVERSARY. Dec 20, 1881. Wesley Branch Rickey, Baseball Hall of Fame player, manager and executive born at Lucasville, OH. Rickey was baseball's most innovative general manager. He invented the farm system, instituted unique training and teaching methods and, most prominently, signed Jackie Robinson to play major league baseball with the Brooklyn Dodgers. Inducted into the Hall of Fame in 1967. Died at Columbia, MO, Dec 9, 1965.

SACAGAWEA: DEATH ANNIVERSARY. Dec 20, 1812. As a young Shoshone Indian woman, Sacagawea in 1805 (with her two-month-old son strapped to her back) traveled with the Lewis and Clark expedition, serving as an interpreter. It is said that the expedition could not have succeeded without her aid. She was born about 1787 and died at Fort Manuel on the Missouri River, Dec 20, 1812. Few other women have been so often honored. There are statues, fountains and memorials of her, and her name has been given to a mountain peak. In 2000 the US Mint issued a $1 coin honoring her.

SOUTH CAROLINA: SECESSION ANNIVERSARY. Dec 20, 1860. South Carolina's legislature voted to secede from the US, the first state to do so. Within six weeks, five more states seceded. On Feb 4, 1861, representatives from the six states met at Montgomery, AL, to establish a government and on Feb 9 Jefferson Davis was elected president of the Confederate States of America. By June 1861, 11 states had seceded.

US INVASION OF PANAMA: ANNIVERSARY. Dec 20, 1989. The US launched operation "Just Cause," invading Panama in an attempt to seize Manuel Noriega and bring him to justice for narcotics trafficking. Seven months after Noriega had ruled unfavorable election results null and void, the US toppled the Noriega government and oversaw the installation of Guillermo Endara as president. Although the initial military action was declared a success, Noriega eluded capture. He surrendered to US troops on Jan 4, 1990, and was tried, convicted and imprisoned in the US.

VIRGINIA COMPANY EXPEDITION TO AMERICA: 400th ANNIVERSARY. Dec 20, 1606. Three small ships, the *Susan Constant*, the *Godspeed* and the *Discovery*, commanded by Captain Christopher Newport, departed London, England, bound for America, where the royally chartered Virginia Company's approximately 120 persons established the first permanent English settlement in what is now the United States at Jamestown, VA, May 14, 1607.

BIRTHDAYS TODAY

Jenny Agutter, 54, actress (Emmy for "The Snow Goose"), born London, England, Dec 20, 1952.

Uri Geller, 60, psychic, clairvoyant, born Tel Aviv, Israel, Dec 20, 1946.

John Hillerman, 74, actor ("The Betty White Show," "Magnum, PI"), born Denison, TX, Dec 20, 1932.

David Levine, 80, artist, caricaturist (*New York Review of Books*), born Brooklyn, NY, Dec 20, 1926.

Sonny Perdue, 60, Governor of Georgia (R), born Perry, GA, Dec 20, 1946.

John Spencer, 60, actor ("The West Wing," "LA Law"), born New York, NY, Dec 20, 1946.

William Julius Wilson, 71, sociologist, educator, writer (*When Work Disappears*), born Derry Township, PA, Dec 20, 1935.

DECEMBER 21 — THURSDAY
Day 355 — 10 Remaining

BÖLL, HEINRICH: BIRTH ANNIVERSARY. Dec 21, 1917. German novelist, winner of the 1972 Nobel Prize for Literature, author of some 20 books including *Billiards at Half-Past Nine, The Clown* and *Group Portrait with Lady*, was born at Cologne, Germany. He died near Bonn, Germany, July 16, 1985.

DISRAELI, BENJAMIN: BIRTH ANNIVERSARY. Dec 21, 1804. British novelist and statesman, born at London and died there Apr 19, 1881. "No government," he wrote, "can be long secure without a formidable opposition."

ELVIS PRESLEY MEETS PRESIDENT NIXON: ANNIVERSARY. Dec 21, 1970. After writing President Richard M. Nixon offering to be a "Federal Agent-at-Large" to fight drug abuse and the drug culture, Elvis Presley met with Nixon at the White House on this date. Presley was not made a federal agent, but the two men had a cordial meeting. The photograph of them shaking hands is the most requested reproduction from the National Archives (more than the Bill of Rights or the US Constitution).

FIRST CROSSWORD PUZZLE: ANNIVERSARY. Dec 21, 1913. The first crossword puzzle was compiled by Arthur Wynne and published in a supplement to the *New York World*.

December 2006	S	M	T	W	T	F	S
						1	2
	3	4	5	6	7	8	9
	10	11	12	13	14	15	16
	17	18	19	20	21	22	23
	24	25	26	27	28	29	30
	31						

FOREFATHERS' DAY. Dec 21. Observed mainly in New England in commemoration of landing at Plymouth Rock on this day in 1620.

GIBSON, JOSH: BIRTH ANNIVERSARY. Dec 21, 1912. Joshua (Josh) Gibson, Baseball Hall of Fame catcher born at Buena Vista, GA, is regarded as the greatest slugger to play in the Negro Leagues and perhaps the greatest ballplayer ever. Gibson starred with the Pittsburgh Crawfords. His long home runs are the stuff of legend. Inducted into the Hall of Fame in 1972. Died at Pittsburgh, PA, Jan 20, 1947.

HUMBUG DAY. Dec 21. Allows all those preparing for Christmas to vent their frustrations. 12 "humbugs" allowed. [©2003 by WH.] For info: Thomas & Ruth Roy, Wellcat Holidays, 2418 Long Ln, Lebanon, PA 17046. Phone: (717) 279-0184. E-mail: info@wellcat.com. Web: www.wellcat.com.

PAN AMERICAN FLIGHT 103 EXPLOSION: ANNIVERSARY. Dec 21, 1988. Pan Am World Airways Flight 103 exploded in midair and crashed into the heart of Lockerbie, Scotland, the result of a terrorist bombing. The 259 passengers and crew members and 11 persons on the ground were killed in the disaster. The tragedy raised questions about security and the notification of passengers in the event of threatened flights. In the resultant investigation it was revealed that government agencies and the airline had known that the flight was possibly the target of a terrorist attack.

PARKINSON, JAMES: DEATH ANNIVERSARY. Dec 21, 1824. The remarkable English physician and paleontologist who first described the "shaking palsy" later had it named for him—Parkinson's disease. He was the author of numerous books and articles on a variety of subjects. His *Organic Remains of a Former World* is called the first attempt to give a scientific account of fossils. Under oath, Parkinson declared that he was a member of the group that hatched the "Pop-gun Plot" to assassinate King George III in a theater, using a poisoned dart for the deed. Parkinson was born at London about 1755, and died there, Dec 21, 1824.

PHILEAS FOGG WINS A WAGER DAY. Dec 21. Anniversary, from Jules Verne's *Around the World in Eighty Days*, of the winning of Phileas Fogg's wager, on Dec 21, 1872, when Fogg walked into the saloon of the Reform Club at London, announcing "Here I am, gentlemen!" exactly 79 days, 23 hours, 59 minutes and 59 seconds after starting his trip "around the world in 80 days," to win his £20,000 wager. See also: "Phileas Fogg's Wager Day" (Oct 2).

PILGRIM LANDING: ANNIVERSARY. Dec 21, 1620. According to Governor William Bradford's *History of Plymouth Plantation*, "On Munday," [Dec 21, 1620, New Style] the Pilgrims, aboard the *Mayflower*, reached Plymouth, MA, "sounded ye harbor, and founde it fitt for shipping; and marched into ye land, & founde diverse cornfields, and ye best they could find, and ye season & their presente necessitie made them glad to accepte of it. . . . And after wards tooke better view of ye place, and resolved wher to pitch their dwelling; and them and their goods." Plymouth Rock, the legendary place of landing since it first was "identified" in 1769, nearly 150 years after the landing, has been a historic shrine since. The landing anniversary is observed in much of New England as Forefathers' Day. See also: "Forefathers' Day" (Dec 21).

SHERMAN TAKES SAVANNAH: ANNIVERSARY. Dec 21, 1864. Despite efforts by Confederate General William Hardee to defend the city of Savannah, GA, Southern troops were forced to pull out of the city, and on this date Union forces under William Tecumseh Sherman captured the town. By marching from Atlanta to the coast at Savannah, Sherman had cut the lower South off from the center.

SNOW WHITE AND THE SEVEN DWARFS FILM PREMIERE: ANNIVERSARY. Dec 21, 1937. America's first full-length animated feature film (and also the first Technicolor feature) premiered on this date at the Carthay Circle Theater, Hollywood, CA. The labor of love from Walt Disney—who for years wanted to create a feature-length cartoon—involved more than 750 artists and 1,500 colors in four years of development. The film features the classic songs "Some Day My Prince Will Come" and "Whistle While You Work." Walt Disney received a special Oscar for *Snow White*—along with seven miniature Oscars.

SPACE MILESTONE: *APOLLO 8* (US). Dec 21, 1968. First moon voyage launched, manned by Colonel Frank Borman, Captain James A. Lovell, Jr and Major William A. Anders. Orbited moon Dec 24, returned to Earth Dec 27. First men to orbit the moon and see the side of the moon away from Earth.

STALIN, JOSEPH: BIRTH ANNIVERSARY. Dec 21, 1879. Russian dictator whose family name was Dzhugashvili, was born at Gori, Georgia. One of the most powerful and most feared men of the 20th century, Stalin died (of a stroke) at the Kremlin, at Moscow, Mar 5, 1953.

SZOLD, HENRIETTA: BIRTH ANNIVERSARY. Dec 21, 1860. Teacher, writer, social worker, organizer and pioneer Zionist, Henrietta Szold is best remembered as founder and first president of Hadassah, the Women's Zionist Organization of America. Born at Baltimore, MD, she was influenced by her father Rabbi Benjamin Szold, an active and vocal abolitionist. She established the first "night school" at Baltimore, focused on teaching English and job skills to immigrants. Her trip to Palestine in 1910 sparked the genesis of Hadassah. While there, Szold was alarmed by the lack of social, medical and educational services and returned with the idea that a national women's Zionist organization must be formed to carry out practical projects. The "Mother of Social Service in Palestine," Szold died at Jerusalem, Feb 13, 1945. See also: "Hadassah: Anniversary" (Feb 24).

WORLD PEACE DAY/WINTER SOLSTICE. Dec 21. A day on which bells throughout the world will be rung along with prayers for world peace. The Middle East and Iraq will be the main focal point this year. Choose peace now. Annually, on the winter solstice. For info: Donald L. Orne, PO Box 225, Marblehead, MA 01945. Phone: (781) 631-0786. E-mail: don@yingcom .com. Web: www.yingcom.com.

YALDA. Dec 21. Yalda, the longest night of the year, is celebrated by Iranians. The ceremony has an Indo-Iranian origin, where Light and Good were considered to struggle against Darkness and Evil. With fires burning and lights lit, family and friends gather to stay up through the night helping the sun in its battle against darkness. They recite poetry, tell stories and eat special fruits and nuts until the sun, triumphant, reappears in the morning.

YULE. Dec 21. (Also called Alban Arthan.) One of the "Lesser Sabbats" during the Wiccan year, Yule marks the death of the Sun-God and his rebirth from the Earth Goddess. Annually, on the winter solstice.

ZAPPA, FRANK: BIRTH ANNIVERSARY. Dec 21, 1940. Rock musician and composer, Zappa was noted for his satire and as a leading advocate against censorship of contemporary music. He formed the group Mothers of Invention. Born at Baltimore, MD, he died Dec 4, 1993, at Los Angeles, CA, at age 52.

BIRTHDAYS TODAY

Tina Brown, 53, former *New Yorker* editor, born London, England, Dec 21, 1953.
Andy Dick, 41, actor ("NewsRadio"), born Charleston, SC, Dec 21, 1965.
Phil Donahue, 71, former TV talk-show host ("Donahue"), born Cleveland, OH, Dec 21, 1935.
Christine Marie (Chris) Evert, 52, sportscaster, former tennis player, born Ft Lauderdale, FL, Dec 21, 1954.
Jane Fonda, 69, actress (Oscars for *Klute, Coming Home; Julia, On Golden Pond*), born New York, NY, Dec 21, 1937.
Samuel L. Jackson, 58, actor (*Pulp Fiction, Jurassic Park*), born Washington, DC, Dec 21, 1948.
Jane Kaczmarek, 51, actress ("Malcolm in the Middle"), born Milwaukee, WI, Dec 21, 1955.
Joe Paterno, 80, college football coach, born Brooklyn, NY, Dec 21, 1926.

Ray Romano, 49, comedian, actor ("Everybody Loves Raymond"), born Queens, NY, Dec 21, 1957.
Kiefer Sutherland, 40, actor ("24," *Flatliners, A Few Good Men*), born London, England, Dec 21, 1966.
Michael Tilson Thomas, 62, conductor, pianist, organist, born Hollywood, CA, Dec 21, 1944.
Andrew James (Andy) Van Slyke, 46, former baseball player, born Utica, NY, Dec 21, 1960.
Karrie Webb, 32, golfer, born Ayr, Queensland, Australia, Dec 21, 1974.
Paul Winchell, 84, ventriloquist, actor, born New York, NY, Dec 21, 1922.

DECEMBER 22 — FRIDAY
Day 356 — 9 Remaining

ABILITIES DAY. Dec 22. Celebrates all people with disabilities and their caregivers. To celebrate this day wear a white ribbon. For info: Paul Cannaday, 4971 Wixson Rd, Croswell, MI 48422. Phone: (810) 679-0236. E-mail: paulc@greatlakes.net. Web: www .disabilitygrapevine.com.

ASHCROFT, PEGGY: BIRTH ANNIVERSARY. Dec 22, 1907. British actress Dame Edith Margaret Emily Ashcroft was born at Croyden, England. In addition to her many accolades on the British stage she won an Oscar for her supporting role in *Passage to India* (1985) and a special British Olivier Award for lifetime achievement in 1991. She died June 14, 1991, at London, England.

CAPRICORN, THE GOAT. Dec 22–Jan 19. In the astronomical and astrological zodiac that divides the sun's apparent orbit into 12 segments, the period Dec 22–Jan 19 is identified, traditionally, as the sun sign of Capricorn, the goat. The ruling planet is Saturn.

"DING DONG SCHOOL" TV PREMIERE: ANNIVERSARY. Dec 22, 1952. Named by a three-year-old after watching a test broadcast of the opening sequence (a hand ringing a bell), "Ding Dong School" was one of the first children's educational series. Miss Frances (Dr. Frances Horwich, head of Roosevelt College's education department at Chicago) was the host of this weekday show.

ELLERY, WILLIAM: BIRTH ANNIVERSARY. Dec 22, 1727. Signer of the Declaration of Independence, born at Newport, RI, and died there Feb 15, 1820.

FIRST GORILLA BORN IN CAPTIVITY: 50th BIRTH ANNIVERSARY. Dec 22, 1956. "Colo" was born at the Columbus, OH, zoo, weighing in at 3¼ pounds, the first gorilla born in captivity.

OGLETHORPE, JAMES EDWARD: BIRTH ANNIVERSARY. Dec 22, 1696. English general, author and colonizer of Georgia. Founder of the city of Savannah. Oglethorpe was born at London. He died June 30, 1785, at Cranham Hall, Essex, England.

PUCCINI, GIACOMO: BIRTH ANNIVERSARY. Dec 22, 1858. Italian composer of such operas as *La Boheme* and *Madame Butterfly*. Born at Lucca, Tuscany, Italy, he died Nov 29, 1924, at Brussels, Belgium.

ROBINSON, EDWIN ARLINGTON: BIRTH ANNIVERSARY. Dec 22, 1869. Three-time Pulitzer Prize winner best known for his short dramatic poems, including "Richard Cory" and "Miniver Cheevy." Born at Head Tide, ME, and died at Los Angeles, CA, Apr 6, 1935.

WINTER. Dec 22–Mar 20, 2007. In the Northern Hemisphere winter begins today with the winter solstice, at 7:22 PM, EST. Note that in the Southern Hemisphere today is the beginning of summer. Between Equator and Arctic Circle the sunrise and sunset points on the horizon are farthest south for the year and daylight length is minimum (ranging from 12 hours, 8 minutes, at the equator to zero at the Arctic Circle).

BIRTHDAYS TODAY

Barbara Billingsley, 84, actress ("Leave It to Beaver," *Airplane!*), born Los Angeles, CA, Dec 22, 1922.

Steven Norman (Steve) Carlton, 62, Hall of Fame baseball player, born Miami, FL, Dec 22, 1944.

Hector Elizondo, 70, actor (*Pretty Woman, Frankie and Johnny,* "Chicago Hope"), born New York, NY, Dec 22, 1936.

Ralph Fiennes, 44, actor (*Schindler's List, The English Patient*), born Suffolk, England, Dec 22, 1962.

Steve Garvey, 58, former baseball player, born Tampa, FL, Dec 22, 1948.

Robin Gibb, 57, singer, musician (The Bee Gees), born Manchester, England, Dec 22, 1949.

Claudia Alta (Lady Bird) Johnson, 94, former First Lady, widow of Lyndon B. Johnson, 36th president of the US, born Karnack, TX, Dec 22, 1912.

Diane K. Sawyer, 60, journalist ("60 Minutes," "Prime Time Live"), born Glasgow, KY, Dec 22, 1946.

Jan Stephenson, 55, golfer, born Sydney, Australia, Dec 22, 1951.

DECEMBER 23 — SATURDAY
Day 357 — 8 Remaining

FEDERAL RESERVE SYSTEM: ANNIVERSARY. Dec 23, 1913. Established pursuant to authority contained in the Federal Reserve Act of Dec 23, 1913, the system serves as the nation's central bank, with the responsibility for execution of monetary policy. It is called on to contribute to the strength and vitality of the US economy, in part by influencing the lending and investing activities of commercial banks and the cost and availability of money and credit.

FIRST NONSTOP FLIGHT AROUND THE WORLD WITHOUT REFUELING: ANNIVERSARY. Dec 23, 1987. Dick Rutan and Jeana Yeager set a new world record of 216 hours of continuous flight, breaking their own record of 111 hours set July 15, 1986. The aircraft *Voyager* departed from Edwards Air Force Base in California, Dec 14, 1987, and landed Dec 23, 1987. The journey covered 24,986 miles at an official speed of 115 miles per hour.

JAPAN: BIRTHDAY OF THE EMPEROR. Dec 23. National Day. Holiday honoring Emperor Akihito, born in 1933.

December 2006	S	M	T	W	T	F	S
						1	2
	3	4	5	6	7	8	9
	10	11	12	13	14	15	16
	17	18	19	20	21	22	23
	24	25	26	27	28	29	30
	31						

METRIC CONVERSION ACT: ANNIVERSARY. Dec 23, 1975. The Congress of the US passed Public Law 94–168, known as the Metric Conversion Act of 1975. This act declares that the SI (International System of Units) will be this country's basic system of measurement and establishes the United States Metric Board, which is responsible for the planning, coordination and implementation of the nation's voluntary conversion to SI. (Congress had authorized the metric system as a legal system of measurement in the US by an act passed July 28, 1866. In 1875, the US became one of the original signers of the Treaty of the Metre, which established an international metric system.)

MEXICO: FEAST OF THE RADISHES. Dec 23. Oaxaca. Figurines of people and animals cleverly carved out of radishes are sold during festivities.

MONROE, HARRIET: BIRTH ANNIVERSARY. Dec 23, 1860. American poet, editor and founder of *Poetry* magazine. Born at Chicago, IL. Died Sept 26, 1936, at Arequipa, Peru.

SMITH, JOSEPH, JR: BIRTH ANNIVERSARY. Dec 23, 1805. The founding prophet of The Church of Jesus Christ of Latter-day Saints was born at Sharon, VT. He was assassinated by an armed mob on June 27, 1844, at Carthage, IL. See also: "Smith, Joseph, Jr, and Hyrum: Death Anniversary" (June 27).

TOJO HIDEKI EXECUTION: ANNIVERSARY. Dec 23, 1948. Tojo Hideki, prime minister of Japan from Oct 16, 1941, until his resignation July 19, 1944. After Japan's surrender in August 1945, Tojo was arrested as a war criminal, tried by a military tribunal and sentenced to death Nov 12, 1948. Born at Tokyo, Japan, Dec 30, 1884, Tojo was hanged (with six other Japanese wartime military leaders) at Sugamo Prison, Tokyo, Dec 23, 1948, the sentence being carried out by the US 8th Army.

TRANSISTOR UNVEILED: ANNIVERSARY. Dec 23, 1947. John Bardeen, Walter Brattain and William Shockley of Bell Laboratories shared the 1956 Nobel Prize for their invention of the transistor, which led to a revolution in communications and electronics. It was smaller, lighter, more durable, more reliable and generated less heat than the vacuum tube that had been used up to this time.

BIRTHDAYS TODAY

Akihito, 73, Emperor of Japan, born Tokyo, Japan, Dec 23, 1933.

Robert Bly, 80, author (*Iron John: A Book About Men; What Have I Ever Lost by Dying?*), born Madison, MN, Dec 23, 1926.

Scott Gomez, 27, hockey player, born Anchorage, AK, Dec 23, 1979.

Jose Greco, 88, dancer, born Abruzzi, Italy, Dec 23, 1918.

Corey Haim, 35, actor (*Murphy's Romance, The Lost Boys*), born Toronto, ON, Canada, Dec 23, 1971.

James Joseph (Jim) Harbaugh, 43, former football player, born Toledo, OH, Dec 23, 1963.

Susan Lucci, 57, actress ("All My Children," *Mafia Princess*), born Westchester, NY, Dec 23, 1949.

Gerald O'Loughlin, 85, actor ("The Rookies," "Our House"), born New York, NY, Dec 23, 1921.

DECEMBER 24 — SUNDAY

Day 358 — 7 Remaining

***AIDA* PREMIERE: ANNIVERSARY.** Dec 24, 1871. Giuseppe Verdi's opera *Aida* premiered at Cairo. It was commissioned by the Khedive of Egypt to celebrate the opening of the Suez Canal.

ARNOLD, MATTHEW: BIRTH ANNIVERSARY. Dec 24, 1822. English poet and essayist, born at Laleham, England. Died Apr 15, 1888, at Liverpool, England. "One has often wondered," he wrote in *Culture and Anarchy*, "whether upon the whole earth there is anything so unintelligent, so unapt to perceive how the world is really going, as an ordinary young Englishman of our upper class."

AUSTRIA: "SILENT NIGHT, HOLY NIGHT" CELEBRATIONS. Dec 24. Oberndorf, Hallein and Wagrain, Salzburg, Austria. Commemorating the creation of the Christmas carol here in 1818.

CARSON, CHRISTOPHER "KIT": BIRTH ANNIVERSARY. Dec 24, 1809. American frontiersman, soldier, trapper, guide and Indian agent best known as Kit Carson. Born at Madison County, KY, he died at Fort Lyon, CO, May 23, 1868.

CHRISTMAS BELLS RING AGAIN IN ST. BASIL'S: ANNIVERSARY. Dec 24, 1990. For the first time since the death of Lenin in 1924, the bells of St. Basil's Cathedral, on Red Square in Moscow, rang to celebrate Christmas.

CHRISTMAS EVE. Dec 24. Family gift-giving occasion in many Christian countries.

CHRISTMAS EVE TORCHLIGHT PARADE. Dec 24. Winter Park Resort, Winter Park, CO. One of Winter Park Resort's most beloved traditions, highlighted by Santa Claus leading a procession of torch-bearing skiers down Lower Hughes trail under a spectacular fireworks display. Est attendance: 1,500. For info: Winter Park Resort, PO Box 36, Winter Park, CO 80482. Phone: (970) 726-1564. Fax: (970) 726-1572. E-mail: wpinfo@mail.ski winterpark.com. Web: winterparkresort.com.

FIRST SURFACE-TO-SURFACE GUIDED MISSILE: ANNIVERSARY. Dec 24, 1942. German rocket engineer Wernher von Braun launched the first surface-to-surface guided missile. Buzz bombs, a form of guided missile, were used by Germany against Great Britain starting Sept 8, 1944. On Feb 24, 1949, the first rocket to reach outer space (an altitude of 25 miles) was fired. The two-stage rocket, a Wac Corporal set in the nose of a German V-2, was launched from the White Sands Proving Grounds, NM, by a team of scientists headed by von Braun.

GARDNER, AVA: BIRTH ANNIVERSARY. Dec 24, 1922. Actress and leading sex symbol of the 1940s and '50s, Ava Lavinia Gardner was born at Smithfield, NC. Among Gardner's numerous movies are *The Barefoot Contessa*, *Bhowani Junction*, *The Sun Also Rises* and *The Life and Times of Judge Roy Bean*. Gardner was married to Mickey Rooney (1942–43), Artie Shaw (1945–46) and Frank Sinatra (1951–57). Died at London, England, Jan 25, 1990.

HUGHES, HOWARD ROBARD: BIRTH ANNIVERSARY. Dec 24, 1905. Wealthy American industrialist, aviator and movie producer who spent his latter years as a recluse. Born at Houston, TX, he died in airplane en route from Acapulco, Mexico, to Houston, Apr 5, 1976.

JOULE, JAMES PRESCOTT: BIRTH ANNIVERSARY. Dec 24, 1818. English physicist and inventor after whom Joule's Law (the first law of thermodynamics) was named was born at Salford, Lancashire, England. The unit of measurement of the mechnical equivalent of heat is known as the Joule. He died at Cheshire, England, Oct 11, 1889.

LIBYA: INDEPENDENCE DAY. Dec 24. Libya gained its independence from Italy in 1951.

"THE PERRY COMO SHOW" TV PREMIERE: ANNIVERSARY. Dec 24, 1948. Singer Perry Como hosted "The Chesterfield Supper Club" when it came to TV from radio. Also featured were the Mitchell Ayres Orchestra and the Fontane Sisters. The show was retitled "The Perry Como Show" during 1955–59 and then "The Kraft Music Hall" during 1959–63. The Ray Charles Singers and the Louis DaPron Dancers were featured. Como's theme song was "Dream Along with Me."

BIRTHDAYS TODAY

Diedrich Bader, 40, actor ("The Drew Carey Show"), born Alexandria, VA, Dec 24, 1966.

Mary Higgins Clark, 75, author (*Where Are the Children?*, *Silent Night*), born New York, NY, Dec 24, 1931.

Ricky Martin, 35, singer, actor ("General Hospital"), born Enrique José Martín, San Juan, Puerto Rico, Dec 24, 1971.

Ryan Seacrest, 32, television host ("American Idol"), radio personality ("America's Top 40"), born Atlanta, GA, Dec 24, 1974.

Jeff Sessions, 60, US Senator (R, Alabama), born Hybart, AL, Dec 24, 1946.

DECEMBER 25 — MONDAY

Day 359 — 6 Remaining

A'PHABET DAY. Dec 25. Also known as "No-L" Day, this celebration is for people who do not want to send Christmas cards but who want to greet their friends; so they send out cards listing the letters of the alphabet in order, but with a gap where L would be. For info: Bob Birch, The Puns Corps, 3108 Dashiell Rd, Falls Church, VA 22042. Phone: (703) 533-3668.

BARTON, CLARA: BIRTH ANNIVERSARY. Dec 25, 1821. Clarissa Harlowe Barton, American nurse and philanthropist, founder of the American Red Cross, was born at Oxford, MA. In 1881, she became first president of the American Red Cross (founded May 21, 1881). She died at Glen Echo, MD, Apr 12, 1912.

BOGART, HUMPHREY: BIRTH ANNIVERSARY. Dec 25, 1899. American stage and screen actor, Humphrey DeForest Bogart was born at New York, NY. Among his best remembered films are: *The African Queen*, *The Maltese Falcon*, *Casablanca* and *To Have and Have Not*. Bogart died Jan 14, 1957, at Hollywood, CA.

BOOTH, EVANGELINE CORY: BIRTH ANNIVERSARY. Dec 25, 1865. Salvation Army general, active in England, Canada and the US. Author and composer of songs, Booth was born at London, England. She died at Hartsdale, NY, July 17, 1950.

CALLOWAY, CAB: BIRTH ANNIVERSARY. Dec 25, 1907. American singer and bandleader Cabell Calloway was born at Rochester, NY. George Gershwin modeled the part of Sportin' Life in *Porgy and Bess* (1935) after this jazz singer who also played the role across the US until 1956. He is best known for his song "Minnie the Moocher" (1931). He died Nov 18, 1994, at Hockessin, DE.

CEAUSESCU, NICOLAE: DEATH ANNIVERSARY. Dec 25, 1989. On Christmas evening a broadcast of a Christmas symphony on state-run television was interrupted with the report that Romanian president Nicolae Ceausescu and his wife had been executed, bringing to an end the last hard-line regime in the Soviet bloc. Ceausescu's downfall began when he ordered members of his black-shirted state police, the Securitate, to use force to quell a disturbance in the town of Timisorara. The brutal crackdown led to estimates of as many as 4,500 killed. Ceausescu's rule was marked by corruption, deprivation and terror.

CHRISTMAS. Dec 25. Christian festival commemorating the birth of Jesus of Nazareth. Most popular of Christian observances, Christmas as a Feast of the Nativity dates from the 4th century. Although Jesus's birth date is not known, the Western church selected Dec 25 for the feast, possibly to counteract the non-Christian festivals of that approximate date. Many customs from non-Christian festivals (Roman Saturnalia, Mithraic sun's birthday, Teutonic yule, Druidic and other winter solstice rites) have been adopted as part of the Christmas celebration (lights, mistletoe, holly and ivy, holiday tree, wassailing and gift giving, for example). Some Orthodox churches celebrate Christmas Jan 7 based on the "old calendar" (Julian). Theophany (recognition of the divinity of Jesus) is observed on this date and also on Jan 6, especially by the Eastern Orthodox Church.

CHRISTMAS FIRESIDE CHAT WARNING: ANNIVERSARY. Dec 25, 1943. In his Christmas message to the American people, Franklin D. Roosevelt warned, "The war is now reaching the stage when we shall have to look forward to large casualty lists—dead, wounded and missing. War entails just that. There is no easy road to victory. And the end is not yet in sight."

CUBA: CHRISTMAS RETURNS: ANNIVERSARY. Dec 25, 1998. Christmas was celebrated in Cuba after Fidel Castro's government announced that it was again a regular holiday in the Cuban calendar. In 1997 the government had granted a Christmas holiday in deference to Pope John Paul II who was visiting the island the next month. Christmas had been abolished as a holiday in Cuba in 1969.

FARLEY, CAL: BIRTH ANNIVERSARY. Dec 25, 1895. Cal Farley, known as "America's Greatest Foster Father," started Cal Farley's Boys Ranch in 1939 with nine boys. The ranch has grown into a modern community of 441 boys (and girls since 1992), which has housed and educated more than 4,000 boys and girls over the years. Cal Farley was born at Saxton, IA; he died Feb 19, 1967, at Boys Ranch, TX.

FIRST INDOOR BASEBALL GAME: ANNIVERSARY. Dec 25, 1888. Long before the domed stadiums of the late 20th century, a large building at the state fairgrounds in Philadelphia,

PA, was the site of the first indoor baseball game. 2,000 spectators watched the Downtowners beat the Uptowners, 6–1.

IT'S ABOUT TIME WEEK!. Dec 25–31. Innovative week dedicated to time-to-give, time-to-live and time-to-remember. Encourages creativity applied to problems and honors pioneers and partnerships in research, ideas and services for "ABetterWay; ABetterWorld." Awards to pioneers and partnerships. Send nominations by October. For info: The ForGoodnessSake! Center, 427 E 7th St, Michigan City, IN 46360. E-mail: ForGood@adsnet.com.

JINNAH, MOHAMMED ALI (QAID-E-AZAM): BIRTH ANNIVERSARY. Dec 25, 1876. The founder of the Islamic Republic of Pakistan, Mohammed Ali Jinnah was born at Karachi, then part of India. When Pakistan became an independent political entity (Aug 15, 1947), Jinnah became its first governor general. He was given the title Qaid-e-Azam (Great Leader) in 1947. He died at Karachi, Sept 11, 1948. This day is a holiday in Pakistan.

"METROPOLITAN OPERA RADIO BROADCASTS" PREMIERE: 75th ANNIVERSARY. Dec 25, 1931. On Christmas Day 1931, the Metropolitan Opera of New York City broadcast an entire opera, *Hansel and Gretel*, on the NBC radio network—the first time this had ever been done. This broadcast was the first of an ongoing radio series of Saturday matinees. On Dec 7, 1940, Texaco (now ChevronTexaco) became a sponsor and began the longest continuous sponsorship in broadcast history—a sponsorship that ended after the 2003–2004 season. For decades, the Metropolitan Opera radio broadcasts have introduced opera to new fans far from New York. Today, the broadcasts are heard internationally in 42 countries.

"THE STEVE ALLEN SHOW" TV PREMIERE: ANNIVERSARY. Dec 25, 1950. Talented actor, comedian, singer and musician, Steve Allen hosted a number of variety shows from 1950 to 1969 (with a few breaks in between to host specials and "The Tonight Show"). For two years, his television show was similar to his radio show and featured singer Peggy Lee, announcer Bern Bennett and Llemuel the llama. His next show competed with Ed Sullivan's show, though Allen's stressed comedy. Some of his "funnymen" were Don Knotts; Tom Poston; Louis Nye; Gabe Dell; Pat Harrington, Jr; Dayton Allen and Bill Dana. His other shows included a talk show, a game show, a comedy show, an educational music show and a flashback-comedy show.

STOCK EXCHANGE HOLIDAY (CHRISTMAS DAY). Dec 25. The holiday schedules for the various exchanges are subject to change if relevant rules, regulations or exchange policies are revised. If you have questions, phone: American Stock Exchange (212) 306-1000, Chicago Board of Options Exchange (312) 786-5600, Chicago Board of Trade (312) 435-3500, NASDAQ Stock Market (646) 441-5200, New York Stock Exchange (212) 656-3000, Pacific Stock Exchange (415) 393-4000, Philadelphia Stock Exchange (215) 496-5000.

TAIWAN: CONSTITUTION DAY. Dec 25. National holiday. Commemorates the adoption of the 1946 constitution.

UNITED KINGDOM: CHRISTMAS HOLIDAY. Dec 25. Bank and public holiday in England, Wales, Scotland and Northern Ireland.

WASHINGTON CROSSES THE DELAWARE: ANNIVERSARY. Dec 25, 1776. One of the most famous events of the American Revolution happened on a bleak Christmas night, during driving snow. General George Washington led 2,400 men across the Delaware River at McConkey's Ferry, Bucks County, PA, to conduct a surprise attack on Hessian troops at Trenton, NJ. Local fishermen conducted the troops across the river, finally assembling at 3:00 AM on the other side. Washington achieved victory at Trenton, a key event that changed the course of the war to the rebelling colonists' favor.

WEST, REBECCA: BIRTH ANNIVERSARY. Dec 25, 1892. English author, literary critic, prizewinning journalist and noted feminist, Dame Rebecca West was born Cicely Isabel Fairfield at London, England. She died there Mar 15, 1983.

December 2006

S	M	T	W	T	F	S
					1	2
3	4	5	6	7	8	9
10	11	12	13	14	15	16
17	18	19	20	21	22	23
24	25	26	27	28	29	30
31						

BIRTHDAYS TODAY

Jimmy Buffett, 60, singer ("Margaritaville"), songwriter, born Pascagoula, MS, Dec 25, 1946.

Lawrence Richard (Larry) Csonka, 60, Hall of Fame football player, born Stow, OH, Dec 25, 1946.

Rickey Henley Henderson, 48, baseball player, born Chicago, IL, Dec 25, 1958.

Annie Lennox, 52, singer (Eurythmics, "Sweet Dreams Are Made of This"), born Aberdeen, Scotland, Dec 25, 1954.

Barbara Mandrell, 58, singer ("I Was Country When Country Wasn't Cool"), born Houston, TX, Dec 25, 1948.

Gary Sandy, 61, actor ("All That Glitters," "WKRP in Cincinnati"), born Dayton, OH, Dec 25, 1945.

Hanna Schygulla, 63, actress (*The Marriage of Maria Braun, Berlin Alexanderplatz*), born Kattowitz, Germany, Dec 25, 1943.

Mary Elizabeth (Sissy) Spacek, 57, actress (Oscar for *Coal Miner's Daughter; Missing*), born Quitman, TX, Dec 25, 1949.

DECEMBER 26 — TUESDAY

Day 360 — 5 Remaining

ALLEN, STEVE: BIRTH ANNIVERSARY. Dec 26, 1921. American entertainer and TV pioneer, Steve Allen created the original "Tonight" show for NBC in 1953. Also known as a composer and the author of more than 40 books, he was born at New York, NY, Dec 26, 1921. He died at Encino, CA, Oct 30, 2000.

BABBAGE, CHARLES: BIRTH ANNIVERSARY. Dec 26, 1792. English mathematician, born at Teignmouth, England. He developed the principles on which modern computers are designed. Babbage died at London, England, Oct 18, 1871.

BAHAMAS: JUNKANOO. Dec 26. Kaleidoscope of sound and spectacle combining a bit of Mardi Gras, mummers' parade and ancient African tribal rituals. Revelers in colorful costumes parade through the streets to sounds of cowbells, goat skin drums and many other homemade instruments. Always on Boxing Day.

BOXING DAY. Dec 26. Ordinarily observed on the first day after Christmas. A legal holiday in Canada, the United Kingdom and many other countries. Formerly (according to Robert Chambers) a day when Christmas gift boxes were "regularly expected by a postman, the lamplighter, the dustman and generally by all those functionaries who render services to the public at large, without receiving payment therefore from any individual." When Boxing Day falls on a Saturday or Sunday, the Monday or Tuesday immediately following may be proclaimed or observed as a bank or public holiday.

BOXING DAY AT THE HEMINGWAY BIRTHPLACE. Dec 26. Hemingway Birthplace, Oak Park, IL. The Hemingway family celebrated Boxing Day with extended family, eating special foods, listening to Gilbert and Sullivan and sharing literary works and poetry. The Ernest Hemingway Foundation of Oak Park will re-create this holiday celebration with English tea, music, horse and carriage rides and dramatic readings of Christmas tales. For info: The Ernest Hemingway Foundation, PO Box 2222, Oak Park, IL 60303-2222. Phone: (708) 848-2222. Fax: (708) 386-2952. E-mail: ehfop@sbcglobal.net. Web: www.ehfop.org.

CLERC, LAURENT: BIRTH ANNIVERSARY. Dec 26, 1785. The first deaf teacher in America, Laurent Clerc assisted Thomas Hopkins Gallaudet in establishing the first public school for the deaf, Connecticut Asylum for the Education and Instruction of Deaf and Dumb Persons (now the American School for the Deaf), at Hartford, CT, in 1817. For 41 years Clerc trained new teachers in the use of sign language and in methods of teaching the deaf. Clerc was born at LaBalme, France, and died July 18, 1869.

DAYTONA KART WEEK BY COMETIC GASKET. Dec 26–30. Daytona International Speedway, Daytona Beach, FL. World Karting Association races. For info: Daytona International Speedway, PO Box 2801, Daytona Beach, FL 32120-2801. Phone: (800) PIT-SHOP. Web: www.daytonainternationalspeedway.com.

HOLIDAY MAGIC. Dec 26–Jan 1, 2007. Mystic, CT. Everyone pays reduced admission and enjoys a full day of crafts, entertainment and the lore of the sea. Est attendance: 3,000. For info: Mystic Seaport, 75 Greenmanville Ave, Box 6000, Mystic, CT 06355. Phone: (860) 572-5315 or (888) 973-2767. Web: www.mysticseaport.org.

IRELAND: DAY OF THE WREN. Dec 26. Dingle Peninsula. Masked revelers and musicians go from door to door asking for money. Traditional day and night of public merrymaking.

KWANZAA. Dec 26–Jan 1, 2007. American black family observance created in 1966 by Dr. Maulana Karenga in recognition of traditional African harvest festivals. This seven-day festival stresses unity of the black family, with a harvest feast (karamu) on the first day and a day of meditation on the final one. Kwanzaa means "first fruit" in Swahili.

LOVERA, JUAN: BIRTH ANNIVERSARY. Dec 26, 1778. Venezuelan "Artist of Independence," whose best-known canvases commemorate the independence dates of Apr 19, 1810, and July 5, 1811. Known as the founder of historical painting in Venezuela. Died in 1841 (exact date unknown).

LUXEMBOURG: BLESSING OF THE WINE. Dec 26. Greiveldange, Luxembourg. Winemakers parade to the church, where a barrel of wine is blessed.

MADD'S NEW YEAR'S DESIGNATE A DRIVER CAMPAIGN. Dec 26–31. Mothers Against Drunk Driving (MADD) asks motorists to designate a nondrinking driver before the celebrations begin on New Year's Eve (and for any celebration year-round). As part of its Designate a Driver Campaign, MADD offers a free Safe Party Guide in English and Spanish. For info: Mothers Against Drunk Driving (MADD). Phone: (800) GET-MADD. Web: www.madd.org.

MAO TSE-TUNG: BIRTH ANNIVERSARY. Dec 26, 1893. Chinese librarian, teacher, communist revolutionist and "founding father" of the People's Republic of China, born at Hunan Province, China. Died at Beijing, Sept 9, 1976.

MILLER, HENRY (VALENTINE): BIRTH ANNIVERSARY. Dec 26, 1891. Controversial American novelist (*Tropic of Cancer*), born at New York, NY. Died at Pacific Palisades, CA, June 7, 1980.

NATIONAL WHINER'S DAY™. Dec 26. A day dedicated to whiners, especially those who return Christmas gifts and need lots of attention. People are encouraged to be happy about what they do have, rather than unhappy about what they don't have. The most famous whiner(s) of the year will be announced. Nominations accepted through Dec 15. For more info, please send SASE to: Kevin C. Zaborney, 2023 Vickory Rd, Caro, MI 48723. Phone: (989) 673-6696. E-mail: revkev@avci.net. Web: www.geocities.com/hugging_whining.

NELSON, THOMAS: BIRTH ANNIVERSARY. Dec 26, 1738. Merchant and signer of the Declaration of Independence, born at Yorktown, VA. Died at Hanover County, VA, Jan 4, 1789.

RADIUM DISCOVERED: ANNIVERSARY. Dec 26, 1898. French scientists Pierre and Marie Curie discovered the element radium, for which they later won the Nobel Prize for Physics.

SAINT STEPHEN'S DAY. Dec 26. One of the seven deacons named by the apostles to distribute alms. Died during 1st century. Feast Day is Dec 26 and is observed as a public holiday in Austria and the Republic of Ireland.

SECOND DAY OF CHRISTMAS. Dec 26. Observed as holiday in many countries.

SHENANDOAH NATIONAL PARK ESTABLISHED: ANNIVERSARY. Dec 26, 1935. Area of Blue Ridge Mountains of Virginia, originally authorized May 22, 1926, was established as a national park. For further park info: Shenandoah Natl Park, Rte 4, Box 348, Luray, VA 22835.

SLOVENIA: INDEPENDENCE DAY. Dec 26. National holiday. Commemorates 1990 announcement of separation from the Yugoslav Union.

SOUNDS OF THE SEASON: A HOLIDAY CONCERT. Dec 26–27. Ash Lawn–Highland, Home of President James Monroe, Charlottesville, VA. Seasonal music, candlelight house tour and cider. Est attendance: 150. For info: Ash Lawn–Highland, 1000 James Monroe Parkway, Charlottesville, VA 22902. Phone: (434) 293-9539. Fax: (434) 293-8000. E-mail: info@ashlawnhigh land.org. Web: www.ashlawnhighland.org.

SOUTH AFRICA: DAY OF GOODWILL. Dec 26. National holiday. Replaces Boxing Day.

SUMATRAN-ANDAMAN EARTHQUAKE AND TSUNAMIS: ANNIVERSARY. Dec 26, 2004. One of the strongest and most lethal earthquakes of modern history unleashed tsunami waves that devastated coasts all around the Indian Ocean, where it was centered. An estimated 250,000 people died, with thousands missing and millions displaced. With a magnitude in the range of 9.3, this was the second-strongest earthquake of all time. The power was the equivalent of a 100 gigaton bomb, and its action vibrated the entire planet. The Earth spun faster and the day was fractionally shortened as a result. This was also the longest lasting earthquake recorded, with a length of about 10 minutes as opposed to the more typical few seconds.

UNITED KINGDOM: BOXING DAY BANK HOLIDAY. Dec 26. Bank and public holiday in England, Wales, Scotland and Northern Ireland.

BIRTHDAYS TODAY

Evan Bayh, 51, US Senator (D, Indiana), born Shirkleville, IN, Dec 26, 1955.

Susan Butcher, 52, sled dog racer, born Cambridge, MA, Dec 26, 1954.

Gray Davis, 64, former Governor of California (D), born the Bronx, NY, Dec 26, 1942.

Carlton Ernest Fisk, 59, Hall of Fame baseball player, born Bellows Falls, VT, Dec 26, 1947.

Marcelo Rios, 31, tennis player, born Santiago, Chile, Dec 26, 1975.

Osborne Earl (Ozzie) Smith, 52, Hall of Fame baseball player, born Mobile, AL, Dec 26, 1954.

December 2006	S	M	T	W	T	F	S
						1	2
	3	4	5	6	7	8	9
	10	11	12	13	14	15	16
	17	18	19	20	21	22	23
	24	25	26	27	28	29	30
	31						

Phil Spector, 66, music producer, born New York, NY, Dec 26, 1940.

Richard Widmark, 92, actor (*Kiss of Death, Madigan*), born Sunrise, MN, Dec 26, 1914.

DECEMBER 27 — WEDNESDAY
Day 361 — 4 Remaining

CAYLEY, GEORGE: BIRTH ANNIVERSARY. Dec 27, 1773. Aviation pioneer Sir George Cayley, English scientist and inventor, was a theoretician who designed airplanes, helicopters and gliders. He is credited as the father of aerodynamics and he was the pilot of the world's first manned glider flight. Born at Scarborough, Yorkshire, England, he died at Brompton Hall, Yorkshire, Dec 15, 1857.

DIETRICH, MARLENE: BIRTH ANNIVERSARY. Dec 27, 1901. Born at Berlin, Germany, Dietrich enrolled in Max Reinhardt's drama school. Her first big break was in 1930 when Josef Von Sternberg cast her in *The Blue Angel*, the first talkie made in Germany. A year later, she and Sternberg moved to Hollywood and began a string of six films together with *Morocco*, the only film for which she received an Academy Award nomination. Some of her other films were *Destry Rides Again, Around the World in 80 Days, Touch of Evil, Judgment at Nuremberg* and *Witness for the Prosecution*. During the 1950s she was a cabaret singer in a stage revue that toured the globe. Dietrich died May 6, 1992, at Paris, France.

"HOWDY DOODY" TV PREMIERE: ANNIVERSARY. Dec 27, 1947. The first popular children's show was brought to TV by Bob Smith and was one of the first regular NBC shows to be shown in color. It was set in the circus town of Doodyville. Children sat in the bleachers' "Peanut Gallery" and participated in activities such as songs and stories. Human characters were Buffalo Bob (Bob Smith), the silent clown Clarabell (Bob Keeshan, Bobby Nicholson and Lew Anderson), storekeeper Cornelius Cobb (Nicholson), Chief Thunderthud (Bill LeCornec), Princess Summerfall Winterspring (Judy Tyler and Linda Marsh), Bison Bill (Ted Brown) and wrestler Ugly Sam (Dayton Allen). Puppet costars included Howdy Doody, Phineas T. Bluster, Dilly Dally, Flub-a-Dub, Captain Scuttlebutt, Double Doody and Heidi Doody. The filmed adventures of Gumby were also featured. In the final episode, Clarabell broke his long silence to say, "Goodbye, kids."

KEPLER, JOHANNES: BIRTH ANNIVERSARY. Dec 27, 1571. One of the world's greatest astronomers, called "the father of modern astronomy," German mathematician Johannes Kepler was born at Württemberg, Germany; he died at Regensburg, Germany, Nov 15, 1630.

MOON PHASE: FIRST QUARTER. Dec 27. Moon enters First Quarter phase at 9:48 AM, EST.

PASTEUR, LOUIS: BIRTH ANNIVERSARY. Dec 27, 1822. French chemist-bacteriologist born at Dole, Jura, France. Died at Villeneuve l'Etang, France, Sept 28, 1895. Discoverer of prophylactic inoculation against rabies. Pasteurization process named for him.

RADIO CITY MUSIC HALL: ANNIVERSARY. Dec 27, 1932. Radio City Music Hall, at New York City, opened on this date.

SAINT JOHN, APOSTLE-EVANGELIST: FEAST DAY. Dec 27. Son of Zebedee, Galilean fisherman, and Salome. Died about AD 100. Roman Rite Feast Day is Dec 27. (Observed May 8 by Byzantine Rite.)

SALK, LEE: BIRTH ANNIVERSARY. Dec 27, 1926. American child psychologist Lee Salk was born at New York, NY. He became well known for proving the calming effect of a mother's heartbeat on a newborn infant. Salk's warning during the 1970s that women should not abandon full-time childrearing was met with wide opposition, especially from working mothers. He died May 2, 1992, at New York, NY.

BIRTHDAYS TODAY

Gerard Depardieu, 58, actor (*The Return of Martin Guerre, Cyrano de Bergerac*), born Chateauroux, France, Dec 27, 1948.

Tovah Feldshuh, 54, actress (*Holocaust*), born New York, NY, Dec 27, 1952.

Bernard Lanvin, 71, fashion designer, born Neuilly, France, Dec 27, 1935.

Cokie Roberts, 63, news correspondent, born New Orleans, LA, Dec 27, 1943.

Anna Russell, 95, comedienne, born London, England, Dec 27, 1911.

DECEMBER 28 — THURSDAY

Day 362 — 3 Remaining

AUSTRALIA: PROCLAMATION DAY. Dec 28. Observed in South Australia.

ENDANGERED SPECIES ACT: ANNIVERSARY. Dec 28, 1973. President Richard Nixon signed the Endangered Species Act into law.

HOLY INNOCENTS DAY (CHILDERMAS). Dec 28. Commemoration of the massacre of children at Bethlehem, ordered by King Herod who wanted to destroy, among them, the infant Savior. Early and medieval accounts claimed as many as 144,000 victims, but more recent writers, noting that Bethlehem was a very small town, have revised the estimates of the number of children killed to between 6 and 20.

IOWA: ADMISSION DAY: ANNIVERSARY. Dec 28. Became 29th state in 1846.

MESSINA EARTHQUAKE: ANNIVERSARY. Dec 28, 1908. Messina, Sicily. The ancient town of Messina was struck by an earthquake. Nearly 80,000 persons died in the disaster, and half of the town's buildings were destroyed.

MOLSON, JOHN: BIRTH ANNIVERSARY. Dec 28, 1763. John Molson, an orphan, left his home at Lincolnshire, England, to settle in Montreal in 1782. He soon acquired a brewery and became patriarch of the Molson brewery family. Born at Lincolnshire, he died at Montreal, QC, Canada, Jan 11, 1836.

PACIFIC LIFE HOLIDAY BOWL PARADE AND GAME. Dec 28. Parade along Harbor Drive; game at Qualcomm Stadium, San Diego, CA. The televised parade, the morning of the Pacific Life Holiday Bowl football game (teams picked from Pac-10 and Big 12), features floats, marching bands, giant balloons and unique specialty units. Parade at 10 AM, kickoff for game is 5 PM. Est attendance: 160,000. For info: Mark Neville, Holiday Bowl, PO Box 601400, San Diego, CA 92160-1400. Phone: (619) 283-5808. Fax: (619) 281-7947. Web: www.pacificlifeholidaybowl.com.

PLEDGE OF ALLEGIANCE RECOGNIZED: ANNIVERSARY. Dec 28, 1945. The US Congress officially recognized the Pledge of Allegiance and urged its frequent recitation in America's schools. The pledge was composed in 1892 by Francis Bellamy, a Baptist minister. At the time, Bellamy was chairman of a committee of state school superintendents of education, and several public schools adopted his pledge as part of the Columbus Day quadricentennial celebration that year. In 1954 the Knights of Columbus persuaded Congress to add the words "under God" to the pledge. In 2002 a federal appeals court found the pledge unconstitutional for use in public schools due to the "under God" phrase.

POOR RICHARD'S ALMANACK: ANNIVERSARY. Dec 28, 1732. The *Pennsylvania Gazette* carried the first known advertisement for the first issue of *Poor Richard's Almanack* by Richard Saunders (Benjamin Franklin) for the year 1733. The advertisement promised "many pleasant and witty verses, jests and sayings . . . new fashions, games for kisses . . . men and melons . . . breakfast in bed, &c." America's most famous almanac, *Poor Richard's* was published through the year 1758 and has been imitated many times since.

VICE PRESIDENTIAL RESIGNATION: ANNIVERSARY. Dec 28, 1832. John C. Calhoun, who had served as vice president of the US under two presidents (John Quincy Adams and Andrew Jackson), Mar 4, 1825–Dec 28, 1832, finding himself in growing disagreement with President Jackson, resigned the office of vice president, the first to do so. He spent most of his subsequent political life as a US senator from South Carolina.

WILSON, WOODROW: 150th BIRTH ANNIVERSARY. Dec 28, 1856. The 28th president of the US was born Thomas Woodrow Wilson at Staunton, VA. Twice elected president (1912 and 1916), it was Wilson who said, "The world must be made safe for democracy," as he asked the Congress to declare war on Germany, Apr 2, 1917. His first wife, Ellen, died Aug 6, 1914, and he married Edith Bolling Galt, Dec 18, 1915. He suffered a paralytic stroke, Sept 16, 1919, never regaining his health. There were many speculations about who (possibly Mrs Wilson?) was running the government during his illness. His second term of office ended Mar 3, 1921, and he died at Washington, DC, Feb 3, 1924.

BIRTHDAYS TODAY

Ray Bourque, 46, former hockey player, born Montreal, QC, Canada, Dec 28, 1960.

Malcolm Gets, 42, actor ("Caroline in the City"), born near Gainesville, FL, Dec 28, 1964.

Hubert Myatt (Hubie) Green III, 60, golfer, born Birmingham, AL, Dec 28, 1946.

Johnny Isakson, 62, US Senator (R, Georgia), born Atlanta, Ga, Dec 28, 1944.

Lou Jacobi, 93, actor (*Irma La Douce*), born Toronto, ON, Canada, Dec 28, 1913.

Tim Johnson, 60, US Senator (D, South Dakota), born Canton, SD, Dec 28, 1946.

Patrick Rafter, 34, tennis player, born Mount Isa, Queensland, Australia, Dec 28, 1972.

Todd Richards, 37, Olympic snowboarder, born Worcester, MA, Dec 28, 1969.

Maggie Smith, 72, actress (Oscars for *The Prime of Miss Jean Brodie* and *California Suite*; Tony for *Lettice & Lovage*), born Ilford, England, Dec 28, 1934.

Denzel Washington, 52, actor (*The Hurricane, Malcolm X*; Oscars for *Training Day* and *Glory*), born Mount Vernon, NY, Dec 28, 1954.

Edgar Winter, 60, singer, musician (*Edgar Winter's White Trash, They Only Come Out at Night*), born Beaumont, TX, Dec 28, 1946.

DECEMBER 29 — FRIDAY

Day 363 — 2 Remaining

CASALS, PABLO: BIRTH ANNIVERSARY. Dec 29, 1876. Famed cellist Pablo Carlos Salvador Defillio de Casals was born at Venrell, Spain, and died at Rio Pedros, Puerto Rico, Oct 22, 1973.

GLADSTONE, WILLIAM EWART: BIRTH ANNIVERSARY. Dec 29, 1809. English statesman and author for whom the Gladstone (luggage) bag was named. Inspiring orator, eccentric individual, intensely loved or hated by all who knew him (cheered from the streets and jeered from the balconies), Gladstone is said to have left more writings (letters, diaries, journals, books) than any other major English politician. However, his preoccupation with the charitable rehabilitation of prostitutes was perhaps easily misunderstood. Born at Liverpool, England, he was four times Britain's prime minister. Gladstone died at Hawarden, Wales, May 19, 1898.

JOHNSON, ANDREW: BIRTH ANNIVERSARY. Dec 29, 1808. Seventeenth president of the US, Andrew Johnson, proprietor of a tailor shop at Laurens, SC, before he entered politics, was born at Raleigh, NC. Upon Abraham Lincoln's assassination Johnson became president. He was the first president to be impeached by the House and was acquitted Mar 26, 1868, by the Senate. After his term of office as president (Apr 15, 1865–Mar 3, 1869) he made several unsuccessful attempts to win public office. Finally he was elected to the US Senate from Tennessee and served in the Senate from Mar 4, 1875, until his death at Carter's Station, TN, July 31, 1875.

NEW YEAR'S EVE TRAIL RIDE AND PARTY. Dec 29–Jan 1, 2007. Spirit of the Suwannee Music Park and Campground, Live Oak, FL. Enjoy trail riding in the cool and mild warm weather, good food, music, dancing and fun. For info: Spirit of the Suwannee Music Park and Campground, 3076 95th Dr, Live Oak, FL 32060. Phone: (386) 364-1683. Web: www.musiclives here.com.

NO INTERRUPTIONS DAY. Dec 29. On this day there shall be no interruptions! At work we will minimize or eliminate interruptions to our thought processes or tasks we are performing. At home we will silence and shut down all devices that interrupt us so we can devote ourselves to our families or to ourselves. This is a day for quiet and/or focus. It is a day to renew our energies to prepare ourselves for the new calendar year ahead. For info: Sylvia Henderson, Springboard Training, PO Box 588, Olney, MD 20830-0588. Phone: (301) 260-1538. E-mail: admin@spring boardtraining.com. Web: www.springboardtraining.com.

RASPUTIN, GRIGORI EFIMOVICH: 90th ASSASSINATION ANNIVERSARY. Dec 29, 1916. Russian monk and mystic, born Grigori Efimovich Novjkh, about 1871, at Siberia. Rasputin gained great influence with Russian emperor Nicholas II and the empress Alexandra, urging severe measures in dealing with the peasant masses, virtually dictating government policy. Notoriously dissolute and corrupt, Rasputin was said to have possessed hypnotic powers. He claimed divine inspiration and the ability to perform miracles. His name became synonymous with corruption and evil, and he was called the "plague pot" of Russia. In fact, Rasputin was a nickname from the Russian word *rasputny*, meaning debauched, profligate, licentious. When an attempt to poison him failed, he was shot to death and his body dropped through a hole in the ice into the Neva River. It was recovered three days later and buried in a silver casket at Tsarkoe Selo. The imperial government was crushed by the 1917 Revolution within a year of his death.

SAINT THOMAS OF CANTERBURY: FEAST DAY. Dec 29. Thomas, Archbishop of Canterbury, was born at London in 1118 and was murdered at the Canterbury Cathedral on this date in 1170.

SUN BOWL. Dec 29. Sun Bowl Stadium, El Paso, TX. 72nd annual. Sponsored by Vitalis. For info: Sun Bowl Assn, 4150 Pinnacle St, Ste 100, El Paso, TX 79902. Phone: (800) 915-BOWL. Web: www.sunbowl.org.

TEXAS: ADMISSION DAY: ANNIVERSARY. Dec 29. Became 28th state in 1845.

TICK TOCK DAY. Dec 29. Time runs out! All those dreams you've had, all those fantasies? It's time, friend. Do it! Annually, Dec 29. [©2003 by WH.] For info: Thomas & Ruth Roy, Wellcat Holidays, 2418 Long Ln, Lebanon, PA 17046. Phone: (717) 279-0184. E-mail: info@wellcat.com. Web: www.wellcat.com.

WOUNDED KNEE MASSACRE: ANNIVERSARY. Dec 29, 1890. Anniversary of the massacre of more than 200 Native American men, women and children by the US 7th Cavalry at Wounded Knee Creek, SD. Government efforts to suppress a ceremonial religious practice, the Ghost Dance (which called for a messiah who would restore the bison to the plains, make the white men disappear and bring back the old Native American way of life), had resulted in the death of Sitting Bull, Dec 15, 1890, which further inflamed the disgruntled Native Americans and culminated in the slaughter at Wounded Knee, Dec 29.

YMCA ORGANIZED: ANNIVERSARY. Dec 29, 1851. The first US branch of the Young Men's Christian Association was organized at Boston. It was modeled on an organization begun at London in 1844.

BIRTHDAYS TODAY

Patricia Clarkson, 47, actress (*Pieces of April, The Station Agent*), born New Orleans, LA, Dec 29, 1959.

Ted Danson, 59, actor ("Cheers," "Becker," *Three Men and a Baby*), born San Diego, CA, Dec 29, 1947.

Marianne Faithfull, 60, singer ("As Tears Go By," "Summer Nights"), actress, born London, England, Dec 29, 1946.

Thomas Edwin Jarriel, 72, broadcast journalist, born LaGrange, GA, Dec 29, 1934.

Jason Kreis, 34, soccer player, born Omaha, NE, Dec 29, 1972.

Jude Law, 34, actor (*The Talented Mr Ripley*), born London, England, Dec 29, 1972.

Mary Tyler Moore, 70, actress (two Emmys for "The Dick Van Dyke Show"; three Emmys for "The Mary Tyler Moore Show"; *Ordinary People*), born Brooklyn, NY, Dec 29, 1936.

Jon Polito, 56, actor ("Homicide"), born Philadelphia, PA, Dec 29, 1950.

Paula Poundstone, 47, comedienne, born Sudbury, MA, Dec 29, 1959.

Jon Voight, 68, actor (*Midnight Cowboy, Deliverance*), born Yonkers, NY, Dec 29, 1938.

Andy Wachowski, 39, filmmaker with brother Larry Wachowski (*The Matrix*), born Chicago, IL, Dec 29, 1967.

Season's Greetings

DECEMBER 30 — SATURDAY
Day 364 — 1 Remaining

FALLING NEEDLES FAMILY FEST. Dec 30. Now that the yuletide tree's been up for weeks and hasn't been watered since a couple of days before Christmas, gather the gang around and watch the needles gently fall one by one. Live it up! Dance barefoot! [©2003 by WH.] For info: Thomas & Ruth Roy, Wellcat Holidays, 2418 Long Ln, Lebanon, PA 17046. Phone: (717) 279-0184. E-mail: info@wellcat.com. Web: www.wellcat.com.

GUGGENHEIM, SIMON: BIRTH ANNIVERSARY. Dec 30, 1867. American capitalist and philanthropist, born at Philadelphia, PA. He established, in memory of his son, the John Simon Guggenheim Memorial Foundation, in 1925. Died Nov 2, 1941, at New York, NY.

KIPLING, RUDYARD: BIRTH ANNIVERSARY. Dec 30, 1865. English poet, novelist and short story writer, Nobel Prize laureate, Kipling was born at Bombay, India. After working as a journalist at India, he traveled around the world. He married an American and lived in Vermont for several years. Kipling is best known for his children's stories, such as the *Jungle Book* and *Just So Stories* and poems such as "The Ballad of East and West" and "If." He died at London, England, Jan 18, 1936.

LEACOCK, STEPHEN: BIRTH ANNIVERSARY. Dec 30, 1869. Canadian economist and humorist, born at Swanmore, Hampshire, England. Died Mar 28, 1944, at Toronto, Canada. "Lord Ronald. . .," he wrote in *Nonsense Novels*, "flung himself upon his horse and rode madly off in all directions."

December 2006	S	M	T	W	T	F	S
						1	2
	3	4	5	6	7	8	9
	10	11	12	13	14	15	16
	17	18	19	20	21	22	23
	24	25	26	27	28	29	30
	31						

"LET'S MAKE A DEAL" TV PREMIERE: ANNIVER-SARY. Dec 30, 1963. Monty Hall hosted this outrageous and no-skill-required game show. Audience members, many of whom wore costumes, were selected to sit in the trading area, and some were picked to "make a deal" with Hall by trading something of their own for something they were offered. Sometimes prizes were worthless ("zonks"). At the end of the show, the two people who had won the most were given the option to trade their winnings for a chance at the "Big Deal," hidden behind one of three doors. The most recent revival (1990–91) was hosted by Bob Hilton.

MONITOR SINKS: ANNIVERSARY. Dec 30, 1862. The Union ironclad ship USS *Monitor* (which achieved fame after its battle with the *Merrimac*) sank off Cape Hatteras during a storm. Sixteen of its crew were lost. See also: "Battle of the *Monitor* and the *Merrimac*: Anniversary" (Mar 9).

PARKS, BERT: BIRTH ANNIVERSARY. Dec 30, 1914. Bert Parks was born at Atlanta, GA. An actor whose career spanned radio, film, television and Broadway, his name became synonymous with the Miss America pageant, which he emceed for 25 years, ending in 1980. Parks made a special return appearance for the 1990 pageant, once again singing his signature song "There She Is." He died Feb 2, 1992, at La Jolla, CA.

PHILIPPINES: RIZAL DAY. Dec 30. National holiday. Commemorates martyrdom of Dr. Jose Rizal in 1896.

"THE ROY ROGERS SHOW" TV PREMIERE: 55th ANNIVERSARY. Dec 30, 1951. This very popular TV western starred Roy Rogers and his wife, Dale Evans, as themselves. It also featured Pat Brady as Rogers's sidekick who rode a jeep named Nellybelle, the singing group Sons of the Pioneers, Rogers's horse Trigger, Evans's horse Buttermilk and a German shepherd named Bullet. This half-hour show was especially popular with young viewers.

USSR ESTABLISHED: ANNIVERSARY. Dec 30, 1922. After the Russian revolution of 1917 and the subsequent three-year civil war, the Union of Soviet Socialist Republics (or Soviet Union) was founded, a confederation of Russia, Byelorussia, the Ukraine and the Transcaucasian Federation. It was the first state in the world to be based on Marxist communism. The Soviet Union was dissolved Dec 8, 1991. See also: "Soviet Union Dissolved" (Dec 8).

VAN FLEET, JO: BIRTH ANNIVERSARY. Dec 30, 1922. Actress (Oscar for *East of Eden*; "Cinderella"), born at Oakland, CA. Died June 10, 1996.

YAWM ARAFAT: THE STANDING AT ARAFAT. Dec 30. Islamic calendar date: Dhu-Hijjah 9, 1427. The day when people on the Hajj (pilgrimage to Mecca) assemble for "the Standing" at the plain of Arafat at Mina, Saudi Arabia, near Mecca. This gathering is a foreshadowing of the Day of Judgment. Different methods for "anticipating" the visibility of the new moon crescent at Mecca are used by different Muslim groups. US date may vary. Began at sunset the preceding day.

BIRTHDAYS TODAY

Joseph Bologna, 68, actor, writer (*The Big Bus, My Favorite Year, Blame It on Rio*), born Brooklyn, NY, Dec 30, 1938.

James Burrows, 66, director ("Cheers," "Taxi"), born Los Angeles, CA, Dec 30, 1940.

Bo Diddley, 78, singer, songwriter ("Who Do You Love," "I'm a Man"), musician, born McCombs, MS, Dec 30, 1928.

Eliza Dushku, 26, actress ("Buffy the Vampire Slayer," "Angel"), born Boston, MA, Dec 30, 1980.

LeBron James, 22, basketball player, born Akron, OH, Dec 30, 1984.

Davy Jones, 60, actor, singer (The Monkees, "Daydream Believer"), born Manchester, England, Dec 30, 1946.

Sanford (Sandy) Koufax, 71, Hall of Fame baseball player, former sportscaster, born Brooklyn, NY, Dec 30, 1935.

Kristin Kreuk, 24, actress ("Smallville"), born Vancouver, BC, Canada, Dec 30, 1982.

Matt Lauer, 49, news anchor ("Today"), born New York, NY, Dec 30, 1957.

Kenyon Martin, 29, basketball player, born Saginaw, MI, Dec 30, 1977.

Michael Nesmith, 64, singer, songwriter (The Monkees), director, born Houston, TX, Dec 30, 1942.

Patti Smith, 60, singer ("Because the Night"), born Chicago, IL, Dec 30, 1946.

Russ Tamblyn, 71, actor ("Twin Peaks," *Peyton Place, West Side Story*), born Los Angeles, CA, Dec 30, 1935.

Concetta Tomei, 61, actress ("Providence," "China Beach"), born Kenosha, WI, Dec 30, 1945.

Tracey Ullman, 47, actress, singer ("The Tracey Ullman Show," *I Love You to Death*), born Buckinghamshire, England, Dec 30, 1959.

Meredith Vieira, 55, television journalist ("The View," "60 Minutes"), born Providence, RI, Dec 30, 1951.

Eldrick (Tiger) Woods, 31, golfer, born Cypress, CA, Dec 30, 1975.

DECEMBER 31 — SUNDAY
Day 365 — 0 Remaining

CANADA: FIRST NIGHTS. Dec 31. These Canadian cities have First Night celebrations: Banff, Drayton Valley, Edmonton and Red Deer, Alberta; Kamloops and Whistler, British Columbia; Yellowknife, Northwest Territories; and Chatham-Kent, Hamilton, Kingston, Peterborough and Toronto, Ontario. For info: First Night Intl, 84 Court St, Ste 507, Binghamton, NY 13901. Phone: (607) 772-3597. Fax: (607) 772-6305. Web: www.firstnight.com.

DENVER, JOHN: BIRTH ANNIVERSARY. Dec 31, 1943. Born Henry John Deutschendorf at Roswell, NM, this singer-songwriter ("Rocky Mountain High," "Sunshine on My Shoulder") died in a plane crash off the coast of California, Oct 12, 1997.

EID-AL-ADHA: FEAST OF THE SACRIFICE. Dec 31. Islamic calendar date: Dhu-Hijjah 10, 1427. Commemorates Abraham's willingness to sacrifice his son Ishmael in obedience to God. It is part of the Hajj (pilgrimage to Mecca). The day begins with the sacrifice of an animal in remembrance of the Angel Gabriel's substitution of a lamb as Abraham's offering. One-third of the meat is given to the poor and the rest is shared with friends and family. Celebrated with gifts and general merrymaking, the festival usually continues for several days. It is celebrated as Tabaski in Benin, Burkina Faso, Guinea, Guinea-Bissau, Ivory Coast, Mali, Niger and Senegal; as Hari Raya Hajj in Southeast Asia and as Kurban Bayram in Turkey and Bosnia. Different methods for "anticipating" the visibility of the moon crescent at Mecca are used by different Muslim groups. US date may vary. Began at sunset the preceding day.

FIRST BANK OPENS IN US: 225th ANNIVERSARY. Dec 31, 1781. The first modern bank in the US, the Bank of North America, was organized by Robert Morris and received its charter from the Confederation Congress. It began operations Jan 7, 1782, at Philadelphia.

FIRST NIGHT ALBANY. Dec 31. Downtown Albany, NY. A New Year's Eve celebration of the arts in multiple locations downtown with music, dancing, children's events and fireworks. Annually, on New Year's Eve. Est attendance: 10,000. For info: City of Albany Office of Special Events, City Hall, 4th Fl, Eagle St, Albany, NY 12207. Phone: (518) 434-2032. Fax: (518) 426-0759. E-mail: info@albanyevents.org. Web: www.albanyevents.org.

Health, Peace, and sweet content be yours. —Shakespeare

FIRST NIGHT ASHEVILLE. Dec 31. Asheville, NC. This alcohol-free celebration of art, music and entertainment includes approximately 15 indoor venues featuring magic, drama and dance, as well as interactive games and children's activities. The grand finale includes live music and a countdown to midnight that culminates with a spectacular fireworks show. Est attendance: 10,000. For info: Paul Clarke, Festival Coord, Asheville Parks & Rec/First Night, PO Box 7148, Asheville, NC 28802-7148. Phone: (828) 259-5800. Fax: (828) 259-5606.

FIRST NIGHT BOSTON. Dec 31. Boston, MA. The largest New Year's arts festival in North America, First Night Boston has grown to be a highly anticipated tradition. The festival features more than 1,000 artists in 250 performances and exhibitions in 50 venues throughout downtown Boston, a Mardi Gras-style Grand Procession, large-scale ice sculptures, music, dance, theater, family entertainment, fireworks at midnight and much more! Boston was the site of the first First Night in 1976. Est attendance: 1,000,000. For info: First Night, Inc, 31 Saint James Ave, Ste 949, Boston, MA 02116. Phone: (617) 542-1399. Fax: (617) 426-9531. E-mail: info@firstnight.org. Web: www.firstnight.org.

FIRST NIGHTS. Dec 31. The following US cities have First Night celebrations: Mobile, AL; Fayetteville, AR; Bakersfield, Escondido, Fullerton, Martinez, Monterey, San Diego, San Luis Obispo, Santa Barbara, Santa Cruz, Santa Fe Springs, Santa Rosa, Stockton and Whittier, CA; Fort Collins and Pikes Peak, CO; Cheshire, Danbury, Hartford, Torrington and Westport/Weston, CT; Dover and Wilmington, DE; Delray Beach, Dunedin, Fort Walton Beach, Miami Beach and St. Petersburg, FL; Athens, Gainesville, Golden Isles, Macon and Savannah, GA; Boise and Idaho Falls, ID; Aurora, Bloomington/Normal, Centralia, Evanston, Pontiac, River Bend, Rockford and Springfield, IL; Evansville, IN; Owensboro, KY; Annapolis, Frederick, Montgomery County and Talbot, MD; Beverly, Boston, Chatham, Fall River, Martha's Vineyard, New Bedford, Northampton, Pittsfield, Quincy, Sharon, Sturbridge, Twin Cities and Worcester, MA; Jackson, MS; Cadillac and Birmingham, MI; St. Paul, MN; Columbia and Springfield, MO; Flathead and Missoula, MT; Portsmouth and Wolfeboro, NH; Bridgewater/Raritan/Somerville, Flemington, Haddonfield, Manasquan, Maplewood/South Orange, Montclair, Moorestown, Morris County, Mount Holly, Newark, Ocean City, Ocean County, Red Bank, Ridgewood, Summit, Teaneck and Westfield, NJ; Albany, Binghamton, Buffalo, Gloversville/Johnstown, Greenport, Middletown, New York City, Nyack, Oneonta, Saratoga, Sayville, Staten Island, Syracuse and Watertown, NY; Asheville and Raleigh, NC; Grand Forks, ND; Akron, Canfield, Columbus, Toledo and Youngstown, OH; Eugene and Salem, OR; Bethlehem, Bloomsburg, Bradford, Bristol, Carlisle, Doylestown, Erie,

Hanover, Newtown, Norwin, Oil City, Philipsburg, Pittsburgh, Scranton, State College, Warren and York, PA; Providence and Westerly, RI; Charleston and Varnville, SC; Yankton, SD; Kingsport, TN; The Woodlands, TX; Ogden, Provo, Salt Lake City and St. George, UT; Bennington, Burlington, Montpelier, Rutland and St. Johnsbury, VT; Augusta, Blacksburg, Charlottesville, Fredericksburg, Harrisonburg, Leesburg, Warrenton, Williamsburg and Winchester, VA; Tacoma and Tri-Cities, WA; and Morgantown, WV. For info: First Night Intl, 84 Court St, Ste 507, Binghamton, NY 13901. Phone: (607) 772-3597. Fax: (607) 772-6305. Web: www.firstnight.com.

JAPAN: NAMAHAGE. Dec 31. Oga Peninsula, Akita Prefecture, Japan. In the evening, groups of "Namahage" men disguised as devils make door-to-door visits, growling, "Any good-for-nothing fellow hereabout?" The object of this annual event is to give sluggards an opportunity to change their minds and become diligent. Otherwise, according to legend, they will be punished by devils.

LEAP SECOND ADJUSTMENT TIME. Dec 31. One of the times that have been favored for the addition or subtraction of a second from clock time (to coordinate atomic and astronomical time). The determination to adjust is made by the International Earth Rotation Service of the International Bureau of Weights and Measures, at Paris, France. See also: "Leap Seconds" (see Contents).

MAKE UP YOUR MIND DAY. Dec 31. A day for all those people who have a hard time making up their minds. Make a decision today and follow through with it! Annually, Dec 31. For info: A.C. Vierow and M.A. Dufour, Box 71, Clio, MI 48420-0071.

MARSHALL, GEORGE CATLETT: BIRTH ANNIVERSARY. Dec 31, 1880. Chairman of the newly formed Joint Chiefs of Staff Committee throughout the US's involvement in WWII, General George Marshall was born at Uniontown, PA. He accompanied Roosevelt or represented the US at most Allied war conferences. He served as secretary of state and was designer of the Marshall Plan after the war. Died Oct 16, 1959, at Washington, DC.

MATISSE, HENRI: BIRTH ANNIVERSARY. Dec 31, 1869. Painter born at Le Cateau, France. Matisse also designed textiles and stained-glass windows. Died at Nice, France, Nov 3, 1954.

NEW YEAR'S EVE. Dec 31. The last evening of the Gregorian calendar year, traditionally a night for merrymaking to welcome in the new year.

NEW YEAR'S FEST. Dec 31. Kalamazoo, MI. Kalamazoo comes alive as families, teens and seniors come downtown to welcome the New Year. Featuring more than 25 different artists, performances are hosted in 11 different indoor sites throughout downtown Kalamazoo. The cultural celebration offers music, theater, puppetry, dance, mime and storytelling. Artists come from throughout the Midwest to join in this nonalcoholic celebration. Est attendance: 6,500. For info: Deborah Droppers, New Year's Fest, Inc, 346 W Michigan Ave, Kalamazoo, MI 49007. Phone: (269) 388-2830. E-mail: EventKzoo@chartermi.net. Web: www.eventkalamazoo.com.

NIXON, JOHN: DEATH ANNIVERSARY. Dec 31, 1808. Revolutionary patriot and businessman, Commander of the Philadelphia City Guard, born 1733 (exact date unknown). Appointed to conduct the first public reading of the Declaration of Independence, July 8, 1776. Died at Philadelphia, PA.

	S	M	T	W	T	F	S
December						1	2
	3	4	5	6	7	8	9
2006	10	11	12	13	14	15	16
	17	18	19	20	21	22	23
	24	25	26	27	28	29	30
	31						

OCEAN DANCE. Dec 31–Jan 1, 2007. Hollywood, FL. A free two-day celebration of dance featuring a critically acclaimed dance company with performances on the beach. Est attendance: 50,000. For info: Art & Culture Center of Hollywood, 1650 Harrison St, Hollywood, FL 33020. Phone: (954) 921-3274. E-mail: pr@artandculturecenter.org. Web: www.artandculturecenter.org.

ONE VOICE. Dec 31. A reading of the Universal Peace Covenant at the turning of the New Year, beginning at midnight on Dec 31, 2006. In conjunction with the Universal Hour of Peace, the School of Metaphysics invites people all around the world to create a peace wave by reading this document, penned in 1996 by more than two dozen spiritual teachers ages 20 to 70, from varied cultures and walks of life. The Universal Peace Covenant is available in several languages at www.peacedome.org or you can write to have a copy sent to you. For info: School of Metaphysics, 163 Moon Valley Rd, Windyville, MO 65783. Phone: (417) 345-8411. E-mail: som@som.org.

PANAMA: ASSUMES CONTROL OF CANAL: ANNIVERSARY. Dec 31, 1999. With the expiration of the Panama Canal Treaty of 1979 at noon, the Republic of Panama assumed full responsibility for the canal and the US Panama Canal Commission ceased to exist.

SAINT SYLVESTER'S DAY. Dec 31. Observed in Belgium, Germany, France, Switzerland. Commemorates death of Pope Sylvester I in 335. Feasting, particularly upon "St. Sylvester's Carp."

SAMOA: SAMOAN FIRE DANCE. Dec 31. New Year's Eve is occasion for Samoan bamboo fireworks, singing and traditional performances such as the Samoan Fire Dance.

SCOTLAND: HOGMANAY. Dec 31. The Scottish New Year celebrations date from ancient pagan times. Hogmanay (no one is sure the origin of the name) traditions include fireworks and torch-lit processions in the cities and bonfires in the rural areas. "First footing" is still observed: it is believed to be good luck for the first foot over the threshold to be that of a dark-haired stranger bearing a piece of coal, shortbread or whiskey. After the midnight chimes, everyone sings "Auld Lang Syne."

UNIVERSAL HOUR OF PEACE. Dec 31. Begins at 11:30 PM on Dec 31, 2006, and ends at 12:30 AM on Jan 1, 2007. An hour dedicated to creating peace throughout our planet. Every man, woman and child is asked to spend the hour in meditation, prayer, conversation, listening to beautiful music or whatever helps them concentrate on peace. The simple truth is "living peaceably begins by thinking peacefully." To add your name to the "Millions for Peace" list, e-mail your name, city, state/country to peace@som.org. An hour-long cassette tape of the Universal Peace Covenant voiced in seven languages is available at no charge by contacting SOM. One hour of peace, a world of difference. For info: Dr. Barbara Condron, Intl Coordinator, School of Metaphysics, World HQ, 163 Moon Valley Rd, Windyville, MO 65783. Phone: (417) 345-8411. Fax: (417) 345-6668. E-mail: peace@som.org. Web: www.som.org.

WORLD PEACE MEDITATION. Dec 31. An opportunity for people around the world to focus their thoughts and energy on peace. The event is observed internationally, beginning at noon Greenwich Mean Time (GMT) and lasting one hour (7 AM–8 AM, EST). For info: Quartus Foundation, PO Box 1768, Boerne, TX 78006. Phone: (830) 249-3985. Fax: (830) 249-3318. E-mail: quartus@quartus.org. Web: www.quartus.org.

BIRTHDAYS TODAY

Sir Anthony Hopkins, 69, actor (*The Silence of the Lambs, Legends of the Fall*), born Port Talbot, South Wales, UK, Dec 31, 1937.

Val Kilmer, 47, actor (*Batman Forever, Top Secret, The Doors, Heat*), born Los Angeles, CA, Dec 31, 1959.

Ben Kingsley, 63, actor (Oscar for *Gandhi; Sexy Beast, Schindler's List*), born Krishna Bhanji at Yorkshire, England, Dec 31, 1943.

Tim Matheson, 58, actor (*Animal House*, "The Virginian," "Bonanza"), born Los Angeles, CA, Dec 31, 1948.

Sarah Miles, 65, actress (*The Servant, Blow-Up, Hope and Glory*), born Ingatestone, England, Dec 31, 1941.

Bebe Neuwirth, 48, actress ("Cheers," "Frasier"; stage: *Chicago*), born Newark, NJ, Dec 31, 1958.

Odetta, 76, folksinger, musician, born Odetta Homes Felious Gordon at Birmingham, AL, Dec 31, 1930.

James Remar, 53, actor (*48 Hrs, Drugstore Cowboy*), born Boston, MA, Dec 31, 1953.

Donna Summer, 58, singer ("Bad Girls"), born LaDonna Andrea Gaines at Boston, MA, Dec 31, 1948.

Diane Halfin von Furstenberg, 61, fashion designer, author, born Brussels, Belgium, Dec 31, 1945.

See ya next year!

☆ *Chase's 2006 Calendar of Events* ☆

CALENDAR INFORMATION FOR THE YEAR 2006

Time shown is Eastern Standard Time. All dates are given in terms of the Gregorian calendar.
(Based in part on information prepared by the Nautical Almanac Office, US Naval Observatory.)

ERAS	YEAR	BEGINS
Byzantine	7515	Sept 14
Jewish*	5767	Sept 23
Chinese (Year of the Dog)	4704	Jan 29
Roman (AUC)	2759	Jan 14
Nabonassar	2755	Apr 23
Japanese (Heisei)	18	Jan 1
Grecian (Seleucidae)	2318	Sept 14
		(or Oct 14)
Indian (Saka)	1928	Mar 22
Diocletian	1723	Sept 11
Islamic (Hegira)**	1427	Jan 30

*Year begins the previous day at sunset.
**Year begins the previous evening at moon crescent.

RELIGIOUS CALENDARS

Epiphany	Jan 6
Shrove Tuesday	Feb 28
Ash Wednesday	Mar 1
Lent	Mar 1–Apr 15
Palm Sunday	Apr 9
Good Friday	Apr 14
Easter	Apr 16
Ascension Day	May 25
Whit Sunday (Pentecost)	June 4
Trinity Sunday	June 11
First Sunday in Advent	Dec 3
Christmas Day	Dec 25

Eastern Orthodox Church Observances

Great Lent begins	Mar 6
Pascha (Easter)	Apr 23
Ascension	June 1
Pentecost	June 11

Jewish Holy Days*

Purim	Mar 14
Passover (1st day)	Apr 13
Shavuot	June 2–3
Tisha B'av	Aug 3
Rosh Hashanah (New Year)	Sept 23–24
Yom Kippur	Oct 2
Succoth	Oct 7–12
Chanukah	Dec 16–Dec 23

*All Jewish holy days begin the previous day at sundown.

Islamic Holy Days**

Islamic New Year (1427)	Jan 31
First Day of Ramadan (1427)	Sept 24
Eid-Al-Fitr (1427)	Oct 24

**All Islamic holy days begin the previous evening at moon crescent.

CIVIL CALENDAR—USA—2006

New Year's Day	Jan 1
Martin Luther King's Birthday (obsvd)	Jan 16
Lincoln's Birthday	Feb 12
Washington's Birthday (obsvd)/Presidents' Day	Feb 20
Memorial Day (obsvd)	May 29
Independence Day	July 4
Labor Day	Sept 4
Columbus Day (obsvd)	Oct 9
General Election Day	Nov 7
Veterans Day	Nov 11
Thanksgiving Day	Nov 23

Other Days Widely Observed in US—2006

Groundhog Day (Candlemas)	Feb 2
St. Valentine's Day	Feb 14
St. Patrick's Day	Mar 17
Mother's Day	May 14
Flag Day	June 14
Father's Day	June 18
National Grandparents Day	Sept 10
Hallowe'en	Oct 31

CIVIL CALENDAR—CANADA—2006

Victoria Day	May 22
Canada Day	July 1
Labor Day	Sept 4
Thanksgiving Day	Oct 9
Remembrance Day	Nov 11
Boxing Day	Dec 26

CIVIL CALENDAR—MEXICO—2006

New Year's Day	Jan 1
Constitution Day	Feb 5
Benito Juarez Birthday	Mar 21
Labor Day	May 1
Battle of Puebla Day (Cinco de Mayo)	May 5
Independence Day*	Sept 16
Dia de La Raza	Oct 12
Mexican Revolution Day	Nov 20
Guadalupe Day	Dec 12

*Celebration begins Sept 15 at 11:00 P.M.

CIVIL CALENDAR—UNITED KINGDOM—2006

Accession of Queen Elizabeth II	Feb 6
St. David (Wales)	Mar 1
Commonwealth Day	Mar 13
St. Patrick (Ireland)	Mar 17
Birthday of Queen Elizabeth II	Apr 21
St. George (England)	Apr 23
Coronation Day	June 2
The Queen's Official Birthday (tentative)	June 10
Birthday of Prince Philip, Duke of Edinburgh	June 10
Remembrance Sunday	Nov 12
Birthday of the Prince of Wales	Nov 14
St. Andrew (Scotland)	Nov 30

BANK AND PUBLIC HOLIDAYS—UNITED KINGDOM—2006

(Observed during 2006 in England and Wales, Scotland
and Northern Ireland unless otherwise indicated)

New Year	Jan 1
Bank Holiday (Scotland)	Jan 2
St. Patrick's Day (Northern Ireland)	Mar 17
Good Friday	Apr 14
Easter Monday (except Scotland)	Apr 17
May Day Bank Holiday	May 1
Spring Bank Holiday	May 29
Orangeman's Day (Battle of the Boyne) (Northern Ireland)	July 12
Summer Bank Holiday (Scotland)	Aug 7
Summer Bank Holiday (except Scotland)	Aug 28
Christmas Day Holiday	Dec 25
Boxing Day Holiday	Dec 26

SEASONS

Spring (Vernal Equinox)	Mar 20, 1:26 PM, EST
Summer (Summer Solstice)	June 21, 8:26 AM, EDT
Autumn (Autumnal Equinox)	Sept 23, 12:03 AM, EDT
Winter (Winter Solstice)	Dec 21, 7:22 PM, EST

DAYLIGHT SAVING TIME SCHEDULE—2006

Sunday, Apr 2, 2:00 AM–Sunday, Oct 29, 2:00 AM—in all time zones.

CHRONOLOGICAL CYCLES

Dominical Letter	A
Epact	*
Golden Number (Lunar Cycle)	XII
Julian Period (year of)	6719
Roman Indiction	14
Solar Cycle	27

☆ *Chase's 2006 Calendar of Events* ☆

CALENDAR INFORMATION FOR THE YEAR 2007

Time shown is Eastern Standard Time. All dates are given in terms of the Gregorian calendar.

(Based in part on information prepared by the Nautical Almanac Office, US Naval Observatory.)

ERAS	YEAR	BEGINS
Byzantine	7516	Sept 14
Jewish*	5768	Sept 13
Chinese (Year of the Boar)	4705	Feb 18
Roman (AUC)	2760	Jan 14
Nabonassar	2756	Apr 23
Japanese (Heisei)	19	Jan 1
Grecian (Seleucidae)	2319	Sept 14
		(or Oct 14)
Indian (Saka)	1929	Mar 22
Diocletian	1724	Sept 11
Islamic (Hegira)**	1428	Jan 20

*Year begins the previous day at sunset.
**Year begins the previous evening at moon crescent.

RELIGIOUS CALENDARS

Epiphany	Jan 6
Shrove Tuesday	Feb 20
Ash Wednesday	Feb 21
Lent	Feb 21–Apr 7
Palm Sunday	Apr 1
Good Friday	Apr 6
Easter	Apr 8
Ascension Day	May 17
Whit Sunday (Pentecost)	May 27
Trinity Sunday	June 3
First Sunday in Advent	Dec 2
Christmas Day	Dec 25

Eastern Orthodox Church Observances

Great Lent begins	Feb 19
Pascha (Easter)	Apr 8
Ascension	May 17
Pentecost	May 27

Jewish Holy Days*

Purim	Mar 4
Passover (1st day)	Apr 3
Shavuot	May 23–24
Tisha B'av	July 24
Rosh Hashanah (New Year)	Sept 13–14
Yom Kippur	Sept 22
Succoth	Sept 27–Oct 2
Chanukah	Dec 5–12

*All Jewish holy days begin the previous day at sundown.

Islamic Holy Days**

Islamic New Year (1428)	Jan 20
First Day of Ramadan (1428)	Sept 13
Eid-Al-Fitr (1428)	Oct 13

**All Islamic holy days begin the previous evening at moon crescent.

CIVIL CALENDAR—USA—2007

New Year's Day	Jan 1
Martin Luther King's Birthday (obsvd)	Jan 15
Lincoln's Birthday	Feb 12
Washington's Birthday (obsvd)/Presidents' Day	Feb 19
Memorial Day (obsvd)	May 28
Independence Day	July 4
Labor Day	Sept 3
Columbus Day (obsvd)	Oct 8
General Election Day	Nov 6
Veterans Day	Nov 11
Thanksgiving Day	Nov 22

Other Days Widely Observed in US—2007

Groundhog Day (Candlemas)	Feb 2
St. Valentine's Day	Feb 14
St. Patrick's Day	Mar 17
Mother's Day	May 13
Flag Day	June 14
Father's Day	June 17
National Grandparents Day	Sept 9
Hallowe'en	Oct 31

CIVIL CALENDAR—CANADA—2007

Victoria Day	May 21
Canada Day	July 1
Labor Day	Sept 3
Thanksgiving Day	Oct 8
Remembrance Day	Nov 11
Boxing Day	Dec 26

CIVIL CALENDAR—MEXICO—2007

New Year's Day	Jan 1
Constitution Day	Feb 5
Benito Juarez Birthday	Mar 21
Labor Day	May 1
Battle of Puebla Day (Cinco de Mayo)	May 5
Independence Day*	Sept 16
Dia de La Raza	Oct 12
Mexican Revolution Day	Nov 20
Guadalupe Day	Dec 12

*Celebration begins Sept 15 at 11:00 P.M.

CIVIL CALENDAR—UNITED KINGDOM—2007

Accession of Queen Elizabeth II	Feb 6
St. David (Wales)	Mar 1
Commonwealth Day	Mar 12
St. Patrick (Ireland)	Mar 17
Birthday of Queen Elizabeth II	Apr 21
St. George (England)	Apr 23
Coronation Day	June 2
The Queen's Official Birthday (tentative)	June 9
Birthday of Prince Philip, Duke of Edinburgh	June 10
Remembrance Sunday	Nov 11
Birthday of the Prince of Wales	Nov 14
St. Andrew (Scotland)	Nov 30

BANK AND PUBLIC HOLIDAYS—UNITED KINGDOM—2007

(Observed during 2007 in England and Wales, Scotland
and Northern Ireland unless otherwise indicated)

New Year	Jan 1
Bank Holiday (Scotland)	Jan 2
St. Patrick's Day (Northern Ireland)	Mar 17
Good Friday	Apr 6
Easter Monday (except Scotland)	Apr 9
May Day Bank Holiday	May 7
Spring Bank Holiday	May 28
Orangeman's Day (Battle of the Boyne) (Northern Ireland)	July 12
Summer Bank Holiday (Scotland)	Aug 6
Summer Bank Holiday (except Scotland)	Aug 27
Christmas Day Holiday	Dec 25
Boxing Day Holiday	Dec 26

SEASONS

Spring (Vernal Equinox)	Mar 20, 8:07 PM, EDT
Summer (Summer Solstice)	June 21, 2:06 PM, EDT
Autumn (Autumnal Equinox)	Sept 23, 5:51 AM, EDT
Winter (Winter Solstice)	Dec 22, 1:08 AM, EST

DAYLIGHT SAVING TIME SCHEDULE—2007*

Sunday, Mar 11, 2:00 AM–Sunday, Nov 4, 2:00 AM—in all time zones.

*Extended per the Energy Policy Act of 2005.

CHRONOLOGICAL CYCLES

Dominical Letter	G
Epact	11
Golden Number (Lunar Cycle)	XIII
Julian Period (year of)	6720
Roman Indiction	15
Solar Cycle	28

CALENDAR INFORMATION FOR THE YEAR 2008

Time shown is Eastern Standard Time. All dates are given in terms of the Gregorian calendar.

(Based in part on information prepared by the Nautical Almanac Office, US Naval Observatory.)

ERAS	YEAR	BEGINS
Byzantine	7517	Sept 14
Jewish*	5769	Sept 30
Chinese (Year of the Rat)	4706	Feb 7
Roman (AUC)	2761	Jan 14
Nabonassar	2757	Apr 23
Japanese (Heisei)	20	Jan 1
Grecian (Seleucidae)	2320	Sept 14 (or Oct 14)
Indian (Saka)	1930	Mar 22
Diocletian	1725	Sept 11
Islamic (Hegira)**	1429	Jan 10

*Year begins the previous day at sunset.
**Year begins the previous evening at moon crescent.

RELIGIOUS CALENDARS

Epiphany	Jan 6
Shrove Tuesday	Feb 5
Ash Wednesday	Feb 6
Lent	Feb 6–Mar 22
Palm Sunday	Mar 16
Good Friday	Mar 21
Easter	Mar 23
Ascension Day	May 1
Whit Sunday (Pentecost)	May 11
Trinity Sunday	May 18
First Sunday in Advent	Nov 30
Christmas Day	Dec 25

Eastern Orthodox Church Observances

Great Lent begins	Mar 10
Pascha (Easter)	Apr 27
Ascension	June 5
Pentecost	June 15

Jewish Holy Days*

Purim	Mar 21
Passover (1st day)	Apr 20
Shavuot	June 9–10
Tisha B'av	Aug 10
Rosh Hashanah (New Year)	Sept 30–Oct 1
Yom Kippur	Oct 9
Succoth	Oct 14–20
Chanukah	Dec 22–29

*All Jewish holy days begin the previous day at sundown.

Islamic Holy Days**

Islamic New Year (1429)	Jan 10
First Day of Ramadan (1429)	Sept 2
Eid-Al-Fitr (1429)	Oct 2

**All Islamic holy days begin the previous evening at moon crescent.

CIVIL CALENDAR—USA—2008

New Year's Day	Jan 1
Martin Luther King's Birthday (obsvd)	Jan 21
Lincoln's Birthday	Feb 12
Washington's Birthday (obsvd)/Presidents' Day	Feb 18
Memorial Day (obsvd)	May 26
Independence Day	July 4
Labor Day	Sept 1
Columbus Day (obsvd)	Oct 13
General Election Day	Nov 4
Veterans Day	Nov 11
Thanksgiving Day	Nov 27

Other Days Widely Observed in US—2008

Groundhog Day (Candlemas)	Feb 2
St. Valentine's Day	Feb 14
St. Patrick's Day	Mar 17
Mother's Day	May 11
Flag Day	June 14
Father's Day	June 15
National Grandparents Day	Sept 7
Hallowe'en	Oct 31

CIVIL CALENDAR—CANADA—2008

Victoria Day	May 19
Canada Day	July 1
Labor Day	Sept 1
Thanksgiving Day	Oct 13
Remembrance Day	Nov 11
Boxing Day	Dec 26

CIVIL CALENDAR—MEXICO—2008

New Year's Day	Jan 1
Constitution Day	Feb 5
Benito Juarez Birthday	Mar 21
Labor Day	May 1
Battle of Puebla Day (Cinco de Mayo)	May 5
Independence Day*	Sept 16
Dia de La Raza	Oct 12
Mexican Revolution Day	Nov 20
Guadalupe Day	Dec 12

*Celebration begins Sept 15 at 11:00 P.M.

CIVIL CALENDAR—UNITED KINGDOM—2008

Accession of Queen Elizabeth II	Feb 6
St. David (Wales)	Mar 1
Commonwealth Day	Mar 10
St. Patrick (Ireland)	Mar 17
Birthday of Queen Elizabeth II	Apr 21
St. George (England)	Apr 23
Coronation Day	June 2
The Queen's Official Birthday (tentative)	June 14
Birthday of Prince Philip, Duke of Edinburgh	June 10
Remembrance Sunday	Nov 9
Birthday of the Prince of Wales	Nov 14
St. Andrew (Scotland)	Nov 30

BANK AND PUBLIC HOLIDAYS—UNITED KINGDOM—2008

(Observed during 2008 in England and Wales, Scotland and Northern Ireland unless otherwise indicated)

New Year	Jan 1
Bank Holiday (Scotland)	Jan 2
St. Patrick's Day (Northern Ireland)	Mar 17
Good Friday	Mar 21
Easter Monday (except Scotland)	Mar 24
May Day Bank Holiday	May 5
Spring Bank Holiday	May 26
Orangeman's Day (Battle of the Boyne) (Northern Ireland)	July 12
Summer Bank Holiday (Scotland)	Aug 4
Summer Bank Holiday (except Scotland)	Aug 25
Christmas Day Holiday	Dec 25
Boxing Day Holiday	Dec 26

SEASONS

Spring (Vernal Equinox)	Mar 20, 1:48 AM, EDT
Summer (Summer Solstice)	June 20, 7:59 PM, EDT
Autumn (Autumnal Equinox)	Sept 22, 11:44 AM, EDT
Winter (Winter Solstice)	Dec 21, 7:04 AM, EST

DAYLIGHT SAVING TIME SCHEDULE—2008*

Sunday, Mar 9, 2:00 AM–Sunday, Nov 2, 2:00 AM—in all time zones.

*Extended per the Energy Policy Act of 2005.

CHRONOLOGICAL CYCLES

Dominical Letter	FE
Epact	22
Golden Number (Lunar Cycle)	XIV
Julian Period (year of)	6721
Roman Indiction	1
Solar Cycle	1

Perpetual Calendar, 1753–2100

A perpetual calendar lets you find the day of the week for any date in any year. Since January 1 may fall on any of the seven days of the week, and may be a leap or non-leap year, 14 different calendars are possible. The number next to each year corresponds to one of the 14 calendars. Calendar 1 will be used in 2006; calendar 2 will be used in 2007.

Year	No.	Year	No.	Year	No.	Year	No.	Year	No.	Year	No.	Year	No.	Year	No.	Year	No.
1753	2	1792	8	1831	7	1870	7	1909	6	1948	12	1987	5	2026	5	2065	5
1754	3	1793	3	1832	8	1871	1	1910	7	1949	7	1988	13	2027	6	2066	6
1755	4	1794	4	1833	3	1872	9	1911	1	1950	1	1989	1	2028	14	2067	7
1756	12	1795	5	1834	4	1873	4	1912	9	1951	2	1990	2	2029	2	2068	8
1757	7	1796	13	1835	5	1874	5	1913	4	1952	10	1991	3	2030	3	2069	3
1758	1	1797	1	1836	13	1875	6	1914	5	1953	5	1992	11	2031	4	2070	4
1759	2	1798	2	1837	1	1876	14	1915	6	1954	6	1993	6	2032	12	2071	5
1760	10	1799	3	1838	2	1877	2	1916	14	1955	7	1994	7	2033	7	2072	13
1761	5	1800	4	1839	3	1878	3	1917	2	1956	8	1995	1	2034	1	2073	1
1762	6	1801	5	1840	11	1879	4	1918	3	1957	3	1996	9	2035	2	2074	2
1763	7	1802	6	1841	6	1880	12	1919	4	1958	4	1997	4	2036	10	2075	3
1764	8	1803	7	1842	7	1881	7	1920	12	1959	5	1998	5	2037	5	2076	11
1765	3	1804	8	1843	1	1882	1	1921	7	1960	13	1999	6	2038	6	2077	6
1766	4	1805	3	1844	9	1883	2	1922	1	1961	1	2000	14	2039	7	2078	7
1767	5	1806	4	1845	4	1884	10	1923	2	1962	2	2001	2	2040	8	2079	1
1768	13	1807	5	1846	5	1885	5	1924	10	1963	3	2002	3	2041	3	2080	9
1769	1	1808	13	1847	6	1886	6	1925	5	1964	11	2003	4	2042	4	2081	4
1770	2	1809	1	1848	14	1887	7	1926	6	1965	6	2004	12	2043	5	2082	5
1771	3	1810	2	1849	2	1888	8	1927	7	1966	7	2005	7	2044	13	2083	6
1772	11	1811	3	1850	3	1889	3	1928	8	1967	1	2006	1	2045	1	2084	14
1773	6	1812	11	1851	4	1890	4	1929	3	1968	9	2007	2	2046	2	2085	2
1774	7	1813	6	1852	12	1891	5	1930	4	1969	4	2008	10	2047	3	2086	3
1775	1	1814	7	1853	7	1892	13	1931	5	1970	5	2009	5	2048	11	2087	4
1776	9	1815	1	1854	1	1893	1	1932	13	1971	6	2010	6	2049	6	2088	12
1777	4	1816	9	1855	2	1894	2	1933	1	1972	14	2011	7	2050	7	2089	7
1778	5	1817	4	1856	10	1895	3	1934	2	1973	2	2012	8	2051	1	2090	1
1779	6	1818	5	1857	5	1896	11	1935	3	1974	3	2013	3	2052	9	2091	2
1780	14	1819	6	1858	6	1897	6	1936	11	1975	4	2014	4	2053	4	2092	10
1781	2	1820	14	1859	7	1898	7	1937	6	1976	12	2015	5	2054	5	2093	5
1782	3	1821	2	1860	8	1899	1	1938	7	1977	7	2016	13	2055	6	2094	6
1783	4	1822	3	1861	3	1900	2	1939	1	1978	1	2017	1	2056	14	2095	7
1784	12	1823	4	1862	4	1901	3	1940	9	1979	2	2018	2	2057	2	2096	8
1785	7	1824	12	1863	5	1902	4	1941	4	1980	10	2019	3	2058	3	2097	3
1786	1	1825	7	1864	13	1903	5	1942	5	1981	5	2020	11	2059	4	2098	4
1787	2	1826	1	1865	1	1904	13	1943	6	1982	6	2021	6	2060	12	2099	5
1788	10	1827	2	1866	2	1905	1	1944	14	1983	7	2022	7	2061	7	2100	6
1789	5	1828	10	1867	3	1906	2	1945	2	1984	8	2023	1	2062	1		
1790	6	1829	5	1868	11	1907	4	1946	3	1985	3	2024	2	2063	3		
1791	7	1830	6	1869	6	1908	11	1947	4	1986	4	2025	4	2064	10		

Calendar 1 — 2006

JAN
```
 S  M  T  W  T  F  S
 1  2  3  4  5  6  7
 8  9 10 11 12 13 14
15 16 17 18 19 20 21
22 23 24 25 26 27 28
29 30 31
```

FEB
```
 S  M  T  W  T  F  S
             1  2  3  4
 5  6  7  8  9 10 11
12 13 14 15 16 17 18
19 20 21 22 23 24 25
26 27 28
```

MAR
```
 S  M  T  W  T  F  S
          1  2  3  4
 5  6  7  8  9 10 11
12 13 14 15 16 17 18
19 20 21 22 23 24 25
26 27 28 29 30 31
```

APR
```
 S  M  T  W  T  F  S
                   1
 2  3  4  5  6  7  8
 9 10 11 12 13 14 15
16 17 18 19 20 21 22
23 24 25 26 27 28 29
30
```

MAY
```
 S  M  T  W  T  F  S
    1  2  3  4  5  6
 7  8  9 10 11 12 13
14 15 16 17 18 19 20
21 22 23 24 25 26 27
28 29 30 31
```

JUNE
```
 S  M  T  W  T  F  S
             1  2  3
 4  5  6  7  8  9 10
11 12 13 14 15 16 17
18 19 20 21 22 23 24
25 26 27 28 29 30
```

JULY
```
 S  M  T  W  T  F  S
                   1
 2  3  4  5  6  7  8
 9 10 11 12 13 14 15
16 17 18 19 20 21 22
23 24 25 26 27 28 29
30 31
```

AUG
```
 S  M  T  W  T  F  S
          1  2  3  4  5
 6  7  8  9 10 11 12
13 14 15 16 17 18 19
20 21 22 23 24 25 26
27 28 29 30 31
```

SEPT
```
 S  M  T  W  T  F  S
                1  2
 3  4  5  6  7  8  9
10 11 12 13 14 15 16
17 18 19 20 21 22 23
24 25 26 27 28 29 30
```

OCT
```
 S  M  T  W  T  F  S
 1  2  3  4  5  6  7
 8  9 10 11 12 13 14
15 16 17 18 19 20 21
22 23 24 25 26 27 28
29 30 31
```

NOV
```
 S  M  T  W  T  F  S
          1  2  3  4
 5  6  7  8  9 10 11
12 13 14 15 16 17 18
19 20 21 22 23 24 25
26 27 28 29 30
```

DEC
```
 S  M  T  W  T  F  S
                1  2
 3  4  5  6  7  8  9
10 11 12 13 14 15 16
17 18 19 20 21 22 23
24 25 26 27 28 29 30
31
```

Calendar 2 — 2007

JAN
```
 S  M  T  W  T  F  S
    1  2  3  4  5  6
 7  8  9 10 11 12 13
14 15 16 17 18 19 20
21 22 23 24 25 26 27
28 29 30 31
```

FEB
```
 S  M  T  W  T  F  S
          1  2  3
 4  5  6  7  8  9 10
11 12 13 14 15 16 17
18 19 20 21 22 23 24
25 26 27 28
```

MAR
```
 S  M  T  W  T  F  S
          1  2  3
 4  5  6  7  8  9 10
11 12 13 14 15 16 17
18 19 20 21 22 23 24
25 26 27 28 29 30 31
```

APR
```
 S  M  T  W  T  F  S
 1  2  3  4  5  6  7
 8  9 10 11 12 13 14
15 16 17 18 19 20 21
22 23 24 25 26 27 28
29 30
```

MAY
```
 S  M  T  W  T  F  S
       1  2  3  4  5
 6  7  8  9 10 11 12
13 14 15 16 17 18 19
20 21 22 23 24 25 26
27 28 29 30 31
```

JUNE
```
 S  M  T  W  T  F  S
                1  2
 3  4  5  6  7  8  9
10 11 12 13 14 15 16
17 18 19 20 21 22 23
24 25 26 27 28 29 30
```

JULY
```
 S  M  T  W  T  F  S
 1  2  3  4  5  6  7
 8  9 10 11 12 13 14
15 16 17 18 19 20 21
22 23 24 25 26 27 28
29 30 31
```

AUG
```
 S  M  T  W  T  F  S
             1  2  3  4
 5  6  7  8  9 10 11
12 13 14 15 16 17 18
19 20 21 22 23 24 25
26 27 28 29 30 31
```

SEPT
```
 S  M  T  W  T  F  S
                   1
 2  3  4  5  6  7  8
 9 10 11 12 13 14 15
16 17 18 19 20 21 22
23 24 25 26 27 28 29
30
```

OCT
```
 S  M  T  W  T  F  S
    1  2  3  4  5  6
 7  8  9 10 11 12 13
14 15 16 17 18 19 20
21 22 23 24 25 26 27
28 29 30 31
```

NOV
```
 S  M  T  W  T  F  S
          1  2  3
 4  5  6  7  8  9 10
11 12 13 14 15 16 17
18 19 20 21 22 23 24
25 26 27 28 29 30
```

DEC
```
 S  M  T  W  T  F  S
                   1
 2  3  4  5  6  7  8
 9 10 11 12 13 14 15
16 17 18 19 20 21 22
23 24 25 26 27 28 29
30 31
```

Calendar 3

JAN

S	M	T	W	T	F	S
		1	2	3	4	5
6	7	8	9	10	11	12
13	14	15	16	17	18	19
20	21	22	23	24	25	26
27	28	29	30	31		

FEB

S	M	T	W	T	F	S
					1	2
3	4	5	6	7	8	9
10	11	12	13	14	15	16
17	18	19	20	21	22	23
24	25	26	27	28		

MAR

S	M	T	W	T	F	S
					1	2
3	4	5	6	7	8	9
10	11	12	13	14	15	16
17	18	19	20	21	22	23
24	25	26	27	28	29	30
31						

APR

S	M	T	W	T	F	S
	1	2	3	4	5	6
7	8	9	10	11	12	13
14	15	16	17	18	19	20
21	22	23	24	25	26	27
28	29	30				

MAY

S	M	T	W	T	F	S
			1	2	3	4
5	6	7	8	9	10	11
12	13	14	15	16	17	18
19	20	21	22	23	24	25
26	27	28	29	30	31	

JUNE

S	M	T	W	T	F	S
						1
2	3	4	5	6	7	8
9	10	11	12	13	14	15
16	17	18	19	20	21	22
23	24	25	26	27	28	29
30						

JULY

S	M	T	W	T	F	S
	1	2	3	4	5	6
7	8	9	10	11	12	13
14	15	16	17	18	19	20
21	22	23	24	25	26	27
28	29	30	31			

AUG

S	M	T	W	T	F	S
				1	2	3
4	5	6	7	8	9	10
11	12	13	14	15	16	17
18	19	20	21	22	23	24
25	26	27	28	29	30	31

SEPT

S	M	T	W	T	F	S
1	2	3	4	5	6	7
8	9	10	11	12	13	14
15	16	17	18	19	20	21
22	23	24	25	26	27	28
29	30					

OCT

S	M	T	W	T	F	S
		1	2	3	4	5
6	7	8	9	10	11	12
13	14	15	16	17	18	19
20	21	22	23	24	25	26
27	28	29	30	31		

NOV

S	M	T	W	T	F	S
					1	2
3	4	5	6	7	8	9
10	11	12	13	14	15	16
17	18	19	20	21	22	23
24	25	26	27	28	29	30

DEC

S	M	T	W	T	F	S
1	2	3	4	5	6	7
8	9	10	11	12	13	14
15	16	17	18	19	20	21
22	23	24	25	26	27	28
29	30	31				

Calendar 4

JAN

S	M	T	W	T	F	S
			1	2	3	4
5	6	7	8	9	10	11
12	13	14	15	16	17	18
19	20	21	22	23	24	25
26	27	28	29	30	31	

FEB

S	M	T	W	T	F	S
						1
2	3	4	5	6	7	8
9	10	11	12	13	14	15
16	17	18	19	20	21	22
23	24	25	26	27	28	

MAR

S	M	T	W	T	F	S
						1
2	3	4	5	6	7	8
9	10	11	12	13	14	15
16	17	18	19	20	21	22
23	24	25	26	27	28	29
30	31					

APR

S	M	T	W	T	F	S
		1	2	3	4	5
6	7	8	9	10	11	12
13	14	15	16	17	18	19
20	21	22	23	24	25	26
27	28	29	30			

MAY

S	M	T	W	T	F	S
				1	2	3
4	5	6	7	8	9	10
11	12	13	14	15	16	17
18	19	20	21	22	23	24
25	26	27	28	29	30	31

JUNE

S	M	T	W	T	F	S
1	2	3	4	5	6	7
8	9	10	11	12	13	14
15	16	17	18	19	20	21
22	23	24	25	26	27	28
29	30					

JULY

S	M	T	W	T	F	S
		1	2	3	4	5
6	7	8	9	10	11	12
13	14	15	16	17	18	19
20	21	22	23	24	25	26
27	28	29	30	31		

AUG

S	M	T	W	T	F	S
					1	2
3	4	5	6	7	8	9
10	11	12	13	14	15	16
17	18	19	20	21	22	23
24	25	26	27	28	29	30
31						

SEPT

S	M	T	W	T	F	S
	1	2	3	4	5	6
7	8	9	10	11	12	13
14	15	16	17	18	19	20
21	22	23	24	25	26	27
28	29	30				

OCT

S	M	T	W	T	F	S
			1	2	3	4
5	6	7	8	9	10	11
12	13	14	15	16	17	18
19	20	21	22	23	24	25
26	27	28	29	30	31	

NOV

S	M	T	W	T	F	S
						1
2	3	4	5	6	7	8
9	10	11	12	13	14	15
16	17	18	19	20	21	22
23	24	25	26	27	28	29
30						

DEC

S	M	T	W	T	F	S
	1	2	3	4	5	6
7	8	9	10	11	12	13
14	15	16	17	18	19	20
21	22	23	24	25	26	27
28	29	30	31			

Calendar 5

JAN

S	M	T	W	T	F	S
				1	2	3
4	5	6	7	8	9	10
11	12	13	14	15	16	17
18	19	20	21	22	23	24
25	26	27	28	29	30	31

FEB

S	M	T	W	T	F	S
1	2	3	4	5	6	7
8	9	10	11	12	13	14
15	16	17	18	19	20	21
22	23	24	25	26	27	28

MAR

S	M	T	W	T	F	S
1	2	3	4	5	6	7
8	9	10	11	12	13	14
15	16	17	18	19	20	21
22	23	24	25	26	27	28
29	30	31				

APR

S	M	T	W	T	F	S
			1	2	3	4
5	6	7	8	9	10	11
12	13	14	15	16	17	18
19	20	21	22	23	24	25
26	27	28	29	30		

MAY

S	M	T	W	T	F	S
					1	2
3	4	5	6	7	8	9
10	11	12	13	14	15	16
17	18	19	20	21	22	23
24	25	26	27	28	29	30
31						

JUNE

S	M	T	W	T	F	S
	1	2	3	4	5	6
7	8	9	10	11	12	13
14	15	16	17	18	19	20
21	22	23	24	25	26	27
28	29	30				

JULY

S	M	T	W	T	F	S
			1	2	3	4
5	6	7	8	9	10	11
12	13	14	15	16	17	18
19	20	21	22	23	24	25
26	27	28	29	30	31	

AUG

S	M	T	W	T	F	S
						1
2	3	4	5	6	7	8
9	10	11	12	13	14	15
16	17	18	19	20	21	22
23	24	25	26	27	28	29
30	31					

SEPT

S	M	T	W	T	F	S
		1	2	3	4	5
6	7	8	9	10	11	12
13	14	15	16	17	18	19
20	21	22	23	24	25	26
27	28	29	30			

OCT

S	M	T	W	T	F	S
				1	2	3
4	5	6	7	8	9	10
11	12	13	14	15	16	17
18	19	20	21	22	23	24
25	26	27	28	29	30	31

NOV

S	M	T	W	T	F	S
1	2	3	4	5	6	7
8	9	10	11	12	13	14
15	16	17	18	19	20	21
22	23	24	25	26	27	28
29	30					

DEC

S	M	T	W	T	F	S
		1	2	3	4	5
6	7	8	9	10	11	12
13	14	15	16	17	18	19
20	21	22	23	24	25	26
27	28	29	30	31		

Calendar 6

JAN

S	M	T	W	T	F	S
					1	2
3	4	5	6	7	8	9
10	11	12	13	14	15	16
17	18	19	20	21	22	23
24	25	26	27	28	29	30
31						

FEB

S	M	T	W	T	F	S
	1	2	3	4	5	6
7	8	9	10	11	12	13
14	15	16	17	18	19	20
21	22	23	24	25	26	27
28						

MAR

S	M	T	W	T	F	S
	1	2	3	4	5	6
7	8	9	10	11	12	13
14	15	16	17	18	19	20
21	22	23	24	25	26	27
28	29	30	31			

APR

S	M	T	W	T	F	S
				1	2	3
4	5	6	7	8	9	10
11	12	13	14	15	16	17
18	19	20	21	22	23	24
25	26	27	28	29	30	

MAY

S	M	T	W	T	F	S
						1
2	3	4	5	6	7	8
9	10	11	12	13	14	15
16	17	18	19	20	21	22
23	24	25	26	27	28	29
30	31					

JUNE

S	M	T	W	T	F	S
		1	2	3	4	5
6	7	8	9	10	11	12
13	14	15	16	17	18	19
20	21	22	23	24	25	26
27	28	29	30			

JULY

S	M	T	W	T	F	S
				1	2	3
4	5	6	7	8	9	10
11	12	13	14	15	16	17
18	19	20	21	22	23	24
25	26	27	28	29	30	31

AUG

S	M	T	W	T	F	S
1	2	3	4	5	6	7
8	9	10	11	12	13	14
15	16	17	18	19	20	21
22	23	24	25	26	27	28
29	30	31				

SEPT

S	M	T	W	T	F	S
			1	2	3	4
5	6	7	8	9	10	11
12	13	14	15	16	17	18
19	20	21	22	23	24	25
26	27	28	29	30		

OCT

S	M	T	W	T	F	S
					1	2
3	4	5	6	7	8	9
10	11	12	13	14	15	16
17	18	19	20	21	22	23
24	25	26	27	28	29	30
31						

NOV

S	M	T	W	T	F	S
	1	2	3	4	5	6
7	8	9	10	11	12	13
14	15	16	17	18	19	20
21	22	23	24	25	26	27
28	29	30				

DEC

S	M	T	W	T	F	S
			1	2	3	4
5	6	7	8	9	10	11
12	13	14	15	16	17	18
19	20	21	22	23	24	25
26	27	28	29	30	31	

Year 7

JAN

S	M	T	W	T	F	S
						1
2	3	4	5	6	7	8
9	10	11	12	13	14	15
16	17	18	19	20	21	22
23	24	25	26	27	28	29
30	31					

FEB

S	M	T	W	T	F	S
				1	2	3
4	5	6	7	8	9	10
11	12	13	14	15	16	17
18	19	20	21	22	23	24
25	26	27	28			

FEB

S	M	T	W	T	F	S
				1	2	3
4	5	6	7	8	9	10
11	12	13	14	15	16	17
18	19	20	21	22	23	24
25	26	27	28			

Calendar 11

JAN
S	M	T	W	T	F	S
				1	2	3	4
5	6	7	8	9	10	11
12	13	14	15	16	17	18
19	20	21	22	23	24	25
26	27	28	29	30	31	

FEB
S	M	T	W	T	F	S
						1
2	3	4	5	6	7	8
9	10	11	12	13	14	15
16	17	18	19	20	21	22
23	24	25	26	27	28	29

MAR
S	M	T	W	T	F	S
1	2	3	4	5	6	7
8	9	10	11	12	13	14
15	16	17	18	19	20	21
22	23	24	25	26	27	28
29	30	31				

APR
S	M	T	W	T	F	S
				1	2	3	4
5	6	7	8	9	10	11
12	13	14	15	16	17	18
19	20	21	22	23	24	25
26	27	28	29	30		

MAY
S	M	T	W	T	F	S
					1	2
3	4	5	6	7	8	9
10	11	12	13	14	15	16
17	18	19	20	21	22	23
24	25	26	27	28	29	30
31						

JUNE
S	M	T	W	T	F	S
	1	2	3	4	5	6
7	8	9	10	11	12	13
14	15	16	17	18	19	20
21	22	23	24	25	26	27
28	29	30				

JULY
S	M	T	W	T	F	S
				1	2	3	4
5	6	7	8	9	10	11
12	13	14	15	16	17	18
19	20	21	22	23	24	25
26	27	28	29	30	31	

AUG
S	M	T	W	T	F	S
						1
2	3	4	5	6	7	8
9	10	11	12	13	14	15
16	17	18	19	20	21	22
23	24	25	26	27	28	29
30	31					

SEPT
S	M	T	W	T	F	S
	1	2	3	4	5	
6	7	8	9	10	11	12
13	14	15	16	17	18	19
20	21	22	23	24	25	26
27	28	29	30			

OCT
S	M	T	W	T	F	S
					1	2	3
4	5	6	7	8	9	10
11	12	13	14	15	16	17
18	19	20	21	22	23	24
25	26	27	28	29	30	31

NOV
S	M	T	W	T	F	S
1	2	3	4	5	6	7
8	9	10	11	12	13	14
15	16	17	18	19	20	21
22	23	24	25	26	27	28
29	30					

DEC
S	M	T	W	T	F	S
	1	2	3	4	5	
6	7	8	9	10	11	12
13	14	15	16	17	18	19
20	21	22	23	24	25	26
27	28	29	30	31		

Calendar 12

JAN
S	M	T	W	T	F	S
					1	2	3
4	5	6	7	8	9	10
11	12	13	14	15	16	17
18	19	20	21	22	23	24
25	26	27	28	29	30	31

FEB
S	M	T	W	T	F	S
1	2	3	4	5	6	7
8	9	10	11	12	13	14
15	16	17	18	19	20	21
22	23	24	25	26	27	28
29						

MAR
S	M	T	W	T	F	S
	1	2	3	4	5	6
7	8	9	10	11	12	13
14	15	16	17	18	19	20
21	22	23	24	25	26	27
28	29	30	31			

APR
S	M	T	W	T	F	S
					1	2	3
4	5	6	7	8	9	10
11	12	13	14	15	16	17
18	19	20	21	22	23	24
25	26	27	28	29	30	

MAY
S	M	T	W	T	F	S
						1
2	3	4	5	6	7	8
9	10	11	12	13	14	15
16	17	18	19	20	21	22
23	24	25	26	27	28	29
30	31					

JUNE
S	M	T	W	T	F	S
		1	2	3	4	5
6	7	8	9	10	11	12
13	14	15	16	17	18	19
20	21	22	23	24	25	26
27	28	29	30			

JULY
S	M	T	W	T	F	S
					1	2	3
4	5	6	7	8	9	10
11	12	13	14	15	16	17
18	19	20	21	22	23	24
25	26	27	28	29	30	31

AUG
S	M	T	W	T	F	S
1	2	3	4	5	6	7
8	9	10	11	12	13	14
15	16	17	18	19	20	21
22	23	24	25	26	27	28
29	30	31				

SEPT
S	M	T	W	T	F	S
			1	2	3	4
5	6	7	8	9	10	11
12	13	14	15	16	17	18
19	20	21	22	23	24	25
26	27	28	29	30		

OCT
S	M	T	W	T	F	S
						1	2
3	4	5	6	7	8	9
10	11	12	13	14	15	16
17	18	19	20	21	22	23
24	25	26	27	28	29	30
31						

NOV
S	M	T	W	T	F	S
	1	2	3	4	5	6
7	8	9	10	11	12	13
14	15	16	17	18	19	20
21	22	23	24	25	26	27
28	29	30				

DEC
S	M	T	W	T	F	S
			1	2	3	4
5	6	7	8	9	10	11
12	13	14	15	16	17	18
19	20	21	22	23	24	25
26	27	28	29	30	31	

Calendar 13

JAN
S	M	T	W	T	F	S
						1	2
3	4	5	6	7	8	9
10	11	12	13	14	15	16
17	18	19	20	21	22	23
24	25	26	27	28	29	30
31						

FEB
S	M	T	W	T	F	S
	1	2	3	4	5	6
7	8	9	10	11	12	13
14	15	16	17	18	19	20
21	22	23	24	25	26	27
28	29					

MAR
S	M	T	W	T	F	S
		1	2	3	4	5
6	7	8	9	10	11	12
13	14	15	16	17	18	19
20	21	22	23	24	25	26
27	28	29	30	31		

APR
S	M	T	W	T	F	S
						1	2
3	4	5	6	7	8	9
10	11	12	13	14	15	16
17	18	19	20	21	22	23
24	25	26	27	28	29	30

MAY
S	M	T	W	T	F	S
1	2	3	4	5	6	7
8	9	10	11	12	13	14
15	16	17	18	19	20	21
22	23	24	25	26	27	28
29	30	31				

JUNE
S	M	T	W	T	F	S
			1	2	3	4
5	6	7	8	9	10	11
12	13	14	15	16	17	18
19	20	21	22	23	24	25
26	27	28	29	30		

JULY
S	M	T	W	T	F	S
						1	2
3	4	5	6	7	8	9
10	11	12	13	14	15	16
17	18	19	20	21	22	23
24	25	26	27	28	29	30
31						

AUG
S	M	T	W	T	F	S
	1	2	3	4	5	6
7	8	9	10	11	12	13
14	15	16	17	18	19	20
21	22	23	24	25	26	27
28	29	30	31			

SEPT
S	M	T	W	T	F	S
				1	2	3
4	5	6	7	8	9	10
11	12	13	14	15	16	17
18	19	20	21	22	23	24
25	26	27	28	29	30	

OCT
S	M	T	W	T	F	S
						1
2	3	4	5	6	7	8
9	10	11	12	13	14	15
16	17	18	19	20	21	22
23	24	25	26	27	28	29
30	31					

NOV
S	M	T	W	T	F	S
		1	2	3	4	5
6	7	8	9	10	11	12
13	14	15	16	17	18	19
20	21	22	23	24	25	26
27	28	29	30			

DEC
S	M	T	W	T	F	S
				1	2	3
4	5	6	7	8	9	10
11	12	13	14	15	16	17
18	19	20	21	22	23	24
25	26	27	28	29	30	31

Calendar 14

JAN
S	M	T	W	T	F	S
						1
2	3	4	5	6	7	8
9	10	11	12	13	14	15
16	17	18	19	20	21	22
23	24	25	26	27	28	29
30	31					

FEB
S	M	T	W	T	F	S
		1	2	3	4	5
6	7	8	9	10	11	12
13	14	15	16	17	18	19
20	21	22	23	24	25	26
27	28	29				

MAR
S	M	T	W	T	F	S
			1	2	3	4
5	6	7	8	9	10	11
12	13	14	15	16	17	18
19	20	21	22	23	24	25
26	27	28	29	30	31	

APR
S	M	T	W	T	F	S
						1
2	3	4	5	6	7	8
9	10	11	12	13	14	15
16	17	18	19	20	21	22
23	24	25	26	27	28	29
30						

MAY
S	M	T	W	T	F	S
	1	2	3	4	5	6
7	8	9	10	11	12	13
14	15	16	17	18	19	20
21	22	23	24	25	26	27
28	29	30	31			

JUNE
S	M	T	W	T	F	S
				1	2	3
4	5	6	7	8	9	10
11	12	13	14	15	16	17
18	19	20	21	22	23	24
25	26	27	28	29	30	

JULY
S	M	T	W	T	F	S
						1
2	3	4	5	6	7	8
9	10	11	12	13	14	15
16	17	18	19	20	21	22
23	24	25	26	27	28	29
30	31					

AUG
S	M	T	W	T	F	S
		1	2	3	4	5
6	7	8	9	10	11	12
13	14	15	16	17	18	19
20	21	22	23	24	25	26
27	28	29	30	31		

SEPT
S	M	T	W	T	F	S
					1	2
3	4	5	6	7	8	9
10	11	12	13	14	15	16
17	18	19	20	21	22	23
24	25	26	27	28	29	30

OCT
S	M	T	W	T	F	S
1	2	3	4	5	6	7
8	9	10	11	12	13	14
15	16	17	18	19	20	21
22	23	24	25	26	27	28
29	30	31				

NOV
S	M	T	W	T	F	S
			1	2	3	4
5	6	7	8	9	10	11
12	13	14	15	16	17	18
19	20	21	22	23	24	25
26	27	28	29	30		

DEC
S	M	T	W	T	F	S
					1	2
3	4	5	6	7	8	9
10	11	12	13	14	15	16
17	18	19	20	21	22	23
24	25	26	27	28	29	30
31						

☆ *Chase's 2006 Calendar of Events* ☆

NATIONAL DAYS OF THE WORLD FOR 2006

(Compiled from publications of the U.S. Department of State, the United Nations and from information received from the countries listed.)

Most nations set aside one or more days each year as national public holidays, often recognizing the anniversary of the attainment of independence, or the birthday of the country's ruler. Below, the national days are listed alphabetically. It should be noted that in some countries the Gregorian Calendar date of observance varies from year to year. See the Index and the main chronology for further details of observance, and for numerous holidays in addition to the national days listed here.

Afghanistan . . . Aug 19	Ghana . . . Mar 6	Norway . . . May 17
Albania . . . Nov 28	Greece . . . Mar 25	Oman . . . Nov 18
Algeria . . . Nov 1	Grenada . . . Feb 7	Pakistan . . . Mar 23
Andorra . . . Sept 8	Guatemala . . . Sept 15	Panama . . . Nov 3
Angola . . . Nov 11	Guinea . . . Oct 2	Papua New Guinea . . . Sept 16
Antigua and Barbuda . . . Nov 1	Guinea-Bissau . . . Sept 24	Paraguay . . . May 15
Argentina . . . May 25	Guyana . . . Feb 23	Peru . . . July 28
Armenia . . . Sept 21	Haiti . . . Jan 1	Philippines . . . June 12
Australia . . . Jan 26	Holy See . . . Oct 22	Poland . . . May 3
Austria . . . Oct 26	Honduras . . . Sept 15	Portugal . . . June 10
Azerbaijan . . . May 28	Hungary . . . Aug 20	Qatar . . . Sept 3
Bahamas . . . July 10	Iceland . . . June 17	Romania . . . Dec 1
Bahrain . . . Dec 16	India . . . Jan 26	Russian Federation . . . June 12
Bangladesh . . . Mar 26	Indonesia . . . Aug 17	Rwanda . . . July 1
Barbados . . . Nov 30	Iran . . . Apr 1	Saint Christopher (St Kitts) and Nevis . . . Sept 19
Belarus . . . July 3	Iraq . . . Apr 9	Saint Lucia . . . Feb 22
Belgium . . . July 21	Ireland . . . Mar 17	Saint Vincent and the Grenadines . . . Oct 27
Belize . . . Sept 21	Israel . . . May 3	Samoa . . . June 1
Benin . . . Aug 1	Italy . . . June 2	San Marino . . . Sept 3
Bhutan . . . Dec 17	Jamaica . . . Aug 1	Sao Tome and Principe . . . July 12
Bolivia . . . Aug 6	Japan . . . Dec 23	Saudi Arabia . . . Sept 23
Bosnia and Herzegovina . . . Nov 25	Jordan . . . May 25	Senegal . . . Apr 4
Botswana . . . Sept 30	Kazakhstan . . . Oct 25	Serbia and Montenegro . . . Apr 27
Brazil . . . Sept 7	Kenya . . . Dec 12	Seychelles . . . June 18
Brunei Darussalam . . . Feb 23	Kiribati . . . July 12	Sierra Leone . . . Apr 27
Bulgaria . . . Mar 3	Korea, Democratic People's Republic of . . . Sept 9	Singapore . . . Aug 9
Burkina Faso . . . Dec 11	Korea, Republic of . . . Aug 15	Slovakia . . . Sept 1
Burundi . . . July 1	Kuwait . . . Feb 25	Slovenia . . . June 25
Cambodia . . . Nov 9	Kyrgyzstan . . . Aug 31	Solomon Islands . . . July 7
Cameroon . . . May 20	Lao People's Democratic Republic . . . Dec 2	Somalia . . . July 1
Canada . . . July 1	Latvia . . . Nov 18	South Africa . . . Apr 27
Cape Verde . . . July 5	Lebanon . . . Nov 22	Spain . . . Oct 12
Central African Republic . . . Dec 1	Lesotho . . . Oct 4	Sri Lanka . . . Feb 4
Chad . . . Aug 11	Liberia . . . July 26	Sudan . . . Jan 1
Chile . . . Sept 18	Libya . . . Sept 1	Suriname . . . Nov 25
China . . . Oct 1	Liechtenstein . . . Aug 15	Swaziland . . . Sept 6
Colombia . . . July 20	Lithuania . . . Feb 16	Sweden . . . June 6
Comoros . . . July 6	Luxembourg . . . June 23	Switzerland . . . Aug 1
Congo . . . Aug 15	Macedonia, Former Yugoslav Republic of . . . Aug 2	Syrian Arab Republic . . . Apr 17
Congo, Democratic Republic of . . . June 30	Madagascar . . . June 26	Taiwan . . . Oct 10
Costa Rica . . . Sept 15	Malawi . . . July 6	Tajikistan . . . Sept 9
Cote D'Ivoire . . . Aug 7	Malaysia . . . Aug 31	Tanzania, United Republic of . . . Apr 26
Croatia . . . June 25	Maldives . . . July 26	Thailand . . . Dec 5
Cuba . . . Jan 1	Mali . . . Sept 22	Togo . . . Apr 27
Cyprus . . . Oct 1	Malta . . . Sept 21	Tonga . . . June 4
Czech Republic . . . Oct 28	Marshall Islands . . . May 1	Trinidad and Tobago . . . Aug 31
Denmark . . . June 5	Mauritania . . . Nov 28	Tunisia . . . Mar 20
Djibouti . . . June 27	Mauritius . . . Mar 12	Turkey . . . Oct 29
Dominica . . . Nov 3	Mexico . . . Sept 16	Turkmenistan . . . Oct 27
Dominican Republic . . . Feb 27	Micronesia (Federated States of) . . . May 10	Tuvalu . . . Oct 1
East Timor . . . Nov 28	Moldova, Republic of . . . Aug 27	Uganda . . . Oct 9
Ecuador . . . Aug 10	Monaco . . . Nov 19	Ukraine . . . Aug 24
Egypt . . . July 23	Mongolia . . . July 11	United Arab Emirates . . . Dec 2
El Salvador . . . Sept 15	Morocco . . . July 30	United Kingdom* . . . June 10
Equatorial Guinea . . . Oct 12	Mozambique . . . June 25	United States of America . . . July 4
Eritrea . . . May 24	Myanmar . . . Jan 4	Uruguay . . . Aug 25
Estonia . . . Feb 24	Namibia, Republic of . . . Mar 21	Uzbekistan . . . Sept 1
Ethiopia . . . May 28	Nauru . . . Jan 31	Vanuatu . . . July 30
Fiji . . . Oct 10	Nepal . . . July 7	Venezuela . . . July 5
Finland . . . Dec 6	Netherlands . . . Apr 30	Vietnam . . . Sept 2
France . . . July 14	New Zealand . . . Feb 6	Yemen . . . May 22
Gabon . . . Mar 12	Nicaragua . . . Sept 15	Zambia . . . Oct 24
Gambia . . . Feb 18	Niger . . . Dec 18	Zimbabwe . . . Apr 18
Georgia . . . May 26	Nigeria . . . Oct 1	
Germany . . . Oct 3		*Trooping the Colour—Queen's official birthday.

SELECTED SPECIAL YEARS: 1972–2006

As sponsored by the United Nations

Intl Book Year: 1972
World Population Year: 1974
Intl Women's Year: 1975
Intl Year of the Child: 1979
Intl Year for Disabled Persons: 1981
World Communications Year: 1983
Intl Youth Year: 1985
Intl Year of Peace: 1986
Intl Year of Shelter for the Homeless: 1987
Year of the Reader: 1987
Year of the Young Reader: 1989
Intl Space Year: 1992
Intl Year for World's Indigenous Peoples: 1993
Intl Year of the Family: 1994
Year for Tolerance: 1995
Intl Year for Eradication of Poverty: 1996
Intl Year of the Ocean: 1998
Intl Year of Older Persons: 1999
Intl Year for the Culture of Peace: 2000
Intl Year of Thanksgiving: 2000
Intl Year of Volunteers: 2001
Year of Dialogue Among Civilizations: 2001
Intl Decade for a Culture of Peace: 2001–10
Intl Year of Mobilization Against Racism: 2001
Intl Year of Mountains: 2002
Intl Year of Ecotourism: 2002
Literacy Decade: Education for All: 2003–2012
Intl Year of Freshwater: 2003
Intl Year of Rice: 2004
Intl Year to Commemorate the Struggle Against Slavery and Its Abolition: 2004
Intl Year of Microcredit: 2005
Intl Year for Sports and Physical Education: 2005
Intl Year of Deserts and Desertification: 2006

CHINESE CALENDAR

The Chinese lunar year is divided into 12 months of 29 or 30 days. The calendar is adjusted to the length of the solar year by the addition of extra months at regular intervals. The years are arranged in major cycles of 60 years. Each successive year is named after one of 12 animals. These 12-year cycles are continuously repeated.

Year	Animal
2002	Horse
2003	Sheep (Goat)
2004	Monkey
2005	Rooster
2006	Dog
2007	Boar (Pig)
2008	Rat
2009	Ox
2010	Tiger
2011	Hare
2012	Dragon
2013	Snake

WEDDING ANNIVERSARY GIFTS

Anniversary	Gift
1st	paper, plastics, clocks
2nd	cotton, china, calico
3rd	leather, crystal, glass
4th	books, electrical appliances, silk, fruit, flowers
5th	wood, silverware
6th	sugar, candy, wood, iron
7th	wool, copper, desk sets
8th	bronze, pottery, linens, laces, electrical appliances
9th	pottery, willow, leather
10th	tin, aluminum, diamond jewelry
11th	steel, fashion jewelry, accessories
12th	silk, linen, pearls, colored gems
13th	lace, textiles, furs
14th	ivory, gold jewelry
15th	crystal, watches, glass
16th	silver hollowware
17th	furniture
18th	porcelain
19th	bronze
20th	china, platinum
21st	brass, nickel
22nd	copper
23rd	silver plate
24th	musical instruments
25th	silver
26th	original pictures
27th	sculpture
28th	orchids
29th	new furniture
30th	pearl, diamond
31st	time pieces
32nd	conveyances (including automobiles)
33rd	amethyst
34th	opal
35th	coral, jade
36th	bone china
37th	alabaster
38th	beryl, tourmaline
39th	lace
40th	ruby
41st	land
42nd	improved real estate
43rd	trips
44th	groceries
45th	sapphire
46th	original poetry tributes
47th	books
48th	optical (spectacles, microscopes, telescopes)
49th	luxuries of any kind
50th	gold
55th	emerald
60th	diamond
75th	diamond

Standard Time = Universal Time + value from table

	h m			h m
Z	0		N	−1
A	+1		O	−2
B	+2		P	−3
C	+3		P*	−3 30
C*	+3 30		Q	−4
D	+4		R	−5
D*	+4 30		S	−6
E	+5		T	−7
E*	+5 30		U	−8
F	+6		U*	−8 30
F*	+6 30		V	−9
G	+7		V*	−9 30
H	+8		W	−10
I	+9		X	−11
I*	+9 30		Y	−12
K	+10			
K*	+10 30			
L	+11			
L*	+11 30			
M	+12			
M*	+13			
M†	+14			

‡ No Standard Time legally adopted

STANDARD TIME ZONES
Corrected to April 2001
Zone boundaries are approximate

Daylight Saving Time (*Summer Time*),
usually one hour in advance of Standard
Time, is kept in some places

Map outline © Mountain High Maps
Compiled by HM Nautical Almanac Office

International Date Line

‡

Reprinted from *Astronomical Phenomena for the Year 2002*, prepared jointly by the Nautical Almanac Office of the US Naval Observatory and Her Majesty's Nautical Almanac Office of the Royal Greenwich Observatory.

UNIVERSAL, STANDARD AND DAYLIGHT TIMES

Universal Time (UT) is also known as Greenwich Mean Time (GMT) and is the standard time of the Greenwich meridian (0° of longitude). A time given in UT may be converted to local mean time by the addition of east longitude (or the subtraction of west longitude), where the longitude of the place is expressed in time-measure at the rate of one hour for every 15°. Local clock times may differ from standard times, especially in summer when clocks are often advanced by one hour ("daylight saving" or "summer" time).

The time used in this book is Eastern Standard Time. The following table provides conversion between Universal Time and all Time Zones in the United States. An asterisk denotes that the time is on the preceding day.

Universal Time	Eastern Daylight Time	Eastern Standard Time and Central Daylight Time	Central Standard Time and Mountain Daylight Time	Mountain Standard Time and Pacific Daylight Time	Pacific Standard Time
0ʰ	* 8 P. M.	* 7 P. M.	* 6 P. M.	* 5 P. M.	* 4 P. M.
1	* 9	* 8	* 7	* 6	* 5
2	*10	* 9	* 8	* 7	* 6
3	*11 P. M.	*10	* 9	* 8	* 7
4	0 Midnight	*11 P. M.	*10	* 9	* 8
5	1 A. M.	0 Midnight	*11 P. M.	*10	* 9
6	2	1 A. M.	0 Midnight	*11 P. M.	*10
7	3	2	1 A. M.	0 Midnight	*11 P. M.
8	4	3	2	1 A. M.	0 Midnight
9	5	4	3	2	1 A. M.
10	6	5	4	3	2
11	7	6	5	4	3
12	8	7	6	5	4
13	9	8	7	6	5
14	10	9	8	7	6
15	11 A. M.	10	9	8	7
16	12 Noon	11 A. M.	10	9	8
17	1 P. M.	12 Noon	11 A. M.	10	9
18	2	1 P. M.	12 Noon	11 A. M.	10
19	3	2	1 P. M.	12 Noon	11 A. M.
20	4	3	2	1 P. M.	12 Noon
21	5	4	3	2	1 P. M.
22	6	5	4	3	2
23	7 P. M.	6 P. M.	5 P. M.	4 P. M.	3 P. M.

The longitudes of the standard meridians for the standard time zones are:

Eastern . . . . . 75° West   Central . . . . . 90° West   Mountain . . . . . 105° West   Pacific . . . . . 120° West

LEAP SECONDS

The information below is developed by the editors from data supplied by the US Naval Observatory.

Because of Earth's slightly erratic rotation and the need for greater precision in time measurement it has become necessary to add a "leap second" from time to time to man's clocks to coordinate them with astronomical time. Rotation of the Earth has been slowing since 1900, making an astronomical second longer than an atomic second. Since 1972, by international agreement, adjustments have been made to keep astronomical and atomic clocks within 0.9 second of each other. The determination to add (or subtract) seconds is made by the Central Bureau of the International Earth Rotation Service, in Paris. Preferred times for adjustment have been June 30 and December 31, but any time may be designated by the International Earth Rotation Service. The first such adjustment was made in 1972, and as of July 1, 2005, a total of 22 leap seconds had been added. The additions have been made at 23:59:60 UTC (Coordinated Universal Time) = 6:59:60 EST (Eastern Standard Time). Leap seconds have been inserted into the UTC time scale on the following dates:

June 30, 1972	Dec 31, 1977	June 30, 1985	June 30, 1994
Dec 31, 1972	Dec 31, 1978	Dec 31, 1987	Dec 31, 1995
Dec 31, 1973	Dec 31, 1979	Dec 31, 1989	June 30, 1997
Dec 31, 1974	June 30, 1981	Dec 31, 1990	Dec 31, 1998
Dec 31, 1975	June 30, 1982	June 30, 1992	
Dec 31, 1976	June 30, 1983	June 30, 1993	

ASTRONOMICAL PHENOMENA
FOR THE YEARS 2006–2008

All dates are given in terms of Eastern Standard or Daylight Time and the Gregorian calendar.

(Based in part on information prepared by the Nautical Almanac Office, US Naval Observatory.)

2006
PRINCIPAL PHENOMENA
EARTH

Perihelion . . . . Jan 4
Aphelion . . . . July 3
Equinoxes . . . . Mar 20, Sept 23
Solstices . . . . June 21, Dec 22

PHASES OF THE MOON

New Moon	First Quarter	Full Moon	Last Quarter
	Jan 6	Jan 14	Jan 22
Jan 29	Feb 5	Feb 12	Feb 21
Feb 27	Mar 6	Mar 14	Mar 22
Mar 29	Apr 5	Apr 13	Apr 20
Apr 27	May 5	May 13	May 20
May 27	June 3	June 11	June 18
June 25	July 3	July 10	July 17
July 25	Aug 2	Aug 9	Aug 15
Aug 23	Aug 31	Sept 7	Sept 14
Sept 22	Sept 30	Oct 6	Oct 13
Oct 22	Oct 29	Nov 5	Nov 12
Nov 20	Nov 28	Dec 4	Dec 12
Dec 20	Dec 27		

ECLIPSES

Penumbral eclipse of the Moon . . . . Mar 14
Total eclipse of the Sun . . . . Mar 29
Partial eclipse of the Moon . . . . Sept 7
Annular eclipse of the Sun . . . . Sept 22

VISIBILITY OF PLANETS
IN MORNING AND EVENING TWILIGHT

	Morning	Evening
Venus	June 15–Dec 31	Jan 1–June 2
Mars	Oct 30–Dec 31	Jan 1–July 31
Jupiter	Jan 1–Mar 4, Oct 5–Dec 31	Mar 4–Sept 8
Saturn	July 27–Dec 31	Jan 1–June 20

2007
PRINCIPAL PHENOMENA
EARTH

Perihelion . . . . Jan 3
Aphelion . . . . July 6
Equinoxes . . . . Mar 20, Sept 23
Solstices . . . . June 21, Dec 22

PHASES OF THE MOON

New Moon	First Quarter	Full Moon	Last Quarter
		Jan 3	Jan 11
Jan 18	Jan 25	Feb 2	Feb 10
Feb 17	Feb 24	Mar 3	Mar 11
Mar 18	Mar 25	Apr 2	Apr 10
Apr 17	Apr 24	May 2	May 10
May 16	May 23	May 31	June 8
June 14	June 22	June 30	July 7
July 14	July 22	July 29	Aug 5
Aug 12	Aug 20	Aug 28	Sept 3
Sept 11	Sept 19	Sept 26	Oct 3
Oct 11	Oct 19	Oct 26	Nov 1
Nov 9	Nov 17	Nov 24	Dec 1
Dec 9	Dec 17	Dec 23	Dec 31

ECLIPSES

Total eclipse of the Moon . . . . Mar 3
Partial eclipse of the Sun . . . . Mar 19
Total eclipse of the Moon . . . . Aug 28
Partial eclipse of the Sun . . . . Sept 11

2008
PRINCIPAL PHENOMENA
EARTH

Perihelion . . . . Jan 2
Aphelion . . . . July 4
Equinoxes . . . . Mar 20, Sept 22
Solstices . . . . June 20, Dec 21

PHASES OF THE MOON

New Moon	First Quarter	Full Moon	Last Quarter
Jan 8	Jan 15	Jan 22	Jan 30
Feb 6	Feb 13	Feb 20	Feb 28
Mar 7	Mar 14	Mar 21	Mar 29
Apr 5	Apr 12	Apr 20	Apr 28
May 5	May 11	May 19	May 27
June 3	June 10	June 18	June 26
July 2	July 10	July 18	July 25
Aug 1	Aug 8	Aug 16	Aug 23
Aug 30	Sept 7	Sept 15	Sept 22
Sept 29	Oct 7	Oct 14	Oct 21
Oct 28	Nov 5	Nov 13	Nov 19
Nov 27	Dec 5	Dec 12	Dec 19
Dec 27			

ECLIPSES

Annular eclipse of the Sun . . . . Feb 6
Total eclipse of the Moon . . . . Feb 21
Total eclipse of the Sun . . . . Aug 1
Partial eclipse of the Moon . . . . Aug 16

THE NAMING OF HURRICANES

(Compiled from information issued by the US Department of Commerce,
National Oceanic and Atmospheric Administration.)

Why are hurricanes named? Experience shows that the use of short, distinctive names greatly reduces confusion when two or more tropical storms occur at the same time. The use of easily remembered names in written and spoken communication is quicker and less subject to error than the older, more cumbersome latitude-longitude identification methods, advantages which are especially important in exchanging detailed storm information between hundreds of widely scattered stations, airports, coastal bases and ships at sea.

The practice of naming hurricanes began hundreds of years ago, but only relatively recently did they begin to be named solely for women. During World War II forecasters and meteorologists began using female names for storms in weather map discussions, and in 1953 the US weather services adopted the practice, creating a new international phonetic alphabet of women's names from A–W to name hurricanes. In 1978 men's names were also introduced into the storm lists.

Because hurricanes affect other nations and are tracked by their weather services, the lists have an international flavor. Names are agreed upon during international meetings of the World Meteorological Organization by the nations involved, and can be retired and replaced with new names in the event of particularly severe storms.

The National Hurricane Center near Miami, FL, keeps a constant watch on oceanic storm-breeding areas for tropical disturbances that may herald the formation of a hurricane. If a disturbance intensifies into a tropical storm—with rotary circulation and wind speeds above 39 miles per hour—the Center will give the storm a name from one of six lists. The Atlantic and Eastern Pacific lists are rotated year by year so that the 2006 set, for example, will be used again to name storms in 2012.

The lists of names for Central Pacific and Western Pacific hurricanes (tropical cyclones) are not rotated on a yearly basis. Meteorologists follow each list until all those names have been used, then go on to the next list. The name of a particularly severe storm is retired and replaced. For example, Iniki—the name of the hurricane that devastated Hawaii—has been replaced with Iolana on List 2.

ATLANTIC HURRICANE NAMES

2006	2007	2008
Alberto	Andrea	Arthur
Beryl	Barry	Bertha
Chris	Chantal	Cristobal
Debby	Dean	Dolly
Ernesto	Erin	Edouard
Florence	Felix	Fay
Gordon	Gabrielle	Gustav
Helene	Humberto	Hanna
Isaac	Ingrid	Ike
Joyce	Jerry	Josephine
Kirk	Karen	Kyle
Leslie	Lorenzo	Laura
Michael	Melissa	Marco
Nadine	Noel	Nana
Oscar	Olga	Omar
Patty	Pablo	Paloma
Rafael	Rebekah	Rene
Sandy	Sebastien	Sally
Tony	Tanya	Teddy
Valerie	Van	Vicky
William	Wendy	Wilfred

EASTERN PACIFIC HURRICANE NAMES

2006	2007	2008
Aletta	Alvin	Alma
Bud	Barbara	Boris
Carlotta	Cosme	Cristina
Daniel	Dalila	Douglas
Emilia	Erick	Elida
Fabio	Flossie	Fausto
Gilma	Gil	Genevieve
Hector	Henriette	Hernan
Ileana	Ivo	Iselle
John	Juliette	Julio
Kristy	Kiko	Karina
Lane	Lorena	Lowell
Miriam	Mañuel	Marie
Norman	Narda	Norbert
Olivia	Octave	Odile
Paul	Priscilla	Polo
Rosa	Raymond	Rachel
Sergio	Sonia	Simon
Tara	Tico	Trudy
Vicente	Velma	Vance
Willa	Wallis	Winnie
Xavier	Xina	Xavier
Yolanda	York	Yolanda
Zeke	Zelda	Zeke

If more than 24 tropical cyclones occur in a year, then the Greek alphabet will be used following Zelda or Zeke.

CENTRAL PACIFIC TROPICAL CYCLONE NAMES

LIST 1	LIST 3
Akoni (ah-KOH-nee)	Alika (ah-LEE-kah)
Ema (EH-ma)	Ele (EH-leh)
Hana (HAH-nah)	Huko (HOO-koh)
IO (EE-oo)	Ioke (ee-OH-keh)
Keli (KEH-lee)	Kika (KEE-kah)
Lala (LAH-lah)	Lana (LAH-nah)
Moke (MOH-keh)	Maka (MAH-kah)
Nele (NEH-leh)	Neki (NEH-kee)
Oka (OH-kah)	Oleka (oh-LEH-kah)
Peke (PEH-keh)	Peni (PEH-nee)
Uleki (oo-LEH-kee)	Ulia (oo-LEE-ah)
Wila (VEE-lah)	Wali (WAH-lee)

LIST 2	LIST 4
Aka (AH-kah)	Ana (AH-nah)
Ekeka (eh-KEH-kah)	Ela (EH-lah)
Hali (HAH-lee)	Halola (hah-LOH-lah)
Iolana (ee-OH-lah-nah)	Iune (ee-OO-neh)
Keoni (keh-OH-nee)	Kimo (KEE-moh)
Li (LEE)	Loke (LOH-keh)
Mele (MEH-leh)	Malia (mah-LEE-ah)
Nona (NOH-nah)	Niala (nee-AH-lah)
Oliwa (oh-LEE-vah)	Oko (OH-koh)
Paka (PAH-hak)	Pali (PAH-lee)
Upana (oo-PAH-nah)	Ulika (oo-LEE-kah)
Wene (WEH-neh)	Walaka (wah-LAH-kah)

In Hawaiian, all letters are pronounced, including double or triple vowels.

WESTERN PACIFIC TROPICAL CYCLONE NAMES

LIST 1	LIST 2	LIST 3	LIST 4	LIST 5
Damrey	Kong-rey	Nakri	Krovanh	Sarika
Longwang	Yutu	Fengshen	Dujuan	Haima
Kirogi	Toraji	Kalmaegi	Maemi	Meari
Kai-Tak	Man-yi	Fung-wong	Choi-wan	Ma-on
Tenbin	Usagi	Kanmuri	Koppu	Tokage
Bolaven	Pabuk	Phanfone	Ketsana	Nock-ten
Chanchu	Wutip	Vongfong	Parma	Muifa
Jelawat	Sepat	Rusa	Melor	Merbok
Ewinlar	Fitow	Sinlaku	Nepartak	Nanmadol
Bilis	Danas	Hagupit	Lupit	Talas
Gaemi	Nari	Changmi	Sudal	Noru
Prapiroon	Vipa	Megkhla	Nida	Kularb
Maria	Francisco	Higos	Omais	Roke
Saomai	Lekima	Bavi	Conson	Sonca
Bopha	Krosa	Maysak	Chanthu	Nesat
Wukong	Haiyan	Haishen	Dianmu	Haitang
Sonamu	Podul	Pongsona	Mindule	Nalgae
Shanshan	Lingling	Yanyan	Tingting	Banyan
Yagi	Kaziki	Kuzira	Kompasu	Washi
Xangsane	Faxai	Chan-hom	Namtheun	Matsa
Bebinca	Vamei	Linfa	Malou	Sanvu
Rumbia	Tapah	Nangka	Meranti	Mawar
Soulik	Mitag	Soudelor	Rananin	Guchol
Cimaron	Hagibis	Imbudo	Malakas	Talim
Chebi	Noguri	Koni	Megi	Nabi
Durian	Ramasoon	Hanuman	Chaba	Khanun
Utor	Chataan	Etau	Kodo	Vicete
Trami	Halong	Vamco	Songda	Saola

☆ *Chase's 2006 Calendar of Events* ☆
SOME FACTS ABOUT THE PRESIDENTS

Name	Birthdate, Place	Party	Tenure	Died	First Lady	Vice President
1. George Washington	2/22/1732, Westmoreland Cnty, VA	Federalist	1789–1797	12/14/1799	Martha Dandridge Custis	John Adams
2. John Adams	10/30/1735, Braintree (Quincy), MA	Federalist	1797–1801	7/4/1826	Abigail Smith	Thomas Jefferson
3. Thomas Jefferson	4/13/1743, Shadwell, VA	Democratic-Republican	1801–1809	7/4/1826	Martha Wayles Skelton	Aaron Burr, 1801–05 George Clinton, 1805–09
4. James Madison	3/16/1751, Port Conway, VA	Democratic-Republican	1809–1817	6/28/1836	Dolley Payne Todd	George Clinton, 1809–12 Elbridge Gerry, 1813–14(?)
5. James Monroe	4/28/1758, Westmoreland Cnty, VA	Democratic-Republican	1817–1825	7/4/1831	Elizabeth Kortright	Daniel D. Tompkins
6. John Q. Adams	7/11/1767, Braintree (Quincy), MA	Democratic-Republican	1825–1829	2/23/1848	Louisa Catherine Johnson	John C. Calhoun
7. Andrew Jackson	3/15/1767, Waxhaw Settlement, SC	Democrat	1829–1837	6/8/1845	Mrs. Rachel Donelson Robards	John C. Calhoun, 1829–32 Martin Van Buren, 1833–37
8. Martin Van Buren	12/5/1782, Kinderhook, NY	Democrat	1837–1841	7/24/1862	Hannah Hoes	Richard M. Johnson
9. William H. Harrison	2/9/1773, Charles City Cnty, VA	Whig	1841	4/4/1841†	Anna Symmes	John Tyler
10. John Tyler	3/29/1790, Charles City Cnty, VA	Whig	1841–1845	1/18/1862	Letitia Christian Julia Gardiner	
11. James K. Polk	11/2/1795, near Pineville, NC	Democrat	1845–1849	6/15/1849	Sarah Childress	George M. Dallas
12. Zachary Taylor	11/24/1784, Barboursville, VA	Whig	1849–1850	7/9/1850†	Margaret Mackall Smith	Millard Fillmore
13. Millard Fillmore	1/7/1800, Locke, NY	Whig	1850–1853	3/8/1874	Abigail Powers Mrs. Caroline Carmichael McIntosh	
14. Franklin Pierce	11/23/1804, Hillsboro, NH	Democrat	1853–1857	10/8/1869	Jane Means Appleton	William R. D. King
15. James Buchanan	4/23/1791, near Mercersburg, PA	Democrat	1857–1861	6/1/1868		John C. Breckinridge
16. Abraham Lincoln	2/12/1809, near Hodgenville, KY	Republican	1861–1865	4/15/1865*	Mary Todd	Hannibal Hamlin, 1861–65 Andrew Johnson, 1865
17. Andrew Johnson	12/29/1808, Raleigh, NC	Democrat	1865–1869	7/31/1875	Eliza McCardle	
18. Ulysses S. Grant	4/27/1822, Point Pleasant, OH	Republican	1869–1877	7/23/1885	Julia Boggs Dent	Schuyler Colfax, 1869–73 Henry Wilson, 1873–75
19. Rutherford B. Hayes	10/4/1822, Delaware, OH	Republican	1877–1881	1/17/1893	Lucy Ware Webb	William A. Wheeler
20. James A. Garfield	11/19/1831, Orange, OH	Republican	1881	9/19/1881*	Lucretia Rudolph	Chester A. Arthur
21. Chester A. Arthur	10/5/1829, Fairfield, VT	Republican	1881–1885	11/18/1886	Ellen Lewis Herndon	
22. Grover Cleveland	3/18/1837, Caldwell, NJ	Democrat	1885–1889	6/24/1908	Frances Folsom	Thomas A. Hendricks, 1885
23. Benjamin Harrison	8/20/1833, North Bend, OH	Republican	1889–1893	3/13/1901	Caroline Lavinia Scott Mrs. Mary Dimmick	Levi P. Morton
24. Grover Cleveland	3/18/1837, Caldwell, NJ	Democrat	1893–1897	6/24/1908	Frances Folsom	Adlai Stevenson, 1893–97

Name	Birthdate, Place	Party	Tenure	Died	First Lady	Vice President
25. William McKinley	1/29/1843, Niles, OH	Republican	1897–1901	9/14/1901*	Ida Saxton	Garret A. Hobart, 1897–99 Theodore Roosevelt, 1901
26. Theodore Roosevelt	10/27/1858, New York, NY	Republican	1901–1909	1/6/1919	Alice Hathaway Lee Edith Kermit Carow	Charles W. Fairbanks
27. William H. Taft	9/15/1857, Cincinnati, OH	Republican	1909–1913	3/8/1930	Helen Herron	James S. Sherman
28. Woodrow Wilson	12/28/1856, Staunton, VA	Democrat	1913–1921	2/3/1924	Ellen Louise Axson Edith Bolling Galt	Thomas R. Marshall
29. Warren G. Harding	11/2/1865, near Corsica, OH	Republican	1921–1923	8/2/1923†	Florence Kling DeWolfe	Calvin Coolidge
30. Calvin Coolidge	7/4/1872, Plymouth Notch, VT	Republican	1923–1929	1/5/1933	Grace Anna Goodhue	Charles G. Dawes
31. Herbert C. Hoover	8/10/1874, West Branch, IA	Republican	1929–1933	10/20/1964	Lou Henry	Charles Curtis
32. Franklin D. Roosevelt	1/30/1882, Hyde Park, NY	Democrat	1933–1945	4/12/1945†	Eleanor Roosevelt	John N. Garner, 1933–41 Henry A. Wallace, 1941–45 Harry S. Truman, 1945
33. Harry S. Truman	5/8/1884, Lamar, MO	Democrat	1945–1953	12/26/1972	Elizabeth Virginia (Bess) Wallace	Alben W. Barkley
34. Dwight D. Eisenhower	10/14/1890, Denison, TX	Republican	1953–1961	3/28/1969	Mamie Geneva Doud	Richard M. Nixon
35. John F. Kennedy	5/29/1917, Brookline, MA	Democrat	1961–1963	11/22/1963*	Jacqueline Lee Bouvier	Lyndon B. Johnson
36. Lyndon B. Johnson	8/27/1908, near Stonewall, TX	Democrat	1963–1969	1/22/1973	Claudia Alta (Lady Bird) Taylor	Hubert H. Humphrey
37. Richard M. Nixon	1/9/1913, Yorba Linda, CA	Republican	1969–1974**	4/22/1994	Thelma Catherine (Pat) Ryan	Spiro T. Agnew, 1969–73 Gerald R. Ford, 1973–74
38. Gerald R. Ford	7/14/1913, Omaha, NE	Republican	1974–1977		Elizabeth (Betty) Bloomer	Nelson A. Rockefeller
39. James E. Carter, Jr	10/1/1924, Plains, GA	Democrat	1977–1981		Rosalynn Smith	Walter F. Mondale
40. Ronald W. Reagan	2/6/1911, Tampico, IL	Republican	1981–1989	6/5/2004	Nancy Davis	George H. W. Bush
41. George H. W. Bush	6/12/1924, Milton, MA	Republican	1989–1993		Barbara Pierce	J. Danforth Quayle
42. William J. Clinton	8/19/1946, Hope, AR	Democrat	1993–2001		Hillary Rodham	Albert Gore, Jr.
43. George W. Bush	7/6/1946, New Haven, CT	Republican	2001–		Laura Welch	Richard Cheney

*assassinated while in office
** resigned Aug 9, 1974
†died while in office—nonviolently

PRESIDENTIAL PROCLAMATIONS
ISSUED, JANUARY 9, 2004–JUNE 19, 2005

No. Title, Observance Dates, (Date of signing).

2004

7749 National Mentoring Month, 2004: January (Jan 9, 2004)

7750 To Suspend Entry as Immigrants or Nonimmigrants of Persons Engaged in or Benefiting from Corruption (Jan 12, 2004)

7751 Martin Luther King, Jr, Federal Holiday, 2004: Jan 19, 2004 (Jan 15, 2004)

7752 National Sanctity of Human Life Day, 2004: Jan 18, 2004 (Jan 15, 2004)

7753 Religious Freedom Day, 2004: Jan 16, 2004 (Jan 16, 2004)

7754 American Heart Month, 2004: February (Feb 2, 2004)

7755 National Consumer Protection Awareness Week, 2004: Feb 1–7, 2004 (Feb 2, 2004)

7756 National African American History Month, 2004: February (Feb 3, 2004)

7757 Expanding the Scope of the National Emergency and Invocation of Emergency Authority Relating to the Regulation of the Anchorage and Movement of Vessels into Cuban Territorial Waters (Feb 26, 2004)

7758 To Modify Duty-Free Treatment Under the Generalized System of Preferences (Mar 1, 2004)

7759 American Red Cross Month, 2004: March (Mar 3, 2004)

7760 Irish American Heritage Month, 2004: March (Mar 5, 2004)

7761 Women's History Month, 2004: March (Mar 5, 2004)

7762 Save Your Vision Week, 2004: Mar 7–13, 2004 (Mar 5, 2004)

7763 National Poison Prevention Week, 2004: Mar 21–27, 2004 (Mar 19, 2004)

7764 Greek Independence Day: A National Day of Celebration of Greek and American Democracy, 2004: Mar 25, 2004 (Mar 25, 2004)

7765 Cancer Control Month, 2004: April (Apr 2, 2004)

7766 National Child Abuse Prevention Month, 2004: April (Apr 2, 2004)

7767 Education and Sharing Day, U.S.A., 2004: Apr 2, 2004 (Apr 2, 2004)

7768 National D.A.R.E. (Drug Abuse Resistance Education) Day, 2004: Apr 8, 2004 (Apr 7, 2004)

7769 National Donate Life Month, 2004: April (Apr 8, 2004)

7770 National Former Prisoner of War Recognition Day, 2004: Apr 9, 2004 (Apr 9, 2004)

7771 Pan American Day and Pan American Week, 2004: Apr 14, 2004 and Apr 11–17, 2004 (Apr 13, 2004)

7772 National Park Week, 2004: Apr 18–25, 2004 (Apr 16, 2004)

7773 National Volunteer Week, 2004: Apr 18–24, 2004 (Apr 16, 2004)

7774 National Crime Victim's Rights Week, 2004: Apr 18–24, 2004 (Apr 17, 2004)

7775 Jewish Heritage Week, 2004: Apr 25–May 2, 2004 (Apr 23, 2004)

7776 Older Americans Month, 2004: May (Apr 30, 2004)

7777 National Charter Schools Week, 2004: May 2–8, 2004 (Apr 30, 2004)

7778 Law Day, U.S.A., 2004: May 1, 2004 (Apr 30, 2004)

7779 Loyalty Day, 2004: May 1, 2004 (Apr 30, 2004)

7780 National Day of Prayer, 2004: May 6, 2004 (Apr 30, 2004)

7781 Asian/Pacific American Heritage Month, 2004: May (May 2, 2004)

7782 National Physical Fitness and Sports Month, 2004: May (May 7, 2004)

7783 Mother's Day, 2004: May 9, 2004 (May 7, 2004)

7784 Peace Officers Memorial Day and Police Week, 2004: May 15, 2004 and May 9–15, 2004 (May 7, 2004)

No. Title, Observance Dates, (Date of signing).

7785 National Defense Transportation Day and National Transportation Week, 2004: May 21, 2004 and May 16–22, 2004 (May 14, 2004)

7786 National Hurricane Preparedness Week, 2004: May 16–22, 2004 (May 14, 2004)

7787 Small Business Week, 2004: May 16–22, 2004 (May 14, 2004)

7788 World Trade Week, 2004: May 16–22, 2004 (May 14, 2004)

7789 National Maritime Day, 2004: May 22, 2004 (May 21, 2004)

7790 National Safe Boating Week, 2004: May 22–28, 2004 (May 21, 2004)

7791 Prayer for Peace, Memorial Day, 2004: May 31, 2004 (May 26, 2004)

7792 D-Day National Remembrance Day, 2004: June 5, 2004 (June 5, 2004)

7793 National Child's Day, 2004: June 6, 2004 (June 5, 2004)

7794 Announcing the Death of Ronald Reagan, June 5, 2004 (June 6, 2004)

7795 Great Outdoors Month, 2004: June (June 4, 2004)

7796 Flag Day and National Flag Week, 2004: June 14, 2004 and June 13–19, 2004 (June 12, 2004)

7797 Father's Day, 2004: June 20, 2004 (June 19, 2004)

7798 Black Music Month, 2004: June (June 22, 2004)

7799 National HIV Testing Day, 2004: June 27, 2004 (June 26, 2004)

7800 To Modify Duty-Free Treatment Under the Generalized System of Preferences (June 30, 2004)

7801 Returning the Flag of the United States to Full-Staff (July 2, 2004)

7802 Captive Nations Week, 2004: July 18–24, 2004 (July 16, 2004)

7803 Parents' Day, 2004: July 25, 2004 (July 23, 2004)

7804 Anniversary of the Americans with Disabilities Act, 2004: July 26, 2004 (July 26, 2004)

7805 National Airborne Day, 2004: Aug 16, 2004 (Aug 16, 2004)

7806 Women's Equality Day, 2004: Aug 26, 2004 (Aug 26, 2004)

7807 Minority Enterprise Development Week, 2004: Sept 5–11, 2004 (Sept 4, 2004)

7808 To Modify the Generalized System of Preferences, and for Other Purposes (Sept 7, 2004)

7809 National Alcohol and Drug Addiction Recovery Month, 2004: September (Sept 10, 2004)

7810 National Ovarian Cancer Awareness Month, 2004: September (Sept 10, 2004)

7811 National Days of Prayer and Remembrance, 2004: Sept 10–12, 2004 (Sept 10, 2004)

7812 Patriot Day, 2004: Sept 11, 2004 (Sept 10, 2004)

7813 National Prostate Cancer Awareness Month, 2004: September (Sept 14, 2004)

7814 National Historically Black Colleges and Universities Week, 2004: Sept 12–18, 2004 (Sept 14, 2004)

7815 National POW/MIA Recognition Day, 2004: Sept 14, 2004 (Sept 14, 2004)

7816 National Hispanic Heritage Month, 2004: Sept 15–Oct 15, 2004 (Sept 17, 2004)

7817 Citizenship Day and Constitution Week, 2004: Sept 17, 2004 and Sept 17–23, 2004 (Sept 17, 2004)

7818 National Farm Safety and Health Week, 2004: Sept 19–25, 2004 (Sept 20, 2004)

7819 National Employer Support of the Guard and Reserve Week, 2004: Sept 26–Oct 2, 2004 (Sept 21, 2004)

7820 Family Day, 2004: Sept 27, 2004 (Sept 24, 2004)

7821 Gold Star Mother's Day, 2004: Sept 26, 2004 (Sept 25, 2004)

7822 National Hunting and Fishing Day, 2004: Sept 25, 2004 (Sept 24, 2004)

☆ *Chase's 2006 Calendar of Events* ☆

No. Title, Observance Dates, (Date of signing).

7823 National Breast Cancer Awareness Month, 2004: October (Oct 1, 2004)
7824 Fire Prevention Week, 2004: Oct 3–9, 2004 (Oct 4, 2004)
7825 Child Health Day, 2004: Oct 4, 2004 (Oct 4, 2004)
7826 To Implement the 2004 United States–Israel Agreement on Trade in Agricultural Products (Oct 4, 2004)
7827 German-American Day, 2004: Oct 6, 2004 (Oct 6, 2004)
7828 Leif Erikson Day, 2004: Oct 9, 2004 (Oct 7, 2004)
7829 Columbus Day, 2004: Oct 11, 2004 (Oct 11, 2004)
7830 General Pulaski Memorial Day, 2004: Oct 11, 2004 (Oct 11, 2004)
7831 National School Lunch Week, 2004: Oct 10–16, 2004 (Oct 12, 2004)
7832 National Mammography Day, 2004: Oct 15, 2004 (Oct 15, 2004)
7833 White Cane Safety Day, 2004: Oct 15, 2004 (Oct 15, 2004)
7834 National Character Counts Week, 2004: Oct 17–23, 2004 (Oct 18, 2004)
7835 National Disability Employment Awareness Month, 2004: October (Oct 20, 2004)
7836 National Forest Products Week, 2004: Oct 17–23, 2004 (Oct 20, 2004)
7837 United Nations Day, 2004: Oct 24, 2004 (Oct 24, 2004)
7838 National Adoption Month, 2004: November (Nov 4, 2004)
7839 National Alzheimer's Disease Awareness Month, 2004: November (Nov 4, 2004)
7840 National American Indian Heritage Month, 2004: November (Nov 4, 2004)
7841 National Diabetes Month, 2004: November (Nov 4, 2004)
7842 National Family Caregivers Month, 2004: November (Nov 4, 2004)
7843 National Hospice Month, 2004: November (Nov 4, 2004)
7844 Veteran's Day and National Veteran's Awareness Week, 2003: Nov 11 and Nov 7–13, 2004 (Nov 9, 2004)
7845 World Freedom Day, 2004: Nov 9, 2004 (Nov 9, 2004)
7846 America Recycles Day, 2004: Nov 15, 2004 (Nov 15, 2004)
7847 National Farm-City Week, 2004: Nov 19–25, 2004 (Nov 19, 2004)
7848 National Family Week, 2004: Nov 21–27, 2004 (Nov 23, 2004)
7849 Thanksgiving Day, 2004: Nov 25, 2004 (Nov 23, 2004)
7850 World AIDS Day, 2004: Dec 1, 2004 (Dec 1, 2004)
7851 National Drunk and Drugged Driving Prevention Month, 2004: December (Dec 2, 2004)
7852 National Pearl Harbor Remembrance Day, 2004: Dec 7, 2004 (Dec 6, 2004)
7853 To Take Certain Actions Under the African Growth and Opportunity Act with Respect to Burkina Faso (Dec 10, 2004)
7854 Human Rights Day, Bill of Rights Day and Human Rights Week, 2004: Dec 10, Dec 15, and Dec 10–17, 2004 (Dec 10, 2004)
7855 60th Anniversary of the Battle of the Bulge (Dec 15, 2004)
7856 Wright Brothers Day, 2004: Dec 17, 2004 (Dec 17, 2004)
7857 To Implement the United States-Australia Free Trade Agreement (Dec 20, 2004)
7858 To Take Certain Actions Under the African Growth and Opportunity Act (Dec 21, 2004)

2005

7859 Honoring the Memory of the Indian Ocean Earthquake and Tsunamis (Jan 1, 2005)
7860 To Extend the Nondiscriminatory Trade Treatment to the Products of Armenia (Jan 7, 2005)
7861 National Mentoring Month, 2005: January (Jan 12, 2005)
7862 Martin Luther King, Jr, Federal Holiday, 2005: Jan 17, 2005 (Jan 14, 2005)
7863 National Sanctity of Human Life Day, 2005: Jan 16, 2005 (Jan 14, 2005)
7864 Religious Freedom Day, 2005: Jan 16, 2005 (Jan 14, 2005)
7865 60th Anniversary of the Liberation of the Auschwitz Concentration Camp, 2005: Jan 27, 2005 (Jan 25, 2005)

No. Title, Observance Dates, (Date of signing).

7866 American Heart Month, 2005: February (Feb 1, 2005)
7867 Centennial of the Forest Service, 2005: Feb 1, 2005 (Feb 1, 2005)
7868 National African American History Month, 2005: February (Feb 7, 2005)
7869 National Consumer Protection Week, 2005: Feb 6–12, 2005 (Feb 7, 2005)
7870 Modifying Rules of Origin Under the North American Free Trade Agreement, 2005 (Feb 9, 2005)
7871 American Red Cross Month, 2005: March (Feb 28, 2005)
7872 Women's History Month, 2005: March (Mar 2, 2005)
7873 Irish-American Heritage Month, 2005: March (Mar 4, 2005)
7874 Save Your Vision Week, 2005: Mar 6–12, 2005 (Mar 4, 2005)
7875 National Poison Prevention Week, 2005: Mar 20–26, 2005 (Mar 18, 2005)
7876 Greek Independence Day, 2005: Mar 25, 2005 (Mar 24, 2005)
7877 National Crime Victims' Rights Week, 2005: Apr 10–16, 2005 (Mar 31, 2005)
7878 National Child Abuse Prevention Month, 2005: April (Apr 5, 2005)
7879 National Donate Life Month, 2005: April (Apr 1, 2005)
7880 National Former Prisoner of War Recognition Day, 2005: Apr 9, 2005 (Apr 1, 2005)
7881 Honoring the Memory of Pope John Paul II (Apr 2, 2005)
7882 Pan American Day and Pan American Week, 2005: Apr 14, 2005 and Apr 10–16, 2005 (Apr 5, 2005)
7883 National D.A.R.E. (Drug Abuse Resistance Education) Day, 2005: Apr 14, 2005 (Apr 5, 2005)
7884 Cancer Control Month, 2005: April (Apr 5, 2005)
7885 National Volunteer Week, 2005: Apr 17–23, 2005 (Apr 14, 2005)
7886 Small Business Week, 2005: Apr 24–30, 2005 (Apr 14, 2005)
7887 National Park Week, 2005: Apr 18–24, 2005 (Apr 15, 2005)
7888 Education and Sharing Day, U.S.A., 2005: Apr 20, 2005 (Apr 19, 2005)
7889 National Physical Fitness and Sports Month, 2005: May (Apr 20, 2005)
7890 National Charter Schools Week, 2005: May 1–7, 2005 (Apr 28, 2005)
7891 Law Day, U.S.A., 2005: May 1, 2005 (Apr 29, 2005)
7892 Loyalty Day, 2005: May 1, 2005 (Apr 29, 2005)
7893 National Observance of the 60th Anniversary of the End of World War II, 2005 (May 3, 2005)
7894 Asian/Pacific American Heritage Month, 2005: May (May 3, 2005)
7895 Older Americans Month, 2005: May (May 3, 2005)
7896 National Day of Prayer, 2005: May 5, 2005 (May 3, 2005)
7897 Mother's Day, 2005: May 8, 2005 (May 5, 2005)
7898 Jewish Heritage Week, 2005: May 8–15, 2005 (May 5, 2005)
7899 National Hurricane Preparedness Week, 2005: May 15–21, 2005 (May 10, 2005)
7900 World Trade Week, 2005: May 15–21, 2005 (May 12, 2005)
7901 Peace Officers Memorial Day and Police Week, 2005: May 15, 2005 and May 15–21, 2005 (May 13, 2005)
7902 National Defense Transportation Day and National Transportation Week, 2005: May 20, 2005 and May 15–21, 2005 (May 13, 2005)
7903 National Safe Boating Week, 2005: May 21–27, 2005 (May 19, 2005)
7904 National Maritime Day, 2005: May 22, 2005 (May 19, 2005)
7905 Prayer for Peace, Memorial Day, 2005: May 30, 2005 (May 20, 2005)
7906 National Homeownership Month, 2005: June (May 25, 2005)
7907 Black Music Month, 2005: June (June 1, 2005)
7908 Great Outdoors Month, 2005: June (June 2, 2005)
7909 National Child's Day, 2005: June 5, 2005 (June 3, 2005)
7910 Flag Day and National Flag Week, 2005: June 14, 2005 and June 12–18, 2005 (June 10, 2005)
7911 Father's Day, 2005: June 19, 2005 (June 16, 2005)

SOME FACTS ABOUT THE UNITED STATES

State	Capital	Popular name	Area (sq. mi.)	State bird	State flower	State tree	Admitted to the Union	Order of Admission
Alabama	Montgomery	Cotton or Yellowhammer State; or Heart of Dixie	51,609	Yellowhammer	Camellia	Southern pine (Longleaf pine)	1819	22
Alaska	Juneau	Last Frontier	591,004	Willow ptarmigan	Forget-me-not	Sitka spruce	1959	49
Arizona	Phoenix	Grand Canyon State	114,000	Cactus wren	Saguaro (giant cactus)	Palo Verde	1912	48
Arkansas	Little Rock	The Natural State	53,187	Mockingbird	Apple blossom	Pine	1836	25
California	Sacramento	Golden State	158,706	California valley quail	Golden poppy	California redwood	1850	31
Colorado	Denver	Centennial State	104,091	Lark bunting	Rocky Mountain columbine	Blue spruce	1876	38
Connecticut	Hartford	Constitution State	5,018	Robin	Mountain laurel	White oak	1788	5
Delaware	Dover	First State	2,044	Blue hen chicken	Peach blossom	American holly	1787	1
Florida	Tallahassee	Sunshine State	58,664	Mockingbird	Orange blossom	Cabbage (sabal) palm	1845	27
Georgia	Atlanta	Empire State of the South	58,910	Brown thrasher	Cherokee rose	Live oak	1788	4
Hawaii	Honolulu	Aloha State	6,471	Nene (Hawaiian goose)	Hibiscus	Kukui	1959	50
Idaho	Boise	Gem State	83,564	Mountain bluebird	Syringa (mock orange)	Western white pine	1890	43
Illinois	Springfield	Prairie State	56,345	Cardinal	Native violet	White oak	1818	21
Indiana	Indianapolis	Hoosier State	36,185	Cardinal	Peony	Tulip tree or yellow poplar	1816	19
Iowa	Des Moines	Hawkeye State	56,275	Eastern goldfinch	Wild rose	Oak	1846	29
Kansas	Topeka	Sunflower State	82,277	Western meadowlark	Sunflower	Cottonwood	1861	34
Kentucky	Frankfort	Bluegrass State	40,409	Kentucky cardinal	Goldenrod	Kentucky coffeetree	1792	15
Louisiana	Baton Rouge	Pelican State	47,752	Pelican	Magnolia	Bald cypress	1812	18
Maine	Augusta	Pine Tree State	33,265	Chickadee	White pine cone and tassel	White pine	1820	23
Maryland	Annapolis	Old Line State	10,577	Baltimore oriole	Black-eyed Susan	White oak	1788	7
Massachusetts	Boston	Bay State	8,284	Chickadee	Mayflower	American elm	1788	6
Michigan	Lansing	Wolverine State	58,527	Robin	Apple blossom	White pine	1837	26
Minnesota	St. Paul	North Star State	84,402	Common loon	Pink and white lady's-slipper	Norway, or red, pine	1858	32
Mississippi	Jackson	Magnolia State	47,689	Mockingbird	Magnolia	Magnolia	1817	20
Missouri	Jefferson City	Show Me State	69,697	Bluebird	Hawthorn	Flowering dogwood	1821	24
Montana	Helena	Treasure State	147,046	Western meadowlark	Bitterroot	Ponderosa pine	1889	41
Nebraska	Lincoln	Cornhusker State	77,355	Western meadowlark	Goldenrod	Cottonwood	1867	37
Nevada	Carson City	Silver State	110,540	Mountain bluebird	Sagebrush	Single-leaf piñon	1864	36
New Hampshire	Concord	Granite State	9,304	Purple finch	Purple lilac	White birch	1788	9
New Jersey	Trenton	Garden State	7,787	Eastern goldfinch	Purple violet	Red oak	1787	3
New Mexico	Santa Fe	Land of Enchantment	121,593	Roadrunner	Yucca flower	Piñon, or nut pine	1912	47

☆ Chase's 2006 Calendar of Events ☆

State	Capital	Popular name	Area (sq. mi.)	State bird	State flower	State tree	Admitted to the Union	Order of Admission
New York	Albany	Empire State	49,108	Bluebird	Rose	Sugar maple	1788	11
North Carolina	Raleigh	Tar Heel State or Old North State	52,669	Cardinal	Dogwood	Pine	1789	12
North Dakota	Bismarck	Peace Garden State	70,702	Western meadowlark	Wild prairie rose	American elm	1889	39
Ohio	Columbus	Buckeye State	41,330	Cardinal	Scarlet carnation	Buckeye	1803	17
Oklahoma	Oklahoma City	Sooner State	69,956	Scissortail flycatcher	Mistletoe	Redbud	1907	46
Oregon	Salem	Beaver State	97,073	Western meadowlark	Oregon grape	Douglas fir	1859	33
Pennsylvania	Harrisburg	Keystone State	45,308	Ruffed grouse	Mountain laurel	Hemlock	1787	2
Rhode Island	Providence	Ocean State	1,212	Rhode Island Red	Violet	Red maple	1790	13
South Carolina	Columbia	Palmetto State	31,113	Carolina wren	Carolina jessamine	Palmetto	1788	8
South Dakota	Pierre	Sunshine State	77,116	Ring-necked pheasant	American pasqueflower	Black Hills spruce	1889	40
Tennessee	Nashville	Volunteer State	42,114	Mockingbird	Iris	Tulip poplar	1796	16
Texas	Austin	Lone Star State	266,807	Mockingbird	Bluebonnet	Pecan	1845	28
Utah	Salt Lake City	Beehive State	84,899	Sea Gull	Sego lily	Blue spruce	1896	45
Vermont	Montpelier	Green Mountain State	9,614	Hermit thrush	Red clover	Sugar maple	1791	14
Virginia	Richmond	Old Dominion	40,767	Cardinal	Dogwood	Dogwood	1788	10
Washington	Olympia	Evergreen State	68,139	Willow goldfinch	Coast rhododendron	Western hemlock	1889	42
West Virginia	Charleston	Mountain State	24,231	Cardinal	Rhododendron	Sugar maple	1863	35
Wisconsin	Madison	Badger State	56,153	Robin	Wood violet	Sugar maple	1848	30
Wyoming	Cheyenne	Equality State	97,809	Meadowlark	Indian paintbrush	Cottonwood	1890	44

STATE & TERRITORY ABBREVIATIONS: UNITED STATES

Alabama . . . . AL	Kentucky . . . . KY	Oklahoma . . . . OK
Alaska . . . . AK	Louisiana . . . . LA	Oregon . . . . OR
Arizona . . . . AZ	Maine . . . . ME	Pennsylvania . . . . PA
Arkansas . . . . AR	Maryland . . . . MD	Puerto Rico . . . . PR
American Samoa . . . . AS	Massachusetts . . . . MA	Rhode Island . . . . RI
California . . . . CA	Michigan . . . . MI	South Carolina . . . . SC
Colorado . . . . CO	Minnesota . . . . MN	South Dakota . . . . SD
Connecticut . . . . CT	Mississippi . . . . MS	Tennessee . . . . TN
Delaware . . . . DE	Missouri . . . . MO	Texas . . . . TX
District of Columbia . . . . DC	Montana . . . . MT	Utah . . . . UT
Florida . . . . FL	Nebraska . . . . NE	Vermont . . . . VT
Georgia . . . . GA	Nevada . . . . NV	Virginia . . . . VA
Guam . . . . GU	New Hampshire . . . . NH	Virgin Islands VI
Hawaii . . . . HI	New Jersey . . . . NJ	Washington . . . . WA
Idaho . . . . ID	New Mexico . . . . NM	West Virginia . . . . WV
Illinois IL	New York . . . . NY	Wisconsin . . . . WI
Indiana . . . . IN	North Carolina . . . . NC	Wyoming . . . . WY
Iowa . . . . IA	North Dakota . . . . ND	
Kansas . . . . KS	Ohio . . . . OH	

STATE GOVERNORS/US SENATORS/US SUPREME COURT

GOVERNORS
Name (Party, State)

Bob Riley (R, AL)*
Frank Murkowski (R, AK)*
Janet Napolitano (D, AZ)*
Mike Huckabee (R, AR)*
Arnold Schwarzenegger (R, CA)*
Bill Owens (R, CO)*
M. Jodi Rell (R, CT)*
Ruth Ann Minner (D, DE)
Jeb Bush (R, FL)*
Sonny Perdue (R, GA)*
Linda Lingle (R, HI)*
Dirk Kempthorne (R, ID)*
Rod Blagojevich (D, IL)*
Mitchell Daniels (R, IN)
Tom Vilsack (D, IA)*
Kathleen Sebelius (D, KS)*
Ernie Fletcher (R, KY)
Kathleen Blanco (D, LA)
John Baldacci (D, ME)*
Robert Ehrlich, Jr (R, MD)*
Mitt Romney (R, MA)*
Jennifer Granholm (D, MI)*
Tim Pawlenty (R, MN)*
Haley Barbour (R, MS)
Matt Blunt (R, MO)
Brian Schweitzer (D, MT)
David Heineman (R, NE)*
Kenny Guinn (R, NV)*
John Lynch (D, NH)*
Richard J. Codey (D, NJ)†
Bill Richardson (D, NM)*
George Pataki (R, NY)*
Mike Easley (D, NC)
John Hoeven (R, ND)
Bob Taft (R, OH)*
Brad Henry (D, OK)*
Ted Kulongoski (D, OR)*
Ed Rendell (D, PA)*
Donald Carcieri (R, RI)*
Mark Sanford (R, SC)*
Mike Rounds (R, SD)*
Phil Bredesen (D, TN)*
Rick Perry (R, TX)*
Jon Huntsman, Jr (R, UT)
Jim Douglas (R, VT)*
Mark Warner (R, VA)
Christine Gregoire (D, WA)
Joe Manchin III (D, WV)
Jim Doyle (D, WI)*
Dave Freudenthal (D, WY)*

Office holders were current as of July 2005. Elections will take place in November 2006 for those seats marked with a *.

† Serving as Acting Governor until January 2006.

SENATORS
Name (Party, State)

Jeff Sessions (R, AL)
Richard C. Shelby (R, AL)
Ted Stevens (R, AK)
Lisa Murkowski (R, AK)
Jon Kyl (R, AZ)*
John McCain (R, AZ)
Blanche Lambert Lincoln (D, AR)
Mark Pryor (D, AR)
Dianne Feinstein (D, CA)*
Barbara Boxer (D, CA)
Wayne Allard (R, CO)
Ken Salazar (D, CO)
Christopher J. Dodd (D, CT)
Joseph I. Lieberman (D, CT)*
Thomas Carper (D, DE)*
Joseph R. Biden, Jr (D, DE)
Mel Martinez (R, FL)
Bill Nelson (D, FL)*
Saxby Chambliss (R, GA)
Johnny Isakson (R, GA)
Daniel K. Inouye (D, HI)
Daniel K. Akaka (D, HI)*
Larry E. Craig (R, ID)
Michael Crapo (R, ID)
Richard J. Durbin (D, IL)
Barack Obama (D, IL)
Richard G. Lugar (R, IN)*
Evan Bayh (D, IN)
Charles E. Grassley (R, IA)
Tom Harkin (D, IA)
Sam Brownback (R, KS)
Pat Roberts (R, KS)
Jim Bunning (R, KY)
Mitch McConnell (R, KY)
Mary L. Landrieu (D, LA)
David Vitter (R, LA)
Susan M. Collins (R, ME)
Olympia J. Snowe (R, ME)*
Paul S. Sarbanes (D, MD)*
Barbara A. Mikulski (D, MD)
Edward M. Kennedy (D, MA)*
John F. Kerry (D, MA)
Debbie Stabenow (D, MI)*
Carl Levin (D, MI)
Mark Dayton (D, MN)*
Norm Coleman (R, MN)
Thad Cochran (R, MS)
Trent Lott (R, MS)*
Jim Talent (R, MO)*
Christopher S. Bond (R, MO)
Max S. Baucus (D, MT)
Conrad Burns (R, MT)*
Chuck Hagel (R, NE)*
Ben Nelson (D, NE)
Harry M. Reid (D, NV)
John Ensign (R, NV)*
John Sununu (R, NH)
Judd Gregg (R, NH)

Frank Lautenberg (D, NJ)
Jon Corzine (D, NJ)*
Pete V. Domenici (R, NM)
Jeff Bingaman (D, NM)*
Hillary Rodham Clinton (D, NY)*
Charles E. Schumer (D, NY)
Elizabeth Dole (R, NC)
Richard Burr (R, NC)
Kent Conrad (D, ND)*
Byron L. Dorgan (D, ND)
George Voinovich (R, OH)
Mike DeWine (R, OH)*
James M. Inhofe (R, OK)
Tom Coburn (R, OK)
Gordon Smith (R, OR)
Ron Wyden (D, OR)
Arlen Specter (R, PA)
Rick Santorum (R, PA)*
Jack Reed (D, RI)
Lincoln Chafee (R, RI)*
Lindsey Graham (R, SC)
Jim DeMint (R, SC)
Tim Johnson (D, SD)
John R. Thune (R, SD)
William Frist (R, TN)*
Lamar Alexander (R, TN)
John Cornyn (R, TX)
Kay Bailey Hutchison (R, TX)*
Orrin G. Hatch (R, UT)*
Robert F. Bennett (R, UT)
Patrick J. Leahy (D, VT)
James M. Jeffords (I, VT)*
John W. Warner (R, VA)
George Allen (R, VA)*
Maria Cantwell (D, WA)*
Patty Murray (D, WA)
Robert C. Byrd (D, WV)*
John D. Rockefeller IV (D, WV)
Herbert H. Kohl (D, WI)*
Russell D. Feingold (D, WI)
Michael B. Enzi (R, WY)
Craig Thomas (R, WY)*

SUPREME COURT JUSTICES
Name (Appointed by, Year)

William H. Rehnquist, Chief Justice (Reagan, 1986)
John P. Stevens (Ford, 1975)
Sandra Day O'Connor (Reagan, 1981)*
Antonin Scalia (Reagan, 1986)
Anthony M. Kennedy (Reagan, 1988)
David H. Souter (G.H.W. Bush, 1990)
Clarence Thomas (G.H.W. Bush, 1991)
Ruth Bader Ginsburg (Clinton, 1993)
Stephen G. Breyer (Clinton, 1994)

*Announced retirement on July 1, 2005. Her replacement had not been named at press time.

SOME FACTS ABOUT CANADA

Province/Territory	Capital	Population*	Flower	Land/Fresh Water (sq. mi.)	Total Area
Alberta	Edmonton	2,974,807	Wild Rose	248,000/7,541	255,541
British Columbia	Victoria	3,907,738	Pacific dogwood	357,216/7,548	364,764
Manitoba	Winnipeg	1,119,583	Prairie crocus	213,729/36,387	250,116
New Brunswick	Fredericton	729,498	Purple violet	27,587/563	28,150
Newfoundland & Labrador	St. John's	513,930	Pitcher plant	144,343/12,100	156,543
Northwest Territories	Yellowknife	37,360	Mountain avens	456,791/62,943	519,734
Nova Scotia	Halifax	908,007	Mayflower	20,593/752	21,345
Nunavut	Iqaluit	26,745	Purple saxifrage	747,537/60,648	808,185
Ontario	Toronto	11,410,046	White trillium	354,341/61,256	415,599
Prince Edward Island	Charlottetown	135,294	Lady's-slipper	2,185/0	2,185
Quebec	Quebec City	7,237,479	White garden lily	527,079/68,313	595,391
Saskatchewan	Regina	978,933	Western red lily	228,445/22,921	251,366
Yukon Territory	Whitehorse	28,674	Fireweed	183,163/3,109	186,272

*Based on the 2001 Canadian Census

PROVINCE & TERRITORY ABBREVIATIONS: CANADA

Alberta	AB	Northwest Territories	NT	Prince Edward Island	PE
British Columbia	BC	Nova Scotia	NS	Quebec	QC
Manitoba	MB	Nunavut	NU	Saskatchewan	SK
New Brunswick	NB	Ontario	ON	Yukon Territory	YT
Newfoundland & Labrador	NF				

SOME FACTS ABOUT MEXICO

State	Abbreviation	Capital	Population*	Area (sq. mi.)
Aguascalientes	Ags.	Aguascalientes	944,285	2,156
Baja California	B.C.	Mexicali	2,487,367	27,655
Baja California Sur	B.C.S.	La Paz	424,041	27,979
Campeche	Camp.	Campeche	690,689	19,672
Chiapas	Chis.	Tuxtla Gutiérrez	3,920,892	28,732
Chihuahua	Chih.	Chihuahua	3,052,907	94,831
Coahuila	Coah.	Saltillo	2,298,070	58,067
Colima	Col.	Colima	542,627	2010
Distrito Federal	D.F.	Mexico City	8,605,239	573
Durango	Dgo.	Durango	1,448,661	47,691
Guanajuato	Gto.	Guanajuato	4,663,032	11,805
Guerrero	Gro.	Chilpancingo	3,079,649	24,887
Hidalgo	Hgo.	Pachuca	2,235,591	8058
Jalisco	Jal.	Guadalajara	6,322,002	31,152
México	Mex.	Toluca	13,096,686	8,268
Michoacán	Mich.	Morelia	3,985,667	23,202
Morelos	Mor.	Cuernavaca	1,555,296	1,917
Nayarit	Nay.	Tepic	920,185	10,547
Nuevo León	N.L.	Monterrey	3,834,141	25,136
Oaxaca	Oax.	Oaxaca	3,438,765	36,375
Puebla	Pue.	Puebla	5,076,686	13,126
Querétaro	Qro.	Querétaro	1,404,306	4,432
Quintana Roo	Q.R.	Chetumal	874,963	19,630
San Luis Potosí	S.L.P.	San Luis Potosí	2,229,360	24,417
Sinaloa	Sin.	Culiacán	2,536,844	22,582
Sonora	Son.	Hermosillo	2,216,969	70,484
Tabasco	Tab.	Villahermosa	1,891,829	9,783
Tamaulipas	Tamps.	Ciudad Victoria	2,753,222	30,734
Tlaxcala	Tlax.	Tlaxcala	962,646	1,555
Veracruz	Ver.	Jalapa	6,908,975	27,759
Yucatán	Yuc.	Mérida	1,658,210	14,868
Zacatecas	Zac.	Zacatecas	1,353,610	28,125

*Based on the 2000 Mexican Census

☆ *Chase's 2006 Calendar of Events* ☆

2006 Special Months

For more information on these special months, see the listing on the first day of the month (unless specified otherwise).

January

Be On-Purpose Month, Natl
Book Blitz Month
Business Success Resolutions Month, Intl
Celebration of Life Month
Cervical Cancer Screening Month
Clean Up Your Computer Month, Natl
Coffee Gourmet International Month
Creativity Month, Intl
Family Fit Lifestyle Month
Financial Wellness Month
Get Organized Month, Natl
Glaucoma Awareness Month, Natl
Hot Tea Month, Natl
Life Balance Month, Intl
Mailorder Gardening Month, Natl
Mentoring Month, Natl
Oatmeal Month
Personal Self-Defense Awareness Month, Natl
Poverty in America Awareness Month, Natl
Quality of Life Month, Intl
Radon Action Month, Natl
Returns Month, Natl
Slow Cooking Month, Natl
Wealth Mentality Month, Intl
Yours, Mine and Ours Month, Natl

February

AMD/Low Vision Awareness Month
American Heart Month
Bake for Family Fun Month
Bird Feeding Month, Natl
Black History Month, Natl
Boost Self-Esteem Month, Intl
Cherry Month, Natl
Children's Dental Health Month, Natl
Expect Success Month, Intl
February Is Fabulous Florida Strawberry Month
Get to Know an Independent Real Estate Broker Month, Natl
Hot Breakfast Month, Natl
Library Lovers' Month
Marfan Syndrome Awareness Month
North Carolina Sweetpotato Month
Parent Leadership Month, Natl
Pet Dental Health Month, Natl
Plant the Seeds of Greatness Month
Relationship Wellness Month
Return Shopping Carts to the Supermarket Month
Senior Independence Month, Natl
Time Management Month, Natl
Weddings Month, Natl
Wise Health Care Consumer Month
Youth Leadership Month

March

American Red Cross Month
Athletic Training Month, Natl
Caffeine Awareness Month, Natl
Chronic Fatigue Syndrome Awareness Month, Natl
Collision Awareness Month, Natl
Colorectal Cancer Awareness Month, Natl
Craft Month, Natl
Ethics Awareness Month, Natl
Eye Donor Month, Natl
Frozen Food Month, Natl
Honor Society Awareness Month
Humorists Are Artists Month
Ideas Month, Intl

Irish-American Heritage Month
Kidney Month, Natl
Listening Awareness Month, Intl
Mental Retardation Awareness Month
Mirth Month, Intl
Multiple Sclerosis Education and Awareness Month, Natl
Music in our Schools Month
Nutrition Month{r}, Natl
On-Hold Month, Natl
Optimism Month
Play-the-Recorder Month
Poison Prevention Awareness Month
Save Your Vision Month
Small Press Month
Spiritual Wellness Month
Talk with Your Teen About Sex Month, Natl
Umbrella Month, Natl
Vulvar Health Awareness Month
Women's History Month, Natl
Workplace Eye Health and Safety Month
Youth Art Month

March–April

Deaf History Month (Mar 13–Apr 15)

April

Alcohol Awareness Month
Appreciate Diversity Month
Autism Awareness Month, Natl
Cancer Control Month
Car Care Month, Natl
Child Abuse Prevention Month, Natl
Couple Appreciation Month
Customer Loyalty Month, Intl
Daffynitions Month, Intl
Decorating Month, Natl
Donate Life Month, Natl
Fresh Florida Tomato Month
Grange Month
Holy Humor Month
Humor Month, Natl
Informed Woman Month
Injury Prevention Month
Jazz Appreciation Month
Kite Month, Natl
Knuckles Down Month, Natl
Landscape Architecture Month, Natl
Month of the Young Child{r}
Occupational Therapy Month, Natl
Parkinson's Awareness Month, Natl
Pecan Month, Natl
Pet First Aid Awareness Month, Natl
Pharmacists War on Diabetes
Physical Wellness Month
Poetry Month, Natl
Prepare Your Home to Be Sold Month, Natl
Prevention of Animal Cruelty Month
Rosacea Awareness Month
School Library Media Month
Sexual Assault Awareness and Prevention Month, Natl
Sexually Transmitted Diseases (STDs) Education and Awareness Month, Natl
Southern Belles Month
Straw Hat Month
Stress Awareness Month
Twit Award Month, Intl
Women's Eye Health and Safety Month
Workplace Conflict Awareness Month
World Habitat Awareness Month
Youth Sports Safety Month, Natl

May

Allergy/Asthma Awareness Month, Natl
Arthritis Month, Natl
Asian Pacific American Heritage Month
Awareness of Medical Orphans Month
Barbecue Month, Natl
Better Hearing and Speech Month
Bike Month, Natl
Business Image Improvement Month, Intl
Clean Air Month
Correct Posture Month, Natl
Creative Beginnings Month
Egg Month, Natl
Family Wellness Month
Fibromyalgia Education and Awareness Month
Freedom Shrine Month
Get Caught Reading Month
Good Car-Keeping Month, Natl
Haitian Heritage Month
Hamburger Month, Natl
Heal the Children Month
Healthy Vision Month
Hepatitis Awareness Month, Natl
Huntington's Disease Awareness Month
Law Enforcement Appreciation Month in Florida
Melanoma/Skin Cancer Detection and Prevention Month
More than Just a Pretty Face Month
Motorcycle Safety Month
Mental Health Month, Natl
Moving Month, Natl
Neurofibromatosis Awareness Month, Natl
Older Americans Month, Natl
Osteoporosis Awareness and Prevention Month, Natl
Personal History Month
Physical Fitness and Sports Month, Natl
Prepare to Buy a Home Month, Natl
Preservation Month, Natl
Revise Your Work Schedule Month
Salsa Month, Natl
Scholarship Month, Natl
Sight-Saving/Ultraviolet Awareness Month, Natl
Smile Month, Natl
Strike Out Strokes Month
Stroke Awareness Month, Natl
Victorious Woman Month, Intl
Women's Health Care Month
Young Achiever Month

May–June

Family Month, Natl (May 14–June 18)
Prepare Tomorrow's Parents Month (May 14–June 18)

June

Accordion Awareness Month, Natl
Adopt-a-Shelter-Cat Month
Aphasia Awareness Month, Natl
Cancer from the Sun Month
Candy Month, Natl
Celibacy Awareness Month
Child Vision Awareness Month
Children's Awareness Month
Dairy Alternatives Month
Effective Communications Month
Entrepreneurs "Do It Yourself" Marketing Month
Fireworks Safety Months
Gay and Lesbian Pride Month
GLBT Book Month, Natl
Iced Tea Month, Natl
June Dairy Month
June Is Perennial Gardening Month
June Is Turkey Lovers' Month
Men's Month, Intl
Pharmacists Declare War on Alcoholism Month
Potty Training Awareness Month
Professional Wellness Month
Rebuild Your Life Month
Rivers Month, Natl
Rose Month, Natl
Safety Month, Natl
Soul Food Month, Natl
Sports America Kids Month
Steakhouse Month, Natl
Student Safety Month
Vision Research Month

July

Baked Bean Month, Natl
Bioterrorism/Disaster Education and Awareness Month
Blondie and Deborah Harry Month, Intl
Blueberries Month, Natl
Cell Phone Courtesy Month
"Doghouse Repairs" Month, Natl
Family Reunion Month
Grilling Month, Natl
Herbal/Prescription Awareness Month
Home Inspector Appreciation Month, Natl
Horseradish Month, Natl
Hot Dog Month, Natl
Purposeful Parenting Month, Natl
Recreation and Parks Month, Natl
Roots and Branches Month
Smart Irrigation Month
Social Wellness Month
Wheelchair Beautification Month, Natl
Women's Motorcycle Month

August

Black Business Month
Cataract Awareness Month
Children's Eye Health and Safety Month
Children's Vision and Learning Month
Family Meal Month
Get Ready for Kindergarten Month
Happiness Happens Month
Immunization Awareness Month, Natl
Inventors' Month{r}, Natl
Spinal Muscular Atrophy Awareness Month
Win with Civility Month, Natl

September

Alcohol and Drug Addiction Recovery Month, Natl
Attention Deficit Hyperactivity Disorder Month
Baby Safety Month
Backpack Safety America Month
Be Kind to Editors and Writers Month

Biscuit Month, Natl
Chicken Month, Natl
Children's Good Manners Month
Civics Awareness Month, Natl
College Savings Month
Coupon Month, Natl
Fall Hat Month
5-A-Day Month, Natl
Go Wild During California Wild Rice Month
Gynecologic Cancer Awareness Month
Honey Month, Natl
Library Card Sign-Up Month
Menopause Awareness Month
Metaphysical Awareness Month
Mushroom Month, Natl
Organic Harvest Month, Natl
Osteopathic Medicine Month, Natl
Ovarian Cancer Awareness Month, Natl
Pediatric Cancer Awareness Month
Pediculosis Prevention Month, Natl
People Skills Month, Intl
Piano Month, Natl
Pleasure Your Mate Month
Potato Month, Natl
Preparedness Month, Natl
Reunion Planning Month
Rice Month, Natl
School Success Month, Natl
Sea Cadet Month
Self-Awareness Month, Intl
Self-Improvement Month
September Is Healthy Aging{r} Month
Shameless Promotion Month
Skin Care Awareness Month, Natl
Southern Gospel Music Month
Sports and Home Eye Health and Safety Month
Strategic Thinking Month, Intl
Subliminal Communications Month
United Planet Month
Update Your Resume Month
Very Important Parents (VIP) Month{tm}, Natl

September–October

Hispanic Heritage Month, Natl (Sept 15– Oct 15)

October

Adopt-a-Shelter-Dog Month
Animal Safety and Protection Month, Natl
Billiard Awareness Month
Book Month, Natl
Breast Cancer Awareness Month, Natl
Celebrate Sun Dried Tomatoes Month
Celiac Disease Awareness Month
Children's Magazine Month
Chili Month, Natl
Church Safety and Security Month
Class Reunion Month
Communicate with Your Kid Month, Natl
Construction Toy Month, Natl
Cookie Month, Natl
Crime Prevention Month, Natl
Dental Hygiene Month, Natl
Depression Education and Awareness Month, Natl
Disability Employment Awareness Month, Natl
Diversity Awareness Month
Domestic Violence Awareness Month, Natl
Down Syndrome Month, Natl
Eat Better, Eat Together Month
Emotional Wellness Month
Family Sexuality Education Month, Natl

"Gain the Inside Advantage" Month, Natl
Gay and Lesbian History Month
German-American Heritage Month
Go Hog Wild—Eat Country Ham Month
Go on a Field Trip Month, Natl
Halloween Safety Month
Health Literacy Month
Long Term Care Planning Month
Medical Librarians Month, Natl
Organize Your Medical Information Month
Orthodontic Health Month, Natl
Pajama Month, Natl
Physical Therapy Month, Natl
Polish American Heritage Month
Popcorn Poppin' Month, Natl
Pork Month, Natl
Positive Attitude Month
Reading Group Month, Natl
Rett Syndrome Awareness Month
Right-Brainers Rule Month
Roller Skating Month, Natl
RSV Awareness Month, Natl
Sarcastics Awareness Month, Natl
Seafood Month, Natl
Self-Promotion Month
Spina Bifida Awareness Month, Natl
Spinach Lovers Month
Spinal Health Month, Natl
Starman Month, Intl
Strategic Planning Month, Intl
Sudden Infant Death Syndrome Awareness Month, Natl
Talk About Prescriptions Month
Toilet Tank Repair Month, Natl
Vegetarian Month
Women's Small Business Month
Workplace Politics Awareness Month

November

Adoption Month, Natl
AIDS Awareness Month, Natl
Alzheimer's Disease Month, Natl
American Diabetes Month
American Indian Heritage Month, Natl
Aviation History Month
Celebrate Empty Nester Month
COPD Awareness Month, Natl
Diabetic Eye Disease Month
Epilepsy Awareness Month
Family Caregivers Month, Natl
Family Stories Month
Georgia Pecan Month, Natl
Hospice Month, Natl
I Am So Thankful Month
Inspirational Role Models Month, Natl
Lifewriting Month, Natl
Lung Cancer Awareness Month
Marrow Awareness Month, Natl
Microfinance Month, Intl
Peanut Butter Lovers' Month
Pomegranate Month, Natl
Prematurity Awareness Month
Roasting Month, Natl
Vegan Month

December

Bingo's Birthday Month
Colorectal Cancer Education and Awareness Month
Drunk and Drugged Driving Prevention Month, Natl
Identity Theft Prevention and Awareness Month
Safe Toys and Gifts Month
Sign Up for Summer Camp Month, Natl
Spiritual Literacy Month
Stress-Free Family Holidays Month, Natl
Tie Month, Natl
Universal Human Rights Month

THE NATIONAL FILM REGISTRY

Under the terms of the National Film Preservation Act, each year the Librarian of Congress names 25 "culturally, historically or aesthetically" significant motion pictures to the Registry. The list is designed to reflect the full breadth and diversity of America's film heritage, thus increasing public awareness of the richness of American cinema and the need for its preservation. A film must be at least ten years old to be considered. These are the 2004 additions to the archive; the full list can be found at www.loc.gov/film/titles.html.

Ben Hur (1959)
The Blue Bird (1918)
A Bronx Morning (1931)
Clash of the Wolves (1925)
The Court Jester (1956)
D.O.A. (1950)
Daughters of the Dust (1991)
Duck and Cover (1951)
Empire (1964)
Enter the Dragon (1973)
Eraserhead (1978)
Garlic Is as Good as Ten Mothers (1980)
Going My Way (1944)
Jailhouse Rock (1957)
Kannapolis, NC (1941)
Lady Helen's Escapade (1909)
The Nutty Professor (1963)
OffOn (1968)
Popeye the Sailor Meets Sinbad the Sailor (1936)
Pups Is Pups (Our Gang, 1930)
Schindler's List (1993)
Seven Brides for Seven Brothers (1954)
Swing Time (1936)
There It Is (1928)
Unforgiven (1992)

THE NATIONAL RECORDING REGISTRY

Founded in 2002 by the National Recording Preservation Board at the Library of Congress, the National Recording Registry maintains and preserves sound recordings and collections of sound recordings that are culturally, historically or aesthetically significant. These are the 2004 additions to the archive; the full list can be found at www.loc.gov/rr/record/nrpb.

"Gypsy Love Song," performed by Eugene Cowles (1898)
"Some of These Days," performed by Sophie Tucker (1911)
"The Castles in Europe One-Step (Castle House Rag)," performed by Europe's Society Orchestra (1914)
"Swanee," performed by Al Jolson (1920)
Armistice Day radio broadcast by Woodrow Wilson (1923)
"See See Rider Blues," performed by Gertrude "Ma" Rainey (1923)
"Charleston," performed by the Golden Gate Orchestra (1925)
"Fascinating Rhythm" from *Lady, Be Good!*, performed by Fred and Adele Astaire with George Gershwin on piano (1926)
NBC radio broadcast coverage of Charles A. Lindbergh's arrival and reception in Washington, D.C. (1927)
"Stardust," performed by Hoagy Carmichael (1927)
"Blue Yodel (T for Texas)," performed by Jimmie Rodgers (1927)
"Ain't Misbehavin'," performed by Thomas "Fats" Waller (1929)
"Gregorio Cortez," performed by Trovadores Regionales (1929)

Sergei Rachmaninoff: *Piano Concerto No. 2 in C minor*, performed by Sergei Rachmaninoff on piano; conducted by Leopold Stokowski, with the Philadelphia Orchestra (1929)
"The Suncook Town Tragedy," performed by Mabel Wilson Tatro of Springfield, VT (July 1930)
Rosina Cohen oral narrative, as recorded by Lorenzo D. Turner (1932)
"Stormy Weather," performed by Ethel Waters (1933)
"Body and Soul," performed by Coleman Hawkins (1939)
Sergey Prokofiev: *Peter and the Wolf*, conducted by Serge Koussevitzky, narrated by Richard Hale, with the Boston Symphony Orchestra (1939)
"In the Mood," performed by Glenn Miller and His Orchestra (1939)
Edward R. Murrow radio broadcasts from the Battle of Britain and other bombings of London (1940)
We Hold These Truths, radio broadcast (1941)
Peter Ilich Tchaikovsky: *Piano Concerto No. 1, op. 23, B-flat minor*, performed by Vladimir Horowitz on piano; conducted by Arturo Toscanini, with the NBC Symphony Orchestra (1943)
"Down by the Riverside," performed by Sister Rosetta Tharpe (1944)
U.S. Highball (A Musical Account of a Transcontinental Hobo Trip), performed and recorded by Harry Partch with the Gate 5 Ensemble (1946)
Four Saints in Three Acts, performed by members of original 1934 cast, composed by Virgil Thomson (1947)
"Manteca," performed by the Dizzy Gillespie Big Band with Chano Pozo (1947)
Jack Benny radio program, show of March 28, 1948
"Foggy Mountain Breakdown," performed by Lester Flatt and Earl Scruggs (1949)
"Lovesick Blues," performed by Hank Williams (1949)
Guys and Dolls, recorded by the original Broadway cast (1950)
"Old Soldiers Never Die," General Douglas MacArthur's Farewell Address to Congress (1951)
Songs by Tom Lehrer, recorded by Tom Lehrer (1953)
"I'm Your Hoochie Coochie Man," performed by Muddy Waters (1954)
"Earth Angel (Will You Be Mine)," performed by The Penguins (1954)
Tuskegee Institute Choir Sings Spirituals, performed by the Tuskegee Institute Choir, directed by William L. Dawson (1955)
Messiah, conducted by Eugene Ormandy, the Mormon Tabernacle Choir with the Philadelphia Orchestra, Richard Condie, choir director (1958)
Giant Steps, performed by John Coltrane (1959)
Drums of Passion, performed by Michael Babatunde Olatunji (1960)
Peace Be Still, performed by James Cleveland (1962)
"The Girl from Ipanema," performed by Stan Getz, Joao Gilberto, Antonio Carlos Jobim and Astrud Gilberto (1963)
Live at the Apollo, performed by James Brown (1965)
Pet Sounds, performed by The Beach Boys (1966)
King James version of the Bible, read by Alexander Scourby (1966)
Remarks by Apollo 11 astronaut Neil Armstrong, broadcast from the moon (1969)
The Allman Brothers Band at Fillmore East, performed by the Allman Brothers Band (1971)
Star Wars, the original film soundtrack composed and conducted by John Williams (1977)
Recordings of Asian elephants by Katharine B. Payne (1984)
Fear of a Black Planet, performed by Public Enemy (1989)
Nevermind, performed by Nirvana (1991)

MAJOR AWARDS: ENTERTAINMENT

2005 ACADEMY AWARDS
77th Annual, for 2004 Achievement

Picture: *Million Dollar Baby*
Director: Clint Eastwood, *Million Dollar Baby*
Actor: Jamie Foxx, *Ray*
Actress: Hilary Swank, *Million Dollar Baby*
Supporting Actor: Morgan Freeman, *Million Dollar Baby*
Supporting Actress: Cate Blanchett, *The Aviator*
Original Screenplay: Charlie Kaufman, *Eternal Sunshine of the Spotless Mind*
Adapted Screenplay: Alexander Payne and Jim Taylor, *Sideways*
Foreign Language Film: *The Sea Inside* (Spain)
Animated Feature: *The Incredibles*
Animated Short Film: "Ryan"
Live Action Short Film: "Wasp"
Documentary Feature: *Born into Brothels*
Documentary Short Subject: "Mighty Times: The Children's March"
Film Editing: Thelma Schoonmaker, *The Aviator*
Costume Design: Sandy Powell, *The Aviator*
Cinematography: Robert Richardson, *The Aviator*
Art Direction: Dante Ferretti (Art Direction), Francesca Lo Schiavo (Set Decoration), *The Aviator*
Visual Effects: John Dykstra, Scott Stokdyk, Anthony LaMolinara and John Frazier, *Spider-Man 2*
Makeup: Valli O'Reilly and Bill Corso, *Lemony Snicket's A Series of Unfortunate Events*
Sound Mixing: Scott Millan, Greg Orloff, Bob Beemer and Steve Cantamessa, *Ray*
Sound Editing: Michael Silvers and Randy Thom, *The Incredibles*
Original Score: Jan A.P. Kaczmarek, *Finding Neverland*
Original Song: Jorge Drexler, "Al Otro Lado Del Río" from *The Motorcycle Diaries*
Lifetime Achievement Award: Sidney Lumet

2005 GOLDEN GLOBE AWARDS
62nd Annual, For 2004 Achievement

MOVIES
Drama: *The Aviator*
Musical or Comedy: *Sideways*
Director: Clint Eastwood, *Million Dollar Baby*
Actor, Drama: Leonardo DiCaprio, *The Aviator*
Actress, Drama: Hilary Swank, *Million Dollar Baby*
Actor, Musical or Comedy: Jamie Foxx, *Ray*
Actress, Musical or Comedy: Annette Bening, *Being Julia*
Supporting Actor: Clive Owen, *Closer*
Supporting Actress: Natalie Portman, *Closer*
Screenplay: Alexander Payne and Jim Taylor, *Sideways*
Foreign Language Film: *The Sea Inside*, Spain
Original Score: Howard Shore, *The Aviator*
Original Song: Mick Jagger and David A. Stewart, "Old Habits Die Hard," *Alfie*

TELEVISION
Series, Drama: "Nip/Tuck"
Series, Musical or Comedy: "Desperate Housewives"
Miniseries or TV Movie: *The Life and Death of Peter Sellers*
Actor, Series, Drama: Ian McShane, "Deadwood"
Actress, Series, Drama: Mariska Hargitay, "Law & Order: Special Victims Unit"
Actor, Series, Musical or Comedy: Jason Bateman, "Arrested Development"
Actress, Series, Musical or Comedy: Teri Hatcher, "Desperate Housewives"
Actor, Miniseries or TV Movie: Geoffrey Rush, *The Life and Death of Peter Sellers*
Actress, Miniseries or TV Movie: Glenn Close, *The Lion in Winter*
Actor, Supporting Role: William Shatner, "Boston Legal"
Actress, Supporting Role: Anjelica Huston, *Iron Jawed Angel*

2005 SUNDANCE FILM FESTIVAL AWARDS
24th Annual

Dramatic Grand Jury Prize: *Forty Shades of Blue*
Documentary Grand Jury Prize: *Why We Fight*
Dramatic Audience Award: *Hustle and Flow*
Documentary Audience Award: *Murderball*
World Cinema Dramatic Grand Jury Prize: *The Hero* (Angola/Portugal/France)
World Cinema Documentary Grand Jury Prize: *Shape of the Moon* (The Netherlands)
World Cinema Audience Award, Dramatic: *Brothers* (Denmark)
World Cinema Audience Award, Documentary: *Shake Hands with the Devil: The Journey of Roméo Dallaire* (Canada)
Directing Award, Dramatic: Noah Baumbach, *The Squid and the Whale*
Directing Award, Documentary: Jeff Feuerzeig, *The Devil and Daniel Johnston*
Excellence in Cinemetography Award, Dramatic: Amelia Vincent, *Hustle and Flow*
Excellence in Cinemetography Award, Documentary: Gary Griffin, *The Education of Shelby Knox*
Waldo Salt Screenwriting Award: Noah Baumbach, *The Squid and the Whale*
Special Jury Prizes, Dramatic: *Me and You and Everyone We Know* and *Brick*
Special Jury Prizes, World Cinema Dramatic: *The Forest for the Trees* and *Live-In Maid*

Special Jury Prize, Dramatic, for Acting: Amy Adams for *Junebug*; Lou Pucci for *Thumbsucker*
Special Jury Prize, Documentary: *After Innocence*
Special Jury Prizes, World Cinema Documentary: *Wall* and *The Liberace of Baghdad*
Jury Prizes in Short Filmmaking: "Family Portrait" and "Bullets in the Hood: A Bed-Stuy Story"
Jury Prize in International Short Filmmaking: "Wasp"
Alfred P. Sloan Prize: *Grizzly Man*

CANNES FILM FESTIVAL
58th Annual

Palme d'Or (Golden Palm): *The Child*
Grand Prix: *Broken Flowers*
Jury Prize: *Shanghai Dreams*
Best Short Film: *Wayfarers*
Best Actress: Hanna Laslo, *Free Zone*
Best Actor: Tommy Lee Jones, *The Three Burials of Melquiades Estrada*
Best Director: Michael Haneke, *Hidden*
Best Screenplay: Guillermo Arriaga, *The Three Burials of Melquiades Estrada*
Camera d'Or (Golden Camera): TIE: Miranda July, *Me and You and Everyone We Know*, and Vimukthi Jayasundara, *The Forsaken Land*

TONY AWARDS
59th Annual, for 2004–2005
Achievement

Play: *Doubt*
Musical: *Monty Python's Spamalot*
Book of a Musical: Rachel Sheinkin, *The 25th Annual Putnam County Spelling Bee*
Original Musical Score: Adam Guettel, *The Light in the Piazza*
Revival of a Play: *Glengarry Glen Ross*
Revival of a Musical: *La Cage aux Folles*
Special Theatrical Event: *Billy Crystal 700 Sundays*
Director of a Play: Doug Hughes, *Doubt*
Director of a Musical: Mike Nichols, *Monty Python's Spamalot*
Leading Actor in a Play: Bill Irwin, *Who's Afraid of Virginia Woolf?*
Leading Actress in a Play: Cherry Jones, *Doubt*
Leading Actor in a Musical: Norbert Leo Butz, *Dirty Rotten Scoundrels*
Leading Actress in a Musical: Victoria Clark, *The Light in the Piazza*
Featured Actor in a Play: Liev Schreiber, *Glengarry Glen Ross*
Featured Actress in a Play: Adriane Lenox, *Doubt*
Featured Actor in a Musical: Dan Fogler, *The 25th Annual Putnam County Spelling Bee*
Featured Actress in a Musical: Sara Ramirez, *Monty Python's Spamalot*
Scenic Design of a Play: Scott Pask, *The Pillowman*
Scenic Design of a Musical: Michael Yeargan, *The Light in the Piazza*
Costume Design of a Play: Jess Goldstein, *The Rivals*

Costume Design of a Musical: Catherine Zuber, *The Light in the Piazza*
Lighting Design of a Play: Brian MacDevitt, *The Pillowman*
Lighting Design of a Musical: Christopher Akerlind, *The Light in the Piazza*
Choreography: Jerry Mitchell, *La Cage aux Folles*
Orchestration: Ted Sperling, Adam Guettel and Bruce Coughlin, *The Light in the Piazza*
Special Award for Lifetime Achievement: Edward Albee
Special Award for Regional Theater: Theatre de la Jeune Lune, Minneapolis, MN

2004 PRIME TIME EMMY AWARDS
(Major Categories)
56th Annual

Drama: "The Sopranos," HBO
Comedy: "Arrested Development," Fox
Miniseries: *Angels in America*, HBO
Made-for-Television Movie: *Something the Lord Made*, HBO
Variety, Music or Comedy Series: "The Daily Show with Jon Stewart," Comedy Central
Variety, Music or Comedy Special: "Elaine Stritch: At Liberty," HBO
Children's Program: "Happy to be Nappy and Other Stories of Me," HBO
Animated Program (Less Than One Hour): "Samurai Jack: The Birth of Evil," Cartoon Network
Animated Program (One Hour or More): "Star Wars: Clone Wars," Cartoon Network
Reality Program: "Queer Eye for the Straight Guy," Bravo
Reality/Competition Program: "The Amazing Race," CBS
Nonfiction Program (Special Class): "New York City Ballet—Lincoln Center Celebrates Balanchine 100," PBS
Nonfiction Series: "American Masters," PBS
Nonfiction Special: "The Forgetting: A Portrait of Alzheimer's," PBS
Lead Actress in a Drama Series: Allison Janney, "The West Wing," NBC

Lead Actor in a Drama Series: James Spader, "The Practice," ABC

Lead Actress in a Comedy Series: Sarah Jessica Parker, "Sex and the City," HBO

Lead Actor in a Comedy Series: Kelsey Grammer, "Frasier," NBC

Lead Actress in a Miniseries or TV Movie: Meryl Streep, *Angels in America,* HBO

Lead Actor in a Miniseries or TV Movie: Al Pacino, *Angels in America,* HBO

Supporting Actress in a Drama Series: Drea de Matteo, "The Sopranos," HBO

Supporting Actor in a Drama Series: Michael Imperioli, "The Sopranos," HBO

Supporting Actress in a Comedy Series: Cynthia Nixon, "Sex and the City," HBO

Supporting Actor in a Comedy Series: David Hyde Pierce, "Frasier," NBC

Supporting Actress in a Miniseries or TV Movie: Mary-Louise Parker, *Angels in America,* HBO

Supporting Actor in a Miniseries or TV Movie: Jeffrey Wright, *Angels in America,* HBO

Guest Actress in a Drama Series: Sharon Stone, "The Practice," ABC

Guest Actor in a Drama Series: William Shatner, "The Practice," ABC

Guest Actress in a Comedy Series: Laura Linney, "Frasier," NBC

Guest Actor in a Comedy Series: John Turturro, "Monk," USA

Performance in a Variety, Music or Comedy Program: Elaine Stritch, "Elaine Stritch: At Liberty," HBO

Drama Series Directing: Walter Hill, "Deadwood," HBO

Comedy Series Directing: Joe Russo and Anthony Russo, "Arrested Development," Fox

Variety, Music or Comedy Program Directing: Louis J. Horvitz, "The 76th Annual Academy Awards," ABC

Miniseries or TV Movie Directing: Mike Nichols, *Angels in America,* HBO

Nonfiction Directing: Kate Davis, "Jockey," HBO

Drama Series Writing: Terence Winter, "The Sopranos: Long Term Parking," HBO

Comedy Series Writing: Mitchell Hurwitz, "Arrested Development," Fox

Variety, Music or Comedy Program Writing: David Javerbaum, Jon Stewart, et al, "The Daily Show With Jon Stewart," Comedy Central

Miniseries or TV Movie Writing: Tony Kushner, *Angels in America,* HBO

Nonfiction Writing: Susan Lacy and Stephen Stept, "American Masters, Judy Garland: By Myself," PBS

2005 DAYTIME EMMY AWARDS (Major Categories) 32nd Annual

Drama: "General Hospital," ABC

Lead Actress in a Drama Series: Erika Slezak, "One Life to Live," ABC

Lead Actor in a Drama Series: Christian Jules LeBlanc, "The Young and the Restless," CBS

Supporting Actress in a Drama Series: Natalia Livingston, "General Hospital," ABC

Supporting Actor in a Drama Series: Greg Rikaart, "The Young and the Restless," CBS

Younger Actress in a Drama Series: Eden Riegel, "All My Children," ABC

Younger Actor in a Drama Series: David Lago, "The Young and the Restless," CBS

Drama Series Writing Team: "As the World Turns," CBS

Drama Series Directing Team: "General Hospital," ABC

Preschool Children's Series: "Sesame Street," PBS

Children's Series: "Reading Rainbow," PBS

Performer in a Children's Series: Kevin Clash, "Sesame Street," PBS

Children's Series Writing Team: "Reading Rainbow," PBS

Children's Series Directing Team: "Sesame Street," PBS

Children's Animated Program: "Peep and the Big Wide World," TLC

Performer in an Animated Program: Henry Winkler, "Clifford's Puppy Days," PBS

Children's Special: "Mighty Times: The Legacy of Rosa Parks," HBO

Performer in a Children's Special: Stockard Channing, "Jack," SHO

Special Class Animated Program: "Rolie Polie Olie," DIS

Special Class Series: "Starting Over," syndicated

Special Class Special: "9/11 Memorial from Ground Zero," syndicated

Special Class Writing Team: "The Ellen DeGeneres Show," syndicated

Special Class Directing: Gary Halvorson, "78th Annual Macy's Thanksgiving Day Parade," NBC

Talk Show: "The Ellen DeGeneres Show," syndicated

Talk Show Host: Ellen DeGeneres, "The Ellen DeGeneres Show," syndicated

Talk Show Directing: Lenn Goodside, "The Ellen DeGeneres Show," syndicated

Game Show: "Jeopardy!," syndicated

Game Show Host: Meredith Vieira, "Who Wants to Be a Millionaire," syndicated

Game Show Directing: Matthew Cohen, "Who Wants to Be a Millionaire," syndicated

Service Show: "Martha Stewart Living," syndicated

Service Show Host: TIE: Bobby Flay, "Boy Meets Grill," FOOD, and Michael Chiarello, "Easy Entertaining with Michael Chiarello," FOOD

Service Show Directing: Natalie Gustafson, "Easy Entertaining with Michael Chiarello," FOOD

2005 GRAMMY AWARDS

Record of the Year: "Here We Go Again," Ray Charles and Norah Jones

Album of the Year: *Genius Loves Company*, Ray Charles and various artists

Song of the Year: "Daughters," John Mayer (John Mayer)

Best New Artist: Maroon5

Best Female Pop Vocal Performance: "Sunrise," Norah Jones

Best Male Pop Vocal Performance: "Daughters," John Mayer

Best Pop Performance by a Duo or Group with Vocal: "Heaven," Los Lonely Boys

Best Pop Collaboration with Vocals: "Here We Go Again," Ray Charles and Norah Jones

Best Pop Instrumental Performance: "11th Commandment," Ben Harper

Best Pop Instrumental Album: *Henry Mancini: Pink Guitar*, various artists

Best Pop Vocal Album: *Genius Loves Company*, Ray Charles and various artists

Best Dance Recording: "Toxic," Britney Spears

Best Electronic/Dance Album: *Kish Kash*, Basement Jaxx

Best Traditional Pop Vocal Album: *Stardust. . . The Great American Songbook Volume III*, Rod Stewart

Best Solo Rock Vocal Performance: "Code of Silence," Bruce Springsteen

Best Rock Performance by a Duo or Group with Vocal: "Vertigo," U2

Best Hard Rock Performance: "Slither," Velvet Revolver

Best Metal Performance: "Whiplash," Motörhead

Best Rock Instrumental Performance: "Mrs. O'Leary's Cow," Brian Wilson

Best Rock Song: "Vertigo," Bono, Adam Clayton, The Edge and Larry Mullen (U2)

Best Rock Album: *American Idiot*, Green Day

Best Alternative Music Album: *A Ghost Is Born*, Wilco

Best Female R&B Vocal Performance: "If I Ain't Got You," Alicia Keys

Best Male R&B Vocal Performance: "Call My Name," Prince

Best R&B Performance by a Duo or Group with Vocal: "My Boo," Usher and Alicia Keys

Best Traditional R&B Vocal Performance: "Musicology," Prince

Best Urban/Alternative Performance: "Cross My Mind," Jill Scott

Best R&B Song: "You Don't Know My Name," Alicia Keys, Harold Lilly and Kanye West (Alicia Keys)

Best R&B Album: *The Diary of Alicia Keys*, Alicia Keys

Best Contemporary R&B Album: *Confessions*, Usher

Best Rap Solo Performance: "99 Problems," Jay-Z

Best Rap Performance by a Duo or Group: "Let's Get It Started," The Black Eyed Peas

Best Rap/Sung Collaboration: "Yeah!," Usher featuring Lil Jon and Ludacris

Best Rap Song: "Jesus Walks," Miri Ben Ari, C. Smith and Kanye West (Kanye West)

Best Rap Album: *The College Dropout*, Kanye West

Best Female Country Vocal Performance: "Redneck Woman," Gretchen Wilson

Best Male Country Vocal Performance: "Live Like You Were Dying," Tim McGraw

Best Country Performance by a Duo or Group with Vocal: "Top of the World," Dixie Chicks

Best Country Collaboration with Vocals: "Portland Oregon," Loretta Lynn and Jack White

Best Country Instrumental Performance: "Earl's Breakdown," Nitty Gritty Dirt Band featuring Earl Scruggs, Randy Scruggs, Vassar Clements and Jerry Douglas

Best Country Song: "Live Like You Were Dying," Tim Nichols and Craig Wiseman (Tim McGraw)

Best Country Album: *Van Lear Rose*, Loretta Lynn

Best Bluegrass Album: *Brand New Strings*, Ricky Skaggs and Kentucky Thunder

Best New Age Album: *Returning*, Will Ackerman

Best Contemporary Jazz Album: *Unspeakable*, Bill Frisell

Best Jazz Vocal Album: *R.S.V.P. (Rare Songs, Very Personal)*, Nancy Wilson

Best Jazz Instrumental Solo: "Speak Like a Child," Herbie Hancock, soloist

Best Jazz Instrumental Album, Individual or Group: *Illuminations*, McCoy Tyner with Gary Bartz, Terence Blanchard, Christian McBride and Lewis Nash

Best Large Jazz Ensemble Album: *Concert in the Garden*, Maria Schneider Orchestra

Best Latin Jazz Album: *Land of the Sun*, Charlie Haden

Best Rock Gospel Album: *Wire*, Third Day

Best Pop/Contemporary Gospel Album: *All Things New*, Steven Curtis Chapman

Best Southern, Country or Bluegrass Gospel Album: *Worship & Faith*, Randy Travis

Best Traditional Soul Gospel Album: *There Will Be a Light*, Ben Harper and The Blind Boys of Alabama

Best Contemporary Soul Gospel Album: *Nothing Without You*, Smokie Norful

Best Gospel Album by a Choir or Chorus: *Live. . . This is Your House*, Carol Cymbala, choir director; The Brooklyn Tabernacle Choir

Best Latin Pop Album: *Amar Sin Mentiras*, Marc Anthony

Best Latin Rock/Alternative Album: *Street Signs*, Ozomatli

Best Traditional Tropical Latin Album: *¡Ahora Sí!*, Israel López "Cachao"

Best Salsa/Merengue Album: *Across 110th Street*, Spanish Harlem Orchestra Featuring Ruben Blades

Best Mexican/Mexican-American Album: *Intimamente*, Intocable

Best Tejano Album: *Polkas, Gritos y Acordeónes*, David Lee Garza, Joel Guzman and Sunny Sauceda

Best Traditional Blues Album: *Blues to the Bone*, Etta James

Best Contemporary Blues Album: *Keep It Simple*, Keb' Mo'

Best Traditional Folk Album: *Beautiful Dreamer—The Songs of Stephen Foster*, various artists

Best Contemporary Folk Album: *The Revolution Starts. . . . Now*, Steve Earle

Best Native American Music Album: *Cedar Dream Songs*, Bill Miller

Best Reggae Album: *True Love*, Toots & The Maytals

Best Hawaiian Music Album: *Slack Key Guitar Volume 2*, various artists

Best Traditional World Music Album: *Raise Your Spirits Higher*, Ladysmith Black Mambazo

Best Contemporary World Music Album: *Egypt*, Youssou N'Dour

Best Polka Album: *Let's Kiss: 25th Anniversary Album*, Brave Combo

Best Musical Album for Children: *cELLAbration! A Tribute to Ella Jenkins*, various artists

Best Spoken Word Album for Children: *The Train They Call the City of New Orleans*, Tom Chapin

Best Spoken Word Album: *My Life* (Bill Clinton), Bill Clinton

Best Comedy Album: *The Daily Show with Jon Stewart Presents. . . . America: A Citizen's Guide to Democracy Inaction*, Jon Stewart and the Cast of "The Daily Show"

Best Musical Show Album: *Wicked*

Best Compilation Soundtrack Album for a Motion Picture, Television or Other Visual Media: *Garden State*, various artists

Best Score Soundtrack Album for a Motion Picture, Television or Other Visual Media: *The Lord of the Rings—The Return of the King*, Howard Shore

Best Song Written for a Motion Picture, Television or Other Visual Media: "Into the West" (from *The Lord of the Rings—The Return of the King*), Annie Lennox, Howard Shore and Fran Walsh, songwriters (Annie Lennox)

Best Instrumental Composition: "Merengue," Paquito D'Rivera, composer (Yo-Yo Ma)

Best Instrumental Arrangement: "Past Present & Future," Slide Hampton, arranger (The Vanguard Jazz Orchestra)

Best Instrumental Arrangement with Accompanying Vocal(s): "Over the Rainbow," Victor Vanacore, arranger (Ray Charles and Johnny Mathis)

Best Recording Package: *A Ghost Is Born*, Peter Buchanan-Smith and Dan Nadel, art directors (Wilco)

Best Boxed or Special Limited Edition Recording Package: *Once in a Lifetime*, Stefan Sagmeister, art director (Talking Heads)

Best Album Notes: *The Complete Columbia Recordings of Woody Herman and His Orchestra and Woodchoppers (1945–1947)*, Loren Schoenberg, album notes writer (Woody Herman and His Orchestra)

Best Historical Album: *Night Train to Nashville: Music City Rhythm & Blues, 1945–1970*

Best Engineered Album, Non-Classical: *Genius Loves Company*, Robert Fernandez, John Harris, Terry Howard, Pete Karam, Joel Moss, Seth Presant, Al Schmitt and Ed Thacker, engineers (Ray Charles and various artists)

Producer of the Year, Non-Classical: John Shanks

Best Remixed Recording, Non-Classical: *It's My Life (Jacques Lu Cont's Thin White Duke Mix)*, Jacques Lu Cont, remixer (No Doubt)

Best Surround Sound Album: *Genius Loves Company* (Ray Charles and various artists)

Best Engineered Album, Classical: *Higdon: City Scape; Concerto for Orchestra*, Jack Renner, engineer (Robert Spano)

Classical Producer of the Year: David Frost

Best Classical Album: *Adams: On the Transmigration of Souls*, Lorin Maazel, conductor; John Adams and Lawrence Rock, producers (Brooklyn Youth Chorus and New York Choral Artists; New York Philharmonic)

Best Orchestral Performance: *Adams: On the Transmigration of Souls*, Lorin Maazel, conductor; Brooklyn Youth Chorus and New York Choral Artists; New York Philharmonic

Best Opera Recording: *Mozart: Le Nozze Di Figaro*, René Jacobs, conductor; Patrizia Ciofi, Véronique Gens, Simon Keenlyside, Angelika Kirchschlager and Lorenzo Regazzo; Concerto Köln

Best Choral Performance: *Berlioz: Requiem*, Robert Spano, conductor; Norman Mackenzie, choir director; Frank Lopardo, tenor, Atlanta Symphony Orchestra Chorus, Atlanta Symphony Orchestra

Best Instrumental Soloist(s) Performance (with Orchestra): *Previn: Violin Concerto "Anne-Sophie"/Bernstein: Serenade*, André Previn, conductor; Anne-Sophie Mutter, violin

Best Instrumental Soloist Performance (without Orchestra): *Aire Latino (Morel, Villa-Lobos, Ponce, etc.)*, David Russell, guitar

Best Chamber Music Performance: *Prokofiev: Cinderella—Suite for Two Pianos/Ravel: Ma Mère L'Oye*, Martha Argerich, piano, and Mikhail Pletnev, piano

Best Small Ensemble Album Performance: *Carlos Chávez—Complete Chamber Music, Volume 2*, Jeff von der Schmidt, conductor; Southwest Chamber Music

Best Classical Vocal Performance: *Ives: Songs*, Susan Graham, mezzo soprano

Best Classical Contemporary Composition: *Adams: On the Transmigration of Souls*, John Adams

Best Classical Crossover Album: *LAGQ's Guitar Heroes*, Los Angeles Guitar Quartet

Best Music Video, Short Form: *Vertigo*, U2; Alex & Martin, video director; Grace Bodie, video producer

Best Music Video, Long Form: *Concert for George*, various artists; David Leland, video director; Ray Cooper, Olivia Harrison and Jon Kamen, video producers

2004 AMERICAN MUSIC AWARDS
32nd Annual

Pop/Rock
Male Artist: Usher
Female Artist: Sheryl Crow
Band, Duo or Group: OutKast
Album: *Confessions*, Usher

Soul/Rhythm & Blues
Male Artist: Usher
Female Artist: Alicia Keys
Album: *Confessions*, Usher

Country
Male Artist: Toby Keith
Female Artist: Reba McEntire
Band, Duo or Group: Brooks & Dunn
Album: *Shock'n Y'All*, Toby Keith

Rap/Hip-Hop
Male Artist: Jay-Z
Band, Duo or Group: OutKast
Album: *Speakerboxxx/The Love Below*, OutKast

Latin
Artist: Marc Anthony

Adult Contemporary
Artist: Sheryl Crow

Alternative
Artist: Linkin Park

Contemporary Inspirational
Artist: MercyMe

Breakthrough Favorite New Artist
Gretchen Wilson

Award of Merit
Bon Jovi

T-Mobile Text-In Award
Kenny Chesney

2005 DOVE AWARDS
36th Annual, Presented by the Gospel Music Association

Song of the Year: "Who Am I," Mark Hall
Songwriter of the Year: Mark Hall
Male Vocalist of the Year: Jeremy Camp
Female Vocalist of the Year: Nicole C. Mullen
Group of the Year: Casting Crowns
Artist of the Year: Switchfoot
New Artist of the Year: Building 429
Producer of the Year: Ed Cash
Rap/Hip Hop Recorded Song: "Hittin' Curves," Grits
Rap/Hip Hop Album: *Welcome to Diverse City*, tobyMac
Modern Rock Recorded Song: "Control," MuteMath
Modern Rock Album: *Fight the Tide*, Sanctus Real
Rock Recorded Song: "Stay," Jeremy Camp
Rock Album: *Day of Fire*, Day of Fire
Rock/Contemporary Recorded Song: "Dare You to Move," Switchfoot
Rock/Contemporary Album: *Wire*, Third Day
Pop/Contemporary Recorded Song: "Who Am I," Casting Crowns
Pop/Contemporary Album: *Undone*, MercyMe
Inspirational Recorded Song: "Voice of Truth," Casting Crowns
Inspirational Album: *Hiding Place*, Selah
Southern Gospel Recorded Song: "He Came Looking for Me," The Crabb Family
Southern Gospel Album: *Driven*, The Crabb Family

Bluegrass Recorded Song: "Heroes," The Isaacs
Bluegrass Album: *Angels Gathering Flowers*, The Lewis Family
Country Recorded Song: "Forever," The Crabb Family
Country Album: *Passing Through*, Randy Travis
Urban Recorded Song: "You Don't Know," Kierra Kiki Sheard
Urban Album: *Everyday People*, Nicole C. Mullen
Traditional Gospel Recorded Song: "Through the Fire," The Crabb Family featuring Donnie McClurkin
Traditional Gospel Album: *A Tribute to Mahalia Jackson*, Lynda Randle
Contemporary Gospel Recorded Song: "Again I Say Rejoice," Israel & New Breed
Contemporary Gospel Album: *Live from Another Level*, Israel & New Breed
Praise and Worship Album: *Arriving*, Chris Tomlin
Instrumental Album: *The Passion of the Christ Original Motion Picture Soundtrack*, various
Children's Music Album: *Angel Alert!*, various
Spanish Language Album: *Te Amo Dios*, Praise Street Worship Band
Special Event Album: *The Passion of the Christ: Songs*, various
Musical: *Emmanuel—Celebrating Heaven's Child*, Joel Lindsey
Youth/Children's Musical: *Fear Not Factor*, Dennis Allen and Nan Allen
Choral Collection: *Live. . . This Is Your House*, Carol Cymbala
Worship Song: "Blessed Be Your Name," Matt Redman and Beth Redman
Recorded Music Packaging: *Happy*, Jan Cook, Tim Frank, Emily West, Clark Hook and Susan Levy
Short Form Music Video: "Dare You to Move," Switchfoot
Long Form Music Video: *Switchfoot Live in San Diego*, Switchfoot

2004 COUNTRY MUSIC AWARDS
38th Annual

Entertainer of the Year: Kenny Chesney
Male Vocalist of the Year: Keith Urban
Female Vocalist of the Year: Martina McBride
Horizon Award: Gretchen Wilson
Vocal Group of the Year: Rascal Flatts
Vocal Duo of the Year: Brooks & Dunn
Single of the Year: "Live Like You Were Dying," Tim McGraw; Byron Gallimore, Tim McGraw and Darran Smith, producers
Album of the Year: *When the Sun Goes Down*, Kenny Chesney; Buddy Cannon and Kenny Chesney, producers
Song of the Year: "Live Like You Were Dying," Tim Nichols and Craig Wiseman
Musical Event of the Year: Brad Paisley featuring Alison Krauss: "Whiskey Lullaby"
Musician of the Year: Dann Huff, guitar
Music Video of the Year: "Whiskey Lullaby," Brad Paisley and Alison Krauss

MAJOR AWARDS: LITERATURE AND HUMANITIES

NOBEL PRIZES
2004 Recipients

Awarded each October, the Nobel Prizes are highly prestigious international awards given yearly since 1901, named for founder Alfred E. Nobel. The prize consists of a medal, a personal diploma, and a prize amount. Details can be found at www.nobel.se.

Peace: Wangari Maathai
Physics: David J. Gross, H. David Politzer and Frank Wilczek
Chemistry: Aaron Ciechanover, Avram Hershko and Irwin Rose
Physiology or Medicine: Richard Axel and Linda B. Buck
Literature: Elfriede Jelinek
Economics: Finn E. Kydland and Edward C. Prescott

2005 PULITZER PRIZES

THE ARTS
Fiction: *Gilead*, Marilynne Robinson
Drama: *Doubt, a Parable*, John Patrick Shanley
History: *Washington's Crossing*, David Hackett Fischer
Biography: *De Kooning: An American Master*, Mark Stevens and Annalyn Swan
Poetry: *Delights & Shadows*, Ted Kooser
General Nonfiction: *Ghost Wars: The Secret History of the CIA, Afghanistan and Bin Laden, from the Soviet Invasion to September 10, 2001*, Steve Coll
Music: *Second Concerto for Orchestra*, Steven Stucky

JOURNALISM
Public Service: *The Los Angeles Times*
Breaking News Reporting: Staff, *The Star-Ledger*, Newark, NJ
Investigative Reporting: Nigel Jaquiss, *Willamette Week*, Portland, OR
Explanatory Reporting: Gareth Cook, *The Boston Globe*
Beat Reporting: Amy Dockser Marcus, *The Wall Street Journal*
National Reporting: Walt Bogdanich, *The New York Times*
International Reporting: Dele Olojede, *Newsday*; Kim Murphy, *The Los Angeles Times*
Feature Writing: Julia Keller, *Chicago Tribune*
Commentary: Connie Schultz, *The Plain Dealer*, Cleveland, OH
Criticism: Joe Morgenstern, *The Wall Street Journal*
Editorial Writing: Tom Philp, *The Sacramento Bee*
Breaking News Photography: Staff, The Associated Press
Feature Photography: Deanne Fitzmaurice, *The San Francisco Chronicle*

2004 NATIONAL ENDOWMENT AWARDS
Awarded November 17, 2004

2004 National Medal of Arts:
Andrew W. Mellon Foundation, philanthropic organization
Ray Bradbury, author
Carlisle Floyd, opera composer
Frederick Hart, sculptor
Anthony Hecht, poet
John Ruthven, wildlife artist
Vincent Scully, architectural historian and educator
Twyla Tharp, choreographer, artistic director and dancer

2004 National Medal of Humanities:
Marva Collins, educator
Gertrude Himmelfarb, historian, author and educator
Hilton Kramer, art critic
Madeleine L'Engle, author
Harvey Mansfield, political scientist
John Searle, philosopher and educator
Shelby Steele, author and educator
The United States Capitol Historical Society, preservation society

2004 PEABODY AWARDS
64th Annual

"On the Media," WNYC Radio, National Public Radio, New York
"Studio 360 American Icons: Melville's Moby Dick," WNYC Radio, Public Radio International, New York
"The War in Iraq," National Public Radio, Washington, DC
"Leonard Bernstein: An American Life," CultureWorks and the WFMT Radio Network
"Let the Good Times Roll," The Rhythm and Blues Foundation, Washington, DC, Public Radio International
"To the Best of Our Knowledge," Wisconsin Public Radio, Public Radio International
"The Darfur Crisis," BBC Television News, London, UK
"MOSAIC: World News from the Middle East," Link TV, San Francisco, CA
"State of Denial," WFAA-TV, Dallas, TX
"Friends in High Places," WTVF-TV, Nashville, TN
Chesapeake Bay Pollution Investigation, WBAL-TV, Baltimore, MD
"60 Minutes II": "Abuse at Abu Ghraib," CBS News
"Black Sky: The Race for Space," Discovery Channel and Vulcan Productions in association with Gemini Productions and Antenna Films
"Bus 174," Zendo Entertainment in association with Cinemax Reel Life
"Balseros," Televisio de Catalunya, Bausan Films in association with Cinemax Reel Life
"Beah: A Black Woman Speaks," Clinica Estetico and LisaGay Inc. in association with HBO
"Something the Lord Made," A Cort/Madden Production in association with HBO Films
"Deadwood," Red Board Productions and Paramount Television in association with HBO Entertainment
"The N-Word," TRIO and Post Consumer Media
"American Experience: Tupperware!," Filmmakers Collaborative, Blueberry Hill Productions for American Experience/WGBH
"Rwanda—Do Scars Ever Fade?," Bill Brummel Productions for The History Channel
"The Age of Wal-Mart: Inside America's Most Powerful Company," CNBC
"The Daily Show with Jon Stewart: Indecision 2004," Comedy Central
"Human Cargo," Howe Sound Films and Force Four Entertainment in association with the Canadian Broadcasting Corporation
"State of Play," An Endor Production in association with the BBC, BBC America
"The Kumars at No. 42," Hat Trick Productions, BBC America
"Nursery Tap, Hip to Toe," Nursery Tap, LLC
"The Suffering of Sudan," Channel One Network
"Takalani Sesame Presents": "talk to me. . . ," Sesame Workshop (USA) and Kwasukasukela (South Africa)
"The Bully Project," WITI-TV, Milwaukee, WI
"Univision Communications, Salud es Vida . . . Entérate! (Lead a Healthy Life . . . Get the Facts!)," Univision, Miami, FL
Grant Tinker

2004 GEORGE POLK AWARDS

Awarded for special achievement in journalism.

Economic Reporting: Ellen E. Schultz and Theo Francis, *The Wall Street Journal*
Foreign Reporting: Paisley Dodds, The Associated Press
Labor Reporting: Justin Pritchard, The Associated Press
Local Reporting: Tim Novak and Steve Warmbir, *Chicago Sun-Times*
Magazine Reporting: Seymour M. Hersh, *The New Yorker*
Military Reporting: Diana B. Henriques, *The New York Times*
National Reporting: Walt Bogdanich, *The New York Times*
Regional Reporting: *The Press Democrat*, Santa Rosa, CA
Sports Reporting: Mark Fainaru-Wada and Lance Williams, *San Francisco Chronicle*
State Reporting: John Hill and Dorothy Korber, *The Sacramento Bee*
Television Reporting: Diane Sawyer and Robbie Gordon, *PrimeTime Live*, ABC News
War Reporting: Dexter Filkins, *The New York Times*
Career Award: Bill Moyers

2004 WEBBY AWARDS
8th Annual

Activism: Tolerance.org—www.tolerance.org
Best Practices: Google—www.google.com
Broadband: P.O.V.-Borders: Environment—www.pbs.org/pov/borders
Commerce: iTunes Music Store—www.apple.com/itunes/store/shop.html
Community: Wikipedia—www.wikipedia.org
Education: BBC—Human Body—www.bbc.co.uk/science/humanbody
Fashion: colette—www.colette.fr
Film: Fog of War—www.sonyclassics.com/fogofwar/index
Finance: U.S. Securities and Exchange Commission—www.sec.gov
Games: Yohoho! Puzzle Pirates—www.puzzlepirates.com
Government and Law: HealthyOntario.com—www.healthyontario.com
Health: KidsHealth—KidsHealth.org
Humor: The Onion—www.theonion.com
Living: Epicurious.com—www.epicurious.com
Music: iTunes Music Store—www.apple.com/itunes/store
Net Art: Access—www.accessproject.net
News: BBC News—www.bbc.co.uk/news
Personal: RAKU-GAKI.COM—www.raku-gaki.com
Politics: Meetup—www.meetup.com
Print & Zines: {fray}—www.fray.com
Radio: KEXP Radio Online—www.kexp.org
Science: Exploratorium—www.exploratorium.edu
Services: Google—www.google.com
Spirituality: GraceCathedral.org—www.GraceCathedral.org
Sports: BBC Sport—www.bbc.co.uk/sport
Technical Achievement: Map24—www.map24.com
Travel: IgoUgo—www.igougo.com
TV: PBS.org—www.pbs.org
Weird: Car Stuck Girls—www.carstuckgirls.com
Youth: WIRETAP—www.wiretapmag.org

NATIONAL BOOK AWARDS 2004

Given annually by the National Book Foundation.

Fiction: *The News from Paraguay*, Lily Tuck
Nonfiction: *Arc of Justice: A Saga of Race, Civil Rights, and Murder in the Jazz Age*, Kevin Boyle
Poetry: *Door in the Mountain: New and Collected Poems, 1965–2003*, Jean Valentine
Young People's Literature: *Godless*, Pete Hautman

THE NATIONAL BOOK CRITICS CIRCLE AWARDS 2004

Fiction: *Gilead*, Marilynne Robinson
General Nonfiction: *The Reformation: A History*, Diarmaid MacCulloch
Biography/Autobiography: *De Kooning: An American Master*, Mark Stevens and Annalyn Swan
Poetry: *The School Among the Ruins*, Adrienne Rich
Criticism: *Where You're At: Notes from the Frontline of a Hip-Hop Planet*, Patrick Neate

PEN/FAULKNER AWARD FOR FICTION 2005

An award given by an organization of writers to honor their peers.

Winner
Ha Jin, *War Trash*
Finalists
Edwidge Danticat, *The Dew Breaker*
Marilynne Robinson, *Gilead*
Jerome Charyn, *The Green Lantern: A Romance of Stalinist Russia*
Steve Yarbrough, *Prisoners of War*

THE BOOK SENSE BOOK OF THE YEAR 2005

Formerly known as the ABBY (American Booksellers Book of the Year), this award is given annually by the American Booksellers Association.

Adult Fiction: *Jonathan Strange & Mr. Norrell*, Susanna Clarke
Adult Nonfiction: *Shadow Divers: The True Adventure of Two Americans Who Risked Everything to Solve One of the Last Mysteries of World War II*, Robert Kurson
Children's Illustrated: *Duck for President*, Doreen Cronin, illustrated by Betsy Lewin
Children's Literature: *Chasing Vermeer*, Blue Balliett, illustrated by Brett Helquist

THE MAN BOOKER PRIZE 2004

Sponsored by Booker Prize Foundation and the Man Group in the United Kingdom, this award is given annually to the best full-length novel written in English by a citizen of the U.K., the Commonwealth, Eire, Pakistan, or South Africa.

Winner
The Line of Beauty, Alan Hollinghurst
Shortlisted Titles
Bitter Fruit, Achmat Dangor
The Electric Michelangelo, Sarah Hall
Cloud Atlas, David Mitchell
The Master, Colm Tóibín
I'll Go to Bed at Noon, Gerard Woodward

THE MAN BOOKER INTERNATIONAL PRIZE

A new prize from the sponsors of the Man Booker Prize, awarded biennially for a body of literature. Open to authors of all nationalities whose work has been either written or translated widely into English.

2005 Recipient: Ismail Kadare of Albania.

ORANGE PRIZE FOR FICTION 2005

Celebrating the excellence of women's writing.

We Need to Talk About Kevin, Lionel Shriver

WHITBREAD BOOK AWARDS 2004

Awards given to celebrate the most enjoyable British writing of the year.

Novel: *Small Island*, Andrea Levy
First Novel: *Eve Green*, Susan Fletcher
Poetry: *Roberts Corpus*, Michael Symmons
Biography: *My Heart Is My Own: The Life of Mary Queen of Scots*, John Guy
Children's Book: *Not the End of the World*, Geraldine McCaughrean
Book of the Year: *Small Island*, Andrea Levy

THE KORET JEWISH BOOK AWARDS 2005

Given annually to the most outstanding books on aspects of Jewish life.

Fiction: *The Persistence of Memory*, Tony Eprile
History: *Mothers and Children: Jewish Family Life in Medieval Europe*, Elisheva Baumgarten
Biography, Autobiography and Literary Studies: *A Tale of Love and Darkness*, Amos Oz, translated from the Hebrew by Nicolas de Lange
Philosophy and Thought: *Wrestling with God and Men: Homosexuality in the Jewish Tradition*, Rabbi Steven Greenberg
Children's Literature: *The Cats in Krasinski Square*, Karen Hesse, illustrated by Wendy Watson
Translation and Commentary: *The Five Books of Moses*, Robert Alter

THE JAMES BEARD FOUNDATION/KITCHENAID BOOK AWARDS 2005

Given annually by the James Beard Foundation to the best original, English-language books on culinary topics published in the previous year.

Baking and Desserts: *A Blessing of Bread: Recipes and Rituals, Memories and Mitzvah*, Maggie Glezer
Cooking from a Professional Point of View: *John Ash Cooking One on One: Private Lessons in Simple, Contemporary Foods from a Master Teacher*, John Ash and Amy Mintzer
Entertaining and Special Occasions: *Serena, Food and Stories*, Serena Bass
Focus on Health: *The New Mayo Clinic Cookbook*, Maureen Callahan, R.D., and Cheryl Forberg, R.D.
Food of the Americas: *Food of the Americas Cookbook: Native Recipes and Traditions*, Fernando and Marlene Divina
General: *Weir Cooking in the City*, Joanne Weir
International: *Provence Cookbook*, Patricia Wells
Photography: *Bouchon*, Deborah Jones, photographer; Thomas Keller, author
Reference: *On Food and Cooking*, Harold McGee
Single Subject: *All About Braising*, Molly Stevens
Vegetarian *Olive Trees and Honey: A Treasury of Vegetarian Recipes from Jewish Communities Around the World*, Gil Marks
Wines and Spirits: *Scotch Whisky*, Charles MacLean
Writing on Food: *Last Chance to Eat*, Gina Mallet
Kitchenaid Cookbook Hall of Fame: *The Great Scandinavian Baking Book*, Beatrice Ojakangas
Kitchenaid Cookbook of the Year: *Rick Stein's Complete Seafood*, Rick Stein

2005 AMERICAN LIBRARY ASSOCIATION AWARDS FOR CHILDREN'S BOOKS

NEWBERY MEDAL Given to the author of the most distinguished contribution to American literature for children published in 2004:
Winner
Cynthia Kadohata, author, *Kira-Kira*
Honor Books
Gary D. Schmidt, author, *Lizzie Bright and the Buckminster Boy*
Gennifer Choldenko, author, *Al Capone Does My Shirts*
Russell Freedman, author, *The Voice That Challenged a Nation: Marian Anderson and the Struggle for Equal Rights*

CALDECOTT MEDAL Given to the illustrator of the most distinguished American picture book for children published in 2004:
Winner
Kevin Henkes, illustrator and author, *Kitten's First Full Moon*
Honor Books
Barbara Lehman, illustrator and author, *The Red Book*
E.B. Lewis, illustrator, *Coming on Home Soon*, written by Jacqueline Woodson
Mo Willems, illustrator and author, *Knuffle Bunny: A Cautionary Tale*

CORETTA SCOTT KING AWARD For outstanding books by African American authors and illustrators:
Winners
Toni Morrison, author, *Remember: The Journey to School Integration*
Kadir Nelson, illustrator, *Ellington Was Not a Street*, written by Ntozake Shange
Honor Books—Authors
Sheila P. Moses, *The Legend of Buddy Bush*
Sharon G. Flake, *Who Am I Without Him*
Marilyn Nelson, *Fortune's Bones: The Manumission Requiem*
Honor Books—Illustrators
Jerry Pinkney, *God Bless the Child*, written by Billie Holiday and Arthur Herzog, Jr
Leo and Diane Dillon, *The People Could Fly: The Picture Book*, written by Virginia Hamilton
John Steptoe New Talent Award
For narrative: Barbara Hathaway, *Missy Violet and Me*
For illustration: Frank Morrison, *Jazzy Miz Mozetta*, written by Brenda C. Roberts

MICHAEL L. PRINTZ AWARD For excellence in writing literature for young adults:
Winner
Meg Rosoff, author, *How I Live Now*
Honor Books
Kenneth Oppel, author, *Airborn*
Gary D. Schmidt, author, *Lizzie Bright and the Buckminster Boy*
Allan Stratton, author, *Chanda's Secrets*

ROBERT F. SIBERT AWARD For most distinguished informational book for children published in 2004:
Winner
Russell Freedman, author, *The Voice That Challenged a Nation: Marian Anderson and the Struggle for Equal Rights*
Honor Books
Barbara Kerley, author, *Walt Whitman: Words for America*, illustrated by Brian Selznick
Sy Montgomery, author, *The Tarantula Scientist*, illustrated by Nic Bishop
James Rumford, author, *Sequoyah: The Cherokee Man Who Gave His People Writing*, illustrated by Anna Sixkiller Huckaby

MARGARET A. EDWARDS AWARD For lifetime achievement in writing books for young adults:
Francesca Lia Block, recipient

LAURA INGALLS WILDER MEDAL For an author or illustrator whose books, published in the United States, have made, over a period of years, a substantial and lasting contribution to literature for children:
Laurence Yep, recipient

MILDRED L. BATCHELDER AWARD For the best children's book in English translation (first published in a foreign country) published in the US:
Winner
Delacorte Press/Random House Children's Books, publisher, *The Shadows of Ghadames*, written by Joëlle Stolz, translated from French by Catherine Temerson
Honor Books
Farrar, Straus and Giroux, publisher, *The Crow-Girl: The Children of Crow Cove*, written by Bodil Bredsdorff, translated from Danish by Faith Ingwersen
A Richard Jackson Book, Atheneum Books for Young Readers, publisher, *Danial Half Human and the Good Nazi*, written by David Chotjewitz, translated from German by Doris Orgel

ANDREW CARNEGIE MEDAL FOR EXCELLENCE IN CHILDREN'S VIDEO
Paul R. Gagne and Melissa Reilly, producers, *The Dot*, based on the book written and illustrated by Peter H. Reynolds

MAY HILL ARBUTHNOT LECTURE AWARD
Russell Freedman, recipient

THE LAMBDA LITERARY AWARDS

17th annual awards given by the Lambda Literary Foundation to recognize excellence in lesbian/gay/bisexual/transgender (LGBT) literature, for works published in 2004.

Gay Men's Fiction: *The Master*, Colm Tóibín
Lesbian Fiction: *A Seahorse Year*, Stacey D'Erasmo
Debut Gay Men's Fiction: *Clay's Way*, Blair Mastbaum
Debut Lesbian Fiction: *Crybaby Butch*, Judith Frank
Gay Men's Poetry: *Written in Water*, Luis Cernuda
Lesbian Poetry: *Sweet to Burn*, Beverly Burch
Gay Men's Mystery: *Flight of the Aquavit*, Anthony Bidulka
Lesbian Mystery: *Hancock Park*, Katherine V. Forrest
Biography: *Warrior Poet: A Biography of Audre Lorde*, Alexis De Veaux
Memoir/Autobiography: *Name All the Animals*, Alison Smith
Anthology (Fiction): *Fresh Men: New Voices in Gay Fiction*, selected by Edmund White, edited by Donald Weise
Anthology (Nonfiction): *I Do/I Don't: Queers on Marriage*, edited by Greg Wharton and Ian Philips
Humor: *Dress Your Family in Corduroy and Denim*, David Sedaris
Drama: *I Am My Own Wife*, Doug Wright
Science Fiction/Fantasy/Horror: *The Ordinary*, Jim Grimsley
Spirituality: *Jesus and the Shamanic Tradition of Same-Sex Love*, Will Roscoe
Visual Arts/Photography: *At Ease: Navy Men of World War II*, Evan Bachner
Children/Young Adult: *So Hard to Say*, Alex Sanchez
Erotica: *Best Gay Erotica 2005*, edited by Richard Labonte
Transgender: *The Gender Frontier*, Mariette Pathy Allen
Romance: *Almost Like Being in Love*, Steven Kluger
LGBT Studies: *For the Love of Women: Gender, Identity, and Same-Sex Relations in a Greek Provincial Town*, Elisabeth Kirtsoglou

LGBT Independent Press: Bella Books
Lambda Literary Foundation Pioneer Award: Blanche Weisen Cooke
Lambda Literary Foundation Bridge Builders Award: Eve Ensler, author of *The Vagina Monologues*

THE EDGAR AWARDS 2005

The Mystery Writers of America honor the best in mystery fiction and nonfiction produced in the previous year. Named in honor of Edgar Allan Poe.

Best Novel: *California Girl*, T. Jefferson Parker
Best First Novel by an American Author: *Country of Origin*, Don Lee
Best Paperback Original: *The Confession*, Domenic Stansberry
Best Critical/Biographical Work: *The New Annotated Sherlock Holmes: The Complete Short Stories*, edited by Leslie S. Klinger
Best Fact Crime: *Conviction: Solving the Moxley Muders: A Reporter and a Detective's Twenty-Year Search for Justice*, Leonard Levitt
Best Short Story: "Something About a Scar," Laurie Lynn Drummond
Best Young Adult: *In Darkness, Death*, Dorothy and Thomas Hoobler
Best Juvenile: *Chasing Vermeer*, Blue Balliett
Best Play: *Spatter Pattern (Or, How I Got Away With It)*, Neal Bell
Best Television Episode Teleplay: "Law & Order: Criminal Intent": "Want," Elizabeth Benjamin
Best Television Feature or Mini-Series Teleplay: *State of Play*, Paul Abbott
Best Motion Picture Screenplay: *A Very Long Engagement*, Jean-Pierre Jeunet
Grand Master: Marcia Muller
Robert L. Fish Award: "Can't Catch Me," Thomas Morrissey
Ellery Queen Award: Carolyn Marino, VP/Executive Editor, HarperCollins
Raven Award: Cape Cod Mystery Theatre; DorothyL listserv; Murder by the Book, Houston, TX
Simon & Schuster–Mary Higgins Clark Award: *Grave Endings*, Rochelle Krich
Special Awards: David Chase, writer/producer of "The Sopranos," "The Rockford Files" and "Kolchak: The Night Stalker;" Tom Fontana, writer/producer of "Homicide: Life on the Street," "Oz" and "The Jury"

THE HUGO AWARDS 2004

Also known as the Science Fiction Achievement Award, given annually by the World Science Fiction Society. 51st annual awards.

Best Novel: *Paladin of Souls*, Lois McMaster Bujold
Best Novella: "The Cookie Monster," Vernor Vinge
Best Novelette: "Legions in Time," Michael Swanwick
Best Related Book: *The Chelsea Awards for Science Fiction and Fantasy Art: A Retrospective*, John Grant, Elizabeth L. Humphrey and Pamela D. Scoville
Best Short Story: "A Study in Emerald," Neil Gaiman
John W. Campbell Award for Best New Writer: Jay Lake

THE NEBULA AWARDS 2004

40th annual awards given by Science Fiction and Fantasy Writers of America, Inc.

Novel: *Paladin of Souls*, Lois McMaster Bujold
Novella: "The Green Leopard Plague," Walter Jon Williams
Novelette: "Basement Magic," Ellen Klages
Script: *The Lord of the Rings: The Return of the King*, Fran Walsh, Philippa Boyens and Peter Jackson
Short Story: "Coming to Terms," Eileen Gunn

INDEX

Aames—Agriculture

Aames, Willie: Birth, Jul 15
Aaron, Hank: Birth, Feb 5
Aaron, Hank: Home Run Record: Anniv, Apr 8
Abbado, Claudio: Birth, Jun 26
Abbott and Costello Show TV Premiere: Anniv, Dec 5
Abbott, Berenice: Birth Anniv, Jul 17
Abbott, Jim: Birth, Sep 19
Abdul, Paula: Birth, Jun 19
Abdul-Jabbar, Kareem: Birth, Apr 16
Aberdeen Intl Youth Fest (Aberdeen, Scotland), Aug 2
Abilities Day, Dec 22
Abolition Society Founded, First American: Anniv, Apr 14
Abortion Counseling, Supreme Court Upholds Ban: Anniv, May 23
Abortion First Legalized: Anniv, Apr 25
Abortion: Roe v Wade Supreme Court Decision: Anniv, Jan 22
Abraham, F. Murray: Birth, Oct 24
Abuse: Heal the Children Month, May 1
Abused Women and Children's Awareness Day, Jun 11
Academy Awards Presentation, Mar 5
Academy Awards, First: Anniv, May 16
Acadia Natl Park Established: Anniv, Jan 1
According to Hoyle Day, Aug 29
Accordion Awareness Month, Intl, Jun 1
Accordion Chmpshp, Kimberley Intl (Kimberley, BC, Canada), Jul 3
Accordion Fest, Sata-Hame (Ikaalinen, Finland), Jun 27
Ace, Goodman: Birth Anniv, Jan 15
Achelis, Elisabeth: Birth Anniv, Jan 24
Ackland, Joss: Birth, Feb 29
ACL Awareness Among Young Women Day, Accelerate, Apr 5
Act Happy Day, Mar 20
Acuff, Roy: Birth Anniv, Sep 15
Adams County Fair/Rodeo (Hettinger, ND), Aug 3
Adams, Abigail: Birth Anniv, Nov 22
Adams, Ansel: Birth Anniv, Feb 20
Adams, Brooke: Birth, Feb 8
Adams, Bryan: Birth, Nov 5
Adams, Don: Birth, Apr 19
Adams, Edie: Birth, Apr 16
Adams, Joey Lauren: Birth, Jan 6
Adams, John Quincy: Birth Anniv, Jul 11
Adams, John Quincy: Returns to Congress: Anniv, Mar 4
Adams, John, and Jefferson, Thomas: Death Anniv, Jul 4
Adams, John: Birth Anniv, Oct 30
Adams, Louisa Catherine Johnson: Birth Anniv, Feb 12
Adams, Maud: Birth, Feb 12
Adams, Samuel: Birth Anniv, Sep 27
Adams, Scott: Birth, Jun 8
Addams Family TV Premiere: Anniv, Sep 18
Addams, Charles: Birth Anniv, Jan 7
Addams, Jane: Birth Anniv, Sep 6
Adding Machine, Patent Issued for First: Anniv, Oct 11
Addison, Joseph: Birth Anniv, May 1
Adjani, Isabelle: Birth, Jun 27
Administrative Professionals Day, Apr 26
Administrative Professionals Intl Conv (New Orleans, LA), Jul 23
Administrative Professionals Week, Apr 23
Admission Day Holiday (HI), Aug 18
Adolfo: Birth, Feb 15
Adopt-A-Shelter-Cat Month, Jun 1
Adoption Month, Natl, Nov 1
Adoption Week, Natl, Nov 1
Adult Immunization Awareness Week, Natl, Sep 24
Advent, First Sunday of, Dec 3
Adventures of Ellery Queen TV Premiere: Anniv, Oct 14
Advertising: Mobius Awards (Los Angeles, CA), Feb 10
Aebleskiver Days (Tyler, MN), Jul 21
Affleck, Ben: Birth, Aug 15
Afghanistan
   Fall of Kabul: Anniv, Nov 13
   Independence Day, Aug 19
   Soviet Troop Withdrawal Deadline, Feb 15
AFL Founded: Anniv, Dec 8
AFL-CIO Founded: Anniv, Dec 5
Africa Industrialization Day (UN), Nov 20
African American

African American History Month, Natl, Feb 1
African Methodist Episcopal Church Organized: Anniv, Apr 9
African-American Coaches Day, Feb 2
Alpha Kappa Alpha Sorority Founded: Anniv, Jan 15
Amistad Seized: Anniv, Aug 29
Anderson, Marian: Birth Anniv, Feb 27
Anderson, Marian: Easter Concert: Anniv, Apr 9
Ashford, Emmett: Birth Anniv, Nov 23
Attack on Fort Wagner: Anniv, Jul 19
Black Business Month, Aug 1
Black History Month at Tuskegee Univ (Tuskegee, AL), Feb 1
Black History Month, Natl, Feb 1
Black Love Day, Feb 13
Black Page Appointed US House: Anniv, Apr 9
Black Poetry Day, Oct 18
Black Press Day: Anniv of First Black Newspaper in US, Mar 16
Black Senate Page Appointed: Anniv, Apr 8
Black Single Parents' Week, Jun 4
Blacks Ruled Eligible to Vote: Anniv, Apr 3
Bolin, Jane M.: Birth, Apr 11
Brown, Jesse Leroy: Birth Anniv, Oct 13
Chisholm, Shirley: Birth Anniv, Nov 30
Civil Rights Act of 1964: Anniv, Jul 2
Civil Rights Bill of 1866: Anniv, Apr 9
Civil Rights Workers Found Slain: Anniv, Aug 4
Cole, Nat "King": Birth Anniv, Mar 17
Coleman, Bessie: Birth Anniv, Jan 26
Cullen, Countee: Birth Anniv, May 30
Davis, Benjamin O., Jr: Birth Anniv, Dec 18
Desegregation, US Army First: Anniv, Jul 26
Dorothy Porter Wesley Lecture (Washington, DC), Apr 21
Dred Scott Decision: Anniv, Mar 6
Drew, Charles: Birth Anniv, Jun 3
Ella Fitzgerald Wins Apollo Amateur Night: Anniv, Nov 21
Emancipation of 500: Anniv, Aug 1
Escape to Freedom (F. Douglass): Anniv, Sep 3
First American Abolition Society Founded: Anniv, Apr 14
First Black Governor Elected: Anniv, Nov 7
First Black Plays in NBA Game: Anniv, Oct 31
First Black Receives Congressional Medal: Anniv, May 23
First Black Serves in US House of Representatives: Anniv, Dec 12
First Black Southern Lt Gov: Anniv, Jan 11
First Black US Cabinet Member: Anniv, Jan 18
First Black US State's Attorney: Anniv, Jul 6
First Natl Convention for Blacks: Anniv, Sep 15
Forten, James: Birth Anniv, Sep 2
Foster, Andrew: Birth Anniv, Sep 17
Frederick Douglass Speaks: Anniv, Aug 11
Freedom Riders: Anniv, May 4
Gibbs, Mifflin Wister: Birth Anniv, Apr 28
Greensboro Sit-in: Anniv, Feb 1
Harlem Globetrotters Play First Game: Anniv, Jan 7
Harris, Patricia Roberts: Birth Anniv, May 31
Historically Black Colleges and Universities Week, Natl (Pres Proc), Sep 17
Hughes, Langston: Birth Anniv, Feb 1
Jackie Robinson Breaks Baseball Color Line: Anniv, Apr 15
Joplin, Scott: Birth Anniv, Nov 24
Juneteenth, Jun 19
King Awarded Nobel Peace Prize: Anniv, Oct 14
King, Martin Luther, Jr: Birth Anniv, Jan 15
Kunta Kinte Heritage Festival (Crownsville, MD), Aug 12
Kwanzaa Fest, Dec 26
Links, Inc: Anniv, Nov 9
Little Rock Nine: Anniv, Sep 4
Malcolm X Assassinated: Anniv, Feb 21
Malcolm X: Birth Anniv, May 19
Marian Anderson Performs with Metropolitan Opera: Anniv, Jan 7
Marshall, Thurgood: Birth Anniv, Jul 2
Marshall, Thurgood: Resigns from Supreme Court: Anniv, Jun 27
Marshall, Thurgood: Sworn in to Supreme Court: Anniv, Oct 2
Martin Luther King Jr Day (Charlottesville, VA), Jan 16
McDaniel, Hattie: Birth Anniv, Jun 10
Medgar Evers Assassinated: Anniv, Jun 13
Meredith (James) Enrolls at Ole Miss: Anniv, Sep 30

Million Man March: Anniv, Oct 16
Minority Enterprise Development Week (Pres Proc), Sep 10
Montgomery Boycott Arrests: Anniv, Feb 22
Montgomery Bus Boycott Begins: Anniv, Dec 5
Montgomery Bus Boycott Ends: Anniv, Dec 20
Motley, Constance Baker: Birth, Sep 14
NAACP Founded: Anniv, Feb 12
New York Slave Revolt: Anniv, Apr 7
Niagara Movement Founded: Anniv, Jul 11
Ralph Bunche Awarded Nobel Peace Prize: Anniv, Dec 10
Robinson Named First Black Manager: Anniv, Oct 3
Robinson, Roscoe, Jr: Birth Anniv, Oct 11
Rosa Parks Day, Dec 1
Saint Louis Race Riots: Anniv, Jul 2
Scottsboro Trial: Anniv, Apr 6
16th Street Baptist Church Bombing: Anniv, Sep 15
Soul Food Month, Natl, Jun 1
Spelman College Established: Anniv, Apr 11
Stokes Becomes First Black Mayor in US: Anniv, Nov 13
Tanner, Henry Ossawa: Birth Anniv, Jun 21
Truth, Sojourner: Death Anniv, Nov 26
Tubman, Harriet: Death Anniv, Mar 10
Tuskegee Airmen Activated: Anniv, Mar 22
Tuskegee Institute Opening: Anniv, Jul 4
Tuskegee University 125th Anniv (Tuskegee, AL), Apr 2
Wheatley, Phillis: Death Anniv, Dec 5
Wheatley, Phillis: Poetry Collection Published: Anniv, Sep 1
Zora Neale Hurston Fest (Eatonville, FL), Jan 25
African American History Month, Natl, Feb 1
African Methodist Episcopal Church Organized: Anniv, Apr 9
African Natl Congress Ban Lifted, Feb 2
African-American Coaches Day, Feb 2
Agassi, Andre: Birth, Apr 29
Agassiz, Louis: Birth Anniv, May 28
Agee, James: Birth Anniv, Nov 27
Aggie Muster, Apr 21
Agnew Resignation: Anniv, Oct 10
Agnew, Spiro: Birth Anniv, Nov 9
Agriculture (including state and county fairs)
   Acton Fair (Acton, ME), Aug 24
   Agriculture Day, Natl, Mar 20
   Agriculture Week, Natl, Mar 19
   Agrifair (Abbotsford, BC, Canada), Aug 3
   Alabama Natl Fair (Montgomery, AL), Oct 6
   Alaska State Fair (Palmer, AK), Aug 24
   Arkansas State Fair (Little Rock, AR), Oct 13
   Bangor State Fair (Bangor, ME), Jul 28
   Barn Day (Filley, NE), Jul 16
   Big E (West Springfield, MA), Sep 15
   Black Hills Stock Show and Rodeo (Rapid City, SD), Jan 27
   Blue Hill Fair (Blue Hill, ME), Aug 31
   Broome County Fair (Whitney Point, NY), Jul 25
   Calgary Stampede (Calgary, AB, Canada), Jul 7
   California State Fair (Sacramento, CA), Aug 11
   Canadian Western Agribition (Regina, SK, Canada), Nov 20
   Champlain Valley Fair (Essex Junction, VT), Aug 26
   Clinton County Corn Fest (Wilmington, OH), Sep 8
   Coe Hill Agricultural Fair (Coe Hill, ON, Canada), Aug 18
   Colorado State Fair (Pueblo, CO), Aug 25
   Columbia County Fair (Chatham, NY), Aug 30
   Comal County Fair (New Braunfels, TX), Sep 26
   Common Ground Country Fair (Unity, ME), Sep 22
   Corn Palace Fest (Mitchell, SD), Aug 30
   Dairy Expo, World (Madison, WI), Oct 3
   Delaware State Fair (Harrington, DE), Jul 20
   Delmarva Chicken Fest (Snow Hill, MD), Jun 23
   Eastern Idaho State Fair (Blackfoot, ID), Sep 2
   Eighteenth-Century Threshing Day (McLean, VA), Nov 19
   Eighteenth-Century Wheat Harvest (McLean, VA), Jun 25
   Fairfest (Hastings, NE), Jul 26
   Farm Animals Awareness Week, Natl, Sep 17
   Farm Safety Week, Natl (Pres Proc), Sep 17
   Farm Sanctuary Hoedown (Watkins Glen, NY), Aug 5
   Farm Toy Show & Auction (Sauk Centre, MN), Feb 11
   Farm-City Week, Natl (Pres Proc), Nov 17
   Florida State Fair (Tampa, FL), Feb 9
   Fryeburg Fair (Fryeburg, ME), Oct 1

Garfield County Fair (Burwell, NE), **Jul 26**
Gateway Farm Expo (Kearney, NE), **Nov 15**
Georgia Natl Fair (Perry, GA), **Oct 6**
Grange Month, **Apr 1**
Harvard Milk Days Fest (Harvard, IL), **Jun 2**
Hood River County Fair (Hood River, OR), **Jul 26**
Husker Harvest Days (Grand Island, NE), **Sep 12**
Illinois State Fair (Springfield, IL), **Aug 11**
Indiana State Fair (Indianapolis, IN), **Aug 9**
Iowa State Fair (Des Moines, IA), **Aug 10**
Johnson County 4H and FFA Fair (Iowa City, IA), **Jul 24**
Kansas State Fair (Hutchinson, KS), **Sep 8**
Kentucky State Fair (Louisville, KY), **Aug 17**
Lee County Cotton Fest and Agricultural Fair (Bishopville, SC), **Oct 6**
Livestock Show, Rio Grande Valley (Mercedes, TX), **Mar 11**
Louisiana, State Fair of (Shreveport, LA), **Oct 26**
Makoti Threshing Bee Show (Makoti, ND), **Oct 6**
Marion County Fair (Salem, OR), **Jul 6**
Maryland State Fair (Timonium, MD), **Aug 25**
McHenry County Fair (Woodstock, IL), **Aug 2**
Michigan State Fair (Detroit, MI), **Aug 9**
Mid-South Fair (Memphis, TN), **Sep 22**
Minnesota State Fair (St. Paul, MN), **Aug 24**
Mississippi State Fair (Jackson, MS), **Oct 4**
Missouri State Fair (Sedalia, MO), **Aug 10**
Montana State Fair (Great Falls, MT), **Jul 28**
Montana Winter Fair (Lewistown, MT), **Jan 25**
Montgomery County Agricultural Fair (Gaithersburg, MD), **Aug 11**
Morrill Land Grant Act Passed: Anniv, **Jul 1**
Nebraska State Fair (Lincoln, NE), **Aug 26**
Nevada State Fair (Reno, NV), **Aug 17**
New Jersey State Fair/Sussex Farm and Horse Show (Augusta, NJ), **Aug 4**
New York State Fair (Syracuse, NY), **Aug 24**
North Carolina State Fair (Raleigh, NC), **Oct 13**
North Central Missouri Fair (Trenton, MO), **Aug 1**
North Dakota State Fair (Minot, ND), **Jul 21**
Northeast Montana Threshing Bee/Antique Show (Culbertson, MT), **Sep 23**
Northeastern Wisconsin Antique Power and Machinery Show Thresheree (Sturgeon Bay, WI), **Aug 18**
Northern Intl Livestock Expo (Billings, MT), **Oct 18**
No-Tillage Conference, Natl (St. Louis, MO), **Jan 11**
Ohio State Fair (Columbus, OH), **Aug 2**
Oklahoma State Fair (Oklahoma City, OK), **Sep 14**
Old Tyme Farm Days (Live Oak, FL), **Nov 23**
Oregon State Fair (Salem, OR), **Aug 25**
Organic Harvest Month, Natl, **Sep 1**
Ozark Empire Fair (Springfield, MO), **Jul 28**
Ozark Fall Farmfest (Springfield, MO), **Oct 6**
Penn State's Agri Progress Days (Rock Springs, PA), **Aug 15**
Pennsylvania Farm Show, **Jan 7**
Red River Valley Fair (Fargo, ND), **Jun 16**
Rice Month, Natl, **Sep 1**
Rochester Fair (Rochester, NH), **Sep 15**
Rockbridge Regional Fair (Lexington, VA), **Jul 18**
Rotary Tiller Race, World Chmpshp/Purplehull Pea Fest (Emerson, AR), **Jun 23**
Royal Bath and West Show (Shepton Mallet, Somerset, England), **May 30**
Ruffin, Edmund: Birth Anniv, **Jan 5**
Rural Life Sunday, **May 21**
Scotts Bluff County Fair (Mitchell, NE), **Aug 14**
Seed to Stalk (Williamsburg, VA), **Aug 1**
Sheep to Shawl Festival (Savannah, GA), **Mar 25**
Sioux Empire Fair (Sioux Falls, SD), **Aug 8**
Sioux Empire Farm Show (Sioux Falls, SD), **Jan 24**
Sodbuster Days—Harvest (Fort Ransom, ND), **Sep 9**
Sonoma-Marin Fair (Petaluma, CA), **Jun 21**
Sorghum Day Fest (Wewoka, OK), **Oct 28**
South Carolina State Fair (Columbia, SC), **Oct 5**
South Dakota State Fair (Huron, SD), **Sep 2**
South Mountain Fair (Gettysburg, PA), **Aug 23**
Southeast Missouri District Fair (Cape Girardeau, MO), **Sep 9**
Southwestern Expo Livestock Show/Rodeo (Fort Worth, TX), **Jan 13**
State Fair of Texas (Dallas, TX), **Sep 29**
Swap Meet and Tractor Show (Washington, KS), **Jun 3**
Tennessee State Fair (Nashville, TN), **Sep 8**
Texas-Oklahoma Fair (Wichita Falls, TX), **Sep 12**
Texoma Farm and Ranch Show (Wichita Falls, TX), **Feb 15**
Traditional Plowing Match (Woodstock, VT), **May 7**
Upper Canada Village (Morrisburg, ON, Canada), **May 20**
Utah State Fair (Salt Lake City, UT), **Sep 7**
Vermont State Fair (Rutland, VT), **Sep 1**

Virginia, State Fair of (Richmond, VA), **Sep 21**
West Virginia State Fair (Lewisburg, WV), **Aug 11**
Western Idaho Fair (Boise, ID), **Aug 18**
Western Washington Fair (Puyallup, WA), **Sep 8**
Winter Show (Valley City, ND), **Mar 7**
Wisconsin State Fair (Milwaukee, WI), **Aug 3**
World Ag Expo (Tulare, CA), **Feb 14**
World Beef Expo/Harvest Fair (Milwaukee, WI), **Sep 21**
Wyoming State Fair & Rodeo (Douglas, WY), **Aug 12**
Aguilera, Christina: Birth, **Dec 18**
Agutter, Jenny: Birth, **Dec 20**
Aida Premieres: Anniv, **Dec 24**
AIDS
  Awareness Month, Natl, **Nov 1**
  Condom Week, Natl, **Feb 14**
  First Noted: Anniv, **Jun 5**
  World AIDS Day (Pres Proc), **Dec 1**
  World AIDS Day (UN), **Dec 1**
Aiello, Danny, Jr: Birth, **Jun 20**
Aiken, Conrad: Birth Anniv, **Aug 5**
Aikman, Troy: Birth, **Nov 21**
Ailey, Alvin: Birth Anniv, **Jan 5**
Aimee, Anouk: Birth, **Apr 27**
Ainge, Danny: Birth, **Mar 17**
Air Conditioning Appreciation Days, **Jul 3**
Air Force Academy, US, Established: Anniv, **Apr 1**
Ajaye, Franklyn: Birth, **May 13**
Akaka, Daniel K.: Birth, **Sep 11**
AKC/Eukanuba Natl Chmpshp (Tampa Bay and St. Petersburg, FL), **Jan 14**
Akers, Michelle: Birth, **Feb 1**
Akihito: Birth, **Dec 23**
Al Qaeda: Attack on America: Anniv, **Sep 11**
Al Qaeda: Fall of Kabul: Anniv, **Nov 13**
Al Qaeda: London Terrorist Bombings: Anniv, **Jul 7**
Al Qaeda: Madrid Train Bombings: Anniv, **Mar 11**
Alabama
  Admission Day, **Dec 14**
  Alabama Coastal Cleanup (Mobile), **Sep 16**
  Alabama Renaissance Faire (Florence), **Oct 21**
  American Indian Heritage Day, **Oct 9**
  Battle of Mobile Bay: Anniv, **Aug 5**
  Black History Month at Tuskegee Univ (Tuskegee), **Feb 1**
  Chilton County Peach Fest (Clanton), **Jun 18**
  Christmas on the River (Demopolis), **Nov 26**
  Commemoration of 1997 Presidential Apology for USPHS Syphilis Study (Tuskegee), **May 16**
  Confederate Memorial Day, **Apr 24**
  DeSoto Caverns Park Fall Native American Dance Fest (Childersburg), **Sep 23**
  DeSoto Caverns Park Spring Native American Dance & Crafts Fest (Childersburg), **Apr 1**
  Do Dah Day (Birmingham), **May 6**
  Fireworks Celebration (Demopolis), **Jul 4**
  First Monday Trade Days (Scottsboro), **Jan 1**
  Helen Keller Fest (Tuscumbia), **Jun 22**
  Joe Cain Procession (Mobile), **Feb 26**
  Longhorn World Chmpshp Rodeo (Huntsville), **Mar 3**
  NAIA Men's & Women's Tennis Chmpshps (Mobile), **May 15**
  NAIA Softball Chmpshp (Decatur), **May 19**
  National Fair (Montgomery), **Oct 6**
  Panoply (Huntsville), **Apr 28**
  Riley, Bob: Birth, **Oct 3**
  River City Rumble Boat Races (Demopolis), **Jul 15**
  Senior Bowl Football Game (Mobile), **Jan 28**
  Sessions, Jeff: Birth, **Dec 24**
  Shelby, Richard C.: Birth, **May 6**
  Siege of Bridgeport (Bridgeport), **Mar 17**
  Southern Appalachian Dulcimer Fest (McCalla), **May 6**
  Spirit of Freedom Celebration (Florence), **Jul 4**
  Tennessee Valley Old Time Fiddlers Conv (Athens), **Oct 6**
  Trail of Tears Commemoration (Waterloo), **Sep 16**
  Tuskegee University 125th Anniv (Tuskegee), **Apr 2**
  W.C. Handy Fest (Florence), **Jul 23**
Alamo: Anniv of the Fall, **Mar 6**
Alaska
  Admission Day, **Jan 3**
  Alascattalo Day (Anchorage), **Nov 25**
  Alaska Day, **Oct 18**
  Alaska Flag Day Celebration, **Jul 9**
  Anvil Mountain Run (Nome), **Jul 4**
  Blueberry Arts Fest (Ketchikan), **Aug 5**
  Carrs/Safeway Great Alaska Shootout (Anchorage), **Nov 21**
  Earthquake Strikes Alaska: Anniv, **Mar 27**
  Fairbanks Summer Arts Fest (Fairbanks), **Jul 16**
  Fest of the North (Ketchikan), **Feb 1**
  59 Min 37 Sec Anvil Mountain Challenge (Nome), **Sep 7**

  Gigglefeet Dance Fest (Ketchikan), **Aug 4**
  Great Bathtub Race (Nome), **Sep 4**
  Iditarod Trail Sled Dog Race (Anchorage), **Mar 4**
  Kodiak Crab Fest (Kodiak), **May 25**
  Midnight Sun Baseball Game (Fairbanks), **Jun 21**
  Midnight Sun Fest (Nome), **Jun 17**
  Miss Alaska Scholarship Pageant (Anchorage), **Jun 16**
  Murkowski, Frank Hughes: Birth, **Mar 28**
  Murkowski, Lisa: Birth, **May 22**
  Music in the Park (Anchorage), **Jun 2**
  National Parks Established: Anniv, **Dec 2**
  Nenana Tripod Raising Fest (Nenana), **Mar 4**
  Polar Bear Swim (Nome), **Jun 17**
  Poorman's Paradise Gold Panner Contest (Nome), **Jul 20**
  Seward's Day, **Mar 27**
  Sled Dogs Save Nome: Anniv, **Feb 2**
  Snake River Duck Race (Nome), **Sep 4**
  Snowshoe Chmpshps, US Natl (Anchorage), **Mar 24**
  State Fair (Palmer), **Aug 24**
  Stevens, Ted: Birth, **Nov 18**
  Summer Music Fest (Sitka), **Jun 2**
  Tsunami, Highest Recorded in History: Anniv, **Jul 9**
  Yukon Quest Intl 1,000-Mile Sled Dog Race (Fairbanks), **Feb 11**
Alba, Jessica: Birth, **Apr 28**
Albania: Independence Day, **Nov 28**
Albany Riverfront Jazz Fest (Albany, NY), **Sep 9**
Albee, Edward: Birth, **Mar 12**
Alberghetti, Anna Maria: Birth, **May 15**
Albert, Edward: Birth, **Feb 20**
Albert, Marv: Birth, **Jun 12**
Albom, Mitch: Birth, **May 23**
Albright, Madeleine: Birth, **May 15**
Albuquerque Intl Balloon Fiesta (Albuquerque, NM), **Sep 30**
Alcohol and Drug Addiction Recovery Month, Natl, **Sep 1**
Alcohol, Alcoholism
  Alcohol and Other Drug-Related Birth Defects Week, Natl, **May 7**
  Alcohol-Free Weekend, **Apr 7**
  Alcoholics Anonymous: Founding Anniv, **Jun 10**
  Awareness Month, **Apr 1**
  MADD's Tie One On for Safety, **Nov 16**
  Pharmacists Declare War on Alcoholism, **Jun 1**
  Screening Day, Natl, **Apr 6**
  Women's Christian Temperance Union: Anniv, **Nov 19**
Alcott, Amy Strum: Birth, **Feb 22**
Alcott, Louisa May: Birth Anniv, **Nov 29**
Alda, Alan: Birth, **Jan 28**
Aldrin, Edwin "Buzz": Birth, **Jan 20**
Aleichem, Sholem: Birth Anniv, **Feb 18**
Alexander, Jane: Birth, **Oct 28**
Alexander, Jason: Birth, **Sep 23**
Alexander, Lamar: Birth, **Jul 30**
Alexis, Kim: Birth, **Jul 15**
Alfonso, Kristian: Birth, **Sep 5**
Alfonzo, Edgardo: Birth, **Nov 8**
Alfred Hitchcock Presents TV Premiere: Anniv, **Oct 2**
Alger, Horatio, Jr: Birth Anniv, **Jan 13**
Algeria
  Independence Day, **Jul 5**
  Revolution Day, **Nov 1**
Algonquin Mill Fall Fest (Carrollton, OH), **Oct 13**
Ali, Muhammad: Birth, **Jan 17**
Ali, Muhammad: Clay Becomes Heavyweight Champ: Anniv, **Feb 25**
Ali, Muhammad: Stripped of Title: Anniv, **Apr 30**
Alice TV Premiere: Anniv, **Aug 31**
All Fools' Day, **Apr 1**
All Hallows, **Nov 1**
All Hallows Eve, **Oct 31**
All in the Family TV Premiere: Anniv, **Jan 12**
All My Children TV Premiere: Anniv, **Jan 5**
All Saints' Day, **Nov 1**
All Souls' Day, **Nov 2**
All the News That's Fit to Print: Anniv, **Feb 10**
Allanson, Susie: Birth, **Mar 17**
Allard, Wayne: Birth, **Dec 2**
Allen, Byron: Birth, **Apr 22**
Allen, Chad: Birth, **Jun 5**
Allen, Debbie: Birth, **Jan 16**
Allen, Deborah: Birth, **Sep 30**
Allen, Ethan: Birth Anniv, **Jan 21**
Allen, George: Birth, **Mar 8**
Allen, Joan: Birth, **Aug 20**
Allen, Karen: Birth, **Oct 5**
Allen, Marcus: Birth, **Mar 26**
Allen, Nancy: Birth, **Jun 24**
Allen, Ray: Birth, **Jul 20**
Allen, Rex, Days (Willcox, AZ), **Oct 6**
Allen, Steve: Birth Anniv, **Dec 26**
Allen, Tim: Birth, **Jun 13**

Allen—Antiques

Allen, Woody: Birth, Dec 1
Allergy/Asthma Awareness Month, Natl, May 1
Alley, Kirstie: Birth, Jan 12
Allilueva, Svetlana: Birth, Feb 28
Allman, Gregg: Birth, Dec 8
All-Northwest Barbershop Ballad Contest (Forest Grove, OR), Mar 3
All-Star Game, First Major League Baseball, Jul 6
All-Star Game, Major League Baseball (Pittsburgh, PA), Jul 11
Allyson, June: Birth, Oct 7
Almanack, Poor Richard's: Anniv, Dec 28
Alomar, Roberto: Birth, Feb 5
Alou, Moises: Birth, Jul 3
Alpert, Herb: Birth, Mar 31
Alpha Kappa Alpha Sorority Founded: Anniv, Jan 15
Alphabet Day (Korea), Oct 9
Alston, Charles H.: Birth Anniv, Nov 28
Alt, Carol: Birth, Dec 1
Altamont Concert: Anniv, Dec 6
Altman, Robert: Birth, Feb 20
Alvin Show TV Premiere: Anniv, Oct 4
Alzheimer, Alois: Birth Anniv, Jun 14
Alzheimer's Disease Month, Natl, Nov 1
AMA Founded: Anniv, May 5
AMD/Low Vision Awareness Month, Feb 1
Ameche, Don: Birth Anniv, May 31
America Recycles Day, Nov 15
America the Beautiful Published, Jul 4
American Bandstand TV Premiere: Anniv, Aug 5
American Bandstand: Dick Clark Retires: Anniv, Mar 23
American Council on Education Annual Mtg (Los Angeles, CA), Feb 11
American Crossword Puzzle Tournament (Stamford, CT), Mar 24
American Dental Assn: Annual Session (Las Vegas, NV), Oct 16
American Dietetic Assn Food & Nutrition Conf & Expo (Honolulu, HI), Sep 16
American Education Week, Nov 12
American Federation of Labor Founded: Anniv, Dec 8
American Flight Crashes at O'Hare: Anniv, May 25
American Historical Assn Annual Mtg (Philadelphia, PA), Jan 5
American History Essay Contest, Aug 1
American Idol TV Premiere: Anniv, Jun 11
American Indian Heritage Day (AL), Oct 9
American Indian Heritage Month, Natl, Nov 1
American Library Assn Annual Conf (New Orleans, LA), Jun 22
American Library Assn Founded: Anniv, Oct 6
American Massage Therapy Assn, Natl Conv (Atlanta, GA), Oct 11
American Psychological Assn Annual Meeting (New Orleans, LA), Aug 10
American Red Cross: Founding Anniv, May 21
American Samoa
    Park of American Samoa Authorized, Natl: Anniv, Oct 31
    White Sunday, Oct 8
American Top 40 Radio Program: Anniv, Jul 4
Americans with Disabilities Act: Anniv, Jul 26
America's Cup: Intl Yacht Race: Anniv, Aug 22
America's First Department Store (Salt Lake City, UT), Oct 16
America's Kids Day, Jun 25
Ames, Bruce N.: Birth, Dec 16
Amis, Kingsley: Birth Anniv, Apr 16
Amis, Martin: Birth, Aug 25
Amis, Suzy: Birth, Jan 5
Amish Acres Arts & Crafts Fest (Nappanee, IN), Aug 10
Amistad Seized: Anniv, Aug 29
Amnesty for Polygamists: Anniv, Jan 4
Amos 'n' Andy TV Premiere: Anniv, Jun 28
Amos, Tori: Birth, Aug 22
Ampere, Andre: Birth Anniv, Jan 22
Amtrak: Anniv, May 1
Amundsen, Roald: Birth Anniv, Jul 16
Ancestor Appreciation Day, Sep 27
Andersen, Hans Christian: Birth Anniv, Apr 2
Anderson, Dame Judith: Birth Anniv, Feb 10
Anderson, George Lee (Sparky): Birth, Feb 22
Anderson, Gillian: Birth, Aug 9
Anderson, Harry: Birth, Oct 14
Anderson, Helen E.M.: First Woman US Alzheimer Ambassador: Anniv, Oct 28
Anderson, Ian: Birth, Aug 10
Anderson, Jack: Birth, Oct 19
Anderson, Kevin: Birth, Jan 13
Anderson, Loni: Birth, Aug 5
Anderson, Louie: Birth, Mar 23
Anderson, Lynn: Birth, Sep 26
Anderson, Marian: Birth Anniv, Feb 27

Anderson, Marian: Easter Concert: Anniv, Apr 9
Anderson, Marion: Performs with Metropolitan Opera: Anniv, Jan 7
Anderson, Melissa Sue: Birth, Sep 26
Anderson, Pamela: Birth, Jul 1
Anderson, Paul Thomas: Birth, Jun 26
Anderson, Richard Dean: Birth, Jan 23
Anderson, Sherwood: Birth Anniv, Sep 13
Anderson, Wes: Birth, May 1
Andersson, Bibi: Birth, Nov 11
Andorra: National Holiday, Sep 8
Andrea Doria Sinks: Anniv, Jul 25
Andree, Salomon A.: Birth Anniv, Oct 18
Andress, Ursula: Birth, Mar 19
Andretti, Mario: Birth, Feb 28
Andretti, Michael: Birth, Oct 5
Andrew, Prince: Birth, Feb 19
Andrews, Julie: Birth, Oct 1
Andrews, Julie: Sound of Music Film Premiere: Anniv, Mar 2
Andy Griffith Show TV Premiere: Anniv, Oct 3
Andy Williams Show TV Premiere: Anniv, Jul 2
Anesthetic First Used in Surgery: Anniv, Mar 30
Angel Day, Be an, Aug 22
Angel, Vanessa: Birth, Nov 10
Angelou, Maya: Birth, Apr 4
Anglund, Joan Walsh: Birth, Jan 3
Angola
    Armed Struggle Day, **Feb 4**
    Day of the National Hero, **Sep 17**
    Independence Day, **Nov 11**
Animals. See also Dogs; Horses; Pets; Rats; Sled Dogs
    Adopt-A-Shelter-Cat Month, **Jun 1**
    Adopt-A-Shelter-Dog Month, **Oct 1**
    AFRMA Display & Show (Costa Mesa, CA), **Jul 7**
    AFRMA Display at America's Family Pet Expo (Costa Mesa, CA), **Apr 14**
    Animal Cruelty/Human Violence Awareness Week, **Apr 16**
    Animal Poison Prevention Week, Natl, **Mar 20**
    Animal Safety and Protection Month, **Oct 1**
    Animal Shelter Appreciation Week, Natl, **Nov 5**
    Answer Your Cat's Question Day, **Jan 22**
    Bark in the Park (Chicago, IL), **May 6**
    Barnegat Bay Crab Race and Fest (Seaside Heights, NJ), **Aug 27**
    Be Kind to Animals Week, **May 1**
    Blessing of Animals at the Cathedral (Mexico), **Jan 17**
    Boo at the Zoo (Cleveland, OH), **Oct 19**
    Buffalo Auction (Custer, SD), **Nov 18**
    Buffalo Roundup (Custer, SD), **Oct 2**
    Burro Race (Leadville, CO), **Aug 6**
    Buzzard Day Fest (Glendive, MT), **Jun 10**
    Cloning of an Adult Animal, First: Anniv, **Feb 23**
    Cow Appreciation Day (Woodstock, VT), **Jul 15**
    Cow Milked While Flying: Anniv, **Feb 18**
    Crufts Dog Show (Birmingham, England), **Mar 9**
    Day of the Seal Celebration, Intl (Point Pleasant Beach, NJ), **Mar 18**
    Dog Bite Prevention Week, Natl, **May 21**
    Dog Day, Natl, **Aug 26**
    Elephant Appreciation Day, **Sep 22**
    Elephant Roundup at Surin (Thailand), **Nov 18**
    Faith City Kennel Club Dog Show (Wichita Falls, TX), **Mar 4**
    Fancy Rat and Mouse Annual Show (Riverside, CA), **Jan 14**
    Farm Animals Awareness Week, Natl, **Sep 17**
    Farm Sanctuary Hoedown (Watkins Glen, NY), **Aug 5**
    Farm Sanctuary's Annual Pignic (Watkins Glen, NY), **Jul 4**
    Field Trial Chmpshp, Natl (Bird Dogs) (Grand Junction, TN), **Feb 13**
    First US Zoo: Anniv (Philadelphia, PA), **Jul 1**
    Fish Amnesty Day, **Sep 23**
    Give Wildlife a Brake! Week, **Oct 23**
    Go Fetch! Natl Food Drive for Homeless Animals, **May 1**
    Goat Days (Millington, TN), **Sep 8**
    Gorilla Born in Captivity, First: Anniv, **Dec 22**
    Grand American Coon Hunt (Orangeburg, SC), **Jan 6**
    Hairball Awareness Day, Natl, **Apr 28**
    Happy Mew Year for Cats Day, **Jan 2**
    Haute Dog Charity Easter Parade (Long Beach, CA), **Apr 16**
    Haute Dog Charity Howl'oween Parade (Long Beach, CA), **Oct 29**
    Hedgehog Day, **Feb 2**
    Ho Sheep Market (Denmark), **Aug 26**
    Holistic Pet Day, Natl, **Aug 30**
    Homeless Animals Day, Natl/Candlelight Vigils, **Aug 19**
    Hug Your Cat Day, **May 19**
    Humane Society of the US: Anniv, **Nov 22**

Jumbo the Elephant Arrives in America: Anniv, Apr 9
Jumping Frog Jubilee/Calaveras Fair (Angel Camp, CA), May 18
Koko the Gorilla: Birth, Jul 4
Lizard Race, World's Greatest (Lovington, NM), Jul 4
Miss Crustacean/Ocean City Creep (Ocean City, NJ), Aug 2
Moth-er Day, Mar 14
Mule Day, Oct 26
Mule Day (Columbia, TN), Mar 30
North Star Classic (Valley City, ND), Dec 1
Operation Santa Paws, Dec 1
Penguin Awareness Day (Point Pleasant Beach, NJ), Jan 14
Pet Dental Health Month, Natl, Feb 1
Pet First Aid Awareness Month, Natl, Apr 1
Pet Owners Independence Day, Apr 18
Pet Week, Natl, May 7
Pig Day, Natl, Mar 1
Prevention of Animal Cruelty Month, Apr 1
Professional Pet Sitters Week, Mar 5
Rabbit Week, Natl, Jul 15
Rattlesnake Derby (Mangum, OK), Apr 28
Reptile Awareness Day (Point Pleasant Beach, NJ), Oct 21
Respect for Chickens Day, Intl, May 4
Riverfest (Columbus, GA), Apr 28
Save the Florida Panther Day, Mar 18
Save the Rhino Day, May 1
Sea Monkey Day, Intl, May 16
Seal, Intl Day of the, Mar 22
Seeing Eye Established: Anniv, Jan 29
Shamu's Birthday, Sep 26
Sheep Herding with Border Collies (Woodstock, VT), Sep 17
Snake Hunt (Cross Fork, PA), Jun 24
Spay Day USA, Feb 28
Squirrel Appreciation Day, Jan 21
Squirrel Awareness Week, Oct 1
Stock Dog Trials & Farm Fest, US Open (Dawsonville, GA), Oct 6
Take Your Dog to Work Day, Jun 23
Taylor Horsefest (Taylor, ND), Jul 22
Toad Suck Daze (Conway, AR), May 5
Turkey Vultures Return to the Living Sign (Canisteo, NY), Mar 11
Turtle Races (Danville, IL), Jun 10
Wayne Chicken Days (Wayne, NE), Jul 7
Westminster Kennel Club Dog Show (New York, NY), Feb 13
What If Cats and Dogs Had Opposable Thumbs Day, Mar 3
White Cloud Days (Jamestown, ND), Jul 6
Wild Horse Chasing (Japan), Jul 23
Wildlife Week, Natl, Apr 23
Wishbones for Pets, Oct 15
Woolly Worm Fest (Banner Elk, NC), Oct 21
World Farm Animals Day, Oct 2
World Habitat Awareness Month, Apr 1
World Turtle Day, May 23
Animation: Bugs Bunny's Debut: Anniv, Apr 30
Aniston, Jennifer: Birth, Feb 11
Anka, Paul: Birth, Jul 30
Annan, Kofi: Birth, Apr 8
Annapolis Convention: Anniv, Sep 11
Anne, Princess: Birth, Aug 15
Annenberg, Walter: Birth Anniv, Mar 13
Annie Oakley Days (Greenville, OH), Jul 28
Ann-Margret: Birth, Apr 28
Annunciation, Feast of, Mar 25
Another Look Unlimited Day, Sep 5
Another World TV Premiere: Anniv, May 4
Anson, Cap: Birth Anniv, Apr 17
Anspach, Susan: Birth, Nov 23
Answer Your Cat's Question Day, Jan 22
Ant, Adam: Birth, Nov 3
Antarctica: Shackleton, Ernest: Birth Anniv, Feb 15
Anthem Day, Natl, Mar 3
Anthony, Carmelo: Birth, May 29
Anthony, Marc: Birth, Sep 16
Anthony, Susan B.: Day, Feb 15
Anthony, Susan B.: Fined for Voting: Anniv, Jun 6
Antietam, Battle of: Anniv, Sep 17
Antigua and Barbuda
    August Monday, **Aug 7**
    Independence Day, **Nov 1**
Antique Power Exhibition (Burton, OH), Jul 28
Antiques
    Antique Marine Engine Exposition (Mystic, CT), **Aug 19**
    Antique Show (Somerset, PA), **Aug 12**
    Antiques & Collectibles Show & Sale, Mid-Summer (Millville, NJ), **Jul 29**
    Antiques at Memorial Day (Cape May, NJ), **May 28**
    Antiques on the Diamond (Ligonier, PA), **Jun 10**

Arizona Antique Show/Sale (Yuma, AZ), **Jan 7**
Art & Antiques at the American Club (Kohler, WI), **Mar 11**
Charlestown Intl Antiques Show (Charleston, SC), **Mar 17**
Chelsea Antiques Fair (London, England), **Sep 15**
Chester Antiques and Fine Art Show (Cheshire, England), **Feb 16**
Collectables-Antiques-Craft-Flea Market Sale (Sauk Centre, MN), **Jul 15**
Cotton Pickin' Fair (Gay, GA), **May 6**
Gettysburg Outdoor Antique Show (Gettysburg, PA), **May 20**
Gettysburg Outdoor Antique Show (Gettysburg, PA), **Sep 23**
Kane County Flea Market (St. Charles, IL), **Jan 7**
Landon Azalea Garden Fest/Antique Show (Bethesda, MD), **May 5**
Lucky May Show and Sale (Chapel Hill, NC), **May 5**
Mid-Winter Antiques Show (Millville, NJ), **Feb 4**
New Oxford Outdoor Antique Show (New Oxford, PA), **Jun 17**
Old Time Antiques & Collectibles Faire (Toms River, NJ), **Sep 2**
Pec Thing (Pecatonica, IL), **May 20**
Petersfield Antiques Fair (Petersfield, England), **Feb 10**
Vegaspex (Las Vegas, NV), **May 26**
West London Antiques & Fine Art Fair (London, England), **Jan 13**
Anti-Saloon League Founded: Anniv, May 24
Anton, Susan: Birth, Oct 12
Antonioni, Michelangelo: Birth, Sep 29
Anwar, Gabrielle: Birth, Feb 4
Anxiety Disorders Screening Day, Natl, May 3
ANZAC Day, Apr 25
Apache Wars Began: Anniv, Feb 4
Apartheid Law, South Africa Repeals Last: Anniv, Jun 17
Apgar, Virginia: Birth Anniv, Jun 7
A'phabet Day, Dec 25
Aphasia Awareness Month, Natl, Jun 1
Aphelion, Earth at, Jul 3
Aplastic Anemia Awareness Week, Natl, Dec 1
Apollo I: Spacecraft Fire: Anniv, Jan 27
Appert, Nicolas: Birth Anniv, Oct 23
Apple Blossom Fest (Annapolis Valley, NS, Canada), May 31
Apple Blossom Fest (Gettysburg, PA), **May 6**
Apple Blossom Fest, Washington State (Wenatchee, WA), Apr 27
Apple Butter Makin' Days (Mount Vernon, MO), Oct 13
Apple Butter Stirrin' (Coshocton, OH), Oct 20
Apple Fest (Topeka, KS), Oct 1
Apple Fest, Jackson County (Jackson, OH), Sep 19
Apple Fest, Kentucky (Paintsville, KY), Oct 6
Apple Fest, Vermont (Springfield, VT), Oct 7
Apple Harvest Fest (Gettysburg, PA), Oct 7
Apple II Computer Released: Anniv, Jun 5
Apple, Fiona: Birth, Sep 13
Applegate, Christina: Birth, Nov 25
Applejack Fest (Nebraska City, NE), Sep 16
Apples: Eat an Apple Day, Intl, Sep 15
Appleseed Days, Johnny (Lake City, MN), Oct 1
Appleseed, Johnny: Birth Anniv, Sep 26
Appleseed: Johnny Appleseed Day, Mar 11
Appreciate Diversity Month, Apr 1
April Fools' Day, Apr 1
Aquarius Begins, Jan 20
Aquino, Benigno: Assassination Anniv, Aug 21
Aquino, Corazon: Birth, Jan 25
Arab Oil Embargo Lifted: Anniv, Mar 13
Arab-Israeli War (Yom Kippur War), Oct 6
Arafat Returns to Palestine: Anniv, Jul 1
Arafat, Yasser: Birth Anniv, Aug 24
Arbor Day (Arizona), Apr 28
Arbor Day (Florida), Jan 20
Arbor Day Fest (Nebraska City, NE), Apr 28
Arbor Day, Natl, Apr 28
Arcadia Daze (Arcadia, MI), Jul 21
Archeology
  Aztec Calendar Stone Discovery: Anniv, **Dec 17**
  Iceman Mummy Discovered: Anniv, **Sep 19**
  King Tut Tomb Discovery: Anniv, **Nov 4**
  Statue of Ramses II Unearthed: Anniv, **Nov 30**
  Sutton Hoo Ship Burial Discovered: Anniv, **May 11**
Archer, Anne: Birth, Aug 25
Arches Natl Park Established: Anniv, Nov 12
Archibald, Nate: Birth, Sep 2
Architecture: First Skyscraper: Anniv, May 1
Area Codes Introduced: Anniv, Nov 10
Argentina
  Death Anniversary of San Martin, **Aug 17**
  Falkland Islands War: Anniv, **Apr 2**
  Flag Day, **Jun 20**

Independence Day, Jul 9
Revolution Day, May 25
Aries Begins, Mar 21
Arizona
  Admission Day: Anniv, **Feb 14**
  All States Picnic (Yuma), **Jan 3**
  American Family Day, **Aug 6**
  Americana Indian and Western Art Show/Sale (Yuma), **Jan 27**
  Apache Wars Began: Anniv, **Feb 4**
  Arbor Day, **Apr 28**
  Arizona Antique Show/Sale (Yuma), **Jan 7**
  Arizona Renaissance Fest (Apache Junction), **Feb 11**
  Benson Antique Tractor Pull & Engine Show (Benson), **Feb 18**
  Butterfield Overland Stage Days (Benson), **Oct 7**
  Colorado River Crossing Balloon Festival (Yuma), **Nov 17**
  Constitution Commemoration Day, **Sep 17**
  Cowboy Hall of Fame Ceremony (Willcox), **Oct 5**
  Desert Foothills Musicfest (Carefree), **Feb 7**
  Doll Show (Yuma), **Feb 4**
  Fest of the West, Natl, and Log Home Show (Scottsdale), **Mar 16**
  Fiesta De Los Vaqueros (Tucson), **Feb 18**
  Four Corner States Bluegrass Fest (Wickenburg), **Nov 10**
  Gold Rush Days (Wickenburg), **Feb 10**
  Grand Canyon Natl Park Established: Anniv, **Feb 26**
  Kyl, Jon: Birth, **Apr 25**
  Lost Dutchman Days (Apache Junction), **Feb 24**
  McCain, John Sidney, III: Birth, **Aug 29**
  Midnight at the Oasis (Yuma), **Mar 3**
  Miss Arizona Pageant (Gilbert), **Jun 22**
  Napolitano, Janet: Birth, **Nov 29**
  Petrified Forest Natl Park Established: Anniv, **Dec 9**
  Rex Allen Days (Willcox), **Oct 6**
  RV Workers and Workampers Day (Quartzsite), **Jan 20**
  Scottsdale Culinary Fest (Scottsdale), **Apr 18**
  Sedona Arts Fest (West Sedona), **Oct 7**
  Sonora Showcase (Yuma), **Jan 24**
  Southwest Senior Chmpshp (Yuma), **Jan 17**
  Tempe Spring Fest of Arts (Tempe), **Mar 31**
  Tostitos Fiesta Bowl (Tempe), **Jan 2**
  Tucson Intl Mariachi Conf (Tucson), **Apr 24**
  US Mid-Amateur (Golf) Chmpshp (Flagstaff), **Sep 9**
  Wings Over Willcox—Sandhill Crane Celebration (Willcox), **Jan 12**
  Winterfest (Flagstaff), **Feb 1**
  Yuma Home Show (Yuma), **Jan 13**
  Yuma Square and Round Dance Fest (Yuma), **Feb 10**
Arkansas
  Admission Day: Anniv, **Jun 15**
  Bluegrass Fest (Hope), **May 12**
  Chicken and Egg Fest (Prescott), **Jun 2**
  Chuckwagon Races, Natl Chmpshp (Clinton), **Sep 1**
  Clothesline Fair (Prairie Grove), **Sep 2**
  Dermott's Annual Crawfish Fest (Dermott), **May 19**
  Duck-Calling Contest/Wings Over Prairie Fest (Stuttgart), **Nov 24**
  Eagles Et Cetera Fest (Bismarck), **Jan 27**
  Fordyce on the Cotton Belt Fest (Fordyce), **Apr 17**
  Great Arkansas Pig-Out (Morrilton), **Aug 4**
  Homefest (Bald Knob), **May 11**
  Hope Watermelon Fest (Hope), **Aug 10**
  Hot Springs Natl Park Established: Anniv, **Mar 4**
  Huckabee, Mike: Birth, **Aug 24**
  Lincoln, Blanche Lambert: Birth, **Sep 30**
  Magnolia Blossom Fest (Magnolia), **May 19**
  NCAA Indoor Track/Field Chmpshps (Fayetteville), **Mar 10**
  Ozark UFO Conf (Eureka Springs), **Apr 14**
  Petit Jean Antique Auto Show/Swap Meet (Morrilton), **Jun 13**
  Petit Jean Fall Antique Auto Swap Meet (Morrilton), **Sep 20**
  Pryor, Mark: Birth, **Jan 10**
  Quadrangle Fest (Texarkana), **Sep 9**
  Riverfest (Little Rock), **May 26**
  Rotary Tiller Race, World Chmpshp/Purplehull Pea Fest (Emerson), **Jun 23**
  State Fair and Livestock Show (Little Rock), **Oct 13**
  Steak Cook-off World Chmpshp (Magnolia), **May 20**
  Toad Suck Daze (Conway), **May 5**
  White River Water Carnival (Batesville), **Jul 29**
Arkin, Adam: Birth, Aug 19
Arkin, Alan: Birth, Mar 26
Arlen, Harold: Birth Anniv, Feb 15
Armani, Giorgio: Birth, Jul 11
Armatrading, Joan: Birth, Dec 9

Armed Forces Day (Egypt), Oct 6
Armed Forces Day (Pres Proc), May 20
Armed Forces Unified: Anniv, Jul 26
Armenia
  Armenian Church Christmas, **Jan 6**
  Armenian Martyrs Day, **Apr 24**
  Earthquake of 1988: Anniv, **Dec 7**
  Independence Day, **Sep 21**
Armistice Day, Nov 11
Armistice Day: See Veterans Day, Nov 11
Armstrong, BJ: Birth, Sep 9
Armstrong, Darrell: Birth, Jun 22
Armstrong, Lance: Birth, Sep 18
Armstrong, Louis: Birth Anniv, Aug 4
Armstrong, Neil: Birth, Aug 5
Armstrong, Trace: Birth, Oct 5
Armstrong-Jones, Anthony: Birth, Mar 7
Army, US: Established: Anniv, Jun 14
Army, US: First Desegregation: Anniv, Jul 26
Army-Navy Game, First: Anniv, Nov 29
Arnaz, Desi, Jr: Birth, Jan 19
Arnaz, Desi: Birth Anniv, Mar 2
Arnaz, Lucie: Birth, Jul 17
Arness, James: Birth, May 26
Arnold, Benedict: Birth Anniv, Jan 14
Arnold, Eddy: Birth, May 15
Arnold, Henry "Hap": Birth Anniv, Jun 25
Arnold, Matthew: Birth Anniv, Dec 24
Arnold, Sir Malcolm: Birth, Oct 21
Arnold, Tom: Birth, Mar 6
Arquette, Courteney Cox: Birth, Jun 15
Arquette, David: Birth, Sep 8
Arquette, Patricia: Birth, Apr 8
Arquette, Rosanna: Birth, Aug 10
Arrington, LaVar: Birth, Jun 20
Arsenio Hall Show TV Premiere: Anniv, Jan 3
Art Deco Weekend (Miami Beach, FL), Jan 13
Art Linkletter's House Party TV Premiere: Anniv, Sep 1
Arthritis Month, Natl, May 1
Arthur Murray Party TV Premiere: Anniv, Jul 20
Arthur, Beatrice: Birth, May 13
Arthur, Chester A.: Birth Anniv, Oct 5
Arthur, Ellen: Birth Anniv, Aug 30
Arthur, Jean: Birth Anniv, Oct 17
Articles of Confederation: Ratification Anniv, Mar 1
Articles of Peace: Anniv, Nov 30
Artists of America Day, Jun 1
Arts and Crafts. See also Quilt
  Adelphian Club Christmas Bazaar (Kennett, MO), **Dec 2**
  Alpenfest (Gaylord, MI), **Jul 11**
  American Club Teddy Bear and Doll Classic (Kohler, WI), **Feb 26**
  Amish Acres Arts & Crafts Fest (Nappanee, IN), **Aug 10**
  Appalachian Potters Market (Marion, NC), **Nov 18**
  Artists in the Park (Wolfeboro, NH), **Aug 16**
  Arts & Crafts Fest (Loveladies, NJ), **Jul 29**
  Belsnickel Craft Show (Boyertown, PA), **Nov 24**
  Berea Craft Fest (Berea, KY), **Jul 14**
  Blue Claw Crab Craft Show & Crab Race (Harvey Cedars, NJ), **Aug 19**
  Blue Ridge Folklife Fest (Ferrum, VA), **Oct 28**
  Boardwalk Art Show & Fest (Virginia Beach, VA), **Jun 15**
  Cambridge Pottery Fest and US Pottery Games (Cambridge, WI), **Jun 10**
  Capitol Hill People's Fair (Denver, CO), **Jun 3**
  Catoctin ColorFest Arts/Crafts (Thurmont, MD), **Oct 14**
  Catonsville Arts & Crafts Fest (Catonsville, MD), **Sep 10**
  Children's Craft Day, Natl, **Mar 14**
  Chimneyville Crafts Fest (Jackson, MS), **Dec 2**
  Christkindl Market (Canton, OH), **Nov 10**
  Christmas Craft Show (Aiken, SC), **Dec 1**
  Christmas Craft Show (York, PA), **Dec 10**
  Clothesline Fair (Prairie Grove, AR), **Sep 2**
  Corn Hill Arts Fest (Rochester, NY), **Jul 8**
  Country Affair (Menomonee Falls, WI), **Oct 21**
  Country Fest and Auction (Deep Creek Lake, MD), **Aug 26**
  Craft & Hobby Assn Conv & Trade Show (Las Vegas, NV), **Jan 30**
  Craft Day by the Bay (Harvey Cedars, NJ), **Jul 1**
  Craft Fair of the Southern Highlands (Asheville, NC), **Jul 20**
  Craft Month, Natl, **Mar 1**
  Craftsmen's Christmas Classic Arts & Crafts Fest (Greensboro, NC), **Nov 24**
  Craftsmen's Christmas Classic Arts & Crafts Fest (Richmond, VA), **Nov 3**
  Craftsmen's Classic Arts & Crafts Fest (Richmond, VA), **Mar 10**
  Craftsmen's Classic Arts & Crafts Fest (Chantilly, VA), **Mar 24, Oct 20**

Arts and Crafts (cont'd)—Auberjonois

Craftsmen's Classic Arts & Crafts Fest (Columbia, SC), **Mar 3**
Craftsmen's Classic Arts & Crafts Fest (Greensboro, NC), **Mar 31**
Craftsmen's Classic Arts & Crafts Fest (Myrtle Beach, SC), **Aug 4**
Craftsmen's Classic Arts & Crafts Fest (Roanoke, VA), **Sep 29**
Dyersville Fest of the Arts (Dyersville, IA), **Sep 23**
Easter Craft Show (York, PA), **Feb 12**
Faire on the Square Art & Craft Fair (Baraboo, WI), **May 20**
Fall Country Jamboree (Barberville, FL), **Nov 4**
Fall Fest of Arts and Crafts (Washington, MO), **Sep 23**
Fallasburg Fall Fest (Lowell, MI), **Sep 23**
Fargo's Downtown Street Fair (Fargo, ND), **Jul 20**
Fest of Fine Craft (Millville, NJ), **Oct 7**
Fest of the Little Hills (St. Charles, MO), **Aug 18**
Fest-in-the-Park (Nutley, NJ), **Sep 10**
Festival 2006: Fest of Fine Arts and Fine Crafts (Dalton, GA), **Sep 16**
Frankfort Fall Fest (Frankfort, IL), **Sep 2**
Gift Fest, Intl (Fairfield, PA), **Nov 9**
Gift of the Waters Pageant & Art Fest in the Park (Thermopolis, WY), **Aug 4**
Great Mississippi River Arts/Crafts Fest (Hannibal, MO), **May 27**
Greater Pittsburgh Arts & Crafts Holiday Spectacular (Greensburg, PA), **Nov 10**
Harborfest (South Haven, MI), **Jun 16**
Heritage Days Fest (Cumberland, MD), **Jun 10**
Holiday Craft Show (York, PA), **Oct 15**
Iroquois Indian Fest (Howes Cave, NY), **Sep 2**
Jay Peak Annual Arts & Crafts Fair (Jay, VT), **Oct 7**
Jours de Fete (Ste. Genevieve, MO), **Aug 12**
Keystone Country Fest (Altoona, PA), **Sep 8**
Lavallette Heritage Arts & Crafts Show (Lavallette, NJ), **Jul 30**
League of NH Craftsmen Annual Craftsmen's Fair (Newbury, NH), **Aug 5**
Liberty Spring on the Square Festival (Liberty, MO), **May 20**
Little Falls Arts/Crafts (Little Falls, MN), **Sep 9**
Lovington Fall Arts/Crafts Fest (Lovington, NM), **Nov 4**
Main Street Fest (Franklin, TN), **Apr 29**
Maritime Gig Fest (Gig Harbor, WA), **Jun 3**
Meet the Artists & Artisans Show (Milford Green, CT), **May 13**
Melrose Plantation Arts/Crafts Fest (Melrose, LA), **Jun 10**
Midsummer Nights' Fair (Norman, OK), **Jul 14**
Missouri Day Fest (Trenton, MO), **Oct 19**
Mossy Creek Barnyard Fest (Warner Robins, GA), **Apr 22**
Mount Pleasant Glass & Ethnic Fest (Mount Pleasant, PA), **Sep 22**
New Beginning Fest (Coffeyville, KS), **Apr 28**
Ocean County Wildfowl Art & Decoy Show (Toms River, NJ), **Feb 11**
Original Raggedy Ann & Andy Fest (Arcola, IL), **Jun 10**
Palm Harbor Arts/Crafts/Music Fest (Palm Harbor, FL), **Dec 2**
Peddler's Village Scarecrow Contest and Outdoor Display (Lahaska, PA), **Sep 11**
Pennsylvania Arts & Crafts Christmas Fest (Washington, PA), **Oct 20**
Pennsylvania Arts & Crafts Colonial Fest (Greensburg, PA), **Sep 1**
Pennsylvania Arts & Crafts Mother's Day Fest (Uniontown, PA), **May 12**
Pittsburgh Arts & Crafts Spring Fever Fest (Greensburg, PA), **Mar 24**
Pocono State Craft Fair (Shawnee-on-the-Delaware, PA), **Aug 26**
Powers' Crossroads Country Fair/Art Fest (Newnan, GA), **Sep 2**
Quilting Day, Natl, **Mar 18**
Scrapbook Day, Natl, **May 6**
Sedona Arts Fest (West Sedona, AZ), **Oct 7**
Sharon on the Green Arts and Crafts Fair (Sharon, CT), **Aug 5**
Sheep to Shawl Festival (Savannah, GA), **Mar 25**
Sheyenne Valley Arts/Crafts (Fort Ransom, ND), **Sep 23**
South Mountain Fair (Gettysburg, PA), **Aug 23**
Southeastern Wildlife Expo (Charleston, SC), **Feb 17**
Spinning and Weaving Week, **Oct 2**
Spring Arts Fest (Gainesville, FL), **Apr 1**
Spring Craft Celebration (Richboro, PA), **May 20**
Spring Craft Show (York, PA), **Apr 9**
Springs Folk Fest (Springs, PA), **Oct 6**
State Craft Fair (Lancaster, PA), **Jul 28**
Sugarloaf Art Fair (Novi, MI), **Apr 21, Oct 20**

Sugarloaf Crafts Fest (Chantilly, VA), **Jan 27, May 5, Dec 8**
Sugarloaf Crafts Fest (Fort Washington, PA), **Mar 17, Oct 27**
Sugarloaf Crafts Fest (Gaithersburg, MD), **Apr 7, Oct 13, Nov 16**
Sugarloaf Crafts Fest (Manassas, VA), **Sep 8**
Sugarloaf Crafts Fest (Secaucus, NJ), **Nov 3**
Sugarloaf Crafts Fest (Somerset, NJ), **Mar 10**
Sugarloaf Crafts Fest (Timonium, MD), **Apr 28, Oct 6**
Summer Craft Show (York, PA), **Jul 16**
Swappin' Meetin' (Cumberland, KY), **Oct 6**
TACA Fall Craft Fair (Chattanooga, TN), **Sep 30**
TACA Fall Craft Fair (Nashville, TN), **Sep 22**
Tarpon Springs Fine Arts Fest (Tarpon Springs, FL), **Apr 8**
Tempe Spring Fest of Arts (Tempe, AZ), **Mar 31**
Totah Fest (Farmington, NM), **Sep 2**
Virginia Spring Show (Richmond, VA), **Mar 9**
Ward World Chmpshp Waterfowl Carving Competition (Ocean City, MD), **Apr 28**
Waterfowl Fest (Easton, MD), **Nov 10**
Wichita West Spring Arts/Crafts Show (Wichita Falls, TX), **Mar 25**
Winfield Art-in-the-Park Fest (Winfield, KS), **Oct 7**
Wisconsin Holiday Market (Kohler, WI), **Nov 10**
Wyandotte Heritage Days (Wyandotte, MI), **Sep 9**
Wyandotte Street Fair (Wyandotte, MI), **Jul 12**
Yukon Sourdough Rendezvous (Whitehorse, YT, Canada), **Feb 23**

Arts, Fine and Performing; Art Shows
Affaire in Gardens, Beverly Hills (Beverly Hills, CA), **May 20**
Americana Indian and Western Art Show/Sale (Yuma, AZ), **Jan 27**
Ann Arbor Summer Art Fair (Ann Arbor, MI), **Jul 19**
Ann Arbor Winter Art Fair (Ann Arbor, MI), **Nov 11**
Art Deco Weekend (Miami Beach, FL), **Jan 13**
Art Fair & Winefest (Washington, MO), **May 19**
Art Fair (Rhinelander, WI), **Jun 10**
Art Fair on the Square (Madison, WI), **Jul 8**
Art Festival (Harvey Cedars, NJ), **Jul 16**
Art in the Garden (Washington, PA), **Sep 9**
Artown (Reno, NV), **Jul 1**
Arts & Crafts Fest (Stone Mountain Village, GA), **Jun 17**
Arts in the Park (Kalispell, MT), **Jul 21**
Arts/Quincy Riverfest (Quincy, IL), **Sep 17**
Ballet Introduced to the US: Anniv, **Feb 7**
Bay Harbor Summer Art Fair (Bay Harbor, MI), **Aug 5**
Buffalo Roundup Arts Fest (Custer, SD), **Sep 30**
Bumbershoot: The Seattle Arts Fest (Seattle, WA), **Sep 1**
C.M. Russell Auction Orig Western Art (Great Falls, MT), **Mar 15**
Cartoonists Against Crime Day, **Oct 25**
Cartoonists Day, **May 5**
Cellular South Gum Tree Fest (Tupelo, MS), **May 13**
Chautauqua of the Arts (Greensburg, IN), **Sep 16**
Chelsea Art Fair (London, England), **Apr 20**
City of London Fest (London, England), **Jun 26**
Day With(out) Art, **Dec 1**
Decoy and Wildlife Art Show (Clayton, NY), **Jul 14**
Dogwood Arts Fest (Knoxville, TN), **Apr 5**
Downtown Fest/Art Show (Gainesville, FL), **Nov 4**
European Fine Art Fair (Maastricht, Netherlands), **Mar 10**
Fairbanks Summer Arts Fest (Fairbanks, AK), **Jul 16**
Fest of the North (Ketchikan, AK), **Feb 1**
Festival 2006: Fest of Fine Arts and Fine Crafts (Dalton, GA), **Sep 16**
Fine Art & Crafts Show (Lahaska, PA), **Jun 3**
Foothills Art Fest (Jackson, OH), **Oct 13**
Geneva Arts Fair (Geneva, IL), **Jul 22**
Grant Wood Art Fest (Stone City–Anamosa, IA), **Jun 11**
Inspire Your Heart with the Arts Day, **Jan 31**
Iroquois Arts Showcase (Howes Cave, NY), **May 27**
Kohler Arts Center's Outdoor Arts Fest (Sheboygan, WI), **Jul 15**
Little Red School House Annual Art Fair (Willow Springs, IL), **Oct 1**
Meet the Artists & Artisans Show (Milford Green, CT), **May 13**
Mural-in-a-Day (Toppenish, WA), **Jun 3**
Museum of Contemporary Art Studio Tour (Fort Collins, CO), **Sep 16**
Northwest Folklife Fest (Seattle, WA), **May 26**
Panoply (Huntsville, AL), **Apr 28**
Red Cloud Indian Art Show (Pine Ridge, SD), **Jun 4**
Riverfest (Little Rock, AR), **May 26**
Rockport Art Fest (Rockport, TX), **Jul 1**

Russell, Charles M.: Birth Anniv, **Mar 19**
Sidewalk Art Fest (Bangor, ME), **Aug 5**
Sidewalk Art Fest (Portland, ME), **Aug 26**
Spring Gala (Lovington, NM), **May 6**
Three Rivers Fest (Fort Wayne, IN), **Jul 8**
Westmoreland Arts & Heritage Fest (Greensburg, PA), **Jul 1**
Wildflower Fest of the Arts (Dahlonega, GA), **May 20**
Youth Art Month, **Mar 1**
Aruba: Flag Day, **Mar 18**
As The World Turns TV Premiere: Anniv, **Apr 2**
As Young as You Feel Day, **Mar 22**
Asarah B'Tevet, **Jan 10**
Ascension Day, **May 25**
Ascension of Baha'u'llah, **May 29**
Ash Wednesday, **Mar 1**
Ashanti: Birth, **Oct 13**
Ashcroft, Peggy: Birth Anniv, **Dec 22**
Ashe, Arthur: Birth Anniv, **Jul 10**
Asher, Jane: Birth, **Apr 5**
Ashford, Emmett: Birth Anniv, **Nov 23**
Ashford, Evelyn: Birth, **Apr 15**
Ashford, Nickolas: Birth, **May 4**
Ashley, Elizabeth: Birth, **Aug 30**
Ashura: Tenth Day (Islamic), **Feb 9**
Asian Games (Doha, Qatar), **Dec 1**
Asian Pacific American Heritage Month (Pres Proc), **May 1**
Asimov, Isaac: Birth Anniv, **Jan 2**
Asner, Ed: Birth, **Nov 15**
Aspen Music Fest (Aspen, CO), **Jun 19**
AspenCash Motorcycle Rally (Ruidoso, NM), **May 18**
Aspinwall Crosses US on Horseback: Anniv, **Jul 8**
Assante, Armand: Birth, **Oct 4**
Assassination Attempt: Pope John Paul II: Anniv, **May 13**
Assassinations Report, Committee on: Anniv, **Mar 29**
Assisted Living Week, Natl, **Sep 10**
Association Week in Chicagoland (Chicago, IL), **Jun 19**
Assumption of the Virgin Mary, **Aug 15**
Astaire, Fred: Birth Anniv, **May 10**
Astin, John: Birth, **Mar 30**
Astin, MacKenzie: Birth, **May 12**
Astin, Sean: Birth, **Feb 25**
Astor Place Riot: Anniv, **May 10**
Astor, Brooke: Birth, **Mar 30**
Astrology
Aquarius, **Jan 20**
Aries, **Mar 21**
Cancer, **Jun 21**
Capricorn, **Dec 22**
Gemini, **May 21**
Leo, **Jul 23**
Libra, **Sep 23**
Pisces, **Feb 20**
Sagittarius, **Nov 22**
Scorpio, **Oct 23**
Taurus, **Apr 20**
Virgo, **Aug 23**
Astronomers Find New Solar System: Anniv, **Apr 15**
Astronomy Day, **May 6**
Astronomy Week, **May 1**
AT&T Divestiture: Anniv, **Jan 8**
Ataturk, Mustafa Kemal: Birth Anniv, **Mar 12**
Atchison, David R.: Birth Anniv, **Aug 11**
Atherton, William: Birth, **Jul 30**
Athletic Training Month, Natl, **Mar 1**
Atkins, Christopher: Birth, **Feb 21**
Atkinson, Rowan: Birth, **Jan 6**
Atlantic Charter Signing: Anniv, **Aug 14**
Atlantic Telegraph Cable Laid: Anniv, **Jul 27**
Atlas, Charles: Birth Anniv, **Oct 30**
Atler, Vanessa: Birth, **Feb 17**
Atomic Bomb Dropped on Hiroshima: Anniv, **Aug 6**
Atomic Bomb Dropped on Nagasaki: Anniv, **Aug 9**
Atomic Bomb Tested: Anniv, **Jul 16**
Atomic Plant Begun, Oak Ridge: Anniv, **Aug 1**
Atomic Power Plant Accident, Fermi: Anniv, **Oct 5**
Attack on America: Anniv, **Sep 11**
Attack on America: Fall of Kabul: Anniv, **Nov 13**
Attacks Against America: Libraries Remember, **Sep 11**
Attenborough, David: Birth, **May 8**
Attenborough, Sir Richard: Birth, **Aug 29**
Attend Your Grandchild's Birth Day, Natl, **Sep 29**
Attention Deficit Hyperactivity Disorder Month, **Sep 1**
Attlee, Clement Richard: Birth Anniv, **Jan 3**
Attucks, Crispus: Day, **Mar 5**
Atwood, Margaret: Birth, **Nov 18**
Auberjonois, Rene: Birth, **Jun 1**

Auctioneers Day, Natl, **Apr 15**
Auden, W.H.: Birth Anniv, **Feb 2**
Audubon, John J.: Birth Anniv, **Apr 26**
Auerbach, Arnold "Red": Birth, **Sep 20**
Augusta Futurity (Augusta, GA), **Jan 26**
Aung San Suu Kyi: Birth, **Jun 19**
Aura Awareness Day, Intl, **Nov 25**
Auschwitz Liberated: Anniv, **Jan 27**
Austen, Jane: Birth Anniv, **Dec 16**
Austin, Stephen F.: Birth Anniv, **Nov 3**
Austin, Tracy: Birth, **Dec 12**
Australia
   ANZAC Day, **Apr 25**
   Australia Day, **Jan 26**
   Canberra Day, **Mar 20**
   Commonwealth Formed: Anniv, **Jan 1**
   Commonwealth Games (Melbourne), **Mar 15**
   Eight Hour Day (Labor Day), **Mar 6**
   Ned Kelly's Last Stand: Anniv, **Jun 27**
   Picnic Day, **Aug 7**
   Proclamation Day, **Dec 28**
   Recreation Day, **Nov 6**
   Sorry Day, **May 26**
Austria
   Fasching, **Feb 27**
   Fasching Sunday, **Feb 26**
   Invaded by Nazi Germany: Anniv, **Mar 12**
   Krampuslauf, **Dec 5**
   Mozart 2006, **Jan 27**
   National Day, **Oct 26**
   Saint Stephen's Day, **Dec 26**
   Silent Night, Holy Night Celebrations, **Dec 24**
Authors' Day, Natl, **Nov 1**
Autism Awareness Month, Natl, **Apr 1**
Autism: COSAC Annual Conference, **May 19**
Automatic Toll Collection Machine, First: Anniv, **Nov 19**
Automobile Speed Reduction: Anniv, **Nov 25**
Automobiles (including shows, races, etc)
   AMA Grand National Kickoff (Daytona Beach, FL), **Mar 9**
   AMA Natl Hot Shoe Dirt Track Race (Daytona Beach, FL), **Mar 8**
   Antique and Classic Car Show (Bennington, VT), **Sep 14**
   Antiques by the Bay (St. Ignace, MI), **Jun 16**
   Automotion (Wisconsin Dells, WI), **May 20**
   Automotive Service Professionals Week, Natl, **Jun 11**
   Bud Pole Day for the Daytona 500 (Daytona Beach, FL), **Feb 12**
   Budweiser Shootout at Daytona NEXTEL Cup Series Race (Daytona Beach, FL), **Feb 11**
   Car Care Month, Natl, **Apr 1**
   Center of Nation All-Car Rally (Belle Fourche, SD), **Jun 10**
   Collision Awareness Month, Natl, **Mar 1**
   Concours d'Elegance (Forest Grove, OR), **Jul 16**
   Corvette and High Performance Meet (Puyallup, WA), **Feb 11**
   Corvette Show (Mackinaw City, MI), **Aug 25**
   Crown Royal Intl Race of Champions (Daytona Beach, FL), **Feb 17**
   Cruisin' Downtown (Toms River, NJ), **Jun 14**
   Daytona 200 by Honda Qualifying Day (Daytona Beach, FL), **Mar 8**
   Daytona 500 (Daytona Beach, FL), **Feb 19**
   Daytona Kart Week (Daytona Beach, FL), **Dec 26**
   Daytona Turkey Run (Daytona Beach, FL), **Nov 23**
   55 mph Speed Limit: Anniv, **Jan 2**
   First Car Insurance: Anniv, **Feb 1**
   Ford Mustang Day, Intl, **Apr 17**
   4-Wheel Drive Jamboree (Springfield, MO), **May 6**
   Gatorade Duel Qualifying Races (Daytona Beach, FL), **Feb 16**
   Good Car-Keeping Month, Natl, **May 1**
   Hershey's 300 NASCAR Busch Series Race (Daytona Beach, FL), **Feb 18**
   Hot August Nights (Reno and Sparks, NV), **Jul 29**
   Hot Times Downtown Wilber Car and Truck Show (Wilber, NE), **Jun 3**
   Indianapolis 500: Anniv, **May 30**
   Indianapolis 500-Mile Race (Indianapolis, IN), **May 28**
   Interstate Highway System Born: Anniv, **Jun 29**
   KRXL Car Cruise (Kirksville, MO), **Aug 5**
   Kustom Kemps Car Show (Biglerville, PA), **Jun 9**
   London/Brighton Veteran Car Run (London, England), **Nov 5**
   Lost in the '50s (Sandpoint, ID), **May 19**
   MADD's Tie One On for Safety, **Nov 16**
   Magic Dragon Street Meet Nationals & ExtremeCar Shows (Lake Ozark, MO), **May 5**
   Medford Cruise (Medford, OR), **Jun 16**
   Mid-America Natl Street Rod Assn Car Show (Springfield, MO), **May 26**
   Midnight at the Oasis (Yuma, AZ), **Mar 3**
   Model T Introduced: Anniv, **Oct 1**

   NASCAR Craftsman Truck Series 250 (Daytona Beach, FL), **Feb 17**
   NC RV and Camping Show (Charlotte, NC), **Jan 20**
   NC RV and Camping Show (Greensboro, NC), **Jan 6**
   NC RV and Camping Show (Raleigh, NC), **Feb 10**
   On the Waterfront Swap Meet/Car Show (St. Ignace, MI), **Sep 15**
   Ozark Antique Auto Club Swap Meet (Springfield, MO), **Aug 25**
   Pepsi 400 NASCAR NEXTEL Cup Series (Daytona, FL), **Jul 1**
   Petit Jean Antique Auto Show/Swap Meet (Morrilton, AR), **Jun 13**
   Petit Jean Fall Antique Auto Swap Meet (Morrilton, AR), **Sep 20**
   Portland Historic Races (Portland, OR), **Jul 7**
   Rally of the Tall Pines (Bancroft, ON, Canada), **Nov 11**
   Richard Crane Memorial Truck Show (St. Ignace, MI), **Sep 15**
   Rolex 24 at Daytona (Daytona, FL), **Feb 4**
   Show of Wheels (Lovington, NM), **Feb 18**
   St. Ignace Auto Show (St. Ignace, MI), **Jun 22**
   Street Machine Fall Nationals (Springfield, MO), **Sep 15**
   Streetscene (Covington, VA), **Aug 12**
   Woodie Wagon Day, Natl, **Jul 15**
   World of Wheels (Wichita Falls, TX), **Feb 3**
Autumn Begins, **Sep 23**
Autumn Market Fair, Eighteenth-Century (McLean, VA), **Oct 21**
Avalon, Frankie: Birth, **Sep 18**
Avedon, Richard: Birth Anniv, **May 15**
Aviation; Aviation History; Air Shows; Airplane Fly-ins
   Abbotsford Intl Airshow (Abbotsford, BC, Canada), **Aug 11**
   Amelia Earhart Atlantic Crossing: Anniv, **May 20**
   Amelia Earhart Disappears: Anniv, **Jul 2**
   American Flight Crashes at O'Hare: Anniv, **May 25**
   Aviation Day, Natl (Pres Proc), **Aug 19**
   Aviation History Month, **Nov 1**
   Aviation in America: Anniv, **Jan 9**
   Aviation Week, Natl, **Aug 14**
   Balloon Crossing of Atlantic: Anniv, **Aug 17**
   Berlin Airlift: Anniv, **Jun 24**
   Campbell Becomes First American Air ACE: Anniv, **Apr 14**
   Canary Islands Plane Disaster: Anniv, **Mar 27**
   Cayley, George: Birth Anniv, **Dec 27**
   Championship Air Races, Natl (Reno, NV), **Sep 13**
   China Clipper: Anniv, **Nov 22**
   Civil Air Patrol Founded: Anniv, **Dec 1**
   Civil Aviation Day, Intl (UN), **Dec 7**
   Cleveland Natl Air Show (Cleveland, OH), **Sep 2**
   Coleman, Bessie: Birth Anniv, **Jan 26**
   EAA Airventure Oshkosh (Oshkosh, WI), **Jul 24**
   Earhart, Amelia: Birth Anniv, **Jul 24**
   First Airplane Crossing English Channel: Anniv, **Jul 25**
   First Airship Crossing of Atlantic: Anniv, **Jul 6**
   First Balloon Flight Across English Channel: Anniv, **Jan 7**
   First Balloon Flight: Anniv, **Jun 5**
   First Concorde Flight: Anniv, **Jan 21**
   First Fatal Aviation Accident: Anniv, **Jun 15**
   First Flight Anniv Celebration (Kill Devil Hills, NC), **Dec 17**
   First Flight Attendant: Anniv, **May 15**
   First Flight into the Stratosphere: Anniv, **May 27**
   First Free Flight by a Woman: Anniv, **Jun 4**
   First Manned Balloon Flight: Anniv, **Oct 15**
   First Man-Powered Flight Across English Channel: Anniv, **Jun 12**
   First Man-Powered Flight: Anniv, **Aug 23**
   First Nonstop Flight of World/No Refueling: Anniv, **Dec 23**
   First Nonstop Transatlantic Flight: Anniv, **Jun 14**
   First Round-the-World Balloon Flight: Anniv, **Mar 21**
   First Scheduled Transcontinental Flight: Anniv, **Jan 25**
   First Solo Round-the-World Balloon Flight: Anniv, **Jul 2**
   Frequent Flyer Day, Natl, **May 1**
   Frequent Flyer Program Debuts: Anniv, **May 1**
   Hindenburg Disaster: Anniv, **May 6**
   Iran Air Flight 655 Disaster, **Jul 3**
   Johnson, Amy: Flight Anniv, **May 5**
   Kennedy Intl Airport Dedication: Anniv, **Jul 31**
   Lady Be Good Lost: Anniv, **Apr 4**
   Levine, Charles A.: Death Anniv, **Dec 6**
   Lindbergh Flight: Anniv, **May 20**
   Lindbergh, Charles A.: Birth Anniv, **Feb 4**
   Mint Julep Scale Meet (Falls of Rough, KY), **May 19**

   Montgolfier, Jacques: Birth Anniv, **Jan 7**
   Pan Am Circles Earth: Anniv, **Jan 6**
   Pan Am Flight 103 Explosion: Anniv, **Dec 21**
   Post, Wiley: Birth Anniv, **Nov 22**
   Quad City Air Show (Davenport, IA), **Jun 24**
   Sikorsky, Igor: Birth Anniv, **May 25**
   Solo Transatlantic Balloon Crossing: Anniv, **Sep 14**
   Sound Barrier Broken: Anniv, **Oct 14**
   Spruce Goose Flight: Anniv, **Nov 2**
   Stearman Fly-In Days, Natl (Galesburg, IL), **Sep 4**
   Streeter, Ruth Cheney: Birth Anniv, **Oct 2**
   Tuskegee Airmen Activated: Anniv, **Mar 22**
   US Air Force Academy Established: Anniv, **Apr 1**
   US Air Force Established: Anniv, **Sep 18**
   Wright Brothers Day (Pres Proc), **Dec 17**
   Wright Brothers First Powered Flight: Anniv, **Dec 17**
   Wrong Way Corrigan Day, **Jul 17**
Awkward Moments Day, **Mar 18**
Aykroyd, Dan: Birth, **Jul 1**
Aylesworth, Reiko: Birth, **Dec 9**
Aylwin, Patricio: Military Dictatorship Ended, **Dec 15**
Azalea Fest (Muskogee, OK), **Apr 3**
Azalea Fest, Brookings-Harbor (Brookings, OR), **May 26**
Azaria, Hank: Birth, **Apr 25**
Azerbaijan
   Day of the Republic, **May 28**
   Independence Day, **Oct 18**
   Martyrs' Day, **Jan 20**
Aznavour, Charles: Birth, **May 22**
Aztec Calendar Stone Discovery: Anniv, **Dec 17**
Azzi, Jennifer: Birth, **Aug 31**

Bab, Birth of the (Baha'i): Anniv, **Oct 20**
Babbage, Charles: Birth Anniv, **Dec 26**
Babenco, Hector: Birth, **Feb 7**
Baby Boomer Born, First, **Jan 1**
Baby Boomers Recognition Day, **Jun 21**
Baby Food Fest, Natl (Fremont, MI), **Jul 18**
Baby Safety Month, **Sep 1**
Babysitter Safety Day, **Mar 4**
Babysitters Day, Natl, **May 13**
Bacall, Lauren: Birth, **Sep 16**
Bach Fest (Leipzig, Germany), **May 27**
Bach, Catherine: Birth, **Mar 1**
Bach, Johann Sebastian: Birth Anniv, **Mar 21**
Bacharach, Burt: Birth, **May 12**
Bachelor Father TV Premiere: Anniv, **Sep 15**
Bachelors Day, **Feb 1**
Back Week, Natl Save Your, **Oct 23**
Backpack Safety America Month, **Sep 1**
Backus, Jim: Birth Anniv, **Feb 25**
Backyard Games Week, Natl, **May 22**
Bacon, Francis: Birth Anniv, **Jan 22**
Bacon, Kevin: Birth, **Jul 8**
Bacon's Rebellion, Jamestown Burned By: Anniv, **Sep 19**
Bad Day Day, Have a, **Nov 19**
Bad Poetry Day, **Aug 18**
Baden-Powell, Robert: Birth Anniv, **Feb 22**
Bader, Diedrich: Birth, **Dec 24**
Badlands Natl Park Established: Anniv, **Nov 10**
Badminton Horse Trials (Badminton, England), **May 4**
Badminton: Scottish Intl Chmpshp (Edinburgh, Scotland), **Nov 23**
Badu, Erykah: Birth, **Feb 26**
Baer, Max, Jr: Birth, **Dec 4**
Baez, Joan: Birth, **Jan 9**
Bagwell, Jeff: Birth, **May 27**
Baha'i
   American Baha'i Community: Anniv, **Jun 5**
   Ascension of Baha'u'llah, **May 29**
   Baha'i New Year's Day: Naw-Ruz, **Mar 21**
   Birth of Baha'u'llah, **Nov 12**
   Birth of the Bab, **Oct 20**
   Declaration of the Bab, **May 23**
   Fest of Ridvan, **Apr 21**
   Martyrdom of the Bab, **Jul 9**
   Race Unity Day, **Jun 11**
Bahamas
   Discovery Day, **Oct 12**
   Emancipation Day, **Aug 7**
   Fox Hill Day (Nassau), **Aug 8**
   Independence Day, **Jul 10**
   Junkanoo, **Dec 26**
   Labor Day, **Jun 2**
Bahrain: Independence Day, **Dec 16**
Bailey, F. Lee: Birth, **Jun 10**
Bailey, Pearl Mae: Birth Anniv, **Mar 29**
Baines, Harold: Birth, **Mar 15**
Baio, Scott: Birth, **Sep 22**
Baisakhi: Vaisakhi (India), **Apr 14**
Baiul, Oksana: Birth, **Nov 16**
Bake for Family Fun Month, **Feb 1**
Baked Bean Month, Natl, **Jul 1**

Baker—Bay

Baker, Anita: Birth, Jan 26
Baker, Carroll: Birth, May 28
Baker, Diane: Birth, Feb 25
Baker, Joe Don: Birth, Feb 12
Baker, Josephine: Birth Anniv, Jun 3
Baker, Kathy: Birth, Jun 8
Baker, Russell: Birth, Aug 14
Baker, Vin: Birth, Nov 23
Bakker, Jim: Birth, Jan 2
Bakula, Scott: Birth, Oct 9
Balance Awareness Week, Sep 18
Balanchine, George: Birth Anniv, Jan 22
Balboa: Pacific Ocean Discovered: Anniv, Sep 25
Bald and Be Free Day, Be, Oct 14
Bald Eagle Appreciation Days (Keokuk, IA), Jan 21
Bald Is Beautiful Convention (Morehead City, NC), Sep 8
Baldacci, John: Birth, Jan 30
Baldwin, Adam: Birth, Feb 27
Baldwin, Alec: Birth, Apr 3
Baldwin, Caroline: First Woman Dr. Science: Anniv, Jun 20
Baldwin, James: Birth Anniv, Aug 2
Baldwin, Roger Nash: Birth Anniv, Jan 21
Baldwin, Stephen: Birth, May 12
Baldwin, William: Birth, Feb 21
Bale, Christian: Birth, Jan 30
Balfour, Eric: Birth, Apr 24
Bali Terrorist Bombing: Anniversary, Oct 12
Ball, Lucille: Birth Anniv, Aug 6
Ballesteros, Seve: Birth, Apr 9
Ballet Introduced to the US: Anniv, Feb 7
Ballet: Rite of Spring Premiere and Riot: Anniv, May 29
Balloons, Hot-Air
   Albuquerque Intl Balloon Fiesta (Albuquerque, NM), Sep 30
   Aviation in America: Anniv, Jan 9
   Balloon Crossing of Atlantic: Anniv, Aug 17
   Balloons Around the World, Oct 4
   Colorado River Crossing Balloon Festival (Yuma, AZ), Nov 17
   Columbus Fest/Hot Air Balloon Regatta (Columbus, KS), Oct 6
   Creston/Southwest Iowa Balloon Days (Creston, IA), Sep 15
   Farmington Invitational Balloon Fest (Farmington, NM), May 27
   First Balloon Flight Across English Channel: Anniv, Jan 7
   First Balloon Flight: Anniv, Jun 5
   First Balloon Honeymoon: Anniv, Jun 20
   First Flight into the Stratosphere: Anniv, May 27
   First Manned Flight: Anniv, Oct 15
   First Round-the-World Balloon Flight: Anniv, Mar 21
   First Solo Round-the-World Balloon Flight: Anniv, Jul 2
   Great Wellsville Balloon Rally (Wellsville, NY), Jul 21
   Macon, GA's Cherry Blossom Fest, Intl (Macon, GA), Mar 17
   Re/Max Ballunar Liftoff Festival (Houston, TX), Aug 24
   Rocky Mountain Balloon Fest (Denver, CO), Aug 25
   Solo Transatlantic Balloon Crossing: Anniv, Sep 14
   Telluride Balloon Fest (Telluride, CO), Jun 2
Ball-Point Pen Patented: Anniv, Jun 10
Balzac, Honore De: Birth Anniv, May 20
Bamboo Celebration Day, Aug 20
Banana Split Fest (Wilmington, OH), Jun 9
Bancroft, George: Birth Anniv, Oct 3
Band Fest, Great American Brass (Danville, KY), Jun 10
Banderas, Antonio: Birth, Aug 10
Banerjee, Victor: Birth, Oct 15
Banff Mountain Book Fest (Banff, AB, Canada), Nov 1
Banff Mountain Film Fest (Banff, AB, Canada), Nov 3
Bangladesh
   Independence Day, Mar 26
   Martyrs Day, Feb 21
   Solidarity Day, Nov 7
   Victory Day, Dec 16
Banjo: Guthrie Jazz Banjo Fest (Guthrie, OK), May 26
Bank Holiday, Spring (United Kingdom), May 29
Bank Holiday, Summer (Scotland), Aug 7
Bank Holiday, Summer (United Kingdom), Aug 28
Bank Opens in US, First: Anniv, Dec 31
Banks, Ernie: Birth, Jan 31
Banks, Tyra: Birth, Dec 4
Banned Books Week, Sep 23
Banneker, Benjamin: Birth Anniv, Nov 9
Bannister Breaks Four-Minute Mile: Anniv, May 6

Bannister, Dr. Roger: Birth, Mar 23
Bar Assn, American Founding: Anniv, Aug 21
Bar Code Introduced: Anniv, Jun 26
Barak, Ehud: Birth, Feb 12
Baraka, Imamu Amiri: Birth, Oct 7
Baranski, Christine: Birth, May 2
Barbados: Independence Day, Nov 30
Barbeau, Adrienne: Birth, Jun 11
Barbecue Month, Natl, May 1
Barbed Wire Swap/Sell (LaCrosse, KS), May 5
Barber, Frances: Birth, May 13
Barber, Red: Birth Anniv, Feb 17
Barber, Red: First Baseball Games Televised: Anniv, Aug 26
Barbershop Quartet Day, Apr 11
Barbershop: SPEBSQSA Convention (Jacksonville, FL), Jan 15
Barbie and Barney Backlash Day, Dec 16
Barbie Debuts: Anniv, Mar 9
Barbosa, Jose Celso: Birth Anniv, Jul 27
Barbour, Haley: Birth, Oct 22
Bardem, Javier: Birth, Mar 1
Bardot, Brigitte: Birth, Sep 28
Barenboim, Daniel: Birth, Nov 15
Barista Chmpshp, World (Berne, Switzerland), May 19
Barker, Bob: Birth, Dec 12
Barkin, Ellen: Birth, Apr 16
Barkley, Alben: Birth Anniv, Nov 24
Barkley, Charles: Birth, Feb 20
Barnaby Jones TV Premiere: Anniv, Jan 28
Barnard, Christiaan: Birth Anniv, Nov 8
Barnard, Christiaan: First Heart Transplant: Anniv, Dec 3
Barnes, Clive: Birth, May 13
Barnes, Joanna: Birth, Nov 15
Barnesville Pumpkin Fest (Barnesville, OH), Sep 21
Barney & Friends TV Premiere: Anniv, Apr 6
Barney Miller TV Premiere: Anniv, Jan 23
Barnum, Phineas Taylor: Birth Anniv, Jul 5
Baron Bliss Day (Belize), Mar 9
Barrel Race, Josey's World Champion Junior (Marshall, TX), May 5
Barrett, Rona: Birth, Oct 8
Barrie, Barbara: Birth, May 23
Barris, Chuck: Birth, Jun 3
Barrow, Clyde: Bonnie and Clyde: Death Anniv, May 23
Barry, Dave: Birth, Jul 3
Barry, Gene: Birth, Jun 14
Barry, John: Death Anniv, Sep 13
Barrymore, Drew: Birth, Feb 22
Barrymore, Ethel: Birth Anniv, Aug 15
Barrymore, John: Birth Anniv, Feb 15
Barrymore, Lionel: Birth Anniv, Apr 28
Barth, John: Birth, May 27
Bartholdi, Frederic A.: Birth Anniv, Apr 2
Bartholomew, Freddie: Birth Anniv, Mar 28
Bartlett, John: Birth Anniv, Jun 14
Bartlett, Josiah: Birth Anniv, Nov 21
Bartok, Bela: Birth Anniv, Mar 25
Bartoli, Cecilia: Birth, Jun 4
Barton, Clara: American Red Cross Founding Anniv, May 21
Barton, Clara: Birth Anniv, Dec 25
Barton, Mischa: Birth, Jan 24
Baryshnikov, Mikhail: Birth, Jan 27
Bascom, Earl W.: Birth Anniv, Jun 19
Bascom, Florence: Birth Anniv, Jul 14
Bascom, George N.: Birth Anniv, Apr 24
Bascom, Texas Rose: Birth Anniv, Feb 25
Baseball. See also Softball
   Ashford, Emmett: Birth Anniv, Nov 23
   Babe Ruth Calls His Shot?: Anniv, Oct 1
   Babe Ruth's First Major League Home Run: Anniv, May 6
   Babe Ruth's First Pro Homer: Anniv, Sep 5
   Baseball Declared Nonessential: Anniv, Jul 20
   Baseball First Played Under Lights: Anniv, May 24
   Baseball Hall of Fame Dedicated, Natl: Anniv, Jun 12
   Baseball's Greatest Dispute: Anniv, Sep 23
   Baseball's Sad Lexicon Published: Anniv, Jul 10
   Bell, James: Birth Anniv, May 17
   Big Ten Baseball Tournament, May 24
   Bonds Breaks Home Run Record, Oct 5
   Caray, Harry: Birth Anniv, Mar 14
   Cobb, Ty: Birth Anniv, Dec 18
   Designated Hitter Rule Adopted: Anniv, Jan 11
   Doubleday, Abner: Birth Anniv, Jun 26
   First Baseball Games Televised: Anniv, Aug 26
   First Baseball Strike Ends: Anniv, Apr 13
   First Indoor Game: Anniv, Dec 25
   First Perfect Game: Anniv, Jun 12
   Gehrig, Lou: Birth Anniv, Jun 19
   Gibson, Josh: Birth, Dec 21
   Greenberg, Hank: Birth Anniv, Jan 1

   Hall of Fame's Charter Members: Anniv, Feb 2
   Home Run Record: Anniv, Apr 8
   Jackie Robinson Breaks Baseball Color Line: Anniv, Apr 15
   Ladies' Day Initiated in Baseball: Anniv, Jun 16
   Little League Baseball Week, Natl, Jun 12
   Little League World Series (Williamsport, PA), Aug 18
   Major League Baseball First All-Star Game: Anniv, Jul 6
   Major League's First Double Header, Sep 25
   Maris Breaks Ruth Home Run Record: Anniv, Oct 1
   Martin, Billy: Birth Anniv, May 16
   McGwire Breaks Home Run Record: Anniv, Sep 8
   Midnight Sun Baseball Game (Fairbanks, AK), Jun 21
   Mighty Casey Has Struck Out: Anniv, Jun 3
   MLB All-Star Game (Pittsburgh, PA), Jul 11
   NAIA Baseball World Series (Lewiston, ID), May 26
   NCAA Div I Men's College World Series (Baseball Chmpshp) (Omaha, NE), Jun 16
   President Taft Opens Baseball Season: Anniv, Apr 14
   Robinson Named First Black Manager: Anniv, Oct 3
   Tinker to Evers to Chance: First Double Play Anniv, Sep 15
   Tinker, Joe: Birth Anniv, Jul 27
   Young, Cy: Birth Anniv, Mar 29
Bashoff, Blake: Birth, May 30
Basinger, Kim: Birth, Dec 8
Basketball
   Basketball Created: Anniv, Dec 1
   Big 12 Men's Basketball Chmpshp (Dallas, TX), Mar 9
   Big 12 Women's Basketball Tournament (Dallas, TX), Mar 7
   Big Ten Men's Basketball Tournament (Indianapolis, IN), Mar 9
   Big Ten Women's Basketball Tournament (Indianapolis, IN), Mar 2
   Carrs/Safeway Great Alaska Shootout (Anchorage, AK), Nov 21
   Chicago Bulls Third Straight Title for the Second Time, Jun 14
   First Black Plays in NBA Game: Anniv, Oct 31
   First Shattered Backboard: Anniv, Nov 5
   First Women's Collegiate Basketball Game: Anniv, Mar 22
   Harlem Globetrotters Play First Game: Anniv, Jan 7
   NAIA Div I Men's Basketball Chmpshp (Kansas City, MO), Mar 15
   NAIA Div I Women's Basketball Chmpshp (Jackson, TN), Mar 15
   NAIA Div II Men's Basketball Chmpshp (Point Lookout, MO), Mar 8
   NAIA Div II Women's Basketball Chmpshp (Sioux City, IA), Mar 8
   NBA All-Star Weekend (Houston, TX), Feb 17
   NCAA Div I Men's Basketball Chmpshp (Indianapolis, IN), Apr 1
   NJCAA Div II Men's Natl Basketball Finals (Danville, IL), Mar 22
Bassett, Angela: Birth, Aug 16
Bassey, Shirley: Birth, Jan 8
Bastille Day (France), Jul 14
Bastille Day Celebration (Boston, MA), Jul 14
Bataan Death March: Anniv, Apr 10
Bateman, Jason: Birth, Jan 14
Bateman, Justine: Birth, Feb 19
Bates, Kathy: Birth, Jun 28
Bathtub Party Day, Dec 5
Bathtub Race, Great (Nome, AK), Sep 4
Batman Debuts: Anniv, May 1
Batman TV Premiere: Anniv, Jan 12
Battier, Shane: Birth, Sep 9
Battle of Blue Licks Celebration (Mount Olivet, KY), Aug 19
Battle of Brandywine: Anniv, Sep 11
Battle of Britain Day (United Kingdom), Sep 15
Battle of Britain Week (United Kingdom), Sep 10
Battle of Bushy Run Reenactment (Harrison City, PA), Aug 5
Battle of Germantown Reenactment (Philadelphia, PA), Oct 7
Battle of Kursk: Anniv, Jul 12
Battle of Lexington and Concord: Anniv, Apr 19
Battle of Little Bighorn: Anniv, Jun 25
Battle of Midway: Anniv, Jun 4
Battle, Kathleen: Birth, Aug 13
Baucus, Max: Birth, Dec 11
Baum, L. Frank.: Birth Anniv, May 15
Baxter, Meredith: Birth, Jun 21
Bay Harbor Summer Art Fair (Bay Harbor, MI), Aug 5
Bay of Pigs Invasion Launched: Anniv, Apr 17

Bay to Breakers Race (San Francisco, CA), May 19
Bayfest (Corpus Christi, TX), Sep 29
Bayh, Evan: Birth, Dec 26
Baylor, Don: Birth, Jun 28
Baylor, Elgin Gay: Birth, Sep 16
Baywatch TV Premiere: Anniv, Apr 23
BCS Natl Chmpshp Game: Nokia Sugar Bowl, Jan 2
Be an Angel Day, Aug 22
Be Bald and Be Free Day, Oct 14
Be Electrific Day, Feb 11
Be Kind to Animals Week, May 1
Be Kind to Humankind Week, Aug 25
Be Late for Something Day, Sep 5
Be Nice to New Jersey Week, Jul 2
Beach Party (Deadwood, SD), Mar 11
Beadle, George: Birth Anniv, Oct 22
Beals, Jennifer: Birth, Dec 19
Bean Throwing Fest (Japan), Feb 3
Bean, Alan: Birth, Mar 15
Bean, Andy: Birth, Mar 13
Bean, Orson: Birth, Jul 22
Bean, Sean: Birth, Apr 17
Beard, Charles: Birth Anniv, Nov 27
Beard, James: Birth Anniv, May 5
Beardsley, Aubrey V.: Birth Anniv, Aug 21
Bearse, Amanda: Birth, Aug 9
Beasley, Allyce: Birth, Jul 6
Beasley, DaMarcus: Birth, May 24
Beat the Clock TV Premiere: Anniv, Mar 23
Beatles, The
   Appear on The Ed Sullivan Show: Anniv, Feb 9
   Bed-in for Peace: Anniv, Mar 25
   Break Up: Anniv, Apr 10
   Harrison, George: Birth Anniv, Feb 25
   John Lennon Shot: Anniv, Dec 8
   Last Concert: Anniv, Jan 30
   Lennon, John: Birth Anniv, Oct 9
   McCartney, Paul: Birth, Jun 18
   Sgt Pepper's Lonely Hearts Club Band Released: Anniv, Jun 1
   Starr, Ringo: Birth, Jul 7
   Take Over Music Charts: Anniv, Apr 4
Beatrix, Queen: Birth, Jan 31
Beatty, Ned: Birth, Jul 6
Beatty, Warren: Birth, Mar 30
Beaufort Scale Day, May 7
Beaumont, William: Birth Anniv, Nov 21
Beauregard, Genl: Battle of Shiloh: Anniv, Apr 6
Beauty and the Beast TV Premiere: Anniv, Sep 25
Beauty Contests, Pageants
   First Miss America: Anniv, Sep 8
   Miss Alaska Scholarship Pageant (Anchorage, AK), Jun 16
   Miss American Rose Day, Oct 20
   Miss Arizona Pageant (Gilbert, AZ), Jun 22
   Miss Delaware Pageant (Rehoboth Beach, DE), Jun 9
   Miss Iowa Scholarship Pageant (Eldridge, IA), Jun 8
   Miss Louisiana Pageant (Monroe, LA), Jun 15
   Miss Mississippi Pageant (Vicksburg, MS), Jun 21
   Miss New Mexico Scholarship Pageant (Alamogordo, NM), Jun 9
   Miss Ohio Pageant (Mansfield, OH), Jun 14
   Miss Oregon Scholarship Pageant (Seaside, OR), Jun 25
   Miss South Carolina Pageant (Spartanburg, SC), Jul 4
   Miss South Carolina Teen Competition (Spartanburg, SC), Jun 26
   Miss Tennessee Pageant (Jackson, TN), Jun 21
   Miss Virginia Pageant (Roanoke, VA), Jun 22
   Miss Wisconsin Pageant (Oshkosh, WI), Jun 22
Parks, Bert: Birth Anniv, Dec 30
Beauty: Turn Beauty Inside Out Day, May 17
Beauvais-Nilon, Garcelle: Birth, Nov 26
Beavers, Louise: Birth Anniv, Mar 8
Beck, John: Birth, Jan 28
Becker, Boris: Birth, Nov 22
Beckett, Samuel: Birth Anniv, Apr 13
Beckham, David: Birth, May 2
Beckham, Victoria Adams: Birth, Apr 17
Beckinsale, Kate: Birth, Jul 26
Bed and Breakfast: Country Inn, Bed and Breakfast Day, Oct 1
Bedard, Irene: Birth, Jul 22
Bedelia, Bonnie: Birth, Mar 25
Bed-in for Peace: Anniv, Mar 25
Bednarik, Chuck: Birth, May 1
Beecher, Catharine Esther: Birth Anniv, Sep 6
Beecher, Henry W.: Birth Anniv, Jun 24
Beef Empire Days (Garden City, KS), May 30
Beer; Beer-related Events
   Beer Day (Iceland), Mar 1
   Beer Fest (Luxembourg), Jul 16
   Brewers Fest, Oregon (Portland, OR), Jul 27

   Craft Brewers Conf & BrewExpo America (Seattle, WA), Apr 11
   Great American Beer Fest (Denver, CO), Sep 28
   Memorabilia: Winterfest (Burton, MI), Jan 21
   Telluride Blues & Brews Festival (Telluride, CO), Sep 15
Beethoven, Ludwig van: Birth Anniv, Dec 16
Beethoven's Ninth Symphony Premiere: Anniv, May 7
Beggar's Night, Oct 31
Begin, Menachem: Birth Anniv, Aug 16
Begley, Ed, Jr: Birth, Sep 16
Behan, Brendan: Birth Anniv, Feb 9
Behar, Joy: Birth, Oct 7
Beirut Terrorist Attack: Anniv, Oct 23
Belafonte, Harry: Birth, Mar 1
Belafonte-Harper, Shari: Birth, Sep 22
Belarus
   Constitution Day, Mar 15
   Independence Day, Jul 3
Bele Chere (Asheville, NC), Jul 28
Belfour, Ed: Birth, Apr 21
Belgium
   Dynasty Day, Nov 15
   Historical Procession (Tournai), Sep 10
   Lover's Fair, Dec 7
   Military Music Fest, Jun 11
   National Holiday, Jul 21
   Nuts Fair (Bastogne), Dec 18
   Ommegang Pageant, Jul 6
   Play of St. Evermaar, May 1
   Procession of Golden Chariot (Mons), Jun 2
   Procession of the Holy Blood, May 25
   Wedding of the Giants, Aug 27
Believe It or Not TV Premiere: Anniv, Mar 1
Belize
   Baron Bliss Day, Mar 9
   Columbus Day, Oct 12
   Commonwealth Day, May 24
   Garifuna Day, Nov 19
   Independence Day, Sep 21
   Saint George's Caye Day, Sep 10
Bell, Alexander Graham: Birth Anniv, Mar 3
Bell, Catherine: Birth, Aug 14
Bell, James: Birth Anniv, May 17
Bell, Jay: Birth, Dec 11
Bellamy, Ralph: Birth Anniv, Jun 17
Belle, Albert: Birth, Aug 25
Bellow, Saul: Birth Anniv, Jun 10
Belmondo, Jean-Paul: Birth, Apr 9
Belmont Stakes (Belmont Park, NY), Jun 10
Belote, Melissa: Birth, Oct 16
Beltane, Apr 30
Belushi, Jim: Birth, Jun 15
Belushi, John: Birth Anniv, Jan 24
Belzer, Richard: Birth, Aug 4
Benatar, Pat: Birth, Jan 10
Bench, Johnny: Birth, Dec 7
Benchley, Peter: Birth, May 8
Benedict XVI, Pope: Birth, Apr 16
Benedict, Paul: Birth, Sep 17
Benes, Andy: Birth, Aug 20
Benet, William Rose: Birth Anniv, Feb 2
Ben-Gurion, David: Birth Anniv, Oct 16
Benigni, Roberto: Birth, Oct 27
Benin: Independence Day, Aug 1
Bening, Annette: Birth, May 29
Benjamin Franklin Tercentenary, Jan 17
Benjamin, Richard: Birth, May 22
Bennett, Arnold: Birth Anniv, May 27
Bennett, Cornelius: Birth, Aug 25
Bennett, Joan: Birth Anniv, Feb 27
Bennett, Richard Bedford: Birth Anniv, Jul 3
Bennett, Robert F.: Birth, Sep 18
Bennett, Tony: Birth, Aug 3
Bennington Battle Day, Aug 16
Benny, Jack: Birth Anniv, Feb 14
Benson, George: Birth, Mar 22
Benson, Robby: Birth, Jan 21
Bentley, Edmund Clerihew: Clerihew Day, Jul 10
Benton Neighbor Day (Benton, MO), Sep 1
Benton, Thomas Hart: Birth Anniv, Apr 15
Berenger, Tom: Birth, May 31
Berenson, Marisa: Birth, Feb 15
Berenson, Red: Birth, Dec 8
Bergen, Candice: Birth, May 9
Bergen, Edgar: Birth Anniv, Feb 16
Bergen, Polly: Birth, Jul 14
Bergeron, Tom: Birth, May 6
Bergin, Michael: Birth, Mar 19
Bergman, Ingmar: Birth, Jul 14
Bergman, Ingrid: Birth & Death Anniv, Aug 29
Bergman, Peter: Birth, Jun 11
Bergson, Henri: Birth Anniv, Oct 18
Berkeley, Busby: Birth Anniv, Nov 29
Berkoff, Steven: Birth, Aug 3
Berle, Milton: Birth Anniv, Jul 12
Berlin Airlift: Anniv, Jun 24

Berlin International Film Fest (Berlin, Germany), Feb 9
Berlin Wall Erected: Anniv, Aug 13
Berlin Wall Opened: Anniv, Nov 9
Berlin Wall: Tear Down This Wall Speech: Anniv, Jun 12
Berlin, Irving: Birth Anniv, May 11
Berman, Shelley: Birth, Feb 3
Bermuda Colonized by English: Anniv, Mar 12
Bermuda: Peppercorn Ceremony, Apr 23
Bernard, Carlos: Birth, Oct 12
Bernard, Crystal: Birth, Sep 30
Berne Swiss Days (Berne, IN), Jul 27
Berners-Lee, Tim: Birth, Jun 8
Bernhard, Sandra: Birth, Jun 6
Bernsen, Corbin: Birth, Sep 7
Bernstein, Carl: Birth, Feb 14
Bernstein, Leonard: Birth Anniv, Aug 25
Berra, Yogi: Birth, May 12
Berridge, Elizabeth: Birth, May 2
Berry, Chuck: Birth, Oct 18
Berry, Halle: Birth, Aug 14
Berry, Ken: Birth, Nov 3
Bertinelli, Valerie: Birth, Apr 23
Bertolucci, Bernardo: Birth, Mar 16
Best Friend's Day, Aug 15
Bethune, Mary McLeod: Birth Anniv, Jul 10
Bethune, Norman: Birth Anniv, Mar 3
Bettis, Jerome: Birth, Feb 16
Beverly Hillbillies TV Premiere: Anniv, Sep 26
Bewick, Thomas: Birth Anniv, Aug 12
Bewitched TV Premiere: Anniv, Sep 17
Bezos, Jeff: Birth, Jan 12
Bhopal Poison Gas Disaster: Anniv, Dec 3
Bhutan
   Coronation Day, Jun 2
   Natl Day, Jun 25
Bhutto, Benazir: Birth, Jun 21
Bialik, Mayim: Birth, Dec 12
Bibby, Mike: Birth, May 13
Bible Week, Natl, Nov 19
Bichette, Dante: Birth, Nov 18
Bicycle
   Big Mac Shoreline Fall Scenic Bike Tour (Mackinaw City, MI), Sep 16
   Bike Month, Natl, May 1
   Bike to Work Day, Natl, May 19
   Bike Van Buren (Van Buren County, IA), Aug 19
   Borneo Rhino Challenge (Malaysia), May 14
   Great Peanut Tour (Skippers, VA), Sep 7
   Hotter 'n Hell Hundred Bike Race/Fest (Wichita Falls, TX), Aug 24
   Leadville Trail 100 Bike Race (Leadville, CO), Aug 12
   Perry's "BRR" (Bike Ride to Rippey) (Perry, IA), Feb 4
   RAGBRAI—Register's Bicycle Ride Across Iowa (Des Moines, IA), Jul 23
   Tour de Cure (Diabetes), Apr 1
   Tour de France, Jul 1
   Tour of Somerville (Somerville, NJ), May 29
Biddle, Nicholas: Birth Anniv, Jan 8
Biden, Joe: Birth, Nov 20
Biel, Jessica: Birth, Mar 3
Bifocals at the Monitor Liberation Day, Dec 1
Big Bend Natl Park Established: Anniv, Jun 12
Big Bertha Paris Gun: Anniv, Mar 23
Big E, The (West Springfield, MA), Sep 15
Big Island Rendezvous & Fest (Albert Lea, MN), Oct 7
Big Top TV Premiere: Anniv, Jul 1
Big Valley Jamboree (Camrose, AB, Canada), Aug 4
Big Whopper Liar's Contest (New Harmony, IN), Sep 10
Big Wind: Anniv, Apr 12
Biggio, Craig: Birth, Dec 14
Biggs, E. Power: Birth Anniv, Mar 29
Biggs, Jason: Birth, May 12
Bike to Work Day, Natl, May 19
Bikel, Theodore: Birth, May 2
Bikini Debuted: Anniv, Jul 5
Bill of Rights: Anniv, Dec 15
Bill of Rights: Anniv of First State Ratification, Nov 20
Bill of Rights: Day (Pres Proc), Dec 15
Bill of Rights: Proposal, Jun 8
Bill of Rights: Religious Freedom Week, Sep 22
Bill, Tony: Birth, Aug 23
Billiard Awareness Month, Oct 1
Billingsley, Barbara: Birth, Dec 22
Billington, James Hadley: Birth, Jun 1
Billy the Kid: Birth Anniv, Nov 23
Bingaman, Jeff: Birth, Oct 3
Bingo's Birthday Month, Dec 1
Binoche, Juliette: Birth, Mar 9
Biodiesel Day, Natl (Rudolph Diesel Birth Anniv), Mar 18

Biographers—Bombing

Biographers Day, May 16
Biological Clock Gene Discovered: Anniv, Apr 28
Biological Diversity, Intl Day for (UN), May 22
Bioterrorism/Disaster Education and Awareness Month, Jul 1
Bird, Larry: Birth, Dec 7
Birds
　Bald Eagle Appreciation Days (Keokuk, IA), Jan 21
　Bird Feeding Month, Natl, Feb 1
　Birds & Blossoms Spring Nature Fest (Norfolk, VA), May 11
　Crane Watch (Kearney, NE), Mar 1
　Curlew Day, Mar 16
　Down East Spring Birding Fest (Eastport, Whiting, Lubec, ME), May 26
　Duck-Calling Contest/Wings Over Prairie (Stuttgart, AR), Nov 24
　Eagle Day at the Lake (Kansas City, KS), Jan 21
　Eagle Days (Junction City, KS), Jan 14
　Eagle Days in Springfield (Springfield, MO), Jan 21
　Eagles Et Cetera Fest (Bismarck, AR), Jan 27
　Fall in Love with Fond du Lac (Fond du Lac, WI), Sep 1
　Great Backyard Bird Count, Feb 17
　Hummer/Bird Celebration (Rockport, Fulton, TX), Sep 14
　Kirtland, Jared: Birth Anniv, Nov 10
　Migratory Bird Celebration, Intl (Chincoteague, VA), May 13
　Migratory Bird Day, Intl, May 13
　Picatinny Peak Fall Hawkwatch (Dover, NJ), Sep 1
　South Texas Wildlife and Birding Fest (Kingsville, TX), Nov 17
　Swallows Depart San Juan Capistrano (CA), Oct 23
　Swallows Return to San Juan Capistrano (CA), Mar 19
　Waterfowl Fest (Easton, MD), Nov 10
　Wings Over the Platte Spring Migration Fest (Grand Island, NE), Feb 18
　Wings Over Willcox—Sandhill Crane Celebration (Willcox, AZ), Jan 12
Birdseye, Clarence: Birth Anniv, Dec 9
Birkebeiner, American (Cable to Hayward, WI), Feb 23
Birkin, Jane: Birth, Dec 14
Birmingham (AL) Resistance: Anniv, Apr 3
Birmingham Riot: Anniv (England), Jul 14
Birney, David: Birth, Apr 23
Birth Control Clinic Opened, First: Anniv, Oct 16
Birth Control Pills Sold: Anniv, Aug 18
Birthday of Mother's Whistler, May 18
Biscayne Natl Park Established: Anniv, Jun 28
Biscuit Month, Natl, Sep 1
Bishop, Elvin: Birth, Oct 21
Bishop, Joey: Birth, Feb 3
Bison-Ten-Yell Day, Sep 2
Bisset, Jacqueline: Birth, Sep 13
Bissett, Josie: Birth, Oct 5
Bjork: Birth, Nov 21
Black Cow Created: Anniv, Aug 19
Black Friday, Nov 24
Black Hills Stock Show and Rodeo (Rapid City, SD), Jan 27
Black History Month, Natl, Feb 1
Black Love Day, Feb 13
Black Nazarene Fiesta (Philippines), Jan 1
Black Nazarene, Feast of the (Philippines), Jan 9
Black Poetry Day, Oct 18
Black Press Day: Anniv of the First Black Newspaper, Mar 16
Black Single Parents' Week, Jun 4
Black Walnut Fest (Stockton, MO), Sep 20
Black, Clint: Birth, Feb 4
Black, Debbie: Birth, Jul 29
Black, Karen: Birth, Jul 1
Black, Lewis: Birth, Aug 30
Black, Shirley Temple: Birth, Apr 23
Blackmun, Harry A.: Birth Anniv, Nov 12
Blackout, East Coast: Anniv, Nov 9
Blackstone, William: Birth Anniv, Mar 5
Blackwell, Elizabeth, Awarded MD: Anniv, Jan 23
Blackwell, Elizabeth: Birth Anniv, Feb 3
Blades, Ruben: Birth, Jul 16
Blagojevich, Rod: Birth, Dec 10
Blah Blah Blah Day, Apr 17
Blaine, David: Birth, Apr 4
Blair, Bonnie: Birth, Mar 18
Blair, Linda: Birth, Jan 22
Blair, Tony: Birth, May 6
Blake, Eubie: Birth Anniv, Feb 7
Blake, Robert: Birth, Sep 18
Blake, William: Birth Anniv, Nov 28
Blakely, Susan: Birth, Sep 7
Blakey, Art: Birth Anniv, Oct 11
Blame Someone Else Day, Jan 13
Blanchett, Cate: Birth, May 14
Blanco, Kathleen: Birth, Dec 15

Blanda, George: Birth, Sep 17
Blass, Bill: Birth Anniv, Jun 22
Blatty, William: Birth, Jan 7
Bledel, Alexis: Birth, Sep 16
Bledsoe, Drew: Birth, Feb 14
Bledsoe, Tempestt: Birth, Aug 1
Bleeth, Yasmine: Birth, Jun 14
Bleriot, Louis: Birth Anniv, Jul 1
Blessing of Animals at the Cathedral (Mexico), Jan 17
Blethyn, Brenda: Birth, Feb 20
Blige, Mary J.: Birth, Jan 11
Bliss, Lizzie: Birth Anniv, Apr 11
Blizzard, Great of '88: Anniv, Mar 12
Blondie and Deborah Harry Month, Intl, Jul 1
Blondin, Charles: Birth Anniv, Feb 28
Blondin, Charles: Conquest of Niagara Falls: Anniv, Jun 30
Bloodworth-Thomason, Linda: Birth, Apr 15
Bloody Sunday (Northern Ireland): Anniv, Jan 30
Bloom, Claire: Birth, Feb 15
Bloom, Harold: Birth, Jul 11
Bloom, Orlando: Birth, Jan 13
Bloomberg, Michael: Birth, Feb 14
Bloomer, Amelia Jenks: Birth Anniv, May 27
Bloomsday: Anniv, Jun 16
Blue Claw Crab Craft Show & Crab Race (Harvey Cedars, NJ), Aug 19
Blue Hill Fair (Blue Hill, ME), Aug 31
Blue Ribbon Week, Natl (Child Abuse), Apr 2
Blue Ridge Folklife Fest (Ferrum, VA), Oct 28
Blueberries Month, Natl, Jul 1
Blueberry Arts Fest (Ketchikan, AK), Aug 5
Blueberry Fest (Montrose, PA), Aug 4
Blueberry Fest, Natl (South Haven, MI), Aug 10
Bluegrass. See also Fiddlers
　Bluegrass Fest (Alta, WY), Aug 11
　Bluegrass Fest (Hope, AR), May 12
　Bluegrass Fest, Ocean County (Waretown, NJ), Sep 10
　Fest of the Bluegrass (Lexington, KY), Jun 8
　Four Corner States Bluegrass Fest (Wickenburg, AZ), Nov 11
　Gettysburg Bluegrass Fest (Gettysburg, PA), May 18
　Gettysburg Fall Bluegrass Fest (Gettysburg, PA), Aug 24
　Homeplace Fest (Waretown, NJ), Nov 18
　Kentucky State Chmpshp Fiddler's Contest (Falls of Rough, KY), Jul 21
　Ladies of Country Music Show (Waretown, NJ), Jun 24
　Lil Margaret's Bluegrass and Old-Time Music Fest (Leonardtown, MD), Aug 10
　Lonesome River Band Music Fest (Live Oak, FL), Apr 6
　Nova Scotia Oldtime Music Fest (Stewiacke, NS), Jul 28
　Ocean County Bluegrass Fest (Waretown, NJ), Feb 5
　Old Fiddlers' Conv (Galax, VA), Aug 7
　Old-Time Fiddlers' Jamboree (Smithville, TN), Jun 30
　Polk County Ramp Tramp Fest (Benton, TN), Apr 22
　Red, White & Bluegrass (Hollywood, FL), May 12
　Thomas Point Beach Bluegrass Fest (Brunswick, ME), Aug 31
Blues Fest, Chicago (Chicago, IL), Jun 1
Bluford, Guion S., Jr: Birth, Nov 22
Blume, Judy: Birth, Feb 12
Blunt, Matt: Birth, Nov 20
Bly, Nellie: Around the World in 72 Days: Anniv, Jan 25
Bly, Nellie: Birth Anniv, May 5
Bly, Robert: Birth, Dec 23
Boats, Ships, Things That Float. See also Rowing
　Antique/Classic Boat Rendezvous (Mystic, CT), Jul 22
　Art Armada (Sheboygan, WI), Jul 4
　Big Ten Women's Rowing (Minneapolis, MN), Apr 29
　Burlington Steamboat Days/Music Fest (Burlington, IA), Jun 13
　Calgary Boat/Sportsmen's Show (Calgary, AB, Canada), Feb 9
　Canoe, Capstan & Cargo (Williamsburg and Yorktown, VA), Jun 1
　Civil War Submarine Attack: Anniv, Oct 5
　Classic Boat Fest (Victoria, BC, Canada), Sep 1
　Classic Boat Show (Tuckerton, NJ), Aug 19
　Commencement Bay Maritime Fest (Tacoma, WA), Sep 16
　Coshocton Canal Fest (Coshocton, OH), Aug 19
　Devizes/Westminster Intl Canoe Race (Devizes, England), Apr 14
　Edmund Fitzgerald Sinking: Anniv, Nov 10

　First American to Circumnavigate Earth: Anniv, Apr 10
　Fort Lauderdale Intl Boat Show (Fort Lauderdale, FL), Oct 26
　Frenchman Rows Across Pacific: Anniv, Nov 21
　Fulton Sails Steamboat: Anniv, Aug 17
　Grand Rapids Boat Show (Grand Rapids, MI), Feb 15
　Halifax, Nova Scotia, Destroyed: Anniv, Dec 6
　Head of the River Race (London, England), Mar 25
　Henley Royal Regatta (Henley-on-Thames, England), Jun 28
　Historical Regatta (Venice, Italy), Sep 3
　Louisiana Sportsmen's Show (New Orleans, LA), Mar 8
　Loyalty Days and Seafair Fest (Newport, OR), May 4
　Maritime Heritage Fest (St. Mary's City, MD), Jun 17
　Merrimac Destroyed: Anniv, May 11
　Miami Intl Boat/Sailboat Show (Miami Beach, FL), Feb 16
　Milwaukee Boat Show (Milwaukee, WI), Jan 20
　Monitor Sinking: Anniv, Dec 30
　New Orleans Boat Show (New Orleans, LA), Feb 8
　Newport Intl Boat Show (Newport, RI), Sep 14
　Ohio River Sternwheel Fest (Marietta, OH), Sep 8
　Ottawa Boat/Sportsmen's Show (Ottawa, ON, Canada), Feb 23
　Palio del Golfo (La Spezia, Italy), Aug 13
　Queen Mary, RMS: Anniv, May 27
　Remember the Maine Day, Feb 15
　River City Rumble Boat Races (Demopolis, AL), Jul 15
　Royal George Sinks: Anniv, Aug 29
　Safe Boating Week, Natl, May 20
　Safe Boating Week, Natl (Pres Proc), May 20
　Sailfest (Island Heights, NJ), Sep 8
　San Diego Boat Show (San Diego, CA), Jan 5
　Schroders London Boat Show (London, England), Jan 5
　Sea Music Fest (Mystic, CT), Jun 8
　Seattle Boat Show (Seattle, WA), Jan 13
　Skandia Cowes Week (Isle of Wight), Jul 29
　Small Craft Weekend (Mystic, CT), Jun 3
　SOS Adopted: Anniv, Nov 3
　South Jersey Canoe/Kayak Classic (Lakewood, NJ), Jun 3
　Spanish War/Maine Memorial Day, Feb 15
　Sternwheeler Days (Cascade Locks, OR), Jun 23
　Toms River Seaport Society Wood Boat Fest (Toms River, NJ), Jul 8
　Tybee 500 (Hollywood, FL, and Tybee Island, GA), May 6
　Ultimate Fishing Show (Novi, MI), Jan 12
　Vancouver Intl Boat Show (Vancouver, BC, Canada), Feb 8
　Washington Boat Show (Washington, DC), Feb 22
　White River Water Carnival (Batesville, AR), Jul 29
　Whitewater Wednesday (Kernville, CA), Jun 21
　Windjammer Days (Boothbay Harbor, ME), Jun 27
　Winterfest Boat Parade (Fort Lauderdale, FL), Dec 16
　Yacht Race, Intl: Anniv, Aug 22
Bob Hope Show TV Premiere: Anniv, Oct 12
Bob Newhart Show TV Premiere: Anniv, Oct 10
Bob Wills Day (Turkey, TX), Apr 29
Bochco, Steven: Birth, Dec 16
Bock, Jerry: Birth, Nov 23
Bocuse, Paul: Birth, Feb 11
Bodman, Samuel: Birth, Nov 26
Boer War: Anniv, Oct 12
Boff, Leonardo: Birth, Dec 14
Bogart, Humphrey: Birth Anniv, Dec 25
Bogdanovich, Peter: Birth, Jul 30
Boggs, Wade: Birth, Jun 15
Bogosian, Eric: Birth, Apr 24
Bogues, Muggsy: Birth, Jan 9
Boitano, Brian: Birth, Oct 22
Bol, Manute: Birth, Oct 16
Bold and the Beautiful TV Premiere: Anniv, Mar 23
Boleyn, Anne: Execution Anniv, May 19
Bolin, Jane M.: Birth, Apr 11
Bolivar, Simon: Birth Anniv, Jul 24
Bolivar, Simon: Death Anniv, Dec 17
Bolivia
　Alacitis Fair, Jan 24
　Independence Day, Aug 6
　La Paz Day, Jul 16
Boll, Heinrich: Birth Anniv, Dec 21
Bolles, Don: Death Anniv, Jun 13
Bollingen Prize Award: Anniv, Feb 19
Bologna, Joseph: Birth, Dec 30
Bolton, Michael: Birth, Feb 27
Bombeck, Erma: Birth Anniv, Feb 21
Bombing, Oklahoma City: Anniv, Apr 19
Bombing, World Trade Center: Anniv, Feb 26

Bon Fest (Feast of Lanterns) (Japan), Jul 13
Bon Jovi, Jon: Birth, Mar 2
Bonaduce, Danny: Birth, Aug 13
Bonaparte, Napoleon: Birth Anniv, Aug 15
Bond, Carrie Jacobs: Birth Anniv, Aug 11
Bond, Christopher S.: Birth, Mar 6
Bond, Julian: Birth, Jan 14
Bonds Breaks Home Run Record: Anniv, Oct 5
Bonds, Barry: Birth, Jul 24
Bonds, Gary U.S.: Birth, Jun 6
Bonerz, Peter: Birth, Aug 6
Bonet, Lisa: Birth, Nov 16
Bonham Carter, Helena: Birth, May 26
Bonheur, Rosa: Birth Anniv, Mar 16
Bonilla, Bobby: Birth, Feb 23
Bonnie and Clyde: Death Anniv, May 23
Bonnie Blue Natl Horse Show (Lexington, VA), May 10
Bono: Birth, May 10
Bonsall, Brian: Birth, Dec 3
Bonza Bottler Day, Jan 1, Feb 2, Mar 3, Apr 4, May 5, Jun 6, Jul 7, Aug 8, Sep 9, Oct 10, Nov 11, Dec 12
Book and Copyright Day, World (UN), Apr 23
Book Month, Natl, Oct 1
Books for Treats Day (San Jose, CA), Oct 31
Books. See also Library/Librarians
  Appreciate a Dragon Day, Jan 16
  Authors' Day, Natl, Nov 1
  Banff Mountain Book Fest (Banff, AB, Canada), Nov 1
  Banned Books Week, Sep 23
  Bible Week, Natl, Nov 19
  Biographers Day, May 16
  Book Blitz Month, Jan 1
  Book Day (Spain), Apr 23
  Book Month, Natl, Oct 1
  BookExpo America (Washington, DC), May 19
  Children's Authors & Illustrators Week, Feb 5
  Children's Book Day, Intl, Apr 2
  Children's Book Week, Natl, Nov 13
  Copyright Law Passed: Anniv, May 31
  Copyright Revision Law: Anniv, Jan 1
  Cyberspace Coined: Neuromancer Publication Anniv, Oct 1
  Dictionary Day, Oct 16
  Farmer's Almanac Editor Ray Geiger: Birth Anniv, Sep 18
  First Dictionary of American English Published: Anniv, Apr 14
  Frankfurt Book Fair (Frankfurt, Germany), Oct 4
  Get Caught Reading Month, May 1
  Gettysburg Civil War Book Fair (Gettysburg, PA), Jun 30
  Ghostwriters Week, Natl, Mar 1
  GLBT Book Month, Natl, Jun 1
  Gone with the Wind Published: Anniv, May 19
  Grapes of Wrath Published: Anniv, Apr 14
  Guadalajara Intl Book Fair (Guadalajara, Mexico), Nov 25
  Gutenberg Bible Published: Anniv, Sep 30
  Joy of Cooking Publication Anniv, Nov 30
  Joy of Sex Published: Anniv, Oct 1
  King James Bible Published: Anniv, May 2
  Literature Fest (Norfolk, NE), Jul 29
  London Book Fair (London, England), Mar 5
  Lord of the Rings, First Part Published: Anniv, Jul 19
  Maltese Falcon: Publication Anniv, Feb 14
  Melville (Moby-Dick) Marathon (Mystic, CT), Jul 31
  Newberry Library's Annual Book Fair (Chicago, IL), Jul 28
  On the Origin of Species Published: Anniv, Nov 22
  Paperback Books Introduced: Anniv, Jul 30
  R.E.A.D. in America Day (Washington, DC), Sep 23
  Read an E-Book Week, Mar 5
  Reading Group Month, Natl, Oct 1
  Reading Is Fun Week, May 14
  Return the Borrowed Books Week, Mar 1
  Romance Reader's Luncheon (Portland, OR), Apr 22
  Small Press Month, Mar 1
  Southern Fest of Books (Memphis, TN), Oct 13
  Teen Read Week, Oct 15
  Young Reader's Day, Natl, Nov 14
Boom Box Parade (Willimantic, CT), Jul 4
Boom Days (Leadville, CO), Aug 4
Boomer Bonus Day, Apr 1
Boone, Bret: Birth, Apr 6
Boone, Daniel: Battle of Blue Licks Celebration (Mount Olivet, KY), Aug 19
Boone, Daniel: Birth Anniv, Nov 2
Boone, Daniel: Boone Day, Jun 7
Boone, Debbie: Birth, Sep 22
Boone, Pat: Birth, Jun 1
Boonesborough Days (Boonsboro, MD), Sep 9
Boorman, John: Birth, Jan 18

Boosler, Elayne: Birth, Aug 18
Booth, Edwin: Birth Anniv, Nov 13
Booth, Evangeline: Birth Anniv, Dec 25
Booth, John Wilkes, Escape Route Tour (Clinton, MD), Apr 15
Booth, Shirley: Birth Anniv, Aug 30
Booth, William: Birth Anniv, Apr 10
Borden, Lizzie, Verdict: Anniv, Jun 20
Borden, Sir Robert Laird: Birth Anniv, Jun 26
Boreanaz, David: Birth, May 16
Borg, Bjorn: Birth, Jun 6
Borges, Jorge Luis: Birth Anniv, Aug 24
Borglum, Gutzon: Birth Anniv, Mar 25
Borgnine, Ernest: Birth, Jan 24
Borman, Frank: Birth, Mar 14
Borneo Rhino Challenge (Malaysia), May 14
Bosley, Tom: Birth, Oct 1
Bosnia and Herzegovina
  Independence Day, Mar 1
  National Day, Nov 25
Boss Day, Natl, Oct 16
Boss/Employee Exchange Day, Natl, Sep 11
Boston Fire: Anniv, Nov 9
Boston Harborfest (Boston, MA), Jun 28
Boston Marathon (Boston, MA), Apr 17
Boston Massacre: Anniv, Mar 5
Boston Public Library: Anniv, Apr 3
Boston Tea Party: Anniv, Dec 16
Bostwick, Barry: Birth, Feb 24
Boswell, James: Birth Anniv, Oct 29
Bosworth, Kate: Birth, Jan 2
Botswana
  Independence Day, Sep 30
  Sir Seretse Khama Day, Jul 1
Bottled Water Week, Sep 17
Bottoms, Timothy: Birth, Aug 30
Boucher, Brian: Birth, Jan 2
Boulez, Pierre: Birth, Mar 26
Bounty, Mutiny on the: Anniv, Apr 28
Bourke-White, Margaret: Birth Anniv, Jun 14
Bourque, Ray: Birth, Dec 28
Boutros-Ghali, Boutros: Birth, Nov 14
Bowditch, Nathaniel: Birth Anniv, Mar 26
Bowdler's Day, Jul 11
Bowe, Riddick: Birth, Aug 10
Bowen, Julie: Birth, Mar 3
Bowie, David: Birth, Jan 8
Bowman, Scotty: Birth, Sep 18
Boxer, Barbara: Birth, Nov 11
Boxing
  Clay Becomes Heavyweight Champ: Anniv, Feb 25
  Corbett-Fitzsimmons Title Fight: Anniv, Mar 17
  Corbett-Sullivan Prize Fight: Anniv, Sep 7
  First US Heavyweight Champ Defeated: Anniv, Dec 10
  Johnson, John (Jack) Arthur: Birth Anniv, Mar 31
  Long Count Day, Sep 22
  Louis v Braddock/Schmeling Fight Anniv, Jun 22
  Louis, Joe: Birth Anniv, May 13
  Muhammad Ali Stripped of Title: Anniv, Apr 30
Boxing Day (United Kingdom), Dec 26
Boxing Day Bank Holiday (United Kingdom), Dec 26
Boxleitner, Bruce: Birth, May 12
Boy George: Birth, Jun 14
Boy Scouts of America Founded: Anniv, Feb 8
Boy Scouts: Baden-Powell, Robert: Birth Anniv, Feb 22
Boycott, Charles C.: Birth Anniv, Mar 12
Boyd, Belle: Birth Anniv, May 9
Boyd, William: Birth Anniv, Jun 5
Boyer, Charles: Birth Anniv, Aug 28
Boyle, Lara Flynn: Birth, Mar 24
Boyle, Peter: Birth, Oct 18
Boyle, Robert: Birth Anniv, Jan 25
Boyle, T. Coraghessan: Birth, Dec 2
Boys' Clubs Founded: Anniv, May 19
Bracco, Lorraine: Birth, Oct 2
Brackett Day, Joseph, May 6
Bradbury, Ray: Birth, Aug 22
Braddock, James: Birth Anniv, Jun 7
Bradford, Barbara Taylor: Birth, May 10
Bradford, William: Birth Anniv, Mar 19
Bradlee, Benjamin: Birth, Aug 26
Bradley, Bill: Birth, Jul 28
Bradley, Ed: Birth, Jun 22
Bradshaw, Terry: Birth, Sep 2
Bradstreet: Anne Bradstreet Day, Sep 16
Brady Bunch TV Premiere: Anniv, Sep 26
Brady, Mathew: First Presidential Photograph: Anniv, Feb 14
Brady, Sarah: Birth, Feb 6
Brady, Tom: Birth, Aug 3
Braff, Zach: Birth, Apr 6
Braga, Sonia: Birth, Jun 16
Brahms Requiem Premiere: Anniv, Apr 10
Braille, Louis: Birth Anniv, Jan 4
Brain Awareness Week, Intl, Mar 13

Branagh, Kenneth: Birth, Dec 10
Branch Davidian Fire at Waco: Anniv, Apr 19
Brand, Elton: Birth, Mar 11
Brand, Oscar: Birth, Feb 7
Brandauer, Klaus Maria: Birth, Jun 22
Brandeis, Louis D.: Birth Anniv, Nov 13
Brando, Marlon: Birth Anniv, Apr 3
Brando, Marlon: Godfather Film Premiere: Anniv, Mar 15
Brandt, Willy: Birth Anniv, Dec 18
Brandy: Birth, Feb 11
Branson Fest (Branson, MO), Apr 4
Branson Veterans Homecoming (Branson, MO), Nov 5
Brasilia Inaugurated: Anniv, Apr 21
Bratt, Benjamin: Birth, Dec 16
Braugher, Andre: Birth, Jul 1
Braxton, Carter: Birth Anniv, Sep 10
Braxton, Toni: Birth, Oct 7
Brazil
  Carnival, Feb 25
  Cirio de Nazare, Oct 8
  Discovery of Brazil Day, Apr 22
  Fest of Penha (Rio de Janeiro), Oct 1
  Independence Day, Sep 7
  Independence Week, Sep 1
  Nosso Senhor Do Bonfim Fest, Jan 20
  Republic Day, Nov 15
  San Sebastian's Day, Jan 20
  Tiradentes Day, Apr 21
Brazleton, T. Berry: Birth, May 10
Brazzi, Rossano: Birth Anniv, Sep 18
Breach of Promise Suit, First US: Anniv, Jun 14
Bread Day, Homemade, Nov 17
Bread Pudding Recipe Exchange, May 1
Breakfast Club Radio Premiere: Anniv, Jun 23
Bream, Julian: Birth, Jul 15
Breast Cancer Awareness Month, Natl, Oct 1
Breast Cancer Awareness Month, Natl (Pres Proc), Oct 1
Breast Cancer: Pajama Month, Natl, Oct 1
Breathed, Berke: Birth, Jun 21
Brecht, Bertolt: Birth Anniv, Feb 10
Breckinridge, John Cabell: Birth Anniv, Jan 21
Bredesen, Phil: Birth, Nov 21
Brennan, Eileen: Birth, Sep 3
Brennan, William: Birth Anniv, Apr 25
Brenneman, Amy: Birth, Jun 22
Brenner, David: Birth, Feb 4
Brent, Margaret: Demands a Political Voice: Anniv, Jan 21
Brett, George: Birth, May 15
Brewer, Theresa: Birth, May 7
Breweriana: Summerswap (Frankenmuth, MI), Jul 15
Brewers Fest, Oregon (Portland, OR), Jul 27
Breyer, Stephen G.: Birth, Aug 15
Brezhnev, Leonid: Birth Anniv, Dec 19
Brickell, Edie: Birth, Mar 10
Brickhouse, Jack: Birth Anniv, Jan 24
Bridal Expo (Santa Cruz, CA), Jan 29
Bridge Day (Fayetteville, WV), Oct 21
Bridge Fest, Covered (Washington County, PA), Sep 16
Bridge Fest, Parke County Covered (Rockville, IN), Oct 13
Bridge over the Neponset: Anniv, Apr 1
Bridgeport, Siege of (Bridgeport, AL), Mar 17
Bridger, Jim: Birth Anniv, Mar 17
Bridges, Beau: Birth, Dec 9
Bridges, Jeff: Birth, Dec 4
Bridges, Todd: Birth, May 27
Brimley, Wilford: Birth, Sep 27
Brinkley, Christie: Birth, Feb 2
Brinkley, David: Birth Anniv, Jul 10
Brisebois, Danielle: Birth, Jun 28
Britain Declares War on Germany: Anniv, Sep 3
British and World Marbles Chmpshp, Apr 14
British Museum: Anniv, Jan 15
British North America Act: Anniv, Mar 29
British Open (Open Chmpshp) (Hoylake, England), Jul 20
Brittany, Morgan: Birth, Dec 5
Britten, (Edward) Benjamin: Birth Anniv, Nov 22
Broadbent, Jim: Birth, May 24
Broadway: Oklahoma! Premiere: Anniv, Mar 31
Brock, Lou: Birth, Jun 18
Broderick, Matthew: Birth, Mar 21
Brodeur, Martin: Birth, May 6
Brody, Adam: Birth, Dec 15
Brody, Adrien: Birth, Apr 14
Brokaw, Tom: Birth, Feb 6
Brolin, James: Birth, Jul 18
Brolin, Josh: Birth, Feb 12
Bronson, Charles: Birth Anniv, Nov 3
Bronte, Charlotte: Birth Anniv, Apr 21
Bronte, Emily: Birth Anniv, Jul 30
Brook, Peter: Birth, Mar 21

Brookfield Summer Fun Days (Brookfield, MO), Jun 15
Brooklyn Bridge Opened: Anniv, May 24
Brooks, Albert: Birth, Jul 22
Brooks, Garth: Birth, Feb 7
Brooks, James David: Birth Anniv, Oct 18
Brooks, James L.: Birth, May 9
Brooks, Jason: Birth, May 10
Brooks, Louise: Birth Anniv, Nov 14
Brooks, Mel: Birth, Jun 28
Brooks, Phillips: Birth Anniv, Dec 13
Brosnan, Pierce: Birth, May 16
Brother's Day, May 24
Brothers, Joyce: Birth, Sep 20
Brothers: Siblings Day, Natl, Apr 10
Brougham, Henry P.: Birth Anniv, Sep 19
Brown v Board of Education: Anniv, May 17
Brown, Bobby: Birth, Feb 5
Brown, Bryan: Birth, Jun 23
Brown, Curtis, Jr: Birth, Mar 11
Brown, Helen Gurley: Birth, Feb 18
Brown, James: Birth, May 3
Brown, Jesse Leroy: Birth Anniv, Oct 13
Brown, Jim: Birth, Feb 17
Brown, John: Birth Anniv, May 9
Brown, John: Execution Anniv, Dec 2
Brown, John: Raid Anniv, Oct 16
Brown, Louise: First Test-Tube Baby: Birth, Jul 25
Brown, Tina: Birth, Dec 21
Brown, Tony: Birth, Apr 11
Brownback, Sam: Birth, Sep 12
Browne, Jackson: Birth, Oct 9
Browne, Thomas: Birth Anniv, Oct 19
Browning, Elizabeth Barrett: Birth Anniv, Mar 6
Browning, John Moses: Birth Anniv, Jan 21
Browning, Robert: Birth Anniv, May 7
Brownmiller, Susan: Birth, Feb 15
Broz, Josip "Tito": Birth Anniv, May 25
Brubeck, Dave: Birth, Dec 6
Bruce, Isaac: Birth, Nov 10
Bruce, Lenny: Birth Anniv, Oct 13
Bruckner, Anton: Birth Anniv, Sep 4
Brummell, Beau: Birth Anniv, Jun 7
Brunei: National Day, Feb 23
Brunell, Mark: Birth, Sep 17
Brutus Day, Mar 15
Bryan, William Jennings: Birth Anniv, Mar 19
Bryan, Zachery Ty: Birth, Oct 9
Bryant, Anita: Birth, Mar 25
Bryant, Kobe: Birth, Aug 23
Bryant, William C.: Birth Anniv, Nov 3
Bryce Canyon Natl Park Established: Anniv, Jan 1
Bryson, Peabo: Birth, Apr 13
Bubba Day, Natl, Jun 2
Bubble Gum Day, Feb 1
Bubble Week, Natl, Mar 20
Bubble Wrap Appreciation Day, Jan 30
Buchanan, James: Birth Anniv, Apr 23
Buchanan, Patrick: Birth, Nov 2
Buchwald, Art: Birth, Oct 20
Buck Rogers TV Premiere: Anniv, Apr 15
Buck, Pearl S.: Birth Anniv, Jun 26
Buckingham, Lindsey: Birth, Oct 3
Buckley, Betty: Birth, Jul 3
Buckley, William F., Jr: Birth, Nov 24
Buckner, Bill: Birth, Dec 14
Buckwheat Fest, Preston County (Kingwood, WV), Sep 28
Buddha: Birth Anniv, Apr 8
Buddha: Birthday (China), May 5
Buell, Marjorie H.: Birth Anniv, Dec 11
Buffalo Auction (Custer, SD), Nov 18
Buffalo Bill (William F. Cody): Birth Anniv, Feb 26
Buffalo Days Celebration (Luverne, MN), Jun 2
Buffalo Roundup (Custer, SD), Sep 29
Buffalo Roundup Arts Fest (Custer, SD), Sep 30
Buffett, Jimmy: Birth, Dec 25
Buffy the Vampire Slayer TV Premiere: Anniv, Mar 10
Bugs Bunny's Debut: Anniv, Apr 30
Buhl Day (Sharon, PA), Sep 4
Building on Faith Week, Habitat for Humanity Intl's, Sep 10
Bujold, Genevieve: Birth, Jul 1
Bulgaria
    Babin Den (Day of the Midwives), **Jan 23**
    Culture Day, **May 24**
    Hristo Botev Day, **Jun 2**
    Liberation Day, **Mar 3**
    Saint Lasarus's Day, **Apr 1**
    Unification Day, **Sep 6**
    Viticulturists' Day, **Feb 14**
Bullfinch Exchange Fest (Japan), Jan 7
Bullnanza (Guthrie, OK), Jan 27
Bullock, Sandra: Birth, Jul 26
Bullwinkle Show: Rocky and His Friends TV Premiere: Anniv, Nov 19

Bullying: Freedom from Bullies Week, Oct 16
Bumbershoot: The Seattle Arts Fest (Seattle, WA), Sep 1
Bun Day (Iceland), Feb 27
Bunche, Ralph: Awarded Nobel Peace Prize: Anniv, Dec 10
Bunche, Ralph: Birth Anniv, Aug 7
Bunker Hill Day (Suffolk County, MA), Jun 17
Bunning, Jim: Birth, Oct 23
Bunsen Burner Day, Mar 31
Bunsen, Robert: Birth, Mar 31
Bunyan, John: Birth Anniv, Nov 28
Buonarroti, Michelangelo: Birth Anniv, Mar 6
Buoniconti, Nick: Birth, Dec 15
Burbank, Luther: Birth Anniv, Mar 7
Burdon, Eric: Birth, Apr 5
Bure, Candace Cameron: Birth, Apr 6
Bure, Pavel: Birth, Mar 31
Bureau of Indian Affairs Established, Mar 11
Bureau of Internal Revenue Established: Anniv, Jul 1
Burger, Warren E.: Birth Anniv, Sep 17
Burgess, Anthony: Birth Anniv, Feb 25
Burghoff, Gary: Birth, May 24
Burgoo Fest (Utica, IL), Oct 8
Burk, Martha (Calamity Jane): Death Anniv, Aug 1
Burke, Christopher: Birth, Aug 26
Burke, Delta: Birth, Jul 30
Burke, Edmund: Birth Anniv, Jan 12
Burkina Faso
    National Day, Dec 11
    Republic Day, Aug 5
    Revolution Day, Aug 4
Burnett, Carol: Birth, Apr 26
Burnham, Daniel: Birth Anniv, Sep 4
Burnquist, Bob: Birth, Oct 10
Burns and Allen Show TV Premiere: Anniv, Oct 12
Burns, Conrad: Birth, Jan 25
Burns, George: Birth Anniv, Jan 20
Burns, Ken: Birth, Jul 29
Burns, Robert: Birth Anniv, Jan 25
Burr, Aaron: Birth Anniv, Feb 6
Burr, Aaron: Duel with Alexander Hamilton: Anniv, Jul 11
Burr, Raymond: Birth Anniv, May 21
Burr, Richard: Birth, Nov 30
Burro Race (Leadville, CO), Aug 6
Burroughs, Edgar Rice: Birth Anniv, Sep 1
Burroughs, John: Birth Anniv, Apr 3
Burrows, James: Birth, Dec 30
Bursting Day (Iceland), Feb 28
Burstyn, Ellen: Birth, Dec 7
Burton, LeVar: Birth, Feb 16
Burton, Richard: Birth Anniv, Nov 10
Burton, Tim: Birth, Aug 25
Burundi
    Assassination of the Hero of the Nation Day, Oct 13
    Independence Day, Jul 1
Buscemi, Steve: Birth, Dec 13
Busey, Gary: Birth, Jun 29
Busfield, Timothy: Birth, Jun 12
Bush, Barbara Pierce: Birth, Jun 8
Bush, George H.W. and Barbara, Wedding: Anniv, Jan 6
Bush, George Herbert Walker: Birthday, Jun 12
Bush, George W. and Laura, Wedding: Anniv, Nov 5
Bush, George W.: Birthday, Jul 6
Bush, George W.: Supreme Court Rules for Bush: Anniv, Dec 12
Bush, Jeb: Birth, Feb 11
Bush, Kate: Birth, Jul 30
Bush, Laura: Birthday, Nov 4
Business (including business history, skills, workplace life, types of). See also Careers
    American Business Women's Day, Sep 22
    AT&T Divestiture: Anniv, Jan 8
    Be Heard Day, Natl, Mar 7
    Better Business Communication Day, Jan 23
    Black Business Month, Aug 1
    Boss/Employee Exchange Day, Natl, Sep 11
    Bring Your Teddy Bear to Work Day, Natl, Oct 11
    Build Your Business with Business Cards Week, Oct 8
    Business Image Improvement Month, Intl, May 1
    Business of America Quotation: Anniv, Jan 17
    Business Resolutions Month, Intl, Jan 1
    Business Women's Week, Natl, Oct 16
    Celebrate Micro Small & Home Business Week, Oct 16
    Clean-Off-Your-Desk Day, Natl, Jan 9
    Companies That Care Day, Mar 16
    Computer Security Day, Nov 30
    Craft Brewers Conf & BrewExpo America (Seattle, WA), Apr 11
    Credit Union Week, Intl, Oct 15

Customer Loyalty Month, Intl, **Apr 1**
Customer Service Day, **Jan 17**
Enron Files for Bankruptcy: Anniv, **Dec 2**
Entrepreneurs "Do It Yourself" Marketing Month, **Jun 1**
Ethics Awareness Month, Natl, **Mar 1**
Fair Trade Day, World, **May 13**
Families in Business Week, **Jun 12**
Federal Govt Seizure of Steel Mills: Anniv, **Apr 8**
Five-Dollar-a-Day Minimum Wage: Anniv, **Jan 5**
Fun at Work Day, **Jan 27**
Fun at Work Day, Natl, **Apr 6**
Get to Know Your Customer Day, **Jan 19**
Getting World to Beat a Path to Your Door Week, **Oct 15**
Google Founded: Anniv, **Sep 7**
Home-Based Business Week, **Oct 8**
Independent Retailers Week, Natl, **Jul 16**
Innovation Week Intl, **Apr 23**
Irrational Exuberance Enters Lexicon: Anniv, **Dec 5**
Just Say No to PowerPoint Week, **Feb 6**
Laugh and Get Rich Day, **Feb 8**
Laugh at Work Week, **Apr 1**
Leadership Success Day, **Feb 7**
Leadership Week Intl, **Apr 10**
Ludlow Mine Incident: Anniv, **Apr 20**
Mail-Order Catalog: Anniv, **Aug 18**
Microfinance Month, Intl, **Nov 1**
Mom and Pop Business Owners Day, Natl, **Mar 29**
Montgomery Ward Seized: Anniv, **Apr 26**
Networking Week, Natl, **Apr 10**
New York Stock Exchange: Anniv, **May 17**
On-Hold Month, Natl, **Mar 1**
Printing Week, Intl, **Jan 15**
Professional Wellness Month, **Jun 1**
Publicity for Profit Week, **Feb 1**
Recess at Work Day, **Jun 15**
Revise Your Work Schedule Month, **May 1**
Scrapbooking Industry Day, Intl, **Mar 4**
Shameless Promotion Month, **Sep 1**
Smith, Adam: Birth Anniv, **Jun 5**
Stay Home Because You're Well Day, **Nov 30**
Stop the Bad Service Day, **Mar 1**
Strategic Planning Month, Intl, **Oct 1**
Subliminal Communications Month, **Sep 1**
Support Your Local Chamber of Commerce Day, Natl, **Oct 18**
Synergy Week Intl, **Oct 22**
Take Our Daughters and Sons to Work Day, **Apr 27**
Thank-Your-Customers Week, Natl, **Jan 9**
Tourism Week, Natl, **May 13**
Triangle Shirtwaist Fire: Anniv, **Mar 25**
Women's Ecommerce Day, Intl, **Sep 19**
Women's Leadership Conference, Natl (Anaheim, CA), **Sep 28**
Women's Small Business Month, **Oct 1**
Work from Home Week, Natl, **Oct 1**
Work Like a Dog Day, **Aug 4**
Workplace Conflict Awareness Month, **Apr 1**
Workplace Napping Day, Natl, **Apr 3**
Workplace Politics Awareness Month, **Oct 1**
Butcher, Susan: Birth, Dec 26
Butkus, Dick: Birth, Dec 9
Butler, Benjamin: Farragut Captures New Orleans: Anniv, Apr 25
Butler, Brett: Birth, Jan 30
Butler, Dan: Birth, Dec 2
Butler, Samuel: Birth Anniv, Dec 4
Button, Dick: Birth, Jul 18
Buttons, Red: Birth, Feb 5
Butts, Alfred M.: Birth Anniv, Apr 13
Buy Nothing Day, Nov 24
Buzzi, Ruth: Birth, Jul 24
Bynes, Amanda: Birth, Apr 3
Byrd, Robert C.: Birth, Nov 20
Byrne, David: Birth, May 14
Byrne, Gabriel: Birth, May 12
Byrnes, Edd: Birth, Jul 30
Byron, George Gordon: Birth Anniv, Jan 22

Caan, James: Birth, Mar 26
Cabinet, US: Perkins, Frances (1st Woman Appointed), Mar 4
Cable Car Patent: Anniv, Jan 17
Cabrillo Day (CA), Sep 28
Cabrillo Fest (San Diego, CA), Sep 29
Cabrini, Mother Frances Xavier: Anniv, Jul 7
Caesar, Sid: Birth, Sep 8
Caesarean Section, First: Anniv, Jan 14
Caffeine Awareness Month, Natl, Mar 1
Cage, John: Birth Anniv, Sep 5
Cage, Nicolas: Birth, Jan 7
Cagney & Lacey TV Premiere: Anniv, Mar 25
Cahn, Sammy: Birth Anniv, Jun 18
Cain, Dean: Birth, Jul 31
Caine, Michael: Birth, Mar 14

Cal Farley's Boys Ranch Rodeo (Boys Ranch, TX), **Sep 2**
Calabro, Thomas: Birth, **Feb 3**
Calamity Jane (Martha Burk): Death Anniv, **Aug 1**
Calder, Alexander: Birth Anniv, **Jul 22**
Caldwell, Sarah: Birth, **Mar 6**
Caldwell, Zoe: Birth, **Sep 14**
Calendar Adjustment Day: Anniv, **Sep 2**
Calendar Day, Gregorian, **Feb 24**
Calendar Stone, Aztec, Discovery: Anniv, **Dec 17**
Calhoun, John C.: Birth Anniv, **Mar 18**
Calhoun, John C.: VP Resignation: Anniv, **Dec 28**
California
  Admission Day, **Sep 9**
  Aerospace Walk of Honor (Lancaster), **Sep 16**
  AFRMA Display & Show (Costa Mesa), **Jul 7**
  AFRMA Display at America's Family Pet Expo (Costa Mesa), **Apr 14**
  American Council on Education Annual Mtg (Los Angeles), **Feb 11**
  Bay to Breakers Race (San Francisco), **May 19**
  Beverly Hills Affaire in Gardens (Beverly Hills), **May 20**
  Blessing of the Fishing Fleet (San Francisco), **Oct 1**
  Bob Hope Chrysler Golf Classic (La Quinta), **Jan 16**
  Books for Treats Day (San Jose), **Oct 31**
  Boxer, Barbara: Birth, **Nov 11**
  Bridal Expo (Santa Cruz), **Jan 29**
  Cabrillo Day, **Sep 28**
  Cabrillo Fest (San Diego), **Sep 29**
  Calaveras Fair/Jumping Frog Jubilee (Angel Camp), **May 18**
  California Artichoke Fest (Castroville), **May 20**
  California Gold Discovery: Anniv, **Jan 24**
  California Poppy Fest (Lancaster), **Apr 22**
  California State Fair (Sacramento), **Aug 11**
  Carlsbad Marathon (Carlsbad), **Jan 15**
  Cesar Chavez Day, **Mar 31**
  Channel Islands Natl Park Established: Anniv, **Mar 5**
  Chinese New Year Fest (San Francisco), **Jan 21**
  Chinese New Year Golden Dragon Parade & Fest (Los Angeles), **Feb 4**
  Clam Chowder Cookoff (Santa Cruz), **Feb 25**
  Date Fest, Natl (Indio), **Feb 17**
  Davis, Gray: Birth, **Dec 26**
  Day of the Horse, Natl, **Dec 9**
  Disneyland Opened: Anniv, **Jul 17**
  Farmers Market (El Centro), **Jan 21**
  Feinstein, Dianne: Birth, **Jun 22**
  Festival of Children (Costa Mesa), **Sep 1**
  Fiesta La Ballona (Culver City), **Aug 26**
  Fortune Cookie Day (San Francisco), **Sep 13**
  Gilroy Garlic Fest (Gilroy), **Jul 28**
  Go Wild During California Wild Rice Month, **Sep 1**
  Golden Gate Bridge Opened: Anniv, **May 27**
  Grubstake Days (Yucca Valley), **May 25**
  Harvest Wine Celebration (Livermore), **Sep 3**
  Haute Dog Charity Easter Parade (Long Beach), **Apr 16**
  Haute Dog Charity Howl'oween Parade (Long Beach), **Oct 29**
  Huck Finn's Jubilee (Victorville), **Jun 16**
  Hypnosis Federation Conf, Intl (Los Angeles), **Aug 4**
  Invisible Chronic Illness Awareness Week, Natl (San Diego), **Sep 11**
  Kraft Nabisco Chmpshp (Rancho Mirage), **Mar 27**
  Lassen Volcanic Natl Park Established: Anniv, **Aug 9**
  Laura Ingalls Wilder Gingerbread Sociable (Pomona), **Feb 4**
  Long Beach Bayou Fest (Long Beach), **Jun 23**
  Los Angeles Founded: Anniv, **Sep 4**
  Los Angeles Riots: Anniv, **Apr 29**
  Mainly Mozart Fest (San Diego), **Jun 1**
  Mission San Carlos Borromeo de Carmelo: Founding Anniv, **Jun 3**
  Mobius Awards (Los Angeles), **Feb 10**
  Monterey Jazz Fest (Monterey), **Sep 15**
  Morro Bay Harbor Fest (Morro Bay), **Oct 7**
  Mother Goose Parade (El Cajon), **Nov 19**
  Mozart Fest (San Luis Obispo), **Jul 14**
  MS Walk (San Jose and Monterey), **Apr 1**
  NCAA Div I Men's and Women's Track Chmpshps (Sacramento), **Jun 7**
  NCAA Div I Women's Tennis Chmpshps (Stanford), **May 18**
  Nixon Birthday Holiday (Yorba Linda), **Jan 9**
  Pacific DanceSport Chmpshps (Los Angeles), **Nov 3**
  Pacific Life Holiday Bowl Parade/Game (San Diego), **Dec 28**
  Pasadena Doo Dah Parade (Pasadena), **Nov 19**
  Proposition 13: Anniv, **Jun 6**

Rat and Mouse Annual Show, Fancy (Riverside), **Jan 14**
  Redwood Natl Park Established: Anniv, **Oct 2**
  Rideshare Week, **Oct 2**
  Rose Bowl Game (Pasadena), **Jan 4**
  Sacramento Jazz Jubilee (Sacramento), **May 26**
  San Diego Boat Show (San Diego), **Jan 5**
  San Francisco Silent Film Fest (San Francisco), **Jul 14**
  Santa by Stage Coach Parade (El Centro), **Dec 2**
  Schwarzenegger, Arnold: Birth, **Jul 30**
  Sequoia and Kings Canyon Natl Park Established: Anniv, **Sep 25**
  Snowbirds Pancake Breakfast (El Centro), **Jan 14**
  Sonoma Valley Harvest Wine Auction (Sonoma), **Sep 1**
  Sonoma-Marin Fair (Petaluma), **Jun 21**
  Southern California Firestorms: Anniv, **Oct 25**
  Stamp Expo (Anaheim), **May 5, Sep 8**
  Stamp Expo (Los Angeles), **Mar 31**
  Stamp Expo (Pasadena), **Feb 17, May 19, Jun 30**
  Stamp Expo (Sherman Oaks), **Jun 16**
  Stamp Expo America (Anaheim), **Nov 10**
  Stamp Expo USA (Anaheim), **Feb 10**
  Stamp Expo: Anaheim (Anaheim), **Oct 6**
  Stamp Expo: California (Pasadena), **Nov 17**
  Stamp Expo: South (Anaheim), **Apr 28**
  Starman Family-Con 2006 (Hollywood), **Sep 15**
  Swallows Depart from San Juan Capistrano, **Oct 23**
  Swallows Return to San Juan Capistrano, **Mar 19**
  Tamale Fiesta (El Centro), **Dec 2**
  Taste of Morgan Hill (Morgan Hill), **Sep 23**
  Tournament of Roses Parade (Pasadena), **Jan 2**
  US Intl Film/Video Awards (Los Angeles), **Jun 2**
  Viva El Mariachi Fest (Fresno), **Mar 26**
  Whiskey Flat Days (Kernville), **Feb 17**
  Whitewater Wednesday (Kernville), **Jun 21**
  Women's Leadership Conference, Natl (Anaheim), **Sep 28**
  World Ag Expo (Tulare), **Feb 14**
  Yosemite Natl Park Established: Anniv, **Oct 1**
Call In Single Day, Natl, **Feb 14**
Callas, Maria: Birth Anniv, **Dec 2**
Callas, Maria: Last Performance: Anniv, **Jul 5**
Callow, Simon: Birth, **Jun 15**
Calloway, Cab: Birth Anniv, **Dec 25**
Calvin, John: Birth Anniv, **Jul 10**
Cambodia
  Constitutional Declaration Day, **Sep 24**
  Falls to the Khmer Rouge: Anniv, **Apr 17**
  Independence Day, **Nov 9**
  Invaded by US: Anniv, **Apr 30**
  Peace Treaty Day, **Oct 23**
  Pol Pot Overthrown: Anniv, **Jan 7**
Camden, Battle of: Anniv, **Aug 16**
Cameron, James: Birth, **Aug 16**
Cameron, James: Titanic Released: Anniv, **Dec 19**
Cameron, Kirk: Birth, **Oct 12**
Cameroon
  National Holiday: Anniv, **May 20**
  Volcanic Eruption: Anniv, **Aug 22**
  Youth Day, **Feb 11**
CAMEX (Houston, TX), **Mar 3**
Camp David Accord Signed: Anniv, **Mar 26**
Camp Fire Birthday Week, **Mar 13**
Camp Fire Founders Day, **Mar 17**
Camp Month, Natl Sign Up for Summer, **Dec 1**
Camp, Walter: Birth Anniv, **Apr 7**
Campanella, Roy: Birth Anniv, **Nov 19**
Campbell, Billy: Birth, **Jul 7**
Campbell, Christian: Birth, **May 12**
Campbell, Douglas: Becomes First American Air ACE: Anniv, **Apr 14**
Campbell, Earl: Birth, **Mar 29**
Campbell, Glen: Birth, **Apr 22**
Campbell, Kim: Birth, **Mar 10**
Campbell, Kim: Canada's First Woman Prime Minister: Anniv, **Jun 25**
Campbell, Malcolm: Birth Anniv, **Mar 11**
Campbell, Naomi: Birth, **May 22**
Campbell, Neve: Birth, **Oct 3**
Campion, Jane: Birth, **Apr 30**
Campos, Bruno: Birth, **Dec 3**
Camus, Albert: Birth Anniv, **Nov 7**
Canada
  Abbotsford Berry Fest (Abbotsford, BC), **Jul 7**
  Abbotsford Intl Airshow (Abbotsford, BC), **Aug 11**
  Agrifair (Abbotsford, BC), **Aug 3**
  Apple Blossom Fest (Annapolis Valley, NS), **May 31**
  Bancroft Frosty Frolics (Bancroft, ON), **Feb 12**
  Banff Mountain Book Fest (Banff, AB), **Nov 1**
  Banff Mountain Film Fest (Banff, AB), **Nov 3**
  Big Valley Jamboree (Camrose, AB), **Aug 4**
  Brantford's Elvis Festival (Brantford, ON), **Aug 24**
  British North America Act: Anniv, **Mar 29**

  Calgary Boat/Sportsmen's Show (Calgary, AB), **Feb 9**
  Calgary Folk Fest (Calgary, AB), **Jul 27**
  Calgary Stampede (Calgary, AB), **Jul 7**
  Canada Day, **Jul 1**
  Canada Day Celebration (Ottawa, ON), **Jul 1**
  Canada Day Celebrations (Squamish, BC), **Jul 1**
  Canada Day Party in the Park (Bancroft, ON), **Jul 1**
  Canada's Natl Ukrainian Fest (Dauphin, MB), **Aug 4**
  Canadian Open Fiddle Chmpshp (Shelburne, ON), **Aug 9**
  Canadian Tulip Fest (Ottawa, ON), **May 4**
  Canadian Western Agribition (Regina, SK), **Nov 20**
  Canmore Folk Music Fest (Canmore, AB), **Aug 5**
  Cisco Systems Ottawa Bluesfest (Ottawa, ON), **Jul 7**
  Civic Holiday, **Aug 7**
  Classic Boat Fest (Victoria, BC), **Sep 1**
  CN Tower: Anniv, **Jun 26**
  Coe Hill Agricultural Fair (Coe Hill, ON), **Aug 18**
  Constitution Act: Anniv, **Apr 18**
  Country Good Times (Wilberforce, ON), **Jul 14**
  Daylight Saving Time Begins, **Apr 2**
  Daylight Saving Time Ends, **Oct 29**
  Drowning Prevention Day, Natl, **Jul 22**
  Edmonton Folk Music Fest (Edmonton, AB), **Aug 10**
  Edmonton Intl Fringe Theatre Fest (Edmonton, AB), **Aug 17**
  Elmira Maple Syrup Fest (Elmira, ON), **Apr 1**
  Family Day in Alberta, **Feb 20**
  First Nights, **Dec 31**
  First Woman Prime Minister: Anniv, **Jun 25**
  Folklorama—Canada's Cultural Celebration (Winnipeg, MB), **Aug 6**
  Great Rendezvous (Thunder Bay, ON), **Jun 29**
  Guelph Spring Fest (Guelph, ON), **Apr 28**
  Halifax Intl Busker Fest (Halifax, NS), **Aug 10**
  Halifax, Nova Scotia, Destroyed: Anniv, **Dec 6**
  Harrison Fest of Arts (Harrison Hot Springs, BC), **Jul 8**
  Heritage Days (Chatham, ON), **Oct 7**
  Immigrants' Day, **May 22**
  Inuit Territory Approved: Anniv, **Nov 3**
  Just for Laughs Fest (Montreal, QC), **Jul 13**
  Kimberley Intl Accordion Chmpshp (Kimberley, BC), **Jul 3**
  Klondike Eldorado Gold Discovery: Anniv, **Aug 31**
  Klondike Gold Discovery: Anniv, **Aug 16**
  Labor Day, **Sep 4**
  Maple Fest of Nova Scotia (Northern Nova Scotia), **Mar 18**
  Maple Leaf Flag Adopted: Anniv, **Feb 15**
  Masters (Calgary, AB), **Sep 6**
  Maynooth Madness (Maynooth, ON), **Sep 1**
  Mineral Capital Rock Show (Bancroft, ON), **Jul 22**
  Mineral Collecting Field Trips (Bancroft, ON), **Jul 4**
  Montreal Hunting, Fishing & Camping Show (Montreal, QC), **Feb 23**
  Morden Corn/Apple Fest (Morden, MB), **Aug 25**
  Mourning, Natl Day of, **Apr 28**
  Multicultural Fest (Dartmouth, NS), **Jun 16**
  National Tournament (Calgary, AB), **Jun 7**
  Newfoundland Discovery Day, **Jun 26**
  Newfoundland: Saint George's Day, **Apr 24**
  North American Tournament (Calgary, AB), **Jul 5**
  North America's Coldest Recorded Temperature: Anniv, **Feb 3**
  Nova Scotia Bluegrass/Oldtime Music Fest (Stewiacke, NS), **Jul 28**
  Nova Scotia Intl Tattoo (Halifax, NS), **Jul 1**
  Nova Scotia's Gem and Mineral Show (Parrsboro, NS), **Aug 18**
  Nunavut Independence: Anniv, **Apr 1**
  Ojibwa Keeshigun (Thunder Bay, ON), **Aug 19**
  Oktoberfest (Kitchener/Waterloo, ON), **Oct 6**
  Ontario Winter Carnival Bon Soo (Sault Ste. Marie, ON), **Jan 27**
  Organizing Week, Natl, **May 1**
  Ottawa Boat/Sportsmen's Show (Ottawa, ON), **Feb 23**
  Ottawa Folk Fest (Ottawa, ON), **Aug 24**
  Persons Day, **Oct 18**
  Pioneer Days (Steinbach, MB), **Aug 4**
  Quebec City Hunting, Fishing & Camping Show (Quebec City, QC), **Mar 16**
  Rally of the Tall Pines (Bancroft, ON), **Nov 18**
  Remembrance Day, **Nov 11**
  Rockhound Gemboree (Bancroft, ON), **Jul 27**
  Saint Jean-Baptiste Day (Quebec, QC), **Jun 24**
  Saint Swithun's Celebration (Toronto, ON), **Jul 15**
  Sam Steele Days (Cranbrook, BC), **Jun 15**
  Shelburne County Lobster Fest (Shelburne County, NS), **Jun 1**
  Siege at Kanata (Brantford, ON), **Aug 12**
  Thanksgiving Day, **Oct 9**

Canada (cont'd)—Cates

Thunder Bay Chamber of Commerce Trade Show (Thunder Bay, ON), **May 4**
Toronto Intl Film Fest (Toronto, ON), **Sep 7**
Toronto Ski, Snowboard and Travel Show (Toronto, ON), **Oct 12**
Toronto Sportsmen's Show (Toronto, ON), **Mar 15**
Upper Canada Village (Morrisburg, ON), **May 20**
Vancouver Folk Music Fest (Vancouver, BC), **Jul 14**
Vancouver Intl Boat Show (Vancouver, BC), **Feb 8**
Victoria Day, **May 22**
Winnipeg Fringe Theatre Fest (Winnipeg, MB), **Jul 19**
Winnipeg Intl Children's Fest (Winnipeg, MB), **Jun 8**
Winterlude (Ottawa, ON), **Feb 3**
World Future Society Annual Conf (Toronto, ON), **Jul 28**
Yukon Discovery Day, **Aug 14**
Yukon Gold Panning (Dawson City, YT), **Jul 1**
Yukon Order of Pioneers: Anniv, **Dec 1**
Yukon Quest Intl 1,000-Mile Sled Dog Race (Whitehorse, YT), **Feb 11**
Yukon River Bathtub Race (Whitehorse, YT), **Aug 18**
Yukon Sourdough Rendezvous (Whitehorse, YT), **Feb 23**
Canadian Pacific RR: Transcontinental Completion Anniv, **Nov 7**
Canal Fest, Coshocton (Coshocton, OH), **Aug 19**
Canaletto, Giovanni Antonio: Birth Anniv, **Oct 18**
Canary Islands Plane Disaster: Anniv, **Mar 27**
Cancer (Zodiac) Begins, **Jun 21**
Cancer Control Month (Pres Proc), **Apr 1**
Cancer from the Sun Month, **Jun 1**
Cancer Survivors Day, Natl, **Jun 4**
Candid Camera TV Premiere: Anniv, **Aug 10**
Candlemas Day (Presentation of the Lord), **Feb 2**
Candy Month, Natl, **Jun 1**
Candy, John: Birth Anniv, **Oct 31**
Caniff, Milton: Birth Anniv, **Feb 28**
Cannes Film Fest (Cannes, France), **May 17**
Canning: Appert, Nicholas: Birth Anniv, **Oct 23**
Cannon, Annie Jump: Birth Anniv, **Dec 11**
Cannon, Dyan: Birth, **Jan 4**
Canoe, Capstan & Cargo (Williamsburg and Yorktown, VA), **Jun 1**
Canova, Diana: Birth, **Jun 2**
Canseco, Jose, Jr: Birth, **Jul 2**
Cantinflas: Birth Anniv, **Aug 12**
Cantrell, Lana: Birth, **Aug 7**
Cantwell, Maria: Birth, **Oct 13**
Capa, Robert: Birth Anniv, **Oct 22**
Cape Verde: National Day, **Jul 5**
Capek, Karel: Robot Enters World Lexicon: Anniv, **Jan 25**
Capital One Bowl (Orlando, FL), **Jan 2**
Capitol Cornerstone Laid, US: Anniv, **Sep 18**
Capitol Reef Natl Park Established: Anniv, **Dec 18**
Capone, Al: Birth Anniv, **Jan 17**
Capote, Truman: Birth Anniv, **Sep 30**
Capp, Al: Birth Anniv, **Sep 28**
Capra, Frank: Birth Anniv, **May 18**
Capriati, Jennifer: Birth, **Mar 29**
Capricorn Begins, **Dec 22**
Capshaw, Kate: Birth, **Nov 3**
Captain Kangaroo TV Premiere: Anniv, **Oct 3**
Captain Kangaroo: Keeshan, Bob: Birth Anniv, **Jun 27**
Captain Midnight TV Premiere: Anniv, **Sep 4**
Captain Video and His Video Rangers TV Premiere: Anniv, **Jun 27**
Captive Nations Week (Pres Proc), **Jul 16**
Car Care Month, Natl, **Apr 1**
Car Talk Natl Radio Premiere: Anniv, **Oct 31**
Cara, Irene: Birth, **Mar 18**
Carabao Fest (Philippines), **May 14**
Caraway, Hattie Wyatt: Birth Anniv, **Feb 1**
Caraway, Hattie Wyatt: First Elected Woman Senator: Anniv, **Jan 12**
Caray, Harry: Birth Anniv, **Mar 14**
Carbon-14 Dating Inventor (Libby): Birth Anniv, **Dec 17**
Carbonell, Nestor: Birth, **Dec 1**
Carcieri, Donald: Birth, **Dec 16**
Cardellini, Linda: Birth, **Jun 25**
Cardin, Pierre: Birth, **Jul 7**
Cardinale, Claudia: Birth, **Apr 15**
Care Sunday (England), **Apr 2**
Careers (employment, employees, occupations, professions). See also Business, Labor
Administrative Professionals Day, **Apr 26**
Administrative Professionals Intl Conv (New Orleans, LA), **Jul 23**
Administrative Professionals Week, **Apr 23**
American Society of Assn Executives Mtg/Expo (Boston, MA), **Aug 19**

Appreciate Your Plumbing, Heating and Cooling Professionals Week, **Jun 18**
Auctioneers Day, Natl, **Apr 15**
Automotive Service Professionals Week, Natl, **Jun 11**
Be Kind to Editors and Writers Month, **Sep 1**
Boss Day, Natl, **Oct 16**
Celebrate Job Loss Week, **Oct 23**
Columnist's Day, Natl, **Jun 27**
Companies That Care Day, **Mar 16**
Cranky Coworkers Day, **Oct 27**
Custodial Workers Day, Natl, **Oct 2**
Disability Employment Awareness Month, Natl, **Oct 1**
Emergency Nurses Day, **Oct 11**
Emergency Nurses Week, **Oct 8**
Engineers Week, Natl, **Feb 19**
Executive Coaching Day, **May 1**
Exhibitor Appreciation Week, **Aug 7**
Explore Your Career Options Week, **Apr 10**
Extraordinary Work Team Recognition Day, **Dec 4**
Family, Career and Community Leaders of America Natl Leadership Mtg (Nashville, TN), **Jul 9**
Family, Career and Community Leaders Week, Natl, **Feb 12**
First Flight Attendant: Anniv, **May 15**
Flexible Work Arrangements Week, **May 7**
Freedom from Bullies Week, **Oct 16**
Freelance Writers Appreciation Week, **Feb 6**
Get Paid to Shop Week, **Feb 5**
Goodwill Industries Week, **May 7**
Groundhog Job Shadow Day, **Feb 2**
Gruntled Workers Day, **Jul 13**
Hairstylist Day, **Apr 28**
Handshake Day, Natl, **Jun 28**
Home Inspector Appreciation Month, Natl, **Jul 1**
Hospital Admitting Clerks Day, **Apr 7**
Labor Day, **Sep 4**
Labor Day, **May 1**
Leave the Office Earlier Day, Natl, **Jun 2**
Legal Assistants Day, **Mar 26**
Meeting Planners Appreciation Day, Natl, **May 3**
Mom and Pop Business Owners Day, Natl, **Mar 29**
Nightshift Workers Day, Natl, **May 10**
Nurse Anesthetists Week, Natl, **Jan 22**
Nurses Day and Week, Natl, **May 6**
Nursing Assistants Day and Week, Natl, **Jun 15**
Nursing Conf on Pediatric Primary Care (Washington, DC), **Apr 5**
Occupational Therapy Month, Natl, **Apr 1**
Pastoral Care Week, **Oct 22**
Pawnbrokers Day, Natl, **Dec 6**
Payroll Week, Natl, **Sep 4**
Peace Officer Memorial Day, Natl, **May 15**
Perioperative (OR) Nurse Week, **Nov 12**
Physician Assistants Day, **Oct 6**
Police Week, Natl, **May 14**
Professional Pet Sitters Week, **Mar 5**
Receptionists Day, Natl, **May 12**
Salesperson's Day, Natl, **Mar 3**
Solo-Preneuring Week, **Jan 22**
Substitute Teacher Appreciation Week, **Sep 18**
Tailors Day, Natl, **Jun 7**
Take Our Daughters and Sons to Work Day, **Apr 27**
Thank You, School Librarian Day, **Apr 5**
Third Shift Workers Day, Natl, **May 10**
TV Talk-Show Host Day, **Oct 23**
Update Your References Week, **May 1**
Update Your Resume Month, **Sep 1**
Waitstaff Day, Natl, **May 21**
Weatherman's Day, **Feb 5**
Wordsmith Day, **May 3**
Work at Home Moms Week, **May 14**
Workers Memorial Day, **Apr 28**
Working Women's Day, Intl, **Mar 8**
Workplace Conflict Awareness Month, **Apr 1**
Carew, Rod: Birth, **Oct 1**
Carey, Drew: Birth, **May 23**
Carey, Mariah: Birth, **Mar 27**
Caribbean or Caricom Day, **Jul 3**
Caricom or Caribbean Day, **Jul 3**
Carillon Fest, Intl (Springfield, IL), **Jun 4**
Car-Keeping Month, Natl Feel Good, **May 1**
Carleton, Will: Birth Anniv, **Oct 21**
Carlin, George: Birth, **May 12**
Carlisle, Belinda: Birth, **Aug 17**
Carlisle, Kitty: Birth, **Sep 3**
Carlsbad Caverns Natl Park Established: Anniv, **May 14**
Carlson, Chester: Birth Anniv, **Feb 8**
Carlton, Steve: Birth, **Dec 22**
Carlyle, Robert: Birth, **Apr 14**
Carlyle, Thomas: Birth Anniv, **Dec 4**
Carmichael, Hoagie: Birth Anniv, **Nov 22**
Carnegie, Andrew: Birth Anniv, **Nov 25**
Carnegie, Dale: Birth Anniv, **Nov 24**
Carnes, Kim: Birth, **Jul 20**

Carney, Art: Birth Anniv, **Nov 4**
Carney, William: First Black Receives Congressional Medal: Anniv, **May 23**
Carnival, **Feb 27**
Carnival (Malta), **Feb 25**
Carnival (Port of Spain, Trinidad and Tobago), **Feb 27**
Carnival de Ponce (Ponce, PR), **Feb 22**
Carnival Season, **Jan 6**
Carnival Week (Milan, Italy), **Feb 26**
Carnovsky, Morris: Birth Anniv, **Sep 5**
Caro, Robert A.: Birth, **Oct 30**
Carol Burnett Show TV Premiere: Anniv, **Sep 11**
Caroline, Princess: Birth, **Jan 23**
Caron, Leslie: Birth, **Jul 1**
Carousel: Santa Cruz Beach Looff Carousel: Anniv, **Aug 3**
Carpenter Ant Awareness Week, **Jun 18**
Carpenter, John: Birth, **Jan 16**
Carpenter, Mary Chapin: Birth, **Feb 21**
Carper, Tom: Birth, **Jan 23**
Carr, Gerald Paul: Birth, **Aug 22**
Carr, Vikki: Birth, **Jul 19**
Carradine, David: Birth, **Dec 8**
Carradine, John: Birth Anniv, **Feb 5**
Carradine, Keith: Birth, **Aug 8**
Carreras, Jose: Birth, **Dec 5**
Carrere, Tia: Birth, **Jan 2**
Carrey, Jim: Birth, **Jan 17**
Carroll, Charles: Birth Anniv, **Sep 19**
Carroll, Diahann: Birth, **Jul 17**
Carroll, Lewis: Birth Anniv. See Dodgson, Charles, **Jan 27**
Carroll, Pat: Birth, **May 5**
Carry a Tune Week, Natl, **Oct 1**
Carsey, Marcy: Birth, **Nov 21**
Carson, Johnny: Birth Anniv, **Oct 23**
Carson, Johnny: Final Show, **May 22**
Carson, Kit: Birth Anniv, **Dec 24**
Carson, Lisa Nicole: Birth, **Jul 12**
Carson, Rachel: Birth Anniv, **May 27**
Carson, Rachel: Silent Spring Publication: Anniv, **Apr 13**
Carter, Chris: Birth, **Oct 13**
Carter, Cris: Birth, **Nov 25**
Carter, Dixie: Birth, **May 25**
Carter, Gary: Birth, **Apr 8**
Carter, Hodding, III: Birth, **Apr 7**
Carter, Jimmy and Rosalynn, Wedding Anniv, **Jul 7**
Carter, Jimmy: Birthday, **Oct 1**
Carter, Lynda: Birth, **Jul 24**
Carter, Robert III: Emancipation of 500: Anniv, **Aug 1**
Carter, Rosalynn: Birth, **Aug 18**
Carter, Vince: Birth, **Jan 26**
Cartier, Jacques: Death Anniv, **Sep 1**
Cartier-Bresson, Henri: Birth Anniv, **Aug 22**
Cartoonists Against Crime Day, **Oct 25**
Cartoonists Day, **May 5**
Cartoons: Bugs Bunny's Debut: Anniv, **Apr 30**
Cartwright, Angela: Birth, **Sep 9**
Cartwright, Edmund: Birth Anniv, **Apr 24**
Caruso, David: Birth, **Jan 7**
Caruso, Enrico: Birth Anniv, **Feb 25**
Carvel, Tom: Birth Anniv, **Jul 14**
Carver, George Washington: Death Anniv, **Jan 5**
Carver, Raymond: Birth Anniv, **May 25**
Carvey, Dana: Birth, **Jun 2**
Casablanca Premiere: Anniv, **Nov 26**
Casady, Jack: Birth, **Apr 13**
Casals, Pablo: Birth Anniv, **Dec 29**
Casanova, Giovanni: Birth Anniv, **Apr 2**
Case, Steve: Birth, **Aug 21**
Case/Zippo Intl Swap Meet (Bradford, PA), **Jul 21**
Casey at the Bat: Mighty Casey Has Struck Out: Anniv, **Jun 3**
Casey, Bernie: Birth, **Jun 8**
Casey, Sean: Birth, **Jul 2**
Cash, Johnny: Birth Anniv, **Feb 26**
Cash, Johnny: Plays at Folsom Prison: Anniv, **Jan 13**
Cash, June Carter: Birth Anniv, **Jun 23**
Cash, Pat: Birth, **May 27**
Cassatt, Mary: Birth Anniv, **May 22**
Cassel, Seymour: Birth, **Jan 22**
Cassidy, Butch (Robert Leroy Parker): Birth Anniv, **Apr 13**
Cassidy, David: Birth, **Apr 12**
Cassidy, Joanna: Birth, **Aug 2**
Cassidy, Patrick: Birth, **Jan 4**
Cassidy, Shaun: Birth, **Sep 27**
Cassini, Oleg: Birth, **Apr 11**
Cassini-Huygens Reaches Saturn, **Jul 1**
Castro, Fidel: Birth, **Aug 13**
Cat Herders Day, **Dec 15**
Cataract Awareness Month, **Aug 1**
Cates, Phoebe: Birth, **Jul 16**

Cathedral: Cologne Cathedral Completion: Anniv, Aug 14
Cather, Willa: Birth Anniv, Dec 7
Cathode-Ray Tube Patented: Anniv, Dec 20
Catholic Educational Assn Conv/Expo, Natl (New Orleans, LA), Apr 18
Catholic Hour TV Premiere: Anniv, Jan 4
Catholic Schools Week, Jan 29
Catlin, George: Birth Anniv, Jul 26
Cats Premieres: Anniv, Oct 7
Cats: Hairball Awareness Day, Natl, Apr 28
Cats: Hug Your Cat Day, May 19
Catt, Carrie Lane Chapman: Birth Anniv, Jan 9
Cattrall, Kim: Birth, Aug 21
Cauthen, Steve: Birth, May 1
Cavalcade of Stars TV Premiere: Anniv, Jun 4
Cavanagh, Tom: Birth, Oct 26
Cavett, Dick: Birth, Nov 19
Cavoukian, Raffi: Birth, Jul 8
Caxton, William: Birth Anniv, Aug 13
Caxton's "Mirror of the World" Translation: Anniv, Mar 8
Cayley, George: Birth Anniv, Dec 27
Cazenove, Christopher: Birth, Dec 17
CBS Evening News TV Premiere: Anniv, May 3
CD Player Debuts: Anniv, Oct 1
Ceausescu, Nicolae: Death Anniv, Dec 25
Ceccato, Aldo: Birth, Feb 18
Cedric the Entertainer: Birth, Apr 24
Celebrate Your Elected Officials Day, May 19
Celebrate Your Name Week, Mar 5
Celebration of Life Day, Jan 22
Celebration of Life Month, Jan 1
Celebration of Life Week, Jan 1
Celebration of Love Week, Feb 12
Celebration of the Senses, Jun 24
Celebrations: Don't Wait—Celebrate! Week, Aug 7
Celiac Disease Awareness Month, Oct 1
Celibacy Awareness Month, Jun 1
Cell Phone Courtesy Month, Jul 1
Cellophane Tape Patented: Anniv, May 27
Cellucci, A. Paul: Birth, Apr 24
Celtic Fest, Southern Maryland (St. Leonard, MD), Apr 29
Census, First US: Anniv, Aug 1
Central African Republic
   Boganda Day, Mar 29
   Independence Day, Aug 13
   National Day, Dec 4
Cermak, Anton J.: Assassination Anniv, Feb 15
Cervantes Saavedra, Miguel de: Death Anniv, Apr 23
Cervical Cancer Screening Month, Jan 1
Cetera, Peter: Birth, Sep 13
Cezanne, Paul: Birth Anniv, Jan 19
Chabrol, Claude: Birth, Jun 24
Chad
   African Freedom Day, May 25
   Independence Day, Aug 11
   Republic Day, Nov 28
Chadds Ford Days (Chadds Ford, PA), Sep 9
Chafee, Lincoln: Birth, Mar 26
Chalke, Sarah: Birth, Aug 27
Challenger Space Shuttle Explosion: Anniv, Jan 28
Chamberlain, Richard: Birth, Mar 31
Chamberlain, Wilt: Birth Anniv, Aug 21
Chambers, Tom: Birth, Jun 21
Chambersfest (Chambersburg, PA), Jul 14
Chambliss, Saxby: Birth, Nov 10
Champion of the Month, Jan 15
Champion, Marge: Birth, Sep 2
Chan, Jackie: Birth, Apr 7
Chance, Frank: Baseball's Sad Lexicon Published: Anniv, Jul 10
Chancellor, John: Birth Anniv, Jul 14
Chandler, Chris: Birth, Oct 12
Chandler, Kyle: Birth, Sep 17
Chandler, Raymond: Birth Anniv, Jul 23
Chanel, Coco: Birth Anniv, Aug 19
Chaney, Goodman, Schwerner: Civil Rights Workers Slain, Aug 4
Chaney, Lon, Jr: Birth Anniv, Feb 10
Chaney, Lon: Birth Anniv, Apr 1
Chang, Michael: Birth, Feb 22
Change: Take Charge of Change Week, Jul 9
Channel Islands Natl Park Established: Anniv, Mar 5
Channing, Carol: Birth, Jan 31
Channing, Stockard: Birth, Feb 13
Channing, William Ellery: Birth Anniv, Apr 7
Chanukah, Dec 16
Chao, Elaine: Birth, Mar 26
Chapin, Harry: Birth Anniv, Dec 7
Chaplin, Charles: Birth Anniv, Apr 16
Chaplin, Charlie: Tramp Debuts: Anniv, Feb 7
Chaplin, Geraldine: Birth, Jul 31

Chapman, John (Johnny Appleseed): Birth Anniv, Sep 26
Chapman, John: Death Anniv: Johnny Appleseed Day, Mar 11
Chapman, John: Johnny Appleseed Fest (Fort Wayne, IN), Sep 16
Chapman, Tracy: Birth, Mar 30
Character Counts Week, Natl (Pres Proc), Oct 15
Charisse, Cyd: Birth, Mar 8
Charles I: Execution Anniv, Jan 30
Charles II: Restoration and Birth Anniv, May 29
Charles, Prince: Birth, Nov 14
Charles, Ray: Birth Anniv, Sep 23
Charleston Earthquake: Anniv, Aug 31
Charlie the Tuna: Sorry Charlie Day, Apr 1
Charlie's Angels TV Premiere: Anniv, Sep 22
Charo: Birth, Mar 13
Charro Days Fiesta (Brownsville, TX; Matamoros, Mexico), Feb 23
Charvet, David: Birth, May 15
Chase, Chevy: Birth, Oct 8
Chase, Harrison, V.: Birth Anniv, Aug 17
Chase, Helen M.: Birth, Dec 4
Chase, Salmon Portland: Birth Anniv, Jan 13
Chase, Samuel: Birth Anniv, Apr 17
Chase, Sylvia: Birth, Feb 23
Chase, William D.: Birth, Apr 8
Chase's 2006 Calendar of Events Published, Oct 9
Chase's Calendar Deadline Approaching, Mar 6
Chase's Calendar of Events: Birthday, Dec 4
Chastain, Brandi: Birth, Jul 21
Chateaubriand, Francois Rene de: Birth Anniv, Sep 4
Chatterton, Thomas: Birth Anniv, Nov 20
Chaucer, Geoffrey: Death Anniv, Oct 25
Chauvin Day, Aug 15
Chavez, Cesar Estrada: Birth Anniv, Mar 31
Cheadle, Don: Birth, Nov 29
Check Your Batteries Day, Apr 2
Checker, Chubby: Birth, Oct 3
Checkers Day, Sep 23
Cheer Coach Day, Jun 3
Cheerleading Week, Natl, Mar 6
Cheers TV Premiere: Anniv, Sep 30
Cheese Fest, Great Wisconsin (Little Chute, WI), Jun 2
Chekhov, Anton Pavlovich: Birth Anniv, Jan 29
Chelios, Chris: Birth, Jan 25
Chelsea Antiques Fair (London, England), Sep 15
Chemistry Week, Natl, Oct 22
Chen, Joan: Birth, Apr 26
Cheney, Lynne: Birthday, Aug 14
Cheney, Richard (Dick): Birthday, Jan 30
Cheng Huang: Birth Anniv Celebration (Taiwan), Jun 8
Chenoweth, Kristin: Birth, Jul 24
Cher: Birth, May 20
Chernobyl Nuclear Reactor Disaster: Anniv, Apr 26
Cherokee Rose Fest (Gilmer, TX), May 20
Cherokee Strip Celebration (Perry, OK), Sep 16
Cherokee Strip Day (OK), Sep 16
Cherry Blossom Fest (Washington, DC), Mar 25
Cherry Blossom Fest, Macon, GA's Intl, Mar 17
Cherry Month, Natl, Feb 1
Cherry Pit Spitting Chmpshp, Intl (Eau Claire, MI), Jul 1
Chertoff, Michael: Birth, Nov 28
Chesapeake-Leopard Affair: Anniv, Jun 22
Chesnut, Mary Boykin Miller: Birth Anniv, Mar 31
Chesnutt, Charles W.: Birth Anniv, Jun 20
Chess: First Computer Chess Victory: Anniv, Feb 10
Chesterton, Gilbert: Birth Anniv, May 29
Chestnut Week, Natl, Oct 8
Chiang Kai-Shek Day (Taiwan), Oct 31
Chiang Kai-Shek: Birth Anniv, Oct 31
Chicago Bulls: Third Straight Title for the Second Time, Jun 14
Chicago Cubs: Baseball's Sad Lexicon Published: Anniv, Jul 10
Chicago Cubs: Tinker to Evers to Chance: First Double Play Anniv, Sep 15
Chicago Fire, Great: Anniv, Oct 8
Chicago Flag Exhibit Controversy: Anniv, Feb 17
Chicago Flood, Great: Anniv, Apr 13
Chicago Gospel Music Fest (Chicago, IL), Jun 9
Chicago Jazz Fest (Chicago, IL), Aug 31
Chicago Marathon, The LaSalle Bank (Chicago, IL), Oct 22
Chicago, Judy: Birth, Jul 20
Chicago, Univ of, First Day Classes: Anniv, Oct 1
Chicago: Incorporated as City: Anniv, Mar 4
Chicken and Egg Fest (Prescott, AR), Jun 2
Chicken Boy's Birthday, Sep 1
Chicken Days, Wayne (Wayne, NE), Jul 7
Chicken Lady Day, Natl, Nov 4

Chicken Month, Natl, Sep 1
Chicken Wing Society Cook-off, Great Intl (Reno, NV), Jul 1
Chickens: Respect for Chickens Day, Intl, May 4
Chief Joseph Surrender: Anniv, Oct 5
Chiklis, Michael: Birth, Aug 30
Child Abuse Prevention Month, Apr 1
Child Abuse Prevention Month, Natl (Pres Proc), Apr 1
Child, Julia: Birth Anniv, Aug 15
Child, Julia: French Chef TV Premiere: Anniv, Feb 11
Child, Lydia Maria: Birth Anniv, Feb 11
Childermas, Dec 28
Children
   Absolutely Incredible Kid Day, Mar 16
   Abused Women and Children's Awareness Day, Jun 11
   Adoption Month, Natl, Nov 1
   Alcohol and Other Drug-Related Birth Defects Week, Natl, May 7
   All-American Soap Box Derby (Akron, OH), Jul 29
   America's Kids Day, Jun 25
   Andersen, Hans Christian: Birth Anniv, Apr 2
   Appreciate a Dragon Day, Jan 16
   Attention Deficit Hyperactivity Disorder Month, Sep 1
   Australia: Sorry Day, May 26
   Baby Safety Month, Sep 1
   Babysitter Safety Day, May 4
   Babysitters Day, Natl, May 13
   Backpack Safety America Month, Sep 1
   Baraboo Circus Heritage (Baraboo, WI), May 19
   Blue Ribbon Week, Natl (Child Abuse), Apr 2
   Boy Scouts of America Founded: Anniv, Feb 8
   Camp Fire Birthday Week, Mar 13
   Camp Fire Founders Day, Mar 17
   Child Abuse Prevention Month, Apr 1
   Child Abuse Prevention Month, Natl, Apr 1
   Child Abuse Prevention Month, Natl (Pres Proc), Apr 1
   Child Health Day (Pres Proc), Oct 2
   Child Safety Council Founded, Natl: Anniv, Nov 9
   Child Vision Awareness Month, Jun 1
   Childhood Depression Awareness Day, May 9
   Childhood Injury Prevention Week, Natl, Sep 1
   Children and Police Day, Natl, May 19
   Children with Alopecia Day, Apr 14
   Children's Awareness Memorial Day, Jun 4
   Children's Awareness Month, Jun 1
   Children's Book Day, Intl, Apr 2
   Children's Book Week, Natl, Nov 13
   Children's Celebration (Springfield, OR), Jul 8
   Children's Day (FL), Apr 11
   Children's Day (Japan), May 5
   Children's Day (MA), Jun 11
   Children's Day (South Korea), May 5
   Children's Day (Woodstock, VT), Aug 26
   Children's Day, Intl (China), Jun 1
   Children's Day/Natl Sovereignty (Turkey), Apr 23
   Children's Dental Health Month, Natl, Feb 1
   Children's Eye Health and Safety Month, Aug 1
   Children's Good Manners Month, Sep 1
   Children's Magazine Month, Oct 1
   Children's Party at Green Animals (Newport, RI), Jul 14
   Children's Sunday, Jun 11
   Children's Vision and Learning Month, Aug 1
   Circus City Fest (Peru, IN), Jul 15
   Communicate with Your Kid Month, Natl, Oct 1
   Construction Toy Month, Natl, Oct 1
   Davidson Fellows Award Reception (Washington, DC), Sep 27
   Day of Natl Concern about Young People and Gun Violence, Oct 18
   Dr. Seuss (Theodor Geisel): Birth Anniv, Mar 2
   Family Day—A Day to Eat Dinner with Your Children, Sep 25
   Family Month, Natl, May 14
   Festival of Children (Costa Mesa, CA), Sep 1
   Firepup's Birthday, Oct 1
   Get Ready for Kindergarten Month, Aug 1
   Gifted Children Conv, Natl Assn (Charlotte, NC), Nov 1
   Girl Scout Week, Mar 12
   Girl Scouts Founding: Anniv, Mar 12
   Heal the Children Month, May 1
   Innocent Children Victims of Aggression, Intl Day of, Jun 4
   Johnson County 4H and FFA Fair (Iowa City, IA), Jul 24
   Keep Kids Creative Week, Natl, Sep 24
   Kids Care Week, Oct 22
   Kids' Goal Setting Week, Nov 6
   KidsDay, Natl, Aug 6
   KidSpree (Aurora, CO), Jul 15
   Kiwanis Kids' Day, Natl, Sep 23
   Library Card Sign-up Month, Sep 1

Children (cont'd)—Christmas

Little League Baseball Week, Natl, **Jun 12**
Little League Baseball World Series (Williamsport, PA), **Aug 18**
Love Our Children Day, Natl, **Apr 1**
Missing Children's Day, Natl, **May 25**
Mother Goose Day, **May 1**
Multicultural American Child Awareness Day, **Jun 11**
Music in Our Schools Month, **Mar 1**
National Children's Memorial Day, **Dec 10**
National Communicate with Your Baby Day, **Dec 5**
No Homework Day, **May 6**
Pediatric Cancer Awareness Month, **Sep 1**
Pediatric Nurse Practitioner Week, **Mar 30**
Playground Safety Week, Natl, **Apr 24**
Potty Training Awareness Month, **Jun 1**
Prematurity Awareness Day, **Nov 1**
President's Environmental Youth Award Natl Competition, **Jul 31**
R.E.A.D. in America Day (Washington, DC), **Sep 23**
Read Across America Day, **Mar 2**
Read Me Week (TN), **Feb 27**
RSV Awareness Month, Natl, **Oct 1**
Safe Toys and Gifts Month, **Dec 1**
School Breakfast Week, Natl, **Mar 6**
School Lunch Week, Natl, **Oct 9**
Sea Cadet Month, **Sep 1**
Send a Kid to Kamp Radiothon (Lexington, KY), **May 6**
Sign Up for Summer Camp Month, Natl, **Dec 1**
Spank Out Day USA, **Apr 30**
Spelling Bee Finals, Natl, **May 31**
Spina Bifida Awareness Month, Natl, **Oct 1**
Sports America Kids Month, **Jun 1**
Stepparents' Week, **Jun 1**
Stories Day, **Apr 5**
Student Safety Month, **Jun 1**
Sudden Infant Death Syndrome Awareness Month, Natl, **Oct 1**
Summer Reading Club (El Paso, TX), **Jun 3**
Super Scout Sunday (Springfield, MO), **May 13**
Swedish Language and Culture Day Camp (Cambridge, MN), **Aug 21**
Take a Kid Fishing Weekend (St. Paul, MN), **Jun 9**
Talk With Your Teen About Sex Month, Natl, **Mar 1**
Teach Children to Save Day, Natl, **Apr 25**
Tooth Fairy Day, Natl, **Feb 28**
Truancy Law: Anniv, **Apr 12**
Universal Children's Day (UN), **Nov 20**
Universal Children's Week, **Oct 1**
Vegetarian Resource Group's Essay Contest for Kids, **May 1**
Very Important Parents Month, Natl, **Sep 1**
Video Games Day, **Sep 12**
White Sunday (Samoa, American Samoa), **Oct 8**
Window Safety Week, Natl, **Apr 23**
Winnipeg Intl Children's Fest (Winnipeg, MB, Canada), **Jun 8**
World Breastfeeding Week, **Aug 1**
Young Achievers Month, **May 1**
Young Child, Month of the (MI), **Apr 1**
Young Child, Week of the, **Apr 2**
Young People's Poetry Week, **Apr 10**
Young Reader's Day, Natl, **Nov 14**
Youth Art Month, **Mar 1**
Youth Cowboy Poetry Gathering (Boys Ranch, TX), **Jun 8**
Youth Day (Cameroon), **Feb 11**
Youth Day (Taiwan), **Mar 29**
Youth Day (Zambia), **Aug 7**
Youth Leadership Month, **Feb 1**
Youth Service Day, Natl, **Apr 21**
Children's Authors & Illustrators Week, Feb 5
Children's Craft Day, Natl, Mar 14
Children's Memorial Day, Natl, Dec 10
Chile
Battle of Iquique, **May 21**
Independence Day, **Sep 18**
Military Dictatorship Ended: Anniv, **Dec 15**
National Month, **Sep 1**
Strongest Earthquake of the 20th Century: Anniv, **May 22**
Chili Cook-off, State Chmpshp (Roanoke, VA), May 6
Chili Cookoff/Quail-Egg Eat, Prairie Dog (Grand Prairie, TX), Apr 8
Chili Day, Natl, Feb 23
Chili Month, Natl, Oct 1
Chimborazo Day, Jun 3
Chimney Safety Wk, Natl, Sep 24
China Beach TV Premiere: Anniv, Apr 26
China Clipper: Anniv, Nov 22
China, People's Republic of
Birthday of Confucius (Observance), **Oct 18**
Birthday of Lord Buddha, **May 5**
Canton Autumn Trade Fair, **Oct 15**
Canton Spring Trade Fair, **Apr 15**

Central China Flood: Anniv, **Jun 25**
Chung Yeung Fest (or Double Nine Fest), **Oct 30**
Double Seven Fest, **Jul 31**
Double Tenth Day, **Oct 10**
Dragon Boat Fest, **May 31**
Fest of Hungry Ghosts, **Aug 8**
Half-Year Day, **Jul 1**
International Children's Day, **Jun 1**
Lantern Fest, **Feb 12**
Macau Day, **Jun 24**
Macau Reverts to Chinese Control: Anniv, **Dec 20**
Moon Fest (Mid-Autumn Fest), **Oct 6**
National Day, **Oct 1**
Qing Ming Fest or Tomb Sweeping Day, **Apr 5**
Shanghai Communique: Anniv, **Feb 27**
Sun Yat-Sen Birth Anniv, **Nov 12**
Tiananmen Square Massacre: Anniv, **Jun 4**
Youth Day, **May 4**
China: Taiwan Expelled from UN: Anniv, Oct 25
Chinese Nationalists Move to Formosa: Anniv, Dec 8
Chinese New Year, Jan 29
Chinese New Year Golden Dragon Parade & Fest (Los Angeles, CA), Feb 4
Chipotle Day, Totally, May 5
CHiPs TV Premiere: Anniv, Sep 15
Chirac, Jacques: Birth, Nov 29
Chisholm, Shirley: Birth Anniv, Nov 30
Cho, Margaret: Birth, Dec 5
Chocolate Fest (Galesburg, IL), Feb 10
Chokachi, David: Birth, Jan 16
Chong, Tommy: Birth, May 24
Chou En-Lai: Death Anniv, Jan 8
Chow Yun-Fat: Birth, May 18
Chretien, Jean: Birth, Jan 11
Christ, Circumcision of, Jan 1
Christensen, Hayden: Birth, Apr 19
Christian Leadership Week Intl, Sep 17
Christian Unity, Week of, Jan 18
Christianity Week, Consider, Apr 2
Christie, Agatha: Birth Anniv, Sep 15
Christie, Julie: Birth, Apr 14
Christie, Lou: Birth, Feb 19
Christmas
Adelphian Club Christmas Bazaar (Kennett, MO), **Dec 2**
Adoration Parade (Branson, MO), **Dec 3**
Andrews COC Holly Jolly Weekend (Andrews, TX), **Nov 30**
Armenian Christmas, **Jan 6**
BCHS Christmas Open House (Ainsworth, NE), **Dec 3**
Black Friday, **Nov 24**
Boxing Day at the Hemingway Birthplace (Oak Park, IL), **Dec 26**
Christmas, **Dec 25**
Christmas at Union Station (Omaha, NE), **Nov 24**
Christmas Bells Ring Again (CIS): Anniv, **Dec 24**
Christmas Candlelight House Tours (Cape May, NJ), **Dec 2**
Christmas Candlelight Tour (Bardstown, KY), **Nov 24**
Christmas Candlelight Tour (Fredericksburg, VA), **Dec 9**
Christmas Candlelightings (Coshocton, OH), **Dec 2**
Christmas Craft Show (Aiken, SC), **Dec 1**
Christmas Craft Show (York, PA), **Dec 10**
Christmas Epiphany Celebration (Isanti, MN), **Jan 8**
Christmas Eve, **Dec 24**
Christmas Eve Torchlight Parade (Winter Park, CO), **Dec 24**
Christmas Fest of Lights (Natchitoches, LA), **Dec 1**
Christmas Gift and Hobby Show (Indianapolis, IN), **Nov 8**
Christmas Greens Show (Salem, OR), **Dec 1**
Christmas Greetings from Space: Anniv, **Dec 19**
Christmas in Roseland (Shreveport, LA), **Nov 24**
Christmas in the Villages (Van Buren County, IA), **Dec 2**
Christmas Magic (Wichita Falls, TX), **Nov 3**
Christmas New Orleans Style (New Orleans, LA), **Dec 1**
Christmas on the Prairie (Wahoo, NE), **Dec 2**
Christmas on the River (Demopolis, AL), **Nov 26**
Christmas Seal Campaign, **Oct 1**
Christmas Stroll Weekend (Nantucket Island, MA), **Dec 1**
Christmas to Remember (Laurel, MT), **Dec 3**
Christmas Traditions (St. Charles, MO), **Nov 24**
Christmas Walk and House Tour (Geneva, IL), **Dec 1**
Clute's Christmas in the Park (Clute, TX), **Dec 5**
Colonial Christmas (Williamsburg, VA), **Dec 16**
Colonial Christmas at Wormsloe (Savannah, GA), **Dec 10**
Community Carol Singing (Mystic, CT), **Dec 17**
Country Christmas (Cambridge, WI), **Dec 2**

Craftsmen's Christmas Classic Arts & Crafts Fest (Columbia, SC), **Nov 10**
Craftsmen's Christmas Classic Arts & Crafts Fest (Greensboro, NC), **Nov 24**
Craftsmen's Christmas Classic Arts & Crafts Fest (Richmond, VA), **Nov 3**
Cuba: Christmas Returns: Anniv, **Dec 25**
Cut Your Own Christmas Tree (Charlottesville, VA), **Nov 24**
Dear Santa Letter Week, **Nov 5**
Dickens' Christmas Extravaganza (Cape May, NJ), **Dec 3**
Dickens of a Christmas (Franklin, TN), **Dec 9**
Dickens of a Christmas at Mount Hope Mansion (Manheim, PA), **Nov 24**
Dickens Village Fest (Garrison, ND), **Nov 24**
Eighteenth-Century Christmas Wassail (McLean, VA), **Dec 10**
Electric Light Parade (Lovington, NM), **Dec 4**
Ethnic Holiday Fest (Omaha, NE), **Dec 1**
Falling Needles Family Fest, **Dec 30**
Family Christmas at Benjamin Harrison Home (Indianapolis, IN), **Nov 20**
Fantasy of Lights (Wichita Falls, TX), **Dec 1**
Frankfurt Christmas Market (Frankfurt, Germany), **Nov 25**
Garden of Lights (Muskogee, OK), **Nov 23**
Garden of Lights (Norfolk, VA), **Nov 23**
Gettysburg Holiday Fest (Gettysburg, PA), **Nov 24**
Gingerbread House Day, **Dec 12**
Gingerbread on Parade (Omaha, NE), **Nov 27**
Grand Illumination (Lahaska, PA), **Nov 17**
Heritage Christmas (Lindsborg, KS), **Nov 2**
Historical Society Tour of Homes (Crawfordsville, IN), **Dec 10**
Holiday Happiness (Upper Arlington, OH), **Dec 2**
Holiday House Tours (Charlottesville, VA), **Dec 10**
Holiday Lights on the Lake (Altoona, PA), **Nov 23**
Holiday Magic (Aurora, IL), **Nov 24**
Holiday Market (Greensboro, NC), **Nov 3**
Holiday Tour of Homes (Natchitoches, LA), **Dec 6**
Holidays in the City Grand Illumination Parade (Norfolk, VA), **Nov 18**
Hollywood Beach Candy Cane Parade (Hollywood, FL), **Dec 2**
Homesteaders Holiday (Greeley, CO), **Dec 2**
Humbug Day, **Dec 21**
Jinglebell Journey (Mount Wolf, PA), **Dec 3**
Jule Fest (Elk Horn, IA), **Nov 24**
La Posada de Kingsville/Celebration of Lights (Kingsville, TX), **Nov 17**
Lantern Light Tours (Mystic, CT), **Dec 1**
LeMoyne House Candlelight Christmas Tours (Washington, PA), **Dec 2**
Liberace Museum Christmas Tree Lighting (Las Vegas, NV), **Dec 7**
Light of the World Christmas Pageant (Minden, NE), **Nov 25**
Lights of Blacklands (TX), **Dec 1**
Longwood Gardens Christmas Display (Kennett Square, PA), **Nov 23**
Mayor's Christmas Tree (Kansas City, MO), **Nov 24**
Natchitoches Fest of Lights (Natchitoches, LA), **Nov 18**
Navidades (Puerto Rico), **Dec 15**
Nordic Yulefest (Seattle, WA), **Nov 18**
Norskedalen's Old-Fashioned Christmas (Coon Valley, WI), **Dec 2**
Norwegian Christmas (Brooklyn Park, MN), **Dec 2**
Operation Santa Paws, **Dec 1**
Ozark Mountain Christmas/Branson Fest of Lights (Branson, MO), **Nov 1**
Parade of Lights (Kingsville, TX), **Dec 2**
Peddler's Village Gingerbread House Competition & Display (Lahaska, PA), **Nov 17**
Pennsylvania Arts & Crafts Christmas Fest (Washington, PA), **Oct 20**
Philippines: Christmas Observance, **Dec 16**
Plaza Lights (Kansas City, MO), **Nov 23**
Polish Christmas Open House (Philadelphia, PA), **Dec 9**
Quincy Preserves Christmas Candlelight Tour (Quincy, IL), **Dec 10**
Recipe Greetings for the Holidays, **Dec 1**
Rockefeller Center Christmas Tree Lighting (New York, NY), **Nov 28**
Russia: Christmas Day, **Jan 7**
Saint Nicholas Day, **Dec 6**
Saint Olaf Christmas Fest (Northfield, MN), **Nov 30**
Salt Lake's Family Christmas Gift Show (Sandy, UT), **Nov 4**
Santa by Stage Coach Parade (El Centro, CA), **Dec 2**
Shaker Christmas Fair (New Gloucester, ME), **Dec 2**
Shopping Reminder Day, **Nov 25**

Silent Night, Holy Night Celebrations (Austria), **Dec 24**
Sounds of Season: Holiday Concert (Charlottesville, VA), **Dec 26**
Suwannee Lights (Live Oak, FL), **Dec 1**
Territorial Christmas Celebration (Guthrie, OK), **Nov 25**
34th St Express (Boston, MA), **Dec 9**
Thomasville's Victorian Christmas (Thomasville, GA), **Dec 14**
Three Kings Day, **Jan 6**
Tie Month, Natl, **Dec 1**
Twelve Villages of Christmas (Washington County, KS), **Dec 1**
Victorian Christmas Celebration (Cumberland, MD), **Nov 24**
Victorian Christmas Home Tour (Leadville, CO), **Dec 1**
Victorian Christmas Sleighbell Parade (Manistee, MI), **Dec 1**
Victorian Christmas Tours at Frank Lloyd Wright Home (Oak Park, IL), **Dec 9**
Virginia Christmas Show (Richmond, VA), **Nov 2**
Wassail Celebration (Woodstock, VT), **Dec 8**
Whiner's Day, Natl, **Dec 26**
Winterfest (Luverne, MN), **Dec 1**
Wisconsin Holiday Market (Kohler, WI), **Nov 10**
Wolf Point's Annual Christmas Parade (Wolf Point, MT), **Dec 1**
Wonderland of Lights (Marshall, TX), **Nov 22**
Christo: Birth, **Jun 13**
Christopher, Dennis: Birth, **Dec 2**
Christopher, William: Birth, **Oct 20**
Chronic Fatigue Syndrome Awareness Month, Natl, **Mar 1**
Chuckwagon Races, Natl Chmpshp (Clinton, AR), **Sep 1**
Chung Yeung Fest (China), **Oct 30**
Chung Yuan Fest (China), **Aug 8**
Chung, Connie: Birth, **Aug 20**
Church and Synagogue Library Assn Conf (Greensboro, NC), **Jul 30**
Church of England Ordains Women Priests: Anniv, **Mar 12**
Church of Jesus Christ of Latter-day Saints: Anniv, **Apr 6**
Church Safety and Security Month, **Oct 1**
Church, Charlotte: Birth, **Feb 21**
Church, Thomas Haden: Birth, **Jun 17**
Churchill, Randolph Henry Spencer: Birth Anniv, **Feb 13**
Churchill, Winston: Birth Anniv, **Nov 30**
Churchill, Winston: Day, **Apr 9**
Chusok, **Oct 6**
CIA Agent Arrested as Spy: Anniv, **Feb 21**
Ciardi, John: Birth Anniv, **Jun 24**
Cibrian, Eddie: Birth, **Jun 18**
Cigarette Advertising Banned: Anniv, **Apr 1**
Cigarettes Reported Hazardous: Anniv, **Jan 11**
Cinco de Mayo (Mexico), **May 5**
Cinco de Mayo Fest (Portland, OR), **May 4**
Circumcision of Christ, **Jan 1**
Circus
Baraboo Circus Heritage (Baraboo, WI), **May 19**
Circus City Fest (Peru, IN), **Jul 15**
Circus Train Wreck: Anniv, **Jun 22**
Emmett Kelly Clown Fest (Houston, MO), **May 5**
Greatest Show on Earth: Anniv, **Mar 28**
Jumbo the Elephant Arrives in America: Anniv, **Apr 9**
Kelly, Emmett: Birth Anniv, **Dec 9**
Citizen Kane Premiere: Anniv, **May 1**
Citizenship Day (Pres Proc), **Sep 17**
Civics Awareness Month, Natl, **Sep 1**
Civil Air Patrol Founded: Anniv, **Dec 1**
Civil Aviation Day, Intl (UN), **Dec 7**
Civil Rights
Anderson, Marian: Easter Concert: Anniv, **Apr 9**
Birmingham Resistance: Anniv, **Jul 19**
Blacks Ruled Eligible to Vote: Anniv, **Apr 3**
Brown v Board of Education: Anniv, **May 17**
Civil Rights Act of 1964: Anniv, **Jul 2**
Civil Rights Act of 1968: Anniv, **Apr 11**
Civil Rights Bill of 1866: Anniv, **Apr 9**
Civil Rights Workers Found Slain: Anniv, **Aug 4**
Dred Scott Decision: Anniv, **Mar 6**
Freedom Riders: Anniv, **May 4**
Greensboro Sit-in: Anniv, **Feb 1**
Little Rock Nine: Anniv, **Sep 4**
March on Washington: Anniv, **Aug 28**
Meredith (James) Enrolls at Ole Miss: Anniv, **Sep 30**
Montgomery Bus Boycott Ends: Anniv, **Dec 20**
Montgomery Bus Boycott: Anniv, **Dec 5**
Poll Tax Outlawed: Anniv, **Apr 8**
Rosa Parks Day, **Dec 1**
Saint Louis Race Riots: Anniv, **Jul 2**
Selma Civil Rights March: Anniv, **Mar 21**

16th Street Baptist Church Bombing: Anniv, **Sep 15**
24th Amendment (Eliminated Poll Taxes), **Jan 23**
Civil Service Created: Anniv, **Jan 16**
Civil War, American
Amnesty Issued for Southern Rebels: Anniv, **May 29**
Attack on Fort Sumter: Anniv, **Apr 12**
Attack on Fort Wagner: Anniv, **Jul 19**
Battle of Antietam: Anniv, **Sep 17**
Battle of Bull Run: Anniv, **Jul 21**
Battle of Chattanooga: Anniv, **Nov 24**
Battle of Cold Harbor: Anniv, **Jun 3**
Battle of Gettysburg: Anniv, **Jul 1**
Battle of La Glorietta Pass: Anniv, **Mar 28**
Battle of Mobile Bay: Anniv, **Aug 5**
Battle of Nashville: Anniv, **Dec 16**
Battle of Shiloh: Anniv, **Apr 6**
Battle of Spotsylvania: Anniv, **May 12**
Battle of the Wilderness: Anniv, **May 5**
Bread Riot at Richmond: Anniv, **Apr 2**
Burgoo Fest (Utica, IL), **Oct 8**
Civil War Days (Chesapeake, VA), **Sep 9**
Civil War Ending: Anniv, **Apr 9**
Civil War Peace Talks: Anniv, **Feb 3**
Civil War Reenactment (Coshocton, OH), **Jul 15**
Civil War Reenactment (Keokuk, IA), **Apr 21**
Civil War Relic/Collectors Show (Gettysburg, PA), **Jun 23**
Civil War Submarine Attack: Anniv, **Oct 5**
Davis, Jefferson: Inauguration: Anniv, **Feb 18**
Defeat at Five Forks: Anniv, **Apr 1**
Doubleday, Abner: Birth Anniv, **Jun 26**
Fall of Richmond: Anniv, **Apr 3**
Farragut Captures New Orleans: Anniv, **Apr 25**
First Black Receives Congressional Medal: Anniv, **May 23**
Fort Sumter Returned to Union Control: Anniv, **Feb 17**
Fort Sumter Shelled by North: Anniv, **Aug 17**
Fredericksburg Heritage Fest (Fredericksburg, VA), **Jul 4**
Gettysburg Address Memorial Ceremony (Gettysburg, PA), **Nov 19**
Gettysburg Civil War Book Fair (Gettysburg, PA), **Jun 30**
Gettysburg Civil War Heritage Days (Gettysburg, PA), **Jun 24**
Grant Commissioned Commander: Anniv, **Mar 9**
Hunter Frees the Slaves: Anniv, **May 9**
John Wilkes Booth Escape Route Tour (Clinton, MD), **Apr 15**
Johnson Impeachment Proceedings: Anniv, **Feb 24**
Last Formal Surrender of Confederate Troops: Anniv, **Jun 23**
Lincoln Approves 13th Amendment (Freedom Day), **Feb 1**
Lincoln Assassination Anniv, **Apr 14**
Lincoln Assassination Conspirators Hanging, **Jul 7**
Lincoln Signs Income Tax: Anniv, **Jul 1**
Lincoln's Gettysburg Address: Anniv, **Nov 19**
Massacre at Fort Pillow: Anniv, **Apr 12**
Memorial Day Ceremonies (Andersonville, GA), **May 28**
Memorial Day Parade and Ceremonies (Gettysburg, PA), **May 29**
Merrimac Destroyed: Anniv, **May 11**
Monitor Sinking: Anniv, **Dec 30**
Natural Bridge Battle (Tallahassee, FL), **Mar 4**
Peninsula Campaign Intensified: Anniv, **May 9**
Quantrill's Raid on Lawrence, KS: Anniv, **Aug 21**
Raid on Richmond: Anniv, **Mar 1**
Remembrance Day (Gettysburg, PA), **Nov 18**
Rock of Chickamauga: Anniv, **Sep 20**
Ruffin, Edmund: Birth Anniv, **Jan 5**
Seven Days Campaign: Anniv, **Jun 25**
Sherman Enters Atlanta: Anniv, **Sep 2**
Sherman Takes Savannah: Anniv, **Dec 21**
South Carolina: Secession Anniv, **Dec 20**
Sultana Explosion: Anniv, **Apr 27**
Surrender at Durham Station: Anniv, **Apr 18**
Surrender of Fort Donelson: Anniv, **Feb 16**
Union Officers Escape Libby Prison: Anniv, **Feb 9**
Vicksburg Surrenders: Anniv, **Jul 3**
Wade-Davis Reconstruction Bill: Anniv, **May 4**
Civility Month, Natl Win with, **Aug 1**
Claiborne, Liz: Birth, **Mar 31**
Clam Chowder Cookoff (Santa Cruz, CA), **Feb 25**
Clancy, Tom: Birth, **Apr 12**
Clapp, Gordon: Birth, **Sep 24**
Clapton, Eric: Birth, **Mar 30**
Clark, Abraham: Birth Anniv, **Feb 15**
Clark, Barney: Artificial Heart Transplant: Anniv, **Dec 2**
Clark, Barney: Death Anniv, **Mar 23**
Clark, Dave: Birth, **Dec 15**
Clark, Dick: American Bandstand TV Premiere: Anniv, **Aug 5**
Clark, Dick: Birth, **Nov 30**

Clark, Dick: Retires from American Bandstand: Anniv, **Mar 23**
Clark, George R: Birth Anniv, **Nov 19**
Clark, Mark: Birth Anniv, **May 1**
Clark, Mary Higgins: Birth, **Dec 24**
Clark, Petula: Birth, **Nov 15**
Clark, Roy: Birth, **Apr 15**
Clark, Susan: Birth, **Mar 8**
Clark, William: Birth Anniv, **Aug 1**
Clarke, Arthur C.: Birth, **Dec 16**
Clarkson, Patricia: Birth, **Dec 29**
Class Reunion Month, **Oct 1**
Clay (Muhammad Ali) Becomes Heavyweight Champ: Anniv, **Feb 25**
Clay, Cassius, Jr (Muhammad Ali): Birth, **Jan 17**
Clay, Henry: Birth Anniv, **Apr 12**
Clayburgh, Jill: Birth, **Apr 30**
Clayton, Adam: Birth, **Mar 13**
Clean Air Act Passed by Congress: Anniv, **Dec 17**
Clean Air Month, **May 1**
Clean Hands Week, Natl, **Sep 17**
Clean Up Your Computer Month, Natl, **Jan 1**
Clean-Off-Your-Desk Day, Natl, **Jan 9**
Clear Lake Crawfish Fest (Seabrook, TX), **Apr 1**
Cleary, Beverly: Birth, **Apr 12**
Cleese, John: Birth, **Oct 27**
Clemens, Roger: Birth, **Aug 4**
Clemens, Samuel (Mark Twain): Birth Anniv, **Nov 30**
Clemente, Roberto: Birth Anniv, **Aug 18**
Clements, George Harold: Birth, **Jan 26**
Clemons, Clarence: Birth, **Jan 11**
Clemson, Thomas: Birth Anniv, **Jul 1**
Clerc, Laurent: Birth Anniv, **Dec 26**
Clerc-Gallaudet Week, **Dec 3**
Clergy: Pastoral Care Week, **Oct 22**
Clerihew Day (Edmund Bentley Clerihew Birth Anniv), **Jul 10**
Cleveland Home and Garden Show (Cleveland, OH), **Feb 4**
Cleveland Natl Air Show (Cleveland, OH), **Sep 2**
Cleveland, Esther: First White House Presidential Baby, **Aug 30**
Cleveland, Frances: Birth Anniv, **Jul 21**
Cleveland, Grover: Birth Anniv, **Mar 18**
Cleveland, Grover: Cleveland's Secret Surgery: Anniv, **Jul 1**
Cleveland, Grover: Second Inauguration: Anniv, **Mar 4**
Cliburn, Van: Birth, **Jul 12**
Cliche Day, **Nov 3**
Cliché Week, Sports, **Jul 9**
Clijsters, Kim: Birth, **Jun 8**
Cline, Patsy: Birth Anniv, **Sep 8**
Clinton, Bill and Hillary, Wedding: Anniv, **Oct 11**
Clinton, Bill: "Meaning of 'Is' Is": Anniv, **Aug 17**
Clinton, George: Birth Anniv, **Jul 26**
Clinton, Hillary Rodham: Birth, **Oct 26**
Clinton, William Jefferson: Birthday, **Aug 19**
Clinton, William: Impeachment Proceedings: Anniv, **Dec 20**
Clinton, William: Military Ban on Homosexuals Eased, **Jan 29**
Clodagh: Birth, **Oct 8**
Cloning of an Adult Animal, First: Anniv, **Feb 23**
Clooney, George: Birth, **May 6**
Clooney, Rosemary: Birth Anniv, **May 23**
Close, Glenn: Birth, **Mar 19**
Clothesline Fair (Prairie Grove, AR), **Sep 2**
Clothesline Week, Intl, **Jun 3**
Clower, Jerry: Birth, **Sep 28**
Clowns: Grimaldi, Joseph: Birth Anniv, **Dec 18**
Clowns: Kelly, Emmett: Birth Anniv, **Dec 9**
Clute's Christmas in the Park (Clute, TX), **Dec 5**
Clymer, George: Birth Anniv, **Mar 16**
CN Tower: Anniv, **Jun 26**
CNN Debuted: Anniv, **Jun 1**
Coaching; Coaching Events
African-American Coaches Day, **Feb 2**
Cheer Coach Day, **Jun 3**
Coaching Week, Intl, **Feb 5**
Executive Coaching Day, **May 1**
Life Coach Recognition Week, **May 8**
Natl Soccer Coaches Assn of America Natl Conv (Philadelphia, PA), **Jan 18**
Coal Miner Days (Novinger, MO), **May 28**
Coast Guard Day, **Aug 4**
Coastal Cleanup, Intl, **Sep 16**
Coats & Toys for Kids Day (ME), **Dec 2**
Cobb, Tyrus "Ty": Birth Anniv, **Dec 18**
Cobblestone Fest (Falls City, NE), **Aug 18**
Coburn, James: Birth Anniv, **Aug 31**
Coburn, Tom: Birth, **Mar 14**
Cochise: Death Anniv, **Jun 8**
Cochran, Jacqueline: Death Anniv, **Aug 9**
Cochran, Thad: Birth, **Dec 7**
Cocker, Joe: Birth, **May 20**

Codey—Connecticut

Codey, Richard J.: Birth, **Nov 27**
Cody, William F. "Buffalo Bill": Birth Anniv, **Feb 26**
Coen, Ethan: Birth, **Sep 21**
Coen, Joel: Birth, **Nov 29**
Coffee Gourmet Intl Month, **Jan 1**
Coffee, World of/World Barista Chmpshp (Berne, Switzerland), **May 19**
Cohen, Leonard: Birth, **Sep 21**
Cohen, Rob: Birth, **Mar 12**
Cohen, Sasha: Birth, **Oct 26**
Cohocton Fall Foliage Fest (Cohocton, NY), **Oct 6**
Coin Flip For Benjamin Franklin's 300th Birthday, **Jan 17**
Coin Week, Natl, **Apr 16**
Coins Stamped "In God We Trust": Anniv, **Apr 22**
Colantoni, Enrico: Birth, **Feb 14**
Colbert, Claudette: Birth Anniv, **Sep 13**
Colbert, Claudette: It Happened One Night Film Release: Anniv, **Feb 22**
Cold War: Treaty Signed to Mark End: Anniv, **Nov 19**
Cole, Nat "King": Birth Anniv, **Mar 17**
Cole, Natalie: Birth, **Feb 6**
Coleman, Bessie: Birth Anniv, **Jan 26**
Coleman, Dabney: Birth, **Jan 3**
Coleman, Derrick: Birth, **Jun 21**
Coleman, Gary: Birth, **Feb 8**
Coleman, Norm: Birth, **Aug 17**
Coleman, Ornette: Birth, **Mar 19**
Coleman, Signy: Birth, **Jul 4**
Coleridge, Samuel: Birth Anniv, **Oct 21**
Coles, Joanna: Birth, **Aug 11**
Colfax, Schuyler: Birth Anniv, **Mar 23**
Collectables-Antiques-Craft-Flea Market Sale (Sauk Centre, MN), **Jul 15**
College Cup (NCAA Div I Men's Soccer Chmpshp), **Dec 1**
College Cup (NCAA Div I Women's Soccer Chmpshp), **Dec 1**
College Savings Month, **Sep 1**
Collette, Toni: Birth, **Nov 1**
Collins, Eileen: Birth, **Nov 19**
Collins, Gary: Birth, **Apr 30**
Collins, Jackie: Birth, **Oct 4**
Collins, Joan: Birth, **May 23**
Collins, Judy: Birth, **May 1**
Collins, Michael: Birth, **Oct 31**
Collins, Pauline: Birth, **Sep 3**
Collins, Phil: Birth, **Jan 30**
Collins, Stephen: Birth, **Oct 1**
Collins, Susan M.: Birth, **Dec 7**
Collins, Wilkie: Birth Anniv, **Jan 8**
Collinsworth, Cris: Birth, **Jan 27**
Collision Awareness Month, Natl, **Mar 1**
Collison, Nick: Birth, **Oct 26**
Cologne Cathedral Completion: Anniv, **Aug 14**
Colombia
  Battle of Boyaca Day, **Aug 7**
  Cartagena Independence Day, **Nov 11**
  Independence Day, **Jul 20**
Colonial Christmas (Williamsburg, VA), **Dec 16**
Color Day, Natl, **Oct 22**
Color TV Broadcast, First: Anniv, **Jun 25**
Colorado
  Abortion First Legalized: Anniv, **Apr 25**
  Admission Day, **Aug 1**
  Allard, Wayne: Birth, **Dec 2**
  Aspen Music Fest (Aspen), **Jun 19**
  Bolder Boulder 10k (Boulder), **May 29**
  Boom Days (Leadville), **Aug 4**
  Burro Race (Leadville), **Aug 6**
  Capitol Hill People's Fair (Denver), **Jun 3**
  Christmas Eve Torchlight Parade (Winter Park), **Dec 24**
  Coca–Cola Spring Splash (Winter Park), **Apr 16**
  Colorado Brewers' Fest (Fort Collins), **Jun 24**
  Colorado Country Christmas Holiday Gift Show (Denver), **Nov 3**
  Colorado Day, **Aug 7**
  Colorado Shakespeare Fest (Boulder), **Jun 30**
  Emma Crawford Fest and Memorial Coffin Race (Manitou Springs), **Oct 28**
  Fourth of July Celebration (Aurora), **Jul 4**
  Great American Beer Fest (Denver), **Sep 28**
  Great Fruitcake Toss (Manitou Springs), **Jan 7**
  Homesteaders Holiday (Greeley), **Dec 2**
  KidSpree (Aurora), **Jul 15**
  Leadville Trail 100 Bike Race (Leadville), **Aug 12**
  Leadville Trail 100 Ultramarathon (Leadville), **Aug 18**
  Longs Peak Scottish/Irish Highland Fest (Estes Park), **Sep 7**
  Mesa Verde Natl Park Established: Anniv, **Jun 29**
  Museum of Contemporary Art Studio Tour (Fort Collins), **Sep 16**
  NCAA Men's & Women's Skiing Chmpshps (Steamboat Springs), **Mar 8**

New West Fest (Fort Collins), **Aug 19**
Owens, Bill: Birth, **Oct 22**
Potato Day Fest (Greeley), **Sep 9**
Pumpkin Fest (Aurora), **Oct 14**
Rocky Mountain Balloon Fest (Denver), **Aug 25**
Rocky Mountain Natl Park Established: Anniv, **Jan 26**
Salazar, Ken: Birth, **Mar 2**
State Fair (Pueblo), **Aug 25**
Summerset Fest (Littleton), **Sep 15**
Taste of Colorado (Denver), **Sep 1**
Telluride Balloon Fest (Telluride), **Jun 2**
Telluride Blues & Brews Festival (Telluride), **Sep 15**
Telluride Film Fest (Telluride), **Sep 1**
Telluride Jazz Celebration (Telluride), **Aug 4**
Telluride Mushroom Fest (Telluride), **Aug 17**
Telluride Wine Fest (Telluride), **Jun 22**
US Women's Amateur Public Links Chmpshp (Pueblo), **Jun 20**
Victorian Christmas Home Tour (Leadville), **Dec 1**
Wells Fargo Bank Cup (Winter Park), **Feb 24**
Western Stock Show and Rodeo, Natl (Denver), **Jan 7**
Colorado River Crossing Balloon Festival (Yuma, AZ), **Nov 17**
Colorectal Cancer Awareness Month, Natl, **Mar 1**
Colorectal Cancer Awareness Month, Natl (Pres Proc), **Mar 1**
Colorectal Cancer Education/Awareness Month, **Dec 1**
Colter, Jessi: Birth, **May 25**
Coltrane, Robbie: Birth, **Mar 30**
Columbia Space Shuttle Disaster: Anniv, **Feb 1**
Columbian Exposition Opening: Anniv, **May 1**
Columbian Exposition, Closing: Anniv, **Oct 30**
Columbine High School Killings: Anniv, **Apr 20**
Columbo TV Premiere: Anniv, **Sep 15**
Columbus Day Parade and Italian Fest, Ocean County (Seaside Heights, NJ), **Oct 6**
Columbus, Christopher
  Columbus Day (Observed), **Oct 9**
  Columbus Day (Traditional), **Oct 12**
  Columbus Day, Natl (Pres Proc), **Oct 9**
  Columbus Sails for New World: Anniv, **Aug 3**
  Columbus's Last Voyage to New World: Anniv, **Sep 18**
  Discovery of Jamaica by: Anniv, **May 4**
Columnist's Day, Natl, **Jun 27**
Comaneci, Nadia: Birth, **Nov 12**
Comaneci, Nadia: First Perfect Score in Olympic History: Anniv, **Jul 18**
Combs, Holly Marie: Birth, **Dec 3**
Combs, Sean "Puffy": Birth, **Nov 4**
Come and Take It Festival (Gonzales, TX), **Oct 6**
COMECON and Warsaw Pact Disband: Anniv, **Jun 28**
Comet, Closest Approach to Earth: Anniv, **Feb 20**
Comics (Newspaper and Comic Books)
  Batman Debuts: Anniv, **May 1**
  Caniff, Milton: Birth Anniv, **Feb 28**
  Capp, Al: Birth Anniv, **Sep 28**
  Crankshaft: Anniv, **Aug 31**
  Dick Tracy Debuts: Anniv, **Oct 4**
  Eisner, Will: Birth Anniv, **Mar 6**
  First Newspaper Comic Strip: Anniv, **Oct 18**
  Funky Winkerbean: Anniv, **Mar 27**
  Garfield: Birthday, **Jun 19**
  Gould, Chester: Birth Anniv, **Nov 20**
  Gray, Harold Lincoln: Birth Anniv, **Jan 20**
  Herriman, George: Birth Anniv, **Aug 22**
  Kelly, Walt: Birth Anniv, **Aug 25**
  King, Frank: Birth Anniv, **Apr 9**
  Messick, Dale: Birth Anniv, **Apr 11**
  Odie: Birthday, **Aug 8**
  Outcault, Richard Felton: Birth Anniv, **Jan 14**
  Peanuts Debuts: Anniv, **Oct 2**
  Popeye Debuts: Anniv, **Jan 17**
  Schulz, Charles: Birth Anniv, **Nov 26**
  Superman Debuts: Anniv, **Jun 1**
  Wallet, Skeezix: Birth, **Feb 14**
  Young, Chic: Birth Anniv, **Jan 9**
Coming Out Day, Natl, **Oct 11**
Commercial Bank, First US: Anniv, **Jan 7**
Commodore Perry Day, **Apr 10**
Common Prayer Day (Denmark), **May 12**
Common Sense Published: Anniv, **Jan 10**
Commoner, Barry: Birth, **May 28**
Commonwealth Day (Belize), **May 24**
Commonwealth Day (United Kingdom), **Mar 13**
Commonwealth Games (Melbourne, Australia), **Mar 15**
Communications
  Better Conversation Week, **Nov 20**
  Communicate with Your Baby Day, Natl, **Dec 5**
  Communicate with Your Kid Month, Natl, **Oct 1**
  Communication Day, Better Business, **Jan 23**
  Communication Week, World, **Nov 1**
  Communications Month, Effective, **Jun 1**

Electronic Communications Week, **Apr 24**
Freedom from Fear of Speaking Week, **Jul 2**
Speak Up and Succeed Day, Natl, **Jan 24**
Subliminal Communications Month, **Sep 1**
Telecommunication Day, World (UN), **May 17**
Communist Manifesto Published: Anniv, **Feb 26**
Communist Party Suspended, Soviet: Anniv, **Aug 29**
Community Spirit Days, **Apr 1**
Comoros: Independence Day, **Jul 6**
Companies That Care Day, **Mar 16**
Compliment Day, Natl, **Jan 25**
Compliment-Your-Mirror Day, **Jul 3**
Computer
  Apple II Computer Released: Anniv, **Jun 5**
  Babbage, Charles: Birth Anniv, **Dec 26**
  Bifocals at the Monitor Liberation Day, **Dec 1**
  Cathode-Ray Tube Patented: Anniv, **Dec 20**
  Clean Up Your Computer Month, Natl, **Jan 1**
  Computer Security Day, **Nov 30**
  Eckert, J. Presper, Jr: Birth Anniv, **Apr 9**
  ENIAC Introduced: Anniv, **Feb 14**
  First Computer Chess Victory: Anniv, **Feb 10**
  Google Founded: Anniv, **Sep 7**
  IBM PC Introduced: Anniv, **Aug 12**
  Internet Created: Anniv, **Oct 29**
  Internet Moms Week, Intl, **Mar 12**
  Lotus 1-2-3 Released: Anniv, **Jan 26**
  Macintosh Debuts: Anniv, **Jan 25**
  Microsoft Releases Windows: Anniv, **Nov 10**
  Name Your PC Day, **Nov 20**
  Race Your Mouse Around the Icons Day, **Aug 28**
  Read an E-Book Week, **Mar 5**
  Shareware Day, Intl, **Dec 9**
  Take Your Webmaster to Lunch Day, **Jul 6**
  World Wide Web: Anniv, **Aug 1**
Conaway, Jeff: Birth, **Oct 5**
Concorde Flight, First: Anniv, **Jan 21**
Concours d'Elegance (Forest Grove, OR), **Jul 16**
Condom Week, Natl, **Feb 14**
Cone, David: Birth, **Jan 2**
Confederate Decoration Day (TN), **Jun 3**
Confederate Heroes Day (TX), **Jan 19**
Confederate Memorial Day (AL), **Apr 24**
Confederate Memorial Day (FL, GA), **Apr 26**
Confederate Memorial Day (KY, LA, TN), **Jun 3**
Confederate Memorial Day (MS), **Apr 24**
Confederate Memorial Day (NC, SC), **May 10**
Confederation, Articles of: Ratification Anniv, **Mar 1**
Confucius: Birthday and Teacher's Day (Taiwan), **Sep 28**
Confucius: Birthday Observance (China), **Oct 18**
Congenital Heart Defect Awareness Week, **Feb 7**
Congo (Brazzaville)
  Day of Natl Reconciliation, **Jun 10**
  National Holiday, **Aug 15**
Congo (Dem Rep of the)
  Independence Day, **Jun 30**
Congress, US
  Adams, John Quincy: Returns to Congress: Anniv, **Mar 4**
  Assembles (US), **Jan 3**
  Brawl in US House of Representatives, First: Anniv, **Jan 30**
  Congressional Page, First Female: Anniv, **Jan 3**
  First Black Serves in US House of Representatives: Anniv, **Dec 12**
  First Meeting under Constitution: Anniv, **Mar 4**
  First Meets at Washington: Anniv, **Nov 21**
  House of Representatives, First Quorum: Anniv, **Apr 1**
  Sumner Attacked in the Senate: Anniv, **May 22**
  Woman Runs the US House of Representatives: Anniv, **Jun 20**
Connecticut
  American Crossword Puzzle Tournament (Stamford), **Mar 24**
  Antique Marine Engine Exposition (Mystic), **Aug 19**
  Antique/Classic Boat Rendezvous (Mystic), **Jul 22**
  Boom Box Parade (Willimantic), **Jul 4**
  Community Carol Singing (Mystic), **Dec 17**
  Connecticut Early Music Fest (New London), **Jun 9**
  Connecticut Storytelling Fest (New London), **Apr 28**
  Constitution Ratification: Anniv, **Jan 9**
  Dodd, Christopher J.: Birth, **May 27**
  Holiday Magic (Mystic), **Dec 26**
  Lantern Light Tours (Mystic), **Dec 1**
  Levitt Pavilion Performing Arts/Music Fest (Westport), **Jun 25**
  Lieberman, Joseph: Birth, **Feb 24**
  Litchfield Open House Tour (Litchfield), **Jul 7**
  Lobsterfest (Mystic), **May 27**
  Meet the Artists & Artisans Show (Milford Green), **May 13**
  Melville (Moby-Dick) Marathon (Mystic), **Jul 31**
  Mystic Seaport Field Days (Mystic), **Nov 24**

Mystic Seaport Independence Day Celebration (Mystic), **Jul 4**
Nathan Hale Fife and Drum Muster (Coventry), **Jul 22**
Norwalk Seaport Oyster Fest (Norwalk), **Sep 8**
Odyssey—A Greek Fest (Orange), **Sep 1**
Rell, M. Jodi: Birth, **Jun 16**
Road Church Country Fair (Stonington), **Sep 16**
Road Church Missionary Fair (Stonington), **May 13**
Sea Harvest (Mystic), **Oct 7**
Sea Music Fest (Mystic), **Jun 8**
Sharon on the Green Arts and Crafts Fair (Sharon), **Aug 5**
Small Craft Weekend (Mystic), **Jun 3**
Supreme Court Strikes Down Law Banning Contraception: Anniv, **Jun 7**
Tellabration! An Evening of Storytelling for Grown-Ups, **Nov 17**
Whippoorwill Morgan Horse Open Barn (Old Lyme), **May 27**
Whippoorwill Morgan Horse Versatility Event (Old Lyme), **Sep 9**
Woodstock Fair (Woodstock), **Sep 1**
Connelly, Jennifer: Birth, **Dec 12**
Connery, Sean: Birth, **Aug 25**
Connick, Harry, Jr: Birth, **Sep 11**
Connolly, Maureen: Birth Anniv, **Sep 17**
Connors, Chuck: Birth Anniv, **Apr 10**
Connors, Chuck: First Shattered Backboard: Anniv, **Nov 5**
Connors, Jimmy: Birth, **Sep 2**
Connors, Mike: Birth, **Aug 15**
Conrad, Joseph: Birth Anniv, **Dec 3**
Conrad, Kent: Birth, **Mar 12**
Conrad, Robert: Birth, **Mar 1**
Conroy, Pat: Birth, **Oct 26**
Constable, John: Birth Anniv, **Jun 11**
Constantinople Falls to the Turks: Anniv, **May 29**
Constitution Week: Pledge Across America, **Sep 22**
Constitution, US
  11th Amendment Ratified (States' Sov), **Feb 7**
  12th Amendment Ratified (Electoral College Modified), **Jun 15**
  13th Amendment Ratified (Abolished Slavery), **Dec 6**
  14th Amendment Ratified (Citizenship), **Jul 9**
  15th Amendment Ratified (Voting Rights), **Feb 3**
  16th Amendment Ratified (Income Tax), **Feb 3**
  17th Amendment Ratified (Direct Election of Senators), **Apr 8**
  18th Amendment Ratified (Prohibition), **Jan 16**
  19th Amendment Ratified (Women's Right to Vote), **Aug 18**
  20th Amendment Ratified (Inaugural, Congress opening dates), **Jan 23**
  21st Amendment Ratified (Prohibition Repealed), **Dec 5**
  22nd Amendment Ratified (Two-Term Limit), **Feb 27**
  23rd Amendment Ratified (DC Residents Right to Vote), **Mar 29**
  24th Amendment Ratified (Eliminated Poll Taxes), **Jan 23**
  25th Amendment Ratified (Pres Succession, Disability), **Feb 10**
  26th Amendment Ratified (Voting Age to 18), **Jul 1**
  27th Amendment Ratified (No Midterm Congressional Pay Raises), **May 7**
  Bill of Rights: Anniv of First State Ratification, **Nov 20**
  Constitution of the US: Anniv, **Sep 17**
  Constitution Week (Pres Proc), **Sep 17**
  Constitution Week, Natl, **Sep 17**
  Constitutional Convention: Anniv, **May 25**
  Equal Rights Amendment Sent to States for Ratification, **Mar 22**
  Federalist Papers: Anniv, **Oct 27**
  Presidential Succession Act: Anniv, **Jul 18**
  Religious Freedom Day, **Jan 16**
  Takes Effect: Anniv, **Jul 2**
  Women's Suffrage Amendment Introduced: Anniv, **Jan 10**
Consumer Awareness Week, **Apr 16**
Consumer Electronics Show, Intl (Las Vegas, NV), **Jan 5**
Consumer Protection Week, Natl (Pres Proc), **Feb 5**
Consumerism: Buy Nothing Day, **Nov 24**
Conti, Bill: Birth, **Apr 13**
Conti, Tom: Birth, **Nov 22**
Continental Congress Assembly, First: Anniv, **Sep 5**
Contraband Days (Lake Charles, LA), **May 2**
Construction Toy Month, Natl, **Oct 1**
Conversation Week, Better, **Nov 20**

Converse, Frank: Birth, **May 22**
Converse, Harriet: White Woman Made Indian Chief: Anniv, **Sep 18**
Conway, Gary: Birth, **Feb 4**
Conway, Kevin: Birth, **May 29**
Conway, Tim: Birth, **Dec 15**
Coogan, Keith: Birth, **Jan 13**
Cook Something Bold and Pungent Day, **Nov 8**
Cook, James: Birth Anniv, **Oct 27**
Cook, Rachael Leigh: Birth, **Oct 4**
Cooke, Alistair: Birth Anniv, **Nov 20**
Cooke, Alistair: Letter from America Radio Premiere: Anniv, **Mar 24**
Cookie Cutter Week, **Dec 1**
Cookie Month, Natl, **Oct 1**
Cooking: Joy of Cooking Publication Anniv, **Nov 30**
Coolidge, Calvin: Birth Anniv, **Jul 4**
Coolidge, Calvin: Business of America Quotation: Anniv, **Jan 17**
Coolidge, Grace: Birth Anniv, **Jan 3**
Coolidge, Rita: Birth, **May 1**
Coon Hunt, Grand American (Orangeburg, SC), **Jan 6**
Cooney, Gerry: Birth, **Aug 24**
Cooney, Joan Ganz: Birth, **Nov 30**
Cooper, Alice: Birth, **Feb 4**
Cooper, Bradley: Birth, **Jan 5**
Cooper, Cynthia: Birth, **Apr 14**
Cooper, D.B., Hijacking: Anniv, **Nov 24**
Cooper, Gary: Birth Anniv, **May 7**
Cooper, Jackie: Birth, **Sep 15**
Cooper, James Fenimore: Birth Anniv, **Sep 15**
Cooper, Justin: Birth, **Nov 17**
Cooper, L. Gordon: Birth, **Mar 6**
Cooperatives, Intl Day of (UN), **Jul 1**
COPD Awareness Month, Natl, **Nov 1**
Copernicus, Nicolaus: Birth Anniv, **Feb 19**
Copland, Aaron: Birth Anniv, **Nov 14**
Copperfield, David: Birth, **Sep 16**
Coppola, Francis Ford: Birth, **Apr 7**
Coppola, Francis Ford: Godfather Film Premiere: Anniv, **Mar 15**
Copyright Law Passed: Anniv, **May 31**
Copyright Revision Law: Anniv, **Jan 1**
Coral Sea, Battle of: Anniv, **May 8**
Coray, Melissa Burton: Birth Anniv, **Mar 2**
Corbett-Fitzsimmons Title Fight: Anniv, **Mar 17**
Corbett-Sullivan Prize Fight: Anniv, **Sep 7**
Corbin, Barry: Birth, **Oct 16**
Corea, Chick: Birth, **Jun 12**
Corelli, Arcangelo: Birth Anniv, **Feb 17**
Corley, Pat: Birth, **Jun 1**
Corman, Roger: Birth, **Apr 5**
Corn Fest, Sun Prairie's Sweet (Sun Prairie, WI), **Aug 17**
Corn Palace Fest (Mitchell, SD), **Aug 30**
Cornwall: Saint Piran's Day, **Mar 5**
Cornwell, Patricia: Birth, **Jun 9**
Cornyn, John: Birth, **Feb 2**
Corpus Christi, **Jun 15**
Corpus Christi (US): Observance, **Jun 18**
Corrigan, Mairead: Birth, **Jan 27**
Corrigan, Wrong Way Day, **Jul 17**
Cort, Bud: Birth, **Mar 29**
Cortes Conquers Mexico: Anniv, **Nov 8**
Cortese, Dan: Birth, **Sep 14**
Cortese, Valentina: Birth, **Jan 1**
Corvette and High Performance Meet (Puyallup, WA), **Feb 11**
Corvette Show (Mackinaw City, MI), **Aug 25**
Corzine, Jon: Birth, **Jan 1**
Cosby Show TV Premiere: Anniv, **Sep 20**
Cosby, Bill: Birth, **Jul 12**
Cosell, Howard: Birth Anniv, **Mar 25**
Cosmopolite's Day, **Oct 8**
Costa Rica
  Feast of Our Lady of Angels, **Aug 2**
  Guanacaste Day, **Jul 25**
  Independence Day, **Sep 15**
  Juan Santamaria Day, **Apr 11**
Costas, Bob: Birth, **Mar 22**
Costello, Elvis: Birth, **Aug 25**
Costello, Lou: Birth Anniv, **Mar 6**
Costner, Kevin: Birth, **Jan 18**
Cote D'Ivoire
  Commemoration Day, **Dec 7**
  National Day, **Aug 7**
Cotten, Joseph: Birth Anniv, **May 15**
Cotton Bowl Classic (Dallas, TX), **Jan 2**
Cotton Pickin' Fair (Gay, GA), **May 6**
Coulter, Ann: Birth, **Dec 8**
Council of Nicaea I: Anniv, **May 20**
Counseling Week, Natl School, **Feb 6**
Country Day, Colton (Colton, NY), **Jul 15**
Country Good Times (Wilberforce, ON), **Jul 14**
Country Ham Days, Marion County (Lebanon, KY), **Sep 22**

Country-Western
  Acuff, Roy: Birth Anniv, **Sep 15**
  Johnny Cash at Folsom Prison: Anniv, **Jan 13**
  Twitty, Conway: Birth Anniv, **Sep 1**
  Williams, Hank, Sr: Birth Anniv, **Sep 17**
  Wills, Bob: Birth Anniv, **Mar 6**
Coup Attempt in the Soviet Union: Anniv, **Aug 19**
Couple Appreciation Month, **Apr 1**
Couples, Fred: Birth, **Oct 3**
Coupon Month, Natl, **Sep 1**
Courageous Follower Day, **Mar 4**
Couric, Katie: Birth, **Jan 7**
Court TV Debut: Anniv, **Jul 1**
Courtenay, Tom: Birth, **Feb 25**
Courtesy Day, Natl Common, **Mar 22**
Cousins Day, **Jul 24**
Cousteau, Jacques: Birth Anniv, **Jun 11**
Cousy, Bob: Birth, **Aug 9**
Covered Bridge Fest (Washington County, PA), **Sep 16**
Cow Chip-Throwing Chmpshp, World (Beaver, OK), **Apr 15**
Coward, Noel: Birth Anniv, **Dec 16**
Cowboy State Sports Fest (Casper, WY), **Feb 4**
Cowboys, Frontier, Old West
  American Legacy (Mandan, ND), **Jul 28**
  Annie Oakley Days (Greenville, OH), **Jul 28**
  Bannack Days (Bannack, MT), **Jul 15**
  Bascom, Texas Rose: Birth Anniv, **Feb 25**
  Butterfield Overland Stage Days (Benson, AZ), **Oct 7**
  Calamity Jane (Martha Burk): Death Anniv, **Aug 1**
  Carson City Rendezvous (Carson City, NV), **Jun 9**
  Cherokee Strip Celebration (Perry, OK), **Sep 16**
  Come and Take It Fest (Gonzales, TX), **Oct 6**
  Cowboy Hall of Fame Ceremony (Willcox, AZ), **Oct 5**
  Cowboy Poetry Gathering, Natl (Elko, NV), **Jan 28**
  Cowboy Poetry Gathering, Texas (Alpine, TX), **Feb 24**
  Cowboy Poetry Gathering, Youth (Boys Ranch, TX), **Jun 8**
  Defeat of Jesse James Days (Northfield, MN), **Sep 6**
  Dodge City Days (Dodge City, KS), **Jul 28**
  Fest of the West, Natl, and Log Home Show (Scottsdale, AZ), **Mar 16**
  Fiesta Bullwhacker/Wild West Show (Olathe, KS), **Sep 23**
  Gold Rush Days (Wickenburg, AZ), **Feb 10**
  Gunfight at the OK Corral: Anniv, **Oct 26**
  Oakley, Annie: Birth Anniv, **Aug 13**
  Oregon Trail Days (Gering, NE), **Jul 13**
  Pendleton Round-Up (Pendleton, OR), **Sep 9**
  Pony Express Fest (Hanover, KS), **Aug 27**
  Reenactment of Cowtown's Last Gunfight (Fort Worth, TX), **Feb 8**
  Rex Allen Days (Willcox, AZ), **Oct 6**
  River City Roundup (Omaha, NE), **Sep 28**
  Russell, Charles M.: Birth Anniv, **Mar 19**
  Santa-Cali-Gon Days Fest (Independence, MO), **Sep 1**
  Stagecoach Days (Marshall, TX), **May 20**
  Texas Ranch Roundup (Wichita Falls, TX), **Aug 18**
  Trails West! (St. Joseph, MO), **Aug 18**
  Western Days (Elgin, TX), **Jun 20**
Cow-Chip Throw, Wisconsin (Prairie du Sac, WI), **Sep 1**
Cowher, Bill: Birth, **May 8**
Cox, Bobby: Birth, **May 21**
Cox, Ronny: Birth, **Jul 23**
Craddock, Billy "Crash": Birth, **Jun 16**
Craft & Hobby Assn Conv & Trade Show (Las Vegas, NV), **Jan 30**
Craig, Larry E.: Birth, **Jul 20**
Cranberry Fest, Warrens (Warrens, WI), **Sep 22**
Crandall, Prudence: Birth Anniv, **Sep 3**
Crane, Stephen: Birth Anniv, **Nov 1**
Crankshaft: Anniv, **Aug 31**
Cranky Coworkers Day, **Oct 27**
Cranmer, Thomas: Birth Anniv, **Jul 2**
Cranston, Bryan: Birth, **Mar 7**
Crapo, Michael: Birth, **May 20**
Crapper, Thomas: Death Anniv, **Jan 27**
Crater Lake Natl Park Established: Anniv, **May 22**
Crater Lake Rim Runs and Marathon (Klamath Falls, OR), **Aug 12**
Crater, Judge Joseph F.: Disappearance Anniv, **Aug 6**
Craven, Wes: Birth, **Aug 2**
Crawfish Fest, Dermott's Annual (Dermott, AR), **May 19**
Crawford, Cindy: Birth, **Feb 20**
Crawford, Joan: Birth Anniv, **Mar 23**
Crawford, Michael: Birth, **Jan 19**
Crawford, Wahoo Sam: Birth Anniv, **Apr 18**
Crawfordsville Strawberry Fest (Crawfordsville, IN), **Jun 9**

Cray, Robert: Birth, Aug 1
Crayfish Premiere (Sweden), Aug 9
Create a Great Funeral Day, Oct 30
Creative Beginnings Month, May 1
Creative Frugality Week, Natl, Jan 22
Creativity Month, Intl, Jan 1
Creativity: Date to Create, The, Aug 8
Creativity: Swap Ideas Day, Sep 10
Credit Union Act: Anniv, Jun 26
Credit Union Day, Intl, Oct 19
Credit Union Law, First US: Anniv, Apr 6
Credit Union Week, Intl, Oct 15
Credit: Get Smart About Credit Day, Oct 19
Creeley, Robert: Birth, May 21
Cremation, America's First: Anniv, Dec 9
Crenshaw, Ben: Birth, Jan 11
Cribb, Tom: First US Heavyweight Defeated:
  Anniv, Dec 10
Crichton, Michael: Birth, Oct 23
Crick, Francis: Birth Anniv, Jun 8
Crime
  Billy the Kid: Birth Anniv, Nov 23
  Bonnie and Clyde: Death Anniv, May 23
  Borden, Lizzie, Verdict: Anniv, Jun 20
  Capone, Al: Birth Anniv, Jan 17
  Columbine High School Killings: Anniv, Apr 20
  Crime Prevention Month, Natl, Oct 1
  Crime Victims' Rights Week, Natl (Pres Proc),
    Apr 16
  D.B. Cooper Hijacking: Anniv, Nov 24
  Dillinger, John: Death Anniv, Jul 22
  Electrocution for Death Penalty, First: Anniv, Aug 6
  Harry Thaw Shoots Stanford White: Anniv, Jun 25
  Identity Theft Prevention and Awareness Month,
    Dec 1
  Jack the Ripper Letter: Anniv, Sep 27
  Miranda Decision: Anniv, Jun 13
  Ned Kelly's Last Stand: Anniv, Jun 27
  Siegel, Bugsy: Birth Anniv, Feb 28
  Stockholm Syndrome Bank Robbery: Anniv,
    Aug 23
  Ten Most Wanted List Debuts: Anniv, Mar 14
  Valentine's Day Massacre: Anniv, Feb 14
  Whitechapel Murders Begin: Anniv, Aug 31
Crimean War Began: Anniv, Oct 16
Crispus Attucks Day, Mar 5
Crist, Judith: Birth, May 22
Croatia
  Antifascist Struggle Day, Jun 22
  Homeland Thanksgiving Day, Aug 5
  Statehood Day, Jun 25
Crockett, David: Birth Anniv, Aug 17
Cromwell, James: Birth, Jan 27
Cronenberg, David: Birth, May 15
Cronkite, Walter: Birth, Nov 4
Croquet, Wicket World of (Indianapolis, IN),
  Jun 10
Crosby, Cathy Lee: Birth, Dec 2
Crosby, David: Birth, Aug 14
Crosby, Harry L. "Bing": Birth Anniv, May 3
Crosby, Mary: Birth, Sep 14
Crosby, Norm: Birth, Sep 15
Cross, Marcia: Birth, Mar 25
Crossword Puzzle, First: Anniv, Dec 21
Crouse, Lindsay: Birth, May 12
Crow, Sheryl: Birth, Feb 11
Crowded Nest Awareness Day, Jun 12
Crowe, Cameron: Birth, Jul 13
Crowe, Russell: Birth, Apr 7
Crudup, Billy: Birth, Jul 8
Cruelty Month, Prevention of Animal, Apr 1
Crufts Dog Show (Birmingham, England), Mar 9
Cruikshank, George: Birth Anniv, Sep 27
Cruise, Tom: Birth, Jul 3
Cruz, Celia: Birth Anniv, Oct 21
Cruz, Penelope: Birth, Apr 28
Cryer, Jon: Birth, Apr 16
Crystal, Billy: Birth, Mar 14
CSI: Crime Scene Investigation TV Premiere:
  Anniv, Oct 6
Csonka, Larry: Birth, Dec 25
Cuba
  Anniversary of the Revolution, Jan 1
  Bay of Pigs Invasion Launched: Anniv, Apr 17
  Beginning of Independence Wars Day, Oct 10
  Christmas Returns: Anniv, Dec 25
  Cuban Missile Crisis: Anniv, Oct 22
  Liberation Day, Jan 1
  National Day, Jul 26
Cuckoo Dancing Week, Jan 11
Culkin, Macaulay: Birth, Aug 26
Cullen, Countee: Birth Anniv, May 30
Culligan, Emmett J.: Birth Anniv, Mar 5
Cullum, John: Birth, Mar 2
Culp, Robert: Birth, Aug 16
Cultural Diversity for Dialogue and Development,
  World Day for (UN), May 21
Cumming, Alan: Birth, Jan 27

Cummings, Quinn: Birth, Aug 13
Cummings, Robert: Birth Anniv, Jun 9
Cummings, Terry: Birth, Mar 15
Cunningham, Glenn: Birth Anniv, Aug 4
Cunningham, Merce: Birth, Apr 16
Cunningham, Randall: Birth, Mar 27
Curacao
  Animals' Day, Sep 4
  Curacao Day, Jul 26
  Kingdom Day and Antillean Flag Day, Dec 15
  Memorial Day, May 4
Curie, Marie: Birth Anniv, Nov 7
Curlew Day, Mar 16
Curling Is Cool Day, Feb 23
Curry, Mark: Birth, Jun 1
Curry, Tim: Birth, Apr 19
Curtin, Jane: Birth, Sep 6
Curtis Cup (Bandon, OR), Jul 29
Curtis, Charles: Birth Anniv, Jan 25
Curtis, Jamie Lee: Birth, Nov 22
Curtis, Tony: Birth, Jun 3
Curtiss, Glenn: Birth Anniv, May 21
Curwood Festival (Owosso, MI), Jun 1
Cusack, Joan: Birth, Oct 11
Cusack, John: Birth, Jun 28
Custer Battlefield Becomes Little Bighorn
  Battlefield: Anniv, Nov 26
Custer, George: Battle of Little Bighorn: Anniv,
  Jun 25
Custer: Little Bighorn Days (Hardin, MT), Jun 21
Custodial Workers Day, Natl, Oct 2
Customer Day, Get to Know Your, Jan 19
Customer Loyalty Month, Intl, Apr 1
Customer Service Day, Jan 17
Customer Service: Stop the Bad Service Day,
  Mar 1
Customers Week, Natl Thank-Your-, Jan 9
Cut Your Energy Costs Day, Natl, Jan 10
Cuthbert, Elisha: Birth, Nov 30
Cyberspace Coined: Anniv, Oct 1
Cyprus
  Independence Day, Oct 1
  Procession of Icon of St. Lazarus, Apr 15
  Saint Paul's Feast, Jun 28
Cyrus, Billy Ray: Birth, Aug 25
Czar Nicholas II and Family Executed: Anniv,
  Jul 17
Czech Republic
  Commemoration Day, Jul 6
  Foundation of the Republic, Oct 28
  Liberation Day, May 8
  Prague Autumn Intl Music Fest, Sep 12
  Teachers' Day, Mar 28
Czechoslovakia
  Clarkson Czech Fest (Clarkson, NE), Jun 23
  Czech Days (Tabor, SD), Jun 16
  Czechoslovakia Ends Communist Rule: Anniv,
    Nov 29
  Czechoslovakian Fest, Natl (Wilber, NE), Aug 4
  Czech-Slovak Divorce: Anniv, Jan 1
  Rape of Lidice: Anniv, Jun 10
  Westfest (West, TX), Sep 2

D.A.R.E. Day, Natl (Pres Proc), Apr 13
D'Abo, Olivia: Birth, Jan 22
Daffodil Fest Weekend (Nantucket Island, MA),
  Apr 28
Daffynitions Month, Intl, Apr 1
Dafoe, Willem: Birth, Jul 22
Daguerre, Louis: Birth Anniv, Nov 18
Dahl, Arlene: Birth, Aug 11
Dahl, Roald: Birth Anniv, Sep 13
Dahl, Steve: Birth, Nov 20
Dailey, Irene: Birth, Sep 12
Dailey, Janet: Birth, May 21
Dairy Alternatives Month, Jun 1
Dairy Expo, World (Madison, WI), Oct 3
Dairy Month, June, Jun 1
Dakides, Tara: Birth, Aug 20
Dalai Lama Flees Tibet: Anniv, Mar 31
Dalai Lama: Birth, Jul 6
Daley, John: Birth, Jul 20
Daley, Richard M.: Birth, Apr 24
Dali, Salvador: Birth Anniv, May 11
Dallas Cup (Frisco, TX), Apr 9
Dallas TV Premiere: Anniv, Apr 2
Dallas, George: Birth Anniv, Jul 10
Dalton Defenders Day (Coffeyville, KS), Oct 6
Dalton, John: Birth Anniv, Sep 6
Dalton, Timothy: Birth, Mar 21
Daltrey, Roger: Birth, Mar 1
Daly, Carson: Birth, Jun 22
Daly, Chuck: Birth, Jul 20
Daly, John: Birth, Apr 28
Daly, Timothy: Birth, Mar 1
Daly, Tyne: Birth, Feb 21
Damian, Michael: Birth, Apr 26
Damon, Matt: Birth, Oct 8

Damone, Vic: Birth, Jun 12
Dana, Bill: Birth, Oct 5
Dance
  Ailey, Alvin: Birth Anniv, Jan 5
  Balanchine, George: Birth Anniv, Jan 22
  Ballet Introduced to US: Anniv, Feb 7
  Dance Day, Natl, Mar 21
  Duncan, Isadora: Birth Anniv, May 27
  English Riviera Dance Fest (Torquay, England),
    Jun 2
  Folkmoot USA (Waynesville, NC), Jul 17
  Fonteyn, Margot: Birth Anniv, May 18
  Fosse, Bob: Birth Anniv, Jun 23
  Gigglefeet Dance Fest (Ketchikan, AK), Aug 4
  Graham, Martha: Birth Anniv, May 11
  Kuopio Dance Fest (Kuopio, Finland), Jun 15
  Martha Graham's First Solo: Anniv, Apr 18
  Merrie Monarch Fest & Hula Competition (Hilo, HI),
    Apr 16
  Ocean Dance (Hollywood, FL), Dec 31
  Pacific DanceSport Chmpshps (Los Angeles, CA),
    Nov 3
  Rite of Spring Premiere and Riot: Anniv, May 29
  Robinson, Bill "Bojangles": Birth Anniv, May 25
  Shrewsbury Intl Music Fest (Shropshire, England),
    Jun 30
  Tap Dance Day, Natl, May 25
  World Folkfest (Springville, UT), Jul 8
  Yuma Square and Round Dance Fest (Yuma, AZ),
    Feb 10
Dance, Charles: Birth, Oct 10
Dandridge, Dorothy: Birth Anniv, Nov 9
Danes, Claire: Birth, Apr 12
D'Angelo, Beverly: Birth, Nov 15
Daniel Boone Pioneer Festival (Winchester, KY),
  Sep 1
Daniel Boone TV Premiere: Anniv, Sep 24
Daniel, Beth: Birth, Oct 14
Daniels, Charlie: Birth, Oct 28
Daniels, Jeff: Birth, Feb 19
Daniels, Mitchell: Birth, Apr 7
Daniels, William: Birth, Mar 31
Danish
  Aebleskiver Days (Tyler, MN), Jul 21
  Tivoli Fest (Elk Horn, IA), May 27
Danner, Blythe: Birth, Feb 3
Danson, Ted: Birth, Dec 29
Dante Alighieri: Death Anniv, Sep 14
Danza, Tony: Birth, Apr 21
Darby, Kim: Birth, Jul 8
Dare, Virginia: Birth Anniv, Aug 18
Dark Day in New England: Anniv, May 19
Dark Shadows TV Premiere: Anniv, Jun 27
Darren, James: Birth, Jun 8
Darrow, Clarence, Death Commemoration
  (Chicago, IL), Mar 13
Darrow, Clarence: Birth Anniv, Apr 18
Darwin Day, Feb 12
Darwin, Charles Robert: Birth Anniv, Feb 12
Darwin, Charles: On the Origin of Species
  Published: Anniv, Nov 22
Daschle, Thomas: Birth, Dec 9
Dassehra (India), Oct 2
Date Fest, Natl (Indio, CA), Feb 17
Dating Game TV Premiere: Anniv, Dec 20
Daumier, Honore: Birth Anniv, Feb 26
Davenport, Lindsay: Birth, Jun 8
David, Keith: Birth, Jun 4
Davidovich, Lolita: Birth, Jul 15
Davidson, John: Birth, Dec 13
Davies, Jeremy: Birth, Oct 28
Davies, Laura: Birth, Oct 5
Davies, Marion: Birth Anniv, Jan 3
Davis, Al: Birth, Jul 4
Davis, Angela: Birth, Jan 26
Davis, Bette: Birth Anniv, Apr 5
Davis, Clifton: Birth, Oct 4
Davis, Eric: Birth, May 29
Davis, Geena: Birth, Jan 21
Davis, Gray: Birth, Dec 26
Davis, Jefferson: Birth Anniv, Jun 3
Davis, Jefferson: Bread Riot Richmond: Anniv,
  Apr 2
Davis, Jefferson: Inauguration: Anniv, Feb 18
Davis, Jim: Birth, Jul 28
Davis, Jr, Benjamin O.: Birth Anniv, Dec 18
Davis, Judy: Birth, Apr 23
Davis, Mac: Birth, Jan 21
Davis, Miles: Birth Anniv, May 25
Davis, Ossie: Birth Anniv, Dec 18
Davis, Paige: Birth, Oct 15
Davis, Sammy, Jr: Birth Anniv, Dec 8
Davis, Terrell: Birth, Oct 28
Davison, Bruce: Birth, Jun 28
Davis-Voss, Sammi: Birth, Jun 21
Davy Crockett TV Premiere: Anniv, Dec 15
Dawber, Pam: Birth, Oct 18
Dawes, Charles: Birth Anniv, Aug 27

Cray—Dawes

Dawson, Andre: Birth, Jul 10
Dawson, Dermontti: Birth, Jun 17
Dawson, Richard: Birth, Nov 20
Dawson, Rosario: Birth, May 9
Day of Natl Concern about Young People and Gun Violence, Oct 18
Day of Peace, Intl, Sep 21
Day of Prayer and Action for Human Habitat, Intl, Sep 17
Day of Reason, Natl, May 4
Day of the Five Billion: Anniv, Jul 11
Day of the Race: See Columbus Day, Oct 12
Day of the Six Billion: Anniv, Oct 12
Day With(out) Art, Dec 1
Day, Doris: Birth, Apr 3
Day-Lewis, Daniel: Birth, Apr 29
Daylight Savings Time: Workplace Napping Day, Natl, Apr 3
Dayne, Taylor: Birth, Mar 7
Days of Our Lives TV Premiere: Anniv, Nov 8
Dayton, Mark: Birth, Jan 26
D-Day: Anniv, Jun 6
De Bont, Jan: Birth, Oct 22
De Carlo, Yvonne: Birth, Sep 1
De Forest, Lee: Birth Anniv, Aug 26
De Gaulle, Charles: Birth Anniv, Nov 22
de Havilland, Olivia: Birth, Jul 1
de Klerk, Frederik Willem: Birth, Mar 18
de la Hoya, Oscar: Birth, Feb 4
De La Renta, Oscar: Birth, Jul 22
De Laurentiis, Dino: Birth, Aug 8
de Matteo, Drea: Birth, Jan 19
De Mille, Cecil B.: Birth Anniv, Aug 12
De Mornay, Rebecca: Birth, Aug 29
De Niro, Robert: Birth, Aug 17
De Palma, Brian: Birth, Sep 11
De Rita, Joe: Birth Anniv, Jul 12
De Sade, Donatien: Birth Anniv, Jun 2
De Young, Cliff: Birth, Feb 12
Deaf Awareness Week, Sep 24
Deaf Conference, Natl Assn of the (New Orleans, LA), Jul 11
Deaf Day, Mother, Father, Apr 30
Deaf History Month, Mar 13
Deaf, First School for: Anniv, Apr 15
Dean, Dizzy: Birth Anniv, Jan 16
Dean, Howard: Birth, Nov 17
Dean, James, Birthday Celebration (Fairmont, IN), Feb 4
Dean, James: Birth Anniv, Feb 8
Dean, James: Death Anniv, Sep 30
Dean, James: Fairmount Fest/Remembering (Fairmount, IN), Sep 22
Dean, Jimmy: Birth, Aug 10
Dean, John: Birth, Oct 14
Dear Diary Day, Sep 22
Dear Santa Letter Week, Nov 5
Death of a Salesman Premiere: Anniv, Feb 10
Death Penalty Banned: Anniv, Jun 29
Death/Duty Day, Nov 11
Death: Funeral Service Education Week, Feb 6
DeBakey, Michael: Birth, Sep 7
DeBarge, Eldra: Birth, Jun 4
Debs, Eugene V: Birth Anniv, Nov 5
Debussy, Claude: Birth Anniv, Aug 22
Decatur, Stephen: Birth Anniv, Jan 5
Decide to Be Married Day, Jun 27
Decisions: Make Up Your Mind Day, Dec 31
Declaration of Independence
  Approval and Signing: Anniv, Jul 4
  First Public Reading: Anniv, Jul 8
  Official Signing: Anniv, Aug 2
  Resolution: Anniv, Jul 2
Declaration of the Bab, May 23
Decorating Month, Natl, Apr 1
Decoration Day (Memorial Day), May 29
Decoy and Wildlife Art Show (Clayton, NY), Jul 14
Decter, Midge: Birth, Jul 25
Dee, Ruby: Birth, Oct 27
Deep Impact Smashes into Tempel 1, Jul 4
Deepavali (India), Oct 21
Deerfield Massacre: Anniv (Feb 29), Feb 1
Dees, Rick: Birth, Mar 14
Def, Mos: Birth, Dec 11
Defenders Day, Sep 12
Defense Transportation Day, Natl (Pres Proc), May 19
DeFrantz, Anita L.: Birth, Oct 4
Degas, Edgar: Birth Anniv, Jul 19
DeGeneres, Ellen: Birth, Jan 26
DeHaven, Gloria: Birth, Jul 23
Del Toro, Benicio: Birth, Feb 19
Delaney, Kim: Birth, Nov 29
Delano, Jane: Birth Anniv, Mar 26
Delany, Dana: Birth, Mar 13
Delaware
  Biden, Joe: Birth, Nov 20
  Carper, Tom: Birth, Jan 23

Delaware State Fair (Harrington), Jul 20
  Minner, Ruth Ann: Birth, Jan 17
  Miss Delaware Pageant (Rehoboth Beach), Jun 9
  Nanticoke Indian Powwow (Millsboro), Sep 9
  Point-to-Point (Wilmington), May 7
  Ratification Day, Dec 7
  Return Day (Georgetown), Nov 9
  Sea Witch Halloween Fest (Rehoboth Beach/Dewey Beach), Oct 28
Delgado, Carlos: Birth, Jun 25
DeLillo, Don: Birth, Nov 20
Delmonico, Lorenzo: Birth Anniv, Mar 13
DeLuise, Dom: Birth, Aug 1
DeMille, Agnes: Birth Anniv, Sep 18
DeMint, Jim: Birth, Sep 2
Demme, Jonathan: Birth, Feb 22
Dempsey, Jack: Birth Anniv, Jun 24
Dempsey, Jack: Long Count Day, Sep 22
Dempsey, Patrick: Birth, Jan 13
DeMunn, Jeffrey: Birth, Apr 25
Denali Natl Park: Anniv, Dec 2
Dench, Judi: Birth, Dec 9
Deneuve, Catherine: Birth, Oct 22
Deng, Luol: Birth, Apr 16
Denim Day, Lee Natl, Oct 6
Denmark
  Aalborg and Rebild Fest (Aalborg and Rebild), Jul 2
  Common Prayer Day, May 12
  Constitution Day, Jun 5
  Ho Sheep Market, Aug 26
  Midsummer Eve, Jun 23
  Queen Margrethe's Birthday, Apr 16
  Tivoli Gardens Season (Copenhagen), May 1
  Viking Fest (Frederiksund), Jun 23
Dennehy, Brian: Birth, Jul 9
Dennis, Sandy: Birth Anniv, Apr 27
Dent, Bucky: Birth, Nov 25
Dental Drill Patent: Anniv, Jan 26
Dental Health Month, Natl Children's, Feb 1
Dental Hygiene Month, Natl, Oct 1
Dental: Flossing Day, Natl, Nov 24
Dentistry: Root Canal Appreciation Day, May 10
Denton, James: Birth, Jan 20
Denver, Bob: Birth, Jan 9
Denver, John: Birth Anniv, Dec 31
Depardieu, Gerard: Birth, Dec 27
Depp, Johnny: Birth, Jun 9
DePreist, James (Anderson): Birth, Nov 21
Depression Education and Awareness Month, Natl, Oct 1
Depression Screening Day, Natl, Oct 5
Derek, Bo: Birth, Nov 20
Dern, Bruce: Birth, Jun 4
Dern, Laura: Birth, Feb 10
Derrida, Jacques: Birth Anniv, Jul 15
Dershowitz, Alan: Birth, Sep 1
Descartes, Rene: Birth, Mar 31
Descendants Day, Jun 24
Desegregation, US Army First: Anniv, Jul 26
Desert Shield: Anniv, Aug 7
Desert Storm: Ground War Begins: Anniv, Feb 23
Desert Storm: Kuwait Liberated: Anniv, Feb 27
Desert Storm: Persian Gulf War Begins: Anniv, Jan 16
Deserts and Desertification, Intl Year of (UN), Jan 1
DeShannon, Jackie: Birth, Aug 21
Designated Hitter Rule Adopted: Anniv, Jan 11
DeSoto Caverns Park Fall Native American Dance Fest (Childersburg, AL), Sep 23
DeSoto Caverns Park Spring Native American Dance & Crafts Fest (Childersburg, AL), Apr 1
Des'ree: Birth, Nov 30
Detroit (MI): Anniv, Jul 24
Devane, William: Birth, Sep 5
Development Information Day, World (UN), Oct 24
Devers, Gail: Birth, Nov 19
Devil's Night, Oct 30
DeVito, Danny: Birth, Nov 17
Devlin, Bernadette: Birth, Apr 23
DeVoe, Ronald: Birth, Feb 17
Dewey Defeats Truman Headline: Anniv, Nov 3
Dewey, John: Birth Anniv, Oct 20
Dewey, Melvil: Birth Anniv, Dec 10
Dewhurst, Colleen: Birth Anniv, Jun 3
DeWine, Mike: Birth, Jan 5
Dewitt, Joyce: Birth, Apr 23
Dey, Susan: Birth, Dec 10
Dia de la Raza (Mexico), Oct 12
Dia de la Raza: See Columbus Day, Oct 12
Diabetes Assn Alert Day, American, Mar 28
Diabetes Month, American, Nov 1
Diabetes, Dollars Against (DAD's) Day, Jun 16
Diabetic Eye Disease Month, Nov 1
Diallo, Mamadou: Birth, Aug 28
Diamond, Dustin: Birth, Jan 7
Diamond, Neil: Birth, Jan 24

Diana, Princess of Wales: Birth Anniv, Jul 1
Diary Day, Dear, Sep 22
Diaz, Cameron: Birth, Aug 30
DiCaprio, Leonardo: Birth, Nov 11
Dice Day, Natl, Dec 4
Dicing for Bibles (Huntingdonshire, England), Jun 5
Dick Cavett Show TV Premiere: Anniv, Mar 4
Dick Tracy Debuts: Anniv, Oct 4
Dick Van Dyke Show TV Premiere: Anniv, Oct 3
Dick, Andy: Birth, Dec 21
Dickens' Christmas Extravaganza (Cape May, NJ), Dec 3
Dickens of a Christmas (Franklin, TN), Dec 9
Dickens on the Strand (Galveston, TX), Dec 1
Dickens, Charles: Birth Anniv, Feb 7
Dickerson, Eric: Birth, Sep 2
Dickinson, Angie: Birth, Sep 30
Dickinson, Emily: Birth Anniv, Dec 10
Dictionary Day, Oct 16
Dictionary of American English Published, First: Anniv, Apr 14
Diddley, Bo: Birth, Dec 30
Didion, Joan: Birth, Dec 5
Didrikson, Babe: See under Zaharias, Jun 26
Diefenbaker, John: Birth Anniv, Sep 18
Diego, Jose de: Birth Anniv, Apr 16
Dien Bien Phu Falls: Anniv, May 7
Diesel Engine Patented: Anniv, Feb 23
Diesel, Rudolph: Natl Biodiesel Day, Mar 18
Diesel, Vin: Birth, Jul 18
Dietrich, Marlene: Birth Anniv, Dec 27
Diets, Dieting (including weight loss and weight issues). See also Health
  Diet Resolution Week, Jan 1
  Dietary Managers Assn Mtg/Expo (Milwaukee, WI), Jul 16
  Family Fit Lifestyle Month, Jan 1
  Healthy Weight Week, Jan 15
  Lose Weight/Feel Great Week, Natl, Jan 1
  No Diet Day, May 6
  Rid the World of Fad Diets/Gimmicks Day, Jan 17
  Women's Healthy Weight Day, Jan 19
DiFranco, Ani: Birth, Sep 23
Diggs, Taye: Birth, Jan 2
Diller, Phyllis: Birth, Jul 17
Dillinger, John: Death Anniv, Jul 22
Dillman, Bradford: Birth, Apr 14
Dillon, Kevin: Birth, Aug 19
Dillon, Matt: Birth, Feb 18
Dillon, Melinda: Birth, Oct 13
DiMaggio, Joe: Birth Anniv, Nov 25
Dimpled Chad Day, Jan 4
DiMucci, Dion: Birth, Jul 18
Dinah Shore Show TV Premiere: Anniv, Nov 27
Ding Dong School TV Premiere: Anniv, Dec 22
Ding Ling: Death Anniv, Mar 4
Dining Out for Life (Atlanta, GA), Apr 27
Dinkins, David: Birth, Jul 10
Dinosaur Roundup Rodeo (Vernal, UT), Jul 12
Dion, Celine: Birth, Mar 30
Dionne Quintuplets: Birth, May 28
Dior, Christian: Birth Anniv, Jan 21
Disabled
  Abilities Day, Dec 22
  Americans with Disabilities Act: Anniv, Jul 26
  Bell, Alexander Graham: Birth Anniv, Mar 3
  Clerc-Gallaudet Week, Dec 3
  Deaf Awareness Week, Sep 24
  Deaf History Month, Mar 13
  Disability Employment Awareness Month, Natl, Oct 1
  Disability Employment Awareness Month, Natl (Pres Proc), Oct 1
  Disabled Persons, Intl Day of (UN), Dec 3
  First School for Deaf: Anniv, Apr 15
  Fishing Has No Boundaries (Hayward, WI), May 19
  Fishing Has No Boundaries (Monticello, IN), May 20
  Goodwill Industries Week, May 7
  Helen Keller's Miracle: Anniv, Apr 5
  Mother, Father Deaf Day, Apr 30
  National Association of the Deaf Conf (New Orleans, LA), Jul 11
  Rehabilitation Awareness Celebration, Natl, Sep 17
  Seeing Eye Established: Anniv, Jan 29
  Special Olympics Day, Jul 20
  Special Olympics Winter Games (McHenry, MD), Feb 26
  Special Recreation Day, Jul 2
  Special Recreation Week, Jul 2
  Therapeutic Recreation Week, Natl, Jul 9
  Travelers with Disabilities Awareness Week, Nov 26
  Wells Fargo Bank Cup (Winter Park, CO), Feb 24
Disarmament Week (UN), Oct 24
Discotheque Bombing: Anniv, Apr 5
Discoverers' Day (Hawaii), Oct 9

Discovery Launches Satellite: Anniv, Nov 7
Dishonor List, New Year's, Jan 1
Disney World Opened: Anniv, Oct 1
Disney, Walt: Birth Anniv, Dec 5
Disneyland Opened: Anniv, Jul 17
Disraeli, Benjamin: Birth Anniv, Dec 21
Distinguished Service Medal: Anniv, Mar 7
Ditka, Mike: Birth, Oct 18
Divac, Vlade: Birth, Feb 3
Diversity Awareness Month, Oct 1
Diversity Day, Natl, Oct 6
Diversity Month, Appreciate, Apr 1
Diwali (India), Oct 21
Dix, Dorothea L.: Birth Anniv, Apr 4
Dixie, Holiday in (Shreveport and Bossier City, LA), Apr 21
Dixon, Donna: Birth, Jul 20
Dixon, Willie: Birth Anniv, Jul 1
Djibouti: Independence Day, Jun 27
Do Dah Day (Birmingham, AL), May 6
Do It Day (aka Fight Procrastination Day), Sep 6
Dobson, Kevin: Birth, Mar 18
Doctorow, E.L.: Birth, Jan 6
Doctor-Patient Trust Day, Mar 17
Doctors' Day, Mar 30
Doctors TV Premiere: Anniv, Apr 1
Dodd, Christopher J.: Birth, May 27
Dodge Poetry Fest (NJ), Sep 28
Dodgson, Charles Lutwidge: Birth Anniv, Jan 27
Dog Day Road Race (Harvey Cedars, NJ), Aug 20
Dog Days, Jul 3
Doghouse Repairs Month, Natl, Jul 1
Dogs. See also Sled Dogs
    Adopt-A-Shelter-Dog Month, Oct 1
    AKC/Eukanuba Natl Chmpshp (Tampa Bay and St. Petersburg, FL), Jan 14
    Bark in the Park (Chicago, IL), May 6
    Crufts Dog Show (Birmingham, England), Mar 9
    Dog Bite Prevention Week, Natl, May 21
    Dog Day, Natl, Aug 26
    Faith City Kennel Club Dog Show (Wichita Falls, TX), Mar 4
    Field Trial Chmpshp, Natl (Bird Dogs) (Grand Junction, TN), Feb 13
    Haute Dog Charity Easter Parade (Long Beach, CA), Apr 16
    Haute Dog Charity Howl'oween Parade (Long Beach, CA), Oct 29
    Laika: Sputnik 2, Nov 3
    Scoop the Poop Week, Natl, Apr 24
    Sled Dogs Save Nome: Anniv, Feb 2
    Stock Dog Trials & Farm Fest, US Open (Dawsonville, GA), Oct 6
    Take Your Dog to Work Day, Jun 23
    Westminster Kennel Club Dog Show (New York, NY), Feb 13
    What If Cats and Dogs Had Opposable Thumbs Day, Mar 3
    Woofstock (Wichita, KS), Oct 7
Dogwood Arts Fest (Knoxville, TN), Apr 5
Doherty, Shannen: Birth, Apr 12
Dolby, Ray: Birth, Jan 18
Dole, Elizabeth: Birth, Jul 29
Dole, Robert J.: Birth, Jul 22
Dolenz, Micky: Birth, Mar 8
Doll Classic, American Club's Teddy Bear and (Kohler, WI), Feb 26
Doll Fest (Japan), Mar 3
Doll Show (Yuma, AZ), Feb 4
Doll, Kewpie: Rose C. O'Neill: Birth Anniv, Jun 25
Dollars Against Diabetes (DAD's) Day, Jun 16
Domenici, Pete V.: Birth, May 7
Domestic Violence Awareness Month, Oct 1
Domestic Violence Awareness Month, Natl, Oct 1
Domingo, Placido: Birth, Jan 21
Dominica: National Day, Nov 3
Dominican Republic
    Independence Day, Feb 27
    National Holiday, Jan 26
    Restoration of the Republic, Aug 16
Domino, Fats: Birth, Feb 26
Donahue, Elinor: Birth, Apr 19
Donahue, Phil: Birth, Dec 21
Donald Duck: Birth, Jun 9
Donaldson, Sam: Birth, Mar 11
Donate a Day's Wages to Charity Day, May 10
Donate Life Month (Pres Proc), Apr 1
Donate Life Month, Natl, Apr 1
Donizetti's "Lucia Di Lammermoor" Premiere: Anniv, Sep 26
Donna Reed Performing Arts Fest (Denison, IA), Jun 19
Donnelly, Donal: Birth, Jul 6
Donner Party Famine: Anniv, Oct 28
Donny and Marie TV Premiere: Anniv, Jan 16
D'Onofrio, Vincent: Birth, Jun 30
Donor Sabbath, Natl, Nov 10
Donovan, Landon: Birth, Mar 4

Donovan, Tate: Birth, Sep 25
Donovan: Birth, Feb 10
Don't Step on a Bee Day, Jul 10
Don't Wait—Celebrate! Week, Aug 7
Dooley, Paul: Birth, Feb 22
Doolittle, Eliza: Day, May 20
Doolittle, James Harold: Birth Anniv, Dec 14
Dorgan, Byron L.: Birth, May 14
Dormition of Theotokos, Aug 15
Dorsett, Tony: Birth, Apr 7
Dorsey, Thomas A.: Birth, Jul 1
Dostoyevsky, Fyodor M: Birth Anniv, Nov 11
Double Nine Fest (China), Oct 30
Double Seven Fest (China), Jul 31
Double Tenth Day (China), Oct 10
Doubleday, Abner: Birth Anniv, Jun 26
Douglas, Illeana: Birth, Jul 25
Douglas, Jim: Birth, Jun 21
Douglas, Kirk: Birth, Dec 9
Douglas, Michael: Birth, Sep 25
Douglas, Mike: Birth, Aug 11
Douglas, Sherman: Birth, Sep 15
Douglas, Virginia O'Hanlon: Death Anniv, May 13
Douglas, William O.: Birth Anniv, Oct 16
Douglass, Frederick
    Death Anniv, Feb 20
    Escape to Freedom: Anniv, Sep 3
    Frederick Douglass Speaks: Anniv, Aug 11
Dourdan, Gary: Birth, Dec 11
Dourif, Brad: Birth, Mar 18
Dow, Tony: Birth, Apr 13
Dowie, John: Birth Anniv, May 25
Dow-Jones Biggest Drop: Anniv, Oct 19
Dow-Jones Industrial Average: Anniv, Oct 7
Dow-Jones Tops 1,000: Anniv, Nov 14
Dow-Jones Tops 3,000: Anniv, Apr 17
Dow-Jones Tops 5,000: Anniv, Nov 21
Dow-Jones Tops 6,000: Anniv, Oct 14
Dow-Jones Tops 10,000: Anniv, Mar 29
Dow-Jones Tops 11,000: Anniv, May 3
Down Syndrome Month, Natl, Oct 1
Down, Lesley-Anne: Birth, Mar 17
Downey, Robert, Jr: Birth, Apr 4
Downey, Roma: Birth, May 6
Downs, Hugh: Birth, Feb 14
Doyle, Jim: Birth, Nov 23
Doyle, Sir Arthur Conan: Birth Anniv, May 22
Dr. Who TV Premiere: Anniv, Nov 23
Drabble, Margaret: Birth, Jun 5
Dracula Premiere: Anniv, Feb 12
Dragnet TV Premiere: Anniv, Dec 16
Dragon Boat Fest (China), May 31
Dragon, Daryl: Birth, Aug 27
Dragons: Appreciate a Dragon Day, Jan 16
Dream 2006 Day, Mar 11
Dream Hotline, Natl, Apr 28
Dred Scott Decision: Anniv, Mar 6
Dreiser, Theodore: Birth Anniv, Aug 27
Drescher, Fran: Birth, Sep 30
Dresden Firebombing, Feb 13
Drew, Charles: Birth Anniv, Jun 3
Drew, Elizabeth: Birth, Nov 16
Drexler, Clyde Austin: Birth, Jun 22
Dreyfuss, Richard: Birth, Oct 29
Drinking Age: Minimum Legal at 21: Anniv, Jul 17
Drinking Straw Patented: Anniv, Jan 3
Drive-In Movie Opens, First: Anniv, Jun 6
Driver, Minnie: Birth, Jan 31
Drive-Thru Day, Natl, Jul 24
Drowning Prevention Day, Natl (Canada), Jul 22
Drucker, Peter: Birth, Nov 19
Drug Abuse/Illicit Trafficking, Intl Day Against (UN), Jun 26
Drugs: Just Pray No: Worldwide Weekend Prayer, Apr 23
Drunk and Drugged Driving Prevention Month, Natl (Pres Proc), Dec 1
Drysdale, Don: Birth Anniv, Jul 23
Dubcek, Alexander: Birth Anniv, Nov 27
DuBois, Ja'net: Birth, Aug 5
DuBois, W.E.B.: Birth Anniv, Feb 23
DuBois, W.E.B.: Niagara Movement Founded: Anniv, Jul 11
Duchovny, David: Birth, Aug 7
Duck-Calling Contest, World Chmpshp (Stuttgart, AR), Nov 24
Duff, Hilary: Birth, Sep 28
Duff, Howard: Birth Anniv, Nov 24
Duffy, Julia: Birth, Jun 27
Duffy, Patrick: Birth, Mar 17
Dugan, Dennis: Birth, Sep 5
Dukakis, Michael: Birth, Nov 3
Dukakis, Olympia: Birth, Jun 20
Duke, Patty: Birth, Dec 14
Dukes of Hazzard TV Premiere: Anniv, Jan 26
Dulcimer Days (Coshocton, OH), May 19
Dulcimer Fest, Southern Appalachian (McCalla, AL), May 6

Dullea, Keir: Birth, May 30
Dumars, Joe: Birth, May 24
Dumas, Alexandre (Fils): Birth Anniv, Jul 27
Dumas, Alexandre: Birth Anniv, Jul 24
Dumb Week (Greece), Apr 9
Dump Your "Significant Jerk" Day, Feb 7
Dunant, Jean Henri: Birth Anniv, May 8
Dunaway, Faye: Birth, Jan 14
Duncan, Isadora: Birth Anniv, May 27
Duncan, Sandy: Birth, Feb 20
Duncan, Tim: Birth, Apr 25
Dunkirk Evacuated: Anniv, May 26
Dunn, Adam: Birth, Nov 9
Dunn, Nora: Birth, Apr 29
Dunn, Shannon: Birth, Nov 26
Dunn, Warrick: Birth, Jan 5
Dunne, Griffin: Birth, Jun 8
Dunne, Philip: Birth Anniv, Feb 11
Dunst, Kirsten: Birth, Apr 30
Duran Duran Appreciation Day, Natl, Aug 10
Duran, Roberto: Birth, Jun 16
Durang, Christopher: Birth, Jan 2
Durant, Will: Birth Anniv, Nov 5
Durant, William: Birth Anniv, Dec 8
Durante, Jimmy: Birth Anniv, Feb 10
Durbin, Deanna: Birth, Dec 4
Durbin, Richard J.: Birth, Nov 21
Durer, Albrecht: Birth Anniv, May 21
Durning, Charles: Birth, Feb 28
Durocher, Leo: Birth Anniv, Jul 27
Dushku, Eliza: Birth, Dec 30
Dussault, Nancy: Birth, Jun 30
Duston, Hannah: American Heroine Rewarded: Anniv, Jun 8
Dutoit, Charles: Birth, Oct 7
Dutton, Charles S.: Birth, Jan 30
Duval, David: Birth, Nov 9
Duvall, Robert: Birth, Jan 5
Duvall, Shelley: Birth, Jul 7
Dvorak, Anton: New World Symphony Premiere: Anniv, Dec 16
Dykstra, Lenny: Birth, Feb 10
Dylan, Bob: Birth, May 24
Dynasty TV Premiere: Anniv, Jan 12
Dysart, Richard: Birth, Mar 30

E, Sheila: Birth, Dec 12
Eads, George: Birth, Mar 1
Eagle Days in Springfield (Springfield, MO), Jan 21
Eagles Et Cetera Fest (Bismarck, AR), Jan 27
Earhart, Amelia, Atlantic Crossing: Anniv, May 20
Earhart, Amelia: Birth Anniv, Jul 24
Earhart, Amelia: Disappears: Anniv, Jul 2
Early America Historical Fair (Albert Lea, MN), Feb 11
Earmuffs Patented: Anniv, Mar 13
Earnhardt, Dale, Jr: Birth, Oct 10
Earnhardt, Dale: Birth Anniv, Apr 29
Earp Brothers (Wyatt, Morgan, Virgil): Gunfight at the OK Corral: Anniv, Oct 26
Earp, Wyatt: Birth Anniv, Mar 19
Earth at Aphelion, Jul 3
Earth at Perihelion, Jan 4
Earth Day, Apr 22
Earthquake
    Calabria (Italy) Earthquake: Anniv, Dec 16
    Earthquake Jolts Philippines: Anniv, Jul 16
    Earthquake of 1988, Armenian: Anniv, Dec 7
    Earthquake Strikes Alaska: Anniv, Mar 27
    Indian Earthquake, Jan 26
    Japan Suffers Major Quake: Anniv, Jan 17
    Lisbon: Anniv, Nov 1
    Mexico City Earthquake: Anniv, Sep 19
    Missouri Earthquakes: Anniv, Dec 6
    Plymouth Plantation: Anniv, Jun 1
    Richter Scale Day, Apr 26
    San Francisco 1906 Earthquake: Anniv, Apr 18
    San Francisco 1989 Earthquake: Anniv, Oct 17
    Southern California: Anniv, Jan 17
    Strongest Earthquake of the 20th Century: Anniv, May 22
    Sumatran-Andaman Earthquake and Tsunamis: Anniv, Dec 26
    Turkish Earthquake: Anniv, Aug 17
Earth's Rotation Proved: Anniv, Jan 8
Easley, Mike: Birth, Mar 23
East Coast Blackout: Anniv, Nov 9
East Texas Poultry Fest (Center, TX), Oct 5
East Timor: Independence: Anniv, May 20
Easter
    Bunny Bop and Hop (Aiken, SC), Apr 15
    Chincoteague Easter Decoy Show (Chincoteague Island, VA), Apr 14
    Easter Egg Hunt (Rockford, OH), Apr 15
    Easter Even, Apr 15
    Easter Monday, Apr 17

Easter Monday Bank Holiday (United Kingdom), **Apr 17**
Easter Sunday, **Apr 16**
Easter Sundays Through the Year 2009, **Apr 16**
Easter Sunrise Service (Chimney Rock, NC), **Apr 16**
Haute Dog Charity Easter Parade (Long Beach, CA), **Apr 16**
Holy Humor Month, **Apr 1**
Holy Week, **Apr 9**
Longwood Gardens Easter Display (Kennett Square, PA), **Apr 8**
Lucerne Fest, Ostern (Lucerne, Switzerland), **Apr 1**
Megga Hunt (Springfield, OR), **Apr 15**
Moravian Easter Resurrection Service (Winston-Salem, NC), **Apr 16**
Orthodox Easter Sunday, **Apr 23**
Passion Week, **Mar 13**
Passiontide, **Apr 2**
White House Easter Egg Roll (Washington, DC), **Apr 17**
White House Easter Egg Roll: Anniv, **Apr 2**
Easter Rising (Ireland), Apr 24
Easton, Sheena: Birth, Apr 27
Eastport "Old Home Week" Celebration (Eastport, ME), Jul 1
Eastwood, Clint: Birth, May 31
Eat Better, Eat Together Month, Oct 1
Eat Dessert First Week, May 1
Eat What You Want Day, May 11
Eating Disorders Awareness Week, Natl, Feb 26
Ebersole, Christine: Birth, Feb 21
Ebert, Roger: Birth, Jun 18
Ebsen, Buddy: Birth Anniv, Apr 2
Eckersley, Dennis: Birth, Oct 3
Eckert, J. Presper, Jr: Birth Anniv, Apr 9
Eckstine, Billy: Birth Anniv, Jul 8
Eclipses
  Annular Solar Eclipse, **Sep 22**
  Partial Lunar Eclipse, **Sep 7**
  Penumbral Lunar Eclipse, **Mar 14**
  Total Solar Eclipse, **Mar 29**
Eco, Umberto: Birth, Jan 5
Ecommerce Day, Intl Women's, Sep 19
Ecuador
  Battle of Pichincha, **May 24**
  Day of Quito, **Dec 6**
  Independence Day, **Aug 10**
Ed Sullivan Show TV Premiere: Anniv, Jun 20
Ed Sullivan Show: The Beatles Appear: Anniv, Feb 9
Eddy, Duane: Birth, Apr 26
Eddy, Mary Baker: Birth Anniv, Jul 16
Edelman, Marian Wright: Birth, Jun 6
Eden, Barbara: Birth, Aug 23
Ederle, Gertrude: Birth Anniv, Oct 23
Ederle, Gertrude: Swims English Channel: Anniv, Aug 6
Edge of Night TV Premiere: Anniv, Apr 2
Edge, The: Birth, Aug 8
Edison, Thomas
  Birth Anniv, **Feb 11**
  Black Maria Studio: Anniv, **Feb 1**
  Death Anniv, **Oct 18**
  First Electric Lighting: Anniv, **Sep 4**
  Incandescent Lamp Demonstrated: Anniv, **Oct 21**
  Record of a Sneeze: Anniv, **Feb 2**
Edison, Thomas: Be Electrific Day, Feb 11
Editing: Word Nerd Day, Jan 9
Editors and Writers Month, Be Kind to, Sep 1
Edmonds, Kenneth (Babyface): Birth, Apr 10
Edmonton Intl Fringe Theatre Fest (Edmonton, AB, Canada), Aug 17
Edmund Fitzgerald Beacon Lighting (Two Harbors, MN), Nov 10
Edmund Fitzgerald Sinking: Anniv, Nov 10
Education and Sharing Day (Pres Proc), Mar 27
Education, Learning, Schools
  American Council on Education Annual Mtg (Los Angeles, CA), **Feb 11**
  American Education Week, **Nov 12**
  Banned Books Week, **Sep 23**
  Bubble Gum Day, **Feb 1**
  Catholic Educational Assn Conv/Expo, Natl (New Orleans, LA), **Apr 18**
  Catholic Schools Week, **Jan 29**
  Chemistry Week, Natl, **Oct 22**
  Children's Book Day, Intl, **Apr 2**
  College Savings Month, **Sep 1**
  Education Assn Meeting, Natl (Orlando, FL), **Jun 30**
  Educational Support Personnel Day, Natl, **Nov 15**
  Eliza Doolittle Day, **May 20**
  Family Literacy Day, Natl, **Nov 1**
  Fashion Show (Milwaukee, WI), **May 5**
  Froebel, Friedrich: Birth Anniv, **Apr 21**
  Geographic Bee Finals, Natl (Washington, DC), **May 23**
  Geographic Bee, School Level, Natl, **Jan 3**
  Geographic Bee, State Level, Natl, **Mar 31**
  Get Ready for Kindergarten Month, **Aug 1**
  Get Smart about Credit Day, **Oct 19**
  Gifted Children Conv, Natl Assn (Charlotte, NC), **Nov 1**
  Go on a Field Trip Month, Natl, **Oct 1**
  Groundhog Job Shadow Day, **Feb 2**
  Harvard Univ Founded: Anniv, **Oct 28**
  Historically Black Colleges and Universities Week, Natl (Pres Proc), **Sep 17**
  Honor Society Awareness Month, **Mar 1**
  Introduce a Girl to Engineering Day, **Feb 23**
  Kindergarten Day, **Apr 21**
  Learning Disabilities Assn Intl Conf (New Orleans, LA), **Mar 1**
  Library Week, Natl, **Apr 2**
  Literacy Day, Intl (UN), **Sep 8**
  Mentoring Month, Natl, **Jan 1**
  Metric Week, Natl, **Oct 8**
  MiAEYC Early Childhood Conference (Grand Rapids, MI), **Mar 30**
  Mole Day, Natl, **Oct 23**
  Morrill Land Grant Act Passed: Anniv, **Jul 1**
  Mount Holyoke College Founded, **Nov 8**
  Museum Day, Intl, **May 18**
  Music in Our Schools Month, **Mar 1**
  Newspaper in Education Week, **Mar 6**
  Paraprofessional Appreciation Day, **Apr 5**
  Parents as Teachers Day, Natl, **Nov 8**
  Peabody, Elizabeth Palmer: Birth Anniv, **May 16**
  PTA Founders' Day, Natl, **Feb 17**
  PTA Teacher Appreciation Week, Natl, **May 7**
  Public School, First in America: Anniv, **Apr 23**
  Read Across America Day, **Mar 2**
  Read Me Week (TN), **Feb 27**
  Reading Is Fun Week, **May 14**
  Scholarship Month, Natl, **May 1**
  School Bus Safety Week, Natl, **Oct 15**
  School Counseling Week, Natl, **Feb 6**
  School for Deaf Founded, First: Anniv, **Apr 15**
  School Library Media Month, **Apr 1**
  School Lunch Week, Natl, **Oct 9**
  School Nurse Day, Natl, **May 10**
  School Principals' Day, **May 1**
  School Spirit Season, Intl, **Apr 30**
  School Success Month, Natl, **Sep 1**
  Self-Improvement Month, **Sep 1**
  Self-University Week, **Sep 1**
  Special Education Day, **Dec 2**
  Spelling Bee Finals, Natl, **May 31**
  Spelman College Established: Anniv, **Apr 11**
  Student Government Day (MA), **Apr 7**
  Substitute Teacher Appreciation Week, **Sep 18**
  Sullivan, Anne: Birth Anniv, **Apr 14**
  Sunday School Teacher Appreciation Day, **Oct 15**
  Teacher Appreciation Week, **May 7**
  Teacher Day, Natl, **May 9**
  Teachers' Day (Czech Republic), **Mar 28**
  Thank You, School Librarian Day, **Apr 5**
  Truancy Law: Anniv, **Apr 12**
  Tuskegee Institute Opening: Anniv, **Jul 4**
  Tutor Appreciation Day, **Apr 8**
  Univ of Chicago First Day of Classes, **Oct 1**
  World Teachers' Day (UN), **Oct 5**
  Yale Univ Founded: Anniv, **Oct 16**
  Young Child, Week of the, **Apr 2**
  Young Reader's Day, Natl, **Nov 14**
Edward D. Jones: Birth Anniv, Oct 7
Edward VIII: Abdication Anniv, Dec 11
Edward, Jonathan: Birth Anniv, Oct 5
Edward, Prince: Birth, Mar 10
Edwards, Anthony: Birth, Jul 19
Edwards, Blake: Birth, Jul 26
Edwards, Douglas: Birth Anniv, Jul 14
Edwards, Harry: Birth, Nov 22
Edwards, John: Birth, Jun 10
Edwards, Vince: Birth Anniv, Jul 9
Effectiveness Week, Natl, May 15
Egg Month, Natl, May 1
Egg Races (Switzerland), Apr 17
Egg Roll, White House Easter Egg Roll: Anniv, Apr 2
Egg Salad Week, Apr 17
Eggar, Samantha: Birth, Mar 5
Eggert, Nicole: Birth, Jan 13
Eggsibit (Phillipsburg, NJ), Apr 1
Egypt
  Armed Forces Day, **Oct 6**
  Camp David Accord Signed: Anniv, **Mar 26**
  Evacuation Day, **Jun 18**
  Revolution Day, **Jul 23**
  Sinai Day, **Apr 25**
  Statue of Ramses II Unearthed: Anniv, **Nov 30**
  Suez Canal Formal Opening: Anniv, **Nov 17**
  Suez Canal Opens: Anniv, **Mar 7**
Ehrlich, Paul: Birth, May 29
Ehrlich, Robert, Jr: Birth, Nov 25

Eichhorn, Lisa: Birth, Feb 4
Eid-al-Adha: Feast of the Sacrifice (Muslim), Jan 10, Dec 31
Eid-al-Fitr: Celebrating the Fast (Muslim), Oct 24
Eiffel Tower: Anniv (Paris, France), Mar 31
Eiffel, Alexandre Gustave: Birth Anniv, Dec 15
Eight Is Enough TV Premiere: Anniv, Mar 15
Eikenberry, Jill: Birth, Jan 21
Einstein on Wine (Tampa, FL), Feb 4
Einstein, Albert: Birth Anniv, Mar 14
Einstein, Albert: Russell-Einstein Manifesto: Anniv, Jul 9
Eisenhower, David: Birth, Apr 1
Eisenhower, Dwight: Birth Anniv, Oct 14
Eisenhower, Dwight: Ike's Farewell (military-industrial warning): Anniv, Jan 17
Eisenhower, Mamie Doud: Birth Anniv, Nov 14
Eisenhower: Interstate Highway System Born: Anniv, Jun 29
Eisenstaedt, Alfred: Birth Anniv, Dec 6
Eisner, Michael: Birth, Mar 7
Eisner, Will: Birth Anniv, Mar 6
Ekberg, Anita: Birth, Sep 29
Ekland, Britt: Birth, Oct 6
El Salvador
  Day of the First Shout for Independence, **Nov 5**
  Day of the Soldier, **May 7**
  Independence Day, **Sep 15**
  National Day of Peace, **Jan 16**
Eldard, Ron: Birth, Feb 20
Eldon Turkey Fest (Eldon, MO), Oct 14
Eleanor Roosevelt Day (Menlo, WA), Aug 12
Elections, Caucuses, Political Conventions
  Dimpled Chad Day, **Jan 4**
  Election Day, US, **Nov 7**
  Last Week to Register to Vote in US General Elections, **Oct 1**
  Return Day (Georgetown, DE), **Nov 9**
  Supreme Court Rules for Bush: Anniv, **Dec 12**
Electra, Carmen: Birth, Apr 20
Electric Lighting, First: Anniv, Sep 4
Electricity: Incandescent Lamp Demonstrated: Anniv, Oct 21
Electrocution for Death Penalty, First: Anniv, Aug 6
Electronic Communications Week, Apr 24
Electronic Greetings Day, Nov 29
Elephant Appreciation Day, Sep 22
Elephant Roundup at Surin (Thailand), Nov 18
Elephants: Jumbo Arrives in America: Anniv, Apr 9
Elfman, Jenna: Birth, Sep 30
Eliot, George: Birth Anniv, Nov 22
Eliot, John: Birth Anniv, Aug 5
Eliot, T.S.: Birth Anniv, Sep 26
Elizabeth I, Queen: Accession Anniv, Nov 17
Elizabeth I, Queen: Birth Anniv, Sep 7
Elizabeth II, Queen: Accession Anniv, Feb 6
Elizabeth II, Queen: Agrees to Pay Taxes, Nov 26
Elizabeth II, Queen: Birth, Apr 21
Elizabeth II: Marriage of Elizabeth and Philip: Anniv, Nov 20
Elizabeth, the Queen Mother: Birth Anniv, Aug 4
Elizondo, Hector: Birth, Dec 22
Elkin, Stanley: Birth Anniv, May 11
Ellerbee, Linda: Birth, Aug 15
Ellery, William: Birth Anniv, Dec 22
Ellington, Duke: Birth Anniv, Apr 29
Elliott, Bill: Birth, Oct 8
Elliott, Chris: Birth, May 31
Elliott, David James: Birth, Sep 21
Elliott, Missy: Birth, Jul 1
Elliott, Sam: Birth, Aug 9
Elliott, Sean: Birth, Feb 2
Ellis Island Family History Day, Apr 17
Ellis Island Opened: Anniv, Jan 1
Ellison, Ralph Waldo: Birth Anniv, Mar 1
Ellsberg, Daniel: Birth, Apr 7
Ellsworth, Oliver: Birth Anniv, Apr 29
Els, Ernie: Birth, Oct 17
Elvis Presley Remembered (St. Louis, MO), Aug 12
Elvis Week (Memphis, TN), Aug 8
Elway, John: Birth, Jun 28
Elwes, Cary: Birth, Oct 26
Emaishen (Luxembourg), Apr 17
Emancipation Day (Texas), Jun 19
Emancipation of 500: Anniv, Aug 1
Emancipation Proclamation Takes Effect: Anniv, Jan 1
Emancipation Proclamation: Anniv, Sep 22
Embassy Seizure, US, in Teheran: Anniv, Nov 4
Embrace Your Geekness Day, Jul 13
Emergency Nurses Day, Oct 11
Emergency Nurses Week, Oct 8
Emergency TV Premiere: Anniv, Jan 22
Emerson, Ralph Waldo: Birth Anniv, May 25
Eminem: Birth, Oct 17

Emmerich—Evers

Emmerich, Roland: Birth, Nov 10
Emmett Kelly Clown Fest (Houston, MO), May 5
Emmett, Daniel D.: Birth Anniv, Oct 29
Emotional Wellness Month, Oct 1
Empowerment Week, Women's Self-, Jan 2
Empty Nester Month, Celebrate, Nov 1
Enberg, Dick: Birth, Jan 9
Endangered Species Act: Anniv, Dec 28
Energy Management Is a Family Affair, Oct 1
Energy: Cut Your Energy Costs Day, Natl, Jan 10
Engineering: Introduce a Girl to Day, Feb 23
Engineers Week, Natl, Feb 19
England
  Badminton Horse Trials (Badminton), May 4
  Beatles Fest (Liverpool), Aug 25
  Birmingham Riot: Anniv, Jul 14
  Blackpool Illuminations (Blackpool, Lancashire),
    Sep 1
  British Air Raid on Berlin: Anniv, Jan 16
  British and World Marbles Chmpshp, Apr 14
  British Museum: Anniv, Jan 15
  Care Sunday, Apr 2
  Charles II: Restoration and Birth Anniv, May 29
  Chelsea Antiques Fair (London), Sep 15
  Chelsea Art Fair (London), Apr 20
  Chelsea Flower Show (London), May 23
  Cheltenham Hunt Fest (Prestbury), Mar 14
  Chester Antiques and Fine Art Show (Cheshire),
    Feb 16
  Christmas Holiday, Dec 25
  City of London Fest (London), Jun 26
  Crufts Dog Show (Birmingham), Mar 9
  Derby, The, Jun 10
  Devizes/Westminster Intl Canoe Race (Devizes),
    Apr 14
  Dicing for Bibles, Jun 5
  English Riviera Dance Fest (Torquay), Jun 2
  Exeter Fest (Exeter), Jun 16
  George VI's Coronation: Anniv, May 12
  Great Britain Formed: Anniv, May 1
  Great Fire of London: Anniv, Sep 2
  Guy Fawkes Day, Nov 5
  Hallaton Bottle Kicking (Hallaton), Apr 17
  Hampton Court Palace Flower Show Charity Gala
    Preview (East Molesey, Surrey), Jul 3
  Harrogate Autumn Flower Show (Harrogate, N
    Yorkshire), Sep 15
  Harrogate Spring Flower Show (Harrogate, N
    Yorkshire), Apr 27
  Head of the River Race (London), Mar 25
  Helston Furry Dance, May 6
  Henley Royal Regatta (Henley-on-Thames), Jun 28
  Jersey Battle of Flowers (St. Lawrence, Channel
    Islands), Aug 10
  Last Hurrah for British Hong Kong, Jun 30
  Lawn Tennis Chmpshps at Wimbledon (London),
    Jun 26
  London Book Fair (London), Mar 5
  London Terrorist Bombings: Anniv, Jul 7
  London/Brighton Veteran Car Run (London), Nov 5
  Lord Mayor's Show (London), Nov 11
  Marriage of Elizabeth and Philip: Anniv, Nov 20
  Mothering Sunday, Mar 26
  New Year's Day Parade (London), Jan 1
  Nottingham Goose Fair (Nottingham), Oct 4
  Open Golf Chmpshp (British Open) (Hoylake),
    Jul 20
  Petersfield Antiques Fair (Petersfield), Feb 10
  Plough Monday, Jan 9
  Queen Elizabeth I: Birth Anniv, Sep 7
  RAF Bombs Hitler Celebration: Anniv, Jan 30
  Remembrance Sunday (London), Nov 12
  Royal Ascot, Jun 20
  Royal Bath and West Show (Shepton Mallet,
    Somerset), May 30
  Royal George Sinks: Anniv, Aug 29
  Royal Windsor Horse Show (Windsor), May 11
  Saint George: Feast Day, Apr 23
  Schroders London Boat Show (London), Jan 5
  Scotland Yard First Appearance Anniv, Sep 29
  Shrewsbury Intl Music Fest (Shropshire), Jun 30
  Shrovetide Pancake Race (Olney,
    Buckinghamshire), Feb 28
  Skandia Cowes Week (Isle of Wight), Jul 29
  Slave Trade Abolished: Anniv, Mar 25
  Trooping Colours/Queen's Official Birthday, Jun 10
  Walter Plinge Day, Dec 2
  Ways With Words Literature Fest (Dartington),
    Jul 7
  West London Antiques & Fine Art Fair (London),
    Jan 13
  Words by the Water: A Cumbrian Literature Fest
    (Lake District), Mar 10
English Channel, First Airplane Crossing: Anniv,
  Jul 25
English Channel, First Man-Powered Flight
  Across: Anniv, Jun 12

English Colony in North America, First: Anniv,
  Aug 5
ENIAC Computer Introduced: Anniv, Feb 14
Enigma Machine, British Capture of: Anniv, May 9
Eno, Brian: Birth, May 15
Enron Files for Bankruptcy: Anniv, Dec 2
Ensign, John: Birth, Mar 25
Entebbe, Raid on: Anniv, Jul 3
Enthusiasm Week, Intl, Sep 1
Entrepreneurs "Do It Yourself" Marketing Month,
  Jun 1
Environment Day, World (UN), Jun 5
Environment
  Alabama Coastal Cleanup (Mobile, AL), Sep 16
  America Recycles Day, Nov 15
  Arbor Day, Natl, Apr 28
  Bike to Work Day, Natl, May 19
  Biodiesel Day, Natl (Rudolph Diesel Birth Anniv),
    Mar 18
  Biological Diversity, Intl Day for (UN), May 22
  Cattus Island Nature Fest (Toms River, NJ), Oct 1
  Celebrate Earth Day Weekend (Point Pleasant
    Beach, NJ), Apr 22
  Chernobyl Reactor Disaster: Anniv, Apr 26
  Clean Air Act Passed by Congress: Anniv, Dec 17
  Clean Air Month, May 1
  Clothesline Week, Intl, Jun 3
  Coastal Cleanup, Intl, Sep 16
  Day for Preventing the Exploitation of the
    Environment in War and Armed Conflict, Intl
    (UN), Nov 6
  Earth Day, Apr 22
  Earth Day Community Fest (St. Louis, MO), Apr 23
  Endangered Species Act: Anniv, Dec 28
  Environmental Policy Act, Natl, Jan 1
  Exxon Valdez Oil Spill: Anniv, Mar 24
  Greenpeace Founded: Anniv, Sep 15
  International Day for Preservation of the Ozone
    Layer (UN), Sep 16
  Japan Agrees to End Use of Drift Nets: Anniv,
    Nov 26
  Mother Ocean Day, May 13
  Natural Disaster Reduction, Intl Day for (UN),
    Oct 11
  Pee on Earth Day, Jun 21
  President's Environmental Youth Award Natl
    Competition, Jul 31
  Rainbow Warrior Sinking: Anniv, Jul 10
  Rainforest Week, Natl, Oct 16
  Rivers Month, Natl, Jun 1
  Rural Life Sunday, May 21
  Sierra Club Founded: Anniv, May 28
  Silent Spring Publication: Anniv, Apr 13
  Smart Irrigation Month, Jul 1
  Trails Day, Natl, Jun 3
  Water Pollution Control Act: Anniv, Oct 18
  Water, World Day for (UN), Mar 22
  Week of Ocean Fest Sea-Son, Natl (Fort
    Lauderdale, FL), Mar 4
  Week of the Ocean, Natl, Apr 2
  World Day to Combat Desertification and Drought
    (UN), Jun 17
  World Environment Day (UN), Jun 5
Enzi, Michael B.: Birth, Feb 1
Ephron, Nora: Birth, May 19
Epilepsy Awareness Month, Nov 1
Epiphany (Twelfth Day), Jan 6
Episcopal Bishop, First Woman: Anniv, Feb 11
Epitaph Day, Plan Your, Nov 2
Epps, Omar: Birth, Jul 23
Equal Rights Party Founding: Anniv, Sep 20
Equatorial Guinea
  Armed Forces Day, Aug 3
  Constitution Day, Aug 15
  Independence Day, Oct 12
Equinox, Autumn, Sep 23
Equinox, Spring, Mar 20
ER TV Premiere: Anniv, Sep 19
Eradication of Poverty, Intl Day for (UN), Oct 17
Erasmus, Desiderius: Birth Anniv, Oct 28
Erdrich, Louise: Birth, Jun 7
Erie Canal: Anniv, Oct 26
Erikson, Leif: Day (Iceland), Oct 9
Erikson, Leif: Day (Pres Proc), Oct 9
Eritrea: Independence Day, May 24
Eritrea: Timket (Epiphany), Jan 19
Ermey, R. Lee: Birth, Mar 24
Ernie Kovacs TV Premiere: Anniv, May 14
Erving, Julius: Birth, Feb 22
Escoffier, Georges: Birth Anniv, Oct 28
Esiason, Boomer: Birth, Apr 17
Esposito, Giancarlo: Birth, Apr 26
Esposito, Phil: Birth, Feb 20
Essay Contest, American History, Aug 1
Estefan, Emilio: Birth, Mar 4
Estefan, Gloria: Birth, Sep 1
Estes, Rob: Birth, Jul 22
Estevez, Emilio: Birth, May 12

Estonia
  Baltic States' Independence Recognized: Anniv,
    Sep 6
  Day of National Rebirth, Nov 16
  Independence Day, Feb 24
  Victory Day, Jun 23
Estrada, Erik: Birth, Mar 16
Etheridge, Melissa: Birth, May 29
Ethics Awareness Month, Natl, Mar 1
Ethiopia
  Adwa Day, Mar 2
  National Day, May 28
  New Year's Day, Sep 11
  Patriots Victory Day, May 5
  Timket (Epiphany), Jan 19
  True Cross Day, Sep 27
Ethnic Awareness Program (Macon, GA), Apr 26
Ethnic Observances. See also nationality names
  Aebleskiver Days (Tyler, MN), Jul 21
  Asian Pacific American Heritage Month (Pres
    Proc), May 1
  Cabrillo Fest (San Diego, CA), Sep 29
  Canada's Natl Ukrainian Fest (Dauphin, MB,
    Canada), Aug 4
  Central Nebraska Ethnic Fest (Grand Island, NE),
    Jul 28
  Chinese New Year Fest (San Francisco, CA),
    Jan 21
  Czech Days (Tabor, SD), Jun 16
  Dalesburg Midsummer Fest (Vermillion, SD),
    Jun 23
  German-American Day, Natl, Oct 6
  German-American Heritage Month, Oct 1
  Haitian Heritage Month, May 1
  Heritagefest (New Ulm, MN), Jul 14
  Herrinfesta Italiana (Herrin, IL), May 25
  Hispanic Heritage Month, Sep 15
  Holiday Folk Fair Intl (Milwaukee, WI), Nov 17
  Hollywood Beach Latin Fest (Hollywood, FL),
    Aug 13
  Irish-American Heritage Month, Mar 1
  Italian Fest and Columbus Day Parade, Ocean
    County (Seaside Heights, NJ), Sep 3
  Jours de Fete (Ste. Genevieve, MO), Aug 12
  Midsummer Day/Eve Celebrations, Jun 23
  Polish American Heritage Month, Oct 1
  Polish Christmas Open House (Philadelphia, PA),
    Dec 9
  Pulaski Day Parade (Philadelphia, PA), Oct 1
  Saint Paul's Feast, Jun 28
  Saint Piran's Day (Cornish) Celebration (Kansas
    City, MO), Mar 4
  Scandinavian Fest (Edison, NJ), Sep 3
  Swedish Days (Geneva, IL), Jun 20
  Tivoli Fest (Elk Horn, IA), May 27
  West Virginia Italian Heritage Fest (Clarksburg,
    WV), Sep 1
  Westfest (Czech) (West, TX), Sep 2
  Wilhelm Tell Fest (New Glarus, WI), Sep 1
Etiquette
  Cell Phone Courtesy Month, Jul 1
  Children's Good Manners Month, Sep 1
  Civility Month, Natl Win with, Aug 1
  Common Courtesy Day, Natl, Mar 22
  Electronic Communications Week, Apr 24
  Etiquette Week, Natl, May 21
  Fresh Breath Day, Natl, Aug 6
  I Forgot Day, Jul 2
  Thank You Days, Intl, Jan 11
  Thanks for All the Gifts Week, Aug 13
  Thank-Your-Customers Week, Natl, Jan 9
  Toad Hollow Day of Thank You, Jun 20
Eubanks, Bob: Birth, Jan 8
Eubanks, Kevin: Birth, Nov 15
Euro Introduced: Anniv, Jan 1
Europe: Summer Daylight-Saving Time, Mar 26
European Union Established: Anniv, Nov 1
European Union: Schuman Plan Anniv, May 9
Evacuation Day (Boston, MA), Mar 17
Evacuation Day (Egypt), Jun 18
Evangelista, Linda: Birth, Jun 10
Evans, Bob: Birth, May 30
Evans, Chick: Birth Anniv, Jul 18
Evans, Heloise Cruse: Birth, Apr 15
Evans, Linda: Birth, Nov 18
Evans, Sara: Birth, Feb 5
Evening at Pops TV Premiere: Anniv, Jul 12
Everest Summit Reached: Anniv, May 29
Everest: First Woman to Climb: Anniv, May 16
Everett, Chad: Birth, Jun 11
Everett, Rupert: Birth, May 29
Everglades Natl Park Established: Anniv, Dec 6
Everly, Don: Birth, Feb 1
Everly, Phil: Birth, Jan 19
Evers, Johnny: Baseball's Sad Lexicon
  Published: Anniv, Jul 10
Evers, Johnny: Birth Anniv, Jul 21
Evers, Medgar, Assassinated: Anniv, Jun 13

Evert, Chris: Birth, Dec 21
Everybody's Day Fest (Thomasville, NC), Sep 30
Evigan, Greg: Birth, Oct 14
Ewell, Tom: Birth Anniv, Apr 29
Ewing, Patrick: Birth, Aug 5
Exchange Club Birthday, Natl, Mar 27
Exchange Club: Freedom Shrine Month, May 1
Execution: First Criminal in American Colonies: Anniv, Sep 30
Executive Coaching Day, May 1
Executives, American Society of Assn: Mtg/Expo (Boston, MA), Aug 19
Exhibitor Appreciation Week, Aug 7
Expect Success Month, Intl, Feb 1
Explore Your Career Options Week, Apr 10
Explosion of the Cart (Florence, Italy), Apr 16
Explosion: Halifax, Nova Scotia, Destroyed: Anniv, Dec 6
Explosion: Texas City Disaster: Anniv, Apr 16
Extraordinary Work Team Recognition Day, Dec 4
Extraterrestrial Culture Day (New Mexico), Feb 9
Extreme Sports (Parachuting, etc.)
  Bridge Day (Fayetteville, WV), Oct 21
  Freefall Conv, World (Rantoul, IL), Aug 4
  Ironman Triathlon World Chmpshp (Kailua-Kona, HI), Oct 14
  Nissan Xterra World Chmpshp (Maui, HI), Oct 29
  Powered Parachute Fly-in (Columbus, KS), Sep 21
Exxon Valdez Oil Spill: Anniv, Mar 24
Eye Donor Month, Natl, Mar 1
Eye Health and Safety Month, Children's, Aug 1
Eye Health and Safety Month, Women's, Apr 1
Eyes: Healthy Vision Month, May 1

Fabares, Shelley: Birth, Jan 19
Faberge, Carl: Birth Anniv, May 30
Fabian: Birth, Feb 6
Fabio: Birth, Mar 15
Fabray, Nanette: Birth, Oct 27
Face the Nation TV Premiere: Anniv, Nov 7
Facts of Life TV Premiere: Anniv, Aug 24
Fahrenheit, Gabriel D.: Birth Anniv, May 14
Fain, Sammy: Birth Anniv, Jun 17
Fair Trade Day, World, May 13
Fair, First Annual, in America: Anniv, Sep 30
Fair, Lorrie: Birth, Aug 5
Fairbanks, Charles W.: Birth Anniv, May 11
Fairbanks, Douglas: Birth Anniv, May 23
Fairchild, David G.: Birth Anniv, Apr 7
Fairchild, Morgan: Birth, Feb 3
Faithfull, Marianne: Birth, Dec 29
Fake Howard Hughes Biography: Anniv, Jan 9
Falana, Lola: Birth, Sep 11
Falco, Edie: Birth, Jul 5
Falcon Crest TV Premiere: Anniv, Dec 4
Faldo, Nick: Birth, Jul 18
Falk, Peter: Birth, Sep 16
Falkland Islands War: Anniv, Apr 2
Fall Fest of Arts and Crafts (Washington, MO), Sep 23
Fall Fest of Leaves (Ross County, OH), Oct 20
Fall Fest, Belle Meade Plantation (Nashville, TN), Sep 16
Fall Fest, Wo-Zha-Wa (Wisconsin Dells, WI), Sep 15
Fall Fiesta (Andrews, TX), Sep 22
Fall Hat Month, Sep 1
Fall in Love with Fond du Lac (Fond du Lac, WI), Sep 1
Fall of Kabul: Anniv, Nov 13
Fall of the Alamo: Anniv, Mar 6
Fall on Nantucket (Nantucket Island, MA), Oct 1
Falling Needles Family Fest, Dec 30
Fallon, Jimmy: Birth, Sep 19
Fallows, James: Birth, Aug 2
Falwell, Jerry: Birth, Aug 11
Family Feud TV Premiere: Anniv, Jul 12
Family Ties TV Premiere: Anniv, Sep 22
Family TV Premiere: Anniv, Mar 9
Family. See also Romance
  Absolutely Incredible Kid Day, Mar 16
  Adoption Week, Natl, Nov 1
  American Family Day, Aug 6
  Ancestor Appreciation Day, Sep 27
  Attend Your Grandchild's Birth Day, Natl, Sep 29
  Bake for Family Fun Month, Feb 1
  Black Single Parents' Week, Jun 4
  Brother's Day, May 24
  Canada: Family Day in Alberta, Feb 20
  Celebrate Empty Nester Month, Nov 1
  Child Abuse Prevention Month, Apr 1
  Communicate with Your Kid Month, Natl, Oct 1
  Cousins Day, Jul 24
  Crowded Nest Awareness Day, Jun 12
  Descendants Day, Jun 24
  Eat Better, Eat Together Month, Oct 1
  Ellis Island Family History Day, Apr 17
  Energy Management Is a Family Affair, Oct 1

Families in Business Week, Jun 12
Families, Intl Day of (UN), May 15
Family Awareness Day, Jun 18
Family Caregivers Month, Natl, Nov 1
Family Caregivers Month, Natl (Pres Proc), Nov 1
Family Day (TN), Aug 27
Family Day in Nevada, Nov 24
Family Day—A Day to Eat Dinner with Your Children, Sep 25
Family Fit Lifestyle Month, Jan 1
Family Health and Fitness Days—USA, Sep 30
Family History Day, Jun 14
Family Literacy Day, Natl, Nov 1
Family Meal Month, Aug 1
Family Month, Natl, May 14
Family Reunion Month, Jul 1
Family Sexuality Education Month, Natl, Oct 1
Family Stories Month, Nov 1
Family Volunteer Day, Natl, Nov 18
Family Week, Natl, May 7
Family Week, Natl (Pres Proc), Nov 19
Family Wellness Month, May 1
Family, Career and Community Leaders of America Natl Leadership Mtg (Nashville, TN), Jul 9
Family, Career and Community Leaders of America Week, Natl, Feb 12
Family-Leave Bill: Anniv, Feb 5
Father-Daughter Take a Walk Together Day, Jul 7
Father's Day, Jun 18
Father's Day (Pres Proc), Jun 18
Forgive Mom & Dad Day, Mar 18
Game & Puzzle Week, Natl, Nov 19
Genealogy Day, Mar 11
Gorgeous Grandma Day, Jul 23
Grandparents' Day, Natl, Sep 10
Hugging Day, Natl, Jan 21
Husband Appreciation Day, Apr 15
Husband Caregiver Day, Jun 18
Immunization Awareness Month, Natl, Aug 1
Intergeneration Day, Oct 1
Internet Moms Week, Intl, Mar 12
KidsDay, Natl, Aug 6
Knights of Columbus Family Week, Aug 12
Lifewriting Month, Natl, Nov 1
Love Our Children Day, Natl, Apr 1
Married to a Scorpio Support Day, Nov 18
Michigan's Grandparents and Grandchildren Day, Mar 18
Million Minute Family Challenge™, Sep 1
Mother-in-Law Day, Oct 22
Mother's Day, May 14
Moving Month, Natl, May 1
Orlando Family Spring Break (Orlando, FL), Mar 1
Parent Leadership Month, Natl, Feb 1
Parents as Teachers Day, Natl, Nov 8
Parents' Day (Pres Proc), Jul 23
Personal History Month, May 1
Please Take My Children to Work Day, Jun 26
Prepare Tomorrow's Parents Month, May 14
Purposeful Parenting Month, Natl, Jul 1
Respect for Parents Day, Aug 1
Second Honeymoon Weekend, Feb 17
Siblings Day, Natl, Apr 10
Sisters' Day, Aug 6
Stepparents' Week, Jun 1
Stress-Free Family Holidays Month, Natl, Dec 1
Take Our Daughters and Sons to Work Day, Apr 27
Talk With Your Teen About Sex Month, Natl, Mar 1
TV Turnoff Week, Natl, Apr 24
Unassisted Homebirth Week, Natl, Jul 1
Universal Children's Week, Oct 1
Universal Family Week, May 14
Universal Father's Week, Jun 18
Very Important Parents Month, Natl, Sep 1
Visit Your Relatives Day, May 18
Weddings Month, Natl, Feb 1
Work@Home Father's Day, Jun 16
World Marriage Day, Feb 12
Write to Your Father Day, Jun 11
Yours, Mine and Ours Month, Natl, Jan 1
Famous Preston Night Rodeo (Preston, ID), Jul 28
Faneuil Hall Opened to the Public: Anniv, Sep 24
Fantasy Fest (Key West, FL), Oct 20
Fantasy Island TV Premiere: Anniv, Jan 28
Faraday, Michael: Birth Anniv, Sep 22
Farentino, James: Birth, Feb 24
Fargas, Antonio: Birth, Aug 14
Fargo, Donna: Birth, Nov 10
Farina, Dennis: Birth, Feb 29
Farley, Cal: Birth Anniv, Dec 25
Farm Safety Week, Natl (Pres Proc), Sep 17
Farm Toy Show, Natl (Dyersville, IA), Nov 3
Farm-City Week, Natl (Pres Proc), Nov 17
Farmer, James: Birth Anniv, Jan 12
Farmer, Philip Jose: Birth, Jan 26

Farmers & Threshermens Jubilee (New Centerville, PA), Sep 6
Farmington Country Days (Farmington, MO), Jun 2
Farnsworth, Philo: Birth Anniv, Aug 19
Farr, Jamie: Birth, Jul 1
Farragut, David: Battle of Mobile Bay: Anniv, Aug 5
Farragut, David: Birth Anniv, Jul 5
Farragut, David: Farragut Captures New Orleans: Anniv, Apr 25
Farrakhan, Louis: Birth, May 11
Farrell, Colin: Birth, May 31
Farrell, James T.: Birth Anniv, Feb 27
Farrell, Mike: Birth, Feb 6
Farrell, Terry: Birth, Nov 19
Farrell, Will: Birth, Jul 16
Farrier's Week, Natl, Jul 9
Farrow, Mia: Birth, Feb 9
Fasching (Germany, Austria), Feb 27
Fasching Sunday (Germany, Austria), Feb 26
Fashion; Fashion Shows
  Adolfo: Birth, Feb 15
  Blass, Bill: Birth Anniv, Jun 22
  Cardin, Pierre: Birth, Jul 7
  Cassini, Oleg: Birth, Apr 11
  Chanel, Coco: Birth Anniv, Aug 19
  De La Renta, Oscar: Birth, Jul 22
  Dior, Christian: Birth Anniv, Jan 21
  Fashion Show (Milwaukee, WI), May 5
  Givenchy, Hubert de: Birth, Feb 21
  Intimate Apparel Market Week, Jan 9
  Kamali, Norma: Birth, Jun 27
  Karan, Donna: Birth, Oct 2
  Lacroix, Christian: Birth, May 17
  Lagerfeld, Karl: Birth, Sep 10
  McCartney, Stella: Birth, Sep 13
  Saint Laurent, Yves: Birth, Aug 1
  Schiaparelli, Elsa: Birth Anniv, Sep 10
  Secondhand Wardrobe Day, Natl, Jan 5
  Underwear Day, Natl, Aug 9
Fast of Esther: Ta'anit Esther, Mar 13
Fast of Gedalya, Sep 25
Fat Albert and the Cosby Kids TV Premiere: Anniv, Sep 9
Father-Daughter Take a Walk Together Day, Jul 7
Father's Day, Jun 18
Father's Day (Pres Proc), Jun 18
Fatima, Pilgrimage to (Portugal), May 12
Faulk, Marshall: Birth, Feb 26
Faulkner, William: Birth Anniv, Sep 25
Fauset, Jessie Redmon: Birth Anniv, Apr 26
Faustino, David: Birth, Mar 3
Favre, Brett: Birth, Oct 10
Fawcett, Farrah: Birth, Feb 2
Fawkes, Guy: Day (England), Nov 5
FBI: First Female FBI Agents: Anniv, Oct 25
FBI: Hoover, J. Edgar: Birth Anniv, Jan 1
Feast of Lanterns (Bon Fest) (Japan), Jul 13
Feast of St. Paul's Shipwreck (Valletta, Malta), Feb 10
Feast of the Immaculate Conception, Dec 8
Feast of the Incappucciati (Gradoli, Italy), Feb 23
Feast of the Redeemer (Venice, Italy), Jul 16
Federal Communications Commission Created: Anniv, Feb 26
Federal Credit Union Act: Anniv, Jun 26
Federal Reserve System: Anniv, Dec 23
Federalist Papers: Anniv, Oct 27
FedEx Orange Bowl (Miami, FL), Jan 3
Fedorov, Sergei: Birth, Dec 13
Feiffer, Jules: Birth, Jan 26
Feingold, Russell D.: Birth, Mar 2
Feinstein, Alan: Birth, Sep 8
Feinstein, Dianne: Birth, Jun 22
Feinstein, Michael: Birth, Sep 7
Feld, Eliot: Birth, Jul 5
Feldman, Corey: Birth, Jul 16
Feldon, Barbara: Birth, Mar 12
Feldshuh, Tovah: Birth, Dec 27
Feliciano, Jose: Birth, Sep 10
Felker, Clay S.: Birth, Oct 2
Feller, Bob: Birth, Nov 3
Fellini, Federico: Birth Anniv, Jan 20
Fell's Point Fun Fest (Baltimore, MD), Oct 7
Felt, W. Mark: Birth, Aug 17
Feltsman, Vladimir: Birth, Jan 8
Feminine Mystique Published: Anniv, Feb 19
Fender, Freddy: Birth, Jun 4
Fenn, Sherilyn: Birth, Feb 1
Fenwick, Millicent: Birth Anniv, Feb 25
Ferber, Edna: Birth Anniv, Aug 15
Ferguson, Maynard: Birth, May 4
Ferlinghetti, Lawrence: Birth, Mar 24
Fermi Atomic Power Plant: Accident Anniv, Oct 5
Fermi, Enrico: Birth Anniv, Sep 29
Fernandez, Giselle: Birth, May 15
Ferrante, Arthur: Birth, Sep 7

Ferraro—Florida

Ferraro, Geraldine: Birth, Aug 26
Ferrell, Conchata: Birth, Mar 28
Ferrer, Jose: Birth Anniv, Jan 8
Ferrer, Mel: Birth, Aug 25
Ferrer, Miguel: Birth, Feb 7
Ferrigno, Lou: Birth, Nov 9
Ferris Wheel Day, Feb 14
Ferry, Bryan: Birth, Sep 26
Fest of the Sea (Point Pleasant Beach, NJ),
  Sep 16
Fest of the West, Natl, and Log Home Show
  (Scottsdale, AZ), Mar 16
Festifall (Point Marion, PA), Sep 24
Fey, Tina: Birth, May 18
Fiber Arts: Convergence 2006 (Grand Rapids,
  MI), Jun 25
Fiber Festival, Michigan (Allegan, MI), Aug 16
Fibromyalgia Education & Awareness Month,
  May 1
Fiddlers. See also Bluegrass
  Canadian Open Fiddle Chmpshp (Shelburne, ON,
    Canada), Aug 9
  Fiddle Chmpshp, Louisiana State (Natchitoches,
    LA), Jul 21
  Fiddler's Frolics (Hallettsville, TX), Apr 27
  Kentucky State Fiddler's Chmpshp (Falls of Rough,
    KY), Jul 21
  Old Fiddlers' Conv (Galax, VA), Aug 7
  Old-Time Fiddlers' Contest and Fest, Natl (Weiser,
    ID), Jun 19
  Old-Time Fiddlers' Contest, Intl (Dunseith, ND),
    Jun 8
  Tennessee Valley Old Time Fiddlers Conv (Athens,
    AL), Oct 6
Field Trial Chmpshp (Bird Dogs), Natl (Grand
  Junction, TN), Feb 13
Field, Sally: Birth, Nov 6
Field, Shirley-Anne: Birth, Jun 27
Fielder, Cecil: Birth, Sep 21
Fields, Kim: Birth, May 12
Fields, W.C.: Birth Anniv, Jan 29
Fiennes, Joseph: Birth, May 27
Fiennes, Ralph: Birth, Dec 22
Fierstein, Harvey: Birth, Jun 6
Fiesta Bowl (Tempe, AZ), Jan 2
Fiesta La Ballona (Culver City, CA), Aug 26
Fiesta San Antonio (San Antonio, TX), Apr 21
FIFA World Cup (Germany), Jun 9
Fig Week, Natl, Nov 1
Figure Skating: Skating Week, Natl, Jan 14
Fiji: Independence Day, Oct 10
Filene, Edward Albert: Birth Anniv, Sep 3
Files Week, Natl Love Your, Sep 17
Filipina-American Recognition Day, Aug 9
Fillmore, Abigail P.: Birth Anniv, Mar 13
Fillmore, Caroline: Birth Anniv, Oct 21
Fillmore, Millard: Birth Anniv, Jan 7
Film
  Academy Awards Presentation, Mar 5
  Academy Awards, First: Anniv, May 16
  Ann Arbor Film Fest (Ann Arbor, MI), Mar 21
  Banff Mountain Film Fest (Banff, AB, Canada),
    Nov 3
  Berlin International Film Fest (Berlin, Germany),
    Feb 9
  Black Maria Studio: Anniv, Feb 1
  Bugs Bunny's Debut: Anniv, Apr 30
  Cannes Film Fest (Cannes, France), May 17
  Casablanca Premiere: Anniv, Nov 26
  Chaplin's Tramp Debuts: Anniv, Feb 7
  Chicago Intl Film Fest (Chicago, IL), Oct 5
  Citizen Kane Premiere: Anniv, May 1
  Dracula Premiere: Anniv, Feb 12
  First Drive-In Movie Opens: Anniv, Jun 6
  First Movie Theater Opens: Anniv, Apr 23
  Godfather Film Premiere: Anniv, Mar 15
  Gone with the Wind Premiere: Anniv, Dec 15
  It Happened One Night Release: Anniv, Feb 22
  It's a Wonderful Life Premiere: Anniv, Dec 20
  Jaws Release: Anniv, Jun 20
  KidFilm® Fest (Dallas, TX), Jan 9
  King Kong Premiere: Anniv, Mar 2
  Lumiere, Auguste: Birth Anniv, Oct 19
  Lumiere, Louis: Birth Anniv, Oct 5
  Marilyn Monroe's First Screen Test: Anniv, Jul 19
  New York Film Fest (New York, NY), Sep 29
  Psycho Premiere: Anniv, Jun 16
  Record of a Sneeze: Anniv, Feb 2
  Riefenstahl, Leni: Birth Anniv, Aug 22
  Roger Ebert's Overlooked Film Fest (Champaign,
    IL), Apr 26
  San Francisco Silent Film Fest (San Francisco,
    CA), Jul 14
  Sheik Film Release: Anniv, Nov 20
  Singin' in the Rain Premiere: Anniv, Mar 27
  Slamdance (Park City, UT), Jan 19
  Snow White and the Seven Dwarfs Film Premiere:
    Anniv, Dec 21

Sound of Music Premiere: Anniv, Mar 2
Star Wars Released: Anniv, May 25
Sundance Film Fest (Park City, UT), Jan 19
Telluride Film Fest (Telluride, CO), Sep 1
Titanic Released: Anniv, Dec 19
Toronto Intl Film Fest (Toronto, ON, Canada),
  Sep 7
Tribeca Film Fest (New York, NY), Apr 25
2001: A Space Odyssey Premiere: Anniv, Apr 3
US Intl Film/Video Awards (Los Angeles, CA),
  Jun 2
USA Film Fest (Dallas, TX), Apr 20
Valentino (Rudolph) Memorial Service, Aug 23
Wildlife Film Fest, Intl (Missoula, MT), Apr 29
Wizard of Oz Fest (Chesterton, IN), Sep 15
Wizard of Oz Released: Anniv, Aug 25
Final Four: NCAA Div I Men's Basketball
  Chmpshp (Indianapolis, IN), Apr 1
Financial Panic of 1873: Anniv, Sep 20
Financial Planning Week, Oct 2
Financial Wellness Month, Jan 1
Fine, Larry: Birth Anniv, Oct 5
Finland
  Flag Day, Jun 4
  Independence Day: Anniv, Dec 6
  Jazz Fest, Intl (Pori), Jul 15
  Jyvaskyla Arts Fest (Jyvaskyla), Jul 11
  Kuopio Dance Fest (Kuopio), Jun 15
  Lahti Organ Fest (Lahti), Aug 6
  Sata-Hame Accordion Fest (Ikaalinen), Jun 27
  Time of Music (Viitasaari), Jul 4
  Turku Music Fest (Turku), Aug 11
Finney, Albert: Birth, May 9
Fiorentino, Linda: Birth, Mar 9
Fire
  Apollo Spacecraft Fire: Anniv, Jan 27
  Fire Prevention Week, Oct 8
  Fire Prevention Week (Pres Proc), Oct 8
  Great Chicago Fire: Anniv, Oct 8
  Great Fire of London: Anniv, Sep 2
  Great Michigan Fire of 1881: Anniv, Sep 5
  Peshtigo (WI) Forest Fire: Anniv, Oct 8
  Southern California Firestorms: Anniv, Oct 25
  Triangle Shirtwaist Fire: Anniv, Mar 25
Fire Safety Council, Natl: Anniv, Dec 7
Fireant Fest (Marshall, TX), Oct 14
Firepup's Birthday, Oct 1
Fireside Chat, FDR's First: Anniv, Mar 12
Fireside Theatre TV Premiere: Anniv, Apr 5
Firestone, Harvey: Birth Anniv, Dec 20
Fireworks on the Fjord (Poulsbo, WA), Jul 3
Fireworks Safety Month, Jun 1
First American to Orbit Earth: Anniv, Feb 20
First Baby Boomer Born: Anniv, Jan 1
First Baseball Strike Ends: Anniv, Apr 13
First Black Southern Lt Gov: Anniv, Jan 11
First Car Insurance: Anniv, Feb 1
First Elected Woman Senator: Anniv, Jan 12
First Indoor Baseball Game: Anniv, Dec 25
First Man in Space: Anniv, Apr 12
First Manned Private Spaceflight: Anniv, Jun 21
First Monday Trade Days (Scottsboro, AL), Jan 1
First Moon Landing: Anniv, Jul 20
First Nights, Dec 31
First Perfect Game: Anniv, Jun 12
First Perfect Score in Olympic History: Anniv,
  Jul 18
First Roller Coaster Opens: Anniv, Jun 13
First Round-the-World Balloon Flight: Anniv,
  Mar 21
First Salem Witches Arrested: Anniv, Feb 1
First Scheduled Radio Broadcast: Anniv, Nov 2
First Scheduled Television Broadcast: Anniv,
  Jul 1
First Secret Service Agent to Die in the Line of
  Duty: Anniv, Sep 3
First Session of the Supreme Court: Anniv, Feb 1
First Solo Round-the-World Balloon Flight: Anniv,
  Jul 2
First Tourist in Space, Apr 28
First Tuxedo Created, Oct 10
First UN General Assembly: Anniv, Jan 10
First US Chamber of Commerce Founded: Anniv,
  Apr 5
First Woman British Prime Minister: Anniv, May 4
First Woman in Space: Anniv, Jun 16
First Woman to Climb Mount Everest: Anniv,
  May 16
First Women's Collegiate Basketball Game:
  Anniv, Mar 22
Firth, Colin: Birth, Sep 10
Fiscal Year, US Federal, Oct 1
Fischer, Bobby: Birth, Mar 9
Fish Amnesty Day, Sep 23
Fishburne, Laurence: Birth, Jul 30
Fisher, Carrie: Birth, Oct 21
Fisher, Eddie: Birth, Aug 10
Fisher, Joely: Birth, Oct 29

Fishing
  Blessing of the Fishing Fleet (San Francisco, CA),
    Oct 1
  Boca Grande Tarpon Tournament (Boca Grande,
    FL), Jun 27
  Fish Amnesty Day, Sep 23
  Fishing Contest (Lakewood, NJ), May 6
  Fishing Has No Boundaries (Hayward, WI), May 19
  Fishing Has No Boundaries (Monticello, IN),
    May 20
  Hodag Muskie Challenge (Rhinelander, WI),
    Sep 15
  Hunting and Fishing Day, Natl (Pres Proc), Sep 23
  Ice Fishing Contest (Fort Peck, MT), Feb 11
  Long Beach Island Surf Fishing Tournament (Long
    Beach Island, NJ), Oct 7
  Montana Governor's Cup Walleye Tournament (Fort
    Peck, MT), Jul 6
  Montreal Hunting, Fishing & Camping Show
    (Montreal, QC, Canada), Feb 23
  Morro Bay Harbor Fest (Morro Bay, CA), Oct 7
  Ottawa Boat/Sportsmen's Show (Ottawa, ON,
    Canada), Feb 23
  Palmetto Sportsmen's Classic (Columbia, SC),
    Mar 24
  Prospect Park Fishing Contest (Brooklyn, NY),
    Jul 18
  Take a Kid Fishing Weekend (St. Paul, MN), Jun 9
  Ultimate Fishing Show (Novi, MI), Jan 12
  Ultimate Sport & RV Show (Grand Rapids, MI),
    Mar 16
  Walton, Izaak: Birth Anniv, Aug 9
  World Famous Fish House Parade (Aitkin, MN),
    Nov 24
Fisk, Carlton: Birth, Dec 26
Fiske, Minnie M.: Birth Anniv, Dec 19
Fitness, Physical, and Sports Month, Natl, May 1
Fitzgerald, Edward: Birth Anniv, Mar 31
Fitzgerald, Ella: Birth Anniv, Apr 25
Fitzgerald, Ella: Wins Apollo Amateur Night:
  Anniv, Nov 21
Fitzgerald, F. Scott: Birth Anniv, Sep 24
Fitzgerald, Frances: Birth, Oct 21
5-a-Day Month, Natl, Sep 1
Five Billion, Day of the: Anniv, Jul 11
Flack, Roberta: Birth, Feb 10
Flag Act of 1818: Anniv, Apr 4
Flag Day (Pres Proc), Jun 14
Flag Day USA, Pause for Pledge, Natl, Jun 14
Flag Day: Anniv of the Stars and Stripes, Jun 14
Flag Exhibit Controversy, Chicago: Anniv, Feb 17
Flag Week, Natl (Pres Proc), Jun 11
Flagg, Fannie: Birth, Sep 21
Flaherty, Joe: Birth, Jun 21
Flaherty, Robert J.: Birth Anniv, Feb 16
Flannery, Susan: Birth, Jul 31
Flatley, Michael: Birth, Jul 16
Flaubert, Gustave: Birth Anniv, Dec 12
Flax Scutching Fest (Stahlstown, PA), Sep 9
Fleetwood, Mick: Birth, Jun 24
Fleming, Alexander: Birth Anniv, Aug 6
Fleming, Ian: Birth Anniv, May 28
Fleming, Peggy: Birth, Jul 27
Fleming, Rhonda: Birth, Aug 10
Fletcher, Ernie: Birth, Nov 12
Fleury, Theo: Birth, Jun 29
Flexible Work Arrangements Week, May 7
Flight Attendant, First: Anniv, May 15
Flintstones TV Premiere: Anniv, Sep 30
Flipper TV Premiere: Anniv, Sep 19
Flirting Week, Intl, Feb 13
Flockhart, Calista: Birth, Nov 11
Flood Victims Relief: Anniv, Aug 12
Flood, Curt: Birth Anniv, Jan 18
Flood, Great Chicago: Anniv, Apr 13
Flood, Johnstown: Anniv, May 31
Floral Design Day, Feb 28
Florida
  Acquired by US: Anniv, Feb 22
  Admission Day, Mar 3
  AHRMA Vintage Motorcycle Races (Daytona
    Beach), Mar 6
  AKC/Eukanuba Natl Chmpshp (Tampa Bay and St.
    Petersburg), Jan 14
  AMA Grand National Kickoff (Daytona Beach),
    Mar 9
  AMA Natl Hot Shoe Dirt Track Race (Daytona
    Beach), Mar 8
  Arbor Day, Jan 20
  Art Deco Weekend (Miami Beach), Jan 13
  Biketoberfest (Daytona Beach), Oct 19
  Biscayne Natl Park Established: Anniv, Jun 28
  Boca Grande Tarpon Tournament (Boca Grande),
    Jun 27
  Bon Fest (Delray Beach), Aug 12
  Bud Pole Day for the Daytona 500 (Daytona
    Beach), Feb 12

Budweiser Shootout at Daytona NEXTEL Cup Series Race (Daytona Beach), **Feb 11**
Bush, Jeb: Birth, **Feb 11**
Canadafest (Hollywood), **Jan 28**
Capital One Bowl (Orlando), **Jan 2**
Children's Day, **Apr 11**
Confederate Memorial Day, **Apr 26**
Crown Royal Intl Race of Champions (Daytona Beach), **Feb 17**
Daytona 200 by Honda Classic (Daytona Beach), **Mar 11**
Daytona 200 by Honda Qualifying Day (Daytona Beach), **Mar 8**
Daytona 500 (Daytona Beach), **Feb 19**
Daytona Kart Week (Daytona Beach), **Dec 26**
Daytona Supercross by Honda (Daytona Beach), **Mar 10**
Daytona Turkey Run (Daytona Beach), **Nov 23**
Disney World Opened: Anniv, **Oct 1**
Downtown Fest/Art Show (Gainesville), **Nov 4**
Dr. Martin Luther King, Jr, Celebration (Hollywood), **Jan 13**
Easter Beach Run (Daytona Beach), **Apr 15**
Education Assn Meeting, Natl (Orlando), **Jun 30**
Einstein on Wine (Tampa), **Feb 4**
Everglades Natl Park Established: Anniv, **Dec 6**
Fall Country Jamboree (Barberville), **Nov 4**
Fall Cycle Scene Motorcycle Races (Daytona Beach), **Oct 19**
Fall Suwannee River Gospel Jubilee (Live Oak), **Oct 4**
Fantasy Fest (Key West), **Oct 20**
February Is Fabulous Florida Strawberry Month, **Feb 1**
FedEx Orange Bowl (Miami), **Jan 3**
Florida Folk Fest (White Springs), **May 26**
Ford Chmpshp at Doral (Miami), **Mar 1**
Fort Lauderdale Intl Boat Show (Fort Lauderdale), **Oct 26**
Fourth of July Celebration (Live Oak), **Jul 1**
Gasparilla Extravaganza and Pirate Fest (Tampa), **Jan 21**
Gatorade Duel Qualifying Races (Daytona Beach), **Feb 16**
Grandmother's Day, **Oct 8**
Hatsume Fair (Delray Beach), **Feb 25**
Hershey's 300 NASCAR Busch Series Race (Daytona Beach), **Feb 18**
Hispanic Heritage Fest (Miami), **Oct 8**
Hoggetowne Medieval Faire (Gainesville), **Jan 28**
Hollywood Beach Candy Cane Parade (Hollywood), **Dec 2**
Hollywood Beach Latin Fest (Hollywood), **Aug 13**
Hometown Family Fourth (Hollywood), **Jul 4**
Isle of Eight Flags Shrimp Fest (Fernandina Beach), **May 5**
July 4th Family Celebration (Fort Lauderdale), **Jul 4**
Kissimmee Slough Shootout and Rendezvous (Big Cypress Reservation), **Feb 3**
Kuumba on the Beach (Hollywood), **Apr 15**
Labor Day Picnic (Live Oak), **Sep 1**
Law Enforcement Appreciation Month, **May 1**
Lonesome River Band Music Fest (Live Oak), **Apr 6**
Magnolia Fest (Live Oak), **Oct 19**
Mardi Gras Fiesta Tropicale (Hollywood), **Feb 24**
Maroone Hispanicfest (Hollywood), **Apr 16**
Martinez, Mel: Birth, **Oct 23**
Memorial Day Getaway (Live Oak), **May 26**
Miami Intl Boat/Sailboat Show (Miami Beach), **Feb 16**
NAIA Men's Soccer Natl Chmpshps (Daytona Beach), **Nov 15**
NASCAR Craftsman Truck Series 250 (Daytona Beach), **Feb 17**
Natural Bridge Battle (Tallahassee), **Mar 4**
Nelson, Bill: Birth, **Sep 29**
New Year's Eve Trail Ride and Party (Live Oak), **Dec 29**
Ocean Dance (Hollywood), **Dec 31**
Old Tyme Farm Days (Live Oak), **Nov 23**
Orlando Family Spring Break (Orlando), **Mar 1**
Outback Bowl (Tampa), **Jan 2**
Palm Harbor Arts/Crafts/Music Fest (Palm Harbor), **Dec 2**
Pan-American Day, **Apr 14**
Pascua Florida Day, **Apr 2**
Patriot's Day, **Apr 19**
Pepsi 400 NASCAR NEXTEL Cup Series (Daytona), **Jul 1**
Poetry Day, **May 25**
Ponce de Leon Discovers Florida: Anniv, **Apr 2**
Red, White & Bluegrass (Hollywood), **May 12**
Rolex 24 at Daytona (Daytona Beach), **Feb 4**
Saint Petersburg Fest of States (St. Petersburg), **Mar 31**
Save the Florida Panther Day, **Mar 18**

Seminole Tribe Festival, Powwow and Rodeo (Hollywood), **Feb 10**
Seminole Tribe of Florida Legally Established: Anniv, **Aug 21**
Sizzlin' Summer Garage Sale (Live Oak), **Aug 5**
South Florida Senior Games (Hollywood), **Jan 25**
Southeast Florida Scottish Fest & Games (Coral Springs), **Mar 4**
SPEBSQSA (Barbershop Quartet) Mid-Winter Conv (Jacksonville), **Jan 15**
Speech-Language-Hearing Conv, American (Miami), **Nov 16**
Spring Arts Fest (Gainesville), **Apr 1**
Spring Suwannee River Gospel Jubilee (Live Oak), **Jun 14**
St. Patrick's Day Parade & Fest (Hollywood), **Mar 12**
State Fair (Tampa), **Feb 9**
Strawberry Fest (Plant City), **Mar 2**
SunFest (West Palm Beach), **May 3**
Suwannee Lights (Live Oak), **Dec 1**
Suwannee Spring Fest (Live Oak), **Mar 23**
Tarpon Springs Fine Arts Fest (Tarpon Springs), **Apr 8**
Teacher's Day, **May 19**
Trail Ride Gathering, Natl (Live Oak), **Nov 4**
Tybee 500 (Hollywood and Tybee Island, GA), **May 6**
Week of Ocean Fest Sea-Son, Natl (Fort Lauderdale), **Mar 4**
Winterfest Boat Parade (Fort Lauderdale), **Dec 16**
Zora Neale Hurston Fest (Eatonville), **Jan 25**
Flossing Day, Natl, Nov 24
Flowers, Flower Shows
Albany Tulip Fest (Albany, NY), **May 12**
American Rose Society Fall Natl Conv (Dallas, TX), **Oct 13**
Azalea Fest (Muskogee, OK), **Apr 3**
California Poppy Fest (Lancaster, CA), **Apr 22**
Camellia Sasanqua Days (Fort Valley, GA), **Nov 1**
Canadian Tulip Fest (Ottawa, ON, Canada), **May 4**
Chelsea Flower Show (London, England), **May 23**
Cherry Blossom Fest (Washington, DC), **Mar 25**
Daffodil Fest Weekend (Nantucket Island, MA), **Apr 28**
Daylily Extravaganza (Fort Valley, GA), **Jun 1**
Fest of Camellias (Fort Valley, GA), **Feb 1**
Floral Design Day, **Feb 28**
Flower Fest (Japan), **Apr 8**
Hampton Court Palace Flower Show Charity Gala Preview (East Molesey, Surrey, England), **Jul 3**
Harrogate Autumn Flower Show (Harrogate, England), **Sep 15**
Harrogate Spring Flower Show (Harrogate, England), **Apr 27**
Holland Tulip Time Fest (Holland, MI), **May 6**
Indiana Flower and Patio Show (Indianapolis, IN), **Mar 11**
Iris Fest (Sumter, SC), **May 25**
Jersey Battle of Flowers (St. Lawrence, Channel Islands), **Aug 10**
Landon Azalea Garden Fest/Antiques (Bethesda, MD), **May 5**
Lei Day (Hawaii), **May 1**
Lilac Fest (Mackinac Island, MI), **Jun 9**
Lilac Fest (Rochester, NY), **May 1**
Longwood Gardens Acres of Spring (Kennett Square, PA), **Apr 22**
Longwood Gardens Christmas Display (Kennett Square, PA), **Nov 23**
Longwood Gardens Chrysanthemum Fest (Kennett Square, PA), **Oct 28**
Longwood Gardens Welcome Spring (Kennett Square, PA), **Jan 21**
Macon, GA's Cherry Blossom Fest, Intl (Macon, GA), **Mar 17**
Magnolia Blossom Fest (Magnolia, AR), **May 19**
Marigold Fest (Pekin, IL), **Sep 8**
Maryland Home and Garden Show (Baltimore, MD), **Mar 3**
Maymont Flower & Garden Show (Richmond, VA), **Feb 9**
Mother's Day Annual Rhododendron Show (Portland, OR), **May 13**
Orchid Show (St. Louis, MO), **Jan 28**
Pella Tulip Time Fest (Pella, IA), **May 4**
Philadelphia Flower Show (Philadelphia, PA), **Mar 5**
Poinsettia Day, **Dec 12**
Portland Rose Fest (Portland, OR), **Jun 1**
QCCA Regional Lawn, Garden and Flower Show (Rock Island, IL), **Mar 2**
Rhododendron Fest (Florence, OR), **May 19**
Rose Month, Natl, **Jun 1**
Skagit Valley Tulip Fest (Burlington, WA), **Apr 1**
South Carolina Fest of Flowers (Greenwood, SC), **Jun 16**

South Carolina Fest of Roses (Orangeburg, SC), **Apr 21**
Take Your Houseplants for a Walk Day, **Jul 27**
Tournament of Roses Parade (Pasadena, CA), **Jan 2**
Washington Home & Garden Show (Washington, DC), **Feb 9**
Wildflower Week, Natl, **May 1**
Yellow Daisy Fest (Stone Mountain, GA), **Sep 7**
Floyd, William: Birth Anniv, **Dec 17**
Flutie, Doug: Birth, **Oct 23**
Flying Nun TV Premiere: Anniv, **Sep 7**
Flynt, Larry: Birth, **Nov 1**
Foch, Nina: Birth, **Apr 20**
Fodor, Eugene: Birth Anniv, **Oct 14**
Fogelberg, Dan: Birth, **Aug 13**
Fogg, Phileas: Wager Day, **Oct 2**
Fogg, Phileas: Wins a Wager Day, **Dec 21**
Foley, Dave: Birth, **Jan 4**
Folger, Henry C.: Birth Anniv, **Jun 18**
Foliage Fest, Northeast Kingdom Fall (Walden, VT), **Oct 2**
Folk Fair Intl, Holiday (Milwaukee, WI), **Nov 17**
Folk Fest, Florida (White Springs, FL), **May 26**
Folkfest, World (Springville, UT), **Jul 8**
Folklife Fest (Monroe, LA), **Sep 9**
Folklife Fest, Autumn Historic (Hannibal, MO), **Oct 21**
Folklife Fest, Texas (San Antonio, TX), **Jun 8**
Folklorama—Canada's Cultural Celebration (Winnipeg, MB, Canada), **Aug 6**
Folkmoot USA: The NC Intl Folk Fest (Waynesville, NC), **Jul 17**
Follett, Ken: Birth, **Jun 5**
Fonda, Bridget: Birth, **Jan 27**
Fonda, Henry: Birth Anniv, **May 16**
Fonda, Jane: Birth, **Dec 21**
Fonda, Peter: Birth, **Feb 23**
Fonteyn, Margot: Birth Anniv, **May 18**
Food and Beverage-Related Events and Observances
Abbotsford Berry Fest (Abbotsford, BC, Canada), **Jul 7**
All About Apples (Woodstock, VT), **Sep 24**
American Dietetic Assn Food & Nutrition Conf & Expo (Honolulu, HI), **Sep 16**
Anti-Saloon League Founded: Anniv, **May 24**
Appert, Nicholas: Birth Anniv, **Oct 23**
Apple Butter Fest (Berkeley Springs, WV), **Oct 7**
Apple Butter Makin' Days (Mount Vernon, MO), **Oct 13**
Apple Butter Stirrin' (Coshocton, OH), **Oct 20**
Apple Fest (Lahaska, PA), **Nov 4**
Apple Fest (Topeka, KS), **Oct 1**
Apple Fest, Kentucky (Paintsville, KY), **Oct 6**
Apple Fest, Vermont (Springfield, VT), **Oct 7**
Apple Harvest Fest (Gettysburg, PA), **Oct 7**
Apple Saturdays (New Gloucester, ME), **Sep 23**
Applejack Fest (Nebraska City, NE), **Sep 16**
Art Fair & Winefest (Washington, MO), **May 19**
Association for Dressings & Sauces Annual Meeting (Asheville, NC), **Oct 15**
Baby Food Fest, Natl (Fremont, MI), **Jul 18**
Bake for Family Fun Month, **Feb 1**
Baked Bean Month, Natl, **Jul 1**
Banana Split Fest (Wilmington, OH), **Jun 9**
Barbecue Month, Natl, **May 1**
Beef Empire Days (Garden City, KS), **May 30**
Beer Day (Iceland), **Mar 1**
Biscuit Month, Natl, **Sep 1**
Black Cow Created: Anniv, **Aug 19**
Black Walnut Fest (Stockton, MO), **Sep 20**
Blueberries Month, Natl, **Jul 1**
Blueberry Arts Fest (Ketchikan, AK), **Aug 5**
Blueberry Fest (Montrose, PA), **Aug 4**
Blueberry Fest, Natl (South Haven, MI), **Aug 10**
Bottled Water Week, **Sep 17**
Braham Pie Day (Braham, MN), **Aug 4**
Bread Pudding Recipe Exchange, **May 1**
Brewers Fest, Oregon (Portland, OR), **Jul 27**
Bubble Gum Day, **Feb 1**
Buffalo Wallow Chili Cookoff (Custer, SD), **Oct 1**
Bun Day (Iceland), **Feb 27**
Burgoo Fest (Utica, IL), **Oct 8**
Caffeine Awareness Month, Natl, **Mar 1**
California Artichoke Fest (Castroville, CA), **May 20**
Canadafest (Hollywood, FL), **Jan 28**
Candy Month, Natl, **Jun 1**
Cape May Food & Wine Fest (Cape May, NJ), **Sep 16**
Celebrate Sun Dried Tomatoes Month, **Oct 1**
Cheese Fest, Great Wisconsin (Little Chute, WI), **Jun 2**
Cherry Month, Natl, **Feb 1**
Cherry Pit Spitting Chmpshp, Intl (Eau Claire, MI), **Jul 1**
Chestnut Week, Natl, **Oct 8**
Chicken Fest, Delmarva (Snow Hill, MD), **Jun 23**

Food and Beverage (cont'd)—Footbag

Chicken Month, Natl, **Sep 1**
Chili Cook-off, State Chmpshp (Roanoke, VA), **May 6**
Chili Day, Natl, **Feb 23**
Chili Month, Natl, **Oct 1**
Chilton County Peach Fest (Clanton, AL), **Jun 18**
Chocolate Fest (Galesburg, IL), **Feb 10**
Clam Chowder Cookoff (Santa Cruz, CA), **Feb 25**
Clam Fest, Yarmouth (Yarmouth, ME), **Jul 21**
Clear Lake Crawfish Fest (Seabrook, TX), **Apr 1**
Clinton County Corn Fest (Wilmington, OH), **Sep 8**
Coffee Gourmet Intl Month, **Jan 1**
Colorado Brewers' Fest (Fort Collins, CO), **Jun 24**
Cook Something Bold and Pungent Day, **Nov 8**
Cookie Cutter Week, **Dec 1**
Cookie Month, Natl, **Oct 1**
Country Ham Days, Marion County (Lebanon, KY), **Sep 22**
Crab and Steak Dinner (Cornelius, OR), **Jan 21**
Crawfish Fest, Dermott's Annual (Dermott, AR), **May 19**
Crawfordsville Strawberry Fest (Crawfordsville, IN), **Jun 9**
Crayfish Premiere (Sweden), **Aug 9**
Dairy Alternatives Month, **Jun 1**
Dairy Month, June, **Jun 1**
Dandelion May Fest (Dover, OH), **May 5**
Date Fest, Natl (Indio, CA), **Feb 17**
Diet Resolution Week, **Jan 1**
Drive-Thru Day, Natl, **Jul 24**
Eat an Apple Day, Intl, **Sep 16**
Eat Dessert First Week, **May 1**
Eat What You Want Day, **May 11**
Egg Month, Natl, **May 1**
Egg Salad Week, **Apr 17**
Einstein on Wine (Tampa, FL), **Feb 4**
Eldon Turkey Fest (Eldon, MO), **Oct 14**
Electra Goat BBQ Cook-Off (Electra, TX), **May 12**
Elmira Maple Syrup Fest (Elmira, ON, Canada), **Apr 1**
Escoffier, Georges: Birth Anniv, **Oct 28**
Fall on Nantucket (Nantucket Island, MA), **Oct 1**
Family Meal Month, **Aug 1**
Feast of the Ramson (Richwood, WV), **Apr 22**
February Is Fabulous Florida Strawberry Month, **Feb 1**
Fig Week, Natl, **Nov 1**
First McDonald's Opens: Anniv, **Apr 15**
5-A-Day Month, Natl, **Sep 1**
Florida Strawberry Fest (Plant City, FL), **Mar 2**
Food Bank Week, Natl, **Oct 15**
Foods/Feasts of Colonial Virginia (Williamsburg, VA), **Nov 23**
Fortune Cookie Day, **Sep 13**
French Chef TV Premiere: Anniv, **Feb 11**
Fresh Squeezed Juice Week, Natl, **Jan 15**
Frozen Food Month, Natl, **Mar 1**
Fulton Oysterfest (Fulton, TX), **Mar 2**
Georgia Pecan Month, Natl, **Nov 1**
Gilroy Garlic Fest (Gilroy, CA), **Jul 28**
Gingerbread House Competition, Natl (Asheville, NC), **Nov 13**
Gingerbread House Day, **Dec 12**
Go Hog Wild—Eat Country Ham Month, **Oct 1**
Go Wild During California Wild Rice Month, **Sep 1**
Grape Jamboree, Geneva Area (Geneva, OH), **Sep 23**
Great American Beer Fest (Denver, CO), **Sep 28**
Great American Low-Cholesterol, Low-Fat Pizza Bake, **Sep 1**
Great American Meatout, **Mar 18**
Great Arkansas Pig-Out (Morrilton, AR), **Aug 4**
Great Fruitcake Toss (Manitou Springs, CO), **Jan 7**
Great Intl Chicken Wing Society Cook-off (Reno, NV), **Jul 1**
Great Peanut Tour (Skippers, VA), **Sep 7**
Grilling Month, Natl, **Jul 1**
Gumbo Fest (Bridge City, LA), **Nov 3**
Hamburger Month, Natl, **May 1**
Hard Crab Derby and Fair, Natl (Crisfield, MD), **Sep 1**
Harvest Weekends (Bryan, TX), **Jul 22**
Harvest Wine Celebration (Livermore, CA), **Sep 3**
Hearth and Home in Early Maryland (St. Mary's City, MD), **Nov 24**
Herb Fest (Mattoon, IL), **Apr 29**
Herrinfesta Italiana (Herrin, IL), **May 25**
Highland County Maple Fest (Highland County, VA), **Mar 11**
Hog Capital of the World Fest (Kewanee, IL), **Sep 1**
Homemade Bread Day, **Nov 17**
Honey Month, Natl, **Sep 1**
Hope Watermelon Fest (Hope, AR), **Aug 10**
Horseradish Fest (Collinsville, IL), **Jun 10**
Horseradish Month, Natl, **Jul 1**
Hot Breakfast Month, Natl, **Feb 1**
Hot Dog Month, Natl, **Jul 1**

Hot Dog Night (Luverne, MN), **Jul 13**
Hot Tea Month, Natl, **Jan 1**
Ice Cream Cone: Anniv, **Sep 22**
Ice Cream Day, Natl, **Jul 16**
Ice Cream Days (Le Mars, IA), **Jun 15**
Ice Cream Fest, Old-Fashioned (Utica, OH), **May 27**
Ice Cream Social (Indianapolis, IN), **Jul 4**
Iced Tea Month, Natl, **Jun 1**
Isle of Eight Flags Shrimp Fest (Fernandina Beach, FL), **May 5**
Jackson County Apple Fest (Jackson, OH), **Sep 19**
Jell-O Week, **Feb 12**
June Is Turkey Lovers' Month, **Jun 1**
Kentucky Bourbon Fest (Bardstown, KY), **Sep 13**
Kodiak Crab Fest (Kodiak, AK), **May 25**
Kool-Aid Days (Hastings, NE), **Aug 11**
La Tomatina (Spain), **Aug 30**
Leitersburg Peach Fest (Leitersburg, MD), **Aug 12**
Lobster Fest, Maine (Rockland, ME), **Aug 2**
Lobsterfest (Mystic, CT), **May 27**
Long Beach Island Chowder Cook-Off (Beach Haven, NJ), **Sep 30**
Louisiana Peach Fest (Ruston, LA), **Jun 22**
Machias Wild Blueberry Fest (Machias, ME), **Aug 17**
Maple Fest of Nova Scotia (Northern Nova Scotia, Canada), **Mar 18**
Maple Syrup Saturday (Appleton, WI), **Mar 18**
Mardi Gras Fiesta Tropicale (Hollywood, FL), **Feb 24**
Marion Popcorn Fest (Marion, OH), **Sep 7**
Marriage of the Port Ceremony (Bryan, TX), **Feb 11**
Marshall County Blueberry Fest (Plymouth, IN), **Sep 1**
Men Make Dinner Day, Natl, **Nov 2**
Messina Hof's Wine Premiere (Bryan, TX), **Nov 18**
Mint Fest, Saint Johns (St. Johns, MI), **Aug 11**
Mitchell Persimmon Fest (Mitchell, IN), **Sep 22**
Morden Corn/Apple Fest (Morden, MB, Canada), **Aug 25**
More Herbs, Less Salt Day, **Aug 29**
Morel Mushroom Fest (Muscoda, WI), **May 19**
Morton Pumpkin Fest (Morton, IL), **Sep 13**
Mudbug Madness (Shreveport, LA), **May 25**
Mushroom Fest (Kennett Square, PA), **Sep 9**
Mushroom Fest (Telluride, CO), **Aug 17**
Mushroom Month, Natl, **Sep 1**
Mustard Day, Natl, **Aug 5**
Newport Seafood and Wine Fest (Newport, OR), **Feb 24**
No Salt Week, **Oct 2**
North Carolina Apple Fest (Hendersonville, NC), **Sep 1**
North Carolina SweetPotato Month, **Feb 1**
Norwalk Seaport Oyster Fest (Norwalk, CT), **Sep 8**
Nugget Best in the West Rib Cook-Off (Sparks, NV), **Aug 31**
Nuts Fair (Bastogne, Belgium), **Dec 18**
Oatmeal Month, **Jan 1**
October Frozen & Refrigerated Food Fest, **Oct 1**
Onion Market (Zibelemärit, Switzerland), **Nov 27**
Organic Harvest Month, Natl, **Sep 1**
Oyster Fest (Chincoteague Island, VA), **Oct 7**
Oyster Fest, St. Mary's County (Leonardtown, MD), **Oct 21**
Paczki Day, **Feb 28**
Pancake Day, Intl (Liberal, KS), **Feb 28**
Pancake Week, Natl, **Feb 26**
Payson Golden Onion Days (Payson, UT), **Sep 1**
Peanut Butter Lover's Month, **Nov 1**
Pecan Day, **Mar 25**
Pecan Month, Natl, **Apr 1**
Personal Chef Day, Natl, **Jul 15**
Polk County Ramp Tramp Fest (Benton, TN), **Apr 22**
Pomegranate Month, Natl, **Nov 1**
Popcorn Fest (Valparaiso, IN), **Sep 9**
Popcorn Poppin' Month, Natl, **Oct 1**
Pork Month, Natl, **Oct 1**
Potato Blossom Fest, Maine (Fort Fairfield, ME), **Jul 7**
Potato Bowl USA (Grand Forks, ND), **Sep 5**
Potato Day Fest (Greeley, CO), **Sep 9**
Potato Feast Days (Houlton, ME), **Aug 18**
Potato Month, Natl, **Sep 1**
Poteet Strawberry Fest (Poteet, TX), **Apr 7**
Prairie Dog Chili Cookoff (Grand Prairie, TX), **Apr 8**
Pumpkin Pie Day, **Nov 21**
Pumpkin Show, Circleville (Circleville, OH), **Oct 18**
Ranch Hand Breakfast (Kingsville, TX), **Nov 18**
Recipe Greetings for the Holidays, **Dec 1**
Return Shopping Carts to the Supermarket Month, **Feb 1**
Rhubarb Fest (Intercourse, PA), **May 19**
Ribfest (Kalamazoo, MI), **Aug 3**

Rice God, Day of the (Chiyoda, Japan), **Jun 4**
Rice Month, Natl, **Sep 1**
Rice Planting Fest (Osaka, Japan), **Jun 14**
Riverfest (Columbus, GA), **Apr 28**
Roasting Month, Natl, **Nov 1**
Rochesterfest (Rochester, MN), **Jun 17**
Rockport Seafair (Rockport, TX), **Oct 6**
Salsa Month, Natl, **May 1**
Sandwich Day, **Nov 3**
Saveur Texas Hill Country Wine & Food Fest (Austin, TX), **Apr 6**
Schmeckfest (Freeman, SD), **Mar 24**
School Breakfast Week, Natl, **Mar 6**
Scottsdale Culinary Fest (Scottsdale, AZ), **Apr 18**
Sea Harvest (Mystic, CT), **Oct 7**
Seafood Month, Natl, **Oct 1**
Seven Sweets & Sours Fest (Intercourse, PA), **Sep 15**
Shelburne County Lobster Fest (Shelburne County, NS, Canada), **Jun 1**
Shrimp and Petroleum Fest, Louisiana (Morgan City, LA), **Aug 31**
Shrimp Fest, Low Country (McClellanville, SC), **May 6**
Sinkie Day, **Nov 24**
Slow Cooking Month, **Jan 1**
Sneak Some Zucchini onto Your Neighbors' Porch Night, **Aug 8**
Solo Diners Eat Out Week, **Feb 1**
Sonoma Valley Harvest Wine Auction (Sonoma, CA), **Sep 1**
Soul Food Month, Natl, **Jun 1**
Sour Herring Premiere (Sweden), **Aug 17**
Spinach Lovers Month, **Oct 1**
Steak Cook-off, World Chmpshp (Magnolia, AR), **May 20**
Steakhouse Month, Natl, **Jun 1**
Strawberry Fest (Lahaska, PA), **May 6**
Sun Prairie's Sweet Corn Fest (Sun Prairie, WI), **Aug 17**
Sweetcorn Fest, Natl (Hoopeston, IL), **Aug 31**
Tacoma Holiday Food and Gift Fest (Tacoma, WA), **Oct 25**
Tamale Fiesta (El Centro, CA), **Dec 2**
Taste of Cincinnati (Cincinnati, OH), **May 27**
Taste of Colorado (Denver, CO), **Sep 1**
Taste of Madison (Madison, WI), **Sep 2**
Taste of Morgan Hill (Morgan Hill, CA), **Sep 23**
Taste of the Town (Wichita Falls, TX), **Mar 7**
Telluride Wine Fest (Telluride, CO), **Jun 22**
3-A-Day Week, **Mar 3**
Tomato Month, Fresh Florida, **Apr 1**
Totally Chipotle Day, **May 5**
Turkey Rama (McMinnville, OR), **Jul 13**
Turkey-Free Thanksgiving, **Nov 23**
University Kiwanis Pancake Fest (Wichita Falls, TX), **Jan 28**
Vegan Month, **Nov 1**
Vegan World Day, **Jun 21**
Vegetarian Day, World, **Oct 1**
Vegetarian Month, **Oct 1**
Verboort Sausage and Kraut Dinner (Forest Grove, OR), **Nov 4**
Vermont Maple Fest (St. Albans, VT), **Apr 28**
Vinegar Day, **Jun 17**
Virginia Peanut Fest (Emporia, VA), **Sep 22**
Virginia Wine Fest (Charlottesville, VA), **May 20**
Waffle Week, Natl, **Sep 3**
Warrens Cranberry Fest (Warrens, WI), **Sep 22**
Washington State Apple Blossom Fest (Wenatchee, WA), **Apr 27**
Watermelon Fest (Rush Springs, OK), **Aug 12**
Watermelon Thump (Luling, TX), **Jun 22**
World Beef Expo/Harvest Fair (Milwaukee, WI), **Sep 21**
World Chmpshp BBQ Goat Cook-off (Brady, TX), **Sep 2**
World Egg Day, **Oct 13**
World Food Day, **Oct 16**
World Food Day (UN), **Oct 16**
World Licorice Day, **Apr 12**
World of Coffee/World Barista Chmpshp (Berne, Switzerland), **May 19**
World's Biggest Fish Fry (Paris, TN), **Apr 24**
World's Largest Breakfast Table (Battle Creek, MI), **Jun 10**
Yambilee, Louisiana (Opelousas, LA), **Oct 25**
Food and Drug Interaction Education and Awareness Week, Oct 17
Food Bank Week, Natl, Oct 15
Food Drive: Stamp Out Hunger—NALC National Food Drive, May 13
Food Fight, World's Largest: La Tomatina (Spain), Aug 30
Food Stamps Authorized: Anniv, Sep 11
Footbag Chmpshps, World (Frankfurt, Germany), Jul 24

Football
Camp, Walter: Birth Anniv, **Apr 7**
Capital One Bowl (Orlando, FL), **Jan 2**
Fabulous 1890s Weekend (Mansfield, PA), **Sep 29**
FedEx Orange Bowl (Miami, FL), **Jan 3**
First Army-Navy Game: Anniv, **Nov 29**
First Night Football Game (Mansfield, PA), **Sep 28**
First Play-by-Play Football Game Broadcast, **Nov 23**
First Super Bowl: Anniv, **Jan 15**
Football League, Natl, Formed: Anniv, **Sep 17**
Hula Bowl (Honolulu, HI), **Jan 21**
Monday Night Football TV Premiere: Anniv, **Sep 21**
NAIA Div II Football Chmpshp Game (Hardin County, TN), **Dec 16**
Nokia Sugar Bowl (New Orleans, LA), **Jan 2**
Oil Bowl Football Classic (Wichita Falls, TX), **Jun 17**
Outback Bowl (Tampa, FL), **Jan 2**
Pacific Life Holiday Bowl Parade/Game (San Diego, CA), **Dec 28**
PSFCA East West All-Star Game (Altoona, PA), **Jun 24**
Rose Bowl Game (Pasadena, CA), **Jan 4**
SBC Cotton Bowl Classic (Dallas, TX), **Jan 2**
Senior Bowl Football Game (Mobile, AL), **Jan 28**
Sun Bowl (El Paso, TX), **Dec 29**
Super Bowl (Detroit, MI), **Feb 5**
Tostitos Fiesta Bowl (Tempe, AZ), **Jan 2**
Unitas, Johnny: Birth Anniv, **May 7**
Women's Pro Football Day, **Aug 5**
Foothills Art Fest (Jackson, OH), **Oct 13**
For Pete's Sake Day, **Feb 26**
Forbes, Malcolm: Birth Anniv, **Aug 19**
Forbes, Michelle: Birth, **Feb 17**
Forbes, Steve: Birth, **Jul 18**
Ford, Eileen: Birth, **Mar 25**
Ford, Elizabeth (Betty): Birth, **Apr 8**
Ford, Faith: Birth, **Sep 14**
Ford, Gerald: Assassination Attempts: Anniv, **Sep 5**
Ford, Gerald: Birthday, **Jul 14**
Ford, Gerald: Veep Day, **Aug 9**
Ford, Gerald: Vice Presidential Swearing In: Anniv, **Dec 6**
Ford, Glenn: Birth, **May 1**
Ford, Harrison: Birth, **Jul 13**
Ford, Henry: Birth Anniv, **Jul 30**
Ford, John: Birth Anniv, **Feb 1**
Ford, Richard: Birth, **Feb 16**
Ford, Whitey: Birth, **Oct 21**
Forefathers' Day, **Dec 21**
Foreman, George: Birth, **Jan 10**
Forest Craft/Scenic Drive Fest (Van Buren County, IA), **Oct 14**
Forest Products Week, Natl (Pres Proc), **Oct 15**
Forgive Mom & Dad Day, **Mar 18**
Forman, Milos: Birth, **Feb 18**
Former Prisoner of War Recognition Day, Natl (Pres Proc), **Apr 9**
Forrest, Nathan Bedford: Birth Anniv, **Jul 13**
Forsberg, Peter: Birth, **Jul 20**
Forster, E.M.: Birth Anniv, **Jan 1**
Forster, Robert: Birth, **Jul 13**
Forsyth, Frederick: Birth, **Aug 25**
Forsythe, John: Birth, **Jan 29**
Fort Ligonier Days (Ligonier, PA), **Oct 13**
Fort Moore Established: Anniv, **Apr 24**
Fort Sumter Shelled by North: Anniv, **Aug 17**
Fort Union Trading Post Rendezvous (Williston, ND), **Jun 15**
Fortas, Abe: Birth Anniv, **Jun 19**
Forten, James: Birth Anniv, **Sep 2**
Fortune Cookie Day, **Sep 13**
48 Hours TV Premiere: Anniv, **Jan 19**
Fosse, Bob: Birth Anniv, **Jun 23**
Fossey, Dian: Birth Anniv, **Jan 16**
Foster, Andrew "Rube": Birth Anniv, **Sep 17**
Foster, Jodie: Birth, **Nov 19**
Foster, Meg: Birth, **May 14**
Foster, Stephen: Birth Anniv, **Jul 4**
Foucault, Jean: Earth's Rotation Proved: Anniv, **Jan 8**
Foudy, Julie: Birth, **Jan 27**
Foundation Day, Natl (Japan), **Feb 11**
Founders' Day (Toms River, NJ), **Jun 10**
Founder's Day Corn Roast (Forest Grove, OR), **Sep 17**
Fountain, Pete: Birth, **Jul 3**
Fountains, Longwood Gardens Fest of (Kennett Square, PA), **May 27**
Four Chaplains Memorial Day, **Feb 3**
Fox, Bernard: Birth, **May 11**
Fox, Edward: Birth, **Apr 13**
Fox, James: Birth, **May 19**
Fox, Jorja: Birth, **Jul 7**
Fox, Matthew: Birth, **Jul 14**
Fox, Michael J.: Birth, **Jun 9**

Fox, Terry: Birth Anniv, **Jul 28**
Fox, Vicente: Birth, **Jul 2**
Foxfield Races (Charlottesville, VA), **Apr 29**
Foxworthy, Jeff: Birth, **Sep 6**
Foxx, Jamie: Birth, **Dec 13**
Foxx, Redd: Birth Anniv, **Dec 9**
Foyt, A.J.: Birth, **Jan 16**
Fraggle Rock TV Premiere: Anniv, **Sep 12**
Frampton, Peter: Birth, **Apr 22**
France
Bastille Day, **Jul 14**
Cannes Film Fest (Cannes), **May 17**
Eiffel Tower: Anniv (Paris), **Mar 31**
Nice Carnival, **Feb 17**
Night Watch, **Jul 13**
Tour de France, **Jul 1**
Victory Day, **May 8**
Franciosa, Anthony: Birth, **Oct 25**
Francis, Anne: Birth, **Sep 16**
Francis, Connie: Birth, **Dec 12**
Francis, Genie: Birth, **May 26**
Francis, Ron: Birth, **Mar 1**
Franco, James: Birth, **Apr 19**
Frank, Anne, Diary: Last Entry: Anniv, **Aug 1**
Frank, Anne: Birth Anniv, **Jun 12**
Frankel, Max: Birth, **Apr 3**
Franken, Al: Birth, **May 21**
Frankenstein Friday, **Oct 27**
Frankfurt Book Fair (Frankfurt, Germany), **Oct 4**
Franklin Day, Joe, **Mar 9**
Franklin Prefers Turkey: Anniv, **Jan 26**
Franklin, Aretha: Birth, **Mar 25**
Franklin, Benjamin
Birth Anniv, **Jan 17**
Coin Flip for 300th Birthday, **Jan 17**
Poor Richard's Almanack: Anniv, **Dec 28**
Tercentenary, **Jan 17**
Franklin, Bonnie: Birth, **Jan 6**
Franklin, Pamela: Birth, **Feb 4**
Franks, Tommy: Birth, **Jun 17**
Franz, Arthur: Birth, **Feb 29**
Franz, Dennis: Birth, **Oct 28**
Franzen, Jonathan: Birth, **Aug 17**
Fraser, Brendan: Birth, **Dec 3**
Frasier TV Premiere: Anniv, **Sep 16**
Frazier, Joe: Birth, **Jan 12**
Frazier, Sheila E.: Birth, **Nov 13**
Freberg, Stan: Birth, **Aug 7**
Fred Waring Show TV Premiere: Anniv, **Apr 17**
Freedom Day: Anniv, **Feb 1**
Freedom of Information Day, **Mar 16**
Freedom Riders: Anniv, **May 4**
Freedom Shrine Month, **May 1**
Freedom Week, **Jul 4**
Freedom Week, Religious, **Sep 22**
Freefall Conv, World (Rantoul, IL), **Aug 4**
Freelance Writers Appreciation Week, **Feb 6**
Freeman, Al, Jr: Birth, **Mar 21**
Freeman, Morgan: Birth, **Jun 1**
Freer, Charles L.: Birth Anniv, **Feb 25**
Freethinker's Day, **Jan 29**
Frelich, Phyllis: Birth, **Feb 29**
French and Indian War, Treaty of Paris Ends: Anniv, **Feb 10**
French Chef TV Premiere: Anniv, **Feb 11**
French Polynesia: Hawaiki Nui Va'a Race, **Oct 18**
French Quarter Fest (New Orleans, LA), **Apr 20**
French West Indies
Carnival (Martinique), **Feb 25**
French, Daniel C.: Birth Anniv, **Apr 20**
Frenchman Rows Across Pacific: Anniv, **Nov 21**
Frequent Flyer Day, Natl, **May 1**
Frequent Flyer Program Debuts: Anniv, **May 1**
Fresh Breath Day, Natl, **Aug 6**
Fresh Squeezed Juice Week, Natl, **Jan 15**
Freud, Sigmund: Birth Anniv, **May 6**
Freudenthal, Dave: Birth, **Oct 12**
Frey, Glenn: Birth, **Nov 6**
Fricke, Janie: Birth, **Dec 19**
Fricker, Brenda: Birth, **Feb 17**
Friday the Thirteenth, **Jan 13**
Friedan, Betty: Birth, **Feb 4**
Friedel, Brad: Birth, **May 18**
Friedkin, William: Birth, **Aug 29**
Friedle, Will: Birth, **Aug 11**
Friedman, Milton: Birth, **Jul 31**
Friends TV Premiere: Anniv, **Sep 22**
Friendship Week, Intl, **Feb 19**
Friendship: Girlfriend's Day, **Aug 1**
Friendship: New Friends, Old Friends Week, Natl, **May 21**
Frisch, Max: Birth Anniv, **May 15**
Frist, William: Birth, **Feb 22**
Froebel, Friedrich: Birth Anniv, **Apr 21**
Frog Jumping Jubilee/Calaveras Fair (Angel Camp, CA), **May 18**
Frontier Address, Turner's: Anniv, **Jul 12**
Frontline TV Premiere: Anniv, **Jan 17**

Frost, David: Birth, **Apr 7**
Frost, Robert: Birth Anniv, **Mar 26**
Frozen Food Month, Natl, **Mar 1**
Frugal Fun Day, Intl, **Oct 7**
Fruitcake Toss, Great (Manitou Springs, CO), **Jan 7**
Fry, Elizabeth: Birth Anniv, **May 21**
Fry, Stephen: Birth, **Aug 24**
Frye, Soleil Moon: Birth, **Aug 6**
Fuentes, Daisy: Birth, **Nov 17**
Fugitive TV Premiere: Anniv, **Sep 17**
Fulbright, J. William: Birth Anniv, **Nov 9**
Fuller, Alfred Carl: Birth Anniv, **Jan 13**
Fuller, Bobby: Death Anniv, **Jul 18**
Fuller, Buckminster: Birth Anniv, **Jul 12**
Fuller, Margaret: Birth Anniv, **May 23**
Fuller, Melville Weston: Birth Anniv, **Feb 11**
Fulton, Robert: Birth Anniv, **Nov 14**
Fulton, Robert: Sails Steamboat: Anniv, **Aug 17**
Fun at Work Day, **Jan 27**
Fun at Work Day, Natl, **Apr 6**
Fun Day, Natl, **Apr 1**
Fun Facts About Names Day, **Mar 6**
Funeral Day, Create a Great, **Oct 30**
Funeral for Ol' Man Winter, Wayne State Univ (Detroit, MI), **Apr 5**
Funeral Service Education Week, **Feb 6**
Funicello, Annette: Birth, **Oct 22**
Funky Winkerbean: Anniv, **Mar 27**
Fur Trade, Voyageurs
Big Island Rendezvous & Fest (Albert Lea, MN), **Oct 7**
Fest of Adventures (Aitkin, MN), **Sep 16**
Fort Union Trading Post Rendezvous (Williston, ND), **Jun 15**
Great Rendezvous (Thunder Bay, ON, Canada), **Jun 29**
Mountain Man Rendezvous (Cataldo, ID), **Aug 18**
Prairie Villa Rendezvous (Prairie du Chien, WI), **Jun 15**
Tetonkaha Rendezvous (Lake Benton, MN), **Aug 11**
White Oak Rendezvous (Deer River, MN), **Aug 4**
Furcal, Rafael: Birth, **Aug 24**
Furlong, Edward: Birth, **Aug 2**
Furnishings Market, Intl Home (High Point, NC), **Apr 27**

Gable, Clark: Birth Anniv, **Feb 1**
Gable, Clark: Gone with the Wind Film Premiere: Anniv, **Dec 15**
Gable, Clark: It Happened One Night Film Release: Anniv, **Feb 22**
Gabon: Independence Day, **Aug 17**
Gabon: National Day, **Mar 12**
Gabor, Zsa Zsa: Birth, **Feb 6**
Gabriel, Peter: Birth, **Feb 13**
Gagarin, Yuri A.: Birth Anniv, **Mar 9**
Gage, Nicholas: Birth, **Jul 23**
Gagne, Eric: Birth, **Jan 7**
Gagne, Simon: Birth, **Feb 29**
Gail, Max: Birth, **Apr 5**
Gain the Inside Advantage Month, Natl, **Oct 1**
Gaines, Ernest J.: Birth, **Jan 15**
Gaines, William M.: Birth Anniv, **Mar 1**
Gainsborough, Thomas: Birth Anniv, **May 14**
Gal, Uzi: Birth Anniv, **Dec 15**
Galbraith, John Kenneth: Birth, **Oct 15**
Gale, Robert: Birth, **Oct 11**
Galecki, Johnny: Birth, **Apr 30**
Galilei, Galileo: Birth Anniv, **Feb 15**
Gallagher, Peter: Birth, **Aug 19**
Gallaudet, Thomas Hopkins: Birth Anniv, **Dec 10**
Galligan, Zach: Birth, **Feb 14**
Gallo, Frank: Birth, **Jan 13**
Galveston Historic Homes Tour (Galveston Island, TX), **May 6**
Galveston, TX Hurricane: Anniv, **Sep 8**
Galway, James: Birth, **Dec 8**
Gambia: Independence Day, **Feb 18**
Gambill, Jan-Michael: Birth, **Jun 3**
Gambon, Michael: Birth, **Oct 19**
Game & Puzzle Week, Natl, **Nov 19**
Games, Multisport Competitions
Asian Games (Doha, Qatar), **Dec 1**
Badger State Summer Games (Madison, WI), **Jun 16**
Badger State Winter Games (Wausau, WI), **Jan 27**
Big Sky State Games (Billings, MT), **Jul 14**
Commonwealth Games (Melbourne, Australia), **Mar 15**
Cowboy State Sports Fest (Casper, WY), **Feb 4**
Dice Day, Natl, **Dec 4**
Gay Games (Chicago, IL), **Jul 15**
Maine Highland Games (Brunswick, ME), **Aug 19**
Paralympic Games (Turin, Italy), **Mar 10**
Simplot Games (Pocatello, ID), **Feb 16**
State Games of Oregon (Portland, OR), **Jul 7**

Games (cont'd)—GI

Wicket World of Croquet (Indianapolis, IN), **Jun 10**
Winter Games of Idaho (ID), **Feb 1**
Winter Olympiad (Turin, Italy), **Feb 10**
Games: Backyard Games Week, Natl, **May 22**
Gandhi, Mohandas, Assassinated: Anniv, Jan 30
Gandhi, Mohandas: Birth Anniv, Oct 2
Gandhi, Mohandas: Makes Salt: Anniv, Apr 6
Gandhi, Rajiv, Assassinated: Anniv, May 21
Gandolfini, James: Birth, Sep 18
Ganz, Bruno: Birth, Mar 22
Garage Sale Day, Natl, **Aug 12**
Garagiola, Joe: Birth, Feb 12
Garber, Victor: Birth, Mar 16
Garbo, Greta: Birth Anniv, Sep 18
Garcia, Andy: Birth, Apr 12
Garcia, Jeff: Birth, Feb 24
Garcia, Jerry: Birth Anniv, Aug 1
Garcia, Sergio: Birth, Jan 9
Garcia-Marquez, Gabriel: Birth, Mar 6
Garciaparra, Nomar: Birth, Jul 23
Garden
  Bamboo Celebration Day, **Aug 20**
  Ford Field Home & Garden Show (Detroit, MI), **Mar 10**
  Garden Week, Natl, **Apr 9**
  Gardenfest at Longwood Gardens (Kennett Square, PA), **Sep 9**
  Historic Garden Week (Virginia), **Apr 22**
  Home and Garden Fest (Wichita Falls, TX), **Feb 25**
  June Is Perennial Gardening Month, **Jun 1**
  Landscape Architecture Month, Natl, **Apr 1**
  Longwood Gardens Autumn's Colors (Kennett Square, PA), **Oct 7**
  Mailorder Gardening Month, Natl, **Jan 1**
  National City Cleveland Home and Garden Show (Cleveland, OH), **Feb 4**
  QCCA Regional Lawn, Garden and Flower Show (Rock Island, IL), **Mar 2**
  Savannah Tour of Homes and Gardens (Savannah, GA), **Mar 23**
  Spring Gardener's Market and Plant Sale (Norfolk, VA), **May 12**
  Washington Home & Garden Show (Washington, DC), **Feb 9**
  Wisconsin Spring Garden Market (Kohler, WI), **Apr 8**
Gardenia, Vincent: Birth Anniv, Jan 7
Gardner, Ava: Birth Anniv, Dec 24
Gardner, Erle Stanley: Birth Anniv, Jul 17
Gardner, Randy: Birth, Dec 2
Garfield, Allen: Birth, Nov 22
Garfield, James A.: Birth Anniv, Nov 19
Garfield, James: Assassination Anniv, Jul 2
Garfield, Lucretia R.: Birth Anniv, Apr 19
Garfield: Birthday, Jun 19
Garfunkel, Art: Birth, Nov 5
Garland, Beverly: Birth, Oct 17
Garland, Judy: Birth Anniv, Jun 10
Garland, Judy: Wizard of Oz Released: Anniv, Aug 25
Garner, James: Birth, Apr 7
Garner, Jennifer: Birth, Apr 17
Garner, John Nance: Birth Anniv, Nov 22
Garnett, Kevin: Birth, May 19
Garofalo, Janeane: Birth, Sep 28
Garr, Teri: Birth, Dec 11
Garrett, Brad: Birth, Apr 14
Garrick, David: Birth Anniv, Feb 19
Garrison, William Lloyd: Birth Anniv, Dec 12
Garth, Jennie: Birth, Apr 3
Garvey, Steve: Birth, Dec 22
Gasol, Pau: Birth, Jul 6
Gasoline Alley Creator: King, Frank: Birth Anniv, Apr 9
Gates of the Arctic Natl Park: Anniv, Dec 2
Gates, Bill: Birth, Oct 28
Gates, David: Birth, Dec 11
Gates, Henry Louis, Jr: Birth, Sep 16
Gatlin, Larry: Birth, May 2
Gauguin, Paul: Birth Anniv, Jun 7
Gautier, Dick: Birth, Oct 30
Gay & Lesbian
  Coming Out Day, Natl, **Oct 11**
  First US Same-sex Marriages: Anniv, **May 17**
  Gay and Lesbian History Month, **Oct 1**
  Gay and Lesbian Pride Month, **Jun 1**
  Gay and Lesbian Pride Parade (Chicago, IL), **Jun 25**
  Gay Games (Chicago, IL), **Jul 15**
  GLBT Book Month, Natl, **Jun 1**
  Military Ban on Homosexuals Eased, **Jan 29**
  Stonewall Riot: Anniv, **Jun 28**
Gayle, Crystal: Birth, Jan 9
Gaynor, Janet: Birth Anniv, Oct 6
Gaynor, Mitzi: Birth, Sep 4
Gazzara, Ben: Birth, Aug 28
Geary, Anthony: Birth, May 29
Gedalya, Fast of, Sep 25

Geeson, Judy: Birth, Sep 10
Geffen, David: Birth, Feb 21
Gehrig, Lou: Birth Anniv, Jun 19
Gehry, Frank: Birth, Feb 28
Geiger, Matt: Birth, Sep 10
Geiger, Ray: Birth Anniv, Sep 18
Geisel, Theodor "Dr. Seuss": Birth Anniv, Mar 2
Gelbart, Larry: Birth, Feb 25
Geldof, Bob: Birth, Oct 5
Gellar, Sarah Michelle: Birth, Apr 14
Geller, Uri: Birth, Dec 20
Gem and Mineral Show, Nova Scotia's (Parrsboro, NS, Canada), **Aug 18**
Gemini Begins, May 21
Gene Autry Show TV Premiere: Anniv, Jul 23
Genealogy Day, Mar 11
Genealogy: Ellis Island Family History Day, Apr 17
General Election Day (US), Nov 7
General Electric Theater TV Premiere: Anniv, Feb 1
General Hospital TV Premiere: Anniv, Apr 1
General Motors: Founding Anniv, Sep 16
Geneva Accords: Anniv, Jul 20
Genocide Convention: Anniv, Dec 9
Gentle Ben TV Premiere: Anniv, Sep 10
Gentry, Bobbie: Birth, Jul 27
Geode Fest/Rocktober (Keokuk, IA), **Oct 6**
Geoffreys, Stephen: Birth, Nov 22
Geographers Annual Mtg, Assn of American (Chicago, IL), **Mar 7**
Geographic Bee Finals, Natl (Washington, DC), **May 23**
Geographic Bee, School Level, Natl, Jan 3
Geographic Bee, State Level, Natl, Mar 31
George Gobel Show TV Premiere: Anniv, Oct 2
George III: Birth Anniv, Jun 4
George Spelvin Day, Nov 15
George VI's Coronation: Anniv, May 12
George, Jeff: Birth, Dec 8
George, Melissa: Birth, Aug 6
George, Phyllis: Birth, Jun 24
George, Susan: Birth, Jul 26
Georgia
  AIDS Walk Atlanta (Atlanta), **Oct 15**
  American Massage Therapy Assn, Natl Conv (Atlanta), **Oct 11**
  Arts & Crafts Fest (Stone Mountain Village), **Jun 17**
  Atlanta Marathon and Half Marathon (Atlanta), **Nov 23**
  Augusta Futurity (Augusta), **Jan 26**
  Camellia Sasanqua Days (Fort Valley), **Nov 1**
  Chambliss, Saxby: Birth, **Nov 10**
  Colonial Christmas at Wormsloe (Savannah), **Dec 10**
  Colonial Faire and Muster (Savannah), **Feb 4**
  Concerts By the Springs (Atlanta), **May 21**
  Confederate Memorial Day, **Apr 26**
  Cotton Pickin' Fair (Gay), **May 6**
  Daylily Extravaganza (Fort Valley), **Jun 1**
  Dining Out for Life (Atlanta), **Apr 27**
  1836 Encampment (Lumpkin), **May 27**
  Ethnic Awareness Program (Macon), **Apr 26**
  FDR Commemorative Ceremony (Warm Springs), **Apr 12**
  Fest of Camellias (Fort Valley), **Feb 1**
  Festival 2006: Fest of Fine Arts and Fine Crafts (Dalton), **Sep 16**
  Friendly Forest Halloween Hike (Savannah), **Oct 27**
  Georgia National Fair (Perry), **Oct 6**
  Georgia Pecan Month, Natl, **Nov 1**
  Georgia Renaissance Spring Fest (Atlanta), **Apr 15**
  Ghostly Gathering (Atlanta), **Oct 27**
  Isakson, Johnny: Birth, **Dec 28**
  Macon, GA's Cherry Blossom Fest, Intl (Macon), **Mar 17**
  May Day (Lumpkin), **May 5**
  Memorial Day Ceremonies (Andersonville), **May 28**
  Mossy Creek Barnyard Fest (Warner Robins), **Apr 22**
  Mountain Fair (Hiawassee), **Jul 19**
  NCAA Men's Div I Swimming/Diving Chmpshps (Atlanta), **Mar 23**
  NCAA Women's Div I Swimming/Diving Chmpshps (Athens), **Mar 16**
  Peachtree Road Race (Atlanta), **Jul 4**
  Perdue, Sonny: Birth, **Dec 20**
  Powers' Crossroads Country Fair/Art Fest (Newnan), **Sep 2**
  Pro-Am Snipe Excursion and Hunt (Moultrie), **Apr 1**
  Ratification Day, **Jan 2**
  Rhododendron Fest (Hiawassee), **May 12**
  Riverfest (Columbus), **Apr 28**
  Sandy Springs Festival (Atlanta), **Sep 16**

  Savannah Tour of Homes and Gardens (Savannah), **Mar 23**
  Sheep to Shawl Festival (Savannah), **Mar 25**
  Sherman Enters Atlanta: Anniv, **Sep 2**
  Sherman Takes Savannah: Anniv, **Dec 21**
  Southern Cyclone: Anniv, **Aug 24**
  Steeplechase at Callaway Gardens (Pine Mountain), **Nov 4**
  Thomasville's Victorian Christmas (Thomasville), **Dec 14**
  Tools and Skills That Built the Colony (Savannah), **Sep 2**
  Tybee 500 (Tybee Island), **May 6**
  US Open Stock Dog Trials & Farm Fest (Dawsonville), **Oct 6**
  War of Jenkin's Ear: Living History (Savannah), **May 27**
  Warm Springs Thanksgiving (Warm Springs), **Nov 18**
  Wildflower Fest of the Arts (Dahlonega), **May 20**
  WSB-TV Salute 2 America Parade (Atlanta), **Jul 4**
  Yellow Daisy Fest (Stone Mountain), **Sep 7**
Georgia (Europe): Independence Restoration Day, **May 26**
Georgia (Europe): Soviet Georgia Votes Independence, **Mar 31**
Gerard, Gil: Birth, Jan 23
Gere, Richard: Birth, Aug 29
German. See also Octoberfest; Oktoberfest
  Deutsch Country Days (Marthaville, MO), **Oct 21**
  German-American Day, Natl, **Oct 6**
  German-American Heritage Month, **Oct 1**
  Germanfest (Fort Wayne, IN), **Jun 4**
  Hanover Dutch Fest (Hanover, PA), **Jul 28**
  Oktoberfest (New Ulm, MN), **Oct 6**
  Schmeckfest (Freeman, SD), **Mar 24**
Germany
  Bach Fest (Leipzig), **May 27**
  Berlin Airlift: Anniv, **Jun 24**
  Berlin International Film Fest (Berlin), **Feb 9**
  Berlin Wall Opened: Anniv, **Nov 9**
  Buss und Bettag, **Nov 22**
  Capital Returns to Berlin: Anniv, **Sep 1**
  Day of Remembrance for Victims of Nazism, **Jan 27**
  Dresden Firebombing, **Feb 13**
  Erntedankfest, **Oct 1**
  Fasching, **Feb 27**
  Fasching Sunday, **Feb 26**
  Footbag Chmpshps, World (Frankfurt), **Jul 24**
  Frankfurt Book Fair (Frankfurt), **Oct 4**
  Frankfurt Christmas Market (Frankfurt), **Nov 25**
  German Plebiscite: Anniv, **Aug 19**
  German Surrender at Stalingrad: Anniv, **Feb 2**
  Hamburg Harbor Birthday, **May 7**
  Invades Poland: Anniv, **Sep 1**
  Kristallnacht: Anniv, **Nov 9**
  Munich Fasching Carnival, **Jan 7**
  Nuremberg War Crimes Trial: Anniv, **Nov 20**
  Red Army Departs Berlin: Anniv, **Jun 11**
  Reunification: Anniv, **Oct 3**
  Totensonntag, **Nov 26**
  Volkstrauertag, **Nov 19**
  Wagner Festspiele (Bayreuth), **Jul 25**
  Waldchestag (Frankfurt), **Jun 6**
  Wilhelm II Abdicates: Anniv, **Nov 9**
  World Cup (Berlin), **Jun 9**
Geronimo: Death Anniv, Feb 17
Gerry, Elbridge: Birth Anniv, Jul 17
Gershwin, George: Birth Anniv, Sep 26
Gershwin, Ira: Birth Anniv, Dec 6
Gertz, Jami: Birth, Oct 28
Get a Different Name Day, Feb 13
Get Organized Month, Natl, Jan 1
Get Out of the Doghouse Day, Natl, Jul 17
Get Smart TV Premiere: Anniv, Sep 18
Get to Know an Independent Real Estate Broker Month, Natl, Feb 1
Gets, Malcolm: Birth, Dec 28
Getty, Balthazar: Birth, Jan 22
Getty, Estelle: Birth, Jul 25
Gettysburg Address Memorial Ceremony (Gettysburg, PA), **Nov 19**
Gettysburg Address, Lincoln's: Anniv, **Nov 19**
Gettysburg Bluegrass Fest (Gettysburg, PA), **May 18**
Gettysburg Outdoor Antique Show (Gettysburg, PA), **May 20**
Getz, Stan: Birth Anniv, Feb 2
Ghana
  Independence Day, **Mar 6**
  Republic Day, **Jul 1**
  Revolution Day, **Jun 4**
Ghost Tours (New Hope, PA), **Jun 3**
Ghostley, Alice: Birth, Aug 14
Ghosts, Fest of Hungry (China), **Aug 8**
Ghostwriters Week, Natl, **Mar 1**
GI Day, Hug a, **Mar 4**

Giamatti, Bartlett: Birth Anniv, Apr 4
Giamatti, Paul: Birth, Jun 6
Giambi, Jason: Birth, Jan 8
Giannini, Giancarlo: Birth, Aug 1
Gibb, Barry: Birth, Sep 1
Gibb, Robin: Birth, Dec 22
Gibbon, Edward: Birth Anniv, Apr 27
Gibbons, Leeza: Birth, Mar 26
Gibbs, Joe Jackson: Birth, Nov 25
Gibbs, Marla: Birth, Jun 14
Gibbs, Mifflin Wister: Birth Anniv, Apr 28
Gibran, Kahlil: Birth Anniv, Jan 6
Gibson, Althea: Birth Anniv, Aug 25
Gibson, Bob: Birth, Nov 9
Gibson, Debbie: Birth, Aug 31
Gibson, Henry: Birth, Sep 21
Gibson, Josh: Birth Anniv, Dec 21
Gibson, Kirk: Birth, May 28
Gibson, Mel: Birth, Jan 3
Gibson, Thomas: Birth, Jul 3
Gibson, William: Cyberspace Coined: Anniv, Oct 1
Gielgud, Sir John: Birth Anniv, Apr 14
Gifford, Frank: Birth, Aug 16
Gifford, Kathie Lee: Birth, Aug 16
Gift Fest, Intl (Fairfield, PA), Nov 9
Gifted Children Conv, Natl Assn (Charlotte, NC), Nov 1
Giguere, Jean-Sebastien: Birth, May 16
Gilbert, John: Birth Anniv, Jul 10
Gilbert, Melissa: Birth, May 8
Gilbert, Sara: Birth, Jan 29
Gilbert, Sir William: Birth Anniv, Nov 18
Gilford, Jack: Birth Anniv, Jul 25
Gillars, Mildred E.: Death Anniv, Jun 25
Gillespie, Dizzy: Birth Anniv, Oct 21
Gilley, Mickey: Birth, Mar 9
Gilliam, Armon: Birth, May 28
Gilliam, Terry: Birth, Nov 22
Gilligan's Island TV Premiere: Anniv, Sep 26
Gillis, Margaret: Birth, Jul 9
Gilmore, Artis: Birth, Sep 21
Gilmour, Dave: Birth, Mar 6
Gilpin, Peri: Birth, May 27
Gilroy Garlic Fest (Gilroy, CA), Jul 28
Gimme A Break! TV Premiere: Anniv, Oct 29
Gingerbread House Competition, Natl (Asheville, NC), Nov 13
Gingerbread House Day, Dec 12
Gingerbread on Parade (Omaha, NE), Nov 27
Ginsberg, Allen: Birth Anniv, Jun 3
Ginsburg, Ruth Bader: Birth, Mar 15
Ginza Holiday: Japanese Cultural Fest (Chicago, IL), Aug 11
Girl Scout Week, Mar 12
Girl Scouts Founding: Anniv, Mar 12
Girlfriend's Day, Aug 1
Girls and Women in Sports Day, Natl, Feb 1
Gish, Lillian: Birth Anniv, Oct 14
Giuliani, Rudolph: Birth, May 28
Give Wildlife a Brake! Week, Oct 23
Givenchy, Hubert de: Birth, Feb 21
Givens, Robin: Birth, Nov 27
Glacier Bay Natl Park: Anniv, Dec 2
Glacier Natl Park: Anniv, May 11
Gladstone, William: Birth Anniv, Dec 29
Glaser, Paul Michael: Birth, Mar 25
Glass Fest, Elwood (Elwood, IN), Aug 18
Glass, Ira: Birth, Mar 3
Glass, Philip: Birth, Jan 31
Glass, Ron: Birth, Jul 10
Glaucoma Awareness Month, Natl, Jan 1
Glavine, Tom: Birth, Mar 25
GLBT Book Month, Natl, Jun 1
Gleason, Jackie: Birth Anniv, Feb 26
Glenn, John: Birth, Jul 18
Glenn, Scott: Birth, Jan 26
Gless, Sharon: Birth, May 31
Glover, Crispin: Birth, Apr 20
Glover, Danny: Birth, Jul 22
Glover, John: Birth, Aug 7
Glover, Savion: Birth, Nov 19
Go Fetch! Natl Food Drive for Homeless Animals, May 1
Go Hog Wild—Eat Country Ham Month, Oct 1
Go On a Field Trip Month, Natl, Oct 1
Goals, Goal Setting (personal and professional growth)
Be On-Purpose Month, Natl, Jan 1
Build a Better Image Week, Sep 17
Business Resolutions Month, Intl, Jan 1
Do It Day (aka Fight Procrastination Day), Sep 6
Effectiveness Week, Natl, May 15
Kick-Butt Day, Natl, Oct 9
Kids' Goal Setting Week, Nov 6
New Year's Resolutions Week, Jan 1
Plant the Seeds of Greatness Month, Feb 1
Second Half of the New Year Day, Jul 1

Single-Tasking Day, Feb 21
Take a New Year's Resolution to Stop Smoking, Dec 10
Toss Away the "Could Haves" and "Should Haves" Day, Jul 15
Goat Cook-off, World Chmpshp BBQ/Crafts Fair (Brady, TX), Sep 2
God Bless America First Performed: Anniv, Nov 11
Godard, Jean Luc: Birth, Dec 3
Goddard Day: Anniv, Mar 16
Goddard, Robert H.: Birth Anniv, Oct 5
Godfather Film Premiere: Anniv, Mar 15
Godwin, Mary. See Wollstonecraft, Mary: Birth Anniv, Apr 27
Godwin, William: Birth Anniv, Mar 3
Goebbels, Paul Josef: Birth Anniv, Oct 29
Goethals, George W.: Birth Anniv, Jun 29
Goethe, Johann W.: Birth Anniv, Aug 28
Gogol, Nikolai: Birth Anniv, Mar 31
Gold Discovery Days (Custer, SD), Jul 21
Gold Discovery, California: Anniv, Jan 24
Gold Discovery, Klondike Eldorado: Anniv, Aug 31
Gold Discovery, Klondike: Anniv, Aug 16
Gold Rush Days (Wickenburg, AZ), Feb 10
Gold Rush: Whiskey Flat Days (Kernville, CA), Feb 17
Gold Star Mother's Day (Pres Proc), Sep 24
Gold, Missy: Birth, Jul 14
Gold, Tracey: Birth, May 16
Goldberg, Rube: Birth Anniv, Jul 4
Goldberg, Whoopi: Birth, Nov 13
Goldbergs TV Premiere: Anniv, Jan 17
Goldblum, Jeff: Birth, Oct 22
Golden Aspen Motorcycle Rally (Ruidoso, NM), Sep 13
Golden Gate Bridge Opened: Anniv, May 27
Golden Girls TV Premiere: Anniv, Sep 14
Golden Rule Week, Apr 1
Golden Spike Driving: Anniv, May 10
Golding, Sir William: Birth Anniv, Sep 19
Goldman, William: Birth, Aug 12
Goldsmith, Oliver: Birth Anniv, Nov 10
Goldwyn, Samuel: Birth Anniv, Aug 17
Goldwyn, Tony: Birth, May 20
Golf
Big 12 Men's Chmpshp (Tulsa, OK), Apr 24
Big 12 Women's Golf Chmpshp (Lincoln, NE), Apr 17
Big Ten Men's Golf Chmpshps (Evanston, IL), May 5
Big Ten Women's Chmpshps (Bloomington, IN), Apr 28
Bob Hope Chrysler Classic (La Quinta, CA), Jan 16
Chicago Golf Club: Anniv, Jul 18
Curtis Cup (Bandon, OR), Jul 29
First PGA Championship: Anniv, Apr 10
Ford Chmpshp at Doral (Miami, FL), Mar 1
Hogan, Ben: Birth Anniv, Aug 13
Jones Wins First Grand Slam: Anniv, Jul 12
Jones, Bobby: Birth Anniv, Mar 17
Kraft Nabisco Chmpshp (Rancho Mirage, CA), Mar 27
NAIA Men's Golf Chmpshps, May 16
NAIA Women's Natl Chmpshps (South Bend, IN), May 23
NCAA Div I Men's Golf Chmpshps (Sunriver, OR), May 31
NCAA Div I Women's Golf Chmpshps (Columbus, OH), May 23
Open Golf Chmpshp (British Open) (Hoylake, England), Jul 20
Ouimet, Francis DeSales: Birth Anniv, May 8
PGA Chmpshp (Medinah, IL), Aug 14
PGA Founded: Anniv, Jan 17
PGA Seniors' Chmpshp (Edmond, OK), May 22
Ryder Cup Matches (Straffan, Ireland), Sep 22
Sarazen, Gene: Birth Anniv, Feb 27
Snead, Sam: Birth Anniv, May 27
Southwest Senior Chmpshp (Yuma, AZ), Jan 17
Texas-Oklahoma Junior Golf Tournament (Wichita Falls, TX), Jun 26
US Amateur Chmpshp (Chaska, MN), Aug 21
US Amateur Public Links Chmpshp (Bremerton, WA), Jul 10
US Mid-Amateur Chmpshp (Flagstaff, AZ), Sep 9
US Open Chmpshp (Mamaroneck, NY), Jun 15
US Senior Open (Golf) Chmpshp (Hutchinson, KS), Jul 6
US Women's Amateur Chmpshp (North Plains, OR), Aug 7
US Women's Amateur Public Links Chmpshp (Pueblo, CO), Jun 20
US Women's Open Chmpshp (Newport, RI), Jun 29

USGA Senior Amateur Chmpshp (Newburgh, IN), Sep 16
Zaharias, Mildred Babe Didrikson: Birth Anniv, Jun 26
Golino, Valeria: Birth, Oct 22
Gomez, Scott: Birth, Dec 23
Gompers, Samuel: Birth Anniv, Jan 27
Gone with the Wind Film Premiere: Anniv, Dec 15
Gone with the Wind Published: Anniv, May 19
Gong Show TV Premiere: Anniv, Jun 14
Gonzales, Alberto: Birth, Aug 4
Gonzales, Pancho: Birth Anniv, May 9
Gonzalez, Juan: Birth, Oct 16
Good Friday, Apr 14
Good Friday Bank Holiday (United Kingdom), Apr 14
Good Friday Peace Agreement in Northern Ireland: Anniv, Apr 10
Good Morning America TV Premiere: Anniv, Nov 6
Good Samaritan Involvement Day, Mar 13
Good Sex! with Dr. Ruth Westheimer TV Premiere: Anniv, Aug 27
Good Times TV Premiere: Anniv, Feb 1
Goodall, Jane: Birth, Apr 3
Gooden, Dwight: Birth, Nov 16
Goodeve, Grant: Birth, Jul 6
Gooding, Cuba, Jr: Birth, Jan 2
Goodman, Benny: Birth Anniv, May 30
Goodman, Ellen: Birth, Apr 11
Goodman, John: Birth, Jun 20
Goodson, Mark: Birth Anniv, Jan 24
Goodwill Industries Week, May 7
Goodwill: Helms, Edgar J.: Birth Anniv, Jan 19
Goof-Off Day, Intl, Mar 22
Google Founded: Anniv, Sep 7
Goolagong, Evonne: Birth, Jul 31
Goorjian, Michael: Birth, Feb 4
Gorbachev, Mikhail: Birth, Mar 2
Gordimer, Nadine: Birth, Nov 20
Gordon, Jeff: Birth, Aug 4
Gordon, Keith: Birth, Feb 3
Gordone, Charles: Birth Anniv, Oct 12
Gordon-Levitt, Joseph: Birth, Feb 17
Gordy, Berry, Jr: Birth, Nov 28
Gore, Al: Birth, Mar 31
Gore, Lesley: Birth, May 2
Gore, Tipper: Birth, Aug 19
Gorgas, William Crawford: Birth Anniv, Oct 3
Gorgeous Grandma Day, Jul 23
Gorilla Born in Captivity, First: Anniv, Dec 22
Gorillas: Koko: Birth, Jul 4
Gorme, Eydie: Birth, Aug 16
Gortner, Marjoe: Birth, Jan 14
Gospel. See also Music
Chicago Gospel Music Fest (Chicago, IL), Jun 9
Dorsey, Thomas A.: Birth Anniv, Jul 1
Jackson, Mahalia: Birth Anniv, Oct 26
Singing on the Mountain (Linville, NC), Jun 25
Southern Gospel Music Month, Sep 1
Gossage, Goose: Birth, Jul 5
Gosselaar, Mark-Paul: Birth, Mar 1
Gossett, Louis, Jr: Birth, May 27
Gottlieb, Robert: Birth, Apr 29
Gottschalk, Louis Moreau: Birth Anniv, May 8
Gould, Chester: Birth Anniv, Nov 20
Gould, Elliott: Birth, Aug 29
Gould, Harold: Birth, Dec 10
Gould, Stephen Jay: Birth Anniv, Sep 10
Goulet, Robert: Birth, Nov 26
Goya, Francisco Jose de: Birth Anniv, Mar 30
Grace, Mark: Birth, Jun 28
Grace, Topher: Birth, Jul 19
Grady, Don: Birth, Jun 8
Graf, Steffi: Birth, Jun 14
Graffman, Gary: Birth, Oct 14
Grafton, Sue: Birth, Apr 24
Graham, Billy: Birth, Nov 7
Graham, Calvin "Baby Vet": Birth Anniv, Apr 3
Graham, Heather: Birth, Jan 29
Graham, Lauren: Birth, Mar 16
Graham, Lindsey: Birth, Jul 9
Graham, Martha: Birth Anniv, May 11
Graham, Martha: First Solo: Anniv, Apr 18
Graham, Otto: Birth, Dec 6
Grahame, Kenneth: Birth Anniv, Mar 8
Grammer, Kelsey: Birth, Feb 21
Grammy Awards, Feb 8
Granato, Cammi: Birth, Mar 25
Grand Canyon Natl Park Established: Anniv, Feb 26
Grand Militia Muster (St. Mary's City, MD), Oct 21
Grand Ole Opry Broadcast, First: Anniv, Dec 10
Grand Teton Music Fest (Teton Village, WY), Jul 4
Grand Teton Natl Park Established: Anniv, Feb 1
Grandmother's Day in Florida, Oct 8
Grandparents' Day, Natl, Sep 10
Grandy, Fred: Birth, Jun 29

Grange Founding, Natl: Anniv, Dec 4
Grange Month, Apr 1
Grange, Red: Birth Anniv, Jun 13
Granholm, Jennifer: Birth, Feb 5
Grant, Amy: Birth, Nov 25
Grant, Cary: Birth Anniv, Jan 18
Grant, Harvey: Birth, Jul 4
Grant, Horace: Birth, Jul 4
Grant, Hugh: Birth, Sep 9
Grant, Jennifer: Birth, Feb 26
Grant, Julia Dent: Birth Anniv, Jan 26
Grant, Richard E.: Birth, May 5
Grant, Ulysses S.
  Battle of Chattanooga: Anniv, Nov 24
  Battle of Cold Harbor: Anniv, Jun 3
  Battle of Shiloh: Anniv, Apr 6
  Battle of Spotsylvania: Anniv, May 12
  Battle of the Wilderness: Anniv, May 5
  Birth Anniv, Apr 27
  Commissioned Commander: Anniv, Mar 9
  Speech of Apology: Anniv, Dec 5
  Surrender of Fort Donelson: Anniv, Feb 16
  Vicksburg Surrenders: Anniv, Jul 3
Grantsville Days (Grantsville, MD), Jun 23
Grape Jamboree, Geneva Area (Geneva, OH), Sep 23
Grapes of Wrath Published: Anniv, Apr 14
Grass Is Always Browner on the Other Side of the Fence Day, Mar 30
Grass, Gunter: Birth, Oct 16
Grassle, Karen: Birth, Feb 25
Grassley, Charles: Birth, Sep 17
Gratitude: I Am So Thankful Month, Nov 1
Gratton, Chris: Birth, Jul 5
Graves' Disease Awareness Week, Jan 9
Graves, Peter: Birth, Mar 18
Graves, Rupert: Birth, Jun 30
Gray, Asa: Birth Anniv, Nov 18
Gray, Erin: Birth, Jan 7
Gray, Harold Lincoln: Birth Anniv, Jan 20
Gray, Linda: Birth, Sep 12
Gray, Macy: Birth, Dec 6
Gray, Robert, Circumnavigates the Earth: Anniv, Apr 10
Grayson, Kathryn: Birth, Feb 9
Great American Meatout, Mar 18
Great American Smokeout, Nov 16
Great American Smokeout Day, Natl (Pres Proc), Nov 16
Great American Warm-Up, Nov 10
Great Backyard Bird Count, Feb 17
Great Britain Formed: Anniv, May 1
Great (Holy) Week, Apr 9
Great NY State Snow & Track Expo (Albany, NY), Nov 4
Great Outdoors Show, Northeast (Albany, NY), Mar 17
Great Smoky Mountains Natl Park Established: Anniv, Jun 15
Great Wellsville Balloon Rally (Wellsville, NY), Jul 21
Greatest Show on Earth Formed: Anniv, Mar 28
Greco, Buddy: Birth, Aug 14
Greco, Jose: Birth, Dec 23
Greece
  Dumb Week, Apr 9
  Independence Day, Mar 25
  Midwife's Day or Women's Day, Jan 8
  Ochi Day, Oct 28
Greek Culture Event: Odyssey—A Greek Fest (Orange, CT), Sep 1
Greek Independence Day (Pres Proc), Mar 25
Greeley, Father Andrew: Birth, Feb 5
Greeley, Horace: Birth Anniv, Feb 3
Green Monday, Mar 6
Green, Al: Birth, Apr 13
Green, Brian: Birth, Jul 15
Green, Hetty: Birth Anniv, Nov 21
Green, Hubie: Birth, Dec 28
Green, Seth: Birth, Feb 8
Greenberg, Hank: Birth Anniv, Jan 1
Greene, Bob: Birth, Mar 10
Greene, Graham: Birth Anniv, Oct 2
Greene, Nathaniel: Birth Anniv, Aug 7
Greene, Shecky: Birth, Apr 8
Greenfield, Jeff: Birth, Jun 10
Greenland: National Day, Jun 21
Greenpeace Founded: Anniv, Sep 15
Greenpeace: Rainbow Warrior Sinking: Anniv, Jul 10
Greensboro Sit-in: Anniv, Feb 1
Greenspan, Alan: Birth, Mar 6
Greenspan, Alan: Irrational Exuberance Enters Lexicon: Anniv, Dec 5
Greenwich Mean Time Begins: Anniv, Sep 25
Greenwood, Joan: Birth Anniv, Mar 4
Greer, Germaine: Birth, Jan 29
Gregg, Judd: Birth, Feb 14

Gregoire, Christine: Birth, Mar 24
Gregorian Calendar Adjustment: Anniv, Oct 4
Gregorian Calendar Day, Feb 24
Gregory, Bettina: Birth, Jun 4
Gregory, Cynthia: Birth, Jul 8
Gregory, Dick: Birth, Oct 12
Greist, Kim: Birth, May 12
Grenada
  Emancipation Day, Aug 7
  Independence Day, Feb 7
  Invasion by US: Anniv, Oct 25
Grenadines and Saint Vincent: Independence Day, Oct 27
Gretzky, Wayne: Birth, Jan 26
Grey, Jennifer: Birth, Mar 26
Grey, Joel: Birth, Apr 11
Grey, Zane: Birth Anniv, Jan 31
Grieco, Richard: Birth, Mar 23
Grieg, Edvard: Birth Anniv, Jun 15
Grieg, Edvard: Birth Anniv Celebration (Norway), Jun 15
Grier, David Alan: Birth, Jun 30
Grier, Pam: Birth, May 26
Grier, Roosevelt (Rosey): Birth, Jul 14
Griese, Bob: Birth, Feb 3
Grieve, Ben: Birth, May 4
Griffey, Ken: Birth, Nov 21
Griffin, John H.: Birth Anniv, Jun 16
Griffin, Kathy: Birth, Nov 4
Griffin, Merv: Birth, Jul 6
Griffith, Andy, Show TV Premiere: Anniv, Oct 3
Griffith, Andy: Birth, Jun 1
Griffith, D.W.: Birth Anniv, Jan 22
Griffith, Melanie: Birth, Aug 9
Griffith, Yolanda: Birth, Mar 1
Griffiths, Martha: Speech Against Sex Discrimination, Feb 8
Grilling Month, Natl, Jul 1
Grimaldi, Joseph: Birth Anniv, Dec 18
Grimes, Gary: Birth, Jun 2
Grimke, Sarah: Birth Anniv, Nov 26
Grimm, Jacob: Birth Anniv, Jan 4
Grimm, Wilhelm: Birth Anniv, Feb 24
Grint, Rupert: Birth, Aug 24
Grisham, John: Birth, Feb 8
Grodin, Charles: Birth, Apr 21
Groening, Matt: Birth, Feb 15
Gross, Mary: Birth, Mar 25
Gross, Michael: Birth, Jun 21
Grotius, Hugo: Birth Anniv, Apr 10
Grouch Day, Natl, Oct 15
Ground Zero Recovery and Cleanup Ends: Anniv, May 30
Groundhog Day, Feb 2
Groundhog Day (Punxsutawney, PA), Feb 2
Groundhog Day (Sun Prairie, WI), Feb 2
Groundhog Days (Woodstock, IL), Jan 28
Groundhog Fest (Punxsutawney, PA), Jul 2
Groundhog Job Shadow Day, Feb 2
Groundhog Run (Kansas City, MO), Jan 29
Grubstake Days (Yucca Valley, CA), May 25
Grump Out, Great American, May 31
Gruntled Workers Day, Jul 13
Guadalajara Intl Book Fair (Guadalajara, Mexico), Nov 25
Guadalcanal, Allies Retake: Anniv, Feb 9
Guadalupe Hidalgo, Treaty of: Anniv, Feb 2
Guadalupe Natl Park Established: Anniv, Sep 30
Guadalupe, Day of Our Lady of, Dec 12
Guam
  Discovery Day, Mar 6
  Lady of Camarin Day, Dec 8
  Liberation Day, Jul 21
  Magellan Day, Mar 6
  Spanish-American War: Surrender, to US: Anniv, Jun 20
Guatemala
  Armed Forces Day, Jun 30
  Independence Day, Sep 15
  Kite Fest of Santiago Sacatepequez, Nov 1
  Revolution Day, Oct 20
Guccione, Bob: Birth, Dec 17
Guernica Massacre: Anniv, Apr 26
Guerrero, Vladimir: Birth, Feb 9
Guest, Christopher: Birth, Feb 5
Guest, Edgar A.: Birth Anniv, Aug 20
Guest, Lance: Birth, Jul 21
Guggenheim, Simon: Birth Anniv, Dec 30
Gugliotta, Tom: Birth, Dec 19
Guiding Light TV Premiere: Anniv, Jun 26
Guidry, Ron: Birth, Aug 28
Guilfoyle, Paul: Birth, Jul 12
Guillaume, Robert: Birth, Nov 30
Guillotin, Joseph: Birth Anniv, May 28
Guinea: Anniversary of the Second Republic, Apr 3
Guinea: Independence Day, Oct 2
Guinea-Bissau

Colonization Martyr's Day, Aug 3
Independence Day, Sep 24
National Holiday, Sep 12
Natl Heroes Day, Jan 20
Readjustment Movement's Day, Nov 14
Guinn, Kenny: Birth, Aug 24
Guinness, Sir Alec: Birth Anniv, Apr 2
Guisewite, Cathy Lee: Birth, Sep 5
Gulf of Tonkin Resolution: Anniv, Aug 7
Gullikson Foundation Week, May 1
Gumbel, Bryant: Birth, Sep 29
Gumbel, Greg: Birth, May 3
Gumbo Fest (Bridge City, LA), Nov 3
Gumby Show TV Premiere: Anniv, Mar 16
Gun Shows, Sales, Competition
  Ocean County Decoy/Gun Show (Tuckerton, NJ), Sep 30
  Texas Collectors' Gun & Knife Show (Wichita Falls, TX), Jan 28
  Walsh Invitational Rifle Tournament (Cincinnati, OH), Nov 3
Gunn, Moses: Birth Anniv, Oct 2
Gunpowder Plot Trial: Anniv, Jan 27
Guns: Day of Natl Concern about Young People and Gun Violence, Oct 18
Gunsmoke TV Premiere: Anniv, Sep 10
Gutenberg Bible Published: Anniv, Sep 30
Guterson, David: Birth, May 4
Guth, Alan: Birth, Feb 27
Guthrie, Arlo: Birth, Jul 10
Guthrie, Janet: Birth, Mar 7
Guthrie, Woody: Birth Anniv, Jul 14
Gutierrez, Carlos: Birth, Nov 4
Guttenberg, Steve: Birth, Aug 24
Guy, Jasmine: Birth, Mar 10
Guyana: National Day, Feb 23
Gwathmey, Charles: Birth, Jun 19
Gwinnett, Button: Death Anniv, May 16
Gwynn, Tony: Birth, May 9
Gwynne, Fred: Birth Anniv, Jul 10
Gyllenhall, Jake: Birth, Dec 19
Gyllenhall, Maggie: Birth, Nov 16
Gymnastics (competitions, championships, etc)
  Big 12 Women's Chmpshp (Lincoln, NE), Mar 25
  Big Ten Men's Chmpshps (Iowa City, IA), Mar 24
  Big Ten Women's Chmpshps (East Lansing, MI), Mar 25
  National Collegiate Women's (Corvallis, OR), Apr 20
Gynecologic Cancer Awareness Month, Sep 1
Gypsy Rose Lee (Rose L Hovick): Birth Anniv, Feb 9

Haas, Lukas: Birth, Apr 16
Habitat Day, World (UN), Oct 2
Habitat for Humanity Intl's Building on Faith Week, Sep 10
Hackman, Gene: Birth, Jan 30
Hadassah: Anniv, Feb 24
Haden, Pat: Birth, Jan 23
Hagar, Sammy: Birth, Oct 13
Hagel, Chuck: Birth, Oct 4
Hagerty, Julie: Birth, Jun 15
Haggard, Merle: Birth, Apr 6
Hagler, Marvelous Marvin: Birth, May 23
Hagman, Larry: Birth, Sep 21
Haid, Charles: Birth, Jun 2
Haim, Corey: Birth, Dec 23
Hair Broadway Opening: Anniv, Mar 28
Hairball Awareness Day, Natl, Apr 28
Hairstylist Day, Apr 28
Haiti
  Ancestors' Day, Jan 2
  Army Day, Nov 18
  Discovery Day: Anniv, Dec 5
  Flag and University Day, May 18
  Independence Day, Jan 1
Haitian Heritage Month, May 1
HAL (computer): Birth, Jan 12
Halas, George: Birth Anniv, Feb 2
Halberstam, David: Birth, Apr 10
Halcyon Days, Dec 15
Hale, Barbara: Birth, Apr 18
Hale, Nathan: Birth Anniv, Jun 6
Haleakala Natl Park Established: Anniv, Sep 30
Haley, Alex Palmer: Birth Anniv, Aug 11
Halfway Point of 2006, Jul 2
Halifax Busker Fest, Intl (Halifax, NS, Canada), Aug 10
Halifax Independence Day (NC), Apr 12
Hall, Anthony Michael: Birth, Apr 14
Hall, Arsenio: Birth, Feb 12
Hall, Daryl: Birth, Oct 11
Hall, Deidre: Birth, Oct 31
Hall, Donald A.: Birth, Sep 20
Hall, Edd: Birth, Dec 7
Hall, Lyman: Birth Anniv, Apr 12
Hall, Monty: Birth, Aug 25

Hall, Tom T.: Birth, May 25
Halley, Edmund: Birth Anniv, Nov 8
Hallmark Hall of Fame TV Premiere: Anniv, Jan 6
Halloween
  Boo at the Zoo (Cleveland, OH), Oct 19
  Books for Treats Day (San Jose, CA), Oct 31
  Devil's Night, Oct 30
  Emma Crawford Fest and Memorial Coffin Race (Manitou Springs, CO), Oct 28
  Family Halloween, A (Woodstock, VT), Oct 29
  Fantasy Fest (Key West, FL), Oct 20
  Frankenstein Friday, Oct 27
  Friendly Forest Halloween Hike (Savannah, GA), Oct 27
  Ghostly Gathering (Atlanta, GA), Oct 27
  Halloween (Arapahoe, NE), Oct 31
  Hallowe'en or All Hallow's Eve, Oct 31
  Halloween Parade (Toms River, NJ), Oct 31
  Halloween Safety Month, Oct 1
  Haunted Refrigerator Night, Oct 30
  Haunted Seaport (Tuckerton, NJ), Oct 28
  Haute Dog Charity Howl'oween Parade (Long Beach, CA), Oct 29
  Knock-Knock Day, Natl, Oct 31
  Literally, A Haunted House (New Albany, IN), Oct 6
  Magic Day, Oct 31
  Monster Myths by Moonlight (Milford, KS), Oct 14
  Samhain, Oct 31
  Scare a Friend Day, Oct 31
  Scared Silly: Halloween in Prospect Park (Brooklyn, NY), Oct 28
  Sea Witch Halloween Fest (Rehoboth Beach/Dewey Beach, DE), Oct 28
  Trick or Treat or Beggar's Night, Oct 31
  UNICEF Day, Natl (Pres Proc), Oct 31
  Wisconsin Dells Autumn Harvest Fest (Wisconsin Dells, WI), Oct 21
  WMAS Annual Halloween Ball (Springfield, MA), Oct 28
Halsey, William "Bull": Birth Anniv, Oct 30
Ham: Go Hog Wild—Eat Country Ham Month, Oct 1
Hamburger Hill, Battle of: Anniversary, May 11
Hamburger Month, Natl, May 1
Hamel, Veronica: Birth, Nov 20
Hamill, Mark: Birth, Sep 25
Hamilton, Alexander: Birth Anniv, Jan 11
Hamilton, Alexander: Duel with Aaron Burr: Anniv, Jul 11
Hamilton, Alice: Birth Anniv, Feb 27
Hamilton, George: Birth, Aug 12
Hamilton, Jane: Birth, Jul 13
Hamilton, Linda: Birth, Sep 26
Hamilton, Scott: Birth, Aug 28
Hamlin, Hannibal: Birth Anniv, Aug 27
Hamlin, Harry: Birth, Oct 30
Hamlisch, Marvin: Birth, Jun 2
Hamm, Mia: Birth, May 17
Hamm, Morgan: Birth, Sep 24
Hamm, Paul: Birth, Sep 24
Hammer, Armand: Birth Anniv, May 21
Hammer, M.C.: Birth, Mar 30
Hammerstein II, Oscar: Oklahoma! Broadway Premiere: Anniv, Mar 31
Hammett, Dashiell: Birth Anniv, May 27
Hammett, Dashiell: Maltese Falcon: Publication Anniv, Feb 14
Hammon, Jupiter: Birth Anniv, Oct 17
Hammond, Darrell: Birth, Oct 8
Hampton, James: Birth, Jul 9
Hampton, Lionel: Birth Anniv, Apr 20
Hampton, Mike: Birth, Sep 9
Hancock, Herbie: Birth, Apr 12
Hancock, John: Birth Anniv, Jan 23
Hancock, Winfield Scott: Birth Anniv, Feb 14
Handel, George Frederick: Birth Anniv, Feb 23
Handel, George Frederick: Premiere of Messiah: Anniv, Apr 13
Handshake Day, Natl, Jun 28
Handwriting Analysis Week, Natl, Jan 22
Handwriting Day, Natl, Jan 23
Handy, W.C., Fest (Florence, AL), Jul 23
Handy, William C.: Birth Anniv, Nov 16
Hang Around Victor Day (Victor, NY), Sep 9
Hangul (Korea), Oct 9
Hanks, Tom: Birth, Jul 9
Hanna, William: Birth Anniv, Jul 14
Hannah, Daryl: Birth, Dec 3
Hannukah: See Chanukah, Dec 16
Hansberry, Lorraine: Birth Anniv, May 19
Hansen, Beck: Birth, Jul 8
Hansom, Joseph: Birth Anniv, Oct 26
Hanson, Howard: Birth Anniv, Oct 28
Hanson, Isaac: Birth, Nov 17
Happiness Happens Day, Aug 8
Happiness Happens Month, Aug 1
Happiness: Hunt for Happiness Week, Jan 15

Happy Birthday to "Happy Birthday to You", Jun 27
Happy Days TV Premiere: Anniv, Jan 15
Happy Mew Year for Cats Day, Jan 2
Harbaugh, Jim: Birth, Dec 23
Hard Crab Derby and Fair, Natl (Crisfield, MD), Sep 1
Hardaway, Penny: Birth, Jul 18
Hardaway, Tim: Birth, Sep 1
Harden, Marcia Gay: Birth, Aug 14
Harding, Florence: Birth Anniv, Aug 15
Harding, Tonya: Birth, Nov 12
Harding, Warren G.: Birth Anniv, Nov 2
Harding, Warren G.: First Radio Broadcast, Jun 14
Hardison, Kadeem: Birth, Jul 24
Hardy, Oliver: Birth Anniv, Jan 18
Harewood, Dorian: Birth, Aug 6
Hargitay, Mariska: Birth, Jan 23
Harkin, Thomas R.: Birth, Nov 19
Harlem Globetrotters Play First Game: Anniv, Jan 7
Harmon, Angie: Birth, Aug 10
Harmon, Mark: Birth, Sep 2
Harmonic Convergence: Anniv, Aug 16
Harmonica Competition, Louisiana State (Spring Fest) (Marthaville, LA), Apr 28
Harper, Jessica: Birth, Oct 10
Harper, Valerie: Birth, Aug 22
Harrelson, Woody: Birth, Jul 23
Harrington, Pat, Jr: Birth, Aug 13
Harris, Ed: Birth, Nov 28
Harris, Emmylou: Birth, Apr 2
Harris, Franco: Birth, Mar 7
Harris, Joel Chandler: Birth Anniv, Dec 9
Harris, Julie: Birth, Dec 2
Harris, Lou: Birth, Jan 6
Harris, Mel: Birth, Jul 12
Harris, Neil Patrick: Birth, Jun 15
Harris, Patricia Roberts: Birth Anniv, May 31
Harris, Richard: Birth Anniv, Oct 1
Harris, Roy: Birth Anniv, Feb 12
Harrison, Anna: Birth Anniv, Jul 25
Harrison, Benjamin, Family Christmas at Home (Indianapolis, IN), Nov 20
Harrison, Benjamin: Birth Anniv, Aug 20
Harrison, Benjamin: Birth Celeb (Indianapolis, IN), Aug 20
Harrison, Benjamin: Presidents' Day: Live from Delaware St (Indianapolis, IN), Feb 20
Harrison, Caroline L.S.: Birth Anniv, Oct 1
Harrison, George: Birth Anniv, Feb 25
Harrison, Gregory: Birth, May 31
Harrison, Mary: Birth Anniv, Apr 30
Harrison, Rex: Birth Anniv, Mar 5
Harrison, William Henry: Birth Anniv, Feb 9
Harrold, Kathryn: Birth, Aug 2
Harry Thaw Shoots Stanford White: Anniv, Jun 25
Harry, Debbie: Birth, Jul 1
Harry, Deborah, and Blondie Month, Intl, Jul 1
Harry, Prince: Birth, Sep 15
Hart, Charles: Birth, Jun 3
Hart, Gary: Birth, Nov 28
Hart, John: Death Anniv, May 11
Hart, Mary: Birth, Nov 8
Hart, Melissa Joan: Birth, Apr 18
Harte, Bret: Birth Anniv, Aug 25
Hartley, Mariette: Birth, Jun 21
Hartman Black, Lisa: Birth, Jun 1
Hartman, David: Birth, May 19
Hartnett, Josh: Birth, Jul 21
Hartville Annual Fall Fest (Hartville, MO), Oct 21
Haru-No-Yabuiri (Japan), Jan 16
Harvard Univ Founded: Anniv, Oct 28
Harvard, John: Day, Nov 26
Harvest Fest (Hood River, OR), Oct 20
Harvest Moon, Sep 7
Harvest Weekends (Bryan, TX), Jul 22
Harvey, Paul: Birth, Sep 4
Harvey, Steve: Birth, Nov 23
Harvey, William: Birth Anniv, Apr 1
Harwell, Ernie: Birth, Jan 25
Hasek, Dominik: Birth, Jan 29
Hasenfus, Eugene, Captured: Anniv, Oct 5
Hasselhoff, David: Birth, Jul 17
Hastert, Dennis: Birth, Jan 2
Hat Month, Fall, Sep 1
Hat Month, Straw, Apr 1
Hatch, Orrin: Birth, Mar 22
Hatcher, Teri: Birth, Dec 8
Hate Week, Apr 4
Hatfield-McCoy Feud Erupts: Anniv, Aug 7
Hatsume Fair (Delray Beach, FL), Feb 25
Hauer, Rutger: Birth, Jan 23
Haunted Refrigerator Night, Oct 30
Hauptmann Execution: Anniv, Apr 3
Have a Bad Day Day, Nov 19
Have Gun Will Travel TV Premiere: Anniv, Sep 14

Havel, Vaclav: Birth, Oct 5
Havers, Nigel: Birth, Nov 6
Havlicek, John: Birth, Apr 8
Havoc, June: Birth, Nov 8
Hawaii
  Admission Day Holiday, Aug 18
  Akaka, Daniel K.: Birth, Sep 11
  American Dietetic Assn Food & Nutrition Conf & Expo (Honolulu), Sep 16
  Discoverers' Day, Oct 9
  Haleakala Natl Park Established: Anniv, Sep 30
  Hawaii Statehood: Anniv, Aug 21
  Hawaii Volcanoes Natl Park Established: Anniv, Aug 1
  Hula Bowl (Honolulu), Jan 21
  Inouye, Daniel: Birth, Sep 7
  Ironman Triathlon World Chmpshp (Kailua-Kona), Oct 14
  King Kamehameha I Day, Jun 11
  KWXX Ho'olaula'a (Hilo), Sep 30
  Lei Day, May 1
  Lingle, Linda: Birth, Jun 4
  Merrie Monarch Fest (Hilo), Apr 16
  Nissan Xterra World Chmpshp (Maui), Oct 29
  Prince Jonah Kuhio Kalanianole Day, Mar 26
  Queen Liliuokalani Deposed: Anniv, Jan 17
  Triple Crown of Surfing (Oahu), Nov 13
  Waikiki Roughwater Swim (Honolulu), Sep 3
Hawaii Annexed by US: Anniv, Jul 7
Hawaii Five-O TV Premiere: Anniv, Sep 26
Hawaiki Nui Va'a Race (French Polynesia), Oct 18
Hawk, Tony: Birth, May 12
Hawke, Ethan: Birth, Nov 6
Hawking, Stephen: Birth, Jan 8
Hawkins, Hersey: Birth, Sep 29
Hawn, Goldie: Birth, Nov 21
Haworth, Cheryl Ann: Birth, Apr 18
Hawthorne, Nathaniel: Birth Anniv, Jul 4
Hayakawa, Samuel: Birth, Jul 18
Hayden, Tom: Birth, Dec 11
Haydn, Franz Joseph: Birth Anniv, Mar 31
Hayek, Salma: Birth, Sep 2
Hayes, Helen: Birth Anniv, Oct 10
Hayes, Ira Hamilton: Birth Anniv, Jan 12
Hayes, Isaac: Birth, Aug 20
Hayes, Lucy: Birth Anniv, Aug 28
Hayes, Rutherford B.: Birth Anniv, Oct 4
Hayes, Sean P.: Birth, Jun 26
Haymarket Pardon: Anniv, Jun 26
Haymarket Square Riot: Anniv, May 4
Hay-on-Wye Fest of Literature (Hay-on-Wye, Wales), May 26
Hays, Robert: Birth, Jul 24
Haysbert, Dennis: Birth, Jun 2
Hazel TV Premiere: Anniv, Sep 28
Headache Awareness Week, Natl, Jun 4
Headache Foundation Fundraiser, Natl (New York, NY), May 6
Headly, Glenne: Birth, Mar 13
Heald, Anthony: Birth, Aug 25
Healing from the Inside Out, Mar 5
Health and Welfare
  Accelerate ACL Awareness Among Young Women Day, Apr 5
  Act Happy Day, Mar 20
  Adoption Week, Natl, Nov 1
  Adult Immunization Awareness Week, Natl, Sep 24
  AIDS Awareness Month, Natl, Nov 1
  AIDS First Noted: Anniv, Jun 5
  AIDS Walk Atlanta (Atlanta, GA), Oct 15
  Alcohol and Drug Addiction Recovery Month, Natl, Sep 1
  Alcohol and Other Drug-Related Birth Defects Week, Natl, May 7
  Alcohol Awareness Month, Apr 1
  Alcohol Screening Day, Natl, Apr 6
  Alcohol-Free Weekend, Apr 7
  Allergy/Asthma Awareness Month, Natl, May 1
  Alzheimer's Disease Month, Natl, Nov 1
  AMA Founded: Anniv, May 5
  AMD/Low Vision Awareness Month, Feb 1
  American Dental Assn: Annual Session (Las Vegas, NV), Oct 16
  American Massage Therapy Assn, Natl Conv (Atlanta, GA), Oct 11
  American Red Cross: Founding Anniv, May 21
  Anesthetic First Used in Surgery: Anniv, Mar 30
  Anxiety Disorders Screening Day, Natl, May 3
  Aphasia Awareness Month, Natl, Jun 1
  Aplastic Anemia Awareness Week, Natl, Dec 1
  Arthritis Month, Natl, May 1
  Artificial Heart Transplant: Anniv, Dec 2
  Assisted Living Week, Natl, Sep 10
  Athletic Training Month, Natl, Mar 1
  Attention Deficit Hyperactivity Disorder Month, Sep 1
  Autism Awareness Month, Natl, Apr 1
  Awareness of Medical Orphans Month, May 1

Health (cont'd)—Heche

Backpack Safety America Month, **Sep 1**
Balance Awareness Week, **Sep 18**
Better Hearing and Speech Month, **May 1**
Birth Control Clinic Opened, First: Anniv, **Oct 16**
Birth Control Pills Sold: Anniv, **Aug 18**
Brain Awareness Week, Intl, **Mar 13**
Breast Cancer Awareness Month, Natl, **Oct 1**
Breast Cancer Awareness Month, Natl (Pres Proc), **Oct 1**
Caesarean Section, First: Anniv, **Jan 14**
Caffeine Awareness Month, Natl, **Mar 1**
Cancer Control Month (Pres Proc), **Apr 1**
Cancer from the Sun Month, **Jun 1**
Cancer Survivors Day, Natl, **Jun 4**
Cataract Awareness Month, **Aug 1**
Celiac Disease Awareness Month, **Oct 1**
Cervical Cancer Screening Month, **Jan 1**
Child Health Day (Pres Proc), **Oct 2**
Child Vision Awareness Month, **Jun 1**
Childhood Depression Awareness Day, **May 9**
Children with Alopecia Day, **Apr 14**
Children's Dental Health Month, Natl, **Feb 1**
Children's Eye Health and Safety Month, **Aug 1**
Children's Vision and Learning Month, **Aug 1**
Christmas Seal Campaign, **Oct 1**
Chronic Fatigue Syndrome Awareness Month, Natl, **Mar 1**
Cigarettes Reported Hazardous: Anniv, **Jan 11**
Clean Air Month, **May 1**
Clean Hands Week, Natl, **Sep 17**
Colorectal Cancer Awareness Month, Natl, **Mar 1**
Colorectal Cancer Education/Awareness Month, **Dec 1**
Condom Week, Natl, **Feb 14**
Congenital Heart Defect Awareness Week, **Feb 7**
COPD Awareness Month, Natl, **Nov 1**
Correct Posture Month, Natl, **May 1**
COSAC Annual Conference, **May 19**
Dairy Alternatives Month, **Jun 1**
Deaf History Month, **Mar 13**
Dental Hygiene Month, Natl, **Oct 1**
Depression Education and Awareness Month, Natl, **Oct 1**
Depression Screening Day, Natl, **Oct 5**
Diabetes Assn Alert Day, American, **Mar 28**
Diabetes Month, American, **Nov 1**
Diabetic Eye Disease Month, **Nov 1**
Diet Resolution Week, **Jan 1**
Doctor-Patient Trust Day, **Mar 17**
Doctors' Day, **Mar 30**
Dollars Against Diabetes (DAD's) Day, **Jun 16**
Donate Life Month (Pres Proc), **Apr 1**
Donate Life Month, Natl, **Apr 1**
Donor Sabbath, Natl, **Nov 10**
Down Syndrome Month, Natl, **Oct 1**
Eat Better, Eat Together Month, **Oct 1**
Eating Disorders Awareness Week, Natl, **Feb 26**
Emotional Wellness Month, **Oct 1**
Epilepsy Awareness Month, **Nov 1**
Eye Donor Month, Natl, **Mar 1**
Family Fit Lifestyle Month, **Jan 1**
Family Health and Fitness Days—USA, **Sep 30**
Family Sexuality Education Month, Natl, **Oct 1**
Fibromyalgia Education & Awareness Month, **May 1**
5-A-Day Month, Natl, **Sep 1**
Flossing Day, Natl, **Nov 24**
Food and Drug Interaction Education and Awareness Week, **Oct 17**
Fresh Breath Day, Natl, **Aug 6**
Glaucoma Awareness Month, Natl, **Jan 1**
Goof-Off Day, Intl, **Mar 22**
Graves' Disease Awareness Week, **Jan 9**
Great American Low-Cholesterol, Low-Fat Pizza Bake, **Sep 1**
Great American Smokeout, **Nov 16**
Great American Smokeout Day, Natl (Pres Proc), **Nov 16**
Gynecologic Cancer Awareness Month, **Sep 1**
Handwriting Analysis Week, Natl, **Jan 22**
Have a Heart Day, Natl, **Feb 14**
Headache Awareness Week, Natl, **Jun 4**
Headache Foundation Fundraiser, Natl (New York, NY), **May 6**
Health and Happiness with Hypnosis Day, **Jul 25**
Health Education Week, Natl, **Oct 16**
Health Literacy Month, **Oct 1**
Healthy Vision Month, **May 1**
Healthy Weight Week, **Jan 15**
Heart Failure Awareness Week, **Feb 12**
Heart Month, American, **Feb 1**
Heart Month, American (Pres Proc), **Feb 1**
Heart Transplant, First: Anniv, **Dec 3**
Help Someone See Week (Rockford, OH), **Mar 6**
Hepatitis Awareness Month, Natl, **May 1**
Herbal/Prescription Interaction Awareness Month, **Jul 1**
HIV Testing Day, Natl, **Jun 27**

Hospice Month, Natl, **Nov 1**
Hunger Awareness Day, Natl, **Jun 6**
Huntington's Disease Awareness Month, **May 1**
Hypnosis Federation Conf, Intl (Los Angeles, CA), **Aug 4**
I Love My Dentist Day, **Jun 2**
Immunization Awareness Month, Natl, **Aug 1**
Infection Prevention Week, **Oct 16**
Infertility Survival Day, Natl, **May 7**
Injury Prevention Month, **Apr 1**
Insulin First Isolated: Anniv, **Jul 27**
Invisible Chronic Illness Awareness Week, Natl (San Diego, CA), **Sep 11**
Jackie Mayer Rehab Center Day (OH), **Oct 6**
Jerry Lewis Muscular Dystrophy Association Telethon, **Sep 3**
Kidney Month, Natl, **Mar 1**
Lee Natl Denim Day, **Oct 6**
Lister, Joseph: Birth Anniv, **Apr 5**
Long Term Care Planning Month, **Oct 1**
Lose Weight/Feel Great Week, Natl, **Jan 1**
Lung Cancer Awareness Month, **Nov 1**
Lupus Alert Day, **Apr 1**
Lupus Awareness Campaign, **Oct 1**
Mammography Day, Natl, **Oct 20**
Marfan Syndrome Awareness Month, **Feb 1**
Marrow Awareness Month, Natl, **Nov 1**
Massage Therapy Awareness Week, Natl, **Oct 22**
Medical Group Practice Week, Natl, **Jan 23**
Medical Patient Advocacy Week, Natl, **Apr 2**
Medicare: Anniv, **Jul 1**
Medication Safety Week, **Apr 1**
Melanoma Monday, **May 1**
Melanoma/Skin Cancer Detection and Prevention Month, **May 1**
Menopause Awareness Month, **Sep 1**
Mental Health Month, Natl, **May 1**
Mental Illness Awareness Week, **Oct 1**
Mental Retardation Awareness Month, **Mar 1**
More Herbs, Less Salt Day, **Aug 29**
More Than Just a Pretty Face Month, **May 1**
MS Walk (San Jose and Monterey, CA), **Apr 1**
Multiple Sclerosis Awareness Week, **Mar 13**
Multiple Sclerosis Education & Awareness Month, Natl, **Mar 1**
Neurofibromatosis Awareness Month, Natl, **May 1**
No Diet Day, **May 6**
Nuclear Medicine Week, **Oct 1**
Nurse Anesthetists Week, Natl, **Jan 22**
Nurses Day and Week, Natl, **May 6**
Nursing Assistants Day and Week, Natl, **Jun 15**
Nursing Conf on Pediatric Primary Care (Washington, DC), **Apr 5**
Nursing Home Week, Natl, **May 14**
Nutrition Month, Natl, **Mar 1**
Occupational Therapy Month, Natl, **Apr 1**
Open-Heart Surgery, First: Anniv, **Jul 9**
Organize Your Medical Information Month, **Oct 1**
Orthodonic Health Month, Natl, **Oct 1**
Osteopathic Medicine Month, Natl, **Sep 1**
Osteoporosis Awareness and Prevention Month, Natl, **May 1**
Ovarian Cancer Awareness Month, **Sep 1**
Ovarian Cancer Awareness Month, Natl (Pres Proc), **Sep 1**
Pandemic of 1918 Hits US: Anniv, **Mar 11**
Parkinson's Awareness Month, Natl, **Apr 1**
Patient Recognition Week, Natl, **Feb 1**
PCOS Awareness Day, **Sep 18**
Pediatric Cancer Awareness Month, **Sep 1**
Pediatric Nurse Practitioner Week, **Mar 30**
Pediculosis Prevention Month, Natl, **Sep 1**
Perioperative (OR) Nurse Week, **Nov 12**
Personal Training Week, Natl, **Apr 16**
Pharmacists Declare War on Alcoholism, **Jun 1**
Pharmacists' War on Diabetes, **Apr 1**
Physical Fitness and Sports Month, Natl, **May 1**
Physical Therapy Month, Natl, **Oct 1**
Physical Wellness Month, **Apr 1**
Physician Assistants Day, **Oct 6**
Poison Prevention Awareness Month, **Mar 1**
Poison Prevention Week, Natl, **Mar 19**
Polio Vaccine: Anniv, **Apr 12**
Prematurity Awareness Day, **Nov 1**
Prescription Errors Education & Awareness Week, **Oct 24**
Prostate Cancer Awareness Week, **Sep 17**
Public Health Week, Natl, **Apr 2**
Purposeful Parenting Month, Natl, **Jul 1**
Race for the Cure (Pittsburgh, PA), **May 14**
Radon Action Month, Natl, **Jan 1**
Rebuild Your Life Month, **Jun 1**
Red Cross Month, **Mar 1**
Red Cross Month, American (Pres Proc), **Mar 1**
Rehabilitation Awareness Celebration, Natl, **Sep 17**
Relaxation Day, Natl, **Aug 15**
Restless Leg Syndrome (RLS) Education and Awareness Week, **Jul 18**

Rett Syndrome Awareness Month, **Oct 1**
Rid the World of Fad Diets/Gimmicks Day, **Jan 17**
Root Canal Appreciation Day, **May 10**
Rosacea Awareness Month, **Apr 1**
RSV Awareness Month, Natl, **Oct 1**
Save Your Back Week, Natl, **Oct 23**
Save Your Smile Week, Natl, **Aug 20**
Save Your Vision Month, **Mar 1**
Save Your Vision Week (Pres Proc), **Mar 7**
School Breakfast Week, Natl, **Mar 6**
Senior Health and Fitness Day, Natl, **May 31**
September Is Healthy Aging Month, **Sep 1**
Sexually Transmitted Diseases (STDs) Awareness Month, Natl, **Apr 1**
Sight-Saving/Ultraviolet Awareness Month, Natl, **May 1**
Simplify Your Life Week, **Aug 1**
Skin Care Awareness Month, Natl, **Sep 1**
Sleep Awareness Week, Natl, **Mar 27**
Smallpox Vaccine Discovered: Anniv, **May 14**
Smile Month, Natl, **May 1**
Social Security Act: Anniv, **Aug 14**
Special Recreation Week, **Jul 2**
Speech-Language-Hearing Conv, American (Miami, FL), **Nov 16**
Spina Bifida Awareness Month, Natl, **Oct 1**
Spinal Health Month, Natl, **Oct 1**
Spinal Muscular Atrophy Awareness Month, **Aug 1**
Sports & Home Eye Health and Safety Month, **Sep 1**
Stay Out of the Sun Day, **Jul 3**
Stress Awareness Day, Natl, **Apr 18**
Stress Awareness Month, **Apr 1**
Strike Out Strokes Day, **May 1**
Stroke Awareness Month, Natl, **May 1**
Stuttering Awareness Day, Intl, **Oct 22**
Stuttering Awareness Week, Natl, **May 8**
Successful Antirabies Inoculation, First: Anniv, **Jul 6**
Sudden Infant Death Syndrome Awareness Month, Natl, **Oct 1**
Suicide Prevention Week, Natl, **Sep 10**
Take a New Year's Resolution to Stop Smoking, **Dec 10**
Talk About Prescriptions Month, **Oct 1**
Testicular Cancer Awareness Week, **Apr 1**
Test-Tube Baby: Birth, **Jul 25**
Therapeutic Recreation Week, Natl, **Jul 9**
3-A-Day Week, **Mar 3**
Tim & Tom Gullikson Foundation Week, **May 1**
Tour de Cure (Diabetes), **Apr 1**
Vegetarian Month, **Oct 1**
Vision Research Month, **Jun 1**
Vitamin C Isolated: Anniv, **Apr 4**
Volunteer Week, Natl, **Apr 23**
Volunteers Week, Intl, **Jun 1**
Vulvar Health Awareness Month, **Mar 1**
Walk Days, Intl, **Apr 30**
Wear Red Day, **Feb 3**
Wheelchair Beautification Month, Natl, **Jul 1**
White Cane Safety Day (Pres Proc), **Oct 15**
Wise Health Care Consumer Month, **Feb 1**
WOC Nurse Week, **Apr 17**
Women's Eye Health and Safety Month, **Apr 1**
Women's Health and Fitness Day, Natl, **Sep 27**
Women's Health Care Month, **May 1**
Women's Healthy Weight Day, **Jan 19**
Women's Heart Health Day, **Feb 1**
Women's Heart Week, **Feb 1**
Women's Nutrition Week, Natl, **Apr 9**
Workplace Eye Health and Safety Month, **Mar 1**
World AIDS Day (Pres Proc), **Dec 1**
World AIDS Day (UN), **Dec 1**
World Breastfeeding Week, **Aug 1**
World Food Day (UN), **Oct 16**
World Health Day (UN), **Apr 7**
World Mental Health Day (UN), **Oct 10**
World No-Tobacco Day (UN), **May 31**
World Red Cross Day, **May 8**
World Tuberculosis Day, **Mar 24**
Young Child, Month of the (MI), **Apr 1**
Youth Sports Safety Month, Natl, **Apr 1**
Heard, John: Birth, Mar 7
Hearing and Speech Month, Better, May 1
Hearn, Lafcadio: Birth Anniv, Jun 27
Hearst, William R.: Birth Anniv, Apr 29
Heart
Congenital Heart Defect Awareness Week, **Feb 7**
Heart Day, Natl Have a, **Feb 14**
Heart Failure Awareness Week, **Feb 12**
Heart Health Day, Women's, **Feb 1**
Heart Health: Wear Red Day, **Feb 3**
Heart Month, American, **Feb 1**
Heart Month, American (Pres Proc), **Feb 1**
Heatherton, Joey: Birth, Sep 14
Heaton, Patricia: Birth, Mar 4
Hebron Massacre: Anniv, Feb 25
Heche, Anne: Birth, May 25

Hecht, Ben: Birth Anniv, Feb 28
Heckerling, Amy: Birth, May 7
Hedgehog Day, Feb 2
Hee Haw TV Premiere: Anniv, Jun 15
Hefner, Christie: Birth, Nov 8
Hefner, Hugh: Birth, Apr 9
Heiden, Eric: Birth, Jun 14
Heimlich Maneuver Introduced: Anniv, Jun 1
Heine, Heinrich: Birth Anniv, Dec 13
Heineman, Dave: Birth, May 12
Hejduk, Milan: Birth, Feb 14
Helgenberger, Marg: Birth, Nov 16
Hellman, Lillian: Birth Anniv, Jun 20
Hello Day, World, Nov 21
Hell's Angels: Altamont Concert: Anniv, Dec 6
Helmond, Katherine: Birth, Jul 5
Helms, Edgar J.: Birth Anniv, Jan 19
Helms, Jesse: Birth, Oct 18
Helmsley, Leona: Birth, Jul 4
Heloise: Birth, Apr 15
Helton, Todd: Birth, Aug 20
Hemingway Birthday Colloquium (Oak Park, IL),
  Jul 21
Hemingway, Ernest: Birth Anniv, Jul 21
Hemingway, Ernest: Boxing Day at Birthplace
  (Oak Park, IL), Dec 26
Hemingway, Mariel: Birth, Nov 22
Hemsley, Sherman: Birth, Feb 1
Henderson, Florence: Birth, Feb 14
Henderson, Rickey: Birth, Dec 25
Henderson, Skitch: Birth, Jan 27
Hendricks, Thomas A: Birth Anniv, Sep 17
Hendrix, Jimi: Birth Anniv, Nov 27
Henie, Sonja: Birth Anniv, Apr 8
Henin-Hardenne, Justine: Birth, Jun 1
Henley, Don: Birth, Jul 22
Henman, Tim: Birth, Sep 6
Henner, Marilu: Birth, Apr 6
Hennessy, Jill: Birth, Nov 25
Henried, Paul: Birth Anniv, Jan 10
Henriksen, Lance: Birth, May 5
Henry, Brad: Birth, Jul 10
Henry, Joseph: Birth Anniv, Dec 17
Henry, Justin: Birth, May 25
Henry, O. (William S. Porter): Birth Anniv, Sep 11
Henry, O.: Museum Pun-Off (Austin, TX), May 6
Henry, Patrick: Birth Anniv, May 29
Henson, Jim: Birth Anniv, Sep 24
Henson, John: Birth, Jul 11
Henson, Matthew A.: Birth Anniv, Aug 8
Hentoff, Nat: Birth, Jun 10
Hepatitis Awareness Month, Natl, May 1
Hepburn, Audrey: Birth Anniv, May 4
Hepburn, Katharine: Birth, May 12
Herb Fest (Mattoon, IL), Apr 29
Herbal/Prescription Interaction Awareness
  Month, Jul 1
Heritage Day Fest (Lavallette, NJ), Sep 9
Heritage Days Fest (Cumberland, MD), Jun 10
Heritage Week (New Harmony, IN), Apr 17
Heritagefest (New Ulm, MN), Jul 14
Herman, Alexis: Birth, Jul 16
Herman, Jerry: Birth, Jul 10
Hermit, Robert the: Death Anniv, Apr 1
Hernandez, Keith: Birth, Oct 20
Hernandez, Orlando: Birth, Oct 11
Heroes: Inspirational Role Models Month, Natl,
  Nov 1
Herriman, George: Birth Anniv, Aug 22
Herriot, James: Birth Anniv, Oct 3
Herrmann, Edward: Birth, Jul 21
Hersey, John: Birth Anniv, Jun 17
Hersh, Seymour: Birth, Apr 8
Hershey, Barbara: Birth, Feb 5
Hershiser, Orel: Birth, Sep 16
Herzl, Theodor: Birth Anniv, May 20
Herzog, Chaim: Birth Anniv, Sep 17
Hess, Rudolf: Birth Anniv, Apr 26
Hesseman, Howard: Birth, Feb 27
Heston, Charlton: Birth, Oct 4
Hewes, Joseph: Birth Anniv, Jan 23
Hewitt, Don: Birth, Dec 14
Hewitt, Jennifer Love: Birth, Feb 21
Hewitt, Lleyton: Birth, Feb 24
Heyerdahl, Thor: Birth Anniv, Oct 6
Heyward, Thomas: Birth Anniv, Jul 28
Hiawatha Pageant, Song of (Pipestone, MN),
  Jul 21
Hickman, Darryl: Birth, Jul 28
Hickman, Dwayne: Birth, May 18
Hickok, Wild Bill: Birth Anniv, May 27
Hicks, Catherine: Birth, Aug 6
Higgins, David Anthony: Birth, Dec 9
Higginson, Bobby: Birth, Aug 18
Highlights Foundation Writer's Workshop
  (Chautauqua, NY), Jul 15
Hightower, Jim: Birth, Jan 11
Highway Numbers Introduced: Anniv, Mar 2

Hijuelos, Oscar: Birth, Aug 24
Hill Street Blues TV Premiere: Anniv, Jan 15
Hill, Anita: Birth, Jul 30
Hill, Arthur: Birth, Aug 1
Hill, Bernard: Birth, Dec 17
Hill, Dule: Birth, May 3
Hill, Faith: Birth, Sep 21
Hill, Grant: Birth, Oct 5
Hill, Lauryn: Birth, May 25
Hill, Mildred J.: Happy Birthday to "Happy
  Birthday to You", Jun 27
Hill, Patty Smith: Birth Anniv, Mar 27
Hill, Steven: Birth, Feb 24
Hillary, Sir Edmund: Birth, Jul 20
Hillary, Sir Edmund: Everest Summit Reached:
  Anniv, May 29
Hillerman, John: Birth, Dec 20
Hillman, Chris: Birth, Dec 4
Hilton, Paris: Birth, Feb 17
Hinamatsuri (Japan), Mar 3
Hindenburg Disaster: Anniv, May 6
Hindu: Dassehra, Oct 2
Hindu: Diwali, Oct 21
Hindu: Holi, Mar 14
Hines, Gregory: Birth Anniv, Feb 14
Hingis, Martina: Birth, Sep 30
Hinske, Eric: Birth, Aug 5
Hirohito, Emperor: Birth Anniv, Apr 29
Hiroshima Day, Aug 6
Hirsch, Elroy "Crazylegs": Birth, Jun 17
Hirsch, Judd: Birth, Mar 15
Hirschfeld, Al: Birth Anniv, Jun 21
Hispanic
  Charro Days Fiesta (Brownsville, TX; Matamoros,
    Mexico), **Feb 23**
  Cinco de Mayo (Mexico), **May 5**
  Cinco de Mayo Fest (Portland, OR), **May 4**
  Hispanic Heritage Fest (Miami, FL), **Oct 8**
  Hispanic Heritage Month, Natl (Pres Proc), **Sep 15**
  League of United Latin American Citizens (LULAC)
    Founded: Anniv, **Feb 17**
  Maroone Hispanicfest (Hollywood, FL), **Apr 16**
  Mexican Fiesta Internacional (Milwaukee, WI),
    Aug 25
  Tucson Intl Mariachi Conf (Tucson, AZ), **Apr 24**
  Viva El Mariachi Fest (Fresno, CA), **Mar 26**
  Viva! Chicago Latin Music Fest (Chicago, IL),
    Aug 26
  Zoot Suit Riots: Anniv, **Jun 3**
Historical Fest, Fort Sisseton (Lake City, SD),
  Jun 3
Historical Re-enactment: Siege at Kanata
  (Brantford, ON, Canada), Aug 12
Historically Black Colleges and Universities
  Week, Natl (Pres Proc), Sep 17
History Alive! (Norfolk, VA), Oct 6
History Meets the Arts (Gettysburg, PA), Apr 21
Hitchcock, Alfred: Birth Anniv, Aug 13
Hitchcock, Alfred: Psycho Film Premiere: Anniv,
  Jun 16
Hite, Shere: Birth, Nov 2
Hitler Celebration, RAF Bombs: Anniv, Jan 30
Hitler Youth Deployed: Anniv, Jan 26
Hitler, Adolf: Birth Anniv, Apr 20
Hitler, Adolf: German Plebiscite: Anniv, Aug 19
Hitler, Adolf: Gersdorff Assassination Attempt:
  Anniv, Mar 21
Hitler, Adolf: Operation Flash: Anniv, Mar 13
HIV Testing Day, Natl, Jun 27
Ho Chi Minh: Birth Anniv, May 19
Ho, Don: Birth, Aug 13
Hoban, James: Death Anniv, Dec 8
Hobart, Garret A.: Birth Anniv, Jun 3
Hobbit Day, Sep 22
Hobo Convention, Natl (Britt, IA), Aug 10
Hockey (Field, Ice)
  Hockey Mask Invented: Anniv, **Nov 1**
  Miracle on Ice: US Team Defeats USSR: Anniv,
    Feb 22
  NCAA Div I Men's Chmpshp (Milwaukee, WI),
    Apr 6
  NCAA Div III Field Hockey Chmpshp (Geneva,
    NY), **Nov 17**
Hockney, David: Birth, Jul 9
Hodag Muskie Challenge (Rhinelander, WI),
  Sep 15
Hodge, Patricia: Birth, Sep 29
Hoeven, John: Birth, Mar 13
Hoffa, James: Disappearance Anniv, Jul 30
Hoffman, Abbie: Birth Anniv, Nov 30
Hoffman, Alice: Birth, Mar 16
Hoffman, Dustin: Birth, Aug 8
Hoffman, Mat: Birth, Jan 9
Hog Capital of the World Fest (Kewanee, IL),
  Sep 1
Hogan, Ben: Birth Anniv, Aug 13
Hogan, Hulk: Birth, Aug 11
Hogan, Paul: Birth, Oct 8

Hogarth, William: Birth Anniv, Nov 10
Hogeye Fest (Elgin, TX), Oct 28
Hogmanay (Scottish New Year), Dec 31
Hoiby, Lee: Birth, Feb 17
Holbrook, Hal: Birth, Feb 17
Holden, William: Birth Anniv, Apr 17
Holdsclaw, Chamique: Birth, Aug 9
Holi (India), Mar 14
Holiday Bowl Parade/Game, Pacific Life (San
  Diego, CA), Dec 28
Holiday, Make Up Your Own, Mar 26
Holiday, Billie: Birth Anniv, Apr 7
Holiday, First US by Presidential Proclamation:
  Anniv, Nov 26
Holistic Pet Day, Natl, Aug 30
Holland Tunnel: Anniv, Nov 13
Holliday, Doc: Gunfight at the OK Corral: Anniv,
  Oct 26
Holliday, Polly: Birth, Jul 2
Holliger, Heinz: Birth, May 21
Hollings, Ernest F.: Birth, Jan 1
Holly, Buddy: Birth Anniv, Sep 7
Holly, Buddy: Day the Music Died: Death Anniv,
  Feb 3
Holly, Lauren: Birth, Oct 28
Hollyhock Fest (Kyoto, Japan), May 15
Hollywood Squares TV Premiere: Anniv, Oct 17
Holm, Celeste: Birth, Apr 29
Holm, Ian: Birth, Sep 12
Holmes, Katie: Birth, Dec 18
Holmes, Oliver W.: Birth Anniv, Aug 29
Holmes, Oliver Wendell: Old Ironsides Saved by
  Poem: Anniv, Sep 16
Holmes, Rupert: Birth, Feb 24
Holmgren, Mike: Birth, Jun 15
Holocaust Day (Israel), Apr 25
Holocaust Museum Opens, US: Anniv, Apr 26
Holtz, Lou: Birth, Jan 6
Holy Humor Month, Apr 1
Holy Innocents Day, Dec 28
Holy See: National Holiday, Oct 22
Holy Thursday, Apr 13
Holy Week, Apr 9
Holyfield, Evander: Birth, Oct 19
Home Improvement Time, Apr 1
Home Improvement TV Premiere: Anniv, Sep 17
Home Inspector Appreciation Month, Natl, Jul 1
Home Office Safety and Security Week, Jan 8
Home Office Week, Improve Your, Oct 9
Home Office: Organize Your Home Office Day,
  Mar 14
Home Office: Work from Home Week, Natl, Oct 1
Home Owners Loan Act: Anniv, Jun 13
Home Run Record: Anniv, Apr 8
Home Sewing Machine Patented: Anniv, Aug 12
Home Shows and Tours
  Fest of Houses and Gardens (Charleston, SC),
    Mar 16
  Fredericksburg Day (Fredericksburg, VA), **Apr 18**
  Galveston Historic Homes Tour (Galveston Island,
    TX), **May 6**
  Great Northeast Home Show (Albany, NY), **Feb 10**
  Holiday Tour of Homes (Natchitoches, LA), **Dec 6**
  Home Furnishings Market, Intl (High Point, NC),
    Apr 27
  Home Improvement Show, Milwaukee/NARI (West
    Allis, WI), **Feb 9**
  Litchfield Open House Tour (Litchfield, CT), **Jul 7**
  Maryland Home and Garden Show (Baltimore,
    MD), **Mar 3**
  Mother's Day Housewalk (Evanston, IL), **May 14**
  Natchez Fall Pilgrimage (Natchez, MS), **Sep 30**
  Natchez Spring Pilgrimage (Natchez, MS), **Mar 10**
  Natchitoches Historic Pilgrimage (Natchitoches,
    LA), **Oct 14**
  National City Cleveland Home and Garden Show
    (Cleveland, OH), **Feb 4**
  New England Home Show (Boston, MA), **Feb 25**
  Original Massachusetts Home & Garden Show
    (West Springfield, MA), **Mar 23**
  Quincy Preserves Fall Architectural Tour (Quincy,
    IL), **Oct 21**
  Savannah Tour of Homes and Gardens (Savannah,
    GA), **Mar 23**
  Seashore Open House Tour (Loveladies, NJ),
    Aug 2
  Spring Fest (Cape May, NJ), **Apr 21**
  Stone House Day (Hurley, NY), **Jul 8**
  Victorian Christmas Home Tour (Leadville, CO),
    Dec 1
  Wright, Frank Lloyd: Wright Plus (Oak Park, IL),
    May 20
  Yuma Home Show (Yuma, AZ), **Jan 13**
Home: Decorating Month, Natl, Apr 1
Home: Organize Your Home Day, Jan 9
Home: Prepare Your Home To Be Sold Month,
  Natl, Apr 1
Home-Based Business Week, Oct 8

Homebirth—Humor

Homebirth Week, Natl Unassisted, Jul 1
Homefest (Bald Knob, AR), May 11
Homeless Animals Day, Natl, Aug 19
Homeowner's Day, New, May 1
Homer, Louise Dilworth: Birth Anniv, Apr 28
Homer, Winslow: Birth Anniv, Feb 24
Homestead Act: Anniv, May 20
Homestead Days (Beatrice, NE), Jun 14
Homesteader Harvest Fest (Brandon, SD), Sep 10
Honda, Soichiro: Birth Anniv, Nov 17
Honduras
  Dia De Las Americas, Apr 14
  Francisco Morazan Holiday, Oct 3
  Hurricane Mitch: Anniv, Oct 27
  Independence Day, Sep 15
Honest Abe Awards: Natl Honesty Day, Apr 30
Honesty Day, Natl, Apr 30
Honey Month, Natl, Sep 1
Honeymoon Weekend, Second, Feb 17
Honeymoon, First Balloon: Anniv, Jun 20
Hong Kong
  Last Hurrah for British, Jun 30
  Lease Anniv, Jun 9
  Liberation Day, Aug 28
Honor Society Awareness Month, Mar 1
Hoodie-Hoo Day, Northern Hemisphere, Feb 20
Hoof-Care Summit, Intl (Cincinnati, OH), Jan 31
Hooks, Jan: Birth, Apr 23
Hooks, Kevin: Birth, Sep 19
Hooks, Robert: Birth, Apr 18
Hooper, William: Birth Anniv, Jun 17
Hoover, Herbert: Birth Anniv, Aug 10
Hoover, Herbert: Day (IA), Aug 13
Hoover, J. Edgar: Birth Anniv, Jan 1
Hoover, Lou H.: Birth Anniv, Mar 29
Hopalong Cassidy TV Premiere: Anniv, Jun 24
Hope, Bob: Birth Anniv, May 29
Hope, Bob: Chrysler Golf Classic (La Quinta, CA), Jan 16
Hope, Leslie: Birth, May 6
Hopkins, Bo: Birth, Feb 2
Hopkins, Sir Anthony: Birth, Dec 31
Hopkins, Stephen: Birth Anniv, Mar 7
Hopkins, Telma: Birth, Oct 28
Hopkinson, Francis: Birth Anniv, Sep 21
Hopper, Dennis: Birth, May 17
Hopper, Grace: Birth Anniv, Dec 9
Horn, Paul: Birth, Mar 17
Hornacek, John: Birth, May 3
Horne, Lena: Birth, Jun 30
Horne, Marilyn: Birth, Jan 16
Horowitz, Vladimir: Birth Anniv, Oct 1
Horrocks, Jane: Birth, Jan 18
Horseradish Month, Natl, Jul 1
Horses
  Augusta Futurity (Augusta, GA), Jan 26
  Badminton Horse Trials (Badminton, England), May 4
  Belmont Stakes (Belmont Park, NY), Jun 10
  Belmont Stakes, First Running of: Anniv, Jun 19
  Bonnie Blue Natl Horse Show (Lexington, VA), May 10
  Breeder's Cup (Louisville, KY), Nov 4
  Britt Draft Horse Show (Britt, IA), Sep 1
  Celebration of the Horse (Houston, TX), Jul 14
  Central Montana Fair (Lewistown, MT), Jul 26
  Cheltenham Hunt Fest (Prestbury, England), Mar 14
  Chincoteague Pony Penning (Chincoteague Island, VA), Jul 26
  Day of the Horse, Natl, Dec 9
  Derby, The (Epsom Downs, England), Jun 10
  Farrier's Week, Natl, Jul 9
  First Kentucky Derby: Anniv, May 17
  Foxfield Races (Charlottesville, VA), Apr 29
  Gold Cup, Intl (The Plains, VA), Oct 15
  Hoof-Care Summit, Intl (Cincinnati, OH), Jan 31
  Iron Horse Outraced by Horse: Anniv, Sep 18
  Kentucky Derby (Louisville, KY), May 6
  Kentucky Derby Fest (Louisville, KY), Apr 21
  Kentucky State Fair (Louisville, KY), Aug 17
  Masters (Calgary, AB, Canada), Sep 6
  Miles City Bucking Horse Sale (Miles City, MT), May 19
  Missouri State Chmpshp Racking Horse Show (Dexter, MO), Jun 3
  National Tournament (Calgary, AB, Canada), Jun 7
  New Jersey State Fair/Sussex Farm and Horse Show (Augusta, NJ), Aug 4
  North American Tournament (Calgary, AB, Canada), Jul 5
  Palio (Siena, Italy), Jul 2
  Point-to-Point (Wilmington, DE), May 7
  Pony Express Fest (Hanover, KS), Aug 27
  Pony Express, Inauguration of: Anniv, Apr 3
  Preakness Stakes (Baltimore, MD), May 20
  Preakness Stakes: Anniv, May 27
  Royal Ascot (Ascot, Berkshire, England), Jun 20
  Royal Windsor Horse Show (Windsor, England), May 11
  Sandpoint Saddle Club Horse Show (Sandpoint, ID), Jun 17
  Seabiscuit Defeats War Admiral: Anniv, Nov 1
  Steeplechase at Callaway Gardens (Pine Mountain, GA), Nov 4
  Strawberry Hill Races (Richmond, VA), Apr 15
  Taylor Horsefest (Taylor, ND), Jul 22
  Tennessee Walking Horse Natl Celeb (Shelbyville, TN), Aug 23
  Trail Ride Gathering, Natl (Live Oak, FL), Nov 4
  Upperville Colt/Horse Show (Upperville, VA), Jun 5
  Virginia Gold Cup (Warrenton, VA), May 6
  West Allis Western Days Family Jamboree (West Allis, WI), Jun 15
  Whippoorwill Morgan Horse Open Barn (Old Lyme, CT), May 27
  Whippoorwill Morgan Horse Versatility Event (Old Lyme, CT), Sep 9
Horseshoe Tournament, Head-of-the-Mon-River (Fairmont, WV), May 27
Horsley, Lee: Birth, May 15
Hoskins, Bob: Birth, Oct 26
Hospice Month, Natl, Nov 1
Hospital Admitting Clerks Day, Apr 7
Hossa, Marian: Birth, Jan 12
Hostage Released, Last American: Anniv, Dec 4
Hostos, Eugenio Maria: Birth Anniv, Jan 11
Hot Breakfast Month, Natl, Feb 1
Hot Dog Month, Natl, Jul 1
Hot Dog Night (Luverne, MN), Jul 13
Hot Enough for Ya Day, Jul 23
Hot Springs Natl Park Established: Anniv, Mar 4
Houdini, Harry: Birth Anniv, Mar 24
Houdini, Harry: Death Anniv, Oct 31
Houdini, Harry: Magic Day, Oct 31
House of Representatives, First Black Serves in: Anniv, Dec 12
House of Representatives, First Brawl: Anniv, Jan 30
House of Representatives, First Quorum: Anniv, Apr 1
Houseman, John: Birth Anniv, Sep 22
Houseplants: Take Your Houseplants for a Walk Day, Jul 27
Housework Day, No, Apr 7
Housing: Habitat for Humanity Intl's Building on Faith Week, Sep 10
Houston Marathon (Houston, TX), Jan 15
Houston, Sam: Birth Anniv, Mar 2
Houston, Whitney: Birth, Aug 9
Hovick, Rose L. (Gypsy Rose Lee): Birth Anniv, Feb 9
Howard, Curly: Birth Anniv, Oct 22
Howard, Juwan: Birth, Feb 7
Howard, Ken: Birth, Mar 28
Howard, Leslie: Birth Anniv, Apr 3
Howard, Moe: Birth Anniv, Jun 19
Howard, Robert: Birth Anniv, Jan 22
Howard, Ron: Birth, Mar 1
Howard, Shemp: Birth Anniv, Mar 17
Howard, Susan: Birth, Jan 28
Howard, Traylor: Birth, Jun 14
Howard, Trevor: Birth Anniv, Sep 29
Howdy Doody TV Premiere: Anniv, Dec 27
Howe, Elias: Birth Anniv, Jul 9
Howe, Gordie: Birth, Mar 31
Howell, C. Thomas: Birth, Dec 7
Howes, Sally Ann: Birth, Jul 20
Hoyle, Edmund: Death Anniv, Aug 29
Hu, Kelly: Birth, Feb 13
Hubbard, Elbert: Birth Anniv, Jun 19
Hubbard, L. Ron: Birth Anniv, Mar 13
Hubble Space Telescope Deployed: Anniv, Apr 25
Hubble, Edwin Powell: Birth Anniv, Nov 20
Huck Finn's Jubilee (Victorville, CA), Jun 16
Huckabee, Mike: Birth, Aug 24
Hudson, Ernie: Birth, Dec 17
Hudson, Kate: Birth, Apr 19
Huerta, Dolores: Birth, Apr 10
Huffman, Felicity: Birth, Dec 9
Hug a GI Day, Mar 4
Hug an Australian Day, Apr 26
Hug Holiday Week, Natl, May 7
Hugging Day, Natl, Jan 21
Hughes, Barnard: Birth, Jul 16
Hughes, Charles E.: Birth Anniv, Apr 11
Hughes, Finola: Birth, Oct 29
Hughes, Howard: Birth Anniv, Dec 24
Hughes, John: Birth, Feb 18
Hughes, Langston: Birth Anniv, Feb 1
Hughes, Sarah: Birth, May 2
Hughley, D.L.: Birth, Mar 6
Hugo, Victor: Birth Anniv, Feb 26
Hula Bowl (Honolulu, HI), Jan 21
Hula Dancing: Merrie Monarch Fest & Hula Competition (Hilo, HI), Apr 16
Hula in the Coola Day, Feb 1
Hulce, Thomas: Birth, Dec 6
Hull House Opens: Anniv, Sep 18
Hull, Bobby: Birth, Jan 3
Hull, Brett: Birth, Aug 9
Hull, Cordell: Birth Anniv, Oct 2
Hull, John: First Mint in America: Anniv, Jun 10
Human Genome Mapped: Anniv, Jun 26
Human Relations. See also Romance
  American Red Cross: Founding Anniv, May 21
  Be an Angel Day, Aug 22
  Be Kind to Humankind Week, Aug 25
  Black History Month, Natl, Feb 1
  Blame Someone Else Day, Jan 13
  Celebration of Life Day, Jan 22
  Celebration of Love Week, Feb 12
  Coaching Week, Intl, Feb 5
  Compliment Day, Natl, Jan 25
  Day of Prayer and Action for Human Habitat, Intl, Sep 17
  Diversity Awareness Month, Oct 1
  Doghouse Repairs Month, Natl, Jul 1
  Donate a Day's Wages to Charity Day, May 10
  Emancipation Proclamation: Anniv, Sep 22
  Eradication of Poverty, Intl Day for (UN), Oct 17
  Ethics Awareness Month, Natl, Mar 1
  Etiquette Week, Natl, May 21
  First Natl Convention for Blacks: Anniv, Sep 15
  First US Breach of Promise Suit: Anniv, Jun 14
  Fourteen Points Proposed: Anniv, Jan 8
  Freedom Week, Jul 4
  Friendship Week, Intl, Feb 19
  Get Out of the Doghouse Day, Natl, Jul 17
  Good Neighbor Day, Natl, Sep 24
  Good Samaritan Involvement Day, Mar 13
  Great American Grump Out, May 31
  Great American Warm-Up, Nov 10
  Honesty Day, Natl, Apr 30
  Hug Holiday Week, Natl, May 7
  Human Rights Day (Pres Proc), Dec 10
  Human Rights Day (UN), Dec 10
  Human Rights Month, Universal, Dec 1
  Human Rights Week (Pres Proc), Dec 10
  I Want You to Be Happy Day, Mar 3
  Joygerm Day, Natl, Jan 8
  Kindness Day, World, Nov 13
  Kiss-and-Make-Up-Day, Aug 25
  Language Week, Intl, Dec 15
  League of Nations: Anniv, Jan 10
  Lost Penny Day, Feb 12
  Lumpy Rug Day, May 3
  Magic of Differences™ Week, Oct 23
  New Friends, Old Friends Week, Natl, May 21
  No Bully Week, Natl, Sep 11
  Pay-a-Compliment Day, Feb 6
  Peace Corps Founded: Anniv, Mar 1
  Peace, Friendship and Good Will Week, Oct 25
  Pen-Friends Week Intl, May 1
  Poverty in America Awareness Month, Natl, Jan 1
  Quality of Life Month, Intl, Jan 1
  Race Relations Day, Feb 14
  Race Unity Day, Jun 11
  Ralph Bunche Awarded Nobel Peace Prize: Anniv, Dec 10
  Reconciliation Day, Apr 2
  Red Cross Day, World, May 8
  Religion Day, World, Jan 15
  Religious Freedom Week, Sep 22
  Roots and Branches Month, Jul 1
  Salvation Army Founder's Day, Apr 10
  Salvation Army in US: Anniv, Mar 10
  Senior Independence Month, Natl, Feb 1
  Spring Fever Week, Natl, Mar 20
  Swap Ideas Day, Sep 10
  Thank You Days, Intl, Jan 11
  Toad Hollow Day of Encouragement, Jan 26
  Tolerance Week, Dec 1
  Turn Beauty Inside Out Day, May 17
  United Planet Month, Sep 1
  Universal Family Week, May 14
  Universal Hour of Peace, Dec 31
  Universal Human Beings Week, Mar 1
  Volunteer Week, Natl, Apr 23
  Volunteers Week, Intl, Jun 1
  World Day of Prayer, Mar 3
  World Hello Day, Nov 21
Human Spirit Day, World, Feb 17
Humane Society of the US: Anniv, Nov 22
Humbug Day, Dec 21
Hummel, Sister Maria Innocentia: Birth Anniv, May 21
Humor, Comedy
  Abet and Aid Punsters Day, Nov 8
  Alascattalo Day (Anchorage, AK), Nov 25
  A'phabet Day, Dec 25
  Bubba Day, Natl, Jun 2
  Daffynitions Month, Intl, Apr 1
  Gaines, William M.: Birth Anniv, Mar 1

Holy Humor Month, **Apr 1**
Humor Month, Natl, **Apr 1**
Humorists Are Artists Month (HAAM), **Mar 1**
Just for Laughs Fest (Montreal, QC, Canada), **Jul 13**
Kurtzman, Harvey: Birth Anniv, **Oct 3**
Laugh at Work Week, **Apr 1**
Loosen Up, Lighten Up Day, **Nov 14**
Love May Make World Go Round but Laughter Keeps Us from Getting Dizzy Week, **Feb 8**
Mirth Month, Intl, **Mar 1**
Moment of Laughter Day, **Apr 14**
O. Henry Museum Pun-Off (Austin, TX), **May 6**
SCUD Day, **Jul 8**
Someday We'll Laugh About This Week, **Jan 2**
Twit Award Month, Intl, **Apr 1**
HUMOResilience Workshop (Lake George, NY), **Oct 27**
Humperdinck, Engelbert: Birth, **May 3**
Humphrey, Hubert: Birth Anniv, **May 27**
Humphrey, Terin: Birth, **Aug 14**
Humphries, Barry: Birth, **Feb 17**
Hungary
  Anniversary of the 1848 Revolution, **Mar 15**
  Anniversary of the 1956 Revolution, **Oct 23**
  Hungary Declares Independence: Anniv, **Oct 23**
  St. Stephen's Day, **Aug 20**
Hunger Awareness Day, Natl, **Jun 6**
Hungerford, Margaret Wolfe: Duchess Who Wasn't Day, **Aug 27**
Hunnicutt, Gayle: Birth, **Feb 6**
Hunt, Bonnie: Birth, **Sep 22**
Hunt, Helen: Birth, **Jun 15**
Hunt, Lamar: Birth, **Aug 2**
Hunt, Linda: Birth, **Apr 2**
Hunter, Catfish: Birth Anniv, **Apr 8**
Hunter, David: Hunter Frees the Slaves: Anniv, **May 9**
Hunter, Holly: Birth, **Mar 20**
Hunter, Rachel: Birth, **Sep 9**
Hunter, Tab: Birth, **Jul 11**
Hunter-Gault, Charlayne: Birth, **Feb 27**
Hunter's Moon, **Oct 6**
Hunters' Moon, Feast of (Lafayette, IN), **Oct 7**
Hunting and Fishing Day, Natl (Pres Proc), **Sep 23**
Hunting: Cheltenham Hunt Fest (Prestbury, England), **Mar 14**
Huntington, Samuel: Birth Anniv, **Jul 3**
Huntington's Disease Awareness Month, **May 1**
Huntsman, Jr, John: Birth Anniv, **Mar 26**
Huppert, Isabelle: Birth, **Mar 16**
Hurley, Elizabeth: Birth, **Jun 10**
Hurricanes, Tornados, Cyclones, Typhoons
  Atlantic, Caribbean and Gulf Hurricane Season, **Jun 1**
  Central Pacific Hurricane Season, **Jun 1**
  Eastern Pacific Hurricane Season, **May 15**
  Galveston, TX: Anniv, **Sep 8**
  Hurricane Agnes: Anniv, **Jun 21**
  Hurricane Hugo Hits American Coast: Anniv, **Sep 21**
  Hurricane Mitch: Anniv, **Oct 27**
  Hurricane Supplication Day (Virgin Islands), **Jul 24**
  Hurricane Thanksgiving Day (Virgin Islands), **Oct 16**
  Port Royal (Jamaica) Hurricane: Anniv, **Aug 28**
  Southern Cyclone: Anniv, **Aug 24**
  Texas Panhandle Tornado: Anniv, **Apr 9**
  Western Pacific Hurricane Season, **Jan 1**
Hurston, Zora Neale: Birth Anniv, **Jan 7**
Hurston, Zora: Zora Neale Hurston Fest (Eatonville, FL), **Jan 25**
Hurt, John: Birth, **Jan 22**
Hurt, Mary Beth: Birth, **Sep 26**
Hurt, William: Birth, **Mar 20**
Hus, John: Commemoration Day (Czech), **Jul 6**
Husband Appreciation Day, **Apr 15**
Husband Caregiver Day, **Jun 18**
Husky, Ferlin: Birth, **Dec 3**
Hussein, King of Jordan: Birth Anniv, **Nov 14**
Hussein, Saddam: Birth, **Apr 28**
Hussein, Saddam: Operation Iraqi Freedom: Anniv, **Mar 19**
Hussey, Olivia: Birth, **Apr 17**
Huston, Anjelica: Birth, **Jul 8**
Huston, John: Birth Anniv, **Aug 5**
Hutchins, Robert Maynard: Birth Anniv, **Jan 17**
Hutchinson, Anne: Memorial Day (Portsmouth, RI), **Apr 30**
Hutchison, Kay Bailey: Birth, **Jul 22**
Hutton, Betty: Birth, **Feb 26**
Hutton, Lauren: Birth, **Nov 17**
Hutton, Timothy: Birth, **Aug 16**
Huxley, Aldous: Birth Anniv, **Jul 26**
Huygens, Christiaan: Birth Anniv, **Apr 14**
Hynde, Chrissie: Birth, **Sep 7**

Hypnosis Federation Conf, Intl (Los Angeles, CA), **Aug 4**
Hypnosis: Health and Happiness with Hypnosis Day, **Jul 25**

I Am So Thankful Month, **Nov 1**
I Love Lucy TV Premiere: Anniv, **Oct 15**
I Need a Patch for That Day, **May 21**
I Spy TV Premiere: Anniv, **Sep 15**
I Want You to Be Happy Day, **Mar 3**
Iacocca, Lee: Birth, **Oct 15**
IBM PC Introduced: Anniv, **Aug 12**
Ibsen, Henrik: Birth Anniv, **Mar 20**
Ice Cream Cone: Anniv, **Sep 22**
Ice Cream Day, Natl, **Jul 16**
Ice Cream Days (Le Mars, IA), **Jun 15**
Ice Cream Fest, Old-Fashioned (Utica, OH), **May 27**
Ice Cream Social (Indianapolis, IN), **Jul 4**
Ice Fest (Ligonier, PA), **Jan 28**
Ice T: Birth, **Feb 16**
Icebox Days (International Falls, MN), **Jan 12**
Iced Tea Month, Natl, **Jun 1**
Iceland
  August Holiday, **Aug 7**
  Beer Day, **Mar 1**
  Bun Day, **Feb 27**
  Bursting Day, **Feb 28**
  First Day of Summer, **Apr 20**
  Independence Day, **Jun 17**
  Laki Volcano Eruption: Anniv, **Jun 8**
  Leif Erikson Day, **Oct 9**
  University Students' Celebration, **Dec 1**
Iceman Mummy Discovered: Anniv, **Sep 19**
Idaho
  Admission Day, **Jul 3**
  Coeur d'Alene Tribal Pilgrimage (Cataldo), **Aug 15**
  Craig, Larry E.: Birth, **Jul 20**
  Crapo, Michael: Birth, **May 20**
  Eastern Idaho State Fair (Blackfoot), **Sep 2**
  Festival at Sandpoint (Sandpoint), **Aug 3**
  Kempthorne, Dirk: Birth, **Oct 29**
  Lewis & Clark Bicentennial Natl Signature Event: Among the Niimiipuu (Lewiston), **Jun 14**
  Lionel Hampton Jazz Fest (Moscow), **Feb 22**
  Lost in the '50s (Sandpoint), **May 19**
  Mountain Man Rendezvous (Cataldo), **Aug 18**
  NAIA Baseball World Series (Lewiston), **May 26**
  Old Mission Historic Skills Fair (Cataldo), **Jul 9**
  Old-Time Fiddlers' Contest and Fest, Natl (Weiser), **Jun 19**
  Sandpoint Saddle Club Horse Show (Sandpoint), **Jun 17**
  Shakespeare Fest (Boise), **Jun 2**
  Simplot Games (Pocatello), **Feb 16**
  Snake River Stampede (Nampa), **Jul 18**
  That Famous Preston Night Rodeo (Preston), **Jul 28**
  Wells Fargo Boulder Mountain Tour (Sun Valley), **Feb 4**
  Western Idaho Fair (Boise), **Aug 18**
  Winter Games of Idaho, **Feb 1**
Ideas Month, Intl, **Mar 1**
Identity Theft Prevention and Awareness Month, **Dec 1**
Ides of March, **Mar 15**
Iditarod Trail Sled Dog Race (Anchorage, AK), **Mar 4**
Idle, Eric: Birth, **Mar 29**
Idol, Billy: Birth, **Nov 30**
Ifans, Rhys: Birth, **Jul 22**
Ig Nobel Prize Ceremony (Cambridge, MA), **Oct 5**
Iglesias, Enrique: Birth, **May 8**
Iglesias, Julio: Birth, **Sep 23**
Ilitch, Mike: Birth, **Jul 20**
Illinden: Saint Elias Day: Macedonian Uprising: Anniv, **Aug 2**
Illinois
  Admission Day, **Dec 3**
  Arcola Broom Corn Fest (Arcola), **Sep 8**
  Arts/Quincy Riverfest (Quincy), **Sep 17**
  Association Week in Chicagoland (Chicago), **Jun 19**
  Bark in the Park (Chicago), **May 6**
  Big Ten Men's Golf Chmpshps (Evanston), **May 5**
  Big Ten Men's Tennis Chmpshp (Urbana), **Apr 27**
  Blagojevich, Rod: Birth, **Dec 10**
  Bon Odori Fest of the Lanterns (Chicago), **Jul 8**
  Boxing Day at the Hemingway Birthplace (Oak Park), **Dec 26**
  Burgoo Fest (Utica), **Oct 8**
  Carillon Fest, Intl (Springfield), **Jun 4**
  Chicago Blues Fest (Chicago), **Jun 1**
  Chicago Golf Club: Anniv, **Jul 18**
  Chicago Gospel Music Fest (Chicago), **Jun 9**

  Chicago Intl Film Fest (Chicago), **Oct 5**
  Chicago Jazz Fest (Chicago), **Aug 31**
  Chocolate Fest (Galesburg), **Feb 10**
  Christmas Walk and House Tour (Geneva), **Dec 1**
  City of Chicago Incorporated: Anniv, **Mar 4**
  Clarence Darrow Death Commemoration (Chicago), **Mar 13**
  Closing of Columbian Exposition: Anniv, **Oct 30**
  Columbian Exposition Opening: Anniv, **May 1**
  Decatur Celebration (Decatur), **Aug 4**
  Downtown Alive! (Aurora), **Jun 9**
  Durbin, Richard J.: Birth, **Nov 21**
  Fest of the Vine (Geneva), **Sep 8**
  Fourth of July Patriotic Concert & Fireworks (Aurora), **Jul 4**
  Frankfort Fall Fest (Frankfort), **Sep 2**
  Freedom Fest (Mahomet), **Jul 4**
  Friends of Lake Forest Library Book Sale (Lake Forest), **Sep 15**
  Galesburg Railroad Days (Galesburg), **Jun 24**
  Gay and Lesbian Pride Parade (Chicago), **Jun 25**
  Gay Games (Chicago), **Jul 15**
  Geneva Arts Fair (Geneva), **Jul 22**
  Geographers Annual Mtg, Assn of American (Chicago), **Mar 7**
  Ginza Holiday: Japanese Cultural Fest (Chicago), **Aug 11**
  Great Chicago Flood: Anniv, **Apr 13**
  Great River Tug Fest (Port Byron), **Aug 11**
  Groundhog Days (Woodstock), **Jan 28**
  Hankfest (Chicago), **Sep 16**
  Harold Washington Elected Chicago's First Black Mayor: Anniv, **Apr 11**
  Harvard Milk Days Fest (Harvard), **Jun 2**
  Haymarket Pardon: Anniv, **Jun 26**
  Haymarket Square Riot: Anniv, **May 4**
  Hemingway Birthday Colloquium (Oak Park), **Jul 21**
  Herb Fest (Mattoon), **Apr 29**
  Herrinfesta Italiana (Herrin), **May 25**
  Hog Capital of the World Fest (Kewanee), **Sep 1**
  Holiday Magic (Aurora), **Nov 24**
  Horseradish Fest (Collinsville), **Jun 10**
  Illinois Snow Sculpting Competition (Rockford), **Jan 18**
  Illinois State Fair (Springfield), **Aug 11**
  Jubilee Days Fest (Zion), **Sep 2**
  Kane County Flea Market (St. Charles), **Jan 7**
  Knox County Scenic Drive (Galesburg), **Oct 7**
  LaSalle Bank Chicago Marathon, (Chicago), **Oct 22**
  Little Red School House Annual Art Fair (Willow Springs), **Oct 1**
  Lockport Old Canal Days (Lockport), **Jun 16**
  Marigold Fest (Pekin), **Sep 8**
  McHenry County Fair (Woodstock), **Aug 2**
  Memorial Day Parade (Aurora), **May 29**
  Morton Pumpkin Fest (Morton), **Sep 13**
  Mother's Day Housewalk (Evanston), **May 14**
  Newberry Library's Annual Book Fair (Chicago), **Jul 28**
  Newspaper Assn of America Conv (Chicago), **Apr 2**
  NJCAA Div II Men's Natl Basketball Finals (Danville), **Mar 22**
  Obama, Barack: Birth, **Aug 4**
  On the Waterfront (Rockford), **Aug 31**
  Original Raggedy Ann & Andy Fest (Arcola), **Jun 10**
  Party in the Plaza (Aurora), **Jun 7**
  Pec Thing (Pecatonica), **May 20**
  PGA Golf Chmpshp (Medinah), **Aug 14**
  QCCA Regional Lawn, Garden and Flower Show (Rock Island), **Mar 2**
  Quincy Preserves Christmas Candlelight Tour (Quincy), **Dec 10**
  Quincy Preserves Fall Architectural Tour (Quincy), **Oct 21**
  Radiological Society of North America Scientific Assembly and Annual Mtg (Chicago), **Nov 26**
  Roger Ebert's Overlooked Film Fest (Champaign), **Apr 26**
  Scarecrow Fest (St. Charles), **Oct 6**
  Shakespeare Fest (Bloomington), **Jun 29**
  Special Kids Day (Elmhurst), **Dec 6**
  Spoon River Valley Scenic Drive (Lewistown), **Oct 7**
  Stearman Fly-In Days, Natl (Galesburg), **Sep 4**
  Superman Celebration (Metropolis), **Jun 8**
  Swedish Days (Geneva), **Jun 20**
  Sweetcorn Fest, Natl (Hoopeston), **Aug 31**
  Turtle Races (Danville), **Jun 10**
  Victorian Christmas Tours at Frank Lloyd Wright Home (Oak Park), **Dec 9**
  Viva! Chicago Latin Music Fest (Chicago), **Aug 26**

Illinois (cont'd)—Iran

World Chmpshp Old-Time Piano Playing Contest (Peoria), **May 26**
World Freefall Convention (Rantoul), **Aug 4**
World's Largest Easter Egg Hunt (Rockford), **Mar 26**
Wright, Frank Lloyd: Wright Plus (Oak Park), **May 20**
I'm Not Going to Take It Anymore Day, Jan 7
Image Week, Build a Better, Sep 17
Iman: Birth, Jul 25
Imbolc, Feb 2
Immaculate Conception, Feast of, Dec 8
Immigrants' Day (Canada), May 22
Immigration: Ellis Island Opened: Anniv, Jan 1
Immunization Awareness Month, Natl, Aug 1
Impeachment: Clinton Proceedings: Anniv, Dec 20
Impeachment: Johnson Proceedings: Anniv, Feb 24
Imperioli, Michael: Birth, Jan 1
Imus, Don: Birth, Jul 23
Imus, Don: Imus in the Morning Radio Premiere: Anniv, Dec 2
In Living Color TV Premiere: Anniv, Apr 15
In the Heat of the Night TV Premiere: Anniv, Mar 6
Inane Answering Message Day, Jan 30
Inauguration Day, Old, Mar 4
Incandescent Lamp Demonstarted: Anniv, Oct 21
Income Tax Birthday, Feb 3
Income Tax Due Date, Quarterly Estimated Federal, Jan 17, Apr 17, Jun 15, Sep 15
Income Tax Pay Day, Apr 15
Income Tax Pay Day: This Is Really It, Apr 17
Income Tax: Anniv, Mar 8
Inconvenience Yourself Day, Feb 22
Incredible Hulk TV Premiere: Anniv, Mar 10
Independence Day (Russia), Jun 12
Independence Day, US (Fourth of July)
  Aalborg and Rebild Fest (Aalborg and Rebild, Denmark), **Jul 2**
  Andrews 4th of July Festivities (Andrews, TX), **Jul 3**
  Boom Box Parade (Willimantic, CT), **Jul 4**
  Bristol Civic, Military/Firemen's Parade (Bristol, RI), **Jul 4**
  Calithumpian Parade (Biwabik, MN), **Jul 4**
  Celebration on the Cane (Natchitoches, LA), **Jul 4**
  Dam Experience (Warsaw, MO), **Jul 1**
  Declaration of Independence Approval and Signing: Anniv, **Jul 4**
  Firestorm (Altoona, PA), **Jul 4**
  Fireworks Celebration (Demopolis, AL), **Jul 4**
  Fireworks on the Fjord (Poulsbo, WA), **Jul 3**
  Fourth of July Celebration (Hettinger, ND), **Jul 1**
  Fourth of July Celebration (Live Oak, FL), **Jul 1**
  Fourth of July Fireworks (Mackinaw City, MI), **Jul 4**
  Fourth of July Patriotic Concert & Fireworks (Aurora, IL), **Jul 4**
  Fredericksburg Heritage Fest (Fredericksburg, VA), **Jul 4**
  Freedom Days (Farmington, NM), **Jul 1**
  Freedom Fest (Mahomet, IL), **Jul 4**
  Hometown Family Fourth (Hollywood, FL), **Jul 4**
  Hood River Old-Fashioned Fourth of July (Hood River, OR), **Jul 4**
  Independence Day Celebration (Catonsville, MD), **Jul 4**
  Independence Day Concert and Fireworks (Wheeling, WV), **Jul 4**
  Independence Extravaganza (Lavallette, NJ), **Jul 2**
  Monett Fourth of July (Monett, MO), **Jul 4**
  Mount Rushmore July 4 Celebration (Mount Rushmore, SD), **Jul 3**
  Mystic Seaport Independence Day Celebration (Mystic, CT), **Jul 4**
  Old Glory Jubilee (Elsberry, MO), **Jul 4**
  Old Vermont Fourth (Woodstock, VT), **Jul 4**
  Red, White and Boom (Columbus, OH), **Jul 3**
  Road to Independence (Yorktown, VA), **Jul 2**
  Spamtown USA Freedom Fest (Austin, MN), **Jul 1**
  Star Spangled Sparks (Sparks, NV), **Jul 4**
  WSB-TV Salute 2 America Parade (Atlanta, GA), **Jul 4**
Independence Sunday (IA), Jul 2
Independence-from-Meat Day, Jul 4
India
  Bhopal Poison Gas Disaster: Anniv, **Dec 3**
  Children's Day, **Nov 14**
  Dassehra, **Oct 2**
  Deepavali (Diwali), **Oct 21**
  Gandhi, Mohandas: Assassination Anniv, **Jan 30**
  Gandhi, Mohandas: Birth Anniv, **Oct 2**
  Gandhi, Mohandas: Makes Salt: Anniv, **Apr 6**
  Guru Nanak's Birth Anniv, **Nov 5**
  Holi, **Mar 14**
  Independence Day, **Aug 15**
  Indian Earthquake, **Jan 26**

New Year's Day, **Mar 22**
Rajiv Gandhi Assassinated: Anniv, **May 21**
Republic Day, **Jan 26**
Vaisakhi, **Apr 14**
Indian Ocean Earthquake and Tsunamis: Anniv, Dec 26
Indian Saint, First: Anniv, Jul 31
Indiana
  Admission Day, **Dec 11**
  Amish Acres Arts & Crafts Fest (Nappanee), **Aug 10**
  Bayh, Evan: Birth, **Dec 26**
  Benjamin Harrison Day (Indianapolis), **Mar 3**
  Benjamin Harrison's Birthday Celeb (Indianapolis), **Aug 20**
  Berne Swiss Days (Berne), **Jul 27**
  Big Ten Men's Basketball Tournament (Indianapolis), **Mar 9**
  Big Ten Men's Swimming/Diving Chmpshps (Bloomington), **Feb 23**
  Big Ten Men's/Women's Cross Country Chmpshps (Bloomington), **Oct 29**
  Big Ten Women's Basketball Tournament (Indianapolis), **Mar 2**
  Big Ten Women's Golf Chmpshps (Bloomington), **Apr 28**
  Big Ten Wrestling Chmpshps (Bloomington), **Mar 2**
  Big Whopper Liar's Contest (New Harmony), **Sep 16**
  Chautauqua of the Arts (Greensburg), **Sep 16**
  Christmas Gift and Hobby Show (Indianapolis), **Nov 8**
  Circus City Fest (Peru), **Jul 15**
  Crawfordsville Strawberry Fest (Crawfordsville), **Jun 9**
  Daniels, Mitchell: Birth, **Apr 7**
  Dean, James, Birthday Celebration (Fairmont), **Feb 4**
  Elwood Glass Fest (Elwood), **Aug 18**
  Fairmount Fest/Remembering James Dean (Fairmount), **Sep 22**
  Family Christmas at Benjamin Harrison Home (Indianapolis), **Nov 20**
  Feast of the Hunters' Moon (Lafayette), **Oct 7**
  Fishing Has No Boundaries (Monticello), **May 20**
  Fulton County Historical Power Show (Rochester), **Jun 16**
  Germanfest (Fort Wayne), **Jun 4**
  Ghost Tales of the White House (Indianapolis), **Oct 27**
  Heritage Week (New Harmony), **Apr 17**
  Historical Society Christmas Tour of Homes (Crawfordsville), **Dec 11**
  Ice Cream Social (Indianapolis), **Jul 4**
  Indiana Flower and Patio Show (Indianapolis), **Mar 11**
  Indianapolis Senior Expo (Indianapolis), **Oct 5**
  Indy 500-Mile Race (Indianapolis), **May 28**
  Johnny Appleseed Fest (Fort Wayne), **Sep 16**
  Literally, A Haunted House (New Albany), **Oct 6**
  Lugar, Richard G.: Birth, **Apr 4**
  Marshall County Blueberry Fest (Plymouth), **Sep 1**
  Mississinewa 1812 (Marion), **Oct 13**
  Mitchell Persimmon Fest (Mitchell), **Sep 22**
  NAIA Women's Natl Chmpshps (South Bend), **May 23**
  NCAA Div I Men's Basketball Chmpshp (Indianapolis), **Apr 1**
  Parke County Covered Bridge Fest (Rockville), **Oct 13**
  Popcorn Fest (Valparaiso), **Sep 9**
  Presidents' Day: Live from Delaware St (Indianapolis), **Feb 20**
  Primary Day: Live from Delaware St (Indianapolis), **May 2**
  Redbud Trail Rendezvous (Rochester), **Apr 29**
  Scott County Courtfest (Scottsburg), **Sep 9**
  State Fair (Indianapolis), **Aug 9**
  Three Rivers Fest (Fort Wayne), **Jul 8**
  Trail of Courage Living-History Fest (Rochester), **Sep 16**
  USGA Senior Amateur (Golf) Chmpshp (Newburgh), **Sep 16**
  Wicket World of Croquet (Indianapolis), **Jun 10**
  Wizard of Oz Fest (Chesterton), **Sep 15**
Indiana, Robert: Birth, Sep 13
Indianapolis 500: Anniv, May 30
Indianapolis Sunk: Anniv, Jul 29
Indonesia
  Independence Day, **Aug 17**
  Kartini Day, **Apr 21**
Infection Prevention Week, Oct 16
Infertility Survival Day, Natl, May 7
Informed Woman Month, Apr 1
Ingels, Marty: Birth, Mar 9
Ingram, James: Birth, Feb 16
Inhofe, James M.: Birth, Nov 17
Injury Prevention Month, Apr 1

Inkster, Juli: Birth, Jun 24
Inn: Country Inn, Bed and Breakfast Day, Oct 1
Innergize Day, Sep 24
Innes, Laura: Birth, Aug 16
Innovation Week Intl, Apr 23
Inouye, Daniel: Birth, Sep 7
INPEX, Jun 7
Insects: Carpenter Ant Awareness Week, Jun 18
Insulin First Isolated: Anniv, Jul 27
Intergeneration Day, Oct 1
International Workers of the World (IWW) Founded: Anniv, Jun 27
Internet Created: Anniv, Oct 29
Internet Moms Week, Intl, Mar 12
Interstate Highway System Born: Anniv, Jun 29
Intimate Apparel Market Week, Jan 9
Introduce a Girl to Engineering Day, Feb 23
Inventors Congress, Minnesota (Redwood Falls, MN), Jun 8
Inventors Hall of Fame, Woman Inducted to: Anniv, May 18
Inventors' Month, Natl, Aug 1
Iowa
  Admission Day, **Dec 28**
  Bald Eagle Appreciation Days (Keokuk), **Jan 21**
  Big 12 Wrestling Chmpshp (Ames), **Mar 4**
  Big Ten Men's Gymnastics Chmpshps (Iowa City), **Mar 24**
  Big Ten Men's Indoor Track/Field Chmpshps (Iowa City), **Feb 25**
  Big Ten Women's Soccer Tournament (Iowa City), **Nov 2**
  Big Ten Women's Tennis Chmpshp (Iowa City), **Apr 27**
  Bike Van Buren (Van Buren County), **Aug 19**
  Bix Beiderbecke Mem Jazz Fest (Davenport), **Jul 27**
  Britt Draft Horse Show (Britt), **Sep 1**
  Burlington Steamboat Days/Amer Music Fest (Burlington), **Jun 13**
  Christmas in the Villages (Van Buren County), **Dec 2**
  Civil War Reenactment (Keokuk), **Apr 21**
  Creston/Southwest Iowa Balloon Days (Creston), **Sep 15**
  Donna Reed Performing Arts Fest (Denison), **Jun 19**
  Dyersville Fest of the Arts (Dyersville), **Sep 23**
  Forest Craft/Scenic Drive Fest (Van Buren County), **Oct 14**
  Glenn Miller Birthplace Society Fest (Clarinda), **Jun 8**
  Grant Wood Art Fest (Stone City–Anamosa), **Jun 11**
  Grassley, Charles: Birth, **Sep 17**
  Great River Tug Fest (LeClaire), **Aug 11**
  Harkin, Thomas R.: Birth, **Nov 19**
  Herbert Hoover Day, **Aug 13**
  Hobo Convention, Natl (Britt), **Aug 10**
  Ice Cream Days (Le Mars), **Jun 15**
  Independence Sunday, **Jul 2**
  Iowa Storytelling Fest (Clear Lake), **Jul 21**
  Johnson County 4H and FFA Fair (Iowa City), **Jul 24**
  Jule Fest (Elk Horn), **Nov 24**
  Miss Iowa Scholarship Pageant (Eldridge), **Jun 8**
  NAIA Div II Women's Basketball Chmpshp (Sioux City), **Mar 8**
  Old Threshers Reunion (Mount Pleasant), **Aug 31**
  Old-Time Country Music Contest, Fest & Expo, Natl (Missouri Valley), **Aug 28**
  Pella Tulip Time Fest (Pella), **May 4**
  Perry's "BRR" (Bike Ride to Rippey) (Perry), **Feb 4**
  Quad City Air Show (Davenport), **Jun 24**
  RAGBRAI—Register's Bicycle Ride Across Iowa (Des Moines), **Jul 23**
  Rocktober Geode Fest (Keokuk), **Oct 6**
  State Fair, Iowa (Des Moines), **Aug 10**
  Summer Farm Toy Show (Dyersville), **Jun 2**
  Ten Thousand Crestonians (Creston), **Jul 1**
  Tivoli Fest (Elk Horn), **May 27**
  Vilsack, Tom: Birth, **Dec 13**
  Wrestling Chmpshps, NAIA (Sioux City), **Mar 3**
Iowa, Explosion on USS: Anniv, Apr 19
Iran
  Fifteenth of Khordad, **Jun 5**
  Iran Air Flight 655 Disaster, **Jul 3**
  Iran-Iraq War: Anniv, **Sep 22**
  Islamic Republic Day, **Apr 1**
  Khomeini: Death Anniv, **Jun 3**
  National Day, **Feb 11**
  National Day of Oil, **Mar 19**
  New Year (Noruz), **Mar 21**
  Seizure of US Embassy: Anniv, **Nov 4**
  Teheran Conference: Anniv, **Nov 28**
  Yalda, **Dec 21**
Iran Hostages: US Attempt To Free: Anniv, Apr 24

Iraq
Congress Authorized Force Against Iraq: Anniv, **Jan 12**
Desert Shield: Anniv, **Aug 7**
Ground War Against Iraq Begins: Anniv, **Feb 23**
Iran-Iraq War: Anniv, **Sep 22**
Iraq Invades Kuwait: Anniv, **Aug 2**
National Day, **Apr 9**
Operation Iraqi Freedom: Anniv, **Mar 19**
Persian Gulf War Begins: Anniv, **Jan 16**
Ireland
Bank Holiday, **Jun 3, Aug 5, Oct 28**
Bloomsday: Anniv, **Jun 16**
Day of the Wren, **Dec 26**
Easter Rising, **Apr 24**
Ivy Day, **Oct 6**
May Day Bank Holiday, **May 6**
National Day, **Mar 17**
Ryder Cup Matches (Straffan, County Kildare), **Sep 22**
Saint Stephen's Day, **Dec 26**
World Book Day, **Mar 2**
Ireland, Kathy: Birth, Mar 8
Ireland, Patricia: Birth, Oct 19
Iris Fest (Sumter, SC), May 25
Irish-American Heritage Month, Mar 1
Iron Curtain Speech: Anniv, Mar 5
Ironman Triathlon World Chmpshp (Kailua-Kona, HI), Oct 14
Irons, Jeremy: Birth, Sep 19
Ironside TV Premiere: Anniv, Sep 14
Irrational Exuberance Enters Lexicon: Anniv, Dec 5
Irrigation Show, Intl (San Antonio, TX), Nov 5
Irrigation: Smart Irrigation Month, Jul 1
Irving, Amy: Birth, Sep 10
Irving, Clifford: Fake Howard Hughes Biography: Anniv, Jan 9
Irving, John: Birth, Mar 2
Irving, Washington: Birth Anniv, Apr 3
Irwin Earns 1st Medal of Honor: Anniv, Feb 13
Irwin, Bill: Birth, Apr 11
Irwin, Hale S.: Birth, Jun 3
Irwin, Steve: Birth, Feb 22
Isaak, Chris: Birth, Jun 26
Isakson, Johnny: Birth, Dec 28
Isherwood, Christopher: Birth Anniv, Aug 26
Ishii, Kazuhiro: Birth, Sep 9
Ising, Rudolf C.: Birth Anniv, Aug 7
Isle of Man: Tynwald Day, Jul 5
Isle Royale Natl Park Established: Anniv, Apr 3
Isozaki, Arata: Birth, Jul 23
Isra al Mi'raj: Ascent of Prophet Muhammad, Aug 21
Israel
Arafat Returns to Palestine: Anniv, **Jul 1**
Camp David Accord Signed: Anniv, **Mar 26**
Hashoah/Holocaust Day, **Apr 25**
Hebron Massacre: Anniv, **Feb 25**
Independence Day (Yom Ha'atzma'ut), **May 3**
Israeli Siege of Suez City Ends: Anniv, **Jan 28**
Jerusalem Day (Yom Yerushalayim), **May 26**
Remembrance Day (Yom Ha'zikkaron), **May 2**
Israeli Olympiad Massacre: Anniv, Sep 5
Issaquah Salmon Days Festival (Issaquah, WA), Oct 7
It Happened One Night Film Release: Anniv, Feb 22
It Takes a Thief TV Premiere: Anniv, Jan 9
Italian Heritage Fest, West Virginia (Clarksburg, WV), Sep 1
Italy
Battle of San Pietro Anniv, **Dec 15**
Calabria Earthquake: Anniv, **Dec 16**
Calcio Fiorentino (Florence), **Jun 24**
Carnival Week (Milan), **Feb 26**
Epiphany Fair (Rome), **Jan 5**
Explosion of the Cart (Florence), **Apr 16**
Feast of the Incappucciati (Gradoli), **Feb 23**
Feast of the Redeemer (Venice), **Jul 16**
Fest of St. Efisio (Cagliari), **May 1**
Gioco Del Ponte (Pisa), **Jun 4**
Giostra della Quintana (Foligno), **Sep 10**
Historical Regatta (Venice), **Sep 3**
Joust of the Quintana (Ascoli/Piceno), **Aug 6**
Joust of the Saracen (Arezzo), **Sep 3**
La Befana, **Jan 6**
Liberation Day, **Apr 25**
Mussolini Ousted: Anniv, **Jul 25**
Palio (Siena), **Jul 2**
Palio Dei Balestrieri (Gubbio), **May 28**
Palio del Golfo (La Spezia), **Aug 13**
Paralympic Games (Turin), **Mar 10**
Procession of Addolorata and Mysteries (Taranto), **Apr 13**
Purgatory Banquet (Gradoli), **Mar 1**
Republic Day, **Jun 2**
Stresa Music Weeks (Stresa), **Jul 26**

Victory Day, **Nov 4**
Wedding of the Sea (Venice), **May 28**
Winter Olympiad (Turin), **Feb 10**
It's a Wonderful Life Film Premiere: Anniv, Dec 20
It's About Time Week, Dec 25
Ivanek, Zeljko: Birth, Aug 15
I've Got a Secret TV Premiere: Anniv, Jun 19
Iverson, Allen: Birth, Jun 7
Ives, Burl: Birth Anniv, Jun 14
Ivey, Judith: Birth, Sep 4
Ivy Day (Ireland), Oct 6
Iwo Jima Day: Anniv, Feb 23

Jack Benny Program TV Premiere: Anniv, Oct 28
Jack the Ripper Letter: Anniv, Sep 27
Jackie Mayer Rehab Center Day (Sandusky, OH), Oct 6
Jackson, Andrew: Battle of New Orleans: Anniv, Jan 8
Jackson, Andrew: Birth Anniv, Mar 15
Jackson, Anne: Birth, Sep 3
Jackson, Bo: Birth, Nov 30
Jackson, Glenda: Birth, May 9
Jackson, Jackie: Birth, May 4
Jackson, Janet: Birth, May 16
Jackson, Jermaine: Birth, Dec 11
Jackson, Jesse: Birth, Oct 8
Jackson, Joe: Birth, Aug 11
Jackson, Jonathan: Birth, May 11
Jackson, Joshua: Birth, Jun 11
Jackson, Kate: Birth, Oct 29
Jackson, Mahalia: Birth Anniv, Oct 26
Jackson, Marlon: Birth, Mar 12
Jackson, Michael: Birth, Aug 29
Jackson, Peter: Birth, Oct 31
Jackson, Phil: Birth, Sep 17
Jackson, Rachel D.: Birth Anniv, Jun 15
Jackson, Randy: Birth, Oct 29
Jackson, Reggie: Birth, May 18
Jackson, Samuel L.: Birth, Dec 21
Jackson, Shirley Ann: Birth, Aug 6
Jackson, Stonewall: Birthday Celebration, Jan 21
Jackson, Stonewall: Lee-Jackson Day, Jan 13
Jackson, Thomas J. "Stonewall": Birth Anniv, Jan 21
Jackson, Tito: Birth, Oct 15
Jackson, Victoria: Birth, Aug 2
Jacob, Irene: Birth, Jul 15
Jacobi, Derek: Birth, Oct 22
Jacobi, Lou: Birth, Dec 28
Jacoby, Scott: Birth, Nov 19
Jaeger, Andrea: Birth, Jun 4
Jagger, Bianca: Birth, May 2
Jagger, Dean: Birth Anniv, Nov 7
Jagger, Mick: Birth, Jul 26
Jagr, Jaromir: Birth, Feb 15
Jahn, Helmut: Birth, Jan 1
Jakes, John: Birth, Mar 31
Jamaica
Abolition of Slavery, **Aug 1**
Discovery by Columbus: Anniv, **May 4**
Independence Day, **Aug 7**
Maroon Fest, **Jan 6**
National Heroes Day, **Oct 16**
Port Royal Hurricane: Anniv, **Aug 28**
James, Henry: Birth Anniv, Apr 15
James, Jesse: Birth Anniv, Sep 5
James, John: Birth, Apr 18
James, Kevin: Birth, Apr 26
James, LeBron: Birth, Dec 30
James, P.D.: Birth, Aug 3
James, Sonny: Birth, May 1
James, William: Birth Anniv, Jan 11
Jamestown Burned by Bacon's Rebellion: Anniv, Sep 19
Jamestown Landing Day (Williamsburg, VA), May 13
Jamestown, VA: Founding Anniv, May 14
Jamieson, Bob: Birth, Feb 1
Jamison, Judith: Birth, May 10
Janis, Byron: Birth, Mar 24
Janney, Allison: Birth, Nov 19
Jansen, Dan: Birth, Jun 17
Japan
Autumnal Equinox Day, **Sep 23**
Battle of Bismarck Sea: Anniv, **Mar 2**
Bean Throwing Fest (Setsubun), **Feb 3**
Birthday of the Emperor, **Dec 23**
Bon Fest (Feast of Lanterns), **Jul 13**
Children's Day, **May 5**
Chrysanthemum Day, **Sep 9**
Coming-of-Age Day, **Jan 9**
Constitution Memorial Day, **May 3**
Cormorant Fishing Fest, **May 11**
Culture Day, **Nov 3**
Day of the Rice God (Chiyoda), **Jun 4**
Doll Fest (Hinamatsuri), **Mar 3**
Flower Fest (Hana Matsuri), **Apr 8**

Foundation Day, Natl, **Feb 11**
Golden Week Holidays, **Apr 29**
Greenery Day, **Apr 29**
Ha-Ri-Ku-Yo (Needle Mass), **Feb 8**
Haru-No-Yabuiri, **Jan 16**
Health-Sports Day, **Oct 9**
Hiroshima Day, **Aug 6**
Hollyhock Fest (Kyoto), **May 15**
Japan Agrees to End Use of Drift Nets: Anniv, **Nov 26**
Japan Bombed: Anniv, **Apr 18**
Japanese Era New Year, **Jan 1**
Kakizome, **Jan 2**
Kanto Earthquake Memorial Day, **Sep 1**
Labor Thanksgiving Day, **Nov 23**
Marine Day, **Jul 20**
Moment of Silence (Nagasaki), **Aug 9**
Mount Ogura Plane Crash: Anniv, **Aug 12**
Namahage, **Dec 31**
Nanakusa, **Jan 7**
Newspaper Week, **Oct 1**
Peace Fest (Hiroshima), **Aug 6**
Respect for the Aged Day, **Sep 15**
Rice Planting Fest (Osaka), **Jun 14**
Roughhouse Fest, **Oct 14**
Shichi-Go-San, **Nov 15**
Snow Fest, **Feb 8**
Soma No Umaoi (Wild Horse Chasing), **Jul 23**
Suffers Major Earthquake: Anniv, **Jan 17**
Tanabata (Star Fest), **Jul 7**
Usokae (Bullfinch Exchange Fest), **Jan 7**
Vernal Equinox Day, **Mar 20**
Water-Drawing Fest, **Mar 1**
Japanese
Bon Fest (Delray Beach, FL), **Aug 12**
Bon Odori Fest of Lanterns (Chicago, IL), **Jul 8**
Ginza Holiday (Chicago, IL), **Aug 11**
Hatsume Fair (Delray Beach, FL), **Feb 25**
Japanese Fest (St. Louis, MO), **Sep 2**
Japanese Attack on US Mainland: Anniv, Feb 23
Japanese Internment (WWII): Anniv, Feb 19
Jarman, Claude, Jr: Birth, Sep 27
Jarreau, Al: Birth, Mar 12
Jarrett, Dale: Birth, Nov 26
Jarriel, Thomas Edwin: Birth, Dec 29
Jarvik, Robert: Birth, May 11
Jarvis, Gregory B.: Birth Anniv, Aug 24
Jaws Film Release: Anniv, Jun 20
Jay, John: Birth Anniv, Dec 12
Jazz and Blues
Albany Riverfront Jazz Fest (Albany, NY), **Sep 9**
All That Jazz Weekend (Asheville, NC), **Jan 27**
Bix Beiderbecke Mem Jazz Fest (Davenport, IA), **Jul 27**
Charlie Parker at the LA Philharmonic: Anniv, **Mar 25**
Chicago Blues Fest (Chicago, IL), **Jun 1**
Chicago Jazz Fest (Chicago, IL), **Aug 31**
Davis, Miles: Birth Anniv, **May 25**
Guthrie Jazz Banjo Fest (Guthrie, OK), **May 26**
Jazz Day, Intl, **May 27**
Jazz Fest, Intl (Pori, Finland), **Jul 15**
Lionel Hampton Jazz Fest (Moscow, ID), **Feb 22**
Medford Jazz Jubilee (Medford, OR), **Oct 13**
Monterey Jazz Fest (Monterey, CA), **Sep 15**
Natchitoches Jazz Fest (Natchitoches, LA), **Apr 1**
New Orleans Jazz/Heritage Fest (New Orleans, LA), **Apr 28**
North Sea Jazz Fest (The Hague, Netherlands), **Jul 14**
Parker, Charlie: Birth Anniv, **Aug 29**
Ra, Sun: Birth Anniv, **May 22**
Red Wine and Blues Fest (Tuckerton, NJ), **Jul 15**
Sacramento Jazz Jubilee (Sacramento, CA), **May 26**
San Sebastian Jazz Fest (San Sebastian, Spain), **Jul 22**
Satchmo Summerfest (New Orleans, LA), **Aug 3**
Snowbird, Utah Jazz & Blues Festival (Snowbird, UT), **Jul 28**
SunFest (West Palm Beach, FL), **May 3**
Taste of the Blue Ridge Blues & Jazz Fest (Roanoke, VA), **Sep 9**
Telluride Jazz Celebration (Telluride, CO), **Aug 4**
Ziegler Kettle Moraine Jazz Fest (West Bend, WI), **Sep 8**
Jazz Appreciation Month, Apr 1
Jeffers, Robinson: Birth Anniv, Jan 10
Jefferson Davis Day (Confederate Memorial Day, KY), Jun 3
Jefferson, Joseph: Birth Anniv, Feb 20
Jefferson, Martha: Birth Anniv, Oct 19
Jefferson, Richard: Birth, Jun 21
Jefferson, Thomas, and Adams, John: Death Anniv, Jul 4
Jefferson, Thomas: Birth Anniv, Apr 13
Jefferson, Thomas: Birth Anniv (Pres Proc), Apr 13

Jeffersons—Kansas

Jeffersons TV Premiere: Anniv, Jan 18
Jeffords, James M.: Birth, May 11
Jeffries, John: Weatherman's Day, Feb 5
Jemison, Mae: Birth, Oct 17
Jenkins, Stephan: Birth, Sep 27
Jenkins's Ear Day, Apr 9
Jenner, Bruce: Birth, Oct 28
Jenner, Edward: Birth Anniv, May 17
Jennings, Jason: Birth, Jul 17
Jeopardy TV Premiere: Anniv, Mar 30
Jerry Lewis Muscular Dystrophy Association Telethon, Sep 3
Jesse James Days, Defeat of (Northfield, MN), Sep 6
Jeter, Derek: Birth, Jun 26
Jetsons TV Premiere: Anniv, Sep 23
Jett, Joan: Birth, Sep 22
Jewel: Birth, May 23
Jewish Heritage Week (Pres Proc), Apr 30
Jewish Observances
    Asarah B'Tevet, Jan 10
    Chanukah, Dec 16
    Fast of Gedalya, Sep 25
    Fast of Tammuz, Jul 13
    Hadassah: Anniv, Feb 24
    Israel Yom Ha'atzma'ut (Independence Day), May 3
    Kristallnacht: Anniv, Nov 9
    Lag B'Omer, May 16
    Liberation of Buchenwald: Anniv, Apr 11
    Passover Begins, Apr 12
    Pesach (Passover), Apr 13
    Purim, Mar 14
    Rosh Hashanah (New Year), Sep 23
    Rosh Hashanah Begins, Sep 22
    Shabbat Across America, Mar 3
    Shavuot, Jun 2
    Shavuot Begins, Jun 1
    Shemini Atzeret, Oct 14
    Simchat Torah, Oct 15
    Sukkot Begins, Oct 6
    Sukkot/Succoth/Feast of Tabernacles, Oct 7
    Ta'anit Esther (Fast of Esther), Mar 13
    Tisha B'Av (Fast of Ab), Aug 3
    Tu B'Shvat, Feb 13
    US Holocaust Museum Opens: Anniv, Apr 26
    Warsaw Ghetto Revolt: Anniv, Apr 19
    Yom Hashoah/Holocaust Day (Israel), Apr 25
    Yom Kippur, Oct 2
    Yom Kippur Begins, Oct 1
Jewison, Norman: Birth, Jul 21
Jillette, Penn: Birth, Mar 5
Jillian, Ann: Birth, Jan 29
Jimmy Durante Show TV Premiere: Anniv, Oct 2
Jinnah, Mohammed Ali: Birth Anniv, Dec 25
Joan of Arc: Birth Anniv, Jan 6
Jobs, Steven: Birth, Feb 24
Joe Cain Procession (Mobile, AL), Feb 26
Joel, Billy: Birth, May 9
Johanns, Mike: Birth, Aug 18
Johansson, Scarlett: Birth, Nov 22
John Parker Day, Apr 19
John, Elton: Birth, Mar 25
John, Tommy: Birth, May 22
Johnny Appleseed Day, Mar 11
Johnny Appleseed Days (Lake City, MN), Oct 1
Johnny Appleseed Fest (Fort Wayne, IN), Sep 16
Johns, Glynis: Birth, Oct 5
Johns, Jasper: Birth, May 15
Johnson, Amy: Flight Anniv, May 5
Johnson, Andrew, Impeachment Proceedings: Anniv, Feb 24
Johnson, Andrew: Birth Anniv, Dec 29
Johnson, Arte: Birth, Jan 20
Johnson, Ban: Birth Anniv, Jan 6
Johnson, Betsy: Birth, Aug 10
Johnson, Clark: Birth, Sep 10
Johnson, Davey: Birth, Jan 30
Johnson, Don: Birth, Dec 15
Johnson, Eliza M.: Birth Anniv, Oct 4
Johnson, Jimmy: Birth, Mar 31
Johnson, John (Jack) Arthur: Birth Anniv, Mar 31
Johnson, Kevin: Birth, Mar 4
Johnson, Keyshawn: Birth, Jul 22
Johnson, Lady Bird: Birth, Dec 22
Johnson, Lyndon B.: Birth Anniv, Aug 27
Johnson, Lyndon B.: Monday Holiday Law: Anniv, Jun 28
Johnson, Lyndon B.: Civil Rights Act of 1968: Anniv, Apr 11
Johnson, Magic: Birth, Aug 14
Johnson, Michael: Birth, Sep 13
Johnson, Nick: Birth, Sep 19
Johnson, Phillip: Birth Anniv, Jul 8
Johnson, Randy: Birth, Sep 10
Johnson, Richard M.: Birth Anniv, Oct 17
Johnson, Robert: Birth Anniv, May 8
Johnson, Samuel: Birth Anniv, Sep 18

Johnson, Tim: Birth, Dec 28
Johnson, Virginia: Birth, Feb 11
Johnson, William H.: Birth Anniv, Mar 18
Johnston, Joseph: Birth Anniv, Feb 3
Johnston, Joseph: Surrender at Durham Station: Anniv, Apr 18
Johnston, Kristen: Birth, Sep 20
Johnstown Flood of 1889 Commemoration (Johnstown, PA), May 27
Johnstown Flood: Anniv, May 31
Join Hands Day, May 6
Jolie, Angelina: Birth, Jun 4
Jolson, Al: Birth Anniv, May 26
Jones Reynolds, Star: Birth, Mar 24
Jones, Andruw: Birth, Apr 23
Jones, Bobby: Birth Anniv, Mar 17
Jones, Bobby: Wins First Grand Slam: Anniv, Jul 12
Jones, Casey: Birth Anniv, Mar 14
Jones, Chipper: Birth, Apr 24
Jones, Chuck: Birth Anniv, Sep 21
Jones, Cobi: Birth, Jun 16
Jones, Davy: Birth, Dec 30
Jones, Dean: Birth, Jan 25
Jones, Eddie: Birth, Oct 20
Jones, Edward "Too Tall": Birth, Feb 23
Jones, George: Birth, Sep 12
Jones, Grace: Birth, May 19
Jones, Howard: Birth, Feb 23
Jones, James Earl: Birth, Jan 17
Jones, Jeffrey: Birth, Sep 28
Jones, Jennifer: Birth, Mar 2
Jones, Jenny: Birth, Jun 7
Jones, John Paul: Birth Anniv, Jul 6
Jones, K.C.: Birth, May 25
Jones, Leroi: See Amiri Baraka: Birth, Oct 7
Jones, Marion: Birth, Oct 12
Jones, Mary H.: Birth Anniv, May 1
Jones, Norah: Birth, Mar 30
Jones, Quincy: Birth, Mar 14
Jones, Ricki Lee: Birth, Nov 8
Jones, Sam J.: Birth, Aug 12
Jones, Shirley: Birth, Mar 31
Jones, Terry: Birth, Feb 1
Jones, Tom: Birth, Jun 7
Jones, Tommy Lee: Birth, Sep 15
Jonestown Massacre: Anniv, Nov 18
Jong, Erica: Birth, Mar 26
Jonson, Ben: Birth Anniv, Jun 11
Joplin, Janis: Birth Anniv, Jan 19
Joplin, Scott: Birth Anniv, Nov 24
Jordan
    Accession Day, Jun 9
    Great Arab Revolt and Army Day, Jun 10
    Independence Day, May 25
    King Hussein: Birth Anniv, Nov 14
    King's Birthday, Jan 30
Jordan, Michael: Birth, Feb 17
Jordan, Neil: Birth, Feb 25
Jordan, Vernon, Jr: Birth, Aug 15
Joseph, Chief, Surrender: Anniv, Oct 5
Joseph, Chief: Death Anniv, Sep 21
Jouett, Jack: Ride Anniv, Jun 3
Joule, James: Birth Anniv, Dec 24
Journalism
    All the News That's Fit to Print: Anniv, Feb 10
    Around the World in 72 Days: Anniv, Jan 25
    Beginning of the Penny Press: Anniv, Sep 3
    Bolles, Don: Death Anniv, Jun 13
    Brinkley, David: Birth Anniv, Jul 10
    Columnist's Day, Natl, Jun 27
    Dewey Defeats Truman Headline: Anniv, Nov 3
    First American Daily Newspaper Published: Anniv, May 30
    First American Newspaper: Anniv, Sep 25
    First Magazine Published in America: Anniv, Feb 13
    First Newspaper Comic Strip: Anniv, Oct 18
    First Photos Used in a Newspaper Report: Anniv, Jul 1
    First Televised Presidential News Conf: Anniv, Jan 25
    Japan: Newspaper Week, Oct 1
    Life Magazine Debuts: Anniv, Nov 23
    NAB/National Broadcasters Conv (Las Vegas, NV), Apr 22
    New York Times First Published: Anniv, Sep 18
    New York Weekly Journal First Issue: Anniv, Nov 5
    New Yorker Published: Anniv, Feb 21
    Newspaper Carrier Day, Sep 4
    Newspaper in Education Week, Mar 6
    Newspaper Week, Natl, Oct 1
    Nixon's Last Press Conf: Anniv, Nov 7
    Obituary Writers' Intl Conference, Great (Las Vegas, NV), Jun 15
    People Magazine: Anniv, Mar 4
    Pulitzer, Joseph: Birth Anniv, Apr 10
    Pyle, Ernest: Birth Anniv, Aug 3

    Thomas, Lowell: Birth Anniv, Apr 6
    Time Magazine First Published: Anniv, Mar 3
    UN: World Press Freedom Day, May 3
    USA Today First Published: Anniv, Sep 15
    Zenger, John P.: Arrest Anniv, Nov 17
Joust of the Quintana (Ascoli/Piceno, Italy), Aug 6
Joy of Cooking: Publication Anniv, Nov 30
Joy of Sex Published: Anniv, Oct 1
Joy, Robert: Birth, Aug 17
Joyce, James: Birth Anniv, Feb 2
Joyce, James: Bloomsday: Anniv, Jun 16
Joygerm Day, Natl, Jan 8
Joyner-Kersee, Jackie: Birth, Mar 3
Juarez, Benito: Birth Anniv, Mar 21
Jubilee Days Fest (Zion, IL), Sep 2
Judd, Ashley: Birth, Apr 19
Judd, Naomi: Birth, Jan 11
Judd, Wynonna: Birth, May 30
Judgment Day, Jan 17
Juggling Day, World, Jun 17
Jule Fest (Elk Horn, IA), Nov 24
Julia, Raul: Birth Anniv, Mar 9
Julian, Percy: Birth Anniv, Apr 11
Jumbo the Elephant Arrives in America: Anniv, Apr 9
June Is Perennial Gardening Month, Jun 1
June Is Turkey Lovers' Month, Jun 1
Juneteenth, Jun 19
Junkanoo (Bahamas), Dec 26
Jupiter Effect: Anniv, Mar 10
Jupiter, Comet Crashes into: Anniv, Jul 16
Jurgensen, Sonny: Birth, Aug 23
Jury, First All-Woman: Anniv, Sep 22
Just for Laughs Fest (Montreal, QC, Canada), Jul 13
Just Pray No: Worldwide Weekend Prayer, Apr 23
Just, Ernest E.: Birth Anniv, Aug 14
Justice, David: Birth, Apr 14
Justice, US Dept of: Anniv, Jun 22

Kaczmarek, Jane: Birth, Dec 21
Kahanamoku, Duke: Birth Anniv, Aug 24
Kahlo, Frida: Birth Anniv, Jul 6
Kalb, Marvin: Birth, Jun 9
Kamali, Norma: Birth, Jun 27
Kamehameha Day (HI), Jun 11
Kanakaredes, Melina: Birth, Apr 23
Kanawa, Kiri Te: Birth, Mar 6
Kander, John: Birth, Mar 18
Kane, Bob: Batman Debuts: Anniv, May 1
Kane, Carol: Birth, Jun 18
Kansas
    Admission Day, Jan 29
    Apple Fest (Topeka), Oct 1
    Barbed Wire Swap/Sell (LaCrosse), May 5
    Beef Empire Days (Garden City), May 30
    Brownback, Sam: Birth, Sep 12
    Columbus Day Fest/Hot Air Balloon Regatta (Columbus), Oct 6
    Dalton Defenders Day (Coffeyville), Oct 6
    Dodge City Days (Dodge City), Jul 28
    Eagle Day at the Lake (Kansas City), Jan 21
    Eagle Days (Junction City), Jan 14
    Fiesta Bullwhacker/Wild West Show (Olathe), Sep 23
    Guitar Flat-Picking Chmpshps/Walnut Valley Fest, Natl (Winfield), Sep 14
    Heritage Christmas (Lindsborg), Dec 2
    Hoisington Celebration (Hoisington), Sep 1
    Inter-State Fair/Rodeo (Coffeyville), Aug 12
    Kansas City Renaissance Fest (Bonner Springs), Sep 2
    Little Balkans Days (Pittsburg), Aug 31
    Mennonite Relief Sale (Hutchinson), Apr 7
    Monster Myths by Moonlight (Milford), Oct 14
    NAIA Women's Soccer Natl Chmpshps (Olathe), Nov 15
    New Beginning Fest (Coffeyville), Apr 28
    Orphan Train Heritage Society Reunion (Concordia), Jun 9
    Oz Fest (Liberal), Oct 13
    Pancake Day, Intl (Liberal), Feb 28
    Pony Express Fest (Hanover), Aug 27
    Powered Parachute Fly-in (Columbus), Sep 21
    Quantrill's Raid on Lawrence, KS: Anniv, Aug 21
    Roberts, Pat: Birth, Apr 20
    Salter Elected First Woman Mayor in US: Anniv, Apr 4
    Sibelius, Kathleen: Birth, May 15
    State Fair (Hutchinson), Sep 8
    Swap Meet and Tractor Show (Washington), Jun 3
    Twelve Villages of Christmas (Washington County), Dec 1
    US Senior Open (Golf) Chmpshp (Hutchinson), Jul 6
    Winfield Art-in-the-Park Fest (Winfield), Oct 7
    Woofstock (Wichita), Oct 7

Kansas City Hotel Disaster: Anniv, Jul 17
Kaplan, Gabe: Birth, Mar 31
Kapoor, Shashi: Birth, Mar 18
Karan, Donna: Birth, Oct 2
Karaoke Week, Natl, Apr 23
Kariya, Paul: Birth, Oct 16
Karloff, Boris: Birth Anniv, Nov 23
Karn, Richard: Birth, Feb 17
Karras, Alex: Birth, Jul 15
Kasdan, Lawrence: Birth, Jan 14
Kasem, Casey: Birth, Apr 27
Kasparov, Garry: Birth, Apr 13
Kasparov, Garry: First Computer Chess Victory: Anniv, Feb 10
Katmai Natl Park: Anniv, Dec 2
Katt, William: Birth, Feb 16
Kauffmann, Stanley J.: Birth, Apr 24
Kaufmann, Christine: Birth, Jan 11
Kavner, Julie: Birth, Sep 7
Kaye, Danny: Birth Anniv, Jan 18
Kazakhstan
   Constitution Day, Aug 31
   Independence Day, Oct 25
Kazan, Elia: Birth Anniv, Sep 7
Kazan, Lainie: Birth, May 15
Kazurinsky, Tim: Birth, Mar 3
Keach, Stacy, Jr: Birth, Jun 2
Keane, Bil: Birth, Oct 5
Keaton, Buster: Birth Anniv, Oct 4
Keaton, Diane: Birth, Jan 5
Keaton, Michael: Birth, Sep 9
Keats, John: Birth Anniv, Oct 31
Keegan, Andrew: Birth, Jan 29
Keene, Donald: Birth, Jun 18
Keener, Catherine: Birth, Mar 26
Keep Kids Creative Week, Natl, Sep 24
Keeshan, Bob: Birth Anniv, Jun 27
Keillor, Garrison: Birth, Aug 7
Keitel, Harvey: Birth, May 13
Keith, David: Birth, May 8
Keller, Helen, Fest (Tuscumbia, AL), Jun 22
Keller, Helen: Birth Anniv, Jun 27
Keller, Helen: Miracle: Anniv, Apr 5
Kellerman, Sally: Birth, Jun 2
Kelley, Kitty: Birth, Apr 4
Kelly, Emmett: Birth Anniv, Dec 9
Kelly, Gene: Birth Anniv, Aug 23
Kelly, Gene: Singin' in the Rain Film Premiere: Anniv, Mar 27
Kelly, Grace: Birth Anniv, Nov 12
Kelly, Ned: Last Stand: Anniv, Jun 27
Kelly, Walt: Birth Anniv, Aug 25
Kelsey, Linda: Birth, Jul 28
Kemble, Fanny: Birth Anniv, Nov 27
Kemmler, William: First Electrocution for Death Penalty: Anniv, Aug 6
Kemp, Jack: Birth, Jul 13
Kemp, Shawn: Birth, Nov 26
Kempthorne, Dirk: Birth, Oct 29
Kenai Fjords Natl Park: Anniv, Dec 2
Keneally, Thomas: Birth, Oct 7
Kennan, George: Birth Anniv, Feb 16
Kennedy Intl Airport Dedication: Anniv, Jul 31
Kennedy, Anthony M.: Birth, Jul 23
Kennedy, Cortez: Birth, Aug 23
Kennedy, Edward Moore: Birth, Feb 22
Kennedy, Ethel: Birth, Apr 11
Kennedy, George: Birth, Feb 18
Kennedy, Jamie: Birth, May 25
Kennedy, John F., Jr: Birth Anniv, Nov 25
Kennedy, John Fitzgerald
   Assassination Anniv, Nov 22
   Birth Anniv, May 29
   Committee on Assassinations Report, Mar 29
   First Televised Presidential Debate: Anniv, Sep 26
   First Televised Presidential News Conf: Anniv, Jan 25
   Profiles in Courage Published: Anniv, Jan 1
   Warren Commission Report Anniv, Sep 27
Kennedy, Robert
   Assassination Anniv, Jun 5
   Birth Anniv, Nov 20
   Committee on Assassinations Report, Mar 29
Kennedy, William: Birth, Jan 16
Kennerly, David Hume: Birth, Mar 9
Kenny G: Birth, Jun 6
Kensit, Patsy: Birth, Mar 4
Kent State Students' Memorial Day, May 4
Kent, Jeff: Birth, Mar 7
Kentucky
   Admission Day, Jun 1
   American Quilter's Society Show (Paducah), Apr 26
   Battle of Blue Licks Celebration (Mount Olivet), Aug 19
   Berea Craft Fest (Berea), Jul 14
   Boone Day, Jun 7
   Breeder's Cup (Louisville), Nov 4

Bunning, Jim: Birth, Oct 23
   Christmas Candlelight Tour (Bardstown), Nov 24
   Confederate Memorial Day, Jun 3
   Daniel Boone Pioneer Festival (Winchester), Sep 1
   Everly Brothers/Central City Rock 'n Roll Cruise-In and Concert (Central City), Sep 1
   Fancy Farm Picnic (Fancy Farm), Aug 5
   Fest of the Bluegrass (Lexington), Jun 8
   Fletcher, Ernie: Birth, Nov 12
   Great American Brass Band Fest (Danville), Jun 10
   Indian Artifact Show (Owensboro), Aug 4
   Kentucky Apple Fest (Paintsville), Oct 6
   Kentucky Bourbon Fest (Bardstown), Sep 13
   Kentucky Derby (Louisville), May 6
   Kentucky Derby Fest (Louisville), Apr 21
   Kentucky State Chmpshp Fiddler's Contest (Falls of Rough), Jul 21
   Lincoln's Birthplace Cabin Wreath Laying (Hodgenville), Feb 12
   Maifest (Covington), May 19
   Mammoth Cave Natl Park Established: Anniv, Jul 1
   Marion County Country Ham Days (Lebanon), Sep 22
   McConnell, Mitch: Birth, Feb 20
   Memory Days (Grayson), May 20
   Mint Julep Scale Meet (Falls of Rough), May 19
   NAIA Men's and Women's Cross Country Natl Chmpshps (Louisville), Nov 18
   Oktoberfest (Covington), Sep 8
   River Raid Renaissance Fest and Goettafest (Covington), Jun 17
   Running of the Rodents (Louisville), Apr 10
   Sawyer/Louisville Landsharks Triathlon (Louisville), Aug 5
   Send a Kid to Kamp Radiothon (Lexington), May 6
   State Fair (Louisville), Aug 17
   Surrender of Fort Donelson: Anniv, Feb 16
   Swappin' Meetin' (Cumberland), Oct 6
   Williamsburg Old-Fashioned Trading Days (Williamsburg), Sep 7
Kentucky Derby, First: Anniv, May 17
Kenya
   Jamhuri Day, Dec 12
   Kenyatta Day, Oct 20
   Madaraka Day, Jun 1
Kepler, Johannes: Birth Anniv, Dec 27
Kercheval, Ken: Birth, Jul 15
Kern, Jerome: Birth Anniv, Jan 27
Kerns, Joanna: Birth, Feb 12
Kerouac, Jack: Birth Anniv, Mar 12
Kerr, Deborah: Birth, Sep 30
Kerr, Steve: Birth, Sep 27
Kerrigan, Nancy: Birth, Oct 13
Kerry, John F.: Birth, Dec 11
Kerwin, Brian: Birth, Oct 25
Kerwin, Lance: Birth, Nov 6
Kewpie Doll: Rose C. O'Neill: Birth Anniv, Jun 25
Key, Francis Scott: Birth Anniv, Aug 1
Key, Francis Scott: Star-Spangled Banner Inspired: Anniv, Sep 13
Keynes, John Maynard: Birth Anniv, Jun 5
Keys, Alicia: Birth, Jan 25
KGB Founder Statue Dismantled: Anniv, Aug 22
Khachaturian, Aram: Birth Anniv, Jun 6
Khan, Chaka: Birth, Mar 23
Khomeini, Ayatollah: Death Anniv, Jun 3
Kick-Butt Day, Natl, Oct 9
Kidd, Jason: Birth, Mar 23
Kidd, Michael: Birth, Aug 12
Kidder, Margot: Birth, Oct 17
KidFilm® Fest (Dallas, TX), Jan 9
Kidman, Nicole: Birth, Jun 20
Kidnapping, Lindbergh: Anniv, Mar 1
Kidney Month, Natl, Mar 1
Kids Care Week, Oct 22
Kids' Day, Kiwanis, Natl, Sep 23
Kids' Goal Setting Week, Nov 6
KidsDay, Natl, Aug 6
KidSpree, Jul 15
Kiel, Richard: Birth, Sep 13
Kilborn, Craig: Birth, Aug 24
Killebrew, Harmon: Birth, Jun 29
Killy, Jean-Claude: Birth, Aug 30
Kilmer, Joyce: Birth Anniv, Dec 6
Kilmer, Val: Birth, Dec 31
Kilpatrick, James: Birth, Nov 1
Kim Il Sung: Death Anniv, Jul 8
Kimbrough, Charles: Birth, May 23
Kimmel, Jimmy: Birth, Nov 13
Kind, Richard: Birth, Nov 22
Kindergarten Day, Apr 21
Kindergarten: Get Ready for Kindergarten Month, Aug 1
Kindness Day, World, Nov 13
King Family Show TV Premiere: Anniv, Jan 23
King James Bible Published: Anniv, May 2
King Kong Film Premiere: Anniv, Mar 2

King Tut Tomb Discovery: Anniv, Nov 4
King, B.B.: Birth, Sep 16
King, Ben E.: Birth, Sep 28
King, Bille Jean, Wins Battle of Sexes: Anniv, Sep 20
King, Billie Jean: Birth, Nov 22
King, Carole: Birth, Feb 9
King, Coretta Scott: Birth, Apr 27
King, Don: Birth, Aug 20
King, Frank: Birth Anniv, Apr 9
King, Larry: Birth, Nov 19
King, Martin Luther, Jr
   Assassination Anniv, Apr 4
   Awarded Nobel Peace Prize: Anniv, Oct 14
   Birth Anniv, Jan 15
   Birthday Observed, Jan 16
   Committee on Assassinations Report, Mar 29
   March on Washington: Anniv, Aug 28
   Martin Luther King, Jr, Federal Holiday, Jan 16
   Opposes Vietnam War: Anniv, Apr 4
   Stock Exchange Holiday, Jan 16
King, Perry: Birth, Apr 30
King, Rodney: Los Angeles Riots: Anniv, Apr 29
King, Stephen: Birth, Sep 21
King, W.L. MacKenzie: Birth Anniv, Dec 17
King, Wayne: Birth Anniv, Feb 16
King, William R.: Birth Anniv, Apr 7
Kingsley, Ben: Birth, Dec 31
Kingston, Alex: Birth, Mar 11
Kingsville Intl Young Performers' Competitions (Kingsville, TX), Apr 6
Kinnear, Greg: Birth, Jun 17
Kinney, Kathy: Birth, Nov 3
Kinsey, Alfred: Birth Anniv, Jun 23
Kinski, Nastassja: Birth, Jan 24
Kipling, Rudyard: Birth Anniv, Dec 30
Kirby, Bruno: Birth, Apr 28
Kiribati: Independence Day, Jul 12
Kirshner, Don: Birth, Apr 17
Kirtland, Jared: Birth Anniv, Nov 10
Kiss-and-Make-Up-Day, Aug 25
Kissimmee Slough Shootout and Rendezvous (Big Cypress Reservation, FL), Feb 3
Kissinger, Henry: Birth, May 27
Kite Flying Day, Mar 27
Kite, Tom: Birth, Dec 9
Kites, Kite-Flying
   Frankenmuth Skyfest (Frankenmuth, MI), May 7
   Kite Fest of Santiago Sacatepequez (Guatemala), Nov 1
   Kite Flying Day, Mar 27
   Kite Month, Natl, Apr 1
Kitt, Eartha: Birth, Jan 17
Kiwanis
   Kiwanis Intl: Anniv, Jan 21
   Kiwanis Kids' Day, Natl, Sep 23
   Kiwanis Prayer Week, May 14
Klein, Calvin: Birth, Nov 19
Klein, Robert: Birth, Feb 8
Kliban, B(ernard): Birth Anniv, Jan 1
Kline, Kevin: Birth, Oct 24
Klondike Days (Eagle River, WI), Feb 18
Klondike Eldorado Gold Discovery: Anniv, Aug 31
Klondike Gold Discovery: Anniv, Aug 16
Klugman, Jack: Birth, Apr 27
Knievel, Evel: Birth, Oct 17
Knight, Bobby: Birth, Oct 25
Knight, Gladys: Birth, May 28
Knight, O. Raymond: Birth Anniv, Apr 8
Knight, Shirley: Birth, Jul 5
Knightley, Keira: Birth, Mar 26
Knights of Columbus Family Week, Aug 12
Knights of Columbus Founder's Day, Mar 29
Knights of Pythias: Founding Anniv, Feb 19
Knock-Knock Day, Natl, Oct 31
Knotts, Don: Birth, Jul 21
Knowles, Beyonce: Birth, Sep 4
Knox County Scenic Drive (Galesburg, IL), Oct 7
Knuckles Down Month, Natl, Apr 1
Kobuk Valley Natl Park: Anniv, Dec 2
Koch, Edward: Birth, Dec 12
Koenig, Walter: Birth, Sep 14
Koestler, Arthur: Birth Anniv, Sep 5
Kohl, Herb: Birth, Feb 7
Koko the Gorilla: Birth, Jul 4
Kokoschka, Oskar: Birth Anniv, Mar 1
Kolzig, Olaf: Birth, Apr 6
Koop, C. Everett: Birth, Oct 14
Kopell, Bernie: Birth, Jun 21
Koppel, Ted: Birth, Feb 8
Korbut, Olga: Birth, May 16
Korea
   Alphabet Day (Hangul), Oct 9
   Chusok, Oct 6
   Constitution Day, Jul 17
   Independence Day, Aug 15
   Korea, North and South, End War: Anniv, Dec 13

Korea (cont'd)—Lee

Korean Air Lines Flight 007 Disaster: Anniv, **Sep 1**
Korean War Armistice: Anniv, **Jul 27**
Korean War Began: Anniv, **Jun 25**
Memorial Day, **Jun 6**
National Day, **Sep 9**
National Foundation, **Oct 3**
Samiljol (Independence Movement Day), **Mar 1**
Seoul Recaptured by UN Forces, **Mar 14**
Tano Day, **May 31**
Korean War Veterans Armistice Day, Natl (Pres Proc), **Jul 27**
Korman, Harvey: Birth, **Feb 15**
Kosar, Bernie: Birth, **Nov 25**
Kosciusko, Thaddeus: Birth Anniv, **Feb 4**
Kotto, Yaphet: Birth, **Nov 15**
Koufax, Sandy: Birth, **Dec 30**
Kournikova, Anna: Birth, **Jun 7**
Kovacs, Ernie: Birth Anniv, **Jan 23**
Kozak, Harley Jane: Birth, **Jan 28**
Krabbe, Jeroen: Birth, **Dec 5**
Kraft Nabisco Chmpshp (Rancho Mirage, CA), **Mar 27**
Kraft Television Theatre TV Premiere: Anniv, **May 7**
Krakatoa Eruption: Anniv, **Aug 26**
Krall, Diana: Birth, **Nov 16**
Krampuslauf (Austria), **Dec 5**
Krantz, Judith: Birth, **Jan 9**
Krassner, Paul: Birth, **Apr 9**
Krause, Peter: Birth, **Aug 12**
Kravitz, Lenny: Birth, **May 26**
Kreis, Jason: Birth **Dec 29**
Kreuk, Kristin: Birth, **Dec 30**
Kreutzmann, Bill, Jr: Birth, **Jun 7**
Krige, Alice: Birth, **Jun 28**
Krim, Mathilde: Birth, **Jul 9**
Kristallnacht: Anniv, **Nov 9**
Kristofferson, Kris: Birth, **Jun 22**
Kroft, Steve: Birth **Aug 22**
Krone, Julie: Birth, **Jul 24**
Krupp, Alfried: Birth Anniv, **Aug 13**
Kubek, Tony: Birth, **Oct 12**
Kubrick, Stanley: Birth Anniv, **Jul 26**
Kudrow, Lisa: Birth **Jul 30**
Kuhn, Bowie: Birth, **Oct 28**
Kuhn, Margaret: Birth Anniv, **Aug 3**
Kukla, Fran and Ollie TV Premiere: Anniv, **Nov 29**
Kulongoski, Ted: Birth, **Nov 5**
Kung Fu TV Premiere: Anniv, **Oct 1**
Kunis, Mila: Birth **Aug 14**
Kunta Kinte Heritage Festival (Crownsville, MD), **Aug 12**
Kupets, Courtney: Birth, **Jul 27**
Kuralt, Charles: Birth Anniv, **Sep 10**
Kurban Bayram: See Eid-al-Adha, **Jan 10**
Kurban Bayram: See Eid-al-Adha, **Dec 31**
Kurosawa, Akira: Birth Anniv, **Mar 23**
Kurri, Jari: Birth, **May 18**
Kurtis, Bill: Birth, **Sep 21**
Kurtz, Swoosie: Birth, **Sep 6**
Kurtzman, Harvey: Birth Anniv, **Oct 3**
Kustom Kemps of America Car Show (Biglerville, PA), **Jun 9**
Kutcher, Ashton: Birth, **Feb 7**
Kutner, Luis: Birth Anniv, **Jun 9**
Kuumba on the Beach (Hollywood, FL), **Apr 15**
Kuwait
  Iraq Invades Kuwait: Anniv, **Aug 2**
  Kuwait Liberated: Anniv, **Feb 27**
  National Day, **Feb 25**
Kwan, Michelle: Birth, **Jul 7**
Kwanzaa, **Dec 26**
Kyl, Jon: Birth, **Apr 25**
Kyrgyzstan: Independence Day, **Aug 31**
Kyser, Kay: Birth Anniv, **Jun 18**

La Befana (Italy), **Jan 6**
La Guardia, Fiorello: Birth Anniv, **Dec 11**
LA Law TV Premiere: Anniv, **Oct 3**
La Placa, Alison: Birth, **Dec 16**
La Russa, Tony, Jr: Birth, **Oct 4**
La Salle, Eriq: Birth, **Jul 23**
LaBelle, Patti: Birth, **May 24**
Labonte, Bobby: Birth, **May 8**
Labor Day Picnic (Live Oak, FL), **Sep 1**
Labor. See also Careers
  AFL Founded: Anniv, **Dec 8**
  AFL-CIO Founded: Anniv, **Dec 5**
  Day of the Holy Cross, **May 3**
  Five-Dollar-a-Day Minimum Wage: Anniv, **Jan 5**
  Haymarket Pardon: Anniv, **Jun 26**
  Haymarket Square Riot: Anniv, **May 4**
  International Workers of the World (IWW) Founded: Anniv, **Jun 27**
  Jones, Mary H.: Birth Anniv, **May 1**
  Labor Day, **Sep 4**
  Labor Day, **May 1**
  Labor Day (Bahamas), **Jun 2**

Labor Relations Act, Natl: Anniv, **Jul 5**
Ludlow Mine Incident: Anniv, **Apr 20**
Montgomery Ward Seized: Anniv, **Apr 26**
Murray, Philip: Birth Anniv, **May 25**
Schneiderman, Rose: Birth Anniv, **Apr 6**
Lachey, Nick: Birth, **Nov 9**
Lacoste, Rene: Birth Anniv, **Jul 2**
Lacroix, Christian: Birth, **May 17**
Lacrosse: NCAA Division I Women's Chmpshp (Boston, MA), **May 26**
Ladd, Cheryl: Birth, **Jul 12**
Ladd, David Alan: Birth, **Feb 5**
Ladd, Diane: Birth, **Nov 29**
Ladies' Day Initiated in Baseball: Anniv, **Jun 16**
Laennec, Rene: Birth Anniv, **Feb 17**
Laettner, Christian: Birth, **Aug 17**
Lafayette, Marquis de: Birth Anniv, **Sep 6**
Laffer, Arthur: Birth, **Aug 14**
LaFleur, Guy: Birth, **Sep 20**
Lag B'Omer, **May 16**
Lagerfeld, Karl: Birth, **Sep 10**
Lagerlof, Selma: Birth Anniv, **Nov 20**
Lahti, Christine: Birth, **Apr 4**
Lailat ul Qadr: (Islamic) Night of Power, **Oct 14**
Laimbeer, Bill, Jr: Birth, **May 19**
Laine, Frankie: Birth, **Mar 30**
Lake Clark Natl Park: Anniv, **Dec 2**
Lake Fest, Virginia (Clarksville, VA), **Jul 13**
Lake, Ricki: Birth, **Sep 21**
Laker, Freddie: Birth, **Aug 6**
Lalas, Alexi: Birth, **Jun 1**
Lamas, Lorenzo: Birth, **Jan 20**
Lamb, Charles: Birth Anniv, **Feb 10**
Lambert, Christopher: Birth, **Mar 29**
Lamour, Dorothy: Birth Anniv, **Dec 10**
Lancaster, Burt: Birth Anniv, **Nov 2**
Land Mine Ban: Anniv, **Mar 1**
Landau, Martin: Birth, **Jun 20**
Landers, Ann: Birth Anniv, **Jul 4**
Landesberg, Steve: Birth, **Nov 3**
Landis, Kenesaw: Birth Anniv, **Nov 20**
Lando, Joe: Birth, **Dec 9**
Landon, Michael, Jr: Birth, **Jun 20**
Landon, Michael: Birth Anniv, **Oct 31**
Landrieu, Mary L.: Birth, **Nov 23**
Landscape Architecture Month, Natl, **Apr 1**
Landsgemeinde (Switzerland), **Apr 30**
Lane, Diane: Birth, **Jan 22**
Lane, Mark: Birth, **Feb 24**
Lane, Nathan: Birth, **Feb 3**
lang, k.d.: Birth, **Nov 2**
Lang, Stephen: Birth, **Jul 11**
Lange, Hope: Birth, **Nov 28**
Lange, Jessica: Birth, **Apr 20**
Langella, Frank: Birth, **Jan 1**
Langer, A.J.: Birth, **May 22**
Langer, Susanne: Birth Anniv, **Dec 20**
Langley, Samuel Pierpont: Birth Anniv, **Aug 22**
Langston, Mark: Birth, **Aug 20**
Lansbury, Angela: Birth, **Oct 16**
Lansing, Sherry: Birth, **Jul 31**
Lansky, Aaron: Birth, **Jul 17**
Lantz, Walter: Birth Anniv, **Apr 27**
Lanvin, Bernard: Birth, **Dec 27**
Laos: Natl Holiday, **Dec 2**
Lappe, Frances Moore: Birth, **Feb 10**
Lardner, Ring Jr: Birth Anniv, **Aug 19**
Lardner, Ring: Birth Anniv, **Mar 6**
Laredo, Ruth: Birth, **Nov 20**
Largent, Steve: Birth, **Sep 28**
Larkin, Barry: Birth, **Apr 28**
Larroquette, John: Birth, **Nov 25**
Larry King Show TV Premiere: Anniv, **Mar 13**
Larson, Gary: Birth, **Aug 14**
Lasek, Bucky: Birth, **Dec 3**
Laser Patented: Anniv, **Mar 22**
Lasorda, Tommy: Birth, **Sep 22**
Lassen Volcanic Natl Park Established: Anniv, **Aug 9**
Lasser, Louise: Birth, **Apr 11**
Lassie TV Premiere: Anniv, **Sep 12**
Late Night with David Letterman TV Premiere: Anniv, **Feb 1**
Lathrop, Julia C.: Birth Anniv, **Jun 29**
Latvia
  Baltic States' Independence Recognized: Anniv, **Sep 6**
  Independence Day, **Nov 18**
  John's Day (Midsummer Night Day), **Jun 24**
Lauder, Estee: Birth Anniv, **Jul 1**
Lauer, Andy: Birth, **Jun 19**
Lauer, Matt: Birth, **Dec 30**
Laugh and Get Rich Day, **Feb 8**
Laugh at Work Week, **Apr 1**
Laugh-In TV Premiere: Anniv, **Jan 22**
Lauper, Cyndi: Birth, **Jun 20**
Laura Ingalls Wilder Pageant (De Smet, SD), **Jul 7**

Laurel and Hardy: Cuckoo Dancing Week, **Jan 11**
Laurel, Stan: Birth Anniv, **Jun 16**
Lauren, Ralph: Birth, **Oct 14**
Lauria, Dan: Birth, **Apr 12**
Laurie, Piper: Birth, **Jan 22**
Laurier, Sir Wilfred: Birth Anniv, **Nov 20**
Lautenberg, Frank: Birth, **Jan 23**
Lauter, Ed: Birth, **Oct 30**
Lavallette Heritage Arts & Crafts Show (Lavallette, NJ), **Jul 30**
Laver, Rod: Birth, **Aug 9**
Laverne and Shirley TV Premiere: Anniv, **Jan 27**
Lavin, Linda: Birth, **Oct 15**
Lavoisier, Antoine: Execution Anniv, **May 8**
Law & Order TV Premiere: Anniv, **Sep 13**
Law Day, USA (Pres Proc), **May 1**
Law Enforcement Appreciation Month in Florida, **May 1**
Law, John Philip: Birth, **Sep 7**
Law, Jude: Birth, **Dec 29**
Law: Mansfield, Arabella: Birth Anniv, **May 23**
Lawless, Lucy: Birth, **Mar 29**
Lawn Mower Race, Sta-Bil Natl Chmpshp (Mansfield, OH), **Sep 2**
Lawrence (of Arabia), T.E.: Birth Anniv, **Aug 16**
Lawrence Welk Show TV Premiere: Anniv, **Jul 2**
Lawrence, Carol: Birth, **Sep 5**
Lawrence, David H.: Birth Anniv, **Sep 11**
Lawrence, Jacob: Birth Anniv, **Sep 7**
Lawrence, James: Birth Anniv, **Oct 1**
Lawrence, Joey: Birth, **Apr 20**
Lawrence, Martin: Birth, **Apr 16**
Lawrence, Sharon: Birth, **Jun 29**
Lawrence, Steve: Birth, **Jul 8**
Lawrence, Vicki: Birth, **Mar 26**
Lazar, Irving ("Swifty"): Birth Anniv, **Mar 28**
Lazarus Saturday, **Apr 15**
Lazarus, Procession of Icon of Saint (Cyprus), **Apr 15**
Le Mat, Paul: Birth, **Sep 22**
Leach, Robin: Birth, **Aug 29**
Leachman, Cloris: Birth, **Apr 30**
Leacock, Stephen: Birth Anniv, **Dec 30**
Leadership Success Day, **Feb 7**
Leadership Week Intl, **Feb 5**
Leadership: Courageous Follower Day, **Mar 4**
League of Nations: Anniv, **Jan 10**
League of United Latin American Citizens (LULAC) Founded: Anniv, **Feb 17**
League of Women Voters Formed: Anniv, **Feb 14**
Leahy, Patrick J.: Birth, **Mar 31**
Leakey, Richard E.: Birth, **Dec 19**
Lean, Sir David: Birth Anniv, **Mar 25**
Leap Second Adjustment Time, **Jun 30, Dec 31**
Leap Year Day, **Feb 1**
Leap Year: Bachelors Day, **Feb 1**
Lear, Edward: Birth Anniv, **May 12**
Lear, Evelyn: Birth, **Jan 18**
Lear, Norman: Birth, **Jul 27**
Learned, Michael: Birth, **Apr 9**
Learning Disabilities Assn Intl Conf (New Orleans, LA), **Mar 1**
Leary, Timothy Francis: Birth Anniv, **Oct 22**
Leaud, Jean-Pierre: Birth, **May 5**
Leave It to Beaver TV Premiere: Anniv, **Oct 4**
Leave the Office Earlier Day, Natl, **Jun 2**
Leavitt, Mike: Birth, **Feb 11**
Lebanon
  Independence Day, **Nov 22**
  Last American Hostage Released: Anniv, **Dec 4**
  Palestinian Massacre: Anniv, **Sep 16**
  St. Maron's Day, **Feb 9**
LeBlanc, Matt: Birth, **Jul 25**
LeBon, Simon: Birth, **Oct 27**
Lebowitz, Fran: Birth, **Oct 27**
LeCarre, John: Birth, **Oct 19**
Ledger, Heath: Birth, **Apr 4**
Lee, Ang: Birth, **Oct 23**
Lee, Ann: Birth Anniv, **Feb 1**
Lee, Brenda: Birth, **Dec 11**
Lee, Bruce: Birth Anniv, **Nov 27**
Lee, Christopher: Birth, **May 27**
Lee, Francis Lightfoot: Birth Anniv, **Oct 14**
Lee, Harper: Birth, **Apr 28**
Lee, Michele: Birth, **Jun 24**
Lee, Peggy: Birth Anniv, **May 26**
Lee, Pinky (Pincus Leff): Birth Anniv, **May 2**
Lee, Richard Henry: Birth Anniv, **Jan 20**
Lee, Robert E.
  Battle of Spotsylvania: Anniv, **May 12**
  Battle of the Wilderness: Anniv, **May 5**
  Birth Anniv, **Jan 19**
  Defeat at Five Forks: Anniv, **Apr 1**
  Fall of Richmond: Anniv, **Apr 3**
  Lee-Jackson Day, **Jan 13**
  Seven Days Campaign: Anniv, **Jun 25**
Lee, Spike: Birth, **Mar 20**

Leetch, Brian: Birth, Mar 3
Leeves, Jane: Birth, Apr 18
Legal Assistants Day, Mar 26
Legrand, Michel: Birth, Feb 24
LeGuin, Ursula K.: Birth, Oct 21
Leguizamo, John: Birth, Jul 22
Lehrer, James: Birth, May 19
Lehrer, Tom: Birth, Apr 9
Lei Day (Hawaii), May 1
Leibman, Ron: Birth, Oct 11
Leif Ericson Day Celebration (Philadelphia, PA), Oct 9
Leigh, Janet: Birth Anniv, Jul 6
Leigh, Janet: Psycho Film Premiere: Anniv, Jun 16
Leigh, Jennifer Jason: Birth, Feb 5
Leigh, Vivian: Gone with the Wind Film Premiere: Anniv, Dec 15
Leland, David: Birth, Apr 20
LeMay, Curtis: Birth Anniv, Nov 15
Lemieux, Mario: Birth, Oct 5
Lemmon, Jack: Birth Anniv, Feb 8
Lemon, Meadowlark: Birth, Apr 25
LeMond, Greg: Birth, Jun 26
LeMoyne House Candlelight Christmas Tours (Washington, PA), Dec 2
Lendl, Ivan: Birth, Mar 7
L'Enfant, Pierre C.: Birth Anniv, Aug 2
L'Engle, Madeleine: Birth, Nov 29
Lenin, Nikolai: Birth Anniv, Apr 22
Lennon, John: Bed-in for Peace: Anniv, Mar 25
Lennon, John: Birth Anniv, Oct 9
Lennon, John: Death Anniv, Dec 8
Lennon, Julian: Birth, Apr 8
Lennox, Annie: Birth, Dec 25
Leno, Jay: Birth, Apr 28
Lent, Mar 1
Lent, Orthodox, Mar 6
Lenz, Kay: Birth, Mar 4
Leo Begins, Jul 23
Leonard, Elmore: Birth, Oct 11
Leonard, Justin: Birth, Jun 15
Leonard, Robert Sean: Birth, Feb 28
Leonard, Sugar Ray: Birth, May 17
Leonardo Da Vinci: Death Anniv, May 2
Leoni, Tea: Birth, Feb 25
Leopold, Aldo: Aldo Leopold Weekend (WI), Mar 3
Lerner, Michael: Birth, Jun 22
Leroux, Charles: Last Jump: Anniv, Sep 12
Leslie, Lisa: Birth, Jul 7
Lesotho
  Army Day, Jan 20
  Independence Day, Oct 4
  Moshoeshoe's Day, Mar 12
  Tree Planting Day, Natl, Mar 21
Lester, Mark: Birth, Jul 11
Lester, Richard: Birth, Jan 19
Let It Go Day, Jun 23
Lethem, Jonathan: Birth, Feb 19
Let's Make a Deal TV Premiere: Anniv, Dec 30
Letter from America Radio Premiere: Anniv, Mar 24
Letterman, David: Birth, Apr 12
Letter-Writing Week, Universal, Jan 8
Leutze, Emanuel: Birth Anniv, May 24
Levin, Carl: Birth, Jun 28
Levine, Charles A.: Death Anniv, Dec 6
Levine, David: Birth, Dec 20
Levine, Irving R.: Birth, Aug 26
Levine, James: Birth, Jun 23
Levinson, Barry: Birth, Apr 6
Levy, Eugene: Birth, Dec 17
Lewis & Clark Expedition
  Among the Niimiipuu (Lewiston, ID), Jun 14
  Clark on the Yellowstone (Billings, MT), Jul 22
  Clark, William: Birth Anniv, Aug 1
  Confluence with Destiny (St. Louis, MO), Sep 23
  Expedition Commissioned: Anniv, Jan 18
  Expedition Reaches the Pacific Ocean: Anniv, Nov 16
  Expedition Returns: Anniv, Sep 23
  Expedition Sets Out: Anniv, May 14
  Lewis and Clark Days (Washburn, ND), Jun 16
  Lewis and Clark Heritage Days (St. Charles, MO), May 20
  Lewis, Meriwether: Birth Anniv, Aug 18
  Reunion at the Home of Sakakawea (New Town, ND), Aug 17
  Sacagawea: Death Anniv, Dec 20
Lewis, Anthony: Birth, Mar 27
Lewis, C.S.: Birth Anniv, Nov 29
Lewis, Carl: Birth, Jul 1
Lewis, Clea: Birth, Jul 19
Lewis, Emmanuel: Birth, Mar 9
Lewis, Francis: Birth Anniv, Mar 21
Lewis, Gary: Birth, Jul 31
Lewis, Huey: Birth, Jul 5

Lewis, Jerry Lee: Birth, Sep 29
Lewis, Jerry: Birth, Mar 16
Lewis, John L.: Birth Anniv, Feb 12
Lewis, Juliette: Birth, Jun 21
Lewis, Meriwether: Birth Anniv, Aug 18
Lewis, Ramsey: Birth, May 27
Lewis, Sinclair: Birth Anniv, Feb 7
Lewis, Sinclair: Sinclair Lewis Days (Sauk Centre, MN), Jul 9
Lewis, Vicki: Birth, Mar 17
Li, Jet: Birth, Apr 26
Liar's Contest, Big Whopper (New Harmony, IN), Sep 16
Libby, Willard F.: Birth Anniv, Dec 17
Liberace
  Birth Anniv, May 16
  Birthday Celebration & Play-A-Like Competition (Las Vegas, NV), May 13
  Museum Christmas Tree Lighting (Las Vegas, NV), Dec 7
  TV Show Premiere: Anniv, Jul 1
Liberation Day (Poland), Jan 17
Liberia
  Flag Day, Aug 24
  J.J. Roberts Day, Mar 15
  National Day, Jul 26
Liberty Day, Mar 23
Libra Begins, Sep 23
Libraries Remember, Sep 11
Library/Librarians
  American Library Assn Annual Conf (New Orleans, LA), Jun 22
  Boston Public Library: Anniv, Apr 3
  Church/Synagogue Library Assn Conf (Greensboro, NC), Jul 30
  Federation of Library Assns Annual Conf, Intl (Seoul, South Korea), Aug 20
  First Presidential Library: Anniv, Nov 19
  Freedom of Information Day, Mar 16
  Friends of Lake Forest Library Book Sale (Lake Forest, IL), Sep 15
  Library Assn, American: Founding, Oct 6
  Library Card Sign-up Month, Sep 1
  Library Legislative Day, May 1
  Library Lovers' Month, Feb 1
  Library of Congress: Anniv, Apr 24
  Library Week, Natl, Apr 2
  Medical Librarians Month, Natl, Oct 1
  New York Public Library: Anniv, May 23
  School Library Media Month, Apr 1
  Teen Read Week, Oct 15
  Thank You, School Librarian Day, Apr 5
Libya
  British Bases Evacuation Day, Mar 28
  Evacuation Day, Jun 11
  Independence Day, Dec 24
  Revolution Day, Sep 1
License Plates, First: Anniv, Apr 25
Lichtenstein, Roy: Birth Anniv, Oct 27
Licorice Day, World, Apr 12
Liddy, G. Gordon: Birth, Nov 30
Lieberman, Joseph: Birth, Feb 24
Liebling, A.J.: Birth Anniv, Oct 18
Liechtenstein: National Day, Aug 15
Life Balance Month, Intl, Jan 1
Life Coach Recognition Week, May 8
Life Magazine Debuts: Anniv, Nov 23
Life Month, Celebration of, Jan 1
Life Week, Celebration of, Jan 1
Lifewriting Month, Natl, Nov 1
Light the Night for Sight, May 1
Light, Judith: Birth, Feb 9
Lightfoot, Gordon: Birth, Nov 17
Ligonier Highland Games (Ligonier, PA), Sep 8
Lil Margaret's Bluegrass and Old-Time Music Fest (Leonardtown, MD), Aug 10
Lilac Fest (Mackinac Island, MI), Jun 9
Liliuokalani Deposed, Queen: Anniv, Jan 17
Lillard, Matthew: Birth, Jan 24
Lilly, Evangeline: Birth, Aug 3
Lilly, William: Birth Anniv, Apr 30
Limbaugh, Rush, Natl Radio Show Premiere: Anniv, Aug 1
Limbaugh, Rush: Birth, Jan 12
Limerick Day, May 12
Lincoln, Abraham
  Assassination Anniv, Apr 14
  Assassination Conspirators Hanging, Jul 7
  Birth Anniv, Feb 12
  Birthday Observance (OR), Feb 6
  Emancipation Proclamation Takes Effect: Anniv, Jan 1
  Emancipation Proclamation: Anniv, Sep 22
  Gettysburg Address: Anniv, Nov 19
  Lincoln Memorial Dedication: Anniv, May 30
  Lincoln's Birthplace Cabin Wreath Laying (Hodgenville, KY), Feb 12
  Lost Penny Day, Feb 12

Peninsula Campaign Intensified: Anniv, May 9
Signs Income Tax: Anniv, May 9
Lincoln, Blanche Lambert: Birth, Sep 30
Lincoln, Mary Todd: Birth Anniv, Dec 13
Lind, Jenny: Birth Anniv, Oct 6
Lind, Jenny: US Premiere, Sep 11
Lindbergh Flight: Anniv, May 20
Lindbergh Kidnapping: Anniv, Mar 1
Lindbergh Kidnapping: Hauptmann Execution: Anniv, Apr 3
Lindbergh, Anne M.: Birth Anniv, Jun 22
Lindbergh, Charles A.: Birth Anniv, Feb 4
Linden, Hal: Birth, Mar 20
Lindros, Eric: Birth, Feb 28
Lindsay, Robert: Birth, Dec 12
Lingle, Linda: Birth, Jun 4
Linn-Baker, Mark: Birth, Jun 17
Linney, Laura: Birth, Feb 5
Liotta, Ray: Birth, Dec 18
Lipinski, Tara: Birth, Jun 10
Lippman, Walter: Birth Anniv, Sep 23
Lips Appreciation Day, Mar 16
Lipton, Peggy: Birth, Aug 30
Lisbon Earthquake: Anniv, Nov 1
Lisi, Virna: Birth, Nov 8
Listening Awareness Month, Intl, Mar 1
Lister, Joseph: Birth Anniv, Apr 5
Liston, Sonny: Birth Anniv, May 8
Liszt, Franz: Birth Anniv, Oct 22
Litchfield Open House Tour (Litchfield, CT), Jul 7
Literacy Day, Intl (UN), Sep 8
Literacy: Stories Day, Apr 5
Literature
  American Poet Laureate Establishment: Anniv, Dec 20
  Amis, Kingsley: Birth Anniv, Apr 16
  Anne Bradstreet Day, Sep 16
  Asimov, Isaac: Birth Anniv, Jan 2
  Authors' Day, Natl, Nov 1
  Bad Poetry Day, Aug 18
  Be Kind to Editors and Writers Month, Sep 1
  Beckett, Samuel: Birth Anniv, Apr 13
  Biographers Day, May 16
  Black Poetry Day, Oct 18
  Bollingen Prize Award: Anniv, Feb 19
  Buck, Pearl S.: Birth Anniv, Jun 26
  Child, Lydia Maria: Birth Anniv, Feb 11
  Cooper, James Fenimore: Birth Anniv, Sep 15
  Dickens, Charles: Birth Anniv, Feb 7
  Edgar Allan Poe Fest (Manheim, PA), Oct 27
  Eliot, T.S.: Birth Anniv, Sep 26
  Eliza Doolittle Day, May 20
  Emerson, Ralph Waldo: Birth Anniv, May 25
  First Magazine Published in America: Anniv, Feb 13
  Grapes of Wrath Published: Anniv, Apr 14
  Hay-on-Wye Fest of Literature (Hay-on-Wye, Wales), May 26
  Hobbit Day, Sep 22
  I Love to Write Day, Nov 15
  Laura Ingalls Wilder Gingerbread Sociable (Pomona, CA), Feb 4
  Merriam, Eve: Birth Anniv, Jul 19
  Mystery Series Week, Oct 1
  Orwell, George: Birth Anniv, Jun 25
  P.V. Helmerich Distinguished Author Award (Tulsa, OK), Dec 1
  Poe, Edgar Allan: Birth Anniv, Jan 19
  Poetry Month, Natl, Apr 1
  Pulitzer Prizes First Awarded: Anniv, Jun 4
  Silent Spring Publication: Anniv, Apr 13
  Smith, Thorne: Birth Anniv, Mar 27
  Stowe, Harriet Beecher: Birth Anniv, Jun 14
  Texas Book Fest (Austin, TX), Oct 27
  The Duchess Who Wasn't Day, Aug 27
  Tolkien Week, Sep 17
  Tolkien, J.R.R.: Birth Anniv, Jan 3
  Underdog Day, Dec 15
  Vercors, Jean: Birth Anniv, Feb 26
  Ways With Words Literature Fest (Dartington, England), Jul 7
  Wheatley, Phillis: Death Anniv, Dec 5
  White, E.B.: Birth Anniv, Jul 11
  Whitman, Walt: Birth Anniv, May 31
  Wilde, Oscar: Birth Anniv, Oct 16
  Words by the Water: A Cumbrian Literature Fest (Lake District, England), Mar 10
  Zora Neale Hurston Fest (Eatonville, FL), Jan 25
Lithgow, John: Birth, Oct 19
Lithuania
  Baltic States' Independence Recognized: Anniv, Sep 6
  Day of Statehood, Jul 6
  Independence Day, Feb 16
  Restitution of Independence Day, Mar 11
Little Bighorn Days (Hardin, MT), Jun 21
Little House on the Prairie TV Premiere: Anniv, Sep 11

Little League—Lyon

Little League Baseball Week, Natl (Pres Proc), Jun 12
Little League Baseball World Series (Williamsport, PA), Aug 18
Little Orphan Annie: Gray, Harold Lincoln: Birth Anniv, Jan 20
Little Richard: Birth, Dec 5
Little Rock Nine: Anniv, Sep 4
Little, Cleavon: Birth Anniv, Jun 1
Little, Malcolm: Assassination Anniv, Feb 21
Little, Rich: Birth, Nov 26
Liu, Lucy: Birth, Dec 2
Live Aid Concerts: Anniv, Jul 13
Livermore, Mary: Birth Anniv, Dec 19
Livestock Show, Rio Grande Valley (Mercedes, TX), Mar 11
Livestock Show/Rodeo, Southwestern Expo (Fort Worth, TX), Jan 13
Livingston, Philip: Birth Anniv, Jan 15
Livingston, Robert: Birth Anniv, Nov 27
Livingston, Stanley: Birth, Nov 24
Livingstone, David: Birth Anniv, Mar 19
Livingstone, Stanley Finds: Anniv, Nov 10
Lizard Race, World's Greatest (Lovington, NM), Jul 4
Lloyd Webber, Andrew: Birth, Mar 22
Lloyd, Christopher: Birth, Oct 22
Lloyd, Emily: Birth, Sep 29
Lloyd, Eric: Birth, May 19
Lloyd, Harold: Birth Anniv, Apr 20
Lloyd, Sabrina: Birth, Nov 20
Lobo, Rebecca: Birth, Oct 6
Lobster Fest, Maine (Rockland, ME), Aug 2
Lobsterfest (Mystic, CT), May 27
Locke, John: Birth Anniv, Aug 29
Locke, Sondra: Birth, May 28
Lockhart, June: Birth, Jun 25
Lockhart, Keith: Birth, Nov 7
Locklear, Heather: Birth, Sep 25
Lockport Old Canal Days (Lockport, IL), Jun 16
Lockwood, Belva A. Bennett: Birth Anniv, Oct 24
Lockwood, Gary: Birth, Feb 21
Locust Plague of 1874: Anniv, Jul 20
Loewy, Raymond: Birth Anniv, Nov 5
Lofgren, Nils: Birth, Jun 21
Lofton, James: Birth, Jul 5
Lofton, Kenny: Birth, May 31
Log Cabin Day (Michigan), Jun 25
Log Home Show and Natl Fest of the West (Scottsdale, AZ), Mar 16
Loggia, Robert: Birth, Jan 3
Logging and Timber Industry; Logger Competition
  Logging Museum Fest Days (Rangeley, ME), Jul 28
  Lumberjack World Chmpshps (Hayward, WI), Jul 28
  Maynooth Madness (Maynooth, ON, Canada), Sep 1
  Paul Bunyan Show (Nelsonville, OH), Oct 6
  Tupper Lake Woodsmen's Days (Tupper Lake, NY), Jul 8
Loggins, Kenny: Birth, Jan 7
Lohan, Lindsay: Birth, Jul 2
Lollobrigida, Gina: Birth, Jul 4
Loloma, Charles: Birth Anniv, Jun 9
Lombardi, Vince: Birth Anniv, Jun 11
Lombroso, Cesare: Birth Anniv, Nov 18
London Book Fair (London, England), Mar 5
London Terrorist Bombings: Anniv, Jul 7
London to Brighton Veteran Car Run (England), Nov 5
London, Jack: Birth Anniv, Jan 12
London, Jeremy: Birth, Nov 7
Lone Ranger TV Premiere: Anniv, Sep 15
Long Beach Bayou Fest (Long Beach, CA), Jun 23
Long Count Day, Sep 22
Long Term Care Planning Month, Oct 1
Long, Crawford: First Use Anesthetic (Doctor's Day), Mar 30
Long, Howie: Birth, Jan 6
Long, Huey P.: Day, Aug 30
Long, Shelley: Birth, Aug 23
Longest Dam Run (Fort Peck, MT), Jun 17
Longest War in History Ends: Anniv, Feb 5
Longfellow, Henry Wadsworth: Birth Anniv, Feb 27
Longoria, Eva: Birth, Mar 15
Longwood Gardens Autumn's Colors (Kennett Square, PA), Oct 7
Longwood Gardens Easter Display (Kennett Square, PA), Apr 8
Longwood Gardens Welcomes Spring (Kennett Square, PA), Jan 21
Longyear, John M.: Birth Anniv, Apr 15
Looff Carousel, Santa Cruz Beach: Anniv, Aug 3
Look Up and Live TV Premiere: Anniv, Jan 3

Loomis Day, May 30
Loos, Anita: Birth Anniv, Apr 26
Loosen Up, Lighten Up Day, Nov 14
Lopez, Alfonso Raymond (Al): Birth, Aug 20
Lopez, Javy: Birth, Nov 5
Lopez, Jennifer: Birth, Jul 24
Lopez, Mario: Birth, Oct 10
Lopez, Nancy: Birth, Jan 6
Lopez, Trini: Birth, May 15
Lopiano, Donna: Birth, Sep 11
Lord Mayor's Show (London, England), Nov 11
Lord of the Rings, First Part Published: Anniv, Jul 19
Lord, Jack: Hawaii Five-O TV Premiere: Anniv, Sep 26
Loren, Sophia: Birth, Sep 20
Loretta Young Show TV Premiere: Anniv, Sep 20
Loring, Gloria: Birth, Dec 10
Los Angeles (CA) Founded: Anniv, Sep 4
Los Angeles, CA: Chicken Boy's Birthday, Sep 1
Lose Weight/Feel Great Week, Natl, Jan 1
Lost Dutchman Days (Apache Junction, AZ), Feb 24
Lost Penny Day, Feb 12
Lott, Ronnie: Birth, May 8
Lott, Trent: Birth, Oct 9
Lotus 1-2-3 Released: Anniv, Jan 26
Loudon, Dorothy: Birth, Sep 17
Louganis, Greg: Birth, Jan 29
Loughlin, Lori: Birth, Jul 28
Louis v Braddock/Schmeling Fight Anniv, Jun 22
Louis, Joe: Birth Anniv, May 13
Louis-Dreyfus, Julia: Birth, Jan 13
Louise, Tina: Birth, Feb 11
Louisiana
  Adai Caddo Indian Nation Pow Wow (Marthaville), Oct 21
  Administrative Professionals Intl Conv (New Orleans), Jul 23
  Admission Day, Apr 30
  American Library Assn Conf (New Orleans), Jun 22
  American Psychological Assn Annual Meeting (New Orleans), Aug 10
  Blanco, Kathleen: Birth, Dec 15
  Catholic Educational Assn Conv/Expo, Natl (New Orleans), Apr 18
  Celebration on the Cane (Natchitoches), Jul 4
  Christmas Fest of Lights (Natchitoches), Dec 1
  Christmas in Roseland (Shreveport), Nov 24
  Christmas New Orleans Style (New Orleans), Dec 1
  Contraband Days (Lake Charles), May 2
  Deaf Conference, Natl Assn of the (New Orleans), Jul 11
  Farragut Captures New Orleans: Anniv, Apr 25
  Folklife Fest (Monroe), Sep 9
  French Quarter Fest (New Orleans), Apr 20
  Gumbo Fest (Bridge City), Nov 3
  Holiday in Dixie (Shreveport and Bossier City), Apr 21
  Holiday Tour of Homes (Natchitoches), Dec 6
  Huey P. Long Day, Aug 30
  Landrieu, Mary L.: Birth, Nov 23
  Learning Disabilities Assn Intl Conf (New Orleans), Mar 1
  Louisiana Purchase Day, Apr 30
  Louisiana State Fiddle Chmpshp (Natchitoches), Jul 21
  Louisiana Yambilee (Opelousas), Oct 25
  Lousiana Sportsmen's Show (New Orleans), Mar 8
  Marksville Easter Egg Knocking Contest (Marksville), Apr 16
  Melrose Plantation Arts/Crafts Fest (Melrose), Jun 10
  Miss Louisiana Pageant (Monroe), Jun 15
  Mudbug Madness (Shreveport), May 25
  Natchitoches Fest of Lights (Natchitoches), Nov 18
  Natchitoches Historic Pilgrimage (Natchitoches), Oct 14
  Natchitoches Jazz Fest (Natchitoches), Apr 1
  Natchitoches/NW State Univ Folk Fest (Natchitoches), Jul 21
  New Orleans Boat Show (New Orleans), Feb 8
  New Orleans Jazz/Heritage Fest (New Orleans), Apr 28
  Nokia Sugar Bowl (New Orleans), Jan 2
  Peach Fest, Louisiana (Ruston), Jun 22
  Saint Patrick's Day Parade (Baton Rouge), Mar 18
  Satchmo Summerfest (New Orleans), Aug 3
  Shrimp and Petroleum Fest, Louisiana (Morgan City), Aug 31
  Spring Fest (Marthaville), Apr 28
  State Fair of Louisiana (Shreveport), Oct 26
  Twin Cities Janus Mardi Gras Parade (Monroe), Feb 18
  Veterans Day Celebration (Mamou), Nov 11
  Vitter, David: Birth, May 3

Lousma, Jack: Birth, Feb 29
Love a Mensch Week, Feb 6
Love Boat TV Premiere: Anniv, Sep 24
Love Is a Many Splendored Thing TV Premiere: Anniv, Sep 18
Love Litigating Lawyers Day, Aug 31
Love May Make World Go Round but Laughter Keeps Us from Getting Dizzy, Feb 8
Love Week, Celebration of, Feb 12
Love, Courtney: Birth, Jul 9
Love, Davis, III: Birth, Apr 13
Love, Mike: Birth, Mar 15
Lovecraft, H.P.: Birth Anniv, Aug 20
Lovejoy, Elijah P.: Birth Anniv, Nov 9
Loveladies Fair (Loveladies, NJ), Jun 3
Lovell, James: Birth, Mar 25
Lovera, Juan: Birth Anniv, Dec 26
Lovell, Amy: Birth Anniv, Feb 9
Lovell, Carey: Birth, Feb 11
Lovell, James R.: Birth Anniv, Feb 22
Lovell, Percival: Birth Anniv, Mar 13
Loy, Myrna: Birth Anniv, Aug 2
Loyalty Day (Pres Proc), May 1
Loyalty Days/Seafair Fest (Newport, OR), May 4
Lucas, George: Birth, May 14
Lucas, Josh: Birth, Mar 26
Lucci, Susan: Birth, Dec 23
Luce, Clare Boothe: Birth Anniv, Mar 10
Luce, Henry: Birth Anniv, Apr 3
Lucid, Shannon: Birth, Jan 14
Luckinbill, Laurence: Birth, Nov 21
Ludendorff, Erich: Birth Anniv, Apr 9
Ludington Carferry Fest (Ludington, MI), Jun 15
Luft, Lorna: Birth, Nov 21
Lugar, Richard G.: Birth, Apr 4
Lughnasadh, Aug 1
Lugosi, Bela: Birth Anniv, Oct 20
Lugosi, Bela: Dracula Premiere: Anniv, Feb 12
LULAC (League of United Latin American Citizens) Founded: Anniv, Feb 17
Lully, Jean Baptiste: Birth Anniv, Nov 28
Lumberjack World Chmpshps (Hayward, WI), Jul 28
Lumet, Sidney: Birth, Jun 25
Lumiere, Auguste: Birth Anniv, Oct 19
Lumiere, Louis: Birth Anniv, Oct 5
Lumpy Rug Day, May 3
Lunch Prowl Week, Sep 18
Lunden, Joan: Birth, Sep 19
Lundgren, Dolph: Birth, Nov 3
Luner, Jamie: Birth, May 12
Lung Assn, American: Christmas Seal Campaign, Oct 1
Lung Cancer Awareness Month, Nov 1
Lunsford, Bascom Lamar: Birth Anniv, Mar 21
Lupercalia, Feb 15
LuPone, Patti: Birth, Apr 21
Lupus Alert Day, Apr 1
Lupus Awareness Campaign, Oct 1
Lurie, Alison: Birth, Sep 3
Lusitania Sinking: Anniv, May 7
Luther, Martin: Birth Anniv, Nov 10
Luxembourg
  Beer Fest, Jul 16
  Blessing of the Wine (Greiveldange), Dec 26
  Bretzelsonndeg (Pretzel Sunday), Mar 26
  Burgsonndeg, Mar 5
  Candlemas, Feb 2
  Emaishen, Apr 17
  Ettelbruck Remembrance Day, Jul 6
  Liberation Ceremony, Sep 9
  National Holiday, Jun 23
  Osweiler, Mar 27
  Schuebermess (Shepherd's Fair), Aug 20
Luyts, Jan: Birth Anniv, Sep 19
Lydon, Johnny (Rotten): Birth, Jan 31
Lyman, Dorothy: Birth, Apr 18
Lynch, David: Birth, Jan 20
Lynch, John: Birth, Nov 25
Lynch, Kelly: Birth, Jan 31
Lynch, Thomas: Birth Anniv, Aug 5
Lynley, Carol: Birth, Feb 13
Lynn, Jonathan: Birth, Apr 3
Lynn, Loretta: Birth, Apr 14
Lyon, Mary: Birth Anniv, Feb 28
Lyon, Sue: Birth, Jul 10

M*A*S*H Final Episode: Anniv, Feb 28
M*A*S*H TV Premiere: Anniv, Sep 17
Ma, Yo-Yo: Birth, Oct 7
Maass, Clara: Birth Anniv, Jun 28
Mabon, Sep 23
Mac, Bernie: Birth, Oct 5
MacArthur Returns: US Landing on Leyte, Philippines: Anniv, Oct 20
MacArthur, Douglas: Birth Anniv, Jan 26
MacArthur, James: Birth, Dec 8
Macau: Reverts to Chinese Control: Anniv, Dec 20
Macaulay, Thomas B.: Birth Anniv, Oct 25
Macchio, Ralph: Birth, Nov 4
MacCorkindale, Simon: Birth, Feb 12
MacDonald, Anne Thompson: Death Anniv, Oct 12
MacDonald, John A.: Birth Anniv, Jan 11
Macdonald, Norm: Birth, Oct 17
MacDowell, Andie: Birth, Apr 21
Macedonia
    Independence Day, Sep 8
    National Day, Aug 2
Macedonian Uprising: Saint Elias Day: Anniv, Aug 2
MacFadden, Bernarr: Birth Anniv, Aug 16
MacGraw, Ali: Birth, Apr 1
Machias Wild Blueberry Fest (Machias, ME), Aug 17
Machiavelli, Niccolo: Birth Anniv, May 3
MacInnis, Al: Birth, Jul 11
Macintosh Debuts: Anniv, Jan 25
MacKenzie, Alexander: Birth Anniv, Jan 28
Mackie, Bob: Birth, Mar 24
Mackinac Bridge Walk (St. Ignace, MI), Sep 4
MacLachlan, Kyle: Birth, Feb 22
MacLaine, Shirley: Birth, Apr 24
MacLeish, Archibald: Birth Anniv, May 7
MacLeish, Rod: Birth, Jan 15
MacMurray, Fred: Birth Anniv, Aug 30
MacNeil, Robert: Birth, Jan 19
MacNeil-Lehrer Newshour TV Premiere: Anniv, Sep 5
MacNelly, Jeff: Birth Anniv, Sep 17
MacNicol, Peter: Birth, Apr 10
Macpherson, Elle: Birth, Mar 29
MacRae, Sheila: Birth, Sep 24
Macy, William H.: Birth, Mar 13
Mad Magazine: Gaines, William M.: Birth Anniv, Mar 1
Mad Magazine: Kurtzman, Harvey: Birth Anniv, Oct 3
Madagascar
    Commemoration Day, Mar 29
    Independence Day, Jun 26
Madama Butterfly Premiere: Anniv, Feb 17
MADD: New Year's Designate a Driver Campaign, Dec 26
MADD: Tie One On for Safety, Nov 16
Madden, John: Birth, Apr 10
Maddux, Greg: Birth, Apr 14
Madigan, Amy: Birth, Sep 11
Madison, Dolly: Birth Anniv, May 20
Madison, James: Birth Anniv, Mar 16
Madonna: Birth, Aug 16
Madrid Train Bombings: Anniv, Mar 11
Madsen, Michael: Birth, Sep 25
Madsen, Virginia: Birth, Sep 11
Maffia, Roma: Birth, May 31
Magazine Month, Children's, Oct 1
Magazine, First Published in America: Anniv, Feb 13
Magellan, Ferdinand: Death Anniv, Apr 27
Magic Day, Oct 31
Magic of Differences™ Week, Oct 23
Magic Week, Intl, Oct 25
Magic: Robert-Houdin, Jean Eugene: Birth Anniv, Dec 6
Magna Carta Day, Jun 15
Magnolia Blossom Fest (Magnolia, AR), May 19
Magnum, PI TV Premiere: Anniv, Dec 11
Magnuson, Ann: Birth, Jan 4
Maguire, Tobey: Birth, Jun 27
Maher, Bill: Birth, Jan 20
Mahoney: John: Birth, Jun 20
Maifest (Covington, KY), May 19
Maifest (Hermann, MO), May 20
Mail: Pony Express, Inauguration of: Anniv, Apr 3
Mail: V-Mail Delivery: Anniv, Jun 22
Mailer, Norman: Birth, Jan 31
Mail-Order Catalog: Anniv, Aug 18
Mailorder Gardening Month, Natl, Jan 1
Maiman, Theodore: Birth, Jul 11
Maine
    Acadia Natl Park Established: Anniv, Jan 1
    Acton Fair (Acton), Aug 24
    Admission Day, Mar 15
    Apple Saturdays (New Gloucester), Sep 23
    Baldacci, John: Birth, Jan 30

Bangor State Fair (Bangor), Jul 28
Blue Hill Fair (Blue Hill), Aug 31
Chester Greenwood Day Parade (Farmington), Dec 2
Coats & Toys for Kids Day, Dec 2
Collins, Susan M.: Birth, Dec 7
Common Ground Country Fair (Unity), Sep 22
Down East Spring Birding Fest (Eastport, Whiting, Lubec), May 26
Eastport "Old Home Week" Celebration (Eastport), Jul 1
Fryeburg Fair (Fryeburg), Oct 1
Island Falls Summerfest (Island Falls), Jul 29
Island Falls Winterfest (Island Falls), Feb 10
Logging Museum Fest Days (Rangeley), Jul 28
Machias Wild Blueberry Fest (Machias), Aug 17
Maine Highland Games (Brunswick), Aug 19
Maine Law: Anniv, Jun 2
Maine Lobster Fest (Rockland), Aug 2
Maine Potato Blossom Fest (Fort Fairfield), Jul 7
Margaretta Days (Machias), Jun 8
MooseStompers Weekend (Houlton), Feb 3
Patriot's Day, Apr 17
Potato Feast Days (Houlton), Aug 18
Shaker Christmas Fair (New Gloucester), Dec 2
Shaker Museum Opening Day (New Gloucester), May 26
Sidewalk Art Fest (Bangor), Aug 5
Sidewalk Art Fest (Portland), Aug 26
Skowhegan State Fair (Skowhegan), Aug 10
Snowe, Olympia J.: Birth, Feb 21
Thomas Point Beach Bluegrass Fest (Brunswick), Aug 31
West Quoddy Head Light Keepers Association Anniv Celebration (Lubec), Jun 17
Windjammer Days (Boothbay Harbor), Jun 27
Yarmouth Clam Fest (Yarmouth), Jul 21
Majerle, Dan: Birth, Sep 9
Major League Baseball All-Star Game (Pittsburgh, PA), Jul 11
Major, John: Birth, Mar 29
Majors, Lee: Birth, Apr 23
Make a Difference Day, Oct 28
Make Room for Daddy TV Premiere: Anniv, Sep 29
Make Up Your Mind Day, Dec 31
Make Up Your Own Holiday Day, Mar 26
Makeba, Miriam: Birth, Mar 4
Makepeace, Chris: Birth, Apr 22
Malawi
    Freedom Day, Jun 14
    John Chilembwe Day, Jan 16
    Martyr's Day, Mar 3
    Republic Day, Jul 6
Malaysia
    Borneo Rhino Challenge, May 14
    Freedom Day, Aug 31
    Head of State's Official Birthday, Jun 3
Malcolm X: Assassination Anniv, Feb 21
Malcolm X: Birth Anniv, May 19
Malden, Karl: Birth, Mar 22
Maldives
    National Day, Jul 26
    Republic Day, Nov 11
Maleska, Eugene T.: Birth Anniv, Jan 6
Mali: Independence Day, Sep 22
Malick, Wendie: Birth, Dec 13
Malkovich, John: Birth, Dec 9
Malle, Louis: Birth Anniv, Oct 30
Mallory, George L.: Birth Anniv, Jun 18
Malone, Dorothy: Birth, Jan 30
Malone, Karl: Birth, Jul 24
Malone, Moses: Birth, Mar 23
Maloney, Janel: Birth, Oct 3
Malta
    Carnival, Feb 25
    Feast of St. Paul's Shipwreck (Valletta), Feb 10
    Independence Day, Sep 21
    Mnarja, Jun 22
    National Day, Jun 7
    Republic Day, Dec 13
    Siege Broken: Anniv, Sep 8
Maltese Falcon: Publication Anniv, Feb 14
Malthus, Thomas: Birth Anniv, Feb 17
Maltin, Leonard: Birth, Dec 18
Mama TV Premiere: Anniv, Jul 1
Mamet, David: Birth, Nov 30
Mammography Day, Natl, Oct 20
Mammoth Cave Natl Park Established: Anniv, Jul 1
Man Day, Feb 12
Mananitas, Las (Ponce, Puerto Rico), Dec 12
Manchester, Melissa: Birth, Feb 15
Manchin III, Joe: Birth, Aug 24
Mancini, Henry: Birth Anniv, Apr 16
Mandan, Robert: Birth, Feb 2
Mandarich, Tony: Birth, Sep 23
Mandel, Howie: Birth, Nov 29

Mandela, Nelson
    Arrest Anniv, Aug 4
    Birth, Jul 18
    Inauguration Anniv, May 10
    Prison Release Anniv, Feb 11
Mandrell, Barbara: Birth, Dec 25
Mandrell, Louise: Birth, Jul 13
Manet, Edouard: Birth Anniv, Jan 23
Mangano, Silvana: Birth Anniv, Apr 21
Mangione, Chuck: Birth, Nov 29
Manheim, Camryn: Birth, Mar 8
Manilow, Barry: Birth, Jun 17
Manistee Natl Forest Fest (Manistee), Jun 29
Mankiewicz, Joseph L.: Birth Anniv, Feb 11
Mankiller, Wilma: Birth, Nov 18
Mann, Horace: Birth Anniv, May 4
Mann, James: Birth Anniv, Oct 20
Mann, Marty: Birth Anniv, Oct 15
Manners, Miss (Judith Martin): Birth, Sep 13
Manning, Danny: Birth, May 17
Manning, Peyton: Birth, Mar 24
Mannix TV Premiere: Anniv, Sep 16
Manoff, Dinah: Birth, Jan 25
Man-Powered Flight, First: Anniv, Aug 23
Mansfield, Arabella: Birth Anniv, May 23
Manson, Patrick: Birth Anniv, Oct 3
Manstein, Erich von: Birth Anniv, Nov 24
Mantegna, Joe: Birth, Nov 13
Mantle, Mickey: Birth Anniv, Oct 20
Mantooth, Randolph: Birth, Sep 19
Mao Tse-Tung: Birth Anniv, Dec 26
Mao Tse-Tung: Death Anniv, Sep 9
Maple Fest, Highland County (Highland County, VA), Mar 11
Maple Syrup Saturday (Appleton, WI), Mar 18
Maples, Marla: Birth, Oct 27
Mappelthorpe, Robert: Birth Anniv, Nov 4
Maradona, Diego: Birth, Oct 30
Marathon, Battle of: Anniv, Sep 9
Marathon, Historic Runs: Anniv, Sep 2
Marbles
    Marble Meet, Northeast (Marlborough, MA), Oct 7
    Marble Weekend (Millville, NJ), Jun 24
    Marbles Chmpshp, British and World (England), Apr 14
National Knuckles Down Month, Apr 1
Marbury, Stephon: Birth, Feb 20
Marceau, Marcel: Birth, Mar 22
Marceau, Sophie: Birth, Nov 17
March, Fredric: Birth Anniv, Aug 8
Marchand, Nancy: Birth Anniv, Jun 19
Marciano, Rocky: Birth Anniv, Sep 1
Marconi, Guglielmo: Birth Anniv, Apr 25
Marcos, Ferdinand: Birth Anniv, Sep 11
Marcovicci, Andrea: Birth, Nov 18
Mardi Gras, Feb 28
Mardi Gras in Branson (Branson, MO), Jun 8
Marfan Syndrome Awareness Month, Feb 1
Margaretta Days (Machias, ME), Jun 8
Margolin, Stuart: Birth, Jan 31
Margulies, Julianna: Birth, Jun 8
Mariachi Conf, Tucson Intl (Tucson, AZ), Apr 24
Marie Antoinette: Execution Anniv, Oct 16
Marilyn Monroe's First Screen Test: Anniv, Jul 19
Marin, Cheech: Birth, Jul 13
Marinaro, Ed: Birth, Mar 31
Marine Corps Birthday: Anniv, Nov 10
Marino, Dan: Birth, Sep 15
Mario Day, Mar 10
Marion Popcorn Fest (Marion, OH), Sep 7
Maris Breaks Ruth Home Run Record: Anniv, Oct 1
Maris, Roger: Birth Anniv, Sep 10
Maritime Day, Natl, May 22
Maritime Day, Natl (Pres Proc), May 22
Markert, Russell: Birth Anniv, Aug 31
Marketing: Entrepreneurs "Do It Yourself" Marketing Month, Jun 1
Markham, Monte: Birth, Jun 21
Marley, Bob: Birth Anniv, Feb 6
Maroon Fest (Jamaica), Jan 6
Marquette, Jacques: Birth Anniv, Jun 1
Marriage Day, World, Feb 12
Marriage of Elizabeth and Philip: Anniv, Nov 20
Marriage: Loving v Virginia: Anniv, Jun 12
Marriage: Proposal Day!, Mar 20
Married to a Scorpio Support Day, Nov 18
Married With Children TV Premiere: Anniv, Apr 5
Marrow Awareness Month, Natl, Nov 1
Marsalis, Branford: Birth, Aug 26
Marsalis, Wynton: Birth, Oct 18
Marsh, Jean: Birth, Jul 1
Marshall County Blueberry Fest (Plymouth, IN), Sep 1
Marshall Islands: National Day, May 1
Marshall Plan: Anniv, Apr 3
Marshall, Garry: Birth, Nov 13
Marshall, George: Birth Anniv, Dec 31

Marshall—McKinley

Marshall, John: Appointed Chief Justice: Anniv, Jan 20
Marshall, John: Birth Anniv, Sep 24
Marshall, Penny: Birth, Oct 15
Marshall, Peter: Birth, Mar 30
Marshall, Thomas Riley: Birth Anniv, Mar 14
Marshall, Thurgood: Birth Anniv, Jul 2
Marshall, Thurgood: Resigns from Supreme Court: Anniv, Jun 27
Marshall, Thurgood: Sworn in to Supreme Court: Anniv, Oct 2
Marti, Jose Julian: Birth Anniv, Jan 28
Martin Z. Mollusk Day (Ocean City, NJ), May 4
Martin, Andrea: Birth, Jan 15
Martin, Ann: Birth, Aug 12
Martin, Billy: Birth Anniv, May 16
Martin, Chris: Birth, Mar 2
Martin, Curtis: Birth, May 1
Martin, Dean: Birth Anniv, Jun 7
Martin, Dick: Birth, Jan 30
Martin, Jesse L.: Birth, Jan 18
Martin, Judith: Birth, Sep 13
Martin, Kellie: Birth, Oct 16
Martin, Kenyon: Birth, Dec 30
Martin, Mary: Birth Anniv, Dec 1
Martin, Pamela Sue: Birth, Jan 5
Martin, Paul: Birth, Aug 28
Martin, Ricky: Birth, Dec 24
Martin, Steve: Birth, Aug 14
Martinez, Edgar: Birth, Jan 2
Martinez, Jose: Birth, May 14
Martinez, Mel: Birth, Oct 23
Martinez, Pedro: Birth, Oct 25
Martinez, Tino: Birth, Dec 7
Martinique: Mount Pelee Eruption: Anniv, May 8
Martinmas, Nov 11
Martinmas Goose (Switzerland), Nov 11
Martino, Al: Birth, Oct 7
Martyrs Day (Bangladesh), Feb 21
Martyrs' Day (Panama), Jan 9
Marvell, Andrew: Birth Anniv, Mar 31
Marx, Groucho: Birth Anniv, Oct 2
Marx, Harpo: Birth Anniv, Nov 23
Marx, Karl: Birth Anniv, May 5
Marx, Richard: Birth, Sep 16
Mary Tyler Moore Show TV Premiere: Anniv, Sep 19
Mary, Queen of Scots: Execution Anniv, Feb 8
Maryland
  Adopts Articles of Confederation: Anniv, Jan 30
  Boonesborough Days (Boonsboro), Sep 9
  Catoctin ColorFest Arts/Crafts (Thurmont), Oct 14
  Catonsville Arts & Crafts Fest (Catonsville), Sep 10
  Celtic Fest, Southern Maryland (St. Leonard), Apr 29
  Chestertown Tea Party Fest (Chestertown), May 27
  Country Fest and Auction (Deep Creek Lake), Aug 26
  Defenders Day, Sep 12
  Delmarva Chicken Fest (Snow Hill), Jun 23
  Ehrlich, Robert, Jr: Birth, Nov 25
  Fairmount Academy 1800s Fest (Fairmount), May 27
  Fell's Point Fun Fest (Baltimore), Oct 7
  Grand Militia Muster (St. Mary's City), Oct 21
  Grantsville Days (Grantsville), Jun 23
  Hard Crab Derby and Fair, Natl (Crisfield), Sep 1
  Hearth and Home in Early Maryland (St. Mary's City), Nov 24
  Heritage Days Fest (Cumberland), May 20
  Independence Day Celebration (Catonsville), Jul 4
  John Wilkes Booth Escape Route Tour (Clinton), Apr 15
  Kunta Kinte Heritage Festival (Crownsville), Aug 12
  Landon Azalea Garden Fest/Antique Show (Bethesda), May 5
  Leitersburg Peach Fest (Leitersburg), Aug 12
  Lil Margaret's Bluegrass and Old-Time Music Fest (Leonardtown), Aug 10
  Maritime Heritage Fest (St. Mary's City), Jun 17
  Maryland Constitution Ratification: Anniv, Apr 28
  Maryland Day, Mar 25
  Maryland Day (St. Mary's City), Mar 26
  Maryland Home and Garden Show (Baltimore), Mar 3
  Maryland Renaissance Fest (Annapolis), Aug 26
  Mikulski, Barbara Ann: Birth, Jul 20
  Montgomery County Agricultural Fair (Gaithersburg), Aug 11
  Preakness Stakes (Baltimore), May 20
  Sarbanes, Paul S.: Birth, Feb 3
  Special Olympics Winter Games (McHenry), Feb 26
  St. Mary's County Oyster Fest (Leonardtown), Oct 21

State Fair (Timonium), Aug 25
Sugarloaf Crafts Fest (Gaithersburg), Apr 7, Oct 13, Nov 16
Sugarloaf Crafts Fest (Timonium), Apr 28, Oct 6
Tidewater Archaeology Dig (St. Mary's City), Jul 29
Towsontown Spring Fest (Towson), May 6
Victorian Christmas Celebration (Cumberland), Nov 24
Ward World Chmpshp Waterfowl Carving Competition (Ocean City), Apr 28
Waterfowl Fest (Easton), Nov 10
Woodland Indian Discovery Day (St. Mary's City), Sep 9
Mason, Bobbie Ann: Birth, May 1
Mason, Dave: Birth, May 10
Mason, Jackie: Birth, Jun 9
Mason, Marsha: Birth, Apr 3
Massachusetts
  American Heroine Rewarded: Anniv, Jun 8
  American Society of Assn Executives Mtg/Expo (Boston), Aug 19
  Bastille Day Celebration (Boston), Jul 14
  Big E (West Springfield), Sep 15
  Boston Fire: Anniv, Nov 9
  Boston Harborfest (Boston), Jun 28
  Boston Marathon (Boston), Apr 17
  Boston Public Library: Anniv, Apr 3
  Bridge over the Neponset: Anniv, Apr 1
  Bunker Hill Day (Suffolk County), Jun 17
  Children's Day, Jun 11
  Christmas Stroll Weekend (Nantucket Island), Dec 1
  Daffodil Fest Weekend (Nantucket Island), Apr 28
  Deerfield Massacre: Anniv (Feb 29), Feb 1
  Evacuation Day (Boston), Mar 17
  Fall on Nantucket (Nantucket Island), Oct 1
  First Night (Boston), Dec 31
  Haitian Heritage Month, May 1
  Ig Nobel Prize Ceremony (Cambridge), Oct 5
  Kennedy, Edward Moore: Birth, Feb 22
  Kerry, John F.: Birth, Dec 11
  NCAA Division I Women's Lacrosse Chmpshp (Boston), May 26
  New England Home Show (Boston), Feb 25
  Northeast Marble Meet (Marlborough), Oct 7
  Original Massachusetts Home & Garden Show (West Springfield), Mar 23
  Patriot's Day, Apr 17
  Plymouth Plantation Earthquake: Anniv, Jun 1
  Railroad and Hobby Show (Springfield), Jan 28
  Ratification Day, Feb 6
  Romney, Mitt: Birth, Mar 12
  Sandcastle & Sculpture Day (Nantucket Island), Aug 19
  Student Government Day, Apr 7
  34th St Express (Boston), Dec 9
  WMAS Annual Halloween Ball (Springfield), Oct 28
  WMAS Valentine's Ball (Springfield), Feb 10
Massacre at Fort Pillow: Anniv, Apr 12
Massage Therapy Awareness Week, Natl, Oct 22
Massey, Anna: Birth, Aug 11
Masterpiece Theatre TV Premiere: Anniv, Jan 10
Masters, Ben: Birth, May 6
Masters, Edgar L.: Birth Anniv, Aug 23
Masterson, Bat: Birth Anniv, Nov 27
Masterson, Christopher: Birth, Jan 22
Masterson, Mary Stuart: Birth, Jun 28
Mastrantonio, Mary Elizabeth: Birth, Nov 17
Mastroeni, Pablo: Birth, Aug 29
Mastroianni, Marcello: Birth Anniv, Sep 28
Masur, Richard: Birth, Nov 20
Mata Hari: Birth Anniv, Aug 7
Matanzas Mule Day, Apr 27
Mathematics: Intl Congress of Mathematicians (Madrid, Spain), Aug 22
Mathers, Jerry: Birth, Jun 2
Mathers, Marshall (Eminem): Birth, Oct 17
Matheson, Tim: Birth, Dec 31
Mathewson, Christy: Birth Anniv, Aug 12
Mathias, Bob: Birth, Nov 17
Mathis, Johnny: Birth, Sep 30
Matisse, Henri: Birth Anniv, Dec 31
Matlin, Marlee: Birth, Aug 24
Matson, Boyd: Birth, Apr 26
Matsui, Hideki: Birth, Jun 12
Matthau, Walter: Birth Anniv, Oct 1
Matthews, Dave: Birth, Jan 9
Matthews, DeLane: Birth, Aug 7
Mattingly, Don: Birth, Apr 20
Maude TV Premiere: Anniv, Sep 12
Maugham, W. Somerset: Birth Anniv, Jan 25
Maundy Thursday (Holy Thursday), Apr 13
Maura, Carmen: Birth, Sep 15
Mauritania: Independence Day, Nov 28
Mauritius: Independence Day, Mar 12
Maury, Matthew Fontaine: Birth Anniv, Jan 14
Maverick TV Premiere: Anniv, Sep 22

Mawlid al Nabi: Birthday of Prophet Muhammad, Apr 11
Max, Peter: Birth, Oct 19
Maxwell, James Clerk: Birth Anniv, Nov 13
Maxwell, Robert: Death Anniv, Nov 5
May Day, May 1
May Day (Lumpkin, GA), May 5
May Day Bank Holiday (United Kingdom), May 1
May in Montclair (Montclair Township, NJ), May 1
May Ray Day, May 19
May, Elaine: Birth, Apr 21
Mayall, John: Birth, Nov 29
Mayer, Maria Goeppert: Birth Anniv, Jun 28
Mayflower Day, Sep 16
Maymont Flower & Garden Show (Richmond, VA), Feb 9
Mayo, Charles: Birth Anniv, Jul 19
Mayo, William J.: Birth Anniv, Jun 29
Mayron, Melanie: Birth, Oct 20
Mays, Willie: Birth, May 6
Mazowiecki, Tadeusz: Poland: Solidarity Founded, Aug 31
Mazursky, Paul: Birth, Apr 25
McAliskey, Bernadette Devlin: Birth, Apr 23
McArdle, Andrea: Birth, Nov 4
McAuliffe, Christa: Birth Anniv, Sep 2
McBride, Brian: Birth, Jun 19
McBride, Martina: Birth, Jul 29
McBride, Patricia: Birth, Aug 23
McCain, John Sidney, III: Birth, Aug 29
McCallum, David: Birth, Sep 19
McCarthy Silenced by Senate: Anniv, Dec 2
McCarthy, Andrew: Birth, Nov 29
McCarthy, Cormac: Birth, Jul 20
McCarthy, Eugene: Birth, Mar 29
McCarthy, Jenny: Birth, Nov 1
McCarthy, Kevin: Birth, Feb 15
McCartney, Paul: Beatles Break Up: Anniv, Apr 10
McCartney, Paul: Birth, Jun 18
McCartney, Stella: Birth, Sep 13
McCianahan, Rue: Birth, Feb 21
McClure, Marc: Birth, Mar 31
McClurg, Edie: Birth, Jul 23
McConaughey, Matthew: Birth, Nov 4
McConnell, Mitch: Birth, Feb 20
McCoo, Marilyn: Birth, Sep 30
McCormack, Eric: Birth, Apr 18
McCormick, Cyrus H.: Birth Anniv, Feb 15
McCormick, Pat: Birth, Jul 17
McCourt, Frank: Birth, Aug 19
McCoy-Hatfield Feud Erupts: Anniv, Aug 7
McCrea, Joel: Birth Anniv, Nov 5
McDaniel, Hattie: Birth Anniv, Jun 10
McDermott, Dylan: Birth, Oct 26
McDonald's Opens, First : Anniv, Apr 15
McDormand, Frances: Birth, Jun 23
McDowell, Jack Burns: Birth, Jan 16
McDowell, Malcolm: Birth, Jun 13
McEnroe, John Patrick, Jr: Birth, Feb 16
McEntire, Reba: Birth, Mar 28
McEwan, Ian: Birth, May 21
McEwen, Mark: Birth, Sep 16
McFarland, George (Spanky): Birth Anniv, Oct 2
McFerrin, Bobby: Birth, Mar 11
McGavin, Darren: Birth, May 7
McGillis, Kelly: Birth, Jul 9
McGinley, John: Birth, Aug 3
McGinley, Ted: Birth, May 30
McGoohan, Patrick: Birth, Mar 19
McGovern, Elizabeth: Birth, Jul 18
McGovern, George: Birth, Jul 19
McGovern, Maureen: Birth, Jul 27
McGowan, Rose: Birth, Sep 5
McGrady, Tracy: Birth, May 24
McGrath, Mark: Birth, Mar 15
McGraw, Dr. Phil: Birth, Sep 1
McGraw, John: Birth Anniv, Apr 7
McGraw, Tim: Birth, May 1
McGregor, Ewan: Birth, Mar 31
McGriff, Fred: Birth, Oct 31
McGuffey, William H.: Birth Anniv, Sep 23
McGuinn, Roger: Birth, Jul 13
McGwire Breaks Home Run Record: Anniv, Sep 8
McGwire, Mark: Birth, Oct 1
McHale, Kevin: Birth, Dec 19
McInerney, Jay: Birth, Jan 13
McKay, Jim: Birth, Sep 24
McKean, Michael: Birth, Oct 17
McKean, Thomas: Birth Anniv, Mar 19
McKellar, Danica: Birth, Jan 3
McKellen, Sir Ian: Birth, May 25
McKenzie, Benjamin: Birth, Sep 12
McKeon, Doug: Birth, Jun 10
McKeon, Nancy: Birth, Apr 4
McKeon, Philip: Birth, Nov 11
McKinley, Ida Saxton: Birth Anniv, Jun 8
McKinley, Morganfield (Muddy Waters): Birth Anniv, Apr 4

McKinley, William: Birth Anniv, Jan 29
McKinley, William: Death Anniv, Sep 14
McKnight, Brian: Birth, Jun 5
McKuen, Rod: Birth, Apr 29
McLachlan, Sarah: Birth, Jan 28
McLaughlin, John: Birth, Mar 29
McLean, Don: Birth, Oct 2
McLuhan, Marshall: Birth Anniv, Jul 21
McMahon, Ed: Birth, Mar 6
McMahon, Jim: Birth, Aug 21
McMahon, Julian: Birth, Jul 27
McMillan, Terry: Birth, Oct 18
McMurtry, Larry: Birth, Jun 3
McNair, Barbara: Birth, Mar 4
McNair, Ronald E.: Birth Anniv, Oct 12
McNamara, Robert S.: Birth, Jun 9
McNichol, Jimmy: Birth, Jul 2
McNichol, Kristy: Birth, Sep 11
McPartland, Marian: Birth, Mar 20
McRae, Carmen: Birth Anniv, Apr 8
McRaney, Gerald: Birth, Aug 19
McShane, Ian: Birth, Sep 29
McTeer, Janet: Birth, May 8
McVie, Christine: Birth, Jul 12
Mead, Margaret: Birth Anniv, Dec 16
Meadows, Jayne: Birth, Sep 27
Meaney, Colm: Birth, May 30
Means, Russell: Birth, Nov 10
Meany, George: Birth Anniv, Aug 16
Meara, Anne: Birth, Sep 20
Mears, Rick: Birth, Dec 3
Meat Loaf: Birth, Sep 27
Mecklenburg Day (NC), May 20
Medal of Honor, First World War II: Anniv, Feb 10
Medal of Honor, Irwin Earns 1st: Anniv, Feb 13
Medical Group Practice Week, Natl, Jan 23
Medical Librarians Month, Natl, Oct 1
Medical Orphans Month, Awareness of, May 1
Medical Patient Advocacy Week, Natl, Apr 2
Medical School for Women Opened: Anniv, Nov 1
Medicare: Anniv, Jul 1
Medication Safety Week, Apr 1
Medieval Fair (Norman, OK), Mar 31
Medieval Faire, Hoggetowne (Gainesville, FL), Jan 28
Meditation, World Peace, Annual, Dec 31
Meet a Mate Week, Jun 12
Meet the Press TV Premiere: Anniv, Nov 6
Meeting Planners Appreciation Day, Natl, May 3
Mehta, Zubin: Birth, Apr 29
Meier, Garry: Birth, Dec 2
Meir, Golda: Birth Anniv, May 3
Mekka, Eddie: Birth, Jun 14
Melanoma Monday, May 1
Melanoma/Skin Cancer Detection and Prevention Month, May 1
Mellencamp, John: Birth, Oct 7
Mellon, Andrew W.: Birth Anniv, Mar 24
Meloni, Christopher: Birth, Apr 2
Melvill, Michael: First Manned Private Spaceflight: Anniv, Jun 21
Melville (Moby-Dick) Marathon (Mystic, CT), Jul 31
Melville, Herman: Birth Anniv, Aug 1
Melvin, Allan: Birth, Feb 18
Memento Mori, Jan 3
Memorial Day (Observed), May 29
Memorial Day (Pres Proc), May 29
Memorial Day (Traditional), May 30
Memorial Day Ceremonies (Andersonville, GA), May 28
Memorial Day Getaway (Live Oak, FL), May 26
Memorial Day Parade and Ceremonies (Gettysburg, PA), May 29
Memory Day, Mar 21
Memory Days (Grayson, KY), May 20
Men Make Dinner Day, Natl, Nov 2
Mencken, Henry Louis: Birth Anniv, Sep 12
Mendel, Gregor Johann: Birth Anniv, Jul 22
Mendes, Sergio: Birth, Feb 11
Menendez de Aviles, Pedro: Birth Anniv, Feb 15
Menken, Alan: Birth, Jul 22
Mennonite Relief Sale (Hutchinson, KS), Apr 7
Menopause Awareness Month, Sep 1
Menopause Day, World, Oct 18
Menotti, Gian Carlo: Birth, Jul 7
Men's Month, Intl, Jun 1
Mensch Week, Love a, Feb 6
Mental Health Month, Natl, May 1
Mental Illness Awareness Week, Oct 1
Mental Retardation Awareness Month, Mar 1
Mentoring Month, Natl, Jan 1
Menzies, Robert: Birth Anniv, Dec 20
Meramec Community Fair (Sullivan, MO), Jun 22
Mercator, Gerhardus: Birth Anniv, Mar 5
Mercer, John Herndon (Johnny): Birth Anniv, Nov 18
Merchant, Natalie: Birth, Oct 26

Mercouri, Melina: Birth Anniv, Oct 18
Meredith (James) Enrolls at Ole Miss: Anniv, Sep 30
Meredith, Burgess: Birth Anniv, Nov 16
Meredith, Don: Birth, Apr 10
Meriwether, Lee: Birth, May 27
Merkerson, S. Epatha: Birth, Nov 28
Merman, Ethel: Birth Anniv, Jan 16
Merriam, Eve: Birth Anniv, Jul 19
Merrie Monarch Fest & Hula Competition (Hilo, HI), Apr 16
Merrill, Dina: Birth, Dec 9
Merrimac Destroyed: Anniv, May 11
Merv Griffin Show TV Premiere: Anniv, Oct 1
Mesa Verde Natl Park Established: Anniv, Jun 29
Mesmer, Friedrich: Birth Anniv, May 23
Messiah, Premiere of: Anniv, Apr 13
Messick, Dale: Birth Anniv, Apr 11
Messier, Mark: Birth, Jan 18
Messina Earthquake Anniv, Dec 28
Messina Hof's Wine Premiere (Bryan, TX), Nov 18
Messina, Jim: Birth, Dec 5
Messing, Debra: Birth, Aug 15
Metaphysical Awareness Month, Sep 1
Metcalf, Laurie: Birth, Jun 16
Metcalfe, Jesse: Birth, Dec 9
Meteor Showers, Perseid, Aug 9
Meteorological Day, World (UN), Mar 23
Metheny, Pat: Birth, Aug 12
Metric Conversion Act: Anniv, Dec 23
Metric System Developed: Anniv, Apr 7
Metric Week, Natl, Oct 8
Metropolitan Opera House: Opening Anniv, Oct 22
Metropolitan Opera Natl Council Auditions Finals (New York, NY), Mar 19
Metropolitan Opera Radio Broadcasts Premiere: Anniv, Dec 25
Mexican Fiesta Internacional (Milwaukee, WI), Aug 25
Mexican War Declared: Anniv, May 13
Mexico
  Battle of Puebla: Anniv, May 5
  Benito Juarez : Birth Anniv, Mar 21
  Blessing of Animals at Cathedral, Jan 17
  Cinco de Mayo, May 5
  Constitution Day, Feb 5
  Cortes Conquers Mexico: Anniv, Nov 8
  Day of the Dead, Nov 1
  Day of the Holy Cross, May 3
  Dia de la Candelaria, Feb 2
  Dia de la Raza, Oct 12
  Feast of Our Lady of Solitude, Dec 18
  Feast of the Radishes (Oaxaca), Dec 23
  Flag Day, Feb 24
  Guadalajara Intl Book Fair (Guadalajara), Nov 25
  Guadalupe Day, Dec 12
  Independence Day, Sep 16
  Mainly Mozart Fest (Baja California), Jun 1
  Mexico City Earthquake: Anniv, Sep 19
  Posadas, Dec 16
  Postman's Day, Nov 12
  President's State of the Union Address, Sep 1
  Revolution Day, Nov 20
  San Isidro Day, May 15
  Sonora Showcase (Yuma, AZ), Jan 24
  Treaty of Guadalupe Hidalgo (with US): Anniv, Feb 2
  Zapatista Rebellion: Anniv, Jan 1
Mfume, Kweisi: Birth, Oct 24
Miami Intl Boat/Sailboat Show (Miami Beach, FL), Feb 16
Mice: AFRMA Display & Show (Costa Mesa, CA), Jul 7
Mice: AFRMA Display at America's Family Pet Expo (Costa Mesa, CA), Apr 14
Michael, George: Birth, Jun 25
Michaelmas, Sep 29
Michaels, Lorne: Birth, Nov 17
Michelangelo: Birth Anniv, Mar 6
Michele, Michael: Birth, Aug 30
Michelin, Andre: Birth Anniv, Jan 16
Michelson, Albert: First US Scientist Receives Nobel Prize: Anniv, Dec 10
Michener, James: Birth Anniv, Feb 3
Michigan
  Admission Day, Jan 26
  Alma Highland Fest and Games (Alma), May 27
  Alpenfest (Gaylord), Jul 11
  Ann Arbor Film Fest (Ann Arbor), Mar 21
  Ann Arbor Summer Art Fair (Ann Arbor), Jul 19
  Ann Arbor Winter Art Fair (Ann Arbor), Nov 11
  Antiques by the Bay (St. Ignace), Jun 16
  Arcadia Daze (Arcadia), Jul 21
  Baby Food Fest, Natl (Fremont), Jul 18
  Battle Creek Cereal Fest (with World's Largest Breakfast Table) (Battle Creek), Jun 10
  Bay Harbor Summer Art Fair (Bay Harbor), Aug 5

  Big Mac Shoreline Fall Scenic Bike Tour (Mackinaw City), Sep 16
  Big Ten Field Hockey Tournament (Ann Arbor), Nov 3
  Big Ten Men's Soccer Chmpshp (East Lansing), Nov 9
  Blueberry Fest, Natl (South Haven), Aug 10
  Cherry Pit Spitting Chmpshp, Intl (Eau Claire), Jul 1
  Convergence 2006 (Grand Rapids), Jun 25
  Corvette Show (Mackinaw City), Aug 25
  Curwood Fest (Owosso), Jun 1
  Detroit Founded: Anniv, Jul 24
  Do-Dah Parade (Kalamazoo), Jun 3
  Fallasburg Fall Fest (Lowell), Sep 23
  Ford Field Home & Garden Show (Detroit), Mar 10
  Fourth of July Fireworks (Mackinaw City), Jul 4
  Frankenmuth Skyfest (Frankenmuth), May 7
  Grand Rapids Boat Show (Grand Rapids), Feb 15
  Grandparents and Grandchildren Day, Mar 18
  Granholm, Jennifer: Birth, Feb 5
  Great Fire of 1881: Anniv, Sep 5
  Gymnastics Chmpshps, Big Ten Women's (East Lansing), Mar 25
  Harborfest (South Haven), Jun 16
  Holland Tulip Time Fest (Holland), May 6
  Isle Royale Natl Park Established: Anniv, Apr 3
  KCQ Country Music Fest (Saginaw), Jun 17
  Lakestore Half-Marathon (Ludington), Jun 17
  Levin, Carl: Birth, Jun 28
  Lilac Fest (Mackinac Island), Jun 9
  Log Cabin Day, Jun 25
  Longhorn Chmpshp Rodeo (Auburn Hills), Feb 17
  Ludington Carferry Fest (Ludington), Jun 15
  Mackinac Bridge Walk (St. Ignace), Sep 4
  Manistee Natl Forest Fest (Manistee), Jun 29
  MiAEYC Early Childhood Conference (Grand Rapids), Mar 30
  Michigan Fiber Festival (Allegan), Aug 16
  Michigan Storytellers Fest (Flint), Jul 7
  Midwinter's Day Celebration (Ann Arbor), Feb 6
  Month of the Young Child, Apr 1
  New Year's Fest (Kalamazoo), Dec 31
  On the Waterfront Swap Meet/Car Show (St. Ignace), Sep 15
  Ribfest (Kalamazoo), Aug 3
  Richard Crane Memorial Truck Show (St. Ignace), Sep 15
  Riverwalk Fest (Lowell), Jul 7
  Saint Johns Mint Fest (St. Johns), Aug 11
  Silver Bells in the City (Lansing), Nov 17
  Snowman Burning (Sault Ste. Marie), Mar 20
  St. Ignace Auto Show (St. Ignace), Jun 22
  Stabenow, Debbie: Birth, Apr 29
  State Fair (Detroit), Aug 9
  Sugarloaf Art Fair (Novi), Apr 21, Oct 20
  Summerswap (Frankenmuth), Jul 15
  Super Bowl (Detroit), Feb 5
  Tip-Up Town USA (Houghton Lake), Jan 21
  Ultimate Fishing Show (Novi), Jan 12
  Ultimate Sport & RV Show (Grand Rapids), Mar 16
  Victorian Christmas Sleighbell Parade (Manistee), Dec 1
  Wayne State Univ: Funeral for Winter (Detroit), Apr 5
  Winterfest (Burton), Jan 21
  Wyandotte Heritage Days (Wyandotte), Sep 9
  Wyandotte Street Art Fair (Wyandotte), Jul 12
  Zehnder's Snowfest (Frankenmuth), Jan 25
Mickelson, Phil: Birth, Jun 16
Mickey Mouse Club TV Premiere: Anniv, Oct 3
Mickey Mouse's Birthday, Nov 18
Micro Small & Home Business Week, Celebrate, Oct 16
Microfinance Month, Intl, Nov 1
Micronesia, Federated States of: Constitution Day, May 10
Micronesia, Federated States of: Independence Day, Nov 3
Microsoft Releases Windows: Anniv, Nov 10
Mid-Autumn Fest (China), Oct 6
Middleton, Arthur: Birth Anniv, Jun 26
Midler, Bette: Birth, Dec 1
Midnight Sun Baseball Game (Fairbanks, AK), Jun 21
Midnight Sun Fest (Nome, AK), Jun 17
Midori: Birth, Oct 25
Mid-South Fair (Memphis, TN), Sep 22
Midsummer (Wiccan), Jun 21
Midsummer Day/Eve Celebrations, Jun 23
Midsummer Nights' Fair (Norman, OK), Jul 14
Midwife's Day (Greece), Jan 8
Midwinter's Day Celebration (Ann Arbor, MI), Feb 6
Mighty Mouse Playhouse TV Premiere: Anniv, Dec 10
Migrants Day, Intl (UN), Dec 18
Migratory Bird Day, Intl, May 13

Mikita, Stan: Birth, May 20
Mikulski, Barbara Ann: Birth, Jul 20
Mikulski, Barbara: Polish-American in the House: Anniv, Jan 4
Milano, Alyssa: Birth, Dec 19
Milbrett, Tiffeny: Birth, Oct 23
Miles, Sarah: Birth, Dec 31
Miles, Sylvia: Birth, Sep 9
Miles, Vera: Birth, Aug 23
Military Dictatorship Ended in Chile: Anniv, Dec 15
Military Through the Ages (Williamsburg, VA), Mar 18
Milk Days Fest, Harvard (Harvard, IL), Jun 2
Millay, Edna St. Vincent: Birth Anniv, Feb 22
Millennium Summit, UN: Anniv, Sep 6
Miller, Arthur: Birth Anniv, Oct 17
Miller, Arthur: Death of a Salesman Premiere: Anniv, Feb 10
Miller, Barry: Birth, Feb 6
Miller, Christa: Birth, May 28
Miller, Dennis: Birth, Nov 3
Miller, Glenn: Birth Anniv, Mar 1
Miller, Glenn: Birthplace Society Fest (Clarinda, IA), Jun 8
Miller, Henry: Birth Anniv, Dec 26
Miller, Jonny Lee: Birth, Nov 15
Miller, Penelope Ann: Birth, Jan 13
Miller, Reggie: Birth, Aug 24
Miller, Roger: Birth Anniv, Jan 2
Miller, Shannon: Birth, Mar 10
Miller, Steve: Birth, Oct 5
Miller's, Joe: Joke Day, Aug 16
Millett, Kate: Birth, Sep 14
Million Man March: Anniv, Oct 16
Million Minute Family Challenge™, Sep 1
Million Mom March: Anniv, May 14
Millionaire TV Premiere: Anniv, Jan 19
Mills, Donna: Birth, Dec 11
Mills, Florence: Birth Anniv, Jan 25
Mills, Hayley: Birth, Apr 18
Mills, John: Birth Anniv, Feb 22
Mills, Juliet: Birth, Nov 21
Milne, A.A.: Birth Anniv (Pooh Day), Jan 18
Milsap, Ronnie: Birth, Jan 16
Milton Berle Show: Texaco Star Theater, Sep 21
Milton, John: Birth Anniv, Dec 9
Milwaukee Irish Fest (Milwaukee, WI), Aug 17
Mimieux, Yvette: Birth, Jan 8
Mims, Marilyn: Birth, Sep 8
Mind Day, Make Up Your, Dec 31
Mineral Collecting Field Trips (Bancroft, ON, Canada), Jul 4
Mineta, Norman: Birth, Nov 12
Ming, Yao: Birth, Sep 12
Minghella, Anthony: Birth, Jan 6
Mining: Boom Days (Leadville, CO), Aug 4
Minnelli, Liza: Birth, Mar 12
Minner, Ruth Ann: Birth, Jan 17
Minnesota
    Admission Day, May 11
    Aebleskiver Days (Tyler), Jul 21
    American Nurses Assn Conv (Minneapolis), Jun 25
    Big Island Rendezvous & Fest (Albert Lea), Oct 7
    Big Ten Women's Rowing (Minneapolis), Apr 29
    Braham Pie Day (Braham), Aug 4
    Buffalo Days Celebration (Luverne), Jun 2
    Calithumpian Parade (Biwabik), Jul 4
    Christmas Epiphany Celebration (Isanti), Jan 8
    Coleman, Norm: Birth, Aug 17
    Dayton, Mark: Birth, Jan 26
    Defeat of Jesse James Days (Northfield), Sep 6
    Early America Historical Fair (Albert Lea), Feb 11
    Edmund Fitzgerald Beacon Lighting (Two Harbors), Nov 10
    Farm Toy Show & Auction (Sauk Centre), Feb 11
    Fest of Adventures (Aitkin), Sep 16
    Fest of Nations (St. Paul), May 4
    Heritagefest (New Ulm), Jul 14
    Hot Dog Night (Luverne), Jul 13
    Icebox Days (International Falls), Jan 12
    Inventors Congress (Redwood Falls), Jun 8
    Johnny Appleseed Days (Lake City), Oct 1
    King Turkey Days (Worthington), Sep 16
    Little Falls Arts/Crafts (Little Falls), Sep 9
    Minnesota Renaissance Fest (Shakopee), Aug 12
    Nobel Conference (St. Peter), Oct 3
    Norwegian Christmas (Brooklyn Park), Dec 2
    Oktoberfest (New Ulm), Oct 6
    Old Time School (Cambridge), Jun 3
    Paul Bunyan Sled Dog Races, Mutt Races (Bemidji), Feb 25
    Pawlenty, Tim: Birth, Nov 1
    Rochesterfest (Rochester), Jun 17
    Saint Olaf Christmas Fest (Northfield), Nov 30
    Saint Paul Winter Carnival (St. Paul), Jan 27
    Scandinavian Hjemkomst Fest (Moorhead), Jun 23
    Sinclair Lewis Days (Sauk Centre), Jul 9

Song of Hiawatha Pageant (Pipestone), Jul 21
South St. Paul Kaposia Days (South St. Paul), Jun 23
Spamtown USA Freedom Fest (Austin), Jul 1
State Fair (St. Paul), Aug 24
Swedish Language and Culture Day Camp (Cambridge), Aug 21
Take a Kid Fishing Weekend (St. Paul), Jun 9
Tall Timber Days Fest (Grand Rapids), Aug 5
Tetonkaha Rendezvous (Lake Benton), Aug 11
Tri-State Band Fest (Luverne), Sep 30
US Amateur (Golf) Chmpshp (Chaska), Aug 21
Voyageurs Natl Park Established: Anniv, Apr 8
Water Ski Days (Lake City), Jun 23
White Oak Rendezvous (Deer River), Aug 4
Windsurfing Regatta/Unvarnished Music Fest (Worthington), Jun 9
Winterfest (Luverne), Dec 1
World Famous Fish House Parade (Aitkin), Nov 24
Minority Enterprise Development Week (Pres Proc), Sep 10
Minow, Newton: Birth, Jan 17
Minow, Newton: Vast Wasteland Speech: Anniv, May 9
Mint Julep Scale Meet (Falls of Rough, KY), May 19
Mint, US: Anniv, Apr 2
Miou-Miou: Birth, Feb 22
Mir Space Station, Feb 20
Mirabel Sisters Murdered: Anniv, Nov 25
Miracle on Ice: US Hockey Team Defeats USSR: Anniv, Feb 22
Miranda Decision: Anniv, Jun 13
Mirra, Dave: Birth, Apr 4
Mirren, Helen: Birth, Jul 26
Mirror of the World Translation, Caxton's: Anniv, Mar 8
Mirth Month, Intl, Mar 1
Mischief Night, Nov 4
Miss America Pageant, First: Anniv, Sep 8
Miss American Rose Day, Oct 20
Missile (Titan II) Explosion: Anniv, Sep 19
Missile, First Surface-to-Surface Missile: Anniv, Dec 24
Missing Children's Day, Natl, May 25
Missing Persons Day, New York State (Albany, NY), Apr 6
Mission Delores Founding: Anniv, Oct 9
Mission San Antonio de Padua: Founding Anniv, Jul 14
Mission San Carlos Borromeo de Carmelo: Founding Anniv, Jun 3
Mission San Diego de Alcala: Founding Anniv, Jul 16
Mission San Gabriel Archangel: Founding Anniv, Sep 8
Mission San Juan Capistrano: Founding Anniv, Nov 1
Mission San Luis Obispo de Tolosa: Founding Anniv, Sep 1
Mission San Luis Rey de Francia: Founding Anniv, Jun 13
Mission Santa Barbara: Founding Anniv, Dec 4
Mission Santa Clara de Asis: Founding Anniv, Jan 12
Mission: Impossible TV Premiere: Anniv, Sep 17
Missionary Fair, Road Church (Stonington, CT), May 13
Mississinewa 1812 (Marion, IN), Oct 13
Mississippi
    Admission Day, Dec 10
    Barbour, Haley: Birth, Oct 22
    Cellular South Gum Tree Fest (Tupelo), May 13
    Chimneyville Crafts Fest (Jackson), Dec 2
    Civil Rights Workers Found Slain: Anniv, Aug 4
    Cochran, Thad: Birth, Dec 7
    Confederate Memorial Day, Apr 24
    Lott, Trent: Birth, Oct 9
    Meredith (James) Enrolls at Ole Miss: Anniv, Sep 30
    Miss Mississippi Pageant (Vicksburg), Jun 21
    Natchez Fall Pilgrimage (Natchez), Sep 30
    Natchez Powwow (Natchez), Mar 25
    Natchez Spring Pilgrimage (Natchez), Mar 10
    Neshoba County Fair (Philadelphia), Jul 21
    State Fair (Jackson), Oct 4
    Vicksburg Surrenders: Anniv, Jul 3
Mississippi River Valley Scenic Drive (Cape Girardeau, MO), Apr 22
Missouri
    Adelphian Club Christmas Bazaar (Kennett), Dec 2
    Admission Day, Aug 10
    Adoration Parade (Branson), Dec 3
    American Assn for the Advancement of Science Mtg (St. Louis), Feb 16
    Apple Butter Makin' Days (Mount Vernon), Oct 13
    Art Fair & Winefest (Washington), May 19
    Autumn Historic Folklife Fest (Hannibal), Oct 21

Benton Neighbor Day (Benton), Sep 1
Big 12 Men's & Women's Swimming Chmpshp (Columbia), Feb 22
Big Muddy Folk Music Fest (Boonville), Apr 7
Black Walnut Fest (Stockton), Sep 20
Blueberry Hill Open Dart Tournament (St. Louis), Apr 28
Blunt, Matt: Birth, Nov 20
Bond, Christopher S.: Birth, Mar 6
Branson Fest (Branson), Apr 4
Brookfield Summer Fun Days (Brookfield), Jun 15
Christmas Traditions (St. Charles), Nov 24
Coal Miner Days (Novinger), May 28
Cow Milked While Flying: Anniv, Feb 18
Dam Experience (Warsaw), Jul 1
Deutsch Country Days (Marthasville), Oct 21
Dogwood Festival (Camdenton), Apr 20
Eagle Days in Springfield (Springfield), Jan 21
Earth Day Community Fest (St. Louis), Apr 23
Earthquakes: Anniv, Dec 6
Eldon Turkey Fest (Eldon), Oct 14
Elvis Presley Remembered (St. Louis), Aug 12
Emmett Kelly Clown Fest (Houston), May 5
Fall Fest (Monett), Sep 16
Fall Fest of Arts and Crafts (Washington), Sep 23
Farmington Country Days (Farmington), Jun 2
Festival of the Little Hills (St. Charles), Aug 18
4-Wheel Drive Jamboree (Springfield), May 6
Fourth of July Celebration (Trenton), Jul 2
Great Mississippi River Arts/Crafts Fest (Hannibal), May 27
Greater Springfield Garage Sale (Springfield), Jan 28
Groundhog Run (Kansas City), Jan 29
Hartville Annual Fall Fest (Hartville), Oct 21
Heritage Day (Houston), Sep 16
Japanese Fest (St. Louis), Sep 2
Jours de Fete (Ste. Genevieve), Aug 12
KRXL Car Cruise (Kirksville), Aug 5
Lewis and Clark Bicentennial Natl Signature Event: Confluence with Destiny (St. Louis), Sep 23
Lewis and Clark Heritage Days (St. Charles), May 20
Liberty Fall Festival (Liberty), Sep 22
Liberty Spring on the Square Festival (Liberty), May 20
Magic Dragon Street Meet Nationals & Extreme Car Shows (Lake Ozark), May 5
Maifest (Hermann), May 20
Mardi Gras in Branson (Branson), Jun 8
Mayor's Christmas Tree (Kansas City), Nov 24
Meramec Community Fair (Sullivan), Jun 22
Mid-America Natl Street Rod Assn Car Show (Springfield), May 26
Mississippi River Valley Scenic Drive (Cape Girardeau), Apr 22
Missouri Day, Oct 18
Missouri Day Fest (Trenton), Oct 19
Missouri River Fest of Arts (Boonville), Aug 25
Missouri State Chmpshp Racking Horse Show (Dexter), Jun 3
Monett Fourth of July (Monett), Jul 4
NAIA Div I Men's Basketball Chmpshp (Kansas City), Mar 15
NAIA Div II Men's Basketball Chmpshp (Point Lookout), Mar 8
NAIA Natl Men's and Women's Swimming/Diving Chmpshps (St. Peters), Mar 1
North Central Missouri Fair (Trenton), Aug 1
Northeast Missouri Triathlon (Kirksville), Sep 10
No-Tillage Conference, Natl (St. Louis), Jan 11
Oktoberfest (St. Charles), Oct 7
Old Glory Jubilee (Elsberry), Jul 4
Orchid Show (St. Louis), Jan 28
Osage River Mountain Man Fest and Black Powder Shoot (Lake Ozark), Sep 15
Ozark Antique Auto Club Swap Meet (Springfield), Aug 25
Ozark Empire Fair (Springfield), Jul 28
Ozark Fall Farmfest (Springfield), Oct 6
Ozark Mountain Christmas/Branson Fest of Lights (Branson), Nov 1
Plaza Lights (Kansas City), Nov 23
Prairie Day (Diamond), Sep 9
Richmond's Mushroom Fest (Richmond), May 5
Saint Louis Race Riots: Anniv, Jul 2
Saint Piran's Day Celebration (Kansas City), Mar 4
Santa-Cali-Gon-Days Fest (Independence), Sep 1
Southeast Missouri District Fair (Cape Girardeau), Sep 9
State Fair (Sedalia), Aug 10
Strawberry Fest (Independence), Jun 3
Street Machine Fall Nationals (Springfield), Sep 15
Super Scout Sunday (Springfield), May 13
Talent, Jim: Birth, Oct 18

Texas County Fair/Old Settlers Reunion (Houston), **Aug 1**
Tom Sawyer Days, Natl (Hannibal), **Jul 1**
Trails West! (St. Joseph), **Aug 18**
Missouri Compromise: Anniv, **Mar 3**
Mister Rogers' Neighborhood TV Premiere: Anniv, **May 22**
Mitchell, Andrea: Birth, **Oct 30**
Mitchell, Chad: Birth, **Dec 5**
Mitchell, James: Birth, **Feb 29**
Mitchell, Joni: Birth, **Nov 7**
Mitchell, Margaret: Birth Anniv, **Nov 8**
Mitchell, Margaret: Gone with the Wind Published: Anniv, **May 19**
Mitchell, Maria: Birth Anniv, **Aug 1**
Mitchum, Robert: Birth Anniv, **Aug 6**
Mix, Tom: Birth Anniv, **Jan 6**
Mize, Larry: Birth, **Sep 23**
Mobius Awards (Los Angeles, CA), **Feb 10**
Mobius, August: Birth Anniv, **Nov 17**
Moby: Birth, **Sep 11**
Moby-Dick (Melville) Marathon (Mystic, CT), **Jul 31**
Moceanu, Dominique: Birth, **Sep 30**
Mochrie, Colin: Birth, **Nov 30**
Modano, Mike: Birth, **Jun 7**
Model Airplane: Mint Julep Scale Meet (Falls of Rough, KY), **May 19**
Model Railroad Show (Wheeling, WV), **Jan 14**
Model T Introduced: Anniv, **Oct 1**
Modine, Matthew: Birth, **Mar 22**
Moffo, Anna: Birth, **Jun 27**
Mohr, Jay: Birth, **Aug 23**
Moldova
  Independence Day, **Aug 27**
  National Language Day, **Aug 31**
Mole Day, Natl, **Oct 23**
Moliere Day: Baptism Anniv, **Jan 15**
Molina, Alfred: Birth, **May 24**
Molineaux, Tom: First US Heavyweight Defeated: Anniv, **Dec 10**
Molitor, Paul: Birth, **Aug 22**
Moll, Richard: Birth, **Jan 13**
Molson, John: Birth Anniv, **Dec 28**
Mom and Pop Business Owners Day, Natl, **Mar 29**
Moment of Frustration Scream Day, Intl, **Oct 12**
Moment of Laughter Day, **Apr 14**
Moment of Silence (Nagasaki, Japan), **Aug 9**
Monaco: National Holiday, **Nov 19**
Monaghan, Dominic: Birth, **Dec 8**
Mondale, Walter Frederick (Fritz): Birth, **Jan 5**
Monday Holiday Law: Anniv, **Jun 28**
Monday Night Football TV Premiere: Anniv, **Sep 21**
Monday: Natl Thank God It's Monday! Day, **Jan 9**
Mondesi, Raul: Birth, **Mar 12**
Monet, Claude: Birth Anniv, **Nov 14**
Money, Eddie: Birth, **Mar 2**
Money, Paper, Issued: Anniv, **Mar 10**
Mongolia
  National Holiday, **Jul 11**
  Republic Day, **Nov 26**
Monica: Birth, **Oct 24**
Monitor Sinking: Anniv, **Dec 30**
Monk, Art: Birth, **Dec 5**
Monkees TV Premiere: Anniv, **Sep 12**
Monkey Trial: John T. Scopes Birth Anniv, **Aug 3**
Monopoly Invented: Anniv, **Mar 7**
Monroe Doctrine: Anniv, **Dec 2**
Monroe, Elizabeth K.: Birth Anniv, **Jun 30**
Monroe, Harriet: Birth Anniv, **Dec 23**
Monroe, James: Birthday Celebration (Charlottesville, VA), **Apr 28**
Monroe, James: Birth Anniv, **Apr 28**
Monroe, Marilyn: Birth Anniv, **Jun 1**
Monroe, Marilyn: First Screen Test: Anniv, **Jul 19**
Montagnier, Luc: Birth, **Aug 18**
Montaigne, Michel de: Birth Anniv, **Feb 28**
Montalban, Ricardo: Birth, **Nov 20**
Montana
  Admission Day, **Nov 8**
  Arts in the Park (Kalispell), **Jul 21**
  Bannack Days (Bannack), **Jul 15**
  Battle of Little Bighorn: Anniv, **Jun 25**
  Baucus, Max: Birth, **Dec 11**
  Beartooth Run (Red Lodge), **Jun 24**
  Big Sky State Games (Billings), **Jul 14**
  Burns, Conrad: Birth, **Jan 25**
  Buzzard Day Fest (Glendive), **Jun 10**
  C.M. Russell Auction Orig Western Art (Great Falls), **Mar 15**
  Central Montana Fair (Lewistown), **Jul 26**
  Christmas to Remember (Laurel), **Dec 3**
  Ennis Rodeo & Parade (Ennis), **Jul 3**
  Glacier Natl Park: Anniv, **May 11**
  Helena Railroad Fair (Helena), **Apr 30**
  Ice Fishing Contest (Fort Peck), **Feb 11**

Lewis & Clark Bicentennial Natl Signature Event: Clark on the Yellowstone (Billings), **Jul 22**
  Little Bighorn Days (Hardin), **Jun 21**
  Livingston Roundup & PRCA Rodeo (Livingston), **Jul 2**
  Longest Dam Run (Fort Peck), **Jun 17**
  Mai Wah Society Chinese Lunar New Year Parade (Butte), **Feb 4**
  Miles City Bucking Horse Sale (Miles City), **May 19**
  Montana Governor's Cup Walleye Tournament (Fort Peck), **Jul 6**
  Montana Winter Fair (Lewistown), **Jan 25**
  Nordicfest (Libby), **Sep 8**
  Northeast Montana Threshing Bee/Antique Show (Culbertson), **Sep 23**
  Northern Intl Livestock Expo (Billings), **Oct 18**
  NRA/NWRA Rodeo Finals (Billings), **Feb 17**
  Schweitzer, Brian: Birth, **Sep 5**
  State Fair (Great Falls), **Jul 28**
  Tamarack Time (Bigfork), **Oct 14**
  Wild Horse Stampede (Wolf Point), **Jul 6**
  Wildlife Film Fest, Intl (Missoula), **Apr 29**
  Wolf Point's Annual Christmas Parade (Wolf Point), **Dec 1**
Montana, Joe: Birth, **Jun 11**
Montand, Yves: Birth Anniv, **Oct 13**
Monterey Jazz Fest (Monterey, CA), **Sep 15**
Montessori, Maria: Birth Anniv, **Aug 31**
Montgolfier, Jacques: Birth Anniv, **Jan 7**
Montgolfier, Joseph M.: Birth Anniv, **Aug 26**
Montgomery Boycott Arrests: Anniv, **Feb 22**
Montgomery Bus Boycott Begins: Anniv, **Dec 5**
Montgomery Bus Boycott Ends: Anniv, **Dec 20**
Montgomery, Belinda: Birth, **Jul 23**
Montgomery, Bernard Law: Birth Anniv, **Nov 17**
Montgomery, Poppy: Birth, **Jun 19**
Montoya, Carlos: Birth Anniv, **Dec 3**
Montserrat: Volcano Erupts: Anniv, **Jun 25**
Monty Python's Flying Circus TV Premiere: Anniv, **Oct 5**
Moody, Helen Wills: Birth Anniv, **Oct 6**
Moog, Robert: Birth, **May 23**
Moon Day (First Moon Landing), **Jul 20**
Moon Fest (China), **Oct 6**
Moon Phases
  First Quarter, Jan 6, Feb 5, Mar 6, Apr 5, May 5, Jun 3, Jul 3, Aug 2, Aug 31, Sep 30, Oct 29, Nov 28, Dec 27
  Full Moon, Jan 14, Feb 12, Mar 14, Apr 13, May 13, Jun 11, Jul 10, Aug 9, Sep 7, Oct 6, Nov 5, Dec 4
  Last Quarter, Jan 22, Feb 21, Mar 22, Apr 20, May 20, Jun 18, Jul 17, Aug 15, Sep 14, Oct 13, Nov 12, Dec 12
  New Moon, Jan 29, Feb 27, Mar 29, Apr 27, May 27, Jun 25, Jul 25, Aug 23, Sep 22, Oct 22, Nov 20, Dec 20
Moon, Harvest, **Sep 7**
Moon, Hunter's, **Oct 6**
Moon, Warren: Birth, **Nov 18**
Moonlighting TV Premiere: Anniv, **Mar 3**
Moore, Archie: Birth Anniv, **Dec 13**
Moore, Clement: Birth Anniv, **Jul 15**
Moore, Demi: Birth, **Nov 11**
Moore, Dudley: Birth Anniv, **Apr 19**
Moore, Garry: Birth Anniv, **Jan 31**
Moore, Henry: Birth Anniv, **Jul 30**
Moore, Julia A. Davis: Birth Anniv, **Dec 1**
Moore, Julianne: Birth, **Dec 3**
Moore, Lenny: Birth, **Nov 25**
Moore, Mary Tyler: Birth, **Dec 29**
Moore, Melba: Birth, **Oct 29**
Moore, Michael: Birth, **Apr 23**
Moore, Roger: Birth, **Oct 14**
Moore, Shemar: Birth, **Apr 20**
Moore, Terry: Birth, **Jan 7**
MooseStompers Weekend (Houlton, ME), **Feb 3**
Morales, Esai: Birth, **Oct 1**
Moran, Erin: Birth, **Oct 18**
Moranis, Rick: Birth, **Apr 18**
Moravian Easter Resurrection Service (Winston-Salem, NC), **Apr 16**
Morazan, Francisco: Holiday (Honduras), **Oct 3**
More Herbs, Less Salt Day, **Aug 29**
More than Just a Pretty Face Month, **May 1**
More, Sir Thomas: Birth Anniv, **Feb 7**
Moreau, Jeanne: Birth, **Jan 23**
Moreno, Rita: Birth, **Dec 11**
Morgan, Harry: Birth, **Apr 10**
Morgan, Jaye P.: Birth, **Dec 3**
Morgan, Joe: Birth, **Sep 19**
Morgan, John P.: Birth Anniv, **Apr 17**
Morgan, Michele: Birth, **Feb 29**
Moriarty, Cathy: Birth, **Nov 29**
Moriarty, Michael: Birth, **Apr 5**
Morione's Fest (Marinduque Island, Philippines), **Apr 13**
Morissette, Alanis: Birth, **Jun 1**

Morita, Pat: Birth, **Aug 28**
Morley, Robert: Birth Anniv, **May 26**
Mormon
  Amnesty for Polygamists: Anniv, **Jan 4**
  Church of Jesus Christ of Latter-day Saints: Anniv, **Apr 6**
  Female Relief Society of Nauvoo: Anniv, **Mar 17**
  Mormon Battalion Arrival in California: Anniv, **Jan 29**
  Mormon Choir First Performs: Anniv, **Aug 22**
  Nauvoo Legion Chartered: Anniv, **Feb 3**
  Pioneer Day, **Jul 24**
Morocco
  Anniversary of the Green March, **Nov 6**
  Independence Day, **Jan 11**
  National Day, **May 23**
  Revolution of the King and the People, **Aug 20**
  Youth Day, **Jul 9**
Morrill Land Grant Act Passed: Anniv, **Jul 1**
Morris, Esther Hobart McQuigg: Birth Anniv, **Aug 8**
Morris, Garrett: Birth, **Feb 1**
Morris, Jack: Birth, **May 16**
Morris, Kathryn: Birth, **Jan 28**
Morris, Lewis: Birth Anniv, **Apr 8**
Morris, Mark: Birth, **Aug 29**
Morris, Robert: Birth Anniv, **Jan 31**
Morris, William: Birth Anniv, **Mar 24**
Morrison, Jim: Birth Anniv, **Dec 8**
Morrison, Jim: Death Anniv, **Jul 3**
Morrison, Toni: Birth, **Feb 18**
Morrison, Van: Birth, **Aug 31**
Morro Bay Harbor Fest (Morro Bay, CA), **Oct 7**
Morrow, Rob: Birth, **Sep 21**
Morse, David: Birth, **Oct 11**
Morse, Robert: Birth, **May 18**
Morse, Samuel F.: Birth Anniv, **Apr 27**
Morse, Samuel F.: Opens First US Telegraph Line: Anniv, **May 24**
Mortensen, Viggo: Birth, **Oct 20**
Morton, Jelly Roll: Birth Anniv, **Sep 20**
Morton, Joe: Birth, **Oct 18**
Morton, Levi P.: Birth Anniv, **May 16**
Moscow Soccer Tragedy: Anniv, **Oct 20**
Moscow, Nixon First American President to Visit: Anniv, **May 22**
Moses, Anna: Grandma Moses Day, **Sep 7**
Moses, Edwin: Birth, **Aug 31**
Moshoeshoe's Day (Lesotho), **Mar 12**
Mosquito Fest, Great Texas (Clute, TX), **Jul 27**
Moss, Randy: Birth, **Feb 13**
Moth-er Day, **Mar 14**
Mother Goose Day, **May 1**
Mother Goose Parade (El Cajon, CA), **Nov 19**
Mother Language Day, Intl, **Feb 21**
Mother Ocean Day, **May 13**
Mother Teresa: Birth Anniv, **Aug 27**
Mother, Father Deaf Day, **Apr 30**
Mothering Sunday (England), **Mar 26**
Mother-in-Law-Day, **Oct 22**
Mother's Day, **May 14**
Mother's Day (Pres Proc), **May 14**
Mothers Day at the Wall (Washington, DC), **May 14**
Mother's Day Housewalk (Evanston, IL), **May 14**
Motley, Constance Baker: Birth, **Sep 14**
Motor Voter Bill Signed: Anniv, **May 20**
Motorcycle
  AHRMA Vintage Motorcycle Races (Daytona Beach, FL), **Mar 6**
  AspenCash Motorcycle Rally (Ruidoso, NM), **May 18**
  Biketoberfest (Daytona Beach, FL), **Oct 19**
  Daytona 200 by Honda Classic (Daytona Beach, FL), **Mar 11**
  Daytona Supercross by Honda (Daytona Beach, FL), **Mar 11**
  Fall Cycle Scene Motorcycle Races (Daytona Beach, FL), **Oct 19**
  Golden Aspen Motorcycle Rally (Ruidoso, NM), **Sep 13**
  Motorcycle Safety Month, **May 1**
  Sturgis Rally (Sturgis, SD), **Aug 7**
  Trail of Tears Commemoration (Waterloo, AL), **Sep 16**
  Women's Motorcycle Month, **Jul 1**
Mott, Lucretia (Coffin): Birth Anniv, **Jan 3**
Mott, Stewart Rawlings: Birth, **Dec 4**
Moulin, Jean: Death Anniv, **Jul 8**
Mount Everest Summit Reached: Anniv, **May 29**
Mount Everest, First Woman to Climb: Anniv, **May 16**
Mount Holyoke College Founded: Anniv, **Nov 8**
Mount Ogura Plane Crash: Anniv, **Aug 12**
Mount Pelee Eruption: Anniv, **May 8**
Mount Rainier Natl Park: Anniv, **Mar 2**
Mount Rushmore Completion: Anniv, **Oct 31**

Mount Rushmore—Music

Mount Rushmore July 4 Celebration (Mount Rushmore, SD), **Jul 3**
Mount Saint Helens Eruption: Anniv, **May 18**
Mountain Dance and Folk Fest (Asheville, NC), **Aug 3**
Mountain Day, Intl (UN), **Dec 11**
Mountain Fair (Hiawassee, GA), **Jul 19**
Mountain Glory Fest (Marion, NC), **Oct 14**
Mountain Man Rendezvous (Cataldo, ID), **Aug 18**
Mountbatten, Louis: Assassination Anniv, **Aug 27**
Mourning, Alonzo: Birth, **Feb 8**
Move Hollywood & Broadway to Lebanon, PA, Day, **Feb 5**
Movie Theater Opens, First : Anniv, **Apr 23**
Moving Month, Natl, **May 1**
Moya, Carlos: Birth, **Aug 27**
Moyers, Bill: Birth, **Jun 5**
Mozambique
    Armed Forces Day, **Sep 24**
    Heroes' Day, **Feb 3**
    Independence Day, **Jun 25**
Mozart 2006 (Austria), **Jan 27**
Mozart Fest (San Luis Obispo, CA), **Jul 14**
Mozart Fest, Mainly (San Diego, CA), **Jun 1**
Mozart Intl Fest (Bartlesville, OK), **Jun 9**
Mozart, Wolfgang Amadeus: Birth Anniv, **Jan 27**
Mr Peepers TV Premiere: Anniv, **Jul 3**
Mr Wizard TV Premiere: Anniv, **Mar 3**
MTV Premiere: Anniv, **Aug 1**
Mudbug Madness (Shreveport, LA), **May 25**
Mudd Day, **Dec 20**
Mudd, Roger: Birth, **Feb 9**
Muddy Frogwater Country Classic Fest (Milton-Freewater, OR), **Aug 18**
Muhammad: Isra al Mi'raj: Ascent of Prophet, **Aug 21**
Muhammad: Mawlid al Nabi: Birth of Muhammad, **Apr 11**
Muharram: See Islamic New Year, **Jan 31**
Muir, John: Birth Anniv, **Apr 21**
Muldaur, Diana: Birth, **Aug 19**
Muldaur, Maria: Birth, **Sep 12**
Mule Day, **Oct 26**
Mule Day (Columbia, TN), **Mar 30**
Mulgrew, Kate: Birth, **Apr 29**
Mulhern, Matt: Birth, **Jul 21**
Mulholland, Terry: Birth, **Mar 9**
Mull, Martin: Birth, **Aug 18**
Mullally, Megan: Birth, **Nov 12**
Mullen, Larry: Birth, **Oct 31**
Mulligan Day, **Oct 17**
Mulligan, Gerry: Birth Anniv, **Apr 6**
Mullin, Chris: Birth, **Jul 30**
Mulroney, Brian: Birth, **Mar 20**
Mulroney, Dermot: Birth, **Oct 31**
Multicultural American Child Awareness Day, **Jun 11**
Multicultural Fest (Dartmouth, NS, Canada), **Jun 16**
Multiple Sclerosis Awareness Week, **Mar 13**
Multiple Sclerosis Education & Awareness Month, Natl, **Mar 1**
Mummies: Iceman Discovered: Anniv, **Sep 19**
Mummies: King Tut Tomb Discovery: Anniv, **Nov 4**
Mumy, Bill: Birth, **Feb 1**
Muniz, Frankie: Birth, **Dec 5**
Munoz-Rivera, Luis: Birth Anniv, **Jul 17**
Munsel, Patrice: Birth, **May 14**
Munsters TV Premiere: Anniv, **Sep 24**
Muppet Show Premiere: Anniv, **Sep 13**
Muppets: Henson, Jim: Birth Anniv, **Sep 24**
Mural-in-a-Day (Toppenish, WA), **Jun 3**
Murder, She Wrote TV Premiere: Anniv, **Sep 30**
Murdoch, Rupert: Birth, **Mar 11**
Murkowski, Frank Hughes: Birth, **Mar 28**
Murkowski, Lisa: Birth, **May 22**
Murphy Brown TV Premiere: Anniv, **Nov 14**
Murphy, Audie: Birth Anniv, **Jun 20**
Murphy, Ben: Birth, **Mar 6**
Murphy, Brittany: Birth, **Nov 10**
Murphy, Dale: Birth, **Mar 12**
Murphy, Eddie: Birth, **Apr 3**
Murphy, Michael: Birth, **May 5**
Murray, Anne: Birth, **Jun 20**
Murray, Bill: Birth, **Sep 21**
Murray, Chad Michael: Birth, **Aug 24**
Murray, Don: Birth, **Jul 31**
Murray, Eddie: Birth, **Feb 24**
Murray, Jan: Birth, **Oct 4**
Murray, Ken: Birth Anniv, **Jul 14**
Murray, Patty: Birth, **Oct 11**
Murray, Philip: Birth Anniv, **May 25**
Musburger, Brent: Birth, **May 26**
Museum Day, Intl, **May 18**
Musgrave, Storey: Birth, **Aug 19**
Mushroom Fest (Kennett Square, PA), **Sep 9**
Mushroom Fest, Richmond's (Richmond, MO), **May 5**

Mushroom Fest, Telluride (Telluride, CO), **Aug 17**
Mushroom Month, Natl, **Sep 1**
Musial, Stan: Birth, **Nov 21**
Music. See also Bluegrass, Country & Western, Fiddlers, Gospel, Jazz and Blues, Rock 'n' Roll
    Aberdeen Intl Youth Fest (Aberdeen, Scotland), **Aug 2**
    Accordion Awareness Month, Intl, **Jun 1**
    Accordion Chmpshp, Kimberley Intl (Kimberley, BC, Canada), **Jul 3**
    Accordion Fest, Sata-Hame (Ikaalinen, Finland), **Jun 27**
    Albany Alive at Five (Albany, NY), **Jun 1**
    All That Jazz Weekend (Asheville, NC), **Jan 27**
    All-Northwest Barbershop Ballad Contest (Forest Grove, OR), **Mar 3**
    Altamont Concert: Anniv, **Dec 6**
    America the Beautiful Published, **Jul 4**
    Anderson, Marian: Easter Concert: Anniv, **Apr 9**
    Ash Lawn Opera Fest (Charlottesville, VA), **Jul 10**
    Aspen Music Fest (Aspen, CO), **Jun 19**
    Bach Fest (Leipzig, Germany), **May 27**
    Barbershop Quartet Day, **Apr 11**
    Beatles Fest (Liverpool, England), **Aug 25**
    Beatles Last Concert: Anniv, **Jan 30**
    Beethoven's Ninth Symphony Premiere: Anniv, **May 7**
    Big Muddy Folk Music Fest (Boonville, MO), **Apr 7**
    Big Valley Jamboree (Camrose, AB, Canada), **Aug 4**
    Blondie and Deborah Harry Month, Intl, **Jul 1**
    Brahms Requiem Premiere: Anniv, **Apr 10**
    Branson Fest (Branson, MO), **Apr 4**
    Brass Band Festival (Gettysburg, PA), **Jun 15**
    Burlington Steamboat Days/Music Fest (Burlington, IA), **Jun 13**
    Calgary Folk Fest (Calgary, AB, Canada), **Jul 27**
    Canmore Folk Music Fest (Canmore, AB, Canada), **Aug 5**
    Cape May Music Fest (Cape May, NJ), **May 21**
    Carillon Fest, Intl (Springfield, IL), **Jun 4**
    Carry a Tune Week, Natl, **Oct 1**
    Celtic Classic Highland Games & Fest (Bethlehem, PA), **Sep 29**
    Celtic Fest, Southern Maryland (St. Leonard, MD), **Apr 29**
    Chicago Gospel Music Fest (Chicago, IL), **Jun 9**
    Chicago Jazz Fest (Chicago, IL), **Aug 31**
    Cisco Systems Ottawa Bluesfest (Ottawa, ON, Canada), **Jul 7**
    Concerts By the Springs (Atlanta, GA), **May 21**
    Connecticut Early Music Fest (New London, CT), **Jun 9**
    Day the Music Died (Holly, Richardson, Valens: Death Anniv), **Feb 3**
    Desert Foothills Musicfest (Carefree, AZ), **Feb 7**
    Downtown Fest/Art Show (Gainesville, FL), **Nov 4**
    Dulcimer Days (Coshocton, OH), **May 19**
    Duran Duran Appreciation Day, Natl, **Aug 10**
    Eastern Music Fest (Greensboro, NC), **Jun 24**
    Edinburgh Intl Fest (Edinburgh, Scotland), **Aug 13**
    Edmonton Folk Music Fest (Edmonton, AB, Canada), **Aug 10**
    Everly Brothers/Central City Rock 'n Roll Cruise-In and Concert (Central City, KY), **Sep 1**
    Exeter Fest (Exeter, England), **Jun 16**
    Falcon Ridge Folk Fest (Hillsdale, NY), **Jul 20**
    Fall Suwannee River Gospel Jubilee (Live Oak, FL), **Oct 4**
    Festival at Sandpoint (Sandpoint, ID), **Aug 3**
    Fiddler's Frolics (Hallettsville, TX), **Apr 27**
    First Grand Ole Opry Broadcast: Anniv, **Dec 10**
    Glenn Miller Birthplace Society Fest (Clarinda, IA), **Jun 8**
    God Bless America First Performed: Anniv, **Nov 11**
    Grammy Awards, **Feb 8**
    Grand Teton Music Fest (Teton Village, WY), **Jul 4**
    Great American Brass Band Fest (Danville, KY), **Jun 10**
    Guelph Spring Fest (Guelph, ON, Canada), **Apr 28**
    Guitar Flat-Picking Chmpshps, Natl (Winfield, KS), **Sep 14**
    Hankfest (Chicago, IL), **Sep 16**
    Happy Birthday to "Happy Birthday to You", **Jun 27**
    Harrison Fest of Arts (Harrison Hot Springs, BC, Canada), **Jul 8**
    Heritage Craft and Olde-Time Music Fest (Coshocton, OH), **Jun 17**
    Hodag Country Fest (Rhinelander, WI), **Jul 13**
    Homeplace Fest (Waretown, NJ), **Nov 18**
    Hot August Nights (Reno and Sparks, NV), **Jul 29**
    Jazz Appreciation Month, **Apr 1**
    Jazz Day, Intl, **May 27**
    Joseph Brackett Day, **May 6**
    Karaoke Week, Natl, **Apr 23**
    KCQ Country Music Fest (Saginaw, MI), **Jun 17**
    Kingsville Intl Young Performers' Competitions (Kingsville, TX), **Apr 6**

    Kuopio Dance Fest (Kuopio, Finland), **Jun 15**
    Ladies of Country Music Show (Waretown, NJ), **Jun 24**
    Lahti Organ Fest (Lahti, Finland), **Aug 6**
    Levitt Pavilion Performing Arts/Music Fest (Westport, CT), **Jun 25**
    Liberace Birthday Celebration & Play-A-Like Competition (Las Vegas, NV), **May 13**
    Live Aid Concerts: Anniv, **Jul 13**
    Llangollen Intl Musical Eisteddfod (Llangollen, Wales), **Jul 4**
    Lucerne Fest, Ostern (Lucerne, Switzerland), **Apr 1**
    Lucerne Fest, Piano (Lucerne, Switzerland), **Nov 21**
    Lucerne Fest, Sommer (Lucerne, Switzerland), **Aug 11**
    Madrigal Dinner and Concert (Milwaukee, WI), **Dec 2**
    Magnolia Fest (Live Oak, FL), **Oct 19**
    Mainly Mozart Fest (San Diego, CA), **Jun 1**
    Mardi Gras Fiesta Tropicale (Hollywood, FL), **Feb 24**
    Memorial Day Getaway (Live Oak, FL), **May 26**
    Midnight at the Oasis (Yuma, AZ), **Mar 3**
    Military Music Fest (Belgium), **Jun 11**
    Missouri Day Fest (Trenton, MO), **Oct 19**
    Missouri River Fest of Arts (Boonville, MO), **Aug 25**
    Mormon Choir First Performs: Anniv, **Aug 22**
    Mozart Fest (San Luis Obispo, CA), **Jul 14**
    Music Camp, Intl (Dunseith, ND), **Jun 11**
    Music in Our Schools Month, **Mar 1**
    Music in the Park (Anchorage, AK), **Jun 2**
    Musikfest (Bethlehem, PA), **Aug 4**
    National Eisteddfod of Wales (Swansea, Wales), **Aug 5**
    New World Symphony Premiere: Anniv, **Dec 16**
    Newport Music Fest (Newport, RI), **Jul 7**
    OK Mozart Intl Fest (Bartlesville, OK), **Jun 9**
    Old Stoughton (MA) Musical Society: Anniv, **Nov 7**
    Old-Time Country Music Contest, Fest & Expo, Natl (Missouri Valley, IA), **Aug 28**
    On the Waterfront (Rockford, IL), **Aug 31**
    One-Hit Wonder Day, Natl, **Sep 25**
    Oregon Bach Fest (Eugene, OR), **Jun 30**
    Ottawa Folk Fest (Ottawa, ON, Canada), **Aug 24**
    Party in the Plaza (Aurora, IL), **Jun 7**
    Piano Month, Natl, **Sep 1**
    Piano Playing Contest, World Chmpshp Old-Time (Peoria, IL), **May 26**
    Play-the-Recorder Month, **Mar 1**
    Pop Music Chart Introduced: Anniv, **Jan 4**
    Porter, Cole: Birth Anniv, **Jun 9**
    Prague Autumn Intl Music Fest (Czech Republic), **Sep 12**
    Premiere of Handel's Messiah: Anniv, **Apr 13**
    Quirky Country Music Song Titles Day, **Mar 27**
    Red River Valley Fair (Fargo, ND), **Jun 16**
    Rounds Resounding Day, **Aug 1**
    Saint Olaf Christmas Fest (Northfield, MN), **Nov 30**
    Saint Petersburg Fest of States (St. Petersburg, FL), **Mar 31**
    Santa Fe Chamber Music Fest (Santa Fe, NM), **Jul 16**
    Saxophone Day, **Nov 6**
    Sea Music Fest (Mystic, CT), **Jun 8**
    Shrewsbury Intl Music Fest (Shropshire, England), **Jun 30**
    Silent Record Week, **Jan 1**
    Sing-Out Day, Intl, **Sep 15**
    Songwriter's Show (Waretown, NJ), **Mar 18**
    South by Southwest (Austin, TX), **Mar 10**
    Southern Appalachian Dulcimer Fest (McCalla, AL), **May 6**
    Southern Gospel Music Month, **Sep 1**
    SPEBSQSA (Barbershop Quartet) Conv (Jacksonville, FL), **Jan 15**
    Spoleto Fest USA (Charleston, SC), **May 26**
    Spring Suwannee River Gospel Jubilee (Live Oak, FL), **Jun 14**
    Stars and Stripes Forever Day, **May 14**
    Strauss, Richard G.: Birth Anniv, **Jun 11**
    Stresa Music Weeks (Stresa, Italy), **Jul 26**
    Summer Music Fest (Sitka, AK), **Jun 2**
    Summerfest (Milwaukee, WI), **Jun 29**
    Suwannee Spring Fest (Live Oak, FL), **Mar 23**
    Tennessee Fall Homecoming (Norris, TN), **Oct 11**
    Tennessee Valley Old Time Fiddlers Conv (Athens, AL), **Oct 6**
    Time of Music (Viitasaari, Finland), **Jul 4**
    Traditional Sousa Concert (Kohler, WI), **Jul 4**
    Tri-State Band Fest (Luverne, MN), **Sep 30**
    Tucson Intl Mariachi Conf (Tucson, AZ), **Apr 24**
    Turku Music Fest (Turku, Finland), **Aug 11**
    Vancouver Folk Music Fest (Vancouver, BC, Canada), **Jul 14**
    Vietnam Moratorium Concert: Anniv, **Mar 28**
    Vinyl Record Day, **Aug 12**

Viva El Mariachi Fest (Fresno, CA), **Mar 26**
Viva! Chicago Latin Music Fest (Chicago, IL), **Aug 26**
W.C. Handy Fest (Florence, AL), **Jul 23**
Wagner Festspiele (Bayreuth, Germany), **Jul 25**
Wills, Bob: Birth Anniv, **Mar 6**
Windsurfing Regatta/Unvarnished Music Fest (Worthington, MN), **Jun 9**
Muslim Observances
  Ashura: Tenth Day, **Feb 9**
  Eid-al-Adha: Feast of the Sacrifice, **Jan 10, Dec 31**
  Eid-al-Fitr: Celebrating the Fast, **Oct 24**
  Isra al Mi'raj: Ascent of Prophet Muhammad, **Aug 21**
  Lailat ul Qadr: The Night of Power, **Oct 14**
  Mawlid al Nabi: Birthday of Prophet Muhammad, **Apr 11**
  Muharram (New Year), **Jan 31**
  Rabi' I: Month of the Migration, **Mar 31**
  Ramadan: Islamic Month of Fasting, **Sep 24**
  Yawm Arafat: The Standing at Arafat, **Jan 9, Dec 30**
Mussina, Mike: Birth, **Dec 8**
Mussolini Ousted: Anniv, **Jul 25**
Mussolini, Benito: Birth Anniv, **Jul 29**
Mustang: Intl Ford Mustang Day, **Apr 17**
Mustard Day, Natl, **Aug 5**
Mutiny on the Bounty: Anniv, **Apr 28**
Mutombo, Dikembe: Birth, **Jun 25**
Muybridge, Eadweard: Birth Anniv, **Apr 9**
My Friend Flicka TV Premiere: Anniv, **Feb 10**
My Lai Massacre: Anniv, **Mar 16**
My Little Margie TV Premiere: Anniv, **Jun 15**
My Way Day, **Feb 17**
Myanmar
  Independence Day, **Jan 4**
  Resistance Day, **Mar 27**
  Union Day, **Feb 12**
Myers, Mike: Birth, **May 25**
Myers, Russell: Birth, **Oct 9**
Myerson, Bess: Birth, **Jul 16**
Mystery Series Week, **Oct 1**

NAACP Founded: Anniv, **Feb 12**
Nabokov, Evgeni: Birth, **Jul 25**
Nabors, Jim: Birth, **Jun 12**
Nader, Ralph: Birth, **Feb 27**
Nafels Pilgrimage (Canton Glarus, Switzerland), **Apr 6**
NAFTA Signed: Anniv, **Dec 8**
Nagra, Parminder K.: Birth, **Oct 5**
Nagurski, Bronko: Birth Anniv, **Nov 3**
Naismith, James: Birth Anniv, **Nov 6**
Najimy, Kathy: Birth, **Feb 6**
NALC National Food Drive (Stamp Out Hunger), **May 13**
Namath, Joe: Birth, **May 31**
Name That Tune TV Premiere: Anniv, **Jul 6**
Names
  Celebrate Your Name Week, **Mar 5**
  Fun Facts About Names Day, **Mar 6**
  Get a Different Name Day, **Feb 13**
  Learn What Your Name Means Day, **Mar 8**
  Middle Name Pride Day, **Mar 10**
  Name Your PC Day, **Nov 20**
  Namesake Day, **Mar 5**
  Nametag Day, **Mar 9**
  Unique Names Day, **Mar 7**
  Z Day, **Jan 1**
Namibia
  Heroes' Day, **Aug 26**
  Independence Day, **Mar 21**
Nanak, Guru: Birth Anniv, **Nov 5**
Nanakusa (Japan), **Jan 7**
Nanticoke Indian Powwow (Millsboro, DE), **Sep 9**
Napolitano, Janet: Birth, **Nov 29**
Napping Day, Natl Workplace, **Apr 3**
Nash, Graham: Birth, **Feb 2**
Nash, Ogden: Birth Anniv, **Aug 19**
Nast, Thomas: Birth Anniv, **Sep 27**
Nastase, Ilie: Birth, **Jul 19**
Nat King Cole TV Premiere: Anniv, **Nov 5**
Natchez Fall Pilgrimage (Natchez, MS), **Sep 30**
Natchez Spring Pilgrimage (Natchez, MS), **Mar 10**
Natchitoches Historic Pilgrimage (Natchitoches, LA), **Oct 14**
Natchitoches Jazz Fest (Natchitoches, LA), **Apr 1**
Natchitoches/NW State Univ Folk Fest (Natchitoches, LA), **Jul 21**
Nathan Hale Fife and Drum Muster (Coventry, CT), **Jul 22**
Nation, Carry: Birth Anniv, **Nov 25**
National Bank, First Chartered by Congress: Anniv, **Feb 25**
National Broadcasters Conv (Las Vegas, NV), **Apr 22**
National Park Week (Pres Proc), **Apr 16**

Nations, Fest of (St. Paul, MN), **May 4**
Native-American
  Adai Caddo Indian Nation Pow Wow (Marthaville, LA), **Oct 21**
  American Indian Heritage Day (AL), **Oct 9**
  American Indian Heritage Month, Natl, **Nov 1**
  Americana Indian and Western Art Show/Sale (Yuma, AZ), **Jan 27**
  Apache Wars Began: Anniv, **Feb 4**
  Battle of Little Bighorn: Anniv, **Jun 25**
  Bureau of Indian Affairs Established, **Mar 11**
  Chief Joseph Surrender: Anniv, **Oct 5**
  Cochise: Death Anniv, **Jun 8**
  Coeur d'Alene Tribal Pilgrimage (Cataldo, ID), **Aug 15**
  Crow Reservation Opened for Settlement: Anniv, **Oct 15**
  Custer Battlefield Becomes Little Bighorn: Anniv, **Nov 26**
  DeSoto Caverns Park Fall Native American Dance Fest (Childersburg, AL), **Sep 23**
  DeSoto Caverns Park Spring Native American Dance & Crafts Fest (Childersburg, AL), **Apr 1**
  Gift of the Waters Pageant & Art Fest in the Park (Thermopolis, WY), **Aug 4**
  Hayes, Ira Hamilton: Birth Anniv, **Jan 12**
  Indian Artifact Show (Owensboro, KY), **Aug 4**
  Indian Powwow, Natl Chmpsh (Grand Prairie, TX), **Sep 8**
  Iroquois Arts Showcase (Howes Cave, NY), **May 27**
  Iroquois Indian Fest (Howes Cave, NY), **Sep 2**
  Joseph, Chief: Death Anniv, **Sep 21**
  Kiamichi Owa-Chito Fest of the Forest (Broken Bow, OK), **Jun 16**
  Kissimmee Slough Shootout and Rendezvous (Big Cypress Reservation, FL), **Feb 3**
  Last Formal Surrender of Confederate Troops: Anniv, **Jun 23**
  Loloma, Charles: Birth Anniv, **Jun 9**
  Makah Days (Neah Bay, WA), **Aug 25**
  Mescalero Apache Maiden's Puberty Rites (Mescalero, NM), **Jul 1**
  Minority Enterprise Development Week (Pres Proc), **Sep 10**
  Nanticoke Indian Powwow (Millsboro, DE), **Sep 9**
  Natchez Powwow (Natchez, MS), **Mar 25**
  Native American Citizenship Day, **Jun 15**
  Native Americans' Day (SD), **Oct 9**
  Occoneechee State Park Native American Fest and Pow Wow (Clarksville, VA), **May 13**
  Oconaluftee Indian Village (Cherokee, NC), **May 15**
  Ojibwa Keeshigun (Thunder Bay, ON, Canada), **Aug 19**
  Osceola: Death Anniv, **Jan 30**
  Pendleton Round-Up (Pendleton, OR), **Sep 9**
  Pocahontas: Death Anniv, **Mar 21**
  Red Cloud Indian Art Show (Pine Ridge, SD), **Jun 4**
  Red Cloud: Death Anniv, **Dec 10**
  Rights Recognized: Anniv, **May 12**
  Sedona Arts Fest (West Sedona, AZ), **Oct 7**
  Seminole Tribe Festival, Powwow and Rodeo (Hollywood, FL), **Feb 10**
  Seminole Tribe of Florida Legally Established: Anniv, **Aug 21**
  Sitting Bull: Death Anniv, **Dec 15**
  Tecumseh! Epic Outdoor Drama (Chillicothe, OH), **Jun 9**
  Totah Fest (Farmington, NM), **Sep 2**
  Trail of Courage Living-History Fest (Rochester, IN), **Sep 16**
  Trail of Tears Commemoration (Waterloo, AL), **Sep 16**
  United Tribes Powwow (Bismarck, ND), **Sep 7**
  White Woman Made Indian Chief: Anniv, **Sep 18**
  Woodland Indian Discovery Day (St. Mary's City, MD), **Sep 9**
  Wounded Knee Massacre: Anniv, **Dec 29**
NATO Forces Attack Yugoslavia: Anniv, **Mar 25**
NATO Planes Down Serb Jets: Anniv, **Feb 28**
NATO: Anniv, **Apr 4**
Natural Bridges Natl Monument: Anniv, **Apr 16**
Nature Photography Day, **Jun 15**
Naughton, David: Birth, **Feb 13**
Naughton, James: Birth, **Dec 6**
Nauru: National Day, **Jan 31**
Nautilus: First Nuclear-Powered Submarine Voyage: Anniv, **Jan 17**
Nauvoo Legion Chartered: Anniv, **Feb 3**
Navratilova, Martina: Birth, **Oct 18**
Navy Birthday, **Oct 13**
Navy Day, **Oct 27**
Neal, Patricia: Birth, **Jan 20**
Nealon, Kevin: Birth, **Nov 18**
Near Miss Day, **Mar 23**
Neas, Ralph: Birth, **May 14**

Nebraska
  Admission Day, **Mar 1**
  Applejack Fest (Nebraska City), **Sep 16**
  Arbor Day Fest (Nebraska City), **Apr 28**
  Barn Day (Filley), **Jul 16**
  BCHS Christmas Open House (Ainsworth), **Dec 3**
  Big 12 Men's and Women's Indoor Track Chmpshps (Lincoln), **Feb 24**
  Big 12 Women's Golf Chmpshp (Lincoln), **Apr 17**
  Big 12 Women's Gymnastics Chmpshp (Lincoln), **Mar 25**
  Central Nebraska Ethnic Fest (Grand Island), **Jul 28**
  Christmas at Union Station (Omaha), **Nov 24**
  Christmas on the Prairie (Wahoo), **Dec 2**
  Clarkson Czech Fest (Clarkson), **Jun 23**
  Clearwater Chamber of Commerce Rodeo (Clearwater), **Jun 23**
  Cobblestone Fest (Falls City), **Aug 18**
  Crane Watch (Kearney), **Mar 1**
  Czechoslovakian Fest, Natl (Wilber), **Aug 4**
  Ethnic Holiday Fest (Omaha), **Dec 1**
  Fairfest (Hastings), **Jul 26**
  Garfield County Fair (Burwell), **Jul 26**
  Gateway Farm Expo (Kearney), **Nov 15**
  Gingerbread on Parade (Omaha), **Nov 27**
  Hagel, Chuck: Birth, **Oct 4**
  Halloween (Arapahoe), **Oct 31**
  Heineman, Dave: Birth, **May 12**
  Homestead Days (Beatrice), **Jun 14**
  Hot Times Downtown Wilber Car and Truck Show (Wilber), **Jun 3**
  Husker Harvest Days (Grand Island), **Sep 12**
  Kool-Aid Days (Hastings), **Aug 11**
  Lavitsef (Norfolk), **Sep 23**
  Light of the World Christmas Pageant (Minden), **Nov 25**
  Lisco Old-timers Day (Lisco), **Sep 10**
  Literature Fest (Norfolk), **Jul 29**
  NCAA Div I Men's College World Series (Baseball Chmpshp) (Omaha), **Jun 16**
  Nebraska State Fair (Lincoln), **Aug 26**
  Nebraska's Big Rodeo (Burwell), **Jul 27**
  Nelson, Ben: Birth, **May 17**
  Oregon Trail Days (Gering), **Jul 13**
  Oregon Trail Rodeo (Hastings), **Sep 1**
  Prairie Pioneer Days (Arapahoe), **Jul 4**
  River City Roundup (Omaha), **Sep 28**
  Scotts Bluff County Fair (Mitchell), **Aug 14**
  Shakespeare on the Green (Omaha), **Jun 22**
  Wayne Chicken Days (Wayne), **Jul 7**
  Willow Tree Fest (Gordon), **Sep 9**
  Wings Over the Platte Spring Migration Fest (Grand Island), **Feb 18**
Neeson, Liam: Birth, **Jun 7**
Nehru, Jawaharlal: Birth Anniv, **Nov 14**
Neighbor Day (RI), **May 21**
Neighbor Day, Natl Good, **Sep 24**
Neill, Sam: Birth, **Sep 14**
Neither Snow Nor Rain Day: Anniv, **Sep 7**
Nelligan, Kate: Birth, **Mar 16**
Nelson, Barry: Birth, **Apr 16**
Nelson, Ben: Birth, **May 17**
Nelson, Bill: Birth, **Sep 29**
Nelson, Cindy: Birth, **Aug 19**
Nelson, Craig T.: Birth, **Apr 4**
Nelson, David: Birth, **Oct 24**
Nelson, Horatio: Birth Anniv, **Sep 29**
Nelson, Judd: Birth, **Nov 28**
Nelson, Thomas: Birth Anniv, **Dec 26**
Nelson, Willie: Birth, **Apr 30**
Nelson: Ozzie and Harriet Show Debut: Anniv, **Oct 8**
Nemec, Corin: Birth, **Nov 5**
Nemerov, Howard: Birth Anniv, **Feb 1**
Nenana Tripod Raising Fest (Nenana, AK), **Mar 4**
Nepal
  Democracy Day, Natl, **Feb 18**
  King's Birthday National Holiday, **Jul 7**
  National Unity Day, **Jan 11**
Neptune Discovery: Anniv, **Sep 23**
Neptune Fest Boardwalk Weekend (Virginia Beach, VA), **Sep 29**
Nerve Gas Attack on Japanese Subway: Anniv, **Mar 20**
Neshoba County Fair (Philadelphia, MS), **Jul 21**
Nesmith, Michael: Birth, **Dec 30**
Ness, Eliot: Birth Anniv, **Apr 19**
Netherlands
  European Fine Art Fair (Maastricht), **Mar 10**
  Liberation Day, **May 5**
  Midwinter Horn Blowing, **Dec 3**
  National Windmill Day, **May 13**
  Netherlands-United States: Diplomatic Anniv, **Apr 19**
  North Sea Jazz Fest (The Hague), **Jul 14**
  Prinsjesdag (Parliament opening), **Sep 19**
  Queen's Birthday, **Apr 30**

☆ *Chase's 2006 Calendar of Events* ☆

Netherlands (cont'd)—New York

Relief of Leiden, **Oct 3**
Scilly Isles Peace Anniv, **Apr 17**
Networking Week, Natl, Apr 10
Neuharth, Allen: Birth, Mar 22
Neurofibromatosis Awareness Month, Natl, May 1
Neuromancer Publication Anniv (Cyberspace Coined), Oct 1
Neutrality Appeal, American: Anniv, Aug 18
Neuwirth, Bebe: Birth, Dec 31
Nevada
Admission Day, **Oct 31**
American Dental Assn: Annual Session (Las Vegas), **Oct 16**
Artown (Reno), **Jul 1**
Carson City Library Foundation Oktoberfest (Carson City), **Oct 7**
Carson City Rendezvous (Carson City), **Jun 9**
Championship Air Races, Natl (Reno), **Sep 13**
Consumer Electronics Show, Intl (Las Vegas, NV), **Jan 5**
Cowboy Poetry Gathering, Natl (Elko), **Jan 28**
Craft & Hobby Assn Conv & Trade Show (Las Vegas), **Jan 30**
Ensign, John: Birth, **Mar 25**
Family Day, **Nov 24**
Great Intl Chicken Wing Society Cook-off (Reno), **Jul 1**
Guinn, Kenny: Birth, **Aug 24**
Hot August Nights (Reno and Sparks), **Jul 29**
Liberace Birthday Celebration & Play-A-Like Competition (Las Vegas), **May 13**
Liberace Museum Christmas Tree Lighting (Las Vegas), **Dec 7**
NAB/National Broadcasters Conv (Las Vegas), **Apr 22**
Nevadapex Coin and Stamp Expo (Laughlin), **Jan 6**
Nugget Best in the West Rib Cook-Off (Sparks), **Aug 31**
Reid, Harry: Birth, **Dec 2**
Reno Birthday, **May 9**
Star Spangled Sparks (Sparks), **Jul 4**
State Fair (Reno), **Aug 17**
Vegaspex (Las Vegas), **May 26**
Neville, Aaron: Birth, Jan 24
Nevis: Independence Day, Sep 19
New Beginning Fest (Coffeyville, KS), Apr 28
New England Home Show (Boston, MA), Feb 25
New England, Dark Day in: Anniv, May 19
New Friends, Old Friends Week, Natl, May 21
New Hampshire
Artists in the Park (Wolfeboro), **Aug 16**
Gregg, Judd: Birth, **Feb 14**
League of NH Craftsmen Annual Craftsmen's Fair (Newbury), **Aug 5**
Lynch, John: Birth, **Nov 25**
New Hampshire Highland Games (Contoocook), **Sep 22**
Ratification Day, **Jun 21**
Rochester Fair (Rochester), **Sep 15**
Sununu, John: Birth, **Sep 10**
New Jersey
Antiques at Memorial Day (Cape May), **May 28**
Art Festival (Harvey Cedars), **Jul 16**
Arts & Crafts Fest (Loveladies), **Jul 29**
Barnegat Bay Crab Race and Fest (Seaside Heights), **Aug 27**
Baymen's Seafood and Music Fest (Tuckerton), **Jun 24**
Be Nice to New Jersey Week, **Jul 2**
Black Maria Studio: Anniv, **Feb 1**
Blue Claw Crab Craft Show & Crab Race (Harvey Cedars), **Aug 19**
Cape May Food & Wine Fest (Cape May), **Sep 16**
Cape May Kids Playhouse (Cape May), **Jul 3**
Cape May Music Fest (Cape May), **May 21**
Cattus Island Nature Fest (Toms River), **Oct 1**
Celebrate Earth Day (Point Pleasant Beach), **Apr 22**
Christmas Candlelight House Tours (Cape May), **Dec 2**
Classic Boat Show (Tuckerton), **Aug 19**
Codey, Richard J.: Birth, **Nov 27**
Colonial Day (Tuckerton), **Oct 14**
Corzine, Jon: Birth, **Jan 1**
Craft Day by the Bay (Harvey Cedars), **Jul 1**
Cruisin' Downtown (Toms River), **Jun 14**
Crustacean Beauty Pageant/Ocean City Creep (Ocean City), **Aug 2**
Day of the Seal Celebration, Intl (Point Pleasant Beach), **Mar 18**
Dickens' Christmas Extravaganza (Cape May), **Dec 3**
Dodge Poetry Fest, **Sep 28**
Dog Day Road Race (Harvey Cedars), **Aug 20**
Eggsibit (Phillipsburg), **Apr 1**
Father's Day Celebration (Point Pleasant Beach), **Jun 18**

Fest of Fine Craft (Millville), **Oct 7**
Fest-in-the-Park (Nutley), **Sep 10**
Festival of the Sea (Point Pleasant Beach), **Sep 16**
Fishing Contest (Lakewood), **May 6**
Founders' Day (Toms River), **Jun 10**
Halloween Parade (Toms River), **Oct 31**
Haunted Seaport (Tuckerton), **Oct 28**
Heritage Day Fest (Lavallette), **Sep 9**
Homeplace Fest (Waretown), **Nov 18**
Independence Extravaganza (Lavallette), **Jul 2**
Ladies of Country Music Show (Waretown), **Jun 24**
Lautenberg, Frank: Birth, **Jan 23**
Lavallette Heritage Arts & Crafts Show (Lavallette), **Jul 30**
Long Beach Island Chowder Cook-Off (Beach Haven), **Sep 30**
Long Beach Island Surf Fishing Tournament (Long Beach Island), **Oct 7**
Loveladies Fair (Loveladies), **Jun 3**
Manahawkin Good Ol' Days (Manahawkin), **Sep 2**
Marble Weekend (Millville), **Jun 24**
Martin Z. Mollusk Day (Ocean City), **May 4**
May in Montclair (Montclair Township), **May 1**
Mid-Summer Antiques & Collectibles Show & Sale (Millville), **Jul 29**
Mid-Winter Antiques Show (Millville), **Feb 4**
Mother's Day Celebration (Point Pleasant Beach), **May 14**
Museum of American Glass Mid-Winter Exhibit (Millville), **Jan 14**
New Jersey State Fair/Sussex Farm and Horse Show (Augusta), **Aug 4**
Ocean County Bluegrass Fest (Waretown), **Feb 5, Sep 10**
Ocean County Columbus Day Parade and Italian Fest (Seaside Heights), **Oct 6**
Ocean County Decoy/Gun Show (Tuckerton), **Sep 30**
Ocean County Wildfowl Art & Decoy Show (Toms River), **Feb 11**
Old Time Antiques & Collectibles Faire (Toms River), **Sep 2**
Penguin Awareness Day (Point Pleasant Beach), **Jan 14**
Picatinny Peak Fall Hawkwatch (Dover), **Sep 1**
Pine Barrens Jamboree (Waretown), **Oct 7**
Ratification Day: Anniv, **Dec 18**
Red Wine and Blues Fest (Tuckerton), **Jul 15**
Reptile Awareness Day (Point Pleasant Beach), **Oct 21**
Sailfest (Island Heights), **Sep 8**
Saint Ann's Italian Street Fest (Hoboken), **Jul 21**
Scandinavian Fest (Edison), **Sep 3**
Seashore Open House Tour (Loveladies), **Aug 2**
Shark Awareness Day (Point Pleasant Beach), **Jul 15**
Songwriter's Show (Waretown), **Mar 18**
South Jersey Canoe/Kayak Classic (Lakewood), **Jun 3**
Spring Fest (Cape May), **Apr 21**
Suffragists' Voting Attempt: Anniv, **Nov 19**
Sugarloaf Crafts Fest (Secaucus), **Nov 3**
Sugarloaf Crafts Fest (Somerset), **Mar 10**
Toms River Canoe Race (Toms River), **Sep 30**
Toms River Seaport Society Wood Boat Fest (Toms River), **Jul 8**
Tour of Somerville (Somerville), **May 29**
Victorian Sherlock Holmes Weekend (Cape May), **Mar 3**
Victorian Week (Cape May), **Oct 6**
Weird Contest Week (Ocean City), **Aug 14**
Wings 'n' Water Fest (Stone Harbor), **Sep 16**
New Mexico
Admission Day, **Jan 6**
Albuquerque Intl Balloon Fiesta (Albuquerque), **Sep 30**
AspenCash Motorcycle Rally (Ruidoso), **May 18**
Bingaman, Jeff: Birth, **Oct 3**
Carlsbad Caverns Natl Park Established: Anniv, **May 14**
Domenici, Pete V.: Birth, **May 7**
Electric Light Parade (Lovington), **Dec 4**
Extraterrestrial Culture Day, **Feb 9**
Farmington Invitational Balloon Fest (Farmington), **May 27**
Freedom Days (Farmington), **Jul 1**
Golden Aspen Motorcycle Rally (Ruidoso), **Sep 13**
Lovington Fall Arts/Crafts Fest (Lovington), **Nov 4**
Mescalero Apache Maiden's Puberty Rites (Mescalero), **Jul 1**
Miss New Mexico Scholarship Pageant (Alamogordo), **Jun 9**
Obituary Writers' Intl Conference, Great (Las Vegas), **Jun 15**
Outdoor Summer Theater (Farmington), **Jun 14**
Richardson, Bill: Birth, **Nov 15**
Santa Fe Chamber Music Fest (Santa Fe), **Jul 16**
Show of Wheels (Lovington), **Feb 18**

Shuttle Camp (Alamogordo), **Jun 5**
Spring Gala (Lovington), **May 6**
Totah Fest (Farmington), **Sep 2**
World's Greatest Lizard Race (Lovington), **Jul 4**
New Orleans, Battle of: Anniv, Jan 8
New World Symphony Premiere: Anniv, Dec 16
New Year
Chinese New Year, **Jan 29**
Chinese New Year Fest (San Francisco, CA), **Jan 21**
Ethiopia: New Year's Day, **Sep 11**
First Night (Boston, MA), **Dec 31**
First Night Albany (Albany, NY), **Dec 31**
First Night Asheville (Asheville, NC), **Dec 31**
First Nights (Canada), **Dec 31**
First Nights (US), **Dec 31**
Hogmanay (Scotland), **Dec 31**
India: New Year's Day, **Mar 22**
Iranian New Year (Persian), **Mar 21**
Japanese Era New Year, **Jan 1**
MADD's New Year's Designate a Driver Campaign, **Dec 26**
Muharram (Islamic New Year), **Jan 31**
Naw-Ruz (Baha'i New Year's Day), **Mar 21**
New Year's Day, **Jan 1**
New Year's Day (Gregorian), **Jan 1**
New Year's Day Observance (Russia), **Jan 1**
New Year's Day Parade (London, England), **Jan 1**
New Year's Dishonor List, **Jan 1**
New Year's Eve, **Dec 31**
New Year's Eve Trail Ride and Party (Live Oak, FL), **Dec 29**
New Year's Fest (Kalamazoo, MI), **Dec 31**
New Year's Resolutions Week, **Jan 1**
Old New Year's Day, **Mar 25**
Rosh Hashanah (Jewish New Year), **Sep 23**
Russia: Old New Year's Eve, **Jan 13**
Sinhala and Tamil New Year (Sri Lanka), **Apr 13**
Songkran Fest (Thailand), **Apr 13**
Stock Exchange Holiday, **Jan 2**
United Kingdom New Year's Holiday, **Jan 1**
New York
Albany Alive at Five (Albany), **Jun 1**
Albany Riverfront Jazz Fest (Albany), **Sep 9**
Albany Tulip Fest (Albany), **May 12**
Belmont Stakes (Belmont Park), **Jun 10**
Belmont Stakes, First Running of: Anniv, **Jun 19**
Brooklyn Bridge Opened: Anniv, **May 24**
Broome County Fair (Whitney Point), **Jul 25**
Clinton, Hillary Rodham: Birth, **Oct 26**
Cohocton Fall Foliage Fest (Cohocton), **Oct 6**
Colton Country Day (Colton), **Jul 15**
Columbia County Fair (Chatham), **Aug 30**
Corn Hill Arts Fest (Rochester), **Jul 8**
Decoy and Wildlife Art Show (Clayton), **Jul 14**
Falcon Ridge Folk Fest (Hillsdale), **Jul 20**
Farm Sanctuary Hoedown (Watkins Glen), **Aug 5**
Farm Sanctuary's Annual Pignic (Watkins Glen), **Jul 4**
First Night Albany (Albany), **Dec 31**
Great Northeast Home Show (Albany), **Feb 10**
Great NY State Snow & Track Expo (Albany), **Nov 4**
Great Wellsville Balloon Rally (Wellsville), **Jul 21**
Hang Around Victor Day (Victor), **Sep 9**
Highlights Foundation Writer's Workshop (Chautauqua), **Jul 15**
HUMOResilience Workshop (Lake George), **Oct 27**
Iroquois Arts Showcase (Howes Cave), **May 27**
Iroquois Indian Fest (Howes Cave), **Sep 2**
Johnson City Field Days (Johnson City), **Sep 1**
Lilac Fest (Rochester), **May 12**
Macy's Thanksgiving Day Parade (New York), **Nov 23**
Metropolitan Opera Natl Council Auditions Finals (New York), **Mar 19**
NCAA Div III Field Hockey Chmpshp (Geneva), **Nov 17**
New York City Marathon (New York), **Nov 5**
New York City Subway: Anniv, **Oct 27**
New York Film Fest (New York), **Sep 29**
New York Public Library: Anniv, **May 23**
New York State Missing Persons Day (Albany), **Apr 6**
New York Subway Accident: Anniv, **Nov 2**
New York Times Travel Show (New York), **Feb 24**
Northeast Great Outdoors Show (Albany), **Mar 17**
Pataki, George: Birth, **Jun 24**
Prospect Park Fishing Contest (Brooklyn), **Jul 18**
Ratification Day, **Jul 26**
Renaissance Fest (Sterling), **Jul 1**
Rockefeller Center Christmas Tree Lighting (New York), **Nov 28**
Saint Patrick's Day Parade (Hornell), **Mar 18**
Saint Patrick's Day Parade (New York), **Mar 17**
Saranac Lake Winter Carnival (Saranac Lake), **Feb 3**

Scared Silly: Halloween in Prospect Park (Brooklyn), **Oct 28**
Schumer, Charles E.: Birth, **Nov 23**
Stamp & Coin Expo (New York), **Apr 21**
State Fair (Syracuse), **Aug 24**
Stationery Show, Natl (New York), **May 21**
Stone House Day (Hurley), **Jul 8**
Thousand Islands Quilt Show (Clayton), **Jul 21**
Toy Tips Executive Toy Test (New York), **Sep 1**
Tribeca Film Fest (New York, NY), **Apr 25**
Tupper Lake Woodsmen's Days (Tupper Lake), **Jul 8**
US Open (Golf) Chmpshp (Mamaroneck), **Jun 15**
Westminster Kennel Club Dog Show (New York), **Feb 13**
You Gotta Have Park (Brooklyn), **May 13**
New York Stock Exchange Established: Anniv, May 17
New York Times First Published: Anniv, Sep 18
New York Weekly First Issue: Anniv, Nov 5
New Yorker Published: Anniv, Feb 21
New Yorker: Addams, Charles: Birth Anniv, Jan 7
New Zealand
ANZAC Day, **Apr 25**
Labor Day, **Oct 23**
New Zealand First Sighted by Europeans, **Dec 13**
Otago/Southland Provincial Anniv, **Mar 23**
Waitangi Day, **Feb 6**
Newberry Library's Annual Book Fair (Chicago, IL), Jul 28
Newby, Marcia: Birth, Mar 8
Newcomb, Simon: Birth Anniv, Mar 12
Newhart TV Premiere: Anniv, Oct 25
Newhart, Bob: Birth, Sep 5
Newhouse, Samuel: Birth Anniv, May 24
Newlywed Game TV Premiere: Anniv, Jul 11
Newman, Barry: Birth, Nov 7
Newman, Edwin: Birth, Jan 25
Newman, Laraine: Birth, Mar 2
Newman, Paul: Birth, Jan 26
Newman, Randy: Birth, Nov 28
Newmar, Julie: Birth, Aug 16
Newport Seafood and Wine Fest (Newport, OR), Feb 24
Newspaper Assn of America Conv (Chicago, IL), Apr 2
Newspaper Week (Japan), Oct 1
Newspaper Week, Natl, Oct 1
Newspaper, First American: Anniv, Sep 25
Newton, Isaac: Birth Anniv, Jan 4
Newton, Juice: Birth, Feb 18
Newton, Thandie: Birth, Nov 6
Newton, Wayne: Birth, Apr 3
Newton-John, Olivia: Birth, Sep 26
NEXTEL Cup, Daytona 500 NASCAR (Daytona Beach, FL), Feb 19
Nez Perce: Chief Joseph Surrender: Anniv, Oct 5
Niagara Falls Runs Dry: Anniv, Mar 29
Niagara Falls, Charles Blondin's Conquest of: Anniv, Jun 30
Niagara Movement Founded: Anniv, Jul 11
Nicaragua
Battle of San Jacinto Day, **Sep 14**
Civil War Truce: Anniv, **Apr 19**
Independence Day, **Sep 15**
National Liberation Day, **Jul 19**
Nicholas II and Family Executed: Anniv, Jul 17
Nicholas, Denise: Birth, Jul 12
Nichols, Mike: Birth, Nov 6
Nichols, Stephen: Birth, Feb 19
Nicholson, Jack: Birth, Apr 22
Nicholson, Jim: Birth, Feb 6
Nick at Nite: Anniv, Jul 1
Nickelodeon Premiere: Anniv, Apr 2
Nickerson, Camille ("Louisiana Lady"): Birth Anniv, Mar 30
Nicklaus, Jack: Birth, Jan 21
Nicks, Stevie: Birth, May 26
Nidetch, Jean: Birth, Oct 12
Nielsen, Arthur Charles: Birth Anniv, Sep 5
Nielsen, Leslie: Birth, Feb 11
Nietzsche, Friedrich Wilhelm: Birth Anniv, Oct 15
Nieuwendyk, Joe: Birth, Sep 10
Niger: Independence Day, Aug 3
Niger: Republic Day, Dec 18
Nigeria: Independence Day, Oct 1
Night Court TV Premiere: Anniv, Jan 4
Night Out, Natl, Aug 1
Night Watch (France), Jul 13
Nightingale, Florence: Birth Anniv, May 12
Nightshift Workers Day, Natl, May 10
Nijinsky, Vaslav: Rite of Spring Premiere and Riot: Anniv, May 29
Nimoy, Leonard: Birth, Mar 26
Nininger, Alexander, Jr: First WWII Medal of Honor, Feb 10
Nissan Xterra World Chmpshp (Maui, HI), Oct 29
Nixon Birthday Holiday (Yorba Linda, CA), Jan 9

Nixon, Cynthia: Birth, Apr 9
Nixon, John: Death Anniv, Dec 31
Nixon, Pat: Birth Anniv, Mar 16
Nixon, Richard M.
Birth Anniv, **Jan 9**
Checkers Day, **Sep 23**
First American Pres to Visit Moscow, **May 22**
First Televised Presidential Debate: Anniv, **Sep 26**
Last Press Conf: Anniv, **Nov 7**
Meets Elvis Presley: Anniv, **Dec 21**
Moscow Communique: Anniv, **May 29**
Nixon's Rejection of Senate Order: Anniv, **Jan 4**
Pardoned: Anniv, **Sep 8**
Presidential Resignation: Anniversary, **Aug 9**
Saturday Night Massacre, **Oct 20**
Shanghai Communique: Anniv, **Feb 27**
Trip to China: Anniv, **Feb 21**
No Bully Week, Natl, Sep 11
No Homework Day, May 6
No Housework Day, Apr 7
No Interruptions Day, Dec 29
No Socks Day, May 8
Noah, Yannick: Birth, May 18
Nobel Conference (St. Peter, MN), Oct 3
Nobel Prize Ceremonies (Oslo, Norway/Stockholm, Sweden), Dec 10
Nobel Prize, First US Scientist Receives: Anniv, Dec 10
Nobel, Alfred: Birth Anniv, Oct 21
Noiret, Philippe: Birth, Oct 1
Nokia Sugar Bowl (New Orleans, LA), Jan 2
Nolte, Nick: Birth, Feb 8
Nomo, Hideo: Birth, Aug 31
Noone, Kathleen: Birth, Jan 8
Nordic: Tivoli-Viking Days at the Nordic Heritage Museum (Seattle, WA), Jul 8
Nordicfest (Libby, MT), Sep 8
Norgay, Tensing: Everest Summit Reached: Anniv, May 29
Noriega, Manuel: US Invasion of Panama: Anniv, Dec 20
Norman, Greg: Birth, Feb 10
Norman, Jessye: Birth, Sep 15
Norris, Chuck: Birth, Mar 10
Norskedalen's Midsummer Fest (Coon Valley, WI), Jun 24
Norskedalen's Old-Fashioned Christmas (Coon Valley, WI), Dec 2
North Atlantic Treaty Ratified: Anniv, Apr 4
North Carolina
All That Jazz Weekend (Asheville), **Jan 27**
Appalachian Potters Market (Marion), **Nov 18**
Association for Dressings & Sauces Annual Meeting (Asheville), **Oct 15**
Bald Is Beautiful Convention (Morehead City), **Sep 8**
Bele Chere (Asheville), **Jul 28**
Burr, Richard: Birth, **Nov 30**
Church/Synagogue Library Assn Conf (Greensboro), **Jul 30**
Confederate Memorial Day, **May 10**
Craft Fair of the Southern Highlands (Asheville), **Jul 20**
Craftsmen's Classic Arts & Crafts Fest (Greensboro), **Mar 31, Nov 24**
Dole, Elizabeth: Birth, **Jul 29**
Easley, Mike: Birth, **Mar 23**
Easter Sunrise Service (Chimney Rock), **Apr 16**
Eastern Music Fest (Greensboro), **Jun 24**
Everybody's Day Fest (Thomasville), **Sep 30**
First Night Asheville (Asheville), **Dec 31**
Folkmoot USA: The NC Intl Folk Fest (Waynesville), **Jul 17**
Gifted Children Conv, Natl Assn (Charlotte), **Nov 1**
Gingerbread House Competition, Natl (Asheville), **Nov 13**
Great Smoky Mountains Natl Park Established: Anniv, **Jun 15**
Halifax Independence Day, **Apr 12**
Holiday Market (Greensboro), **Nov 3**
Home Furnishings Market, Intl (High Point), **Apr 27**
Longhorn World Chmpshp Rodeo (Winston-Salem), **Feb 24**
Lucky May Show and Sale (Chapel Hill), **May 5**
Mecklenburg Day, **May 20**
Moravian Easter Resurrection Service (Winston-Salem), **Apr 16**
Mountain Dance and Folk Fest (Asheville), **Aug 3**
Mountain Glory Fest (Marion), **Oct 14**
NC RV and Camping Show (Charlotte), **Jan 20**
NC RV and Camping Show (Greensboro), **Jan 6**
NC RV and Camping Show (Raleigh), **Feb 10**
North Carolina Apple Fest (Hendersonville), **Sep 1**
North Carolina SweetPotato Month, **Feb 1**
Oconaluftee Indian Village (Cherokee), **May 15**
Ratification Day, **Nov 21**
Singing on the Mountain (Linville), **Jun 25**
Soldiers' Reunion Celebration (Newton), **Aug 17**

State Fair (Raleigh), **Oct 13**
Surrender at Durham Station: Anniv, **Apr 18**
Valle County Fair (Valle Crucis), **Oct 21**
Whistlers Convention, Intl (Louisburg), **Apr 19**
Woolly Worm Fest (Banner Elk), **Oct 21**
North Cascades Natl Park Established: Anniv, Oct 2
North Dakota
Adams County Fair/Rodeo (Hettinger), **Aug 3**
Admission Day, **Nov 2**
American Legacy (Mandan), **Jul 28**
Conrad, Kent: Birth, **Mar 12**
Dickens Village Fest (Garrison), **Nov 24**
Dorgan, Byron L.: Birth, **May 14**
Fargo's Downtown Street Fair (Fargo), **Jul 20**
Fort Union Trading Post Rendezvous (Williston), **Jun 15**
Fourth of July Celebration (Hettinger), **Jul 1**
Hoeven, John: Birth, **Mar 13**
Killdeer Mountain Roundup Rodeo Days (Killdeer), **Jul 3**
Lewis & Clark Bicentennial Natl Signature Event: Reunion at the Home of Sakakawea (New Town), **Aug 17**
Lewis and Clark Days (Washburn), **Jun 16**
Makoti Threshing Bee Show (Makoti), **Oct 6**
Music Camp, Intl (Dunseith), **Jun 11**
Norsk Hostfest (Minot), **Oct 10**
North Star Classic (Valley City), **Dec 1**
Old-Time Fiddlers' Contest, Intl (Dunseith), **Jun 8**
Potato Bowl USA (Grand Forks), **Sep 5**
Red River Valley Fair (Fargo), **Jun 16**
Sheyenne Valley Arts/Crafts Fest (Fort Ransom), **Sep 23**
Sodbuster Days (Fort Ransom), **Jul 8**
Sodbuster Days—Harvest (Fort Ransom), **Sep 9**
State Fair (Minot), **Jul 21**
Taylor Horsefest (Taylor), **Jul 22**
Theodore Roosevelt Natl Park Established: Anniv, **Apr 25**
United Tribes Powwow (Bismarck), **Sep 7**
White Cloud Days (Jamestown), **Jul 6**
Winter Show (Valley City), **Mar 7**
North Pole Discovered: Anniv, Apr 6
North Pole, Solo Trip to: Anniv, Apr 22
North Sea Oil Rig Disaster: Anniv, Mar 27
North, Oliver Laurence: Birth, Oct 7
North, Sheree: Birth, Jan 17
Northern Exposure TV Premiere: Anniv, Jul 12
Northern Hemisphere Hoodie-Hoo Day, Feb 20
Northern Ireland
Bloody Sunday: Anniv, **Jan 30**
Christmas Holiday, **Dec 25**
Good Friday Peace Agreement: Anniv, **Apr 10**
Orangemen's Day, **Jul 12**
Saint Patrick's Day, **Mar 17**
Northern Pacific Railroad Completed: Anniv, Sep 8
Northwest Folklife Fest (Seattle, WA), May 26
Northwest Ordinance: Anniv, Jul 13
Norton, Edward: Birth, Aug 18
Norton, Gale: Birth, Mar 11
Norton, Ken: Birth, Aug 9
Norton, Mary: Birth Anniv, Dec 10
Noruz (Iranian New Year), Mar 21
Norville, Deborah: Birth, Aug 8
Norwalk Seaport Oyster Fest (Norwalk, CT), Sep 8
Norway
Constitution or Independence Day, **May 17**
Edvard Grieg Birth Anniv Celebration, **Jun 15**
Midnight Sun at North Cape, **May 14**
Nobel Prize Awards Ceremony (Oslo), **Dec 10**
Olsok Eve, **Jul 29**
Pageantry in Oslo (Oslo), **Oct 2**
Tyvendedagen, **Jan 13**
Norwegian
Norsk Hostfest (Minot, ND), **Oct 10**
Norwegian Christmas (Brooklyn Park, MN), **Dec 2**
Nosso Senhor Do Bonfim Fest (Brazil), Jan 20
Nostradamus: Birth Anniv, Dec 14
Noth, Chris: Birth, Nov 13
Nothing Day, Natl, Jan 16
Nouri, Michael: Birth, Dec 9
Nova Scotia Bluegrass/Oldtime Music Fest (Stewiacke, NS), Jul 28
Nova Scotia Intl Tattoo (Halifax, NS, Canada), Jul 1
Novak, Kim: Birth, Feb 13
Novello, Antonia: Birth, Aug 23
Novello, Don: Birth, Jan 1
NOW Founded: Anniv, Jun 30
Nowitzki, Dirk: Birth, Jun 19
Nuclear Chain Reaction, First Self-Sustaining: Anniv, Dec 2
Nuclear Medicine Week, Oct 1
Nuclear Power Plant Accident, Three Mile Island: Anniv, Mar 28

Nuclear Weapons—Opera

Nuclear Weapons: Russell-Einstein Manifesto: Anniv, Jul 9
Nuclear-Free World, First Step Toward a: Anniv, Dec 8
Nuclear-Powered Submarine Voyage, First: Anniv, Jan 17
Nude Recreation Week, Jul 10
Nugent, Ted: Birth, Dec 13
Nunavut Independence: Anniv, Apr 1
Nuremberg War Crimes Trial (Germany): Anniv, Nov 20
Nureyev, Rudolf: Birth Anniv, Mar 17
Nurses, Nursing. See also Health
    American Nurses Assn Conv (Minneapolis, MN), Jun 25
    Delano, Jane: Birth Anniv, Mar 26
    Emergency Nurses Day, Oct 11
    Emergency Nurses Week, Oct 8
    Nurse Anesthetists Week, Natl, Jan 22
    Nurses Day and Week, Natl, May 6
    Nursing Assistants Day and Week, Natl, Jun 15
    Nursing Conf on Pediatric Primary Care (Washington, DC), Apr 5
    Perioperative (OR) Nurse Week, Nov 12
    School Nurse Day, Natl, May 10
Nursing Home Week, Natl, May 14
Nutrition Month, Natl, Mar 1
Nutrition Week, Natl Women's, Apr 9
Nutrition: Eat Better, Eat Together Month, Oct 1
Nutt Day, Emma M., Sep 1
Nuyen, France: Birth, Jul 31
Nykvist, Sven Vilhem: Birth, Dec 3
Nylon Stockings: Anniv, May 15
NYPD Blue TV Premiere: Anniv, Sep 21
Nyquist, Ryan: Birth, Mar 6

O.K. First Appearance in Print: Anniv, Mar 23
Oakley, Annie: Birth Anniv, Aug 13
Oakley, Charles: Birth, Dec 18
Oates, John: Birth, Apr 7
Oates, Joyce Carol: Birth, Jun 16
Oatmeal Fest (Bertram/Oatmeal, TX), Sep 1
Oatmeal Month, Jan 1
Obama, Barack: Birth, Aug 4
Obituary Writers' Intl Conference, Great (Las Vegas, NM), Jun 15
O'Brian, Hugh: Birth, Apr 19
O'Brien, Conan: Birth, Apr 18
O'Brien, Edna: Birth, Dec 15
O'Brien, Margaret: Birth, Jan 15
O'Brien, Tim: Birth, Oct 1
O'Casey, Sean: Birth Anniv, Mar 30
Occoneechee State Park Native American Fest and Pow Wow (Clarksville, VA), May 13
Occupational Therapy Month, Natl, Apr 1
Ocean Dance (Hollywood, FL), Dec 31
Ocean Fest Sea-Son, Natl Week of (Fort Lauderdale, FL), Mar 4
Ocean, Billy: Birth, Jan 21
Oconaluftee Indian Village (Cherokee, NC), May 15
O'Connell, Daniel: Birth Anniv, Aug 6
O'Connor, Carroll: Birth Anniv, Aug 2
O'Connor, Donald: Birth Anniv, Aug 28
O'Connor, Donald: Singin' in the Rain Film Premiere: Anniv, Mar 27
O'Connor, Frances: Birth, Jun 12
O'Connor, Glynnis: Birth, Nov 19
O'Connor, Sandra Day: Birth, Mar 26
O'Connor, Sandra Day: First Woman Supreme Court Justice: Anniv, Sep 25
O'Connor, Sinead: Birth, Dec 8
October Frozen & Refrigerated Foods Fest, Oct 1
October War (Yom Kippur War), Oct 6
Octoberfest (Appleton, WI), Sep 30
O'Dell, William "Spike": Birth, May 21
Odets, Clifford: Birth Anniv, Jul 18
Odetta: Birth, Dec 31
Odie: Birthday, Aug 8
Odometer Invented: Anniv, May 12
O'Donnell, Chris: Birth, Jun 26
O'Donnell, Rosie: Birth, Mar 21
Ogden, Jonathan: Birth, Jul 31
Ogden Day, Feb 12
Oglethorpe, James: Birth Anniv, Dec 22
O'Grady, Gail: Birth, Jan 23
Oh, Sandra: Birth, Nov 30
O'Hara, Catherine: Birth, Mar 4
O'Hara, Maureen: Birth, Aug 17
O'Higgins, Bernardo: Birth Anniv, Aug 20
Ohio
    Admission Day, Mar 1
    Algonquin Mill Fall Fest (Carrollton), Oct 13
    All-American Soap Box Derby (Akron), Jul 29
    Annie Oakley Days (Greenville), Jul 28
    Antique Power Exhibition (Burton), Jul 28
    Anti-Saloon League Founded: Anniv (Oberlin), May 24

Apple Butter Stirrin' (Coshocton), Oct 20
Banana Split Fest (Wilmington), Jun 9
Barnesville Pumpkin Fest (Barnesville), Sep 21
Boo at the Zoo (Cleveland), Oct 19
Christkindl Market (Canton), Nov 10
Christmas Candlelightings (Coshocton), Dec 2
Circleville Pumpkin Show (Circleville), Oct 18
Civil War Reenactment (Coshocton), Jul 15
Cleveland Home and Garden Show (Cleveland), Feb 4
Cleveland Natl Air Show (Cleveland), Sep 2
Clinton County Corn Fest (Wilmington), Jun 9
Coshocton Canal Fest (Coshocton), Aug 19
Dandelion May Fest (Dover), May 5
DeWine, Mike: Birth, Jan 5
Dulcimer Days (Coshocton), May 19
Easter Egg Hunt (Rockford), Apr 15
Fall Fest of Leaves (Ross County), Oct 20
Foothills Art Fest (Jackson), Oct 13
Geneva Area Grape Jamboree (Geneva), Sep 23
Help Someone See Week (Rockford), Mar 6
Heritage Craft and Olde-Time Music Fest (Coshocton), Jun 17
Holiday Happiness (Upper Arlington), Dec 2
Hoof-Care Summit, Intl (Cincinnati), Jan 31
Jackson County Apple Fest (Jackson), Sep 19
Lawn Mower Race, Sta-Bil Natl Chmpshp (Mansfield), Sep 2
Longhorn World Chmpshp Rodeo (Cincinnati), Jan 27
Longhorn World Chmpshp Rodeo (Columbus), Feb 3
Longhorn World Chmpshp Rodeo (Dayton), Feb 10
Marion Popcorn Fest (Marion), Sep 7
Miss Ohio Pageant (Mansfield), Jun 14
NCAA Div I Women's Golf Chmpshps (Columbus), May 23
Ohio River Sternwheel Fest (Marietta), Sep 8
Ohio State Fair (Columbus), Aug 2
Paul Bunyan Show (Nelsonville), Oct 6
Red, White and Boom (Columbus), Jul 3
Stokes Becomes First Black Mayor in US: Anniv, Nov 13
Swiss Fest (Sugarcreek), Sep 29
Taft, Bob: Birth, Jan 8
Taste of Cincinnati (Cincinnati), May 27
Tecumseh! Epic Outdoor Drama (Chillicothe), Jun 9
Twins Day Fest (Twinsburg), Aug 4
Utica Old-Fashioned Ice Cream Fest (Utica), May 27
Voinovich, George V.: Birth, Jul 15
Walsh Invitational Rifle Tournament (Cincinnati), Nov 3
Women's Big Ten Swimming/Diving Chmpshps (Columbus), Feb 15
Oil Embargo Lifted, Arab: Anniv, Mar 13
Oil Well, First Commercial: Anniv, Aug 27
OK Corral, Gunfight: Anniv, Oct 26
Okafor, Emeka: Birth, Sep 28
O'Keefe, Michael: Birth, Apr 24
O'Keeffe, Georgia: Birth Anniv, Nov 15
Oklahoma
    Admission Day, Nov 16
    Azalea Fest (Muskogee), Apr 3
    Big 12 Men's Golf Chmpshp (Tulsa), Apr 24
    Big 12 Women's Softball Chmpshp (Oklahoma City), May 10
    Bullnanza (Guthrie), Jan 27
    Cherokee Strip Celebration (Perry), Sep 16
    Cherokee Strip Day, Sep 16
    Coburn, Tom: Birth, Mar 14
    Eighty-Niner Celebration (Guthrie), Apr 18
    Garden of Lights (Muskogee), Nov 23
    Green Country RV & Boat Show (Tulsa), Mar 3
    Guthrie Jazz Banjo Fest (Guthrie), May 26
    Henry, Brad: Birth, Jul 10
    Historical Day, Oct 10
    Inhofe, James M.: Birth, Nov 17
    Kiamichi Owa-Chito Fest of the Forest (Broken Bow), Jun 16
    Land Rush Begins, Apr 22
    Last Formal Surrender of Confederate Troops: Anniv, Jun 23
    Longhorn World Chmpshp Rodeo (Tulsa), Jan 20
    Medieval Fair (Norman), Mar 31
    Midsummer Nights' Fair (Norman), Jul 14
    NCAA Div I Softball Chmpshp (Oklahoma City), Jun 1
    NCAA Div I Wrestling Chmpshps (Oklahoma City), Mar 16
    OK Mozart Intl Fest (Bartlesville), Jun 9
    Oklahoma City Bombing: Anniv, Apr 19
    Oklahoma Day, Apr 22
    Oklahoma State Fair (Oklahoma City), Sep 14
    P.V. Helmerich Distinguished Author Award (Tulsa), Dec 1
    PGA Seniors' Chmpshp (Edmond), May 22

Rattlesnake Derby (Mangum), Apr 28
Sorghum Day Fest (Wewoka), Oct 28
Territorial Christmas Celebration (Guthrie), Nov 25
Tulsa Boat, Sport & Travel Show (Tulsa), Jan 30
Watermelon Fest (Rush Springs), Aug 12
World Cow Chip-Throwing Chmpshp (Beaver), Apr 15
Oklahoma City Bombing: Anniv, Apr 19
Oklahoma! Broadway Premiere: Anniv, Mar 31
Oktoberfest (Covington, KY), Sep 8
Oktoberfest (New Ulm, MN), Oct 6
Oktoberfest (Snowbird, UT), Aug 26
Oktoberfest (St. Charles, MO), Oct 7
Oktoberfest, Carson City Library Foundation (Carson City, NV), Oct 7
Oktoberfest, Rhinelander's (Rhinelander, WI), Oct 6
Olajuwon, Hakeem: Birth, Jan 21
Old Inauguration Day, Mar 4
Old Ironsides Launched: Anniversary, Oct 21
Old Ironsides Saved by Poem: Anniv, Sep 16
Old New Year's Day, Mar 25
Old Red Courthouse Dedication and Opening of Old Red Museum (Dallas, TX), Jul 1
Old Stoughton (MA) Musical Society: Anniv, Nov 7
Old Threshers Reunion (Mount Pleasant, IA), Aug 31
Old Time School (Cambridge, MN), Jun 3
Oldenburg, Claes: Birth, Jan 28
Older Americans Month, Natl (Pres Proc), May 1
Oldest Man in Space: Discovery, Oct 29
Oldman, Gary: Birth, Mar 21
Old-Time Country Music Contest, Fest & Expo, Natl (Missouri Valley, IA), Aug 28
Old-Time Fiddlers' Jamboree (Smithville, TN), Jun 30
Olerud, John: Birth, Aug 5
Olin, Ken: Birth, Jul 30
Oliphant, Pat: Birth, Jul 24
Olive Branch Petition: Anniv, Jul 8
Oliver, Jamie: Birth, May 27
Olivier, Laurence: Birth Anniv, May 22
Olmos, Edward James: Birth, Feb 24
Olmsted, Frederick L.: Birth Anniv, Apr 26
O'Loughlin, Gerald: Birth, Dec 23
Olowokandi, Michael: Birth, Apr 3
Olsen, Ashley: Birth, Jun 13
Olsen, Mary-Kate: Birth, Jun 13
Olsen, Merlin: Birth, Sep 15
Olympic Games
    First Modern Olympics Began: Anniv, Apr 6
    First Perfect Score: Anniv, Jul 18
    First Winter Olympics: Anniv, Jan 25
    Israeli Olympiad Massacre: Anniv, Sep 5
    Paralympic Games (Turin, Italy), Mar 10
    Special Olympics Day, Jul 20
    Special Olympics Winter Games (McHenry, MD), Feb 26
    Winter (Turin, Italy), Feb 10
Olympic Natl Park Established: Anniv, Jun 29
Oman: National Holiday, Nov 18
Omarr, Sydney: Birth Anniv, Aug 5
Omnibus TV Premiere: Anniv, Nov 9
On the Origin of Species Published: Anniv, Nov 22
Onassis, Aristotle: Birth Anniv, Jan 7
Onassis, Jacqueline Kennedy: Birth Anniv, Jul 28
One Day at a Time TV Premiere: Anniv, Dec 16
One Life to Live TV Premiere: Anniv, Jul 15
One Voice, Dec 31
O'Neal, Jermaine: Birth, Oct 13
O'Neal, Ryan: Birth, Apr 20
O'Neal, Shaquille: Birth, Mar 6
O'Neal, Tatum: Birth, Nov 5
One-Hit Wonder Day, Natl, Sep 25
O'Neill, Ed: Birth, Apr 12
O'Neill, Eugene: Birth Anniv, Oct 16
O'Neill, Jennifer: Birth, Feb 20
O'Neill, Rose Cecil: Birth Anniv, Jun 25
On-Hold Month, Natl, Mar 1
Onizuka, Ellison S.: Birth Anniv, Jun 24
Ono, Yoko: Bed-in for Peace: Anniv, Mar 25
Ono, Yoko: Birth, Feb 18
Ontkean, Michael: Birth, Jan 24
Open an Umbrella Indoors Day, Natl, Mar 13
Open-Heart Surgery, First: Anniv, Jul 9
Opera
    Aida Premieres: Anniv, Dec 24
    Callas's Last Performance: Anniv, Jul 5
    Donizetti's "Lucia Di Lammermoor" Premiere: Anniv, Sep 26
    Madama Butterfly Premiere: Anniv, Feb 17
    Marian Anderson Performs with Metropolitan Opera: Anniv, Jan 7
    Metropolitan Opera House: Opening Anniv, Oct 22
    Metropolitan Opera Natl Council Auditions Finals (New York, NY), Mar 19

Metropolitan Opera Radio Broadcasts Premiere: Anniv, **Dec 25**
Opera Debut in the Colonies: Anniv, **Feb 8**
Ponselle, Rosa: Birth Anniv, **Jan 22**
Puccini, Giacomo: Birth Anniv, **Dec 22**
Verdi, Giuseppi: Birth Anniv, **Oct 10**
Wagner, Richard: Birth Anniv, **May 22**
Operation Iraqi Freedom: Anniv, Mar 19
Oprah Winfrey Show TV Premiere: Anniv, Sep 8
Optimism Month, Mar 1
Orange Bowl (Miami, FL), Jan 3
Orangemen's Day (Northern Ireland), Jul 12
Orbach, Jerry: Birth Anniv, Oct 20
Orchid Show (St. Louis, MO), Jan 28
Ordonez, Reynaldo: Birth, Nov 11
Oregon
  Admission Day, **Feb 14**
  All-Northwest Barbershop Ballad Contest (Forest Grove), **Mar 3**
  Brookings-Harbor Azalea Fest (Brookings), **May 26**
  Children's Celebration (Springfield), **Jul 8**
  Christmas Greens Show (Salem), **Dec 1**
  Cinco de Mayo Fest (Portland), **May 4**
  Collegiate Women's Gymnastics, Natl (Corvallis), **Apr 20**
  Columbia River Cross Channel Swim (Hood River), **Sep 4**
  Concours d'Elegance (Forest Grove), **Jul 16**
  Crab and Steak Dinner (Cornelius), **Jan 21**
  Crater Lake Natl Park Established: Anniv, **May 22**
  Crater Lake Rim Runs and Marathon (Klamath Falls), **Aug 12**
  Curtis Cup (Bandon), **Jul 29**
  Founder's Day Corn Roast (Forest Grove), **Sep 17**
  Hangover Handicap Run (Klamath Falls), **Jan 1**
  Holiday Ale Fest (Portland), **Dec 1**
  Hood River County Fair (Hood River), **Jul 26**
  Hood River Old-Fashioned Fourth of July (Hood River), **Jul 4**
  Hood River Valley Harvest Fest (Hood River), **Oct 20**
  Kulongoski, Ted: Birth, **Nov 5**
  Lincoln, Abraham: Birthday Observance, **Feb 6**
  Loyalty Days/Seafair Fest (Newport), **May 4**
  Marion County Fair (Salem), **Jul 6**
  Medford Cruise (Medford), **Jun 16**
  Medford Jazz Jubilee (Medford), **Oct 13**
  Megga Hunt (Springfield), **Apr 15**
  Miss Oregon Scholarship Pageant (Seaside), **Jun 25**
  Mother's Day Annual Rhododendron Show (Portland), **May 13**
  Mount Hood Railroad Season (Hood River), **Apr 1**
  Muddy Frogwater Country Classic Fest (Milton-Freewater), **Aug 18**
  NCAA Div I Men's Golf Chmpshps (Sunriver), **May 31**
  Newport Seafood and Wine Fest (Newport), **Feb 24**
  Oregon Bach Fest (Eugene), **Jun 30**
  Oregon Brewers Fest (Portland), **Jul 27**
  Oregon State Fair (Salem), **Aug 25**
  Pendleton Round-Up (Pendleton), **Sep 9**
  Portland Historic Races (Portland), **Jul 7**
  Portland Rose Fest (Portland), **Jun 1**
  Portland's Birthday, **Apr 6**
  Rhododendron Fest (Florence), **May 19**
  Romance Reader's Luncheon (Portland), **Apr 22**
  Saint Urho's Day (Hood River), **Mar 16**
  Shakespeare Fest (Ashland), **Feb 24**
  Sherwood Robin Hood Fest (Sherwood), **Jul 21**
  Smith, Gordon: Birth, **May 25**
  South Coast Writer's Conf (Gold Beach), **Feb 17**
  State Games of Oregon (Portland), **Jul 7**
  Sternwheeler Days (Cascade Locks), **Jun 23**
  Turkey Rama (McMinnville), **Jul 13**
  US Women's Amateur (Golf) Chmpshp (North Plains), **Aug 7**
  Verboort Sausage and Kraut Dinner (Forest Grove), **Nov 4**
  Wyden, Ron: Birth, **May 3**
Oregon Trail: Pony Express Fest (Hanover, KS), Aug 27
Organic Act Day (US Virgin Islands), Jun 19
Organization of American States Founded: Anniv, Apr 30
Organization, Organizing
  Clean-Off-Your-Desk Day, Natl, **Jan 9**
  Garage Sale Day, Natl, **Aug 12**
  Get Organized Month, Natl, **Jan 1**
  Love Your Files Week, Natl, **Sep 17**
  Organize Your Home Day, **Jan 9**
  Organize Your Home Office Day, **Mar 14**
  Organize Your Medical Information Month, **Oct 1**
  Organizing Week, Natl (Canada), **May 1**
  Single-Tasking Day, **Feb 21**
Orlando, Tony: Birth, Apr 3
Ormond, Julia: Birth, Jan 4

Orphan Train Heritage Society Reunion (Concordia, KS), Jun 9
Orr, Bobby: Birth, Mar 20
Orthodontic Health Month, Natl, Oct 1
Orthodox Christian Observances
  Ascension Day, **Jun 1**
  Cheesefare Sunday, **Mar 5**
  Dormition of Theotokos, **Aug 15**
  Dumb Week (Greece), **Apr 9**
  Easter Sunday, **Apr 23**
  Festival of All Saints, **Jun 18**
  Green Monday, **Mar 6**
  Lazarus Saturday, **Apr 15**
  Lent, **Mar 6**
  Meatfare Sunday, **Feb 26**
  Palm Sunday, **Apr 16**
  Pentecost, **Jun 11**
  Roman Catholic/Eastern Orthodox Meeting: Anniv, **Jan 5**
Orwell, George: Birth Anniv, Jun 25
Osage River Mountain Man Fest and Black Powder Shoot (Lake Ozark, MO), Sep 15
Osborne, Jeffrey: Birth, Mar 9
Osbourne, Ozzy: Birth, Dec 3
Oscars Presentation, Mar 5
Osceola: Death Anniv, Jan 30
Osgood, Charles: Birth, Jan 8
O'Shea, Milo: Birth, Jun 2
Osment, Haley Joel: Birth, Apr 10
Osmond, Donny: Birth, Dec 9
Osmond, Marie: Birth, Oct 13
Ostara, Mar 20
Osteopathic Medicine Month, Natl, Sep 1
Osteoporosis Awareness and Prevention Month, Natl, May 1
Oswalt, Roy: Birth, Aug 29
O'Toole, Annette: Birth, Apr 1
O'Toole, Peter: Birth, Aug 2
Ott, Melvin (Mel): Birth Anniv, Mar 2
Ottawa Bluesfest, Cisco Systems (Ottawa, ON, Canada), Jul 7
Ouimet, Francis DeSales: Birth Anniv, May 8
Our Miss Brooks TV Premiere: Anniv, Oct 3
Outback Bowl (Tampa, FL), Jan 2
Outcault, Richard Felton: Birth Anniv, Jan 14
Outrigger Canoes: Hawaiki Nui Va'a Race (French Polynesia), Oct 18
Ovarian Cancer Awareness Month, Sep 1
Ovarian Cancer Awareness Month, Natl (Pres Proc), Sep 1
Overall, Park: Birth, Mar 15
Overlooked Film Fest (Champaign, IL), Apr 26
Overseas Chinese Day (Taiwan), Oct 21
Owen Marshall: Counselor at Law TV Premiere: Anniv, Sep 16
Owen, Clive: Birth, Oct 3
Owen, Michael: Birth, Dec 14
Owen, Robert: Birth Anniv, May 14
Owens, Bill: Birth, Oct 22
Owens, Buck: Birth, Aug 12
Owens, Gary: Birth, May 10
Owens, Jesse: Birth Anniv, Sep 12
Owens, Jesse: Greatest Day in Track and Field: Anniv, May 25
Oxenberg, Catherine: Birth, Sep 22
Oyster Fest, St. Mary's County (Leonardtown, MD), Oct 21
Oz Fest (Liberal, KS), Oct 13
Oz, Frank: Birth, May 24
Ozark Empire Fair (Springfield, MO), Jul 28
Ozark Jubilee TV Premiere: Anniv, Jan 22
Ozawa, Seiji: Birth, Sep 1
Ozick, Cynthia: Birth, Apr 17
Ozzie and Harriet Show Radio Debut: Anniv, Oct 8
Ozzie and Harriet TV Premiere: Anniv, Oct 3

Paar, Jack: Birth Anniv, May 1
Paca, William: Birth Anniv, Oct 31
Pace, Orlando: Birth, Nov 4
Pacific DanceSport Chmpshps (Los Angeles, CA), Nov 3
Pacific Ocean Discovered: Anniv, Sep 25
Pacific: Eastern Pacific Hurricane Season, May 15
Pacing the Bounds (Liestal, Switzerland), May 22
Pacino, Al: Birth, Apr 25
Paczki Day, Feb 28
Paderewski, Ignace J: Birth Anniv, Nov 6
Paganini, Nicolo: Birth Anniv, Oct 27
Page, Patti: Birth, Nov 8
Pagett, Nicola: Birth, Jun 15
Paglia, Camille: Birth, Apr 2
Paige, Janis: Birth, Sep 16
Paige, Satchel: Birth Anniv, Jul 7
Paine, Robert Treat: Birth Anniv, Mar 11
Paine, Thomas: Birth Anniv, Jan 29
Paine, Thomas: Freethinker's Day, Jan 29

Pajama Month, Natl, Oct 1
Pajamas: Wear Your Pajamas To Work Day, Natl, Apr 18
Pak, Se Ri: Birth, Sep 28
Pakistan
  Defense of Pakistan Day, **Sep 6**
  Founder's Death Anniv (Qaid-e-Azam), **Sep 11**
  Independence Day, **Aug 14**
  Jinnah, Mohammed Ali (Qaid-e-Azam): Birth Anniv, **Dec 25**
  Republic Day, **Mar 23**
Palance, Jack: Birth, Feb 18
Palestinian Massacre: Anniv, Sep 16
Palestinian People, Intl Day of Solidarity with (UN), Nov 29
Palffy, Ziggy: Birth, May 5
Palin, Michael: Birth, May 5
Palm Harbor Arts/Crafts/Music Fest (Palm Harbor, FL), Dec 2
Palm Sunday, Apr 9
Palm Sunday, Orthodox, Apr 16
Palme, Olof: Assassination Anniv, Feb 28
Palmeiro, Rafael: Birth, Sep 24
Palmer, Alice Freeman: Birth Anniv, Feb 21
Palmer, Arnold: Birth, Sep 10
Palmer, Betsy: Birth, Nov 1
Palmer, Jim: Birth, Oct 15
Palmer, Lilli: Birth Anniv, May 24
Palminteri, Chazz: Birth, May 15
Palomares Hydrogen Bomb Accident: Anniv, Jan 17
Paltrow, Gwyneth: Birth, Sep 28
Pan Am Circles Earth: Anniv, Jan 6
Pan American Flight 103 Explosion: Anniv, Dec 21
Pan American Week (Pres Proc), Apr 9
Panama
  Assumes Control of Canal: Anniv, **Dec 31**
  First Shout of Independence, **Nov 10**
  Flag Day, **Nov 4**
  Independence Day, **Nov 3**
  Independence from Spain Day, **Nov 28**
  Martyrs' Day, **Jan 9**
  Panama City Foundation Day, **Aug 15**
  US Invasion of Panama: Anniv, **Dec 20**
Panama Canal Opens: Anniv, Aug 15
Pan-American Day (Pres Proc), Apr 14
Pan-American Day in Florida, Apr 14
Pancake Day, Intl (Liberal, KS), Feb 28
Pancake Week, Natl, Feb 26
Pandemic of 1918 Hits US: Anniv, Mar 11
Panic Day, Mar 9
Panizzi, Anthony: Birth Anniv, Sep 16
Pankin, Stuart: Birth, Apr 8
Pankow, John: Birth, Apr 18
Panoply (Huntsville, AL), Apr 28
Panther Day, Save the Florida, Mar 18
Pantoliano, Joe: Birth, Sep 12
Papua New Guinea: Independence Day, Sep 16
Paper Money Issued: Anniv, Mar 10
Paperback Books Introduced: Anniv, Jul 30
Papp, Joseph: Birth Anniv, Jun 22
Papua New Guinea: Independence Day, Sep 16
Paquin, Anna: Birth, Jul 24
Parachute: Powered Fly-in (Columbus, KS), Sep 21
Parades
  Boom Box Parade (Willimantic, CT), **Jul 4**
  Bristol Civic, Military/Firemen's Parade (Bristol, RI), **Jul 4**
  Calithumpian Parade (Biwabik, MN), **Jul 4**
  Canadian Tulip Fest (Ottawa, ON, Canada), **May 4**
  Chester Greenwood Day Parade (Farmington, ME), **Dec 2**
  Chinese New Year Golden Dragon Parade & Fest (Los Angeles, CA), **Feb 4**
  Christmas on the River (Demopolis, AL), **Nov 26**
  Do Dah Day (Birmingham, AL), **May 6**
  Do-Dah Parade (Kalamazoo, MI), **Jun 3**
  Dodge City Days (Dodge City, KS), **Jul 28**
  Electric Light Parade (Lovington, NM), **Dec 4**
  Ennis Rodeo & Parade (Ennis, MT), **Jul 3**
  Fantasy of Light Parade (Wheeling, WV), **Nov 17**
  Fredericksburg Heritage Fest (Fredericksburg, VA), **Jul 4**
  Gasparilla Extravaganza and Pirate Fest (Tampa, FL), **Jan 21**
  George Washington Birthday (Alexandria, VA), **Feb 20**
  Halloween Parade (Toms River, NJ), **Oct 31**
  Holidays in the City Grand Illumination Parade (Norfolk, VA), **Nov 18**
  Hollywood Beach Candy Cane Parade (Hollywood, FL), **Dec 2**
  Jersey Battle of Flowers (St. Lawrence, Channel Islands), **Aug 10**
  Joe Cain Procession (Mobile, AL), **Feb 26**
  Macy's Thanksgiving Day Parade (New York, NY), **Nov 23**

Parades (cont'd)—Pennsylvania

Mai Wah Society Chinese Lunar New Year Parade (Butte, MT), **Feb 4**
Marigold Fest (Pekin, IL), **Sep 8**
Memorial Day Parade (Aurora, IL), **May 29**
Memorial Day Parade and Ceremonies (Gettysburg, PA), **May 29**
Mother Goose Parade (El Cajon, CA), **Nov 19**
Mummers Parade (Philadelphia, PA), **Jan 1**
New Year's Day Parade (London, England), **Jan 1**
Oktoberfest (Kitchener/Waterloo, ON, Canada), **Oct 6**
Pacific Life Holiday Bowl Parade (San Diego, CA), **Dec 28**
Pasadena Doo Dah Parade (Pasadena, CA), **Nov 19**
Pro-Am Snipe Excursion and Parade (Moultrie, GA), **Apr 1**
Pulaski Day Parade (Philadelphia, PA), **Oct 1**
Rhododendron Fest Grand Floral Parade (Florence, OR), **May 19**
Saint Patrick's Day Parade (Baton Rouge, LA), **Mar 18**
Saint Patrick's Day Parade (Hornell, NY), **Mar 18**
Saint Patrick's Day Parade (New York, NY), **Mar 17**
Saint Patrick's Day Parade (Roanoke, VA), **Mar 17**
Santa by Stage Coach Parade (El Centro, CA), **Dec 2**
Three Rivers Fest (Fort Wayne, IN), **Jul 8**
Tournament of Roses Parade (Pasadena, CA), **Jan 2**
Twin Cities Janus Mardi Gras Parade (Monroe, LA), **Feb 18**
Victorian Christmas Sleighbell Parade (Manistee, MI), **Dec 1**
West Allis Western Days Family Jamboree (West Allis, WI), **Jun 15**
Wild Horse Stampede (Wolf Point, MT), **Jul 6**
Wolf Point's Annual Christmas Parade (Wolf Point, MT), **Dec 1**
World Famous Fish House Parade (Aitkin, MN), **Nov 24**
Paraguay
Battle of Boqueron Day, **Sep 29**
Independence Day, **May 15**
National Heroes' Day, **Mar 1**
Peace with Bolivia Day, **Jun 12**
Paralympic Games (Turin, Italy), **Mar 10**
Paranormal Day, **May 3**
Paraprofessional Appreciation Day, **Apr 5**
Parcells, Bill: Birth, **Aug 22**
Pare, Michael: Birth, **Oct 9**
Parent Leadership Month, Natl, **Feb 1**
Parent, Bernie: Birth, **Apr 3**
Parents as Teachers Day, Natl, **Nov 8**
Parents' Day (Pres Proc), **Jul 23**
Parents: Prepare Tomorrow's Parents Month, **May 14**
Paretsky, Sara: Birth, **Jun 8**
Paris, Treaty of, Ends American Rev, **Sep 3**
Parish, Robert: Birth, **Aug 30**
Parker Day, John, **Apr 19**
Parker, Bonnie: Bonnie and Clyde: Death Anniv, **May 23**
Parker, Charlie: at the LA Philharmonic: Anniv, **Mar 25**
Parker, Charlie: Birth Anniv, **Aug 29**
Parker, Charlie: First Recorded: Anniv, **Apr 30**
Parker, Dave: Birth, **Jun 9**
Parker, Eleanor: Birth, **Jun 26**
Parker, Fess: Birth, **Aug 16**
Parker, George: Death Anniv, **Mar 17**
Parker, Jameson: Birth, **Nov 18**
Parker, Mary-Louise: Birth, **Aug 2**
Parker, Robert Leroy (Butch Cassidy): Birth Anniv, **Apr 13**
Parker, Sarah Jessica: Birth, **Mar 25**
Parker, Tony: Birth, **May 17**
Parker, Trey: Birth, **May 30**
Parkins, Barbara: Birth, **May 22**
Parkinson, James: Death Anniv, **Dec 21**
Parkinson's Awareness Month, Natl, **Apr 1**
Parkman, Francis: Birth Anniv, **Sep 16**
Parks Month, Natl Recreation and, **Jul 1**
Parks, Bert: Birth Anniv, **Dec 30**
Parks, Gordon: Birth, **Nov 30**
Parks, Michael: Birth, **Apr 4**
Parks, Rosa: Birth, **Feb 4**
Parks, Rosa: Day, **Dec 1**
Parnell, Charles S.: Birth Anniv, **Jun 27**
Parry, William: Birth Anniv, **Dec 19**
Parseghian, Ara: Birth, **May 10**
Parsons, Estelle: Birth, **Nov 20**
Parsons, Louella: Birth Anniv, **Aug 6**
Particularly Preposterous Packaging Day, **Aug 7**
Parton, Dolly: Birth, **Jan 19**
Pascal, Blaise: Birth Anniv, **Jun 19**
Pascua Florida Day (FL), **Apr 2**

Passion Week, **Mar 13**
Passiontide, **Apr 2**
Passover, **Apr 13**
Passover Begins, **Apr 12**
Passport Presentation (Russia), **Jan 2**
Pasternak, Boris: Birth Anniv, **Feb 10**
Pasteur, Louis: Birth Anniv, **Dec 27**
Pasteur, Louis: First Successful Antirabies Inoculation, **Jul 6**
Pastoral Care Week, **Oct 22**
Pat Boone Show TV Premiere: Anniv, **Oct 3**
Pataki, George: Birth, **Jun 24**
Patent Issued for First Adding Machine: Anniv, **Oct 11**
Patent Office Opens, US: Anniv, **Jul 31**
Paterno, Joe: Birth, **Dec 21**
Patient Recognition Week, Natl, **Feb 1**
Patinkin, Mandy: Birth, **Nov 30**
Patric, Jason: Birth, **Jun 27**
Patrick, Dan: Birth, **May 15**
Patriot Day, **Sep 11**
Patriot's Day (MA, ME), **Apr 17**
Patriot's Day in Florida, **Apr 19**
Patterson, Floyd: Birth, **Jan 4**
Patterson, James: Birth, **Mar 22**
Patton, George S, Jr: Birth Anniv, **Nov 11**
Patton, Will: Birth, **Jun 14**
Paul Bunyan Show (Nelsonville, OH), **Oct 6**
Paul, Adrian: Birth, **May 29**
Paul, Alexandra: Birth, **Jul 29**
Paul, Alice: Birth Anniv, **Jan 11**
Paul, Les: Birth, **Jun 9**
Pauley, Jane: Birth, **Oct 31**
Paulus, Friedrich: Birth Anniv, **Sep 23**
Pause for Pledge (Natl Flag Day USA), **Jun 14**
Pavan, Marisa: Birth, **Jun 19**
Pavarotti, Luciano: Birth, **Oct 12**
Pavlova, Anna: Birth Anniv, **Feb 12**
Pawlenty, Tim: Birth, **Nov 1**
Pawnbrokers Day, Natl, **Dec 6**
Paxson, John: Birth, **Sep 29**
Paxton, Bill: Birth, **May 17**
Pay-A-Compliment Day, **Feb 6**
Paymer, David: Birth, **Aug 30**
Payne, John H.: Birth Anniv, **Jun 9**
Payroll Week, Natl, **Sep 4**
Pays, Amanda: Birth, **Jun 6**
Payton, Gary: Birth, **Jul 23**
Peña, Elizabeth: Birth, **Sep 23**
Peabody, Elizabeth Palmer: Birth Anniv, **May 16**
Peabody, George: Birth Anniv, **Feb 18**
Peace
Annual World Peace Meditation, **Dec 31**
Day of Peace, Intl, **Sep 21**
Disarmament Week (UN), **Oct 24**
Dream Day, **Mar 11**
Peace Covenant, Universal: One Voice, **Dec 31**
Peace Fest (Hiroshima, Japan), **Aug 6**
Peace Officer Memorial Day (Pres Proc), **May 15**
Peace, Friendship and Good Will Week, **Oct 25**
Versailles Peace Conference (WWI): Anniv, **Jan 18**
World Hello Day, **Nov 21**
Peace Corps Day, **Mar 7**
Peace Corps Founded: Anniv, **Mar 1**
Peace Rose Introduced to World: Anniv, **Apr 29**
Peacekeepers, Intl Day of (UN), **May 29**
Peach Fest, Leitersburg (Leitersburg, MD), **Aug 12**
Peach Fest, Louisiana (Ruston, LA), **Jun 22**
Peachtree Road Race (Atlanta, GA), **Jul 4**
Peale, Anna Claypoole: Birth Anniv, **Mar 6**
Peale, Charles W.: Birth Anniv, **Apr 15**
Peale, James: Death Anniv, **May 24**
Peale, Norman Vincent: Birth Anniv, **May 31**
Peanut Butter Lover's Month, **Nov 1**
Peanuts Debuts: Anniv, **Oct 2**
Pearl Harbor Day, **Dec 7**
Pearl Harbor Remembrance Day, Natl (Pres Proc), **Dec 7**
Pearl, Daniel: Birth Anniv, **Oct 10**
Pearl, Minnie: Birth Anniv, **Oct 25**
Pearse, Richard: Flight Anniv, **Mar 31**
Pearson, Lester B.: Birth Anniv, **Apr 23**
Peary, Robert E.: Birth Anniv, **May 6**
Peary, Robert E.: North Pole Discovered: Anniv, **Apr 6**
Pecan Day, **Mar 25**
Pecan Month, Natl, **Apr 1**
Peck, Annie S.: Birth Anniv, **Oct 19**
Peck, Gregory: Birth Anniv, **Apr 5**
Peddler's Village Gingerbread House Competition & Display (Lahaska, PA), **Nov 17**
Peddler's Village Scarecrow Contest and Outdoor Display (Lahaska, PA), **Sep 11**
Peddler's Village Scarecrow Fest (Lahaska, PA), **Sep 16**
Pediatric Cancer Awareness Month, **Sep 1**
Pediatric Nurse Practitioner Week, **Mar 30**

Pediculosis Prevention Month, Natl, **Sep 1**
Pee on Earth Day, **Jun 21**
Peel, Robert: Birth Anniv, **Feb 5**
Peet, Amanda: Birth, **Jan 11**
Peete, Calvin: Birth, **Jul 18**
Pele Scores 1,000th Goal: Anniv, **Nov 19**
Pele: Birth, **Oct 23**
Pencil Patented: Anniv, **Mar 30**
Penderecki, Krzysztof: Birth, **Nov 23**
Pendergrass, Teddy: Birth, **Mar 26**
Pendleton, Austin: Birth, **Mar 27**
Pen-Friends Week Intl, **May 1**
Penguin Awareness Day (Point Pleasant Beach, NJ), **Jan 14**
Penguin Plunge (Jamestown, RI), **Jan 1**
Penn, Arthur Heller: Birth, **Sep 27**
Penn, Irving: Birth, **Jun 16**
Penn, John: Birth Anniv, **May 6**
Penn, Sean: Birth, **Aug 17**
Penn, William: Birth Anniv, **Oct 14**
Penn, William: Pennsylvania Deeded to: Anniv, **Mar 4**
Penniman, Little Richard: Birth, **Dec 5**
Pennington, Ty: Birth, **Oct 19**
Pennsylvania
American Historical Assn Annual Mtg (Philadelphia), **Jan 5**
Antique Show (Somerset), **Aug 12**
Antiques on the Diamond (Ligonier), **Jun 10**
Apple Blossom Fest (Gettysburg), **May 6**
Apple Fest (Lahaska), **Nov 4**
Apple Harvest Fest (Gettysburg), **Oct 7**
Art in the Garden (Washington), **Sep 9**
Battle of Bushy Run Reenactment (Harrison City), **Aug 5**
Battle of Germantown Reenactment (Philadelphia), **Oct 7**
Battle of Gettysburg: Anniv, **Jul 1**
Belsnickel Craft Show (Boyertown), **Nov 24**
Benjamin Franklin Tercentenary (Philadelphia), **Jan 17**
Blueberry Fest (Montrose), **Aug 4**
Buhl Day (Sharon), **Sep 4**
Celtic Classic Highland Games & Fest (Bethlehem), **Sep 29**
Celtic Fling (Manheim), **Jun 24**
Chadds Ford Days (Chadds Ford), **Sep 9**
Chambersfest (Chambersburg), **Jul 14**
Christmas Craft Show (York), **Dec 10**
Civil War Relic/Collectors Show (Gettysburg), **Jun 23**
Covered Bridge Fest (Washington County), **Sep 16**
Dickens of a Christmas at Mount Hope Mansion (Manheim), **Nov 24**
Easter Craft Show (York), **Feb 12**
Edgar Allan Poe Evermore (Manheim), **Oct 27**
Eisenhower Fifties Weekend (Gettysburg), **Jun 17**
Eisenhower World War II Weekend (Gettysburg), **Sep 16**
Fabulous 1890s Weekend (Mansfield), **Sep 29**
Farm Show, **Jan 7**
Farmers & Threshermens Jubilee (New Centerville), **Sep 6**
Festifall (Point Marion), **Sep 24**
Fine Art & Crafts Show (Lahaska), **Jun 3**
Firestorm (Altoona), **Jul 4**
First American Abolition Society Founded: Anniv, **Apr 14**
First Commercial Oil Well: Anniv, **Aug 27**
First Natl Convention for Blacks: Anniv, **Sep 15**
First Night Football Game (Mansfield), **Sep 28**
First US Zoo: Anniv (Philadelphia), **Jul 1**
Flax Scutching Fest (Stahlstown), **Sep 9**
Fort Ligonier Days (Ligonier), **Oct 13**
Garden Fest (Chestnut Hill), **May 7**
Gardenfest at Longwood Gardens (Kennett Square), **Sep 9**
Gettysburg Address Memorial Ceremony (Gettysburg), **Nov 19**
Gettysburg Bluegrass Fest (Gettysburg), **May 18**
Gettysburg Brass Band Festival (Gettysburg), **Jun 15**
Gettysburg Civil War Book Fair (Gettysburg), **Jun 30**
Gettysburg Civil War Heritage Days (Gettysburg), **Jun 24**
Gettysburg Fall Bluegrass Fest (Gettysburg), **Aug 24**
Gettysburg Holiday Fest (Gettysburg), **Nov 24**
Gettysburg Outdoor Antique Show (Gettysburg), **May 20, Sep 23**
Ghost Tours (New Hope), **Jun 3**
Gift Fest, Intl (Fairfield), **Nov 9**
Grand Illumination (Lahaska), **Nov 17**
Great Flood of 1889 Commemoration (Johnstown), **May 27**
Greater Pittsburgh Arts & Crafts Holiday Spectacular (Greensburg), **Nov 10**

Greater Pittsburgh Renaissance Fest (West Newton), **Aug 12**
Groundhog Day in Punxsutawney, PA (Punxsutawney), **Feb 2**
Hanover Dutch Fest (Hanover), **Jul 28**
History Meets the Arts (Gettysburg), **Apr 21**
Holiday Craft Show (York), **Oct 15**
Holiday Lights on the Lake (Altoona), **Nov 23**
Ice Fest (Ligonier), **Jan 28**
INPEX (Pittsburgh), **Jun 7**
Jinglebell Journey (Mount Wolf), **Dec 3**
Johnstown Flood: Anniv, **May 31**
Keystone Country Fest (Altoona), **Sep 8**
Kustom Kemps Car Show (Biglerville), **Jun 9**
Leif Ericson Day Celebration (Philadelphia), **Oct 9**
LeMoyne House Candlelight Christmas Tours (Washington), **Dec 2**
Ligonier Highland Games (Ligonier), **Sep 8**
Little League Baseball World Series (Williamsport), **Aug 18**
Longwood Gardens Acres of Spring (Kennett Square), **Apr 22**
Longwood Gardens Autumn's Colors (Kennett Square), **Oct 7**
Longwood Gardens Christmas Display (Kennett Square), **Nov 23**
Longwood Gardens Chrysanthemum Fest (Kennett Square), **Oct 28**
Longwood Gardens Easter Display (Kennett Square), **Apr 8**
Longwood Gardens Fest of Fountains (Kennett Square), **May 27**
Longwood Gardens Welcome Spring (Kennett Square), **Jan 21**
Major League Baseball All-Star Game (Pittsburgh), **Jul 11**
Memorial Day Parade and Ceremonies (Gettysburg), **May 29**
Mount Pleasant Glass & Ethnic Fest (Mount Pleasant), **Sep 22**
Mummers Parade (Philadelphia), **Jan 1**
Mushroom Fest (Kennett Square), **Sep 9**
Musikfest (Bethlehem), **Aug 4**
National Soccer Coaches Assn of America Natl Conv (Philadelphia), **Jan 18**
New Oxford Outdoor Antique Show (New Oxford), **Jun 17**
Peddler's Village Gingerbread House Competition & Display (Lahaska), **Nov 17**
Peddler's Village Quilt Competition/Display (Lahaska), **Jan 16**
Peddler's Village Scarecrow Contest and Outdoor Display (Lahaska), **Sep 11**
Peddler's Village Scarecrow Fest (Lahaska), **Sep 16**
Penn State's Agri Progress Days (Rock Springs), **Aug 15**
Pennsylvania Arts & Crafts Christmas Fest (Washington), **Oct 20**
Pennsylvania Arts & Crafts Colonial Fest (Greensburg), **Sep 1**
Pennsylvania Arts & Crafts Mother's Day Fest (Uniontown), **May 12**
Pennsylvania Deeded to William Penn: Anniv, **Mar 4**
Pennsylvania Renaissance Faire (Manheim), **Aug 12**
Pennsylvania RV & Camping Show (Hershey), **Sep 11**
Philadelphia Flower Show (Philadelphia), **Mar 5**
Pittsburgh Arts & Crafts Spring Fever Fest (Greensburg), **Mar 24**
Pocono State Craft Fair (Shawnee-on-the-Delaware), **Aug 26**
Polish Christmas Open House (Philadelphia), **Dec 9**
PSFCA East West All-Star Game (Altoona), **Jun 24**
Pulaski Day Parade (Philadelphia), **Oct 1**
Punxsutawney Groundhog Fest (Punxsutawney), **Jul 2**
Quilt Odyssey (Hershey), **Jul 27**
Race for the Cure (Pittsburgh), **May 14**
Rain Day (Waynesburg), **Jul 29**
Ratification Day, **Dec 12**
Remembrance Day (Gettysburg), **Nov 18**
Rendell, Ed: Birth, **Jan 5**
Rhubarb Fest (Intercourse), **May 19**
Santorum, Rick: Birth, **May 10**
Seneca Falls Survivor Votes: Anniv (Philadelphia), **Nov 2**
Seven Sweets & Sours Fest (Intercourse), **Sep 15**
Slow Pitch Softball Tournament (Williamsport), **Jul 7**
Snake Hunt (Cross Fork), **Jun 24**
South Mountain Fair (Gettysburg), **Aug 23**
Specter, Arlen: Birth, **Feb 12**
Spring Craft Celebration (Richboro), **May 20**
Spring Craft Show (York), **Apr 9**

Springs Folk Fest (Springs), **Oct 6**
State Craft Fair (Lancaster), **Jul 28**
Storytelling Historical Walk Around Washington (Washington), **May 20**
Strawberry Fest (Lahaska), **May 6**
Sugarloaf Crafts Fest (Fort Washington), **Mar 17, Oct 27**
Summer Craft Show (York), **Jul 16**
Westmoreland Arts & Heritage Fest (Greensburg), **Jul 1**
York Intl Postcard Fair (York), **Nov 17**
Zippo/Case Intl Swap Meet (Bradford), **Jul 21**
Pennsylvania Ave Closed: Anniv, **May 20**
Penny Press, Beginning of the: Anniv, **Sep 3**
Pentagon Completed: Anniv, **Jan 15**
Pentagon, Vietnam War Protestors Storm Pentagon: Anniv, **Oct 21**
Pentecost, **Jun 4**
People Magazine: Anniv, **Mar 4**
People Skills Month, Intl, **Sep 1**
Pepitone, Joe: Birth, **Oct 9**
Pepper, Barry: Birth, **Apr 4**
Pepper, Claude Denson: Birth Anniv, **Sep 8**
Peppercorn Ceremony (Bermuda), **Apr 23**
Pepys, Samuel: Birth Anniv, **Feb 23**
Perdue, Sonny: Birth, **Dec 20**
Perdue, Will: Birth, **Aug 29**
Perez, Rosie: Birth, **Sep 6**
Perez, Tony: Birth, **May 14**
Perigean Spring Tides, **Jan 29, Feb 27, Sep 7, Oct 6**
Perihelion, Earth at, **Jan 4**
Perioperative (OR) Nurse Week, **Nov 12**
Perkins, Anthony: Birth Anniv, **Apr 4**
Perkins, Anthony: Psycho Film Premiere: Anniv, **Jun 16**
Perkins, Elizabeth: Birth, **Nov 18**
Perkins, Frances: Appointed to Cabinet, **Mar 4**
Perkins, Frances: Birth Anniv, **Apr 10**
Perkins, Millie: Birth, **May 12**
Perkins, Sam: Birth, **Jun 14**
Perlman, Itzhak: Birth, **Aug 31**
Perlman, Rhea: Birth, **Mar 31**
Perlman, Ron: Birth, **Apr 13**
Perot, H. Ross: Birth, **Jun 27**
Perreau, Gigi: Birth, **Feb 6**
Perrine, Valerie: Birth, **Sep 3**
Perry Como Show TV Premiere: Anniv, **Dec 24**
Perry Mason TV Premiere: Anniv, **Sep 21**
Perry, Gaylord Jackson: Birth, **Sep 15**
Perry, Jeff: Birth, **Aug 16**
Perry, Luke: Birth, **Oct 11**
Perry, Matthew: Birth, **Aug 19**
Perry, Matthew: Commodore Perry Day: Birth Anniv, **Apr 10**
Perry, Oliver H.: Birth Anniv, **Aug 23**
Perry, Rick: Birth, **Mar 4**
Perry, Steve: Birth, **Jan 22**
Perry, William "The Refrigerator": Birth, **Dec 16**
Perseid Meteor Showers, **Aug 9**
Pershing, John J.: Birth Anniv, **Sep 13**
Persian Gulf War
  Begins: Anniv, **Jan 16**
  Desert Shield: Anniv, **Aug 7**
  Ground War Begins: Anniv, **Feb 23**
  Kuwait Liberated: Anniv, **Feb 27**
Persimmon Fest, Mitchell (Mitchell, IN), **Sep 22**
Person, Chuck Connors: Birth, **Jun 27**
Personal Chef Day, Natl, **Jul 15**
Personal Finance
  Achieve Financial Independence Week, **Oct 15**
  Financial Wellness Month, **Jan 1**
  Get Smart About Credit Day, **Oct 19**
  Teach Children to Save Day, Natl, **Apr 25**
  Wealth Mentality Month, Intl, **Jan 1**
Personal History Month, **May 1**
Personal Self-Defense Awareness Month, Natl, **Jan 1**
Personal Training Week, Natl, **Apr 16**
Peru
  Countryman's Day, **Jun 24**
  Day of National Honor, **Oct 9**
  Independence Day, **Jul 28**
  Saint Rose of Lima Day, **Aug 30**
Pesach (Passover), **Apr 13**
Pesach Begins, **Apr 12**
Pesci, Joe: Birth, **Feb 9**
Pescow, Donna: Birth, **Mar 24**
Peshtigo Forest Fire: Anniv, **Oct 8**
Peter and Paul Day, Saint, **Jun 29**
Peter I: Birth Anniv, **May 30**
Peters, Bernadette: Birth, **Feb 28**
Peters, Roberta: Birth, **May 4**
Petersen, Paul: Birth, **Sep 23**
Petersen, William: Birth, **Feb 21**
Peterson, Cassandra: Birth, **Sep 17**
Peterson, Roger Tory: Birth Anniv, **Aug 28**
Peterson, Seth: Birth, **Aug 16**

Petrified Forest Natl Park Established: Anniv, **Dec 9**
Petroleum Fest, Louisiana Shrimp and (Morgan City, LA), **Aug 31**
Pets (see also Animals; Dogs; Horses; Rats)
  Holistic Pet Day, Natl, **Aug 30**
  Pet Dental Health Month, Natl, **Feb 1**
  Pet First Aid Awareness Month, Natl, **Apr 1**
  Pet Owners Independence Day, **Apr 18**
  Pet Week, Natl, **May 7**
  Professional Pet Sitters Week, **Mar 5**
  Wishbones for Pets, **Oct 15**
Pettit, Bob: Birth, **Dec 12**
Petty, Richard: Birth, **Jul 2**
Petty, Tom: Birth, **Oct 20**
Pfeiffer, Michelle: Birth, **Apr 29**
Phair, Liz: Birth, **Apr 17**
Pharmacists Declare War on Alcoholism, **Jun 1**
Pharmacists' War on Diabetes, **Apr 1**
Phil Donahue Show, The: Anniv, **Nov 6**
Phil Silvers Show TV Premiere: Anniv, **Sep 20**
Philadelphia Flower Show, **Mar 5**
Philadelphia Police Bombing: Anniv, **May 13**
Philatelic Exhibition, World (Washington, DC), **May 27**
Philbin, Regis: Birth, **Aug 25**
Philip, King: Assassination Anniv, **Aug 12**
Philip, Prince: Birth, **Jun 10**
Philippines
  Aquino, Benigno: Assassination Anniv, **Aug 21**
  Ati-Atihan Fest, **Jan 21**
  Bataan Day: Anniv, **Apr 9**
  Black Nazarene Fiesta, **Jan 1**
  Bonifacio Day, **Nov 30**
  Carabao Fest, **May 14**
  Christmas Observance, **Dec 16**
  Earthquake Jolts: Anniv, **Jul 16**
  Feast of Our Lady of Peace/Good Voyage, **May 1**
  Feast of the Black Nazarene, **Jan 9**
  Fil-American Friendship Day, **Jul 4**
  Holy Week, **Apr 9**
  Independence Day, **Jun 12**
  Morione's Fest (Marinduque Island), **Apr 13**
  Mount Pinatubo Erupts in Philippines: Anniv, **Jun 11**
  National Heroes' Day, **Aug 27**
  Philippine Independence: Anniv, **Mar 24**
  Rizal Day, **Dec 30**
  Santacruzan, **May 1**
  Simbang Gabi, **Dec 16**
  US Military Leaves, **Nov 24**
Phillips, Bobbie: Birth, **Jan 29**
Phillips, Chynna: Birth, **Feb 12**
Phillips, Julianne: Birth, **May 13**
Phillips, Lou Diamond: Birth, **Feb 17**
Phillips, Mackenzie: Birth, **Nov 10**
Phillips, Michelle: Birth, **Jun 4**
Phillips, Stone: Birth, **Dec 2**
Phillips, Wendy: Birth, **Jan 2**
Photography
  Abbott, Berenice: Birth Anniv, **Jul 17**
  Bourke-White, Margaret: Birth Anniv, **Jun 14**
  First Photos Used in a Newspaper Report: Anniv, **Jul 1**
  First Picture of Earth from Space: Anniv, **Aug 7**
  First Presidential Photograph: Anniv, **Feb 14**
  Nature Photography Day, **Jun 15**
Physical Fitness and Sports Month, Natl, **May 1**
Physical Therapy Month, Natl, **Oct 1**
Physical Wellness Month, **Apr 1**
Physician Assistants Day, **Oct 6**
Piano Competitions and Performances
  Lucerne Fest, Piano (Lucerne, Switzerland), **Nov 21**
  Piano Month, Natl, **Sep 1**
  World Chmpshp Old-Time Piano Playing (Peoria, IL), **May 26**
Piazza, Mike: Birth, **Sep 4**
Piazzetta, Giovanni Battista: Birth Anniv, **Feb 13**
Picasso, Pablo: Birth Anniv, **Oct 25**
Picatinny Peak Fall Hawkwatch (Dover, NJ), **Sep 1**
Piccard, Auguste: Birth Anniv, **Jan 28**
Piccard, Jacques: Birth, **Jul 28**
Piccard, Jean Felix: Birth Anniv, **Jan 28**
Piccard, Jeannette Ridlon: Birth Anniv, **Jan 5**
Pickett, Bill: Birth Anniv, **Dec 5**
Pickett, George: Defeat at Five Forks: Anniv, **Apr 1**
Pickett, Wilson: Birth, **Mar 18**
Pickett's Charge: Battle of Gettysburg: Anniv, **Jul 1**
Picnic, All States (Yuma, AZ), **Jan 3**
Pidgeon, Walter: Birth Anniv, **Sep 23**
Pied Piper of Hamelin: Anniv, **Jul 22**
Pied Piper: Rat-Catchers Day, **Jul 22**
Pierce, David Hyde: Birth, **Apr 3**
Pierce, Franklin: Birth Anniv, **Nov 23**
Pierce, Jane: Birth Anniv, **Mar 12**

Pierce—Presley

Pierce, Paul: Birth, Oct 13
Pietz, Amy: Birth, Mar 6
Pig Day, Natl, Mar 1
Pigott-Smith, Tim: Birth, May 13
Pilates Day, Intl, May 6
Pileggi, Mitch: Birth, Apr 5
Pilgrim Landing: Anniv, Dec 21
Pinchot, Bronson: Birth, May 20
Pine Barrens Jamboree (Waretown, NJ), Oct 7
Piniella, Lou: Birth, Aug 28
Pinkerton, Allan: Birth Anniv, Aug 25
Pinkett Smith, Jada: Birth, Sep 18
Pinochet, Augusto: Military Dictatorship Ended, Dec 15
Pinter, Harold: Birth, Oct 10
Pinzon, Martin: Arrival Anniv, Mar 1
Pioneer Days (Steinbach, MB, Canada), Aug 4
Pippen, Scottie: Birth, Sep 25
Piquet, Nelson: Birth, Aug 17
Pirate Day, Talk Like a, Sep 19
Pisces Begins, Feb 20
Piscopo, Joe: Birth, Jun 17
Pisier, Marie-France: Birth, May 10
Pitcher, Molly: Birth Anniv, Oct 13
Pitlochry Festival Theatre Season (Scotland), Apr 1
Pitt, Brad: Birth, Dec 18
Pitt, William: Birth Anniv, May 28
Pittsburgh Arts & Crafts Spring Fever Fest (Greensburg, PA), Mar 24
Piven, Jeremy: Birth, Jul 26
Pizarro, Francesco: Death Anniv, Jun 26
Place, Mary Kay: Birth, Sep 23
Plan a Solo Vacation Day, Mar 1
Planck, Max: Birth Anniv, Apr 23
Planet Pluto Discovery: Anniv, Feb 18
Plant Appreciation Day, Intl, Apr 13
Plant the Seeds of Greatness Month, Feb 1
Plant, Robert: Birth, Aug 20
Platt, Oliver: Birth, Jan 12
Play Days, Sep 5
Play Presented in North American Colonies, First: Anniv, Aug 27
Playboy First Published: Anniv, Dec 1
Player, Gary: Birth, Nov 1
Playground Safety Week, Natl, Apr 24
Play-the-Recorder Month, Mar 1
Please Take My Children to Work Day, Jun 26
Pleasure Your Mate Month, Sep 1
Pledge Across America, Sep 22
Pledge of Allegiance Recognized: Anniv, Dec 28
Pledge of Allegiance, Pause for (Natl Flag Day USA), Jun 14
Pleshette, Suzanne: Birth, Jan 31
Plimpton, George: Birth Anniv, Mar 18
Plimpton, Martha: Birth, Nov 16
Plimsoll Day, Feb 10
Plough Monday (England), Jan 9
Plumb, Eve: Birth, Apr 29
Plumbing, Heating and Cooling Professionals Week, Jun 18
Plummer, Amanda: Birth, Mar 23
Plummer, Christopher: Birth, Dec 13
Plushenko, Evgeny: Birth, Nov 3
Pluto Discovery, Planet: Anniv, Feb 18
Plutonium First Weighed: Anniv, Aug 20
Plymouth Plantation Earthquake: Anniv, Jun 1
Pocahontas: Death Anniv, Mar 21
Poe, Edgar Allan, Evermore (Manheim, PA), Oct 27
Poe, Edgar Allan: Birth Anniv, Jan 19
Poe, Edgar Allan: Raven Published: Anniv, Jan 29
Poehler, Amy: Birth, Sep 16
Poetry
    American Poet Laureate Establishment: Anniv, Dec 20
    Bad Poetry Day, Aug 18
    Baseball's Sad Lexicon Published: Anniv, Jul 10
    Cowboy Poetry Gathering, Natl (Elko, NV), Jan 28
    Cullen, Countee: Birth Anniv, May 30
    Dodge Poetry Fest (NJ), Sep 28
    Hammon, Jupiter: Birth Anniv, Oct 17
    Limerick Day, May 12
    Mighty Casey Has Struck Out: Anniv, Jun 3
    Poetry Contest (El Paso, TX), Jan 1
    Poetry Day in Florida, May 25
    Poetry Month, Natl, Apr 1
    Poet's Day, Aug 21
    Raven Published: Anniv, Jan 29
    Texas Cowboy Poetry Gathering (Alpine, TX), Feb 24
    Wheatley, Phillis: Death Anniv, Dec 5
    Wheatley, Phillis: Poetry Collection Published: Anniv, Sep 1
    Young People's Poetry Week, Apr 10
    Youth Cowboy Poetry Gathering (Boys Ranch, TX), Jun 8
Poinsett, Joel Roberts: Death Anniv, Dec 12

Poinsettia Day, Dec 12
Pointer, Bonnie: Birth, Jul 11
Poison Prevention Awareness Month, Mar 1
Poison Prevention Week, Natl, Mar 19
Poison Prevention Week, Natl (Pres Proc), Mar 19
Poitier, Sidney: Birth, Feb 20
Pol Pot Overthrown: Anniv, Jan 7
Poland
    Constitution Day, May 3
    Germany Invades: Anniv, Sep 1
    Independence Day, Nov 11
    Liberation Day, Jan 17
    Solidarity Founded Anniv, Aug 31
    Solidarity Granted Legal Status: Anniv, Apr 17
Polanski, Roman: Birth, Aug 18
Polar Bear Swim (Nome, AK), Jun 17
Polar Bear Swim (Sheboygan, WI), Jan 1
Police
    Children and Police Day, Natl, May 19
    Peace Officer Memorial Day (Pres Proc), May 15
    Peace Officer Memorial Day, Natl, May 15
    Police Officers Who Gave Their Lives in the Line of Duty Week, Apr 29
    Police Week (Pres Proc), May 14
    Police Week, Natl, May 14
Polio Vaccine: Anniv, Apr 12
Polish
    Polish American Heritage Month, Oct 1
    Polish-American in the House (Mikulski): Anniv, Jan 4
Polito, Jon: Birth, Dec 29
Polk, James: Birth Anniv, Nov 2
Polk, James: First Presidential Photograph: Anniv, Feb 14
Polk, Sarah Childress: Birth Anniv, Sep 4
Poll Tax Outlawed: Anniv, Apr 8
Pollack, Sydney: Birth, Jul 1
Pollak, Kevin: Birth, Oct 30
Pollan, Tracy: Birth, Jun 22
Pollard, Michael J.: Birth, May 30
Polycystic Ovarian Syndrome Awareness Day, Sep 18
Polygamists, Amnesty for: Anniv, Jan 4
Pomegranate Month, Natl, Nov 1
Pompeii Destroyed (Vesuvius Day): Anniv, Aug 24
Ponce de Leon Discovers Florida: Anniv, Apr 2
Ponselle, Rosa: Birth Anniv, Jan 22
Ponti, Carlo: Birth, Dec 11
Pony Express, Inauguration of: Anniv, Apr 3
Pooh Day (A.A. Milne Birth Anniv), Jan 18
Poole, Cecil: First Black US State's Attorney: Anniv, Jul 6
Poor Richard's Almanack: Anniv, Dec 28
Pop Music Chart Introduced: Anniv, Jan 4
Pop, Iggy: Birth, Apr 21
Popcorn Fest (Valparaiso, IN), Sep 9
Popcorn Poppin' Month, Natl, Oct 1
Pope, Alexander: Birth Anniv, May 21
Pope, John: Birth Anniv, Mar 16
Popes, Roman Catholic
    Benedict XV: Birth Anniv, Nov 21
    Benedict XVI: Birth, Apr 16
    Benedict XVI: Election Anniv, Apr 19
    John Paul I: Birth Anniv, Oct 17
    John Paul II: Assassination Attempt: Anniv, May 13
    John Paul II: Birth Anniv, May 18
    John Paul II: Death Anniv, Apr 2
    John XXIII: Birth Anniv, Nov 25
    Paul VI: Birth Anniv, Sep 26
    Pius XI: Birth Anniv, May 31
    Pius XII: Birth Anniv, Mar 2
    Saint Pius X: Birth Anniv, Jun 2
Popeye Debuts: Anniv, Jan 17
Population Day, World (UN), Jul 11
Population: Day of Five Billion: Anniv, Jul 11
Population: Day of the Six Billion: Anniv, Oct 12
Pork Month, Natl, Oct 1
Porter, Cole: Birth Anniv, Jun 9
Porter, Katherine Anne: Birth Anniv, May 15
Porter, Sylvia: Birth Anniv, Jun 18
Porter, Terry: Birth, Apr 8
Porter, William S. (O. Henry): Birth Anniv, Sep 11
Portman, Natalie: Birth, Jun 9
Portugal
    Day of Portugal, Jun 10
    Independence Day, Dec 1
    Liberty Day, Apr 25
    Lisbon Earthquake: Anniv, Nov 1
    Pilgrimage to Fatima, May 12
    Republic Day, Oct 5
    Saint Anthony of Padua: Feast Day, Jun 13
Posey, Parker: Birth, Nov 8
Positive Attitude Month, Oct 1
Post Day, World (UN), Oct 9
Post, Emily: Birth Anniv, Oct 30
Post, Markie: Birth, Nov 4

Post, Wiley: Birth Anniv, Nov 22
Postcard Shows
    Postcard Week, Natl, May 7
    York Intl Postcard Fair (York, PA), Nov 17
Postell, Ashley: Birth, Jun 9
Postlethwaite, Pete: Birth, Feb 7
Postman's Day (Mexico), Nov 12
Postmaster General Established, US: Anniv, Sep 22
Poston, Tom: Birth, Oct 17
Posture Month, Natl Correct, May 1
Potato Blossom Fest, Maine (Fort Fairfield, ME), Jul 7
Potato Bowl USA (Grand Forks, ND), Sep 5
Potato Feast Days (Houlton, ME), Aug 18
Potato Month, Natl, Sep 1
Potomac Celtic Festival (Leesburg, VA), Jun 10
Potsdam Declaration: Anniv, Jul 26
Potter, Beatrix: Birth Anniv, Jul 28
Potters Market, Appalachian (Marion, NC), Nov 18
Potts, Annie: Birth, Oct 28
Potty Training Awareness Month, Jun 1
Pound, Ezra: Birth Anniv, Oct 30
Pound, Ezra: Bollingen Prize Award, Feb 19
Poundstone, Paula: Birth, Dec 29
Poverty in America Awareness Month, Natl, Jan 1
Poverty, War on: Anniv, Jan 8
Povich, Maury: Birth, Jan 17
POW/MIA Recognition Day, Natl (Pres Proc), Sep 15
Powell, Colin: Birth, Apr 5
Powell, Cristen: Birth, Mar 22
Powell, Jane: Birth, Apr 1
Powell, John W.: Birth Anniv, Mar 24
Powell, Lewis F., Jr: Birth Anniv, Sep 19
Power Show, Fulton County Historical (Rochester, IN), Jun 16
Power, Tyrone: Birth Anniv, May 5
PowerPoint Week, Just Say No to, Feb 6
Powers, Francis Gary: Birth Anniv, Aug 17
Powers, Francis Gary: U-2 Incident: Anniv, May 1
Powers, Stefanie: Birth, Nov 2
Prague Autumn Intl Music Fest (Czech Republic), Sep 12
Prairie Day (Diamond, MO), Sep 9
Prairie Home Companion Premiere: Anniv, Feb 17
Prairie Pioneer Days (Arapahoe, NE), Jul 4
Prayer
    Just Pray No: Worldwide Weekend Prayer, Apr 23
    Kiwanis Prayer Week, May 14
    National Day of Prayer (Pres Proc), May 4
    Supreme Court Bans School Prayer: Anniv, Jun 25
    World Day of Prayer, Mar 3
Preakness Stakes (Baltimore, MD), May 20
Preakness Stakes: Anniv, May 27
Prematurity Awareness Day, Nov 1
Prentiss, Paula: Birth, Mar 4
Prepare to Buy a Home Month, Natl, May 1
Prepare Tomorrow's Parents Month, May 14
Prepare Your Home to Be Sold Month, Natl, Apr 1
Preparedness Month, Natl, Sep 1
Prescott, William: Birth Anniv, Feb 20
Prescription Errors Education & Awareness Week, Oct 24
Prescriptions Month, Talk About, Oct 1
Presentation of the Lord (Candlemas Day), Feb 2
Preservation Month, Natl, May 1
Preservation of the Ozone Layer, Intl Day for (UN), Sep 16
President Occupies the White House: Anniv, Nov 1
Presidential Debate, First Televised: Anniv, Sep 26
Presidential Inaugural Ball: Anniv, May 7
Presidential Inauguration Anniv, George Washington, Apr 30
Presidential Inauguration, G. Cleveland's Second: Anniv, Mar 4
Presidential Photograph, First: Anniv, Feb 14
Presidential Resignation: Anniversary, Aug 9
Presidential Telecast, First: Anniv, Apr 30
Presidential Visit to Moscow, First American: Anniv, May 22
Presidents' Day, Feb 20
President's Environmental Youth Award Natl Competition, Jul 31
Presley, Elvis
    Birth Anniv, Jan 8
    Brantford's Elvis Fest (Brantford, ON, Canada), Aug 24
    Death Anniv, Aug 16
    Elvis Presley Blvd Named: Anniv, Jun 29
    Elvis Presley Remembered (St. Louis, MO), Aug 12
    Elvis Presley's Birthday Celebration (Memphis, TN), Jan 6
    Elvis Week (Memphis, TN), Aug 8

First Concert Appearance: Anniv, **Jul 30**
First Single Released: Anniv, **Jul 19**
Meets President Nixon: Anniv, **Dec 21**
Presley, Lisa Marie: Birth, **Feb 1**
Presley, Priscilla: Birth, **May 24**
Press Freedom Day, World (UN), **May 3**
Pressman, Lawrence: Birth, **Jul 10**
Preston, Billy: Birth, **Sep 9**
Preston, Kelly: Birth, **Oct 13**
Prevention of Eye Injuries Awareness Week, Natl, **Jun 27**
Previn, Andre: Birth, **Apr 6**
Price Is Right TV Premiere: Anniv, **Nov 26**
Price, Alan: Birth, **Apr 19**
Price, Leontyne: Birth, **Feb 10**
Price, Ray: Birth, **Jan 12**
Price, Vincent: Birth Anniv, **May 27**
Price, William Mark: Birth, **Feb 15**
Pride, Charley: Birth, **Mar 18**
Priesand, Sally: First Woman Rabbi in US: Anniv, **Jun 3**
Priestley, Jason: Birth, **Aug 28**
Priestly, Joseph: Birth Anniv, **Mar 13**
Prime Meridian Set: Anniv, **Nov 1**
Primetime Live TV Premiere: Anniv, **Aug 3**
Primus, Barry: Birth, **Feb 16**
Prince Harry: Birth, **Sep 15**
Prince Jonah Kuhio Kalanianole Day (HI), **Mar 26**
Prince Rainier: Birth Anniv, **May 31**
Prince William: Birth, **Jun 21**
Prince: Birth, **Jun 7**
Princeton, USS, Explosion: Anniv, **Feb 28**
Principal, Victoria: Birth, **Jan 3**
Principals' Day, School, **May 1**
Prine, Andrew: Birth, **Feb 14**
Printing Week, Intl, **Jan 15**
Prinze, Freddie, Jr: Birth, **Mar 8**
Prison, Union Officers Escape Libby: Anniv, **Feb 9**
Prisoner of War Recognition Day, Natl Former (Pres Proc), **Apr 9**
Prisoner TV Premiere: Anniv, **Jun 1**
Pro Sports Wives Day, **Feb 11**
Problem-Solving: It's About Time Week, **Dec 25**
Probst, Jeff: Birth, **Oct 26**
Procession of the Addolorata and Mysteries (Taranto, Italy), **Apr 13**
Procession of the Holy Blood (Belgium), **May 25**
Procrastination Week, Natl, **Mar 6**
Procrastination: Do It Day (aka Fight Procrastination Day), **Sep 6**
Professional Speakers Day, **Aug 7**
Professional Wellness Month, **Jun 1**
Profiles in Courage Published: Anniv, **Jan 1**
Prohibition (18th) Amendment: Anniv, **Jan 16**
Prohibition Act Veto Overridden, Wilson's: Anniv, **Oct 28**
Prohibition Repealed: 21st Amendment Ratified, **Dec 5**
Prohibition: Maine Law: Anniv, **Jun 2**
Promotion Month, Shameless, **Sep 1**
Pronger, Chris: Birth, **Oct 10**
Proposal Day!, **Mar 20**
Proposition 13: Anniv, **Jun 6**
Prosky, Robert: Birth, **Dec 13**
Prospect Park: You Gotta Have Park (Brooklyn, NY), **May 13**
Prostate Cancer Awareness Week, **Sep 17**
Proulx, E. Annie: Birth, **Aug 22**
Proust, Marcel: Birth Anniv, **Jul 10**
Prout, Mary Ann: Birth Anniv, **Feb 14**
Prowse, Juliet: Birth Anniv, **Sep 25**
Pryce, Jonathan: Birth, **Jun 1**
Pryor, Mark: Birth, **Jan 10**
Pryor, Richard: Birth, **Dec 1**
Psychic Sunday, **Aug 6**
Psychic Week, **Aug 7**
Psycho Film Premiere: Anniv, **Jun 16**
PTA Founders' Day, Natl, **Feb 17**
PTA Teacher Appreciation Week, Natl, **May 7**
Public Health Week, Natl, **Apr 2**
Public Radio, Natl: Anniv, **May 3**
Public Relations: Getting World to Beat Path to Door Week, **Oct 15**
Public School, First in America: Anniv, **Apr 23**
Public Service Day (UN), **Jun 23**
Public Speaking: Freedom from Fear of Speaking Week, **Jul 2**
Public Television Debuts: Anniv, **Nov 3**
Publicity for Profit Week, **Feb 1**
Publishing: Small Press Month, **Mar 1**
Puccini, Giacomo: Birth Anniv, **Dec 22**
Puccini, Giacomo: Madama Butterfly Premiere: Anniv, **Feb 17**
Puckett, Kirby: Birth, **Mar 14**
Pueblo, USS, Seized by North Korea: Anniv, **Jan 23**

Puente, Tito: Birth Anniv, **Apr 20**
Puerto Rico
  Barbosa, Jose Celso: Birth Anniv, **Jul 27**
  Carnival de Ponce (Ponce), **Feb 22**
  Constitution Day, **Jul 25**
  Diego, Jose de: Birth Anniv, **Apr 16**
  Discovery Day, **Nov 19**
  Emancipation Day, **Mar 22**
  Hostos, Eugenio Maria: Birth Anniv, **Jan 11**
  Las Mananitas, **Dec 12**
  Loiza Aldea Fiesta, **Jul 25**
  Munoz-Rivera Day, **Jul 17**
  Navidades, **Dec 15**
Pujols, Albert: Birth, **Jan 16**
Pulaski, Casimir: Birth Anniv, **Mar 4**
Pulaski, Casimir: Memorial Day (Pres Proc), **Oct 11**
Pulitzer Prizes First Awarded: Anniv, **Jun 4**
Pulitzer, Joseph: Birth Anniv, **Apr 10**
Pulliam, Keshia Knight: Birth, **Apr 9**
Pullman, Bill: Birth, **Dec 17**
Pullman, George: Birth Anniv, **Mar 3**
Pumpkin Fest (Aurora, CO), **Oct 14**
Pumpkin Fest, Morton (Morton, IL), **Sep 13**
Pumpkin Pie Day, **Nov 21**
Pumpkin Show, Circleville (Circleville, OH), **Oct 18**
Punctuation Day, Natl, **Sep 24**
Punsters Day, Abet and Aid, **Nov 8**
Purcell, Henry: Death Anniv, **Nov 21**
Purcell, Sarah: Birth, **Oct 8**
Purgatory Banquet (Gradoli, Italy), **Mar 1**
Purim, **Mar 14**
Purl, Linda: Birth, **Sep 2**
Purple Heart: Anniv, **Aug 7**
Pursuit of Happiness Week, **Nov 8**
Push-Button Telephone Debuts: Anniv, **Nov 18**
Pushkin, Alexander: Birth Anniv, **Jun 6**
Putin, Vladimir: Birth, **Oct 7**
Puyallup Spring Fair (Puyallup, WA), **Apr 20**
Pyle, Ernest: Birth Anniv, **Aug 3**
Pynchon, Thomas: Birth, **May 8**
Pyramid Fests, **Apr 9**

Qatar: Asian Games (Doha), **Dec 1**
Qatar: Independence Day, **Sep 3**
Qing Ming Fest or Tomb Sweeping Day, **Apr 5**
Quadrangle Fest (Texarkana, AR and TX), **Sep 9**
Quaid, Dennis: Birth, **Apr 9**
Quaid, Randy: Birth, **Oct 1**
Quality of Life Month, Intl, **Jan 1**
Quantrill's Raid on Lawrence, KS: Anniv, **Aug 21**
Quark, Physicists Discover Top: Anniv, **Apr 23**
Quasthoff, Thomas: Birth, **Nov 9**
Quayle, Dan: Birth, **Feb 4**
Quebec City Hunting, Fishing & Camping Show (Quebec City, QC, Canada), **Mar 16**
Queen Elizabeth I: Accession Anniv, **Nov 17**
Queen Elizabeth I: Birth Anniv, **Sep 7**
Queen Elizabeth II: Accession Anniv, **Feb 6**
Queen Elizabeth II: Agrees to Pay Taxes: Anniv, **Nov 26**
Queen for a Day TV Premiere: Anniv, **Jan 3**
Queen Latifah: Birth, **Mar 18**
Queen Mary, RMS: Anniv, **May 27**
Queen Victoria: Death Anniv, **Jan 22**
Queen's Official Birthday, **Jun 12**
Queen's Official Birthday/Trooping Colours (England), **Jun 10**
Quilt (quilts, quilting, quilt shows)
  American Heritage Quilt Show (Staunton, VA), **Sep 24**
  American Quilter's Society Quilt Exposition (Nashville, TN), **Aug 23**
  Peddler's Village Quilt Competition/Display (Lahaska, PA), **Jan 16**
  Quilt Odyssey (Hershey, PA), **Jul 27**
  Quilt Show (Woodstock, VT), **Jul 29**
  Quilter's Society Show, American (Paducah, KY), **Apr 26**
  Quilting Day, Natl, **Mar 18**
  Thousand Islands Quilt Show (Clayton, NY), **Jul 21**
Quincy TV Premiere: Anniv, **Oct 3**
Quinlan, Karen Ann: Birth Anniv, **Mar 29**
Quinlan, Kathleen: Birth, **Nov 19**
Quinn, Aidan: Birth, **Mar 8**
Quinn, Anthony: Birth Anniv, **Apr 21**
Quinn, Jane Bryant: Birth, **Feb 5**
Quirky Country Music Song Titles Day, **Mar 27**
Quiz Kids TV Premiere: Anniv, **Jul 6**

R.E.A.D. in America Day (Washington, DC), **Sep 23**
Ra, Sun: Birth Anniv, **May 22**
Rabbi: First Woman Rabbi in US: Anniv, **Jun 3**
Rabbit Week, Natl, **Jul 15**
Rabe, David: Birth, **Mar 10**
Rabi' I: Month of the Migration (Islamic), **Mar 31**

Rabinowitz, Solomon: Birth Anniv, **Feb 18**
Race for the Cure (Pittsburgh, PA), **May 14**
Race Relations Day, **Feb 14**
Race Riots, Saint Louis: Anniv, **Jul 2**
Race Unity Day, **Jun 11**
Race Your Mouse Around the Icons Day, **Aug 28**
Racial Discrimination, Intl Day for Elimination of (UN), **Mar 21**
Racism/Racial Discrimination, Solidarity Against (UN), **Mar 21**
Radcliffe, Ann: Birth Anniv, **Jul 9**
Radcliffe, Daniel: Birth, **Jul 23**
Radio
  American Top 40: Anniv, **Jul 4**
  Breakfast Club Premiere: Anniv, **Jun 23**
  Car Talk Natl Premiere: Anniv, **Oct 31**
  Federal Communications Commission Created: Anniv, **Feb 26**
  First Play-by-Play Football Game Broadcast, **Nov 23**
  First Radio Broadcast of a Prizefight: Anniv, **Sep 6**
  First Scheduled Radio Broadcast: Anniv, **Nov 2**
  Howard Stern Show Radio Premiere: Anniv, **Nov 18**
  Imus in the Morning Radio Premiere: Anniv, **Dec 2**
  Letter from America Premiere: Anniv, **Mar 24**
  Loomis Day, **May 30**
  Metropolitan Opera Radio Broadcasts Premiere: Anniv, **Dec 25**
  National Traffic Directors Day, **Nov 2**
  Ozzie and Harriet Show Debut: Anniv, **Oct 8**
  Prairie Home Companion Premiere: Anniv, **Feb 17**
  Public Radio, Natl: Anniv, **May 3**
  Radio Broadcast by a President, First, **Jun 14**
  Radio Broadcasting: Anniv, **Jan 13**
  Radio Commercials: Anniv, **Aug 28**
  Rest of the Story Premiere: Anniv, **May 10**
  Rush Limbaugh Show Natl Radio Premiere: Anniv, **Aug 1**
  Shadow Premiere: Anniv, **Jul 31**
  Transistor Unveiled: Anniv, **Dec 23**
  War of the Worlds Broadcast: Anniv, **Oct 30**
  Wolfman Jack: Birth Anniv, **Jan 21**
  Your Hit Parade Radio Premiere: Anniv, **Apr 12**
Radio City Music Hall: Anniv, **Dec 27**
Radiological Society of North America Scientific Assembly and Annual Mtg (Chicago, IL), **Nov 26**
Radishes, Feast of (Oaxaca, Mexico), **Dec 23**
Radium Discovered: Anniv, **Dec 26**
Radner, Gilda: Birth Anniv, **Jun 28**
Radon Action Month, Natl, **Jan 1**
Radosavljevic, Predrag: Birth, **Jun 24**
Radziwill, Lee: Birth, **Mar 3**
Rae, Charlotte: Birth, **Apr 22**
Rafalski, Brian: Birth, **Sep 28**
Raffi: Birth, **Jul 8**
Raffin, Deborah: Birth, **Mar 13**
Raffles, Stamford: Birth Anniv, **Jul 5**
Rafter, Patrick: Birth, **Dec 28**
RAGBRAI—Register's Bicycle Ride Across Iowa (Des Moines, IA), **Jul 23**
Raggedy Ann & Andy Fest, Original (Arcola, IL), **Jun 10**
Ragsdale, William: Birth, **Jan 19**
Raid on Entebbe: Anniv, **Jul 3**
Raid on Richmond: Anniv, **Mar 1**
Railroad
  Amtrak: Anniv, **May 1**
  Antique Power Exhibition (Burton, OH), **Jul 28**
  Circus Train Wreck: Anniv, **Jun 22**
  Fordyce on the Cotton Belt Fest (Fordyce, AR), **Apr 17**
  Galesburg Railroad Days (Galesburg, IL), **Jun 24**
  Golden Spike Driving: Anniv, **May 10**
  Helena Railroad Fair (Helena, MT), **Apr 30**
  Iron Horse Outraced by Horse: Anniv, **Sep 18**
  Model Railroad Show (Wheeling, WV), **Jan 14**
  Mount Hood Railroad Season (Hood River, OR), **Apr 1**
  New York City Subway: Anniv, **Oct 27**
  Northern Pacific Railroad Completed: Anniv, **Sep 8**
  Railroad and Hobby Show (Springfield, MA), **Jan 28**
  34th St Express (Boston, MA), **Dec 9**
  Transcontinental US Railway Completion: Anniv, **Aug 15**
Rain Day (Waynesburg, PA), **Jul 29**
Rainbow Warrior Sinking: Anniv, **Jul 10**
Rainer, Luise: Birth, **Jan 12**
Raines, Tim: Birth, **Sep 16**
Rainey, Joseph: First Black in US House of Reps: Anniv, **Dec 12**
Rainey, Ma (Gertrude B.): Birth Anniv, **Apr 3**
Rainforest Week, World, **Oct 16**
Rainier, Prince: Birth Anniv, **May 31**
Raitt, Bonnie: Birth, **Nov 8**
Ram, Jagjivan: Birth Anniv, **Apr 1**

Ramadan: Islamic Month of Fasting, Sep 24
Rameau, Jean P.: Birth Anniv, Sep 25
Ramirez, Manny: Birth, May 30
Ramis, Harold: Birth, Nov 21
Ramo, Roberta Cooper: Birth, Aug 8
Rampling, Charlotte: Birth, Feb 5
Ramses II Unearthed, Statue of: Anniv, Nov 30
Ramson, Feast of the (Richwood, WV), Apr 22
Ranch Roundup, Texas (Wichita Falls, TX), Aug 18
Rand, Ayn: Birth Anniv, Feb 2
Rand, Sally: Birth Anniv, Apr 3
Randall, Tony: Birth Anniv, Feb 26
Randolph, Peyton: Death Anniv, Oct 22
Rankin, Jeannette: Birth Anniv, Jun 11
Raphael, Sally Jessy: Birth, Feb 25
Raphael: Birth Anniv, Apr 6
Rashad, Ahmad: Birth, Nov 19
Rashad, Phylicia: Birth, Jun 19
Rasputin, Grigori: Assassination Anniv, Dec 29
Rather, Dan: Birth, Oct 31
Ratification Day, Jan 14
Rats (see also Animals; Mice; Pets)
    AFRMA Display & Show (Costa Mesa, CA), Jul 7
    AFRMA Display at America's Family Pet Expo (Costa Mesa, CA), Apr 14
    Pied Piper of Hamelin: Anniv, Jul 22
    Rat and Mouse Annual Show, Fancy (Riverside, CA), Jan 14
    Rat-Catchers Day, Jul 22
Rattle, Simon: Birth, Jan 19
Rattlesnake Roundup, World's Largest (Sweetwater, TX), Mar 10
Ratzenberger, John: Birth, Apr 6
Ratzinger, Joseph: Pope Benedict XVI: Election Anniv, Apr 19
Rauh, Joseph L., Jr: Birth Anniv, Jan 3
Rauschenberg, Robert: Birth, Oct 22
Raven Published: Anniv, Jan 29
Raver, Kim: Birth, Mar 15
Rawhide TV Premiere: Anniv, Jan 9
Rawlings, Marjorie Kinnan: Birth Anniv, Aug 8
Rawls, Lou: Birth, Dec 1
Ray Day, May, May 19
Ray, Satyajit: Birth Anniv, May 2
Raye, Martha: Birth Anniv, Aug 27
Razor, Electric, First Marketed: Anniv, Mar 18
Rea, Stephen: Birth, Oct 31
Read Across America Day, Mar 2
Read an E-Book Week, Mar 5
Read Me Week (TN), Feb 27
Read, Allen, Discovers O.K. Origin: Anniv, Mar 23
Read, George: Birth Anniv, Sep 18
Reader's Day, Natl Young, Nov 14
Reading Groups Month, Natl, Oct 1
Reading Is Fun Week, May 14
Reading: Banned Books Week, Sep 23
Reading: Get Caught Reading Month, May 1
Reagan, Nancy: Birth, Jul 6
Reagan, Ronald Prescott: Birth, May 20
Reagan, Ronald Wilson
    And Nancy Davis: Wedding Anniv, Mar 4
    Assassination Attempt On: Anniv, Mar 30
    Birth Anniv, Feb 6
    Tear Down This Wall Speech: Anniv, Jun 12
Real Estate
    Get to Know an Independent Real Estate Broker Month, Natl, Feb 1
    Home Inspector Appreciation Month, Natl, Jul 1
    Prepare to Buy a Home Month, Natl, May 1
    Prepare Your Home to Be Sold Month, Natl, Apr 1
Real McCoys TV Premiere: Anniv, Oct 3
Real People TV Premiere: Anniv, Apr 18
Reasoner, Harry: Birth Anniv, Apr 17
Rebuild Your Life Month, Jun 1
Rebuilding Day, Natl, Apr 29
Receptionists Day, Natl, May 12
Recess at Work Day, Jun 15
Recipe Greetings for the Holidays, Dec 1
Reckell, Peter: Birth, May 7
Reconciliation Day, Apr 2
Recreation and Parks Month, Natl, Jul 1
Recreation Week, Special, Jul 2
Red Army Departs Berlin: Anniv, Jun 11
Red Cloud Indian Art Show (Pine Ridge, SD), Jun 4
Red Cloud: Death Anniv, Dec 10
Red Cross Day, World, May 8
Red Cross Month, Mar 1
Red Cross Month, American (Pres Proc), Mar 1
Red Skelton Show TV Premiere: Anniv, Sep 30
Reddy, Helen: Birth, Oct 25
Redford, Robert: Birth, Aug 18
Redgrave, Lynn: Birth, Mar 8
Redgrave, Vanessa: Birth, Jan 30
Redwood Natl Park Established: Anniv, Oct 2
Reece, Gabrielle: Birth, Jan 6

Reed, Donna: It's a Wonderful Life Film Premiere: Anniv, Dec 20
Reed, Jack: Birth, Nov 12
Reed, Jerry: Birth, Mar 20
Reed, Pamela: Birth, Apr 2
Reed, Rex: Birth, Oct 2
Reed, Walter: Birth Anniv, Sep 13
Reed, Willis: Birth, Jun 25
Reenactments (Historical, Military)
    Battle of Bushy Run Reenactment (Harrison City, PA), Aug 5
    Battle of Germantown Reenactment (Philadelphia, PA), Oct 7
    Civil War Reenactment (Coshocton, OH), Jul 15
    Civil War Reenactment (Keokuk, IA), Apr 21
    Military Through the Ages (Williamsburg, VA), Mar 18
    Natural Bridge Battle (Tallahassee, FL), Mar 4
    Reenactment of Cowtown's Last Gunfight (Fort Worth, TX), Feb 8
    Siege of Bridgeport (Bridgeport, AL), Mar 17
Reese, Della: Birth, Jul 6
Reese, Pee Wee: Birth Anniv, Jul 23
Reeve, Christopher: Birth Anniv, Sep 25
Reeves, Jim: Birth Anniv, Aug 20
Reeves, Keanu: Birth, Sep 2
Reeves, Martha: Birth, Jul 18
Refired, not Retired, Day, Mar 1
Reformation Day, Oct 31
Reformation Sunday, Oct 29
Refugee Day, World (UN), Jun 20
Rehabilitation Awareness Celebration, Natl, Sep 17
Rehnquist, William: Birth, Oct 1
Reid, Harry: Birth, Dec 2
Reid, Tara: Birth, Nov 8
Reid, Tim: Birth, Dec 19
Reiki, World Day of, Aug 15
Reilly, Charles Nelson: Birth, Jan 13
Reiner, Carl: Birth, Mar 20
Reiner, Rob: Birth, Mar 6
Reinhold, Judge: Birth, May 21
Reinking, Ann: Birth, Nov 10
Reiser, Paul: Birth, Mar 30
Reitman, Ivan: Birth, Oct 26
Rejection Awareness Week, Feb 7
Relationship Wellness Month, Feb 1
Relaxation Day, Natl, Aug 15
Religion Day, World, Jan 15
Religion: Sunday School Teacher Appreciation Day, Oct 15
Religious Freedom Day, Jan 16
Religious Freedom Day (Pres Proc), Jan 16
Religious Freedom Week, Sep 22
Rell, M. Jodi: Birth, Jun 16
Remar, James: Birth, Dec 31
Rembrandt: Birth Anniv, Jul 15
Remember the Maine Day, Feb 15
Remembrance Day (Canada), Nov 11
Remembrance Day (Gettysburg, PA), Nov 18
Remembrance Sunday (England), Nov 12
Remick, Lee: Birth Anniv, Dec 14
Remington Steele TV Premiere: Anniv, Oct 1
Remington, Frederic S.: Birth Anniv, Oct 4
Remini, Leah: Birth, Jun 15
Renaissance Fairs
    Alabama Renaissance Faire (Florence, AL), Oct 21
    Arizona Renaissance Fest (Apache Junction, AZ), Feb 11
    Georgia Renaissance Spring Fest (Atlanta, GA), Apr 15
    Greater Pittsburgh Renaissance Fest (West Newton, PA), Aug 12
    Kansas City Renaissance Fest (Bonner Springs, KS), Sep 2
    Maryland Renaissance Fest (Annapolis, MD), Aug 26
    Minnesota Renaissance Fest (Shakopee, MN), Aug 12
    Pennsylvania Renaissance Faire (Manheim, PA), Aug 12
    Sterling Renaissance Fest (Sterling, NY), Jul 1
Rendell, Ed: Birth, Jan 5
Rendezvous, Great (Thunder Bay, ON, Canada), Jun 29
Rendezvous, Redbud Trail (Rochester, IN), Apr 29
Renfro, Brad: Birth, Jul 25
Reno, Janet: Birth, Jul 21
Renoir, Pierre: Birth Anniv, Feb 25
Reptile Awareness Day (Point Pleasant Beach, NJ), Oct 21
Republican Party Formed: Anniv, Jul 6
Republican Symbol: Anniv, Nov 7
Research Council, Natl: First Meeting: Anniv, Sep 20
Resnik, Judith A.: Birth Anniv, Apr 5
Resolutions: Second Half of the New Year Day, Jul 1

Respect for Parents Day, Aug 1
Respect for the Aged Day (Japan), Sep 15
Respighi, Ottorino: Birth Anniv, Jul 9
Rest of the Story Radio Premiere: Anniv, May 10
Restless Leg Syndrome (RLS) Education and Awareness Week, Jul 18
Resurrect Romance Week, Natl, Aug 13
Retailers Week, Natl Independent, Jul 16
Retrocession Day (Taiwan), Oct 25
Rett Syndrome Awareness Month, Oct 1
Retton, Mary Lou: Birth, Jan 24
Return Day (Georgetown, DE), Nov 9
Return Shopping Carts to the Supermarket Month, Feb 1
Return the Borrowed Books Week, Mar 1
Returns Month, Natl, Jan 1
Reuben, Gloria: Birth, Jun 9
Reunification of Germany: Anniv, Oct 3
Reunion Planning Month, Sep 1
Reunions: Class Reunion Month, Oct 1
Reunions: Family Reunion Month, Jul 1
Reuther, Walter: Birth Anniv, Sep 1
Revere, Anne: Birth Anniv, Jun 25
Revere, Paul: Birth, Jan 7
Revere, Paul: Birth Anniv, Jan 1
Revere, Paul: Ride Anniv, Apr 18
Revolution, American
    Battle of Blue Licks Celebration (Mount Olivet, KY), Aug 19
    Battle of Brandywine: Anniv, Sep 11
    Battle of Germantown Reenactment (Philadelphia, PA), Oct 7
    Battle of Lexington and Concord: Anniv, Apr 19
    Bennington Battle Day, Aug 16
    Boston Tea Party: Anniv, Dec 16
    Camden, Battle of: Anniv, Aug 16
    Cessation of Hostilities: Anniv, Jan 20
    Chestertown Tea Party Fest (Chestertown, MD), May 27
    Evacuation Day (Boston, MA), Mar 17
    Great Britain-US: Articles of Peace: Anniv, Nov 30
    Hale, Nathan: Birth Anniv, Jun 6
    Henry, Patrick: Birth Anniv, May 29
    Independence Day (US), Jul 4
    John Parker Day, Apr 19
    Liberty Day, Mar 23
    Middleton, Arthur: Birth Anniv, Jun 26
    Nathan Hale Fife and Drum Muster (Coventry, CT), Jul 22
    Olive Branch Petition: Anniv, Jul 8
    Paris, Treaty of: Signing Anniv, Sep 3
    Paul Revere's Ride: Anniv, Apr 18
    Road to Independence (Yorktown, VA), Jul 2
    Salvador, Francis: Death Anniv, Jul 31
    Sampson, Deborah: Birth Anniv, Dec 17
    Shays Rebellion: Anniv, Aug 29
    Washington Crosses the Delaware: Anniv, Dec 25
    Washington, George: Takes Command of Continental Army, Jul 3
    Yorktown Day, Oct 19
    Yorktown Day (Yorktown, VA), Oct 19
    Yorktown Victory Day (VA), Oct 9
Revolution, Russian: Anniv, Nov 7
Revson, Charles: Birth Anniv, Oct 11
Rex Allen Days (Willcox, AZ), Oct 6
Rey, Margaret: Birth Anniv, May 16
Reyna, Claudio: Birth, Jul 20
Reynolds, Burt: Birth, Feb 11
Reynolds, Debbie: Birth, Apr 1
Reynolds, Debbie: Singin' in the Rain Film Premiere: Anniv, Mar 27
Reynolds, Joshua: Birth Anniv, Jul 16
Reynolds, Star Jones: Birth, Mar 24
Reznor, Trent: Birth, May 17
Rhames, Ving: Birth, May 12
Rhinelander's Oktoberfest (Rhinelander, WI), Oct 6
Rhino Challenge, Borneo (Malaysia), May 14
Rhino Day, Save the, May 1
Rhode Island
    Anne Hutchinson Memorial Day (Portsmouth), Apr 30
    Bristol Civic, Military/Firemen's Parade (Bristol), Jul 4
    Carcieri, Donald: Birth, Dec 16
    Chafee, Lincoln: Birth, Mar 26
    Children's Party at Green Animals (Newport), Jul 14
    Independence Day, May 4
    Neighbor Day, May 21
    New England Mid-winter Surfing Chmpshp (Narragansett), Feb 18
    Newport Intl Boat Show (Newport), Sep 14
    Newport Music Fest (Newport), Jul 7
    Newport Winter Fest (Newport), Feb 17
    Penguin Plunge (Jamestown), Jan 1
    Ratification Day, May 29
    Reed, Jack: Birth, Nov 12

US Women's Open Chmpshp (Newport), **Jun 29**
Victory Day, **Aug 14**
Voters Reject Constitution: Anniv, **Mar 24**
Rhodes, Cecil: Birth Anniv, Jul 5
Rhodes, Cynthia: Birth, Nov 21
Rhododendron Fest (Florence, OR), May 19
Rhododendron Fest (Hiawassee, GA), May 12
Rhubarb Fest (Intercourse, PA), May 19
Rhue, Madlyn: Birth, Oct 3
Ricardo, David: Birth Anniv, Apr 19
Ricci, Christina: Birth, Feb 12
Rice Month, Natl, Sep 1
Rice, Anne: Birth, Oct 4
Rice, Condoleezza: Birth, Nov 14
Rice, Glen: Birth, May 28
Rice, Jerry Lee: Birth, Oct 13
Rice, Jim: Birth, Mar 8
Rice, Tim: Birth, Nov 10
Rich, Adam: Birth, Oct 12
Richard, Rocket: Birth Anniv, Aug 4
Richards, Denise: Birth, Feb 17
Richards, Keith: Birth, Dec 18
Richards, Michael: Birth, Aug 24
Richards, Todd: Birth, Dec 28
Richardson, Bill: Birth, Nov 15
Richardson, J.P. (Big Bopper): Day the Music Died: Death Anniv, Feb 3
Richardson, Joely: Birth, Jan 9
Richardson, Miranda: Birth, Mar 3
Richardson, Natasha: Birth, May 11
Richardson, Patricia: Birth, Feb 23
Richie, Lionel: Birth, Jun 20
Richie, Nicole: Birth, Sep 21
Richmond, Lee: First Perfect Game: Anniv, Jun 12
Richmond, Mitch: Birth, Jun 30
Richter Scale Day, Apr 26
Richter, Andy: Birth, Oct 28
Richter, Mike: Birth, Sep 22
Rickenbacker, Edward V.: Birth Anniv, Oct 8
Rickey, Branch: Birth Anniv, Dec 20
Rickles, Don: Birth, May 8
Rickover, Hyman George: Birth Anniv, Jan 27
Riddles, Libby: Birth, Apr 1
Ride, Sally K.: Birthday, May 26
Ridgeley, Andrew: Birth, Jan 26
Ridgway, Matthew Bunker: Birth Anniv, Mar 3
Riefenstahl, Leni: Birth Anniv, Aug 22
Riegert, Peter: Birth, Apr 11
Riel, Louis: Hanging Anniv, Nov 16
Rifkin, Ron: Birth, Oct 31
Rifle Tournament, Walsh Invitational (Cincinnati, OH), Nov 3
Rigby, Cathy: Birth, Dec 12
Rigg, Diana: Birth, Jul 20
Riggs, Bobby: Billie Jean King Wins: Anniv, Sep 20
Right-Brainers Rule Month, Oct 1
Riley, Bob: Birth, Oct 3
Riley, James Whitcomb: Death Anniv, Jul 22
Riley, Pat: Birth, Mar 20
Rimes, LeAnn: Birth, Aug 28
Ringgold, Faith: Birth, Oct 8
Ringwald, Molly: Birth, Feb 18
Rios, Marcelo: Birth, Dec 26
Riot Act: Anniv, Jul 20
Riot, Watts: Anniv, Aug 11
Ripa, Kelly: Birth, Oct 2
Ripken, Cal, Jr: Birth, Aug 24
Ripper, Jack the: Letter: Anniv, Sep 27
Ripper, Jack the: Whitechapel Murders Begin: Anniv, Aug 31
Rite of Spring Premiere and Riot: Anniv, May 29
Ritt, Martin: Birth Anniv, Mar 2
River Raid Renaissance Fest and Goettafest (Covington, KY), Jun 17
Rivera, Chita: Birth, Jan 23
Rivera, Diego: Birth Anniv, Dec 8
Rivera, Geraldo: Birth, Jul 4
Rivera, Mariano: Birth, Nov 29
Riverbend Fest (Chattanooga, TN), Jun 9
Riverfest (LaCrosse, WI), Jun 30
Rivers Month, Natl, Jun 1
Rivers, Glenn: Birth, Oct 13
Rivers, Joan: Birth, Jun 8
Rivers, Johnny: Birth, Nov 7
Rizzuto, Phil: Birth, Sep 25
Roach, Hal: Birth Anniv, Jan 14
Roasting Month, Natl, Nov 1
Robards, Jason: Birth Anniv, Jul 26
Robbins, Jerome: Birth Anniv, Oct 11
Robbins, Tim: Birth, Oct 16
Robert the Hermit: Death Anniv, Apr 1
Robert-Houdin, Jean Eugene: Birth Anniv, Dec 6
Robert's Rules Day, May 2
Roberts, Cokie: Birth, Dec 27
Roberts, Doris: Birth, Nov 4
Roberts, Eric: Birth, Apr 18

Roberts, Julia: Birth, Oct 28
Roberts, Nora: Birth, Oct 10
Roberts, Oral: Birth, Jan 24
Roberts, Pat: Birth, Apr 20
Roberts, Pernell: Birth, May 18
Roberts, Tony: Birth, Oct 22
Robertson, Cliff: Birth, Sep 9
Robertson, Oscar Palmer: Birth, Nov 24
Robertson, Pat: Birth, Mar 22
Robertson, Robbie: Birth, Jul 5
Robeson, Paul: Birth Anniv, Apr 9
Robin Hood Fest, Sherwood (Sherwood, OR), Jul 21
Robinson Crusoe Day, Feb 1
Robinson, Bill "Bojangles": Birth Anniv, May 25
Robinson, Brooks: Birth, May 18
Robinson, Cliff: Birth, Dec 16
Robinson, David: Birth, Aug 6
Robinson, Eddie: Birth, Feb 13
Robinson, Edwin Arlington: Birth Anniv, Dec 22
Robinson, Frank: Birth, Aug 31
Robinson, Frank: Named First Black Manager: Anniv, Oct 3
Robinson, Glenn: Birth, Jan 10
Robinson, Jackie: Birth Anniv, Jan 31
Robinson, Jackie: Breaks Baseball Color Line: Anniv, Apr 15
Robinson, Roscoe, Jr: Birth Anniv, Oct 11
Robinson, Smokey: Birth, Feb 19
Robinson, Sugar Ray: Birth Anniv, May 3
Robot Enters World Lexicon: Anniv, Jan 25
Robot Homicide, First: Anniv, Jul 21
Rocco, Alex: Birth, Feb 29
Rochester Fair (Rochester, NH), Sep 15
Rochon, Lela: Birth, Apr 17
Rock Show, Mineral Capital (Bancroft, ON, Canada), Jul 22
Rock, Chris: Birth, Feb 7
Rockbridge Community Fest (Lexington, VA), Aug 19
Rockefeller, Abby Greene Aldrich: Birth Anniv, Oct 26
Rockefeller, David: Birth, Jun 12
Rockefeller, John D., IV: Birth, Jun 18
Rockefeller, Nelson: Birth Anniv, Jul 8
Rockhound Gemboree (Bancroft, ON, Canada), Jul 27
Rockne, Knute: Birth Anniv, Mar 4
Rockne, Knute: Death Anniv, Mar 31
Rocks: Geode Fest (Keokuk, IA), Oct 6
Rockwell, Norman: Birth Anniv, Feb 3
Rockwell, Norman: First Post Cover: Anniv, May 20
Rockwell, Norman: Self-Portrait: Anniv, Oct 8
Rocky and His Friends TV Premiere: Anniv, Nov 19
Rocky Mountain Natl Park Established: Anniv, Jan 26
Roddenberry, Gene: Birth Anniv, Aug 19
Roddick, Andy: Birth, Aug 30
Rodents, Running of the (Louisville, KY), Apr 10
Rodeo
  Adams County Fair/Rodeo (Hettinger, ND), **Aug 3**
  Beef Empire Days (Garden City, KS), **May 30**
  Black Hills Roundup (Belle Fourche, SD), **Jul 2**
  Black Hills Stock Show and Rodeo (Rapid City, SD), **Jan 27**
  Bullnanza (Guthrie, OK), **Jan 27**
  Cal Farley's Boys Ranch Rodeo (Boys Ranch, TX), **Sep 2**
  Calgary Stampede (Calgary, AB, Canada), **Jul 7**
  Central Montana Fair (Lewistown, MT), **Jul 26**
  Cheyenne Frontier Days (Cheyenne, WY), **Jul 21**
  Clearwater Chamber of Commerce Rodeo (Clearwater, NE), **Jun 23**
  Dinosaur Roundup Rodeo (Vernal, UT), **Jul 12**
  Eighty-Niner Celebration (Guthrie, OK), **Apr 18**
  Ennis Rodeo & Parade (Ennis, MT), **Jul 3**
  Fiesta De Los Vaqueros (Tucson, AZ), **Feb 18**
  Houston Livestock Show/Rodeo (Houston, TX), **Feb 28**
  Inter-State Fair/Rodeo (Coffeyville, KS), **Aug 12**
  Killdeer Mountain Roundup Rodeo Days (Killdeer, ND), **Jul 3**
  Livingston Roundup & PRCA Rodeo (Livingston, MT), **Jul 2**
  Longhorn Chmpshp Finals Rodeo (Murfreesboro, TN), **Nov 9**
  Longhorn Chmpshp Rodeo (Auburn Hills, MI), **Feb 17**
  Longhorn World Chmpshp Rodeo (Chattanooga, TN), **Mar 10**
  Longhorn World Chmpshp Rodeo (Cincinnati, OH), **Jan 27**
  Longhorn World Chmpshp Rodeo (Columbus, OH), **Feb 3**
  Longhorn World Chmpshp Rodeo (Dayton, OH), **Feb 10**

  Longhorn World Chmpshp Rodeo (Huntsville, AL), **Mar 3**
  Longhorn World Chmpshp Rodeo (Tulsa, OK), **Jan 20**
  Longhorn World Chmpshp Rodeo (Winston-Salem, NC), **Feb 24**
  Lost Dutchman Days (Apache Junction, AZ), **Feb 24**
  Nebraska's Big Rodeo (Burwell, NE), **Jul 27**
  NRA/NWRA Rodeo Finals (Billings, MT), **Feb 17**
  Oregon Trail Rodeo (Hastings, NE), **Sep 1**
  Pendleton Round-Up (Pendleton, OR), **Sep 9**
  Ranching Heritage Fest, South Texas (Kingsville, TX), **Mar 3**
  Red River Rodeo (Wichita Falls, TX), **Jun 7**
  River City Roundup (Omaha, NE), **Sep 28**
  Scotts Bluff County Fair (Mitchell, NE), **Aug 14**
  Seminole Tribe Festival, Powwow and Rodeo (Hollywood, FL), **Feb 10**
  Snake River Stampede (Nampa, ID), **Jul 18**
  Southwestern Expo Livestock Show/Rodeo (Fort Worth, TX), **Jan 13**
  Texas Ranch Roundup (Wichita Falls, TX), **Aug 18**
  That Famous Preston Night Rodeo (Preston, ID), **Jul 28**
  Utah State Fair (Salt Lake City, UT), **Sep 7**
  Western Stock Show and Rodeo, Natl (Denver, CO), **Jan 7**
  Wild Horse Stampede (Wolf Point, MT), **Jul 6**
Rodgers, Richard: Oklahoma! Broadway Premiere: Anniv, Mar 31
Rodin, Auguste: Birth Anniv, Nov 12
Rodman, Dennis: Birth, May 13
Rodney, Caesar: Birth Anniv, Oct 7
Rodriguez, Alex: Birth, Jul 27
Rodriguez, Ivan "Pudge": Birth, Nov 30
Rodriguez, Juan "Chi-Chi": Birth, Oct 23
Rodriguez, Robert: Birth, Jun 20
Roe v Wade Decision: Anniv, Jan 22
Roentgen, Wilhelm K.: Birth Anniv, Mar 27
Roeper, Richard: Birth, Oct 17
Rogation Sunday, May 21
Roger Ebert's Overlooked Film Fest (Champaign, IL), Apr 26
Rogers, Edith Nourse: Birth Anniv, Mar 19
Rogers, Fred: Birth Anniv, Mar 20
Rogers, Ginger: Birth Anniv, Jul 16
Rogers, Kenny: Birth, Aug 21
Rogers, Mimi: Birth, Jan 27
Rogers, Roy: Birth Anniv, Nov 5
Rogers, Wayne: Birth, Apr 7
Rogers, Will: Birth Anniv, Nov 4
Roget, Peter Mark: Birth Anniv, Jan 18
Roker, Al: Birth, Aug 20
Role Model Month, Natl Inspirational, Nov 1
Rolen, Scott: Birth, Apr 4
Roller Coaster, First, Opens: Anniv, Jun 13
Roller Skating Month, Natl, Oct 1
Rolling Stones: Altamont Concert: Anniv, Dec 6
Rollins, Jimmy: Birth, Nov 27
Roman Catholic/Eastern Orthodox Meeting: Anniv, Jan 5
Roman Catholic: New Catechism: Anniv, Nov 16
Romance (including dating, love, relationships)
  Call In Single Day, Natl, **Feb 14**
  Couple Appreciation Month, **Apr 1**
  Decide to Be Married Day, **Jun 27**
  Dump Your "Significant Jerk" Day, **Feb 7**
  Flirting Week, Intl, **Feb 13**
  Kiss-and-Make-Up-Day, **Aug 25**
  Love a Mensch Week, **Feb 6**
  Lunch Prowl Week, **Sep 18**
  Meet a Mate Week, **Jun 12**
  Pleasure Your Mate Month, **Sep 1**
  Proposal Day!, **Mar 20**
  Rejection Awareness Week, **Feb 7**
  Relationship Wellness Month, **Feb 1**
  Resurrect Romance Week, Natl, **Aug 13**
  Singles Week, Natl, **Sep 17**
  Valentine's Day, **Feb 14**
  Weddings Month, Natl, **Feb 1**
  Wife Appreciation Day, **Sep 16**
  World Marriage Day, **Feb 12**
Romania
  Ceausescu, Nicolae: Death Anniv, **Dec 25**
  National Day, **Dec 1**
  Surrender to USSR: Anniv, **Aug 23**
Romano, Ray: Birth, Dec 21
Rombauer, Irma: Joy of Cooking Publication Anniv, Nov 30
Rome Executions: Anniv, Mar 25
Rome Liberated: Anniv, Jun 4
Rome, Sack of: Anniv, May 6
Rome: Birthday (Italy), Apr 21
Romero Barcelo, Carlos: Birth, Sep 4
Romijn, Rebecca: Birth, Nov 6
Rommel, Erwin: Birth Anniv, Nov 15
Romney, Mitt: Birth, Mar 12

Ronaldo—Safety

Ronaldo: Birth, Sep 22
Ronstadt, Linda: Birth, Jul 15
Room of One's Own Day, Jan 25
Rooney, Andy: Birth, Jan 14
Rooney, Mickey: Birth, Sep 23
Roosevelt, Alice: Birth Anniv, Jul 29
Roosevelt, Edith: Birth Anniv, Aug 6
Roosevelt, Eleanor, Day (Menlo, WA), Aug 12
Roosevelt, Eleanor: Birth Anniv, Oct 11
Roosevelt, Franklin Delano
    Birth Anniv, Jan 30
    Christmas Fireside Chat Warning: Anniv, Dec 25
    Death Anniv, Apr 12
    Elected to Fourth Term: Anniv, Nov 7
    FDR Commemorative Ceremony (Warm Springs,
        GA), Apr 12
    First Fireside Chat: Anniv, Mar 12
    First Presidential Telecast: Anniv, Apr 30
    Unconditional Surrender Statement: Anniv, Jan 24
    US Bank Holiday: Anniv, Mar 5
    Warm Springs Thanksgiving (Warm Springs, GA),
        Nov 18
Roosevelt, Theodore: Birth Anniv, Oct 27
Roosevelt, Theodore: First Secret Service Agent
    to Die in the Line of Duty: Anniv, Sep 3
Root Canal Appreciation Day, May 10
Roots and Branches Month, Jul 1
Rosacea Awareness Month, Apr 1
Rose Bowl Game (Pasadena, CA), Jan 4
Rose Fest, Portland (Portland, OR), Jun 1
Rose Month, Natl, Jun 1
Rose, Billy: Birth Anniv, Sep 6
Rose, Charlie: Birth, Jan 5
Rose, Jalen: Birth, Jan 30
Rose, Peace: Introduced to World: Anniv, Apr 29
Rose, Pete: Birth, Apr 14
Roseanne TV Premiere: Anniv, Oct 18
Roseanne: Birth, Nov 3
Rosenbaum, Michael: Birth, Jul 11
Rosenberg Execution: Anniv, Jun 19
Roses Parade, Tournament of (Pasadena, CA),
    Jan 2
Roses, South Carolina Fest of (Orangeburg, SC),
    Apr 21
Rosh Hashanah, Sep 23
Rosh Hashanah Begins, Sep 22
Ross, Betsy: Birth Anniv, Jan 1
Ross, Diana: Birth, Mar 26
Ross, George: Birth Anniv, May 10
Ross, Katharine: Birth, Jan 29
Ross, Marion: Birth, Oct 25
Ross, Nellie Tayloe: Birth Anniv, Nov 29
Ross, Nellie Tayloe: Wyoming Inaugurates 1st US
    Woman Gov: Anniv, Jan 5
Rossellini, Isabella: Birth, Jun 18
Rossetti, Christina: Birth Anniv, Dec 5
Rossner, Judith: Birth, Mar 1
Rossovich, Rick: Birth, Aug 28
Rossum, Emmy: Birth, Sep 12
Rostropovich, Mstislav Leopoldovich: Birth,
    Mar 27
Rotary Tiller Race, World Chmpshp/Purplehull
    Pea Fest (Emerson, AR), Jun 23
Roth, David Lee: Birth, Oct 10
Roth, Philip: Birth, Mar 19
Roth, Tim: Birth, May 14
Roughhouse Fest (Japan), Oct 14
Rounds Resounding Day, Aug 1
Rounds, Mike: Birth, Oct 24
Roundtree, Richard: Birth, Sep 7
Rourke, Mickey: Birth, Sep 16
Rousseau, Henri: Birth Anniv, May 20
Rousseau, Jean J.: Birth Anniv, Jun 28
Rowan and Martin's Laugh-In, Jan 22
Rowlands, Gena: Birth, Jun 19
Rowling, J.K.: Birth, Jul 31
Roy Rogers Show TV Premiere: Anniv, Dec 30
Roy, Patrick: Birth, Oct 5
Royko, Mike: Birth Anniv, Sep 19
Rozelle, Pete: Birth Anniv, Mar 1
Rozier, Jean Francois Pilatre de: First Fatal
    Aviation Accident: Anniv, Jun 15
RSV Awareness Month, Natl, Oct 1
Rubens, Paul: Birth, Aug 27
Rubens, Peter P.: Birth Anniv, Jun 28
Rubik, Erno: Birth, Jul 13
Ruble Becomes Convertible: Anniv, Jul 1
Ruck, Alan: Birth, Jul 1
Rucker, Darius: Birth, May 13
Rudd, Paul: Birth, Apr 6
Rudner, Rita: Birth, Sep 17
Rudolph, Maya: Birth, Jul 27
Rudolph, Wilma: Birth Anniv, Jun 23
Ruffin, Davis Eli (David): Birth Anniv, Jan 18
Ruffin, Edmund: Birth Anniv, Jan 5
Rukeyser, Louis: Birth, Jan 30
Rumsfeld, Donald: Birth, Jul 9
Rundgren, Todd: Birth, Jun 22

Running
    Al's Memorial Run & Walk (Milwaukee, WI), Sep 30
    Anvil Mountain Run (Nome, AK), Jul 4
    Atlanta Marathon and Half Marathon (Atlanta, GA),
        Nov 23
    Bay to Breakers Race (San Francisco, CA),
        May 19
    Beartooth Run (Red Lodge, MT), Jun 24
    Big Ten Men's/Women's Cross Country Chmpshps
        (Bloomington, IN), Oct 29
    Bolder Boulder 10k (Boulder, CO), May 29
    Boston Marathon (Boston, MA), Apr 17
    California Artichoke Fest (Castroville, CA), May 20
    Carlsbad Marathon (Carlsbad, CA), Jan 15
    Crater Lake Rim Runs and Marathon (Klamath
        Falls, OR), Aug 12
    Dog Day Road Race (Harvey Cedars, NJ), Aug 20
    Easter Beach Run (Daytona Beach, FL), Apr 15
    Egg Races (Switzerland), Apr 17
    59 Min 37 Sec Anvil Mountain Challenge (Nome,
        AK), Sep 7
    Groundhog Run (Kansas City, MO), Jan 29
    Hangover Handicap Run (Klamath Falls, OR),
        Jan 1
    Historic Marathon Runs: Anniv, Sep 2
    Houston Marathon (Houston, TX), Jan 15
    Lakestride Half-Marathon (Ludington, MI), Jun 17
    LaSalle Bank Chicago Marathon (Chicago, IL),
        Oct 22
    Leadville Trail 100 Ultramarathon (Leadville, CO),
        Aug 18
    Longest Dam Run (Fort Peck, MT), Jun 17
    Mad City Marathon (Madison, WI), May 28
    New York City Marathon (New York, NY), Nov 5
    Peachtree Road Race (Atlanta, GA), Jul 4
    Romp in the Swamp Fun Walk (Appleton, WI),
        Oct 21
Runyan, Damon: Birth Anniv, Oct 4
RuPaul: Birth, Nov 17
Rural Life Sunday, May 21
Rush, Barbara: Birth, Jan 4
Rush, Benjamin: Birth Anniv, Jan 4
Rush, Geoffrey: Birth, Jul 6
Rush, William: Death Anniv, Jan 17
Rushdie, Salman, Death Sentence: Anniv, Feb 14
Rushdie, Salman: Birth, Jun 19
Rusk, (David) Dean: Birth Anniv, Feb 9
Russell, Anna: Birth, Dec 27
Russell, Bill: Birth, Feb 12
Russell, Charles M.: Birth Anniv, Mar 19
Russell, Jane: Birth, Jun 21
Russell, Keri: Birth, Mar 23
Russell, Kurt: Birth, Mar 17
Russell, Leon: Birth, Apr 2
Russell, Lillian: Birth Anniv, Dec 4
Russell, Mark: Birth, Aug 23
Russell, Nipsey: Birth, Oct 13
Russell, Theresa: Birth, Mar 20
Russell-Einstein Manifesto: Anniv, Jul 9
Russert, Tim: Birth, May 7
Russia
    Army and Navy Day, Feb 23
    Baltic States' Independence Recognized: Anniv,
        Sep 6
    Battle of Stalingrad Begins: Anniv, Aug 22
    Boris Yeltsin Inaugurated: Anniv, Jul 10
    Christmas Bells Ring Again: Anniv, Dec 24
    Christmas Day, Jan 7
    COMECON and Warsaw Pact Disband: Anniv,
        Jun 28
    Constitution Day, Dec 12
    Coup Attempt in the Soviet Union: Anniv, Aug 19
    Czar Nicholas II and Family Executed: Anniv,
        Jul 17
    Day of National Reconciliation and Agreement,
        Nov 7
    German Surrender at Stalingrad: Anniv, Feb 2
    Great October Socialist Revolution: Anniv, Nov 7
    Independence Day, Jun 12
    International Labor Day, May 1
    KGB Founder Statue Dismantled: Anniv, Aug 22
    New Year's Day Observance, Jan 1
    October Revolution, Nov 7
    Old New Year's Eve, Jan 13
    Passport Presentation, Jan 2
    Ruble Becomes Convertible: Anniv, Jul 1
    Saint Petersburg Founded: Anniv, May 27
    Saint Petersburg Massacre: Anniv, Jan 9
    Saint Petersburg Name Restored: Anniv, Sep 6
    Soviet Communist Party Suspended: Anniv,
        Aug 29
    Soviet Cosmonaut Returns to New Country: Anniv,
        Mar 26
    Soviet Union Dissolved: Anniv, Dec 8
    Soviet Union Invaded: Anniv, Jun 22
    USSR Established: Anniv, Dec 30
    Victory Day, May 9
    Women's Day, Intl, Mar 8

Russo, Rene: Birth, Feb 17
Russo, Richard: Birth, Jul 15
Rustin, Bayard: Birth Anniv, Mar 17
Ruth, George Herman
    Babe Ruth Day: Anniv, Apr 27
    Baseball Hall of Fame's Charter Members: Anniv,
        Feb 2
    Birth Anniv, Feb 6
    Calls His Shot?: Anniv, Oct 1
    Death Anniv, Aug 16
    Debut in Majors: Anniv, Jul 11
    First Major League Home Run: Anniv, May 6
    First Pro Homer: Anniv, Sep 5
    House That Ruth Built: Anniv, Apr 18
    Last Game as Yankee: Anniv, Sep 30
    Pitching Debut: Anniv, Apr 22
    Sets Home Run Record: Anniv, Sep 30
Rutherford, Ernest: Birth Anniv, Aug 30
Rutledge, Edward: Birth Anniv, Nov 23
Rutledge, John: Death Anniv, Jul 18
Ruttan, Susan: Birth, Sep 16
RV Lifestyle Week, Apr 23
RV Workers and Workampers Day (Quartzsite,
    AZ), Jan 20
Rwanda
    Genocide Remembrance Day, Apr 7
    Independence Day, Jul 1
    Republic Day, Sep 25
    Tragedy in Rwanda: Anniv, Apr 6
Ryan, Jeri: Birth, Feb 22
Ryan, Meg: Birth, Nov 19
Ryan, Nolan: Birth, Jan 31
Ryan's Hope TV Premiere: Anniv, Jul 7
Rydell, Bobby: Birth, Apr 26
Ryder Cup Matches (Straffan, Ireland), Sep 22
Ryder, Albert Pinkham: Birth Anniv, Mar 19
Ryder, Winona: Birth, Oct 29

Saarinen, Eero: Birth Anniv, Aug 20
Saarinen, Eliel: Birth Anniv, Aug 20
Sabathia, C.C.: Birth, Jul 21
Sabatini, Gabriela: Birth, May 16
Sabato, Antonio, Jr: Birth, Feb 29
Saberhagen, Bret: Birth, Apr 11
Sabin, Albert Bruce: Birth Anniv, Aug 26
Sacagawea: Death Anniv, Dec 20
Sacagawea: Reunion at the Home of Sakakawea
    (New Town, ND), Aug 17
Sacco-Vanzetti Memorial Day, Aug 23
Sacramento Jazz Jubilee (Sacramento, CA),
    May 26
Sadat, Anwar El: Assassination Anniv, Oct 6
Sadie Hawkins Day, Nov 4
Safe Boating Week, Natl, May 20
Safer, Morley: Birth, Nov 8
Safety Pin Patented: Anniv, Apr 10
Safety Razor Patented: Anniv, Dec 2
Safety. See also Crime
    Automobile Speed Reduction: Anniv, Nov 25
    Baby Safety Month, Sep 1
    Babysitter Safety Day, Mar 4
    Cartoonists Against Crime Day, Oct 25
    Check Your Batteries Day, Apr 2
    Child Safety Council Founded, Natl: Anniv, Nov 9
    Childhood Injury Prevention Week, Natl, Sep 1
    Children and Police Day, Natl, May 19
    Chimney Safety Week, Natl, Sep 24
    Church Safety and Security Month, Oct 1
    Collision Awareness Month, Natl, Mar 1
    Crime Prevention Month, Natl, Oct 1
    Day of Natl Concern about Young People and Gun
        Violence, Oct 18
    Drowning Prevention Day, Natl (Canada), Jul 22
    Drunk and Drugged Driving Prevention Month, Natl
        (Pres Proc), Dec 1
    Farm Safety Week, Natl (Pres Proc), Sep 17
    Fire Prevention Week, Oct 8
    Fire Prevention Week (Pres Proc), Oct 8
    Fire Safety Council, Natl: Anniv, Dec 7
    Firepup's Birthday, Oct 1
    Fireworks Safety Months, Jun 1
    Halloween Safety Month, Oct 1
    Heimlich Maneuver Introduced: Anniv, Jun 1
    Home Office Safety and Security Week, Jan 8
    Identity Theft Prevention and Awareness Month,
        Dec 1
    Light the Night for Sight, May 1
    MADD's New Year's Designate a Driver Campaign,
        Dec 26
    MADD's Tie One On for Safety, Nov 16
    Missing Children's Day, Natl, May 25
    Motorcycle Safety Month, May 1
    Night Out, Natl, Aug 1
    Personal Self-Defense Awareness Month, Natl,
        Jan 1
    Playground Safety Week, Natl, Apr 24
    Poison Prevention Week, Natl, Mar 19
    Poison Prevention Week, Natl (Pres Proc), Mar 19

☆ *Chase's 2006 Calendar of Events* ☆   Index

Preparedness Month, Natl, **Sep 1**
Prevention of Eye Injuries Awareness Week, Natl, **Jun 27**
Safe Boating Week, Natl, **May 20**
Safe Boating Week, Natl (Pres Proc), **May 20**
Safe Toys and Gifts Month, **Dec 1**
Safety Month, Natl, **Jun 1**
Safetypup's Birthday, **Feb 12**
Sexual Assault Awareness and Prevention Month, Natl, **Apr 1**
SOS Adopted: Anniv, **Nov 3**
Sports & Home Eye Health and Safety Month, **Sep 1**
Student Safety Month, **Jun 1**
Workers Memorial Day, **Apr 28**
Youth Sports Safety Month, Natl, **Apr 1**
Safire, William: Birth, **Dec 17**
Sagal, Katey: Birth, **Nov 18**
Sagan, Carl: Birth Anniv, **Nov 9**
Sager, Carole Bayer: Birth, **Mar 8**
Saget, Bob: Birth, **May 17**
Sagittarius Begins, **Nov 22**
Sahl, Mort: Birth, **May 11**
Saint Ann's Italian Street Fest (Hoboken, NJ), **Jul 21**
Saint Aubin, Helen "Callaghan": Birth Anniv, **Mar 13**
Saint Bartholomew's Day Massacre: Anniv, **Aug 24**
Saint Basil's Cathedral: Christmas Bells Again: Anniv, **Dec 24**
Saint Christopher: Independence Day, **Sep 19**
Saint Elias Day: Macedonian Uprising: Anniv, **Aug 2**
Saint Elsewhere TV Premiere: Anniv, **Oct 26**
Saint Eustatius, West Indies: Statia and America Day, **Nov 16**
Saint George's Day (Newfoundland, Canada), **Apr 24**
Saint Gotthard Auto Tunnel: Opening Anniv, **Sep 5**
Saint James, Susan: Birth, **Aug 14**
Saint Lasarus' Day (Bulgaria), **Apr 1**
Saint Laurent, Yves: Birth, **Aug 1**
Saint Lawrence Seaway Act: Anniv, **May 13**
Saint Lawrence Seaway: Dedication Anniv, **Jun 26**
Saint Lucia: Independence Day, **Feb 22**
Saint Olaf Christmas Fest (Northfield, MN), **Nov 30**
Saint Patrick's Day (Northern Ireland), **Mar 17**
Saint Patrick's Day Parade (Baton Rouge, LA), **Mar 18**
Saint Patrick's Day Parade (Hornell, NY), **Mar 18**
Saint Patrick's Day Parade (New York, NY), **Mar 17**
Saint Patrick's Day Parade (Roanoke, VA), **Mar 17**
Saint Paul's Feast (Cyprus), **Jun 28**
Saint Petersburg Founded: Anniv, **May 27**
Saint Petersburg Massacre: Anniv, **Jan 9**
Saint Petersburg Name Restored: Anniv, **Sep 6**
Saint Piran's Day Celebration (Kansas City, MO), **Mar 4**
Saint Swithun's Celebration (Toronto, ON, Canada), **Jul 15**
Saint Vincent and the Grenadines: Independence Day, **Oct 27**
Saint, Eva Marie: Birth, **Jul 4**
Sainte-Marie, Buffy: Birth, **Feb 20**
Saint-Gaudens, Augustus: Birth Anniv, **Mar 1**
Saints, Saints' Days
  Anthony's Day, **Jan 17**
  Andrew's Day, **Nov 30**
  Anthony of Padua: Feast Day (Portugal), **Jun 13**
  Apollinaris: Feast Day, **Jul 23**
  Augustine of Canterbury, Feast of, **May 26**
  Augustine, Feast of, **Aug 28**
  Barbara's Day, **Dec 4**
  Basil's Day, **Jan 1**
  Bernard of Montjoux: Feast Day, **May 28**
  Catherine of Siena: Feast Day, **Apr 29**
  Catherine's Day, **Nov 25**
  Cecilia: Feast Day, **Nov 22**
  Clare of Assisi: Feast Day, **Aug 11**
  Crispin's Day, **Oct 25**
  David's Day (Wales), **Mar 1**
  Edward, The Confessor: Feast Day, **Oct 13**
  Frances of Rome: Feast Day, **Mar 9**
  Frances Xavier Cabrini: Birth Anniv, **Jul 15**
  Francis of Assisi: Feast Day, **Oct 4**
  Gabriel: Feast Day, **Mar 24**
  George: Feast Day (England), **Apr 23**
  Gudula: Feast Day, **Jan 8**
  Ignatius of Loyola, Feast of, **Jul 31**
  Isidro Day (Mexico), **May 15**
  James Day (Spain), **Jul 25**
  Januarius: Feast Day, **Sep 19**
  Jerome, Feast of, **Sep 30**
  Joan of Arc: Feast Day, **May 30**

John Nepomucene Neumann: Birth Anniv, **Mar 28**
John of Capistrano: Death Anniv, **Oct 23**
John the Baptist Day, **Jun 24**
John, Apostle-Evangelist: Feast Day, **Dec 27**
Jude's Day, **Oct 28**
Lucia Day (Sweden), **Dec 13**
Luke: Feast Day, **Oct 18**
Martin's Day (Sweden), **Nov 11**
Nicholas Day, **Dec 6**
Oswald of Worcester Feast Day, **Feb 28**
Patrick's Day, **Mar 17**
Peter and Paul Day, **Jun 29**
Peter's Day (Turkey), **Jun 29**
Piran's Day, **Mar 5**
Pius X: Birth Anniv, **Jun 2**
Sebastian's Day (Brazil), **Jan 20**
Stephen's Day, **Dec 26**
Swithin's Day, **Jul 15**
Sylvester's Day, **Dec 31**
Thomas of Canterbury: Feast Day, **Dec 29**
Valentine's Day, **Feb 14**
Vincent De Paul: Feast Day, **Sep 27**
Vincent De Paul: Old Feast Day, **Jul 19**
Vincent: Feast Day, **Jan 22**
Sajak, Pat: Birth, **Oct 26**
Sakharov, Andrei Dmitriyevich: Birth Anniv, **May 21**
Sakic, Joe: Birth, **Jul 7**
Salaam, Rashaan: Birth, **Oct 8**
Salazar, Alberto: Birth, **Aug 7**
Salazar, Ken: Birth, **Mar 2**
Saldana, Theresa: Birth, **Aug 20**
Salem Witch Hysteria Begins: Anniv, **Mar 1**
Salem Witch Trials Begin: Anniv, **Jun 2**
Sales, Soupy: Birth, **Jan 8**
Salesperson's Day, Natl, **Mar 3**
Salinger, J.D.: Birth, **Jan 1**
Salisbury, Harrison: Birth Anniv, **Nov 14**
Salk, Jonas: Birth Anniv, **Oct 28**
Salk, Lee: Birth Anniv, **Dec 27**
Salomon, Haym: Death Anniv, **Jan 6**
Salsa Month, Natl, **May 1**
Salt, Jennifer: Birth, **Sep 4**
Salt: No Salt Week, **Oct 2**
Salter, Susanna, Elected 1st Woman Mayor in US: Anniv, **Apr 4**
Salvador, Francis: Death Anniv, **Jul 31**
Salvation Army Founder's Day, **Apr 10**
Salvation Army in US: Anniv, **Mar 10**
Salvation Army: Booth, William: Birth Anniv, **Apr 10**
Sambora, Richie: Birth, **Jul 11**
Same-sex Marriages, First US: Anniv, **May 17**
Samhain, **Oct 31**
Samms, Emma: Birth, **Aug 28**
Sammy Kaye Show TV Premiere: Anniv, **Jul 28**
Samoa
  ANZAC Day, **Apr 25**
  Arbor Day, **Nov 3**
  Independence Day, **Jun 1**
  Samoan Fire Dance, **Dec 31**
  White Sunday, **Oct 8**
Samoa, American: Flag Day, **Apr 17**
Sampras, Pete: Birth, **Aug 12**
Sampson, Deborah: Birth Anniv, **Dec 17**
Sampson, Ralph: Birth, **Jul 7**
Samuelson, Joan Benoit: Birth, **May 16**
San Francisco 1906 Earthquake: Anniv, **Apr 18**
San Francisco 1989 Earthquake: Anniv, **Oct 17**
San Francisco Silent Film Fest (San Francisco, CA), **Jul 14**
San Giacomo, Laura: Birth, **Nov 14**
San Isidro Day (Mexico), **May 15**
San Jacinto Day (TX), **Apr 21**
San Marino: National Day, **Sep 3**
San Sebastian's Day (Brazil), **Jan 20**
Sanborn, David: Birth, **Jul 30**
Sand, George: Birth Anniv, **Jul 1**
Sand, Paul: Birth, **Mar 5**
Sanda, Dominique: Birth, **Mar 11**
Sandberg, Ryne: Birth, **Sep 18**
Sandburg, Carl: Birth Anniv, **Jan 6**
Sandcastle Day, **Aug 17**
Sanders, Barry: Birth, **Jul 16**
Sanders, Colonel Harland David: Birth Anniv, **Sep 9**
Sanders, Deion: Birth, **Aug 9**
Sanders, Jay O.: Birth, **Apr 16**
Sanders, Reggie: Birth, **Dec 1**
Sanders, Richard: Birth, **Aug 23**
Sandino, Cesar: Assassination Anniv, **Feb 21**
Sandler, Adam: Birth, **Sep 9**
Sands, Tommy: Birth, **Aug 27**
Sandwich Day: John Montague Birth Anniv, **Nov 3**
Sandy Springs Festival (Atlanta, GA), **Sep 16**
Sandy, Gary: Birth, **Dec 25**
Sandys, Edwin: Birth Anniv, **Dec 9**

Sanford and Son TV Premiere: Anniv, **Jan 14**
Sanford, Mark: Birth, **May 28**
Sanger, Margaret (Higgins): Birth Anniv, **Sep 14**
Santa Fe Chamber Music Fest, **Jul 16**
Santa Lucia Day (Sweden), **Dec 13**
Santa-Cali-Gon Days Fest (Independence, MO), **Sep 1**
Santana, Carlos: Birth, **Jul 20**
Santayana, George: Birth Anniv, **Dec 16**
Santiago, Benito: Birth, **Mar 9**
Santiago, Saundra: Birth, **Apr 13**
Santorum, Rick: Birth, **May 10**
Sao Tome and Principe: Independence Day, **Jul 12**
Sarah, Duchess of York: Birth, **Oct 15**
Sarandon, Chris: Birth, **Jul 24**
Sarandon, Susan: Birth, **Oct 4**
Sarazen, Gene: Birth Anniv, **Feb 27**
Sarbanes, Paul S.: Birth, **Feb 3**
Sarcastics Month, Natl, **Oct 1**
Sargent, John Singer: Birth Anniv, **Jan 12**
Saroyan, William: Birth Anniv, **Aug 31**
Sarrazin, Michael: Birth, **May 22**
Sarto, Andrea Del: Birth Anniv, **Jul 14**
Sartre, Jean-Paul: Birth Anniv, **Jun 21**
Sasaki, Kazuhiro: Birth, **Feb 22**
Sassoon, Vidal: Birth, **Jan 17**
Satisfied Staying Single Day, **Feb 11**
Saturday Night Live TV Premiere: Anniv, **Oct 11**
Saturday Night Massacre, **Oct 20**
Saturn: Cassini-Huygens Reaches, **Jul 1**
Saturnalia, **Dec 17**
Saudi Arabia: Kingdom Unification, **Sep 23**
Sauntering Day, World, **Jun 19**
Savage, Ben: Birth, **Sep 13**
Savage, Fred: Birth, **Jul 9**
Savage, John: Birth, **Aug 25**
Savant, Doug: Birth, **Jun 21**
Savant, Marilyn vos: Birth, **Aug 11**
Save the Rhino Day, **May 1**
Save Your Back Week, Natl, **Oct 23**
Save Your Home Week, **Mar 12**
Save Your Smile Week, Natl, **Aug 20**
Save Your Vision Month, **Mar 1**
Save Your Vision Week (Pres Proc), **Mar 7**
Savings and Loan: Home Owners Loan Act: Anniv, **Jun 13**
Sawa, Devon: Birth, **Sep 7**
Sawyer, Diane K.: Birth, **Dec 22**
Sax, Adolphe: Birth Anniv (Saxophone Day), **Nov 6**
Saxon, John: Birth, **Aug 5**
Saxophone Day, **Nov 6**
Sayer, Leo: Birth, **May 21**
Sayers, Gale: Birth, **May 30**
SBC Cotton Bowl Classic (Dallas, TX), **Jan 2**
Scacchi, Greta: Birth, **Feb 18**
Scaggs, Boz: Birth, **Jun 8**
Scalia, Antonin: Birth, **Mar 11**
Scaliger, Joseph J.: Birth Anniv, **Aug 4**
Scandinavian Hjemkomst Fest (Moorhead, MN), **Jun 23**
Scare a Friend Day, **Oct 31**
Scarecrow and Mrs King TV Premiere: Anniv, **Oct 3**
Scarecrow Fest (St. Charles, IL), **Oct 6**
Scarlatti, Domenico: Birth Anniv, **Oct 26**
Scarry, Richard M.: Birth Anniv, **Jun 5**
Scharansky, Natan (Anatoly): Birth, **Jan 20**
Scheider, Roy: Birth, **Nov 10**
Schell, Maximilian: Birth, **Dec 8**
Schembechler, Bo: Birth, **Apr 1**
Schiaparelli, Elsa: Birth Anniv, **Sep 10**
Schieffer, Bob: Birth, **Feb 25**
Schiff, Richard: Birth, **May 27**
Schiffer, Claudia: Birth, **Aug 25**
Schilling, Curt: Birth, **Nov 14**
Schirra, Wally: Birth, **Mar 12**
Schlafly, Phyllis: Birth, **Aug 15**
Schlatter, Charlie: Birth, **May 1**
Schlesinger, Arthur Meier, Jr: Birth, **Oct 15**
Schlitz Playhouse of Stars TV Premiere: Anniv, **Oct 5**
Schmeling, Max: Birth Anniv, **Sep 28**
Schmidt, Mike: Birth, **Sep 27**
Schneider, John: Birth, **Apr 8**
Schneider, Maria: Birth, **Mar 27**
Schneider, Rob: Birth, **Oct 31**
Schneiderman, Rose: Birth Anniv, **Apr 6**
Schnitzler, Arthur: Birth Anniv, **May 15**
Scholarship Month, Natl, **May 1**
Schools
  Breakfast Week, Natl, **Mar 6**
  Counseling Week, Natl, **Feb 6**
  Library Media Month, **Apr 1**
  Principals' Day, **May 1**
  School Bus Safety Week, Natl, **Oct 15**
  School Lunch Week, Natl, **Oct 9**

Schools (cont'd)—Shannon

School Lunch Week, Natl (Pres Proc), **Oct 8**
School Nurse Day, Natl, **May 10**
Spirit Season, Intl, **Apr 30**
Success Month, Natl, **Sep 1**
Thank You, School Librarian Day, **Apr 5**
Schopenhauer, Arthur: Birth Anniv, **Feb 22**
Schorr, Daniel: Birth, **Aug 31**
Schrempf, Detlef: Birth, **Jan 21**
Schroder, Rick: Birth, **Apr 13**
Schroeder, Gerhard: Birth, **Apr 7**
Schroeder, Patricia: Birth, **Jun 30**
Schubert, Franz: Birth Anniv, **Jan 31**
Schuck, John: Birth, **Feb 4**
Schultz, Dwight: Birth, **Nov 24**
Schulz, Charles: Birth Anniv, **Nov 26**
Schuman Plan Anniv: European Union, **May 9**
Schuman, William Howard: Birth Anniv, **Aug 4**
Schumer, Charles E.: Birth, **Nov 23**
Schurz, Carl: Birth Anniv, **Mar 2**
Schutz, Heinrich: Birth Anniv, **Oct 8**
Schwartzman, Jason: Birth, **Jun 26**
Schwarzenegger, Arnold: Birth, **Jul 30**
Schwarzkopf, Norman H.: Birth, **Aug 22**
Schweitzer, Albert: Birth Anniv, **Jan 14**
Schweitzer, Brian: Birth, **Sep 5**
Schwenkfelder Thanksgiving, **Sep 24**
Schwikert, Tasha: Birth, **Nov 21**
Schwimmer, David: Birth, **Nov 12**
Schygulla, Hanna: Birth, **Dec 25**
Scialfa, Patty: Birth, **Jul 29**
Science
American Assn for the Advancement of Science Annual Mtg (St. Louis, MO), **Feb 16**
Astronomy Day, **May 6**
Astronomy Week, **May 1**
Biological Clock Gene Discovered: Anniv, **Apr 28**
Brain Awareness Week, Intl, **Mar 13**
Bunsen Burner Day, **Mar 31**
Cellophane Tape Patented: Anniv, **May 27**
Chemistry Week, Natl, **Oct 22**
Cloning of an Adult Animal, First: Anniv, **Feb 23**
Congress of Mathematicians, Intl (Madrid, Spain), **Aug 22**
Darwin Day, **Feb 12**
Diesel Engine Patented: Anniv, **Feb 23**
Earth's Rotation Proved: Anniv, **Jan 8**
First Self-Sustaining Nuclear Chain Reaction: Anniv, **Dec 2**
First US Scientist Receives Nobel Prize: Anniv, **Dec 10**
Geographers Annual Mtg, Assn of American (Chicago, IL), **Mar 7**
Human Genome Mapped: Anniv, **Jun 26**
Ig Nobel Prize Ceremony (Cambridge, MA), **Oct 5**
INPEX (Pittsburgh, PA), **Jun 7**
Laser Patented: Anniv, **Mar 22**
Metric Conversion Act: Anniv, **Dec 23**
Metric System Developed: Anniv, **Apr 7**
Mole Day, Natl, **Oct 23**
Nobel Conference (St. Peter, MN), **Oct 3**
Nuclear Medicine Week, **Oct 1**
Odometer Invented: Anniv, **May 12**
Physicists Discover Top Quark: Anniv, **Apr 23**
Plutonium First Weighed: Anniv, **Aug 20**
Radiological Society of North America Scientific Assembly and Annual Mtg (Chicago, IL), **Nov 26**
Radium Discovered: Anniv, **Dec 26**
Science Fest, Edinburgh Intl (Edinburgh, Scotland), **Apr 7**
Sky Awareness Week, **Apr 23**
Vitamin C Isolated: Anniv, **Apr 4**
Woman Inducted to Natl Inventors Hall of Fame: Anniv, **May 18**
X-Ray Discovery Day: Anniv, **Nov 8**
Science Fiction
Asimov, Isaac: Birth Anniv, **Jan 2**
Cyberspace Coined: Neuromancer Publication Anniv, **Oct 1**
Robot Enters World Lexicon: Anniv, **Jan 25**
Star Trek TV Premiere: Anniv, **Sep 8**
Star Wars Released: Anniv, **May 25**
2001: A Space Odyssey Premiere: Anniv, **Apr 3**
X-Files TV Premiere: Anniv, **Sep 10**
Sciorra, Annabella: Birth, **Mar 24**
Scobee, Francis R.: Birth Anniv, **May 19**
Scofield, Paul: Birth, **Jan 21**
Scoggins, Tracy: Birth, **Nov 13**
Scolari, Peter: Birth, **Sep 12**
Scooby-Doo, Where Are You? TV Premiere: Anniv, **Sep 13**
Scoop the Poop Week, Natl, **Apr 24**
Scopes, John T.: Birth Anniv, **Aug 3**
Scorpio Begins, **Oct 23**
Scorsese, Martin: Birth, **Nov 17**
Scotland
Aberdeen Intl Youth Fest (Aberdeen), **Aug 2**
Bannockburn Day, **Jun 24**

Braemar Royal Highland Gathering (Braemar), **Sep 2**
Burns' Nights, **Jan 25**
Christmas Holiday, **Dec 25**
Edinburgh Intl Fest (Edinburgh), **Aug 13**
Edinburgh Intl Science Fest (Edinburgh), **Apr 7**
Edinburgh Military Tattoo (Edinburgh), **Aug 4**
Hogmanay, **Dec 31**
Mary, Queen of Scots: Execution Anniv, **Feb 8**
New Year's Bank Holiday, **Jan 2**
Pitlochry Fest Theatre Season, **Apr 1**
Scottish Intl Badminton Chmpsh (Edinburgh), **Nov 23**
Summer Bank Holiday, **Aug 7**
Tartan Day, **Apr 6**
Up Helly Aa, **Jan 31**
Scotland Yard First Appearance Anniv, **Sep 29**
Scott County Courtfest, **Sep 9**
Scott Thomas, Kristin: Birth, **May 24**
Scott, Campbell: Birth, **Jul 19**
Scott, Ridley: Birth, **Nov 30**
Scott, Robert: Birth Anniv, **Jun 6**
Scott, Sir Walter: Birth Anniv, **Aug 15**
Scott, Willard: Birth, **Mar 7**
Scott, Winfield: Birth Anniv, **Jun 13**
Scottish
Alma Highland Fest/Games (Alma, MI), **May 27**
Celtic Fling (Manheim, PA), **Jun 24**
Ligonier Highland Games (Ligonier, PA), **Sep 8**
Longs Peak Scottish/Irish Highland Fest (Estes Park, CO), **Sep 7**
New Hampshire Highland Games (Contoocook, NH), **Sep 22**
Richmond Highland Games/Celtic Fest (Richmond, VA), **Oct 21**
Southeast Florida Fest & Games (Coral Springs, FL), **Mar 4**
Scotto, Renata: Birth, **Feb 24**
Scottsboro Trial: Anniv, **Apr 6**
Scottsdale Culinary Fest (Scottsdale, AZ), **Apr 18**
Scout Sunday, Super (Springfield, MO), **May 13**
Scout Week, Girl, **Mar 12**
Scowcroft, Brent: Birth, **Mar 19**
Scrabble Inventor: Butts, Alfred M.: Birth Anniv, **Apr 13**
Scrapbook Day, Natl, **May 6**
Scrapbooking Industry Day, Intl, **Mar 4**
Scruggs, Earl: Birth, **Jan 6**
Scuba Diving: Seaspace (Houston, TX), **Jun 24**
SCUD Day (Savor the Comic, Unplug the Drama), **Jul 8**
Scully, Vin: Birth, **Nov 29**
Scurry, Briana: Birth, **Sep 7**
Sea Cadet Month, **Sep 1**
Sea Monkey Day, Intl, **May 16**
Seabiscuit Defeats War Admiral: Anniv, **Nov 1**
Seaborg, Glen: Plutonium First Weighed: Anniv, **Aug 20**
Seacrest, Ryan: Birth, **Dec 24**
Seafair (Seattle, WA), **Jul 1**
Seafood Month, Natl, **Oct 1**
Seagal, Steven: Birth, **Apr 10**
Seal, Intl Day of the, **Mar 22**
Seal: Birth, **Feb 19**
Search for Tomorrow TV Premiere: Anniv, **Sep 3**
Seaspace (Houston, TX), **Jun 24**
Seaver, Tom: Birth, **Nov 17**
Second Day of Christmas, **Dec 26**
Second Half of the New Year Day, **Jul 1**
Secondhand Wardrobe Day, Natl, **Jan 5**
Secor, Kyle: Birth, **May 31**
Secret Agent TV Premiere: Anniv, **Apr 5**
Secret Service Agent, First to Die in the Line of Duty: Anniv, **Sep 3**
Secret Storm TV Premiere: Anniv, **Feb 1**
Secretaries Day: See Administrative Professionals Day, **Apr 26**
Secretaries Week: See Administrative Professionals Week, **Apr 23**
Securities and Exchange Commission Created: Anniv, **Jun 6**
Sedaka, Neil: Birth, **Mar 13**
Sedgwick, Kyra: Birth, **Aug 19**
See It Now TV Premiere: Anniv, **Nov 18**
Seeger, Pete: Birth, **May 3**
Seeing Eye Established: Anniv, **Jan 29**
Segal, Erich: Birth, **Jun 16**
Segal, George: Birth, **Feb 13**
Segar, E.C.: Birth Anniv, **Dec 8**
Seger, Bob: Birth, **May 6**
Sehorn, Jason: Birth, **Apr 15**
Seibert, Florence: Birth Anniv, **Oct 6**
Seidelman, Susan: Birth, **Dec 11**
Seikaly, Rony: Birth, **May 10**
Seinfeld TV Premiere: Anniv, **May 31**
Seinfeld, Jerry: Birth, **Apr 29**
Selanne, Teemu: Birth, **Jul 3**
Selby, David: Birth, **Feb 5**

Selena: Birth Anniv, **Apr 16**
Seles, Monica: Birth, **Dec 2**
Self Awareness Month, Intl, **Sep 1**
Self-Esteem Month, Intl Boost Your, **Feb 1**
Self-Improvement Month, **Sep 1**
Self-Promotion Month, **Oct 1**
Self-Renewal Day, **Feb 2**
Self-University Week, **Sep 1**
Selfridge, Thomas E.: Death Anniv, **Sep 17**
Selig, Bud: Birth, **Jul 30**
Sellecca, Connie: Birth, **May 25**
Selleck, Tom: Birth, **Jan 29**
Sellers, Peter: Birth Anniv, **Sep 8**
Selma Civil Rights March: Anniv, **Mar 21**
Selznick, David: Gone with the Wind Film Premiere: Anniv, **Dec 15**
Seminole Tribe of Florida Legally Established: Anniv, **Aug 21**
Semmes, Raphael: Birth Anniv, **Sep 27**
Senate Quorum, First: Anniv, **Apr 6**
Senate: Black Page Appointed: Anniv, **Apr 8**
Sendak, Maurice: Birth, **Jun 10**
Senegal: Independence Day, **Apr 4**
Senior Citizens
All States Picnic (Yuma, AZ), **Jan 3**
Assisted Living Week, Natl, **Sep 10**
Family Caregivers Month, Natl, **Nov 1**
First Social Security Check Issued: Anniv, **Jan 31**
Indianapolis Senior Expo (Indianapolis, IN), **Oct 5**
Lisco Old-timers Day (Lisco, NE), **Sep 10**
Medicare: Anniv, **Jul 1**
Older Americans Month, Natl, **May 1**
Older Persons, Intl Day of (UN), **Oct 1**
Senior Health and Fitness Day, Natl, **May 31**
Senior Independence Month, Natl, **Feb 1**
September Is Healthy Aging Month, **Sep 1**
Shut-In Visitation Day, Natl, **Feb 11**
South Florida Senior Games (Hollywood, FL), **Jan 25**
Southwest Senior Chmpsh (Yuma, AZ), **Jan 17**
Wellderly Day, **Mar 20**
Senses, Celebration of the, **Jun 24**
Seoul Recaptured by UN Forces, **Mar 14**
Separation of Church & State Day, **Oct 28**
Sequim Irrigation Fest (Sequim), **May 6**
Sequoia and Kings Canyon Natl Park Established: Anniv, **Sep 25**
Serbia and Montenegro: National Day, **Apr 27**
Sgt Pepper's Lonely Hearts Club Band Released: Anniv, **Jun 1**
Serkin, Peter: Birth, **Jul 24**
Servan-Schreiber, Jean-Claude: Birth, **Apr 11**
Service Day, Stop the Bad (Customer), **Mar 1**
Service, Robert William: Birth Anniv, **Jan 16**
Sesame Street TV Premiere: Anniv, **Nov 10**
Sessions, Jeff: Birth, **Dec 24**
Seton, Elizabeth Ann Bayley: Feast Day, **Jan 4**
Seton, Elizabeth Ann: Canonization Anniv, **Sep 14**
Setsubun (Japan), **Feb 3**
Seurat, Georges: Birth Anniv, **Dec 2**
Sevareid, Eric: Birth Anniv, **Nov 26**
Sevareid, Doc: Birth, **Jul 7**
Sew Be It! Day, **Sep 10**
Seward's Day (AK), **Mar 27**
Sex and the City TV Premiere: Anniv, **Jun 6**
Sex Discrimination, Martha Griffiths Speaks Out Against, **Feb 8**
Sex Month, Natl Talk With Your Teen About, **Mar 1**
Sex: Joy of Sex Published: Anniv, **Oct 1**
Sexual Assault Awareness and Prevention Month, Natl, **Apr 1**
Sexuality Education Month, Natl Family, **Oct 1**
Sexually Transmitted Diseases (STDs) Awareness Month, Natl, **Apr 1**
Seychelles
Constitution Day, **Jun 18**
Independence Day, **Jun 29**
Seymour, Jane: Birth, **Feb 15**
Shabbat Across America, **Mar 3**
Shackelford, Ted: Birth, **Jun 23**
Shackleton, Ernest: Birth Anniv, **Feb 15**
Shadow Radio Premiere: Anniv, **Jul 31**
Shaffer, Paul: Birth, **Nov 28**
Shakespeare Fest, Colorado (Boulder, CO), **Jun 30**
Shakespeare Fest, Illinois (Bloomington, IL), **Jun 29**
Shakespeare Fest, Oregon (Ashland, OR), **Feb 24**
Shakespeare, William: Birth and Death Anniv, **Apr 23**
Shakira: Birth, **Feb 9**
Shalhoub, Tony: Birth, **Oct 9**
Shamu's Birthday, **Sep 26**
Shandling, Garry: Birth, **Nov 29**
Shange, Ntozake: Birth, **Oct 18**
Shannon, Molly: Birth, **Sep 16**

Shanty Days (Algoma, WI), Aug 11
Sharapova, Maria: Birth, Apr 19
Shareware Day, Intl, Dec 9
Sharif, Omar: Birth, Apr 10
Shark Awareness Day (Point Pleasant Beach, NJ), Jul 15
Sharon on the Green Arts and Crafts Fair (Sharon, CT), Aug 5
Shatner, William: Birth, Mar 22
Shaughnessy, Charles: Birth, Feb 9
Shaver, Helen: Birth, Feb 24
Shavuot, Jun 2
Shavuot Begins, Jun 1
Shaw, Artie: Birth, May 23
Shaw, George Bernard: Birth Anniv, Jul 26
Shaw, Patty Hearst: Birth, Feb 20
Shawn, Ted: Birth Anniv, Oct 21
Shawn, William: Birth Anniv, Aug 31
Shays Rebellion: Anniv, Aug 29
Sheedy, Ally: Birth, Jun 13
Sheehy, Gail: Birth, Nov 27
Sheen, Charlie: Birth, Sep 3
Sheen, Martin: Birth, Aug 3
Sheep Market, Ho (Denmark), Aug 26
Sheffield, Gary: Birth, Nov 18
Sheik Film Release: Anniv, Nov 20
Shelby, Richard C.: Birth, May 6
Sheldon, Sidney: Birth, Feb 11
Shelley, Mary Wollstonecraft: Birth Anniv, Aug 30
Shelley, Percy Bysshe: Birth Anniv, Aug 4
Shemini Atzeret, Oct 14
Shenandoah Natl Park Established: Anniv, Dec 26
Shepard, Alan: Birth Anniv, Nov 18
Shepard, Sam: Birth, Nov 5
Shepherd, Cybill: Birth, Feb 18
Shepherd's Fair/Schuebermess (Luxembourg), Aug 20
Sheridan, Jamey: Birth, Jul 12
Sheridan, Nicollette: Birth, Nov 21
Sheridan, Richard B.: Birth Anniv, Oct 30
Sherman Enters Atlanta: Anniv, Sep 2
Sherman, Bobby: Birth, Jul 22
Sherman, James S.: Birth Anniv, Oct 24
Sherman, Roger: Birth Anniv, Apr 19
Sherman, William Tecumseh
   Birth Anniv, Feb 8
   Surrender at Durham Station: Anniv, **Apr 18**
   Takes Savannah: Anniv, **Dec 21**
   War is Hell: Anniv, **Jun 19**
Sherwood, Brad: Birth, Nov 24
Sherwood, Madeline: Birth, Nov 13
She's Funny That Way Day, Natl, Mar 31
Shields, Brooke: Birth, May 31
Shilts, Randy: Birth Anniv, Aug 8
Shire, Talia: Birth, Apr 25
Shirer, William L.: Birth Anniv, Feb 23
Shirley Temple Theatre TV Premiere: Anniv, Sep 18
Shoemaker-Levy: Comet Crashes into Jupiter: Anniv, Jul 16
Shopping Carts to the Supermarket Month, Return, Feb 1
Shopping Reminder Day, Nov 25
Shopping: Buy Nothing Day, Nov 24
Shore, Dinah: Birth Anniv, Mar 1
Shore, Pauly: Birth, Feb 1
Short, Martin: Birth, Mar 26
Shorter, Wayne: Birth, Aug 25
Shostakovich, Dmitri: Birth Anniv, Sep 25
Show and Tell Day at Work, Jan 8
Show of Wheels (Lovington, NM), Feb 18
Show, Grant: Birth, Feb 27
Shrimp and Petroleum Fest, Louisiana (Morgan City, LA), Aug 31
Shrimp Fest, Isle of Eight Flags (Fernandina Beach, FL), May 5
Shriver, Eunice Mary Kennedy: Birth, Jul 10
Shriver, Maria: Birth, Nov 6
Shriver, Pam: Birth, Jul 4
Shrove Monday, Feb 27
Shrove Tuesday, Feb 28
Shrove Tuesday: Pancake Week, Natl, Feb 26
Shrovetide, Feb 26
Shue, Andrew: Birth, Feb 19
Shue, Elisabeth: Birth, Oct 6
Shula, Don: Birth, Jan 4
Shuster, Joe: Superman Debuts: Anniv, Jun 1
Shut-In Visitation Day, Natl, Feb 11
Shuttle Camp (Alamogordo, NM), Jun 5
Sibelius, Kathleen: Birth, May 15
Siberian Explosion: Anniversary, Jun 30
Siblings Day, Natl, Apr 10
Sidney, Philip: Birth Anniv, Nov 30
Siegel, Bugsy: Birth Anniv, Feb 28
Siegel, Jerry: Superman Debuts: Anniv, Jun 1
Siegmeister, Elie: Birth Anniv, Jan 15
Sierra Club Founded: Anniv, May 28
Sierra Leone: Independence Day, Apr 27

Sierra Leone: National Holiday, Apr 19
Sight-Saving/Ultraviolet Awareness Month, Natl, May 1
Sikh: Vaisakhi (India), Apr 14
Sikorsky, Igor: Birth Anniv, May 25
Silent Film Fest, San Francisco (San Francisco, CA), Jul 14
Silent Record Week, Jan 1
Silent Spring Publication: Anniv, Apr 13
Sills, Beverly: Birth, May 25
Silver Bells in the City (Lansing, MI), Nov 17
Silver, Joel: Birth, Jul 14
Silver, Ron: Birth, Jul 2
Silverman, Fred: Birth, Sep 13
Silverman, Jonathan: Birth, Aug 5
Silverstein, Shel: Birth Anniv, Oct 18
Silverstone, Alicia: Birth, Oct 4
Simchat Torah, Oct 15
Simenon, Georges: Birth Anniv, Feb 12
Simmons, Gene: Birth, Aug 25
Simmons, J.K.: Birth, Jan 9
Simmons, Jean: Birth, Jan 31
Simmons, Joseph "Run": Birth, Nov 14
Simmons, Richard: Birth, Jul 12
Simms, Hilda: Birth Anniv, Apr 15
Simms, Phil: Birth, Nov 3
Simon, Carly: Birth, Jun 25
Simon, Neil: Birth, Jul 4
Simon, Paul: Birth, Oct 13
Simone, Nina: Birth Anniv, Feb 21
Simplify Your Life Week, Aug 1
Simplon Tunnel Opening: Anniv, May 19
Simpson, Jessica: Birth, Jul 10
Simpson, O.J.: Birth, Jul 9
Simpsons TV Premiere: Anniv, Dec 17
Sinai Day (Egypt), Apr 25
Sinatra, Frank: Birth Anniv, Dec 12
Sinatra, Nancy: Birth, Jun 8
Sinbad: Birth, Nov 10
Sinclair Lewis Days (Sauk Centre, MN), Jul 9
Sinclair, Upton: Birth Anniv, Sep 20
Sinden, Donald: Birth, Oct 9
Singapore
   National Day, **Aug 9**
   Vesak Day, **May 10**
Singh, Vijay: Birth, Feb 22
Singin' in the Rain Film Premiere: Anniv, Mar 27
Singing Telegram: Anniv, Jul 28
Single: Satisfied Staying Single Day, Feb 11
Singles Week, Natl, Sep 17
Singletary, Mike: Birth, Oct 9
Single-Tasking Day, Feb 21
Singleton, John: Birth, Jan 6
Singleton, Raynoma Gordy: Birth, Mar 8
Sing-Out Day, Intl, Sep 15
Sinise, Gary: Birth, Mar 17
Sinkie Day, Nov 24
Sioux Empire Fair (Sioux Falls, SD), Aug 8
Sioux Empire Farm Show (Sioux Falls, SD), Jan 24
Sirani, Elisabetta: Birth Anniv, Jan 8
Sirica, John: Birth Anniv, Mar 19
Sirk, Douglas: Birth Anniv, Apr 26
Sisley, Alfred: Birth Anniv, Oct 30
Sisters' Day, Aug 6
Sisters: Siblings Day, Natl, Apr 10
Sitting Bull: Death Anniv, Dec 15
Six Million Dollar Man TV Premiere: Anniv, Oct 20
$64,000 Question TV Premiere: Anniv, Jun 7
16th Street Baptist Church Bombing: Anniv, Sep 15
Sixty Minutes TV Premiere: Anniv, Sep 24
Skaggs, Ricky: Birth, Jul 18
Skagit Valley Tulip Fest (Burlington, WA), Apr 1
Skating (Ice, Inline, Roller)
   National Roller Skating Month, **Oct 1**
   Skating Week, Natl, **Jan 14**
Skeptics' Days, Intl, Jan 13
Skerritt, Tom: Birth, Aug 25
Skiing
   American Birkebeiner (Cable to Hayward, WI), **Feb 23**
   NCAA Men's & Women's Skiing Chmpshps (Steamboat Springs, CO), **Mar 8**
   Toronto Ski, Snowboard and Travel Show (Toronto, ON, Canada), **Oct 12**
   Wells Fargo Bank Cup (Winter Park, CO), **Feb 24**
   Wells Fargo Boulder Mountain Tour (Sun Valley, ID), **Feb 4**
Skin Care Awareness Month, Natl, Sep 1
Skin: Rosacea Awareness Month, Apr 1
Skinner, B.F.: Birth Anniv, Mar 20
Skowhegan State Fair (Skowhegan, ME), Aug 10
Sky Awareness Week, Apr 23
Sky King TV Premiere: Anniv, Sep 16
Skye, Ione: Birth, Sep 4
Skylab Falls to Earth, Jul 11
Skyscraper, First: Anniv, May 1

Slamdance (Park City, UT), Jan 19
Slater, Christian: Birth, Aug 18
Slater, Helen: Birth, Dec 15
Slave Revolt, New York: Anniv, Apr 7
Slavery Abolished in District of Columbia: Anniv, Apr 16
Slavery, Abolition of (Jamaica), Aug 1
Slavery: First American Abolition Society Founded: Anniv, Apr 14
Slavery: Remembrance of the Slave Trade and its Abolition, Intl Day for the (UN), Aug 23
Slayton, Donald "Deke" K.: Birth Anniv, Mar 1
Sled Dogs
   Bancroft Frosty Frolics (Bancroft, ON, Canada), **Feb 12**
   Iditarod Trail Sled Dog Race (Anchorage, AK), **Mar 4**
   Klondike Days (Eagle River, WI), **Feb 18**
   Paul Bunyan Sled Dog Races (Bemidji, MN), **Feb 25**
   Sled Dogs Save Nome: Anniv, **Feb 2**
   Yukon Quest Intl 1,000-Mile Sled Dog Race (Whitehorse, YT, Canada), **Feb 11**
Sleep Awareness Week, Natl, Mar 27
Sleidanus, Johannes: Death Anniv, Oct 31
Slezak, Erika: Birth, Aug 5
Slick, Grace: Birth, Oct 30
Sloane, Hans: Birth Anniv, Apr 16
Slovakia
   Constitution Day, **Sep 1**
   Czech-Slovak Divorce: Anniv, **Jan 1**
   Liberation Day, **May 8**
   National Uprising Day, **Aug 29**
   St. Cyril and Methodius Day, **Jul 5**
Slovenia
   Culture Day, **Feb 8**
   Independence Day, **Dec 26**
   Insurrection Day, **Apr 27**
   National Day, **Jun 25**
Slovenian: St. Cyril's Parish Fest (Sheboygan, WI), Jul 16
Slovik, Eddie: Execution Anniv, Jan 31
Slovo, Joe: Birth Anniv, May 23
Slow Cooking Month, Jan 1
Slow Pitch Softball Tournament (Williamsport, PA), Jul 7
Slugs Return from Capistrano Day, May 28
Small Press Month, Mar 1
Smallpox Vaccine Discovered: Anniv, May 14
Smart, Jean: Birth, Sep 13
Smile Month, Natl, May 1
Smiley, Jane: Birth, Sep 26
Smirnoff, Yakov: Birth, Jan 24
Smith Day, Natl, Jan 6
Smith, Adam: Birth Anniv, Jun 5
Smith, Bessie: Birth Anniv, Apr 15
Smith, Bubba: Birth, Feb 28
Smith, Charles Martin: Birth, Oct 30
Smith, Emmitt: Birth, May 15
Smith, Gordon: Birth, May 25
Smith, Holland: Birth Anniv, Apr 20
Smith, Jaclyn: Birth, Oct 26
Smith, James: Death Anniv, Jul 11
Smith, Jedediah Strong: Birth Anniv, Jan 6
Smith, Joseph, Jr. and Hyrum: Death Anniv, Jun 27
Smith, Joseph, Jr: Birth Anniv, Dec 23
Smith, Kate: Birth Anniv, May 1
Smith, Kate: God Bless America First Performed: Anniv, Nov 11
Smith, Kurtwood: Birth, Jul 3
Smith, Liz: Birth, Feb 2
Smith, Maggie: Birth, Dec 28
Smith, Margaret: Birth Anniv, Dec 14
Smith, Michael J.: Birth Anniv, Apr 30
Smith, Ozzie: Birth, Dec 26
Smith, Patti: Birth, Dec 30
Smith, Red: Birth Anniv, Sep 25
Smith, Robert: Alcoholics Anonymous: Founding Anniv, Jun 10
Smith, Sammi: Birth, Aug 5
Smith, Steve: Birth, Mar 31
Smith, Thorne: Birth Anniv, Mar 27
Smith, Will: Birth, Sep 25
Smithson, James: Death Anniv, Jun 27
Smithsonian Institution Founded: Anniv, Aug 10
Smitrovich, Bill: Birth, May 16
Smits, Jimmy: Birth, Jul 9
Smits, Rik: Birth, Aug 23
Smokeout, Great American, Nov 16
Smoking, Take a New Year's Resolution to Stop Smoking, Dec 10
Smoltz, John: Birth, May 15
Smothers Brothers Fired: Anniv, Apr 4
Smothers, Dick: Birth, Nov 20
Smothers, Tom: Birth, Feb 2
Snake Hunt (Cross Fork, PA), Jun 24
Snake River Duck Race (Nome, AK), Sep 4

Snake—Space Milestones

Snake River Stampede (Nampa, ID), Jul 18
Snead, Sam: Birth Anniv, May 27
Sneak Some Zucchini onto Your Neighbors' Porch Night, Aug 8
Snider, Dee: Birth, Mar 15
Snipe Excursion and Hunt, Pro-Am (Moultrie, GA), Apr 1
Snipes, Wesley: Birth, Jul 31
Snodgrass, W.D.: Birth, Jan 5
Snow Fest (Japan), Feb 8
Snow Plow Mailbox Hockey Day, Jan 23
Snow Sculpting Competition (Rockford, IL), Jan 18
Snow White and the Seven Dwarfs Film Premiere: Anniv, Dec 21
Snow, John: Birth, Aug 2
Snow, Phoebe: Birth, Jul 17
Snowbirds Pancake Breakfast (El Centro, CA), Jan 14
Snowe, Olympia J.: Birth, Feb 21
Snowman Burning (Sault Ste. Marie, MI), Mar 20
Snowshoe Chmpshps, US Natl (Anchorage, AK), Mar 24
Snyder, Tom: Birth, May 12
Soap Box Derby, All-American (Akron, OH), Jul 29
Soap TV Premiere: Anniv, Sep 13
Sobieski, Leelee: Birth, Jun 10
Soccer
    Big Ten Men's Soccer Chmpshp (East Lansing, MI), Nov 9
    Big Ten Women's Soccer Tournament (Iowa City, IA), Nov 2
    Dallas Cup (Frisco, TX), Apr 9
    NAIA Men's & Women's Natl Chmpshps, Nov 15
    National Soccer Coaches Assn of America Natl Conv (Philadelphia, PA), Jan 18
    NCAA Div I Men's Soccer Chmpshp, Dec 1
    NCAA Div I Women's Soccer Chmpshp, Dec 1
    Pele Scores 1,000th Goal: Anniv, Nov 19
    Soccer Tragedy (Belgium): Anniv, May 29
    Soccer Tragedy, Moscow: Anniv, Oct 20
    World Cup (Germany), Jun 9
    World Cup Inaugurated: Anniv, Jul 13
Social Security Act: Anniv, Aug 14
Social Security Check Issued, First: Anniv, Jan 31
Social Wellness Month, Jul 1
Sodbuster Days (Fort Ransom, ND), Jul 8
Soderbergh, Steven: Birth, Jan 14
Softball. See also Baseball
    Big 12 Women's Softball Chmpshp (Oklahoma City), May 10
    Big Ten Softball Tournament, May 11
    NAIA Softball Chmpshp (Decatur, AL), May 19
    NCAA Div I Softball Chmpshp (Oklahoma City), Jun 1
    Slow Pitch Softball Tournament (Williamsport, PA), Jul 7
    365-Inning Softball Game: Anniv, Aug 14
Soil Stewardship Sunday: See Rural Life Sunday, May 21
Soldiers' Reunion Celebration (Newton, NC), Aug 17
Solemnity of Mary, Jan 1
Solidarity Granted Legal Status: Anniv, Apr 17
Solidarity with Palestinian People, Intl Day of (UN), Nov 29
Solidarity with the Peoples of Non-Self-Governing Territories, Week of (UN), May 25
Solo Diners Eat Out Week, Feb 1
Solomon Islands: Independence Day, Jul 7
Solo-Preneuring Week, Jan 22
Solstice, Summer, Jun 21
Solstice, Winter, Dec 22
Solti, Georg: Birth Anniv, Oct 21
Solzhenitsyn, Aleksandr: Birth, Dec 11
Somalia: National Day, Jul 1
Someday, Sep 15
Someday We'll Laugh About This Week, Jan 2
Somers, Suzanne: Birth, Oct 16
Sommer, Elke: Birth, Nov 5
Sondheim, Stephen: Birth, Mar 22
Sonora Showcase (Yuma, AZ), Jan 24
Sopranos TV Premiere: Anniv, Jan 13
Sorbo, Kevin: Birth, Sep 24
Sorenstam, Annika: Birth, Oct 9
Sorghum Day Fest (Wewoka, OK), Oct 28
Soriano, Alfonso: Birth, Jan 7
Soros, George: Birth, Aug 12
Sorry Charlie Day, Apr 1
Sorvino, Paul: Birth, Apr 13
SOS Adopted: Anniv, Nov 3
Sosa, Sammy: Birth, Nov 12
Soul Food Month, Natl, Jun 1
Soul, David: Birth, Aug 28
Sound Barrier Broken: Anniv, Oct 14
Sound of Music Film Premiere: Anniv, Mar 2

Sounds of Season: Holiday Concert (Charlottesville, VA), Dec 26
Soupy Sales TV Premiere: Anniv, Jul 4
Sour Herring Premiere (Sweden), Aug 17
Sourest Day, Oct 25
Sousa, John P.: Birth Anniv, Nov 6
Sousa: Stars and Stripes Forever Day, May 14
Souter, David H.: Birth, Sep 17
South Africa
    African Natl Congress Ban Lifted: Anniv, Feb 2
    Boer War: Anniv, Oct 12
    Day of Goodwill, Dec 26
    Family Day, Apr 17
    Freedom Day, Apr 27
    Heritage Day, Sep 24
    Human Rights Day, Mar 21
    Mandela Inauguration: Anniv, May 10
    Multiracial Elections: Anniv, Apr 26
    National Women's Day, Aug 9
    New Constitution: Anniv, Nov 18
    Reconciliation Day, Dec 16
    Repeals Last Apartheid Law: Anniv, Jun 17
    Whites Vote to End Minority Rule: Anniv, Mar 17
    Youth Day, Jun 16
South by Southwest (Austin, TX), Mar 10
South Carolina
    Attack on Fort Sumter: Anniv, Apr 12
    Attack on Fort Wagner: Anniv, Jul 19
    Bunny Bop and Hop (Aiken), Apr 15
    Charleston Earthquake: Anniv, Aug 31
    Charlestown Intl Antiques Show (Charleston), Mar 17
    Christmas Craft Show (Aiken), Dec 1
    Confederate Memorial Day, May 10
    Craftsmen's Christmas Classic Arts & Crafts Fest (Columbia), Nov 10
    Craftsmen's Classic Arts & Crafts Fest (Columbia), Mar 3
    Craftsmen's Classic Arts & Crafts Fest (Myrtle Beach), Aug 4
    DeMint, Jim: Birth, Sep 2
    Festival of Houses and Gardens (Charleston), Mar 16
    Fort Sumter Returned to Union Control: Anniv, Feb 17
    Fort Sumter Shelled by North: Anniv, Aug 17
    Graham, Lindsey: Birth, Jul 9
    Grand American Coon Hunt (Orangeburg), Jan 6
    Historic Pendleton Spring Jubilee (Pendleton), Apr 1
    Iris Fest (Sumter), May 25
    Lee County Cotton Fest and Agricultural Fair (Bishopville), Oct 6
    Low Country Shrimp Fest (McClellanville), May 6
    Miss South Carolina Pageant (Spartanburg), Jul 4
    Miss South Carolina Teen Competition (Spartanburg), Jun 26
    Palmetto Sportsmen's Classic (Columbia), Mar 24
    Ratification Day, May 23
    Sanford, Mark: Birth, May 28
    Secession Anniv, Dec 20
    South Carolina Fest of Flowers (Greenwood), Jun 16
    South Carolina Fest of Roses (Orangeburg), Apr 21
    Southeastern Wildlife Expo (Charleston), Feb 17
    Southern Cyclone: Anniv, Aug 24
    Spoleto Fest USA (Charleston), May 26
    Sporting Goods Assn Mgmt Conf, Natl (Hilton Head), May 7
    State Fair (Columbia), Oct 5
South Coast Writer's Conf (Gold Beach, OR), Feb 17
South Dakota
    Admission Day, Nov 2
    Badlands Natl Park Established: Anniv, Nov 10
    Beach Party (Deadwood), Mar 11
    Black Hills Passion Play (Spearfish), Jun 1
    Black Hills Roundup (Belle Fourche), Jul 2
    Black Hills Stock Show and Rodeo (Rapid City), Jan 27
    Buffalo Roundup (Custer), Oct 2
    Buffalo Roundup Arts Fest (Custer), Sep 30
    Buffalo Wallow Chili Cookoff (Custer), Oct 1
    Center of Nation All-Car Rally (Belle Fourche), Jun 10
    Corn Palace Fest (Mitchell), Aug 30
    Custer State Park Buffalo Auction (Custer), Nov 18
    Czech Days (Tabor), Jun 16
    Dalesburg Midsummer Fest (Vermillion), Jun 23
    Fort Sisseton Historical Fest (Lake City), Jun 3
    Gold Discovery Days (Custer), Jul 21
    Homesteader Harvest Fest (Brandon), Sep 10
    Johnson, Tim: Birth, Dec 28
    Laura Ingalls Wilder Pageant (De Smet), Jul 7
    Mount Rushmore July 4 Celebration (Mount Rushmore), Jul 3
    Native Americans' Day, Oct 9

Prairie Village Jamboree (Madison), Aug 25
Red Cloud Indian Art Show (Pine Ridge), Jun 4
Rounds, Mike: Birth, Oct 24
Schmeckfest (Freeman), Mar 24
Sioux Empire Fair (Sioux Falls), Aug 8
Sioux Empire Farm Show (Sioux Falls), Jan 24
State Fair (Huron), Sep 2
Sturgis Rally (Sturgis), Aug 7
Thune, John R.: Birth, Jan 7
Wind Cave Natl Park Established: Anniv, Jan 3
South Korea
    Armed Forces Day, Oct 1
    Children's Day, May 5
    Federation of Library Assns Annual Conf, Intl (Seoul), Aug 20
South Pole Discovery: Anniv, Dec 14
South Texas Ranching Heritage Fest (Kingsville, TX), Mar 3
South Texas Wildlife and Birding Fest (Kingsville, TX), Nov 17
Southeast Missouri District Fair (Cape Girardeau, MO), Sep 9
Southeastern Wildlife Expo (Charleston, SC), Feb 17
Southern Belles Month, Apr 1
Southern Fest of Books (Memphis, TN), Oct 13
Southern Hemisphere Hoodie-Hoo Day, Aug 23
Soviet Georgia Votes Independence: Anniv, Mar 31
Soviet Union Invaded: Anniv, Jun 22
Sowerby, Leo: Birth Anniv, May 1
Soyinka, Wole: Birth, Jul 13
Space (excluding Space Milestones)
    Aerospace Walk of Honor (Lancaster, CA), Sep 16
    Apollo I: Spacecraft Fire: Anniv, Jan 27
    Astronomers Find New Solar System: Anniv, Apr 15
    Challenger Space Shuttle Explosion: Anniv, Jan 28
    Christmas Greetings from Space: Anniv, Dec 19
    Closest Approach of a Comet to Earth: Anniv, Feb 20
    Comet Crashes into Jupiter: Anniv, Jul 16
    Gagarin, Yuri: Birth Anniv, Mar 9
    Jupiter Effect: Anniv, Mar 10
    NASA Established: Anniv, Jul 29
    Near Miss Day, Mar 23
    Ozark UFO Conf (Eureka Springs, AR), Apr 14
    Shuttle Camp (Alamogordo, NM), Jun 5
    Soviet Cosmonaut Returns to New Country: Anniv, Mar 26
    Space Shuttle Columbia Disaster: Anniv, Feb 1
    Titan 34-D Rocket Failure: Anniv, Apr 18
    Windstorms Discovered: Anniv, Nov 7
    World Space Week (UN), Oct 4
Space Milestones
    Year 1 (1957)
        Sputnik 1, Oct 4
        Sputnik 2, Nov 3
    Year 2 (1958)
        Explorer 1, Jan 31
        Vanguard 1, Mar 17
        Atlas—Christmas Greetings from Space, Dec 19
    Year 3 (1959)
        Luna 1, Jan 2
        First Picture of Earth from Space, Aug 7
        Luna 2, Sept 12
        Luna 3, Oct 4
    Year 4 (1960)
        Echo 1, Aug 12
        Sputnik 5, Aug 19
    Year 5 (1961)
        Project Mercury Test, Jan 31
        Vostok 1, Apr 12
        Freedom 7, May 5
        Vostok 2, Aug 6
    Year 6 (1962)
        Friendship 7, Feb 20
        Aurora 7, May 24
        Telstar, July 10
        Vostok 3, Aug 11
    Year 7 (1963)
        Faith 7, May 15
        Vostok 6, June 16
    Year 8 (1964)
        Mariner 4, Nov 28
    Year 9 (1965)
        Voskhod 2, Mar 18
        Gemini 3, June 3
        Gemini 5, Aug 21
        Pegasus 1, Sept 17
        Venera 3, Nov 16
    Year 10 (1966)
        Luna 9, Jan 31
        Gemini 8, Mar 16
        Gemini 12, Nov 11
    Year 11 (1967)
        Venera 4, June 12
        Mariner 5, June 14

Year 12 (1968)
OGO 5, **Mar 4**
Soyuz 3, **Oct 26**
Apollo 8, **Dec 21**
Year 13 (1969)
Soyuz 4, **Jan 14**
Apollo 10, **May 18**
Apollo 11, **July 16**
Moon Day, **July 20**
Apollo 12, **Nov 14**
Year 14 (1970)
Osumi, **Feb 11**
Apollo 13, **Apr 11**
China 1, **Apr 24**
Space Rescue Agreement, **Oct 28**
Year 15 (1971)
Apollo 14, **Jan 31**
Salyut, **Apr 19**
Soyuz 10, **Apr 23**
Mars 2 and Mars 3, **May 19**
Mariner 9, **May 30**
Soyuz 11, **June 6**
Apollo 15, **July 26**
Intelsat 4 F-3, **Dec 19**
Year 16 (1972)
Pioneer 10, **Mar 2**
Venera 8, **Mar 27**
Apollo 16, **Apr 16**
Copernicus OAO 4, **Apr 21**
Apollo 17, **Dec 7**
Year 17 (1973)
Skylab, **May 14**
Skylab 2, **May 25**
Skylab 3, **July 28**
Intelsat-4 F-7, **Aug 23**
Soyuz 12, **Sept 27**
Skylab 4, **Nov 16**
Year 19 (1975)
Soyuz 17, **Jan 10**
Venera 9 and 10, **June 8**
Apollo-Soyuz Test Project, **July 17**
Viking 1 and 2, **Aug 20**
Year 20 (1976)
Soyuz 21, **July 6**
Year 21 (1977)
Cosmos 954 Falls, **Jan 24**
Enterprise, **Aug 12**
Voyager 2, **Aug 20**
Voyager 1, **Sept 5**
Salyut 6, **Sept 29**
Soyuz 26, **Dec 10**
Year 22 (1978)
Cosmos 954, **Jan 24**
Soyuz 27, **Jan 10**
Soyuz 28, **Mar 2**
Pioneer Venus 1, **May 20**
Pioneer Venus, **Aug 8**
Soyuz 31, **Aug 26**
Pegasus 1, **Sept 17**
Year 23 (1979)
Soyuz 32, **Feb 25**
Skylab Falls to Earth, **July 11**
Year 24 (1980)
SMM, **Feb 14**
Soyuz 35, **Apr 9**
Soyuz T-2, **June 5**
Rohini 1, **July 18**
Soyuz 37, **July 23**
Soyuz T-3, **Nov 27**
Year 25 (1981)
Columbia STS-1, **Apr 12**
Ariane, **June 19**
Columbia STS-2, **Nov 12**
Year 26 (1982)
Kosmos 1383, **July 1**
Soyuz T-7, **Aug 19**
Columbia STS-5, **Nov 11**
Year 27 (1983)
NOAA 8, **Mar 28**
Challenger STS-6, **Apr 4**
Challenger STS-7, **June 18**
Challenger STS-8, **Aug 30**
Columbia STS-9, **Nov 28**
Year 28 (1984)
Challenger STS-10, **Feb 3**
Soyuz T-12, **July 17**
Discovery, **Aug 30**
Challenger STS 41-G, **Oct 5**
Vega 1, **Dec 15**
Year 29 (1985)
Discovery, **Jan 24**
Arabsat-1, **Feb 8**
Brasilsat 1, **Feb 8**
Discovery, **Apr 12**
Challenger STS 51-B, **Apr 29**
Year 30 (1986)
Mir Space Station, **Feb 20**
Titan 34-D, **Apr 18**

Delta 3914 Rocket Failure, **May 3**
Year 31 (1987)
Soyuz TM-3, **July 22**
Ariane-3, **Sept 15**
Year 32 (1988)
Phobos 2, **July 12**
Discovery, **Sept 29**
Buran, **Nov 15**
Year 33 (1989)
Atlantis, **May 4**
Voyager 2 Reaches Neptune, **Aug 24**
Year 34 (1990)
First Soviet Commercial Satellite, **Feb 11**
Hubble Space Telescope, **Apr 25**
Year 36 (1992)
Endeavour, **May 13**
Year 39 (1995)
Atlantis Docks with Mir, **June 29**
Galileo, **Dec 7**
Record Time, **Mar 22**
Year 41 (1997)
Mars Pathfinder, **July 4**
Mars Global Surveyor, **Sept 11**
Cassini, **Oct 15**
Year 42 (1998)
Lunar Explorer, **Jan 6**
Discovery: Oldest Man in Space, **Oct 29**
International Space Station Launch, **Dec 4**
Year 43 (1999)
Stardust, **Feb 7**
Columbia: First Female Commander, **July 23**
Year 44 (2000)
Endeavour Mapping Mission, **Feb 11**
Near Orbits Asteroid, **Feb 14**
100th Space Shuttle Flight, **Oct 11**
ISS Inhabited, **Nov 2**
Year 45 (2001)
100th Spacewalk, **Feb 14**
Mir Abandoned, **Mar 23**
Mars Odyssey, **Apr 7**
First Tourist in Space, **Apr 28**
Genesis, **Aug 8**
Helios Solar Wing, **Aug 13**
Year 48 (2004)
Mars Exploration Rover Spirit, **Jan 3**
First Manned Private Spaceflight, **June 21**
Cassini-Huygens Reaches Saturn, **July 1**
Year 49 (2005)
Deep Impact Smashes into Tempel 1, **July 4**
Spacek, Sissy: Birth, **Dec 25**
Spacey, Kevin: Birth, **Jul 26**
Spade, David: Birth, **Jul 22**
Spader, James: Birth, **Feb 7**
Spahn, Warren: Birth, **Apr 23**
Spain
Book Day and Lover's Day, **Apr 23**
Canary Islands Plane Disaster: Anniv, **Mar 27**
Civil War Begins: Anniv, **Jul 18**
Constitution Day, **Dec 6**
Fiesta de Las Fallas (Valencia), **Mar 12**
International Congress of Mathematicians (Madrid), **Aug 22**
La Tomatina, **Aug 30**
Madrid Train Bombings: Anniv, **Mar 11**
National Holiday, **Oct 12**
Running of the Bulls, **Jul 7**
Saint James Day, **Jul 25**
San Sebastian Jazz Fest (San Sebastian), **Jul 22**
Spain Captures Granada: Anniv, **Jan 2**
Spanish Flu: Pandemic of 1918 Hits US: Anniv, Mar 11
Spanish-American War
Maine Memorial Day, **Feb 15**
Matanzas Mule Day, **Apr 27**
Remember the Maine Day, **Feb 15**
Spanish-American War: Surrender of Guam to US: Anniv, **Jun 20**
Treaty of Paris Signed: Anniv, **Dec 10**
Spank Out Day USA, Apr 30
Spano, Vincent: Birth, **Oct 18**
Spassky, Boris: Birth, **Jan 30**
Spay Day USA, Feb 28
Speak Up and Succeed Day, Natl, Jan 24
Speaking: Freedom from Fear of Speaking Week, Jul 2
Speaking: Professional Speakers Day, Aug 7
Spears, Britney: Birth, **Dec 2**
Special Education Day, Dec 2
Special Kids Day (Elmhurst, IL), Dec 6
Special Olympics Day, Jul 20
Special Olympics Winter Games (McHenry, MD), Feb 24
Special Recreation Day, Jul 2
Specter, Arlen: Birth, **Feb 12**
Spector, Phil: Birth, **Dec 26**
Speech Month, Better Hearing and, May 1
Speech-Language-Hearing Conv, American (Miami, FL), Nov 16

Spelling Bee Finals, Natl, **May 31**
Spelling, Aaron: Birth, **Apr 22**
Spelling, Tori: Birth, **May 16**
Spellings, Margaret: Birth, **Nov 30**
Spelman College Established: Anniv, **Apr 11**
Spelvin, George: Day, **Nov 15**
Spencer, John: Birth, **Dec 20**
Spengler, Oswald: Birth Anniv, **May 29**
Spielberg, Steven: Birth, **Dec 18**
Spielberg, Steven: Jaws Film Release: Anniv, **Jun 20**
Spillane, Mickey: Birth, **Mar 9**
Spina Bifida Awareness Month, Natl, **Oct 1**
Spinach Lovers Month, **Oct 1**
Spinal Health Month, Natl, **Oct 1**
Spinal Muscular Atrophy Awareness Month, **Aug 1**
Spinks, Leon: Birth, **Jul 11**
Spinks, Michael: Birth, **Jul 13**
Spinning and Weaving Week, **Oct 2**
Spinoza, Baruch: Birth Anniv, **Nov 24**
Spirit of Freedom Celebration (Florence, AL), **Jul 4**
Spiritual Literacy Month, **Dec 1**
Spiritual Wellness Month, **Mar 1**
Spitz, Mark: Birth, **Feb 10**
Splurge Day, Natl, **Jun 18**
Spock, Benjamin: Birth Anniv, **May 2**
Spoleto Fest USA (Charleston, SC), **May 26**
Spoon River Valley Scenic Drive (Lewistown, IL), **Oct 7**
Spoon River Valley: Knox County Scenic Drive (Galesburg, IL), **Oct 7**
Spooner, William: Birth Anniv, **Jul 22**
Spooner's Day, **Jul 22**
Sporting Goods Assn Mgmt Conf, Natl (Hilton Head, SC), **May 7**
Sports America Kids Month, **Jun 1**
Sports Cliché Week, **Jul 9**
Sports Show, Milwaukee Journal Sentinel (Milwaukee, WI), **Mar 10**
Sports, Physical Fitness and, Month, Natl, **May 1**
Sportsmen's Show, Toronto (Toronto, ON, Canada), **Mar 15**
Spradlin, G.D.: Birth, **Aug 31**
Sprewell, Latrell: Birth, **Sep 8**
Spring Begins, **Mar 20**
Spring Fest, Towsontown (Towson, MD), **May 6**
Spring Fever Week, Natl, **Mar 20**
Spring Gala (Lovington, NM), **May 6**
Spring Market Fair, Eighteenth-Century (McLean, VA), **May 20**
Spring Suwannee River Gospel Jubilee (Live Oak, FL), **Jun 14**
Springer, Jerry: Birth, **Feb 13**
Springfield, Rick: Birth, **Aug 23**
Springs Folk Fest (Springs, PA), **Oct 6**
Springsteen, Bruce: Birth, **Sep 23**
Spruce Goose Flight: Anniv, **Nov 2**
Spurrier, Steve: Birth, **Apr 20**
Sputnik 1: Anniv, **Oct 4**
Squirrel Appreciation Day, **Jan 21**
Squirrel Awareness Week, **Oct 1**
Sri Lanka
Independence Day, **Feb 4**
National Heroes Day, **May 22**
Sinhala and Tamil New Year, **Apr 13**
St. John, Jill: Birth, **Aug 19**
St. Laurent, Louis Stephen: Birth Anniv, **Feb 1**
Stabenow, Debbie: Birth, **Apr 29**
Stackhouse, Jerry: Birth, **Nov 5**
Stade, Frederica von: Birth, **Jun 1**
Stagecoach Days (Marshall, TX), **May 20**
Stagg, Amos Alonzo: Birth Anniv, **Aug 16**
Stahl, Lesley: Birth, **Dec 16**
Staley, Dawn: Birth, **May 4**
Stalin, Joseph: Birth Anniv, **Dec 21**
Stalingrad, German Surrender at: Anniv, **Feb 2**
Stallone, Sylvester: Birth, **Jul 6**
Stamos, John: Birth, **Aug 19**
Stamp Out Hunger—NALC National Food Drive, **May 13**
Stamp, Terence: Birth, **Jul 22**
Stamps
Nevadapex Coin and Stamp Expo (Laughlin, NV), **Jan 6**
Postage Stamps, First US: Anniv, **Jul 1**
Stamp & Coin Expo (New York, NY), **Apr 21**
Stamp Expo (Anaheim, CA), **May 5, Sep 8**
Stamp Expo (Los Angeles, CA), **Mar 31**
Stamp Expo (Pasadena, CA), **Feb 17, May 19, Jun 30**
Stamp Expo (Sherman Oaks, CA), **Jun 16**
Stamp Expo America (Anaheim, CA), **Nov 10**
Stamp Expo USA (Anaheim, CA), **Feb 10**
Stamp Expo: Anaheim (Anaheim, CA), **Oct 6**
Stamp Expo: California (Pasadena, CA), **Nov 17**

☆ Chase's 2006 Calendar of Events ☆

Stamps (cont'd)—Sullivan

Stamp Expo: South (Anaheim, CA), **Apr 28**
Washington 2006—World Philatelic Exhibition (Washington, DC), **May 27**
Standard Time Act, US: Anniv, Mar 19
Standing Bear: Native American Rights Recognized: Anniv, May 12
Stanhope, Philip D.: Birth Anniv, Sep 22
Stanley Finds Livingstone: Anniv, Nov 10
Stanley, Henry Morton: Birth Anniv, Jan 28
Stanton, Elizabeth Cady: Birth Anniv, Nov 12
Stanton, Harry Dean: Birth, Jul 14
Stanwyck, Barbara: Birth Anniv, Jul 16
Stapleton, Jean: Birth, Jan 19
Stapleton, Maureen: Birth, Jun 21
Star Fest (Tanabata) (Japan), Jul 7
Star Trek TV Premiere: Anniv, Sep 8
Star Wars Released: Anniv, May 25
Stark, USS Attacked: Anniv, May 17
Starker, Janos: Birth, Jul 5
Starman Family-Con 2006 (Hollywood, CA), Sep 15
Starman Month, Intl, Oct 1
Starr, Bart: Birth, Jan 9
Starr, Ringo: Birth, Jul 7
Stars and Stripes Forever Day, May 14
Star-Spangled Banner Inspired: Anniv, Sep 13
State Dept Founded, US: Anniv, Jul 27
State Fairs
  Alabama Natl Fair (Montgomery, AL), Oct 6
  Alaska State Fair (Palmer, AK), Aug 24
  Arkansas State Fair (Little Rock, AR), Oct 13
  Bangor State Fair (Bangor, ME), Jul 28
  California State Fair (Sacramento, CA), Aug 11
  Colorado State Fair (Pueblo, CO), Aug 25
  Delaware State Fair (Harrington, DE), Jul 20
  Eastern Idaho State Fair (Blackfoot, ID), Sep 2
  Florida State Fair (Tampa, FL), Feb 9
  Georgia National Fair (Perry, GA), Oct 6
  Illinois State Fair (Springfield, IL), Aug 11
  Indiana State Fair (Indianapolis, IN), Aug 9
  Iowa State Fair (Des Moines, IA), Aug 10
  Kansas State Fair (Hutchinson, KS), Sep 8
  Kentucky State Fair (Louisville, KY), Aug 17
  Louisiana, State Fair of (Shreveport, LA), Oct 26
  Maryland State Fair (Timonium, MD), Aug 25
  Michigan State Fair (Detroit, MI), Aug 9
  Minnesota State Fair (St. Paul, MN), Aug 24
  Mississippi State Fair (Jackson, MS), Oct 4
  Missouri State Fair (Sedalia, MO), Aug 10
  Montana State Fair (Great Falls, MT), Jul 28
  Nebraska State Fair (Lincoln, NE), Aug 26
  Nevada State Fair (Reno, NV), Aug 17
  New Jersey State Fair/Sussex Farm and Horse Show (Augusta, NJ), Aug 4
  New York State Fair (Syracuse, NY), Aug 24
  North Carolina State Fair (Raleigh, NC), Oct 13
  North Dakota State Fair (Minot, ND), Jul 21
  Ohio State Fair (Columbus, OH), Aug 2
  Oklahoma State Fair (Oklahoma City, OK), Sep 14
  Oregon State Fair (Salem, OR), Aug 25
  South Carolina State Fair (Columbia, SC), Oct 5
  South Dakota State Fair (Huron, SD), Sep 2
  State Fair of Texas (Dallas, TX), Sep 29
  Tennessee State Fair (Nashville, TN), Sep 8
  Utah State Fair (Salt Lake City, UT), Sep 7
  Vermont State Fair (Rutland, VT), Sep 1
  Virginia, State Fair of (Richmond, VA), Sep 21
  West Virginia State Fair (Lewisburg, WV), Aug 11
  Western Idaho Fair (Boise, ID), Aug 18
  Wisconsin State Fair (Milwaukee, WI), Aug 3
  Wyoming State Fair & Rodeo (Douglas, WY), Aug 12
Stationery Show, Natl (New York, NY), May 21
Statue of Liberty: Dedication Anniv, Oct 28
Staub, Rusty: Birth, Apr 1
Staubach, Roger: Birth, Feb 5
Staunton, Imelda: Birth, Jan 9
Stay Home Because You're Well Day, Nov 30
Stay Out of the Sun Day, Jul 3
Steakhouse Month, Natl, Jun 1
Stealth Bomber Flight: Anniv, Jul 17
Steel Mills, Fed Govt Seizure: Anniv, Apr 8
Steel, Danielle: Birth, Aug 14
Steele, Tommy: Birth, Dec 17
Steenburgen, Mary: Birth, Feb 8
Steeplechase at Callaway Gardens (Pine Mountain, GA), Nov 4
Stefani, Gwen: Birth, Oct 3
Steichen, Edward: Birth Anniv, Mar 27
Steig, William: Birth Anniv, Nov 14
Steiger, Rod: Birth Anniv, Apr 17
Stein, Ben: Birth, Nov 25
Stein, Gertrude: Birth Anniv, Feb 3
Steinberg, David: Birth, Aug 9
Steinbrenner, George: Birth, Jul 4
Steinem, Gloria: Birth, Mar 25
Stella, Frank: Birth, May 12
Stendhal: Birth Anniv, Jan 23

Stengel, Casey: Birth Anniv, Jul 30
Stephens, James: Birth, May 18
Stephenson, George: Birth Anniv, Jun 9
Stephenson, Jan: Birth, Dec 22
Stepmothers Day, May 1
Stepparents' Week, Jun 1
Sterling Renaissance Fest (Sterling, NY), Jul 1
Stern, Daniel: Birth, Aug 28
Stern, Howard: Birth, Jan 12
Stern, Howard: Radio Show Premiere: Anniv, Nov 18
Sterne, Laurence: Birth Anniv, Nov 24
Sternhagen, Frances: Birth, Jan 13
Sternwheel Fest, Ohio River (Marietta, OH), Sep 8
Steve Allen Show TV Premiere: Anniv, Dec 25
Stevens, Cat: Birth, Jul 21
Stevens, Connie: Birth, Aug 8
Stevens, Fisher: Birth, Nov 27
Stevens, John Paul: Birth, Apr 20
Stevens, Stella: Birth, Oct 1
Stevens, Ted: Birth, Nov 18
Stevenson, Adlai: Birth Anniv, Oct 23
Stevenson, Adlai: Birth Anniv, Feb 5
Stevenson, Alexandra: Birth, Dec 15
Stevenson, Parker: Birth, Jun 4
Stevenson, Robert Louis: Birth Anniv, Nov 13
Stewart, Don: Birth, Nov 14
Stewart, Earnie: Birth, Mar 28
Stewart, French: Birth, Feb 20
Stewart, Jackie: Birth, Jun 11
Stewart, James: Birth Anniv, May 20
Stewart, James: It's a Wonderful Life Film Premiere: Anniv, Dec 20
Stewart, Jon: Birth, Nov 28
Stewart, Kordell: Birth, Oct 16
Stewart, Martha: Birth, Aug 3
Stewart, Patrick: Birth, Jul 13
Stewart, Potter: Birth Anniv, Jan 23
Stewart, Rod: Birth, Jan 10
Stiers, David Ogden: Birth, Oct 31
Stiles, Julia: Birth, Mar 28
Stiles, Ryan: Birth, Apr 22
Still Need To Do Day, Dec 29
Still, Valerie: Birth, May 14
Stiller, Ben: Birth, Nov 30
Stiller, Jerry: Birth, Jun 8
Stills, Stephen: Birth, Jan 3
Stilts: Walk on Stilts Day, Jul 27
Stine, R.L.: Birth, Oct 8
Sting (Gordon Sumner): Birth, Oct 2
Stipe, Michael: Birth, Jan 4
Stock Exchange Holiday, Jan 2, Jan 16, Feb 20, Apr 14, May 29, Jul 4, Sep 4, Nov 23, Dec 25
Stock Exchange, NY, Established: Anniv, May 17
Stock Market Crash (1929): Anniv, Oct 29
Stock Market Crash of 1893: Anniv, May 5
Stock Market Panic: Anniv, Oct 24
Stockholm Syndrome Bank Robbery: Anniv, Aug 23
Stockings, Nylon: Anniv, May 15
Stocks: Dow-Jones Biggest Drop: Anniv, Oct 19
Stocks: Dow-Jones Industrial Average: Anniv, Oct 7
Stocks: Dow-Jones Tops 1,000: Anniv, Nov 14
Stocks: Dow-Jones Tops 3,000: Anniv, Apr 17
Stocks: Dow-Jones Tops 5,000: Anniv, Nov 21
Stocks: Dow-Jones Tops 6,000: Anniv, Oct 14
Stocks: Dow-Jones Tops 10,000: Anniv, Mar 29
Stocks: Dow-Jones Tops 11,000: Anniv, May 3
Stockton, David: Birth, Nov 2
Stockton, John: Birth, Mar 26
Stockton, Richard: Birth Anniv, Oct 1
Stockwell, Dean: Birth, Mar 5
Stockwell, John: Birth, Mar 25
Stojakovic, Peja: Birth, Jun 9
Stojko, Elvis: Birth, Mar 22
Stokes, Carl: Becomes First Black Mayor in US: Anniv, Nov 13
Stoltz, Eric: Birth, Sep 30
Stone, Dee Wallace: Birth, Dec 14
Stone, Harlan Fiske: Birth Anniv, Oct 11
Stone, Lucy: Birth Anniv, Aug 13
Stone, Oliver: Birth, Sep 15
Stone, Sharon: Birth, Mar 10
Stone, Sly: Birth, Mar 15
Stone, Steve: Birth, Jul 14
Stone, Thomas: Death Anniv, Oct 5
Stonewall Riot: Anniv, Jun 28
Stookey, Noel Paul: Birth, Nov 30
Stoppard, Tom: Birth, Jul 3
Storey, David: Birth, Jul 13
Stories Day, Apr 5
Storm, Gale: Birth, Apr 5
Story, Joseph: Birth Anniv, Sep 18
Storytelling
  Connecticut Storytelling Fest (New London, CT), Apr 28
  Iowa Storytelling Fest (Clear Lake, IA), Jul 21

Michigan Storytellers Fest (Flint, MI), Jul 7
Smoky Mountains Storytelling Fest (Pigeon Forge, TN), Feb 2
Storytelling Fest, Natl (Jonesborough, TN), Oct 6
Storytelling Historical Walk Around Washington (Washington, PA), May 20
Stotz, Carl E.: Birth Anniv, Feb 20
Stoudamire, Damon: Birth, Sep 3
Stowe, Harriet Beecher: Birth Anniv, Jun 14
Stowe, Madeleine: Birth, Aug 18
Stradivari, Antonio: Death Anniv, Dec 18
Strait, George: Birth, May 18
Straith, Claire: Birth Anniv, Aug 30
Strang, James Jesse: Birth Anniv, Mar 21
Strange, Curtis: Birth, Jan 30
Strassman, Marcia: Birth, Apr 28
Strategic Planning Month, Intl, Oct 1
Strategic Thinking Month, Intl, Sep 1
Stratemeyer, Edward L.: Birth Anniv, Oct 4
Strathairn, David: Birth, Jan 26
Stratton, Dorothy C.: Birth Anniv, Mar 24
Strauss, Levi: Birth Anniv, Feb 26
Strauss, Peter: Birth, Feb 20
Strauss, Richard G.: Birth Anniv, Jun 11
Stravinsky, Igor F.: Birth Anniv, Jun 17
Stravinsky, Igor: Rite of Spring Premiere and Riot: Anniv, May 29
Straw Hat Month, Apr 1
Strawberry Fest (Independence, MO), Jun 3
Strawberry Fest (Plant City, FL), Mar 2
Strawberry Fest, Poteet (Poteet, TX), Apr 7
Strawberry Hill Races (Richmond, VA), Apr 15
Strawberry Month, February Is Fabulous Florida, Feb 1
Strawberry, Darryl: Birth, Mar 12
Streep, Meryl: Birth, Jun 22
Street Machine Fall Nationals (Springfield, MO), Sep 15
Street, Picabo: Birth, Apr 3
Streetcar Named Desire Broadway Opening: Anniv, Dec 3
Streeter, Ruth Cheney: Birth Anniv, Oct 2
Streisand, Barbra: Birth, Apr 24
Stresa Music Weeks (Stresa, Italy), Jul 26
Stress Awareness Day, Natl, Apr 18
Stress Awareness Month, Apr 1
Stress Management: Zero-Tasking Day, Oct 30
Stress: Life Balance Month, Intl, Jan 1
Stress-Free Family Holidays Month, Natl, Dec 1
Strickland, Rod: Birth, Jul 11
Strike It Rich TV Premiere: Anniv, May 7
Strindberg, August: Birth Anniv, Jan 22
Stringfield, Sherry: Birth, Jun 24
Stritch, Elaine: Birth, Feb 2
Stroke Awareness Month, Natl, May 1
Strokes Day, Strike Out, May 1
Strong, Rider: Birth, Dec 11
Stroud, Don: Birth, Sep 1
Strug, Kerri: Birth, Nov 19
Struthers, Sally: Birth, Jul 28
Stuart, Gilbert: Birth Anniv, Dec 3
Student Government Day (MA), Apr 7
Student Safety Month, Jun 1
Students' Memorial Day, Kent State, May 4
Stupid Guy Thing Day, Jun 22
Sturges, John: Birth Anniv, Jan 3
Sturgis Rally and Races, Aug 7
Stuttering Awareness Day, Intl, Oct 22
Stuttering Awareness Week, Natl, May 8
Styron, William: Birth, Jun 11
Subliminal Communications Month, Sep 1
Submarine: First Nuclear-Powered Voyage: Anniv, Jan 17
Substitute Teacher Appreciation Week, Sep 18
Subway Accident, New York: Anniv, Nov 2
Subway, New York City: Subway Anniv, Oct 27
Succoth, Oct 7
Suchet, David: Birth, May 2
Sudan
  Independence Day, Jan 1
  Revolution Day, Jun 30
Sudden Infant Death Syndrome Awareness Month, Natl, Oct 1
Suez Canal Formal Opening: Anniv, Nov 17
Suez Canal Opens: Anniv, Mar 7
Suez Canal: Evacuation Day (Egypt), Jun 18
Suffrage Parade Attacked, Woman: Anniv, Mar 3
Sugar Bowl, Nokia (New Orleans, LA), Jan 2
Suicide Prevention Week, Natl, Sep 10
Sukkot, Oct 7
Sukkot Begins, Oct 6
Sullivan, Anne: Birth Anniv, Apr 14
Sullivan, Anne: Helen Keller's Miracle: Anniv, Apr 5
Sullivan, Arthur: Birth Anniv, May 13
Sullivan, Ed: Birth Anniv, Sep 28
Sullivan, Erik Per: Birth, Jul 12
Sullivan, Louis: Birth Anniv, Sep 3

Sullivan, Susan: Birth, Nov 18
Sultana Explosion: Anniv, Apr 27
Sulzberger, Arthur O.: Birth, Sep 22
Sumac, Yma: Birth, Sep 10
Sumatran-Andaman Earthquake and Tsunamis: Anniv, Dec 26
Summer Arrival: Martin Z. Mollusk Day (Ocean City, NJ), May 4
Summer Begins, Jun 21
Summer Daylight-Saving Time (Europe), Mar 26
Summer Farm Toy Show (Dyersville, IA), Jun 2
Summer Market Fair, Eighteenth-Century (McLean, VA), Jul 15
Summer Music Fest (Sitka, AK), Jun 2
Summer Time (United Kingdom), Mar 27
Summer, Donna: Birth, Dec 31
Summerfest (Milwaukee, WI), Jun 29
Summers, Lawrence: Birth, Nov 30
Summitt, Patricia (Pat): Birth, Jun 14
Sumner, Charles, Attacked in the Senate: Anniv, May 22
Sumner, Gordon (Sting): Birth, Oct 2
Sun Bowl (El Paso, TX), Dec 29
Sun Yat-Sen: Birth Anniv, Nov 12
Sun Yat-Sen: Death Anniv, Mar 12
Sundance Film Festival (Park City, UT), Jan 19
Sunday School Teacher Appreciation Day, Oct 15
Sunday, Billy: Birth Anniv, Nov 19
Sununu, John: Birth, Sep 10
Super Bowl (Detroit, MI), Feb 5
Super Bowl, First: Anniv, Jan 15
Superman Celebration (Metropolis, IL), Jun 8
Superman Debuts: Anniv, Jun 1
Support Your Local Chamber of Commerce Day, Natl, Oct 18
Supreme Court
  Abortion Notification Ruling: Anniv, Jun 25
  Bans School Prayer: Anniv, Jun 25
  Brown v Board of Education: Anniv, May 17
  Dred Scott Decision: Anniv, Mar 6
  First Session of: Anniv, Feb 1
  First Woman Justice: Anniv, Sep 25
  Loving v Virginia: Anniv, Jun 12
  Miranda Decision: Anniv, Jun 13
  Roe v Wade Decision: Anniv, Jan 22
  Rules for Bush: Anniv, Dec 12
  Strikes Down Connecticut Law Banning Contraception: Anniv, Jun 7
  Term Begins, Oct 2
  Thurgood Marshall Resigns: Anniv, Jun 27
  Upholds Ban on Abortion Counseling: Anniv, May 23
  Upholds Right to Die: Anniv, Jun 25
  Woman Presides Over: Anniv, Apr 3
Surfing
  Kahanamoku, Duke: Birth Anniv, Aug 24
  New England Mid-winter (Narragansett, RI), Feb 18
  Triple Crown of Surfing (Oahu, HI), Nov 13
Suriname
  Independence Day, Nov 25
  Liberation Day, Jul 1
Surratt, Mary: Lincoln Assassination Conspirators Hanging, Jul 7
Survivor TV Premiere: Anniv, May 31
Susskind, David: Birth Anniv, Dec 19
Sutcliffe, Rick: Birth, Jun 21
Sutherland, Donald: Birth, Jul 17
Sutherland, Joan: Birth, Nov 7
Sutherland, Kiefer: Birth, Dec 21
Sutter, John A.: Birth Anniv, Feb 15
Sutton Hoo Ship Burial Discovered: Anniv, May 11
Suvari, Mena: Birth, Feb 9
Suzman, Janet: Birth, Feb 9
Suzuki, Ichiro: Birth, Oct 22
Svenson, Bo: Birth, Feb 13
Swallows Depart from San Juan Capistrano (CA), Oct 23
Swallows Return to San Juan Capistrano (CA), Mar 19
Swank, Hilary: Birth, Jul 30
Swanson, Gloria: Birth Anniv, Mar 27
Swanson, Kristy: Birth, Dec 19
Swappin' Meetin' (Cumberland, KY), Oct 6
Swayze, John Cameron: Birth Anniv, Apr 4
Swayze, Patrick: Birth, Aug 18
Swaziland
  Independence Day, Sep 6
  King's Birthday, Apr 19
  National Flag Day, Apr 25
Sweat, Keith: Birth, Jul 22
Sweden
  All Saints' Day, Nov 4
  Crayfish Premiere, Aug 9
  Feast of Valborg, Apr 30
  Flag Day, Jun 6
  Gustavus Adolphus Day, Nov 6

  Linnaeus Day (Stenbrohult), May 23
  Midsummer, Jun 23
  Nobel Prize Awards Ceremony (Stockholm), Dec 10
  Saint Knut's Day, Jan 13
  Saint Martin's Day, Nov 11
  Santa Lucia Day, Dec 13
  Sour Herring Premiere, Aug 17
Swedenborg, Emanuel: Birth Anniv, Jan 29
Swedish Language and Culture Day Camp (Cambridge, MN), Aug 21
Sweeney, D.B.: Birth, Nov 14
Sweetcorn Fest, Natl (Hoopeston, IL), Aug 31
Sweetest Day, Oct 21
Swift, Jonathan: Birth Anniv, Nov 30
Swimming and Diving
  Big 12 Men's & Women's Swimming Chmpshp (Columbia, MO), Feb 22
  Big Ten Men's Swimming/Diving Chmpshps (Bloomington, IN), Feb 23
  Columbia River Cross Channel Swim (Hood River, OR), Sep 4
  First Woman Swims English Channel: Anniv, Aug 6
  Kahanamoku, Duke: Birth Anniv, Aug 24
  NAIA Natl Men's and Women's Swimming/Diving Chmpshps (St. Peters, MO), Mar 1
  NCAA Men's Div I Swimming/Diving Chmpshps (Atlanta, GA), Mar 23
  NCAA Women's Div I Swimming/Diving Chmpshps (Athens, GA), Mar 16
  Penguin Plunge (Jamestown, RI), Jan 1
  Polar Bear Swim (Nome, AK), Jan 1
  Polar Bear Swim (Sheboyan, WI), Jan 1
  Swimming School Opens, First US, Jul 23
  Waikiki Roughwater Swim (Honolulu, HI), Sep 3
  Weissmuller, Johnny: Birth Anniv, Jun 2
  Women's Big Ten Swimming/Diving Chmpshps (Columbus, OH), Feb 15
Swiss Fest, Ohio (Sugarcreek, OH), Sep 29
Swit, Loretta: Birth, Nov 4
Switzerland
  Berchtoldstag, Jan 2
  Chalandra Marz, Mar 1
  Confederation Day, Aug 1
  Dornach Battle Commemoration, Jul 23
  Egg Races, Apr 17
  Homstrom (Scuol), Feb 5
  Landsgemeinde, Apr 30
  Lucerne Fest, Ostern (Lucerne), Apr 1
  Lucerne Fest, Piano (Lucerne), Nov 21
  Lucerne Fest, Sommer (Lucerne), Aug 11
  Martinmas Goose, Nov 11
  Meitlisunntig, Jan 8
  Morat Battle: Anniv, Jun 22
  Nafels Pilgrimage (Canton Glarus), Apr 6
  Onion Market (Zibelemarit), Nov 27
  Pacing the Bounds (Liestal), May 22
  Saint Gotthard Auto Tunnel Opened: Anniv, Sep 5
  Sempach Battle Commemoration, Jul 10
  World of Coffee/World Barista Championship (Berne), May 19
Swoopes, Sheryl: Birth, Mar 25
Synergy Week Intl, Oct 22
Synge, John M.: Birth Anniv, Apr 16
Syrian Arab Republic
  Independence Day, Apr 17
  Revolution Day, Mar 8
Szold, Henrietta: Birth Anniv, Dec 21

T, Mr: Birth, May 21
Ta'anit Esther (Fast of Esther), Mar 13
Tabaski: See Eid-al-Adha, Jan 10
Tabaski: See Eid-al-Adha, Dec 31
Tabei, Junko: Birth, Sep 22
Tabei, Junko: First Woman to Climb Mount Everest, May 16
Tabernacles, Feast of: First Day, Oct 7
Tabori, Kristoffer: Birth, Aug 4
Tacoma Holiday Food and Gift Fest (Tacoma, WA), Oct 25
Taft, Bob: Birth, Jan 8
Taft, Helen Herron: Birth Anniv, Jan 2
Taft, William H.: Birth Anniv, Sep 15
Taft, William: Opens Baseball Season: Anniv, Apr 14
Tagore, Rabindranath: Birth Anniv, May 6
Tailors Day, Natl, Jun 7
Taiwan
  Birthday of Cheng Huang, Jun 8
  Birthday of Kuan Yin, Goddess of Mercy, Mar 18
  Cheng Cheng Kung Landing Day, Apr 29
  Chiang Kai-Shek Day, Oct 31
  Confucius's Birthday and Teachers' Day, Sep 28
  Constitution Day, Dec 25
  Double Tenth Day, Oct 10
  Expelled from UN: Anniv, Oct 25
  Foundation Days, Jan 1
  Overseas Chinese Day, Oct 21

  Retrocession Day, Oct 25
  Tomb-Sweeping Day, Natl, Apr 5
  Youth Day, Mar 29
Tajikistan: Independence Day, Sep 9
Take a Wild Guess Day, Natl, Apr 15
Take Back Your Time Week, Natl, Jan 24
Take Our Daughters and Sons to Work Day, Apr 27
Take Your Webmaster to Lunch Day, Jul 6
Talent Scouts TV Premiere: Anniv, Dec 6
Talent, Jim: Birth, Oct 18
Tales of Wells Fargo TV Premiere: Anniv, Mar 18
Talese, Gay: Birth, Feb 7
Talk Like a Pirate Day, Sep 19
Tall Timber Days Fest (Grand Rapids, MN), Aug 5
Tallchief, Maria: Birth, Jan 24
Tamale Fiesta (El Centro, CA), Dec 2
Tamarack Time (Bigfork, MT), Oct 14
Tamblyn, Amber: Birth, May 14
Tamblyn, Russ: Birth, Dec 30
Tambor, Jeffrey: Birth, Jul 8
Tammuz, Fast of, Jul 13
Tan, Amy: Birth, Feb 19
Tandy, Jessica: Streetcar Named Desire Broadway Opening: Anniv, Dec 3
Taney, Roger B.: Birth Anniv, Mar 17
Tanner, Henry Ossawa: Birth Anniv, Jun 21
Tano Day (Korea), May 31
Tanzania
  Farmers' Day, Aug 8
  Independence and Republic Day, Dec 9
  Saba Saba Day, Jul 7
  Union Day, Apr 26
  Zanzibar Revolution Day, Jan 12
Tap Dance Day, Natl, May 25
Tarantino, Quentin: Birth, Mar 27
Tarbell, Ida M.: Birth Anniv, Nov 5
Tarkenton, Fran: Birth, Feb 3
Tarkington, Booth: Birth Anniv, Jul 29
Tartan Day, Apr 6
Tarzan TV Premiere: Anniv, Sep 8
Tasso, Torquato: Birth Anniv, Mar 11
Tattoo, Nova Scotia Intl (Halifax, NS, Canada), Jul 1
Taurus Begins, Apr 20
Tax Freedom Day, Apr 18
Tax, Income, Pay Day, Apr 15
Tax, Income, Pay Day: This Is Really It, Apr 17
Taylor, Billy: Birth, Jul 24
Taylor, Delores: Birth, Sep 27
Taylor, Elizabeth: Birth, Feb 27
Taylor, Frederick W.: Birth Anniv, Mar 20
Taylor, George: Death Anniv, Feb 23
Taylor, Holland: Birth, Jan 14
Taylor, James: Birth, Mar 12
Taylor, Lawrence: Birth, Feb 4
Taylor, Lili: Birth, Feb 20
Taylor, Lucy Hobbs: Birth Anniv, Mar 14
Taylor, Margaret S.: Birth Anniv, Sep 21
Taylor, Meshach: Birth, Apr 11
Taylor, Paul: Birth, Jul 29
Taylor, Renee: Birth, Mar 19
Taylor, Rod: Birth, Jan 11
Taylor, Zachary: Birth Anniv, Nov 24
Taylor-Young, Leigh: Birth, Jan 25
Tchaikovsky, Peter Ilich: Birth Anniv, May 7
Tea Month, Natl Hot, Jan 1
Tea Party Fest, Chestertown (Chestertown, MD), May 27
Teach Children to Save Day, Natl, Apr 25
Teacher Appreciation Week, May 7
Teacher Appreciation Week, Natl PTA, May 7
Teacher Day, Natl, May 9
Teacher's Day in Florida, May 19
Teachers' Day, Confucius's Birthday and (Taiwan), Sep 28
Teachers' Day, World (UN), Oct 5
Tear Down This Wall Speech: Anniv, Jun 12
Tebaldi, Renata: Birth, Jan 2
Technology Day, Trial, Jun 7
Tecumseh: Death Anniv, Oct 5
Tecumseh: Epic Outdoor Drama (Chillicothe, OH), Jun 9
Ted Mack's Original Amateur Hour TV Premiere: Anniv, Jan 18
Teddy Bear and Doll Classic, American Club (Kohler, WI), Feb 26
Teddy Bear Day, Natl American, Nov 14
Teddy Bear to Work Day, Natl Bring Your, Oct 11
Teen Read Week, Oct 15
Teflon Invented: Anniv, Apr 6
Teicher, Louis: Birth, Aug 24
Teilhard De Chardin, Pierre: Birth Anniv, May 1
Telecommunication Day, World (UN), May 17
Telecommuter Appreciation Week, Feb 26
Telegram, Singing: Anniv, Jul 28
Telegraph Line, Morse Opens First US: Anniv, May 24

Telegraph—Television

Telegraph, Atlantic Cable Laid: Anniv, Jul 27
Telephone
Area Codes Introduced: Anniv, **Nov 10**
AT&T Divestiture: Anniv, **Jan 8**
Bell, Alexander Graham: Birth Anniv, **Mar 3**
First Telephone Operator: Emma M. Nutt Day,
Sep 1
Inane Answering Message Day, **Jan 30**
Invention: Anniv, **Mar 10**
On-Hold Month, Natl, **Mar 1**
Push-Button Debuts: Anniv, **Nov 18**
Television
Abbott and Costello Show TV Premiere: Anniv,
Dec 5
Addams Family Premiere: Anniv, **Sep 18**
Adventures of Ellery Queen Premiere: Anniv,
Oct 14
Alfred Hitchcock Presents Premiere: Anniv, **Oct 2**
Alice Premiere: Anniv, **Aug 31**
All in the Family Premiere: Anniv, **Jan 12**
All My Children Premiere: Anniv, **Jan 5**
Alvin Show Premiere: Anniv, **Oct 4**
American Bandstand Premiere: Anniv, **Aug 5**
American Idol Premiere: Anniv, **Jun 11**
Amos 'n' Andy Premiere: Anniv, **Jun 28**
Andy Griffith Show Premiere: Anniv, **Oct 3**
Andy Williams Show Premiere: Anniv, **Jul 2**
Another World Premiere: Anniv, **May 4**
Arsenio Hall Show Premiere: Anniv, **Jan 3**
Art Linkletter's House Party Premiere: Anniv,
Sep 1
Arthur Murray Party Premiere: Anniv, **Jul 20**
As The World Turns Premiere: Anniv, **Apr 2**
Bachelor Father Premiere: Anniv, **Sep 15**
Barnaby Jones Premiere: Anniv, **Jan 28**
Barney & Friends Premiere: Anniv, **Apr 6**
Barney Miller Premiere: Anniv, **Jan 23**
Batman Premiere: Anniv, **Jan 12**
Baywatch Premiere: Anniv, **Apr 23**
Beat the Clock Premiere: Anniv, **Mar 23**
Beauty and the Beast Premiere: Anniv, **Sep 25**
Believe It or Not Premiere: Anniv, **Mar 1**
Beverly Hillbillies Premiere: Anniv, **Sep 26**
Bewitched Premiere: Anniv, **Sep 17**
Big Top Premiere: Anniv, **Jul 1**
Bob Hope Show Premiere: Anniv, **Oct 12**
Bob Newhart Show Premiere: Anniv, **Oct 10**
Bold and the Beautiful Premiere: Anniv, **Mar 23**
Brady Bunch Premiere: Anniv, **Sep 26**
Buck Rogers Premiere: Anniv, **Apr 15**
Buffy the Vampire Slayer Premiere: Anniv, **Mar 10**
Burns and Allen Show Premiere: Anniv, **Oct 12**
Cagney & Lacey Premiere: Anniv, **Mar 25**
Candid Camera Premiere: Anniv, **Aug 10**
Captain Kangaroo Premiere: Anniv, **Oct 3**
Captain Midnight Premiere: Anniv, **Sep 4**
Captain Video and His Video Rangers Premiere:
Anniv, **Jun 27**
Carol Burnett Show Premiere: Anniv, **Sep 11**
Cathode-Ray Tube Patented: Anniv, **Dec 20**
Catholic Hour Premiere: Anniv, **Jan 4**
Cavalcade of Stars Premiere: Anniv, **Jun 4**
CBS Evening News Premiere: Anniv, **May 3**
Charlie's Angels Premiere: Anniv, **Sep 22**
Cheers Premiere: Anniv, **Sep 30**
China Beach Premiere: Anniv, **Apr 26**
CHiPs Premiere: Anniv, **Sep 15**
CNN Debuted: Anniv, **Jun 1**
Columbo Premiere: Anniv, **Sep 15**
Cosby Show Premiere: Anniv, **Sep 20**
Court TV Debut: Anniv, **Jul 1**
CSI: Crime Scene Investigation Premiere: Anniv,
Oct 6
Dallas Premiere: Anniv, **Apr 2**
Daniel Boone Premiere: Anniv, **Sep 24**
Dark Shadows Premiere: Anniv, **Jun 27**
Dating Game Premiere: Anniv, **Dec 20**
Davy Crockett Premiere: Anniv, **Dec 15**
Days of Our Lives Premiere: Anniv, **Nov 8**
Dick Cavett Show Premiere: Anniv, **Mar 4**
Dick Clark Retires from American Bandstand:
Anniv, **Mar 23**
Dick Van Dyke Show Premiere: Anniv, **Oct 3**
Dinah Shore Show Premiere: Anniv, **Nov 27**
Ding Dong School Premiere: Anniv, **Dec 22**
Doctors Premiere: Anniv, **Apr 1**
Donny and Marie Premiere: Anniv, **Jan 16**
Dr. Who Premiere: Anniv, **Nov 23**
Dragnet Premiere: Anniv, **Dec 16**
Dukes of Hazzard Premiere: Anniv, **Jan 26**
Dynasty Premiere: Anniv, **Jan 12**
Ebert & Roeper and the Movies (Sneak Previews):
Anniv, **Oct 12**
Ed Sullivan Show Premiere: Anniv, **Jun 20**
Edge of Night Premiere: Anniv, **Apr 2**
Eight Is Enough Premiere: Anniv, **Mar 15**
Emergency Premiere: Anniv, **Jan 22**
ER Premiere: Anniv, **Sep 19**

Ernie Kovacs Premiere: Anniv, **May 14**
Evening at Pops Premiere: Anniv, **Jul 12**
Face the Nation Premiere: Anniv, **Nov 7**
Facts of Life Premiere: Anniv, **Aug 24**
Falcon Crest Premiere: Anniv, **Dec 4**
Family Feud Premiere: Anniv, **Jul 12**
Family Premiere: Anniv, **Mar 9**
Family Ties Premiere: Anniv, **Sep 22**
Fantasy Island Premiere: Anniv, **Jan 28**
Farnsworth, Philo: Birth Anniv, **Aug 19**
Fat Albert and the Cosby Kids Premiere: Anniv,
Sep 9
Fireside Theatre Premiere: Anniv, **Apr 5**
First Baseball Games Televised: Anniv, **Aug 26**
First Color TV Broadcast: Anniv, **Jun 25**
First Presidential Telecast: Anniv, **Apr 30**
First Scheduled Television Broadcast: Anniv, **Jul 1**
First Televised Presidential Debate: Anniv, **Sep 26**
First Televised Presidential News Conf: Anniv,
Jan 25
Flintstones TV Premiere: Anniv, **Sep 30**
Flipper Premiere: Anniv, **Sep 19**
Flying Nun Premiere: Anniv, **Sep 7**
48 Hours Premiere: Anniv, **Jan 19**
Fraggle Rock Premiere: Anniv, **Sep 12**
Frasier Premiere: Anniv, **Sep 16**
Fred Waring Show Premiere: Anniv, **Apr 17**
French Chef Premiere: Anniv, **Feb 11**
Friends Premiere: Anniv, **Sep 22**
Frontline Premiere: Anniv, **Jan 17**
Fugitive Premiere: Anniv, **Sep 17**
Gene Autry Show Premiere: Anniv, **Jul 23**
General Electric Theater Premiere: Anniv, **Feb 1**
General Hospital Premiere: Anniv, **Apr 1**
Gentle Ben Premiere: Anniv, **Sep 10**
George Gobel Show Premiere: Anniv, **Oct 2**
Get Smart Premiere: Anniv, **Sep 18**
Gilligan's Island Premiere: Anniv, **Sep 26**
Gimme A Break! Premiere: Anniv, **Oct 29**
Goldbergs Premiere: Anniv, **Jan 17**
Golden Girls Premiere: Anniv, **Sep 14**
Gong Show Premiere: Anniv, **Jun 14**
Good Morning America Premiere: Anniv, **Nov 6**
Good Sex! with Dr. Ruth Westheimer Premiere:
Anniv, **Aug 27**
Good Times Premiere: Anniv, **Feb 1**
Guiding Light Premiere: Anniv, **Jun 26**
Gumby Show Premiere: Anniv, **Mar 16**
Gunsmoke Premiere: Anniv, **Sep 10**
Hallmark Hall of Fame Premiere: Anniv, **Jan 6**
Happy Days Premiere: Anniv, **Jan 15**
Have Gun Will Travel Premiere: Anniv, **Sep 14**
Hawaii Five-O Premiere: Anniv, **Sep 26**
Hazel Premiere: Anniv, **Sep 28**
Hee Haw Premiere: Anniv, **Jun 15**
Hill Street Blues Premiere: Anniv, **Jan 15**
Hollywood Squares Premiere: Anniv, **Oct 17**
Home Improvement Premiere: Anniv, **Sep 17**
Hopalong Cassidy Premiere: Anniv, **Jun 24**
Howdy Doody Premiere: Anniv, **Dec 27**
I Love Lucy Premiere: Anniv, **Oct 15**
I Spy Premiere: Anniv, **Sep 15**
In Living Color Premiere: Anniv, **Apr 15**
In the Heat of the Night Premiere: Anniv, **Mar 6**
Incredible Hulk Premiere: Anniv, **Mar 10**
Ironside Premiere: Anniv, **Sep 14**
It Takes a Thief Premiere: Anniv, **Jan 9**
I've Got a Secret Premiere: Anniv, **Jun 19**
Jack Benny Program Premiere: Anniv, **Oct 28**
Jeffersons Premiere: Anniv, **Jan 18**
Jeopardy Premiere: Anniv, **Mar 30**
Jetsons Premiere: Anniv, **Sep 23**
Jimmy Durante Show Premiere: Anniv, **Oct 2**
Joe Franklin Day, **Mar 9**
Johnny Carson's Final Show, **May 22**
King Family Show Premiere: Anniv, **Jan 23**
Kraft Television Theatre Premiere: Anniv, **May 7**
Kukla, Fran and Ollie Premiere: Anniv, **Nov 29**
Kung Fu Premiere: Anniv, **Oct 1**
LA Law Premiere: Anniv, **Oct 3**
Larry King Show Premiere: Anniv, **Mar 13**
Lassie Premiere: Anniv, **Sep 12**
Late Night with David Letterman Premiere: Anniv,
Feb 1
Laugh-In Premiere: Anniv, **Jan 22**
Laverne and Shirley Premiere: Anniv, **Jan 27**
Law & Order Premiere: Anniv, **Sep 13**
Lawrence Welk Show Premiere: Anniv, **Jul 2**
Leave It to Beaver Premiere: Anniv, **Oct 4**
Let's Make a Deal Premiere: Anniv, **Dec 30**
Liberace Show Premiere: Anniv, **Jul 1**
Little House on the Prairie Premiere: Anniv, **Sep 11**
Lone Ranger Premiere: Anniv, **Sep 15**
Look Up and Live Premiere: Anniv, **Jan 3**
Loretta Young Show Premiere: Anniv, **Sep 20**
Love Boat Premiere: Anniv, **Sep 24**
Love Is a Many Splendored Thing Premiere: Anniv,
Sep 18

Love of Life Premiere: Anniv, **Sep 24**
M*A*S*H Final Episode: Anniv, **Feb 28**
M*A*S*H Premiere: Anniv, **Sep 17**
MacNeil-Lehrer Newshour Premiere: Anniv, **Sep 5**
Magnum, PI Premiere: Anniv, **Dec 11**
Make Room for Daddy Premiere: Anniv, **Sep 29**
Mama Premiere: Anniv, **Jul 1**
Mannix Premiere: Anniv, **Sep 16**
Married With Children Premiere: Anniv, **Apr 5**
Mary Tyler Moore Show Premiere: Anniv, **Sep 19**
Masterpiece Theatre Premiere: Anniv, **Jan 10**
Maude Premiere: Anniv, **Sep 12**
Maverick Premiere: Anniv, **Sep 22**
Meet the Press Premiere: Anniv, **Nov 6**
Merv Griffin Show Premiere: Anniv, **Oct 1**
Mickey Mouse Club Premiere: Anniv, **Oct 3**
Mighty Mouse Playhouse Premiere: Anniv, **Dec 10**
Millionaire Premiere: Anniv, **Jan 19**
Minow, Newton: Birth, **Jan 17**
Mission: Impossible Premiere: Anniv, **Sep 17**
Mister Rogers' Neighborhood Premiere: Anniv,
May 22
Monday Night Football Premiere: Anniv, **Sep 21**
Monkees Premiere: Anniv, **Sep 12**
Monty Python's Flying Circus: Anniv, **Oct 5**
Moonlighting Premiere: Anniv, **Mar 3**
Mr Peepers Premiere: Anniv, **Jul 3**
Mr Wizard Premiere: Anniv, **Mar 3**
MTV Premiere: Anniv, **Aug 1**
Munsters Premiere: Anniv, **Sep 24**
Muppet Show Premiere: Anniv, **Sep 13**
Murder, She Wrote Premiere: Anniv, **Sep 30**
Murphy Brown Premiere: Anniv, **Nov 14**
My Friend Flicka Premiere: Anniv, **Feb 10**
My Little Margie Premiere: Anniv, **Jun 15**
Name That Tune Premiere: Anniv, **Jul 6**
Nat King Cole Show Premiere: Anniv, **Nov 5**
National Traffic Directors Day, **Nov 2**
Newhart Premiere: Anniv, **Oct 25**
Newlywed Game Premiere: Anniv, **Jul 11**
Nick at Nite: Anniv, **Jul 1**
Nickelodeon Premiere: Anniv, **Apr 2**
Nielsen, Arthur Charles: Birth Anniv, **Sep 5**
Night Court Premiere: Anniv, **Jan 4**
Northern Exposure Premiere: Anniv, **Jul 12**
NYPD Blue Premiere: Anniv, **Sep 21**
Omnibus Premiere: Anniv, **Nov 9**
One Day at a Time Premiere: Anniv, **Dec 16**
One Life to Live Premiere: Anniv, **Jul 15**
Oprah Winfrey Show Premiere: Anniv, **Sep 8**
Our Miss Brooks Premiere: Anniv, **Oct 3**
Owen Marshall: Counselor at Law Premiere: Anniv,
Sep 16
Ozark Jubilee Premiere: Anniv, **Jan 22**
Ozzie and Harriet Premiere: Anniv, **Oct 3**
Pat Boone Show Premiere: Anniv, **Oct 3**
Perry Como Show Premiere: Anniv, **Dec 24**
Perry Mason Premiere: Anniv, **Sep 21**
Phil Donahue Show, The: Anniv, **Nov 6**
Phil Silvers Show Premiere: Anniv, **Sep 20**
Price Is Right Premiere: Anniv, **Nov 26**
Primetime Live Premiere: Anniv, **Aug 3**
Prisoner Premiere: Anniv, **Jun 1**
Public Television Debuts: Anniv, **Nov 3**
Queen for a Day Premiere: Anniv, **Jan 3**
Quincy Premiere: Anniv, **Oct 3**
Quiz Kids Premiere: Anniv, **Jul 6**
Rawhide Premiere: Anniv, **Jan 9**
Real McCoys Premiere: Anniv, **Oct 3**
Real People Premiere: Anniv, **Apr 18**
Red Skelton Show Premiere: Anniv, **Sep 30**
Remington Steele Premiere: Anniv, **Oct 1**
Rocky and His Friends Premiere: Anniv, **Nov 19**
Rogers, Fred: Birth Anniv, **Mar 20**
Roseanne Premiere: Anniv, **Oct 18**
Roy Rogers Show Premiere: Anniv, **Dec 30**
Ryan's Hope Premiere: Anniv, **Jul 7**
Saint Elsewhere Premiere: Anniv, **Oct 26**
Sammy Kaye Show Premiere: Anniv, **Jul 28**
Sanford and Son Premiere: Anniv, **Jan 14**
Saturday Night Live Premiere: Anniv, **Oct 11**
Scarecrow and Mrs King Premiere: Anniv, **Oct 3**
Schlitz Playhouse of Stars Premiere: Anniv, **Oct 5**
Scooby-Doo, Where Are You? Premiere: Anniv,
Sep 13
Search for Tomorrow Premiere: Anniv, **Sep 3**
Secret Agent Premiere: Anniv, **Apr 5**
Secret Storm Premiere: Anniv, **Feb 1**
See It Now Premiere: Anniv, **Nov 18**
Seinfeld Premiere: Anniv, **May 31**
Sesame Street Premiere: Anniv, **Nov 10**
Sex and the City Premiere: Anniv, **Jun 6**
Shirley Temple Theatre Premiere: Anniv, **Sep 18**
Simpsons Premiere: Anniv, **Dec 17**
Six Million Dollar Man Premiere: Anniv, **Oct 20**
$64,000 Question Premiere: Anniv, **Jun 7**
Sixty Minutes Premiere: Anniv, **Sep 24**
Sky King Premiere: Anniv, **Sep 16**

Smothers Brothers Fired: Anniv, **Apr 4**
Sneak Previews Premiere: Anniv, **Oct 12**
Soap Premiere: Anniv, **Sep 13**
Sopranos Premiere: Anniv, **Jan 13**
Soupy Sales Show Premiere: Anniv, **Jul 4**
Star Trek Premiere: Anniv, **Sep 8**
Starman Month, Intl, **Oct 1**
Steve Allen Show Premiere: Anniv, **Dec 25**
Strike It Rich Premiere: Anniv, **May 7**
Survivor Premiere: Anniv, **May 31**
Talent Scouts Premiere: Anniv, **Dec 6**
Tales of Wells Fargo Premiere: Anniv, **Mar 18**
Tarzan Premiere: Anniv, **Sep 8**
Ted Mack's Original Amateur Hour Premiere: Anniv,
Jan 18
Television Academy Hall of Fame First Inductees,
Mar 4
Texaco Star Theater Premiere: Anniv, **Sep 21**
That Girl Premiere: Anniv, **Sep 8**
3rd Rock from the Sun Premiere: Anniv, **Jan 9**
Thirtysomething Premiere: Anniv, **Sep 29**
This Is Your Life Premiere: Anniv, **Oct 1**
Three's Company Premiere: Anniv, **Mar 15**
To Tell the Truth Premiere: Anniv, **Dec 18**
Today Premiere: Anniv, **Jan 14**
Tom Corbett, Space Cadet Premiere: Anniv, **Oct 1**
Tonight Show Premiere: Anniv, **Sep 27**
Tracey Ullman Show Premiere: Anniv, **Apr 5**
Truth or Consequences Premiere: Anniv, **Sep 7**
TV Talk-Show Host Day, **Oct 23**
20/20 Premiere: Anniv, **Jun 6**
Twenty Questions Premiere: Anniv, **Nov 26**
Twilight Zone Premiere: Anniv, **Oct 2**
Upstairs, Downstairs Premiere: Anniv, **Oct 10**
Vast Wasteland Speech: Anniv, **May 9**
Virginian Premiere: Anniv, **Sep 19**
Wagon Train Premiere: Anniv, **Sep 18**
Walt Disney Premiere: Anniv, **Oct 27**
Waltons Premiere: Anniv, **Sep 14**
Welcome Back, Kotter Premiere: Anniv, **Sep 9**
Welk, Lawrence: Birth Anniv, **Mar 11**
What's My Line Premiere: Anniv, **Feb 2**
Wheel of Fortune Premiere: Anniv, **Jan 6**
Wonder Years Premiere: Anniv, **Mar 15**
World Television Day (UN), **Nov 21**
Wyatt Earp Premiere: Anniv, **Sep 6**
X-Files Premiere: Anniv, **Sep 10**
You Are There Premiere: Anniv, **Feb 1**
You Bet Your Life Premiere: Anniv, **Oct 5**
Young and the Restless Premiere: Anniv, **Mar 26**
Your Hit Parade Premiere: Anniv, **Oct 7**
Your Show of Shows Premiere: Anniv, **Feb 25**
Zane Grey Theater Premiere: Anniv, **Oct 5**
Zoo Parade Premiere: Anniv, **May 28**
**Tellabration! An Evening of Storytelling for
Grown-Ups (CT), Nov 17**
Teller, Edward: Birth Anniv, Jan 15
Teller: Birth, Feb 14
**Telluride Blues & Brews Festival (Telluride, CO),
Sep 15**
Telluride Wine Fest (Telluride, CO), Jun 22
Telstar: Space Milestone: Anniv, Jul 10
**Temperance Union, Women's Christian: Anniv,
Nov 19**
**Temperature, North America's Coldest Recorded:
Anniv, Feb 3**
Temple, Shirley: Birth, Apr 23
Ten Most Wanted List Debuts: Anniv, Mar 14
Ten-Four Day, Oct 4
Tennant, Victoria: Birth, Sep 30
Tennessee
Admission Day, **Jun 1**
Alexander, Lamar: Birth, **Jul 30**
American Quilter's Society Quilt Exposition
(Nashville), **Aug 23**
Battle of Chattanooga: Anniv, **Nov 24**
Battle of Nashville: Anniv, **Dec 16**
Battle of Shiloh: Anniv, **Apr 6**
Belle Meade Plantation Fall Fest (Nashville),
Sep 16
Bredesen, Phil: Birth, **Nov 21**
Dickens of a Christmas (Franklin), **Dec 9**
Dogwood Arts Fest (Knoxville), **Apr 5**
Elvis Presley's Birthday Celebration (Memphis),
Jan 6
Elvis Week (Memphis), **Aug 8**
Family Day, **Aug 27**
Family, Career and Community Leaders of America
Natl Leadership Meeting (Nashville), **Jul 9**
Field Trial Chmpshp, Natl (Bird Dogs) (Grand
Junction), **Feb 13**
First Grand Ole Opry Broadcast: Anniv, **Dec 10**
Frist, William: Birth, **Feb 22**
Goat Days (Millington), **Sep 8**
Great Smoky Mountains Natl Park Established:
Anniv, **Jun 15**
Longhorn Chmpshp Finals Rodeo (Murfreesboro),
Nov 9

Longhorn World Chmpshp Rodeo (Chattanooga),
Mar 10
Main Street Fest (Franklin), **Apr 29**
Mid-South Fair (Memphis), **Sep 22**
Miss Tennessee Pageant (Jackson), **Jun 21**
Mule Day (Columbia), **Mar 30**
NAIA Div I Women's Basketball Chmpshp
(Jackson), **Mar 15**
Oak Ridge Atomic Plant Begun: Anniv, **Aug 1**
Old-Time Fiddlers' Jamboree (Smithville), **Jun 30**
Polk County Ramp Tramp Fest (Benton), **Apr 22**
Riverbend Fest (Chattanooga), **Jun 9**
Rock of Chickamauga: Anniv, **Sep 20**
Scopes Trial (Dayton), **Jul 14**
Secret City Festival (Oak Ridge), **Jun 16**
Smoky Mountains Storytelling Fest (Pigeon Forge),
Feb 2
Southern Fest of Books (Memphis), **Oct 13**
State Fair (Nashville), **Sep 8**
Storytelling Fest, Natl (Jonesborough), **Oct 6**
TACA Fall Craft Fair (Chattanooga), **Sep 30**
TACA Fall Craft Fair (Nashville), **Sep 22**
Tennessee Fall Homecoming (Norris), **Oct 11**
Tennessee Walking Horse Natl Celebration
(Shelbyville), **Aug 23**
World's Biggest Fish Fry (Paris), **Apr 24**
Tenney, Jon: Birth, Dec 16
Tenniel, John: Birth Anniv, Feb 28
Tennille, Toni: Birth, May 8
Tennis
Big 12 Men's & Women's Tennis Chmpshps (Waco,
TX), **Apr 27**
Big Ten Men's Tennis Chmpshp (Urbana, IL),
Apr 27
Big Ten Women's Tennis Chmpshp (Iowa City, IA),
Apr 27
Lacoste, Rene: Birth Anniv, **Jul 2**
Lawn Tennis Chmpshps at Wimbledon (London,
England), **Jun 26**
NAIA Men's & Women's Tennis Chmpshps (Mobile,
AL), **May 15**
NCAA Div I Women's Tennis Chmpshps (Stanford,
CA), **May 18**
Tennyson, Alfred, Lord: Birth Anniv, Aug 6
Teresa, Mother: Birth Anniv, Aug 27
Tereshkova-Nikolaeva, Valentina: Birth, Mar 6
Terkel, Studs: Birth, May 16
**Territorial Christmas Celebration (Guthrie, OK),
Nov 25**
Terrorism: Madrid Train Bombings: Anniv, Mar 11
Terry, Ellen: Birth Anniv, Feb 27
Tesh, John: Birth, Jul 9
Testaverde, Vinny: Birth, Nov 13
Test-Tube Baby: Birth, Jul 25
Testicular Cancer Awareness Week, Apr 1
Tet Offensive Begins: Anniv, Jan 30
Tet: See Chinese New Year, Jan 29
**Tetonkaha Rendezvous (Lake Benton, MN),
Aug 11**
Texaco Star Theater TV Premiere: Anniv, Sep 21
Texas
Admission Day, **Dec 29**
Aggie Muster (College Station), **Apr 21**
American Rose Society Fall Natl Conv (Dallas),
Oct 13
Andrews 4th of July Festivities (Andrews, TX),
Jul 3
Andrews COC Holly Jolly Weekend (Andrews),
Nov 30
Bayfest (Corpus Christi), **Sep 29**
Big 12 Men's & Women's Outdoor Track/Field
Chmpshps (Waco), **May 12**
Big 12 Men's & Women's Tennis Chmpshps
(Waco), **Apr 27**
Big 12 Men's Basketball Chmpshp (Dallas), **Mar 9**
Big 12 Women's Basketball Tournament (Dallas),
Mar 7
Big Bend Natl Park Established: Anniv, **Jun 12**
Bob Wills Day (Turkey), **Apr 29**
Boys Ranch Rodeo (Boys Ranch), **Sep 2**
Branch Davidian Fire at Waco: Anniv, **Apr 19**
CAMEX (Houston), **Mar 3**
Celebration of the Horse (Houston), **Jul 14**
Charro Days Fiesta (Brownsville), **Feb 23**
Cherokee Rose Fest (Gilmer), **May 20**
Chili Cookoff/Quail-Egg Eat, Prairie Dog (Grand
Prairie), **Apr 8**
Christmas Magic (Wichita Falls), **Nov 3**
Clear Lake Crawfish Fest (Seabrook), **Apr 1**
Clute's Christmas in the Park (Clute), **Dec 5**
Comal County Fair (New Braunfels), **Sep 26**
Come and Take It Fest (Gonzales), **Oct 6**
Communitywide Garage Sale (Elgin), **May 6**
Confederate Heroes Day, **Jan 19**
Cornyn, John: Birth, **Feb 2**
Cowboy Poetry Gathering (Alpine), **Feb 24**
Dallas Cup (Frisco), **Apr 9**
Dickens on the Strand (Galveston), **Dec 1**

East Texas Poultry Fest (Center), **Oct 5**
East Texas Yamboree (Gilmer), **Oct 18**
Electra Goat BBQ Cook-Off (Electra), **May 12**
Elgin Market Days (Elgin), **Feb 4**
Emancipation Day, **Jun 19**
Faith City Kennel Club Dog Show (Wichita Falls),
Mar 4
Fall Citywide Garage Sale (Electra), **Oct 7**
Fall Fiesta (Andrews), **Sep 22**
Fantasy of Lights (Wichita Falls), **Dec 1**
Fiddler's Frolics (Hallettsville), **Apr 27**
Fiesta San Antonio (San Antonio), **Apr 21**
Fireant Fest (Marshall), **Oct 14**
Fulton Oysterfest (Fulton), **Mar 2**
Galveston Historic Homes Tour (Galveston Island),
May 6
Galveston Hurricane: Anniv, **Sep 8**
Great Texas Mosquito Fest (Clute), **Jul 27**
Guadalupe Natl Park Established: Anniv, **Sep 30**
Harvest Weekends (Bryan), **Jul 22**
Hogeye Fest (Elgin), **Oct 28**
Home and Garden Fest (Wichita Falls), **Feb 25**
Hotter 'n Hell Hundred Bike Race/Fest (Wichita
Falls), **Aug 24**
Houston Livestock Show/Rodeo (Houston), **Feb 28**
Houston Marathon (Houston), **Jan 15**
Hummer/Bird Celebration (Rockport, Fulton),
Sep 14
Hutchison, Kay Bailey: Birth, **Jul 22**
Independence Day, **Mar 2**
Indian Powwow, Natl Chmpshp (Grand Prairie),
Sep 8
Irrigation Show, Intl (San Antonio), **Nov 5**
Josey's World Champion Junior Barrel Race
(Marshall), **May 5**
Juneteenth, **Jun 19**
KidFilm® Fest (Dallas), **Jan 9**
Kingsville Intl Young Performers' Competitions
(Kingsville), **Apr 6**
La Posada de Kingsville/Celebration of Lights
(Kingsville), **Nov 17**
Lights of Blacklands, **Dec 1**
Marriage of the Port Ceremony (Bryan), **Feb 11**
Messina Hof's Wine Premiere (Bryan), **Nov 18**
NBA All-Star Weekend (Houston), **Feb 17**
O. Henry Museum Pun-Off (Austin), **May 6**
Oatmeal Fest (Bertram/Oatmeal), **Sep 1**
Oil Bowl Football Classic (Wichita Falls), **Jun 17**
Old Red Courthouse Dedication and Opening of
Old Red Museum (Dallas), **Jul 1**
Parade of Lights (Kingsville), **Dec 2**
Perry, Rick: Birth, **Mar 4**
Poetry Contest (El Paso), **Jun 1**
Poteet Strawberry Fest (Poteet), **Apr 7**
Quadrangle Fest (Texarkana), **Sep 9**
Ranch Hand Breakfast (Kingsville), **Nov 18**
Ranching Heritage Fest, South Texas (Kingsville),
Mar 3
Re/Max Ballunar Liftoff Festival (Houston), **Aug 24**
Red River Rodeo (Wichita Falls), **Jun 7**
Reenactment of Cowtown's Last Gunfight (Fort
Worth), **Feb 8**
Rio Grande Valley Livestock Show (Mercedes),
Mar 11
Rockport Art Fest (Rockport), **Jul 1**
Rockport Seafair (Rockport), **Oct 6**
San Jacinto Day, **Apr 21**
Saveur Texas Hill Country Wine & Food Fest
(Austin), **Apr 6**
SBC Cotton Bowl Classic (Dallas), **Jan 2**
Seaspace (Houston), **Jun 24**
South by Southwest (Austin), **Mar 10**
South Texas Wildlife and Birding Fest (Kingsville),
Nov 17
Southwestern Expo Livestock Show/Rodeo (Fort
Worth), **Jan 13**
Spring Swing City Garage Sale (Electra), **Apr 1**
Stagecoach Days (Marshall), **May 20**
State Fair (Dallas), **Sep 29**
Summer Reading Club (El Paso), **Jun 3**
Sun Bowl (El Paso), **Dec 29**
Taste of the Town (Wichita Falls), **Mar 7**
Texas Book Fest (Austin), **Oct 27**
Texas City Disaster: Anniv, **Apr 16**
Texas Collectors' Gun & Knife Show (Wichita
Falls), **Jan 28**
Texas Folklife Fest (San Antonio), **Jun 8**
Texas Panhandle Tornado: Anniv, **Apr 9**
Texas Ranch Roundup (Wichita Falls), **Aug 18**
Texas-Oklahoma Fair (Wichita Falls), **Sep 12**
Texas-Oklahoma Junior Golf Tournament (Wichita
Falls), **Jun 26**
Texoma Farm and Ranch Show (Wichita Falls),
Feb 15
University Kiwanis Pancake Fest (Wichita Falls),
Jan 28
USA Film Fest (Dallas), **Apr 20**
Washington's Birthday Celeb (Laredo), **Jan 26**

Texas (cont'd)—Toynbee

Watermelon Thump (Luling), **Jun 22**
Western Days (Elgin), **Jun 20**
Westfest (West), **Sep 2**
Wichita West Spring Arts/Crafts Show (Wichita Falls), **Mar 25**
Wonderland of Lights (Marshall), **Nov 22**
World Chmpshp BBQ Goat Cook-off/Crafts Fair (Brady), **Sep 2**
World of Wheels (Wichita Falls), **Feb 3**
World's Largest Rattlesnake Roundup (Sweetwater), **Mar 10**
Youth Cowboy Poetry Gathering (Boys Ranch), **Jun 8**
Texas County Fair/Old Settlers Reunion (Houston, MO), **Aug 1**
Thackeray, William: Birth Anniv, **Jul 18**
Thailand
  Birth of the Queen, **Aug 12**
  Chakri Day, **Apr 6**
  Chulalongkorn Day, **Oct 23**
  Constitution Day, **Dec 10**
  Coronation Day, **May 5**
  Elephant Roundup at Surin, **Nov 18**
  King's Birthday and National Day, **Dec 5**
  Midyear Day (Half-Year Day), **Jul 1**
  Songkran Fest, **Apr 13**
Thank God It's Monday! Day, Natl, **Jan 9**
Thank You Days, Intl, **Jan 11**
Thanks for All the Gifts Week, **Aug 13**
Thanksgiving Day, **Nov 23**
Thanksgiving Day (Canada), **Oct 9**
Thanksgiving Day (Pres Proc), **Nov 23**
Thanksgiving, Turkey-Free, **Nov 23**
Tharp, Twyla: Birth, **Jul 1**
That Girl TV Premiere: Anniv, **Sep 8**
That Sucks Day, **Apr 15**
Thatcher, Margaret: Birth, **Oct 13**
Thatcher, Margaret: First Woman British Prime Minister: Anniv, **May 4**
Thayer, Ernest L.: Birth Anniv, **Aug 14**
Thayer, Sylvanus: Birth Anniv, **Jun 9**
Theater. See also Opera
  Astor Place Riot: Anniv, **May 10**
  Black Hills Passion Play (Spearfish, SD), **Jun 1**
  Cats Premieres: Anniv, **Oct 7**
  Colorado Shakespeare Fest (Boulder, CO), **Jun 30**
  Coward, Noel: Birth Anniv, **Dec 16**
  Death of a Salesman Premiere: Anniv, **Feb 10**
  Donna Reed Performing Arts Fest (Denison, IA), **Jun 19**
  Edinburgh Intl Fest (Edinburgh, Scotland), **Aug 13**
  Edmonton Intl Fringe Theatre Fest (Edmonton, AB, Canada), **Aug 17**
  First Actor to Perform in Two Cities Same Day: Anniv, **Feb 10**
  First Play Presented in North American Colonies: Anniv, **Aug 27**
  First Tony Awards Presented: Anniv, **Apr 6**
  George Spelvin Day, **Nov 15**
  Hair Broadway Opening: Anniv, **Mar 28**
  Harrison Fest of Arts (Harrison Hot Springs, BC, Canada), **Jul 8**
  Idaho Shakespeare Fest (Boise, ID), **Jun 2**
  Illinois Shakespeare Fest (Bloomington, IL), **Jun 29**
  Laura Ingalls Wilder Pageant (De Smet, SD), **Jul 7**
  Odets, Clifford: Birth Anniv, **Jul 18**
  Oklahoma! Broadway Premiere: Anniv, **Mar 31**
  Outdoor Summer Theater (Farmington, NM), **Jun 14**
  Papp, Joseph: Birth Anniv, **Jun 22**
  Pitlochry Fest Theatre Season (Scotland), **Apr 1**
  Scopes Trial (Dayton, TN), **Jul 14**
  Shakespeare Fest (Ashland, OR), **Feb 24**
  Shakespeare on the Green (Omaha, NE), **Jun 22**
  Song of Hiawatha Pageant (Pipestone, MN), **Jul 21**
  Streetcar Named Desire Broadway Opening: Anniv, **Dec 3**
  Tecumseh! Epic Outdoor Drama (Chillicothe, OH), **Jun 9**
  Theater in North America, First Performance: Anniv, **Apr 30**
  Walter Plinge Day (England), **Dec 2**
  Williams, Tennessee: Birth Anniv, **Mar 26**
  Winnipeg Fringe Theatre Fest (Winnipeg, MB, Canada), **Jul 19**
Theisman, Joe: Birth, **Sep 9**
Theodore Roosevelt Natl Park Established: Anniv, **Apr 25**
Theodosius I: Birth Anniv, **Jan 11**
Therapeutic Recreation Week, Natl, **Jul 9**
Theron, Charlize: Birth, **Aug 7**
Theroux, Paul: Birth, **Apr 10**
Thewlis, David: Birth, **Mar 20**
3rd Rock from the Sun TV Premiere: Anniv, **Jan 9**
Thible, Marie: First Free Flight by a Woman: Anniv, **Jun 4**
Thicke, Alan: Birth, **Mar 1**
Thiessen, Tiffani-Amber: Birth, **Jan 23**

Thinking, Intl Strategic, Month, **Sep 1**
Thinnes, Roy: Birth, **Apr 6**
Third Punic War: Ends: Anniv, **Feb 5**
Third Shift Workers Day, Natl, **May 10**
Third World Day: Anniv, **Apr 18**
Thirtysomething TV Premiere: Anniv, **Sep 29**
This Is Your Life TV Premiere: Anniv, **Oct 1**
Thomas Crapper Day, **Jan 27**
Thomas, B.J.: Birth, **Aug 7**
Thomas, Betty: Birth, **Jul 27**
Thomas, Clarence: Birth, **Jun 23**
Thomas, Craig: Birth, **Feb 17**
Thomas, Danny: Birth Anniv, **Jan 6**
Thomas, Dylan: Birth Anniv, **Oct 27**
Thomas, Frank: Birth, **May 27**
Thomas, Heather: Birth, **Sep 8**
Thomas, Helen: Birth, **Aug 4**
Thomas, Henry: Birth, **Sep 8**
Thomas, Isaiah: Birth Anniv, **Jan 30**
Thomas, Isiah: Birth, **Apr 30**
Thomas, Jonathan Taylor: Birth, **Sep 8**
Thomas, Kurt: Birth, **Mar 29**
Thomas, Lowell: Birth Anniv, **Apr 6**
Thomas, Marlo: Birth, **Nov 21**
Thomas, Martha Carey: Birth Anniv, **Jan 2**
Thomas, Michael Tilson: Birth, **Dec 21**
Thomas, Philip Michael: Birth, **May 26**
Thomas, Richard: Birth, **Jun 13**
Thomas, Robert B.: Birth Anniv, **Apr 24**
Thomas, Sean Patrick: Birth, **Dec 17**
Thome, Jim: Birth, **Aug 27**
Thompson, Emma: Birth, **Apr 14**
Thompson, Fred: Birth, **Aug 19**
Thompson, Hunter S.: Birth Anniv, **Jul 18**
Thompson, Jack: Birth, **Aug 31**
Thompson, John: Birth, **Sep 2**
Thompson, LaMarcus: First Roller Coaster Opens: Anniv, **Jun 13**
Thompson, Lea: Birth, **May 31**
Thompson, Sada: Birth, **Sep 27**
Thomson, Charles: Birth Anniv, **Nov 29**
Thoreau, Henry David: Birth Anniv, **Jul 12**
Thorne-Smith, Courtney: Birth, **Nov 8**
Thornton, Billy Bob: Birth, **Aug 4**
Thornton, Matthew: Death Anniv, **Jun 24**
Thorpe, James: Birth Anniv, **May 28**
3-a-Day Week, **Mar 3**
Three Kings Day, **Jan 6**
Three Stooges
  De Rita, Joe: Birth Anniv, **Jul 12**
  Fine, Larry: Birth Anniv, **Oct 5**
  Howard, Curly: Birth Anniv, **Oct 22**
  Howard, Moe: Birth Anniv, **Jun 19**
  Howard, Shemp: Birth Anniv, **Mar 17**
Three's Company TV Premiere: Anniv, **Mar 15**
Threshing Bee Show, Makoti (ND), **Oct 6**
Threshing Bee, Norskedalen's (Coon Valley, WI), **Sep 23**
Thumb, Tom: Birth Anniv, **Jan 4**
Thune, John R.: Birth, **Jan 7**
Thurber, James: Birth Anniv, **Dec 8**
Thurman, Uma: Birth, **Apr 29**
Thurmond, Nate: Birth, **Jul 25**
Thurmond, Strom: Birth Anniv, **Dec 5**
Tiananmen Square Massacre: Anniv, **Jun 4**
Tiara Day, Intl, **May 24**
Tibet: Dalai Lama Flees Tibet: Anniv, **Mar 31**
Ticotin, Rachel: Birth, **Nov 1**
Tides, Perigean Spring, **Jan 29, Feb 27, Sep 7, Oct 6**
Tidewater Archaeology Dig (St. Mary's City, MD), **Jul 29**
Tie Month, Natl, **Dec 1**
Tierney, Gene: Birth Anniv, **Nov 20**
Tierney, Maura: Birth, **Feb 3**
Tiffany, Charles L.: Birth Anniv, **Feb 15**
Tiffany, Louis C.: Birth Anniv, **Feb 18**
Tiffin, Pamela: Birth, **Oct 13**
Tighe, Kevin: Birth, **Aug 13**
Tilbrook, Glenn: Birth, **Aug 31**
Tilden, Bill: Birth Anniv, **Feb 10**
Till, Emmett: Death Anniv, **Aug 28**
Tillis, Mel: Birth, **Aug 8**
Tilly, Jennifer: Birth, **Sep 16**
Tilly, Meg: Birth, **Feb 14**
Time Magazine First Published: Anniv, **Mar 3**
Time Management
  It's About Time Week, **Dec 25**
  Month, Natl, **Feb 1**
  Revise Your Work Schedule Month, **May 1**
  Take Back Your Time Week, Natl, **Jan 24**
  Zero-Tasking Day, **Oct 30**
Time; Calendars
  Daylight Saving Time Begins, **Apr 2**
  Daylight Saving Time Ends, **Oct 29**
  Greenwich Mean Time Begins: Anniv, **Sep 25**
  Leap Second Adjustment Time, **Jun 30, Dec 31**
  Prime Meridian Set: Anniv, **Nov 1**

Summer Daylight-Saving Time (Europe), **Mar 26**
Summer Time (United Kingdom), **Mar 27**
Time Zone Plan, US Uniform: Anniv, **Nov 18**
US Standard Time Act: Anniv, **Mar 19**
War Time: Anniv, **Feb 9**
Tin Can Patent: Anniv, **Jan 19**
Tinker to Evers to Chance Lines in "Baseball's Sad Lexicon" First Published: Anniv, **Jul 10**
Tinker, Grant: Birth, **Jan 11**
Tinker, Joe: Birth Anniv, **Jul 27**
Tinsley, Jamaal: Birth, **Feb 28**
Tip-Up Town USA (Houghton Lake, MI), **Jan 21**
Tisch, Laurence: Birth, **Mar 5**
Tisha B'Av (Fast of Ab), **Aug 3**
Titan II Missile Explosion: Anniv, **Sep 19**
Titanic (Film) Released: Anniv, **Dec 19**
Titanic Discovered: Anniv, **Sep 1**
Titanic, Sinking of the: Anniv, **Apr 15**
Tito (Josip Broz): Birth Anniv, **May 25**
Tittle, Y.A.: Birth, **Oct 24**
Tivoli Gardens Season (Copenhagen, Denmark), **May 1**
Tivoli-Viking Days at the Nordic Heritage Museum (Seattle, WA), **Jul 8**
Tkachuk, Keith: Birth, **Mar 28**
To Tell the Truth TV Premiere: Anniv, **Dec 18**
Toad Hollow Day of Encouragement, **Jan 26**
Toad Hollow Day of Thank You, **Jun 20**
Toad Hollow Week, Natl, **Mar 14**
Toad Suck Daze (Conway, AR), **May 5**
Tobacco Harvest (McLean, VA), **Aug 27**
Tobago
  Emancipation Day, **Aug 1**
  Independence Day, **Aug 31**
  Spiritual Baptist Liberation Shouter Day, **Mar 30**
Tobolowsky, Stephen: Birth, **May 30**
Tocqueville, Alexis de: Birth Anniv, **Jul 29**
Today TV Premiere: Anniv, **Jan 14**
Todd, Beverly: Birth, **Jul 11**
Toffler, Alvin: Birth, **Oct 4**
Togo
  Independence Day, **Apr 27**
  Liberation Day, **Jan 13**
Toilet Tank Repair Month, Natl, **Oct 1**
Tojo Hideki: Execution Anniv, **Dec 23**
Tolerance Week, **Dec 1**
Tolerance, Intl Day for (UN), **Nov 16**
Tolkan, James: Birth, **Jun 20**
Tolkien Week, **Sep 17**
Tolkien, J.R.R.: Birth Anniv, **Jan 3**
Tolkien, J.R.R.: Hobbit Day, **Sep 22**
Tolkien, J.R.R.: Lord of the Rings, First Part Published: Anniv, **Jul 19**
Toll Collection Machine, First Automatic: Anniv, **Nov 19**
Tolstoy, Leo: Birth Anniv, **Sep 9**
Tom Corbett, Space Cadet TV Premiere: Anniv, **Oct 1**
Tom Sawyer Days, Natl (Hannibal, MO), **Jul 1**
Tomatina, La (Spain), **Aug 30**
Tomato Month, Fresh Florida, **Apr 1**
Tomatoes, Celebrate Sun Dried, Month, **Oct 1**
Tomb Sweeping Day (China), **Apr 5**
Tomb-Sweeping Day, Natl (Taiwan), **Apr 5**
Tomczak, Mike: Birth, **Oct 23**
Tomei, Concetta: Birth, **Dec 30**
Tomei, Marisa: Birth, **Dec 4**
Tomjanovich, Rudy: Birth, **Nov 24**
Tomlin, Lily: Birth, **Sep 1**
Tomlinson, LaDanian: Birth, **Jun 23**
Tompkins, Daniel D.: Birth Anniv, **Jun 21**
Tonga: Emancipation Day, **Jun 4**
Tonight Show TV Premiere: Anniv, **Sep 27**
Tony Awards Presented, First: Anniv, **Apr 6**
Toomey, William: Birth, **Jan 10**
Tooth Fairy Day, Natl, **Feb 28**
Tork, Peter: Birth, **Feb 13**
Torn, Rip: Birth, **Feb 6**
Torquemada, Tomas de: Death Anniv, **Sep 16**
Torre, Joe: Birth, **Jul 18**
Toscanini, Arturo: Birth Anniv, **Mar 25**
Toss Away the "Could Haves" and "Should Haves" Day, **Jul 15**
Tostitos Fiesta Bowl (Tempe, AZ), **Jan 2**
Totenberg, Nina: Birth, **Jan 14**
Toulouse-Lautrec, Henri de: Birth Anniv, **Nov 24**
Tour de France, **Jul 1**
Tourism Day, World, **Sep 27**
Tourism Week, Natl, **May 13**
Town Criers Day, Intl, **Jul 10**
Town Meeting Day (Vermont), **Mar 7**
Towne, Benjamin: First American Daily Newspaper: Anniv, **May 30**
Townsend, Robert: Birth, **Feb 6**
Townshend, Pete: Birth, **May 19**
Toy Show, Natl Farm (Dyersville, IA), **Nov 3**
Toy Tips Executive Toy Test (New York, NY), **Sep 1**
Toynbee, Arnold J.: Birth Anniv, **Apr 14**

Toys: Farm Toy Show & Auction (Sauk Centre, MN), Feb 11
Tracey Ullman Show TV Premiere: Anniv, Apr 5
Track and Field
Bannister Breaks Four-Minute Mile: Anniv, **May 6**
Big 12 Men's and Women's Indoor Track Chmpshps (Lincoln, NE), **Feb 24**
Big 12 Men's and Women's Outdoor Track/Field Chmpshps (Waco, TX), **May 12**
Big Ten Men's and Women's Outdoor Track/Field Chmpshps, **May 12**
Big Ten Men's Indoor Track/Field Chmpshps (Iowa City, IA), **Feb 25**
Big Ten Women's Indoor Track/Field Chmpshps, **Feb 25**
Jesse Owens' Remarkable Records: Anniv, **May 25**
NAIA Men's and Women's Cross Country Natl Chmpshps (Louisville, KY), **Nov 18**
NAIA Men's and Women's Indoor Track/Field Chmpshps, **Mar 2**
NAIA Men's and Women's Outdoor Track/Field Chmpshps, **May 25**
NCAA Div I Men's and Women's Track Chmpshps (Sacramento, CA), **Jun 7**
NCAA Indoor Track/Field Chmpshps (Fayetteville, AR), **Mar 10**
Simplot Games (Pocatello, ID), **Feb 16**
Tracy, Spencer: Birth Anniv, Apr 5
Trade Days, First Monday (Scottsboro, AL), Jan 1
Trade Fair, Canton Autumn (China), Oct 15
Trade Week, World (Pres Proc), May 21
Trafalgar, Battle of: Anniv, Oct 21
Trail of Courage Living-History Fest (Rochester, IN), Sep 16
Trail of Tears Commemoration (Waterloo, AL), Sep 16
Trails Day, Natl, Jun 3
Transatlantic Flight, First Nonstop: Anniv, Jun 14
Transatlantic Phoning: Anniv, Jan 7
Transcontinental Flight, First Scheduled: Anniv, Jan 25
Transfer Day (US Virgin Islands), Mar 31
Transistor Unveiled: Anniv, Dec 23
Transportation Week, Natl (Pres Proc), May 14
Travalena, Fred: Birth, Oct 6
Travanti, Daniel J.: Birth, Mar 7
Travel Show, New York Times (New York, NY), Feb 24
Travelers with Disabilities Awareness Week, Nov 26
Travers, Mary: Birth, Nov 7
Travis, Nancy: Birth, Sep 21
Travis, Randy: Birth, May 4
Travolta, John: Birth, Feb 18
Treasury Dept, US: Anniv, Sep 2
Treaty of Guadalupe Hidalgo: Anniv, Feb 2
Treaty of Paris Ends French and Indian War: Anniv, Feb 10
Trebek, Alex: Birth, Jul 22
Tree Planting Day, Natl (Lesotho), Mar 21
Trelawney, Edward J.: Birth Anniv, Nov 13
Trevino, Lee: Birth, Dec 1
Trial Technology Day, Jun 7
Triangle Shirtwaist Fire: Anniv, Mar 25
Triathlon
Ironman Triathlon World Chmpshp (Kailua-Kona, HI), **Oct 14**
Northeast Missouri Triathlon (Kirksville, MO), **Sep 10**
Sawyer/Louisville Landsharks Triathlon (Louisville, KY), **Aug 5**
Tribeca Film Fest (New York, NY), Apr 29
Trick or Treat Night, Oct 31
Trillin, Calvin: Birth, Dec 5
Trinidad
Carnival (Port of Spain), **Feb 27**
Emancipation Day, **Aug 1**
Independence Day, **Aug 31**
Indian Arrival Day (Port of Spain), **May 30**
Spiritual Baptist Liberation Shouter Day, **Mar 30**
Trinity Sunday, Jun 11
Tripplehorn, Jeanne: Birth, Jun 10
Tritt, Travis: Birth, Feb 9
Triumph of the Will (Riefenstahl, Leni: Birth Anniv), Aug 22
Trivia Contest, World's Largest (Stevens Point, WI), Apr 7
Trivia Day, Jan 4
Trollope, Anthony: Birth Anniv, Apr 24
Truancy Law: Anniv, Apr 12
Trudeau, Garry: Birth, Jul 21
Trudeau, Pierre Elliott: Birth Anniv, Oct 18
True Confessions Day, Mar 15
Truffaut, Francois: Birth Anniv, Feb 6
Truman Doctrine: Anniv, May 22
Truman, Bess (Elizabeth): Birth Anniv, Feb 13
Truman, Harry S: Birth Anniv, May 8

Truman, Harry S: Dewey Defeats Truman Headline: Anniv, Nov 3
Trumbull, Jonathan: Birth Anniv, Oct 12
Trump, Donald: Birth, Jun 14
Trust Your Intuition Day, May 10
Truth or Consequences TV Premiere: Anniv, Sep 7
Truth, Sojourner: Death Anniv, Nov 26
Tsunami, Highest Recorded in History: Anniv, Jul 9
Tu B'Shvat, Feb 13
Tubb, Ernest: Birth Anniv, Feb 9
Tubman, Harriet: Death Anniv, Mar 10
Tucci, Stanley: Birth, Jan 11
Tucker, Chris: Birth, Aug 31
Tucker, Michael: Birth, Feb 6
Tucker, Tanya: Birth, Oct 10
Tug Fest, Great River (Port Byron, IL; LeClaire, IA), Aug 11
Tulip Fest, Albany (Albany, NY), May 12
Tulip Time Fest, Holland (Holland, MI), May 6
Tulip Time Fest, Pella (Pella, IA), May 4
Tulsa Boat, Sport & Travel Show (Tulsa, OK), Jan 30
Tune, Tommy: Birth, Feb 28
Tunie, Tamara: Birth, Mar 14
Tunisia
Independence Day, **Mar 20**
Martyrs' Day, **Apr 9**
Republic Day, **Jul 25**
Tree Fest, **Nov 12**
Women's Day, **Aug 13**
Tunney, Gene: Long Count Day, Sep 22
Tunney, James Joseph (Gene): Birth Anniv, May 25
Turgeon, Pierre: Birth, Aug 29
Turkey
Constantinople Falls to the Turks: Anniv, **May 29**
National Sovereignty/Children's Day, **Apr 23**
Republic Day, **Oct 29**
Saint Peter's Day, **Jun 29**
Turkish Earthquake: Anniv, **Aug 17**
Victory Day, **Aug 30**
Youth and Sports Day, **May 19**
Turkey Days, King (Worthington, MN), Sep 16
Turkey Lovers' Month, June Is, Jun 1
Turkey Rama (McMinnville, OR), Jul 13
Turkey Vultures Return to the Living Sign (Canisteo, NY), Mar 11
Turkey-Free Thanksgiving, Nov 23
Turkmenistan
Independence Day, **Oct 27**
Neutrality Day, **Dec 12**
Revival and Unity Day, **May 18**
Turkoglu, Hedo: Birth, Mar 19
Turlington, Christy: Birth, Jan 2
Turn Beauty Inside Out Day, May 17
Turner, Ike: Birth, Nov 5
Turner, Janine: Birth, Dec 6
Turner, John Napier: Birth, Jun 7
Turner, Kathleen: Birth, Jun 19
Turner, Ted: Birth, Nov 19
Turner, Tina: Birth, Nov 26
Turner's Frontier Address: Anniv, Jul 12
Turtle Day, World, May 23
Turtle Races (Danville, IL), Jun 10
Turturro, John: Birth, Feb 28
Turturro, Nick: Birth, Jan 29
Tushingham, Rita: Birth, Mar 14
Tuskegee Airmen Activated: Anniv, Mar 22
Tuskegee Institute Opening: Anniv, Jul 4
Tuskegee Univ 125th Anniv (Tuskegee, AL), Apr 2
Tuskegee Univ: Black History Month (Tuskegee, AL), Feb 1
Tussaud, Marie: Birth Anniv, Dec 7
Tut, King: Tomb Discovery Anniv, Nov 4
Tutor Appreciation Day, Apr 8
Tutu, Desmond: Birth, Oct 7
Tuvalu: National Holiday, Oct 1
Tuxedo, First Created, Oct 10
TV Turnoff Week, Natl, Apr 24
Twain, Mark (Samuel Clemens): Birth Anniv, Nov 30
Twain, Mark: Natl Tom Sawyer Days (Hannibal, MO), Jul 1
Twain, Shania: Birth, Aug 28
20/20 TV Premiere: Anniv, Jun 6
Tweed Day, Apr 3
Tweed, Shannon: Birth, Mar 10
Twelfth Day (Epiphany), Jan 6
Twelfth Night, Jan 5
Twellman, Taylor: Birth, Feb 29
Twenty Questions TV Premiere: Anniv, Nov 26
Twiggy: Birth, Sep 19
Twilight Zone TV Premiere: Anniv, Oct 2
Twins Day Fest (Twinsburg, OH), Aug 4
Twit Award Month, Intl, Apr 1

Twitty, Conway: Birth Anniv, Sep 1
2001: A Space Odyssey Premiere: Anniv, Apr 3
Tybee 500 (Hollywood, FL, and Tybee Island, GA), May 6
Tyler, Aisha: Birth, Sep 18
Tyler, Anne: Birth, Oct 25
Tyler, John: Birth Anniv, Mar 29
Tyler, Julia G.: Birth Anniv, May 4
Tyler, Letitia Christian: Birth Anniv, Nov 12
Tyler, Liv: Birth, Jul 1
Tyler's Cabinet Resigns: Anniv, Sep 11
Tynan, Ronan: Birth, May 14
Tynwald Day (Isle of Man), Jul 5
Typewriter, First: Anniv, Jun 23
Tyson, Cicely: Birth, Dec 19
Tyson, Mike: Birth, Jun 30

U-2 Incident: Anniv, May 1
Ueberroth, Peter: Birth, Sep 2
Uecker, Bob: Birth, Jan 26
Uganda
Independence Day, **Oct 9**
Liberation Day, **Apr 11**
Uggams, Leslie: Birth, May 25
Ukraine
Chernobyl Reactor Disaster: Anniv, **Apr 26**
Independence Day, **Aug 24**
October Revolution, **Nov 7**
Odessa Retaken Anniv, **Apr 10**
Ukrainian Day, **Jan 22**
Ullman, Tracey: Birth, Dec 30
Ullmann, Liv: Birth, Dec 16
Ulrich, Skeet: Birth, Jan 20
Ultimate Sport & RV Show (Grand Rapids, MI), Mar 16
Ultraviolet Awareness/Sight-Saving Month, Natl, May 1
Umbrella Month, Natl, Mar 1
Umbrella: Open an Umbrella Indoors Day, Natl, Mar 13
Underdog Day, Dec 15
Underground America Day, May 14
Underwear Day, Natl, Aug 9
Underwood, Blair: Birth, Aug 25
UNESCO: Anniv, Nov 4
UNICEF (UN): Anniv, Dec 11
Union of Soviet Socialist Republics
Coup Attempt in the Soviet Union: Anniv, **Aug 19**
Moscow Communique: Anniv, **May 29**
Saint Petersburg Name Restored: Anniv, **Sep 6**
Soviet Union Dissolved: Anniv, **Dec 8**
Troop Withdrawal/Afghanistan Deadline, **Feb 15**
Union, Gabrielle: Birth, Oct 29
Unitas, Johnny: Birth Anniv, May 7
United Arab Emirates
National Day (Independence), **Dec 2**
United Kingdom. See also individual countries
Accession of Queen Elizabeth II: Anniv, **Feb 6**
Battle of Britain Day, **Sep 15**
Battle of Britain Week, **Sep 10**
Boxing Day, **Dec 26**
Boxing Day Bank Holiday, **Dec 26**
Commonwealth Day, **Mar 13**
Coronation Day, **Jun 2**
Easter Monday Bank Holiday, **Apr 17**
Good Friday Bank Holiday, **Apr 14**
Holocaust Memorial Day, **Jan 27**
May Day Bank Holiday, **May 1**
New Year's Holiday, **Jan 1**
Spring Bank Holiday, **May 29**
Summer Bank Holiday, **Aug 28**
Summer Time, **Mar 27**
World Book Day, **Mar 2**
United Nations
Abolition of Slavery, Intl Day for the, **Dec 2**
Africa Industrialization Day, **Nov 20**
AIDS Day, World, **Dec 1**
Biological Diversity, Intl Day for, **May 22**
Charter Signed: Anniv, **Jun 26**
Civil Aviation Day, Intl, **Dec 7**
Cooperatives, Intl Day of, **Jul 1**
Day for Preventing the Exploitation of the Environment in War and Armed Conflict, Intl, **Nov 6**
Day for Women's Rights & Intl Peace, **Mar 8**
Disabled Persons, Intl Day of, **Dec 3**
Disarmament Week, **Oct 24**
Drug Abuse/Illicit Trafficking, Intl Day Against, **Jun 26**
Elimination of Violence against Women, Intl Day for the, **Nov 25**
Eradication of Poverty, Intl Day for, **Oct 17**
Families, Intl Day of, **May 15**
First General Assembly: Anniv, **Jan 10**
General Assembly Opening Day, **Sep 19**
Human Rights Day, **Dec 10**
Innocent Children Victims of Aggression, Intl Day of, **Jun 4**

United Nations (cont'd)—Utah

International Day for Preservation of the Ozone Layer, **Sep 16**
International Day for Tolerance, **Nov 16**
International Day of Peace, **Sep 21**
International Day of United Nations Peacekeepers, **May 29**
Land Mine Ban: Anniv, **Mar 1**
Literacy Day, Intl, **Sep 8**
Migrants Day, Intl, **Dec 18**
Millennium Summit: Anniv, **Sep 6**
Mother Language Day, Intl, **Feb 21**
Mountain Day, Intl, **Dec 11**
Natural Disaster Reduction, Intl Day for, **Oct 11**
Older Persons, Intl Day of, **Oct 1**
Public Service Day, **Jun 23**
Racial Discrimination, Intl Day for Elimination of, **Mar 21**
Racism/Racial Discrimination, Solidarity Against, **Mar 21**
Remembrance of the Slave Trade and its Abolition, Intl Day for the, **Aug 23**
Revokes Resolution on Zionism: Anniv, **Dec 16**
Solidarity with Palestinian People, Intl Day of, **Nov 29**
Taiwan Expelled: Anniv, **Oct 25**
Telecommunication Day, World, **May 17**
UNESCO: Anniv, **Nov 4**
UNICEF Day, Natl (Pres Proc), **Oct 31**
UNICEF: Anniv, **Dec 11**
United Nations Day, **Oct 24**
United Nations Day (Pres Proc), **Oct 24**
Universal Children's Day, **Nov 20**
Victims of Torture, Intl Day in Support of, **Jun 26**
Volunteer Day for Economic/Social Dvmt, Intl, **Dec 5**
Water, World Day for, **Mar 22**
Week of Solidarity with the Peoples of Non-Self-Governing Territories, **May 25**
World Book and Copyright Day, **Apr 23**
World Day for Cultural Diversity for Dialogue and Development, **May 21**
World Day to Combat Desertification and Drought, **Jun 17**
World Development Information Day, **Oct 24**
World Environment Day, **Jun 5**
World Food Day, **Oct 16**
World Habitat Day, **Oct 2**
World Health Day, **Apr 7**
World Health Organization: Anniv, **Apr 7**
World Maritime Day, **Sep 25**
World Mental Health Day, **Oct 10**
World Meteorological Day, **Mar 23**
World No-Tobacco Day, **May 31**
World Population Day, **Jul 11**
World Post Day, **Oct 9**
World Press Freedom Day, **May 3**
World Refugee Day, **Jun 20**
World Space Week, **Oct 4**
World Teachers' Day, **Oct 5**
World Television Day, **Nov 21**
World Tuberculosis Day, **Mar 24**
World's Indigenous People, Intl Day of the, **Aug 9**
Year of Deserts and Desertification, Intl, **Jan 1**
Youth Day, Intl, **Aug 12**
United Planet Month, Sep 1
United States (government and history)
Air Force Established: Anniv, **Sep 18**
Armed Forces Unified: Anniv, **Jul 26**
Army Established: Anniv, **Jun 14**
Attack on America: Anniv, **Sep 11**
Attack on the USS Liberty: Anniv, **Jun 8**
Attempt To Free Iran Hostages: Anniv, **Apr 24**
Bank Bailout Bill: Anniv, **Nov 27**
Bank Holiday: Anniv, **Mar 5**
Bureau of Indian Affairs Established, **Mar 11**
Capitol Cornerstone Laid: Anniv, **Sep 18**
Civil Rights Act of 1964: Anniv, **Jul 2**
Civil Rights Act of 1968: Anniv, **Apr 11**
Clinton Impeachment Proceedings: Anniv, **Dec 20**
Coins Stamped "In God We Trust": Anniv, **Apr 22**
Congress Assembles, **Jan 3**
Congress Authorized Force Against Iraq: Anniv, **Jan 12**
Congress First Meets at Washington: Anniv, **Nov 21**
Congress: First Meeting under Constitution: Anniv, **Mar 4**
Constitution of the US: Anniv, **Sep 17**
Customs: Anniv, **Aug 1**
Daylight Saving Time Begins, **Apr 2**
Daylight Saving Time Ends, **Oct 29**
Death Penalty Banned: Anniv, **Jun 29**
Declaration of Independence Approval and Signing: Anniv, **Jul 4**
Dept of Justice: Anniv, **Jun 22**
Dept of State Founded: Anniv, **Jul 27**
Distinguished Service Medal: Anniv, **Mar 7**

District of Columbia Establishing Legislation: Anniv, **Jul 16**
Dred Scott Decision: Anniv, **Mar 6**
Family-Leave Bill: Anniv, **Feb 5**
Federal Communications Commission Created: Anniv, **Feb 26**
Federal Credit Union Act: Anniv, **Jun 26**
Federal Govt Seizure of Steel Mills: Anniv, **Apr 8**
Female House Page, First Formal: Anniv, **May 14**
55 mph Speed Limit: Anniv, **Jan 2**
First Brawl in US House of Representatives: Anniv, **Jan 30**
First Census: Anniv, **Aug 1**
First Elected Woman Senator: Anniv, **Jan 12**
First Mint in America: Anniv, **Jun 10**
First US Government Building: Anniv, **Jul 31**
First Woman US Ambassador Appointed: Anniv, **Oct 28**
Flood Victims Relief: Anniv, **Aug 12**
General Election Day, **Nov 7**
Gerald Ford: Assassination Attempts: Anniv, **Sep 5**
Great Seal of the US: Authorization Anniv, **Jan 28**
Great Seal of the US: First Use Anniv, **Sep 16**
Great Seal of the US: Proposed: Anniv, **Jul 4**
Ground War Against Iraq Begins: Anniv, **Feb 23**
Home Owners Loan Act: Anniv, **Jun 13**
Hostages in Iran Released: Anniv, **Jan 20**
Income Tax: Anniv, **Mar 8**
Independence Day, **Jul 4**
Invasion of Panama: Anniv, **Dec 20**
Irwin Earns 1st Medal of Honor: Anniv, **Feb 13**
Japan Bombed: Anniv, **Apr 18**
Japanese Internment: Anniv, **Feb 19**
Johnson Impeachment Proceedings: Anniv, **Feb 24**
Kuwait Liberated: Anniv, **Feb 27**
Labor Relations Act, Natl: Anniv, **Jul 5**
Lewis & Clark Expedition Commissioned: Anniv, **Jan 18**
Lewis & Clark Expedition Returns: Anniv, **Sep 23**
Lewis and Clark Expedition Sets Out: Anniv, **May 14**
Library of Congress: Anniv, **Apr 24**
Lincoln Signs Income Tax: Anniv, **Jul 1**
Military Ban on Homosexuals Eased: Anniv, **Jan 29**
Moscow Communique: Anniv, **May 29**
Motor Voter Bill Signed: Anniv, **May 20**
NAFTA Signed: Anniv, **Dec 8**
Native American Rights Recognized: Anniv, **May 12**
Nixon's Trip to China: Anniv, **Feb 21**
Nuclear-Free World, First Step Toward a: Anniv, **Dec 8**
Operation Iraqi Freedom: Anniv, **Mar 19**
Paper Money Issued: Anniv, **Mar 10**
Peace Corps Founded: Anniv, **Mar 1**
Persian Gulf War Begins: Anniv, **Jan 16**
Philippine Independence: Anniv, **Mar 24**
Pony Express, Inauguration of: Anniv, **Apr 3**
Postmaster General Established: Anniv, **Sep 22**
President Occupies the White House, **Nov 1**
Presidential Succession Act: Anniv, **Jul 18**
Ratification Day, **Jan 14**
Sanctions Against South Africa Lifted: Anniv, **Jul 10**
Securities and Exchange Commission Created: Anniv, **Jun 6**
Senate Quorum: Anniv, **Apr 6**
Shanghai Communique: Anniv, **Feb 27**
Standard Time Act: Anniv, **Mar 19**
Sumner Attacked in the Senate: Anniv, **May 22**
Supreme Court Abortion Notification Ruling: Anniv, **Jun 25**
Supreme Court Bans School Prayer: Anniv, **Jun 25**
Supreme Court Right to Die Ruling: Anniv, **Jun 25**
Supreme Court Upholds Ban on Abortion Counseling: Anniv, **May 23**
Treasury Department: Anniv, **Sep 2**
Treaty of Guadalupe Hidalgo (with Mexico): Anniv, **Feb 2**
Truman Doctrine: Anniv, **May 22**
Tyler's Cabinet Resigns: Anniv, **Sep 11**
Uniform Time Zone Plan: Anniv, **Nov 18**
US Capital Established at NYC: Anniv, **Sep 13**
US Enters WWI: Anniv, **Apr 6**
US Mint: Anniv, **Apr 2**
US Takes Out Its First Loan: Anniv, **Sep 18**
Vietnam Peace Agreement Signed: Anniv, **Jan 27**
Vietnam War Protestors Storm Pentagon: Anniv, **Oct 21**
Voting Rights Act Signed: Anniv, **Aug 6**
WAAC: Anniv, **May 14**
War Department: Establishment Anniv, **Aug 7**
War of 1812: Declaration Anniv, **Jun 18**
War on Poverty: Anniv, **Jan 8**
Washington Crosses the Delaware: Anniv, **Dec 25**
Water Pollution Control Act: Anniv, **Oct 18**
White House Easter Egg Roll: Anniv, **Apr 2**

Woman Runs the US House of Representatives: Anniv, **Jun 20**
Write to Congress Day, Natl, **Jan 3**
UNIVAC Computer: Anniv, Jun 14
Universal Children's Day (UN), Nov 20
Universal Father's Week, Jun 18
Universal Hour of Peace, Dec 31
Universal Human Rights Month, Dec 1
Universal Letter-Writing Week, Jan 8
Unser, Al, Jr: Birth, Apr 19
Unser, Al: Birth, May 29
Unser, Bobby: Birth, Feb 20
Up Helly Aa (Scotland), Jan 31
Update Your References Week, May 1
Update Your Resume Month, Sep 1
Updike, John: Birth, Mar 18
Upjohn, Richard: Birth Anniv, Jan 22
Upshaw, Dawn: Birth, Jul 17
Upshaw, Gene: Birth, Aug 15
Upstairs, Downstairs TV Premiere: Anniv, Oct 10
Upsy Daisy Day, Jun 8
Uranus, Discovery of Planet: Anniv, Mar 13
Uris, Leon: Birth Anniv, Aug 3
Urlacher, Brian: Birth, May 25
Uruguay
Artigas Day, **Jun 19**
Battle of Las Piedras Day, **May 18**
Constitution Day, **Jul 18**
Independence Day, **Aug 25**
Landing of the 33 Patriots, **Apr 19**
US Air Force Academy Established: Anniv, Apr 1
US Amateur (Golf) Chmpshp (Chaska, MN), Aug 21
US Amateur Public Links (Golf) Chmpshp (Bremerton, WA), Jul 10
US and Vatican Reestablish Diplomatic Relations: Anniv, Jan 10
US House, Black Page Appointed: Anniv, Apr 9
US Mid-Amateur (Golf) Chmpshp (Flagstaff, AZ), Sep 9
US Military Academy Founded: Anniv, Mar 16
US Natl Snow Sculpting Competition (Lake Geneva, WI), Feb 1
US Naval Academy Founded: Anniv, Oct 10
US Navy: Authorization Anniv, Oct 13
US Open (Golf) Chmpshp (Mamaroneck, NY), Jun 15
US Senior Open (Golf) Chmpshp (Hutchinson, KS), Jul 6
US Virgin Islands
Danish West Indies Emancipation Day, **Jul 3**
Liberty Day, **Nov 1**
National Park Established: Anniv, **Aug 2**
Organic Act Day, **Jun 19**
Transfer Day, **Mar 31**
US Women's Amateur (Golf) Chmpshp (North Plains, OR), Aug 7
US Women's Amateur Public Links (Golf) Chmpshp (Pueblo, CO), Jun 20
US Women's Open (Golf) Chmpshp (Newport, RI), Jun 29
USA Film Fest (Dallas, TX), Apr 20
USA Today First Published: Anniv, Sep 15
USGA Senior Amateur (Golf) Chmpshp (Newburgh, IN), Sep 16
Usher: Birth, Oct 14
USO Birthday, Feb 4
USS Constitution Launched: Anniversary, Oct 21
USS Constitution Saved by Poem: Anniv, Sep 16
USS Iowa, Explosion on: Anniv, Apr 19
USS Liberty, Attack on: Anniv, Jun 8
USS Princeton Explosion: Anniv, Feb 28
USS Pueblo Seized: Anniv, Jan 23
USS Stark Attacked: Anniv, May 17
USSR Established: Anniv, Dec 30
Ustinov, Peter: Birth Anniv, Apr 16
Usui, Mikao. See World Day of Reiki, Aug 15
Utah
Admission Day, **Jan 4**
America's First Department Store (Salt Lake City), **Oct 16**
Arches Natl Park Established: Anniv, **Nov 12**
Bennett, Robert F.: Birth, **Sep 18**
Bryce Canyon Natl Park Established: Anniv, **Jan 1**
Capitol Reef Natl Park Established: Anniv, **Dec 18**
Dinosaur Roundup Rodeo (Vernal), **Jul 12**
Hatch, Orrin: Birth, **Mar 22**
Huntsman, Jr, John: Birth, **Mar 26**
Jell-O Week, **Feb 12**
Payson Golden Onion Days (Payson), **Sep 1**
Pioneer Day, **Jul 24**
Salt Lake's Family Christmas Gift Show (Sandy), **Nov 10**
Slamdance (Park City), **Jan 19**
Snowbird Jazz & Blues Festival (Snowbird), **Jul 28**
Snowbird Oktoberfest, **Aug 26**
State Fair (Salt Lake City), **Sep 7**
Sundance Film Fest (Park City), **Jan 19**

Utah Women Given Vote: Anniv, **Feb 12**
Walker, Olene: Birth, **Nov 15**
World Folkfest (Springville), **Jul 8**
Zion Natl Park Established: Anniv, **Nov 19**
Utley, Garrick: Birth, **Nov 19**
Uzbekistan
   Army Day, **Jan 14**
   Constitution Day, **Dec 8**
   Day of Memory and Honor, **May 9**
   Independence Day, **Sep 1**

Vaccaro, Brenda: Birth, **Nov 18**
Vachon, Rogie: Birth, **Sep 8**
Vaisakhi (India), **Apr 14**
Valderrama, Carlos: Birth, **Sep 2**
Valens, Richie: Day the Music Died: Death Anniv, **Feb 3**
Valentine, Bobby: Birth, **May 13**
Valentine, Karen: Birth, **May 25**
Valentine, Scott: Birth, **Jun 3**
Valentine's Ball, WMAS's (Springfield, MA), **Feb 10**
Valentine's Day, **Feb 14**
Valentine's Day Massacre: Anniv, **Feb 14**
Valentine's Day, Chinese (Double Seven Fest), **Jul 31**
Valentino (Rudolph) Memorial Service, **Aug 23**
Valentino, Rudolph: Birth Anniv, **May 6**
Valentino, Rudolph: Sheik Film Release: Anniv, **Nov 20**
Valenzuela, Fernando: Birth, **Nov 1**
Vallee, Rudy: Birth Anniv, **Jul 28**
Valli, Frankie: Birth, **May 3**
Van Ark, Joan: Birth, **Jun 16**
Van Brocklin, Norm: Birth Anniv, **Mar 15**
Van Buren, Abigail: Birth, **Jul 4**
Van Buren, Hannah Hoes: Birth Anniv, **Mar 8**
Van Buren, Martin: Birth Anniv, **Dec 5**
Van Cleef, Lee: Birth Anniv, **Jan 9**
Van Damme, Jean-Claude: Birth, **Oct 18**
Van Der Beek, James: Birth, **Mar 8**
Van Devere, Trish: Birth, **Mar 9**
Van Doren, Mamie: Birth, **Feb 6**
Van Dyke, Dick: Birth, **Dec 13**
Van Dyke, Jerry: Birth, **Jul 27**
Van Exel, Nick: Birth, **Nov 27**
Van Fleet, Jo: Birth Anniv, **Dec 30**
Van Gogh, Vincent: Birth Anniv, **Mar 30**
Van Gundy, Jeff: Birth, **Jan 19**
Van Halen, Eddie: Birth, **Jan 26**
Van Heusen, Jimmy: Birth Anniv, **Jan 26**
Van Horn, Keith: Birth, **Oct 23**
Van Patten, Dick: Birth, **Dec 9**
Van Patten, Joyce: Birth, **Mar 9**
Van Peebles, Mario: Birth, **Jan 15**
Van Peebles, Melvin: Birth, **Aug 21**
Van Slyke, Andy: Birth, **Dec 21**
Vancouver, George: Birth Anniv, **Jun 22**
Vanderbilt, Gloria: Birth, **Feb 20**
Vanilla Ice: Birth, **Oct 31**
Vanuatu: Independence Day, **Jul 30**
Vardalos, Nia: Birth, **Sep 24**
Vatican and US Reestablish Diplomatic Relations: Anniv, **Jan 10**
Vatican City: Independence Anniv, **Feb 11**
Vatican Council II: Anniv, **Oct 11**
Vaughan Williams, Ralph: Birth Anniv, **Oct 12**
Vaughan, Sarah: Birth Anniv, **Mar 27**
Vaughn, Robert: Birth, **Nov 22**
Vaughn, Vince: Birth, **Mar 28**
VCR Introduced: Anniv, **Jun 7**
V-E Day, **May 8**
Veblen, Thorstein: Birth Anniv, **Jul 30**
Veeck, Bill: Birth Anniv, **Feb 9**
Veep Day, **Aug 9**
Vega, Suzanne: Birth, **Jul 11**
Vegan Month, **Nov 1**
Vegan World Day, **Jun 21**
Vegetarian Day, World, **Oct 1**
Vegetarian Month, **Oct 1**
Vegetarian Resource Group's Essay Contest for Kids, **May 1**
Vegetarianism: Independence-from-Meat Day, **Jul 4**
Vegetarianism: Natl Have-A-Heart Day, **Feb 14**
VelJohnson, Reginald: Birth, **Aug 16**
Venezuela
   Battle of Carabobo Day, **Jun 24**
   Independence Day, **Jul 5**
Ventura, Jesse: Birth, **Jul 15**
Ventura, Robin: Birth, **Jul 14**
Verboort Sausage and Kraut Dinner (Forest Grove, OR), **Nov 4**
Vercors, Jean: Birth Anniv, **Feb 26**
Verdi, Giuseppi: Birth Anniv, **Oct 10**
Verdon, Gwen: Birth Anniv, **Jan 13**
Vereen, Ben: Birth, **Oct 10**
Vermeil, Dick: Birth, **Oct 30**

Vermont
   Admission Day, **Mar 4**
   All About Apples (Woodstock), **Sep 24**
   Antique/Classic Car Show (Bennington), **Sep 14**
   Brookfield Ice Harvest (Brookfield), **Jan 28**
   Champlain Valley Fair (Essex Junction), **Aug 26**
   Children's Day (Woodstock), **Aug 26**
   Cow Appreciation Day (Woodstock), **Jul 15**
   Douglas, Jim: Birth, **Jun 21**
   Family Halloween, A (Woodstock), **Oct 29**
   Harvest Celebration (Woodstock), **Oct 7**
   Jay Peak Annual Arts & Crafts Fair (Jay), **Oct 7**
   Jeffords, James M.: Birth, **May 11**
   Leahy, Patrick J.: Birth, **Mar 31**
   Northeast Kingdom Fall Foliage Fest (Walden), **Oct 2**
   Old Vermont Fourth (Woodstock), **Jul 4**
   Pumpkin Day (Woodstock), **Sep 30**
   Quilt Show (Woodstock), **Jul 29**
   Sheep Herding with Border Collies (Woodstock), **Sep 17**
   State Fair (Rutland), **Sep 1**
   Town Meeting Day, **Mar 7**
   Traditional Plowing Match (Woodstock), **May 7**
   Vermont Apple Fest (Springfield), **Oct 7**
   Vermont Maple Fest (St. Albans), **Apr 28**
   Wassail Celebration (Woodstock), **Dec 8**
Verne, Jules: Birth Anniv, **Feb 8**
Verrazano Day, **Apr 17**
Versailles Peace Conference: Anniv, **Jan 18**
Vesak, Day of: See Birthday of the Buddha, **Apr 8**
Vesey, Denmark: Death Anniv, **Jul 2**
Vespucci, Amerigo: Birth Anniv, **Mar 9**
Vesuvius Day, **Aug 24**
Veterans
   ANZAC Day, **Apr 25**
   Branson Veterans Homecoming (Branson, MO), **Nov 5**
   Pearl Harbor Remembrance Day, Natl (Pres Proc), **Dec 7**
   Remembrance Day (Gettysburg, PA), **Nov 18**
   Soldiers' Reunion Celebration (Newton, NC), **Aug 17**
   Veterans Bonus Army Eviction: Anniv, **Jul 28**
   Veterans Day, **Nov 11**
   Veterans Day (Pres Proc), **Nov 11**
   Veterans Day Celebration (Mamou, LA), **Nov 11**
   Veterans of Foreign Wars Established: Anniv, **Sep 29**
   VFW Ladies Auxiliary Organized: Anniv, **Sep 17**
   Vietnam Veterans Memorial Statue Unveiling: Anniv, **Nov 9**
   Women's War Memorial Dedicated: Anniv, **Nov 11**
Vice Presidential Resignation: Anniv, **Dec 28**
Vice-Presidential Candidate, First Woman: Anniv, **Jul 19**
Victims of Torture, Intl Day in Support of (UN), **Jun 26**
Victor Emmanuel III: Birth Anniv, **Nov 11**
Victor, James: Birth, **Jul 27**
Victoria Day (Canada), **May 22**
Victorian Sherlock Holmes Weekend (Cape May, NJ), **Mar 3**
Victorian Week (Cape May, NJ), **Oct 6**
Victory Day (RI), **Aug 14**
Victory in Europe Day, **May 8**
Vidal, Gore: Birth, **Oct 3**
Video Games Day, **Sep 12**
Vieira, Meredith: Birth, **Dec 30**
Vietnam
   Ho Chi Minh: Birth Anniv, **May 19**
   Liberation Day, **Apr 30**
   National Holiday, **Feb 3**
Vietnam War (US undeclared)
   Battle of Hamburger Hill: Anniv, **May 11**
   Cambodia Invaded by US: Anniv, **Apr 30**
   Dien Bien Phu Falls: Anniv, **May 7**
   Gulf of Tonkin Resolution: Anniv, **Aug 7**
   Independence Day, **Sep 2**
   King Opposes Vietnam War: Anniv, **Apr 4**
   My Lai Massacre: Anniv, **Mar 16**
   Saigon Falls to Vietcong: Anniv, **Apr 30**
   Tet Offensive Begins, **Jan 30**
   Vietnam and US Resume Relations: Anniv, **May 26**
   Vietnam Conflict Begins [with French]: Anniv, **Aug 22**
   Vietnam Moratorium Concert: Anniv, **Mar 28**
   Vietnam Peace Agreement Signed: Anniv, **Jan 27**
   Vietnam Veterans Memorial Statue Unveiling: Anniv, **Nov 9**
   Vietnam War Protestors Storm Pentagon: Anniv, **Oct 21**
   Women's War Memorial Dedicated: Anniv, **Nov 11**
Vigoda, Abe: Birth, **Feb 24**
Viking Fest (Frederiksund, Denmark), **Jun 23**
Viking: Up Helly Aa (Scotland), **Jan 31**
Vila, Bob: Birth, **Jun 20**
Vilas, Guillermo: Birth, **Aug 17**

Villeneueve, Jacques: Birth, **Apr 9**
Vilsack, Tom: Birth, **Dec 13**
Vincent, Fay: Birth, **May 29**
Vincent, Jan-Michael: Birth, **Jul 15**
Vinegar Day, **Jun 17**
Vinson, Fred M.: Birth Anniv, **Jan 22**
Vinton, Bobby: Birth, **Apr 16**
Vinyl Record Day, **Aug 12**
Violence, YWCA Week Without, **Oct 15**
Virchow, Rudolf: Birth Anniv, **Oct 13**
Virgen de la Guadalupe: Las Mananitas (Ponce, Puerto Rico), **Dec 12**
Virgin Islands
   Hurricane Supplication Day, **Jul 24**
   Hurricane Thanksgiving Day, **Oct 16**
   Puerto Rico Friendship Day, **Oct 9**
Virginia
   Allen, George: Birth, **Mar 8**
   American Heritage Quilt Show (Staunton), **Sep 24**
   Ash Lawn Opera Fest (Charlottesville), **Jul 10**
   Battle of Bull Run: Anniv, **Jul 21**
   Battle of Cold Harbor: Anniv, **Jun 3**
   Battle of Spotsylvania: Anniv, **May 12**
   Battle of the Wilderness: Anniv, **May 5**
   Birds & Blossoms Spring Nature Fest (Norfolk), **May 11**
   Blue Ridge Folklife Fest (Ferrum), **Oct 28**
   Boardwalk Art Show & Fest (Virginia Beach), **Jun 15**
   Bonnie Blue Natl Horse Show (Lexington), **May 10**
   Bread Riot at Richmond: Anniv, **Apr 2**
   Canoe, Capstan & Cargo (Williamsburg and Yorktown), **Jun 1**
   Chincoteague Easter Decoy Show (Chincoteague Island), **Apr 14**
   Chincoteague Pony Penning (Chincoteague Island), **Jul 25**
   Christmas Candlelight Tour (Fredericksburg), **Dec 9**
   Civil War Days (Chesapeake), **Sep 9**
   Civil War Peace Talks: Anniv, **Feb 3**
   Colonial Christmas (Williamsburg), **Dec 16**
   Craftsmen's Christmas Classic Arts & Crafts Fest (Richmond), **Nov 3**
   Craftsmen's Classic Arts & Crafts Fest (Chantilly), **Mar 24, Oct 20**
   Craftsmen's Classic Arts & Crafts Fest (Richmond), **Mar 10**
   Craftsmen's Classic Arts & Crafts Fest (Roanoke), **Sep 29**
   Cut Your Own Christmas Tree (Charlottesville), **Nov 24**
   Defeat at Five Forks: Anniv, **Apr 1**
   Eighteenth-Century Autumn Market Fair (McLean), **Oct 21**
   Eighteenth-Century Christmas Wassail (McLean), **Dec 10**
   Eighteenth-Century Spring Market Fair (McLean), **May 20**
   Eighteenth-Century Summer Market Fair (McLean), **Jul 15**
   Eighteenth-Century Threshing Day (McLean), **Nov 19**
   Eighteenth-Century Wheat Harvest (McLean), **Jun 25**
   Fall of Richmond: Anniv, **Apr 3**
   First US Breach of Promise Suit: Anniv, **Jun 14**
   Foods/Feasts of Colonial Virginia (Williamsburg), **Nov 23**
   Foxfield Races (Charlottesville), **Apr 29**
   Fredericksburg Day (Fredericksburg), **Apr 18**
   Fredericksburg Heritage Fest (Fredericksburg), **Jul 4**
   Garden of Lights (Norfolk), **Nov 23**
   George Washington Birthday Parade (Alexandria), **Feb 20**
   Gold Cup, Intl (The Plains), **Oct 15**
   Great Peanut Tour (Skippers), **Sep 7**
   Highland County Maple Fest (Highland County), **Mar 11**
   Historic Garden Week, **Apr 22**
   History Alive! (Norfolk), **Oct 6**
   Holiday House Tours (Charlottesville), **Dec 10**
   Holidays in the City Grand Illumination Parade (Norfolk), **Nov 18**
   James Monroe Birthday Celebration (Charlottesville), **Apr 28**
   Jamestown Landing Day (Williamsburg), **May 13**
   Lee-Jackson Day, **Jan 13**
   Martin Luther King Jr Day (Charlottesville), **Jan 16**
   Maymont Flower & Garden Show (Richmond), **Feb 9**
   Migratory Bird Celebration, Intl (Chincoteague), **May 13**
   Military Through the Ages (Williamsburg), **Mar 18**
   Miss Virginia Pageant (Roanoke), **Jun 22**
   Neptune Fest Boardwalk Weekend (Virginia Beach), **Sep 29**

Virginia (cont'd)—Washington

Occoneechee State Park Native American Fest and Pow Wow (Clarksville), **May 13**
Old Fiddlers' Conv (Galax), **Aug 7**
Oyster Fest (Chincoteague Island), **Oct 7**
Peninsula Campaign Intensified: Anniv, **May 9**
Potomac Celtic Fest (Leesburg), **Jun 10**
Presidents' Day at Ash Lawn-Highland (Charlottesville), **Feb 20**
Raid on Richmond: Anniv, **Mar 1**
Ratification Day, **Jun 25**
Richmond Highland Games/Celtic Fest (Richmond), **Oct 21**
Road to Independence (Yorktown), **Jul 2**
Rockbridge Community Fest (Lexington), **Aug 19**
Rockbridge Regional Fair (Lexington), **Jul 18**
Saint Patrick's Day Parade (Roanoke), **Mar 17**
Seed to Stalk (Williamsburg), **Aug 1**
Seven Days Campaign: Anniv, **Jun 25**
Shenandoah Natl Park Established: Anniv, **Dec 26**
Sounds of Season: Holiday Concert (Charlottesville), **Dec 26**
Spring Gardener's Market and Plant Sale (Norfolk), **May 12**
State Chmpshp Chili Cook-off (Roanoke), **May 6**
State Fair (Richmond), **Sep 21**
Stonewall Jackson's Birthday Celebration (Lexington), **Jan 21**
Strawberry Hill Races (Richmond), **Apr 15**
Streetscene (Covington), **Aug 12**
Sugarloaf Crafts Fest (Chantilly), **Jan 27, May 5, Dec 8**
Sugarloaf Crafts Fest (Manassas), **Sep 8**
Taste of the Blue Ridge Blues & Jazz Fest (Roanoke), **Sep 9**
Tobacco Harvest (McLean), **Aug 27**
Union Officers Escape Libby Prison: Anniv, **Feb 9**
Upperville Colt/Horse Show (Upperville), **Jun 5**
Virginia Christmas Show (Richmond), **Nov 2**
Virginia Gold Cup (Warrenton), **May 6**
Virginia Lake Fest (Clarksville), **Jul 13**
Virginia Peanut Fest (Emporia), **Sep 22**
Virginia Spring Show (Richmond), **Mar 9**
Virginia Wine Fest (Charlottesville), **May 20**
Warner, John: Birth, **Feb 18**
Warner, Mark: Birth, **Dec 15**
Yorktown Day (Yorktown), **Oct 19**
Yorktown Victory Day, **Oct 9**
Virginia Company Expedition to America: Anniv, Dec 20
Virginia Plan Proposed: Anniv, May 29
Virginian TV Premiere: Anniv, Sep 19
Virgo Begins, Aug 23
Vision and Learning Month, Children's, Aug 1
Vision Research Month, Jun 1
Vision, Healthy, Month, May 1
Vision: AMD/Low Vision Awareness Month, Feb 1
Visit Your Relatives Day, May 18
Visnjic, Goran: Birth, **Sep 9**
Vitale, Dick: Birth, **Jun 9**
Vitamin C Isolated: Anniv, Apr 4
Viticulturist's Day (Bulgaria), Feb 14
Vitter, David: Birth, **May 3**
Vitti, Monica: Birth, **Nov 3**
Viva! Chicago Latin Music Fest (Chicago, IL), Aug 26
V-J Day (Announcement), Aug 14
V-J Day (Ratification), Sep 2
V-Mail Delivery: Anniv, Jun 22
Voight, Jon: Birth, **Dec 29**
Voinovich, George V.: Birth, **Jul 15**
Volcanoes
Cameroon: Eruption: Anniv, **Aug 22**
Laki Volcano Eruption: Anniv, **Jun 8**
Montserrat: Volcano Erupts: Anniv, **Jun 25**
Mount Pelee Eruption: Anniv, **May 8**
Mount Pinatubo Erupts in Philippines: Anniv, **Jun 11**
Mount Saint Helens Eruption: Anniv, **May 18**
Vesuvius Day (Pompeii Destroyed): Anniv, **Aug 24**
Volksfest (New Glarus, WI), Aug 6
Volleyball: NAIA Women's Volleyball Chmpshp (San Diego, CA), Nov 30
Voltaire: Birth Anniv, Nov 21
Volunteers, Volunteering
Community Spirit Days, **Apr 1**
Family Volunteer Day, Natl, **Nov 18**
Join Hands Day, **May 6**
Make a Difference Day, **Oct 28**
Volunteer Day for Economic/Social Dvmt, Intl (UN), **Dec 5**
Volunteer Week, Natl, **Apr 23**
Volunteer Week, Natl (Pres Proc), **Apr 16**
Volunteers Week, Intl, **Jun 1**
Von Braun: First Surface-to-Surface Missile: Anniv, Dec 24
von Furstenberg, Diane: Birth, **Dec 31**
Von Oy, Jenna: Birth, **May 2**

Von Richtofen: Red Baron Shot Down: Anniv, Apr 21
Von Steuben, Baron Friedrich: Birth Anniv, Sep 17
Von Sydow, Max: Birth, Apr 10
Vonnegut, Kurt, Jr: Birth, Nov 11
Voting
Blacks Ruled Eligible to Vote: Anniv, **Apr 3**
Last Week to Register to Vote in US General Elections, **Oct 1**
League of Women Voters Formed: Anniv, **Feb 14**
Motor Voter Bill Signed: Anniv, **May 20**
Suffragists' Voting Attempt: Anniv, **Nov 19**
Susan B. Anthony Fined for Voting, **Jun 6**
Voting Age Changed (26th Amendment): Anniv, **Jul 1**
Voting Rights Act Signed: Anniv, **Aug 6**
Women Denied Vote: Anniv, **Jan 12**
Women's Rights Convention Held (Seneca Falls): Anniv, **Jul 19**
Women's Suffrage Amendment Introduced: Anniv, **Jan 10**
Vox Populi Day, Nov 11
Voyageurs Natl Park Established: Anniv, Apr 8

Wachowski, Andy: Birth, **Dec 29**
Wachowski, Larry: Birth, **Jun 21**
Wade, Dwyane: Birth, **Jan 17**
Wade, Virginia: Birth, **Jul 10**
Wadlow, Robert Pershing: Birth Anniv, **Feb 22**
Waffle Week, Natl, Sep 3
Waggoner, Lyle: Birth, **Apr 13**
Wagner, Billy: Birth, **Jun 25**
Wagner, Honus: Birth Anniv, **Feb 24**
Wagner, Jack P.: Birth, **Oct 3**
Wagner, Kurt: Birth, **Jun 22**
Wagner, Lindsay: Birth, **Jun 22**
Wagner, Richard: Birth Anniv, **May 22**
Wagner, Robert: Birth, **Feb 10**
Wagon Train TV Premiere: Anniv, Sep 18
Wagoner, Porter: Birth, **Aug 12**
Wahl, Ken: Birth, **Dec 11**
Wahlberg, Donnie: Birth, **Aug 17**
Wahlberg, Mark: Birth, **Jun 5**
Waikiki Roughwater Swim (Honolulu, HI), Sep 3
Waitangi Day (New Zealand), Feb 6
Waite, Morrison R.: Birth Anniv, **Nov 29**
Waite, Terry: Birth, **May 31**
Waits, Tom: Birth, **Dec 7**
Waitstaff Day, Natl, May 21
Waitz, Grete: Birth, **Oct 1**
Walden, Narada Michael: Birth, **Apr 23**
Walden, Robert: Birth, **Sep 25**
Waldseemuller, Martin: Remembrance Day, Apr 25
Wales
Christmas Holiday, **Dec 25**
Hay-on-Wye Fest of Literature (Hay-on-Wye), **May 26**
Llangollen Intl Musical Eisteddfod (Llangollen, Denbighshire), **Jul 4**
National Eisteddfod of Wales (Swansea), **Aug 5**
Saint David's Day, **Mar 1**
Walesa, Lech: Birth, **Sep 29**
Walesa, Lech: Solidarity Founded Anniv, Aug 31
Walk on Stilts Day, Jul 27
Walk on Your Wild Side Day, Apr 12
Walken, Christopher: Birth, **Mar 31**
Walker, Alice: Birth, **Feb 9**
Walker, Ally: Birth, **Aug 25**
Walker, Antoine: Birth, **Aug 12**
Walker, Clint: Birth, **May 30**
Walker, Doak: Birth Anniv, **Jan 1**
Walker, Herschel: Birth, **Mar 3**
Walker, Jimmie: Birth, **Jun 25**
Walker, Larry: Birth, **Dec 1**
Walker, Mary E.: Birth Anniv, **Nov 26**
Walker, Mort: Birth, **Sep 3**
Walker, Olene: Birth, **Nov 15**
Walking
Mackinac Bridge Walk (St. Ignace, MI), **Sep 4**
Sauntering Day, World, **Jun 19**
Walk Days, Intl, **Apr 30**
Wallace, Chris: Birth, **Oct 12**
Wallace, George, Shot: Anniv, May 15
Wallace, Henry A.: Birth Anniv, **Oct 7**
Wallace, Mike: Birth, **May 9**
Wallace, Rasheed: Birth, **Sep 17**
Wallace, Rusty: Birth, **Aug 14**
Wallach, Eli: Birth, **Dec 7**
Wallenberg, Raoul: Birth Anniv, Aug 5
Wallet, Skeezix: Birth, **Feb 14**
Walpurgis Night, Apr 30
Walsh, Dylan: Birth, **Nov 17**
Walsh, M. Emmet: Birth, **Mar 22**
Walt Disney TV Premiere: Anniv, Oct 27
Walter Plinge Day (England), Dec 2
Walter, Jessica: Birth, **Jan 31**
Walters, Barbara: Birth, **Sep 25**

Walters, Julie: Birth, **Feb 22**
Walton, Bill: Birth, **Nov 5**
Walton, George: Death Anniv, **Feb 2**
Walton, Izaak: Birth Anniv, **Aug 9**
Walton, Sam: Birth Anniv, **Mar 29**
Waltons TV Premiere: Anniv, Sep 14
Waltrip, Darrell: Birth, **Feb 5**
Wambaugh, Joseph: Birth, **Jan 22**
Wang, Garrett: Birth, **Dec 15**
Wapner, Joseph: Birth, **Nov 15**
War Crimes Trial (Japan): Anniv, Jan 19
War Criminals (German) Execution: Anniv, Oct 16
War is Hell: Anniv, Jun 19
War of 1812: Declaration Anniv, Jun 18
War of the Worlds Broadcast: Anniv, Oct 30
War on Poverty Anniv, Jan 8
War Time: Anniv, Feb 9
Ward, Burt: Birth, **Jul 6**
Ward, Montgomery, Seized: Anniv, Apr 26
Ward, Rachel: Birth, **Sep 12**
Ward, Sela: Birth, **Jul 11**
Ward, Simon: Birth, **Oct 19**
Warden, Jack: Birth, **Sep 18**
Warfield, Marsha: Birth, **Mar 5**
Warner Weather Quotation: Anniv, Aug 24
Warner, Charles Dudley: Birth Anniv, **Sep 12**
Warner, David: Birth, **Jul 29**
Warner, John: Birth, **Feb 18**
Warner, Malcolm-Jamal: Birth, **Aug 18**
Warner, Mark: Birth, **Dec 15**
Warren Commission Report: Anniv, Sep 27
Warren, Earl: Birth Anniv, **Mar 19**
Warren, Lesley Ann: Birth, **Aug 16**
Warren, Michael: Birth, **Mar 5**
Warren, Robert Penn: Birth Anniv, **Apr 24**
Warrens Cranberry Fest (Warrens, WI), Sep 22
Warwick, Dionne: Birth, **Dec 12**
Washington
Admission Day, **Nov 11**
Bumbershoot: The Seattle Arts Fest (Seattle), **Sep 1**
Cantwell, Maria: Birth, **Oct 13**
Commencement Bay Maritime Fest (Tacoma), **Sep 16**
Corvette and High Performance Meet (Puyallup), **Feb 11**
Craft Brewers Conf & BrewExpo America (Seattle), **Apr 11**
Eleanor Roosevelt Day (Menlo), **Aug 12**
Fireworks on the Fjord (Poulsbo), **Jul 3**
Gregoire, Christine: Birth, **Mar 24**
Issaquah Salmon Days Festival (Issaquah), **Oct 7**
Makah Days (Neah Bay), **Aug 25**
Maritime Gig Fest (Gig Harbor), **Jun 3**
Mount Rainier Natl Park: Anniv, **Mar 2**
Mural-in-a-Day (Toppenish), **Jun 3**
Murray, Patty: Birth, **Oct 11**
Nordic Yulefest (Seattle), **Nov 18**
North Cascades Natl Park Established: Anniv, **Oct 2**
Northwest Folklife Fest (Seattle), **May 26**
Olympic Natl Park Established: Anniv, **Jun 29**
Puyallup Spring Fair (Puyallup), **Apr 20**
Seafair (Seattle), **Jul 1**
Seattle Boat Show (Seattle), **Jan 13**
Sequim Irrigation Fest (Sequim), **May 6**
Skagit Valley Tulip Fest (Burlington), **Apr 1**
Tacoma Holiday Food and Gift Fest (Tacoma), **Oct 25**
Tivoli-Viking Days at the Nordic Heritage Museum (Seattle), **Jul 8**
US Amateur Public Links (Golf) Chmpshp (Bremerton), **Jul 10**
Washington State Apple Blossom Fest (Wenatchee), **Apr 27**
Western Washington Fair (Puyallup), **Sep 8**
Washington 2006—World Philatelic Exhibition (Washington, DC), May 27
Washington, Booker T.: Birth Anniv, Apr 5
Washington, Denzel: Birth, Dec 28
Washington, District of Columbia
BookExpo America, **May 19**
Cherry Blossom Fest, **Mar 25**
Davidson Fellows Award Reception, **Sep 27**
District-Establishing Legislation: Anniv, **Jul 16**
Dorothy Porter Wesley Lecture, **Apr 21**
Geographic Bee Finals, Natl, **May 23**
Invasion Anniv, **Aug 24**
Mothers Day at the Wall, **May 14**
Nursing Conf on Pediatric Primary Care, **Apr 5**
R.E.A.D. in America Day, **Sep 23**
Spelling Bee Finals, Natl, **May 31**
Vietnam Veterans Memorial Statue Unveiling: Anniv, **Nov 9**
Washington 2006—World Philatelic Exhibition, **May 27**
Washington Boat Show, **Feb 22**

Washington Home & Garden Show, **Feb 9**
Washington Monument Dedicated: Anniv, **Feb 21**
White House Easter Egg Roll, **Apr 17**
Women's War Memorial Dedicated: Anniv, **Nov 11**
Washington, George
  Address to Continental Army Officers: Anniv, **Mar 15**
  Birth Anniv, **Feb 22**
  Birthday Observance (Legal Holiday), **Feb 20**
  Birthday Parade (Alexandria, VA), **Feb 20**
  Crosses the Delaware: Anniv, **Dec 25**
  Presidential Inauguration Anniv, **Apr 30**
  Takes Command of Continental Army: Anniv, **Jul 3**
  Washington's Birthday Celeb (Laredo, TX), **Jan 26**
  White House Cornerstone Laid: Anniv, **Oct 13**
Washington, Harold: Birth Anniv, **Apr 15**
Washington, Harold: Elected Chicago's First Black Mayor: Anniv, **Apr 11**
Washington, Martha: Birth Anniv, **Jun 21**
Wasserstein, Wendy: Birth, **Oct 18**
Wasson, Craig: Birth, **Mar 15**
Watanabe, Ken: Birth, **Oct 21**
Water Ski Days (Lake City, MN), **Jun 23**
Water, Bottled, Week, Sep 17
Water, World Day for (UN), Mar 22
Water-Drawing Fest (Japan), Mar 1
Waterfowl Fest (Easton, MD), Nov 10
Watergate Day, Jun 17
Waterloo, Battle of: Anniv, **Jun 18**
Watermelon Fest (Rush Springs, OK), Aug 12
Watermelon Fest, Hope (Hope, AR), Aug 10
Watermelon Thump (Luling, TX), Jun 22
Waters, Ethel: Birth Anniv, **Oct 31**
Waters, John: Birth, **Apr 22**
Waters, Muddy: Birth Anniv, **Apr 4**
Waterston, Sam: Birth, **Nov 15**
Watie, Stand: Birth Anniv, **Dec 12**
Watley, Jody: Birth, **Jan 30**
Watson, Doc: Birth, **Mar 2**
Watson, Emily: Birth, **Jan 14**
Watson, Emma: Birth, **Apr 15**
Watson, James: Birth, **Apr 6**
Watson, Tom: Birth, **Sep 4**
Watt, James: Birth Anniv, **Jan 19**
Wattleton, Alyce Faye: Birth, **Jul 8**
Watts Riot: Anniv, **Aug 11**
Watts, Andre: Birth, **Jun 20**
Watts, Charlie: Birth, **Jun 2**
Watts, Rolonda: Birth, **Jul 12**
Wave All Your Fingers at Your Neighbor Day, Feb 7
Wayans, Damon: Birth, **Sep 4**
Wayans, Keenen Ivory: Birth, **Jun 8**
Wayans, Marlon: Birth, **Jul 23**
Wayans, Shawn: Birth, **Jan 19**
Wayne, John: Birth Anniv, **May 26**
Wayne, Mad Anthony: Birth Anniv, **Jan 1**
Wealth Mentality Month, Intl, Jan 1
Wear Red Day, Feb 3
Weather
  Great Blizzard of '88: Anniv, **Mar 12**
  Meteorological Day, World (UN), **Mar 23**
  North America's Coldest Recorded Temperature: Anniv, **Feb 3**
  Warmest Year on Record Declared, **Jan 11**
  Warner Quotation: Anniv, **Aug 24**
  Weatherman's Day, **Feb 5**
Weathers, Carl: Birth, **Jan 14**
Weaver, Dennis: Birth, **Jun 4**
Weaver, Fritz: Birth, **Jan 19**
Weaver, Robert C.: First Black US Cabinet Member: Anniv, **Jan 18**
Weaver, Sigourney: Birth, **Oct 8**
Weaving Week, Spinning and, Oct 2
Webb, Karrie: Birth, **Dec 21**
Webb, Spud: Birth, **Jul 13**
Webber, Chris: Birth, **Mar 1**
Weber, Carl Maria Von: Birth Anniv, **Nov 18**
Weber, Steven: Birth, **Mar 4**
Webster, Daniel: Birth Anniv, **Jan 18**
Webster, Noah: Birth Anniv, **Oct 16**
Webster-Ashburton Treaty Signed: Anniv, **Aug 9**
Wedding of the Giants (Belgium), Aug 27
Wedding of the Sea (Venice, Italy), May 28
Wedding: Bill and Hillary Clinton: Anniv, **Oct 11**
Wedding: Bush, George H.W. and Barbara: Anniv, **Jan 6**
Wedding: Bush, George W. and Laura, Wedding: Anniv, **Nov 5**
Wedding: Jimmy and Rosalynn Carter: Anniv, **Jul 7**
Weddings Month, Natl, Feb 1
Weddings: Santa Cruz Bridal Expo (Santa Cruz, CA), Jan 29
Wedgwood, Josiah: Birth Anniv, **Jul 12**
Week of the Ocean, Natl, Apr 2
Weems, Mason L. (Parson): Birth Anniv, **Oct 11**
Wegman, William: Birth, **Dec 2**

Weights and Measures Day, May 20
Weil, Andrew: Birth, **Jun 8**
Weinberg, Max M.: Birth, **Apr 13**
Weir, Bob: Birth, **Oct 16**
Weir, Peter: Birth, **Aug 21**
Weird Contest Week (Ocean City, NJ), Aug 14
Weiskopf, Tom: Birth, **Nov 9**
Weiss, Michael T.: Birth, **Feb 2**
Weiss, Michael: Birth, **Aug 2**
Weissmuller, Johnny: Birth Anniv, **Jun 2**
Weisz, Rachel: Birth, **Mar 7**
Weitz, Bruce: Birth, **May 27**
Weizmann, Chaim: Birth Anniv, **Nov 27**
Welch, Jack: Birth, **Nov 19**
Welch, Raquel: Birth, **Sep 5**
Welcome Back, Kotter TV Premiere: Anniv, **Sep 9**
Welcomegiving Day, You're, Nov 24
Weld, Tuesday: Birth, **Aug 27**
Welfare: See Health and Welfare, Aug 14
Welk, Lawrence: Birth Anniv, **Mar 11**
Wellderly Day, Mar 20
Weller, Peter: Birth, **Jun 24**
Welles, Orson: Birth Anniv, **May 6**
Welles, Orson: Citizen Kane Premiere: Anniv, **May 1**
Welles, Orson: The Shadow Radio Premiere: Anniv, **Jul 31**
Welling, Tom: Birth, **Apr 26**
Wells, H.G.: Birth Anniv, **Sep 21**
Wells, Ida B.: Birth Anniv, **Jul 16**
Wells, Kitty: Birth, **Aug 30**
Wells, Mary: Birth Anniv, **May 13**
Wen, Ming-Na: Birth, **Nov 20**
Wendt, George: Birth, **Oct 17**
Wenner, Jann: Birth, **Jan 7**
Werfel, Franz: Birth Anniv, **Sep 10**
Wesley, John: Birth Anniv, **Jun 17**
West Virginia
  Admission Day, **Jun 20**
  Apple Butter Fest (Berkeley Springs), **Oct 7**
  Bridge Day (Fayetteville), **Oct 21**
  Byrd, Robert C.: Birth, **Nov 20**
  Fantasy of Light Parade (Wheeling), **Nov 17**
  Feast of the Ramson (Richwood), **Apr 22**
  Head-of-the-Mon-River Horseshoe Tournament (Fairmont), **May 27**
  Hilltop Fest (Huntington), **Sep 9**
  Independence Day Concert and Fireworks (Wheeling), **Jul 4**
  Manchin III, Joe: Birth, **Aug 24**
  Model Railroad Show (Wheeling), **Jan 14**
  Preston County Buckwheat Fest (Kingwood), **Sep 28**
  Rockefeller, John D., IV: Birth, **Jun 18**
  State Fair (Lewisburg), **Aug 11**
  West Virginia Italian Heritage Fest (Clarksburg), **Sep 1**
West, Adam: Birth, **Sep 19**
West, Dottie: Birth Anniv, **Oct 11**
West, Rebecca: Birth Anniv, **Dec 25**
Western Stock Show and Rodeo, Natl (Denver, CO), Jan 7
Westheimer, Dr. Ruth: Birth, **Jun 4**
Westinghouse, George: Birth Anniv, **Oct 6**
Westminster Kennel Club Dog Show (New York, NY), Feb 13
Wettig, Patricia: Birth, **Dec 4**
Whales: Shamu's Birthday, Sep 26
Whalin, Justin: Birth, **Sep 6**
Whalley, Joanne: Birth, **Aug 25**
Wharton, Edith: Birth Anniv, **Jan 24**
What Do You Love About America Day, Nov 22
What You Think Upon Grows Day, May 31
What's My Line TV Premiere: Anniv, **Feb 2**
Wheatley, Phillis: Death Anniv, **Dec 5**
Wheatley, Phillis: Poetry Collection Published: Anniv, **Sep 1**
Wheaton, Wil: Birth, **Jul 29**
Wheel of Fortune TV Premiere: Anniv, **Jan 6**
Wheelchair Beautification Month, Natl, Jul 1
Wheeler, William A.: Birth Anniv, **Jun 30**
Whelchel, Lisa: Birth, **May 29**
Whiner's Day, Natl, Dec 26
Whipple, William: Birth Anniv, **Jan 14**
Whiskey Flat Days (Kernville, CA), Feb 17
Whistler, James: Birth Anniv, **Jul 10**
Whistlers Convention, Intl (Louisburg, NC), Apr 19
Whitaker, Forest: Birth, **Jul 15**
White Cane Safety Day (Pres Proc), Oct 15
White House Cornerstone Laid: Anniv, **Oct 13**
White House Easter Egg Roll (Washington, DC), Apr 17
White House: Pennsylvania Ave Closed: Anniv, **May 20**
White Oak Rendezvous (Deer River, MN), Aug 4
White Shirt Day, Feb 11
White Sunday (Samoa, American Samoa), Oct 8

White, Betty: Birth, **Jan 17**
White, Byron R.: Birth Anniv, **Jun 8**
White, Charles: Birth Anniv, **Apr 2**
White, E.B.: Birth Anniv, **Jul 11**
White, Edward Douglass: Birth Anniv, **Nov 3**
White, Gilbert: Birth Anniv, **Jul 18**
White, Jaleel: Birth, **Nov 27**
White, Stanford: Birth Anniv, **Nov 9**
White, Vanna: Birth, **Feb 18**
Whitechapel Murders Begin: Anniv, **Aug 31**
Whitelaw, Billie: Birth, **Jun 6**
Whitfield, Lynn: Birth, **May 6**
Whiting, Margaret: Birth, **Jul 22**
Whitman, Christine T.: Birth, **Sep 26**
Whitman, Slim (Otis): Birth, **Jan 20**
Whitman, Stuart: Birth, **Feb 1**
Whitman, Walt: Birth Anniv, **May 31**
Whitmire, Kathryn: Birth, **Aug 15**
Whitmonday, Jun 5
Whitney, Eli: Birth Anniv, **Dec 8**
Whitsunday, Jun 4
Whittier, John Greenleaf: Birth Anniv, **Dec 17**
Wiccan Observances
  Beltane, **Apr 30**
  Imbolc, **Feb 2**
  Lughnasadh, **Aug 1**
  Mabon, **Sep 23**
  Midsummer, **Jun 21**
  Ostara, **Mar 20**
  Samhain, **Oct 31**
  Yule, **Dec 21**
Wicker, Tom: Birth, **Jun 18**
Widmark, Richard: Birth, **Dec 26**
Wiesel, Elie: Birth, **Sep 30**
Wiest, Dianne: Birth, **Mar 28**
Wife Appreciation Day, Sep 16
Wiggin, Kate Douglas: Birth Anniv, **Sep 28**
Wilbur, Richard: Birth, **Mar 1**
Wilby, James: Birth, **Feb 20**
Wilcox, Dave: Birth, **Sep 29**
Wilde, Oscar: Birth Anniv, **Oct 16**
Wilder Pageant, Laura Ingalls (De Smet, SD), Jul 7
Wilder, Billy: Birth Anniv, **Jun 22**
Wilder, Gene: Birth, **Jun 11**
Wilder, L. Douglas: First Black Governor Elected: Anniv, **Nov 7**
Wilder, Laura Ingalls Gingerbread Sociable (Pomona, CA), Feb 4
Wilder, Thornton: Birth Anniv, **Apr 17**
Wildflower Fest of the Arts (Dahlonega, GA), May 20
Wildflower Week, Natl, May 1
Wildfowl Art & Decoy Show, Ocean County (Toms River, NJ), Feb 11
Wildlife Week, Natl, Apr 23
Wilhelm Tell Fest (New Glarus, WI), Sep 1
Wilkins, Roy: Birth Anniv, **Aug 30**
Wilkinson, Tom: Birth, **Dec 12**
Will Rogers Day, Nov 4
Will, George F.: Birth, **May 4**
Willard, Archibald M.: Birth Anniv, **Aug 22**
Willard, Emma Hart: Birth Anniv, **Feb 23**
Willard, Frances E.C.: Birth Anniv, **Sep 28**
William the Conqueror: Death Anniv, **Sep 9**
William, Prince: Birth, **Jun 21**
Williams, Andy: Birth, **Dec 3**
Williams, Archie: Birth Anniv, **May 1**
Williams, Bernie: Birth, **Sep 13**
Williams, Billy Dee: Birth, **Apr 6**
Williams, Cindy: Birth, **Aug 22**
Williams, Clarence, III: Birth, **Aug 21**
Williams, Curtis: Birth, **Dec 11**
Williams, Deniece: Birth, **Jun 3**
Williams, Esther: Birth, **Aug 8**
Williams, Hank, Jr: Birth, **May 26**
Williams, Hank, Sr: Birth Anniv, **Sep 17**
Williams, Hank, Sr: Hankfest (Chicago, IL), Sep 16
Williams, Jayson: Birth, **Feb 22**
Williams, Jimy: Birth, **Oct 4**
Williams, JoBeth: Birth, **Dec 6**
Williams, John: Birth, **Feb 8**
Williams, Mason: Birth, **Aug 24**
Williams, Matt: Birth, **Nov 28**
Williams, Michelle: Birth, **Sep 9**
Williams, Montel: Birth, **Jul 3**
Williams, Paul: Birth, **Sep 19**
Williams, Robin: Birth, **Jul 21**
Williams, Serena: Birth, **Sep 26**
Williams, Ted: Birth Anniv, **Aug 30**
Williams, Tennessee: Birth Anniv, **Mar 26**
Williams, Tennessee: Streetcar Named Desire Broadway Opening: Anniv, **Dec 3**
Williams, Treat: Birth, **Dec 1**
Williams, Vanessa: Birth, **Mar 18**
Williams, Venus: Birth, **Jun 17**
Williams, William: Birth Anniv, **Apr 8**

Williamson—Women

Williamson, Fred: Birth, Mar 5
Williamson, Nicol: Birth, Sep 14
Willis, Bruce: Birth, Mar 19
Willkie, Wendell L.: Birth Anniv, Feb 18
Willow Tree Fest (Gordon, NE), Sep 9
Wills, Bob: Birth Anniv, Mar 6
Wills, Bob: Day (Turkey, TX), Apr 29
Wills, Garry: Birth, May 22
Willson, Meredith: Birth Anniv, May 18
Wilson, Ann: Birth, Jun 19
Wilson, August: Birth, Apr 27
Wilson, Blaine: Birth, Aug 3
Wilson, Brian: Birth, Jun 20
Wilson, Carnie: Birth, Apr 29
Wilson, Cassandra: Birth, Dec 4
Wilson, Edith: Birth Anniv, Oct 15
Wilson, Elizabeth: Birth, Apr 4
Wilson, Ellen L.: Birth Anniv, May 15
Wilson, Ellis: Birth Anniv, Apr 30
Wilson, Harold: Birth Anniv, Mar 11
Wilson, Henry: Birth Anniv, Feb 16
Wilson, James: Birth Anniv, Sep 14
Wilson, Luke: Birth, Sep 21
Wilson, Mary: Birth, Mar 4
Wilson, Nancy: Birth, Feb 20
Wilson, Owen: Birth, Nov 18
Wilson, Tom: Birth, Aug 1
Wilson, William G.: Alcoholics Anonymous:
   Founding Anniv, Jun 10
Wilson, William Julius: Birth, Dec 20
Wilson, Woodrow: Birth Anniv, Dec 28
Wilson, Woodrow: Fourteen Points Proposed:
   Anniv, Jan 8
Wilson's Volstead Prohibition Act Veto
   Overridden: Anniv, Oct 28
Wimbledon: Lawn Tennis Chmpshps at (London,
   England), Jun 26
Winchell, Paul: Birth, Dec 21
Winchell, Walter: Birth Anniv, Apr 7
Wind Cave Natl Park Established: Anniv, Jan 3
Windjammer Days (Boothbay Harbor, ME), Jun 27
Windmill Day, Natl (Netherlands), May 13
Windom, William: Birth, Sep 28
Window Safety Week, Natl, Apr 23
Windsor, Duke of, Marriage: Anniv, Jun 3
Wine, Blessing of the (Greiveldange,
   Luxembourg), Dec 26
Wine: Telluride Wine Fest (Telluride, CO), Jun 22
Winfield, Dave: Birth, Oct 3
Winfrey, Oprah: Birth, Jan 29
Winger, Debra: Birth, May 17
Wings 'n' Water Fest (Stone Harbor, NJ), Sep 16
Wings Over the Platte Spring Migration Fest
   (Grand Island, NE), Feb 18
Wings Over Willcox—Sandhill Crane Celebration
   (Willcox, AZ), Jan 12
Winkler, Henry: Birth, Oct 30
Winningham, Mare: Birth, May 16
Winslet, Kate: Birth, Oct 5
Winter Begins, Dec 22
Winter Festivals and Celebrations
   Badger State Winter Games (Wausau, WI), **Jan 27**
   Brookfield Ice Harvest (Brookfield, VT), **Jan 28**
   Illinois Snow Sculpting Competition (Rockford, IL),
      Jan 18
   Newport Winter Fest (Newport, RI), **Feb 17**
   Saint Paul Winter Carnival (St. Paul, MN), **Jan 27**
   Snowman Burning (Sault Ste. Marie, MI), **Mar 20**
   Tip-Up Town USA (Houghton Lake, MI), **Jan 21**
   US Natl Snow Sculpting Competition (Lake
      Geneva, WI), **Feb 1**
   Winter Carnival Bon Soo (Sault Ste. Marie, ON,
      Canada), **Jan 27**
   Winter Fest (New Glarus, WI), **Jan 13**
   Winterfest (Flagstaff, AZ), **Feb 1**
   Winterfest (Luverne, MN), **Dec 1**
   Winterlude (Ottawa, ON, Canada), **Feb 3**
   Wisconsin Dells Flake Out Fest (Wisconsin Dells,
      WI), **Jan 21**
   Zehnder's Snowfest (Frankenmuth, MI), **Jan 25**
Winter Olympiad (Turin, Italy), Feb 10
Winter Olympics, First: Anniv, Jan 25
Winter Solstice: Yalda (Iran), Dec 21
Winter, Alex: Birth, Jul 17
Winter, Edgar: Birth, Dec 28
Winter, Johnny: Birth, Feb 23
Winter: Funeral for Ol' Man Winter at Wayne State
   Univ (Detroit, MI), Apr 5
Winterlude (Ottawa, ON, Canada), Feb 3
Winters, Jonathan: Birth, Nov 11
Winters, Shelley: Birth, Aug 18
Winthrop, John: Birth Anniv, Jan 12
Winwood, Steve: Birth, May 12
Wisconsin
   Admission Day, **May 29**
   Aldo Leopold Weekend, **Mar 3**
   Al's Memorial Run & Walk (Milwaukee), **Sep 30**
   American Birkebeiner (Cable to Hayward), **Feb 23**

American Club Teddy Bear and Doll Classic
   (Kohler), **Feb 26**
Art & Antiques at the American Club (Kohler),
   Mar 11
Art Armada (Sheboygan), **Jul 4**
Art Fair (Rhinelander), **Jun 10**
Art Fair on the Square (Madison), **Jul 8**
Automotion (Wisconsin Dells), **May 20**
Badger State Summer Games (Madison), **Jun 16**
Badger State Winter Games (Wausau), **Jan 27**
Baraboo Circus Heritage (Baraboo), **May 19**
Cambridge Pottery Fest and US Pottery Games
   (Cambridge), **Jun 10**
Country Affair (Menomonee Falls), **Oct 21**
Country Christmas (Cambridge), **Dec 2**
Dietary Managers Assn Mtg/Expo (Milwaukee),
   Jul 16
Doyle, Jim: Birth, **Nov 23**
Ducktona 500 (Sheboygan Falls), **Jul 2**
EAA Airventure Oshkosh (Oshkosh), **Jul 24**
Faire on the Square Art & Craft Fair (Baraboo),
   May 20
Fall in Love with Fond du Lac (Fond du Lac),
   Sep 1
Fashion Show (Milwaukee), **May 5**
Feingold, Russell D.: Birth, **Mar 2**
Fishing Has No Boundaries (Hayward), **May 19**
Great Wisconsin Cheese Fest (Little Chute), **Jun 2**
Groundhog Day in Sun Prairie (Sun Prairie), **Feb 2**
Hodag Country Fest (Rhinelander), **Jul 13**
Hodag Muskie Challenge (Rhinelander), **Sep 15**
Holiday Folk Fair Intl (Milwaukee), **Nov 17**
Home Improvement Show, Milwaukee/NARI (West
   Allis), **Feb 9**
Klondike Days (Eagle River), **Feb 18**
Kohl, Herb: Birth, **Feb 7**
Kohler Arts Center's Outdoor Arts Fest
   (Sheboygan), **Jul 15**
Lumberjack World Chmpshps (Hayward), **Jul 28**
Mad City Marathon (Madison), **May 28**
Madrigal Dinner and Concert (Milwaukee), **Dec 2**
Maple Syrup Saturday (Appleton), **Mar 18**
Mexican Fiesta Internacional (Milwaukee), **Aug 25**
Milwaukee Boat Show (Milwaukee), **Jan 20**
Milwaukee Irish Fest (Milwaukee), **Aug 17**
Milwaukee Journal Sentinel Sports Show
   (Milwaukee), **Mar 10**
Miss Wisconsin Pageant (Oshkosh), **Jun 22**
Morel Mushroom Fest (Muscoda), **May 19**
NCAA Div I Men's Ice Hockey Chmpshp
   (Milwaukee), **Apr 6**
Norskedalen's Midsummer Fest (Coon Valley),
   Jun 24
Norskedalen's Old-Fashioned Christmas (Coon
   Valley), **Dec 2**
Norskedalen's Threshing Bee (Coon Valley),
   Sep 23
Northeastern Wisconsin Antique Power and
   Machinery Show Thresheree (Sturgeon Bay),
   Aug 18
Octoberfest (Appleton), **Sep 30**
Polar Bear Swim (Sheboygan), **Jan 1**
Prairie Villa Rendezvous (Prairie du Chien), **Jun 15**
Rhinelander's Oktoberfest (Rhinelander), **Oct 6**
Riverfest (LaCrosse), **Jun 30**
Romp in the Swamp Fun Walk (Appleton), **Oct 21**
Saint Cyril's Parish Fest (Sheboygan), **Jul 16**
Shanty Days (Algoma), **Aug 11**
Spring Garden Market (Kohler), **Apr 8**
State Fair (Milwaukee), **Aug 3**
Summerfest (Milwaukee), **Jun 29**
Sun Prairie's Sweet Corn Fest (Sun Prairie),
   Aug 17
Taste of Madison (Madison), **Sep 2**
Traditional Sousa Concert (Kohler), **Jul 4**
US Natl Snow Sculpting Competition (Lake
   Geneva), **Feb 1**
Volksfest (New Glarus), **Aug 6**
Warrens Cranberry Fest (Warrens), **Sep 22**
West Allis Western Days Family Jamboree (West
   Allis), **Jun 15**
Wilhelm Tell Fest (New Glarus), **Sep 1**
Winter Fest (New Glarus), **Jan 13**
Wisconsin Cow-Chip Throw (Prairie du Sac), **Sep 1**
Wisconsin Dells Autumn Harvest Fest (Wisconsin
   Dells), **Oct 21**
Wisconsin Dells Flake Out Fest (Wisconsin Dells),
   Jan 21
Wisconsin Holiday Market (Kohler), **Nov 10**
World Beef Expo/Harvest Fair (Milwaukee), **Sep 21**
World Dairy Expo (Madison), **Oct 3**
World's Largest Trivia Contest (Stevens Point),
   Apr 7
Wo-Zha-Wa Fall Fest (Wisconsin Dells), **Sep 15**
Ziegler Kettle Moraine Jazz Fest (West Bend),
   Sep 8
Wise Health Care Consumer Month, Feb 1
Wise, Robert: Birth, Sep 10

Wise, Thomas J.: Birth Anniv, Oct 7
Wishbones for Pets, Oct 15
Witches: First in Salem Arrested: Anniv, Feb 1
Witches: Salem Hysteria Begins: Anniv, Mar 1
Witches: Salem Trials Begin: Anniv, Jun 2
Witherspoon, John: Birth Anniv, Feb 5
Witherspoon, Reese: Birth, Mar 22
Witt, Alicia: Birth, Aug 21
Witt, Katarina: Birth, Dec 3
Witt, Paul Junger: Birth, Mar 20
Wizard of Oz Fest (Chesterton, IN), Sep 15
Wizard of Oz Film Released: Anniv, Aug 25
WMAS Annual Halloween Ball (Springfield, MA),
   Oct 28
Wodehouse, P.G.: Birth Anniv, Oct 15
Wojtyla: Pope John Paul II: Birth Anniv, May 18
Wojtyla: Pope John Paul II: Death Anniv, Apr 2
Wolcott, Oliver: Birth Anniv, Nov 20
Wolf, Peter: Birth, Mar 7
Wolf, Scott: Birth, Jun 4
Wolfe, James: Birth Anniv, Jan 2
Wolfe, Tom: Birth, Mar 2
Wolff, Geoffrey: Birth, Nov 5
Wolff, Josh: Birth, Feb 25
Wolfman Jack: Birth Anniv, Jan 21
Wollstonecraft, Mary: Birth Anniv, Apr 27
Women
   Abused Women and Children's Awareness Day,
      Jun 11
   Accelerate ACL Awareness Among Young Women
      Day, **Apr 5**
   Alpha Kappa Alpha Sorority Founded: Anniv,
      Jan 15
   American Heroine Rewarded: Anniv, **Jun 8**
   Around the World in 72 Days: Anniv, **Jan 25**
   Aspinwall Crosses US on Horseback: Anniv, **Jul 8**
   Be Heard Day, Natl, **Mar 7**
   Billie Jean King Wins Battle of Sexes: Anniv,
      Sep 20
   Blackwell, Elizabeth, Awarded MD: Anniv, **Jan 23**
   Bloomer, Amelia Jenks: Birth Anniv, **May 27**
   Breast Cancer Awareness Month, Natl, **Oct 1**
   Business Women's Day, American, **Sep 22**
   Business Women's Week, Natl, **Oct 16**
   Canada: Persons Day, **Oct 18**
   Canada's First Woman Prime Minister: Anniv,
      Jun 25
   Cervical Cancer Screening Month, **Jan 1**
   Day for Women's Rights & Intl Peace (UN), **Mar 8**
   Elimination of Violence against Women, Intl Day for
      the (UN), **Nov 25**
   English Channel, First Woman Swims: Anniv,
      Aug 6
   Equal Rights Party Founding: Anniv, **Sep 20**
   Female House Page, First Formal: Anniv, **May 14**
   Female Relief Society of Nauvoo: Anniv, **Mar 17**
   Feminine Mystique Published: Anniv, **Feb 19**
   Fibromyalgia Education & Awareness Month,
      May 1
   First All-Woman Jury: Anniv, **Sep 22**
   First American Woman in Space: Anniv, **Jun 18**
   First Doctor of Science Degree Earned by a
      Woman, **Jun 20**
   First Elected Woman Senator: Anniv, **Jan 12**
   First Episcopal Bishop: Anniv, **Feb 11**
   First Female Congressional Page: Anniv, **Jan 3**
   First Female FBI Agents: Anniv, **Oct 25**
   First Free Flight by a Woman: Anniv, **Jun 4**
   First to Climb Mount Everest, **May 16**
   First US Woman Governor Inaugurated, **Jan 5**
   First Woman in Space: Space Milestone, **Jun 16**
   First Woman Rabbi in US: Anniv, **Jun 3**
   First Woman to Walk in Space, **Jul 17**
   First Woman US Ambassador Appointed: Anniv,
      Oct 28
   First Woman Vice-Presidential Candidate: Anniv,
      Jul 19
   First Women's Collegiate Basketball Game: Anniv,
      Mar 2
   Friedan, Betty: Birth, **Feb 4**
   Fuller, Margaret: Birth Anniv, **May 23**
   Girlfriend's Day, **Aug 1**
   Girls and Women in Sports Day, Natl, **Feb 1**
   Gynecologic Cancer Awareness Month, **Sep 1**
   Informed Woman Month, **Apr 1**
   Introduce a Girl to Engineering Day, **Feb 23**
   Ladies' Day Initiated in Baseball: Anniv, **Jun 16**
   League of Women Voters Formed: Anniv, **Feb 14**
   Links, Inc: Anniv, **Nov 9**
   Mansfield, Arabella: Birth Anniv, **May 23**
   Margaret Brent Demands a Political Voice: Anniv,
      Jan 21
   Martha Griffiths Speech Against Sex
      Discrimination, **Feb 8**
   Mayer, Maria G.: Birth Anniv, **Jun 28**
   Medical School Opened: Anniv, **Nov 1**
   Meitlisunntig (Switzerland), **Jan 8**
   Merriam, Eve: Birth Anniv, **Jul 19**

Million Mom March: Anniv, **May 14**
National Women's Day (South Africa), **Aug 9**
19th Amendment Ratified, **Aug 18**
NOW Founded: Anniv, **Jun 30**
PCOS Awareness Day, **Sep 18**
Perkins, Frances (1st Woman Appointed to US Cabinet), **Mar 4**
Personal Self-Defense Awareness Month, Natl, **Jan 1**
Pocahontas: Death Anniv, **Mar 21**
Pro Sports Wives Day, **Feb 11**
Queen Liliuokalani Deposed: Anniv, **Jan 17**
Russia: Women's Day, Intl, **Mar 8**
Salter Elected First Woman Mayor in US: Anniv, **Apr 4**
Seneca Falls Survivor Votes: Anniv, **Nov 2**
She's Funny That Way Day, Natl, **Mar 31**
Southern Belles Month, **Apr 1**
Stupid Guy Thing Day, **Jun 22**
Suffrage Parade Attacked: Anniv, **Mar 3**
Suffragists' Voting Attempt: Anniv, **Nov 19**
Supreme Court Abortion Notification Ruling: Anniv, **Jun 25**
Susan B. Anthony Fined for Voting, **Jun 6**
Tiara Day, Intl, **May 24**
Tubman, Harriet: Death Anniv, **Mar 10**
Universal Women's Week, **Mar 8**
Utah Women Given Vote: Anniv, **Feb 12**
Victorious Woman Month, Intl, **May 1**
Vulvar Health Awareness Month, **Mar 1**
WAAC: Anniv, **May 14**
White Woman Made Indian Chief: Anniv, **Sep 18**
Woman Inducted to Natl Inventors Hall of Fame: Anniv, **May 18**
Woman Presides Over US Supreme Court: Anniv, **Apr 3**
Woman Runs the US House of Representatives: Anniv, **Jun 20**
Women Denied Vote: Anniv, **Jan 12**
Women's Ecommerce Day, Intl, **Sep 19**
Women's Equality Day, **Aug 26**
Women's Equality Day (Pres Proc), **Aug 26**
Women's Eye Health and Safety Month, **Apr 1**
Women's Friendship Day, **Sep 17**
Women's Hall of Fame, Natl: Dedication Anniv, **Jul 21**
Women's Health and Fitness Day, Natl, **Sep 27**
Women's Health Care Month, **May 1**
Women's Healthy Weight Day, **Jan 19**
Women's Heart Health Day, **Feb 1**
Women's Heart Week, **Feb 1**
Women's History Month (Pres Proc), **Mar 1**
Women's History Month, Natl, **Mar 1**
Women's Leadership Conference, Natl (Anaheim, CA), **Sep 28**
Women's Motorcycle Month, **Jul 1**
Women's Nutrition Week, Natl, **Apr 9**
Women's Pro Football Day, **Aug 5**
Women's Rights Convention Held (Seneca Falls): Anniv, **Jul 19**
Women's Self-Empowerment Week, **Jan 2**
Women's Small Business Month, **Oct 1**
Women's Suffrage Amendment Introduced: Anniv, **Jan 10**
Work at Home Moms Week, **May 14**
Working Women's Day, Intl, **Mar 8**
World Menopause Day, **Oct 18**
Women's Intl Cup (Golf): See Curtis Cup, Jul 29
Wonder Years TV Premiere: Anniv, Mar 15
Wonder, Stevie: Birth, May 13
Wonderful Weirdos Day, Sep 9
Wood, Elijah: Birth, Jan 28
Wood, Grant, Art Fest (Stone City–Anamosa, IA), Jun 11
Wood, Grant: Birth Anniv, Feb 13
Wood, Kerry: Birth, Jun 16
Wood, Ron: Birth, Jun 1
Woodard, Alfre: Birth, Nov 8
Woodhull, Victoria C.: Birth Anniv, Sep 23
Woodie Wagon Day, Natl, Jul 15
Woodland Indian Discovery Day (St. Mary's City, MD), Sep 9
Woodruff, Judy: Birth, Nov 20
Woods, Eldrick (Tiger): Birth, Dec 30
Woods, Granville T.: Birth Anniv, Apr 23
Woods, James: Birth, Apr 18
Woodson, Carter Godwin: Birth Anniv, Dec 19
Woodstock Fair (Woodstock, CT), Sep 1
Woodstock: Anniv, Aug 15
Woodward, Bob: Birth, Mar 26
Woodward, Edward: Birth, Jun 1
Woodward, Joanne: Birth, Feb 27
Woodward, Robert B.: Birth Anniv, Apr 10
Woofstock (Wichita, KS), Oct 7
Woolery, Chuck: Birth, Mar 16
Woolf, Virginia: Birth Anniv, Jan 25
Woolly Worm Fest (Banner Elk, NC), Oct 21
Woolworths Opened: Anniv, Feb 22

Wopat, Tom: Birth, Sep 9
Word Nerd Day, Jan 9
Word Origins
   Cyberspace Coined: Neuromancer Publication Anniv, **Oct 1**
   O.K. First Appearance in Print: Anniv, **Mar 23**
   Robot Enters World Lexicon: Anniv, **Jan 25**
Words by the Water: A Cumbrian Literature Fest (Lake District, England), Mar 10
Wordsmith Day, May 3
Wordsworth, William: Birth Anniv, Apr 7
Work at Home Moms Week, May 14
Work from Home Week, Natl, Oct 1
Work Like a Dog Day, Aug 4
Work Schedule Month, Revise Your, May 1
Work@Home Father's Day, Jun 16
Workers Memorial Day, Apr 28
Working Women's Day, Intl, Mar 8
Workplace Conflict Awareness Month, Apr 1
Workplace Eye Health and Safety Month, Mar 1
Workplace Politics Awareness Month, Oct 1
World AIDS Day (Pres Proc), Dec 1
World Book Day (UK and Ireland), Mar 2
World Breastfeeding Week, Aug 1
World Communion Sunday, Oct 1
World Cup (Germany), Jun 9
World Cup Inaugurated: Anniv, Jul 13
World Day of Prayer, Mar 3
World Egg Day, Oct 13
World Farm Animals Day, Oct 2
World Food Day, Oct 16
World Future Society Annual Conf (Chicago), Jul 28
World Habitat Awareness Month, Apr 1
World Health Organization: Anniv, Apr 7
World Human Spirit Day, Feb 17
World Juggling Day, Jun 17
World Maritime Day (UN), Sep 25
World Peace Day, Dec 21
World Smile Day, Oct 6
World Tourism Day, Sep 27
World Trade Center Attack (9-11): Anniv, Sep 11
World Trade Center Bombing of 1993: Anniv, Feb 26
World Trade Center Recovery and Cleanup Ends: Anniv, May 30
World Trade Week (Pres Proc), May 21
World Turtle Day, May 23
World War I
   Alvin C. York Day, **Oct 8**
   ANZAC Day, **Apr 25**
   Armistice: Anniv, **Nov 11**
   Baseball Declared Nonessential: Anniv, **Jul 20**
   Battle of Amiens, Second: Anniv, **Aug 8**
   Battle of Cambrai–Saint Quentin: Anniv, **Sep 27**
   Battle of Gallipoli, **Apr 25**
   Battle of Lys River: Anniv, **Apr 7**
   Battle of Meuse-Argonne Forest: Anniv, **Sep 26**
   Battle of Saint-Mihiel: Anniv, **Sep 12**
   Battle of Somme, Second: Anniv, **Mar 21**
   Battle of the Marne: Anniv, **Jul 15**
   Battle of Verdun, **Feb 21**
   Battle of Vittorio Veneto: Anniv, **Oct 24**
   Begins: Anniv, **Jul 28**
   Big Bertha Paris Gun: Anniv, **Mar 23**
   Campbell Becomes First American Air ACE: Anniv, **Apr 14**
   Coal Conservation Ordered: Anniv, **Jan 16**
   Death/Duty Day, **Nov 11**
   Fourteen Points Proposed: Anniv, **Jan 8**
   German Revolution of 1918: Anniv, **Oct 28**
   Ludendorff, Erich: Birth Anniv, **Apr 9**
   Mata Hari: Birth Anniv, **Aug 7**
   Neutrality Appeal, American: Anniv, **Aug 18**
   Red Baron Shot Down: Anniv, **Apr 21**
   Treaty of Versailles: Anniv, **Jun 28**
   US Enters WWI: Anniv, **Apr 6**
   Versailles Peace Conference: Anniv, **Jan 18**
   Veterans Bonus Army Eviction: Anniv, **Jul 28**
   Wilhelm II Abdicates: Anniv, **Nov 9**
World War II
   Allied Invasion of Sicily: Anniv, **Jul 10**
   Allied Landings in South of France: Anniv, **Aug 15**
   Allies Capture Monte Cassino: Anniv, **May 18**
   Allies Retake Guadalcanal: Anniv, **Feb 9**
   Allies Take New Guinea: Anniv, **Jan 22**
   Allies Take Palermo: Anniv, **Jul 22**
   America Enters World War II, **Dec 8**
   Arnold, Henry H.: Birth Anniv, **Jun 25**
   Atomic Bomb Dropped on Hiroshima: Anniv, **Aug 6**
   Atomic Bomb Dropped on Nagasaki: Anniv, **Aug 9**
   Atomic Bomb Tested: Anniv, **Jul 16**
   Attempt on Hitler's Life: Anniv, **Jul 20**
   Auschwitz Liberated: Anniv, **Jan 27**
   Austria Invaded by Nazi Germany: Anniv, **Mar 12**
   Bataan Death March: Anniv, **Apr 10**
   Battle of Bismarck Sea: Anniv, **Mar 2**
   Battle of Coral Sea: Anniv, **May 8**

   Battle of Kursk: Anniv, **Jul 12**
   Battle of Leyte Gulf: Anniv, **Oct 23**
   Battle of Midway: Anniv, **Jun 4**
   Battle of Okinawa Begins: Anniv, **Apr 1**
   Battle of Okinawa Ends: Anniv, **Jun 21**
   Battle of Philippine Sea, **Jun 19**
   Battle of Salerno: Anniv, **Sep 9**
   Battle of San Pietro: Anniv, **Dec 15**
   Battle of Stalingrad Begins: Anniv, **Aug 22**
   Battle of Tarawa-Makin: Anniv, **Nov 20**
   Battle of the Aleutian Islands: Anniv, **May 30**
   Battle of the Bulge: Anniv, **Dec 16**
   Begins: Germany Invades Poland: Anniv, **Sep 1**
   Berlin Surrenders: Anniv, **May 2**
   Britain Declares War on Germany: Anniv, **Sep 3**
   British Air Raid on Berlin: Anniv, **Jan 16**
   British Capture Enigma Machine: Anniv, **May 9**
   Christmas Fireside Chat Warning: Anniv, **Dec 25**
   Civil Air Patrol Founded: Anniv, **Dec 1**
   Clark, Mark: Birth Anniv, **May 1**
   Corsica Liberated: Anniv, **Oct 4**
   Czechoslovakia: Rape of Lidice: Anniv, **Jun 10**
   Davis, Benjamin O., Jr: Birth Anniv, **Dec 18**
   D-Day: Anniv, **Jun 6**
   De Gaulle, Charles: Birth Anniv, **Nov 22**
   Diary of Anne Frank: Last Entry: Anniv, **Aug 1**
   Dresden Firebombing, **Feb 13**
   Dunkirk Evacuated: Anniv, **May 26**
   East Meets West: Anniv, **Apr 25**
   FDR's Unconditional Surrender Statement: Anniv, **Jan 24**
   First Medal of Honor: Anniv, **Feb 10**
   First Surface-to-Surface Missile: Anniv, **Dec 24**
   Four Chaplains Memorial Day, **Feb 3**
   German Surrender at Stalingrad: Anniv, **Feb 2**
   Germany's First Surrender: Anniv, **May 7**
   Germany's Second Surrender: Anniv, **May 8**
   Gersdorff Hitler Assassination Attempt: Anniv, **Mar 21**
   Gilbert Islands Taken: Anniv, **Nov 23**
   Gillars, Mildred E.: Death Anniv, **Jun 25**
   Graham, Calvin "Baby Vet": Birth Anniv, **Apr 3**
   Gypsy Condemnation Order: Anniv, **Nov 15**
   Halsey, William "Bull": Birth Anniv, **Oct 30**
   Hamburg Firestorm: Anniv, **Jul 28**
   Hitler Youth Deployed: Anniv, **Jan 26**
   Howard, Leslie: Birth Anniv, **Apr 3**
   Indianapolis Sunk: Anniv, **Jul 29**
   Italy Surrenders: Anniv, **Sep 3**
   Iwo Jima Day: Anniv, **Feb 23**
   Japan Bombed: Anniv, **Apr 18**
   Japanese Attack US Mainland: Anniv, **Feb 23**
   Japanese Internment: Anniv, **Feb 19**
   Japan's Unconditional Surrender: Anniv, **Aug 10**
   Kristallnacht: Anniv, **Nov 9**
   Krupp, Alfried: Birth Anniv, **Aug 13**
   Lady Be Good Lost: Anniv, **Apr 4**
   Leningrad Liberated: Anniv, **Jan 27**
   Liberation of Buchenwald: Anniv, **Apr 11**
   Liberation of Dachau: Anniv, **Apr 29**
   MacArthur Returns: US Landing on Leyte, Philippines: Anniv, **Oct 20**
   Manstein, Erich von: Birth Anniv, **Nov 24**
   Marshall, George C.: Birth Anniv, **Dec 31**
   Montgomery, Bernard Law: Birth Anniv, **Nov 17**
   Moulin, Jean: Death Anniv, **Jul 8**
   Mussolini Executed: Anniv, **Apr 28**
   Mussolini Ousted: Anniv, **Jul 25**
   Napalm Used: Anniv, **Jul 11**
   Nimitz, Chester: Birth Anniv, **Feb 24**
   Oak Ridge Atomic Plant Begun: Anniv, **Aug 1**
   Odessa Retaken: Anniv, **Apr 10**
   Operation Flash: Anniv, **Mar 13**
   Operation Overcast, **Jul 6**
   Paris Liberated: Anniv, **Aug 25**
   Paulus, Friedrich: Birth Anniv, **Sep 23**
   Peace Rose Introduced to World: Anniv, **Apr 29**
   Pearl Harbor Day, **Dec 7**
   Potsdam Declaration: Anniv, **Jul 26**
   RAF Bombs Hitler Celebration: Anniv, **Jan 30**
   RAF Bombs Ruhr Dams: Anniv, **May 16**
   RAF Jams Nazi Radar: Anniv, **Jul 24**
   Raising Flag on Iwo Jima: Hayes, Ira: Birth Anniv, **Jan 12**
   Remagen Bridge Capture: Anniv, **Mar 7**
   Ridgway, Matthew Bunker: Birth Anniv, **Mar 3**
   Rogers, Edith Nourse: Birth Anniv, **Mar 19**
   Romania Surrender to USSR: Anniv, **Aug 23**
   Rome Executions: Anniv, **Mar 25**
   Rome Liberated: Anniv, **Jun 4**
   Rommel, Erwin: Birth Anniv, **Nov 15**
   Roosevelt, Franklin D.: Death Anniv, **Apr 12**
   Russia: Victory Day, **May 9**
   Smith, Holland: Birth Anniv, **Apr 20**
   Soviet Union Invaded: Anniv, **Jun 22**
   Stratton, Dorothy C.: Birth Anniv, **Mar 24**
   Teheran Conference: Anniv, **Nov 28**
   Tokyo Blanket Bombing: Anniv, **Mar 9**

World War II (cont'd)—Zukerman

Truman Doctrine: Anniv, **May 22**
Tunis Campaign Victory: Anniv, **May 13**
Tuskegee Airmen Activated: Anniv, **Mar 22**
US Forces Land in Mindoro, Philippines: Anniv, **Dec 15**
US Landing on Iwo Jima: Anniv, **Feb 19**
US Landing on Luzon: Anniv, **Jan 9**
US Landing on Saipan, **Jun 15**
US Landing on the Admiralty Islands: Anniv, **Feb 1**
US Troops Enter Germany: Anniv, **Sep 15**
V-E Day, **May 8**
V-J Day (Announcement), **Aug 14**
V-J Day (Ratification), **Sep 2**
V-Mail Delivery: Anniv, **Jun 22**
WAAC: Anniv, **May 14**
War Time: Anniv, **Feb 9**
Warsaw Ghetto Revolt: Anniv, **Apr 19**
Warsaw Uprising: Anniv, **Aug 1**
Yalta Agreement Signed: Anniv, **Feb 11**
Yamamoto, Isoroku: Birth Anniv, **Apr 4**
World Wide Web: Anniv, Aug 1
World's End Day, Oct 22
World's Indigenous People, Intl Day of the (UN), Aug 9
Worley, Jo Anne: Birth, Sep 6
Woronov, Mary: Birth, Dec 8
Worthy, James: Birth, Feb 27
Wouk, Herman: Birth, May 27
Wound Ostomy and Continence Nurse Week, Apr 17
Wounded Knee Massacre: Anniv, Dec 29
Wozniak, Stephen: Birth, Aug 11
Wrangell-Saint Elias Natl Park: Anniv, Dec 2
Wray, Fay: Birth Anniv, Sep 15
Wray, Fay: King Kong Film Premiere: Anniv, Mar 2
Wren, Christopher: Birth Anniv, Oct 20
Wren, Day of the (Ireland), Dec 26
Wrestling
    Big 12 Chmpshp (Ames, IA), **Mar 4**
    Big Ten Chmpshps (Bloomington, IN), **Mar 2**
    NCAA Div I Wrestling Chmpshps (Oklahoma City, OK), **Mar 16**
    Wrestling Chmpshps, NAIA (Sioux City, IA), **Mar 3**
Wright Brothers Day (Pres Proc), Dec 17
Wright Brothers First Powered Flight: Anniv, Dec 17
Wright Brothers: First Flight 100th Anniv Celeb (Kill Devil Hills, NC), Dec 17
Wright, Amy: Birth, Apr 15
Wright, Frank Lloyd: Birth Anniv, Jun 8
Wright, Frank Lloyd: Wright Plus (Oak Park, IL), May 20
Wright, Gary: Birth, Apr 26
Wright, Orville: Birth Anniv, Aug 19
Wright, Richard: Birth Anniv, Sep 4
Wright, Rick: Birth, Jul 28
Wright, Robin: Birth, Apr 8
Wright, Steven: Birth, Dec 6
Wright, Wilbur: Birth Anniv, Apr 16
Writing. See also Journalism
    Freelance Writers Appreciation Week, **Feb 6**
    Ghostwriters Week, Natl, **Mar 1**
    Highlights Foundation Writer's Workshop (Chautauqua, NY), **Jul 15**
    I Love To Write Day, **Nov 15**
    Lifewriting Month, Natl, **Nov 1**
    Obituary Writers' Intl Conference, Great (Las Vegas, NM), **Jun 15**
    Word Nerd Day, **Jan 9**
    Wordsmith Day, **May 3**
    Write a Letter of Appreciation Week, Natl, **Mar 1**
    Write to Congress Day, Natl, **Jan 3**
    Write to Your Father Day, **Jun 11**
Wuhl, Robert: Birth, Oct 9
Wyatt Earp TV Premiere: Anniv, Sep 6
Wyatt, Jane: Birth, Aug 12
Wyden, Ron: Birth, May 3
Wyle, Noah: Birth, Jun 4
Wyman, Bill: Birth, Oct 24
Wyman, Jane: Birth, Jan 4
Wyoming
    Admission Day, **Jul 10**
    Bluegrass Fest (Alta), **Aug 11**
    Cheyenne Frontier Days (Cheyenne), **Jul 21**
    Cowboy State Games Sports Fest (Casper), **Feb 4**
    Enzi, Michael B.: Birth, **Feb 1**
    First US Woman Governor Inaugurated, **Jan 5**
    Fort Bridger Rendezvous (Fort Bridger), **Sep 1**
    Freudenthal, Dave: Birth, **Oct 12**
    Gift of the Waters Pageant & Art Fest in the Park (Thermopolis), **Aug 4**
    Grand Teton Music Fest (Teton Village), **Jul 4**
    Grand Teton Natl Park Established: Anniv, **Feb 1**
    River Regalia (Thermopolis), **Aug 12**
    State Fair & Rodeo (Douglas), **Aug 12**
    Thomas, Craig: Birth, **Feb 17**
Wythe, George: Death Anniv, Jun 8

X-Files TV Premiere: Anniv, Sep 10
X-Ray Discovery Day: Anniv, Nov 8

Yacht Race, Intl: Anniv, Aug 22
Yagudin, Alexei: Birth, Mar 18
Yalda (Iran), Dec 21
Yale Univ Founded: Anniv, Oct 16
Yale, Linus: Birth Anniv, Apr 4
Yalow, Rosalyn: Birth, Jul 19
Yalta Agreement Signed: Anniv, Feb 11
Yamaguchi, Kristi: Birth, Jul 12
Yamamoto, Isoroku: Birth Anniv, Apr 4
Yambilee, Louisiana (Opelousas, LA), Oct 25
Yamboree, East Texas (Gilmer, TX), Oct 18
Yankee Stadium Opens, Apr 18
Yankovic, Weird Al: Birth, Oct 23
Yanni: Birth, Nov 14
Yarborough, Cale: Birth, Mar 27
Yarrow, Peter: Birth, May 31
Yasbeck, Amy: Birth, Sep 12
Yastrzemski, Carl: Birth, Aug 22
Yawm Arafat (Islamic): The Standing at Arafat, Jan 9, Dec 30
Yeager, Chuck: Birth, Feb 13
Yearwood, Trisha: Birth, Sep 19
Yeats, William B.: Birth Anniv, Jun 13
Yell "Fudge" at the Cobras in North America Day, Jun 2
Yellow Daisy Fest (Stone Mountain, GA), Sep 7
Yellow Kid: First Newspaper Comic Strip: Anniv, Oct 18
Yellowstone Natl Park Established: Anniv, Mar 1
Yeltsin, Boris, Inaugurated Russian President: Anniv, Jul 10
Yemen: Natl Day, May 22
Yeoh, Michelle: Birth, Aug 6
Yevtushenko, Yevgeny: Birth, Jul 18
YMCA Organized: Anniv, Dec 29
Yoakam, Dwight: Birth, Oct 23
Yom Hashoah (Israel), Apr 25
Yom Kippur, Oct 2
Yom Kippur Begins, Oct 1
Yom Kippur War, Oct 6
York, Alvin C.: Day, Oct 8
York, Michael: Birth, Mar 27
York, Susannah: Birth, Jan 9
Yorktown Day, Oct 19
Yorktown Day (Yorktown, VA), Oct 19
Yorktown Victory Day (VA), Oct 9
Yosemite Natl Park Established: Anniv, Oct 1
Yothers, Tina: Birth, May 5
You Are There TV Premiere: Anniv, Feb 1
You Bet Your Life TV Premiere: Anniv, Oct 5
You Gotta Have Park (Brooklyn, NY), May 13
Young Achievers Month, May 1
Young and the Restless TV Premiere: Anniv, Mar 26
Young, Andrew: Birth, Mar 12
Young, Brigham: Anniv of Last Marriage, Apr 6
Young, Brigham: Birth Anniv, Jun 1
Young, Burt: Birth, Apr 30
Young, Chic: Birth Anniv, Jan 9
Young, Chris: Birth, Apr 28
Young, Cy: Birth Anniv, Mar 29
Young, Loretta: Birth Anniv, Jan 6
Young, Neil: Birth, Nov 12
Young, Paul: Birth, Jan 17
Young, Sean: Birth, Nov 20
Young, Steve: Birth, Oct 11
Yount, Robin: Birth, Sep 16
Your Hit Parade Radio Premiere: Anniv, Apr 12
Your Hit Parade TV Premiere: Anniv, Oct 7
Your Show of Shows TV Premiere: Anniv, Feb 25
You're Welcomegiving Day, Nov 24
Yours, Mine and Ours Month, Natl, Jan 1
Youth Art Month, Mar 1
Youth Day (Cameroon), Feb 11
Youth Day (People's Republic of China), May 4
Youth Day, Intl (UN), Aug 12
Youth Leadership Month, Feb 1
Youth Service Day, Natl, Apr 21
Youth Sports Safety Month, Natl, Apr 1
Yu, Jessica: Birth, Feb 14
Yugoslavia
    Civil War: Anniv, **Jun 25**
    NATO Forces Attack: Anniv, **Mar 25**
    Slovenia and Croatia Independence: Anniv, **Jun 25**
    Tito (Josip Broz): Birth Anniv, **May 25**
Yukon Gold Panning (Dawson City, YT, Canada), Jul 1
Yukon Quest Intl 1,000-Mile Sled Dog Race (Fairbanks, AK), Feb 11
Yukon River Bathtub Race (Whitehorse, YT, Canada), Aug 18
Yule (Wiccan), Dec 21
YWCA Week Without Violence, Oct 15
Yzerman, Steve: Birth, May 9

Z Day, Jan 1
Zadora, Pia: Birth, May 4
Zaharias, Mildred Babe Didrikson: Birth Anniv, Jun 26
Zahn, Paula: Birth, Feb 24
Zahn, Steve: Birth, Nov 13
Zaire: Congo (Dem Rep of the): Independence Day, Jun 30
Zambia
    African Freedom Day, **May 25**
    Heroes Day, **Jul 3**
    Independence Day, **Oct 23**
    Unity Day, **Jul 4**
    Youth Day, **Aug 7**
Zane Grey TV Premiere: Anniv, Oct 5
Zane, Billy: Birth, Feb 24
Zanuck, Darryl F.: Birth Anniv, Sep 5
Zappa, Dweezil: Birth, Sep 5
Zappa, Frank: Birth Anniv, Dec 21
Zeffirelli, Franco: Birth, Feb 12
Zellweger, Renee: Birth, Apr 25
Zemeckis, Robert: Birth, May 14
Zenger, John P.: Arrest Anniv, Nov 17
Zerbe, Anthony: Birth, May 20
Zero-Tasking Day, Oct 30
Zeta-Jones, Catherine: Birth, Sep 25
Zetkin, Clara: Birth Anniv, Jul 5
Zhang, Ziyi: Birth, Feb 9
Ziegler Kettle Moraine Jazz Fest (West Bend, WI), Sep 8
Zimbabwe
    Heroes' Day, **Aug 11**
    Independence Day, **Apr 18**
Zimbalist, Efrem, Jr: Birth, Nov 30
Zimbalist, Stephanie: Birth, Oct 6
Zimmer, Don: Birth, Jan 17
Zion Natl Park Established: Anniv, Nov 19
Zionism, UN Revokes Resolution on: Anniv, Dec 16
Zip Codes Inaugurated: Anniv, Jul 1
Zipper Patented: Anniv, Apr 29
Zippo/Case Intl Swap Meet (Bradford, PA), Jul 21
Zoeller, Fuzzy: Birth, Nov 11
Zola, Emile: Birth Anniv, Apr 2
Zolotow, Charlotte: Birth, Jun 26
Zoo
    Boo at the Zoo (Cleveland, OH), **Oct 19**
    First US Zoo: Anniv (Philadelphia, PA), **Jul 1**
Zoo Parade TV Premiere: Anniv, May 28
Zoot Suit Riots: Anniv, Jun 3
Zucker, David: Birth, Oct 6
Zucker, Jerry: Birth, Mar 11
Zukerman, Pinchas: Birth, Jul 16

Yes! Please send me additional copies of *Chase's 2006 Calendar of Events*.

Ship to _____

Address _____

City, State, Zip _____

Phone ( ) _____

Please send me _____ copies of the 2006 edition of
CHASE'S CALENDAR OF EVENTS at $64.95 each (0-07-146110-8) $_____

Add applicable sales tax for all states **except** AK, DE, MT, NH, OR $_____

Shipping & Handling: Add $5.00 for the first copy,
$3.50 for each additional copy $_____

                                                              Total $_____

☐ Check or money order enclosed payable to: The McGraw-Hill Companies

Charge my ☐ Visa ☐ MasterCard ☐ American Express ☐ Discover Card

Acct. # _____ Exp. Date ____/____

X _____
            Signature (if charging to bankcard)

Name (please print) _____

STANDING ORDER AUTHORIZATION

To make sure that I receive each year's new edition, please accept this Standing Order Authorization to ship me ____ copies of Chase's Calendar of Events beginning with the 2006 edition. Bill me at the address shown at the top of this order form. I understand that I may cancel my Standing Order at any time.

X _____
            Signature   Date

                                              ( )
_____
Name (please print)   Phone

GUARANTEE: Any book you order is unconditionally guaranteed and may be returned within 10 days of receipt for full refund.

Prices subject to change without notice.   9353

Mail to: **McGraw-Hill Customer Service**
P.O. Box 545
Blacklick, OH 43004-0545

Phone: (800) 722-4726 • Fax: (614) 755-5645 • Website: www.chases.com

There is no charge for being listed in **Chase's**. Use the form below to submit new entries for forthcoming editions of **Chase's Calendar of Events**. Background information about your entry is also appreciated. Please be sure your dates are confirmed for 2007, or clearly indicate if dates are tentative. Use a separate sheet for each entry submitted. Information selected by the editors may be used and publicized through their books, electronic formats, syndicated services and/or other related products and services. The editors reserve the right to select and edit information received. Please mail all information to: Calendar Editor, Chase's Calendar of Events, McGraw-Hill, 130 E. Randolph St., Ste 900, Chicago, IL 60601.

☞**DEADLINE FOR 2007 EDITION: APRIL 15, 2006.**   PLEASE TYPE OR PRINT VERY CLEARLY.

1. Exact name of entry:

2. Exact INCLUSIVE DATES for 2007:

3. If applicable, estimated attendance (one figure—grand total all days):

4. Location (site [not address], city and state):

5. Brief description:

6. Formula—ONLY if used to set date(s) each year (Example: Annually, the third Monday in May):

7. For public use, complete contact info to be printed in book—name, address, phone, fax, e-mail, web.

8. For Chase's staff use, complete mailing address to send our update form to you next year—name, title or department, organization name, address—as well as a name, phone and e-mail of person we can contact with questions about your entry:

9. Person furnishing information: (print) _____ (sign) _____

10. PLEASE CIRCLE THE EXACT INCLUSIVE DATES FOR YOUR 2007 EVENT ON THE CALENDAR BELOW.

2007
Key dates

M. L. King Birthday, Jan 15	Passover, Apr 3	Summer, June 21	Yom Kippur, Sept 22
Chinese New Year, Feb 18	Easter, Apr 8	Labor Day, Sept 3	Columbus Day, Oct 8
Washington's Birthday, Feb 19	Mother's Day, May 13	Ramadan, Sept 12	Thanksgiving, Nov 22
Lent begins, Feb 21	Memorial Day, May 28	Rosh Hashanah, Sept 13–14	Chanukah, Dec 5–12
Spring, Mar 20	Father's Day, June 17	Autumn, Sept 23	Winter, Dec 22

2007

JAN
S M T W T F S
1 2 3 4 5 6
7 8 9 10 11 12 13
14 15 16 17 18 19 20
21 22 23 24 25 26 27
28 29 30 31

APR
S M T W T F S
1 2 3 4 5 6 7
8 9 10 11 12 13 14
15 16 17 18 19 20 21
22 23 24 25 26 27 28
29 30

JULY
S M T W T F S
1 2 3 4 5 6 7
8 9 10 11 12 13 14
15 16 17 18 19 20 21
22 23 24 25 26 27 28
29 30 31

OCT
S M T W T F S
1 2 3 4 5 6
7 8 9 10 11 12 13
14 15 16 17 18 19 20
21 22 23 24 25 26 27
28 29 30 31

FEB
S M T W T F S
1 2 3
4 5 6 7 8 9 10
11 12 13 14 15 16 17
18 19 20 21 22 23 24
25 26 27 28

MAY
S M T W T F S
1 2 3 4 5
6 7 8 9 10 11 12
13 14 15 16 17 18 19
20 21 22 23 24 25 26
27 28 29 30 31

AUG
S M T W T F S
1 2 3 4
5 6 7 8 9 10 11
12 13 14 15 16 17 18
19 20 21 22 23 24 25
26 27 28 29 30 31

NOV
S M T W T F S
1 2 3
4 5 6 7 8 9 10
11 12 13 14 15 16 17
18 19 20 21 22 23 24
25 26 27 28 29 30

MAR
S M T W T F S
1 2 3
4 5 6 7 8 9 10
11 12 13 14 15 16 17
18 19 20 21 22 23 24
25 26 27 28 29 30 31

JUNE
S M T W T F S
1 2
3 4 5 6 7 8 9
10 11 12 13 14 15 16
17 18 19 20 21 22 23
24 25 26 27 28 29 30

SEPT
S M T W T F S
1
2 3 4 5 6 7 8
9 10 11 12 13 14 15
16 17 18 19 20 21 22
23 24 25 26 27 28 29
30

DEC
S M T W T F S
1
2 3 4 5 6 7 8
9 10 11 12 13 14 15
16 17 18 19 20 21 22
23 24 25 26 27 28 29
30 31

Note: This page may be photocopied in order to submit additional event entries to **Chase's 2007 Calendar of Events**